POCKET CRIMINAL CODE

2020

CARSWELL

POCKET CRIMINAL CODE

2020

With Forms of Charges from
The Police Officers Manual
by Gary P. Rodrigues, B.A., LL.B.,
of the Ontario Bar

Incorporating R.S.C. 1985
and subsequent amendments

A cataloguing record for this publication is available from Library and Archives Canada.

ISSN 0841-6214

978-0-7798-9033-0 (2020 edition)

Printed in the United States by Thomson Reuters.

THOMSON REUTERS CANADA, A DIVISION OF THOMSON REUTERS CANADA LIMITED

One Corporate Plaza
2075 Kennedy Road
Toronto, Ontario
M1T 3V4

Customer Support
1-416-609-3800 (Toronto & International)
1-800-387-5164 (Toll Free Canada & U.S.)
Fax 1-416-298-5082 (Toronto)
Fax 1-877-750-9041 (Toll Free Canada Only)
Email CustomerSupport.LegalTaxCanada@TR.com

PREFACE

The *2020 Pocket Criminal Code* incorporates the following legislative developments that occurred since publication of the last edition. Amendments not in force as of September 19, 2019 appear in the work as shaded text.

[1] On June 21, 2018, the *Expungement of Historically Unjust Convictions Act*, S.C. 2018, c. 11 (former Bill C-66) received Royal Assent and came into force. This Act amended three sections of the *Criminal Code.*

[2] On June 21, 2018, *An Act to amend the Criminal Code (offences related to conveyances) and to make consequential amendments to other Acts*, S.C. 2018, c. 21 (former Bill C-46) received Royal Assent. Its Part 1 came into force upon Royal Assent, and its Part 2 came into force on December 18, 2018.

[3] On June 21, 2018, the *Cannabis Act*, S.C. 2018, c. 16 (former Bill C-45) and the *Budget Implementation Act, 2018, No. 1*, S.C. 2018, c. 12 (former Bill C-74) received Royal Assent, and their amendments to the *Criminal Code* came into force on October 17, 2018, pursuant to Order in Council SI/2018-52. The *Cannabis Act*, selected sections of which have been introduced with this edition, also amended the *Controlled Drugs and Substances Act*, the *Firearms Act* and the *Youth Criminal Justice Act*.

[4] On December 13, 2018, the *Act to amend the Export and Import Permits Act and the Criminal Code (amendments permitting the accession to the Arms Trade Treaty and other amendments)*, S.C. 2018, c. 26 (former Bill C-47) received Royal Assent, with the aim to come into force on a day to be fixed by order of the Governor in Council.

[5] On December 13, 2018, the *Budget Implementation Act, 2018, No. 2*, S.C. 2018, c. 27 (former Bill C-86) received Royal Assent and came into force. This act amended two sections of the *Criminal Code.*

[6] On December 13, 2018, the *Act to amend the Criminal Code and the Department of Justice Act and to make consequential amendments to another Act*, S.C. 2018, c. 29 (former Bill C-51) received Royal Assent and came into force. Its numerous amendments aim to enhance and to update Code provisions deemed obsolete, redundant or risky in light of the *Canadian Charter of Rights and Freedoms*, as well as to modify particular Code provisions relating to sexual assault.

[7] On June 21, 2019, the *Act to amend the Criminal Code, the Youth Criminal Justice Act and other Acts*, S.C. 2019, c. 25 (former Bill C-75) received Royal Assent, with its amendments coming into force on one of June 21, July 21, September 19, and December 18, 2019. Its numerous amendments aim to achieve a variety of objectives including

- the modernization and enhancement of interim release provisions with special focus on Aboriginal accuseds, offenders from vulnerable populations, and those who commit violent acts against intimate partners;

• the provision of a judicial referral hearing to deal with failure-to-comply and failure-to-appear offences;

• the abolition of peremptory challenges of jurors and modification of the process for challenging jurors for cause;

• the restriction of preliminary inquiries to offences punishable for terms of fourteen years or more; and

• the re-introduction of the Victim Surcharge regime, which now permits the court to adjust amounts owing in the event of undue hardship or disproportionality.

[8] On June 21, 2019, the *Act to amend certain Acts and Regulations in relation to firearms*, S.C. 2019, c. 9 (former Bill C-71), received Royal Assent, with some of its amendments to the *Criminal Code* and the *Firearms Act* having come into force on that date.

[9] On June 21, 2019, the *Act to amend the Criminal Code and other Acts (ending the captivity of whales and dolphins)*, S.C. 2019, c. 11 (former Bill S-203), and the *Act to amend the Criminal Code (bestiality and animal fighting)*, S.C. 2019, c. 17 (former Bill C-84), received Royal Assent and came into immediate effect.

[10] On June 21, 2019, amendments to the *Criminal Code* and the *Canada Evidence Act* were introduced by an *Act respecting national security matters*, S.C. 2019, c. 13 (former Bill C-59), and by an *Act to amend the National Defence Act and to make related and consequential amendments to other Acts*, S.C. 2019, c. 15 (former Bill C-77). Although both received Royal Assent on that date, only the *Act respecting national security matters* had come into force by the date of publication of this edition.

[11] On June 21, 2019, the *Criminal Code* was also amended by the *Budget Implementation Act, 2019, No. 1*, S.C. 2019, c. 29 (former Bill C-97) — the addition of recklessness to the description of the offence of laundering proceeds of crime came into effect on that date.

[12] While the index has been fully updated to reflect all amendments, the forms of charges underwent its annual update prior to the amendments of June 21, 2019 (see items 7 through 11 above) — please be mindful of these amendments when consulting these precedents.

SUMMARY TABLE OF CONTENTS

TABLE OF CONTENTS

CRIMINAL CODE

SHORT TITLE

INTERPRETATION (SS. 2–3)

PART I (SS. 3.1–45)

General

Parties to Offences

Protection of Persons Administering and Enforcing the Law

Suppression of Riots

Self-Induced Intoxication

Defence of Person

Defence of Property

Protection of Persons in Authority

PART II — OFFENCES AGAINST PUBLIC ORDER (SS. 46–83)

Treason and other Offences against the Queen's Authority and Person

Prohibited Acts

Official Documents

Part II.1 — Terrorism (ss. 83.01–83.33)

Offences relating to Lost, Destroyed or Defaced Weapons, etc.

Prohibition Orders

Limitations on Access

Search and Seizure

Exempted Persons

General

PART IV — OFFENCES AGAINST THE ADMINISTRATION OF LAW AND JUSTICE (SS. 118–149)

Interpretation

Corruption and Disobedience

Misleading Justice

Escapes and Rescues

PART V — SEXUAL OFFENCES, PUBLIC MORALS AND DISORDERLY CONDUCT (SS. 150–182)

Interpretation

Sexual Offences

Suicide

Kidnapping, Trafficking in Persons, Hostage Taking and Abduction

Commodification of Sexual Activity

PART VIII.1 — OFFENCES RELATING TO CONVEYANCES (SS. 320.11–320.4)

PART IX — OFFENCES AGAINST RIGHTS OF PROPERTY (SS. 321–378)

Falsification of Books and Documents

Identity Theft and Identity Fraud

Forgery of Trademarks and Trade Descriptions

Wreck

Public Stores

Search, Seizure and Detention of Proceeds of Crime

Forfeiture of Proceeds of Crime

Disclosure Provisions

Specific Rules of Forfeiture

Regulations

PART XIII — ATTEMPTS — CONSPIRACIES — ACCESSORIES (SS. 463–467.2)

PART XIV — JURISDICTION (SS. 468–482.1)

General

Special Jurisdiction

Rules of Court

PART XV — SPECIAL PROCEDURE AND POWERS (SS. 483–492.2)

General Powers of Certain Officials

Evidence on Trial

Children and Young Persons

Corroboration

Verdicts

Previous Convictions

Jurisdiction

Formal Defects in Jury Process

PART XX.1 — MENTAL DISORDER (SS. 672.1–672.95)

Interpretation

Assessment Orders

Dispositions by a Court or Review Board

Terms of Dispositions

High-Risk Accused

Dual Status Offenders

Appeals

Review of Dispositions

Power to Compel Appearance

[Heading added 2005, c. 22, s. 31.]

Stay of Proceedings

[Heading added 2005, c. 22, s. 33.]

Interprovincial Transfers

SCHEDULE TO PART XXII.1 — OFFENCES IN RESPECT OF WHICH A REMEDIATION AGREEMENT MAY BE ENTERED INTO

PART XXIII — SENTENCING (SS. 716–751.1)

Part XXVII — Summary Convictions (ss. 785–840)

SI/85-201 — Approved Breath Analysis Instruments Order

Short Title

Approved Instruments

SI/85-200 — Approved Screening Devices Order

Short Title

Approved Screening Devices

2005-37 — Order Approving Blood Sample Containers

2018-179 — Approved Drug Screening Equipment Order

2018-148 — Blood Drug Concentration Regulations

2008-196 — Evaluation of Impaired Operation (Drugs and Alcohol) Regulations

98-462 — Regulations Prescribing Certain Firearms and Other Weapons, Components and Parts of Weapons, Accessories, Cartridge Magazines, Ammunition and Projectiles as Prohibited, Restricted or Non-Restricted

98-466 — Regulations Prescribing Public Officers

2002-284 — Regulations Establishing a List of Entities

SI/2012-103 — Order Accepting the Recommendation of the Minister of Public Safety and Emergency Preparedness Concerning the Two-year Review of the List of Entities

2015-24 — Order Accepting the Recommendation of the Minister of Public Safety and Emergency Preparedness Concerning the Two-Year Review of the List set out in the Regulations Establishing a List of Entities

2010-161 — Regulations Prescribing Certain Offences to be Serious Offences

2014-304 — Samples of Bodily Substances Regulations

Coming Into Force

CANADA EVIDENCE ACT

SHORT TITLE

PART I — (SS. 2–42)

Application

Witnesses

Oaths and Solemn Affirmations

Judicial Notice

Documentary Evidence

CANADIAN BILL OF RIGHTS

CANADIAN VICTIMS BILL OF RIGHTS

Part V — Administrative Orders for Contraventions of Designated Regulations (ss. 33–43)

Part VI — General (ss. 44–60)

CRIMINAL RECORDS ACT

DNA IDENTIFICATION ACT

FIREARMS ACT

2006-95 — Order Declaring an Amnesty Period (2006)

2014-56 — Order Declaring an Amnesty Period (2014)

2018-46 — Order Declaring an Amnesty Period (2018)

Identification of Criminals Act

Interpretation Act

AN ACT RESPECTING THE MANDATORY REPORTING OF INTERNET CHILD PORNOGRAPHY BY PERSONS WHO PROVIDE AN INTERNET SERVICE

Sex Offender Information Registration Act

Effect of Termination of Youth Sentence

PART 5 — CUSTODY AND SUPERVISION (SS. 83–109)

PART 6 — PUBLICATION, RECORDS AND INFORMATION (SS. 110–129)

Protection of Privacy of Young Persons

Fingerprints and Photographs

Records That May Be Kept

Evidence

Forms, Regulations and Rules of Court

Agreements with Provinces

Programs

PART 8 — TRANSITIONAL PROVISIONS (SS. 158–165)

PART 9 — CONSEQUENTIAL AMENDMENTS, REPEAL AND COMING INTO FORCE (SS. 166–200)

Consequential Amendments

Repeal

Coming into Force

Table of Concordance

Editor's note: Current to May 15, 2019.

R.S.C. 1970, c. C-34	R.S.C. 1985, c. C-46
C-34	C-46
1	1
2	2
2“court of criminal jurisdiction”	2“court of criminal jurisdiction”
2“magistrate”	2“magistrate” [rep. R.S. 1985, c. 27 (1st. Supp.), s. 2(4)]
2“motor vehicle”	2“motor vehicle”
2“peace officer”	2“peace officer”
(d.1)	(e)
(e)	(f)
(f)	(g)
2“railway equipment”	2“railway equipment”
2“superior court of criminal juridiction”	2“superior court of criminal jurisdiction”
(c)	(c)
(d)	(e)
(e)	(d)
(f)	(f)
(g)	(g)
2.1	3
Part I	Part I
3(1)	—
3(2)	4(1)
3(3)	4(2)
3(4)	4(3)

R.S.C. 1970, c. C-34	R.S.C. 1985, c. C-46
3(5)	4(4)
3(6)	4(5)
3(7)	4(6)
3(8)	4(7)
4	5
5	6
6	7
6(1.1)	7(2)
6(1.2)	7(3)
6(1.3)	7(3.1)
6(1.4)	7(3.2) [rep. 2013, c. 13, s. 3(2)]
6(1.5)	7(3.3) [rep. 2013, c. 13, s. 3(2)]
6(1.6)	7(3.4) [rep. 2013, c. 13, s. 3(2)]
6(1.7)	7(3.5) [rep. 2013, c. 13, s. 3(2)]
6(1.8)	7(3.6) [rep. 2013, c. 13, s. 3(2)]
6(1.9)	7(3.7) [rep. 2013, c. 13, s. 3(2)]
6(1.91)	7(3.71)
6(1.92)	7(3.72)
6(1.93)	7(3.73)
6(1.94)	7(3.74)
6(1.95)	7(3.75)
6(1.96)	7(3.76)

R.S.C. 1970, c. C-34	R.S.C. 1985, c. C-46
6(1.97)	7(3.77)
6(2)	7(4)
6(3)	7(5)
6(3.1)	7(5.1)
6(4)	7(6)
6(5)	7(7)
6(6)	7(8)
6(7)	7(9)
6(8)	7(10)
6(9)	7(11)
7	8
7(1)(a)	8(1)(b)
7(1)(b)	8(1)(a)
8	9
9	10
10	11
11	12
12	13
13	—
14	14
15	15
16	16
17	17
18	18
19	19
20	20
21	21
22	22
23(1)	23(1)
23(2)	23(2) [rep. 2000, c. 12, s. 92]
23.1	23.1 [en. R.S. 1985, c. 24 (2nd Supp.), s. 45]
24	24
25	25
26	26
27	27

R.S.C. 1970, c. C-34	R.S.C. 1985, c. C-46
28	28
29	29
30	30
31	31
32	32
33	33
34	34
35	35
36	36 [rep. 2012, c. 9, s. 2]
37	37 [rep. 2012, c. 9, s. 2]
38	38 [rep. 2012, c. 9, s. 2]
39	39 [rep. 2012, c. 9, s. 2]
40	40 [rep. 2012, c. 9, s. 2]
41	41 [rep. 2012, c. 9, s. 2]
42	42 [rep. 2012, c. 9, s. 2]
43	43
44	44 [rep. 2001, c. 26, s. 294]
45	45
Part II	Part II
46	46
47	47
48	48
49	—
50	50
51	51
52	52
53	53
54	54
55	55
56	—
57	56
58	57
59	58

R.S.C. 1970, c. C-34	R.S.C. 1985, c. C-46
60	59
61	60
62	61
63	62
64	63
65	64
66	65
67	66
68	67
69	68
70	69
71	70
72	—
73	72
74	73
75	74
76	75
76.1	76
76.2	77
76.3	78
77	79
78	80
79	81
80	82
81	83
Part II.1	Part III

(Note: Part III, R.S.C. 1985, c. C-46 replaced by S.C. 1995, c. 39. See the end of this Table for a Table of Equivalent Sections.)

R.S.C. 1970, c. C-34	R.S.C. 1985, c. C-46
82	84
83	85
84	86
85	87
86	88
87	89
88	90
88(1)	90(1)
88(2)	90(2)
88(3)	90(3)
88(4)	90(4)
89	91
90	92
91	93
92	94
93	95
94	96
95	97
96	98
97	99
98	100
98(11)"appeal court"	100(11) "appeal court"
(a)	(d)
(b)	(b.1) [rep. 1992, c. 51, s. 33(1)]
(b.1)	(a)
(c)	(b)
(d)	(c)
(e)	—
(f)	(e)
99	101
100	102
101	103
102	104
103	105
104	106
104(1)	106(1)
104(2)	106(2)
104(3)	106(4)
104(4)	106(5)
104(5)	106(6)
104(6)	106(7)
104(7)	106(8)
104(8)	106(9)
104(9)	106(10)
104(10)	106(11)
104(11)	106(12)
104(12)	106(13)

R.S.C. 1970, c. C-34	R.S.C. 1985, c. C-46	R.S.C. 1970, c. C-34	R.S.C. 1985, c. C-46
105	107	131	143
106	108	132	144
106.1	109	133	145
106.2	110	133(7)	145(7) [rep. 1985, c. 27 (1st Supp.), s. 20(2)]
106.3	111	134	146
106.4	112	135	147
106.5	113	136	148
106.6	114	137	149
106.7	115	Part IV	Part V
106.8	116	138	150
106.9	117	139	150.1
Part III	Part IV	140	151
107	118	142–145	—
108	119	146	153
109	120	147	154 [rep. R.S. 1985, c. 19 (3rd Supp.), s. 1]
110	121	148–149	—
111	122	150	155
112	123	151–153	156–158 [rep. 1985, c. 19 (3rd Supp.), s. 2]
113	124	154	159
114	125	155	160
115	126	156	—
116	127	157–158	161–162 [rep. 1985, c. 19 (3rd Supp.), s. 4]
117	128	159	163
118	129	159(1)	163(1)
119	130	159(2)	163(2)
120	131	159(3)	163(3)
121	132	159(4)	163(4)
122	133	159(5)	163(5)
122.1	134		
123	135 [rep. R.S. 1985, c. 27 (1st. Supp.), s. 17]		
124	136		
125	137		
126	138		
127	139		
128	140		
129	141		
130	142		

R.S.C. 1970, c. C-34	R.S.C. 1985, c. C-46
159(6)	163(6) [rep. 1993, c. 46, s. 1]
159(7)	—
159(8)	163(8)
160	164
160(8)"court"	164(8)"court"
(a)	(a)
(a.1)	(b)
(b)	(c)
(c)	(d)
161	—
162	166 [rep. 1994, c. 44, s. 9]
163	167
164	—
165	169
166	170
167	171
168	172
168(1)	172(1)
168(2)	172(2) [rep. R.S. 1985, c. 19 (3rd Supp.), s. 6]
168(3)	172(3)
168(4)	172(4)
169	173
169(1)	173(1)
169(2)	173(2)
170	174
171	175
172	176
173	177
174	—
175	179
175(1)(a)	—
175(1)(b)	—
175(1)(c)	—
175(1)(d)	179(1)(a)
175(1)(e)	179(1)(b)
175(2)	179(2)
175(3)	—
176	180
177	181
178	182
Part IV.1	Part VI
178.1	183
178.1"offence"	183"offence"
178.11	184
178.11(1)	184(1)
178.11(2)	184(2)
178.11(3)	184(3) [rep. 1993, c. 40, s. 3(3); re-en. 2004, c. 12, s. 4(2)]
178.12	185
178.12(1)(e.1)	185(1)(f)
178.12(1)(f)	185(1)(g)
178.12(1)(g)	185(1)(h)
178.13	186
178.13(1.1)	186(2)
178.13(1.2)	186(3)
178.13(2)	186(4)
178.13(2.1)	186(5)
178.13(3)	186(6)
178.13(4)	186(7)
178.14	187
178.15	188
178.15(1)	188(1)
178.15(2)	188(2)
178.15(3)	188(3) [rep. 1993, c. 40, s. 8]
178.15(4)(a)	188(4)(a)
178.15(4)(b)	188(4)(b)
178.15(4)(b.1)	188(4)(e.1)
178.15(4)(c)	188(4)(f.1)
178.15(4)(c.1)	188(4)(d)
178.15(4)(c.2)	188(4)(c)
178.15(4)(d)	188(4)(e)

R.S.C. 1970, c. C-34	R.S.C. 1985, c. C-46
178.15(4)(e)	188(4)(f)
178.15(4)(f)	188(4)(g)
178.15(4)(g)	188(4)(h)
178.16	189
178.16(1)	189(1) [rep. 1993, c. 40, s. 10]
178.16(2)	189(2) [rep. 1993, c. 40, s. 10]
178.16(3)	189(3) [rep. 1993, c. 40, s. 10]
178.16(3.1)	189(4) [rep. 1993, c. 40, s. 10(1)]
178.16(4)	189(5)
178.16(5)	189(6)
178.17	190
178.18	191
178.19	192
178.2	193
178.2(2)(e)	193(2)(e)
178.21	194
178.22	195
178.22(2)(g.1)	195(2)(h)
178.22(2)(h)	195(2)(i)
178.22(2)(i)	195(2)(j)
178.22(2)(j)	195(2)(k)
178.22(2)(k)	195(2)(l)
178.22(2)(l)	195(2)(m)
178.22(2)(m)	195(2)(n)
178.23	196
178.23(1)	196(1)
178.23(2)	—
178.23(3)	196(2)
178.23(4)	196(3)
178.23(5)	196(4)
Part V	Part VII
179	197
180	—

R.S.C. 1970, c. C-34	R.S.C. 1985, c. C-46
181	199
182–183	—
184	200 [rep. R.S. 1985, c. 27 (1st Supp.), s. 30]
185	201
186	202
187	203
188	204
188(6.1)	204(7)
188(6.2)	204(8)
188(6.3)	204(8.1)
188(7)	204(9)
188(7.1)	204(9.1)
188(8)	204(10)
188(9)	204(11)
188.1	205 [rep. 1985, c. 52 (1st Supp.), s.1]
189	206
190	207
191	208 [rep. R.S. 1985, c. 27 (1st Supp.), s. 32]
192	209
193	210
194	211
195	212 [rep., with heading, 2014, c. 25, s. 13]
195(2)–(4)	212
195.1	213
Part VI	Part VIII
196	214
196“operate”	214“operate”
197	215
198	216
199	217
200	218
201	—
202	219

R.S.C. 1970, c. C-34	R.S.C. 1985, c. C-46	R.S.C. 1970, c. C-34	R.S.C. 1985, c. C-46
203	220	231	247
204	221	232	248
205	222	233	—
206	223	233(1)(d)	—
207	224	234	—
208	225	235	—
209	226	235(1)(c)	—
210	227 [rep. 1999, c. 5, s. 9(1)]	235(2)(c)	—
		235(3)	—
211	228	236	—
212	229	237	—
213	230	238	—
214	231	238(2)	—
214(1)	231(1)	238(6)	—
214(2)	231(2)	239	—
214(3)	231(3)	240	—
214(4)	231(4)	240.1	—
214(5)	231(5)	241	—
214(6)	231(6) [rep. R.S. 1985, c. 27 (1st Supp.), s. 35]	241(1)(a)	—
		242	—
		242(1)	—
		242(2)	—
214(7)	231(7)	242(4)	—
215	232	242(5)(a)	—
216	233	243	—
217	234	243.1	—
218	235	243.2	262
219	236	243.3	263
220	237	243.4	264.1
221	238	244	265
222	239	245	266
223	240	245.1	267
224	241	245.2	268
225	—	245.3	269
226	242	245.4	269.1
227	243	246	270
228	244	246.1	271
229	245	246.1(1)	271(1)
230	246		

R.S.C. 1970, c. C-34	R.S.C. 1985, c. C-46
246.1(2)	271(2) [rep. R.S. 1985, c. 19 (3rd Supp.), s. 10]
246.2	272
246.3	273
246.4	274
246.5	275
246.6	276
246.6(1)	276(1)
246.7	277
246.8	278
247	279
247.1	279.1 [en. R.S. 1985, c. 27 (1st Supp.), s. 40]
248	—
249	280
250	281
250.1	282
250.2	283
250.3	284
250.4	285
250.5	286
251	287
251(6)"Minister of Health"	287(6) "Minister of Health"
(a)	(a)
(a.1)	(d)
(b)	(c)
(c)	(b)
(d)	(e)
252	—
253	289 [rep. R.S. 1985, s. 27 (1st Supp.), s. 41]
254	290
255	291
256	292
257	293
258	294

R.S.C. 1970, c. C-34	R.S.C. 1985, c. C-46
259	295
260	—
261	297
262	298
263	299
264	300
265	301
266	302
267	303
268	304
269	305
270	306
271	307
272	308
273	309
274	310
275	311
276	312
277	313
278	314
279	315
280	316
281	317
281.1	318
281.2	319
281.3	320
281.3(8) "court"	320(8) "court"
(a)	(a)
(a.1)	(b)
(b)	(c)
(c)	(d)
281.3(8)"judge"	320(8) "judge"
Part VII	Part IX
282	321
283	322
284	323
285	324
286	325

R.S.C. 1970, c. C-34	R.S.C. 1985, c. C-46
287	326 [rep. 2014, c. 31, s. 14(2)]
287.1	327
288	328
289	329 [rep. 2000, ch. 12, s. 94]
290	330
291	331
292	332
293	333
294	334
295	335
295(1)	335(1)
295(2)	335(2)
296	336
297	—
298	338
298(1.1)	338(2)
298(2)	338(3)
298(3)	338(4)
299	339
300	340
301	341
301.1	342
301.1(1)	342(1)
301.1(2)	342(2)
301.1(3)	342(3) [rep. R.S. 1985, c. 27 (1st Supp.), s. 44]
301.2	342.1 [en. R.S. 1985, c. 27 (1st Supp.), s. 45]
302	343
303	344
304	345
305	346
305.1	347
306	348
306(3)	—
306(4)	348(3)
307	349
308	350
309	351
310	352
311	353
312	354
313	355
314	356
315	357
316	358
317	—
318	—
319	361
320	362
321	363
322	364
323	—
324	366
325	367
325(1)	367(1)
325(2)	367(2) [rep. 1994, c. 44, s. 24]
326	368
327	369
328	—
329	—
330	372
331	373 [rep. R.S. 1985, c. 27 (1st Supp.), s. 53]
332	374
333	375
334	376
335	377
336	378
Part VIII	Part X
337	379
338	380
339	381

R.S.C. 1970, c. C-34	R.S.C. 1985, c. C-46	R.S.C. 1970, c. C-34	R.S.C. 1985, c. C-46
340	382	380	422
341	383	381	423
342	384	381.1	424
343	385	382	425
344	386	383	426
345	387	384	—
346	388	Part IX	Part XI
347	389	385	428
348	390	386	429
349	391	387	430
350	392	387.1	431
351	393	388	432 [rep. R.S. 1985, c. 27 (1st Supp.), s. 58]
352	394		
353	395		
354	396	389	433
355	397	390	434
356	398	391	435
357	399	392	436
358	400	393	437
359	401	394	438
360	—	395	439
361	403	396	440
362	—	397	441
363	405	398	442
364	406	399	443
365	407	400	—
366	408	401	445
367	409	402	446
368	410	403	447
369	411	404–405	–
370	412	Part X	Part XII
371	—	406	448
372	414	407	449
373	415	408	450
374	416	409	451
375	417	410	452
376	418	411	453
377	419	412	454
378	420	413	455
379	421	414	456

R.S.C. 1970, c. C-34	R.S.C. 1985, c. C-46	R.S.C. 1970, c. C-34	R.S.C. 1985, c. C-46
415	457	420.18	462.38 [en. R.S. 1985, c. 42 (4th Supp.), s.2]
416	458		
417	459		
418	460	420.19	462.39 [en. R.S. 1985, c. 42 (4th Supp.), s.2]
419	461		
420	462		
Part X.1	—	420.2	462.4 [en. R.S. 1985, c. 42 (4th Supp.), s.2]
420.1	—		
420.2	—		
Part X.1	Part XII.2		
420.1	462.3 [en. R.S. 1985, c. 42 (4th Supp.), s.2]	420.21	462.41 [en. R.S. 1985, c. 42 (4th Supp.), s.2]
420.11	462.31 [en. R.S. 1985, c. 42 (4th Supp.), s.2]	420.22	462.42 [en. R.S. 1985, c. 42 (4th Supp.), s.2]
420.12	462.32 [en. R.S. 1985, c. 42 (4th Supp.), s.2]	420.23	462.43 [en. R.S. 1985, c. 42 (4th Supp.), s.2]
420.13	462.33 [en. R.S. 1985, c. 42 (4th Supp.), s.2]	420.24	462.44 [en. R.S. 1985, c. 42 (4th Supp.), s.2]
420.14	462.34 [en. R.S. 1985, c. 42 (4th Supp.), s.2]	420.25	462.45 [en. R.S. 1985, c. 42 (4th Supp.), s.2]
420.15	462.35 [en. R.S. 1985, c. 42 (4th Supp.), s.2]	420.26	462.46 [en. R.S. 1985, c. 42 (4th Supp.), s.2]
420.16	462.36 [en. R.S. 1985, c. 42 (4th Supp.), s.2]	420.27	462.47 [en. R.S. 1985, c. 42 (4th Supp.), s.2]
420.17	462.37 [en. R.S. 1985, c. 42 (4th Supp.), s.2]	420.28	462.48 [en. R.S. 1985, c. 42 (4th Supp.), s.2]

R.S.C. 1970, c. C-34	R.S.C. 1985, c. C-46
420.29	462.49 [en. R.S. 1985, c. 42 (4th Supp.), s.2]
420.3	462.5 [en. R.S. 1985, c. 42 (4th Supp.), s.2]
Part XI	Part XIII
421	463
422	464
423	465
423(1)(c)	—
423(1)(d)	465(1)(c)
423(1)(e)	465(1)(d)
423(2)	465(2) [rep. R.S. 1985, c. 27 (1st Supp.), s. 61(3)]
423(3)	465(3)
423(4)	465(4)
423(5)	465(5)
423(6)	465(7)
424	466
425	467
Part XII	Part XIV
426	468
427	469
428	470
429	471
429.1	472 [rep. 1985, c. 27 (1st Supp.), s. 63]
430	473
431	474
431.1	475
432	476
433	477
434	478
435	479
436	480

R.S.C. 1970, c. C-34	R.S.C. 1985, c. C-46
437	481
438	482
438(1.1)	482(2)
438(2)	482(3)
438(3)	–
438(4)	482(4)
438(5)	482(5)
Part XIII	Part XV
439	483
440	484
440.1	485
440.2	485.1 [en. R.S. 1985, c. 27 (1st Supp.), s. 67]
441	—
442	486
442(1)	486(1)
442(2.1)	486(2.1)
442(2.2)	486(2.2)
442(3)	486(3)
442(3.1)	486(4)
442(4)	486(5)
442(5)	486(6) [rep. R.S. 1985, c. 19 (3rd Supp.), s. 14(2)]
443	487
443.1	487.1 [en. R.S. 1985, c. 27 (1st Supp.), s. 69]
443.2	487.2 [en. R.S. 1985, c. 27 (1st Supp.), s. 69]
444	488
444.1	488.1 [en. R.S. 1985, c. 27 (1st Supp.), s. 71]
445	489
445.1	489.1 [en. R.S. 1985, c. 27 (1st Supp.), s. 72]
446	490

R.S.C. 1970, c. C-34	R.S.C. 1985, c. C-46
446.1	491
446.2	491.1 [en. R.S. 1985, c. 27 (1st Supp.), s. 74]
446.3	491.2 [en. R.S. 1985, c. 23 (1st Supp.), s. 2]
447	492
Part XIV	Part XVI
448	493
448"judge	493"judge"
(b)	(b)
	(c) N.S. [rep. 1992, c. 51, s. 37]
(c) N.S., Man., B.C.	(d) N.S., Man., B.C.
(d) Nfld.	(d) Nfld.
(d.1) N.B., Alta., Sask.	(d) N.B., Alta., Sask.
(e) P.E.I.	(d) P.E.I.
(e) Y.T., N.W.T.	(e) Y.T., N.W.T.
449	494
450	495
451	496
452	497
453	498
453.1	499
453.2	500
453.3	501
453.4	502
454	503
454(1.1)	503(2)
454(2)	503(3)
454(2.1)	503(3.1)
454(3)	503(4)
454(4)	503(5)
455	504
455.1	505
455.2	506

R.S.C. 1970, c. C-34	R.S.C. 1985, c. C-46
455.3	507
455.4	508
455.5	509
455.6	510
456	511
456.1	512
456.2	513
456.3	514
457	515
457(2)(c.1)	515(2)(d)
457(2)(d)	515(2)(e)
457(2.1)	515(2.1)
457(3)	515(3)
457(4)	515(4)
457(5)	515(5)
457(5.1)	515(6)
457(5.2)	515(7)
457(5.3)	515(8)
457(6)	515(9)
457(7)	515(10)
457(8)	515(11)
457.1	516
457.2	517
457.3	518
457.4	519
457.5	520
457.6	521
457.7	522
457.7(2.1)	522(3)
457.7(2.2)	522(4)
457.7(3)	522(5)
457.7(4)	522(6)
457.8	523
458	524
458(4.1)	524(5)
458(4.2)	524(6)
458(4.3)	524(7)
458(5)	524(8)
458(5.1)	524(9)
458(6)	524(10)

R.S.C. 1970, c. C-34	R.S.C. 1985, c. C-46	R.S.C. 1970, c. C-34	R.S.C. 1985, c. C-46
458(7)	524(11)	470	542
458(8)	524(12)	471	543
458(9)	524(13)	471.1	544
459	525	472	545
459.1	526	473	546
460	527	474	547
461	528	474.1	547.1 [en. R.S. 1985, c. 27 (1st Supp.), s. 100]
462	529 [rep. 1994, c. 44, s. 52]	475	548
Part XIV.1	Part XVII	476	549
462.1	530	477	550
462.11	530.1 [en. R.S. 1985, c. 31 (4th Supp.), s. 94]	478	551
462.2	531	479–481	—
462.3	532	Part XVI	Part XIX
462.4	533	482	552
Part XV	Part XVIII	482"judge"	552"judge"
463	535	(a)	(a)
464	536	(b)	(b)
465	537	(c)	(c)
465(1)(a)	—	(c.1)	(d)
465(1)(b)	537(1)(a)	(d)	(g)
465(1)(c)	537(1)(b)	(e)	(e)
465(1)(d)	537(1)(c)	(f)	(h)
465(1)(e)	537(1)(d)	(g) Nfld.	(f) Nfld.
465(1)(f)	537(1)(e)	(h) P.E.I.	(f) P.E.I.
465(1)(g)	—	(h) Y.T., N.W.T.	(i) Y.T., N.W.T.
465(1)(h)	537(1)(f)	(i) "magistrate"	(i) "magistrate" [rep. R.S. 1985, c. 27, (1st Supp.), s. 103(2)]
465(1)(i)	537(1)(g)	483	553
465(1)(j)	537(1)(h)	484	554
465(1)(k)	537(1)(i)	484(1)	554(1)
465(2)–(4)	537(2)–(4) [rep. 1991, c. 43, s. 9, Sch. item 3(2)]	484(2)	554(2) [rep. R.S. 1985, c. 27 (1st Supp.), s. 105)]
466	538		
467	539		
468	540		
469	541		

R.S.C. 1970, c. C-34	R.S.C. 1985, c. C-46
484(3)	554(3) [rep. R.S. 1985, c. 27 (1st Supp.), s. 105)]
484(4)	554(4) [rep. R.S. 1985, c. 27 (1st Supp.), s. 105)]
485	555
486	556
487	557
488	558
489	559
490	560
490(1)	560(1)
490(2)	560(2)
490(3)	560(3)
490(4)	560(4)
490(5)	560(5) [rep. R.S. 1985, c. 27 (1st Supp.), s. 109(2)]
491	561
492	562
493	563
494	564 [rep. R.S. 1985, c. 27 (1st Supp.), s. 110]
495	565
496	566
497	567
498	568
499	569 [rep. R.S. 1985, c. 27 (1st Supp.), s. 111]
500	570
501	571
502	572
503	573 [rep. R.S. 1985, c. 27 (1st Supp.), s. 113]
Part XVII	Part XX
504	574
505	575 [rep. R.S. 1985, c. 27 (1st Supp.), s. 113]
506	576
507	577
507.1	578
508	579
509	580
510	581
511	582
512	583
513	584
514	585
515	586
516	587
517	588
518	589
519	590
520	591
521	592
522	593
523–525	594–596 [rep. R.S. 1985, c. 27 (1st Supp.), s. 120]
526	597
526.1	598
527	599
527(1)	599(1)
527(1.1)	599(2) [rep. R.S. 1985, c. 1 (4th Supp.), s. 16]
527(2)	599(3)
527(3)	599(4)
527(4)	599(5)
528	600
529	601

R.S.C. 1970, c. C-34	R.S.C. 1985, c. C-46
530	602 [rep. R.S. 1985, c. 27 (1st Supp.), s. 124]
531	603
532	604 [rep. 1997, c. 18, s. 69]
533	605
533.1	625.1 [en. R.S. 1985, c. 27 (1st Supp.), s. 127]
534	606
535	607
535(6)	607(6)
536	608
537	609
538	610
539	611
540	612
541	613
542–547	614–619 [rep. 1991, c. 43, s. 3]
549	621
550	622
551	623
552	624
553	625
553.1	625.1
554	626
555	627 [rep. R.S. 1985, c. 2 (1st Supp.), ss. 1 and 3]
556	—
557	628 [rep. R.S. 1985, c. 27 (1st Supp.), s. 129]
558	629
559	630
560	631
561	632
562	633

R.S.C. 1970, c. C-34	R.S.C. 1985, c. C-46
563	634
564 [rep. 1977–78, c. 36, s. 4]	635 [rep. R.S. 1985, c. 2 (1st Supp.), s. 2]
—	635 [en. 1992, c. 41, s. 2]
565	636 [rep. 1992, c. 41, s. 2]
566	637 [rep. 1992, c. 41, s. 2]
567	638
568	639
569	640
570	641
571	642
572	643
573	644
574	645
575	646
576	647
576.1	648
576.2	649
577	650
578	651
579	652
580	653
581	654
582	655
583	656
584	657
584.1	657.1 [en. R.S. 1985, c. 23 (4th Supp.), s. 3]
585	658
586	659 [rep. R.S. 1985, c. 19 (3rd Supp.), s. 15]
—	659 [en. 1993, c. 45, s. 9]
587	660

R.S.C. 1970, c. C-34	R.S.C. 1985, c. C-46
588	661
589	662
590	663
591	664
592	665 [rep. 1995, c. 22, s. 3]
593	666
594	667
594(3.1)	667(4)
594(4)	667(5)
595	668 [rep. 1995, c. 22, s. 4]
596	669 [rep. 1995, c. 22, s. 4]
597	669.1 [en. R.S. 1985, c. 27 (1st Supp.), s. 137]
597.1	669.2 [en. R.S. 1985, c. 27 (1st Supp.), s. 137]
598	670
599	671
600	672
Part XVIII	Part XXI
601	673
601"sentence"	673 "sentence"
602	674
603	675
603(1.1)	675(2)
603(2)	675(3)
603(3)	675(4)
604	—
605	676
606	677
607	678
607.1	678.1 [en. R.S. 1985, c. 27 (1st Supp.), s. 140]
608	679
608.1	680
608.2	681 [rep. 1991, c. 43, s. 9, Sch., item 7]
609	682
610	683
610(5)	683(5)
611	684
612	685
613	686
614	687
615	688
616	689
616(1)	689(1)
617	690 [rep. 2002, c. 13, s. 70]
618	691
618(1)(b)	691(1)(b)
619	—
620	692
620(3)(b)	692(3)(b)
621	693
621(1)	693(1)
622	694
622.1	694.1 [en. R.S. 1985, c. 34 (3rd Supp.), s. 13]
622.2	694.2 [en. R.S. 1985, c. 34 (3rd Supp.), s. 13]
623	695
624	696
Part XIX	Part XXII
625	697
626	698
627	699
628	700
629	701
630	702
631	703

R.S.C. 1970, c. C-34	**R.S.C. 1985, c. C-46**
631.1	703.1 [en. R.S. 1985, c. 27 (1st Supp.), s. 149]
631.2	703.2 [en. R.S. 1985, c. 27 (1st Supp.), s. 149]
632	704
633	705
634	706
635	707
636	708
637	709
638	710
639	711
640	712
640(1)	712(1)
640(2)	712(2)
640(3)	712(3) [rep. R.S. 1985, c. 27 (1st Supp.), s. 153]
641	713
642	714
643	715
643.1	715.1 [en. R.S. 1985, c. 19 (3rd Supp.), s. 16]
Part XX	Part XXIII

(Note: Part XXIII, R.S.C. 1985, c. 46 replaced by S.C. 1995, c. 22. See the end of this Table for a Table of Equivalent Sections.)

R.S.C. 1970, c. C-34	**R.S.C. 1985, c. C-46**
644	716
645	717
646	718
646.1	718.1 [en. R.S. 1985, c. 27 (1st Supp.), s. 156]
647	719
648	720
649	721
650	722
651	723
652	724
653	725
654	726
655	727 [rep. R.S. 1985, c. 27 (1st Supp.), s. 160]
656	728
657	729
658	730
659	731
659(1)	731(1)
659(2)	731(2)
659(3)	731(3)
659(4)	731(4)
659(5)	731(5)
659(6)	731(6) [rep. 1992, c. 20, s. 200(1)]
659(6.1)	731(7) [rep. 1992, c. 20, s. 200(1)]
659(7)	731(8)
—	731.1 [en. 1992, c. 20, s. 201]
660	732
660.1	733
661	734
662	735
662(1.1)	735(1.1)
662(1.2)	735(1.2)
662(1.3)	735(1.3)
662(1.4)	735(1.4)
662(2)	735(2)
662.1	736
663	737
664	738
665	739
666	740

R.S.C. 1970, c. C-34	R.S.C. 1985, c. C-46
667	741 [rep. R.S. 1985, c. 27 (1st Supp.), s. 164]
668	741.1 [rep. R.S. 1985, c. 24 (2nd Supp.), s. 47]
—	741.2 [en. 1992, c. 20, s. 203]
669	742
—	742.1 [en. 1992, c. 11, s. 16]
670	743
—	743.1 [en. 1992, c. 11, s. 16]
671	744
—	744.1 [en. 1992, c. 11, s. 16]
672	745
672(6)(a)	745(6)
672(6)(a)(i)	745(6)(e)
672(6)(a)(ii)	745(6)(c)
672(6)(a)(iii)	745(6)(d)
672(6)(a)(iv)	—
672(6)(a)(v)	745(6)(a)
672(6)(a)(vi)	745(6)(b)
672(6)(b)	745(6)(f) part
672(6)(c)	745(6)(f) part
673	746
674	747
675–681	—
682	748
682(3.1)	748(4)
682(3.2)	748(5)
682(4)	748(6)
683	749
685	750
686	751

R.S.C. 1970, c. C-34	R.S.C. 1985, c. C-46
Part XXI	Part XXIV
687	752
688	753
689	754
690	755
691 [rep. 1997, c. 17, s. 5]	756
692	757
693	758
694	759
695	760
695.1	761
Part XXII	Part XXV
696	762
697	763
698	764
699	765
700	766
701	767
701.1	767.1 [en. R.S. 1985, c. 27 (1st Supp.), s. 167]
702	768
703	769
704	770
705	771
706	772
707	773
Part XXIII	Part XXVI
708	774
709	775
710	776
711	777
712	778
713	779
714	780
715	781
716	782
717	783
718	—

R.S.C. 1970, c. C-34	R.S.C. 1985, c. C-46	R.S.C. 1970, c. C-34	R.S.C. 1985, c. C-46
719	784	733	798
Part XXIV	Part XXVII	734	799
720	785	735	800
721	786	736	801
722	787	736(1)	801(1)
722(1)	787(1)	736(2)	801(2)
722(2)	787(2)	736(3)	801(3)
722(3)–(11)	787(3)–(11) [rep. R.S. 1985, c. 27 (1st Supp.), s. 171]	736(4)	801(4) [rep. R.S. 1985, c. 27 (1st Supp.), s. 177(2)]
723	788	736(5)	801(5) [rep. R.S. 1985, c. 27 (1st Supp.), s. 177(2)
724	789		
725	790		
725(1)	790(1)	737	802
725(2)	790(2)	738	803
725(3)	790(3) [rep. R.S. 1985, c. 27 (1st Supp.), s. 172]	738(2)	—
		738(3)	803(2)
		738(3.1)	803(3)
725(4)	790(4) [rep. R.S. 1985, c. 27 (1st Supp.), s. 172]	738(4)	803(4)
		738(5)–(8)	803(5)–(8) [rep. 1991, c. 43, s. 9, Sch., item 11]
725(5)	—		
726	791 [rep. R.S. 1985, c. 27 (1st Supp.), s. 173]	739	804
		740	805 [rep. R.S. 1985, c. 27 (1st Supp.), s. 179]
727	—		
728	792 [rep. 1985, c. 27 (1st Supp.), s. 174]	741	806
		742	807
		743	808
729	793 [rep. 1985, c. 27 (1st Supp.), s. 175]	744	809
		745	810
		746	811
730	794	747	812
731	795		
732	796 [rep. 1985, c. 27 (1st Supp.), s. 176]	747"appeal court"	812 "appeal court"
		747(a)	812(f)
732.1	797 [rep. 1985, c. 27 (1st Supp.), s. 176]	747(b)	812(g)
		747(c)	812(c)
		747(d)	812(b)

R.S.C. 1970, c. C-34	R.S.C. 1985, c. C-46
747(e)	812(a)
747(f)	812(d)
747(g)	—
747(h)	812(e) [rep. 1992, c. 51, s. 43(2)]
747(i)	812(h)
748	813
749	814
750	815
751	—
752	816
752.1	817
752.2	818
752.3	819
753	820
754	821
755	822
755.1	823 [rep. 1991, c. 43, s. 9, Sch., item 14]
756	824
757	825
758	826
759	827
760	828
761	829
762	830
763	831
764	832
765	833
766	834
767	835
768	836
769	837
770	838
771	839
772	840
—	841–848 [en. 2002, c. 13, s. 84]

R.S.C. 1970, c. C-34	R.S.C. 1985, c. C-46
773	846 [en. 2002, c. 13, s. 84]
773(3)	841(3) [en. 2002, c. 13, s. 84]
Part XXV	Part XXVIII
Forms 1–2	Forms 1–2
Form 3	Form 3 [rep. R.S. 1985, c. 27 (1st Supp.), s. 184(2)]
Form 4	Form 4
Form 5	Form 5
Form 5.1	Form 5.1 [en. R.S. 1985, c. 27 (1st Supp.), s. 184(3)]
Form 5.2	Form 5.2 [en. R.S. 1985, c. 27 (1st Supp.), s. 184(3)]
Form 5.3	Form 5.3 [en. R.S. 1985, c. 42 (4th Supp.), s. 6]
Form 6	Form 6
Form 7	Form 7
Form 8	Form 8
Form 8.1	Form 9
Form 8.2	Form 10
Form 8.3	Form 11
Form 9	Form 12
Form 9.1	Form 13
Form 9.2	Form 14
Form 10	Form 15
Form 11	Form 16
Form 12	Form 17
Form 13	Form 18
Form 14	Form 19
Form 15	—
Form 16	Form 20
Form 17	—

R.S.C. 1970, c. C-34	R.S.C. 1985, c. C-46	R.S.C. 1970, c. C-34	R.S.C. 1985, c. C-46
Form 18	Form 21	Form 33	Form 37
Form 19	Form 22	Form 34	Form 38
Form 20	Form 23	Form 35	Form 39
Form 21	Form 24	Form 36	Form 40
Form 22	Form 25	Form 37	Form 41
Form 23	Form 26	Form 38	Form 42
Form 24	Form 27	Form 39	Form 43
Form 25	Form 28	Forms 40–41	—
Form 25.1	Form 29	Form 42	Form 44
Form 26	Form 30	Form 43	Form 45
Form 27	Form 31	Form 44	Form 46
Form 28	Form 32	Form 45	Form 47 [en. R.S. 1985, c. 42 (4th Supp.), s.8]
Form 29	Form 33		
Form 30	Form 34		
Form 31	Form 35		
Form 32	Form 36	774	—

Part III: Firearms and Other Weapons

Table of Equivalent Sections

The Firearms Act, S.C. 1995, c. 39 repeals and replaces Part III of the Criminal Code. What follows is a table of equivalent sections and subsections which identify, insofar as possible, the substantive correspondence between sections and subsections of the new and old Part III. Note that certain of the provisions of the old Part III also correspond to the provisions of the Firearms Act itself.

Part III S.C. 1995, c. 39	Part III R.S.C. 1985, c. C-46 (prior to enactment of S.C. 1995, c. 39)	Part III S.C. 1995, c. 39	Part III R.S.C. 1985, c. C-46 (prior to enactment of S.C. 1995, c. 39)
84(1)	84(1)	88	87
84(2)	84(1.1)	89	88
84(3)	84(2)	90	89
84(3.1)	—	91(1)	—
84(4)	—	91(2), (3)	90(1); 91(1)
85	85	91(4)(a)	90(3.1); 91(4)(b)
86(1)	86(2)		
86(2)	86(3)	91(4)(b)	91(4)(c)
86(3)	86(2), (3)	91(5)	—
87	86(1)	92(1)	—

Part III S.C. 1995, c. 39	**Part III R.S.C. 1985, c. C-46 (prior to enactment of S.C. 1995, c. 39)**
92(2), (3)	91(1)
92(4)	91(4)
92(5), (6)	—
93	91(2)
94(1), (2)	90(2); 91(3)
94(3)	—
94(4)	90(4); 91(5)
94(5)	—
95	—
96	—
97	—
98	—
99	93; 94; 95; 96; 97
100	—
101	93(1); 94; 95; 96; 97
102	95.1
103	95(1)
104	95(1); 96(3); 97(3)
105(1)	104(1), (2); 105(2), (8)
105(2)	104(5); 105(8)
106	105(2); 105(8)
107	—
108	104(3), (3.1), (4), (5)
109	100(1), (1.1), (1.3)
110	100(2), (2.1), (3)
111(1)	100(4)
111(2)	100(5)
111(3)	100(6)
111(4)	100(9)
111(5)	100(7)
111(7)	—
111(8)–(10)	100(10)
111(11)	100(11)
112	—
113	100(1.1), (1.2)
114	—
115	100(13)
116	100(7.1)
117	—
117.01	100(12); 103(10)
117.011	—
117.012	—
117.02	101
117.03	102
117.04	103(1), (2), (3), (3.1)
117.05(1)	103(4)
117.05(2)	103(4.1)
117.05(3)	103(5)
117.05(4)	103(6)
117.05(5)	—
117.05(6)	—
117.05(7)-(9)	103(8)
117.06(1)	103(7)
117.06(2)	103(7.1)
117.07	92; 98(1), (3)
117.08	92; 98(2)
117.09(1), (2)	91(6); 99
117.09(3)	–
117.09(4), (5), (6), (7)	92(2); 98(3)
117.1	–
117.11	115(1)
117.12	115(2)

Part III S.C. 1995, c. 39	Part III R.S.C. 1985, c. C-46 (prior to enactment of S.C. 1995, c. 39)	Part III S.C. 1995, c. 39	Part III R.S.C. 1985, c. C-46 (prior to enactment of S.C. 1995, c. 39)
117.13	–	117.15	116; 84(1)"prohibited weapon"; "restrictred weapon"
117.14	91.1		

Part XXIII: Sentencing

Table of Equivalent Sections

Bill C-41 (1995, c. 22) repealed and replaced the whole of Part XXIII of the Criminal Code, R.S.C. 1985, c. C-46. The substance of many of the sections of Part XXIII as it existed prior to the proclamation of Bill C-41 (1995, c. 22) was carried over into the new Part XXIII, but because many new sections were introduced, a complete renumbering of sections was required. What follows is a table of equivalent sections and subsections, which identifies, insofar as possible, the substantive correspondence between sections and subsections, of the "new" and "old" Part XXIII.

While the amendments flowing from 1995, c. 22 have now been fully integrated into the infobases of the Criminal Law Partner, the Table of Equivalent Sections and Subsections in Part XXIII of the Code is reproduced here for ease of reference:

Part XXIII S.C. 1995, c. 22 "New" section	Part XXIII R.S.C. 1985, c. C-46 Prior equivalent section/subsection	Part XXIII S.C. 1995, c. 22 "New" section	Part XXIII R.S.C. 1985, c. C-46 Prior equivalent section/subsection
716	716	718.3(4)	717(4)
717	—	718.3(5)(not in force at date of publication)	—
717.1	—		
717.2	—		
717.3	—	719	721
717.4	—	720	—
718	—	721	735
718.1	—	721(1)	735(1)
718.2	—	721(2)	—
718.3	717	721(3)	—
718.3(1)	717(1)	721(4)	—
718.3(2)	717(2)	722	735
718.3(3)	717(3)	722(1)	735(1.1)

Part XXIII S.C. 1995, c. 22 "New" section	Part XXIII R.S.C. 1985, c. C-46 Prior equivalent section/subsection
722(2)	735(1.2)
722(3)	735(1.3)
722(4)	735(1.4)
722.1	735(2)
723	—
724	—
725	—
726	—
726.1	—
726.2	—
727	—
728	—
729	—
730	736
731	737
731(1)(a)	737(1)(a)
731(2)	—
731.1	—
732	737
732(1)	737(1)(c)
732(2)	—
732(3)	—
732.1	737
732.1(1)	—
732.1(2)(a)	737(2)
732.1(2)(b)	737(2)
732.1(2)(c)	— [cf. 737(2)(f)]
732.1(3)(a)	737(2)(a)
732.1(3)(b)	737(2)(f)
732.1(3)(c)(i)	737(2)(c)
732.1(3)(c)(ii)	—
732.1(3)(d)	737(2)(d)
732.1(3)(e)	737(2)(b)
732.1(3)(f)	—
732.1(3)(g)	—

Part XXIII S.C. 1995, c. 22 "New" section	Part XXIII R.S.C. 1985, c. C-46 Prior equivalent section/subsection
732.1(3)(h)	737(2)(h)
732.1(4)	737(3)
732.1(5)(a)(i)	737(4)(b)
732.1(5)(a)(ii)	—
732.1(5)(a)(iii)	—
732.1(5)(b)	—
732.2	738
732.2(1)(a)	738(1)(a)
732.2(1)(b)	738(1)(b)
732.3(1)(c)	—
732.2(2)(a)	738(2)(a)
732.2(2)(b)	738(2)(b)
732.2(3)	738(3)
732.2(4)	—
732.2(5)	738(4)
732.2(6)	738(5)
733	739
733(1)(a) [probation officer]	739(1) [prosecutor]
733(1)(b)	739(1)(b)
733(2)	739(2)
733.1	740
733.1(1)(a)	—
733.1(1)(b)	740(1)
733.1(2)	740(2)
734	718
734(1) [offence]	718(1) [indictable offence, five years or less]
734(2)	—
734(3)	—
734(4)	—
734(5)	—
734(6)	— [cf. 725(3); 726(3)]
734(7)	—

Part XXIII S.C. 1995, c. 22 "New" section	Part XXIII R.S.C. 1985, c. C-46 Prior equivalent section/subsection	Part XXIII S.C. 1995, c. 22 "New" section	Part XXIII R.S.C. 1985, c. C-46 Prior equivalent section/subsection
734.1	—	735	719
734.2	—	735(1)	719
734.3	— [cf. 718(11)]	735(2) [civil court with jurisdiction]	720 [superior court]
734.4	723	736	718.1
734.5	—	737	727.9
734.6	724	738	725
734.6(1)(a) [default of payment of fine]	724(1) [fine]	738(1)(a)	725(1)
		738(1)(b)	—
734.6(1)(b) [forfeiture not paid; any other method provided by law]	724(1) [forfeiture; civil proceedings]	738(1)(c)	—
		738(2)	—
		739	726
		739(a)	726(1)
734.6(1)(c) [A.G. of province]	724(1) [Her Majesty]	739(b)	—
		740	—
		741	726
734.6(1)(d) [A.G. of Canada]	724(1) [Her Majesty]	741(1) [civil court with jurisdiction]	726(2) [superior court]
734.6(1) [filing of order in civil court with jurisdiction]	—	741(2)	726(3); 725(3)
		741.1	—
		741.2	—
		742	—
734.6(2)	—	742.1	—
734.7	718	742.2	—
734.7(1)(a)	718(7)	742.3	—
734.7(1)(b)	—	742.4	—
734.7(2)	718(8)	742.5	—
734.7(3)	—	742.6	—
734.7(4)	—	742.7	—
734.8	722	743	730
734.8(1)	722(5)	743.1	731
734.8(2)	722(1)	743.1(1)	731(1)
734.8(3)	722(2)	743.1(2)	731(2)
734.8(4)	722(3)	743.1(3)	731(3)
734.8(5)	722(4)	743.1(4)	731(4)

Part XXIII S.C. 1995, c. 22 "New" section	Part XXIII R.S.C. 1985, c. C-46 Prior equivalent section/subsection
743.1(5)	731(5)
743.1(6)	731(8)
743.2	731.1
743.3	732(1)
743.4	733
743.5	741.1
743.6	741.2
743.6(1)	741.2
743.6(2)	—
744	734
745	742
745(a)	742(a)
745(b)	742(a.1)
745(c)	742(b)
745(d)	742(c)
745.1	742.1
745.2	743
745.3	743.1
745.4	744
745.5	744.1
745.6	745
745.6(2)(a)	745(2)
745.6(2)(b)	745(2)
745.6(2)(c)	745(2)
745.6(2)(d)	—
745.6(2)(e)	745(2)
745.6(3)	—
745.6(4)	745(3)
745.6(5)	745(4)
745.6(6)	745(5)
745.6(7)	745(6)
745.6(8)	745(7)
746	746
746.1	747
746.1(1)	747(1)
746.1(2)	747(2)
746.1(3)	747(2.1)
(Note: ss. 747 to 747.8 repealed before coming into force, S.C. 2005, c. 22, s. 39)	
748	749
748.1	750
749	751
750	748
750(1) [two years or more]	748(1) [exceeding five years]
750(2)	748(2)
750(3)	748(3)
750(4)	748(4)
750(5)	748(5)
750(6)	748(6)
751	728
751.1	729

CRIMINAL CODE

An Act respecting the criminal law

Revised Statutes of Canada, 1985

Chapter C-46

CRIMINAL CODE

An Act respecting the criminal law

Revised Statutes of Canada, 1985
Chapter C–46
and Amendments

An Act respecting the criminal law

R.S.C. 1985, c. C-46, as am. R.S.C. 1985, c. 2 (1st Supp.), ss. 1–3; R.S.C. 1985, c. 11 (1st Supp.), s. 2; R.S.C. 1985, c. 27 (1st Supp.), ss. 1–187, 203 [s. 36 as it enacts s. 258(1)(c)(i), 258(1)(g)(iii)(A) of the *Criminal Code* repealed before coming into force 2008, c. 20, s. 3.]; R.S.C. 1985, c. 31 (1st Supp.), s. 61; R.S.C. 1985, c. 47 (1st Supp.), s. 1; R.S.C. 1985, c. 51 (1st Supp.), s. 1; R.S.C. 1985, c. 52 (1st Supp.), ss. 1–3; R.S.C. 1985, c. 1 (2nd Supp.), s. 213; R.S.C. 1985, c. 24 (2nd Supp.), ss. 45–47; R.S.C. 1985, c. 27 (2nd Supp.), s. 10; R.S.C. 1985, c. 35 (2nd Supp.), s. 34; R.S.C. 1985, c. 10 (3rd Supp.), ss. 1, 2; R.S.C. 1985, c. 19 (3rd Supp.), ss. 1–16; R.S.C. 1985, c. 30 (3rd Supp.), ss. 1, 2; R.S.C. 1985, c. 34 (3rd Supp.), ss. 9–13; R.S.C. 1985, c. 1 (4th Supp.), ss. 13–18, 45; R.S.C. 1985, c. 23 (4th Supp.), ss. 1–8; R.S.C. 1985, c. 29 (4th Supp.), s. 17; R.S.C. 1985, c. 30 (4th Supp.), s. 45; R.S.C. 1985, c. 31 (4th Supp.), ss. 94–97; R.S.C. 1985, c. 32 (4th Supp.), ss. 55–62; R.S.C. 1985, c. 40 (4th Supp.), s. 2; R.S.C. 1985, c. 42 (4th Supp.), ss. 1–8; R.S.C. 1985, c. 50 (4th Supp.), s. 1; S.C. 1989, c. 2, s. 1; 1990, c. 15, s. 1; 1990, c. 16, ss. 2–7; 1990, c. 17, ss. 7–15; 1990, c. 44, s. 15; 1991, c. 1, s. 28; 1991, c. 4, ss. 1, 2; 1991, c. 28, ss. 6–12; 1991, c. 40, ss. 1–41; 1991, c. 43, ss. 1–10 [s. 4 as it enacts ss. 672.64–672.66 of the *Criminal Code*, 10(8) not in force at date of publication. Repealed 2005, c. 22, ss. 24, 43(3).]; 1992, c. 1, s. 58; 1992, c. 11, ss. 14–18; 1992, c. 20, ss. 199–204, 215, 216, 228, 229; 1992, c. 21, s. 9; 1992, c. 22, s. 12; 1992, c. 27, s. 90; 1992, c. 38; 1992, c. 41; 1992, c. 47, ss. 68–72 [Amended 1994, c. 44, s. 94; 1996, c. 7, s. 38.]; 1992, c. 51, ss. 32–43, 67; 1993, c. 7; 1993, c. 25, ss. 93–96; 1993, c. 28, s. 78 (Sched. III, items 25–37 [items 25(2), 27–29, 31, 32, 34, 35.1–36 repealed 1999, c. 3, s. 12 (Sched., items 5–9).]); 1993, c. 34, s. 59(1); 1993, c. 37; 1993, c. 40; 1993, c. 45; 1993, c. 46; 1994, c. 12, s. 1; 1994, c. 13, s. 7; 1994, c. 38, ss. 14, 25; 1994, c. 44, ss. 1–84; 1995, c. 5, s. 25(1)(g); 1995, c. 19, ss. 37–41; 1995, c. 22, ss. 1–12, 14, 15, 19–24 [s. 6 as it enacts ss. 718.3(5), 747–747.8 of the *Criminal Code* not in force at date of publication; s. 718.3(5) repealed 1999, c. 5, s. 30; ss. 747–747.8 repealed 2005, c. 22, s. 39.] [s. 7(2) conditions not yet satisfied. Repealed 2005, c. 22, s. 44.]; 1995, c. 27, ss. 1, 3; 1995, c. 29, ss. 39, 40; 1995, c. 32, s. 1; 1995, c. 39, ss. 138–157, 188–190; 1995, c. 42, ss. 73–78, 86, 87; 1996, c. 8, s. 32; 1996, c. 16, s. 60; 1996, c. 19, ss. 65–76, 93.3; 1996, c. 31, ss. 68–72; 1996, c. 34, ss. 1–8 [ss. 1, 2(1), 3–5 repealed before coming into force 2008, c. 20, s. 3.]; 1997, c. 9, s. 124 [Conditions not yet satisfied. Repealed 2005, c. 22, s. 62.]; 1997, c. 16, ss. 1–7; 1997, c. 17, ss. 1–10; 1997, c. 18, ss. 2–115, 139.1, 140, 141 [ss. 106, 107 repealed before coming into force 2008, c. 20, s. 3.]; 1997, c. 23, ss. 1–20, 26, 27; 1997, c. 30, ss. 1–3; 1997, c. 39, ss. 1–3; 1998, c. 7, ss. 2, 3; 1998, c. 9, ss. 2–8; 1998, c. 15, s. 20; 1998, c. 30, ss. 14, 16; 1998, c. 34, ss. 8, 9, 11; 1998, c. 35, ss. 119–121; 1998, c. 37, ss. 15–24; 1999, c. 2, s. 47; 1999, c. 3, ss. 25–58; 1999, c. 5, ss. 1–47, 51, 52; 1999, c. 17, s. 120; 1999, c. 18, ss. 92–95; 1999, c. 25 [s. 29(2) conditions not yet satisfied. Repealed 2005, c. 22, s. 46.]; 1999, c. 28, ss. 155, 156; 1999, c. 31, ss. 67–69; 1999, c. 32, ss. 1–6; 1999, c. 33, s. 346; 1999, c. 35, s. 11; 2000, c. 1, s. 9; 2000, c. 2; 2000, c. 10, ss. 13–24; 2000, c. 12, ss. 91–95; 2000, c. 17, s. 89; 2000, c. 24, ss. 42–46; s. 43 am. 2001, c. 34, s. 36; 2000, c. 25; 2001, c. 26, s. 294; 2001, c. 27, ss. 244–247 [s. 245 not in force at date of publication. Repealed 2004, c. 15, s. 110.] [s. 246 repealed 2001, c. 32, s. 81(3)(d).]; 2001, c. 32, ss. 1–46.1, 81(2), 82 [ss. 1(1), (6), 3, 9(1), 12(5), 31(3), 44, 82(2), (3): (Fr.).] [s. 81(2) conditions not yet satisfied. Repealed 2004, c. 15, s. 109.] [s. 82(3) conditions not yet satisfied.]; 2001, c. 37; 2001, c. 41, ss. 2–23, 31–34, 80, 126, 130(7.1), 133(1), (2), (5), (8)–(11), (13)–(19), 143; 2002, c. 1, ss. 175–186; 2002, c. 7, ss. 137–150; 2002, c. 13, ss. 2–86 [ss. 5(1), 16, 86: (Fr.).]; 2002, c. 22, ss. 324–327, 409(2)(b) [s. 326 repealed 2002, c. 22, s. 409(2)(a); s. 327 repealed 2002, c. 22, s. 409(6).]; 2003, c. 8, ss. 2–8 [s. 8 not in force at date of publication. Repealed 2012, c. 1, s. 47.]; 2003, c. 21; 2003, c. 22, s. 224(z.23); 2004, c. 3; 2004, c. 10, ss. 20, 21; 2004, c. 12, ss. 1–7, 8 (Fr.), 9–17; 2004, c. 14; 2004, c. 15, ss. 32, 108; 2005, c. 10, ss. 18–25, 34(1)(f); 2005, c. 22, ss. 1–8, 9 (Fr.), 10–26, 27(1) (Fr.), (2), 28–34, 35 (Fr.), 36–41, 42 (Fr.), 64(2); 2005, c. 25, ss. 1, 2 (Fr.), 3–13, 30.1 [ss. 1(5.1), (6.1), 7, 30.1 repealed 2007, c. 22, ss. 2, 4, 6; s. 4 amended 2007, c. 22, s. 3.]; 2005, c. 32, ss. 1–7, 8(1) (Fr.), (2)–(5), 9–25; 2005, c. 38, ss. 58, 138(e), 140(b); 2005, c. 40, ss. 1–3, 7; 2005, c. 43, ss. 1–7, 8(3), 9(2); 2005, c. 44, ss. 1, 2 (Fr.), 3–12; 2006, c. 9, s. 246; 2006, c. 14, ss. 1, 2, 3(1) (Fr.), (2), (3), 4–7; 2007, c. 5, ss. 11–20, 21(1) (Fr.), (2), 22–29, 30(1) (Fr.), (2), (3), 31; 2007, c. 9; 2007, c. 12; 2007, c. 13; 2007, c. 20; 2007, c. 22, ss. 7–26, 47; 2007, c. 28; 2008, c. 6, ss. 2–23, 24(1), (2), (3) (Fr.), (4)–(9), 25–44, 45(1), (2), (3) (Fr.), 46, 47, 48(1), (2) (Fr.), 49–54, 61, 62 [s. 35 amended 2008, c. 6, s. 63(2).]; 2008, c. 12; 2008, c. 18, ss. 1–26, 27 (Fr.), 28–45.1 [s. 7 amended 2008, c. 18, s. 45.2.]; 2009, c. 2, s. 442; 2009, c. 22; 2009, c. 28; 2009, c. 29; 2010, c. 3; 2010, c. 14, ss. 2–11; 2010, c. 17, ss. 2–27; 2010, c. 19; 2010, c. 20; 2011, c. 2, ss. 2–5; 2011, c. 5, ss. 2–5; 2011, c. 6; 2011, c. 7, ss. 2–7, 8(1) (Fr.) (2), (3), 9–13; 2011, c. 16, ss. 2, 3 (Fr.), 4–16; 2012, c. 1, ss. 10–21, 22(1), (2), (3) (Fr.), 23–38, 141(1) (Fr.), (2), (3), (4) (Fr.), 142–147, 160(c), 200, 201 (Fr.); 2012, c. 6, ss. 2–8; 2012, c. 9; 2012, c. 15; 2012, c. 19, s. 371; 2012, c. 29; 2013, c. 8; 2013, c. 9, ss. 2, 3(1) (Fr.), (2), 4–16; 2013, c. 11; 2013, c. 13; 2013, c. 15; 2013, c. 19; 2013, c. 24, s. 117 (Fr.); 2013, c. 32; 2013, c. 40, s. 174; 2014, c. 6, ss. 2–5, 6(1) (Fr.), (2), 7(1)–(3), (4) (Fr.), (5), 8–10, 11(1) (Fr.), (2), 12–20; 2014, c. 9; 2014, c. 10; 2014, c. 17, ss. 1–16; 2014, c. 20, s. 366(1); 2014, c. 21, ss. 1–4; 2014, c. 23; 2014, c. 25, ss. 2–33, 46(2)–(7), 48(5), (6); 2014, c. 31, ss. 2–13, 14(1) (Fr.), (2), 15–26; 2014, c. 32, s. 59; 2014, c. 39, s. 171; 2015, c. 1; 2015, c. 3, ss. 44–51, 52 (Fr.), 53, 54 (Fr.), 55–59; 2015, c. 13, ss. 3–36 [ss. 5(1), 18(3) repealed 2014, c. 25, s. 48(3), (8).]; 2015, c. 16, ss. 1, 2 (Fr.), 3, 4 [s. 3 not in force at date of publication.] [Amended 2019, c. 25, s. 386.]; 2015, c. 20, ss. 15–27, 34(2)–(4), 35, 38 [s. 27(2) repealed 2015, c. 20, s. 37(3).]; 2015, c. 23, ss. 2–19, 30, 31, 33 [ss. 30, 31 not in force at date of publication.]; 2015, c. 27, ss. 18–34; 2015, c. 29, ss. 6–12; 2015, c. 34; 2016, c. 3, ss. 1–6; 2017, c. 7, ss. 54, 55 (Fr.), 56, 57 (Fr.), 58, 59(1), (2) (Fr.), 60(1), (2) (Fr.), 61, 62 (Fr.), 63 (Fr.), 64–68, 69 (Fr.); 2017, c. 13, ss. 3, 4; 2017, c. 22, s. 3; 2017, c. 23; 2017, c. 27, ss. 61, 62 [Not in force at date of publication.]; 2017, c. 33, s. 255; 2018, c. 11, ss. 27–29; 2018, c. 12, ss. 114, 403–405; 2018, c. 16, ss. 190, 207–225 [s. 190 conditions not yet satisfied.]; 2018, c. 21, ss. 1–9, 12–23, 24 (Fr.), 25–31; 2018, c. 26, s. 23; 2018, c. 27, ss. 28, 686; 2018, c. 29, ss. 1–8, 9(1)–(8), (9) (Fr.), (10), (11) (Fr.), (12), 10(1)–(2.1), (3) (Fr.), (4)–(6), 11–18, 19(1)–(2.1), (3) (Fr.), 20–68, 69(1), (2) (Fr.), 70(1), (2) (Fr.), 71, 72; 2019, c. 9, ss. 16–18 [ss. 16, 18 not in force at date of publication.]; 2019, c. 11, s. 2; 2019, c. 13, ss. 140–145; 146(1), (2) (Fr.), (3), 147–154; 2019, c. 14, s. 58.3; 2019, c. 15, s. 47 [Not in force at date of publication.]; 2019, c. 16, ss. 122–124; 2019, c. 17; 2019, c. 25, ss. 1–33, 34(1) (Fr.), (2), 35–51, 52(1) (Fr.), (2), 53–238, 239(1), (2) (Fr.), (3)–(5), (6) (Fr.), 240–244, 245(1), (2) (Fr.), (3) (Fr.), (4), 246–253, 254(1)–(3), (4) (Fr.), (5), 255(1), (2) (Fr.), (3)–(5), 256–264, 265(1), (2) (Fr.), (3), 266–285, 286(1)–(3), (4) (Fr.), 287, 288, 289(Fr.), 290–317.1, 318(1), (2) (Fr.), (3), 319(1), (2) (Fr.), (3) (Fr.), (4), 320–353, 402(11)(b)–(e), (14), 403(10.1), 404(2) [ss. 1(3), 5, 24, 30–32, 47, 91, 157(2), 182, 187(1), 209–215, 217–224, 225(1), (3)–(7), 226–236, 245(4), 248, 249, 254(2), (3), 255(3), 260(2), 264, 266, 276, 279, 280, 281(3), (4), 287, 288, 295–297, 300, 303, 304, 308–313, 323–328, 334(3), 335, 336(2), 337, 345(2), 348(3), 349(3) to come into force December 18, 2019.] [s. 89 repealed before coming into force 2019, c. 25, ss. 402(4), (6), (9).] [s. 178 repealed before coming into force 2019, c. 25, s. 401(2).] [ss. 85–88 repealed before coming into force 2019, c. 25, s. 402(11)(a).] [ss. 38(2), 116(2), 158(2), 295 repealed before coming into force 2019, c. 25, s. 403(6), (11), (20), (25).]; 2019, c. 29, ss. 103, 121 (Fr.).

Short Title

1. Short title — This Act may be cited as the *Criminal Code*.

Interpretation (ss. 2–3)

2. Definitions — In this Act,

"Act" includes

(a) an Act of Parliament,

(b) an Act of the legislature of the former Province of Canada,

(c) an Act of the legislature of a province, and

(d) an Act or ordinance of the legislature of a province, territory or place in force at the time that province, territory or place became a province of Canada;

Proposed Addition — 2 "appearance notice"

"appearance notice" means a notice in Form 9 issued by a peace officer;

2019, c. 25, s. 1(3) [To come into force December 18, 2019.]

"associated personnel" means persons who are

(a) assigned by a government or an intergovernmental organization with the agreement of the competent organ of the United Nations,

(b) engaged by the Secretary-General of the United Nations, by a specialized agency of the United Nations or by the International Atomic Energy Agency, or

(c) deployed by a humanitarian non-governmental organization or agency under an agreement with the Secretary-General of the United Nations, by a specialized agency of the United Nations or by the International Atomic Energy Agency,

to carry out activities in support of the fulfilment of the mandate of a United Nations operation;

"Attorney General"

(a) with respect to proceedings to which this Act applies, means the Attorney General or Solicitor General of the province in which those proceedings are taken and includes his or her lawful deputy or, if those proceedings are referred to in subsection 2.3(1), the Attorney General of Canada or the Attorney General or Solicitor General of the province in which those proceedings are taken and includes the lawful deputy of any of them,

(b) means the Attorney General of Canada and includes his or her lawful deputy with respect to

(i) Yukon, the Northwest Territories and Nunavut, or

(ii) proceedings commenced at the instance of the Government of Canada and conducted by or on behalf of that Government in respect of an offence under any Act of Parliament — other than this Act or the *Canada Elections Act* — or any regulation made under such an Act, and

(c) means the Director of Public Prosecutions appointed under subsection 3(1) of the *Director of Public Prosecutions Act* with respect to proceedings in relation to an offence under the *Canada Elections Act*;

[Editor's Note: Section 137(1) of 2002, c. 7 purported to amend the definition of Attorney General by replacing subparagraph (b)(i) thereof, with the intent of replacing the words "the Yukon Territory" with the word "Yukon". By the time 2002, c. 7 received Royal Assent, however, the definition as a whole had been replaced by 2001, c. 41, s. 2, and no longer contained a subparagraph (b)(i). Accordingly, the amendment would appear to be null.]

"audioconference" means any means of telecommunication that allows the judge or justice and any individual to communicate orally in a proceeding;

"bank-note" includes any negotiable instrument

(a) issued by or on behalf of a person carrying on the business of banking in or out of Canada, and

(b) issued under the authority of Parliament or under the lawful authority of the government of a state other than Canada,

intended to be used as money or as the equivalent of money, immediately on issue or at some time subsequent thereto, and includes bank bills and bank post bills;

"bodily harm" means any hurt or injury to a person that interferes with the health or comfort of the person and that is more than merely transient or trifling in nature;

"Canadian Forces" means the armed forces of Her Majesty raised by Canada;

"cattle" means neat cattle or an animal of the bovine species by whatever technical or familiar name it is known, and includes any horse, mule, ass, pig, sheep or goat;

"clerk of the court" includes a person, by whatever name or title he may be designated, who from time to time performs the duties of a clerk of the court;

"common-law partner", in relation to an individual, means a person who is cohabiting with the individual in a conjugal relationship, having so cohabited for a period of at least one year;

"complainant" means the victim of an alleged offence;

"counsel" means a barrister or solicitor, in respect of the matters or things that barristers and solicitors, respectively, are authorized by the law of a province to do or perform in relation to legal proceedings;

"count" means a charge in an information or indictment;

"court of appeal" means, in all provinces, the Court of Appeal;

"court of criminal jurisdiction" means

(a) a court of general or quarter sessions of the peace, when presided over by a Superior Court judge,

(a.1) in the Province of Quebec, the Court of Quebec, the municipal court of Montreal and the municipal court of Quebec,

(b) a provincial court judge or judge acting under Part XIX, and

(c) in the Province of Ontario, the Ontario Court of Justice;

"criminal organization" has the same meaning as in subsection 467.1(1);

"criminal organization offence" means

(a) an offence under section 467.11, 467.111, 467.12 or 467.13, or a serious offence committed for the benefit of, at the direction of, or in association with, a criminal organization, or

(b) a conspiracy or an attempt to commit, being an accessory after the fact in relation to, or any counselling in relation to, an offence referred to in paragraph (*a*);

"day" means the period between six o'clock in the forenoon and nine o'clock in the afternoon of the same day;

"document of title to goods" includes a bought and sold note, bill of lading, warrant, certificate or order for the delivery or transfer of goods or any other valuable thing, and any other document used in the ordinary course of business as evidence of the possession or control of goods, authorizing or purporting to authorize, by endorsement or by delivery, the person in possession of the document to transfer or receive any goods thereby represented or therein mentioned or referred to;

"document of title to lands" includes any writing that is or contains evidence of the title, or any part of the title, to real property or to any interest in real property, and any notarial or registrar's copy thereof and any duplicate instrument, memorial, certificate or document authorized or required by any law in force in any part of Canada with respect to registration of titles that relates to title to real property or to any interest in real property;

"dwelling-house" means the whole or any part of a building or structure that is kept or occupied as a permanent or temporary residence, and includes

(a) a building within the curtilage of a dwelling-house that is connected to it by a doorway or by a covered and enclosed passage-way, and

(b) a unit that is designed to be mobile and to be used as a permanent or temporary residence and that is being used as such a residence;

"environment" means the components of the Earth and includes

(a) air, land and water,

(b) all layers of the atmosphere,

(c) all organic and inorganic matter and living organisms, and

(d) the interacting natural systems that include components referred to in paragraphs (a) to (c);

"every one", **"person"** and **"owner"**, and similar expressions, include Her Majesty and an organization;

"explosive substance" includes

(a) anything intended to be used to make an explosive substance,

(b) anything, or any part thereof, used or intended to be used, or adapted to cause, or to aid in causing an explosion in or with an explosive substance, and

(c) an incendiary grenade, fire bomb, molotov cocktail or other similar incendiary substance or device and a delaying mechanism or other thing intended for use in connection with such a substance or device;

"feeble-minded person" [Repealed 1991, c. 43, s. 9, Sched., item 1.]

"firearm" means a barrelled weapon from which any shot, bullet or other projectile can be discharged and that is capable of causing serious bodily injury or death to a person, and includes any frame or receiver of such a barrelled weapon and anything that can be adapted for use as a firearm;

"government or public facility" means a facility or conveyance, whether permanent or temporary, that is used or occupied in connection with their official duties by representatives of a state, members of a government, members of a legislature, members of the judiciary, or officials or employees of a state or of any other public authority or public entity, or by officials or employees of an intergovernmental organization;

"Her Majesty's Forces" means the naval, army and air forces of Her Majesty wherever raised, and includes the Canadian Forces;

"highway" means a road to which the public has the right of access, and includes bridges over which or tunnels through which a road passes;

"indictment" includes

(a) information or a count therein,

(b) a plea, replication or other pleading, and

(c) any record;

"internationally protected person" means

(a) a head of state, including any member of a collegial body that performs the functions of a head of state under the constitution of the state concerned, a head of a government or a minister of foreign affairs, whenever that person is in a state other than the state in which he holds that position or office,

(b) a member of the family of a person described in paragraph (*a*) who accompanies that person in a state other than the state in which that person holds that position or office,

(c) a representative or an official of a state or an official or agent of an international organization of an intergovernmental character who, at the time when and at the place where an offence referred to in subsection 7(3) is committed against his person or any property referred to in section 431 that is used by him, is entitled, pursuant to international law, to special protection from any attack on his person, freedom or dignity, or

(d) a member of the family of a representative, official or agent described in paragraph (*c*) who forms part of his household, if the representative, official or agent, at the time when and at the place where any offence referred to in subsection 7(3) is committed against the member of his family or any property referred to in section 431 that is used by that member, is entitled, pursuant to international law, to special protection from any attack on his person, freedom or dignity;

Proposed Addition — 2 "intimate partner"

"intimate partner" with respect to a person, includes their current or former spouse, common-law partner and dating partner;

2019, c. 25, s. 1(3) [To come into force December 18, 2019.]

"justice" means a justice of the peace or a provincial court judge, and includes two or more justices where two or more justices are, by law, required to act or, by law, act or have jurisdiction;

"justice system participant" means

(a) a member of the Senate, of the House of Commons, of a legislative assembly or of a municipal council,

(b) a person who plays a role in the administration of criminal justice, including

(i) the Minister of Public Safety and Emergency Preparedness and a Minister responsible for policing in a province,

(ii) a prosecutor, a lawyer, a member of the Chambre des notaires du Québec and an officer of a court,

(iii) a judge and a justice,

(iv) a juror and a person who is summoned as a juror,

(v) an informant, a prospective witness, a witness under subpoena and a witness who has testified,

(vi) a peace officer within the meaning of any of paragraphs (b), (c), (d), (e) and (g) of the definition "peace officer",

(vii) a civilian employee of a police force,

(viii) a person employed in the administration of a court,

(viii.1) a public officer within the meaning of subsection 25.1(1) and a person acting at the direction of such an officer,

(ix) an employee of the Canada Revenue Agency who is involved in the investigation of an offence under an Act of Parliament,

(ix.1) an employee of the Canada Border Services Agency who is involved in the investigation of an offence under an Act of Parliament,

(x) an employee of a federal or provincial correctional service, a parole supervisor and any other person who is involved in the administration of a sentence under the supervision of such a correctional service and a person who conducts disciplinary hearings under the *Corrections and Conditional Release Act*, and

(xi) an employee and a member of the Parole Board of Canada and of a provincial parole board; and

(c) a person who plays a role in respect of proceedings involving

(i) security information,

(ii) criminal intelligence information,

(iii) information that would endanger the safety of any person if it were disclosed,

(iv) information that is obtained in confidence from a source in Canada, the government of a foreign state, an international organization of states or an institution of such a government or international organization, or

(v) potentially injurious information or sensitive information as those terms are defined in section 38 of the *Canada Evidence Act*;

"magistrate" [Repealed R.S.C. 1985, c. 27 (1st Supp.), s. 2(4).]

"mental disorder" means a disease of the mind;

"military" shall be construed as relating to all or any of the Canadian Forces;

"military law" includes all laws, regulations or orders relating to the Canadian Forces;

"motor vehicle" means a vehicle that is drawn, propelled or driven by any means other than muscular power, but does not include railway equipment;

"municipality" includes the corporation of a city, town, village, county, township, parish or other territorial or local division of a province, the inhabitants of which are incorporated or are entitled to hold property collectively for a public purpose;

"newly-born child" means a person under the age of one year;

"night" means the period between nine o'clock in the afternoon and six o'clock in the forenoon of the following day;

"nuclear facility" means

(a) any nuclear reactor, including a reactor installed on a vessel, vehicle, aircraft or space object for use as an energy source in order to propel the vessel, vehicle, aircraft or space object or for any other purpose, and

(b) any plant or conveyance used for the production, storage, processing or transport of nuclear material or radioactive material;

"nuclear material" means

(a) plutonium, except plutonium with an isotopic concentration of plutonium-238 that is greater than 80%,

(b) uranium-233,

(c) uranium containing uranium-233 or uranium-235 or both in an amount such that the abundance ratio of the sum of those isotopes to the isotope uranium-238 is greater than 0.72%,

(d) uranium with an isotopic concentration equal to that occurring in nature, except uranium in the form of ore or ore-residue, and

(e) any substance containing any material described in paragraphs (a) to (d);

"offence-related property" means any property, within or outside Canada,

(a) by means or in respect of which an indictable offence under this Act or the *Corruption of Foreign Public Officials Act* is committed,

(b) that is used in any manner in connection with the commission of such an offence, or

(c) that is intended to be used for committing such an offence;

"offender" means a person who has been determined by a court to be guilty of an offence, whether on acceptance of a plea of guilty or on a finding of guilt;

"offensive weapon" has the same meaning as "weapon";

"organization" means

(a) a public body, body corporate, society, company, firm, partnership, trade union or municipality, or

(b) an association of persons that

(i) is created for a common purpose,

(ii) has an operational structure, and

(iii) holds itself out to the public as an association of persons;

"peace officer" includes

(a) a mayor, warden, reeve, sheriff, deputy sheriff, sheriff's officer and justice of the peace,

(b) a member of the Correctional Service of Canada who is designated as a peace officer pursuant to Part I of the *Corrections and Conditional Release Act*, and a warden, deputy warden, instructor, keeper, jailer, guard and any other officer or permanent employee of a prison other than a penitentiary as defined in Part I of the *Corrections and Conditional Release Act*,

(c) a police officer, police constable, bailiff, constable, or other person employed for the preservation and maintenance of the public peace or for the service or execution of civil process,

(c.1) a designated officer as defined in section 2 of the *Integrated Cross-border Law Enforcement Operations Act*, when

(i) participating in an integrated cross-border operation, as defined in section 2 of that Act, or

(ii) engaging in an activity incidental to such an operation, including travel for the purpose of participating in the operation and appearances in court arising from the operation;

(d) an officer within the meaning of the *Customs Act*, the *Excise Act* or the *Excise Act, 2001*, or a person having the powers of such an officer, when performing any duty in the administration of any of those Acts,

(d.1) an officer authorized under subsection 138(1) of the *Immigration and Refugee Protection Act*,

(e) a person designated as a fishery guardian under the *Fisheries Act* when performing any duties or functions under that Act and a person designated as a fishery officer under the *Fisheries Act* when performing any duties or functions under that Act or the *Coastal Fisheries Protection Act*,

(f) the pilot in command of an aircraft

(i) registered in Canada under regulations made under the *Aeronautics Act*, or

(ii) leased without crew and operated by a person who is qualified under regulations made under the *Aeronautics Act* to be registered as owner of an aircraft registered in Canada under those regulations,

while the aircraft is in flight, and

(g) officers and non-commissioned members of the Canadian Forces who are

(i) appointed for the purposes of section 156 of the *National Defence Act*, or

(ii) employed on duties that the Governor in Council, in regulations made under the *National Defence Act* for the purposes of this paragraph, has prescribed to be of such a kind as to necessitate that the officers and non-commissioned members performing them have the powers of peace officers;

"prison" includes a penitentiary, common jail, public or reformatory prison, lock-up, guard-room or other place in which persons who are charged with or convicted of offences are usually kept in custody;

"property" includes

(a) real and personal property of every description and deeds and instruments relating to or evidencing the title or right to property, or giving a right to recover or receive money or goods,

(b) property originally in the possession or under the control of any person, and any property into or for which it has been converted or exchanged and anything acquired at any time by the conversion or exchange, and

(c) any postal card, postage stamp or other stamp issued or prepared for issue under the authority of Parliament or the legislature of a province for the payment to the Crown or a corporate body of any fee, rate or duty, whether or not it is in the possession of the Crown or of any person;

"prosecutor" means the Attorney General or, where the Attorney General does not intervene, means the person who institutes proceedings to which this Act applies, and includes counsel acting on behalf of either of them;

"provincial court judge" means a person appointed or authorized to act by or pursuant to an Act of the legislature of a province, by whatever title that person may be designated, who has the power and authority of two or more justices of the peace and includes the lawful deputy of that person;

"public department" means a department of the Government of Canada or a branch thereof or a board, commission, corporation or other body that is an agent of Her Majesty in right of Canada;

"public officer" includes

(a) an officer of customs or excise,

(b) an officer of the Canadian Forces,

(c) an officer of the Royal Canadian Mounted Police, and

(d) any officer while the officer is engaged in enforcing the laws of Canada relating to revenue, customs, excise, trade or navigation;

"public stores" includes any personal property that is under the care, supervision, administration or control of a public department or of any person in the service of a public department;

"radioactive material" means any material that emits one or more types of ionizing radiation, such as alpha or beta particles, neutrons and gamma rays, and that is capable of, owing to its radiological or fissile properties, causing death, serious bodily harm or substantial damage to property or the environment;

"railway equipment" means

(a) any machine that is constructed for movement exclusively on lines of railway, whether or not the machine is capable of independent motion, or

(b) any vehicle that is constructed for movement both on and off lines of railway while the adaptations of that vehicle for movement on lines of railway are in use;

Proposed Addition — 2 "recognizance", "release order"

"recognizance" means a recognizance in Form 32 entered into before a judge or justice;

"release order" means an order in Form 11 made by a **"judge"** as defined in section 493 or a justice;

2019, c. 25, s. 1(3) [To come into force December 18, 2019.]

"representative", in respect of an organization, means a director, partner, employee, member, agent or contractor of the organization;

"senior officer" means a representative who plays an important role in the establishment of an organization's policies or is responsible for managing an important aspect of the organization's activities and, in the case of a body corporate, includes a director, its chief executive officer and its chief financial officer;

"serious offence" has the same meaning as in subsection 467.1(1);

"steal" means to commit theft;

"street racing" [Repealed 2018, c. 21, s. 12.]

Proposed Addition — 2 "summons"

"summons" means a summons in Form 6 issued by a judge or justice or by the **"chairperson"** of a *Review Board* as defined in subsection 672.1(1);

2019, c. 25, s. 1(3) [To come into force December 18, 2019.]

"superior court of criminal jurisdiction" means

(a) in the Province of Ontario, the Court of Appeal or the Superior Court of Justice,

(b) in the Province of Quebec, the Superior Court,

(c) in the Provinces of Nova Scotia, British Columbia and Prince Edward Island, the Court of Appeal or the Supreme Court,

(d) in the Provinces of New Brunswick, Manitoba, Saskatchewan and Alberta, the Court of Appeal or the Court of Queen's Bench,

(e) in the Province of Newfoundland and Labrador, Yukon and the Northwest Territories, the Supreme Court, and

(f) in Nunavut, the Nunavut Court of Justice;

(g) and (h) [Repealed 2015, c. 3, s. 44(3).]

"territorial division" includes any province, county, union of counties, township, city, town, parish or other judicial division or place to which the context applies;

"terrorism offence" means

(a) an offence under any of sections 83.02 to 83.04 or 83.18 to 83.23,

(b) an indictable offence under this or any other Act of Parliament committed for the benefit of, at the direction of or in association with a terrorist group,

(c) an indictable offence under this or any other Act of Parliament where the act or omission constituting the offence also constitutes a terrorist activity, or

(d) a conspiracy or an attempt to commit, or being an accessory after the fact in relation to, or any counselling in relation to, an offence referred to in paragraph (a), (b) or (c);

"terrorist activity" has the same meaning as in subsection 83.01(1);

"terrorist group" has the same meaning as in subsection 83.01(1);

"testamentary instrument" includes any will, codicil or other testamentary writing or appointment, during the life of the testator whose testamentary disposition it purports to be and after his death, whether it relates to real or personal property or to both;

"trustee" means a person who is declared by any Act to be a trustee or is, by the law of a province, a trustee, and, without restricting the generality of the foregoing, includes a trustee on an express trust created by deed, will or instrument in writing, or by parol;

Proposed Addition — 2 "undertaking"

"undertaking" means, unless a contrary intention appears, an undertaking in Form 10 given to a peace officer;

2019, c. 25, s. 1(3) [To come into force December 18, 2019.]

"unfit to stand trial" means unable on account of mental disorder to conduct a defence at any stage of the proceedings before a verdict is rendered or to instruct counsel to do so, and, in particular, unable on account of mental disorder to

(a) understand the nature or object of the proceedings,

(b) understand the possible consequences of the proceedings, or

(c) communicate with counsel;

"United Nations operation" means an operation that is established by the competent organ of the United Nations in accordance with the Charter of the United Nations and is conducted under United Nations authority and control, if the operation is for the purpose of maintaining or restoring international peace and security or if the Security Council or the General Assembly of the United Nations has declared, for the purposes of the *Convention on the Safety of United Nations and Associated Personnel*, that there exists an exceptional risk to the safety of the personnel participating in the operation. It does not include an operation authorized by the Security Council as an enforcement action under Chapter VII of the Charter of the United Nations in which any of the personnel are engaged as combatants against organized armed forces and to which the law of international armed conflict applies;

"United Nations personnel" means

(a) persons who are engaged or deployed by the Secretary-General of the United Nations as members of the military, police or civilian components of a United Nations operation, or

(b) any other officials or experts who are on mission of the United Nations or one of its specialized agencies or the International Atomic Energy Agency and who are present in an official capacity in the area where a United Nations operation is conducted;

"valuable mineral" means a mineral of a value of at least $100 per kilogram, and includes precious metals, diamonds and other gemstones and any rock or ore that contains those minerals;

"valuable security" includes

(a) an order, exchequer acquittance or other security that entitles or evidences the title of any person

(i) to a share or interest in a public stock or fund or in any fund of a body corporate, company or society, or

(ii) to a deposit in a financial institution,

(b) any debenture, deed, bond, bill, note, warrant, order or other security for money or for payment of money,

(c) a document of title to lands or goods wherever situated,

(d) a stamp or writing that secures or evidences title to or an interest in a chattel personal, or that evidences delivery of a chattel personal, and

(e) a release, receipt, discharge or other instrument evidencing payment of money;

"victim" means a person against whom an offence has been committed, or is alleged to have been committed, who has suffered, or is alleged to have suffered, physical or emotional harm, property damage or economic loss as the result of the commission or alleged commission of the offence and includes, for the purposes of sections 672.5, 722 and 745.63, a person who has suffered physical or emotional harm, property damage or economic loss as the result of the commission of an offence against any other person;

"videoconference" means any means of telecommunication that allows the judge, justice or **"chairperson"** of a *Review Board*, as defined in subsection 672.1(1), and any individual to engage in simultaneous visual and oral communication in a proceeding;

"weapon" means any thing used, designed to be used or intended for use

(a) in causing death or injury to any person, or

(b) for the purpose of threatening or intimidating any person and, without restricting the generality of the foregoing, includes a firearm and, for the purposes of sections 88, 267 and 272, any thing used, designed to be used or intended for use in binding or tying up a person against their will;

"wreck" includes the cargo, stores and tackle of a vessel and all parts of a vessel separated from the vessel, and the property of persons who belong to, are on board or have quitted a vessel that is wrecked, stranded or in distress at any place in Canada;

"writing" includes a document of any kind and any mode in which, and any material on which, words or figures, whether at length or abridged, are written, printed or otherwise expressed, or a map or plan is inscribed.

R.S.C. 1985, c. 11 (1st Supp.), s. 2(1) (Sched, item 1(1)); R.S.C. 1985, c. 27 (1st Supp.), ss. 2, 203; R.S.C. 1985, c. 31 (1st Supp.), s. 61 (Sched. II, item 2); R.S.C. 1985, c. 1 (2nd Supp.), s. 213(4) (Sched. IV, item 1); R.S.C. 1985, c. 27 (2nd Supp.), s. 10 (Sched., item 6); R.S.C. 1985, c. 35 (2nd Supp.), s. 34; R.S.C. 1985, c. 32 (4th Supp.), s. 55; R.S.C. 1985, c. 40 (4th Supp.), s. 2; 1990, c. 17, s. 7; 1991, c. 1, s. 28; 1991, c. 40, s. 1; 1991, c. 43, ss. 1, 9 (Sched., item 1); 1992, c. 20, s. 216(1)(a); 1992, c. 51, s. 32; 1993, c. 28, s. 78 (Sched. III, item 25) [Repealed in part 1999, c. 3, s. 12 (Sched., item 5).]; 1993, c. 34, s. 59(1); 1994, c. 44, s. 2; 1995, c. 29, ss. 39, 40; 1995, c. 39, s. 138; 1997, c. 23, s. 1; 1998, c. 30, s. 14(d); 1999, c. 3, s. 25; 1999, c. 5, s. 1; 1999, c. 25, s. 1; 1999, c. 28, s. 155; 2000, c. 12, s. 91; 2001, c. 32, s. 1 [Amended 2001, c. 41, s. 131.]; 2001, c. 41, s. 2; 2002, c. 7, s. 137(2); 2002, c. 22, s. 324; 2003, c. 21, s. 1; 2004, c. 3, s. 1; 2005, c. 10, s. 34(1)(f)(i); 2005, c. 38, s. 58; 2005, c. 40, ss. 1, 7; 2006, c. 14, s. 1; 2007, c. 13, s. 1; 2012, c. 1, s. 160(c)(i); 2012, c. 19, s. 371; 2013, c. 13, s. 2; 2014, c. 17, s. 1; 2014, c. 23, s. 2; 2014, c. 25, s. 2; 2015, c. 3, s. 44; 2015, c. 13, s. 3; 2015, c. 20, s. 15; 2018, c. 21, s. 12; 2019, c. 13, s. 140; 2019, c. 25, s. 1(1), (2)

2.1 Further definitions — firearms — In this Act, **"ammunition"**, **"antique firearm"**, **"automatic firearm"**, **"cartridge magazine"**, **"cross-bow"**, **"handgun"**, **"imitation firearm"**, **"prohibited ammunition"**, **"prohibited device"**, **"prohibited firearm"**, **"prohibited weapon"**, **"replica firearm"**, **"restricted firearm"** and **"restricted weapon"**, as well as **"authorization"**, **"licence"** and **"registration certificate"** when used in relation to those words and expressions, have the same meaning as in subsection 84(1).

2009, c. 22, s. 1

2.2 (1) Acting on victim's behalf — For the purposes of sections 606, 672.5, 715.37, 722, 737.1 and 745.63, any of the following individuals may act on the victim's behalf if the victim is dead or incapable of acting on their own behalf:

(a) the victim's spouse, or if the victim is dead, their spouse at the time of death;

(b) the victim's common-law partner, or if the victim is dead, their common-law partner at the time of death;

(c) a relative or dependant of the victim;

(d) an individual who has in law or fact custody, or is responsible for the care or support, of the victim; and

(e) an individual who has in law or fact custody, or is responsible for the care or support, of a dependant of the victim.

(2) Exception — An individual is not entitled to act on a victim's behalf if the individual is an accused in relation to the offence or alleged offence that resulted in the victim suffering harm or loss or is an individual who is found guilty of that offence or who is found not criminally responsible on account of mental disorder or unfit to stand trial in respect of that offence.

2015, c. 13, s. 4; 2018, c. 12, s. 403

2.3 (1) Concurrent jurisdiction — The proceedings for the purposes of paragraph (a) of the definition **"Attorney General"** in section 2 are

(a) proceedings in relation to an offence under subsection 7(2.01), (2.3) or (2.31) or section 57, 58, 83.12, 103, 104, 121.1, 380, 382, 382.1, 400, 424.1, 431.1, 467.11 or 467.111 or in relation to any terrorism offence;

(b) proceedings in relation to an offence against a member of United Nations personnel or associated personnel under section 235, 236, 266 to 269, 269.1, 271 to 273, 279 or 279.1;

(c) proceedings in relation to an offence referred to in subsection 7(3.71) or in relation to an offence referred to in paragraph (a) of the definition "terrorist activity" in subsection 83.01(1) if the act or omission constituting the offence was committed outside Canada and is deemed under any of subsections 7(2), (2.1) to (2.21), (3), (3.1), (3.72) and (3.73) to have been committed in Canada;

(d) proceedings in relation to an offence if the act or omission constituting the offence is a terrorist activity referred to in paragraph (b) of the definition "terrorist activity" in subsection 83.01(1) and was committed outside Canada and is deemed by virtue of subsection 7(3.74) or (3.75) to have been committed in Canada;

(e) a proceeding in relation to an offence under section 811 that arises out of a breach of a recognizance made under section 810.01 or 810.011, if he or she has given consent to the information referred to in those sections; and

(f) proceedings under section 83.13, 83.14, 83.222, 83.223 or 83.3.

(2) For greater certainty — Attorney General of Canada — For greater certainty, the Attorney General of Canada or his or her lawful deputy may, in respect of an offence referred to in subsection (1) or an offence under any Act of Parliament — other than this Act or the *Canada Elections Act* — or any regulation made under such an Act, exercise all the powers and perform all the duties and functions assigned to the Attorney General by or under this Act, and those powers include the power to commence and to conduct

(a) a proceeding for conspiring or attempting to commit such an offence or for being an accessory after the fact or counselling a person to be a party to such an offence;

(b) a proceeding in relation to a criminal organization offence that arises out of conduct that relates, in whole or in part, to any offence for which he or she has the power to commence and to conduct a proceeding;

(c) a proceeding in relation to an offence referred to in section 354, 355.2, 355.4 or 462.31 that arises out of conduct that relates, in whole or in part, to any offence for which he or she has the power to commence and to conduct a proceeding or out of any act or omission that, if it had occurred in Canada, would have constituted such an offence;

(d) a proceeding for the breach of any court order made in the course of a proceeding commenced or conducted by him or her;

(e) a proceeding for the failure to comply with any condition associated with the release of a person by a peace officer or other competent authority — including a condition to appear at a specified time and place — in relation to any offence for which he or she has the power to commence and to conduct a proceeding; and

(f) any ancillary proceedings in relation to any offence for which he or she has the power to commence and to conduct a proceeding.

(3) For greater certainty — Director of Public Prosecutions — For greater certainty, in respect of an offence under the *Canada Elections Act*, the Director of Public Prosecutions, subject to the *Director of Public Prosecutions Act*, exercises the powers and performs the duties and functions of the Attorney General of Canada referred to in subsection (2).

2019, c. 25, s. 2 [Amended 2019, c. 25, s. 404(2).]

3. Descriptive cross references — Where, in any provision of this Act, a reference to another provision of this Act or a provision of any other Act is followed by words in parenthesis that are or purport to be descriptive of the subject-matter of the provision referred to, the words in parenthesis form no part of the provision in which they occur but shall be deemed to have been inserted for convenience of reference only.

PART I (SS. 3.1–45)

General

3.1 (1) Effect of judicial acts — Unless otherwise provided or ordered, anything done by a court, justice or judge is effective from the moment it is done, whether or not it is reduced to writing.

(2) Clerk of the court — Unless otherwise provided or ordered, if anything is done from the bench by a court, justice or judge and it is reduced to writing, the clerk of the court may sign the writing.

2002, c. 13, s. 2; 2019, c. 25, s. 3

4. (1) Postcard a chattel, value — For the purposes of this Act, a postal card or stamp referred to in paragraph (*c*) of the definition "property" in section 2 shall be deemed to be a chattel and to be equal in value to the amount of the postage, rate or duty expressed on its face.

(2) Value of valuable security — For the purposes of this Act, the following rules apply for the purpose of determining the value of a valuable security where value is material:

(a) where the valuable security is one mentioned in paragraph (*a*) or (*b*) of the definition "valuable security" in section 2, the value is the value of the share, interest, deposit or unpaid money, as the case may be, that is secured by the valuable security;

(b) where the valuable security is one mentioned in paragraph (*c*) or (*d*) of the definition "valuable security" in section 2, the value is the value of the lands, goods, chattel personal or interest in the chattel personal, as the case may be; and

(c) where the valuable security is one mentioned in paragraph (*e*) of the definition "valuable security" in section 2, the value is the amount of money that has been paid.

(3) **Possession** — For the purposes of this Act,

(a) a person has anything in **"possession"** when he has it in his personal possession or knowingly

(i) has it in the actual possession or custody of another person, or

(ii) has it in any place, whether or not that place belongs to or is occupied by him, for the use or benefit of himself or of another person; and

(b) where one of two or more persons, with the knowledge and consent of the rest, has anything in his custody or possession, it shall be deemed to be in the custody and possession of each and all of them.

(4) **Expressions taken from other acts** — Where an offence that is dealt with in this Act relates to a subject that is dealt with in another Act, the words and expressions used in this Act with respect to that offence have, subject to this Act, the meaning assigned to them in that other Act.

(5) **Sexual intercourse** — For the purposes of this Act, sexual intercourse is complete on penetration to even the slightest degree, notwithstanding that seed is not emitted.

(6) **Proof of notifications and service of documents** — For the purposes of this Act, the service of any document and the giving or sending of any notice may be proved

(a) by oral evidence given under oath by, or by the affidavit or solemn declaration of, the person claiming to have served, given, or sent it; or

(b) in the case of a peace officer, by a statement in writing certifying that the document was served or the notice was given or sent by the peace officer, and such a statement is deemed to be a statement made under oath.

(6.1) **Proof of service in accordance with provincial laws** — Despite subsection (6), the service of documents may be proved in accordance with the laws of a province relating to offences created by the laws of that province.

(7) **Attendance for examination** — Despite subsection (6) or (6.1), the court may require the person who appears to have signed an affidavit, a solemn declaration or a statement in accordance with that subsection to appear before it for examination or cross-examination in respect of the issue of proof of service or of the giving or sending of any notice.

(8) **Means of telecommunication** — For greater certainty, for the purposes of this Act, if the elements of an offence contain an explicit or implicit element of communication without specifying the means of communication, the communication may also be made by a means of telecommunication.

R.S.C. 1985, c. 27 (1st Supp.), s. 3; 1994, c. 44, s. 3; 1997, c. 18, s. 2; 2008, c. 18, s. 1; 2014, c. 31, s. 2

5. **Canadian Forces not affected** — Nothing in this Act affects any law relating to the government of the Canadian Forces.

6. (1) **Presumption of innocence** — Where an enactment creates an offence and authorizes a punishment to be imposed in respect of that offence,

(a) a person shall be deemed not to be guilty of the offence until he is convicted or discharged under section 730 of the offence; and

(b) a person who is convicted or discharged under section 730 of the offence is not liable to any punishment in respect thereof other than the punishment prescribed by this Act or by the enactment that creates the offence.

(2) **Offences outside Canada** — Subject to this Act or any other Act of Parliament, no person shall be convicted or discharged under section 730 of an offence committed outside Canada.

(3) **Definition of "enactment"** — In this section **"enactment"** means

(a) an Act of Parliament, or

(b) an Act of the legislature of a province that creates an offence to which Part XXVII applies,

or any regulation made thereunder.

R.S.C. 1985, c. 27 (1st Supp.), s. 4; 1995, c. 22, ss. 10, 18

7. (1) **Offences committed on aircraft** — Notwithstanding anything in this Act or any other Act, every one who

(a) on or in respect of an aircraft

(i) registered in Canada under regulations made under the *Aeronautics Act*, or

(ii) leased without crew and operated by a person who is qualified under regulations made under the *Aeronautics Act* to be registered as owner of an aircraft registered in Canada under those regulations,

while the aircraft is in flight, or

(b) on any aircraft, while the aircraft is in flight if the flight terminated in Canada,

commits an act or omission in or outside Canada that if committed in Canada would be an offence punishable by indictment shall be deemed to have committed that act or omission in Canada.

(2) **Idem** — Notwithstanding this Act or any other Act, every one who

(a) on an aircraft, while the aircraft is in flight, commits an act or omission outside Canada that if committed in Canada or on an aircraft registered in

Canada under regulations made under the *Aeronautics Act* would be an offence against section 76 or paragraph 77(a),

(b) in relation to an aircraft in service, commits an act or omission outside Canada that if committed in Canada would be an offence against any of paragraphs 77(c), (d) or (g),

(c) in relation to an air navigation facility used in international air navigation, commits an act or omission outside Canada that if committed in Canada would be an offence against paragraph 77(e),

(d) at or in relation to an airport serving international civil aviation, commits an act or omission outside Canada that if committed in Canada would be an offence against paragraph 77(b) or (f), or

(e) commits an act or omission outside Canada that if committed in Canada would constitute a conspiracy or an attempt to commit an offence referred to in this subsection, or being an accessory after the fact or counselling in relation to such an offence,

shall be deemed to have committed that act or omission in Canada if the person is, after the commission thereof, present in Canada.

(2.01) Offences in relation to cultural property — Despite anything in this Act or any other Act, a person who commits an act or omission outside Canada that if committed in Canada would constitute an offence under section 322, 341, 344, 380, 430 or 434 in relation to cultural property as defined in Article 1 of the Convention, or a conspiracy or an attempt to commit such an offence, or being an accessory after the fact or counselling in relation to such an offence, is deemed to have committed that act or omission in Canada if the person

(a) is a Canadian citizen;

(b) is not a citizen of any state and ordinarily resides in Canada; or

(c) is a permanent resident within the meaning of subsection 2(1) of the *Immigration and Refugee Protection Act* and is, after the commission of the act or omission, present in Canada.

(2.02) Definition of "Convention" — For the purpose of subsection (2.01), **"Convention"** means the Convention for the Protection of Cultural Property in the Event of Armed Conflict, done at The Hague on May 14, 1954. Article 1 of the Convention is set out in the schedule to the *Cultural Property Export and Import Act*.

(2.1) Offences against fixed platforms or international maritime navigation — Notwithstanding anything in this Act or any other Act, every one who commits an act or omission outside Canada against or on board a fixed platform attached to the continental shelf of any state or against or on board a ship navigating or scheduled to navigate beyond the territorial sea of any state, that if committed in Canada would constitute an offence against, a conspiracy or an attempt to commit an offence against, or being an accessory after the fact or counselling in relation to an offence against, section 78.1, shall be deemed to commit that act or omission in Canada if it is committed

(a) against or on board a fixed platform attached to the continental shelf of Canada;

(b) against or on board a ship registered or licensed, or for which an identification number has been issued, pursuant to any Act of Parliament;

(c) by a Canadian citizen;

(d) by a person who is not a citizen of any state and who ordinarily resides in Canada;

(e) by a person who is, after the commission of the offence, present in Canada;

(f) in such a way as to seize, injure or kill, or threaten to injure or kill, a Canadian citizen; or

(g) in an attempt to compel the Government of Canada to do or refrain from doing any act.

(2.2) **Offences against fixed platforms or navigation in the internal waters or territorial sea of another state** — Notwithstanding anything in this Act or any other Act, every one who commits an act or omission outside Canada against or on board a fixed platform not attached to the continental shelf of any state or against or on board a ship not navigating or scheduled to navigate beyond the territorial sea of any state, that if committed in Canada would constitute an offence against, a conspiracy or an attempt to commit an offence against, or being an accessory after the fact or counselling in relation to an offence against, section 78.1, shall be deemed to commit that act or omission in Canada

(a) if it is committed as described in any of paragraphs (2.1)(b) to (g); and

(b) if the offender is found in the territory of a state, other than the state in which the act or omission was committed, that is

(i) a party to the Convention for the Suppression of Unlawful Acts against the Safety of Maritime Navigation, done at Rome on March 10, 1988, in respect of an offence committed against or on board a ship, or

(ii) a party to the Protocol for the Suppression of Unlawful Acts against the Safety of Fixed Platforms Located on the Continental Shelf, done at Rome on March 10, 1988, in respect of an offence committed against or on board a fixed platform.

(2.21) **Nuclear terrorism offence committed outside Canada** — Despite anything in this Act or any other Act, everyone who commits an act or omission outside Canada that if committed in Canada would constitute an offence under any of sections 82.3 to 82.6, or a conspiracy or attempt to commit such an offence, or being an accessory after the fact or counselling in relation to such an offence, is deemed to have committed that act or omission in Canada if

(a) the act or omission is committed on a ship that is registered or licensed, or for which an identification number has been issued, under any Act of Parliament;

(b) the act or omission is committed on an aircraft that

(i) is registered in Canada under regulations made under the *Aeronautics Act*, or

(ii) is leased without crew and operated by a person who is qualified under regulations made under the *Aeronautics Act* to be registered as owner of an aircraft in Canada under those regulations;

(c) the person who commits the act or omission is a Canadian citizen; or

(d) the person who commits the act or omission is, after the commission of the act or omission, present in Canada.

(2.3) Space Station — Canadian crew members — Despite anything in this Act or any other Act, a Canadian crew member who, during a space flight, commits an act or omission outside Canada that if committed in Canada would constitute an indictable offence is deemed to have committed that act or omission in Canada, if that act or omission is committed

(a) on, or in relation to, a flight element of the Space Station; or

(b) on any means of transportation to or from the Space Station.

(2.31) Space Station — crew members of Partner States — Despite anything in this Act or any other Act, a crew member of a Partner State who commits an act or omission outside Canada during a space flight on, or in relation to, a flight element of the Space Station or on any means of transportation to and from the Space Station that if committed in Canada would constitute an indictable offence is deemed to have committed that act or omission in Canada, if that act or omission

(a) threatens the life or security of a Canadian crew member; or

(b) is committed on or in relation to, or damages, a flight element provided by Canada.

(2.32) [Repealed 2019, c. 25, s. 4(1).]

(2.33) Consent of Attorney General of Canada — No proceedings in relation to an offence referred to in subsection (2.3) or (2.31) may be instituted without the consent of the Attorney General of Canada.

(2.34) Definitions — The definitions in this subsection apply in this subsection and in subsections (2.3) and (2.31).

"Agreement" has the same meaning as in section 2 of the *Civil International Space Station Agreement Implementation Act*.

"Canadian crew member" means a crew member of the Space Station who is

(a) a Canadian citizen; or

(b) a citizen of a foreign state, other than a Partner State, who is authorized by Canada to act as a crew member for a space flight on, or in relation to, a flight element.

"crew member of a Partner State" means a crew member of the Space Station who is

(a) a citizen of a Partner State; or

(b) a citizen of a state, other than that Partner State, who is authorized by that Partner State to act as a crew member for a space flight on, or in relation to, a flight element.

"flight element" means a Space Station element provided by Canada or by a Partner State under the Agreement and under any memorandum of understanding or other implementing arrangement entered into to carry out the Agreement.

"Partner State" means a State, other than Canada, who contracted to enter into the Agreement and for which the Agreement has entered into force in accordance with article 25 of the Agreement.

"space flight" means the period that begins with the launching of a crew member of the Space Station, continues during their stay in orbit and ends with their landing on earth.

"Space Station" means the civil international Space Station that is a multi-use facility in low-earth orbit, with flight elements and dedicated ground elements provided by, or on behalf of, the Partner States.

(3) Offence against internationally protected person — Notwithstanding anything in this Act or any other Act, every one who, outside Canada, commits an act or omission against the person of an internationally protected person or against any property referred to in section 431 used by that person that, if committed in Canada, would be an offence against any of sections 235, 236, 266, 267, 268, 269, 269.1, 271, 272, 273, 279, 279.1, 280 to 283, 424 and 431 is deemed to commit that act or omission in Canada if

(a) the act or omission is committed on a ship that is registered or licensed, or for which an identification number has been issued, pursuant to any Act of Parliament;

(b) the act or omission is committed on an aircraft

(i) registered in Canada under regulations made under the *Aeronautics Act*, or

(ii) leased without crew and operated by a person who is qualified under regulations made under the *Aeronautics Act* to be registered as owner of an aircraft in Canada under those regulations;

(c) the person who commits the act or omission is a Canadian citizen or is, after the act or omission has been committed, present in Canada; or

(d) the act or omission is against

(i) a person who enjoys the status of an internationally protected person by virtue of the functions that person performs on behalf of Canada, or

(ii) a member of the family of a person described in subparagraph (i) who qualifies under paragraph (*b*) or (*d*) of the definition "internationally protected person" in section 2.

(3.1) Offence of hostage taking — Notwithstanding anything in this Act or any other Act, every one who, outside Canada, commits an act or omission that if committed in Canada would be an offence against section 279.1 shall be deemed to commit that act or omission in Canada if

(a) the act or omission is committed on a ship that is registered or licensed, or for which an identification number has been issued, pursuant to any Act of Parliament;

(b) the act or omission is committed on an aircraft

(i) registered in Canada under regulations made under the *Aeronautics Act*, or

(ii) leased without crew and operated by a person who is qualified under regulations made under the *Aeronautics Act* to be registered as owner of an aircraft in Canada under such regulations;

(c) the person who commits the act or omission

(i) is a Canadian citizen, or

(ii) is not a citizen of any state and ordinarily resides in Canada;

(d) the act or omission is committed with intent to induce Her Majesty in right of Canada or of a province to commit or cause to be committed any act or omission;

(e) a person taken hostage by the act or omission is a Canadian citizen; or

(f) the person who commits the act or omission is, after the commission thereof, present in Canada.

(3.2) to (3.6) [Repealed 2013, c. 13, s. 3(2).]

(3.7) Jurisdiction — Notwithstanding anything in this Act or any other Act, every one who, outside Canada, commits an act or omission that, if committed in Canada, would constitute an offence against, a conspiracy or an attempt to commit an offence against, being an accessory after the fact in relation to an offence against, or any counselling in relation to an offence against, section 269.1 shall be deemed to commit that act or omission in Canada if

(a) the act or omission is committed on a ship that is registered or licensed, or for which an identification number has been issued, pursuant to any Act of Parliament;

(b) the act or omission is committed on an aircraft

(i) registered in Canada under regulations made under the *Aeronautics Act*, or

(ii) leased without crew and operated by a person who is qualified under regulations made under the *Aeronautics Act* to be registered as owner of an aircraft in Canada under those regulations;

(c) the person who commits the act or omission is a Canadian citizen;

(d) the complainant is a Canadian citizen; or

(e) the person who commits the act or omission is, after the commission thereof, present in Canada.

(3.71) Offence against United Nations or associated personnel — Notwithstanding anything in this Act or any other Act, every one who, outside Canada, commits an act or omission against a member of United Nations personnel or associated personnel or against property referred to in section 431.1 that, if committed in Canada, would constitute an offence against, a conspiracy or an attempt to commit an offence against, or being an accessory after the fact or counselling in relation to an offence against, section 235, 236, 266, 267, 268, 269, 269.1, 271, 272, 273, 279, 279.1, 424.1 or 431.1 is deemed to commit that act or omission in Canada if

(a) the act or omission is committed on a ship that is registered or licensed, or for which an identification number has been issued, under an Act of Parliament;

(b) the act or omission is committed on an aircraft

(i) registered in Canada under regulations made under the *Aeronautics Act*, or

(ii) leased without crew and operated by a person who is qualified under regulations made under the *Aeronautics Act* to be registered as owner of an aircraft in Canada under those regulations;

(c) the person who commits the act or omission

(i) is a Canadian citizen, or

(ii) is not a citizen of any state and ordinarily resides in Canada;

(d) the person who commits the act or omission is, after the commission of the act or omission, present in Canada;

(e) the act or omission is committed against a Canadian citizen; or

(f) the act or omission is committed with intent to compel the Government of Canada or of a province to do or refrain from doing any act.

(3.72) Offence involving explosive or other lethal device — Notwithstanding anything in this Act or any other Act, every one who, outside Canada, commits an act or omission that, if committed in Canada, would constitute an offence against, a conspiracy or an attempt to commit an offence against, or being an accessory after the fact or counselling in relation to an offence against, section 431.2 is deemed to commit that act or omission in Canada if

(a) the act or omission is committed on a ship that is registered or licensed, or for which an identification number has been issued, under any Act of Parliament;

(b) the act or omission is committed on an aircraft

(i) registered in Canada under regulations made under the *Aeronautics Act*,

(ii) leased without crew and operated by a person who is qualified under regulations made under the *Aeronautics Act* to be registered as owner of an aircraft in Canada under those regulations, or

(iii) operated for or on behalf of the Government of Canada;

(c) the person who commits the act or omission

(i) is a Canadian citizen, or

(ii) is not a citizen of any state and ordinarily resides in Canada;

(d) the person who commits the act or omission is, after the commission of the act or omission, present in Canada;

(e) the act or omission is committed against a Canadian citizen;

(f) the act or omission is committed with intent to compel the Government of Canada or of a province to do or refrain from doing any act; or

(g) the act or omission is committed against a Canadian government or public facility located outside Canada.

(3.73) Offence relating to financing of terrorism — Notwithstanding anything in this Act or any other Act, every one who, outside Canada, commits an act or omission that, if committed in Canada, would constitute an offence against, a conspiracy or an attempt to commit an offence against, or being an accessory after the fact or counselling in relation to an offence against, section 83.02 is deemed to commit the act or omission in Canada if

(a) the act or omission is committed on a ship that is registered or licensed, or for which an identification number has been issued, under an Act of Parliament;

(b) the act or omission is committed on an aircraft

(i) registered in Canada under regulations made under the *Aeronautics Act*, or

(ii) leased without crew and operated by a person who is qualified under regulations made under the *Aeronautics Act* to be registered as the owner of an aircraft in Canada under those regulations;

(c) the person who commits the act or omission

(i) is a Canadian citizen, or

(ii) is not a citizen of any state and ordinarily resides in Canada;

(d) the person who commits the act or omission is, after its commission, present in Canada;

(e) the act or omission is committed for the purpose of committing an act or omission referred to in paragraph 83.02(a) or (b) in order to compel the Government of Canada or of a province to do or refrain from doing any act;

(f) the act or omission is committed for the purpose of committing an act or omission referred to in paragraph 83.02(a) or (b) against a Canadian government or public facility located outside Canada; or

(g) the act or omission is committed for the purpose of committing an act or omission referred to in paragraph 83.02(a) or (b) in Canada or against a Canadian citizen.

(3.74) Terrorism offence committed outside Canada — Notwithstanding anything in this Act or any other Act, every one who commits an act or omission outside Canada that, if committed in Canada, would be a terrorism offence, other than an offence under section 83.02 or an offence referred to in paragraph (a) of the definition "terrorist activity" in subsection 83.01(1), is deemed to have committed that act or omission in Canada if the person

(a) is a Canadian citizen;

(b) is not a citizen of any state and ordinarily resides in Canada; or

(c) is a permanent resident within the meaning of subsection 2(1) of the *Immigration and Refugee Protection Act* and is, after the commission of the act or omission, present in Canada.

(3.75) Terrorist activity committed outside Canada — Notwithstanding anything in this Act or any other Act, every one who commits an act or omission outside Canada that, if committed in Canada, would be an indictable offence and would also constitute a terrorist activity referred to in paragraph (b) of the definition "terrorist activity" in subsection 83.01(1) is deemed to commit that act or omission in Canada if

(a) the act or omission is committed against a Canadian citizen;

(b) the act or omission is committed against a Canadian government or public facility located outside Canada; or

(c) the act or omission is committed with intent to compel the Government of Canada or of a province to do or refrain from doing any act.

(3.76) and (3.77) [Repealed 2000, c. 24, s. 42.]

(4) Offences by public service employees — Every one who, while employed as an employee within the meaning of the *Public Service Employment Act* in a place outside Canada, commits an act or omission in that place that is an offence under the laws of that place and that, if committed in Canada, would be an offence punishable by indictment shall be deemed to have committed that act or omission in Canada.

(4.1) Offence in relation to sexual offences against children — Notwithstanding anything in this Act or any other Act, every one who, outside Canada, commits an act or omission that if committed in Canada would be an offence against section 151, 152, 153 or 155, subsection 160(2) or (3), section 163.1, 170, 171, 171.1, 172.1, 172.2 or 173 or subsection 286.1(2) shall be deemed to commit that act or omission in Canada if the person who commits the act or omission is a Canadian citizen or a **"permanent resident"** within the meaning of subsection 2(1) of the *Immigration and Refugee Protection Act.*

(4.11) Offence in relation to trafficking in persons — Notwithstanding anything in this Act or any other Act, every one who, outside Canada, commits an act or omission that if committed in Canada would be an offence against section 279.01, 279.011, 279.02 or 279.03 shall be deemed to commit that act or omission in Canada if the person who commits the act or omission is a Canadian citizen or a permanent resident within the meaning of subsection 2(1) of the *Immigration and Refugee Protection Act.*

(4.2) [Repealed 2002, c. 13, s. 3(2).]

(4.3) Consent of Attorney General — Proceedings with respect to an act or omission deemed to have been committed in Canada under subsection (4.1) may only be instituted with the consent of the Attorney General.

(5) Jurisdiction — Where a person is alleged to have committed an act or omission that is an offence by virtue of this section, proceedings in respect of that offence may, whether or not that person is in Canada, be commenced in any territorial division in Canada and the accused may be tried and punished in respect of that offence in the same manner as if the offence had been committed in that territorial division.

(5.1) Appearance of accused at trial — For greater certainty, the provisions of this Act relating to

(a) requirements that an accused appear at and be present during proceedings, and

(b) the exceptions to those requirements,

apply to proceedings commenced in any territorial division pursuant to subsection (5).

(6) If previously tried outside Canada — If a person is alleged to have committed an act or omission that is an offence by virtue of this section and that person has been tried and dealt with outside Canada in respect of the offence in such a manner that, if that person had been tried and dealt with in Canada, they would be able to plead *autrefois acquit, autrefois convict*, pardon or an expungement order under the *Expungement of Historically Unjust Convictions Act*, that person shall be deemed to have been so tried and dealt with in Canada.

(7) If accused not Canadian citizen — If the accused is not a Canadian citizen, no proceedings in respect of which courts have jurisdiction by virtue of this section shall be continued unless the consent of the Attorney General of Canada is obtained not later than eight days after the proceedings are commenced.

(8) Definition of "flight" and "in flight" — For the purposes of this section, of the definition "peace officer" in section 2 and of sections 27.1, 76 and 77, **"flight"** means the act of flying or moving through the air and an aircraft is deemed to be in flight from the time when all external doors are closed following embarkation until the later of

(a) the time at which any such door is opened for the purpose of disembarkation, and

(b) where the aircraft makes a forced landing in circumstances in which the owner or operator thereof or a person acting on behalf of either of them is not in control of the aircraft, the time at which control of the aircraft is restored to the owner or operator thereof or a person acting on behalf of either of them.

(9) Definition of "in service" — For the purposes of this section and section 77, an aircraft shall be deemed to be in service from the time when pre-flight preparation of the aircraft by ground personnel or the crew thereof begins for a specific flight until

(a) the flight is cancelled before the aircraft is in flight,

(b) twenty-four hours after the aircraft, having commenced the flight, lands, or

(c) the aircraft, having commenced the flight, ceases to be in flight,

whichever is the latest.

(10) Certificate as evidence — In any proceedings under this Act, a certificate purporting to have been issued by or under the authority of the Minister of Foreign

Affairs is admissible in evidence without proof of the signature or authority of the person appearing to have signed it and, in the absence of evidence to the contrary, is proof of the facts it states that are relevant to the question of whether any person is a member of United Nations personnel, a member of associated personnel or a person who is entitled under international law to protection from attack or threat of attack against his or her person, freedom or dignity.

(11) Idem — A certificate purporting to have been issued by or under the authority of the Minister of Foreign Affairs stating

(a) that at a certain time any state was engaged in an armed conflict against Canada or was allied with Canada in an armed conflict,

(b) that at a certain time any convention, treaty or other international agreement was or was not in force and that Canada was or was not a party thereto, or

(c) that Canada agreed or did not agree to accept and apply the provisions of any convention, treaty or other international agreement in an armed conflict in which Canada was involved,

is admissible in evidence in any proceedings under this Act without proof of the signature or authority of the person appearing to have issued it, and is proof of facts so stated.

R.S.C. 1985, c. 27 (1st Supp.), s. 5; R.S.C. 1985, c. 10 (3rd Supp.), s. 1; R.S.C. 1985, c. 30 (3rd Supp.), s. 1(1), (3); 1992, c. 1, s. 58(1) (Sched. I, items 1(1), (2)); 1993, c. 7, s. 1; 1995, c. 5, s. 25(1)(g); 1997, c. 16, s. 1; 1999, c. 35, s. 11; 2000, c. 24, s. 42; 2001, c. 27, s. 244; 2001, c. 41, ss. 3, 126(2); 2002, c. 13, s. 3; 2004, c. 12, s. 1; 2005, c. 40, s. 2; 2012, c. 1, s. 10; 2012, c. 15, s. 1; 2013, c. 9, s. 2; 2013, c. 13, s. 3; 2014, c. 25, s. 3; 2018, c. 11, s. 27; 2019, c. 25, s. 4

8. (1) Application to territories — The provisions of this Act apply throughout Canada except

(a) in Yukon, in so far as they are inconsistent with the *Yukon Act*;

(b) in the Northwest Territories, in so far as they are inconsistent with the *Northwest Territories Act*; and

(c) in Nunavut, in so far as they are inconsistent with the *Nunavut Act*.

(2) Application of criminal law of England — The criminal law of England that was in force in a province immediately before April 1, 1955 continues in force in the province except as altered, varied, modified or affected by this Act or any other Act of the Parliament of Canada.

(3) Common law principles continued — Every rule and principle of the common law that renders any circumstance a justification or excuse for an act or a defence to a charge continues in force and applies in respect of proceedings for an offence under this Act or any other Act of Parliament except in so far as they are altered by or are inconsistent with this Act or any other Act of Parliament.

1993, c. 28, s. 78 (Sched. III, item 26); 2002, c. 7, s. 138

9. Criminal offences to be under law of Canada — Notwithstanding anything in this Act or any other Act, no person shall be convicted or discharged under section 730

(a) of an offence at common law,

(b) of an offence under an Act of the Parliament of England, or of Great Britain, or of the United Kingdom of Great Britain and Ireland, or

(c) of an offence under an Act or ordinance in force in any province, territory or place before that province, territory or place became a province of Canada,

but nothing in this section affects the power, jurisdiction or authority that a court, judge, justice or provincial court judge had, immediately before April 1, 1955, to impose punishment for contempt of court.

R.S.C. 1985, c. 27 (1st Supp.), s. 6; 1995, c. 22, ss. 10, 18

10. (1) Appeal — Where a court, judge, justice or provincial court judge summarily convicts a person for a contempt of court committed in the face of the court and imposes punishment in respect thereof, that person may appeal

(a) from the conviction; or

(b) against the punishment imposed.

(2) Idem — Where a court or judge summarily convicts a person for a contempt of court not committed in the face of the court and punishment is imposed in respect thereof, that person may appeal

(a) from the conviction; or

(b) against the punishment imposed.

(3) Part XXI applies — An appeal under this section lies to the court of appeal of the province in which the proceedings take place, and, for the purposes of this section, the provisions of Part XXI apply, with such modifications as the circumstances require.

R.S.C. 1985, c. 27 (1st Supp.), s. 203

11. Civil remedy not suspended — No civil remedy for an act or omission is suspended or affected by reason that the act or omission is a criminal offence.

12. Offence punishable under more than one Act — Where an act or omission is an offence under more than one Act of Parliament, whether punishable by indictment or on summary conviction, a person who does the act or makes the omission is, unless a contrary intention appears, subject to proceedings under any of those Acts, but is not liable to be punished more than once for the same offence.

13. Child under twelve — No person shall be convicted of an offence in respect of an act or omission on his part while that person was under the age of twelve years.

14. Consent to death — No person is entitled to consent to have death inflicted on them, and such consent does not affect the criminal responsibility of any person who inflicts death on the person who gave consent.

2016, c. 3, s. 1

15. Obedience to *de facto* law — No person shall be convicted of an offence in respect of an act or omission in obedience to the laws for the time being made and enforced by persons in *de facto* possession of the sovereign power in and over the place where the act or omission occurs.

16. (1) Defence of mental disorder — No person is criminally responsible for an act committed or an omission made while suffering from a mental disorder that rendered the person incapable of appreciating the nature and quality of the act or omission or of knowing that it was wrong.

(2) Presumption — Every person is presumed not to suffer from a mental disorder so as to be exempt from criminal responsibility by virtue of subsection (1), until the contrary is proved on the balance of probabilities.

(3) Burden of proof — The burden of proof that an accused was suffering from a mental disorder so as to be exempt from criminal responsibility is on the party that raises the issue.

1991, c. 43, s. 2

17. Compulsion by threats — A person who commits an offence under compulsion by threats of immediate death or bodily harm from a person who is present when the offence is committed is excused for committing the offence if the person believes that the threats will be carried out and if the person is not a party to a conspiracy or association whereby the person is subject to compulsion, but this section does not apply where the offence that is committed is high treason or treason, murder, piracy, attempted murder, sexual assault, sexual assault with a weapon, threats to a third party or causing bodily harm, aggravated sexual assault, forcible abduction, hostage taking, robbery, assault with a weapon or causing bodily harm, aggravated assault, unlawfully causing bodily harm, arson or an offence under sections 280 to 283 (abduction and detention of young persons).

R.S.C. 1985, c. 27 (1st Supp.), s. 40(2)

18. Compulsion of spouse — No presumption arises that a married person who commits an offence does so under compulsion by reason only that the offence is committed in the presence of the spouse of that married person.

19. Ignorance of the law — Ignorance of the law by a person who commits an offence is not an excuse for committing that offence.

20. Certain acts on holidays valid — A warrant or summons that is authorized by this Act or an appearance notice, promise to appear, undertaking or recognizance issued, given or entered into in accordance with Part XVI, XXI or XXVII may be issued, executed, given or entered into, as the case may be, on a holiday.

Proposed Amendment — 20

20. Certain acts on holidays valid — A warrant, summons, appearance notice, undertaking, release order or recognizance that is authorized by this Act may be executed, issued, given or entered into, as the case may be, on a holiday.

2019, c. 25, s. 5 [To come into force December 18, 2019.]

Parties to Offences

21. (1) Parties to offence — Every one is a party to an offence who

(a) actually commits it;

(b) does or omits to do anything for the purpose of aiding any person to commit it; or

(c) abets any person in committing it.

(2) Common intention — Where two or more persons form an intention in common to carry out an unlawful purpose and to assist each other therein and any one of them, in carrying out the common purpose, commits an offence, each of them who knew or ought to have known that the commission of the offence would be a probable consequence of carrying out the common purpose is a party to that offence.

22. (1) Person counselling offence — Where a person counsels another person to be a party to an offence and that other person is afterwards a party to that offence, the person who counselled is a party to that offence, notwithstanding that the offence was committed in a way different from that which was counselled.

(2) Idem — Every one who counsels another person to be a party to an offence is a party to every offence that the other commits in consequence of the counselling that the person who counselled knew or ought to have known was likely to be committed in consequence of the counselling.

(3) Definition of "counsel" — For the purposes of this Act, **"counsel"** includes procure, solicit or incite.

R.S.C. 1985, c. 27 (1st Supp.), s. 7(1)

22.1 Offences of negligence — organizations — In respect of an offence that requires the prosecution to prove negligence, an organization is a party to the offence if

(a) acting within the scope of their authority

(i) one of its representatives is a party to the offence, or

(ii) two or more of its representatives engage in conduct, whether by act or omission, such that, if it had been the conduct of only one representative, that representative would have been a party to the offence; and

(b) the senior officer who is responsible for the aspect of the organization's activities that is relevant to the offence departs — or the senior officers, collectively, depart — markedly from the standard of care that, in the circumstances, could reasonably be expected to prevent a representative of the organization from being a party to the offence.

2003, c. 21, s. 2

22.2 Other offences — organizations — In respect of an offence that requires the prosecution to prove fault — other than negligence — an organization is a party to the offence if, with the intent at least in part to benefit the organization, one of its senior officers

(a) acting within the scope of their authority, is a party to the offence;

(b) having the mental state required to be a party to the offence and acting within the scope of their authority, directs the work of other representatives of the organization so that they do the act or make the omission specified in the offence; or

(c) knowing that a representative of the organization is or is about to be a party to the offence, does not take all reasonable measures to stop them from being a party to the offence.

2003, c. 21, s. 2

23. (1) Accessory after the fact — An accessory after the fact to an offence is one who, knowing that a person has been a party to the offence, receives, comforts or assists that person for the purpose of enabling that person to escape.

(2) [Repealed 2000, c. 12, s. 92.]

2000, c. 12, s. 92

23.1 Where one party cannot be convicted — For greater certainty, sections 21 to 23 apply in respect of an accused notwithstanding the fact that the person whom the accused aids or abets, counsels or procures or receives, comforts or assists cannot be convicted of the offence.

R.S.C. 1985, c. 24 (2nd Supp.), s. 45

24. (1) Attempts — Every one who, having an intent to commit an offence, does or omits to do anything for the purpose of carrying out his intention is guilty of an attempt to commit the offence whether or not it was possible under the circumstances to commit the offence.

(2) Question of law — The question whether an act or omission by a person who has an intent to commit an offence is or is not mere preparation to commit the offence, and too remote to constitute an attempt to commit the offence, is a question of law.

Protection of Persons Administering and Enforcing the Law

25. (1) Protection of persons acting under authority — Every one who is required or authorized by law to do anything in the administration or enforcement of the law

(a) as a private person,

(b) as a peace officer or public officer,

(c) in aid of a peace officer or public officer, or

(d) by virtue of his office,

is, if he acts on reasonable grounds, justified in doing what he is required or authorized to do and in using as much force as is necessary for that purpose.

(2) Idem — Where a person is required or authorized by law to execute a process or to carry out a sentence, that person or any person who assists him is, if that person acts in good faith, justified in executing the process or in carrying out the sentence notwithstanding that the process or sentence is defective or that it was issued or imposed without jurisdiction or in excess of jurisdiction.

(3) When not protected — Subject to subsections (4) and (5), a person is not justified for the purposes of subsection (1) in using force that is intended or is likely to cause death or grievous bodily harm unless the person believes on reasonable grounds that it is necessary for the self-preservation of the person or the preservation of any one under that person's protection from death or grievous bodily harm.

(4) When protected — A peace officer, and every person lawfully assisting the peace officer, is justified in using force that is intended or is likely to cause death or grievous bodily harm to a person to be arrested, if

(a) the peace officer is proceeding lawfully to arrest, with or without warrant, the person to be arrested;

(b) the offence for which the person is to be arrested is one for which that person may be arrested without warrant;

(c) the person to be arrested takes flight to avoid arrest;

(d) the peace officer or other person using the force believes on reasonable grounds that the force is necessary for the purpose of protecting the peace officer, the person lawfully assisting the peace officer or any other person from imminent or future death or grievous bodily harm; and

(e) the flight cannot be prevented by reasonable means in a less violent manner.

(5) Power in case of escape from penitentiary — A peace officer is justified in using force that is intended or is likely to cause death or grievous bodily harm against an inmate who is escaping from a penitentiary within the meaning of subsection 2(1) of the *Corrections and Conditional Release Act*, if

(a) the peace officer believes on reasonable grounds that any of the inmates of the penitentiary pose a threat of death or grievous bodily harm to the peace officer or any other person; and

(b) the escape cannot be prevented by reasonable means in a less violent manner.

1994, c. 12, s. 1

25.1 (1) Definitions — The following definitions apply in this section and sections 25.2 to 25.4.

"competent authority" means, with respect to a public officer or a senior official,

(a) in the case of a member of the Royal Canadian Mounted Police, the Minister of Public Safety and Emergency Preparedness, personally;

(b) in the case of a member of a police service constituted under the laws of a province, the Minister responsible for policing in the province, personally; and

(c) in the case of any other public officer or senior official, the Minister who has responsibility for the Act of Parliament that the officer or official has the power to enforce, personally.

("autorité compétente")

"public officer" means a peace officer, or a public officer who has the powers of a peace officer under an Act of Parliament. *("fonctionnaire public")*

"senior official" means a senior official who is responsible for law enforcement and who is designated under subsection (5). *("fonctionnaire supérieur")*

(2) Principle — It is in the public interest to ensure that public officers may effectively carry out their law enforcement duties in accordance with the rule of law and, to that end, to expressly recognize in law a justification for public officers and other persons acting at their direction to commit acts or omissions that would otherwise constitute offences.

(3) Designation of public officers — A competent authority may designate public officers for the purposes of this section and sections 25.2 to 25.4.

(3.1) Condition — civilian oversight — A competent authority referred to in paragraph (a) or (b) of the definition of that term in subsection (1) may not designate any public officer under subsection (3) unless there is a public authority composed of persons who are not peace officers that may review the public officer's conduct.

(3.2) Declaration as evidence — The Governor in Council or the lieutenant governor in council of a province, as the case may be, may designate a person or body as a public authority for the purposes of subsection (3.1), and that designation is conclusive evidence that the person or body is a public authority described in that subsection.

(4) Considerations — The competent authority shall make designations under subsection (3) on the advice of a senior official and shall consider the nature of the duties performed by the public officer in relation to law enforcement generally, rather than in relation to any particular investigation or enforcement activity.

(5) Designation of senior officials — A competent authority may designate senior officials for the purposes of this section and sections 25.2 to 25.4.

(6) Emergency designation — A senior official may designate a public officer for the purposes of this section and sections 25.2 to 25.4 for a period of not more than 48 hours if the senior official is of the opinion that

(a) by reason of exigent circumstances, it is not feasible for the competent authority to designate a public officer under subsection (3); and

(b) in the circumstances of the case, the public officer would be justified in committing an act or omission that would otherwise constitute an offence.

The senior official shall without delay notify the competent authority of the designation.

(7) Conditions — A designation under subsection (3) or (6) may be made subject to conditions, including conditions limiting

(a) the duration of the designation;

(b) the nature of the conduct in the investigation of which a public officer may be justified in committing, or directing another person to commit, acts or omissions that would otherwise constitute an offence; and

(c) the acts or omissions that would otherwise constitute an offence and that a public officer may be justified in committing or directing another person to commit.

(8) Justification for acts or omissions — A public officer is justified in committing an act or omission — or in directing the commission of an act or omission under subsection (10) — that would otherwise constitute an offence if the public officer

(a) is engaged in the investigation of an offence under, or the enforcement of, an Act of Parliament or in the investigation of criminal activity;

(b) is designated under subsection (3) or (6); and

(c) believes on reasonable grounds that the commission of the act or omission, as compared to the nature of the offence or criminal activity being investigated, is reasonable and proportional in the circumstances, having regard to such matters as the nature of the act or omission, the nature of the investigation and the reasonable availability of other means for carrying out the public officer's law enforcement duties.

(9) Requirements for certain acts — No public officer is justified in committing an act or omission that would otherwise constitute an offence and that would be likely to result in loss of or serious damage to property, or in directing the commission of an act or omission under subsection (10), unless, in addition to meeting the conditions set out in paragraphs (8)(a) to (c), he or she

(a) is personally authorized in writing to commit the act or omission — or direct its commission — by a senior official who believes on reasonable grounds that committing the act or omission, as compared to the nature of the offence or criminal activity being investigated, is reasonable and proportional in the circumstances, having regard to such matters as the nature of the act or omission, the nature of the investigation and the reasonable availability of other means for carrying out the public officer's law enforcement duties; or

(b) believes on reasonable grounds that the grounds for obtaining an authorization under paragraph (a) exist but it is not feasible in the circumstances to obtain the authorization and that the act or omission is necessary to

(i) preserve the life or safety of any person,

(ii) prevent the compromise of the identity of a public officer acting in an undercover capacity, of a confidential informant or of a person acting covertly under the direction and control of a public officer, or

(iii) prevent the imminent loss or destruction of evidence of an indictable offence.

(10) Person acting at direction of public officer — A person who commits an act or omission that would otherwise constitute an offence is justified in committing it if

(a) a public officer directs him or her to commit that act or omission and the person believes on reasonable grounds that the public officer has the authority to give that direction; and

(b) he or she believes on reasonable grounds that the commission of that act or omission is for the purpose of assisting the public officer in the public officer's law enforcement duties.

(11) Limitation — Nothing in this section justifies

(a) the intentional or criminally negligent causing of death or bodily harm to another person;

(b) the wilful attempt in any manner to obstruct, pervert or defeat the course of justice; or

(c) conduct that would violate the sexual integrity of an individual.

(12) Protection, defences and immunities unaffected — Nothing in this section affects the protection, defences and immunities of peace officers and other persons recognized under the law of Canada.

(13) Compliance with requirements — Nothing in this section relieves a public officer of criminal liability for failing to comply with any other requirements that govern the collection of evidence.

(14) Exception — *Controlled Drugs and Substances Act* and *Cannabis Act* — Nothing in this section justifies a public officer or a person acting at his or her direction in committing an act or omission — or a public officer in directing the commission of an act or omission — that constitutes an offence under a provision of Part I of the *Controlled Drugs and Substances Act* or of the regulations made under it or a provision of Division 1 of Part 1 of the *Cannabis Act*.

2001, c. 32, s. 2; 2005, c. 10, s. 34(1)(f)(ii); 2018, c. 16, s. 207

25.2 Public officer to file report — Every public officer who commits an act or omission — or directs the commission by another person of an act or omission — under paragraph 25.1(9)(a) or (b) shall, as soon as is feasible after the commission of the act or omission, file a written report with the appropriate senior official describing the act or omission.

2001, c. 32, s. 2

25.3 (1) Annual report — Every competent authority shall publish or otherwise make available to the public an annual report for the previous year that includes, in respect of public officers and senior officials designated by the competent authority,

(a) the number of designations made under subsection 25.1(6) by the senior officials;

(b) the number of authorizations made under paragraph 25.1(9)(a) by the senior officials;

(c) the number of times that acts and omissions were committed in accordance with paragraph 25.1(9)(b) by the public officers;

(d) the nature of the conduct being investigated when the designations referred to in paragraph (a) or the authorizations referred to in paragraph (b) were made or when the acts or omissions referred to in paragraph (c) were committed; and

(e) the nature of the acts or omissions committed under the designations referred to in paragraph (a), under the authorizations referred to in paragraph (b) and in the manner described in paragraph (c).

(2) Limitation — The annual report shall not contain any information the disclosure of which would

(a) compromise or hinder an ongoing investigation of an offence under an Act of Parliament;

(b) compromise the identity of a public officer acting in an undercover capacity, of a confidential informant or of a person acting covertly under the direction and control of a public officer;

(c) endanger the life or safety of any person;

(d) prejudice a legal proceeding; or

(e) otherwise be contrary to the public interest.

2001, c. 32, s. 2

25.4 (1) Written notification to be given — When a public officer commits an act or omission — or directs the commission by another person of an act or omission — under paragraph 25.1(9)(a) or (b), the senior official with whom the public officer files a written report under section 25.2 shall, as soon as is feasible after the report is filed, and no later than one year after the commission of the act or omission, notify in writing any person whose property was lost or seriously damaged as a result of the act or omission.

(2) Limitation — The competent authority may authorize the senior official not to notify the person under subsection (1) until the competent authority is of the opinion that notification would not

(a) compromise or hinder an ongoing investigation of an offence under an Act of Parliament;

(b) compromise the identity of a public officer acting in an undercover capacity, of a confidential informant or of a person acting covertly under the direction and control of a public officer;

(c) endanger the life or safety of any person;

(d) prejudice a legal proceeding; or

(e) otherwise be contrary to the public interest.

2001, c. 32, s. 2

26. Excessive force — Every one who is authorized by law to use force is criminally responsible for any excess thereof according to the nature and quality of the act that constitutes the excess.

27. Use of force to prevent commission of offence — Every one is justified in using as much force as is reasonably necessary

(a) to prevent the commission of an offence

(i) for which, if it were committed, the person who committed it might be arrested without warrant, and

(ii) that would be likely to cause immediate and serious injury to the person or property of anyone, or

(b) to prevent anything being done that, on reasonable grounds, he believes would, if it were done, be an offence mentioned in paragraph (*a*).

27.1 (1) Use of force on board an aircraft — Every person on an aircraft in flight is justified in using as much force as is reasonably necessary to prevent the commission of an offence against this Act or another Act of Parliament that the person believes on reasonable grounds, if it were committed, would be likely to cause immediate and serious injury to the aircraft or to any person or property therein.

(2) Application of this section — This section applies in respect of any aircraft in flight in Canadian airspace and in respect of any aircraft registered in Canada in accordance with the regulations made under the *Aeronautics Act* in flight outside Canadian airspace.

2004, c. 12, s. 2

28. (1) Arrest of wrong person — Where a person who is authorized to execute a warrant to arrest believes, in good faith and on reasonable grounds, that the person whom he arrests is the person named in the warrant, he is protected from criminal responsibility in respect thereof to the same extent as if that person were the person named in the warrant.

(2) Person assisting — Where a person is authorized to execute a warrant to arrest,

(a) every one who, being called on to assist him, believes that the person in whose arrest he is called on to assist is the person named in the warrant, and

(b) every keeper of a prison who is required to receive and detain a person who he believes has been arrested under the warrant,

is protected from criminal responsibility in respect thereof to the same extent as if that person were the person named in the warrant.

29. (1) Duty of person arresting — It is the duty of every one who executes a process or warrant to have it with him, where it is feasible to do so, and to produce it when requested to do so.

(2) Notice — It is the duty of every one who arrests a person, whether with or without a warrant, to give notice to that person, where it is feasible to do so, of

(a) the process or warrant under which he makes the arrest; or

(b) the reason for the arrest.

(3) Failure to comply — Failure to comply with subsection (1) or (2) does not of itself deprive a person who executes a process or warrant, or a person who makes an arrest, or those who assist them, of protection from criminal responsibility.

30. Preventing breach of peace — Every one who witnesses a breach of the peace is justified in interfering to prevent the continuance or renewal thereof and may detain any person who commits or is about to join in or to renew the breach of the peace, for the purpose of giving him into the custody of a peace officer, if he uses no more force than is reasonably necessary to prevent the continuance or renewal of the breach of the peace or than is reasonably proportioned to the danger to be apprehended from the continuance or renewal of the breach of the peace.

31. (1) Arrest for breach of peace — Every peace officer who witnesses a breach of the peace and every one who lawfully assists the peace officer is justified in arresting any person whom he finds committing the breach of the peace or who, on reasonable grounds, the peace officer believes is about to join in or renew the breach of the peace.

(2) Giving person in charge — Every peace officer is justified in receiving into custody any person who is given into his charge as having been a party to a breach of the peace by one who has, or who on reasonable grounds the peace officer believes has, witnessed the breach of the peace.

Suppression of Riots

32. (1) Use of force to suppress riot — Every peace officer is justified in using or in ordering the use of as much force as the peace officer believes, in good faith and on reasonable grounds,

(a) is necessary to suppress a riot; and

(b) is not excessive, having regard to the danger to be apprehended from the continuance of the riot.

(2) Person bound by military law — Every one who is bound by military law to obey the command of his superior officer is justified in obeying any command given by his superior officer for the suppression of a riot unless the order is manifestly unlawful.

(3) **Obeying order of peace officer** — Every one is justified in obeying an order of a peace officer to use force to suppress a riot if

(a) he acts in good faith; and

(b) the order is not manifestly unlawful.

(4) **Apprehension of serious mischief** — Every one who, in good faith and on reasonable grounds, believes that serious mischief will result from a riot before it is possible to secure the attendance of a peace officer is justified in using as much force as he believes in good faith and on reasonable grounds,

(a) is necessary to suppress the riot; and

(b) is not excessive, having regard to the danger to be apprehended from the continuance of the riot.

(5) **Question of law** — For the purposes of this section, the question whether an order is manifestly unlawful or not is a question of law.

33. (1) **Duty of officers if rioters do not disperse** — Where the proclamation referred to in section 67 has been made or an offence against paragraph 68(*a*) or (*b*) has been committed, it is the duty of a peace officer and of a person who is lawfully required by him to assist, to disperse or to arrest persons who do not comply with the proclamation.

(2) **Protection of officers** — No civil or criminal proceedings lie against a peace officer or a person who is lawfully required by a peace officer to assist him in respect of any death or injury that by reason of resistance is caused as a result of the performance by the peace officer or that person of a duty that is imposed by subsection (1).

(3) **Section not restrictive** — Nothing in this section limits or affects any powers, duties or functions that are conferred or imposed by this Act with respect to the suppression of riots.

Self-Induced Intoxication

33.1 (1) **When defence not available** — It is not a defence to an offence referred to in subsection (3) that the accused, by reason of self-induced intoxication, lacked the general intent or the voluntariness required to commit the offence, where the accused departed markedly from the standard of care as described in subsection (2).

(2) **Criminal fault by reason of intoxication** — For the purposes of this section, a person departs markedly from the standard of reasonable care generally recognized in Canadian society and is thereby criminally at fault where the person, while in a state of self-induced intoxication that renders the person unaware of, or incapable of consciously controlling, their behaviour, voluntarily or involuntarily interferes or threatens to interfere with the bodily integrity of another person.

(3) Application — This section applies in respect of an offence under this Act or any other Act of Parliament that includes as an element an assault or any other interference or threat of interference by a person with the bodily integrity of another person.

1995, c. 32, s. 1

Defence of Person

34. (1) Defence — use or threat of force — A person is not guilty of an offence if

(a) they believe on reasonable grounds that force is being used against them or another person or that a threat of force is being made against them or another person;

(b) the act that constitutes the offence is committed for the purpose of defending or protecting themselves or the other person from that use or threat of force; and

(c) the act committed is reasonable in the circumstances.

(2) Factors — In determining whether the act committed is reasonable in the circumstances, the court shall consider the relevant circumstances of the person, the other parties and the act, including, but not limited to, the following factors:

(a) the nature of the force or threat;

(b) the extent to which the use of force was imminent and whether there were other means available to respond to the potential use of force;

(c) the person's role in the incident;

(d) whether any party to the incident used or threatened to use a weapon;

(e) the size, age, gender and physical capabilities of the parties to the incident;

(f) the nature, duration and history of any relationship between the parties to the incident, including any prior use or threat of force and the nature of that force or threat;

(f.1) any history of interaction or communication between the parties to the incident;

(g) the nature and proportionality of the person's response to the use or threat of force; and

(h) whether the act committed was in response to a use or threat of force that the person knew was lawful.

(3) No defence — Subsection (1) does not apply if the force is used or threatened by another person for the purpose of doing something that they are required or authorized by law to do in the administration or enforcement of the law, unless the person who commits the act that constitutes the offence believes on reasonable grounds that the other person is acting unlawfully.

2012, c. 9, s. 2

Defence of Property

[Heading added 2012, c. 9, s. 2.]

35. (1) Defence — property — A person is not guilty of an offence if

(a) they either believe on reasonable grounds that they are in peaceable possession of property or are acting under the authority of, or lawfully assisting, a person whom they believe on reasonable grounds is in peaceable possession of property;

(b) they believe on reasonable grounds that another person

(i) is about to enter, is entering or has entered the property without being entitled by law to do so,

(ii) is about to take the property, is doing so or has just done so, or

(iii) is about to damage or destroy the property, or make it inoperative, or is doing so;

(c) the act that constitutes the offence is committed for the purpose of

(i) preventing the other person from entering the property, or removing that person from the property, or

(ii) preventing the other person from taking, damaging or destroying the property or from making it inoperative, or retaking the property from that person; and

(d) the act committed is reasonable in the circumstances.

(2) No defence — Subsection (1) does not apply if the person who believes on reasonable grounds that they are, or who is believed on reasonable grounds to be, in peaceable possession of the property does not have a claim of right to it and the other person is entitled to its possession by law.

(3) No defence — Subsection (1) does not apply if the other person is doing something that they are required or authorized by law to do in the administration or enforcement of the law, unless the person who commits the act that constitutes the offence believes on reasonable grounds that the other person is acting unlawfully.

2012, c. 9, s. 2

36 and 37. [Repealed 2012, c. 9, s. 2.]

Heading and ss. 38 to 42. [Repealed 2012, c. 9, s. 2.]

Protection of Persons in Authority

43. Correction of child by force — Every schoolteacher, parent or person standing in the place of a parent is justified in using force by way of correction toward a pupil or child, as the case may be, who is under his care, if the force does not exceed what is reasonable under the circumstances.

44. [Repealed 2001, c. 26, s. 294.]

45. Surgical operations — Every one is protected from criminal responsibility for performing a surgical operation on any person for the benefit of that person if

(a) the operation is performed with reasonable care and skill; and

(b) it is reasonable to perform the operation, having regard to the state of health of the person at the time the operation is performed and to all the circumstances of the case.

PART II — OFFENCES AGAINST PUBLIC ORDER (SS. 46–83)

Treason and other Offences against the Queen's Authority and Person

46. (1) High treason — Every one commits high treason who, in Canada,

(a) kills or attempts to kill Her Majesty, or does her any bodily harm tending to death or destruction, maims or wounds her, or imprisons or restrains her;

(b) levies war against Canada or does any act preparatory thereto; or

(c) assists an enemy at war with Canada, or any armed forces against whom Canadian Forces are engaged in hostilities, whether or not a state of war exists between Canada and the country whose forces they are.

(2) Treason — Every one commits treason who, in Canada,

(a) uses force or violence for the purpose of overthrowing the government of Canada or a province;

(b) without lawful authority, communicates or makes available to an agent of a state other than Canada, military or scientific information or any sketch, plan, model, article, note or document of a military or scientific character that he knows or ought to know may be used by that state for a purpose prejudicial to the safety or defence of Canada;

(c) conspires with any person to commit high treason or to do anything mentioned in paragraph *(a)*;

(d) forms an intention to do anything that is high treason or that is mentioned in paragraph *(a)* and manifests that intention by an overt act; or

(e) conspires with any person to do anything mentioned in paragraph *(b)* or forms an intention to do anything mentioned in paragraph *(b)* and manifests that intention by an overt act.

(3) Canadian citizen — Notwithstanding subsection (1) or (2), a Canadian citizen or a person who owes allegiance to Her Majesty in right of Canada,

(a) commits high treason if, while in or out of Canada, he does anything mentioned in subsection (1); or

(b) commits treason if, while in or out of Canada, he does anything mentioned in subsection (2).

(4) Overt act — Where it is treason to conspire with any person, the act of conspiring is an overt act of treason.

47. (1) Punishment for high treason — Every one who commits high treason is guilty of an indictable offence and shall be sentenced to imprisonment for life.

(2) Punishment for treason — Every one who commits treason is guilty of an indictable offence and liable

(a) to be sentenced to imprisonment for life if he is guilty of an offence under paragraph 46(2)(*a*), (*c*) or (*d*);

(b) to be sentenced to imprisonment for life if he is guilty of an offence under paragraph 46(2)(*b*) or (*e*) committed while a state of war exists between Canada and another country; or

(c) to be sentenced to imprisonment for a term not exceeding fourteen years if he is guilty of an offence under paragraph 46(2)(*b*) or (*e*) committed while no state of war exists between Canada and another country.

(3) Corroboration — No person shall be convicted of high treason or treason on the evidence of only one witness, unless the evidence of that witness is corroborated in a material particular by evidence that implicates the accused.

(4) Minimum punishment — For the purposes of Part XXIII, the sentence of imprisonment for life prescribed by subsection (1) is a minimum punishment.

48. (1) Limitation — No proceedings for an offence of treason as defined by paragraph 46(2)(*a*) shall be commenced more than three years after the time when the offence is alleged to have been committed.

(2) Information for treasonable words — No proceedings shall be commenced under section 47 in respect of an overt act of treason expressed or declared by open and considered speech unless

(a) an information setting out the overt act and the words by which it was expressed or declared is laid under oath before a justice within six days after the time when the words are alleged to have been spoken; and

(b) a warrant for the arrest of the accused is issued within ten days after the time when the information is laid.

Prohibited Acts

49. [Repealed 2018, c. 29, s. 1.]

50. (1) Assisting alien enemy to leave Canada, or omitting to prevent treason — Every one commits an offence who

(a) incites or willfully assists a subject of

(i) a state that is at war with Canada, or

(ii) a state against whose forces Canadian Forces are engaged in hostilities, whether or not a state of war exists between Canada and the state whose forces they are,

to leave Canada without the consent of the Crown, unless the accused establishes that assistance to the state referred to in subparagraph (i) or the forces of the state referred to in subparagraph (ii), as the case may be, was not intended thereby; or

(b) knowing that a person is about to commit high treason or treason does not, with all reasonable dispatch, inform a justice of the peace or other peace officer thereof or make other reasonable efforts to prevent that person from committing high treason or treason.

(2) **Punishment** — Every one who commits an offence under subsection (1) is guilty of an indictable offence and liable to imprisonment for a term not exceeding fourteen years.

51. Intimidating Parliament or legislature — Every one who does an act of violence in order to intimidate Parliament or the legislature of a province is guilty of an indictable offence and liable to imprisonment for a term not exceeding fourteen years.

52. (1) Sabotage — Every person is guilty of an indictable offence and liable to imprisonment for a term of not more than 10 years or is guilty of an offence punishable on summary conviction who does a prohibited act for a purpose prejudicial to

(a) the safety, security or defence of Canada, or

(b) the safety or security of the naval, army or air forces of any state other than Canada that are lawfully present in Canada.

(2) **"prohibited act"** — In this section, **"prohibited act"** means an act or omission that

(a) impairs the efficiency or impedes the working of any vessel, vehicle, aircraft, machinery, apparatus or other thing; or

(b) causes property, by whomever it may be owned, to be lost, damaged or destroyed.

(3) **Saving** — No person does a prohibited act within the meaning of this section by reason only that

(a) he stops work as a result of the failure of his employer and himself to agree on any matter relating to his employment;

(b) he stops work as a result of the failure of his employer and a bargaining agent acting on his behalf to agree on any matter relating to his employment; or

(c) he stops work as a result of his taking part in a combination of workmen or employees for their own reasonable protection as workmen or employees.

(4) Idem — No person does a prohibited act within the meaning of this section by reason only that he attends at or near or approaches a dwelling-house or place for the purpose only of obtaining or communicating information.

2019, c. 25, s. 6

53. Inciting to mutiny — Every one who

(a) attempts, for a traitorous or mutinous purpose, to seduce a member of the Canadian Forces from his duty and allegiance to Her Majesty, or

(b) attempts to incite or to induce a member of the Canadian Forces to commit a traitorous or mutinous act,

is guilty of an indictable offence and liable to imprisonment for a term not exceeding fourteen years.

54. Assisting deserter — Every one who aids, assists, harbours or conceals a person who he knows is a deserter or absentee without leave from the Canadian Forces is guilty of an offence punishable on summary conviction, but no proceedings shall be instituted under this section without the consent of the Attorney General of Canada.

55. Evidence of overt acts — In proceedings for an offence against any provision in section 47 or sections 50 to 53, evidence of an overt act is not admissible unless that overt act is set out in the indictment or unless the evidence is otherwise relevant as tending to prove an overt act that is set out in the indictment.

2018, c. 29, s. 2

56. Offences in relation to members of R.C.M.P. — Every one who wilfully

(a) persuades or counsels a member of the Royal Canadian Mounted Police to desert or absent himself without leave,

(b) aids, assists, harbours or conceals a member of the Royal Canadian Mounted Police who he knows is a deserter or absentee without leave, or

(c) aids or assists a member of the Royal Canadian Mounted Police to desert or absent himself without leave, knowing that the member is about to desert or absent himself without leave,

is guilty of an offence punishable on summary conviction.

R.S.C. 1985, c. 27 (1st Supp.), s. 8

Official Documents

[Heading amended 2009, c. 28, s. 1.]

56.1 (1) Identity documents — Every person commits an offence who, without lawful excuse, procures to be made, possesses, transfers, sells or offers for sale an identity document that relates or purports to relate, in whole or in part, to another person.

(2) For greater certainty — For greater certainty, subsection (1) does not prohibit an act that is carried out

(a) in good faith, in the ordinary course of the person's business or employment or in the exercise of the duties of their office;

(b) for genealogical purposes;

(c) with the consent of the person to whom the identity document relates or of a person authorized to consent on behalf of the person to whom the document relates, or of the entity that issued the identity document; or

(d) for a legitimate purpose related to the administration of justice.

(3) Definition of "identity document" — For the purposes of this section, **"identity document"** means a Social Insurance Number card, a driver's licence, a health insurance card, a birth certificate, a death certificate, a passport as defined in subsection 57(5), a document that simplifies the process of entry into Canada, a certificate of citizenship, a document indicating immigration status in Canada, a certificate of Indian status or an employee identity card that bears the employee's photograph and signature, or any similar document, issued or purported to be issued by a department or agency of the federal government or of a provincial or foreign government.

(4) Punishment — Every person who commits an offence under subsection (1)

(a) is guilty of an indictable offence and liable to imprisonment for a term of not more than five years; or

(b) is guilty of an offence punishable on summary conviction.

2009, c. 28, s. 1

57. (1) Forgery of or uttering forged passport — Every one who, while in or out of Canada,

(a) forges a passport, or

(b) knowing that a passport is forged

(i) uses, deals with or acts on it, or

(ii) causes or attempts to cause any person to use, deal with, or act on it, as if the passport were genuine,

is guilty of an indictable offence and liable to imprisonment for a term not exceeding fourteen years.

(2) False statement in relation to passport — Every one who, while in or out of Canada, for the purpose of procuring a passport for himself or any other person or for the purpose of procuring any material alteration or addition to any such passport, makes a written or an oral statement that he knows is false or misleading

(a) is guilty of an indictable offence and liable to imprisonment for a term not exceeding two years; or

(b) is guilty of an offence punishable on summary conviction.

(3) **Possession of forged, etc., passport** — Every person who, without lawful excuse, has in their possession a forged passport or a passport in respect of which an offence under subsection (2) has been committed is guilty of

(a) an indictable offence and liable to imprisonment for a term of not more than five years; or

(b) an offence punishable on summary conviction.

(4) **Special provisions applicable** — For the purposes of proceedings under this section,

(a) the place where a passport was forged is not material; and

(b) the definition "false document" in section 321, and section 366, apply with such modifications as the circumstances require.

(5) **Definition of "passport"** — In this section, **"passport"** has the same meaning as in section 2 of the *Canadian Passport Order*.

(6) **Jurisdiction** — Where a person is alleged to have committed, while out of Canada, an offence under this section, proceedings in respect of that offence may, whether or not that person is in Canada, be commenced in any territorial division in Canada and the accused may be tried and punished in respect of that offence in the same manner as if the offence had been committed in that territorial division.

(7) **Appearance of accused at trial** — For greater certainty, the provisions of this Act relating to

(a) requirements that an accused appear at and be present during proceedings, and

(b) the exceptions to those requirements,

apply to proceedings commenced in any territorial division pursuant to subsection (6).

R.S.C. 1985, c. 27 (1st Supp.), s. 9; 1994, c. 44, s. 4; 1995, c. 5, s. 25(1)(g); 2013, c. 40, s. 174; 2018, c. 29, s. 3; 2019, c. 25, s. 7

58. (1) Fraudulent use of certificate of citizenship — Every person is guilty of an indictable offence and liable to imprisonment for a term of not more than two years or is guilty of an offence punishable on summary conviction who, while in or outside Canada,

(a) uses a certificate of citizenship or a certificate of naturalization for a fraudulent purpose, or

(b) being a person to whom a certificate of citizenship or a certificate of naturalization has been granted, knowingly parts with the possession of that certificate with intent that it should be used for a fraudulent purpose.

(2) **Definition of "certificate of citizenship" and "certificate of naturalization"** — In this section, **"certificate of citizenship"** and **"certificate of naturalization"** respectively, mean a certificate of citizenship and a certificate of naturalization as defined by the *Citizenship Act*.

2019, c. 25, s. 8

Sedition

59. (1) Seditious words — Seditious words are words that express a seditious intention.

(2) Seditious libel — A seditious libel is a libel that expresses a seditious intention.

(3) Seditious conspiracy — A seditious conspiracy is an agreement between two or more persons to carry out a seditious intention.

(4) Seditious intention — Without limiting the generality of the meaning of the expression **"seditious intention"**, every one shall be presumed to have a seditious intention who

(a) teaches or advocates, or

(b) publishes or circulates any writing that advocates,

the use, without the authority of law, of force as a means of accomplishing a governmental change within Canada.

60. Exception — Notwithstanding subsection 59(4), no person shall be deemed to have a seditious intention by reason only that he intends, in good faith,

(a) to show that Her Majesty has been misled or mistaken in her measures;

(b) to point out errors or defects in

(i) the government or constitution of Canada or a province,

(ii) Parliament or the legislature of a province, or

(iii) the administration of justice in Canada;

(c) to procure, by lawful means, the alteration of any matter of government in Canada; or

(d) to point out, for the purpose of removal, matters that produce or tend to produce feelings of hostility and ill-will between different classes of persons in Canada.

61. Punishment of seditious offences — Every one who

(a) speaks seditious words,

(b) publishes a seditious libel, or

(c) is a party to a seditious conspiracy,

is guilty of an indictable offence and liable to imprisonment for a term not exceeding fourteen years.

62. (1) Offences in relation to military forces — Every person is guilty of an indictable offence and liable to imprisonment for a term of not more than five years or is guilty of an offence punishable on summary conviction who intentionally

(a) interferes with, impairs or influences the loyalty or discipline of a member of a force,

(b) publishes, edits, issues, circulates or distributes a writing that advises, counsels or urges insubordination, disloyalty, mutiny or refusal of duty by a member of a force, or

(c) advises, counsels, urges or in any manner causes insubordination, disloyalty, mutiny or refusal of duty by a member of a force.

(2) "member of a force" — In this section, **"member of a force"** means a member of

(a) the Canadian Forces; or

(b) the naval, army or air forces of a state other than Canada that are lawfully present in Canada.

2019, c. 25, s. 9

Unlawful Assemblies and Riots

63. (1) Unlawful assembly — An unlawful assembly is an assembly of three or more persons who, with intent to carry out any common purpose, assemble in such a manner or so conduct themselves when they are assembled as to cause persons in the neighbourhood of the assembly to fear, on reasonable grounds, that they

(a) will disturb the peace tumultuously; or

(b) will by that assembly needlessly and without reasonable cause provoke other persons to disturb the peace tumultuously.

(2) Lawful assembly becoming unlawful — Persons who are lawfully assembled may become an unlawful assembly if they conduct themselves with a common purpose in a manner that would have made the assembly unlawful if they had assembled in that manner for that purpose.

(3) Exception — Persons are not unlawfully assembled by reason only that they are assembled to protect the dwelling-house of any one of them against persons who are threatening to break and enter it for the purpose of committing an indictable offence therein.

64. Riot — A riot is an unlawful assembly that has begun to disturb the peace tumultuously.

65. (1) Punishment of rioter — Every person who takes part in a riot is guilty of

(a) an indictable offence and liable to imprisonment for a term of not more than two years; or

(b) an offence punishable on summary conviction.

(2) Concealment of identity — Every person who commits an offence under subsection (1) while wearing a mask or other disguise to conceal their identity without lawful excuse is guilty of

(a) an indictable offence and liable to imprisonment for a term of not more than 10 years; or

(b) an offence punishable on summary conviction.

2013, c. 15, s. 2; 2019, c. 25, s. 10

66. (1) Punishment for unlawful assembly — Every one who is a member of an unlawful assembly is guilty of an offence punishable on summary conviction.

(2) Concealment of identity — Every person who commits an offence under subsection (1) while wearing a mask or other disguise to conceal their identity without lawful excuse is guilty of

(a) an indictable offence and liable to imprisonment for a term not exceeding five years; or

(b) an offence punishable on summary conviction.

2013, c. 15, s. 3

67. Reading proclamation — A person who is

(a) a justice, mayor or sheriff, or the lawful deputy of a mayor or sheriff,

(b) a warden or deputy warden of a prison, or

(c) the institutional head of a penitentiary, as those expressions are defined in subsection 2(1) of the *Corrections and Conditional Release Act*, or that person's deputy,

who receives notice that, at any place within the jurisdiction of the person, twelve or more persons are unlawfully and riotously assembled together shall go to that place and, after approaching as near as is safe, if the person is satisfied that a riot is in progress, shall command silence and thereupon make or cause to be made in a loud voice a proclamation in the following words or to the like effect: Her Majesty the Queen charges and commands all persons being assembled immediately to disperse and peaceably to depart to their habitations or to their lawful business on the pain of being guilty of an offence for which, on conviction, they may be sentenced to imprisonment for life. GOD SAVE THE QUEEN.

1994, c. 44, s. 5

68. Offences related to proclamation — Every one is guilty of an indictable offence and liable to imprisonment for life who

(a) opposes, hinders or assaults, wilfully and with force, a person who begins to make or is about to begin to make or is making the proclamation referred to in section 67 so that it is not made;

(b) does not peaceably disperse and depart from a place where the proclamation referred to in section 67 is made within thirty minutes after it is made; or

(c) does not depart from a place within thirty minutes when he has reasonable grounds to believe that the proclamation referred to in section 67 would have been made in that place if some person had not opposed, hindered or assaulted, wilfully and with force, a person who would have made it.

69. Neglect by peace officer — A peace officer who receives notice that there is a riot within their jurisdiction and, without reasonable excuse, fails to take all reasonable steps to suppress the riot is guilty of

(a) an indictable offence and liable to imprisonment for a term of not more than two years; or

(b) an offence punishable on summary conviction.

2019, c. 25, s. 11

Unlawful Drilling

70. (1) Orders by Governor in Council — The Governor in Council may by proclamation, make orders

(a) to prohibit assemblies, without lawful authority, of persons for the purpose

(i) of training or drilling themselves,

(ii) of being trained or drilled to the use of arms, or

(iii) of practising military exercises; or

(b) to prohibit persons when assembled for any purpose from training or drilling themselves or from being trained or drilled.

(2) General or special order — An order that is made under subsection (1) may be general or may be made applicable to particular places, districts or assemblies to be specified in the order.

(3) Punishment — Every person who contravenes an order made under this section is guilty of

(a) an indictable offence and liable to imprisonment for a term of not more than five years; or

(b) an offence punishable on summary conviction.

2019, c. 25, s. 12

Heading and s. 71. [Repealed 2018, c. 29, s. 4.]

Forcible Entry and Detainer

72. (1) Forcible entry — A person commits forcible entry when that person enters real property that is in the actual and peaceable possession of another in a manner that is likely to cause a breach of the peace or reasonable apprehension of a breach of the peace.

(1.1) Matters not material — For the purposes of subsection (1), it is immaterial whether or not a person is entitled to enter the real property or whether or not that person has any intention of taking possession of the real property.

(2) Forcible detainer — A person commits forcible detainer when, being in actual possession of real property without colour of right, he detains it in a manner that is likely to cause a breach of the peace or reasonable apprehension of a breach of the peace, against a person who is entitled by law to possession of it.

(3) Questions of law — The questions whether a person is in actual and peaceable possession or is in actual possession without colour of right are questions of law.

R.S.C. 1985, c. 27 (1st Supp.), s. 10

73. Punishment — Every person who commits forcible entry or forcible detainer is guilty of

(a) an indictable offence and liable to imprisonment for a term of not more than two years; or

(b) an offence punishable on summary conviction.

R.S.C. 1985, c. 27 (1st Supp.), s. 11; 1992, c. 1, s. 58(1) (Sched. I, item 2); 2019, c. 25, s. 13

Piracy

74. (1) Piracy by law of nations — Every one commits piracy who does any act that, by the law of nations, is piracy.

(2) Punishment — Every one who commits piracy while in or out of Canada is guilty of an indictable offence and liable to imprisonment for life.

75. Piratical acts — Every one who, while in or out of Canada,

(a) steals a Canadian ship,

(b) steals or without lawful authority throws overboard, damages or destroys anything that is part of the cargo, supplies or fittings in a Canadian ship,

(c) does or attempts to do a mutinous act on a Canadian ship, or

(d) counsels a person to do anything mentioned in paragraph *(a)*, *(b)* or *(c)*,

is guilty of an indictable offence and liable to imprisonment for a term not exceeding fourteen years.

R.S.C. 1985, c. 27 (1st Supp.), s. 7(3)

Offences Against Air or Maritime Safety

76. Hijacking — Every one who, unlawfully, by force or threat thereof, or by any other form of intimidation, seizes or exercises control of an aircraft with intent

(a) to cause any person on board the aircraft to be confined or imprisoned against his will,

(b) to cause any person on board the aircraft to be transported against his will to any place other than the next scheduled place of landing of the aircraft,

(c) to hold any person on board the aircraft for ransom or to service against his will, or

(d) to cause the aircraft to deviate in a material respect from its flight plan,

is guilty of an indictable offence and liable to imprisonment for life.

77. Endangering safety of aircraft or airport — Every one who,

(a) on board an aircraft in flight, commits an act of violence against a person that is likely to endanger the safety of the aircraft,

(b) using a weapon, commits an act of violence against a person at an airport serving international civil aviation that causes or is likely to cause serious injury or death and that endangers or is likely to endanger safety at the airport,

(c) causes damage to an aircraft in service that renders the aircraft incapable of flight or that is likely to endanger the safety of the aircraft in flight,

(d) places or causes to be placed on board an aircraft in service anything that is likely to cause damage to the aircraft, that will render it incapable of flight or that is likely to endanger the safety of the aircraft in flight,

(e) causes damage to or interferes with the operation of any air navigation facility where the damage or interference is likely to endanger the safety of an aircraft in flight,

(f) using a weapon, substance or device, destroys or causes serious damage to the facilities of an airport serving international civil aviation or to any aircraft not in service located there, or causes disruption of services of the airport, that endangers or is likely to endanger safety at the airport, or

(g) endangers the safety of an aircraft in flight by communicating to any other person any information that the person knows to be false,

is guilty of an indictable offence and liable to imprisonment for life.

1993, c. 7, s. 3

78. (1) Offensive weapons and explosive substances — Every one, other than a peace officer engaged in the execution of his duty, who takes on board a civil aircraft an offensive weapon or any explosive substance

(a) without the consent of the owner or operator of the aircraft or of a person duly authorized by either of them to consent thereto, or

(b) with the consent referred to in paragraph (*a*) but without complying with all terms and conditions on which the consent was given,

is guilty of an indictable offence and liable to imprisonment for a term not exceeding fourteen years.

(2) Definition of "civil aircraft" — For the purposes of this section, **"civil aircraft"** means all aircraft other than aircraft operated by the Canadian Forces, a police force in Canada or persons engaged in the administration or enforcement of the *Customs Act*, the *Excise Act* or the *Excise Act, 2001*.

R.S.C. 1985, c. 1 (2nd Supp.), s. 213(3) (Sched. III, item 1); 2002, c. 22, s. 325

78.1 (1) Seizing control of ship or fixed platform — Every one who seizes or exercises control over a ship or fixed platform by force or threat of force or by any other form of intimidation is guilty of an indictable offence and liable to imprisonment for life.

(2) Endangering safety of ship or fixed platform — Every one who

(a) commits an act of violence against a person on board a ship or fixed platform,

(b) destroys or causes damage to a ship or its cargo or to a fixed platform,

(c) destroys or causes serious damage to or interferes with the operation of any maritime navigational facility, or

(d) places or causes to be placed on board a ship or fixed platform anything that is likely to cause damage to the ship or its cargo or to the fixed platform,

where that act is likely to endanger the safe navigation of a ship or the safety of a fixed platform, is guilty of an indictable offence and liable to imprisonment for life.

(3) False communication — Every one who communicates information that endangers the safe navigation of a ship, knowing the information to be false, is guilty of an indictable offence and liable to imprisonment for life.

(4) Threats causing death or injury — Every one who threatens to commit an offence under paragraph (2)(*a*), (b) or (*c*) in order to compel a person to do or refrain from doing any act, where the threat is likely to endanger the safe navigation of a ship or the safety of a fixed platform, is guilty of an indictable offence and liable to imprisonment for life.

(5) Definitions — In this section,

"fixed platform" means an artificial island or a marine installation or structure that is permanently attached to the seabed for the purpose of exploration or exploitation of resources or for other economic purposes;

"ship" means every description of vessel not permanently attached to the seabed, other than a warship, a ship being used as a naval auxiliary or for customs or police purposes or a ship that has been withdrawn from navigation or is laid up.

1993, c. 7, s. 4

Dangerous Materials and Devices

[Heading amended 2013, c. 13, s. 4.]

79. Duty of care re explosive — Every one who has an explosive substance in his possession or under his care or control is under a legal duty to use reasonable care to prevent bodily harm or death to persons or damage to property by that explosive substance.

80. Breach of duty — Every one who, being under a legal duty within the meaning of section 79, fails without lawful excuse to perform that duty, is guilty of an indictable offence and, if as a result an explosion of an explosive substance occurs that

(a) causes death or is likely to cause death to any person, is liable to imprisonment for life; or

(b) causes bodily harm or damage to property or is likely to cause bodily harm or damage to property, is liable to imprisonment for a term not exceeding fourteen years.

81. (1) Using explosives — Every one commits an offence who

(a) does anything with intent to cause an explosion of an explosive substance that is likely to cause serious bodily harm or death to persons or is likely to cause serious damage to property;

(b) with intent to do bodily harm to any person

(i) causes an explosive substance to explode,

(ii) sends or delivers to a person or causes a person to take or receive an explosive substance or any other dangerous substance or thing, or

(iii) places or throws anywhere or at or on a person a corrosive fluid, explosive substance or any other dangerous substance or thing;

(c) with intent to destroy or damage property without lawful excuse, places or throws an explosive substance anywhere; or

(d) makes or has in his possession or has under his care or control any explosive substance with intent thereby

(i) to endanger life or to cause serious damage to property, or

(ii) to enable another person to endanger life or to cause serious damage to property.

(2) Punishment — Every one who commits an offence under subsection (1) is guilty of an indictable offence and liable

(a) for an offence under paragraph (1)(*a*) or (*b*), to imprisonment for life, or

(b) for an offence under paragraph (1)(*c*) or (*d*), to imprisonment for a term not exceeding fourteen years.

82. (1) Possession of explosive — Every person who, without lawful excuse, makes or has in their possession or under their care or control any explosive substance is guilty of

(a) an indictable offence and liable to imprisonment for a term of not more than five years; or

(b) an offence punishable on summary conviction.

(2) Possession in association with criminal organization — Every person who, without lawful excuse, makes or has in their possession or under their care or control any explosive substance for the benefit of, at the direction of or in association with a criminal organization is guilty of an indictable offence and liable to imprisonment for a term of not more than 14 years.

R.S.C. 1985, c. 27 (1st Supp.), s. 12; 1997, c. 23, s. 2; 2018, c. 29, s. 5; 2019, c. 25, s. 14

82.1 Sentences to be served consecutively — A sentence imposed on a person for an offence under subsection 82(2) shall be served consecutively to any other punishment imposed on the person for an offence arising out of the same event or series of events and to any other sentence to which the person is subject at the time the sentence is imposed on the person for an offence under subsection 82(2).

1997, c. 23, s. 2

82.2 Definition of "device" — For the purposes of sections 82.3 to 82.5, **"device"** means any of the following:

(a) a nuclear explosive device;

(b) a device that disperses radioactive material;

(c) a device that emits ionizing radiation and that is capable of causing death, serious bodily harm or substantial damage to property or the environment.

2013, c. 13, s. 5

82.3 Possession, etc., of nuclear material, radioactive material or device — Everyone who, with intent to cause death, serious bodily harm or substantial damage to property or the environment, makes a device or possesses, uses, transfers, exports, imports, alters or disposes of nuclear material, radioactive material or a device or commits an act against a nuclear facility or an act that causes serious interference with or serious disruption of its operations, is guilty of an indictable offence and liable to imprisonment for life.

2013, c. 13, s. 5

82.4 Use or alteration of nuclear material, radioactive material or device — Everyone who, with intent to compel a person, government or international organization to do or refrain from doing any act, uses or alters nuclear material, radioactive material or a device or commits an act against a nuclear facility or an act that causes serious interference with or serious disruption of its operations, is guilty of an indictable offence and liable to imprisonment for life.

2013, c. 13, s. 5

82.5 Commission of indictable offence to obtain nuclear material, etc. — Everyone who commits an indictable offence under this or any other Act of Parliament, with intent to obtain nuclear material, radioactive material or a device or to obtain access to a nuclear facility, is guilty of an indictable offence and is liable to imprisonment for life.

2013, c. 13, s. 5

82.6 Threats — Everyone who threatens to commit an offence under any of sections 82.3 to 82.5 is guilty of an indictable offence and is liable to imprisonment for a term of not more than 14 years.

2013, c. 13, s. 5

82.7 Armed forces — For greater certainty, sections 82.3 to 82.6 do not apply to an act that is committed during an armed conflict and that, at the time and in the place of its commission, is in accordance with customary international law or conventional international law applicable to the conflict, or to activities undertaken by military forces of a state in the exercise of their official duties, to the extent that those activities are governed by other rules of international law.

2013, c. 13, s. 5

Prize Fights

83. (1) Engaging in prize fight — Every one who

(a) engages as a principal in a prize fight,

(b) advises, encourages or promotes a prize fight, or

(c) is present at a prize fight as an aid, second, surgeon, umpire, backer or reporter,

is guilty of an offence punishable on summary conviction.

(2) Definition of "prize fight" — In this section, **"prize fight"** means an encounter or fight with fists, hands or feet between two persons who have met for that purpose by previous arrangement made by or for them, but does not include

(a) a contest between amateur athletes in a combative sport with fists, hands or feet held in a province if the sport is on the programme of the International Olympic Committee or the International Paralympic Committee and, in the case where the province's lieutenant governor in council or any other person or body specified by him or her requires it, the contest is held with their permission;

(b) a contest between amateur athletes in a combative sport with fists, hands or feet held in a province if the sport has been designated by the province's lieutenant governor in council or by any other person or body specified by him or her and, in the case where the lieutenant governor in council or other specified person or body requires it, the contest is held with their permission;

(c) a contest between amateur athletes in a combative sport with fists, hands or feet held in a province with the permission of the province's lieutenant governor in council or any other person or body specified by him or her; and

(d) a boxing contest or mixed martial arts contest held in a province with the permission or under the authority of an athletic board, commission or similar body established by or under the authority of the province's legislature for the control of sport within the province.

R.S.C. 1985, c. 27 (1st Supp.), s. 186; 2013, c. 19, s. 1

PART II.1 — TERRORISM (SS. 83.01–83.33)

Interpretation

[Heading added 2001, c. 41, s. 4.]

83.01 (1) Definitions — The following definitions apply in this Part.

"Canadian" means a Canadian citizen, a permanent resident within the meaning of subsection 2(1) of the *Immigration and Refugee Protection Act* or a body corporate incorporated and continued under the laws of Canada or a province. *("Canadien")*

"entity" means a person, group, trust, partnership or fund or an unincorporated association or organization. *("entité")*

"listed entity" means an entity on a list established by the Governor in Council under section 83.05. *("entité inscrite")*

"terrorist activity" means

(a) an act or omission that is committed in or outside Canada and that, if committed in Canada, is one of the following offences:

(i) the offences referred to in subsection 7(2) that implement the *Convention for the Suppression of Unlawful Seizure of Aircraft*, signed at The Hague on December 16, 1970,

(ii) the offences referred to in subsection 7(2) that implement the *Convention for the Suppression of Unlawful Acts against the Safety of Civil Aviation*, signed at Montreal on September 23, 1971,

(iii) the offences referred to in subsection 7(3) that implement the *Convention on the Prevention and Punishment of Crimes against Internationally Protected Persons, including Diplomatic Agents*, adopted by the General Assembly of the United Nations on December 14, 1973,

(iv) the offences referred to in subsection 7(3.1) that implement the *International Convention against the Taking of Hostages*, adopted by the General Assembly of the United Nations on December 17, 1979,

(v) the offences referred to in subsection 7(2.21) that implement the Convention on the Physical Protection of Nuclear Material, done at Vienna and New York on March 3, 1980, as amended by the Amendment to the Convention on the Physical Protection of Nuclear Material, done at Vienna on July 8, 2005 and the International Convention for the Suppression of Acts of Nuclear Terrorism, done at New York on September 14, 2005,

(vi) the offences referred to in subsection 7(2) that implement the *Protocol for the Suppression of Unlawful Acts of Violence at Airports Serving International Civil Aviation*, supplementary to the *Convention for the Suppression of Unlawful Acts against the Safety of Civil Aviation*, signed at Montreal on February 24, 1988,

(vii) the offences referred to in subsection 7(2.1) that implement the *Convention for the Suppression of Unlawful Acts against the Safety of Maritime Navigation*, done at Rome on March 10, 1988,

(viii) the offences referred to in subsection 7(2.1) or (2.2) that implement the *Protocol for the Suppression of Unlawful Acts against the Safety of Fixed Platforms Located on the Continental Shelf*, done at Rome on March 10, 1988,

(ix) the offences referred to in subsection 7(3.72) that implement the *International Convention for the Suppression of Terrorist Bombings*, adopted by the General Assembly of the United Nations on December 15, 1997, and

(x) the offences referred to in subsection 7(3.73) that implement the *International Convention for the Suppression of the Financing of Terrorism*, adopted by the General Assembly of the United Nations on December 9, 1999, or

(b) an act or omission, in or outside Canada,

(i) that is committed

(A) in whole or in part for a political, religious or ideological purpose, objective or cause, and

(B) in whole or in part with the intention of intimidating the public, or a segment of the public, with regard to its security, including its economic security, or compelling a person, a government or a domestic or an international organization to do or to refrain from doing any act, whether the public or the person, government or organization is inside or outside Canada, and

(ii) that intentionally

(A) causes death or serious bodily harm to a person by the use of violence,

(B) endangers a person's life,

(C) causes a serious risk to the health or safety of the public or any segment of the public,

(D) causes substantial property damage, whether to public or private property, if causing such damage is likely to result in the conduct or harm referred to in any of clauses (A) to (C), or

(E) causes serious interference with or serious disruption of an essential service, facility or system, whether public or private, other than as a result of advocacy, protest, dissent or stoppage of work that is not intended to result in the conduct or harm referred to in any of clauses (A) to (C),

and includes a conspiracy, attempt or threat to commit any such act or omission, or being an accessory after the fact or counselling in relation to any such act or omission, but, for greater certainty, does not include an act or omission that is committed during an armed conflict and that, at the time and in the place of its commission, is in accordance with customary international law or conventional international law applicable to the conflict, or the activities undertaken by military forces of a state in the exercise of their official duties, to the extent that those activities are governed by other rules of international law. (*"activité terroriste"*)

"terrorist group" means

(a) an entity that has as one of its purposes or activities facilitating or carrying out any terrorist activity, or

(b) a listed entity,

and includes an association of such entities. (*"groupe terroriste"*)

(1.1) For greater certainty — For greater certainty, the expression of a political, religious or ideological thought, belief or opinion does not come within paragraph (b) of the definition **"terrorist activity"** in subsection (1) unless it constitutes an act or omission that satisfies the criteria of that paragraph.

(1.2) For greater certainty — For greater certainty, a suicide bombing is an act that comes within paragraph (a) or (b) of the definition "terrorist activity" in subsection (1) if it satisfies the criteria of that paragraph.

(2) Facilitation — For the purposes of this Part, facilitation shall be construed in accordance with subsection 83.19(2).

2001, c. 41, ss. 4, 126(3); 2010, c. 19, s. 1; 2013, c. 13, s. 6

Financing of Terrorism

[Heading added 2001, c. 41, s. 4.]

83.02 Providing or collecting property for certain activities — Every person is guilty of an indictable offence and liable to imprisonment for a term of not more than 10 years who, directly or indirectly, wilfully and without lawful justification or excuse, provides or collects property intending that it be used or knowing that it will be used, in whole or in part, in order to carry out

(a) an act or omission that constitutes an offence referred to in subparagraphs (a)(i) to (ix) of the definition of "terrorist activity" in subsection 83.01(1), or

(b) any other act or omission intended to cause death or serious bodily harm to a civilian or to any other person not taking an active part in the hostilities in a situation of armed conflict, if the purpose of that act or omission, by its nature or context, is to intimidate the public, or to compel a government or an international organization to do or refrain from doing any act.

2001, c. 41, s. 4; 2019, c. 25, s. 15

83.03 Providing, making available, etc., property or services for terrorist purposes — Every person is guilty of an indictable offence and liable to imprisonment for a term of not more than 10 years who, directly or indirectly, collects property, provides or invites a person to provide, or makes available property or financial or other related services

(a) intending that they be used, or knowing that they will be used, in whole or in part, for the purpose of facilitating or carrying out any terrorist activity, or for the purpose of benefiting any person who is facilitating or carrying out such an activity, or

(b) knowing that, in whole or part, they will be used by or will benefit a terrorist group.

2001, c. 41, s. 4; 2019, c. 25, s. 16

83.04 Using or possessing property for terrorist purposes — Every person is guilty of an indictable offence and liable to imprisonment for a term of not more than 10 years who

(a) uses property, directly or indirectly, in whole or in part, for the purpose of facilitating or carrying out a terrorist activity, or

(b) possesses property intending that it be used or knowing that it will be used, directly or indirectly, in whole or in part, for the purpose of facilitating or carrying out a terrorist activity.

2001, c. 41, s. 4; 2019, c. 25, s. 17

List of Entities

[Heading added 2001, c. 41, s. 4.]

83.05 (1) Establishment of list — The Governor in Council may, by regulation, establish a list on which the Governor in Council may place any entity if, on the recommendation of the Minister of Public Safety and Emergency Preparedness, the Governor in Council is satisfied that there are reasonable grounds to believe that

(a) the entity has knowingly carried out, attempted to carry out, participated in or facilitated a terrorist activity; or

(b) the entity has knowingly acted on behalf of, at the direction of or in association with an entity referred to in paragraph (a).

(1.1) Recommendation — The Minister may make a recommendation referred to in subsection (1) only if he or she has reasonable grounds to believe that the entity to which the recommendation relates is an entity referred to in paragraph (1)(a) or (b).

(1.2) Amendment to name of listed entity — The Minister may, by regulation,

(a) change the name of a listed entity, or add to the list any other name by which a listed entity may also be or have been known, if the Minister has reasonable grounds to believe that the listed entity is using a name that is not on the list; and

(b) delete from the list any other name by which a listed entity may also have been known, if the entity is no longer using that name.

(2) Application to Minister — On application in writing by a listed entity to be removed from the list, the Minister shall decide whether the applicant should remain a listed entity or whether the Minister should recommend to the Governor in Council that the applicant be removed from the list, taking into account the grounds set out in subsection (1).

(3) Deeming — If the Minister does not make a decision on the application referred to in subsection (2) within 90 days after receipt of the application, or within any longer period that may be agreed to in writing by the Minister and the applicant, the Minister is deemed to have decided that the applicant should remain a listed entity.

(4) Notice of the decision to the applicant — The Minister shall give notice without delay to the applicant of any decision taken or deemed to have been taken respecting the application referred to in subsection (2).

(5) Judicial review — Within 60 days after the receipt of the notice of the decision referred to in subsection (4), the applicant may apply to a judge for judicial review of the decision.

(6) Reference — When an application is made under subsection (5), the judge shall, without delay

(a) examine, in private, any security or criminal intelligence reports considered in the making of the decision on whether the applicant should remain a listed entity and hear any other evidence or information that may be presented by or on behalf of the Minister and may, at his or her request, hear all or part of that evidence or information in the absence of the applicant and any counsel representing the applicant, if the judge is of the opinion that the disclosure of the information would injure national security or endanger the safety of any person;

(b) provide the applicant with a statement summarizing the information available to the judge so as to enable the applicant to be reasonably informed of the reasons for the decision, without disclosing any information the disclosure of which would, in the judge's opinion, injure national security or endanger the safety of any person;

(c) provide the applicant with a reasonable opportunity to be heard; and

(d) determine whether the decision is reasonable on the basis of the information available to the judge and, if found not to be reasonable, order that the applicant no longer be a listed entity.

(6.1) Evidence — The judge may receive into evidence anything that, in the opinion of the judge, is reliable and appropriate, even if it would not otherwise be admissible under Canadian law, and may base his or her decision on that evidence.

(7) Publication — The Minister shall cause to be published, without delay, in the *Canada Gazette* notice of a final order of a court that the applicant no longer be a listed entity.

(8) New application — A listed entity may not make another application under subsection (2) except if, since the time when the entity made its last application,

(a) there has been a material change in its circumstances; or

(b) the Minister has completed a review under subsection (8.1) with respect to that entity.

(8.1) Review — listed entity — The Minister shall review whether there are still reasonable grounds, as set out in subsection (1), for an entity to be a listed entity and make a recommendation to the Governor in Council as to whether the entity should remain a listed entity

(a) within five years after

(i) the day on which this subsection comes into force, if the entity is a listed entity on that day, or

(ii) the day on which the entity is added to the list, if the entity is added to the list after the day on which this subsection comes into force; and

(b) subsequently, within five years after the most recent recommendation made under this subsection with respect to the entity.

(9) Validity — Reviews undertaken under subsection (8.1) do not affect the validity of the list.

(10) Publication — The Minister shall cause notice of the results of every review of a listed entity undertaken under subsection (8.1) to be published in the *Canada Gazette* within five years after the review is completed.

(11) Definition of "judge" — In this section, **"judge"** means the Chief Justice of the Federal Court or a judge of that Court designated by the Chief Justice.

2001, c. 41, ss. 4, 143; 2005, c. 10, ss. 18, 34(1)(f)(iii); 2019, c. 13, s. 141

83.06 (1) Admission of foreign information obtained in confidence — For the purposes of subsection 83.05(6), in private and in the absence of the applicant or any counsel representing it,

(a) the Minister of Public Safety and Emergency Preparedness may make an application to the judge for the admission of information obtained in confidence from a government, an institution or an agency of a foreign state, from an international organization of states or from an institution or an agency of an international organization of states; and

(b) the judge shall examine the information and provide counsel representing the Minister with a reasonable opportunity to be heard as to whether the information is relevant but should not be disclosed to the applicant or any counsel representing it because the disclosure would injure national security or endanger the safety of any person.

(2) Return of information — The information shall be returned to counsel representing the Minister and shall not be considered by the judge in making the determination under paragraph 83.05(6)(d), if

(a) the judge determines that the information is not relevant;

(b) the judge determines that the information is relevant but should be summarized in the statement to be provided under paragraph 83.05(6)(b); or

(c) the Minister withdraws the application.

(3) Use of information — If the judge decides that the information is relevant but that its disclosure would injure national security or endanger the safety of persons, the information shall not be disclosed in the statement mentioned in paragraph 83.05(6)(b), but the judge may base the determination under paragraph 83.05(6)(d) on it.

2001, c. 41, s. 4; 2005, c. 10, s. 19

83.07 (1) Mistaken identity — An entity whose name is the same as or similar to a name, appearing on the list, of a listed entity and who claims not to be that listed entity may apply in writing to the Minister of Public Safety and Emergency Preparedness for a certificate stating that it is not that listed entity.

(2) Issuance of certificate — The Minister shall, within 30 days after receiving the application, issue a certificate if he or she is satisfied that the applicant is not that listed entity.

2001, c. 41, s. 4; 2005, c. 10, s. 20; 2019, c. 13, s. 142

Freezing of Property

[Heading added 2001, c. 41, s. 4.]

83.08 (1) Freezing of property — No person in Canada and no Canadian outside Canada shall knowingly

(a) deal directly or indirectly in any property that is owned or controlled by or on behalf of a terrorist group;

(b) enter into or facilitate, directly or indirectly, any transaction in respect of property referred to in paragraph (a); or

(c) provide any financial or other related services in respect of property referred to in paragraph (a) to, for the benefit of or at the direction of a terrorist group.

(2) No civil liability — A person who acts reasonably in taking, or omitting to take, measures to comply with subsection (1) shall not be liable in any civil action arising from having taken or omitted to take the measures, if they took all reasonable steps to satisfy themselves that the relevant property was owned or controlled by or on behalf of a terrorist group.

2001, c. 41, s. 4; 2013, c. 9, s. 3(2)

83.09 (1) Exemptions — The Minister of Public Safety and Emergency Preparedness, or a person designated by him or her, may authorize any person in Canada or any Canadian outside Canada to carry out a specified activity or transaction that is prohibited by section 83.08, or a class of such activities or transactions.

(2) Ministerial authorization — The Minister, or a person designated by him or her, may make the authorization subject to any terms and conditions that are required in their opinion and may amend, suspend, revoke or reinstate it.

(3) Existing equities maintained — All secured and unsecured rights and interests in the frozen property that are held by persons, other than terrorist groups or their agents, are entitled to the same ranking that they would have been entitled to had the property not been frozen.

(4) Third party involvement — If a person has obtained an authorization under subsection (1), any other person involved in carrying out the activity or transaction, or class of activities or transactions, to which the authorization relates is not subject to sections 83.08, 83.1 and 83.11 if the terms or conditions of the authorization that are imposed under subsection (2), if any, are met.

2001, c. 41, s. 4; 2005, c. 10, s. 21

83.1 (1) Disclosure — Every person in Canada and every Canadian outside Canada shall disclose without delay to the Commissioner of the Royal Canadian Mounted Police or to the Director of the Canadian Security Intelligence Service

(a) the existence of property in their possession or control that they know is owned or controlled by or on behalf of a terrorist group; and

(b) information about a transaction or proposed transaction in respect of property referred to in paragraph (a).

(2) Immunity — No criminal or civil proceedings lie against a person for disclosure made in good faith under subsection (1).

2001, c. 41, s. 4; 2013, c. 9, s. 4

83.11 (1) Audit — The following entities must determine on a continuing basis whether they are in possession or control of property owned or controlled by or on behalf of a listed entity:

(a) authorized foreign banks within the meaning of section 2 of the *Bank Act* in respect of their business in Canada, or banks to which that Act applies;

(b) cooperative credit societies, savings and credit unions and caisses populaires regulated by a provincial Act and associations regulated by the *Cooperative Credit Associations Act*;

(c) foreign companies within the meaning of subsection 2(1) of the *Insurance Companies Act* in respect of their insurance business in Canada;

(c.1) companies, provincial companies and societies within the meaning of subsection 2(1) of the *Insurance Companies Act*;

(c.2) fraternal benefit societies regulated by a provincial Act in respect of their insurance activities, and insurance companies and other entities engaged in the business of insuring risks that are regulated by a provincial Act;

(d) companies to which the *Trust and Loan Companies Act* applies;

(e) trust companies regulated by a provincial Act;

(f) loan companies regulated by a provincial Act; and

(g) entities authorized under provincial legislation to engage in the business of dealing in securities, or to provide portfolio management or investment counselling services.

(2) Monthly report — Subject to the regulations, every entity referred to in paragraphs (1)(a) to (g) must report, within the period specified by regulation or, if no period is specified, monthly, to the principal agency or body that supervises or regulates it under federal or provincial law either

(a) that it is not in possession or control of any property referred to in subsection (1), or

(b) that it is in possession or control of such property, in which case it must also report the number of persons, contracts or accounts involved and the total value of the property.

(3) Immunity — No criminal or civil proceedings lie against a person for making a report in good faith under subsection (2).

(4) Regulations — The Governor in Council may make regulations

(a) excluding any entity or class of entities from the requirement to make a report referred to in subsection (2), and specifying the conditions of exclusion; and

(b) specifying a period for the purposes of subsection (2).

2001, c. 41, s. 4

83.12 (1) Offences — freezing of property, disclosure or audit — Every person who contravenes any of sections 83.08, 83.1 and 83.11 is guilty of an offence and liable

(a) on conviction on indictment, to imprisonment for a term of not more than 10 years; or

(b) on summary conviction, to a fine of not more than $100,000 or to imprisonment for a term of not more than two years less a day, or to both.

(2) [Repealed 2013, c. 9, s. 5.]

2001, c. 41, s. 4; 2013, c. 9, s. 5; 2019, c. 25, s. 18

Seizure and Restraint of Property

[Heading added 2001, c. 41, s. 4.]

83.13 (1) Seizure and restraint of assets — Where a judge of the Federal Court, on an *ex parte* application by the Attorney General, after examining the application in private, is satisfied that there are reasonable grounds to believe that there is in any building, receptacle or place any property in respect of which an order of forfeiture may be made under subsection 83.14(5), the judge may issue

(a) if the property is situated in Canada, a warrant authorizing a person named therein or a peace officer to search the building, receptacle or place for that property and to seize that property and any other property in respect of which that person or peace officer believes, on reasonable grounds, that an order of forfeiture may be made under that subsection; or

(b) if the property is situated in or outside Canada, a restraint order prohibiting any person from disposing of, or otherwise dealing with any interest in, that property other than as may be specified in the order.

(1.1) Contents of application — An affidavit in support of an application under subsection (1) may be sworn on information and belief, and, notwithstanding the *Federal Court Rules, 1998*, no adverse inference shall be drawn from a failure to provide evidence of persons having personal knowledge of material facts.

(2) Appointment of manager — On an application under subsection (1), at the request of the Attorney General, if a judge is of the opinion that the circumstances so require, the judge may

(a) appoint a person to take control of, and to manage or otherwise deal with, all or part of the property in accordance with the directions of the judge; and

(b) require any person having possession of that property to give possession of the property to the person appointed under paragraph (a).

(3) Appointment of Minister of Public Works and Government Services — When the Attorney General of Canada so requests, a judge appointing a person under subsection (2) shall appoint the Minister of Public Works and Government Services.

(4) Power to manage — The power to manage or otherwise deal with property under subsection (2) includes

(a) the power to make an interlocutory sale of perishable or rapidly depreciating property;

(b) the power to destroy, in accordance with subsections (5) to (8), property that has little or no value; and

(c) the power to have property, other than real property or a conveyance, forfeited to Her Majesty in accordance with subsection (8.1).

(5) Application for destruction order — Before a person who is appointed to manage property destroys property that has little or no value, they shall apply to a judge of the Federal Court for a destruction order.

(6) Notice — Before making a destruction order, a judge shall require notice in accordance with subsection (7) to be given to and may hear any person who, in the judge's opinion, appears to have a valid interest in the property.

(7) Manner of giving notice — A notice shall

(a) be given in the manner that the judge directs or that may be specified in the rules of the Federal Court; and

(b) specify the effective period of the notice that the judge considers reasonable or that may be set out in the rules of the Federal Court.

(8) Destruction order — A judge shall order that the property be destroyed if they are satisfied that the property has little or no financial or other value.

(8.1) Forfeiture order — On application by a person who is appointed to manage the property, a judge of the Federal Court shall order that the property, other than real property or a conveyance, be forfeited to Her Majesty to be disposed of or otherwise dealt with in accordance with the law if

(a) a notice is given or published in the manner that the judge directs or that may be specified in the rules of the Federal Court;

(b) the notice specifies a period of 60 days during which a person may make an application to the judge asserting their interest in the property; and

(c) during that period, no one makes such an application.

(9) When management order ceases to have effect — A management order ceases to have effect when the property that is the subject of the management order is returned in accordance with the law, destroyed or forfeited to Her Majesty.

(9.1) For greater certainty — For greater certainty, if property that is the subject of a management order is sold, the management order applies to the net proceeds of the sale.

(10) Application to vary — The Attorney General may at any time apply to a judge of the Federal Court to cancel or vary an order or warrant made under this section, other than an appointment made under subsection (3).

(11) Procedure — Subsections 462.32(4) and (6), sections 462.34 to 462.35 and 462.4, subsection 487(3) and section 488 apply, with any modifications that the circumstances require, to a warrant issued under paragraph (1)(a). Any peace officer who executes the warrant must have authority to act as a peace officer in the place where it is executed.

(12) Procedure — Subsections 462.33(4) and (6) to (11) and sections 462.34 to 462.35 and 462.4 apply, with such modifications as the circumstances require, to an order issued under paragraph (1)(b).

2001, c. 41, s. 4; 2017, c. 7, s. 54; 2019, c. 25, s. 19

Forfeiture of Property

[Heading added 2001, c. 41, s. 4.]

83.14 (1) Application for order of forfeiture — The Attorney General may make an application to a judge of the Federal Court for an order of forfeiture in respect of

(a) property owned or controlled by or on behalf of a terrorist group; or

(b) property that has been or will be used, in whole or in part, to facilitate or carry out a terrorist activity.

(2) Contents of application — An affidavit in support of an application by the Attorney General under subsection (1) may be sworn on information and belief, and, notwithstanding the *Federal Court Rules, 1998*, no adverse inference shall be drawn from a failure to provide evidence of persons having personal knowledge of material facts.

(3) Respondents — The Attorney General is required to name as a respondent to an application under subsection (1) only those persons who are known to own or control the property that is the subject of the application.

(4) Notice — The Attorney General shall give notice of an application under subsection (1) to named respondents in such a manner as the judge directs or as provided in the rules of the Federal Court.

(5) Granting of forfeiture order — If a judge is satisfied on a balance of probabilities that property is property referred to in paragraph (1)(a) or (b), the judge shall order that the property be forfeited to Her Majesty to be disposed of as the Attorney General directs or otherwise dealt with in accordance with the law.

(5.1) Use of proceeds — Any proceeds that arise from the disposal of property under subsection (5) may be used to compensate victims of terrorist activities and to fund anti-terrorist initiatives in accordance with any regulations made by the Governor in Council under subsection (5.2).

(5.2) Regulations — The Governor in Council may make regulations for the purposes of specifying how the proceeds referred to in subsection (5.1) are to be distributed.

(6) Order refusing forfeiture — Where a judge refuses an application under subsection (1) in respect of any property, the judge shall make an order that describes the property and declares that it is not property referred to in that subsection.

(7) Notice — On an application under subsection (1), a judge may require notice to be given to any person who, in the opinion of the Court, appears to have an interest in the property, and any such person shall be entitled to be added as a respondent to the application.

(8) Third party interests — If a judge is satisfied that a person referred to in subsection (7) has an interest in property that is subject to an application, has exercised reasonable care to ensure that the property would not be used to facilitate or carry out a terrorist activity, and is not a member of a terrorist group, the judge shall order that the interest is not affected by the forfeiture. Such an order shall declare the nature and extent of the interest in question.

(9) Dwelling-house — Where all or part of property that is the subject of an application under subsection (1) is a dwelling-house, the judge shall also consider

(a) the impact of an order of forfeiture on any member of the immediate family of the person who owns or controls the dwelling-house, if the dwelling-house was the member's principal residence at the time the dwelling-house was ordered restrained or at the time the forfeiture application was made and continues to be the member's principal residence; and

(b) whether the member appears innocent of any complicity or collusion in the terrorist activity.

(10) Motion to vary or set aside — A person who claims an interest in property that was forfeited and who did not receive notice under subsection (7) may bring a motion to the Federal Court to vary or set aside an order made under subsection (5) not later than 60 days after the day on which the forfeiture order was made.

(11) No extension of time — The Court may not extend the period set out in subsection (10).

2001, c. 41, s. 4

83.15 Disposition of property — Subsection 462.42(6) and sections 462.43 and 462.46 apply, with such modifications as the circumstances require, to property subject to a warrant or restraint order issued under subsection 83.13(1) or ordered forfeited under subsection 83.14(5).

2001, c. 41, s. 4

83.16 (1) Interim preservation rights — Pending any appeal of an order made under section 83.14, property restrained under an order issued under section 83.13 shall continue to be restrained, property seized under a warrant issued under that section shall continue to be detained, and any person appointed to manage, control or otherwise deal with that property under that section shall continue in that capacity.

(2) Appeal of refusal to grant order — Section 462.34 applies, with such modifications as the circumstances require, to an appeal taken in respect of a refusal to grant an order under subsection 83.14(5).

2001, c. 41, s. 4

83.17 (1) Other forfeiture provisions unaffected — This Part does not affect the operation of any other provision of this or any other Act of Parliament respecting the forfeiture of property.

(2) Priority for restitution to victims of crime — Property is subject to forfeiture under subsection 83.14(5) only to the extent that it is not required to satisfy the operation of any other provision of this or any other Act of Parliament respecting restitution to, or compensation of, persons affected by the commission of offences.

2001, c. 41, s. 4

Participating, Facilitating, Instructing and Harbouring

[Heading added 2001, c. 41, s. 4.]

83.18 (1) Participation in activity of terrorist group — Every person who knowingly participates in or contributes to, directly or indirectly, any activity of a terrorist group for the purpose of enhancing the ability of any terrorist group to facilitate or carry out a terrorist activity is guilty of an indictable offence and liable to imprisonment for a term of not more than 10 years.

(2) Prosecution — An offence may be committed under subsection (1) whether or not

(a) a terrorist group actually facilitates or carries out a terrorist activity;

(b) the participation or contribution of the accused actually enhances the ability of a terrorist group to facilitate or carry out a terrorist activity; or

(c) the accused knows the specific nature of any terrorist activity that may be facilitated or carried out by a terrorist group.

(3) Meaning of participating or contributing — Participating in or contributing to an activity of a terrorist group includes

(a) providing, receiving or recruiting a person to receive training;

(b) providing or offering to provide a skill or an expertise for the benefit of, at the direction of or in association with a terrorist group;

(c) recruiting a person in order to facilitate or commit

(i) a terrorism offence, or

(ii) an act or omission outside Canada that, if committed in Canada, would be a terrorism offence;

(d) entering or remaining in any country for the benefit of, at the direction of or in association with a terrorist group; and

(e) making oneself, in response to instructions from any of the persons who constitute a terrorist group, available to facilitate or commit

(i) a terrorism offence, or

(ii) an act or omission outside Canada that, if committed in Canada, would be a terrorism offence.

(4) Factors — In determining whether an accused participates in or contributes to any activity of a terrorist group, the court may consider, among other factors, whether the accused

(a) uses a name, word, symbol or other representation that identifies, or is associated with, the terrorist group;

(b) frequently associates with any of the persons who constitute the terrorist group;

(c) receives any benefit from the terrorist group; or

(d) repeatedly engages in activities at the instruction of any of the persons who constitute the terrorist group.

2001, c. 41, s. 4; 2019, c. 25, s. 20

83.181 Leaving Canada to participate in activity of terrorist group — Every person who leaves or attempts to leave Canada, or goes or attempts to go on board a conveyance with the intent to leave Canada, for the purpose of committing an act or omission outside Canada that, if committed in Canada, would be an offence under subsection 83.18(1) is guilty of an indictable offence and liable to imprisonment for a term of not more than 10 years.

2013, c. 9, s. 6; 2019, c. 25, s. 21

83.19 (1) Facilitating terrorist activity — Every one who knowingly facilitates a terrorist activity is guilty of an indictable offence and liable to imprisonment for a term not exceeding fourteen years.

(2) Facilitation — For the purposes of this Part, a terrorist activity is facilitated whether or not

(a) the facilitator knows that a particular terrorist activity is facilitated;

(b) any particular terrorist activity was foreseen or planned at the time it was facilitated; or

(c) any terrorist activity was actually carried out.

2001, c. 41, s. 4

83.191 Leaving Canada to facilitate terrorist activity — Everyone who leaves or attempts to leave Canada, or goes or attempts to go on board a conveyance with the intent to leave Canada, for the purpose of committing an act or omission outside Canada that, if committed in Canada, would be an offence under subsection 83.19(1) is guilty of an indictable offence and liable to imprisonment for a term of not more than 14 years.

2013, c. 9, s. 7

83.2 Commission of offence for terrorist group — Every one who commits an indictable offence under this or any other Act of Parliament for the benefit of, at the direction of or in association with a terrorist group is guilty of an indictable offence and liable to imprisonment for life.

2001, c. 41, s. 4

83.201 Leaving Canada to commit offence for terrorist group — Everyone who leaves or attempts to leave Canada, or goes or attempts to go on board a conveyance with the intent to leave Canada, for the purpose of committing an act or omission outside Canada that, if committed in Canada, would be an indictable offence under this or any other Act of Parliament for the benefit of, at the direction of or in association with a terrorist group is guilty of an indictable offence and liable to imprisonment for a term of not more than 14 years.

2013, c. 9, s. 8

83.202 Leaving Canada to commit offence that is terrorist activity — Everyone who leaves or attempts to leave Canada, or goes or attempts to go on board a conveyance with the intent to leave Canada, for the purpose of committing an act or omission outside Canada that, if committed in Canada, would be an indictable offence under this or any other Act of Parliament if the act or omission constituting the offence also constitutes a terrorist activity is guilty of an indictable offence and liable to imprisonment for a term of not more than 14 years.

2013, c. 9, s. 8

83.21 (1) Instructing to carry out activity for terrorist group — Every person who knowingly instructs, directly or indirectly, any person to carry out any activity for the benefit of, at the direction of or in association with a terrorist group, for the purpose of enhancing the ability of any terrorist group to facilitate or carry out a terrorist activity, is guilty of an indictable offence and liable to imprisonment for life.

(2) Prosecution — An offence may be committed under subsection (1) whether or not

(a) the activity that the accused instructs to be carried out is actually carried out;

(b) the accused instructs a particular person to carry out the activity referred to in paragraph (a);

(c) the accused knows the identity of the person whom the accused instructs to carry out the activity referred to in paragraph (a);

(d) the person whom the accused instructs to carry out the activity referred to in paragraph (a) knows that it is to be carried out for the benefit of, at the direction of or in association with a terrorist group;

(e) a terrorist group actually facilitates or carries out a terrorist activity;

(f) the activity referred to in paragraph (a) actually enhances the ability of a terrorist group to facilitate or carry out a terrorist activity; or

(g) the accused knows the specific nature of any terrorist activity that may be facilitated or carried out by a terrorist group.

2001, c. 41, s. 4

83.22 (1) Instructing to carry out terrorist activity — Every person who knowingly instructs, directly or indirectly, any person to carry out a terrorist activity is guilty of an indictable offence and liable to imprisonment for life.

(2) Prosecution — An offence may be committed under subsection (1) whether or not

(a) the terrorist activity is actually carried out;

(b) the accused instructs a particular person to carry out the terrorist activity;

(c) the accused knows the identity of the person whom the accused instructs to carry out the terrorist activity; or

(d) the person whom the accused instructs to carry out the terrorist activity knows that it is a terrorist activity.

2001, c. 41, s. 4

83.221 (1) Counselling commission of terrorism offence — Every person who counsels another person to commit a terrorism offence without identifying a specific terrorism offence is guilty of an indictable offence and is liable to imprisonment for a term of not more than five years.

(2) Application — An offence may be committed under subsection (1) whether or not a terrorism offence is committed by the person who is counselled.

2015, c. 20, s. 16; 2019, c. 13, s. 143

83.222 (1) Warrant of seizure — A judge who is satisfied by information on oath that there are reasonable grounds to believe that any publication, copies of which are kept for sale or distribution in premises within the court's jurisdiction, is terrorist propaganda may issue a warrant authorizing seizure of the copies.

(2) Summons to occupier — Within seven days after the day on which the warrant is issued, the judge shall issue a summons to the premises' occupier requiring the occupier to appear before the court and to show cause why the matter seized should not be forfeited to Her Majesty.

(3) Owner and author may appear — The owner and the author of the matter seized and alleged to be terrorist propaganda may appear and be represented before the court in order to oppose the making of an order for the forfeiture of the matter.

(4) Order of forfeiture — If the court is satisfied, on a balance of probabilities, that the publication is terrorist propaganda, it may make an order declaring that the matter be forfeited to Her Majesty, for disposal as the Attorney General may direct.

(5) Disposal of matter — If the court is not satisfied that the publication is terrorist propaganda, it may order that the matter be restored to the person from whom it was seized without delay after the time for final appeal has expired.

(6) Appeal — An appeal lies from an order made under subsection (4) or (5) by any person who appeared before the court, on any ground of appeal that involves a question of law or fact alone, or a question of mixed law and fact, as if it were an appeal against conviction or against a judgment or verdict of acquittal, as the case may be, on a question of law alone under Part XXI, and sections 673 to 696 apply with any modifications that the circumstances require.

(7) Consent — No proceeding under this section shall be instituted without the Attorney General's consent.

(8) Definitions — The following definitions apply in this section.

"court" has the same meaning as in subsection 320(8). *("tribunal")*

"judge" has the same meaning as in subsection 320(8). *("juge")*

"terrorist propaganda" means any writing, sign, visible representation or audio recording that counsels the commission of a terrorism offence. *("propagande terroriste")*

2015, c. 20, s. 16; 2019, c. 13, s. 144

83.223 (1) Order to computer system's custodian — If a judge is satisfied by information on oath that there are reasonable grounds to believe that there is material — that is terrorist propaganda or computer data that makes terrorist propaganda available — stored on and made available to the public through a computer system that is within the court's jurisdiction, the judge may order the computer system's custodian to

(a) give an electronic copy of the material to the court;

(b) ensure that the material is no longer stored on and made available through the computer system; and

(c) provide the information that is necessary to identify and locate the person who posted the material.

(2) Notice to person who posted material — Within a reasonable time after receiving the information referred to in paragraph (1)(c), the judge shall cause notice to be given to the person who posted the material, giving that person the opportunity to appear and be represented before the court and to show cause why the material should not be deleted. If the person cannot be identified or located or does not reside in Canada, the judge may order the computer system's custodian to post the text of the notice at the location where the material was previously stored and made available, until the time set for the appearance.

(3) Person who posted material may appear — The person who posted the material may appear and be represented before the court in order to oppose the making of an order under subsection (5).

(4) Non-appearance — If the person who posted the material does not appear before the court, the court may proceed to hear and determine the proceedings in the absence of the person as fully and effectually as if the person had appeared.

(5) Order of deletion — If the court is satisfied, on a balance of probabilities, that the material is available to the public and is terrorist propaganda or computer data that makes terrorist propaganda available, it may order the computer system's custodian to delete the material.

(6) Destruction of electronic copy — When the court makes the order for the deletion of the material, it may order the destruction of the electronic copy in the court's possession.

(7) Return of material — If the court is not satisfied that the material is available to the public and is terrorist propaganda or computer data that makes terrorist propaganda available, the court shall order that the electronic copy be returned to the computer system's custodian and terminate the order under paragraph (1)(b).

(8) Appeal — An appeal lies from an order made under subsection (5) or (6) by any person who appeared before the court, on any ground of appeal that involves a question of law or fact alone, or a question of mixed law and fact, as if it were an appeal against conviction or against a judgment or verdict of acquittal, as the case may be, on a question of law alone under Part XXI, and sections 673 to 696 apply with any modifications that the circumstances require.

(9) Consent — No proceeding under this section shall be instituted without the Attorney General's consent.

(10) When order takes effect — No order made under any of subsections (5) to (7) takes effect until the time for final appeal has expired.

(11) Definitions — The following definitions apply in this section.

"computer data" has the same meaning as in subsection 342.1(2). *("données informatiques")*

"computer system" has the same meaning as in subsection 342.1(2). *("ordinateur")*

"court" has the same meaning as in subsection 320(8). *("tribunal")*

"data" [Repealed 2015, c. 20, s. 35(d).]

"judge" has the same meaning as in subsection 320(8). *("juge")*

"terrorist propaganda" has the same meaning as in subsection 83.222(8). *("propagande terroriste")*

2015, c. 20, ss. 16, 35

83.23 (1) Concealing person who carried out terrorist activity — Every person who knowingly harbours or conceals another person whom they know to be a person who has carried out a terrorist activity, for the purpose of enabling that other person to facilitate or carry out any terrorist activity, is guilty of

(a) an indictable offence and liable to imprisonment for a term of not more than 14 years, if the person who is harboured or concealed carried out a terrorist activity that is a terrorism offence for which that person is liable to imprisonment for life; and

(b) an indictable offence and liable to imprisonment for a term of not more than 10 years, if the person who is harboured or concealed carried out a terrorist activity that is a terrorism offence for which that person is liable to any other punishment.

(2) Concealing person who is likely to carry out terrorist activity — Every person who knowingly harbours or conceals another person whom they know to be a person who is likely to carry out a terrorist activity, for the purpose of enabling that other person to facilitate or carry out any terrorist activity, is guilty of an indictable offence and liable to imprisonment for a term of not more than 10 years.

2001, c. 41, s. 4; 2013, c. 9, s. 9; 2019, c. 25, s. 22

Hoax Regarding Terrorist Activity

[Heading added 2004, c. 15, s. 32.]

83.231 (1) Hoax — terrorist activity — Every one commits an offence who, without lawful excuse and with intent to cause any person to fear death, bodily harm, substantial damage to property or serious interference with the lawful use or operation of property,

(a) conveys or causes or procures to be conveyed information that, in all the circumstances, is likely to cause a reasonable apprehension that terrorist activity is occurring or will occur, without believing the information to be true; or

(b) commits an act that, in all the circumstances, is likely to cause a reasonable apprehension that terrorist activity is occurring or will occur, without believing that such activity is occurring or will occur.

(2) Punishment — Every one who commits an offence under subsection (1) is guilty of

(a) an indictable offence and liable to imprisonment for a term not exceeding five years; or

(b) an offence punishable on summary conviction.

(3) Causing bodily harm — Every one who commits an offence under subsection (1) and thereby causes bodily harm to any other person is guilty of

(a) an indictable offence and liable to imprisonment for a term not exceeding ten years; or

(b) an offence punishable on summary conviction.

(4) Causing death — Every one who commits an offence under subsection (1) and thereby causes the death of any other person is guilty of an indictable offence and liable to imprisonment for life.

2004, c. 15, s. 32; 2019, c. 25, s. 23

Proceedings and Aggravated Punishment

[Heading added 2001, c. 41, s. 4.]

83.24 Attorney General's consent — Proceedings in respect of a terrorism offence or an offence under section 83.12 shall not be commenced without the consent of the Attorney General.

2001, c. 41, s. 4

83.25 (1) Jurisdiction — Where a person is alleged to have committed a terrorism offence or an offence under section 83.12, proceedings in respect of that offence may, whether or not that person is in Canada, be commenced at the instance of the Government of Canada and conducted by the Attorney General of Canada or counsel acting on his or her behalf in any territorial division in Canada, if the offence is alleged to have occurred outside the province in which the proceedings are commenced, whether or not proceedings have previously been commenced elsewhere in Canada.

(2) Trial and punishment — An accused may be tried and punished in respect of an offence referred to in subsection (1) in the same manner as if the offence had been committed in the territorial division where the proceeding is conducted.

2001, c. 41, s. 4

83.26 Sentences to be served consecutively — A sentence, other than one of life imprisonment, imposed on a person for an offence under any of sections 83.02 to 83.04 and 83.18 to 83.23 shall be served consecutively to

(a) any other punishment imposed on the person, other than a sentence of life imprisonment, for an offence arising out of the same event or series of events; and

(b) any other sentence, other than one of life imprisonment, to which the person is subject at the time the sentence is imposed on the person for an offence under any of those sections.

2001, c. 41, s. 4

83.27 (1) Punishment for terrorist activity — Notwithstanding anything in this Act, a person convicted of an indictable offence, other than an offence for which a sentence of imprisonment for life is imposed as a minimum punishment, where the act or omission constituting the offence also constitutes a terrorist activity, is liable to imprisonment for life.

(2) Offender must be notified — Subsection (1) does not apply unless the prosecutor satisfies the court that the offender, before making a plea, was notified that the application of that subsection would be sought.

2001, c. 41, s. 4

Heading and ss. 83.28 and 83.29 [Repealed 2019, c. 13, s. 145.]

Recognizance with Conditions

[Heading added 2001, c. 41, s. 4.]

83.3 (1) Attorney General's consent — The Attorney General's consent is required before a peace officer may lay an information under subsection (2).

(2) Terrorist activity — Subject to subsection (1), a peace officer may lay an information before a provincial court judge if the peace officer

(a) believes on reasonable grounds that a terrorist activity may be carried out; and

(b) suspects on reasonable grounds that the imposition of a recognizance with conditions on a person, or the arrest of a person, is necessary to prevent the carrying out of the terrorist activity.

(3) Appearance — The judge who receives the information may cause the person to appear before any provincial court judge.

(4) Arrest without warrant — Despite subsections (2) and (3), a peace officer may arrest a person without a warrant and cause the person to be detained in custody, in order to bring them before a provincial court judge in accordance with subsection (6), if

(a) either

(i) the grounds for laying an information referred to in paragraphs (2)(a) and (b) exist but, by reason of exigent circumstances, it would be impracticable to lay an information under subsection (2), or

(ii) an information has been laid under subsection (2) and a summons has been issued; and

(b) the peace officer suspects on reasonable grounds that the detention of the person in custody is necessary to prevent a terrorist activity.

(5) Duty of peace officer — If a peace officer arrests a person without a warrant in the circumstance described in subparagraph (4)(a)(i), the peace officer shall, within the time prescribed by paragraph (6)(a) or (b),

(a) lay an information in accordance with subsection (2); or

(b) release the person.

(6) When person to be taken before judge — Unless a peace officer, or an officer in charge as defined in Part XVI, is satisfied that a person should be released from custody unconditionally before their appearance before a provincial court judge in accordance with the rules in paragraph (a) or (b), and so releases the person, the person detained in custody shall be taken before a provincial court judge in accordance with the following rules:

Proposed Amendment — 83.3(6) opening words

(6) When person to be taken before judge — Unless a peace officer is satisfied that a person should be released from custody without conditions before their appearance before a provincial court judge in accordance with the rules in paragraph (a) or (b), and so releases the person, the person detained in custody shall be taken before a provincial court judge in accordance with the following rules:

2019, c. 25, s. 24 [To come into force December 18, 2019.]

(a) if a provincial court judge is available within 24 hours after the person has been arrested, the person shall be taken before a provincial court judge without unreasonable delay and in any event within that period; and

(b) if a provincial court judge is not available within 24 hours after the person has been arrested, the person shall be taken before a provincial court judge as soon as feasible.

(7) How person dealt with — When a person is taken before a provincial court judge under subsection (6),

(a) if an information has not been laid under subsection (2), the judge shall order that the person be released; or

(b) if an information has been laid under subsection (2),

(i) the judge shall order that the person be released unless the peace officer who laid the information shows cause why the person's detention in custody is justified on one or more of the following grounds:

(A) the detention is necessary to ensure the person's appearance before a provincial court judge in order to be dealt with in accordance with subsection (8),

(B) the detention is necessary for the protection or safety of the public, including any witness, having regard to all the circumstances including

(I) the likelihood that, if the person is released from custody, a terrorist activity will be carried out, and

(II) any substantial likelihood that the person will, if released from custody, interfere with the administration of justice, and

(C) the detention is necessary to maintain confidence in the administration of justice, having regard to all the circumstances, including the apparent strength of the peace officer's grounds under subsection (2), and the gravity of any terrorist activity that may be carried out, and

(ii) the judge may adjourn the matter for a hearing under subsection (8) but, if the person is not released under subparagraph (i), the adjournment may not exceed 48 hours.

(7.1) Adjournment under subparagraph (7)(b)(ii) — If a judge has adjourned the matter under subparagraph (7)(b)(ii) and the person remains in custody at the end of the period of adjournment, the person shall be taken before a provincial court judge who

(a) shall order that the person be released unless a peace officer shows cause why the person's detention in custody is justified on one or more of the grounds set out in clauses (7)(b)(i)(A) to (C) and satisfies the judge that the investigation in relation to which the person is detained is being conducted diligently and expeditiously; and

(b) may adjourn the matter for a hearing under subsection (8) but, if the person is not released under paragraph (a), the adjournment may not exceed 48 hours.

(7.2) Adjournment under paragraph (7.1)(b) — If a judge has adjourned the matter under paragraph (7.1)(b) and the person remains in custody at the end of the period of adjournment, the person shall be taken before a provincial court judge who

(a) shall order that the person be released unless a peace officer shows cause why the person's detention in custody is justified on one or more of the grounds set out in clauses (7)(b)(i)(A) to (C) and satisfies the judge that the investigation in relation to which the person is detained is being conducted diligently and expeditiously; and

(b) may adjourn the matter for a hearing under subsection (8) but, if the person is not released under paragraph (a), the adjournment may not exceed 48 hours.

(8) Hearing before judge — The judge before whom the person appears in accordance with subsection (3)

(a) may, if the judge is satisfied by the evidence adduced that the peace officer has reasonable grounds for the suspicion, order that the person enter into a recognizance, with or without sureties, to keep the peace and be of good behaviour for a period of not more than 12 months and to comply with any other reasonable conditions prescribed in the recognizance, including the conditions set out in subsections (10), (11.1) and (11.2), that the judge considers desirable for preventing the carrying out of a terrorist activity; and

(b) if the person was not released under subparagraph (7)(b)(i) or paragraph (7.1)(a) or (7.2)(a), shall order that the person be released, subject to the recognizance, if any, ordered under paragraph (a).

(8.1) Duration extended — However, if the judge is also satisfied that the person was convicted previously of a terrorism offence, the judge may order that the person enter into the recognizance for a period of not more than two years.

(9) Refusal to enter into recognizance — The judge may commit the person to prison for a term not exceeding 12 months if the person fails or refuses to enter into the recognizance.

(10) Conditions — firearms — Before making an order under paragraph (8)(a), the judge shall consider whether it is desirable, in the interests of the safety of the person or of any other person, to include as a condition of the recognizance that the person be prohibited from possessing any firearm, crossbow, prohibited weapon, restricted weapon, prohibited device, ammunition, prohibited ammunition or explosive substance, or all of those things, for any period specified in the recognizance, and if the judge decides that it is so desirable, they shall add the condition to the recognizance.

(11) Surrender, etc. — If the judge adds the condition described in subsection (10) to a recognizance, they shall specify in it the manner and method by which

(a) the things referred to in that subsection that are in the person's possession shall be surrendered, disposed of, detained, stored or dealt with; and

(b) the authorizations, licences and registration certificates that are held by the person shall be surrendered.

(11.1) Condition — passport — The judge shall consider whether it is desirable, to prevent the carrying out of a terrorist activity, to include in the recognizance a condition that the person deposit, in the specified manner, any passport or other travel document issued in their name that is in their possession or control. If the judge decides that it is desirable, the judge shall add the condition to the recognizance and specify the period during which it applies.

(11.2) Condition — specified geographic area — The judge shall consider whether it is desirable, to prevent the carrying out of a terrorist activity, to include in the recognizance a condition that the person remain within a specified geographic area unless written permission to leave that area is obtained from the judge or any individual designated by the judge. If the judge decides that it is desirable, the judge shall add the condition to the recognizance and specify the period during which it applies.

(12) Reasons — If the judge does not add a condition described in subsection (10), (11.1) or (11.2) to a recognizance, the judge shall include in the record a statement of the reasons for not adding it.

(13) Variance of conditions — The judge, or any other judge of the same court, may, on application of the peace officer, the Attorney General or the person, vary the conditions fixed in the recognizance.

(14) Other provisions to apply — Subsections 810(4) and (5) apply, with any necessary modifications, to proceedings under this section.

2001, c. 41, s. 4; 2013, c. 9, s. 10; 2015, c. 20, s. 17; 2019, c. 13, s. 146(1), (3)

83.31 (1) and (1.1) [Repealed 2019, c. 13, s. 147.]

(2) Annual report (section 83.3) — The Attorney General of Canada shall prepare and cause to be laid before Parliament and the Attorney General of every province shall publish or otherwise make available to the public an annual report for the previous year on the operation of section 83.3 that includes

(a) the number of consents to lay an information that were sought, and the number that were obtained, by virtue of subsections 83.3(1) and (2);

(b) the number of cases in which a summons or a warrant of arrest was issued for the purposes of subsection 83.3(3);

(c) the number of cases in which a person was not released under subsection 83.3(7), (7.1) or (7.2) pending a hearing;

(d) the number of cases in which an order to enter into a recognizance was made under paragraph 83.3(8)(a), and the types of conditions that were imposed;

(e) the number of times that a person failed or refused to enter into a recognizance, and the term of imprisonment imposed under subsection 83.3(9) in each case; and

(f) the number of cases in which the conditions fixed in a recognizance were varied under subsection 83.3(13).

(3) Annual report (section 83.3) — The Minister of Public Safety and Emergency Preparedness shall prepare and cause to be laid before Parliament and the Minister responsible for policing in every province shall publish or otherwise make available to the public an annual report for the previous year on the operation of section 83.3 that includes

(a) the number of arrests without warrant that were made under subsection 83.3(4) and the period of the arrested person's detention in custody in each case; and

(b) the number of cases in which a person was arrested without warrant under subsection 83.3(4) and was released

(i) by a peace officer under paragraph 83.3(5)(b), or

(ii) by a judge under paragraph 83.3(7)(a), (7.1)(a) or (7.2)(a).

(3.1) Opinions — The Attorney General of Canada and the Minister of Public Safety and Emergency Preparedness shall include in their annual reports under subsections (2) and (3), respectively, their opinion, supported by reasons, on whether the operation of section 83.3 should be extended.

(4) Limitation — The annual report shall not contain any information the disclosure of which would

(a) compromise or hinder an ongoing investigation of an offence under an Act of Parliament;

(b) endanger the life or safety of any person;

(c) prejudice a legal proceeding; or

(d) otherwise be contrary to the public interest.

2001, c. 41, s. 4; 2005, c. 10, s. 34(1)(f)(iv); 2013, c. 9, s. 11; 2015, c. 20, s. 18; 2019, c. 13, s. 147

83.32 (1) Sunset provision — Section 83.3 ceases to have effect at the end of the fifth anniversary of the day on which the *National Security Act, 2017* receives royal assent unless, before the end of that fifth anniversary, the operation of that section is extended by resolution — whose text is established under subsection (2) — passed by both Houses of Parliament in accordance with the rules set out in subsection (3).

(1.1) Review — A comprehensive review of section 83.3 and its operation shall be undertaken by any committee of the Senate, of the House of Commons or of both Houses of Parliament that may be designated or established by the Senate or the House of Commons, or by both Houses of Parliament, as the case may be, for that purpose.

(1.2) Report — The committee shall, no later than one year before the fifth anniversary referred to subsection (1), submit a report on the review to the appropriate House of Parliament, or to both Houses, as the case may be, including its recommendation with respect to extending the operation of section 83.3.

(2) Order in council — The Governor in Council may, by order, establish the text of a resolution that provides for the extension of the operation of section 83.3 and that specifies the period of the extension, which may not exceed five years from the first day on which the resolution has been passed by both Houses of Parliament.

(3) Rules — A motion for the adoption of the resolution may be debated in both Houses of Parliament but may not be amended. At the conclusion of the debate, the Speaker of the House of Parliament shall immediately put every question necessary to determine whether or not the motion is concurred in.

(4) Subsequent extensions — The operation of section 83.3 may be further extended in accordance with this section, but

(a) the reference to "at the end of the fifth anniversary of the day on which the *National Security Act, 2017* receives royal assent unless, before the end of that fifth anniversary" in subsection (1) is to be read as a reference to "on the expiry of the most recent extension under this section unless, before that extension expires"; and

(b) the reference to "the fifth anniversary referred to subsection (1)" in subsection (1.2) is to be read as a reference to "the expiry of the most recent extension under this section".

(5) [Repealed 2019, c. 13, s. 148(2).]

2001, c. 41, s. 4; 2013, c. 9, s. 12; 2019, c. 13, s. 148

83.33 (1) [Repealed 2019, c. 13, s. 149.]

(2) Transitional provision — section 83.3 — In the event that section 83.3 ceases to have effect in accordance with section 83.32, a person detained in custody under section 83.3 shall be released when that section ceases to have effect, except that subsections 83.3(7) to (14) continue to apply to a person who was taken before a judge under subsection 83.3(6) before section 83.3 ceased to have effect.

2001, c. 41, s. 4; 2013, c. 9, s. 13; 2019, c. 13, s. 149

PART III — FIREARMS AND OTHER WEAPONS (SS. 84–117.15)

Interpretation

84. (1) Definitions — In this Part,

"ammunition" means a cartridge containing a projectile designed to be discharged from a firearm and, without restricting the generality of the foregoing, includes a caseless cartridge and a shot shell;

"antique firearm" means

(a) any firearm manufactured before 1898 that was not designed to discharge rim-fire or centre-fire ammunition and that has not been redesigned to discharge such ammunition, or

(b) any firearm that is prescribed to be an antique firearm;

"authorization" means an authorization issued under the *Firearms Act*;

"automatic firearm" means a firearm that is capable of, or assembled or designed and manufactured with the capability of, discharging projectiles in rapid succession during one pressure of the trigger;

"cartridge magazine" means a device or container from which ammunition may be fed into the firing chamber of a firearm;

"chief firearms officer" means a chief firearms officer as defined in subsection 2(1) of the *Firearms Act*;

"Commissioner of Firearms" means the Commissioner of Firearms appointed under section 81.1 of the *Firearms Act*;

"cross-bow" means a device with a bow and a bowstring mounted on a stock that is designed to propel an arrow, a bolt, a quarrel or any similar projectile on a trajectory guided by a barrel or groove and that is capable of causing serious bodily injury or death to a person;

"export" means export from Canada and, for greater certainty, includes the exportation of goods from Canada that are imported into Canada and shipped in transit through Canada;

"firearms officer" means a firearms officer as defined in subsection 2(1) of the *Firearms Act*;

"handgun" means a firearm that is designed, altered or intended to be aimed and fired by the action of one hand, whether or not it has been redesigned or subsequently altered to be aimed and fired by the action of both hands;

"imitation firearm" means any thing that imitates a firearm, and includes a replica firearm;

"import" means import into Canada and, for greater certainty, includes the importation of goods into Canada that are shipped in transit through Canada and exported from Canada;

"licence" means a licence issued under the *Firearms Act*;

"non-restricted firearm" means

(a) a firearm that is neither a prohibited firearm nor a restricted firearm, or

(b) a firearm that is prescribed to be a non-restricted firearm;

Proposed Amendment — 84(1) "non-restricted firearm"

"non-restricted firearm" means a firearm that is neither a prohibited firearm nor a restricted firearm;

2019, c. 9, s. 16 [Not in force at date of publication.]

"prescribed" means prescribed by the regulations;

"prohibited ammunition" means ammunition, or a projectile of any kind, that is prescribed to be prohibited ammunition;

"prohibited device" means

(a) any component or part of a weapon, or any accessory for use with a weapon, that is prescribed to be a prohibited device,

(b) a handgun barrel that is equal to or less than 105 mm in length, but does not include any such handgun barrel that is prescribed, where the handgun barrel is for use in international sporting competitions governed by the rules of the International Shooting Union,

(c) a device or contrivance designed or intended to muffle or stop the sound or report of a firearm,

(d) a cartridge magazine that is prescribed to be a prohibited device, or

(e) a replica firearm;

"prohibited firearm" means

(a) a handgun that

(i) has a barrel equal to or less than 105 mm in length, or

(ii) is designed or adapted to discharge a 25 or 32 calibre cartridge,

but does not include any such handgun that is prescribed, where the handgun is for use in international sporting competitions governed by the rules of the International Shooting Union,

(b) a firearm that is adapted from a rifle or shotgun, whether by sawing, cutting or any other alteration, and that, as so adapted,

(i) is less than 660 mm in length, or

(ii) is 660 mm or greater in length and has a barrel less than 457 mm in length,

(c) an automatic firearm, whether or not it has been altered to discharge only one projectile with one pressure of the trigger, or

(d) any firearm that is prescribed to be a prohibited firearm;

"prohibited weapon" means

(a) a knife that has a blade that opens automatically by gravity or centrifugal force or by hand pressure applied to a button, spring or other device in or attached to the handle of the knife, or

(b) any weapon, other than a firearm, that is prescribed to be a prohibited weapon;

"prohibition order" means an order made under this Act or any other Act of Parliament prohibiting a person from possessing any firearm, cross-bow, prohibited weapon, restricted weapon, prohibited device, ammunition, prohibited ammunition or explosive substance, or all such things;

"Registrar" means the Registrar of Firearms appointed under section 82 of the *Firearms Act*;

"registration certificate" means a registration certificate issued under the *Firearms Act*;

"replica firearm" means any device that is designed or intended to exactly resemble, or to resemble with near precision, a firearm, and that itself is not a firearm, but does not include any such device that is designed or intended to exactly resemble, or to resemble with near precision, an antique firearm;

"restricted firearm" means

(a) a handgun that is not a prohibited firearm,

(b) a firearm that

(i) is not a prohibited firearm,

(ii) has a barrel less than 470 mm in length, and

(iii) is capable of discharging centre-fire ammunition in a semi-automatic manner,

(c) a firearm that is designed or adapted to be fired when reduced to a length of less than 660 mm by folding, telescoping or otherwise, or

(d) a firearm of any other kind that is prescribed to be a restricted firearm;

"restricted weapon" means any weapon, other than a firearm, that is prescribed to be a restricted weapon;

"superior court" means

(a) in Ontario, the Superior Court of Justice, sitting in the region, district or county or group of counties where the relevant adjudication was made,

(b) in Quebec, the Superior Court,

(c) in New Brunswick, Manitoba, Saskatchewan and Alberta, the Court of Queen's Bench,

(d) in Nova Scotia, British Columbia, Prince Edward Island and a territory, the Supreme Court, and

(e) in Newfoundland and Labrador, the Trial Division of the Supreme Court;

"transfer" means sell, provide, barter, give, lend, rent, send, transport, ship, distribute or deliver.

(2) Barrel length — For the purposes of this Part, the length of a barrel of a firearm is

(a) in the case of a revolver, the distance from the muzzle of the barrel to the breach end immediately in front of the cylinder, and

(b) in any other case, the distance from the muzzle of the barrel to and including the chamber,

but does not include the length of any component, part or accessory including any component, part or accessory designed or intended to suppress the muzzle flash or reduce recoil.

(3) Certain weapons deemed not to be firearms — For the purposes of sections 91 to 95, 99 to 101, 103 to 107 and 117.03 of this Act and the provisions of the *Firearms Act*, the following weapons are deemed not to be firearms;

(a) any antique firearm;

(b) any device that is

(i) designed exclusively for signalling, for notifying of distress, for firing blank cartridges or for firing stud cartridges, explosive-driven rivets or other industrial projectiles, and

(ii) intended by the person in possession of it to be used exclusively for the purpose for which it is designed;

(c) any shooting device that is

(i) designed exclusively for the slaughtering of domestic animals, the tranquillizing of animals or the discharging of projectiles with lines attached to them, and

(ii) intended by the person in possession of it to be used exclusively for the purpose for which it is designed; and

(d) any other barrelled weapon, where it is proved that the weapon is not designed or adapted to discharge

(i) a shot, bullet or other projectile at a muzzle velocity exceeding 152.4 m per second or at a muzzle energy exceeding 5.7 Joules, or

(ii) a shot, bullet or other projectile that is designed or adapted to attain a velocity exceeding 152.4 m per second or an energy exceeding 5.7 Joules.

(3.1) Exceptions — antique firearms — Notwithstanding subsection (3), an antique firearm is a firearm for the purposes of regulations made under paragraph 117(*h*) of the *Firearms Act* and subsection 86(2) of this Act.

(4) Meaning of "holder" — For the purposes of this Part, a person is the **"holder"** of

(a) an authorization or a licence if the authorization or licence has been issued to the person and the person continues to hold it; and

(b) a registration certificate for a firearm if

(i) the registration certificate has been issued to the person and the person continues to hold it, or

(ii) the person possesses the registration certificate with the permission of its lawful holder.

(5) Subsequent offences — In determining, for the purpose of subsection 85(3), 95(2), 99(2), 100(2) or 103(2), whether a convicted person has committed a second or subsequent offence, if the person was earlier convicted of any of the following offences, that offence is to be considered as an earlier offence:

(a) an offence under section 85, 95, 96, 98, 98.1, 99, 100, 102 or 103 or subsection 117.01(1);

(b) an offence under section 244 or 244.2; or

(c) an offence under section 220, 236, 239, 272 or 273, subsection 279(1) or section 279.1, 344 or 346 if a firearm was used in the commission of the offence.

However, an earlier offence shall not be taken into account if 10 years have elapsed between the day on which the person was convicted of the earlier offence and the day on which the person was convicted of the offence for which sentence is being imposed, not taking into account any time in custody.

(6) Sequence of convictions only — For the purposes of subsection (5), the only question to be considered is the sequence of convictions and no consideration shall be given to the sequence of commission of offences or whether any offence occurred before or after any conviction.

1995, c. 39, s. 139; 1998, c. 30, s. 16; 2003, c. 8, s. 2; 2008, c. 6, s. 2; 2009, c. 22, s. 2; 2015, c. 3, s. 45; 2015, c. 27, s. 18

Use Offences

85. (1) Using firearm in commission of offence — Every person commits an offence who uses a firearm, whether or not the person causes or means to cause bodily harm to any person as a result of using the firearm,

(a) while committing an indictable offence, other than an offence under section 220 (criminal negligence causing death), 236 (manslaughter), 239 (attempted murder), 244 (discharging firearm with intent), 244.2 (discharging firearm — recklessness), 272 (sexual assault with a weapon) or 273 (aggravated sexual assault), subsection 279(1) (kidnapping) or section 279.1 (hostage taking), 344 (robbery) or 346 (extortion);

(b) while attempting to commit an indictable offence; or

(c) during flight after committing or attempting to commit an indictable offence.

(2) Using imitation firearm in commission of offence — Every person commits an offence who uses an imitation firearm

(a) while committing an indictable offence,

(b) while attempting to commit an indictable offence, or

(c) during flight after committing or attempting to commit an indictable offence,

whether or not the person causes or means to cause bodily harm to any person as a result of using the imitation firearm.

(3) Punishment — Every person who commits an offence under subsection (1) or (2) is guilty of an indictable offence and liable

(a) in the case of a first offence, except as provided in paragraph (b), to imprisonment for a term not exceeding fourteen years and to a minimum punishment of imprisonment for a term of one year; and

(b) in the case of a second or subsequent offence, to imprisonment for a term not exceeding 14 years and to a minimum punishment of imprisonment for a term of three years.

(c) [Repealed 2008, c. 6, s. 3(2).]

(4) Sentences to be served consecutively — A sentence imposed on a person for an offence under subsection (1) or (2) shall be served consecutively to any other punishment imposed on the person for an offence arising out of the same event or series of events and to any other sentence to which the person is subject at the time the sentence is imposed on the person for an offence under subsection (1) or (2).

1995, c. 39, s. 139; 2003, c. 8, s. 3; 2008, c. 6, s. 3; 2009, c. 22, s. 3

86. (1) Careless use of firearm, etc. — Every person commits an offence who, without lawful excuse, uses, carries, handles, ships, transports or stores a firearm, a prohibited weapon, a restricted weapon, a prohibited device or any ammunition or prohibited ammunition in a careless manner or without reasonable precautions for the safety of other persons.

(2) **Contravention of storage regulations, etc.** — Every person commits an offence who contravenes a regulation made under paragraph 117(*h*) of the *Firearms Act* respecting the storage, handling, transportation, shipping, display, advertising and mail-order sales of firearms and restricted weapons.

(3) **Punishment** — Every person who commits an offence under subsection (1) or (2)

(a) is guilty of an indictable offence and liable to imprisonment

(i) in the case of a first offence, for a term not exceeding two years, and

(ii) in the case of a second or subsequent offence, for a term not exceeding five years; or

(b) is guilty of an offence punishable on summary conviction.

1995, c. 39, ss. 139, 163

87. (1) **Pointing a firearm** — Every person commits an offence who, without lawful excuse, points a firearm at another person, whether the firearm is loaded or unloaded.

(2) **Punishment** — Every person who commits an offence under subsection (1)

(a) is guilty of an indictable offence and liable to imprisonment for a term not exceeding five years; or

(b) is guilty of an offence punishable on summary conviction.

1995, c. 39, s. 139

Possession Offences

88. (1) **Possession of weapon for dangerous purpose** — Every person commits an offence who carries or possesses a weapon, an imitation of a weapon, a prohibited device or any ammunition or prohibited ammunition for a purpose dangerous to the public peace or for the purpose of committing an offence.

(2) **Punishment** — Every person who commits an offence under subsection (1)

(a) is guilty of an indictable offence and liable to imprisonment for a term not exceeding ten years; or

(b) is guilty of an offence punishable on summary conviction.

1995, c. 39, s. 139

89. (1) **Carrying weapon while attending public meeting** — Every person commits an offence who, without lawful excuse, carries a weapon, a prohibited device or any ammunition or prohibited ammunition while the person is attending or is on the way to attend a public meeting.

(2) **Punishment** — Every person who commits an offence under subsection (1) is guilty of an offence punishable on summary conviction.

1995, c. 39, s. 139

90. (1) Carrying concealed weapon — Every person commits an offence who carries a weapon, a prohibited device or any prohibited ammunition concealed, unless the person is authorized under the *Firearms Act* to carry it concealed.

(2) Punishment — Every person who commits an offence under subsection (1)

(a) is guilty of an indictable offence and liable to imprisonment for a term not exceeding five years; or

(b) is guilty of an offence punishable on summary conviction.

1995, c. 39, s. 139

91. (1) Unauthorized possession of firearm — Subject to subsection (4), every person commits an offence who possesses a prohibited firearm, a restricted firearm or a non-restricted firearm without being the holder of

(a) a licence under which the person may possess it; and

(b) in the case of a prohibited firearm or a restricted firearm, a registration certificate for it.

(2) Unauthorized possession of prohibited weapon or restricted weapon — Subject to subsection (4), every person commits an offence who possesses a prohibited weapon, a restricted weapon, a prohibited device, other than a replica firearm, or any prohibited ammunition, without being the holder of a licence under which the person may possess it.

(3) Punishment — Every person who commits an offence under subsection (1) or (2)

(a) is guilty of an indictable offence and liable to imprisonment for a term not exceeding five years; or

(b) is guilty of an offence punishable on summary conviction.

(4) Exceptions — Subsections (1) and (2) do not apply to

(a) a person who possesses a prohibited firearm, a restricted firearm, a non-restricted firearm, a prohibited weapon, a restricted weapon, a prohibited device or any prohibited ammunition while the person is under the direct and immediate supervision of a person who may lawfully possess it, for the purpose of using it in a manner in which the supervising person may lawfully use it; or

(b) a person who comes into possession of a prohibited firearm, a restricted firearm, a non-restricted firearm, a prohibited weapon, a restricted weapon, a prohibited device or any prohibited ammunition by the operation of law and who, within a reasonable period after acquiring possession of it,

(i) lawfully disposes of it, or

(ii) obtains a licence under which the person may possess it and, in the case of a prohibited firearm or a restricted firearm, a registration certificate for it.

(5) [Repealed 2012, c. 6, s. 2(3).]

1995, c. 39, s. 139; 2008, c. 6, s. 4; 2012, c. 6, s. 2; 2015, c. 27, s. 19

91.1 [Repealed 1995, c. 39, s. 139.]

92. (1) Possession of firearm knowing its possession is unauthorized — Subject to subsection (4), every person commits an offence who possesses a prohibited firearm, a restricted firearm or a non-restricted firearm knowing that the person is not the holder of

(a) a licence under which the person may possess it; and

(b) in the case of a prohibited firearm or a restricted firearm, a registration certificate for it.

(2) Possession of prohibited weapon, device or ammunition knowing its possession is unauthorized — Subject to subsection (4), every person commits an offence who possesses a prohibited weapon, a restricted weapon, a prohibited device, other than a replica firearm, or any prohibited ammunition knowing that the person is not the holder of a licence under which the person may possess it.

(3) Punishment — Every person who commits an offence under subsection (1) or (2) is guilty of an indictable offence and liable

(a) in the case of a first offence, to imprisonment for a term not exceeding ten years;

(b) in the case of a second offence, to imprisonment for a term not exceeding ten years and to a minimum punishment of imprisonment for a term of one year; and

(c) in the case of a third or subsequent offence, to imprisonment for a term not exceeding ten years and to a minimum punishment of imprisonment for a term of two years less a day.

(4) Exceptions — Subsections (1) and (2) do not apply to

(a) a person who possesses a prohibited firearm, a restricted firearm, a non-restricted firearm, a prohibited weapon, a restricted weapon, a prohibited device or any prohibited ammunition while the person is under the direct and immediate supervision of a person who may lawfully possess it, for the purpose of using it in a manner in which the supervising person may lawfully use it; or

(b) a person who comes into possession of a prohibited firearm, a restricted firearm, a non-restricted firearm, a prohibited weapon, a restricted weapon, a prohibited device or any prohibited ammunition by the operation of law and who, within a reasonable period after acquiring possession of it,

(i) lawfully disposes of it, or

(ii) obtains a licence under which the person may possess it and, in the case of a prohibited firearm or a restricted firearm, a registration certificate for it.

(5) and (6) [Repealed 2012, c. 6, s. 3(3).]

1995, c. 39, s. 139; 2008, c. 6, s. 5; 2012, c. 6, s. 3; 2015, c. 27, s. 20

93. (1) Possession at unauthorized place — Subject to subsection (3), every person commits an offence who, being the holder of an authorization or a licence under which the person may possess a prohibited firearm, a restricted firearm, a non-restricted firearm, a prohibited weapon, a restricted weapon, a prohibited device or prohibited ammunition, possesses them at a place that is

(a) indicated on the authorization or licence as being a place where the person may not possess it;

(b) other than a place indicated on the authorization or licence as being a place where the person may possess it; or

(c) other than a place where it may be possessed under the *Firearms Act*.

(2) Punishment — Every person who commits an offence under subsection (1)

(a) is guilty of an indictable offence and liable to imprisonment for a term not exceeding five years; or

(b) is guilty of an offence punishable on summary conviction.

(3) Exception — Subsection (1) does not apply to a person who possesses a replica firearm.

1995, c. 39, s. 139; 2008, c. 6, s. 6; 2015, c. 27, s. 21

94. (1) Unauthorized possession in motor vehicle — Subject to subsections (3) and (4), every person commits an offence who is an occupant of a motor vehicle in which the person knows there is a prohibited firearm, a restricted firearm, a non-restricted firearm, a prohibited weapon, a restricted weapon, a prohibited device, other than a replica firearm, or any prohibited ammunition, unless

(a) in the case of a prohibited firearm, a restricted firearm or a non-restricted firearm,

(i) the person or any other occupant of the motor vehicle is the holder of

(A) a licence under which the person or other occupant may possess the firearm, and

(B) in the case of a prohibited firearm or a restricted firearm, an authorization and a registration certificate for it,

(ii) the person had reasonable grounds to believe that any other occupant of the motor vehicle was the holder of

(A) a licence under which that other occupant may possess the firearm, and

(B) in the case of a prohibited firearm or a restricted firearm, an authorization and a registration certificate for it, or

(iii) the person had reasonable grounds to believe that any other occupant of the motor vehicle was a person who could not be convicted of an offence under this Act by reason of sections 117.07 to 117.1 or any other Act of Parliament; and

(b) in the case of a prohibited weapon, a restricted weapon, a prohibited device or any prohibited ammunition,

(i) the person or any other occupant of the motor vehicle is the holder of an authorization or a licence under which the person or other occupant may transport the prohibited weapon, restricted weapon, prohibited device or prohibited ammunition, or

(ii) the person had reasonable grounds to believe that any other occupant of the motor vehicle was

(A) the holder of an authorization or a licence under which the other occupant may transport the prohibited weapon, restricted weapon, prohibited device or prohibited ammunition, or

(B) a person who could not be convicted of an offence under this Act by reason of sections 117.07 to 117.1 or any other Act of Parliament.

(2) **Punishment** — Every person who commits an offence under subsection (1)

(a) is guilty of an indictable offence and liable to imprisonment for a term not exceeding ten years; or

(b) is guilty of an offence punishable on summary conviction.

(3) **Exception** — Subsection (1) does not apply to an occupant of a motor vehicle who, on becoming aware of the presence of the firearm, weapon, device or ammunition in the motor vehicle, attempted to leave the motor vehicle, to the extent that it was feasible to do so, or actually left the motor vehicle.

(4) **Exception** — Subsection (1) does not apply to an occupant of a motor vehicle when the occupant or any other occupant of the motor vehicle is a person who came into possession of the firearm, weapon, device or ammunition by the operation of law.

(5) [Repealed 2012, c. 6, s. 4(3).]

1995, c. 39, s. 139; 2008, c. 6, s. 7; 2012, c. 6, s. 4; 2015, c. 27, s. 22

95. (1) **Possession of prohibited or restricted firearm with ammunition** — Subject to subsection (3), every person commits an offence who, in any place, possesses a loaded prohibited firearm or restricted firearm, or an unloaded prohibited firearm or restricted firearm together with readily accessible ammunition that is capable of being discharged in the firearm, without being the holder of

(a) an authorization or a licence under which the person may possess the firearm in that place; and

(b) the registration certificate for the firearm.

(2) **Punishment** — Every person who commits an offence under subsection (1)

(a) is guilty of an indictable offence and liable to imprisonment for a term not exceeding 10 years and to a minimum punishment of imprisonment for a term of

(i) in the case of a first offence, three years, and

(ii) in the case of a second or subsequent offence, five years; or

(b) is guilty of an offence punishable on summary conviction.

(3) **Exception** — Subsection (1) does not apply to a person who is using the firearm under the direct and immediate supervision of another person who is lawfully

entitled to possess it and is using the firearm in a manner in which that other person may lawfully use it.

1995, c. 39, s. 139; 2008, c. 6, s. 8; 2012, c. 6, s. 5; 2019, c. 25, s. 25

96. (1) Possession of weapon obtained by commission of offence — Subject to subsection (3), every person commits an offence who possesses a firearm, a prohibited weapon, a restricted weapon, a prohibited device or any prohibited ammunition that the person knows was obtained by the commission in Canada of an offence or by an act or omission anywhere that, if it had occurred in Canada, would have constituted an offence.

(2) Punishment — Every person who commits an offence under subsection (1)

(a) is guilty of an indictable offence and liable to imprisonment for a term not exceeding ten years and to a minimum punishment of imprisonment for a term of one year; or

(b) is guilty of an offence punishable on summary conviction.

(3) Exception — Subsection (1) does not apply to a person who comes into possession of anything referred to in that subsection by the operation of law and who lawfully disposes of it within a reasonable period after acquiring possession of it.

1995, c. 39, s. 139; 2019, c. 25, s. 26

97. [Repealed 1995, c. 39, s. 139.]

98. (1) Breaking and entering to steal firearm — Every person commits an offence who

(a) breaks and enters a place with intent to steal a firearm located in it;

(b) breaks and enters a place and steals a firearm located in it; or

(c) breaks out of a place after

(i) stealing a firearm located in it, or

(ii) entering the place with intent to steal a firearm located in it.

(2) Definitions of "break" and "place" — In this section, **"break"** has the same meaning as in section 321, and **"place"** means any building or structure — or part of one — and any motor vehicle, vessel, aircraft, railway vehicle, container or trailer.

(3) Entrance — For the purposes of this section,

(a) a person enters as soon as any part of his or her body or any part of an instrument that he or she uses is within any thing that is being entered; and

(b) a person is deemed to have broken and entered if he or she

(i) obtained entrance by a threat or an artifice or by collusion with a person within, or

(ii) entered without lawful justification or excuse by a permanent or temporary opening.

(4) **Punishment** — Every person who commits an offence under subsection (1) is guilty of an indictable offence and liable to imprisonment for life.

1995, c. 39, s. 139; 2008, c. 6, s. 9

98.1 **Robbery to steal firearm** — Every person who commits a robbery within the meaning of section 343 with intent to steal a firearm or in the course of which he or she steals a firearm commits an indictable offence and is liable to imprisonment for life.

2008, c. 6, s. 9

Trafficking Offences

99. (1) **Weapons trafficking** — Every person commits an offence who

(a) manufactures or transfers, whether or not for consideration, or

(b) offers to do anything referred to in paragraph (*a*) in respect of

a prohibited firearm, a restricted firearm, a non-restricted firearm, a prohibited weapon, a restricted weapon, a prohibited device, any ammunition or any prohibited ammunition knowing that the person is not authorized to do so under the *Firearms Act* or any other Act of Parliament or any regulations made under any Act of Parliament.

(2) **Punishment — firearm** — Every person who commits an offence under subsection (1) when the object in question is a prohibited firearm, a restricted firearm, a non-restricted firearm, a prohibited device, any ammunition or any prohibited ammunition is guilty of an indictable offence and liable to imprisonment for a term not exceeding 10 years and to a minimum punishment of imprisonment for a term of

(a) in the case of a first offence, three years; and

(b) in the case of a second or subsequent offence, five years.

(3) **Punishment — other cases** — In any other case, a person who commits an offence under subsection (1) is guilty of an indictable offence and liable to imprisonment for a term not exceeding 10 years and to a minimum punishment of imprisonment for a term of one year.

1995, c. 39, s. 139; 2008, c. 6, s. 10; 2015, c. 27, s. 23

100. (1) **Possession for purpose of weapons trafficking** — Every person commits an offence who possesses a prohibited firearm, a restricted firearm, a non-restricted firearm, a prohibited weapon, a restricted weapon, a prohibited device, any ammunition or any prohibited ammunition for the purpose of

(a) transferring it, whether or not for consideration, or

(b) offering to transfer it,

knowing that the person is not authorized to transfer it under the *Firearms Act* or any other Act of Parliament or any regulations made under any Act of Parliament.

(2) **Punishment — firearm** — Every person who commits an offence under subsection (1) when the object in question is a prohibited firearm, a restricted firearm, a non-restricted firearm, a prohibited device, any ammunition or any prohibited am-

munition is guilty of an indictable offence and liable to imprisonment for a term not exceeding 10 years and to a minimum punishment of imprisonment for a term of

(a) in the case of a first offence, three years; and

(b) in the case of a second or subsequent offence, five years.

(3) Punishment — other cases — In any other case, a person who commits an offence under subsection (1) is guilty of an indictable offence and liable to imprisonment for a term not exceeding 10 years and to a minimum punishment of imprisonment for a term of one year.

1995, c. 39, s. 139; 1996, c. 19, s. 65; 2008, c. 6, s. 11; 2015, c. 27, s. 24

101. (1) Transfer without authority — Every person commits an offence who transfers a prohibited firearm, a restricted firearm, a non-restricted firearm, a prohibited weapon, a restricted weapon, a prohibited device, any ammunition or any prohibited ammunition to any person otherwise than under the authority of the *Firearms Act* or any other Act of Parliament or any regulations made under an Act of Parliament.

(2) Punishment — Every person who commits an offence under subsection (1)

(a) is guilty of an indictable offence and liable to imprisonment for a term not exceeding five years; or

(b) is guilty of an offence punishable on summary conviction.

1995, c. 39, s. 139; 2015, c. 27, s. 25

Assembling Offence

102. (1) Making automatic firearm — Every person commits an offence who, without lawful excuse, alters a firearm so that it is capable of, or manufactures or assembles any firearm that is capable of, discharging projectiles in rapid succession during one pressure of the trigger.

(2) Punishment — Every person who commits an offence under subsection (1)

(a) is guilty of an indictable offence and liable to imprisonment for a term not exceeding ten years and to a minimum punishment of imprisonment for a term of one year, or

(b) is guilty of an offence punishable on summary conviction.

1995, c. 39, s. 139; 2019, c. 25, s. 27

Export and Import Offences

103. (1) Importing or exporting knowing it is unauthorized — Every person commits an offence who imports or exports

(a) a prohibited firearm, a restricted firearm, a non-restricted firearm, a prohibited weapon, a restricted weapon, a prohibited device or any prohibited ammunition, or

(b) any component or part designed exclusively for use in the manufacture of or assembly into an automatic firearm, knowing that the person is not authorized to do so under the *Firearms Act* or any other Act of Parliament or any regulations made under an Act of Parliament.

(2) **Punishment — firearm** — Every person who commits an offence under subsection (1) when the object in question is a prohibited firearm, a restricted firearm, a non-restricted firearm, a prohibited device or any prohibited ammunition is guilty of an indictable offence and liable to imprisonment for a term not exceeding 10 years and to a minimum punishment of imprisonment for a term of

(a) in the case of a first offence, three years; and

(b) in the case of a second or subsequent offence, five years.

(2.1) **Punishment — other cases** — In any other case, a person who commits an offence under subsection (1) is guilty of an indictable offence and liable to imprisonment for a term not exceeding 10 years and to a minimum punishment of imprisonment for a term of one year.

(3) [Repealed 2019, c. 25, s. 28.]

1995, c. 39, s. 139; 2008, c. 6, s. 12; 2015, c. 27, s. 26; 2019, c. 25, s. 28

104. (1) **Unauthorized importing or exporting** — Every person commits an offence who imports or exports

(a) a prohibited firearm, a restricted firearm, a non-restricted firearm, a prohibited weapon, a restricted weapon, a prohibited device or any prohibited ammunition, or

(b) any component or part designed exclusively for use in the manufacture of or assembly into an automatic firearm,

otherwise than under the authority of the *Firearms Act* or any other Act of Parliament or any regulations made under an Act of Parliament.

(2) **Punishment** — Every person who commits an offence under subsection (1)

(a) is guilty of an indictable offence and liable to imprisonment for a term not exceeding five years; or

(b) is guilty of an offence punishable on summary conviction.

(3) [Repealed 2019, c. 25, s. 29.]

1995, c. 39, s. 139; 2015, c. 27, s. 27; 2019, c. 25, s. 29

Offences relating to Lost, Destroyed or Defaced Weapons, etc.

105. (1) **Losing or finding** — Every person commits an offence who

(a) having lost a prohibited firearm, a restricted firearm, a non-restricted firearm, a prohibited weapon, a restricted weapon, a prohibited device, any prohibited ammunition, an authorization, a licence or a registration certificate, or having had it stolen from the person's possession, does not with reasonable despatch report the loss to a peace officer, to a firearms officer or a chief firearms officer; or

(b) on finding a prohibited firearm, a restricted firearm, a non-restricted firearm, a prohibited weapon, a restricted weapon, a prohibited device or any prohibited ammunition that the person has reasonable grounds to believe has been lost or abandoned, does not with reasonable despatch deliver it to a peace officer, a firearms officer or a chief firearms officer or report the finding to a peace officer, a firearms officer or a chief firearms officer.

(2) Punishment — Every person who commits an offence under subsection (1)

(a) is guilty of an indictable offence and liable to imprisonment for a term not exceeding five years; or

(b) is guilty of an offence punishable on summary conviction.

1995, c. 39, ss. 139, 164; 2015, c. 27, s. 28

106. (1) Destroying — Every person commits an offence who

(a) after destroying any prohibited firearm, restricted firearm, prohibited weapon, restricted weapon, prohibited device or prohibited ammunition, or

(b) on becoming aware of the destruction of any prohibited firearm, restricted firearm, prohibited weapon, restricted weapon, prohibited device or prohibited ammunition that was in the person's possession before its destruction,

does not with reasonable despatch report the destruction to a peace officer, firearms officer or chief firearms officer.

(2) Punishment — Every person who commits an offence under subsection (1)

(a) is guilty of an indictable offence and liable to imprisonment for a term not exceeding five years; or

(b) is guilty of an offence punishable on summary conviction.

1995, c. 39, s. 139; 2012, c. 6, s. 6

107. (1) False statements — Every person commits an offence who knowingly makes, before a peace officer, firearms officer or chief firearms officer, a false report or statement concerning the loss, theft or destruction of a prohibited firearm, a restricted firearm, a non-restricted firearm, a prohibited weapon, a restricted weapon, a prohibited device, any prohibited ammunition, an authorization, a licence or a registration certificate.

(2) Punishment — Every person who commits an offence under subsection (1)

(a) is guilty of an indictable offence and liable to imprisonment for a term not exceeding five years; or

(b) is guilty of an offence punishable on summary conviction.

(3) Definition of "report" or "statement" — In this section, **"report"** or **"statement"** means an assertion of fact, opinion, belief or knowledge, whether material or not and whether admissible or not.

1995, c. 39, s. 139; 2015, c. 27, s. 29

108. (1) Tampering with serial number — Every person commits an offence who, without lawful excuse,

(a) alters, defaces or removes a serial number on a firearm; or

(b) possesses a firearm knowing that the serial number on it has been altered, defaced or removed.

(2) Punishment — Every person who commits an offence under subsection (1)

(a) is guilty of an indictable offence and liable to imprisonment for a term not exceeding five years; or

(b) is guilty of an offence punishable on summary conviction.

(3) Exception — No person is guilty of an offence under paragraph (1)(b) by reason only of possessing a prohibited firearm or restricted firearm the serial number on which has been altered, defaced or removed, if that serial number has been replaced and a registration certificate in respect of the firearm has been issued setting out a new serial number for the firearm.

(4) Evidence — In proceedings for an offence under subsection (1), evidence that a person possesses a firearm the serial number on which has been wholly or partially obliterated otherwise than through normal use over time is, in the absence of evidence to the contrary, proof that the person possesses the firearm knowing that the serial number on it has been altered, defaced or removed.

1995, c. 39, s. 139; 2012, c. 6, s. 7; 2018, c. 29, s. 6

Prohibition Orders

109. (1) Mandatory prohibition order — Where a person is convicted, or discharged under section 730, of

(a) an indictable offence in the commission of which violence against a person was used, threatened or attempted and for which the person may be sentenced to imprisonment for ten years or more,

(a.1) an indictable offence in the commission of which violence was used, threatened or attempted against

(i) the person's current or former intimate partner,

Proposed Amendment — 109(1)(a.1)(i)

(i) the person's intimate partner,

2019, c. 25, s. 30 [To come into force December 18, 2019.]

(ii) a child or parent of the person or of anyone referred to in subparagraph (i), or

(iii) any person who resides with the person or with anyone referred to in subparagraph (i) or (ii),

(b) an offence under subsection 85(1) (using firearm in commission of offence), subsection 85(2) (using imitation firearm in commission of offence), 95(1) (possession of prohibited or restricted firearm with ammunition), 99(1) (weapons trafficking), 100(1) (possession for purpose of weapons trafficking), 102(1) (making automatic firearm), 103(1) (importing or exporting knowing it is unauthorized) or section 264 (criminal harassment),

(c) an offence relating to the contravention of subsection 5(1) or (2), 6(1) or (2) or 7(1) of the *Controlled Drugs and Substances Act*,

(c.1) an offence relating to the contravention of subsection 9(1) or (2), 10(1) or (2), 11(1) or (2), 12(1), (4), (5), (6) or (7), 13(1) or 14(1) of the *Cannabis Act*, or

(d) an offence that involves, or the subject-matter of which is, a firearm, a cross-bow, a prohibited weapon, a restricted weapon, a prohibited device, any ammunition, any prohibited ammunition or an explosive substance and, at the time of the offence, the person was prohibited by any order made under this Act or any other Act of Parliament from possessing any such thing,

the court that sentences the person or directs that the person be discharged, as the case may be, shall, in addition to any other punishment that may be imposed for that offence or any other condition prescribed in the order of discharge, make an order prohibiting the person from possessing any firearm, cross-bow, prohibited weapon, restricted weapon, prohibited device, ammunition, prohibited ammunition and explosive substance during the period specified in the order as determined in accordance with subsection (2) or (3), as the case may be.

(2) Duration of prohibition order — first offence — An order made under subsection (1) shall, in the case of a first conviction for or discharge from the offence to which the order relates, prohibit the person from possessing

(a) any firearm, other than a prohibited firearm or restricted firearm, and any cross-bow, restricted weapon, ammunition and explosive substance during the period that

(i) begins on the day on which the order is made, and

(ii) ends not earlier than ten years after the person's release from imprisonment after conviction for the offence or, if the person is not then imprisoned or subject to imprisonment, after the person's conviction for or discharge from the offence; and

(b) any prohibited firearm, restricted firearm, prohibited weapon, prohibited device and prohibited ammunition for life.

(3) Duration of prohibition order — subsequent offences — An order made under subsection (1) shall, in any case other than a case described in subsection (2), prohibit the person from possessing any firearm, cross-bow, restricted weapon, ammunition and explosive substance for life.

(4) Definition of "release from imprisonment" — In subparagraph (2)(a)(ii), **"release from imprisonment"** means release from confinement by reason of expiration of sentence, commencement of statutory release or grant of parole.

(4.1) to (4.3) [Repealed 1995, c. 39, s. 139.]

(5) Application of ss. 113 to 117 — Sections 113 to 117 apply in respect of every order made under subsection (1).

1991, c. 40, s. 21; 1995, c. 39, ss. 139, 190(d); 1996, c. 19, s. 65.1; 2003, c. 8, s. 4; 2015, c. 27, s. 30; 2018, c. 16, s. 208

109.1 [Repealed 1995, c. 39, s. 139.]

110. (1) Discretionary prohibition order — Where a person is convicted, or discharged under section 730, of

(a) an offence, other than an offence referred to in any of paragraphs 109(1)(a) to (c.1), in the commission of which violence against a person was used, threatened or attempted, or

(b) an offence that involves, or the subject-matter of which is, a firearm, a cross-bow, a prohibited weapon, a restricted weapon, a prohibited device, ammunition, prohibited ammunition or an explosive substance and, at the time of the offence, the person was not prohibited by any order made under this Act or any other Act of Parliament from possessing any such thing,

the court that sentences the person or directs that the person be discharged, as the case may be, shall, in addition to any other punishment that may be imposed for that offence or any other condition prescribed in the order of discharge, consider whether it is desirable, in the interests of the safety of the person or of any other person, to make an order prohibiting the person from possessing any firearm, cross-bow, prohibited weapon, restricted weapon, prohibited device, ammunition, prohibited ammunition or explosive substance, or all such things, and where the court decides that it is so desirable, the court shall so order.

(2) Duration of prohibition order — An order made under subsection (1) against a person begins on the day on which the order is made and ends not later than ten years after the person's release from imprisonment after conviction for the offence to which the order relates or, if the person is not then imprisoned or subject to imprisonment, after the person's conviction for or discharge from the offence.

(2.1) Exception — Despite subsection (2), an order made under subsection (1) may be imposed for life or for any shorter duration if, in the commission of the offence, violence was used, threatened or attempted against

(a) the person's current or former intimate partner;

Proposed Amendment — 110(2.1)(a)

(a) the person's intimate partner;

2019, c. 25, s. 31 [To come into force December 18, 2019.]

(b) a child or parent of the person or of anyone referred to in paragraph (a); or

(c) any person who resides with the person or with anyone referred to in paragraph (a) or (b).

(3) Reasons — Where the court does not make an order under subsection (1), or where the court does make such an order but does not prohibit the possession of everything referred to in that subsection, the court shall include in the record a statement of the court's reasons for not doing so.

(4) Definition of "release from imprisonment" — In subsection (2), **"release from imprisonment"** means release from confinement by reason of expiration of sentence, commencement of statutory release or grant of parole.

(5) Application of ss. 113 to 117 — Sections 113 to 117 apply in respect of every order made under subsection (1).

1995, c. 39, ss. 139, 190(e); 2015, c. 27, s. 31; 2018, c. 16, s. 209

110.1 Definition of "intimate partner" — In sections 109 and 110, **"intimate partner"** includes a spouse, a common-law partner and a dating partner.

Proposed Repeal — 110.1

110.1 [Repealed 2019, c. 25, s. 32. To come into force December 18, 2019.]

2015, c. 27, s. 32

111. (1) Application for prohibition order — A peace officer, firearms officer or chief firearms officer may apply to a provincial court judge for an order prohibiting a person from possessing any firearm, cross-bow, prohibited weapon, restricted weapon, prohibited device, ammunition, prohibited ammunition or explosive substance, or all such things, where the peace officer, firearms officer or chief firearms officer believes on reasonable grounds that it is not desirable in the interests of the safety of the person against whom the order is sought or of any other person that the person against whom the order is sought should possess any such thing.

(2) Date for hearing and notice — On receipt of an application made under subsection (1), the provincial court judge shall fix a date for the hearing of the application and direct that notice of the hearing be given, in such manner as the provincial court judge may specify, to the person against whom the order is sought.

(3) Hearing of application — Subject to subsection (4), at the hearing of an application made under subsection (1), the provincial court judge shall hear all relevant evidence presented by or on behalf of the applicant and the person against whom the order is sought.

(4) Where hearing may proceed *ex parte* — A provincial court judge may proceed *ex parte* to hear and determine an application made under subsection (1) in the absence of the person against whom the order is sought in the same circumstances as those in which a summary conviction court may, under Part XXVII, proceed with a trial in the absence of the defendant.

(5) Prohibition order — Where, at the conclusion of a hearing of an application made under subsection (1), the provincial court judge is satisfied that the circumstances referred to in that subsection exist, the provincial court judge shall make an order prohibiting the person from possessing any firearm, cross-bow, prohibited weapon, restricted weapon, prohibited device, ammunition, prohibited ammunition or explosive substance, or all such things, for such period, not exceeding five years, as is specified in the order, beginning on the day on which the order is made.

(6) Reasons — Where a provincial court judge does not make an order under subsection (1), or where a provincial court judge does make such an order but does not prohibit the possession of everything referred to in that subsection, the provincial court judge shall include in the record a statement of the court's reasons.

(7) **Application of ss. 113 to 117** — Sections 113 to 117 apply in respect of every order made under subsection (5).

(8) **Appeal by person or Attorney General** — Where a provincial court judge makes an order under subsection (5), the person to whom the order relates, or the Attorney General, may appeal to the superior court against the order.

(9) **Appeal by Attorney General** — Where a provincial court judge does not make an order under subsection (5), the Attorney General, may appeal to the superior court against the decision not to make an order.

(10) **Application of Part XXVII to appeals** — The provisions of Part XXVII, except sections 785 to 812, 816 to 819 and 829 to 838, apply in respect of an appeal made under subsection (8) or (9), with such modifications as the circumstances require and as if each reference in that Part to the appeal court were a reference to the superior court.

(11) **Definition of "provincial court judge"** — In this section and sections 112, 117.011 and 117.012, **"provincial court judge"** means a provincial court judge having jurisdiction in the territorial division where the person against whom the application for an order was brought resides.

1995, c. 39, s. 139

112. Revocation of prohibition order under s. 111(5) — A provincial court judge may, on application by the person against whom an order is made under subsection 111(5), revoke the order if satisfied that the circumstances for which it was made have ceased to exist.

1995, c. 39, s. 139

113. (1) Lifting of prohibition order for sustenance or employment — Where a person who is or will be a person against whom a prohibition order is made establishes to the satisfaction of a competent authority that

(a) the person needs a firearm or restricted weapon to hunt or trap in order to sustain the person or the person's family, or

(b) a prohibition order against the person would constitute a virtual prohibition against employment in the only vocation open to the person,

the competent authority may, notwithstanding that the person is or will be subject to a prohibition order, make an order authorizing a chief firearms officer or the Registrar to issue, in accordance with such terms and conditions as the competent authority considers appropriate, an authorization, a licence or a registration certificate, as the case may be, to the person for sustenance or employment purposes.

(2) **Factors** — A competent authority may make an order under subsection (1) only after taking the following factors into account;

(a) the criminal record, if any, of the person;

(b) the nature and circumstances of the offence, if any, in respect of which the prohibition order was or will be made; and

(c) the safety of the person and of other persons.

(3) Effect of order — Where an order is made under subsection (1),

(a) an authorization, a licence or a registration certificate may not be denied to the person in respect of whom the order was made solely on the basis of a prohibition order against the person or the commission of an offence in respect of which a prohibition order was made against the person; and

(b) an authorization and a licence may, for the duration of the order, be issued to the person in respect of whom the order was made only for sustenance or employment purposes and, where the order sets out terms and conditions, only in accordance with those terms and conditions, but, for greater certainty, the authorization or licence may also be subject to terms and conditions set by the chief firearms officer that are not inconsistent with the purpose for which it is issued and any terms and conditions set out in the order.

(4) When order can be made — For greater certainty, an order under subsection (1) may be made during proceedings for an order under subsection 109(1), 110(1), 111(5), 117.05(4) or 515(2), paragraph 732.1(3)(d) or subsection 810(3).

(5) Meaning of "competent authority" — In this section, **"competent authority"** means the competent authority that made or has jurisdiction to make the prohibition order.

1995, c. 39, ss. 139, 190(f)

114. Requirement to surrender — A competent authority that makes a prohibition order against a person may, in the order, require the person to surrender to a peace officer, a firearms officer or a chief firearms officer

(a) any thing the possession of which is prohibited by the order that is in the possession of the person on the commencement of the order, and

(b) every authorization, licence and registration certificate relating to any thing the possession of which is prohibited by the order that is held by the person on the commencement of the order.

and where the competent authority does so, it shall specify in the order a reasonable period for surrendering such things and documents and during which section 117.01 does not apply to that person.

1995, c. 39, s. 139

115. (1) Forfeiture — Unless a prohibition order against a person specifies otherwise, every thing the possession of which is prohibited by the order is forfeited to Her Majesty if, on the commencement of the order, the thing is in the person's possession or has been seized and detained by, or surrendered to, a peace officer.

(1.1) Exception — Subsection (1) does not apply in respect of an order made under section 515.

(2) Disposal — Every thing forfeited to Her Majesty under subsection (1) shall be disposed of or otherwise dealt with as the Attorney General directs.

1995, c. 39, s. 139; 2003, c. 8, s. 5; 2019, c. 9, s. 17

116. (1) Authorizations revoked or amended — Subject to subsection (2), every authorization, licence and registration certificate relating to any thing the possession of which is prohibited by a prohibition order and issued to a person against whom the prohibition order is made is, on the commencement of the prohibition order, revoked, or amended, as the case may be, to the extent of the prohibitions in the order.

(2) Duration of revocation or amendment — orders under section 515 — An authorization, a licence and a registration certificate relating to a thing the possession of which is prohibited by an order made under section 515 is revoked, or amended, as the case may be, only in respect of the period during which the order is in force.

1995, c. 39, s. 139; 2003, c. 8, s. 6

117. Return to owner — Where the competent authority that makes a prohibition order or that would have had jurisdiction to make the order is, on application for an order under this section, satisfied that a person, other than the person against whom a prohibition order was or will be made,

(a) is the owner of any thing that is or may be forfeited to Her Majesty under subsection 115(1) and is lawfully entitled to possess it, and

(b) in the case of a prohibition order under subsection 109(1) or 110(1), had no reasonable grounds to believe that the thing would or might be used in the commission of the offence in respect of which the prohibition order was made,

the competent authority shall order that the thing be returned to the owner or the proceeds of any sale of the thing be paid to that owner or, if the thing was destroyed, that an amount equal to the value of the thing be paid to the owner.

1995, c. 39, s. 139

117.01 (1) Possession contrary to order — Subject to subsection (4), every person commits an offence who possesses a firearm, a cross-bow, a prohibited weapon, a restricted weapon, a prohibited device, any ammunition, any prohibited ammunition or an explosive substance while the person is prohibited from doing so by any order made under this Act or any other Act of Parliament.

(2) Failure to surrender authorization, etc. — Every person commits an offence who wilfully fails to surrender to a peace officer, a firearms officer or a chief firearms officer any authorization, licence or registration certificate held by the person when the person is required to do so by any order made under this Act or any other Act of Parliament.

(3) Punishment — Every person who commits an offence under subsection (1) or (2)

(a) is guilty of an indictable offence and liable to imprisonment for a term not exceeding ten years; or

(b) is guilty of an offence punishable on summary conviction.

(4) Exception — Subsection (1) does not apply to a person who possessed a firearm in accordance with an authorization or licence issued to the person as the result of an order made under subsection 113(1).

1995, c. 39, s. 139

Limitations on Access

117.011 (1) Application for order — A peace officer, firearms officer or chief firearms officer may apply to a provincial court judge for an order under this section where the peace officer, firearms officer or chief firearms officer believes on reasonable grounds that

(a) the person against whom the order is sought cohabits with, or is an associate of, another person who is prohibited by any order made under this Act or any other Act of Parliament from possessing any firearm, cross-bow, prohibited weapon, restricted weapon, prohibited device, ammunition, prohibited ammunition or explosive substance, or all such things; and

(b) the other person would or might have access to any such thing that is in the possession of the person against whom the order is sought.

(2) Date for hearing and notice — On receipt of an application made under subsection (1), the provincial court judge shall fix a date for the hearing of the application and direct that notice of the hearing be given, in such manner as the provincial court judge may specify, to the person against whom the order is sought.

(3) Hearing of application — Subject to subsection (4), at the hearing of an application made under subsection (1), the provincial court judge shall hear all relevant evidence presented by or on behalf of the applicant and the person against whom the order is sought.

(4) Where hearing may proceed *ex parte* — A provincial court judge may proceed *ex parte* to hear and determine an application made under subsection (1) in the absence of the person against whom the order is sought in the same circumstances as those in which a summary conviction court may, under Part XXVII, proceed with a trial in the absence of the defendant.

(5) Order — Where, at the conclusion of a hearing of an application made under subsection (1), the provincial court judge is satisfied that the circumstances referred to in that subsection exist, the provincial court judge shall make an order in respect of the person against whom the order was sought imposing such terms and conditions on the person's use and possession of anything referred to in subsection (1) as the provincial court judge considers appropriate.

(6) Terms and conditions — In determining terms and conditions under subsection (5), the provincial court judge shall impose terms and conditions that are the least intrusive as possible, bearing in mind the purpose of the order.

(7) Appeal by person or Attorney General — Where a provincial court judge makes an order under subsection (5), the person to whom the order relates, or the Attorney General, may appeal to the superior court against the order.

(8) Appeal by Attorney General — Where a provincial court judge does not make an order under subsection (5), the Attorney General may appeal to the superior court against the decision not to make an order.

(9) Application of Part XXVII to appeals — The provisions of Part XXVII, except sections 785 to 812, 816 to 819 and 829 to 838, apply in respect of an appeal made under subsection (7) or (8), with such modifications as the circumstances require and as if each reference in that Part to the appeal court were a reference to the superior court.

1995, c. 39, s. 139

117.012 Revocation of order under s. 117.011 — A provincial court judge may, on application by the person against whom an order is made under subsection 117.011(5), revoke the order if satisfied that the circumstances for which it was made have ceased to exist.

1995, c. 39, s. 139

Search and Seizure

117.02 (1) Search and seizure without warrant where offence committed — Where a peace officer believes on reasonable grounds

(a) that a weapon, an imitation firearm, a prohibited device, any ammunition, any prohibited ammunition or an explosive substance was used in the commission of an offence, or

(b) that an offence is being committed, or has been committed, under any provision of this Act that involves, or the subject-matter of which is, a firearm, an imitation firearm, a cross-bow, a prohibited weapon, a restricted weapon, a prohibited device, ammunition, prohibited ammunition or an explosive substance,

and evidence of the offence is likely to be found on a person, in a vehicle or in any place or premises other than a dwelling-house, the peace officer may, where the conditions for obtaining a warrant exist but, by reason of exigent circumstances, it would not be practicable to obtain a warrant, search, without warrant, the person, vehicle, place or premises, and seize any thing by means of or in relation to which that peace officer believes on reasonable grounds the offence is being committed or has been committed.

(2) Disposition of seized things — Any thing seized pursuant to subsection (1) shall be dealt with in accordance with sections 490 and 491.

1995, c. 39, s. 139

117.03 (1) Seizure on failure to produce authorization — Despite section 117.02, a peace officer who finds

(a) a person in possession of a prohibited firearm, a restricted firearm or a non-restricted firearm who fails, on demand, to produce, for inspection by the peace officer, an authorization or a licence under which the person may lawfully possess the firearm and, in the case of a prohibited firearm or a restricted firearm, a registration certificate for it, or

(b) a person in possession of a prohibited weapon, a restricted weapon, a prohibited device or any prohibited ammunition who fails, on demand, to produce, for inspection by the peace officer, an authorization or a licence under which the person may lawfully possess it, may seize the firearm, prohibited weapon, restricted weapon, prohibited device or prohibited ammunition unless its possession by the person in the circumstances in which it is found is authorized by any provision of this Part, or the person is under the direct and immediate supervision of another person who may lawfully possess it.

(2) Return of seized thing on production of authorization — If a person from whom any thing is seized under subsection (1) claims the thing within 14 days after the seizure and produces for inspection by the peace officer by whom it was seized, or any other peace officer having custody of it,

(a) a licence under which the person is lawfully entitled to possess it, and

(b) in the case of a prohibited firearm or a restricted firearm, an authorization and registration certificate for it,

the thing shall without delay be returned to that person.

(3) Forfeiture of seized thing — Where any thing seized pursuant to subsection (1) is not claimed and returned as and when provided by subsection (2), a peace officer shall forthwith take the thing before a provincial court judge, who may, after affording the person from whom it was seized or its owner, if known, an opportunity to establish that the person is lawfully entitled to possess it, declare it to be forfeited to Her Majesty, to be disposed of or otherwise dealt with as the Attorney General directs.

1995, c. 39, s. 139; 2012, c. 6, s. 8; 2015, c. 27, s. 33

117.04 (1) Application for warrant to search and seize — Where, pursuant to an application made by a peace officer with respect to any person, a justice is satisfied by information on oath that there are reasonable grounds to believe that the person possesses a weapon, a prohibited device, ammunition, prohibited ammunition or an explosive substance in a building, receptacle or place and that it is not desirable in the interests of the safety of the person, or of any other person, for the person to possess the weapon, prohibited device, ammunition, prohibited ammunition or explosive substance, the justice may issue a warrant authorizing a peace officer to search the building, receptacle or place and seize any such thing, and any authorization, licence or registration certificate relating to any such thing, that is held by or in the possession of the person.

(2) Search and seizure without warrant — Where, with respect to any person, a peace officer is satisfied that there are reasonable grounds to believe that it is not desirable, in the interests of the safety of the person or any other person, for the person to possess any weapon, prohibited device, ammunition, prohibited ammunition or explosive substance, the peace officer may, where the grounds for obtaining a warrant under subsection (1) exist but, by reason of a possible danger to the safety of that person or any other person, it would not be practicable to obtain a warrant, search for and seize any such thing, and any authorization, licence or registration certificate relating to any such thing, that is held by or in the possession of the person.

(3) Return to justice — A peace officer who executes a warrant referred to in subsection (1) or who conducts a search without a warrant under subsection (2) shall forthwith make a return to the justice who issued the warrant or, if no warrant was issued, to a justice who might otherwise have issued a warrant, showing

(a) in the case of an execution of a warrant, the things or documents, if any, seized and the date of execution of the warrant; and

(b) in the case of a search conducted without a warrant, the grounds on which it was concluded that the peace officer was entitled to conduct the search, and the things or documents, if any, seized.

(4) Authorizations etc., revoked — Where a peace officer who seizes any thing under subsection (1) or (2) is unable at the time of the seizure to seize an authorization or a licence under which the person from whom the thing was seized may possess the thing and, in the case of a seized firearm, a registration certificate for the firearm, every authorization, licence and registration certificate held by the person is, as at the time of the seizure, revoked.

1995, c. 39, s. 139; 2004, c. 12, s. 3

117.05 (1) Application for disposition — Where any thing or document has been seized under subsection 117.04(1) or (2), the justice who issued the warrant authorizing the seizure or, if no warrant was issued, a justice who might otherwise have issued a warrant, shall, on application for an order for the disposition of the thing or document so seized made by a peace officer within thirty days after the date of execution of the warrant or of the seizure without a warrant, as the case may be, fix a date for the hearing of the application and direct that notice of the hearing be given to such persons or in such manner as the justice may specify.

(2) *Ex parte* hearing — A justice may proceed *ex parte* to hear and determine an application made under subsection (1) in the absence of the person from whom the thing or document was seized in the same circumstances as those in which a summary conviction court may, under Part XXVII, proceed with a trial in the absence of the defendant.

(3) Hearing of application — At the hearing of an application made under subsection (1), the justice shall hear all relevant evidence, including evidence respecting the value of the thing in respect of which the application was made.

(4) Forfeiture and prohibition order on finding — Where, following the hearing of an application made under subsection (1), the justice finds that it is not desirable in the interests of the safety of the person from whom the thing was seized or of any other person that the person should possess any weapon, prohibited device, ammunition, prohibited ammunition and explosive substance, or any such thing, the justice shall

(a) order that any thing seized by forfeited to Her Majesty or be otherwise disposed of; and

(b) where the justice is satisfied that the circumstances warrant such an action, order that the possession by that person of any weapon, prohibited device, ammunition, prohibited ammunition and explosive substance, or of any such thing, be prohibited during any period, not exceeding five years, that is specified in the order, beginning on the making of the order.

(5) Reasons — Where a justice does not make an order under subsection (4), or where a justice does make such an order but does not prohibit the possession of all of the things referred to in that subsection, the justice shall include in the record a statement of the justice's reasons.

(6) Application of ss. 113 to 117 — Sections 113 to 117 apply in respect of every order made under subsection (4).

(7) Appeal by person — Where a justice makes an order under subsection (4) in respect of a person, or in respect of any thing that was seized from a person, the person may appeal to the superior court against the order.

(8) Appeal by Attorney General — Where a justice does not make a finding as described in subsection (4) following the hearing of an application under subsection (1), or makes the finding but does not make an order to the effect described in paragraph (4)(b), the Attorney General may appeal to the superior court against the failure to make the finding or to make an order to the effect so described.

(9) Application of Part XXVII to appeals — The provisions of Part XXVII, except sections 785 to 812, 816 to 819 and 829 to 838, apply in respect of an appeal made under subsection (7) or (8) with such modifications as the circumstances require and as if each reference in that Part to the appeal court were a reference to the superior court.

1995, c. 39, s. 139

117.06 (1) Where no finding or application — Any thing or document seized pursuant to subsection 117.04(1) or (2) shall be returned to the person from whom it was seized if

(a) no application is made under subsection 117.05(1) within thirty days after the date of execution of the warrant or of the seizure without a warrant, as the case may be; or

(b) an application is made under subsection 117.05(1) within the period referred to in paragraph (a), and the justice does not make a finding as described in subsection 117.05(4).

(2) Restoration of authorizations — Where, pursuant to subsection (1), any thing is returned to the person from whom it was seized and an authorization, a licence or a registration certificate, as the case may be, is revoked pursuant to subsection 117.04(4), the justice referred to in paragraph (1)(b) may order that the revocation be reversed and that the authorization, licence or registration certificate be restored.

1995, c. 39, s. 139

Exempted Persons

117.07 (1) Public officers — Notwithstanding any other provision of this Act, but subject to section 117.1, no public officer is guilty of an offence under this Act or the *Firearms Act* by reason only that the public officer

(a) possesses a firearm, a prohibited weapon, a restricted weapon, a prohibited device, any prohibited ammunition or an explosive substance in the course of or for the purpose of the public officer's duties or employment;

(b) manufactures or transfers, or offers to manufacture or transfer, a firearm, a prohibited weapon, a restricted weapon, a prohibited device, any ammunition or any prohibited ammunition in the course of the public officer's duties or employment;

(c) exports or imports a firearm, a prohibited weapon, a restricted weapon, a prohibited device or any prohibited ammunition in the course of the public officer's duties or employment;

(d) exports or imports a component or part designed exclusively for use in the manufacture of or assembly into an automatic firearm in the course of the public officer's duties or employment;

(e) in the course of the public officer's duties or employment, alters a firearm so that it is capable of, or manufactures or assembles any firearm with intent to produce a firearm that is capable of, discharging projectiles in rapid succession during one pressure of the trigger;

(f) fails to report the loss, theft or finding of any firearm, prohibited weapon, restricted weapon, prohibited device, ammunition, prohibited ammunition or explosive substance that occurs in the course of the public officer's duties or employment or the destruction of any such thing in the course of the public officer's duties or employment; or

(g) alters a serial number on a firearm in the course of the public officer's duties or employment.

(2) Definition of "public officer" — In this section, **"public officer"** means

(a) a peace officer;

(b) a member of the Canadian Forces or of the armed forces of a state other than Canada who is attached or seconded to any of the Canadian Forces;

(c) an operator of a museum established by the Chief of the Defence Staff or a person employed in any such museum;

(d) a member of a cadet organization under the control and supervision of the Canadian Forces;

(e) a person training to become a police officer or a peace officer under the control and supervision of

(i) a police force, or

(ii) a police academy or similar institution designated by the Attorney General of Canada or the lieutenant governor in council of a province;

(f) a member of a visiting force, within the meaning of section 2 of the *Visiting Forces Act*, who is authorized under paragraph 14(a) of that Act to possess and carry explosives, ammunition and firearms;

(g) a person, or member of a class of persons, employed in the federal public administration or by the government of a province or municipality who is prescribed to be a public officer; or

(h) the Commissioner of Firearms, the Registrar, a chief firearms officer, any firearms officer and any person designated under section 100 of the *Firearms Act*.

1995, c. 39, s. 139; 2003, c. 8, s. 7; 2003, c. 22, s. 224(z.23)

Proposed Addition — 117.071

117.071 Preclearance officers — Despite any other provision of this Act, but subject to section 117.1, no **"preclearance officer"**, as defined in section 5 of the *Preclearance Act, 2016*, is guilty of an offence under this Act or the *Firearms Act* by reason only that the preclearance officer

(a) possesses a firearm, a prohibited weapon, a restricted weapon, a prohibited device or any prohibited ammunition in the course of or for the purpose of their duties or employment;

(b) transfers or offers to transfer a firearm, a prohibited weapon, a restricted weapon, a prohibited device, any ammunition or any prohibited ammunition in the course of their duties or employment;

(c) exports or imports a firearm, a prohibited weapon, a restricted weapon, a prohibited device or any prohibited ammunition in the course of their duties or employment; or

(d) fails to report the loss, theft or finding of any firearm, prohibited weapon, restricted weapon, prohibited device, ammunition, prohibited ammunition or explosive substance that occurs in the course of their duties or employment or the destruction of any such thing in the course of their duties or employment.

2017, c. 27, s. 61 [Not in force at date of publication.]

117.08 Individuals acting for police force, Canadian Forces and visiting forces — Notwithstanding any other provision of this Act, but subject to section 117.1, no individual is guilty of an offence under this Act or the *Firearms Act* by reason only that the individual

(a) possesses a firearm, a prohibited weapon, a restricted weapon, a prohibited device, any prohibited ammunition or an explosive substance,

(b) manufactures or transfers, or offers to manufacture or transfer, a firearm, a prohibited weapon, a restricted weapon, a prohibited device, any ammunition or any prohibited ammunition,

(c) exports or imports a firearm, a prohibited weapon, a restricted weapon, a prohibited device or any prohibited ammunition,

(d) exports or imports a component or part designed exclusively for use in the manufacture of or assembly into an automatic firearm,

(e) alters a firearm so that it is capable of, or manufactures or assembles any firearm with intent to produce a firearm that is capable of, discharging projectiles in rapid succession during one pressure of the trigger,

(f) fails to report the loss, theft or finding of any firearm, prohibited weapon, restricted weapon, prohibited device, ammunition, prohibited ammunition or explosive substance or the destruction of any such thing, or

(g) alters a serial number on a firearm,

if the individual does so on behalf of, and under the authority of, a police force, the Canadian Forces, a visiting force, within the meaning of section 2 of the *Visiting Forces Act*, or a department of the Government of Canada or of a province.

1995, c. 39, s. 139

117.09 (1) Employees of business with licence — Notwithstanding any other provision of this Act, but subject to section 117.1, no individual who is the holder of a licence to possess and acquire restricted firearms and who is employed by a business as defined in subsection 2(1) of the *Firearms Act* that itself is the holder of a licence that authorizes the business to carry out specified activities in relation to prohibited firearms, prohibited weapons, prohibited devices or prohibited ammunition is guilty of an offence under this Act or the *Firearms Act* by reason only that the individual, in the course of the individual's duties or employment in relation to those specified activities,

(a) possesses a prohibited firearm, a prohibited weapon, a prohibited device or any prohibited ammunition;

(b) manufactures or transfers, or offers to manufacture or transfer, a prohibited weapon, a prohibited device or any prohibited ammunition;

(c) alters a firearm so that it is capable of, or manufactures or assembles any firearm with intent to produce a firearm that is capable of, discharging projectiles in rapid succession during one pressure of the trigger, or

(d) alters a serial number on a firearm.

(2) Employees of business with licence — Notwithstanding any other provision of this Act, but subject to section 117.1, no individual who is employed by a business as defined in subsection 2(1) of the *Firearms Act* that itself is the holder of a licence is guilty of an offence under this Act or the *Firearms Act* by reason only that the individual, in the course of the individual's duties or employment, possesses, manufactures or transfers, or offers to manufacture or transfer, a partially manufactured barrelled weapon that, in its unfinished state, is not a barrelled weapon from which any shot, bullet or other projectile can be discharged and that is capable of causing serious bodily injury or death to a person.

(3) Employees of carriers — Notwithstanding any other provision of this Act, but subject to section 117.1, no individual who is employed by a carrier, as defined in subsection 2(1) of the *Firearms Act*, is guilty of an offence under this Act or that Act by reason only that the individual, in the course of the individual's duties or employment, possesses any firearm, cross-bow, prohibited weapon, restricted weapon, prohibited device, ammunition or prohibited ammunition or transfers, or offers to transfer any such thing.

(4) Employees of museums handling functioning imitation antique firearm — Notwithstanding any other provision of this Act, but subject to section 117.1, no individual who is employed by a museum as defined in subsection 2(1) of the *Firearms Act* that itself is the holder of a licence is guilty of an offence under this Act or the *Firearms Act* by reason only that the individual, in the course of the individual's duties or employment, possesses or transfers a firearm that is designed or intended to exactly resemble, or to resemble with near precision, an antique firearm if the individual has been trained to handle and use such a firearm.

(5) Employees of museums handling firearms generally — Notwithstanding any other provision of this Act, but subject to section 117.1, no individual who is employed by a museum as defined in subsection 2(1) of the *Firearms Act* that itself is the holder of a licence is guilty of an offence under this Act or the *Firearms Act* by reason only that the individual possesses or transfers a firearm in the course of the individual's duties or employment if the individual is designated, by name, by a provincial minister within the meaning of subsection 2(1) of the *Firearms Act*.

(6) Public safety — A provincial minister shall not designate an individual for the purpose of subsection (5) where it is not desirable, in the interests of the safety of any person, to designate the individual.

(7) Conditions — A provincial minister may attach to a designation referred to in subsection (5) any reasonable condition that the provincial minister considers desirable in the particular circumstances and in the interests of the safety of any person.

1995, c. 39, s. 139

117.1 Restriction — Sections 117.07 to 117.09 do not apply if the public officer or the individual is subject to a prohibition order and acts contrary to that order or to an authorization or a licence issued under the authority of an order made under subsection 113(1).

1995, c. 39, s. 139

General

117.11 Onus on the accused — Where, in any proceedings for an offence under any of sections 89, 90, 91, 93, 97, 101, 104 and 105, any question arises as to whether a person is the holder of an authorization, a licence or a registration certificate, the onus is on the accused to prove that the person is the holder of the authorization, licence or registration certificate.

1995, c. 39, s. 139

117.12 (1) Authorizations, etc. as evidence — In any proceedings under this Act or any other Act of Parliament, a document purporting to be an authorization, a licence or a registration certificate is evidence of the statements contained therein.

(2) Certified copies — In any proceedings under this Act or any other Act of Parliament, a copy of any authorization, licence or registration certificate is, if certified as a true copy by the Registrar or a chief firearms officer, admissible in evidence and, in the absence of evidence to the contrary, has the same probative force as the authorization, licence or registration certificate would have had if it had been proved in the ordinary way.

1995, c. 39, s. 139

117.13 (1) Certificate of analyst — A certificate purporting to be signed by an analyst stating that the analyst has analyzed any weapon, prohibited device, ammunition, prohibited ammunition or explosive substance, or any part or component of such a thing, and stating the results of the analysis is evidence in any proceedings in relation to any of those things under this Act or under section 19 of the *Export and Import Permits Act* in relation to subsection 15(2) of that Act without proof of the signature or official character of the person appearing to have signed the certificate.

(2) Attendance of analyst — The party against whom a certificate of an analyst is produced may, with leave of the court, require the attendance of the analyst for the purposes of cross-examination.

(3) Notice of intention to produce certificate — No certificate of an analyst may be admitted in evidence unless the party intending to produce it has, before the trial, given to the party against whom it is intended to be produced reasonable notice of that intention together with a copy of the certificate.

(4) and (5) [Repealed 2008, c. 18, s. 2.]

1995, c. 39, s. 139; 2008, c. 18, s. 2

117.14 (1) Amnesty period — The Governor in Council may, by order, declare for any purpose referred to in subsection (2) any period as an amnesty period with respect to any weapon, prohibited device, prohibited ammunition, explosive substance or component or part designed exclusively for use in the manufacture of or assembly into an automatic firearm.

(2) Purposes of amnesty period — An order made under subsection (1) may declare an amnesty period for the purpose of

(a) permitting any person in possession of any thing to which the order relates to do anything provided in the order, including, without restricting the generality of the foregoing, delivering the thing to a peace officer, a firearms officer or a chief firearms officer, registering it, destroying it or otherwise disposing of it; or

(b) permitting alterations to be made to any prohibited firearm, prohibited weapon, prohibited device or prohibited ammunition to which the order relates so that it no longer qualifies as a prohibited firearm, a prohibited weapon, a prohibited device or prohibited ammunition, as the case may be.

(3) Reliance on amnesty period — No person who, during an amnesty period declared by an order made under subsection (1) and for a purpose described in the order, does anything provided for in the order, is, by reason only of the fact that the person did that thing, guilty of an offence under this Part.

(4) Proceedings are a nullity — Any proceedings taken under this Part against any person for anything done by the person in reliance of this section are a nullity.

1995, c. 39, s. 139

117.15 (1) Regulations — Subject to subsection (2), the Governor in Council may make regulations prescribing anything that by this Part is to be or may be prescribed.

(2) Restriction — In making regulations, the Governor in Council may not prescribe any thing to be a prohibited firearm, a restricted firearm, a prohibited weapon, a restricted weapon, a prohibited device or prohibited ammunition if, in the opinion of the Governor in Council, the thing to be prescribed is reasonable for use in Canada for hunting or sporting purposes.

(3) Non-restricted firearm — Despite the definitions "prohibited firearm" and "restricted firearm" in subsection 84(1), a firearm that is prescribed to be a non-restricted firearm is deemed not to be a prohibited firearm or a restricted firearm.

Proposed Repeal — 117.15(3)

(3) [Repealed 2019, c. 9, s. 18. Not in force at date of publication.]

(4) Restricted firearm — Despite the definition "prohibited firearm" in subsection 84(1), a firearm that is prescribed to be a restricted firearm is deemed not to be a prohibited firearm.

Proposed Repeal — 117.15(4)

(4) [Repealed 2019, c. 9, s. 18. Not in force at date of publication.]

1995, c. 39, s. 139; 2015, c. 27, s. 34

Part IV — Offences Against the Administration of Law and Justice (ss. 118–149)

Interpretation

118. Definitions — In this Part

"evidence" or **"statement"** means an assertion of fact, opinion, belief or knowledge whether material or not and whether admissible or not;

"government" means

(a) the Government of Canada,

(b) the government of a province, or

(c) Her Majesty in right of Canada or a province;

"judicial proceeding" means a proceeding

(a) in or under the authority of a court of justice,

(b) before the Senate or House of Commons or a committee of the Senate or House of Commons, or before a legislative council, legislative assembly or house of assembly or a committee thereof that is authorized by law to administer an oath,

(c) before a court, judge, justice, provincial court judge or coroner,

(d) before an arbitrator or umpire, or a person or body of persons authorized by law to make an inquiry and take evidence therein under oath, or

(e) before a tribunal by which a legal right or legal liability may be established,

whether or not the proceeding is invalid for want of jurisdiction or for any other reason;

"office" includes

(a) an office or appointment under the government,

(b) a civil or military commission, and

(c) a position or an employment in a public department;

"official" means a person who

(a) holds an office, or

(b) is appointed or elected to discharge a public duty;

"witness" means a person who gives evidence orally under oath or by affidavit in a judicial proceeding, whether or not he is competent to be a witness, and includes a child of tender years who gives evidence but does not give it under oath, because, in the opinion of the person presiding, the child does not understand the nature of an oath.

R.S.C. 1985, c. 27 (1st Supp.), ss. 15, 203; 2007, c. 13, s. 2

Corruption and Disobedience

119. (1) Bribery of judicial officers, etc. — Every one is guilty of an indictable offence and liable to imprisonment for a term not exceeding fourteen years who

(a) being the holder of a judicial office, or being a member of Parliament or of the legislature of a province, directly or indirectly, corruptly accepts, obtains, agrees to accept or attempts to obtain, for themselves or another person, any money, valuable consideration, office, place or employment in respect of anything done or omitted or to be done or omitted by them in their official capacity, or

(b) directly or indirectly, corruptly gives or offers to a person mentioned in paragraph (a), or to anyone for the benefit of that person, any money, valuable consideration, office, place or employment in respect of anything done or omitted or to be done or omitted by that person in their official capacity.

(2) Consent of Attorney General — No proceedings against a person who holds a judicial office shall be instituted under this section without the consent in writing of the Attorney General of Canada.

2007, c. 13, s. 3

120. Bribery of officers — Every one is guilty of an indictable offence and liable to imprisonment for a term not exceeding fourteen years who

(a) being a justice, police commissioner, peace officer, public officer or officer of a juvenile court, or being employed in the administration of criminal law, directly or indirectly, corruptly accepts, obtains, agrees to accept or attempts to obtain, for themselves or another person, any money, valuable consideration, office, place or employment with intent

(i) to interfere with the administration of justice,

(ii) to procure or facilitate the commission of an offence, or

(iii) to protect from detection or punishment a person who has committed or who intends to commit an offence; or

(b) directly or indirectly, corruptly gives or offers to a person mentioned in paragraph (a), or to anyone for the benefit of that person, any money, valuable consideration, office, place or employment with intent that the person should do anything mentioned in subparagraph (a)(i), (ii) or (iii).

2007, c. 13, s. 4

121. (1) Frauds on the government — Every one commits an offence who

(a) directly or indirectly

(i) gives, offers, or agrees to give or offer to an official or to any member of his family, or to any one for the benefit of an official, or

(ii) being an official, demands, accepts or offers or agrees to accept from any person for himself or another person,

a loan, reward, advantage or benefit of any kind as consideration for cooperation, assistance, exercise of influence or an act or omission in connection with

(iii) the transaction of business with or any matter of business relating to the government, or

(iv) a claim against Her Majesty or any benefit that Her Majesty is authorized or is entitled to bestow,

whether or not, in fact, the official is able to cooperate, render assistance, exercise influence or do or omit to do what is proposed, as the case may be;

(b) having dealings of any kind with the government, directly or indirectly pays a commission or reward to or confers an advantage or benefit of any kind on an employee or official of the government with which the dealings take place, or to any member of the employee's or official's family, or to anyone for the benefit of the employee or official, with respect to those dealings, unless the person has the consent in writing of the head of the branch of government with which the dealings take place;

(c) being an official or employee of the government, directly or indirectly demands, accepts or offers or agrees to accept from a person who has dealings with the government a commission, reward, advantage or benefit of any kind for themselves or another person, unless they have the consent in writing of the head of the branch of government that employs them or of which they are an official;

(d) having or pretending to have influence with the government or with a minister of the government or an official, directly or indirectly demands, accepts or offers or agrees to accept, for themselves or another person, a reward, advantage or benefit of any kind as consideration for cooperation, assistance, exercise of influence or an act or omission in connection with

(i) anything mentioned in subparagraph (a)(iii) or (iv), or

(ii) the appointment of any person, including themselves, to an office;

(e) directly or indirectly gives or offers, or agrees to give or offer, to a minister of the government or an official, or to anyone for the benefit of a minister or an official, a reward, advantage or benefit of any kind as consideration for cooperation, assistance, exercise of influence, or an act or omission, by that minister or official, in connection with

(i) anything mentioned in subparagraph (a)(iii) or (iv), or

(ii) the appointment of any person, including themselves, to an office; or

(f) having made a tender to obtain a contract with the government,

(i) directly or indirectly gives or offers, or agrees to give or offer, to another person who has made a tender, to a member of that person's family or to another person for the benefit of that person, a reward, advantage or benefit of any kind as consideration for the withdrawal of the tender of that person, or

(ii) directly or indirectly demands, accepts or offers or agrees to accept from another person who has made a tender a reward, advantage or benefit of any kind for themselves or another person as consideration for the withdrawal of their own tender.

(2) **Contractor subscribing to election fund** — Every one commits an offence who, in order to obtain or retain a contract with the government, or as a term of any such contract, whether express or implied, directly or indirectly subscribes or gives, or agrees to subscribe or give, to any person any valuable consideration

(a) for the purpose of promoting the election of a candidate or a class or party of candidates to Parliament or the legislature of a province; or

(b) with intent to influence or affect in any way the result of an election conducted for the purpose of electing persons to serve in Parliament or the legislature of a province.

(3) **Punishment** — Every person who commits an offence under this section is guilty of

(a) an indictable offence and liable to imprisonment for a term of not more than five years; or

(b) an offence punishable on summary conviction.

2007, c. 13, s. 5; 2019, c. 25, s. 33

121.1 (1) **Selling, etc., of tobacco products and raw leaf tobacco** — No person shall sell, offer for sale, transport, deliver, distribute or have in their possession for the purpose of sale a tobacco product, or raw leaf tobacco that is not packaged, unless it is stamped. The terms **"tobacco product"**, **"raw leaf tobacco"**, **"packaged"** and **"stamped"** have the same meanings as in section 2 of the *Excise Act, 2001*.

(2) Exceptions — subsections 30(2) and 32(2) and (3) of *Excise Act, 2001* — Subsection (1) does not apply in any of the circumstances described in any of subsections 30(2) and 32(2) and (3) of the *Excise Act, 2001*.

(3) Exception — section 31 of *Excise Act, 2001* — A tobacco grower does not contravene subsection (1) by reason only that they have in their possession raw leaf tobacco described in paragraph 31(a), (b) or (c) of the *Excise Act, 2001*.

(4) Punishment — Every person who contravenes subsection (1)

(a) is guilty of an indictable offence and liable to imprisonment for a term of not more than five years and, if the amount of tobacco product is 10,000 cigarettes or more or 10 kg or more of any other tobacco product, or the amount of raw leaf tobacco is 10 kg or more,

(i) in the case of a second offence, to a minimum punishment of imprisonment for a term of 90 days,

(ii) in the case of a third offence, to a minimum punishment of imprisonment for a term of 180 days, and

(iii) in the case of a fourth or subsequent offence, to a minimum punishment of imprisonment for a term of two years less a day; or

(b) is guilty of an offence punishable on summary conviction.

(5) Subsequent offences — For the purpose of determining whether a convicted person has committed a second or subsequent offence, an offence under this section for which the person was previously convicted is considered to be an earlier offence whether it was prosecuted by indictment or by way of summary conviction proceedings.

2014, c. 23, s. 3; 2019, c. 25, s. 34(2)

122. Breach of trust by public officer — Every official who, in connection with the duties of their office, commits fraud or a breach of trust, whether or not the fraud or breach of trust would be an offence if it were committed in relation to a private person, is guilty of

(a) an indictable offence and liable to imprisonment for a term of not more than five years; or

(b) an offence punishable on summary conviction.

2019, c. 25, s. 35

123. (1) Municipal corruption — Every person is guilty of an indictable offence and liable to imprisonment for a term of not more than five years or is guilty of an offence punishable on summary conviction who directly or indirectly gives, offers or agrees to give or offer to a municipal official or to anyone for the benefit of a municipal official — or, being a municipal official, directly or indirectly demands, accepts or offers or agrees to accept from any person for themselves or another person — a loan, reward, advantage or benefit of any kind as consideration for the official

(a) to abstain from voting at a meeting of the municipal council or a committee of the council;

(b) to vote in favour of or against a measure, motion or resolution;

(c) to aid in procuring or preventing the adoption of a measure, motion or resolution; or

(d) to perform or fail to perform an official act.

(e) and (f) [Repealed 2007, c. 13, s. 6.]

(2) Influencing municipal official — Every person is guilty of an indictable offence and liable to imprisonment for a term of not more than five years or is guilty of an offence punishable on summary conviction who influences or attempts to influence a municipal official to do anything mentioned in paragraphs (1)(a) to (d) by

(a) suppression of the truth, in the case of a person who is under a duty to disclose the truth;

(b) threats or deceit; or

(c) any unlawful means.

(3) "municipal official" — In this section **"municipal official"** means a member of a municipal council or a person who holds an office under a municipal government.

R.S.C. 1985, c. 27 (1st Supp.), s. 16; 2007, c. 13, s. 6; 2019, c. 25, s. 36

124. Selling or purchasing office — Every person is guilty of an indictable offence and liable to imprisonment for a term of not more than five years or is guilty of an offence punishable on summary conviction who

(a) purports to sell or agrees to sell an appointment to or resignation from an office, or a consent to any such appointment or resignation, or receives or agrees to receive a reward or profit from the purported sale thereof, or

(b) purports to purchase or gives a reward or profit for the purported purchase of any such appointment, resignation or consent, or agrees or promises to do so.

2019, c. 25, s. 37

125. Influencing or negotiating appointments or dealing in offices — Every person is guilty of an indictable offence and liable to imprisonment for a term of not more than five years or is guilty of an offence punishable on summary conviction who

(a) receives, agrees to receive, gives or procures to be given, directly or indirectly, a reward, advantage or benefit of any kind as consideration for cooperation, assistance or exercise of influence to secure the appointment of any person to an office,

(b) solicits, recommends or negotiates in any manner with respect to an appointment to or resignation from an office, in expectation of a direct or indirect reward, advantage or benefit, or

(c) keeps without lawful authority a place for transacting or negotiating any business relating to

(i) the filling of vacancies in offices,

(ii) the sale or purchase of offices, or

(iii) appointments to or resignations from offices.

2018, c. 29, s. 7; 2019, c. 25, s. 38

126. (1) Disobeying a statute — Every person who, without lawful excuse, contravenes an Act of Parliament by intentionally doing anything that it forbids or by intentionally omitting to do anything that it requires to be done is, unless a punishment is expressly provided by law, guilty of

(a) an indictable offence and liable to imprisonment for a term of not more than two years; or

(b) an offence punishable on summary conviction.

(2) Attorney General of Canada may act — Any proceedings in respect of a contravention of or conspiracy to contravene an Act mentioned in subsection (1), other than this Act, may be instituted at the instance of the Government of Canada and conducted by or on behalf of that Government.

127. (1) Disobeying order of court — Every one who, without lawful excuse, disobeys a lawful order made by a court of justice or by a person or body of persons authorized by any Act to make or give the order, other than an order for the payment of money, is, unless a punishment or other mode of proceeding is expressly provided by law, guilty of

(a) an indictable offence and liable to imprisonment for a term not exceeding two years; or

(b) an offence punishable on summary conviction.

(2) Attorney General of Canada may act — Where the order referred to in subsection (1) was made in proceedings instituted at the instance of the Government of Canada and conducted by or on behalf of that Government, any proceedings in respect of a contravention of or conspiracy to contravene that order may be instituted and conducted in like manner.

2005, c. 32, s. 1

128. Misconduct of officers executing process — Every peace officer or coroner is guilty of an indictable offence and liable to imprisonment for a term of not more than two years or is guilty of an offence punishable on summary conviction who, being entrusted with the execution of a process, intentionally

(a) misconducts himself in the execution of the process, or

(b) makes a false return to the process.

2019, c. 25, s. 40

129. Offences relating to public or peace officer — Every one who

(a) resists or wilfully obstructs a public officer or peace officer in the execution of his duty or any person lawfully acting in aid of such an officer,

(b) omits, without reasonable excuse, to assist a public officer or peace officer in the execution of his duty in arresting a person or in preserving the peace, after having reasonable notice that he is required to do so, or

(c) resists or wilfully obstructs any person in the lawful execution of a process against lands or goods or in making a lawful distress or seizure,

is guilty of

(d) an indictable offence and liable to imprisonment for a term not exceeding two years, or

(e) an offence punishable on summary conviction.

130. (1) Personating peace officer — Everyone commits an offence who

(a) falsely represents himself to be a peace officer or a public officer; or

(b) not being a peace officer or public officer, uses a badge or article of uniform or equipment in a manner that is likely to cause persons to believe that he is a peace officer or a public officer, as the case may be.

(2) Punishment — Everyone who commits an offence under subsection (1)

(a) is guilty of an indictable offence and liable to imprisonment for a term of not more than five years; or

(b) is guilty of an offence punishable on summary conviction.

2009, c. 28, s. 2

130.1 Aggravating circumstance — If a person is convicted of an offence under section 130, the court imposing the sentence on the person shall consider as an aggravating circumstance the fact that the accused personated a peace officer or a public officer, as the case may be, for the purpose of facilitating the commission of another offence.

2014, c. 10, s. 1

Misleading Justice

131. (1) Perjury — Subject to subsection (3), every one commits perjury who, with intent to mislead, makes before a person who is authorized by law to permit it to be made before him, a false statement under oath or solemn affirmation, by affidavit, solemn declaration or deposition or orally, knowing that the statement is false.

(1.1) Video links, etc. — Subject to subsection (3), every person who gives evidence under subsection 46(2) of the *Canada Evidence Act*, or gives evidence or a statement pursuant to an order made under section 22.2 of the *Mutual Legal Assistance in Criminal Matters Act,* commits perjury who, with intent to mislead, makes a false statement knowing that it is false, whether or not the false statement was made under oath or solemn affirmation in accordance with subsection (1), so long as the false statement was made in accordance with any formalities required by the law of the place outside Canada in which the person is virtually present or heard.

(2) Idem — Subsection (1) applies whether or not a statement referred to in that subsection is made in a judicial proceeding.

(3) Application — Subsections (1) and (1.1) do not apply to a statement referred to in either of those subsections that is made by a person who is not specially permitted, authorized or required by law to make that statement.

R.S.C. 1985, c. 27 (1st Supp.), s. 17; 1999, c. 18, s. 92

132. Punishment — Every one who commits perjury is guilty of an indictable offence and liable to imprisonment for a term not exceeding fourteen years.

R.S.C. 1985, c. 27 (1st Supp.), s. 17; 1998, c. 35, s. 119

133. Corroboration — No person shall be convicted of an offence under section 132 on the evidence of only one witness unless the evidence of that witness is corroborated in a material particular by evidence that implicates the accused.

R.S.C. 1985, c. 27 (1st Supp.), s. 17

134. (1) Idem — Subject to subsection (2), every one who, not being specially permitted, authorized or required by law to make a statement under oath or solemn affirmation, makes such a statement, by affidavit, solemn declaration or deposition or orally before a person who is authorized by law to permit it to be made before him, knowing that the statement is false, is guilty of an offence punishable on summary conviction.

(2) Application — Subsection (1) does not apply to a statement referred to in that subsection that is made in the course of a criminal investigation.

R.S.C. 1985, c. 27 (1st Supp.), s. 17

135. [Repealed R.S.C. 1985, c. 27 (1st Supp.), s. 17.]

136. (1) Witness giving contradictory evidence — Every one who, being a witness in a judicial proceeding, gives evidence with respect to any matter of fact or knowledge and who subsequently, in a judicial proceeding, gives evidence that is contrary to his previous evidence is guilty of an indictable offence and liable to imprisonment for a term not exceeding fourteen years, whether or not the prior or later evidence or either is true, but no person shall be convicted under this section unless the court, judge or provincial court judge, as the case may be, is satisfied beyond a reasonable doubt that the accused, in giving evidence in either of the judicial proceedings, intended to mislead.

(1.1) Evidence in specific cases — Evidence given under section 714.1, 714.2 or 714.3 or under subsection 46(2) of the *Canada Evidence Act* or evidence or a statement given under an order made under section 22.2 of the *Mutual Legal Assistance in Criminal Matters Act* is deemed to be evidence given by a witness in a judicial proceeding for the purposes of subsection (1).

(2) **"Evidence"** — Notwithstanding the definition "evidence" in section 118, **"evidence"**, for the purposes of this section, does not include evidence that is not material.

(2.1) **Proof of former trial** — Where a person is charged with an offence under this section, a certificate specifying with reasonable particularity the proceeding in which that person is alleged to have given the evidence in respect of which the offence is charged, is evidence that it was given in a judicial proceeding, without proof of the signature or official character of the person by whom the certificate purports to be signed if it purports to be signed by the clerk of the court or other official having the custody of the record of that proceeding or by his lawful deputy.

(3) **Consent required** — No proceedings shall be instituted under this section without the consent of the Attorney General.

R.S.C. 1985, c. 27 (1st Supp.), ss. 18, 203; 1999, c. 18, s. 93; 2019, c. 25, s. 41

137. Fabricating evidence — Every one who, with intent to mislead, fabricates anything with intent that it shall be used as evidence in a judicial proceeding, existing or proposed, by any means other than perjury or incitement to perjury is guilty of an indictable offence and liable to imprisonment for a term not exceeding fourteen years.

138. Offences relating to affidavits — Every person is guilty of an indictable offence and liable to imprisonment for a term of not more than two years or is guilty of an offence punishable on summary conviction who

(a) signs a writing that purports to be an affidavit or statutory declaration and to have been sworn or declared before him when the writing was not so sworn or declared or when he knows that he has no authority to administer the oath or declaration,

(b) uses or offers for use any writing purporting to be an affidavit or statutory declaration that he knows was not sworn or declared, as the case may be, by the affiant or declarant or before a person authorized in that behalf, or

(c) signs as affiant or declarant a writing that purports to be an affidavit or statutory declaration and to have been sworn or declared by him, as the case may be, when the writing was not so sworn or declared.

2019, c. 25, s. 42

139. (1) Obstructing justice — Every one who wilfully attempts in any manner to obstruct, pervert or defeat the course of justice in a judicial proceeding,

(a) by indemnifying or agreeing to indemnify a surety, in any way and either in whole or in part, or

(b) where he is a surety, by accepting or agreeing to accept a fee or any form of indemnity whether in whole or in part from or in respect of a person who is released or is to be released from custody,

is guilty of

(c) an indictable offence and is liable to imprisonment for a term not exceeding two years, or

(d) an offence punishable on summary conviction.

(2) Idem — Every person who intentionally attempts in any manner other than a manner described in subsection (1) to obstruct, pervert or defeat the course of justice is guilty of

(a) an indictable offence and liable to imprisonment for a term of not more than 10 years; or

(b) an offence punishable on summary conviction.

(3) Idem — Without restricting the generality of subsection (2), every one shall be deemed wilfully to attempt to obstruct, pervert or defeat the course of justice who in a judicial proceeding, existing or proposed,

(a) dissuades or attempts to dissuade a person by threats, bribes or other corrupt means from giving evidence;

(b) influences or attempts to influence by threats, bribes or other corrupt means a person in his conduct as a juror; or

(c) accepts or obtains, agrees to accept or attempts to obtain a bribe or other corrupt consideration to abstain from giving evidence, or to do or to refrain from doing anything as a juror.

2019, c. 25, s. 43

140. (1) Public mischief — Every one commits public mischief who, with intent to mislead, causes a peace officer to enter on or continue an investigation by

(a) making a false statement that accuses some other person of having committed an offence;

(b) doing anything that is intended to cause some other person to be suspected of having committed an offence that the other person has not committed, or to divert suspicion from himself;

(c) reporting that an offence has been committed when it has not been committed; or

(d) reporting or in any other way making it known or causing it to be made known that he or some other person has died when he or that other person has not died.

(2) Punishment — Every one who commits public mischief

(a) is guilty of an indictable offence and liable to imprisonment for a term not exceeding five years; or

(b) is guilty of an offence punishable on summary conviction.

R.S.C. 1985, c. 27 (1st Supp.), s. 19

141. (1) Compounding indictable offence — Every person who asks for or obtains or agrees to receive or obtain any valuable consideration for themselves or any other person by agreeing to compound or conceal an indictable offence is guilty of

(a) an indictable offence and liable to imprisonment for a term of not more than two years; or

(b) an offence punishable on summary conviction.

(2) Exception for diversion agreements — No offence is committed under subsection (1) where valuable consideration is received or obtained or is to be received or obtained under an agreement for compensation or restitution or personal services that is

(a) entered into with the consent of the Attorney General; or

(b) made as part of a program, approved by the Attorney General, to divert persons charged with indictable offences from criminal proceedings.

R.S.C. 1985, c. 27 (1st Supp.), s. 19; 2019, c. 25, s. 44

142. Corruptly taking reward for recovery of goods — Every person who corruptly accepts any valuable consideration, directly or indirectly, under pretence or on account of helping any person to recover anything obtained by the commission of an indictable offence is guilty of

(a) an indictable offence and liable to imprisonment for a term of not more than five years; or

(b) an offence punishable on summary conviction.

2019, c. 25, s. 45

143. [Repealed 2018, c. 29, s. 8.]

Escapes and Rescues

144. Prison breach — Every person is guilty of an indictable offence and liable to imprisonment for a term of not more than 10 years or is guilty of an offence punishable on summary conviction who

(a) by force or violence breaks a prison with intent to set at liberty himself or any other person confined therein, or

(b) with intent to escape forcibly breaks out of, or makes any breach in, a cell or other place within a prison in which he is confined.

2019, c. 25, s. 46

145. (1) Escape and being at large without excuse — Every person is guilty of an indictable offence and liable to imprisonment for a term of not more than two years or is guilty of an offence punishable on summary conviction who

(a) escapes from lawful custody, or

(b) is, before the expiration of a term of imprisonment to which they were sentenced, at large in or out of Canada without lawful excuse.

Proposed Amendment — 145(1)

(1) Escape and being at large without excuse — Every person who escapes from lawful custody or who is, before the expiration of a term of imprisonment to which they were sentenced, at large in or outside Canada without lawful excuse, is guilty of

(a) an indictable offence and liable to imprisonment for a term of not more than two years; or

(b) an offence punishable on summary conviction.

2019, c. 25, s. 47(1) [To come into force December 18, 2019.]

(2) Failure to attend court — Every person is guilty of an indictable offence and liable to imprisonment for a term of not more than two years or is guilty of an offence punishable on summary conviction who,

(a) being at large on their undertaking or recognizance given to or entered into before a justice or judge, fails, without lawful excuse, to attend court in accordance with the undertaking or recognizance; or

(b) having appeared before a court, justice or judge, fails, without lawful excuse, to attend court as subsequently required by the court, justice or judge or to surrender themselves in accordance with an order of the court, justice or judge, as the case may be.

Proposed Amendment — 145(2)

(2) Failure to attend court or surrender — Every person is guilty of an indictable offence and liable to imprisonment for a term not exceeding two years or is guilty of an offence punishable on summary conviction who,

(a) is at large on a release order and who fails, without lawful excuse, to attend court in accordance with the release order;

(b) having appeared before a court, justice or judge, fails, without lawful excuse, to subsequently attend court as required by the court, justice or judge; or

(c) fails to surrender themselves in accordance with an order of the court, justice or judge, as the case may be.

2019, c. 25, s. 47(1) [To come into force December 18, 2019.]

(3) Failure to comply with condition of undertaking or recognizance — Every person who is at large on an undertaking or recognizance given to or entered into before a justice or judge and is bound to comply with a condition of that undertaking or recognizance, and every person who is bound to comply with a direction under subsection 515(12) or 522(2.1) or an order under subsection 516(2), and who fails, without lawful excuse, to comply with the condition, direction or order is guilty of

(a) an indictable offence and is liable to imprisonment for a term not exceeding two years; or

(b) an offence punishable on summary conviction.

Proposed Amendment — 145(3)

(3) Failure to comply with appearance notice or summons — Every person who is named in an appearance notice that has been confirmed by a justice under section 508 or who is served with a summons and who fails, without lawful excuse, to appear at the time and place stated in the notice or the summons, as the case may be, for the purposes of the *Identification of Criminals Act*, or to attend court in accordance with the notice or the summons, as the case may be, is guilty of

(a) an indictable offence and liable to imprisonment for a term of not more than two years; or

(b) an offence punishable on summary conviction.

2019, c. 25, s. 47(1) [To come into force December 18, 2019.]

(4) Failure to appear or to comply with summons — Every person who is served with a summons and who fails, without lawful excuse, to appear at the time and place stated in it for the purposes of the *Identification of Criminals Act* or to attend court in accordance with it, is guilty of

(a) an indictable offence and is liable to imprisonment for a term not exceeding two years; or

(b) an offence punishable on summary conviction.

Proposed Amendment — 145(4)

(4) Failure to comply with undertaking — Every person is guilty of an indictable offence and liable to imprisonment for a term of not more than two years or an offence punishable on summary conviction who,

(a) is at large on an undertaking and who fails, without lawful excuse, to comply with a condition of that undertaking; or

(b) is at large on an undertaking that has been confirmed by a justice under section 508 and who fails, without lawful excuse, to appear at the time and place stated in the undertaking for the purposes of the *Identification of Criminals Act* or to attend court in accordance with the undertaking.

2019, c. 25, s. 47(1) [To come into force December 18, 2019.]

(5) Failure to comply with appearance notice or promise to appear — Every person who is named in an appearance notice or promise to appear, or in a recognizance entered into before an officer in charge or another peace officer, that has been confirmed by a justice under section 508 and who fails, without lawful excuse, to appear at the time and place stated in it for the purposes of the *Identification of Criminals Act*, or to attend court in accordance with it, is guilty of

(a) an indictable offence and is liable to imprisonment for a term not exceeding two years; or

(b) an offence punishable on summary conviction.

Proposed Amendment — 145(5)

(5) Failure to comply with order — Every person is guilty of an indictable offence and liable to imprisonment for a term of not more than two years, or is guilty of an offence punishable on summary conviction, who

(a) is at large on a release order and who fails, without lawful excuse, to comply with a condition of that release order other than the condition to attend court; or

(b) is bound to comply with an order under subsection 515(12), 516(2) or 522(2.1) and who fails, without lawful excuse, to comply with that order.

2019, c. 25, s. 47(1) [To come into force December 18, 2019.]

(5.1) Failure to comply with conditions of undertaking — Every person who, without lawful excuse, fails to comply with any condition of an undertaking entered into under subsection 499(2) or 503(2.1)

(a) is guilty of an indictable offence and is liable to imprisonment for a term not exceeding two years; or

(b) is guilty of an offence punishable on summary conviction.

Proposed Repeal — 145(5.1)

(5.1) [Repealed 2019, c. 25, s. 47(1). To come into force December 18, 2019.]

(6) Idem — For the purposes of subsection (5), it is not a lawful excuse that an appearance notice, promise to appear or recognizance states defectively the substance of the alleged offence.

Proposed Amendment — 145(6)

(6) Not an excuse — For the purposes of subsections (3) and (4), it is not a lawful excuse that an appearance notice or undertaking states defectively the substance of the alleged offence.

2019, c. 25, s. 47(1) [To come into force December 18, 2019.]

(7) [Repealed R.S.C. 1985, c. 27 (1st Supp.), s. 20(2).]

(8) Election of Crown under *Contraventions Act* — For the purposes of subsections (3) to (5), it is a lawful excuse to fail to comply with a condition of an undertaking or recognizance or to fail to appear at a time and place stated in a summons, an appearance notice, a promise to appear or a recognizance for the purposes of the *Identification of Criminals Act* if before the failure the Attorney General, within the meaning of the *Contraventions Act*, makes an election under section 50 of that Act.

Proposed Amendment — 145(8)

(8) Election of Crown under *Contraventions Act* — For the purposes of paragraph (2)(a) and subsections (3) to (5), it is a lawful excuse to fail to attend court in accordance with a summons, appearance notice, undertaking or release order, to comply with a condition of an undertaking or release order or to fail to appear at the time and place stated in a summons, an appearance notice or an undertaking for the purposes of the *Identification of Criminals Act* if — before the failure — the **"Attorney General"**, within the meaning of the *Contraventions Act*, makes an election under section 50 of that Act.

2019, c. 25, s. 47(2) [To come into force December 18, 2019.]

(9) Proof of certain facts by certificate — In any proceedings under subsection (2), (4) or (5), a certificate of the clerk of the court or a judge of the court before which the accused is alleged to have failed to attend or of the person in charge of the place at which it is alleged the accused failed to attend for the purposes of the *Identification of Criminals Act* stating that,

(a) in the case of proceedings under subsection (2), the accused gave or entered into an undertaking or recognizance before a justice or judge and failed to attend court in accordance therewith or, having attended court, failed to attend court thereafter as required by the court, justice or judge or to surrender in accordance with an order of the court, justice or judge, as the case may be,

(b) in the case of proceedings under subsection (4), a summons was issued to and served on the accused and the accused failed to attend court in accordance therewith or failed to appear at the time and place stated therein for the purposes of the *Identification of Criminals Act*, as the case may be, and

(c) in the case of proceedings under subsection (5), the accused was named in an appearance notice, a promise to appear or a recognizance entered into before an officer in charge or another peace officer, that was confirmed by a justice under section 508, and the accused failed to appear at the time and place stated therein for the purposes of the *Identification of Criminals Act*, failed to attend court in accordance therewith or, having attended court, failed to attend court thereafter as required by the court, justice or judge, as the case may be,

is evidence of the statements contained in the certificate without proof of the signature or the official character of the person appearing to have signed the certificate.

Proposed Amendment — 145(9)

(9) Proof of certain facts by certificate — In any proceedings under subsections (2) to (4), a certificate of the clerk of the court or a judge of the court before which the accused is alleged to have failed to attend or of the person in charge of the place at which it is alleged the accused failed to attend for the purposes of the *Identification of Criminals Act* is evidence of the statements contained in the certificate without proof of the signature or the official character of the person appearing to have signed the certificate if the certificate states that,

(a) in the case of proceedings under subsection (2), the accused failed to attend court as required by the release order or, having attended court, failed to subsequently attend court as required by the court, judge or justice or failed to surrender in accordance with an order of the court, judge or justice, as the case may be;

(b) in the case of proceedings under subsection (3), the accused was named in an appearance notice that was confirmed by a justice under section 508 and the accused failed to attend court in accordance with the notice or failed to appear at the time and place stated in the notice for the purposes of the *Identification of Criminals Act*, as the case may be;

(c) in the case of proceedings under subsection (3), a summons was issued to and served on the accused and the accused failed to attend court in accordance with the summons or failed to appear at the time and place stated in the summons for the purposes of the *Identification of Criminals Act*, as the case may be; and

(d) in the case of proceedings under subsection (4), the accused was at large on an undertaking that was confirmed by a justice under section 508, and the accused failed to attend court in accordance with the undertaking or failed to appear at the time and place stated in the undertaking for the purposes of the *Identification of Criminals Act*, as the case may be.

2019, c. 25, s. 47(2) [To come into force December 18, 2019.]

(10) Attendance and right to cross-examination — An accused against whom a certificate described in subsection (9) is produced may, with leave of the court, require the attendance of the person making the certificate for the purposes of cross-examination.

(11) Notice of intention to produce — No certificate shall be received in evidence pursuant to subsection (9) unless the party intending to produce it has, before the trial, given to the accused reasonable notice of his intention together with a copy of the certificate.

R.S.C. 1985, c. 27 (1st Supp.), s. 20; 1992, c. 47, s. 68 [Amended 1996, c. 7, s. 38.]; 1994, c. 44, s. 8; 1997, c. 18, s. 3; 2008, c. 18, s. 3; 2018, c. 29, s. 9(1)–(8), (10), (12)

146. Permitting or assisting escape — Every person is guilty of an indictable offence and liable to imprisonment for a term of not more than two years or is guilty of an offence punishable on summary conviction who

(a) permits a person whom he has in lawful custody to escape, by failing to perform a legal duty,

(b) conveys or causes to be conveyed into a prison anything, with intent to facilitate the escape of a person imprisoned therein, or

(c) directs or procures, under colour of pretended authority, the discharge of a prisoner who is not entitled to be discharged.

2019, c. 25, s. 48

147. Rescue or permitting escape — Every person is guilty of an indictable offence and liable to imprisonment for a term of not more than five years or is guilty of an offence punishable on summary conviction who

(a) rescues any person from lawful custody or assists any person in escaping or attempting to escape from lawful custody,

(b) being a peace officer, wilfully permits a person in his lawful custody to escape, or

(c) being an officer of or an employee in a prison, wilfully permits a person to escape from lawful custody therein.

2019, c. 25, s. 49

148. Assisting prisoner of war to escape — Every person is guilty of an indictable offence and liable to imprisonment for a term of not more than five years or is guilty of an offence punishable on summary conviction who knowingly

(a) assists a prisoner of war in Canada to escape from a place where he is detained, or

(b) assists a prisoner of war, who is permitted to be at large on parole in Canada, to escape from the place where he is at large on parole.

2019, c. 25, s. 50

149. (1) Service of term for escape — Notwithstanding section 743.1, a court that convicts a person for an escape committed while undergoing imprisonment may order that the term of imprisonment be served in a penitentiary, even if the time to be served is less than two years.

(2) Definition of "escape" — In this section, **"escape"** means breaking prison, escaping from lawful custody or, without lawful excuse, being at large before the expiration of a term of imprisonment to which a person has been sentenced.

R.S.C. 1985, c. 27 (1st Supp.), s. 203; 1992, c. 20, s. 199; 1995, c. 22, ss. 1, 10 (Sched. I, item 11)

PART V — SEXUAL OFFENCES, PUBLIC MORALS AND DISORDERLY CONDUCT (SS. 150–182)

Interpretation

150. Definitions — In this Part,

"guardian" includes any person who has in law or in fact the custody or control of another person;

"public place" includes any place to which the public have access as of right or by invitation, express or implied;

"theatre" includes any place that is open to the public where entertainments are given, whether or not any charge is made for admission.

Sexual Offences

150.1 (1) Consent no defence — Subject to subsections (2) to (2.2), when an accused is charged with an offence under section 151 or 152 or subsection 153(1), 160(3) or 173(2) or is charged with an offence under section 271, 272 or 273 in respect of a complainant under the age of 16 years, it is not a defence that the complainant consented to the activity that forms the subject-matter of the charge.

(2) Exception — complainant aged 12 or 13 — When an accused is charged with an offence under section 151 or 152, subsection 173(2) or section 271 in respect of a complainant who is 12 years of age or more but under the age of 14 years, it is a defence that the complainant consented to the activity that forms the subject-matter of the charge if the accused

(a) is less than two years older than the complainant; and

(b) is not in a position of trust or authority towards the complainant, is not a person with whom the complainant is in a relationship of dependency and is not in a relationship with the complainant that is exploitative of the complainant.

(2.1) Exception — complainant aged 14 or 15 — If an accused is charged with an offence under section 151 or 152, subsection 173(2) or section 271 in respect of a complainant who is 14 years of age or more but under the age of 16 years, it is a defence that the complainant consented to the activity that forms the subject-matter of the charge if the accused

(a) is less than five years older than the complainant; and

(b) is not in a position of trust or authority towards the complainant, is not a person with whom the complainant is in a relationship of dependency and is not in a relationship with the complainant that is exploitative of the complainant.

(2.2) Exception for transitional purposes — When the accused referred to in subsection (2.1) is five or more years older than the complainant, it is a defence that the complainant consented to the activity that forms the subject-matter of the charge if, on the day on which this subsection comes into force,

(a) the accused is the common-law partner of the complainant, or has been cohabiting with the complainant in a conjugal relationship for a period of less than one year and they have had or are expecting to have a child as a result of the relationship; and

(b) the accused is not in a position of trust or authority towards the complainant, is not a person with whom the complainant is in a relationship of dependency and is not in a relationship with the complainant that is exploitative of the complainant.

(2.3) Exception for transitional purposes — If, immediately before the day on which this subsection comes into force, the accused referred to in subsection (2.1) is married to the complainant, it is a defence that the complainant consented to the activity that forms the subject-matter of the charge.

(3) Exemption for accused aged twelve or thirteen — No person aged twelve or thirteen years shall be tried for an offence under section 151 or 152 or subsection 173(2) unless the person is in a position of trust or authority towards the complainant, is a person with whom the complainant is in a relationship of dependency or is in a relationship with the complainant that is exploitative of the complainant.

(4) Mistake of age — It is not a defence to a charge under section 151 or 152, subsection 160(3) or 173(2), or section 271, 272 or 273 that the accused believed that the complainant was 16 years of age or more at the time the offence is alleged to have been committed unless the accused took all reasonable steps to ascertain the age of the complainant.

(5) Idem — It is not a defence to a charge under section 153, 170, 171 or 172 or subsection 286.1(2), 286.2(2) or 286.3(2) that the accused believed that the complainant was 18 years of age or more at the time the offence is alleged to have been committed unless the accused took all reasonable steps to ascertain the age of the complainant.

(6) Mistake of age — An accused cannot raise a mistaken belief in the age of the complainant in order to invoke a defence under subsection (2) or (2.1) unless the accused took all reasonable steps to ascertain the age of the complainant.

R.S.C. 1985, c. 19 (3rd Supp.), s. 1; 2005, c. 32, s. 2; 2008, c. 6, ss. 13, 54(a); 2014, c. 25, s. 4; 2015, c. 29, s. 6; 2019, c. 25, s. 51

151. Sexual interference — Every person who, for a sexual purpose, touches, directly or indirectly, with a part of the body or with an object, any part of the body of a person under the age of 16 years

(a) is guilty of an indictable offence and is liable to imprisonment for a term of not more than 14 years and to a minimum punishment of imprisonment for a term of one year; or

(b) is guilty of an offence punishable on summary conviction and is liable to imprisonment for a term of not more than two years less a day and to a minimum punishment of imprisonment for a term of 90 days.

R.S.C. 1985, c. 19 (3rd Supp.), s. 1; 2005, c. 32, s. 3; 2008, c. 6, s. 54(b); 2012, c. 1, s. 11; 2015, c. 23, s. 2

152. Invitation to sexual touching — Every person who, for a sexual purpose, invites, counsels or incites a person under the age of 16 years to touch, directly or indirectly, with a part of the body or with an object, the body of any person, including the body of the person who so invites, counsels or incites and the body of the person under the age of 16 years,

(a) is guilty of an indictable offence and is liable to imprisonment for a term of not more than 14 years and to a minimum punishment of imprisonment for a term of one year; or

(b) is guilty of an offence punishable on summary conviction and is liable to imprisonment for a term of not more than two years less a day and to a minimum punishment of imprisonment for a term of 90 days.

R.S.C. 1985, c. 19 (3rd Supp.), s. 1; 2005, c. 32, s. 3; 2008, c. 6, s. 54(b); 2012, c. 1, s. 12; 2015, c. 23, s. 3

153. (1) Sexual exploitation — Every person commits an offence who is in a position of trust or authority towards a young person, who is a person with whom the young person is in a relationship of dependency or who is in a relationship with a young person that is exploitative of the young person, and who

(a) for a sexual purpose, touches, directly or indirectly, with a part of the body or with an object, any part of the body of the young person; or

(b) for a sexual purpose, invites, counsels or incites a young person to touch, directly or indirectly, with a part of the body or with an object, the body of any person, including the body of the person who so invites, counsels or incites and the body of the young person.

(1.1) Punishment — Every person who commits an offence under subsection (1)

(a) is guilty of an indictable offence and is liable to imprisonment for a term of not more than 14 years and to a minimum punishment of imprisonment for a term of one year; or

(b) is guilty of an offence punishable on summary conviction and is liable to imprisonment for a term of not more than two years less a day and to a minimum punishment of imprisonment for a term of 90 days.

(1.2) Inference of sexual exploitation — A judge may infer that a person is in a relationship with a young person that is exploitative of the young person from the nature and circumstances of the relationship, including

(a) the age of the young person;

(b) the age difference between the person and the young person;

(c) the evolution of the relationship; and

(d) the degree of control or influence by the person over the young person.

(2) Definition of "young person" — In this section, **"young person"** means a person 16 years of age or more but under the age of eighteen years.

R.S.C. 1985, c. 19 (3rd Supp.), s. 1; 2005, c. 32, s. 4; 2008, c. 6, s. 54(c); 2012, c. 1, s. 13; 2015, c. 23, s. 4

153.1 (1) Sexual exploitation of person with disability — Every person who is in a position of trust or authority towards a person with a mental or physical disability or who is a person with whom a person with a mental or physical disability is in a relationship of dependency and who, for a sexual purpose, counsels or incites that person to touch, without that person's consent, his or her own body, the body of the person who so counsels or incites, or the body of any other person, directly or indirectly, with a part of the body or with an object, is guilty of

(a) an indictable offence and liable to imprisonment for a term not exceeding five years; or

(b) an offence punishable on summary conviction.

(2) Definition of "consent" — Subject to subsection (3), **"consent"** means, for the purposes of this section, the voluntary agreement of the complainant to engage in the sexual activity in question.

(2.1) Consent — Consent must be present at the time the sexual activity in question takes place.

(2.2) Question of law — The question of whether no consent is obtained under subsection (3) or (4) or 265(3) is a question of law.

(3) When no consent obtained — For the purposes of this section, no consent is obtained if

(a) the agreement is expressed by the words or conduct of a person other than the complainant;

(a.1) the complainant is unconscious;

(b) the complainant is incapable of consenting to the activity for any reason other than the one referred to in paragraph (a.1);

(c) the accused counsels or incites the complainant to engage in the activity by abusing a position of trust, power or authority;

(d) the complainant expresses, by words or conduct, a lack of agreement to engage in the activity; or

(e) the complainant, having consented to engage in sexual activity, expresses, by words or conduct, a lack of agreement to continue to engage in the activity.

(4) **Subsection (3) not limiting** — Nothing in subsection (3) shall be construed as limiting the circumstances in which no consent is obtained.

(5) **When belief in consent not a defence** — It is not a defence to a charge under this section that the accused believed that the complainant consented to the activity that forms the subject-matter of the charge if

(a) the accused's belief arose from

(i) the accused's self-induced intoxication,

(ii) the accused's recklessness or wilful blindness, or

(iii) any circumstance referred to in subsection (3) or (4) or 265(3) in which no consent is obtained;

(b) the accused did not take reasonable steps, in the circumstances known to the accused at the time, to ascertain that the complainant was consenting; or

(c) there is no evidence that the complainant's voluntary agreement to the activity was affirmatively expressed by words or actively expressed by conduct.

(6) **Accused's belief as to consent** — If an accused alleges that he or she believed that the complainant consented to the conduct that is the subject-matter of the charge, a judge, if satisfied that there is sufficient evidence and that, if believed by the jury, the evidence would constitute a defence, shall instruct the jury, when reviewing all the evidence relating to the determination of the honesty of the accused's belief, to consider the presence or absence of reasonable grounds for that belief.

1998, c. 9, s. 2; 2018, c. 29, s. 10(1)–(2.1), (4)–(6); 2019, c. 25, s. 52(2)

154. [Repealed R.S.C. 1985, c. 19 (3rd Supp.), s. 1.]

155. (1) Incest — Every one commits **"incest"** who, knowing that another person is by blood relationship his or her parent, child, brother, sister, grandparent or grandchild, as the case may be, has sexual intercourse with that person.

(2) **Punishment** — Everyone who commits incest is guilty of an indictable offence and is liable to imprisonment for a term of not more than 14 years and, if the other person is under the age of 16 years, to a minimum punishment of imprisonment for a term of five years.

(3) **Defence** — No accused shall be determined by a court to be guilty of an offence under this section if the accused was under restraint, duress or fear of the person with whom the accused had the sexual intercourse at the time the sexual intercourse occurred.

(4) "brother", "sister" — In this section, **"brother"** and **"sister"**, respectively, include half-brother and half-sister.

R.S.C. 1985, c. 27 (1st Supp.), s. 21; 2012, c. 1, s. 14

156. Historical offences — No person shall be convicted of any sexual offence under this Act as it read from time to time before January 4, 1983 unless the conduct alleged would be an offence under this Act if it occurred on the day on which the charge was laid.

2019, c. 25, s. 53

157 and 158. [Repealed R.S.C. 1985, c. 19 (3rd Supp.), s. 2.]

159. [Repealed 2019, c. 25, s. 54.]

160. (1) Bestiality — Every person who commits bestiality is guilty of an indictable offence and is liable to imprisonment for a term not exceeding ten years or is guilty of an offence punishable on summary conviction.

(2) Compelling the commission of bestiality — Every person who compels another to commit bestiality is guilty of an indictable offence and is liable to imprisonment for a term not exceeding ten years or is guilty of an offence punishable on summary conviction.

(3) Bestiality in presence of or by child — Despite subsection (1), every person who commits bestiality in the presence of a person under the age of 16 years, or who incites a person under the age of 16 years to commit bestiality,

(a) is guilty of an indictable offence and is liable to imprisonment for a term of not more than 14 years and to a minimum punishment of imprisonment for a term of one year; or

(b) is guilty of an offence punishable on summary conviction and is liable to imprisonment for a term of not more than two years less a day and to a minimum punishment of imprisonment for a term of six months.

(4) Order of prohibition or restitution — The court may, in addition to any other sentence that it may impose under any of subsections (1) to (3),

(a) make an order prohibiting the accused from owning, having the custody or control of or residing in the same premises as an animal during any period that the court considers appropriate but, in the case of a second or subsequent offence, for a minimum of five years; and

(b) on application of the Attorney General or on its own motion, order that the accused pay to a person or an organization that has taken care of an animal as a result of the commission of the offence the reasonable costs that the person or organization incurred in respect of the animal, if the costs are readily ascertainable.

(5) Breach of order — Every person who contravenes an order made under paragraph (4)(a) is guilty of an offence punishable on summary conviction.

(6) Application — Sections 740 to 741.2 apply, with any modifications that the circumstances require, to orders made under paragraph (4)(b).

(7) Definition of "bestiality" — In this section, **"bestiality"** means any contact, for a sexual purpose, with an animal.

R.S.C. 1985, c. 19 (3rd Supp.), s. 3; 2008, c. 6, s. 54(d); 2012, c. 1, s. 15; 2015, c. 23, s. 5; 2019, c. 17, s. 1

161. (1) Order of prohibition — When an offender is convicted, or is discharged on the conditions prescribed in a probation order under section 730, of an offence referred to in subsection (1.1) in respect of a person who is under the age of 16 years, the court that sentences the offender or directs that the accused be discharged, as the case may be, in addition to any other punishment that may be imposed for that offence or any other condition prescribed in the order of discharge, shall consider making and may make, subject to the conditions or exemptions that the court directs, an order prohibiting the offender from

(a) attending a public park or public swimming area where persons under the age of 16 years are present or can reasonably be expected to be present, or a daycare centre, schoolground, playground or community centre;

(a.1) being within two kilometres, or any other distance specified in the order, of any dwelling-house where the victim identified in the order ordinarily resides or of any other place specified in the order;

(b) seeking, obtaining or continuing any employment, whether or not the employment is remunerated, or becoming or being a volunteer in a capacity, that involves being in a position of trust or authority towards persons under the age of 16 years;

(c) having any contact — including communicating by any means — with a person who is under the age of 16 years, unless the offender does so under the supervision of a person whom the court considers appropriate; or

(d) using the Internet or other digital network, unless the offender does so in accordance with conditions set by the court.

(1.1) Offences — The offences for the purpose of subsection (1) are

(a) an offence under section 151, 152 or 155, subsection 160(2) or (3), section 163.1, 170, 171, 171.1, 172.1 or 172.2, subsection 173(2), section 271, 272, 273 or 279.011, subsection 279.02(2) or 279.03(2), section 280 or 281 or subsection 286.1(2), 286.2(2) or 286.3(2);

(b) an offence under section 144 (rape), 145 (attempt to commit rape), 149 (indecent assault on female), 156 (indecent assault on male) or 245 (common assault) or subsection 246(1) (assault with intent) of the *Criminal Code*, chapter C-34 of the Revised Statutes of Canada, 1970, as it read immediately before January 4, 1983;

(c) an offence under subsection 146(1) (sexual intercourse with a female under 14) or section 153 (sexual intercourse with step-daughter), 155 (buggery or bestiality), 157 (gross indecency), 166 (parent or guardian procuring defilement) or 167 (householder permitting defilement) of the *Criminal Code*, chapter C-34 of the Revised Statutes of Canada, 1970, as it read immediately before January 1, 1988; or

(d) an offence under subsection 212(1) (procuring), 212(2) (living on the avails of prostitution of person under 18 years), 212(2.1) (aggravated offence in relation to living on the avails of prostitution of person under 18 years) or 212(4) (prostitution of person under 18 years) of this Act, as it read from time to time before the day on which this paragraph comes into force.

(2) **Duration of prohibition** — The prohibition may be for life or for any shorter duration that the court considers desirable and, in the case of a prohibition that is not for life, the prohibition begins on the later of

(a) the date on which the order is made; and

(b) where the offender is sentenced to a term of imprisonment, the date on which the offender is released from imprisonment for the offence, including release on parole, mandatory supervision or statutory release.

(3) **Court may vary order** — A court that makes an order of prohibition or, where the court is for any reason unable to act, another court of equivalent jurisdiction in the same province, may, on application of the offender or the prosecutor, require the offender to appear before it at any time and, after hearing the parties, that court may vary the conditions prescribed in the order if, in the opinion of the court, the variation is desirable because of changed circumstances after the conditions were prescribed.

(4) **Offence** — Every person who is bound by an order of prohibition and who does not comply with the order is guilty of

(a) an indictable offence and is liable to imprisonment for a term of not more than four years; or

(b) an offence punishable on summary conviction.

1993, c. 45, s. 1; 1995, c. 22, s. 18 (Sched. IV, item 26); 1997, c. 18, s. 4; 1999, c. 31, s. 67; 2002, c. 13, s. 4; 2005, c. 32, s. 5; 2008, c. 6, s. 54(e); 2012, c. 1, s. 16; 2014, c. 21, s. 1; 2014, c. 25, s. 5; 2015, c. 23, s. 6; 2019, c. 25, s. 55

162. (1) **Voyeurism** — Every one commits an offence who, surreptitiously, observes — including by mechanical or electronic means — or makes a visual recording of a person who is in circumstances that give rise to a reasonable expectation of privacy, if

(a) the person is in a place in which a person can reasonably be expected to be nude, to expose his or her genital organs or anal region or her breasts, or to be engaged in explicit sexual activity;

(b) the person is nude, is exposing his or her genital organs or anal region or her breasts, or is engaged in explicit sexual activity, and the observation or recording is done for the purpose of observing or recording a person in such a state or engaged in such an activity; or

(c) the observation or recording is done for a sexual purpose.

(2) **Definition of "visual recording"** — In this section, **"visual recording"** includes a photographic, film or video recording made by any means.

(3) Exemption — Paragraphs (1)(a) and (b) do not apply to a peace officer who, under the authority of a warrant issued under section 487.01, is carrying out any activity referred to in those paragraphs.

(4) Printing, publication, etc., of voyeuristic recordings — Every one commits an offence who, knowing that a recording was obtained by the commission of an offence under subsection (1), prints, copies, publishes, distributes, circulates, sells, advertises or makes available the recording, or has the recording in his or her possession for the purpose of printing, copying, publishing, distributing, circulating, selling or advertising it or making it available.

(5) Punishment — Every one who commits an offence under subsection (1) or (4)

(a) is guilty of an indictable offence and liable to imprisonment for a term not exceeding five years; or

(b) is guilty of an offence punishable on summary conviction.

(6) Defence — No person shall be convicted of an offence under this section if the acts that are alleged to constitute the offence serve the public good and do not extend beyond what serves the public good.

(7) Question of law, motives — For the purposes of subsection (6),

(a) it is a question of law whether an act serves the public good and whether there is evidence that the act alleged goes beyond what serves the public good, but it is a question of fact whether the act does or does not extend beyond what serves the public good; and

(b) the motives of an accused are irrelevant.

2005, c.32, s. 6

162.1 (1) Publication, etc., of an intimate image without consent — Everyone who knowingly publishes, distributes, transmits, sells, makes available or advertises an intimate image of a person knowing that the person depicted in the image did not give their consent to that conduct, or being reckless as to whether or not that person gave their consent to that conduct, is guilty

(a) of an indictable offence and liable to imprisonment for a term of not more than five years; or

(b) of an offence punishable on summary conviction.

(2) Definition of "intimate image" — In this section, **"intimate image"** means a visual recording of a person made by any means including a photographic, film or video recording,

(a) in which the person is nude, is exposing his or her genital organs or anal region or her breasts or is engaged in explicit sexual activity;

(b) in respect of which, at the time of the recording, there were circumstances that gave rise to a reasonable expectation of privacy; and

(c) in respect of which the person depicted retains a reasonable expectation of privacy at the time the offence is committed.

(3) Defence — No person shall be convicted of an offence under this section if the conduct that forms the subject-matter of the charge serves the public good and does not extend beyond what serves the public good.

(4) Question of fact and law, motives — For the purposes of subsection (3),

(a) it is a question of law whether the conduct serves the public good and whether there is evidence that the conduct alleged goes beyond what serves the public good, but it is a question of fact whether the conduct does or does not extend beyond what serves the public good; and

(b) the motives of an accused are irrelevant.

2014, c. 31, s. 3

162.2 (1) Prohibition order — When an offender is convicted, or is discharged on the conditions prescribed in a probation order under section 730, of an offence referred to in subsection 162.1(1), the court that sentences or discharges the offender, in addition to any other punishment that may be imposed for that offence or any other condition prescribed in the order of discharge, may make, subject to the conditions or exemptions that the court directs, an order prohibiting the offender from using the Internet or other digital network, unless the offender does so in accordance with conditions set by the court.

(2) Duration of prohibition — The prohibition may be for any period that the court considers appropriate, including any period to which the offender is sentenced to imprisonment.

(3) Court may vary order — A court that makes an order of prohibition or, if the court is for any reason unable to act, another court of equivalent jurisdiction in the same province may, on application of the offender or the prosecutor, require the offender to appear before it at any time and, after hearing the parties, that court may vary the conditions prescribed in the order if, in the opinion of the court, the variation is desirable because of changed circumstances after the conditions were prescribed.

(4) Offence — Every person who is bound by an order of prohibition and who does not comply with the order is guilty of

(a) an indictable offence and is liable to imprisonment for a term of not more than four years; or

(b) an offence punishable on summary conviction.

2014, c. 31, s. 3; 2015, c. 23, s. 33; 2019, c. 25, s. 56

Offences Tending to Corrupt Morals

163. (1) Obscene materials — Every person commits an offence who makes, prints, publishes, distributes, circulates or has in their possession for the purpose of publication, distribution or circulation any obscene written matter, picture, model, phonograph record or any other obscene thing.

(2) **Idem** — Every person commits an offence who knowingly, without lawful justification or excuse,

(a) sells, exposes to public view or has in their possession for that purpose any obscene written matter, picture, model, phonograph record or any other obscene thing; or

(b) publicly exhibits a disgusting object or an indecent show.

(c) and (d) [Repealed 2018, c. 29, s. 11(3).]

(3) **Defence of public good** — No person shall be convicted of an offence under this section if the public good was served by the acts that are alleged to constitute the offence and if the acts alleged did not extend beyond what served the public good.

(4) **Question of law and question of fact** — For the purposes of this section, it is a question of law whether an act served the public good and whether there is evidence that the act alleged went beyond what served the public good, but it is a question of fact whether the acts did or did not extend beyond what served the public good.

(5) **Motives irrelevant** — For the purposes of this section, the motives of an accused are irrelevant.

(6) [Repealed 1993, c. 46, s. 1(2).]

(7) [Repealed 2018, c. 29, s. 11(4).]

(8) **Obscene publication** — For the purposes of this Act, any publication a dominant characteristic of which is the undue exploitation of sex, or of sex and any one or more of the following subjects, namely, crime, horror, cruelty and violence, shall be deemed to be obscene.

1993, c. 46, s. 1; 2018, c. 29, s. 11

163.1 (1) **Definition of "child pornography"** — In this section, **"child pornography"** means

(a) a photographic, film, video or other visual representation, whether or not it was made by electronic or mechanical means,

(i) that shows a person who is or is depicted as being under the age of eighteen years and is engaged in or is depicted as engaged in explicit sexual activity, or

(ii) the dominant characteristic of which is the depiction, for a sexual purpose, of a sexual organ or the anal region of a person under the age of eighteen years;

(b) any written material, visual representation or audio recording that advocates or counsels sexual activity with a person under the age of eighteen years that would be an offence under this Act;

(c) any written material whose dominant characteristic is the description, for a sexual purpose, of sexual activity with a person under the age of eighteen years that would be an offence under this Act; or

(d) any audio recording that has as its dominant characteristic the description, presentation or representation, for a sexual purpose, of sexual activity with a person under the age of eighteen years that would be an offence under this Act.

(2) **Making child pornography** — Every person who makes, prints, publishes or possesses for the purpose of publication any child pornography is guilty of an indictable offence and liable to imprisonment for a term of not more than 14 years and to a minimum punishment of imprisonment for a term of one year.

(3) **Distribution, etc. of child pornography** — Every person who transmits, makes available, distributes, sells, advertises, imports, exports or possesses for the purpose of transmission, making available, distribution, sale, advertising or exportation any child pornography is guilty of an indictable offence and liable to imprisonment for a term of not more than 14 years and to a minimum punishment of imprisonment for a term of one year.

(4) **Possession of child pornography** — Every person who possesses any child pornography is guilty of

(a) an indictable offence and is liable to imprisonment for a term of not more than 10 years and to a minimum punishment of imprisonment for a term of one year; or

(b) an offence punishable on summary conviction and is liable to imprisonment for a term of not more than two years less a day and to a minimum punishment of imprisonment for a term of six months.

(4.1) **Accessing child pornography** — Every person who accesses any child pornography is guilty of

(a) an indictable offence and is liable to imprisonment for a term of not more than 10 years and to a minimum punishment of imprisonment for a term of one year; or

(b) an offence punishable on summary conviction and is liable to imprisonment for a term of not more than two years less a day and to a minimum punishment of imprisonment for a term of six months.

(4.2) **Interpretation** — For the purposes of subsection (4.1), a person accesses child pornography who knowingly causes child pornography to be viewed by, or transmitted to, himself or herself.

(4.3) **Aggravating factor** — If a person is convicted of an offence under this section, the court that imposes the sentence shall consider as an aggravating factor the fact that the person committed the offence with intent to make a profit.

(5) **Defences** — It is not a defence to a charge under subsection (2) in respect of a visual representation that the accused believed that a person shown in the representation that is alleged to constitute child pornography was or was depicted as being eighteen years of age or more unless the accused took all reasonable steps to ascertain the age of that person and took all reasonable steps to ensure that, where the person was eighteen years of age or more, the representation did not depict that person as being under the age of eighteen years.

(6) Defence — No person shall be convicted of an offence under this section if the act that is alleged to constitute the offence

(a) has a legitimate purpose related to the administration of justice or to science, medicine, education or art; and

(b) does not pose an undue risk of harm to persons under the age of eighteen years.

(7) Question of law — For greater certainty, for the purposes of this section, it is a question of law whether any written material, visual representation or audio recording advocates or counsels sexual activity with a person under the age of eighteen years that would be an offence under this Act.

1993, c. 46, s. 2; 2002, c. 13, s. 5(2)–(4); 2005, c. 32, s. 7; 2012, c. 1, s. 17; 2015, c. 23, s. 7

164. (1) Warrant of seizure — A judge may issue a warrant authorizing seizure of copies of a recording, a publication, a representation or any written material, if the judge is satisfied by information on oath that there are reasonable grounds to believe that

(a) the recording, copies of which are kept for sale or distribution in premises within the jurisdiction of the court, is a voyeuristic recording;

(b) the recording, copies of which are kept for sale or distribution in premises within the jurisdiction of the court, is an intimate image;

(c) the publication, copies of which are kept for sale or distribution in premises within the jurisdiction of the court, is **"obscene"**, within the meaning of subsection 163(8);

(d) the representation, written material or recording, copies of which are kept in premises within the jurisdiction of the court, is child pornography as defined in section 163.1; or

(e) the representation, written material or recording, copies of which are kept in premises within the jurisdiction of the court, is an advertisement of sexual services.

(2) Summons to occupier — Within seven days of the issue of a warrant under subsection (1), the judge shall issue a summons to the occupier of the premises requiring him to appear before the court and show cause why the matter seized should not be forfeited to Her Majesty.

(3) Owner and maker may appear — The owner and the maker of the matter seized under subsection (1), and alleged to be obscene, child pornography, a voyeuristic recording, an intimate image or an advertisement of sexual services, may appear and be represented in the proceedings to oppose the making of an order for the forfeiture of the matter.

(4) Order of forfeiture — If the court is satisfied, on a balance of probabilities, that the publication, representation, written material or recording referred to in subsection (1) is obscene, child pornography, a voyeuristic recording, an intimate image or an advertisement of sexual services, it may make an order declaring the matter forfeited to Her Majesty in right of the province in which the proceedings take place, for disposal as the Attorney General may direct.

(5) Disposal of matter — If the court is not satisfied that the publication, representation, written material or recording referred to in subsection (1) is obscene, child pornography, a voyeuristic recording, an intimate image or an advertisement of sexual services, it shall order that the matter be restored to the person from whom it was seized without delay after the time for final appeal has expired.

(6) Appeal — An appeal lies from an order made under subsection (4) or (5) by any person who appeared in the proceedings

(a) on any ground of appeal that involves a question of law alone,

(b) on any ground of appeal that involves a question of fact alone, or

(c) on any ground of appeal that involves a question of mixed law and fact,

as if it were an appeal against conviction or against a judgment or verdict of acquittal, as the case may be, on a question of law alone under Part XXI and sections 673 to 696 apply with such modifications as the circumstances require.

(7) Consent — If an order is made under this section by a judge in a province with respect to one or more copies of a publication, a representation, written material or a recording, no proceedings shall be instituted or continued in that province under section 162, 162.1, 163, 163.1 or 286.4 with respect to those or other copies of the same publication, representation, written material or recording without the consent of the Attorney General.

(8) Definitions — In this section

"advertisement of sexual services" means any material — including a photographic, film, video, audio or other recording, made by any means, a visual representation or any written material — that is used to advertise sexual services contrary to section 286.4.

"court" means

(a) in the Province of Quebec, the Court of Quebec, the municipal court of Montreal and the municipal court of Quebec,

(a.1) in the Province of Ontario, the Superior Court of Justice,

(b) in the Provinces of New Brunswick, Manitoba, Saskatchewan and Alberta, the Court of Queen's Bench,

(c) in the Province of Newfoundland and Labrador, the Trial Division of the Supreme Court,

(c.1) [Repealed 1992, c. 51, s. 34.]

(d) in the Provinces of Nova Scotia, British Columbia and Prince Edward Island, in Yukon and in the Northwest Territories, the Supreme Court, and

(e) in Nunavut, the Nunavut Court of Justice;

"crime comic" [Repealed 2018, c. 29, s. 12(3).]

"intimate image" has the same meaning as in subsection 162.1(2).

"judge" means a judge of a court.

"voyeuristic recording" means a visual recording within the meaning of subsection 162(2) that is made as described in subsection 162(1).

R.S.C. 1985, c. 27 (2nd Supp.), s. 10 (Sched., item 6); R.S.C. 1985, c. 40 (4th Supp.), s. 2; 1990, c. 16, s. 3; 1990, c. 17, s. 9; 1992, c. 1, s. 58(1) (Sched. 1, item 3); 1992, c. 51, s. 34; 1993, c. 28, s. 78 (Sched. III, item 28) [Repealed 1999, c. 3, s. 12 (Sched., item 6).]; 1993, c. 46, s. 3; 1997, c. 18, s. 5; 1998, c. 30, s. 14(d); 1999, c. 3, s. 27; 2002, c. 7, s. 139; 2002, c. 13, s. 6; 2005, c. 32, s. 8(2)–(5); 2014, c. 25, ss. 6, 46(2)–(4); 2014, c. 31, s. 4; 2015, c. 3, s. 46; 2018, c. 29, s. 12

164.1 (1) Warrant of seizure — If a judge is satisfied by information on oath that there are reasonable grounds to believe that there is material — namely, child pornography as defined in section 163.1, a voyeuristic recording, an intimate image or an advertisement of sexual services as defined in 164(8) or computer data as defined in subsection 342.1(2) that makes child pornography, a voyeuristic recording, an intimate image or an advertisement of sexual services available — that is stored on and made available through a computer system as defined in subsection 342.1(2) that is within the jurisdiction of the court, the judge may order the custodian of the computer system to

(a) give an electronic copy of the material to the court;

(b) ensure that the material is no longer stored on and made available through the computer system; and

(c) provide the information necessary to identify and locate the person who posted the material.

(2) Notice to person who posted the material — Within a reasonable time after receiving the information referred to in paragraph (1)(c), the judge shall cause notice to be given to the person who posted the material, giving that person the opportunity to appear and be represented before the court, and show cause why the material should not be deleted. If the person cannot be identified or located or does not reside in Canada, the judge may order the custodian of the computer system to post the text of the notice at the location where the material was previously stored and made available, until the time set for the appearance.

(3) Person who posted the material may appear — The person who posted the material may appear and be represented in the proceedings in order to oppose the making of an order under subsection (5).

(4) Non-appearance — If the person who posted the material does not appear for the proceedings, the court may proceed *ex parte* to hear and determine the proceedings in the absence of the person as fully and effectually as if the person had appeared.

(5) Order — If the court is satisfied, on a balance of probabilities, that the material is child pornography as defined in section 163.1, a voyeuristic recording, an intimate image or an advertisement of sexual services as defined in subsection 164(8) or computer data as defined in subsection 342.1(2) that makes child pornography, the voyeuristic recording, the intimate image or the advertisement of sexual services available, it may order the custodian of the computer system to delete the material.

(6) Destruction of copy — When the court makes the order for the deletion of the material, it may order the destruction of the electronic copy in the court's possession.

(7) Return of material — If the court is not satisfied that the material is child pornography as defined in 163.1, a voyeuristic recording, an intimate image or an advertisement of sexual services as defined in subsection 164(8) or computer data as defined in subsection 342.1(2) that makes child pornography, the voyeuristic recording, the intimate image or the advertisement of sexual services available, the court shall order that the electronic copy be returned to the custodian of the computer system and terminate the order under paragraph (1)(b).

(8) Other provisions to apply — Subsections 164(6) to (8) apply, with any modifications that the circumstances require, to this section.

(9) When order takes effect — No order made under subsections (5) to (7) takes effect until the time for final appeal has expired.

2002, c. 13, s. 7; 2005, c. 32, s. 9; 2014, c. 25, ss. 7, 46(5)–(7); 2014, c. 31, s. 5

164.2 (1) Forfeiture after conviction — On application of the Attorney General, a court that convicts a person of an offence under section 162.1, 163.1, 172.1 or 172.2, in addition to any other punishment that it may impose, may order that anything — other than real property — be forfeited to Her Majesty and disposed of as the Attorney General directs if it is satisfied, on a balance of probabilities, that the thing

(a) was used in the commission of the offence; and

(b) is the property of

(i) the convicted person or another person who was a party to the offence, or

(ii) a person who acquired the thing from a person referred to in subparagraph (i) under circumstances that give rise to a reasonable inference that it was transferred for the purpose of avoiding forfeiture.

(2) Third party rights — Before making an order under subsection (1), the court shall cause notice to be given to, and may hear, any person whom it considers to have an interest in the thing, and may declare the nature and extent of the person's interest in it.

(3) Right of appeal — third party — A person who was heard in response to a notice given under subsection (2) may appeal to the court of appeal against an order made under subsection (1).

(4) Right of appeal — Attorney General — The Attorney General may appeal to the court of appeal against the refusal of a court to make an order under subsection (1).

(5) Application of Part XXI — Part XXI applies, with any modifications that the circumstances require, with respect to the procedure for an appeal under subsections (3) and (4).

2002, c. 13, s. 7; 2008, c. 18, s. 4; 2012, c. 1, s. 18; 2014, c. 31, s. 6

164.3 (1) Relief from forfeiture — Within thirty days after an order under subsection 164.2(1) is made, a person who claims an interest in the thing forfeited may apply in writing to a judge for an order under subsection (4).

(2) **Hearing of application** — The judge shall fix a day — not less than thirty days after the application is made — for its hearing.

(3) **Notice to Attorney General** — At least fifteen days before the hearing, the applicant shall cause notice of the application and of the hearing day to be served on the Attorney General.

(4) **Order** — The judge may make an order declaring that the applicant's interest in the thing is not affected by the forfeiture and declaring the nature and extent of the interest if the judge is satisfied that the applicant

(a) was not a party to the offence; and

(b) did not acquire the thing from a person who was a party to the offence under circumstances that give rise to a reasonable inference that it was transferred for the purpose of avoiding forfeiture.

(5) **Appeal to court of appeal** — A person referred to in subsection (4) or the Attorney General may appeal to the court of appeal against an order made under that subsection. Part XXI applies, with any modifications that the circumstances require, with respect to the procedure for an appeal under this subsection.

(6) **Powers of Attorney General** — On application by a person who obtained an order under subsection (4), made after the expiration of the time allowed for an appeal against the order and, if an appeal is taken, after it has been finally disposed of, the Attorney General shall direct that

(a) the thing be returned to the person; or

(b) an amount equal to the value of the extent of the person's interest, as declared in the order, be paid to the person.

2002, c. 13, s. 7

165. [Repealed 2018, c. 29, s. 13.]

166. [Repealed 1994, c. 44, s. 9.]

167. (1) Immoral theatrical performance — Every one commits an offence who, being the lessee, manager, agent or person in charge of a theatre, presents or gives or allows to be presented or given therein an immoral, indecent or obscene performance, entertainment or representation.

(2) **Person taking part** — Every one commits an offence who takes part or appears as an actor, a performer or an assistant in any capacity, in an immoral, indecent or obscene performance, entertainment or representation in a theatre.

168. (1) Mailing obscene matter — Every one commits an offence who makes use of the mails for the purpose of transmitting or delivering anything that is obscene, indecent, immoral or scurrilous.

(2) Exceptions — Subsection (1) does not apply to a person who

(a) prints or publishes any matter for use in connection with any judicial proceedings or communicates it to persons who are concerned in the proceedings;

(b) prints or publishes a notice or report under the direction of a court; or

(c) prints or publishes any matter

(i) in a volume or part of a genuine series of law reports that does not form part of any other publication and consists solely of reports of proceedings in courts of law, or

(ii) in a publication of a technical character that is intended, in good faith, for circulation among members of the legal or medical profession.

1999, c. 5, s. 2

169. Punishment — Every one who commits an offence under section 163, 165, 167 or 168 is guilty of

(a) an indictable offence and is liable to imprisonment for a term not exceeding two years; or

(b) an offence punishable on summary conviction.

1999, c. 5, s. 3

170. Parent or guardian procuring sexual activity — Every parent or guardian of a person under the age of 18 years who procures the person for the purpose of engaging in any sexual activity prohibited by this Act with a person other than the parent or guardian is guilty of an indictable offence and liable to imprisonment for a term of not more than 14 years and to a minimum punishment of imprisonment for a term of one year.

R.S.C. 1985, c. 19 (3rd Supp.), s. 5; 2005, c. 32, s. 9.1; 2008, c. 6, s. 54(f); 2012, c. 1, s. 19; 2015, c. 23, s. 8

171. Householder permitting prohibited sexual activity — Every owner, occupier or manager of premises, or any other person who has control of premises or assists in the management or control of premises, who knowingly permits a person under the age of 18 years to resort to or to be in or on the premises for the purpose of engaging in any sexual activity prohibited by this Act is guilty of an indictable offence and liable to imprisonment for a term of not more than 14 years and to a minimum punishment of imprisonment for a term of one year.

R.S.C. 1985, c. 19 (3rd Supp.), s. 5; 2005, c. 32, s. 9.1; 2008, c. 6, s. 54(g); 2012, c. 1, s. 20; 2015, c. 23, s. 9

171.1 (1) Making sexually explicit material available to child — Every person commits an offence who transmits, makes available, distributes or sells sexually explicit material to

(a) a person who is, or who the accused believes is, under the age of 18 years, for the purpose of facilitating the commission of an offence with respect to that person under subsection 153(1), section 155, 163.1, 170, 171 or 279.011 or subsection 279.02(2), 279.03(2), 286.1(2), 286.2(2) or 286.3(2);

(b) a person who is, or who the accused believes is, under the age of 16 years, for the purpose of facilitating the commission of an offence under section 151 or 152, subsection 160(3) or 173(2) or section 271, 272, 273 or 280 with respect to that person; or

(c) a person who is, or who the accused believes is, under the age of 14 years, for the purpose of facilitating the commission of an offence under section 281 with respect to that person.

(2) **Punishment** — Every person who commits an offence under subsection (1)

(a) is guilty of an indictable offence and is liable to imprisonment for a term of not more than 14 years and to a minimum punishment of imprisonment for a term of six months; or

(b) is guilty of an offence punishable on summary conviction and is liable to imprisonment for a term of not more than two years less a day and to a minimum punishment of imprisonment for a term of 90 days.

(3) **Presumption** — Evidence that the person referred to in paragraph (1)(a), (b) or (c) was represented to the accused as being under the age of 18, 16 or 14 years, as the case may be, is, in the absence of evidence to the contrary, proof that the accused believed that the person was under that age.

(4) **No defence** — It is not a defence to a charge under paragraph (1)(a), (b) or (c) that the accused believed that the person referred to in that paragraph was at least 18, 16 or 14 years of age, as the case may be, unless the accused took reasonable steps to ascertain the age of the person.

(5) **Definition of "sexually explicit material"** — In subsection (1), **"sexually explicit material"** means material that is not child pornography, as defined in subsection 163.1(1), and that is

(a) a photographic, film, video or other visual representation, whether or not it was made by electronic or mechanical means,

(i) that shows a person who is engaged in or is depicted as engaged in explicit sexual activity, or

(ii) the dominant characteristic of which is the depiction, for a sexual purpose, of a person's genital organs or anal region or, if the person is female, her breasts;

(b) written material whose dominant characteristic is the description, for a sexual purpose, of explicit sexual activity with a person; or

(c) an audio recording whose dominant characteristic is the description, presentation or representation, for a sexual purpose, of explicit sexual activity with a person.

2012, c. 1, s. 21; 2014, c. 25, s. 8; 2015, c. 23, s. 10

172. (1) **Corrupting children** — Every person who, in the home of a child, participates in adultery or sexual immorality or indulges in habitual drunkenness or any

other form of vice, and by doing so endangers the morals of the child or renders the home an unfit place for the child to be in, is guilty of

(a) an indictable offence and liable to imprisonment for a term of not more than two years; or

(b) an offence punishable on summary conviction.

(2) [Repealed R.S.C. 1985, c. 19 (3rd Supp.), s. 6.]

(3) Definition of "child" — For the purposes of this section, **"child"** means a person who is or appears to be under the age of eighteen years.

(4) Who may institute prosecutions — No proceedings shall be commenced under subsection (1) without the consent of the Attorney General, unless they are instituted by or at the instance of a recognized society for the protection of children or by an officer of a juvenile court.

R.S.C. 1985, c. 19 (3rd Supp.), s. 6; 2019, c. 25, s. 57

172.1 (1) Luring a child — Every person commits an offence who, by a means of telecommunication, communicates with

(a) a person who is, or who the accused believes is, under the age of 18 years, for the purpose of facilitating the commission of an offence with respect to that person under subsection 153(1), section 155, 163.1, 170, 171 or 279.011 or subsection 279.02(2), 279.03(2), 286.1(2), 286.2(2) or 286.3(2);

(b) a person who is, or who the accused believes is, under the age of 16 years, for the purpose of facilitating the commission of an offence under section 151 or 152, subsection 160(3) or 173(2) or section 271, 272, 273 or 280 with respect to that person; or

(c) a person who is, or who the accused believes is, under the age of 14 years, for the purpose of facilitating the commission of an offence under section 281 with respect to that person.

(2) Punishment — Every person who commits an offence under subsection (1)

(a) is guilty of an indictable offence and is liable to imprisonment for a term of not more than 14 years and to a minimum punishment of imprisonment for a term of one year; or

(b) is guilty of an offence punishable on summary conviction and is liable to imprisonment for a term of not more than two years less a day and to a minimum punishment of imprisonment for a term of six months.

(3) Presumption re age — Evidence that the person referred to in paragraph (1)(a), (b) or (c) was represented to the accused as being under the age of eighteen years, sixteen years or fourteen years, as the case may be, is, in the absence of evidence to the contrary, proof that the accused believed that the person was under that age.

(4) No defence — It is not a defence to a charge under paragraph (1)(a), (b) or (c) that the accused believed that the person referred to in that paragraph was at least eighteen years of age, sixteen years or fourteen years of age, as the case may be, unless the accused took reasonable steps to ascertain the age of the person.

2002, c. 13, s. 8; 2007, c. 20, s. 1; 2008, c. 6, s. 14; 2012, c. 1, s. 22(1), (2); 2014, c. 25, s. 9; 2015, c. 23, s. 11

Disorderly Conduct

172.2 (1) Agreement or arrangement — sexual offence against child — Every person commits an offence who, by a means of telecommunication, agrees with a person, or makes an arrangement with a person, to commit an offence

(a) under subsection 153(1), section 155, 163.1, 170, 171 or 279.011 or subsection 279.02(2), 279.03(2), 286.1(2), 286.2(2) or 286.3(2) with respect to another person who is, or who the accused believes is, under the age of 18 years;

(b) under section 151 or 152, subsection 160(3) or 173(2) or section 271, 272, 273 or 280 with respect to another person who is, or who the accused believes is, under the age of 16 years; or

(c) under section 281 with respect to another person who is, or who the accused believes is, under the age of 14 years.

(2) Punishment — Every person who commits an offence under subsection (1)

(a) is guilty of an indictable offence and is liable to imprisonment for a term of not more than 14 years and to a minimum punishment of imprisonment for a term of one year; or

(b) is guilty of an offence punishable on summary conviction and is liable to imprisonment for a term of not more than two years less a day and to a minimum punishment of imprisonment for a term of six months.

(3) Presumption — Evidence that the person referred to in paragraph (1)(a), (b) or (c) was represented to the accused as being under the age of 18, 16 or 14 years, as the case may be, is, in the absence of evidence to the contrary, proof that the accused believed that the person was under that age.

(4) No defence — It is not a defence to a charge under paragraph (1)(a), (b) or (c) that the accused believed that the person referred to in that paragraph was at least 18, 16 or 14 years of age, as the case may be, unless the accused took reasonable steps to ascertain the age of the person.

(5) No defence — It is not a defence to a charge under paragraph (1)(a), (b) or (c)

(a) that the person with whom the accused agreed or made an arrangement was a peace officer or a person acting under the direction of a peace officer; or

(b) that, if the person with whom the accused agreed or made an arrangement was a peace officer or a person acting under the direction of a peace officer, the person referred to in paragraph (1)(a), (b) or (c) did not exist.

2012, c. 1, s. 23; 2014, c. 25, s. 10; 2015, c. 23, s. 12

173. (1) Indecent acts — Everyone who wilfully does an indecent act in a public place in the presence of one or more persons, or in any place with intent to insult or offend any person,

(a) is guilty of an indictable offence and is liable to imprisonment for a term of not more than two years; or

(b) is guilty of an offence punishable on summary conviction.

(2) Exposure — Every person who, in any place, for a sexual purpose, exposes his or her genital organs to a person who is under the age of 16 years

(a) is guilty of an indictable offence and is liable to imprisonment for a term of not more than two years and to a minimum punishment of imprisonment for a term of 90 days; or

(b) is guilty of an offence punishable on summary conviction and is liable to imprisonment for a term of not more than six months and to a minimum punishment of imprisonment for a term of 30 days.

R.S.C. 1985, c. 19 (3rd Supp.), s. 7; 2008, c. 6, s. 54(h); 2010, c. 17, s. 2; 2012, c. 1, s. 23; 2019, c. 25, s. 58

174. (1) Nudity — Every one who, without lawful excuse,

(a) is nude in a public place, or

(b) is nude and exposed to public view while on private property, whether or not the property is his own,

is guilty of an offence punishable on summary conviction.

(2) Nude — For the purposes of this section, a person is nude who is so clad as to offend against public decency or order.

(3) Consent of Attorney General — No proceedings shall be commenced under this section without the consent of the Attorney General.

175. (1) Causing disturbance, indecent exhibition, loitering, etc. — Every one who

(a) not being in a dwelling-house, causes a disturbance in or near a public place,

(i) by fighting, screaming, shouting, swearing, singing or using insulting or obscene language,

(ii) by being drunk, or

(iii) by impeding or molesting other persons,

(b) openly exposes or exhibits an indecent exhibition in a public place,

(c) loiters in a public place and in any way obstructs persons who are in that place, or

(d) disturbs the peace and quiet of the occupants of a dwelling-house by discharging firearms or by other disorderly conduct in a public place or who, not being an occupant of a dwelling-house comprised in a particular building or structure, disturbs the peace and quiet of the occupants of a dwelling-house comprised in the building or structure by discharging firearms or by other disorderly conduct in any part of a building or structure to which, at the time of such conduct, the occupants of two or more dwelling-houses comprised in the building or structure have access as of right or by invitation, express or implied,

is guilty of an offence punishable on summary conviction.

(2) Evidence of peace officer — In the absence of other evidence, or by way of corroboration of other evidence, a summary conviction court may infer from the evidence of a peace officer relating to the conduct of a person or persons, whether ascertained or not, that a disturbance described in paragraph (1)(a) or (d) or an obstruction described in paragraph (1)(c) was caused or occurred.

1997, c. 18, s. 6

176. (1) Obstructing or violence to or arrest of officiating clergyman — Every person is guilty of an indictable offence and liable to imprisonment for a term of not more than two years or is guilty of an offence punishable on summary conviction who

(a) by threats or force, unlawfully obstructs or prevents or endeavours to obstruct or prevent an officiant from celebrating a religious or spiritual service or performing any other function in connection with their calling, or

(b) knowing that an officiant is about to perform, is on their way to perform or is returning from the performance of any of the duties or functions mentioned in paragraph (a)

(i) assaults or offers any violence to them, or

(ii) arrests them on a civil process, or under the pretence of executing a civil process.

(2) Disturbing religious worship or certain meetings — Every one who wilfully disturbs or interrupts an assemblage of persons met for religious worship or for a moral, social or benevolent purpose is guilty of an offence punishable on summary conviction.

(3) Idem — Every one who, at or near a meeting referred to in subsection (2), wilfully does anything that disturbs the order or solemnity of the meeting is guilty of an offence punishable on summary conviction.

2018, c. 29, s. 13.1; 2019, c. 25, s. 59

177. Trespassing at night — Every person who, without lawful excuse, loiters or prowls at night on the property of another person near a dwelling-house situated on that property is guilty of an offence punishable on summary conviction.

2018, c. 29, s. 14

178. [Repealed 2018, c. 29, s. 14.]

179. [Repealed 2019, c. 25, s. 60.]

Nuisances

180. (1) Common nuisance — Every person is guilty of an indictable offence and liable to imprisonment for a term of not more than two years or is guilty of an offence punishable on summary conviction who commits a common nuisance and by doing so

(a) endangers the lives, safety or health of the public, or

(b) causes physical injury to any person.

(2) Definition — For the purposes of this section, every one commits a common nuisance who does an unlawful act or fails to discharge a legal duty and thereby

(a) endangers the lives, safety, health, property or comfort of the public; or

(b) obstructs the public in the exercise or enjoyment of any right that is common to all the subjects of Her Majesty in Canada.

2019, c. 25, s. 61

181. [Repealed 2019, c. 25, s. 62.]

182. Dead body — Every person is guilty of an indictable offence and liable to imprisonment for a term of not more than five years or is guilty of an offence punishable on summary conviction who

(a) neglects, without lawful excuse, to perform any duty that is imposed on him by law or that he undertakes with reference to the burial of a dead human body or human remains, or

(b) improperly or indecently interferes with or offers any indignity to a dead human body or human remains, whether buried or not.

2019, c. 25, s. 63

PART VI — INVASION OF PRIVACY (SS. 183–196.1)

Definitions

183. Definitions — In this Part,

"authorization" means an authorization to intercept a private communication given under section 186 or subsection 184.2(3), 184.3(6) or 188(2);

"electro-magnetic, acoustic, mechanical or other device" means any device or apparatus that is used or is capable of being used to intercept a private communication, but does not include a hearing aid used to correct subnormal hearing of the user to not better than normal hearing;

"intercept" includes listen to, record or acquire a communication or acquire the substance, meaning or purport thereof;

"offence" means an offence contrary to, any conspiracy or attempt to commit or being an accessory after the fact in relation to an offence contrary to, or any counselling in relation to an offence contrary to

(a) any of the following provisions of this Act, namely,

(i) section 47 (high treason),

(ii) section 51 (intimidating Parliament or a legislature),

(iii) section 52 (sabotage),

(iii.1) section 56.1 (identity documents),

(iv) section 57 (forgery, etc.),

(v) section 61 (sedition),

(vi) section 76 (hijacking),

(vii) section 77 (endangering safety of aircraft or airport),

(viii) section 78 (offensive weapons, etc., on aircraft),

(ix) section 78.1 (offences against maritime navigation or fixed platforms),

(x) section 80 (breach of duty),

(xi) section 81 (using explosives),

(xii) section 82 (possessing explosives),

(xii.01) section 82.3 (possession, etc., of nuclear material, radioactive material or device),

(xii.02) section 82.4 (use or alteration of nuclear material, radioactive material or device),

(xii.03) section 82.5 (commission of indictable offence to obtain nuclear material, etc.),

(xii.04) section 82.6 (threats),

(xii.1) section 83.02 (providing or collecting property for certain activities),

(xii.2) section 83.03 (providing, making available, etc., property or services for terrorist purposes),

(xii.3) section 83.04 (using or possessing property for terrorist purposes),

(xii.4) section 83.18 (participation in activity of terrorist group),

(xii.41) section 83.181 (leaving Canada to participate in activity of terrorist group),

(xii.5) section 83.19 (facilitating terrorist activity),

(xii.51) section 83.191 (leaving Canada to facilitate terrorist activity),

(xii.6) section 83.2 (commission of offence for terrorist group),

(xii.61) section 83.201 (leaving Canada to commit offence for terrorist group), (xii.62) section 83.202 (leaving Canada to commit offence that is terrorist activity),

(xii.7) section 83.21 (instructing to carry out activity for terrorist group),

(xii.8) section 83.22 (instructing to carry out terrorist activity),

(xii.81) section 83.221 (counselling commission of terrorism offence),

(xii.9) section 83.23 (harbouring or concealing),

(xii.91) section 83.231 (hoax — terrorist activity),

(xiii) section 96 (possession of weapon obtained by commission of offence),

(xiii.1) section 98 (breaking and entering to steal firearm),

(xiii.2) section 98.1 (robbery to steal firearm),

(xiv) section 99 (weapons trafficking),

(xv) section 100 (possession for purpose of weapons trafficking),

(xvi) section 102 (making automatic firearm),

(xvii) section 103 (importing or exporting knowing it is unauthorized),

(xviii) section 104 (unauthorized importing or exporting),

(xix) section 119 (bribery, etc.),

(xx) section 120 (bribery, etc.),

(xxi) section 121 (fraud on government),

(xxii) section 122 (breach of trust),

(xxiii) section 123 (municipal corruption),

(xxiv) section 132 (perjury),

(xxv) section 139 (obstructing justice),

(xxvi) section 144 (prison breach),

(xxvii) subsection 145(1) (escape, etc.),

(xxvii.1) section 162 (voyeurism),

(xxvii.2) section 162.1 (intimate image),

(xxviii) subsection 163(1) (obscene materials),

(xxix) section 163.1 (child pornography),

(xxix.1) section 170 (parent or guardian procuring sexual activity),

(xxix.2) section 171 (householder permitting sexual activity),

(xxix.3) section 171.1 (making sexually explicit material available to child),

(xxix.4) section 172.1 (luring a child),

(xxix.5) section 172.2 (agreement or arrangement — sexual offence against child),

(xxx) section 184 (unlawful interception),

(xxxi) section 191 (possession of intercepting device),

(xxxii) subsection 201(1) (keeping gaming or betting house),

(xxxiii) paragraph 202(1)(e) (pool-selling, etc.),

(xxxiv) [Repealed 2019, c. 25, s. 63.1]

(xxxv) to (xxxviii) [Repealed 2014, c. 25, s. 11(1).]

(xxxix) section 235 (murder),

(xxxix.1) section 244 (discharging firearm with intent),

(xxxix.2) section 244.2 (discharging firearm — recklessness),

(xl) section 264.1 (uttering threats),

(xli) section 267 (assault with a weapon or causing bodily harm),

(xlii) section 268 (aggravated assault),

(xliii) section 269 (unlawfully causing bodily harm),

(xliii.1) section 270.01 (assaulting peace officer with weapon or causing bodily harm),

(xliii.2) section 270.02 (aggravated assault of peace officer),

(xliv) section 271 (sexual assault),

(xlv) section 272 (sexual assault with a weapon, threats to a third party or causing bodily harm),

(xlvi) section 273 (aggravated sexual assault),

(xlvii) section 279 (kidnapping),

(xlvii.1) section 279.01 (trafficking in persons),

(xlvii.11) section 279.011 (trafficking of a person under the age of eighteen years),

(xlvii.2) section 279.02 (material benefit),

(xlvii.3) section 279.03 (withholding or destroying documents),

(xlviii) section 279.1 (hostage taking),

(xlix) section 280 (abduction of person under sixteen),

(l) section 281 (abduction of person under fourteen),

(li) section 282 (abduction in contravention of custody order or parenting order),

(lii) section 283 (abduction),

(lii.1) 286.1 (obtaining sexual services for consideration),

(lii.2) 286.2 (material benefit from sexual services),

(lii.3) 286.3 (procuring),

(lii.4) 286.4 (advertising sexual services),

(liii) section 318 (advocating genocide),

(liv) section 327 (possession of device to obtain telecommunication facility or service),

(liv.1) section 333.1 (motor vehicle theft),

(lv) section 334 (theft),

(lvi) section 342 (theft, forgery, etc., of credit card),

(lvi.1) section 342.01 (instruments for copying credit card data or forging or falsifying credit cards),

(lvii) section 342.1 (unauthorized use of computer),

(lviii) section 342.2 (possession of device to obtain unauthorized use of computer system or to commit mischief),

(lix) section 344 (robbery),

(lx) section 346 (extortion),

(lxi) section 347 (criminal interest rate),

(lxii) section 348 (breaking and entering),

(lxii.1) section 353.1 (tampering with vehicle identification number),

(lxiii) section 354 (possession of property obtained by crime),

(lxiii.1) section 355.2 (trafficking in property obtained by crime),

(lxiii.2) section 355.4 (possession of property obtained by crime — trafficking),

(lxiv) section 356 (theft from mail),

(lxv) section 367 (forgery),

(lxvi) section 368 (use, trafficking or possession of forged document),

(lxvi.1) section 368.1 (forgery instruments),

(lxvii) section 372 (false information),

(lxviii) section 380 (fraud),

(lxix) section 381 (using mails to defraud),

(lxx) section 382 (fraudulent manipulation of stock exchange transactions),

(lxx.1) subsection 402.2(1) (identity theft),

(lxx.2) subsection 402.2(2) (trafficking in identity information),

(lxx.3) section 403 (identity fraud),

(lxxi) section 423.1 (intimidation of justice system participant or journalist),

(lxxii) section 424 (threat to commit offences against internationally protected person),

(lxxii.1) section 424.1 (threat against United Nations or associated personnel),

(lxxiii) section 426 (secret commissions),

(lxxiv) section 430 (mischief),

(lxxv) section 431 (attack on premises, residence or transport of internationally protected person),

(lxxv.1) section 431.1 (attack on premises, accommodation or transport of United Nations or associated personnel),

(lxxv.2) subsection 431.2(2) (explosive or other lethal device), (lxxvi) section 433 (arson),

(lxxvii) section 434 (arson),

(lxxviii) section 434.1 (arson),

(lxxix) section 435 (arson for fraudulent purpose),

(lxxx) section 449 (making counterfeit money),

(lxxxi) section 450 (possession, etc., of counterfeit money),

(lxxxii) section 452 (uttering, etc., counterfeit money),

(lxxxiii) section 462.31 (laundering proceeds of crime),

(lxxxiv) subsection 462.33(11) (acting in contravention of restraint order),

(lxxxv) section 467.11 (participation in criminal organization),

(lxxxv.1) section 467.111 (recruitment of members — criminal organization),

(lxxxvi) section 467.12 (commission of offence for criminal organization), or

(lxxxvii) section 467.13 (instructing commission of offence for criminal organization),

(b) section 198 (fraudulent bankruptcy) of the *Bankruptcy and Insolvency Act*,

(b.1) any of the following provisions of the *Biological and Toxin Weapons Convention Implementation Act*, namely,

(i) section 6 (production, etc., of biological agents and means of delivery), or

(ii) section 7 (unauthorized production, etc., of biological agents),

(b.2) any of the following provisions of the *Cannabis Act*, namely,

(i) section 9 (distribution and possession for purpose of distributing),

(ii) section 10 (selling and possession for purpose of selling),

(iii) section 11 (importing and exporting and possession for purpose of exporting),

(iv) section 12 (production),

(v) section 13 (possession, etc., for use in production or distribution of illicit cannabis), or

(vi) section 14 (use of young person),

(c) any of the following provisions of the *Competition Act*, namely,

(i) section 45 (conspiracies, agreements or arrangements between competitors),

(ii) section 47 (bid-rigging), or

(iii) subsection 52.1(3) (deceptive telemarketing),

(d) any of the following provisions of the *Controlled Drugs and Substances Act*, namely,

(i) section 5 (trafficking),

(ii) section 6 (importing and exporting),

(iii) section 7 (production), or

(iv) section 7.1 (possession, sale, etc., for use in production or trafficking),

(d.1) section 42 (offences related to infringement of copyright) of the *Copyright Act*,

(e) section 3 (bribing a foreign public official) of the *Corruption of Foreign Public Officials Act*,

(e.1) the *Crimes Against Humanity and War Crimes Act*,

(f) either of the following provisions of the *Customs Act*, namely,

(i) section 153 (false statements), or

(ii) section 159 (smuggling),

(g) any of the following provisions of the *Excise Act, 2001*, namely,

(i) section 214 (unlawful production, sale, etc., of tobacco, alcohol or cannabis),

(ii) section 216 (unlawful possession of tobacco product),

(iii) section 218 (unlawful possession, sale, etc., of alcohol),

(iii.1) section 218.1 (unlawful possession, sale, etc., of unstamped cannabis),

(iv) section 219 (falsifying or destroying records),

(v) section 230 (possession of property obtained by excise offences), or

(vi) section 231 (laundering proceeds of excise offences),

(h) any of the following provisions of the *Export and Import Permits Act*, namely,

(i) section 13 (export or attempt to export),

(ii) section 14 (import or attempt to import),

(ii.1) section 14.2 (broker or attempt to broker),

(iii) section 15 (diversion, etc.),

(iv) section 16 (no transfer of permits),

(v) section 17 (false information), or

(vi) section 18 (aiding and abetting),

(i) any of the following provisions of the *Immigration and Refugee Protection Act*, namely,

(i) section 117 (organizing entry into Canada),

(ii) section 118 (trafficking in persons),

(iii) section 119 (disembarking persons at sea),

(iv) section 122 (offences related to documents),

(v) section 126 (counselling misrepresentation), or

(vi) section 129 (offences relating to officers),

(j) any offence under the *Security of Information Act*, or

(k) section 51.01 (offences related to goods, labels, packaging or services) of the *Trademarks Act*,

and includes any other offence that there are reasonable grounds to believe is a criminal organization offence or any other offence that there are reasonable grounds to believe is an offence described in paragraph (b) or (c) of the definition "terrorism offence" in section 2;

"police officer" means any officer, constable or other person employed for the preservation and maintenance of the public peace;

"private communication" means any oral communication, or any telecommunication, that is made by an originator who is in Canada or is intended by the originator to be received by a person who is in Canada and that is made under circumstances in which it is reasonable for the originator to expect that it will not be intercepted by any person other than the person intended by the originator to receive it, and includes any radio-based telephone communication that is treated electronically or otherwise for the purpose of preventing intelligible reception by any person other than the person intended by the originator to receive it;

"public switched telephone network" means a telecommunication facility the primary purpose of which is to provide a land line-based telephone service to the public for compensation;

"radio-based telephone communication" means any radiocommunication within the meaning of the *Radiocommunication Act* that is made over apparatus that is used primarily for connection to a public switched telephone network;

"sell" includes offer for sale, expose for sale, have in possession for sale or distribute or advertise for sale;

"solicitor" means, in the Province of Quebec, an advocate or a notary and, in any other province, a barrister or solicitor.

R.S.C. 1985, c. 27 (1st Supp.), ss. 7(2)(a), 23; R.S.C. 1985, c. 1 (2nd Supp.), s. 213(1) (Sched. I, item 2); R.S.C. 1985, c. 1 (4th Supp.), s. 13; R.S.C. 1985, c. 29 (4th Supp.), s. 17; R.S.C. 1985, c. 42 (4th Supp.), s. 1; 1991, c. 28, s. 12; 1992, c. 27, s. 90; 1993, c. 7, s. 5; 1993, c. 25, s. 94; 1993, c. 40, s. 1; 1993, c. 46, s. 4; 1995, c. 39, s. 140; 1996, c. 19, s. 66; 1997, c. 18, s. 7; 1997, c. 23, s. 3; 1998, c. 34, s. 8; 1999, c. 2, s. 47; 1999, c. 5, s. 4; 2000, c. 24, s. 43 (amended 2001, c. 34, s. 36); 2001, c. 32, s. 4; 2001, c. 41, ss. 5, 31, 133(2), (5); 2002, c. 22, s. 409(2)(b); 2004, c. 15, s. 108; 2005, c. 32, s. 10; 2005, c. 43, s. 1; 2008, c. 6, s. 15; 2009, c. 2, s. 442; 2009, c. 22, s. 4; 2009, c. 28, s. 3; 2010, c. 3, s. 1; 2010, c. 14, s. 2; 2012, c. 1, s. 24; 2013, c. 8, s. 2; 2013, c. 9, s. 14; 2013, c. 13, s. 7; 2014, c. 17, s. 2; 2014, c. 20, s. 366(1); 2014, c. 25, s. 11; 2014, c. 31, s. 7; 2014, c. 32, s. 59; 2015, c. 20, s. 19; 2017, c. 7, s. 56; 2018, c. 12, s. 114; 2018, c. 16, s. 210; 2018, c. 26, s. 23; 2018, c. 29, s. 15; 2019, c. 13, s. 150; 2019, c. 16, s. 122; 2019, c. 25, s. 63.1

183.1 Consent to interception — Where a private communication is originated by more than one person or is intended by the originator thereof to be received by more than one person, a consent to the interception thereof by any one of those persons is sufficient consent for the purposes of any provision of this Part.

1993, c. 40, s. 2

Interception of Communications

184. (1) Interception — Every person who, by means of any electromagnetic, acoustic, mechanical or other device, knowingly intercepts a private communication is guilty of

(a) an indictable offence and liable to imprisonment for a term of not more than five years; or

(b) an offence punishable on summary conviction.

(2) Saving provision — Subsection (1) does not apply to

(a) a person who has the consent to intercept, express or implied, of the originator of the private communication or of the person intended by the originator thereof to receive it;

(b) a person who intercepts a private communication in accordance with an authorization or pursuant to section 184.4 or any person who in good faith aids in any way another person who the aiding person believes on reasonable grounds is acting with an authorization or pursuant to section 184.4;

(c) a person engaged in providing a telephone, telegraph or other communication service to the public who intercepts a private communication,

(i) if the interception is necessary for the purpose of providing the service,

(ii) in the course of service observing or random monitoring necessary for the purpose of mechanical or service quality control checks, or

(iii) if the interception is necessary to protect the person's rights or property directly related to providing the service;

(d) an officer or servant of Her Majesty in right of Canada who engages in radio frequency spectrum management, in respect of a private communication intercepted by that officer or servant for the purpose of identifying, isolating or preventing an unauthorized or interfering use of a frequency or of a transmission; or

(e) a person, or any person acting on their behalf, in possession or control of a computer system, as defined in subsection 342.1(2), who intercepts a private communication originating from, directed to or transmitting through that computer system, if the interception is reasonably necessary for

(i) managing the quality of service of the computer system as it relates to performance factors such as the responsiveness and capacity of the system as well as the integrity and availability of the system and data, or

(ii) protecting the computer system against any act that would be an offence under subsection 342.1(1) or 430(1.1).

(3) Use or retention — A private communication intercepted by a person referred to in paragraph (2)(e) can be used or retained only if

(a) it is essential to identify, isolate or prevent harm to the computer system; or

(b) it is to be disclosed in circumstances referred to in subsection 193(2).

1993, c. 40, s. 3; 2004, c. 12, s. 4; 2019, c. 25, s. 64

184.1 (1) Interception to prevent bodily harm — An agent of the state may intercept, by means of any electro-magnetic, acoustic, mechanical or other device, a private communication if

(a) either the originator of the private communication or the person intended by the originator to receive it has consented to the interception;

(b) the agent of the state believes on reasonable grounds that there is a risk of bodily harm to the person who consented to the interception; and

(c) the purpose of the interception is to prevent the bodily harm.

(2) Admissibility of intercepted communication — The contents of a private communication that is obtained from an interception pursuant to subsection (1) are inadmissible as evidence except for the purposes of proceedings in which actual, attempted or threatened bodily harm is alleged, including proceedings in respect of an application for an authorization under this Part or in respect of a search warrant or a warrant for the arrest of any person.

(3) Destruction of recording and transcripts — The agent of the state who intercepts a private communication pursuant to subsection (1) shall, as soon as is practicable in the circumstances, destroy any recording of the private communication that is obtained from an interception pursuant to subsection (1), any full or partial transcript of the recording and any notes made by that agent of the private communication if nothing in the private communication suggests that bodily harm, attempted bodily harm or threatened bodily harm has occurred or is likely to occur.

(4) Definition of "agent of the state" — For the purposes of this section, **"Agent of the state"** means

(a) a peace officer; and

(b) a person acting under the authority of, or in cooperation with, a peace officer.

1993, c. 40, s. 4

184.2 (1) Interception with consent — A person may intercept, by means of any electro-magnetic, acoustic, mechanical or other device, a private communication where either the originator of the private communication or the person intended by the originator to receive it has consented to the interception and an authorization has been obtained pursuant to subsection (3).

(2) Application for authorization — An application for an authorization under this section shall be made by a peace officer, or a public officer who has been appointed or designated to administer or enforce any federal or provincial law and whose duties include the enforcement of this or any other Act of Parliament, ex parte and in writing to a provincial court judge, a judge of a superior court of criminal jurisdiction or a judge as defined in section 552, and shall be accompanied by an affidavit, which may be sworn on the information and belief of that peace officer or public officer or of any other peace officer or public officer, deposing to the following matters:

(a) that there are reasonable grounds to believe that an offence against this or any other Act of Parliament has been or will be committed;

(b) the particulars of the offence;

(c) the name of the person who has consented to the interception;

(d) the period for which the authorization is requested; and

(e) in the case of an application for an authorization where an authorization has previously been granted under this section or section 186, the particulars of the authorization.

(3) **Judge to be satisfied** — An authorization may be given under this section if the judge to whom the application is made is satisfied that

(a) there are reasonable grounds to believe that an offence against this or any other Act of Parliament has been or will be committed;

(b) either the originator of the private communication or the person intended by the originator to receive it has consented to the interception; and

(c) there are reasonable grounds to believe that information concerning the offence referred to in paragraph (a) will be obtained through the interception sought.

(4) **Content and limitation of authorization** — An authorization given under this section shall

(a) state the offence in respect of which private communications may be intercepted;

(b) state the type of private communication that may be intercepted;

(c) state the identity of the persons, if known, whose private communications are to be intercepted, generally describe the place at which private communications may be intercepted, if a general description of that place can be given, and generally describe the manner of interception that may be used;

(d) contain the terms and conditions that the judge considers advisable in the public interest; and

(e) be valid for the period, not exceeding sixty days, set out therein.

(5) **Related warrant or order** — A judge who gives an authorization under this section may, at the same time, issue a warrant or make an order under any of sections 487, 487.01, 487.014 to 487.018, 487.02, 492.1 and 492.2 if the judge is of the opinion that the requested warrant or order is related to the execution of the authorization.

1993, c. 40, s. 4; 2014, c. 31, s. 8

184.3 (1) Application by means of telecommunication — Notwithstanding section 184.2, an application for an authorization under subsection 184.2(2) may be made ex parte to a provincial court judge, a judge of a superior court of criminal jurisdiction or a judge as defined in section 552, by telephone or other means of telecommunication, if it would be impracticable in the circumstances for the applicant to appear personally before a judge.

(2) **Application** — An application for an authorization made under this section shall be on oath and shall be accompanied by a statement that includes the matters referred to in paragraphs 184.2(2)(a) to (e) and that states the circumstances that make it impracticable for the applicant to appear personally before a judge.

(3) **Recording** — The judge shall record, in writing or otherwise, the application for an authorization made under this section and, on determination of the application, shall cause the writing or recording to be placed in the packet referred to in subsection 187(1) and sealed in that packet, and a recording sealed in a packet shall be treated as if it were a document for the purposes of section 187.

(4) **Oath** — For the purposes of subsection (2), an oath may be administered by telephone or other means of telecommunication.

(5) **Alternative to oath** — An applicant who uses a means of telecommunication that produces a writing may, instead of swearing an oath for the purposes of subsection (2), make a statement in writing stating that all matters contained in the application are true to the knowledge or belief of the applicant and such a statement shall be deemed to be a statement made under oath.

(6) **Authorization** — Where the judge to whom an application is made under this section is satisfied that the circumstances referred to in paragraphs 184.2(3)(a) to (c) exist and that the circumstances referred to in subsection (2) make it impracticable for the applicant to appear personally before a judge, the judge may, on such terms and conditions, if any, as are considered advisable, give an authorization by telephone or other means of telecommunication for a period of up to thirty-six hours.

(7) **Giving authorization** — Where a judge gives an authorization by telephone or other means of telecommunication, other than a means of telecommunication that produces a writing,

(a) the judge shall complete and sign the authorization in writing, noting on its face the time, date and place at which it is given;

(b) the applicant shall, on the direction of the judge, complete a facsimile of the authorization in writing, noting on its face the name of the judge who gave it and the time, date and place at which it was given; and

(c) the judge shall, as soon as is practicable after the authorization has been given, cause the authorization to be placed in the packet referred to in subsection 187(1) and sealed in that packet.

(8) **Giving authorization where telecommunication produces writing** — Where a judge gives an authorization by a means of telecommunication that produces a writing, the judge shall

(a) complete and sign the authorization in writing, noting on its face the time, date and place at which it is given;

(b) transmit the authorization by the means of telecommunication to the applicant, and the copy received by the applicant shall be deemed to be a facsimile referred to in paragraph (7)(b); and

(c) as soon as is practicable after the authorization has been given, cause the authorization to be placed in the packet referred to in subsection 187(1) and sealed in that packet.

1993, c. 40, s. 4

184.4 Immediate interception — imminent harm — A police officer may intercept, by means of any electro-magnetic, acoustic, mechanical or other device, a private communication if the police officer has reasonable grounds to believe that

(a) the urgency of the situation is such that an authorization could not, with reasonable diligence, be obtained under any other provision of this Part;

(b) the interception is immediately necessary to prevent an offence that would cause serious harm to any person or to property; and

(c) either the originator of the private communication or the person intended by the originator to receive it is the person who would commit the offence that is likely to cause the harm or is the victim, or intended victim, of the harm.

1993, c. 40, s. 4; 2013, c. 8, s. 3

184.5 (1) Interception of radio-based telephone communications — Every person who intercepts, by means of any electro-magnetic, acoustic, mechanical or other device, maliciously or for gain, a radio-based telephone communication, if the originator of the communication or the person intended by the originator of the communication to receive it is in Canada, is guilty of

(a) an indictable offence and liable to imprisonment for a term of not more than five years; or

(b) an offence punishable on summary conviction.

(2) Other provisions to apply — Section 183.1, subsection 184(2) and sections 184.1 to 190 and 194 to 196 apply, with such modifications as the circumstances require, to interceptions of radio-based telephone communications referred to in subsection (1).

1993, c. 40, s. 4; 2019, c. 25, s. 65

184.6 One application for authorization sufficient — For greater certainty, an application for an authorization under this Part may be made with respect to both private communications and radio-based telephone communications at the same time.

1993, c. 40, s. 4

185. (1) Application for authorization — An application for an authorization to be given under section 186 shall be made *ex parte* and in writing to a judge of a superior court of criminal jurisdiction or a judge as defined in section 552 and shall be signed by the Attorney General of the province in which the application is made or the Minister of Public Safety and Emergency Preparedness or an agent specially designated in writing for the purposes of this section by

(a) the Minister personally or the Deputy Minister of Public Safety and Emergency Preparedness personally, if the offence under investigation is one in respect of which proceedings, if any, may be instituted at the instance of the Government of Canada and conducted by or on behalf of the Attorney General of Canada, or

(b) the Attorney General of a province personally or the Deputy Attorney General of a province personally, in any other case,

and shall be accompanied by an affidavit, which may be sworn on the information and belief of a peace officer or public officer deposing to the following matters:

(c) the facts relied on to justify the belief that an authorization should be given together with particulars of the offence,

(d) the type of private communication proposed to be intercepted,

(e) the names, addresses and occupations, if known, of all persons, the interception of whose private communications there are reasonable grounds to believe may assist the investigation of the offence, a general description of the nature and location of the place, if known, at which private communications are proposed to be intercepted and a general description of the manner of interception proposed to be used,

(f) the number of instances, if any, on which an application has been made under this section in relation to the offence and a person named in the affidavit pursuant to paragraph (*e*) and on which the application was withdrawn or no authorization was given, the date on which each application was made and the name of the judge to whom each application was made,

(g) the period for which the authorization is requested, and

(h) whether other investigative procedures have been tried and have failed or why it appears they are unlikely to succeed or that the urgency of the matter is such that it would be impractical to carry out the investigation of the offence using only other investigative procedures.

(1.1) Exception for criminal organizations and terrorist groups — Notwithstanding paragraph (1)(h), that paragraph does, not apply where the application for an authorization is in relation to

(a) an offence under section 467.11, 467.111, 467.12 or 467.13;

(b) an offence committed for the benefit of, at the direction of or in association with a criminal organization; or

(c) a terrorism offence.

(2) Extension of period for notification — An application for an authorization may be accompanied by an application, personally signed by the Attorney General of the province in which the application for the authorization is made or the Minister of Public Safety and Emergency Preparedness if the application for the authorization is made by him or on his behalf, to substitute for the period mentioned in subsection 196(1) such longer period not exceeding three years as is set out in the application.

(3) Where extension to be granted — Where an application for an authorization is accompanied by an application referred to in subsection (2), the judge to whom the applications are made shall first consider the application referred to in subsection (2) and where, on the basis of the affidavit in support of the application for the authorization and any other affidavit evidence submitted in support of the application referred to in subsection (2), the judge is of the opinion that the interests of justice warrant the granting of the application, he shall fix a period, not exceeding three years, in substitution for the period mentioned in subsection 196(1).

(4) Where extension not granted — Where the judge to whom an application for an authorization and an application referred to in subsection (2) are made refuses to fix a period in substitution for the period mentioned in subsection 196(1) or where the judge fixes a period in substitution therefor that is less than the period set out in the application referred to in subsection (2), the person appearing before the judge on the application for the authorization may withdraw the application for the authorization and thereupon the judge shall not proceed to consider the application for the authorization or to give the authorization and shall return to the person appearing before him on the application for the authorization both applications and all other material pertaining thereto.

1993, c. 40, s. 5; 1997, c. 18, s. 8; 1997, c. 23, s. 4; 2001, c. 32, s. 5; 2001, c. 41, ss. 6, 133(8); 2005, c. 10, ss. 22, 34(1)(f)(v); 2014, c. 17, s. 3

186. (1) Judge to be satisfied — An authorization under this section may be given if the judge to whom the application is made is satisfied

(a) that it would be in the best interests of the administration of justice to do so; and

(b) that other investigative procedures have been tried and have failed, other investigative procedures are unlikely to succeed or the urgency of the matter is such that it would be impractical to carry out the investigation of the offence using only other investigative procedures.

(1.1) Exception for criminal organizations and terrorism offences — Notwithstanding paragraph (1)(b), that paragraph does not apply where the judge is satisfied that the application for an authorization is in relation to

(a) an offence under section 467.11, 467.111, 467.12 or 467.13;

(b) an offence committed for the benefit of, at the direction of or in association with a criminal organization; or

(c) a terrorism offence.

(2) Where authorization not to be given — No authorization may be given to intercept a private communication at the office or residence of a solicitor, or at any other place ordinarily used by a solicitor and by other solicitors for the purpose of consultation with clients, unless the judge to whom the application is made is satisfied that there are reasonable grounds to believe that the solicitor, any other solicitor practising with him, any person employed by him or any other such solicitor or a member of the solicitor's household has been or is about to become a party to an offence.

(3) Terms and conditions — Where an authorization is given in relation to the interception of private communications at a place described in subsection (2), the judge by whom the authorization is given shall include therein such terms and conditions as he considers advisable to protect privileged communications between solicitors and clients.

(4) Content and limitation of authorization — An authorization shall

(a) state the offence in respect of which private communications may be intercepted;

(b) state the type of private communication so that may be intercepted;

(c) state the identity of the persons, if known, whose private communications are to be intercepted, generally describe the place at which private communications may be intercepted, if a general description of that place can be given, and generally describe the manner of interception that may be used;

(d) contain such terms and conditions as the judge considers advisable in the public interest; and

(e) be valid for the period, not exceeding sixty days, set out therein.

(5) Persons designated — The Minister of Public Safety and Emergency Preparedness or the Attorney General, as the case may be, may designate a person or persons who may intercept private communications under authorizations.

(5.1) Installation and removal of device — For greater certainty, an authorization that permits interception by means of an electro-magnetic, acoustic, mechanical or other device includes the authority to install, maintain or remove the device covertly.

(5.2) Removal after expiry of authorization — On an *ex parte* application, in writing, supported by affidavit, the judge who gave an authorization referred to in subsection (5.1) or any other judge having jurisdiction to give such an authorization may give a further authorization for the covert removal of the electro-magnetic, acoustic, mechanical or other device after the expiry of the original authorization

(a) under any terms or conditions that the judge considers advisable in the public interest; and

(b) during any specified period of not more than sixty days.

(6) Renewal of authorization — Renewals of an authorization may be given by a judge of a superior court of criminal jurisdiction or a judge as defined in section 552 on receipt by him or her of an *ex parte* application in writing signed by the Attorney General of the province in which the application is made or the Minister of Public Safety and Emergency Preparedness — or an agent specially designated in writing for the purposes of section 185 by the Minister or the Attorney General, as the case may be — accompanied by an affidavit of a peace officer or public officer deposing to the following matters:

(a) the reason and period for which the renewal is required,

(b) full particulars, together with times and dates, when interceptions, if any, were made or attempted under the authorization, and any information that has been obtained by any interception, and

(c) the number of instances, if any, on which, to the knowledge and belief of the deponent, an application has been made under this subsection in relation to the same authorization and on which the application was withdrawn or no renewal was given, the date on which each application was made and the name of the judge to whom each application was made, and supported by such other information as the judge may require.

(7) Renewal — A renewal of an authorization may be given if the judge to whom the application is made is satisfied that any of the circumstances described in subsection (1) still obtain, but no renewal shall be for a period exceeding sixty days.

(8) Related warrant or order — A judge who gives an authorization under this section may, at the same time, issue a warrant or make an order under any of sections 487, 487.01, 487.014 to 487.018, 487.02, 492.1 and 492.2 if the judge is of the opinion that the requested warrant or order is related to the execution of the authorization.

1993, c. 40, s. 6; 1997, c. 23, s. 5; 1999, c. 5, s. 5; 2001, c. 32, s. 6; 2001, c. 41, ss. 6.1, 133(8.1); 2005, c. 10, ss. 23, 34(1)(f)(vi); 2014, c. 17, s. 4; 2014, c. 31, s. 9

186.1 Time limitation in relation to criminal organizations and terrorism offences — Notwithstanding paragraphs 184.2(4)(e) and 186(4)(e) and subsection 186(7), an authorization or any renewal of an authorization may be valid for one or more periods specified in the authorization exceeding sixty days, each not exceeding one year, where the authorization is in relation to

(a) an offence under section 467.11, 467.111, 467.12 or 467.13;

(b) an offence committed for the benefit of, at the direction of or in association with a criminal organization; or

(c) a terrorism offence.

1997, c. 23, s. 6; 2001, c. 32, s. 7; 2001, c. 41, ss. 7, 133(9); 2014, c. 17, s. 5

187. (1) Manner in which application to be kept secret — All documents relating to an application made pursuant to any provision of this Part are confidential and, subject to subsection (1.1), shall be placed in a packet and sealed by the judge to whom the application is made immediately on determination of the application, and that packet shall be kept in the custody of the court in a place to which the public has no access or in such other place as the judge may authorize and shall not be dealt with except in accordance with subsections (1.2) to (1.5).

(1.1) Exception — An authorization given under this Part need not be placed in the packet except where, pursuant to subsection 184.3(7) or (8), the original authorization is in the hands of the judge, in which case that judge must place it in the packet and the facsimile remains with the applicant.

(1.2) Opening for further applications — The sealed packet may be opened and its contents removed for the purpose of dealing with an application for a further authorization or with an application for renewal of an authorization.

(1.3) Opening on order of judge — A provincial court judge, a judge of a superior court of criminal jurisdiction or a judge as defined in section 552 may order that the sealed packet be opened and its contents removed for the purpose of copying and examining the documents contained in the packet.

(1.4) Opening on order of trial judge — A judge or provinical court judge before whom a trial is to be held and who has jurisdiction in the province in which an authorization was given may order that the sealed packet be opened and its contents removed for the purpose of copying and examining the documents contained in the packet if

(a) any matter relevant to the authorization or any evidence obtained pursuant to the authorization is in issue in the trial; and

(b) the accused applies for such an order for the purpose of consulting the documents to prepare for trial.

(1.5) **Order for destruction of documents** — Where a sealed packet is opened, its contents shall not be destroyed except pursuant to an order of a judge of the same court as the judge who gave the authorization.

(2) **Order of judge** — An order under subsection (1.2), (1.3), (1.4) or (1.5) made with respect to documents relating to an application made pursuant to section 185 or subsection 186(6) or 196(2) may only be made after the Attorney General or the Minister of Public Safety and Emergency Preparedness by whom or on whose authority the application for the authorization to which the order relates was made has been given an opportunity to be heard.

(3) **Idem** — An order under subsection (1.2), (1.3), (1.4) or (1.5) made with respect to documents relating to an application made pursuant to subsection 184.2(2) or section 184.3 may only be made after the Attorney General has been given an opportunity to be heard.

(4) **Editing of copies** — Where a prosecution has been commenced and an accused applies for an order for the copying and examination of documents pursuant to subsection (1.3) or (1.4), the judge shall not, notwithstanding those subsections, provide any copy of any document to the accused until the prosecutor has deleted any part of the copy of the document that the prosecutor believes would be prejudicial to the public interest, including any part that the prosecutor believes could

(a) compromise the identity of any confidential informant;

(b) compromise the nature and extent of ongoing investigations;

(c) endanger persons engaged in particular intelligence-gathering techniques and thereby prejudice future investigations in which similar techniques would be used; or

(d) prejudice the interests of innocent persons.

(5) **Accused to be provided with copies** — After the prosecutor has deleted the parts of the copy of the document to be given to the accused under subsection (4), the accused shall be provided with an edited copy of the document.

(6) **Original documents to be returned** — After the accused has received an edited copy of a document, the prosecutor shall keep a copy of the original document, and an edited copy of the document and the original document shall be returned to the packet and the packet resealed.

(7) **Deleted parts** — An accused to whom an edited copy of a document has been provided pursuant to subsection (5) may request that the judge before whom the trial is to be held order that any part of the document deleted by the prosecutor be made available to the accused, and the judge shall order that a copy of any part that, in the opinion of the judge, is required in order for the accused to make full answer

and defence and for which the provision of a judicial summary would not be sufficient, be made available to the accused.

(8) **Documents to be kept secret — related warrant or order** — The rules provided for in this section apply to all documents relating to a request for a related warrant or order referred to in subsection 184.2(5), 186(8) or 188(6) with any necessary modifications.

R.S.C. 1985, c. 27 (1st Supp.), s. 24; 1993, c. 40, s. 7; 2005, c. 10, s. 24; 2014, c. 31, s. 10

188. (1) Applications to specially appointed judges — Notwithstanding section 185, an application made under that section for an authorization may be made *ex parte* to a judge of a superior court of criminal jurisdiction, or a judge as defined in section 552, designated from time to time by the Chief Justice, by a peace officer specially designated in writing, by name or otherwise, for the purposes of this section by

(a) the Minister of Public Safety and Emergency Preparedness, if the offence is one in respect of which proceedings, if any, may be instituted by the Government of Canada and conducted by or on behalf of the Attorney General of Canada, or

(b) the Attorney General of a province, in respect of any other offence in the province,

if the urgency of the situation requires interception of private communications to commence before an authorization could, with reasonable diligence, be obtained under section 186.

(2) **Authorizations in emergency** — Where the judge to whom an application is made pursuant to subsection (1) is satisfied that the urgency of the situation requires that interception of private communications commence before an authorization could, with reasonable diligence, be obtained under section 186, he may, on such terms and conditions, if any, as he considers advisable, give an authorization in writing for a period of up to thirty-six hours.

(3) [Repealed 1993, c. 40, s. 8.]

(4) **Definition of "chief justice"** — In this section, **"Chief Justice"** means

(a) in the Province of Ontario, the Chief Justice of the Ontario Court;

(b) in the Province of Quebec, the Chief Justice of the Superior Court;

(c) in the Provinces of Nova Scotia, British Columbia and Prince Edward Island, and in the Yukon and the Northwest Territories, the Chief Justice of the Supreme Court;

(d) in the Provinces of New Brunswick, Manitoba, Saskatchewan and Alberta, the Chief Justice of the Court of Queen's Bench;

(e) in the Province of Newfoundland and Labrador, the Chief Justice of the Supreme Court, Trial Division; and

(f) in Nunavut, the Chief Justice of the Nunavut Court of Justice.

(5) **Inadmissibility of evidence** — The trial judge may deem inadmissible the evidence obtained by means of an interception of a private communication pursuant

to a subsequent authorization given under this section, where he finds that the application for the subsequent authorization was based on the same facts, and involved the interception of the private communications of the same person or persons, or related to the same offence, on which the application for the original authorization was based.

(6) Related warrant or order — A judge who gives an authorization under this section may, at the same time, issue a warrant or make an order under any of sections 487, 487.01, 487.014 to 487.018, 487.02, 492.1 and 492.2 if the judge is of the opinion that the requested warrant or order is related to the execution of the authorization, that the urgency of the situation requires the warrant or the order and that it can be reasonably executed or complied with within 36 hours.

R.S.C. 1985, c. 27 (1st Supp.), s. 25; R.S.C. 1985, c. 27 (2nd Supp.), s. 10 (Sched., item 6); 1990, c. 17, s. 10; 1992, c. 1, s. 58(1) (Sched. I, item 4); 1992, c. 51, s. 35; 1993, c. 28, s. 78 (Sched. III, item 29) [Repealed 1999, c. 3, s. 12 (Sched., item 6).]; 1993, c. 40, s. 8; 1999, c. 3, s. 28; 2002, c. 7, s. 140; 2005, c. 10, s. 34(1)(f)(vii); 2014, c. 31, s. 11; 2015, c. 3, s. 47; 2017, c. 33, s. 255

188.1 Execution in Canada — An authorization given under section 184.2, 184.3, 186 or 188 may be executed at any place in Canada. Any peace officer who executes the authorization must have authority to act as a peace officer in the place where it is executed.

1993, c. 40, s. 9; 2019, c. 25, s. 66

188.2 No civil or criminal liability — No person who acts in accordance with an authorization or under section 184.1 or 184.4 or who aids, in good faith, a person who he or she believes on reasonable grounds is acting in accordance with an authorization or under one of those sections incurs any criminal or civil liability for anything reasonably done further to the authorization or to that section.

1993, c. 40, s. 9

189. (1) to (4) [Repealed 1993, c. 40, s. 10(1).]

(5) Notice of intention to produce evidence — The contents of a private communication that is obtained from an interception of the private communication pursuant to any provision of, or pursuant to an authorization given under, this Part shall not be received in evidence unless the party intending to adduce it has given to the accused reasonable notice of the intention together with

(a) a transcript of the private communication, where it will be adduced in the form of a recording, or a statement setting out full particulars of the private communication, where evidence of the private communication will be given *viva voce*; and

(b) a statement respecting the time, place and date of the private communication and the parties thereto, if known.

(6) Privileged evidence — Any information obtained by an interception that, but for the interception, would have been privileged remains privileged and inadmissible as evidence without the consent of the person enjoying the privilege.

R.S.C. 1985, c. 27 (1st Supp.), s. 203; 1993, c. 40, s. 10

190. Further particulars — Where an accused has been given notice pursuant to subsection 189(5), any judge of the court in which the trial of the accused is being or is to be held may at any time order that further particulars be given of the private communication that is intended to be adduced in evidence.

191. (1) Possession, etc. — Every person who possesses, sells or purchases any electro-magnetic, acoustic, mechanical or other device or any component of it knowing that its design renders it primarily useful for surreptitious interception of private communications is guilty of

(a) an indictable offence and liable to imprisonment for a term of not more than two years; or

(b) an offence punishable on summary conviction.

(2) Exemptions — Subsection (1) does not apply to

(a) a police officer in possession of a device or component described in subsection (1) in the course of his employment;

(b) a person in possession of such a device or component for the purpose of using it in an interception made or to be made in accordance with an authorization;

(b.1) a person in possession of such a device or component under the direction of a police officer in order to assist that officer in the course of his duties as a police officer;

(c) an officer or a servant of Her Majesty in right of Canada or a member of the Canadian Forces in possession of such a device or component in the course of his duties as such an officer, servant or member, as the case may be; and

(d) any other person in possession of such a device or component under the authority of a licence issued by the Minister of Public Safety and Emergency Preparedness.

(3) Terms and conditions of licence — A licence issued for the purpose of paragraph (2)(d) may contain such terms and conditions relating to the possession, sale or purchase of a device or component described in subsection (1) as the Minister of Public Safety and Emergency Preparedness may prescribe.

R.S.C. 1985, c. 27 (1st Supp.), s. 26; 2005, c. 10, s. 34(1)(f)(viii); 2013, c. 8, s. 4; 2019, c. 25, s. 67

192. (1) Forfeiture — Where a person is convicted of an offence under section 184 or 191, any electro-magnetic, acoustic, mechanical or other device by means of which the offence was committed or the possession of which constituted the offence, on the conviction, in addition to any punishment that is imposed, may be ordered forfeited to Her Majesty whereupon it may be disposed of as the Attorney General directs.

(2) Limitation — No order for forfeiture shall be made under subsection (1) in respect of telephone, telegraph or other communication facilities or equipment owned by a person engaged in providing telephone, telegraph or other communication service to the public or forming part of the telephone, telegraph or other communication service or system of that person by means of which an offence under section 184 has been committed if that person was not a party to the offence.

193. (1) Disclosure of information — If a private communication has been intercepted by means of an electro-magnetic, acoustic, mechanical or other device without the consent, express or implied, of the originator of that communication or of the person intended by the originator to receive it, every person commits an offence who, without the express consent of the originator of that communication or of the person intended to receive it, knowingly

(a) uses or discloses the private communication or any part of it or the substance, meaning or purpose of it or of any part of it, or

(b) discloses the existence of the private communication.

(1.1) Punishment — Every person who commits an offence under subsection (1) is guilty of

(a) an indictable offence and liable to imprisonment for a term of not more than two years; or

(b) an offence punishable on summary conviction.

(2) Exemptions — Subsection (1) does not apply to a person who discloses a private communication or any part thereof or the substance, meaning or purport thereof or of any part thereof or who discloses the existence of a private communication

(a) in the course of or for the purpose of giving evidence in any civil or criminal proceedings or in any other proceedings in which the person may be required to give evidence on oath;

(b) in the course of or for the purpose of any criminal investigation if the private communication was lawfully intercepted;

(c) in giving notice under section 189 or furnishing further particulars pursuant to an order under section 190;

(d) in the course of the operation of

(i) a telephone, telegraph or other communication service to the public,

(ii) a department or an agency of the Government of Canada, or

(iii) services relating to the management or protection of a computer system, as defined in subsection 342.1(2),

if the disclosure is necessarily incidental to an interception described in paragraph 184(2)(c), (d) or (e);

(e) where disclosure is made to a peace officer or prosecutor in Canada or to a person or authority with responsibility in a foreign state for the investigation or prosecution of offences and is intended to be in the interests of the administration of justice in Canada or elsewhere; or

(f) where the disclosure is made to the Director of the Canadian Security Intelligence Service or to an employee of the Service for the purpose of enabling the Service to perform its duties and functions under section 12 of the *Canadian Security Intelligence Service Act*.

(3) Publishing of prior lawful disclosure — Subsection (1) does not apply to a person who discloses a private communication or any part thereof or the substance, meaning or purport thereof or of any part thereof or who discloses the existence of a private communication where that which is disclosed by him was, prior to the disclosure, lawfully disclosed in the course of or for the purpose of giving evidence in proceedings referred to in paragraph (2)(*a*).

R.S.C. 1985, c. 30 (4th Supp.), s. 45; 1993, c. 40, s. 11; 2004, c. 12, s. 5; 2019, c. 25, s. 68

193.1 (1) Disclosure of information received from interception of radio-based telephone communications — Every person who knowingly uses or discloses a radio-based telephone communication or who knowingly discloses the existence of such a communication is guilty of an indictable offence and liable to imprisonment for a term of not more than two years or is guilty of an offence punishable on summary conviction, if

(a) the originator of the communication or the person intended by the originator of the communication to receive it was in Canada when the communication was made;

(b) the communication was intercepted by means of an electromagnetic, acoustic, mechanical or other device without the consent, express or implied, of the originator of the communication or of the person intended by the originator to receive the communication; and

(c) the person does not have the express or implied consent of the originator of the communication or of the person intended by the originator to receive the communication.

(2) Other provisions to apply — Subsections 193(2) and (3) apply, with such modifications as the circumstances require, to disclosures of radio-based telephone communications.

1993, c. 40, s. 12; 2019, c. 25, s. 69

194. (1) Damages — Subject to subsection (2), a court that convicts an accused of an offence under section 184, 184.5, 193 or 193.1 may, on the application of a person aggrieved, at the time sentence is imposed, order the accused to pay to that person an amount not exceeding five thousand dollars as punitive damages.

(2) No damages where civil proceedings commenced — No amount shall be ordered to be paid under subsection (1) to a person who has commenced an action under Part II of the *Crown Liability Act*.

(3) Judgment may be registered — Where an amount that is ordered to be paid under subsection (1) is not paid forthwith, the applicant may, by filing the order, enter as a judgment, in the superior court of the province in which the trial was held, the amount ordered to be paid, and that judgment is enforceable against the accused in the same manner as if it were a judgment rendered against the accused in that court in civil proceedings.

(4) Moneys in possession of accused may be taken — All or any part of an amount that is ordered to be paid under subsection (1) may be taken out of moneys found in the possession of the accused at the time of his arrest, except where there is a dispute respecting ownership of or right of possession to those moneys by claimants other than the accused.

1993, c. 40, s. 13

195. (1) Annual report — The Minister of Public Safety and Emergency Preparedness shall, as soon as possible after the end of each year, prepare a report relating to

(a) authorizations for which that Minister and agents specially designated in writing by that Minister for the purposes of section 185 applied and the interceptions made under those authorizations in the immediately preceding year;

(b) authorizations given under section 188 for which peace officers specially designated by that Minister for the purposes of that section applied and the interceptions made under those authorizations in the immediately preceding year; and

(c) interceptions made under section 184.4 in the immediately preceding year if the interceptions relate to an offence for which proceedings may be commenced by the Attorney General of Canada.

(2) Information respecting authorizations — sections 185 and 188 — The report shall, in relation to the authorizations and interceptions referred to in paragraphs (1)(a) and (b), set out

(a) the number of applications made for authorizations;

(b) the number of applications made for renewal of authorizations;

(c) the number of applications referred to in paragraphs (a) and (b) that were granted, the number of those applications that were refused and the number of applications referred to in paragraph (a) that were granted subject to terms and conditions;

(d) the number of persons identified in an authorization against whom proceedings were commenced at the instance of the Attorney General of Canada in respect of

(i) an offence specified in the authorization,

(ii) an offence other than an offence specified in the authorization but in respect of which an authorization may be given, and

(iii) an offence in respect of which an authorization may not be given;

(e) the number of persons not identified in an authorization against whom proceedings were commenced at the instance of the Attorney General of Canada in respect of

(i) an offence specified in such an authorization,

(ii) an offence other than an offence specified in such an authorization but in respect of which an authorization may be given, and

(iii) an offence other than an offence specified in such an authorization and for which no such authorization may be given,

and whose commission or alleged commission of the offence became known to a peace officer as a result of an interception of a private communication under an authorization;

(f) the average period for which authorizations were given and for which renewals thereof were granted;

(g) the number of authorizations that, by virtue of one or more renewals thereof, were valid for more than sixty days, for more than one hundred and twenty days, for more than one hundred and eighty days and for more than two hundred and forty days;

(h) the number of notifications given pursuant to section 196;

(i) the offences in respect of which authorizations were given, specifying the number of authorizations given in respect of each of those offences;

(j) a description of all classes of places specified in authorizations and the number of authorizations in which each of those classes of places was specified;

(k) a general description of the methods of interception involved in each interception under an authorization;

(l) the number of persons arrested whose identity became known to a peace officer as a result of an interception under an authorization;

(m) the number of criminal proceedings commenced at the instance of the Attorney General of Canada in which private communications obtained by interception under an authorization were adduced in evidence and the number of those proceedings that resulted in a conviction; and

(n) the number of criminal investigations in which information obtained as a result of the interception of a private communication under an authorization was used although the private communication was not adduced in evidence in criminal proceedings commenced at the instance of the Attorney General of Canada as a result of the investigations.

(2.1) Information respecting interceptions — section 184.4 — The report shall, in relation to the interceptions referred to in paragraph (1)(c), set out

(a) the number of interceptions made;

(b) the number of parties to each intercepted private communication against whom proceedings were commenced in respect of the offence that the police officer sought to prevent in intercepting the private communication or in respect of any other offence that was detected as a result of the interception;

(c) the number of persons who were not parties to an intercepted private communication but whose commission or alleged commission of an offence became known to a police officer as a result of the interception of a private communication, and against whom proceedings were commenced in respect of the offence that the police officer sought to prevent in intercepting the private communication or in respect of any other offence that was detected as a result of the interception;

(d) the number of notifications given under section 196.1;

(e) the offences in respect of which interceptions were made and any other offences for which proceedings were commenced as a result of an interception, as well as the number of interceptions made with respect to each offence;

(f) a general description of the methods of interception used for each interception;

(g) the number of persons arrested whose identity became known to a police officer as a result of an interception;

(h) the number of criminal proceedings commenced in which private communications obtained by interception were adduced in evidence and the number of those proceedings that resulted in a conviction;

(i) the number of criminal investigations in which information obtained as a result of the interception of a private communication was used even though the private communication was not adduced in evidence in criminal proceedings commenced as a result of the investigations; and

(j) the duration of each interception and the aggregate duration of all the interceptions related to the investigation of the offence that the police officer sought to prevent in intercepting the private communication.

(3) Other information — The report shall, in addition to the information referred to in subsections (2) and (2.1), set out

(a) the number of prosecutions commenced against officers or servants of Her Majesty in right of Canada or members of the Canadian Forces for offences under section 184 or 193; and

(b) a general assessment of the importance of interception of private communications for the investigation, detection, prevention and prosecution of offences in Canada.

(4) Report to be laid before Parliament — The Minister of Public Safety and Emergency Preparedness shall cause a copy of each report prepared by him under subsection (1) to be laid before Parliament forthwith on completion thereof, or if Parliament is not then sitting, on any of the first fifteen days next thereafter that Parliament is sitting.

(5) Report by Attorneys General — The Attorney General of each province shall, as soon as possible after the end of each year, prepare and publish or otherwise make available to the public a report relating to

(a) authorizations for which the Attorney General and agents specially designated in writing by the Attorney General for the purposes of section 185 applied and to the interceptions made under those authorizations in the immediately preceding year;

(b) authorizations given under section 188 for which peace officers specially designated by the Attorney General for the purposes of that section applied and to the interceptions made under those authorizations in the immediately preceding year; and

(c) interceptions made under section 184.4 in the immediately preceding year, if the interceptions relate to an offence not referred to in paragraph (1)(c).

The report must set out, with any modifications that the circumstances require, the information described in subsections (2) to (3).

R.S.C. 1985, c. 27 (1st Supp.), s. 27; 2005, c. 10, s. 34(1)(f)(ix), (x); 2013, c. 8, s. 5; 2015, c. 20, s. 20

196. (1) Written notification to be given — The Attorney General of the province in which an application under subsection 185(1) was made or the Minister of Public Safety and Emergency Preparedness if the application was made by or on behalf of that Minister shall, within 90 days after the period for which the authorization was given or renewed or within such other period as is fixed pursuant to subsection 185(3) or subsection (3) of this section, notify in writing the person who was the object of the interception pursuant to the authorization and shall, in a manner prescribed by regulations made by the Governor in Council, certify to the court that gave the authorization that the person has been so notified.

(2) Extension of period for notification — The running of the 90 days referred to in subsection (1), or of any other period fixed pursuant to subsection 185(3) or subsection (3) of this section, is suspended until any application made by the Attorney General or the Minister to a judge of a superior court of criminal jurisdiction or a judge as defined in section 552 for an extension or a subsequent extension of the period for which the authorization was given or renewed has been heard and disposed of.

(3) Where extension to be granted — Where the judge to whom an application referred to in subsection (2) is made, on the basis of an affidavit submitted in support of the application, is satisfied that

(a) the investigation of the offence to which the authorization relates, or

(b) a subsequent investigation of an offence listed in section 183 commenced as a result of information obtained from the investigation referred to in paragraph (*a*),

is continuing and is of the opinion that the interests of justice warrant the granting of the application, the judge shall grant an extension, or a subsequent extension, of the period, each extension not to exceed three years.

(4) Application to be accompanied by affidavit — An application pursuant to subsection (2) shall be accompanied by an affidavit deposing to

(a) the facts known or believed by the deponent and relied on to justify the belief that an extension should be granted; and

(b) the number of instances, if any, on which an application has, to the knowledge or belief of the deponent, been made under that subsection in relation to the particular authorization and on which the application was withdrawn or the application was not granted, the date on which each application was made and the judge to whom each application was made.

(5) Exception for criminal organizations and terrorist groups — Notwithstanding subsections (3) and 185(3), where the judge to whom an application referred to in subsection (2) or 185(2) is made, on the basis of an affidavit submitted in support of the application, is satisfied that the investigation is in relation to

(a) an offence under section 467.11, 467.111, 467.12 or 467.13,

(b) an offence committed for the benefit of, at the direction of or in association with a criminal organization, or

(c) a terrorism offence,

and is of the opinion that the interests of justice warrant the granting of the application, the judge shall grant an extension, or a subsequent extension, of the period, but no extension may exceed three years.

R.S.C. 1985, c. 27 (1st Supp.), s. 28; 1993, c. 40, s. 14; 1997, c. 23, s. 7; 2001, c. 32, s. 8; 2001, c. 41, ss. 8, 133(10); 2005, c. 10, s. 25; 2014, c. 17, s. 6

196.1 (1) Written notice — interception in accordance with section 184.4 — Subject to subsections (3) and (5), the Attorney General of the province in which a police officer intercepts a private communication under section 184.4 or, if the interception relates to an offence for which proceedings may be commenced by the Attorney General of Canada, the Minister of Public Safety and Emergency Preparedness shall give notice in writing of the interception to any person who was the object of the interception within 90 days after the day on which it occurred.

(2) Extension of period for notification — The running of the 90-day period or of any extension granted under subsection (3) or (5) is suspended until any application made by the Attorney General of the province or the Minister to a judge of a superior court of criminal jurisdiction or a judge as defined in section 552 for an extension or a subsequent extension of the period has been heard and disposed of.

(3) Where extension to be granted — The judge to whom an application under subsection (2) is made shall grant an extension or a subsequent extension of the 90-day period — each extension not to exceed three years — if the judge is of the opinion that the interests of justice warrant granting the application and is satisfied, on the basis of an affidavit submitted in support of the application, that one of the following investigations is continuing:

(a) the investigation of the offence to which the interception relates; or

(b) a subsequent investigation of an offence commenced as a result of information obtained from the investigation referred to in paragraph (a).

(4) Application to be accompanied by affidavit — An application shall be accompanied by an affidavit deposing to

(a) the facts known or believed by the deponent and relied on to justify the belief that an extension should be granted; and

(b) the number of instances, if any, on which an application has, to the knowledge or belief of the deponent, been made under subsection (2) in relation to the particular interception and on which the application was withdrawn or the application was not granted, the date on which each application was made and the judge to whom each application was made.

(5) Exception — criminal organization or terrorism offence — Despite subsection (3), the judge to whom an application under subsection (2) is made shall grant an extension or a subsequent extension of the 90-day period — each extension not to exceed three years — if the judge is of the opinion that the interests of justice warrant granting the application and is satisfied, on the basis of an affidavit submitted in support of the application, that the interception of the communication relates to an investigation of

(a) an offence under section 467.11, 467.12 or 467.13;

(b) an offence committed for the benefit of, at the direction of or in association with a criminal organization; or

(c) a terrorism offence.

2013, c. 8, s. 6

PART VII — DISORDERLY HOUSES, GAMING AND BETTING (SS. 197–213)

Interpretation

197. (1) Definitions — In this Part

"bet" means a bet that is placed on any contingency or event that is to take place in or out of Canada, and without restricting the generality of the foregoing, includes a bet that is placed on any contingency relating to a horse-race, fight, match or sporting event that is to take place in or out of Canada;

"common bawdy-house" [Repealed 2019, c. 25, s. 69.1(1).]

"common betting house" means a place that is opened, kept or used for the purpose of

(a) enabling, encouraging or assisting persons who resort thereto to bet between themselves or with the keeper, or

(b) enabling any person to receive, record, register, transmit or pay bets or to announce the results of betting;

"common gaming house" means a place that is

(a) kept for gain to which persons resort for the purpose of playing games, or

(b) kept or used for the purpose of playing games

(i) in which a bank is kept by one or more but not all of the players,

(ii) in which all or any portion of the bets on or proceeds from a game is paid, directly or indirectly, to the keeper of the place,

(iii) in which, directly or indirectly, a fee is charged to or paid by the players for the privilege of playing or participating in a game or using gaming equipment, or

(iv) in which the chances of winning are not equally favourable to all persons who play the game, including the person, if any, who conducts the game;

"disorderly house" means a common betting house or a common gaming house;

"game" means a game of chance or mixed chance and skill;

"gaming equipment" means anything that is or may be used for the purpose of playing games or for betting;

"keeper" includes a person who

(a) is an owner or occupier of a place,

(b) assists or acts on behalf of an owner or occupier of a place,

(c) appears to be, or to assist or act on behalf of an owner or occupier of a place,

(d) has the care or management of a place, or

(e) uses a place permanently or temporarily, with or without the consent of the owner or occupier;

"place" includes any place, whether or not

(a) it is covered or enclosed,

(b) it is used permanently or temporarily, or

(c) any person has an exclusive right of user with respect to it;

"prostitute" [Repealed 2014, c. 25, s. 12(1).]

"public place" includes any place to which the public have access as of right or by invitation, express or implied.

(2) Exception — A place is not a common gaming house within the meaning of paragraph (*a*) or subparagraph (*b*)(ii) or (iii) of the definition "common gaming house" in subsection (1) while it is occupied and used by an incorporated genuine social club or branch thereof, if

(a) the whole or any portion of the bets on or proceeds from games played therein is not directly or indirectly paid to the keeper thereof; and

(b) no fee is charged to persons for the right or privilege of participating in the games played therein other than under the authority of and in accordance with the terms of a licence issued by the Attorney General of the province in which the place is situated or by such other person or authority in the province as may be specified by the Attorney General thereof.

(3) Onus — The onus of proving that, by virtue of subsection (2), a place is not a common gaming house is on the accused.

(4) Effect when game partly played on premises — A place may be a common gaming house notwithstanding that

(a) it is used for the purpose of playing part of a game and another part of the game is played elsewhere;

(b) the stake that is played for is in some other place, or

(c) it is used on only one occasion in the manner described in paragraph (*b*) of the definition "common gaming house" in subsection (1), if the keeper or any person acting on behalf of or in concert with the keeper has used another place on another occasion in the manner described in that paragraph.

R.S.C. 1985, c. 27 (1st Supp.), s. 29; 2014, c. 25, s. 12; 2019, c. 25, s. 69.1

Presumptions

198. [Repealed 2018, c. 29, s. 16.]

Search

199. (1) Warrant to search — A justice who is satisfied by information on oath that there are reasonable grounds to believe that an offence under section 201, 202, 203, 206 or 207 is being committed at any place within the jurisdiction of the justice may issue a warrant authorizing a peace officer to enter and search the place by day or night and seize anything found in that place that may be evidence that an offence under section 201, 202, 203, 206 or 207, as the case may be, is being committed at that place, and to take into custody all persons who are found in or at that place and requiring those persons and things to be brought before that justice or before another justice having jurisdiction, to be dealt with according to law.

(2) Search without warrant, seizure and arrest — A peace officer may, whether or not he is acting under a warrant issued pursuant to this section, take into custody any person whom he finds keeping a common gaming house and any person whom he finds therein, and may seize anything that may be evidence that such an offence is being committed and shall bring those persons and things before a justice having jurisdiction, to be dealt with according to law.

(3) Disposal of property seized — Except where otherwise expressly provided by law, a court, judge, justice or provincial court judge before whom anything that is seized under this section is brought may declare that the thing is forfeited, in which case it shall be disposed of or dealt with as the Attorney General may direct if no person shows sufficient cause why it should not be forfeited.

(4) When declaration or direction may be made — No declaration or direction shall be made pursuant to subsection (3) in respect of anything seized under this section until

(a) it is no longer required as evidence in any proceedings that are instituted pursuant to the seizure; or

(b) the expiration of thirty days from the time of seizure where it is not required as evidence in any proceedings.

(5) Conversion into money — The Attorney General may, for the purpose of converting anything forfeited under this section into money, deal with it in all respects as if he were the owner thereof.

(6) Telephones exempt from seizure — Nothing in this section or in section 489 authorizes the seizure, forfeiture or destruction of telephone, telegraph or other communication facilities or equipment that may be evidence of or that may have been used in the commission of an offence under section 201, 202, 203, 206 or 207 and that is owned by a person engaged in providing telephone, telegraph or other communication service to the public or forming part of the telephone, telegraph or other communication service or system of that person.

(7) Exception — Subsection (6) does not apply to prohibit the seizure, for use as evidence, of any facility or equipment described in that subsection that is designed or adapted to record a communication.

R.S.C. 1985, c. 27 (1st Supp.), s. 203; 1994, c. 44, s. 10; 2019, c. 25, s. 69.2

Obstruction

200. [Repealed R.S.C. 1985, c. 27 (1st Supp.), s. 30.]

Gaming and Betting

201. (1) Keeping gaming or betting house — Every person who keeps a common gaming house or common betting house is guilty of

(a) an indictable offence and liable to imprisonment for a term of not more than two years; or

(b) an offence punishable on summary conviction.

(2) Person found in or owner permitting use — Every one who

(a) is found, without lawful excuse, in a common gaming house or common betting house, or

(b) as owner, landlord, lessor, tenant, occupier or agent, knowingly permits a place to be let or used for the purposes of a common gaming house or common betting house,

is guilty of an offence punishable on summary conviction.

2019, c. 25, s. 70

202. (1) Betting, pool-selling, book-making, etc. — Every one commits an offence who

(a) uses or knowingly allows a place under his control to be used for the purposes of recording or registering bets or selling a pool;

(b) imports, makes, buys, sells, rents, leases, hires or keeps, exhibits, employs or knowingly allows to be kept, exhibited or employed in any place under his control any device or apparatus for the purpose of recording or registering bets or selling a pool, or any machine or device for gambling or betting;

(c) has under his control any money or other property relating to a transaction that is an offence under this section;

(d) records or registers bets or sells a pool;

(e) engages in book-making or pool-selling, or in the business or occupation of betting, or makes any agreement for the purchase or sale of betting or gaming privileges, or for the purchase or sale of information that is intended to assist in book-making, pool-selling or betting;

(f) prints, provides or offers to print or provide information intended for use in connection with book-making, pool-selling or betting on any horse-race, fight, game or sport, whether or not it takes place in or outside Canada or has or has not taken place;

(g) imports or brings into Canada any information or writing that is intended or is likely to promote or be of use in gambling, book-making, pool-selling or betting on a horse-race, fight, game or sport, and where this paragraph applies it is immaterial

(i) whether the information is published before, during or after the race, fight, game or sport, or

(ii) whether the race, fight, game or sport takes place in Canada or elsewhere,

but this paragraph does not apply to a newspaper, magazine or other periodical published in good faith primarily for a purpose other than the publication of such information;

(h) advertises, prints, publishes, exhibits, posts up, or otherwise gives notice of any offer, invitation or inducement to bet on, to guess or to foretell the results of a contest, or a result of or contingency relating to any contest;

(i) wilfully and knowingly sends, transmits, delivers or receives any message that conveys any information relating to book-making, pool-selling, betting or wagering, or that is intended to assist in book-making, pool-selling, betting or wagering; or

(j) aids or assists in any manner in anything that is an offence under this section.

(2) Punishment — Every one who commits an offence under this section is guilty of an indictable offence and liable

(a) for a first offence, to imprisonment for not more than two years;

(b) for a second offence, to imprisonment for not more than two years and not less than fourteen days; and

(c) for each subsequent offence, to imprisonment for not more than two years and not less than three months.

2008, c. 18, s. 5

203. Placing bets on behalf of others — Every one who

(a) places or offers or agrees to place a bet on behalf of another person for a consideration paid or to be paid by or on behalf of that other person,

(b) engages in the business or practice of placing or agreeing to place bets on behalf of other persons, whether for a consideration or otherwise, or

(c) holds himself out or allows himself to be held out as engaging in the business or practice of placing or agreeing to place bets on behalf of other persons, whether for a consideration or otherwise,

is guilty of an indictable offence and liable

(d) for a first offence, to imprisonment for not more than two years,

(e) for a second offence, to imprisonment for not more than two years and not less than fourteen days, and

(f) for each subsequent offence, to imprisonment for not more than two years and not less than three months.

204. (1) Exemption — Sections 201 and 202 do not apply to

(a) any person or association by reason of his or their becoming the custodian or depository of any money, property or valuable thing staked, to be paid to

(i) the winner of a lawful race, sport, game or exercise,

(ii) the owner of a horse engaged in a lawful race, or

(iii) the winner of any bets between not more than ten individuals;

(b) a private bet between individuals not engaged in any way in the business of betting;

(c) bets made or records of bets made through the agency of a pari-mutuel system on running, trotting or pacing horse-races if

(i) the bets or records of bets are made on the race-course of an association in respect of races conducted at that race-course or another race-course in or out of Canada, and, in the case of a race conducted on a race-course situated outside Canada, the governing body that regulates the race has been certified as acceptable by the Minister of Agriculture and Agri-Food or a person designated by that Minister pursuant to subsection (8.1) and that Minister or person has permitted pari-mutuel betting in Canada on the race pursuant to that subsection, and

(ii) the provisions of this section and the regulations are complied with.

(1.1) Exception — For greater certainty, a person may, in accordance with the regulations, do anything described in section 201 or 202, if the person does it for the purposes of legal pari-mutuel betting.

(2) Presumption — For the purposes of paragraph (1)(c), bets made, in accordance with the regulations, in a betting theatre referred to in paragraph (8)(e), or by any means of telecommunication to the race-course of an association or to such a betting theatre, are deemed to be made on the race-course of the association.

(3) Operation of pari-mutuel system — No person or association shall use a pari-mutuel system of betting in respect of a horse-race unless the system has been approved by and its operation is carried on under the supervision of an officer appointed by the Minister of Agriculture and Agri-Food.

(4) Supervision of pari-mutuel system — Every person or association operating a pari-mutuel system of betting in accordance with this section in respect of a horse-race, whether or not the person or association is conducting the race-meeting at which the race is run, shall pay to the Receiver General in respect of each individual pool of the race and each individual feature pool one-half of one per cent, or such greater fraction not exceeding one per cent as may be fixed by the Governor in Council, of the total amount of money that is bet through the agency of the pari-mutuel system of betting.

(5) Percentage that may be deducted and retained — Where any person or association becomes a custodian or depository of any money, bet or stakes under a pari-mutuel system in respect of a horse-race, that person or association shall not deduct or retain any amount from the total amount of money, bets or stakes unless it does so pursuant to subsection (6).

(6) Idem — An association operating a pari-mutuel system of betting in accordance with this section in respect of a horse-race, or any other association or person acting on its behalf, may deduct and retain from the total amount of money that is bet through the agency of the pari-mutuel system, in respect of each individual pool of each race or each individual feature pool, a percentage not exceeding the percentage prescribed by the regulations plus any odd cents over any multiple of five cents in the amount calculated in accordance with the regulations to be payable in respect of each dollar bet.

(7) Stopping of betting — Where an officer appointed by the Minister of Agriculture and Agri-Food is not satisfied that the provisions of this section and the regulations are being carried out in good faith by any person or association in relation to a race meeting, he may, at any time, order any betting in relation to the race meeting to be stopped for any period that he considers proper.

(8) Regulations — The Minister of Agriculture and Agri-Food may make regulations

(a) prescribing the maximum number of races for each race-course on which a race meeting is conducted, in respect of which a pari-mutuel system of betting may be used for the race meeting or on any one calendar day during the race meeting, and the circumstances in which the Minister of Agriculture and Agri-Food or a person designated by him for that purpose may approve of the use of that system in respect of additional races on any race-course for a particular race meeting or on a particular day during the race meeting;

(b) prohibiting any person or association from using a pari-mutuel system of betting for any race-course on which a race meeting is conducted in respect of more than the maximum number of races prescribed pursuant to paragraph (*a*) and the additional races, if any, in respect of which the use of a pari-mutuel system of betting has been approved pursuant to that paragraph;

(c) prescribing the maximum percentage that may be deducted and retained pursuant to subsection (6) by or on behalf of a person or association operating a pari-mutuel system of betting in respect of a horse-race in accordance with this section and providing for the determination of the percentage that each such person or association may deduct and retain;

(d) respecting pari-mutuel betting in Canada on horse-races conducted on a race-course situated outside Canada; and

(e) authorizing pari-mutuel betting and governing the conditions for pari-mutuel betting, including the granting of licences therefor, that is conducted by an association in a betting theatre owned or leased by the association in a province in which the Lieutenant Governor in Council, or such other person or authority in the province as may be specified by the Lieutenant Governor in Council thereof, has issued a licence to that association for the betting theatre.

(8.1) Approvals — The Minister of Agriculture and Agri-Food or a person designated by that Minister may, with respect to a horse-race conducted on a race-course situated outside Canada,

(a) certify as acceptable, for the purposes of this section, the governing body that regulates the race; and

(b) permit pari-mutuel betting in Canada on the race.

(9) Regulations — The Minister of Agriculture and Agri-Food may make regulations respecting

(a) the supervision and operation of pari-mutuel systems related to race meetings, and the fixing of the dates on which and the places at which an association may conduct such meetings;

(b) the method of calculating the amount payable in respect of each dollar bet;

(c) the conduct of race-meetings in relation to the supervision and operation of pari-mutuel systems, including photo-finishes, video patrol and the testing of bodily substances taken from horses entered in a race at such meetings, including, in the case of a horse that dies while engaged in racing or immediately before or after the race, the testing of any tissue taken from its body;

(d) the prohibition, restriction or regulation of

(i) the possession of drugs or medicaments or of equipment used in the administering of drugs or medicaments at or near race-courses, or

(ii) the administering of drugs or medicaments to horses participating in races run at a race meeting during which a pari-mutuel system of betting is used; and

(e) the provision, equipment and maintenance of accommodation, services or other facilities for the proper supervision and operation of pari-mutuel systems related to race meetings, by associations conducting those meetings or by other associations.

(9.1) 900 metre zone — For the purposes of this section, the Minister of Agriculture and Agri-Food may designate, with respect to any race-course, a zone that shall be deemed to be part of the race-course, if

(a) the zone is immediately adjacent to the race-course;

(b) the farthest point of that zone is no more than 900 metres from the nearest point on the race track of the race-course; and

(c) all real property situated in that zone is owned or leased by the person or association that owns or leases the race-course.

(10) Contravention — Every person who contravenes or fails to comply with any of the provisions of this section or of any regulations made under this section is guilty of

(a) an indictable offence and is liable to imprisonment for a term not exceeding two years, or

(b) an offence punishable on summary conviction.

(11) Definition of "association" — For the purposes of this section **"association"** means an association incorporated by or pursuant to an Act of the Parliament or of the legislature of a province that owns or leases a race-course and conducts horse-races in the ordinary course of its business and, to the extent that the applicable legislation requires that the purposes of the association be expressly stated in its constating instrument, having as one of its purposes the conduct of horse-races.

R.S.C. 1985, c. 47 (1st Supp.), s. 1; 1989, c. 2, s. 1; 1994, c. 38, ss. 14, 25(1)(g); 2008, c. 18, s. 6

205. [Repealed R.S.C. 1985, c. 52 (1st Supp.), s. 1.]

206. (1) Offence in relation to lotteries and games of chance — Every person is guilty of an indictable offence and liable to imprisonment for a term of not more than two years or is guilty of an offence punishable on summary conviction who

(a) makes, prints, advertises or publishes, or causes or procures to be made, printed, advertised or published, any proposal, scheme or plan for advancing, lending, giving, selling or in any way disposing of any property by lots, cards, tickets or any mode of chance whatever;

(b) sells, barters, exchanges or otherwise disposes of, or causes or procures, or aids or assists in, the sale, barter, exchange or other disposal of, or offers for sale, barter or exchange, any lot, card, ticket or other means or device for advancing, lending, giving, selling or otherwise disposing of any property by lots, tickets or any mode of chance whatever;

(c) knowingly sends, transmits, mails, ships, delivers or allows to be sent, transmitted, mailed, shipped or delivered, or knowingly accepts for carriage or transport or conveys any article that is used or intended for use in carrying out any device, proposal, scheme or plan for advancing, lending, giving, selling or otherwise disposing of any property by any mode of chance whatever;

(d) conducts or manages any scheme, contrivance or operation of any kind for the purpose of determining who, or the holders of what lots, tickets, numbers or chances, are the winners of any property so proposed to be advanced, lent, given, sold or disposed of;

(e) conducts, manages or is a party to any scheme, contrivance or operation of any kind by which any person, on payment of any sum of money, or the giving of any valuable security, or by obligating himself to pay any sum of money or give any valuable security, shall become entitled under the scheme, contrivance or operation to receive from the person conducting or managing the scheme, contrivance or operation, or any other person, a larger sum of money or amount of valuable security than the sum or amount paid or given, or to be paid or given, by reason of the fact that other persons have paid or given, or obligated themselves to pay or give any sum of money or valuable security under the scheme, contrivance or operation;

(f) disposes of any goods, wares or merchandise by any game of chance or any game of mixed chance and skill in which the contestant or competitor pays money or other valuable consideration;

(g) induces any person to stake or hazard any money or other valuable property or thing on the result of any dice game, three-card monte, punch board, coin table or on the operation of a wheel of fortune;

(h) for valuable consideration carries on or plays or offers to carry on or to play, or employs any person to carry on or play in a public place or a place to which the public have access, the game of three-card monte;

(i) receives bets of any kind on the outcome of a game of three-card monte; or

(j) being the owner of a place, permits any person to play the game of three-card monte therein.

(2) "three-card monte" — In this section **"three-card monte"** means the game commonly known as three-card monte and includes any other game that is similar to it, whether or not the game is played with cards and notwithstanding the number of cards or other things that are used for the purpose of playing.

(3) Exemption for fairs — Paragraphs (1)(*f*) and (*g*), in so far as they do not relate to a dice game, three-card monte, punch board or coin table, do not apply to the board of an annual fair or exhibition, or to any operator of a concession leased by that board within its own grounds and operated during the fair or exhibition on those grounds.

(3.1) Definition of "fair or exhibition" — For the purposes of this section, **"fair or exhibition"** means an event where agricultural or fishing products are presented or where activities relating to agriculture or fishing take place.

(4) Offence — Every one who buys, takes or receives a lot, ticket or other device mentioned in subsection (1) is guilty of an offence punishable on summary conviction.

(5) Lottery sale void — Every sale, loan, gift, barter or exchange of any property, by any lottery, ticket, card or other mode of chance depending on or to be determined by chance or lot, is void, and all property sold, lent, given, bartered or exchanged is forfeited to Her Majesty.

(6) *Bona fide* exception — Subsection (5) does not affect any right or title to property acquired by any *bona fide* purchaser for valuable consideration without notice.

(7) Foreign lottery included — This section applies to the printing or publishing, or causing to be printed or published, of any advertisement, scheme, proposal or plan of any foreign lottery, and the sale or offer for sale of any ticket, chance or share, in any such lottery, or the advertisement for sale of such ticket, chance or share, and the conducting or managing of any such scheme, contrivance or operation for determining the winners in any such lottery.

(8) Saving — This section does not apply to

(a) the division by lot or chance of any property by joint tenants or tenants in common, or persons having joint interests in any such property; or

(b) [Repealed 1999, c. 28, s. 156.]

(c) bonds, debentures, debenture stock or other securities recallable by drawing of lots and redeemable with interest and providing for payment of premiums on redemption or otherwise.

R.S.C. 1985, c. 52 (1st Supp.), s. 2; 1999, c. 28, s. 156; 2019, c. 25, s. 71

207. (1) Permitted lotteries — Notwithstanding any of the provisions of this Part relating to gaming and betting, it is lawful

(a) for the government of a province, either alone or in conjunction with the government of another province, to conduct and manage a lottery scheme in that province, or in that and the other province, in accordance with any law enacted by the legislature of that province;

(b) for a charitable or religious organization, pursuant to a licence issued by the Lieutenant Governor in Council of a province or by such other person or authority in the province as may be specified by the Lieutenant Governor in Council thereof, to conduct and manage a lottery scheme in that province if the proceeds from the lottery scheme are used for a charitable or religious object or purpose;

(c) for the board of a fair or of an exhibition or an operator of a concession leased by that board, to conduct and manage a lottery scheme in a province where the Lieutenant Governor in Council of the province or such other person or authority in the province as may be specified by the Lieutenant Governor in Council thereof has

(i) designated that fair or exhibition as a fair or exhibition where a lottery scheme may be conducted and managed, and

(ii) issued a licence for the conduct and management of a lottery scheme to that board or operator;

(d) for any person, pursuant to a licence issued by the Lieutenant Governor in Council of a province or by such other person or authority in the province as may be specified by the Lieutenant Governor in Council thereof, to conduct and manage a lottery scheme at a public place of amusement in that province if

(i) the amount or value of each prize awarded does not exceed five hundred dollars, and

(ii) the money or other valuable consideration paid to secure a chance to win a prize does not exceed two dollars;

(e) for the government of a province to agree with the government of another province that lots, cards or tickets in relation to a lottery scheme that is by any of paragraphs *(a)* to *(d)* authorized to be conducted and managed in that other province may be sold in the province;

(f) for any person, pursuant to a licence issued by the Lieutenant Governor in Council of a province or such other person or authority in the province as may be designated by the Lieutenant Governor in Council thereof, to conduct and manage in the province a lottery scheme that is authorized to be conducted and managed in one or more other provinces where the authority by which the lottery scheme was first authorized to be conducted and managed consents thereto;

(g) for any person, for the purpose of a lottery scheme that is lawful in a province under any of paragraphs *(a)* to *(f)*, to do anything in the province, in accordance with the applicable law or licence, that is required for the conduct, management or operation of the lottery scheme or for the person to participate in the scheme; and

(h) for any person to make or print anywhere in Canada or to cause to be made or printed anywhere in Canada anything relating to gaming and betting that is to be used in a place where it is or would, if certain conditions provided by law are met, be lawful to use such a thing, or to send, transmit, mail, ship, deliver or allow to be sent, transmitted, mailed, shipped or delivered or to accept for carriage or transport or convey any such thing where the destination thereof is such a place.

(2) Terms and conditions of licence — Subject to this Act, a licence issued by or under the authority of the Lieutenant Governor in Council of a province as described in paragraph (1)(*b*), (*c*), (*d*), or (*f*) may contain such terms and conditions relating to the conduct, management and operation of or participation in the lottery scheme to which the licence relates as the Lieutenant Governor in Council of that province, the person or authority in the province designated by the Lieutenant Governor in Council thereof or any law enacted by the legislature of that province may prescribe.

(3) Offence — Every one who, for the purposes of a lottery scheme, does anything that is not authorized by or pursuant to a provision of this section

(a) in the case of the conduct, management or operation of that lottery scheme

(i) is guilty of an indictable offence and liable to imprisonment for a term not exceeding two years, or

(ii) is guilty of an offence punishable on summary conviction; or

(b) in the case of participating in that lottery scheme, is guilty of an offence punishable on summary conviction.

(4) Definition of "lottery scheme" — In this section, **"lottery scheme"** means a game or any proposal, scheme, plan, means, device, contrivance or operation described in any of paragraphs 206(1)(*a*) to (*g*), whether or not it involves betting, pool selling or a pool system of betting other than

(a) three-card monte, punch board or coin table;

(b) bookmaking, pool selling or the making or recording of bets, including bets made through the agency of a pool or pari-mutuel system, on any race or fight, or on a single sport event or athletic contest; or

(c) for the purposes of paragraphs (1)(b) to (f), a game or proposal, scheme, plan, means, device, contrivance or operation described in any of paragraphs 206(1)(a) to (g) that is operated on or through a computer, video device, slot machine or a dice game.

(4.01) Definition of "slot machine" — In paragraph 4(c), **"slot machine"** means any automatic machine or slot machine, other than any automatic machine or slot machine that dispenses as prizes only one or more free games on that machine, that

(a) is used or intended to be used for any purpose other than selling merchandise or services; or

(b) is used or intended to be used for the purpose of selling merchandise or services if

(i) the result of one of any number of operations of the machine is a matter of chance or uncertainty to the operator,

(ii) as a result of a given number of successive operations by the operator, the machine produces different results, or

(iii) on any operation of the machine, it discharges or emits a slug or token.

(4.1) Exception — charitable or religious organization — The use of a computer for the sale of a ticket, selection of a winner or the distribution of a prize in a raffle, including a 50/50 draw, is excluded from paragraph (4)(c) in so far as the raffle is authorized under paragraph (1)(b) and the proceeds are used for a charitable or religious object or purpose.

(5) Exception re: pari-mutuel betting — For greater certainty, nothing in this section shall be construed as authorizing the making or recording of bets on horse-races through the agency of a pari-mutuel system other than in accordance with section 204.

R.S.C. 1985, c. 27 (1st Supp.), s. 31; R.S.C. 1985, c. 52 (1st Supp.), s. 3; 1999, c. 5, s. 6; 2014, c. 39, s. 171; 2018, c. 29, s. 17

207.1 (1) Exemption — lottery scheme on an international cruise ship — Despite any of the provisions of this Part relating to gaming and betting, it is lawful for the owner or operator of an international cruise ship, or their agent, to conduct, manage or operate and for any person to participate in a lottery scheme during a voyage on an international cruise ship when all of the following conditions are satisfied:

(a) all the people participating in the lottery scheme are located on the ship;

(b) the lottery scheme is not linked, by any means of communication, with any lottery scheme, betting, pool selling or pool system of betting located off the ship;

(c) the lottery scheme is not operated within five nautical miles of a Canadian port at which the ship calls or is scheduled to call; and

(d) the ship is registered

(i) in Canada and its entire voyage is scheduled to be outside Canada, or

(ii) anywhere, including Canada, and its voyage includes some scheduled voyaging within Canada and the voyage

(A) is of at least forty-eight hours duration and includes some voyaging in international waters and at least one non-Canadian port of call including the port at which the voyage begins or ends, and

(B) is not scheduled to disembark any passengers at a Canadian port who have embarked at another Canadian port, without calling on at least one non-Canadian port between the two Canadian ports.

(2) **Paragraph 207(1)(h) and subsection 207(5) apply** — For greater certainty, paragraph 207(1)(h) and subsection 207(5) apply for the purposes of this section.

(3) **Offence** — Every one who, for the purpose of a lottery scheme, does anything that is not authorized by this section

(a) in the case of the conduct, management or operation of the lottery scheme,

(i) is guilty of an indictable offence and liable to imprisonment for a term of not more than two years, or

(ii) is guilty of an offence punishable on summary conviction; and

(b) in the case of participating in the lottery scheme, is guilty of an offence punishable on summary conviction.

(4) **Definitions** — The definitions in this subsection apply in this section

"international cruise ship" means a passenger ship that is suitable for continuous ocean voyages of at least forty-eight hours duration, but does not include such a ship that is used or fitted for the primary purpose of transporting cargo or vehicles.

"lottery scheme" means a game or any proposal, scheme, plan, means, device, contrivance or operation described in any of paragraphs 206(1)(a) to (g), whether or not it involves betting, pool selling or a pool system of betting. It does not include

(a) three-card monte, punch board or coin table; or

(b) bookmaking, pool selling or the making or recording of bets, including bets made through the agency of a pool or pari-mutuel system, on any race or fight, or on a single sporting event or athletic contest.

1999, c. 5, s. 7

208. [Repealed R.S.C. 1985, c. 27 (1st Supp.), s. 32.]

209. Cheating at play — Every person who, with intent to defraud any person, cheats while playing a game or in holding the stakes for a game or in betting is guilty of

(a) an indictable offence and liable to imprisonment for a term of not more than two years; or

(b) an offence punishable on summary conviction.

2019, c. 25, s. 72

Heading and ss. 210 and 211. [Repealed 2019, c. 25, s. 73.]

Heading and s. 212. [Repealed 2014, c. 25, s. 13.]

Offences in Relation to Offering, Providing or Obtaining Sexual Services for Consideration

[Heading amended 2014, c. 25, s. 14.]

213. (1) Stopping or impeding traffic — Everyone is guilty of an offence punishable on summary conviction who, in a public place or in any place open to public view, for the purpose of offering, providing or obtaining sexual services for consideration,

(a) stops or attempts to stop any motor vehicle, or

(b) impedes the free flow of pedestrian or vehicular traffic or ingress to or egress from premises adjacent to that place.

(c) [Repealed 2014, c. 25, s. 15(2).]

(1.1) Communicating to provide sexual services for consideration — Everyone is guilty of an offence punishable on summary conviction who communicates with any person — for the purpose of offering or providing sexual services for consideration — in a public place, or in any place open to public view, that is or is next to a school ground, playground or daycare centre.

(2) Definition of "public place" — In this section, **"public place"** includes any place to which the public have access as of right or by invitation, express or implied, and any motor vehicle located in a public place or in any place open to public view.

R.S.C. 1985, c. 51 (1st Supp.), s. 1; 2014, c. 25, s. 15

PART VIII — OFFENCES AGAINST THE PERSON AND REPUTATION (SS. 214–320.1)

Interpretation

214. Definitions — In this Part,

"abandon" or **"expose"** includes

(a) a wilful omission to take charge of a child by a person who is under a legal duty to do so, and

(b) dealing with a child in a manner that is likely to leave that child exposed to risk without protection;

"aircraft" [Repealed 2018, c. 21, s. 13.]

"form of marriage" includes a ceremony of marriage that is recognized as valid

(a) by the law of the place where it was celebrated, or

(b) by the law of the place where an accused is tried, notwithstanding that it is not recognized as valid by the law of the place where it was celebrated;

"guardian" includes a person who has in law or in fact the custody or control of a child.

"operate" [Repealed 2018, c. 21, s. 13.]

"vessel" [Repealed 2018, c. 21, s. 13.]

R.S.C. 1985, c. 27 (1st Supp.), s. 33; R.S.C. 1985, c. 32 (4th Supp.), s. 56; 2002, c. 13, s. 9; 2018, c. 21, s. 13

Duties Tending to Preservation of Life

215. (1) Duty of persons to provide necessaries — Every one is under a legal duty

(a) as a parent, foster parent, guardian or head of a family, to provide necessaries of life for a child under the age of sixteen years;

(b) to provide necessaries of life to their spouse or common-law partner; and

(c) to provide necessaries of life to a person under his charge if that person

(i) is unable, by reason of detention, age, illness, mental disorder or other cause, to withdraw himself from that charge, and

(ii) is unable to provide himself with necessaries of life.

(2) Offence — Every person commits an offence who, being under a legal duty within the meaning of subsection (1), fails without lawful excuse to perform that duty, if

(a) with respect to a duty imposed by paragraph (l)(a) or (b),

(i) the person to whom the duty is owed is in destitute or necessitous circumstances, or

(ii) the failure to perform the duty endangers the life of the person to whom the duty is owed, or causes or is likely to cause the health of that person to be endangered permanently; or

(b) with respect to a duty imposed by paragraph (1)(c), the failure to perform the duty endangers the life of the person to whom the duty is owed or causes or is likely to cause the health of that person to be injured permanently.

(3) Punishment — Every one who commits an offence under subsection (2)

(a) is guilty of an indictable offence and liable to imprisonment for a term not exceeding five years; or

(b) is guilty of an offence punishable on summary conviction.

(4) Presumptions — For the purpose of proceedings under this section,

(a) [Repealed 2000, c. 12, s. 93(2).]

(b) evidence that a person has in any way recognized a child as being his child is, in the absence of any evidence to the contrary, proof that the child is his child;

(c) evidence that a person has failed for a period of one month to make provision for the maintenance of any child of theirs under the age of sixteen years is, in the absence of any evidence to the contrary, proof that the person has failed without lawful excuse to provide necessaries of life for the child; and

(d) the fact that a spouse or common-law partner or child is receiving or has received necessaries of life from another person who is not under a legal duty to provide them is not a defence.

1991, c. 43, s. 9 (Sched., item 2); 2000, c. 12, ss. 93, 95(a); 2005, c. 32, s. 11; 2018, c. 29, s. 18; 2019, c. 25, s. 74

216. Duty of persons undertaking acts dangerous to life — Every one who undertakes to administer surgical or medical treatment to another person or to do any other lawful act that may endanger the life of another person is, except in cases of necessity, under a legal duty to have and to use reasonable knowledge, skill and care in so doing.

217. Duty of persons undertaking acts — Every one who undertakes to do an act is under a legal duty to do it if an omission to do the act is or may be dangerous to life.

217.1 Duty of persons directing work — Every one who undertakes, or has the authority, to direct how another person does work or performs a task is under a legal duty to take reasonable steps to prevent bodily harm to that person, or any other person, arising from that work or task.

2003, c. 21, s. 3

218. Abandoning child — Every one who unlawfully abandons or exposes a child who is under the age of ten years, so that its life is or is likely to be endangered or its health is or is likely to be permanently injured,

(a) is guilty of an indictable offence and liable to imprisonment for a term not exceeding five years; or

(b) is guilty of an offence punishable on summary conviction.

2005, c. 32, s. 12; 2019, c. 25, s. 75

Criminal Negligence

219. (1) Criminal negligence — Every one is criminally negligent who

(a) in doing anything, or

(b) in omitting to do anything that it is his duty to do,

shows wanton or reckless disregard for the lives or safety of other persons.

(2) "duty" — For the purposes of this section, **"duty"** means a duty imposed by law.

220. Causing death by criminal negligence — Every person who by criminal negligence causes death to another person is guilty of an indictable offence and liable

(a) where a firearm is used in the commission of the offence, to imprisonment for life and to a minimum punishment of imprisonment for a term of four years; and

(b) in any other case, to imprisonment for life.

1995, c. 39, s. 141

221. Causing bodily harm by criminal negligence — Every person who by criminal negligence causes bodily harm to another person is guilty of

(a) an indictable offence and liable to imprisonment for a term of not more than 10 years; or

(b) an offence punishable on summary conviction.

2019, c. 25, s. 76

Homicide

222. (1) Homicide — A person commits homicide when, directly or indirectly, by any means, he causes the death of a human being.

(2) Kinds of homicide — Homicide is culpable or not culpable.

(3) Non culpable homicide — Homicide that is not culpable is not an offence.

(4) Culpable homicide — Culpable homicide is murder or manslaughter or infanticide.

(5) Idem — A person commits culpable homicide when he causes the death of a human being,

(a) by means of an unlawful act,

(b) by criminal negligence,

(c) by causing that human being, by threats or fear of violence or by deception, to do anything that causes his death, or

(d) by wilfully frightening that human being, in the case of a child or sick person.

(6) Exception — Notwithstanding anything in this section, a person does not commit homicide within the meaning of this Act by reason only that he causes the death of a human being by procuring, by false evidence, the conviction and death of that human being by sentence of the law.

223. (1) When child becomes human being — A child becomes a human being within the meaning of this Act when it has completely proceeded, in a living state, from the body of its mother whether or not

(a) it has breathed,

(b) it has an independent circulation, or

(c) the navel string is severed.

(2) Killing child — A person commits homicide when he causes injury to a child before or during its birth as a result of which the child dies after becoming a human being.

224. Death which might have been prevented — Where a person, by an act or omission, does any thing that results in the death of a human being, he causes the death of that human being notwithstanding that death from that cause might have been prevented by resorting to proper means.

225. Death from treatment of injury — Where a person causes to a human being a bodily injury that is of itself of a dangerous nature and from which death results, he causes the death of that human being notwithstanding that the immediate cause of death is proper or improper treatment that is applied in good faith.

226. Acceleration of death — Where a person causes to a human being a bodily injury that results in death, he causes the death of that human being notwithstanding that the effect of the bodily injury is only to accelerate his death from a disease or disorder arising from some other cause.

227. (1) Exemption for medical assistance in dying — No medical practitioner or nurse practitioner commits culpable homicide if they provide a person with medical assistance in dying in accordance with section 241.2.

(2) Exemption for person aiding practitioner — No person is a party to culpable homicide if they do anything for the purpose of aiding a medical practitioner or nurse practitioner to provide a person with medical assistance in dying in accordance with section 241.2.

(3) Reasonable but mistaken belief — For greater certainty, the exemption set out in subsection (1) or (2) applies even if the person invoking it has a reasonable but mistaken belief about any fact that is an element of the exemption.

(4) Non-application of section 14 — Section 14 does not apply with respect to a person who consents to have death inflicted on them by means of medical assistance in dying provided in accordance with section 241.2.

(5) Definitions — In this section, **"medical assistance in dying"**, **"medical practitioner"** and **"nurse practitioner"** have the same meanings as in section 241.1.

2016, c. 3, s. 2

228. Killing by influence on the mind — No person commits culpable homicide where he causes the death of a human being

(a) by any influence on the mind alone, or

(b) by any disorder or disease resulting from influence on the mind alone,

but this section does not apply where a person causes the death of a child or sick person by wilfully frightening him.

Murder, Manslaughter and Infanticide

229. Murder — Culpable homicide is murder

(a) where the person who causes the death of a human being

(i) means to cause his death, or

(ii) means to cause him bodily harm that he knows is likely to cause his death, and is reckless whether death ensues or not;

(b) where a person, meaning to cause death to a human being or meaning to cause him bodily harm that he knows is likely to cause his death, and being reckless whether death ensues or not, by accident or mistake causes death to another human being, notwithstanding that he does not mean to cause death or bodily harm to that human being; or

(c) if a person, for an unlawful object, does anything that they know is likely to cause death, and by doing so causes the death of a human being, even if they desire to effect their object without causing death or bodily harm to any human being.

2019, c. 25, s. 77

230. [Repealed 2019, c. 25, s. 78.]

231. (1) Classification of murder — Murder is first degree murder or second degree murder.

(2) Planned and deliberate murder — Murder is first degree murder when it is planned and deliberate.

(3) Contracted murder — Without limiting the generality of subsection (2), murder is planned and deliberate when it is committed pursuant to an arrangement under which money or anything of value passes or is intended to pass from one person to another, or is promised by one person to another, as consideration for that other's causing or assisting in causing the death of anyone or counselling another person to do any act causing or assisting in causing that death.

(4) Murder of peace officer, etc. — Irrespective of whether a murder is planned and deliberate on the part of any person, murder is first degree murder when the victim is

(a) a police officer, police constable, constable, sheriff, deputy sheriff, sheriff's officer or other person employed for the preservation and maintenance of the public peace, acting in the course of his duties;

(b) a warden, deputy warden, instructor, keeper, jailer, guard or other officer or a permanent employee of a prison, acting in the course of his duties; or

(c) a person working in a prison with the permission of the prison authorities and acting in the course of his work therein.

(5) Hijacking, sexual assault or kidnapping — Irrespective of whether a murder is planned and deliberate on the part of any person, murder is first degree murder in respect of a person when the death is caused by that person while committing or attempting to commit an offence under one of the following sections:

(a) section 76 (hijacking an aircraft);

(b) section 271 (sexual assault);

(c) section 272 (sexual assault with a weapon, threats to a third party or causing bodily harm);

(d) section 273 (aggravated sexual assault);

(e) section 279 (kidnapping and forcible confinement); or

(f) section 279.1 (hostage taking).

(6) Criminal harassment — Irrespective of whether a murder is planned and deliberate on the part of any person, murder is first degree murder when the death is caused by that person while committing or attempting to commit an offence under section 264 and the person committing that offence intended to cause the person murdered to fear for the safety of the person murdered or the safety of anyone known to the person murdered.

(6.01) Murder — terrorist activity — Irrespective of whether a murder is planned and deliberate on the part of a person, murder is first degree murder when the death is caused by that person while committing or attempting to commit an indictable offence under this or any other Act of Parliament if the act or omission constituting the offence also constitutes a terrorist activity.

(6.1) Murder — criminal organization — Irrespective of whether a murder is planned and deliberate on the part of a person, murder is first degree murder when

(a) the death is caused by that person for the benefit of, at the direction of or in association with a criminal organization; or

(b) the death is caused by that person while committing or attempting to commit an indictable offence under this or any other Act of Parliament for the benefit of, at the direction of or in association with a criminal organization.

(6.2) Intimidation — Irrespective of whether a murder is planned and deliberate on the part of a person, murder is first degree murder when the death is caused by that person while committing or attempting to commit an offence under section 423.1.

(7) Second degree murder — All murder that is not first degree murder is second degree murder.

R.S.C. 1985, c. 27 (1st Supp.), ss. 7(2), 35, 40(2) (Sched. I, item 3); 1997, c. 16, s. 3; 1997, c. 23, s. 8; 2001, c. 32, s. 9(2); 2001, c. 41, s. 9; 2009, c. 22, s. 5

232. (1) Murder reduced to manslaughter — Culpable homicide that otherwise would be murder may be reduced to manslaughter if the person who committed it did so in the heat of passion caused by sudden provocation.

(2) What is provocation — Conduct of the victim that would constitute an indictable offence under this Act that is punishable by five or more years of imprisonment and that is of such a nature as to be sufficient to deprive an ordinary person of the power of self-control is provocation for the purposes of this section, if the accused acted on it on the sudden and before there was time for their passion to cool.

(3) Questions of fact — For the purposes of this section, the questions

(a) whether the conduct of the victim amounted to provocation under subsection (2), and

(b) whether the accused was deprived of the power of self-control by the provocation that he alleges he received, are questions of fact, but no one shall be deemed to have given provocation to another by doing anything that he had a legal right to do, or by doing anything that the accused incited him to do in order to provide the accused with an excuse for causing death or bodily harm to any human being.

(4) **Death during illegal arrest** — Culpable homicide that otherwise would be murder is not necessarily manslaughter by reason only that it was committed by a person who was being arrested illegally, but the fact that the illegality of the arrest was known to the accused may be evidence of provocation for the purpose of this section.

2015, c. 29, s. 7

233. **Infanticide** — A female person commits infanticide when by a wilful act or omission she causes the death of her newly-born child, if at the time of the act or omission she is not fully recovered from the effects of giving birth to the child and by reason thereof or of the effect of lactation consequent on the birth of the child her mind is then disturbed.

234. **Manslaughter** — Culpable homicide that is not murder or infanticide is manslaughter.

235. (1) **Punishment for murder** — Every one who commits first degree murder or second degree murder is guilty of an indictable offence and shall be sentenced to imprisonment for life.

(2) **Minimum punishment** — For the purposes of Part XXIII, the sentence of imprisonment for life prescribed by this section is a minimum punishment.

236. **Manslaughter** — Every person who commits manslaughter is guilty of an indictable offence and liable

(a) where a firearm is used in the commission of the offence, to imprisonment for life and to a minimum punishment of imprisonment for a term of four years; and

(b) in any other case, to imprisonment for life.

1995, c. 39, s. 142

237. **Punishment for infanticide** — Every female person who commits infanticide is guilty of

(a) an indictable offence and liable to imprisonment for a term of not more than five years; or

(b) an offence punishable on summary conviction.

2019, c. 25, s. 79

238. (1) **Killing unborn child in act of birth** — Every one who causes the death, in the act of birth, of any child that has not become a human being, in such a manner that, if the child were a human being, he would be guilty of murder, is guilty of an indictable offence and liable to imprisonment for life.

(2) **Saving** — This section does not apply to a person who, by means that, in good faith, he considers necessary to preserve the life of the mother of a child, causes the death of that child.

239. (1) **Attempt to commit murder** — Every person who attempts by any means to commit murder is guilty of an indictable offence and liable

(a) if a restricted firearm or prohibited firearm is used in the commission of the offence or if any firearm is used in the commission of the offence and the offence is committed for the benefit of, at the direction of, or in association with, a criminal organization, to imprisonment for life and to a minimum punishment of imprisonment for a term of

(i) in the case of a first offence, five years, and

(ii) in the case of a second or subsequent offence, seven years;

(a.1) in any other case where a firearm is used in the commission of the offence, to imprisonment for life and to a minimum punishment of imprisonment for a term of four years; and

(b) in any other case, to imprisonment for life.

(2) **Subsequent offences** — In determining, for the purpose of paragraph (1)(a), whether a convicted person has committed a second or subsequent offence, if the person was earlier convicted of any of the following offences, that offence is to be considered as an earlier offence:

(a) an offence under this section;

(b) an offence under subsection 85(1) or (2) or section 244 or 244.2; or

(c) an offence under section 220, 236, 272 or 273, subsection 279(1) or section 279.1, 344 or 346 if a firearm was used in the commission of the offence.

However, an earlier offence shall not be taken into account if 10 years have elapsed between the day on which the person was convicted of the earlier offence and the day on which the person was convicted of the offence for which sentence is being imposed, not taking into account any time in custody.

(3) **Sequence of convictions only** — For the purposes of subsection (2), the only question to be considered is the sequence of convictions and no consideration shall be given to the sequence of commission of offences or whether any offence occurred before or after any conviction.

1995, c. 39, s. 143; 2008, c. 6, s. 16; 2009, c. 22, s. 6

240. **Accessory after fact to murder** — Every one who is an accessory after the fact to murder is guilty of an indictable offence and liable to imprisonment for life.

Suicide

241. (1) Counselling or aiding suicide — Everyone is guilty of an indictable offence and liable to imprisonment for a term of not more than 14 years who, whether suicide ensues or not,

(a) counsels a person to die by suicide or abets a person in dying by suicide; or

(b) aids a person to die by suicide.

(2) Exemption for medical assistance in dying — No medical practitioner or nurse practitioner commits an offence under paragraph (1)(b) if they provide a person with medical assistance in dying in accordance with section 241.2.

(3) Exemption for person aiding practitioner — No person is a party to an offence under paragraph (1)(b) if they do anything for the purpose of aiding a medical practitioner or nurse practitioner to provide a person with medical assistance in dying in accordance with section 241.2.

(4) Exemption for pharmacist — No pharmacist who dispenses a substance to a person other than a medical practitioner or nurse practitioner commits an offence under paragraph (1)(b) if the pharmacist dispenses the substance further to a prescription that is written by such a practitioner in providing medical assistance in dying in accordance with section 241.2.

(5) Exemption for person aiding patient — No person commits an offence under paragraph (1)(b) if they do anything, at another person's explicit request, for the purpose of aiding that other person to self-administer a substance that has been prescribed for that other person as part of the provision of medical assistance in dying in accordance with section 241.2.

(5.1) Clarification — For greater certainty, no social worker, psychologist, psychiatrist, therapist, medical practitioner, nurse practitioner or other health care professional commits an offence if they provide information to a person on the lawful provision of medical assistance in dying.

(6) Reasonable but mistaken belief — For greater certainty, the exemption set out in any of subsections (2) to (5) applies even if the person invoking the exemption has a reasonable but mistaken belief about any fact that is an element of the exemption.

(7) Definitions — In this section, **"medical assistance in dying"**, **"medical practitioner"**, **"nurse practitioner"** and **"pharmacist"** have the same meanings as in section 241.1.

R.S.C. 1985, c. 27 (1st Supp.), s. 7(3); 2016, c. 3, s. 3

Medical Assistance in Dying

[Heading added 2016, c. 3, s. 3.]

241.1 Definitions — The following definitions apply in this section and in sections 241.2 to 241.4.

"medical assistance in dying" means

(a) the administering by a medical practitioner or nurse practitioner of a substance to a person, at their request, that causes their death; or

(b) the prescribing or providing by a medical practitioner or nurse practitioner of a substance to a person, at their request, so that they may self-administer the substance and in doing so cause their own death.

("aide médicale à mourir")

"medical practitioner" means a person who is entitled to practise medicine under the laws of a province. *("médecin")*

"nurse practitioner" means a registered nurse who, under the laws of a province, is entitled to practise as a nurse practitioner — or under an equivalent designation — and to autonomously make diagnoses, order and interpret diagnostic tests, prescribe substances and treat patients. *("infirmier praticien")*

"pharmacist" means a person who is entitled to practise pharmacy under the laws of a province. *("pharmacien")*

2016, c. 3, s. 3

241.2 (1) Eligibility for medical assistance in dying — A person may receive medical assistance in dying only if they meet all of the following criteria:

(a) they are eligible — or, but for any applicable minimum period of residence or waiting period, would be eligible — for health services funded by a government in Canada;

(b) they are at least 18 years of age and capable of making decisions with respect to their health;

(c) they have a grievous and irremediable medical condition;

(d) they have made a voluntary request for medical assistance in dying that, in particular, was not made as a result of external pressure; and

(e) they give informed consent to receive medical assistance in dying after having been informed of the means that are available to relieve their suffering, including palliative care.

(2) Grievous and irremediable medical condition — A person has a grievous and irremediable medical condition only if they meet all of the following criteria:

(a) they have a serious and incurable illness, disease or disability;

(b) they are in an advanced state of irreversible decline in capability;

(c) that illness, disease or disability or that state of decline causes them enduring physical or psychological suffering that is intolerable to them and that cannot be relieved under conditions that they consider acceptable; and

(d) their natural death has become reasonably foreseeable, taking into account all of their medical circumstances, without a prognosis necessarily having been made as to the specific length of time that they have remaining.

(3) Safeguards — Before a medical practitioner or nurse practitioner provides a person with medical assistance in dying, the medical practitioner or nurse practitioner must

(a) be of the opinion that the person meets all of the criteria set out in subsection (1);

(b) ensure that the person's request for medical assistance in dying was

(i) made in writing and signed and dated by the person or by another person under subsection (4), and

(ii) signed and dated after the person was informed by a medical practitioner or nurse practitioner that the person has a grievous and irremediable medical condition;

(c) be satisfied that the request was signed and dated by the person — or by another person under subsection (4) — before two independent witnesses who then also signed and dated the request;

(d) ensure that the person has been informed that they may, at any time and in any manner, withdraw their request;

(e) ensure that another medical practitioner or nurse practitioner has provided a written opinion confirming that the person meets all of the criteria set out in subsection (1);

(f) be satisfied that they and the other medical practitioner or nurse practitioner referred to in paragraph (e) are independent;

(g) ensure that there are at least 10 clear days between the day on which the request was signed by or on behalf of the person and the day on which the medical assistance in dying is provided or — if they and the other medical practitioner or nurse practitioner referred to in paragraph (e) are both of the opinion that the person's death, or the loss of their capacity to provide informed consent, is imminent — any shorter period that the first medical practitioner or nurse practitioner considers appropriate in the circumstances;

(h) immediately before providing the medical assistance in dying, give the person an opportunity to withdraw their request and ensure that the person gives express consent to receive medical assistance in dying; and

(i) if the person has difficulty communicating, take all necessary measures to provide a reliable means by which the person may understand the information that is provided to them and communicate their decision.

(4) Unable to sign — If the person requesting medical assistance in dying is unable to sign and date the request, another person — who is at least 18 years of age, who understands the nature of the request for medical assistance in dying and who does not know or believe that they are a beneficiary under the will of the person making the request, or a recipient, in any other way, of a financial or other material benefit resulting from that person's death — may do so in the person's presence, on the person's behalf and under the person's express direction.

(5) Independent witness — Any person who is at least 18 years of age and who understands the nature of the request for medical assistance in dying may act as an independent witness, except if they

(a) know or believe that they are a beneficiary under the will of the person making the request, or a recipient, in any other way, of a financial or other material benefit resulting from that person's death;

(b) are an owner or operator of any health care facility at which the person making the request is being treated or any facility in which that person resides;

(c) are directly involved in providing health care services to the person making the request; or

(d) directly provide personal care to the person making the request.

(6) Independence — medical practitioners and nurse practitioners — The medical practitioner or nurse practitioner providing medical assistance in dying and the medical practitioner or nurse practitioner who provides the opinion referred to in paragraph (3)(e) are independent if they

(a) are not a mentor to the other practitioner or responsible for supervising their work;

(b) do not know or believe that they are a beneficiary under the will of the person making the request, or a recipient, in any other way, of a financial or other material benefit resulting from that person's death, other than standard compensation for their services relating to the request; or

(c) do not know or believe that they are connected to the other practitioner or to the person making the request in any other way that would affect their objectivity.

(7) Reasonable knowledge, care and skill — Medical assistance in dying must be provided with reasonable knowledge, care and skill and in accordance with any applicable provincial laws, rules or standards.

(8) Informing pharmacist — The medical practitioner or nurse practitioner who, in providing medical assistance in dying, prescribes or obtains a substance for that purpose must, before any pharmacist dispenses the substance, inform the pharmacist that the substance is intended for that purpose.

(9) Clarification — For greater certainty, nothing in this section compels an individual to provide or assist in providing medical assistance in dying.

2016, c. 3, s. 3

241.3 Failure to comply with safeguards — A medical practitioner or nurse practitioner who, in providing medical assistance in dying, knowingly fails to comply with all of the requirements set out in paragraphs 241.2(3)(b) to (i) and subsection 241.2(8) is guilty of

(a) an indictable offence and liable to imprisonment for a term of not more than five years; or

(b) an offence punishable on summary conviction.

2016, c. 3, s. 3; 2019, c. 25, s. 80

241.31 (1) Filing information — medical practitioner or nurse practitioner — Unless they are exempted under regulations made under subsection (3), a medical practitioner or nurse practitioner who receives a written request for medical assistance in dying must, in accordance with those regulations, provide the information required by those regulations to the recipient designated in those regulations.

(2) Filing information — pharmacist — Unless they are exempted under regulations made under subsection (3), a pharmacist who dispenses a substance in connection with the provision of medical assistance in dying must, in accordance with those regulations, provide the information required by those regulations to the recipient designated in those regulations.

(3) Regulations — The Minister of Health must make regulations that he or she considers necessary

(a) respecting the provision and collection, for the purpose of monitoring medical assistance in dying, of information relating to requests for, and the provision of, medical assistance in dying, including

(i) the information to be provided, at various stages, by medical practitioners or nurse practitioners and by pharmacists, or by a class of any of them,

(ii) the form, manner and time in which the information must be provided,

(iii) the designation of a person as the recipient of the information, and

(iv) the collection of information from coroners and medical examiners;

(b) respecting the use of that information, including its analysis and interpretation, its protection and its publication and other disclosure;

(c) respecting the disposal of that information; and

(d) exempting, on any terms that may be specified, a class of persons from the requirement set out in subsection (1) or (2).

(3.1) Guidelines — information on death certificates — The Minister of Health, after consultation with representatives of the provincial governments responsible for health, must establish guidelines on the information to be included on death certificates in cases where medical assistance in dying has been provided, which may include the way in which to clearly identify medical assistance in dying as the manner of death, as well as the illness, disease or disability that prompted the request for medical assistance in dying.

(4) Offence and punishment — A medical practitioner or nurse practitioner who knowingly fails to comply with subsection (1), or a pharmacist who knowingly fails to comply with subsection (2),

(a) is guilty of an indictable offence and liable to a term of imprisonment of not more than two years; or

(b) is guilty of an offence punishable on summary conviction.

(5) Offence and punishment — Everyone who knowingly contravenes the regulations made under subsection (3)

(a) is guilty of an indictable offence and liable to a term of imprisonment of not more than two years; or

(b) is guilty of an offence punishable on summary conviction.

2016, c. 3, s. 4

241.4 (1) Forgery — Everyone commits an offence who commits forgery in relation to a request for medical assistance in dying.

(2) Destruction of documents — Everyone commits an offence who destroys a document that relates to a request for medical assistance in dying with intent to interfere with

(a) another person's access to medical assistance in dying;

(b) the lawful assessment of a request for medical assistance in dying;

(c) another person invoking an exemption under any of subsections 227(1) or (2), 241(2) to (5) or 245(2); or

(d) the provision by a person of information under section 241.31.

(3) Punishment — Everyone who commits an offence under subsection (1) or (2) is guilty of

(a) an indictable offence and liable to imprisonment for a term of not more than five years; or

(b) an offence punishable on summary conviction.

(4) Definition of "document" — In subsection (2), **"document"** has the same meaning as in section 321.

2016, c. 3, ss. 3, 5; 2019, c. 25, s. 81

Neglect in Child-birth and Concealing Dead Body

242. Neglect to obtain assistance in childbirth — A female person who, being pregnant and about to be delivered, with intent that the child shall not live or with intent to conceal the birth of the child, fails to make provision for reasonable assistance in respect of her delivery is, if the child is permanently injured as a result of the failure or dies immediately before, during or in a short time after birth, as a result of the failure, guilty of

(a) an indictable offence and liable to imprisonment for a term of not more than five years; or

(b) an offence punishable on summary conviction.

2019, c. 25, s. 82

243. Concealing body of child — Every person who in any manner disposes of the dead body of a child, with intent to conceal the fact that its mother has been delivered of it, whether the child died before, during or after birth, is guilty of

(a) an indictable offence and liable to imprisonment for a term of not more than two years; or

(b) an offence punishable on summary conviction.

2019, c. 25, s. 82

Bodily Harm and Acts and Omissions Causing Danger to the Person

244. (1) Discharging firearm with intent — Every person commits an offence who discharges a firearm at a person with intent to wound, maim or disfigure, to endanger the life of or to prevent the arrest or detention of any person — whether or not that person is the one at whom the firearm is discharged.

(2) Punishment — Every person who commits an offence under subsection (1) is guilty of an indictable offence and liable

(a) if a restricted firearm or prohibited firearm is used in the commission of the offence or if the offence is committed for the benefit of, at the direction of, or in association with, a criminal organization, to imprisonment for a term not exceeding 14 years and to a minimum punishment of imprisonment for a term of

(i) in the case of a first offence, five years, and

(ii) in the case of a second or subsequent offence, seven years; and

(b) in any other case, to imprisonment for a term not exceeding 14 years and to a minimum punishment of imprisonment for a term of four years.

(3) Subsequent offences — In determining, for the purpose of paragraph (2)(a), whether a convicted person has committed a second or subsequent offence, if the person was earlier convicted of any of the following offences, that offence is to be considered as an earlier offence:

(a) an offence under this section;

(b) an offence under subsection 85(1) or (2) or section 244.2; or

(c) an offence under section 220, 236, 239, 272 or 273, subsection 279(1) or section 279.1, 344 or 346 if a firearm was used in the commission of the offence.

However, an earlier offence shall not be taken into account if 10 years have elapsed between the day on which the person was convicted of the earlier offence and the day on which the person was convicted of the offence for which sentence is being imposed, not taking into account any time in custody.

(4) Sequence of convictions only — For the purposes of subsection (3), the only question to be considered is the sequence of convictions and no consideration shall be given to the sequence of commission of offences or whether any offence occurred before or after any conviction.

1995, c. 39, s. 144; 2008, c. 6, s. 17; 2009, c. 22, s. 7

244.1 Causing bodily harm with intent — air gun or pistol — Every person who, with intent

(a) to wound, maim or disfigure any person,

(b) to endanger the life of any person, or

(c) to prevent the arrest or detention of any person,

discharges an air or compressed gas gun or pistol at any person, whether or not that person is the person mentioned in paragraph (*a*), (*b*) or (*c*), is guilty of an indictable offence and liable to imprisonment for a term not exceeding fourteen years.

1995, c. 39, s. 144

244.2 (1) Discharging firearm — recklessness — Every person commits an offence

(a) who intentionally discharges a firearm into or at a place, knowing that or being reckless as to whether another person is present in the place; or

(b) who intentionally discharges a firearm while being reckless as to the life or safety of another person.

(2) Definition of "place" — For the purpose of paragraph (1)(a), **"place"** means any building or structure — or part of one — or any motor vehicle, vessel, aircraft, railway vehicle, container or trailer.

(3) Punishment — Every person who commits an offence under subsection (1) is guilty of an indictable offence and

(a) if a restricted firearm or prohibited firearm is used in the commission of the offence or if the offence is committed for the benefit of, at the direction of or in association with a criminal organization, is liable to imprisonment for a term of not more than 14 years and to a minimum punishment of imprisonment for a term of

(i) five years, in the case of a first offence, and

(ii) seven years, in the case of a second or subsequent offence; and

(b) in any other case, is liable to imprisonment for a term of not more than 14 years and to a minimum punishment of imprisonment for a term of four years.

(4) Subsequent offences — In determining, for the purpose of paragraph (3)(a), whether a convicted person has committed a second or subsequent offence, if the person was earlier convicted of any of the following offences, that offence is to be considered as an earlier offence:

(a) an offence under this section;

(b) an offence under subsection 85(1) or (2) or section 244; or

(c) an offence under section 220, 236, 239, 272 or 273, subsection 279(1) or section 279.1, 344 or 346 if a firearm was used in the commission of the offence.

However, an earlier offence shall not be taken into account if 10 years have elapsed between the day on which the person was convicted of the earlier offence and the day on which the person was convicted of the offence for which sentence is being imposed, not taking into account any time in custody.

(5) **Sequence of convictions only** — For the purpose of subsection (4), the only question to be considered is the sequence of convictions and no consideration shall be given to the sequence of commission of offences or whether any offence occurred before or after any conviction.

2009, c. 22, s. 8

245. (1) Administering noxious thing — Every person who administers or causes to be administered to any other person or causes any other person to take poison or any other destructive or noxious thing is guilty

(a) of an indictable offence and liable to imprisonment for a term of not more than 14 years, if they did so with intent to endanger the life of or to cause bodily harm to that person; or

(b) of an indictable offence and liable to imprisonment for a term of not more than two years or of an offence punishable on summary conviction, if they did so with intent to aggrieve or annoy that person.

(2) **Exemption** — Subsection (1) does not apply to

(a) a medical practitioner or nurse practitioner who provides medical assistance in dying in accordance with section 241.2; and

(b) a person who does anything for the purpose of aiding a medical practitioner or nurse practitioner to provide medical assistance in dying in accordance with section 241.2.

(3) **Definitions** — In subsection (2), **"medical assistance in dying"**, **"medical practitioner"** and **"nurse practitioner"** have the same meanings as in section 241.1.

2016, c. 3, s. 6; 2019, c. 25, s. 83

246. Overcoming resistance to commission of offence — Every one who, with intent to enable or assist himself or another person to commit an indictable offence,

(a) attempts, by any means, to choke, suffocate or strangle another person, or by any means calculated to choke, suffocate or strangle, attempts to render another person insensible, unconscious or incapable of resistance, or

(b) administers, or causes to be administered to any person, or attempts to administer to any person, or causes or attempts to cause any person to take a stupefying or overpowering drug, matter or thing,

is guilty of an indictable offence and liable to imprisonment for life.

247. (1) Traps likely to cause bodily harm — Every person is guilty of an indictable offence and liable to imprisonment for a term of not more than five years or is guilty of an offence punishable on summary conviction who with intent to cause death or bodily harm to a person, whether ascertained or not,

(a) sets or places a trap, device or other thing that is likely to cause death or bodily harm to a person; or

(b) being in occupation or possession of a place, knowingly permits such a trap, device or other thing to remain in that place.

(2) Bodily harm — Every person who commits an offence under subsection (1), and by doing so causes bodily harm to any other person, is guilty of

(a) an indictable offence and liable to imprisonment for a term of not more than 10 years; or

(b) an offence punishable on summary conviction.

(3) Offence-related place — Every person who commits an offence under subsection (1), in a place kept or used for the purpose of committing another indictable offence, is guilty of

(a) an indictable offence and liable to imprisonment for a term of not more than 10 years; or

(b) an offence punishable on summary conviction.

(4) Offence related place — bodily harm — Every one who commits an offence under subsection (1), in a place kept or used for the purpose of committing another indictable offence, and thereby causes bodily harm to a person is guilty of an indictable offence and liable to a term of imprisonment not exceeding fourteen years.

(5) Death — Every one who commits an offence under subsection (1) and thereby causes the death of any other person is guilty of an indictable offence and liable to imprisonment for life.

2004, c. 12, s. 6; 2019, c. 25, s. 84

248. Interfering with transportation facilities — Every one who, with intent to endanger the safety of any persons, places anything on or does anything to any property that is used for or in connection with the transportation of persons or goods by land, water or air that is likely to cause death or bodily harm to persons is guilty of an indictable offence and liable to imprisonment for life.

Heading and ss. 249 to 261. [Repealed 2018, c. 21, s. 14.]

262. Impeding attempt to save life — Every person is guilty of an indictable offence and liable to imprisonment for a term of not more than 10 years or is guilty of an offence punishable on summary conviction who

(a) prevents or impedes or attempts to prevent or impede any person who is attempting to save his own life, or

(b) without reasonable cause prevents or impedes or attempts to prevent or impede any person who is attempting to save the life of another person.

2019, c. 25, s. 90

263. (1) Duty to safeguard opening in ice — Every one who makes or causes to be made an opening in ice that is open to or frequented by the public is under a legal duty to guard it in a manner that is adequate to prevent persons from falling in by accident and is adequate to warn them that the opening exists.

(2) Excavation on land — Every one who leaves an excavation on land that he owns or of which he has charge or supervision is under a legal duty to guard it in a manner that is adequate to prevent persons from falling in by accident and is adequate to warn them that the excavation exists.

(3) Offences — Every one who fails to perform a duty imposed by subsection (1) or (2) is guilty of

(a) manslaughter, if the death of any person results therefrom;

(b) an offence under section 269, if bodily harm to any person results therefrom; or

(c) an offence punishable on summary conviction.

264. (1) Criminal harassment — No person shall, without lawful authority and knowing that another person is harassed or recklessly as to whether the other person is harassed, engage in conduct referred to in subsection (2) that causes that other person reasonably, in all the circumstances, to fear for their safety or the safety of anyone known to them.

(2) Prohibited conduct — The conduct mentioned in subsection (1) consists of

(a) repeatedly following from place to place the other person or anyone known to them;

(b) repeatedly communicating with, either directly or indirectly, the other person or anyone known to them;

(c) besetting or watching the dwelling-house, or place where the other person, or anyone known to them, resides, works, carries on business or happens to be; or

(d) engaging in threatening conduct directed at the other person or any member of their family.

(3) Punishment — Every person who contravenes this section is guilty of

(a) an indictable offence and is liable to imprisonment for a term not exceeding ten years; or

(b) an offence punishable on summary conviction.

(4) Factors to be considered — Where a person is convicted of an offence under this section, the court imposing the sentence on the person shall consider as an aggravating factor that, at the time the offence was committed, the person contravened

(a) the terms or conditions of an order made pursuant to section 161 or a recognizance entered into pursuant to section 810, 810.1 or 810.2; or

(b) the terms or conditions of any other order or recognizance made or entered into under the common law or a provision of this or any other Act of

Parliament or of a province that is similar in effect to an order or recognizance referred to in paragraph (*a*).

Proposed Amendment — 264(4)(b)

(b) the terms or conditions of any other order or recognizance, or of an undertaking, made or entered into under the common law, this Act or any other Act of Parliament or of a provincial legislature that is similar in effect to an order or recognizance referred to in paragraph (a).

2019, c. 25, s. 91 [To come into force December 18, 2019.]

(5) Reasons — Where the court is satisfied of the existence of an aggravating factor referred to in subsection (4), but decides not to give effect to it for sentencing purposes, the court shall give reasons for its decision.

R.S.C. 1985, c. 27 (1st Supp.), s. 37; 1993, c. 45, s. 2; 1997, c. 16, s. 4; 1997, c. 17, s. 9(3); 2002, c. 13, s. 10

Assaults

264.1 (1) Uttering threats — Every one commits an offence who, in any manner, knowingly utters, conveys or causes any person to receive a threat

(a) to cause death or bodily harm to any person;

(b) to burn, destroy or damage real or personal property; or

(c) to kill, poison or injure an animal or bird that is the property of any person.

(2) Punishment — Every one who commits an offence under paragraph (1)(*a*) is guilty of

(a) an indictable offence and liable to imprisonment for a term not exceeding five years; or

(b) an offence punishable on summary conviction.

(3) Idem — Every one who commits an offence under paragraph (1)(*b*) or (*c*)

(a) is guilty of an indictable offence and liable to imprisonment for a term not exceeding two years; or

(b) is guilty of an offence punishable on summary conviction.

R.S.C. 1985, c. 27 (1st Supp.), s. 38; 1994, c. 44, s. 16; 2019, c. 25, s. 92

265. (1) Assault — A person commits an **assault** when

(a) without the consent of another person, he applies force intentionally to that other person, directly or indirectly;

(b) he attempts or threatens, by an act or a gesture, to apply force to another person, if he has, or causes that other person to believe on reasonable grounds that he has, present ability to effect his purpose; or

(c) while openly wearing or carrying a weapon or an imitation thereof, he accosts or impedes another person or begs.

(2) **Application** — This section applies to all forms of assault, including sexual assault, sexual assault with a weapon, threats to a third party or causing bodily harm and aggravated sexual assault.

(3) **Consent** — For the purposes of this section, no consent is obtained where the complainant submits or does not resist by reason of

(a) the application of force to the complainant or to a person other than the complainant;

(b) threats or fear of the application of force to the complainant or to a person other than the complainant;

(c) fraud; or

(d) the exercise of authority.

(4) **Accused's belief as to consent** — Where an accused alleges that he believed that the complainant consented to the conduct that is the subject-matter of the charge, a judge, if satisfied that there is sufficient evidence and that, if believed by the jury, the evidence would constitute a defence, shall instruct the jury, when reviewing all the evidence relating to the determination of the honesty of the accused's belief, to consider the presence or absence of reasonable grounds for that belief.

266. **Assault** — Every one who commits an assault is guilty of

(a) an indictable offence and is liable to imprisonment for a term not exceeding five years; or

(b) an offence punishable on summary conviction.

267. **Assault with a weapon or causing bodily harm** — Every person is guilty of an indictable offence and liable to imprisonment for a term of not more than 10 years or is guilty of an offence punishable on summary conviction who, in committing an assault,

(a) carries, uses or threatens to use a weapon or an imitation thereof,

(b) causes bodily harm to the complainant, or

(c) chokes, suffocates or strangles the complainant.

1994, c. 44, s. 17; 2019, c. 25, s. 93

268. (1) **Aggravated assault** — Every one commits an aggravated assault who wounds, maims, disfigures or endangers the life of the complainant.

(2) **Punishment** — Every one who commits an aggravated assault is guilty of an indictable offence and liable to imprisonment for a term not exceeding fourteen years.

(3) **Excision** — For greater certainty, in this section, **"wounds"** or **"maims"** includes to excise, infibulate or mutilate, in whole or in part, the labia majora, labia minora or clitoris of a person, except where

(a) a surgical procedure is performed, by a person duly qualified by provincial law to practise medicine, for the benefit of the physical health of the person or for the purpose of that person having normal reproductive functions or normal sexual appearance or function; or

(b) the person is at least eighteen years of age and there is no resulting bodily harm.

(4) Consent — For the purposes of this section and section 265, no consent to the excision, infibulation or mutilation, in whole or in part, of the labia majora, labia minora or clitoris of a person is valid, except in the cases described in paragraphs (3)(*a*) and (*b*).

1997, c. 16, s. 5

269. Unlawfully causing bodily harm — Every one who unlawfully causes bodily harm to any person is guilty of

(a) an indictable offence and liable to imprisonment for a term not exceeding ten years; or

(b) an offence punishable on summary conviction.

1994, c. 44, s. 18; 2019, c. 25, s. 94

269.01 (1) Aggravating circumstance — assault against a public transit operator — When a court imposes a sentence for an offence referred to in paragraph 264.1(1)(a) or any of sections 266 to 269, it shall consider as an aggravating circumstance the fact that the victim of the offence was, at the time of the commission of the offence, a public transit operator engaged in the performance of his or her duty.

(2) Definitions — The following definitions apply in this section.

"public transit operator" means an individual who operates a vehicle used in the provision of passenger transportation services to the public, and includes an individual who operates a school bus. *("conducteur de véhicule de transport en commun")*

"vehicle" includes a bus, paratransit vehicle, licensed taxi cab, train, subway, tram and ferry. *("véhicule")*

2015, c. 1, s. 1

269.1 (1) Torture — Every official, or every person acting at the instigation of or with the consent or acquiescence of an official, who inflicts torture on any other person is guilty of an indictable offence and is liable to imprisonment for a term not exceeding fourteen years.

(2) Definitions — For the purposes of this section,

"official" means

(a) a peace officer,

(b) a public officer,

(c) a member of the Canadian Forces, or

(d) any person who may exercise powers, pursuant to a law in force in a foreign state, that would, in Canada be exercised by a person referred to in paragraph (*a*), (*b*), or (*c*),

whether the person exercises powers in Canada or outside Canada;

"torture" means any act or omission by which severe pain or suffering, whether physical or mental, is intentionally inflicted on a person

(a) for a purpose including

(i) obtaining from the person or from a third person information or a statement,

(ii) punishing the person for an act that the person or a third person has committed or is suspected of having committed, and

(iii) intimidating or coercing the person or a third person, or

(b) for any reason based on discrimination of any kind,

but does not include any act or omission arising only from, inherent in or incidental to lawful sanctions.

(3) No defence — It is no defence to a charge under this section that the accused was ordered by a superior or a public authority to perform the act or omission that forms the subject-matter of the charge or that the act or omission is alleged to have been justified by exceptional circumstances, including a state of war, a threat of war, internal political instability or any other public emergency.

(4) Evidence — In any proceedings over which Parliament has jurisdiction, any statement obtained as a result of the commission of an offence under this section is inadmissible in evidence except as evidence that the statement was so obtained.

R.S.C. 1985, c. 10 (3rd Supp.), s. 2

270. (1) Assaulting a peace officer — Every one commits an offence who

(a) assaults a public officer or peace officer engaged in the execution of his duty or a person acting in aid of such an officer;

(b) assaults a person with intent to resist or prevent the lawful arrest or detention of himself or another person; or

(c) assaults a person

(i) who is engaged in the lawful execution of a process against lands or goods or in making a lawful distress or seizure, or

(ii) with intent to rescue anything taken under lawful process, distress or seizure.

(2) Punishment — Every one who commits an offence under subsection (1) is guilty of

(a) an indictable offence and is liable to imprisonment for a term not exceeding five years; or

(b) an offence punishable on summary conviction.

270.01 (1) Assaulting peace officer with weapon or causing bodily harm — Everyone commits an offence who, in committing an assault referred to in section 270,

(a) carries, uses or threatens to use a weapon or an imitation of one; or

(b) causes bodily harm to the complainant.

(2) Punishment — Everyone who commits an offence under subsection (1) is guilty of

(a) an indictable offence and liable to imprisonment for a term of not more than 10 years; or

(b) an offence punishable on summary conviction.

2009, c. 22, s. 9; 2019, c. 25, s. 95

270.02 Aggravated assault of peace officer — Everyone who, in committing an assault referred to in section 270, wounds, maims, disfigures or endangers the life of the complainant is guilty of an indictable offence and liable to imprisonment for a term of not more than 14 years.

2009, c. 22, s. 9

270.03 Sentences to be served consecutively — A sentence imposed on a person for an offence under subsection 270(1) or 270.01(1) or section 270.02 committed against a law enforcement officer, as defined in subsection 445.01(4), shall be served consecutively to any other punishment imposed on the person for an offence arising out of the same event or series of events.

2015, c. 34, s. 2

270.1 (1) Disarming a peace officer — Every one commits an offence who, without the consent of a peace officer, takes or attempts to take a weapon that is in the possession of the peace officer when the peace officer is engaged in the execution of his or her duty.

(2) Definition of "weapon" — For the purpose of subsection (1), **"weapon"** means any thing that is designed to be used to cause injury or death to, or to temporarily incapacitate, a person.

(3) Punishment — Every one who commits an offence under subsection (1) is guilty of

(a) an indictable offence and liable to imprisonment for a term of not more than five years; or

(b) an offence punishable on summary conviction.

2002, c. 13, s. 11; 2019, c. 25, s. 96

271. Sexual assault — Everyone who commits a sexual assault is guilty of

(a) an indictable offence and is liable to imprisonment for a term of not more than 10 years or, if the complainant is under the age of 16 years, to imprisonment for a term of not more than 14 years and to a minimum punishment of imprisonment for a term of one year; or

(b) an offence punishable on summary conviction and is liable to imprisonment for a term of not more than 18 months or, if the complainant is under the age of 16 years, to imprisonment for a term of not more than two years less a day and to a minimum punishment of imprisonment for a term of six months.

R.S.C. 1985, c. 19 (3rd Supp.), s. 10; 1994, c. 44, s. 19; 2012, c. 1, s. 25; 2015, c. 23, s. 14

272. (1) Sexual assault with a weapon, threats to a third party or causing bodily harm — Every person commits an offence who, in committing a sexual assault,

(a) carries, uses or threatens to use a weapon or an imitation of a weapon;

(b) threatens to cause bodily harm to a person other than the complainant;

(c) causes bodily harm to the complainant;

(c.1) chokes, suffocates or strangles the complainant; or

(d) is a party to the offence with any other person.

(2) Punishment — Every person who commits an offence under subsection (1) is guilty of an indictable offence and liable

(a) if a restricted firearm or prohibited firearm is used in the commission of the offence or if any firearm is used in the commission of the offence and the offence is committed for the benefit of, at the direction of, or in association with, a criminal organization, to imprisonment for a term not exceeding 14 years and to a minimum punishment of imprisonment for a term of

(i) in the case of a first offence, five years, and

(ii) in the case of a second or subsequent offence, seven years;

(a.1) in any other case where a firearm is used in the commission of the offence, to imprisonment for a term not exceeding 14 years and to a minimum punishment of imprisonment for a term of four years;

(a.2) if the complainant is under the age of 16 years, to imprisonment for life and to a minimum punishment of imprisonment for a term of five years; and

(b) in any other case, to imprisonment for a term not exceeding fourteen years.

(3) Subsequent offences — In determining, for the purpose of paragraph (2)(a), whether a convicted person has committed a second or subsequent offence, if the person was earlier convicted of any of the following offences, that offence is to be considered as an earlier offence:

(a) an offence under this section;

(b) an offence under subsection 85(1) or (2) or section 244 or 244.2; or

(c) an offence under section 220, 236, 239 or 273, subsection 279(1) or section 279.1, 344 or 346 if a firearm was used in the commission of the offence.

However, an earlier offence shall not be taken into account if 10 years have elapsed between the day on which the person was convicted of the earlier offence and the day on which the person was convicted of the offence for which sentence is being imposed, not taking into account any time in custody.

(4) Sequence of convictions only — For the purposes of subsection (3), the only question to be considered is the sequence of convictions and no consideration shall be given to the sequence of commission of offences or whether any offence occurred before or after any conviction.

1995, c. 39, s. 145; 2008, c. 6, s. 28; 2009, c. 22, s. 10; 2012, c. 1, s. 26; 2015, c. 23, s. 15; 2019, c. 25, s. 97

273. (1) Aggravated sexual assault — Every one commits an aggravated sexual assault who, in committing a sexual assault, wounds, maims, disfigures or endangers the life of the complainant.

(2) Aggravated sexual assault — Every person who commits an aggravated sexual assault is guilty of an indictable offence and liable

(a) if a restricted firearm or prohibited firearm is used in the commission of the offence or if any firearm is used in the commission of the offence and the offence is committed for the benefit of, at the direction of, or in association with, a criminal organization, to imprisonment for life and to a minimum punishment of imprisonment for a term of

(i) in the case of a first offence, five years, and

(ii) in the case of a second or subsequent offence, seven years;

(a.1) in any other case where a firearm is used in the commission of the offence, to imprisonment for life and to a minimum punishment of imprisonment for a term of four years;

(a.2) if the complainant is under the age of 16 years, to imprisonment for life and to a minimum punishment of imprisonment for a term of five years; and

(b) in any other case, to imprisonment for life.

(3) Subsequent offences — In determining, for the purpose of paragraph (2)(a), whether a convicted person has committed a second or subsequent offence, if the person was earlier convicted of any of the following offences, that offence is to be considered as an earlier offence:

(a) an offence under this section;

(b) an offence under subsection 85(1) or (2) or section 244 or 244.2; or

(c) an offence under section 220, 236, 239 or 272, subsection 279(1) or section 279.1, 344 or 346 if a firearm was used in the commission of the offence.

However, an earlier offence shall not be taken into account if 10 years have elapsed between the day on which the person was convicted of the earlier offence and the day on which the person was convicted of the offence for which sentence is being imposed, not taking into account any time in custody.

(4) Sequence of convictions only — For the purposes of subsection (3), the only question to be considered is the sequence of convictions and no consideration shall be given to the sequence of commission of offences or whether any offence occurred before or after any conviction.

1995, c. 39, s. 146; 2008, c. 6, s. 29; 2009, c. 22, s. 11; 2012, c. 1, s. 27

273.1 (1) Meaning of "consent" — Subject to subsection (2) and subsection 265(3), **"consent"** means, for the purposes of sections 271, 272 and 273, the voluntary agreement of the complainant to engage in the sexual activity in question.

(1.1) Consent — Consent must be present at the time the sexual activity in question takes place.

(1.2) Question of law — The question of whether no consent is obtained under subsection 265(3) or subsection (2) or (3) is a question of law.

(2) No consent obtained — For the purpose of subsection (1), no consent is obtained if

(a) the agreement is expressed by the words or conduct of a person other than the complainant;

(a.1) the complainant is unconscious;

(b) the complainant is incapable of consenting to the activity for any reason other than the one referred to in paragraph (a.1);

(c) the accused induces the complainant to engage in the activity by abusing a position of trust, power or authority;

(d) the complainant expresses, by words or conduct, a lack of agreement to engage in the activity; or

(e) the complainant, having consented to engage in sexual activity, expresses, by words or conduct, a lack of agreement to continue to engage in the activity.

(3) Subsection (2) not limiting — Nothing in subsection (2) shall be construed as limiting the circumstances in which no consent is obtained.

1992, c. 38, s. 1; 2018, c. 29, s. 19(1)–(2.1)

273.2 Where belief in consent not a defence — It is not a defence to a charge under section 271, 272 or 273 that the accused believed that the complainant consented to the activity that forms the subject-matter of the charge, where

(a) the accused's belief arose from

(i) the accused's self-induced intoxication,

(ii) the accused's recklessness or wilful blindness, or

(iii) any circumstance referred to in subsection 265(3) or 273.1(2) or (3) in which no consent is obtained;

(b) the accused did not take reasonable steps, in the circumstances known to the accused at the time, to ascertain that the complainant was consenting; or

(c) there is no evidence that the complainant's voluntary agreement to the activity was affirmatively expressed by words or actively expressed by conduct.

1992, c. 38, s. 1; 2018, c. 29, s. 20

273.3 (1) Removal of child from Canada — No person shall do anything for the purpose of removing from Canada a person who is ordinarily resident in Canada and who is

(a) under the age of 16 years, with the intention that an act be committed outside Canada that if it were committed in Canada would be an offence against section 151 or 152 or subsection 160(3) or 173(2) in respect of that person;

(b) 16 years of age or more but under the age of eighteen years, with the intention that an act be committed outside Canada that if it were committed in Canada would be an offence against section 153 in respect of that person;

(c) under the age of eighteen years, with the intention that an act be committed outside Canada that if it were committed in Canada would be an offence against section 155, subsection 160(2) or section 170, 171, 267, 268, 269, 271, 272 or 273 in respect of that person; or

(d) under the age of 18 years, with the intention that an act be committed outside Canada that, if it were committed in Canada, would be an offence against section 293.1 in respect of that person or under the age of 16 years, with the intention that an act be committed outside Canada that, if it were committed in Canada, would be an offence against section 293.2 in respect of that person.

(2) Punishment — Every person who contravenes this section is guilty of

(a) an indictable offence and is liable to imprisonment for a term not exceeding five years; or

(b) an offence punishable on summary conviction.

1993, c. 45, s. 3; 1997, c. 18, s. 13; 2008, c. 6, s. 54(i); 2015, c. 29, s. 8; 2019, c. 25, s. 98

274. Corroboration not required — If an accused is charged with an offence under section 151, 152, 153, 153.1, 155, 160, 170, 171, 172, 173, 271, 272, 273, 286.1, 286.2 or 286.3, no corroboration is required for a conviction and the judge shall not instruct the jury that it is unsafe to find the accused guilty in the absence of corroboration.

R.S.C. 1985, c. 19 (3rd Supp.), s. 11; 2002, c. 13, s. 12; 2014, c. 25, s. 16; 2019, c. 25, s. 99

275. Rules respecting recent complaint abrogated — The rules relating to evidence of recent complaint are hereby abrogated with respect to offences under sections 151, 152, 153, 153.1 and 155, subsections 160(2) and (3) and sections 170, 171, 172, 173, 271, 272 and 273.

R.S.C. 1985, c. 19 (3rd Supp.), s. 11; 2002, c. 13, s. 12; 2019, c. 25, s. 99

276. (1) Evidence of complainant's sexual activity — In proceedings in respect of an offence under section 151, 152, 153, 153.1 or 155, subsection 160(2) or (3) or section 170, 171, 172, 173, 271, 272 or 273, evidence that the complainant has engaged in sexual activity, whether with the accused or with any other person, is not admissible to support an inference that, by reason of the sexual nature of that activity, the complainant

(a) is more likely to have consented to the sexual activity that forms the subject-matter of the charge; or;

(b) is less worthy of belief.

(2) Conditions for admissibility — In proceedings in respect of an offence referred to in subsection (1), evidence shall not be adduced by or on behalf of the accused that the complainant has engaged in sexual activity other than the sexual activity that forms the subject-matter of the charge, whether with the accused or with any other person, unless the judge, provincial court judge or justice determines, in accordance with the procedures set out in sections 278.93 and 278.94, that the evidence

(a) is not being adduced for the purpose of supporting an inference described in subsection (1);

(b) is relevant to an issue at trial; and

(c) is of specific instances of sexual activity; and

(d) has significant probative value that is not substantially outweighed by the danger of prejudice to the proper administration of justice.

(3) Factors that judge must consider — In determining whether evidence is admissible under subsection (2), the judge, provincial court judge or justice shall take into account

(a) the interests of justice, including the right of the accused to make a full answer and defence;

(b) society's interest in encouraging the reporting of sexual assault offences;

(c) whether there is a reasonable prospect that the evidence will assist in arriving at a just determination in the case;

(d) the need to remove from the fact-finding process any discriminatory belief or bias;

(e) the risk that the evidence may unduly arouse sentiments of prejudice, sympathy or hostility in the jury;

(f) the potential prejudice to the complainant's personal dignity and right of privacy;

(g) the right of the complainant and of every individual to personal security and to the full protection and benefit of the law; and

(h) any other factor that the judge, provincial court judge or justice considers relevant.

(4) Interpretation — For the purpose of this section, **"sexual activity"** includes any communication made for a sexual purpose or whose content is of a sexual nature.

R.S.C. 1985, c. 19 (3rd Supp.), s. 12; 1992, c. 38, s. 2; 2002, c. 13, s. 13; 2018, c. 29, s. 21; 2019, c. 25, s. 100

276.1 to 276.5 [Repealed 2018, c. 29, s. 22.]

277. Reputation evidence — In proceedings in respect of an offence under section 151, 152, 153, 153.1 or 155, subsection 160(2) or (3) or section 170, 171, 172, 173, 271, 272 or 273, evidence of sexual reputation, whether general or specific, is not admissible for the purpose of challenging or supporting the credibility of the complainant.

R.S.C. 1985, c. 19 (3rd Supp.), s. 13; 2002, c. 13, s. 14; 2019, c. 25, s. 101

278. Spouse may be charged — A husband or wife may be charged with an offence under section 271, 272 or 273 in respect of his or her spouse, whether or not the spouses were living together at the time the activity that forms the subject-matter of the charge occurred.

278.1 Definition of "record" — For the purposes of sections 278.2 to 278.92, **"record"** means any form of record that contains personal information for which there is a reasonable expectation of privacy and includes medical, psychiatric, therapeutic, counselling, education, employment, child welfare, adoption and social services records, personal journals and diaries, and records containing personal information the production or disclosure of which is protected by any other Act of Parliament or a provincial legislature, but does not include records made by persons responsible for the investigation or prosecution of the offence.

1997, c. 30, s. 1; 2018, c. 29, s. 23

278.2 (1) Production of record to accused — Except in accordance with sections 278.3 to 278.91, no record relating to a complainant or a witness shall be produced to an accused in any proceedings in respect of any of the following offences or in any proceedings in respect of two or more offences at least one of which is any of the following offences:

(a) an offence under section 151, 152, 153, 153.1, 155, 160, 170, 171, 172, 173, 213, 271, 272, 273, 279.01, 279.011, 279.02, 279.03, 286.1, 286.2 or 286.3; or

(b) any offence under this Act, as it read from time to time before the day on which this paragraph comes into force, if the conduct alleged would be an offence referred to in paragraph (a) if it occurred on or after that day.

(c) [Repealed 2014, c. 25, s. 17(3).]

(2) Application of provisions — Section 278.1, this section and sections 278.3 to 278.91 apply where a record is in the possession or control of any person, including the prosecutor in the proceedings, unless, in the case of a record in the possession or control of the prosecutor, the complainant or witness to whom the record relates has expressly waived the application of those sections.

(3) Duty of prosecutor to give notice — In the case of a record in respect of which this section applies that is in the possession or control of the prosecutor, the prosecutor shall notify the accused that the record is in the prosecutor's possession but, in doing so, the prosecutor shall not disclose the record's contents.

1997, c. 30, s. 1; 1998, c. 9, s. 3; 2014, c. 25, ss. 17, 48(5); 2015, c. 13, s. 5(2); 2019, c. 25, s. 102

278.3 (1) Application for production — An accused who seeks production of a record referred to in subsection 278.2(1) must make an application to the judge before whom the accused is to be, or is being, tried.

(2) No application in other proceedings — For greater certainty, an application under subsection (1) may not be made to a judge or justice presiding at any other proceedings, including a preliminary inquiry.

(3) Form and content of application — An application must be made in writing and set out

(a) particulars identifying the record that the accused seeks to have produced and the name of the person who has possession or control of the record; and

(b) the grounds on which the accused relies to establish that the record is likely relevant to an issue at trial or to the competence of a witness to testify.

(4) Insufficient grounds — Any one or more of the following assertions by the accused are not sufficient on their own to establish that the record is likely relevant to an issue at trial or to the competence of a witness to testify:

(a) that the record exists;

(b) that the record relates to medical or psychiatric treatment, therapy or counselling that the complainant or witness has received or is receiving;

(c) that that record relates to the incident that is the subject-matter of the proceedings;

(d) that the record may disclose a prior inconsistent statement of the complainant or witness;

(e) that the record may relate to the credibility of the complainant or witness;

(f) that the record may relate to the reliability of the testimony of the complainant or witness merely because the complainant or witness has received or is receiving psychiatric treatment, therapy or counselling;

(g) that the record may reveal allegations of sexual abuse of the complainant by a person other than the accused;

(h) that the record relates to the sexual activity of the complainant with any person, including the accused;

(i) that the record relates to the presence or absence of a recent complaint;

(j) that the record relates to the complainant's sexual reputation; or

(k) that the record was made close in time to a complaint or to the activity that forms the subject-matter of the charge against the accused.

(5) Service of application and subpoena — The accused shall serve the application on the prosecutor, on the person who has possession or control of the record, on the complainant or witness, as the case may be, and on any other person to whom, to the knowledge of the accused, the record relates, at least 60 days before the hearing referred to in subsection 278.4(1) or any shorter interval that the judge may allow in the interests of justice. The accused shall also serve a subpoena issued under Part XXII in Form 16.1 on the person who has possession or control of the record at the same time as the application is served.

(6) Service on other persons — The judge may at any time order that the application be served on any person to whom the judge considers the record may relate.

1997, c. 30, s. 1; 2015, c. 13, s. 6; 2018, c. 29, s. 24

278.4 (1) Hearing *in camera* — The judge shall hold a hearing *in camera* to determine whether to order the person who has possession or control of the record to produce it to the court for review by the judge.

(2) Persons who may appear at hearing — The person who has possession or control of the record, the complainant or witness, as the case may be, and any other person to whom the record relates may appear and make submissions at the hearing, but they are not compellable as witnesses at the hearing.

(2.1) Right to counsel — The judge shall, as soon as feasible, inform any person referred to in subsection (2) who participates in the hearing of their right to be represented by counsel.

(3) Costs — No order for costs may be made against a person referred to in subsection (2) in respect of their participation in the hearing.

1997, c. 30, s. 1; 2015, c. 13, s. 7

278.5 (1) Judge may order production of record for review — The judge may order the person who has possession or control of the record to produce the record or part of the record to the court for review by the judge if, after the hearing referred to in subsection 278.4(1), the judge is satisfied that

(a) the application was made in accordance with subsections 278.3(2) to (6);

(b) the accused has established that the record is likely relevant to an issue at trial or to the competence of a witness to testify; and

(c) the production of the record is necessary in the interests of justice.

(2) Factors to be considered — In determining whether to order the production of the record or part of the record for review pursuant to subsection (1), the judge shall consider the salutary and deleterious effects of the determination on the accused's right to make a full answer and defence and on the right to privacy, personal security and equality of the complainant or witness, as the case may be, and of any other person to whom the record relates. In particular, the judge shall take the following factors into account:

(a) the extent to which the record is necessary for the accused to make a full answer and defence;

(b) the probative value of the record;

(c) the nature and extent of the reasonable expectation of privacy with respect to the record;

(d) whether production of the record is based on a discriminatory belief or bias;

(e) the potential prejudice to the personal dignity and right to privacy of any person to whom the record relates;

(f) society's interest in encouraging the reporting of sexual offences;

(g) society's interest in encouraging the obtaining of treatment by complainants of sexual offences; and

(h) the effect of the determination on the integrity of the trial process.

1997, c. 30, s. 1; 2015, c. 13, s. 8

278.6 (1) Review of record by judge — Where the judge has ordered the production of the record or part of the record for review, the judge shall review it in the absence of the parties in order to determine whether the record or part of the record should be produced to the accused.

(2) Hearing *in camera* — The judge may hold a hearing *in camera* if the judge considers that it will assist in making the determination.

(3) Provisions re hearing — Subsections 278.4(2) to (3) apply in the case of a hearing under subsection (2).

1997, c. 30, s. 1; 2015, c. 13, s. 9

278.7 (1) Judge may order production of record to accused — Where the judge is satisfied that the record or part of the record is likely relevant to an issue at trial or to the competence of a witness to testify and its production is necessary in the interests of justice, the judge may order that the record or part of the record that is likely relevant be produced to the accused, subject to any conditions that may be imposed pursuant to subsection (3).

(2) Factors to be considered — In determining whether to order the production of the record or part of the record to the accused, the judge shall consider the salutary and deleterious effects of the determination on the accused's right to make a full answer and defence and on the right to privacy, personal security and equality of the complainant or witness, as the case may be, and of any other person to whom the record relates and, in particular, shall take the factors specified in paragraphs 278.5(2)(a) to (h) into account.

(3) Conditions on production — If the judge orders the production of the record or part of the record to the accused, the judge may impose conditions on the production to protect the interests of justice and, to the greatest extent possible, the privacy, personal security and equality interests of the complainant or witness, as the case may be, and of any other person to whom the record relates, including, for example, the following conditions:

(a) that the record be edited as directed by the judge;

(b) that a copy of the record, rather than the original, be produced;

(c) that the accused and counsel for the accused not disclose the contents of the record to any other person, except with the approval of the court;

(d) that the record be viewed only at the offices of the court;

(e) that no copies of the record be made or that restrictions be imposed on the number of copies of the record that may be made; and

(f) that information regarding any person named in the record, such as their address, telephone number and place of employment, be severed from the record.

(4) **Copy to prosecutor** — Where the judge orders the production of the record or part of the record to the accused, the judge shall direct that a copy of the record or part of the record be provided to the prosecutor, unless the judge determines that it is not in the interests of justice to do so.

(5) **Record not to be used in other proceedings** — The record or part of the record that is produced to the accused pursuant to an order under subsection (1) shall not be used in any other proceedings.

(6) **Retention of record by court** — Where the judge refuses to order the production of the record or part of the record to the accused, the record or part of the record shall, unless a court orders otherwise, be kept in a sealed package by the court until the later of the expiration of the time for any appeal and the completion of any appeal in the proceedings against the accused, whereupon the record or part of the record shall be returned to the person lawfully entitled to possession or control of it.

1997, c. 30, s. 1; 2015, c. 13, s. 10

278.8 (1) **Reasons for decision** — The judge shall provide reasons for ordering or refusing to order the production of the record or part of the record pursuant to subsection 278.5(1) or 278.7(1).

(2) **Record of reasons** — The reasons referred to in subsection (1) shall be entered in the record of the proceedings or, where the proceedings are not recorded, shall be provided in writing.

1997, c. 30, s. 1

278.9 (1) **Publication prohibited** — No person shall publish in any document, or broadcast or transmit in any way, any of the following:

(a) the contents of an application made under section 278.3;

(b) any evidence taken, information given or submissions made at a hearing under subsection 278.4(1) or 278.6(2); or

(c) the determination of the judge pursuant to subsection 278.5(1) or 278.7(1) and the reasons provided pursuant to section 278.8, unless the judge, after taking into account the interests of justice and the right to privacy of the person to whom the record relates, orders that the determination may be published.

(2) **Offence** — Every person who contravenes subsection (1) is guilty of an offence punishable on summary conviction.

1997, c. 30, s. 1; 2005, c. 32, s. 14

278.91 **Appeal** — For the purposes of sections 675 and 676, a determination to make or refuse to make an order pursuant to subsection 278.5(1) or 278.7(1) is deemed to be a question of law.

1997, c. 30, s. 1

278.92 (1) **Admissibility — accused in possession of records relating to complainant** — Except in accordance with this section, no record relating to a complainant that is in the possession or control of the accused — and which the accused intends to adduce — shall be admitted in evidence in any proceedings in respect of any of the following offences or in any proceedings in respect of two or more offences at least one of which is any of the following offences:

(a) an offence under section 151, 152, 153, 153.1, 155, 160, 170, 171, 172, 173, 213, 271, 272, 273, 279.01, 279.011, 279.02, 279.03, 286.1, 286.2 or 286.3; or

(b) any offence under this Act, as it read from time to time before the day on which this paragraph comes into force, if the conduct alleged would be an offence referred to in paragraph (a) if it occurred on or after that day.

(2) Requirements for admissibility — The evidence is inadmissible unless the judge, provincial court judge or justice determines, in accordance with the procedures set out in sections 278.93 and 278.94,

(a) if the admissibility of the evidence is subject to section 276, that the evidence meets the conditions set out in subsection 276(2) while taking into account the factors set out in subsection (3); or

(b) in any other case, that the evidence is relevant to an issue at trial and has significant probative value that is not substantially outweighed by the danger of prejudice to the proper administration of justice.

(3) Factors that judge shall consider — In determining whether evidence is admissible under subsection (2), the judge, provincial court judge or justice shall take into account

(a) the interests of justice, including the right of the accused to make a full answer and defence;

(b) society's interest in encouraging the reporting of sexual assault offences;

(c) society's interest in encouraging the obtaining of treatment by complainants of sexual offences;

(d) whether there is a reasonable prospect that the evidence will assist in arriving at a just determination in the case;

(e) the need to remove from the fact-finding process any discriminatory belief or bias;

(f) the risk that the evidence may unduly arouse sentiments of prejudice, sympathy or hostility in the jury;

(g) the potential prejudice to the complainant's personal dignity and right of privacy;

(h) the right of the complainant and of every individual to personal security and to the full protection and benefit of the law; and

(i) any other factor that the judge, provincial court judge or justice considers relevant.

2018, c. 29, s. 25; 2019, c. 25, s. 403(10.1)

278.93 (1) Application for hearing — sections 276 and 278.92 — Application may be made to the judge, provincial court judge or justice by or on behalf of the accused for a hearing under section 278.94 to determine whether evidence is admissible under subsection 276(2) or 278.92(2).

(2) **Form and content of application** — An application referred to in subsection (1) must be made in writing, setting out detailed particulars of the evidence that the accused seeks to adduce and the relevance of that evidence to an issue at trial, and a copy of the application must be given to the prosecutor and to the clerk of the court.

(3) **Jury and public excluded** — The judge, provincial court judge or justice shall consider the application with the jury and the public excluded.

(4) **Judge may decide to hold hearing** — If the judge, provincial court judge or justice is satisfied that the application was made in accordance with subsection (2), that a copy of the application was given to the prosecutor and to the clerk of the court at least seven days previously, or any shorter interval that the judge, provincial court judge or justice may allow in the interests of justice and that the evidence sought to be adduced is capable of being admissible under subsection 276(2), the judge, provincial court judge or justice shall grant the application and hold a hearing under section 278.94 to determine whether the evidence is admissible under subsection 276(2) or 278.92(2).

2018, c. 29, s. 25

278.94 (1) **Hearing — jury and public excluded** — The jury and the public shall be excluded from a hearing to determine whether evidence is admissible under subsection 276(2) or 278.92(2).

(2) **Complainant not compellable** — The complainant is not a compellable witness at the hearing but may appear and make submissions.

(3) **Right to counsel** — The judge shall, as soon as feasible, inform the complainant who participates in the hearing of their right to be represented by counsel.

(4) **Judge's determination and reasons** — At the conclusion of the hearing, the judge, provincial court judge or justice shall determine whether the evidence, or any part of it, is admissible under subsection 276(2) or 278.92(2) and shall provide reasons for that determination, and

(a) if not all of the evidence is to be admitted, the reasons must state the part of the evidence that is to be admitted;

(b) the reasons must state the factors referred to in subsection 276(3) or 278.92(3) that affected the determination; and

(c) if all or any part of the evidence is to be admitted, the reasons must state the manner in which that evidence is expected to be relevant to an issue at trial.

(5) **Record of reasons** — The reasons provided under subsection (4) shall be entered in the record of the proceedings or, if the proceedings are not recorded, shall be provided in writing.

2018, c. 29, s. 25

278.95 (1) Publication prohibited — A person shall not publish in any document, or broadcast or transmit in any way, any of the following:

(a) the contents of an application made under subsection 278.93;

(b) any evidence taken, the information given and the representations made at an application under section 278.93 or at a hearing under section 278.94;

(c) the decision of a judge or justice under subsection 278.93(4), unless the judge or justice, after taking into account the complainant's right of privacy and the interests of justice, orders that the decision may be published, broadcast or transmitted; and

(d) the determination made and the reasons provided under subsection 278.94(4), unless

(i) that determination is that evidence is admissible, or

(ii) the judge or justice, after taking into account the complainant's right of privacy and the interests of justice, orders that the determination and reasons may be published, broadcast or transmitted.

(2) Offence — Every person who contravenes subsection (1) is guilty of an offence punishable on summary conviction.

2018, c. 29, s. 25

278.96 Judge to instruct jury — re use of evidence — If evidence is admitted at trial on the basis of a determination made under subsection 278.94(4), the judge shall instruct the jury as to the uses that the jury may and may not make of that evidence.

2018, c. 29, s. 25

278.97 Appeal — For the purposes of sections 675 and 676, a determination made under subsection 278.94(4) shall be deemed to be a question of law.

2018, c. 29, s. 25

Kidnapping, Trafficking in Persons, Hostage Taking and Abduction

[Heading amended 2005, c. 43, s. 2.]

279. (1) Kidnapping — Every person commits an offence who kidnaps a person with intent

(a) to cause the person to be confined or imprisoned against the person's will;

(b) to cause the person to be unlawfully sent or transported out of Canada against the person's will; or

(c) to hold the person for ransom or to service against the person's will.

(1.1) Punishment — Every person who commits an offence under subsection (1) is guilty of an indictable offence and liable

(a) if a restricted firearm or prohibited firearm is used in the commission of the offence or if any firearm is used in the commission of the offence and the offence is committed for the benefit of, at the direction of, or in association with, a criminal organization, to imprisonment for life and to a minimum punishment of imprisonment for a term of

(i) in the case of a first offence, five years, and

(ii) in the case of a second or subsequent offence, seven years;

(a.1) in any other case where a firearm is used in the commission of the offence, to imprisonment for life and to a minimum punishment of imprisonment for a term of four years;

(a.2) if the person referred to in paragraph (1)(a), (b) or (c) is under 16 years of age, to imprisonment for life and, unless the person who commits the offence is a parent, guardian or person having the lawful care or charge of the person referred to in that paragraph, to a minimum punishment of imprisonment for a term of five years; and

(b) in any other case, to imprisonment for life.

(1.2) Subsequent offences — In determining, for the purpose of paragraph (1.1)(a), whether a convicted person has committed a second or subsequent offence, if the person was earlier convicted of any of the following offences, that offence is to be considered as an earlier offence:

(a) an offence under subsection (1);

(b) an offence under subsection 85(1) or (2) or section 244 or 244.2; or

(c) an offence under section 220, 236, 239, 272, 273, 279.1, 344 or 346 if a firearm was used in the commission of the offence.

However, an earlier offence shall not be taken into account if 10 years have elapsed between the day on which the person was convicted of the earlier offence and the day on which the person was convicted of the offence for which sentence is being imposed, not taking into account any time in custody.

(1.21) Factors to consider — In imposing a sentence under paragraph (1.1)(a.2), the court shall take into account the age and vulnerability of the victim.

(1.3) Sequence of convictions only — For the purposes of subsection (1.2), the only question to be considered is the sequence of convictions and no consideration shall be given to the sequence of commission of offences or whether any offence occurred before or after any conviction.

(2) Forcible confinement — Every one who, without lawful authority, confines, imprisons or forcibly seizes another person is guilty of

(a) an indictable offence and liable to imprisonment for a term not exceeding ten years; or

(b) an offence punishable on summary conviction.

(3) [Repealed 2018, c. 29, s. 26.]

R.S.C. 1985, c. 27 (1st Supp.), s. 39; 1995, c. 39, s. 147; 1997, c. 18, s. 14; 2008, c. 6, s. 30; 2009, c. 22, s. 12; 2013, c. 32, s. 1; 2018, c. 29, s. 26; 2019, c. 25, s. 103

279.01 (1) Trafficking in persons — Every person who recruits, transports, transfers, receives, holds, conceals or harbours a person, or exercises control, direction or influence over the movements of a person, for the purpose of exploiting them or facilitating their exploitation is guilty of an indictable offence and liable

(a) to imprisonment for life and to a minimum punishment of imprisonment for a term of five years if they kidnap, commit an aggravated assault or aggravated sexual assault against, or cause death to, the victim during the commission of the offence; or

(b) to imprisonment for a term of not more than 14 years and to a minimum punishment of imprisonment for a term of four years in any other case.

(2) **Consent** — No consent to the activity that forms the subject-matter of a charge under subsection (1) is valid.

(3) **Presumption** — For the purposes of subsections (1) and 279.011(1), evidence that a person who is not exploited lives with or is habitually in the company of a person who is exploited is, in the absence of evidence to the contrary, proof that the person exercises control, direction or influence over the movements of that person for the purpose of exploiting them or facilitating their exploitation.

2005, c. 43, s. 3; 2014, c. 25, s. 18; 2015, c. 16, s. 1

279.011 (1) **Trafficking of a person under the age of eighteen years** — Every person who recruits, transports, transfers, receives, holds, conceals or harbours a person under the age of eighteen years, or exercises control, direction or influence over the movements of a person under the age of eighteen years, for the purpose of exploiting them or facilitating their exploitation is guilty of an indictable offence and liable

(a) to imprisonment for life and to a minimum punishment of imprisonment for a term of six years if they kidnap, commit an aggravated assault or aggravated sexual assault against, or cause death to, the victim during the commission of the offence; or

(b) to imprisonment for a term of not more than fourteen years and to a minimum punishment of imprisonment for a term of five years, in any other case.

(2) **Consent** — No consent to the activity that forms the subject-matter of a charge under subsection (1) is valid.

2010, c. 3, s. 2

279.02 (1) **Material benefit — trafficking** — Every person who receives a financial or other material benefit, knowing that it is obtained by or derived directly or indirectly from the commission of an offence under subsection 279.01(1), is guilty of

(a) an indictable offence and liable to imprisonment for a term of not more than 10 years; or

(b) an offence punishable on summary conviction.

(2) **Material benefit — trafficking of person under 18 years** — Everyone who receives a financial or other material benefit, knowing that it is obtained by or derived directly or indirectly from the commission of an offence under subsection 279.011(1), is guilty of an indictable offence and liable to imprisonment for a term

of not more than 14 years and to a minimum punishment of imprisonment for a term of two years.

2005, c. 43, s. 3; 2010, c. 3, s. 3; 2014, c. 25, s. 19; 2019, c. 25, s. 104

279.03 (1) Withholding or destroying documents — trafficking — Every person who, for the purpose of committing or facilitating an offence under subsection 279.01(1), conceals, removes, withholds or destroys any travel document that belongs to another person or any document that establishes or purports to establish another person's identity or immigration status — whether or not the document is of Canadian origin or is authentic — is guilty of

(a) an indictable offence and liable to imprisonment for a term of not more than five years; or

(b) an offence punishable on summary conviction.

(2) Withholding or destroying documents — trafficking of person under 18 years — Everyone who, for the purpose of committing or facilitating an offence under subsection 279.011(1), conceals, removes, withholds or destroys any travel document that belongs to another person or any document that establishes or purports to establish another person's identity or immigration status — whether or not the document is of Canadian origin or is authentic — is guilty of an indictable offence and liable to imprisonment for a term of not more than 10 years and to a minimum punishment of imprisonment for a term of one year.

2005, c. 43, s. 3; 2010, c. 3, s. 3; 2014, c. 25, s. 19; 2019, c. 25, s. 105

279.04 (1) Exploitation — For the purposes of sections 279.01 to 279.03, a person exploits another person if they cause them to provide, or offer to provide, labour or a service by engaging in conduct that, in all the circumstances, could reasonably be expected to cause the other person to believe that their safety or the safety of a person known to them would be threatened if they failed to provide, or offer to provide, the labour or service.

(2) Factors — In determining whether an accused exploits another person under subsection (1), the Court may consider, among other factors, whether the accused

(a) used or threatened to use force or another form of coercion;

(b) used deception; or

(c) abused a position of trust, power or authority.

(3) Organ or tissue removal — For the purposes of sections 279.01 to 279.03, a person exploits another person if they cause them, by means of deception or the use or threat of force or of any other form of coercion, to have an organ or tissue removed.

2005, c. 43, s. 3; 2012, c. 15, s. 2

Proposed Addition — 279.05

279.05 Sentences to be served consecutively — A sentence imposed on a person for an offence under sections 279.01 to 279.03 shall be served consecutively to any other punishment imposed on the person for an offence arising out of the same event or series of events and to any other sentence to which the person is subject at the time the sentence is imposed on the person for an offence under any of those sections.

2015, c. 16, s. 3 [Not in force at date of publication.]

279.1 (1) Hostage taking — Everyone takes a person hostage who — with intent to induce any person, other than the hostage, or any group of persons or any state or international or intergovernmental organization to commit or cause to be committed any act or omission as a condition, whether express or implied, of the release of the hostage —

(a) confines, imprisons, forcibly seizes or detains that person; and

(b) in any manner utters, conveys or causes any person to receive a threat that the death of, or bodily harm to, the hostage will be caused or that the confinement, imprisonment or detention of the hostage will be continued.

(2) Hostage-taking — Every person who takes a person hostage is guilty of an indictable offence and liable

(a) if a restricted firearm or prohibited firearm is used in the commission of the offence or if any firearm is used in the commission of the offence and the offence is committed for the benefit of, at the direction of, or in association with, a criminal organization, to imprisonment for life and to a minimum punishment of imprisonment for a term of

(i) in the case of a first offence, five years, and

(ii) in the case of a second or subsequent offence, seven years;

(a.1) in any other case where a firearm is used in the commission of the offence, to imprisonment for life and to a minimum punishment of imprisonment for a term of four years; and

(b) in any other case, to imprisonment for life.

(2.1) Subsequent offences — In determining, for the purpose of paragraph (2)(a), whether a convicted person has committed a second or subsequent offence, if the person was earlier convicted of any of the following offences, that offence is to be considered as an earlier offence:

(a) an offence under this section;

(b) an offence under subsection 85(1) or (2) or section 244 or 244.2; or

(c) an offence under section 220, 236, 239, 272 or 273, subsection 279(1) or section 344 or 346 if a firearm was used in the commission of the offence.

However, an earlier offence shall not be taken into account if 10 years have elapsed between the day on which the person was convicted of the earlier offence and the day on which the person was convicted of the offence for which sentence is being imposed, not taking into account any time in custody.

(2.2) Sequence of convictions only — For the purposes of subsection (2.1), the only question to be considered is the sequence of convictions and no consideration shall be given to the sequence of commission of offences or whether any offence occurred before or after any conviction.

(3) [Repealed 2018, c. 29, s. 27.]

R.S.C. 1985, c. 27 (1st Supp.), s. 40(1); 1995, c. 39, s. 148; 2008, c. 6, s. 31; 2009, c. 22, s. 13; 2018, c. 29, s. 27

280. (1) Abduction of person under age of 16 — Every person who, without lawful authority, takes or causes to be taken a person under the age of 16 years out of the possession of and against the will of the parent or guardian of that person or of any other person who has the lawful care or charge of that person is guilty of

(a) an indictable offence and liable to imprisonment for a term of not more than five years; or

(b) an offence punishable on summary conviction.

(2) Definition of "guardian" — In this section and sections 281 to 283, **"guardian"** includes any person who has in law or in fact the custody or control of another person.

2019, c. 25, s. 106

281. Abduction of person under age of 14 — Every person who, not being the parent, guardian or person having the lawful care or charge of a person under the age of 14 years, unlawfully takes, entices away, conceals, detains, receives or harbours that person with intent to deprive a parent or guardian, or any other person who has the lawful care or charge of that person, of the possession of that person is guilty of

(a) an indictable offence and liable to imprisonment for a term of not more than 10 years; or

(b) an offence punishable on summary conviction.

2019, c. 25, s. 107

282. (1) Abduction in contravention of custody or parenting order — Every one who, being the parent, guardian or person having the lawful care or charge of a child under the age of 14 years, takes, entices away, conceals, detains, receives or harbours that child, in contravention of a custody order or a parenting order made by a court anywhere in Canada, with intent to deprive a parent or guardian, or any other person who has the lawful care or charge of that child, of the possession of that child is guilty of

(a) an indictable offence and is liable to imprisonment for a term not exceeding ten years; or

(b) an offence punishable on summary conviction.

(2) If no belief in validity of custody order or parenting order — If a count charges an offence under subsection (1) and the offence is not proven only because the accused did not believe that there was a valid custody order or parenting order but the evidence does prove an offence under section 283, the accused may be convicted of an offence under that section.

1993, c. 45, s. 4; 2019, c. 16, s. 123

283. (1) Abduction — Everyone who, being the parent, guardian or person having the lawful care or charge of a child under the age of 14 years, takes, entices away, conceals, detains, receives or harbours that child, whether or not there is an order referred to in subsection 282(1) in respect of the child, with intent to deprive a parent, guardian or any other person who has the lawful care or charge of that child, of the possession of that child, is guilty of

(a) an indictable offence and is liable to imprisonment for a term not exceeding ten years; or

(b) an offence punishable on summary conviction.

(2) Consent required — No proceedings may be commenced under subsection (1) without the consent of the Attorney General or counsel instructed by him for that purpose.

1993, c. 45, s. 5; 2019, c. 16, s. 124

284. Defence — No one shall be found guilty of an offence under sections 281 to 283 if he establishes that the taking, enticing away, concealing, detaining, receiving or harbouring of any young person was done with the consent of the parent, guardian or other person having the lawful possession, care or charge of that young person.

285. Defence — No one shall be found guilty of an offence under sections 280 to 283 if the court is satisfied that the taking, enticing away, concealing, detaining, receiving or harbouring of any young person was necessary to protect the young person from danger of imminent harm or if the person charged with the offence was escaping from danger of imminent harm.

1993, c. 45, s. 6

286. No defence — In proceedings in respect of an offence under sections 280 to 283, it is not a defence to any charge that a young person consented to or suggested any conduct of the accused.

Commodification of Sexual Activity

[Heading added 2014, c. 25, s. 20.]

286.1 (1) Obtaining sexual services for consideration — Everyone who, in any place, obtains for consideration, or communicates with anyone for the purpose of obtaining for consideration, the sexual services of a person is guilty of

(a) an indictable offence and liable to imprisonment for a term of not more than five years and a minimum punishment of,

(i) in the case where the offence is committed in a public place, or in any place open to public view, that is or is next to a park or the grounds of a school or religious institution or that is or is next to any other place where persons under the age of 18 can reasonably be expected to be present,

(A) for a first offence, a fine of $2,000, and

(B) for each subsequent offence, a fine of $4,000, or

(ii) in any other case,

(A) for a first offence, a fine of $1,000, and

(B) for each subsequent offence, a fine of $2,000; or

(b) an offence punishable on summary conviction and liable to a fine of not more than $5,000 or to imprisonment for a term of not more than two years less a day, or to both, and to a minimum punishment of,

(i) in the case referred to in subparagraph (a)(i),

(A) for a first offence, a fine of $1,000, and

(B) for each subsequent offence, a fine of $2,000, or

(ii) in any other case,

(A) for a first offence, a fine of $500, and

(B) for each subsequent offence, a fine of $1,000.

(2) **Obtaining sexual services for consideration from person under 18 years** — Everyone who, in any place, obtains for consideration, or communicates with anyone for the purpose of obtaining for consideration, the sexual services of a person under the age of 18 years is guilty of an indictable offence and liable to imprisonment for a term of not more than 10 years and to a minimum punishment of imprisonment for a term of

(a) for a first offence, six months; and

(b) for each subsequent offence, one year.

(3) **Subsequent offences** — In determining, for the purpose of subsection (2), whether a convicted person has committed a subsequent offence, if the person was earlier convicted of any of the following offences, that offence is to be considered as an earlier offence:

(a) an offence under that subsection; or

(b) an offence under subsection 212(4) of this Act, as it read from time to time before the day on which this subsection comes into force.

(4) **Sequence of convictions only** — In determining, for the purposes of this section, whether a convicted person has committed a subsequent offence, the only question to be considered is the sequence of convictions and no consideration shall be given to the sequence of commission of offences, whether any offence occurred before or after any conviction or whether offences were prosecuted by indictment or by way of summary conviction proceedings.

(5) **Definitions of "place" and "public place"** — For the purposes of this section, **"place"** and **"public place"** have the same meaning as in subsection 197(1).

2014, c. 25, s. 20; 2019, c. 25, s. 108

286.2 (1) **Material benefit from sexual services** — Every person who receives a financial or other material benefit, knowing that it is obtained by or derived directly or indirectly from the commission of an offence under subsection 286.1(1), is guilty of

(a) an indictable offence and liable to imprisonment for a term of not more than 10 years; or

(b) an offence punishable on summary conviction.

(2) **Material benefit from sexual services provided by person under 18 years** — Everyone who receives a financial or other material benefit, knowing that it is obtained by or derived directly or indirectly from the commission of an offence under subsection 286.1(2), is guilty of an indictable offence and liable to imprisonment for a term of not more than 14 years and to a minimum punishment of imprisonment for a term of two years.

(3) **Presumption** — For the purposes of subsections (1) and (2), evidence that a person lives with or is habitually in the company of a person who offers or provides sexual services for consideration is, in the absence of evidence to the contrary, proof that the person received a financial or other material benefit from those services.

(4) **Exception** — Subject to subsection (5), subsections (1) and (2) do not apply to a person who receives the benefit

(a) in the context of a legitimate living arrangement with the person from whose sexual services the benefit is derived;

(b) as a result of a legal or moral obligation of the person from whose sexual services the benefit is derived;

(c) in consideration for a service or good that they offer, on the same terms and conditions, to the general public; or

(d) in consideration for a service or good that they do not offer to the general public but that they offered or provided to the person from whose sexual services the benefit is derived, if they did not counsel or encourage that person to provide sexual services and the benefit is proportionate to the value of the service or good.

(5) **No exception** — Subsection (4) does not apply to a person who commits an offence under subsection (1) or (2) if that person

(a) used, threatened to use or attempted to use violence, intimidation or coercion in relation to the person from whose sexual services the benefit is derived;

(b) abused a position of trust, power or authority in relation to the person from whose sexual services the benefit is derived;

(c) provided a drug, alcohol or any other intoxicating substance to the person from whose sexual services the benefit is derived for the purpose of aiding or abetting that person to offer or provide sexual services for consideration;

(d) engaged in conduct, in relation to any person, that would constitute an offence under section 286.3; or

(e) received the benefit in the context of a commercial enterprise that offers sexual services for consideration.

(6) Aggravating factor — If a person is convicted of an offence under this section, the court that imposes the sentence shall consider as an aggravating factor the fact that that person received the benefit in the context of a commercial enterprise that offers sexual services for consideration.

2014, c. 25, s. 20; 2019, c. 25, s. 109

286.3 (1) Procuring — Everyone who procures a person to offer or provide sexual services for consideration or, for the purpose of facilitating an offence under subsection 286.1(1), recruits, holds, conceals or harbours a person who offers or provides sexual services for consideration, or exercises control, direction or influence over the movements of that person, is guilty of an indictable offence and liable to imprisonment for a term of not more than 14 years.

(2) Procuring — person under 18 years — Everyone who procures a person under the age of 18 years to offer or provide sexual services for consideration or, for the purpose of facilitating an offence under subsection 286.1(2), recruits, holds, conceals or harbours a person under the age of 18 who offers or provides sexual services for consideration, or exercises control, direction or influence over the movements of that person, is guilty of an indictable offence and liable to imprisonment for a term of not more than 14 years and to a minimum punishment of imprisonment for a term of five years.

2014, c. 25, s. 20

286.4 Advertising sexual services — Everyone who knowingly advertises an offer to provide sexual services for consideration is guilty of

(a) an indictable offence and liable to imprisonment for a term of not more than five years; or

(b) an offence punishable on summary conviction.

2014, c. 25, s. 20; 2019, c. 25, s. 110

286.5 (1) Immunity — material benefit and advertising — No person shall be prosecuted for

(a) an offence under section 286.2 if the benefit is derived from the provision of their own sexual services; or

(b) an offence under section 286.4 in relation to the advertisement of their own sexual services.

(2) Immunity — aiding, abetting, etc. — No person shall be prosecuted for aiding, abetting, conspiring or attempting to commit an offence under any of sections 286.1 to 286.4 or being an accessory after the fact or counselling a person to be a party to such an offence, if the offence relates to the offering or provision of their own sexual services.

2014, c. 25, s. 20

Abortion

287. [Repealed 2019, c. 25, s. 111.]

288. [Repealed 2018, c. 29, s. 28.]

Venereal Diseases

289. [Repealed R.S.C. 1985, c. 27 (1st Supp.), s. 41.]

Offences Against Conjugal Rights

290. (1) Bigamy — Every one commits **"bigamy"** who

(a) in Canada,

(i) being married, goes through a form of marriage with another person,

(ii) knowing that another person is married, goes through a form of marriage with that person, or

(iii) on the same day or simultaneously, goes through a form of marriage with more than one person; or

(b) being a Canadian citizen resident in Canada leaves Canada with intent to do anything mentioned in subparagraphs (*a*)(i) to (iii) and, pursuant thereto, does outside Canada anything mentioned in those subparagraphs in circumstances mentioned therein.

(2) Matters of defence — No person commits bigamy by going through a form of marriage if

(a) that person in good faith and on reasonable grounds believes that his spouse is dead,

(b) the spouse of that person has been continuously absent from him for seven years immediately preceding the time when he goes through the form of marriage, unless he knew that his spouse was alive at any time during those seven years,

(c) that person has been divorced from the bond of the first marriage, or

(d) the former marriage has been declared void by a court of competent jurisdiction.

(3) Incompetency no defence — Where a person is alleged to have committed bigamy, it is not a defence that the parties would, if unmarried, have been incompetent to contract marriage under the law of the place where the offence is alleged to have been committed.

(4) Validity presumed — Every marriage or form of marriage shall, for the purpose of this section, be deemed to be valid unless the accused establishes that it was invalid.

(5) Act or omission by accused — No act or omission on the part of an accused who is charged with bigamy invalidates a marriage or form of marriage that is otherwise valid.

291. (1) Punishment — Every person who commits bigamy is guilty of

(a) an indictable offence and liable to imprisonment for a term of not more than five years; or

(b) an offence punishable on summary conviction.

(2) Certificate of marriage — For the purposes of this section, a certificate of marriage issued under the authority of law is evidence of the marriage or form of marriage to which it relates without proof of the signature or official character of the person by whom it purports to be signed.

2019, c. 25, s. 112

292. (1) Procuring feigned marriage — Every person who procures or knowingly aids in procuring a feigned marriage between themselves and another person is guilty of

(a) an indictable offence and liable to imprisonment for a term of not more than five years; or

(b) an offence punishable on summary conviction.

(2) Corroboration — No person shall be convicted of an offence under this section on the evidence of only one witness unless the evidence of that witness is corroborated in a material particular by evidence that implicates the accused.

2019, c. 25, s. 113

293. (1) Polygamy — Every person is guilty of an indictable offence and liable to imprisonment for a term of not more than five years or is guilty of an offence punishable on summary conviction who

(a) practises or enters into or in any manner agrees or consents to practise or enter into any form of polygamy or any kind of conjugal union with more than one person at the same time, whether or not it is by law recognized as a binding form of marriage; or

(b) celebrates, assists or is a party to a rite, ceremony, contract or consent that purports to sanction a relationship mentioned in paragraph (a).

(2) Evidence in case of polygamy — Where an accused is charged with an offence under this section, no averment or proof of the method by which the alleged relationship was entered into, agreed to or consented to is necessary in the indictment or on the trial of the accused, nor is it necessary on the trial to prove that the persons who are alleged to have entered into the relationship had or intended to have sexual intercourse.

2019, c. 25, s. 114

293.1 Forced marriage — Every person who celebrates, aids or participates in a marriage rite or ceremony knowing that one of the persons being married is marrying against their will is guilty of

(a) an indictable offence and liable to imprisonment for a term of not more than five years; or

(b) an offence punishable on summary conviction.

2015, c. 29, s. 9; 2019, c. 25, s. 115

293.2 Marriage under age of 16 years — Every person who celebrates, aids or participates in a marriage rite or ceremony knowing that one of the persons being married is under the age of 16 years is guilty of

(a) an indictable offence and liable to imprisonment for a term of not more than five years; or

(b) an offence punishable on summary conviction.

2015, c. 29, s. 9; 2019, c. 25, s. 115

Unlawful Solemnization of Marriage

294. Pretending to solemnize marriage — Every person is guilty of an indictable offence and liable to imprisonment for a term of not more than two years or is guilty of an offence punishable on summary conviction who

(a) solemnizes or pretends to solemnize a marriage without lawful authority; or

(b) procures a person to solemnize a marriage knowing that he is not lawfully authorized to solemnize the marriage.

2018, c. 29, s. 29; 2019, c. 25, s. 116

295. Marriage contrary to law — Every person who, being lawfully authorized to solemnize marriage, knowingly solemnizes a marriage in contravention of federal law or the laws of the province in which the marriage is solemnized is guilty of

(a) an indictable offence and liable to imprisonment for a term of not more than two years; or

(b) an offence punishable on summary conviction.

2015, c. 29, s. 10; 2019, c. 25, s. 117

Heading and s. 296. [Repealed 2018, c. 29, s. 30.]

Defamatory Libel

297. Definition of "newspaper" — In sections 303, 304 and 308, **"newspaper"** means any paper, magazine or periodical containing public news, intelligence or reports of events, or any remarks or observations thereon, printed for sale and published periodically or in parts or numbers, at intervals not exceeding thirty-one days between the publication of any two such papers, parts or numbers, and any paper, magazine or periodical printed in order to be dispersed and made public, weekly or more often, or at intervals not exceeding thirty-one days, that contains advertisements, exclusively or principally.

298. (1) Definition — A **"defamatory libel"** is matter published, without lawful justification or excuse, that is likely to injure the reputation of any person by exposing him to hatred, contempt or ridicule, or that is designed to insult the person of or concerning whom it is published.

(2) Mode of expression — A defamatory libel may be expressed directly or by insinuation or irony

(a) in words legibly marked on any substance, or

(b) by any object signifying a defamatory libel otherwise than by words.

299. Publishing — A person publishes a libel when he

(a) exhibits it in public,

(b) causes it to be read or seen, or

(c) shows or delivers it, or causes it to be shown or delivered, with intent that it should be read or seen by any person other than the person whom it defames.

2018, c. 29, s. 31

300. Punishment of libel known to be false — Every person who publishes a defamatory libel that they know is false is guilty of

(a) an indictable offence and liable to imprisonment for a term of not more than five years; or

(b) an offence punishable on summary conviction.

2019, c. 25, s. 118

301. Punishment for defamatory libel — Every person who publishes a defamatory libel is guilty of

(a) an indictable offence and liable to imprisonment for a term of not more than two years; or

(b) an offence punishable on summary conviction.

2019, c. 25, s. 118

302. (1) Extortion by libel — Every one commits an offence who, with intent

(a) to extort money from any person, or

(b) to induce a person to confer on or procure for another person an appointment or office of profit or trust,

publishes or threatens to publish or offers to abstain from publishing or to prevent the publication of a defamatory libel.

(2) Idem — Every one commits an offence who, as the result of the refusal of any person to permit money to be extorted or to confer or procure an appointment or office of profit or trust, publishes or threatens to publish a defamatory libel.

(3) Punishment — Every person who commits an offence under this section is guilty of

(a) an indictable offence and liable to imprisonment for a term of not more than five years; or

(b) an offence punishable on summary conviction.

2019, c. 25, s. 119

303. (1) Proprietor of newspaper presumed responsible — The proprietor of a newspaper shall be deemed to publish defamatory matter that is inserted and published therein, unless he proves that the defamatory matter was inserted in the newspaper without his knowledge and without negligence on his part.

(2) General authority to manager when negligence — Where the proprietor of a newspaper gives to a person general authority to manage or conduct the newspaper as editor or otherwise, the insertion by that person of defamatory matter in the newspaper shall, for the purposes of subsection (1), be deemed not to be negligence on the part of the proprietor unless it is proved that

(a) he intended the general authority to include authority to insert defamatory matter in the newspaper; or

(b) he continued to confer general authority after he knew that it had been exercised by the insertion of defamatory matter in the newspaper.

(3) Selling newspapers — No person shall be deemed to publish a defamatory libel by reason only that he sells a number or part of a newspaper that contains a defamatory libel, unless he knows that the number or part contains defamatory matter or that defamatory matter is habitually contained in the newspaper.

304. (1) Selling book containing defamatory libel — No person shall be deemed to publish a defamatory libel by reason only that he sells a book, magazine, pamphlet or other thing, other than a newspaper that contains defamatory matter if, at the time of the sale, he does not know that it contains the defamatory matter.

(2) Sale by servant — Where a servant, in the course of his employment, sells a book, magazine, pamphlet or other thing, other than a newspaper, the employer shall be deemed not to publish any defamatory matter contained therein unless it is proved that the employer authorized the sale knowing that

(a) defamatory matter was contained therein; or

(b) defamatory matter was habitually contained therein, in the case of a periodical.

305. Publishing proceedings of courts of justice — No person shall be deemed to publish a defamatory libel by reason only that he publishes defamatory matter

(a) in a proceeding held before or under the authority of a court exercising judicial authority; or

(b) in an inquiry made under the authority of an Act or by order of Her Majesty, or under the authority of a public department or a department of the government of a province.

306. Parliamentary papers — No person shall be deemed to publish a defamatory libel by reason only that he

(a) publishes to the Senate or House of Commons or to a legislature of a province defamatory matter contained in a petition to the Senate or House of Commons or to the legislature of a province, as the case may be;

(b) publishes by order or under the authority of the Senate or House of Commons or of the legislature of a province a paper containing defamatory matter; or

(c) publishes, in good faith and without ill-will to the person defamed, an extract from or abstract of a petition or paper mentioned in paragraph (*a*) or (*b*).

307. (1) Fair reports of Parliamentary or judicial proceedings — No person shall be deemed to publish a defamatory libel by reason only that he publishes in good faith, for the information of the public, a fair report of the proceedings of the Senate or House of Commons or the legislature of a province, or a committee thereof, or of the public proceedings before a court exercising judicial authority, or publishes, in good faith, any fair comment on any such proceedings.

(2) Divorce proceedings an exception — This section does not apply to a person who publishes a report of evidence taken or offered in any proceeding before the Senate or House of Commons or any committee thereof, on a petition or bill relating to any matter of marriage or divorce, if the report is published without authority from or leave of the House in which the proceeding is held or is contrary to any rule, order or practice of that House.

308. Fair report of public meeting — No person shall be deemed to publish a defamatory libel by reason only that he publishes in good faith, in a newspaper, a fair report of the proceedings of any public meeting if

(a) the meeting is lawfully convened for a lawful purpose and is open to the public;

(b) the report is fair and accurate;

(c) the publication of the matter complained of is for the public benefit; and

(d) he does not refuse to publish in a conspicuous place in the newspaper a reasonable explanation or contradiction by the person defamed in respect of the defamatory matter.

309. Public benefit — No person shall be deemed to publish a defamatory libel by reason only that he publishes defamatory matter that, on reasonable grounds, he believes is true, and that is relevant to any subject of public interest, the public discussion of which is for the public benefit.

310. Fair comment on public person or work of art — No person shall be deemed to publish a defamatory libel by reason only that he publishes fair comments

(a) on the public conduct of a person who takes part in public affairs; or

(b) on a published book or other literary production, or on any composition or work of art or performance publicly exhibited, or on any other communication made to the public on any subject, if the comments are confined to criticism thereof.

311. When truth a defence — No person shall be deemed to publish a defamatory libel where he proves that the publication of the defamatory matter in the manner in which it was published was for the public benefit at the time when it was published and that the matter itself was true.

312. Publication invited or necessary — No person shall be deemed to publish a defamatory libel by reason only that he publishes defamatory matter

(a) on the invitation or challenge of the person in respect of whom it is published, or

(b) that it is necessary to publish in order to refute defamatory matter published in respect of him by another person,

if he believes that the defamatory matter is true and it is relevant to the invitation, challenge or necessary refutation, as the case may be, and does not in any respect exceed what is reasonably sufficient in the circumstances.

313. Answer to inquiries — No person shall be deemed to publish a defamatory libel by reason only that he publishes, in answer to inquiries made to him, defamatory matter relating to a subject-matter in respect of which the person by whom or on whose behalf the inquiries are made has an interest in knowing the truth or who, on reasonable grounds, the person who publishes the defamatory matter believes has such an interest, if

(a) the matter is published, in good faith, for the purpose of giving information in answer to the inquiries;

(b) the person who publishes the defamatory matter believes that it is true;

(c) the defamatory matter is relevant to the inquiries; and

(d) the defamatory matter does not in any respect exceed what is reasonably sufficient in the circumstances.

314. Giving information to person interested — No person shall be deemed to publish a defamatory libel by reason only that he publishes to another person defamatory matter for the purpose of giving information to that person with respect to a subject-matter in which the person to whom the information is given has, or is believed on reasonable grounds by the person who gives it to have, an interest in knowing the truth with respect to that subject-matter if

(a) the conduct of the person who gives the information is reasonable in the circumstances;

(b) the defamatory matter is relevant to the subject-matter; and

(c) the defamatory matter is true, or if it is not true, is made without ill-will toward the person who is defamed and is made in the belief, on reasonable grounds, that it is true.

315. Publication in good faith for redress of wrong — No person shall be deemed to publish a defamatory libel by reason only that he publishes defamatory matter in good faith for the purpose of seeking remedy or redress for a private or public wrong or grievance from a person who has, or who on reasonable grounds he believes has, the right or is under an obligation to remedy or redress the wrong or grievance, if

(a) he believes that the defamatory matter is true;

(b) the defamatory matter is relevant to the remedy or redress that is sought; and

(c) the defamatory matter does not in any respect exceed what is reasonably sufficient in the circumstances.

316. (1) Proving publication by order of legislature — An accused who is alleged to have published a defamatory libel may, at any stage of the proceedings, adduce evidence to prove that the matter that is alleged to be defamatory was contained in a paper published by order or under the authority of the Senate or House of Commons or the legislature of a province.

(2) Directing verdict — Where at any stage in proceedings referred to in subsection (1) the court, judge, justice or provincial court judge is satisfied that the matter alleged to be defamatory was contained in a paper published by order or under the authority of the Senate or House of Commons or the legislature of a province, he shall direct a verdict of not guilty to be entered and shall discharge the accused.

(3) Certificate of order — For the purposes of this section, a certificate under the hand of the Speaker or clerk of the Senate or House of Commons or the legislature of a province to the effect that the matter that is alleged to be defamatory was contained in a paper published by order or under the authority of the Senate, House of Commons or the legislature of a province, as the case may be, is conclusive evidence thereof.

R.S.C. 1985, c. 27 (1st Supp.), s. 203

Verdicts

317. Verdicts in cases of defamatory libel — Where, on the trial of an indictment for publishing a defamatory libel, a plea of not guilty is pleaded, the jury that is sworn to try the issue may give a general verdict of guilty or not guilty on the whole matter put in issue on the indictment, and shall not be required or directed by the judge to find the defendant guilty merely on proof of publication by the defendant of the alleged defamatory libel, and of the sense ascribed thereto in the indictment, but the judge may, in his discretion, give a direction or opinion to the jury on the matter in issue as in other criminal proceedings, and the jury may, on the issue, find a special verdict.

Hate Propaganda

318. (1) Advocating genocide — Every person who advocates or promotes genocide is guilty of an indictable offence and liable to imprisonment for a term of not more than five years.

(2) Definition of "genocide" — In this section **"genocide"** means any of the following acts committed with intent to destroy in whole or in part any identifiable group, namely,

(a) killing members of the group; or

(b) deliberately inflicting on the group conditions of life calculated to bring about its physical destruction.

(3) Consent — No proceeding for an offence under this section shall be instituted without the consent of the Attorney General.

(4) Definition of "identifiable group" — In this section, **"identifiable group"** means any section of the public distinguished by colour, race, religion, national or ethnic origin, age, sex, sexual orientation, gender identity or expression, or mental or physical disability.

2004, c. 14, s. 1; 2014, c. 31, s. 12; 2017, c. 13, s. 3; 2019, c. 25, s. 120

319. (1) Public incitement of hatred — Every one who, by communicating statements in any public place, incites hatred against any identifiable group where such incitement is likely to lead to a breach of the peace is guilty of

(a) an indictable offence and is liable to imprisonment for a term not exceeding two years; or

(b) an offence punishable on summary conviction.

(2) Wilful promotion of hatred — Every one who, by communicating statements, other than in private conversation, wilfully promotes hatred against any identifiable group is guilty of

(a) an indictable offence and is liable to imprisonment for a term not exceeding two years; or

(b) an offence punishable on summary conviction.

(3) Defences — No person shall be convicted of an offence under subsection (2)

(a) if he establishes that the statements communicated were true;

(b) if, in good faith, the person expressed or attempted to establish by an argument an opinion on a religious subject or an opinion based on a belief in a religious text;

(c) if the statements were relevant to any subject of public interest, the discussion of which was for the public benefit, and if on reasonable grounds he believed them to be true; or

(d) if, in good faith, he intended to point out, for the purpose of removal, matters producing or tending to produce feelings of hatred towards an identifiable group in Canada.

(4) Forfeiture — Where a person is convicted of an offence under section 318 or subsection (1) or (2) of this section, anything by means of or in relation to which the offence was committed, on such conviction, may, in addition to any other punishment imposed, be ordered by the presiding provincial court judge or judge to be forfeited to Her Majesty in right of the province in which that person is convicted, for disposal as the Attorney General may direct.

(5) Exemption from seizure of communication facilities — Subsections 199(6) and (7) apply with such modifications as the circumstances require to section 318 or subsection (1) or (2) of this section.

(6) Consent — No proceeding for an offence under subsection (2) shall be instituted without the consent of the Attorney General.

(7) Definitions — In this section,

"communicating" includes communicating by telephone, broadcasting or other audible or visible means;

"identifiable group" has the same meaning as in section 318;

"public place" includes any place to which the public have access as of right or by invitation, express or implied;

"statements" includes words spoken or written or recorded electronically or electro-magnetically or otherwise, and gestures, signs or other visible representations.

R.S.C. 1985, c. 27 (1st Supp.), s. 203; 2004, c. 14, s. 2

320. (1) Warrant of seizure — A judge who is satisfied by information on oath that there are reasonable grounds for believing that any publication, copies of which are kept for sale or distribution in premises within the jurisdiction of the court, is hate propaganda shall issue a warrant under his hand authorizing seizure of the copies.

(2) Summons to occupier — Within seven days of the issue of a warrant under subsection (1), the judge shall issue a summons to the occupier of the premises requiring him to appear before the court and show cause why the matter seized should not be forfeited to Her Majesty.

(3) Owner and author may appear — The owner and the author of the matter seized under subsection (1) and alleged to be hate propaganda may appear and be represented in the proceedings in order to oppose the making of an order for the forfeiture of the matter.

(4) Order of forfeiture — If the court is satisfied that the publication referred to in subsection (1) is hate propaganda, it shall make an order declaring the matter forfeited to Her Majesty in right of the province in which the proceedings take place, for disposal as the Attorney General may direct.

(5) Disposal of matter — If the court is not satisfied that the publication referred to in subsection (1) is hate propaganda, it shall order that the matter be restored to the person from whom it was seized forthwith after the time for final appeal has expired.

(6) Appeal — An appeal lies from an order made under subsection (4) or (5) by any person who appeared in the proceedings

(a) on any ground of appeal that involves a question of law alone,

(b) on any ground of appeal that involves a question of fact alone, or

(c) on any ground of appeal that involves a question of mixed law and fact,

as if it were an appeal against conviction or against a judgment or verdict of acquittal, as the case may be, on a question of law alone under Part XXI, and sections 673 to 696 apply with such modifications as the circumstances require.

(7) Consent — No proceeding under this section shall be instituted without the consent of the Attorney General.

(8) Definitions — In this section

"court" means

(a) in the Province of Quebec, the Court of Quebec;

(a.1) in the Province of Ontario, the Superior Court of Justice;

(b) in the Provinces of New Brunswick, Manitoba, Saskatchewan and Alberta, the Court of Queen's Bench;

(c) in the Province of Newfoundland and Labrador, the Supreme Court, Trial Division,

(c.1) [Repealed 1992, c. 51, s. 36.]

(d) in the Provinces of Nova Scotia, British Columbia and Prince Edward Island, in Yukon and in the Northwest Territories, the Supreme Court, and

(e) in Nunavut, the Nunavut Court of Justice;

"genocide" has the same meaning as it has in section 318;

"hate propaganda" means any writing, sign or visible representation that advocates or promotes genocide or the communication of which by any person would constitute an offence under section 319;

"judge" means a judge of a court.

R.S.C. 1985, c. 27 (2nd Supp.), s. 10 (Sched., item 6(9)); R.S.C. 1985, c. 40 (4th Supp.), s. 2 (Sched., item 1(3), (4)); 1990, c. 16, s. 4; 1990, c. 17, s. 11; 1992, c. 1, s. 58(1) (Sched. I, item 6); 1992, c. 51, s. 36; 1993, c. 28, s. 78 (Sched. III, item 31); 1998, c. 30, s. 14(d); 1999, c. 3, s. 29; 2002, c. 7, s. 142; 2015, c. 3, s. 49

320.1 (1) Warrant of seizure — If a judge is satisfied by information on oath that there are reasonable grounds to believe that there is material that is hate propaganda within the meaning of subsection 320(8) or computer data within the meaning of subsection 342.1(2) that makes hate propaganda available, that is stored on and made available to the public through a computer system within the meaning of subsection 342.1(2) that is within the jurisdiction of the court, the judge may order the custodian of the computer system to

(a) give an electronic copy of the material to the court;

(b) ensure that the material is no longer stored on and made available through the computer system; and

(c) provide the information necessary to identify and locate the person who posted the material.

(2) Notice to person who posted the material — Within a reasonable time after receiving the information referred to in paragraph (1)(c), the judge shall cause notice to be given to the person who posted the material, giving that person the opportunity to appear and be represented before the court and show cause why the material should not be deleted. If the person cannot be identified or located or does not reside in Canada, the judge may order the custodian of the computer system to post the text of the notice at the location where the material was previously stored and made available, until the time set for the appearance.

(3) **Person who posted the material may appear** — The person who posted the material may appear and be represented in the proceedings in order to oppose the making of an order under subsection (5).

(4) **Non-appearance** — If the person who posted the material does not appear for the proceedings, the court may proceed *ex parte* to hear and determine the proceedings in the absence of the person as fully and effectually as if the person had appeared.

(5) **Order** — If the court is satisfied, on a balance of probabilities, that the material is available to the public and is hate propaganda within the meaning of subsection 320(8) or computer data within the meaning of subsection 342.1(2) that makes hate propaganda available, it may order the custodian of the computer system to delete the material.

(6) **Destruction of copy** — When the court makes the order for the deletion of the material, it may order the destruction of the electronic copy in the court's possession.

(7) **Return of material** — If the court is not satisfied that the material is available to the public and is hate propaganda within the meaning of subsection 320(8) or computer data within the meaning of subsection 342.1(2) that makes hate propaganda available, the court shall order that the electronic copy be returned to the custodian and terminate the order under paragraph (1)(b).

(8) **Other provisions to apply** — Subsections 320(6) to (8) apply, with any modifications that the circumstances require, to this section.

(9) **When order takes effect** — No order made under subsections (5) to (7) takes effect until the time for final appeal has expired.

2001, c. 41, s. 10; 2014, c. 31, s. 13

PART VIII.1 — OFFENCES RELATING TO CONVEYANCES (SS. 320.11–320.4)

[Heading added 2018, c. 21, s. 15.]

Interpretation

[Heading added 2018, c. 21, s. 15.]

320.11 Definitions — The following definitions apply in this Part.

"analyst" means a person who is, or a person who is a member of a class of persons that is, designated by the Attorney General under subparagraph 320.4(b)(ii) or paragraph 320.4(c). *("analyste")*

"approved container" means a container that is designed to receive a sample of a person's blood for analysis and that is approved by the Attorney General of Canada under paragraph 320.39(d). *("contenant approuvé")*

"approved drug screening equipment" means equipment that is designed to ascertain the presence of a drug in a person's body and that is approved by the Attorney General of Canada under paragraph 320.39(b). *("matériel de détection des drogues approuvé")*

"approved instrument" means an instrument that is designed to receive and make an analysis of a sample of a person's breath to determine their blood alcohol concentration and that is approved by the Attorney General of Canada under paragraph 320.39(c). *("éthylomètre approuvé")*

"approved screening device" means a device that is designed to ascertain the presence of alcohol in a person's blood and that is approved by the Attorney General of Canada under paragraph 320.39(a). *("appareil de détection approuvé")*

"conveyance" means a motor vehicle, a vessel, an aircraft or railway equipment. *("moyen de transport")*

"evaluating officer" means a peace officer who has the qualifications prescribed by regulation that are required in order to act as an evaluating officer. *("agent évaluateur")*

"operate" means

(a) in respect of a motor vehicle, to drive it or to have care or control of it;

(b) in respect of a vessel or aircraft, to navigate it, to assist in its navigation or to have care or control of it; and

(c) in respect of railway equipment, to participate in the direct control of its motion, or to have care or control of it as a member of the equipment's crew, as a person who acts in lieu of a member of the equipment's crew by remote control, or otherwise.

("conduire")

"qualified medical practitioner" means a person who is qualified under provincial law to practise medicine. *("médecin qualifié")*

"qualified technician" means

(a) in respect of breath samples, a person who is designated by the Attorney General under paragraph 320.4(a); and

(b) in respect of blood samples, a person who is, or a person who is a member of a class of persons that is, designated by the Attorney General under subparagraph 320.4(b)(i).

("technicien qualifié")

"vessel" includes a hovercraft. *("bateau")*

2018, c. 21, s. 15

Recognition and Declaration

[Heading added 2018, c. 21, s. 15.]

320.12 Recognition and declaration — It is recognized and declared that

(a) operating a conveyance is a privilege that is subject to certain limits in the interests of public safety that include licensing, the observance of rules and sobriety;

(b) the protection of society is well served by deterring persons from operating conveyances dangerously or while their ability to operate them is impaired by alcohol or a drug, because that conduct poses a threat to the life, health and safety of Canadians;

(c) the analysis of a sample of a person's breath by means of an approved instrument produces reliable and accurate readings of blood alcohol concentration; and

(d) an evaluation conducted by an evaluating officer is a reliable method of determining whether a person's ability to operate a conveyance is impaired by a drug or by a combination of alcohol and a drug.

2018, c. 21, s. 15

Offences and Punishment

[Heading added 2018, c. 21, s. 15.]

320.13 (1) Dangerous operation — Everyone commits an offence who operates a conveyance in a manner that, having regard to all of the circumstances, is dangerous to the public.

(2) Operation causing bodily harm — Everyone commits an offence who operates a conveyance in a manner that, having regard to all of the circumstances, is dangerous to the public and, as a result, causes bodily harm to another person.

(3) Operation causing death — Everyone commits an offence who operates a conveyance in a manner that, having regard to all of the circumstances, is dangerous to the public and, as a result, causes the death of another person.

2018, c. 21, s. 15

320.14 (1) Operation while impaired — Everyone commits an offence who

(a) operates a conveyance while the person's ability to operate it is impaired to any degree by alcohol or a drug or by a combination of alcohol and a drug;

(b) subject to subsection (5), has, within two hours after ceasing to operate a conveyance, a blood alcohol concentration that is equal to or exceeds 80 mg of alcohol in 100 mL of blood;

(c) subject to subsection (6), has, within two hours after ceasing to operate a conveyance, a blood drug concentration that is equal to or exceeds the blood drug concentration for the drug that is prescribed by regulation; or

(d) subject to subsection (7), has, within two hours after ceasing to operate a conveyance, a blood alcohol concentration and a blood drug concentration that is equal to or exceeds the blood alcohol concentration and the blood drug concentration for the drug that are prescribed by regulation for instances where alcohol and that drug are combined.

(2) **Operation causing bodily harm** — Everyone commits an offence who commits an offence under subsection (1) and who, while operating the conveyance, causes bodily harm to another person.

(3) **Operation causing death** — Everyone commits an offence who commits an offence under subsection (1) and who, while operating the conveyance, causes the death of another person.

(4) **Operation — low blood drug concentration** — Subject to subsection (6), everyone commits an offence who has, within two hours after ceasing to operate a conveyance, a blood drug concentration that is equal to or exceeds the blood drug concentration for the drug that is prescribed by regulation and that is less than the concentration prescribed for the purposes of paragraph (1)(c).

(5) **Exception — alcohol** — No person commits an offence under paragraph (1)(b) if

(a) they consumed alcohol after ceasing to operate the conveyance;

(b) after ceasing to operate the conveyance, they had no reasonable expectation that they would be required to provide a sample of breath or blood; and

(c) their alcohol consumption is consistent with their blood alcohol concentration as determined in accordance with subsection 320.31(1) or (2) and with their having had, at the time when they were operating the conveyance, a blood alcohol concentration that was less than 80 mg of alcohol in 100 mL of blood.

(6) **Exception — drugs** — No person commits an offence under paragraph (1)(c) or subsection (4) if

(a) they consumed the drug after ceasing to operate the conveyance; and

(b) after ceasing to operate the conveyance, they had no reasonable expectation that they would be required to provide a sample of a bodily substance.

(7) **Exception — combination of alcohol and drug** — No person commits an offence under paragraph (1)(d) if

(a) they consumed the drug or the alcohol or both after ceasing to operate the conveyance;

(b) after ceasing to operate the conveyance, they had no reasonable expectation that they would be required to provide a sample of a bodily substance; and

(c) their alcohol consumption is consistent with their blood alcohol concentration as determined in accordance with subsection 320.31(1) or (2) and with their having had, at the time when they were operating the conveyance, a blood alcohol concentration less than the blood alcohol concentration established under paragraph 320.38(c).

2018, c. 21, s. 15

320.15 (1) Failure or refusal to comply with demand — Everyone commits an offence who, knowing that a demand has been made, fails or refuses to comply, without reasonable excuse, with a demand made under section 320.27 or 320.28.

(2) Accident resulting in bodily harm — Everyone commits an offence who commits an offence under subsection (1) and who, at the time of the failure or refusal, knows that, or is reckless as to whether, they were involved in an accident that resulted in bodily harm to another person.

(3) Accident resulting in death — Everyone commits an offence who commits an offence under subsection (1) and who, at the time of the failure or refusal, knows that, or is reckless as to whether, they were involved in an accident that resulted in the death of another person or in bodily harm to another person whose death ensues.

(4) Only one conviction — A person who is convicted of an offence under this section is not to be convicted of another offence under this section with respect to the same transaction.

2018, c. 21, s. 15

320.16 (1) Failure to stop after accident — Everyone commits an offence who operates a conveyance and who at the time of operating the conveyance knows that, or is reckless as to whether, the conveyance has been involved in an accident with a person or another conveyance and who fails, without reasonable excuse, to stop the conveyance, give their name and address and, if any person has been injured or appears to require assistance, offer assistance.

(2) Accident resulting in bodily harm — Everyone commits an offence who commits an offence under subsection (1) and who at the time of committing the offence knows that, or is reckless as to whether, the accident resulted in bodily harm to another person.

(3) Accident resulting in death — Everyone commits an offence who commits an offence under subsection (1) and who, at the time of committing the offence, knows that, or is reckless as to whether, the accident resulted in the death of ano8ther person or in bodily harm to another person whose death ensues.

2018, c. 21, s. 15

320.17 Flight from peace officer — Everyone commits an offence who operates a motor vehicle or vessel while being pursued by a peace officer and who f ails, without reasonable excuse, to stop the motor vehicle or vessel as soon as is reasonable in the circumstances.

2018, c. 21, s. 15

320.18 (1) Operation while prohibited — Everyone commits an offence who operates a conveyance while prohibited from doing so

(a) by an order made under this Act; or

(b) by any other form of legal restriction imposed under any other Act of Parliament or under provincial law in respect of a conviction under this Act or a discharge under section 730.

(2) Exception — No person commits an offence under subsection (1) arising out of the operation of a motor vehicle if they are registered in an alcohol ignition interlock device program established under the law of the province in which they reside and they comply with the conditions of the program.

2018, c. 21, s. 15

320.19 (1) Punishment — Every person who commits an offence under subsection 320.14(1) or 320.15(1) is guilty of

(a) an indictable offence and liable to imprisonment for a term of not more than 10 years and to a minimum punishment of,

(i) for a first offence, a fine of $1,000,

(ii) for a second offence, imprisonment for a term of 30 days, and

(iii) for each subsequent offence, imprisonment for a term of 120 days; or

(b) an offence punishable on summary conviction and liable to a fine of not more than $5,000 or to imprisonment for a term of not more than two years less a day, or to both, and to a minimum punishment of,

(i) for a first offence, a fine of $1,000,

(ii) for a second offence, imprisonment for a term of 30 days, and

(iii) for each subsequent offence, imprisonment for a term of 120 days.

(2) Summary conviction — Everyone who commits an offence under subsection 320.14(4) is liable on summary conviction to a fine of not more than $1,000.

(3) Minimum fines for high blood alcohol concentrations — Despite subparagraphs (1)(a)(i) and (b)(i), every person who commits an offence under paragraph 320.14(1)(b) is liable, for a first offence, to

(a) a fine of not less than $1,500, if the person's blood alcohol concentration is equal to or exceeds 120 mg of alcohol in 100 mL of blood but is less than 160 mg of alcohol in 100 mL of blood; and

(b) a fine of not less than $2,000, if the person's blood alcohol concentration is equal to or exceeds 160 mg of alcohol in 100 mL of blood.

(4) Minimum fine — subsection 320.15(1) — Despite subparagraphs (1)(a)(i) and (b)(i), every person who commits an offence under subsection 320.15(1) is liable, for a first offence, to a fine of not less than $2,000.

(5) Punishment — dangerous operation and other offences — Every person who commits an offence under subsection 320.13(1) or 320.16(1), section 320.17 or subsection 320.18(1) is guilty of

(a) an indictable offence and liable to imprisonment for a term of not more than 10 years; or

(b) an offence punishable on summary conviction.

2018, c. 21, s. 15; 2019, c. 25, s. 402(11)(b)–(d)

320.2 Punishment in case of bodily harm — Every person who commits an offence under subsection 320.13(2), 320.14(2), 320.15(2) or 320.16(2) is guilty of

(a) an indictable offence and liable to imprisonment for a term of not more than 14 years and to a minimum punishment of,

(i) for a first offence, a fine of $1,000,

(ii) for a second offence, imprisonment for a term of 30 days, and

(iii) for each subsequent offence, imprisonment for a term of 120 days; or

(b) an offence punishable on summary conviction and liable to a fine of not more than $5,000 or to imprisonment for a term of not more than two years less a day, or to both, and to the minimum punishments set out in subparagraphs (a)(i) to (iii).

2018, c. 21, s. 15; 2019, c. 25, s. 402(11)(e)

320.21 Punishment in case of death — Everyone who commits an offence under subsection 320.13(3), 320.14(3), 320.15(3) or 320.16(3) is liable on conviction on indictment to imprisonment for life and to a minimum punishment of,

(a) for a first offence, a fine of $1,000;

(b) for a second offence, imprisonment for a term of 30 days; and

(c) for each subsequent offence, imprisonment for a term of 120 days.

2018, c. 21, s. 15

320.22 Aggravating circumstances for sentencing purposes — A court imposing a sentence for an offence under any of sections 320.13 to 320.18 shall consider, in addition to any other aggravating circumstances, the following:

(a) the commission of the offence resulted in bodily harm to, or the death of, more than one person;

(b) the offender was operating a motor vehicle in a race with at least one other motor vehicle or in a contest of speed, on a street, road or highway or in another public place;

(c) a person under the age of 16 years was a passenger in the conveyance operated by the offender;

(d) the offender was being remunerated for operating the conveyance;

(e) the offender's blood alcohol concentration at the time of committing the offence was equal to or exceeded 120 mg of alcohol in 100 mL of blood;

(f) the offender was operating a large motor vehicle; and

(g) the offender was not permitted, under a federal or provincial Act, to operate the conveyance.

2018, c. 21, s. 15

320.23 (1) Delay of sentencing — The court may, with the consent of the prosecutor and the offender, and after considering the interests of justice, delay sentencing of an offender who has been found guilty of an offence under subsection 320.14(1) or 320.15(1) to allow the offender to attend a treatment program approved by the province in which the offender resides. If the court delays sentencing, it shall make an order prohibiting the offender from operating, before sentencing, the type of conveyance in question, in which case subsections 320.24(6) to (9) apply.

(2) Exception to minimum punishment — If the offender successfully completes the treatment program, the court is not required to impose the minimum punishment under section 320.19 or to make a prohibition order under section 320.24, but it shall not direct a discharge under section 730.

2018, c. 21, s. 15

320.24 (1) Mandatory prohibition order — If an offender is found guilty of an offence under subsection 320.14(1) or 320.15(1), the court that sentences the offender shall, in addition to any other punishment that may be imposed for that offence, make an order prohibiting the offender from operating the type of conveyance in question during a period to be determined in accordance with subsection (2).

(2) Prohibition period — The prohibition period is

(a) for a first offence, not less than one year and not more than three years, plus the entire period to which the offender is sentenced to imprisonment;

(b) for a second offence, not less than two years and not more than 10 years, plus the entire period to which the offender is sentenced to imprisonment; and

(c) for each subsequent offence, not less than three years, plus the entire period to which the offender is sentenced to imprisonment.

(3) Discretionary order of prohibition — low blood drug concentration — If an offender is found guilty of an offence under subsection 320.14(4), the court that sentences the offender may, in addition to any other punishment that may be imposed for that offence, make an order prohibiting the offender from operating the type of conveyance in question during a period of not more than one year.

(4) Discretionary order of prohibition — other offences — If an offender is found guilty of an offence under section 320.13, subsection 320.14(2) or (3), 320.15(2) or (3) or under any of sections 320.16 to 320.18, the court that sentences the offender may, in addition to any other punishment that may be imposed for that offence, make an order prohibiting the offender from operating the type of conveyance in question during a period to be determined in accordance with subsection (5).

(5) Prohibition period — The prohibition period is

(a) if the offender is liable to imprisonment for life in respect of that offence, of any duration that the court considers appropriate, plus the entire period to which the offender is sentenced to imprisonment;

(b) if the offender is liable to imprisonment for more than five years but less than life in respect of that offence, not more than 10 years, plus the entire period to which the offender is sentenced to imprisonment; and

(c) in any other case, not more than three years, plus the entire period to which the offender is sentenced to imprisonment.

(5.1) Effect of order — Subject to subsection (9), a prohibition order takes effect on the day that it is made.

(6) Obligation of court — A court that makes a prohibition order under this section shall cause the order to be read by or to the offender or a copy of the order to be given to the offender.

(7) Validity of prohibition order not affected — A failure to comply with subsection (6) does not affect the validity of the prohibition order.

(8) Application — public place — A prohibition order in respect of a motor vehicle applies only to its operation on a street, road or highway or in any other public place.

(9) Consecutive prohibition periods — If the offender is, at the time of the commission of the offence, subject to an order made under this Act prohibiting the offender from operating a conveyance, a court that makes a prohibition order under this section that prohibits the offender from operating the same type of conveyance may order that the prohibition order be served consecutively to that order.

(10) Minimum absolute prohibition period — A person may not be registered in an alcohol ignition interlock device program referred to in subsection 320.18(2) until the expiry of

(a) in the case of a first offence, a period, if any, that may be fixed by order of the court;

(b) in the case of a second offence, a period of three months after the day on which the sentence is imposed or any longer period that may be fixed by order of the court; and

(c) in the case of a subsequent offence, a period of six months after the day on which the sentence is imposed or any longer period that may be fixed by order of the court.

2018, c. 21, s. 15

320.25 (1) Stay of order pending appeal — Subject to subsection (2), if an appeal is taken against a conviction or sentence for an offence under any of sections 320.13 to 320.18, a judge of the court to which the appeal is taken may direct that the prohibition order under section 320.24 arising out of the conviction shall, on any conditions that the judge imposes, be stayed pending the final disposition of the appeal or until otherwise ordered by that court.

(2) **Appeals to Supreme Court of Canada** — In the case of an appeal to the Supreme Court of Canada, a direction may be made only by a judge of the court from which the appeal was taken.

(3) **Effect of conditions** — The imposition of conditions on a stay of a prohibition order does not operate to decrease the prohibition period provided in the prohibition order.

2018, c. 21, s. 15

320.26 **Earlier and subsequent offences** — In determining, for the purpose of imposing a sentence for an offence under subsection 320.14(1) or 320.15(1), whether the offence is a second, third or subsequent offence, any of the following offences for which the offender was previously convicted is considered to be an earlier offence:

(a) an offence under any of subsections 320.14(1) to (3) or section 320.15; or

(b) an offence under any of sections 253, 254 and 255, as those sections read from time to time before the day on which this section comes into force.

2018, c. 21, s. 15

Investigative Matters

[Heading added 2018, c. 21, s. 15.]

320.27 (1) **Testing for presence of alcohol or drug** — If a peace officer has reasonable grounds to suspect that a person has alcohol or a drug in their body and that the person has, within the preceding three hours, operated a conveyance, the peace officer may, by demand, require the person to comply with the requirements of either or both of paragraphs (a) and (b) in the case of alcohol or with the requirements of either or both of paragraphs (a) and (c) in the case of a drug:

(a) to immediately perform the physical coordination tests prescribed by regulation and to accompany the peace officer for that purpose;

(b) to immediately provide the samples of breath that, in the peace officer's opinion, are necessary to enable a proper analysis to be made by means of an approved screening device and to accompany the peace officer for that purpose;

(c) to immediately provide the samples of a bodily substance that, in the peace officer's opinion, are necessary to enable a proper analysis to be made by means of approved drug screening equipment and to accompany the peace officer for that purpose.

(2) **Mandatory alcohol screening** — If a peace officer has in his or her possession an approved screening device, the peace officer may, in the course of the lawful exercise of powers under an Act of Parliament or an Act of a provincial legislature or arising at common law, by demand, require the person who is operating a motor vehicle to immediately provide the samples of breath that, in the peace officer's opinion, are necessary to enable a proper analysis to be made by means of that device and to accompany the peace officer for that purpose.

2018, c. 21, s. 15

320.28 (1) Samples of breath or blood — alcohol — If a peace officer has reasonable grounds to believe that a person has operated a conveyance while the person's ability to operate it was impaired to any degree by alcohol or has committed an offence under paragraph 320.14(1)(b), the peace officer may, by demand made as soon as practicable,

(a) require the person to provide, as soon as practicable,

(i) the samples of breath that, in a qualified technician's opinion, are necessary to enable a proper analysis to be made by means of an approved instrument, or

(ii) if the peace officer has reasonable grounds to believe that, because of their physical condition, the person may be incapable of providing a sample of breath or it would be impracticable to take one, the samples of blood that, in the opinion of the qualified medical practitioner or qualified technician taking the samples, are necessary to enable a proper analysis to be made to determine the person's blood alcohol concentration; and

(b) require the person to accompany the peace officer for the purpose of taking samples of that person's breath or blood.

(2) Evaluation and samples of blood — drugs — If a peace officer has reasonable grounds to believe that a person has operated a conveyance while the person's ability to operate it was impaired to any degree by a drug or by a combination of alcohol and a drug, or has committed an offence under paragraph 320.14(1)(c) or (d) or subsection 320.14(4), the peace officer may, by demand, made as soon as practicable, require the person to comply with the requirements of either or both of paragraphs (a) and (b):

(a) to submit, as soon as practicable, to an evaluation conducted by an evaluating officer to determine whether the person's ability to operate a conveyance is impaired by a drug or by a combination of alcohol and a drug, and to accompany the peace officer for that purpose; or

(b) to provide, as soon as practicable, the samples of blood that, in the opinion of the qualified medical practitioner or qualified technician taking the samples, are necessary to enable a proper analysis to be made to determine the person's blood drug concentration, or the person's blood drug concentration and blood alcohol concentration, as the case may be, and to accompany the peace officer for that purpose.

(3) Samples of breath — alcohol — An evaluating officer who has reasonable grounds to suspect that a person has alcohol in their body may, if a demand was not made under subsection (1), by demand made as soon as practicable, require the person to provide, as soon as practicable, the samples of breath that, in a qualified technician's opinion, are necessary to enable a proper analysis to be made by means of an approved instrument.

(4) Samples of bodily substances — If, on completion of the evaluation, the evaluating officer has reasonable grounds to believe that one or more of the types of drugs set out in subsection (5) — or that a combination of alcohol and one or more of those types of drugs — is impairing the person's ability to operate a conveyance, the evaluating officer shall identify the type or types of drugs in question and may, by demand made as soon as practicable, require the person to provide, as soon as practicable,

(a) a sample of oral fluid or urine that, in the evaluating officer's opinion, is necessary to enable a proper analysis to be made to ascertain the presence in the person's body of one or more of the types of drugs set out in subsection (5); or

(b) the samples of blood that, in the opinion of the qualified medical practitioner or qualified technician taking the samples, are necessary to enable a proper analysis to be made to ascertain the presence in the person's body of one or more of the types of drugs set out in subsection (5) or to determine the person's blood drug concentration for one or more of those types of drugs.

(5) **Types of drugs** — For the purpose of subsection (4), the types of drugs are the following:

(a) a depressant;

(b) an inhalant;

(c) a dissociative anaesthetic;

(d) cannabis;

(e) a stimulant;

(f) a hallucinogen; or

(g) a narcotic analgesic.

(6) **Condition** — A sample of blood may be taken from a person under this section only by a qualified medical practitioner or a qualified technician, and only if they are satisfied that taking the sample would not endanger the person's health.

(7) **Approved containers** — A sample of blood shall be received into an approved container that shall be subsequently sealed.

(8) **Retained sample** — A person who takes samples of blood under this section shall cause one of the samples to be retained for the purpose of analysis by or on behalf of the person from whom the blood samples were taken.

(9) **Validity of analysis not affected** — A failure to comply with subsection (7) or (8) does not by itself affect the validity of the taking of the sample or of an analysis made of the sample.

(10) **Release of retained sample** — A judge of a superior court of criminal jurisdiction or a court of criminal jurisdiction shall, on the summary application of the person from whom samples of blood were taken under this section, made within six months after the day on which the samples were taken, order the release of any sample that was retained to the person for the purpose of examination or analysis, subject to any terms that the judge considers appropriate to ensure that the sample is safeguarded and preserved for use in any proceedings in respect of which it was taken.

2018, c. 21, s. 15

320.29 (1) **Warrants to obtain blood samples** — A justice may issue a warrant authorizing a peace officer to require a qualified medical practitioner or a qualified technician to take the samples of a person's blood that, in the opinion of the practitioner or technician taking the samples, are necessary to enable a proper analysis to be made to determine the person's blood alcohol concentration or blood drug concentration, or both, if the justice is satisfied, on an information on oath in Form 1 or on an information on oath submitted to the justice by telephone or other means of telecommunication, that

(a) there are reasonable grounds to believe that the person has, within the preceding eight hours, operated a conveyance that was involved in an accident that resulted in bodily harm to themselves or another person or in the death of another person;

(b) there are reasonable grounds to suspect that the person has alcohol or a drug in their body; and

(c) a qualified medical practitioner is of the opinion that

(i) by reason of any physical or mental condition of the person, the person is unable to consent to the taking of samples of their blood, and

(ii) the taking of samples of the person's blood will not endanger their health.

(2) Form — A warrant issued under subsection (1) may be in Form 5 or 5.1, varied to suit the case.

(3) Procedure — telephone or other means of telecommunication — Section 487.1 applies, with any modifications that the circumstances require, in respect of an application for a warrant that is submitted by telephone or other means of telecommunication.

(4) Duration of warrant — Samples of blood may be taken from a person under a warrant issued under subsection (1) only during the time that a qualified medical practitioner is satisfied that the conditions referred to in subparagraphs (1)(c)(i) and (ii) continue to exist.

(5) Copy or facsimile to person — If a warrant issued under subsection (1) is executed, the peace officer shall, as soon as practicable, give a copy of it — or, in the case of a warrant issued by telephone or other means of telecommunication, a facsimile — to the person from whom the samples of blood are taken.

(6) Taking of samples — Subsections 320.28(7) to (10) apply with respect to the taking of samples of blood under this section.

2018, c. 21, s. 15

320.3 Testing blood — drug or alcohol — Samples of a person's blood that are taken for the purposes of this Part may be analyzed to determine the person's blood alcohol concentration or blood drug concentration, or both.

2018, c. 21, s. 15

Evidentiary Matters

[Heading added 2018, c. 21, s. 15.]

320.31 (1) Breath samples — If samples of a person's breath have been received into an approved instrument operated by a qualified technician, the results of the analyses of the samples are conclusive proof of the person's blood alcohol concentration at the time when the analyses were made if the results of the analyses are the same — or, if the results of the analyses are different, the lowest of the results is conclusive proof of the person's blood alcohol concentration at the time when the analyses were made — if

(a) before each sample was taken, the qualified technician conducted a system blank test the result of which is not more than 10 mg of alcohol in 100 mL of blood and a system calibration check the result of which is within 10% of the target value of an alcohol standard that is certified by an analyst;

(b) there was an interval of at least 15 minutes between the times when the samples were taken; and

(c) the results of the analyses, rounded down to the nearest multiple of 10 mg, did not differ by more than 20 mg of alcohol in 100 mL of blood.

(2) Blood samples — concentration when sample taken — The result of an analysis made by an analyst of a sample of a person's blood is proof of their blood alcohol concentration or their blood drug concentration, as the case may be, at the time when the sample was taken in the absence of evidence tending to show that the analysis was performed improperly.

(3) Evidence not included — Evidence of the following does not constitute evidence tending to show that an analysis of a sample of a person's blood was performed improperly:

(a) the amount of alcohol or a drug that they consumed;

(b) the rate at which the alcohol or the drug would have been absorbed or eliminated by their body; or

(c) a calculation based on the evidence referred to in paragraphs (a) and (b) of what their blood alcohol concentration or blood drug concentration would have been at the time the sample was taken.

(4) Presumption — blood alcohol concentration — For the purpose of paragraphs 320.14(1)(b) and (d), if the first of the samples of breath was taken, or the sample of blood was taken, more than two hours after the person ceased to operate the conveyance and the person's blood alcohol concentration was equal to or exceeded 20 mg of alcohol in 100 mL of blood, the person's blood alcohol concentration within those two hours is conclusively presumed to be the concentration established in accordance with subsection (1) or (2), as the case may be, plus an additional 5 mg of alcohol in 100 mL of blood for every interval of 30 minutes in excess of those two hours.

(5) Admissibility of evaluating officer's opinion — An evaluating officer's opinion relating to the impairment, by a type of drug that they identified, or by a combination of alcohol and that type of drug, of a person's ability to operate a conveyance is admissible in evidence without qualifying the evaluating officer as an expert.

(6) **Presumption — drug** — If the analysis of a sample provided under subsection 320.28(4) demonstrates that the person has a drug in their body that is of a type that the evaluating officer has identified as impairing the person's ability to operate a conveyance, that drug — or, if the person has also consumed alcohol, the combination of alcohol and that drug — is presumed, in the absence of evidence to the contrary, to be the drug, or the combination of alcohol and that drug, that was present in the person's body at the time when the person operated the conveyance and, on proof of the person's impairment, to have been the cause of that impairment.

(7) **Admissibility of result of analysis** — The result of an analysis of a sample of a person's breath, blood, urine, sweat or other bodily substance that they were not required to provide under this Part may be admitted in evidence even if the person was not warned before they provided the sample that they were not required to do so or that the result of the analysis of the sample might be used in evidence.

(8) **Evidence of failure to provide sample** — Unless a person is required to provide a sample of a bodily substance under this Part, evidence that they failed or refused to provide a sample for analysis or that a sample was not taken is not admissible and the failure, refusal or fact that a sample was not taken shall not be the subject of comment by any person in any proceedings under this Part.

(9) **Admissibility of statement** — A statement made by a person to a peace officer, including a statement compelled under a provincial Act, is admissible in evidence for the purpose of justifying a demand made under section 320.27 or 320.28.

(10) **Evidence of failure to comply with demand** — In any proceedings in respect of an offence under section 320.14, evidence that the accused, without reasonable excuse, failed or refused to comply with a demand made under section 320.27 or 320.28 is admissible and the court may draw an inference adverse to the accused from that evidence.

2018, c. 21, s. 15

320.32 (1) **Certificates** — A certificate of an analyst, qualified medical practitioner or qualified technician made under this Part is evidence of the facts alleged in the certificate without proof of the signature or the official character of the person who signed the certificate.

(2) **Notice of intention to produce certificate** — No certificate shall be received in evidence unless the party intending to produce it has, before the trial, given to the other party reasonable notice of their intention to produce it and a copy of the certificate.

(3) **Attendance and cross-examination** — A party against whom the certificate is produced may apply to the court for an order requiring the attendance of the person who signed the certificate for the purposes of cross-examination.

(4) **Form and content of application** — The application shall be made in writing and set out the likely relevance of the proposed cross-examination with respect

to the facts alleged in the certificate. A copy of the application shall be given to the prosecutor at least 30 days before the day on which the application is to be heard.

(5) Time of hearing — The hearing of the application shall be held at least 30 days before the day on which the trial is to be held.

(6) Certificate admissible in evidence — In proceedings in respect of an offence under subsection 320.18(1), the following certificates are evidence of the facts alleged in them without proof of the signature or official character of the person who signed them:

(a) a certificate setting out with reasonable particularity that the person named in it is prohibited from operating a motor vehicle in the province specified in the certificate, signed by the person who is responsible for the registration of motor vehicles in that province or any person authorized by the responsible person to sign it; and

(b) a certificate setting out with reasonable particularity that the person named in it is prohibited from operating a conveyance other than a motor vehicle, signed by the Minister of Transport or any person authorized by him or her to sign it.

(7) Onus — If it is proved that a prohibition under paragraph 320.18(1)(b) has been imposed on a person and that notice of the prohibition has been mailed to them at their last known address, that person is, beginning on the tenth day after the day on which the notice is mailed, in the absence of evidence to the contrary, presumed to have received the notice and to have knowledge of the prohibition, of the date of its commencement and of its duration.

2018, c. 21, s. 15

320.33 Printout from approved instrument — A document that is printed out from an approved instrument and signed by a qualified technician who certifies it to be the printout produced by the approved instrument when it made an analysis of a sample of a person's breath is evidence of the facts alleged in the document without proof of the signature or official character of the person who signed it.

2018, c. 21, s. 15

320.34 (1) Disclosure of information — In proceedings in respect of an offence under section 320.14, the prosecutor shall disclose to the accused, with respect to any samples of breath that the accused provided under section 320.28, information sufficient to determine whether the conditions set out in paragraphs 320.31(1)(a) to (c) have been met, namely:

(a) the results of the system blank tests;

(b) the results of the system calibration checks;

(c) any error or exception messages produced by the approved instrument at the time the samples were taken;

(d) the results of the analysis of the accused's breath samples; and

(e) a certificate of an analyst stating that the sample of an alcohol standard that is identified in the certificate is suitable for use with an approved instrument.

(2) Application for further disclosure — The accused may apply to the court for a hearing to determine whether further information should be disclosed.

(3) Form and content of application — The application shall be in writing and set out detailed particulars of the information that the accused seeks to have disclosed and the likely relevance of that information to determining whether the approved instrument was in proper working order. A copy of the application shall be given to the prosecutor at least 30 days before the day on which the application is to be heard.

(4) Time of hearing — The hearing of the application shall be held at least 30 days before the day on which the trial is to be held.

(5) For greater certainty — For greater certainty, nothing in this section limits the disclosure to which the accused may otherwise be entitled.

2018, c. 21, s. 15

320.35 Presumption of operation — In proceedings in respect of an offence under section 320.14 or 320.15, if it is proved that the accused occupied the seat or position ordinarily occupied by a person who operates a conveyance, the accused is presumed to have been operating the conveyance unless they establish that they did not occupy that seat or position for the purpose of setting the conveyance in motion.

2018, c. 21, s. 15

General Provisions

[Heading added 2018, c. 21, s. 15.]

320.36 (1) Unauthorized use of bodily substance — No person shall use a bodily substance obtained under this Part for any purpose other than for an analysis under this Part.

(2) Unauthorized use or disclosure of results — No person shall use, disclose or allow the disclosure of the results obtained under this Part of any evaluation, physical coordination test or analysis of a bodily substance, except for the purpose of the administration or enforcement of a federal or provincial Act related to drugs and/or alcohol and/or to the operation of a motor vehicle, vessel, aircraft or railway equipment.

(3) Exception — The results of an evaluation, test or analysis referred to in subsection (2) may be disclosed to the person to whom they relate, and may be disclosed to any other person if the results are made anonymous and the disclosure is made for statistical or research purposes.

(4) Offence — Everyone who contravenes subsection (1) or (2) commits an offence punishable on summary conviction.

2018, c. 21, s. 15

320.37 (1) Refusal to take sample — No qualified medical practitioner or qualified technician shall be found guilty of an offence by reason only of their refusal to take a sample of blood from a person for the purposes of this Part if they have a reasonable excuse for refusing to do so.

(2) No liability — No qualified medical practitioner, and no qualified technician, who takes a sample of blood from a person under this Part incurs any liability for doing anything necessary to take the sample that was done with reasonable care and skill.

2018, c. 21, s. 15

320.38 Regulations — The Governor in Council may make regulations

(a) prescribing the qualifications required for a peace officer to act as an evaluating officer and respecting the training of evaluating officers;

(b) prescribing the blood drug concentration for a drug for the purpose of paragraph 320.14(1)(c);

(c) prescribing a blood alcohol concentration and a blood drug concentration for a drug for the purposes of paragraph 320.14(1)(d);

(d) prescribing the blood drug concentration for a drug for the purpose of subsection 320.14(4);

(e) prescribing the physical coordination tests to be conducted under paragraph 320.27(1)(a); and

(f) prescribing the tests to be conducted and procedures to be followed during an evaluation under paragraph 320.28(2)(a) and the forms to be used in recording the results of the evaluation.

2018, c. 21, s. 15

320.39 Approval — Attorney General of Canada — The Attorney General of Canada may, by order, approve

(a) a device that is designed to ascertain the presence of alcohol in a person's blood;

(b) equipment that is designed to ascertain the presence of a drug in a person's body;

(c) an instrument that is designed to receive and make an analysis of a sample of a person's breath to determine their blood alcohol concentration; and

(d) a container that is designed to receive a sample of a person's blood for analysis.

2018, c. 21, s. 15

320.4 Designation — Attorney General — The Attorney General may designate

(a) a person as qualified, for the purposes of this Part, to operate an approved instrument;

(b) a person or class of persons as qualified, for the purposes of this Part,

(i) to take samples of blood, or

(ii) to analyze samples of bodily substances; and

(c) a person or class of persons as qualified, for the purposes of this Part, to certify that an alcohol standard is suitable for use with an approved instrument.

2018, c. 21, s. 15

Part IX — Offences Against Rights of Property (SS. 321–378)

Interpretation

321. Definitions — In this Part,

"break" means

(a) to break any part, internal or external, or

(b) to open any thing that is used or intended to be used to close or to cover an internal or external opening;

"credit card" means any card, plate, coupon book or other device issued or otherwise distributed for the purpose of being used

(a) on presentation to obtain, on credit, money, goods, services or any other thing of value, or

(b) in an automated teller machine, a remote service unit or a similar automated banking device to obtain any of the services offered through the machine, unit or device;

"document" means any paper, parchment or other material on which is recorded or marked anything that is capable of being read or understood by a person, computer system or other device, and includes a credit card, but does not include trademarks on articles of commerce or inscriptions on stone or metal or other like material;

"exchequer bill" means a bank note, bond, note, debenture or security that is issued or guaranteed by Her Majesty under the authority of Parliament or the legislature of a province;

"exchequer bill paper" means paper that is used to manufacture exchequer bills;

"false document" means a document

(a) the whole or a material part of which purports to be made by or on behalf of a person

(i) who did not make it or authorize it to be made, or

(ii) who did not in fact exist,

(b) that is made by or on behalf of the person who purports to make it but is false in some material particular,

(c) that is made in the name of an existing person, by him or under his authority, with a fraudulent intention that it should pass as being made by a person, real or fictitious, other than the person who makes it or under whose authority it is made;

"revenue paper" means paper that is used to make stamps, licences or permits or for any purpose connected with the public revenue.

R.S.C. 1985, c. 27 (1st Supp.), s. 42; 2014, c. 20, s. 366(1)

Theft

322. (1) Theft — Every one commits theft who fraudulently and without colour of right takes, or fraudulently and without colour of right converts to his use or to the use of another person, anything, whether animate or inanimate, with intent,

(a) to deprive, temporarily or absolutely, the owner of it, or a person who has a special property or interest in it, of the thing or of his property or interest in it;

(b) to pledge it or deposit it as security;

(c) to part with it under a condition with respect to its return that the person who parts with it may be unable to perform; or

(d) to deal with it in such a manner that it cannot be restored in the condition in which it was at the time it was taken or converted.

(2) Time when theft completed — A person commits theft when, with intent to steal anything, he moves it or causes it to move or to be moved, or begins to cause it to become movable.

(3) Secrecy — A taking or conversion of anything may be fraudulent notwithstanding that it is effected without secrecy or attempt at concealment.

(4) Purpose of taking — For the purposes of this Act, the question whether anything that is converted is taken for the purpose of conversion, or whether it is, at the time it is converted, in the lawful possession of the person who converts it is not material.

(5) Wild living creature — For the purposes of this section, a person who has a wild living creature in captivity shall be deemed to have a special property or interest in it while it is in captivity and after it has escaped from captivity.

323. (1) Oysters — Where oysters and oyster brood are in oyster beds, layings or fisheries that are the property of any person and are sufficiently marked out or known as the property of that person, that person shall be deemed to have a special property or interest in them.

(2) Oyster bed — An indictment is sufficient if it describes an oyster bed, laying or fishery by name or in any other way, without stating that it is situated in a particular territorial division.

324. Theft by bailee of things under seizure — Every one who is a bailee of anything that is under lawful seizure by a peace officer or public officer in the execution of the duties of his office, and who is obliged by law or agreement to produce and deliver it to that officer or to another person entitled thereto at a certain time and place, or on demand, steals it if he does not produce and deliver it in accordance with his obligation, but he does not steal it if his failure to produce and deliver it is not the result of a wilful act or omission by him.

325. Agent pledging goods, when not theft — A factor or an agent does not commit theft by pledging or giving a lien on goods or documents of title to goods that are entrusted to him for the purpose of sale or for any other purpose, if the pledge or lien is for an amount that does not exceed the sum of

(a) the amount due to him from his principal at the time the goods or documents are pledged or the lien is given; and

(b) the amount of any bill of exchange that he has accepted for or on account of his principal.

326. (1) Theft of telecommunication service — Every one commits theft who fraudulently, maliciously, or without colour of right,

(a) abstracts, consumes or uses electricity or gas or causes it to be wasted or diverted; or

(b) uses any telecommunication facility or obtains any telecommunication service.

(2) [Repealed 2014, c. 31, s. 14(2).]

327. (1) Possession of device to obtain use of telecommunication facility or service — Every person who, without lawful excuse, makes, possesses, sells, offers for sale, imports, obtains for use, distributes or makes available a device that is designed or adapted primarily to use a telecommunication facility or obtain a telecommunication service without payment of a lawful charge, knowing that the device has been used or is intended to be used for that purpose, is

(a) guilty of an indictable offence and liable to imprisonment for a term of not more than two years; or

(b) guilty of an offence punishable on summary conviction.

(2) Forfeiture — If a person is convicted of an offence under subsection (1) or paragraph 326(1)(b), in addition to any punishment that is imposed, any device in relation to which the offence was committed or the possession of which constituted the offence may be ordered forfeited to Her Majesty and may be disposed of as the Attorney General directs.

(3) Limitation — No order for forfeiture is to be made in respect of telecommunication facilities or equipment by means of which an offence under subsection (1) is committed if they are owned by a person engaged in providing a telecommunication service to the public or form part of such a person's telecommunication service or system and that person is not a party to the offence.

(4) Definition of "device" — In this section, **"device"** includes

(a) a component of a device; and

(b) a computer program within the meaning of subsection 342.1(2).

2014, c. 31, s. 15; 2018, c. 29, s. 32

328. Theft by or from person having special property or interest — A person may be convicted of theft notwithstanding that anything that is alleged to have been stolen was stolen

(a) by the owner of it from a person who has a special property or interest in it;

(b) by a person who has a special property or interest in it from the owner of it;

(c) by a lessee of it from his reversioner;

(d) by one of several joint owners, tenants in common or partners of or in it from the other persons who have an interest in it; or

(e) by the representatives of an organization from the organization.

2003, c. 21, s. 4

329. [Repealed 2000, c. 12, s. 94.]

330. (1) Theft by person required to account — Every one commits theft who, having received anything from any person on terms that require him to account for or pay it or the proceeds of it or a part of the proceeds to that person or another person, fraudulently fails to account for or pay it or the proceeds of it or the part of the proceeds of it accordingly.

(2) Effect of entry in account — Where subsection (1) otherwise applies, but one of the terms is that the thing received or the proceeds or part of the proceeds of it shall be an item in a debtor and creditor account between the person who receives the thing and the person to whom he is to account for or to pay it, and that the latter shall rely only on the liability of the other as his debtor in respect thereof, a proper entry in that account of the thing received or the proceeds or part of the proceeds of it, as the case may be, is a sufficient accounting therefor, and no fraudulent conversion of the thing or the proceeds or part of the proceeds of it thereby accounted for shall be deemed to have taken place.

331. Theft by person holding power of attorney — Every one commits theft who, being entrusted, whether solely or jointly with another person, with a power of attorney for the sale, mortgage, pledge or other disposition of real or personal property, fraudulently sells, mortgages, pledges or otherwise disposes of the property or any part of it, or fraudulently converts the proceeds of a sale, mortgage, pledge or other disposition of the property, or any part of the proceeds, to a purpose other than that for which he was entrusted by the power of attorney.

332. (1) Misappropriation of money held under direction — Every one commits theft who, having received, either solely or jointly with another person, money or valuable security or a power of attorney for the sale of real or personal property, with a direction that the money or a part of it, or the proceeds or a part of the proceeds of the security or the property shall be applied to a purpose or paid to a person specified in the direction, fraudulently and contrary to the direction applies to any other purpose or pays to any other person the money or proceeds or any part of it.

(2) Effect of entry in account — This section does not apply where a person who receives anything mentioned in subsection (1) and the person from whom he receives it deal with each other on such terms that all money paid to the former would, in the absence of any such direction, be properly treated as an item in a debtor and creditor account between them, unless the direction is in writing.

333. Taking ore for scientific purpose — No person commits theft by reason only that he takes, for the purpose of exploration or scientific investigation, a specimen of ore or mineral from land that is not enclosed and is not occupied or worked as a mine, quarry or digging.

333.1 (1) Motor vehicle theft — Everyone who commits theft is, if the property stolen is a motor vehicle, guilty of an offence and liable

(a) on proceedings by way of indictment, to imprisonment for a term of not more than 10 years, and to a minimum punishment of imprisonment for a term of six months in the case of a third or subsequent offence under this subsection; or

(b) on summary conviction, to imprisonment for a term of not more than two years less a day.

(2) Subsequent offences — For the purpose of determining whether a convicted person has committed a third or subsequent offence, an offence for which the person was previously convicted is considered to be an earlier offence whether it was prosecuted by indictment or by way of summary conviction proceedings.

2010, c. 14, s. 3; 2019, c. 25, s. 121

334. Punishment for theft — Except where otherwise provided by law, every one who commits theft

(a) if the property stolen is a testamentary instrument or the value of what is stolen is more than $5,000, is guilty of

(i) an indictable offence and liable to imprisonment for a term of not more than 10 years, or

(ii) an offence punishable on summary conviction; or

(b) if the value of what is stolen is not more than $5,000, is guilty

(i) of an indictable offence and is liable to imprisonment for a term not exceeding two years, or

(ii) of an offence punishable on summary conviction.

R.S.C. 1985, c. 27 (1st Supp.), s. 43; 1994, c. 44, s. 20; 2019, c. 25, s. 122

Offences Resembling Theft

335. (1) Taking motor vehicle or vessel or found therein without consent — Subject to subsection (1.1), every one who, without the consent of the owner, takes a motor vehicle or vessel with intent to drive, use, navigate or operate it or cause it to be driven, used, navigated or operated, or is an occupant of a motor vehicle or vessel knowing that it was taken without the consent of the owner, is guilty of an offence punishable on summary conviction.

(1.1) Exception — Subsection (1) does not apply to an occupant of a motor vehicle or vessel who, on becoming aware that it was taken without the consent of the owner, attempted to leave the motor vehicle or vessel, to the extent that it was feasible to do so, or actually left the motor vehicle or vessel.

(2) Definition of "vessel" — For the purposes of subsection (1), **"vessel"** has the same meaning as in section 320.11.

R.S.C. 1985, c. 1 (4th Supp.), s. 15; 1997, c. 18, s. 15; 2018, c. 21, s. 16

336. Criminal breach of trust — Every one who, being a trustee of anything for the use or benefit, whether in whole or in part, of another person, or for a public or charitable purpose, converts, with intent to defraud and in contravention of his trust, that thing or any part of it to a use that is not authorized by the trust is guilty of an indictable offence and liable to imprisonment for a term not exceeding fourteen years.

337. [Repealed 2018, c. 29, s. 33.]

338. (1) Fraudulently taking cattle or defacing brand — Every person is guilty of an indictable offence and liable to imprisonment for a term of not more than five years or is guilty of an offence punishable on summary conviction who, without the consent of the owner,

(a) fraudulently takes, holds, keeps in his possession, conceals, receives, appropriates, purchases or sells cattle that are found astray, or

(b) fraudulently, in whole or in part,

(i) obliterates, alters or defaces a brand or mark on cattle, or

(ii) makes a false or counterfeit brand or mark on cattle.

(2) Punishment for theft of cattle — Every person who commits theft of cattle is guilty of

(a) an indictable offence and liable to imprisonment for a term of not more than 10 years; or

(b) an offence punishable on summary conviction.

(3) Evidence of property in cattle — In any proceedings under this Act, evidence that cattle are marked with a brand or mark that is recorded or registered in accordance with any Act is, in the absence of any evidence to the contrary, proof that the cattle are owned by the registered owner of that brand or mark.

(4) Presumption from possession — Where an accused is charged with an offence under subsection (1) or (2), the burden of proving that the cattle came lawfully into the possession of the accused or his employee or into the possession of another person on behalf of the accused is on the accused, if the accused is not the registered owner of the brand or mark with which the cattle are marked, unless it appears that possession of the cattle by an employee of the accused or by another person on behalf of the accused was without the knowledge and authority, sanction or approval of the accused.

2019, c. 25, s. 123

339. (1) Taking possession, etc., of drift timber — Every person is guilty of an indictable offence and liable to imprisonment for a term of not more than five years or is guilty of an offence punishable on summary conviction who, without the consent of the owner,

(a) fraudulently takes, holds, keeps in their possession, conceals, receives, appropriates, purchases or sells any lumber or lumbering equipment that is found adrift, cast ashore or lying on or embedded in the bed or bottom, or on the bank or beach, of a river, stream or lake in Canada, or in the harbours or any of the coastal waters of Canada;

(b) removes, alters, obliterates or defaces a mark or number on such lumber or lumbering equipment; or

(c) refuses to deliver such lumber or lumbering equipment up to the owner or to the person in charge of it on behalf of the owner or to a person authorized by the owner to receive it.

(2) Dealer in second-hand goods — Every one who, being a dealer in second-hand goods of any kind, trades or traffics in or has in his possession for sale or traffic any lumbering equipment that is marked with the mark, brand, registered timber mark, name or initials of a person, without the written consent of that person, is guilty of an offence punishable on summary conviction.

(3) Search for timber unlawfully detained — A peace officer who suspects, on reasonable grounds, that any lumber owned by any person and bearing the registered timber mark of that person is kept or detained in or on any place without the knowledge or consent of that person, may enter into or on that place to ascertain whether or not it is detained there without the knowledge or consent of that person.

(4) Evidence of property in timber — Where any lumber or lumbering equipment is marked with a timber mark or a boom chain brand registered under any Act, the mark or brand is, in proceedings under subsection (1), and, in the absence of any evidence to the contrary, proof that it is the property of the registered owner of the mark or brand.

(5) Presumption from possession — Where an accused or his servants or agents are in possession of lumber or lumbering equipment marked with the mark, brand, registered timber mark, name or initials of another person, the burden of proving that it came lawfully into his possession or into possession of his servants or agents is, in proceedings under subsection (1), on the accused.

(6) Definitions — In this section

"coastal waters of Canada" includes all of Queen Charlotte Sound, all the Strait of Georgia and the Canadian waters of the Strait of Juan de Fuca;

"lumber" means timber, mast, spar, shingle bolt, sawlog or lumber of any description;

"lumbering equipment" includes a boom chain, chain, line and shackle.

2019, c. 25, s. 124

340. Destroying documents of title — Every person is guilty of an indictable offence and liable to imprisonment for a term of not more than 10 years or is guilty of an offence punishable on summary conviction who, for a fraudulent purpose, destroys, cancels, conceals or obliterates

(a) a document of title to goods or lands,

(b) a valuable security or testamentary instrument, or

(c) a judicial or official document.

2019, c. 25, s. 125

341. Fraudulent concealment — Every person who, for a fraudulent purpose, takes, obtains, removes or conceals anything is guilty of

(a) an indictable offence and liable to imprisonment for a term of not more than two years; or

(b) an offence punishable on summary conviction.

2019, c. 25, s.126

342. (1) Theft, forgery, etc., of credit card — Every person who

(a) steals a credit card,

(b) forges or falsifies a credit card,

(c) possesses, uses or traffics in a credit card or a forged or falsified credit card, knowing that it was obtained, made or altered

(i) by the commission in Canada of an offence, or

(ii) by an act or omission anywhere that, if it had occurred in Canada, would have constituted an offence, or

(d) uses a credit card knowing that it has been revoked or cancelled,

is guilty of

(e) an indictable offence and is liable to imprisonment for a term not exceeding ten years, or

(f) an offence punishable on summary conviction.

(2) Jurisdiction — An accused who is charged with an offence under subsection (1) may be tried and punished by any court having jurisdiction to try that offence in the place where the offence is alleged to have been committed or in the place where the accused is found, is arrested or is in custody, but where the place where the accused is found, is arrested or is in custody is outside the province in which the offence is alleged to have been committed, no proceedings in respect of that offence shall be commenced in that place without the consent of the Attorney General of that province.

(3) Unauthorized use of credit card data — Every person who, fraudulently and without colour of right, possesses, uses, traffics in or permits another person to use credit card data, including personal authentication information, whether or not the data is authentic, that would enable a person to use a credit card or to obtain the services that are provided by the issuer of a credit card to credit card holders is guilty of

(a) an indictable offence and is liable to imprisonment for a term not exceeding ten years; or

(b) an offence punishable on summary conviction.

(4) **Definitions** — In this section,

"personal authentication information" means a personal identification number or any other password or information that a credit card holder creates or adopts to be used to authenticate his or her identity in relation to the credit card; *("authentifiant personnel")*

"traffic" means, in relation to a credit card or credit card data, to sell, export from or import into Canada, distribute or deal with in any other way. *("trafic")*

R.S.C. 1985, c. 27 (1st Supp.), s. 44; 1997, c. 18, s. 16; 2009, c. 28, s. 4

342.01 (1) **Instruments for copying credit card data or forging or falsifying credit cards** — Every person is guilty of an indictable offence and liable to imprisonment for a term of not more than 10 years, or is guilty of an offence punishable on summary conviction, who, without lawful justification or excuse, makes, repairs, buys, sells, exports from Canada, imports into Canada or possesses any instrument, device, apparatus, material or thing that they know has been used or know is adapted or intended for use

(a) in the copying of credit card data for use in the commission of an offence under subsection 342(3); or

(b) in the forging or falsifying of credit cards.

(c) and (d) [Repealed 2009, c. 28, s. 5.]

(2) **Forfeiture** — Where a person is convicted of an offence under subsection (1), any instrument, device, apparatus, material or thing in relation to which the offence was committed or the possession of which constituted the offence may, in addition to any other punishment that may be imposed, be ordered forfeited to Her Majesty, whereupon it may be disposed of as the Attorney General directs.

(3) **Limitation** — No order of forfeiture may be made under subsection (2) in respect of any thing that is the property of a person who was not a party to the offence under subsection (1).

1997, c. 18, s. 17; 2009, c. 28, s. 5

342.1 (1) **Unauthorized use of computer** — Everyone is guilty of an indictable offence and liable to imprisonment for a term of not more than 10 years, or is guilty of an offence punishable on summary conviction who, fraudulently and without colour of right,

(a) obtains, directly or indirectly, any computer service;

(b) by means of an electro-magnetic, acoustic, mechanical or other device, intercepts or causes to be intercepted, directly or indirectly, any function of a computer system;

(c) uses or causes to be used, directly or indirectly, a computer system with intent to commit an offence under paragraph (a) or (b) or under section 430 in relation to computer data or a computer system; or

(d) uses, possesses, traffics in or permits another person to have access to a computer password that would enable a person to commit an offence under paragraph (a), (b) or (c).

(2) **Definitions** — In this section,

"computer data" means representations, including signs, signals or symbols, that are in a form suitable for processing in a computer system;

"computer password" means any computer data by which a computer service or computer system is capable of being obtained or used;

"computer program" means computer data representing instructions or statements that, when executed in a computer system, causes the computer system to perform a function;

"computer service" includes data processing and the storage or retrieval of computer data;

"computer system" means a device that, or a group of interconnected or related devices one or more of which,

(a) contains computer programs or other computer data, and

(b) by means of computer programs,

(i) performs logic and control, and

(ii) may perform any other function;

"data" [Repealed 2014, c. 31, s. 16(2).]

"electro-magnetic, acoustic, mechanical or other device" means any device or apparatus that is used or is capable of being used to intercept any function of a computer system, but does not include a hearing aid used to correct subnormal hearing of the user to not better than normal hearing;

"function" includes logic, control, arithmetic, deletion, storage and retrieval and communication or telecommunication to, from or within a computer system;

"intercept" includes listen to or record a function of a computer system, or acquire the substance, meaning or purport thereof;

"traffic" means, in respect of a computer password, to sell, export from or import into Canada, distribute or deal with in any other way.

R.S.C. 1985, c. 27 (1st Supp.), s. 45; 1997, c. 18, s. 18; 2014, c. 31, s. 16

342.2 (1) **Possession of device to obtain unauthorized use of computer system or to commit mischief** — Every person who, without lawful excuse, makes, possesses, sells, offers for sale, imports, obtains for use, distributes or makes available a device that is designed or adapted primarily to commit an offence under section 342.1 or 430, knowing that the device has been used or is intended to be used to commit such an offence, is

(a) guilty of an indictable offence and liable to imprisonment for a term of not more than two years; or

(b) guilty of an offence punishable on summary conviction.

(2) Forfeiture — If a person is convicted of an offence under subsection (1), in addition to any punishment that is imposed, any device in relation to which the offence was committed or the possession of which constituted the offence may be ordered forfeited to Her Majesty and may be disposed of as the Attorney General directs.

(3) Limitation — No order of forfeiture may be made under subsection (2) in respect of any thing that is the property of a person who was not a party to the offence under subsection (1).

(4) Definition of "device" — In this section, **"device"** includes

(a) a component of a device; and

(b) a computer program within the meaning of subsection 342.1(2).

1997, c. 18, s. 19; 2014, c. 31, s. 17; 2018, c. 29, s. 34

Robbery and Extortion

343. Robbery — Every one commits robbery who

(a) steals, and for the purpose of extorting whatever is stolen or to prevent or overcome resistance to the stealing, uses violence or threats of violence to a person or property;

(b) steals from any person and, at the time he steals or immediately before or immediately thereafter, wounds, beats, strikes or uses any personal violence to that person;

(c) assaults any person with intent to steal from him; or

(d) steals from any person while armed with an offensive weapon or imitation thereof.

344. (1) Robbery — Every person who commits robbery is guilty of an indictable offence and liable

(a) if a restricted firearm or prohibited firearm is used in the commission of the offence or if any firearm is used in the commission of the offence and the offence is committed for the benefit of, at the direction of, or in association with, a criminal organization, to imprisonment for life and to a minimum punishment of imprisonment for a term of

(i) in the case of a first offence, five years, and

(ii) in the case of a second or subsequent offence, seven years;

(a.1) in any other case where a firearm is used in the commission of the offence, to imprisonment for life and to a minimum punishment of imprisonment for a term of four years; and

(b) in any other case, to imprisonment for life.

(2) Subsequent offences — In determining, for the purpose of paragraph (1)(a), whether a convicted person has committed a second or subsequent offence, if the person was earlier convicted of any of the following offences, that offence is to be considered as an earlier offence:

(a) an offence under this section;

(b) an offence under subsection 85(1) or (2) or section 244 or 244.2; or

(c) an offence under section 220, 236, 239, 272 or 273, subsection 279(1) or section 279.1 or 346 if a firearm was used in the commission of the offence.

However, an earlier offence shall not be taken into account if 10 years have elapsed between the day on which the person was convicted of the earlier offence and the day on which the person was convicted of the offence for which sentence is being imposed, not taking into account any time in custody.

(3) Sequence of convictions only — For the purposes of subsection (2), the only question to be considered is the sequence of convictions and no consideration shall be given to the sequence of commission of offences or whether any offence occurred before or after any conviction.

1995, c. 39, s. 149; 2008, c. 6, s. 32; 2009, c. 22, s. 14

345. Stopping mail with intent — Every one who stops a mail conveyance with intent to rob or search it is guilty of an indictable offence and liable to imprisonment for life.

346. (1) Extortion — Every one commits extortion who, without reasonable justification or excuse and with intent to obtain anything, by threats, accusations, menaces or violence induces or attempts to induce any person, whether or not he is the person threatened, accused or menaced or to whom violence is shown, to do anything or cause anything to be done.

(1.1) Extortion — Every person who commits extortion is guilty of an indictable offence and liable

(a) if a restricted firearm or prohibited firearm is used in the commission of the offence or if any firearm is used in the commission of the offence and the offence is committed for the benefit of, at the direction of, or in association with, a criminal organization, to imprisonment for life and to a minimum punishment of imprisonment for a term of

(i) in the case of a first offence, five years, and

(ii) in the case of a second or subsequent offence, seven years;

(a.1) in any other case where a firearm is used in the commission of the offence, to imprisonment for life and to a minimum punishment of imprisonment for a term of four years; and

(b) in any other case, to imprisonment for life.

(1.2) Subsequent offences — In determining, for the purpose of paragraph (1.1)(a), whether a convicted person has committed a second or subsequent offence, if the person was earlier convicted of any of the following offences, that offence is to be considered as an earlier offence:

(a) an offence under this section;

(b) an offence under subsection 85(1) or (2) or section 244 or 244.2; or

(c) an offence under section 220, 236, 239, 272 or 273, subsection 279(1) or section 279.1 or 344 if a firearm was used in the commission of the offence.

However, an earlier offence shall not be taken into account if 10 years have elapsed between the day on which the person was convicted of the earlier offence and the day on which the person was convicted of the offence for which sentence is being imposed, not taking into account any time in custody.

(1.3) Sequence of convictions only — For the purposes of subsection (1.2), the only question to be considered is the sequence of convictions and no consideration shall be given to the sequence of commission of offences or whether any offence occurred before or after any conviction.

(2) Saving — A threat to institute civil proceedings is not a threat for the purposes of this section.

R.S.C. 1985, c. 27 (1st Supp.), s. 46; 1995, c. 39, s. 150; 2008, c. 6, s. 33; 2009, c. 22, s. 15

Criminal Interest Rate

347. (1) Criminal interest rate — Despite any other Act of Parliament, every one who enters into an agreement or arrangement to receive interest at a criminal rate, or receives a payment or partial payment of interest at a criminal rate, is

(a) guilty of an indictable offence and liable to imprisonment for a term not exceeding five years; or

(b) guilty of an offence punishable on summary conviction and liable to a fine of not more than $25,000 or to imprisonment for a term of not more than two years less a day, or to both.

(c) and (d) [Repealed 2007, c. 9, s. 1.]

(2) Definitions — In this section,

"credit advanced" means the aggregate of the money and the monetary value of any goods, services or benefits actually advanced or to be advanced under an agreement or arrangement minus the aggregate of any required deposit balance and any fee, fine, penalty, commission and other similar charge or expense directly or indirectly incurred under the original or any collateral agreement or arrangement;

"criminal rate" means an effective annual rate of interest calculated in accordance with generally accepted actuarial practices and principles that exceeds sixty per cent on the credit advanced under an agreement or arrangement;

"insurance charge" means the cost of insuring the risk assumed by the person who advances or is to advance credit under an agreement or arrangement, where the face amount of the insurance does not exceed the credit advanced;

"interest" means the aggregate of all charges and expenses, whether in the form of a fee, fine, penalty, commission or other similar charge or expense or in any other form, paid or payable for the advancing of credit under an agreement or arrangement, by or on behalf of the person to whom the credit is or is to be advanced, irrespective of the person to whom any such charges and expenses are or are to be paid or payable, but does not include any repayment of credit advanced or any insurance charge, official fee, overdraft charge, required deposit balance or, in the case of a mortgage transaction, any amount required to be paid on account of property taxes;

"official fee" means a fee required by law to be paid to any governmental authority in connection with perfecting any security under an agreement or arrangement for the advancing of credit;

"overdraft charge" means a charge not exceeding five dollars for the creation of or increase in an overdraft, imposed by a credit union or caisse populaire the membership of which is wholly or substantially comprised of natural persons or a deposit taking institution the deposits in which are insured, in whole or in part, by the Canada Deposit Insurance Corporation or guaranteed, in whole or in part, by the Quebec Deposit Insurance Board;

"required deposit balance" means a fixed or an ascertainable amount of the money actually advanced or to be advanced under an agreement or arrangement that is required, as a condition of the agreement or arrangement, to be deposited or invested by or on behalf of the person to whom the advance is or is to be made and that may be available, in the event of his defaulting in any payment, to or for the benefit of the person who advances or is to advance the money.

(3) Presumption — Where a person receives a payment or partial payment of interest at a criminal rate, he shall, in the absence of evidence to the contrary, be deemed to have knowledge of the nature of the payment and that it was received at a criminal rate.

(4) Proof of effective annual rate — In any proceedings under this section, a certificate of a Fellow of the Canadian Institute of Actuaries stating that he has calculated the effective annual rate of interest on any credit advanced under an agreement or arrangement and setting out the calculations and the information on which they are based is, in the absence of evidence to the contrary, proof of the effective annual rate without proof of the signature or official character of the person appearing to have signed the certificate.

(5) Notice — A certificate referred to in subsection (4) shall not be received in evidence unless the party intending to produce it has given to the accused or defendant reasonable notice of that intention together with a copy of the certificate.

(6) Cross examination with leave — An accused or a defendant against whom a certificate referred to in subsection (4) is produced may, with leave of the court, require the attendance of the actuary for the purposes of cross-examination.

(7) Consent required for proceedings — No proceedings shall be commenced under this section without the consent of the Attorney General.

(8) Application — This section does not apply to any transaction to which the *Tax Rebate Discounting Act* applies.

2007, c. 9, s. 1; 2019, c. 25, s. 127

347.1 (1) Definitions — The following definitions apply in subsection (2).

"interest" has the same meaning as in subsection 347(2). *("intérêts")*

"payday loan" means an advancement of money in exchange for a post-dated cheque, a pre-authorized debit or a future payment of a similar nature but not for any guarantee, suretyship, overdraft protection or security on property and not through a margin loan, pawnbroking, a line of credit or a credit card. *("prêt sur salaire")*

(2) Non-application — Section 347 and section 2 of the *Interest Act* do not apply to a person, other than a financial institution within the meaning of paragraphs (a) to (d) of the definition "financial institution" in section 2 of the *Bank Act*, in respect of a payday loan agreement entered into by the person to receive interest, or in respect of interest received by that person under the agreement, if

(a) the amount of money advanced under the agreement is $1,500 or less and the term of the agreement is 62 days or less;

(b) the person is licensed or otherwise specifically authorized under the laws of a province to enter into the agreement; and

(c) the province is designated under subsection (3).

(3) Designation of province — The Governor in Council shall, by order and at the request of the lieutenant governor in council of a province, designate the province for the purposes of this section if the province has legislative measures that protect recipients of payday loans and that provide for limits on the total cost of borrowing under the agreements.

(4) Revocation — The Governor in Council shall, by order, revoke the designation made under subsection (3) if requested to do so by the lieutenant governor in council of the province or if the legislative measures described in that subsection are no longer in force in that province.

2007, c. 9, s. 2

Breaking and Entering

348. (1) Breaking and entering with intent, committing offence or breaking out — Every one who

(a) breaks and enters a place with intent to commit an indictable offence therein,

(b) breaks and enters a place and commits an indictable offence therein, or

(c) breaks out of a place after

(i) committing an indictable offence therein, or

(ii) entering the place with intent to commit an indictable offence therein, is guilty

(d) if the offence is committed in relation to a dwelling-house, of an indictable offence and liable to imprisonment for life, and

(e) if the offence is committed in relation to a place other than a dwelling-house, of an indictable offence and liable to imprisonment for a term not exceeding ten years or of an offence punishable on summary conviction.

(2) **Presumptions** — For the purposes of proceedings under this section, evidence that an accused

(a) broke and entered a place or attempted to break and enter a place is, in the absence of any evidence to the contrary, proof that he broke and entered the place or attempted to do so, as the case may be, with intent to commit an indictable offence therein; or

(b) broke out of a place is, in the absence of any evidence to the contrary, proof that he broke out after

(i) committing an indictable offence therein, or

(ii) entering with intent to commit an indictable offence therein.

(3) **Definition of "place"** — For the purposes of this section, and section 351, **"place"** means

(a) a dwelling-house;

(b) a building or structure or any part thereof, other than a dwelling-house;

(c) a railway vehicle, a vessel, an aircraft or a trailer; or

(d) a pen or an enclosure in which fur-bearing animals are kept in captivity for breeding or commercial purposes.

R.S.C. 1985, c. 27 (1st Supp.), s. 47; 1997, c. 18, s. 20

348.1 Aggravating circumstance — home invasion — If a person is convicted of an offence under section 98 or 98.1, subsection 279(2) or section 343, 346 or 348 in relation to a dwelling-house, the court imposing the sentence on the person shall consider as an aggravating circumstance the fact that the dwelling-house was occupied at the time of the commission of the offence and that the person, in committing the offence,

(a) knew that or was reckless as to whether the dwelling-house was occupied; and

(b) used violence or threats of violence to a person or property.

2002, c. 13, s. 15; 2008, c. 6, s. 34

349. (1) Being unlawfully in dwelling-house — Every person who, without lawful excuse, enters or is in a dwelling-house with intent to commit an indictable offence in it is guilty of an indictable offence and liable to imprisonment for a term of not more than 10 years or of an offence punishable on summary conviction.

(2) **Presumption** — For the purposes of proceedings under this section, evidence that an accused, without lawful excuse, entered or was in a dwelling-house is, in the

absence of any evidence to the contrary, proof that he entered or was in the dwelling-house with intent to commit an indictable offence therein.

1997, c. 18, s. 21; 2018, c. 29, s. 35

350. Entrance — For the purposes of sections 348 and 349,

(a) a person enters as soon as any part of his body or any part of an instrument that he uses is within any thing that is being entered; and

(b) a person shall be deemed to have broken and entered if

(i) he obtained entrance by a threat or artifice or by collusion with a person within, or

(ii) he entered without lawful justification or excuse by a permanent or temporary opening.

2018, c. 29, s. 36

351. (1) Possession of break-in instrument — Every person who, without lawful excuse, has in their possession any instrument suitable for the purpose of breaking into any place, motor vehicle, vault or safe knowing that the instrument has been used or is intended to be used for that purpose,

(a) is guilty of an indictable offence and liable to imprisonment for a term not exceeding ten years; or

(b) is guilty of an offence punishable on summary conviction.

(2) Disguise with intent — Every person who, with intent to commit an indictable offence, has their face masked or coloured or is otherwise disguised is guilty of

(a) an indictable offence and liable to imprisonment for a term of not more than 10 years; or

(b) an offence punishable on summary conviction.

R.S.C. 1985, c. 27 (1st Supp.), s. 48; 2008, c. 18, s. 9; 2018, c. 29, s. 37; 2019, c. 25, s. 128

352. Possession of instruments for breaking into coin-operated or currency exchange devices — Every person who, without lawful excuse, has in their possession any instrument suitable for the purpose of breaking into a coin-operated device or a currency exchange device, knowing that the instrument has been used or is or was intended to be used for that purpose, is guilty of

(a) an indictable offence and liable to imprisonment for a term of not more than two years; or

(b) an offence punishable on summary conviction.

2018, c. 29, s. 38; 2019, c. 25, s. 129

353. (1) Selling, etc., automobile master key — Every person is guilty of an indictable offence and liable to imprisonment for a term of not more than two years or is guilty of an offence punishable on summary conviction who

(a) sells, offers for sale or advertises in a province an automobile master key otherwise than under the authority of a licence issued by the Attorney General of that province, or

(b) purchases or has in his possession in a province an automobile master key otherwise than under the authority of a licence issued by the Attorney General of that province.

(1.1) Exception — A police officer specially authorized by the chief of the police force to possess an automobile master key is not guilty of an offence under subsection (1) by reason only that the police officer possesses an automobile master key for the purposes of the execution of the police officer's duties.

(2) Terms and conditions of licence — A licence issued by the Attorney General of a province as described in paragraph (1)(*a*) or (*b*) may contain such terms and conditions relating to the sale, offering for sale, advertising, purchasing, having in possession or use of an automobile master key as the Attorney General of that province may prescribe.

(2.1) Fees — The Attorney General of a province may prescribe fees for the issue or renewal of licences as described in paragraph (1)(*a*) or (*b*).

(3) Record to be kept — Every one who sells an automobile master key

(a) shall keep a record of the transaction showing the name and address of the purchaser and particulars of the licence issued to the purchaser as described in paragraph (1)(*b*); and

(b) shall produce the record for inspection at the request of a peace officer.

(4) Failure to comply with subsection (3) — Every one who fails to comply with subsection (3) is guilty of an offence punishable on summary conviction.

(5) Definitions — The definitions in this subsection apply in this section.

"automobile master key" includes a key, pick, rocker key or other instrument designed or adapted to operate the ignition or other switches or locks of a series of motor vehicles.

"licence" includes any authorization.

1997, c. 18, s. 22; 2019, c. 25, s. 130

353.1 (1) Tampering with vehicle identification number — Every person commits an offence who, without lawful excuse, wholly or partially alters, removes or obliterates a vehicle identification number on a motor vehicle.

(2) Definition of "vehicle identification number" — For the purpose of this section, **"vehicle identification number"** means any number or other mark placed on a motor vehicle for the purpose of distinguishing it from other similar motor vehicles.

(3) Exception — Despite subsection (1), it is not an offence to wholly or partially alter, remove or obliterate a vehicle identification number on a motor vehicle during regular maintenance or any repair or other work done on the vehicle for a legitimate purpose, including a modification of the vehicle.

(4) Punishment — Every person who commits an offence under subsection (1)

(a) is guilty of an indictable offence and liable to imprisonment for a term of not more than five years; or

(b) is guilty of an offence punishable on summary conviction.

2010, c. 14, s. 4

Possession and Trafficking

[Heading amended 2010, c. 14, s. 5.]

354. (1) Possession of property obtained by crime — Every one commits an offence who has in his possession any property or thing or any proceeds of any property or thing knowing that all or part of the property or thing or of the proceeds was obtained by or derived directly or indirectly from

(a) the commission in Canada of an offence punishable by indictment; or

(b) an act or omission anywhere that, if it had occurred in Canada, would have constituted an offence punishable by indictment.

(2) Obliterated vehicle identification number — In proceedings in respect of an offence under subsection (1), evidence that a person has in their possession a motor vehicle the vehicle identification number of which has been wholly or partially removed or obliterated or a part of a motor vehicle being a part bearing a vehicle identification number that has been wholly or partially removed or obliterated is, in the absence of any evidence to the contrary, proof that the motor vehicle or part, as the case may be, was obtained,

(a) by the commission in Canada of an offence punishable by indictment; or

(b) by an act or omission anywhere that, if it had occurred in Canada, would have constituted an offence punishable by indictment.

(3) "vehicle identification number" defined — For the purposes of subsection (2), **"vehicle identification number"** means any number or other mark placed on a motor vehicle for the purpose of distinguishing the motor vehicle from other similar motor vehicles.

(4) Exception — A peace officer or a person acting under the direction of a peace officer is not guilty of an offence under this section by reason only that the peace officer or person possesses property or a thing or the proceeds of property or a thing mentioned in subsection (1) for the purposes of an investigation or otherwise in the execution of the peace officer's duties.

1997, c. 18, s. 23; 2018, c. 29, s. 39

355. Punishment — Every one who commits an offence under section 354

(a) if the subject matter of the offence is a testamentary instrument or the value of the subject matter of the offence is more than $5,000, is guilty of

(i) an indictable offence and liable to imprisonment for a term of not more than 10 years, or

(ii) an offence punishable on summary conviction; or

(b) if the value of the subject matter of the offence is not more than $5,000, is guilty

(i) of an indictable offence and is liable to imprisonment for a term not exceeding two years, or

(ii) of an offence punishable on summary conviction.

R.S.C. 1985, c. 27 (1st Supp.), s. 49; 1994, c. 44, s. 21; 2019, c. 25, s. 131

355.1 Definition of "traffic" — For the purposes of sections 355.2 and 355.4, **"traffic"** means to sell, give, transfer, transport, export from Canada, import into Canada, send, deliver or deal with in any other way, or to offer to do any of those acts.

2010, c. 14, s. 6

355.2 Trafficking in property obtained by crime — Everyone commits an offence who traffics in any property or thing or any proceeds of any property or thing knowing that all or part of the property, thing or proceeds was obtained by or derived directly or indirectly from

(a) the commission in Canada of an offence punishable by indictment; or

(b) an act or omission anywhere that, if it had occurred in Canada, would have constituted an offence punishable by indictment.

2010, c. 14, s. 6

355.3 *In rem* prohibition — The importation into Canada or exportation from Canada of any property or thing or any proceeds of any property or thing is prohibited if all or part of the property, thing or proceeds was obtained by or derived directly or indirectly from

(a) the commission in Canada of an offence punishable by indictment; or

(b) an act or omission anywhere that, if it had occurred in Canada, would have constituted an offence punishable by indictment.

2010, c. 14, s. 6

355.4 Possession of property obtained by crime — trafficking — Everyone commits an offence who has in their possession, for the purpose of trafficking, any property or thing or any proceeds of any property or thing knowing that all or part of the property, thing or proceeds was obtained by or derived directly or indirectly from

(a) the commission in Canada of an offence punishable by indictment; or

(b) an act or omission anywhere that, if it had occurred in Canada, would have constituted an offence punishable by indictment.

2010, c. 14, s. 6

355.5 Punishment — Everyone who commits an offence under section 355.2 or 355.4

(a) is, if the value of the subject matter of the offence is more than $5,000, guilty of an indictable offence and liable to imprisonment for a term of not more than 14 years; or

(b) is, if the value of the subject matter of the offence is not more than $5,000,

(i) guilty of an indictable offence and liable to imprisonment for a term of not more than five years, or

(ii) guilty of an offence punishable on summary conviction.

2010, c. 14, s. 6

356. (1) Theft from mail — Everyone commits an offence who

(a) steals

(i) anything sent by post, after it is deposited at a post office and before it is delivered, or after it is delivered but before it is in the possession of the addressee or of a person who may reasonably be considered to be authorized by the addressee to receive mail,

(ii) a bag, sack or other container or covering in which mail is conveyed, whether or not it contains mail, or

(iii) a key suited to a lock adopted for use by the Canada Post Corporation;

(a.1) with intent to commit an offence under paragraph (a), makes, possesses or uses a copy of a key suited to a lock adopted for use by the Canada Post Corporation, or a key suited to obtaining access to a receptacle or device provided for the receipt of mail;

(b) has in their possession anything that they know has been used to commit an offence under paragraph (a) or (a.1) or anything in respect of which they know that such an offence has been committed; or

(c) fraudulently redirects, or causes to be redirected, anything sent by post.

(2) Allegation of value not necessary — In proceedings for an offence under this section it is not necessary to allege in the indictment or to prove on the trial that anything in respect of which the offence was committed had any value.

(3) Punishment — Everyone who commits an offence under subsection (1)

(a) is guilty of an indictable offence and liable to imprisonment for a term of not more than 10 years; or

(b) is guilty of an offence punishable on summary conviction.

2009, c. 28, s. 6

357. Bringing into Canada property obtained by crime — Every person who brings into or has in Canada anything that they have obtained outside Canada by an act that, if it had been committed in Canada, would have been the offence of theft or an offence under section 342 or 354 is guilty of

(a) an indictable offence and liable to imprisonment for a term of not more than 10 years; or

(b) an offence punishable on summary conviction.

R.S.C. 1985, c. 27 (1st Supp.), s. 50; 2019, c. 25, s. 132

358. Having in possession when complete — For the purposes of sections 342 and 354 and paragraph 356(1)(*b*), the offence of having in possession is complete when a person has, alone or jointly with another person, possession of or control over anything mentioned in those sections or when he aids in concealing or disposing of it, as the case may be.

R.S.C. 1985, c. 27 (1st Supp.), s. 50

359 and 360. [Repealed 2018, c. 29, s. 40.]

False Pretences

361. (1) False pretence — A false pretence is a representation of a matter of fact either present or past, made by words or otherwise, that is known by the person who makes it to be false and that is made with a fraudulent intent to induce the person to whom it is made to act on it.

(2) Exaggeration — Exaggerated commendation or depreciation of the quality of anything is not a false pretence unless it is carried to such an extent that it amounts to a fraudulent misrepresentation of fact.

(3) Question of fact — For the purposes of subsection (2), it is a question of fact whether commendation or depreciation amounts to a fraudulent misrepresentation of fact.

362. (1) False pretence or false statement — Every one commits an offence who

(a) by a false pretence, whether directly or through the medium of a contract obtained by a false pretence, obtains anything in respect of which the offence of theft may be committed or causes it to be delivered to another person;

(b) obtains credit by a false pretence or by fraud;

(c) knowingly makes or causes to be made, directly or indirectly, a false statement in writing with intent that it should be relied on, with respect to the financial condition or means or ability to pay of himself or herself or any person or organization that he or she is interested in or that he or she acts for, for the purpose of procuring, in any form whatever, whether for his or her benefit or the benefit of that person or organization,

(i) the delivery of personal property,

(ii) the payment of money,

(iii) the making of a loan,

(iv) the grant or extension of credit,

(v) the discount of an account receivable, or

(vi) the making, accepting, discounting or endorsing of a bill of exchange, cheque, draft or promissory note; or

(d) knowing that a false statement in writing has been made with respect to the financial condition or means or ability to pay of himself or herself or another person or organization that he or she is interested in or that he or she acts for, procures on the faith of that statement, whether for his or her benefit or for the benefit of that person or organization, anything mentioned in subparagraphs (c)(i) to (vi).

(2) Punishment — Every one who commits an offence under paragraph (1)(*a*)

(a) if the property obtained is a testamentary instrument or the value of what is obtained is more than $5,000, is guilty of

(i) an indictable offence and liable to imprisonment for a term of not more than 10 years, or

(ii) an offence punishable on summary conviction; or

(b) if the value of what is obtained is not more than $5,000, is guilty

(i) of an indictable offence and is liable to imprisonment for a term not exceeding two years, or

(ii) of an offence punishable on summary conviction.

(3) Idem — Every person who commits an offence under paragraph (1)(b), (c) or (d) is guilty of

(a) an indictable offence and liable to imprisonment for a term of not more than 10 years; or

(b) an offence punishable on summary conviction.

(4) Presumption from cheque issued without funds — Where, in proceedings under paragraph (1)(*a*), it is shown that anything was obtained by the accused by means of a cheque that, when presented for payment within a reasonable time, was dishonoured on the ground that no funds or insufficient funds were on deposit to the credit of the accused in the bank or other institution on which the cheque was drawn, it shall be presumed to have been obtained by a false pretence, unless the court is satisfied by evidence that when the accused issued the cheque he believed on reasonable grounds that it would be honoured if presented for payment within a reasonable time after it was issued.

(5) Definition of "cheque" — In this section, **"cheque"** includes, in addition to its ordinary meaning, a bill of exchange drawn on any institution that makes it a business practice to honour bills of exchange or any particular kind thereof drawn on it by depositors.

R.S.C. 1985, c. 27 (1st Supp.), s. 52; 1994, c. 44, s. 22; 2003, c. 21, s. 5; 2019, c. 25, s. 133

363. Obtaining execution of valuable security by fraud — Every person is guilty of an indictable offence and liable to imprisonment for a term of not more than five years or is guilty of an offence punishable on summary conviction who, with intent to defraud or injure another person, by a false pretence causes or induces any person

(a) to execute, make, accept, endorse or destroy the whole or any part of a valuable security, or

(b) to write, impress or affix a name or seal on any paper or parchment in order that it may afterwards be made or converted into or used or dealt with as a valuable security.

2019, c. 25, s. 134

364. (1) Fraudulently obtaining food, beverage or accommodation — Every one who fraudulently obtains food, a beverage or accommodation at any place that is in the business of providing those things is guilty of an offence punishable on summary conviction.

(2) Presumption — In proceedings under this section, evidence that the accused obtained food, a beverage or accommodation at a place that is in the business of providing those things and did not pay for it and

(a) made a false or fictitious show or pretence of having baggage,

(b) had any false or pretended baggage,

(c) surreptitiously removed or attempted to remove his baggage or any material part of it,

(d) absconded or surreptitiously left the premises,

(e) knowingly made a false statement to obtain credit or time for payment, or

(f) offered a worthless cheque, draft or security in payment for the food, beverage or accommodation,

is, in the absence of any evidence to the contrary, proof of fraud.

(3) Definition of "cheque" — In this section **"cheque"** includes, in addition to its ordinary meaning, a bill of exchange drawn on any institution that makes it a business practice to honour bills of exchange or any particular kind thereof drawn on it by depositors.

1994, c. 44, s. 23

365. [Repealed 2018, c. 29, s. 41.]

Forgery and Offences Resembling Forgery

366. (1) Forgery — Every one commits forgery who makes a false document, knowing it to be false, with intent

(a) that it should in any way be used or acted on as genuine, to the prejudice of any one whether within Canada or not, or

(b) that a person should be induced, by the belief that it is genuine, to do or to refrain from doing anything, whether within Canada or not.

(2) Making false document — Making a false document includes

(a) altering a genuine document in any material part;

(b) making a material addition to a genuine document or adding to it a false date, attestation, seal or other thing that is material; or

(c) making a material alteration in a genuine document by erasure, obliteration, removal or in any other way.

(3) When forgery complete — Forgery is complete as soon as a document is made with the knowledge and intent referred to in subsection (1), notwithstanding that the person who makes it does not intend that any particular person should use or act on it as genuine or be induced, by the belief that it is genuine, to do or refrain from doing anything.

(4) Forgery complete though document incomplete — Forgery is complete notwithstanding that the false document is incomplete or does not purport to be a document that is binding in law, if it is such as to indicate that it was intended to be acted on as genuine.

(5) Exception — No person commits forgery by reason only that the person, in good faith, makes a false document at the request of a police force, the Canadian Forces or a department or agency of the federal government or of a provincial government.

2009, c. 28, s. 7

367. Punishment for forgery — Every one who commits forgery

(a) is guilty of an indictable offence and liable to imprisonment for a term not exceeding ten years; or

(b) is guilty of an offence punishable on summary conviction.

1994, c. 44, s. 24; 1997, c. 18, s. 24

368. (1) Use, trafficking or possession of forged document — Everyone commits an offence who, knowing or believing that a document is forged,

(a) uses, deals with or acts on it as if it were genuine;

(b) causes or attempts to cause any person to use, deal with or act on it as if it were genuine;

(c) transfers, sells or offers to sell it or makes it available, to any person, knowing that or being reckless as to whether an offence will be committed under paragraph (a) or (b); or

(d) possesses it with intent to commit an offence under any of paragraphs (a) to (c).

(1.1) Punishment — Everyone who commits an offence under subsection (1)

(a) is guilty of an indictable offence and liable to imprisonment for a term of not more than 10 years; or

(b) is guilty of an offence punishable on summary conviction.

(2) Wherever forged — For the purposes of proceedings under this section, the place where a document was forged is not material.

1997, c. 18, s. 25; 2009, c. 28, s. 8

368.1 Forgery instruments — Everyone is guilty of an indictable offence and liable to imprisonment for a term of not more than 14 years, or is guilty of an offence punishable on summary conviction, who, without lawful authority or excuse, makes, repairs, buys, sells, exports from Canada, imports into Canada or possesses any instrument, device, apparatus, material or thing that they know has been used or know is adapted or intended for use by any person to commit forgery.

2009, c. 28, s. 9

368.2 Public officers acting in the course of their duties or employment — No public officer, as defined in subsection 25.1(1), is guilty of an offence under any of sections 366 to 368.1 if the acts alleged to constitute the offence were committed by the public officer for the sole purpose of establishing or maintaining a covert identity for use in the course of the public officer's duties or employment.

2009, c. 28, s. 9

369. Exchequer bill paper, public seals, etc. — Everyone is guilty of an indictable offence and liable to imprisonment for a term of not more than 14 years who, without lawful authority or excuse,

(a) makes, uses or possesses

(i) any exchequer bill paper, revenue paper or paper that is used to make bank-notes, or

(ii) any paper that is intended to resemble paper mentioned in subparagraph (i); or

(b) makes, reproduces or uses a public seal of Canada or of a province, or the seal of a public body or authority in Canada or of a court of law.

(c) [Repealed 2009, c. 28, s. 9.]

2009, c. 28, s. 9

370 and 371. [Repealed 2018, c. 29, s. 42.]

372. (1) False information — Everyone commits an offence who, with intent to injure or alarm a person, conveys information that they know is false, or causes such information to be conveyed by letter or any means of telecommunication.

(2) Indecent communications — Everyone commits an offence who, with intent to alarm or annoy a person, makes an indecent communication to that person or to any other person by a means of telecommunication.

(3) Harassing communications — Everyone commits an offence who, without lawful excuse and with intent to harass a person, repeatedly communicates, or causes repeated communications to be made, with them by a means of telecommunication.

(4) Punishment — Everyone who commits an offence under this section is

(a) guilty of an indictable offence and liable to imprisonment for a term of not more than two years; or

(b) guilty of an offence punishable on summary conviction.

2014, c. 31, s. 18

373. [Repealed R.S.C. 1985, c. 27 (1st Supp.), s. 53.]

374. Drawing document without authority, etc. — Every one who

(a) with intent to defraud and without lawful authority makes, executes, draws, signs, accepts or endorses a document in the name or on the account of another person by procuration or otherwise, or

(b) makes use of or utters a document knowing that it has been made, executed, signed, accepted or endorsed with intent to defraud and without lawful authority, in the name or on the account of another person, by procuration or otherwise,

is guilty of an indictable offence and liable to imprisonment for a term not exceeding fourteen years.

375. Obtaining, etc., by instrument based on forged document — Every one who demands, receives or obtains anything, or causes or procures anything to be delivered or paid to any person under, on or by virtue of any instrument issued under the authority of law, knowing that it is based on a forged document, is guilty of an indictable offence and liable to imprisonment for a term not exceeding fourteen years.

376. (1) Counterfeiting stamp, etc. — Every person is guilty of an indictable offence and liable to imprisonment for a term of not more than 14 years who

(a) fraudulently uses, mutilates, affixes, removes or counterfeits a stamp or part thereof,

(b) knowingly and without lawful excuse has in their possession

(i) a counterfeit stamp or a stamp that has been fraudulently mutilated, or

(ii) anything bearing a stamp of which a part has been fraudulently erased, removed or concealed, or

(c) without lawful excuse makes or knowingly has in their possession a die or instrument that is capable of making the impression of a stamp or part of a stamp.

(2) Counterfeiting mark — Every one who, without lawful authority,

(a) makes a mark,

(b) sells, or exposes for sale, or has in his possession a counterfeit mark,

(c) affixes a mark to anything that is required by law to be marked, branded, sealed or wrapped other than the thing to which the mark was originally affixed or was intended to be affixed, or

(d) affixes a counterfeit mark to anything that is required by law to be marked, branded, sealed or wrapped,

is guilty of an indictable offence and liable to imprisonment for a term not exceeding fourteen years.

(3) Definitions — In this section

"mark" means a mark, brand, seal, wrapper or design used by or on behalf of

(a) the Government of Canada or a province,

(b) the government of a state other than Canada, or

(c) any department, board, commission or agent established by a government mentioned in paragraph (*a*) or (*b*) in connection with the service or business of that government;

"stamp" means an impressed or adhesive stamp used for the purpose of revenue by the Government of Canada or of a province or by the government of a state other than Canada.

2018, c. 29, s. 43

377. (1) Damaging documents — Every person is guilty of an indictable offence and liable to imprisonment for a term of not more than five years or is guilty of an offence punishable on summary conviction who unlawfully

(a) destroys, defaces or injures a register, or any part of a register of births, baptisms, marriages, deaths or burials that is required or authorized by law to be kept in Canada, or a copy or any part of a copy of such a register that is required by law to be transmitted to a registrar or other officer,

(b) inserts or causes to be inserted in a register or copy referred to in paragraph (*a*) an entry, that he knows is false, of any matter relating to a birth, baptism, marriage, death or burial, or erases any material part from that register or copy,

(c) destroys, damages or obliterates an election document or causes an election document to be destroyed, damaged or obliterated, or

(d) makes or causes to be made an erasure, alteration or interlineation in or on an election document.

(2) Definition of "election document" — In this section, **"election document"** means any document or writing issued under the authority of an Act of Parliament or the legislature of a province with respect to an election held pursuant to the authority of that Act.

2019, c. 25, s. 135

378. Offences in relation to registers — Every person is guilty of an indictable offence and liable to imprisonment for a term of not more than five years or is guilty of an offence punishable on summary conviction who

(a) being authorized or required by law to make or issue a certified copy of, extract from or certificate in respect of a register, record or document, knowingly makes or issues a false certified copy, extract or certificate,

(b) not being authorized or required by law to make or issue a certified copy of, extract from or certificate in respect of a register, record or document, fraudulently makes or issues a copy, extract or certificate that purports to be certified as authorized or required by law, or

(c) being authorized or required by law to make a certificate or declaration concerning any particular required for the purpose of making entries in a register, record or document, knowingly and falsely makes the certificate or declaration.

2019, c. 25, s. 136

Part X — Fraudulent Transactions Relating to Contracts and Trade (ss. 379–427)

Interpretation

379. Definition of "goods" — In this Part, **"goods"** means anything that is the subject of trade or commerce.

2018, c. 29, s. 43.1

Fraud

380. (1) Fraud — Every one who, by deceit, falsehood or other fraudulent means, whether or not it is a false pretence within the meaning of this Act, defrauds the public or any person, whether ascertained or not, of any property, money or valuable security or any service,

(a) is guilty of an indictable offence and liable to a term of imprisonment not exceeding fourteen years, where the subject-matter of the offence is a testamentary instrument or the value of the subject-matter of the offence exceeds five thousand dollars; or

(b) is guilty

(i) of an indictable offence and is liable to imprisonment for a term not exceeding two years, or

(ii) of an offence punishable on summary conviction,

where the value of the subject-matter of the offence does not exceed five thousand dollars.

(1.1) Minimum punishment — When a person is prosecuted on indictment and convicted of one or more offences referred to in subsection (1), the court that imposes the sentence shall impose a minimum punishment of imprisonment for a term of two years if the total value of the subject-matter of the offences exceeds one million dollars.

(2) Affecting public market — Every one who, by deceit, falsehood or other fraudulent means, whether or not it is a false pretence within the meaning of this Act, with intent to defraud, affects the public market price of stocks, shares, merchandise or anything that is offered for sale to the public is guilty of an indictable offence and liable to imprisonment for a term not exceeding fourteen years.

R.S.C. 1985, c. 27 (1st Supp.), s. 54; 1994, c. 44, s. 25; 1997, c. 18, s. 26; 2004, c. 3, s. 2; 2011, c. 6, s. 2

380.1 (1) Sentencing — aggravating circumstances — Without limiting the generality of section 718.2, where a court imposes a sentence for an offence referred to in section 380, 382, 382.1 or 400, it shall consider the following as aggravating circumstances:

(a) the magnitude, complexity, duration or degree of planning of the fraud committed was significant;

(b) the offence adversely affected, or had the potential to adversely affect, the stability of the Canadian economy or financial system or any financial market in Canada or investor confidence in such a financial market;

(c) the offence involved a large number of victims;

(c.1) the offence had a significant impact on the victims given their personal circumstances including their age, health and financial situation;

(d) in committing the offence, the offender took advantage of the high regard in which the offender was held in the community;

(e) the offender did not comply with a licensing requirement, or professional standard, that is normally applicable to the activity or conduct that forms the subject-matter of the offence; and

(f) the offender concealed or destroyed records related to the fraud or to the disbursement of the proceeds of the fraud.

(1.1) **Aggravating circumstance — value of the fraud** — Without limiting the generality of section 718.2, when a court imposes a sentence for an offence referred to in section 382, 382.1 or 400, it shall also consider as an aggravating circumstance the fact that the value of the fraud committed exceeded one million dollars.

(2) **Non-mitigating factors** — When a court imposes a sentence for an offence referred to in section 380, 382, 382.1 or 400, it shall not consider as mitigating circumstances the offender's employment, employment skills or status or reputation in the community if those circumstances were relevant to, contributed to, or were used in the commission of the offence.

(3) **Record of proceedings** — The court shall cause to be stated in the record the aggravating and mitigating circumstances it took into account when determining the sentence.

2004, c. 3, s. 3; 2011, c. 6, s. 3

380.2 (1) Prohibition order — When an offender is convicted, or is discharged on the conditions prescribed in a probation order under section 730, of an offence referred to in subsection 380(1), the court that sentences or discharges the offender, in addition to any other punishment that may be imposed for that offence or any other condition prescribed in the order of discharge, may make, subject to the conditions or exemptions that the court directs, an order prohibiting the offender from seeking, obtaining or continuing any employment, or becoming or being a volunteer in any capacity, that involves having authority over the real property, money or valuable security of another person.

(2) **Duration** — The prohibition may be for any period that the court considers appropriate, including any period to which the offender is sentenced to imprisonment.

(3) **Court may vary order** — A court that makes an order of prohibition or, if the court is for any reason unable to act, another court of equivalent jurisdiction in the same province, may, on application of the offender or the prosecutor, require the offender to appear before it at any time and, after hearing the parties, that court may

vary the conditions prescribed in the order if, in the opinion of the court, the variation is desirable because of changed circumstances.

(4) Offence — Every person who is bound by an order of prohibition and who does not comply with the order is guilty of

(a) an indictable offence and is liable to imprisonment for a term not exceeding two years; or

(b) an offence punishable on summary conviction.

2011, c. 6, s. 4

380.3 and 380.4 [Repealed 2015, c. 13, s. 11.]

381. Using mails to defraud — Every person who makes use of the mails for the purpose of transmitting or delivering letters or circulars concerning schemes devised or intended to deceive or defraud the public, or for the purpose of obtaining money under false pretences, is guilty of

(a) an indictable offence and liable to imprisonment for a term of not more than two years; or

(b) an offence punishable on summary conviction.

2019, c. 25, s. 137

382. Fraudulent manipulation of stock exchange transactions — Every person is guilty of an indictable offence and liable to imprisonment for a term of not more than 10 years or is guilty of an offence punishable on summary conviction who, through the facility of a stock exchange, curb market or other market, with intent to create a false or misleading appearance of active public trading in a security or with intent to create a false or misleading appearance with respect to the market price of a security,

(a) effects a transaction in the security that involves no change in the beneficial ownership thereof,

(b) enters an order for the purchase of the security, knowing that an order of substantially the same size at substantially the same time and at substantially the same price for the sale of the security has been or will be entered by or for the same or different persons, or

(c) enters an order for the sale of the security, knowing that an order of substantially the same size at substantially the same time and at substantially the same price for the purchase of the security has been or will be entered by or for the same or different persons.

2004, c. 3, s. 4; 2019, c. 25, s. 138

382.1 (1) Prohibited insider trading — Every person is guilty of an indictable offence and liable to imprisonment for a term of not more than 10 years or is guilty of an offence punishable on summary conviction who, directly or indirectly, buys or sells a security, knowingly using inside information that they

(a) possess by virtue of being a shareholder of the issuer of that security;

(b) possess by virtue of, or obtained in the course of, their business or professional relationship with that issuer;

(c) possess by virtue of, or obtained in the course of, a proposed takeover or reorganization of, or amalgamation, merger or similar business combination with, that issuer;

(d) possess by virtue of, or obtained in the course of, their employment, office, duties or occupation with that issuer or with a person referred to in paragraphs (a) to (c); or

(e) obtained from a person who possesses or obtained the information in a manner referred to in paragraphs (a) to (d).

(2) Tipping — Except when necessary in the course of business, a person who knowingly conveys inside information that they possess or obtained in a manner referred to in subsection (1) to another person, knowing that there is a risk that the person will use the information to buy or sell, directly or indirectly, a security to which the information relates, or that they may convey the information to another person who may buy or sell such a security, is guilty of

(a) an indictable offence and liable to imprisonment for a term not exceeding five years; or

(b) an offence punishable on summary conviction.

(3) Saving — For greater certainty, an act is not an offence under this section if it is authorized or required, or is not prohibited, by any federal or provincial Act or regulation applicable to it.

(4) Definition of "inside information" — In this section, **"inside information"** means information relating to or affecting the issuer of a security or a security that they have issued, or are about to issue, that

(a) has not been generally disclosed; and

(b) could reasonably be expected to significantly affect the market price or value of a security of the issuer.

2004, c. 3, s. 5; 2019, c. 25, s. 139

383. (1) Gaming in stocks or merchandise — Every person is guilty of an indictable offence and liable to imprisonment for a term of not more than five years or is guilty of an offence punishable on summary conviction who, with intent to make gain or profit by the rise or fall in price of the stock of an incorporated or unincorporated company or undertaking, whether in or outside Canada, or of any goods, wares or merchandise,

(a) makes or signs, or authorizes to be made or signed, any contract or agreement, oral or written, purporting to be for the purchase or sale of shares of stock or goods, wares or merchandise, without the *bona fide* intention of acquiring the shares, goods, wares or merchandise or of selling them, as the case may be, or

(b) makes or signs, or authorizes to be made or signed, any contract or agreement, oral or written, purporting to be for the sale or purchase of shares of stock or goods, wares or merchandise in respect of which no delivery of the thing sold or purchased is made or received, and without the *bona fide* intention of making or receiving delivery thereof, as the case may be,

This section does not apply if a broker, on behalf of a purchaser, receives delivery, even if the broker retains or pledges what is delivered as security for the advance of the purchase money or any part of it.

(2) **Onus** — Where, in proceedings under this section, it is established that the accused made or signed a contract or an agreement for the sale or purchase of shares of stock or goods, wares or merchandise, or acted, aided or abetted in the making or signing thereof, the burden of proof of a *bona fide* intention to acquire or to sell the shares, goods, wares or merchandise or to deliver or to receive delivery thereof, as the case may be, lies on the accused.

2019, c. 25, s. 140

384. (1) **Broker reducing stock by selling for their own account** — Every person commits an offence who, being an individual, or a member or employee of a partnership, or a director, officer or employee of a corporation, if they or the partnership or corporation is employed as a broker by any customer to buy and carry on margin any shares of an incorporated or unincorporated company or undertaking, whether in or outside Canada, later sells or causes to be sold shares of the company or undertaking for any account in which they or their firm or a partner of the firm or the corporation or a director of the corporation has a direct or indirect interest, if the effect of the sale is, otherwise than unintentionally, to reduce the amount of those shares in the hands of the broker or under their control in the ordinary course of business below the amount of those shares that the broker should be carrying for all customers.

(2) **Punishment** — Every person who commits an offence under subsection (1) is guilty of

(a) an indictable offence and liable to imprisonment for a term of not more than five years; or

(b) an offence punishable on summary conviction.

2019, c. 25, s. 141

385. (1) **Fraudulent concealment of title documents** — Every person is guilty of an indictable offence and liable to imprisonment for a term of not more than two years or is guilty of an offence punishable on summary conviction who, being a vendor, mortgagor or hypothecary debtor of property or a chose in action or an incorporeal right or being a lawyer or notary for or agent or mandatary of a vendor, mortgagor or hypothecary debtor of property, a chose in action or incorporeal right, is served with a written demand for an abstract of title by or on behalf of the purchaser, mortgagee or hypothecary creditor before the completion of the purchase, mortgage or hypothec, and who

(a) with intent to defraud and for the purpose of inducing the purchaser, mortgagee or hypothecary creditor to accept the title offered or produced to them, conceals from them any settlement, deed, will or other instrument or act material to the title, or any encumbrance on the title, or

(b) falsifies any pedigree on which the title depends.

(2) Consent required — No proceedings shall be instituted under this section without the consent of the Attorney General.

2019, c. 25, s. 142

386. Fraudulent registration of title — Every person is guilty of an indictable offence and liable to imprisonment for a term of not more than five years or is guilty of an offence punishable on summary conviction who, as principal, agent or mandatary in a proceeding to register title to real property or immovable property, or in a transaction relating to real property or immovable property that is or is proposed to be registered, knowingly and with intent to deceive,

(a) makes a material false statement or representation,

(b) suppresses or conceals from a judge or registrar, or any person employed by or assisting the registrar, any material document, fact, matter or information, or

(c) is privy to anything mentioned in paragraph (*a*) or (*b*).

2019, c. 25, s. 143

387. Fraudulent sale of real property — Every person who, knowing of an unregistered prior sale or of an existing unregistered grant, mortgage, hypothec, lien or encumbrance of or on real property, fraudulently sells the property or any part of it is guilty of

(a) an indictable offence and liable to imprisonment for a term of not more than two years; or

(b) an offence punishable on summary conviction.

2019, c. 25, s. 144

388. Misleading receipt — Every person is guilty of an indictable offence and liable to imprisonment for a term of not more than two years or is guilty of an offence punishable on summary conviction who knowingly,

(a) with intent to mislead, injure or defraud any person, whether or not that person is known to him, gives to a person anything in writing that purports to be a receipt for or an acknowledgment of property that has been delivered to or received by him, before the property referred to in the purported receipt or acknowledgment has been delivered to or received by him, or

(b) accepts, transmits or uses a purported receipt or acknowledgment to which paragraph (*a*) applies.

2019, c. 25, s. 145

389. (1) Fraudulent disposal of goods on which money advanced — Every person is guilty of an indictable offence and liable to imprisonment for a term of not more than two years or is guilty of an offence punishable on summary conviction who

(a) having shipped or delivered to the keeper of a warehouse or to a factor, an agent or a carrier anything on which the consignee thereof has advanced money or has given valuable security, thereafter, with intent to deceive, defraud or injure the consignee, disposes of it in a manner that is different from and inconsistent with any agreement that has been made in that behalf between him and the consignee, or

(b) knowingly and wilfully aids or assists any person to make a disposition of anything to which paragraph (*a*) applies for the purpose of deceiving, defrauding or injuring the consignee,

(2) Saving — No person is guilty of an offence under this section where, before disposing of anything in a manner that is different from and inconsistent with any agreement that has been made in that behalf between him and the consignee, he pays or tenders to the consignee the full amount of money or valuable security that the consignee has advanced.

2019, c. 25, s. 146

390. Fraudulent receipts under *Bank Act* — Every person is guilty of an indictable offence and liable to imprisonment for a term of not more than two years or is guilty of an offence punishable on summary conviction who

(a) knowingly makes a false statement in any receipt, certificate or acknowledgment for anything that may be used for a purpose mentioned in the *Bank Act*; or

(b) knowingly, after either giving to another person or after a person employed by them has, to their knowledge, given to another person, or after obtaining and endorsing or assigning to another person, any receipt, certificate or acknowledgment for anything that may be used for a purpose mentioned in the *Bank Act*, without the consent in writing of the holder or endorsee or the production and delivery of the receipt, certificate or acknowledgment, alienates or parts with, or does not deliver to the holder or owner the property mentioned in the receipt, certificate or acknowledgment.

2019, c. 25, s. 147

391. [Repealed 2003, c. 21, s. 6.]

392. Disposal of property to defraud creditors — Every person is guilty of an indictable offence and liable to imprisonment for a term of not more than two years or is guilty of an offence punishable on summary conviction who,

(a) with intent to defraud his creditors,

(i) makes or causes to be made any gift, conveyance, assignment, sale, transfer or delivery of his property, or

(ii) removes, conceals or disposes of any of his property, or

(b) with intent that any one should defraud his creditors, receives any property by means of or in relation to which an offence has been committed under paragraph (*a*).

2019, c. 25, s. 148

393. (1) Fraud in relation to fares, etc. — Every person whose duty it is to collect a fare, toll, ticket or admission and who intentionally does any of the following is guilty of an indictable offence and liable to imprisonment for a term of not more than two years or is guilty of an offence punishable on summary conviction:

(a) fails to collect it,

(b) collects less than the proper amount payable in respect thereof, or

(c) accepts any valuable consideration for failing to collect it or for collecting less than the proper amount payable in respect thereof.

(2) Idem — Every person is guilty of an indictable offence and liable to imprisonment for a term of not more than two years or is guilty of an offence punishable on summary conviction who gives or offers to a person whose duty it is to collect a fare, toll, ticket or admission fee any valuable consideration

(a) for failing to collect it, or

(b) for collecting an amount less than the amount payable in respect thereof.

(3) Fraudulently obtaining transportation — Every one who, by any false pretence or fraud, unlawfully obtains transportation by land, water or air is guilty of an offence punishable on summary conviction.

2019, c. 25, s. 149

394. (1) Fraud in relation to valuable minerals — No person who is the holder of a lease or licence issued under an Act relating to the mining of valuable minerals, or by the owner of land that is supposed to contain valuable minerals, shall

(a) by a fraudulent device or contrivance, defraud or attempt to defraud any person of

(i) any valuable minerals obtained under or reserved by the lease or licence, or

(ii) any money or valuable interest or thing payable in respect of valuable minerals obtained or rights reserved by the lease or licence; or

(b) fraudulently conceal or make a false statement with respect to the amount of valuable minerals obtained under the lease or licence.

(2) Sale of valuable minerals — No person, other than the owner or the owner's agent or someone otherwise acting under lawful authority, shall sell any valuable mineral that is unrefined, partly refined, uncut or otherwise unprocessed.

(3) Purchase of valuable minerals — No person shall buy any valuable mineral that is unrefined, partly refined, uncut or otherwise unprocessed from anyone who the person has reason to believe is not the owner or the owner's agent or someone otherwise acting under lawful authority.

(4) Presumption — In any proceeding in relation to subsection (2) or (3), in the absence of evidence raising a reasonable doubt to the contrary, it is presumed that

(a) in the case of a sale, the seller is not the owner of the valuable mineral or the owner's agent or someone otherwise acting under lawful authority; and

(b) in the case of a purchase, the purchaser, when buying the valuable mineral, had reason to believe that the seller was not the owner of the mineral or the owner's agent or someone otherwise acting under lawful authority.

(5) **Offence** — A person who contravenes subsection (1), (2) or (3) is guilty of

(a) an indictable offence and liable to imprisonment for a term of not more than five years; or

(b) an offence punishable on summary conviction.

(6) **Forfeiture** — If a person is convicted of an offence under this section, the court may order anything by means of or in relation to which the offence was committed, on such conviction, to be forfeited to Her Majesty.

(7) **Exception** — Subsection (6) does not apply to real property other than real property built or significantly modified for the purpose of facilitating the commission of an offence under this section.

R.S.C. 1985, c. 27 (1st Supp.), s. 186; 1999, c. 5, s. 10; 2019, c. 25, s. 150

394.1 (1) Possession of stolen or fraudulently obtained valuable minerals — No person shall possess any valuable mineral that is unrefined, partly refined, uncut or otherwise unprocessed that has been stolen or dealt with contrary to section 394.

(2) **Evidence** — Reasonable grounds to believe that the valuable mineral has been stolen or dealt with contrary to section 394 are, in the absence of evidence raising a reasonable doubt to the contrary, proof that the valuable mineral has been stolen or dealt with contrary to section 394.

(3) **Offence** — A person who contravenes subsection (1) is guilty of

(a) an indictable offence and liable to imprisonment for a term of not more than five years; or

(b) an offence punishable on summary conviction.

(4) **Forfeiture** — If a person is convicted of an offence under this section, the court may, on that conviction, order that anything by means of or in relation to which the offence was committed be forfeited to Her Majesty.

(5) **Exception** — Subsection (4) does not apply to real property, other than real property built or significantly modified for the purpose of facilitating the commission of an offence under subsection (3).

1999, c. 5, s. 10; 2019, c. 25, s. 151

395. (1) Search for valuable minerals — If an information in writing is laid under oath before a justice by a peace officer or by a public officer who has been appointed or designated to administer or enforce a federal or provincial law and whose duties include the enforcement of this Act or any other Act of Parliament and the justice is satisfied that there are reasonable grounds to believe that, contrary to this Act or any other Act of Parliament, any valuable mineral is deposited in a place or held by a person, the justice may issue a warrant authorizing a peace officer or a public officer, if the public officer is named in it, to search any of the places or persons mentioned in the information.

(1.1) **Execution in Canada** — A warrant issued under subsection (1) may be executed at any place in Canada. A public officer named in the warrant, or any peace officer, who executes the warrant must have authority to act in that capacity in the place where the warrant is executed.

(2) Power to seize — Where, on search, anything mentioned in subsection (1) is found, it shall be seized and carried before the justice who shall order

(a) that it be detained for the purposes of an inquiry or a trial; or

(b) if it is not detained for the purposes of an inquiry or a trial,

(i) that it be restored to the owner, or

(ii) that it be forfeited to Her Majesty in right of the province in which the proceedings take place if the owner cannot be ascertained.

(3) Appeal — An appeal lies from an order made under paragraph (2)(*b*) in the manner in which an appeal lies in summary conviction proceedings under Part XXVII and the provisions of that Part relating to appeals apply to appeals under this subsection.

1999, c. 5, s. 11; 2019, c. 25, s. 152

396. (1) Offences in relation to mines — Every person is guilty of an indictable offence and liable to imprisonment for a term of not more than 10 years or is guilty of an offence punishable on summary conviction who

(a) adds anything to or removes anything from any existing or prospective mine, mining claim or oil well with a fraudulent intent to affect the result of an assay, a test or a valuation that has been made or is to be made with respect to the mine, mining claim or oil well, or

(b) adds anything to, removes anything from or tampers with a sample or material that has been taken or is being or is about to be taken from any existing or prospective mine, mining claim or oil well for the purpose of being assayed, tested or otherwise valued, with a fraudulent intent to affect the result of the assay, test or valuation.

(2) Presumption — For the purposes of proceedings under subsection (1), evidence that

(a) something has been added to or removed from anything to which subsection (1) applies, or

(b) anything to which subsection (1) applies has been tampered with,

is, in the absence of any evidence to the contrary, proof of a fraudulent intent to affect the result of an assay, test or a valuation.

2019, c. 25, s. 153

Falsification of Books and Documents

397. (1) Books and documents — Every person is guilty of an indictable offence and liable to imprisonment for a term of not more than five years or is guilty of an offence punishable on summary conviction who, with intent to defraud,

(a) destroys, mutilates, alters, falsifies or makes a false entry in a book, paper, writing, valuable security or document, or

(b) omits a material particular from, or alters a material particular in, a book, paper, writing, valuable security or document.

(2) Privy — Every person who, with intent to defraud their creditors, is privy to the commission of an offence under subsection (1) is guilty of

(a) an indictable offence and liable to imprisonment for a term of not more than five years; or

(b) an offence punishable on summary conviction.

2019, c. 25, s. 154

398. Falsifying employment record — Every one who, with intent to deceive, falsifies an employment record by any means, including the punching of a time clock, is guilty of an offence punishable on summary conviction.

399. False return by public officer — Every person is guilty of an indictable offence and liable to imprisonment for a term of not more than five years or is guilty of an offence punishable on summary conviction who, being entrusted with the receipt, custody or management of any part of the public revenues, knowingly furnishes a false statement or return of

(a) any sum of money collected by him or entrusted to his care, or

(b) any balance of money in his hands or under his control.

2019, c. 25, s. 155

400. (1) False prospectus, etc. — Every person is guilty of an indictable offence and liable to imprisonment for a term of not more than 10 years or is guilty of an offence punishable on summary conviction who makes, circulates or publishes a prospectus, a statement or an account, whether written or oral, that they know is false in a material particular, with intent

(a) to induce persons, whether ascertained or not, to become shareholders or partners in a company,

(b) to deceive or defraud the members, shareholders or creditors, whether ascertained or not, of a company, or

(c) to induce any person to

(i) entrust or advance anything to a company, or

(ii) enter into any security for the benefit of a company.

(2) Definition of "company" — In this section, **"company"** means a syndicate, body corporate or company, whether existing or proposed to be created.

1994, c. 44, s. 26; 2019, c. 25, s. 156

401. (1) Obtaining carriage by false billing — Every one who, by means of a false or misleading representation, knowingly obtains or attempts to obtain the carriage of anything by any person into a country, province, district or other place, whether or not within Canada, where the importation or transportation of it is, in the circumstances of the case, unlawful is guilty of an offence punishable on summary conviction.

(2) Forfeiture — Where a person is convicted of an offence under subsection (1), anything by means of or in relation to which the offence was committed, on such conviction, in addition to any punishment that is imposed, is forfeited to Her Majesty and shall be disposed of as the court may direct.

402. [Repealed 2018, c. 29, s. 44.]

Identity Theft and Identity Fraud

[Heading amended 2009, c. 28, s. 10.]

402.1 Definition of "identity information" — For the purposes of sections 402.2 and 403, **"identity information"** means any information — including biological or physiological information — of a type that is commonly used alone or in combination with other information to identify or purport to identify an individual, including a fingerprint, voice print, retina image, iris image, DNA profile, name, address, date of birth, written signature, electronic signature, digital signature, user name, credit card number, debit card number, financial institution account number, passport number, Social Insurance Number, health insurance number, driver's licence number or password.

2009, c. 28, s. 10

402.2 (1) Identity theft — Every person commits an offence who obtains or possesses another person's identity information with intent to use it to commit an indictable offence that includes fraud, deceit or falsehood as an element of the offence.

(2) Trafficking in identity information — Everyone commits an offence who transmits, makes available, distributes, sells or offers for sale another person's identity information, or has it in their possession for any of those purposes, knowing that or being reckless as to whether the information will be used to commit an indictable offence that includes fraud, deceit or falsehood as an element of the offence.

(3) Clarification — For the purposes of subsections (1) and (2), an indictable offence referred to in either of those subsections includes an offence under any of the following sections:

(a) section 57 (forgery of or uttering forged passport);

(b) section 58 (fraudulent use of certificate of citizenship);

(c) section 130 (personating peace officer);

(d) section 131 (perjury);

(e) section 342 (theft, forgery, etc., of credit card);

(f) section 362 (false pretence or false statement);

(g) section 366 (forgery);

(h) section 368 (use, trafficking or possession of forged document);

(i) section 380 (fraud); and

(j) section 403 (identity fraud).

(4) Jurisdiction — An accused who is charged with an offence under subsection (1) or (2) may be tried and punished by any court having jurisdiction to try that offence in the place where the offence is alleged to have been committed or in the place where the accused is found, is arrested or is in custody. However, no proceeding in respect of the offence shall be commenced in a province without the consent of the Attorney General of that province if the offence is alleged to have been committed outside that province.

(5) Punishment — Everyone who commits an offence under subsection (1) or (2)

(a) is guilty of an indictable offence and liable to imprisonment for a term of not more than five years; or

(b) is guilty of an offence punishable on summary conviction.

2009, c. 28, s. 10; 2018, c. 29, s. 45

403. (1) Identity fraud — Everyone commits an offence who fraudulently personates another person, living or dead,

(a) with intent to gain advantage for themselves or another person;

(b) with intent to obtain any property or an interest in any property;

(c) with intent to cause disadvantage to the person being personated or another person; or

(d) with intent to avoid arrest or prosecution or to obstruct, pervert or defeat the course of justice.

(2) Clarification — For the purposes of subsection (1), personating a person includes pretending to be the person or using the person's identity information — whether by itself or in combination with identity information pertaining to any person — as if it pertains to the person using it.

(3) Punishment — Everyone who commits an offence under subsection (1)

(a) is guilty of an indictable offence and liable to imprisonment for a term of not more than 10 years; or

(b) is guilty of an offence punishable on summary conviction.

1994, c. 44, s. 27; 2009, c. 28, s. 10

404. [Repealed 2018, c. 29, s. 46.]

405. Acknowledging instrument in false name — Every person who, without lawful authority or excuse, acknowledges, in the name of another person before a court or a judge or other person authorized to receive the acknowledgment, a recognizance of bail, confession of judgment, consent to judgment or judgment, deed or other instrument or act is guilty of

Proposed Amendment — 405 opening words

405. Acknowledging instrument in false name — Every person who, without lawful authority or excuse, acknowledges, in the name of another person before a court or a judge or other person authorized to receive the acknowledgment, a recognizance, undertaking, release order, confession of judgment, consent to judgment or judgment, deed or other instrument or act is guilty of

2019, c. 25, s. 157(2) [To come into force December 18, 2019.]

(a) an indictable offence and liable to imprisonment for a term of not more than five years; or

(b) an offence punishable on summary conviction.

2018, c. 29, s. 46; 2019, c. 25, s. 157(1)

Forgery of Trademarks and Trade Descriptions

[Heading amended 2014, c. 20 s. 366(1).]

406. Forging trademark — For the purposes of this Part, every one forges a trademark who

(a) without the consent of the proprietor of the trademark, makes or reproduces in any manner that trademark or a mark so nearly resembling it as to be calculated to deceive; or

(b) falsifies, in any manner, a genuine trademark.

407. Offence — Every one commits an offence who, with intent to deceive or defraud the public or any person, whether ascertained or not, forges a trademark.

408. Passing off — Every one commits an offence who, with intent to deceive or defraud the public or any person, whether ascertained or not,

(a) passes off other wares or services as and for those ordered or required; or

(b) makes use, in association with wares or services, of any description that is false in a material respect regarding

(i) the kind, quality, quantity or composition,

(ii) the geographical origin, or

(iii) the mode of the manufacture, production or performance

of those wares or services.

409. (1) Instruments for forging trademark — Every one commits an offence who makes, has in his possession or disposes of a die, block, machine or other instrument designed or intended to be used in forging a trademark.

(2) Saving — No person shall be convicted of an offence under this section where he proves that he acted in good faith in the ordinary course of his business or employment.

410. Other offences in relation to trademarks — Every one commits an offence who, with intent to deceive or defraud,

(a) defaces, conceals or removes a trademark or the name of another person from anything without the consent of that other person; or

(b) being a manufacturer, dealer, trader or bottler, fills any bottle or siphon that bears the trademark or name of another person, without the consent of that other person, with a beverage, milk, by-product of milk or other liquid commodity for the purpose of sale or traffic.

411. Used goods sold without disclosure — Every one commits an offence who sells, exposes or has in his possession for sale, or advertises for sale, goods that have been used, reconditioned or remade and that bear the trademark or the tradename of another person, without making full disclosure that the goods have been reconditioned, rebuilt or remade for sale and that they are not then in the condition in which they were originally made or produced.

412. (1) Punishment — Every one who commits an offence under section 407, 408, 409, 410 or 411 is guilty of

(a) an indictable offence and is liable to imprisonment for a term not exceeding two years; or

(b) an offence punishable on summary conviction.

(2) Forfeiture — Anything by means of or in relation to which a person commits an offence under section 407, 408, 409, 410 or 411 is, unless the court otherwise orders, forfeited on the conviction of that person for that offence.

413. [Repealed 2018, c. 29, s. 47.]

414. Presumption from port of shipment — Where, in proceedings under this Part, the alleged offence relates to imported goods, evidence that the goods were shipped to Canada from a place outside Canada is, in the absence of any evidence to the contrary, proof that the goods were made or produced in the country from which they were shipped.

Wreck

415. Offences in relation to wreck — Every one who

(a) secretes wreck, defaces or obliterates the marks on wreck, or uses any means to disguise or conceal the fact that anything is wreck, or in any manner conceals the character of wreck, from a person who is entitled to inquire into the wreck,

(b) receives wreck, knowing that it is wreck, from a person other than the owner thereof or a receiver of wreck, and does not within forty-eight hours thereafter inform the receiver of wreck thereof,

(c) offers wreck for sale or otherwise deals with it, knowing that it is wreck, and not having a lawful authority to sell or deal with it,

(d) keeps wreck in his possession knowing that it is wreck, without lawful authority to keep it, for any time longer than the time reasonably necessary to deliver it to the receiver of wreck, or

(e) boards, against the will of the master, a vessel that is wrecked, stranded or in distress unless he is a receiver of wreck or a person acting under orders of a receiver of wreck,

is guilty of

(f) an indictable offence and is liable to imprisonment for a term not exceeding two years, or

(g) an offence punishable on summary conviction.

Public Stores

416. Distinguishing mark on public stores — The Governor in Council may, by notice to be published in the *Canada Gazette*, prescribe distinguishing marks that are appropriate for use on public stores to denote the property of Her Majesty therein, whether the stores belong to Her Majesty in right of Canada or to Her Majesty in any other right.

417. (1) Applying or removing marks without authority — Every person is guilty of an indictable offence and liable to imprisonment for a term of not more than two years or is guilty of an offence punishable on summary conviction who,

(a) without lawful authority applies a distinguishing mark to anything, or

(b) with intent to conceal the property of Her Majesty in public stores, removes, destroys or obliterates, in whole or in part, a distinguishing mark.

(2) Unlawful transactions in public stores — Every person who, without lawful authority, receives, possesses, keeps, sells or delivers public stores that they know bear a distinguishing mark is guilty of

(a) an indictable offence and is liable to imprisonment for a term not exceeding two years; or

(b) an offence punishable on summary conviction.

(3) Definition of "distinguishing mark" — For the purposes of this section, **"distinguishing mark"** means a distinguishing mark that is appropriated for use on public stores pursuant to section 416.

2018, c. 29, s. 48; 2019, c. 25, s. 158

418. (1) Selling defective stores to Her Majesty — Every one who knowingly sells or delivers defective stores to Her Majesty or commits fraud in connection with the sale, lease or delivery of stores to Her Majesty or the manufacture of stores for Her Majesty is guilty of an indictable offence and liable to imprisonment for a term not exceeding fourteen years.

(2) Offences by representatives — Every one who, being a representative of an organization that commits, by fraud, an offence under subsection (1),

(a) knowingly takes part in the fraud, or

(b) knows or has reason to suspect that the fraud is being committed or has been or is about to be committed and does not inform the responsible government, or a department thereof, of Her Majesty,

is guilty of an indictable offence and liable to imprisonment for a term not exceeding fourteen years.

2003, c. 21, s. 6.1

419. Unlawful use of military uniforms or certificates — Every person is guilty of an offence punishable on summary conviction who, without lawful authority,

(a) wears a uniform of the Canadian Forces or any other naval, army or air force or a uniform that is so similar to the uniform of any of those forces that it is likely to be mistaken therefor,

(b) wears a distinctive mark relating to wounds received or service performed in war, or a military medal, ribbon, badge, chevron or any decoration or order that is awarded for war services, or any imitation thereof, or any mark or device or thing that is likely to be mistaken for any such mark, medal, ribbon, badge, chevron, decoration or order,

(c) has in his possession a certificate of discharge, certificate of release, statement of service or identity card from the Canadian Forces or any other naval, army or air force that has not been issued to and does not belong to him, or

(d) has in his possession a commission or warrant or a certificate of discharge, certificate of release, statement of service or identity card issued to an officer or a person in or who has been in the Canadian Forces or any other naval, army or air force, that contains any alteration that is not verified by the initials of the officer who issued it, or by the initials of an officer thereto lawfully authorized.

2018, c. 29, s. 49

420. (1) Military stores — Every one who buys, receives or detains from a member of the Canadian Forces or a deserter or an absentee without leave therefrom any military stores that are owned by Her Majesty or for which the member, deserter or absentee without leave is accountable to Her Majesty is guilty of

(a) an indictable offence and is liable to imprisonment for a term not exceeding five years; or

(b) an offence punishable on summary conviction.

(2) Exception — No person shall be convicted of an offence under this section where he establishes that he did not know and had no reason to suspect that the military stores in respect of which the offence was committed were owned by Her Majesty or were military stores for which the member, deserter or absentee without leave was accountable to Her Majesty.

421. (1) Evidence of enlistment — In proceedings under sections 417 to 420, evidence that a person was at any time performing duties in the Canadian Forces is, in the absence of any evidence to the contrary, proof that his enrolment in the Canadian Forces prior to that time was regular.

(2) **Presumption when accused a dealer in stores** — An accused who is charged with an offence under subsection 417(2) shall be presumed to have known that the stores in respect of which the offence is alleged to have been committed bore a distinguishing mark within the meaning of that subsection at the time the offence is alleged to have been committed if he was, at that time, in the service or employment of Her Majesty or was a dealer in marine stores or in old metals.

Breach of Contract, Intimidation and Discrimination Against Trade Unionists

422. (1) Criminal breach of contract — Every one who wilfully breaks a contract, knowing or having reasonable cause to believe that the probable consequences of doing so, whether alone or in combination with others, will be

(a) to endanger human life,

(b) to cause serious bodily injury,

(c) to expose valuable property, real or personal, to destruction or serious injury,

(d) to deprive the inhabitants of a city or place, or part thereof, wholly or to a great extent, of their supply of light, power, gas or water, or

(e) to delay or prevent the running of any locomotive engine, tender, freight or passenger train or car, on a railway that is a common carrier,

is guilty of

(f) an indictable offence and is liable to imprisonment for a term not exceeding five years, or

(g) an offence punishable on summary conviction.

(2) **Saving** — No person wilfully breaks a contract within the meaning of subsection (1) by reason only that

(a) being the employee of an employer, he stops work as a result of the failure of his employer and himself to agree on any matter relating to his employment, or,

(b) being a member of an organization of employees formed for the purpose of regulating relations between employers and employees, he stops work as a result of the failure of the employer and a bargaining agent acting on behalf of the organization to agree on any matter relating to the employment of members of the organization,

if, before the stoppage of work occurs, all steps provided by law with respect to the settlement of industrial disputes are taken and any provision for the final settlement of differences, without stoppage of work, contained in or by law deemed to be contained in a collective agreement is complied with and effect given thereto.

(3) **Consent required** — No proceedings shall be instituted under this section without the consent of the Attorney General.

423. (1) Intimidation — Every one is guilty of an indictable offence and liable to imprisonment for a term of not more than five years or is guilty of an offence punishable on summary conviction who, wrongfully and without lawful authority, for the purpose of compelling another person to abstain from doing anything that he or she has a lawful right to do, or to do anything that he or she has a lawful right to abstain from doing,

(a) uses violence or threats of violence to that person or their intimate partner or children, or injures the person's property;

(b) intimidates or attempts to intimidate that person or a relative of that person by threats that, in Canada or elsewhere, violence or other injury will be done to or punishment inflicted on him or her or a relative of his or hers, or that the property of any of them will be damaged;

(c) persistently follows that person;

(d) hides any tools, clothes or other property owned or used by that person, or deprives him or her of them or hinders him or her in the use of them;

(e) with one or more other persons, follows that person, in a disorderly manner, on a highway;

(f) besets or watches the place where that person resides, works, carries on business or happens to be; or

(g) blocks or obstructs a highway.

(2) Exception — A person who attends at or near or approaches a dwelling-house or place, for the purpose only of obtaining or communicating information, does not watch or beset within the meaning of this section.

2000, c. 12, s. 95(b); 2001, c. 32, s. 10; 2019, c. 25, s. 159

423.1 (1) Intimidation of a justice system participant or a journalist — No person shall, without lawful authority, engage in any conduct with the intent to provoke a state of fear in

(a) a group of persons or the general public in order to impede the administration of criminal justice;

(b) a justice system participant in order to impede him or her in the performance of his or her duties; or

Proposed Amendment — 423.1(1)(b)

(b) a justice system participant or military justice system participant in order to impede him or her in the performance of his or her duties; or

2019, c. 15, s. 47(1) [Not in force at date of publication.]

(c) a journalist in order to impede him or her in the transmission to the public of information in relation to a criminal organization.

(2) [Repealed 2015, c. 13, s. 12(2).]

(3) Punishment — Every person who contravenes this section is guilty of an indictable offence and is liable to imprisonment for a term of not more than fourteen years.

Proposed Addition — 423.1(4)

(4) Definition of "military justice system participant" — In this section, **"military justice system participant"** has the same meaning as in subsection 2(1) of the *National Defence Act*.

2019, c. 15, s. 47(2) [Not in force at date of publication.]

2001, c. 32, s. 11; 2015, c. 13, s. 12

424. Threat against internationally protected person — Every person who threatens to commit an offence under section 235, 236, 266, 267, 268, 269, 269.1, 271, 272, 273, 279 or 279.1 against an internationally protected person or who threatens to commit an offence under section 431 is guilty of

(a) an indictable offence and liable to imprisonment for a term of not more than five years; or

(b) an offence punishable on summary conviction.

R.S.C. 1985, c. 27 (1st Supp.), s. 55; 2001, c. 41, s. 11; 2019, c. 25, s. 160

424.1 Threat against United Nations or associated personnel — Every person who, with intent to compel any person, group of persons, state or any international or intergovernmental organization to do or refrain from doing any act, threatens to commit an offence under section 235, 236, 266, 267, 268, 269, 269.1, 271, 272, 273, 279 or 279.1 against a member of United Nations personnel or associated personnel or threatens to commit an offence under section 431.1 is guilty of

(a) an indictable offence and liable to imprisonment for a term of not more than 10 years; or

(b) an offence punishable on summary conviction.

2001, c. 41, s. 11; 2019, c. 25, s. 160

425. Offences by employers — Every one who, being an employer or the agent of an employer, wrongfully and without lawful authority

(a) refuses to employ or dismisses from his employment any person for the reason only that the person is a member of a lawful trade union or of a lawful association or combination of workmen or employees formed for the purpose of advancing, in a lawful manner, their interests and organized for their protection in the regulation of wages and conditions of work,

(b) seeks by intimidation, threat of loss of position or employment, or by causing actual loss of position or employment, or by threatening or imposing any pecuniary penalty, to compel workmen or employees to abstain from belonging to a trade union, association or combination to which they have a lawful right to belong, or

(c) conspires, combines, agrees or arranges with any other employer or his agent to do anything mentioned in paragraph *(a)* or *(b)*,

is guilty of an offence punishable on summary conviction.

425.1 (1) Threats and retaliation against employees — No employer or person acting on behalf of an employer or in a position of authority in respect of an employee of the employer shall take a disciplinary measure against, demote, terminate or otherwise adversely affect the employment of such an employee, or threaten to do so,

(a) with the intent to compel the employee to abstain from providing information to a person whose duties include the enforcement of federal or provincial law, respecting an offence that the employee believes has been or is being committed contrary to this or any other federal or provincial Act or regulation by the employer or an officer or employee of the employer or, if the employer is a corporation, by one or more of its directors; or

(b) with the intent to retaliate against the employee because the employee has provided information referred to in paragraph (a) to a person whose duties include the enforcement of federal or provincial law.

(2) Punishment — Any one who contravenes subsection (1) is guilty of

(a) an indictable offence and liable to imprisonment for a term not exceeding five years; or

(b) an offence punishable on summary conviction.

2004, c. 3, s. 6

Secret Commissions

426. (1) Secret commissions — Every one commits an offence who

(a) directly or indirectly, corruptly gives, offers or agrees to give or offer to an agent or to anyone for the benefit of the agent — or, being an agent, directly or indirectly, corruptly demands, accepts or offers or agrees to accept from any person, for themselves or another person — any reward, advantage or benefit of any kind as consideration for doing or not doing, or for having done or not done, any act relating to the affairs or business of the agent's principal, or for showing or not showing favour or disfavour to any person with relation to the affairs or business of the agent's principal; or

(b) with intent to deceive a principal, gives to an agent of that principal, or, being an agent, uses with intent to deceive his principal, a receipt, account or other writing

(i) in which the principal has an interest,

(ii) that contains any statement that is false or erroneous or defective in any material particular, and

(iii) that is intented to mislead the principal.

(2) Privity to offence — Every one commits an offence who is knowingly privy to the commission of an offence under subsection (1).

(3) Punishment — A person who commits an offence under this section is guilty of

(a) an indictable offence and liable to imprisonment for a term of not more than five years; or

(b) an offence punishable on summary conviction.

(4) Definitions of "agent" and "principal" — In this section **"agent"** includes an employee, and **"principal"** includes an employer.

R.S.C. 1985, c. 27 (1st Supp.), s. 56; 2007, c. 13, s. 7; 2019, c. 25, s. 161

Heading and s. 427. [Repealed 2018, c. 29, s. 50.]

PART XI — WILFUL AND FORBIDDEN ACTS IN RESPECT OF CERTAIN PROPERTY (SS. 428–447.1)

Interpretation

428. "Property" — In this Part, **"property"** means real or personal corporeal property.

429. (1) Wilfully causing event to occur — Every one who causes the occurrence of an event by doing an act or by omitting to do an act that it is his duty to do, knowing that the act or omission will probably cause the occurrence of the event and being reckless whether the event occurs or not, shall be deemed, for the purposes of this Part, wilfully to have caused the occurrence of the event.

(2) Colour of right — A person shall not be convicted of an offence under sections 430 to 446 if they act with legal justification or excuse or colour of right.

(3) Interest — Where it is an offence to destroy or to damage anything,

(a) the fact that a person has a partial interest in what is destroyed or damaged does not prevent him from being guilty of the offence if he caused the destruction or damage; and

(b) the fact that a person has a total interest in what is destroyed or damaged does not prevent him from being guilty of the offence if he caused the destruction or damage with intent to defraud.

2018, c. 29, s. 51

Mischief

430. (1) Mischief — Every one commits mischief who wilfully

(a) destroys or damages property;

(b) renders property dangerous, useless, inoperative or ineffective;

(c) obstructs, interrupts or interferes with the lawful use, enjoyment or operation of property; or

(d) obstructs, interrupts or interferes with any person in the lawful use, enjoyment or operation of property.

(1.1) Mischief in relation to computer data — Everyone commits mischief who wilfully

(a) destroys or alters computer data;

(b) renders computer data meaningless, useless or ineffective;

(c) obstructs, interrupts or interferes with the lawful use of computer data; or

(d) obstructs, interrupts or interferes with a person in the lawful use of computer data or denies access to computer data to a person who is entitled to access to it.

(2) **Punishment** — Every one who commits mischief that causes actual danger to life is guilty of an indictable offence and liable to imprisonment for life.

(3) **Idem** — Every one who commits mischief in relation to property that is a testamentary instrument or the value of which exceeds five thousand dollars

(a) is guilty of an indictable offence and liable to imprisonment for a term not exceeding ten years; or

(b) is guilty of an offence punishable on summary conviction.

(4) **Idem** — Every one who commits mischief in relation to property, other than property described in subsection (3),

(a) is guilty of an indictable offence and liable to imprisonment for a term not exceeding two years; or

(b) is guilty of an offence punishable on summary conviction.

(4.1) **Mischief relating to religious property, educational institutions, etc.** — Everyone who commits mischief in relation to property described in any of paragraphs (4.101)(a) to (d), if the commission of the mischief is motivated by bias, prejudice or hate based on colour, race, religion, national or ethnic origin, age, sex, sexual orientation, gender identity or expression or mental or physical disability,

(a) is guilty of an indictable offence and liable to imprisonment for a term not exceeding ten years; or

(b) is guilty of an offence punishable on summary conviction.

(4.101) **Definition of "property"** — For the purposes of subsection (4.1), **"property"** means

(a) a building or structure, or part of a building or structure, that is primarily used for religious worship — including a church, mosque, synagogue or temple — , an object associated with religious worship located in or on the grounds of such a building or structure, or a cemetery;

(b) a building or structure, or part of a building or structure, that is primarily used by an **"identifiable group"** as defined in subsection 318(4) as an educational institution — including a school, daycare centre, college or university — , or an object associated with that institution located in or on the grounds of such a building or structure;

(c) a building or structure, or part of a building or structure, that is primarily used by an **"identifiable group"** as defined in subsection 318(4) for administrative, social, cultural or sports activities or events — including a town hall, community centre, playground or arena — , or an object associated with such an activity or event located in or on the grounds of such a building or structure; or

(d) a building or structure, or part of a building or structure, that is primarily used by an **"identifiable group"** as defined in subsection 318(4) as a residence for seniors or an object associated with that residence located in or on the grounds of such a building or structure.

(4.11) Mischief relating to war memorials — Everyone who commits mischief in relation to property that is a building, structure or part thereof that primarily serves as a monument to honour persons who were killed or died as a consequence of a war, including a war memorial or cenotaph, or an object associated with honouring or remembering those persons that is located in or on the grounds of such a building or structure, or a cemetery is guilty of an indictable offence or an offence punishable on summary conviction and liable,

(a) whether the offence is prosecuted by indictment or punishable on summary conviction, to the following minimum punishment, namely,

(i) for a first offence, to a fine of not less than $1,000,

(ii) for a second offence, to imprisonment for not less than 14 days, and

(iii) for each subsequent offence, to imprisonment for not less than 30 days;

(b) if the offence is prosecuted by indictment, to imprisonment for a term not exceeding 10 years; and

(c) if the offence is punishable on summary conviction, to imprisonment for a term of not more than two years less a day.

(4.2) Mischief in relation to cultural property — Every one who commits mischief in relation to cultural property as defined in Article 1 of the Convention for the Protection of Cultural Property in the Event of Armed Conflict, done at The Hague on May 14, 1954, as set out in the schedule to the *Cultural Property Export and Import Act*,

(a) is guilty of an indictable offence and liable to imprisonment for a term not exceeding ten years; or

(b) is guilty of an offence punishable on summary conviction.

(5) Mischief in relation to computer data — Everyone who commits mischief in relation to computer data

(a) is guilty of an indictable offence and liable to imprisonment for a term not exceeding ten years; or

(b) is guilty of an offence punishable on summary conviction.

(5.1) Offence — Everyone who wilfully does an act or wilfully omits to do an act that it is their duty to do, if that act or omission is likely to constitute mischief causing actual danger to life, or to constitute mischief in relation to property or computer data,

(a) is guilty of an indictable offence and liable to imprisonment for a term not exceeding five years; or

(b) is guilty of an offence punishable on summary conviction.

(6) Saving — No person commits mischief within the meaning of this section by reason only that

(a) he stops work as a result of the failure of his employer and himself to agree on any matter relating to his employment;

(b) he stops work as a result of the failure of his employer and a bargaining agent acting on his behalf to agree on any matter relating to his employment; or

(c) he stops work as a result of his taking part in a combination of workmen or employees for their own reasonable protection as workmen or employees.

(7) Idem — No person commits mischief within the meaning of this section by reason only that he attends at or near or approaches a dwelling-house or place for the purpose only of obtaining or communicating information.

(8) Definition of "computer data" — In this section, **"computer data"** has the same meaning as in subsection 342.1(2).

R.S.C. 1985, c. 27 (1st Supp.), s. 57; 1994, c. 44, s. 28; 2001, c. 41, s. 12; 2005, c. 40, s. 3; 2014, c. 9, s. 1; 2014, c. 31, s. 19; 2017, c. 23, ss. 1, 2; 2019, c. 25, s. 162

431. Attack on premises, residence or transport of internationally protected person — Every one who commits a violent attack on the official premises, private accommodation or means of transport of an internationally protected person that is likely to endanger the life or liberty of such a person is guilty of an indictable offence and liable to imprisonment for a term of not more than fourteen years.

R.S.C. 1985, c. 27 (1st Supp.), s. 58; 2001, c. 41, s. 13

431.1 Attack on premises, accommodation or transport of United Nations or associated personnel — Every one who commits a violent attack on the official premises, private accommodation or means of transport of a member of United Nations personnel or associated personnel that is likely to endanger the life or liberty of such a person is guilty of an indictable offence and liable to imprisonment for a term of not more than fourteen years.

2001, c. 41, s. 13

431.2 (1) Definitions — The following definitions apply in this section.

"explosive or other lethal device" means

(a) an explosive or incendiary weapon or device that is designed to cause, or is capable of causing, death, serious bodily injury or substantial material damage; or

(b) a weapon or device that is designed to cause, or is capable of causing, death, serious bodily injury or substantial material damage through the release, dissemination or impact of toxic chemicals, biological agents or toxins or similar substances, or radiation or radioactive material.

("engin explosif ou autre engin meurtrier")

"infrastructure facility" means a publicly or privately owned facility that provides or distributes services for the benefit of the public, including services relating to water, sewage, energy, fuel and communications. *("infrastructure")*

"military forces of a state" means the armed forces that a state organizes, trains and equips in accordance with the law of the state for the primary purpose of national defence or national security, and every person acting in support of those armed forces who is under their formal command, control and responsibility. *("forces armées d'un État")*

"place of public use" means those parts of land, a building, street, waterway or other location that are accessible or open to members of the public, whether on a continuous, periodic or occasional basis, and includes any commercial, business, cultural, historical, educational, religious, governmental, entertainment, recreational or other place that is accessible or open to the public on such a basis. *("lieu public")*

"public transportation system" means a publicly or privately owned facility, conveyance or other thing that is used in connection with publicly available services for the transportation of persons or cargo. *("système de transport public")*

(2) **Explosive or other lethal device** — Every one who delivers, places, discharges or detonates an explosive or other lethal device to, into, in or against a place of public use, a government or public facility, a public transportation system or an infrastructure facility, either with intent to cause death or serious bodily injury or with intent to cause extensive destruction of such a place, system or facility that results in or is likely to result in major economic loss, is guilty of an indictable offence and liable to imprisonment for life.

(3) **Armed forces** — For greater certainty, subsection (2) does not apply to an act or omission that is committed during an armed conflict and that, at the time and in the place of its commission, is in accordance with customary international law or conventional international law applicable to the conflict, or to activities undertaken by military forces of a state in the exercise of their official duties, to the extent that those activities are governed by other rules of international law.

2001, c. 41, s. 13

432. (1) **Unauthorized recording of a movie** — A person who, without the consent of the theatre manager, records in a movie theatre a performance of a cinematographic work within the meaning of section 2 of the *Copyright Act* or its soundtrack

(a) is guilty of an indictable offence and liable to imprisonment for a term of not more than two years; or

(b) is guilty of an offence punishable on summary conviction.

(2) **Unauthorized recording for purpose of sale, etc.** — A person who, without the consent of the theatre manager, records in a movie theatre a performance of a cinematographic work within the meaning of section 2 of the *Copyright*

Act or its soundtrack for the purpose of the sale, rental or other commercial distribution of a copy of the cinematographic work

(a) is guilty of an indictable offence and liable to imprisonment for a term of not more than five years; or

(b) is guilty of an offence punishable on summary conviction.

(3) Forfeiture — In addition to any punishment that is imposed on a person who is convicted of an offence under this section, the court may order that anything that is used in the commission of the offence be forfeited to Her Majesty in right of the province in which the proceedings are taken. Anything that is forfeited may be disposed of as the Attorney General directs.

(4) Forfeiture — limitation — No order may be made under subsection (3) in respect of anything that is the property of a person who is not a party to the offence.

2007, c. 28, s. 1

Arson and Other Fires

433. Arson — disregard for human life — Every person who intentionally or recklessly causes damage by fire or explosion to property, whether or not that person owns the property, is guilty of an indictable offence and liable to imprisonment for life where

(a) the person knows that or is reckless with respect to whether the property is inhabited or occupied; or

(b) the fire or explosion causes bodily harm to another person.

1990, c. 15, s. 1

434. Arson — damage to property — Every person who intentionally or recklessly causes damage by fire or explosion to property that is not wholly owned by that person is guilty of an indictable offence and liable to imprisonment for a term not exceeding fourteen years.

1990, c. 15, s. 1

434.1 Arson — own property — Every person who intentionally or recklessly causes damage by fire or explosion to property that is owned, in whole or in part, by that person is guilty of an indictable offence and liable to imprisonment for a term not exceeding fourteen years, where the fire or explosion seriously threatens the health, safety or property of another person.

1990, c. 15, s. 1

435. (1) Arson for fraudulent purpose — Every person who, with intent to defraud any other person, causes damage by fire or explosion to property, whether or not that person owns, in whole or in part, the property, is guilty of

(a) an indictable offence and liable to imprisonment for a term of not more than 10 years; or

(b) an offence punishable on summary conviction.

(2) Holder or beneficiary of fire insurance policy — Where a person is charged with an offence under subsection (1), the fact that the person was the holder of or was named as a beneficiary under a policy of fire insurance relating to the property in respect of which the offence is alleged to have been committed is a fact from which intent to defraud may be inferred by the court.

1990, c. 15, s. 1; 2019, c. 25, s. 163

436. (1) Arson by negligence — Every person who owns, in whole or in part, or controls property and who, as a result of a marked departure from the standard of care that a reasonably prudent person would use to prevent or control the spread of fires or to prevent explosions, is a cause of a fire or explosion in that property that causes bodily harm to another person or damage to property is guilty of

(a) an indictable offence and liable to imprisonment for a term of not more than five years; or

(b) an offence punishable on summary conviction.

(2) Non-compliance with prevention laws — Where a person is charged with an offence under subsection (1), the fact that the person has failed to comply with any law respecting the prevention or control of fires or explosions in the property is a fact from which a marked departure from the standard of care referred to in that subsection may be inferred by the court.

1990, c. 15, s. 1; 2019, c. 25, s. 164

436.1 Possession of incendiary material — Every person who possesses any incendiary material, incendiary device or explosive substance for the purpose of committing an offence under any of sections 433 to 436 is guilty of

(a) an indictable offence and liable to imprisonment for a term of not more than five years; or

(b) an offence punishable on summary conviction.

1990, c. 15, s. 1; 2019, c. 25, s. 165

Other Interference with Property

437. False alarm of fire — Every one who wilfully, without reasonable cause, by outcry, ringing bells, using a fire alarm, telephone or telegraph, or in any other manner, makes or circulates or causes to be made or circulated an alarm of fire is guilty of

(a) an indictable offence and is liable to imprisonment for a term not exceeding two years; or

(b) an offence punishable on summary conviction.

438. (1) Interfering with saving of wrecked vessel — Every person is guilty of an indictable offence and liable to imprisonment for a term of not more than five years or is guilty of an offence punishable on summary conviction who intentionally prevents or impedes, or who intentionally endeavours to prevent or impede,

(a) the saving of a vessel that is wrecked, stranded, abandoned or in distress, or

(b) a person who attempts to save a vessel that is wrecked, stranded, abandoned or in distress,

(2) Interfering with saving of wreck — Every one who wilfully prevents or impedes or wilfully endeavours to prevent or impede the saving of wreck is guilty of an offence punishable on summary conviction.

2019, c. 25, s. 166

439. (1) Interfering with marine signal, etc. — Every one who makes fast a vessel or boat to a signal, buoy or other sea-mark that is used for purposes of navigation is guilty of an offence punishable on summary conviction.

(2) Idem — Every person who intentionally alters, removes or conceals a signal, buoy or other sea-mark that is used for purposes of navigation is guilty of

(a) an indictable offence and liable to imprisonment for a term of not more than 10 years; or

(b) an offence punishable on summary conviction.

2019, c. 25, s. 167

440. Removing natural bar without permission — Every person who knowingly and without the written permission of the Minister of Transport removes any stone, wood, earth or other material that forms a natural bar necessary to the existence of a public harbour, or that forms a natural protection to such a bar, is guilty of

(a) an indictable offence and liable to imprisonment for a term of not more than two years; or

(b) an offence punishable on summary conviction.

2019, c. 25, s. 168

441. Occupant injuring building — Every person who, intentionally and to the prejudice of a mortgagee, a hypothecary creditor or an owner, pulls down, demolishes or removes all or any part of a dwelling-house or other building of which they are in possession or occupation, or severs from the freehold any fixture fixed to it or from the immovable property any movable property permanently attached or joined to the immovable property, is guilty of

(a) an indictable offence and liable to imprisonment for a term of not more than five years; or

(b) an offence punishable on summary conviction.

2019, c. 25, s. 168

442. Interfering with boundary lines — Every one who wilfully pulls down, defaces, alters or removes anything planted or set up as the boundary line or part of the boundary line of land is guilty of an offence punishable on summary conviction.

443. (1) Interfering with international boundary marks, etc. — Every person is guilty of an indictable offence and liable to imprisonment for a term of not more than five years or is guilty of an offence punishable on summary conviction who intentionally pulls down, defaces, alters or removes

(a) a boundary mark lawfully placed to mark an international, provincial, county or municipal boundary, or

(b) a boundary mark lawfully placed by a land surveyor to mark any limit, boundary or angle of a concession, range, lot or parcel of land.

(2) Saving provision — A land surveyor does not commit an offence under subsection (1) where, in his operations as a land surveyor,

(a) he takes up, when necessary, a boundary mark mentioned in paragraph (1)(b) and carefully replaces it as it was before he took it up, or

(b) he takes up a boundary mark mentioned in paragraph (1)(b) in the course of surveying for a highway or other work that, when completed, will make it impossible or impracticable for that boundary mark to occupy its original position, and he establishes a permanent record of the original position sufficient to permit that position to be ascertained.

2019, c. 25, s. 169

Animals

[Heading amended 2018, c. 29, s. 52.]

444. [Repealed 2018, c. 29, s. 52.]

445. (1) Injuring or endangering other animals — Every one commits an offence who, wilfully and without lawful excuse,

(a) kills, maims, wounds, poisons or injures dogs, birds or animals that are kept for a lawful purpose; or

(b) places poison in such a position that it may easily be consumed by dogs, birds or animals that are kept for a lawful purpose.

(2) Punishment — Every one who commits an offence under subsection (1) is guilty of

(a) an indictable offence and liable to imprisonment for a term of not more than five years; or

(b) an offence punishable on summary conviction and liable to a fine of not more than $10,000 or to imprisonment for a term of not more than two years less a day, or to both.

2008, c. 12, s. 1; 2018, c. 29, s. 53; 2019, c. 25, s. 170

445.01 (1) Killing or injuring certain animals — Every one commits an offence who, wilfully and without lawful excuse, kills, maims, wounds, poisons or injures a law enforcement animal while it is aiding a law enforcement officer in carrying out that officer's duties, a military animal while it is aiding a member of the Canadian Forces in carrying out that member's duties or a service animal.

(2) Punishment — Every one who commits an offence under subsection (1) is guilty of

(a) an indictable offence and liable to imprisonment for a term of not more than five years and, if a law enforcement animal is killed in the commission of the offence, to a minimum punishment of imprisonment for a term of six months; or

(b) an offence punishable on summary conviction and liable to a fine of not more than $10,000 or to imprisonment for a term of not more than two years less a day, or to both.

(3) Sentences to be served consecutively — A sentence imposed on a person for an offence under subsection (1) committed against a law enforcement animal shall be served consecutively to any other punishment imposed on the person for an offence arising out of the same event or series of events.

(4) Definitions — The following definitions apply in this section.

"law enforcement animal" means a dog or horse that is trained to aid a law enforcement officer in carrying out that officer's duties. *("animal d'assistance policière")*

"law enforcement officer" means a police officer, a police constable or any person referred to in paragraph (b), (c.1), (d), (d.1), (e) or (g) of the definition "peace officer" in section 2. *("agent de contrôle d'application de la loi")*

"military animal" means an animal that is trained to aid a member of the Canadian Forces in carrying out that member's duties. *("animal d'assistance militaire")*

"service animal" means an animal that is required by a person with a disability for assistance and is certified, in writing, as having been trained by a professional service animal institution to assist a person with a disability. *("animal d'assistance")*

2015, c. 34, s. 3; 2019, c. 25, s. 171

Cruelty to Animals

[Heading added 2008, c. 12, s. 1.]

445.1 (1) Causing unnecessary suffering — Every one commits an offence who

(a) wilfully causes or, being the owner, wilfully permits to be caused unnecessary pain, suffering or injury to an animal or a bird;

(b) in any manner encourages, aids, promotes, arranges, assists at, receives money for or takes part in

(i) the fighting or baiting of animals or birds, or

(ii) the training, transporting or breeding of animals or birds for the purposes of subparagraph (i);

(c) wilfully, without reasonable excuse, administers a poisonous or an injurious drug or substance to a domestic animal or bird or an animal or a bird wild by nature that is kept in captivity or, being the owner of such an animal or a bird, wilfully permits a poisonous or an injurious drug or substance to be administered to it;

(d) promotes, arranges, conducts, assists in, receives money for or takes part in any meeting, competition, exhibition, pastime, practice, display or event at or in the course of which captive birds are liberated by hand, trap, contrivance or any other means for the purpose of being shot when they are liberated; or

(e) being the owner, occupier or person in charge of any premises, permits the premises or any part thereof to be used for a purpose mentioned in paragraph (d).

(2) **Punishment** — Every one who commits an offence under subsection (1) is guilty of

(a) an indictable offence and liable to imprisonment for a term of not more than five years; or

(b) an offence punishable on summary conviction and liable to a fine of not more than $10,000 or to imprisonment for a term of not more than two years less a day, or to both.

(3) **Failure to exercise reasonable care as evidence** — For the purposes of proceedings under paragraph (1)(a), evidence that a person failed to exercise reasonable care or supervision of an animal or a bird thereby causing it pain, suffering or injury is, in the absence of any evidence to the contrary, proof that the pain, suffering or injury was caused or was permitted to be caused wilfully, as the case may be.

(4) **Presence at baiting as evidence** — For the purpose of proceedings under paragraph (1)(b), evidence that an accused was present at the fighting or baiting of animals or birds is, in the absence of any evidence to the contrary, proof that he or she encouraged, aided or assisted at the fighting or baiting.

2008, c. 12, s. 1; 2019, c. 17, s. 2; 2019, c. 25, s. 172

445.2 (1) **Definition of "cetacean"** — In this section, **"cetacean"** includes any member of the cetacean order, including a whale, dolphin or porpoise.

(2) **Offence** — Subject to subsections (2.1) to (3.1), every person commits an offence who

(a) owns, has the custody of or controls a cetacean that is kept in captivity;

(b) breeds or impregnates a cetacean; or

(c) possesses or seeks to obtain reproductive materials of cetaceans, including sperm or an embryo.

(2.1) **Exception — gestation** — If a cetacean is gestating on the day on which this subsection comes into force, paragraphs (2)(b) and (c) do not apply in respect of that cetacean for the period in which it gestates that includes the day on which this subsection comes into force.

(2.2) **Exception — offspring** — Paragraph (2)(a) does not apply to the offspring of a cetacean if that offspring was born immediately after a gestational period that included the day on which this subsection came into force.

(3) Exception — Paragraph (2)(a) does not apply to a person who

(a) owns, has the custody of or controls a cetacean that is kept in captivity at the coming into force of this section and remains continuously in captivity thereafter;

(b) has the custody of or controls a cetacean that is kept in captivity for the purpose of providing it with assistance or care or to rehabilitate it following an injury or another state of distress; or

(c) is authorized to keep a cetacean in captivity in the best interests of the cetacean's welfare pursuant to a licence issued by the Lieutenant Governor in Council of a province or by such other person or authority in the province as may be specified by the Lieutenant Governor in Council.

(3.1) Exception — Subsection (2) does not apply to a person who is conducting scientific research pursuant to a licence issued by the Lieutenant Governor in Council of a province or by such other person or authority in the province as may be specified by the Lieutenant Governor in Council.

(4) Exception — authorization — Every person commits an offence who promotes, arranges, conducts, assists in, receives money for or takes part in any meeting, competition, exhibition, pastime, practice, display or event at or in the course of which captive cetaceans are used, in Canada, for performance for entertainment purposes, unless the performance is authorized under a licence issued by the Lieutenant Governor in Council of a province or by an authority in the province as may be specified by the Lieutenant Governor in Council.

(5) Punishment — Every one who commits an offence under subsection (2) or (4) is guilty of an offence punishable on summary conviction and liable to a fine not exceeding $200,000.

2019, c. 11, s. 2; 2019, c. 14, s. 58.3

[Heading repealed 2008, c. 12, s. 1.]

446. (1) Causing damage or injury — Every one commits an offence who

(a) by wilful neglect causes damage or injury to animals or birds while they are being driven or conveyed; or

(b) being the owner or the person having the custody or control of a domestic animal or a bird or an animal or a bird wild by nature that is in captivity, abandons it in distress or wilfully neglects or fails to provide suitable and adequate food, water, shelter and care for it.

(2) Punishment — Every one who commits an offence under subsection (1) is guilty of

(a) an indictable offence and liable to imprisonment for a term of not more than two years; or

(b) an offence punishable on summary conviction.

(3) Failure to exercise reasonable care as evidence — For the purposes of proceedings under paragraph (1)(a), evidence that a person failed to exercise reasonable care or supervision of an animal or a bird thereby causing it damage or injury is, in the absence of any evidence to the contrary, proof that the damage or injury was caused by wilful neglect.

(4) to (6) [Repealed 2008, c. 12, s. 1.]

2008, c. 12, s. 1; 2019, c. 25, s. 173

447. (1) Arena for animal fighting — Everyone commits an offence who builds, makes, maintains or keeps an arena for animal fighting on premises that he or she owns or occupies, or allows such an arena to be built, made, maintained or kept on such premises.

(2) Punishment — Every one who commits an offence under subsection (1) is guilty of

(a) an indictable offence and liable to imprisonment for a term of not more than five years; or

(b) an offence punishable on summary conviction and liable to a fine of not more than $10,000 or to imprisonment for a term of not more than two years less a day, or to both.

(3) [Repealed 2019, c. 17, s. 3(2).]

2008, c. 12, s. 1; 2019, c. 17, s. 3; 2019, c. 25, s. 174

447.1 (1) Order of prohibition or restitution — The court may, in addition to any other sentence that it may impose under subsection 445(2), 445.1(2), 446(2) or 447(2),

(a) make an order prohibiting the accused from owning, having the custody or control of or residing in the same premises as an animal or a bird during any period that the court considers appropriate but, in the case of a second or subsequent offence, for a minimum of five years; and

(b) on application of the Attorney General or on its own motion, order that the accused pay to a person or an organization that has taken care of an animal or a bird as a result of the commission of the offence the reasonable costs that the person or organization incurred in respect of the animal or bird, if the costs are readily ascertainable.

(2) Breach of order — Every one who contravenes an order made under paragraph (1)(a) is guilty of an offence punishable on summary conviction.

(3) Application — Sections 740 to 741.2 apply, with any modifications that the circumstances require, to orders made under paragraph (1)(b).

2008, c. 12, s. 1; 2018, c. 29, s. 54

PART XII — OFFENCES RELATING TO CURRENCY (SS. 448–462)

Interpretation

448. Definitions — In this Part,

"counterfeit money" includes

(a) false coin or false paper money that resembles or is apparently intended to resemble or pass for a current coin or current paper money,

(b) a forged bank note or forged blank bank note, whether complete or incomplete,

(c) a genuine coin or genuine paper money that is prepared or altered to resemble or pass for a current coin or current paper money of a higher denomination,

(d) a current coin from which the milling is removed by filing or cutting the edges and on which new milling is made to restore its appearance,

(e) a coin cased with gold, silver or nickel, as the case may be, that is intended to resemble or pass for a current gold, silver or nickel coin, and

(f) a coin or a piece of metal or mixed metals washed or coloured by any means with a wash or material capable of producing the appearance of gold, silver or nickel and that is intended to resemble or pass for a current gold, silver or nickel coin;

"counterfeit token of value" means a counterfeit excise stamp, postage stamp or other evidence of value, by whatever technical, trivial or deceptive designation it may be described, and includes genuine coin or paper money that has no value as money;

"current" means lawfully current in Canada or elsewhere by virtue of a law, proclamation or regulation in force in Canada or elsewhere as the case may be;

"utter" includes sell, pay, tender and put off.

Making

449. Making — Every one who makes or begins to make counterfeit money is guilty of an indictable offence and liable to imprisonment for a term not exceeding fourteen years.

Possession

450. Possession, etc., of counterfeit money — Every person is guilty of an indictable offence and liable to imprisonment for a term of not more than 14 years who, without lawful justification or excuse,

(a) buys, receives or offers to buy or receive counterfeit money;

(b) has in their custody or possession counterfeit money; or

(c) introduces counterfeit money into Canada.

2018, c. 29, s. 55

451. Having clippings, etc. — Every person who, without lawful justification or excuse, has in their custody or possession gold or silver filings, clippings or bullion or gold or silver in dust, solution or otherwise, produced or obtained by impairing, diminishing or lightening a current gold or silver coin, knowing that it has been so produced or obtained, is guilty of

(a) an indictable offence and liable to imprisonment for a term of not more than five years; or

(b) an offence punishable on summary conviction.

2018, c. 29, s. 56; 2019, c. 25, s. 175

Uttering

452. Uttering, etc., counterfeit money — Every person is guilty of an indictable offence and liable to imprisonment for a term of not more than 14 years who, without lawful justification or excuse,

(a) utters or offers to utter counterfeit money or uses counterfeit money as if it were genuine, or

(b) exports, sends or takes counterfeit money out of Canada.

2018, c. 29, s. 57

453. Uttering coin — Every person is guilty of an indictable offence and liable to imprisonment for a term of not more than two years or is guilty of an offence punishable on summary conviction who, with intent to defraud, knowingly utters

(a) a coin that is not current, or

(b) a piece of metal or mixed metals that resembles in size, figure or colour a current coin for which it is uttered.

2019, c. 25, s. 176

454. Slugs and tokens — Every person is guilty of an offence punishable on summary conviction who, without lawful excuse, manufactures, produces, sells or has in their possession anything that is intended to be fraudulently used in substitution for a coin or token of value that any coin or token-operated device is designed to receive.

2018, c. 29, s. 58

Defacing or Impairing

455. Clipping and uttering clipped coin — Every one who

(a) impairs, diminishes or lightens a current gold or silver coin with intent that it should pass for a current gold or silver coin, or

(b) utters a coin, knowing that it has been impaired, diminished or lightened contrary to paragraph (a),

is guilty of an indictable offence and liable to imprisonment for a term not exceeding fourteen years.

456. Defacing current coins — Every one who

(a) defaces a current coin, or

(b) utters a current coin that has been defaced,

is guilty of an offence punishable on summary conviction.

457. (1) Likeness of bank-notes — No person shall make, publish, print, execute, issue, distribute or circulate, including by electronic or computer-assisted means, anything in the likeness of

(a) a current bank-note; or

(b) an obligation or a security of a government or bank.

(2) Exception — Subsection (1) does not apply to

(a) the Bank of Canada or its employees when they are carrying out their duties;

(b) the Royal Canadian Mounted Police or its members or employees when they are carrying out their duties; or

(c) any person acting under a contract or licence from the Bank of Canada or Royal Canadian Mounted Police.

(3) Offence — A person who contravenes subsection (1) is guilty of an offence punishable on summary conviction.

(4) Defence — No person shall be convicted of an offence under subsection (3) in relation to the printed likeness of a Canadian bank-note if it is established that the length or width of the likeness is less than three-fourths or greater than one-and-one-half times the length or width, as the case may be, of the bank-note and

(a) the likeness is in black-and-white only; or

(b) the likeness of the bank-note appears on only one side of the likeness.

1999, c. 5, s. 12

Instruments or Materials

458. Making, having or dealing in instruments for counterfeiting — Every person who, without lawful justification or excuse, makes, repairs, buys, sells or has in their custody or possession any machine, engine, tool, instrument, material or other thing that they know has been used or is adapted and intended for use in making counterfeit money or counterfeit tokens of value, is guilty of an indictable offence and liable to imprisonment for a term of not more than 14 years.

2018, c. 29, s. 59

459. Conveying instruments for coining out of mint — Every person is guilty of an indictable offence and liable to imprisonment for a term of not more than 14 years who, without lawful justification or excuse, knowingly conveys out of any of Her Majesty's mints in Canada,

(a) any machine, engine, tool, instrument, material or thing used or employed in connection with the manufacture of coins,

(b) a useful part of anything mentioned in paragraph (a), or

(c) coin, bullion, metal or a mixture of metals.

2018, c. 29, s. 60

Advertising and Trafficking in Counterfeit Money or Counterfeit Tokens of Value

460. (1) Advertising and dealing in counterfeit money, etc. — Every person is guilty of an indictable offence and liable to imprisonment for a term of not more than five years or is guilty of an offence punishable on summary conviction who

(a) by an advertisement or any other writing, offers to sell, procure or dispose of counterfeit money or counterfeit tokens of value or to give information with respect to the manner in which or the means by which counterfeit money or counterfeit tokens of value may be sold, procured or disposed of, or

(b) purchases, obtains, negotiates or otherwise deals with counterfeit tokens of value, or offers to negotiate with a view to purchasing or obtaining them.

(2) Fraudulent use of money genuine but valueless — No person shall be convicted of an offence under subsection (1) in respect of genuine coin or genuine paper money that has no value as money unless, at the time when the offence is alleged to have been committed, he knew that the coin or paper money had no value as money and he had a fraudulent intent in his dealings with or with respect to the coin or paper money.

2019, c. 25, s. 177

Special Provisions as to Proof

461. (1) When counterfeit complete — Every offence relating to counterfeit money or counterfeit tokens of value shall be deemed to be complete notwithstanding that the money or tokens of value in respect of which the proceedings are taken are not finished or perfected or do not copy exactly the money or tokens of value that they are apparently intended to resemble or for which they are apparently intended to pass.

(2) Certificate of examiner of counterfeit — In any proceedings under this Part, a certificate signed by a person designated as an examiner of counterfeit by the Minister of Public Safety and Emergency Preparedness, stating that any coin, paper money or bank note described therein is counterfeit money or that any coin, paper money or bank note described therein is genuine and is or is not, as the case may be, current in Canada or elsewhere, is evidence of the statements contained in the certificate without proof of the signature or official character of the person appearing to have signed the certificate.

(3) Notice of intention to produce certificate — No certificate shall be received in evidence unless the party intending to produce it has, before the trial, given to the other party reasonable notice of their intention and a copy of the certificate.

(4) Attendance and cross-examination — A party against whom the certificate is produced may, with leave of the court, require the attendance of the person who signed the certificate for the purposes of cross-examination.

1992, c. 1, s. 58(1) (Sched. I, item 7); 2005, c. 10, s. 34(1)(f)(xi); 2018, c. 21, s. 17

Forfeiture

462. (1) Ownership — Counterfeit money, counterfeit tokens of value and anything that is used or is intended to be used to make counterfeit money or counterfeit tokens of value belong to Her Majesty.

(2) Seizure — A peace officer may seize and detain

(a) counterfeit money,

(b) counterfeit tokens of value, and

(c) machines, engines, tools, instruments, materials or things that have been used or that have been adapted and are intended for use in making counterfeit money or counterfeit tokens of value,

and anything seized shall be sent to the Minister of Finance to be disposed of or dealt with as he may direct, but anything that is required as evidence in any proceedings shall not be sent to the Minister until it is no longer required in those proceedings.

PART XII.1

Headings and ss. 462.1 and 462.2 [Repealed 2018, c. 16, s. 211.]

PART XII.2 — PROCEEDS OF CRIME (SS. 462.3–462.5)

Interpretation

462.3 (1) Definitions — In this Part,

"designated substance offence" [Repealed, 2001, c. 32, s. 12(3).]

"designated offence" means

(a) any offence that may be prosecuted as an indictable offence under this or any other Act of Parliament, other than an indictable offence prescribed by regulation, or

(b) a conspiracy or an attempt to commit, being an accessory after the fact in relation to, or any counselling in relation to, an offence referred to in paragraph (a);

("infraction désignée")

"enterprise crime offence" [Repealed, 2001, c. 32, s. 12(2).]

"judge" means a judge as defined in section 552 or a judge of a superior court of criminal jurisdiction;

"proceeds of crime" means any property, benefit or advantage, within or outside Canada, obtained or derived directly or indirectly as a result of

(a) the commission in Canada of a designated offence, or

(b) an act or omission anywhere that, if it had occurred in Canada, would have constituted a designated offence.

("produits de la criminalité")

(2) Regulations — The Governor in Council may make regulations prescribing indictable offences that are excluded from the definition "designated offence" in subsection (1).

(3) and (4) [Repealed 2019, c. 25, s. 179.]

R.S.C. 1985, c. 42 (4th Supp.), s. 2; 1993, c. 25, s. 95; 1993, c. 37, s. 32; 1993, c. 46, s. 5; 1994, c. 44, s. 29; 1995, c. 39, s. 151; 1996, c. 19, ss. 68, 70(a), (b); 1997, c. 18, s. 27; 1997, c. 23, s. 9; 1998, c. 34, ss. 9, 11; 1999, c. 5, ss. 13, 52; 2001, c. 32, s. 12(1)–(4), (6), (7); 2001, c. 41, ss. 14, 33; 2005, c. 44, s. 1; 2010, c. 14, s. 7; 2019, c. 25, s. 179

Offence

462.31 (1) Laundering proceeds of crime — Every one commits an offence who uses, transfers the possession of, sends or delivers to any person or place, transports, transmits, alters, disposes of or otherwise deals with, in any manner and by any means, any property or any proceeds of any property with intent to conceal or convert that property or those proceeds, knowing or believing that, or being reckless as to whether, all or a part of that property or of those proceeds was obtained or derived directly or indirectly as a result of

(a) the commission in Canada of a designated offence; or

(b) an act or omission anywhere that, if it had occurred in Canada, would have constituted a designated offence.

(2) Punishment — Every one who commits an offence under subsection (1)

(a) is guilty of an indictable offence and liable to imprisonment for a term not exceeding ten years; or

(b) is guilty of an offence punishable on summary conviction.

(3) Exception — A peace officer or a person acting under the direction of a peace officer is not guilty of an offence under subsection (1) if the peace officer or person does any of the things mentioned in that subsection for the purposes of an investigation or otherwise in the execution of the peace officer's duties.

R.S.C. 1985, c. 42 (4th Supp.), s. 2; 1996, c. 19, s. 70(c); 1997, c. 18, s. 28; 2001, c. 32, s. 13; 2019, c. 29, s. 103

Search, Seizure and Detention of Proceeds of Crime

462.32 (1) Special search warrant — Subject to subsection (3), if a judge, on application of the Attorney General, is satisfied by information on oath in Form 1 that there are reasonable grounds to believe that there is in any building, receptacle or place, within the province in which the judge has jurisdiction or any other province, any property in respect of which an order of forfeiture may be made under subsection 462.37(1) or (2.01) or 462.38(2), in respect of a designated offence alleged to have been committed within the province in which the judge has jurisdiction, the judge may issue a warrant authorizing a person named in the warrant or a peace officer to search the building, receptacle or place for that property and to seize that property and any other property in respect of which that person or peace officer believes, on reasonable grounds, that an order of forfeiture may be made under that subsection.

(2) Procedure — An application for a warrant under subsection (1) may be made *ex parte*, shall be made in writing and shall include a statement as to whether any previous applications have been made under subsection (1) with respect to the property that is the subject of the application.

(2.1) Execution in Canada — A warrant issued under subsection (1) may be executed at any place in Canada. Any peace officer who executes the warrant must have authority to act as a peace officer in the place where it is executed.

(2.2) [Repealed 2019, c. 25, s. 180.]

(3) Other provisions to apply — Subsections 487(2.1) to (3) and section 488 apply, with any modifications that the circumstances require, to a warrant issued under this section.

(4) Detention and record of property seized — Every person who executes a warrant issued by a judge under this section shall

(a) detain or cause to be detained the property seized, taking reasonable care to ensure that the property is preserved so that it may be dealt with in accordance with the law;

(b) as soon as practicable after the execution of the warrant but within a period not exceeding seven days thereafter, prepare a report in Form 5.3, identifying the property seized and the location where the property is being detained, and cause the report to be filed with the clerk of the court; and

(c) cause a copy of the report to be provided, on request, to the person from whom the property was seized and to any other person who, in the opinion of the judge, appears to have a valid interest in the property.

(4.1) Return of proceeds — Subject to this or any other Act of Parliament, a peace officer who has seized anything under a warrant issued by a judge under this section may, with the written consent of the Attorney General, on being issued a receipt for it, return the thing seized to the person lawfully entitled to its possession, if

(a) the peace officer is satisfied that there is no dispute as to who is lawfully entitled to possession of the thing seized;

(b) the peace officer is satisfied that the continued detention of the thing seized is not required for the purpose of forfeiture; and

(c) the thing seized is returned before a report is filed with the clerk of the court under paragraph (4)(b).

(5) Notice — Before issuing a warrant under this section in relation to any property, a judge, may require notice to be given to and may hear any person who, in the opinion of the judge, appears to have a valid interest in the property unless the judge is of the opinion that giving such notice before the issuance of the warrant would result in the disappearance, dissipation or reduction in value of the property or otherwise affect the property so that all or a part thereof could not be seized pursuant to the warrant.

(6) Undertakings by Attorney General — Before issuing a warrant under this section, a judge shall require the Attorney General to give such undertakings as the judge considers appropriate with respect to the payment of damages or costs, or both, in relation to the issuance and execution of the warrant.

R.S.C. 1985, c. 42 (4th Supp.), s. 2; 1997, c. 18, s. 29; 2001, c. 32, s. 14; 2005, c. 44, s. 3; 2019, c. 25, s. 180

462.33 (1) Application for restraint order — The Attorney General may make an application in accordance with subsection (2) for a restraint order under subsection (3) in respect of any property.

(2) Procedure — An application made under subsection (1) for a restraint order under subsection (3) in respect of any property may be made *ex parte* and shall be made in writing to a judge and be accompanied by an affidavit sworn on the information and belief of the Attorney General or any other person deposing to the following matters, namely,

(a) the offence or matter under investigation;

(b) the person who is believed to be in possession of the property;

(c) the grounds for the belief that an order of forfeiture may be made under subsection 462.37(1) or (2.01) or 462.38(2) in respect of the property;

(d) a description of the property; and

(e) whether any previous applications have been made under this section with respect to the property.

(3) Restraint order — A judge who hears an application for a restraint order made under subsection (1) may — if the judge is satisfied that there are reasonable grounds to believe that there exists, within the province in which the judge has jurisdiction or any other province, any property in respect of which an order of forfeiture may be made under subsection 462.37(1) or (2.01) or 462.38(2), in respect of a designated offence alleged to have been committed within the province in which the judge has jurisdiction — make an order prohibiting any person from disposing of, or otherwise dealing with any interest in, the property specified in the order otherwise than in the manner that may be specified in the order.

(3.01) Effect of order — A restraint order issued under subsection (1) has effect throughout Canada.

(3.1) Property outside Canada — A restraint order may be issued under this section in respect of property situated outside Canada, with any modifications that the circumstances require.

(4) Idem — An order made by a judge under subsection (3) may be subject to such reasonable conditions as the judge thinks fit.

(5) Notice — Before making an order under subsection (3) in relation to any property, a judge may require notice to be given to and may hear any person who, in the opinion of the judge, appears to have a valid interest in the property unless the judge is of the opinion that giving such notice before making the order would result in the disappearance, dissipation or reduction in value of the property or otherwise affect the property so that all or a part thereof could not be subject to an order of forfeiture under subsection 462.37(1) or (2.01) or 462.38(2).

(6) Order in writing — An order made under subsection (3) shall be made in writing.

(7) Undertakings by Attorney General — Before making an order under subsection (3), a judge shall require the Attorney General to give such undertakings as the judge considers appropriate with respect to the payment of damages or costs, or both, in relation to

(a) the making of an order in respect of property situated within or outside Canada; and

(b) the execution of an order in respect of property situated within Canada.

(8) Service of order — A copy of an order made by a judge under subsection (3) shall be served on the person to whom the order is addressed in such manner as the judge directs or as may be prescribed by rules of court.

(9) Registration of order — A copy of an order made under subsection (3), shall be registered against any property in accordance with the laws of the province in which the property is situated.

(10) Continues in force — An order made under subsection (3) remains in effect until

(a) it is revoked or varied under subsection 462.34(4) or revoked under paragraph 462.43(a);

(b) it ceases to be in force under section 462.35; or

(c) an order of forfeiture or restoration of the property is made under subsection 462.37(1) or (2.01), 462.38(2) or 462.41(3) or any other provision of this or any other Act of Parliament.

(11) Offence — Any person on whom an order made under subsection (3) is served in accordance with this section and who, while the order is in force, acts in contravention of or fails to comply with the order is guilty of an indictable offence or an offence punishable on summary conviction.

R.S.C. 1985, c. 42 (4th Supp.), s. 2; 1993, c. 37, s. 21; 1996, c. 16, s. 60(1)(d); 1997, c. 18, s. 30; 2001, c. 32, s. 15; 2005, c. 44, s. 4; 2019, c. 25, s. 181

462.331 (1) Management order — With respect to property seized under section 462.32 or restrained under section 462.33, other than a **"controlled substance"**, within the meaning of the *Controlled Drugs and Substances Act*, or **"cannabis"**, as defined in subsection 2(1) of the *Cannabis Act*, on application of the Attorney General or of any other person with the written consent of the Attorney General, if a judge is of the opinion that the circumstances so require, the judge may

(a) appoint a person to take control of and to manage or otherwise deal with all or part of the property in accordance with the directions of the judge; and

(b) require any person having possession of that property to give possession of the property to the person appointed under paragraph (a).

(2) Appointment of Minister of Public Works and Government Services — When the Attorney General of Canada so requests, a judge appointing a person under subsection (1) shall appoint the Minister of Public Works and Government Services.

(3) Power to manage — The power to manage or otherwise deal with property under subsection (1) includes

(a) the power to make an interlocutory sale of perishable or rapidly depreciating property;

(b) the power to destroy, in accordance with subsections (4) to (7), property that has little or no value; and

(c) the power to have property, other than real property or a conveyance, forfeited to Her Majesty in accordance with subsection (7.1).

(4) Application for destruction order — Before a person who is appointed to manage property destroys property that has little or no value, they shall apply to a court for a destruction order.

(5) Notice — Before making a destruction order, a court shall require notice in accordance with subsection (6) to be given to and may hear any person who, in the court's opinion, appears to have a valid interest in the property.

(6) Manner of giving notice — A notice shall

(a) be given in the manner that the court directs or that may be specified in the rules of the court; and

(b) specify the effective period of the notice that the court considers reasonable or that may be set out in the rules of the court.

(7) Destruction order — A court shall order that the property be destroyed if it is satisfied that the property has little or no financial or other value.

(7.1) Forfeiture order — On application by a person who is appointed to manage the property, a court shall order that the property, other than real property or a conveyance, be forfeited to Her Majesty to be disposed of or otherwise dealt with in accordance with the law if

(a) a notice is given or published in the manner that the court directs or that may be specified in the rules of the court;

(b) the notice specifies a period of 60 days during which a person may make an application to the court asserting their interest in the property; and

(c) during that period, no one makes such an application.

(8) When management order ceases to have effect — A management order ceases to have effect when the property that is the subject of the management order is returned in accordance with the law, destroyed or forfeited to Her Majesty.

(8.1) For greater certainty — For greater certainty, if property that is the subject of a management order is sold, the management order applies to the net proceeds of the sale.

(9) Application to vary conditions — The Attorney General may at any time apply to the judge to cancel or vary any condition to which a management order is subject but may not apply to vary an appointment made under subsection (2).

2001, c. 32, s. 16; 2017, c. 7, s. 58; 2018, c. 16, s. 212

462.34 (1) Application for review of special warrants and restraint orders — Any person who has an interest in property that was seized under a warrant issued pursuant to section 462.32 or in respect of which a restraint order was made under subsection 462.33(3) may, at any time, apply to a judge

(a) for an order under subsection (4); or

(b) for permission to examine the property.

(2) Notice to Attorney General — Where an application is made under paragraph (1)(a),

(a) the application shall not, without the consent of the Attorney General, be heard by a judge unless the applicant has given to the Attorney General at least two clear days notice in writing of the application; and

(b) the judge may require notice of the application to be given to and may hear any person who, in the opinion of the judge, appears to have a valid interest in the property.

(3) Terms of examination order — A judge may, on an application made to the judge under paragraph (1)(b), order that the applicant be permitted to examine property subject to such terms as appear to the judge to be necessary or desirable to ensure that the property is safeguarded and preserved for any purpose for which it may subsequently be required.

(4) Order of restoration of property or revocation or variation of order — On an application made to a judge under paragraph (1)(a) in respect of any property and after hearing the applicant and the Attorney General and any other person to whom notice was given pursuant to paragraph (2)(b), the judge may order that the property or a part thereof be returned to the applicant or, in the case of a restraint order made under subsection 462.33(3), revoke the order, vary the order to exclude the property or any interest in the property or part thereof from the application of the order or make the order subject to such reasonable conditions as the judge thinks fit,

(a) if the applicant enters into a recognizance before the judge, with or without sureties, in such amount and with such conditions, if any, as the judge directs and, where the judge considers it appropriate, deposits with the judge such sum of money or other valuable security as the judge directs;

(b) if the conditions referred to in subsection (6) are satisfied; or

(c) for the purpose of

(i) meeting the reasonable living expenses of the person who was in possession of the property at the time the warrant was executed or the order was made or any person who, in the opinion of the judge, has a valid interest in the property and of the dependants of that person,

(ii) meeting the reasonable business and legal expenses of a person referred to in subparagraph (i), or

(iii) permitting the use of the property in order to enter into a recognizance under Part XVI,

Proposed Amendment — 462.34(4)(c)(iii)

(iii) permitting the use of the property in relation to an undertaking or release order,

2019, c. 25, s. 182(1) [To come into force December 18, 2019.]

if the judge is satisfied that the applicant has no other assets or means available for the purposes set out in this paragraph and that no other person appears to be the lawful owner of or lawfully entitled to possession of the property.

(5) Hearing — For the purpose of determining the reasonableness of legal expenses referred to in subparagraph (4)(*c*)(ii), a judge shall hold an *in camera* hearing, without the presence of the Attorney General, and shall take into account the legal aid tariff of the province.

(5.1) Expenses — For the purpose of determining the reasonableness of expenses referred to in paragraph (4)(*c*), the Attorney General may

(a) at the hearing of the application, make representations as to what would constitute the reasonableness of the expenses, other than legal expenses; and

(b) before or after the hearing of the application held *in camera* pursuant to subsection (5), make representations as to what would constitute reasonable legal expenses referred to in subparagraph (4)(c)(ii).

(5.2) Taxing legal fees — The judge who made an order under paragraph (4)(*c*) may, and on the application of the Attorney General shall, tax the legal fees forming part of the legal expenses referred to in subparagraph (4)(*c*)(ii) and, in so doing, shall take into account

(a) the value of property in respect of which an order of forfeiture may be made;

(b) the complexity of the proceedings giving rise to those legal expenses;

(c) the importance of the issues involved in those proceedings;

(d) the duration of any hearings held in respect of those proceedings;

(e) whether any stage of those proceedings was improper or vexatious;

(f) any representations made by the Attorney General; and

(g) any other relevant matter.

(6) Conditions to be satisfied — An order under paragraph (4)(b) in respect of property may be made by a judge if the judge is satisfied

(a) where the application is made by

(i) a person charged with a designated offence, or

(ii) any person who acquired title to or a right of possession of that property from a person referred to in subparagraph (i) under circumstances that give rise to a reasonable inference that the title or right was transferred from that person for the purpose of avoiding the forfeiture of the property,

that a warrant should not have been issued pursuant to section 462.32 or a restraint order under subsection 462.33(3) should not have been made in respect of that property, or

(b) in any other case, that the applicant is the lawful owner of or lawfully entitled to possession of the property and appears innocent of any complicity in a designated offence or of any collusion in relation to such an offence, and that no other person appears to be the lawful owner of or lawfully entitled to possession of the property,

and that the property will no longer be required for the purpose of any investigation or as evidence in any proceeding.

(7) Saving provision — Sections 354, 355.2 and 355.4 do not apply to a person who comes into possession of any property that, by virtue of an order made under paragraph (4)(c), was returned to any person after having been seized or was excluded from the application of a restraint order made under subsection 462.33(3).

(8) Form of recognizance — A recognizance entered into pursuant to paragraph (4)(a) may be in Form 32.

Proposed Repeal — 462.34(8)

(8) [Repealed 2019, c. 25, s. 182(2). To come into force December 18, 2019.]

R.S.C. 1985, c. 42 (4th Supp.), s. 2; 1996, c. 19, ss. 69, 70(d), (e); 1997, c. 18, s. 31, 140(d)(i); 2001, c. 32, s. 17; 2010, c. 14, s. 8

462.341 Application of property restitution provisions — Subsection 462.34(2), paragraph 462.34(4)(c) and subsections 462.34(5), (5.1) and (5.2) apply, with any modifications that the circumstances require, to a person who has an interest in money or bank-notes that are seized under this Act, the *Controlled Drugs and Substances Act* or the *Cannabis Act* and in respect of which proceedings may be taken under subsection 462.37(1) or (2.01) or 462.38(2).

1997, c. 18, ss. 32, 140(a); 1999, c. 5, s. 14; 2005, c. 44, s. 5; 2018, c. 16, s. 213

462.35 (1) Expiration of special warrants and restraint orders — Subject to this section, where property has been seized under a warrant issued pursuant to section 462.32 or a restraint order has been made under section 462.33 in relation to property, the property may be detained or the order may continue in force, as the case may be, for a period not exceeding six months from the seizure or the making of the order, as the case may be.

(2) Where proceedings instituted — The property may continue to be detained, or the order may continue in force, for a period that exceeds six months if proceedings are instituted in respect of which the thing detained may be forfeited.

(3) Where application made — The property may continue to be detained or the order may continue in force for a period or periods that exceed six months if the continuation is, on application made by the Attorney General, ordered by a judge, where the judge is satisfied that the property is required, after the expiration of the period or periods, for the purpose of section 462.37 or 462.38 or any other provision of this or any other Act of Parliament respecting forfeiture or for the purpose of any investigation or as evidence in any proceeding.

R.S.C. 1985, c. 42 (4th Supp.), s. 2; 1997, c. 18, s. 33

462.36 Forwarding to clerk where accused to stand trial — Where a judge issues a warrant under section 462.32 or makes a restraint order under section 462.33 in respect of any property, the clerk of the court shall, when an accused is ordered to stand trial for a designated offence, cause to be forwarded to the clerk of the court to which the accused has been ordered to stand trial a copy of the report filed pursuant to paragraph 462.32(4)(b) or of the restraint order in respect of the property.

R.S.C. 1985, c. 42 (4th Supp.), s. 2; 2001, c. 32, s. 18

Forfeiture of Proceeds of Crime

462.37 (1) Order of forfeiture of property — Subject to this section and sections 462.39 to 462.41, if an offender is convicted, or discharged under section 730, of a designated offence and the court imposing sentence on or discharging the offender, on application of the Attorney General, is satisfied, on a balance of probabilities, that any property is proceeds of crime obtained through the commission of the designated offence, the court shall order that the property be forfeited to Her Majesty to be disposed of as the Attorney General directs or otherwise dealt with in accordance with the law.

(2) Proceeds of crime — other offences — If the evidence does not establish to the satisfaction of the court that property in respect of which an order of forfeiture would otherwise be made under subsection (1) was obtained through the commission of the designated offence of which the offender is convicted or discharged, but the court is satisfied, beyond a reasonable doubt, that the property is proceeds of crime, the court may make an order of forfeiture under subsection (1) in relation to that property.

(2.01) Order of forfeiture — particular circumstances — A court imposing sentence on an offender convicted of an offence described in subsection (2.02) shall, on application of the Attorney General and subject to this section and sections 462.4 and 462.41, order that any property of the offender that is identified by the Attorney General in the application be forfeited to Her Majesty to be disposed of as the Attorney General directs or otherwise dealt with in accordance with the law if the court is satisfied, on a balance of probabilities, that

(a) within 10 years before the proceedings were commenced in respect of the offence for which the offender is being sentenced, the offender engaged in a pattern of criminal activity for the purpose of directly or indirectly receiving a material benefit, including a financial benefit; or

(b) the income of the offender from sources unrelated to designated offences cannot reasonably account for the value of all the property of the offender.

(2.02) Offences — The offences are the following:

(a) a criminal organization offence punishable by five or more years of imprisonment;

(b) an offence under section 5, 6 or 7 of the *Controlled Drugs and Substances Act* — or a conspiracy or an attempt to commit, being an accessory after the fact in relation to, or any counselling in relation to an offence under any of those sections — prosecuted by indictment;

(c) an offence under subsection 9(1) or (2), 10(1) or (2), 11(1) or (2), 12(1), (4), (5), (6) or (7), 13(1) or 14(1) of the *Cannabis Act* — or a conspiracy or an attempt to commit, being an accessory after the fact in relation to, or any counselling in relation to an offence under any of those subsections — prosecuted by indictment; and

(d) an offence under any of sections 279.01 to 279.03.

(2.03) Offender may establish that property is not proceeds of crime — A court shall not make an order of forfeiture under subsection (2.01) in respect of any property that the offender establishes, on a balance of probabilities, is not proceeds of crime.

(2.04) Pattern of criminal activity — In determining whether the offender has engaged in a pattern of criminal activity described in paragraph (2.01)(a), the court shall consider

(a) the circumstances of the offence for which the offender is being sentenced;

(b) any act or omission — other than an act or omission that constitutes the offence for which the offender is being sentenced — that the court is satisfied, on a balance of probabilities, was committed by the offender and constitutes an offence punishable by indictment under any Act of Parliament;

(c) any act or omission that the court is satisfied, on a balance of probabilities, was committed by the offender and is an offence in the place where it was committed and, if committed in Canada, would constitute an offence punishable by indictment under any Act of Parliament; and

(d) any other factor that the court considers relevant.

(2.05) Conditions — pattern of criminal activity — A court shall not determine that an offender has engaged in a pattern of criminal activity unless the court is satisfied, on a balance of probabilities, that the offender committed, within the period referred to in paragraph (2.01)(a),

(a) acts or omissions — other than an act or omission that constitutes the offence for which the offender is being sentenced — that constitute at least two serious offences or one criminal organization offence;

(b) acts or omissions that are offences in the place where they were committed and, if committed in Canada, would constitute at least two serious offences or one criminal organization offence; or

(c) an act or omission described in paragraph (a) that constitutes a serious offence and an act or omission described in paragraph (b) that, if committed in Canada, would constitute a serious offence.

(2.06) **Application under subsection (1) not prevented** — Nothing in subsection (2.01) shall be interpreted as preventing the Attorney General from making an application under subsection (1) in respect of any property.

(2.07) **Exception** — A court may, if it considers it in the interests of justice, decline to make an order of forfeiture against any property that would otherwise be subject to forfeiture under subsection (2.01). The court shall give reasons for its decision.

(2.1) **Property outside Canada** — An order may be issued under this section in respect of property situated outside Canada, with any modifications that the circumstances require.

(3) **Fine instead of forfeiture** — If a court is satisfied that an order of forfeiture under subsection (1) or (2.01) should be made in respect of any property of an offender but that the property or any part of or interest in the property cannot be made subject to an order, the court may, instead of ordering the property or any part of or interest in the property to be forfeited, order the offender to pay a fine in an amount equal to the value of the property or the part of or interest in the property. In particular, a court may order the offender to pay a fine if the property or any part of or interest in the property

(a) cannot, on the exercise of due diligence, be located;

(b) has been transferred to a third party;

(c) is located outside Canada;

(d) has been substantially diminished in value or rendered worthless; or

(e) has been commingled with other property that cannot be divided without difficulty.

(4) **Imprisonment in default of payment of fine** — Where a court orders an offender to pay a fine pursuant to subsection (3), the court shall

(a) impose, in default of payment of that fine, a term of imprisonment

(i) not exceeding six months, where the amount of the fine does not exceed ten thousand dollars,

(ii) of not less than six months and not exceeding twelve months, where the amount of the fine exceeds ten thousand dollars but does not exceed twenty thousand dollars,

(iii) of not less than twelve months and not exceeding eighteen months, where the amount of the fine exceeds twenty thousand dollars but does not exceed fifty thousand dollars,

(iv) of not less than eighteen months and not exceeding two years, where the amount of the fine exceeds fifty thousand dollars but does not exceed one hundred thousand dollars,

(v) of not less than two years and not exceeding three years, where the amount of the fine exceeds one hundred thousand dollars but does not exceed two hundred and fifty thousand dollars,

(vi) of not less than three years and not exceeding five years, where the amount of the fine exceeds two hundred and fifty thousand dollars but does not exceed one mllion dollars, or

(vii) of not less than five years and not exceeding ten years, where the amount of the fine exceeds one million dollars; and

(b) direct that the term of imprisonment imposed pursuant to paragraph (*a*) be served consecutively to any other term of imprisonment imposed on the offender or that the offender is then serving.

(5) **Fine option not available to offender** — Section 736 does not apply to an offender against whom a fine is imposed pursuant to subsection (3).

R.S.C. 1985, c. 42 (4th Supp.), s. 2; 1995, c. 22, s. 18; 2001, c. 32, s. 19; 2005, c. 44, s. 6; 2015, c. 16, s. 4; 2017, c. 7, s. 59(1); 2018, c. 16, ss. 214, 225

462.371 (1) **Definition of "order"** — In this section, **"order"** means an order made under section 462.37 or 462.38.

(2) **Execution** — An order may be executed anywhere in Canada.

(3) **Filing of order from another province** — Where the Attorney General of a province in which property that is the subject of an order made in another province is situated receives a certified copy of the order and files it with the superior court of criminal jurisdiction of the province in which the property is situated, the order shall be entered as a judgment of that court.

(4) **Attorney General of Canada** — Where the Attorney General of Canada receives a certified copy of an order made in a province in respect of property situated in another province and files the order with the superior court of criminal jurisdiction of the province in which the property is situated, the order shall be entered as a judgment of the court.

(5) **Effect of registered order** — An order has, from the date it is filed in a court of a province under subsection (3) or (4), the same effect as if it had been an order originally made by that court.

(6) **Notice** — Where an order has been filed in a court under subsection (3) or (4), it shall not be executed before notice in accordance with subsection 462.41(2) is given to every person who, in the opinion of the court, appears to have a valid interest in the property.

(7) **Application of section 462.42** — Section 462.42 applies, with such modifications as the circumstances require, in respect of a person who claims an interest in property that is the subject of an order filed under subsection (3) or (4).

(8) **Application under section 462.42 to be made in one province** — No person may make an application under section 462.42 in relation to property that is the subject of an order filed under subsection (3) or (4) if that person has previously made an application in respect of the same property in another province.

(9) **Finding in one court binding** — The finding by a court of a province in relation to property that is the subject of an order filed under subsection (3) or (4) as to whether or not an applicant referred to in subsection 462.42(4) is affected by the forfeiture referred to in that subsection or declaring the nature and extent of the interest of the applicant under that subsection is binding on the superior court of criminal jurisdiction of the province where the order is entered as a judgment.

1997, c. 18, s. 34

462.38 (1) Application for forfeiture — Where an information has been laid in respect of a designated offence, the Attorney General may make an application to a judge for an order of forfeiture under subsection (2) in respect of any property.

(2) **Order of forfeiture of property** — Subject to sections 462.39 to 462.41, where an application is made to a judge under subsection (1), the judge shall, if the judge is satisfied that

(a) any property is, beyond a reasonable doubt, proceeds of crime,

(b) that property was obtained through the commission of a designated offence in respect of which proceedings were commenced, and

(c) the accused charged with the offence referred to in paragraph (*b*) has died or absconded,

order that the property be forfeited to Her Majesty to be disposed of as the Attorney General directs or otherwise dealt with in accordance with the law.

(2.1) **Property outside Canada** — An order may be issued under this section in respect of property situated outside Canada, with any modifications that the circumstances require.

(3) **Person deemed absconded** — For the purposes of this section, a person shall be deemed to have absconded in connection with a designated offence if

(a) an information has been laid alleging the commission of the offence by the person,

(b) a warrant for the arrest of the person or a summons in respect of an organization has been issued in relation to that information, and

(c) reasonable attempts to arrest the person pursuant to the warrant or to serve the summons have been unsuccessful during the period of six months commencing on the day the warrant or summons was issued, or, in the case of a person who is not or never was in Canada, the person cannot be brought within that period to the jurisdiction in which the warrant or summons was issued, and the person shall be deemed to have so absconded on the last day of that period of six months.

R.S.C. 1985, c. 42 (4th Supp.), s. 2; 1997, c. 18, s. 35(2); 2001, c. 32, s. 20; 2003, c. 21, s. 7; 2017, c. 7, s. 60(1)

462.39 Inference — For the purpose of subsection 462.37(1) or 462.38(2), the court may infer that property was obtained or derived as a result of the commission of a designated offence where evidence establishes that the value, after the commission of that offence, of all the property of the person alleged to have committed the offence exceeds the value of all the property of that person before the commission of that offence and the court is satisfied that the income of that person from sources unrelated to designated offences committed by that person cannot reasonably account for such an increase in value.

R.S.C. 1985, c. 42 (4th Supp.), s. 2; 1996, c. 19, s. 70(f); 2001, c. 32, s. 21

462.4 Voidable transfers — A court may,

(a) prior to ordering property to be forfeited under subsection 462.37(1) or (2.01) or 462.38(2), and

(b) in the case of property in respect of which a restraint order was made under section 462.33, where the order was served in accordance with subsection 462.33(8),

set aside any conveyance or transfer of the property that occurred after the seizure of the property or the service of the order under section 462.33, unless the conveyance or transfer was for valuable consideration to a person acting in good faith.

R.S.C. 1985, c. 42 (4th Supp.), s. 2; 1997, c. 18, s. 36; 2005, c. 44, s. 7

462.41 (1) Notice — Before making an order under subsection 462.37(1) or (2.01) or 462.38(2) in relation to any property, a court shall require notice in accordance with subsection (2) to be given to and may hear any person who, in the opinion of the court, appears to have a valid interest in the property.

(2) Manner of giving notice — A notice shall

(a) be given in the manner that the court directs or that may be specified in the rules of the court;

(b) specify the period that the court considers reasonable or that may be set out in the rules of the court during which a person may make an application to the court asserting their interest in the property; and

(c) set out the designated offence charged and a description of the property.

(3) Order of restoration of property — Where a court is satisfied that any person, other than

(a) a person who is charged with, or was convicted of, a designated offence, or

(b) a person who acquired title to or a right of possession of that property from a person referred to in paragraph *(a)* under circumstances that give rise to a reasonable inference that the title or right was transferred for the purpose of avoiding the forfeiture of the property, is the lawful owner or is lawfully entitled to possession of any property or any part thereof that would otherwise be forfeited pursuant to subsection 462.37(1) or (2.01) or 462.38(2) and that the person appears innocent of any complicity in an offence referred to in paragraph (*a*) or of any collusion in relation to such an offence, the court may order that the property or part thereof be returned to that person.

R.S.C. 1985, c. 42 (4th Supp.), s. 2; 1996, c. 19, s. 70(g); 1997, c. 18, ss. 37, 140(d)(ii); 2001, c. 32, s. 22; 2005, c. 44, s. 8; 2017, c. 7, s. 61

462.42 (1) Application by person claiming interest for relief from forfeiture — Any person who claims an interest in property that is forfeited to Her Majesty under subsection 462.37(1) or (2.01) or 462.38(2) may, within thirty days after the forfeiture, apply by notice in writing to a judge for an order under subsection (4) unless the person is

(a) a person who is charged with, or was convicted of, a designated offence that resulted in the forfeiture; or

(b) a person who acquired title to or a right of possession of the property from a person referred to in paragraph (a) under circumstances that give rise to a reasonable inference that the title or right was transferred from that person for the purpose of avoiding the forfeiture of the property.

(2) Fixing day for hearing — The judge to whom an application is made under subsection (1) shall fix a day not less than thirty days after the date of filing of the application for the hearing thereof.

(3) Notice — An applicant shall serve a notice of the application made under subsection (1) and of the hearing thereof on the Attorney General at least fifteen days before the day fixed for the hearing.

(4) Order declaring interest not subject to forfeiture — Where, on the hearing of an application made under subsection (1), the judge is satisfied that the applicant is not a person referred to in paragraph (1)(a) or (b) and appears innocent of any complicity in any designated offence that resulted in the forfeiture or of any collusion in relation to any such offence, the judge may make an order declaring that the interest of the applicant is not affected by the forfeiture and declaring the nature and extent of the interest.

(5) Appeal from order under subsection (4) — An applicant or the Attorney General may appeal to the court of appeal from an order under subsection (4) and the provisions of Part XXI with respect to procedure on appeals apply, with such modifications as the circumstances require, to appeals under this subsection.

(6) Return of property — The Attorney General shall, on application made to the Attorney General by any person who has obtained an order under subsection (4) and where the periods with respect to the taking of appeals from that order have expired and any appeal from that order taken under subsection (5) has been determined,

(a) direct that the property or the part thereof to which the interest of the applicant relates be returned to the applicant; or

(b) direct that an amount equal to the value of the interest of the applicant, as declared in the order, be paid to the applicant.

R.S.C. 1985, c. 42 (4th Supp.), s. 2; 1996, c. 19, s. 70(h), (i); 1997, c. 18, s. 38(1), 140(d)(iii); 2001, c. 32, s. 23; 2005, c. 44, s. 9

462.43 (1) Residual disposal of property seized or dealt with pursuant to special warrants or restraint orders — Where property has been seized under a warrant issued pursuant to section 462.32, a restraint order has been made under section 462.33 in relation to any property or a recognizance has been entered into pursuant to paragraph 462.34(4)(*a*) in relation to any property and a judge, on application made to the judge by the Attorney General or any person having an interest in the property or on the judge's own motion, after notice given to the Attorney General and any other person having an interest in the property, is satisfied that the property will no longer be required for the purpose of section 462.37, 462.38 or any other provision of this or any other Act of Parliament respecting forfeiture or for the purpose of any investigation or as evidence in any proceeding, the judge

(a) in the case of a restraint order, shall revoke the order;

(b) in the case of a recognizance, shall cancel the recognizance; and

(c) in the case of property seized under a warrant issued pursuant to section 462.32 or property under the control of a person appointed pursuant to paragraph 462.331(1)(a),

(i) if possession of it by the person from whom it was taken is lawful, shall order that it be returned to that person,

(ii) if possession of it by the person from whom it was taken is unlawful and the lawful owner or person who is lawfully entitled to its possession is known, shall order that it be returned to the lawful owner or the person who is lawfully entitled to its possession, or

(iii) if possession of it by the person from whom it was taken is unlawful and the lawful owner or person who is lawfully entitled to its possession is not known, may order that it be forfeited to Her Majesty, to be disposed of as the Attorney General directs, or otherwise dealt with in accordance with the law.

(2) Property outside Canada — An order may be issued under this section in respect of property situated outside Canada, with any modifications that the circumstances require.

R.S.C. 1985, c. 42 (4th Supp.), s. 2; 2001, c. 32, s. 24; 2004, c. 12, s. 7

462.44 Appeals from certain orders — Any person who considers that they are aggrieved by an order made under subsection 462.38(2) or 462.41(3) or section 462.43 may appeal from the order as if the order were an appeal against conviction or against a judgment or verdict of acquittal, as the case may be, under Part XXI, and that Part applies, with such modifications as the circumstances require, to such an appeal.

R.S.C. 1985, c. 42 (4th Supp.), s. 2; 1997, c. 18, s. 39

462.45 Suspension of forfeiture pending appeal — Despite anything in this Part, the operation of an order of forfeiture or restoration of property under subsection 462.34(4), 462.37(1) or (2.01), 462.38(2) or 462.41(3) or section 462.43 is suspended pending

(a) any application made in respect of the property under any of those provisions or any other provision of this or any other Act of Parliament that provides for the restoration or forfeiture of such property,

(b) any appeal taken from an order of forfeiture or restoration in respect of the property, or

(c) any other proceeding in which the right of seizure of the property is questioned,

and property shall not be disposed of within thirty days after an order of forfeiture is made under any of those provisions.

R.S.C. 1985, c. 42 (4th Supp.), s. 2; 2005, c. 44, s. 10

462.46 (1) Copies of documents returned or forfeited — If any document is returned or ordered to be returned, forfeited or otherwise dealt with under subsection 462.34(3) or (4), 462.37(1) or (2.01), 462.38(2) or 462.41(3) or section 462.43, the Attorney General may, before returning the document or complying with the order, cause a copy of the document to be made and retained.

(2) Probative force — Every copy made under subsection (1) shall, if certified as a true copy by the Attorney General, be admissible in evidence and, in the absence of evidence to the contrary, shall have the same probative force as the original document would have had if it had been proved in the ordinary way.

R.S.C. 1985, c. 42 (4th Supp.), s. 2; 2005, c. 44, s. 11

Disclosure Provisions

462.47 No civil or criminal liability incurred by informants — For greater certainty but subject to section 241 of the *Income Tax Act*, a person is justified in disclosing to a peace officer or the Attorney General any facts on the basis of which that person reasonably suspects that any property is proceeds of crime or that any person has committed or is about to commit a designated offence.

R.S.C. 1985, c. 42 (4th Supp.), s. 2; 1996, c. 19, s. 70(j); 2001, c. 32, s. 25

462.48 (1) Definition of "designated substance offence" — In this section, **"designated substance offence"** means

(a) an offence under Part I of the *Controlled Drugs and Substances Act*, except subsection 4(1) of that Act;

(a.1) an offence under Division 1 of Part 1 of the *Cannabis Act*, except subsection 8(1) of that Act; or

(b) a conspiracy or an attempt to commit, being an accessory after the fact in relation to, or any counselling in relation to, an offence referred to in paragraph (a) or (a.1).

(c) [Repealed 2001, c. 32, s. 26(1).]

(1.1) Disclosure of income tax information — The Attorney General may make an application in accordance with subsection (2) for an order for disclosure of information under subsection (3), for the purposes of an investigation in relation to

(a) a designated substance offence;

(b) an offence against section 354, 355.2, 355.4 or 462.31 if the offence is alleged to have been committed in relation to any property, thing or proceeds obtained or derived directly or indirectly as a result of

(i) the commission in Canada of a designated substance offence, or

(ii) an act or omission anywhere that, if it had occurred in Canada, would have constituted a designated substance offence;

(c) an offence against section 467.11, 467.111, 467.12 or 467.13, or a conspiracy or an attempt to commit, or being an accessory after the fact in relation to, such an offence; or

(d) a terrorism offence.

(2) Application — An application under subsection (1.1) shall be made *ex parte* in writing to a judge and be accompanied by an affidavit sworn on the information and belief of the Attorney General or a person specially designated by the Attorney General for that purpose deposing to the following matters, namely,

(a) the offence or matter under investigation;

(b) the person in relation to whom the information or documents referred to in paragraph (*c*) are required;

(c) the type of information or book, record, writing, return or other document obtained by or on behalf of the Minister of National Revenue for the purposes of the *Income Tax Act*, Part IX of the *Excise Tax Act* or the *Excise Act, 2001* to which access is sought or that is proposed to be examined or communicated; and

(d) the facts relied on to justify the belief, on reasonable grounds, that the person referred to in paragraph (b) has committed or benefited from the commission of any of the offences referred to in subsection (1.1) and that the information or documents referred to in paragraph (c) are likely to be of substantial value, whether alone or together with other material, to the investigation for the purposes of which the application is made.

(3) Order for disclosure of information — Where the judge to whom an application under subsection (1.1) is made is satisfied

(a) of the matters referred to in paragraph (2)(*d*), and

(b) that there are reasonable grounds for believing that it is in the public interest to allow access to the information or documents to which the application relates, having regard to the benefit likely to accrue to the investigation if the access is obtained,

the judge may, subject to any conditions that the judge considers advisable in the public interest, order the Commissioner of Revenue or any person specially designated in writing by the Commissioner for the purposes of this section

(c) to allow a police officer named in the order access to all such information and documents and to examine them, or

(d) where the judge considers it necessary in the circumstances, to produce all such information and documents to the police officer and allow the police officer to remove the information and documents,

within such period as the judge may specify after the expiration of seven clear days following the service of the order pursuant to subsection (4).

(4) Service of order — A copy of an order made by a judge under subsection (3) shall be served on the person to whom the order is addressed in such manner as the judge directs or as may be prescribed by rules of court.

(5) Extension of period for compliance with order — A judge who makes an order under subsection (3) may, on application of the Minister of National Revenue, extend the period within which the order is to be complied with.

(6) Objection to disclosure of information — The Minister of National Revenue or any person specially designated in writing by that Minister for the purposes of this section may object to the disclosure of any information or document in respect of which an order under subsection (3) has been made by certifying orally or in writing that the information or document should not be disclosed on the ground that

(a) the Minister of National Revenue is prohibited from disclosing the information or document by any bilateral or international treaty, convention or other agreement respecting taxation to which the Government of Canada is signatory;

(b) a privilege is attached by law to the information or document;

(c) the information or document has been placed in a sealed package pursuant to law or an order of a court of competent jurisdiction; or

(d) disclosure of the information or document would not, for any other reason, be in the public interest.

(7) Determination of objection — Where an objection to the disclosure of information or a document is made under subsection (6), the objection may be determined, on application, in accordance with subsection (8), by the Chief Justice of the Federal Court, or by such other judge of that court as the Chief Justice may designate to hear such applications.

(8) Judge may examine information — A judge who is to determine an objection pursuant to subsection (7) may, if the judge considers it necessary to determine the objection, examine the information or document in relation to which the objection is made and shall grant the objection and order that disclosure of the information or document be refused where the judge is satisfied of any of the grounds mentioned in subsection (6).

(9) Limitation period — An application under subsection (7) shall be made within ten days after the objection is made or within such greater or lesser period as the Chief Justice of the Federal Court, or such other judge of that court as the Chief Justice may designate to hear such applications, considers appropriate.

(10) Appeal to federal court of appeal — An appeal lies from a determination under subsection (7) to the Federal Court of Appeal.

(11) Limitation period for appeal — An appeal under subsection (10) shall be brought within ten days from the date of the determination appealed from or within such further time as the Federal Court of Appeal considers appropriate in the circumstances.

(12) Special rules for hearing — An application under subsection (7) or an appeal brought in respect of that application shall

(a) be heard in *camera*; and

(b) on the request of the person objecting to the disclosure of information, be heard and determined in the National Capital Region described in the schedule to the *National Capital Act*.

(13) *Ex parte* representations — During the hearing of an application under subsection (7) or an appeal brought in respect of that application, the person who made the objection in respect of which the application was made or the appeal was brought shall, on the request of that person, be given the opportunity to make representations *ex parte*.

(14) Copies — When any information or document is examined or provided under subsection (3), the person by whom it is examined or to whom it is provided or any officer of the Canada Revenue Agency may make, or cause to be made, one or more copies of it, and any copy purporting to be certified by the Minister of National Revenue or an authorized person to be a copy made under this subsection is evidence of the nature and content of the original information or document and has the same probative force as the original information or document would have had if it had been proved in the ordinary way.

(15) Further disclosure — No person to whom information or documents have been disclosed or provided pursuant to this subsection or pursuant to an order made under subsection (3) shall further disclose the information or documents except for the purposes of the investigation in relation to which the order was made.

(16) Form — An order made under subsection (3) may be in Form 47.

(17) Definition of "police officer" — In this section, **"police officer"** means any officer, constable or other person employed for the preservation and maintenance of the public peace.

R.S.C. 1985, c. 42 (4th Supp.), s. 2; 1994, c. 13, s. 7(1)(b); 1996, c. 19, s. 70(k); 1997, c. 23, s. 10; 1999, c. 17, s. 120; 2001, c. 32, s. 26; 2001, c. 41, ss. 15, 133(11); 2005, c. 38, ss. 138(e), 140(b); 2010, c. 14, s. 9; 2013, c. 9, s. 15; 2014, c. 17, s. 7; 2018, c. 16, s. 215; 2018, c. 27, s. 28

Specific Rules of Forfeiture

462.49 (1) Specific forfeiture provisions unaffected by this part — This Part does not affect the operation of any other provision of this or any other Act of Parliament respecting the forfeiture of property.

(2) Priority for restitution to victims of crime — The property of an offender may be used to satisfy the operation of a provision of this or any other Act of Parliament respecting the forfeiture of property only to the extent that it is not required to satisfy the operation of any other provision of this or any other Act of Parliament respecting the restitution to or compensation of persons affected by the commission of offences.

R.S.C. 1985, c. 42 (4th Supp.), s. 2

Regulations

462.5 Regulations — The Attorney General may make regulations governing the manner of disposing of or otherwise dealing with, in accordance with the law, property, forfeited under this Part.

R.S.C. 1985, c. 42 (4th Supp.), s. 2

PART XIII — ATTEMPTS — CONSPIRACIES — ACCESSORIES (SS. 463–467.2)

463. Attempts, accessories — Except where otherwise expressly provided by law, the following provisions apply in respect of persons who attempt to commit or are accessories after the fact to the commission of offences:

(a) every one who attempts to commit or is an accessory after the fact to the commission of an indictable offence for which, on conviction, an accused is liable to be sentenced to imprisonment for life is guilty of an indictable offence and liable to imprisonment for a term not exceeding fourteen years;

(b) every one who attempts to commit or is an accessory after the fact to the commission of an indictable offence for which, on conviction, an accused is liable to imprisonment for fourteen years or less is guilty of an indictable offence and liable to imprisonment for a term that is one-half of the longest term to which a person who is guilty of that offence is liable;

(c) every one who attempts to commit or is an accessory after the fact to the commission of an offence punishable on summary conviction is guilty of an offence punishable on summary conviction; and

(d) every one who attempts to commit or is an accessory after the fact to the commission of an offence for which the offender may be prosecuted by indictment or for which he is punishable on summary conviction

(i) is guilty of an indictable offence and liable to imprisonment for a term not exceeding a term that is one-half of the longest term to which a person who is guilty of that offence is liable, or

(ii) is guilty of an offence punishable on summary conviction.

R.S.C. 1985, c. 27 (1st Supp.), s. 59; 1998, c. 35, s. 120

464. Counselling offence that is not committed — Except where otherwise expressly provided by law, the following provisions apply in respect of persons who counsel other persons to commit offences, namely,

(a) every one who counsels another person to commit an indictable offence is, if the offence is not committed, guilty of an indictable offence and liable to the same punishment to which a person who attempts to commit that offence is liable; and

(b) every one who counsels another person to commit an offence punishable on summary conviction is, if the offence is not committed, guilty of an offence punishable on summary conviction.

R.S.C. 1985, c. 27 (1st Supp.), s. 60

465. (1) Conspiracy — Except where otherwise expressly provided by law, the following provisions apply in respect of conspiracy:

(a) every one who conspires with any one to commit murder or to cause another person to be murdered, whether in Canada or not, is guilty of an indictable offence and liable to a maximum term of imprisonment for life;

(b) every one who conspires with any one to prosecute a person for an alleged offence, knowing that they did not commit that offence, is guilty of

(i) an indictable offence and liable to imprisonment for a term of not more than 10 years or an offence punishable on summary conviction, if the alleged offence is one for which, on conviction, that person would be liable to be sentenced to imprisonment for life or for a term of not more than 14 years, or

(ii) an indictable offence and liable to imprisonment for a term of not more than five years or an offence punishable on summary conviction, if the alleged offence is one for which, on conviction, that person would be liable to imprisonment for less than 14 years;

(c) every one who conspires with any one to commit an indictable offence not provided for in paragraph (*a*) or (*b*) is guilty of an indictable offence and liable to the same punishment as that to which an accused who is guilty of that offence would, on conviction, be liable; and

(d) every one who conspires with any one to commit an offence punishable on summary conviction is guilty of an offence punishable on summary conviction.

(2) [Repealed R.S.C. 1985, c. 27 (1st Supp.), s. 61(3).]

(3) Conspiracy to commit offences — Every one who, while in Canada, conspires with any one to do anything referred to in subsection (1) in a place outside Canada that is an offence under the laws of that place shall be deemed to have conspired to do that thing in Canada.

(4) Idem — Every one who, while in a place outside Canada, conspires with any one to do anything referred to in subsection (1) in Canada shall be deemed to have conspired in Canada to do that thing.

(5) Jurisdiction — Where a person is alleged to have conspired to do anything that is an offence by virtue of subsection (3) or (4), proceedings in respect of that offence may, whether or not that person is in Canada, be commenced in any territorial division in Canada, and the accused may be tried and punished in respect of that offence in the same manner as if the offence had been committed in that territorial division.

(6) Appearance of accused at trial — For greater certainty, the provisions of this Act relating to

(a) requirements that an accused appear at and be present during proceedings, and

(b) the exceptions to those requirements,

apply to proceedings commenced in any territorial division pursuant to subsection (5).

(7) If previously tried outside Canada — If a person is alleged to have conspired to do anything that is an offence by virtue of subsection (3) or (4) and that person has been tried and dealt with outside Canada in respect of the offence in such a manner that, if the person had been tried and dealt with in Canada, they would be able to plead *autrefois acquit, autrefois convict*, pardon or an expungement order under the *Expungement of Historically Unjust Convictions Act*, the person shall be deemed to have been so tried and dealt with in Canada.

R.S.C. 1985, c. 27 (1st Supp.), s. 61; 1998, c. 35, s. 121; 2018, c. 11, s. 28; 2019, c. 25, s. 183

466. (1) Conspiracy in restraint of trade — A conspiracy in restraint of trade is an agreement between two or more persons to do or to procure to be done any unlawful act in restraint of trade.

(2) Trade union, exception — The purposes of a trade union are not, by reason only that they are in restraint of trade, unlawful within the meaning of subsection (1).

467. (1) Saving — No person shall be convicted of the offence of conspiracy by reason only that he

(a) refuses to work with a workman or for an employer; or

(b) does any act or causes any act to be done for the purpose of a trade combination, unless such act is an offence expressly punishable by law.

(2) "trade combination" — In this section, **"trade combination"** means any combination between masters or workmen or other persons for the purpose of regulating or altering the relations between masters or workmen, or the conduct of a master or workman in or in respect of his business, employment or contract of employment or service.

467.1 (1) Definitions — The following definitions apply in this Act.

"criminal organization" means a group, however organized, that

(a) is composed of three or more persons in or outside Canada; and

(b) has as one of its main purposes or main activities the facilitation or commission of one or more serious offences that, if committed, would likely result in the direct or indirect receipt of a material benefit, including a financial benefit, by the group or by any of the persons who constitute the group.

It does not include a group of persons that forms randomly for the immediate commission of a single offence. *("organisation criminelle")*

"serious offence" means an indictable offence under this or any other Act of Parliament for which the maximum punishment is imprisonment for five years or more, or another offence that is prescribed by regulation. *("infraction grave")*

(2) Facilitation — For the purposes of this section, section 467.11 and 467.111, facilitation of an offence does not require knowledge of a particular offence the commission of which is facilitated, or that an offence actually be committed.

(3) Commission of offence — In this section and in sections 467.11 to 467.13, committing an offence means being a party to it or counselling any person to be a party to it.

(4) Regulations — The Governor in Council may make regulations prescribing offences that are included in the definition "serious offence" in subsection (1).

1997, c. 23, s. 11; 2001, c. 32, s. 27; 2014, c. 17, s. 8

467.11 (1) Participation in activities of criminal organization — Every person who, for the purpose of enhancing the ability of a criminal organization to facilitate or commit an indictable offence under this or any other Act of Parliament, knowingly, by act or omission, participates in or contributes to any activity of the criminal organization is guilty of

(a) an indictable offence and liable to imprisonment for a term of not more than five years; or

(b) an offence punishable on summary conviction.

(2) Prosecution — In a prosecution for an offence under subsection (1), it is not necessary for the prosecutor to prove that

(a) the criminal organization actually facilitated or committed an indictable offence;

(b) the participation or contribution of the accused actually enhanced the ability of the criminal organization to facilitate or commit an indictable offence;

(c) the accused knew the specific nature of any indictable offence that may have been facilitated or committed by the criminal organization; or

(d) the accused knew the identity of any of the persons who constitute the criminal organization.

(3) Factors — In determining whether an accused participates in or contributes to any activity of a criminal organization, the Court may consider, among other factors, whether the accused

(a) uses a name, word, symbol or other representation that identifies, or is associated with, the criminal organization;

(b) frequently associates with any of the persons who constitute the criminal organization;

(c) receives any benefit from the criminal organization; or

(d) repeatedly engages in activities at the instruction of any of the persons who constitute the criminal organization.

2001, c. 32, s. 27; 2019, c. 25, s. 184

467.111 Recruitment of members by a criminal organization — Every person who, for the purpose of enhancing the ability of a criminal organization to facilitate or commit an indictable offence under this Act or any other Act of Parliament, recruits, solicits, encourages, coerces or invites a person to join the criminal organization, is guilty of an indictable offence and liable,

(a) in the case where the person recruited, solicited, encouraged or invited is under 18 years of age, to imprisonment for a term not exceeding five years, and to a minimum punishment of imprisonment for a term of six months; and

(b) in any other case, to imprisonment for a term not exceeding five years.

2014, c. 17, s. 9

467.12 (1) Commission of offence for criminal organization — Every person who commits an indictable offence under this or any other Act of Parliament for the benefit of, at the direction of, or in association with, a criminal organization is guilty of an indictable offence and liable to imprisonment for a term not exceeding fourteen years.

(2) Prosecution — In a prosecution for an offence under subsection (1), it is not necessary for the prosecutor to prove that the accused knew the identity of any of the persons who constitute the criminal organization.

2001, c. 32, s. 27

467.13 (1) Instructing commission of offence for criminal organization — Every person who is one of the persons who constitute a criminal organization and who knowingly instructs, directly or indirectly, any person to commit an offence under this or any other Act of Parliament for the benefit of, at the direction of, or in association with, the criminal organization is guilty of an indictable offence and liable to imprisonment for life.

(2) Prosecution — In a prosecution for an offence under subsection (1), it is not necessary for the prosecutor to prove that

(a) an offence other than the offence under subsection (1) was actually committed;

(b) the accused instructed a particular person to commit an offence; or

(c) the accused knew the identity of all of the persons who constitute the criminal organization.

2001, c. 32, s. 27

467.14 Sentences to be served consecutively — A sentence imposed on a person for an offence under section 467.11, 467.111, 467.12 or 467.13 shall be served consecutively to any other punishment imposed on the person for an offence arising out of the same event or series of events and to any other sentence to which the person is subject at the time the sentence is imposed on the person for an offence under any of those sections.

2001, c. 32, s. 27; 2014, c. 17, s. 10

467.2 [Repealed 2019, c. 25, s. 185.]

Part XIV — Jurisdiction (SS. 468–482.1)

General

468. Superior court of criminal jurisdiction — Every superior court of criminal jurisdiction has jurisdiction to try any indictable offence.

469. Court of criminal jurisdiction — Every court of criminal jurisdiction has jurisdiction to try an indictable offence other than

(a) an offence under any of the following sections:

(i) section 47 (treason),

(ii) [Repealed 2018, c. 29, s. 61.]

(iii) section 51 (intimidating Parliament or a legislature),

(iv) section 53 (inciting to mutiny),

(v) section 61 (seditious offences),

(vi) section 74 (piracy),

(vii) section 75 (piratical acts), or

(viii) section 235 (murder);

(b) **Accessories** — the offence of being an accessory after the fact to high treason or treason or murder;

(c) **Corrupting justice** — an offence under section 119 (bribery) by the holder of a judicial office;

(c.1) **Crimes against humanity** — an offence under any of sections 4 to 7 of the *Crimes Against Humanity and War Crimes Act*;

(d) **Attempts** — the offence of attempting to commit any offence mentioned in subparagraphs (*a*)(i) to (vii); or

(e) **Conspiracy** — the offence of conspiring to commit any offence mentioned in paragraph (*a*).

R.S.C. 1985, c. 27 (1st Supp.), s. 62; 2000, c. 24, s. 44; 2018, c. 29, s. 61

470. Jurisdiction over person — Subject to this Act, every superior court of criminal jurisdiction and every court of criminal jurisdiction that has power to try an indictable offence is competent to try an accused for that offence

(a) if the accused is found, is arrested or is in custody within the territorial jurisdiction of the court; or

(b) if the accused has been ordered to be tried by

(i) that court, or

(ii) any other court, the jurisdiction of which has by lawful authority been transferred to that court.

R.S.C. 1985, c. 27 (1st Supp.), s. 101(3)

471. Trial by jury compulsory — Except where otherwise expressly provided by law, every accused who is charged with an indictable offence shall be tried by a court composed of a judge and jury.

472. [Repealed R.S.C. 1985, c. 27 (1st Supp.), s. 63.]

473. (1) Trial without jury — Notwithstanding anything in this Act, an accused charged with an offence listed in section 469 may, with the consent of the accused and the Attorney General, be tried without a jury by a judge of a superior court of criminal jurisdiction.

(1.1) Joinder of other offences — Where the consent of the accused and the Attorney General is given in accordance with subsection (1), the judge of the superior court of criminal jurisdiction may order that any offence be tried by that judge in conjunction with the offence listed in section 469.

(2) Withdrawal of consent — Notwithstanding anything in this Act, where the consent of an accused and the Attorney General is given in accordance with subsection (1), such consent shall not be withdrawn unless both the accused and the Attorney General agree to the withdrawal.

R.S.C. 1985, c. 27 (1st Supp.), s. 63; 1994, c. 44, s. 30

474. (1) Adjournment when no jury summoned — Where the competent authority has determined that a panel of jurors is not to be summoned for a term or sittings of the court for the trial of criminal cases in any territorial division, the clerk of the court may, on the day of the opening of the term or sittings, if a judge is not present to preside over the court, adjourn the court and the business of the court to a subsequent day.

(2) Adjournment on instructions of judge — A clerk of the court for the trial of criminal cases in any territorial division may, at any time, on the instructions of the presiding judge or another judge of the court, adjourn the court and the business of the court to a subsequent day.

1994, c. 44, s. 31

475. (1) Accused absconding during trial — Notwithstanding any other provision of this Act, where an accused, whether or not he is charged jointly with another, absconds during the course of his trial,

(a) he shall be deemed to have waived his right to be present at his trial, and

(b) the court may

(i) continue the trial and proceed to a judgment or verdict and, if it finds the accused guilty, impose a sentence on him in his absence, or

(ii) if a warrant in Form 7 is issued for the arrest of the accused, adjourn the trial to await his appearance,

but where the trial is adjourned pursuant to subparagraph (*b*)(ii), the court may, at any time, continue the trial if it is satisfied that it is no longer in the interests of justice to await the appearance of the accused.

(2) **Adverse inference** — Where a court continues a trial pursuant to subsection (1), it may draw an inference adverse to the accused from the fact that he has absconded.

(3) **Accused not entitled to re-opening** — Where an accused reappears at his trial that is continuing pursuant to subsection (1), he is not entitled to have any part of the proceedings that was conducted in his absence re-opened unless the court is satisfied that because of exceptional circumstances it is in the interests of justice to re-open the proceedings.

(4) **Counsel for accused may continue to act** — Where an accused has absconded during the course of his trial and the court continues the trial, counsel for the accused is not thereby deprived of any authority he may have to continue to act for the accused in the proceedings.

Special Jurisdiction

476. Special jurisdictions — For the purposes of this Act,

(a) where an offence is committed in or on any water or on a bridge between two or more territorial divisions, the offence shall be deemed to have been committed in any of the territorial divisions;

(b) where an offence is committed on the boundary of two or more territorial divisions or within five hundred metres of any such boundary, or the offence was commenced within one territorial division and completed within another, the offence shall be deemed to have been committed in any of the territorial divisions;

(c) where an offence is committed in or on a vehicle employed in a journey, or on board a vessel employed on a navigable river, canal or inland water, the offence shall be deemed to have been committed in any territorial division through which the vehicle or vessel passed in the course of the journey or voyage on which the offence was committed, and where the center or other part of the road, or navigable river, canal or inland water on which the vehicle or vessel passed in the course of the journey or voyage is the boundary of two of more territorial divisions, the offence shall be deemed to have been committed in any of the territorial divisions;

(d) where an offence is committed in an aircraft in the course of a flight of that aircraft, it shall be deemed to have been committed

(i) in the territorial division in which the flight commenced,

(ii) in any territorial division over which the aircraft passed in the course of the flight, or

(iii) in the territorial division in which the flight ended; and

(e) where an offence is committed in respect of a mail in the course of its door-to-door delivery, the offence shall be deemed to have been committed in any territorial division through which the mail was carried on that delivery.

R.S.C. 1985, c. 27 (1st Supp.), s. 186; 1992, c. 1, s. 58(1) (Sched. I, item 8)

477. (1) Definition of "ship" — In sections 477.1 to 477.4, **"ship"** includes any description of vessel, boat or craft designed, used or capable of being used solely or partly for marine navigation, without regard to method or lack of propulsion.

(2) Saving — Nothing in sections 477.1 to 477.4 limits the operation of any other Act of Parliament or the jurisdiction that a court may exercise apart from those sections.

1990, c. 44, s. 15; 1996, c. 31, s. 67

477.1 Offences outside of Canada — Every person who commits an act or omission that, if it occurred in Canada, would be an offence under a federal law, within the meaning of section 2 of the *Oceans Act*, is deemed to have committed that act or omission in Canada if it is an act or omission

(a) in the exclusive economic zone of Canada that

(i) is committed by a person who is in the exclusive economic zone of Canada in connection with exploring or exploiting, conserving or managing the natural resources, whether living or non-living, of the exclusive economic zone of Canada, and

(ii) is committed by or in relation to a person who is a Canadian citizen or a permanent resident within the meaning of subsection 2(1) of the *Immigration and Refugee Protection Act*;

(b) that is committed in a place in or above the continental shelf of Canada and that is an offence in that place by virtue of section 20 of the *Oceans Act*;

(c) that is committed outside Canada on board or by means of a ship registered or licensed, or for which an identification number has been issued, pursuant to any Act of Parliament;

(d) that is committed outside Canada in the course of hot pursuit; or

(e) that is committed outside the territory of any state by a Canadian citizen.

1990, c. 44, s. 15; 1996, c. 31, s. 68; 2001, c. 27, s. 247

477.2 (1) Consent of Attorney General of Canada — No proceedings in respect of an offence committed in or on the territorial sea of Canada shall be continued unless the consent of the Attorney General of Canada is obtained not later than eight days after the proceedings are commenced, if the accused is not a Canadian citizen and the offence is alleged to have been committed on board any ship registered outside Canada.

(1.1) Exception — Subsection (1) does not apply to proceedings by way of summary conviction.

(2) Consent of Attorney General of Canada — No proceedings in respect of which courts have jurisdiction by virtue only of paragraph 477.1(*a*) or (*b*) shall be continued unless the consent of the Attorney General of Canada is obtained not later than eight days after the proceedings are commenced, if the accused is not a Canadian citizen and the offence is alleged to have been committed on board any ship registered outside Canada.

(3) **Consent of Attorney General of Canada** — No proceedings in respect of which courts have jurisdiction by virtue only of paragraph 477.1(*d*) or (*e*) shall be continued unless the consent of the Attorney General of Canada is obtained not later than eight days after the proceedings are commenced.

(4) **Consent to be filed** — The consent of the Attorney General required by subsection (1), (2) or (3) must be filed with the clerk of the court in which the proceedings have been instituted.

1990, c. 44, s. 15; 1994, c. 44, s. 32; 1996, c. 31, s. 69

477.3 (1) **Exercising powers of arrest, entry, etc.** — Every power of arrest, entry, search or seizure or other power that could be exercised in Canada in respect of an act or omission referred to in section 477.1 may be exercised, in the circumstances referred to in that section,

(a) at the place or on board the ship or marine installation or structure, within the meaning of section 2 of the *Oceans Act*, where the act or omission occurred; or

(b) where hot pursuit has been commenced, at any place on the seas, other than a place that is part of the territorial sea of any other state.

(2) **Arrest, search, seizure, etc.** — A justice or judge in any territorial division in Canada has jurisdiction to authorize an arrest, entry, search or seizure or an investigation or other ancillary matter related to an offence

(a) committed in or on the territorial sea of Canada or any area of the sea that forms part of the internal waters of Canada, or

(b) referred to in section 477.1

in the same manner as if the offence had been committed in that territorial division.

(3) **Limitation** — Where an act or omission that is an offence by virtue only of section 477.1 is alleged to have been committed on board any ship registered outside Canada, the powers referred to in subsection (1) shall not be exercised outside Canada with respect to that act or omission without the consent of the Attorney General of Canada.

1990, c. 44, s. 15; 1996, c. 31, s. 70

477.4 (1) **and** (2) [Repealed 1996, c. 31, s. 71(1).]

(3) **Evidence** — In proceedings in respect of an offence,

(a) a certificate referred to in subsection 23(1) of the *Oceans Act*, or

(b) a certificate issued by or under the authority of the Minister of Foreign Affairs containing a statement that any geographical location specified in the certificate was, at any time material to the proceedings, in an area of a fishing zone of Canada that is not within the internal waters of Canada or the territorial sea of Canada or outside the territory of any state,

is conclusive proof of the truth of the statement without proof of the signature or official character of the person appearing to have issued the certificate.

(4) Certificate cannot be compelled — A certificate referred to in subsection (3) is admissible in evidence in proceedings referred to in that subsection but its production cannot be compelled.

1990, c. 44, s. 15; 1995, c. 5, s. 25(1)(g); 1996, c. 31, s. 71

478. (1) Offence committed entirely in one province — Subject to this Act, a court in a province shall not try an offence committed entirely in another province.

(2) Exception — Every proprietor, publisher, editor or other person charged with the publication of a defamatory libel in a newspaper or with conspiracy to publish a defamatory libel in a newspaper shall be dealt with, indicted, tried and punished in the province where he resides or in which the newspaper is printed.

(3) Idem — An accused who is charged with an offence that is alleged to have been committed in Canada outside the province in which the accused is may, if the offence is not an offence mentioned in section 469 and

(a) in the case of proceedings instituted at the instance of the Government of Canada and conducted by or on behalf of that Government, if the Attorney General of Canada consents, or

(b) in any other case, if the Attorney General of the province where the offence is alleged to have been committed consents,

appear before a court or judge that would have had jurisdiction to try that offence if it had been committed in the province where the accused is, and where the accused consents to plead guilty and pleads guilty to that offence, the court or judge shall determine the accused to be guilty of the offence and impose the punishment warranted by law, but where the accused does not consent to plead guilty and does not plead guilty, the accused shall, if the accused was in custody prior to appearance, be returned to custody and shall be dealt with according to law.

(4) Where accused committed to stand trial — Notwithstanding that an accused described in subsection (3) has been ordered to stand trial or that an indictment has been preferred against the accused in respect of the offence to which he desires to plead guilty, the accused shall be deemed simply to stand charged of that offence without a preliminary inquiry having been conducted or an indictment having been preferred with respect thereto.

(5) "newspaper" — In this section **"newspaper"** has the same meaning that it has in section 297.

R.S.C. 1985, c. 27 (1st Supp.), ss. 64, 101(3); 1994, c. 44, s. 33

479. Offence outstanding in same province — Where an accused is charged with an offence that is alleged to have been committed in the province in which he is, he may, if the offence is not an offence mentioned in section 469, and

(a) in the case of proceedings instituted at the instance of the Government of Canada and conducted by or on behalf of that Government, the Attorney General of Canada consents, or

(b) in any other case, the Attorney General of the province where the offence is alleged to have been committed consents, appear before a court or judge that would have had jurisdiction to try that offence if it had been committed in the place where the accused is, and where the accused consents to plead guilty and pleads guilty to that offence, the court or judge shall determine the accused to be guilty of the offence and impose the punishment warranted by law, but where the accused does not consent to plead guilty and does not plead guilty, the accused shall, if the accused was in custody prior to appearance, be returned to custody and shall be dealt with according to law.

R.S.C. 1985, c. 27 (1st Supp.), s. 65; 1994, c. 44, s. 34

480. (1) Offence in unorganized territory — Where an offence is committed in an unorganized tract of country in any province or on a lake, river or other water therein, not included in a territorial division or in a provisional judicial district, proceedings in respect thereof may be commenced and an accused may be charged, tried and punished in respect thereof within any territorial division or provisional judicial district of the province in the same manner as if the offence had been committed within that territorial division or provisional judicial district.

(2) New territorial division — Where a provisional judicial district or a new territorial division is constituted in an unorganized tract referred to in subsection (1), the jurisdiction conferred by that subsection continues until appropriate provision is made by law for the administration of criminal justice within the provisional judicial district or new territorial division.

481. Offence not in a province — Where an offence is committed in a part of Canada not in a province, proceedings in respect thereof may be commenced and the accused may be charged, tried and punished within any territorial division in any province in the same manner as if that offence had been committed in that territorial division.

481.1 Offence in Canadian waters — Where an offence is committed in or on the territorial sea of Canada or any area of the sea that forms part of the internal waters of Canada, proceedings in respect thereof may, whether or not the accused is in Canada, be commenced and an accused may be charged, tried and punished within any territorial division in Canada in the same manner as if the offence had been committed in that territorial division.

1996, c. 31, s. 72

481.2 Offence outside Canada — Subject to this or any other Act of Parliament, where an act or omission is committed outside Canada and the act or omission is an offence when committed outside Canada under this or any other Act of Parliament, proceedings in respect of the offence may, whether or not the accused is in Canada, be commenced, and an accused may be charged, tried and punished within any territorial division in Canada in the same manner as if the offence had been committed in that territorial division.

1996, c. 31, s. 72; 2008, c. 18, s. 10

481.3 Appearance of accused at trial — For greater certainty, the provisions of this Act relating to

(a) the requirement of the appearance of an accused at proceedings, and

(b) the exceptions to that requirement

apply to proceedings commenced in any territorial division pursuant to section 481, 481.1 or 481.2.

1996, c. 31, s. 72

Rules of Court

482. (1) Power to make rules — Every superior court of criminal jurisdiction and every court of appeal may make rules of court not inconsistent with this or any other Act of Parliament, and any rules so made apply to any prosecution, proceeding, action or appeal, as the case may be, within the jurisdiction of that court, instituted in relation to any matter of a criminal nature or arising from or incidental to any such prosecution, proceeding, action or appeal.

(2) Power to make rules — The following courts may make rules of court not inconsistent with this Act or any other Act of Parliament that are applicable to any prosecution, proceeding, including a preliminary inquiry or proceedings within the meaning of Part XXVII, action or appeal, as the case may be, within the jurisdiction of that court, instituted in relation to any matter of a criminal nature or arising from or incidental to the prosecution, proceeding, action or appeal:

(a) every court of criminal jurisdiction for a province;

(b) every appeal court within the meaning of section 812 that is not a court referred to in subsection (1);

(c) the Ontario Court of Justice;

(d) the Court of Quebec and every municipal court in the Province of Quebec;

(e) the Provincial Court of Nova Scotia;

(f) the Provincial Court of New Brunswick;

(g) the Provincial Court of Manitoba;

(h) the Provincial Court of British Columbia;

(i) the Provincial Court of Prince Edward Island;

(j) the Provincial Court of Saskatchewan;

(k) the Provincial Court of Alberta;

(l) the Provincial Court of Newfoundland and Labrador;

(m) the Territorial Court of Yukon;

(n) the Territorial Court of the Northwest Territories; and

(o) the Nunavut Court of Justice.

(3) Purpose of rules — Rules under subsection (1) or (2) may be made

(a) generally to regulate the duties of the officers of the court and any other matter considered expedient to attain the ends of justice and carry into effect the provisions of the law;

(b) to regulate the sittings of the court or any division thereof, or of any judge of the court sitting in chambers, except in so far as they are regulated by law;

(c) to regulate the pleading, practice and procedure in criminal matters, including pre-hearing conferences held under section 625.1, proceedings with respect to judicial interim release and preliminary inquiries and, in the case of rules under subsection (1), proceedings with respect to *mandamus*, *certiorari*, *habeas corpus*, prohibition and *procedendo* and proceedings on an appeal under section 830; and

(d) to carry out the provisions of this Act relating to appeals from conviction, acquittal or sentence and, without restricting the generality of this paragraph,

(i) for furnishing necessary forms and instructions in relation to notices of appeal or applications for leave to appeal to officials or other persons requiring or demanding them,

(ii) for ensuring the accuracy of notes taken at a trial and the verification of any copy or transcript,

(iii) for keeping writings, exhibits or other things connected with the proceedings on the trial,

(iv) for securing the safe custody of property during the period in which the operation of an order with respect to that property is suspended under subsection 689(1), and

(v) for providing that the Attorney General and counsel who acted for the Attorney General at the trial be supplied with certified copies of writings, exhibits and things connected with the proceedings that are required for the purposes of their duties.

(4) Publication — Rules of court that are made under this section must be published or otherwise made available to the public.

(5) Regulations to secure uniformity — Notwithstanding anything in this section, the Governor in Council may make such provision as he considers proper to secure uniformity in the rules of court in criminal matters, and all uniform rules made under the authority of this subsection prevail and have effect as if enacted by this Act.

R.S.C. 1985, c. 27 (1st Supp.), s. 66; 1994, c. 44, s. 35; 2002, c. 13, s. 17; 2015, c. 3, s. 50; 2019, c. 25, s. 186

482.1 (1) Power to make rules respecting case management — A court referred to in subsection 482(1) or (2) may make rules for case management, including rules

(a) for the determination of any matter that would assist the court in effective and efficient case management;

(b) permitting personnel of the court to deal with administrative matters relating to proceedings out of court if the accused is represented by counsel; and

(c) establishing case management schedules.

(2) Compliance with directions — The parties to a case shall comply with any direction made in accordance with a rule made under subsection (1).

(3) Summons or warrant — If rules are made under subsection (1), a court, justice or judge may issue a summons or warrant to compel the presence of the accused at case management proceedings.

(4) Provisions to apply — Section 512 and subsection 524(1) apply, with any modifications that the circumstances require, to the issuance of a summons or a warrant under subsection (3).

Proposed Amendment — 482.1(4)

(4) Provisions to apply — Sections 512 and 512.3 apply, with any modifications that the circumstances require, to the issuance of a summons or a warrant under subsection (3).

2019, c. 25, s. 187(1) [To come into force December 18, 2019.]

(5) Subsections 482(4) and (5) to apply — Subsections 482(4) and (5) apply, with any modifications that the circumstances require, to rules made under subsection (1).

(6) [Repealed 2019, c. 25, s. 187(2).]

2002, c. 13, s. 18; 2019, c. 25, s. 187(2)

PART XV — SPECIAL PROCEDURE AND POWERS (SS. 483–492.2)

General Powers of Certain Officials

483. Officials with powers of two justices — Every judge or provincial court judge authorized by the law of the province in which he is appointed to do anything that is required to be done by two or more justices may do alone anything that this Act or any other Act of the Parliament authorizes two or more justices to do.

R.S.C. 1985, c. 27 (1st Supp.), s. 203

484. Preserving order in court — Every judge or provincial court judge has the same power and authority to preserve order in a court over which he presides as may be exercised by the superior court of criminal jurisdiction of the province during the sittings thereof.

R.S.C. 1985, c. 27 (1st Supp.), s. 203

485. (1) Procedural irregularities — Jurisdiction over an offence is not lost by reason of the failure of any court, judge, provincial court judge or justice to act in the exercise of that jurisdiction at any particular time, or by reason of a failure to comply with any of the provisions of this Act respecting adjournments or remands.

(1.1) When accused not appearing personally — Jurisdiction over an accused is not lost by reason of the failure of the accused to appear personally, so long as the provisions of this Act or a rule made under section 482 or 482.1 permitting the accused not to appear personally apply.

(2) Summons or warrant — Where jurisdiction over an accused or a defendant is lost and has not been regained, a court, judge, provincial court judge or justice may, within three months after the loss of jurisdiction, issue a summons, or if it or he considers it necessary in the public interest, a warrant for the arrest of the accused or defendant.

(3) Dismissal for want of prosecution — Where no summons or warrant is issued under subsection (2) within the period provided therein, the proceedings shall be deemed to be dismissed for want of prosecution and shall not be recommenced except in accordance with section 485.1.

(4) Adjournment and order — Where, in the opinion of the court, judge, provincial court judge or justice, an accused or a defendant who appears at a proceeding has been misled or prejudiced by reason of any matter referred to in subsection (1), the court, judge, provincial court judge or justice may adjourn the proceeding and may make such order as it or he considers appropriate.

(5) Part XVI to apply — The provisions of Part XVI apply with such modifications as the circumstances require where a summons or warrant is issued under subsection (2).

R.S.C. 1985, c. 27 (1st Supp.), ss. 67, 203; 1997, c. 18, s. 40; 2002, c. 13, s. 19; 2019, c. 25, s. 188

485.1 Recommencement where dismissal for want of prosecution — Where an indictment in respect of a transaction is dismissed or deemed by any provision of this Act to be dismissed for want of prosecution, a new information shall not be laid and a new indictment shall not be preferred before any court in respect of the same transaction without

(a) the personal consent in writing of the Attorney General or Deputy Attorney General, in any prosecution conducted by the Attorney General or in which the Attorney General intervenes; or

(b) the written order of a judge of that court, in any prosecution conducted by a prosecutor other than the Attorney General and in which the Attorney General does not intervene.

R.S.C. 1985, c. 27 (1st Supp.), s. 67

486. (1) Exclusion of public — Any proceedings against an accused shall be held in open court, but the presiding judge or justice may, on application of the prosecutor or a witness or on his or her own motion, order the exclusion of all or any members of the public from the court room for all or part of the proceedings, or order that the witness testify behind a screen or other device that would allow the witness not to be seen by members of the public, if the judge or justice is of the opinion that such an order is in the interest of public morals, the maintenance of order or the proper administration of justice or is necessary to prevent injury to international relations or national defence or national security.

(1.1) Application — The application may be made, during the proceedings, to the presiding judge or justice or, before the proceedings begin, to the judge or justice who will preside at the proceedings or, if that judge or justice has not been determined, to any judge or justice having jurisdiction in the judicial district where the proceedings will take place.

(1.2) to (1.5) [Repealed 2005, c. 32, s. 15.]

(2) Factors to be considered — In determining whether the order is in the interest of the proper administration of justice, the judge or justice shall consider

(a) society's interest in encouraging the reporting of offences and the participation of victims and witnesses in the criminal justice process;

(b) the safeguarding of the interests of witnesses under the age of 18 years in all proceedings;

(c) the ability of the witness to give a full and candid account of the acts complained of if the order were not made;

(d) whether the witness needs the order for their security or to protect them from intimidation or retaliation;

(e) the protection of justice system participants who are involved in the proceedings;

(f) whether effective alternatives to the making of the proposed order are available in the circumstances;

(g) the salutary and deleterious effects of the proposed order; and

(h) any other factor that the judge or justice considers relevant.

(2.1) to (2.3) [Repealed 2005, c. 32, s. 15.]

(3) Reasons to be stated — If an accused is charged with an offence under section 151, 152, 153, 153.1 or 155, subsection 160(2) or (3) or section 163.1, 170, 171, 171.1, 172, 172.1, 172.2, 173, 271, 272, 273, 279.01, 279.011, 279.02, 279.03, 286.1, 286.2 or 286.3 and the prosecutor or the accused applies for an order under subsection (1), the judge or justice shall, if no such order is made, state, by reference to the circumstances of the case, the reason for not making an order.

(3.1) [Repealed 2005, c. 32, s. 15.]

(4) No adverse inference — No adverse inference may be drawn from the fact that an order is, or is not, made under this section.

(4.1) to (5) [Repealed 2005, c. 32, s. 15.]

(6) [Repealed R.S.C. 1985, c. 19 (3rd Supp.), s. 14(2).]

R.S.C. 1985, c. 27 (1st Supp.), s. 203; R.S.C. 1985, c. 19 (3d Supp.), s. 14; R.S.C. 1985, c. 23 (4th Supp.), s. 1; 1992, c. 21, s. 9; 1993, c. 45, s. 7; 1997, c. 16, s. 6; 1999, c. 25, s. 2; 2001, c. 32, s. 29; 2001, c. 41, ss. 16, 34, 133(13), (14); 2002, c. 13, s. 20; 2005, c. 32, s. 15; 2005, c. 43, ss. 4, 8(3)(a); 2010, c. 3, s. 4; 2012, c. 1, s. 28; 2014, c. 25, s. 21; 2015, c. 13, s. 13; 2015, c. 20, s. 21; 2019, c. 25, s. 189

486.1 (1) Support person — witnesses under 18 or who have a disability — In any proceedings against an accused, the judge or justice shall, on application of the prosecutor in respect of a witness who is under the age of 18 years or who has a mental or physical disability, or on application of such a witness, order that a support person of the witness' choice be permitted to be present and to be close to the witness while the witness testifies, unless the judge or justice is of the opinion that the order would interfere with the proper administration of justice.

(2) **Other witnesses** — In any proceedings against an accused, the judge or justice may, on application of the prosecutor in respect of a witness, or on application of a witness, order that a support person of the witness' choice be permitted to be present and to be close to the witness while the witness testifies if the judge or justice is of the opinion that the order would facilitate the giving of a full and candid account by the witness of the acts complained of or would otherwise be in the interest of the proper administration of justice.

(2.1) **Application** — An application referred to in subsection (1) or (2) may be made, during the proceedings, to the presiding judge or justice or, before the proceedings begin, to the judge or justice who will preside at the proceedings or, if that judge or justice has not been determined, to any judge or justice having jurisdiction in the judicial district where the proceedings will take place.

(3) **Factors to be considered** — In determining whether to make an order under subsection (2), the judge or justice shall consider

(a) the age of the witness;

(b) the witness' mental or physical disabilities, if any;

(c) the nature of the offence;

(d) the nature of any relationship between the witness and the accused;

(e) whether the witness needs the order for their security or to protect them from intimidation or retaliation;

(f) society's interest in encouraging the reporting of offences and the participation of victims and witnesses in the criminal justice process; and

(g) any other factor that the judge or justice considers relevant.

(4) **Witness not to be a support person** — The judge or justice shall not permit a witness to be a support person unless the judge or justice is of the opinion that doing so is necessary for the proper administration of justice.

(5) **No communication while testifying** — The judge or justice may order that the support person and the witness not communicate with each other while the witness testifies.

(6) **No adverse inference** — No adverse inference may be drawn from the fact that an order is, or is not, made under this section.

2005, c. 32, s. 15; 2015, c. 13, s. 14

486.2 (1) **Testimony outside court room — witnesses under 18 or who have a disability** — Despite section 650, in any proceedings against an accused, the judge or justice shall, on application of the prosecutor in respect of a witness who is under the age of 18 years or who is able to communicate evidence but may have difficulty doing so by reason of a mental or physical disability, or on application of such a witness, order that the witness testify outside the court room or behind a screen or other device that would allow the witness not to see the accused, unless the judge or justice is of the opinion that the order would interfere with the proper administration of justice.

(2) Other witnesses — Despite section 650, in any proceedings against an accused, the judge or justice may, on application of the prosecutor in respect of a witness, or on application of a witness, order that the witness testify outside the court room or behind a screen or other device that would allow the witness not to see the accused if the judge or justice is of the opinion that the order would facilitate the giving of a full and candid account by the witness of the acts complained of or would otherwise be in the interest of the proper administration of justice.

(2.1) Application — An application referred to in subsection (1) or (2) may be made, during the proceedings, to the presiding judge or justice or, before the proceedings begin, to the judge or justice who will preside at the proceedings or, if that judge or justice has not been determined, to any judge or justice having jurisdiction in the judicial district where the proceedings will take place.

(3) Factors to be considered — In determining whether to make an order under subsection (2), the judge or justice shall consider

(a) the age of the witness;

(b) the witness' mental or physical disabilities, if any;

(c) the nature of the offence;

(d) the nature of any relationship between the witness and the accused;

(e) whether the witness needs the order for their security or to protect them from intimidation or retaliation;

(f) whether the order is needed to protect the identity of a peace officer who has acted, is acting or will be acting in an undercover capacity, or of a person who has acted, is acting or will be acting covertly under the direction of a peace officer;

(f.1) whether the order is needed to protect the witness's identity if they have had, have or will have responsibilities relating to national security or intelligence;

(g) society's interest in encouraging the reporting of offences and the participation of victims and witnesses in the criminal justice process; and

(h) any other factor that the judge or justice considers relevant.

(4) Same procedure for determination — If the judge or justice is of the opinion that it is necessary for a witness to testify in order to determine whether an order under subsection (2) should be made in respect of that witness, the judge or justice shall order that the witness testify in accordance with that subsection.

(5) Conditions of exclusion — A witness shall not testify outside the court room in accordance with an order made under subsection (1) or (2) unless arrangements are made for the accused, the judge or justice and the jury to watch the testimony of the witness by means of closed-circuit television or otherwise and the accused is permitted to communicate with counsel while watching the testimony.

(6) No adverse inference — No adverse inference may be drawn from the fact that an order is, or is not, made under subsection (1) or (2).

(7) and (8) [Repealed 2015, c. 13, s. 15.]

2005, c. 32, s. 15; 2014, c. 17, s. 12; 2015, c. 13, s. 15; 2015, c. 20, s. 38(2)

486.3 (1) Accused not to cross-examine witnesses under 18 — In any proceedings against an accused, the judge or justice shall, on application of the prosecutor in respect of a witness who is under the age of 18 years, or on application of such a witness, order that the accused not personally cross-examine the witness, unless the judge or justice is of the opinion that the proper administration of justice requires the accused to personally conduct the cross-examination. If such an order is made, the judge or justice shall appoint counsel to conduct the cross-examination.

(2) Accused not to cross-examine complainant — certain offences — In any proceedings against an accused in respect of an offence under any of sections 264, 271, 272 and 273, the judge or justice shall, on application of the prosecutor in respect of a witness who is a victim, or on application of such a witness, order that the accused not personally cross-examine the witness, unless the judge or justice is of the opinion that the proper administration of justice requires the accused to personally conduct the cross-examination. If such an order is made, the judge or justice shall appoint counsel to conduct the cross-examination.

(3) Other witnesses — In any proceedings against an accused, the judge or justice may, on application of the prosecutor in respect of a witness who is not entitled to make an application under subsection (1) or (2), or on application of such a witness, order that the accused not personally cross-examine the witness if the judge or justice is of the opinion that the order would allow the giving of a full and candid account from the witness of the acts complained of or would otherwise be in the interest of the proper administration of justice. If the order is made, the judge or justice shall appoint counsel to conduct the cross-examination.

(4) Factors to be considered — In determining whether to make an order under subsection (3), the judge or justice shall consider

(a) the age of the witness;

(b) the witness' mental or physical disabilities, if any;

(c) the nature of the offence;

(d) whether the witness needs the order for their security or to protect them from intimidation or retaliation;

(e) the nature of any relationship between the witness and the accused;

(f) society's interest in encouraging the reporting of offences and the participation of victims and witnesses in the criminal justice process; and

(g) any other factor that the judge or justice considers relevant.

(4.1) Application — An application referred to in any of subsections (1) to (3) may be made during the proceedings to the presiding judge or justice or, before the proceedings begin, to the judge or justice who will preside at the proceedings or, if that judge or justice has not been determined, to any judge or justice having jurisdiction in the judicial district where the proceedings will take place.

(5) No adverse inference — No adverse inference may be drawn from the fact that counsel is, or is not, appointed under this section.

2005, c. 32, s. 15; 2015, c. 13, s. 16

486.31 (1) Non-disclosure of witness' identity — In any proceedings against an accused, the judge or justice may, on application of the prosecutor in respect of a witness, or on application of a witness, make an order directing that any information that could identify the witness not be disclosed in the course of the proceedings if the judge or justice is of the opinion that the order is in the interest of the proper administration of justice.

(2) Hearing may be held — The judge or justice may hold a hearing to determine whether the order should be made, and the hearing may be in private.

(3) Factors to be considered — In determining whether to make the order, the judge or justice shall consider

(a) the right to a fair and public hearing;

(b) the nature of the offence;

(c) whether the witness needs the order for their security or to protect them from intimidation or retaliation;

(d) whether the order is needed to protect the security of anyone known to the witness;

(e) whether the order is needed to protect the identity of a peace officer who has acted, is acting or will be acting in an undercover capacity, or of a person who has acted, is acting or will be acting covertly under the direction of a peace officer;

(e.1) whether the order is needed to protect the witness's identity if they have had, have or will have responsibilities relating to national security or intelligence;

(f) society's interest in encouraging the reporting of offences and the participation of victims and witnesses in the criminal justice process;

(g) the importance of the witness' testimony to the case;

(h) whether effective alternatives to the making of the proposed order are available in the circumstances;

(i) the salutary and deleterious effects of the proposed order; and

(j) any other factor that the judge or justice considers relevant.

(4) No adverse inference — No adverse inference may be drawn from the fact that an order is, or is not, made under this section.

2015, c. 13, s. 17; 2015, c. 20, s. 38(3)

486.4 (1) Order restricting publication — sexual offences — Subject to subsection (2), the presiding judge or justice may make an order directing that any information that could identify the victim or a witness shall not be published in any document or broadcast or transmitted in any way, in proceedings in respect of

(a) any of the following offences:

(i) an offence under section 151, 152, 153, 153.1, 155, 160, 162, 163.1, 170, 171, 171.1, 172, 172.1, 172.2, 173, 213, 271, 272, 273, 279.01, 279.011, 279.02, 279.03, 280, 281, 286.1, 286.2, 286.3, 346 or 347, or

(ii) any offence under this Act, as it read from time to time before the day on which this subparagraph comes into force, if the conduct alleged would be an offence referred to in subparagraph (i) if it occurred on or after that day; or

(iii) [Repealed 2014, c. 25, s. 22(2).]

(b) two or more offences being dealt with in the same proceeding, at least one of which is an offence referred to in paragraph (a).

(2) Mandatory order on application — In proceedings in respect of the offences referred to in paragraph (1)(a) or (b), the presiding judge or justice shall

(a) at the first reasonable opportunity, inform any witness under the age of eighteen years and the victim of the right to make an application for the order; and

(b) on application made by the victim, the prosecutor or any such witness, make the order.

(2.1) Victim under 18 — other offences — Subject to subsection (2.2), in proceedings in respect of an offence other than an offence referred to in subsection (1), if the victim is under the age of 18 years, the presiding judge or justice may make an order directing that any information that could identify the victim shall not be published in any document or broadcast or transmitted in any way.

(2.2) Mandatory order on application — In proceedings in respect of an offence other than an offence referred to in subsection (1), if the victim is under the age of 18 years, the presiding judge or justice shall

(a) as soon as feasible, inform the victim of their right to make an application for the order; and

(b) on application of the victim or the prosecutor, make the order.

(3) Child pornography — In proceedings in respect of an offence under section 163.1, a judge or justice shall make an order directing that any information that could identify a witness who is under the age of eighteen years, or any person who is the subject of a representation, written material or a recording that constitutes child pornography within the meaning of that section, shall not be published in any document or broadcast or transmitted in any way.

(4) Limitation — An order made under this section does not apply in respect of the disclosure of information in the course of the administration of justice when it is not the purpose of the disclosure to make the information known in the community.

2005, c. 32, s. 15; 2005, c. 43, s. 8(3)(b); 2010, c. 3, s. 5; 2012, c. 1, s. 29; 2014, c. 25, ss. 22, 48(6); 2015, c. 13, s. 18(1), (2), (4); 2019, c. 25, s. 190

486.5 (1) Order restricting publication — victims and witnesses — Unless an order is made under section 486.4, on application of the prosecutor in respect of a victim or a witness, or on application of a victim or a witness, a judge or justice may make an order directing that any information that could identify the victim or witness shall not be published in any document or broadcast or transmitted in any way if the judge or justice is of the opinion that the order is in the interest of the proper administration of justice.

(2) **Justice system participants** — On application of the prosecutor in respect of a justice system participant who is involved in proceedings in respect of an offence referred to in subsection (2.1), or on application of such a justice system participant, a judge or justice may make an order directing that any information that could identify the justice system participant shall not be published in any document or broadcast or transmitted in any way if the judge or justice is of the opinion that the order is in the interest of the proper administration of justice.

(2.1) **Offences** — The offences for the purposes of subsection (2) are

(a) an offence under section 423.1, 467.11, 467.111, 467.12 or 467.13, or a serious offence committed for the benefit of, at the direction of, or in association with, a criminal organization;

(b) a terrorism offence;

(c) an offence under subsection 16(1) or (2), 17(1), 19(1), 20(1) or 22(1) of the *Security of Information Act*; or

(d) an offence under subsection 21(1) or section 23 of the *Security of Information Act* that is committed in relation to an offence referred to in paragraph (c).

(3) **Limitation** — An order made under this section does not apply in respect of the disclosure of information in the course of the administration of justice if it is not the purpose of the disclosure to make the information known in the community.

(4) **Application and notice** — An applicant for an order shall

(a) apply in writing to the presiding judge or justice or, if the judge or justice has not been determined, to a judge of a superior court of criminal jurisdiction in the judicial district where the proceedings will take place; and

(b) provide notice of the application to the prosecutor, the accused and any other person affected by the order that the judge or justice specifies.

(5) **Grounds** — An applicant for an order shall set out the grounds on which the applicant relies to establish that the order is necessary for the proper administration of justice.

(6) **Hearing may be held** — The judge or justice may hold a hearing to determine whether an order should be made, and the hearing may be in private.

(7) **Factors to be considered** — In determining whether to make an order, the judge or justice shall consider

(a) the right to a fair and public hearing;

(b) whether there is a real and substantial risk that the victim, witness or justice system participant would suffer harm if their identity were disclosed;

(c) whether the victim, witness or justice system participant needs the order for their security or to protect them from intimidation or retaliation;

(d) society's interest in encouraging the reporting of offences and the participation of victims, witnesses and justice system participants in the criminal justice process;

(e) whether effective alternatives are available to protect the identity of the victim, witness or justice system participant;

(f) the salutary and deleterious effects of the proposed order;

(g) the impact of the proposed order on the freedom of expression of those affected by it; and

(h) any other factor that the judge or justice considers relevant.

(8) **Conditions** — An order may be subject to any conditions that the judge or justice thinks fit.

(9) **Publication prohibited** — Unless the judge or justice refuses to make an order, no person shall publish in any document or broadcast or transmit in any way

(a) the contents of an application;

(b) any evidence taken, information given or submissions made at a hearing under subsection (6); or

(c) any other information that could identify the person to whom the application relates as a victim, witness or justice system participant in the proceedings.

2005, c. 32, s. 15; 2015, c. 13, s. 19

486.6 (1) Offence — Every person who fails to comply with an order made under any of subsections 486.4(1) to (3) or subsection 486.5(1) or (2) is guilty of an offence punishable on summary conviction.

(2) **Application of order** — For greater certainty, an order referred to in subsection (1) applies to prohibit, in relation to proceedings taken against any person who fails to comply with the order, the publication in any document or the broadcasting or transmission in any way of information that could identify a victim, witness or justice system participant whose identity is protected by the order.

2005, c. 32, s. 15; 2019, c. 13, s. 151

486.7 (1) Security of witnesses — In any proceedings against an accused, the presiding judge or justice may, on application of the prosecutor or a witness or on his or her own motion, make any order, other than one that may be made under any of sections 486 to 486.5, if the judge or justice is of the opinion that the order is necessary to protect the security of any witness and is otherwise in the interest of the proper administration of justice.

(2) **Application** — The application may be made, during the proceedings, to the presiding judge or justice or, before the proceedings begin, to the judge or justice who will preside at the proceedings or, if that judge or justice has not been determined, to any judge or justice having jurisdiction in the judicial district where the proceedings will take place.

(3) **Factors to be considered** — In determining whether to make the order, the judge or justice shall consider

(a) the age of the witness;

(b) the witness's mental or physical disabilities, if any;

(c) the right to a fair and public hearing;

(d) the nature of the offence;

(e) whether the witness needs the order to protect them from intimidation or retaliation;

(f) whether the order is needed to protect the security of anyone known to the witness;

(g) society's interest in encouraging the reporting of offences and the participation of victims and witnesses in the criminal justice process;

(h) the importance of the witness's testimony to the case;

(i) whether effective alternatives to the making of the proposed order are available in the circumstances;

(j) the salutary and deleterious effects of the proposed order; and

(k) any other factor that the judge or justice considers relevant.

(4) No adverse inference — No adverse inference may be drawn from the fact that an order is, or is not, made under this section.

2015, c. 20, s. 22

487. (1) Information for search warrant — A justice who is satisfied by information on oath in Form 1 that there are reasonable grounds to believe that there is in a building, receptacle or place

(a) anything on or in respect of which any offence against this Act or any other Act of Parliament has been or is suspected to have been committed,

(b) anything that there are reasonable grounds to believe will afford evidence with respect to the commission of an offence, or will reveal the whereabouts of a person who is believed to have committed an offence, against this Act or any other Act of Parliament,

(c) anything that there are reasonable grounds to believe is intended to be used for the purpose of committing any offence against the person for which a person may be arrested without warrant, or

(c.1) any offence-related property,

may at any time issue a warrant authorizing a peace officer or a public officer who has been appointed or designated to administer or enforce a federal or provincial law and whose duties include the enforcement of this Act or any other Act of Parliament and who is named in the warrant

(d) to search the building, receptacle or place for any such thing and to seize it, and

(e) subject to any other Act of Parliament, to, as soon as practicable, bring the thing seized before, or make a report in respect thereof to, the justice or some other justice for the same territorial division in accordance with section 489.1.

(2) Execution in Canada — A warrant issued under subsection (1) may be executed at any place in Canada. A public officer named in the warrant, or any peace officer, who executes the warrant must have authority to act in that capacity in the place where the warrant is executed.

(2.1) Operation of computer system and copying equipment — A person authorized under this section to search a computer system in a building or place for data may

(a) use or cause to be used any computer system at the building or place to search any data contained in or available to the computer system;

(b) reproduce or cause to be reproduced any data in the form of a print-out or other intelligible output;

(c) seize the print-out or other output for examination or copying; and

(d) use or cause to be used any copying equipment at the place to make copies of the data.

(2.2) Duty of person in possession or control — Every person who is in possession or control of any building or place in respect of which a search is carried out under this section shall, on presentation of the warrant, permit the person carrying out the search

(a) to use or cause to be used any computer system at the building or place in order to search any data contained in or available to the computer system for data that the person is authorized by this section to search for;

(b) to obtain a hard copy of the data and to seize it; and

(c) to use or cause to be used any copying equipment at the place to make copies of the data.

(3) Form — A search warrant issued under this section may be in the form set out as Form 5 in Part XXVIII, varied to suit the case.

(4) [Repealed 2019, c. 25, s. 191(2).]

R.S.C. 1985, c. 27 (1st Supp.), s. 68; 1994, c. 44, s. 36; 1997, c. 18, s. 41; 1997, c. 23, s. 12; 1999, c. 5, s. 16; 2008, c. 18, s. 11; 2019, c. 25, s. 191

487.01 (1) Information for general warrant — A provincial court judge, a judge of a superior court of criminal jurisdiction or a judge as defined in section 552 may issue a warrant in writing authorizing a peace officer to, subject to this section, use any device or investigative technique or procedure or do any thing described in the warrant that would, if not authorized, constitute an unreasonable search or seizure in respect of a person or a person's property if

(a) the judge is satisfied by information on oath in writing that there are reasonable grounds to believe that an offence against this or any other Act of Parliament has been or will be committed and that information concerning the offence will be obtained through the use of the technique, procedure or device or the doing of the thing;

(b) the judge is satisfied that it is in the best interests of the administration of justice to issue the warrant; and

(c) there is no other provision in this or any other Act of Parliament that would provide for a warrant, authorization or order permitting the technique, procedure or device to be used or the thing to be done.

(2) Limitation — Nothing in subsection (1) shall be construed as to permit interference with the bodily integrity of any person.

(3) Search or seizure to be reasonable — A warrant issued under subsection (1) shall contain such terms and conditions as the judge considers advisable to ensure that any search or seizure authorized by the warrant is reasonable in the circumstances.

(4) Video surveillance — A warrant issued under subsection (1) that authorizes a peace officer to observe, by means of a television camera or other similar electronic device, any person who is engaged in activity in circumstances in which the person has a reasonable expectation of privacy shall contain such terms and conditions as the judge considers advisable to ensure that the privacy of the person or of any other person is respected as much as possible.

(5) Other provisions to apply — The definition "offence" in section 183 and sections 183.1, 184.2, 184.3 and 185 to 188.2, subsection 189(5), and sections 190, 193 and 194 to 196 apply, with such modifications as the circumstances require, to a warrant referred to in subsection (4) as though references in those provisions to interceptions of private communications were read as references to observations by peace officers by means of television cameras or similar electronic devices of activities in circumstances in which persons had reasonable expectations of privacy.

(5.1) Notice after covert entry — A warrant issued under subsection (1) that authorizes a peace officer to enter and search a place covertly shall require, as part of the terms and conditions referred to in subsection (3), that notice of the entry and search be given within any time after the execution of the warrant that the judge considers reasonable in the circumstances.

(5.2) Extension of period for giving notice — Where the judge who issues a warrant under subsection (1) or any other judge having jurisdiction to issue such a warrant is, on the basis of an affidavit submitted in support of an application to vary the period within which the notice referred to in subsection (5.1) is to be given, is satisfied that the interests of justice warrant the granting of the application, the judge may grant an extension, or a subsequent extension, of the period, but no extension may exceed three years.

(6) Execution in Canada — A warrant issued under subsection (1) may be executed at any place in Canada. Any peace officer who executes the warrant must have authority to act as a peace officer in the place where it is executed.

(7) Telewarrant provisions to apply — Where a peace officer believes that it would be impracticable to appear personally before a judge to make an application for a warrant under this section, a warrant may be issued under this section on an information submitted by telephone or other means of telecommunication and, for that purpose, section 487.1 applies, with such modifications as the circumstances require, to the warrant.

1993, c. 40, s. 15; 1997, c. 18, s. 42; 1997, c. 23, s. 13; 2019, c. 25, s. 192

487.011 Definitions — The following definitions apply in this section and in sections 487.012 to 487.0199.

"computer data" has the same meaning as in subsection 342.1(2). *("données informatiques")*

"data" means representations, including signs, signals or symbols, that are capable of being understood by an individual or processed by a computer system or other device. *("données")*

"document" means a medium on which data is registered or marked. *("document")*

"judge" means a judge of a superior court of criminal jurisdiction or a judge of the Court of Quebec. *("juge")*

"public officer" means a public officer who is appointed or designated to administer or enforce a federal or provincial law and whose duties include the enforcement of this Act or any other Act of Parliament. *("fonctionnaire public")*

"tracking data" means data that relates to the location of a transaction, individual or thing. *("données de localisation")*

"transmission data" means data that

(a) relates to the telecommunication functions of dialling, routing, addressing or signalling;

(b) is transmitted to identify, activate or configure a device, including a computer program as defined in subsection 342.1(2), in order to establish or maintain access to a telecommunication service for the purpose of enabling a communication, or is generated during the creation, transmission or reception of a communication and identifies or purports to identify the type, direction, date, time, duration, size, origin, destination or termination of the communication; and

(c) does not reveal the substance, meaning or purpose of the communication.

("données de transmission")

2004, c. 3, s. 7; 2014, c. 31, s. 20

487.012 (1) Preservation demand — A peace officer or public officer may make a demand to a person in Form 5.001 requiring them to preserve computer data that is in their possession or control when the demand is made.

(2) Conditions for making demand — The peace officer or public officer may make the demand only if they have reasonable grounds to suspect that

(a) an offence has been or will be committed under this or any other Act of Parliament or has been committed under a law of a foreign state;

(b) in the case of an offence committed under a law of a foreign state, an investigation is being conducted by a person or authority with responsibility in that state for the investigation of such offences; and

(c) the computer data is in the person's possession or control and will assist in the investigation of the offence.

(3) Limitation — A demand may not be made to a person who is under investigation for the offence referred to in paragraph (2)(a).

(4) Expiry and revocation of demand — A peace officer or public officer may revoke the demand by notice given to the person at any time. Unless the demand is revoked earlier, the demand expires

(a) in the case of an offence that has been or will be committed under this or any other Act of Parliament, 21 days after the day on which it is made; and

(b) in the case of an offence committed under a law of a foreign state, 90 days after the day on which it is made.

(5) Conditions in demand — The peace officer or public officer who makes the demand may impose any conditions in the demand that they consider appropriate — including conditions prohibiting the disclosure of its existence or some or all of its contents — and may revoke a condition at any time by notice given to the person.

(6) No further demand — A peace officer or public officer may not make another demand requiring the person to preserve the same computer data in connection with the investigation.

(7) and (8) [Repealed 2014, c. 31, s. 20.]

2004, c. 3, s. 7; 2014, c. 31, s. 20

487.013 (1) Preservation order — computer data — On *ex parte* application made by a peace officer or public officer, a justice or judge may order a person to preserve computer data that is in their possession or control when they receive the order.

(2) Conditions for making order — Before making the order, the justice or judge must be satisfied by information on oath in Form 5.002

(a) that there are reasonable grounds to suspect that an offence has been or will be committed under this or any other Act of Parliament or has been committed under a law of a foreign state, that the computer data is in the person's possession or control and that it will assist in the investigation of the offence; and

(b) that a peace officer or public officer intends to apply or has applied for a warrant or an order in connection with the investigation to obtain a document that contains the computer data.

(3) Offence against law of foreign state — If an offence has been committed under a law of a foreign state, the justice or judge must also be satisfied that a person or authority with responsibility in that state for the investigation of such offences is conducting the investigation.

(4) Form — The order is to be in Form 5.003.

(5) Limitation — A person who is under investigation for an offence referred to in paragraph (2)(a) may not be made subject to an order.

(6) Expiry of order — Unless the order is revoked earlier, it expires 90 days after the day on which it is made.

2004, c. 3, s. 7; 2014, c. 31, s. 20

487.014 (1) General production order — Subject to sections 487.015 to 487.018, on *ex parte* application made by a peace officer or public officer, a justice or judge may order a person to produce a document that is a copy of a document that is in their possession or control when they receive the order, or to prepare and produce a document containing data that is in their possession or control at that time.

(2) Conditions for making order — Before making the order, the justice or judge must be satisfied by information on oath in Form 5.004 that there are reasonable grounds to believe that

(a) an offence has been or will be committed under this or any other Act of Parliament; and

(b) the document or data is in the person's possession or control and will afford evidence respecting the commission of the offence.

(3) Form — The order is to be in Form 5.005.

(4) Limitation — A person who is under investigation for the offence referred to in subsection (2) may not be made subject to an order.

2004, c. 3, s. 7; 2014, c. 31, s. 20

487.015 (1) Production order to trace specified communication — On *ex parte* application made by a peace officer or public officer for the purpose of identifying a device or person involved in the transmission of a communication, a justice or judge may order a person to prepare and produce a document containing transmission data that is related to that purpose and that is, when they are served with the order, in their possession or control.

(2) Conditions for making order — Before making the order, the justice or judge must be satisfied by information on oath in Form 5.004 that there are reasonable grounds to suspect that

(a) an offence has been or will be committed under this or any other Act of Parliament;

(b) the identification of a device or person involved in the transmission of a communication will assist in the investigation of the offence; and

(c) transmission data that is in the possession or control of one or more persons whose identity is unknown when the application is made will enable that identification.

(3) Form — The order is to be in Form 5.006.

(4) Service — A peace officer or public officer may serve the order on any person who was involved in the transmission of the communication and whose identity was unknown when the application was made

(a) within 60 days after the day on which the order is made; or

(b) within one year after the day on which the order is made, in the case of an offence under section 467.11, 467.12 or 467.13, an offence committed for the benefit of, at the direction of or in association with a criminal organization, or a terrorism offence.

(5) **Limitation** — A person who is under investigation for the offence referred to in subsection (2) may not be made subject to an order.

(6) **Report** — A peace officer or public officer named in the order must provide a written report to the justice or judge who made the order as soon as feasible after the person from whom the communication originated is identified or after the expiry of the period referred to in subsection (4), whichever occurs first. The report must state the name and address of each person on whom the order was served, and the date of service.

2004, c. 3, s. 7; 2014, c. 31, s. 20

487.016 (1) **Production order — transmission data** — On *ex parte* application made by a peace officer or public officer, a justice or judge may order a person to prepare and produce a document containing transmission data that is in their possession or control when they receive the order.

(2) **Conditions for making order** — Before making the order, the justice or judge must be satisfied by information on oath in Form 5.004 that there are reasonable grounds to suspect that

(a) an offence has been or will be committed under this or any other Act of Parliament; and

(b) the transmission data is in the person's possession or control and will assist in the investigation of the offence.

(3) **Form** — The order is to be in Form 5.007.

(4) **Limitation** — A person who is under investigation for the offence referred to in subsection (2) may not be made subject to an order.

2004, c. 3, s. 7; 2014, c. 31, s. 20

487.017 (1) **Production order — tracking data** — On *ex parte* application made by a peace officer or public officer, a justice or judge may order a person to prepare and produce a document containing tracking data that is in their possession or control when they receive the order.

(2) **Conditions for making order** — Before making the order, the justice or judge must be satisfied by information on oath in Form 5.004 that there are reasonable grounds to suspect that

(a) an offence has been or will be committed under this or any other Act of Parliament; and

(b) the tracking data is in the person's possession or control and will assist in the investigation of the offence.

(3) **Form** — The order is to be in Form 5.007.

(4) **Limitation** — A person who is under investigation for the offence referred to in subsection (2) may not be made subject to an order.

2004, c. 3, s. 7; 2014, c. 31, s. 20

487.018 (1) Production order — financial data — On *ex parte* application made by a peace officer or public officer, a justice or judge may order a financial institution, as defined in section 2 of the *Bank Act*, or a person or entity referred to in section 5 of the *Proceeds of Crime (Money Laundering) and Terrorist Financing Act*, to prepare and produce a document setting out the following data that is in their possession or control when they receive the order:

(a) either the account number of a person named in the order or the name of a person whose account number is specified in the order;

(b) the type of account;

(c) the status of the account; and

(d) the date on which it was opened or closed.

(2) Identification of person — For the purpose of confirming the identity of a person who is named or whose account number is specified in the order, the order may also require the institution, person or entity to prepare and produce a document setting out the following data that is in their possession or control:

(a) the date of birth of a person who is named or whose account number is specified in the order;

(b) that person's current address; and

(c) any previous addresses of that person.

(3) Conditions for making order — Before making the order, the justice or judge must be satisfied by information on oath in Form 5.004 that there are reasonable grounds to suspect that

(a) an offence has been or will be committed under this or any other Act of Parliament; and

(b) the data is in the possession or control of the institution, person or entity and will assist in the investigation of the offence.

(4) Form — The order is to be in Form 5.008.

(5) Limitation — A financial institution, person or entity that is under investigation for the offence referred to in subsection (3) may not be made subject to an order.

2014, c. 31, s. 20

487.019 (1) Conditions in preservation and production orders — An order made under any of sections 487.013 to 487.018 may contain any conditions that the justice or judge considers appropriate including, in the case of an order made under section 487.014, conditions to protect a privileged communication between a person who is qualified to give legal advice and their client.

(2) Effect of order — The order has effect throughout Canada.

(3) Power to revoke or vary order — On *ex parte* application made by a peace officer or public officer, the justice or judge who made the order — or a judge in the judicial district where the order was made — may, on the basis of an information on oath in Form 5.0081, revoke or vary the order. The peace officer or public officer must give notice of the revocation or variation to the person who is subject to the order as soon as feasible.

2014, c. 31, s. 20; 2019, c. 25, s. 193

487.0191 (1) Order prohibiting disclosure — On *ex parte* application made by a peace officer or public officer, a justice or judge may make an order prohibiting a person from disclosing the existence or some or all of the contents of a preservation demand made under section 487.012 or a preservation or production order made under any of sections 487.013 to 487.018 during the period set out in the order.

(2) Conditions for making order — Before making the order, the justice or judge must be satisfied by information on oath in Form 5.009 that there are reasonable grounds to believe that the disclosure during that period would jeopardize the conduct of the investigation of the offence to which the preservation demand or the preservation or production order relates.

(3) Form — The order is to be in Form 5.0091.

(4) Application to revoke or vary order — A peace officer or a public officer or a person, financial institution or entity that is subject to an order made under subsection (1) may apply in writing to the justice or judge who made the order — or to a judge in the judicial district where the order was made — to revoke or vary the order.

2014, c. 31, s. 20

487.0192 (1) Particulars — production orders — An order made under any of sections 487.014 and 487.016 to 487.018 must require a person, financial institution or entity to produce the document to a peace officer or public officer named in the order within the time, at the place and in the form specified in the order.

(2) Particulars — production order to trace specified communication — An order made under section 487.015 must require a person to produce the document to a peace officer or public officer named in the order as soon as feasible after they are served with the order at the place and in the form specified in the order.

(3) Form of production — For greater certainty, an order under any of sections 487.014 to 487.018 may specify that a document may be produced on or through an electro-magnetic medium.

(4) Non-application — For greater certainty, sections 489.1 and 490 do not apply to a document that is produced under an order under any of sections 487.014 to 487.018.

(5) Probative force of copies — Every copy of a document produced under section 487.014 is admissible in evidence in proceedings under this or any other Act of Parliament on proof by affidavit that it is a true copy and has the same probative force as the document would have if it were proved in the ordinary way.

(6) Canada Evidence Act — A document that is prepared for the purpose of production is considered to be original for the purposes of the *Canada Evidence Act*.

2014, c. 31, s. 20

487.0193 (1) Application for review of production order — Before they are required by an order made under any of sections 487.014 to 487.018 to produce a document, a person, financial institution or entity may apply in writing to the justice or judge who made the order — or to a judge in the judicial district where the order was made — to revoke or vary the order.

(2) Notice required — The person, institution or entity may make the application only if they give notice of their intention to do so to a peace officer or public officer named in the order within 30 days after the day on which the order is made.

(3) No obligation to produce — The person, institution or entity is not required to prepare or produce the document until a final decision is made with respect to the application.

(4) Revocation or variation of order — The justice or judge may revoke or vary the order if satisfied that

(a) it is unreasonable in the circumstances to require the applicant to prepare or produce the document; or

(b) production of the document would disclose information that is privileged or otherwise protected from disclosure by law.

2014, c. 31, s. 20

487.0194 (1) Destruction of preserved computer data and documents — preservation demand — A person to whom a preservation demand is made under section 487.012 shall destroy the computer data that would not be retained in the ordinary course of business and any document that is prepared for the purpose of preserving computer data under that section as soon as feasible after the demand expires or is revoked, unless they are subject to an order made under any of sections 487.013 to 487.017 with respect to the computer data.

(2) Destruction of preserved computer data and documents — preservation order — A person who is subject to a preservation order made under section 487.013 shall destroy the computer data that would not be retained in the ordinary course of business and any document that is prepared for the purpose of preserving computer data under that section as soon as feasible after the order expires or is revoked, unless they are subject to a new preservation order or to a production order made under any of sections 487.014 to 487.017 with respect to the computer data.

(3) Destruction of preserved computer data and documents — production order — A person who is subject to a production order made under any of sections 487.014 to 487.017 with respect to computer data that they preserved under a preservation demand or order made under section 487.012 or 487.013 shall destroy the computer data that would not be retained in the ordinary course of business and any document that is prepared for the purpose of preserving computer data under that section as soon as feasible after the earlier of

(a) the day on which the production order is revoked, and

(b) the day on which a document that contains the computer data is produced under the production order.

(4) Destruction of preserved computer data and documents — warrant — Despite subsections (1) to (3), a person who preserved computer data under a preservation demand or order made under section 487.012 or 487.013 shall destroy the computer data that would not be retained in the ordinary course of business and any document that is prepared for the purpose of preserving computer data under that section when a document that contains the computer data is obtained under a warrant.

2014, c. 31, s. 20

487.0195 (1) For greater certainty — For greater certainty, no preservation demand, preservation order or production order is necessary for a peace officer or public officer to ask a person to voluntarily preserve data that the person is not prohibited by law from preserving or to voluntarily provide a document to the officer that the person is not prohibited by law from disclosing.

(2) No civil or criminal liability — A person who preserves data or provides a document in those circumstances does not incur any criminal or civil liability for doing so.

2014, c. 31, s. 20

487.0196 Self-incrimination — No one is excused from complying with an order made under any of sections 487.014 to 487.018 on the ground that the document that they are required to produce may tend to incriminate them or subject them to a proceeding or penalty. However, no document that an individual is required to prepare may be used or received in evidence against them in a criminal proceeding that is subsequently instituted against them, other than a prosecution for an offence under section 132, 136 or 137.

2014, c. 31, s. 20

487.0197 Offence — preservation demand — A person who contravenes a preservation demand made under section 487.012 without lawful excuse is guilty of an offence punishable on summary conviction and is liable to a fine of not more than $5,000.

2014, c. 31, s. 20

487.0198 Offence — preservation or production order — A person, financial institution or entity that contravenes an order made under any of sections 487.013 to 487.018 without lawful excuse is guilty of an offence punishable on summary conviction and liable to a fine of not more than $250,000 or to imprisonment for a term of not more than two years less a day, or to both.

2014, c. 31, s. 20; 2019, c. 25, s. 194

487.0199 Offence — destruction of preserved data — A person who contravenes section 487.0194 without lawful excuse is guilty of an offence punishable on summary conviction.

2014, c. 31, s. 20

487.02 Assistance order — If an authorization is given under section 184.2, 184.3, 186 or 188 or a warrant is issued under this Act, the judge or justice who gives the authorization or issues the warrant may order a person to provide assistance, if the person's assistance may reasonably be considered to be required to give effect to the authorization or warrant. The order has effect throughout Canada.

1993, c. 40, s. 15; 1997, c. 18, s. 43; 2014, c. 31, s. 20; 2019, c. 25, s. 195

487.021 (1) Review — Within seven years after the coming into force of this section, a comprehensive review of the provisions and operation of sections 487.011 to 487.02 shall be undertaken by such committee of the House of Commons as may be designated or established by the House for that purpose.

(2) Report — The committee referred to in subsection (1) shall, within a year after a review is undertaken pursuant to that subsection or within such further time as the House may authorize, submit a report on the review to the Speaker of the House, including a statement of any changes the committee recommends.

2014, c. 31, s. 20

487.03 [Repealed 2019, c. 25, s. 196.]

Forensic DNA Analysis

487.04 Definitions — In this section and in sections 487.05 to 487.0911,

"adult" has the meaning assigned by subsection 2(1) of the *Youth Criminal Justice Act*;

"designated offence" means a primary designated offence or a secondary designated offence;

"DNA" means deoxyribonucleic acid;

"forensic DNA analysis"

(a) in relation to a bodily substance that is taken from a person in execution of a warrant under section 487.05, means forensic DNA analysis of the bodily substance and the comparison of the results of that analysis with the results of the analysis of the DNA in the bodily substance referred to in paragraph 487.05(1)(b), and includes any incidental tests associated with that analysis, and

(b) in relation to a bodily substance that is provided voluntarily in the course of an investigation of a designated offence or is taken from a person under an order made under section 487.051 or an authorization granted under section 487.055 or 487.091, or to a bodily substance referred to in paragraph 487.05(1)(b), means forensic DNA analysis of the bodily substance;

"primary designated offence" means

(a) an offence under any of the following provisions, namely,

(i) subsection 7(4.1) (offence in relation to sexual offences against children),

(i.1) section 151 (sexual interference),

(i.2) section 152 (invitation to sexual touching),

(i.3) section 153 (sexual exploitation),

(i.4) section 153.1 (sexual exploitation of person with disability),

(i.5) section 155 (incest),

(i.6) subsection 160(2) (compelling the commission of bestiality),

(i.7) subsection 160(3) (bestiality in presence of or by a child),

(i.8) section 163.1 (child pornography),

(i.9) section 170 (parent or guardian procuring sexual activity),

(i.901) section 171.1 (making sexually explicit material available to child),

(i.91) section 172.1 (luring a child),

(i.911) section 172.2 (agreement or arrangement — sexual offence against child),

(i.92) subsection 173(2) (exposure),

(i.93) to (i.96) [Repealed 2014, c. 25, s. 23(1).]

(ii) section 235 (murder),

(iii) section 236 (manslaughter),

(iv) section 239 (attempt to commit murder),

(v) section 244 (discharging firearm with intent),

(vi) section 244.1 (causing bodily harm with intent — air gun or pistol),

(vi.1) section 244.2 (discharging firearm — recklessness),

(vii) paragraph 245(a) (administering noxious thing with intent to endanger life or cause bodily harm),

(viii) section 246 (overcoming resistance to commission of offence),

(ix) section 267 (assault with a weapon or causing bodily harm),

(x) section 268 (aggravated assault),

(xi) section 269 (unlawfully causing bodily harm),

(xi.1) section 270.01 (assaulting peace officer with weapon or causing bodily harm),

(xi.2) section 270.02 (aggravated assault of peace officer),

(xi.3) section 271 (sexual assault),

(xii) section 272 (sexual assault with a weapon, threats to a third party or causing bodily harm),

(xiii) section 273 (aggravated sexual assault),

(xiii.1) subsection 273.3(2) (removal of a child from Canada),

(xiv) section 279 (kidnapping),

(xiv.1) section 279.011 (trafficking — person under 18 years),

(xiv.2) subsection 279.02(2) (material benefit — trafficking of person under 18 years), (xiv.3) subsection 279.03(2) (withholding or destroying documents — trafficking of person under 18 years),

(xiv.4) subsection 286.1(2) (obtaining sexual services for consideration from person under 18 years),

(xiv.5) subsection 286.2(2) (material benefit from sexual services provided by person under 18 years),

(xiv.6) subsection 286.3(2) (procuring — person under 18 years),

(xv) section 344 (robbery), and

(xvi) section 346 (extortion),

(a.1) an offence under any of the following provisions, namely,

(i) section 75 (piratical acts),

(i.01) section 76 (hijacking),

(i.02) section 77 (endangering safety of aircraft or airport),

(i.03) section 78.1 (seizing control of ship or fixed platform),

(i.04) subsection 81(1) (using explosives),

(i.041) section 82.3 (possession, etc., of nuclear material, radioactive material or device),

(i.042) section 82.4 (use or alteration of nuclear material, radioactive material or device),

(i.043) section 82.5 (commission of indictable offence to obtain nuclear material, etc.),

(i.044) section 82.6 (threats),

(i.05) section 83.18 (participation in activity of terrorist group),

(i.051) section 83.181 (leaving Canada to participate in activity of terrorist group),

(i.06) section 83.19 (facilitating terrorist activity),

(i.061) section 83.191 (leaving Canada to facilitate terrorist activity),

(i.07) section 83.2 (commission of offence for terrorist group),

(i.071) section 83.201 (leaving Canada to commit offence for terrorist group),

(i.072) section 83.202 (leaving Canada to commit offence that is terrorist activity),

(i.08) section 83.21 (instructing to carry out activity for terrorist group),

(i.09) section 83.22 (instructing to carry out terrorist activity),

(i.091) section 83.221 (counselling commission of terrorism offence),

(i.1) section 83.23 (harbouring or concealing),

(i.11) to (iii.1) [Repealed 2010, c. 17, s. 3(4).]

(iv) [Repealed 2014, c. 25, s. 23(3).]

(iv.1) to (iv.5) [Repealed 2010, c. 17, s. 3(4).]

(v) [Repealed 2014, c. 25, s. 23(3).]

(v.1) and (v.2) [Repealed 2010, c. 17, s. 3(4).]

(vi) section 233 (infanticide),

(vii) [Repealed 2010, c. 17, s. 3(5).]

(vii.1) section 279.01 (trafficking in persons),

(vii.11) subsection 279.02(1) (material benefit — trafficking),

(vii.12) subsection 279.03(1) (withholding or destroying documents — trafficking),

(viii) section 279.1 (hostage taking),

(viii.1) subsection 286.2(1) (material benefit from sexual services),

(viii.2) subsection 286.3(1) (procuring),

(ix) paragraph 348(1)(d) (breaking and entering a dwelling-house),

(x) section 423.1 (intimidation of a justice system participant or journalist),

(xi) section 431 (attack on premises, residence or transport of internationally protected person),

(xii) section 431.1 (attack on premises, accommodation or transport of United Nations or associated personnel),

(xiii) subsection 431.2(2) (explosive or other lethal device),

(xiv) section 467.11 (participation in activities of criminal organization),

(xiv.1) section 467.111 (recruitment of members — criminal organization),

(xv) section 467.12 (commission of offence for criminal organization), and

(xvi) section 467.13 (instructing commission of offence for criminal organization),

(xvi.1) to (xx) [Repealed 2005, c. 25, s. 1(4).]

(b) an offence under any of the following provisions of the *Criminal Code*, chapter C-34 of the Revised Statutes of Canada, 1970, as they read from time to time before January 4, 1983, namely,

(i) section 144 (rape),

(i.1) section 145 (attempt to commit rape),

(ii) section 146 (sexual intercourse with female under fourteen and between fourteen and sixteen),

(iii) section 148 (sexual intercourse with feeble-minded, etc.),

(iv) section 149 (indecent assault on female),

(v) section 156 (indecent assault on male),

(vi) section 157 (acts of gross indecency), and

(vii) subsection 246(1) (assault with intent) if the intent is to commit an offence referred to in subparagraphs (i) to (vi),

(c) an offence under any of the following provisions of the *Criminal Code*, chapter C-34 of the Revised Statutes of Canada, 1970, as they read from time to time before January 1, 1988:

(i) subsection 146(1) (sexual intercourse with a female under age of 14),

(ii) subsection 146(2) (sexual intercourse with a female between ages of 14 and 16),

(iii) section 153 (sexual intercourse with step-daughter),

(iv) section 157 (gross indecency),

(v) section 166 (parent or guardian procuring defilement), and

(vi) section 167 (householder permitting defilement),

(c.01) an offence under any of the following provisions of the *Criminal Code*, chapter C-34 of the Revised Statutes of Canada, 1970, as enacted by section 19 of *An Act to amend the Criminal Code in relation to sexual offences and other offences against the person and to amend certain other Acts in relation thereto or in consequence thereof*, chapter 125 of the Statutes of Canada, 1980-81-82-83:

(i) section 246.1 (sexual assault),

(ii) section 246.2 (sexual assault with a weapon, threats to a third party or causing bodily harm), and

(iii) section 246.3 (aggravated sexual assault),

(c.02) an offence under any of the following provisions of this Act, as they read from time to time before the day on which this paragraph comes into force:

(i) paragraph 212(1)(i) (stupefying or overpowering for the purpose of sexual intercourse),

(ii) subsection 212(2) (living on the avails of prostitution of person under 18 years),

(iii) subsection 212(2.1) (aggravated offence in relation to living on the avails of prostitution of person under 18 years), and

(iv) subsection 212(4) (prostitution of person under 18 years),

(c.03) an offence under any of paragraphs 212(1)(a) to (h) (procuring) of this Act, as they read from time to time before the day on which this paragraph comes into force,

(c.1) an offence under any of the following provisions of the *Security of Information Act*, namely,

(i) section 6 (approaching, entering, etc., a prohibited place),

(ii) subsection 20(1) (threats or violence), and

(iii) subsection 21(1) (harbouring or concealing), and

(d) an attempt to commit or, other than for the purposes of subsection 487.05(1), a conspiracy to commit an offence referred to in any of paragraphs (a) to (c.03);

"provincial court judge", in relation to a young person, includes a youth justice court judge within the meaning of subsection 2(1) of the *Youth Criminal Justice Act*;

"secondary designated offence" means an offence, other than a primary designated offence, that is

(a) an offence under this Act that may be prosecuted by indictment — or, for section 487.051 to apply, is prosecuted by indictment — for which the maximum punishment is imprisonment for five years or more,

(a.1) an offence under any of the following provisions of the *Cannabis Act* that may be prosecuted by indictment — or, for section 487.051 to apply, is prosecuted by indictment — for which the maximum punishment is imprisonment for five years or more:

(i) section 9 (distribution and possession for purpose of distributing),

(ii) section 10 (selling and possession for purpose of selling),

(iii) section 11 (importing and exporting and possession for purpose of exporting),

(iv) section 12 (production),

(v) section 13 (possession, etc., for use in production or distribution of illicit cannabis), and

(vi) section 14 (use of young person),

(b) an offence under any of the following provisions of the *Controlled Drugs and Substances Act* that may be prosecuted by indictment — or, for section 487.051 to apply, is prosecuted by indictment — for which the maximum punishment is imprisonment for five years or more:

(i) section 5 (trafficking in substance and possession for purpose of trafficking),

(ii) section 6 (importing and exporting), and

(iii) section 7 (production of substance),

(c) an offence under any of the following provisions of this Act:

(i) subsection 52(1) (sabotage),

(i.001) subsection 57(3) (possession of a forged passport),

(i.002) section 62 (offences in relation to military forces),

(i.003) subsection 65(2) (riot — concealing identity),

(i.004) subsection 70(3) (contravening order made by governor in council),

(i.005) subsection 82(1) (explosives, possession without lawful excuse),

(i.006) subsection 121(1) (frauds on the government),

(i.007) subsection 121(2) (contractor subscribing to election fund),

(i.008) section 122 (breach of trust by public officer),

(i.009) subsection 123(1) (municipal corruption),

(i.01) subsection 123(2) (influencing municipal official),

(i.011) section 124 (selling or purchasing office),

(i.012) section 125 (influencing or negotiating appointments or dealings in offices),

(i.013) subsection 139(2) (obstructing justice),

(i.014) section 142 (corruptly taking reward for recovery of goods),

(i.015) section 144 (prison breach),

(i.016) section 145 (escape and being at large without excuse),

(i.1) section 146 (permitting or assisting escape),

(i.2) section 147 (rescue or permitting escape),

(i.3) section 148 (assisting prisoner of war to escape),

(i.4) and (ii) [Repealed 2010, c. 17, s. 3(10).]

(iii) subsection 173(1) (indecent acts),

(iv) section 182 (dead body — neglect to perform duty, improper or indecent interference with),

(iv.1) section 184 (interception of private communication),

(iv.2) section 184.5 (interception of radio-based telephone communications),

(iv.3) section 221 (cause bodily harm by criminal negligence),

(iv.4) section 237 (infanticide),

(iv.5) section 242 (neglect to obtain assistance in child-birth),

(iv.6) subsection 247(1) (traps likely to cause bodily harm),

(iv.7) subsection 247(2) (traps — causing bodily harm),

(iv.8) subsection 247(3) (traps — in a place kept or used for committing other indictable offence),

(iv.9) section 262 (impeding attempt to save life),

(v) section 264 (criminal harassment),

(vi) section 264.1 (uttering threats),

(vii) section 266 (assault),

(viii) section 270 (assaulting a peace officer),

(viii.01) section 280 (abduction of person under 16),

(viii.02) section 281 (abduction of person under 14),

(viii.1) subsection 286.1(1) (obtaining sexual services for consideration),

(viii.11) section 291 (bigamy),

(viii.12) section 292 (procuring feigned marriage),

(viii.13) section 293 (polygamy),

(viii.14) section 293.1 (forced marriage),

(viii.15) section 293.2 (marriage under age of 16 years),

(viii.16) section 300 (publishing defamatory libel known to be false),

(viii.17) section 302 (extortion by libel),

(viii.2) subsection 320.16(1) (failure to stop after accident),

(viii.21) paragraph 334(a) (theft over $5,000 or testamentary instrument),

(viii.22) section 338 (fraudulently taking cattle or defacing brand),

(viii.23) subsection 339(1) (take possession of drift timber, etc.),

(viii.24) section 340 (destroying documents of title),

(ix) paragraph 348(1)(e) (breaking and entering a place other than a dwelling-house),

(x) section 349 (being unlawfully in dwelling-house), and

(x.1) subsection 351(2) (disguise with intent),

(x.11) paragraph 355(a) (possession of property over $5,000 or testamentary instrument),

(x.12) section 357 (bring into Canada property obtained by crime),

(x.13) paragraph 362(2)(a) (false pretence, property over $5,000 or testamentary instrument),

(x.14) subsection 362(3) (obtain credit, etc. by false pretence),

(x.15) section 363 (obtain execution of valuable security by fraud),

(x.16) subsection 377(1) (damaging documents),

(x.17) section 378 (offences in relation to registers),

(x.18) section 382 (manipulation of stock exchange),

(x.19) subsection 382.1(1) (prohibited insider trading),

(x.2) section 383 (gaming in stocks or merchandise),

(x.21) section 384 (broker reducing stock by selling his own account),

(x.22) section 386 (fraudulent registration of title),

(x.23) section 394 (fraud in relation to minerals),

(x.24) section 394.1 (possession of stolen minerals),

(x.25) section 396 (offences in relation to mines),

(x.26) section 397 (falsification of books and documents),

(x.27) section 399 (false return by public officer),

(x.28) section 400 (false prospectus),

(x.29) section 405 (acknowledging instrument in false name),

(xi) section 423 (intimidation),

(xi.1) section 424 (threat against an internationally protected person),

(xi.11) section 424.1 (threat against United Nations or associated personnel),

(xi.12) section 426 (secret commissions),

(xi.13) section 435 (arson for fraudulent purpose),

(xi.14) section 436 (arson by negligence),

(xi.15) section 436.1 (possession incendiary material),

(xi.16) subsection 438(1) (interfering with saving of a wrecked vessel),

(xi.17) subsection 439(2) (interfering with a marine signal),

(xi.18) section 441 (occupant injuring building),

(xi.19) section 443 (interfering with international boundary marks, etc.),

(xi.2) section 451 (having clippings, etc.),

(xi.21) section 460 (advertising and dealing in counterfeit money),

(xi.22) subparagraphs 465(1)(b)(i) and (ii) (conspiracy to prosecute),

(xi.23) section 753.3 (breach of long-term supervision).

(d) an offence under any of the following provisions of the *Criminal Code*, as they read from time to time before July 1, 1990:

(i) section 433 (arson), and

(ii) section 434 (setting fire to other substance),

(d.1) an offence under section 252, as it read from time to time before the day on which section 14 of *An Act to amend the Criminal Code (offences relating to conveyances) and to make consequential amendments to other Acts* comes into force;

(d.2) an offence under any of sections 249, 249.1, 249.2, 249.3, 249.4, 253, 254 and 255, as they read from time to time before the day on which section 14 of *An Act to amend the Criminal Code (offences relating to conveyances) and to make consequential amendments to other Acts* comes into force, that may be prosecuted by indictment or, for section 487.051 to apply, is prosecuted by indictment; and

(e) an attempt to commit or, other than for the purposes of subsection 487.05(1), a conspiracy to commit

(i) an offence referred to in paragraph (a) or (b) — which, for section 487.051 to apply, is prosecuted by indictment, or

(ii) an offence referred to in any of paragraphs (c) to (d.2);

"Young Offenders Act" means chapter Y-1 of the Revised Statutes of Canada, 1985;

"young person" has the meaning assigned by subsection 2(1) of the *Youth Criminal Justice Act* or subsection 2(1) of the *Young Offenders Act*, as the case may be.

1995, c. 27, s. 1; 1998, c. 37, s. 15; 2001, c. 41, s. 17; 2002, c. 1, s. 175; 2005, c. 25, s. 1; 2005, c. 43, ss. 5, 9(2); 2007, c. 22, ss. 8, 47(1); 2008, c. 6, s. 35 [Amended 2008, c. 6, s. 63(2).]; 2009, c. 22, s. 16; 2010, c. 3, s. 6; 2010, c. 17, s. 3; 2012, c. 1, s. 30; 2013, c. 9, s. 16; 2013, c. 13, s. 8; 2014, c. 17, s. 13; 2014, c. 25, s. 23; 2015, c. 20, s. 23; 2018, c. 16, s. 216; 2018, c. 21, s. 18; 2019, c. 13, s. 152; 2019, c. 25, s. 196.1

487.05 (1) Information for warrant to take bodily substances for forensic DNA analysis — A provincial court judge who on *ex parte* application made in Form 5.01 is satisfied by information on oath that there are reasonable grounds to believe

(a) that a designated offence has been committed,

(b) that a bodily substance has been found or obtained

(i) at the place where the offence was committed,

(ii) on or within the body of the victim of the offence,

(iii) on anything worn or carried by the victim at the time when the offence was committed, or

(iv) on or within the body of any person or thing or at any place associated with the commission of the offence,

(c) that a person was a party to the offence, and

(d) that forensic DNA analysis of a bodily substance from the person will provide evidence about whether the bodily substance referred to in paragraph (b) was from that person

and who is satisfied that it is in the best interests of the administration of justice to do so may issue a warrant in Form 5.02 authorizing the taking, from that person, for the purpose of forensic DNA analysis, of any number of samples of one or more bodily substances that is reasonably required for that purpose, by means of the investigative procedures described in subsection 487.06(1).

(2) **Criteria** — In considering whether to issue the warrant, the provincial court judge shall have regard to all relevant matters, including

(a) the nature of the designated offence and the circumstances of its commission; and

(b) whether there is

(i) a peace officer who is able, by virtue of training or experience, to take samples of bodily substances from the person, by means of the investigative procedures described in subsection 487.06(1), or

(ii) another person who is able, by virtue of training or experience, to take, under the direction of a peace officer, samples of bodily substances from the person, by means of those investigative procedures.

(3) **Telewarrant** — Where a peace officer believes that it would be impracticable to appear personally before a judge to make an application for a warrant under this section, a warrant may be issued under this section on an information submitted by telephone or other means of telecommunication and, for that purpose, section 487.1 applies, with such modifications as the circumstances require, to the warrant.

(4) **Execution in Canada** — A warrant issued under subsection (1) may be executed at any place in Canada. Any peace officer who executes the warrant must have authority to act as a peace officer in the place where it is executed.

1995, c. 27, s. 1; 1997, c. 18, s. 44; 1998, c. 37, s. 16; 2019, c. 25, s. 197

487.051 (1) Order — primary designated offences — The court shall make an order in Form 5.03 authorizing the taking of the number of samples of bodily substances that is reasonably required for the purpose of forensic DNA analysis from a person who is convicted, discharged under section 730 or found guilty under the *Youth Criminal Justice Act* or the *Young Offenders Act*, of an offence committed at any time, including before June 30, 2000, if that offence is a primary designated offence within the meaning of paragraphs (a) and (c.02) of the definition "primary designated offence" in section 487.04 when the person is sentenced or discharged.

(2) Order — primary designated offences — The court shall make such an order in Form 5.03 in relation to a person who is convicted, discharged under section 730 or found guilty under the *Youth Criminal Justice Act* or the *Young Offenders Act*, of an offence committed at any time, including before June 30, 2000, if that offence is a primary designated offence within the meaning of any of paragraphs (a.1) to (c.01) and (c.03) to (d) of the definition "primary designated offence" in section 487.04 when the person is sentenced or discharged. However, the court is not required to make the order if it is satisfied that the person has established that the impact of such an order on their privacy and security of the person would be grossly disproportionate to the public interest in the protection of society and the proper administration of justice, to be achieved through the early detection, arrest and conviction of offenders.

(3) Order — persons found not criminally responsible and secondary designated offences — The court may, on application by the prosecutor and if it is satisfied that it is in the best interests of the administration of justice to do so, make such an order in Form 5.04 in relation to

(a) a person who is found not criminally responsible on account of mental disorder for an offence committed at any time, including before June 30, 2000, if that offence is a designated offence when the finding is made; or

(b) a person who is convicted, discharged under section 730 or found guilty under the *Youth Criminal Justice Act* or the *Young Offenders Act*, of an offence committed at any time, including before June 30, 2000, if that offence is a secondary designated offence when the person is sentenced or discharged.

In deciding whether to make the order, the court shall consider the person's criminal record, whether they were previously found not criminally responsible on account of mental disorder for a designated offence, the nature of the offence, the circumstances surrounding its commission and the impact such an order would have on the person's privacy and security of the person and shall give reasons for its decision.

(4) Order to offender — When the court makes an order authorizing the taking of samples of bodily substances, it may make an order in Form 5.041 to require the person to report at the place, day and time set out in the order and submit to the taking of the samples.

1998, c. 37, s. 17; 2002, c. 1, s. 176; 2005, c. 25, s. 3; 2007, c. 22, ss. 9, 47(2); 2014, c. 25, s. 24

487.052 [Repealed 2005, c. 25, s. 4. Amended 2007, c. 22, s. 3.]

487.053 (1) Timing of order — The court may make an order under section 487.051 authorizing the taking of samples of bodily substances when it imposes a sentence on a person, finds the person not criminally responsible on account of mental disorder or directs that they be discharged under section 730.

(2) Hearing — If the court does not consider the matter at that time, it

(a) shall, within 90 days after the day on which it imposes the sentence, makes the finding or directs that the person be discharged, set a date for a hearing to do so;

(b) retains jurisdiction over the matter; and

(c) may require the person to appear by closed-circuit television or videoconference, as long as the person is given the opportunity to communicate privately with counsel if they are represented by counsel.

1998, c. 37, s. 17; 2000, c. 10, s. 14; 2005, c. 25, s. 4 [Amended 2007, c. 22, s. 3.]; 2019, c. 25, s. 198

487.054 Appeal — The offender or the prosecutor may appeal from a decision of the court under any of subsections 487.051(1) to (3).

1998, c. 37, s. 17; 2007, c. 22, s. 10

487.055 (1) Offenders serving sentences — A provincial court judge may, on *ex parte* application made in Form 5.05, authorize in Form 5.06 the taking, for the purpose of forensic DNA analysis, of any number of samples of bodily substances that is reasonably required for that purpose, by means of the investigative procedures described in subsection 487.06(1), from a person who, before June 30, 2000,

(a) had been declared a dangerous offender under Part XXIV;

(b) had been declared a dangerous offender or a dangerous sexual offender under Part XXI of the *Criminal Code*, being chapter C-34 of the Revised Statutes of Canada, 1970, as it read from time to time before January 1, 1988;

(c) had been convicted of murder;

(c.1) had been convicted of attempted murder or conspiracy to commit murder or to cause another person to be murdered and, on the date of the application, is serving a sentence of imprisonment for that offence;

(d) had been convicted of a sexual offence within the meaning of subsection (3) and, on the date of the application, is serving a sentence of imprisonment for that offence; or

(e) had been convicted of manslaughter and, on the date of the application, is serving a sentence of imprisonment for that offence.

(2) Certificate — The application shall be accompanied by a certificate referred to in paragraph 667(1)(a) that establishes that the person is a person referred to in subsection (1). The certificate may be received in evidence without giving the notice referred to in subsection 667(4).

(3) Definition of "sexual offence" — For the purposes of subsection (1), **"sexual offence"** means

(a) an offence under any of the following provisions, namely,

(i) section 151 (sexual interference),

(ii) section 152 (invitation to sexual touching),

(iii) section 153 (sexual exploitation),

(iv) section 155 (incest),

(v) subsection 212(4) (offence in relation to juvenile prostitution),

(vi) section 271 (sexual assault),

(vii) section 272 (sexual assault with a weapon, threats to a third party or causing bodily harm), and

(viii) section 273 (aggravated sexual assault);

(a.1) an offence under subsection 348(1) if the indictable offence referred to in that subsection is a sexual offence within the meaning of paragraph (a), (b), (c) or (d);

(b) an offence under any of the following provisions of the *Criminal Code*, chapter C-34 of the Revised Statutes of Canada, 1970, as they read from time to time before January 4, 1983, namely,

(i) section 144 (rape),

(ii) section 146 (sexual intercourse with female under fourteen or between fourteen and sixteen),

(iii) section 148 (sexual intercourse with feeble-minded, etc.),

(iv) section 149 (indecent assault on female),

(v) section 156 (indecent assault on male), or

(vi) section 157 (acts of gross indecency);

(c) an offence under paragraph 153(1)(a) (sexual intercourse with step-daughter, etc.) of the *Criminal Code*, chapter C-34 of the Revised Statutes of Canada, 1970, as it read from time to time before January 1, 1988; and

(d) an attempt to commit an offence referred to in any of paragraphs (a) to (c).

(3.01) Manner of appearance — The court may require a person who is given notice of an application under subsection (1) and who wishes to appear at the hearing to appear by closed-circuit television or videoconference, as long as the person is given the opportunity to communicate privately with counsel if they are represented by counsel.

(3.1) Criteria — In deciding whether to grant an authorization under subsection (1), the court shall consider the person's criminal record, the nature of the offence and the circumstances surrounding its commission and the impact such an authorization would have on the privacy and security of the person and shall give reasons for its decision.

(3.11) Order — If the court authorizes the taking of samples of bodily substances from a person who is on conditional release and who has appeared at the hearing, it shall make an order in Form 5.041 to require the person to report at the place, day and time set out in the order and submit to the taking of the samples.

(4) Summons — However, if a person who is on conditional release has not appeared at the hearing, a summons in Form 5.061 setting out the information referred to in paragraphs 487.07(1)(b) to (d) shall be directed to them requiring them to report at the place, day and time set out in the summons and submit to the taking of the samples.

(5) Service on individual — The summons shall be accompanied by a copy of the authorization referred to in subsection (1) and be served by a peace officer who shall either deliver it personally to the person to whom it is directed or, if that person cannot conveniently be found, leave it for the person at their latest or usual place of residence with any person found there who appears to be at least sixteen years of age.

(6) [Repealed 2008, c. 18, s. 13.]

(7) to (10) [Repealed 2007, c. 22, s. 11(4).]

1998, c. 37, s. 17; 2000, c. 10, s. 15; 2005, c. 25, s. 5; 2007, c. 22, s. 11; 2008, c. 18, s. 13; 2019, c. 25, s. 199

487.0551 (1) Failure to appear — If a person fails to appear at the place, day and time set out in an order made under subsection 487.051(4) or 487.055(3.11) or in a summons referred to in subsection 487.055(4) or 487.091(3), a justice of the peace may issue a warrant for their arrest in Form 5.062 to allow samples of bodily substances to be taken.

(2) Execution of warrant — The warrant may be executed anywhere in Canada by a peace officer who has jurisdiction in that place or over the person. The warrant remains in force until it is executed.

2007, c. 22, s. 12

487.0552 (1) Failure to comply with order or summons — Every person who, without reasonable excuse, fails to comply with an order made under subsection 487.051(4) or 487.055(3.11) of this Act or under subsection 196.14(4) or 196.24(4) of the *National Defence Act*, or with a summons referred to in subsection 487.055(4) or 487.091(3) of this Act, is guilty of

(a) an indictable offence and liable to imprisonment for a term of not more than two years; or

(b) an offence punishable on summary conviction.

(2) For greater certainty — For greater certainty, a lawful command that prevents a person from complying with an order or summons is a reasonable excuse if, at the time, the person is subject to the Code of Service Discipline within the meaning of subsection 2(1) of the *National Defence Act*.

2007, c. 22, s. 12

487.056 (1) When collection to take place — Samples of bodily substances shall be taken as authorized under section 487.051

(a) at the place, day and time set out in an order made under subsection 487.051(4) or as soon as feasible afterwards; or

(b) in any other case, on the day on which the order authorizing the taking of the samples is made or as soon as feasible afterwards.

(2) When collection to take place — Samples of bodily substances shall be taken as authorized under section 487.055 or 487.091

(a) at the place, day and time set out in an order made under subsection 487.055(3.11) or a summons referred to in subsection 487.055(4) or 487.091(3) or as soon as feasible afterwards; or

(b) in any other case, as soon as feasible after the authorization is granted.

(3) When collection to take place — If a person fails to appear as required by an order made under subsection 487.051(4) or 487.055(3.11) or a summons referred to in subsection 487.055(4) or 487.091(3), samples of bodily substances shall be taken

(a) when the person is arrested under a warrant issued under subsection 487.0551(1) or as soon as feasible afterwards; or

(b) as soon as feasible after the person appears at the place set out in the order or summons if no warrant is issued.

(4) Appeal — Subsections (1) to (3) apply even if the order or authorization to take the samples of bodily substances is appealed.

(5) Collection of samples — A peace officer who is authorized under section 487.051, 487.055 or 487.091 to take samples of bodily substances may cause the samples to be taken in any place in Canada in which the person who is subject to the order or authorization is located.

(6) Who collects samples — The samples shall be taken by a peace officer who has jurisdiction over the person or in the place in which the samples are taken — or a person acting under their direction — who is able, by virtue of training or experience, to take them.

1998, c. 37, s. 17; 2000, c. 10, s. 16; 2002, c. 1, s. 179; 2005, c. 25, s. 6; 2007, c. 22, s. 13

487.057 (1) Report of peace officer — A peace officer who takes samples of bodily substances from a person or who causes a person who is not a peace officer to take samples under their direction shall, as soon as feasible after the samples are taken, make a written report in Form 5.07 and cause the report to be filed with

(a) the provincial court judge who issued the warrant under section 487.05 or granted the authorization under section 487.055 or 487.091 or another judge of that provincial court; or

(b) the court that made the order under section 487.051.

(2) Contents of report — The report shall include

(a) a statement of the time and date the samples were taken; and

(b) a description of the bodily substances that were taken.

(3) Copy of report — A peace officer who takes the samples or causes the samples to be taken under their direction at the request of another peace officer shall send a copy of the report to the other peace officer unless that other peace officer had jurisdiction to take the samples.

1998, c. 37, s. 17; 2000, c. 10, s. 17; 2007, c. 22, s. 14

487.058 No criminal or civil liability — No peace officer, and no person acting under a peace officer's direction, incurs any criminal or civil liability for anything necessarily done with reasonable care and skill in the taking of samples of bodily substances from a person under a warrant issued under section 487.05, an order made under section 487.051 or an authorization granted under section 487.055 or 487.091.

1998, c. 37, s. 17; 2000, c. 10, s. 18; 2007, c. 22, s. 15

487.06 (1) Investigative procedures — A peace officer or a person acting under a peace officer's direction is authorized by a warrant issued under section 487.05, an order made under section 487.051 or an authorization granted under section 487.055 or 487.091 to take samples of bodily substances by any of the following means:

(a) the plucking of individual hairs from the person, including the root sheath;

(b) the taking of buccal swabs by swabbing the lips, tongue and inside cheeks of the mouth to collect epithelial cells; or

(c) the taking of blood by pricking the skin surface with a sterile lancet.

(2) Terms and conditions — The warrant, order or authorization shall include any terms and conditions that the provincial court judge or court, as the case may be, considers advisable to ensure that the taking of the samples authorized by the warrant, order or authorization is reasonable in the circumstances.

(3) Fingerprints — A peace officer who is authorized to take samples of bodily substances from a person by an order made under section 487.051 or an authorization granted under section 487.055 or 487.091, or a person acting under their direction, may take fingerprints from the person for the purpose of the *DNA Identification Act*.

1995, c. 27, s. 1; 1998, c. 37, s. 18; 2000, c. 10, s. 19; 2007, c. 22, s. 16

487.07 (1) Duty to inform — Before taking samples of bodily substances from a person, or causing samples to be taken under their direction, in execution of a warrant issued under section 487.05 or an order made under section 487.051 or under an authorization granted under section 487.055 or 487.091, a peace officer shall inform the person of

(a) the contents of the warrant, order or authorization;

(b) the nature of the investigative procedures by means of which the samples are to be taken;

(c) the purpose of taking the samples;

(d) the authority of the peace officer and any other person under the direction of the peace officer to use as much force as is necessary for the purpose of taking the samples; and

(d.1) [Repealed 2000, c. 10, s. 20(2).]

(e) in the case of samples of bodily substances taken in execution of a warrant,

(i) the possibility that the results of forensic DNA analysis may be used in evidence, and

(ii) if the sample is taken from a young person, the rights of the young person under subsection (4).

(2) **Detention of person** — A person from whom samples of bodily substances are to be taken may

(a) be detained for that purpose for a period that is reasonable in the circumstances; and

(b) be required to accompany a peace officer for that purpose.

(3) **Respect of privacy** — A peace officer who takes samples of bodily substances from a person, or a person who takes such samples under the direction of a peace officer, shall ensure that the person's privacy is respected in a manner that is reasonable in the circumstances.

(4) **Execution of warrant against young person** — A young person against whom a warrant is executed has, in addition to any other rights arising from his or her detention under the warrant,

(a) the right to a reasonable opportunity to consult with, and

(b) the right to have the warrant executed in the presence of

counsel and a parent or, in the absence of a parent, an adult relative or, in the absence of a parent and an adult relative, any other appropriate adult chosen by the young person.

(5) **Waiver of rights of young person** — A young person may waive his or her rights under subsection (4) but any such waiver

(a) must be recorded on audio tape or video tape or otherwise; or

(b) must be made in writing and contain a statement signed by the young person that he or she has been informed of the right being waived.

1995, c. 27, ss. 1, 3; 1998, c. 37, s. 19; 2000, c. 10, s. 20; 2007, c. 22, s. 17

487.071 (1) **Verification** — Before taking samples of bodily substances from a person under an order made under section 487.051 or an authorization granted under section 487.055 or 487.091, a peace officer, or a person acting under their direction, shall verify whether the convicted offenders index of the national DNA data bank, established under the *DNA Identification Act*, contains the person's DNA profile.

(2) **DNA profile in data bank** — If the person's DNA profile is in the convicted offenders index of the national DNA data bank, the peace officer or person acting under their direction shall not take any bodily substances from the person but shall

(a) confirm in writing on the order or authorization that he or she has been advised that the person's DNA profile is in the DNA data bank; and

(b) transmit a copy of the order or authorization containing that confirmation and any other information prescribed by regulations made under the *DNA Identification Act* to the Commissioner of the Royal Canadian Mounted Police.

(3) **DNA profile not in data bank** — If the person's DNA profile is not in the convicted offenders index of the national DNA data bank, the peace officer or per-

son acting under their direction shall execute the order or authorization and transmit to the Commissioner of the Royal Canadian Mounted Police

(a) any bodily substances taken; and

(b) a copy of the order or authorization and any other information prescribed by regulations made under the *DNA Identification Act*.

1998, c. 37, s. 20; 2000, c. 10, s. 21; 2005, c. 25, s. 8; 2007, c. 22, s. 18

487.08 (1) Use of bodily substances — warrant — No person shall use bodily substances that are taken in execution of a warrant under section 487.05 or under section 196.12 of the *National Defence Act* except to use them for the purpose of forensic DNA analysis in the course of an investigation of a designated offence.

(1.1) Use of bodily substances — order, authorization — No person shall use bodily substances that are taken in execution of an order made under section 487.051 of this Act or section 196.14 of the *National Defence Act*, or under an authorization granted under section 487.055 or 487.091 of this Act or section 196.24 of the *National Defence Act*, except to transmit them to the Commissioner of the Royal Canadian Mounted Police for the purpose of forensic DNA analysis in accordance with the *DNA Identification Act*.

(2) Use of results — warrant — No person shall use the results of forensic DNA analysis of bodily substances that are taken in execution of a warrant under section 487.05 or under section 196.12 of the *National Defence Act* except

(a) in the course of an investigation of the designated offence or any other designated offence in respect of which a warrant was issued or a bodily substance was found in the circumstances described in paragraph 487.05(1)(b) or in paragraph 196.12(1)(b) of the *National Defence Act*; or

(b) in any proceeding for such an offence.

(2.1) [Repealed 2005, c. 25, s. 9(2).]

(3) Offence — Every person who contravenes subsection (1) or (2) is guilty of an offence punishable on summary conviction.

(4) Offence — Every person who contravenes subsection (1.1)

(a) is guilty of an indictable offence and liable to imprisonment for a term not exceeding two years; or

(b) is guilty of an offence punishable on summary conviction.

1995, c. 27, s. 1; 1998, c. 37, s. 21; 2000, c. 10, s. 22; 2005, c. 25, s. 9; 2007, c. 22, s. 19; 2019, c. 25, s. 200

487.09 (1) Destruction of bodily substances, etc. — warrant — Subject to subsection (2), bodily substances that are taken from a person in execution of a warrant under section 487.05 and the results of forensic DNA analysis shall be destroyed or, in the case of results in electronic form, access to those results shall be permanently removed, without delay after

(a) the results of that analysis establish that the bodily substance referred to in paragraph 487.05(1)(b) was not from that person;

(b) the person is finally acquitted of the designated offence and any other offence in respect of the same transaction; or

(c) the expiration of one year after

(i) the person is discharged after a preliminary inquiry into the designated offence or any other offence in respect of the same transaction,

(ii) the dismissal, for any reason other than acquittal, or the withdrawal of any information charging the person with the designated offence or any other offence in respect of the same transaction, or

(iii) any proceeding against the person for the offence or any other offence in respect of the same transaction is stayed under section 579 or under that section as applied by section 572 or 795,

unless during that year a new information is laid or an indictment is preferred charging the person with the designated offence or any other offence in respect of the same transaction or the proceeding is recommenced.

(2) **Exception** — A provincial court judge may order that the bodily substances that are taken from a person and the results of forensic DNA analysis not be destroyed during any period that the provincial court judge considers appropriate if the provincial court judge is satisfied that the bodily substances or results might reasonably be required in an investigation or prosecution of the person for another designated offence or of another person for the designated offence or any other offence in respect of the same transaction.

(3) **Destruction of bodily substances, etc. voluntarily given** — Bodily substances that are provided voluntarily by a person and the results of forensic DNA analysis shall be destroyed or, in the case of results in electronic form, access to those results shall be permanently removed, without delay after the results of that analysis establish that the bodily substance referred to in paragraph 487.05(1)(b) was not from that person.

1995, c. 27, s. 1; 1998, c. 37, s. 22

487.091 (1) **Collection of additional bodily substances** — A provincial court judge may, on *ex parte* application made in Form 5.08, authorize in Form 5.09 the taking from a person, for the purpose of forensic DNA analysis, of any number of additional samples of bodily substances that is reasonably required for that purpose, by means of the investigative procedures described in subsection 487.06(1), if

(a) a DNA profile cannot be derived from the bodily substances that were taken from that person under an order made under section 487.051 or an authorization granted under section 487.055; or

(b) the information or bodily substances required by regulations made under the *DNA Identification Act* were not transmitted in accordance with the requirements of the regulations or were lost.

(2) **Reasons** — The application shall state the reasons why a DNA profile cannot be derived from the bodily substances or why the information or bodily substances were not transmitted in accordance with the regulations or were lost.

(3) **Persons not in custody** — If the court authorizes the taking of samples of bodily substances from a person who is not in custody, a summons in Form 5.061

setting out the information referred to in paragraphs 487.07(1)(b) to (d) shall be directed to the person requiring them to report at the place, day and time set out in the summons and submit to the taking of the samples. Subsections 487.055(5) and (6) apply, with any modifications that the circumstances require.

1998, c. 37, s. 23; 2000, c. 10, s. 23; 2005, c. 25, s. 10; 2007, c. 22, s. 20

487.0911 (1) Review by Attorney General — On receipt of a notice from the Commissioner of the Royal Canadian Mounted Police under subsection 5.2(1) of the *DNA Identification Act* that an order made under section 487.051 or an authorization granted under section 487.091 appears to be defective, the Attorney General shall review the order or authorization and the court record.

(2) Clerical error — If the Attorney General is of the opinion that the defect is due to a clerical error, the Attorney General shall

(a) apply, *ex parte*, to the judge who made the order or authorization, or to a judge of the same court, to have it corrected; and

(b) transmit a copy of the corrected order or authorization, if any, to the Commissioner.

(3) Substantive defect — If the Attorney General is of the opinion that the offence referred to in the order or authorization is not a designated offence, the Attorney General shall inform the Commissioner of that opinion.

(4) No defect — If the Attorney General is of the opinion that the offence referred to in the order or authorization is a designated offence, the Attorney General shall transmit that opinion, with written reasons, to the Commissioner.

2005, c. 25, s. 11; 2007, c. 22, s. 21

487.092 (1) Information for impression warrant — A justice may issue a warrant in writing authorizing a peace officer to do any thing, or cause any thing to be done under the direction of the peace officer, described in the warrant in order to obtain any handprint, fingerprint, footprint, foot impression, teeth impression or other print or impression of the body or any part of the body in respect of a person if the justice is satisfied

(a) by information on oath in writing that there are reasonable grounds to believe that an offence against this or any other Act of Parliament has been committed and that information concerning the offence will be obtained by the print or impression; and

(b) that it is in the best interests of the administration of justice to issue the warrant.

(2) Search or seizure to be reasonable — A warrant issued under subsection (1) shall contain such terms and conditions as the justice considers advisable to ensure that any search or seizure authorized by the warrant is reasonable in the circumstances.

(3) Execution in Canada — A warrant issued under subsection (1) may be executed at any place in Canada. Any peace officer who executes the warrant must have authority to act as a peace officer in the place where it is executed.

(4) Telewarrant — Where a peace officer believes that it would be impracticable to appear personally before a justice to make an application for a warrant under this section, a warrant may be issued under this section on an information submitted by telephone or other means of telecommunication and, for that purpose, section 487.1 applies, with such modifications as the circumstances require, to the warrant.

1997, c. 18, s. 45; 1998, c. 37, s. 23; 2019, c. 25, s. 201

Other Provisions Respecting Search Warrants, Preservation Orders and Production Orders

[Heading added 1995, c. 27, s. 1. Amended 2014, c. 31, s. 21.]

487.1 (1) Telewarrants — If a peace officer believes that an indictable offence has been committed and that it would be impracticable to appear personally before a justice to make an application for a warrant in accordance with section 487, the peace officer may submit an information on oath by telephone or other means of telecommunication to a justice designated for the purpose by the chief judge of the provincial court having jurisdiction in the matter.

(2) Information on oath and record — An information submitted by telephone or other means of telecommunication, other than a means of telecommunication that produces a writing, shall be on oath and shall be recorded verbatim by the justice, who shall, as soon as practicable, cause to be filed, with the clerk of the court for the territorial division in which the warrant is intended for execution, the record or a transcription of it, certified by the justice as to time, date and contents.

(2.1) Information submitted by other means of telecommunication — The justice who receives an information submitted by a means of telecommunication that produces a writing shall, as soon as practicable, cause to be filed, with the clerk of the court for the territorial division in which the warrant is intended for execution, the information certified by the justice as to time and date of receipt.

(3) Administration of oath — For the purposes of subsection (2), an oath may be administered by telephone or other means of telecommunication.

(3.1) Alternative to oath — A peace officer who uses a means of telecommunication referred to in subsection (2.1) may, instead of swearing an oath, make a statement in writing stating that all matters contained in the information are true to his or her knowledge and belief and such a statement is deemed to be a statement made under oath.

(4) Contents of information — An information submitted by telephone or other means of telecommunication shall include

(a) a statement of the circumstances that make it impracticable for the peace officer to appear personally before a justice;

(b) a statement of the indictable offence alleged, the place or premises to be searched and the items alleged to be liable to seizure;

(c) a statement of the peace officer's grounds for believing that items liable to seizure in respect of the offence alleged will be found in the place or premises to be searched; and

(d) a statement as to any prior application for a warrant under this section or any other search warrant, in respect of the same matter, of which the peace officer has knowledge.

(5) Issuing warrant — A justice referred to in subsection (1) may issue a warrant to a peace officer conferring the same authority respecting search and seizure as may be conferred by a warrant issued under subsection 487(1) if the justice is satisfied that an information submitted by telephone or other means of telecommunication

(a) is in respect of an indictable offence and conforms to the requirements of subsection (4);

(b) discloses reasonable grounds for dispensing with an information presented personally and in writing; and

(c) discloses reasonable grounds in accordance with paragraph 487(1)(a), (b) or (c), as the case may be, for the issuance of a warrant in respect of an indictable offence.

The justice may require that the warrant be executed within the period that he or she may order.

(6) Formalities respecting warrant and facsimiles — Where a justice issues a warrant by telephone or other means of telecommunication, other than a means of telecommunication that produces a writing,

(a) the justice shall complete and sign the warrant in Form 5.1, noting on its face the time, date and place of issuance;

(b) the peace officer, on the direction of the justice, shall complete, in duplicate, a facsimile of the warrant in Form 5.1, noting on its face the name of the issuing justice and the time, date and place of issuance; and

(c) the justice shall, as soon as practicable after the warrant has been issued, cause the warrant to be filed with the clerk of the court for the territorial division in which the warrant is intended for execution.

(6.1) Issuance of warrant where telecommunication produces writing — Where a justice issues a warrant by a means of telecommunication that produces a writing,

(a) the justice shall complete and sign the warrant in Form 5.1, noting on its face the time, date and place of issuance;

(b) the justice shall transmit the warrant by the means of telecommunication to the peace officer who submitted the information and the copy of the warrant received by the peace officer is deemed to be a facsimile within the meaning of paragraph (6)(b);

(c) the peace officer shall procure another facsimile of the warrant; and

(d) the justice shall, as soon as practicable after the warrant has been issued, cause the warrant to be filed with the clerk of the court for the territorial division in which the warrant is intended for execution.

(7) Providing facsimile — A peace officer who executes a warrant issued by telephone or other means of telecommunication shall, before or as soon as practicable after entering the place or premises to be searched, give a facsimile of the warrant to any person who is present and ostensibly in control of the place or premises.

(8) Affixing facsimile — A peace officer who, in any unoccupied place or premises, executes a warrant issued by telephone or other means of telecommunication shall, on entering or as soon as practicable after entering the place or premises, cause a facsimile of the warrant to be suitably affixed in a prominent place within the place or premises.

(9) Report of peace officer — A peace officer to whom a warrant is issued by telephone or other means of telecommunication shall file a written report with the clerk of the court for the territorial division in which the warrant was intended for execution as soon as practicable but within a period not exceeding seven days after the warrant has been executed, which report shall include

(a) a statement of the time and date the warrant was executed or, if the warrant was not executed, a statement of the reasons why it was not executed;

(b) a statement of the things, if any, that were seized pursuant to the warrant and the location where they are being held; and

(c) a statement of the things, if any, that were seized in addition to the things mentioned in the warrant and the location where they are being held, together with a statement of the peace officer's grounds for believing that those additional things had been obtained by, or used in, the commission of an offence.

(10) Bringing before justice — The clerk of the court shall, as soon as practicable, cause the report, together with the information and the warrant to which it pertains, to be brought before a justice to be dealt with, in respect of the things seized referred to in the report, in the same manner as if the things were seized pursuant to a warrant issued, on an information presented personally by a peace officer, by that justice or another justice for the same territorial division.

(11) Proof of authorization — In any proceeding in which it is material for a court to be satisfied that a search or seizure was authorized by a warrant issued by telephone or other means of telecommunication, the absence of the information or warrant, signed by the justice and carrying on its face a notation of the time, date and place of issuance, is, in the absence of evidence to the contrary, proof that the search or seizure was not authorized by a warrant issued by telephone or other means of telecommunication.

(12) Duplicates and facsimiles acceptable — A duplicate or a facsimile of an information or a warrant has the same probative force as the original for the purposes of subsection (11).

R.S.C. 1985, c. 27 (1st Supp.), s. 69; 1992, c. 1, ss. 58(1) (Sched. I, item 9), 59 (Sched. I, item 18); 1994, c. 44, s. 37; 2018, c. 21, s. 19

487.11 Where warrant not necessary — A peace officer, or a public officer who has been appointed or designated to administer or enforce any federal or provincial law and whose duties include the enforcement of this or any other Act of Parliament, may, in the course of his or her duties, exercise any of the powers described in subsection 487(1) or 492.1(1) without a warrant if the conditions for obtaining a warrant exist but by reason of exigent circumstances it would be impracticable to obtain a warrant.

1997, c. 18, s. 46

487.2 Restriction on publication — If a search warrant is issued under section 487 or 487.1 or a search is made under such a warrant, every one who publishes in any document, or broadcasts or transmits in any way, any information with respect to

(a) the location of the place searched or to be searched, or

(b) the identity of any person who is or appears to occupy or be in possession or control of that place or who is suspected of being involved in any offence in relation to which the warrant was issued,

without the consent of every person referred to in paragraph (b) is, unless a charge has been laid in respect of any offence in relation to which the warrant was issued, guilty of an offence punishable on summary conviction.

R.S.C. 1985, c. 27 (1st Supp.), s. 69; 2005, c. 32, s. 16

487.3 (1) Order denying access to information — On application made at the time an application is made for a warrant under this or any other Act of Parliament, an order under any of sections 487.013 to 487.018 or an authorization under section 529 or 529.4, or at a later time, a justice, a judge of a superior court of criminal jurisdiction or a judge of the Court of Quebec may make an order prohibiting access to, and the disclosure of, any information relating to the warrant, order or authorization on the ground that

(a) the ends of justice would be subverted by the disclosure for one of the reasons referred to in subsection (2) or the information might be used for an improper purpose; and

(b) the reason referred to in paragraph (a) outweighs in importance the access to the information.

(2) Reasons — For the purposes of paragraph (1)(*a*), an order may be made under subsection (1) on the ground that the ends of justice would be subverted by the disclosure

(a) if disclosure of the information would

(i) compromise the identity of a confidential informant,

(ii) compromise the nature and extent of an ongoing investigation,

(iii) endanger a person engaged in particular intelligence-gathering techniques and thereby prejudice future investigations in which similar techniques would be used, or

(iv) prejudice the interests of an innocent person; and

(b) for any other sufficient reason.

(3) Procedure — Where an order is made under subsection (1), all documents relating to the application shall, subject to any terms and conditions that the justice or judge considers desirable in the circumstances, including, without limiting the generality of the foregoing, any term or condition concerning the duration of the prohibition, partial disclosure of a document, deletion of any information or the occurrence of a condition, be placed in a packet and sealed by the justice or judge immediately on determination of the application, and that packet shall be kept in the custody of the court in a place to which the public has no access or in any other place that the justice or judge may authorize and shall not be dealt with except in accordance with the terms and conditions specified in the order or as varied under subsection (4).

(4) Application for variance of order — An application to terminate the order or vary any of its terms and conditions may be made to the justice or judge who made the order or a judge of the court before which any proceedings arising out of the investigation in relation to which the warrant or production order was obtained may be held.

1997, c. 23, s. 14; 1997, c. 39, s. 1; 2004, c. 3, s. 8; 2014, c. 31, s. 22

488. Execution of search warrant — A warrant issued under section 487 or 487.1 shall be executed by day, unless

(a) the justice is satisfied that there are reasonable grounds for it to be executed by night;

(b) the reasonable grounds are included in the information; and

(c) the warrant authorizes that it be executed by night.

R.S.C. 1985, c. 27 (1st Supp.), s. 70; 1997, c. 18, s. 47

488.01 (1) Definitions — The following definitions apply in this section and in section 488.02.

"data" has the same meaning as in section 487.011. *("données")*

"document" has the same meaning as in section 487.011. *("document")*

"journalist" has the same meaning as in subsection 39.1(1) of the *Canada Evidence Act*. *("journaliste")*

"journalistic source" has the same meaning as in subsection 39.1(1) of the *Canada Evidence Act*. *("source journalistique")*

"officer" means a peace officer or public officer. *("fonctionnaire")*

(2) Warrant, authorization and order — Despite any other provision of this Act, if an applicant for a warrant under section 487.01, 487.1, 492.1 or 492.2, a search warrant under this Act, notably under section 487, an authorization under section 184.2, 184.3, 186 or 188, or an order under any of sections 487.014 to 487.017 knows that the application relates to a journalist's communications or an object, document or data relating to or in the possession of a journalist, they shall make an application to a judge of a superior court of criminal jurisdiction or to a judge as defined in section 552. That judge has exclusive jurisdiction to dispose of the application.

(3) **Warrant, authorization and order** — A judge may issue a warrant, authorization or order under subsection (2) only if, in addition to the conditions required for the issue of the warrant, authorization or order, he or she is satisfied that

(a) there is no other way by which the information can reasonably be obtained; and

(b) the public interest in the investigation and prosecution of a criminal offence outweighs the journalist's right to privacy in gathering and disseminating information.

(4) **Special Advocate** — The judge to whom the application for the warrant, authorization or order is made may, in his or her discretion, request that a special advocate present observations in the interests of freedom of the press concerning the conditions set out in subsection (3).

(5) **Offence by journalist — exception** — Subsections (3) and (4) do not apply in respect of an application for a warrant, authorization or order that is made in relation to the commission of an offence by a journalist.

(6) **Offence by journalist — order** — If a warrant, authorization or order referred to in subsection (2) is sought in relation to the commission of an offence by a journalist and the judge considers it necessary to protect the confidentiality of journalistic sources, the judge may order that some or all documents obtained pursuant to the warrant, authorization or order are to be dealt with in accordance with section 488.02.

(7) **Conditions** — The warrant, authorization or order referred to in subsection (2) may contain any conditions that the judge considers appropriate to protect the confidentiality of journalistic sources and to limit the disruption of journalistic activities.

(8) **Powers** — The judge who rules on the application for the warrant, authorization or order referred to in subsection (2) has the same powers, with the necessary adaptations, as the authority who may issue the warrant, authorization or order.

(9) **Discovery of relation to journalist** — If an officer, acting under a warrant, authorization or order referred to in subsection (2) for which an application was not made in accordance with that subsection, becomes aware that the warrant, authorization or order relates to a journalist's communications or an object, document or data relating to or in the possession of a journalist, the officer shall, as soon as possible, make an *ex parte* application to a judge of a superior court of criminal jurisdiction or a judge as defined in section 552 and, until the judge disposes of the application,

(a) refrain from examining or reproducing, in whole or in part, any document obtained pursuant to the warrant, authorization or order; and

(b) place any document obtained pursuant to the warrant, authorization or order in a sealed packet and keep it in a place to which the public has no access.

(10) **Powers of judge** — On an application under subsection (9), the judge may

(a) confirm the warrant, authorization or order if the judge is of the opinion that no additional conditions to protect the confidentiality of journalistic sources and to limit the disruption of journalistic activities should be imposed;

(b) vary the warrant, authorization or order to impose any conditions that the judge considers appropriate to protect the confidentiality of journalistic sources and to limit the disruption of journalistic activities;

(c) if the judge considers it necessary to protect the confidentiality of journalistic sources, order that some or all documents that were or will be obtained pursuant to the warrant, authorization or order are to be dealt with in accordance with section 488.02; or

(d) revoke the warrant, authorization or order if the judge is of the opinion that the applicant knew or ought reasonably to have known that the application for the warrant, authorization or order related to a journalist's communications or an object, document or data relating to or in the possession of a journalist.

2017, c. 22, s. 3

488.02 (1) Documents — Any document obtained pursuant to a warrant, authorization or order issued in accordance with subsection 488.01(3), or that is the subject of an order made under subsection 488.01(6) or paragraph 488.01(10)(c), is to be placed in a packet and sealed by the court that issued the warrant, authorization or order and is to be kept in the custody of the court in a place to which the public has no access or in such other place as the judge may authorize and is not to be dealt with except in accordance with this section.

(2) Notice — No officer is to examine or reproduce, in whole or in part, a document referred to in subsection (1) without giving the journalist and relevant media outlet notice of his or her intention to examine or reproduce the document.

(3) Application — The journalist or relevant media outlet may, within 10 days of receiving the notice referred to in subsection (2), apply to a judge of the court that issued the warrant, authorization or order to issue an order that the document is not to be disclosed to an officer on the grounds that the document identifies or is likely to identity a journalistic source.

(4) Disclosure: prohibition — A document that is subject to an application under subsection (3) is to be disclosed to an officer only following a disclosure order in accordance with paragraph (7)(b).

(5) Disclosure order — The judge may order the disclosure of a document only if he or she is satisfied that

(a) there is no other way by which the information can reasonably be obtained; and

(b) the public interest in the investigation and prosecution of a criminal offence outweighs the journalist's right to privacy in gathering and disseminating information.

(6) Examination — The judge may, if he or she considers it necessary, examine a document to determine whether it should be disclosed.

(7) Order — The judge must,

(a) if he or she is of the opinion that the document should not be disclosed, order that it be returned to the journalist or the media outlet, as the case may be; or

(b) if he or she is of the opinion that the document should be disclosed, order that it be delivered to the officer who gave the notice under subsection (2), subject to such restrictions and conditions as the judge deems appropriate.

2017, c. 22, s. 3

488.1 (1) Definitions — In this section,

"custodian" means a person in whose custody a package is placed pursuant to subsection (2);

"document", for the purposes of this section, has the same meaning as in section 321;

"judge" means a judge of a superior court of criminal jurisdiction of the province where the seizure was made;

"lawyer" means, in the Province of Quebec, an advocate, lawyer or notary and, in any other province, a barrister or solicitor;

"officer" means a peace officer or public officer.

(2) Examination or seizure of certain documents where privilege claimed — Where an officer acting under the authority of this or any other Act of Parliament is about to examine, copy or seize a document in the possession of a lawyer who claims that a named client of his has a solicitor-client privilege in respect of that document, the officer shall, without examining or making copies of the document,

(a) seize the document and place it in a package and suitably seal and identify the package; and

(b) place the package in the custody of the sheriff of the district or county in which the seizure was made or, if there is agreement in writing that a specified person act as custodian, in the custody of that person.

(3) Application to judge — Where a document has been seized and placed in custody under subsection (2), the Attorney General or the client or the lawyer on behalf of the client, may

(a) within fourteen days from the day the document was so placed in custody, apply, on two days notice of motion to all other persons entitled to make application to a judge for an order

(i) appointing a place and a day, not later than twenty-one days after the date of the order, for the determination of the question whether the document should be disclosed, and

(ii) requiring the custodian to produce the document to the judge at that time and place;

(b) serve a copy of the order on all other persons entitled to make application and on the custodian within six days of the date on which it was made; and

(c) if he has proceeded as authorized by paragraph (b), apply, at the appointed time and place, for an order determining the question.

(4) Disposition of application — On an application under paragraph (3)(c), the judge

(a) may, if the judge considers it necessary to determine the question whether the document should be disclosed, inspect the document;

(b) where the judge is of the opinion that it would materially assist him in deciding whether or not the document is privileged, may allow the Attorney General to inspect the document;

(c) shall allow the Attorney General and the person who objects to the disclosure of the document to make representations; and

(d) shall determine the question summarily and,

(i) if the judge is of the opinion that the document should not be disclosed, ensure that it is repackaged and resealed and order the custodian to deliver the document to the lawyer who claimed the solicitor-client privilege or to the client, or

(ii) if the judge is of the opinion that the document should be disclosed, order the custodian to deliver the document to the officer who seized the document or some other person designated by the Attorney General, subject to such restrictions or conditions as the judge deems appropriate,

and shall, at the same time, deliver concise reasons for the determination in which the nature of the document is described without divulging the details thereof.

(5) Privilege continues — Where the judge determines pursuant to paragraph (4)(d) that a solicitor-client privilege exists in respect of a document, whether or not the judge has, pursuant to paragraph (4)(b), allowed the Attorney General to inspect the document, the document remains privileged and inadmissible as evidence unless the client consents to its admission in evidence or the privilege is otherwise lost.

(6) Order to custodian to deliver — Where a document has been seized and placed in custody under subsection (2) and a judge, on the application of the Attorney General, is satisfied that no application has been made under paragraph (3)(a) or that following such an application no further application has been made under paragraph (3)(c), the judge shall order the custodian to deliver the document to the officer who seized the document or to some other person designated by the Attorney General.

(7) Application to another judge — Where the judge to whom an application has been made under paragraph (3)(*c*) cannot act or continue to act under this section for any reason, subsequent applications under that paragraph may be made to another judge.

(8) Prohibition — No officer shall examine, make copies of or seize any document without affording a reasonable opportunity for a claim of solicitor-client privilege to be made under subsection (2).

(9) Authority to make copies — At any time while a document is in the custody of a custodian under this section, a judge may, on an *ex parte* application of a person claiming a solicitor-client privilege under this section, authorize that person to examine the document or make a copy of it in the presence of the custodian or the judge, but any such authorization shall contain provisions to ensure that the document is repackaged and that the package is resealed without alteration or damage.

(10) Hearing in private — An application under paragraph (3)(c) shall be heard in private.

(11) Exception — This section does not apply in circumstances where a claim of solicitor-client privilege may be made under the *Income Tax Act* or under the *Proceeds of Crime (Money Laundering) and Terrorist Financing Act*.

R.S.C. 1985, c. 27 (1st Supp.), s. 71; 2000, c. 17, s. 89; 2001, c. 41, s. 80

489. (1) Seizure of things not specified — Every person who executes a warrant may seize, in addition to the things mentioned in the warrant, any thing that the person believes on reasonable grounds

(a) has been obtained by the commission of an offence against this or any other Act of Parliament;

(b) has been used in the commission of an offence against this or any other Act of Parliament; or

(c) will afford evidence in respect of an offence against this or any other Act of Parliament.

(2) Seizure without warrant — Every peace officer, and every public officer who has been appointed or designated to administer or enforce any federal or provincial law and whose duties include the enforcement of this or any other Act of Parliament, who is lawfully present in a place pursuant to a warrant or otherwise in the execution of duties may, without a warrant, seize any thing that the officer believes on reasonable grounds

(a) has been obtained by the commission of an offence against this or any Act of Parliament;

(b) has been used in the commission of an offence against this or any other Act of Parliament; or

(c) will afford evidence in respect of an offence against this or any other Act of Parliament.

R.S.C. 1985, c. 27 (1st Supp.), s. 72; R.S.C. 1985, c. 42 (4th Supp.), s. 3; 1993, c. 40, s. 16; 1997, c. 18, s. 48

489.1 (1) Restitution of property or report by peace officer — Subject to this or any other Act of Parliament, where a peace officer has seized anything under a warrant issued under this Act or under section 487.11 or 489 or otherwise in the execution of duties under this or any other Act of Parliament, the peace officer shall, as soon as is practicable,

(a) where the peace officer is satisfied,

(i) that there is no dispute as to who is lawfully entitled to possession of the thing seized, and

(ii) that the continued detention of the thing seized is not required for the purposes of any investigation or a preliminary inquiry, trial or other proceeding,

return the thing seized, on being issued a receipt therefor, to the person lawfully entitled to its possession and report to the justice who issued the warrant or some other justice for the same territorial division or, if no warrant was issued, a justice having jurisdiction in respect of the matter, that he has done so; or

(b) where the peace officer is not satisfied as described in subparagraphs (*a*)(i) and (ii),

(i) bring the thing seized before the justice referred to in paragraph (*a*), or

(ii) report to the justice that he has seized the thing and is detaining it or causing it to be detained

to be dealt with by the justice in accordance with subsection 490(1).

(2) **Idem** — Subject to this or any other Act of Parliament, where a person, other than a peace officer, has seized anything under a warrant issued under this Act or under section 487.11 or 489 or otherwise in the execution of duties under this or any other Act of Parliament, that person shall, as soon as is practicable,

(a) bring the thing seized before the justice who issued the warrant, or some other justice for the same territorial division or, if no warrant was issued, before a justice having jurisdiction in respect of the matter, or

(b) report to the justice referred to in paragraph (*a*) that he has seized the thing and is detaining it or causing it to be detained,

to be dealt with by the justice in accordance with subsection 490(1).

(3) **Form** — A report to a justice under this section shall be in the form set out as Form 5.2 in Part XXVIII, varied to suit the case and shall include, in the case of a report in respect of a warrant issued by telephone or other means of telecommunication, the statements referred to in subsection 487.1(9).

R.S.C. 1985, c. 27 (1st Supp.), s. 72; 1993, c. 40, s. 17; 1997, c. 18, s. 49

490. (1) Detention of things seized — Subject to this or any other Act of Parliament, where, pursuant to paragraph 489.1(1)(*b*) or subsection 489.1(2), anything that has been seized is brought before a justice or a report in respect of anything seized is made to a justice, the justice shall,

(a) where the lawful owner or person who is lawfully entitled to possession of the thing seized is known, order it to be returned to that owner or person, unless the prosecutor, or the peace officer or other person having custody of the thing seized, satisfies the justice that the detention of the thing seized is required for the purposes of any investigation or a preliminary inquiry, trial or other proceeding; or

(b) where the prosecutor, or the peace officer or other person having custody of the thing seized, satisfies the justice that the thing seized should be detained for a reason set out in paragraph (*a*), detain the thing seized or order that it be detained, taking reasonable care to ensure that it is preserved until the conclusion of any investigation or until it is required to be produced for the purposes of a preliminary inquiry, trial or other proceeding.

(2) Further detention — Nothing shall be detained under the authority of paragraph (1)(*b*) for a period of more than three months after the day of the seizure, or any longer period that ends when an application made under paragraph (*a*) is decided, unless

(a) a justice, on the making of a summary application to him after three clear days notice thereof to the person from whom the thing detained was seized, is satisfied that, having regard to the nature of the investigation, its further detention for a specified period is warranted and the justice so orders; or

(b) proceedings are instituted in which the thing detained may be required.

(3) Idem — More than one order for further detention may be made under paragraph (2)(*a*) but the cumulative period of detention shall not exceed one year from the day of the seizure, or any longer period that ends when an application made under paragraph (*a*) is decided, unless

(a) a judge of a superior court of criminal jurisdiction or a judge as defined in section 552, on the making of a summary application to him after three clear days notice thereof to the person from whom the thing detained was seized, is satisfied, having regard to the complex nature of the investigation, that the further detention of the thing seized is warranted for a specified period and subject to such other conditions as the judge considers just, and he so orders; or

(b) proceedings are instituted in which the thing detained may be required.

(3.1) Detention without application where consent — A thing may be detained under paragraph (1)(*b*) for any period, whether or not an application for an order under subsection (2) or (3) is made, if the lawful owner or person who is lawfully entitled to possession of the thing seized consents in writing to its detention for that period.

(4) When accused ordered to stand trial — When an accused has been ordered to stand trial, the justice shall forward anything detained pursuant to subsections (1) to (3) to the clerk of the court to which the accused has been ordered to stand trial to be detained by the clerk and disposed of as the court directs.

(5) Where continued detention no longer required — Where at any time before the expiration of the periods of detention provided for or ordered under subsections (1) to (3) in respect of anything seized, the prosecutor, or the peace officer or other person having custody of the thing seized, determines that the continued detention of the thing seized is no longer required for any purpose mentioned in subsection (1) or (4), the prosecutor, peace officer or other person shall apply to

(a) a judge of a superior court of criminal jurisdiction or a judge as defined in section 552, where a judge ordered its detention under subsection (3), or

(b) a justice, in any other case,

who shall, after affording the person from whom the thing was seized or the person who claims to be the lawful owner thereof or person entitled to its possession, if known, an opportunity to establish that he is lawfully entitled to the possession thereof, make an order in respect of the property under subsection (9).

(6) Idem — Where the periods of detention provided for or ordered under subsections (1) to (3) in respect of anything seized have expired and proceedings have not been instituted in which the thing detained may be required, the prosecutor, peace officer or other person shall apply to a judge or justice referred to in paragraph (5)(*a*) or (*b*) in the circumstances set out in that paragraph, for an order in respect of the property under subsection (9) or (9.1).

(7) Application for order of return — A person from whom anything has been seized may, after the expiration of the periods of detention provided for or ordered under subsections (1) to (3) and on three clear days notice to the Attorney General, apply summarily to

(a) a judge of a superior court of criminal jurisdiction or a judge as defined in section 552, where a judge ordered the detention of the thing seized under subsection (3), or

(b) a justice, in any other case,

for an order under paragraph (9)(*c*) that the thing seized be returned to the applicant.

(8) Exception — A judge of a superior court of criminal jurisdiction or a judge as defined in section 552, where a judge ordered the detention of the thing seized under subsection (3), or a justice, in any other case, may allow an application to be made under subsection (7) prior to the expiration of the periods referred to therein where he is satisfied that hardship will result unless such application is so allowed.

(9) Disposal of things seized — Subject to this or any other Act of Parliament, if

(a) a judge referred to in subsection (7), where a judge ordered the detention of anything seized under subsection (3), or

(b) a justice, in any other case,

is satisfied that the periods of detention provided for or ordered under subsections (1) to (3) in respect of anything seized have expired and proceedings have not been instituted in which the thing detained may be required or, where such periods have not expired, that the continued detention of the thing seized will not be required for any purpose mentioned in subsection (1) or (4), he shall

(c) if possession of it by the person from whom it was seized is lawful, order it to be returned to that person; or

(d) if possession of it by the person from whom it was seized is unlawful and the lawful owner or person who is lawfully entitled to its possession is known, order it to be returned to the lawful owner or to the person who is lawfully entitled to its possession,

and may, if possession of it by the person from whom it was seized is unlawful, or if it was seized when it was not in the possession of any person, and the lawful owner or person who is lawfully entitled to its possession is not known, order it to be forfeited to Her Majesty, to be disposed of as the Attorney General directs, or otherwise dealt with in accordance with the law.

(9.1) Exception — Notwithstanding subsection (9), a judge or justice referred to in paragraph (9)(*a*) or (*b*) may, if the periods of detention provided for or ordered under subsections (1) to (3) in respect of a thing seized have expired but proceedings have not been instituted in which the thing may be required, order that the thing continue to be detained for such period as the judge or justice considers necessary if the judge or justice is satisfied

(a) that the continued detention of the thing might reasonably be required for a purpose mentioned in subsection (1) or (4); and

(b) that it is in the interests of justice to do so.

(10) Application by lawful owner — Subject to this or any other Act of Parliament, a person, other than a person who may make an application under subsection (7), who claims to be the lawful owner or person lawfully entitled to possession of anything seized and brought before or reported to a justice under section 489.1 may, at any time, on three clear days notice to the Attorney General and the person from whom the thing was seized, apply summarily to

(a) a judge referred to in subsection (7), where a judge ordered the detention of the thing seized under subsection (3), or

(b) a justice, in any other case,

for an order that the thing detained be returned to the applicant.

(11) Order — Subject to this or any other Act of Parliament, on an application under subsection (10), where a judge or justice is satisfied that

(a) the applicant is the lawful owner or lawfully entitled to possession of the thing seized, and

(b) the periods of detention provided for or ordered under subsections (1) to (3) in respect of the thing seized have expired and proceedings have not been instituted in which the thing detained may be required or, where such periods have not expired, that the continued detention of the thing seized will not be required for any purpose mentioned in subsection (1) or (4),

the judge shall order that

(c) the thing seized be returned to the applicant; or

(d) except as otherwise provided by law, where, pursuant to subsection (9), the thing seized was forfeited, sold or otherwise dealt within such a manner that it cannot be returned to the applicant, the applicant be paid the proceeds of sale or the value of the thing seized.

(12) Detention pending appeal, etc. — Notwithstanding anything in this section, nothing shall be returned, forfeited or disposed of under this section pending any application made, or appeal taken, thereunder in respect of the thing or proceeding in which the right of seizure thereof is questioned or within thirty days after an order in respect of the thing is made under this section.

(13) Copies of documents returned — The Attorney General, the prosecutor or the peace officer or other person having custody of a document seized may, before bringing it before a justice or complying with an order that the document be returned, forfeited or otherwise dealt with under subsection (1), (9) or (11), make or cause to be made, and may retain, a copy of the document.

(14) Probative force — Every copy made under subsection (13) that is certified as a true copy by the Attorney General, the person who made the copy or the person in whose presence the copy was made is admissible in evidence and, in the absence of evidence to the contrary, has the same probative force as the original document would have if it had been proved in the ordinary way.

(15) Access to anything seized — Where anything is detained pursuant to subsections (1) to (3.1), a judge of a superior court of criminal jurisdiction, a judge as defined in section 552 or a provincial court judge may, on summary application on behalf of a person who has an interest in what is detained, after three clear days notice to the Attorney General, order that the person by or on whose behalf the application is made be permitted to examine anything so detained.

(16) Conditions — An order that is made under subsection (15) shall be made on such terms as appear to the judge to be necessary or desirable to ensure that anything in respect of which the order is made is safeguarded and preserved for any purpose for which it may subsequently be required.

(17) Appeal — A person who feels aggrieved by an order made under subsection (8), (9), (9.1) or (11) may appeal from the order

(a) to the court of appeal as defined in section 673 if the order was made by a judge of a superior court of criminal jurisdiction, in which case sections 678 to 689 apply with any modifications that the circumstances require; or

(b) to the appeal court as defined in section 812 in any other case, in which case sections 813 to 828 apply with any modifications that the circumstances require.

(18) Waiver of notice — Any person to whom three days notice must be given under paragraph (2)(a) or (3)(a) or subsection (7), (10) or (15) may agree that the application for which the notice is given be made before the expiration of the three days.

R.S.C. 1985, c. 27 (1st Supp.), s. 73; 1994, c. 44, s. 38; 1997, c. 18, s. 50; 2008, c. 18, s. 14

490.01 Perishable things — Where any thing seized pursuant to this Act is perishable or likely to depreciate rapidly, the person who seized the thing or any other person having custody of the thing

(a) may return it to its lawful owner or the person who is lawfully entitled to possession of it; or

(b) where, on *ex parte* application to a justice, the justice so authorizes, may

(i) dispose of it and give the proceeds of disposition to the lawful owner of the thing seized, if the lawful owner was not a party to an offence in relation to the thing or, if the identity of that lawful owner cannot be reasonably ascertained, the proceeds of disposition are forfeited to Her Majesty, or

(ii) destroy it.

1997, c. 18, s. 51; 1999, c. 5, s. 17

Sex Offender Information

[Heading added 2004, c. 10, s. 20.]

Interpretation

[Heading added 2004, c. 10, s. 20.]

490.011 (1) Definitions — The following definitions apply in this section and in sections 490.012 to 490.032.

"crime of a sexual nature" means a crime referred to in subsection 3(2) of the *Sex Offender Information Registration Act. ("crimes de nature sexuelle")*

"database" has the same meaning as in subsection 3(1) of the *Sex Offender Information Registration Act. ("banque de données")*

"designated offence" means

(a) an offence under any of the following provisions:

(i) subsection 7(4.1) (offence in relation to sexual offences against children),

(ii) section 151 (sexual interference),

(iii) section 152 (invitation to sexual touching),

(iv) section 153 (sexual exploitation),

(v) section 153.1 (sexual exploitation of person with disability),

(vi) section 155 (incest),

(vi.01) subsection 160(1) (bestiality),

(vi.1) subsection 160(2) (compelling the commission of bestiality),

(vii) subsection 160(3) (bestiality in presence of or by a child),

(viii) section 163.1 (child pornography),

(ix) section 170 (parent or guardian procuring sexual activity),

(ix.1) section 171.1 (making sexually explicit material available to child),

(x) section 172.1 (luring a child),

(x.1) section 172.2 (agreement or arrangement — sexual offence against child),

(xi) subsection 173(2) (exposure),

(xii) to (xv) [Repealed 2014, c. 25, s. 25(1).]

(xvi) section 271 (sexual assault),

(xvii) section 272 (sexual assault with a weapon, threats to a third party or causing bodily harm),

(xviii) paragraph 273(2)(a) (aggravated sexual assault — use of a restricted firearm or prohibited firearm or any firearm in connection with criminal organization), (xviii.1) paragraph 273(2)(a.1) (aggravated sexual assault — use of a firearm),

(xix) paragraph 273(2)(b) (aggravated sexual assault),

(xx) subsection 273.3(2) (removal of a child from Canada),

(xxi) section 279.011 (trafficking — person under 18 years),

(xxii) subsection 279.02(2) (material benefit — trafficking of person under 18 years),

(xxiii) subsection 279.03(2) (withholding or destroying documents — trafficking of person under 18 years),

(xxiv) subsection 286.1(2) (obtaining sexual services for consideration from person under 18 years),

(xxv) subsection 286.2(2) (material benefit from sexual services provided by person under 18 years), and

(xxvi) subsection 286.3(2) (procuring — person under 18 years);

(b) an offence under any of the following provisions:

(i) section 162 (voyeurism),

(i.1) subsection 173(1) (indecent acts),

(ii) section 177 (trespassing at night),

(iii) [Repealed 2019, c. 25, s. 202.]

(iii.1) section 231 (murder),

(iv) section 234 (manslaughter),

(v) paragraph 246(b) (overcoming resistance to commission of offence),

(vi) section 264 (criminal harassment),

(vii) section 279 (kidnapping),

(vii.1) section 279.01 (trafficking in persons),

(vii.11) subsection 279.02(1) (material benefit — trafficking),

(vii.12) subsection 279.03(1) (withholding or destroying documents — trafficking),

(viii) section 280 (abduction of a person under age of sixteen),

(ix) section 281 (abduction of a person under age of fourteen),

(ix.1) subsection 286.1(1) (obtaining sexual services for consideration),

(ix.2) subsection 286.2(1) (material benefit from sexual services),

(ix.3) subsection 286.3(1) (procuring),

(x) paragraph 348(1)(d) (breaking and entering a dwelling house with intent to commit an indictable offence),

(xi) paragraph 348(1)(d) (breaking and entering a dwelling house and committing an indictable offence),

(xii) paragraph 348(1)(e) (breaking and entering a place other than a dwelling house with intent to commit an indictable offence), and

(xiii) paragraph 348(1)(e) (breaking and entering a place other than a dwelling house and committing an indictable offence);

(c) an offence under any of the following provisions of the *Criminal Code*, chapter C-34 of the Revised Statutes of Canada, 1970, as they read from time to time before January 4, 1983:

(i) section 144 (rape),

(ii) section 145 (attempt to commit rape),

(iii) section 149 (indecent assault on female),

(iv) section 156 (indecent assault on male), and

(v) subsection 246(1) (assault with intent) if the intent is to commit an offence referred to in any of subparagraphs (i) to (iv);

(c.1) an offence under any of the following provisions of the *Criminal Code*, chapter C-34 of the Revised Statutes of Canada, 1970, as enacted by section 19 of *An Act to amend the Criminal Code in relation to sexual offences and other offences against the person and to amend certain other Acts in relation thereto or in consequence thereof*, chapter 125 of the Statutes of Canada, 1980-81-82-83:

(i) section 246.1 (sexual assault),

(ii) section 246.2 (sexual assault with a weapon, threats to a third party or causing bodily harm), and

(iii) section 246.3 (aggravated sexual assault);

(d) an offence under any of the following provisions of the *Criminal Code*, chapter C-34 of the Revised Statutes of Canada, 1970, as they read from time to time before January 1, 1988:

(i) subsection 146(1) (sexual intercourse with a female under age of fourteen),

(ii) subsection 146(2) (sexual intercourse with a female between ages of fourteen and sixteen),

(iii) section 153 (sexual intercourse with step-daughter),

(iv) section 157 (gross indecency),

(v) section 166 (parent or guardian procuring defilement), and

(vi) section 167 (householder permitting defilement);

(d.1) an offence under any of the following provisions of this Act, as they read from time to time before the day on which this paragraph comes into force:

(i) paragraph 212(1)(i) (stupefying or overpowering for the purpose of sexual intercourse),

(ii) subsection 212(2) (living on the avails of prostitution of person under 18 years),

(iii) subsection 212(2.1) (aggravated offence in relation to living on the avails of prostitution of person under 18 years), and

(iv) subsection 212(4) (prostitution of person under 18 years);

(e) an attempt or conspiracy to commit an offence referred to in any of paragraphs (a), (c), (c.1), (d) and (d.1); or

(f) an attempt or conspiracy to commit an offence referred to in paragraph (b).

("infraction désignée")

"Ontario Act" means *Christopher's Law (Sex Offender Registry), 2000*, S.O. 2000, c. 1. *("loi ontarienne")*

"pardon" means a conditional pardon granted under Her Majesty's royal prerogative of mercy or under section 748 that has not been revoked. *(« pardon »)*

"record suspension" means a record suspension, as defined in subsection 2(1) of the *Criminal Records Act*, that has not been revoked or ceased to have effect. *(« suspension du casier »)*

"registration centre" has the same meaning as in subsection 3(1) of the *Sex Offender Information Registration Act*. *("bureau d'inscription")*

"Review Board" means the Review Board established or designated for a province under subsection 672.38(1). *("commission d'examen")*

"verdict of not criminally responsible on account of mental disorder" means a verdict of not criminally responsible on account of mental disorder within the meaning of subsection 672.1(1) or a finding of not responsible on account of mental disorder within the meaning of subsection 2(1) of the *National Defence Act*, as the case may be. *("verdict de non-responsabilité")*

(2) Interpretation — For the purpose of this section and sections 490.012 to 490.032, a person who is convicted of, or found not criminally responsible on account of mental disorder for, a designated offence does not include a young person

(a) within the meaning of subsection 2(1) of the *Youth Criminal Justice Act* unless they are given an adult sentence within the meaning of that subsection for the offence; or

(b) within the meaning of subsection 2(1) of the *Young Offenders Act*, chapter Y-1 of the Revised Statutes of Canada, 1985, unless they are convicted of the offence in ordinary court within the meaning of that subsection.

2004, c. 10, s. 20; 2005, c. 43, s. 6; 2007, c. 5, s. 11; 2008, c. 6, s. 36; 2010, c. 3, s. 7; 2010, c. 17, s. 4; 2012, c. 1, ss. 31, 141(2), (3); 2014, c. 25, s. 25; 2019, c. 17, s. 4; 2019, c. 25, s. 202

Order to Comply with the *Sex Offender Information Registration Act*

[Heading added 2004, c. 10, s. 20. Amended 2007, c. 5, s. 12.]

490.012 (1) Order — When a court imposes a sentence on a person for an offence referred to in paragraph (a), (c), (c.1), (d), (d.1) or (e) of the definition "designated offence" in subsection 490.011(1) or renders a verdict of not criminally responsible on account of mental disorder for such an offence, it shall make an order in Form 52 requiring the person to comply with the *Sex Offender Information Registration Act* for the applicable period specified in section 490.013.

(2) Order — if intent established — When a court imposes a sentence on a person for an offence referred to in paragraph (b) or (f) of the definition "designated offence" in subsection 490.011(1), it shall, on application of the prosecutor, make an order in Form 52 requiring the person to comply with the *Sex Offender Information Registration Act* for the applicable period specified in section 490.013 if the prosecutor establishes beyond a reasonable doubt that the person committed the offence with the intent to commit an offence referred to in paragraph (a), (c), (c.1), (d), (d.1) or (e) of that definition.

(3) Order — if previous offence established — When a court imposes a sentence on a person for a designated offence in connection with which an order may be made under subsection (1) or (2) or renders a verdict of not criminally responsible on account of mental disorder for such an offence, it shall, on application of the prosecutor, make an order in Form 52 requiring the person to comply with the *Sex Offender Information Registration Act* for the applicable period specified in section 490.013 if the prosecutor establishes that

(a) the person was, before or after the coming into force of this paragraph, previously convicted of, or found not criminally responsible on account of mental disorder for, an offence referred to in paragraph (a), (c), (c.1), (d), (d.1) or (e) of the definition "designated offence" in subsection 490.011(1) or in paragraph (a) or (c) of the definition "designated offence" in section 227 of the *National Defence Act*;

(b) the person was not served with a notice under section 490.021 or 490.02903 or under section 227.08 of the *National Defence Act* in connection with that offence; and

(c) no order was made under subsection (1) or under subsection 227.01(1) of the *National Defence Act* in connection with that offence.

(4) Failure to make order — If the court does not consider the matter under subsection (1) or (3) at that time, the court

(a) shall, within 90 days after the day on which it imposes the sentence or renders the verdict, set a date for a hearing to do so;

(b) retains jurisdiction over the matter; and

(c) may require the person to appear at the hearing by closed-circuit television or videoconference, as long as the person is given the opportunity to communicate privately with counsel if they are represented by counsel.

(5) [Repealed 2010, c. 17, s. 5.]

2004, c. 10, s. 20; 2007, c. 5, s. 13; 2010, c. 17, s. 5; 2014, c. 25, s. 26; 2019, c. 25, s. 203

490.013 (1) Date order begins — An order made under section 490.012 begins on the day on which it is made.

(2) Duration of order — An order made under subsection 490.012(1) or (2)

(a) ends 10 years after it was made if the offence in connection with which it was made was prosecuted summarily or if the maximum term of imprisonment for the offence is two or five years;

(b) ends 20 years after it was made if the maximum term of imprisonment for the offence is 10 or 14 years; and

(c) applies for life if the maximum term of imprisonment for the offence is life.

(2.1) Duration of order — An order made under subsection 490.012(1) applies for life if the person is convicted of, or found not criminally responsible on account of mental disorder for, more than one offence referred to in paragraph (a), (c), (c.1), (d), (d.1) or (e) of the definition "designated offence" in subsection 490.011(1).

(3) Duration of order — An order made under subsection 490.012(1) or (2) applies for life if the person is, or was at any time, subject to an obligation under section 490.019 or 490.02901, under section 227.06 of the *National Defence Act* or under section 36.1 of the *International Transfer of Offenders Act*.

(4) Duration of order — An order made under subsection 490.012(1) or (2) applies for life if the person is, or was at any time, subject to an order made previously under section 490.012 of this Act or section 227.01 of the *National Defence Act*.

(5) Duration of order — An order made under subsection 490.012(3) applies for life.

2004, c. 10, s. 20; 2007, c. 5, s. 14; 2010, c. 17, s. 6; 2014, c. 25, s. 27

490.014 Appeal — The prosecutor, or a person who is subject to an order under subsection 490.012(2), may appeal from a decision of the court under that subsection on any ground of appeal that raises a question of law or of mixed law and fact. The appeal court may dismiss the appeal, or allow it and order a new hearing, quash the order or make an order that may be made under that subsection.

2004, c. 10, s. 20; 2010, c. 17, s. 7

490.015 (1) Application for termination order — A person who is subject to an order may apply for a termination order

(a) if five years have elapsed since the order was made, in the case of an order referred to in paragraph 490.013(2)(a);

(b) if 10 years have elapsed since the order was made, in the case of an order referred to in paragraph 490.013(2)(b); or

(c) if 20 years have elapsed since the order was made, in the case of an order referred to in paragraph 490.013(2)(c) or subsection 490.013(2.1), (3) or (5).

(2) Multiple orders — A person who is subject to more than one order made under section 490.012 of this Act, or under that section and section 227.01 of the *National Defence Act*, may apply for a termination order if 20 years have elapsed since the most recent order was made.

(3) Pardon or record suspension — Despite subsections (1) and (2), a person may apply for a termination order once they receive a pardon or once a record suspension is ordered.

(4) Scope of application — The application shall be in relation to every order that is in effect. If a person is subject to an obligation under section 490.019 or

490.02901, under section 227.06 of the *National Defence Act* or under section 36.1 of the *International Transfer of Offenders Act*, the application shall also be in relation to that obligation.

(5) Re-application — A person whose application is refused may re-apply if five years have elapsed since they made the previous application. They may also re-apply once they receive a pardon or once a record suspension is ordered. However, they may not re-apply under this subsection if an order is made with respect to them under section 490.012 of this Act or section 227.01 of the *National Defence Act* after the previous application was made.

(6) Jurisdiction — The application shall be made to

(a) a superior court of criminal jurisdiction if

(i) one or more of the orders to which it relates were made by such a court under section 490.012, or

(ii) one or more of the orders to which it relates were made under section 227.01 of the *National Defence Act* and the Chief Military Judge does not have jurisdiction to receive the application under subsection 227.03(6) of that Act; or

(b) a court of criminal jurisdiction, in any other case in which the application relates to one or more orders made under section 490.012.

2004, c. 10, s. 20; 2007, c. 5, s. 15; 2010, c. 17, s. 8; 2012, c. 1, s. 142

490.016 (1) Termination order — The court shall make a termination order if it is satisfied that the person has established that the impact on them of continuing an order or an obligation, including on their privacy or liberty, would be grossly disproportionate to the public interest in protecting society through the effective prevention or investigation of crimes of a sexual nature, to be achieved by the registration of information relating to sex offenders under the *Sex Offender Information Registration Act*.

(2) Reasons for decision — The court shall give reasons for its decision.

(3) Requirements relating to notice — If the court makes a termination order, it shall cause the Commissioner of the Royal Canadian Mounted Police and the Attorney General of the province, or the minister of justice of the territory, to be notified of the decision.

2004, c. 10, s. 20; 2007, c. 5, s. 16; 2010, c. 17, s. 9

490.017 (1) Appeal — The prosecutor or the person who applied for a termination order may appeal from a decision made under subsection 490.016(1) on any ground of appeal that raises a question of law or of mixed law and fact. The appeal court may dismiss the appeal, or allow it and order a new hearing, quash the termination order or make an order that may be made under that subsection.

(2) Requirements relating to notice — If the appeal court makes an order that may be made under subsection 490.016(1), it shall cause the Commissioner of the Royal Canadian Mounted Police and the Attorney General of the province, or the minister of justice of the territory, in which the application for the order was made to be notified of the decision.

2004, c. 10, s. 20; 2007, c. 5, s. 17; 2010, c. 17, s. 10

490.018 (1) Requirements relating to notice — When a court or appeal court makes an order under section 490.012, it shall cause

(a) the order to be read by or to the person who is subject to it;

(b) a copy of the order to be given to that person;

(c) that person to be informed of sections 4 to 7.1 of the *Sex Offender Information Registration Act*, sections 490.031 and 490.0311 of this Act and section 119.1 of the *National Defence Act*; and

(d) a copy of the order to be sent to

(i) the Review Board that is responsible for making a disposition with respect to that person, if applicable,

(ii) the person in charge of the place in which that person is to serve the custodial portion of a sentence or is to be detained in custody as part of a disposition under Part XX.1, if applicable,

(iii) the police service whose member charged that person with the offence in connection with which the order is made, and

(iv) the Commissioner of the Royal Canadian Mounted Police.

(2) Endorsement — After paragraphs (1)(a) to (c) have been complied with, the person who is subject to the order shall endorse the order.

(3) Notice on disposition by Review Board — A Review Board shall cause a copy of the order to be given to the person who is subject to it when it directs

(a) under paragraph 672.54(a), that the person be discharged absolutely; or

(b) under paragraph 672.54(b), that the person be discharged subject to conditions, unless the conditions restrict the person's liberty in a manner and to an extent that prevent them from complying with sections 4, 4.1, 4.3 and 6 of the *Sex Offender Information Registration Act*.

(4) Notice before release — The person in charge of the place in which the person is serving the custodial portion of a sentence, or is detained in custody, before their release or discharge shall give the person a copy of the order not earlier than 10 days before their release or discharge.

2004, c. 10, s. 20; 2007, c. 5, s. 18; 2010, c. 17, s. 11

Notice and Obligation to Comply with the *Sex Offender Information Registration Act* — Convictions Before December 15, 2004

[Heading added 2004, c. 10, s. 20. Amended 2007, c. 5, s. 19; 2010, c. 17, s. 12.]

490.019 Obligation to comply — A person who is served with a notice in Form 53 shall comply with the *Sex Offender Information Registration Act* for the applicable period specified in section 490.022 unless a court makes an exemption order under subsection 490.023(2).

2004, c. 10, s. 20

490.02 (1) Persons who may be served — The Attorney General of a province or minister of justice of a territory may serve a person with a notice only if the person was convicted of, or found not criminally responsible on account of mental disorder for, an offence referred to in paragraph (a), (c), (c.1), (d) or (e) of the definition "designated offence" in subsection 490.011(1) and

(a) on the day on which the *Sex Offender Information Registration Act* comes into force, they are subject to a sentence for, or have not received an absolute discharge under Part XX.1 from, the offence; or

(b) in any other case,

(i) their name appears in connection with the offence, immediately before the *Sex Offender Information Registration Act* comes into force, in the sex offender registry established under the Ontario Act, and

(ii) they either were a resident of Ontario at any time between April 23, 2001 and the day on which the *Sex Offender Information Registration Act* comes into force or committed the offence in Ontario.

(2) Exception — A notice shall not be served on a person

(a) if they have been finally acquitted of, or have received a free pardon granted under Her Majesty's royal prerogative of mercy or under section 748 for, every offence in connection with which a notice may be served on them under section 490.021 of this Act or section 227.08 of the *National Defence Act*;

(b) if an application has been made for an order under subsection 490.012(3) of this Act or subsection 227.01(3) of the *National Defence Act* in relation to any offence in connection with which a notice may be served on them under section 490.021 of this Act or section 227.08 of the *National Defence Act*; or

(c) who is referred to in paragraph (1)(b) if they have provided proof of a pardon in accordance with subsection 9(1) of the Ontario Act.

2004, c. 10, s. 20; 2007, c. 5, s. 20

490.021 (1) Period for and method of service — The notice shall be personally served within one year after the day on which the *Sex Offender Information Registration Act* comes into force.

(2) Exception — If a person referred to in paragraph 490.02(1)(a) is unlawfully at large or is in breach of any terms of their sentence or discharge, or of any conditions set under this Act or under Part III of the *National Defence Act*, that relate to residence, the notice may be served by registered mail at their last known address.

(3) Exception — If a person referred to in paragraph 490.02(1)(b) is not in compliance with section 3 of the Ontario Act on the day on which the *Sex Offender Information Registration Act* comes into force, the notice may be served by registered mail at their last known address.

(4) Exception — If a person referred to in paragraph 490.02(1)(b) is in compliance with section 3 and subsection 7(2) of the Ontario Act on the day on which the *Sex Offender Information Registration Act* comes into force but fails to comply with subsection 3(1) or 7(2) of the Ontario Act within one year after that day, the notice shall be served within one year after the day on which they failed to comply and may be served by registered mail at their last known address.

(5) Proof of service — An affidavit of the person who served the notice, sworn before a commissioner or other person authorized to take affidavits, is evidence of the service and the notice if it sets out that

(a) the person who served the notice has charge of the appropriate records and has knowledge of the facts in the particular case;

(b) the notice was personally served on, or mailed to, the person to whom it was directed on a named day; and

(c) the person who served the notice identifies a true copy of the notice as an exhibit attached to the affidavit.

(6) Requirements relating to notice — The person who served the notice shall, without delay, send a copy of the affidavit and the notice to the Attorney General of the province, or the minister of justice of the territory, in which the person was served.

2004, c. 10, s. 20; 2007, c. 5, s. 21(2)

490.022 (1) Date obligation begins — The obligation under section 490.019 begins

(a) either one year after the day on which the person is served with the notice or when an exemption order is refused under subsection 490.023(2), whichever is later; or

(b) when an exemption order is quashed.

(2) Date obligation ends — The obligation ends on the earliest of

(a) the day on which an exemption order is made on an appeal from a decision made under subsection 490.023(2),

(b) the day on which the obligation of a person referred to in paragraph 490.02(1)(b) to comply with section 3 of the Ontario Act ends under paragraph 7(1)(a) of that Act, or

(c) the day on which a person referred to in paragraph 490.02(1)(b) provides satisfactory proof of a pardon or record suspension to a person who collects information, as defined in subsection 3(1) of the *Sex Offender Information Registration Act*, at a registration centre.

(3) Duration of obligation — If none of paragraphs (2)(a) to (c) applies earlier, the obligation

(a) ends 10 years after the person was sentenced, or found not criminally responsible on account of mental disorder, for the offence listed in the notice if the offence was prosecuted summarily or if the maximum term of imprisonment for the offence is two or five years;

(b) ends 20 years after the person was sentenced, or found not criminally responsible on account of mental disorder, for the offence listed in the notice if the maximum term of imprisonment for the offence is 10 or 14 years;

(c) applies for life if the maximum term of imprisonment for the offence listed in the notice is life; or

(d) applies for life if, at any time, the person was convicted of, or found not criminally responsible on account of mental disorder for, more than one offence that is referred to in paragraph (a), (c), (c.1), (d) or (e) of the definition "designated offence" in subsection 490.011(1) of this Act or in paragraph (a) or (c) of the definition "designated offence" in section 227 of the *National Defence Act* and if more than one of those offences is listed in the notice.

2004, c. 10, s. 20; 2007, c. 5, s. 22; 2012, c. 1, s. 143

490.023 (1) Application for exemption order — A person who is not subject to an order under section 490.012 of this Act or section 227.01 of the *National Defence Act* may apply for an order exempting them from the obligation within one year after they are served with a notice under section 490.021 of this Act or section 227.08 of the *National Defence Act*.

(1.1) Jurisdiction — The application shall be made to a court of criminal jurisdiction if

(a) it relates to an obligation under section 490.019 of this Act; or

(b) it relates to an obligation under section 227.06 of the *National Defence Act* and the Chief Military Judge does not have jurisdiction to receive the application under subsection 227.1(2) of that Act.

(2) Exemption order — The court shall make an exemption order if it is satisfied that the person has established that the impact of the obligation on them, including on their privacy or liberty, would be grossly disproportionate to the public interest in protecting society through the effective prevention or investigation of crimes of a sexual nature, to be achieved by the registration of information relating to sex offenders under the *Sex Offender Information Registration Act*.

(3) Reasons for decision — The court shall give reasons for its decision.

(4) Removal of information from database — If the court makes an exemption order, it shall also make an order requiring the Royal Canadian Mounted Police to permanently remove from the database all information that relates to the person that was registered in the database on receipt of the copy of the notice.

2004, c. 10, s. 20; 2007, c. 5, s. 23; 2010, c. 17, s. 13

490.024 (1) Appeal — The Attorney General or the person who applied for an exemption order may appeal from a decision of the court under subsection 490.023(2) on any ground of appeal that raises a question of law or of mixed law and fact. The appeal court may dismiss the appeal, or allow it and order a new hearing, quash the exemption order or make an order that may be made under that subsection.

(2) Removal of information from database — If the appeal court makes an exemption order, it shall also make an order requiring the Royal Canadian Mounted

Police to permanently remove from the database all information that relates to the person that was registered in the database on receipt of the copy of the notice.

2004, c. 10, s. 20; 2010, c. 17, s. 14

490.025 Requirements relating to notice — If a court refuses to make an exemption order or an appeal court dismisses an appeal from such a decision or quashes an exemption order, it shall cause the Commissioner of the Royal Canadian Mounted Police and the Attorney General of the province, or the minister of justice of the territory, in which the application for the order was made to be notified of the decision and shall cause the person who applied for the order to be informed of sections 4 to 7.1 of the *Sex Offender Information Registration Act*, sections 490.031 and 490.0311 of this Act and section 119.1 of the *National Defence Act*.

2004, c. 10, s. 20; 2007, c. 5, s. 24; 2010, c. 17, s. 15

490.026 (1) Application for termination order — A person who is subject to an obligation under section 490.019 may apply for a termination order unless they are also subject to an obligation under section 490.02901, under section 227.06 of the *National Defence Act* or under section 36.1 of the *International Transfer of Offenders Act* — or an order under section 490.012 or under section 227.01 of the *National Defence Act* — that began later.

(2) Time for application — A person may apply for a termination order if the following period has elapsed since they were sentenced, or found not criminally responsible on account of mental disorder, for an offence referred to in paragraph (a), (c), (c.1), (d) or (e) of the definition "designated offence" in subsection 490.011(1) of this Act or in paragraph (a) or (c) of the definition "designated offence" in section 227 of the *National Defence Act*:

(a) five years if the offence was prosecuted summarily or if the maximum term of imprisonment for the offence is two or five years;

(b) 10 years if the maximum term of imprisonment for the offence is 10 or 14 years; or

(c) 20 years if the maximum term of imprisonment for the offence is life.

(3) More than one offence — If more than one offence is listed in the notice served under section 490.021, the person may apply for a termination order if 20 years have elapsed since they were sentenced, or found not criminally responsible on account of mental disorder, for the most recent offence referred to in paragraph (a), (c), (c.1), (d) or (e) of the definition "designated offence" in subsection 490.011(1) of this Act or in paragraph (a) or (c) of the definition "designated offence" in section 227 of the *National Defence Act*.

(4) Pardon or record suspension — Despite subsections (2) and (3), a person may apply for a termination order once they receive a pardon or once a record suspension is ordered.

(5) Re-application — A person whose application is refused may apply again if five years have elapsed since they made the previous application. They may also apply again once they receive a pardon or once a record suspension is ordered. However, they may not apply again if, after the previous application was made, they become subject to an obligation under section 490.02901, under section 227.06

of the *National Defence Act* or under section 36.1 of the *International Transfer of Offenders Act* or to an order under section 490.012 or under section 227.01 of the *National Defence Act*.

(6) Jurisdiction — The application shall be made to a court of criminal jurisdiction if

(a) it relates to an obligation under section 490.019 of this Act; or

(b) it relates to an obligation under section 227.06 of the *National Defence Act* and the Chief Military Judge does not have jurisdiction to receive the application under subsection 227.12(6) of that Act.

2004, c. 10, s. 20; 2007, c. 5, s. 24; 2010, c. 17, s. 16; 2012, c. 1, s. 144

490.027 (1) Termination order — The court shall make an order terminating the obligation if it is satisfied that the person has established that the impact on them of continuing the obligation, including on their privacy or liberty, would be grossly disproportionate to the public interest in protecting society through the effective prevention or investigation of crimes of a sexual nature, to be achieved by the registration of information relating to sex offenders under the *Sex Offender Information Registration Act*.

(2) Reasons for decision — The court shall give reasons for its decision.

(3) Requirements relating to notice — If the court makes a termination order, it shall cause the Commissioner of the Royal Canadian Mounted Police and the Attorney General of the province, or the minister of justice of the territory, to be notified of the decision.

2004, c. 10, s. 20; 2007, c. 5, s. 25; 2010, c. 17, s. 17

490.028 Deemed application — If a person is eligible to apply for both an exemption order under section 490.023 and a termination order under section 490.026 within one year after they are served with a notice under section 490.021 of this Act or section 227.08 of the *National Defence Act*, an application within that period for one order is deemed to be an application for both.

2004, c. 10, s. 20; 2007, c. 5, s. 26

490.029 (1) Appeal — The Attorney General or the person who applied for a termination order may appeal from a decision of the court made under subsection 490.027(1) on any ground of appeal that raises a question of law or of mixed law and fact. The appeal court may dismiss the appeal, or allow it and order a new hearing, quash the termination order or make an order that may be made under that subsection.

(2) Requirements relating to notice — If the appeal court makes an order that may be made under subsection 490.027(1), it shall cause the Commissioner of the Royal Canadian Mounted Police and the Attorney General of the province, or the minister of justice of the territory, in which the application for the order was made to be notified of the decision.

2004, c. 10, s. 20; 2007, c. 5, s. 26; 2010, c. 17, s. 18

Notice and Obligation to Comply with the Sex Offender Information Registration Act — Convictions Outside Canada

[Heading added 2010, c. 17, s. 19.]

490.02901 Obligation — A person who is served with a notice in Form 54 shall comply with the *Sex Offender Information Registration Act* for the applicable period specified in section 490.02904 unless a court makes an exemption order under subsection 490.02905(2).

2010, c. 17, s. 19

490.02902 (1) Persons who may be served — The Attorney General of a province, or the minister of justice of a territory, may serve a person with a notice in Form 54 only if the person arrived in Canada after the coming into force of this subsection and they were convicted of or found not criminally responsible on account of mental disorder for an offence outside Canada — other than a service offence as defined in subsection 2(1) of the *National Defence Act* — that is, in the opinion of the Attorney General or minister of justice, equivalent to an offence referred to in paragraph (a) of the definition "designated offence" in subsection 490.011(1).

(2) Exception — The notice shall not be served on a person who has been acquitted of every offence in connection with which a notice may be served on them under section 490.02903.

2010, c. 17, s. 19

490.02903 (1) Period for and method of service — A notice in Form 54 shall be personally served.

(2) Proof of service — An affidavit of the person who served the notice, sworn before a commissioner or other person authorized to take affidavits, is evidence of the service and the notice if it sets out that

(a) the person who served the notice has charge of the appropriate records and has knowledge of the facts in the particular case;

(b) the notice was personally served on the person to whom it was directed on a named day; and

(c) the person who served the notice identifies a true copy of the notice as an exhibit attached to the affidavit.

(3) Requirements relating to notice — The person who served the notice shall, without delay, send a copy of the affidavit and the notice to the Attorney General of the province, or the minister of justice of the territory, in which the person was served.

2010, c. 17, s. 19

490.02904 (1) When obligation begins — The obligation under section 490.02901 begins on the day on which the person is served with the notice.

(2) When obligation ends — The obligation ends on the day on which an exemption order is made.

(3) Duration of obligation — If subsection (2) does not apply, the obligation

(a) ends 10 years after the person was sentenced or found not criminally responsible on account of mental disorder if the maximum term of imprisonment provided for in Canadian law for the equivalent offence is two or five years;

(b) ends 20 years after the person was sentenced or found not criminally responsible on account of mental disorder if the maximum term of imprisonment provided for in Canadian law for the equivalent offence is 10 or 14 years;

(c) applies for life if the maximum term of imprisonment provided for in Canadian law for the equivalent offence is life; or

(d) applies for life if, before or after the coming into force of this paragraph, the person was convicted of, or found not criminally responsible on account of mental disorder for, more than one offence referred to in paragraph (a), (c), (c.1), (d), (d.1) or (e) of the definition "designated offence" in subsection 490.011(1) or referred to in paragraph (a) or (c) of the definition "designated offence" in section 227 of the *National Defence Act* and if more than one of those offences is listed in the notice.

2010, c. 17, s. 19; 2014, c. 25, s. 28

490.02905 (1) Application for exemption order — A person who is served with a notice in Form 54 under section 490.02903 may apply to a court of criminal jurisdiction for an order exempting them from the obligation within one year after they are served.

(2) Exemption order — The court

(a) shall make an exemption order if it is satisfied that the person has established that

(i) they were not convicted of or found not criminally responsible on account of mental disorder for or were acquitted of the offence in question, or

(ii) the offence in question is not equivalent to an offence referred to in paragraph (a) of the definition "designated offence" in subsection 490.011(1); and

(b) shall order that the notice be corrected if it is satisfied that the offence in question is not equivalent to the offence referred to in the notice but is equivalent to another offence referred to in paragraph (a) of the definition "designated offence" in subsection 490.011(1).

(3) Reasons for decision — The court shall give reasons for its decision.

(4) Removal of information from database — If the court makes an exemption order, it shall also make an order requiring the Royal Canadian Mounted Police to permanently remove from the database all information that relates to the person that was registered in the database on receipt of the copy of the notice.

(5) Notification — If the court makes an order referred to in paragraph (2)(b), it shall cause the Commissioner of the Royal Canadian Mounted Police and the Attorney General of the province, or the minister of justice of the territory, in which the application for the order was made to be notified of the decision.

2010, c. 17, s. 19

490.02906 (1) Appeal — The Attorney General or the person who applied for an exemption order may appeal from a decision under subsection 490.02905(2) on any ground of appeal that raises a question of law or of mixed law and fact. The appeal court may

(a) dismiss the appeal;

(b) allow the appeal and order a new hearing;

(c) quash the exemption order; or

(d) make an order that may be made under that subsection.

(2) Removal of information from database — If an appeal court makes an exemption order, it shall also make an order requiring the Royal Canadian Mounted Police to permanently remove from the database all information that relates to the person that was registered in the database on receipt of the copy of the notice.

2010, c. 17, s. 19

490.02907 Requirements relating to notice — If an appeal court quashes an exemption order, it shall cause the Commissioner of the Royal Canadian Mounted Police and the Attorney General of the province, or the minister of justice of the territory, in which the application for the order was made to be notified of the decision and shall cause the person who applied for the order to be informed of sections 4 to 7.1 of the *Sex Offender Information Registration Act*, sections 490.031 and 490.0311 of this Act and section 119.1 of the *National Defence Act*.

2010, c. 17, s. 19

490.02908 (1) Application for termination order — A person who is subject to an obligation under section 490.02901 may apply to a court of criminal jurisdiction for a termination order unless they are also subject to another obligation under that section — or to an obligation under section 490.019, under section 227.06 of the *National Defence Act* or under section 36.1 of the *International Transfer of Offenders Act* or an order under section 490.012 or under section 227.01 of the *National Defence Act* — that began later.

(2) Time for application — one offence — The person may apply for a termination order if the following period has elapsed since the sentence was imposed or the verdict of not criminally responsible on account of mental disorder was rendered:

(a) five years if the maximum term of imprisonment provided for in Canadian law for the equivalent offence is two or five years;

(b) 10 years if the maximum term of imprisonment provided for in Canadian law for the equivalent offence is 10 or 14 years; or

(c) 20 years if the maximum term of imprisonment provided for in Canadian law for the equivalent offence is life.

(3) Time for application — more than one offence — If more than one offence is listed in the notice served under section 490.02903, the person may apply for a termination order if 20 years have elapsed since the sentence was imposed, or the verdict of not criminally responsible on account of mental disorder was rendered, for the most recent offence.

(4) Re-application — A person whose application is refused may apply again if five years have elapsed since the application was made.

2010, c. 17, s. 19

490.02909 (1) Termination order — The court shall make an order terminating the obligation if it is satisfied that the person has established that the impact on them of continuing the obligation, including on their privacy or liberty, would be grossly disproportionate to the public interest in protecting society through the effective prevention or investigation of crimes of a sexual nature to be achieved by the registration of information relating to sex offenders under the *Sex Offender Information Registration Act*.

(2) Reasons for decision — The court shall give reasons for its decision.

(3) Requirements relating to notice — If the court makes a termination order, it shall cause the Commissioner of the Royal Canadian Mounted Police and the Attorney General of the province, or the minister of justice of the territory, to be notified of the decision.

2010, c. 17, s. 19

490.0291 (1) Appeal — The Attorney General or the person who applied for a termination order may appeal from a decision under subsection 490.02909(1) on any ground of appeal that raises a question of law or of mixed law and fact. The appeal court may dismiss the appeal, allow the appeal and order a new hearing, quash the termination order or make an order that may be made under that subsection.

(2) Requirements relating to notice — If the appeal court makes an order that may be made under subsection 490.02909(1), it shall cause the Commissioner of the Royal Canadian Mounted Police and the Attorney General of the province, or the minister of justice of the territory, in which the application for the order was made to be notified of the decision.

2010, c. 17, s. 19

490.02911 (1) Obligation to advise police service — A person who was convicted of or found not criminally responsible on account of mental disorder for an offence outside Canada shall, if the offence is equivalent to one referred to in paragraph (a) of the definition "designated offence" in subsection 490.011(1), advise a police service within seven days after the day on which they arrive in Canada of that fact and of their name, date of birth, gender and address. They are not required to so advise the police service again unless they are later convicted of or found not criminally responsible on account of mental disorder for another such offence.

(2) Change in address — The person shall, if they are in Canada, advise a police service of a change in address within seven days after the day on which the change is made.

(3) Information to be provided to Attorney General — The police service shall cause the Attorney General of the province, or the minister of justice of the territory, in which it is located to be provided with the information.

(4) Obligation ends — A person's obligation under subsection (2) ends when they are served under section 490.02902 or, if it is earlier, one year after the day on which they advise the police service under subsection (1).

2010, c. 17, s. 19

International Transfer of Offenders Act

[Heading added 2010, c. 17, s. 19.]

490.02912 (1) Application for termination order — A person who is subject to an obligation under section 36.1 of the *International Transfer of Offenders Act* may apply to a court of criminal jurisdiction for a termination order unless they are also subject to an obligation under section 490.019 or 490.02901 or under section 227.06 of the *National Defence Act* — or to an order under section 490.012 or under section 227.01 of the *National Defence Act* — that began later.

(2) Time for application — one offence — The person may apply for a termination order if the following period has elapsed since the sentence was imposed or the verdict of not criminally responsible on account of mental disorder was rendered:

(a) five years if the maximum term of imprisonment provided for in Canadian law for the equivalent offence is two or five years;

(b) 10 years if the maximum term of imprisonment provided for in Canadian law for the equivalent offence is 10 or 14 years; or

(c) 20 years if the maximum term of imprisonment provided for in Canadian law for the equivalent offence is life.

(3) More than one offence — If more than one offence is listed in the copy of the Form 1 that was delivered under subparagraph 8(4)(a)(ii) of the *International Transfer of Offenders Act*, the person may apply for a termination order if 20 years have elapsed since the sentence was imposed, or the verdict of not criminally responsible on account of mental disorder was rendered, for the most recent offence.

(4) Re-application — A person whose application is refused may apply again if five years have elapsed since the application was made.

2010, c. 17, s. 19

490.02913 (1) Termination order — The court shall make an order terminating the obligation if it is satisfied that the person has established that the impact on them of continuing the obligation, including on their privacy or liberty, would be grossly disproportionate to the public interest in protecting society through the effective prevention or investigation of crimes of a sexual nature to be achieved by the registration of information relating to sex offenders under the *Sex Offender Information Registration Act*.

(2) Reasons for decision — The court shall give reasons for its decision.

(3) Requirements relating to notice — If the court makes a termination order, it shall cause the Commissioner of the Royal Canadian Mounted Police and the Attorney General of the province, or the minister of justice of the territory, to be notified of the decision.

2010, c. 17, s. 19

490.02914 (1) Appeal — The Attorney General or the person who applied for a termination order may appeal from a decision under subsection 490.02913(1) on any ground of appeal that raises a question of law or of mixed law and fact. The appeal court may dismiss the appeal, allow the appeal and order a new hearing, quash the termination order or make an order that may be made under that subsection.

(2) Requirements relating to notice — If the appeal court makes an order that may be made under subsection 490.02913(1), it shall cause the Commissioner of the Royal Canadian Mounted Police and the Attorney General of the province, or the minister of justice of the territory, in which the application for the order was made to be notified of the decision.

2010, c. 17, s. 19

490.02915 (1) Notice before release — The person in charge of the place in which a person who is subject to an obligation under section 36.1 of the *International Transfer of Offenders Act* is serving the custodial portion of a sentence, or is detained in custody before their release or discharge, shall give the person a copy of the Form 1 referred to in subsection 490.02912(3) not earlier than 10 days before their release or discharge.

(2) Notice on disposition by Review Board — A Review Board shall cause a copy of the Form 1 to be given to the person when it directs

(a) under paragraph 672.54(a), that the person be discharged absolutely; or

(b) under paragraph 672.54(b), that the person be discharged subject to conditions unless the conditions restrict the person's liberty in a manner and to an extent that prevent them from complying with sections 4, 4.1, 4.3 and 6 of the *Sex Offender Information Registration Act*.

2010, c. 17, s. 19

Disclosure of Information

[Heading added 2004, c. 10, s. 20.]

490.03 (1) Disclosure — The Commissioner of the Royal Canadian Mounted Police or a person authorized by the Commissioner shall, on request, disclose information that is registered in the database or the fact that such information is registered in the database

(a) to the prosecutor if the disclosure is necessary for the purpose of a proceeding under section 490.012; or

(b) to the Attorney General if the disclosure is necessary for the purpose of a proceeding under subsection 490.016(1), 490.023(2), 490.027(1), 490.02905(2), 490.02909(1) or 490.02913(1) or for the purpose of an appeal from a decision made in any of those proceedings or in a proceeding under subsection 490.012(2).

(2) **Disclosure in connection with proceedings** — The Commissioner or that person shall, on request, disclose to the prosecutor or Attorney General the information that is registered in the database relating to a person if the person discloses, in connection with a proceeding or appeal other than one referred to in subsection (1), the fact that information relating to them is registered in the database.

(3) **Disclosure in proceedings** — The prosecutor or the Attorney General may, if the information is relevant to the proceeding, appeal or any subsequent appeal, disclose it to the presiding court.

(4) [Repealed 2007, c. 5, s. 27(2).]

2004, c. 10, s. 20; 2007, c. 5, s. 27; 2010, c. 17, s. 20

Offences

[Heading added 2004, c. 10, s. 20.]

490.031 (1) Offence — Every person who, without reasonable excuse, fails to comply with an order made under section 490.012 or under section 227.01 of the *National Defence Act* or with an obligation under section 490.019 or 490.02901, under section 227.06 of the *National Defence Act* or under section 36.1 of the *International Transfer of Offenders Act* is guilty of an offence and liable

(a) on conviction on indictment, to a fine of not more than $10,000 or to imprisonment for a term of not more than two years, or to both; or

(b) on summary conviction, to a fine of not more than $10,000 or to imprisonment for a term of not more than two years less a day, or to both.

(2) **Reasonable excuse** — For greater certainty, a lawful command that prevents a person from complying with an order or obligation is a reasonable excuse if, at the time, the person is subject to the Code of Service Discipline within the meaning of subsection 2(1) of the *National Defence Act*.

(3) **Proof of certain facts by certificate** — In proceedings under subsection (1), a certificate of a person referred to in paragraph 16(2)(b) of the *Sex Offender Information Registration Act* stating that the sex offender failed to report under section 4, 4.1, 4.2 or 4.3 — or provide information under section 5 or notify a person under subsection 6(1) — of that Act is evidence of the statements contained in it without proof of the signature or official character of the person appearing to have signed it.

Proposed Amendment — 490.031(3)

(3) **Proof of certain facts by certificate** — In proceedings under subsection (1), a certificate of a person referred to in paragraph 16(2)(b) of the *Sex Offender Information Registration Act* stating that the sex offender failed to report under section 4, 4.1, 4.2 or 4.3 — or provide information under section 5 or notify a person under subsection 6(1) or (1.01) — of that Act is evidence of the statements contained in it without proof of the signature or official character of the person appearing to have signed it.

2015, c. 23, s. 30 [Not in force at date of publication.]

(4) **Attendance and cross-examination** — The sex offender named in the certificate may, with the leave of the court, require the attendance of the person who signed it for the purpose of cross-examination.

(5) **Notice of intention to produce** — A certificate is not to be received in evidence unless, before the commencement of the trial, the party who intends to produce it gives the sex offender a copy of it and reasonable notice of their intention to produce it.

2004, c. 10, s. 20; 2007, c. 5, s. 28; 2010, c. 17, s. 21; 2019, c. 25, s. 204

490.0311 **Offence** — Every person who knowingly provides false or misleading information under subsection 5(1) or 6(1) of the *Sex Offender Information Registration Act* is guilty of an offence and liable

Proposed Amendment — 490.0311 opening words

490.0311 **Offence** — Every person who knowingly provides false or misleading information under subsection 5(1) or 6(1) or (1.01) of the *Sex Offender Information Registration Act* is guilty of an offence and liable

2015, c. 23, s. 31 [Not in force at date of publication.]

(a) on conviction on indictment, to a fine of not more than $10,000 or to imprisonment for a term of not more than two years, or to both; or

(b) on summary conviction, to a fine of not more than $10,000 or to imprisonment for a term of not more than two years less a day, or to both.

2007, c. 5, s. 29; 2010, c. 17, s. 22; 2019, c. 25, s. 205

490.0312 **Offence** — Every person who, without reasonable excuse, fails to comply with an obligation under subsection 490.02911(1) or (2) is guilty of an offence punishable on summary conviction.

2010, c. 17, s. 23

Regulations

[Heading added 2004, c. 10, s. 20.]

490.032 **Regulations** — The Governor in Council may make regulations

(a) requiring that additional information be contained in a notice under Form 53 or Form 54; and

(b) prescribing, for one or more provinces, the form and content of that information.

2004, c. 10, s. 20; 2010, c. 17, s. 24

Forfeiture of Offence-related Property

490.1 (1) Order of forfeiture of property on conviction — Subject to sections 490.3 to 490.41, if a person is convicted, or discharged under section 730, of an indictable offence under this Act or the *Corruption of Foreign Public Officials Act* and, on application of the Attorney General, the court is satisfied, on a balance of probabilities, that offence-related property is related to the commission of the offence, the court shall

(a) if the prosecution of the offence was commenced at the instance of the government of a province and conducted by or on behalf of that government, order that the property be forfeited to Her Majesty in right of that province to be disposed of or otherwise dealt with in accordance with the law by the Attorney General or Solicitor General of that province; and

(b) in any other case, order that the property be forfeited to Her Majesty in right of Canada to be disposed of or otherwise dealt with in accordance with the law by the member of the Queen's Privy Council for Canada that is designated by the Governor in Council for the purpose of this paragraph.

(1.1) [Repealed 2001, c. 41, s. 130(7.1).]

(2) Property related to other offences — Subject to sections 490.3 to 490.41, if the evidence does not establish to the satisfaction of the court that property in respect of which an order of forfeiture would otherwise be made under subsection (1) is related to the commission of the indictable offence under this Act or the *Corruption of Foreign Public Officials Act* of which a person is convicted or discharged, but the court is satisfied, beyond a reasonable doubt, that the property is offence-related property, the court may make an order of forfeiture under subsection (1) in relation to that property.

(2.1) Property outside Canada — An order may be issued under this section in respect of property situated outside Canada, with any modifications that the circumstances require.

(3) Appeal — A person who has been convicted of an indictable offence under this Act or the *Corruption of Foreign Public Officials Act*, or the Attorney General, may appeal to the court of appeal from an order or a failure to make an order under subsection (1) as if the appeal were an appeal against the sentence imposed on the person in respect of the offence.

1997, c. 23, s. 15; 2001, c. 32, s. 30; 2001, c. 41, ss. 18, 130(7.1); 2007, c. 13, s. 8; 2017, c. 7, s. 64

490.2 (1) Application for *in rem* forfeiture — If an information has been laid in respect of an indictable offence under this Act or the *Corruption of Foreign Public Officials Act*, the Attorney General may make an application to a judge for an order of forfeiture under subsection (2).

(2) **Order of forfeiture of property** — Subject to sections 490.3 to 490.41, the judge to whom an application is made under subsection (1) shall order that the property that is subject to the application be forfeited and disposed of in accordance with subsection (4) if the judge is satisfied

(a) beyond a reasonable doubt that the property is offence-related property;

(b) that proceedings in respect of an indictable offence under this Act or the *Corruption of Foreign Public Officials Act* in relation to the property were commenced; and

(c) that the accused charged with the offence has died or absconded.

(3) **Accused deemed absconded** — For the purpose of subsection (2), an accused is deemed to have absconded in connection with the indictable offence if

(a) an information has been laid alleging the commission of the offence by the accused,

(b) a warrant for the arrest of the accused has been issued in relation to that information, and

(c) a reasonable attempts to arrest the accused under the warrant have been unsuccessful during a period of six months beginning on the day on which the warrant was issued,

and the accused is deemed to have so absconded on the last day of that six month period.

(4) **Who may dispose of forfeited property** — For the purpose of subsection (2), the judge shall

(a) if the prosecution of the offence was commenced at the instance of the government of a province and conducted by or on behalf of that government, order that the property be forfeited to Her Majesty in right of that province to be disposed of or otherwise dealt with in accordance with the law by the Attorney General or Solicitor General of that province; and

(b) in any other case, order that the property be forfeited to Her Majesty in right of Canada to be disposed of or otherwise dealt with in accordance with the law by the member of the Queen's Privy Council for Canada that is designated by the Governor in Council for the purpose of this paragraph.

(4.1) **Property outside Canada** — An order may be issued under this section in respect of property situated outside Canada, with any modifications that the circumstances require.

(5) **Definition of "judge"** — In this section and sections 490.5 and 490.8, **"judge"** means a judge as defined in section 552 or a judge of a superior court of criminal jurisdiction.

1997, c. 23, s. 15; 2001, c. 32, s. 31(1), (2), (4); 2007, c. 13, s. 9; 2017, c. 7, s. 65

490.3 Voidable transfers — A court may, before ordering that offence-related property be forfeited under subsection 490.1(1) or 490.2(2), set aside any conveyance or transfer of the property that occurred after the seizure of the property, or the making of a restraint order in respect of the property, unless the conveyance or transfer was for valuable consideration to a person acting in good faith.

1997, c. 23, s. 15

490.4 (1) Notice — Before making an order under subsection 490.1(1) or 490.2(2) in relation to any property, a court shall require notice in accordance with subsection (2) to be given to, and may hear, any person who, in the opinion of the court, appears to have a valid interest in the property.

(2) Manner of giving notice — A notice shall

(a) be given in the manner that the court directs or that may be specified in the rules of the court;

(b) specify the period that the court considers reasonable or that may be set out in the rules of the court during which a person may make an application to the court asserting their interest in the property; and

(c) set out the offence charged and a description of the property.

(3) Order of restoration of property — A court may order that all or part of the property that would otherwise be forfeited under subsection 490.1(1) or 490.2(2) be returned to a person — other than a person who was charged with an indictable offence under this Act or the *Corruption of Foreign Public Officials Act* or a person who acquired title to or a right of possession of the property from such a person under circumstances that give rise to a reasonable inference that the title or right was transferred for the purpose of avoiding the forfeiture of the property — if the court is satisfied that the person is the lawful owner or is lawfully entitled to possession of all or part of that property, and that the person appears innocent of any complicity in, or collusion in relation to, the offence.

1997, c. 23, s. 15; 2001, c. 32, s. 32; 2007, c. 13, s. 10; 2017, c. 7, s. 66

490.41 (1) Notice — If all or part of offence-related property that would otherwise be forfeited under subsection 490.1(1) or 490.2(2) is a dwelling-house, before making an order of forfeiture, a court shall require that notice in accordance with subsection (2) be given to, and may hear, any person who resides in the dwelling-house and is a member of the immediate family of the person charged with or convicted of the indictable offence under this Act or the *Corruption of Foreign Public Officials Act* in relation to which the property would be forfeited.

(2) Manner of giving notice — A notice shall

(a) be given in the manner that the court directs or that may be specified in the rules of the court;

(b) specify the period that the court considers reasonable or that may be set out in the rules of the court during which a member of the immediate family who resides in the dwelling-house may make themselves known to the court; and

(c) set out the offence charged and a description of the property.

(3) Non-forfeiture of property — Subject to an order made under subsection 490.4(3), if a court is satisfied that the impact of an order of forfeiture made under subsection 490.1(1) or 490.2(2) would be disproportionate to the nature and gravity of the offence, the circumstances surrounding the commission of the offence and the criminal record, if any, of the person charged with or convicted of the offence, as the case may be, it may decide not to order the forfeiture of the property or part of the property and may revoke any restraint order made in respect of that property or part.

(4) Factors in relation to dwelling-house — Where all or part of the property that would otherwise be forfeited under subsection 490.1(1) or 490.2(2) is a dwelling-house, when making a decision under subsection (3), the court shall also consider

(a) the impact of an order of forfeiture on any member of the immediate family of the person charged with or convicted of the offence, if the dwelling-house was the member's principal residence at the time the charge was laid and continues to be the member's principal residence; and

(b) whether the member referred to in paragraph (a) appears innocent of any complicity in the offence or of any collusion in relation to the offence.

2001, c. 32, s. 33; 2007, c. 13, s. 11; 2017, c. 7, s. 67

490.5 (1) Application — Where any offence-related property is forfeited to Her Majesty pursuant to an order made under subsection 490.1(1) or 490.2(2), any person who claims an interest in the property, other than

(a) in the case of property forfeited pursuant to an order made under subsection 490.1(1), a person who was convicted of the indictable offence in relation to which the property was forfeited,

(b) in the case of property forfeited pursuant to an order made under subsection 490.2(2), a person who was charged with the indictable offence in relation to which the property was forfeited, or

(c) a person who acquired title to or a right of possession of the property from a person referred to in paragraph (*a*) or (*b*) under circumstances that give rise to a reasonable inference that the title or right was transferred from that person for the purpose of avoiding the forfeiture of the property,

may, within thirty days after the forfeiture, apply by notice in writing to a judge for an order under subsection (4).

(2) Fixing day for hearing — The judge to whom an application is made under subsection (1) shall fix a day not less than thirty days after the date of the filing of the application for the hearing of the application.

(3) Notice — An applicant shall serve a notice of the application made under subsection (1) and of the hearing of it on the Attorney General at least fifteen days before the day fixed for the hearing.

(4) Order declaring interest not affected by forfeiture — Where, on the hearing of an application made under subsection (1), the judge is satisfied that the applicant

(a) is not a person referred to in paragraph (1)(a), (b) or (c) and appears innocent of any complicity in any indictable offence that resulted in the forfeiture of the property or of any collusion in relation to such an offence, and

(b) exercised all reasonable care to be satisfied that the property was not likely to have been used in connection with the commission of an unlawful act by the person who was permitted by the applicant to obtain possession of the property or from whom the applicant obtained possession or, where the applicant is a mortgagee or lienholder, by the mortgagor or lien-giver,

the judge may make an order declaring that the interest of the applicant is not affected by the forfeiture and declaring the nature and the extent or value of the interest.

(5) Appeal from order made under subsection (4) — An applicant or the Attorney General may appeal to the court of appeal from an order made under subsection (4), and the provisions of Part XXI with respect to procedure on appeals apply, with any modifications that the circumstances require, in respect of appeals under this subsection.

(6) Return of property — The Attorney General shall, on application made to the Attorney General by any person in respect of whom a judge has made an order under subsection (4), and where the periods with respect to the taking of appeals from that order under subsection (4), and where the periods with respect to the taking of appeals from that order have expired and any appeal from that order taken under subsection (5) has been determined, direct that

(a) the property, or the part of it to which the interest of the applicant relates, be returned to the applicant; or

(b) an amount equal to the value of the interest of the applicant, as declared in the order, be paid to the applicant.

1997, c. 23, s. 15; 2001, c. 32, s. 34

490.6 Appeals from orders under subsection 490.2(2) — Any person who, in their opinion, is aggrieved by an order made under subsection 490.2(2) may appeal from the order as if the order were an appeal against conviction or against a judgment or verdict of acquittal, as the case may be, under Part XXI, and that Part applies, with any modifications that the circumstances require, in respect of such an appeal.

1997, c. 23, s. 15

490.7 Suspension of order pending appeal — Notwithstanding anything in this Act, the operation of an order made in respect of property under subsection 490.1(1), 490.2(2) or 490.5(4) is suspended pending

(a) any application made in respect of the property under of those provisions or any other provision of this or any other Act of Parliament that provides for restoration or forfeiture of the property, or

(b) any appeal taken from an order of forfeiture or restoration in respect of the property,

and the property shall not be disposed of or otherwise dealt with until thirty days have expired after an order is made under any of those provisions.

1997, c. 23, s. 15

490.8 (1) Application for restraint order — The Attorney General may make an application in accordance with this section for a restraint order under this section in respect of any offence-related property.

(2) Procedure — An application made under subsection (1) for a restraint order in respect of any offence-related property may be made *ex parte* and shall be made in writing to a judge and be accompanied by an affidavit sworn on the information and belief of the Attorney General or any other person deposing to the following matters:

(a) the indictable offence to which the offence-related property relates;

(b) the person who is believed to be in possession of the offence-related property; and

(c) a description of the offence-related property.

(3) Restraint order — Where an application for a restraint order is made to a judge under subsection (1), the judge may, if satisfied that there are reasonable grounds to believe that the property is offence-related property, make a restraint order prohibiting any person from disposing of, or otherwise dealing with any interest in, the offence-related property specified in the order otherwise than in the manner that may be specified in the order.

(3.1) Property outside Canada — A restraint order may be issued under this section in respect of property situated outside Canada, with any modifications that the circumstances require.

(4) Conditions — A restraint order made by a judge under this section may be subject to any reasonable conditions that the judge thinks fit.

(5) Order in writing — A restraint order made under this section shall be made in writing.

(6) Service of order — A copy of a restraint order made under this section shall be served on the person to whom the order is addressed in any manner that the judge making the order directs or in accordance with the rules of the court.

(7) Registration of order — A copy of a restraint order made under this section shall be registered against any property in accordance with the laws of the province in which the property is situated.

(8) Order continues in force — A restraint order made under this section remains in effect until

(a) an order is made under subsection 490(9) or (11), 490.4(3) or 490.41(3) in relation to the property; or

(b) an order of forfeiture of the property is made under section 490 or subsection 490.1(1) or 490.2(2).

(9) Offence — Any person on whom a restraint order made under this section is served in accordance with this section and who, while the order is in force, acts in contravention of or fails to comply with the order is guilty of

(a) an indictable offence and liable to imprisonment for a term of not more than five years; or

(b) an offence punishable on summary conviction.

1997, c. 23, s. 15; 2001, c. 32, s. 35; 2019, c. 25, s. 206

490.81 (1) Management order — With respect to offence-related property other than a **"controlled substance"** within the meaning of the *Controlled Drugs and Substances Act* or **"cannabis"** as defined in subsection 2(1) of the *Cannabis Act*, on application of the Attorney General or of any other person with the written consent of the Attorney General, a judge or justice in the case of offence-related property seized under section 487, or a judge in the case of offence-related property restrained under section 490.8, may, if he or she is of the opinion that the circumstances so require,

(a) appoint a person to take control of and to manage or otherwise deal with all or part of the property in accordance with the directions of the judge or justice; and

(b) require any person having possession of that property to give possession of the property to the person appointed under paragraph (a).

(2) Appointment of Minister of Public Works and Government Services — When the Attorney General of Canada so requests, a judge or justice appointing a person under subsection (1) shall appoint the Minister of Public Works and Government Services.

(3) Power to manage — The power to manage or otherwise deal with property under subsection (1) includes

(a) the power to make an interlocutory sale of perishable or rapidly depreciating property;

(b) the power to destroy, in accordance with subsections (4) to (7), property that has little or no value; and

(c) the power to have property, other than real property or a conveyance, forfeited to Her Majesty in accordance with subsection (7.1).

(4) Application for destruction order — Before a person who is appointed to manage property destroys property that has little or no value, they shall apply to a court for a destruction order.

(5) Notice — Before making a destruction order, a court shall require notice in accordance with subsection (6) to be given to and may hear any person who, in the court's opinion, appears to have a valid interest in the property.

(6) Manner of giving notice — A notice shall

(a) be given in the manner that the court directs or that may be specified in the rules of the court; and

(b) specify the effective period of the notice that the court considers reasonable or that may be set out in the rules of the court.

(7) Destruction order — A court shall order that the property be destroyed if it is satisfied that the property has little or no financial or other value.

(7.1) Forfeiture order — On application by a person who is appointed to manage the property, a court shall order that the property, other than real property or a conveyance, be forfeited to Her Majesty to be disposed of or otherwise dealt with in accordance with the law if

(a) a notice is given or published in the manner that the court directs or that may be specified in the rules of the court;

(b) the notice specifies a period of 60 days during which a person may make an application to the court asserting their interest in the property; and

(c) during that period, no one makes such an application.

(8) **When management order ceases to have effect** — A management order ceases to have effect when the property that is the subject of the management order is returned in accordance with the law, destroyed or forfeited to Her Majesty.

(8.1) **For greater certainty** — For greater certainty, if property that is the subject of a management order is sold, the management order applies to the net proceeds of the sale.

(9) **Application to vary conditions** — The Attorney General may at any time apply to the judge or justice to cancel or vary any condition to which a management order is subject, but may not apply to vary an appointment made under subsection (2).

2001, c. 32, s. 36; 2017, c. 7, s. 68; 2018, c. 16, s. 217

490.9 (1) **Sections 489.1 and 490 applicable** — Subject to sections 490.1 to 490.7 sections 489.1 and 490 apply, with any modifications that the circumstances require, to any offence-related property that is the subject of a restraint order made under section 490.8.

(2) **Recognizance** — Where, pursuant to subsection (1), an order is made under paragraph 490(9)(*c*) for the return of any offence-related property that is the subject of a restraint order under section 490.8, the judge or justice making the order may require the applicant for the order to enter into a recognizance before the judge or justice, with or without sureties, in any amount and with any conditions that the judge or justice directs and, where the judge or justice considers it appropriate, require that applicant to deposit with the judge or justice any sum of money or other valuable security that the judge or justice directs.

1997, c. 23, s. 15

491. (1) **Forfeiture of weapons and ammunition** — Subject to subsection (2) where it is determined by a court that

(a) a weapon, an imitation firearm, a prohibited device, any ammunition, any prohibited ammunition or an explosive substance was used in the commission of an offence and that thing has been seized and detained, or

(b) that a person has committed an offence that involves, or the subject-matter of which is, a firearm, a cross-bow, a prohibited weapon, a restricted weapon, a prohibited device, ammunition, prohibited ammunition or an explosive substance and any such thing has been seized and detained,

the thing so seized and detained is forfeited to Her Majesty and shall be disposed of as the Attorney General directs.

(2) Return to lawful owner — If the court by which a determination referred to in subsection (1) is made is satisfied that the lawful owner of any thing that is or may be forfeited to Her Majesty under subsection (1) was not a party to the offence and had no reasonable grounds to believe that the thing would or might be used in the commission of an offence, the court shall order that the thing be returned to that lawful owner, that the proceeds of any sale of the thing be paid to that lawful owner or, if the thing was destroyed, that an amount equal to the value of the thing be paid to the owner.

(3) Application of proceeds — Where any thing in respect of which this section applies is sold, the proceeds of the sale shall be paid to the Attorney General or, where an order is made under subsection (2), to the person who was, immediately prior to the sale, the lawful owner of the thing.

1991, c. 40, s. 30; 1995, c. 39, s. 152

491.1 (1) Order for restitution or forfeiture of property obtained by crime — Where an accused or defendant is tried for an offence and the court determines that an offence has been committed, whether or not the accused has been convicted or discharged under section 730 of the offence, and at the time of the trial any property obtained by the commission of the offence

(a) is before the court or has been detained so that it can be immediately dealt with, and

(b) will not be required as evidence in any other proceedings,

section 490 does not apply in respect of the property and the court shall make an order under subsection (2) in respect of the property.

(2) Idem — In the circumstances referred to in subsection (1), the court shall order, in respect of any property,

(a) if the lawful owner or person lawfully entitled to possession of the property is known, that it be returned to that person; and

(b) if the lawful owner or person lawfully entitled to possession of the property is not known, that it be forfeited to Her Majesty, to be disposed of as the Attorney General directs or otherwise dealt with in accordance with the law.

(3) When certain orders not to be made — An order shall not be made under subsection (2)

(a) in the case of proceedings against a trustee, banker, merchant, attorney, factor, broker or other agent entrusted with the possession of goods or documents of title to goods, for an offence under section 330, 331, 332 or 336; or

(b) in respect of

(i) property to which a person acting in good faith and without notice has acquired lawful title for valuable consideration,

(ii) a valuable security that has been paid or discharged in good faith by a person who was liable to pay or discharge it,

(iii) a negotiable instrument that has, in good faith, been taken or received by transfer or delivery for valuable consideration by a person who had no notice and no reasonable cause to suspect that an offence had been committed, or

(iv) property in respect of which there is a dispute as to ownership or right of possession by claimants other than the accused or defendant.

(4) By whom order executed — An order made under this section shall, on the direction of the court, be executed by the peace officers by whom the process of the court is ordinarily executed.

R.S.C. 1985, c. 27 (1st Supp.), s. 74; 1995, c. 22, s. 18 (Sched. IV, item 26)

491.2 (1) Photographic evidence — Before any property that would otherwise be required to be produced for the purposes of a preliminary inquiry, trial or other proceeding in respect of an offence under section 334, 344, 348, 354, 355.2, 355.4, 362 or 380 is returned or ordered to be returned, forfeited or otherwise dealt with under section 489.1 or 490 or is otherwise returned, a peace officer or any person under the direction of a peace officer may take and retain a photograph of the property.

(2) Certified photograph admissible in evidence — Every photograph of property taken under subsection (1), accompanied by a certificate of a person containing the statements referred to in subsection (3), shall be admissible in evidence and, in the absence of evidence to the contrary, shall have the same probative force as the property would have had if it had been proved in the ordinary way.

(3) Statements made in certificate — For the purposes of subsection (2), a certificate of a person stating that

(a) the person took the photograph under the authority of subsection (1),

(b) the person is a peace officer or took the photograph under the direction of a peace officer, and

(c) the photograph is a true photograph

shall be admissible in evidence and, in the absence of evidence to the contrary, is evidence of the statements contained in the certificate without proof of the signature of the person appearing to have signed the certificate.

(4) Secondary evidence of peace officer — An affidavit or solemn declaration of a peace officer or other person stating that the person has seized property and detained it or caused it to be detained from the time that person took possession of the property until a photograph of the property was taken under subsection (1) and that property was not altered in any manner before the photograph was taken shall be admissible in evidence and, in the absence of evidence to the contrary, is evidence of the statements contained in the affidavit or solemn declaration without proof of the signature or official character of the person appearing to have signed the affidavit or solemn declaration.

(5) Notice of intention to produce certified photograph — Unless the court orders otherwise, no photograph, certificate, affidavit or solemn declaration shall be received in evidence at a trial or other proceeding pursuant to subsection (2), (3) or (4) unless the prosecutor has, before the trial or other proceeding, given to the accused a copy thereof and reasonable notice of intention to produce it in evidence.

(6) Attendance for examination — Notwithstanding subsection (3) or (4), the court may require the person who appears to have signed a certificate, an affidavit or a solemn declaration referred to in that subsection to appear before it for examination or cross-examination in respect of the issue of proof of any of the facts contained in the certificate, affidavit or solemn declaration.

(7) Production of property in court — A court may order any property seized and returned pursuant to section 489.1 or 490 to be produced in court or made available for examination by all parties to a proceeding at a reasonable time and place, notwithstanding that a photograph of the property has been received in evidence pursuant to subsection (2), where the court is satisfied that the interests of justice so require and that it is possible and practicable to do so in the circumstances.

(8) Definition of "photograph" — In this section, **"photograph"** includes a still photograph, a photographic film or plate, a microphotographic film, a photostatic negative, an X-ray film, a motion picture and a videotape.

R.S.C. 1985, c. 23 (4th Supp.), s. 2; 1992, c. 1, s. 58(1) (Sched. I, item 10); 2010, c. 14, s. 10

492. (1) Seizure of explosives — Every person who executes a warrant issued under section 487 or 487.1 may seize any explosive substance that he suspects is intended to be used for an unlawful purpose, and shall, as soon as possible, remove to a place of safety anything that he seizes by virtue of this section and detain it until he is ordered by a judge of a superior court to deliver it to some other person or an order is made pursuant to subsection (2).

(2) Forfeiture — Where an accused is convicted of an offence in respect of anything seized by virtue of subsection (1), it is forfeited and shall be dealt with as the court that makes the conviction may direct.

(3) Application of proceeds — Where anything to which this section applies is sold, the proceeds of the sale shall be paid to the Attorney General.

R.S.C. 1985, c. 27 (1st Supp.), s. 70

492.1 (1) Warrant for tracking device — transactions and things — A justice or judge who is satisfied by information on oath that there are reasonable grounds to suspect that an offence has been or will be committed under this or any other Act of Parliament and that tracking the location of one or more transactions or the location or movement of a thing, including a vehicle, will assist in the investigation of the offence may issue a warrant authorizing a peace officer or a public officer to obtain that tracking data by means of a tracking device.

(2) Warrant for tracking device — individuals — A justice or judge who is satisfied by information on oath that there are reasonable grounds to believe that an offence has been or will be committed under this or any other Act of Parliament and that tracking an individual's movement by identifying the location of a thing that is usually carried or worn by the individual will assist in the investigation of the offence may issue a warrant authorizing a peace officer or a public officer to obtain that tracking data by means of a tracking device.

(3) **Scope of warrant** — The warrant authorizes the peace officer or public officer, or a person acting under their direction, to install, activate, use, maintain, monitor and remove the tracking device, including covertly.

(4) **Conditions** — A warrant may contain any conditions that the justice or judge considers appropriate, including conditions to protect a person's interests.

(5) **Period of validity** — Subject to subsection (6), a warrant is valid for the period specified in it as long as that period ends no more than 60 days after the day on which the warrant is issued.

(6) **Period of validity — organized crime and terrorism offence** — A warrant is valid for the period specified in it as long as that period ends no more than one year after the day on which the warrant is issued, if the warrant relates to

(a) an offence under any of sections 467.11 to 467.13;

(b) an offence committed for the benefit of, at the direction of, or in association with a criminal organization; or

(c) a terrorism offence.

(6.1) **Execution in Canada** — A warrant issued under this section may be executed at any place in Canada. Any public officer or peace officer who executes the warrant must have authority to act in that capacity in the place where the warrant is executed.

(7) **Removal after expiry of warrant** — On *ex parte* application supported by an affidavit, the justice or judge who issued a warrant or another justice or judge who has jurisdiction to issue such warrants may authorize the covert removal of the tracking device after the expiry of the warrant under any conditions that the justice or judge considers advisable in the public interest. The authorization is valid for the period specified in it as long as that period is not more than 90 days.

(8) **Definitions** — The following definitions apply in this section.

"data" means representations, including signs, signals or symbols, that are capable of being understood by an individual or processed by a computer system or other device. *("données")*

"judge" means a judge of a superior court of criminal jurisdiction or a judge of the Court of Quebec. *("juge")*

"public officer" means a public officer who is appointed or designated to administer or enforce a federal or provincial law and whose duties include the enforcement of this or any other Act of Parliament. *("fonctionnaire public")*

"tracking data" means data that relates to the location of a transaction, individual or thing. *("données de localisation")*

"tracking device" means a device, including a computer program within the meaning of subsection 342.1(2), that may be used to obtain or record tracking data or to transmit it by a means of telecommunication. *("dispositif de localisation")*

1993, c. 40, s. 18; 1999, c. 5, s. 18; 2014, c. 31, s. 23; 2019, c. 25, s. 207

492.2 (1) Warrant for transmission data recorder — A justice or judge who is satisfied by information on oath that there are reasonable grounds to suspect that an offence has been or will be committed against this or any other Act of Parliament and that transmission data will assist in the investigation of the offence may issue a warrant authorizing a peace officer or a public officer to obtain the transmission data by means of a transmission data recorder.

(2) Scope of warrant — The warrant authorizes the peace officer or public officer, or a person acting under their direction, to install, activate, use, maintain, monitor and remove the transmission data recorder, including covertly.

(3) Limitation — No warrant shall be issued under this section for the purpose of obtaining tracking data.

(4) Period of validity — Subject to subsection (5), a warrant is valid for the period specified in it as long as that period ends no more than 60 days after the day on which the warrant is issued.

(5) Period of validity — organized crime or terrorism offence — The warrant is valid for the period specified in it as long as that period ends no more than one year after the day on which the warrant is issued, if the warrant relates to

(a) an offence under any of sections 467.11 to 467.13;

(b) an offence committed for the benefit of, at the direction of, or in association with a criminal organization; or

(c) a terrorism offence.

(5.1) Execution in Canada — A warrant issued under subsection (1) may be executed at any place in Canada. Any public officer or peace officer who executes the warrant must have authority to act in that capacity in the place where the warrant is executed.

(6) Definitions — The following definitions apply in this section.

"data" means representations, including signs, signals or symbols, that are capable of being understood by an individual or processed by a computer system or other device. *("données")*

"judge" means a judge of a superior court of criminal jurisdiction or a judge of the Court of Quebec. *("juge")*

"public officer" means a public officer who is appointed or designated to administer or enforce a federal or provincial law and whose duties include the enforcement of this or any other Act of Parliament. *("fonctionnaire public")*

"transmission data" means data that

(a) relates to the telecommunication functions of dialling, routing, addressing or signalling;

(b) is transmitted to identify, activate or configure a device, including a computer program as defined in subsection 342.1(2), in order to establish or maintain access to a telecommunication service for the purpose of enabling a communication, or is generated during the creation, transmission or reception of a communication and identifies or purports to identify the type, direction, date, time, duration, size, origin, destination or termination of the communication; and

(c) does not reveal the substance, meaning or purpose of the communication.

("données de transmission")

"transmission data recorder" means a device, including a computer program within the meaning of subsection 342.1(2), that may be used to obtain or record transmission data or to transmit it by a means of telecommunication. *("enregistreur de données de transmission")*

1993, c. 40, s. 18; 1999, c. 5, s. 19; 2014, c. 31, s. 23; 2019, c. 25, s. 208

PART XVI — COMPELLING APPEARANCE OF AN ACCUSED BEFORE A JUSTICE AND INTERIM RELEASE (SS. 493–529.5)

Interpretation

493. Definitions — In this Part

"accused" includes

(a) a person to whom a peace officer has issued an appearance notice under section 496, and

Proposed Amendment — 493 "accused" (a)

(a) a person to whom a peace officer has issued an appearance notice under section 497, and

2019, c. 25, s. 209(2) [To come into force December 18, 2019.]

(b) a person arrested for a criminal offence;

"appearance notice" means a notice in Form 9 issued by a peace officer;

Proposed Repeal — 493 "appearance notice"

"appearance notice" [Repealed 2019, c. 25, s. 209(1). To come into force December 18, 2019.]

"judge" means

(a) in the Province of Ontario, a judge of the superior court of criminal jurisdiction of the Province,

(b) in the Province of Quebec, a judge of the superior court of criminal jurisdiction of the province or three judges of the Court of Quebec,

(c) [Repealed 1992, c. 51, s. 37.]

(d) in the Provinces of Nova Scotia, New Brunswick, Manitoba, British Columbia, Prince Edward Island, Saskatchewan, Alberta and Newfoundland and

Labrador, a judge of the superior court of criminal jurisdiction of the Province,

(e) in Yukon and the Northwest Territories, a judge of the Supreme Court, and

(f) in Nunavut, a judge of the Nunavut Court of Justice;

"officer in charge" means the officer for the time being in command of the police force responsible for the lock-up or other place to which an accused is taken after arrest or a peace officer designated by him for the purposes of this Part who is in charge of that place at the time an accused is taken to that place to be detained in custody;

Proposed Repeal — 493 "officer in charge"

"officer in charge" [Repealed 2019, c. 25, s. 209(1). To come into force December 18, 2019.]

"promise to appear" means a promise in Form 10;

Proposed Repeal — 493 "promise to appear"

"promise to appear" [Repealed 2019, c. 25, s. 209(1). To come into force December 18, 2019.]

"recognizance", when used in relation to a recognizance entered into before an officer in charge, or other peace officer, means a recognizance in Form 11, and when used in relation to a recognizance entered into before a justice or judge, means a recognizance in Form 32;

Proposed Repeal — 493 "recognizance"

"recognizance" [Repealed 2019, c. 25, s. 209(1). To come into force December 18, 2019.]

"summons" means a summons in Form 6 issued by a justice or a judge;

Proposed Repeal — 493 "summons"

"summons" [Repealed 2019, c. 25, s. 209(1). To come into force December 18, 2019.]

"undertaking" means an undertaking in Form 11.1 or 12;

Proposed Repeal — 493 "undertaking"

"undertaking" [Repealed 2019, c. 25, s. 209(1). To come into force December 18, 2019.]

"warrant", when used in relation to a warrant for the arrest of a person, means a warrant in Form 7 and, when used in relation to a warrant for the committal of a person, means a warrant in Form 8.

R.S.C. 1985, c. 11 (1st Supp.), s. 2(1) (Sched., item 1(3)); R.S.C. 1985, c. 27 (2nd Supp.), s. 10 (Sched., item 6(10)); R.S.C. 1985, c. 40 (4th Supp.), s. 2 (Sched., item 1(5)); 1990, c. 16, s. 5; 1990, c. 17, s. 12; 1992, c. 51, s. 37; 1994, c. 44, s. 39; 1999, c. 3, s. 30; 2002, c. 7, s. 143; 2015, c. 3, s. 51

Proposed Addition — 493.1, 493.2

Principle and Considerations

[Heading added 2019, c. 25, s. 210. To come into force December 18, 2019.]

493.1 Principle of restraint — In making a decision under this Part, a peace officer, justice or judge shall give primary consideration to the release of the accused at the earliest reasonable opportunity and on the least onerous conditions that are appropriate in the circumstances, including conditions that are reasonably practicable for the accused to comply with, while taking into account the grounds referred to in subsection 498(1.1) or 515(10), as the case may be.

2019, c. 25, s. 210 [To come into force December 18, 2019.]

493.2 Aboriginal accused or vulnerable populations — In making a decision under this Part, a peace officer, justice or judge shall give particular attention to the circumstances of

(a) Aboriginal accused; and

(b) accused who belong to a vulnerable population that is overrepresented in the criminal justice system and that is disadvantaged in obtaining release under this Part.

2019, c. 25, s. 210 [To come into force December 18, 2019.]

Arrest without Warrant and Release from Custody

494. (1) Arrest without warrant by any person — Any one may arrest without warrant

(a) a person whom he finds committing an indictable offence; or

(b) a person who, on reasonable grounds, he believes

(i) has committed a criminal offence, and

(ii) is escaping from and freshly pursued by persons who have lawful authority to arrest that person.

(2) Arrest by owner, etc., of property — The owner or a person in lawful possession of property, or a person authorized by the owner or by a person in lawful possession of property, may arrest a person without a warrant if they find them committing a criminal offence on or in relation to that property and

(a) they make the arrest at that time; or

(b) they make the arrest within a reasonable time after the offence is committed and they believe on reasonable grounds that it is not feasible in the circumstances for a peace officer to make the arrest.

(3) **Delivery to peace officer** — Any one other than a peace officer who arrests a person without warrant shall forthwith deliver the person to a peace officer.

(4) **For greater certainty** — For greater certainty, a person who is authorized to make an arrest under this section is a person who is authorized by law to do so for the purposes of section 25.

2012, c. 9, s. 3

495. (1) **Arrest without warrant by peace officer** — A peace officer may arrest without warrant

(a) a person who has committed an indictable offence or who, on reasonable grounds, he believes has committed or is about to commit an indictable offence,

(b) a person whom he finds committing a criminal offence, or

(c) a person in respect of whom he has reasonable grounds to believe that a warrant of arrest or committal, in any form set out in Part XXVIII in relation thereto, is in force within the territorial jurisdiction in which the person is found.

(2) **Limitation** — A peace officer shall not arrest a person without warrant for

(a) an indictable offence mentioned in section 553,

(b) an offence for which the person may be prosecuted by indictment or for which he is punishable on summary conviction, or

(c) an offence punishable on summary conviction,

in any case where

(d) he believes on reasonable grounds that the public interest, having regard to all the circumstances including the need to

(i) establish the identity of the person,

(ii) secure or preserve evidence of or relating to the offence, or

(iii) prevent the continuation or repetition of the offence or the commission of another offence,

may be satisfied without so arresting the person, and

(e) he has no reasonable grounds to believe that, if he does not so arrest the person, the person will fail to attend court in order to be dealt with according to law.

(3) **Consequences of arrest without warrant** — Notwithstanding subsection (2), a peace officer acting under subsection (1) is deemed to be acting lawfully and in the execution of his duty for the purposes of

(a) any proceedings under this or any other Act of Parliament; and

(b) any other proceedings, unless in any such proceedings it is alleged and established by the person making the allegation that the peace officer did not comply with the requirements of subsection (2).

R.S.C. 1985, c. 27 (1st Supp.), s. 75

Proposed Addition — 495.1

495.1 Arrest without warrant — application of section 524 — Despite any other provision in this Act, if a peace officer has reasonable grounds to believe that an accused has contravened or is about to contravene a summons, appearance notice, undertaking or release order that was issued or given to the accused or entered into by the accused, or has committed an indictable offence while being subject to a summons, appearance notice, undertaking or release order, the peace officer may arrest the accused without a warrant for the purpose of taking them before a judge or justice to be dealt with under section 524.

2019, c. 25, s. 211 [To come into force December 18, 2019.]

496. Issue of appearance notice by peace officer — Where, by virtue of subsection 495(2), a peace officer does not arrest a person, he may issue an appearance notice to the person if the offence is

(a) an indictable offence mentioned in section 553,

(b) an offence for which the person may be prosecuted by indictment or for which he is punishable on summary conviction, or

(c) an offence punishable on summary conviction.

Proposed Amendment — 496

496. Appearance notice for judicial referral hearing — If a peace officer has reasonable grounds to believe that a person has failed to comply with a summons, appearance notice, undertaking or release order or to attend court as required and that the failure did not cause a victim physical or emotional harm, property damage or economic loss, the peace officer may, without laying a charge, issue an appearance notice to the person to appear at a judicial referral hearing under section 523.1.

2019, c. 25, s. 212 [To come into force December 18, 2019.]

497. (1) Release from custody by peace officer — Subject to subsection (1.1), if a peace officer arrests a person without warrant for an offence described in paragraph 496(a), (b) or (c), the peace officer shall, as soon as practicable,

(a) release the person from custody with the intention of compelling their appearance by way of summons; or

(b) issue an appearance notice to the person and then release them.

(1.1) Exception — A peace officer shall not release a person under subsection (1) if the peace officer believes, on reasonable grounds,

(a) that it is necessary in the public interest that the person be detained in custody or that the matter of their release from custody be dealt with under another provision of this Part, having regard to all the circumstances including the need to

(i) establish the identity of the person,

(ii) secure or preserve evidence of or relating to the offence,

(iii) prevent the continuation or repetition of the offence or the commission of another offence, or

(iv) ensure the safety and security of any victim of or witness to the offence; or

(b) that if the person is released from custody, the person will fail to attend court in order to be dealt with according to law.

(2) **Where subsection (1) does not apply** — Subsection (1) does not apply in respect of a person who has been arrested without warrant by a peace officer for an offence described in subsection 503(3).

(3) **Consequences of non-release** — A peace officer who has arrested a person without warrant for an offence described in subsection (1) and who does not release the person from custody as soon as practicable in the manner described in that subsection shall be deemed to be acting lawfully and in the execution of the peace officer's duty for the purposes of

(a) any proceedings under this or any other Act of Parliament; and

(b) any other proceedings, unless in any such proceedings it is alleged and established by the person making the allegation that the peace officer did not comply with the requirements of subsection (1).

Proposed Amendment — 497

497. **Issue of appearance notice by peace officer** — If, by virtue of subsection 495(2), a peace officer does not arrest a person, they may issue an appearance notice to the person if the offence is

(a) an indictable offence mentioned in section 553;

(b) an offence for which the person may be prosecuted by indictment or for which they are punishable on summary conviction; or

(c) an offence punishable on summary conviction.

2019, c. 25, s. 212 [To come into force December 18, 2019.]

1999, c. 25, s. 3

498. (1) **Release from custody by officer in charge** — Subject to subsection (1.1), if a person who has been arrested without warrant by a peace officer is taken into custody, or if a person who has been arrested without warrant and delivered to a peace officer under subsection 494(3) or placed in the custody of a peace officer under subsection 163.5(3) of the *Customs Act* is detained in custody under subsection 503(1) for an offence described in paragraph 496(a), (b) or (c), or any other offence that is punishable by imprisonment for five years or less, and has not been

taken before a justice or released from custody under any other provision of this Part, the officer in charge or another peace officer shall, as soon as practicable,

(a) release the person with the intention of compelling their appearance by way of summons;

(b) release the person on their giving a promise to appear;

(c) release the person on the person's entering into a recognizance before the officer in charge or another peace officer without sureties in an amount not exceeding $500 that the officer directs, but without deposit of money or other valuable security; or

(d) if the person is not ordinarily resident in the province in which the person is in custody or does not ordinarily reside within 200 kilometres of the place in which the person is in custody, release the person on the person's entering into a recognizance before the officer in charge or another peace officer without sureties in an amount not exceeding $500 that the officer directs and, if the officer so directs, on depositing with the officer a sum of money or other valuable security not exceeding in amount or value $500, that the officer directs.

Proposed Amendment — 498(1)

(1) Release from custody — arrest without warrant — Subject to subsection (1.1), if a person has been arrested without warrant for an offence, other than one listed in section 469, and has not been taken before a justice or released from custody under any other provision of this Part, a peace officer shall, as soon as practicable, release the person, if

(a) the peace officer intends to compel the person's appearance by way of summons;

(b) the peace officer issues an appearance notice to the person; or

(c) the person gives an undertaking to the peace officer.

2019, c. 25, s. 213(1) [To come into force December 18, 2019.]

Proposed Addition — 498(1.01)

(1.01) Person delivered or detained — Subsection (1) also applies in respect of a person who has been arrested without warrant and delivered to a peace officer under subsection 494(3) or placed in the custody of a peace officer under subsection 163.5(3) of the *Customs Act* and who is detained in custody for an offence other than one listed in section 469 and who has not been taken before a justice or released from custody under any other provision of this Part.

2019, c. 25, s. 213(1) [To come into force December 18, 2019.]

(1.1) Exception — The officer in charge or the peace officer shall not release a person under subsection (1) if the officer in charge or peace officer believes, on reasonable grounds,

Proposed Amendment — 498(1.1) opening words

(1.1) Exception — The peace officer shall not release the person if the peace officer believes, on reasonable grounds,

2019, c. 25, s. 213(2) [To come into force December 18, 2019.]

(a) that it is necessary in the public interest that the person be detained in custody or that the matter of their release from custody be dealt with under another provision of this Part, having regard to all the circumstances including the need to

(i) establish the identity of the person,

(ii) secure or preserve evidence of or relating to the offence,

(iii) prevent the continuation or repetition of the offence or the commission of another offence, or

(iv) ensure the safety and security of any victim of or witness to the offence; or

(b) that, if the person is released from custody, the person will fail to attend court in order to be dealt with according to law.

(2) Where subsection (1) does not apply — Subsection (1) does not apply in respect of a person who has been arrested without warrant by a peace officer for an offence described in subsection 503(3).

Proposed Amendment — 498(2)

(2) When subsections (1) and (1.01) do not apply — Subsections (1) and (1.01) do not apply in respect of a person who has been arrested without warrant by a peace officer for an offence described in subsection 503(3).

2019, c. 25, s. 213(3) [To come into force December 18, 2019.]

(3) Consequences of non-release — An officer in charge or another peace officer who has the custody of a person taken into or detained in custody for an offence described in subsection (1) and who does not release the person from custody as soon as practicable in the manner described in that subsection shall be deemed to be acting lawfully and in the execution of the officer's duty for the purposes of

Proposed Amendment — 498(3) opening words

(3) Consequences of non-release — A peace officer who has arrested a person without a warrant, or who has been given the custody of a person arrested without a warrant, for an offence described in subsection (1), and who does not release the person from custody as soon as practicable in the manner described in that subsection shall be deemed to be acting lawfully and in the execution of the officer's duty for the purposes of

2019, c. 25, s. 213(4) [To come into force December 18, 2019.]

(a) any proceedings under this or any other Act of Parliament; or

(b) any other proceedings, unless in any such proceedings it is alleged and established by the person making the allegation that the officer in charge or other peace officer did not comply with the requirements of subsection (1).

Proposed Amendment — 498(3)(b)

(b) any other proceedings, unless in any such proceedings it is alleged and established by the person making the allegation that the peace officer did not comply with the requirements of subsection (1).

2019, c. 25, s. 213(5) [To come into force December 18, 2019.]

R.S.C. 1985, c. 27 (1st Supp.), s. 186; 1997, c. 18, s. 52; 1998, c. 7, s. 2; 1999, c. 25, ss. 4, 30

499. (1) Release from custody by officer in charge where arrest made with warrant — Where a person who has been arrested with a warrant by a peace officer is taken into custody for an offence other than one mentioned in section 522, the officer in charge may, if the warrant has been endorsed by a justice under subsection 507(6),

(a) release the person on the person's giving a promise to appear;

(b) release the person on the person's entering into a recognizance before the officer in charge without sureties in the amount not exceeding five hundred dollars that the officer in charge directs, but without deposit of money or other valuable security; or

(c) if the person is not ordinarily resident in the province in which the person is in custody or does not ordinarily reside within two hundred kilometres of the place in which the person is in custody, release the person on the person's entering into a recognizance before the officer in charge without sureties in the amount not exceeding five hundred dollars that the officer in charge directs and, if the officer in charge so directs, on depositing with the officer in charge such sum of money or other valuable security not exceeding in amount or value five hundred dollars, as the officer in charge directs.

(2) Additional conditions — In addition to the conditions for release set out in paragraphs (1)(*a*), (*b*) and (*c*), the officer in charge may also require the person to enter into an undertaking in Form 11.1 in which the person, in order to be released, undertakes to do one or more of the following things:

(a) to remain within a territorial jurisdiction specified in the undertaking;

(b) to notify a peace officer or another person mentioned in the undertaking of any change in his or her address, employment or occupation;

(c) to abstain from communicating, directly or indirectly, with any victim, witness or other person identified in the undertaking, or from going to a place specified in the undertaking, except in accordance with the conditions specified in the undertaking;

(d) to deposit the person's passport with the peace officer or other person mentioned in the undertaking;

(e) to abstain from possessing a firearm and to surrender any firearm in the possession of the person and any authorization, licence or registration certificate or other document enabling that person to acquire or possess a firearm;

(f) to report at the times specified in the undertaking to a peace officer or other person designated in the undertaking;

(g) to abstain from

(i) the consumption of alcohol or other intoxicating substances, or

(ii) the consumption of drugs except in accordance with a medical prescription; and

(h) to comply with any other condition specified in the undertaking that the officer in charge considers necessary to ensure the safety and security of any victim of or witness to the offence.

(3) **Application to justice** — A person who has entered into an undertaking under subsection (2) may, at any time before or at his or her appearance pursuant to a promise to appear or recognizance, apply to a justice for an order under subsection 515(1) to replace his or her undertaking, and section 515 applies, with such modifications as the circumstances require, to such a person.

(4) **Application by prosecutor** — Where a person has entered into an undertaking under subsection (2), the prosecutor may

(a) at any time before the appearance of the person pursuant to a promise to appear or recognizance, after three days notice has been given to that person, or

(b) at the appearance

apply to a justice for an order under subsection 515(2) to replace the undertaking, and section 515 applies, with such modifications as the circumstances require, to such a person.

Proposed Amendment — 499

499. Release from custody — arrest with warrant — If a person who has been arrested with a warrant by a peace officer is taken into custody for an offence other than one listed in section 469 and the warrant has been endorsed by a justice under subsection 507(6), a peace officer may release the person, if

(a) the peace officer issues an appearance notice to the person; or

(b) the person gives an undertaking to the peace officer.

2019, c. 25, s. 214 [To come into force December 18, 2019.]

R.S.C. 1985, c. 27 (1st Supp.), s. 186; 1994, c. 44, s. 40; 1997, c. 18, s. 53; 1999, c. 25, s. 5

500. Money or other valuable security to be deposited with justice — If a person has, under paragraph 498(1)(d) or 499(1)(c), deposited any sum of money or other valuable security with the officer in charge, the officer in charge shall, without delay after the deposit, cause the money or valuable security to be delivered to a justice for deposit with the justice.

Proposed Amendment — 500

500. (1) Contents of appearance notice — An appearance notice shall

(a) set out the name, date of birth and contact information of the accused;

(b) set out the substance of the offence that the accused is alleged to have committed;

(c) require the accused to attend court at a time and place to be stated in the notice and to attend afterwards as required by the court; and

(d) indicate if the accused is required to appear at a judicial referral hearing under section 523.1 for a failure under section 496.

(2) Summary of consequences — failure to appear — An appearance notice shall set out a summary of subsections 145(3) and (6), section 512.2 and subsection 524(4) and the possible consequences of a failure to appear at a judicial referral hearing under section 523.1.

(3) Attendance for purposes of *Identification of Criminals Act* — An appearance notice may require the accused to appear at the time and place stated in it for the purposes of the *Identification of Criminals Act*, if the accused is alleged to have committed an indictable offence and, in the case of an offence designated as a contravention under the *Contraventions Act*, the *Attorney General*, within the meaning of that Act, has not made an election under section 50 of that Act.

(4) Signature of accused — An accused shall be requested to sign in duplicate their appearance notice and, whether or not they comply with that request, one of the duplicates shall be given to the accused. If the accused fails or refuses to sign, the lack of their signature does not invalidate the appearance notice.

2019, c. 25, s. 215 [To come into force December 18, 2019.]

1999, c. 5, s. 20; 1999, c. 25, s. 6

501. (1) Contents of appearance notice, promise to appear and recognizance — An appearance notice issued by a peace officer or a promise to appear given to, or a recognizance entered into before, an officer in charge or another peace officer shall

(a) set out the name of the accused;

(b) set out the substance of the offence that the accused is alleged to have committed; and

(c) require the accused to attend court at a time and place to be stated therein and to attend thereafter as required by the court in order to be dealt with according to law.

(2) Idem — An appearance notice issued by a peace officer or a promise to appear given to, or a recognizance entered into before, an officer in charge or another peace officer shall set out the text of subsections 145(5) and (6) and section 502.

(3) Attendance for purposes of *Identification of Criminals Act* — An appearance notice issued by a peace officer or a promise to appear given to, or a recognizance entered into before, an officer in charge or another peace officer may require the accused to appear at a time and place stated in it for the purposes of the *Identification of Criminals Act*, where the accused is alleged to have committed an indictable offence and, in the case of an offence designated as a contravention under the *Contraventions Act*, the Attorney General, within the meaning of that Act has not made an election under section 50 of that Act.

(4) Signature of accused — An accused shall be requested to sign in duplicate his appearance notice, promise to appear or recognizance and, whether or not he complies with that request, one of the duplicates shall be given to the accused, but if the accused fails or refuses to sign, the lack of his signature does not invalidate the appearance notice, promise to appear or recognizance, as the case may be.

(5) [Repealed 2008, c. 18, s. 15.]

Proposed Amendment — 501

501. (1) Contents of undertaking — An undertaking under paragraph 498(1)(c), 499(b) or 503(1.1)(b) must set out

(a) the name, date of birth and contact information of the accused;

(b) the substance of the offence that the accused is alleged to have committed; and

(c) a summary of subsections 145(4) and (6), sections 512 and 512.2 and subsection 524(4).

(2) Mandatory conditions — The undertaking must contain a condition that the accused attend court at the time and place stated in the undertaking and to attend afterwards as required by the court.

(3) Additional conditions — The undertaking may contain one or more of the following conditions, if the condition is reasonable in the circumstances of the offence and necessary, to ensure the accused's attendance in court or the safety and security of any victim of or witness to the offence, or to prevent the continuation or repetition of the offence or the commission of another offence:

(a) report at specified times to the peace officer or other specified person;

(b) remain within a specified territorial jurisdiction;

(c) notify the peace officer or other specified person of any change in their address, employment or occupation;

(d) abstain from communicating, directly or indirectly, with any victim, witness or other person identified in the undertaking, except in accordance with any specified conditions;

(e) abstain from going to any specified place or entering any geographic area related to any person referred to in paragraph (d), except in accordance with any specified conditions;

(f) deposit all their passports with the peace officer or other specified person;

(g) reside at a specified address, be at that address at specified hours and present themselves at the entrance of that residence to a peace officer or other specified person, at the officer's or specified person's request during those hours;

(h) abstain from possessing a firearm, cross-bow, prohibited weapon, restricted weapon, prohibited device, ammunition, prohibited ammunition or explosive substance, and surrender those that are in their possession to the peace officer or other specified person and also any authorization, licence or registration certificate or other document enabling them to acquire or possess them;

(i) promise to pay an amount specified in the undertaking, which shall not be more than $500, if they fail to comply with any condition of the undertaking;

(j) deposit, with the peace officer specified in the undertaking, money or other valuable security whose value does not exceed $500 if, at the time of giving the undertaking, the accused is not ordinarily resident in the province or does not ordinarily reside within 200 kilometres of the place in which they are in custody; and

(k) comply with any other specified condition for ensuring the safety and security of any victim of or witness to the offence.

(4) **Attendance for purposes of *Identification of Criminals Act*** — The undertaking may require the accused to appear at the time and place stated in it for the purposes of the *Identification of Criminals Act* if the accused is alleged to have committed an indictable offence and, in the case of an offence designated as a contravention under the *Contraventions Act*, the *Attorney General*, within the meaning of that Act, has not made an election under section 50 of that Act.

(5) **Money or other valuable security to be deposited with justice** — If the accused has deposited an amount of money or other valuable security with a peace officer, the officer shall, without delay after the deposit, cause the money or valuable security to be delivered to a justice for deposit with the justice.

(6) **Signature of accused** — The accused shall be requested to sign in duplicate their undertaking and, whether or not they comply with that request, one of the duplicates shall be given to them. If they fail or refuse to sign, the lack of their signature does not invalidate the undertaking.

2019, c. 25, s. 215 [To come into force December 18, 2019.]

R.S.C. 1985, c. 27 (1st Supp.), s. 76; 1992, c. 47, s. 69 [Amended 1994, c. 44, s. 94; 1996, c. 7, s. 38.]; 1994, c. 44, s. 41; 2008, c. 18, s. 15

502. Failure to appear — Where an accused who is required by an appearance notice or promise to appear or by a recognizance entered into before an officer in charge or another peace officer to appear at a time and place stated therein for the purposes of the *Identification of Criminals Act* does not appear at that time and place, a justice may, where the appearance notice, promise to appear or recognizance has been confirmed by a justice under section 508, issue a warrant for the arrest of the accused for the offence with which the accused is charged.

Proposed Amendment — 502

502. (1) **Variation of undertaking on consent** — The undertaking in respect of which an accused has been released under section 498, 499 or 503 may, with the written consent of the accused and the prosecutor, be varied and the undertaking so varied is deemed to be an undertaking given under section 498, 499 or 503, as the case may be.

(2) **Replacement by justice of undertaking with order** — The accused or the prosecutor may, in the absence of consent between them, apply to a justice for a release order under subsection 515(1) or (2) to replace an undertaking given by the accused under paragraph 498(1)(c), 499(b) or 503(1.1)(b) with the order. If the prosecutor applies for the order, the prosecutor must provide three days notice to the accused.

2019, c. 25, s. 215 [To come into force December 18, 2019.]

1992, c. 47, s. 70 [Amended 1996, c. 7, s. 38.]; 1997, c. 18, s. 54

Appearance of Accused before Justice

502.1 (1) Appearance of the accused — Except as otherwise provided in this Part, an accused who is required to appear in a proceeding under this Part shall appear personally but may appear by audioconference or videoconference, if arrangements are made with the court in advance and those arrangements are satisfactory to the justice.

(2) Witness in Canada — Despite section 714.1, a witness in Canada who is required to give evidence in a proceeding under this Part may do so by audioconference or videoconference, if it is satisfactory to the justice.

(3) Witness outside Canada — For greater certainty, sections 714.2 to 714.8 apply when a witness outside Canada gives evidence in a proceeding under this Part.

(4) Participants — A **"participant"**, as defined in subsection 715.25(1), who is to participate in a proceeding under this Part shall participate personally but may participate by audioconference or videoconference, if it is satisfactory to the justice.

(5) Justice — The justice who is to preside at a proceeding under this Part shall preside personally but may preside by audioconference or videoconference, if the justice considers it necessary in the circumstances.

2019, c. 25, s. 216

503. (1) Taking before justice — A peace officer who arrests a person with or without warrant or to whom a person is delivered under subsection 494(3) or into whose custody a person is placed under subsection 163.5(3) of the *Customs Act* shall cause the person to be detained in custody and, in accordance with the following provisions, to be taken before a justice to be dealt with according to law:

(a) where a justice is available within a period of twenty-four hours after the person has been arrested by or delivered to the peace officer, the person shall be taken before a justice without unreasonable delay and in any event within that period, and

(b) where a justice is not available within a period of twenty-four hours after the person has been arrested by or delivered to the peace officer, the person shall be taken before a justice as soon as possible,

unless, at any time before the expiration of the time prescribed in paragraph (*a*) or (*b*) for taking the person before a justice,

(c) the peace officer or officer in charge releases the person under any other provision of this Part, or

(d) the peace officer or officer in charge is satisfied that the person should be released from custody, whether unconditionally under subsection (4) or otherwise conditionally or unconditionally, and so releases him.

Proposed Amendment — 503(1)

(1) **Taking before justice** — Subject to the other provisions of this section, a peace officer who arrests a person with or without warrant and who has not released the person under any other provision under this Part shall, in accordance with the following paragraphs, cause the person to be taken before a justice to be dealt with according to law:

(a) if a justice is available within a period of 24 hours after the person has been arrested by the peace officer, the person shall be taken before a justice without unreasonable delay and in any event within that period; and

(b) if a justice is not available within a period of 24 hours after the person has been arrested by the peace officer, the person shall be taken before a justice as soon as possible.

2019, c. 25, s. 217(1) [To come into force December 18, 2019.]

Proposed Addition — 503(1.1)

(1.1) **Re-evaluation of detention** — At any time before the expiry of the time referred to in paragraph (1)(a) or (b), a peace officer who is satisfied that the continued detention of the person in custody for an offence that is not listed in section 469 is no longer necessary shall release the person, if

(a) the peace officer issues an appearance notice to the person; or

(b) the person gives an undertaking to the peace officer.

2019, c. 25, s. 217(1) [To come into force December 18, 2019.]

(2) **Conditional release** — If a peace officer or an officer in charge is satisfied that a person described in subsection (1) should be released from custody conditionally, the officer may, unless the person is detained in custody for an offence mentioned in section 522, release that person on the person's giving a promise to appear or entering into a recognizance in accordance with paragraphs 498(1)(b) to (d) and subsection (2.1).

Proposed Amendment — 503(2)

(2) **Person delivered or in custody** — Subsections (1) and (1.1) also apply to a peace officer to whom a person is delivered under subsection 494(3) or into whose custody a person is placed under subsection 163.5(3) of the *Customs Act*, except that the 24-hour period referred to in paragraphs (1)(a) and (b) begins after the person is delivered to the officer.

2019, c. 25, s. 217(1) [To come into force December 18, 2019.]

(2.1) **Undertaking** — In addition to the conditions referred to in subsection (2), the peace officer or officer in charge may, in order to release the person, require the person to enter into an undertaking in Form 11.1 in which the person undertakes to do one or more of the following things:

(a) to remain within a territorial jurisdiction specified in the undertaking;

(b) to notify the peace officer or another person mentioned in the undertaking of any change in his or her address, employment or occupation;

(c) to abstain from communicating, directly or indirectly, with any victim, witness or other person identified in the undertaking, or from going to a place specified in the undertaking, except in accordance with the conditions specified in the undertaking;

(d) to deposit the person's passport with the peace officer or other person mentioned in the undertaking;

(e) to abstain possessing a firearm and to surrender any firearm in the possession of the person and any authorization, licence or registration certificate or other document enabling that person to acquire or possess a firearm;

(f) to report at the times specified in the undertaking to a peace officer or other person designated in the undertaking;

(g) to abstain from

(i) the consumption of alcohol or other intoxicating substances, or

(ii) the consumption of drugs except in accordance with a medical prescription; or

(h) to comply with any other condition specified in the undertaking that the peace officer or officer in charge considers necessary to ensure the safety and security of any victim of or witness to the offence.

Proposed Repeal — 503(2.1)

(2.1) [Repealed 2019, c. 25, s. 217(1). To come into force December 18, 2019.]

(2.2) Application to justice — A person who has entered into an undertaking under subsection (2.1) may, at any time before or at his or her appearance pursuant to a promise to appear or recognizance, apply to a justice for an order under subsection 515(1) to replace his or her undertaking, and section 515 applies, with such modifications as the circumstances require, to such a person.

Proposed Repeal — 503(2.2)

(2.2) [Repealed 2019, c. 25, s. 217(1). To come into force December 18, 2019.]

(2.3) Application by prosecutor — Where a person has entered into an undertaking under subsection (2.1), the prosecutor may

(a) at any time before the appearance of the person pursuant to a promise to appear or recognizance, after three days notice has been given to that person, or

(b) at the appearance,

apply to justice for an order under subsection 515(2) to replace the undertaking, and section 515 applies, with such modifications as the circumstances require, to such a person.

Proposed Repeal — 503(2.3)

(2.3) [Repealed 2019, c. 25, s. 217(1). To come into force December 18, 2019.]

(3) Remand in custody for return to jurisdiction where offence alleged to have been committed — Where a person has been arrested without warrant for an indictable offence alleged to have been committed in Canada outside the territorial division where the arrest took place, the person shall, within the time prescribed in paragraph (1)(*a*) or (*b*), be taken before a justice within whose jurisdiction the person was arrested unless, where the offence was alleged to have been committed within the province in which the person was arrested, the person was taken before a justice within whose jurisdiction the offence was alleged to have been committed, and the justice within whose jurisdiction the person was arrested

(a) if the justice is not satisfied that there are reasonable grounds to believe that the person arrested is the person alleged to have committed the offence, shall release that person; or

(b) if the justice is satisfied that there are reasonable grounds to believe that the person arrested is the person alleged to have committed the offence, may

(i) remand the person to the custody of a peace officer to await execution of a warrant for his or her arrest in accordance with section 528, but if no warrant is so executed within a period of six days after the time he or she is remanded to such custody, the person in whose custody he or she then is shall release him or her, or

(ii) where the offence was alleged to have been committed within the province in which the person was arrested, order the person to be taken before a justice having jurisdiction with respect to the offence.

(3.1) Interim release — Notwithstanding paragraph (3)(*b*), a justice may, with the consent of the prosecutor, order that the person referred to in subsection (3), pending the execution of a warrant for arrest of that person, be released

(a) unconditionally, or

Proposed Amendment — 503(3.1)(a)

(a) without conditions; or

2019, c. 25, s. 217(2) [To come into force December 18, 2019.]

(b) on any of the following terms to which the prosecutor consents, namely,

(i) giving an undertaking, including an undertaking to appear at a specified time before the court that has jurisdiction with respect to the indictable offence that the person is alleged to have committed, or

(ii) entering into a recognizance described in any of paragraphs 515(2)(*a*) to (*e*)

with such conditions described in subsection 515(4) as the justice considers desirable and to which the prosecutor consents.

Proposed Amendment — 503(3.1)(b)

(b) on the terms of a release order containing any conditions referred to in paragraphs 515(2)(a) to (e) that the justice considers desirable and to which the prosecutor consents.

2019, c. 25, s. 217(3) [To come into force December 18, 2019.]

(4) **Release of person about to commit indictable offence** — A peace officer or officer in charge having the custody of a person who has been arrested without warrant as a person about to commit an indictable offence shall release that person unconditionally as soon as practicable after he is satisfied that the continued detention of that person in custody is no longer necessary in order to prevent the commission by him of an indictable offence.

Proposed Amendment — 503(4)

(4) **Release of person about to commit indictable offence** — A peace officer having the custody of a person who has been arrested without warrant as a person about to commit an indictable offence shall release that person as soon as practicable after the officer is satisfied that the continued detention of that person is no longer necessary in order to prevent that person from committing an indictable offence.

2019, c. 25, s. 217(4) [To come into force December 18, 2019.]

(5) **Consequences of non-release** — Notwithstanding subsection (4), a peace officer or officer in charge having the custody of a person referred to in that subsection who does not release the person before the expiration of the time prescribed in paragraph (1)(a) or (b) for taking the person before the justice shall be deemed to be acting lawfully and in the execution of his duty for the purposes of

Proposed Amendment — 503(5) opening words

(5) **Consequences of non-release** — Despite subsection (4), a peace officer having the custody of a person referred to in that subsection who does not release the person before the expiry of the time prescribed in paragraph (1)(a) or (b) for taking the person before the justice shall be deemed to be acting lawfully and in the execution of the peace officer's duty for the purposes of

2019, c. 25, s. 217(5) [To come into force December 18, 2019.]

(a) any proceedings under this or any other Act of Parliament; or

(b) any other proceedings, unless in such proceedings it is alleged and established by the person making the allegation that the peace officer or officer in charge did not comply with the requirements of subsection (4).

Proposed Amendment — 503(5)(b)

(b) any other proceedings, unless in those proceedings it is alleged and established by the person making the allegation that the peace officer did not comply with the requirements of subsection (4).

2019, c. 25, s. 217(6) [To come into force December 18, 2019.]

R.S.C. 1985, c. 27 (1st Supp.), s. 77; 1994, c. 44, s. 42; 1997, c. 18, s. 55; 1998, c. 7, s. 3; 1999, c. 25, s. 7

Information, Summons and Warrant

504. In what cases justice may receive information — Any one who, on reasonable grounds, believes that a person has committed an indictable offence may lay an information in writing and under oath before a justice, and the justice shall receive the information, where it is alleged

(a) that the person has committed, anywhere, an indictable offence that may be tried in the province in which the justice resides, and that the person

(i) is or is believed to be, or

(ii) resides or is believed to reside,

within the territorial jurisdiction of the justice;

(b) that the person, wherever he may be, has committed an indictable offence within the territorial jurisdiction of the justice;

(c) that the person has, anywhere, unlawfully received property that was unlawfully obtained within the territorial jurisdiction of the justice; or

(d) that the person has in his possession stolen property within the territorial jurisdiction of the justice.

505. Time within which information to be laid in certain cases — Where

(a) an appearance notice has been issued to an accused under section 496, or

(b) an accused has been released from custody under section 497 or 498,

an information relating to the offence alleged to have been committed by the accused or relating to an included or other offence alleged to have been committed by him shall be laid before a justice as soon as practicable thereafter and in any event before the time stated in the appearance notice, promise to appear or recognizance issued to or given or entered into by the accused for his attendance in court.

Proposed Amendment — 505

505. Time within which information to be laid in certain cases — If an appearance notice has been issued to an accused under section 497, or if an accused has been released from custody under section 498 or 503, an information relating to the offence alleged to have been committed by the accused or relating to an included or other offence alleged to have been committed by them shall be laid before a justice as soon as practicable after the issuance or release, and in any event before the time stated in the appearance notice or undertaking for their attendance in court.

2019, c. 25, s. 218 [To come into force December 18, 2019.]

506. Form — An information laid under section 504 or 505 may be in Form 2.

507. (1) Justice to hear informant and witnesses — public prosecutions — Subject to subsection 523(1.1), a justice who receives an information laid under section 504 by a peace officer, a public officer, the Attorney General or the Attorney General's agent, other than an information laid before the justice under section 505, shall, except if an accused has already been arrested with or without a warrant,

(a) hear and consider, *ex parte*,

(i) the allegations of the informant, and

(ii) the evidence of witnesses, where he considers it desirable or necessary to do so; and

(b) where he considers that a case for so doing is made out, issue, in accordance with this section, either a summons or a warrant for the arrest of the accused to compel the accused to attend before him or some other justice for the same territorial division to answer to a charge of an offence.

(2) **Process compulsory** — No justice shall refuse to issue a summons or warrant by reason only that the alleged offence is one for which a person may be arrested without warrant.

(3) **Procedure when witnesses attend** — A justice who hears the evidence of a witness pursuant to subsection (1) shall

(a) take the evidence on oath; and

(b) cause the evidence to be taken in accordance with section 540 in so far as that section is capable of being applied.

(4) **Summons to be issued except in certain cases** — Where the justice considers that a case is made out for compelling an accused to attend before him to answer to a charge of an offence, he shall issue a summons to the accused unless the allegations of the informant or the evidence of any witness or witnesses taken in accordance with subsection (3) disclose reasonable grounds to believe that it is necessary in the public interest to issue a warrant for the arrest of the accused.

(5) **No process in blank** — A justice shall not sign a summons or warrant in blank.

(6) **Endorsement of warrant by justice** — A justice who issues a warrant under this section or section 508 or 512 may, unless the offence is one mentioned in section 522, authorize the release of the accused pursuant to section 499 by making an endorsement on the warrant in Form 29.

Proposed Amendment — 507(6)

(6) **Endorsement of warrant by justice** — A justice who issues a warrant under this section or section 508, 512, 512.1 or 512.2 may, unless the offence is one listed in section 469, authorize the release of the accused under section 499 by making an endorsement on the warrant in Form 29.

2019, c. 25, s. 219 [To come into force December 18, 2019.]

(7) **Promise to appear or recognizance deemed to have been confirmed** — Where, pursuant to subsection (6), a justice authorizes the release of an accused pursuant to section 499, a promise to appear given by the accused or a recognizance entered into by the accused pursuant to that section shall be deemed, for the purposes of subsection 145(5), to have been confirmed by a justice under section 508.

Proposed Amendment — 507(7)

(7) **Undertaking or appearance notice deemed confirmed** — If, under subsection (6), a justice authorizes the release of an accused under section 499, an appearance notice or undertaking referred to in that section shall be deemed, for the

purposes of subsection 145(3) or (4), as the case may be, to have been confirmed by a justice under section 508.

2019, c. 25, s. 219 [To come into force December 18, 2019.]

(8) Issue of summons or warrant — Where, on an appeal from or review of any decision or matter of jurisdiction, a new trial or hearing or a continuance or renewal of a trial or hearing is ordered, a justice may issue either a summons or a warrant for the arrest of the accused in order to compel the accused to attend at the new or continued or renewed trial or hearing.

R.S.C. 1985, c. 27 (1st Supp.), s. 78; 1994, c. 44, s. 43; 2002, c. 13, s. 21

507.1 (1) Referral when private prosecution — A justice who receives an information laid under section 504, other than an information referred to in subsection 507(1), shall refer it to a provincial court judge or, in Quebec, a judge of the Court of Quebec, or to a designated justice, to consider whether to compel the appearance of the accused on the information.

(2) Summons or warrant — A judge or designated justice to whom an information is referred under subsection (1) and who considers that a case for doing so is made out shall issue either a summons or warrant for the arrest of the accused to compel him or her to attend before a justice to answer to a charge of the offence charged in the information.

(3) Conditions for issuance — The judge or designated justice may issue a summons or warrant only if he or she

(a) has heard and considered the allegations of the informant and the evidence of witnesses;

(b) is satisfied that the Attorney General has received a copy of the information;

(c) is satisfied that the Attorney General has received reasonable notice of the hearing under paragraph (a); and

(d) has given the Attorney General an opportunity to attend the hearing under paragraph (a) and to cross-examine and call witnesses and to present any relevant evidence at the hearing.

(4) Appearance of Attorney General — The Attorney General may appear at the hearing held under paragraph (3)(a) without being deemed to intervene in the proceeding.

(5) Information deemed not to have been laid — If the judge or designated justice does not issue a summons or warrant under subsection (2), he or she shall endorse the information with a statement to that effect. Unless the informant, not later than six months after the endorsement, commences proceedings to compel the judge or designated justice to issue a summons or warrant, the information is deemed never to have been laid.

(6) Information deemed not to have been laid — proceedings commenced — If proceedings are commenced under subsection (5) and a summons or warrant is not issued as a result of those proceedings, the information is deemed never to have been laid.

(7) New evidence required for new hearing — If a hearing in respect of an offence has been held under paragraph (3)(a) and the judge or designated justice has not issued a summons or a warrant, no other hearings may be held under that paragraph with respect to the offence or an included offence unless there is new evidence in support of the allegation in respect of which the hearing is sought to be held.

(8) Subsections 507(2) to (8) to apply — Subsections 507(2) to (8) apply to proceedings under this section.

(9) Non-application — informations laid under sections 810 and 810.1 — Subsections (1) to (8) do not apply in respect of an information laid under section 810 or 810.1.

(10) Definition of "designated justice" — In this section, **"designated justice"** means a justice designated for the purpose by the chief judge of the provincial court having jurisdiction in the matter or, in Quebec, a justice designated by the chief judge of the Court of Quebec.

(11) Meaning of "Attorney General" — In this section, **"Attorney General"** includes the Attorney General of Canada and his or her lawful deputy in respect of proceedings that could have been commenced at the instance of the Government of Canada and conducted by or on behalf of that Government.

2002, c. 13, s. 22; 2008, c. 18, s. 16

508. (1) Justice to hear informant and witnesses — A justice who receives an information laid before him under section 505 shall

(a) hear and consider, *ex parte*,

(i) the allegations of the informant, and

(ii) the evidence of witnesses, where he considers it desirable or necessary to do so;

(b) where he considers that a case for so doing is made out, whether the information relates to the offence alleged in the appearance notice, promise to appear or recognizance or to an included or other offence,

(i) confirm the appearance notice, promise to appear or recognizance, as the case may be, and endorse the information accordingly, or

(ii) cancel the appearance notice, promise to appear or recognizance, as the case may be, and issue, in accordance with section 507, either a summons or a warrant for the arrest of the accused to compel the accused to attend before him or some other justice for the same territorial division to answer to a charge of an offence and endorse on the summons or warrant that the appearance notice, promise to appear or recognizance, as the case may be, has been cancelled; and

Proposed Amendment — 508(1)(b)

(b) if the justice considers that a case for so doing is made out, whether the information relates to the offence alleged in the appearance notice or undertaking or to an included or other offence,

(i) confirm the appearance notice or undertaking and endorse the information accordingly, or

(ii) cancel the appearance notice or undertaking and issue, in accordance with section 507, either a summons or a warrant for the arrest of the accused to compel the accused to attend before the justice or some other justice for the same territorial division to answer to a charge of an offence and endorse on the summons or warrant that the appearance notice or undertaking has been cancelled; and

2019, c. 25, s. 220 [To come into force December 18, 2019.]

(c) where he considers that a case is not made out for the purposes of paragraph (*b*), cancel the appearance notice, promise to appear or recognizance, as the case may be, and cause the accused to be notified forthwith of such cancellation.

Proposed Amendment — 508(1)(c)

(c) if the justice considers that a case is not made out for the purposes of paragraph (b), cancel the appearance notice or undertaking and cause the accused to be immediately notified of the cancellation.

2019, c. 25, s. 220 [To come into force December 18, 2019.]

(2) Procedure when witnesses attend — A justice who hears the evidence of a witness pursuant to subsection (1) shall

(a) take the evidence on oath; and

(b) cause the evidence to be taken in accordance with section 540 in so far as that section is capable of being applied.

R.S.C. 1985, c. 27 (1st Supp.), s. 79

508.1 (1) Information laid otherwise than in person — For the purposes of sections 504 to 508, a peace officer may lay an information by any means of telecommunication that produces a writing.

(2) Alternative to oath — A peace officer who uses a means of telecommunication referred to in subsection (1) shall, instead of swearing an oath, make a statement in writing stating that all matters contained in the information are true to the officer's knowledge and belief, and such a statement is deemed to be a statement made under oath.

1997, c. 18, s. 56

509. (1) Summons — A summons issued under this Part shall

(a) be directed to the accused;

(b) set out briefly the offence in respect of which the accused is charged; and

(c) require the accused to attend court at a time and place to be stated therein and to attend thereafter as required by the court in order to be dealt with according to law.

(2) **Service on individual** — A summons shall be served by a peace officer who shall deliver it personally to the person to whom it is directed or, if that person cannot conveniently be found, shall leave it for him at his latest or usual place of abode with an inmate thereof who appears to be at least sixteen years of age.

(3) [Repealed 2008, c. 18, s. 17.]

(4) **Content of summons** — There shall be set out in every summons the text of subsection 145(4) and section 510.

Proposed Amendment — 509(4)

(4) **Summary of certain provisions** — The summons must set out a summary of subsection 145(3), section 512.1 and subsection 524(4).

2019, c. 25, s. 221 [To come into force December 18, 2019.]

(5) **Attendance for purposes of *Identification of Criminals Act*** — A summons may require the accused to appear at a time and place stated in it for the purposes of the *Identification of Criminals Act*, where the accused is alleged to have committed an indictable offence and, in the case of an offence designated as a contravention under the *Contraventions Act*, the Attorney General, within the meaning of that Act, has not made an election under section 50 of that Act.

R.S.C. 1985, c. 27 (1st Supp.), s. 80; 1992, c. 47, s. 71 [Amended 1996, c. 7, s. 38.]; 2008, c. 18, s. 17

510. Failure to appear — Where an accused who is required by a summons to appear at a time and place stated in it for the purposes of the *Identification of Criminals Act* does not appear at that time and place and, in the case of an offence designated as a contravention under the *Contraventions Act*, the Attorney General, within the meaning of that Act, has not made an election under section 50 of that Act, a justice may issue a warrant for the arrest of the accused for the offence with which the accused is charged.

Proposed Repeal — 510

510. [Repealed 2019, c. 25, s. 222. To come into force December 18, 2019.]

1992, c. 47, s. 72 [Amended 1996, c. 7, s. 38.]

511. (1) **Contents of warrant to arrest** — A warrant issued under this Part shall

(a) name or describe the accused;

(b) set out briefly the offence in respect of which the accused is charged; and

(c) order that the accused be forthwith arrested and brought before the judge or justice who issued the warrant or before some other judge or justice having jurisdiction in the same territorial division, to be dealt with according to law.

(2) **No return day** — A warrant issued under this Part remains in force until it is executed, and need not be made returnable at any particular time.

(3) Discretion to postpone execution — Notwithstanding paragraph (1)(*c*), a judge or justice who issues a warrant may specify in the warrant the period before which the warrant shall not be executed, to allow the accused to appear voluntarily before a judge or justice having jurisdiction in the territorial division in which the warrant was issued.

(4) Deemed execution of warrant — Where the accused appears voluntarily for the offence in respect of which the accused is charged, the warrant is deemed to be executed.

R.S.C. 1985, c. 27 (1st Supp.), s. 81; 1997, c. 18, s. 57

512. (1) Certain actions not to preclude issue of warrant — A justice may, where the justice has reasonable and probable grounds to believe that it is necessary in the public interest to issue a summons or a warrant for the arrest of the accused, issue a summons or warrant notwithstanding that

(a) an appearance notice or a promise to appear or a recognizance entered into before an officer in charge or another peace officer has been confirmed or cancelled under subsection 508(1);

Proposed Amendment — 512(1)(a)

(a) an appearance notice or undertaking has been confirmed or cancelled under subsection 508(1);

2019, c. 25, s. 223(1) [To come into force December 18, 2019.]

(b) a summons has previously been issued under subsection 507(4); or

(c) the accused has been released unconditionally or with the intention of compelling his appearance by way of summons.

Proposed Amendment — 512(1)(c)

(c) the accused has been released without conditions or with the intention of compelling their appearance by way of summons.

2019, c. 25, s. 223(2) [To come into force December 18, 2019.]

(2) Warrant in default of appearance — Where

(a) service of a summons is proved and the accused fails to attend court in accordance with the summons,

(b) an appearance notice or a promise to appear or a recognizance entered into before an officer in charge or another peace officer has been confirmed under subsection 508(1) and the accused fails to attend court in accordance therewith in order to be dealt with according to law, or

Proposed Amendment — 512(2)(b)

(b) an appearance notice or undertaking has been confirmed under subsection 508(1) and the accused fails to attend court in accordance with it in order to be dealt with according to law, or

2019, c. 25, s. 223(3) [To come into force December 18, 2019.]

(c) it appears that a summons cannot be served because the accused is evading service, a justice may issue a warrant for the arrest of the accused.

R.S.C. 1985, c. 27 (1st Supp.), s. 82; 1997, c. 18, s. 58

Proposed Addition — 512.1–512.3

512.1 Arrest warrant — failure to appear under summons — If an accused who is required by a summons to appear at the time and place stated in it for the purposes of the *Identification of Criminals Act* does not appear at that time and place and, in the case of an offence designated as a contravention under the *Contraventions Act*, the **"Attorney General"**, within the meaning of that Act, has not made an election under section 50 of that Act, a justice may issue a warrant for the arrest of the accused for the offence with which the accused is charged.

2019, c. 25, s. 224 [To come into force December 18, 2019.]

512.2 Arrest warrant — failure to appear under appearance notice or undertaking — If an accused who is required by an appearance notice or undertaking to appear at the time and place stated in it for the purposes of the *Identification of Criminals Act* does not appear at that time and place, a justice may, if the appearance notice or undertaking has been confirmed by a justice under section 508, issue a warrant for the arrest of the accused for the offence with which the accused is charged.

2019, c. 25, s. 224 [To come into force December 18, 2019.]

512.3 Warrant to appear under section 524 — If a justice is satisfied that there are reasonable grounds to believe that an accused has contravened or is about to contravene any summons, appearance notice, undertaking or release order that was issued or given to the accused or entered into by the accused or has committed an indictable offence while being subject to any summons, appearance notice, undertaking or release order, the justice may issue a warrant for the purpose of taking them before a justice under section 524.

2019, c. 25, s. 224 [To come into force December 18, 2019.]

513. Formalities of warrant — A warrant in accordance with this Part shall be directed to the peace officers within the territorial jurisdiction of the justice, judge or court by whom or by which it is issued.

514. (1) Execution of warrant — A warrant in accordance with this Part may be executed by arresting the accused

(a) wherever he is found within the territorial jurisdiction of the justice, judge or court by whom or by which the warrant was issued; or

(b) wherever he is found in Canada, in the case of fresh pursuit.

(2) By whom warrant may be executed — A warrant in accordance with this Part may be executed by a person who is one of the peace officers to whom it is directed, whether or not the place in which the warrant is to be executed is within the territory for which the person is a peace officer.

Judicial Interim Release

515. (1) Order of release — Subject to this section, where an accused who is charged with an offence other than an offence listed in section 469 is taken before a justice the justice shall, unless a plea of guilty by the accused is accepted, order, in respect of that offence, that the accused be released on his giving an undertaking without conditions, unless the prosecutor, having been given a reasonable opportunity to do so, shows cause, in respect of that offence, why the detention of the accused in custody is justified or why an order under any other provision of this section should be made and where the justice makes an order under any other provision of this section, the order shall refer only to the particular offence for which the accused was taken before the justice.

Proposed Amendment — 515(1)

(1) Release order without conditions — Subject to this section, when an accused who is charged with an offence other than an offence listed in section 469 is taken before a justice, the justice shall, unless a plea of guilty by the accused is accepted, make a release order in respect of that offence, without conditions, unless the prosecutor, having been given a reasonable opportunity to do so, shows cause, in respect of that offence, why the detention of the accused in custody is justified or why an order under any other provision of this section should be made.

2019, c. 25, s. 225(1) [To come into force December 18, 2019.]

(2) Release on undertaking with conditions, etc. — Where the justice does not make an order under subsection (1), he shall, unless the prosecutor shows cause why the detention of the accused is justified, order that the accused be released

(a) on his giving an undertaking with such conditions as the justice directs;

(b) on his entering into a recognizance before the justice, without sureties, in such amount and with such conditions, if any, as the justice directs but without deposit of money or other valuable security;

(c) on his entering into a recognizance before the justice with sureties in such amount and with such conditions, if any, as the justice directs but without deposit of money or other valuable security;

(d) with the consent of the prosecutor, on his entering into a recognizance before the justice, without sureties, in such amount and with such conditions, if any, as the justice directs and on his depositing with the justice such sum of money or other valuable security as the justice directs, or

(e) if the accused is not ordinarily resident in the province in which the accused is in custody or does not ordinarily reside within two hundred kilometres of the place in which he is in custody, on his entering into a recognizance before the justice with or without sureties in such amount and with such conditions, if any, as the justice directs, and on his depositing with the justice such sum of money or other valuable security as the justice directs.

Proposed Amendment — 515(2)

(2) Release order with conditions — If the justice does not make an order under subsection (1), the justice shall, unless the prosecutor shows cause why the detention of the accused is justified, make a release order that sets out the conditions directed by the justice under subsection (4) and, as the case may be,

(a) an indication that the release order does not include any financial obligations;

(b) the accused's promise to pay a specified amount if they fail to comply with a condition of the order;

(c) the obligation to have one or more sureties, with or without the accused's promise to pay a specified amount if they fail to comply with a condition of the order;

(d) the obligation to deposit money or other valuable security in a specified amount or value, with or without the accused's promise to pay a specified amount if they fail to comply with a condition of the order; or

(e) if the accused is not ordinarily resident in the province in which they are in custody or does not ordinarily reside within 200 kilometres of the place in which they are in custody, the obligation to deposit money or other valuable security in a specified amount or value, with or without the accused's promise to pay a specified amount by the justice if they fail to comply with a condition of the order and with or without sureties.

2019, c. 25, s. 225(1) [To come into force December 18, 2019.]

Proposed Addition — 515(2.01)–(2.03)

(2.01) **Imposition of least onerous form of release** — The justice shall not make an order containing the conditions referred to in one of the paragraphs (2)(b) to (e) unless the prosecution shows cause why an order containing the conditions referred to in the preceding paragraphs for any less onerous form of release would be inadequate.

(2.02) **Promise to pay favoured over deposit** — The justice shall favour a promise to pay an amount over the deposit of an amount of money if the accused or the surety, if applicable, has reasonably recoverable assets.

(2.03) **Restraint in use of surety** — For greater certainty, before making an order requiring that the accused have a surety, the justice shall be satisfied that this requirement is the least onerous form of release possible for the accused in the circumstances.

2019, c. 25, s. 225(1) [To come into force December 18, 2019.]

(2.1) **Power of justice to name sureties in order** — Where, pursuant to subsection (2) or any other provision of this Act, a justice, judge or court orders that an accused be released on his entering into a recognizance with sureties, the justice, judge or court may, in the order, name particular persons as sureties.

Proposed Amendment — 515(2.1)

(2.1) **Power of justice — sureties** — If, under subsection (2) or any other provision of this Act, a judge, justice or court makes a release order with a requirement for sureties, the judge, justice or court may name particular persons as sureties.

2019, c. 25, s. 225(1) [To come into force December 18, 2019.]

(2.2) Appearance of the accused — If, by this Act, the appearance of an accused is required for the purposes of judicial interim release, the accused shall appear personally but the justice may allow the accused to appear by videoconference or, subject to subsection (2.3), by audioconference, if the technological means is satisfactory to the justice.

(2.3) When consent required for audioconference — If the accused cannot appear by closed-circuit television or videoconference and the evidence of a witness is to be taken at the appearance, the consent of the prosecutor and the accused is required for the appearance of the accused by audioconference.

(3) Release on undertaking with conditions etc. — The justice shall not make an order under any of paragraphs (2)(b) to (e) unless the prosecution shows cause why an order under the immediately preceding paragraph should not be made.

Proposed Amendment — 515(3)

(3) Factors to consider — In making an order under this section, the justice shall consider any relevant factors, including,

(a) whether the accused is charged with an offence in the commission of which violence was used, threatened or attempted against their intimate partner; or

(b) whether the accused has been previously convicted of a criminal offence.

2019, c. 25, s. 225(3) [To come into force December 18, 2019.]

(4) Conditions authorized — The justice may direct as conditions under subsection (2) that the accused shall do any one or more of the following things as specified in the order:

(a) report at times to be stated in the order to a peace officer or other person designated in the order;

(b) remain within a territorial jurisdiction specified in the order;

(c) notify the peace officer or other person designated under paragraph (a) of any change in his address or his employment or occupation;

(d) abstain from communicating, directly or indirectly, with any victim, witness or other person identified in the order, or refrain from going to any place specified in the order, except in accordance with the conditions specified in the order that the justice considers necessary;

(e) where the accused is the holder of a passport, deposit his passport as specified in the order;

(e.1) comply with any other condition specified in the order that the justice considers necessary to ensure the safety and security of any victim of or witness to the offence; and

(f) comply with such other reasonable conditions specified in the order as the justice considers desirable.

Proposed Amendment — 515(4)

(4) Conditions authorized — When making an order under subsection (2), the justice may direct the accused to comply with one or more of the following conditions specified in the order:

(a) report at specified times to a peace officer, or other person, designated in the order;

(b) remain within a specified territorial jurisdiction;

(c) notify a peace officer or other person designated in the order of any change in their address, employment or occupation;

(d) abstain from communicating, directly or indirectly, with any victim, witness or other person identified in the order, except in accordance with any specified conditions that the justice considers necessary;

(e) abstain from going to any place or entering any geographic area specified in the order, except in accordance with any specified conditions that the justice considers necessary;

(f) deposit all their passports as specified in the order;

(g) comply with any other specified condition that the justice considers necessary to ensure the safety and security of any victim of or witness to the offence; and

(h) comply with any other reasonable conditions specified in the order that the justice considers desirable.

2019, c. 25, s. 225(3) [To come into force December 18, 2019.]

(4.1) Condition prohibiting possession of firearms, etc. — When making an order under subsection (2), in the case of an accused who is charged with

(a) an offence in the commission of which violence against a person was used, threatened or attempted,

(a.1) a terrorism offence,

(b) an offence under section 264 (criminal harassment),

(b.1) an offence under section 423.1 (intimidation of a justice system participant),

(b.2) an offence relating to the contravention of any of sections 9 to 14 of the *Cannabis Act*,

(c) an offence relating to the contravention of any of sections 5 to 7 of the *Controlled Drugs and Substances Act*,

(d) an offence that involves, or the subject-matter of which is, a firearm, a cross-bow, a prohibited weapon, a restricted weapon, a prohibited device, ammunition, prohibited ammunition or an explosive substance, or

(e) an offence under subsection 20(1) of the *Security of Information Act*, or an offence under subsection 21(1) or 22(1) or section 23 of that Act that is committed in relation to on offence under subsection 20(1) of that Act,

the justice shall add to the order a condition prohibiting the accused from possessing a firearm, cross-bow, prohibited weapon, restricted weapon, prohibited device, ammunition, prohibited ammunition or explosive substance, or all those things, until the accused is dealt with according to law unless the justice considers that such a condition is not required in the interests of the safety of the accused or the safety and security of a victim of the offence or of any other person.

(4.11) Surrender, etc. — Where the justice adds a condition described in subsection (4.1) to an order made under subsection (2), the justice shall specify in the order the manner and method by which

(a) the things referred to in subsection (4.1) that are in the possession of the accused shall be surrendered, disposed of, detained, stored or dealt with; and

(b) the authorizations, licences and registration certificates held by the person shall be surrendered.

(4.12) Reasons — Where the justice does not add a condition described in subsection (4.1) to an order made under subsection (2), the justice shall include in the record a statement of the reasons for not adding the condition.

(4.2) Additional conditions — Before making an order under subsection (2), in the case of an accused who is charged with an offence referred to in subsection (4.3), the justice shall consider whether it is desirable, in the interests of the safety and security of any person, particularly a victim of or witness to the offence or a justice system participant, to include as a condition of the order

(a) that the accused abstain from communicating, directly or indirectly, with any victim, witness or other person identified in the order, or refrain from going to any place specified in the order; or

Proposed Amendment — 515(4.2)(a)

(a) that the accused abstain from communicating, directly or indirectly, with any victim, witness or other person identified in the order, except in accordance with any specified conditions that the justice considers necessary;

2019, c. 25, s. 225(4) [To come into force December 18, 2019.]

Proposed Addition — 515(4.2)(a.1)

(a.1) that the accused abstain from going to any place or entering any geographic area specified in the order, except in accordance with any specified conditions that the justice considers necessary; or

2019, c. 25, s. 225(4) [To come into force December 18, 2019.]

(b) that the accused comply with any other condition specified in the order that the justice considers necessary to ensure the safety and security of those persons.

(4.3) Offences — The offences for the purposes of subsection (4.2) are

(a) a terrorism offence;

(b) an offence described in section 264 or 423.1;

(c) an offence in the commission of which violence against a person was used, threatened or attempted; and

(d) an offence under subsection 20(1) of the *Security of Information Act*, or an offence under subsection 21(1) or 22(1) or section 23 of that Act that is committed in relation to an offence under subsection 20(1) of that Act.

(5) Detention in custody — Where the prosecutor shows cause why the detention of the accused in custody is justified, the justice shall order that the accused be detained in custody until he is dealt with according to law and shall include in the record a statement of his reasons for making the order.

(6) Order of detention — Unless the accused, having been given a reasonable opportunity to do so, shows cause why the accused's detention in custody is not justified, the justice shall order, despite any provision of this section, that the accused be detained in custody until the accused is dealt with according to law, if the accused is charged

(a) with an indictable offence, other than an offence listed in section 469,

(i) that is alleged to have been committed while at large after being released in respect of another indictable offence pursuant to the provisions of this Part or section 679 or 680,

(ii) that is an offence under section 467.11, 467.111, 467.12 or 467.13, or a serious offence alleged to have been committed for the benefit of, at the direction of, or in association with, a criminal organization,

(iii) that is an offence under any of sections 83.02 to 83.04 and 83.18 to 83.23 or otherwise is alleged to be a terrorism offence,

(iv) an offence under subsection 16(1) or (2), 17(1), 19(1), 20(1) or 22(1) of the *Security of Information Act*,

Proposed Amendment — 515(6)(a)(iv)

(iv) that is an offence under subsection 16(1) or (2), 17(1), 19(1), 20(1) or 22(1) of the *Security of Information Act*,

2019, c. 25, s. 225(5) [To come into force December 18, 2019.]

(v) an offence under subsection 21(1) or 22(1) or section 23 of the *Security of Information Act* that is committed in relation to on offence referred to in subparagraph (iv),

Proposed Amendment — 515(6)(a)(v)

(v) that is an offence under subsection 21(1) or 22(1) or section 23 of the *Security of Information Act* committed in relation to an offence referred to in subparagraph (iv),

2019, c. 25, s. 225(5) [To come into force December 18, 2019.]

(vi) that is an offence under section 99, 100 or 103,

(vii) that is an offence under section 244 or 244.2, or an offence under section 239, 272 or 273, subsection 279(1) or section 279.1, 344 or 346 that is alleged to have been committed with a firearm, or

(viii) that is alleged to involve, or whose subject-matter is alleged to be, a firearm, a cross-bow, a prohibited weapon, a restricted weapon, a prohibited device, any ammunition or prohibited ammunition or an explosive substance, and that is alleged to have been committed while the accused was under a prohibition order within the meaning of subsection 84(1);

(b) with an indictable offence, other than an offence listed in section 469 and is not ordinarily resident in Canada,

Proposed Addition — 515(6)(b.1)

(b.1) with an offence in the commission of which violence was allegedly used, threatened or attempted against their intimate partner, and the accused has been previously convicted of an offence in the commission of which violence was used, threatened or attempted against any intimate partner of theirs;

2019, c. 25, s. 225(6) [To come into force December 18, 2019.]

(c) with an offence under any of subsections 145(2) to (5) that is alleged to have been committed while he was at large after being released in respect of another offence pursuant to the provisions of this Part or section 679, 680 or 816, or

Proposed Amendment — 515(6)(c)

(c) with an offence under any of subsections 145(2) to (5) that is alleged to have been committed while they were at large after being released in respect of another offence under the provisions of this Part or section 679, 680 or 816; or

2019, c. 25, s. 225(6) [To come into force December 18, 2019.]

(d) with having committed an offence punishable by imprisonment for life under any of sections 5 to 7 of the *Controlled Drugs and Substances Act* or the offence of conspiring to commit such an offence.

(6.1) Reasons — If the justice orders that an accused to whom subsection (6) applies be released, the justice shall include in the record a statement of the justice's reasons for making the order.

(7) Order of release — Where an accused to whom paragraph 6(a), (c) or (d) applies shows cause why the accused's detention in custody is not justified, the justice shall order that the accused be released on giving an undertaking or entering into a recognizance described in any of paragraphs (2)(a) to (e) with the conditions described in subsections (4) to (4.2) or, where the accused was at large on an undertaking or recognizance with conditions, the additional conditions described in subsections (4) to (4.2), that the justice considers desirable, unless the accused, having been given a reasonable opportunity to do so, shows cause why the conditions or additional conditions should not be imposed.

Proposed Amendment — 515(7)

(7) Release order — If an accused to whom subsection (6) applies shows cause why their detention in custody is not justified, the justice shall make a release order under this section. If the accused was already at large on a release order, the new release order may include any additional conditions described in subsections (4) to (4.2) that the justice considers desirable.

2019, c. 25, s. 225(7) [To come into force December 18, 2019.]

(8) Idem — Where an accused to whom paragraph (6)(b) applies shows cause why the accused's detention in custody is not justified, the justice shall order that the accused be released on giving an undertaking or entering into a recognizance described in any of paragraphs (2)(a) to (e) with the conditions, described in subsections (4) to (4.2), that the justice considers desirable.

Proposed Repeal — 515(8)

(8) [Repealed 2019, c. 25, s. 225(7). To come into force December 18, 2019.]

(9) **Sufficiency of record** — For the purposes of subsections (5) and (6), it is sufficient if a record is made of the reasons in accordance with the provisions of Part XVIII relating to the taking of evidence at preliminary inquiries.

(9.1) **Written reasons** — Despite subsection (9), if the justice orders that the accused be detained in custody primarily because of a previous conviction of the accused, the justice shall state that reason, in writing, in the record.

(10) **Justification for detention in custody** — For the purposes of this section, the detention of an accused in custody is justified only on one or more of the following grounds:

(a) where the detention is necessary to ensure his or her attendance in court in order to be dealt with according to law;

(b) where the detention is necessary for the protection or safety of the public, including any victim of or witness to the offence, or any person under the age of 18 years, having regard to all the circumstances including any substantial likelihood that the accused will, if released from custody, commit a criminal offence or interfere with the administration of justice; and

(c) if the detention is necessary to maintain confidence in the administration of justice, having regard to all the circumstances, including

(i) the apparent strength of the prosecution's case,

(ii) the gravity of the offence,

(iii) the circumstances surrounding the commission of the offence, including whether a firearm was used, and

(iv) the fact that the accused is liable, on conviction, for a potentially lengthy term of imprisonment or, in the case of an offence that involves, or whose subject-matter is, a firearm, a minimum punishment of imprisonment for a term of three years or more.

(11) **Detention in custody for offence mentioned in s. 469** — Where an accused who is charged with an offence mentioned in section 469 is taken before a justice, the justice shall order that the accused be detained in custody until he is dealt with according to law and shall issue a warrant in Form 8 for the committal of the accused.

(12) **Order re no communication** — A justice who orders that an accused be detained in custody under this section may include in the order a direction that the accused abstain from communicating, directly or indirectly, with any victim, witness or other person identified in the order, except in accordance with such conditions specified in the order as the justice considers necessary.

(13) **Consideration of victim's safety and security** — A justice who makes an order under this section shall include in the record of the proceedings a statement

that he or she considered the safety and security of every victim of the offence when making the order.

(14) Copy to victim — If an order is made under this section, the justice shall, on request by a victim of the offence, cause a copy of the order to be given to the victim.

R.S.C. 1985, c. 27 (1st Supp.), ss. 83, 186 (Sched. IV, item 7); 1991, c. 40, s. 31; 1993, c. 45, s. 8; 1994, c. 44, s. 44; 1995, c. 39, s. 153; 1996, c. 19, ss. 71, 93.3; 1997, c. 18, s. 59; 1997, c. 23, s. 16; 1999, c. 5, s. 21; 1999, c. 25, s. 8; 2001, c. 32, s. 37; 2001, c. 41, ss. 19, 133(15)–(17); 2008, c. 6, s. 37; 2009, c. 22, s. 17; 2009, c. 29, s. 2; 2010, c. 20, s. 1; 2012, c. 1, s. 32; 2014, c. 17, s. 14; 2015, c. 13, s. 20; 2018, c. 16, s. 218; 2019, c. 25, s. 225(2)

515.1 Variation of undertaking or recognizance — An undertaking or recognizance pursuant to which the accused was released that has been entered into under section 499, 503 or 515 may, with the written consent of the prosecutor, be varied, and where so varied, is deemed to have been entered into pursuant to section 515.

Proposed Amendment — 515.1

515.1 (1) Declaration of surety — Before a judge, justice or court names a particular person as a surety, the person shall provide the judge, justice or court with a signed declaration under oath, solemn declaration or solemn affirmation in Form 12 that sets out

(a) their name, date of birth and contact information;

(b) information demonstrating that they are suitable to act as a surety for the accused, including financial information;

(c) their relationship to the accused;

(d) the name and date of birth of any other accused for whom they act as a surety;

(e) their acknowledgment of the charge, and of any other outstanding charges against the accused and the contents of the accused's criminal record, if any;

(f) their acknowledgment of the amount that they are willing to promise to pay or deposit to the court and that may be forfeited if the accused fails to comply with any condition of the release order;

(g) their acknowledgment that they understand the role and responsibilities of a surety and that they assume these voluntarily; and

(h) a description of the contents of their criminal record and any outstanding charges against them, if any.

(2) Exception — Despite subsection (1), a judge, justice or court may name a person as a surety without a declaration if

(a) the prosecutor consents to it; or

(b) the judge, justice or court is satisfied that

(i) the person cannot reasonably provide a declaration in the circumstances,

(ii) the judge, justice or court has received sufficient information of the kind that would be set out in a declaration to evaluate whether the person is suitable to act as a surety for the accused, and

(iii) the person has acknowleged that they have received sufficient information with respect to the matters referred to in paragraphs (1)(e) to (g) to accept the role and responsibilities of a surety.

(3) Means of telecommunication — A person may provide the judge, justice or court with the declaration referred to in subsection (1) by a means of telecommunication that produces a writing.

2019, c. 25, s. 226 [To come into force December 18, 2019.]

1997, c. 18, s. 60

516. (1) Remand in custody — A justice may, before or at any time during the course of any proceedings under section 515, on application by the prosecutor or the accused, adjourn the proceedings and remand the accused to custody in prison by warrant in Form 19, but no adjournment shall be for more than three clear days except with the consent of the accused.

(2) Detention pending bail hearing — A justice who remands an accused to custody under subsection (1) or subsection 515(11) may order that the accused abstain from communicating, directly or indirectly, with any victim, witness or other person identified in the order, except in accordance with any conditions specified in the order that the justice considers necessary.

Proposed Addition — 516(3)

(3) Duration of order — An order made under subsection (2) remains in force,

(a) until it is varied or revoked;

(b) until an order in respect of the accused is made under section 515;

(c) until the accused is acquitted of the offence, if applicable; or

(d) until the time the accused is sentenced, if applicable.

2019, c. 25, s. 227 [To come into force December 18, 2019.]

1999, c. 5, s. 22; 1999, c. 25, s. 31(3)

517. (1) Order directing matters not to be published for specified period — If the prosecutor or the accused intends to show cause under section 515, he or she shall so state to the justice and the justice may, and shall on application by the accused, before or at any time during the course of the proceedings under that section, make an order directing that the evidence taken, the information given or the representations made and the reasons, if any, given or to be given by the justice shall not be published in any document, or broadcast or transmitted in any way before such time as

(a) if a preliminary inquiry is held, the accused in respect of whom the proceedings are held is discharged; or

(b) if the accused in respect of whom the proceedings are held is tried or committed for trial, the trial is ended.

(2) Failure to comply — Every person who fails, without lawful excuse, to comply with an order made under subsection (1) is guilty of an offence punishable on summary conviction.

(3) [Repealed 2005, c. 32, s. 17(2).]

R.S.C. 1985, c. 27 (1st Supp.), s. 101(2)(a); 2005, c. 32, s. 17; 2018, c. 29, s. 62

518. (1) Inquiries to be made by justice and evidence — In any proceedings under section 515,

(a) the justice may, subject to paragraph (*b*), make such inquiries, on oath or otherwise, of and concerning the accused as he considers desirable;

(b) the accused shall not be examined by the justice or any other person except counsel for the accused respecting the offence with which the accused is charged, and no inquiry shall be made of the accused respecting that offence by way of cross-examination unless the accused has testified respecting the offence;

(c) the prosecutor may, in addition to any other relevant evidence, lead evidence

(i) to prove that the accused has previously been convicted of a criminal offence,

(ii) to prove that the accused has been charged with and is awaiting trial for another criminal offence,

(iii) to prove that the accused has previously committed an offence under section 145, or

(iv) to show the circumstances of the alleged offence, particularly as they relate to the probability of conviction of the accused;

(d) the justice may take into consideration any relevant matters agreed on by the prosecutor and the accused or his counsel;

(d.1) the justice may receive evidence obtained as a result of an interception of a private communication under and within the meaning of Part VI, in writing, orally or in the form of a recording and, for the purposes of this section, subsection 189(5) does not apply to such evidence;

(d.2) the justice shall take into consideration any evidence submitted regarding the need to ensure the safety or security of any victim of or witness to an offence; and

(e) the justice may receive and base his decision on evidence considered credible or trustworthy by him in the circumstances of each case.

(2) Release pending sentence — Where, before or at any time during the course of any proceedings under section 515, the accused pleads guilty and that plea is accepted, the justice may make any order provided for in this Part for the release of the accused until the accused is sentenced.

R.S.C. 1985, c. 27 (1st Supp.), s. 84; 1994, c. 44, s. 45; 1999, c. 25, s. 9

519. (1) Release of accused — Where a justice makes an order under subsection 515(1), (2), (7) or (8),

Proposed Amendment — 519(1) opening words

(1) Release of accused — If a justice makes a release order under section 515,

2019, c. 25, s. 228(1) [To come into force December 18, 2019.]

(a) if the accused thereupon complies with the order, the justice shall direct that the accused be released

(i) forthwith, if the accused is not required to be detained in custody in respect of any other matter, or

(ii) as soon thereafter as the accused is no longer required to be detained in custody in respect of any other matter; and

Proposed Amendment — 519(1)(a)(ii)

(ii) as soon thereafter as the accused is no longer required to be detained in custody in respect of any other matter;

2019, c. 25, s. 228(2) [To come into force December 18, 2019.]

(b) if the accused does not thereupon comply with the order, the justice who made the order or another justice having jurisdiction shall issue a warrant for the committal of the accused and may endorse thereon an authorization to the person having the custody of the accused to release the accused when the accused complies with the order

(i) forthwith after the compliance, if the accused is not required to be detained in custody in respect of any other matter, or

(ii) as soon thereafter as the accused is no longer required to be detained in custody in respect of any other matter

and if the justice so endorses the warrant, he shall attach to it a copy of the order.

Proposed Amendment — 519(1)(b) closing words

and if the justice so endorses the warrant, he shall attach to it a copy of the order; and

2019, c. 25, s. 228(2) [To come into force December 18, 2019.]

Proposed Addition — 519(1)(c)

(c) any condition in the order that an accused abstain from communicating, directly or indirectly, with any victim, witness or other person identified in the order, except in accordance with any specified conditions, is effective from the moment it is made, whether or not the accused has been released from custody.

2019, c. 25, s. 228(2) [To come into force December 18, 2019.]

(2) Discharge from custody — Where the accused complies with an order referred to in paragraph (1)(*b*), and is not required to be detained in custody in respect of any other matter, the justice who made the order or another justice having jurisdiction shall, unless the accused has been or will be released pursuant to an authorization referred to in that paragraph, issue an order for discharge in Form 39.

(3) Warrant for committal — Where the justice makes an order under subsection 515(5) or (6) for the detention of the accused, he shall issue a warrant for the committal of the accused.

R.S.C. 1985, c. 27 (1st Supp.), s. 85

Proposed Addition — 519.1

519.1 Variation of release order with consent — A release order under which an accused has been released under section 515 may be varied with the written consent of the accused, prosecutor and any sureties. The order so varied is considered to be a release order under section 515.

2019, c. 25, s. 229 [To come into force December 18, 2019.]

520. (1) Review of order — If a justice, or a judge of the Nunavut Court of Justice, makes an order under subsection 515(2), (5), (6), (7), (8) or (12) or makes or vacates any order under paragraph 523(2)(*b*), the accused may, at any time before the trial of the charge, apply to a judge for a review of the order.

Proposed Amendment — 520(1)

(1) Review of order — If a justice, or a judge of the Nunavut Court of Justice, makes an order under subsection 515(2), (5), (6), (7), or (12) or makes or vacates any order under paragraph 523(2)(b), the accused may, at any time before the trial of the charge, apply to a judge for a review of the order.

2019, c. 25, s. 230 [To come into force December 18, 2019.]

(2) Notice to prosecutor — An application under this section shall not, unless the prosecutor otherwise consents, be heard by a judge unless the accused has given to the prosecutor at least two clear days notice in writing of the application.

(3) Accused to be present — If the judge so orders or the prosecutor or the accused or his counsel so requests, the accused shall be present at the hearing of an application under this section and, where the accused is in custody, the judge may order, in writing, the person having the custody of the accused to bring him before the court.

(4) Adjournment of proceedings — A judge may, before or at any time during the hearing of an application under this section, on application by the prosecutor or the accused, adjourn the proceedings, but if the accused is in custody no adjournment shall be for more than three clear days except with the consent of the accused.

(5) Failure of accused to attend — Where an accused, other than an accused who is in custody, has been ordered by a judge to be present at the hearing of an application under this section and does not attend the hearing, the judge may issue a warrant for the arrest of the accused.

(6) Execution — A warrant issued under subsection (5) may be executed anywhere in Canada.

(7) Evidence and powers of judge on review — On the hearing of an application under this section, the judge may consider

(a) the transcript, if any, of the proceedings heard by the justice and by any judge who previously reviewed the order made by the justice,

(b) the exhibits, if any, filed in the proceedings before the justice, and

(c) such additional evidence or exhibits as may be tendered by the accused or the prosecutor,

and shall either

(d) dismiss the application, or

(e) if the accused shows cause, allow the application, vacate the order previously made by the justice and make any other order provided for in section 515 that he considers is warranted.

(8) Limitation of further applications — Where an application under this section or section 521 has been heard, a further or other application under this section or section 521 shall not be made with respect to that same accused, except with leave of a judge, prior to the expiration of thirty days from the date of the decision of the judge who heard the previous application.

(9) Application of ss. 517, 518 and 519 — The provisions of sections 517, 518 and 519 apply with such modifications as the circumstances require in respect of an application under this section.

R.S.C. 1985, c. 27 (1st Supp.), s. 86; 1994, c. 44, s. 46; 1999, c. 3, s. 31

521. (1) Review of order — If a justice, or a judge of the Nunavut Court of Justice, makes an order under subsection 515(1), (2), (7), (8) or (12) or makes or vacates any order under paragraph 523(2)(*b*), the prosecutor may, at any time before the trial of the charge, apply to a judge for a review of the order.

Proposed Amendment — 521(1)

(1) Review of order — If a justice, or a judge of the Nunavut Court of Justice, makes an order under subsection 515(1), (2), (7) or (12) or makes or vacates any order under paragraph 523(2)(b), the prosecutor may, at any time before the trial of the charge, apply to a judge for a review of the order.

2019, c. 25, s. 231 [To come into force December 18, 2019.]

(2) Notice to accused — An application under this section shall not be heard by a judge unless the prosecutor has given to the accused at least two clear days notice in writing of the application.

(3) Accused to be present — If the judge so orders or the prosecutor or the accused or his counsel so requests, the accused shall be present at the hearing of an application under this section and, where the accused is in custody, the judge may order, in writing, the person having the custody of the accused to bring him before the court.

(4) Adjournment of proceedings — A judge may, before or at any time during the hearing of an application under this section, on application of the prosecutor or the accused, adjourn the proceedings, but if the accused is in custody no such adjournment shall be for more than three clear days except with the consent of the accused.

(5) Failure of accused to attend — Where an accused, other than an accused who is in custody, has been ordered by a judge to be present at the hearing of an application under this section and does not attend the hearing, the judge may issue a warrant for the arrest of the accused.

(6) Warrant for detention — Where, pursuant to paragraph (8)(*e*), the judge makes an order that the accused be detained in custody until he is dealt with according to law, he shall, if the accused is not in custody, issue a warrant for the committal of the accused.

(7) Execution — A warrant issued under subsection (5) or (6) may be executed anywhere in Canada.

(8) Evidence and powers of judge on review — On the hearing of an application under this section, the judge may consider

(a) the transcript, if any, of the proceedings heard by the justice and by any judge who previously reviewed the order made by the justice,

(b) the exhibits, if any, filed in the proceedings before the justice, and

(c) such additional evidence or exhibits as may be tendered by the prosecutor or the accused,

and shall either

(d) dismiss the application, or

(e) if the prosecutor shows cause, allow the application, vacate the order previously made by the justice and make any other order provided for in section 515 that he considers to be warranted.

(9) Limitation of further applications — Where an application under this section or section 520 has been heard, a further or other application under this section or section 520 shall not be made with respect to the same accused, except with leave of a judge, prior to the expiration of thirty days from the date of the decision of the judge who heard the previous application.

(10) Application of ss. 517, 518 and 519 — The provisions of sections 517, 518 and 519 apply with such modifications as the circumstances require in respect of an application under this section.

R.S.C. 1985, c. 27 (1st Supp.), s. 87; 1994, c. 44, s. 47; 1999, c. 3, s. 32

522. (1) Interim release by judge only — Where an accused is charged with an offence listed in section 469, no court, judge or justice, other than a judge of or a judge presiding in a superior court of criminal jurisdiction for the province in which the accused is so charged, may release the accused before or after the accused has been ordered to stand trial.

(2) Idem — Where an accused is charged with an offence listed in section 469, a judge of or a judge presiding in a superior court of criminal jurisdiction for the province in which the accused is charged shall order that the accused be detained in custody unless the accused, having been given a reasonable opportunity to do so, shows cause why his detention in custody is not justified within the meaning of subsection 515(10).

(2.1) **Order re no communication** — A judge referred to in subsection (2) who orders that an accused be detained in custody under this section may include in the order a direction that the accused abstain from communicating, directly or indirectly, with any victim, witness or other person identified in the order except in accordance with such conditions specified in the order as the judge considers necessary.

(3) **Release of accused** — If the judge does not order that the accused be detained in custody under subsection (2), the judge may order that the accused be released on giving an undertaking or entering into a recognizance described in any of paragraphs 515(2)(a) to (e) with such conditions described in subsections 515(4), (4.1) and (4.2) as the judge considers desirable.

Proposed Amendment — 522(3)

(3) **Release of accused** — If the judge does not order that the accused be detained in custody under subsection (2), the judge may make a release order referred to in section 515.

2019, c. 25, s. 232 [To come into force December 18, 2019.]

(4) **Order not reviewable except under s. 680** — An order made under this section is not subject to review, except as provided in section 680.

(5) **Application of ss. 517, 518 and 519** — The provisions of sections 517, 518 except subsection (2) thereof, and 519 apply with such modifications as the circumstances require in respect of an application for an order under subsection (2).

(6) **Other offences** — Where an accused is charged with an offence mentioned in section 469 and with any other offence, a judge acting under this section may apply the provisions of this Part respecting judicial interim release to that other offence.

R.S.C. 1985, c. 27 (1st Supp.), s. 88; 1991, c. 40, s. 32; 1994, c. 44, s. 48; 1999, c. 25, s. 10

523. (1) **Period for which appearance notice, etc., continues in force** — Where an accused, in respect of an offence with which he is charged, has not been taken into custody or has been released from custody under or by virtue of any provision of this Part, the appearance notice, promise to appear, summons, undertaking or recognizance issued to, given or entered into by the accused continues in force, subject to its terms, and applies in respect of any new information charging the same offence or an included offence that was received after the appearance notice, promise to appear, summons, undertaking or recognizance was issued, given or entered into,

Proposed Amendment — 523(1) opening words

(1) **Period for which appearance notice, etc., continues in force** — If an accused, in respect of an offence with which they are charged, has not been taken into custody or has been released from custody under any provision of this Part, the appearance notice, summons, undertaking or release order issued to, given or entered into by the accused continues in force, subject to its terms, and applies in

respect of any new information charging the same offence or an included offence that was received after the appearance notice, summons, undertaking or release order was issued, given or entered into,

2019, c. 25, s. 233(1) [To come into force December 18, 2019.]

(a) where the accused was released from custody pursuant to an order of a judge made under subsection 522(3), until his trial is completed; or

(b) in any other case,

(i) until his trial is completed, and

(ii) where the accused is, at his trial, determined to be guilty of the offence, until a sentence within the meaning of section 673 is imposed on the accused unless, at the time the accused is determined to be guilty, the court, judge or justice orders that the accused be taken into custody pending such sentence.

(1.1) **Where new information charging same offence** — Where an accused, in respect of an offence with which he is charged, has not been taken into custody or is being detained or has been released from custody under or by virtue of any provision of this Part and after the order for interim release or detention has been made, or the appearance notice, promise to appear, summons, undertaking or recognizance has been issued, given or entered into, a new information charging the same offence or an included offence, is received, section 507 or 508, as the case may be, does not apply in respect of the new information and the order for interim release or detention of the accused and the appearance notice, promise to appear, summons, undertaking or recognizance, if any, applies in respect of the new information.

Proposed Amendment — 523(1.1)

(1.1) **When new information is received** — If an accused is charged with an offence and a new information, charging the same offence or an included offence, is received while the accused is subject to an order for detention, release order, appearance notice, summons or undertaking, section 507 or 508, as the case may be, does not apply in respect of the new information and the order for detention, release order, appearance notice, summons or undertaking applies in respect of the new information.

2019, c. 25, s. 233(2) [To come into force December 18, 2019.]

(1.2) **When direct indictment is preferred charging same offence** — When an accused, in respect of an offence with which the accused is charged, has not been taken into custody or is being detained or has been released from custody under or by virtue of any provision of this Part and after the order for interim release or detention has been made, or the appearance notice, promise to appear, summons, undertaking or recognizance has been issued, given or entered into, and an indictment is preferred under section 577 charging the same offence or an included offence, the order for interim release or detention of the accused and the appearance notice, promise to appear, summons, undertaking or recognizance, if any, applies in respect of the indictment.

Proposed Amendment — 523(1.2)

(1.2) When direct indictment preferred — If an accused is charged with an offence, and an indictment is preferred under section 577 charging the same offence or an included offence while the accused is subject to an order for detention, release order, appearance notice, summons or undertaking, the order for detention, release order, appearance notice, summons or undertaking applies in respect of the indictment.

2019, c. 25, s. 233(2) [To come into force December 18, 2019.]

(2) Order vacating previous order for release or detention — Despite subsections (1) to (1.2),

(a) the court, judge or justice before whom an accused is being tried, at any time,

(b) the justice, on completion of the preliminary inquiry in relation to an offence for which an accused is ordered to stand trial, other than an offence listed in section 469, or

(c) with the consent of the prosecutor and the accused or, where the accused or the prosecutor applies to vacate an order that would otherwise apply pursuant to subsection (1.1), without such consent, at any time

(i) where the accused is charged with an offence other than an offence listed in section 469, the justice by whom an order was made under this Part or any other justice,

(ii) where the accused is charged with an offence listed in section 469, a judge of or a judge presiding in a superior court of criminal jurisdiction for the province, or

(iii) the court, judge or justice before which or whom an accused is to be tried,

may, on cause being shown, vacate any order previously made under this Part for the interim release or detention of the accused and make any other order provided for in this Part for the detention or release of the accused until his trial is completed that the court, judge or justice considers to be warranted.

(3) Provisions applicable to proceedings under subsection (2) — The provisions of sections 517, 518 and 519 apply, with such modifications as the circumstances require, in respect of any proceedings under subsection (2), except that subsection 518(2) does not apply in respect of an accused who is charged with an offence listed in section 469.

R.S.C. 1985, c. 27 (1st Supp.), s. 89; 2011, c. 16, s. 2

Arrest of Accused on Interim Release

[Heading amended to "Proceedings Respecting Failure to Comply with Release Conditions", 2019, c. 25, s. 234. To come into force December 18, 2019.]

Proposed Addition — 523.1

523.1 (1) Judicial referral hearing — When an accused appears before a justice in any of the circumstances described in subsection (2), the justice shall

(a) if the accused was released from custody under an order made under subsection 522(3) by a judge of the superior court of criminal jurisdiction of any province, order that the accused appear before a judge of that court so that the judge may hear the matter; or

(b) in any other case, hear the matter.

(2) Circumstances — The circumstances referred to in subsection (1) are the following:

(a) an appearance notice has been issued to the accused for failing to comply with a summons, appearance notice, undertaking or release order or to attend court as required and the prosecutor seeks a decision under this section; or

(b) a charge has been laid against the accused for the contravention referred to in paragraph (a) and the prosecutor seeks a decision under this section.

(3) Powers — Judge or Justice — If the judge or justice who hears the matter is satisfied that the accused failed to comply with a summons, appearance notice, undertaking or release order or to attend court as required and that the failure did not cause a victim physical or emotional harm, property damage or economic loss, the judge or justice shall review any conditions of release that have been imposed on the accused and may, as the case may be,

(a) take no action;

(b) cancel any other summons, appearance notice, undertaking or release order in respect of the accused and, as the case may be,

(i) make a release order under section 515, or

(ii) if the prosecutor shows cause why the detention of the accused in custody is justified under subsection 515(10), make an order that the accused be detained in custody until the accused is dealt with according to law and if so detained, the judge or justice shall include in the record a statement of the judge's or justice's reasons for making the order; or

(c) remand the accused to custody for the purposes of the *Identification of Criminals Act*.

(4) Dismissal of charge — If a charge has been laid against the accused for the failure referred to in paragraph (2)(a) and the judge or justice, as the case may be, makes a decision under subsection (3), the judge or justice shall also dismiss that charge.

(5) No information or indictment — If the judge or justice makes a decision under subsection (3), no information may be laid nor indictment be preferred against the accused for the failure referred to in paragraph (2)(a).

2019, c. 25, s. 234 [To come into force December 18, 2019.]

524. (1) Issue of warrant for arrest of accused — Where a justice is satisfied that there are reasonable grounds to believe that an accused

(a) has contravened or is about to contravene any summons, appearance notice, promise to appear, undertaking or recognizance that was issued or given to him or entered into by him, or

(b) has committed an indictable offence after any summons, appearance notice, promise to appear, undertaking or recognizance was issued or given to him or entered into by him,

he may issue a warrant for the arrest of the accused.

(2) Arrest of accused without warrant — Notwithstanding anything in this Act, a peace officer who believes on reasonable grounds that an accused

(a) has contravened or is about to contravene any summons, appearance notice, promise to appear, undertaking or recognizance that was issued or given to him or entered into by him, or

(b) has committed an indictable offence after any summons, appearance notice, promise to appear, undertaking or recognizance was issued or given to him or entered into by him,

may arrest the accused without warrant.

(3) Hearing — Where an accused who has been arrested with a warrant issued under subsection (1), or who has been arrested under subsection (2), is taken before a justice, the justice shall

(a) where the accused was released from custody pursuant to an order made under subsection 522(3) by a judge of the superior court of criminal jurisdiction of any province, order that the accused be taken before a judge of that court; or

(b) in any other case, hear the prosecutor and his witnesses, if any, and the accused and his witnesses, if any.

(4) Detention of accused — Where an accused described in paragraph (3)(*a*) is taken before a judge and the judge finds

(a) that the accused has contravened or had been about to contravene his summons, appearance notice, promise to appear, undertaking or recognizance, or

(b) that there are reasonable grounds to believe that the accused has committed an indictable offence after any summons, appearance notice, promise to appear, undertaking or recognizance was issued or given to him or entered into by him,

he shall cancel the summons, appearance notice, promise to appear, undertaking or recognizance and order that the accused be detained in custody unless the accused, having been given a reasonable opportunity to do so, shows cause why his detention in custody is not justified within the meaning of subsection 515(10).

(5) Release of accused — Where the judge does not order that the accused be detained in custody pursuant to subsection (4), he may order that the accused be released on his giving an undertaking or entering into a recognizance described in any of paragraphs 515(2)(*a*) to (*e*) with such conditions described in subsection 515(4) or, where the accused was at large on an undertaking or a recognizance with conditions, such additional conditions, described in subsection 515(4), as the judge considers desirable.

(6) Order not reviewable — Any order made under subsection (4) or (5) is not subject to review, except as provided in section 680.

(7) Release of accused — Where the judge does not make a finding under paragraph (4)(*a*) or (*b*), he shall order that the accused be released from custody.

(8) Powers of justice after hearing — Where an accused described in subsection (3), other than an accused to whom paragraph (*a*) of that subsection applies, is taken before the justice and the justice finds

(a) that the accused has contravened or had been about to contravene his summons, appearance notice, promise to appear, undertaking or recognizance, or

(b) that there are reasonable grounds to believe that the accused has committed an indictable offence after any summons, appearance notice, promise to appear, undertaking or recognizance was issued or given to him or entered into by him,

he shall cancel the summons, appearance notice, promise to appear, undertaking or recognizance and order that the accused be detained in custody unless the accused, having been given a reasonable opportunity to do so, shows cause why his detention in custody is not justified within the meaning of subsection 515(10).

(9) Release of accused — Where the accused shows cause why his detention in custody is not justified within the meaning of subsection 515(10), the justice shall order that the accused be released on his giving an undertaking or entering into a recognizance described in any of paragraphs 515(2)(a) to (e) with such conditions, described in subsection 515(4), as the justice considers desirable.

(10) Reasons — Where the justice makes an order under subsection (9), he shall include in the record a statement of his reasons for making the order, and subsection 515(9) is applicable with such modification as the circumstances require in respect thereof.

(11) Where justice to order that accused be released — Where the justice does not make a finding under paragraph (8)(*a*) or (*b*), he shall order that the accused be released from custody.

(12) Provisions applicable to proceedings under this section — The provisions of sections 517, 518 and 519 apply with such modifications as the circumstances require in respect of any proceedings under this section, except that subsection 518(2) does not apply in respect of an accused who is charged with an offence mentioned in section 522.

(13) Certain provisions applicable to order under this section — Section 520 applies in respect of any order made under subsection (8) or (9) as though the order were an order made by a justice or a judge of the Nunavut Court of Justice under subsection 515(2) or (5), and section 521 applies in respect of any order made under subsection (9) as though the order were an order made by a justice or a judge of the Nunavut Court of Justice under subsection 515(2).

Proposed Amendment — 524

524. (1) Hearing — When an accused is taken before a justice in any of the circumstances described in subsection (2), the justice shall

(a) if the accused was released from custody under an order made under subsection 522(3) by a judge of the superior court of criminal jurisdiction of any province, order that the accused be taken before a judge of that court so that the judge may hear the matter; or

(b) in any other case, hear the matter.

(2) Circumstances — The circumstances referred to in subsection (1) are the following:

(a) the accused has been arrested for the contravention of or having been about to contravene, a summons, appearance notice, undertaking or release order and the prosecutor seeks to have it cancelled under this section; or

(b) the accused has been arrested for having committed an indictable offence while being subject to a summons, appearance notice, undertaking or release order and the prosecutor seeks to have it cancelled under this section.

(3) Cancellation — The judge or justice who hears the matter shall cancel a summons, appearance notice, undertaking or release order in respect of the accused if the judge or justice finds that

(a) the accused has contravened or had been about to contravene the summons, appearance notice, undertaking or release order; or

(b) there are reasonable grounds to believe that the accused has committed an indictable offence while being subject to the summons, appearance notice, undertaking or release order.

(4) Detention — If the judge or justice cancels the summons, appearance notice, undertaking or release order, the judge or justice shall order that the accused be detained in custody unless the accused, having been given a reasonable opportunity to do so, shows cause why their detention in custody is not justified under subsection 515(10).

(5) Release order — If the judge or justice does not order that the accused be detained in custody under subsection (4), the judge or justice shall make a release order referred to in section 515.

(6) Reasons — If the judge or justice makes a release order under subsection (5), the judge or justice shall include in the record a statement of the reasons for making the order, and subsection 515(9) applies with any modifications that the circumstances require.

(7) Release — If the judge or justice does not cancel the summons, appearance notice, undertaking or release order under subsection (3), the judge or justice shall order that the accused be released from custody.

(8) Provisions applicable to proceedings under this section — The provisions of sections 516 to 519 apply with any modifications that the circumstances require in respect of any proceedings under this section, except that subsection 518(2) does not apply in respect of an accused who is charged with an offence mentioned in section 469.

(9) Review — order by judge — An order made under subsection (4) or (5) respecting an accused referred to in paragraph (1)(a) is not subject to review except as provided in section 680.

(10) Review — order of justice — An order made under subsection (4) or (5) respecting an accused other than the accused referred to in paragraph (1)(a), is subject to review under sections 520 and 521 as if the order were made under section 515.

(11) to (13) [Repealed 2019, c. 25, s. 234. To come into force December 18, 2019.]
2019, c. 25, s. 234 [To come into force December 18, 2019.]

1999, c. 3, s. 33

Review of Detention where Trial Delayed

525. (1) Time for application to judge — Where an accused who has been charged with an offence other than an offence listed in section 469 and who is not required to be detained in custody in respect of any other matter is being detained in custody pending his trial for that offence and the trial has not commenced

(a) in the case of an indictable offence, within ninety days from

(i) the day on which the accused was taken before a justice under section 503, or

(ii) where an order that the accused be detained in custody has been made under section 521 or 524, or a decision has been made with respect to a review under section 520, the later of the day on which the accused was taken into custody under that order and the day of the decision, or

(b) in the case of an offence for which the accused is being prosecuted in proceedings by way of summary conviction, within thirty days from

(i) the day on which the accused was taken before a justice under subsection 503(1), or

(ii) where an order that the accused be detained in custody has been made under section 521 or 524, or a decision has been made with respect to a review under section 520, the later of the day on which the accused was taken into custody under that order and the day of the decision,

the person having the custody of the accused shall, forthwith on the expiration of those ninety or thirty days, as the case may be, apply to a judge having jurisdiction in the place in which the accused is in custody to fix a date for a hearing to determine whether or not the accused should be released from custody.

Proposed Amendment — 525(1)

(1) Time for application to judge — The person having the custody of an accused — who has been charged with an offence other than an offence listed in section 469, who is being detained in custody pending their trial for that offence and who is not required to be detained in custody in respect of any other matter — shall apply to a judge having jurisdiction in the place in which the accused is in custody to fix a date for a hearing to determine whether or not the accused should be released from custody, if the trial has not commenced within 90 days from

(a) the day on which the accused was taken before a justice under section 503; or

(b) in the case where an order that the accused be detained in custody has been made under section 521, paragraph 523.1(3)(b)(ii) or section 524, or a decision has been made with respect to a review under section 520, the later of the day on which the accused was taken into custody under that order and the day of the decision.

The person shall make the application immediately after the expiry of those 90 days.

2019, c. 25, s. 235(1) [To come into force December 18, 2019.]

Proposed Addition — 525(1.1)

(1.1) Waiver of right to hearing — However, the person having the custody of the accused is not required to make the application if the accused has waived in writing their right to a hearing and the judge has received the waiver before the expiry of the 90-day period referred to in subsection (1).

2019, c. 25, s. 235(1) [To come into force December 18, 2019.]

(2) Notice of hearing — On receiving an application under subsection (1), the judge shall

(a) fix a date for the hearing described in subsection (1) to be held in the jurisdiction

(i) where the accused is in custody, or

(ii) where the trial is to take place; and

(b) direct that notice of the hearing be given to such persons, including the prosecutor and the accused, and in such manner, as the judge may specify.

(3) Matters to be considered on hearing — On the hearing described in subsection (1), the judge may, in deciding whether or not the accused should be released from custody, take into consideration whether the prosecutor or the accused has been responsible for any unreasonable delay in the trial of the charge.

Proposed Amendment — 525(3)

(3) Cancellation of hearing — The judge may cancel the hearing if the judge receives the accused's waiver before the hearing.

2019, c. 25, s. 235(2) [To come into force December 18, 2019.]

(4) Order — If, following the hearing described in subsection (1), the judge is not satisfied that the continued detention of the accused in custody is justified within the meaning of subsection 515(10), the judge shall order that the accused be released from custody pending the trial of the charge on his giving an undertaking or entering into a recognizance described in any of paragraphs 515(2)(*a*) to (*e*) with such conditions described in subsection 515(4) as the judge considers desirable.

Proposed Amendment — 525(4)

(4) Consideration of proceeding's progression — On the hearing described in subsection (1), the judge shall consider whether the prosecutor or the accused has been responsible for any delay and, if the judge is concerned that the proceedings are progressing slowly and that an unreasonable delay may result, the judge may

(a) give directions for expediting the proceedings; or

(b) require a further hearing under this section within 90 days or any other period that the judge considers appropriate in the circumstances.

2019, c. 25, s. 235(2) [To come into force December 18, 2019.]

(5) Warrant of judge for arrest — Where a judge having jurisdiction in the province where an order under subsection (4) for the release of an accused has been made is satisfied that there are reasonable grounds to believe that the accused

(a) has violated or is about to violate the undertaking or recognizance on which he has been released, or

(b) has, after his release from custody on his undertaking or recognizance, committed an indictable offence,

he may issue a warrant for the arrest of the accused.

Proposed Amendment — 525(5)

(5) Release order — If, following the hearing, the judge is not satisfied that the continued detention of the accused in custody is justified within the meaning of subsection 515(10), the judge shall make a release order referred to in section 515.

2019, c. 25, s. 235(2) [To come into force December 18, 2019.]

(6) Arrest without warrant by peace officer — Notwithstanding anything in this Act, a peace officer who believes on reasonable grounds that an accused who has been released from custody under subsection (4)

(a) has contravened or is about to contravene the undertaking or recognizance on which he has been released, or

(b) has, after his release from custody on his undertaking or recognizance, committed an indictable offence,

may arrest the accused without warrant and take him or cause him to be taken before a judge having jurisdiction in the province where the order for his release was made.

Proposed Amendment — 525(6)

(6) Provisions applicable to proceedings — Sections 495.1, 512.3, 517 to 519 and 524 apply, with any modifications that the circumstances require, in respect of any proceedings under this section.

2019, c. 25, s. 235(2) [To come into force December 18, 2019.]

(7) Hearing and order — A judge before whom an accused is taken pursuant to a warrant issued under subsection (5) or pursuant to subsection (6) may, where the accused shows cause why his detention in custody is not justified within the meaning of subsection 515(10), order that the accused be released on his giving an undertaking or entering into a recognizance described in any of paragraphs 515(2)(*a*) to (*e*) with such conditions, described in subsection 515(4), as the judge considers desirable.

Proposed Amendment — 525(7)

(7) Definition of "judge" in the Province of Quebec — In this section, **"judge"**, in the Province of Quebec,

(a) in the case where the order that the accused be detained in custody has been made by a judge of the superior court of criminal jurisdiction of the Province of Quebec, has the same meaning as in paragraph (b) of the definition "judge" in section 493; and

(b) in any other case, means a judge of the superior court of criminal jurisdiction of the province, a judge of the Court of Quebec or three judges of the Court of Quebec.

2019, c. 25, s. 235(2) [To come into force December 18, 2019.]

(8) Provisions applicable to proceedings — The provisions of sections 517, 518 and 519 apply with such modifications as the circumstances require in respect of any proceedings under this section.

Proposed Repeal — 525(8)

(8) [Repealed 2019, c. 25, s. 235(2). To come into force December 18, 2019.]

(9) Directions for expediting trial — Where an accused is before a judge under any of the provisions of this section, the judge may give directions for expediting the trial of the accused.

Proposed Repeal — 525(9)

(9) [Repealed 2019, c. 25, s. 235(2). To come into force December 18, 2019.]

R.S.C. 1985, c. 27 (1st Supp.), s. 90; 1994, c. 44, s. 49; 1997, c. 18, s. 61

526. Directions for expediting proceedings — Subject to subsection 525(9), a court, judge or justice before which or whom an accused appears pursuant to this Part may give directions for expediting any proceedings in respect of the accused.

Proposed Amendment — 526

526. Directions for expediting proceedings — Subject to subsection 525(4), a court, judge or justice before which or whom an accused appears under this Part may give directions for expediting any proceedings in respect of the accused.

2019, c. 25, s. 236 [To come into force December 18, 2019.]

R.S.C. 1985, c. 27 (1st Supp.), s. 91

Procedure to Procure Attendance of a Prisoner

527. (1) Procuring attendance — A judge of a superior court of criminal jurisdiction may order in writing that a person who is confined in a prison be brought before the court, judge, justice or provincial court judge before whom the prisoner is required to attend, from day to day as may be necessary, if

(a) the applicant for the order sets out the facts of the case in an affidavit and produces the warrant, if any; and

(b) the judge is satisfied that the ends of justice require that an order be made.

(2) Provincial court judge's order — A provincial court judge has the same powers for the purposes of subsection (1) or (7) as a judge has under that subsection where the person whose attendance is required is within the province in which the provincial court judge has jurisdiction.

(3) Conveyance of prisoner — An order that is made under subsection (1) or (2) shall be addressed to the person who has custody of the prisoner, and on receipt thereof that person shall

(a) deliver the prisoner to any person who is named in the order to receive him; or

(b) bring the prisoner before the court, judge, justice or provincial court judge, as the case may be, on payment of his reasonable charges in respect thereof.

(4) Detention of prisoner required as witness — Where the prisoner is required as a witness, the judge or provincial court judge shall direct, in the order, the manner in which the prisoner shall be kept in custody and returned to the prison from which he is brought.

(5) Detention in other cases — Where the appearance of the prisoner is required for the purposes of paragraph (1)(*a*) or (*b*), the judge or provincial court judge shall give appropriate directions in the order with respect to the manner in which the prisoner is

(a) to be kept in custody, if he is committed for trial; or

(b) to be returned, if he is discharged on a preliminary inquiry or if he is acquitted of the charge against him.

(6) Application of sections respecting sentence — Sections 718.3 and 743.1 apply where a prisoner to whom this section applies is convicted and sentenced to imprisonment by the court, judge, justice or provincial court judge.

(7) **Transfer of prisoner** — On application by the prosecutor, a judge of a superior court of criminal jurisdiction may, if a prisoner or a person in the custody of a peace officer consents in writing, order the transfer of the prisoner or other person to the custody of a peace officer named in the order for a period specified in the order, where the judge is satisfied that the transfer is required for the purpose of assisting a peace officer acting in the execution of his or her duties.

(8) **Conveyance of prisoner** — An order under subsection (7) shall be addressed to the person who has custody of the prisoner and on receipt thereof that person shall deliver the prisoner to the peace officer who is named in the order to receive him.

(9) **Return** — When the purposes of any order made under this section have been carried out, the prisoner shall be returned to the place where he was confined at the time the order was made.

R.S.C. 1985, c. 27 (1st Supp.), ss. 92, 101(2)(b), 203; 1994, c. 44, s. 50; 1995, c. 22, s. 10 (Sched. I, item 18); 1997, c. 18, s. 62

Endorsement of Warrant

528. (1) **Endorsing warrant** — Where a warrant for the arrest or committal of an accused, in any form set out in Part XXVIII in relation thereto, cannot be executed in accordance with section 514 or 703, a justice within whose jurisdiction the accused is or is believed to be shall, on application and proof on oath or by affidavit of the signature of the justice who issued the warrant, authorize the arrest of the accused within his jurisdiction by making an endorsement, which may be in Form 28, on the warrant.

(1.1) **Copy of affidavit or warrant** — A copy of an affidavit or warrant submitted by a means of telecommunication that produces a writing has the same probative force as the original for the purposes of subsection (1).

(2) **Effect of endorsement** — An endorsement that is made on a warrant pursuant to subsection (1) is sufficient authority to the peace officers to whom it was originally directed, and to all peace officers within the territorial jurisdiction of the justice by whom it is endorsed, to execute the warrant and to take the accused before the justice who issued the warrant or before any other justice for the same territorial division.

R.S.C. 1985, c. 27 (1st Supp.), s. 93; 1994, c. 44, s. 51

Powers to Enter Dwelling-houses to Carry out Arrests

[Heading added 1997, c. 39, s. 2.]

529. (1) **Including authorization to enter in warrant of arrest** — A warrant to arrest or apprehend a person issued by a judge or justice under this or any other Act of Parliament may authorize a peace officer, subject to subsection (2), to enter a dwelling-house described in the warrant for the purpose of arresting or apprehending the person if the judge or justice is satisfied by information on oath in writing that there are reasonable grounds to believe that the person is or will be present in the dwelling-house.

(2) Execution — An authorization to enter a dwelling-house granted under subsection (1) is subject to the condition that the peace officer may not enter the dwelling-house unless the peace officer has, immediately before entering the dwelling-house, reasonable grounds to believe that the person to be arrested or apprehended is present in the dwelling-house.

1997, c. 39, s. 2

529.1 Warrant to enter dwelling-house — A judge or justice may issue a warrant in Form 7.1 authorizing a peace officer to enter a dwelling-house described in the warrant for the purpose of arresting or apprehending a person identified or identifiable by the warrant if the judge or justice is satisfied by information on oath that there are reasonable grounds to believe that the person is or will be present in the dwelling-house and that

(a) a warrant referred to in this or any other Act of Parliament to arrest or apprehend the person is in force anywhere in Canada;

(b) grounds exist to arrest the person without warrant under paragraph 495(1)(a) or (b) or section 672.91; or

(c) grounds exist to arrest or apprehend without warrant the person under an Act of Parliament, other than this Act.

1997, c. 39, s. 2; 2002, c. 13, s. 23

529.2 Reasonable terms and conditions — Subject to section 529.4, the judge or justice shall include in a warrant referred to in section 529 or 529.1 any terms and conditions that the judge or justice considers advisable to ensure that the entry into the dwelling-house is reasonable in the circumstances.

1997, c. 39, s. 2

529.3 (1) Authority to enter dwelling without warrant — Without limiting or restricting any power a peace officer may have to enter a dwelling-house under this or any other Act or law, the peace officer may enter the dwelling-house for the purpose of arresting or apprehending a person, without a warrant referred to in section 529 or 529.1 authorizing the entry, if the peace officer has reasonable grounds to believe that the person is present in the dwelling-house, and the conditions for obtaining a warrant under section 529.1 exist but by reason of exigent circumstances it would be impracticable to obtain a warrant.

(2) Exigent circumstances — For the purposes of subsection (1), exigent circumstances include circumstances in which the peace officer

(a) has reasonable grounds to suspect that entry into the dwelling-house is necessary to prevent imminent bodily harm or death to any person; or

(b) has reasonable grounds to believe that evidence relating to the commission of an indictable offence is present in the dwelling-house and that entry into the dwelling-house is necessary to prevent the imminent loss or imminent destruction of evidence.

1997, c. 39, s. 2

529.4 (1) Omitting announcement before entry — A judge or justice who authorizes a peace officer to enter a dwelling-house under section 529 or 529.1, or any judge or justice, may authorize the peace officer to enter the dwelling-house without prior announcement if the judge or justice is satisfied by information on oath that there are reasonable grounds to believe that prior announcement of the entry would

(a) expose the peace officer or any other person to imminent bodily harm or death; or

(b) result in the imminent loss or imminent destruction of evidence relating to the commission of an indictable offence.

(2) Execution of authorization — An authorization under this section is subject to the condition that the peace officer may not enter the dwelling-house without prior announcement despite being authorized to do so unless the peace officer has, immediately before entering the dwelling-house,

(a) reasonable grounds to suspect that prior announcement of the entry would expose the peace officer or any other person to imminent bodily harm or death; or

(b) reasonable grounds to believe that prior announcement of the entry would result in the imminent loss or imminent destruction of evidence relating to the commission of an indictable offence.

(3) Exception — A peace officer who enters a dwelling-house without a warrant under section 529.3 may not enter the dwelling-house without prior announcement unless the peace officer has, immediately before entering the dwelling-house,

(a) reasonable grounds to suspect that prior announcement of the entry would expose the peace officer or any other person to imminent bodily harm or death; or

(b) reasonable grounds to believe that prior announcement of the entry would result in the imminent loss or imminent destruction of evidence relating to the commission of an indictable offence.

1997, c. 39, s. 2

529.5 Telewarrant — If a peace officer believes that it would be impracticable in the circumstances to appear personally before a judge or justice to make an application for a warrant under section 529.1 or an authorization under section 529 or 529.4, the warrant or authorization may be issued on an information submitted by telephone or other means of telecommunication and, for that purpose, section 487.1 applies, with any modifications that the circumstances require, to the warrant or authorization.

1997, c. 39, s. 2

PART XVII — LANGUAGE OF ACCUSED (SS. 530–534)

530. (1) Language of accused — On application by an accused whose language is one of the official languages of Canada, made not later than the time of the appearance of the accused at which their trial date is set, a judge, provincial court judge, judge of the Nunavut Court of Justice or justice of the peace shall grant an order directing that the accused be tried before a justice of the peace, provincial court judge, judge or judge and jury, as the case may be, who speak the official language of Canada that is the language of the accused or, if the circumstances warrant, who speak both official languages of Canada.

(2) **Idem** — On application by an accused whose language is not one of the official languages of Canada, made not later than the time of the appearance of the accused at which their trial date is set, a judge, provincial court judge, judge of the Nunavut Court of Justice or justice of the peace may grant an order directing that the accused be tried before a justice of the peace, provincial court judge, judge or judge and jury, as the case may be, who speak the official language of Canada in which the accused, in the opinion of the judge, provincial court judge, judge of the Nunavut Court of Justice or justice of the peace, can best give testimony or, if the circumstances warrant, who speak both official languages of Canada.

(3) **Accused to be advised of right** — The judge, provincial court judge, judge of the Nunavut Court of Justice or justice of the peace before whom an accused first appears shall ensure that they are advised of their right to apply for an order under subsection (1) or (2) and of the time before which such an application must be made.

(4) **Remand** — If an accused fails to apply for an order under subsection (1) or (2) and the judge, provincial court judge, judge of the Nunavut Court of Justice or justice of the peace before whom the accused is to be tried, in this Part referred to as "the court", is satisfied that it is in the best interests of justice that the accused be tried before a justice of the peace, provincial court judge, judge or judge and jury who speak the official language of Canada that is the language of the accused or, if the language of the accused is not one of the official languages of Canada, the official language of Canada in which the accused, in the opinion of the court, can best give testimony, the court may, if it does not speak that language, by order remand the accused to be tried by a justice of the peace, provincial court judge, judge or judge and jury, as the case may be, who speak that language or, if the circumstances warrant, who speak both official languages of Canada.

(5) **Variation of order** — An order under this section that a trial be held in one of the official languages of Canada may, if the circumstances warrant, be varied by the court to require that it be held in both official languages of Canada, and vice versa.

(6) **Circumstances warranting order directing trial in both official languages** — The facts that two or more accused who are to be tried together are each entitled to be tried before a justice of the peace, provincial court judge, judge or judge and jury who speak one of the official languages of Canada and that those official languages are different may constitute circumstances that warrant that an order be granted directing that they be tried before a justice of the peace, provincial court judge, judge or judge and jury who speak both official languages of Canada.

R.S.C. 1985, c. 27 (1st Supp.), ss. 94, 203; 1999, c. 3, s. 34; 2008, c. 18, s. 18; 2019, c. 25, s. 237

530.01 (1) Translation of documents — If an order is granted under section 530, a prosecutor — other than a private prosecutor — shall, on application by the accused,

(a) cause the portions of an information or indictment against the accused that are in an official language that is not that of the accused or that in which the accused can best give testimony to be translated into the other official language; and

(b) provide the accused with a written copy of the translated text at the earliest possible time.

(2) Original version prevails — In the case of a discrepancy between the original version of a document and the translated text, the original version shall prevail.

2008, c. 18, s. 19

530.1 If order granted — If an order is granted under section 530,

(a) the accused and his counsel have the right to use either official language for all purposes during the preliminary inquiry and trial of the accused;

(b) the accused and his counsel may use either official language in written pleadings or other documents used in any proceedings relating to the preliminary inquiry or trial of the accused;

(c) any witness may give evidence in either official language during the preliminary inquiry or trial;

(c.1) the presiding justice or judge may, if the circumstances warrant, authorize the prosecutor to examine or cross-examine a witness in the official language of the witness even though it is not that of the accused or that in which the accused can best give testimony;

(d) the accused has a right to have a justice presiding over the preliminary inquiry who speaks the official language of the accused or both official languages, as the case may be;

(e) the accused has a right to have a prosecutor — other than a private prosecutor — who speaks the official language of the accused or both official languages, as the case may be;

(f) the court shall make interpreters available to assist the accused, his counsel or any witness during the preliminary inquiry or trial;

(g) the record of proceedings during the preliminary inquiry or trial shall include

(i) a transcript of everything that was said during those proceedings in the official language in which it was said,

(ii) a transcript of any interpretation into the other official language of what was said, and

(iii) any documentary evidence that was tendered during those proceedings in the official language in which it was tendered; and

(h) any trial judgment, including any reasons given therefor, issued in writing in either official language, shall be made available by the court in the official language that is the language of the accused.

R.S.C. 1985, c. 31 (4th Supp.), s. 94; 2008, c. 18, s. 20

530.2 (1) Language used in proceeding — If an order is granted directing that an accused be tried before a justice of the peace, provincial court judge, judge or judge and jury who speak both official languages, the justice or judge presiding over a preliminary inquiry or trial may, at the start of the proceeding, make an order setting out the circumstances in which, and the extent to which, the prosecutor and the justice or judge may use each official language.

(2) Right of the accused — Any order granted under this section shall, to the extent possible, respect the right of the accused to be tried in his or her official language.

2008, c. 18, s. 21

531. Change of venue — Despite any other provision of this Act but subject to any regulations made under section 533, if an order made under section 530 cannot be conveniently complied with in the territorial division in which the offence would otherwise be tried, the court shall, except if that territorial division is in the Province of New Brunswick, order that the trial of the accused be held in another territorial division in the same province.

R.S.C. 1985, c. 27 (1st Supp.), s. 203; 2008, c. 18, s. 21

532. Saving — Nothing in this Part or the *Official Languages Act* derogates from or otherwise adversely affects any right afforded by a law of a province in force on the coming into force of this Part in that province or thereafter coming into force relating to the language of proceedings or testimony in criminal matters that is not inconsistent with this Part or that Act.

533. Regulations — The Lieutenant Governor in Council of a province may make regulations generally for carrying into effect the purposes and provisions of this Part in the province and the Commissioner of Yukon, the Commissioner of the Northwest Territories and the Commissioner of Nunavut may make regulations generally for carrying into effect the purposes and provisions of this Part in Yukon, the Northwest Territories and Nunavut, respectively.

1993, c. 28, s. 78 (Sched. III, item 33); 2002, c. 7, s. 144

533.1 (1) Review — Within three years after this section comes into force, a comprehensive review of the provisions and operation of this Part shall be undertaken by any committee of the Senate, of the House of Commons or of both Houses of Parliament that may be designated or established by the Senate or the House of Commons, or by both Houses of Parliament, as the case may be, for that purpose.

(2) Report — The committee referred to in subsection (1) shall, within a year after a review is undertaken under that subsection or within any further time that may be authorized by the Senate, the House of Commons or both Houses of Parliament, as the case may be, submit a report on the review to Parliament, including a statement of any changes that the committee recommends.

2008, c. 18, s. 21.1

534. [Repealed 1997, c. 18, s. 63.]

PART XVIII — PROCEDURE ON PRELIMINARY INQUIRY (SS. 535–551)

Jurisdiction

535. Inquiry by justice — If an accused who is charged with an indictable offence that is punishable by 14 years or more of imprisonment is before a justice and a request has been made for a preliminary inquiry under subsection 536(4) or 536.1(3), the justice shall, in accordance with this Part, inquire into the charge and any other indictable offence, in respect of the same transaction, founded on the facts that are disclosed by the evidence taken in accordance with this Part.

R.S.C. 1985, c. 27 (1st Supp.), s. 96; 2002, c. 13, s. 24; 2019, c. 25, s. 238

536. (1) Remand by justice to provincial court judge in certain cases — Where an accused is before a justice other than a provincial court judge charged with an offence over which a provincial court judge has absolute jurisdiction under section 553, the justice shall remand the accused to appear before a provincial court judge having jurisdiction in the territorial division in which the offence is alleged to have been committed.

(2) Election before justice — 14 years or more of imprisonment — If an accused is before a justice, charged with an indictable offence that is punishable by 14 years or more of imprisonment, other than an offence listed in section 469, the justice shall, after the information has been read to the accused, put the accused to an election in the following words:

> You have the option to elect to be tried by a provincial court judge without a jury and without having had a preliminary inquiry; or you may elect to be tried by a judge without a jury; or you may elect to be tried by a court composed of a judge and jury. If you do not elect now, you are deemed to have elected to be tried by a court composed of a judge and jury. If you elect to be tried by a judge without a jury or by a court composed of a judge and jury or if you are deemed to have elected to be tried by a court composed of a judge and jury, you will have a preliminary inquiry only if you or the prosecutor requests one. How do you elect to be tried?

(2.1) Election before justice — other indictable offences — If an accused is before a justice, charged with an indictable offence — other than an offence that is punishable by 14 years or more of imprisonment, an offence listed in section 469 that is not punishable by 14 years or more of imprisonment or an offence over which a provincial court judge has absolute jurisdiction under section 553 —, the justice shall, after the information has been read to the accused, put the accused to an election in the following words:

> You have the option to elect to be tried by a provincial court judge without a jury; or you may elect to be tried by a judge without a jury; or you may elect to be tried by a court composed of a judge and jury. If you do not elect now, you are deemed to have elected to be tried by a court composed of a judge and jury. How do you elect to be tried?

(3) Procedure where accused elects trial by provincial court judge — Where an accused elects to be tried by a provincial court judge, the justice shall endorse on the information a record of the election and shall

(a) where the justice is not a provincial court judge, remand the accused to appear and plead to the charge before a provincial court judge having jurisdiction in the territorial division in which the offence is alleged to have been committed; or

(b) where the justice is a provincial court judge, call on the accused to plead to the charge and if the accused does not plead guilty, proceed with the trial or fix a time for the trial.

(4) Request for preliminary inquiry — If an accused referred to in subsection (2) elects to be tried by a judge without a jury or by a court composed of a judge and jury or does not elect when put to the election or is deemed under paragraph 565(1)(a) to have elected to be tried by a court composed of a judge and jury, or if an accused is charged with an offence listed in section 469 that is punishable by 14 years or more of imprisonment, the justice shall, subject to section 577, on the request of the accused or the prosecutor made at that time or within the period fixed by rules of court made under section 482 or 482.1 or, if there are no such rules, by the justice, hold a preliminary inquiry into the charge.

(4.1) Endorsement on the information — accused referred to in subsection (2) — If an accused referred to in subsection (2) elects to be tried by a judge without a jury or by a court composed of a judge and jury or does not elect when put to the election or is deemed under paragraph 565(1)(a) to have elected to be tried by a court composed of a judge and jury, the justice shall endorse on the information and, if the accused is in custody, on the warrant of remand, a statement showing

(a) the nature of the election or deemed election of the accused or that the accused did not elect, as the case may be; and

(b) whether the accused or the prosecutor has requested that a preliminary inquiry be held.

(4.11) Endorsement on the information — other accused charged with an offence punishable by 14 years or more of imprisonment — If an accused is before a justice, charged with an offence listed in section 469 that is punishable by 14 years or more of imprisonment, the justice shall endorse on the information and, if the accused is in custody, on the warrant of remand, a statement showing whether the accused or the prosecutor has requested that a preliminary inquiry be held.

(4.12) Endorsement on the information — accused referred to in subsection (2.1) — If an accused referred to in subsection (2.1) elects to be tried by a judge without a jury or by a court composed of a judge and jury or does not elect when put to the election or is deemed under paragraph 565(1)(a) to have elected to be tried by a court composed of a judge and jury, the justice shall endorse on the information and, if the accused is in custody, on the warrant of remand, a statement showing the nature of the election or deemed election of the accused or that the accused did not elect, as the case may be.

(4.2) Preliminary inquiry if two or more accused — If two or more persons are jointly charged in an information and one or more of them make a request for a preliminary inquiry under subsection (4), a preliminary inquiry must be held with respect to all of them.

(4.3) When no request for preliminary inquiry — If no request for a preliminary inquiry is made under subsection (4), the justice shall fix the date for the trial or the date on which the accused must appear in the trial court to have the date fixed.

(5) Jurisdiction — Where a justice before whom a preliminary inquiry is being or is to be held has not commenced to take evidence, any justice having jurisdiction in the province where the offence with which the accused is charged is alleged to have been committed has jurisdiction for the purposes of subsection (4).

R.S.C. 1985, c. 27 (1st Supp.), s. 96; 2002, c. 13, s. 25; 2004, c. 12, s. 9; 2019, c. 25, s. 239(1), (3)–(5)

536.1 (1) Remand by justice — Nunavut — If an accused is before a justice of the peace charged with an indictable offence mentioned in section 553, the justice of the peace shall remand the accused to appear before a judge.

(2) Election before judge or justice of the peace in Nunavut — 14 years or more of imprisonment — If an accused is before a judge or justice of the peace, charged with an indictable offence that is punishable by 14 years or more of imprisonment, other than an offence mentioned in section 469, the judge or justice of the peace shall, after the information has been read to the accused, put the accused to an election in the following words:

> You have the option to elect to be tried by a judge without a jury or to be tried by a court composed of a judge and jury. If you do not elect now, you are deemed to have elected to be tried by a court composed of a judge and jury. If you elect to be tried by a judge without a jury or by a court composed of a judge and jury or if you are deemed to have elected to be tried by a court composed of a judge and jury, you will have a preliminary inquiry only if you or the prosecutor requests one. How do you elect to be tried?

(2.1) Election before judge or justice of the peace in Nunavut — other indictable offences — If an accused is before a judge or justice of the peace, charged with an indictable offence — other than an offence that is punishable by 14 years or more of imprisonment, an offence listed in section 469 that is not punishable by 14 years or more of imprisonment or an offence mentioned in section 553 —

, the judge or justice of the peace shall, after the information has been read to the accused, put the accused to an election in the following words:

> You have the option to elect to be tried by a judge without a jury or to be tried by a court composed of a judge and jury. If you do not elect now, you are deemed to have elected to be tried by a court composed of a judge and jury. How do you elect to be tried?

(3) **Request for preliminary inquiry — Nunavut** — If an accused referred to in subsection (2) elects to be tried by a judge without a jury or by a court composed of a judge and jury or does not elect when put to the election or is deemed under paragraph 565(1)(a) to have elected to be tried by a court composed of a judge and jury or if an accused is charged with an offence listed in section 469 that is punishable by 14 years or more of imprisonment, the justice or judge shall, subject to section 577, on the request of the accused or the prosecutor made at that time or within the period fixed by rules of court made under section 482 or 482.1 or, if there are no such rules, by the judge or justice, hold a preliminary inquiry into the charge.

(4) **Endorsement on the information — accused referred to in subsection (2)** — If an accused referred to in subsection (2) elects to be tried by a judge without a jury or by a court composed of a judge and jury or does not elect when put to the election or is deemed under paragraph 565(1)(a) to have elected to be tried by a court composed of a judge and jury, the justice or judge shall endorse on the information and, if the accused is in custody, on the warrant of remand, a statement showing

(a) the nature of the election or deemed election of the accused or that the accused did not elect, as the case may be; and

(b) whether the accused or the prosecutor has requested that a preliminary inquiry be held.

(4.01) **Endorsement on the information — other accused charged with an offence punishable by 14 years or more of imprisonment** — If an accused is before a judge or justice of the peace, charged with an offence listed in section 469 that is punishable by 14 years or more of imprisonment, the justice or judge shall endorse on the information and, if the accused is in custody, on the warrant of remand, a statement showing whether the accused or the prosecutor has requested that a preliminary inquiry be held.

(4.02) **Endorsement on the information — accused referred to in subsection (2.1)** — If an accused referred to in subsection (2.1) elects to be tried by a judge without a jury or by a court composed of a judge and jury or does not elect when put to the election or is deemed under paragraph 565(1)(a) to have elected to be tried by a court composed of a judge and jury, the justice shall endorse on the information and, if the accused is in custody, on the warrant of remand, a statement showing the nature of the election or deemed election of the accused or that the accused did not elect, as the case may be.

(4.1) **Preliminary inquiry if two or more accused** — If two or more persons are jointly charged in an information and one or more of them make a request for a preliminary inquiry under subsection (3), a preliminary inquiry must be held with respect to all of them.

(4.2) Procedure if accused elects trial by judge — Nunavut — If no request for a preliminary inquiry is made under subsection (3),

(a) if the accused is before a justice of the peace, the justice of the peace shall remand the accused to appear and plead to the charge before a judge; or

(b) if the accused is before a judge, the judge shall

(i) if the accused elects to be tried by a judge without a jury, call on the accused to plead to the charge and if the accused does not plead guilty, proceed with the trial or fix a time for the trial, or

(ii) if the accused elects or is deemed to have elected to be tried by a court composed of a judge and jury, fix a time for the trial.

(5) Jurisdiction — Nunavut — If a justice of the peace before whom a preliminary inquiry is being or is to be held has not commenced to take evidence, any justice of the peace having jurisdiction in Nunavut has jurisdiction for the purpose of subsection (3).

(6) Application to Nunavut — This section, and not section 536, applies in respect of criminal proceedings in Nunavut.

1999, c. 3, s. 35; 2002, c. 13, s. 26; 2004, c. 12, s. 10; 2019, c. 25, s. 240

536.2 Elections and re-elections in writing — An election or a re-election by an accused in respect of a mode of trial may be made by submission of a document in writing without the personal appearance of the accused.

2002, c. 13, s. 27

Procedures before Preliminary Inquiry

[Heading added 2002, c. 13, s. 27.]

536.3 Statement of issues and witnesses — If a request for a preliminary inquiry is made, the prosecutor or, if the request was made by the accused, counsel for the accused shall, within the period fixed by rules of court made under section 482 or 482.1 or, if there are no such rules, by the justice, provide the court and the other party with a statement that identifies

(a) the issues on which the requesting party wants evidence to be given at the inquiry; and

(b) the witnesses that the requesting party wants to hear at the inquiry.

2002, c. 13, s. 27

536.4 (1) Order for hearing — The justice before whom a preliminary inquiry is to be held may order, on application of the prosecutor or the accused or on the justice's own motion, that a hearing be held, within the period fixed by rules of court made under section 482 or 482.1 or, if there are no such rules, by the justice, to

(a) assist the parties to identify the issues on which evidence will be given at the inquiry;

(b) assist the parties to identify the witnesses to be heard at the inquiry, taking into account the witnesses' needs and circumstances; and

(c) encourage the parties to consider any other matters that would promote a fair and expeditious inquiry.

(2) **Agreement to be recorded** — When the hearing is completed, the justice shall record any admissions of fact agreed to by the parties and any agreement reached by the parties.

2002, c. 13, s. 27

536.5 Agreement to limit scope of preliminary inquiry — Whether or not a hearing is held under section 536.4, the prosecutor and the accused may agree to limit the scope of the preliminary inquiry to specific issues. An agreement shall be filed with the court or recorded under subsection 536.4(2), as the case may be.

2002, c. 13, s. 27; 2019, c. 25, s. 241

Powers of Justice

537. (1) Powers of justice — A justice acting under this Part may

(a) adjourn an inquiry from time to time and change the place of hearing, where it appears to be desirable to do so by reason of the absence of a witness, the inability of a witness who is ill to attend at the place where the justice usually sits or for any other sufficient reason;

(b) remand the accused to custody for the purposes of the *Identification of Criminals Act*;

(c) except where the accused is authorized pursuant to Part XVI to be at large, remand the accused to custody in a prison by warrant in Form 19;

(d) resume an inquiry before the expiration of a period for which it has been adjourned with the consent of the prosecutor and the accused or his counsel;

(e) order in writing, in Form 30, that the accused be brought before him, or any other justice for the same territorial division, at any time before the expiration of the time for which the accused has been remanded;

(f) grant or refuse permission to the prosecutor or his counsel to address him in support of the charge, by way of opening or summing up or by way of reply on any evidence that is given on behalf of the accused;

(g) receive evidence on the part of the prosecutor or the accused, as the case may be, after hearing any evidence that has been given on behalf of either of them;

(h) order that no person other than the prosecutor, the accused and their counsel shall have access to or remain in the room in which the inquiry is held, where it appears to him that the ends of justice will be best served by so doing;

(i) regulate the course of the inquiry in any way that appears to the justice to be desirable, including to promote a fair and expeditious inquiry, that is consistent with this Act and that, unless the justice is satisfied that to do so would be contrary to the best interests of the administration of justice, is in accordance with any admission of fact or agreement recorded under subsection 536.4(2) or agreement made under section 536.5;

(j) if the prosecutor and the accused so agree, permit the accused to appear by counsel or by closed-circuit television or videoconference, for any part of the inquiry other than a part in which the evidence of a witness is taken;

(j.1) permit, on the request of the accused, that the accused be out of court during the whole or any part of the inquiry on any conditions that the justice considers appropriate; and

(k) require an accused who is confined in prison to appear by closed-circuit television or videoconference, for any part of the inquiry other than a part in which the evidence of a witness is taken, as long as the accused is given the opportunity to communicate privately with counsel if they are represented by counsel.

(1.01) Power provided under paragraph (1)(i) — For the purpose of paragraph (1)(i), the justice may, among other things, limit the scope of the preliminary inquiry to specific issues and limit the witnesses to be heard on these issues.

(1.02) 715 or 715.01 — If a justice grants a request under paragraph (1)(j.1), the Court must inform the accused that the evidence taken during their absence could still be admissible under section 715 or 715.01.

(1.1) Inappropriate questioning — A justice acting under this Part shall order the immediate cessation of any part of an examination or cross-examination of a witness that is, in the opinion of the justice, abusive, too repetitive or otherwise inappropriate.

(2) Change of venue — Where a justice changes the place of hearing under paragraph (1)(a) to a place in the same province, other than a place in a territorial division in which the justice has jurisdiction, any justice who has jurisdiction in the place to which the hearing is changed may continue the hearing.

(3) and (4) [Repealed 1991, c. 43, s. 9 (Sched., item 3(2)).]

1991, c. 43, s. 9 (Sched., item 3); 1994, c. 44, s. 53; 1997, c. 18, s. 64; 2002, c. 13, s. 28; 2008, c. 18, s. 22; 2019, c. 25, s. 242

538. Organization — Where an accused is an organization, subsections 556(1) and (2) apply with such modifications as the circumstances require.

2003, c. 21, s. 8

Taking Evidence of Witnesses

539. (1) Order restricting publication of evidence taken at preliminary inquiry — Prior to the commencement of the taking of evidence at a preliminary inquiry, the justice holding the inquiry

(a) may, if application therefor is made by the prosecutor, and

(b) shall, if application therefor is made by any of the accused, make an order directing that the evidence taken at the inquiry shall not be published in any document or broadcast or transmitted in any way before such time as, in respect of each of the accused,

(c) he or she is discharged, or

(d) if he or she is ordered to stand trial, the trial is ended.

(2) Accused to be informed of right to apply for order — Where an accused is not represented by counsel at a preliminary inquiry, the justice holding the inquiry shall, prior to the commencement of the taking of evidence at the inquiry, inform the accused of his right to make application under subsection (1).

(3) Failure to comply with order — Every one who fails to comply with an order made pursuant to subsection (1) is guilty of an offence punishable on summary conviction.

(4) [Repealed 2005, c. 32, s. 18(2).]

R.S.C. 1985, c. 27 (1st Supp.), s. 97; 2005, c. 32, s. 18

540. (1) Taking evidence — Where an accused is before a justice holding a preliminary inquiry, the justice shall

(a) take the evidence under oath of the witnesses called on the part of the prosecution, subject to subsection 537(1.01), and allow the accused or counsel for the accused to cross-examine them; and

(b) cause a record of the evidence of each witness to be taken

(i) in legible writing in the form of a deposition, in Form 31, or by a stenographer appointed by him or pursuant to law, or

(ii) in a province where a sound recording apparatus is authorized by or under provincial legislation for use in civil cases, by the type of apparatus so authorized and in accordance with the requirements of the provincial legislation.

(2) Reading and signing depositions — Where a deposition is taken down in writing, the justice shall, in the presence of the accused, before asking the accused if he wishes to call witnesses,

(a) cause the deposition to be read to the witness;

(b) cause the deposition to be signed by the witness; and

(c) sign the deposition himself.

(3) Authentication by justice — Where depositions are taken down in writing, the justice may sign

(a) at the end of each deposition; or

(b) at the end of several or of all the depositions in a manner that will indicate that his signature is intended to authenticate each deposition.

(4) Stenographer to be sworn — Where the stenographer appointed to take down the evidence is not a duly sworn court stenographer, he shall make oath that he will truly and faithfully report the evidence.

(5) Authentication of transcript — Where the evidence is taken down by a stenographer appointed by the justice or pursuant to law, it need not be read to or signed by the witnesses, but, on request of the justice or of one of the parties, shall be transcribed, in whole or in part, by the stenographer and the transcript shall be accompanied by

(a) an affidavit of the stenographer that it is a true report of the evidence; or

(b) a certificate that it is a true report of the evidence if the stenographer is a duly sworn court stenographer.

(6) Transcription of record taken by sound recording apparatus — Where, in accordance with this Act, a record is taken in any proceedings under this Act by a sound recording apparatus, the record so taken shall, on request of the justice or of one of the parties, be dealt with and transcribed, in whole or in part, and the transcription certified and used in accordance with the provincial legislation, with such modifications as the circumstances require mentioned in subsection (1).

(7) Evidence — A justice acting under this Part may receive as evidence any information that would not otherwise be admissible but that the justice considers credible or trustworthy in the circumstances of the case, including a statement that is made by a witness in writing or otherwise recorded.

(8) Notice of intention to tender — Unless the justice orders otherwise, no information may be received as evidence under subsection (7) unless the party has given to each of the other parties reasonable notice of his or her intention to tender it, together with a copy of the statement, if any, referred to in that subsection.

(9) Appearance for examination — The justice shall, on application of a party, require any person whom the justice considers appropriate to appear for examination or cross-examination with respect to information intended to be tendered as evidence under subsection (7).

R.S.C. 1985, c. 27 (1st Supp.), s. 98; 1997, c. 18, s. 65; 2002, c. 13, s. 29; 2019, c. 25, s. 243

541. (1) Hearing of witnesses — When the evidence of the witnesses called on the part of the prosecution has been taken down and, if required by this Part, has been read, the justice shall, subject to this section and subsection 537(1.01), hear the witnesses called by the accused.

(2) Contents of address to accused — Before hearing any witness called by an accused who is not represented by counsel, the justice shall address the accused as follows or to the like effect:

> Do you wish to say anything in answer to these charges or to any other charges which might have arisen from the evidence led by the prosecution? You are not obliged to say anything. but whatever you do say may be given in evidence against you at your trial. You should not make any confession or admission of guilt because of any promise or threat made to you but if you do make any statement it may be given in evidence against you at your trial in spite of the promise or threat.

(3) Statement of accused — Where the accused who is not represented by counsel says anything in answer to the address made by the justice pursuant to subsection (2), the answer shall be taken down in writing and shall be signed by the justice and kept with the evidence of the witnesses and dealt with in accordance with this Part.

(4) **Witnesses for accused** — Where an accused is not represented by counsel, the justice shall ask the accused if he or she wishes to call any witnesses after subsections (2) and (3) have been complied with.

(5) **Depositions of witnesses** — Subject to subsection 537(1.01), the justice shall hear each witness called by the accused who testifies to any matter relevant to the inquiry, and for the purposes of this subsection, section 540 applies with any modifications that the circumstances require.

R.S.C. 1985, c. 27 (1st Supp.), s. 99; 1994, c. 44, s. 54; 2019, c. 25, s. 244

542. (1) Confession or admission of accused — Nothing in this Act prevents a prosecutor giving in evidence at a preliminary inquiry any admission, confession or statement made at any time by the accused that by law is admissible against him.

(2) **Restriction of publication of reports of preliminary inquiry** — Every one who publishes in any document, or broadcasts or transmits in any way, a report that any admission or confession was tendered in evidence at a preliminary inquiry or a report of the nature of such admission or confession so tendered in evidence unless

(a) the accused has been discharged, or

(b) if the accused has been committed for trial, the trial has ended,

is guilty of an offence punishable on summary conviction.

(3) [Repealed 2005, c. 32, s. 19(2).]

R.S.C. 1985, c. 27 (1st Supp.), s. 101(2); 2005, c. 32, s. 19

Remand Where Offence Committed in Another Jurisdiction

543. (1) Order that accused appear or be taken before justice where offence alleged to have been committed — If an accused is charged with an offence alleged to have been committed out of the limits of the jurisdiction in which they have been charged, the justice before whom they appear or are brought may, at any stage of the inquiry after hearing both parties, order the accused to appear or, if the accused is in custody, issue a warrant in Form 15 to convey the accused before a justice who, having jurisdiction in the place where the offence is alleged to have been committed, shall continue and complete the inquiry.

(2) **Transmission of transcript and documents and effect of order or warrant** — Where a justice makes an order or issues a warrant pursuant to subsection (1), he shall cause the transcript of any evidence given before him in the inquiry and all documents that were then before him and that are relevant to the in-

quiry to be transmitted to a justice having jurisdiction in the place where the offence is alleged to have been committed and

(a) any evidence the transcript of which is so transmitted shall be deemed to have been taken by the justice to whom it is transmitted; and

(b) any appearance notice, promise to appear, undertaking or recognizance issued to or given or entered into by the accused under Part XVI shall be deemed to have been issued, given or entered into in the jurisdiction where the offence is alleged to have been committed and to require the accused to appear before the justice to whom the transcript and documents are transmitted at the time provided in the order made in respect of the accused under paragraph (1)(*a*).

Proposed Amendment — 543(2)(b)

(b) any appearance notice, undertaking or release order issued to or given or entered into by the accused shall be deemed to have been issued, given or entered into in the jurisdiction where the offence is alleged to have been committed and to require the accused to appear before the justice to whom the transcript and documents are transmitted at the time provided in the order made in respect of the accused under paragraph (1)(a).

2019, c. 25, s. 245(4) [To come into force December 18, 2019.]

2019, c. 25, s. 245(1)

Absconding Accused

544. (1) Accused absconding during inquiry — Notwithstanding any other provision of this Act, where an accused, whether or not he is charged jointly with another, absconds during the course of a preliminary inquiry into an offence with which he is charged,

(a) he shall be deemed to have waived his right to be present at the inquiry; and

(b) the justice

(i) may continue the inquiry and, when all the evidence has been taken, shall dispose of the inquiry in accordance with section 548, or

(ii) if a warrant is issued for the arrest of the accused, may adjourn the inquiry to await his appearance,

but where the inquiry is adjourned pursuant to subparagraph (*b*)(ii), the justice may continue it at any time pursuant to subparagraph(*b*)(i) if he is satisfied that it would no longer be in the interests of justice to await the appearance of the accused.

(2) Adverse inference — Where the justice continues a preliminary inquiry pursuant to subsection (1), he may draw an inference adverse to the accused from the fact that he has absconded.

(3) Accused not entitled to re-opening — Where an accused reappears at a preliminary inquiry that is continuing pursuant to subsection (1), he is not entitled to have any part of the proceedings that was conducted in his absence re-opened unless the justice is satisfied that because of exceptional circumstances it is in the interests of justice to re-open the inquiry.

(4) Counsel for accused may continue to act — Where the accused has absconded during the course of a preliminary inquiry and the justice continues the inquiry, counsel for the accused is not thereby deprived of any authority he may have to continue to act for the accused in the proceedings.

(5) Accused calling witnesses — If, at the conclusion of the evidence on the part of the prosecution at a preliminary inquiry that has been continued under subsection (1), the accused is absent but their counsel is present, the counsel shall be given an opportunity to call witnesses on behalf of the accused, subject to subsection 537(1.01), and subsection 541(5) applies with any modifications that the circumstances require.

1994, c. 44, s. 55; 2019, c. 25, s. 246

Procedure where Witness Refuses to Testify

545. (1) Witness refusing to be examined — Where a person, being present at a preliminary inquiry and being required by the justice to give evidence,

(a) refuses to be sworn,

(b) having been sworn, refuses to answer the questions that are put to him,

(c) fails to produce any writings that he is required to produce, or

(d) refuses to sign his deposition,

without offering a reasonable excuse for his failure or refusal, the justice may adjourn the inquiry and may, by warrant in Form 20, commit the person to prison for a period not exceeding eight clear days or for the period during which the inquiry is adjourned, whichever is the lesser period.

(2) Further commitment — Where a person to whom subsection (1) applies is brought before the justice on the resumption of the adjourned inquiry and again refuses to do what is required of him, the justice may again adjourn the inquiry for a period not exceeding eight clear days and commit him to prison for the period of adjournment or any part thereof, and may adjourn the inquiry and commit the person to prison from time to time until the person consents to do what is required of him.

(3) Saving — Nothing in this section shall be deemed to prevent the justice from sending the case for trial on any other sufficient evidence taken by him.

Remedial Provisions

546. Irregularity or variance not to affect validity — The validity of any proceeding at or subsequent to a preliminary inquiry is not affected by

(a) any irregularity or defect in the substance or form of the summons or warrant,

(b) any variance between the charge set out in the summons or warrant and the charge set out in the information, or

(c) any variance between the charge set out in the summons, warrant or information and the evidence adduced by the prosecution at the inquiry.

547. Adjournment if accused misled — Where it appears to the justice that the accused has been deceived or misled by any irregularity, defect or variance mentioned in section 546, he may adjourn the inquiry and may remand the accused or grant him interim release in accordance with Part XVI.

547.1 Inability of justice to continue — Where a justice acting under this Part has commenced to take evidence and dies or is unable to continue for any reason, another justice may

(a) continue taking the evidence at the point at which the interruption in the taking of the evidence occurred, where the evidence was recorded pursuant to section 540 and is available; or

(b) commence taking the evidence as if no evidence had been taken, where no evidence was recorded pursuant to section 540 or where the evidence is not available.

R.S.C. 1985, c. 27 (1st Supp.), s. 100

Adjudication and Recognizances

548. (1) Order to stand trial or discharge — When all the evidence has been taken by the justice, he shall,

(a) if in his opinion there is sufficient evidence to put the accused on trial for the offence charged or any other indictable offence in respect of the same transaction, order the accused to stand trial; or

(b) discharge the accused, if in his opinion on the whole of the evidence no sufficient case is made out to put the accused on trial for the offence charged or any other indictable offence in respect of the same transaction.

(2) Endorsing charge — Where the justice orders the accused to stand trial for an indictable offence, other than or in addition to the one with which the accused was charged, the justice shall endorse on the information the charges on which he orders the accused to stand trial.

(2.1) Where accused ordered to stand trial — A justice who orders that an accused is to stand trial has the power to fix the date for the trial or the date on which the accused must appear in the trial court to have that date fixed.

(3) Defect not to affect validity — The validity of an order to stand trial is not affected by any defect apparent on the face of the information in respect of which the preliminary inquiry is held or in respect of any charge on which the accused is ordered to stand trial unless, in the opinion of the court before which an objection to the information or charge is taken, the accused has been misled or prejudiced in his defence by reason of that defect.

R.S.C. 1985, c. 27 (1st Supp.), s. 101(1); 1994, c. 44, s. 56

549. (1) Order to stand trial at any stage of inquiry with consent — Notwithstanding any other provision of this Act, the justice may, at any stage of the preliminary inquiry, with the consent of the accused and the prosecutor, order the accused to stand trial in the court having criminal jurisdiction, without taking or recording any evidence or further evidence.

(1.1) Limited preliminary inquiry — If the prosecutor and the accused agree under section 536.5 to limit the scope of a preliminary inquiry to specific issues, the justice, without taking or recording evidence on any other issues, may order the accused to stand trial in the court having criminal jurisdiction.

(2) Procedure — If an accused is ordered to stand trial under this section, the justice shall endorse on the information a statement of the consent of the accused and the prosecutor, and the accused shall after that be dealt with in all respects as if ordered to stand trial under section 548.

R.S.C. 1985, c. 27 (1st Supp.), s. 101(3); 2002, c. 13, s. 30; 2019, c. 25, s. 247

550. (1) Recognizance of witness — Where an accused is ordered to stand trial, the justice who held the preliminary inquiry may require any witness whose evidence is, in his opinion, material to enter into a recognizance to give evidence at the trial of the accused and to comply with such reasonable conditions prescribed in the recognizance as the justice considers desirable for securing the attendance of the witness to give evidence at the trial of the accused.

(2) Form — The recognizance entered into pursuant to this section may be in Form 32, and may be set out at the end of a deposition or be separate therefrom.

Proposed Amendment — 550(2)

(2) Clarification — A recognizance entered into under this section may be set out at the end of a deposition or be separate from it.

2019, c. 25, s. 248 [To come into force December 18, 2019.]

(3) Sureties or deposit for appearance of witness — A justice may, for any reason satisfactory to him, require any witness entering into a recognizance pursuant to this section.

(a) to produce one or more sureties in such amount as he may direct; or

(b) to deposit with him a sum of money sufficient in his opinion to ensure that the witness will appear and give evidence.

(4) Witness refusing to be bound — Where a witness does not comply with subsection (1) or (3) when required to do so by a justice, he may be committed by the justice, by warrant in Form 24, to a prison in the territorial division where the trial is to be held, there to be kept until he does what is required of him or until the trial is concluded.

(5) Discharge — Where a witness has been committed to prison pursuant to subsection (4), the court before which the witness appears or a justice having jurisdiction in the territorial division where the prison is situated may, by order in Form 39, discharge the witness from custody when the trial is concluded.

R.S.C. 1985, c. 27 (1st Supp.), s. 101(3)

Transmission of Record

551. Transmitting record — Where a justice orders an accused to stand trial, the justice shall forthwith send to the clerk or other proper officer of the court by which the accused is to be tried, the information, the evidence, the exhibits, the statement if any of the accused taken down in writing under section 541, any promise to appear, undertaking or recognizance given or entered into in accordance with Part XVI, or any evidence taken before a coroner, that is in the possession of the justice.

Proposed Amendment — 551

551. Transmission of record by justice — If a justice orders an accused to stand trial, the justice shall immediately send to the clerk or other proper officer of the court by which the accused is to be tried, any information, evidence, exhibits, or statement of the accused taken down in writing in accordance with section 541, any appearance notice, undertaking or release order given by or issued to the accused and any evidence taken before a coroner that is in the possession of the justice.

2019, c. 25, s. 249 [To come into force December 18, 2019.]

R.S.C. 1985, c. 27 (1st Supp.), s. 102

PART XVIII.1 — CASE MANAGEMENT JUDGE (551.1–551.7)

[Heading added 2011, c. 16, s. 4.]

551.1 (1) Appointment — On application by the prosecutor or the accused or on his or her own motion, the Chief Justice or the Chief Judge of the court before which a trial is to be or is being held or the judge that the Chief Justice or the Chief Judge designates may, if he or she is of the opinion that it is necessary for the proper administration of justice, appoint a judge as the case management judge for that trial at any time before the jury selection, if the trial is before a judge and jury, or before the stage at which the evidence on the merits is presented, if the trial is being heard by a judge without a jury or a provincial court judge.

(2) Conference or hearing — The Chief Justice or the Chief Judge or his or her designate may order that a conference between the prosecutor and the accused or counsel for the accused or a hearing be held for the purpose of deciding if it is necessary for the proper administration of justice to proceed with the appointment.

(3) [Repealed 2019, c. 25, s. 250.]

(4) Same judge — The appointment of a judge as the case management judge does not prevent him or her from becoming the judge who hears the evidence on the merits.

2011, c. 16, s. 4; 2019, c. 25, s. 250

551.2 Role — The case management judge shall assist in promoting a fair and efficient trial, including by ensuring that the evidence on the merits is presented, to the extent possible, without interruption.

2011, c. 16, s. 4

551.3 (1) Powers before evidence on merits presented — In performing their duties before the stage of the presentation of the evidence on the merits, the case management judge, as a trial judge, exercises the powers that a trial judge has before that stage in order to assist in promoting a fair and efficient trial, including by

(a) assisting the parties to identify the witnesses to be heard, taking into account the witnesses' needs and circumstances;

(b) encouraging the parties to make admissions and reach agreements;

(c) encouraging the parties to consider any other matters that would promote a fair and efficient trial;

(d) establishing schedules and imposing deadlines on the parties;

(e) hearing guilty pleas and imposing sentences;

(f) assisting the parties to identify the issues that are to be dealt with at the stage at which the evidence on the merits is presented;

(g) subject to section 551.7, adjudicating any issues that can be decided before that stage, including those related to

(i) the disclosure of evidence,

(ii) the admissibility of evidence,

(iii) the *Canadian Charter of Rights and Freedoms*,

(iv) expert witnesses,

(v) the severance of counts, and

(vi) the separation of trials on one or more counts when there is more than one accused; and

(h) ordering, in each case set out in subsection 599(1), that the trial be held in a territorial division in the same province other than that in which the offence would otherwise be tried.

(2) Hearing — The case management judge shall order that a hearing be held for the purpose of exercising the power referred to in paragraph (1)(g).

(3) Power exercised at trial — When the case management judge exercises the power referred to in paragraph (1)(g), he or she is doing so at trial.

(4) Decision binding — A decision that results from the exercise of the power referred to in paragraph (1)(g) is binding on the parties for the remainder of the trial — even if the judge who hears the evidence on the merits is not the same as the case management judge — unless the court is satisfied that it would not be in the interests of justice because, among other considerations, fresh evidence has been adduced.

2011, c. 16, s. 4; 2019, c. 25, s. 251

551.4 (1) Information relevant to presentation of evidence on merits to be part of court record — When the case management judge is of the opinion that the measures to promote a fair and efficient trial that can be taken before the stage of the presentation of the evidence on the merits have been taken — including adjudicating the issues that can be decided — he or she shall ensure that the court record includes information that, in his or her opinion, may be relevant at the stage of the presentation of the evidence on the merits, including

(a) the names of the witnesses to be heard that have been identified by the parties;

(b) any admissions made and agreements reached by the parties;

(c) the estimated time required to conclude the trial;

(d) any orders and decisions; and

(e) any issues identified by the parties that are to be dealt with at the stage of the presentation of the evidence on the merits.

(2) Exception — This section does not apply to a case management judge who also hears the evidence on the merits.

2011, c. 16, s. 4

551.5 Trial continuous — Even if the judge who hears the evidence on the merits is not the same as the case management judge, the trial of an accused shall proceed continuously, subject to adjournment by the court.

2011, c. 16, s. 4

551.6 (1) Issues referred to case management judge — During the presentation of the evidence on the merits, the case management judge shall adjudicate any issue referred to him or her by the judge hearing the evidence on the merits.

(2) Powers at stage of presentation of evidence on merits — For the purposes of adjudicating an issue, the case management judge may exercise the powers of a trial judge.

2011, c. 16, s. 4

551.7 (1) Decision whether to hold joint hearing — If an issue referred to in any of subparagraphs 551.3(1)(g)(i) to (iii) is to be adjudicated in related trials that are to be or are being held in the same province before a court of the same jurisdiction, the Chief Justice or the Chief Judge of that court or his or her designate may, on application by the prosecutor or the accused or on his or her own motion, determine if it is in the interests of justice, including ensuring consistent decisions, to adjudicate that issue at a joint hearing for some or all of those trials.

(2) Considerations — To make the determination, the Chief Justice or the Chief Judge or his or her designate

(a) shall take into account, among other considerations, the degree to which the evidence relating to the issue is similar in the related trials; and

(b) may order that a conference between the prosecutor and the accused or counsel for the accused or a hearing be held.

(3) **Order for joint hearing** — If the Chief Justice or the Chief Judge or his or her designate determines that it is in the interests of justice to adjudicate the issue at a joint hearing for some or all of the related trials, he or she shall issue an order

(a) declaring that a joint hearing be held to adjudicate the issue in the related trials that he or she specifies;

(b) naming the parties who are to appear at the hearing;

(c) appointing a judge to adjudicate the issue; and

(d) designating the territorial division in which the hearing is to be held, if the trials are being held in different territorial divisions.

(4) **Limitation — indictable offence** — However, the order may only be made in respect of a trial for an indictable offence, other than a trial before a provincial court judge, if the indictment has been preferred.

(5) **Order in court record and transmission to parties** — The Chief Justice or the Chief Judge or his or her designate shall cause a copy of the order to be included in the court record of each of the trials specified in the order and to be provided to each of the parties named in it.

(6) **Transmission of court record** — If one of the specified trials is being held in a territorial division other than the one in which the joint hearing will be held, the officer in that territorial division who has custody of the indictment or information and the writings relating to the trial shall, when he or she receives the order, transmit the indictment or information and the writings without delay to the clerk of the court before which the joint hearing is to be held.

(7) **Order to appear at joint hearing** — The judge appointed under the order shall require the parties who are named in it to appear at the joint hearing.

(8) **Removal of prisoner** — The order made under subsection (2) or (3) is sufficient warrant, justification and authority to all sheriffs, keepers of prisons and peace officers for an accused's removal, disposal and reception in accordance with the terms of the order, and the sheriff may appoint and authorize any peace officer to convey the accused to a prison for the territorial division in which the hearing, as the case may be, is to be held.

(9) **Powers of judge** — The judge appointed under the order may, as a trial judge and for the purpose of adjudicating the issue at the joint hearing, exercise the powers of a trial judge.

(10) **Adjudication at trial** — When the judge adjudicates the issue, he or she is doing so at trial.

(11) **Decision in court records and return of documents** — Once the judge has adjudicated the issue, he or she shall cause his or her decision, with reasons, to be included in the court record of each of the related trials in respect of which the joint hearing was held and, in the case of a trial for which an indictment, information or writings were transmitted by an officer under subsection (6), the judge shall have the documents returned to the officer.

2011, c. 16, s. 4

PART XIX — INDICTABLE OFFENCES — TRIAL WITHOUT A JURY (SS. 552–572)

Interpretation

552. Definitions — In this Part,

"judge" means,

(a) in the Province of Ontario, a judge of the superior court of criminal jurisdiction of the Province,

(b) in the Province of Quebec, a judge of the Court of Quebec,

(c) in the Province of Nova Scotia, a judge of the superior court of criminal jurisdiction of the Province,

(d) in the Province of New Brunswick, a judge of the Court of Queen's Bench,

(e) in the Province of British Columbia, the Chief Justice or a puisne judge of the Supreme Court,

(f) in the Province of Prince Edward Island, a judge of the Supreme Court,

(g) in the Province of Manitoba, the Chief Justice, or a puisne judge of the Court of Queen's Bench,

(h) in the Provinces of Saskatchewan and Alberta, a judge of the superior court of criminal jurisdiction of the province,

(h.1) in the Province of Newfoundland and Labrador, a judge of the Trial Division of the Supreme Court,

(i) in Yukon and the Northwest Territories, a judge of the Supreme Court, and

(j) in Nunavut, a judge of the Nunavut Court of Justice.

"magistrate" [Repealed R.S.C. 1985, c. 27 (1st Supp.), s. 103(2).]

R.S.C. 1985, c. 11 (1st Supp.), s. 2; R.S.C. 1985, c. 27 (1st Supp.), s. 103(1); R.S.C. 1985, c. 27 (2nd Supp.), s. 10 (Sched., item 6); R.S.C. 1985, c. 40 (4th Supp.), s. 2; 1990, c. 16, s. 6; 1990, c. 17, s. 13; 1992, c. 51, s. 38; 1993, c. 28, s. 78 (Sched. III, item 34) [Repealed 1999, c. 3, s. 12 (Sched., item 8).]; 1999, c. 3, s. 36; 2002, c. 7, s. 145; 2015, c. 3, s. 53

Jurisdiction of Provincial Court Judges

Absolute Jurisdiction

553. Absolute jurisdiction — The jurisdiction of a provincial court judge, or in Nunavut, of a judge of the Nunavut Court of Justice, to try an accused is absolute and does not depend on the consent of the accused where the accused is charged in an information

(a) with

(i) theft, other than theft of cattle,

(ii) obtaining money or property by false pretences,

(iii) unlawfully having in his possession any property or thing or any proceeds of any property or thing knowing that all or a part of the property or thing or of the proceeds was obtained by or derived directly or indirectly from the commission in Canada of an offence punishable by indictment or an act or omission anywhere that, if it had occurred in Canada, would have constituted an offence punishable by indictment,

(iv) having, by deceit, falsehood or other fraudulent means, defrauded the public or any person, whether ascertained or not, of any property, money or valuable security, or

(v) mischief under subsection 430(4),

where the subject-matter of the offence is not a testamentary instrument and the alleged value of the subject-matter of the offence does not exceed five thousand dollars;

(b) with counselling or with a conspiracy or attempt to commit or with being an accessory after the fact to the commission of

(i) any offence referred to in paragraph (*a*) in respect of the subject-matter and value thereof referred to in that paragraph, or

(ii) any offence referred to in paragraph (*c*); or

(c) with anoffence under

(i) section 201 (keeping gaming or betting house),

(ii) section 202 (betting, pool-selling, book-making, etc.),

(iii) section 203 (placing bets),

(iv) section 206 (lotteries and games of chance),

(v) section 209 (cheating at play),

(vi) [Repealed 2019, c. 25, s. 251.1.]

(vii) [Repealed 2000, c. 25, s. 4.]

(viii) section 393 (fraud in relation to fares),

(viii.01) section 490.031 (failure to comply with order or obligation),

(viii.02) section 490.0311 (providing false or misleading information),

(viii.1) section 811 (breach of recognizance),

(ix) subsection 733.1(1) (failure to comply with probation order), or

(x) paragraph 4(4)(a) of the *Controlled Drugs and Substances Act*.

(xi) [Repealed 2018, c. 16, s. 219.]

R.S.C. 1985, c. 27 (1st Supp.), s. 104; 1992, c. 1, s. 58(1) (Sched. I, item 11); 1994, c. 44, s. 57; 1995, c. 22, s. 2; 1996, c. 19, s. 72; 1997, c. 18, s. 66; 1999, c. 3, s. 37; 2000, c. 25, s. 4; 2010, c. 17, s. 25; 2012, c. 1, s. 33; 2018, c. 16, s. 219; 2019, c. 25, s. 251.1

Provincial Court Judge's Jurisdiction with Consent

554. (1) Trial by provincial court judge with consent — Subject to subsection (2), if an accused is charged in an information with an indictable offence other than an offence that is mentioned in section 469, and the offence is not one over which a provincial court judge has absolute jurisdiction under section 553, a provincial court judge may try the accused if the accused elects to be tried by a provincial court judge.

(2) Nunavut — With respect to criminal proceedings in Nunavut, if an accused is charged in an information with an indictable offence other than an offence that is mentioned in section 469 and the offence is not one over which a judge of the Nunavut Court of Justice has absolute jurisdiction under section 553, a judge of the Nunavut Court of Justice may try the accused if the accused elects to be tried by a judge without a jury.

(3) and (4) [Repealed R.S.C. 1985, c. 27 (1st Supp.), s. 105.]

R.S.C. 1985, c. 27 (1st Supp.), ss. 105, 203; 1999, c. 3, s. 38; 2002, c. 13, s. 31

555. (1) If charge should be prosecuted by indictment — If in any proceedings under this Part an accused is before a provincial court judge and it appears to the provincial court judge that for any reason the charge should be prosecuted in superior court, the provincial court judge may, at any time before the accused has entered a defence, decide not to adjudicate and shall then inform the accused of the decision.

(1.1) Election before justice — If the provincial court judge has decided not to adjudicate, the judge shall put the accused to an election in the following words:

> You have the option to elect to be tried by a superior court judge without a jury or you may elect to be tried by a court composed of a judge and jury. If you do not elect now, you are deemed to have elected to be tried by a court composed of a judge and jury. If you elect to be tried by a judge without a jury or by a court composed of a judge and jury or if you are deemed to have elected to be tried by a court composed of a judge and jury, you will have a preliminary inquiry only if you are entitled to one and you or the prosecutor requests one. How do you elect to be tried?

(1.2) Continuing proceedings — If the accused is entitled to a preliminary inquiry and they or the prosecutor requests one, the provincial court judge shall continue the proceedings as a preliminary inquiry.

(2) If subject matter is testamentary instrument or exceeds $5,000 in value — If an accused is before a provincial court judge, charged with an offence prosecuted by indictment mentioned in paragraph 553(a) or subparagraph 553(b)(i), and, at any time before the provincial court judge makes an adjudication, the evidence establishes that the subject matter of the offence is a testamentary instrument or that its value exceeds $5,000, the provincial court judge shall put the accused to their election in accordance with subsection 536(2.1).

(3) Continuing proceedings — If an accused is put to their election under subsection (1.1) or (2), the following provisions apply:

(a) if the accused elects to be tried by a superior court judge without a jury or a court composed of a judge and jury or does not elect when put to their election, the provincial court judge shall endorse on the information a record of the nature of the election or deemed election; and

(b) if the accused elects to be tried by a provincial court judge, the provincial court judge shall endorse on the information a record of the election and continue with the trial.

R.S.C. 1985, c. 27 (1st Supp.), ss. 106, 203; 1994, c. 44, s. 58; 2002, c. 13, s. 32; 2019, c. 25, s. 252

555.1 (1) If charge should be prosecuted by indictment — Nunavut — If in any criminal proceedings under this Part an accused is before a judge of the Nunavut Court of Justice and it appears to the judge that for any reason the charge should be prosecuted by indictment, the judge may, at any time before the accused has entered a defence, decide not to adjudicate and shall then inform the accused of the decision.

(1.1) Election before justice — If the judge has decided not to adjudicate, the judge shall put the accused to an election in the following words:

> You have the option to elect to be tried by a judge without a jury or to be tried by a court composed of a judge and jury. If you do not elect now, you are deemed to have elected to be tried by a court composed of a judge and jury. If you elect to be tried by a judge without a jury or by a court composed of a judge and jury or if you are deemed to have elected to be tried by a court composed of a judge and jury, you will have a preliminary inquiry only if you are entitled to one and you or the prosecutor requests one. How do you elect to be tried?

(1.2) Continuing proceedings — If the accused is entitled to a preliminary inquiry and they or the prosecutor requests one, the judge shall endorse on the information a record of the nature of the election or deemed election and continue the proceedings as a preliminary inquiry.

(2) If subject-matter is testamentary instrument or exceeds $5,000 in value — Nunavut — If an accused is before a judge of the Nunavut Court of Justice, charged with an offence prosecuted by indictment mentioned in paragraph 553(a) or subparagraph 553(b)(i), and, at any time before the judge makes an adjudication, the evidence establishes that the subject matter of the offence is a testamentary instrument or that its value exceeds $5,000, the judge shall put the accused to their election in accordance with subsection 536.1(2.1).

(3) Continuing proceedings — Nunavut — If an accused is put to their election under subsection (1.1) and no preliminary inquiry is requested, or is put to an election under subsection (2), and elects to be tried by a judge without a jury or a court composed of a judge and jury or does not elect when put to the election, the judge shall endorse on the information a record of the nature of the election or deemed election and continue with the trial.

(4) Application to Nunavut — This section, and not section 555, applies in respect of criminal proceedings in Nunavut.

(5) [Repealed 2019, c. 25, s. 253.]

1999, c. 3, s. 39; 2002, c. 13, s. 33; 2019, c. 25, s. 253

556. (1) Organization — An accused organization shall appear by counsel or agent.

(2) Non-appearance — Where an accused organization does not appear pursuant to a summons and service of the summons on the organization is proved, the provincial court judge or, in Nunavut, the judge of the Nunavut Court of Justice

(a) may, if the charge is one over which the judge has absolute jurisdiction, proceed with the trial of the charge in the absence of the accused organization; and

(b) shall, if the charge is not one over which the judge has absolute jurisdiction, fix the date for the trial or the date on which the accused organization must appear in the trial court to have that date fixed.

(3) Preliminary inquiry not requested — If an accused organization appears and a preliminary inquiry is not requested under subsection 536(4), the provincial court judge shall fix the date for the trial or the date on which the organization must appear in the trial court to have that date fixed.

(4) Preliminary inquiry not requested — Nunavut — If an accused organization appears and a preliminary inquiry is not requested under subsection 536.1(3), the justice of the peace or the judge of the Nunavut Court of Justice shall fix the date for the trial or the date on which the organization must appear in the trial court to have that date fixed.

R.S.C. 1985, c. 27 (1st Supp.), s. 107; 1999, c. 3, s. 40; 2002, c. 13, s. 34; 2003, c. 21, ss. 9, 22

557. Taking evidence — If an accused is tried by a provincial court judge or a judge of the Nunavut Court of Justice in accordance with this Part, the evidence of witnesses for the prosecutor and the accused must be taken in accordance with the provisions of Part XVIII, other than the subsections 540(7) to (9), relating to preliminary inquiries.

R.S.C. 1985, c. 27 (1st Supp.), s. 203; 1999, c. 3, s. 41; 2002, c. 13, s. 35

Jurisdiction of Judges

Judge's Jurisdiction with Consent

558. Trial by judge without a jury — If an accused who is charged with an indictable offence, other than an offence mentioned in section 469, elects under section 536 or 536.1 or re-elects under section 561 or 561.1 to be tried by a judge without a jury, the accused shall, subject to this Part, be tried by a judge without a jury.

R.S.C. 1985, c. 27 (1st Supp.), s. 108; 1999, c. 3, s. 41

559. (1) Court of record — A judge who holds a trial under this Part shall, for all purposes thereof and proceedings connected therewith or relating thereto, be a court of record.

(2) Custody of records — The record of a trial that a judge holds under this Part shall be kept in the court over which the judge presides.

Election

560. (1) Duty of judge — If an accused elects, under section 536 or 536.1, to be tried by a judge without a jury, a judge having jurisdiction shall

(a) on receiving a written notice from the sheriff or other person having custody of the accused stating that the accused is in custody and setting out the nature of the charge against him, or

(b) on being notified by the clerk of the court that the accused is not in custody and of the nature of the charge against him,

fix a time and place for the trial of the accused.

(2) Notice by sheriff, when given — The sheriff or other person having custody of the accused shall give the notice mentioned in paragraph (1)(*a*) within twenty-four hours after the accused is ordered to stand trial, if he is in custody pursuant to that order or if, at the time of the order, he is in custody for any other reason.

(3) Duty of sheriff when date set for trial — Where, pursuant to subsection (1), a time and place is fixed for the trial of an accused who is in custody, the accused

(a) shall be notified forthwith by the sheriff or other person having custody of the accused of the time and place so fixed; and

(b) shall be produced at the time and place so fixed.

(4) Duty of accused when not in custody — Where an accused is not in custody, the duty of ascertaining from the clerk of the court the time and place fixed for the trial, pursuant to subsection (1), is on the accused, and he shall attend for his trial at the time and place so fixed.

(5) [Repealed R.S.C. 1985, c. 27 (1st Supp.), s. 109(2).]

R.S.C. 1985, c. 27 (1st Supp.), ss. 101(3), 109; 1999, c. 3, s. 42; 2002, c. 13, s. 36

561. (1) Right to re-elect — An accused who elects or is deemed to have elected a mode of trial other than trial by a provincial court judge may re-elect,

(a) if the accused is charged with an offence for which a preliminary inquiry has been requested under subsection 536(4),

(i) at any time before or after the completion of the preliminary inquiry, with the written consent of the prosecutor, to be tried by a provincial court judge,

(ii) at any time before the completion of the preliminary inquiry or before the 60th day following the completion of the preliminary inquiry, as of right, another mode of trial other than trial by a provincial court judge, and

(iii) on or after the 60th day following the completion of the preliminary inquiry, any mode of trial with the written consent of the prosecutor; or

(b) if the accused is charged with an offence for which they are not entitled to request a preliminary inquiry or if they did not request a preliminary inquiry under subsection 536(4),

(i) as of right, not later than 60 days before the day first appointed for the trial, another mode of trial other than trial by a provincial court judge, or

(ii) any mode of trial with the written consent of the prosecutor.

(2) **Right to re-elect** — An accused who elects to be tried by a provincial court judge may, not later than 60 days before the day first appointed for the trial, re-elect as of right another mode of trial, and may do so after that time with the written consent of the prosecutor.

(3) **Notice of re-election under paragraph (1)(a)** — If an accused intends to re-elect under paragraph (1)(a) before the completion of the preliminary inquiry, they shall give notice in writing of their intention to re-elect, together with the written consent of the prosecutor, if that consent is required, to the justice presiding at the preliminary inquiry who shall on receipt of the notice,

(a) in the case of a re-election under subparagraph (1)(a)(ii), put the accused to their re-election in the manner set out in subsection (7); or

(b) if the accused intends to re-elect under subparagraph (1)(a)(i) and the justice is not a provincial court judge, notify a provincial court judge or clerk of the court of the accused's intention to re-elect and send to the provincial court judge or clerk the information and any promise to appear, undertaking or recognizance given or entered into in accordance with Part XVI, or any evidence taken before a coroner, that is in the possession of the justice.

Proposed Amendment — 561(3)(b)

(b) if the accused intends to re-elect under subparagraph (1)(a)(i) and the justice is not a provincial court judge, notify a provincial court judge or clerk of the court of the accused's intention to re-elect and send to the provincial court judge or clerk any information, appearance notice, undertaking or release order given by or issued to the accused and any evidence taken before a coroner that is in the possession of the justice.

2019, c. 25, s. 254(2) [To come into force December 18, 2019.]

(4) **Notice of re-election under paragraph (1)(b) or subsection (2)** — If an accused intends to re-elect under paragraph (1)(b) or subsection (2), they shall give notice in writing that they intend to re-elect together with the written consent of the prosecutor, if that consent is required, to the provincial court judge before whom the accused appeared and pleaded or to a clerk of the court.

(5) **Notice and transmitting record** — If an accused intends to re-elect under paragraph (1)(a) after the completion of the preliminary inquiry, they shall give notice in writing that they intend to reelect, together with the written consent of the prosecutor, if that consent is required, to a judge or clerk of the court of the accused's original election who shall, on receipt of the notice,

(a) notify the judge or provincial court judge or clerk of the court by which the accused wishes to be tried of the accused's intention to re-elect; and

(b) send to that judge or provincial court judge or clerk the information, the evidence, the exhibits and the statement, if any, of the accused taken down in writing under section 541 and any promise to appear, undertaking or recognizance given or entered into in accordance with Part XVI, or any evidence taken before a coroner, that is in the possession of the first-mentioned judge or clerk.

Proposed Amendment — 561(5)

(5) Notice and transmitting record — If an accused intends to re-elect under paragraph (1)(a) after the completion of the preliminary inquiry, they shall give notice in writing, together with the written consent of the prosecutor, if that consent is required, to a judge or clerk of the court of the accused's original election. The judge or clerk shall, on receipt of the notice,

(a) notify the judge or provincial court judge or clerk of the court by which the accused wishes to be tried of the accused's intention to re-elect; and

(b) send to that judge or provincial court judge or clerk any information, evidence, exhibits and statement of the accused taken down in writing in accordance with section 541, any appearance notice, undertaking or release order given by or issued to the accused and any evidence taken before a coroner that is in the possession of the first-mentioned judge or clerk.

2019, c. 25, s. 254(3) [To come into force December 18, 2019.]

(6) Time and place for re-election — Where a provincial court judge or judge or clerk of the court is notified under paragraph (3)(*b*) or subsection (4) or (5) that the accused wishes to re-elect, the provincial court judge or judge shall forthwith appoint a time and place for the accused to re-elect and shall cause notice thereof to be given to the accused and the prosecutor.

(7) Proceedings on re-election — The accused shall attend or, if in custody, shall be produced at the time and place appointed under subsection (6) and shall be put to a re-election after

(a) the charge on which the accused has been ordered to stand trial or the indictment, if an indictment has been preferred under section 566, 574 or 577 or is filed with the court before which the indictment is to be preferred under section 577, has been read to the accused; or

(b) the information, in the case of a re-election under paragraph (1)(a), before the completion of the preliminary inquiry, or under paragraph (1)(b) or subsection (2), has been read to the accused.

The accused shall be put to their re-election in the following words or in words to the like effect:

> You have given notice of your intention to re-elect the mode of your trial. You now have the option to do so. How do you intend to reelect?

R.S.C. 1985, c. 27 (1st Supp.), s. 110; 2002, c. 13, s. 37; 2019, c. 25, s. 254(1), (5)

561.1 (1) Right to re-elect with consent — Nunavut — An accused who has elected or is deemed to have elected a mode of trial may re-elect any other mode of trial at any time with the written consent of the prosecutor.

(2) **Right to re-elect before trial — Nunavut** — An accused who has elected or is deemed to have elected a mode of trial but has not requested a preliminary inquiry under subsection 536.1(3) or is not entitled to make such a request under that subsection may, as of right, re-elect to be tried by any other mode of trial at any time up to 60 days before the day first appointed for the trial.

(3) **Right to re-elect at preliminary inquiry — Nunavut** — An accused who has elected or is deemed to have elected a mode of trial and has requested a preliminary inquiry under subsection 536.1(3) may, as of right, reelect to be tried by the other mode of trial at any time before the completion of the preliminary inquiry or before the 60th day after its completion.

(4) **Notice of re-election under subsection (1) or (3) — Nunavut** — If an accused wishes to re-elect under subsection (1) or (3), before the completion of the preliminary inquiry, the accused shall give notice in writing of the wish to re-elect, together with the written consent of the prosecutor, if that consent is required, to the justice of the peace or judge presiding at the preliminary inquiry who shall on receipt of the notice put the accused to a re-election in the manner set out in subsection (9).

(5) **Notice at preliminary inquiry — Nunavut** — If at a preliminary inquiry an accused wishes to re-elect under subsection (1) or (3) to be tried by a judge without a jury but does not wish to request a preliminary inquiry under subsection 536.1(3), the presiding justice of the peace shall notify a judge or a clerk of the Nunavut Court of Justice of the accused's intention to re-elect and send to the judge or clerk the information and any promise to appear, undertaking or recognizance given or entered into in accordance with Part XVI, or any evidence taken before a coroner, that is in the possession of the justice of the peace.

Proposed Amendment — 561.1(5)

(5) **Notice at preliminary inquiry — Nunavut** — If at a preliminary inquiry an accused intends to reelect under subsection (1) or (3) to be tried by a judge without a jury but does not intend to request a preliminary inquiry under subsection 536.1(3), the presiding justice of the peace shall notify a judge or a clerk of the Nunavut Court of Justice of the accused's intention to reelect and send to the judge or clerk any information, appearance notice, undertaking or release order given by or issued to the accused and any evidence taken before a coroner that is in the possession of the justice of the peace.

2019, c. 25, s. 255(3) [To come into force December 18, 2019.]

(6) **Notice when no preliminary inquiry or preliminary inquiry completed — Nunavut** — If an accused who has not requested a preliminary inquiry under subsection 536.1(3), who has had one or who was not entitled to make such a request under that subsection intends to re-elect under this section, the accused shall give notice in writing of the intention to re-elect together with the written consent of the prosecutor, if that consent is required, to the judge before whom the accused appeared and pleaded or to a clerk of the Nunavut Court of Justice.

(7) [Repealed 2002, c. 13, s. 38(2).]

(8) Time and place for re-election — Nunavut — On receipt of a notice given under any of subsections (4) to (7) that the accused wishes to re-elect, a judge shall immediately appoint a time and place for the accused to re-elect and shall cause notice of the time and place to be given to the accused and the prosecutor.

(9) Proceedings on re-election — Nunavut — The accused shall attend or, if in custody, shall be produced at the time and place appointed under subsection (8) and shall be put to a re-election after

(a) the charge on which the accused has been ordered to stand trial has been read to the accused or, if an indictment has been preferred under section 566, 574 or 577 or is filed with the court before which the indictment is to be preferred under section 577, the indictment has been read to the accused; or

(b) the information — in the case of a re-election under subsection (1) or (3), before the completion of the preliminary inquiry, or under subsection (2) — has been read to the accused.

The accused shall be put to their re-election in the following words or in words to the like effect:

> You have given notice of your intention to re-elect the mode of your trial. You now have the option to do so. How do you intend to reelect?

(10) Application to Nunavut — This section, and not section 561, applies in respect of criminal proceedings in Nunavut.

1999, c. 3, s. 43; 2002, c. 13, s. 38; 2019, c. 25, s. 255(1), (4), (5)

562. (1) Proceedings following re-election — If the accused re-elects under subparagraph 561(1)(a)(i) before the completion of the preliminary inquiry, under paragraph 561(1)(a) after the completion of the preliminary inquiry or under paragraph 561(1)(b), the provincial court judge or judge, as the case may be, shall proceed with the trial or appoint a time and place for the trial.

(2) Proceedings following re-election — If the accused re-elects under subparagraph 561(1)(a)(ii) before the completion of the preliminary inquiry, or under subsection 561(2), and requests a preliminary inquiry under subsection 536(4), the justice shall proceed with the preliminary inquiry.

R.S.C. 1985, c. 27 (1st Supp.), s. 110; 2019, c. 25, s. 256

562.1 (1) Proceedings following re-election — Nunavut — If the accused re-elects under subsection 561.1(1) to be tried by a judge without a jury and does not request a preliminary inquiry under subsection 536.1(3), or if the accused re-elects any other mode of trial under subsection 561.1(2) but is not entitled to make a request for a preliminary inquiry under subsection 536.1(3), the judge shall proceed with the trial or appoint a time and place for the trial.

(2) Proceedings following re-election — Nunavut — If the accused re-elects under section 561.1 before the completion of the preliminary inquiry to be tried by a judge without a jury or by a court composed of a judge and jury, and requests a preliminary inquiry under subsection 536.1(3), the justice of the peace or judge shall proceed with the preliminary inquiry.

(3) Application to Nunavut — This section, and not section 562, applies in respect of criminal proceedings in Nunavut.

1999, c. 3, s. 44; 2002, c. 13, s. 39; 2019, c. 25, s. 257

563. Proceedings on re-election to be tried by provincial court judge without jury — Where an accused re-elects under section 561 to be tried by a provincial court judge,

(a) the accused shall be tried on the information that was before the justice at the preliminary inquiry, if applicable, subject to any amendments to the information that may be allowed by the provincial court judge by whom the accused is tried; and

(b) the provincial court judge before whom the re-election is made shall endorse on the information a record of the re-election.

R.S.C. 1985, c. 27 (1st Supp.), s. 110; 2019, c. 25, s. 258

563.1 (1) Proceedings on re-election to be tried by judge without jury — Nunavut — If an accused re-elects under section 561.1 to be tried by a judge without a jury and does not request a preliminary inquiry under subsection 536.1(3) or is not entitled to make such a request under that subsection,

(a) the accused shall be tried on the information that was before the justice of the peace or judge at the preliminary inquiry, if applicable, subject to any amendments that may be allowed by the judge by whom the accused is tried; and

(b) the judge before whom the re-election is made shall endorse on the information a record of the re-election.

(2) Application to Nunavut — This section, and not section 563, applies in respect of criminal proceedings in Nunavut.

1999, c. 3, s. 45; 2002, c. 13, s. 40; 2019, c. 25, s. 259

564. [Repealed R.S.C. 1985, c. 27 (1st Supp.), s. 110.]

565. (1) Election deemed to have been made — If an accused is ordered to stand trial for an offence that, under this Part, may be tried by a judge without a jury, the accused shall, for the purposes of the provisions of this Part relating to election and re-election, be deemed to have elected to be tried by a court composed of a judge and jury if

(a) the justice of the peace, provincial court judge or judge, as the case may be, declined to record the election or re-election of the accused under section 567 or subsection 567.1(1); or

(b) the accused does not elect when put to an election under section 536 or 536.1.

(1.1) [Repealed 2019, c. 25, s. 260(1).]

(2) When direct indictment preferred — If an accused is to be tried after an indictment has been preferred against the accused on the basis of a consent or order given under section 577, the accused is, for the purposes of the provisions of this

Part relating to election and re-election, deemed to have elected to be tried by a court composed of a judge and jury and not to have requested a preliminary inquiry under subsection 536(4) or 536.1(3), if they were entitled to make such a request, and may re-elect to be tried by a judge without a jury without a preliminary inquiry.

(3) Notice of re-election — Where an accused wishes to re-elect under subsection (2), the accused shall give notice in writing that he wishes to re-elect to a judge or clerk of the court where the indictment has been filed or preferred who shall, on receipt of the notice, notify a judge having jurisdiction or clerk of the court by which the accused wishes to be tried of the accused's intention to re-elect and send to that judge or clerk the indictment and any promise to appear, undertaking or recognizance given or entered into in accordance with Part XVI, any summons or warrant issued under section 578, or any evidence taken before a coroner, that is in the possession of the first-mentioned judge or clerk.

Proposed Amendment — 565(3)

(3) Notice of re-election — If an accused intends to re-elect under subsection (2), the accused shall give notice in writing to a judge or clerk of the court where the indictment has been filed or preferred. The judge or clerk shall, on receipt of the notice, notify a judge having jurisdiction or clerk of the court by which the accused wishes to be tried of the accused's intention to re-elect and send to that judge or clerk any indictment, appearance notice, undertaking or release order given by or issued to the accused, any summons or warrant issued under section 578 and any evidence taken before a coroner that is in the possession of the first-mentioned judge or clerk.

2019, c. 25, s. 260(2) [To come into force December 18, 2019.]

(4) Application — Subsections 561(6) and (7), or subsections 561.1(8) and (9), as the case may be, apply to a re-election made under subsection (3).

R.S.C. 1985, c. 27 (1st Supp.), s. 111; 1999, c. 3, s. 46; 2002, c. 13, s. 41; 2008, c. 18, s. 23; 2019, c. 25, s. 260(1)

Trial

566. (1) Indictment — The trial of an accused for an indictable offence, other than a trial before a provincial court judge, shall be on an indictment in writing setting forth the offence with which he is charged.

(2) Preferring indictment — Where an accused elects under section 536 or re-elects under section 561 to be tried by a judge without a jury, an indictment in Form 4 may be preferred.

(3) What counts may be included and who may prefer indictment — Section 574 and subsection 576(1) apply, with such modifications as the circumstances require, to the preferring of an indictment pursuant to subsection (2).

R.S.C. 1985, c. 27 (1st Supp.), s. 111; 1997, c. 18, s. 67

566.1 (1) Indictment — Nunavut — The trial of an accused for an indictable offence, other than an indictable offence referred to in section 553 or an offence in respect of which the accused has elected or re-elected to be tried by a judge without a jury and in respect of which no party has requested a preliminary inquiry under subsection 536.1(3) or was not entitled to make such a request under that subsection, must be on an indictment in writing setting out the offence with which the accused is charged.

(2) **Preferring indictment — Nunavut** — If an accused elects under section 536.1 or re-elects under section 561.1 to be tried by a judge without a jury and one of the parties requests a preliminary inquiry under subsection 536.1(3), an indictment in Form 4 may be preferred.

(3) **What counts may be included and who may prefer indictment — Nunavut** — Section 574 and subsection 576(1) apply, with any modifications that the circumstances require, to the preferring of an indictment under subsection (2).

(4) **Application to Nunavut** — This section, and not section 566, applies in respect of criminal proceedings in Nunavut.

1999, c. 3, s. 47; 2002, c. 13, s. 42; 2019, c. 25, s. 261

General

567. Mode of trial when two or more accused — Despite any other provision of this Part, if two or more persons are jointly charged in an information, unless all of them elect or re-elect or are deemed to have elected the same mode of trial, the justice, provincial court judge or judge may decline to record any election, re-election or deemed election for trial by a provincial court judge or a judge without a jury.

R.S.C. 1985, c. 27 (1st Supp.), s. 111; 2002, c. 13, s. 43

567.1 (1) Mode of trial if two or more accused — Nunavut — Despite any other provision of this Part, if two or more persons are jointly charged in an information, unless all of them elect or re-elect or are deemed to have elected the same mode of trial, the justice of the peace or judge may decline to record any election, re-election or deemed election for trial by a judge without a jury.

(2) **Application to Nunavut** — This section, and not section 567, applies in respect of criminal proceedings in Nunavut.

1999, c. 3, s. 48; 2002, c. 13, s. 43

568. Attorney General may require trial by jury — Even if an accused elects under section 536 or re-elects under section 561 or subsection 565(2) to be tried by a judge or provincial court judge, as the case may be, the Attorney General may require the accused to be tried by a court composed of a judge and jury unless the alleged offence is one that is punishable with imprisonment for five years or less. If the Attorney General so requires, a judge or provincial court judge has no jurisdiction to try the accused under this Part and a preliminary inquiry must be held if requested under subsection 536(4), unless one has already been held or the re-election was made under subsection 565(2).

R.S.C. 1985, c. 27 (1st Supp.), s. 111; 2002, c. 13, s. 43; 2008, c. 18, s. 24

569. (1) Attorney General may require trial by jury — Nunavut — Even if an accused elects under section 536.1 or re-elects under section 561.1 or subsection 565(2) to be tried by a judge without a jury, the Attorney General may require the accused to be tried by a court composed of a judge and jury unless the alleged offence is one that is punishable with imprisonment for five years or less. If the Attorney General so requires, a judge has no jurisdiction to try the accused under this Part and a preliminary inquiry must be held if requested under subsection 536.1(3), unless one has already been held or the re-election was made under subsection 565(2).

(2) Application to Nunavut — This section, and not section 568, applies in respect of criminal proceedings in Nunavut.

1999, c. 3, s. 49; 2002, c. 13, s. 44; 2008, c. 18, s. 24.1

570. (1) Record of conviction or order — If an accused who is tried under this Part is determined by a judge or provincial court judge to be guilty of an offence on acceptance of a plea of guilty or on a finding of guilt, the judge or provincial court judge, as the case may be, shall endorse the information accordingly and shall sentence the accused or otherwise deal with the accused in the manner authorized by law and, on request by the accused, the prosecutor, a peace officer or any other person, a conviction in Form 35 and a certified copy of it, or an order in Form 36 and a certified copy of it, shall be drawn up and the certified copy shall be delivered to the person making the request.

(2) Acquittal and record of acquittal — If an accused who is tried under this Part is found not guilty of an offence with which the accused is charged, the judge or provincial court judge, as the case may be, shall immediately acquit the accused in respect of that offence, an order in Form 37 shall be drawn up and, on request, a certified copy shall be drawn up and delivered to the accused.

(3) Transmission of record — Where an accused elects to be tried by a provincial court judge under this Part, the provincial court judge shall transmit the written charge, the memorandum of adjudication and the conviction, if any, into such custody as the Attorney General may direct.

(4) Proof of conviction order or acquittal — A copy of a conviction in Form 35 or of an order in Form 36 or 37, certified by the judge or by the clerk or other proper officer of the court, or by the provincial court judge, as the case may be, or proved to be a true copy, is, on proof of the identity of the person to whom the conviction or order relates, sufficient evidence in any legal proceedings to prove the conviction of that person or the making of the order against that person or his acquittal, as the case may be, for the offence mentioned in the copy of the conviction or order.

(5) Warrant of committal — If an accused other than an organization is convicted, the judge or provincial court judge, as the case may be, shall issue a warrant of committal in Form 21, and section 528 applies in respect of a warrant of committal issued under this subsection.

(6) Admissibility of certified copy — If a warrant of committal is signed by a clerk of a court, a copy of the warrant of committal, certified by the clerk, is admissible in evidence in any proceeding.

R.S.C. 1985, c. 27 (1st Supp.), ss. 112, 203; 1994, c. 44, s. 59; 2003, c. 21, s. 10; 2019, c. 25, s. 262

571. Adjournment — A judge or provincial court judge acting under this Part may from time to time adjourn a trial until it is finally terminated.

R.S.C. 1985, c. 27 (1st Supp.), s. 203

572. Application of Parts XVI, XVIII, XX and XXIII — The provisions of Part XVI, the provisions of Part XVIII relating to transmission of the record by a provincial court judge where he holds a preliminary inquiry, and the provisions of Parts XX and XXIII, in so far as they are not inconsistent with this Part, apply, with such modifications as the circumstances require to proceedings under this Part.

R.S.C. 1985, c. 27 (1st Supp.), s. 203

PART XIX.1 — NUNAVUT COURT OF JUSTICE (SS. 573–573.2)

573. (1) Nunavut Court of Justice — The powers to be exercised and the duties and functions to be performed under this Act by a court of criminal jurisdiction, a summary conviction court, a judge, a provincial court judge, a justice or a justice of the peace may be exercised or performed by a judge of the Nunavut Court of Justice.

(2) Status when exercising power — A power exercised or a duty or function performed by a judge of the Nunavut Court of Justice under subsection (1) is exercised or performed by that judge as a judge of a superior court.

(3) Interpretation — Subsection (2) does not authorize a judge of the Nunavut Court of Justice who is presiding at a preliminary inquiry to grant a remedy under section 24 of the *Canadian Charter of Rights and Freedoms.*

1999, c. 3, s. 50

573.1 (1) Application for review — Nunavut — An application for review may be made by the Attorney General or the accused, or by any person directly affected by the decision or order, to a judge of the Court of Appeal of Nunavut in respect of a decision or order of a judge of the Nunavut Court of Justice

(a) relating to a warrant or summons;

(b) relating to the conduct of a preliminary inquiry, including an order under subsection 548(1);

(c) relating to a subpoena;

(d) relating to the publication or broadcasting of information or access to the court room for all or part of the proceedings;

(e) to refuse to quash an information or indictment; or

(f) relating to the detention, disposal or forfeiture of any thing seized under a warrant or order.

(2) Limitation — A decision or order may not be reviewed under this section if

(a) the decision or order is of a kind that could only be made in a province or a territory other than Nunavut by a superior court of criminal jurisdiction or a judge as defined in section 552; or

(b) another statutory right of review is available.

(3) Grounds of review — The judge of the Court of Appeal of Nunavut may grant relief under subsection (4) only if the judge is satisfied that

(a) in the case of any decision or order mentioned in subsection (1),

(i) the judge of the Nunavut Court of Justice failed to observe a principle of natural justice or failed or refused to exercise the judge's jurisdiction, or

(ii) the decision or order was made as a result of an irrelevant consideration or for an improper purpose;

(b) in the case of a decision or order mentioned in paragraph (1)(a), that

(i) the judge failed to comply with a statutory requirement for the making of the decision or order,

(ii) the decision or order was made in the absence of any evidence that a statutory requirement for the making of the decision or order was met,

(iii) the decision or order was made as a result of reckless disregard for the truth, fraud, intentional misrepresentation of material facts or intentional omission to state material facts,

(iv) the warrant is so vague or lacking in particularity that it authorizes an unreasonable search, or

(v) the warrant lacks a material term or condition that is required by law;

(c) in the case of a decision or order mentioned in paragraph (1)(b), that the judge of the Nunavut Court of Justice

(i) failed to follow a mandatory provision of this Act relating to the conduct of a preliminary inquiry,

(ii) ordered the accused to stand trial when there was no evidence adduced on which a properly instructed jury acting reasonably could convict, or

(iii) discharged the accused when there was some evidence adduced on which a properly instructed jury acting reasonably could convict;

(d) in the case of a decision or order mentioned in paragraph (1)(c) or (d), that the judge of the Nunavut Court of Justice erred in law;

(e) in the case of a decision or order mentioned in paragraph (1)(e), that

(i) the information or indictment failed to give the accused notice of the charge,

(ii) the judge of the Nunavut Court of Justice did not have jurisdiction to try the offence, or

(iii) the provision creating the offence alleged to have been committed by the accused is unconstitutional; or

(f) in the case of a decision or order mentioned in paragraph (1)(f), that

(i) the judge failed to comply with a statutory requirement for the making of the decision or order,

(ii) the decision or order was made in the absence of any evidence that a statutory requirement for the making of the decision or order was met, or

(iii) the decision or order was made as a result of reckless disregard for the truth, fraud, intentional misrepresentation of material facts or intentional omission to state material facts.

(4) Powers of judge — On the hearing of the application for review, the judge of the Court of Appeal of Nunavut may do one or more of the following:

(a) order a judge of the Nunavut Court of Justice to do any act or thing that the judge or any other judge of that court failed or refused to do or has delayed in doing;

(b) prohibit or restrain a decision, order or proceeding of a judge of the Nunavut Court of Justice;

(c) declare invalid or unlawful, quash or set aside, in whole or in part, a decision, order or proceeding of a judge of the Nunavut Court of Justice;

(d) refer back for determination in accordance with any directions that the judge considers to be appropriate, a decision, order or proceeding of a judge of the Nunavut Court of Justice;

(e) grant any remedy under subsection 24(1) of the *Canadian Charter of Rights and Freedoms*;

(f) refuse to grant any relief if the judge is of the opinion that no substantial wrong or miscarriage of justice has occurred or that the subject-matter of the application should be determined at trial or on appeal; and

(g) dismiss the application.

(5) Interim orders — If an application for review is made, a judge of the Court of Appeal of Nunavut may make any interim order that the judge considers appropriate pending the final disposition of the application for review.

(6) Rules — A person who proposes to make an application for review shall do so in the manner and within the period that may be directed by rules of court, except that a judge of the Court of Appeal of Nunavut may at any time extend any period specified in the rules.

(7) Appeal — An appeal lies to the Court of Appeal of Nunavut against a decision or order made under subsection (4). The provisions of Part XXI apply, with any modifications that the circumstances require, to the appeal.

1999, c. 3, s. 50

573.2 (1) *Habeas corpus* — *Habeas corpus* proceedings may be brought before a judge of the Court of Appeal of Nunavut in respect of an order made or warrant issued by a judge of the Nunavut Court of Justice, except where

(a) the order or warrant is of a kind that could only be made or issued in a province or a territory other than Nunavut by a superior court of criminal jurisdiction or a judge as defined in section 552; or

(b) another statutory right of review or appeal is available.

(2) Exception — Despite subsection (1), *habeas corpus* proceedings may be brought before a judge of the Court of Appeal of Nunavut with respect to an order or warrant of a judge of the Nunavut Court of Justice if the proceedings are brought to challenge the constitutionality of a person's detention or confinement.

(3) Provisions apply — Subsections 784(2) to (6) apply in respect of any proceedings brought under subsection (1) or (2).

1999, c. 3, s. 50

PART XX — PROCEDURE IN JURY TRIALS AND GENERAL PROVISIONS (SS. 574–672)

Preferring Indictment

574. (1) Prosecutor may prefer indictment — Subject to subsection (3), the prosecutor may, whether the charges were included in one information or not, prefer an indictment against any person who has been ordered to stand trial in respect of

(a) any charge on which that person was ordered to stand trial; or

(b) any charge founded on the facts disclosed by the evidence taken on the preliminary inquiry, in addition to or in substitution for any charge on which that person was ordered to stand trial.

(1.1) Preferring indictment when no preliminary inquiry — If a person has not requested a preliminary inquiry under subsection 536(4) or 536.1(3) into the charge or was not entitled to make such a request, the prosecutor may, subject to subsection (3), prefer an indictment against a person in respect of a charge set out in an information or informations, or any included charge, at any time after the person has made an election, re-election or deemed election on the information or informations.

(1.2) Preferring single indictment — If indictments may be preferred under both subsections (1) and (1.1), the prosecutor may prefer a single indictment in respect of one or more charges referred to in subsection (1) combined with one or more charges or included charges referred to in subsection (1.1).

(2) Consent to inclusion of other charges — An indictment preferred under any of subsections (1) to (1.2) may, if the accused consents, include a charge that is not referred to in those subsections, and the offence charged may be dealt with, tried and determined and punished in all respects as if it were an offence in respect of which the accused had been ordered to stand trial. However, if the offence was committed wholly in a province other than that in which the accused is before the court, subsection 478(3) applies.

(3) **Private prosecutor requires consent** — In a prosecution conducted by a prosecutor other than the Attorney General and in which the Attorney General does not intervene, an indictment may not be preferred under any of subsections (1) to (1.2) before a court without the written order of a judge of that court.

R.S.C. 1985, c. 27 (1st Supp.), s. 113; 2002, c. 13, s. 45; 2019, c. 25, s. 263

575. [Repealed R.S.C. 1985, c. 27 (1st Supp.), s. 113.]

576. (1) **Indictment** — Except as provided in this Act, no indictment shall be preferred.

(2) **Criminal information and bill of indictment** — No criminal information shall be laid or granted and no bill of indictment shall be preferred before a grand jury.

(3) **Coroner's inquisition** — No person shall be tried on a coroner's inquisition.

R.S.C. 1985, c. 27 (1st Supp.), s. 114

577. Direct indictments — Despite section 574, an indictment may be preferred even if the accused has not been given the opportunity to request a preliminary inquiry, a preliminary inquiry has been commenced but not concluded or a preliminary inquiry has been held and the accused has been discharged, if

(a) in the case of a prosecution conducted by the Attorney General or one in which the Attorney General intervenes, the personal consent in writing of the Attorney General or Deputy Attorney General is filed in court; or

(b) in any other case, a judge of the court so orders.

R.S.C. 1985, c. 27 (1st Supp.), s. 115; 2002, c. 13, s. 46

578. (1) **Summons or warrant** — Where notice of the recommencement of proceedings has been given pursuant to subsection 579(2) or an indictment has been filed with the court before which the proceedings are to commence or recommence, the court, if it considers it necessary, may issue

(a) a summons addressed to, or

(b) a warrant for the arrest of,

the accused or defendant, as the case may be, to compel him to attend before the court to answer the charge described in the indictment.

(2) **Part XVI to apply** — The provisions of Part XVI apply with such modifications as the circumstances require where a summons or warrant is issued under subsection (1).

R.S.C. 1985, c. 27 (1st Supp.), s. 116

579. (1) **Attorney General may direct stay** — The Attorney General or counsel instructed by him for that purpose may, at any time after any proceedings in relation to an accused or a defendant are commenced and before judgment, direct the clerk or other proper officer of the court to make an entry on the record that the proceedings are stayed by his direction, and such entry shall be made forthwith thereafter, whereupon the proceedings shall be stayed accordingly and any recognizance relating to the proceedings is vacated.

Proposed Amendment — 579(1)

(1) **Attorney General may direct stay** — The Attorney General or counsel instructed by the Attorney General for that purpose may, at any time after any proceedings in relation to an accused or a defendant are commenced and before judgment, direct the clerk or other proper officer of the court to make an entry on the record that the proceedings are stayed by the Attorney General's or counsel's direction, as the case may be, and the entry shall then be made, at which time the proceedings shall be stayed accordingly and any undertaking or release order relating to the proceedings is vacated.

2019, c. 25, s. 264 [To come into force December 18, 2019.]

(2) **Recommencement of proceedings** — Proceedings stayed in accordance with subsection (1) may be recommenced, without laying a new information or preferring a new indictment, as the case may be, by the Attorney General or counsel instructed by him for that purpose giving notice of the recommencement to the clerk of the court in which the stay of the proceedings was entered, but where no such notice is given within one year after the entry of the stay of proceedings, or before the expiration of the time within which the proceedings could have been commenced, whichever is the earlier, the proceedings shall be deemed never to have been commenced.

R.S.C. 1985, c. 27 (1st Supp.), s. 117

Proposed Addition — 579.001

579.001 (1) **Instruction to stay** — The Attorney General or counsel instructed by him or her for that purpose shall, at any time after proceedings in relation to an act or omission of a **"preclearance officer"**, as defined in section 5 of the *Preclearance Act, 2016*, are commenced and before judgment, direct the clerk or other proper officer of the court to make an entry on the record that the proceedings are stayed by direction of the Attorney General if the Government of the United States has provided notice of the exercise of primary criminal jurisdiction under paragraph 14 of Article X of the Agreement.

(2) **Stay** — The clerk or other officer of the court shall make the entry immediately after being so directed, and on the entry being made the proceedings are stayed and any recognizance relating to the proceedings is vacated.

(3) **Recommencement** — The proceedings may be recommenced without laying a new information or preferring a new indictment, if the Attorney General or counsel instructed by him or her gives notice to the clerk or other officer of the court that

(a) the Government of the United States has provided notice of waiver under paragraph 15 of Article X of the Agreement; or

(b) the Government of the United States has declined, or is unable, to prosecute the accused and the accused has returned to Canada.

(4) Proceedings deemed never commenced — However, if the Attorney General or counsel does not give notice under subsection (3) on or before the first anniversary of the day on which the stay of proceedings was entered, the proceedings are deemed never to have been commenced.

(5) Definition of "Agreement" — In this section, **"Agreement"** means the Agreement on Land, Rail, Marine, and Air Transport Preclearance between the Government of Canada and the Government of the United States of America, done at Washington on March 16, 2015.

2017, c. 27, s. 62 [Not in force at date of publication.]

579.01 When Attorney General does not stay proceedings — If the Attorney General intervenes in proceedings and does not stay them under section 579, he or she may, without conducting the proceedings, call witnesses, examine and cross-examine witnesses, present evidence and make submissions.

2002, c. 13, s. 47

579.1 (1) Intervention by Attorney General of Canada or Director of Public Prosecutions — The Attorney General of Canada or the Director of Public Prosecutions appointed under subsection 3(1) of the *Director of Public Prosecutions Act*, or counsel instructed by him or her for that purpose, may intervene in proceedings in the following circumstances:

(a) the proceedings are in respect of an offence for which he or she has the power to commence or to conduct a proceeding;

(b) the proceedings have not been instituted by an Attorney General;

(c) judgment has not been rendered; and

(d) the Attorney General of the province in which the proceedings are taken has not intervened.

(2) Sections 579 and 579.01 to apply — Sections 579 and 579.01 apply, with any modifications that the circumstances require, to proceedings in which the Attorney General of Canada or the Director of Public Prosecutions intervenes under this section.

1994, c. 44, s. 60; 2019, c. 25, s. 265(1), (3)

580. Form of indictment — An indictment is sufficient if it is on paper and is in Form 4.

R.S.C. 1985, c. 27 (1st Supp.), s. 117

General Provisions respecting Counts

581. (1) Substance of offence — Each count in an indictment shall in general apply to a single transaction and shall contain in substance a statement that the accused or defendant committed an indictable offence therein specified.

(2) Form of statement — The statement referred to in subsection (1) may be

(a) in popular language without technical averments or allegations of matters that are not essential to be proved;

(b) in the words of the enactment that describes the offence or declares the matters charged to be an indictable offence; or

(c) in words that are sufficient to give to the accused notice of the offence with which he is charged.

(3) Details of circumstances — A count shall contain sufficient detail of the circumstances of the alleged offence to give to the accused reasonable information with respect to the act or omission to be proved against him and to identify the transaction referred to, but otherwise the absence or insufficiency of details does not vitiate the count.

(4) Indictment for treason — If an accused is charged with an offence under section 47 or sections 50 to 53, every overt act that is to be relied on shall be stated in the indictment.

(5) Reference to section — A count may refer to any section, subsection, paragraph or subparagraph of the enactment that creates the offence charged, and for the purpose of determining whether a count is sufficient, consideration shall be given to any such reference.

(6) General provisions not restricted — Nothing in this Part relating to matters that do not render a count insufficient shall be deemed to restrict or limit the application of this section.

R.S.C. 1985, c. 27 (1st Supp.), s. 118; 2018, c. 29, s. 63

582. High treason and first degree murder — No person shall be convicted for the offence of high treason or first degree murder unless in the indictment charging the offence he is specifically charged with that offence.

583. Certain omissions not grounds for objection — No count in an indictment is insufficient by reason of the absence of details where, in the opinion of the court, the count otherwise fulfils the requirements of section 581 and, without restricting the generality of the foregoing, no count in an indictment is insufficient by reason only that

(a) it does not name the person injured or intended or attempted to be injured;

(b) it does not name the person who owns or has a special property or interest in property mentioned in the count;

(c) it charges an intent to defraud without naming or describing the person whom it was intended to defraud;

(d) it does not set out any writing that is the subject of the charge;

(e) it does not set out the words used where words that are alleged to have been used are the subject of the charge;

(f) it does not specify the means by which the alleged offence was committed;

(g) it does not name or describe with precision any person, place or thing; or

(h) it does not, where the consent of a person, official or authority is required before proceedings may be instituted for an offence, state that the consent has been obtained.

Special Provisions Respecting Counts

584. (1) Sufficiency of count charging libel — No count for publishing a seditious or defamatory libel, or for selling or exhibiting an obscene book, pamphlet, newspaper or other written matter, is insufficient by reason only that it does not set out the words that are alleged to be libellous or the writing that is alleged to be obscene.

(2) Specifying sense — A count for publishing a libel may charge that the published matter was written in a sense that by innuendo made the publication thereof criminal, and may specify that sense without any introductory assertion to show how the matter was written in that sense.

(3) Proof — It is sufficient, on the trial of a count for publishing a libel, to prove that the matter published was libellous, with or without innuendo.

2018, c. 29, s. 64

585. Sufficiency of count charging perjury, etc. — No count that charges

(a) perjury,

(b) the making of a false oath or a false statement,

(c) fabricating evidence, or

(d) procuring the commission of an offence mentioned in paragraph (*a*), (*b*) or (*c*)

is insufficient by reason only that it does not state the nature of the authority of the tribunal before which the oath or statement was taken or made, or the subject of the inquiry, or the words used or the evidence fabricated, or that it does not expressly negative the truth of the words used.

586. Sufficiency of count relating to fraud — No count that alleges false pretences, fraud or any attempt or conspiracy by fraudulent means is insufficient by reason only that it does not set out in detail the nature of the false pretence, fraud or fraudulent means.

Particulars

587. (1) What may be ordered — A court may, where it is satisfied that it is necessary for a fair trial, order the prosecutor to furnish particulars and, without restricting the generality of the foregoing, may order the prosecutor to furnish particulars

(a) of what is relied on in support of a charge of perjury, the making of a false oath or of a false statement, fabricating evidence or counselling the commission of any of those offences;

(b) of any false pretence or fraud that is alleged;

(c) of any alleged attempt or conspiracy by fraudulent means;

(d) setting out the passages in a book, pamphlet, newspaper or other printing or writing that are relied on in support of a charge of selling or exhibiting an obscene book, pamphlet, newspaper, printing or writing;

(e) further describing any writing or words that are the subject of a charge;

(f) further describing the means by which an offence is alleged to have been committed; or

(g) further describing a person, place or thing referred to in an indictment.

(2) **Regard to evidence** — For the purpose of determining whether or not a particular is required, the court may give consideration to any evidence that has been taken.

(3) **Particular** — Where a particular is delivered pursuant to this section,

(a) a copy shall be given without charge to the accused or his counsel,

(b) the particular shall be entered in the record, and

(c) the trial shall proceed in all respects as if the indictment had been amended to conform with the particular.

R.S.C. 1985, c. 27 (1st Supp.), s. 7(2)

Ownership of Property

588. Ownership — The real and personal property of which a person has, by law, the management, control or custody shall, for the purposes of an indictment or proceeding against any other person for an offence committed on or in respect of the property, be deemed to be the property of the person who has the management, control or custody of it.

Joinder or Severance of Counts

589. Count for murder — No count that charges an indictable offence other than murder shall be joined in an indictment to a count that charges murder unless

(a) the count that charges the offence other than murder arises out of the same transaction as a count that charges murder; or

(b) the accused signifies consent to the joinder of the counts.

1991, c. 4, s. 2

590. (1) Offences may be charged in the alternative — A count is not objectionable by reason only that

(a) it charges in the alternative several different matters, acts or omissions that are stated in the alternative in an enactment that describes as an indictable offence the matters, acts or omissions charged in the count; or

(b) it is double or multifarious.

(2) Application to amend or divide counts — An accused may at any stage of his trial apply to the court to amend or to divide a count that

(a) charges in the alternative different matters, acts or omissions that are stated in the alternative in the enactment that describes the offence or declares that the matters, acts or omissions charged are an indictable offence, or

(b) is double or multifarious,

on the ground that, as framed, it embarrasses him in his defence.

(3) Order — The court may, where it is satisfied that the ends of justice require it, order that a count be amended or divided into two or more counts, and thereupon a formal commencement may be inserted before each of the counts into which it is divided.

591. (1) Joinder of counts — Subject to section 589, any number of counts for any number of offences may be joined in the same indictment, but the counts shall be distinguished in the manner shown in Form 4.

(2) Each count separate — Where there is more than one count in an indictment, each count may be treated as a separate indictment.

(3) Severance of accused and counts — The court may, where it is satisfied that the interests of justice so require, order

(a) that the accused or defendant be tried separately on one or more of the counts; and

(b) where there is more than one accused or defendant, that one or more of them be tried separately on one or more of the counts.

(4) Order for severance — An order under subsection (3) may be made before or during the trial but, if the order is made during the trial, the jury shall be discharged from giving a verdict on the counts

(a) on which the trial does not proceed; or

(b) in respect of the accused or defendant who has been granted a separate trial.

(4.1) Delayed enforcement — The court may make an order under subsection (3) that takes effect either at a specified later date or on the occurrence of a specified event if, taking into account, among other considerations, the need to ensure consistent decisions, it is satisfied that it is in the interests of justice to do so.

(4.2) Decisions binding on parties — Unless the court is satisfied that it would not be in the interests of justice, the decisions relating to the disclosure or admissibility of evidence or the *Canadian Charter of Rights and Freedoms* that are made before any order issued under subsection (3) takes effect continue to bind the parties if the decisions are made — or could have been made — before the stage at which the evidence on the merits is presented.

(5) Subsequent procedure — The counts in respect of which a jury is discharged pursuant to paragraph (4)(*a*) may subsequently be proceeded on in all respects as if they were contained in a separate indictment.

(6) Idem — Where an order is made in respect of an accused or defendant under paragraph (3)(*b*), the accused or defendant may be tried separately on the counts in relation to which the order was made as if they were contained in a separate indictment.

R.S.C. 1985, c. 27 (1st Supp.), s. 119; 2011, c. 16, s. 5

Joinder of Accused in Certain Cases

592. Accessories after the fact — Any one who is charged with being an accessory after the fact to any offence may be indicted, whether or not the principal or any other party to the offence has been indicted or convicted or is or is not amenable to justice.

593. (1) Trial of persons jointly — Any number of persons may be charged in the same indictment with an offence under section 354 or 355.4 or paragraph 356(1)(b), even though

(a) the property was had in possession at different times; or

(b) the person by whom the property was obtained

(i) is not indicted with them, or

(ii) is not in custody or is not amenable to justice.

(2) Conviction of one or more — Where, pursuant to subsection (1), two or more persons are charged in the same indictment with an offence referred to in that subsection, any one or more of those persons who separately committed the offence in respect of the property or any part of it may be convicted.

2010, c. 14, s. 11

594 to 596. [Repealed R.S.C. 1985, c. 27 (1st Supp.), s. 120.]

Proceedings when Person Indicted is at Large

597. (1) Bench warrant — Where an indictment has been preferred against a person who is at large, and that person does not appear or remain in attendance for his trial, the court before which the accused should have appeared or remained in attendance may issue a warrant in Form 7 for his arrest.

(2) Execution — A warrant issued under subsection (1) may be executed anywhere in Canada.

(3) Interim release — Where an accused is arrested under a warrant issued under subsection (1), a judge of the court that issued the warrant may order that the accused be released on his giving an undertaking that he will do any one or more of the following things as specified in the order, namely,

(a) report at times to be stated in the order to a peace officer or other person designated in the order;

(b) remain within a territorial jurisdiction specified in the order;

(c) notify the peace officer or other person designated under paragraph (*a*) of any change in his address or his employment or occupation;

(d) abstain from communicating with any witness or other person expressly named in the order except in accordance with such conditions specified in the order as the judge deems necessary;

(e) where the accused is the holder of a passport, deposit his passport as specified in the order; and

(f) comply with such other reasonable conditions specified in the order as the judge considers desirable.

Proposed Amendment — 597(3)

(3) **Interim release** — If an accused is arrested under a warrant issued under subsection (1), a judge of the court that issued the warrant may make a release order referred to in section 515.

2019, c. 25, s. 266 [To come into force December 18, 2019.]

(4) **Discretion to postpone execution** — A judge who issues a warrant may specify in the warrant the period before which the warrant shall not be executed, to allow the accused to appear voluntarily before a judge having jurisdiction in the territorial division in which the warrant was issued.

(5) **Deemed execution of warrant** — Where the accused appears voluntarily for the offence in respect of which the accused is charged, the warrant is deemed to be executed.

R.S.C. 1985, c. 27 (1st Supp.), s. 121; 1997, c. 18, s. 68

598. (1) Election deemed to be waived — Notwithstanding anything in this Act, where a person to whom subsection 597(1) applies has elected or is deemed to have elected to be tried by a court composed of a judge and jury and, at the time he failed to appear or to remain in attendance for his trial, he had not re-elected to be tried by a court composed of a judge without a jury or a provincial court judge without a jury, he shall not be tried by a court composed of a judge and jury unless

(a) he establishes to the satisfaction of a judge of the court in which he is indicted that there was a legitimate excuse for his failure to appear or remain in attendance for his trial; or

(b) the Attorney General requires pursuant to section 568 or 569 that the accused be tried by a court composed of a judge and jury.

(2) **Election deemed to be waived** — An accused who, under subsection (1), may not be tried by a court composed of a judge and jury is deemed to have elected under section 536 or 536.1 to be tried without a jury by a judge of the court where the accused was indicted and section 561 or 561.1, as the case may be, does not apply in respect of the accused.

R.S.C. 1985, c. 27 (1st Supp.), ss. 122, 203; 1999, c. 3, s. 51; 2002, c. 13, s. 48

Change of Venue

599. (1) Reasons for change of venue — A court before which an accused is or may be indicted, at any term or sittings thereof, or a judge who may hold or sit in that court, may at any time before or after an indictment is found, on the application of the prosecutor or the accused, order the trial to be held in a territorial division in the same province other than that in which the offence would otherwise be tried if

(a) it appears expedient to the ends of justice, including

(i) to promote a fair and efficient trial, and

(ii) to ensure the safety and security of a victim or witness or to protect their interests and those of society; or

(b) a competent authority has directed that a jury is not to be summoned at the time appointed in a territorial division where the trial would otherwise by law be held.

(2) [Repealed R.S.C. 1985, c. 1 (4th Supp.), s. 16.]

(3) Conditions as to expense — The court or judge may, in an order made on an application by the prosecutor under subsection (1), prescribe conditions that he thinks proper with respect to the payment of additional expenses caused to the accused as a result of the change of venue.

(4) Transmission of record — Where an order is made under subsection (1), the officer who has custody of the indictment, if any, and the writings and exhibits relating to the prosecution, shall transmit them forthwith to the clerk of the court before which the trial is ordered to be held, and all proceedings in the case shall be held or, if previously commenced, shall be continued in that court.

(5) Idem — Where the writings and exhibits referred to in subsection (4) have not been returned to the court in which the trial was to be held at the time an order is made to change the place of trial, the person who obtains the order shall serve a true copy thereof on the person in whose custody they are and that person shall thereupon transmit them to the clerk of the court before which the trial is to be held.

R.S.C. 1985, c. 1 (4th Supp.), s. 16; 2019, c. 25, s. 267

600. Order is authority to remove prisoner — An order that is made under section 599 is sufficient warrant, justification and authority to all sheriffs, keepers of prisons and peace officers for the removal, disposal and reception of an accused in accordance with the terms of the order, and the sheriff may appoint and authorize any peace officer to convey the accused to a prison in the territorial division in which the trial is ordered to be held.

Amendment

601. (1) Amending defective indictment or count — An objection to an indictment preferred under this Part or to a count in an indictment, for a defect apparent on its face, shall be taken by motion to quash the indictment or count before the accused enters a plea, and, after the accused has entered a plea, only by leave of the court before which the proceedings take place. The court before which an objection is taken under this section may, if it considers it necessary, order the indictment or count to be amended to cure the defect.

(2) Amendment where variance — Subject to this section, a court may, on the trial of an indictment, amend the indictment or a count therein or a particular that is furnished under section 587, to make the indictment, count or particular conform to the evidence, where there is a variance between the evidence and

(a) a count in the indictment as preferred; or

(b) a count in the indictment

(i) as amended, or

(ii) as it would have been if it had been amended in conformity with any particular that has been furnished pursuant to section 587.

(3) Amending indictment — Subject to this section, a court shall, at any stage of the proceedings, amend the indictment or a count therein as may be necessary where it appears

(a) that the indictment has been preferred under a particular Act of Parliament instead of another Act of Parliament;

(b) that the indictment or a count thereof

(i) fails to state or states defectively anything that is requisite to constitute the offence,

(ii) does not negative an exception that should be negatived,

(iii) is in any way defective in substance,

and the matters to be alleged in the proposed amendment are disclosed by the evidence taken on the preliminary inquiry or on the trial; or

(c) that the indictment or a count thereof is in any way defective in form.

(4) Matters to be considered by the court — The court shall, in considering whether or not an amendment should be made to the indictment or a count in it, consider

(a) the matters disclosed by the evidence taken on the preliminary inquiry;

(b) the evidence taken on the trial, if any;

(c) the circumstances of the case;

(d) whether the accused has been misled or prejudiced in his defence by any variance, error or omission mentioned in subsection (2) or (3); and

(e) whether, having regard to the merits of the case, the proposed amendment can be made without injustice being done.

(4.1) Variance not material — A variance between the indictment or a count therein and the evidence taken is not material with respect to

(a) the time when the offence is alleged to have been committed, if it is proved that the indictment was preferred within the prescribed period of limitation, if any; or

(b) the place where the subject-matter of the proceedings is alleged to have arisen, if it is proved that it arose within the territorial jurisdiction of the court.

(5) Adjournment if accused prejudiced — Where, in the opinion of the court, the accused has been misled or prejudiced in his defence by a variance, error or omission in an indictment or a count therein, the court may, if it is of the opinion that the misleading or prejudice may be removed by an adjournment, adjourn the proceedings to a specified day or sittings of the court and may make such an order with respect to the payment of costs resulting from the necessity for amendment as it considers desirable.

(6) Question of law — The question whether an order to amend an indictment or a count thereof should be granted or refused is a question of law.

(7) Endorsing indictment — An order to amend an indictment or a count therein shall be endorsed on the indictment as part of the record and the proceedings shall continue as if the indictment or count had been originally preferred as amended.

(8) Mistakes not material — A mistake in the heading of an indictment shall be corrected as soon as it is discovered but, whether corrected or not, is not material.

(9) Limitation — The authority of a court to amend indictments does not authorize the court to add to the overt acts stated in an indictment for high treason or treason or for an offence against any provision in sections 50, 51 and 53.

(10) Definition of "court" — In this section, **"court"** means a court, judge, justice or provincial court judge acting in summary conviction proceedings or in proceedings on indictment.

(11) Application — This section applies to all proceedings, including preliminary inquiries, with such modifications as the circumstances require.

R.S.C. 1985, c. 27 (1st Supp.), s. 123; 1999, c. 5, s. 23; 2011, c. 16, s. 6; 2018, c. 29, s. 65

602. [Repealed R.S.C. 1985, c. 27 (1st Supp.), s. 124.]

Inspection and Copies of Documents

603. Right of accused — An accused is entitled, after he has been ordered to stand trial or at his trial,

(a) to inspect without charge the indictment, his own statement, the evidence and the exhibits, if any; and

(b) to receive, on payment of a reasonable fee determined in accordance with a tariff of fees fixed or approved by the Attorney General of the province, a copy

(i) of the evidence,

(ii) of his own statement, if any, and

(iii) of the indictment;

but the trial shall not be postponed to enable the accused to secure copies unless the court is satisfied that the failure of the accused to secure them before the trial is not attributable to lack of diligence on the part of the accused.

R.S.C. 1985, c. 27 (1st Supp.), s. 101(2)

604. [Repealed 1997, c. 18, s. 69.]

605. (1) Release of exhibits for testing — A judge of a superior court of criminal jurisdiction or a court of criminal jurisdiction may, on summary application on behalf of the accused or the prosecutor, after three days notice to the accused or prosecutor, as the case may be, order the release of any exhibit for the purpose of a scientific or other test or examination, subject to such terms as appear to be necessary or desirable to ensure the safeguarding of the exhibit and its preservation for use at the trial.

(2) Disobeying orders — Every one who fails to comply with the terms of an order made under subsection (1) is guilty of contempt of court and may be dealt with summarily by the judge or provincial court judge who made the order or before whom the trial of the accused takes place.

R.S.C. 1985, c. 27 (1st Supp.), s. 203

Pleas

606. (1) Pleas permitted — An accused who is called on to plead may plead guilty or not guilty, or the special pleas authorized by this Part and no others.

(1.1) Conditions for accepting guilty plea — A court may accept a plea of guilty only if it is satisfied that

(a) the accused is making the plea voluntarily;

(b) the accused understands

(i) that the plea is an admission of the essential elements of the offence,

(ii) the nature and consequences of the plea, and

(iii) that the court is not bound by any agreement made between the accused and the prosecutor; and

(c) the facts support the charge.

(1.2) Validity of plea — The failure of the court to fully inquire whether the conditions set out in subsection (1.1) are met does not affect the validity of the plea.

(2) Refusal to plead — Where an accused refuses to plead or does not answer directly, the court shall order the clerk of the court to enter a plea of not guilty.

(3) Allowing time — An accused is not entitled as of right to have his trial postponed but the court may, if it considers that the accused should be allowed further time to plead, move to quash, or prepare for his defence or for any other reason, adjourn the trial to a later time in the session or sittings of the court, or to the next of any subsequent session or sittings of the court, on such terms as the court considers proper.

(4) Included or other offence — Notwithstanding any other provision of this Act, where an accused or defendant pleads not guilty of the offence charged but guilty of any other offence arising out of the same transaction, whether or not it is an included offence, the court may, with the consent of the prosecutor, accept that plea of guilty and, if the plea is accepted, the court shall find the accused or defendant not guilty of the offence charged and find him guilty of the offence in respect of which the plea of guilty was accepted and enter those findings in the record of the court.

(4.1) Inquiry of court — murder and serious personal injury offences — If the accused is charged with a serious personal injury offence, as that expression is defined in section 752, or with the offence of murder, and the accused and the prosecutor have entered into an agreement under which the accused will enter a plea of guilty of the offence charged — or a plea of not guilty of the offence charged but guilty of any other offence arising out of the same transaction, whether or not it is an included offence — the court shall, after accepting the plea of guilty, inquire of the prosecutor if reasonable steps were taken to inform the victims of the agreement.

(4.2) Inquiry of court — certain indictable offences — If the accused is charged with an offence, as defined in section 2 of the *Canadian Victims Bill of Rights*, that is an indictable offence for which the maximum punishment is imprisonment for five years or more, and that is not an offence referred to in subsection (4.1), and the accused and the prosecutor have entered into an agreement referred to in subsection (4.1), the court shall, after accepting the plea of guilty, inquire of the prosecutor whether any of the victims had advised the prosecutor of their desire to be informed if such an agreement were entered into, and, if so, whether reasonable steps were taken to inform that victim of the agreement.

(4.3) Duty to inform — If subsection (4.1) or (4.2) applies, and any victim was not informed of the agreement before the plea of guilty was accepted, the prosecutor shall, as soon as feasible, take reasonable steps to inform the victim of the agreement and the acceptance of the plea.

(4.4) Validity of plea — Neither the failure of the court to inquire of the prosecutor, nor the failure of the prosecutor to take reasonable steps to inform the victims of the agreement, affects the validity of the plea.

(5) Video links — For greater certainty, subsections 650(1.1) and (1.2) apply, with any modifications that the circumstances require, to pleas under this section if the accused has agreed to use a means referred to in those subsections.

R.S.C. 1985, c. 27 (1st Supp.), s. 125; 2002, c. 13, s. 49; 2015, c. 13, s. 21; 2019, c. 25, s. 268

607. (1) Special pleas — An accused may plead the special pleas of

(a) *autrefois acquit*;

(b) *autrefois convict*;

(c) pardon; and

(d) an expungement order under the *Expungement of Historically Unjust Convictions Act*.

(2) In case of libel — An accused who is charged with defamatory libel may plead in accordance with sections 611 and 612.

(3) Disposal — The pleas of *autrefois acquit, autrefois convict*, pardon and an expungement order under the *Expungement of Historically Unjust Convictions Act* shall be disposed of by the judge without a jury before the accused is called on to plead further.

(4) Pleading over — When the pleas referred to in subsection (3) are disposed of against the accused, he may plead guilty or not guilty.

(5) Statement sufficient — Where an accused pleads *autrefois acquit* or *autrefois convict*, it is sufficient if he

(a) states that he has been lawfully acquitted, convicted or discharged under subsection 730(1), as the case may be, of the offence charged in the count to which the plea relates; and

(b) indicates the time and place of the acquittal, conviction or discharge under subsection 730(1).

(6) Exception — foreign trials *in absentia* — A person who is alleged to have committed an act or omission outside Canada that is an offence in Canada by virtue of any of subsections 7(2) to (3.1) or (3.7), or an offence under the *Crimes Against Humanity and War Crimes Act*, and in respect of which the person has been tried and convicted outside Canada, may not plead *autrefois convict* with respect to a count that charges that offence if

(a) at the trial outside Canada the person was not present and was not represented by counsel acting under the person's instructions, and

(b) the person was not punished in accordance with the sentence imposed on conviction in respect of the act or omission,

notwithstanding that the person is deemed by virtue of subsection 7(6), or subsection 12(1) of the *Crimes Against Humanity and War Crimes Act*, as the case may be, to have been tried and convicted in Canada in respect of the act or omission.

R.S.C. 1985, c. 27 (1st Supp.), s. 126; R.S.C. 1985, c. 30 (3rd Supp.), s. 2; 1995, c. 22, s. 10; 2000, c. 24, s. 45; 2013, c. 13, s. 9; 2018, c. 11, s. 29

608. Evidence of identity of charges — Where an issue on a plea of *autrefois acquit* or *autrefois convict* is tried, the evidence and adjudication and the notes of the judge and official stenographer on the former trial and the record transmitted to the court pursuant to section 551 on the charge that is pending before that court are admissible in evidence to prove or to disprove the identity of the charges.

609. (1) What determines identity — Where an issue on a plea of *autrefois acquit* or *autrefois convict* to a count is tried and it appears

(a) that the matter on which the accused was given in charge on the former trial is the same in whole or in part as that on which it is proposed to give him in charge, and

(b) that on the former trial, if all proper amendments had been made that might then have been made, he might have been convicted of all the offences of which he may be convicted on the count to which the plea of *autrefois acquit* or *autrefois convict* is pleaded,

the judge shall give judgment discharging the accused in respect of that count.

(2) **Allowance of special plea in part** — The following provisions apply where an issue on a plea of *autrefois acquit* or *autrefois convict* is tried:

(a) where it appears that the accused might on the former trial have been convicted of an offence of which he may be convicted on the count in issue, the judge shall direct that the accused shall not be found guilty of any offence of which he might have been convicted on the former trial; and

(b) where it appears that the accused may be convicted on the count in issue of an offence of which he could not have been convicted on the former trial, the accused shall plead guilty or not guilty with respect to that offence.

610. (1) Circumstances of aggravation — Where an indictment changes substantially the same offence as that charged in an indictment on which an accused was previously convicted or acquitted, but adds a statement of intention or circumstances of aggravation tending, if proved, to increase the punishment, the previous conviction or acquittal bars the subsequent indictment.

(2) **Effect of previous charge of murder or manslaughter** — A conviction or an acquittal on an indictment for murder bars a subsequent indictment for the same homicide charging it as manslaughter or infanticide, and a conviction or acquittal on an indictment for manslaughter or infanticide bars a subsequent indictment for the same homicide charging it as murder.

(3) **Previous charges of first degree murder** — A conviction or an acquittal on an indictment for first degree murder bars a subsequent indictment for the same homicide charging it as second degree murder, and a conviction or acquittal on an indictment for second degree murder bars a subsequent indictment for the same homicide charging it as first degree murder.

(4) **Effect of previous charge of infanticide or manslaughter** — A conviction or an acquittal on an indictment for infanticide bars a subsequent indictment for the same homicide charging it as manslaughter, and a conviction or acquittal on an indictment for manslaughter bars a subsequent indictment for the same homicide charging it as infanticide.

611. (1) Libel, plea of justification — An accused who is charged with publishing a defamatory libel may plead that the defamatory matter published by him was true, and that it was for the public benefit that the matter should have been published in the manner in which and at the time when it was published.

(2) **Where more than one sense alleged** — A plea that is made under subsection (1) may justify the defamatory matter in any sense in which it is specified in the count, or in the sense that the defamatory matter bears without being specified, or separate pleas justifying the defamatory matter in each sense may be pleaded separately to each count as if two libels had been charged in separate counts.

(3) Plea in writing — A plea that is made under subsection (1) shall be in writing and shall set out the particular facts by reason of which it is alleged to have been for the public good that the matter should have been published.

(4) Reply — The prosecutor may in his reply deny generally the truth of a plea that is made under this section.

612. (1) Plea of justification necessary — The truth of the matters charged in an alleged libel shall not be inquired into in the absence of a plea of justification under section 611 unless the accused is charged with publishing the libel knowing it to be false, in which case evidence of the truth may be given to negative the allegation that the accused knew that the libel was false.

(2) Not guilty, in addition — The accused may, in addition to a plea that is made under section 611, plead not guilty and the pleas shall be inquired into together.

(3) Effect of plea on punishment — Where a plea of justification is pleaded and the accused is convicted, the court may, in pronouncing sentence, consider whether the guilt of the accused is aggravated or mitigated by the plea.

613. Plea of not guilty — Any ground of defence for which a special plea is not provided by this Act may be relied on under the plea of not guilty.

614 to 619. [Repealed 1991, c. 43, s. 3.]

Organizations

[Heading amended 2003, c. 21, s. 11.]

620. Appearance by attorney — Every organization against which an indictment is filed shall appear and plead by counsel or agent.

1997, c. 18, s. 70; 2003, c. 21, s. 11

621. (1) Notice to organization — The clerk of the court or the prosecutor may, where an indictment is filed against an organization, cause a notice of the indictment to be served on the organization.

(2) Contents of notice — A notice of an indictment referred to in subsection (1) shall set out the nature and purport of the indictment and advise that, unless the organization appears on the date set out in the notice or the date fixed under subsection 548(2.1), and enters a plea, a plea of not guilty will be entered for the accused by the court, and that the trial of the indictment will be proceeded with as though the organization had appeared and pleaded.

1997, c. 18, s. 71; 2003, c. 21, s. 11

622. Procedure on default of appearance — Where an organization does not appear in accordance with the notice referred to in section 621, the presiding judge may, on proof of service of the notice, order the clerk of the court to enter a plea of not guilty on behalf of the organization, and the plea has the same force and effect as if the organization had appeared by its counsel or agent and pleaded that plea.

1997, c. 18, s. 72; 2003, c. 21, s. 11

623. Trial of organization — Where an organization appears and pleads to an indictment or a plea of not guilty is entered by order of the court under section 622, the court shall proceed with the trial of the indictment and, where the organization is convicted, section 735 applies.

1995, c. 22, s. 10 (Sched. I, item 21); 2003, c. 21, s. 11

Record of Proceedings

624. (1) How recorded — It is sufficient, in making up the record of a conviction or acquittal on an indictment, to copy the indictment and the plea that was pleaded, without a formal caption or heading.

(2) **Record of proceedings** — The court shall keep a record of every arraignment and of proceedings subsequent to arraignment.

625. Form of record in case of amendment — Where it is necessary to draw up a formal record in proceedings in which the indictment has been amended, the record shall be drawn up in the form in which the indictment remained after the amendment, without reference to the fact that the indictment was amended.

Pre-hearing Conference

625.1 (1) **Pre-hearing conference** — Subject to subsection (2), on application by the prosecutor or the accused or on its own motion, the court, or a judge of the court, before which, or the judge, provincial court judge or justice before whom, any proceedings are to be held may order that a conference between the prosecutor and the accused or counsel for the accused, to be presided over by the court, judge, provincial court judge or justice, be held prior to the proceedings to consider the matters that, to promote a fair and expeditious hearing, would be better decided before the start of the proceedings, and other similar matters, and to make arrangements for decisions on those matters.

(2) **Mandatory pre-trial hearing for jury trials** — In any case to be tried with a jury, a judge of the court before which the accused is to be tried shall, before the trial, order that a conference between the prosecutor and the accused or counsel for the accused, to be presided over by a judge of that court, be held in accordance with the rules of court made under sections 482 and 482.1 to consider any matters that would promote a fair and expeditious trial.

R.S.C. 1985, c. 27 (1st Supp.), s. 127; 1997, c. 18, s. 73; 2002, c. 13, s. 50

Juries

626. (1) Qualification of jurors — A person who is qualified as a juror according to, and summoned as a juror in accordance with, the laws of a province is qualified to serve as a juror in criminal proceedings in that province.

(2) No disqualification based on sex — Notwithstanding any law of a province referred to in subsection (1), no person may be disqualified, exempted or excused from serving as a juror in criminal proceedings on the grounds of his or her sex.

R.S.C. 1985, c. 27 (1st Supp.), s. 128

626.1 Presiding judge — The judge before whom an accused is tried may be either the judge who presided over matters pertaining to the selection of a jury before the commencement of a trial or another judge of the same court.

2002, c. 13, s. 51

627. Support for juror with physical disability — The judge may permit a juror with a physical disability who is otherwise qualified to serve as a juror to have technical, personal, interpretative or other support services.

1998, c. 9, s. 4

Challenging the Array

628. [Repealed R.S.C. 1985, c. 27 (1st Supp.), s. 129.]

629. (1) Challenging the jury panel — The accused or the prosecutor may challenge the jury panel only on the ground of partiality, fraud or wilful misconduct on the part of the sheriff or other officer by whom the panel was returned.

(2) In writing — A challenge under subsection (1) shall be in writing and shall state that the person who returned the panel was partial or fraudulent or that he wilfully misconducted himself, as the case may be.

(3) Form — A challenge under this section may be in Form 40.

R.S.C. 1985, c. 27 (1st Supp.), s. 130

630. Trying ground of challenge — Where a challenge is made under section 629, the judge shall determine whether the alleged ground of challenge is true or not, and where he is satisfied that the alleged ground of challenge is true, he shall direct a new panel to be returned.

Empanelling Jury

631. (1) Names of jurors on cards — The name of each juror on a panel of jurors that has been returned, his number on the panel and his address shall be written on a separate card, and all the cards shall, as far as possible, be of equal size.

(2) To be placed in box — The sheriff or other officer who returns the panel shall deliver the cards referred to in subsection (1) to the clerk of the court who shall cause them to be placed together in a box to be provided for the purpose and to be thoroughly shaken together.

(2.1) Alternate jurors — If the judge considers it advisable in the interests of justice to have one or two alternate jurors, the judge shall so order before the clerk of the court draws out the cards under subsection (3) or (3.1).

(2.2) Additional jurors — If the judge considers it advisable in the interests of justice, he or she may order that 13 or 14 jurors, instead of 12, be sworn in accordance with this Part before the clerk of the court draws out the cards under subsection (3) or (3.1).

(3) Cards to be drawn by clerk of court — If the array of jurors is not challenged or the array of jurors is challenged but the judge does not direct a new panel to be returned, the clerk of the court shall, in open court, draw out one after another the cards referred to in subsection (1), call out the number on each card as it is drawn and confirm with the person who responds that he or she is the person whose name appears on the card drawn, until the number of persons who have answered is, in the opinion of the judge, sufficient to provide a full jury and any alternate jurors ordered by the judge after allowing for orders to excuse, challenges and directions to stand by.

(3.1) Exception — The court, or a judge of the court, before which the jury trial is to be held may, if the court or judge is satisfied that it is necessary for the proper administration of justice, order the clerk of the court to call out the name and the number on each card.

(4) Juror and other persons to be sworn — The clerk of the court shall swear each member of the jury, and any alternate jurors, in the order in which his or her card was drawn and shall swear any other person providing technical, personal, interpretative or other support services to a juror with a physical disability.

(5) Drawing additional cards if necessary — If the number of persons who answer under subsection (3) or (3.1) is not sufficient to provide a full jury and the number of alternate jurors ordered by the judge, the clerk of the court shall proceed in accordance with subsections (3), (3.1) and (4) until 12 jurors — or 13 or 14 jurors, as the case may be, if the judge makes an order under subsection (2.2) — and any alternate jurors are sworn.

(6) Ban on publication, limitation to access or use of information — On application by the prosecutor or on its own motion, the court or judge before which a jury trial is to be held may, if the court or judge is satisfied that such an order is necessary for the proper administration of justice, make an order

(a) directing that the identity of a juror or any information that could disclose their identity shall not be published in any document or broadcast or transmitted in any way; or

(b) limiting access to or the use of that information.

R.S.C. 1985, c. 27 (1st Supp.), s. 131; 1992, c. 41, s. 1; 1998, c. 9, s. 5; 2001, c. 32, ss. 38, 82(4); 2002, c. 13, s. 52; 2005, c. 32, s. 20; 2011, c. 16, s. 7

632. Excusing jurors — The judge may, at any time before the commencement of a trial, order that any juror be excused from jury service, whether or not the juror has been called pursuant to subsection 631(3) or (3.1) or any challenge has been made in relation to the juror, for reasons of

(a) personal interest in the matter to be tried;

(b) relationship with the judge presiding over the jury selection process, the judge before whom the accused is to be tried, the prosecutor, the accused, the counsel for the accused or a prospective witness; or

(c) personal hardship or any other reasonable cause that, in the opinion of the judge, warrants that the juror be excused.

1992, c. 41, s. 2; 2001, c. 32, s. 39; 2002, c. 13, s. 53

633. Stand by — The judge may direct a juror who has been called under subsection 631(3) or (3.1) to stand by for reasons of personal hardship, maintaining public confidence in the administration of justice or any other reasonable cause.

1992, c. 41, s. 2; 2001, c. 32, s. 40; 2019, c. 25, s. 269

634. [Repealed 2019, c. 25, s. 269.]

635. (1) Order of challenges — The accused shall be called on before the prosecutor is called on to declare whether the accused challenges the first juror for cause, and after that the prosecutor and the accused shall be called on alternately, in respect of each of the remaining jurors, to first make such a declaration.

(2) Where there are joint trials — Subsection (1) applies where two or more accused are to be tried together, but all of the accused shall exercise the challenges of the defence in turn, in the order in which their names appear in the indictment or in any other order agreed on by them,

(a) in respect of the first juror, before the prosecutor; and

(b) in respect of each of the remaining jurors, either before or after the prosecutor, in accordance with subsection (1).

1992, c. 41, s. 2; 2019, c. 25, s. 270

636 and 637. [Repealed 1992, c. 41, s. 2.]

638. (1) Challenge for cause — A prosecutor or an accused is entitled to any number of challenges on the ground that

(a) the name of a juror does not appear on the panel, but no misnomer or misdescription is a ground of challenge where it appears to the court that the description given on the panel sufficiently designates the person referred to;

(b) a juror is not impartial;

(c) a juror has been convicted of an offence for which they were sentenced to a term of imprisonment of two years or more and for which no pardon or record suspension is in effect;

(d) a juror is not a Canadian citizen;

(e) a juror, even with the aid of technical, personal, interpretative or other support services provided to the juror under section 627, is physically unable to perform properly the duties of a juror; or

(f) a juror does not speak the official language of Canada that is the language of the accused or the official language of Canada in which the accused can best give testimony or both official languages of Canada, where the accused is required by reason of an order under section 530 to be tried before a judge and jury who speak the official language of Canada that is the language of the accused or the official language of Canada in which the accused can best give testimony or who speak both official languages of Canada, as the case may be.

(2) No other ground — No challenge for cause shall be allowed on a ground not mentioned in subsection (1).

(3) and (4) [Repealed 1997, c. 18, s. 74.]

R.S.C. 1985, c. 27 (1st Supp.), s. 132; R.S.C. 1985, c. 31 (4th Supp.), s. 96; 1997, c. 18, s. 74; 1998, c. 9, s. 6; 2019, c. 25, s. 271

639. (1) Challenge in writing — Where a challenge is made on a ground mentioned in section 638, the court may, in its discretion, require the party that challenges to put the challenge in writing.

(2) Form — A challenge may be in Form 41.

(3) Denial — A challenge may be denied by the other party to the proceedings on the ground that it is not true.

640. (1) Determination of challenge for cause — If a challenge is made on a ground mentioned in section 638, the judge shall determine whether the alleged ground is true or not and, if the judge is satisfied that it is true, the juror shall not be sworn.

(2) Exclusion order — On the application of the accused or prosecutor or on the judge's own motion, the judge may order the exclusion of all jurors, sworn and unsworn, from the court room until it is determined whether the ground of challenge is true if the judge is of the opinion that the order is necessary to preserve the impartiality of the jurors.

(2.1) to (4) [Repealed 2019, c. 25, s. 272.]

2008, c. 18, s. 26; 2011, c. 16, s. 9; 2019, c. 25, s. 272

641. (1) Calling persons who have stood by — If a full jury and any alternate jurors have not been sworn and no cards remain to be drawn, the persons who have been directed to stand by shall be called again in the order in which their cards were drawn and shall be sworn, unless excused by the judge or challenged by the accused or the prosecutor.

(2) Other persons becoming available — If, before a person is sworn as a juror under subsection (1), other persons in the panel become available, the prosecutor may require the cards of those persons to be put into and drawn from the box in accordance with section 631, and those persons shall be challenged, directed to stand by, excused or sworn, as the case may be, before the persons who were originally directed to stand by are called again.

1992, c. 41, s. 3; 2001, c. 32, s. 41; 2002, c. 13, s. 55; 2011, c. 16, s. 10

642. (1) Summoning other jurors when panel exhausted — If a full jury and any alternate jurors considered advisable cannot be provided notwithstanding that the relevant provisions of this Part have been complied with, the court may, at the request of the prosecutor, order the sheriff or other proper officer to summon without delay as many persons, whether qualified jurors or not, as the court directs for the purpose of providing a full jury and alternate jurors.

(2) Orally — Jurors may be summoned under subsection (1) by word of mouth, if necessary.

(3) Adding names to panel — The names of the persons who are summoned under this section shall be added to the general panel for the purposes of the trial, and the same proceedings shall be taken with respect to calling and challenging those persons, excusing them and directing them to stand by as are provided in this Part with respect to the persons named in the original panel.

1992, c. 41, s. 4; 2002, c. 13, s. 56

642.1 (1) Substitution of alternate jurors — Alternate jurors shall attend at the commencement of the presentation of the evidence on the merits and, if there is not a full jury present, shall replace any absent juror, in the order in which their cards were drawn under subsection 631(3).

(2) Excusing of alternate jurors — An alternate juror who is not required as a substitute shall be excused.

2002, c. 13, s. 57; 2011, c. 16, s. 11

643. (1) Who shall be the jury — The 12, 13 or 14 jurors who are sworn in accordance with this Part and present at the commencement of the presentation of the evidence on the merits shall be the jury to hear the evidence on the merits.

(1.1) Names of jurors — The name of each juror, including alternate jurors, who is sworn shall be kept apart until the juror is excused or the jury gives its verdict or is discharged, at which time the name shall be returned to the box as often as occasion arises, as long as an issue remains to be tried before a jury.

(2) Same jury may try another issue by consent — The court may try an issue with the same jury in whole or in part that previously tried or was drawn to try another issue, without the jurors being sworn again, but if the prosecutor or the accused objects to any of the jurors or the court excuses any of the jurors, the court shall order those persons to withdraw and shall direct that the required number of cards to make up a full jury be drawn and, subject to the provisions of this Part relating to challenges, orders to excuse and directions to stand by, the persons whose cards are drawn shall be sworn.

(3) Sections directory — Failure to comply with the directions of this section or section 631, 635 or 641 does not affect the validity of a proceeding.
1992, c. 41, s. 5; 2001, c. 32, s. 42; 2002, c. 13, s. 58; 2011, c. 16, s. 12

644. (1) Discharge of juror — Where in the course of a trial the judge is satisfied that a juror should not, by reason of illness or other reasonable cause, continue to act, the judge may discharge the juror.

(1.1) Replacement of juror — A judge may select another juror to take the place of a juror who by reason of illness or other reasonable cause cannot continue to act, if the jury has not yet begun to hear evidence, either by drawing a name from a panel of persons who were summoned to act as jurors and who are available at the court at the time of replacing the juror or by using the procedure referred to in section 642.

(2) Trial may continue — Where in the course of a trial a member of the jury dies or is discharged pursuant to subsection (1), the jury shall, unless the judge otherwise directs and if the number of jurors is not reduced below ten, be deemed to remain properly constituted for all purposes of the trial and the trial shall proceed and a verdict may be given accordingly.

(3) Trial may continue without jury — If in the course of a trial the number of jurors is reduced below 10, the judge may, with the consent of the parties, discharge the jurors, continue the trial without a jury and render a verdict.
1992, c. 41, s. 6; 1997, c. 18, s. 75; 2019, c. 25, s. 273

Trial

645. (1) Trial continuous — The trial of an accused shall proceed continuously subject to adjournment by the court.

(2) Adjournment — The judge may adjourn the trial from time to time in the same sittings.

(3) Formal adjournment unnecessary — No formal adjournment of trial or entry thereof is required.

(4) Questions reserved for decision — A judge, in any case tried without a jury, may reserve final decision on any question raised at the trial, or any matter raised further to a pre-hearing conference, and the decision, when given, shall be deemed to have been given at the trial.

(5) Questions reserved for decision in a trial with a jury — In any case to be tried with a jury, the judge before whom an accused is or is to be tried has jurisdiction, before any juror on a panel of jurors is called pursuant to subsection 631(3) or (3.1) and in the absence of any such juror, to deal with any matter that would ordinarily or necessarily be dealt with in the absence of the jury after it has been sworn.
R.S.C. 1985, c. 27 (1st Supp.), s. 133; 1997, c. 18, s. 76; 2001, c. 32, s. 43

646. Taking evidence — On the trial of an accused for an indictable offence, the evidence of the witnesses for the prosecutor and the accused and the addresses of the prosecutor and the accused or counsel for the accused by way of summing up shall be taken in accordance with the provisions of Part XVIII, other than subsections 540(7) to (9), relating to the taking of evidence at preliminary inquiries.

2002, c. 13, s. 59

647. (1) Separation of jurors — The judge may, at any time before the jury retires to consider its verdict, permit the members of the jury to separate.

(2) Keeping in charge — Where permission to separate under subsection (1) cannot be given or is not given, the jury shall be kept under the charge of an officer of the court as the judge directs, and that officer shall prevent the jurors from communicating with anyone other than himself or another member of the jury without leave of the judge.

(3) Non-compliance with subsection (2) — Failure to comply with subsection (2) does not affect the validity of the proceedings.

(4) Empanelling new jury in certain cases — Where the fact that there has been a failure to comply with this section or section 648 is discovered before the verdict of the jury is returned, the judge may, if he considers that the failure to comply might lead to a miscarriage of justice, discharge the jury and

(a) direct that the accused be tried with a new jury during the same session or sittings of the court; or

(b) postpone the trial on such terms as justice may require.

(5) Refreshment and accommodation — The judge shall direct the sheriff to provide the jurors who are sworn with suitable and sufficient refreshment, food and lodging while they are together until they have given their verdict.

648. (1) Restriction on publication — After permission to separate is given to members of a jury under subsection 647(1), no information regarding any portion of the trial at which the jury is not present shall be published in any document or broadcast or transmitted in any way before the jury retires to consider its verdict.

(2) Offence — Every one who fails to comply with subsection (1) is guilty of an offence punishable on summary conviction.

(3) [Repealed 2005, c. 32, s. 21(2).]

2005, c. 32, s. 21

649. Disclosure of jury proceedings — Every member of a jury, and every person providing technical, personal, interpretative or other support services to a juror with a physical disability, who except for the purposes of

(a) an investigation of an alleged offence under subsection 139(2) in relation to a juror, or

(b) giving evidence in criminal proceedings in relation to such an offence, discloses any information relating to the proceedings of the jury when it was absent from the courtroom that was not subsequently disclosed in open court is guilty of an offence punishable on summary conviction.

1998, c. 9, s. 7

650. (1) Accused to be present — Subject to subsections (1.1) to (2) and section 650.01, an accused, other than an organization, shall be present in court during the whole of his or her trial.

(1.1) Video links — If the court so orders, and if the prosecutor and the accused so agree, the accused may appear by counsel or by closed-circuit television or videoconference, for any part of the trial other than a part in which the evidence of a witness is taken.

(1.2) Video links — If the court so orders, an accused who is confined in prison may appear by closed-circuit television or videoconference, for any part of the trial other than a part in which the evidence of a witness is taken, as long as the accused is given the opportunity to communicate privately with counsel if they are represented by counsel.

(2) Exceptions — The court may

(a) cause the accused to be removed and to be kept out of court, where he misconducts himself by interrupting the proceedings so that to continue the proceedings in his presence would not be feasible;

(b) permit the accused to be out of court during the whole or any part of his trial on such conditions as the court considers proper; or

(c) cause the accused to be removed and to be kept out of court during the trial of an issue as to whether the accused is unfit to stand trial, where it is satisfied that failure to do so might have an adverse effect on the mental condition of the accused.

(3) To make defence — An accused is entitled, after the close of the case for the prosecution, to make full answer and defence personally or by counsel.

1991, c. 43, s. 9 (Sched., item 4); 1994, c. 44, s. 61; 1997, c. 18, s. 77(2); 2002, c. 13, s. 60; 2003, c. 21, s. 12; 2019, c. 25, s. 274

650.01 (1) Designation of counsel of record — An accused may appoint counsel to represent the accused for any proceedings under this Act by filing a designation with the court.

(2) Contents of designation — The designation must contain the name and address of the counsel and be signed by the accused and the designated counsel.

(3) Effect of designation — If a designation is filed,

(a) the accused may appear by the designated counsel without being present for any part of the proceedings, other than

(i) a part during which oral evidence of a witness is taken,

(ii) a part during which jurors are being selected, and

(iii) an application for a writ of *habeas corpus*;

(b) an appearance by the designated counsel is equivalent to the accused's being present, unless the court orders otherwise; and

(c) a plea of guilty may be made, and a sentence may be pronounced, only if the accused is present, unless the court orders otherwise.

(4) When court orders presence of accused — If the court orders the accused to be present otherwise than by appearance by the designated counsel, the court may

(a) issue a summons to compel the presence of the accused and order that it be served by leaving a copy at the address contained in the designation; or

(b) issue a warrant to compel the presence of the accused.

2002, c. 13, s. 61

650.02 Remote appearance — The prosecutor or the counsel designated under section 650.01 may appear before the court by audioconference or videoconference, if the technological means is satisfactory to the court.

2002, c. 13, s. 61; 2019, c. 25, s. 275

650.1 Pre-charge conference — A judge in a jury trial may, before the charge to the jury, confer with the accused or counsel for the accused and the prosecutor with respect to the matters that should be explained to the jury and with respect to the choice of instructions to the jury.

1997, c. 18, s. 78

651. (1) Summing up by prosecutor — Where an accused, or any one of several accused being tried together, is defended by counsel, the counsel shall, at the end of the case for the prosecution, declare whether or not he intends to adduce evidence on behalf of the accused for whom he appears and if he does not announce his intention to adduce evidence, the prosecutor may address the jury by way of summing up.

(2) Summing up by accused — Counsel for the accused or the accused, where he is not defended by counsel, is entitled, if he thinks fit, to open the case for the defence, and after the conclusion of that opening to examine such witnesses as he thinks fit, and when all the evidence is concluded to sum up the evidence.

(3) Accused's right of reply — Where no witnesses are examined for an accused, he or his counsel is entitled to address the jury last, but otherwise counsel for the prosecution is entitled to address the jury last.

(4) Prosecutor's right of reply where more than one accused — Where two or more accused are tried jointly and witnesses are examined for any of them, all the accused or their respective counsel are required to address the jury before it is addressed by the prosecutor.

652. (1) View — The judge may, where it appears to be in the interests of justice, at any time after the jury has been sworn and before it give its verdict, direct the jury to have a view of any place, thing or person, and shall give directions respecting the manner in which, and the persons by whom, the place, thing or person shall be shown to the jury, and may for that purpose adjourn the trial.

(2) Directions to prevent communication — Where a view is ordered under subsection (1), the judge shall give any directions that he considers necessary for the purpose of preventing undue communication by any person with members of the jury, but failure to comply with any directions given under this subsection does not affect the validity of the proceedings.

(3) Who shall attend — Where a view is ordered under subsection (1) the accused and the judge shall attend.

652.1 (1) Trying of issues of indictment by jury — After the charge to the jury, the jury shall retire to try the issues of the indictment.

(2) Reduction of number of jurors to 12 — However, if there are more than 12 jurors remaining, the judge shall identify the 12 jurors who are to retire to consider the verdict by having the number of each juror written on a card that is of equal size, by causing the cards to be placed together in a box that is to be thoroughly shaken together and by drawing one card if 13 jurors remain or two cards if 14 jurors remain. The judge shall then discharge any juror whose number is drawn.

2011, c. 16, s. 13

653. (1) Disagreement of jury — Where the judge is satisfied that the jury is unable to agree on its verdict and that further detention of the jury would be useless, he may in his discretion discharge that jury and direct a new jury to be empanelled during the sittings of the court, or may adjourn the trial on such terms as justice may require.

(2) Discretion not reviewable — A discretion that is exercised under subsection (1) by a judge is not reviewable.

653.1 Mistrial — rulings binding at new trial — In the case of a mistrial, unless the court is satisfied that it would not be in the interests of justice, rulings relating to the disclosure or admissibility of evidence or the *Canadian Charter of Rights and Freedoms* that were made during the trial are binding on the parties in any new trial if the rulings are made — or could have been made — before the stage at which the evidence on the merits is presented.

2011, c. 16, s. 14

654. Proceeding on Sunday, etc., not invalid — The taking of the verdict of a jury and any proceeding incidental thereto is not invalid by reason only that it is done on Sunday or on a holiday.

Evidence on Trial

655. Admissions at trial — Where an accused is on trial for an indictable offence, he or his counsel may admit any fact alleged against him for the purpose of dispensing with proof thereof.

656. Presumption — valuable minerals — In any proceeding in relation to theft or possession of a valuable mineral that is unrefined, partly refined, uncut or otherwise unprocessed by any person actively engaged in or on a mine, if it is established that the person possesses the valuable mineral, the person is presumed, in the absence of evidence raising a reasonable doubt to the contrary, to have stolen or unlawfully possessed the valuable mineral.

1999, c. 5, s. 24

657. Use in evidence of statement by accused — A statement made by an accused under subsection 541(3) and purporting to be signed by the justice before whom it was made may be given in evidence against the accused at his or her trial without proof of the signature of the justice, unless it is proved that the justice by whom the statement purports to be signed did not sign it.

1994, c. 44, s. 62

657.1 (1) Proof of ownership and value of property — In any proceedings, an affidavit or a solemn declaration of a person who claims to be the lawful owner of, or the person lawfully entitled to possession of, property that was the subject-matter of the offence, or any other person who has specialized knowledge of the property or of that type of property, containing the statements referred to in subsection (2), shall be admissible in evidence and, in the absence of evidence to the contrary, is evidence of the statements contained in the affidavit or solemn declaration without proof of the signature of the person appearing to have signed the affidavit or solemn declaration.

(2) Statements to be made — For the purposes of subsection (1), a person shall state in an affidavit or a solemn declaration

(a) that the person is the lawful owner of, or is lawfully entitled to possession of, the property, or otherwise has specialized knowledge of the property or of property of the same type as that property;

(b) the value of the property;

(c) in the case of a person who is the lawful owner of or is lawfully entitled to possession of the property, that the person has been deprived of the property by fraudulent means or otherwise without the lawful consent of the person;

(c.1) in the case of proceedings in respect of an offence under section 342, that the credit card had been revoked or cancelled, is a false document within the meaning of section 321 or that no credit card that meets the exact description of that credit card was ever issued; and

(d) any facts within the personal knowledge of the person relied on to justify the statements referred to in paragraphs (a) to (c.1).

(3) Notice of intention to produce affidavit or solemn declaration — Unless the court orders otherwise, no affidavit or solemn declaration shall be received in evidence pursuant to subsection (1) unless the prosecutor has, before the trial or other proceeding, given to the accused a copy of the affidavit or solemn declaration and reasonable notice of intention to produce it in evidence.

(4) Attendance for examination — Notwithstanding subsection (1), the court may require the person who appears to have signed an affidavit or solemn declaration referred to in that subsection to appear before it for examination or cross-examination in respect of the issue of proof of any of the statements contained in the affidavit or solemn declaration.

R.S.C. 1985, c. 23 (4th Supp.), s. 3; 1994, c. 44, s. 63; 1997, c. 18, s. 79

657.2 (1) Theft and possession — Where an accused is charged with possession of any property obtained by the commission of an offence, evidence of the conviction or discharge of another person of theft of the property is admissible against the accused, and in the absence of evidence to the contrary is proof that the property was stolen.

(2) Accessory after the fact — Where an accused is charged with being an accessory after the fact to the commission of an offence, evidence of the conviction or discharge of another person of the offence is admissible against the accused, and in the absence of evidence to the contrary is proof that the offence was committed.

1997, c. 18, s. 80

657.3 (1) Expert testimony — In any proceedings, the evidence of a person as an expert may be given by means of a report accompanied by the affidavit or solemn declaration of the person, setting out, in particular, the qualifications of the person as an expert if

(a) the court recognizes that person as an expert; and

(b) the party intending to produce the report in evidence has, before the proceeding, given to the other party a copy of the affidavit or solemn declaration and the report and reasonable notice of the intention to produce it in evidence.

(2) Attendance for examination — Notwithstanding subsection (1), the court may require the person who appears to have signed an affidavit or solemn declaration referred to in that subsection to appear before it for examination or cross-examination in respect of the issue of proof of any of the statements contained in the affidavit or solemn declaration or report.

(3) Notice for expert testimony — For the purpose of promoting the fair, orderly and efficient presentation of the testimony of witnesses,

(a) a party who intends to call a person as an expert witness shall, at least thirty days before the commencement of the trial or within any other period fixed by the justice or judge, give notice to the other party or parties of his or her intention to do so, accompanied by

(i) the name of the proposed witness,

(ii) a description of the area of expertise of the proposed witness that is sufficient to permit the other parties to inform themselves about the area of expertise, and

(iii) a statement of the qualifications of the proposed witness as an expert;

(b) in addition to complying with paragraph (a), a prosecutor who intends to call a person as an expert witness shall, within a reasonable period before trial, provide to the other party or parties

(i) a copy of the report, if any, prepared by the proposed witness for the case, and

(ii) if no report is prepared, a summary of the opinion anticipated to be given by the proposed witness and the grounds on which it is based; and

(c) in addition to complying with paragraph (a), an accused, or his or her counsel, who intends to call a person as an expert witness shall, not later than the close of the case for the prosecution, provide to the other party or parties the material referred to in paragraph (b).

(4) If notices not given — If a party calls a person as an expert witness without complying with subsection (3), the court shall, at the request of any other party,

(a) grant an adjournment of the proceedings to the party who requests it to allow him or her to prepare for cross-examination of the expert witness;

(b) order the party who called the expert witness to provide that other party and any other party with the material referred to in paragraph (3)(b); and

(c) order the calling or recalling of any witness for the purpose of giving testimony on matters related to those raised in the expert witness's testimony, unless the court considers it inappropriate to do so.

(5) Additional court orders — If, in the opinion of the court, a party who has received the notice and material referred to in subsection (3) has not been able to prepare for the evidence of the proposed witness, the court may do one or more of the following:

(a) adjourn the proceedings;

(b) order that further particulars be given of the evidence of the proposed witness; and

(c) order the calling or recalling of any witness for the purpose of giving testimony on matters related to those raised in the expert witness's testimony.

(6) Use of material by prosecution — If the proposed witness does not testify, the prosecutor may not produce material provided to him or her under paragraph (3)(c) in evidence without the consent of the accused.

(7) No further disclosure — Unless otherwise ordered by a court, information disclosed under this section in relation to a proceeding may only be used for the purpose of that proceeding.

1997, c. 18, s. 80; 2002, c. 13, s. 62

Children and Young Persons

658. (1) Testimony as to date of birth — In any proceedings to which this Act applies, the testimony of a person as to the date of his or her birth is admissible as evidence of that date.

(2) Testimony of parent — In any proceedings to which this Act applies, the testimony of a parent as to the age of a person of whom he or she is a parent is admissible as evidence of the age of that person.

(3) Proof of age — In any proceedings to which this act applies,

(a) a birth or baptismal certificate or a copy of such a certificate purporting to be certified under the hand of the person in whose custody the certificate is held is evidence of the age of that person; and

(b) an entry or record of an incorporated society or its officers who have had the control or care of a child or young person at or about the time the child or young person was brought to Canada is evidence of the age of the child or young person if the entry or record was made before the time when the offence is alleged to have been committed.

(4) Other evidence — In the absence of any certificate, copy, entry or record mentioned in subsection (3), or in corroboration of any such certificate, copy, entry or record, a jury, judge, justice or provincial court judge, as the case may be, may receive and act on any other information relating to age that they consider reliable.

(5) Inference from appearance — In the absence of other evidence, or by way of corroboration of other evidence, a jury, judge, justice or provincial court judge, as the case may be, may infer the age of a child or young person from his or her appearance.

R.S.C. 1985, c. 27 (1st Supp.), s. 203; 1994, c. 44, s. 64

Corroboration

659. Children's evidence — Any requirement whereby it is mandatory for a court to give the jury a warning about convicting an accused on the evidence of a child is abrogated.

1993, c. 45, s. 9

Verdicts

660. Full offence charged, attempt proved — Where the complete commission of an offence charged is not proved but the evidence establishes an attempt to commit the offence, the accused may be convicted of the attempt.

661. (1) Attempt charged, full offence proved — Where an attempt to commit an offence is charged but the evidence establishes the commission of the complete offence, the accused is not entitled to be acquitted, but the jury may convict him of the attempt unless the judge presiding at the trial, in his discretion, discharges the jury from giving a verdict and directs that the accused be indicted for the complete offence.

(2) Conviction a bar — An accused who is convicted under this section is not liable to be tried again for the offence that he was charged with attempting to commit.

662. (1) Offence charged, part only proved — A count in an indictment is divisible and where the commission of the offence charged, as described in the enactment creating it or as charged in the count, includes the commission of another offence, whether punishable by indictment or on summary conviction, the accused may be convicted

(a) of an offence so included that is proved, notwithstanding that the whole offence that is charged is not proved; or

(b) of an attempt to commit an offence so included.

(2) First degree murder charged — For greater certainty and without limiting the generality of subsection (1), where a count charges first degree murder and the evidence does not prove first degree murder but proves second degree murder or an attempt to commit second degree murder, the jury may find the accused not guilty of first degree murder but guilty of second degree murder or an attempt to commit second degree murder, as the case may be.

(3) Conviction for infanticide or manslaughter on charge of murder — Subject to subsection (4), where a count charges murder and the evidence proves manslaughter or infanticide but does not prove murder, the jury may find the accused not guilty of murder but guilty of manslaughter or infanticide, but shall not on that count find the accused guilty of any other offence.

(4) Conviction for concealing body of child where murder or infanticide charged — Where a count charges the murder of a child or infanticide and the evidence proves the commission of an offence under section 243 but does not prove murder or infanticide, the jury may find the accused not guilty of murder or infanticide, as the case may be, but guilty of an offence under section 243.

(5) Conviction for dangerous operation when another offence charged — For greater certainty, when a count charges an offence under section 220, 221 or 236 arising out of the operation of a conveyance, and the evidence does not prove that offence but proves an offence under section 320.13, the accused may be convicted of an offence under that section.

(6) Conviction for break and enter with intent — Where a count charges an offence under paragraph 98(1)(b) or 348(1)(b) and the evidence does not prove that offence but does prove an offence under, respectively, paragraph 98(1)(a) or 348(1)(a), the accused may be convicted of an offence under that latter paragraph.

R.S.C. 1985, c. 27 (1st Supp.), s. 134; 2000, c. 2, s. 3; 2008, c. 6, s. 38; 2018, c. 21, s. 20

663. No acquittal unless act or omission not wilful — Where a female person is charged with infanticide and the evidence establishes that she caused the death of her child but does not establish that, at the time of the act or omission by which she caused the death of the child,

(a) she was not fully recovered from the effects of giving birth to the child or from the effect of lactation consequent on the birth of the child, and

(b) the balance of her mind was, at that time, disturbed by reason of the effect of giving birth to the child or of the effect of lactation consequent on the birth of the child, she may be convicted unless the evidence establishes that the act or omission was not wilful.

Previous Convictions

664. No reference to previous conviction — No indictment in respect of an offence for which, by reason of previous convictions, a greater punishment may be imposed shall contain any reference to previous convictions.

665. [Repealed 1995, c. 22, s. 3.]

666. Evidence of character — Where, at a trial, the accused adduces evidence of his good character, the prosecutor may, in answer thereto, before a verdict is returned, adduce evidence of the previous conviction of the accused for any offences, including any previous conviction by reason of which a greater punishment may be imposed.

667. (1) Proof of previous conviction — In any proceedings,

(a) a certificate setting out with reasonable particularity the conviction or discharge under section 730, the finding of guilt under the *Young Offenders Act*, chapter Y-1 of the Revised Statutes of Canada, 1985, the finding of guilt under the *Youth Criminal Justice Act* or the conviction and sentence or finding of guilt and sentence in Canada of an offender is, on proof that the accused or defendant is the offender referred to in the certificate, evidence that the accused or defendant was so convicted, so discharged or so convicted and sentenced or found guilty and sentenced, without proof of the signature or the official character of the person appearing to have signed the certificate, if it is signed by

(i) the person who made the conviction, order for the discharge or finding of guilt,

(ii) the clerk of the court in which the conviction, order for the discharge or finding of guilt was made, or

(iii) a fingerprint examiner;

(b) evidence that the fingerprints of the accused or defendant are the same as the fingerprints of the offender whose fingerprints are reproduced in or attached to a certificate issued under subparagraph (a)(iii) is, in the absence of evidence to the contrary, proof that the accused or defendant is the offender referred to in that certificate;

(c) a certificate of a fingerprint examiner stating that he has compared the fingerprints reproduced in or attached to that certificate with the fingerprints reproduced in or attached to a certificate issued under subparagraph (a)(iii) and that they are those of the same person is evidence of the statements contained in the certificate without proof of the signature or the official character of the person appearing to have signed the certificate; and

(d) a certificate under subparagraph (a)(iii) may be in Form 44, and a certificate under paragraph (c) may be in Form 45.

(2) Idem — In any proceedings, a copy of the summary conviction or discharge under section 730 in Canada of an offender, signed by the person who made the conviction or order for the discharge or by the clerk of the court in which the conviction or order for the discharge was made, is, on proof that the accused or defendant is the offender referred to in the copy of the summary conviction, evidence of the conviction or discharge under section 730 of the accused or defendant, without proof of the signature or the official character of the person appearing to have signed it.

(2.1) Proof of identity — In any summary conviction proceedings, where the name of a defendant is similar to the name of an offender referred to in a certificate made under subparagraph (1)(a)(i) or (ii) in respect of a summary conviction or referred to in a copy of a summary conviction mentioned in subsection (2), that similarity of name is, in the absence of evidence to the contrary, evidence that the defendant is the offender referred to in the certificate or the copy of the summary conviction.

(3) Attendance and right to cross-examine — An accused against whom a certificate issued under subparagraph (1)(a)(iii) or paragraph (1)(c) is produced may, with leave of the court, require the attendance of the person who signed the certificate for the purposes of cross-examination.

(4) Notice of intention to produce certificate — No certificate issued under subparagraph (1)(a)(iii) or paragraph (1)(c) shall be received in evidence unless the party intending to produce it has given to the accused reasonable notice of his intention together with a copy of the certificate.

(5) "fingerprint examiner" — In this section **"fingerprint examiner"** means a person designated as such for the purposes of this section by the Minister of Public Safety and Emergency Preparedness.

R.S.C. 1985, c. 27 (1st Supp.), s. 136; 1995, c. 22, s. 10; 2002, c. 1, s. 181; 2005, c. 10, s. 34(1)(f)(xii); 2012, c. 1, s. 200

668 and 669. [Repealed 1995, c. 22, s. 4.]

Jurisdiction

669.1 (1) Jurisdiction — Where any judge, court or provincial court judge by whom or which the plea of the accused or defendant to an offence was taken has not commenced to hear evidence, any judge, court or provincial court judge having jurisdiction to try the accused or defendant has jurisdiction for the purpose of the hearing and adjudication.

(2) Adjournment — Any court, judge or provincial court judge having jurisdiction to try an accused or a defendant, or any clerk or other proper officer of the court, or in the case of an offence punishable on summary conviction, any justice, may, at any time before or after the plea of the accused or defendant is taken, adjourn the proceedings.

R.S.C. 1985, c. 27 (1st Supp.), s. 137

669.2 (1) Continuation of proceedings — Subject to this section, where an accused or a defendant is being tried by

(a) a judge or provincial court judge,

(b) a justice or other person who is, or is a member of, a summary conviction court, or

(c) a court composed of a judge and jury,

as the case may be, and the judge, provincial court judge, justice or other person dies or is for any reason unable to continue, the proceedings may be continued before another judge, provincial court judge, justice or other person, as the case may be, who has jurisdiction to try the accused or defendant.

(2) Where adjudication is made — Where a verdict was rendered by a jury or an adjudication was made by a judge, provincial court judge, justice or other person before whom the trial was commenced, the judge, provincial court judge, justice or other person before whom the proceedings are continued shall, without further election by an accused, impose the punishment or make the order that is authorized by law in the circumstances.

(3) If no adjudication made — Subject to subsections (4) and (5), if the trial was commenced but no adjudication was made or verdict rendered, the judge, provincial court judge, justice or other person before whom the proceedings are continued shall, without further election by an accused, commence the trial again as if no evidence on the merits had been taken.

(4) If no adjudication made — jury trials — If a trial that is before a court composed of a judge and a jury was commenced but no adjudication was made or verdict rendered, the judge before whom the proceedings are continued may, without further election by an accused, continue the trial or commence the trial again as if no evidence on the merits had been taken.

(5) Where trial continued — Where a trial is continued under paragraph (4)(a), any evidence that was adduced before a judge referred to in paragraph (1)(c) is deemed to have been adduced before the judge before whom the trial is continued but, where the prosecutor and the accused so agree, any part of that evidence may be adduced again before the judge before whom the trial is continued.

R.S.C. 1985, c. 27 (1st Supp.), s. 137; 1994, c. 44, s. 65; 2011, c. 16, s. 15

669.3 Jurisdiction when appointment to another court — Where a court composed of a judge and a jury, a judge or a provincial court judge is conducting a trial and the judge or provincial court judge is appointed to another court, he or she continues to have jurisdiction in respect of the trial until its completion.

1994, c. 44, s. 66

Formal Defects in Jury Process

670. Judgment not to be stayed on certain grounds — Judgment shall not be stayed or reversed after verdict on an indictment

(a) by reason of any irregularity in the summoning or empanelling of the jury; or

(b) for the reason that a person who served on the jury was not returned as a juror by a sheriff or other officer.

671. Directions respecting jury or jurors directory — No omission to observe the directions contained in any Act with respect to the qualification, selection, balloting or distribution of jurors, the preparation of the jurors' book, the selecting of jury lists or the drafting of panels from the jury lists is a ground for impeaching or quashing a verdict rendered in criminal proceedings.

672. Saving powers of court — Nothing in this Act alters, abridges or affects any power or authority that a court or judge had immediately before April 1, 1955, or any practice or form that existed immediately before April 1, 1955, with respect to trials by jury, jury process, juries or jurors, except where the power or authority, practice or form is expressly altered by or is inconsistent with this Act.

PART XX.1 — MENTAL DISORDER (SS. 672.1–672.95)

Interpretation

672.1 (1) Definitions — In this Part,

"accused" includes a defendant in summary conviction proceedings and an accused in respect of whom a verdict of not criminally responsible on account of mental disorder has been rendered;

"assessment" means an assessment by a medical practitioner or any other person who has been designated by the Attorney General as being qualified to conduct an assessment of the mental condition of the accused under an assessment order made under section 672.11 or 672.121, and any incidental observation or examination of the accused;

"chairperson" includes any alternate that the chairperson of a Review Board may designate to act on the chairperson's behalf;

"court" includes a summary conviction court as defined in section 785, a judge, a justice and a judge of the court of appeal as defined in section 673;

"disposition" means an order made by a court or Review Board under section 672.54, an order made by a court under section 672.58 or a finding made by a court under subsection 672.64(1);

"dual status offender" means an offender who is subject to a sentence of imprisonment in respect of one offence and a custodial disposition under paragraph 672.54(c) in respect of another offence;

"high-risk accused" means an accused who is found to be a high-risk accused by a court under subsection 672.64(1);

"hospital" means a place in a province that is designated by the Minister of Health for the province for the custody, treatment or assessment of an accused in respect of whom an assessment order, a disposition or a placement decision is made;

"medical practitioner" means a person who is entitled to practise medicine by the laws of a province;

"party", in relation to proceedings of a court or Review Board to make or review a disposition, means

(a) the accused,

(b) the person in charge of the hospital where the accused is detained or is to attend pursuant to an assessment order or a disposition,

(c) an Attorney General designated by the court or Review Board under subsection 672.5(3),

(d) any interested person designated by the court or Review Board under subsection 672.5(4), or

(e) where the disposition is to be made by a court, the prosecutor of the charge against the accused;

"placement decision" means a decision by a Review Board under subsection 672.68(2) as to the place of custody of a dual status offender;

"prescribed" means prescribed by regulations made by the Governor in Council under section 672.95;

"Review Board" means the Review Board established or designated for a province pursuant to subsection 672.38(1);

"verdict of not criminally responsible on account of mental disorder" means a verdict that the accused committed the act or made the omission that formed the basis of the offence with which the accused is charged but is not criminally responsible on account of mental disorder.

(2) Reference — For the purposes of subsections 672.5(3) and (5), paragraph 672.86(1)(b) and subsections 672.86(2) and (2.1), 672.88(2) and 672.89(2), in respect of a territory or proceedings commenced at the instance of the Government of Canada and conducted by or on behalf of that Government, a reference to the Attorney General of a province shall be read as a reference to the Attorney General of Canada.

1991, c. 43, s. 4; 2005, c. 22, s. 1; 2014, c. 6, s. 2

Assessment Orders

672.11 Assessment order — A court having jurisdiction over an accused in respect of an offence may order an assessment of the mental condition of the accused, if it has reasonable grounds to believe that such evidence is necessary to determine

(a) whether the accused is unfit to stand trial;

(b) whether the accused was, at the time of the commission of the alleged offence, suffering from a mental disorder so as to be exempt from criminal responsibility by virtue of subsection 16(1);

(c) whether the balance of the mind of the accused was disturbed at the time of commission of the alleged offence, where the accused is a female person charged with an offence arising out of the death of her newly-born child;

(d) the appropriate disposition to be made, where a verdict of not criminally responsible on account of mental disorder or unfit to stand trial has been rendered in respect of the accused;

(d.1) whether a finding that the accused is a high-risk accused should be revoked under subsection 672.84(3); or

(e) whether an order should be made under section 672.851 for a stay of proceedings, where a verdict of unfit to stand trial has been rendered against the accused.

1991, c. 43, s. 4; 1995, c. 22, s. 10 (Sched. I); 2005, c. 22, s. 2; 2014, c. 6, s. 3

672.12 (1) Where court may order assessment — The court may make an assessment order at any stage of proceedings against the accused of its own motion, on application of the accused or, subject to subsections (2) and (3), on application of the prosecutor.

(2) Limitation on prosecutor's application for assessment of fitness — Where the prosecutor applies for an assessment in order to determine whether the accused is unfit to stand trial for an offence that is prosecuted by way of summary conviction, the court may only order the assessment if

(a) the accused raised the issue of fitness; or

(b) the prosecutor satisfies the court that there are reasonable grounds to doubt that the accused is fit to stand trial.

(3) Limitation on prosecutor's application for assessment — Where the prosecutor applies for an assessment in order to determine whether the accused was suffering from a mental disorder at the time of the offence so as to be exempt from criminal responsibility, the court may only order the assessment if

(a) the accused puts his or her mental capacity for criminal intent into issue; or

(b) the prosecutor satisfies the court that there are reasonable grounds to doubt that the accused is criminally responsible for the alleged offence, on account of mental disorder.

1991, c. 43, s. 4

672.121 Review Board may order assessment — The Review Board that has jurisdiction over an accused found not criminally responsible on account of mental disorder or unfit to stand trial may order an assessment of the mental condition of the accused of its own motion or on application of the prosecutor or the accused, if it has reasonable grounds to believe that such evidence is necessary to

(a) make a recommendation to the court under subsection 672.851(1);

(b) make a disposition under section 672.54 in one of the following circumstances:

(i) no assessment report on the mental condition of the accused is available,

(ii) no assessment of the mental condition of the accused has been conducted in the last twelve months, or

(iii) the accused has been transferred from another province under section 672.86; or

(c) determine whether to refer to the court for review under subsection 672.84(1) a finding that an accused is a high-risk accused.

2005, c. 22, s. 3; 2014, c. 6, s. 4

672.13 (1) Contents of assessment order — An assessment order must specify

(a) the service that or the person who is to make the assessment, or the hospital where it is to be made;

(b) whether the accused is to be detained in custody while the order is in force; and

(c) the period that the order is to be in force, including the time required for the assessment and for the accused to travel to and from the place where the assessment is to be made.

(2) Form — An assessment order may be in Form 48 or 48.1.

1991, c. 43, s. 4; 2005, c. 22, s. 4

672.14 (1) General rule for period — An assessment order shall not be in force for more than thirty days.

(2) Exception in fitness cases — No assessment order to determine whether the accused is unfit to stand trial shall be in force for more than five days, excluding holidays and the time required for the accused to travel to and from the place where the assessment is to be made, unless the accused and the prosecutor agree to a longer period not exceeding thirty days.

(3) Exception for compelling circumstances — Despite subsections (1) and (2), a court or Review Board may make an assessment order that remains in force for sixty days if the court or Review Board is satisfied that compelling circumstances exist that warrant it.

1991, c. 43, s. 4; 2005, c. 22, s. 5

672.15 (1) Extension — Subject to subsection (2), a court or Review Board may extend an assessment order, of its own motion or on the application of the accused or the prosecutor made during or at the end of the period during which the order is in force, for any further period that is required, in its opinion, to complete the assessment of the accused.

(2) Maximum duration of extensions — No extension of an assessment order shall exceed thirty days, and the period of the initial order together with all extensions shall not exceed sixty days.

1991, c. 43, s. 4; 2005, c. 22, s. 6

672.16 (1) Presumption against custody — Subject to subsection (3), an accused shall not be detained in custody under an assessment order of a court unless

(a) the court is satisfied that on the evidence custody is necessary to assess the accused, or that on the evidence of a medical practitioner custody is desirable to assess the accused and the accused consents to custody;

(b) custody of the accused is required in respect of any other matter or by virtue of any other provision of this Act; or

(c) the prosecutor, having been given a reasonable opportunity to do so, shows that detention of the accused in custody is justified on either of the grounds set out in subsection 515(10).

(1.1) Presumption against custody — Review Board — If the Review Board makes an order for an assessment of an accused under section 672.121, the accused shall not be detained in custody under the order unless

(a) the accused is currently subject to a disposition made under paragraph 672.54(c);

(b) the Review Board is satisfied on the evidence that custody is necessary to assess the accused, or that on the evidence of a medical practitioner custody is desirable to assess the accused and the accused consents to custody; or

(c) custody of the accused is required in respect of any other matter or by virtue of any other provision of this Act.

(1.2) Residency as a condition of disposition — Subject to paragraphs (1.1)(b) and (c), if the accused is subject to a disposition made under paragraph 672.54(b) that requires the accused to reside at a specified place, an assessment ordered under section 672.121 shall require the accused to reside at the same place.

(2) Report of medical practitioner — For the purposes of paragraphs (1)(a) and (1.1)(b), if the prosecutor and the accused agree, the evidence of a medical practitioner may be received in the form of a report in writing.

(3) Presumption of custody in certain circumstances — An assessment order made in respect of an accused who is detained under subsection 515(6) or 522(2) shall order that the accused be detained in custody under the same circumstances referred to in that subsection, unless the accused shows that custody is not justified under the terms of that subsection.

1991, c. 43, s. 4; 2005, c. 22, s. 7

672.17 Assessment order takes precedence over bail hearing — During the period that an assessment order made by a court in respect of an accused charged with an offence is in force, no order for the interim release or detention of the accused may be made by virtue of Part XVI or section 679 in respect of that offence or an included offence.

1991, c. 43, s. 4; 2005, c. 22, s. 8

672.18 Application to vary assessment order — Where at any time while an assessment order made by a court is in force the prosecutor or an accused shows cause, the court may vary the terms of the order respecting the interim release or detention of the accused in such manner as it considers appropriate in the circumstances.

1991, c. 43, s. 4

672.19 No treatment order on assessment — No assessment order may direct that psychiatric or any other treatment of the accused be carried out, or direct the accused to submit to such treatment.

1991, c. 43, s. 4

672.191 When assessment completed — An accused in respect of whom an assessment order is made shall appear before the court or Review Board that made the order as soon as practicable after the assessment is completed and not later than the last day of the period that the order is to be in force.

1997, c. 18, s. 81; 2005, c. 22, s. 10

Assessment Reports

672.2 (1) Assessment reports — An assessment order may require the person who makes the assessment to submit in writing an assessment report on the mental condition of the accused.

(2) Assessment report to be filed — An assessment report shall be filed with the court or Review Board that ordered it, within the period fixed by the court or Review Board, as the case may be.

(3) Court to send assessment report to Review Board — The court shall send to the Review Board without delay a copy of any report filed with it pursuant to subsection (2), to assist in determining the appropriate disposition to be made in respect of the accused.

(4) Copies of reports to accused and prosecutor — Subject to subsection 672.51(3), copies of any report filed with a court or Review Board under subsection (2) shall be provided without delay to the prosecutor, the accused and any counsel representing the accused.

1991, c. 43, s. 4; 2005, c. 22, s. 11

Protected Statements

672.21 (1) Definition of "protected statement" — In this section, **"protected statement"** means a statement made by the accused during the course and for the purposes of an assessment or treatment directed by a disposition, to the person specified in the assessment order or the disposition, or to anyone acting under that person's direction.

(2) Protected statements not admissible against accused — No protected statement or reference to a protected statement made by an accused is admissible in evidence, without the consent of the accused, in any proceeding before a court, tribunal, body or person with jurisdiction to compel the production of evidence.

(3) Exceptions — Notwithstanding subsection (2), evidence of a protected statement is admissible for the purpose of

(a) determining whether the accused is unfit to stand trial;

(b) making a disposition or placement decision respecting the accused;

(c) determining, under section 672.84, whether to refer to the court for review a finding that an accused is a high-risk accused or whether to revoke such a finding;

(d) determining whether the balance of the mind of the accused was disturbed at the time of commission of the alleged offence, where the accused is a female person charged with an offence arising out of the death of her newly-born child;

(e) determining whether the accused was, at the time of the commission of an alleged offence, suffering from automatism or a mental disorder so as to be exempt from criminal responsibility by virtue of subsection 16(1), if the accused puts his or her mental capacity for criminal intent into issue, or if the prosecutor raises the issue after verdict;

(f) challenging the credibility of an accused in any proceeding where the testimony of the accused is inconsistent in a material particular with a protected statement that the accused made previously; or

(g) establishing the perjury of an accused who is charged with perjury in respect of a statement made in any proceeding.

1991, c. 43, s. 4; 2005, c. 22, s. 12; 2014, c. 6, s. 5

Fitness to Stand Trial

672.22 Presumption of fitness — An accused is presumed fit to stand trial unless the court is satisfied on the balance of probabilities that the accused is unfit to stand trial.

1991, c. 43, s. 4

672.23 (1) Court may direct issue to be tried — Where the court has reasonable grounds, at any stage of the proceedings before a verdict is rendered, to believe that the accused is unfit to stand trial, the court may direct, of its own motion or on application of the accused or the prosecutor, that the issue of fitness of the accused be tried.

(2) Burden of proof — An accused or a prosecutor who makes an application under subsection (1) has the burden of proof that the accused is unfit to stand trial.

1991, c. 43, s. 4

672.24 (1) Counsel — Where the court has reasonable grounds to believe that an accused is unfit to stand trial and the accused is not represented by counsel, the court shall order that the accused be represented by counsel.

(2) **Counsel fees and disbursements** — Where counsel is assigned pursuant to subsection (1) and legal aid is not granted to the accused pursuant to a provincial legal aid program, the fees and disbursements of counsel shall be paid by the Attorney General to the extent that the accused is unable to pay them.

(3) **Taxation of fees and disbursements** — Where counsel and the Attorney General cannot agree on the fees or disbursements of counsel, the Attorney General or the counsel may apply to the registrar of the court and the registrar may tax the disputed fees and disbursements.

1991, c. 43, s. 4; 1997, c. 18, s. 82

672.25 (1) **Postponing trial of issue** — The court shall postpone directing the trial of the issue of fitness of an accused in proceedings for an offence for which the accused may be prosecuted by indictment or that is punishable on summary conviction, until the prosecutor has elected to proceed by way of indictment or summary conviction.

(2) **Idem** — The court may postpone directing the trial of the issue of fitness of an accused

(a) where the issue arises before the close of the case for the prosecution at a preliminary inquiry, until a time that is not later than the time the accused is called on to answer to the charge; or

(b) where the issue arises before the close of the case for the prosecution at trial, until a time not later than the opening of the case for the defence or, on motion of the accused, any later time that the court may direct.

1991, c. 43, s. 4

672.26 **Trial of issue by judge and jury** — Where an accused is tried or is to be tried before a court composed of a judge and jury,

(a) if the judge directs that the issue of fitness of the accused be tried before the accused is given in charge to a jury for trial on the indictment, a jury composed of the number of jurors required in respect of the indictment in the province where the trial is to be held shall be sworn to try that issue and, with the consent of the accused, the issues to be tried on the indictment; and

(b) if the judge directs that the issue of fitness of the accused be tried after the accused has been given in charge to a jury for trial on the indictment, the jury shall be sworn to try that issue in addition to the issues in respect of which it is already sworn.

1991, c. 43, s. 4

672.27 **Trial of issue by court** — The court shall try the issue of fitness of an accused and render a verdict where the issue arises

(a) in respect of an accused who is tried or is to be tried before a court other than a court composed of a judge and jury; or

(b) before a court at a preliminary inquiry or at any other stage of the proceedings.

1991, c. 43, s. 4

672.28 Proceeding continues where accused is fit — Where the verdict on trial of the issue is that an accused is fit to stand trial, the arraignment, preliminary inquiry, trial or other stage of the proceeding shall continue as if the issue of fitness of the accused had never arisen.

1991, c. 43, s. 4

672.29 Where continued detention in custody — Where an accused is detained in custody on delivery of a verdict that the accused is fit to stand trial, the court may order the accused to be detained in a hospital until the completion of the trial, if the court has reasonable grounds to believe that the accused would become unfit to stand trial if released.

1991, c. 43, s. 4

672.3 Acquittal — Where the court has postponed directing the trial of the issue of fitness of an accused pursuant to subsection 672.25(2) and the accused is discharged or acquitted before the issue is tried, it shall not be tried.

1991, c. 43, s. 4

672.31 Verdict of unfit to stand trial — Where the verdict on trial of the issue is that an accused is unfit to stand trial, any plea that has been made shall be set aside and any jury shall be discharged.

1991, c. 43, s. 4

672.32 (1) Subsequent proceedings — A verdict of unfit to stand trial shall not prevent the accused from being tried subsequently where the accused becomes fit to stand trial.

(2) Burden of proof — The burden of proof that the accused has subsequently become fit to stand trial is on the party who asserts it, and is discharged by proof on the balance of probabilities.

1991, c. 43, s. 4

672.33 (1) *Prima facie* case to be made every two years — The court that has jurisdiction in respect of the offence charged against an accused who is found unfit to stand trial shall hold an inquiry, not later than two years after the verdict is rendered and every two years thereafter until the accused is acquitted pursuant to subsection (6) or tried, to decide whether sufficient evidence can be adduced at that time to put the accused on trial.

(1.1) Extension of time for holding inquiry — Despite subsection (1), the court may extend the period for holding an inquiry where it is satisfied on the basis of an application by the prosecutor or the accused that the extension is necessary for the proper administration of justice.

(2) Court may order inquiry to be held — On application of the accused, the court may order an inquiry under this section to be held at any time if it is satisfied, on the basis of the application and any written material submitted by the accused, that there is reason to doubt that there is a *prima facie* case against the accused.

(3) Burden of proof — At an inquiry under this section, the burden of proof that sufficient evidence can be adduced to put the accused on trial is on the prosecutor.

(4) Admissible evidence at an inquiry — In an inquiry under this section, the court shall admit as evidence

(a) any affidavit containing evidence that would be admissible if the affidavit as a witness in court; or

(b) any certified copy of the oral testimony given at a previous inquiry or hearing held before a court in respect of the offence with which the accused is charged.

(5) Conduct of inquiry — The court may determine the manner in which an inquiry under this section is conducted and may follow the practices and procedures in respect of a preliminary inquiry under Part XVIII where it concludes that the interests of justice so require.

(6) Where prima facie case not made — Where, on the completion of an inquiry under this section, the court is satisfied that sufficient evidence cannot be adduced to put the accused on trial, the court shall acquit the accused.

1991, c. 43, s. 4; 2005, c. 22, s. 13

Verdict of Not Criminally Responsible on Account of Mental Disorder

672.34 Verdict of not criminally responsible on account of mental disorder — Where the jury, or the judge or provincial court judge where there is no jury, finds that an accused committed the act or made the omission that formed the basis of the offence charged, but was at the time suffering from mental disorder so as to be exempt from criminal responsibility by virtue of subsection 16(1), the jury or the judge shall render a verdict that the accused committed the act or made the omission but is not criminally responsible on account of mental disorder.

1991, c. 43, s. 4

672.35 Effect of verdict of not criminally responsible on account of mental disorder — Where a verdict of not criminally responsible on account of mental disorder is rendered, the accused shall not be found guilty or convicted of the offence, but

(a) the accused may plead *autrefois acquit* in respect of any subsequent charge relating to that offence;

(b) any court may take the verdict into account in considering an application for judicial interim release or in considering what dispositions to make or sentence to impose for any other offence; and

(c) the Parole Board of Canada or any provincial parole board may take the verdict into account in considering an application by the accused for parole or for a record suspension under the *Criminal Records Act* in respect of any other offence.

1991, c. 43, s. 4; 2012, c. 1, ss. 145, 160(c)(ii)

672.36 Verdict not a previous conviction — A verdict of not criminally responsible on account of mental disorder is not a previous conviction for the purposes of any offence under any Act of Parliament for which a greater punishment is provided by reason of previous convictions.

1991, c. 43, s. 4

672.37 (1) Definition of "application for federal employment" — In this section, **"application for federal employment"** means an application form relating to

(a) employment in any department, as defined in section 2 of the *Financial Administration Act*;

(b) employment by any Crown corporation as defined in subsection 83(1) of the *Financial Administration Act*;

(c) enrolment in the Canadian Forces; or

(d) employment in connection with the operation of any work, undertaking or business that is within the legislative authority of Parliament.

(2) Application for federal employment — No application for federal employment shall contain any question that requires the applicant to disclose any charge or finding that the applicant committed an offence that resulted in a finding or a verdict of not criminally responsible on account of mental disorder if the applicant was discharged absolutely or is no longer subject to any disposition in respect of that offence.

(3) Punishment — Any person who uses or authorizes the use of an application for federal employment that contravenes subsection (2) is guilty of an offence punishable on summary conviction.

1991, c. 43, s. 4

Review Boards

672.38 (1) Review boards to be established — A Review Board shall be established or designated for each province to make or review dispositions concerning any accused in respect of whom a verdict of not criminally responsible by reason of mental disorder or unfit to stand trial is rendered, and shall consist of not fewer than five members appointed by the lieutenant governor in council of the province.

(2) Treated as provincial board — A Review Board shall be treated as having been established under the laws of the province.

(3) Personal liability — No member of a Review Board is liable for any act done in good faith in the exercise of the member's powers or the performance of the member's duties and functions or for any default or neglect in good faith in the exercise of those powers or the performance of those duties and functions.

1991, c. 43, s. 4; 1997, c. 18, s. 83

672.39 Members of Review Board — A Review Board must have at least one member who is entitled under the laws of a province to practise psychiatry and, where only one member is so entitled, at least one other member must have training and experience in the field of mental health, and be entitled under the laws of a province to practise medicine or psychology.

1991, c. 43, s. 4

672.4 (1) Chairperson of a Review Board — Subject to subsection (2), the chairperson of a Review Board shall be a judge of the Federal Court or of a superior, district or county court of a province, or a person who is qualified for appointment to, or has retired from, such a judicial office.

(2) Transitional — Where the chairperson of a Review Board that was established before the coming into force of subsection (1) is not a judge or other person referred to therein, the chairperson may continue to act until the expiration of his or her term of office if at least one other member of the Review Board is a judge or other person referred to in subsection (1) or is a member of the bar of the province.

1991, c. 43, s. 4

672.41 (1) Quorum of Review Board — Subject to subsection (2), the quorum of a Review Board is constituted by the chairperson, a member who is entitled under the laws of a province to practise psychiatry, and any other member.

(2) Transitional — Where the chairperson of a Review Board that was established before the coming into force of this section is not a judge or other person referred to in subsection 672.4(1), the quorum of the Review Board is constituted by the chairperson, a member who is entitled under the laws of a province to practise psychiatry, and a member who is a person referred to in that subsection or a member of the bar of the province.

1991, c. 43, s. 4

672.42 Majority vote — A decision of a majority of the members present and voting is the decision of a Review Board.

1991, c. 43, s. 4

672.43 Powers of Review Boards — At a hearing held by a Review Board to make a disposition or review a disposition in respect of an accused, the chairperson has all the powers that are conferred by sections 4 and 5 of the *Inquiries Act* on persons appointed as commissioners under Part I of that Act.

1991, c. 43, s. 4

672.44 (1) Rules of Review Board — A Review Board may, subject to the approval of the lieutenant governor in council of the province, make rules providing for the practice and procedure before the Review Board.

(2) Application and publication of rules — The rules made by a Review Board under subsection (1) apply to any proceeding within its jurisdiction, and shall be published in the *Canada Gazette*.

(3) Regulations — Notwithstanding anything in this section, the Governor in Council may make regulations to provide for the practice and procedure before Review Boards, in particular to make the rules of Review Boards uniform, and all regulations made under this subsection prevail over any rules made under subsection (1).

1991, c. 43, s. 4

Disposition Hearings

672.45 (1) Hearing to be held by a court — Where a verdict of not criminally responsible on account of mental disorder or unfit to stand trial is rendered in respect of an accused, the court may of its own motion, and shall on application by the accused or the prosecutor, hold a disposition hearing.

(1.1) Transmittal of transcript to Review Board — If the court does not hold a hearing under subsection (1), it shall send without delay, following the verdict, in original or copied form, any transcript of the court proceedings in respect of the accused, any other document or information related to the proceedings, and all exhibits filed with it, to the Review Board that has jurisdiction in respect of the matter, if the transcript, document, information or exhibits are in its possession.

(2) Disposition to be made — At a disposition hearing, the court shall make a disposition in respect of the accused, if it is satisfied that it can readily do so and that a disposition should be made without delay.

1991, c. 43, s. 4; 2005, c. 22, s. 14

672.46 (1) Status quo pending Review Board hearing — Where the court does not make a disposition in respect of the accused at a disposition hearing, any order for the interim release or detention of the accused or any appearance notice, promise to appear, summons, undertaking or recognizance in respect of the accused that is in force at the time the verdict of not criminally responsible on account of mental disorder or unfit to stand trial is rendered continues in force, subject to its terms, until the Review Board makes a disposition.

(2) Variation of order — Notwithstanding subsection (1), a court may, on cause being shown, vacate any order, appearance notice, promise to appear, summons, undertaking or recognizance referred to in that subsection and make any other order for the interim release or detention of the accused that the court considers to be appropriate in the circumstances, including an order directing that the accused be detained in custody in a hospital pending a disposition by the Review Board in respect of the accused.

Proposed Amendment — 672.46

672.46 (1) Status quo pending Review Board hearing — If the court does not make a disposition in respect of the accused at a disposition hearing, any order for the detention of the accused or any release order, appearance notice, summons or undertaking in respect of the accused that is in force at the time the verdict of not criminally responsible on account of mental disorder or unfit to stand trial is rendered continues in force, subject to its terms, until the Review Board makes a disposition.

(2) Variation — Despite subsection (1), a court may, pending a disposition by the Review Board in respect of the accused, on cause being shown, vacate the detention order, release order, appearance notice, summons or undertaking referred to in that subsection, and make any other order for the detention of the accused or any other release order that the court considers to be appropriate in the circumstances, including an order directing that the accused be detained in custody in a hospital.

2019, c. 25, s. 276 [To come into force December 18, 2019.]

1991, c. 43, s. 4

672.47 (1) Review board to make disposition where court does not — Where a verdict of not criminally responsible on account of mental disorder or unfit to stand trial is rendered and the court makes no disposition in respect of an accused, the Review Board shall, as soon as is practicable but not later than forty-five days after the verdict was rendered, hold a hearing and make a disposition.

(2) Extension of time for hearing — Where the court is satisfied that there are exceptional circumstances that warrant it, the court may extend the time for holding a hearing under subsection (1) to a maximum of ninety days after the verdict was rendered.

(3) Disposition made by court — Where a court makes a disposition under section 672.54 other than an absolute discharge in respect of an accused, the Review Board shall, not later than ninety days after the disposition was made, hold a hearing and make a disposition in respect of the accused.

(4) Exception — high-risk accused — Despite subsections (1) to (3), if the court makes a disposition under subsection 672.64(3), the Review Board shall, not later than 45 days after the day on which the disposition is made, hold a hearing and make a disposition under paragraph 672.54(c), subject to the restrictions set out in that subsection.

(5) Extension of time for hearing — If the court is satisfied that there are exceptional circumstances that warrant it, the court may extend the time for holding a hearing under subsection (4) to a maximum of 90 days after the day on which the disposition is made.

1991, c. 43, s. 4; 2005, c. 22, s. 15; 2014, c. 6, s. 6(2)

672.48 (1) Review board to determine fitness — Where a Review Board holds a hearing to make or review a disposition in respect of an accused who has been found unfit to stand trial, it shall determine whether in its opinion the accused is fit to stand trial at the time of the hearing.

(2) Review board shall send accused to court — If a Review Board determines that the accused is fit to stand trial, it shall order that the accused be sent back to court, and the court shall try the issue and render a verdict.

(3) Chairperson may send accused to court — The chairperson of a Review Board may, with the consent of the accused and the person in charge of the hospital where an accused is being detained, order that the accused be sent back to court for trial of the issue of whether the accused is unfit to stand trial, where the chairperson is of the opinion that

(a) the accused is fit to stand trial, and

(b) the Review Board will not hold a hearing to make or review a disposition in respect of the accused within a reasonable period.

1991, c. 43, s. 4

672.49 (1) **Continued detention in hospital** — In a disposition made pursuant to section 672.47 the Review Board or chairperson may require the accused to continue to be detained in a hospital until the court determines whether the accused is fit to stand trial, if the Review Board or chairperson has reasonable grounds to believe that the accused would become unfit to stand trial if released.

(2) **Copy of disposition to be sent to court** — The Review Board or chairperson shall send a copy of a disposition made pursuant to section 672.47 without delay to the court having jurisdiction over the accused and to the Attorney General of the province where the accused is to be tried.

1991, c. 43, s. 4

672.5 (1) **Procedure at disposition hearing** — A hearing held by a court or Review Board to make or review a disposition in respect of an accused, including a hearing referred to in subsection 672.84(1) or (3), shall be held in accordance with this section.

(2) **Hearing to be informal** — The hearing may be conducted in as informal a manner as is appropriate in the circumstances.

(3) **Attorneys general may be parties** — On application, the court or Review Board shall designate as a party the Attorney General of the province where the disposition is to be made and, where an accused is transferred from another province, the Attorney General of the province from which the accused is transferred.

(4) **Interested person may be a party** — The court or Review Board may designate as a party any person who has a substantial interest in protecting the interests of the accused, if the court or Review Board is of the opinion that it is just to do so.

(5) **Notice of hearing** — Notice of the hearing shall be given to the parties, the Attorney General of the province where the disposition is to be made and, where the accused is transferred to another province, the Attorney General of the province from which the accused is transferred, within the time and in the manner prescribed, or within the time and in the manner fixed by the rules of the court or Review Board.

(5.1) **Notice** — At the victim's request, notice of the hearing and of the relevant provisions of the Act shall be given to the victim within the time and in the manner fixed by the rules of the court or Review Board.

(5.2) **Notice of discharge and intended place of residence** — If the accused is discharged absolutely under paragraph 672.54(a) or conditionally under paragraph 672.54(b), a notice of the discharge and accused's intended place of residence shall, at the victim's request, be given to the victim within the time and in the manner fixed by the rules of the court or Review Board.

(6) Order excluding the public — Where the court or Review Board considers it to be in the best interests of the accused and not contrary to the public interest, the court or Review Board may order the public or any members of the public to be excluded from the hearing or any part of the hearing.

(7) Right to counsel — The accused or any other party has the right to be represented by counsel.

(8) Assigning counsel — If an accused is not represented by counsel, the court or Review Board shall, either before or at the time of the hearing, assign counsel to act for any accused

(a) who has been found unfit to stand trial; or

(b) wherever the interests of justice so require.

(8.1) Counsel fees and disbursements — Where counsel is assigned pursuant to subsection (8) and legal aid is not granted to the accused pursuant to a provincial legal aid program, the fees and disbursements of counsel shall be paid by the Attorney General to the extent that the accused is unable to pay them.

(8.2) Taxation of fees and disbursements — Where counsel and the Attorney General cannot agree on the fees or disbursements of counsel, the Attorney General or the counsel may apply to the registrar of the court and the registrar may tax the disputed fees and disbursements.

(9) Right of accused to be present — Subject to subsection (10), the accused has the right to be present during the whole of the hearing.

(10) Removal or absence of accused — The court or the chairperson of the Review Board may

(a) permit the accused to be absent during the whole or any part of the hearing on such conditions as the court or chairperson considers proper; or

(b) cause the accused to be removed and barred from re-entry for the whole or any part of the hearing

(i) where the accused interrupts the hearing so that to continue in the presence of the accused would not be feasible,

(ii) on being satisfied that failure to do so would likely endanger the life or safety of another person or would seriously impair the treatment or recovery of the accused, or

(iii) in order to hear, in the absence of the accused, evidence, oral or written submissions, or the cross-examination of any witness concerning whether grounds exist for removing the accused pursuant to subparagraph (ii).

(11) Rights of parties at hearing — Any party may adduce evidence, make oral or written submissions, call witnesses and cross-examine any witness called by any other party and, on application, cross-examine any person who made an assessment report that was submitted to the court or Review Board in writing.

(12) Request to compel attendance of witnesses — A party may not compel the attendance of witnesses, but may request the court or the chairperson of the Review Board to do so.

(13) Video links — If the accused so agrees, the court or the chairperson of the Review Board may permit the accused to appear by closed-circuit television or videoconference for any part of the hearing.

(13.1) Adjournment — The Review Board may adjourn the hearing for a period not exceeding thirty days if necessary for the purpose of ensuring that relevant information is available to permit it to make or review a disposition or for any other sufficient reason.

(13.2) Determination of mental condition of the accused — On receiving an assessment report, the court or Review Board shall determine whether, since the last time the disposition in respect of the accused was made or reviewed there has been any change in the mental condition of the accused that may provide grounds for the discharge of the accused under paragraph 672.54(a) or (b) and, if there has been such a change, the court or Review Board shall notify every victim of the offence that they are entitled to file a statement in accordance with subsection (14).

(13.3) Notice to victims — referral of finding to court — If the Review Board refers to the court for review under subsection 672.84(1) a finding that an accused is a high-risk accused, it shall notify every victim of the offence that they are entitled to file a statement with the court in accordance with subsection (14).

(14) Victim impact statement — A victim of the offence may prepare and file with the court or Review Board a written statement describing the physical or emotional harm, property damage or economic loss suffered by the victim as the result of the commission of the offence and the impact of the offence on the victim. Form 48.2 in Part XXVIII, or a form approved by the lieutenant governor in council of the province in which the court or Review Board is exercising its jurisdiction, must be used for this purpose.

(15) Copy of statement — The court or Review Board shall ensure that a copy of any statement filed in accordance with subsection (14) is provided to the accused or counsel for the accused, and the prosecutor, as soon as practicable after a verdict of not criminally responsible on account of mental disorder is rendered in respect of the offence.

(15.1) Presentation of victim statement — The court or Review Board shall, at the request of a victim, permit the victim to read a statement prepared and filed in accordance with subsection (14), or to present the statement in any other manner that the court or Review Board considers appropriate, unless the court or Review Board is of the opinion that the reading or presentation of the statement would interfere with the proper administration of justice.

(15.2) Inquiry by court or Review Board — The court or Review Board shall, as soon as practicable after a verdict of not criminally responsible on account of mental disorder is rendered in respect of an offence and before making a disposition under section 672.45, 672.47 or 672.64, inquire of the prosecutor or a victim of the offence, or any person representing a victim of the offence, whether the victim has been advised of the opportunity to prepare a statement referred to in subsection (14).

(15.3) Adjournment — On application of the prosecutor or a victim or of its own motion, the court or Review Board may adjourn the hearing held under section 672.45, 672.47 or 672.64 to permit the victim to prepare a statement referred to in subsection (14) if the court or Review Board is satisfied that the adjournment would not interfere with the proper administration of justice.

(16) [Repealed 2015, c. 13, s. 22(2).]

1991, c. 43, s. 4; 1997, c. 18, s. 84; 1999, c. 25, s. 11; 2005, c. 22, s. 16; 2014, c. 6, s. 7(1)–(3), (5); 2015, c. 13, s. 22; 2019, c. 25, s. 277

672.501 (1) Order restricting publication — sexual offences — Where a Review Board holds a hearing referred to in section 672.5 in respect of an accused who has been declared not criminally responsible on account of mental disorder or unfit to stand trial for an offence referred to in subsection 486.4(1), the Review Board shall make an order directing that any information that could identify a victim, or a witness who is under the age of eighteen years, shall not be published in any document or broadcast or transmitted in any way.

(2) Order restricting publication — child pornography — Where a Review Board holds a hearing referred to in section 672.5 in respect of an accused who has been declared not criminally responsible on account of mental disorder or unfit to stand trial for an offence referred to in section 163.1, a Review Board shall make an order directing that any information that could identify a witness who is under the age of eighteen years, or any person who is the subject of a representation, written material or a recording that constitutes child pornography within the meaning of section 163.1, shall not be published in any document or broadcast or transmitted in any way.

(3) Order restricting publication — other offences — Where a Review Board holds a hearing referred to in section 672.5 in respect of an accused who has been declared not criminally responsible on account of mental disorder or unfit to stand trial for an offence other than the offences referred to in subsection (1) or (2), on application of the prosecutor, a victim or a witness, the Review Board may make an order directing that any information that could identify the victim or witness shall not be published in any document or broadcast or transmitted in any way if the Review Board is satisfied that the order is necessary for the proper administration of justice.

(4) Order restricting publication — An order made under any of subsections (1) to (3) does not apply in respect of the disclosure of information in the course of the administration of justice if it is not the purpose of the disclosure to make the information known in the community.

(5) Application and notice — An applicant for an order under subsection (3) shall

(a) apply in writing to the Review Board; and

(b) provide notice of the application to the prosecutor, the accused and any other person affected by the order that the Review Board specifies.

(6) Grounds — An applicant for an order under subsection (3) shall set out the grounds on which the applicant relies to establish that the order is necessary for the proper administration of justice.

(7) Hearing may be held — The Review Board may hold a hearing to determine whether an order under subsection (3) should be made, and the hearing may be in private.

(8) Factors to be considered — In determining whether to make an order under subsection (3), the Review Board shall consider

(a) the right to a fair and public hearing;

(b) whether there is a real and substantial risk that the victim or witness would suffer significant harm if their identity were disclosed;

(c) whether the victim or witness needs the order for their security or to protect them from intimidation or retaliation;

(d) society's interest in encouraging the reporting of offences and the participation of victims and witnesses in the criminal justice process;

(e) whether effective alternatives are available to protect the identity of the victim or witness;

(f) the salutary and deleterious effects of the proposed order;

(g) the impact of the proposed order on the freedom of expression of those affected by it; and

(h) any other factor that the Review Board considers relevant.

(9) Conditions — An order made under subsection (3) may be subject to any conditions that the Review Board thinks fit.

(10) Publication of application prohibited — Unless the Review Board refuses to make an order under subsection (3), no person shall publish in any document or broadcast or transmit in any way

(a) the contents of an application;

(b) any evidence taken, information given or submissions made at a hearing under subsection (7); or

(c) any other information that could identify the person to whom the application relates as a victim or witness in the proceedings.

(11) Offence — Every person who fails to comply with an order made under any of subsections (1) to (3) is guilty of an offence punishable on summary conviction.

(12) Application of order — For greater certainty, an order referred to in subsection (11) also prohibits, in relation to proceedings taken against any person who fails to comply with the order, the publication in any document or the broadcasting or transmission in any way of information that could identify a victim or witness whose identity is protected by the order.

2005, c. 22, ss. 17, 64(2)

672.51 (1) Definition of "disposition information" — In this section, **"disposition information"** means all or part of an assessment report submitted to the court or Review Board and any other written information before the court or Review Board about the accused that is relevant to making or reviewing a disposition.

(2) **Disposition information to be made available to parties** — Subject to this section, all disposition information shall be made available for inspection by, and the court or Review Board shall provide a copy of it to, each party and any counsel representing the accused.

(3) **Exception where disclosure dangerous to any person** — The court or Review Board shall withhold some or all of the disposition information from an accused where it is satisfied, on the basis of that information and the evidence or report of the medical practitioner responsible for the assessment or treatment of the accused, that disclosure of the information would be likely to endanger the life or safety of another person or would seriously impair the treatment or recovery of the accused.

(4) **Idem** — Notwithstanding subsection (3), the court or Review Board may release some or all of the disposition information to an accused where the interests of justice make disclosure essential in its opinion.

(5) **Exception where disclosure unnecessary or prejudicial** — The court or Review Board shall withold disposition information from a party other than the accused or an Attorney General, where disclosure to that party, in the opinion of the court or Review Board, is not necessary to the proceeding and may be prejudicial to the accused.

(6) **Exclusion of certain persons from hearing** — A court or Review Board that withholds disposition information from the accused or any other party pursuant to subsection (3) or (5) shall exclude the accused or the other party, as the case may be, from the hearing during

(a) the oral presentation of that disposition information; or

(b) the questioning by the court or Review Board or the cross-examination of any person concerning that disposition information.

(7) **Prohibition of disclosure in certain cases** — No disposition information shall be made available for inspection or disclosed to any person who is not a party to the proceedings

(a) where the disposition information has been withheld from the accused or any other party pursuant to subsection (3) or (5); or

(b) where the court or Review Board is of the opinion that disclosure of the disposition information would be seriously prejudicial to the accused and that, in the circumstances, protection of the accused takes precedence over the public interest in disclosure.

(8) **Idem** — No part of the record of the proceedings in respect of which the accused was excluded pursuant to subparagraph 672.5(10)(*b*)(ii) or (iii) shall be made available for inspection to the accused or to any person who is not a party to the proceedings.

(9) **Information to be made available to specified persons** — Notwithstanding subsections (7) and (8), the court or Review Board may make any disposi-

tion information, or a copy of it, available on request to any person or member of a class of persons

(a) that has a valid interest in the information for research or statistical purposes, where the court or Review Board is satisfied that disclosure is in the public interest;

(b) that has a valid interest in the information for the purposes of the proper administration of justice; or

(c) that the accused requests or authorizes in writing to inspect it, where the court or Review Board is satisfied that the person will not disclose or give to the accused a copy of any disposition information withheld from the accused pursuant to subsection (3), or of any part of the record of proceedings referred to in subsection (8), or that the reasons for withholding that information from the accused no longer exist.

(10) Disclosure for research or statistical purposes — A person to whom the court or Review Board makes disposition information available under paragraph (9)(*a*) may disclose it for research or statistical purposes, but not in any form or manner that could reasonably be expected to identify any person to whom it relates.

(11) Prohibition on publication — No person shall publish in any document or broadcast or transmit in any way

(a) any disposition information that is prohibited from being disclosed pursuant to subsection (7); or

(b) any part of the record of the proceedings in respect of which the accused was excluded pursuant to subparagraph 672.5(10)(*b*)(ii) or (iii).

(12) Powers of courts not limited — Except as otherwise provided in this section, nothing in this section limits the powers that a court may exercise apart from this section.

1991, c. 43, s. 4; 1997, c. 18, s. 85; 2005, c. 22, s. 18; 2005, c. 32, s. 22; 2014, c. 6, s. 8

672.52 (1) Record of proceedings — The court or Review Board shall cause a record of the proceedings of its disposition hearings to be kept, and include in the record any assessment report submitted.

(2) Transmittal of transcript to Review Board — If a court holds a disposition hearing under subsection 672.45(1), whether or not it makes a disposition, it shall send without delay to the Review Board that has jurisdiction in respect of the matter, in original or copied form, a transcript of the hearing, any other document or information related to the hearing, and all exhibits filed with it, if the transcript, document, information or exhibits are in its possession.

(3) Reasons for disposition and copies to be provided — The court or Review Board shall state its reasons for making a disposition in the record of the proceedings, and shall provide every party with a copy of the disposition and those reasons.

1991, c. 43, s. 4; 2005, c. 22, s. 19

672.53 Proceedings not invalid — Any procedural irregularity in relation to a disposition hearing does not affect the validity of the hearing unless it causes the accused substantial prejudice.

1991, c. 43, s. 4

Dispositions by a Court or Review Board

Terms of Dispositions

672.54 Dispositions that may be made — When a court or Review Board makes a disposition under subsection 672.45(2), section 672.47, subsection 672.64(3) or section 672.83 or 672.84, it shall, taking into account the safety of the public, which is the paramount consideration, the mental condition of the accused, the reintegration of the accused into society and the other needs of the accused, make one of the following dispositions that is necessary and appropriate in the circumstances:

(a) where a verdict of not criminally responsible on account of mental disorder has been rendered in respect of the accused and, in the opinion of the court or Review Board, the accused is not a significant threat to the safety of the public, by order, direct that the accused be discharged absolutely;

(b) by order, direct that the accused be discharged subject to such conditions as the court or Review Board considers appropriate; or

(c) by order, direct that the accused be detained in custody in a hospital, subject to such conditions as the court or Review Board considers appropriate.

1991, c. 43, s. 4; 2005, c. 22, s. 20; 2014, c. 6, s. 9

672.5401 Significant threat to safety of public — For the purposes of section 672.54, a significant threat to the safety of the public means a risk of serious physical or psychological harm to members of the public — including any victim of or witness to the offence, or any person under the age of 18 years — resulting from conduct that is criminal in nature but not necessarily violent.

2014, c. 6, s. 10

672.541 Victim impact statement — If a verdict of not criminally responsible on account of mental disorder has been rendered in respect of an accused, the court or Review Board shall

(a) at a hearing held under section 672.45, 672.47, 672.64, 672.81 or 672.82 or subsection 672.84(5), take into consideration any statement filed by a victim in accordance with subsection 672.5(14) in determining the appropriate disposition or conditions under section 672.54, to the extent that the statement is relevant to its consideration of the criteria set out in section 672.54;

(b) at a hearing held under section 672.64 or subsection 672.84(3), take into consideration any statement filed by a victim in accordance with subsection 672.5(14), to the extent that the statement is relevant to its consideration of the criteria set out in subsection 672.64(1) or 672.84(3), as the case may be, in deciding whether to find that the accused is a high-risk accused, or to revoke such a finding; and

(c) at a hearing held under section 672.81 or 672.82 in respect of a high-risk accused, take into consideration any statement filed by a victim in accordance with subsection 672.5(14) in determining whether to refer to the court for review the finding that the accused is a high-risk accused, to the extent that the statement is relevant to its consideration of the criteria set out in subsection 672.84(1).

1999, c. 25, s. 12; 2005, c. 22, s. 21; 2014, c. 6, s. 10

672.542 **Additional conditions — safety and security** — When a court or Review Board holds a hearing referred to in section 672.5, the court or Review Board shall consider whether it is desirable, in the interests of the safety and security of any person, particularly a victim of or witness to the offence or a justice system participant, to include as a condition of the disposition that the accused

(a) abstain from communicating, directly or indirectly, with any victim, witness or other person identified in the disposition, or refrain from going to any place specified in the disposition; or

(b) comply with any other condition specified in the disposition that the court or Review Board considers necessary to ensure the safety and security of those persons.

2014, c. 6, s. 10

672.55 (1) **Treatment not a condition** — No disposition made under section 672.54 shall direct that any psychiatric or other treatment of the accused be carried out or that the accused submit to such treatment except that the disposition may include a condition regarding psychiatric or other treatment where the accused has consented to the condition and the court or Review Board considers the condition to be reasonable and necessary in the interests of the accused.

(2) [Repealed 2005, c. 22, s. 22.]

1991, c. 43, s. 4; 1997, c. 18, s. 86; 2005, c. 22, s. 22

672.56 (1) **Delegated authority to vary restrictions on liberty of accused** — A Review Board that makes a disposition in respect of an accused under paragraph 672.54(*b*) or (*c*) may delegate to the person in charge of the hospital authority to direct that the restrictions on the liberty of the accused be increased or decreased within any limits and subject to any conditions set out in that disposition, and any direction so made is deemed for the purposes of this Act to be a disposition made by the Review Board.

(1.1) **Exception — high-risk accused** — If the accused is a high-risk accused, any direction is subject to the restrictions set out in subsection 672.64(3).

(2) **Notice to accused and Review Board of increase in restrictions** — A person who increases the restrictions on the liberty of the accused significantly pursuant to authority delegated to the person by a Review Board shall

(a) make a record of the increased restrictions on the file of the accused; and

(b) give notice of the increase as soon as is practicable to the accused and, if the increased restrictions remain in force for a period exceeding seven days, to the Review Board.

1991, c. 43, s. 4; 2014, c. 6, s. 11(2)

672.57 Warrant of committal — Where the court or Review Board makes a disposition under paragraph 672.54(*c*), it shall issue a warrant of committal of the accused, which may be in Form 49.

1991, c. 43, s. 4

672.58 Treatment disposition — Where a verdict of unfit to stand trial is rendered and the court has not made a disposition under section 672.54 in respect of an accused, the court may, on application by the prosecutor, by order, direct that treatment of the accused be carried out for a specified period not exceeding sixty days, subject to such conditions as the court considers appropriate and, where the accused is not detained in custody, direct that the accused submit to that treatment by the person or at the hospital specified.

1991, c. 43, s. 4

672.59 (1) Criteria for disposition — No disposition may be made under section 672.58 unless the court is satisfied, on the basis of the testimony of a medical practitioner, that a specific treatment should be administered to the accused for the purpose of making the accused fit to stand trial.

(2) Evidence required — The testimony required by the court for the purposes of subsection (1) shall include a statement that the medical practitioner has made an assessment of the accused and is of the opinion, based on the grounds specified, that

(a) the accused, at the time of the assessment, was unfit to stand trial;

(b) the psychiatric treatment and any other related medical treatment specified by the medical practitioner will likely make the accused fit to stand trial within a period not exceeding sixty days and that without that treatment the accused is likely to remain unfit to stand trial;

(c) the risk of harm to the accused from the psychiatric and other related medical treatment specified is not disproportionate to the benefit anticipated to be derived from it; and

(d) the psychiatric and other related medical treatment specified is the least restrictive and least intrusive treatment that could, in the circumstances, be specified for the purpose referred to in subsection (1), considering the opinions referred to in paragraphs (*b*) and (*c*).

1991, c. 43, s. 4

672.6 (1) Notice required — The court shall not make a disposition under section 672.58 unless the prosecutor notifies the accused, in writing and as soon as practicable, of the application.

(2) Challenge by accused — On receiving the notice referred to in subsection (1), the accused may challenge the application and adduce evidence for that purpose.

1991, c. 43, s. 4; 1997, c. 18, s. 87

672.61 (1) Exception — The court shall not direct, and no disposition made under section 672.58 shall include, the performance of psychosurgery or electro-convulsive therapy or any other prohibited treatment that is prescribed.

(2) Definitions — In this section,

"electro-convulsive therapy" means a procedure for the treatment of certain mental disorders that induces, by electrical stimulation of the brain, a series of generalized convulsions;

"psychosurgery" means any procedure that by direct or indirect access to the brain removes, destroys or interrupts the continuity of histologically normal brain tissue, or inserts indwelling electrodes for pulsed electrical stimulation for the purpose of altering behaviour or treating psychiatric illness, but does not include neurological procedures used to diagnose or treat intractable physical pain, organic brain conditions, or epilepsy, where any of those conditions is clearly demonstrable.

1991, c. 43, s. 4

672.62 (1) Consent of hospital required for treatment — No court shall make a disposition under section 672.58 without the consent of

(a) the person in charge of the hospital where the accused is to be treated; or

(b) the person to whom responsibility for the treatment of the accused is assigned by the court.

(2) Consent of accused not required for treatment — The court may direct that treatment of an accused be carried out pursuant to a disposition made under section 672.58 without the consent of the accused or a person who, according to the laws of the province where the disposition is made, is authorized to consent for the accused.

1991, c. 43, s. 4

672.63 Effective date of disposition — A disposition shall come into force on the day on which it is made or on any later day that the court or Review Board specifies in it, and shall remain in force until the Review Board holds a hearing to review the disposition and makes another disposition.

1991, c. 43, s. 4; 2005, c. 22, s. 23

[Editor's Note: Sections 672.64 to 672.66 of the Criminal Code, *proposed by S.C. 1991, c. 43, would have enacted a regime for the capping of dispositions. They were repealed before they came into force by S.C. 2005, c. 22, s. 24, effective January 2, 2006.]*

High-Risk Accused

[Heading added 2014, c. 6, s. 12.]

672.64 (1) Finding — On application made by the prosecutor before any disposition to discharge an accused absolutely, the court may, at the conclusion of a hearing, find the accused to be a high-risk accused if the accused has been found not criminally responsible on account of mental disorder for a serious personal injury offence, as defined in subsection 672.81(1.3), the accused was 18 years of age or more at the time of the commission of the offence and

(a) the court is satisfied that there is a substantial likelihood that the accused will use violence that could endanger the life or safety of another person; or

(b) the court is of the opinion that the acts that constitute the offence were of such a brutal nature as to indicate a risk of grave physical or psychological harm to another person.

(2) **Factors to consider** — In deciding whether to find that the accused is a high-risk accused, the court shall consider all relevant evidence, including

(a) the nature and circumstances of the offence;

(b) any pattern of repetitive behaviour of which the offence forms a part;

(c) the accused's current mental condition;

(d) the past and expected course of the accused's treatment, including the accused's willingness to follow treatment; and

(e) the opinions of experts who have examined the accused.

(3) **Detention of high-risk accused** — If the court finds the accused to be a high-risk accused, the court shall make a disposition under paragraph 672.54(c), but the accused's detention must not be subject to any condition that would permit the accused to be absent from the hospital unless

(a) it is appropriate, in the opinion of the person in charge of the hospital, for the accused to be absent from the hospital for medical reasons or for any purpose that is necessary for the accused's treatment, if the accused is escorted by a person who is authorized by the person in charge of the hospital; and

(b) a structured plan has been prepared to address any risk related to the accused's absence and, as a result, that absence will not present an undue risk to the public.

(4) **Appeal** — A decision not to find an accused to be a high-risk accused is deemed to be a disposition for the purpose of sections 672.72 to 672.78.

(5) **For greater certainty** — For greater certainty, a finding that an accused is a high-risk accused is a disposition and sections 672.72 to 672.78 apply to it.

2014, c. 6, s. 12

Dual Status Offenders

672.67 (1) **Where court imposes a sentence** — Where a court imposes a sentence of imprisonment on an offender who is, or thereby becomes, a dual status offender, that sentence takes precedence over any prior custodial disposition, pending any placement decision by the Review Board.

(2) **Custodial disposition by court** — Where a court imposes a custodial disposition on an accused who is, or thereby becomes, a dual status offender, the disposi-

tion takes precedence over any prior sentence of imprisonment pending any placement decision by the Review Board.

1991, c. 43, s. 4; 1995, c. 22, s. 10; 2005, c. 22, s. 25

672.68 (1) Definition of "minister" — In this section and in sections 672.69 and 672.7, **"Minister"** means the Minister of Public Safety and Emergency Preparedness or the Minister responsible for correctional services of the province to which a dual status offender may be sent pursuant to a sentence of imprisonment.

(2) Placement decision by Review Board — On application by the Minister or of its own motion, where the Review Board is of the opinion that the place of custody of a dual status offender pursuant to a sentence or custodial disposition made by the court is inappropriate to meet the mental health needs of the offender or to safeguard the well-being of other persons, the Review Board shall, after giving the offender and the Minister reasonable notice, decide whether to place the offender in custody in a hospital or in a prison.

(3) Idem — In making a placement decision, the Review Board shall take into consideration

(a) the need to protect the public from dangerous persons;

(b) the treatment needs of the offender and the availability of suitable treatment resources to address those needs;

(c) whether the offender would consent to or is a suitable candidate for treatment;

(d) any submissions made to the Review Board by the offender or any other party to the proceedings and any assessment report submitted in writing to the Review Board; and

(e) any other factors that the Review Board considers relevant.

(4) Time for making placement decision — The Review Board shall make its placement decision as soon as practicable but not later than thirty days after receiving an application from, or giving notice to, the Minister under subsection (2), unless the Review Board and the Minister agree to a longer period not exceeding sixty days.

(5) Effects of placement decision — Where the offender is detained in a prison pursuant to the placement decision of the Review Board, the Minister is responsible for the supervision and control of the offender.

1991, c. 43, s. 4; 2005, c. 10, s. 34(1)(f)(xiii)

672.69 (1) Minister and Review Board entitled to access — The Minister and the Review Board are entitled to have access to any dual status offender in respect of whom a placement decision has been made, for the purpose of conducting a review of the sentence or disposition imposed.

(2) Review of placement decisions — The Review Board shall hold a hearing as soon as is practicable to review a placement decision, on application by the Minister or the dual status offender who is the subject of the decision, where the Review Board is satisfied that a significant change in circumstances requires it.

(3) Idem — The Review Board may of its own motion hold a hearing to review a placement decision after giving the Minister and the dual status offender who is subject to it reasonable notice.

(4) Minister shall be a party — The Minister shall be a party in any proceedings relating to the placement of a dual status offender.

1991, c. 43, s. 4

672.7 (1) Notice of discharge — Where the Minister or the Review Board intends to discharge a dual status offender from custody, each shall give written notice to the other indicating the time, place and conditions of the discharge.

(2) Warrant of committal — A Review Board that makes a placement decision shall issue a warrant of committal of the accused, which may be in Form 50.

1991, c. 43, s. 4

672.71 (1) Detention to count as service of term — Each day of detention of a dual status offender pursuant to a placement decision or a custodial disposition shall be treated as a day of service of the term of imprisonment, and the accused shall be deemed, for all purposes, to be lawfully confined in a prison.

(2) Disposition takes precedence over probation orders — When a dual status offender is convicted or discharged on the conditions set out in a probation order made under section 730 in respect of an offence but is not sentenced to a term of imprisonment, the custodial disposition in respect of the accused comes into force and, notwithstanding subsection 732.2(1), takes precedence over any probation order made in respect of the offence.

1991, c. 43, s. 4; 1995, c. 22, s. 10

Appeals

672.72 (1) Grounds for appeal — Any party may appeal against a disposition made by a court or a Review Board, or a placement decision made by a Review Board, to the court of appeal of the province where the disposition or placement decision was made on any ground of appeal that raises a question of law or fact alone or of mixed law and fact.

(2) Limitation period for appeal — An appellant shall give notice of an appeal against a disposition or placement decision in the manner directed by the applicable rules of the court within fifteen days after the day on which the appellant receives a copy of the placement decision or disposition and the reasons for it or within any further time that the court of appeal, or a judge of that court, may direct.

(3) Appeal to be heard expeditiously — The court of appeal shall hear an appeal against a disposition or placement decision in or out of the regular sessions of the court, as soon as practicable after the day on which the notice of appeal is given, within any period that may be fixed by the court of appeal, a judge of the court of appeal, or the rules of that court.

1991, c. 43, s. 4; 1997, c. 18, s. 88

672.73 (1) Appeal on the transcript — An appeal against a disposition by a court or Review Board or placement decision by a Review Board shall be based on a transcript of the proceedings and any other evidence that the court of appeal finds necessary to admit in the interests of justice.

(2) Additional evidence — For the purpose of admitting additional evidence under this section, subsections 683(1) and (2) apply, with such modifications as the circumstances require.

1991, c. 43, s. 4

672.74 (1) Notice of appeal to be given to court or Review Board — The clerk of the court of appeal, on receiving notice of an appeal against a disposition or placement decision, shall notify the court or Review Board that made the disposition.

(2) Transmission of records to court of appeal — On receipt of notification under subsection (1), the court or Review Board shall transmit to the court of appeal, before the time that the appeal is to be heard or within any time that the court of appeal or a judge of that court may direct,

(a) a copy of the disposition or placement decision;

(b) all exhibits filed with the court or Review Board or a copy of them; and

(c) all other material in its possession respecting the hearing.

(3) Record to be kept by court of appeal — The clerk of the court of appeal shall keep the material referred to in subsection (2) with the records of the court of appeal.

(4) Appellant to provide transcript of evidence — Unless it is contrary to an order of the court of appeal or any applicable rules of court, the appellant shall provide the court of appeal and the respondent with a transcript of any evidence taken before a court or Review Board by a stenographer or a sound recording apparatus, certified by the stenographer or in accordance with subsection 540(6), as the case may be.

(5) Saving — An appeal shall not be dismissed by the court of appeal by reason only that a person other than the appellant failed to comply with this section.

1991, c. 43, s. 4

672.75 Automatic suspension of certain dispositions — The filing of a notice of appeal against a disposition made under section 672.58 suspends the application of the disposition pending the determination of the appeal.

1991, c. 43, s. 4; 2014, c. 6, s. 13

672.76 (1) Application respecting dispositions under appeal — Any party who gives notice to each of the other parties, within the time and in the manner prescribed, may apply to a judge of the court of appeal for an order under this section respecting a disposition or placement decision that is under appeal.

(2) Discretionary powers respecting suspension of dispositions — On receipt of an application made pursuant to subsection (1) a judge of the court of appeal may, if satisfied that the mental condition of the accused justifies it,

(a) by order, direct that a disposition made under section 672.58 be carried out pending the determination of the appeal, despite section 672.75;

(a.1) by order, direct that a disposition made under paragraph 672.54(a) be suspended pending the determination of the appeal;

(b) by order, direct that the application of a placement decision or a disposition made under paragraph 672.54(*b*) or (*c*) be suspended pending the determination of the appeal;

(c) where the application of a disposition is suspended pursuant to section 672.75 or paragraph (*b*), make any other disposition in respect of the accused that is appropriate in the circumstances, other than a disposition under paragraph 672.54(*a*) or section 672.58, pending the determination of the appeal;

(d) where the application of a placement decision is suspended pursuant to an order made under paragraph (*b*), make any other placement decision that is appropriate in the circumstances, pending the determination of the appeal; and

(e) give any directions that the judge considers necessary for expediting the appeal.

(3) Copy of order to parties — A judge of the court of appeal who makes an order under this section shall send a copy of the order to each of the parties without delay.

1991, c. 43, s. 4; 2014, c. 6, s. 14

672.77 Effect of suspension of disposition — Where the application of a disposition or placement decision appealed from is suspended, a disposition, or in the absence of a disposition any order for the interim release or detention of the accused, that was in effect immediately before the disposition or placement decision appealed from took effect, shall be in force pending the determination of the appeal, subject to any disposition made under paragraph 672.76(2)(*c*).

1991, c. 43, s. 4

672.78 (1) Powers of court of appeal — The court of appeal may allow an appeal against a disposition or placement decision and set aside an order made by the court or Review Board, where the court of appeal is of the opinion that

(a) it is unreasonable or cannot be supported by the evidence;

(b) it is based on a wrong decision on a question of law; or

(c) there was a miscarriage of justice.

(2) Idem — The court of appeal may dismiss an appeal against a disposition or placement decision where the court is of the opinion

(a) that paragraphs (1)(*a*), (*b*) and (*c*) do not apply; or

(b) that paragraph (1)(*b*) may apply, but the court finds that no substantial wrong or miscarriage of justice has occurred.

(3) **Orders that the court may make** — Where the court of appeal allows an appeal against a disposition or placement decision, it may

(a) make any disposition under section 672.54 or any placement decision that the Review Board could have made;

(b) refer the matter back to the court or Review Board for rehearing, in whole or in part, in accordance with any directions that the court of appeal considers appropriate; or

(c) make any other order that justice requires.

1991, c. 43, s. 4; 1997, c. 18, s. 89

672.79 and 672.8 [Repealed 2005, c. 22, s. 26.]

Review of Dispositions

672.81 (1) Mandatory review of dispositions — A Review Board shall hold a hearing not later than twelve months after making a disposition and every twelve months thereafter for as long as the disposition remains in force, to review any disposition that it has made in respect of an accused, other than an absolute discharge under paragraph s. 672.54(*a*).

(1.1) Extension on consent — Despite subsection (1), the Review Board may extend the time for holding a hearing to a maximum of twenty-four months after the making or reviewing of a disposition if the accused is represented by counsel and the accused and the Attorney General consent to the extension.

(1.2) Extension for serious personal violence offence — Despite subsection (1), at the conclusion of a hearing under this section the Review Board may, after making a disposition, extend the time for holding a subsequent hearing under this section to a maximum of twenty-four months if

(a) the accused has been found not criminally responsible for a serious personal injury offence;

(b) the accused is subject to a disposition made under paragraph 672.54(c); and

(c) the Review Board is satisfied on the basis of any relevant information, including disposition information within the meaning of subsection 672.51(1) and an assessment report made under an assessment ordered under paragraph 672.121(a), that the condition of the accused is not likely to improve and that detention remains necessary for the period of the extension.

(1.3) Definition of "serious personal injury offence" — For the purposes of subsection (1.2), **"serious personal injury offence"** means

(a) an indictable offence involving

(i) the use or attempted use of violence against another person, or

(ii) conduct endangering or likely to endanger the life or safety of another person or inflicting or likely to inflict severe psychological damage upon another person; or

(b) an indictable offence referred to in section 151, 152, 153, 153.1, 155, 160, 170, 171, 172, 271, 272 or 273 or an attempt to commit such an offence.

(1.31) Extension on consent — high-risk accused — Despite subsections (1) to (1.2), the Review Board may extend the time for holding a hearing in respect of a high-risk accused to a maximum of 36 months after making or reviewing a disposition if the accused is represented by counsel and the accused and the Attorney General consent to the extension.

(1.32) Extension — no likely improvement — Despite subsections (1) to (1.2), at the conclusion of a hearing under subsection 672.47(4) or this section in respect of a high-risk accused, the Review Board may, after making a disposition, extend the time for holding a subsequent hearing under this section to a maximum of 36 months if the Review Board is satisfied on the basis of any relevant information, including disposition information as defined in subsection 672.51(1) and an assessment report made under an assessment ordered under paragraph 672.121(c), that the accused's condition is not likely to improve and that detention remains necessary for the period of the extension.

(1.4) Notice — If the Review Board extends the time for holding a hearing under subsection (1.2) or (1.32), it shall provide notice of the extension to the accused, the prosecutor and the person in charge of the hospital where the accused is detained.

(1.5) Appeal — A decision by the Review Board to extend the time for holding a hearing under subsection (1.2) or (1.32) is deemed to be a disposition for the purpose of sections 672.72 to 672.78.

(2) Additional mandatory reviews in custody cases — The Review Board shall hold a hearing to review any disposition made under paragraph 672.54(b) or (c) as soon as practicable after receiving notice that the person in charge of the place where the accused is detained or directed to attend requests the review.

(2.1) Review in case of increase on restrictions on liberty — The Review Board shall hold a hearing to review a decision to significantly increase the restrictions on the liberty of the accused, as soon as practicable after receiving the notice referred to in subsection 672.56(2).

(3) Idem — Where an accused is detained in custody pursuant to a disposition made under paragraph 672.54(*c*) and a sentence of imprisonment is subsequently imposed on the accused in respect of another offence, the Review Board shall hold a hearing to review the disposition as soon as is practicable after receiving notice of that sentence.

1991, c. 43, s. 4; 2005, c. 22, s. 27(2); 2014, c. 6, s. 15

672.82 (1) Discretionary review — A Review Board may hold a hearing to review any of its dispositions at any time, of its own motion or at the request of the accused or any other party.

(1.1) Review Board to provide notice — Where a Review Board holds a hearing under subsection (1) of its own motion, it shall provide notice to the prosecutor, the accused and any other party.

(2) Review cancels appeal — Where a party requests a review of a disposition under this section, the party is deemed to abandon any appeal against the disposition taken under section 672.72.

1991, c. 43, s. 4; 2005, c. 22, s. 28

672.83 (1) Disposition by Review Board — At a hearing held pursuant to section 672.81 or 672.82, the Review Board shall, except where a determination is made under subsection 672.48(1) that the accused is fit to stand trial, review the disposition made in respect of the accused and make any other disposition that the Review Board considers to be appropriate in the circumstances.

(2) [Repealed 2005, c. 22, s. 29.]

1991, c. 43, s. 4; 1997, c. 18, s. 90; 2005, c. 22, s. 29

672.84 (1) Review of finding — high-risk accused — If a Review Board holds a hearing under section 672.81 or 672.82 in respect of a high-risk accused, it shall, on the basis of any relevant information, including disposition information as defined in subsection 672.51(1) and an assessment report made under an assessment ordered under paragraph 672.121(c), if it is satisfied that there is not a substantial likelihood that the accused — whether found to be a high-risk accused under paragraph 672.64(1)(a) or (b) — will use violence that could endanger the life or safety of another person, refer the finding for review to the superior court of criminal jurisdiction.

(2) Review of conditions — If the Review Board is not so satisfied, it shall review the conditions of detention imposed under paragraph 672.54(c), subject to the restrictions set out in subsection 672.64(3).

(3) Review of finding by court — If the Review Board refers the finding to the superior court of criminal jurisdiction for review, the court shall, at the conclusion of a hearing, revoke the finding if the court is satisfied that there is not a substantial likelihood that the accused will use violence that could endanger the life or safety of another person, in which case the court or the Review Board shall make a disposition under any of paragraphs 672.54(a) to (c).

(4) Hearing and disposition — Any disposition referred to in subsection (3) is subject to sections 672.45 to 672.47 as if the revocation is a verdict.

(5) Review of conditions — If the court does not revoke the finding, it shall immediately send to the Review Board, in original or copied form, a transcript of the hearing, any other document or information related to the hearing, and all exhibits filed with it, if the transcript, document, information or exhibits are in its possession. The Review Board shall, as soon as practicable but not later than 45 days after the day on which the court decides not to revoke the finding, hold a hearing and review the conditions of detention imposed under paragraph 672.54(c), subject to the restrictions set out in subsection 672.64(3).

(6) Appeal — A decision under subsection (1) about referring the finding to the court for review and a decision under subsection (3) about revoking the finding are deemed to be dispositions for the purpose of sections 672.72 to 672.78.

2005, c. 22, s. 30; 2014, c. 6, s. 16

Power to Compel Appearance

[Heading added 2005, c. 22, s. 31.]

672.85 Bringing accused before Review Board — For the purpose of bringing the accused in respect of whom a hearing is to be held before the Review Board, including in circumstances in which the accused did not attend a previous hearing in contravention of a summons or warrant, the chairperson

(a) shall order the person having custody of the accused to bring the accused to the hearing at the time and place fixed for it; or

(b) may, if the accused is not in custody, issue a summons or warrant to compel the accused to appear at the hearing at the time and place fixed for it.

1991, c. 43, s. 4; 2005, c. 22, s. 32

Stay of Proceedings

[Heading added 2005, c. 22, s. 33.]

672.851 (1) Recommendation by Review Board — The Review Board may, of its own motion, make a recommendation to the court that has jurisdiction in respect of the offence charged against an accused found unfit to stand trial to hold an inquiry to determine whether a stay of proceedings should be ordered if

(a) the Review Board has held a hearing under section 672.81 or 672.82 in respect of the accused; and

(b) on the basis of any relevant information, including disposition information within the meaning of subsection 672.51(1) and an assessment report made under an assessment ordered under paragraph 672.121(a), the Review Board is of the opinion that

(i) the accused remains unfit to stand trial and is not likely to ever become fit to stand trial, and

(ii) the accused does not pose a significant threat to the safety of the public.

(2) Notice — If the Review Board makes a recommendation to the court to hold an inquiry, the Review Board shall provide notice to the accused, the prosecutor and any party who, in the opinion of the Review Board, has a substantial interest in protecting the interests of the accused.

(3) Inquiry — As soon as practicable after receiving the recommendation referred to in subsection (1), the court may hold an inquiry to determine whether a stay of proceedings should be ordered.

(4) Court may act on own motion — A court may, of its own motion, conduct an inquiry to determine whether a stay of proceedings should be ordered if the court is of the opinion, on the basis of any relevant information, that

(a) the accused remains unfit to stand trial and is not likely to ever become fit to stand trial; and

(b) the accused does not pose a significant threat to the safety of the public.

(5) Assessment order — If the court holds an inquiry under subsection (3) or (4), it shall order an assessment of the accused.

(6) Application — Section 672.51 applies to an inquiry of the court under this section.

(7) Stay — The court may, on completion of an inquiry under this section, order a stay of proceedings if it is satisfied

(a) on the basis of clear information, that the accused remains unfit to stand trial and is not likely to ever become fit to stand trial;

(b) that the accused does not pose a significant threat to the safety of the public; and

(c) that a stay is in the interests of the proper administration of justice.

(8) Proper administration of justice — In order to determine whether a stay of proceedings is in the interests of the proper administration of justice, the court shall consider any submissions of the prosecutor, the accused and all other parties and the following factors:

(a) the nature and seriousness of the alleged offence;

(b) the salutary and deleterious effects of the order for a stay of proceedings, including any effect on public confidence in the administration of justice;

(c) the time that has elapsed since the commission of the alleged offence and whether an inquiry has been held under section 672.33 to decide whether sufficient evidence can be adduced to put the accused on trial; and

(d) any other factor that the court considers relevant.

(9) Effect of stay — If a stay of proceedings is ordered by the court, any disposition made in respect of the accused ceases to have effect. If a stay of proceedings is not ordered, the finding of unfit to stand trial and any disposition made in respect of the accused remain in force, until the Review Board holds a disposition hearing and makes a disposition in respect of the accused under section 672.83.

2005, c. 22, s. 33

672.852 (1) Appeal — The Court of Appeal may allow an appeal against an order made under subsection 672.851(7) for a stay of proceedings, if the Court of Appeal is of the opinion that the order is unreasonable or cannot be supported by the evidence.

(2) Effect — If the Court of Appeal allows the appeal, it may set aside the order for a stay of proceedings and restore the finding that the accused is unfit to stand trial and the disposition made in respect of the accused.

2005, c. 22, s. 33

Interprovincial Transfers

672.86 (1) Interprovincial transfers — An accused who is detained in custody or directed to attend at a hospital pursuant to a disposition made by a court or Review Board under paragraph 672.54(*c*) or a court under section 672.58 may be transferred to any other place in Canada where

(a) the Review Board of the province where the accused is detained or directed to attend recommends a transfer for the purpose of the reintegration of the accused into society or the recovery, treatment or custody of the accused; and

(b) the Attorney General of the province to which the accused is being transferred, or an officer authorized by that Attorney General, and the Attorney General of the province from which the accused is being transferred, or an officer authorized by that Attorney General, give their consent.

(2) **Transfer where accused in custody** — Where an accused who is detained in custody is to be transferred, an officer authorized by the Attorney General of the province where the accused is being detained shall sign a warrant specifying the place in Canada to which the accused is to be transferred.

(2.1) **Transfer if accused not in custody** — An accused who is not detained in custody may be transferred to any other place in Canada where

(a) the Review Board of the province from which the accused is being transferred recommends a transfer for the purpose of the reintegration of the accused into society or the recovery or treatment of the accused; and

(b) the Attorney General of the province to which the accused is being transferred, or an officer authorized by that Attorney General, and the Attorney General of the province from which the accused is being transferred, or an officer authorized by that Attorney General, give their consent.

(3) **Order** — Where an accused is being transferred in accordance with subsection (2.1), the Review Board of the province from which the accused is being transferred shall, by order,

(a) direct that the accused be taken into custody and transferred pursuant to a warrant under subsection (2); or

(b) direct that the accused attend at a specified place in Canada, subject to any conditions that the Review Board of the province to or from which the accused is being transferred considers appropriate.

1991, c. 43, s. 4; 2005, c. 22, s. 34

672.87 Delivery and detention of accused — A warrant described in subsection 672.86(2) is sufficient authority

(a) for any person who is responsible for the custody of an accused to have the accused taken into custody and conveyed to the person in charge of the place specified in the warrant; and

(b) for the person specified in the warrant to detain the accused in accordance with any disposition made in respect of the accused under paragraph 672.54(*c*).

1991, c. 43, s. 4

672.88 (1) Review Board of receiving province — The Review Board of the province to which an accused is transferred under section 672.86 has exclusive jurisdiction over the accused, and may exercise the powers and shall perform the duties mentioned in sections 672.5 and 672.81 to 672.84 as if that Review Board had made the disposition in respect of the accused.

(2) Agreement — Notwithstanding subsection (1), the Attorney General of the province to which an accused is transferred may enter into an agreement subject to this Act with the Attorney General of the province from which the accused is transferred, enabling the Review Board of that province to exercise the powers and perform the duties referred to in subsection (1) in respect of the accused, in the circumstances and subject to the terms and conditions set out in agreement.

1991, c. 43, s. 4; 2014, c. 6, s. 17

672.89 (1) Other interprovincial transfers — If an accused who is detained in custody under a disposition made by a Review Board is transferred to another province otherwise than under section 672.86, the Review Board of the province from which the accused is transferred has exclusive jurisdiction over the accused and may continue to exercise the powers and shall continue to perform the duties mentioned in sections 672.5 and 672.81 to 672.84.

(2) Agreement — Notwithstanding subsection (1), the Attorneys General of the provinces to and from which the accused is to be transferred as described in that subsection may, after the transfer is made, enter into an agreement subject to this Act, enabling the Review Board of the province to which an accused is transferred to exercise the powers and perform the duties referred to in subsection (1) in respect of the accused, subject to the terms and conditions and in the circumstances set out in the agreement.

1991, c. 43, s. 4; 2014, c. 6, s. 18

Enforcement of Orders and Regulations

672.9 Execution of warrant anywhere in Canada — Any warrant or process issued in relation to an assessment order or disposition made in respect of an accused may be executed or served in any place in Canada outside the province where the order or disposition was made as if it had been issued in that province.

1991, c. 43, s. 4; 1997, c. 18, s. 91

672.91 Arrest without warrant for contravention of disposition — A peace officer may arrest an accused without a warrant at any place in Canada if the peace officer has reasonable grounds to believe that the accused has contravened or wilfully failed to comply with the assessment order or disposition or any condition of it, or is about to do so.

1991, c. 43, s. 4; 2005, c. 22, s. 36

672.92 (1) Release or delivery of accused subject to paragraph 672.54(b) disposition order — If a peace officer arrests an accused under section 672.91 who is subject to a disposition made under paragraph 672.54(b) or an assessment order, the peace officer, as soon as practicable, may release the accused from custody and

(a) issue a summons or appearance notice compelling the accused's appearance before a justice; and

(b) deliver the accused to the place specified in the disposition or assessment order.

(2) No release — A peace officer shall not release an accused under subsection (1) if the peace officer believes, on reasonable grounds,

(a) that it is necessary in the public interest that the accused be detained in custody having regard to all the circumstances, including the need to

(i) establish the identity of the accused,

(ii) establish the terms and conditions of a disposition made under section 672.54 or of an assessment order,

(iii) prevent the commission of an offence, or

(iv) prevent the accused from contravening or failing to comply with the disposition or assessment order;

(b) that the accused is subject to a disposition or an assessment order of a court, or Review Board, of another province; or

(c) that, if the accused is released from custody, the accused will fail to attend, as required, before a justice.

(3) Accused to be brought before justice — If a peace officer does not release the accused, the accused shall be taken before a justice having jurisdiction in the territorial division in which the accused is arrested, without unreasonable delay and in any event within twenty-four hours after the arrest.

(4) Accused subject to paragraph 672.54(c) disposition order — If a peace officer arrests an accused under section 672.91 who is subject to a disposition under paragraph 672.54(c), the accused shall be taken before a justice having jurisdiction in the territorial division in which the accused is arrested without unreasonable delay and, in any event, within twenty-four hours.

(5) Justice not available — If a justice described in subsection (3) or (4) is not available within twenty-four hours after the arrest, the accused shall be taken before a justice as soon as practicable.

1991, c. 43, s. 4; 2005, c. 22, s. 36

672.93 (1) Where justice to release accused — A justice shall release an accused who is brought before the justice under section 672.92 unless the justice is satisfied that there are reasonable grounds to believe that the accused has contravened or failed to comply with a disposition or an assessment order.

(1.1) Notice — If the justice releases the accused, notice shall be given to the court or Review Board, as the case may be, that made the disposition or assessment order.

(2) Order of justice pending decision of Review Board — If the justice is satisfied that there are reasonable grounds to believe that the accused has contravened or failed to comply with a disposition or an assessment order, the justice, pending a hearing of a Review Board with respect to the disposition or a hearing of a court or Review Board with respect to the assessment order, may make an order that is appropriate in the circumstances in relation to the accused, including an order that the accused be returned to a place that is specified in the disposition or assessment order. If the justice makes an order under this subsection, notice shall be given to the court or Review Board, as the case may be, that made the disposition or assessment order.

1991, c. 43, s. 4; 2005, c. 22, s. 36

672.94 Powers of Review Board — Where a Review Board receives a notice given under subsection 672.93(1.1) or (2), it may exercise the powers and shall perform the duties mentioned in sections 672.5 and 672.81 to 672.83 as if the Review Board were reviewing a disposition.

1991, c. 43, s. 4; 2005, c. 22, s. 36

672.95 Regulations — The Governor in Council may make regulations

(a) prescribing anything that may be prescribed under this Part; and

(b) generally to carry out the purposes and provisions of this Part.

1991, c. 43, s. 4

SCHEDULE TO PART XX.1 [Repealed 2005, c. 22, s. 37.]

PART XXI — APPEALS — INDICTABLE OFFENCES (SS. 673–696)

Interpretation

673. Definitions — In this Part,

"court of appeal" means the court of appeal, as defined by the definition "court of appeal" in section 2, for the province or territory in which the trial of a person by indictment is held;

"indictment" includes an information or charge in respect of which a person has been tried for an indictable offence under Part XIX;

"registrar" means the registrar or clerk of the court of appeal;

"sentence" includes

(a) a declaration made under subsection 199(3),

(b) an order made under subsection 109(1) or 110(1), section 161, subsection 164.2(1) or 194(1), section 259, 261 or 462.37, subsection 491.1(2), 730(1) or 737(2.1) or (3) or section 738, 739, 742.1, 742.3, 743.6, 745.4 or 745.5,

(c) a disposition made under section 731 or 732 or subsection 732.2(3) or (5), 742.4(3) or 742.6(9),

(d) an order made under subsection 16(1) of the *Controlled Drugs and Substances Act*, and

(e) an order made under subsection 94(1) of the *Cannabis Act*;

"trial court" means the court by which an accused was tried and includes a judge or a provincial court judge acting under Part XIX.

R.S.C. 1985, c. 27 (1st Supp.), ss. 138, 203; R.S.C. 1985, c. 23 (4th Supp.), s. 4; R.S.C. 1985, c. 42 (4th Supp.), s. 4; 1991, c. 43, s. 5 [Repealed 1995, c. 22, s. 12.]; 1992, c. 1, s. 58(1) (Sched. 1, item 12); 1993, c. 45, ss. 10, 16, 19; 1995, c. 22, s. 5(1); 1995, c. 39, ss. 155, 190(a); 1996, c. 19, s. 74; 1999, c. 5, ss. 25, 51; 1999, c. 25, ss. 13, 31(5), (8); 2002, c. 13, s. 63; 2005, c. 22, s. 38; 2006, c. 14, s. 6; 2013, c. 11, s. 2; 2018, c. 16, s. 220; 2018, c. 21, s. 21; 2019, c. 25, s. 278

Right of Appeal

674. Procedure abolished — No proceedings other than those authorized by this Part and Part XXVI shall be taken by way of appeal in proceedings in respect of indictable offences.

675. (1) Right of appeal of person convicted — A person who is convicted by a trial court in proceedings by indictment may appeal to the court of appeal

(a) against his conviction

(i) on any ground of appeal that involves a question of law alone,

(ii) on any ground of appeal that involves a question of fact or a question of mixed law and fact, with leave of the court of appeal or a judge thereof or on the certificate of the trial judge that the case is a proper case for appeal, or

(iii) on any ground of appeal not mentioned in subparagraph (i) or (ii) that appears to the court of appeal to be a sufficient ground of appeal, with leave of the court of appeal; or

(b) against the sentence passed by the trial court, with leave of the court of appeal or a judge thereof unless that sentence is one fixed by law.

(1.1) Summary conviction appeals — A person may appeal, pursuant to subsection (1), with leave of the court of appeal or a judge of that court, to that court in respect of a summary conviction or a sentence passed with respect to a summary conviction as if the summary conviction had been a conviction in proceedings by indictment if

(a) there has not been an appeal with respect to the summary conviction;

(b) the summary conviction offence was tried with an indictable offence; and

(c) there is an appeal in respect of the indictable offence.

(2) Appeal against absolute term in excess of 10 years — A person who has been convicted of second degree murder and sentenced to imprisonment for life without eligibility for parole for a specified number of years in excess of ten may appeal to the court of appeal against the number of years in excess of ten of his imprisonment without eligibility for parole.

(2.1) **Appeal against section 743.6 order** — A person against whom an order under section 743.6 has been made may appeal to the court of appeal against the order.

(2.2) **Persons under eighteen** — A person who was under the age of eighteen at the time of the commission of the offence for which the person was convicted of first degree murder or second degree murder and sentenced to imprisonment for life without eligibility for parole until the person has served the period specified by the judge presiding at the trial may appeal to the court of appeal against the number of years in excess of the minimum number of years of imprisonment without eligibility for parole that are required to be served in respect of that person's case.

(2.3) **Appeal against s. 745.51(1) order** — A person against whom an order under subsection 745.51(1) has been made may appeal to the court of appeal against the order.

(3) **Appeals against verdicts based on mental disorder** — Where a verdict of not criminally responsible on account of mental disorder or unfit to stand trial is rendered in respect of a person, that person may appeal to the court of appeal against that verdict on any ground of appeal mentioned in subparagraph (1)(*a*)(i), (ii) or (iii) and subject to the conditions described therein.

(4) **Where application for leave to appeal refused by judge** — Where a judge of the court of appeal refuses leave to appeal under this section otherwise than under paragraph (1)(*b*), the appellant may, by filing notice in writing with the court of appeal within seven days after refusal, have the application for leave to appeal determined by the court of appeal.

1991, c. 43, s. 9 (Sched., item 5); 1995, c. 42, s. 73; 1997, c. 18, s. 92; 1999, c. 31, s. 68; 2002, c. 13, s. 64; 2011, c. 5, s. 2

676. (1) **Right of Attorney General to appeal** — The Attorney General or counsel instructed by him for the purpose may appeal to the court of appeal

(a) against a judgment or verdict of acquittal or a verdict of not criminally responsible on account of mental disorder of a trial court in proceedings by indictment on any ground of appeal that involves a question of law alone;

(b) against an order of a superior court of criminal jurisdiction that quashes an indictment or in any manner refuses or fails to exercise jurisdiction on an indictment;

(c) against an order of a trial court that stays proceedings on an indictment or quashes an indictment; or

(d) with leave of the court of appeal or a judge thereof, against the sentence passed by a trial court in proceedings by indictment, unless that sentence is one fixed by law.

(1.1) **Summary conviction appeals** — The Attorney General or counsel instructed by the Attorney General may appeal, pursuant to subsection (1), with leave of the court of appeal or a judge of that court, to that court in respect of a verdict of acquittal in a summary offence proceeding or a sentence passed with respect to a summary conviction as if the summary offence proceeding was a proceeding by indictment if

(a) there has not been an appeal with respect to the summary conviction;

(b) the summary conviction offence was tried with an indictable offence; and

(c) there is an appeal in respect of the indictable offence.

(2) **Acquittal** — For the purposes of this section, a judgment or verdict of acquittal includes an acquittal in respect of an offence specifically charged where the accused has, on the trial thereof, been convicted or discharged under section 730 of any other offence.

(3) **Appeal against verdict of unfit to stand trial** — The Attorney General or counsel instructed by the Attorney General for the purpose may appeal to the court of appeal against a verdict that an accused is unfit to stand trial, on any ground of appeal that involves a question of law alone.

(4) **Appeal against ineligible parole period** — The Attorney General or counsel instructed by him for the purpose may appeal to the court of appeal in respect of a conviction for second degree murder, against the number of years of imprisonment without eligibility for parole, being less than twenty-five, that has been imposed as a result of that conviction.

(5) **Appeal against decision not to make section 743.6 order** — The Attorney General or counsel instructed by the Attorney General for the purpose may appeal to the court of appeal against the decision of the court not to make an order under section 743.6.

(6) **Appeal against decision not to make s. 745.51(1) order** — The Attorney General or counsel instructed by the Attorney General for the purpose may appeal to the court of appeal against the decision of the court not to make an order under subsection 745.51(1).

R.S.C. 1985, c. 27 (1st Supp.), s. 139; 1991, c. 43, s. 9 (Sched., item 6); 1995, c. 22, s. 10; 1995, c. 42, s. 74; 1997, c. 18, s. 93; 2002, c. 13, s. 65; 2008, c. 18, s. 28; 2011, c. 5, s. 3

676.1 Appeal re costs — A party who is ordered to pay costs may, with leave of the court of appeal or a judge of a court of appeal, appeal the order or the amount of costs ordered.

1997, c. 18, s. 94

677. Specifying grounds of dissent — Where a judge of the court of appeal expresses an opinion dissenting from the judgment of the court, the judgment of the court shall specify any grounds in law on which the dissent, in whole or in part, is based.

1994, c. 44, s. 67

Procedure on Appeals

678. (1) Notice of appeal — An appellant who proposes to appeal to the court of appeal or to obtain the leave of that court to appeal shall give notice of appeal or notice of his application for leave to appeal in such manner and within such period as may be directed by rules of court.

(2) **Extension of time** — The court of appeal or a judge thereof may at any time extend the time within which notice of appeal or notice of an application for leave to appeal may be given.

678.1 **Service where respondent cannot be found** — Where a respondent cannot be found after reasonable efforts have been made to serve him with a notice of appeal or notice of an application for leave to appeal, service of the notice of appeal or the notice of the application for leave to appeal may be effected substitutionally in the manner and within the period directed by a judge of the court of appeal.

R.S.C. 1985, c. 27 (1st Supp.), s. 140

679. (1) **Release pending determination of appeal** — A judge of the court of appeal may, in accordance with this section, release an appellant from custody pending the determination of his appeal if,

(a) in the case of an appeal to the court of appeal against conviction, the appellant has given notice of appeal or, where leave is required, notice of his application for leave to appeal pursuant to section 678;

(b) in the case of an appeal to the court of appeal against sentence only, the appellant has been granted leave to appeal; or

(c) in the case of an appeal or an application for leave to appeal to the Supreme Court of Canada, the appellant has filed and served his notice of appeal or, where leave is required, his application for leave to appeal.

(2) **Notice of application for release** — Where an appellant applies to a judge of the court of appeal to be released pending the determination of his appeal, he shall give written notice of the application to the prosecutor or to such other person as a judge of the court of appeal directs.

(3) **Circumstances in which appellant may be released** — In the case of an appeal referred to in paragraph (1)(*a*) or (*c*), the judge of the court of appeal may order that the appellant be released pending the determination of his appeal if the appellant establishes that

(a) the appeal or application for leave to appeal is not frivolous,

(b) he will surrender himself into custody in accordance with the terms of the order, and

(c) his detention is not necessary in the public interest.

(4) **Idem** — In the case of an appeal referred to in paragraph (1)(*b*), the judge of the court of appeal may order that the appellant be released pending the determination of his appeal or until otherwise ordered by a judge of the court of appeal if the appellant establishes that

(a) the appeal has sufficient merit that, in the circumstances, it would cause unnecessary hardship if he were detained in custody;

(b) he will surrender himself into custody in accordance with the terms of the order; and

(c) his detention is not necessary in the public interest.

(5) Conditions of order — Where the judge of the court of appeal does not refuse the application of the appellant, he shall order that the appellant be released

(a) on his giving an undertaking to the judge, without conditions or with such conditions as the judge directs, to surrender himself into custody in accordance with the order, or

(b) on his entering into a recognizance

(i) with one or more sureties,

(ii) with deposit of money or other valuable security,

(iii) with both sureties and deposit, or

(iv) with neither sureties nor deposit,

in such amount, subject to such conditions, if any, and before such justice as the judge directs,

and the person having the custody of the appellant shall, where the appellant complies with the order, forthwith release the appellant.

Proposed Amendment — 679(5)

(5) Conditions of release order — If the judge of the court of appeal does not refuse the appellant's application, the judge shall make a release order referred to in section 515, the form of which may be adapted to suit the circumstances, which must include a condition that the accused surrender themselves into custody in accordance with the order.

2019, c. 25, s. 279(1) [To come into force December 18, 2019.]

(5.1) Conditions — The judge may direct that the undertaking or recognizance referred to in subsection (5) include the conditions described in subsections 515(4), (4.1) and (4.2) that the judge considers desirable.

Proposed Amendment — 679(5.1)

(5.1) Immediate release of appellant — The person having the custody of the appellant shall, if the appellant complies with the release order, immediately release the appellant.

2019, c. 25, s. 279(1) [To come into force December 18, 2019.]

(6) Application of certain provisions of s. 525 — The provisions of subsections 525(5), (6) and (7) apply with such modification as the circumstances require in respect of a person who has been released from custody under subsection (5) of this section.

Proposed Amendment — 679(6)

(6) Applicable provisions — Sections 495.1, 512.3 and 524 apply, with any modifications that the circumstances require, in respect of any proceedings under this section.

2019, c. 25, s. 279(1) [To come into force December 18, 2019.]

(7) Release or detention pending hearing of reference — If, with respect to any person, the Minister of Justice gives a direction or makes a reference under section 696.3, this section applies to the release or detention of that person pending the hearing and determination of the reference as though that person were an appellant in an appeal described in paragraph (1)(a).

(7.1) Release or detention pending new trial or new hearing — Where, with respect to any person, the court of appeal or the Supreme Court of Canada orders a new trial, section 515 or 522, as the case may be, applies to the release or detention of that person pending the new trial or new hearing as though that person were charged with the offence for the first time, except that the powers of a justice under section 515 or of a judge under section 522 are exercised by a judge of the court of appeal.

(8) Application to appeals on summary conviction proceedings — This section applies to applications for leave to appeal and appeals to the Supreme Court of Canada in summary conviction proceedings.

(9) Form of undertaking or recognizance — An undertaking under this section may be in Form 12 and a recognizance under this section may be in Form 32.

Proposed Repeal — 679(9)

(9) [Repealed 2019, c. 25, s. 279(2). To come into force December 18, 2019.]

(10) Directions for expediting appeal, new trial, etc. — A judge of the court of appeal, where on the application of an appellant he does not make an order under subsection (5) or where he cancels an order previously made under this section, or a judge of the Supreme Court of Canada on application by an appellant in the case of an appeal to that Court, may give such directions as he thinks necessary for expediting the hearing of the appellant's appeal or for expediting the new trial or new hearing or the hearing of the reference, as the case may be.

R.S.C. 1985, c. 27 (1st Supp.), s. 141; 1997, c. 18, s. 95; 1999, c. 25, s. 14; 2002, c. 13, s. 66

680. (1) Review by court of appeal — A decision made by a judge under section 522 or subsection 524(4) or (5) or a decision made by a judge of the court of appeal under section 320.25 or 679 may, on the direction of the chief justice or acting chief justice of the court of appeal, be reviewed by that court and that court may, if it does not confirm the decision,

Proposed Amendment — 680(1) opening words

(1) Review by court of appeal — A decision made by a judge under section 522, a decision made under subsections 524(3) to (5) with respect to an accused referred to in paragraph 524(1)(a) or a decision made by a judge of the court of appeal under section 261 or 679 may, on the direction of the chief justice or acting chief justice of the court of appeal, be reviewed by that court and that court may, if it does not confirm the decision,

2019, c. 25, s. 280 [To come into force December 18, 2019.]

Proposed Amendment — Conditional Amendment — 680(1) opening words

On the first day on which both S.C. 2018, c. 21, s. 22 [In force December 18, 2018.] and S.C. 2019, c. 25, s. 280 [To come into force December 18, 2019.] are in force, the opening words of subsection 680(1) are replaced by the following:

> (1) Review by court of appeal — A decision made by a judge under section 522, a decision made under subsections 524(3) to (5) with respect to an accused referred to in paragraph 524(1)(a) or a decision made by a judge of the court of appeal under section 320.25 or 679 may, on the direction of the chief justice or acting chief justice of the court of appeal, be reviewed by that court and that court may, if it does not confirm the decision,

2019, c. 25, s. 402(14) [Conditions not yet satisfied.]

(a) vary the decision; or

(b) substitute such other decision as, in its opinion, should have been made.

(2) Single judge acting — On consent of the parties, the powers of the court of appeal under subsection (1) may be exercised by a judge of that court.

(3) Enforcement of decision — A decision as varied or substituted under this section shall have effect and may be enforced in all respects as though it were the decision originally made.

R.S.C. 1985, c. 27 (1st Supp.), s. 142; 1994, c. 44, s. 68; 2018, c. 21, s. 22

681. [Repealed 1991, c. 43, s. 9 (Sched., item 7).]

682. (1) Report by judge — Where, under this Part, an appeal is taken or an application for leave to appeal is made, the judge or provincial court judge who presided at the trial shall, at the request of the court of appeal or a judge thereof, in accordance with rules of court, furnish it or him with a report on the case or on any matter relating to the case that is specified in the request.

(2) Transcript of evidence — A copy or transcript of

(a) the evidence taken at the trial,

(b) any charge to the jury and any objections that were made to a charge to the jury,

(c) the reasons for judgment, if any, and

(d) the addresses of the prosecutor and the accused, if a ground for the appeal is based on either of the addresses,

shall be furnished to the court of appeal, except in so far as it is dispensed with by order of a judge of that court.

(3) [Repealed 1997, c. 18, s. 96(2).]

(4) Copies to interested parties — A party to an appeal is entitled to receive, on payment of any charges that are fixed by rules of court, a copy or transcript of any material that is prepared under subsections (1) and (2).

(5) Copy for minister of justice — The Minister of Justice is entitled, on request, to receive a copy or transcript of any material that is prepared under subsections (1) and (2).

R.S.C. 1985, c. 27 (1st Supp.), ss. 143, 203; 1997, c. 18, s. 96

683. (1) Powers of court of appeal — For the purposes of an appeal under this Part, the court of appeal may, where it considers it in the interests of justice,

(a) order the production of any writing, exhibit, or other thing connected with the proceedings;

(b) order any witness who could have been a compellable witness at the trial, whether or not he was called at the trial,

(i) to attend and be examined before the court of appeal, or

(ii) to be examined in the manner provided by rules of court before a judge of the court of appeal, or before any officer of the court of appeal or justice of the peace or other person appointed by the court of appeal for the purposes;

(c) admit, as evidence, an examination that is taken under subparagraph (*b*)(ii);

(d) receive the evidence, if tendered, of any witness, including the appellant, who is a competent but not compellable witness;

(e) order that any question arising on the appeal that

(i) involves prolonged examination of writings or accounts, or scientific or local investigation, and

(ii) cannot in the opinion of the court of appeal conveniently be inquired into before the court of appeal,

be referred for inquiry and report, in the manner provided by rules of court, to a special commissioner appointed by the court of appeal;

(f) act on the report of a commissioner who is appointed under paragraph (*e*) in so far as the court of appeal thinks fit to do so; and

(g) amend the indictment, unless it is of the opinion that the accused has been misled or prejudiced in his defence or appeal.

(2) Parties entitled to adduce evidence and be heard — In proceedings under this section, the parties or their counsel are entitled to examine or cross-examine witnesses and, in an inquiry under paragraph (1)(*e*), are entitled to be present during the inquiry, and to adduce evidence and to be heard.

(2.1) Remote appearance — In proceedings under this section, the court of appeal may order that a party appear by audioconference or videoconference, if the technological means is satisfactory to the court.

(2.2) Virtual presence of witnesses — Sections 714.1 to 714.8 apply, with any modifications that the circumstances require, to examinations and cross-examinations of witnesses under this section.

(2.3) Application of sections 715.25 and 715.26 — Sections 715.25 and 715.26 apply, with any modifications that the circumstances require, to proceedings under this section.

(3) Other powers — A court of appeal may exercise in relation to proceedings in the court, any powers not mentioned in subsection (1) that may be exercised by the court on appeals in civil matters, and may issue any process that is necessary to enforce the orders or sentences of the court, but no costs shall be allowed to the appellant or respondent on the hearing and determination of an appeal or on any proceedings preliminary or incidental thereto.

(4) Execution of process — Any process that is issued by the court of appeal under this section may be executed anywhere in Canada.

(5) Power to order suspension — If an appeal or an application for leave to appeal has been filed in the court of appeal, that court, or a judge of that court, may, when the court, or the judge, considers it to be in the interests of justice, order that any of the following be suspended until the appeal has been determined:

(a) an obligation to pay a fine;

(b) an order of forfeiture or disposition of forfeited property;

(c) an order to make restitution under section 738 or 739;

(d) an obligation to pay a victim surcharge under section 737;

(e) a probation order under section 731; and

(f) a conditional sentence order under section 742.1.

(5.1) Undertaking or recognizance — Before making an order under paragraph (5)(e) or (f), the court of appeal, or a judge of that court, may order the offender to enter into an undertaking or recognizance.

Proposed Amendment — 683(5.1)

(5.1) Release order or recognizance — Before making an order under paragraph (5)(e) or (f), the court of appeal, or a judge of that court, may make a release order or order the offender to enter into a recognizance.

2019, c. 25, s. 281(3) [To come into force December 18, 2019.]

(6) Revocation of suspension order — The court of appeal may revoke any order it makes under subsection (5) where it considers the revocation to be in the interests of justice.

(7) Undertaking or recognizance to be taken into account — If the offender has been ordered to enter into an undertaking or recognizance under subsection (5.1), the court of appeal shall, in determining whether to vary the sentence of the offender, take into account the conditions of that undertaking or recognizance and the period during which they were imposed.

Proposed Amendment — 683(7)

(7) Release order to be taken into account — If the offender is subject to a release order under subsection (5.1), the court of appeal shall, in determining whether to vary the sentence of the offender, take into account the conditions of that order and the period for which they were imposed on the offender.

2019, c. 25, s. 281(4) [To come into force December 18, 2019.]

R.S.C. 1985, c. 27 (1st Supp.), s. 144; R.S.C. 1985, c. 23 (4th Supp.), s. 5; 1995, c. 22, s. 10; 1997, c. 18, ss. 97, 141(b); 1999, c. 25, s. 15; 2002, c. 13, s. 67; 2008, c. 18, s. 29; 2019, c. 25, s. 281(1), (2)

684. (1) Legal assistance for appellant — A court of appeal or a judge of that court may, at any time, assign counsel to act on behalf of an accused who is a party to an appeal or to proceedings preliminary or incidental to an appeal where, in the opinion of the court or judge, it appears desirable in the interests of justice that the accused should have legal assistance and where it appears that the accused has not sufficient means to obtain that assistance.

(2) Counsel fees and disbursements — Where counsel is assigned pursuant to subsection (1) and legal aid is not granted to the accused pursuant to a provincial legal aid program, the fees and disbursements of counsel shall be paid by the Attorney General who is the appellant or respondent, as the case may be, in the appeal.

(3) Taxation of fees and disbursements — Where subsection (2) applies and where counsel and the Attorney General cannot agree on fees or disbursements of counsel, the Attorney General or the counsel may apply to the registrar of the court of appeal and the registrar may tax the disputed fees and disbursements.

R.S.C. 1985, c. 34 (3rd Supp.), s. 9

685. (1) Summary determination of frivolous appeals — Where it appears to the registrar that a notice of appeal, which purports to be on a ground of appeal that involves a question of law alone, does not show a substantial ground of appeal, the registrar may refer the appeal to the court of appeal for summary determination, and, where an appeal is referred under this section, the court of appeal may, if it considers that the appeal is frivolous or vexatious and can be determined without being adjourned for a full hearing, dismiss the appeal summarily, without calling on any person to attend the hearing or to appear for the respondent on the hearing.

(2) Summary determination of appeals filed in error — If it appears to the registrar that a notice of appeal should have been filed with another court, the registrar may refer the appeal to a judge of the court of appeal for summary determination, and the judge may dismiss the appeal summarily without calling on any person to attend the hearing or to appear for the respondent on the hearing.

2008, c. 18, s. 30

Powers of the Court of Appeal

686. (1) Powers — On the hearing of an appeal against a conviction or against a verdict that the appellant is unfit to stand trial or not criminally responsible on account of mental disorder, the court of appeal

(a) may allow the appeal where it is of the opinion that

(i) the verdict should be set aside on the ground that it is unreasonable or cannot be supported by the evidence,

(ii) the judgment of the trial court should be set aside on the ground of a wrong decision on a question of law, or

(iii) on any ground there was a miscarriage of justice;

(b) may dismiss the appeal where

(i) the court is of the opinion that the appellant, although he was not properly convicted on a count or part of the indictment, was properly convicted on another count or part of the indictment,

(ii) the appeal is not decided in favour of the appellant on any ground mentioned in paragraph (*a*),

(iii) notwithstanding that the court is of the opinion that on any ground mentioned in subparagraph (*a*)(ii) the appeal might be decided in favour of the appellant, it is of the opinion that no substantial wrong or miscarriage of justice has occurred, or

(iv) notwithstanding any procedural irregularity at trial, the trial court had jurisdiction over the class of offence of which the appellant was convicted and the court of appeal is of the opinion that the appellant suffered no prejudice thereby;

(c) may refuse to allow the appeal where it is of the opinion that the trial court arrived at a wrong conclusion respecting the effect of a special verdict, may order the conclusion to be recorded that appears to the court to be required by the verdict, and may pass a sentence that is warranted in law in substitution for the sentence passed by the trial court; or

(d) may set aside a conviction and find the appellant unfit to stand trial or not criminally responsible on account of mental disorder and may exercise any of the powers of the trial court conferred by or referred to in section 672.45 in any manner deemed appropriate to the court of appeal in the circumstances.

(e) [Repealed 1991, c. 43, s. 9.]

(2) Order to be made — Where a court of appeal allows an appeal under paragraph (1)(*a*), it shall quash the conviction and

(a) direct a judgment or verdict of acquittal to be entered; or

(b) order a new trial.

(3) Substituting verdict — Where a court of appeal dismisses an appeal under subparagraph (1)(*b*)(i), it may substitute the verdict that in its opinion should have been found and

(a) affirm the sentence passed by the trial court; or

(b) impose a sentence that is warranted in law or remit the matter to the trial court and direct the trial court to impose a sentence that is warranted in law.

(4) Appeal from acquittal — If an appeal is from an acquittal or verdict that the appellant or respondent was unfit to stand trial or not criminally responsible on account of mental disorder, the court of appeal may

(a) dismiss the appeal; or

(b) allow the appeal, set aside the verdict and

(i) order a new trial, or

(ii) except where the verdict is that of a court composed of a judge and jury, enter a verdict of guilty with respect to the offence of which, in its opinion, the accused should have been found guilty but for the error in law, and pass a sentence that is warranted in law, or remit the matter to the trial court and direct the trial court to impose a sentence that is warranted in law.

(5) New trial under Part XIX — Subject to subsection (5.01), if an appeal is taken in respect of proceedings under Part XIX and the court of appeal orders a new trial under this Part, the following provisions apply:

(a) if the accused, in his notice of appeal or notice of application for leave to appeal, requested that the new trial, if ordered, should be held before a court composed of a judge and jury, the new trial shall be held accordingly;

(b) if the accused, in his notice of appeal or notice of application for leave to appeal, did not request that the new trial, if ordered, should be held before a court composed of a judge and jury, the new trial shall, without further election by the accused, be held before a judge or provincial court judge, as the case may be, acting under Part XIX, other than a judge or provincial court judge who tried the accused in the first instance, unless the court of appeal directs that the new trial be held before the judge or provincial court judge who tried the accused in the first instance;

(c) if the court of appeal orders that the new trial shall be held before a court composed of a judge and jury the new trial shall be commenced by an indictment in writing setting forth the offence in respect of which the new trial was ordered; and

(d) notwithstanding paragraph (*a*), if the conviction against which the accused appealed was for an offence mentioned in section 553 and was made by a provincial court judge, the new trial shall be held before a provincial court judge acting under Part XIX, other than the provincial court judge who tried the accused in the first instance, unless the court of appeal directs that the new trial be held before the provincial court judge who tried the accused in the first instance.

(5.01) New trial under Part XIX — Nunavut — If an appeal is taken in respect of proceedings under Part XIX and the Court of Appeal of Nunavut orders a new trial under Part XXI, the following provisions apply:

(a) if the accused, in the notice of appeal or notice of application for leave to appeal, requested that the new trial, if ordered, should be held before a court composed of a judge and jury, the new trial shall be held accordingly;

(b) if the accused, in the notice of appeal or notice of application for leave to appeal, did not request that the new trial, if ordered, should be held before a court composed of a judge and jury, the new trial shall, without further election by the accused, and without a preliminary inquiry, be held before a judge, acting under Part XIX, other than a judge who tried the accused in the first instance, unless the Court of Appeal of Nunavut directs that the new trial be held before the judge who tried the accused in the first instance;

(c) if the Court of Appeal of Nunavut orders that the new trial shall be held before a court composed of a judge and jury, the new trial shall be commenced by an indictment in writing setting forth the offence in respect of which the new trial was ordered; and

(d) despite paragraph (a), if the conviction against which the accused appealed was for an indictable offence mentioned in section 553, the new trial shall be held before a judge acting under Part XIX, other than the judge who tried the accused in the first instance, unless the Court of Appeal of Nunavut directs that the new trial be held before the judge who tried the accused in the first instance.

(5.1) Election if new trial a jury trial — Subject to subsection (5.2), if a new trial ordered by the court of appeal is to be held before a court composed of a judge and jury,

(a) the accused may, with the consent of the prosecutor, elect to have the trial heard before a judge without a jury or a provincial court judge;

(b) the election shall be deemed to be a re-election within the meaning of subsection 561(5); and

(c) subsection 561(5) applies, with such modifications as the circumstances require, to the election.

(5.2) Election if new trial a jury trial — Nunavut — If a new trial ordered by the Court of Appeal of Nunavut is to be held before a court composed of a judge and jury, the accused may, with the consent of the prosecutor, elect to have the trial heard before a judge without a jury. The election shall be deemed to be a re-election within the meaning of subsection 561.1(1), and subsection 561.1(6) applies, with any modifications that the circumstances require, to the election.

(6) Where appeal allowed against verdict of unfit to stand trial — Where a court of appeal allows an appeal against a verdict that the accused is unfit to stand trial, it shall, subject to subsection (7), order a new trial.

(7) Appeal court may set aside verdict of unfit to stand trial — Where the verdict that the accused is unfit to stand trial was returned after the close of the case for the prosecution, the court of appeal may, notwithstanding that the verdict is proper, if it is of the opinion that the accused should have been acquitted at the close of the case for the prosecution, allow the appeal, set aside the verdict and direct a judgment or verdict of acquittal to be entered.

(8) Additional powers — Where a court of appeal exercises any of the powers conferred by subsection (2), (4), (6) or (7), it may make any order, in addition, that justice requires.

R.S.C. 1985, c. 27 (1st Supp.), ss. 145, 203; 1991, c. 43, s. 9 (Sched., item 8); 1997, c. 18, s. 98; 1999, c. 3, s. 52; 1999, c. 5, s. 26; 2019, c. 25, s. 282

687. (1) Powers of court on appeal against sentence — Where an appeal is taken against sentence the court of appeal shall, unless the sentence is one fixed by law, consider the fitness of the sentence appealed against, and may on such evidence, if any, as it thinks fit to require or to receive,

(a) vary the sentence within the limits prescribed by law for the offence of which the accused was convicted; or

(b) dismiss the appeal.

(2) Effect of judgment — A judgment of a court of appeal that varies the sentence of an accused who was convicted has the same force and effect as if it were a sentence passed by the trial court.

688. (1) Right of appellant to attend — Subject to subsection (2), an appellant who is in custody is entitled, if he desires, to be present at the hearing of the appeal.

(2) Appellant represented by counsel — An appellant who is in custody and who is represented by counsel is not entitled to be present

(a) at the hearing of the appeal, where the appeal is on a ground involving a question of law alone,

(b) on an application for leave to appeal, or

(c) on any proceedings that are preliminary or incidental to an appeal,

unless rules of court provide that he is entitled to be present or the court of appeal or a judge thereof gives him leave to be present.

(2.1) Manner of appearance — In the case of an appellant who is in custody and who is entitled to be present at any proceedings on an appeal, the court may order that, instead of the appellant personally appearing,

(a) at an application for leave to appeal or at any proceedings that are preliminary or incidental to an appeal, the appellant appear by audioconference or videoconference, if the technological means is satisfactory to the court; and

(b) at the hearing of the appeal, if the appellant has access to legal advice, they appear by closed-circuit television or videoconference.

(3) Argument may be oral or in writing — An appellant may present his case on appeal and his argument in writing instead of orally, and the court of appeal shall consider any case of argument so presented.

(4) Sentence in absence of appellant — A court of appeal may exercise its power to impose sentence notwithstanding that the appellant is not present.

2002, c. 13, s. 68; 2019, c. 25, s. 283

689. (1) Restitution or forfeiture of property — If the trial court makes an order for compensation or for the restitution of property under section 738 or 739 or an order of forfeiture of property under subsection 164.2(1) or 462.37(1) or (2.01), the operation of the order is suspended

(a) until the expiration of the period prescribed by rules of court for the giving of notice of appeal or of notice of application for leave to appeal, unless the accused waives an appeal; and

(b) until the appeal or application for leave to appeal has been determined, where an appeal is taken or application for leave to appeal is made.

(2) Annulling or varying order — The court of appeal may by order annul or vary an order made by the trial court with respect to compensation or the restitution of property within the limits prescribed by the provision under which the order was made by the trial court, whether or not the conviction is quashed.

R.S.C. 1985, c. 42 (4th Supp.), s. 5; 1995, c. 22, s. 10 (Sched. I, item 30); 2002, c. 13, s. 69; 2005, c. 44, s. 12

Heading and s. 690. [Repealed 2002, c. 13, s. 70.]

Appeals to the Supreme Court of Canada

691. (1) Appeal from conviction — A person who is convicted of an indictable offence and whose conviction is affirmed by the court of appeal may appeal to the Supreme Court of Canada

(a) on any question of law on which a judge of the court of appeal dissents; or

(b) on any question of law, if leave to appeal is granted by the Supreme Court of Canada.

(2) Appeal where acquittal set aside — A person who is acquitted of an indictable offence other than by reason of a verdict of not criminally responsible on account of mental disorder and whose acquittal is set aside by the court of appeal may appeal to the Supreme Court of Canada

(a) on any question of law on which a judge of the court of appeal dissents;

(b) on any question of law, if the Court of Appeal enters a verdict of guilty against the person; or

(c) on any question of law, if leave to appeal is granted by the Supreme Court of Canada.

R.S.C. 1985, c. 34 (3rd Supp.), s. 10; 1991, c. 43, s. 9 (Sched., item 9); 1997, c. 18, s. 99

692. (1) Appeal against affirmation of special verdict of not criminally responsible on account of mental disorder — A person who has been found not criminally responsible on account of mental disorder and

(a) whose verdict is affirmed on that ground by the court of appeal, or

(b) against whom a verdict of guilty is entered by the court of appeal under subparagraph 686(4)(*b*)(ii),

may appeal to the Supreme Court of Canada.

(2) Appeal against affirmation of verdict of unfit to stand trial — A person who is found unfit to stand trial and against whom that verdict is affirmed by the court of appeal may appeal to the Supreme Court of Canada.

(3) Grounds of appeal — An appeal under subsection (1) or (2) may be

(a) on any question of law on which a judge of the court of appeal dissents; or

(b) on any question of law, if leave to appeal is granted by the Supreme Court of Canada.

R.S.C. 1985, c. 34 (3rd Supp.), s. 11; 1991, c. 43, s. 9 (Sched., item 10)

693. (1) Appeal by Attorney General — Where a judgment of a court of appeal sets aside a conviction pursuant to an appeal taken under section 675 or dismisses an appeal taken pursuant to paragraph 676(1)(*a*), (*b*) or (*c*) or subsection 676(3), the Attorney General may appeal to the Supreme Court of Canada

(a) on any question of law on which a judge of the court of appeal dissents, or

(b) on any question of law, if leave to appeal is granted by the Supreme Court of Canada.

(2) Terms — Where leave to appeal is granted under paragraph (1)(*b*), the Supreme Court of Canada may impose such terms as it sees fit.

R.S.C. 1985, c. 27 (1st Supp.), s. 146; R.S.C. 1985, c. 34 (3rd Supp.), s. 12

694. Notice of appeal — No appeal lies to the Supreme Court of Canada unless notice of appeal in writing is served by the appellant on the respondent in accordance with the *Supreme Court Act*.

R.S.C. 1985, c. 34 (3rd Supp.), s. 13

694.1 (1) Legal assistance for accused — The Supreme Court of Canada or a judge thereof may, at any time, assign counsel to act on behalf of an accused who is a party to an appeal to the Court or to proceedings preliminary or incidental to an appeal to the Court where, in the opinion of the Court or judge, it appears desirable in the interests of justice that the accused should have legal assistance and where it appears that the accused has not sufficient means to obtain that assistance.

(2) Counsel fees and disbursements — Where counsel is assigned pursuant to subsection (1) and legal aid is not granted to the accused pursuant to a provincial legal aid program, the fees and disbursements of counsel shall be paid by the Attorney General who is the appellant or respondent, as the case may be, in the appeal.

(3) Taxation of fees and disbursements — Where subsection (2) applies and counsel and the Attorney General cannot agree on fees or disbursements of counsel, the Attorney General or the counsel may apply to the Registrar of the Supreme Court of Canada, and the Registrar may tax the disputed fees and disbursements.

R.S.C. 1985, c. 34 (3rd Supp.), s. 13

694.2 (1) Right of appellant to attend — Subject to subsection (2), an appellant who is in custody and who desires to be present at the hearing of the appeal before the Supreme Court of Canada is entitled to be present at it.

(2) Appellant represented by counsel — An appellant who is in custody and who is represented by counsel is not entitled to be present before the Supreme Court of Canada

(a) on an application for leave to appeal,

(b) on any proceedings that are preliminary or incidental to an appeal, or

(c) at the hearing of the appeal,

unless rules of court provide that entitlement or the Supreme Court of Canada or a judge thereof gives the appellant leave to be present.

R.S.C. 1985, c. 34 (3rd Supp.), s. 13

695. (1) Order of Supreme Court of Canada — The Supreme Court of Canada may, on an appeal under this Part, make any order that the court of appeal might have made and may make any rule or order that is necessary to give effect to its judgment.

(2) Election if new trial — Subject to subsection (3), if a new trial ordered by the Supreme Court of Canada is to be held before a court composed of a judge and jury, the accused may, with the consent of the prosecutor, elect to have the trial heard before a judge without a jury or a provincial court judge. The election is deemed to be a re-election within the meaning of subsection 561(5) and subsections 561(5) to (7) apply to it with any modifications that the circumstances require.

(3) Nunavut — If a new trial ordered by the Supreme Court of Canada is to be held before a court composed of a judge and jury in Nunavut, the accused may, with the consent of the prosecutor, elect to have the trial heard before a judge without a jury. The election is deemed to be a re-election within the meaning of subsection 561.1(6) and subsections 561.1(6) to (9) apply to it with any modifications that the circumstances require.

1999, c. 5, s. 27; 2008, c. 18, s. 31

Appeals by Attorney General of Canada

696. Right of Attorney General of Canada to appeal — The Attorney General of Canada has the same rights of appeal in proceedings instituted at the instance of the Government of Canada and conducted by or on behalf of that Government as the Attorney General of a province has under this Part.

PART XXI.1 — APPLICATIONS FOR MINISTERIAL REVIEW — MISCARRIAGES OF JUSTICE (SS. 696.1–696.6)

[Heading added 2002, c. 13, s. 71.]

696.1 (1) Application — An application for ministerial review on the grounds of miscarriage of justice may be made to the Minister of Justice by or on behalf of a person who has been convicted of an offence under an Act of Parliament or a regulation made under an Act of Parliament or has been found to be a dangerous offender or a long-term offender under Part XXIV and whose rights of judicial review or appeal with respect to the conviction or finding have been exhausted.

(2) Form of application — The application must be in the form, contain the information and be accompanied by any documents prescribed by the regulations.

2002, c. 13, s. 71

696.2 (1) Review of applications — On receipt of an application under this Part, the Minister of Justice shall review it in accordance with the regulations.

(2) Powers of investigation — For the purpose of any investigation in relation to an application under this Part, the Minister of Justice has and may exercise the powers of a commissioner under Part I of the *Inquiries Act* and the powers that may be conferred on a commissioner under section 11 of that Act.

(3) Delegation — Despite subsection 11(3) of the *Inquiries Act*, the Minister of Justice may delegate in writing to any member in good standing of the bar of a province, retired judge or any other individual who, in the opinion of the Minister, has similar background or experience the powers of the Minister to take evidence, issue subpoenas, enforce the attendance of witnesses, compel them to give evidence and otherwise conduct an investigation under subsection (2).

2002, c. 13, s. 71

696.3 (1) Definition of "court of appeal" — In this section, **"the court of appeal"** means the court of appeal, as defined by the definition "court of appeal" in section 2, for the province in which the person to whom an application under this Part relates was tried.

(2) Power to refer — The Minister of Justice may, at any time, refer to the court of appeal, for its opinion, any question in relation to an application under this Part on which the Minister desires the assistance of that court, and the court shall furnish its opinion accordingly.

(3) Powers of Minister of Justice — On an application under this Part, the Minister of Justice may

(a) if the Minister is satisfied that there is a reasonable basis to conclude that a miscarriage of justice likely occurred,

(i) direct, by order in writing, a new trial before any court that the Minister thinks proper or, in the case of a person found to be a dangerous offender or a long-term offender under Part XXIV, a new hearing under that Part, or

(ii) refer the matter at any time to the court of appeal for hearing and determination by that court as if it were an appeal by the convicted person or the person found to be a dangerous offender or a long-term offender under Part XXIV, as the case may be; or

(b) dismiss the application.

(4) No appeal — A decision of the Minister of Justice made under subsection (3) is final and is not subject to appeal.

2002, c. 13, s. 71

696.4 Considerations — In making a decision under subsection 696.3(3), the Minister of Justice shall take into account all matters that the Minister considers relevant, including

(a) whether the application is supported by new matters of significance that were not considered by the courts or previously considered by the Minister in an application in relation to the same conviction or finding under Part XXIV;

(b) the relevance and reliability of information that is presented in connection with the application; and

(c) the fact that an application under this Part is not intended to serve as a further appeal and any remedy available on such an application is an extraordinary remedy.

2002, c. 13, s. 71

696.5 Annual report — The Minister of Justice shall within six months after the end of each financial year submit an annual report to Parliament in relation to applications under this Part.

2002, c. 13, s. 71

696.6 Regulations — The Governor in Council may make regulations

(a) prescribing the form of, the information required to be contained in any documents that must accompany an application under this Part;

(b) prescribing the process of review in relation to applications under this Part, which may include the following stages, namely, preliminary assessment, investigation, reporting on investigation and decision; and

(c) respecting the form and content of the annual report under section 696.5.

2002, c. 13, s. 71

PART XXII — PROCURING ATTENDANCE (SS. 697–715.2)

Application

697. Application — Except where section 527 applies, this Part applies where a person is required to attend to give evidence in a proceeding to which this Act applies.

R.S.C. 1985, c. 27 (1st Supp.), s. 147

Process

698. (1) Subpoena — Where a person is likely to give material evidence in a proceeding to which this Act applies, a subpoena may be issued in accordance with this Part requiring that person to attend to give evidence.

(2) Warrant in form 17 — Where it is made to appear that a person who is likely to give material evidence

(a) will not attend in response to a subpoena if a subpoena is issued, or

(b) is evading service of a subpoena,

a court, justice or provincial court judge having power to issue a subpoena to require the attendance of that person to give evidence may issue a warrant in Form 17 to cause that person to be arrested and to be brought to give evidence.

(3) Subpoena issued first — Except where paragraph (2)(*a*) applies, a warrant in Form 17 shall not be issued unless a subpoena has first been issued.

R.S.C. 1985, c. 27 (1st Supp.), s. 203

699. (1) Who may issue — If a person is required to attend to give evidence before a superior court of criminal jurisdiction, a court of appeal, an appeal court or a court of criminal jurisdiction other than a provincial court judge acting under Part XIX, a subpoena directed to that person shall be issued out of the court before which the attendance of that person is required.

(2) Order of judge — If a person is required to attend to give evidence before a provincial court judge acting under Part XIX or a summary conviction court under Part XXVII or in proceedings over which a justice has jurisdiction, a subpoena directed to the person shall be issued

(a) by a provincial court judge or a justice, where the person whose attendance is required is within the province in which the proceedings were instituted; or

(b) by a provincial court judge or out of a superior court of criminal jurisdiction of the province in which the proceedings were instituted, where the person whose attendance is required is not within the province.

(3) Order of judge — A subpoena shall not be issued out of a superior court of criminal jurisdiction pursuant to paragraph (2)(*b*), except pursuant to an order of a judge of the court made on application by a party to the proceedings.

(4) Seal — A subpoena or warrant that is issued by a court under this Part shall be under the seal of the court and shall be signed by a judge of the court or by the clerk of the court.

(5) Signature — A subpoena or warrant that is issued by a justice or provincial court judge under this Part must be signed by the justice, provincial court judge or the clerk of the court.

(5.1) Sexual offences — Despite anything in subsections (1) to (5), in the case of an offence referred to in subsection 278.2(1), a subpoena requiring a witness to bring to the court a record, the production of which is governed by sections 278.1 to 278.91, must be issued by a judge and signed by the judge or the clerk of the court.

(6) Form of subpoena — Subject to subsection (7), a subpoena issued under this Part may be in Form 16.

(7) Form of subpoena in sexual offences — In the case of an offence referred to in subsection 278.2(1), a subpoena requiring a witness to bring anything to the court shall be in Form 16.1.

R.S.C. 1985, c. 27 (1st Supp.), s. 203; 1994, c. 44, s. 69; 1997, c. 30, s. 2; 1999, c. 5, s. 28; 2019, c. 25, s. 284

700. (1) Contents of subpoena — A subpoena shall require the person to whom it is directed to attend, at a time and place to be stated in the subpoena, to give evidence and, if required, to bring with him anything that he has in his possession or under his control relating to the subject-matter of the proceedings.

(2) Witness to appear and remain — A person who is served with a subpoena issued under this Part shall attend and shall remain in attendance throughout the proceedings unless he is excused by the presiding judge, justice or provincial court judge.

R.S.C. 1985, c. 27 (1st Supp.), ss. 148, 203

700.1 (1) Video links — If a person is to give evidence under section 714.1 or under subsection 46(2) of the *Canada Evidence Act* — or is to give evidence or a statement under an order made under section 22.2 of the *Mutual Legal Assistance in Criminal Matters Act* — at a place within the jurisdiction of a court referred to in subsection 699(1) or (2) where the technology is available, a subpoena shall be issued out of the court to order the person to give that evidence at that place.

(2) Sections of *Criminal Code* — Sections 699, 700 and 701 to 703.2 apply, with any modifications that the circumstances require, to a subpoena issued under this section.

1999, c. 18, s. 94; 2019, c. 25, s. 285

Execution or Service of Process

701. (1) Service — Subject to subsection (2), a subpoena shall be served in a province by a peace officer or any other person who is qualified in that province to serve civil process, in accordance with subsection 509(2), with such modifications as the circumstances require.

(2) Personal service — A subpoena that is issued pursuant to paragraph 699(2)(*b*) shall be served personally on the person to whom it is directed.

(3) [Repealed 2008, c. 18, s. 32.]

1994, c. 44, s. 70; 2008, c. 18, s. 32

701.1 Service in accordance with provincial laws — Despite section 701, in any province, service of a document may be made in accordance with the laws of the province relating to offences created by the laws of that province.

1997, c. 18, s. 100; 2008, c. 18, s. 33

702. (1) Subpoena effective throughout Canada — A subpoena that is issued by a provincial court judge or out of a superior court of criminal jurisdiction, a court of appeal, an appeal court or a court of criminal jurisdiction has effect anywhere in Canada according to its terms.

(2) Subpoena effective throughout province — A subpoena that is issued by a justice has effect anywhere in the province in which it is issued.

R.S.C. 1985, c. 27 (1st Supp.), s. 203; 1994, c. 44, s. 71

703. (1) Warrant effective throughout Canada — Notwithstanding any other provision of this Act, a warrant of arrest or committal that is issued out of a superior court of criminal jurisdiction, a court of appeal, an appeal court within the meaning of section 812 or a court of criminal jurisdiction other than a provincial court judge acting under Part XIX may be executed anywhere in Canada.

(2) Warrant effective in a province — Despite any other provision of this Act but subject to subsections 487.0551(2) and 705(3), a warrant of arrest or committal that is issued by a justice or provincial court judge may be executed anywhere in the province in which it is issued.

R.S.C. 1985, c. 27 (1st Supp.), s. 149; 2007, c. 22, s. 22

703.1 Summons effective throughout Canada — A summons may be served anywhere in Canada and, if served, is effective notwithstanding the territorial jurisdiction of the authority that issued the summons.

R.S.C. 1985, c. 27 (1st Supp.), s. 149

703.2 Service of process on an organization — Where any summons, notice or other process is required to be or may be served on an organization, and no other method of service is provided, service may be effected by delivery

(a) in the case of a municipality, to the mayor, warden, reeve or other chief officer of the municipality, or to the secretary, treasurer or clerk of the municipality; and

(b) in the case of any other organization, to the manager, secretary or other senior officer of the organization or one of its branches.

R.S.C. 1985, c. 27 (1st Supp.), s. 149; 2003, c. 21, s. 13

Defaulting or Absconding Witness

704. (1) Warrant for absconding witness — Where a person is bound by recognizance to give evidence in any proceedings, a justice who is satisfied on information being made before him in writing and under oath that the person is about to abscond or has absconded may issue his warrant in Form 18 directing a peace officer to arrest that person and to bring him before the court, judge, justice or provincial court judge before whom he is bound to appear.

(2) Endorsement of warrant — Section 528 applies, with such modifications as the circumstances require, to a warrant issued under this section.

(3) Copy of information — A person who is arrested under this section is entitled, on request, to receive a copy of the information on which the warrant for his arrest was issued.

R.S.C. 1985, c. 27 (1st Supp.), s. 203

705. (1) Warrant if witness does not attend — If a person who has been served with a subpoena to give evidence in a proceeding does not attend or remain in attendance, the court, judge, justice or provincial court judge before whom that person was required to attend may issue a warrant in Form 17 for the arrest of that person if it is established

(a) that the subpoena has been served in accordance with this Part, and

(b) that the person is likely to give material evidence.

(2) Warrant if witness bound by recognizance — If a person who has been bound by a recognizance to attend to give evidence in any proceeding does not attend or does not remain in attendance, the court, judge, justice or provincial court judge before whom that person was bound to attend may issue a warrant in Form 17 for the arrest of that person.

(3) Warrant effective throughout Canada — A warrant that is issued by a justice or provincial court judge pursuant to subsection (1) or (2) may be executed anywhere in Canada.

R.S.C. 1985, c. 27 (1st Supp.), s. 203; 2019, c. 25, s. 286

706. Order where witness arrested under warrant — Where a person is brought before a court, judge, justice or provincial court judge under a warrant issued pursuant to subsection 698(2), or section 704 or 705, the court, judge, justice or provincial court judge may order that the person

(a) be detained in custody, or

(b) be released on recognizance in Form 32, with or without sureties,

to appear and give evidence when required.

Proposed Amendment — 706

706. If witness arrested under warrant — If a person is brought before a court, judge, provincial court judge or justice under a warrant issued under subsection 698(2) or section 704 or 705, the court, judge, provincial court judge or justice may, so that the person will appear and give evidence when required, order that the person be detained in custody or be released on recognizance, with or without sureties.

2019, c. 25, s. 287 [To come into force December 18, 2019.]

R.S.C. 1985, c. 27 (1st Supp.), s. 203

707. (1) Maximum period for detention of witness — No person shall be detained in custody under the authority of any provision of this Act, for the purpose only of appearing and giving evidence when required as a witness, for any period exceeding thirty days unless prior to the expiration of those thirty days he has been brought before a judge of a superior court of criminal jurisdiction in the province in which he is being detained.

(2) Application by witness to judge — Where at any time prior to the expiration of the thirty days referred to in subsection (1), a witness being detained in custody as described in that subsection applies to be brought before a judge of a court described therein, the judge before whom the application is brought shall fix a time prior to the expiration of those thirty days for the hearing of the application and shall cause notice of the time so fixed to be given to the witness, the person having custody of the witness and such other persons as the judge may specify, and at the time so fixed for the hearing of the application the person having custody of the witness shall cause the witness to be brought before a judge of the court for that purpose.

(3) Review of detention — If the judge before whom a witness is brought under this section is not satisfied that the continued detention of the witness is justified, he shall order him to be discharged, or to be released on recognizance in Form 32, with or without sureties, to appear and to give evidence when required, but if the judge is satisfied that the continued detention of the witness is justified, he may order his continued detention until the witness does what is required of him pursuant to section 550 or the trial is concluded, or until the witness appears and gives evidence when required, as the case may be, except that the total period of detention of the witness from the time he was first detained in custody shall not in any case exceed ninety days.

Proposed Amendment — 707(3)

(3) Review of detention — If the judge before whom a witness is brought under this section is not satisfied that the continued detention of the witness is justified, the judge shall order them to be discharged or to be released on recognizance, with or without sureties, so that the witness will appear and give evidence when required. However, if the judge is satisfied that the continued detention of the witness is justified, the judge may order their continued detention until they do what is required of them under section 550 or the trial is concluded, or until they appear and give evidence when required, except that the total period of detention of the witness from the time they were first detained in custody shall not in any case exceed 90 days.

2019, c. 25, s. 288 [To come into force December 18, 2019.]

708. (1) Contempt — A person who, being required by law to attend or remain in attendance for the purpose of giving evidence, fails, without lawful excuse, to attend or remain in attendance accordingly is guilty of contempt of court.

(2) Punishment — A court, judge, justice or provincial court judge may deal summarily with a person who is guilty of contempt of court under this section and that person is liable to a fine not exceeding one hundred dollars or to imprisonment for a term not exceeding ninety days or to both, and may be ordered to pay the costs that are incident to the service of any process under this Part and to his detention, if any.

(3) Form — A conviction under this section may be in Form 38 and a warrant of committal in respect of a conviction under this section may be in Form 25.

R.S.C. 1985, c. 27 (1st Supp.), s. 203

Electronically Transmitted Copies

708.1 Electronically transmitted copies — A copy of a summons, warrant or subpoena transmitted by a means of telecommunication that produces a writing has the same probative force as the original for the purposes of this Act.

1997, c. 18, s. 101

Evidence on Commission

709. (1) Order appointing commissioner — A party to proceedings by way of indictment or summary conviction may apply for an order appointing a commissioner to take the evidence of a witness who

(a) is, by reason of

(i) physical disability arising out of illness, or

(ii) any other good and sufficient cause,

not likely to be able to attend at the time the trial is held; or

(b) is out of Canada.

(2) Idem — A decision under subsection (1) is deemed to have been made at the trial held in relation to the proceedings mentioned in that subsection.

R.S.C. 1985, c. 27 (1st Supp.), s. 150; 1994, c. 44, s. 72

710. (1) Application where witness is ill — An application under paragraph 709(1)(*a*) shall be made

(a) to a judge of a superior court of the province in which the proceedings are taken,

(b) to a judge of a county or district court in the territorial division in which the proceedings are taken, or

(c) to a provincial court judge, where

(i) at the time the application is made, the accused is before a provincial court judge presiding over a preliminary inquiry under Part XVIII, or

(ii) the accused or defendant is to be tried by a provincial court judge acting under Part XIX or XXVII.

(2) Evidence of medical practitioner — An application under subparagraph 709(1)(a)(i) may be granted on the evidence of a registered medical practitioner.

R.S.C. 1985, c. 27 (1st Supp.), s. 151; 1994, c. 44, s. 73

711. Admitting evidence of witness who is ill — Where the evidence of a witness mentioned in paragraph 709(1)(a) is taken by a commissioner appointed under section 710, it may be admitted in evidence in the proceedings if

(a) it is proved by oral evidence or by affidavit that the witness is unable to attend by reason of death or physical disability arising out of illness or some other good and sufficient cause,

(b) the transcript of the evidence is signed by the commissioner by or before whom it purports to have been taken; and

(c) it is proved to the satisfaction of the court that reasonable notice of the time for taking the evidence was given to the other party, and that the accused or his counsel, or the prosecutor or his counsel, as the case may be, had or might have had full opportunity to cross-examine the witness.

R.S.C. 1985, c. 27 (1st Supp.), s. 152; 1994, c. 44, s. 74; 1997, c. 18, s. 102

712. (1) Application for order when witness out of Canada — An application that is made under paragraph 709(1)(*b*) shall be made

(a) to a judge of a superior court of criminal jurisdiction or of a court of criminal jurisdiction before which the accused is to be tried; or

(b) to a provincial court judge, where the accused or defendant is to be tried by a provincial court judge acting under Part XIX or XXVII.

(2) Admitting evidence of witness out of Canada — Where the evidence of a witness is taken by a commissioner appointed under this section, it may be admitted in evidence in the proceedings.

(3) [Repealed R.S.C. 1985, c. 27 (1st Supp.), s. 153(2).]

R.S.C. 1985, c. 27 (1st Supp.), s. 153; 1994, c. 44, s. 75; 1997, c. 18, s. 103

713. (1) Providing for presence of accused counsel — A judge or provincial court judge who appoints a commissioner may make provision in the order to enable an accused to be present or represented by counsel when the evidence is taken, but failure of the accused to be present or to be represented by counsel in accordance with the order does not prevent the admission of the evidence in the proceedings if the evidence has otherwise been taken in accordance with the order and with this Part.

(2) Return of evidence — An order for the taking of evidence by commission shall indicate the officer of the court to whom the evidence that is taken under the order shall be returned.

R.S.C. 1985, c. 27 (1st Supp.), s. 203; 1997, c. 18, s. 104

713.1 Evidence not excluded — Evidence taken by a commissioner appointed under section 712 shall not be excluded by reason only that it would have been taken differently in Canada, provided that the process used to take the evidence is consistent with the law of the country where it was taken and that the process used to take the evidence was not contrary to the principles of fundamental justice.

1994, c. 44, s. 76

714. Rules and practice same as in civil cases — Except where otherwise provided by this Part or by rules of court, the practice and procedure in connection with the appointment of commissioners under this Part, the taking of evidence by commissioners, the certifying and return thereof and the use of the evidence in the proceedings shall, as far as possible, be the same as those that govern like matters in civil proceedings in the superior court of the province in which the proceedings are taken.

Video and Audio Evidence

714.1 Audioconference and videoconference — witness in Canada — A court may order that a witness in Canada give evidence by audioconference or videoconference, if the court is of the opinion that it would be appropriate having regard to all the circumstances, including

(a) the location and personal circumstances of the witness;

(b) the costs that would be incurred if the witness were to appear personally;

(c) the nature of the witness' anticipated evidence;

(d) the suitability of the location from where the witness will give evidence;

(e) the accused's right to a fair and public hearing;

(f) the nature and seriousness of the offence; and

(g) any potential prejudice to the parties caused by the fact that the witness would not be seen by them, if the court were to order the evidence to be given by audioconference.

1999, c. 18, s. 95; 2019, c. 25, s. 290

714.2 (1) Videoconference — witness outside Canada — A court shall receive evidence given by a witness outside Canada by videoconference, unless one of the parties satisfies the court that the reception of such testimony would be contrary to the principles of fundamental justice.

(2) Notice — A party who wishes to call a witness to give evidence under subsection (1) shall give notice to the court before which the evidence is to be given and the other parties of their intention to do so not less than 10 days before the witness is scheduled to testify.

1999, c. 18, s. 95; 2019, c. 25, s. 290

714.3 Audioconference — witness outside Canada — The court may receive evidence given by a witness outside Canada by audioconference, if the court is of the opinion that it would be appropriate having regard to all the circumstances, including those set out in paragraphs 714.1(a) to (g).

1999, c. 18, s. 95; 2019, c. 25, s. 290

714.4 Reasons — If the court does not make an order under section 714.1 or does not receive evidence under section 714.2 or 714.3, it shall include in the record a statement of the reasons for not doing so.

1999, c. 18, s. 95; 2019, c. 25, s. 290

714.41 Cessation — The court may, at any time, cease the use of the technological means referred to in section 714.1, 714.2 or 714.3 and take any measure that the court considers appropriate in the circumstances to have the witness give evidence.

2019, c. 25, s. 290

714.5 Oath or affirmation — The evidence referred to in section 714.2 or 714.3, that is given by a witness who is outside of Canada, shall be given

(a) under oath or affirmation in accordance with Canadian law;

(b) under oath or affirmation in accordance with the law in the place where the witness is physically present; or

(c) in any other manner that demonstrates that the witness understands that they must tell the truth.

1999, c. 18, s. 95; 2019, c. 25, s. 290

714.6 Other laws about witnesses to apply — When a witness who is outside Canada gives evidence under section 714.2 or 714.3, the evidence is deemed to be given in Canada, and given under oath or affirmation in accordance with Canadian law, for the purposes of the laws relating to evidence, procedure, perjury and contempt of court.

1999, c. 18, s. 95; 2019, c. 25, s. 290

714.7 Costs of technology — Unless the court orders otherwise, a party who calls a witness to give evidence by means of the technology referred to in section 714.1, 714.2 or 714.3 shall pay any costs associated with the use of the technology.

1999, c. 18, s. 95; 2019, c. 25, s. 290

714.8 Consent — Nothing in sections 714.1 to 714.7 is to be construed as preventing a court from receiving evidence by audioconference or videoconference, if the parties so consent.

1999, c. 18, s. 95; 2019, c. 25, s. 290

Evidence Previously Taken

715. (1) Evidence at preliminary inquiry may be read at trial in certain cases — Where, at the trial of an accused, a person whose evidence was given at a previous trial on the same charge, or whose evidence was taken in the investigation of the charge against the accused or on the preliminary inquiry into the charge, refuses to be sworn or to give evidence, or if facts are proved on oath from which it can be inferred reasonably that the person

(a) is dead,

(b) has since become and is insane,

(c) is so ill that he is unable to travel or testify, or

(d) is absent from Canada,

and where it is proved that the evidence was taken in the presence of the accused, it may be admitted as evidence in the proceedings without further proof, unless the accused proves that the accused did not have full opportunity to cross-examine the witness.

(2) Admission of evidence — Evidence that has been taken on the preliminary inquiry or other investigation of a charge against an accused may be admitted as evidence in the prosecution of the accused for any other offence on the same proof and in the same manner in all respects, as it might, according to law, be admitted as evidence in the prosecution of the offence with which the accused was charged when the evidence was taken.

(2.1) Admission of evidence — Despite subsections (1) and (2), evidence that has been taken at a preliminary inquiry in the absence of the accused may be admitted as evidence for the purposes referred to in those subsections if the accused was absent further to the permission of a justice granted under paragraph 537(1)(j.1).

(3) Absconding accused deemed present — For the purposes of this section, where evidence was taken at a previous trial or preliminary hearing or other proceeding in respect of an accused in the absence of the accused, who was absent by reason of having absconded, the accused is deemed to have been present during the taking of the evidence and to have had full opportunity to cross-examine the witness.

(4) Exception — Subsections (1) to (3) do not apply in respect of evidence received under subsection 540(7).

1994, c. 44, s. 77; 1997, c. 18, s. 105; 2002, c. 13, s. 72; 2008, c. 18, s. 34

715.01 (1) Transcript of evidence — Despite section 715, the transcript of testimony given by a **"police officer"**, as defined in section 183, in the presence of an accused during a *voir dire* or preliminary inquiry held in relation to the accused's trial may be received in evidence at that trial.

(2) Notice of intention to produce evidence — No transcript is to be received in evidence unless the party intending to produce it has given to the party against whom it is intended to be produced reasonable notice of that intention together with a copy of the transcript.

(3) Attendance of police officer — The court may require the attendance of the police officer for the purposes of examination or cross-examination, as the case may be.

(4) Admission of evidence — Despite subsection (1), evidence that has been taken at a preliminary inquiry in the absence of an accused may be received in evidence for the purposes referred to in that subsection if the accused's absence was authorized by a justice under paragraph 537(1)(j.1).

(5) Absconding accused deemed present — For the purposes of this section, if evidence was taken during a *voir dire* or preliminary inquiry in the absence of an accused, who was absent by reason of having absconded, the accused is deemed to have been present during the taking of the evidence and to have had full opportunity to cross-examine the witness.

(6) Exception — This section does not apply to any evidence received under subsection 540(7).

2019, c. 25, s. 291

Video-recorded Evidence

[Heading amended 2005, c. 32, s. 23.]

715.1 (1) Evidence of victim or witness under 18 — In any proceeding against an accused in which a victim or other witness was under the age of eighteen years at the time the offence is alleged to have been committed, a video recording made within a reasonable time after the alleged offence, in which the victim or witness describes the acts complained of, is admissible in evidence if the victim or witness, while testifying, adopts the contents of the video recording, unless the presiding judge or justice is of the opinion that admission of the video recording in evidence would interfere with the proper administration of justice.

(2) Order prohibiting use — The presiding judge or justice may prohibit any other use of a video recording referred to in subsection (1).

R.S.C. 1985, c. 19 (3d Supp.), s. 16; 1997, c. 16, s. 7; 2005, c. 32, s. 23

715.2 (1) Evidence of victim or witness who has a disability — In any proceeding against an accused in which a victim or other witness is able to communicate evidence but may have difficulty doing so by reason of a mental or physical disability, a video recording made within a reasonable time after the alleged offence, in which the victim or witness describes the acts complained of, is admissible in evidence if the victim or witness, while testifying, adopts the contents of the video recording, unless the presiding judge or justice is of the opinion that admission of the video recording in evidence would interfere with the proper administration of justice.

(2) Order prohibiting use — The presiding judge or justice may prohibit any other use of a video recording referred to in subsection (1).

1998, c. 9, s. 8; 2005, c. 32, s. 23

PART XXII.01 — REMOTE ATTENDANCE BY CERTAIN PERSONS (SS. 715.21–715.26)

[Heading added 2019, c. 25, s. 292.]

Principles

[Heading added 2019, c. 25, s. 292.]

715.21 Attendance — Except as otherwise provided in this Act, a person who appears at, participates in or presides at a proceeding shall do so personally.

2019, c. 25, s. 292

715.22 Provisions providing for audioconference or videoconference — The purpose of the provisions of this Act that allow a person to appear at, participate in or preside at a proceeding by audioconference or videoconference, in accordance with the rules of court, is to serve the proper administration of justice, including by ensuring fair and efficient proceedings and enhancing access to justice.

2019, c. 25, s. 292

Accused

[Heading added 2019, c. 25, s. 292.]

715.23 (1) Appearance by audioconference or videoconference — Except as otherwise provided in this Act, the court may order an accused to appear by audioconference or videoconference, if the court is of the opinion that it would be appropriate having regard to all the circumstances, including

(a) the location and personal circumstances of the accused;

(b) the costs that would be incurred if the accused were to appear personally;

(c) the suitability of the location from where the accused will appear;

(d) the accused's right to a fair and public hearing; and

(e) the nature and seriousness of the offence.

(2) Reasons — If the court does not make an order under subsection (1) it shall include in the record a statement of the reasons for not doing so.

(3) Cessation — The court may, at any time, cease the use of the technological means referred to in subsection (1) and take any measure that the court considers appropriate in the circumstances to have the accused appear at the proceeding.

2019, c. 25, s. 292

715.24 Accused in prison — Despite anything in this Act, if an accused who is in prison does not have access to legal advice during the proceedings, the court shall, before permitting the accused to appear by videoconference, be satisfied that the accused will be able to understand the proceedings and that any decisions made by the accused during the proceedings will be voluntary.

2019, c. 25, s. 292

Participants

[Heading added 2019, c. 25, s. 292.]

715.25 (1) Definition of "participant" — In this section, **"participant"** means any person, other than an accused, a witness, a juror, a judge or a justice, who may participate in a proceeding.

(2) Participation by audioconference or videoconference — Except as otherwise provided in this Act, the court may order a participant to participate in a proceeding by audioconference or videoconference, if the court is of the opinion that it would be appropriate having regard to all the circumstances, including

(a) the location and personal circumstances of the participant;

(b) the costs that would be incurred if the participant were to participate personally;

(c) the nature of the participation;

(d) the suitability of the location from where the participant will participate;

(e) the accused's right to a fair and public hearing; and

(f) the nature and seriousness of the offence.

(3) Reasons — If the court does not make an order under subsection (2) it shall include in the record a statement of the reasons for not doing so.

(4) Cessation — The court may, at any time, cease the use of the technological means referred to in subsection (2) and take any measure that the court considers appropriate in the circumstances to have the participant participate in the proceeding.

(5) Costs — Unless the court orders otherwise, a party who has a participant participate by audioconference or videoconference shall pay any costs associated with the use of that technology.

2019, c. 25, s. 292

Judge or Justice

[Heading added 2019, c. 25, s. 292.]

715.26 (1) Presiding by audioconference or videoconference — Except as otherwise provided in this Act, the judge or justice may preside at the proceeding by audioconference or videoconference, if the judge or justice considers it necessary having regard to all the circumstances, including

(a) the accused's right to a fair and public hearing;

(b) the nature of the witness' anticipated evidence;

(c) the nature and seriousness of the offence; and

(d) the suitability of the location from where the judge or justice will preside.

(2) Reasons — The judge or justice shall include in the record a statement of the judge or justice's reasons for the decision to preside at the proceeding by audioconference or videoconference.

(3) Cessation — The judge or justice may, at any time, cease the use of the technological means referred to in subsection (1) and take any measure that the judge or justice considers appropriate in the circumstances to preside at the proceeding.

2019, c. 25, s. 292

PART XXII.1 — REMEDIATION AGREEMENTS (SS. 715.3–715.43)

[Heading added 2018, c. 12, s. 404.]

715.3 (1) Definitions — The following definitions apply in this Part.

"court" means a superior court of criminal jurisdiction but does not include a court of appeal. *("tribunal")*

"offence" means any offence listed in the schedule to this Part. *("infraction")*

"organization" has the same meaning as in section 2 but does not include a public body, trade union or municipality. *("organisation")*

"remediation agreement" means an agreement, between an organization accused of having committed an offence and a prosecutor, to stay any proceedings related to that offence if the organization complies with the terms of the agreement. *("accord de réparation")*

"victim" has the same meaning as in section 2 but, with respect to an offence under section 3 or 4 of the *Corruption of Foreign Public Officials Act*, it includes any person outside Canada. *("victime")*

(2) Acting on victim's behalf — For the purposes of this Part, a third party not referred to in section 2.2 may also act on a victim's behalf when authorized to do so by the court, if the victim requests it or the prosecutor deems it appropriate.

2018, c. 12, s. 404

715.31 Purpose — The purpose of this Part is to establish a remediation agreement regime that is applicable to organizations alleged to have committed an offence and that has the following objectives:

(a) to denounce an organization's wrongdoing and the harm that the wrongdoing has caused to victims or to the community;

(b) to hold the organization accountable for its wrongdoing through effective, proportionate and dissuasive penalties;

(c) to contribute to respect for the law by imposing an obligation on the organization to put in place corrective measures and promote a compliance culture;

(d) to encourage voluntary disclosure of the wrongdoing;

(e) to provide reparations for harm done to victims or to the community; and

(f) to reduce the negative consequences of the wrongdoing for persons — employees, customers, pensioners and others — who did not engage in the wrongdoing, while holding responsible those individuals who did engage in that wrongdoing.

2018, c. 12, s. 404

715.32 (1) Conditions for remediation agreement — The prosecutor may enter into negotiations for a remediation agreement with an organization alleged to have committed an offence if the following conditions are met:

(a) the prosecutor is of the opinion that there is a reasonable prospect of conviction with respect to the offence;

(b) the prosecutor is of the opinion that the act or omission that forms the basis of the offence did not cause and was not likely to have caused serious bodily harm or death, or injury to national defence or national security, and was not committed for the benefit of, at the direction of, or in association with, a criminal organization or terrorist group;

(c) the prosecutor is of the opinion that negotiating the agreement is in the public interest and appropriate in the circumstances; and

(d) the Attorney General has consented to the negotiation of the agreement.

(2) Factors to consider — For the purposes of paragraph (1)(c), the prosecutor must consider the following factors:

(a) the circumstances in which the act or omission that forms the basis of the offence was brought to the attention of investigative authorities;

(b) the nature and gravity of the act or omission and its impact on any victim;

(c) the degree of involvement of senior officers of the organization in the act or omission;

(d) whether the organization has taken disciplinary action, including termination of employment, against any person who was involved in the act or omission;

(e) whether the organization has made reparations or taken other measures to remedy the harm caused by the act or omission and to prevent the commission of similar acts or omissions;

(f) whether the organization has identified or expressed a willingness to identify any person involved in wrongdoing related to the act or omission;

(g) whether the organization — or any of its representatives — was convicted of an offence or sanctioned by a regulatory body, or whether it entered into a previous remediation agreement or other settlement, in Canada or elsewhere, for similar acts or omissions;

(h) whether the organization — or any of its representatives — is alleged to have committed any other offences, including those not listed in the schedule to this Part; and

(i) any other factor that the prosecutor considers relevant.

(3) Factors not to consider — Despite paragraph (2)(i), if the organization is alleged to have committed an offence under section 3 or 4 of the *Corruption of Foreign Public Officials Act*, the prosecutor must not consider the national economic interest, the potential effect on relations with a state other than Canada or the identity of the organization or individual involved.

2018, c. 12, s. 404

715.33 (1) Notice to organization — invitation to negotiate — If the prosecutor wishes to negotiate a remediation agreement, they must give the organization written notice of the offer to enter into negotiations and the notice must include

(a) a summary description of the offence to which the agreement would apply;

(b) an indication of the voluntary nature of the negotiation process;

(c) an indication of the legal effects of the agreement;

(d) an indication that, by agreeing to the terms of this notice, the organization explicitly waives the inclusion of the negotiation period and the period during which the agreement is in force in any assessment of the reasonableness of the delay between the day on which the charge is laid and the end of trial;

(e) an indication that negotiations must be carried out in good faith and that the organization must provide all information requested by the prosecutor that the organization is aware of or can obtain through reasonable efforts, including information enabling the identification of any person involved in the act or omission that forms the basis of the offence or any wrongdoing related to that act or omission;

(f) an indication of how the information disclosed by the organization during the negotiations may be used, subject to subsection (2);

(g) a warning that knowingly making false or misleading statements or knowingly providing false or misleading information during the negotiations may lead to the recommencement of proceedings or prosecution for obstruction of justice;

(h) an indication that either party may withdraw from the negotiations by providing written notice to the other party;

(i) an indication that reasonable efforts must be made by both parties to identify any victim as soon as practicable; and

(j) a deadline to accept the offer to negotiate according to the terms of the notice.

(2) Admissions not admissible in evidence — No admission, confession or statement accepting responsibility for a given act or omission made by the organization during the negotiations is admissible in evidence against that organization in any civil or criminal proceedings related to that act or omission, except those contained in the statement of facts or admission of responsibility referred to in paragraphs 715.34(1)(a) and (b), if the parties reach an agreement and it is approved by the court.

2018, c. 12, s. 404

715.34 (1) Mandatory contents of agreement — A remediation agreement must include

(a) a statement of facts related to the offence that the organization is alleged to have committed and an undertaking by the organization not to make or condone any public statement that contradicts those facts;

(b) the organization's admission of responsibility for the act or omission that forms the basis of the offence;

(c) an indication of the obligation for the organization to provide any other information that will assist in identifying any person involved in the act or omission, or any wrongdoing related to that act or omission, that the organization becomes aware of, or can obtain through reasonable efforts, after the agreement has been entered into;

(d) an indication of the obligation for the organization to cooperate in any investigation, prosecution or other proceeding in Canada — or elsewhere if the prosecutor considers it appropriate — resulting from the act or omission, including by providing information or testimony;

(e) with respect to any property, benefit or advantage identified in the agreement that was obtained or derived directly or indirectly from the act or omission, an obligation for the organization to

(i) forfeit it to Her Majesty in right of Canada, to be disposed of in accordance with paragraph 4(1)(b.2) of the *Seized Property Management Act*,

(ii) forfeit it to Her Majesty in right of a province, to be disposed of as the Attorney General directs, or

(iii) otherwise deal with it, as the prosecutor directs;

(f) an indication of the obligation for the organization to pay a penalty to the Receiver General or to the treasurer of a province, as the case may be, for each offence to which the agreement applies, the amount to be paid and any other terms respecting payment;

(g) an indication of any reparations, including restitution consistent with paragraph 738(1)(a) or (b), that the organization is required to make to a victim or a statement by the prosecutor of the reasons why reparations to a victim are not appropriate in the circumstances and an indication of any measure required in lieu of reparations to a victim;

(h) an indication of the obligation for the organization to pay a victim surcharge for each offence to which the agreement applies, other than an offence under section 3 or 4 of the *Corruption of Foreign Public Officials Act*, the amount to be paid and any other terms respecting payment;

(i) an indication of the obligation for the organization to report to the prosecutor on the implementation of the agreement and an indication of the manner in which the report is to be made and any other terms respecting reporting;

(j) an indication of the legal effects of the agreement;

(k) an acknowledgement by the organization that the agreement has been made in good faith and that the information it has provided during the negotiation is accurate and complete and a commitment that it will continue to provide accurate and complete information while the agreement is in force;

(l) an indication of the use that can be made of information obtained as a result of the agreement, subject to subsection (2);

(m) a warning that the breach of any term of the agreement may lead to an application by the prosecutor for termination of the agreement and a recommencement of proceedings;

(n) an indication of the obligation for the organization not to deduct, for income tax purposes, the costs of any reparations or other measures referred to in paragraph (g) or any other costs incurred to fulfil the terms of the agreement;

(o) a notice of the prosecutor's right to vary or terminate the agreement with the approval of the court; and

(p) an indication of the deadline by which the organization must meet the terms of the agreement.

(2) Admissions not admissible in evidence — No admission, confession or statement accepting responsibility for a given act or omission made by the organization as a result of the agreement is admissible in evidence against that organization in any civil or criminal proceedings related to that act or omission, except those contained in the statement of facts and admission of responsibility referred to in paragraphs (1)(a) and (b), if the agreement is approved by the court.

(3) Optional content of agreement — A remediation agreement may include, among other things,

(a) an indication of the obligation for the organization to establish, implement or enhance compliance measures to address any deficiencies in the organization's policies, standards or procedures — including those related to internal control procedures and employee training — that may have allowed the act or omission;

(b) an indication of the obligation for the organization to reimburse the prosecutor for any costs identified in the agreement that are related to its administration and that have or will be incurred by the prosecutor; and

(c) an indication of the fact that an independent monitor has been appointed, as selected with the prosecutor's approval, to verify and report to the prosecutor on the organization's compliance with the obligation referred to in paragraph (a), or any other obligation in the agreement identified by the prosecutor, as well as an indication of the organization's obligations with respect to that monitor, including the obligations to cooperate with the monitor and pay the monitor's costs.

2018, c. 12, s. 404

715.35 Independent monitor — conflict of interest — A candidate for appointment as an independent monitor must notify the prosecutor in writing of any previous or ongoing relationship, in particular with the organization or any of its representatives, that may have a real or perceived impact on the candidate's ability to provide an independent verification.

2018, c. 12, s. 404

715.36 (1) Duty to inform victims — After an organization has accepted the offer to negotiate according to the terms of the notice referred to in section 715.33, the prosecutor must take reasonable steps to inform any victim, or any third party that is acting on the victim's behalf, that a remediation agreement may be entered into.

(2) Interpretation — The duty to inform any victim is to be construed and applied in a manner that is reasonable in the circumstances and not likely to interfere with the proper administration of justice, including by causing interference with prosecutorial discretion or compromising, hindering or causing excessive delay to the negotiation of an agreement or its conclusion.

(3) Reasons — If the prosecutor elects not to inform a victim or third party under subsection (1), they must provide the court, when applying for approval of the agreement, with a statement of the reasons why it was not appropriate to do so in the circumstances.

2018, c. 12, s. 404

715.37 (1) Application for court approval — When the prosecutor and the organization have agreed to the terms of a remediation agreement, the prosecutor must apply to the court in writing for an order approving the agreement.

(2) Coming into force — The coming into force of the agreement is subject to the approval of the court.

(3) Consideration of victims — To determine whether to approve the agreement, the court hearing an application must consider

(a) any reparations, statement and other measure referred to in paragraph 715.34(1)(g);

(b) any statement made by the prosecutor under subsection 715.36(3);

(c) any victim or community impact statement presented to the court; and

(d) any victim surcharge referred to in paragraph 715.34(1)(h).

(4) Victim or community impact statement — For the purpose of paragraph (3)(c), the rules provided for in sections 722 to 722.2 apply, other than subsection 722(6), with any necessary modifications and, in particular,

(a) a victim or community impact statement, or any other evidence concerning any victim, must be considered when determining whether to approve the agreement under subsection (6);

(b) the inquiry referred to in subsection 722(2) must be made at the hearing of the application; and

(c) the duty of the clerk under section 722.1 or subsection 722.2(5) is deemed to be the duty of the prosecutor to make reasonable efforts to provide a copy of the statement to the organization or counsel for the organization as soon as feasible after the prosecutor obtains it.

(5) Victim surcharge — For the purpose of paragraph 715.34(1)(h), the amount of the victim surcharge is 30% of any penalty referred to in paragraph 715.34(1)(f), or any other percentage that the prosecutor deems appropriate in the circumstances, and is payable to the treasurer of the province in which the application for approval referred to in section 715.37 is made.

(6) Approval order — The court must, by order, approve the agreement if it is satisfied that

(a) the organization is charged with an offence to which the agreement applies;

(b) the agreement is in the public interest; and

(c) the terms of the agreement are fair, reasonable and proportionate to the gravity of the offence.

(7) Stay of proceedings — As soon as practicable after the court approves the agreement, the prosecutor must direct the clerk or other proper officer of the court to make an entry on the record that the proceedings against the organization in respect of any offence to which the agreement applies are stayed by that direction and that entry must be made immediately, after which time the proceedings shall be stayed accordingly.

(8) Other proceedings — No other proceedings may be initiated against the organization for the same offence while the agreement is in force.

(9) Limitation period — The running of a limitation period in respect of any offence to which the agreement applies is suspended while the agreement is in force.

2018, c. 12, s. 404

715.38 Variation order — On application by the prosecutor, the court must, by order, approve any modification to a remediation agreement if the court is satisfied that the agreement continues to meet the conditions set out in subsection 715.37(6). On approval, the modification is deemed to form part of the agreement.

2018, c. 12, s. 404

715.39 (1) Termination order — On application by the prosecutor, the court must, by order, terminate the agreement if it is satisfied that the organization has breached a term of the agreement.

(2) Recommencement of proceedings — As soon as the order is made, proceedings stayed in accordance with subsection 715.37(7) may be recommenced, without a new information or a new indictment, as the case may be, by the prosecutor giving notice of the recommencement to the clerk of the court in which the stay of the proceedings was entered.

(3) Stay of proceedings — If no notice is given within one year after the order is made under subsection (1), or before the expiry of the time within which the proceedings could have been commenced, whichever is earlier, the proceedings are deemed never to have been commenced.

2018, c. 12, s. 404

715.4 (1) Order declaring successful completion — On application by the prosecutor, the court must, by order, declare that the terms of the agreement were met if it is satisfied that the organization has complied with the agreement.

(2) Stay of proceedings — The order stays the proceedings against the organization for any offence to which the agreement applies, the proceedings are deemed never to have been commenced and no other proceedings may be initiated against the organization for the same offence.

2018, c. 12, s. 404

715.41 (1) Deadline — The prosecutor must, as soon as practicable after the deadline referred to in paragraph 715.34(1)(p), apply to the court in writing for a variation order under section 715.38, including to extend the deadline, an order terminating the agreement under section 715.39 or an order under section 715.4 declaring that its terms were met and the court may issue any of these orders as it deems appropriate.

(2) Deeming — The agreement is deemed to remain in force until a court issues an order terminating it or declaring that its terms were met.

2018, c. 12, s. 404

715.42 (1) Publication — Subject to subsection (2), the following must be published by the court as soon as practicable:

(a) the remediation agreement approved by the court;

(b) an order made under any of sections 715.37 to 715.41 and the reasons for that order or the reasons for the decision not to make that order; and

(c) a decision made under subsection (2) or (5) and the reasons for that decision.

(2) Decision not to publish — The court may decide not to publish the agreement or any order or reasons referred to in paragraph (1)(b), in whole or in part, if it is satisfied that the non-publication is necessary for the proper administration of justice.

(3) Factors to be considered — To decide whether the proper administration of justice requires making the decision referred to in subsection (2), the court must consider

(a) society's interest in encouraging the reporting of offences and the participation of victims in the criminal justice process;

(b) whether it is necessary to protect the identity of any victims, any person not engaged in the wrongdoing and any person who brought the wrongdoing to the attention of investigative authorities;

(c) the prevention of any adverse effect to any ongoing investigation or prosecution;

(d) whether effective alternatives to the decision referred to in subsection (2) are available in the circumstances;

(e) the salutary and deleterious effects of making the decision referred to in subsection (2); and

(f) any other factor that the court considers relevant.

(4) Conditions — The court may make its decision subject to any conditions that it considers appropriate, including a condition related to the duration of non-publication.

(5) Review of decision — On application by any person, the court must review the decision made under subsection (2) to determine whether the non-publication continues to be necessary for the proper administration of justice. If the court is satisfied that the non-publication is no longer necessary, it must publish the agreement, order or reasons, as the case may be, in whole or in part, as soon as practicable.

2018, c. 12, s. 404; 2018, c. 27, s. 686

715.43 (1) Regulations — On the recommendation of the Minister of Justice, the Governor in Council may make regulations generally for the purposes of carrying out this Part, including regulations respecting

(a) the form of the remediation agreement; and

(b) the verification of compliance by an independent monitor, including

(i) the qualifications for monitors,

(ii) the process to select a monitor,

(iii) the form and content of a conflict of interest notification, and

(iv) reporting requirements.

(2) Amendment of schedule — On the recommendation of the Minister of Justice, the Governor in Council may, by order, amend the schedule by adding or deleting any offence to which a remediation agreement may apply.

(3) Deleting offence — If the Governor in Council orders the deletion of an offence from the schedule to this Part, this Part continues to apply to an organization alleged to have committed that offence if a notice referred to in section 715.33 respecting that offence was sent to the organization before the day on which the order comes into force.

2018, c. 12, s. 404

SCHEDULE TO PART XXII.1 — OFFENCES IN RESPECT OF WHICH A REMEDIATION AGREEMENT MAY BE ENTERED INTO [Heading added 2018, c. 12, s. 405 (Sched. 6).]

(Section 715.3 and subsections 715.32(2) and 715.43(2) and (3))

1 An offence under any of the following provisions of this Act:

(a) section 119 or 120 (bribery of officers);

(b) section 121 (frauds on the government);

(c) section 123 (municipal corruption);

(d) section 124 (selling or purchasing office);

(e) section 125 (influencing or negotiating appointments or dealing in offices);

(f) subsection 139(3) (obstructing justice);

(g) section 322 (theft);

(h) section 330 (theft by person required to account);

(i) section 332 (misappropriation of money held under direction);

(j) section 340 (destroying documents of title);

(k) section 341 (fraudulent concealment);

(l) section 354 (property obtained by crime);

(m) section 362 (false pretence or false statement);

(n) section 363 (obtaining execution of valuable security by fraud);

(o) section 366 (forgery);

(p) section 368 (use, trafficking or possession of forged document);

(q) section 375 (obtaining by instrument based on forged document);

(r) section 378 (offences in relation to registers);

(s) section 380 (fraud);

(t) section 382 (fraudulent manipulation of stock exchange transactions);

(u) section 382.1 (prohibited insider trading);

(v) section 383 (gaming in stocks or merchandise);

(w) section 389 (fraudulent disposal of goods on which money advanced);

(x) section 390 (fraudulent receipts under *Bank Act*);

(y) section 392 (disposal of property to defraud creditors);

(z) section 397 (books and documents);

(z.1) section 400 (false prospectus);

(z.2) section 418 (selling defective stores to Her Majesty); and

(z.3) section 426 (secret commissions);

(z.4) section 462.31 (laundering proceeds of crime).

2 An offence under any of the following provisions of the *Corruption of Foreign Public Officials Act*:

a) section 3 (bribing a foreign public official); and

b) section 4 (maintenance or destruction of books and records to facilitate or hide the bribing of a foreign public official).

3 A conspiracy or an attempt to commit, being an accessory after the fact in relation to, or any counselling in relation to, an offence referred to in section 1 or 2.

2018, c. 12, s. 405 (Sched. 6)

PART XXIII — SENTENCING (SS. 716–751.1)

Interpretation

716. Definitions — In this Part,

"accused" includes a defendant;

"alternative measures" means measures other than judicial proceedings under this Act used to deal with a person who is eighteen years of age or over and alleged to have committed an offence;

"court" means

(a) a superior court of criminal jurisdiction,

(b) a court of criminal jurisdiction,

(c) a justice or provincial court judge acting as a summary conviction court under Part XXVII, or

(d) a court that hears an appeal;

"fine" includes a pecuniary penalty or other sum of money, but does not include restitution.

1995, c. 22, s. 6; 1999, c. 5, s. 29

Alternative Measures

717. (1) When alternative measures may be used — Alternative measures may be used to deal with a person alleged to have committed an offence only if it is not inconsistent with the protection of society and the following conditions are met:

(a) the measures are part of a program of alternative measures authorized by the Attorney General or the Attorney General's delegate or authorized by a person, or a person within a class of persons, designated by the Lieutenant Governor in Council of a province;

(b) the person who is considering whether to use the measures is satisfied that they would be appropriate, having regard to the needs of the person alleged to have committed the offence and the interests of society and of the victim;

(c) the person, having been informed of the alternative measures, fully and freely consents to participate therein;

(d) the person has, before consenting to participate in the alternative measures, been advised of the right to be represented by counsel;

(e) the person accepts responsibility for the act or omission that forms the basis of the offence that the person is alleged to have committed;

(f) there is, in the opinion of the Attorney General or the Attorney General's agent, sufficient evidence to proceed with the prosecution of the offence; and

(g) the prosecution of the offence is not in any way barred at law.

(2) Restriction on use — Alternative measures shall not be used to deal with a person alleged to have committed an offence if the person

(a) denies participation or involvement in the commission of the offence; or

(b) expresses the wish to have any charge against the person dealt with by the court.

(3) Admissions not admissible in evidence — No admission, confession or statement accepting responsibility for a given act or omission made by a person alleged to have committed an offence as a condition of the person being dealt with by alternative measures is admissible in evidence against that person in any civil or criminal proceedings.

(4) No bar to proceedings — The use of alternative measures in respect of a person alleged to have committed an offence is not a bar to proceedings against the person under this Act, but, if a charge is laid against that person in respect of that offence,

(a) where the court is satisfied on a balance of probabilities that the person has totally complied with the terms and conditions of the alternative measures, the court shall dismiss the charge; and

(b) where the court is satisfied on a balance of probabilities that the person has partially complied with the terms and conditions of the alternative measures, the court may dismiss the charge if, in the opinion of the court, the prosecution of the charge would be unfair, having regard to the circumstances and that person's performance with respect to the alternative measures.

(5) Laying of information, etc. — Subject to subsection (4), nothing in this section shall be construed as preventing any person from laying an information, obtaining the issue or confirmation of any process, or proceeding with the prosecution of any offence, in accordance with law.

1995, c. 22, s. 6

717.1 Records of persons dealt with — Sections 717.2 to 717.4 apply only in respect of persons who have been dealt with by alternative measures, regardless of the degree of their compliance with the terms and conditions of the alternative measures.

1995, c. 22, s. 6

717.2 (1) Police records — A record relating to any offence alleged to have been committed by a person, including the original or a copy of any fingerprints or photographs of the person, may be kept by any police force responsible for, or participating in, the investigation of the offence.

(2) Disclosure by peace officer — A peace officer may disclose to any person any information in a record kept pursuant to this section that it is necessary to disclose in the conduct of the investigation of an offence.

(3) Idem — A peace officer may disclose to an insurance company any information in a record kept pursuant to this section for the purpose of investigating any claim arising out of an offence committed or alleged to have been committed by the person to whom the record relates.

1995, c. 22, s. 6

717.3 (1) Government records — A department or agency of any government in Canada may keep records containing information obtained by the department or agency

(a) for the purposes of an investigation of an offence alleged to have been committed by a person;

(b) for use in proceedings against a person under this Act; or

(c) as a result of the use of alternative measures to deal with a person.

(2) Private records — A person or organization may keep records containing information obtained by the person or organization as a result of the use of alternative measures to deal with a person alleged to have committed an offence.

1995, c. 22, s. 6

717.4 (1) Disclosure of records — Any record that is kept pursuant to section 717.2 or 717.3 may be made available to

(a) any judge or court for any purpose relating to proceedings relating to offences committed or alleged to have been committed by the person to whom the record relates;

(b) any peace officer

(i) for the purpose of investigating any offence that the person is suspected on reasonable grounds of having committed, or in respect of which the person has been arrested or charged, or

(ii) for any purpose related to administration of the case to which the record relates;

(c) any member of a department or agency of a government in Canada, or any agent thereof, that is

(i) engaged in the administration of alternative measures in respect of the person, or

(ii) preparing a report in respect of the person pursuant to this Act; or

(d) any other person who is deemed, or any person within a class of persons that is deemed, by a judge of a court to have a valid interest in the record, to the extent directed by the judge, if the judge is satisfied that the disclosure is

(i) desirable in the public interest for research or statistical purposes, or

(ii) desirable in the interest of the proper administration of justice.

(2) Subsequent disclosure — Where a record is made available for inspection to any person under subparagraph (1)(d)(i), that person may subsequently disclose information contained in the record, but may not disclose the information in any form that would reasonably be expected to identify the person to whom it relates.

(3) Information, copies — Any person to whom a record is authorized to be made available under this section may be given any information contained in the record and may be given a copy of any part of the record.

(4) Evidence — Nothing in this section authorizes the introduction into evidence of any part of a record that would not otherwise be admissible in evidence.

(5) Idem — A record kept pursuant to section 717.2 or 717.3 may not be introduced into evidence, except for the purposes set out in paragraph 721(3)(c), more than two years after the end of the period for which the person agreed to participate in the alternative measures.

1995, c. 22, s. 6

Purpose and Principles of Sentencing

718. Purpose — The fundamental purpose of sentencing is to protect society and to contribute, along with crime prevention initiatives, to respect for the law and the maintenance of a just, peaceful and safe society by imposing just sanctions that have one or more of the following objectives:

(a) to denounce unlawful conduct and the harm done to victims or to the community that is caused by unlawful conduct;

(b) to deter the offender and other persons from committing offences;

(c) to separate offenders from society, where necessary;

(d) to assist in rehabilitating offenders;

(e) to provide reparations for harm done to victims or to the community; and

(f) to promote a sense of responsibility in offenders, and acknowledgment of the harm done to victims or to the community.

1995, c. 22, s. 6; 2015, c. 13, s. 23

718.01 Objectives — offences against children — When a court imposes a sentence for an offence that involved the abuse of a person under the age of eighteen years, it shall give primary consideration to the objectives of denunciation and deterrence of such conduct.

2005, c. 32, s. 24

718.02 Objectives — offence against peace officer or other justice system participant — When a court imposes a sentence for an offence under subsection 270(1), section 270.01 or 270.02 or paragraph 423.1(1)(b), the court shall give primary consideration to the objectives of denunciation and deterrence of the conduct that forms the basis of the offence.

2009, c. 22, s. 18

718.03 Objectives — offence against certain animals — When a court imposes a sentence for an offence under subsection 445.01(1), the court shall give primary consideration to the objectives of denunciation and deterrence of the conduct that forms the basis of the offence.

2015, c. 34, s. 4

718.04 Objectives — offence against vulnerable person — When a court imposes a sentence for an offence that involved the abuse of a person who is vulnerable because of personal circumstances — including because the person is Aboriginal and female — the court shall give primary consideration to the objectives of denunciation and deterrence of the conduct that forms the basis of the offence.

2019, c. 25, s. 292.1

718.1 Fundamental principle — A sentence must be proportionate to the gravity of the offence and the degree of responsibility of the offender.

1995, c. 22, s. 6

718.2 Other sentencing principles — A court that imposes a sentence shall also take into consideration the following principles:

(a) a sentence should be increased or reduced to account for any relevant aggravating or mitigating circumstances relating to the offence or the offender, and, without limiting the generality of the foregoing,

(i) evidence that the offence was motivated by bias, prejudice or hate based on race, national or ethnic origin, language, colour, religion, sex, age, mental or physical disability, sexual orientation, or gender identity or expression, or on any other similar factor,

(ii) evidence that the offender, in committing the offence, abused the offender's intimate partner or a member of the victim or the offender's family,

(ii.1) evidence that the offender, in committing the offence, abused a person under the age of eighteen years,

(iii) evidence that the offender, in committing the offence, abused a position of trust or authority in relation to the victim,

(iii.1) evidence that the offence had a significant impact on the victim, considering their age and other personal circumstances, including their health and financial situation,

(iv) evidence that the offence was committed for the benefit of, at the direction of or in association with a criminal organization,

(v) evidence that the offence was a terrorism offence, or

(vi) evidence that the offence was committed while the offender was subject to a conditional sentence order made under section 742.1 or released on parole, statutory release or unescorted temporary absence under the *Corrections and Conditional Release Act;*

shall be deemed to be aggravating circumstances;

(b) a sentence should be similar to sentences imposed on similar offenders for similar offences committed in similar circumstances;

(c) where consecutive sentences are imposed, the combined sentence should not be unduly long or harsh;

(d) an offender should not be deprived of liberty, if less restrictive sanctions may be appropriate in the circumstances; and

(e) all available sanctions, other than imprisonment, that are reasonable in the circumstances and consistent with the harm done to victims or to the community should be considered for all offenders, with particular attention to the circumstances of Aboriginal offenders.

1995, c. 22, s. 6; 1997, c. 23, s. 17; 2000, c. 12, s. 95(c); 2001, c. 41, s. 20; 2005, c. 32, s. 25; 2012, c. 29, s. 2; 2015, c. 13, s. 24; 2015, c. 23, s. 16; 2017, c. 13, s. 4; 2019, c. 25, s. 293

718.201 Additional consideration — increased vulnerability — A court that imposes a sentence in respect of an offence that involved the abuse of an intimate partner shall consider the increased vulnerability of female persons who are victims, giving particular attention to the circumstances of Aboriginal female victims.

2019, c. 25, s. 293.1

Organizations

[Heading added 2003, c. 21, s. 14.]

718.21 Additional factors — A court that imposes a sentence on an organization shall also take into consideration the following factors:

(a) any advantage realized by the organization as a result of the offence;

(b) the degree of planning involved in carrying out the offence and the duration and complexity of the offence;

(c) whether the organization has attempted to conceal its assets, or convert them, in order to show that it is not able to pay a fine or make restitution;

(d) the impact that the sentence would have on the economic viability of the organization and the continued employment of its employees;

(e) the cost to public authorities of the investigation and prosecution of the offence;

(f) any regulatory penalty imposed on the organization or one of its representatives in respect of the conduct that formed the basis of the offence;

(g) whether the organization was — or any of its representatives who were involved in the commission of the offence were — convicted of a similar offence or sanctioned by a regulatory body for similar conduct;

(h) any penalty imposed by the organization on a representative for their role in the commission of the offence;

(i) any restitution that the organization is ordered to make or any amount that the organization has paid to a victim of the offence; and

(j) any measures that the organization has taken to reduce the likelihood of it committing a subsequent offence.

2003, c. 21, s. 14

Punishment Generally

718.3 (1) Degrees of punishment — Where an enactment prescribes different degrees or kinds of punishment in respect of an offence, the punishment to be imposed is, subject to the limitations prescribed in the enactment, in the discretion of the court that convicts a person who commits the offence.

(2) Discretion respecting punishment — Where an enactment prescribes a punishment in respect of an offence, the punishment to be imposed is, subject to the limitations prescribed in the enactment, in the discretion of the court that convicts a person who commits the offence, but no punishment is a minimum punishment unless it is declared to be a minimum punishment.

(3) Imprisonment in default where term not specified — Where an accused is convicted of an offence punishable with both fine and imprisonment and a term of imprisonment in default of payment of the fine is not specified in the enactment that prescribes the punishment to be imposed, the imprisonment that may be imposed in default of payment shall not exceed the term of imprisonment that is prescribed in respect of the offence.

(4) Cumulative punishments — The court that sentences an accused shall consider directing

(a) that the term of imprisonment that it imposes be served consecutively to a sentence of imprisonment to which the accused is subject at the time of sentencing; and

(b) that the terms of imprisonment that it imposes at the same time for more than one offence be served consecutively, including when

(i) the offences do not arise out of the same event or series of events,

(ii) one of the offences was committed while the accused was on judicial interim release, including pending the determination of an appeal, or

(iii) one of the offences was committed while the accused was fleeing from a peace officer.

(5) Cumulative punishments — fines — For the purposes of subsection (4), a term of imprisonment includes imprisonment that results from the operation of subsection 734(4).

(6) Cumulative punishments — youth — For the purposes of subsection (4), a sentence of imprisonment includes

(a) a disposition made under paragraph 20(1)(k) or (k.1) of the *Young Offenders Act*, chapter Y-1 of the Revised Statutes of Canada, 1985;

(b) a youth sentence imposed under paragraph 42(2)(n), (o), (q) or (r) of the *Youth Criminal Justice Act*; and

(c) a sentence that results from the operation of subsection 743.5(1) or (2).

(7) Cumulative punishments — sexual offences against children — When a court sentences an accused at the same time for more than one sexual offence committed against a child, the court shall direct

(a) that a sentence of imprisonment it imposes for an offence under section 163.1 be served consecutively to a sentence of imprisonment it imposes for a sexual offence under another section of this Act committed against a child; and

(b) that a sentence of imprisonment it imposes for a sexual offence committed against a child, other than an offence under section 163.1, be served consecutively to a sentence of imprisonment it imposes for a sexual offence committed against another child other than an offence under section 163.1.

(8) Maximum penalty — intimate partner — If an accused is convicted of an indictable offence in the commission of which violence was used, threatened or attempted against an intimate partner and the accused has been previously convicted of an offence in the commission of which violence was used, threatened or attempted against an intimate partner, the court may impose a term of imprisonment that is more than the maximum term of imprisonment provided for that offence but not more than

(a) five years, if the maximum term of imprisonment for the offence is two years or more but less than five years;

(b) 10 years, if the maximum term of imprisonment for the offence is five years or more but less than 10 years;

(c) 14 years, if the maximum term of imprisonment for the offence is 10 years or more but less than 14 years; or

(d) life, if the maximum term of imprisonment for the offence is 14 years or more and up to imprisonment for life.

1995, c. 22, s. 6; 1997, c. 18, s. 141(c); 1999, c. 5, s. 30; 2002, c. 1, s. 182; 2015, c. 23, s. 17; 2019, c. 25, s. 294

719. (1) Commencement of sentence — A sentence commences when it is imposed, except where a relevant enactment otherwise provides.

(2) Time at large excluded from term of imprisonment — Any time during which a convicted person is unlawfully at large or is lawfully at large on interim release granted pursuant to any provision of this Act does not count as part of any term of imprisonment imposed on the person.

(3) Determination of sentence — In determining the sentence to be imposed on a person convicted of an offence, a court may take into account any time spent in custody by the person as a result of the offence but the court shall limit any credit for that time to a maximum of one day for each day spent in custody.

(3.1) Exception — Despite subsection (3), if the circumstances justify it, the maximum is one and one-half days for each day spent in custody.

(3.2) Reasons — The court shall give reasons for any credit granted and shall cause those reasons to be stated in the record.

(3.3) **Record of proceedings** — The court shall cause to be stated in the record and on the warrant of committal the offence, the amount of time spent in custody, the term of imprisonment that would have been imposed before any credit was granted, the amount of time credited, if any, and the sentence imposed.

(3.4) **Validity not affected** — Failure to comply with subsection (3.2) or (3.3) does not affect the validity of the sentence imposed by the court.

(4) **When time begins to run** — Notwithstanding subsection (1), a term of imprisonment, whether imposed by a trial court or the court appealed to, commences or shall be deemed to be resumed, as the case may be, on the day on which the convicted person is arrested and taken into custody under the sentence.

(5) **When fine imposed** — Notwithstanding subsection (1), where the sentence that is imposed is a fine with a term of imprisonment in default of payment, no time prior to the day of execution of the warrant of committal counts as part of the term of imprisonment.

(6) **Application for leave to appeal** — An application for leave to appeal is an appeal for the purposes of this section.

1995, c. 22, s. 6; 2009, c. 29, s. 3; 2018, c. 29, s. 66

Procedure and Evidence

720. (1) **Sentencing proceedings** — A court shall, as soon as practicable after an offender has been found guilty, conduct proceedings to determine the appropriate sentence to be imposed.

(2) **Court-supervised programs** — The court may, with the consent of the Attorney General and the offender and after considering the interests of justice and of any victim of the offence, delay sentencing to enable the offender to attend a treatment program approved by the province under the supervision of the court, such as an addiction treatment program or a domestic violence counselling program.

1995, c. 22, s. 6; 2008, c. 18, s. 35

721. (1) **Report by probation officer** — Subject to regulations made under subsection (2), where an accused, other than an organization, pleads guilty to or is found guilty of an offence, a probation officer shall, if required to do so by a court, prepare and file with the court a report in writing relating to the accused for the purpose of assisting the court in imposing a sentence or in determining whether the accused should be discharged under section 730.

(2) **Provincial regulations** — The Lieutenant Governor in Council of a province may make regulations respecting the types of offences for which a court may require a report, and respecting the content and form of the report.

(3) **Content of report** — Unless otherwise specified by the court, the report must, wherever possible, contain information on the following matters:

(a) the offender's age, maturity, character, behaviour, attitude and willingness to make amends;

(b) subject to subsection 119(2) of the *Youth Criminal Justice Act*, the history of previous dispositions under the *Young Offenders Act*, chapter Y-1 of the Revised Statutes of Canada, 1985, the history of previous sentences under the *Youth Criminal Justice Act*, and of previous findings of guilt under this Act and any other Act of Parliament;

(c) the history of any alternative measures used to deal with the offender, and the offender's response to those measures; and

(d) any matter required, by any regulation made under subsection (2), to be included in the report.

(4) Idem — The report must also contain information on any other matter required by the court, after hearing argument from the prosecutor and the offender, to be included in the report, subject to any contrary regulation made under subsection (2).

(5) Copy of report — The clerk of the court shall provide a copy of the report, as soon as practicable after filing, to the offender or counsel for the offender, as directed by the court, and to the prosecutor.

1995, c. 22, s. 6; 1999, c. 25, s. 16; 2002, c. 1, s. 183; 2003, c. 21, s. 15

722. (1) Victim impact statement — When determining the sentence to be imposed on an offender or determining whether the offender should be discharged under section 730 in respect of any offence, the court shall consider any statement of a victim prepared in accordance with this section and filed with the court describing the physical or emotional harm, property damage or economic loss suffered by the victim as the result of the commission of the offence and the impact of the offence on the victim.

(2) Inquiry by court — As soon as feasible after a finding of guilt and in any event before imposing sentence, the court shall inquire of the prosecutor if reasonable steps have been taken to provide the victim with an opportunity to prepare a statement referred to in subsection (1).

(2.1) [Repealed 2015, c. 13, s. 25.]

(3) Adjournment — On application of the prosecutor or a victim or on its own motion, the court may adjourn the proceedings to permit the victim to prepare a statement referred to in subsection (1) or to present evidence in accordance with subsection (9), if the court is satisfied that the adjournment would not interfere with the proper administration of justice.

(4) Form — The statement must be prepared in writing, using Form 34.2 in Part XXVIII, in accordance with the procedures established by a program designated for that purpose by the lieutenant governor in council of the province in which the court is exercising its jurisdiction.

(5) Presentation of statement — The court shall, on the request of a victim, permit the victim to present the statement by

(a) reading it;

(b) reading it in the presence and close proximity of any support person of the victim's choice;

(c) reading it outside the court room or behind a screen or other device that would allow the victim not to see the offender; or

(d) presenting it in any other manner that the court considers appropriate.

(6) **Photograph** — During the presentation

(a) the victim may have with them a photograph of themselves taken before the commission of the offence if it would not, in the opinion of the court, disrupt the proceedings; or

(b) if the statement is presented by someone acting on the victim's behalf, that individual may have with them a photograph of the victim taken before the commission of the offence if it would not, in the opinion of the court, disrupt the proceedings.

(7) **Conditions of exclusion** — The victim shall not present the statement outside the court room unless arrangements are made for the offender and the judge or justice to watch the presentation by means of closedcircuit television or otherwise and the offender is permitted to communicate with counsel while watching the presentation.

(8) **Consideration of statement** — In considering the statement, the court shall take into account the portions of the statement that it considers relevant to the determination referred to in subsection (1) and disregard any other portion.

(9) **Evidence concerning victim admissible** — Whether or not a statement has been prepared and filed in accordance with this section, the court may consider any other evidence concerning any victim of the offence for the purpose of determining the sentence to be imposed on the offender or whether the offender should be discharged under section 730.

1995, c. 22, s. 6; 1999, c. 25, s. 17; 2000, c. 12, s. 95(d); 2015, c. 13, s. 25

722.1 **Copy of statement** — The clerk of the court shall provide a copy of a statement referred to in subsection 722(1), as soon as practicable after a finding of guilt, to the offender or counsel for the offender, and to the prosecutor.

1995, c. 22, s. 6; 1999, c. 25, s. 18

722.2 (1) **Community impact statement** — When determining the sentence to be imposed on an offender or determining whether the offender should be discharged under section 730 in respect of any offence, the court shall consider any statement made by an individual on a community's behalf that was prepared in accordance with this section and filed with the court describing the harm or loss suffered by the community as the result of the commission of the offence and the impact of the offence on the community.

(2) **Form** — The statement must be prepared in writing, using Form 34.3 in Part XXVIII, in accordance with the procedures established by a program designated for that purpose by the lieutenant governor in council of the province in which the court is exercising its jurisdiction.

(3) Presentation of statement — The court shall, on the request of the individual making the statement, permit the individual to present the statement by

(a) reading it;

(b) reading it in the presence and close proximity of any support person of the individual's choice;

(c) reading it outside the court room or behind a screen or other device that would allow the individual not to see the offender; or

(d) presenting it in any other manner that the court considers appropriate.

(4) Conditions of exclusion — The individual making the statement shall not present it outside the court room unless arrangements are made for the offender and the judge or justice to watch the presentation by means of closed-circuit television or otherwise and the offender is permitted to communicate with counsel while watching the presentation.

(5) Copy of statement — The clerk of the court shall, as soon as feasible after a finding of guilt, provide a copy of the statement to the offender or counsel for the offender, and to the prosecutor.

1999, c. 25, s. 18; 2015, c. 13, s. 26

723. (1) Submissions on facts — Before determining the sentence, a court shall give the prosecutor and the offender an opportunity to make submissions with respect to any facts relevant to the sentence to be imposed.

(2) Submission of evidence — The court shall hear any relevant evidence presented by the prosecutor or the offender.

(3) Production of evidence — The court may, on its own motion, after hearing argument from the prosecutor and the offender, require the production of evidence that would assist it in determining the appropriate sentence.

(4) Compel appearance — Where it is necessary in the interests of justice, the court may, after consulting the parties, compel the appearance of any person who is a compellable witness to assist the court in determining the appropriate sentence.

(5) Hearsay evidence — Hearsay evidence is admissible at sentencing proceedings, but the court may, if the court considers it to be in the interests of justice, compel a person to testify where the person

(a) has personal knowledge of the matter;

(b) is reasonably available; and

(c) is a compellable witness.

1995, c. 22, s. 6

724. (1) Information accepted — In determining a sentence, a court may accept as proved any information disclosed at the trial or at the sentencing proceedings and any facts agreed on by the prosecutor and the offender.

(2) Jury — Where the court is composed of a judge and jury, the court

(a) shall accept as proven all facts, express or implied, that are essential to the jury's verdict of guilty; and

(b) may find any other relevant fact that was disclosed by evidence at the trial to be proven, or hear evidence presented by either party with respect to that fact.

(3) Disputed facts — Where there is a dispute with respect to any fact that is relevant to the determination of a sentence,

(a) the court shall request that evidence be adduced as to the existence of the fact unless the court is satisfied that sufficient evidence was adduced at the trial;

(b) the party wishing to rely on a relevant fact, including a fact contained in a presentence report, has the burden of proving it;

(c) either party may cross-examine any witness called by the other party;

(d) subject to paragraph (e), the court must be satisfied on a balance of probabilities of the existence of the disputed fact before relying on it in determining the sentence; and

(e) the prosecutor must establish, by proof beyond a reasonable doubt, the existence of any aggravating fact or any previous conviction by the offender.

1995, c. 22, s. 6

725. (1) Other offences — In determining the sentence, a court

(a) shall consider, if it is possible and appropriate to do so, any other offences of which the offender was found guilty by the same court, and shall determine the sentence to be imposed for each of those offences;

(b) shall consider, if the Attorney General and the offender consent, any outstanding charges against the offender to which the offender consents to plead guilty and pleads guilty, if the court has jurisdiction to try those charges, and shall determine the sentence to be imposed for each charge unless the court is of the opinion that a separate prosecution for the other offence is necessary in the public interest;

(b.1) shall consider any outstanding charges against the offender, unless the court is of the opinion that a separate prosecution for one or more of the other offences is necessary in the public interest, subject to the following conditions:

(i) the Attorney General and the offender consent,

(ii) the court has jurisdiction to try each charge,

(iii) each charge has been described in open court,

(iv) the offender has agreed with the facts asserted in the description of each charge, and

(v) the offender has acknowledged having committed the offence described in each charge; and

(c) may consider any facts forming part of the circumstances of the offence that could constitute the basis for a separate charge.

(1.1) Attorney General's consent — For the purpose of paragraphs (1)(b) and (b.1), the Attorney General shall take the public interest into account before consenting.

(2) No further proceedings — The court shall, on the information or indictment, note

(a) any outstanding charges considered in determining the sentence under paragraph (1)(b.1), and

(b) any facts considered in determining the sentence under paragraph (1)(c),

and no further proceedings may be taken with respect to any offence described in those charges or disclosed by those facts unless the conviction for the offence of which the offender has been found guilty is set aside or quashed on appeal.

1995, c. 22, s. 6; 1999, c. 5, s. 31

726. Offender may speak to sentence — Before determining the sentence to be imposed, the court shall ask whether the offender, if present, has anything to say.

1995, c. 22, s. 6

726.1 Relevant information — In determining the sentence, a court shall consider any relevant information placed before it, including any representations or submissions made by or on behalf of the prosecutor or the offender.

1995, c. 22, s. 6

726.2 Reasons for sentence — When imposing a sentence, a court shall state the terms of the sentence imposed, and the reasons for it, and enter those terms and reasons into the record of the proceedings.

1995, c. 22, s. 6

727. (1) Previous conviction — Subject to subsections (3) and (4), where an offender is convicted of an offence for which a greater punishment may be imposed by reason of previous convictions, no greater punishment shall be imposed on the offender by reason thereof unless the prosecutor satisfies the court that the offender, before making a plea, was notified that a greater punishment would be sought by reason thereof.

(2) Procedure — Where an offender is convicted of an offence for which a greater punishment may be imposed by reason of previous convictions, the court shall, on application by the prosecutor and on being satisfied that the offender was notified in accordance with subsection (1), ask whether the offender was previously convicted and, if the offender does not admit to any previous convictions, evidence of previous convictions may be adduced.

(3) Where hearing ex parte — Where a summary conviction court holds a trial pursuant to subsection 803(2) and convicts the offender, the court may, whether or not the offender was notified that a greater punishment would be sought by reason of a previous conviction, make inquiries and hear evidence with respect to previous convictions of the offender and, if any such conviction is proved, may impose a greater punishment by reason thereof.

(4) Organizations — If, under section 623, the court proceeds with the trial of an organization that has not appeared and pleaded and convicts the organization, the court may, whether or not the organization was notified that a greater punishment would be sought by reason of a previous conviction, make inquiries and hear evidence with respect to previous convictions of the organization and, if any such conviction is proved, may impose a greater punishment by reason of that conviction.

(5) Section does not apply — This section does not apply to a person referred to in paragraph 745(b).

1995, c. 22, s. 6; 2003, c. 21, s. 16

728. Sentence justified by any count — Where one sentence is passed on a verdict of guilty on two or more counts of an indictment, the sentence is good if any of the counts would have justified the sentence.

1995, c. 22, s. 6

729. (1) Proof of certificate of analyst — In

(a) a prosecution for failure to comply with a condition in a probation order that the accused not have in possession or use drugs, or

(b) a hearing to determine whether the offender breached a condition of a conditional sentence order that the offender not have in possession or use drugs.

a certificate purporting to be signed by an analyst stating that the analyst has analyzed or examined a substance and stating the result of the analysis or examination is admissible in evidence and, in the absence of evidence to the contrary, is proof of the statements contained in the certificate without proof of the signature or official character of the person appearing to have signed the certificate.

(2) Definition of "analyst" — In this section, **"analyst"** means a person designated as an analyst under the *Controlled Drugs and Substances Act* or the *Cannabis Act*.

(3) Notice of intention to produce certificate — No certificate shall be admitted in evidence unless the party intending to produce it has, before the trial or hearing, as the case may be, given reasonable notice and a copy of the certificate to the party against whom it is to be produced.

(4) and (5) [Repealed 2008, c. 18, s. 36.]

(6) Requiring attendance of analyst — The party against whom a certificate of an analyst is produced may, with leave of the court, require the attendance of the analyst for cross-examination.

1995, c. 22, s. 6; 1999, c. 31, s. 69; 2004, c. 12, s. 11; 2008, c. 18, s. 36; 2018, c. 16, s. 221

729.1 (1) Proof of certificate of analyst — bodily substance — In a prosecution for failure to comply with a condition in a probation order that the accused not consume drugs, alcohol or any other intoxicating substance, or in a hearing to determine whether the offender breached such a condition of a conditional sentence order, a certificate purporting to be signed by an analyst that states that the analyst has analyzed a sample of a bodily substance and that states the result of the analysis is admissible in evidence and, in the absence of evidence to the contrary, is proof of the statements contained in the certificate without proof of the signature or official character of the person who appears to have signed the certificate.

(2) Definition of "analyst" — In this section, **"analyst"** has the same meaning as in section 320.11.

(3) Notice of intention to produce certificate — No certificate shall be admitted in evidence unless the party intending to produce it has, before the trial or hearing, as the case may be, given reasonable notice and a copy of the certificate to the party against whom it is to be produced.

(4) Requiring attendance of analyst — The party against whom a certificate of an analyst is produced may, with leave of the court, require the attendance of the analyst for cross-examination.

2011, c. 7, s. 2; 2018, c. 21, s. 23

Absolute and Conditional Discharges

730. (1) Conditional and absolute discharge — Where an accused, other than an organization, pleads guilty to or is found guilty of an offence, other than an offence for which a minimum punishment is prescribed by law or an offence punishable by imprisonment for fourteen years or for life, the court before which the accused appears may, if it considers it to be in the best interests of the accused and not contrary to the public interest, instead of convicting the accused, by order direct that the accused be discharged absolutely or on the conditions prescribed in a probation order made under subsection 731(2).

(2) Period for which appearance notice, etc., continues in force — Subject to Part XVI, where an accused who has not been taken into custody or who has been released from custody under or by virtue of any provision of Part XVI pleads guilty of or is found guilty of an offence but is not convicted, the appearance notice, promise to appear, summons, undertaking or recognizance issued to or given or entered into by the accused continues in force, subject to its terms, until a disposition in respect of the accused is made under subsection (1) unless, at the time the accused pleads guilty or is found guilty, the court, judge or justice orders that the accused be taken into custody pending such a disposition.

Proposed Amendment — 730(2)

(2) Period for which appearance notice, etc., continues in force — Subject to Part XVI, if an accused who has not been taken into custody or who has been released from custody under any provision of that Part pleads guilty to or is found guilty of an offence but is not convicted, the appearance notice, summons, undertaking or release order issued to, given or entered into by the accused continues in force, subject to its terms, until a disposition in respect of the accused is made under subsection (1) unless, at the time the accused pleads guilty or is found guilty, the court, judge or justice orders that the accused be taken into custody pending such a disposition.

2019, c. 25, s. 296 [To come into force December 18, 2019.]

(3) **Effect of discharge** — Where a court directs under subsection (1) that an offender be discharged of an offence, the offender shall be deemed not to have been convicted of the offence except that

(a) the offender may appeal from the determination of guilt as if it were a conviction in respect of the offence;

(b) the Attorney General and, in the case of summary conviction proceedings, the informant or the informant's agent may appeal from the decision of the court not to convict the offender of the offence as if that decision were a judgment or verdict of acquittal of the offence or a dismissal of the information against the offender; and

(c) the offender may plead autrefois convict in respect of any subsequent charge relating to the offence.

(4) **Where person bound by probation order convicted of offence** — Where an offender who is bound by the conditions of a probation order made at a time when the offender was directed to be discharged under this section is convicted of an offence, including an offence under section 733.1, the court that made the probation order may, in addition to or in lieu of exercising its authority under subsection 732.2(5), at any time when it may take action under that subsection, revoke the discharge, convict the offender of the offence to which the discharge relates and impose any sentence that could have been imposed if the offender had been convicted at the time of discharge, and no appeal lies from a conviction under this subsection where an appeal was taken from the order directing that the offender be discharged.

1995, c. 22, s. 6; 1997, c. 18, s. 141(d); 2003, c. 21, s. 17

Probation

731. (1) **Making of probation order** — Where a person is convicted of an offence, a court may, having regard to the age and character of the offender, the nature of the offence and the circumstances surrounding its commission,

(a) if no minimum punishment is prescribed by law, suspend the passing of sentence and direct that the offender be released on the conditions prescribed in a probation order; or

(b) in addition to fining or sentencing the offender to imprisonment for a term not exceeding two years, direct that the offender comply with the conditions prescribed in a probation order.

(2) **Idem** — A court may also make a probation order where it discharges an accused under subsection 730(1).

1995, c. 22, s. 6

731.1 (1) **Firearm, etc., prohibitions** — Before making a probation order, the court shall consider whether section 109 or 110 is applicable.

(2) **Application of section 109 or 110** — For greater certainty, a condition of a probation order referred to in paragraph 732.1(3)(d) does not affect the operation of section 109 or 110.

1995, c. 22, s. 6; 2002, c. 13, s. 73

732. (1) Intermittent sentence — Where the court imposes a sentence of imprisonment of ninety days or less on an offender convicted of an offence, whether in default of payment of a fine or otherwise, the court may, having regard to the age and character of the offender, the nature of the offence and the circumstances surrounding its commission, and the availability of appropriate accommodation to ensure compliance with the sentence, order

(a) that the sentence be served intermittently at such times as are specified in the order; and

(b) that the offender comply with the conditions prescribed in a probation order when not in confinement during the period that the sentence is being served and, if the court so orders, on release from prison after completing the intermittent sentence.

(2) **Application to vary intermittent sentence** — An offender who is ordered to serve a sentence of imprisonment intermittently may, on giving notice to the prosecutor, apply to the court that imposed the sentence to allow it to be served on consecutive days.

(3) **Court may vary intermittent sentence if subsequent offence** — Where a court imposes a sentence of imprisonment on a person who is subject to an intermittent sentence in respect of another offence, the unexpired portion of the intermittent sentence shall be served on consecutive days unless the court otherwise orders.

1995, c. 22, s. 6

732.1 (1) Definitions — In this section and section 732.2,

"change", in relation to optional conditions, includes deletions and additions;

"optional conditions" means the conditions referred to in subsection (3) or (3.1).

(2) **Compulsory conditions of probation order** — The court shall prescribe, as conditions of a probation order, that the offender do all of the following:

(a) keep the peace and be of good behaviour;

(a.1) abstain from communicating, directly or indirectly, with any victim, witness or other person identified in the order, or refrain from going to any place specified in the order, except in accordance with the conditions specified in the order that the court considers necessary, unless

(i) the victim, witness or other person gives their consent or, if the victim, witness or other person is a minor, the parent or guardian, or any other person who has the lawful care or charge of them, gives their consent, or

(ii) the court decides that, because of exceptional circumstances, it is not appropriate to impose the condition;

Proposed Repeal — 732.1(2)(a.1)

(a.1) [Repealed 2019, c. 25, s. 297(1). To come into force December 18, 2019.]

(b) appear before the court when required to do so by the court; and

(c) notify the court or the probation officer in advance of any change of name or address, and promptly notify the court or the probation officer of any change of employment or occupation.

(2.1) Consent — For the purposes of subparagraph (2)(a.1)(i), the consent is valid only if it is given in writing or in the manner specified in the order.

Proposed Repeal — 732.1(2.1)

(2.1) [Repealed 2019, c. 25, s. 297(2). To come into force December 18, 2019.]

(2.2) Reasons — If the court makes the decision described in subparagraph (2)(a.1)(ii), it shall state the reasons for the decision in the record.

Proposed Repeal — 732.1(2.2)

(2.2) [Repealed 2019, c. 25, s. 297(2). To come into force December 18, 2019.]

(3) Optional conditions of probation order — The court may prescribe, as additional conditions of a probation order, that the offender do one or more of the following:

(a) report to a probation officer

(i) within two working days, or such longer period as the court directs, after the making of the probation order, and

(ii) thereafter, when required by the probation officer and in the manner directed by the probation officer;

Proposed Addition — 732.1(3)(a.1)

(a.1) abstain from communicating, directly or indirectly, with any victim, witness or other person identified in the order or from going to any place or geographic area specified in the order, except in accordance with any specified conditions that the court considers necessary;

2019, c. 25, s. 297(3) [To come into force December 18, 2019.]

(b) remain within the jurisdiction of the court unless written permission to go outside that jurisdiction is obtained from the court or the probation officer;

(c) abstain from the consumption of drugs except in accordance with a medical prescription, of alcohol or of any other intoxicating substance;

(c.1) provide, for the purpose of analysis, a sample of a bodily substance prescribed by regulation on the demand of a peace officer, a probation officer or someone designated under subsection (9) to make a demand, at the place and time and on the day specified by the person making the demand, if that person has reasonable grounds to believe that the offender has breached a condition of the order that requires them to abstain from the consumption of drugs, alcohol or any other intoxicating substance;

(c.2) provide, for the purpose of analysis, a sample of a bodily substance prescribed by regulation at regular intervals that are specified by a probation officer in a notice in Form 51 served on the offender, if a condition of the order requires the offender to abstain from the consumption of drugs, alcohol or any other intoxicating substance;

(d) abstain from owning, possessing or carrying a weapon;

(e) provide for the support or care of dependants;

(f) perform up to 240 hours of community service over a period not exceeding eighteen months;

(g) if the offender agrees, and the subject to the program director's acceptance of the offender, participate actively in a treatment program approved by the province;

(g.1) where the lieutenant governor in council of the province in which the probation order is made has established a program for curative treatment in relation to the consumption of alcohol or drugs, attend at a treatment facility, designated by the lieutenant governor in council of the province, for assessment and curative treatment in relation to the consumption by the offender of alcohol or drugs that is recommended pursuant to the program;

(g.2) where the lieutenant governor in council of the province in which the probation order is made has established a program governing the use of an alcohol ignition interlock device by an offender and if the offender agrees to participate in the program, comply with the program; and

(h) comply with such other reasonable conditions as the court considers desirable, subject to any regulations made under subsection 738(2), for protecting society and for facilitating the offender's successful reintegration into the community.

(3.1) Optional conditions — organization — The court may prescribe, as additional conditions of a probation order made in respect of an organization, that the offender do one or more of the following:

(a) make restitution to a person for any loss or damage that they suffered as a result of the offence;

(b) establish policies, standards and procedures to reduce the likelihood of the organization committing a subsequent offence;

(c) communicate those policies, standards and procedures to its representatives;

(d) report to the court on the implementation of those policies, standards and procedures;

(e) identify the senior officer who is responsible for compliance with those policies, standards and procedures;

(f) provide, in the manner specified by the court, the following information to the public, namely,

(i) the offence of which the organization was convicted,

(ii) the sentence imposed by the court, and

(iii) any measures that the organization is taking — including any policies, standards and procedures established under paragraph (b) — to reduce the likelihood of it committing a subsequent offence; and

(g) comply with any other reasonable conditions that the court considers desirable to prevent the organization from committing subsequent offences or to remedy the harm caused by the offence.

(3.2) **Consideration — organizations** — Before making an order under paragraph (3.1)(b), a court shall consider whether it would be more appropriate for another regulatory body to supervise the development or implementation of the policies, standards and procedures referred to in that paragraph.

(4) **Form and period of order** — A probation order may be in Form 46, and the court that makes the probation order shall specify therein the period for which it is to remain in force.

(5) **Obligations of court** — The court that makes a probation order shall

(a) cause a copy of the order to be given to the offender and, on request, to the victim;

(b) explain the conditions of the order set under subsections (2) to (3.1) and the substance of section 733.1 to the offender;

(c) cause an explanation to be given to the offender of the procedure for applying under subsection 732.2(3) for a change to the optional conditions and of the substance of subsections 732.2(3) and (5); and

(d) take reasonable measures to ensure that the offender understands the order and the explanations.

(6) **For greater certainty** — For greater certainty, a failure to comply with subsection (5) does not affect the validity of the probation order.

(7) **Notice — samples at regular intervals** — The notice referred to in paragraph (3)(c.2) must specify the places and times at which and the days on which the offender must provide samples of a bodily substance under a condition described in that paragraph. The first sample may not be taken earlier than 24 hours after the offender is served with the notice, and subsequent samples must be taken at regular intervals of at least seven days.

(8) **Designations and specifications** — For the purposes of paragraphs (3)(c.1) and (c.2) and subject to the regulations, the Attorney General of a province or the minister of justice of a territory shall, with respect to the province or territory,

(a) designate the persons or classes of persons that may take samples of bodily substances;

(b) designate the places or classes of places at which the samples are to be taken;

(c) specify the manner in which the samples are to be taken;

(d) specify the manner in which the samples are to be analyzed;

(e) specify the manner in which the samples are to be stored, handled and destroyed;

(f) specify the manner in which the records of the results of the analysis of the samples are to be protected and destroyed;

(g) designate the persons or classes of persons that may destroy the samples; and

(h) designate the persons or classes of persons that may destroy the records of the results of the analysis of the samples.

(9) Further designations — For the purpose of paragraph (3)(c.1) and subject to the regulations, the Attorney General of a province or the minister of justice of a territory may, with respect to the province or territory, designate persons or classes of persons to make a demand for a sample of a bodily substance.

(10) Restriction — Samples of bodily substances referred to in paragraphs (3)(c.1) and (c.2) may not be taken, analyzed, stored, handled or destroyed, and the records of the results of the analysis of the samples may not be protected or destroyed, except in accordance with the designations and specifications made under subsection (8).

(11) Destruction of samples — The Attorney General of a province or the minister of justice of a territory, or a person authorized by the Attorney General or minister, shall cause all samples of bodily substances provided under a probation order to be destroyed within the periods prescribed by regulation unless the samples are reasonably expected to be used as evidence in a proceeding for an offence under section 733.1.

(12) Regulations — The Governor in Council may make regulations

(a) prescribing bodily substances for the purposes of paragraphs (3)(c.1) and (c.2);

(b) respecting the designations and specifications referred to in subsections (8) and (9);

(c) prescribing the periods within which samples of bodily substances are to be destroyed under subsection (11); and

(d) respecting any other matters relating to the samples of bodily substances.

1995, c. 22, s. 6; 1999, c. 32, s. 6; 2003, c. 21, s. 18; 2008, c. 18, s. 37; 2011, c. 7, s. 3; 2014, c. 21, s. 2; 2015, c. 13, s. 27

732.11 (1) Prohibition on use of bodily substance — No person shall use a bodily substance provided under a probation order except for the purpose of determining whether an offender is complying with a condition of the order that they abstain from the consumption of drugs, alcohol or any other intoxicating substance.

(2) Prohibition on use or disclosure of result — Subject to subsection (3), no person shall use, disclose or allow the disclosure of the results of the analysis of a bodily substance provided under a probation order.

(3) Exception — The results of the analysis of a bodily substance provided under a probation order may be disclosed to the offender to whom they relate, and may also be used or disclosed in the course of an investigation of, or in a proceeding for, an offence under section 733.1 or, if the results are made anonymous, for statistical or other research purposes.

(4) Offence — Every person who contravenes subsection (1) or (2) is guilty of an offence punishable on summary conviction.

2011, c. 7, s. 4

732.2 (1) Coming into force of order — A probation order comes into force

(a) on the date on which the order is made;

(b) where the offender is sentenced to imprisonment under paragraph 731(1)(b) or was previously sentenced to imprisonment for another offence, as soon as the offender is released from prison or, if released from prison on conditional release, at the expiration of the sentence of imprisonment; or

(c) where the offender is under a conditional sentence order, at the expiration of the conditional sentence order.

(2) Duration of order and limit on term of order — Subject to subsection (5),

(a) where an offender who is bound by a probation order is convicted of an offence, including an offence under section 733.1, or is imprisoned under paragraph 731(1)(b) in default of payment of a fine, the order continues in force except in so far as the sentence renders it impossible for the offender for the time being to comply with the order; and

(b) no probation order shall continue in force for more than three years after the date on which the order came into force.

(3) Changes to probation order — A court that makes a probation order may at any time, on application by the offender, the probation officer or the prosecutor, require the offender to appear before it and, after hearing the offender and one or both of the probation officer and the prosecutor,

(a) make any changes to the optional conditions that in the opinion of the court are rendered desirable by a change in the circumstances since those conditions were prescribed,

(b) relieve the offender, either absolutely or on such terms or for such period as the court deems desirable, of compliance with any optional condition, or

(c) decrease the period for which the probation order is to remain in force,

and the court shall thereupon endorse the probation order accordingly and, if it changes the optional conditions, inform the offender of its action and give the offender a copy of the order so endorsed.

(4) Judge may act in chambers — All the functions of the court under subsection (3) may be exercised in chambers.

(5) Where person convicted of offence — Where an offender who is bound by a probation order is convicted of an offence, including an offence under section 733.1, and

(a) the time within which an appeal may be taken against that conviction has expired and the offender has not taken an appeal,

(b) the offender has taken an appeal against that conviction and the appeal has been dismissed, or

(c) the offender has given written notice to the court that convicted the offender that the offender elects not to appeal the conviction or has abandoned the appeal, as the case may be,

in addition to any punishment that may be imposed for that offence, the court that made the probation order may, on application by the prosecutor, require the offender to appear before it and, after hearing the prosecutor and the offender,

(d) where the probation order was made under paragraph 731(1)(a), revoke the order and impose any sentence that could have been imposed if the passing of sentence had not been suspended, or

(e) make such changes to the optional conditions as the court deems desirable, or extend the period for which the order is to remain in force for such period, not exceeding one year, as the court deems desirable,

and the court shall thereupon endorse the probation order accordingly and, if it changes the optional conditions or extends the period for which the order is to remain in force, inform the offender of its action and give the offender a copy of the order so endorsed.

(6) Compelling appearance of person bound — The provisions of Parts XVI and XVIII with respect to compelling the appearance of an accused before a justice apply, with such modifications as the circumstances require, to proceedings under subsections (3) and (5).

1995, c. 22, s. 6; 2004, c. 12, s. 12

733. (1) Transfer of order — Where an offender who is bound by a probation order becomes a resident of, or is convicted or discharged under section 730 of an offence including an offence under section 733.1 in, a territorial division other than the territorial division where the order was made, on the application of a probation officer, the court that made the order may, subject to subsection (1.1), transfer the order to a court in that other territorial division that would, having regard to the mode of trial of the offender, have had jurisdiciton to make the order in that other territorial division if the offender had been tried and convicted there of the offence in respect of which the order was made, and the order may thereafter be dealt with and enforced by the court to which it is so transferred in all respects as if that court had made the order.

(1.1) Attorney General's consent — The transfer may be granted only with

(a) the consent of the Attorney General of the province in which the probation order was made, if the two territorial divisions are not in the same province; or

(b) the consent of the Attorney General of Canada, if the proceedings that led to the issuance of the probation order were instituted by or on behalf of the Attorney General of Canada.

(2) Where court unable to act — Where a court that has made a probation order or to which a probation order has been transferred pursuant to subsection (1) is for any reason unable to act, the powers of that court in relation to the probation order may be exercised by any other court that has equivalent jurisdiction in the same province.

1995, c. 22, s. 6; 1999, c. 5, s. 32

733.1 (1) Failure to comply with probation order — An offender who is bound by a probation order and who, without reasonable excuse, fails or refuses to comply with that order is guilty of

(a) an indictable offence and is liable to imprisonment for a term of not more than four years; or

(b) an offence punishable on summary conviction.

(2) Where accused may be tried and punished — An accused who is charged with an offence under subsection (1) may be tried and punished by any court having jurisdiction to try that offence in the place where the offence is alleged to have been committed or in the place where the accused is found, is arrested or is in custody, but where the place where the accused is found, is arrested or is in custody is outside the province in which the offence is alleged to have been committed, no proceedings in respect of that offence shall be instituted in that place without the consent of the Attorney General of that province.

1995, c. 22, s. 6; 2015, c. 23, s. 18; 2019, c. 25, s. 298

Fines and Forfeiture

734. (1) Power of court to impose fine — Subject to subsection (2), a court that convicts a person, other than an organization, of an offence may fine the offender by making an order under section 734.1

(a) if the punishment for the offence does not include a minimum term of imprisonment, in addition to or in lieu of any other sanction that the court is authorized to impose; or

(b) if the punishment for the offence includes a minimum term of imprisonment, in addition to any other sanction that the court is required or authorized to impose.

(2) Offender's ability to pay — Except when the punishment for an offence includes a minimum fine or a fine is imposed in lieu of a forfeiture order, a court may fine an offender under this section only if the court is satisfied that the offender is able to pay the fine or discharge it under section 736.

(3) Meaning of default of payment — For the purposes of this section and sections 734.1 to 737, a person is in default of payment of a fine if the fine has not been paid in full by the time set out in the order made under section 734.1.

(4) Imprisonment in default of payment — Where an offender is fined under this section, a term of imprisonment, determined in accordance with subsection (5), shall be deemed to be imposed in default of payment of the fine.

(5) Determination of term — The term of imprisonment referred to in subsection (4) is the lesser of

(a) the number of days that corresponds to a fraction, rounded down to the nearest whole number, of which

(i) the numerator is the unpaid amount of the fine plus the costs and charges of committing and conveying the defaulter to prison, calculated in accordance with regulations made under subsection (7), and

(ii) the denominator is equal to eight times the provincial minimum hourly wage, at the time of default, in the province in which the fine was imposed, and

(b) the maximum term of imprisonment that the court could itself impose on conviction or, if the punishment for the offence does not include a term of imprisonment, five years in the case of an indictable offence or two years less a day in the case of a summary conviction offence.

(6) **Moneys found on offender** — All or any part of a fine imposed under this section may be taken out of moneys found in the possession of the offender at the time of the arrest of the offender if the court making the order, on being satisfied that ownership of or right to possession of those moneys is not disputed by claimants other than the offender, so directs.

(7) **Provincial regulations** — The lieutenant governor in council of a province may make regulations respecting the calculation of the costs and charges referred to in subparagraph (5)(a)(i) and in paragraph 734.8(1)(b).

(8) **Application to other law** — This section and sections 734.1 to 734.8 and 736 apply to a fine imposed under any Act of Parliament, except that subsections (4) and (5) do not apply if the term of imprisonment in default of payment of the fine provided for in that Act or regulation is

(a) calculated by a different method; or

(b) specified, either as a minimum or a maximum.

1995, c. 22, s. 6; 1999, c. 5, s. 33; 2003, c. 21, s. 19; 2008, c. 18, s. 38; 2019, c. 25, s. 299

734.1 Terms of order imposing fine — A court that fines an offender under section 734 shall do so by making an order that clearly sets out

(a) the amount of the fine;

(b) the manner in which the fine is to be paid;

(c) the time or times by which the fine, or any portion thereof, must be paid; and

(d) such other terms respecting the payment of the fine as the court deems appropriate.

1995, c. 22, s. 6

734.2 (1) Obligations of court — A court that makes an order under section 734.1 shall

(a) cause a copy of the order to be given to the offender;

(b) explain the substance of sections 734 to 734.8 and 736 to the offender;

(c) cause an explanation to be given to the offender of the procedure for applying under section 734.3 for a change to the optional conditions and of any available fine option programs referred to in section 736 as well as the procedure to apply for admission to them; and

(d) take reasonable measures to ensure that the offender understands the order and the explanations.

(2) **For greater certainty** — For greater certainty, a failure to comply with subsection (1) does not affect the validity of the order.

1995, c. 22, s. 6; 2008, c. 18, s. 39

734.3 Change in terms of order — A court that makes an order under section 734.1, or a person designated either by name or by title of office by that court, may, on application by or on behalf of the offender, subject to any rules made by the court under section 482 or 482.1, change any term of the order except the amount of the fine, and any reference in this section and sections 734, 734.1, 734.2 and 734.6 to an order shall be read as including a reference to the order as changed under this section.

1995, c. 22, s. 6; 2002, c. 13, s. 74

734.4 (1) Proceeds to go to provincial treasurer — Where a fine or forfeiture is imposed or a recognizance is forfeited and no provision, other than this section, is made by law for the application of the proceeds thereof, the proceeds belong to Her Majesty in right of the province in which the fine or forfeiture was imposed or the recognizance was forfeited, and shall be paid by the person who receives them to the treasurer of that province.

(2) **Proceeds to go to receiver general for Canada** — Where

(a) a fine or forfeiture is imposed

(i) in respect of a contravention of a revenue law of Canada,

(ii) in respect of a breach of duty or malfeasance in office by an officer or employee of the Government of Canada, or

(iii) in respect of any proceedings instituted at the instance of the Government of Canada in which that government bears the costs of prosecution, or

(b) a recognizance in connection with proceedings mentioned in paragraph (a) is forfeited,

the proceeds of the fine, forfeiture or recognizance belong to Her Majesty in right of Canada and shall be paid by the person who receives them to the Receiver General.

(3) **Direction for payment to municipality** — Where a provincial, municipal or local authority bears, in whole or in part, the expense of administering the law under which a fine or forfeiture is imposed or under which proceedings are taken in which a recognizance is forfeited,

(a) the Lieutenant Governor in Council of a province may direct that the proceeds of a fine, forfeiture or recognizance that belongs to Her Majesty in right of the province shall be paid to that authority; and

(b) the Governor in Council may direct that the proceeds of a fine, forfeiture or recognizance that belongs to Her Majesty in right of Canada shall be paid to that authority.

Proposed Amendment — 734.4

734.4 (1) Proceeds to go to provincial treasurer — If a fine or forfeiture is imposed or an amount set out in an undertaking, release order or recognizance is forfeited and no provision, other than this section, is made by law for the application of the proceeds, the proceeds belong to Her Majesty in right of the province in which the fine or forfeiture was imposed or the amount was forfeited, and shall be paid by the person who receives them to the treasurer of that province.

(2) Proceeds to go to Receiver General for Canada — The proceeds described in subsection (1) belong to Her Majesty in right of Canada and must be paid by the person who receives them to the Receiver General if, as the case may be,

(a) the fine or forfeiture is imposed

(i) in respect of a contravention of a revenue law of Canada,

(ii) in respect of a breach of duty or malfeasance in office by an officer or employee of the Government of Canada, or

(iii) in respect of any proceedings instituted at the instance of the Government of Canada in which that government bears the costs of prosecution; or

(b) an amount set out in an undertaking, release order or recognizance is forfeited in connection with proceedings mentioned in paragraph (a).

(3) Direction for payment to municipality — If a provincial, municipal or local authority bears, in whole or in part, the expense of administering the law under which a fine or forfeiture is imposed or under which proceedings are taken in which an amount set out in an undertaking, release order or recognizance is forfeited,

(a) the lieutenant governor in council of a province may direct that the proceeds that belong to Her Majesty in right of the province shall be paid to that authority; and

(b) the Governor in Council may direct that the proceeds that belong to Her Majesty in right of Canada shall be paid to that authority.

2019, c. 25, s. 300 [To come into force December 18, 2019.]

1995, c. 22, s. 6

734.5 Licences, permits, etc. — If an offender is in default of payment of a fine,

(a) where the proceeds of the fine belong to Her Majesty in right of a province by virtue of subsection 734.4(1), the person reponsible, by or under an Act of the legislature of the province, for issuing, renewing or suspending a licence, permit or other similar instrument in relation to the offender may refuse to issue or renew or may suspend the licence, permit or other instrument until the fine is paid in full, proof of which lies on the offender; or

(b) where the proceeds of the fine belong to Her Majesty in right of Canada by virtue of subsection 734.4(2), the person responsible, by or under an Act of Parliament, for issuing or renewing a licence, permit or other similar instrument in relation to the offender may refuse to issue or renew or may suspend the licence, permit or other instrument until the fine is paid in full, proof of which lies on the offender.

1995, c. 22, s. 6; 1999, c. 5, s. 34

734.6 (1) Civil enforcement of fines, forfeiture — Where

(a) an offender is in default of payment of a fine, or

(b) a forfeiture imposed by law is not paid as required by the order imposing it,

then, in addition to any other method provided by law for recovering the fine or forfeiture,

(c) the Attorney General of the province to whom the proceeds of the fine or forfeiture belong, or

(d) the Attorney General of Canada, where the proceeds of the fine or forfeiture belong to Her Majesty in right of Canada,

may, by filing the order, enter as a judgment the amount of the fine or forfeiture, and costs, if any, in any civil court in Canada that has jurisdiction to enter a judgment for that amount.

(2) Effect of filing order — An order that is entered as a judgment under this section is enforceable in the same manner as if it were a judgment obtained by the Attorney General of the province or the Attorney General of Canada, as the case may be, in civil proceedings.

1995, c. 22, s. 6

734.7 (1) Warrant of committal — Where time has been allowed for payment of a fine, the court shall not issue a warrant of committal in default of payment of the fine

(a) until the expiration of the time allowed for payment of the fine in full; and

(b) unless the court is satisfied

(i) that the mechanisms provided by sections 734.5 and 734.6 are not appropriate in the circumstances, or

(ii) that the offender has, without reasonable excuse, refused to pay the fine or discharge it under section 736.

(2) Reasons for committal — Where no time has been allowed for payment of a fine and a warrant committing the offender to prison for default of payment of the fine is issued, the court shall state in the warrant the reason for immediate committal.

(2.1) Period of imprisonment — The period of imprisonment in default of payment of the fine shall be specified in a warrant of committal referred to in subsection (1) or (2).

(3) Compelling appearance of person bound — The provisions of Parts XVI and XVIII with respect to compelling the appearance of an accused before a justice apply, with such modifications as the circumstances require, to proceedings under paragraph (1)(b).

(4) Effect of imprisonment — The imprisonment of an offender for default of payment of a fine terminates the operation of sections 734.5 and 734.6 in relation to that fine.

1995, c. 22, s. 6; 1999, c. 5, s. 35

734.8 (1) Definition of "penalty" — In this section, **"penalty"** means the aggregate of

(a) the fine, and

(b) the costs and charges of committing and conveying the defaulter to prison, calculated in accordance with regulations made under subsection 734(7).

(2) Reduction of imprisonment on part payment — The term of imprisonment in default of payment of a fine shall, on payment of a part of the penalty, whether the payment was made before or after the execution of a warrant of committal, be reduced by the number of days that bears the same proportion to the number of days in the term as the part paid bears to the total penalty.

(3) Minimum that can be accepted — No amount offered in part payment of a penalty shall be accepted after the execution of a warrant of committal unless it is sufficient to secure a reduction of sentence of one day, or a whole number multiple of one day, and no part payment shall be accepted until any fee that is payable in respect of the warrant or its execution has been paid.

(4) To whom payment made — Payment may be made under this section to the person that the Attorney General directs or, if the offender is imprisoned, to the person who has lawful custody of the prisoner or to any other person that the Attorney General directs.

(5) Application of money paid — A payment under this section shall be applied firstly to the payment in full of costs and charges, secondly to the payment in full of any victim surcharge imposed under section 737, and then to payment of any part of the fine that remains unpaid.

1995, c. 22, s. 6; 1999, c. 5, s. 36; 1999, c. 25, s. 19

735. (1) Fines on organizations — An organization that is convicted of an offence is liable, in lieu of any imprisonment that is prescribed as punishment for that offence, to be fined in an amount, except where otherwise provided by law,

(a) that is in the discretion of the court, where the offence is an indictable offence; or

(b) not exceeding one hundred thousand dollars, where the offence is a summary conviction offence.

(1.1) Application of certain provisions — fines — A court that imposes a fine under subsection (1) or under any other Act of Parliament shall make an order that clearly sets out

(a) the amount of the fine;

(b) the manner in which the fine is to be paid;

(c) the time or times by which the fine, or any portion of it, must be paid; and

(d) any other terms respecting the payment of the fine that the court deems appropriate.

(2) **Effect of filing order** — Section 734.6 applies, with any modifications that are required, when an organization fails to pay the fine in accordance with the terms of the order.

1995, c. 22, s. 6; 1999, c. 5, s. 37; 2003, c. 21, s. 20

736. (1) **Fine option program** — An offender who is fined under section 734 may, whether or not the offender is serving a term of imprisonment imposed in default of payment of the fine, discharge the fine in whole or in part by earning credits for work performed during a period not greater than two years in a program established for that purpose by the Lieutenant Governor in Council

(a) of the province in which the fine was imposed, or

(b) of the province in which the offender resides, where an appropriate agreement is in effect between the government of that province and the government of the province in which the fine was imposed,

if the offender is admissible to such a program.

(2) **Credits and other matters** — A program referred to in subsection (1) shall determine the rate at which credits are earned and may provide for the manner of crediting any amounts earned against the fine and any other matters necessary for or incidental to carrying out the program.

(3) **Deemed payment** — Credits earned for work performed as provided by subsection (1) shall, for the purposes of this Act, be deemed to be payment in respect of a fine.

(4) **Federal-provincial agreement** — Where, by virtue of subsection 734.4(2), the proceeds of a fine belong to Her Majesty in right of Canada, an offender may discharge the fine in whole or in part in a fine option program of a province pursuant to subsection (1), where an appropriate agreement is in effect between the government of the province and the Government of Canada.

1995, c. 22, s. 6

737. (1) **Victim surcharge** — An offender who is convicted, or discharged under section 730, of an offence under this Act, the *Controlled Drugs and Substances Act* or the *Cannabis Act* shall pay a victim surcharge for each offence, in addition to any other punishment imposed on the offender.

Proposed Amendment — Conditional Amendment — 737(1)

If Bill C-28 receives Royal Assent, then on the first day on which both subsection 2(1) of that Act and S.C. 2018, c. 16, s. 222 [In force October 17, 2018.] are in force, subsection 737(1) is replaced by the following:

> (1) Victim surcharge — Subject to subsection (1.1), an offender who is convicted, or discharged under section 730, of an offence under this Act, the *Controlled Drugs and Substances Act* or the *Cannabis Act* shall pay a victim surcharge for each offence, in addition to any other punishment imposed on the offender.

2018, c. 16, s. 190 [Conditions not yet satisfied.]

(2) Amount of surcharge — Subject to subsections (2.1) and (3), the amount of the victim surcharge in respect of an offence is

(a) 30% of any fine that is imposed on the offender for the offence; or

(b) if no fine is imposed on the offender for the offence,

(i) $100 in the case of an offence punishable by summary conviction, and

(ii) $200 in the case of an offence punishable by indictment.

(2.1) Exception — Despite subsection (1), the court may, on application of the offender or on its own motion, order an offender to pay no victim surcharge, or to pay a reduced amount, if it is satisfied that the victim surcharge

(a) would cause undue hardship to the offender; or

(b) would not cause undue hardship to the offender but would be disproportionate to the gravity of the offence or the degree of responsibility of the offender.

(2.2) Definition of "undue hardship" — For the purposes of subsection (2.1), **"undue hardship"** means the offender is unable to pay a victim surcharge on account of the offender's precarious financial circumstances, including because of their unemployment, homelessness, lack of assets or significant financial obligations towards their dependants.

(2.3) For greater certainty — For greater certainty, for the purposes of subsection (2.2), the imprisonment of the offender alone does not constitute undue hardship.

(2.4) Reasons — When the court makes an order under subsection (2.1), the court shall state its reasons in the record of the proceedings.

(3) Increase in surcharge — The court may order an offender to pay a victim surcharge in an amount exceeding that set out in subsection (2) if the court considers it appropriate in the circumstances and is satisfied that the offender is able to pay the higher amount.

(4) Time for payment — The victim surcharge imposed in respect of an offence is payable within the time established by the lieutenant governor in council of the province in which the surcharge is imposed. If no time has been so established, the surcharge is payable within a reasonable time after its imposition.

(5) Amounts applied to aid victims — A victim surcharge shall be applied for the purposes of providing such assistance to victims of offences as the lieutenant governor in council of the province in which the surcharge is imposed may direct from time to time.

(6) Notice — The court shall cause to be given to the offender a written notice setting out

(a) the amount of the victim surcharge;

(b) the manner in which the victim surcharge is to be paid;

(c) the time by which the victim surcharge must be paid; and

(d) the procedure for applying for a change in any terms referred to in paragraphs (b) and (c) in accordance with section 734.3.

(7) Enforcement — Subsections 734(3) to (7) and sections 734.3, 734.5, 734.7, 734.8 and 736 apply, with any modifications that the circumstances require, in respect of a victim surcharge imposed under this section and, in particular,

(a) a reference in any of those provisions to "fine", other than in subsection 734.8(5), must be read as if it were a reference to "victim surcharge"; and

(b) the notice provided under subsection (6) is deemed to be an order made under section 734.1.

(8) Application — subsections (2.1) to (2.4) — Subsections (2.1) to (2.4) apply to any offender who is sentenced for an offence under this Act, the *Controlled Drugs and Substances Act* or the *Cannabis Act* that was committed after the day on which those subsections come into force.

(9) [Repealed 2019, c. 25, s. 301.]

(10) [Repealed 2013, c. 11, s. 3(5).]

1995, c. 22, s. 6; 1996, c. 19, s. 75 [Amended 1995, c. 22, s. 18 (Sched. IV, item 15).]; 1999, c. 5, s. 38; 1999, c. 25, s. 20; 2013, c. 11, s. 3; 2015, c. 13, s. 28; 2018, c. 16, s. 222; 2019, c. 25, s. 301

Restitution

737.1 (1) Court to consider restitution order — If an offender is convicted or is discharged under section 730 of an offence, the court that sentences or discharges the offender, in addition to any other measure imposed on the offender, shall consider making a restitution order under section 738 or 739.

(2) Inquiry by court — As soon as feasible after a finding of guilt and in any event before imposing the sentence, the court shall inquire of the prosecutor if reasonable steps have been taken to provide the victims with an opportunity to indicate whether they are seeking restitution for their losses and damages, the amount of which must be readily ascertainable.

(3) Adjournment — On application of the prosecutor or on its own motion, the court may adjourn the proceedings to permit the victims to indicate whether they are seeking restitution or to establish their losses and damages, if the court is satisfied that the adjournment would not interfere with the proper administration of justice.

(4) Form — Victims and other persons may indicate whether they are seeking restitution by completing Form 34.1 in Part XXVIII or a form approved for that purpose by the lieutenant governor in council of the province in which the court is exercising its jurisdiction or by using any other method approved by the court, and, if they are seeking restitution, shall establish their losses and damages, the amount of which must be readily ascertainable, in the same manner.

(5) Reasons — If a victim seeks restitution and the court does not make a restitution order, it shall include in the record a statement of the court's reasons for not doing so.

2015, c. 13, s. 29

738. (1) Restitution to victims of offences — Where an offender is convicted or discharged under section 730 of an offence, the court imposing sentence on or discharging the offender may, on application of the Attorney General or on its own motion, in addition to any other measure imposed on the offender, order that that offender make restitution to another person as follows:

(a) in the case of damage to, or the loss or destruction of, the property of any person as a result of the commission of the offence or the arrest or attempted arrest of the offender, by paying to the person an amount not exceeding the replacement value of the property as of the date the order is imposed, less the value of any part of the property that is returned to that person as of the date it is returned, where the amount is readily ascertainable;

(b) in the case of bodily or psychological harm to any person as a result of the commission of the offence or the arrest or attempted arrest of the offender, by paying to the person an amount not exceeding all pecuniary damages incurred as a result of the harm, including loss of income or support, if the amount is readily ascertainable;

(c) in the case of bodily harm or threat of bodily harm to the offender's intimate partner or child, or any other person, as a result of the commission of the offence or the arrest or attempted arrest of the offender, where the intimate partner, child or other person was a member of the offender's household at the relevant time, by paying to the person in question, independently of any amount ordered to be paid under paragraphs (a) and (b), an amount not exceeding actual and reasonable expenses incurred by that person, as a result of moving out of the offender's household, for temporary housing, food, child care and transportation, where the amount is readily ascertainable;

(d) in the case of an offence under section 402.2 or 403, by paying to a person who, as a result of the offence, incurs expenses to re-establish their identity, including expenses to replace their identity documents and to correct their credit history and credit rating, an amount that is not more than the amount of those expenses, to the extent that they are reasonable, if the amount is readily ascertainable; and

(e) in the case of an offence under subsection 162.1(1), by paying to a person who, as a result of the offence, incurs expenses to remove the intimate image from the Internet or other digital network, an amount that is not more than the amount of those expenses, to the extent that they are reasonable, if the amount is readily ascertainable.

(2) Regulations — The Lieutenant Governor in Council of a province may make regulations precluding the inclusion of provisions on enforcement of restitution orders as an optional condition of a probation order or of a conditional sentence order.

1995, c. 22, s. 6; 2000, c. 12, s. 95(e); 2005, c. 43, s. 7; 2009, c. 28, s. 11; 2014, c. 31, s. 24; 2019, c. 25, s. 302

739. Restitution to persons acting in good faith — Where an offender is convicted or discharged under section 730 of an offence and

(a) any property obtained as a result of the commission of the offence has been conveyed or transferred for valuable consideration to a person acting in good faith and without notice, or

(b) the offender has borrowed money on the security of that property from a person acting in good faith and without notice,

the court may, where that property has been returned to the lawful owner or the person who had lawful possession of that property at the time the offence was committed, order the offender to pay as restitution to the person referred to in paragraph (a) or (b) an amount not exceeding the amount of consideration for that property or the total amount outstanding in respect of the loan, as the case may be.

1995, c. 22, s. 6

739.1 Ability to pay — The offender's financial means or ability to pay does not prevent the court from making an order under section 738 or 739.

2015, c. 13, s. 30

739.2 Payment under order — In making an order under section 738 or 739, the court shall require the offender to pay the full amount specified in the order by the day specified in the order, unless the court is of the opinion that the amount should be paid in instalments, in which case the court shall set out a periodic payment scheme in the order.

2015, c. 13, s. 30

739.3 More than one person — An order under section 738 or 739 may be made in respect of more than one person, in which case the order must specify the amount that is payable to each person. The order may also specify the order of priority in which those persons are to be paid.

2015, c. 13, s. 30

739.4 (1) Public authority — On the request of a person in whose favour an order under section 738 or 739 would be made, the court may make the order in favour of a public authority, designated by the regulations, who is to be responsible for enforcing the order and remitting to the person making the request all amounts received under it.

(2) Orders — The lieutenant governor in council of a province may, by order, designate any person or body as a public authority for the purpose of subsection (1).

2015, c. 13, s. 30

740. Priority to restitution — Where the court finds it applicable and appropriate in the circumstances of a case to make, in relation to an offender, an order of restitution under section 738 or 739, and

(a) an order of forfeiture under this or any other Act of Parliament may be made in respect of property that is the same as property in respect of which the order of restitution may be made, or

(b) the court is considering ordering the offender to pay a fine and it appears to the court that the offender would not have the means or ability to comply with both the order of restitution and the order to pay the fine,

the court shall first make the order of restitution and shall then consider whether and to what extent an order of forfeiture or an order to pay a fine is appropriate in the circumstances.

1995, c. 22, s. 6

741. (1) Enforcing restitution order — An offender who fails to pay all of the amount that is ordered to be paid under section 732.1, 738, 739 or 742.3 by the day specified in the order or who fails to make a periodic payment required under the order is in default of the order and the person to whom the amount, or the periodic payment, as the case may be, was to be made may, by filing the order, enter as a judgment any amount ordered to be paid that remains unpaid under the order in any civil court in Canada that has jurisdiction to enter a judgment for that amount, and that judgment is enforceable against the offender in the same manner as if it were a judgment rendered against the offender in that court in civil proceedings.

(2) Moneys found on offender — All or any part of an amount that is ordered to be paid under section 738 or 739 may be taken out of moneys found in the possession of the offender at the time of the arrest of the offender if the court making the order, on being satisfied that ownership of or right to possession of those moneys is not disputed by claimants other than the offender, so directs.

1995, c. 22, s. 6; 2004, c. 12, s. 13; 2015, c. 13, s. 31

741.1 Notice of orders of restitution — If a court makes an order of restitution under section 738 or 739, it shall cause notice of the content of the order, or a copy of the order, to be given to the person to whom the restitution is ordered to be paid, and if it is to be paid to a public authority designated by regulations made under subsection 739.4(2), to the public authority and the person to whom the public authority is to remit amounts received under the order.

1995, c. 22, s. 6; 2015, c. 13, s. 32

741.2 Civil remedy not affected — A civil remedy for an act or omission is not affected by reason only that an order for restitution under section 738 or 739 has been made in respect of that act or omission.

1995, c. 22, s. 6

Conditional Sentence of Imprisonment

742. Definitions — In sections 742.1 to 742.7,

"change", in relation to optional conditions, includes deletions and additions;

"optional conditions" means the conditions referred to in subsection 742.3(2);

"supervisor" means a person designated by the Attorney General, either by name or by title of office, as a supervisor for the purposes of sections 742.1 to 742.7.

1995, c. 22, s. 6

742.1 Imposing of conditional sentence — If a person is convicted of an offence and the court imposes a sentence of imprisonment of less than two years, the court may, for the purpose of supervising the offender's behaviour in the community, order that the offender serve the sentence in the community, subject to the conditions imposed under section 742.3, if

(a) the court is satisfied that the service of the sentence in the community would not endanger the safety of the community and would be consistent with the fundamental purpose and principles of sentencing set out in sections 718 to 718.2;

(b) the offence is not an offence punishable by a minimum term of imprisonment;

(c) the offence is not an offence, prosecuted by way of indictment, for which the maximum term of imprisonment is 14 years or life;

(d) the offence is not a terrorism offence, or a criminal organization offence, prosecuted by way of indictment, for which the maximum term of imprisonment is 10 years or more;

(e) the offence is not an offence, prosecuted by way of indictment, for which the maximum term of imprisonment is 10 years, that

(i) resulted in bodily harm,

(ii) involved the import, export, trafficking or production of drugs, or

(iii) involved the use of a weapon; and

(f) the offence is not an offence, prosecuted by way of indictment, under any of the following provisions:

(i) section 144 (prison breach),

(ii) section 264 (criminal harassment),

(iii) section 271 (sexual assault),

(iv) section 279 (kidnapping),

(v) section 279.02 (trafficking in persons — material benefit),

(vi) section 281 (abduction of person under fourteen),

(vii) section 333.1 (motor vehicle theft),

(viii) paragraph 334(a) (theft over $5000),

(ix) paragraph 348(1)(e) (breaking and entering a place other than a dwelling-house),

(x) section 349 (being unlawfully in a dwelling-house), and

(xi) section 435 (arson for fraudulent purpose).

1995, c. 22, s. 6; 1997, c. 18, s. 107.1; 2007, c. 12, s. 1; 2012, c. 1, s. 34

742.2 (1) Firearm, etc., prohibitions — Before imposing a conditional sentence under section 742.1, the court shall consider whether section 109 or 110 is applicable.

(2) **Application of section 109 or 110** — For greater certainty, a condition of a conditional sentence order referred to in paragraph 742.3(2)(b) does not affect the operation of section 109 or 110.

1995, c. 22, s. 6; 2002, c. 13, s. 75; 2004, c. 12, s. 14

742.3 (1) **Compulsory conditions of conditional sentence order** — The court shall prescribe, as conditions of a conditional sentence order, that the offender do all of the following:

(a) keep the peace and be of good behaviour;

(b) appear before the court when required to do so by the court;

(c) report to a supervisor

(i) within two working days, or such longer period as the court directs, after the making of the conditional sentence order, and

(ii) thereafter, when required by the supervisor and in the manner directed by the supervisor;

(d) remain within the jurisdiction of the court unless written permission to go outside that jurisdiction is obtained from the court or the supervisor; and

(e) notify the court or the supervisor in advance of any change of name or address, and promptly notify the court or the supervisor of any change of employment or occupation.

(1.1) **Abstain from communicating** — The court shall prescribe, as a condition of a conditional sentence order, that the offender abstain from communicating, directly or indirectly, with any victim, witness or other person identified in the order, or refrain from going to any place specified in the order, except in accordance with the conditions specified in the order that the court considers necessary, unless

(a) the victim, witness or other person gives their consent or, if the victim, witness or other person is a minor, the parent or guardian, or any other person who has the lawful care or charge of them, gives their consent; or

(b) the court decides that, because of exceptional circumstances, it is not appropriate to impose the condition.

Proposed Repeal — 742.3(1.1)

(1.1) [Repealed 2019, c. 25, s. 303(1). To come into force December 18, 2019.]

(1.2) **Consent** — For the purposes of paragraph (1.1)(a), the consent is valid only if it is given in writing or in the manner specified in the order.

Proposed Repeal — 742.3(1.2)

(1.2) [Repealed 2019, c. 25, s. 303(1). To come into force December 18, 2019.]

(1.3) **Reasons** — If the court makes the decision described in paragraph (1.1)(b), it shall state the reasons for the decision in the record.

Proposed Repeal — 742.3(1.3)

(1.3) [Repealed 2019, c. 25, s. 303(1). To come into force December 18, 2019.]

(2) Optional conditions of conditional sentence order — The court may prescribe, as additional conditions of a conditional sentence order, that the offender do one or more of the following:

(a) abstain from the consumption of drugs except in accordance with a medical prescription, of alcohol or of any other intoxicating substance;

(a.1) provide, for the purpose of analysis, a sample of a bodily substance prescribed by regulation on the demand of a peace officer, the supervisor or someone designated under subsection (7) to make a demand, at the place and time and on the day specified by the person making the demand, if that person has reasonable grounds to suspect that the offender has breached a condition of the order that requires them to abstain from the consumption of drugs, alcohol or any other intoxicating substance;

(a.2) provide, for the purpose of analysis, a sample of a bodily substance prescribed by regulation at regular intervals that are specified by the supervisor in a notice in Form 51 served on the offender, if a condition of the order requires the offender to abstain from the consumption of drugs, alcohol or any other intoxicating substance;

Proposed Addition — 742.3(2)(a.3)

(a.3) abstain from communicating, directly or indirectly, with any victim, witness or other person identified in the order or from going to any place or geographic area specified in the order, except in accordance with any specified conditions that the justice considers necessary;

2019, c. 25, s. 303(2) [To come into force December 18, 2019.]

(b) abstain from owning, possessing or carrying a weapon;

(c) provide for the support or care of dependants;

(d) perform up to 240 hours of community service over a period not exceeding eighteen months;

(e) attend a treatment program approved by the province; and

(f) comply with such other reasonable conditions as the court considers desirable, subject to any regulations made under subsection 738(2), for securing the good conduct of the offender and for preventing a repetition by the offender of the same offence or the commission of other offences.

(3) Obligations of court — A court that makes an order under this section shall

(a) cause a copy of the order to be given to the offender and, on request, to the victim;

(b) explain the substance of subsection (1) and sections 742.4 and 742.6 to the offender;

(c) cause an explanation to be given to the offender of the procedure for applying under section 742.4 for a change to the optional conditions; and

(d) take reasonable measures to ensure that the offender understands the order and the explanations.

(4) For greater certainty — For greater certainty, a failure to comply with subsection (3) does not affect the validity of the order.

(5) Notice — samples at regular intervals — The notice referred to in paragraph (2)(a.2) must specify the places and times at which and the days on which the offender must provide samples of a bodily substance under a condition described in that paragraph. The first sample may not be taken earlier than 24 hours after the offender is served with the notice, and subsequent samples must be taken at regular intervals of at least seven days.

(6) Designations and specifications — For the purposes of paragraphs (2)(a.1) and (a.2) and subject to the regulations, the Attorney General of a province or the minister of justice of a territory shall, with respect to the province or territory,

(a) designate the persons or classes of persons that may take samples of bodily substances;

(b) designate the places or classes of places at which the samples are to be taken;

(c) specify the manner in which the samples are to be taken;

(d) specify the manner in which the samples are to be analyzed;

(e) specify the manner in which the samples are to be stored, handled and destroyed;

(f) specify the manner in which the records of the results of the analysis of the samples are to be protected and destroyed;

(g) designate the persons or classes of persons that may destroy the samples; and

(h) designate the persons or classes of persons that may destroy the records of the results of the analysis of the samples.

(7) Further designations — For the purpose of paragraph (2)(a.1) and subject to the regulations, the Attorney General of a province or the minister of justice of a territory may, with respect to the province or territory, designate persons or classes of persons to make a demand for a sample of a bodily substance.

(8) Restriction — Samples of bodily substances referred to in paragraphs (2)(a.1) and (a.2) may not be taken, analyzed, stored, handled or destroyed, and the records of the results of the analysis of the samples may not be protected or destroyed, except in accordance with the designations and specifications made under subsection (6).

(9) Destruction of samples — The Attorney General of a province or the minister of justice of a territory, or a person authorized by the Attorney General or minister, shall cause all samples of bodily substances provided under a conditional sentence order to be destroyed within the periods prescribed by regulation, unless the samples are reasonably expected to be used as evidence in proceedings under section 742.6.

(10) Regulations — The Governor in Council may make regulations

(a) prescribing bodily substances for the purposes of paragraphs (2)(a.1) and (a.2);

(b) respecting the designations and specifications referred to in subsections (6) and (7);

(c) prescribing the periods within which samples of bodily substances are to be destroyed under subsection (9); and

(d) respecting any other matters relating to the samples of bodily substances.

1995, c. 22, s. 6; 2008, c. 18, s. 40; 2011, c. 7, s. 5; 2014, c. 21, s. 3; 2015, c. 13, s. 33

742.31 (1) Prohibition on use of bodily substance — No person shall use a bodily substance provided under a conditional sentence order except for the purpose of determining whether an offender is complying with a condition of the order that they abstain from the consumption of drugs, alcohol or any other intoxicating substance.

(2) Prohibition on use or disclosure of result — Subject to subsection (3), no person shall use, disclose or allow the disclosure of the results of the analysis of a bodily substance provided under a conditional sentence order.

(3) Exception — The results of the analysis of a bodily substance provided under a conditional sentence order may be disclosed to the offender to whom they relate, and may also be used or disclosed in the course of proceedings under section 742.6 or, if the results are made anonymous, for statistical or other research purposes.

(4) Offence — Every person who contravenes subsection (1) or (2) is guilty of an offence punishable on summary conviction.

2011, c. 7, s. 6

742.4 (1) Supervisor may propose changes to optional conditions — Where an offender's supervisor is of the opinion that a change in circumstances makes a change to the optional conditions desirable, the supervisor shall give written notification of the proposed change, and the reasons for it, to the offender, to the prosecutor and to the court.

(2) Hearing — Within seven days after receiving a notification referred to in subsection (1),

(a) the offender or the prosecutor may request the court to hold a hearing to consider the proposed change, or

(b) the court may, of its own initiative, order that a hearing be held to consider the proposed change,

and a hearing so requested or ordered shall be held within thirty days after the receipt by the court of the notification referred to in subsection (1).

(3) Decision at hearing — At a hearing held pursuant to subsection (2), the court

(a) shall approve or refuse to approve the proposed change; and

(b) may make any other change to the optional conditions that the court deems appropriate.

(4) Where no hearing requested or ordered — Where no request or order for a hearing is made within the time period stipulated in subsection (2), the proposed change takes effect fourteen days after the receipt by the court of the notification referred to in subsection (1), and the supervisor shall so notify the offender and file proof of that notification with the court.

(5) Changes proposed by offender or prosecutor — Subsections (1) and (3) apply, with such modifications as the circumstances require, in respect of a change proposed by the offender or the prosecutor to the optional conditions, and in all such cases a hearing must be held, and must be held within thirty days after the receipt by the court of the notification referred to in subsection (1).

(6) Judge may act in chambers — All the functions of the court under this section may be exercised in chambers.

1995, c. 22, s. 6; 1999, c. 5, s. 39

742.5 (1) Transfer of order — Where an offender who is bound by a conditional sentence order becomes a resident of a territorial division, other than the territorial division where the order was made, on the application of a supervisor, the court that made the order may, subject to subsection (1.1), transfer the order to a court in that other territorial division that would, having regard to the mode of trial of the offender, have had jurisdiction to make the order in that other territorial division if the offender had been tried and convicted there of the offence in respect of which the order was made, and the order may thereafter be dealt with and enforced by the court to which it is so transferred in all respects as if that court had made the order.

(1.1) Attorney General's consent — The transfer may be granted only with

(a) the consent of the Attorney General of the province in which the conditional sentence order was made, if the two territorial divisions are not in the same province; or

(b) the consent of the Attorney General of Canada, if the proceedings that led to the issuance of the conditional sentence order were instituted by or on behalf of the Attorney General of Canada.

(2) Where court unable to act — Where a court that has made a conditional sentence order or to which a conditional sentence order has been transferred pursuant to subsection (1) is for any reason unable to act, the powers of that court in relation to the conditional sentence order may be exercised by any other court that has equivalent jurisdiction in the same province.

1995, c. 22, s. 6; 1999, c. 5, s. 40

742.6 (1) Procedure on breach of condition — For the purpose of proceedings under this section,

(a) the provisions of Parts XVI and XVIII with respect to compelling the appearance of an accused before a justice apply, with any modifications that the circumstances require, and any reference in those Parts to committing an offence shall be read as a reference to breaching a condition of a conditional sentence order;

(b) the powers of arrest for breach of a condition are those that apply to an indictable offence, with any modifications that the circumstances require, and subsection 495(2) does not apply;

(c) despite paragraph (a), if an allegation of breach of condition is made, the proceeding is commenced by

(i) the issuance of a warrant for the arrest of the offender for the alleged breach,

(ii) the arrest without warrant of the offender for the alleged breach, or

(iii) the compelling of the offender's appearance in accordance with paragraph (d);

(d) if the offender is already detained or before a court, the offender's appearance may be compelled under the provisions referred to in paragraph (a);

(e) if an offender is arrested for the alleged breach, the peace officer who makes the arrest, the officer in charge or a judge or justice may release the offender and the offender's appearance may be compelled under the provisions referred to in paragraph (a); and

Proposed Amendment — 742.6(1)(e)

(e) if an offender is arrested for the alleged breach, the peace officer who makes the arrest or a judge or justice may release the offender and the offender's appearance may be compelled under the provisions referred to in paragraph (a); and

2019, c. 25, s. 304 [To come into force December 18, 2019.]

(f) any judge of a superior court of criminal jurisdiction or of a court of criminal jurisdiction or any justice of the peace may issue a warrant to arrest no matter which court, judge or justice sentenced the offender, and the provisions that apply to the issuance of telewarrants apply, with any modifications that the circumstances require, as if a breach of condition were an indictable offence.

(2) Interim release — For the purpose of the application of section 515, the release from custody of an offender who is detained on the basis of an alleged breach of a condition of a conditional sentence order shall be governed by subsection 515(6).

(3) Hearing — The hearing of an allegation of a breach of condition shall be commenced within thirty days, or as soon thereafter as is practicable, after

(a) the offender's arrest; or

(b) the compelling of the offender's appearance in accordance with paragraph (1)(d).

(3.1) Place — The allegation may be heard by any court having jurisdiction to hear that allegation in the place where the breach is alleged to have been committed or the offender is found, arrested or in custody.

(3.2) Attorney General's consent — If the place where the offender is found, arrested or in custody is outside the province in which the breach is alleged to have been committed, no proceedings in respect of that breach shall be instituted in that place without

(a) the consent of the Attorney General of the province in which the breach is alleged to have been committed; or

(b) the consent of the Attorney General of Canada, if the proceedings that led to the issuance of the conditional sentence order were instituted by or on behalf of the Attorney General of Canada.

(3.3) Adjournment — A judge may, at any time during a hearing of an allegation of breach of condition, adjourn the hearing for a reasonable period.

(4) Report of supervisor — An allegation of a breach of condition must be supported by a written report of the supervisor, which report must include, where appropriate, signed statements of witnesses.

(5) Admission of report on notice of intent — The report is admissible in evidence if the party intending to produce it has, before the hearing, given the offender reasonable notice and a copy of the report.

(6) and (7) [Repealed 2008, c. 18, s. 41.]

(8) Requiring attendance of supervisor or witness — The offender may, with leave of the court, require the attendance, for cross-examination, of the supervisor or of any witness whose signed statement is included in the report.

(9) Powers of court — Where the court is satisfied, on a balance of probabilities, that the offender has without reasonable excuse, the proof of which lies on the offender, breached a condition of the conditional sentence order, the court may

(a) take no action;

(b) change the optional conditions;

(c) suspend the conditional sentence order and direct

(i) that the offender serve in custody a portion of the unexpired sentence, and

(ii) that the conditional sentence order resume on the offender's release from custody, either with or without changes to the optional conditions; or

(d) terminate the conditional sentence order and direct that the offender be committed to custody until the expiration of the sentence.

(10) Warrant or arrest — suspension of running of conditional sentence order — The running of a conditional sentence order imposed on an offender is suspended during the period that ends with the determination of whether a breach of condition had occurred and begins with the earliest of

(a) the issuance of a warrant for the arrest of the offender for the alleged breach,

(b) the arrest without warrant of the offender for the alleged breach, and

(c) the compelling of the offender's appearance in accordance with paragraph (1)(d).

(11) Conditions continue — If the offender is not detained in custody during any period referred to in subsection (10), the conditions of the order continue to apply, with any changes made to them under section 742.4, and any subsequent breach of those conditions may be dealt with in accordance with this section.

(12) Detention under s. 515(6) — A conditional sentence order referred to in subsection (10) starts running again on the making of an order to detain the offender in custody under subsection 515(6) and, unless section 742.7 applies, continues running while the offender is detained under the order.

(13) Earned remission does not apply — Section 6 of the *Prisons and Reformatories Act* does not apply to the period of detention in custody under subsection 515(6).

(14) Unreasonable delay in execution — Despite subsection (10), if there was unreasonable delay in the execution of a warrant, the court may, at any time, order that any period between the issuance and execution of the warrant that it considers appropriate in the interests of justice is deemed to be time served under the conditional sentence order unless the period has been so deemed under subsection (15).

(15) Allegation dismissed or reasonable excuse — If the allegation is withdrawn or dismissed or the offender is found to have had a reasonable excuse for the breach, the sum of the following periods is deemed to be time served under the conditional sentence order:

(a) any period for which the running of the conditional sentence order was suspended; and

(b) if subsection (12) applies, a period equal to one half of the period that the conditional sentence order runs while the offender is detained under an order referred to in that subsection.

(16) Powers of court — If a court is satisfied, on a balance of probabilities, that the offender has without reasonable excuse, the proof of which lies on the offender, breached a condition of the conditional sentence order, the court may, in exceptional cases and in the interests of justice, order that some or all of the period of suspension referred to in subsection (10) is deemed to be time served under the conditional sentence order.

(17) Considerations — In exercising its discretion under subsection (16), a court shall consider

(a) the circumstances and seriousness of the breach;

(b) whether not making the order would cause the offender undue hardship based on the offender's individual circumstances; and

(c) the period for which the offender was subject to conditions while the running of the conditional sentence order was suspended and whether the offender complied with those conditions during that period.

1995, c. 22, s. 6; 1999, c. 5, s. 41; 2004, c. 12, s. 15; 2008, c. 18, s. 41

742.7 (1) If person imprisoned for new offence — If an offender who is subject to a conditional sentence order is imprisoned as a result of a sentence imposed for another offence, whenever committed, the running of the conditional sentence order is suspended during the period of imprisonment for that other offence.

(2) Breach of condition — If an order is made under paragraph 742.6(9)(c) or (d) to commit an offender to custody, the custodial period ordered shall, unless the court considers that it would not be in the interests of justice, be served consecutively to any other period of imprisonment that the offender is serving when that order is made.

(3) Multiple sentences — If an offender is serving both a custodial period referred to in subsection (2) and any other period of imprisonment, the periods shall, for the purpose of section 743.1 and section 139 of the *Corrections and Conditional Release Act*, be deemed to constitute one sentence of imprisonment.

(4) Conditional sentence order resumes — The running of any period of the conditional sentence order that is to be served in the community resumes upon the release of the offender from prison on parole, on statutory release, on earned remission, or at the expiration of the sentence.

1995, c. 22, s. 6; 1999, c. 5, s. 42; 2004, c. 12, s. 16

Imprisonment

743. Imprisonment when no other provision — Every one who is convicted of an indictable offence for which no punishment is specially provided is liable to imprisonment for a term not exceeding five years.

1995, c. 22, s. 6

743.1 (1) Imprisonment for life or more than two years — Except where otherwise provided, a person who is sentenced to imprisonment for

(a) life,

(b) a term of two years or more, or

(c) two or more terms of less than two years each that are to be served one after the other and that, in the aggregate, amount to two years or more,

shall be sentenced to imprisonment in a penitentiary.

(2) Subsequent term less than two years — Where a person who is sentenced to imprisonment in a penitentiary is, before the expiration of that sentence, sentenced to imprisonment for a term of less than two years, the person shall serve that term in a penitentiary, but if the previous sentence of imprisonment in a penitentiary is set aside, that person shall serve that term in accordance with subsection (3).

(3) Imprisonment for term less than two years — A person who is sentenced to imprisonment and who is not required to be sentenced as provided in subsection (1) or (2) shall, unless a special prison is prescribed by law, be sentenced to imprisonment in a prison or other place of confinement, other than a penitentiary, within the province in which the person is convicted, in which the sentence of imprisonment may be lawfully executed.

(3.1) Long-term supervision — Despite subsection (3), an offender who is subject to long-term supervision under Part XXIV and is sentenced for another offence during the period of the supervision shall be sentenced to imprisonment in a penitentiary.

(4) Sentence to penitentiary of person serving sentence elsewhere — Where a person is sentenced to imprisonment in a penitentiary while the person is lawfully imprisoned in a place other than a penitentiary, that person shall, except where otherwise provided, be sent immediately to the penitentiary, and shall serve in the penitentiary the unexpired portion of the term of imprisonment that the person was serving when sentenced to the penitentiary as well as the term of imprisonment for which that person was sentenced to the penitentiary.

(5) Transfer to penitentiary — Where, at any time, a person who is imprisoned in a prison or place of confinement other than a penitentiary is subject to two or more terms of imprisonment, each of which is for less than two years, that are to be served one after the other, and the aggregate of the unexpired portions of those terms at that time amounts to two years or more, the person shall be transferred to a penitentiary to serve those terms, but if any one or more of such terms is set aside or reduced and the unexpired portions of the remaining term or terms on the day on which that person was transferred under this section amounted to less than two years, that person shall serve that term or terms in accordance with subsection (3).

(6) Newfoundland — For the purposes of subsection (3), "penitentiary" does not, until a day to be fixed by order of the Governor in Council, include the facility mentioned in subsection 15(2) of the *Corrections and Conditional Release Act*.

1995, c. 22, s. 6; 1997, c. 17, s. 1; 2008, c. 6, s. 39

743.2 Report by court to correctional service — A court that sentences or commits a person to penitentiary shall forward to the Correctional Service of Canada its reasons and recommendation relating to the sentence or committal, any relevant reports that were submitted to the court, and any other information relevant to administering the sentence or committal.

1995, c. 22, s. 6

743.21 (1) Non-communication order — The sentencing judge may issue an order prohibiting the offender from communicating, directly or indirectly, with any victim, witness or other person identified in the order during the custodial period of the sentence, except in accordance with any conditions specified in the order that the sentencing judge considers necessary.

(2) Failure to comply with order — Every person who fails, without lawful excuse, to comply with the order

(a) is guilty of an indictable offence and liable to imprisonment for a term not exceeding two years; or

(b) is guilty of an offence punishable on summary conviction.

2008, c. 18, s. 42; 2018, c. 29, s. 67; 2019, c. 25, s. 305

743.3 Sentence served according to regulations — A sentence of imprisonment shall be served in accordance with the enactments and rules that govern the institution to which the prisoner is sentenced.

1995, c. 22, s. 6

743.4 [Repealed 2002, c. 1, s. 184.]

743.5 (1) Transfer of jurisdiction when person already sentenced under *Youth Criminal Justice Act* — If a young person or an adult is or has been sentenced to a term of imprisonment for an offence while subject to a disposition made under paragraph 20(1)(k) or (k.1) of the *Young Offenders Act*, chapter Y-1 of the Revised Statutes of Canada, 1985, or a youth sentence imposed under paragraph 42(2)(n), (o), (q) or (r) of the *Youth Criminal Justice Act*, the remaining portion of the disposition or youth sentence shall be dealt with, for all purposes under this Act or any other Act of Parliament, as if it had been a sentence imposed under this Act.

(2) Transfer of jurisdiction when youth sentence imposed under *Youth Criminal Justice Act* — If a disposition is made under paragraph 20(1)(k) or (k.1) of the *Young Offenders Act*, chapter Y-1 of the Revised Statutes of Canada, 1985, with respect to a person or a youth sentence is imposed on a person under paragraph 42(2)(n), (o), (q) or (r) of the *Youth Criminal Justice Act* while the young person or adult is under sentence of imprisonment imposed under an Act of Parliament other than the *Youth Criminal Justice Act*, the disposition or youth sentence shall be dealt with, for all purposes under this Act or any other Act of Parliament, as if it had been a sentence imposed under this Act.

(3) Sentences deemed to constitute one sentence — section 743.1 — For greater certainty, the following are deemed to constitute one sentence of imprisonment for the purposes of section 139 of the *Corrections and Conditional Release Act*:

(a) for the purposes of subsection (1), the remainder of the youth sentence or disposition and the subsequent term of imprisonment; and

(b) for the purposes of subsection (2), the term of imprisonment and the subsequent youth sentence or disposition.

1995, c. 22, ss. 6, 19(b), 20(b); 2002, c. 1, s. 184; 2008, c. 18, s. 43

Eligibility for Parole

743.6 (1) Power of court to delay parole — Notwithstanding subsection 120(1) of the *Corrections and Conditional Release Act*, where an offender is sentenced, after the coming into force of this section, to a term of imprisonment of two years or more, including a sentence of imprisonment for life imposed otherwise than as a minimum punishment, on conviction for an offence set out in Schedule I or II to that Act that were prosecuted by way of indictment, the court may, if satisfied, having regard to the circumstances of the commission of the offence and the character and circumstances of the offender, that the expression of society's denunciation of the offences or the objective of specific or general deterrence so requires, order that the portion of the sentence that must be served before the offender may be released on full parole is one half of the sentence or ten years, whichever is less.

(1.1) Power of court to delay parole — Notwithstanding section 120 of the *Corrections and Conditional Release Act*, where an offender receives a sentence of imprisonment of two years or more, including a sentence of imprisonment for life imposed otherwise than as a minimum punishment, on conviction for a criminal organization offence other than an offence under section 467.11, 467.111, 467.12 or 467.13, the court may order that the portion of the sentence that must be served before the offender may be released on full parole is one half of the sentence or ten years, whichever is less.

(1.2) Power of court to delay parole — Notwithstanding section 120 of the *Corrections and Conditional Release Act*, where an offender receives a sentence of imprisonment of two years or more, including a sentence of imprisonment for life, on conviction for a terrorism offence or an offence under section 467.11, 467.111, 467.12 or 467.13, the court shall order that the portion of the sentence that must be served before the offender may be released on full parole is one half of the sentence or ten years, whichever is less, unless the court is satisfied, having regard to the circumstances of the commission of the offence and the character and circumstances of the offender, that the expression of society's denunciation of the offence and the objectives of specific and general deterrence would be adequately served by a period of parole ineligibility determined in accordance with the *Corrections and Conditional Release Act*.

(2) Principles that are to guide the court — For greater certainty, the paramount principles that are to guide the court under this section are denunciation and specific or general deterrence, with rehabilitation of the offender, in all cases, being subordinate to those paramount principles.

1995, c. 22, s. 6; 1995, c. 42, s. 86(b); 1997, c. 23, s. 18; 2001, c. 32, s. 45; 2001, c. 41, ss. 21, 133(18); 2014, c. 17, ss. 15, 16

Delivery of Offender to Keeper of Prison

744. Execution of warrant of committal — A peace officer or other person to whom a warrant of committal authorized by this or any other Act of Parliament is directed shall arrest the person named or described therein, if it is necessary to do so in order to take that person into custody, convey that person to the prison mentioned in the warrant and deliver that person, together with the warrant, to the keeper of the prison who shall thereupon give to the peace officer or other person who delivers the prisoner a receipt in Form 43 setting out the state and condition of the prisoner when delivered into custody.

1995, c. 22, s. 6

744.1 [Repealed 1995, c. 22, s. 6.]

Imprisonment for Life

745. Sentence of life imprisonment — Subject to section 745.1, the sentence to be pronounced against a person who is to be sentenced to imprisonment for life shall be

(a) in respect of a person who has been convicted of high treason or first degree murder, that the person be sentenced to imprisonment for life without eligibility for parole until the person has served twenty-five years of the sentence;

(b) in respect of a person who has been convicted of second degree murder where that person has previously been convicted of culpable homicide that is murder, however described in this Act, that the person be sentenced to imprisonment for life without eligibility for parole until the person has served twenty-five years of the sentence;

(b.1) in respect of a person who has been convicted of second degree murder where that person has previously been convicted of an offence under section 4 or 6 of the *Crimes Against Humanity and War Crimes Act* that had as its basis an intentional killing, whether or not it was planned and deliberate, that that person be sentenced to imprisonment for life without eligibility for parole until the person has served twenty-five years of the sentence;

(c) in respect of a person who has been convicted of second degree murder, that the person be sentenced to imprisonment for life without eligibility for parole until the person has served at least ten years of the sentence or such greater number of years, not being more than twenty-five years, as has been substituted therefor pursuant to section 745.4; and

(d) in respect of a person who has been convicted of any other offence, that the person be sentenced to imprisonment for life with normal eligibility for parole.

1995, c. 22, s. 6; 2000, c. 24, s. 46

745.01 (1) Information in respect of parole — Except where subsection 745.6(2) applies, at the time of sentencing under paragraph 745(a), (b) or (c), the judge who presided at the trial of the offender shall state the following, for the record:

> The offender has been found guilty of (*state offence*) and sentenced to imprisonment for life. The offender is not eligible for parole until (*state date*). However, after serving at least 15 years of the sentence, the offender may apply under section 745.6 of the *Criminal Code* for a reduction in the number of years of imprisonment without eligibility for parole. If the jury hearing the application reduces the period of parole ineligibility, the offender may then make an application for parole under the *Corrections and Conditional Release Act* at the end of that reduced period.

(2) Exception — Subsection (1) does not apply if the offender is convicted of an offence committed on or after the day on which this subsection comes into force.

1999, c. 25, s. 21; 2011, c. 2, s. 2

745.1 Persons under eighteen — The sentence to be pronounced against a person who was under the age of eighteen at the time of the commission of the offence for which the person was convicted of first degree murder or second degree murder and who is to be sentenced to imprisonment for life shall be that the person be sentenced to imprisonment for life without eligibility for parole until the person has served

(a) such period between five and seven years of the sentence as is specified by the judge presiding at the trial, or if no period is specified by the judge presiding at the trial, five years, in the case of a person who was under the age of sixteen at the time of the commission of the offence;

(b) ten years, in the case of a person convicted of first degree murder who was sixteen or seventeen years of age at the time of the commission of the offence; and

(c) seven years, in the case of a person convicted of second degree murder who was sixteen or seventeen years of age at the time of the commission of the offence.

1995, c. 22, ss. 6, 21(b)

745.2 Recommendation by jury — Subject to section 745.3, where a jury finds an accused guilty of second degree murder, the judge presiding at the trial shall, before discharging the jury, put to them the following question: You have found the accused guilty of second degree murder and the law requires that I now pronounce a sentence of imprisonment for life against the accused. Do you wish to make any recommendation with respect to the number of years that the accused must serve before the accused is eligible for release on parole? You are not required to make any recommendation but if you do, your recommendation will be considered by me when I am determining whether I should substitute for the ten year period, which the law would otherwise require the accused to serve before the accused is eligible to be considered for release on parole, a number of years that is more than ten but not more than twenty-five.

1995, c. 22, s. 6

745.21 (1) Recommendation by jury — multiple murders — Where a jury finds an accused guilty of murder and that accused has previously been convicted of murder, the judge presiding at the trial shall, before discharging the jury, put to them the following question: You have found the accused guilty of murder. The law requires that I now pronounce a sentence of imprisonment for life against the accused. Do you wish to make any recommendation with respect to the period without eligibility for parole to be served for this murder consecutively to the period without eligibility for parole imposed for the previous murder? You are not required to make any recommendation, but if you do, your recommendation will be considered by me when I make my determination.

(2) Application — Subsection (1) applies to an offender who is convicted of murders committed on a day after the day on which this section comes into force and for which the offender is sentenced under this Act, the *National Defence Act* or the *Crimes Against Humanity and War Crimes Act*.

2011, c. 5, s. 4

745.3 Persons under sixteen — Where a jury finds an accused guilty of first degree murder or second degree murder and the accused was under the age of sixteen at the time of the commission of the offence, the judge presiding at the trial shall, before discharging the jury, put to them the following question: You have found the accused guilty of first degree murder (or second degree murder) and the law requires that I now pronounce a sentence of imprisonment for life against the accused. Do you wish to make any recommendation with respect to the period of imprisonment that the accused must serve before the accused is eligible for release on parole? You are not required to make any recommendation but if you do, your recommendation will be considered by me when I am determining the period of imprisonment that is between five years and seven years that the law would require the accused to serve before the accused is eligible to be considered for release on parole.

1995, c. 22, ss. 6, 22(b)

745.4 Ineligibility for parole — Subject to section 745.5, at the time of the sentencing under section 745 of an offender who is convicted of second degree murder, the judge who presided at the trial of the offender or, if that judge is unable to do so, any judge of the same court may, having regard to the character of the offender, the nature of the offence and the circumstances surrounding its commission, and to the recommendation, if any, made pursuant to section 745.2, by order, substitute for ten years a number of years of imprisonment (being more than ten but nor more than twenty-five) without eligibility for parole, as the judge deems fit in the circumstances.

1995, c. 22, s. 6

745.5 Idem — At the time of the sentencing under section 745.1 of an offender who is convicted of first degree murder or second degree murder and who was under the age of sixteen at the time of the commission of the offence, the judge who presided at the trial of the offender or, if that judge is unable to do so, any judge of the same court, may, having regard to the age and character of the offender, the nature of the offence and the circumstances surrounding its commission, and to the recommendation, if any, made pursuant to section 745.3, by order, decide the period of imprisonment the offender is to serve that is between five years and seven years without eligibility for parole, as the judge deems fit in the circumstances.

1995, c. 22, ss. 6, 23(b)

745.51 (1) Ineligibility for parole — multiple murders — At the time of the sentencing under section 745 of an offender who is convicted of murder and who has already been convicted of one or more other murders, the judge who presided at the trial of the offender or, if that judge is unable to do so, any judge of the same court may, having regard to the character of the offender, the nature of the offence and the circumstances surrounding its commission, and the recommendation, if any, made pursuant to section 745.21, by order, decide that the periods without eligibility for parole for each murder conviction are to be served consecutively.

(2) Reasons — The judge shall give, either orally or in writing, reasons for the decision to make or not to make an order under subsection (1).

(3) Application — Subsections (1) and (2) apply to an offender who is convicted of murders committed on a day after the day on which this section comes into force and for which the offender is sentenced under this Act, the *National Defence Act* or the *Crimes Against Humanity and War Crimes Act*.

2011, c. 5, s. 5

745.6 (1) Application for judicial review — Subject to subsections (2) to (2.6), a person may apply, in writing, to the appropriate Chief Justice in the province in which their conviction took place for a reduction in the number of years of imprisonment without eligibility for parole if the person

(a) has been convicted of murder or high treason;

(a.1) committed the murder or high treason before the day on which this paragraph comes into force;

(b) has been sentenced to imprisonment for life without eligibility for parole until more than fifteen years of their sentence has been served; and

(c) has served at least fifteen years of their sentence.

(2) Exception — multiple murderers — A person who has been convicted of more than one murder may not make an application under subsection (1), whether or not proceedings were commenced in respect of any of the murders before another murder was committed.

(2.1) Less than 15 years of sentence served — A person who is convicted of murder or high treason and who has served less than 15 years of their sentence on the day on which this subsection comes into force may, within 90 days after the day on which they have served 15 years of their sentence, make an application under subsection (1).

(2.2) At least 15 years of sentence served — A person who is convicted of murder or high treason and who has served at least 15 years of their sentence on the day on which this subsection comes into force may make an application under subsection (1) within 90 days after

(a) the end of five years after the day on which the person was the subject of a determination made under subsection 745.61(4) or a determination or conclusion to which subsection 745.63(8) applies; or

(b) the day on which this subsection comes into force, if the person has not made an application under subsection (1).

(2.3) Non-application of subsection (2.2) — Subsection (2.2) has no effect on a determination or decision made under subsection 745.61(3) or (5) or 745.63(3), (5) or (6) as it read immediately before the day on which this subsection comes into force. A person in respect of whom a time is set under paragraph 745.61(3)(a) or 745.63(6)(a) as it read immediately before that day may make an application under subsection (1) within 90 days after the end of that time.

(2.4) Further five-year period if no application made — If the person does not make an application in accordance with subsection (2.1), (2.2) or (2.3), as the case may be, they may make an application within 90 days after the day on which they have served a further five years of their sentence following the 90-day period referred to in that subsection, as the case may be.

(2.5) Subsequent applications — A person who makes an application in accordance with subsection (2.1), (2.2) or (2.3), as the case may be, may make another application under subsection (1) within 90 days after

(a) the end of the time set under paragraph 745.61(3)(a) or 745.63(6)(a), if a time is set under that paragraph; or

(b) the end of five years after the day on which the person is the subject of a determination made under subsection 745.61(4) or a determination or conclusion to which subsection 745.63(8) applies, if the person is the subject of such a determination or conclusion.

(2.6) Subsequent applications — A person who had made an application under subsection (1) as it read immediately before the day on which this subsection comes into force, whose application was finally disposed of on or after that day and who has then made a subsequent application may make a further application in accordance with subsection (2.5), if either paragraph (2.5)(a) or (b) is applicable.

(2.7) The 90-day time limits for the making of any application referred to in subsections (2.1) to (2.5) may be extended by the appropriate Chief Justice, or his or her designate, to a maximum of 180 days if the person, due to circumstances beyond their control, is unable to make an application within the 90-day time limit.

(2.8) If a person convicted of murder does not make an application under subsection (1) within the maximum time period allowed by this section, the Commissioner of Correctional Service Canada, or his or her designate, shall immediately notify in writing a parent, child, spouse or common-law partner of the victim that the convicted person did not make an application. If it is not possible to notify one of the aforementioned relatives, then the notification shall be given to another relative of the victim. The notification shall specify the next date on which the convicted person will be eligible to make an application under subsection (1).

(3) Definition of "appropriate chief justice" — For the purposes of this section and sections 745.61 to 745.64, the **"appropriate Chief Justice"** is

(a) in relation to the Province of Ontario, the Chief Justice of the Ontario Court;

(b) in relation to the Province of Quebec, the Chief Justice of the Superior Court;

(c) in relation to the Province of Newfoundland and Labrador, the Chief Justice of the Supreme Court, Trial Division;

(d) in relation to the Provinces of New Brunswick, Manitoba, Saskatchewan and Alberta, the Chief Justice of the Court of Queen's Bench;

(e) in relation to the Provinces of Nova Scotia, British Columbia and Prince Edward Island, the Chief Justice of the Supreme Court; and

(f) in relation to Yukon, the Northwest Territories and Nunavut, the Chief Justice of the Court of Appeal.

1993, c. 28, s. 78 (Sched. III, item 35) [Amended 1998, c. 15, s. 20.]; 1995, c. 22, s. 6; 1996, c. 34, s. 2(2); 2002, c. 7, s. 146; 2011, c. 2, s. 3; 2015, c. 3, s. 55

745.61 (1) Judicial screening — On receipt of an application under subsection 745.6(1), the appropriate Chief Justice shall determine, or shall designate a judge of the superior court of criminal jurisdiction to determine, on the basis of the following written material, whether the applicant has shown, on a balance of probabilities, that there is a substantial likelihood that the application will succeed:

(a) the application;

(b) any report provided by the Correctional Service of Canada or other correctional authorities; and

(c) any other written evidence presented to the Chief Justice or judge by the applicant or the Attorney General.

(2) Criteria — In determining whether the applicant has shown that there is a substantial likelihood that the application will succeed, the Chief Justice or judge shall consider the criteria set out in paragraphs 745.63(1)(a) to (e), with any modifications that the circumstances require.

(3) Decision re new application — If the Chief Justice or judge determines that the applicant has not shown that there is a substantial likelihood that the application will succeed, the Chief Justice or judge may

(a) set a time, no earlier than five years after the date of the determination, at or after which the applicant may make another application under subsection 745.6(1); or

(b) decide that the applicant may not make another application under that subsection.

(4) If no decision re new application — If the Chief Justice or judge determines that the applicant has not shown that there is a substantial likelihood that the application will succeed but does not set a time for another application or decide that such an application may not be made, the applicant may make another application no earlier than five years after the date of the determination.

(5) Designation of judge to empanel jury — If the Chief Justice or judge determines that the applicant has shown that there is a substantial likelihood that the application will succeed, the Chief Justice shall designate a judge of the superior court of criminal jurisdiction to empanel a jury to hear the application.

1996, c. 34, s. 2(2); 2011, c. 2, s. 4

[Editor's Note: Section 745.61 of the Criminal Code applies in respect of applications for judicial review made after January 9, 1997 in respect of crimes committed before or after that date, unless the applicant has, before that date, made an application under s. 745.6(1) of the Code as it read immediately before that date and the application had not yet been disposed of before that date: see 1996, c. 34, s. 7.]

745.62 (1) Appeal — The applicant or the Attorney General may appeal to the Court of Appeal from a determination or a decision made under section 745.61 on any question of law or fact or mixed law and fact.

(2) Documents to be considered — The appeal shall be determined on the basis of the documents presented to the Chief Justice or judge who made the determination or decision, any reasons for the determination or decision and any other documents that the Court of Appeal requires.

(3) Sections to apply — Sections 673 to 696 apply, with such modifications as the circumstances require.

1996, c. 34, s. 2(2)

[Editor's Note: Section 745.62 of the Criminal Code applies in respect of applications for judicial review made after January 9, 1997, in respect of crimes committed

before or after that date, unless the applicant has, before that date, made an application under s. 745.6(1) of the Code as it read immediately before that date and the application had not yet been disposed of before that date: see 1996, c. 34, s. 7.]

745.63 (1) Hearing of application — The jury empanelled under subsection 745.61(5) to hear the application shall consider the following criteria and determine whether the applicant's number of years of imprisonment without eligibility for parole ought to be reduced:

(a) the character of the applicant;

(b) the applicant's conduct while serving the sentence;

(c) the nature of the offence for which the applicant was convicted;

(d) any information provided by a victim at the time of the imposition of the sentence or at the time of the hearing under this section; and

(e) any other matters that the judge considers relevant in the circumstances.

(1.1) Information provided by victim — Information provided by a victim referred to in paragraph (1)(d) may be provided either orally or in writing, at the discretion of the victim, or in any other manner that the judge considers appropriate.

(2) [Repealed 2015, c. 13, s. 34.]

(3) Reduction — The jury hearing an application under subsection (1) may determine that the applicant's number of years of imprisonment without eligibility for parole ought to be reduced. The determination to reduce the number of years must be by unanimous vote.

(4) No reduction — The applicant's number of years of imprisonment without eligibility for parole is not reduced if

(a) the jury hearing an application under subsection (1) determines that the number of years ought not to be reduced;

(b) the jury hearing an application under subsection (1) concludes that it cannot unanimously determine that the number of years ought to be reduced; or

(c) the presiding judge, after the jury has deliberated for a reasonable period, concludes that the jury is unable to unanimously determine that the number of years ought to be reduced.

(5) Where determination to reduce number of years — If the jury determines that the number of years of imprisonment without eligibility for parole ought to be reduced, the jury may, by a vote of not less than two thirds of the members of the jury,

(a) substitute a lesser number of years of imprisonment without eligibility for parole than that then applicable; or

(b) terminate the ineligibility for parole.

(6) Decision re new application — If the applicant's number of years of imprisonment without eligibility for parole is not reduced, the jury may

(a) set a time, no earlier than five years after the date of the determination or conclusion under subsection (4), at or after which the applicant may make another application under subsection 745.6(1); or

(b) decide that the applicant may not make another application under that subsection.

(7) Two-thirds decision — The decision of the jury under paragraph (6)(*a*) or (*b*) must be made by not less than two thirds of its members.

(8) If no decision re new application — If the jury does not set a date on or after which another application may be made or decide that such an application may not be made, the applicant may make another application no earlier than five years after the date of the determination or conclusion under subsection (4).

1996, c. 34, s. 2(2); 1999, c. 25, s. 22; 2011, c. 2, s. 5; 2015, c. 13, s. 34

[Editor's Note: Section 745.63 of the Criminal Code, other than paragraph 745.63(1)(d), applies in respect of applications for judicial review made after January 9, 1997, in respect of crimes committed before or after that date, unless the applicant has, before that date, made an application under s. 745.6(1) of the Code as it read immediately before that date and the application had not yet been disposed of before that date. Paragraph 745.63(1)(d) applies in respect of hearings held after January 9, 1997, with respect to applications for judicial review in respect of crimes committed before or after that date: see 1996, c. 34, ss. 7, 8 (as amended by 1997, c. 18, s. 139.1).]

745.64 (1) Rules — The appropriate Chief Justice in each province or territory may make such rules as are required for the purposes of sections 745.6 to 745.63.

(1.1) Statutory Instruments Act — The *Statutory Instruments Act* does not apply to those rules.

(2) Territories — When the appropriate Chief Justice is designating a judge of the superior court of criminal jurisdiction, for the purpose of a judicial screening under subsection 745.61(1) or to empanel a jury to hear an application under subsection 745.61(5), in respect of a conviction that took place in Yukon, the Northwest Territories or Nunavut, the appropriate Chief Justice may designate the judge from the Court of Appeal of Yukon, the Northwest Territories or Nunavut, or the Supreme Court of Yukon or the Northwest Territories or the Nunavut Court of Justice, as the case may be.

1996, c. 34, s. 2(2); 1998, c. 15, s. 20 [Repealed 1999, c. 3, s. 12 (Sched., item 9).]; 1999, c. 3, s. 53; 2002, c. 7, s. 147; 2019, c. 25, s. 306

746. Time spent in custody — In calculating the period of imprisonment served for the purposes of section 745, 745.1, 745.4 745.5 or 745.6, there shall be included any time spent in custody between,

(a) in the case of a sentence of imprisonment for life imposed after July 25, 1976, the day on which the person was arrested and taken into custody in respect of the offence for which that person was sentenced to imprisonment for life and the day the sentence was imposed; or

(b) in the case of a sentence of death that has been or is deemed to have been commuted to a sentence of imprisonment for life, the day on which the person was arrested and taken into custody in respect of the offence for which that person was sentenced to death and the day the sentence was commuted or deemed to have been commuted to a sentence of imprisonment for life.

1995, c. 22, ss. 6, 24(b)

746.1 (1) Parole prohibited — Unless Parliament otherwise provides by an enactment making express reference to this section, a person who has been sentenced to imprisonment for life without eligibility for parole for a specified number of years pursuant to this Act shall not be considered for parole or released pursuant to a grant of parole under the *Corrections and Conditional Release Act* or any other Act of Parliament until the expiration or termination of the specified number of years of imprisonment.

(2) Absences with or without escort and day parole — Subject to subsection (3), in respect of a person sentenced to imprisonment for life without eligibility for parole for a specified number of years pursuant to this Act, until the expiration of all but three years of the specified number of years of imprisonment,

(a) no day parole may be granted under the *Corrections and Conditional Release Act*;

(b) no absence without escort may be authorized under that Act or the *Prisons and Reformatories Act*; and

(c) except with the approval of the Parole Board of Canada, no absence with escort otherwise than for medical reasons or in order to attend judicial proceedings or a coroner's inquest may be authorized under either of those Acts.

(3) Young offenders — In the case of any person convicted of first degree murder or second degree murder who was under the age of eighteen at the time of the commission of the offence and who is sentenced to imprisonment for life without eligibility for parole for a specified number of years pursuant to this Act, until the expiration of all but one fifth of the period of imprisonment the person is to serve without eligibility for parole,

(a) no day parole may be granted under the *Corrections and Conditional Release Act*;

(b) no absence without escort may be authorized under that Act or the *Prisons and Reformatories Act*; and

(c) except with the approval of the Parole Board of Canada, no absence with escort otherwise than for medical reasons or in order to attend judicial proceedings or a coroner's inquest may be authorized under either of those Acts.

1995, c. 22, s. 6; 1995, c. 42, s. 87(b); 1997, c. 17, s. 2; 2012, c. 1, s. 160(c)(iii)

[Editor's Note: Sections 747 to 747.8 of the Criminal Code*, as proposed by S.C. 1995, c. 22, s. 6, would have enacted a hospital orders regime. They were repealed before they came into force by S.C. 2005, c. 22, s. 39, effective January 2, 2006.]*

747. [Repealed 1995, c. 22, s. 6.]

Pardons and Remissions

748. (1) To whom pardon may be granted — Her Majesty may extend the royal mercy to a person who is sentenced to imprisonment under the authority of an Act of Parliament, even if the person is imprisoned for failure to pay money to another person.

(2) Free or conditional pardon — The Governor in Council may grant a free pardon or a conditional pardon to any person who has been convicted of an offence.

(3) Effect of free pardon — Where the Governor in Council grants a free pardon to a person, that person shall be deemed thereafter never to have committed the offence in respect of which the pardon is granted.

(4) Punishment for subsequent offence not affected — No free pardon or conditional pardon prevents or mitigates the punishment to which the person might otherwise be lawfully sentenced on a subsequent conviction for an offence other than that for which the pardon was granted.

1995, c. 22, s. 6

748.1 (1) Remission by Governor in Council — The Governor in Council may order the remission, in whole or in part, of a fine or forfeiture imposed under an Act of Parliament, whoever the person may be to whom it is payable or however it may be recoverable.

(2) Terms of remission — An order for remission under subsection (1) may include the remission of costs incurred in the proceedings, but no costs to which a private prosecutor is entitled shall be remitted.

1995, c. 22, s. 6

749. Royal prerogative — Nothing in this Act in any manner limits or affects Her Majesty's royal prerogative of mercy.

1995, c. 22, s. 6

Disabilities

750. (1) Public office vacated for conviction — Where a person is convicted of an indictable offence for which the person is sentenced to imprisonment for two years or more and holds, at the time that person is convicted, an office under the Crown or other public employment, the office or employment forthwith becomes vacant.

(2) When disability ceases — A person to whom subsection (1) applies is, until undergoing the punishment imposed on the person or the punishment substituted therefor by competent authority or receives a free pardon from Her Majesty, incapable of holding any office under the Crown or other public employment, or of being elected or sitting or voting as a member of Parliament or of a legislature or of exercising any right of suffrage.

(3) Disability to contract — No person who is convicted of

(a) an offence under section 121, 124 or 418,

(b) an offence under section 380 committed against her Majesty, or

(c) an offence under paragraph 80(1)(d), subsection 80(2) or section 154.01 of the *Financial Administration Act*,

has, after that conviction, capacity to contract with Her Majesty or to receive any benefit under a contract between Her Majesty and any other person or to hold office under Her Majesty.

(4) Application for restoration of privileges — A person to whom subsection (3) applies may, at any time before a record suspension for which he or she has applied is ordered under the *Criminal Records Act*, apply to the Governor in Council for the restoration of one or more of the capacities lost by the person by virtue of that subsection.

(5) Order of restoration — Where an application is made under subsection (4), the Governor in council may order that the capacities lost by the applicant by virtue of subsection (3) be restored to that applicant in whole or in part and subject to such conditions as the Governor in Council considers desirable in the public interest.

(6) Removal of disability — Where a conviction is set aside by competent authority, any disability imposed by this section is removed.

1995, c. 22, s. 6; 2000, c. 1, s. 9; 2006, c. 9, s. 246; 2012, c. 1, s. 146

Miscellaneous Provisions

751. Costs to successful party in case of libel — The person in whose favour judgment is given in proceedings by indictment for defamatory libel is entitled to recover from the opposite party costs in a reasonable amount to be fixed by order of the court.

1995, c. 22, s. 6

751.1 How recovered — Where costs that are fixed under section 751 are not paid forthwith, the party in whose favour judgment is given may enter judgment for the amount of the costs by filing the order in any civil court of the province in which the trial was held that has jurisdiction to enter a judgment for that amount, and that judgment is enforceable against the opposite party in the same manner as if it were a judgment rendered against that opposite party in that court in civil proceedings.

1995, c. 22, s. 6

PART XXIV — DANGEROUS OFFENDERS AND LONG-TERM OFFENDERS (SS. 752–761)

Interpretation

752. Definitions — In this Part,

"court" means the court by which an offender in relation to whom an application under this Part is made was convicted, or a superior court of criminal jurisdiction;

"designated offence" means

(a) a primary designated offence,

(b) an offence under any of the following provisions:

(i) paragraph 81(1)(a) (using explosives),

(ii) paragraph 81(1)(b) (using explosives),

(iii) section 85 (using firearm or imitation firearm in commission of offence),

(iv) section 87 (pointing firearm),

(iv.1) section 98 (breaking and entering to steal firearm),

(iv.2) section 98.1 (robbery to steal firearm),

(v) section 153.1 (sexual exploitation of person with disability),

(vi) section 163.1 (child pornography),

(vii) section 170 (parent or guardian procuring sexual activity),

(viii) section 171 (householder permitting sexual activity by or in presence of child),

(ix) section 172.1 (luring child),

(ix.1) section 172.2 (agreement or arrangement — sexual offence against child),

(x) to (xii) [Repealed 2014, c. 25, s. 29(1).]

(xiii) section 245 (administering noxious thing),

(xiv) section 266 (assault),

(xv) section 269 (unlawfully causing bodily harm),

(xvi) section 269.1 (torture),

(xvii) paragraph 270(1)(a) (assaulting peace officer),

(xviii) section 273.3 (removal of child from Canada),

(xix) subsection 279(2) (forcible confinement),

(xx) section 279.01 (trafficking in persons),

(xx.1) section 279.011 (trafficking of a person under the age of eighteen years),

(xx.2) section 279.02 (material benefit — trafficking),

(xx.3) section 279.03 (withholding or destroying documents — trafficking),

(xxi) section 279.1 (hostage taking),

(xxii) section 280 (abduction of person under age of 16),

(xxiii) section 281 (abduction of person under age of 14),

(xxiii.1) subsection 286.1(2) (obtaining sexual services for consideration from person under 18 years), (xxiii.2) section 286.2 (material benefit from sexual services),

(xxiii.3) section 286.3 (procuring),

(xxiii.4) section 320.13 (dangerous operation),

(xxiii.5) subsections 320.14(1), (2) and (3) (operation while impaired),

(xxiii.6) section 320.15 (failure or refusal to comply with demand),

(xxiii.7) section 320.16 (failure to stop after accident),

(xxiii.8) section 320.17 (flight from peace officer),

(xxiv) section 344 (robbery), and

(xxv) section 348 (breaking and entering with intent, committing offence or breaking out),

(c) an offence under any of the following provisions of the *Criminal Code*, chapter C-34 of the Revised Statutes of Canada, 1970, as they read from time to time before January 1, 1988:

(i) subsection 146(2) (sexual intercourse with female between ages of 14 and 16),

(ii) section 148 (sexual intercourse with feeble-minded),

(iii) section 166 (parent or guardian procuring defilement), and

(iv) section 167 (householder permitting defilement),

(c.1) an offence under any of the following provisions of this Act, as they read from time to time before the day on which this paragraph comes into force:

(i) subsection 212(1) (procuring),

(ii) subsection 212(2) (living on the avails of prostitution of person under 18 years),

(iii) subsection 212(2.1) (aggravated offence in relation to living on the avails of prostitution of person under 18 years), and

(iv) subsection 212(4) (prostitution of person under 18 years); or

(d) an attempt or conspiracy to commit an offence referred to in paragraph (b), (c) or (c.1);

("infraction désignée")

"long-term supervision" means long-term supervision ordered under subsection 753(4), 753.01(5) or (6) or 753.1(3) or subparagraph 759(3)(a)(i); *("surveillance de longue durée")*

"primary designated offence" means

(a) an offence under any of the following provisions:

(i) section 151 (sexual interference),

(ii) section 152 (invitation to sexual touching),

(iii) section 153 (sexual exploitation),

(iv) section 155 (incest),

(v) section 239 (attempt to commit murder),

(vi) section 244 (discharging firearm with intent),

(vii) section 267 (assault with weapon or causing bodily harm),

(viii) section 268 (aggravated assault),

(ix) section 271 (sexual assault),

(x) section 272 (sexual assault with weapon, threats to third party or causing bodily harm),

(xi) section 273 (aggravated sexual assault), and

(xii) subsection 279(1) (kidnapping),

(b) an offence under any of the following provisions of the *Criminal Code*, chapter C-34 of the Revised Statutes of Canada, 1970, as they read from time to time before January 4, 1983:

(i) section 144 (rape),

(ii) section 145 (attempt to commit rape),

(iii) section 149 (indecent assault on female),

(iv) section 156 (indecent assault on male),

(v) subsection 245(2) (assault causing bodily harm), and

(vi) subsection 246(1) (assault with intent) if the intent is to commit an offence referred to in any of subparagraphs (i) to (v) of this paragraph,

(c) an offence under any of the following provisions of the *Criminal Code*, chapter C-34 of the Revised Statutes of Canada, 1970, as enacted by section 19 of *An Act to amend the Criminal Code in relation to sexual offences and other offences against the person and to amend certain other Acts in relation thereto or in consequence thereof*, chapter 125 of the Statutes of Canada, 1980-81-82-83:

(i) section 246.1 (sexual assault),

(ii) section 246.2 (sexual assault with weapon, threats to third party or causing bodily harm), and

(iii) section 246.3 (aggravated sexual assault),

(d) an offence under any of the following provisions of the *Criminal Code*, chapter C-34 of the Revised Statutes of Canada, 1970, as they read from time to time before January 1, 1988:

(i) subsection 146(1) (sexual intercourse with female under age of 14), and

(ii) paragraph 153(1)(a) (sexual intercourse with step-daughter), or

(e) an attempt or conspiracy to commit an offence referred to in any of paragraphs (a) to (d);

("infraction primaire")

"serious personal injury offence" means

(a) an indictable offence, other than high treason, treason, first degree murder or second degree murder, involving

(i) the use or attempted use of violence against another person, or

(ii) conduct endangering or likely to endanger the life or safety of another person or inflicting or likely to inflict severe psychological damage on another person,

and for which the offender may be sentenced to imprisonment for ten years or more, or

(b) an offence or attempt to commit an offence mentioned in section 271 (sexual assault), 272 (sexual assault with a weapon, threats to a third party or causing bodily harm) or 273 (aggravated sexual assault).

2008, c. 6, ss. 40, 61; 2010, c. 3, s. 8; 2012, c. 1, s. 35; 2014, c. 25, s. 29; 2018, c. 21, s. 25

Dangerous Offenders and Long-Term Offenders

752.01 Prosecutor's duty to advise court — If the prosecutor is of the opinion that an offence for which an offender is convicted is a serious personal injury offence that is a designated offence and that the offender was convicted previously at least twice of a designated offence and was sentenced to at least two years of imprisonment for each of those convictions, the prosecutor shall advise the court, as soon as feasible after the finding of guilt and in any event before sentence is imposed, whether the prosecutor intends to make an application under subsection 752.1(1).

2008, c. 6, s. 41

752.1 (1) Application for remand for assessment — On application by the prosecutor, if the court is of the opinion that there are reasonable grounds to believe that an offender who is convicted of a serious personal injury offence or an offence referred to in paragraph 753.1(2)(a) might be found to be a dangerous offender under section 753 or a long-term offender under section 753.1, the court shall, by order in writing, before sentence is imposed, remand the offender, for a period not exceeding 60 days, to the custody of a person designated by the court who can perform an assessment or have an assessment performed by experts for use as evidence in an application under section 753 or 753.1.

(2) Report — The person to whom the offender is remanded shall file a report of the assessment with the court not later than 30 days after the end of the assessment period and make copies of it available to the prosecutor and counsel for the offender.

(3) Extension of time — On application by the prosecutor, the court may extend the period within which the report must be filed by a maximum of 30 days if the court is satisfied that there are reasonable grounds to do so.

1997, c. 17, s. 4; 2008, c. 6, s. 41

753. (1) Application for finding that an offender is a dangerous offender — On application made under this Part after an assessment report is filed under subsection 752.1(2), the court shall find the offender to be a dangerous offender if it is satisfied

(a) that the offence for which the offender has been convicted is a serious personal injury offence described in paragraph (a) of the definition of that expression in section 752 and the offender constitutes a threat to the life, safety or physical or mental well-being of other persons on the basis of evidence establishing

(i) a pattern of repetitive behaviour by the offender, of which the offence for which he or she has been convicted forms a part, showing a failure to restrain his or her behaviour and a likelihood of causing death or injury to other persons, or inflicting severe psychological damage on other persons, through failure in the future to restrain his or her behaviour,

(ii) a pattern of persistent aggressive behaviour by the offender, of which the offence for which he or she has been convicted forms a part, showing a substantial degree of indifference on the part of the offender respecting the reasonably foreseeable consequences to other persons of his or her behaviour, or

(iii) any behaviour by the offender, associated with the offence for which he or she has been convicted, that is of such a brutal nature as to compel the conclusion that the offender's behaviour in the future is unlikely to be inhibited by normal standards of behavioural restraint; or

(b) that the offence for which the offender has been convicted is a serious personal injury offence described in paragraph (*b*) of the definition of that expression in section 752 and the offender, by his or her conduct in any sexual matter including that involved in the commission of the offence for which he or she has been convicted, has shown a failure to control his or her sexual impulses and a likelihood of causing injury, pain or other evil to other persons through failure in the future to control his or her sexual impulses.

(1.1) Presumption — If the court is satisfied that the offence for which the offender is convicted is a primary designated offence for which it would be appropriate to impose a sentence of imprisonment of two years or more and that the offender was convicted previously at least twice of a primary designated offence and was sentenced to at least two years of imprisonment for each of those convictions, the conditions in paragraph (1)(a) or (b), as the case may be, are presumed to have been met unless the contrary is proved on a balance of probabilities.

(2) Time for making application — An application under subsection (1) must be made before sentence is imposed on the offender unless

(a) before the imposition of sentence, the prosecutor gives notice to the offender of a possible intention to make an application under section 752.1 and an application under subsection (1) not later than six months after that imposition; and

(b) at the time of the application under subsection (1) that is not later than six months after the imposition of sentence, it is shown that relevant evidence that was not reasonably available to the prosecutor at the time of the imposition of sentence became available in the interim.

(3) Application for remand for assessment after imposition of sentence — Notwithstanding subsection 752.1(1), an application under that subsection may be made after the imposition of sentence or after an offender begins to serve the sentence in a case to which paragraphs (2)(*a*) and (*b*) apply.

(4) Sentence for dangerous offender — If the court finds an offender to be a dangerous offender, it shall

(a) impose a sentence of detention in a penitentiary for an indeterminate period;

(b) impose a sentence for the offence for which the offender has been convicted — which must be a minimum punishment of imprisonment for a term of two years — and order that the offender be subject to long-term supervision for a period that does not exceed 10 years; or

(c) impose a sentence for the offence for which the offender has been convicted.

(4.1) Sentence of indeterminate detention — The court shall impose a sentence of detention in a penitentiary for an indeterminate period unless it is satisfied by the evidence adduced during the hearing of the application that there is a reasonable expectation that a lesser measure under paragraph (4)(b) or (c) will adequately protect the public against the commission by the offender of murder or a serious personal injury offence.

(4.2) If application made after sentencing — If the application is made after the offender begins to serve the sentence in a case to which paragraphs (2)(a) and (b) apply, a sentence imposed under paragraph (4)(a), or a sentence imposed and an order made under paragraph 4(b), replaces the sentence that was imposed for the offence for which the offender was convicted.

(5) If offender not found to be dangerous offender — If the court does not find an offender to be a dangerous offender,

(a) the court may treat the application as an application to find the offender to be a long-term offender, section 753.1 applies to the application and the court may either find that the offender is a long-term offender or hold another hearing for that purpose; or

(b) the court may impose sentence for the offence for which the offender has been convicted.

(6) [Repealed 2008, c. 6, s. 42(5).]

1997, c. 17, s. 4; 2008, c. 6, s. 42

753.01 (1) Application for remand for assessment — later conviction — If an offender who is found to be a dangerous offender is later convicted of a serious personal injury offence or an offence under subsection 753.3(1), on application by the prosecutor, the court shall, by order in writing, before sentence is imposed, remand the offender, for a period not exceeding 60 days, to the custody of a person designated by the court who can perform an assessment or have an assessment performed by experts for use as evidence in an application under subsection (4).

(2) Report — The person to whom the offender is remanded shall file a report of the assessment with the court not later than 30 days after the end of the assessment period and make copies of it available to the prosecutor and counsel for the offender.

(3) Extension of time — On application by the prosecutor, the court may extend the period within which the report must be filed by a maximum of 30 days if the court is satisfied that there are reasonable grounds to do so.

(4) Application for new sentence or order — After the report is filed, the prosecutor may apply for a sentence of detention in a penitentiary for an indeterminate period, or for an order that the offender be subject to a new period of long-term supervision in addition to any other sentence that may be imposed for the offence.

(5) Sentence of indeterminate detention — If the application is for a sentence of detention in a penitentiary for an indeterminate period, the court shall impose that sentence unless it is satisfied by the evidence adduced during the hearing of the application that there is a reasonable expectation that a sentence for the offence for which the offender has been convicted — with or without a new period of long-term supervision — will adequately protect the public against the commission by the offender of murder or a serious personal injury offence.

(6) New long-term supervision — If the application is for a new period of long-term supervision, the court shall order that the offender be subject to a new period of long-term supervision in addition to a sentence for the offence for which they have been convicted unless it is satisfied by the evidence adduced during the hearing of the application that there is a reasonable expectation that the sentence alone will adequately protect the public against the commission by the offender of murder or a serious personal injury offence.

2008, c. 6, s. 43

753.02 Victim evidence — Any evidence given during the hearing of an application made under subsection 753(1) by a victim of an offence for which the offender was convicted is deemed also to have been given during any hearing held with respect to the offender under paragraph 753(5)(a) or subsection 753.01(5) or (6).

2008, c. 6, s. 43

753.1 (1) Application for finding that an offender is a long-term offender — The court may, on application made under this Part following the filing of an assessment report under subsection 752.1(2), find an offender to be a long-term offender if it is satisfied that

(a) it would be appropriate to impose a sentence of imprisonment of two years or more for the offence for which the offender has been convicted;

(b) there is a substantial risk that the offender will reoffend; and

(c) there is a reasonable possibility of eventual control of the risk in the community.

(2) Substantial risk — The court shall be satisfied that there is a substantial risk that the offender will reoffend if

(a) the offender has been convicted of an offence under section 151 (sexual interference), 152 (invitation to sexual touching) or 153 (sexual exploitation), subsection 163.1(2) (making child pornography), 163.1(3) (distribution, etc., of child pornography), 163.1(4) (possession of child pornography) or 163.1(4.1) (accessing child pornography), section 170 (parent or guardian procuring sexual activity), 171 (householder permitting sexual activity), 171.1 (making sexually explicit material available to child), 172.1 (luring a child) or 172.2 (agreement or arrangement — sexual offence against child), subsection 173(2) (exposure) or section 271 (sexual assault), 272 (sexual assault with a weapon) 273 (aggravated sexual assault) or 279.011 (trafficking — person under 18 years) or subsection 279.02(2) (material benefit — trafficking of person under 18 years), 279.03(2) (withholding or destroying documents — trafficking of person under 18 years), 286.1(2) (obtaining sexual services for consideration from person under 18 years), 286.2(2) (material benefit from sexual services provided by person under 18 years) or 286.3(2) (procuring — person under 18 years), or has engaged in serious conduct of a sexual nature in the commission of another offence of which the offender has been convicted; and

(b) the offender

(i) has shown a pattern of repetitive behaviour, of which the offence for which he or she has been convicted forms a part, that shows a likelihood of the offender's causing death or injury to other persons or inflicting severe psychological damage on other persons, or

(ii) by conduct in any sexual matter including that involved in the commission of the offence for which the offender has been convicted, has shown a likelihood of causing injury, pain or other evil to other persons in the future through similar offence.

(3) Sentence for long-term offender — If the court finds an offender to be a long-term offender, it shall

(a) impose a sentence for the offence for which the offender has been convicted, which must be a minimum punishment of imprisonment for a term of two years; and

(b) order that the offender be subject to long-term supervision for a period that does not exceed 10 years.

(3.1) Exception–if application made after sentencing — The court may not impose a sentence under paragraph (3)(*a*) and the sentence that was imposed for the offence for which the offender was convicted stands despite the offender's being found to be a long-term offender, if the application was one that

(a) was made after the offender begins to serve the sentence in a case to which paragraphs 753(2)(*a*) and (*b*) apply; and

(b) was treated as an application under this section further to the court deciding to do so under paragraph 753(5)(*a*).

(4) and (5) [Repealed 2008, c. 6, s. 44(2).]

(6) If offender not found to be long-term offender — If the court does not find an offender to be a long-term offender, the court shall impose sentence for the offence for which the offender has been convicted.

1997, c. 17, s. 4; 2002, c. 13, s. 76; 2008, c. 6, s. 44; 2012, c. 1, s. 36; 2014, c. 25, s. 30

753.2 (1) Long-term supervision — Subject to subsection (2), an offender who is subject to long-term supervision shall be supervised in the community in accordance with the *Corrections and Conditional Release Act* when the offender has finished serving

(a) the sentence for the offence for which the offender has been convicted; and

(b) all other sentences for offences for which the offender is convicted and for which sentence of a term of imprisonment is imposed on the offender, either before or after the conviction for the offence referred to in paragraph (*a*).

(2) **Sentence served concurrently with supervision** — A sentence imposed on an offender referred to in subsection (1), other than a sentence that requires imprisonment, is to be served concurrently with the long-term supervision.

(3) **Application for reduction in period of long-term supervision** — An offender who is required to be supervised, a member of the Parole Board of Canada or, on approval of that Board, the offender's parole supervisor, as defined in subsection 99(1) of the *Corrections and Conditional Release Act*, may apply to a superior court of criminal jurisdiction for an order reducing the period of long-term supervision or terminating it on the ground that the offender no longer presents a substantial risk of reoffending and thereby being a danger to the community. The onus of proving that ground is on the applicant.

(4) **Notice to Attorney General** — The applicant must give notice of an application under subsection (3) to the Attorney General at the time the application is made.

1997, c. 17, s. 4; 2008, c. 6, s. 45(1), (2); 2012, c. 1, ss. 147, 160(c)(iv)

753.3 (1) Breach of long-term supervision — An offender who, without reasonable excuse, fails or refuses to comply with long-term supervision is guilty of

(a) an indictable offence and liable to imprisonment for a term of not more than 10 years; or

(b) an offence punishable on summary conviction.

(2) **Where accused may be tried and punished** — An accused who is charged with an offence under subsection (1) may be tried and punished by any court having jurisdiction to try that offence in the place where the offence is alleged to have been committed or in the place where the accused is found, is arrested or is in custody, but if the place where the accused is found, is arrested or is in custody is outside the province in which the offence is alleged to have been committed, no proceedings in respect of that offence shall be instituted in that place without the consent of the Attorney General of that province.

1997, c. 17, s. 4; 2008, c. 6, s. 46; 2019, c. 25, s. 307

753.4 (1) New offence — If an offender who is subject to long-term supervision commits one or more offences under this or any other Act and a court imposes a sentence of imprisonment for the offence or offences, the long-term supervision is interrupted until the offender has finished serving all the sentences, unless the court orders its termination.

(2) Reduction in term of long-term supervision — A court that imposes a sentence of imprisonment under subsection (1) may order a reduction in the length of the period of the offender's long-term supervision.

1997, c. 17, s. 4; 2008, c. 6, s. 47

754. (1) Hearing of application — With the exception of an application for remand for assessment, the court may not hear an application made under this Part unless

(a) the Attorney General of the province in which the offender was tried has, either before or after the making of the application, consented to the application;

(b) at least seven days notice has been given to the offender by the prosecutor, following the making of the application, outlining the basis on which it is intended to found the application; and

(c) a copy of the notice has been filed with the clerk of the court or the provincial court judge, as the case may be.

(2) By court alone — An application under this Part shall be heard and determined by the court without a jury.

(3) When proof unnecessary — For the purposes of an application under this Part, where an offender admits any allegations contained in the notice referred to in paragraph (1)(*b*), no proof of those allegations is required.

(4) Proof of consent — The production of a document purporting to contain any nomination or consent that may be made or given by the Attorney General under this Part and purporting to be signed by the Attorney General is, in the absence of any evidence to the contrary, proof of that nomination or consent without proof of the signature or the official character of the person appearing to have signed the document.

R.S.C. 1985, c. 27 (1st Supp.), s. 203; 2008, c. 6, s. 48(1)

755. (1) Exception to long-term supervision — life sentence — The court shall not order that an offender be subject to long-term supervision if they have been sentenced to life imprisonment.

(2) Maximum length of long-term supervision — The periods of long-term supervision to which an offender is subject at any particular time must not total more than 10 years.

1997, c. 17, s. 5; 2008, c. 6, s. 49

756. [Repealed 1997, c. 17, s. 5.]

757. Evidence of character — Without prejudice to the right of the offender to tender evidence as to their character and repute, if the court thinks fit, evidence of character and repute may be admitted

(a) on the question of whether the offender is or is not a dangerous offender or a long-term offender; and

(b) in connection with a sentence to be imposed or an order to be made under this Part.

1997, c. 17, s. 5; 2008, c. 6, s. 50

758. (1) Presence of accused at hearing of application — The offender shall be present at the hearing of the application under this Part and if at the time the application is to be heard

(a) he is confined in a prison, the court may order, in writing, the person having the custody of the accused to bring him before the court; or

(b) he is not confined in a prison, the court shall issue a summons or a warrant to compel the accused to attend before the court and the provisions of Part XVI relating to summons and warrant are applicable with such modifications as the circumstances require.

(2) Exception — Notwithstanding subsection (1), the court may

(a) cause the offender to be removed and to be kept out of court, where he misconducts himself by interrupting the proceedings so that to continue the proceedings in his presence would not be feasible; or

(b) permit the offender to be out of court during the whole or any part of the hearing on such conditions as the court considers proper.

759. (1) Appeal — offender — An offender who is found to be a dangerous offender or a long-term offender may appeal to the court of appeal from a decision made under this Part on any ground of law or fact or mixed law and fact.

(1.1) [Repealed 2008, c. 6, s. 51.]

(2) Appeal — Attorney General — The Attorney General may appeal to the court of appeal from a decision made under this Part on any ground of law.

(3) Disposition of appeal — The court of appeal may

(a) allow the appeal and

(i) find that an offender is or is not a dangerous offender or a long-term offender or impose a sentence that may be imposed or an order that may be made by the trial court under this Part, or

(ii) order a new hearing, with any directions that the court considers appropriate; or

(b) dismiss the appeal.

(3.1) and (3.2) [Repealed 2008, c. 6, s. 51.]

(4) Effect of decision — A decision of the court of appeal has the same force and effect as if it were a decision of the trial court.

(4.1) to (5) [Repealed 2008, c. 6, s. 51.]

(6) Commencement of sentence — Notwithstanding subsection 719(1), a sentence imposed on an offender by the court of appeal pursuant to this section shall be deemed to have commenced when the offender was sentenced by the court by which he was convicted.

(7) **Part XXI applies re appeals** — The provisions of Part XXI with respect to procedure on appeals apply, with such modifications as the circumstances require, to appeals under this section.

1995, c. 22, s. 10; 1997, c. 17, s. 6; 2008, c. 6, s. 51

760. Disclosure to Correctional Service of Canada — Where a court finds an offender to be a dangerous offender or a long-term offender, the court shall order that a copy of all reports and testimony given by psychiatrists, psychologists, criminologists and other experts and any observations of the court with respect to the reasons for the finding, together with a transcript of the trial of the offender, be forwarded to the Correctional Service of Canada for information.

1997, c. 17, s. 7

761. (1) **Review for parole** — Subject to subsection (2), where a person is in custody under a sentence of detention in a penitentiary for an indeterminate period, the Parole Board of Canada shall, as soon as possible after the expiration of seven years from the day on which that person was taken into custody and not later than every two years after the previous review, review the condition, history and circumstances of that person for the purposes of determining whether he or she should be granted parole under Part II of the *Corrections and Conditional Release Act* and, if so, on what conditions.

(2) **Idem** — Where a person is in custody under a sentence of detention in a penitentiary for an indeterminate period that was imposed before October 15, 1977, the Parole Board of Canada shall, at least once in every year, review the condition, history and circumstances of that person for the purpose of determining whether he should be granted parole under Part II of the *Corrections and Conditional Release Act* and, if so, on what conditions.

1992, c. 20, s. 215(1)(a); 1997, c. 17, s. 8; 2012, c. 1, s. 160(c)(v)

PART XXV — EFFECT AND ENFORCEMENT OF RECOGNIZANCES (SS. 762–773)

[Heading amended to “Effect and Enforcement of Undertakings, Release Orders and Recognizances”, 2019, c. 25, s. 308. To come into force December 18, 2019.]

762. (1) **Applications for forfeiture of recognizances** — Applications for the forfeiture of recognizances shall be made to the courts, designated in column II of the schedule, of the respective provinces designated in column I of the schedule.

Proposed Amendment — 762(1)

(1) **Applications for forfeiture** — Applications for the forfeiture of an amount set out in an undertaking, release order or recognizance must be made to the courts

designated in column II of the schedule of the respective provinces designated in column I of the schedule.

2019, c. 25, s. 309 [To come into force December 18, 2019.]

(2) **Definitions** — In this Part

"clerk of the court" means the officer designated in column III of the schedule in respect of the court designated in column II of the schedule;

"schedule" means the schedule to this Part.

763. **Recognizance binding** — Where a person is bound by recognizance to appear before a court, justice or provincial court judge for any purpose and the session or sittings of that court or the proceedings are adjourned or an order is made changing the place of trial, that person and his sureties continue to be bound by the recognizance in like manner as if it had been entered into with relation to the resumed proceedings or the trial at the time and place at which the proceedings are ordered to be resumed or the trial is ordered to be held.

Proposed Amendment — 763

763. (1) **Undertaking or release order binding on person** — If a person is bound by an undertaking, release order or recognizance to appear before a court, provincial court judge or justice for any purpose and the session or sittings of that court or the proceedings are adjourned or an order is made changing the place of trial, that person and their sureties continue to be bound by the undertaking, release order or recognizance as if it had been entered into or issued with respect to the resumed proceedings or the trial at the time and place at which the proceedings are ordered to be resumed or the trial is ordered to be held.

(2) **Summary of certain provisions** — A summary of section 763 must be set out in any undertaking, release order or recognizance.

2019, c. 25, s. 310 [To come into force December 18, 2019.]

R.S.C. 1985, c. 27 (1st Supp.), s. 203

764. (1) **Responsibility of sureties** — Where an accused is bound by recognizance to appear for trial, his arraignment or conviction does not discharge the recognizance, but it continues to bind him and his sureties, if any, for his appearance until he is discharged or sentenced, as the case may be.

(2) **Committal or new sureties** — Notwithstanding subsection (1), the court, justice or provincial court judge may commit an accused to prison or may require him to furnish new or additional sureties for his appearance until he is discharged or sentenced, as the case may be.

(3) **Effect of committal** — The sureties of the accused who is bound by recognizance to appear for trial are discharged if he is committed to prison pursuant to subsection (2).

(4) Endorsement on recognizance — The provisions of section 763 and subsections (1) to (3) of this section shall be endorsed on any recognizance entered into pursuant to this Act.

Proposed Amendment — 764

764. (1) Undertaking or release order binding on accused — If an accused is bound by an undertaking or release order to appear for trial, their arraignment or conviction does not cancel the undertaking or release order, and it continues to bind them and their sureties for their appearance until the accused is discharged or sentenced, as the case may be.

(2) Committal or new sureties — Despite subsection (1), the court, provincial court judge or justice may commit an accused to prison or may require them to furnish new or additional sureties for their appearance until the accused is discharged or sentenced, as the case may be.

(3) Effect of committal — The sureties of an accused who is bound by a release order to appear for trial are discharged if the accused is committed to prison under subsection (2).

(4) Summary of certain provisions — A summary of subsections (1) to (3) must be set out in any undertaking or release order.

2019, c. 25, s. 310 [To come into force December 18, 2019.]

R.S.C. 1985, c. 27 (1st Supp.), s. 203

765. Effect of subsequent arrest — Where an accused is bound by recognizance to appear for trial, his arrest on another charge does not vacate the recognizance, but it continues to bind him and his sureties, if any, for his appearance until he is discharged or sentenced, as the case may be, in respect of the offence to which the recognizance relates.

Proposed Amendment — 765

765. Effect of subsequent arrest — If an accused is bound by an undertaking or a release order to appear for trial, their arrest on another charge does not cancel the undertaking or release order, and it continues to bind them and their sureties for their appearance until the accused is discharged or sentenced, as the case may be, in respect of the offence to which the undertaking or release order relates.

2019, c. 25, s. 310 [To come into force December 18, 2019.]

766. (1) Render of accused by sureties — A surety for a person who is bound by recognizance to appear may, by an application in writing to a court, justice or provincial court judge, apply to be relieved of his obligation under the recognizance, and the court, justice or provincial court judge shall thereupon issue an order in writing for committal of that person to the prison nearest to the place where he was, under the recognizance, bound to appear.

(2) Arrest — An order under subsection (1) shall be given to the surety and on receipt thereof he or any peace officer may arrest the person named in the order and deliver that person with the order to the keeper of the prison named herein, and the keeper shall receive and imprison that person until he is discharged according to law.

(3) Certificate and entry of render — Where a court, justice or provincial court judge issues an order under subsection (1) and receives from the sheriff a certificate that the person named in the order has been committed to prison pursuant to subsection (2), the court, justice or provincial court judge shall order an entry of the committal to be endorsed on the recognizance.

(4) Discharge of sureties — An endorsement under subsection (3) vacates the recognizance and discharges the sureties.

Proposed Amendment — 766

766. (1) Render of accused by sureties — A surety for a person who is subject to a release order or recognizance may, by an application in writing to a court, provincial court judge or justice, apply to be relieved of their obligation under the release order or recognizance, and the court, provincial court judge or justice shall then make an order in writing for committal of that person to the prison named in that order.

(2) Arrest — An order issued by a court, provincial court judge or justice under subsection (1) must be given to the surety and, on receipt of it, the surety or any peace officer may arrest the person named in the order and deliver that person with the order to the keeper of the prison named in the order, and the keeper shall receive and imprison that person until the person is discharged according to law.

(3) Certificate and entry of render — If a court, provincial court judge or justice issues an order under subsection (1) and receives from the sheriff a certificate that the person named in the order has been committed to prison under subsection (2), the court, provincial court judge or justice shall order an entry of the committal to be endorsed on the release order or recognizance, as the case may be.

(4) Discharge of sureties — An endorsement under subsection (3) cancels the release order or recognizance, as the case may be, and discharges the sureties.

2019, c. 25, s. 310 [To come into force December 18, 2019.]

R.S.C. 1985, c. 27 (1st Supp.), s. 203

767. Render of accused in court by sureties — A surety for a person who is bound by recognizance to appear may bring that person into the court at which he is required to appear at any time during the sittings thereof and before his trial and the surety may discharge his obligation under the recognizance by giving that person into the custody of the court, and the court shall thereupon commit that person to prison until he is discharged according to law.

Proposed Amendment — 767

767. Render of accused in court by sureties — A surety for a person who is subject to a release order or recognizance may bring that person before the court where the person is required to appear or where the person entered into the recognizance at any time during the sittings of that court and before the person's trial, and the surety may discharge their obligation under the release order or recognizance by giving that person into the custody of the court. The court shall then commit that person to prison until the person is discharged according to law.

2019, c. 25, s. 310 [To come into force December 18, 2019.]

767.1 (1) Substitution of surety — Notwithstanding subsection 766(1) and section 767, where a surety for a person who is bound by a recognizance has rendered the person into the custody of a court pursuant to section 767 or applies to be relieved of his obligation under the recognizance pursuant to subsection 766(1), the court, justice or provincial court judge, as the case may be, may, instead of committing or issuing an order for the committal of the person to prison, substitute any other suitable person for the surety under the recognizance.

(2) Signing of recognizance by new sureties — Where a person substituted for a surety under a recognizance pursuant to subsection (1) signs the recognizance, the original surety is discharged, but the recognizance and the order for judicial interim release pursuant to which the recognizance was entered into are not otherwise affected.

Proposed Amendment — 767.1

767.1 (1) Substitution of surety — If a surety for a person who is subject to a release order or recognizance has given the person into the custody of a court under section 767, or a surety applies to be relieved of their obligation under the release order or recognizance under subsection 766(1), the court, justice or provincial court judge, as the case may be, may, instead of committing or issuing an order for the committal of the person to prison, substitute any other suitable person for the surety under the release order or recognizance.

(2) Signing of release order or recognizance by new sureties — If a person substituted for a surety under a release order or recognizance under subsection (1) signs the release order or recognizance, the original surety is discharged, but the release order or recognizance is not otherwise affected.

2019, c. 25, s. 310 [To come into force December 18, 2019.]

R.S.C. 1985, c. 27 (1st Supp.), s. 167

768. Rights of surety preserved — Nothing in this Part limits or restricts any right that a surety has of taking and giving into custody any person for whom, under a recognizance, he is a surety.

Proposed Amendment — 768

768. Rights of surety preserved — Nothing in this Part limits any right that a surety has of taking and giving into custody any person for whom they are a surety under a release order or recognizance.

2019, c. 25, s. 310 [To come into force December 18, 2019.]

769. Application of judicial interim release provisions — Where a surety for a person has rendered him into custody and that person has been committed to prison, the provisions of Parts XVI, XXI and XXVII relating to judicial interim release apply, with such modifications as the circumstances require, in respect of him and he shall forthwith be taken before a justice or judge as an accused charged with an offence or as an appellant, as the case may be, for the purposes of those provisions.

770. (1) Default to be endorsed — Where, in proceedings to which this Act applies, a person who is bound by recognizance does not comply with a condition of the recognizance, a court, justice or provincial court judge having knowledge of the facts shall endorse or cause to be endorsed on the recognizance a certificate in Form 33 setting out

(a) the nature of the default,

(b) the reason for the default, if it is known,

(c) whether the ends of justice have been defeated or delayed by reason of the default, and

(d) the names and addresses of the principal and sureties.

(2) Transmission to clerk of court — A recognizance that has been endorsed pursuant to subsection (1) shall be sent to the clerk of the court and shall be kept by him with the records of the court.

(3) Certificate is evidence — A certificate that has been endorsed on a recognizance pursuant to subsection (1) is evidence of the default to which it relates.

(4) Transmission of deposit — Where, in proceedings to which this section applies, the principal or surety has deposited money as security for the performance of a condition of a recognizance, that money shall be sent to the clerk of the court with the defaulted recognizance, to be dealt with in accordance with this Part.

Proposed Amendment — 770

770. (1) Default to be endorsed — If, in proceedings to which this Act applies, a person who is subject to an undertaking, release order or recognizance does not comply with any of its conditions, a court, provincial court judge or justice having knowledge of the facts shall endorse or cause to be endorsed on the undertaking, release order or recognizance a certificate in Form 33 setting out

(a) the nature of the default;

(b) the reason for the default, if it is known;

(c) whether the ends of justice have been defeated or delayed by reason of the default; and

(d) the names and addresses of the principal and sureties.

(2) Transmission to clerk of court — Once endorsed, the undertaking, release order or recognizance must be sent to the clerk of the court and shall be kept by them with the records of the court.

(3) Certificate is evidence — A certificate that has been endorsed on the undertaking, release order or recognizance is evidence of the default to which it relates.

(4) Transmission of deposit — If, in proceedings to which this section applies, the principal or surety has deposited money as security for the performance of a condition of an undertaking, release order or recognizance, that money must be sent to the clerk of the court with the defaulted undertaking, release order or recognizance, to be dealt with in accordance with this Part.

2019, c. 25, s. 311 [To come into force December 18, 2019.]

R.S.C. 1985, c. 27 (1st Supp.), s. 203; 1997, c. 18, s. 108

771. (1) Proceedings in case of default — Where a recognizance has been endorsed with a certificate pursuant to section 770 and has been received by the clerk of the court pursuant to that section,

(a) a judge of the court shall, on the request of the clerk of the court or the Attorney General or counsel acting on his behalf, fix a time and place for the hearing of an application for the forfeiture of the recognizance; and

(b) the clerk of the court shall, not less than ten days before the time fixed under paragraph (*a*) for the hearing, send by registered mail, or have served in the manner directed by the court or prescribed by the rules of court, to each principal and surety named in the recognizance, directed to the principal or surety at the address set out in the certificate, a notice requiring the person to appear at the time and place fixed by the judge to show cause why the recognizance should not be forfeited.

(2) Order of judge — Where subsection (1) has been complied with, the judge may, after giving the parties an opportunity to be heard, in his discretion grant or refuse the application and make any order with respect to the forfeiture of the recognizance that he considers proper.

(3) Judgment debtors of the crown — Where, pursuant to subsection (2), a judge orders forfeiture of a recognizance, the principal and his sureties become judgment debtors of the Crown, each in the amount that the judge orders him to pay.

(3.1) Order may be filed — An order made under subsection (2) may be filed with the clerk of the superior court and if an order is filed, the clerk shall issue a writ of *fieri facias* in Form 34 and deliver it to the sheriff of each of the territorial divisions in which the principal or any surety resides, carries on business or has property.

(4) Transfer of deposit — Where a deposit has been made by a person against whom an order for forfeiture of a recognizance has been made, no writ of *fieri facias* shall issue, but the amount of the deposit shall be transferred by the person who has custody of it to the person who is entitled by law to receive it.

Proposed Amendment — 771

771. (1) Proceedings in case of default — If an undertaking, release order or recognizance has been endorsed with a certificate and has been received by the clerk of the court,

(a) a judge of the court shall, on the request of the clerk of the court or the Attorney General or counsel acting on the Attorney General's or counsel's behalf, as the case may be, fix a time and place for the hearing of an application for the forfeiture of the amount set out in the undertaking, release order or recognizance; and

(b) the clerk of the court shall, not less than 10 days before the time fixed under paragraph (a) for the hearing, send by registered mail, or have served in the manner directed by the court or prescribed by the rules of court, to each principal and surety, at the address set out in the certificate, a notice requiring the person to appear at the time and place fixed by the judge to show cause why the amount set out in the undertaking, release order or recognizance should not be forfeited.

(2) Order of judge — If subsection (1) has been complied with, the judge may, after giving the parties an opportunity to be heard, in the judge's discretion grant or refuse the application and make any order with respect to the forfeiture of the amount that the judge considers proper.

(3) Judgment debtors of the Crown — If a judge orders forfeiture of the amount set out in the undertaking, release order or recognizance, the principal and their sureties become judgment debtors of the Crown, each in the amount that the judge orders them to pay.

(3.1) Order may be filed — An order made under subsection (2) may be filed with the clerk of the superior court and if one is filed, the clerk shall issue a writ of *fieri facias* in Form 34 and deliver it to the sheriff of each of the territorial divisions in which the principal or any surety resides, carries on business or has property.

(4) Transfer of deposit — If a deposit has been made by a person against whom an order for forfeiture has been made, no writ of *fieri facias* may be issued, but the amount of the deposit must be transferred by the person who has custody of it to the person who is entitled by law to receive it.

2019, c. 25, s. 311 [To come into force December 18, 2019.]

R.S.C. 1985, c. 27 (1st Supp.), s. 168; 1994, c. 44, s. 78; 1999, c. 5, s. 43

772. (1) Levy under writ — Where a writ of *fieri facias* is issued pursuant to section 771, the sheriff to whom it is delivered shall execute the writ and deal with the proceeds thereof in the same manner in which he is authorized to execute and deal with the proceeds of writs of *fieri facias* issued out of superior courts in the province in civil proceedings.

(2) Costs — Where this section applies, the Crown is entitled to the costs of execution and of proceedings incidental thereto that are fixed, in the Province of Quebec, by any tariff applicable in the Superior Court in civil proceedings, and in any other province, by any tariff applicable in the superior court of the province in civil proceedings, as the judge may direct.

773. (1) Committal when writ not satisfied — Where a writ of *fieri facias* has been issued under this Part and it appears from a certificate in a return made by the sheriff that sufficient goods and chattels, lands and tenements cannot be found to satisfy the writ, or that the proceeds of the execution of the writ are not sufficient to satisfy it, a judge of the court may, upon the application of the Attorney General or counsel acting on his behalf, fix a time and place for the sureties to show cause why a warrant of committal should not be issued in respect of them.

(2) Notice — Seven clear days notice of the time and place fixed for the hearing pursuant to subsection (1) shall be given to the sureties.

(3) Hearing — The judge shall, at the hearing held pursuant to subsection (1), inquire into the circumstances of the case and may in his discretion

(a) order the discharge of the amount for which the surety is liable; or

(b) make any order with respect to the surety and to his imprisonment that he considers proper in the circumstances and issue a warrant of committal in Form 27.

(4) Warrant to committal — A warrant of committal issued pursuant to this section authorizes the sheriff to take into custody the person in respect of whom the warrant was issued and to confine him in a prison in the territorial division in which the writ was issued or in the prison nearest to the court, until satisfaction is made or until the period of imprisonment fixed by the judge has expired.

(5) Definition of "Attorney General" — In this section and in section 771, **"Attorney General"** means, where subsection 734.4(2) applies, the Attorney General of Canada.

1995, c. 22, s. 10

SCHEDULE TO PART XXV

(Section 762)

Column I.	Column II.	Column III.
Ontario	A judge of the Court of Appeal in respect of a recognizance for the appearance of a person before the Court	The Registrar of the Court of Appeal
	The Superior Court of Justice in respect of all other recognizances	A Registrar of the Superior Court of Justice

Quebec	The Court of Quebec, Criminal and Penal Division	The Clerk of the Court
Nova Scotia	The Supreme Court	A Prothonotary of the Supreme Court
New Brunswick	The Court of Queen's Bench	The Registrar of the Court of Queen's Bench
British Columbia	The Supreme Court in respect of a recognizance for the appearance of a person before that court or the Court of Appeal	The District Registrar of the Supreme Court
	A Provincial Court in respect of a recognizance for the appearance of a person before a judge of that Court or a justice	The Clerk of the Provincial Court
Prince Edward Island	The Supreme Court	The Prothonotary
Manitoba	The Court of Queen's Bench	The Registrar or a Deputy Registrar of the Court of Queen's Bench
Saskatchewan	The Court of Queen's Bench	The Local Registrar of the of Queen's Bench
Alberta	The Court of Queen's Bench	The Clerk of the Court of Queen's Bench
Newfoundland and Labrador	The Trial Division of the Supreme Court	The Registrar of the Supreme Court
Yukon	The Supreme Court	The Clerk of the Supreme Court
Northwest Territories	The Supreme Court	The Clerk of the Supreme Court
Nunavut	The Nunavut Court of Justice	The Clerk of the Nunavut Court of Justice

Proposed Amendment — Schedule to Part XXV

SCHEDULE TO PART XXV

(Section 762)

Column I.	Column II.	Column III.
Ontario	A judge of the Court of Appeal in respect of a release order or recognizance for the appearance of a person before the Court	The Registrar of the Court of Appeal
	The Superior Court of Justice in respect of undertakings or all other release orders or recognizances	A Registrar of the Superior Court of Justice
Quebec	The Court of Quebec, Criminal and Penal Division	The Clerk of the Court
Nova Scotia	The Supreme Court	A Prothonotary of the Supreme Court
New Brunswick	The Court of Queen's Bench	The Registrar of the Court of Queen's Bench
British Columbia	The Supreme Court in respect of an undertaking, release order or recognizance for the appearance of a person before that court or the Court of Appeal	The District Registrar of the Supreme Court
	A Provincial Court in respect of an undertaking, release order or recognizance for the appearance of a person before a judge of that Court or a justice	The Clerk of the Provincial Court
Prince Edward Island	The Supreme Court	The Prothonotary
Manitoba	The Court of Queen's Bench	The Registrar or a Deputy Registrar of the Court of Queen's Bench

Saskatchewan	The Court of Queen's Bench	The Local Registrar of the of Queen's Bench
Alberta	The Court of Queen's Bench	The Clerk of the Court of Queen's Bench
Newfoundland and Labrador	The Trial Division of the Supreme Court	The Registrar of the Supreme Court
Yukon	The Supreme Court	The Clerk of the Supreme Court
Northwest Territories	The Supreme Court	The Clerk of the Supreme Court
Nunavut	The Nunavut Court of Justice	The Clerk of the Nunavut Court of Justice

2019, c. 25, s. 312 [To come into force December 18, 2019.]

R.S.C. 1985, c. 11 (1st Supp.), s. 2 (Sched., item 1(5)); R.S.C. 1985, c. 27 (1st Supp.), s. 203; R.S.C. 1985, c. 27 (2nd Supp.), s. 10 (Sched., item 6(15)); 1992, c. 1, s. 58(1) (Sched. I, item 15); 1992, c. 51, ss. 40–42; 1993, c. 28, s. 78 (Sched., III, item 35.2) [Amended 1998, c. 15, s. 20; repealed 1999, c. 3, s. 12 (Sched., item 9).]; 1998, c. 30, s. 14(d); 1999, c. 3, s. 54; 1999, c. 5, s. 44; 2002, c. 7, s. 148; 2015, c. 3, ss. 57–59

PART XXVI — EXTRAORDINARY REMEDIES (SS. 774–784)

774. Application of Part — This Part applies to proceedings in criminal matters by way of *certiorari, habeas corpus, mandamus, procedendo* and prohibition.

R.S.C. 1985, c. 27 (1st Supp.), s. 169

774.1 Appearance in person — *habeas corpus* — Despite any other provision of this Act, the person who is the subject of a writ of *habeas corpus* must appear personally in court.

2002, c. 13, s. 77

775. Detention on inquiry to determine legality of imprisonment — Where proceedings to which this Part applies have been instituted before a judge or court having jurisdiction, by or in respect of a person who is in custody by reason that he is charged with or has been convicted of an offence, to have the legality of his imprisonment determined, the judge or court may, without determining the question, make an order for the further detention of that person and direct the judge, justice or provincial court judge under whose warrant he is in custody, or any other judge, justice or provincial court judge to take any proceedings, hear such evidence or do any other thing that, in the opinion of the judge or court, will best further the ends of justice.

R.S.C. 1985, c. 27 (1st Supp.), s. 203

776. Where conviction of order not reviewable — No conviction or order shall be removed by *certiorari*

(a) where an appeal was taken, whether or not the appeal has been carried to a conclusion; or

(b) where the defendant appeared and pleaded and the merits were tried, and an appeal might have been taken, but the defendant did not appeal.

777. (1) Conviction or order remediable, when — No conviction, order or warrant for enforcing a conviction or order shall, on being removed by *certiorari*, be held to be invalid by reason of any irregularity, informality or insufficiency therein, where the court before which or the judge before whom the question is raised, on perusal of the evidence, is satisfied

(a) that an offence of the nature described in the conviction, order or warrant, as the case may be, was committed,

(b) that there was jurisdiction to make the conviction or order or issue the warrant, as the case may be, and

(c) that the punishment imposed, if any, was not in excess of the punishment that might lawfully have been imposed,

but the court or judge has the same powers to deal with the proceedings in the manner that the court or judge considers proper that are conferred on a court to which an appeal might have been taken.

(2) Correcting punishment — Where, in proceedings to which subsection (1) applies, the court or judge is satisfied that a person was properly convicted of an offence but the punishment that was imposed is greater than the punishment that might lawfully have been imposed, the court or judge

(a) shall correct the sentence,

(i) where the punishment is a fine, by imposing a fine that does not exceed the maximum fine that might lawfully have been imposed,

(ii) where the punishment is imprisonment, and the person has not served a term of imprisonment under the sentence that is equal to or greater than the term of imprisonment that might lawfully have been imposed, by imposing a term of imprisonment that does not exceed the maximum term of imprisonment that might lawfully have been imposed, or

(iii) where the punishment is a fine and imprisonment, by imposing a punishment in accordance with subparagraph (i) or (ii), as the case requires; or

(b) shall remit the matter to the convicting judge, justice or provincial court judge and direct him to impose a punishment that is not greater than the punishment that may be lawfully imposed.

(3) Amendment — Where an adjudication is varied pursuant to subsection (1) or (2), the conviction and warrant of committal, if any, shall be amended to conform with the adjudication as varied.

(4) Sufficiency of statement — Any statement that appears in a conviction and is sufficient for the purpose of the conviction is sufficient for the purposes of an information, summons, order or warrant in which it appears in the proceedings.

R.S.C. 1985, c. 27 (1st Supp.), s. 203

778. Irregularities within section 777 — Without restricting the generality of section 777, that section shall be deemed to apply where

(a) the statement of the adjudication or of any other matter or thing is in the past tense instead of in the present tense;

(b) the punishment imposed is less than the punishment that might by law have been imposed for the offence that appears by the evidence to have been committed; or

(c) there has been an omission to negative circumstances, the existence of which would make the act complained of lawful, whether those circumstances are stated by way of exception or otherwise in the provision under which the offence is charged or are stated in another provision.

779. (1) General order for security by recognizance — A court that has authority to quash a conviction, order or other proceeding on *certiorari* may prescribe by general order that no motion to quash any such conviction, order or other proceeding removed to the court by *certiorari*, shall be heard unless the defendant has entered into a recognizance with one or more sufficient sureties, before one or more justices of the territorial division in which the conviction or order was made or before a judge or other officer, or has made a deposit to be prescribed with a condition that the defendant will prosecute the writ of *certiorari* at his own expense, without wilful delay, and, if ordered, will pay to the person in whose favour the conviction, order or other proceeding is affirmed his full costs and charges to be taxed according to the practice of the court where the conviction, order or proceeding is affirmed.

(2) Provisions of Part XXV — The provisions of Part XXV relating to forfeiture of recognizances apply to a recognizance entered into under this section.

Proposed Amendment — 779(2)

(2) Provisions of Part XXV — The provisions of Part XXV relating to forfeiture of an amount set out in a recognizance apply to a recognizance entered into under this section.

2019, c. 25, s. 313 [To come into force December 18, 2019.]

780. Effect of order dismissing application to quash — Where a motion to quash a conviction, order or other proceeding is refused, the order of the court refusing the application is sufficient authority for the clerk of the court forthwith to return the conviction, order or proceeding to the court from which or the person from whom it was removed, and for proceedings to be taken with respect thereto for the enforcement thereof.

781. (1) Want of proof of order in council — No order, conviction or other proceeding shall be quashed or set aside, and no defendant shall be discharged, by reason only that evidence has not been given

(a) of a proclamation or order of the Governor in Council or the lieutenant governor in council;

(b) of rules, regulations or by-laws made by the Governor in Council under an Act of Parliament or by the lieutenant governor in council under an Act of the legislature of the province; or

(c) of the publication of a proclamation, order, rule, regulation or by-law in the *Canada Gazette* or in the official gazette for the province.

(2) Judicial notice — Proclamations, orders, rules, regulations and by-laws mentioned in subsection (1) and the publication thereof shall be judicially noticed.

782. Defect in form — No warrant of committal shall, on *certiorari* or *habeas corpus*, be held to be void by reason only of any defect therein, where

(a) it is alleged in the warrant that the defendant was convicted; and

(b) there is a valid conviction to sustain the warrant.

783. No action against official when conviction, etc., quashed — Where an application is made to quash a conviction, order or other proceeding made or held by a provincial court judge acting under Part XIX or a justice on the ground that he exceeded his jurisdiction, the court to which or the judge to whom the application is made may, in quashing the conviction, order or other proceeding, order that no civil proceedings shall be taken against the justice or provincial court judge or against any officer who acted under the conviction, order or other proceeding or under any warrant issued to enforce it.

R.S.C. 1985, c. 27 (1st Supp.), s. 203

784. (1) Appeal in mandamus etc. — An appeal lies to the court of appeal from a decision granting or refusing the relief sought in proceedings by way of *mandamus, certiorari* or prohibition.

(2) Application of Part XXI — Except as provided in this section, Part XXI applies, with such modifications as the circumstances require, to appeals under this section.

(3) Refusal of application, and appeal — Where an application for a writ of *habeas corpus ad subjiciendum* is refused by a judge of a court having jurisdiction therein, no application may again be made on the same grounds, whether to the same or to another court or judge, unless fresh evidence is adduced, but an appeal from that refusal shall lie to the court of appeal, and where on the appeal the application is refused a further appeal shall lie to the Supreme Court of Canada, with leave of that Court.

(4) Where writ granted — Where a writ of *habeas corpus ad subjiciendum* is granted by any judge, no appeal therefrom shall lie at the instance of any party including the Attorney General of the province concerned or the Attorney General of Canada.

(5) Appeal from judgment on return of writ — Where a judgment is issued on the return of a writ of *habeas corpus ad subjiciendum*, an appeal therefrom lies to the court of appeal, and from a judgment of the court of appeal to the Supreme Court of Canada, with the leave of that court, at the instance of the applicant or the Attorney General of the province concerned or the Attorney General of Canada, but not at the instance of any other party.

(6) Hearing of appeal — An appeal in *habeas corpus* matters shall be heard by the court to which the appeal is directed at an early date, whether in or out of the prescribed sessions of the court.

1997, c. 18, s. 109

PART XXVII — SUMMARY CONVICTIONS (SS. 785–840)

Interpretation

785. Definitions — In this Part,

"clerk of the appeal court" includes a local clerk of the appeal court;

"informant" means a person who lays an information;

"information" includes

(a) a count in an information, and

(b) a complaint in respect of which a justice is authorized by an Act of Parliament or an enactment made thereunder to make an order;

"order" means any order, including an order for the payment of money;

"proceedings" means

(a) proceedings in respect of offences that are declared by an Act of Parliament or an enactment made thereunder to be punishable on summary conviction, and

(b) proceedings where a justice is authorized by an Act of Parliament or an enactment made thereunder to make an order;

"prosecutor" means the Attorney General or where the Attorney General does not intervene, the informant, and includes counsel or an agent acting on behalf of either of them;

"sentence" includes

(a) a declaration made under subsection 199(3),

(b) an order made under subsection 109(1) or 110(1), section 259 or 261, subsection 730(1) or 737(2.1) or (3) or section 738, 739, 742.1 or 742.3,

(c) a disposition made under section 731 or 732 or subsection 732.2(3) or (5), 742.4(3) or 742.6(9);

(d) an order made under subsection 16(1) of the *Controlled Drugs and Substances Act*, and

(e) an order made under subsection 94(1) of the *Cannabis Act*;

"summary conviction court" means a person who has jurisdiction in the territorial division where the subject-matter of the proceedings is alleged to have arisen and who

(a) is given jurisdiction over the proceedings by the enactment under which the proceedings are taken,

(b) is a justice or provincial court judge, where the enactment under which the proceedings are taken does not expressly give jurisdiction to any person or class of persons, or

(c) is a provincial court judge, where the enactment under which the proceedings are taken gives jurisdiction in respect thereof to two or more justices;

"trial" includes the hearing of a complaint.

R.S.C. 1985, c. 27 (1st Supp.), ss. 170, 203; 1992, c. 1, s. 58(1) (Sched. 1, item 16); 1995, c. 22, s. 7; 1995, c. 39, s. 156; 1996, c. 19, s. 76; 1999, c. 25, s. 23; 2002, c. 13, s. 78; 2006, c. 14, s. 7; 2013, c. 11, s. 4; 2018, c. 16, s. 223; 2018, c. 21, s. 26; 2019, c. 25, s. 314

786. (1) Application of Part — Except where otherwise provided by law, this Part applies to proceedings as defined in this Part.

(2) Limitation — No proceedings shall be instituted more than 12 months after the time when the subject matter of the proceedings arose, unless the prosecutor and the defendant so agree.

1997, c. 18, s. 110; 2019, c. 25, s. 315

Punishment

787. (1) General penalty — Unless otherwise provided by law, every person who is convicted of an offence punishable on summary conviction is liable to a fine of not more than $5,000 or to a term of imprisonment of not more than two years less a day, or to both.

(2) Imprisonment in default if not otherwise specified — If the imposition of a fine or the making of an order for the payment of money is authorized by law, but the law does not provide that imprisonment may be imposed in default of payment of the fine or compliance with the order, the court may order that in default of payment of the fine or compliance with the order, as the case may be, the defendant shall be imprisoned for a term of not more than two years less a day.

(3) to (11) [Repealed R.S.C. 1985, c. 27 (1st Supp.), s. 171.]

R.S.C. 1985, c. 27 (1st Supp.), s. 171; 2008, c. 18, s. 44; 2019, c. 25, s. 316

Information

788. (1) Commencement of proceedings — Proceedings under this Part shall be commenced by laying an information in Form 2.

(2) One justice may act before the trial — Notwithstanding any other law that requires an information to be laid before or to be tried by two or more justices, one justice may

(a) receive the information;

(b) issue a summons or warrant with respect to the information; and

(c) do all other things preliminary to the trial.

789. (1) Formalities of information — In proceedings to which this Part applies, an information

(a) shall be in writing and under oath; and

(b) may charge more than one offence or relate to more than one matter of complaint, but where more than one offence is charged or the information relates to more than one matter of complaint, each offence or matter of complaint, as the case may be, shall be set out in a separate count.

(2) No reference to previous convictions — No information in respect of an offence for which, by reason of previous convictions, a greater punishment may be imposed shall contain any reference to previous convictions.

790. (1) Any justice may act before and after trial — Nothing in this Act or any other law shall be deemed to require a justice before whom proceedings are commenced or who issues process before or after the trial to be the justice or one of the justices before whom the trial is held.

(2) Two or more justices — Where two or more justices have jurisdiction with respect to proceedings, they shall be present and act together at the trial, but one justice may thereafter do anything that is required or is authorized to be done in connection with the proceedings.

(3) and (4) [Repealed R.S.C. 1985, c. 27 (1st Supp.), s. 172.]

R.S.C. 1985, c. 27 (1st Supp.), s. 172

791. [Repealed R.S.C. 1985, c. 27 (1st Supp.), s. 173.]

Heading and s. 792. [Repealed R.S.C. 1985, c. 27 (1st Supp.), s. 174.]

Defects and Objections

793. [Repealed R.S.C. 1985, c. 27 (1st Supp.), s. 175.]

794. (1) No need to negative exception, etc. — No exception, exemption, proviso, excuse or qualification prescribed by law is required to be set out or negatived, as the case may be, in an information.

(2) [Repealed 2018, c. 29, s. 68.]

2018, c. 29, s. 68

Application

795. Application of Parts XVI, XVIII, XVIII.1, XX and XX.1 — The provisions of Parts XVI and XVIII with respect to compelling the appearance of an accused before a justice, and the provisions of Parts XVIII.1, XX and XX.1, in so far as they are not inconsistent with this Part, apply, with any necessary modifications, to proceedings under this Part.

R.S.C. 1985, c. 27 (1st Supp.), s. 176; 1991, c. 43, s. 7; 2011, c. 16, s. 16

796 and 797. [Repealed R.S.C. 1985, c. 27 (1st Supp.), s. 176.]

Trial

798. Jurisdiction — Every summary conviction court has jurisdiction to try, determine and adjudge proceedings to which this Part applies in the territorial division over which the person who constitutes that court has jurisdiction.

799. Non-appearance of prosecutor — Where, in proceedings to which this Part applies, the defendant appears for the trial and the prosecutor, having had due notice, does not appear, the summary conviction court may dismiss the information or may adjourn the trial to some other time on such terms as it considers proper.

800. (1) When both parties appear — Where the prosecutor and defendant appear for the trial, the summary conviction court shall proceed to hold the trial.

(2) Counsel or agent — A defendant may appear personally or by counsel or agent, but the summary conviction court may require the defendant to appear personally and may, if it thinks fit, issue a warrant in Form 7 for the arrest of the defendant and adjourn the trial to await his appearance pursuant thereto.

(2.1) Video links — If the summary conviction court so orders and the defendant agrees, the defendant who is confined in prison may appear by closed-circuit television or videoconference, as long as the defendant is given the opportunity to communicate privately with counsel if they are represented by counsel.

(3) Appearance by organization — Where the defendant is an organization, it shall appear by counsel or agent and, if it does not appear, the summary conviction court may, on proof of service of the summons, proceed *ex parte* to hold the trial.

1997, c. 18, s. 111; 2003, c. 21, s. 21; 2019, c. 25, s. 317

801. (1) Arraignment — Where the defendant appears for the trial, the substance of the information laid against him shall be stated to him, and he shall be asked,

(a) whether he pleads guilty or not guilty to the information, where the proceedings are in respect of an offence that is punishable on summary conviction; or

(b) whether he has cause to show why an order should not be made against him, in proceedings where a justice is authorized by law to make an order.

(2) Finding of guilt, conviction or order if charge admitted — Where the defendant pleads guilty or does not show sufficient cause why an order should not be made against him, as the case may be, the summary conviction court shall convict the defendant, discharge the defendant under section 730 or make an order against the defendant accordingly.

(3) Procedure if charge not admitted — Where the defendant pleads not guilty or states that he has cause to show why an order should not be made against him, as the case may be, the summary conviction court shall proceed with the trial, and shall take the evidence of witnesses for the prosecutor and the defendant in accordance with the provisions of Part XVIII relating to preliminary inquiries.

(4) and (5) [Repealed R.S.C. 1985, c. 27 (1st Supp.), s. 177(2).]

R.S.C. 1985, c. 27 (1st Supp.), s. 177; 1995, c. 22, s. 10

802. (1) Right to make full answer and defence — The prosecutor is entitled personally to conduct his case and the defendant is entitled to make his full answer and defence.

(2) Examination of witnesses — The prosecutor or defendant, as the case may be, may examine and cross-examine witnesses personally or by counsel or agent.

(3) On oath — Every witness at a trial in proceedings to which this Part applies shall be examined under oath.

802.1 Limitation on the use of agents — Despite subsections 800(2) and 802(2), a defendant may not appear or examine or cross-examine witnesses by agent if he or she is liable, on summary conviction, to imprisonment for a term of more than six months, unless

(a) the defendant is an organization;

(b) the defendant is appearing to request an adjournment of the proceedings; or

(c) the agent is authorized to do so under a program approved — or criteria established — by the lieutenant governor in council of the province.

2002, c. 13, s. 79; 2019, c. 25, s. 317.1

803. (1) Adjournment — The summary conviction court may, in its discretion, before or during the trial, adjourn the trial to a time and place to be appointed and stated in the presence of the parties or their counsel or agents.

(2) Non-appearance of defendant — If a defendant who is tried alone or together with others does not appear at the time and place appointed for the trial after having been notified of that time and place, or does not appear for the resumption of a trial that has been adjourned in accordance with subsection (1), the summary conviction court

(a) may proceed *ex parte* to hear and determine the proceedings in the absence of that defendant as if they had appeared; or

(b) may, if it thinks fit, issue a warrant in Form 7 for the arrest of that defendant and adjourn the trial to await their appearance under the warrant.

(3) Consent of Attorney General required — If the summary conviction court proceeds in the manner described in paragraph (2)(a), no proceedings under section 145 arising out of the defendant's failure to appear at the time and place appointed for the trial or for the resumption of the trial shall, without the consent of the Attorney General, be instituted or be proceeded with.

(4) Non-appearance of prosecutor — Where the prosecutor does not appear at the time and place appointed for the resumption of an adjourned trial, the summary conviction court may dismiss the information with or without costs.

(5) to (8) [Repealed 1991, c. 43, s. 9 (Sched., item 11).]

1991, c. 43,, s. 9 (Sched., item 11); 1994, c. 44, s. 79; 1997, c. 18, s. 112; 2008, c. 18, s. 45

Adjudication

804. Finding of guilt, conviction, order or dismissal — When the summary conviction court has heard the prosecutor, defendant and witnesses, it shall, after considering the matter, convict the defendant, discharge the defendant under section 730, make an order against the defendant or dismiss the information, as the case may be.

R.S.C. 1985, c. 27 (1st Supp.), s. 178; 1995, c. 22, s. 10

805. [Repealed R.S.C. 1985, c. 27 (1st Supp.), s. 179.]

806. (1) Memo of conviction or order — If a defendant is convicted or an order is made in relation to the defendant, a minute or memorandum of the conviction or order must be made by the summary conviction court indicating that the matter was dealt with under this Part and, on request by the defendant, the prosecutor or any other person, a conviction or order in Form 35 or 36, as the case may be, and a certified copy of the conviction or order must be drawn up and the certified copy must be delivered to the person making the request.

(2) Warrant of committal — Where a defendant is convicted or an order is made against him, the summary conviction court shall issue a warrant of committal in Form 21 or 22, and section 528 applies in respect of a warrant of committal issued under this subsection.

(3) Admissibility of certified copy — If a warrant of committal in Form 21 is signed by a clerk of a court, a copy of the warrant of committal, certified by the clerk, is admissible in evidence in any proceeding.

1994, c. 44, s. 80; 2019, c. 25, s. 318(1), (3)

807. Disposal of penalties when joint offenders — Where several persons join in committing the same offence and on conviction each is adjudged to pay an amount to a person aggrieved, no more shall be paid to that person than an amount equal to the value of the property destroyed or injured or the amount of the injury done, together with costs, if any, and the residue of the amount adjudged to be paid shall be applied in the manner in which other penalties imposed by law are directed to be applied.

808. (1) Order of dismissal — Where the summary conviction court dismisses an information, it may, if requested by the defendant, draw up an order of dismissal, and shall give to the defendant a certified copy of the order of dismissal.

(2) Effect of certificate — A copy of an order of dismissal, certified in accordance with subsection (1) is, without further proof, a bar to any subsequent proceedings against the defendant in respect of the same cause.

809. (1) Costs — The summary conviction court may in its discretion award and order such costs as it considers reasonable and not inconsistent with such of the fees established by section 840 as may be taken or allowed in proceedings before that summary conviction court, to be paid

(a) to the informant by the defendant, where the summary conviction court convicts or makes an order against the defendant; or

(b) to the defendant by the informant, where the summary conviction court dismisses an information.

(2) Order set out — An order under subsection (1) shall be set out in the conviction, order or order of dismissal, as the case may be.

(3) Costs are part of fine — Where a fine or sum of money or both are adjudged to be paid by a defendant and a term of imprisonment in default of payment is imposed, the defendant is, in default of payment, liable to serve the term of imprisonment imposed, and for the purposes of this subsection, any costs that are awarded against the defendant shall be deemed to be part of the fine or sum of money adjudged to be paid.

(4) Where no fine imposed — Where no fine or sum of money is adjudged to be paid by a defendant, but costs are awarded against the defendant or informant, the person who is liable to pay them is, in default of payment, liable to imprisonment for one month.

(5) Definition of "costs" — In this section, **"costs"** includes the costs and charges, after they have been ascertained, of committing and conveying to prison the person against whom costs have been awarded.

Sureties to Keep the Peace

810. (1) If injury or damage feared — An information may be laid before a justice by or on behalf of any person who fears on reasonable grounds that another person

(a) will cause personal injury to them or to their intimate partner or child or will damage their property; or

(b) will commit an offence under section 162.1.

(2) Duty of justice — A justice who receives an information under subsection (1) shall cause the parties to appear before him or before a summary conviction court having jurisdiction in the same territorial division.

(3) Adjudication — If the justice or summary conviction court before which the parties appear is satisfied by the evidence adduced that the person on whose behalf the information was laid has reasonable grounds for the fear, the justice or court may order that the defendant enter into a recognizance, with or without sureties, to keep the peace and be of good behaviour for a period of not more than 12 months.

(3.01) Refusal to enter into recognizance — The justice or summary conviction court may commit the defendant to prison for a term of not more than 12 months if the defendant fails or refuses to enter into the recognizance.

(3.02) Conditions in recognizance — The justice or summary conviction court may add any reasonable conditions to the recognizance that the justice or court considers desirable to secure the good conduct of the defendant, including conditions that require the defendant

(a) to abstain from the consumption of drugs except in accordance with a medical prescription, of alcohol or of any other intoxicating substance;

(b) to provide, for the purpose of analysis, a sample of a bodily substance prescribed by regulation on the demand of a peace officer, a probation officer or someone designated under paragraph 810.3(2)(a) to make a demand, at the place and time and on the day specified by the person making the demand, if that person has reasonable grounds to believe that the defendant has breached a condition of the recognizance that requires them to abstain from the consumption of drugs, alcohol or any other intoxicating substance; or

(c) to provide, for the purpose of analysis, a sample of a bodily substance prescribed by regulation at regular intervals that are specified, in a notice in Form 51 served on the defendant, by a probation officer or a person designated under paragraph 810.3(2)(b) to specify them, if a condition of the recognizance requires the defendant to abstain from the consumption of drugs, alcohol or any other intoxicating substance.

(3.1) Conditions — Before making an order under subsection (3), the justice or the summary conviction court shall consider whether it is desirable, in the interests of the safety of the defendant or any other person, to include as a condition of the recognizance that the defendant be prohibited from possessing any firearm, cross-bow, prohibited weapon, restricted weapon, prohibited device, ammunition, prohibited ammunition or explosive substance, or all such things, for any period specified in the recognizance and, where the justice or summary conviction court decides that it is so desirable, the justice or summary conviction court shall add such a condition to the recognizance.

(3.11) Surrender, etc. — Where the justice or summary conviction court adds a condition described in subsection (3.1) to a recognizance order, the justice or summary conviction court shall specify in the order the manner and method by which

(a) the things referred to in that subsection that are in the possession of the accused shall be surrendered, disposed of, detained, stored or dealt with; and

(b) the authorizations, licences and registration certificates held by the person shall be surrendered.

(3.12) Reasons — Where the justice or summary conviction court does not add a condition described in subsection (3.1) to a recognizance order, the justice or summary conviction court shall include in the record a statement of the reasons for not adding the condition.

(3.2) Supplementary conditions — Before making an order under subsection (3), the justice or the summary conviction court shall consider whether it is desirable, in the interests of the safety of the informant, of the person on whose behalf the information was laid or of that person's intimate partner or child, as the case may be, to add either or both of the following conditions to the recognizance,

(a) a condition prohibiting the defendant from being at, or within a distance specified in the recognizance from, a place specified in the recognizance where the person on whose behalf the information was laid or that person's intimate partner or child, as the case may be, is regularly found; or

(b) a condition prohibiting the defendant from communicating, in whole or in part, directly or indirectly, with the person on whose behalf the information was laid or that person's intimate partner or child, as the case may be.

(4) Form — warrant of committal — A warrant of committal to prison for failure or refusal to enter into the recognizance under subsection (3) may be in Form 23.

(4.1) Modification of recognizance — The justice or the summary conviction court may, on application of the informant or the defendant, vary the conditions fixed in the recognizance.

(5) Procedure — The provisions of this Part apply, with such modifications as the circumstances require, to proceedings under this section.

1991, c. 40, s. 33; 1994, c. 44, s. 81; 1995, c. 22, s. 8; 1995, c. 39, s. 157; 2000, c. 12, s. 95(f), (g); 2011, c. 7, s. 7; 2014, c. 31, s. 25; 2019, c. 25, s. 319(1), (4)

810.01 (1) Fear of certain offences — A person who fears on reasonable grounds that another person will commit an offence under section 423.1 or a criminal organization offence may, with the Attorney General's consent, lay an information before a provincial court judge.

(2) Appearances — A provincial court judge who receives an information under subsection (1) may cause the parties to appear before a provincial court judge.

(3) Adjudication — If the provincial court judge before whom the parties appear is satisfied by the evidence adduced that the informant has reasonable grounds for the fear, the judge may order that the defendant enter into a recognizance to keep the peace and be of good behaviour for a period of not more than 12 months.

(3.1) Duration extended — However, if the provincial court judge is also satisfied that the defendant was convicted previously of an offence referred to in subsection (1), the judge may order that the defendant enter into the recognizance for a period of not more than two years.

(4) Refusal to enter into recognizance — The provincial court judge may commit the defendant to prison for a term not exceeding twelve months if the defendant fails or refuses to enter into the recognizance.

(4.1) Conditions in recognizance — The provincial court judge may add any reasonable conditions to the recognizance that the judge considers desirable for preventing the commission of an offence referred to in subsection (1), including conditions that require the defendant

(a) to participate in a treatment program;

(b) to wear an electronic monitoring device, if the Attorney General makes the request;

(c) to remain within a specified geographic area unless written permission to leave that area is obtained from the judge;

(d) to return to and remain at their place of residence at specified times;

(e) to abstain from the consumption of drugs, except in accordance with a medical prescription, of alcohol or of any other intoxicating substance;

(f) to provide, for the purpose of analysis, a sample of a bodily substance prescribed by regulation on the demand of a peace officer, a probation officer or someone designated under paragraph 810.3(2)(a) to make a demand, at the place and time and on the day specified by the person making the demand, if that person has reasonable grounds to believe that the defendant has breached a condition of the recognizance that requires them to abstain from the consumption of drugs, alcohol or any other intoxicating substance; or

(g) to provide, for the purpose of analysis, a sample of a bodily substance prescribed by regulation at regular intervals that are specified, in a notice in Form 51 served on the defendant, by a probation officer or a person designated under paragraph 810.3(2)(b) to specify them, if a condition of the recognizance requires the defendant to abstain from the consumption of drugs, alcohol or any other intoxicating substance.

(5) Conditions — firearms — The provincial court judge shall consider whether it is desirable, in the interests of the defendant's safety or that of any other person, to prohibit the defendant from possessing any firearm, cross-bow, prohibited weapon, restricted weapon, prohibited device, ammunition, prohibited ammunition or explosive substance, or all of those things. If the judge decides that it is desirable to do so, the judge shall add that condition to the recognizance and specify the period during which the condition applies.

(5.1) Surrender, etc. — If the provincial court judge adds a condition described in subsection (5) to a recognizance, the judge shall specify in the recognizance how the things referred to in that subsection that are in the defendant's possession shall be surrendered, disposed of, detained, stored or dealt with and how the authorizations, licences and registration certificates that are held by the defendant shall be surrendered.

(5.2) Reasons — If the provincial court judge does not add a condition described in subsection (5) to a recognizance, the judge shall include in the record a statement of the reasons for not adding the condition.

(6) Variance of conditions — A provincial court judge may, on application of the informant, the Attorney General or the defendant, vary the conditions fixed in the recognizance.

(7) Other provisions to apply — Subsections 810(4) and (5) apply, with any modifications that the circumstances require, to recognizance made under this section.

(8) Definition of "Attorney General" — With respect to proceedings under this section, **"Attorney General"** means either the Attorney General of Canada or the Attorney General of the province in which those proceedings are taken and includes the lawful deputy of any of them.

1997, c. 23, ss. 19, 26; 2001, c. 32, s. 46 [Amended 2001, c. 41, s. 133(21).]; 2001, c. 41, ss. 22, 133(19); 2002, c. 13, s. 80; 2009, c. 22, s. 19; 2011, c. 7, s. 8(2), (3); 2015, c. 20, s. 24

810.011 (1) Fear of terrorism offence — A person who fears on reasonable grounds that another person may commit a terrorism offence may, with the Attorney General's consent, lay an information before a provincial court judge.

(2) Appearances — The provincial court judge who receives an information under subsection (1) may cause the parties to appear before a provincial court judge.

(3) Adjudication — If the provincial court judge before whom the parties appear is satisfied by the evidence adduced that the informant has reasonable grounds for the fear, the judge may order that the defendant enter into a recognizance, with or without sureties, to keep the peace and be of good behaviour for a period of not more than 12 months.

(4) Duration extended — However, if the provincial court judge is also satisfied that the defendant was convicted previously of a terrorism offence, the judge may order that the defendant enter into the recognizance for a period of not more than five years.

(5) Refusal to enter into recognizance — The provincial court judge may commit the defendant to prison for a term of not more than 12 months if the defendant fails or refuses to enter into the recognizance.

(6) Conditions in recognizance — The provincial court judge may add any reasonable conditions to the recognizance that the judge considers desirable to secure the good conduct of the defendant, including conditions that require the defendant

(a) to participate in a treatment program;

(b) to wear an electronic monitoring device, if the Attorney General makes that request;

(c) to return to and remain at their place of residence at specified times;

(d) to abstain from the consumption of drugs, except in accordance with a medical prescription, of alcohol or of any other intoxicating substance;

(e) to provide, for the purpose of analysis, a sample of a bodily substance prescribed by regulation on the demand of a peace officer, a probation officer or someone designated under paragraph 810.3(2)(a) to make a demand, at the place and time and on the day specified by the person making the demand, if that person has reasonable grounds to believe that the defendant has breached a condition of the recognizance that requires them to abstain from the consumption of drugs, alcohol or any other intoxicating substance; or

(f) to provide, for the purpose of analysis, a sample of a bodily substance prescribed by regulation at regular intervals that are specified, in a notice in Form 51 served on the defendant, by a probation officer or a person designated under paragraph 810.3(2)(b) to specify them, if a condition of the recognizance requires the defendant to abstain from the consumption of drugs, alcohol or any other intoxicating substance.

(7) Conditions — firearms — The provincial court judge shall consider whether it is desirable, in the interests of the defendant's safety or that of any other person, to prohibit the defendant from possessing any firearm, cross-bow, prohibited weapon, restricted weapon, prohibited device, ammunition, prohibited ammunition or explosive substance, or all of those things. If the judge decides that it is desirable to do so, the judge shall add that condition to the recognizance and specify the period during which it applies.

(8) Surrender, etc. — If the provincial court judge adds a condition described in subsection (7) to a recognizance, the judge shall specify in the recognizance how the things referred to in that subsection that are in the defendant's possession shall be surrendered, disposed of, detained, stored or dealt with and how the authorizations, licences and registration certificates that are held by the defendant shall be surrendered.

(9) Condition — passport — The provincial court judge shall consider whether it is desirable, to secure the good conduct of the defendant, to include in the recognizance a condition that the defendant deposit, in the specified manner, any passport or other travel document issued in their name that is in their possession or control. If the judge decides that it is desirable, the judge shall add the condition to the recognizance and specify the period during which it applies.

(10) Condition — specified geographic area — The provincial court judge shall consider whether it is desirable, to secure the good conduct of the defendant, to include in the recognizance a condition that the defendant remain within a specified geographic area unless written permission to leave that area is obtained from the judge or any individual designated by the judge. If the judge decides that it is desirable, the judge shall add the condition to the recognizance and specify the period during which it applies.

(11) Reasons — If the provincial court judge does not add a condition described in subsection (7), (9) or (10) to a recognizance, the judge shall include in the record a statement of the reasons for not adding it.

(12) Variance of conditions — A provincial court judge may, on application of the informant, the Attorney General or the defendant, vary the conditions fixed in the recognizance.

(13) Other provisions to apply — Subsections 810(4) and (5) apply, with any modifications that the circumstances require, to recognizances made under this section.

(14) Definition of "Attorney General" — With respect to proceedings under this section, **"Attorney General"** means either the Attorney General of Canada or the Attorney General of the province in which those proceedings are taken and includes the lawful deputy of any of them.

(15) Annual report — Each year, the Attorney General of Canada shall prepare and cause to be laid before each House of Parliament a report setting out the number of recognizances entered into under this section in the previous year.

2015, c. 20, s. 25; 2019, c. 13, s. 153

810.02 (1) Fear of forced marriage or marriage under age of 16 years — A person who fears on reasonable grounds that another person will commit an offence under paragraph 273.3(1)(d) or section 293.1 or 293.2 may lay an information before a provincial court judge.

(2) Appearances — The judge who receives the information may cause the parties to appear before a provincial court judge.

(3) Adjudication — If the provincial court judge before whom the parties appear is satisfied by the evidence adduced that the informant has reasonable grounds for the fear, the judge may order that the defendant enter into a recognizance to keep the peace and be of good behaviour for a period of not more than 12 months.

(4) Duration extended — However, if the provincial court judge is also satisfied that the defendant was convicted previously of an offence referred to in subsection (1), the judge may order that the defendant enter into the recognizance for a period of not more than two years.

(5) Refusal to enter into recognizance — The provincial court judge may commit the defendant to prison for a term not exceeding 12 months if the defendant fails or refuses to enter into the recognizance.

(6) Conditions in recognizance — The provincial court judge may add any reasonable conditions to the recognizance that the judge considers desirable to secure the good conduct of the defendant, including conditions that

(a) prohibit the defendant from making agreements or arrangements for the marriage, whether in or outside Canada, of the person in respect of whom it is feared that the offence will be committed;

(b) prohibit the defendant from taking steps to cause the person in respect of whom it is feared that the offence will be committed to leave the jurisdiction of the court;

(c) require the defendant to deposit, in the specified manner, any passport or any other travel document that is in their possession or control, whether or not such passport or document is in their name or in the name of any other specified person;

(d) prohibit the defendant from communicating, directly or indirectly, with any specified person, or refrain from going to any specified place, except in accordance with any specified conditions that the judge considers necessary;

(e) require the defendant to participate in a treatment program, including a family violence counselling program;

(f) require the defendant to remain within a specified geographic area unless written permission to leave that area is obtained from the provincial court judge; and

(g) require the defendant to return to and remain at their place of residence at specified times.

(7) Conditions — firearms — The provincial court judge shall consider whether it is desirable, in the interests of the defendant's safety or that of any other person, to prohibit the defendant from possessing any firearm, cross-bow, prohibited weapon, restricted weapon, prohibited device, ammunition, prohibited ammunition or explosive substance, or all of those things. If the judge decides that it is desirable to do so, the judge shall add that condition to the recognizance and specify the period during which the condition applies.

(8) Surrender, etc. — If the provincial court judge adds a condition described in subsection (7) to a recognizance, the judge shall specify in the recognizance how the things referred to in that subsection that are in the defendant's possession are to be surrendered, disposed of, detained, stored or dealt with and how the authorizations, licences and registration certificates that are held by the defendant are to be surrendered.

(9) Variance of conditions — A provincial court judge may, on application of the informant or the defendant, vary the conditions fixed in the recognizance.

2015, c. 29, s. 11

810.1 (1) Where fear of sexual offence — Any person who fears on reasonable grounds that another person will commit an offence under section 151 or 152, subsection 153(1), section 155, subsection 160(2) or (3), section 163.1, 170, 171, 171.1, 172.1 or 172.2, subsection 173(2), section 271, 272, 273 or 279.011, subsection 279.02(2) or 279.03(2), section 280 or 281 or subsection 286.1(2), 286.2(2) or

286.3(2), in respect of one or more persons who are under the age of 16 years, may lay an information before a provincial court judge, whether or not the person or persons in respect of whom it is feared that the offence will be committed are named.

(2) Appearances — A provincial court judge who receives an information under subsection (1) may cause the parties to appear before a provincial court judge.

(3) Adjudication — If the provincial court judge before whom the parties appear is satisfied by the evidence adduced that the informant has reasonable grounds for the fear, the judge may order that the defendant enter into a recognizance to keep the peace and be of good behaviour for a period that does not exceed 12 months.

(3.01) Duration extended — However, if the provincial court judge is also satisfied that the defendant was convicted previously of a sexual offence in respect of a person who is under the age of 16 years, the judge may order that the defendant enter into the recognizance for a period that does not exceed two years.

(3.02) Conditions in recognizance — The provincial court judge may add any reasonable conditions to the recognizance that the judge considers desirable to secure the good conduct of the defendant, including conditions that

(a) prohibit the defendant from having any contact — including communicating by any means — with a person under the age of 16 years, unless the defendant does so under the supervision of a person whom the judge considers appropriate;

(a.1) prohibit the defendant from using the Internet or other digital network, unless the defendant does so in accordance with conditions set by the judge;

(b) prohibit the defendant from attending a public park or public swimming area where persons under the age of 16 years are present or can reasonably be expected to be present, or a daycare centre, schoolground or playground;

(b.1) prohibit the defendant from communicating, directly or indirectly, with any person identified in the recognizance, or refrain from going to any place specified in the recognizance, except in accordance with the conditions specified in the recognizance that the judge considers necessary;

(c) require the defendant to participate in a treatment program;

(d) require the defendant to wear an electronic monitoring device, if the Attorney General makes the request;

(e) require the defendant to remain within a specified geographic area unless written permission to leave that area is obtained from the provincial court judge;

(f) require the defendant to return to and remain at his or her place of residence at specified times;

(g) require the defendant to abstain from the consumption of drugs except in accordance with a medical prescription, of alcohol or of any other intoxicating substance;

(h) require the defendant to provide, for the purpose of analysis, a sample of a bodily substance prescribed by regulation on the demand of a peace officer, a probation officer or someone designated under paragraph 810.3(2)(a) to make a demand, at the place and time and on the day specified by the person making the demand, if that person has reasonable grounds to believe that the defendant has breached a condition of the recognizance that requires them to abstain from the consumption of drugs, alcohol or any other intoxicating substance; or

(i) require the defendant to provide, for the purpose of analysis, a sample of a bodily substance prescribed by regulation at regular intervals that are specified, in a notice in Form 51 served on the defendant, by a probation officer or a person designated under paragraph 810.3(2)(b) to specify them, if a condition of the recognizance requires the defendant to abstain from the consumption of drugs, alcohol or any other intoxicating substance.

(3.03) **Conditions — firearms** — The provincial court judge shall consider whether it is desirable, in the interests of the defendant's safety or that of any other person, to prohibit the defendant from possessing any firearm, cross-bow, prohibited weapon, restricted weapon, prohibited device, ammunition, prohibited ammunition or explosive substance, or all of those things. If the judge decides that it is desirable to do so, the judge shall add that condition to the recognizance and specify the period during which the condition applies.

(3.04) **Surrender, etc.** — If the provincial court judge adds a condition described in subsection (3.03) to a recognizance, the judge shall specify in the recognizance how the things referred to in that subsection that are in the defendant's possession should be surrendered, disposed of, detained, stored or dealt with and how the authorizations, licences and registration certificates that are held by the defendant should be surrendered.

(3.05) **Condition — reporting** — The provincial court judge shall consider whether it is desirable to require the defendant to report to the correctional authority of a province or to an appropriate police authority. If the judge decides that it is desirable to do so, the judge shall add that condition to the recognizance.

(3.1) **Refusal to enter into recognizance** — The provincial court judge may commit the defendant to prison for a term not exceeding twelve months if the defendant fails or refuses to enter into the recognizance.

(4) **Judge may vary recognizance** — A provincial court judge may, on application of the informant or the defendant, vary the conditions fixed in the recognizance.

(5) **Other provisions to apply** — Subsections 810(4) and (5) apply, with such modifications as the circumstances require, to recognizances made under this section.

1993, c. 45, s. 11; 1997, c. 18, s. 113(2); 2002, c. 13, s. 81; 2008, c. 6, ss. 52, 54(j), 62(2); 2011, c. 7, s. 9; 2012, c. 1, s. 37; 2014, c. 21, s. 4; 2014, c. 25, s. 31; 2019, c. 25, s. 320

810.2 (1) Where fear of serious personal injury offence — Any person who fears on reasonable grounds that another person will commit a serious personal injury offence, as that expression is defined in section 752, may, with the consent of the Attorney General, lay an information before a provincial court judge, whether or not the person or persons in respect of whom it is feared that the offence will be committed are named.

(2) Appearances — A provincial court judge who receives an information under subsection (1) may cause the parties to appear before a provincial court judge.

(3) Adjudication — If the provincial court judge before whom the parties appear is satisfied by the evidence adduced that the informant has reasonable grounds for the fear, the judge may order that the defendant enter into a recognizance to keep the peace and be of good behaviour for a period that does not exceed 12 months.

(3.1) Duration extended — However, if the provincial court judge is also satisfied that the defendant was convicted previously of an offence referred to in subsection (1), the judge may order that the defendant enter into the recognizance for a period that does not exceed two years.

(4) Refusal to enter into recognizance — The provincial court judge may commit the defendant to prison for a term not exceeding twelve months if the defendant fails or refuses to enter into the recognizance.

(4.1) Conditions in recognizance — The provincial court judge may add any reasonable conditions to the recognizance that the judge considers desirable to secure the good conduct of the defendant, including conditions that require the defendant

(a) to participate in a treatment program;

(b) to wear an electronic monitoring device, if the Attorney General makes the request;

(c) to remain within a specified geographic area unless written permission to leave that area is obtained from the provincial court judge;

(d) to return to and remain at his or her place of residence at specified times;

(e) to abstain from the consumption of drugs except in accordance with a medical prescription, of alcohol or of any other intoxicating substance;

(f) to provide, for the purpose of analysis, a sample of a bodily substance prescribed by regulation on the demand of a peace officer, a probation officer or someone designated under paragraph 810.3(2)(a) to make a demand, at the place and time and on the day specified by the person making the demand, if that person has reasonable grounds to believe that the defendant has breached a condition of the recognizance that requires them to abstain from the consumption of drugs, alcohol or any other intoxicating substance; or

(g) to provide, for the purpose of analysis, a sample of a bodily substance prescribed by regulation at regular intervals that are specified, in a notice in Form 51 served on the defendant, by a probation officer or a person designated under paragraph 810.3(2)(b) to specify them, if a condition of the recognizance requires the defendant to abstain from the consumption of drugs, alcohol or any other intoxicating substance.

(5) Conditions — firearms — The provincial court judge shall consider whether it is desirable, in the interests of the defendant's safety or that of any other person, to prohibit the defendant from possessing any firearm, cross-bow, prohibited weapon, restricted weapon, prohibited device, ammunition, prohibited ammunition or explosive substance, or all of those things. If the judge decides that it is desirable to do so, the judge shall add that condition to the recognizance and specify the period during which the condition applies.

(5.1) Surrender, etc. — If the provincial court judge adds a condition described in subsection (5) to a recognizance, the judge shall specify in the recognizance how the things referred to in that subsection that are in the defendant's possession should be surrendered, disposed of, detained, stored or dealt with and how the authorizations, licences and registration certificates that are held by the defendant should be surrendered.

(5.2) Reasons — If the provincial court judge does not add a condition described in subsection (5) to a recognizance, the judge shall include in the record a statement of the reasons for not adding the condition.

(6) Condition — reporting — The provincial court judge shall consider whether it is desirable to require the defendant to report to the correctional authority of a province or to an appropriate police authority. If the judge decides that it is desirable to do so, the judge shall add that condition to the recognizance.

(7) Variance of conditions — A provincial court judge may, on application of the informant, of the Attorney General or of the defendant, vary the conditions fixed in the recognizance.

(8) Other provisions to apply — Subsections 810(4) and (5) apply, with such modifications as the circumstances require, to recognizance made under this section.

1997, c. 17, s. 9; 2002, c. 13, s. 82; 2008, c. 6, s. 53; 2011, c. 7, s. 10

810.21 (1) Audioconference or videoconference — If a defendant is required to appear under any of sections 83.3 and 810 to 810.2, a provincial court judge may, on application of the prosecutor, order that the defendant appear by audioconference or videoconference.

(2) Application — Despite section 769, sections 714.1 to 714.8 and Part XXII.01 apply, with any necessary modifications, to proceedings under this section.

2015, c. 20, s. 26; 2019, c. 25, s. 321

810.22 (1) Transfer of order — If a person who is bound by an order under any of sections 83.3 and 810 to 810.2 becomes a resident of — or is charged with, convicted of or discharged under section 730 of an offence, including an offence under section 811, in — a territorial division other than the territorial division in which the order was made, on application of a peace officer or the Attorney General, a provincial court judge may, subject to subsection (2), transfer the order to a provincial court judge in that other territorial division and the order may then be dealt with and enforced by the provincial court judge to whom it is transferred in all respects as if that provincial court judge had made the order.

(2) Attorney General's consent — The transfer may be granted only with

(a) the consent of the Attorney General of the province in which the order was made, if the two territorial divisions are not in the same province; or

(b) the consent of the Attorney General of Canada, if the information that led to the issuance of the order was laid with the consent of the Attorney General of Canada.

(3) If judge unable to act — If the judge who made the order or a judge to whom an order has been transferred is for any reason unable to act, the powers of that judge in relation to the order may be exercised by any other judge of the same court.

2015, c. 20, s. 26

810.3 (1) Samples — designations and specifications — For the purposes of sections 810, 810.01, 810.011, 810.1 and 810.2 and subject to the regulations, the Attorney General of a province or the minister of justice of a territory shall, with respect to the province or territory,

(a) designate the persons or classes of persons that may take samples of bodily substances;

(b) designate the places or classes of places at which the samples are to be taken;

(c) specify the manner in which the samples are to be taken;

(d) specify the manner in which the samples are to be analyzed;

(e) specify the manner in which the samples are to be stored, handled and destroyed;

(f) specify the manner in which the records of the results of the analysis of the samples are to be protected and destroyed;

(g) designate the persons or classes of persons that may destroy the samples; and

(h) designate the persons or classes of persons that may destroy the records of the results of the analysis of the samples.

(2) Further designations — Subject to the regulations, the Attorney General of a province or the minister of justice of a territory may, with respect to the province or territory, designate the persons or classes of persons

(a) to make a demand for a sample of a bodily substance for the purposes of paragraphs 810(3.02)(b), 810.01(4.1)(f), 810.011(6)(e), 810.1(3.02)(h) and 810.2(4.1)(f); and

(b) to specify the regular intervals at which a defendant must provide a sample of a bodily substance for the purposes of paragraphs 810(3.02)(c), 810.01(4.1)(g), 810.011(6)(f), 810.1(3.02)(i) and 810.2(4.1)(g).

(3) Restriction — Samples of bodily substances referred to in sections 810, 810.01, 810.011, 810.1 and 810.2 may not be taken, analyzed, stored, handled or destroyed, and the records of the results of the analysis of the samples may not be protected or destroyed, except in accordance with the designations and specifications made under subsection (1).

(4) Destruction of samples — The Attorney General of a province or the minister of justice of a territory, or a person authorized by the Attorney General or minister, shall cause all samples of bodily substances provided under a recognizance under section 810, 810.01, 810.011, 810.1 or 810.2 to be destroyed within the period prescribed by regulation unless the samples are reasonably expected to be used as evidence in a proceeding for an offence under section 811.

(5) Regulations — The Governor in Council may make regulations

(a) prescribing bodily substances for the purposes of sections 810, 810.01, 810.011, 810.1 and 810.2;

(b) respecting the designations and specifications referred to in subsections (1) and (2);

(c) prescribing the periods within which samples of bodily substances are to be destroyed under subsection (4); and

(d) respecting any other matters relating to the samples of bodily substances.

(6) Notice — samples at regular intervals — The notice referred to in paragraph 810(3.02)(c), 810.01(4.1)(g), 810.011(6)(f), 810.1(3.02)(i) or 810.2(4.1)(g) must specify the places and times at which and the days on which the defendant must provide samples of a bodily substance under a condition described in that paragraph. The first sample may not be taken earlier than 24 hours after the defendant is served with the notice, and subsequent samples must be taken at regular intervals of at least seven days.

2011, c. 7, s. 11; 2015, c. 20, s. 34(2)(a)–(e)

810.4 (1) Prohibition on use of bodily substance — No person shall use a bodily substance provided under a recognizance under section 810, 810.01, 810.011, 810.1 or 810.2 except for the purpose of determining whether a defendant is complying with a condition in the recognizance that they abstain from the consumption of drugs, alcohol or any other intoxicating substance.

(2) Prohibition on use or disclosure of result — Subject to subsection (3), no person shall use, disclose or allow the disclosure of the results of the analysis of a bodily substance provided under a recognizance under section 810, 810.01, 810.011, 810.1 or 810.2.

(3) Exception — The results of the analysis of a bodily substance provided under a recognizance under section 810, 810.01, 810.011, 810.1 or 810.2 may be disclosed to the defendant to whom they relate, and may also be used or disclosed in the course of an investigation of, or in a proceeding for, an offence under section 811 or, if the results are made anonymous, for statistical or other research purposes.

(4) Offence — Every person who contravenes subsection (1) or (2) is guilty of an offence punishable on summary conviction.

2011, c. 7, s. 11; 2015, c. 20, s. 34(2)(f)

810.5 (1) Orders under sections 486 to 486.5 and 486.7 — Sections 486 to 486.5 and 486.7 apply, with any necessary modifications, to proceedings under any of sections 83.3 and 810 to 810.2.

(2) Offence — order restricting publication — Every person who fails to comply with an order made under any of subsections 486.4(1) to (3) or subsection 486.5(1) or (2) in proceedings referred to in subsection (1) is guilty of an offence under section 486.6.

2019, c. 13, s. 154

811. Breach of recognizance — A person bound by a recognizance under any of sections 83.3 and 810 to 810.2 who commits a breach of the recognizance is guilty of

(a) an indictable offence and is liable to imprisonment for a term of not more than four years; or

(b) an offence punishable on summary conviction.

1993, c. 45, s. 11; 1994, c. 44, s. 82; 1997, c. 17, s. 10; 1997, c. 23, ss. 20, 27; 2001, c. 41, s. 23; 2015, c. 20, s. 27(1); 2015, c. 23, s. 19; 2015, c. 29, s. 12; 2019, c. 25, s. 322

811.1 (1) Proof of certificate of analyst — bodily substance — In a prosecution for breach of a condition in a recognizance under section 810, 810.01, 810.011, 810.1 or 810.2 that a defendant not consume drugs, alcohol or any other intoxicating substance, a certificate purporting to be signed by an analyst that states that the analyst has analyzed a sample of a bodily substance and that states the result of the analysis is admissible in evidence and, in the absence of evidence to the contrary, is proof of the statements contained in the certificate without proof of the signature or official character of the person who appears to have signed the certificate.

(2) Definition of "analyst" — In this section, **"analyst"** has the same meaning as in section 320.11.

(3) Notice of intention to produce certificate — No certificate shall be admitted in evidence unless the party intending to produce it has, before the trial, given reasonable notice and a copy of the certificate to the party against whom it is to be produced.

(4) Requiring attendance of analyst — The party against whom a certificate of an analyst is produced may, with leave of the court, require the attendance of the analyst for cross-examination.

2011, c. 7, s. 12; 2015, c. 20, s. 34(3); 2018, c. 21, s. 27

Appeal

812. (1) Definition of "appeal court" — For the purposes of sections 813 to 828 **"appeal court"** means

(a) in the Province of Ontario, the Superior Court of Justice sitting in the region, district or county or group of counties where the adjudication was made;

(b) in the Province of Quebec, the Superior Court;

(c) in the Provinces of Nova Scotia, British Columbia and Prince Edward Island, the Supreme Court;

(d) in the Provinces of New Brunswick, Manitoba, Saskatchewan and Alberta, the Court of Queen's Bench;

(e) [Repealed 1992, c. 51, s. 43(2).]

(f) [Repealed 2015, c. 3, s. 56(2).]

(g) in the Province of Newfoundland and Labrador, the Trial Division of the Supreme Court;

(h) in Yukon and the Northwest Territories, a judge of the Supreme Court; and

(i) in Nunavut, a judge of the Nunavut Court of Justice.

(2) **When appeal court is Court of Appeal of Nunavut** — A judge of the Court of Appeal of Nunavut is the appeal court for the purposes of sections 813 to 828 if the appeal is from a conviction, order, sentence or verdict of a summary conviction court consisting of a judge of the Nunavut Court of Justice.

R.S.C. 1985, c. 11 (1st Supp.), s. 2 (Sched., item 1(6)); R.S.C. 1985, c. 27 (2nd Supp.), s. 10 (Sched., item 6(16)); 1990, c. 16, s. 7; 1990, c. 17, s. 15; 1992, c. 51, s. 43; 1993, c. 28, s. 78 (Sched. III, item 36) [Repealed 1999, c. 3, s. 12 (Sched., item 9).]; 1998, c. 30, s. 14(d); 1999, c. 3, s. 55; 2002, c. 7, s. 149; 2015, c. 3, s. 56

813. Appeal by defendant, informant or Attorney General — Except where otherwise provided by law,

(a) the defendant in proceedings under this Part may appeal to the appeal court

(i) from a conviction or order made against him;

(ii) against a sentence passed on him; or

(iii) against a verdict of unfit to stand trial or not criminally responsible on account of mental disorder; and

(b) the informant, the Attorney General or his agent in proceedings under this Part may appeal to the appeal court

(i) from an order that stays proceedings on an information or dismisses an information,

(ii) against a sentence passed on a defendant; or

(iii) against a verdict of not criminally responsible on account of mental disorder or unfit to stand trial,

and the Attorney General of Canada or his agent has the same rights of appeal in proceedings instituted at the instance of the Government of Canada and conducted by or on behalf of that government as the Attorney General of a province or his agent has under this paragraph.

R.S.C. 1985, c. 27 (1st Supp.), s. 180; 1991, c. 43, s. 9 (Sched., item 12)

814. (1) Manitoba and Alberta — In the Provinces of Manitoba and Alberta, an appeal under section 813 shall be heard at the sittings of the appeal court that is held nearest to the place where the cause of the proceedings arose, but the judge of the appeal court may, on the application of one of the parties, appoint another place for the hearing of the appeal.

(2) **Saskatchewan** — In the Province of Saskatchewan, an appeal under section 813 shall be heard at the sittings of the appeal court at the judicial centre nearest to the place where the adjudication was made, but the judge of the appeal court may, on the application of one of the parties, appoint another place for the hearing of the appeal.

(3) **British Columbia** — In the Province of British Columbia, an appeal under section 813 shall be heard at the sittings of the appeal court that is held nearest to the place where the adjudication was made, but the judge of the appeal court may, on the application of one of the parties, appoint another place for the hearing of the appeal.

(4) **Territories** — In Yukon, the Northwest Territories and Nunavut, an appeal under section 813 shall be heard at the place where the cause of the proceedings arose or at the place nearest to it where a court is appointed to be held.

1993, c. 28, s. 78 (Sched. III, item 37); 2002, c. 7, s. 150

815. (1) **Notice of appeal** — An appellant who proposes to appeal to the appeal court shall give notice of appeal in such manner and within such period as may be directed by rules of court.

(2) **Extension of time** — The appeal court or a judge thereof may extend the time within which notice of appeal may be given.

Interim Release of Appellant

816. (1) **Undertaking or recognizance of appellant** — A person who was the defendant in proceedings before a summary conviction court and by whom an appeal is taken under section 813 shall, if he is in custody, remain in custody unless the appeal court at which the appeal is to be heard orders that the appellant be released

(a) on his giving an undertaking to the appeal court, without conditions or with such conditions as the appeal court directs, to surrender himself into custody in accordance with the order,

(b) on his entering into a recognizance without sureties in such amount, with such conditions, if any, as the appeal court directs, but without deposit of money or other valuable security, or

(c) on his entering into a recognizance with or without sureties in such amount, with such conditions, if any, as the appeal court directs, and on his depositing with that appeal court such sum of money or other valuable security as the appeal court directs,

and the person having the custody of the appellant shall, where the appellant complies with the order, forthwith release the appellant.

(2) **Application of certain provisions of section 525** — The provisions of subsections 525(5), (6) and (7) apply with such modifications as the circumstances require in respect of a person who has been released from custody under subsection (1).

Proposed Amendment — 816

816. (1) Release order — appellant — A person who was the defendant in proceedings before a summary conviction court and who is an appellant under section 813 shall, if they are in custody, remain in custody unless the appeal court at which the appeal is to be heard makes a release order referred to in section 515, the form of which may be adapted to suit the circumstances, which must include the condition that the person surrender themselves into custody in accordance with the order.

(1.1) Release of appellant — The person having the custody of the appellant shall, if the appellant complies with the order, immediately release the appellant.

(2) Applicable provisions — Sections 495.1, 512.3 and 524 apply, with any modifications that the circumstances require, in respect of any proceedings under this section.

2019, c. 25, s. 323 [To come into force December 18, 2019.]

R.S.C. 1985, c. 27 (1st Supp.), s. 181

817. (1) Undertaking or recognizance of prosecutor — The prosecutor in proceedings before a summary conviction court by whom an appeal is taken under section 813 shall, forthwith after filing the notice of appeal and proof of service thereof in accordance with section 815, appear before a justice, and the justice shall, after giving the prosecutor and the respondent a reasonable opportunity to be heard, order that the prosecutor

(a) give an undertaking as prescribed in this section; or

(b) enter into a recognizance in such amount, with or without sureties and with or without deposit of money or other valuable security, as the justice directs.

Proposed Amendment — 817(1)

(1) Recognizance of prosecutor — The prosecutor in proceedings before a summary conviction court by whom an appeal is taken under section 813 shall, immediately after filing the notice of appeal and proof of service of the notice in accordance with section 815, appear before a justice, and the justice shall, after giving the prosecutor and the respondent a reasonable opportunity to be heard, order that the prosecutor enter into a recognizance, with or without sureties, in the amount that the justice directs and with or without the deposit of money or other valuable security that the justice directs.

2019, c. 25, s. 324(1) [To come into force December 18, 2019.]

(2) Condition — The condition of an undertaking or recognizance given or entered into under this section is that the prosecutor will appear personally or by counsel at the sittings of the appeal court at which the appeal is to be heard.

Proposed Amendment — 817(2)

(2) Condition — The condition of a recognizance entered into under this section is that the prosecutor will appear personally or by counsel at the sittings of the appeal court at which the appeal is to be heard.

2019, c. 25, s. 324(1) [To come into force December 18, 2019.]

(3) Appeals by Attorney General — This section does not apply in respect of an appeal taken by the Attorney General or by counsel acting on behalf of the Attorney General.

(4) Form of undertaking or recognizance — An undertaking under this section may be in Form 14 and a recognizance under this section may be in Form 32.

Proposed Repeal — 817(4)

(4) [Repealed 2019, c. 25, s. 324(2). To come into force December 18, 2019.]

818. (1) Application to appeal court for review — Where a justice makes an order under section 817, either the appellant or the respondent may, before or at any time during the hearing of the appeal, apply to the appeal court for a review of the order made by the justice.

(2) Disposition of application by appeal court — On the hearing of an application under this section, the appeal court, after giving the appellant and the respondent a reasonable opportunity to be heard, shall

(a) dismiss the application; or

(b) if the person applying for the review shows cause, allow the application, vacate the order made by the justice and make the order that in the opinion of the appeal court should have been made.

(3) Effect of order — An order made under this section shall have the same force and effect as if it had been made by the justice.

819. (1) Application to fix date for hearing of appeal — Where, in the case of an appellant who has been convicted by a summary conviction court and who is in custody pending the hearing of his appeal, the hearing of his appeal has not commenced within thirty days from the day on which notice of his appeal was given in accordance with the rules referred to in section 815, the person having the custody of the appellant shall, forthwith on the expiration of those thirty days, apply to the appeal court to fix a date for the hearing of the appeal.

(2) Order fixing date — On receiving an application under subsection (1), the appeal court shall, after giving the prosecutor a reasonable opportunity to be heard, fix a date for the hearing of the appeal and give such directions as it thinks necessary for expediting the hearing of the appeal.

820. (1) Payment of fine not a waiver of appeal — A person does not waive his right of appeal under section 813 by reason only that he pays the fine imposed on conviction, without in any way indicating an intention to appeal or reserving the right to appeal.

(2) Presumption — A conviction, order or sentence shall be deemed not to have been appealed against until the contrary is shown.

Procedure on Appeal

821. (1) Notification and transmission of conviction, etc. — Where a notice of appeal has been given in accordance with the rules referred to in section 815, the clerk of the appeal court shall notify the summary conviction court that made the conviction or order appealed from or imposed the sentence appealed against of the appeal and on receipt of the notification that summary conviction court shall transmit the conviction, order or order of dismissal and all other material in its possession in connection with the proceedings to the appeal court before the time when the appeal is to be heard, or within such further time as the appeal court may direct, and the material shall be kept by the clerk of the appeal court with the records of the appeal court.

(2) Saving — An appeal shall not be dismissed by the appeal court by reason only that a person other than the appellant failed to comply with the provisions of this Part relating to appeals.

(3) Appellant to furnish transcript of evidence — Where the evidence on a trial before a summary conviction court has been taken by a stenographer duly sworn or by a sound recording apparatus, the appellant shall, unless the appeal court otherwise orders or the rules referred to in section 815 otherwise provide, cause a transcript thereof, certified by the stenographer or in accordance with subsection 540(6), as the case may be, to be furnished to the appeal court and the respondent for use on the appeal.

822. (1) Certain sections applicable to appeals — Where an appeal is taken under section 813 in respect of any conviction, acquittal, sentence, verdict or order, sections 683 to 689, with the exception of subsections 683(3) and 686(5), apply, with such modifications as the circumstances require.

(2) New trial — Where an appeal court orders a new trial, it shall be held before a summary conviction court other than the court that tried the defendant in the first instance, unless the appeal court directs that the new trial be held before the summary conviction court that tried the defendant in the first instance.

(3) Order of detention or release — Where an appeal court orders a new trial, it may make such order for the release or detention of the appellant pending the trial as may be made by a justice pursuant to section 515 and the order may be enforced in the same manner as if it had been made by a justice under that section, and the provisions of Part XVI apply with such modifications as the circumstances require to the order.

(4) Trial *de novo* — Despite subsections (1) to (3), if an appeal is taken under section 813 and because of the condition of the record of the trial in the summary conviction court or for any other reason, the appeal court, on application of the defendant, the informant, the Attorney General or the Attorney General's agent, is of the opinion that the interests of justice would be better served by hearing and determining the appeal by holding a trial *de novo*, the appeal court may order that the appeal shall be heard by way of trial *de novo* in accordance with any rules that may be made under section 482 or 482.1, and for that purpose the provisions of sections 793 to 809 apply, with any modifications that the circumstances require.

(5) Former evidence — The appeal court may, for the purpose of hearing and determining an appeal under subsection (4), permit the evidence of any witness taken before the summary conviction court to be read if that evidence has been authenticated in accordance with section 540 and if

(a) the appellant and respondent consent,

(b) the appeal court is satisfied that the attendance of the witness cannot reasonably be obtained, or

(c) by reason of the formal nature of the evidence or otherwise the court is satisfied that the opposite party will not be prejudiced,

and any evidence that is read under the authority of this subsection has the same force and effect as if the witness had given the evidence before the appeal court.

(6) Appeal against sentence — Where an appeal is taken under subsection (4) against sentence, the appeal court shall, unless the sentence is one fixed by law, consider the fitness of the sentence appealed against and may, on such evidence, if any, as it thinks fit to require or receive, by order,

(a) dismiss the appeal, or

(b) vary the sentence within the limits prescribed by law for the offence of which the defendant was convicted;

and in making any order under paragraph (*b*) the appeal court may take into account any time spent in custody by the defendant as a result of the offence.

(7) General provisions re appeals — The following provisions apply in respect of appeals under subsection (4):

(a) where an appeal is based on an objection to an information or any process, judgment shall not be given in favour of the appellant

(i) for any alleged defect therein in substance or in form, or

(ii) for any variance between the information or process and the evidence adduced at the trial,

unless it is shown

(iii) that the objection was taken at the trial, and

(iv) that an adjournment of the trial was refused notwithstanding that the variance referred to in subparagraph (ii) had deceived or misled the appellant; and

(b) where an appeal is based on a defect in a conviction or an order, judgment shall not be given in favour of the appellant, but the court shall make an order curing the defect.

1991, c. 43, s. 9 (Sched., item 13); 2002, c. 13, s. 83

823. [Repealed 1991, c. 43, s. 9 (Sched., item 14).]

824. Adjournment — The appeal court may adjourn the hearing of an appeal from time to time as may be necessary.

825. Dismissal for failure to appear or want of prosecution — The appeal court may, on proof that notice of an appeal has been given and that

(a) the appellant has failed to comply with any order made under section 816 or 817 or with the conditions of any undertaking or recognizance given or entered into as prescribed in either of those sections, or

Proposed Amendment — 825(a)

(a) the appellant has failed to comply with the conditions of a release order made under section 816 or of a recognizance entered into under section 817; or

2019, c. 25, s. 325 [To come into force December 18, 2019.]

(b) the appeal has not been proceeded with or has been abandoned,

order that the appeal be dismissed.

826. Costs — Where an appeal is heard and determined or is abandoned or is dismissed for want of prosecution, the appeal court may make any order with respect to costs that it considers just and reasonable.

827. (1) To whom costs payable, and when — Where the appeal court orders the appellant or respondent to pay costs, the order shall direct that the costs be paid to the clerk of the court, to be paid by him to the person entitled to them, and shall fix the period within which the costs shall be paid.

(2) Certificate of non-payment of costs — Where costs are not paid in full within the period fixed for payment and the person who has been ordered to pay them has not been bound by a recognizance to pay them, the clerk of the court shall, on application by the person entitled to the costs, or by any person on his behalf, and on payment of any fee to which the clerk of the court is entitled, issue a certificate in Form 42 certifying that the costs or a part thereof, as the case may be, have not been paid.

(3) Committal — A justice having jurisdiction in the territorial division in which a certificate has been issued under subsection (2) may, on production of the certificate, by warrant in Form 26, commit the defaulter to imprisonment for a term not exceeding one month, unless the amount of the costs and, where the justice thinks fit so to order, the costs of the committal and of conveying the defaulter to prison are sooner paid.

828. (1) Enforcement of conviction or order by court of appeal — A conviction or order made by the appeal court may be enforced

(a) in the same manner as if it had been made by the summary conviction court; or

(b) by process of the appeal court.

(2) Enforcement by justice — Where an appeal taken against a conviction or order adjudging payment of a sum of money is dismissed, the summary conviction court that made the conviction or order or a justice for the same territorial division may issue a warrant of committal as if no appeal had been taken.

(3) Duty of clerk of court — Where a conviction or order that has been made by an appeal court is to be enforced by a justice, the clerk of the appeal court shall send to the justice the conviction or order and all writings relating thereto, except the notice of intention to appeal and any recognizance.

Proposed Amendment — 828(3)

(3) Duty of clerk of court — When a conviction or order that has been made by an appeal court is to be enforced by a justice, the clerk of the appeal court shall send to the justice the conviction or order and all writings relating to that conviction or order, except the notice of intention to appeal and any undertaking, release order or recognizance.

2019, c. 25, s. 326 [To come into force December 18, 2019.]

Summary Appeal on Transcript or Agreed Statement of Facts

829. (1) Definition of "appeal court" — Subject to subsection (2), for the purposes of sections 830 to 838, **"appeal court"** means, in any province, the superior court of criminal jurisdiction for the province.

(2) Nunavut — If the appeal is from a conviction, judgment, verdict or other final order or determination of a summary conviction court consisting of a judge of the Nunavut Court of Justice, **"appeal court"** means a judge of the Court of Appeal of Nunavut.

R.S.C. 1985, c. 27 (1st Supp.), s. 182; 1999, c. 3, s. 56

830. (1) Appeals — A party to proceedings to which this Part applies or the Attorney General may appeal against a conviction, judgment, verdict of acquittal or verdict of not criminally responsible on account of mental disorder or of unfit to stand trial or other final order or determination of a summary conviction court on the ground that

(a) it is erroneous in point of law;

(b) it is in excess of jurisdiction; or

(c) it constitutes a refusal or failure to exercise jurisdiction.

(2) Form of appeal — An appeal under this section shall be based on a transcript of the proceedings appealed from unless the appellant files with the appeal court, within fifteen days of the filing of the notice of appeal, a statement of facts agreed to in writing by the respondent.

(3) Rules for appeals — An appeal under this section shall be made within the period and in the manner directed by any applicable rules of court and where there are no such rules otherwise providing, a notice of appeal in writing shall be served on the respondent and a copy thereof, together with proof of service, shall be filed with the appeal court within thirty days after the date of the conviction, judgment or verdict of acquittal or other final order or determination that is the subject of the appeal.

(4) Rights of Attorney General of Canada — The Attorney General of Canada has the same rights of appeal in proceedings instituted at the instance of the Government of Canada and conducted by or on behalf of that Government as the Attorney General of a province has under this section.

R.S.C. 1985, c. 27 (1st Supp.), s. 182; 1991, c. 43, s. 9 (Sched., item 15)

831. Application — The provisions of sections 816, 817, 819 and 825 apply, with such modifications as the circumstances require, in respect of an appeal under section 830, except that on receiving an application by the person having the custody of an appellant described in section 819 to appoint a date for the hearing of the appeal, the appeal court shall, after giving the prosecutor a reasonable opportunity to be heard, give such directions as it thinks necessary for expediting the hearing of the appeal.

R.S.C. 1985, c. 27 (1st Supp.), s. 182

832. (1) Undertaking or recognizance — When a notice of appeal is filed pursuant to section 830, the appeal court may order that the appellant appear before a justice and give an undertaking or enter into a recognizance as provided in section 816 where the defendant is the appellant, or as provided in section 817, in any other case.

Proposed Amendment — 832(1)

(1) Release order or recognizance — If a notice of appeal is filed under section 830, the appeal court may, if the defendant is the appellant, make a release order as provided in section 816 or, in any other case, order that the appellant appear before a justice and enter into a recognizance as provided in section 817.

2019, c. 25, s. 327 [To come into force December 18, 2019.]

(2) Attorney General — Subsection (1) does not apply where the appellant is the Attorney General or counsel acting on behalf of the Attorney General.

R.S.C. 1985, c. 27 (1st Supp.), s. 182

833. No writ required — No writ of *certiorari* or other writ is required to remove any conviction, judgment, verdict or other final order or determination of a summary conviction court for the purpose of obtaining the judgment, determination or opinion of the appeal court.

R.S.C. 1985, c. 27 (1st Supp.), s. 182; 1991, c. 43, s. 9 (Sched., item 16)

834. (1) Powers of appeal court — When a notice of appeal is filed pursuant to section 830, the appeal court shall hear and determine the grounds of appeal and may

(a) affirm, reverse or modify the conviction, judgment or verdict or other final order or determination, or

(b) remit the matter to the summary conviction court with the opinion of the appeal court,

and may make any other order in relation to the matter or with respect to costs that it considers proper.

(2) **Authority of judge** — Where the authority and jurisdiction of the appeal court may be exercised by a judge of that court, the authority and jurisdiction may, subject to any applicable rules of court, be exercised by a judge of the court sitting in chambers as well in vacation as in term time.

R.S.C. 1985, c. 27 (1st Supp.), s. 182; 1991, c. 43, s. 9 (Sched., item 17)

835. (1) **Enforcement** — Where the appeal court renders its decision on an appeal, the summary conviction court from which the appeal was taken or a justice exercising the same jurisdiction has the same authority to enforce a conviction, order or determination that has been affirmed, modified or made by the appeal court as the summary conviction court would have had if no appeal had been taken.

(2) **Idem** — An order of the appeal court may be enforced by its own process.

R.S.C. 1985, c. 27 (1st Supp.), s. 182

836. **Appeal under section 830** — Every person who appeals under section 830 from any conviction, judgment, verdict or other final order or determination in respect of which that person is entitled to an appeal under section 813 shall be taken to have abandoned all the person's rights of appeal under section 813.

R.S.C. 1985, c. 27 (1st Supp.), s. 182; 1991, c. 43, s. 9 (Sched., item 18)

837. **Appeal barred** — Where it is provided by law that no appeal lies from a conviction or order, no appeal under section 830 lies from such a conviction or order.

R.S.C. 1985, c. 27 (1st Supp.), s. 182

838. **Extension of time** — The appeal court or a judge thereof may at any time extend any time period referred to in section 830, 831 or 832.

R.S.C. 1985, c. 27 (1st Supp.), s. 182

Appeals to Court of Appeal

839. (1) **Appeal on question of law** — Subject to subsection (1.1), an appeal to the court of appeal, as defined in section 673 may, with leave of that court or a judge thereof, be taken on any ground that involves a question of law alone, against

(a) a decision of a court in respect of an appeal under section 822; or

(b) a decision of an appeal court under section 834, except where that court is the court of appeal.

(1.1) **Nunavut** — An appeal to the Court of Appeal of Nunavut may, with leave of that court or a judge of that court, be taken on any ground that involves a question of law alone, against a decision of a judge of the Court of Appeal of Nunavut acting as an appeal court under subsection 812(2) or 829(2).

(2) **Sections applicable** — Sections 673 to 689 apply with such modifications as the circumstances require to an appeal under this section.

(3) Costs — Notwithstanding subsection (2), the court of appeal may make any order with respect to costs that it considers proper in relation to an appeal under this section.

(4) Enforcement of decision — The decision of the court of appeal may be enforced in the same manner as if it had been made by the summary conviction court before which the proceedings were originally heard and determined.

(5) Right of Attorney General of Canada to appeal — The Attorney General of Canada has the same rights of appeal in proceedings instituted at the instance of the Government of Canada and conducted by or on behalf of that Government as the Attorney General of a province has under this Part.

R.S.C. 1985, c. 27 (1st Supp.), s. 183; 1999, c. 3, s. 57

Fees and Allowances

840. (1) Fees and allowances — Subject to subsection (2), the fees and allowances mentioned in the schedule to this Part are the fees and allowances that may be taken or allowed in proceedings before summary conviction courts and justices under this Part.

(2) Order of lieutenant governor in council — The lieutenant governor in council of a province may order that all or any of the fees and allowances mentioned in the schedule to this Part shall not be taken or allowed in proceedings before summary conviction courts and justices under this Part in that province and, when the lieutenant governor in council so orders, he or she may fix any other fees and allowances for any items similar to those mentioned in the schedule, or any other items, to be taken or allowed instead.

1994, c. 44, s. 83; 1997, c. 18, s. 114

SCHEDULE TO PART XXVII

(Section 840)

FEES AND ALLOWANCES THAT MAY BE CHARGED BY SUMMARY CONVICTION COURTS AND JUSTICES

1.	Information	$1.00
2.	Summons or warrant	0.50
3.	Warrant where summons issued in first instance	0.30
4.	Each necessary copy of summons or warrant	0.30
5.	Each subpoena or warrant to or for witnesses	0.30

	(A subpoena may contain any number of names. Only one subpoena may be issued on behalf of a party in any proceeding, unless the summary conviction court or the justice considers it necessary or desirable that more than one subpoena be issued.)	
6.	Information for warrant for witness and warrant for witness	1.00
7.	Each necessary copy of subpoena to or warrant for witness	$0.20
8.	Each recognizance	1.00
9.	Hearing and determining proceeding	1.00
10.	Where hearing lasts more than two hours	2.00
11.	Where two or more justices hear and determine a proceeding, each is entitled to the fee authorized by item 9.	
12.	Each warrant of committal	0.50
13.	Making up record of conviction or order on request of a party to the proceedings	1.00
14.	Copy of a writing other than a conviction or order, on request of a party to the proceedings; for each folio of one hundred words	0.10
15.	Bill of costs, when made out in detail on request of a party to the proceedings	0.20
	(Items 14 and 15 may be charged only where there has been an adjudication.)	
16.	Attending to remand prisoner	1.00
17.	Attending to take recognizance of bail	1.00
	FEES AND ALLOWANCES THAT MAY BE ALLOWED TO PEACE OFFICERS	
18.	Arresting a person on a warrant or without a warrant	1.50
19.	Serving summons or subpoena	0.50
20.	Mileage to serve summons or subpoena or to make an arrest, both ways, for each mile	0.10

	(Where a public conveyance is not used, reasonable costs of transportation may be allowed.)	
21.	Mileage where service cannot be effected on proof of a diligent, attempt to effect service, each way, for each mile	0.10
22.	Returning with prisoner after arrest to take him before a summary conviction court or justice at a place different from the place where the peace officer received the warrant to arrest, if the journey is of necessity over a route different from that taken by the peace officer to make the arrest, each way, for each mile . . .	0.10
23.	Taking a prisoner to prison on remand or committal, each way, for each mile	0.10
	(Where a public conveyance is not used, reasonable costs of may be allowed. No charge may be made under this item in respect of a service for which a charge is made under item 22.)	
24.	Attending summary conviction court or justice on summary conviction proceedings, for each day necessarily employed	2.00
	(No more than $2.00 may be charged under this item in respect of any day notwithstanding the number of proceedings that the peace officer attended on that day before that summary conviction court or justice.)	
	FEES AND ALLOWANCES THAT MAY BE ALLOWED TO WITNESSES	
25.	Each day attending trial	$4.00
26.	Mileage travelled to attend trial, each way, for each mile	0.10
	FEES AND ALLOWANCES THAT MAY BE ALLOWED TO INTERPRETERS	
27.	Each half day attending trial	$2.50

28.	Actual living expenses when away from ordinary place of residence, not to exceed per day	10.00
29.	Mileage travelled to attend trial, each way, for each mile	0.10

Proposed Amendment — Schedule to Part XXVII

SCHEDULE TO PART XXVII

(Section 840)

FEES AND ALLOWANCES THAT MAY BE CHARGED BY SUMMARY CONVICTION COURTS AND JUSTICES

1.	Information	$1.00
2.	Summons or warrant	0.50
3.	Warrant where summons issued in first instance	0.30
4.	Each necessary copy of summons or warrant	0.30
5.	Each subpoena or warrant to or for witnesses	0.30
	(A subpoena may contain any number of names. Only one subpoena may be issued on behalf of a party in any proceeding, unless the summary conviction court or the justice considers it necessary or desirable that more than one subpoena be issued.)	
6.	Information for warrant for witness and warrant for witness	1.00
7.	Each necessary copy of subpoena to or warrant for witness	$0.20
8.	Each release order or recognizance	1.00
9.	Hearing and determining proceeding	1.00
10.	Where hearing lasts more than two hours	2.00
11.	Where two or more justices hear and determine a proceeding, each is entitled to the fee authorized by item 9.	
12.	Each warrant of committal	0.50

13.	Making up record of conviction or order on request of a party to the proceedings	1.00
14.	Copy of a writing other than a conviction or order, on request of a party to the proceedings; for each folio of one hundred words	0.10
15.	Bill of costs, when made out in detail on request of a party to the proceedings	0.20
	(Items 14 and 15 may be charged only where there has been an adjudication.)	
16.	Attending to remand prisoner	1.00
17.	Attending to make a release order or take a recognizance	1.00
	FEES AND ALLOWANCES THAT MAY BE ALLOWED TO PEACE OFFICERS	
18.	Arresting a person on a warrant or without a warrant	1.50
19.	Serving summons or subpoena	0.50
20.	Mileage to serve summons or subpoena or to make an arrest, both ways, for each mile	0.10
	(Where a public conveyance is not used, reasonable costs of transportation may be allowed.)	
21.	Mileage where service cannot be effected on proof of a diligent, attempt to effect service, each way, for each mile	0.10
22.	Returning with prisoner after arrest to take him before a summary conviction court or justice at a place different from the place where the peace officer received the warrant to arrest, if the journey is of necessity over a route different from that taken by the peace officer to make the arrest, each way, for each mile . . .	0.10
23.	Taking a prisoner to prison on remand or committal, each way, for each mile	0.10

	(Where a public conveyance is not used, reasonable costs of may be allowed. No charge may be made under this item in respect of a service for which a charge is made under item 22.)	
24.	Attending summary conviction court or justice on summary conviction proceedings, for each day necessarily employed	2.00
	(No more than $2.00 may be charged under this item in respect of any day notwithstanding the number of proceedings that the peace officer attended on that day before that summary conviction court or justice.)	
	FEES AND ALLOWANCES THAT MAY BE ALLOWED TO WITNESSES	
25.	Each day attending trial	$4.00
26.	Mileage travelled to attend trial, each way, for each mile	0.10
	FEES AND ALLOWANCES THAT MAY BE ALLOWED TO INTERPRETERS	
27.	Each half day attending trial	$2.50
28.	Actual living expenses when away from ordinary place of residence, not to exceed per day	10.00
29.	Mileage travelled to attend trial, each way, for each mile	0.10

2019, c. 25, s. 328 [To come into force December 18, 2019.]

PART XXVIII — MISCELLANEOUS (SS. 841–849)

[Heading amended 2002, c. 13, s. 84.]

Electronic Documents

[Heading amended 2002, c. 13, s. 84.]

841. Definitions — The definitions in this section apply in this section and in sections 842 to 847.

"data" means representations of information or concepts, in any form.

"electronic document" means data that is recorded or stored on any medium in or by a computer system or other similar device and that can be read or perceived by a person or a computer system or other similar device. It includes a display, print-out or other output of the data and any document, record, order, exhibit, notice or form that contains the data.

R.S.C. 1985, c. 31 (4th Supp.), s. 97; 2002, c. 13, s. 84

842. Dealing with data in court — Despite anything in this Act, a court may create, collect, receive, store, transfer, distribute, publish or otherwise deal with electronic documents if it does so in accordance with an Act or with the rules of court.

2002, c. 13, s. 84

843. (1) Transfer of data — Despite anything in this Act, a court may accept the transfer of data by electronic means if the transfer is made in accordance with the laws of the place where the transfer originates or the laws of the place where the data is received.

(2) Time of filing — If a document is required to be filed in a court and the filing is done by transfer of data by electronic means, the filing is complete when the transfer is accepted by the court.

2002, c. 13, s. 84

844. Documents in writing — A requirement under this Act that a document be made in writing is satisfied by the making of the document in electronic form in accordance with an Act or the rules of court.

2002, c. 13, s. 84

845. Signatures — If this Act requires a document to be signed, the court may accept a signature in an electronic document if the signature is made in accordance with an Act or the rules of court.

2002, c. 13, s. 84

846. Oaths — If under this Act an information, an affidavit or a solemn declaration or a statement under oath or solemn affirmation is to be made by a person, the court may accept it in the form of an electronic document if

(a) the person states in the electronic document that all matters contained in the information, affidavit, solemn declaration or statement are true to his or her knowledge and belief;

(b) the person before whom it is made or sworn is authorized to take or receive informations, affidavits, solemn declaration or statements and he or she states in the electronic document that the information, affidavit, solemn declaration or statement was made under oath, solemn declaration or solemn affirmation, as the case may be; and

(c) the electronic document was made in accordance with the laws of the place where it was made.

2002, c. 13, s. 84

847. Copies — Any person who is entitled to obtain a copy of a document from a court is entitled, in the case of a document in electronic form, to obtain a printed copy of the electronic document from the court on payment of a reasonable fee determined in accordance with a tariff of fees fixed or approved by the Attorney General of the relevant province.

2002, c. 13, s. 84

Remote Appearance by Incarcerated Accused

[Heading added 2002, c. 13, s. 84.]

848. [Repealed 2019, c. 25, s. 329.]

Forms

[Heading added 2002, c. 13, s. 84.]

849. (1) Forms — The forms set out in this Part, varied to suit the case, or forms to the like effect are deemed to be good, valid and sufficient in the circumstances for which they are provided.

(2) Seal not required — No justice is required to attach or affix a seal to any writing or process that he or she is authorized to issue and in respect of which a form is provided by this Part.

(3) Official languages — Any pre-printed portions of a form set out in this Part, varied to suit the case, or of a form to the like effect shall be printed in both official languages.

2002, c. 13, s. 84

Form 1 — Information to Obtain a Search Warrant

(Sections 320.29 and 487)

[Reference amended 2018, c. 21, s. 28(a).]

Canada,

Province of ....,

(*territorial division*).

This is the information of A.B., of ...., in the said (*territorial division*), (*occupation*), hereinafter called the informant, taken before me.

The informant says that (*describe things to be searched for and offence in respect of which search is to be made*), and that he believes on reasonable grounds that the said things, or some part of them, are in the (*dwelling-house, etc.*) of C.D., of ...., in the said (*territorial division*). (*Here add the grounds of belief, whatever they may be*).

Wherefore the informant prays that a search warrant may be granted to search the said (*dwelling-house, etc.*) for the said things.

Sworn before me
this .... day of
.........., A.D. ...., ...
at .... (*Signature of Informant*)
....
A Justice of the Peace in and
for ....

2018, c. 21, s. 28(a)

Form 2 — Information

(Section 506 and 788)

Canada,

Province of ....,
(*territorial division*).

This is the information of C.D., of ...., (*occupation*), hereinafter called the informant.

The informant says that (*if the informant has no personal knowledge state that he believes on reasonable grounds and state the offence*).

Sworn before me
this .... day of
.........., A.D. ...., ...
at .... (*Signature of Informant*)
.... A Justice of the
Peace in and for ....

Note: The date of birth of the accused may be mentioned on the information or indictment.

R.S.C. 1985, c. 27 (1st Supp.), s. 184(1)

Form 3 [Repealed R.S.C. 1985, c. 27 (1st Supp.), s. 184(2).]

Form 4 — Heading of Indictment

(Sections 566, 566.1, 580 and 591)

Canada,

Province of ....,
(*territorial division*).

In the (*set out name of the court*) —

Her Majesty the Queen —

against —
(name of accused)
(*Name of accused*) stands charged

1. That he (*state offence*).
2. That he (*state offence*).

Note: The date of birth of the accused may be mentioned on the information or indictment.

Dated this .... day of .... A.D. ...., at ....

. . . . . . *(Signature of signing officer, Agent of Attorney General, etc., as the case may be)*

1999, c. 3, s. 58

Form 5 — Warrant to Search

(Sections 320.29 and 487)

[Reference amended 2018, c. 21, s. 28(b).]

Canada,
Province of ....,
(*territorial division*).

To the peace officers in the said (*territorial division*) or to the (*named public officers)*:

Whereas it appears on the oath of A.B., of .... that there are reasonable grounds for believing that (*describe things to be searched for and offence in respect of which search is to be made*) are in .... at.........., hereinafter called the premises;

This is, therefore, to authorize and require you between the hours of (*as the justice may direct*) to enter into the said premises and to search for the said things and to bring them before me or some other justice.

Dated this .... day of .... A.D. ...., at ....

.... A Justice of the Peace in and for ....

1999, c. 5, s. 45; 2018, c. 21, s. 28(b)

Form 5.001 — Preservation Demand

(Subsection 487.012(1))

Canada,
Province of ....
(*territorial division*)

To (*name of person*), of ....:

Because I have reasonable grounds to suspect that the computer data specified below is in your possession or control and that that computer data

will assist in the investigation of an offence that has been or will be committed under (*specify the provision of the* Criminal Code *or other Act of Parliament*),

(*or*)

will assist in the investigation of an offence that has been committed under (*specify the provision of the law of the foreign state*) that is being conducted by a person or authority, (*name of person or authority*), with responsibility in (*specify the name of the foreign state*) for the investigation of such offences,

you are required to preserve (*specify the computer data*) that is in your possession or control when you receive this demand until (*insert date*) unless, before that date, this demand is revoked or a document that contains that data is obtained under a warrant or an order.

This demand is subject to the following conditions:

If you contravene this demand without lawful excuse, you may be subject to a fine.

You are required to destroy the computer data that would not be retained in the ordinary course of business, and any document that is prepared for the purpose of preserving the computer data, in accordance with section 487.0194 of the *Criminal Code*. If you contravene that provision without lawful excuse, you may be subject to a fine, to imprisonment or to both.

....

(*Signature of peace officer or public officer*)

2014, c. 31, s. 26

Form 5.002 — Information to Obtain a Preservation Order

(Subsection 487.013(2))

Canada,
Province of ....
(*territorial division*)

This is the information of (*name of peace officer or public officer*), of .... ("the informant").

The informant says that they have reasonable grounds to suspect that an offence has been or will be committed under (*specify the provision of the* Criminal Code *or other Act of Parliament*) (*or* has been committed under (*specify the provision of the law of the foreign state*)) and that (*specify the computer data*) is in the possession or control of (*name of the person*) and will assist in the investigation of the offence.

The informant also says that a peace officer or public officer intends to apply or has applied for a warrant or order in connection with the investigation to obtain a document that contains the computer data (*and, if applicable*, and that (*name of person or authority*) is conducting the investigation and has responsibility for the investigation of such offences in (*insert the name of the foreign state*)).

The reasonable grounds are: (*including, if applicable, whether a preservation demand was made under section 487.012 of the* Criminal Code)

The informant therefore requests that (*name of the person*) be ordered to preserve (*specify the computer data*) that is in their possession or control when they receive the order for 90 days after the day on which the order is made.

Sworn before me on (*date*), at (*place*).

....
(*Signature of informant*)

....
(*Signature of justice or judge*)

2014, c. 31, s. 26

Form 5.003 — Preservation Order

(Subsection 487.013(4))

Canada,
Province of ....
(*territorial division*)

To (*name of person*), of ....:

Whereas I am satisfied by information on oath of (*name of peace officer or public officer*), of ....,

(*a*) that there are reasonable grounds to suspect that an offence has been or will be committed under (*specify the provision of the* Criminal Code *or other Act of Parliament*) (*or* has been committed under (*specify the provision of the law of the foreign state*)) and that (*specify the computer data*) is in your possession or control and will assist in the investigation of the offence; and

(*b*) that a peace officer or public officer intends to apply or has applied for a warrant or order to obtain a document that contains the computer data (*and, if applicable*, and that (*name of person or authority*) is conducting the investigation and has responsibility for the investigation of such offences in (*insert the name of the foreign state*));

Therefore, you are required to preserve the specified computer data that is in your possession or control when you receive this order until (*insert date*) unless, before that date, this order is revoked or a document that contains that data is obtained under a warrant or an order.

This order is subject to the following conditions:

If you contravene this order without lawful excuse, you may be subject to a fine, to imprisonment or to both.

You are required to destroy the computer data that would not be retained in the ordinary course of business, and any document that is prepared for the purpose of preserving the computer data, in accordance with section 487.0194 of the *Criminal Code*. If you contravene that provision without lawful excuse, you may be subject to a fine, to imprisonment or to both.

Dated (*date*), at (*place*).

....

(*Signature of justice or judge*)

2014, c. 31, s. 26

Form 5.004 — Information to Obtain a Production Order

(Subsections 487.014(2), 487.015(2), 487.016(2), 487.017(2) and 487.018(3))

Canada,
Province of ....
(*territorial division*)

This is the information of (*name of peace officer or public officer*), of .... ("the informant").

The informant says that they have reasonable grounds to suspect (*or, if the application is for an order under section 487.014 of the* Criminal Code, reasonable grounds to believe)

(*a*) that an offence has been or will be committed under (*specify the provision of the* Criminal Code *or other Act of Parliament*); and

(*b*) (*if the application is for an order under section 487.014 of the* Criminal Code) that (*specify the document or data*) is in the possession or control of (*name of the person*) and will afford evidence respecting the commission of the offence.

(*or*)

(*b*) (*if the application is for an order under section 487.015 of the* Criminal Code) that the identification of a device or person involved in the transmission of (*specify the communication*) will assist in the investigation of the offence and that (*specify the transmission data*) that is in the possession or control of one or more persons whose identity is unknown will enable that identification.

(*or*)

(*b*) (*if the application is for an order under section 487.016 of the* Criminal Code) that (*specify the transmission data*) is in the possession or control of (*name of the person*) and will assist in the investigation of the offence.

(*or*)

(*b*) (*if the application is for an order under section 487.017 of the* Criminal Code) that (*specify the tracking data*) is in the possession or control of (*name of the person*) and will assist in the investigation of the offence.

(*or*)

(*b*) (*if the application is for an order under section 487.018 of the* Criminal Code) that (*specify the data*) is in the possession or control of (*name of the *financial institution, person or entity*) and will assist in the investigation of the offence.

The reasonable grounds are:

The informant therefore requests

(*if the application is for an order under section 487.014 of the* Criminal Code) that (*name of the person*) be ordered to produce a document that is a copy of (*specify the document*) that is in their possession or control when they receive the order (*and/or* to prepare and produce a document containing (*specify the data*) that is in their possession or control when they receive the order).

(*or*)

(*if the application is for an order under section 487.015 of the* Criminal Code) that a person who is served with the order in accordance with subsection 487.015(4) of the *Criminal Code* be ordered to prepare and produce a document containing (*specify the transmission data*) that is in their possession or control when they are served with the order.

(*or*)

(*if the application is for an order under section 487.016 of the* Criminal Code) that (*name of the person*) be ordered to prepare and produce a document containing (*specify the transmission data*) that is in their possession or control when they receive the order.

(*or*)

(*if the application is for an order under section 487.017 of the* Criminal Code) that (*name of the person*) be ordered to prepare and produce a document containing (*specify the tracking data*) that is in their possession or control when they receive the order.

(*or*)

(*if the application is for an order under section 487.018 of the* Criminal Code) that (*name of the financial institution, person or entity*) be ordered to prepare and produce a document setting out (*specify the data*) that is in their possession or control when they receive the order.

Sworn before me on (*date*), at (*place*).

....
(*Signature of informant*)

....
(*Signature of justice or judge*)

2014, c. 31, s. 26

Form 5.005 — Production Order for Documents

(Subsection 487.014(3))

Canada,
Province of ....
(*territorial division*)

To (*name of person*), of ....:

Whereas I am satisfied by information on oath of (*name of peace officer or public officer*), of ...., that there are reasonable grounds to believe that an offence has been or will be committed under (*specify the provision of the* Criminal Code *or other Act of Parliament*) and that (*specify the document or data*) is in your possession or control and will afford evidence respecting the commission of the offence;

Therefore, you are ordered to

produce a document that is a copy of (*specify the document*) that is in your possession or control when you receive this order

(*and/or*)

prepare and produce a document containing (*specify the data*) that is in your possession or control when you receive this order.

The document must be produced to (*name of peace officer or public officer*) within (*time*) at (*place*) in (*form*).

This order is subject to the following conditions:

You have the right to apply to revoke or vary this order.

If you contravene this order without lawful excuse, you may be subject to a fine, to imprisonment or to both.

Dated (*date*), at (*place*).

....

(*Signature of justice or judge*)

2014, c. 31, s. 26

Form 5.006 — Production Order to Trace a Communication

(Subsection 487.015(3))

Canada,
Province of ....
(*territorial division*)

Whereas I am satisfied by information on oath of (*name of peace officer or public officer*), of ...., that there are reasonable grounds to suspect that an offence has been or will be committed under (*specify the provision of the* Criminal Code *or other Act of Parliament*), that the identification of a device or person involved in the transmission of (*specify the communication*) will assist in the investigation of the offence and that one or more persons whose identity was unknown when the application was made have possession or control of (*specify the transmission data*) that will enable that identification;

Therefore, on being served with this order in accordance with subsection 487.015(4) of the *Criminal Code*, you are ordered to prepare and produce a document containing (*specify the transmission data*) that is in your possession or control when you are served with this order.

The document must be produced to (*name of peace officer or public officer*) as soon as feasible at (*place*) in (*form*).

This order is subject to the following conditions:

You have the right to apply to revoke or vary this order.

If you contravene this order without lawful excuse, you may be subject to a fine, to imprisonment or to both.

Dated (*date*), at (*place*).

....

(*Signature of justice or judge*)

Served on (*name of person*) on (*date*), at (*place*).

....

(*Signature of peace officer or public officer*)

....

(*Signature of person served*)

2014, c. 31, s. 26

Form 5.007 — Production Order for Transmission Data or Tracking Data

(Subsections 487.016(3) and 487.017(3))

Canada,

Province of ....

(*territorial division*)

To (*name of person*), of ....:

Whereas I am satisfied by information on oath of (*name of peace officer or public officer*), of ...., that there are reasonable grounds to suspect that an offence has been or will be committed under (*specify the provision of the* Criminal Code *or other Act of Parliament*) and that (*if the order is made under section 487.016 of the* Criminal Code*, specify the transmission data*) (*or, if the order is made under section 487.017 of the* Criminal Code*, specify the tracking data*) is in your possession or control and will assist in the investigation of the offence;

Therefore, you are ordered to prepare and produce a document containing the data specified that is in your possession or control when you receive this order.

The document must be produced to (*name of peace officer or public officer*) within (*time*) at (*place*) in (*form*).

This order is subject to the following conditions:

You have the right to apply to revoke or vary this order.

If you contravene this order without lawful excuse, you may be subject to a fine, to imprisonment or to both.

Dated (*date*), at (*place*).

....

(*Signature of justice or judge*)

2014, c. 31, s. 26

Form 5.008 — Production Order for Financial Data

(Subsection 487.018(4))

Canada,
Province of ....
(*territorial division*)

To (*name of financial institution, person or entity*), of ....:

Whereas I am satisfied by information on oath of (*name of peace officer or public officer*), of ...., that there are reasonable grounds to suspect that an offence has been or will be committed under (*specify the provision of the* Criminal Code *or other Act of Parliament*) and that (*specify the data*) is in your possession or control and will assist in the investigation of the offence;

Therefore, you are ordered to prepare and produce a document setting out (*specify the data*) that is in your possession or control when you receive this order.

The document must be produced to (*name of the peace officer or public officer*) within (*time*) at (*place*) in (*form*).

This order is subject to the following conditions:

You have the right to apply to revoke or vary this order.

If you contravene this order without lawful excuse, you may be subject to a fine, to imprisonment or to both.

Dated (*date*), at (*place*).

....

(*Signature of justice or judge*)

2014, c. 31, s. 26

Form 5.0081 — Information to Revoke or Vary an Order Made under Any of Sections 487.013 to 487.018 of the *Criminal Code*

(Subsection 487.019(3))

Canada,
Province of ....
(*territorial division*)

This is the information of (*name of peace officer or public officer*), of .... ("the informant").

The informant says that on or after (*insert date*) the informant became aware of the following facts that justify the revocation (*or* variation) of an order made on (*insert date*) under (*specify the provision of the* Criminal Code):

....

The informant therefore requests that the order be revoked (*or* be varied as follows: ....).

Sworn before me on (*date*), at (*place*).

....

(*Signature of informant*)

....

(*Signature of justice or judge*)

2014, c. 31, s. 26

Form 5.009 — Information to Obtain a Non-Disclosure Order

(Subsection 487.0191(2))

Canada,
Province of ....
(*territorial division*)

This is the information of (*name of peace officer or public officer*), of .... ("the informant").

The informant says that they have reasonable grounds to believe that the disclosure of the existence (*or* any of the contents *or* any of the following portion or portions) of (*identify the preservation demand made under section 487.012 of the* Criminal Code, *the preservation order made under section 487.013 of that Act or the production order made under any of sections 487.014 to 487.018 of that Act, as the case may be*) during (*identify the period*) would jeopardize the conduct of the investigation of the offence to which it relates:

(*specify portion or portions*)

The reasonable grounds are:

The informant therefore requests an order prohibiting (*name of the person*, financial institution or entity) from disclosing the existence (*or* any of the contents *or* any of the specified portion or portions) of the demand (*or* the order) during a period of (*identify the period*) after the day on which the order is made.

Sworn before me on (*date*), at (*place*).

....

(*Signature of informant*)

....

(*Signature of justice or judge*)

2014, c. 31, s. 26

Form 5.0091 — Non-Disclosure Order

(Subsection 487.0191(3))

Canada,
Province of ....
(*territorial division*)

To (*name of person, financial institution or entity*), of ....:

Whereas I am satisfied by information on oath of (*name of peace officer or public officer*), of ...., that there are reasonable grounds to believe that the disclosure of the existence (*or* any of the contents or any of the portion or portions, specified in the information,) of (*identify the preservation demand made under section 487.012 of the* Criminal Code, *the preservation order made under section 487.013 of that Act or the production order made under any of sections 487.014 to 487.018 of that Act, as the case may be*) during (*identify the period*) would jeopardize the conduct of the investigation of the offence to which it relates;

Therefore, you are prohibited from disclosing the existence (*or* any of the contents *or* any of the following portion or portions) of the demand (*or* the order) during a period of (*identify the period*) after the day on which this order is made.

(*specify portion or portions*)

You have the right to apply to revoke or vary this order.

If you contravene this order without lawful excuse, you may be subject to a fine, to imprisonment or to both.

Dated (*date*), at (*place*).

....
(*Signature of justice or judge*)

2014, c. 31, s. 26

Form 5.01 — Information to Obtain a Warrant to Take Bodily Substances for Forensic DNA Analysis

(Subsection 487.05(1))

Canada,
Province of ....,
(*territorial division*)

This is the information of (*name of peace officer*), (*occupation*), of .... in the said (*territorial division*), hereinafter called the informant, taken before me.

The informant says that he or she has reasonable grounds to believe

(a) that (*offence*), a designated offence within the meaning of section 487.04 of the *Criminal Code*, has been committed;

(b) that a bodily substance has been found

(i) at the place where the offence was committed,

(ii) on or within the body of the victim of the offence,

(iii) on anything worn or carried by the victim at the time when the offence was committed, or

(iv) on or within the body of any person or thing or at any place associated with the commission of the offence;

(c) that (*name of person*) was a party to the offence; and

(d) that forensic DNA analysis of a bodily substance from (*name of person*) will provide evidence about whether the bodily substance referred to in paragraph (b) was from that person.

The reasonable grounds are:

The informant therefore requests that a warrant be issued authorizing the taking from (*name of person*) of the number of samples of bodily substances that are reasonably required for forensic DNA analysis, provided that the person taking the samples is able by virtue of training or experience to take them by means of the investigative procedures described in subsection 487.06(1) of the *Criminal Code* and provided that, if the person taking the samples is not a peace officer, he or she take the samples under the direction of a peace officer.

Sworn to before me
this ....day of.........,
A.D. ...., at ....

....
(*Signature of informant*)

....
(*Signature of provincial court judge*)

1998, c. 37, s. 24

Form 5.02 — Warrant Authorizing the Taking of Bodily Substances for Forensic DNA Analysis

(Subsection 487.05(1))

Canada,
Province of ....,
(*territorial division*)

To the peace officers in (*territorial division*):

Whereas it appears on the oath of (*name of peace officer*) of .... in the said (*territorial division*), that there are reasonable grounds to believe

(a) that (*offence*), a designated offence within the meaning of section 487.04 of the *Criminal Code*, has been committed,

(b) that a bodily substance has been found

(i) at the place where the offence was committed,

(ii) on or within the body of the victim of the offence,

(iii) on anything worn or carried by the victim at the time when the offence was committed, or

(iv) on or within the body of any person or thing or at any place associated with the commission of the offence,

(c) that (*name of person*) was a party to the offence, and

(d) that forensic DNA analysis of a bodily substance from (*name of person*) will provide evidence about whether the bodily substance referred to in paragraph (b) was from that person;

And whereas I am satisfied that it is in the best interests of the administration of justice to issue this warrant;

This is therefore to authorize and require you to take from (*name of person*) or cause to be taken by a person acting under your direction, the number of samples of bodily substances that are reasonably required for forensic DNA analysis, provided that the person taking the samples is able by virtue of training or experience to take them by means of the investigative procedures described in subsection 487.06(1) of the *Criminal Code* and provided that, if the person taking the samples is not a peace officer, he or she take the samples under the direction of a peace officer. This warrant is subject to the following terms and conditions that I consider advisable to ensure that the taking of the samples is reasonable in the circumstances:

Dated this ...... day of ....

A.D. ...., at ....

....

(*Signature of provincial court judge*)

1998, c. 37, s. 24

Form 5.03 — Order Authorizing the Taking of Bodily Substances for Forensic DNA Analysis

(Subsections 487.051(1) and (2))

Canada

Province of ....

(*territorial division*)

To the peace officers in (*territorial division*):

Whereas (*name of person*) has been convicted under the *Criminal Code*, discharged under section 730 of that Act or, in the case of a young person, found guilty under the *Young Offenders Act*, chapter Y-1 of the Revised Statutes of Canada, 1985, or the *Youth Criminal Justice Act* of (*offence*), which, on the day on which the person was sentenced or discharged, was a primary designated offence within the meaning of section 487.04 of the *Criminal Code*;

Therefore, you are authorized to take or cause to be taken from (*name of person*) the number of samples of bodily substances that is reasonably required for forensic DNA analysis, provided that the person taking the samples is able, by virtue of training or experience, to take them by means of the investigative procedures described in subsection 487.06(1) of the *Criminal Code* and that, if the person taking the samples is not a peace officer, they take them under the direction of a peace officer.

This order is subject to the following terms and conditions that the court considers advisable to ensure that the taking of the samples is reasonable in the circumstances:

Dated (*date*).........., at ....(*place*).

(*Signature of judge of the court or clerk of the court*)

1998, c. 37, s. 24; 2002, c. 1, s. 185; 2005, c. 25, s. 12; 2007, c. 22, s. 23; 2019, c. 25, s. 330

Form 5.04 — Order Authorizing the Taking of Bodily Substances for Forensic DNA Analysis

(Subsection 487.051(3))

Canada

Province of ....

(*territorial division*)

To the peace officers in (*territorial division*):

Whereas (*name of person*), in this order called the "person",

(a) has been found not criminally responsible on account of mental disorder for (*offence*), which, on the day on which the finding was made, was a primary designated offence within the meaning of section 487.04 of the *Criminal Code*, or

(b) has been convicted under the *Criminal Code*, discharged under section 730 of that Act or, in the case of a young person, found guilty under the *Young Offenders Act*, chapter Y-1 of the Revised Statutes of Canada, 1985, or the *Youth Criminal Justice Act*, of, or has been found not criminally responsible on account of mental disorder for, (*offence*), which, on the day on which the person was sentenced or discharged or the finding was made, was one of the following secondary designated offences within the meaning of section 487.04 of the *Criminal Code* (*check applicable box*):

❑ (i) an offence under the *Criminal Code* for which the maximum punishment is imprisonment for five years or more and that was prosecuted by indictment,

❑ (i.01) an offence under any of sections 9 to 14 of the *Cannabis Act* for which the maximum punishment is imprisonment for five years or more and that was prosecuted by indictment,

❑ (ii) an offence under any of sections 5 to 7 of the *Controlled Drugs and Substances Act* for which the maximum punishment is imprisonment for five years or more and that was prosecuted by indictment,

❑ (iii) an offence under any of sections 145 to 148, subsection 173(1), sections 264, 264.1, 266 and 270, subsections 286.1(1) and 320.16(1), paragraph 348(1)(e) and sections 349 and 423 of the *Criminal Code*,

❑ (iv) an offence under section 433 or 434 of the *Criminal Code* as that section read from time to time before July 1, 1990,

❑ (iv.1) an offence under section 252 of the *Criminal Code*, as it read from time to time before the day on which section 14 of *An Act to amend the Criminal Code (offences relating to conveyances) and to make consequential amendments to other Acts* comes into force, or

❑ (v) an attempt or a conspiracy to commit an offence referred to in any of subparagraphs (i) to (ii) that was prosecuted by indictment (*or, if applicable*, an attempt or a conspiracy to commit an offence referred to in subparagraph (iii) or (iv));

Whereas the person's criminal record, the nature of the offence, the circumstances surrounding its commission, whether the person was previously found not criminally responsible on account of mental disorder for a designated offence, and the impact that this order would have on the person's privacy and security have been considered by the court;

And whereas the court is satisfied that it is in the best interests of the administration of justice to make this order;

Therefore, you are authorized to take or cause to be taken from (*name of person*) the number of samples of bodily substances that is reasonably required for forensic DNA analysis, provided that the person taking the samples is able, by virtue of training or experience, to take them by means of the investigative procedures described in subsection 487.06(1) of the *Criminal Code* and that, if the person taking the samples is not a peace officer, they take them under the direction of a peace officer.

This order is subject to the following terms and conditions that the court considers advisable to ensure that the taking of the samples is reasonable in the circumstances:

Dated (*date*).........., at ....(*place*).

(*Signature of judge of the court or clerk of the court*)

1998, c. 37, s. 24; 2002, c. 1, s. 186; 2005, c. 25, s. 12; 2007, c. 22, s. 23; 2012, c. 1, s. 38; 2014, c. 25, s. 32; 2018, c. 16, s. 224; 2018, c. 21, s. 29; 2019, c. 25, s. 331

Form 5.041 — Order to a Person to Have Bodily Substances Taken for Forensic DNA Analysis

(Subsections 487.051(4) and 487.055(3.11))

Canada

Province of ....

(*territorial division*)

To A.B., of ....,

Whereas an order has been made under section 487.051, or an authorization has been granted under section 487.055, of the *Criminal Code*, to take from you the number of samples of bodily substances that is reasonably required for forensic DNA analysis;

This is therefore to order you, in Her Majesty's name, to appear on .... (*date*)................................., at.......... (*hour*), at (..........*place*), for the purpose of the taking of bodily substances by means of the investigative procedures set out in subsection 487.06(1) of the *Criminal Code*.

You are warned that failure to appear in accordance with this order may result in a warrant being issued for your arrest under subsection 487.0551(1) of the *Criminal Code*. You are also warned that failure to appear, without reasonable excuse, is an offence under subsection 487.0552(1) of that Act.

Subsection 487.0551(1) of the *Criminal Code* states as follows:

"487.0551 (1) If a person fails to appear at the place, day and time set out in an order made under subsection 487.051(4) or 487.055(3.11) or in a summons referred to in subsection 487.055(4) or 487.091(3), a justice of the peace may issue a warrant for their arrest in Form 5.062 to allow samples of bodily substances to be taken."

Subsection 487.0552(1) of the *Criminal Code* states as follows:

"487.0552 (1) Every person who, without reasonable excuse, fails to comply with an order made under subsection 487.051(4) or 487.055(3.11) of this Act or under subsection 196.14(4) or 196.24(4) of the National Defence Act, or with a summons referred to in subsection 487.055(4) or 487.091(3) of this Act, is guilty of

(a) an indictable offence and liable to imprisonment for a term of not more than two years; or

(b) an offence punishable on summary conviction."

Dated (*date*).........., at ....(*place*).

(*Signature of judge of the court or clerk of the court*)

2007, c. 22, s. 23; 2019, c. 25, s. 332

Form 5.05 — Application for an Authorization to Take Bodily Substances for Forensic DNA Analysis

(Subsection 487.055(1))

Canada

Province of ....

(*territorial division*)

I (*name of peace officer*), (*occupation*), of .... in (*territorial division*), apply for an authorization to take bodily substances for forensic DNA analysis. A certificate referred to in paragraph 667(1)(a) of the *Criminal Code* is filed with this application.

Whereas (*name of offender*), before June 30, 2000,

(a) had been declared a dangerous offender under Part XXIV of the *Criminal Code*,

(b) had been declared a dangerous offender or a dangerous sexual offender under Part XXI of the *Criminal Code*, chapter C-34 of the Revised Statutes of Canada, 1970, as it read from time to time before January 1, 1988,

(c) had been convicted of murder,

(c.1) had been convicted of attempted murder or conspiracy to commit murder or to cause another person to be murdered and is currently serving a sentence of imprisonment for that offence,

(d) had been convicted of a sexual offence within the meaning of subsection 487.055(3) of the *Criminal Code* and is currently serving a sentence of imprisonment for that offence, or

(e) had been convicted of manslaughter and is currently serving a sentence of imprisonment for that offence;

Therefore, I request that an authorization be granted under subsection 487.055(1) of the *Criminal Code* to take from (*name of offender*) the number of samples of bodily substances that is reasonably required for forensic DNA analysis, provided that the person taking the samples is able, by virtue of training or experience, to take them by means of the investigative procedures described in subsection 487.06(1) of the *Criminal Code* and that, if the person taking the samples is not a peace officer, they take them under the direction of a peace officer.

Dated this .... day of ...., A.D. ...., at ....

....

(*Signature of applicant*)

1998, c. 37, s. 24; 2005, c. 25, s. 12; 2007, c. 22, s. 23

Form 5.06 — Authorization to Take Bodily Substances for Forensic DNA Analysis

(Subsection 487.055(1))

Canada

Province of ....

(*territorial division*)

To the peace officers in (*territorial division*):

Whereas (*name of peace officer*), a peace officer in (*territorial division*), has applied for an authorization to take the number of samples of bodily substances from (*name of offender*) that is reasonably required for forensic DNA analysis by means of the investigative procedures described in subsection 487.06(1) of the *Criminal Code*;

Whereas (*name of offender*), before June 30, 2000,

(a) had been declared a dangerous offender under Part XXIV of the *Criminal Code*,

(b) had been declared a dangerous offender or a dangerous sexual offender under Part XXI of the *Criminal Code*, chapter C-34 of the Revised Statutes of Canada, 1970, as it read from time to time before January 1, 1988,

(c) had been convicted of murder,

(c.1) had been convicted of attempted murder or conspiracy to commit murder or to cause another person to be murdered and, on the date of the application, was serving a sentence of imprisonment for that offence,

(d) had been convicted of a sexual offence within the meaning of subsection 487.055(3) of the *Criminal Code* and, on the date of the application, was serving a sentence of imprisonment for that offence, or

(e) had been convicted of manslaughter and, on the date of the application, was serving a sentence of imprisonment for that offence;

And whereas I have considered the offender's criminal record, the nature of the offence, the circumstances surrounding its commission and the impact that this authorization would have on the offender's privacy and security of the person;

Therefore, you are authorized to take those samples or cause them to be taken from (*name of offender*), provided that the person taking the samples is able, by virtue of training or experience, to take them by means of the investigative procedures described in subsection 487.06(1) of the *Criminal Code* and that, if the person taking the samples is not a peace officer, they take them under the direction of a peace officer.

This authorization is subject to the following terms and conditions that I consider advisable to ensure that the taking of the samples is reasonable in the circumstances:

Dated this .... day of ...., A.D., at ....

....

(*Signature of provincial court judge*)

1998, c. 37, s. 24; 2005, c. 25, s. 12; 2007, c. 22, s. 23

Form 5.061 — Summons to a Person to Have Bodily Substances Taken for Forensic DNA Analysis

(Subsections 487.055(4) and 487.091(3))

Canada

Province of ....

(*territorial division*)

To A.B., of ....,

Whereas an authorization has been granted under section 487.055 or 487.091 of the *Criminal Code* to take from you the number of samples of bodily substances that is reasonably required for forensic DNA analysis;

This is therefore to command you, in Her Majesty's name, to appear on ...., the .... day of ...., A.D. ...., at .... o'clock, at ...., for the purpose of the taking of bodily substances by means of the investigative procedures set out in subsection 487.06(1) of the *Criminal Code*. A peace officer, or a person who is acting under a peace officer's direction, who takes the samples of bodily substances may use as much force as necessary to do so.

You are warned that failure to appear in accordance with this summons may result in a warrant being issued for your arrest under subsection 487.0551(1) of the *Criminal Code*. You are also warned that failure to appear, without reasonable excuse, is an offence under subsection 487.0552(1) of that Act.

Subsection 487.0551(1) of the *Criminal Code* states as follows:

"487.0551(1) If a person fails to appear at the place, day and time set out in an order made under subsection 487.051(4) or 487.055(3.11) or in a summons referred to in subsection 487.055(4) or 487.091(3), a justice of the peace may issue a warrant for their arrest in Form 5.062 to allow samples of bodily substances to be taken."

Subsection 487.0552(1) of the *Criminal Code* states as follows:

"487.0552(1) Every person who, without reasonable excuse, fails to comply with an order made under subsection 487.051(4) or 487.055(3.11) of this Act or under subsection 196.14(4) or 196.24(4) of the National Defence Act, or with a summons referred to in subsection 487.055(4) or 487.091(3) of this Act, is guilty of

(a) an indictable offence and liable to imprisonment for a term of not more than two years; or

(b) an offence punishable on summary conviction."

Dated (*date*).........., at ....(*place*).

(*Signature of judge of the court or clerk of the court*)

2007, c. 22, s. 23; 2019, c. 25, s. 333

Form 5.062 — Warrant for Arrest

(Subsection 487.0551(1))

Canada

Province of ....

(*territorial division*)

To the peace officers in (*territorial division*):

This warrant is issued for the arrest of A.B., of ...., (*occupation*), in this warrant called the "offender".

Whereas the offender failed to appear at the place, day and time set out in an order made under subsection 487.051(4) or 487.055(3.11), or in a summons referred to in subsection 487.055(4) or 487.091(3), of the *Criminal Code* to submit to the taking of samples of bodily substances;

This is, therefore, to command you, in Her Majesty's name, to arrest the offender without delay in order to allow the samples of bodily substances to be taken.

Dated this .... day of .... A.D. ...., at ....

....

A Justice of the Peace in and for

....

2005, c. 25, s. 12; 2007, c. 22, s. 23

Form 5.07 — Report to a Provincial Court Judge or the Court

(Subsection 487.057(1))

Canada

Province of ....

(*territorial division*)

[ ] To (*name of judge*), a judge of the provincial court who issued a warrant under section 487.05 or granted an authorization under section 487.055 or 487.091 of the *Criminal Code* or to another judge of that court:

[ ] To the court that made an order under section 487.051 of the *Criminal Code*:

I (*name of peace officer*), declare that (*state here whether the samples were taken under a warrant issued under section 487.05, an order made under section 487.051 or an authorization granted under section 487.055 or 487.091 of the Criminal Code*).

I have (*state here whether you took the samples yourself or caused them to be taken under your direction*) from (*name of offender*) the number of samples of bodily substances that I believe is reasonably required for forensic DNA analysis, in accordance with (*state whether the samples were taken under a warrant issued or an authorization granted by the judge or another judge of the court or an order made by the court*).

The samples were taken on the .... day of ...., A.D. ...., at .... o'clock.

I (*or state the name of the person who took the samples*) took the following samples from (*name of offender*) in accordance with subsection 487.06(1) of the *Criminal Code* and was able, by virtue of training or experience, to do so (*check applicable box*):

[ ] individual hairs, including the root sheath

[ ] epithelial cells taken by swabbing the lips, tongue or inside cheeks of the mouth

[ ] blood taken by pricking the skin surface with a sterile lancet

Any terms or conditions in the (*warrant, order or authorization*) have been complied with.

Dated this .... day of .... A.D. ...., at ....

....

(*Signature of peace officer*)

1998, c. 37, s. 24; 2007, c. 22, s. 24

Form 5.08 — Application for an Authorization to Take Additional Samples of Bodily Substances for Forensic DNA Analysis

(Subsection 487.091(1))

Canada

Province of ....

(*territorial division*)

I (*name of peace officer*), (*occupation*), of .... in (*territorial division*), apply for an authorization to take additional samples of bodily substances for forensic DNA analysis.

Whereas samples of bodily substances were taken from (*name of offender*) for the purpose of forensic DNA analysis under an order made under section 487.051, or an authorization granted under section 487.055, of the *Criminal Code* (*attach a copy of the order or authorization*);

And whereas on (*day/month/year*) it was determined that

(a) a DNA profile could not be derived from the samples for the following reasons:

(b) the information or bodily substances required by regulations made under the *DNA Identification Act* were not transmitted in accordance with the requirements of the regulations or were lost for the following reasons:

Therefore, I request that an authorization be granted under subsection 487.091(1) of the *Criminal Code* to take from (*name of offender*) the number of additional samples of bodily substances that is reasonably required for forensic DNA analysis, provided that the person taking the samples is able, by virtue of training or experience, to take them by means of the investigative procedures described in subsection 487.06(1) of the *Criminal Code* and that, if the person taking the samples is not a peace officer, they take them under the direction of a peace officer.

Dated this .... day of ...., A.D. ...., at ....

....

(*Signature of applicant*)

1998, c. 37, s. 24; 2005, c. 25, s. 13; 2007, c. 22, s. 25

Form 5.09 — Authorization to Take Additional Samples of Bodily Substances for Forensic DNA Analysis

(Subsection 487.091(1))

Canada

Province of ....

(*territorial division*)

To the peace officers in (*territorial division*):

Whereas samples of bodily substances were taken from (*name of offender*) for the purpose of forensic DNA analysis under an order made under section 487.051 or an authorization granted under section 487.055, of the *Criminal Code*;

Whereas on (*day/month/year*) it was determined that

(a) a DNA profile could not be derived from the samples for the following reasons:

(b) the information or bodily substances required by regulations made under the *DNA Identification Act* were not transmitted in accordance with the requirements of the regulations or were lost for the following reasons:

And whereas (*name of peace officer*), a peace officer in (*territorial division*), has applied for an authorization to take the number of additional samples of bodily substances from (*name of offender*) that is reasonably required for forensic DNA analysis by means of the investigative procedures described in subsection 487.06(1) of the *Criminal Code*;

Therefore, you are authorized to take those additional samples, or cause them to be taken, from (*name of offender*), provided that the person taking the samples is able, by virtue of training or experience, to take them by means of the investigative procedures described in subsection 487.06(1) of the *Criminal Code* and that, if the person taking the samples is not a peace officer, they take them under the direction of a peace officer.

This authorization is subject to the following terms and conditions that I consider advisable to ensure that the taking of the samples is reasonable in the circumstances:

Dated this .... day of ...., A.D. ...., at ....

....
(*Signature of provincial court judge*)

1998, c. 37, s. 24; 2005, c. 25, s. 13; 2007, c. 22, s. 25

Form 5.1 — Warrant to Search

(Sections 320.29 and 487.1)

[Reference amended 2018, c. 21, s. 30.]

Canada,

Province of ....,
(*territorial division*).

To A.B. and other peace officers in the (*territorial division in which the warrant is intended for execution*):

Whereas it appears on the oath of A.B., a peace officer in the (*territorial division in which the warrant is intended for execution*), that there are reasonable grounds for dispensing with an information presented personally and in writing; and that there are reasonable grounds for believing that the following things

(*describe things to be searched for*)

relevant to the investigation of the following indictable offence

(*describe offence in respect of which search is to be made*)

are to be found in the following place or premises

(*describe place or premises to be searched*):

This is, therefore, to authorize you to enter the said place or premises between the hours of (*as the justice may direct*) and to search for and seize the said things and to report thereon as soon as practicable but within a period not exceeding seven days after the execution of the warrant to the clerk of the court for the (*territorial division in which the warrant is intended for execution*).

Issued at (*time*) on the (*day*) of (*month*) A.D. (*year*), at (*place*).

.... A Judge of the Provincial Court in and for the Province of (specify province).

To the Occupant: This search warrant was issued by telephone or other means of telecommunication. If you wish to know the basis on which this warrant was issued, you may apply to the clerk of the court for the territorial division in which the warrant was executed, at *address*, to obtain a copy of the information on oath.

You may obtain from the clerk of the court a copy of the report filed by the peace officer who executed this warrant. That report will indicate the things, if any, that were seized and the location where they are being held.

2018, c. 21, s. 30

Form 5.2 — Report to a Justice

(Section 489.1)

Canada,

Province of ....,

(*territorial division*).

To the justice who issued a warrant to the undersigned under section 320.29, 487 or 487.1 of the *Criminal Code* (*or another justice for the same territorial division or, if no warrant was issued, any justice having jurisdiction in respect of the matter*).

I, (*name of the peace officer or other person*) have (*state here whether you have acted under a warrant issued under section 320.29, 487 or 487.1 of the* Criminal Code *or under section 489 of the* Criminal Code *or otherwise in the execution of duties under the* Criminal Code *or other Act of Parliament to be specified*)

1 searched the premises situated at ....; and

2 seized the following things and dealt with them as follows:

Property Seized *(describe each thing seized)*	Disposition *(state, in respect of each thing seized, whether* *(a) it was returned to the person lawfully entitled to its possession, in which case the receipt for it shall be attached to this report; or* *(b) it is being detained to be dealt with according to law, in which case indicate the location and manner in which or, if applicable, the person by whom, it is being detained.*)
1.	....
2.	....
3.	....
4.	....

In the case of a warrant issued by telephone or other means of telecommunication, the statements referred to in subsection 487.1(9) of the *Criminal Code* shall be specified in the report.

Dated (*date*), at (*place*).

....

Signature of the peace officer or other person

R.S.C. 1985, c. 27 (1st Supp.), s. 184(3); 2018, c. 21, s. 31

Form 5.3 — Report to a Judge of Property Seized

(Section 462.32)

Canada

Province of ....,

(territorial division).

To a judge of the court from which the warrant was issued (*specify court*):

I, (*name of the peace officer or other person*) have acted under a warrant issued under section 462.32 of the *Criminal Code* and have

1. searched the premises situated at ....; and
2. seized the following property:

Property Seized (*describe each item of property seized*)	Location (*state, in respect of each item of property seized, the location where it is being detained*).
1.	. . . . . .
2.	. . . . . .
3.	. . . . . .
4.	. . . . . .

Dated this .... day of .... A.D. . . . . at ....

. . . .

Signature of peace officer or other person

R.S.C. 1985, c. 42 (4th Supp.), s. 6

Form 6 — Summons to a Person Charged With an Offence

(Sections 493, 508 and 512)

Canada,

Province of ....,
(*territorial division*).

To A.B., of ...., (*occupation*):

Because you have this day been charged with (*set out briefly the offence in respect of which the accused is charged*);

Therefore, you are ordered, in Her Majesty's name:

(a) to attend court on .... (*date*)................................., at .... (*hour*), at (*place*) .... or before any justice for the (*territorial division*) who is there, and to attend court at any time after as required by the court, in order to be dealt with according to law; and

(b) to appear on ....(*date*).........., at .... (*hour*), at (*place*).........., for the purposes of the *Identification of Criminals Act*. (*Ignore if not filled in*).

You are warned that failure without lawful excuse to attend court in accordance with this summons is an offence under subsection 145(4) of the *Criminal Code*.

Subection 145(4) of the *Criminal Code* states as follows:

"(4) Every person who is served with a summons and who fails, without lawful excuse, to appear at the time and place stated in it for the purposes of the *Identification of Criminals Act* or to attend court in accordance with it, is guilty of

(a) an indictable offence and is liable to imprisonment for a term not exceeding two years; or

(b) an offence punishable on summary conviction."

Section 510 of the *Criminal Code* states as follows:

"510. Where an accused who is required by a summons to appear at a time and place stated therein for the purposes of the *Identification of Criminals Act* does not appear at that time and place, a justice may issue a warrant for the arrest of the accused for the offence with which he is charged."

Dated (*date*).........., at ....(*place*).

(*Signature of judge, justice or clerk of the court*)

Proposed Amendment — Form 6 of Part XXVIII

Form 6 — Summons to a Person Charged with an Offence

(Section 2)

Canada,

Province of ....

(*territorial division*).

To (*name of person*), of ...., born on (*date of birth*):

Because you have this day been charged with (*set out briefly the offence in respect of which the accused is charged*);

Therefore, you are ordered, in Her Majesty's name:

(a) to appear on (*date*) at (*hour*) at (*place*) for the purposes of the *Identification of Criminals Act* (*Ignore, if not filled in*); and

(b) to attend court on (*date*), at (*hour*), at (*place*), or before any justice for the (*territorial division*) who is there, and to attend court at any time after as required by the court, in order to be dealt with according to law.

You are warned that, unless you have a lawful excuse, it is an offence under subsection 145(3) of the *Criminal Code* to fail to appear for the purposes of the *Identification of Criminals Act* or to attend court, as required in this summons.

If you commit an offence under subsection 145(3) of the *Criminal Code*, a warrant for your arrest may be issued (Section 512 or 512.1 of the *Criminal Code*) and you may be liable to a fine or to imprisonment, or to both.

If you do not comply with this summons or are charged with committing an indictable offence after it has been issued to you, this summons may be cancelled and, as a result, you may be detained in custody (Subsection 524(4) of the *Criminal Code*).

Signed on (*date*), at (*place*).

.... (*Signature of judge, justice, clerk of the court or chairperson of the Review Board*)

.... (*Name of the judge, justice or chairperson*)

2019, c. 25, s. 334(3) [To come into force December 18, 2019.]

R.S.C. 1985, c. 27 (1st Supp.), s. 184(4); 2018, c. 29, s. 69(1); 2019, c. 25, s. 334(1), (2)

Form 7 — Warrant for Arrest

(Sections 475, 493, 597, 800 and 803)

Canada,

Province of ....,
(*territorial division*).

To the peace officers in the said (*territorial division*):

This warrant is issued for the arrest of A.B., of ...., (*occupation*), hereinafter called the accused.

Whereas the accused has been charged that (*set out briefly the offence in respect of which the accused is charged*);

And whereas:[1]

(a) there are reasonable grounds to believe that it is necessary in the public interest to issue this warrant for the arrest of the accused [507(4), 512(1)];

(b) the accused failed to attend court in accordance with the summons served on him [512(2)];

(c) (an appearance notice *or* a promise to appear *or* a recognizance entered into before an officer in charge) was confirmed and the accused failed to attend court in accordance therewith [512(2)];

(d) it appears that a summons cannot be served because the accused is evading service [512(2)];

(e) the accused was ordered to be present at the hearing of an application for a review of an order made by a justice and did not attend the hearing [520(5), 521(5)];

(f) there are reasonable grounds to believe that the accused has contravened or is about to contravene the (promise to appear *or* undertaking *or* recognizance) on which he was released [524(1), 525(5), 679(6)];

(g) there are reasonable grounds to believe that the accused has since his release from custody on (a promise to appear *or* an undertaking *or* a recognizance) committed an indictable offence [524(1), 525(5), 679(6)];

(h) the accused was required by (an appearance notice *or* a promise to appear *or* a recognizance entered into before an officer in charge *or* a summons) to attend at a time and place stated therein for the purposes of the *Identification of Criminals Act* and did not appear at that time and place [502, 510];

(i) an indictment has been found against the accused and the accused has not appeared or remained in attendance before the court for his trial [597];

(j)[2]

This is, therefore, to command you, in Her Majesty's name, forthwith to arrest the said accused and to bring him before (*state court, judge or justice*), to be dealt with according to law.

(*Add where applicable*) Whereas there are reasonable grounds to believe that the accused is or will be present in (*here describe dwelling-house*);

This warrant is also issued to authorize you to enter the dwelling-house for the purpose of arresting or apprehending the accused, subject to the condition that you may not enter the dwelling-house unless you have, immediately before entering the dwelling-house, reasonable grounds to believe that the person to be arrested or apprehended is present in the dwelling-house.

---

1 *Initial applicable recital.*

2 *For any case not covered by recitals (a) to (i), insert recital in the words of the statute authorizing the warrant.*

Dated this .... day of .... A.D. ...., at ....

. . . .
Judge, Clerk of the Court,
Provincial Court Judge *or* Justice

Proposed Amendment — Form 7 of Part XXVIII

Form 7 — Warrant for Arrest

(Sections 475, 493, 597, 800 and 803)

Canada,
Province of ....,
(*territorial division*).

To the peace officers in the (*territorial division*):

This warrant is issued for the arrest of (*name of person*), of ...., born on (*date of birth*), referred to in this warrant as the accused.

Because the accused has been charged with (*set out briefly the offence in respect of which the accused is charged*);

And because (*check those that are applicable*):

❑ (a) there are reasonable grounds to believe that it is necessary in the public interest to issue this warrant for the arrest of the accused [507(4), 512(1)];

❑ (b) the accused failed to attend court in accordance with the summons served on the accused [512(2)];

❑ (c) (an appearance notice *or* undertaking) was confirmed and the accused failed to attend court in accordance with it [512(2)];

❑ (d) it appears that a summons cannot be served because the accused is evading service [512(2)];

❑ (e) the accused was ordered to be present at the hearing of an application for a review of an order made by a justice and did not attend the hearing [520(5), 521(5)];

❑ (f) there are reasonable grounds to believe that the accused has contravened or is about to contravene the (summons *or* appearance notice *or* undertaking *or* release order) on which the accused was released [512.3];

❑ (g) there are reasonable grounds to believe that the accused has committed an indictable offence since their release from custody on (summons *or* appearance notice *or* undertaking *or* release order) [512.3];

❑ (h) the accused was required by (appearance notice *or* undertaking *or* summons) to attend at a time and place stated in it for the purposes of the *Identification of Criminals Act* and did not appear at that time and place [512.1, 512.2];

❑ (i) an indictment has been found against the accused and the accused has not appeared or remained in attendance before the court for their trial [597];

❑ (j) (*if none of the above applies, reproduce the provisions of the statute that authorize this warrant*).

Therefore, you are ordered, in Her Majesty's name, to immediately arrest the accused and to bring them before (*state court, judge or justice*), to be dealt with according to law.

❑ (*Check if applicable*) Because there are reasonable grounds to believe that the accused is or will be present in (*specify dwelling-house*), this warrant is also issued to authorize you to enter the dwellinghouse for the purpose of arresting the accused, subject to the condition that you may not enter the dwelling-house unless you have, immediately before entering the dwelling-house, reasonable grounds to believe that the person to be arrested is present in the dwelling-house.

Signed on (*date*), at (*place*).

.... (*Signature of judge, provincial court judge, justice or clerk of the court*)

.... (*Name of the judge, provincial court judge or justice who has issued this warrant*)

2019, c. 25, s. 335 [To come into force December 18, 2019.]

R.S.C. 1985, c. 27 (1st Supp.), s. 203; 1997, c. 39, s. 3; 1999, c. 5, s. 46

Form 7.1 — Warrant to Enter Dwelling-House

(Section 529.1)

Canada,

Province of ....,
(*territorial division*).

To the peace officers in the said (*territorial division*):

This warrant is issued in respect of the arrest of A.B., or a person with the following description ( ), of ...., (*occupation*).

Whereas there are reasonable grounds to believe:[3]

(a) a warrant referred to in this or any other Act of Parliament to arrest or apprehend the person is in force anywhere in Canada;

(b) grounds exist to arrest the person without warrant under paragraph 495(1)(a) or (b) or section 672.91 of the *Criminal Code*; or

(c) grounds exist to arrest or apprehend without warrant the person under an Act of Parliament, other than this Act;

And whereas there are reasonable grounds to believe that the person is or will be present in (*here describe dwelling-house*);

This warrant is issued to authorize you to enter the dwelling-house for the purpose of arresting or apprehending the person.

[3] *Initial applicable recital.*

Dated this .... day of .... A.D. ...., at ....

. . . .

Judge, Clerk of the Court,
Provincial Court Judge or Justice

1997, c. 39, s. 3; 2002, c. 13, s. 85

Form 8 — Warrant for Committal

(Sections 493 and 515)

Canada,

Province of ....,
(*territorial division*).

To the peace officers in the said (*territorial division*) and to the keeper of the (*prison*) at ....:

This warrant is issued for the committal of A.B., of ...., (*occupation*), hereinafter called the accused.

Whereas the accused has been charged that (*set out briefly the offence in respect of which the accused is charged*);

And whereas:[4]

(a) the prosecutor has shown cause why the detention of the accused in custody is justified [515(5)];

(b) an order has been made that the accused be released on (giving an undertaking *or* entering into a recognizance) but the accused has not yet complied with the order [519(1), 520(9), 524(12), 525(8)];[5]

(c) the application by the prosecutor for a review of the order of a justice in respect of the interim release of the accused has been allowed and that order has been vacated, and the prosecutor has shown cause why the detention of the accused in custody is justified [521];

(d) the accused has contravened or was about to contravene his (promise to appear *or* undertaking *or* recognizance) and the same was cancelled, and the detention of the accused in custody is justified or seems proper in the circumstances [524(4), 524(8)];

(e) there are reasonable and probable grounds to believe that the accused has after his release from custody on (a promise to appear *or* an undertaking *or* a recognizance) committed an indictable offence and the detention of the accused in custody is justified or seems proper in the circumstances [524(4), 524(8)];

---

4 *Initial applicable recital.*

5 *If the person having custody of the accused is authorized under paragraph 519(1)(b) to release him upon his complying with an order, endorse the authorization on this warrant and attach a copy of the order.*

(f) the accused has contravened or was about to contravene the (undertaking *or* recognizance) on which he was released and the detention of the accused in custody seems proper in the circumstances [525(7), 679(6)];

(g) there are reasonable grounds to believe that the accused has after his release from custody on (an undertaking *or* a recognizance) committed an indictable offence and the detention of the accused in custody seems proper in the circumstances [525(7), 679(6)];

(h)[6]

This is, therefore, to command you, in Her Majesty's name, to arrest, if necessary, and take the accused and convey him safely to the (*prison*) at ...., and there deliver him to the keeper thereof, with the following precept:

You are ordered to receive the accused in your custody in this prison and keep them safely there until they are delivered by due course of law.

Dated (*date*).........., at ....(*place*).

(*Signature of judge, justice or clerk of the court*)

Proposed Amendment — Form 8 of Part XXVIII

Form 8 — Warrant for Committal

(Sections 493 and 515)

Canada,

Province of ....,

(*territorial division*).

To the peace officers in the (*territorial division*) and to the keeper of the (*prison*) at ....:

This warrant is issued for the committal of (*name of person*), of ...., born on (*date of birth*), referred to in this warrant as the accused.

Because the accused has been charged with (*set out briefly the offence in respect of which the accused is charged*);

And because (*check those that are applicable*):

❑ (a) the prosecutor has shown cause why the detention of the accused in custody is justified [515(5)];

❑ (b) a release order has been issued but the accused has not yet complied with the conditions of the order [519(1), 520(9), 521(10), 524(8), 525(6)];[7]

---

6 *For any case not covered by recitals (a) to (g), insert recital in the words of the statute authorizing the warrant.*

7 *If the person having custody of the accused is authorized under paragraph 519(1)(b) of the* Criminal Code *to release the accused if they comply with a release order, endorse the authorization on this warrant and attach a copy of the order.*

❑ (c) the application by the prosecutor for a review of the release order has been allowed and that release order has been vacated, and the prosecutor has shown cause why the detention of the accused in custody is justified [521];

❑ (d) the accused has contravened or was about to contravene a (summons *or* appearance notice *or* undertaking *or* release order) and it was cancelled, and the detention of the accused in custody is justified [515(10), 523.1(3), 524(3) and (4)];

❑ (e) there are reasonable grounds to believe that the accused has committed an indictable offence after having become subject to the (summons or appearance notice *or* undertaking *or* release order) and the detention of the accused in custody is justified [515(10), 524(3) and (4)];

❑ (f) (*if none of the above applies, reproduce the provisions of the statute that authorize this warrant*).

Therefore, you are ordered, in Her Majesty's name, to arrest the accused and convey them safely to the (*prison*) at ...., and there deliver them to its keeper, with the following order:

You are ordered to receive the accused in your custody in this prison and keep them safely there until they are delivered by due course of law.

Signed on (*date*), at (*place*).

.... (*Signature of judge, justice or clerk of the court*)

.... (*Name of the judge or justice who has issued this warrant*)

2019, c. 25, s. 336(2) [To come into force December 18, 2019.]

R.S.C. 1985, c. 27 (1st Supp.), ss. 184(19), 203; 2019, c. 25, s. 336(1)

Form 9 — Appearance Notice Issued By a Peace Officer to a Person Not Yet Charged With an Offence

(Section 493)

Canada,

Province of ....,

(*territorial division*).

To A.B., of ...., (*occupation*):

You are alleged to have committed (*set out substance of offence*).

1. You are required to attend court on .... day, the .... day of .... A.D. ...., at .... o'clock in the .... noon, in courtroom No. ...., at .... court, in the municipality of.........., and to attend thereafter as required by the court, in order to be dealt with according to law.

2. You are also required to appear on .... day, the .... day of.......... A.D. ...., at .... o'clock in the .... noon, at (*police station*), (*address*), for the purposes of the *Identification of Criminals Act*. (*Ignore, if not filled in*).

You are warned that failure to attend court in accordance with this appearance notice is an offence under subsection 145(5) of the *Criminal Code*.

Subsections 145(5) and (6) of the *Criminal Code* state as follows:

"(5) Every person who is named in an appearance notice or promise to appear, or in a recognizance entered into before an officer in charge or another peace officer, that has been confirmed by a justice under section 508 and who fails, without lawful excuse, to appear at the time and place stated in it for the purposes of the *Identification of Criminals Act*, or to attend court in accordance with it, is guilty of

(a) an indictable offence and is liable to imprisonment for a term not exceeding two years; or

(b) an offence punishable on summary conviction.

(6) For the purposes of subsection (5), it is not a lawful excuse that an appearance notice, promise to appear or recognizance states defectively the substance of the alleged offence."

Section 502 of the *Criminal Code* states as follows:

"502. Where an accused who is required by an appearance notice or promise to appear or by a recognizance entered into before an officer in charge or another peace officer to appear at a time and place stated therein for the purposes of the *Identification of Criminals Act* does not appear at that time and place, a justice may, where the appearance notice, promise to appear or recognizance has been confirmed by a justice under section 508, issue a warrant for the arrest of the accused for the offence with which the accused is charged."

Issued at .... a.m./p.m. this .... day of .... A.D..........., at ....

. . . .
(Signature of peace officer)

. . . .
(Signature of accused)

Proposed Amendment — Form 9 of Part XXVIII

Form 9 — Appearance Notice [Heading amended 2019, c. 25, s. 337. To come into force December 18, 2019.]

(Section 2)

Canada,

Province of ....

(*territorial division*)

1 Identification

Surname: .... Given name(s): ....

Date of Birth: ....

2 Contact Information

....

3 Alleged Offence

You are alleged to have committed (*set out briefly the substance of the offence, including any failure referred to in section 496, that the accused is alleged to have committed*).

❑ (*Check if applicable*) No new charges are being laid against you at this time but you are required to appear at a judicial referral hearing under section 523.1 for a failure under section 496.

4 Conditions

You must attend court as indicated below, and afterwards as required by the court:

Date: ....

Time: ....

Court number: ....

Court address: ....

5 Appearance for the purposes of the Identification of Criminals Act *(*if applicable*)*

❑ You are required to appear on (*date*) at (*hour*) at (*place*) for the purposes of the *Identification of Criminals Act*.

6 Consequence for non-compliance

You are warned that,

(a) in the case where charges have been laid against you, unless you have a lawful excuse, you commit an offence under subsection 145(3) of the *Criminal Code* if you fail to appear for the purposes of the *Identification of Criminals Act* or to attend court, as required in this appearance notice;

(b) in the case where no charges have been laid against you and you fail to appear at a judicial referral hearing under section 523.1, as required in this appearance notice, charges may be laid against you for the alleged offence described in item 3 of this notice.

If you commit an offence under subsection 145(3) of the *Criminal Code*, a warrant for your arrest may be issued (section 512 or 512.2 of the *Criminal Code*) and you may be liable to a fine or to imprisonment, or to both.

It is not a lawful excuse to an offence under subsection 145(3) of the *Criminal Code* that this appearance notice does not accurately describe the offence that you are alleged to have committed (subsection 145(6) of the *Criminal Code*).

If you do not comply with this appearance notice or are charged with committing an indictable offence after you have been released, this appearance notice may be cancelled and, as a result, you may be detained in custody (subsection 524(4) of the *Criminal Code*).

7 Signatures

ACCUSED:

I understand the contents of this appearance notice and agree to comply with it.

Signed on (*date*), at (*place*).

.... (*Signature of accused*)

PEACE OFFICER:

Signed on (*date*), at (*place*).

.... (*Signature of peace officer*)

.... (*Name of the peace officer*)

2019, c. 25, s. 337 [To come into force December 18, 2019.]

1997, c. 18, s. 115; 2018, c. 29, s. 70(1)

Form 10 — Promise to Appear

(Section 493)

Canada,

Province of ....,
(*territorial division*).

I, A.B., of ...., (*occupation*), understand that it is alleged that I have committed (*set out substance of offence*).

In order that I may be released from custody,

1. I promise to attend court on .... day, the .... day of.......... A.D. ...., at .... o'clock in the .... noon, in courtroom No. ...., at court, in the municipality of ...., and to attend thereafter as required by the court, in order to be dealt with according to law.

2. I also promise to appear on .... day, the .... day of.......... A.D. ...., at .... o'clock in the .... noon, at (*police station*), (*address*), for the purposes of the *Identification of Criminals Act*. (*Ignore if not filled in*).

I understand that failure without lawful excuse to attend court in accordance with this promise to appear is an offence under subsection 145(5) of the *Criminal Code*.

Subsections 145(5) and (6) of the *Criminal Code* state as follows:

"(5) Every person who is named in an appearance notice or promise to appear, or in a recognizance entered into before an officer in charge or another peace officer, that has been confirmed by a justice under section 508 and who fails, without lawful excuse, to appear at the time and place stated in it for the purposes of the *Identification of Criminals Act*, or to attend court in accordance with it, is guilty of

(a) an indictable offence and is liable to imprisonment for a term not exceeding two years; or

(b) an offence punishable on summary conviction.

(6) For the purposes of subsection (5), it is not a lawful excuse that an appearance notice, promise to appear or recognizance states defectively the substance of the alleged offence."

Section 502 of the *Criminal Code* states as follows:

"502. Where an accused who is required by an appearance notice or promise to appear or by a recognizance entered into before an officer in charge or another peace officer to appear at a time and place stated therein for the purposes of the *Identification of Criminals Act* does not appear at that time and place, a justice may, where the appearance notice, promise to appear or recognizance has been confirmed by a justice under section 508, issue a warrant for the arrest of the accused for the offence with which the accused is charged."

Dated this .... day of .... A.D. ...., at ....

. . . .
(Signature of accused)

Proposed Amendment — Form 10 of Part XXVIII

Form 10 — Undertaking [Heading amended 2019, c. 25, s. 337. To come into force December 18, 2019.]

(Section 2)

Canada,
Province of ....
(*territorial division*).

1 Identification

Surname: .... Given name(s): ....
Date of Birth: ....

2 Contact Information

....

3 Charge(s)

(*set out briefly the offence in respect of which the accused was charged*)

4 Mandatory Condition

You must attend court as indicated below, and afterwards as required by the court:

Date: ....
Time: ....
Court number: ....
Court address: ....

5 Additional Conditions

You must also comply with any conditions that are indicated below by a check mark (*check only those that are reasonable in the circumstances of the offence and necessary, to ensure the accused's attendance in court or the safety and security of any victim of or witness to the offence, or to prevent the continuation or repetition of the offence or the commission of another offence*):

❑ (a) You must report to (*name or title*) at (*place*) on (*date or dates*).

❑ (b) You must remain within the following territorial jurisdiction: ....

❑ (c) You must notify (*name, title and phone number*) of any change of your (*address, employment or occupation*).

❑ (d) You must not communicate, directly or indirectly, with ...., except in accordance with the following conditions: ....

❑ (e) You must not go to (*places which are related to the person(s) mentioned in the condition set out in paragraph (d)*), except in accordance with the following conditions: ....

❑ (f) You must not enter the areas (*describe in detail the boundaries of the areas related to the person(s) mentioned in the condition set out in paragraph (d)*), except in accordance with the following conditions: ....

❑ (g) You must deposit all your passports with (*name or title*) at (*place*) before (*date*).

❑ (h) You must reside at (*place*), be at that residence between (*hour*) and (*hour*), and present yourself at the entrance of that residence when a peace officer or (*name and title of another person*) requests you to do so within those hours.

❑ (i) You must not possess a firearm, crossbow, prohibited weapon, restricted weapon, prohibited device, ammunition, prohibited ammunition or explosive substance and you must surrender those that are in your possession and also any authorization, licence or registration certificate or other document enabling you to acquire or possess them to (*name or title*) at (*place*).

❑ (j) You promise to pay the amount of .... (*not more than $500*), if you fail to comply with a condition of this undertaking.

❑ (k) You must deposit money or other valuable security whose value is equal to the amount of .... (*not more than $500*) with (*name or title*), because you are not ordinarily resident in the province or do not reside within 200 km of the place in which you are in custody.

❑ (l) You must comply with the following conditions (*conditions for ensuring the safety and security of any victim of or witness to the alleged offence*): ....

6 Appearance for the purposes of the Identification of Criminals Act

❑ You are required to appear on (*date*) at (*hour*) at (*place*) for the purposes of the *Identification of Criminals Act*.

7 Variation and Replacement

The conditions of this undertaking may be varied with the written consent of the prosecutor and yourself. In addition, you or the prosecutor may apply to a justice of the peace to replace this undertaking with a release order under section 515 of the *Criminal Code*.

8 Conditions in effect

The mandatory condition and the conditions indicated by a check mark on this undertaking remain in effect until they are cancelled or changed or until you have been discharged, sentenced or otherwise detained by the court (sections 763 and 764 of the *Criminal Code*).

9 Consequence for non-compliance

You are warned that, unless you have a lawful excuse, you commit an offence under section 145 of the *Criminal Code* if you fail to follow any of the conditions set out in this undertaking, including

(a) to fail to attend court as required;

(b) to fail to appear as required for the purposes of the *Identification of Criminals Act*;

(c) to fail to remain in the territorial jurisdiction specified in section 5 of this undertaking (*if applicable*).

If you commit an offence under section 145 of the *Criminal Code*, a warrant for your arrest may be issued (section 512 or 512.2 of the *Criminal Code*) and you may be liable to a fine or to imprisonment, or to both.

It is not a lawful excuse to an offence under subsection 145(4) of the *Criminal Code* that this undertaking does not accurately describe the offence that you are alleged to have committed (subsection 145(6) of the *Criminal Code*).

If you do not comply with this undertaking or are charged with committing an indictable offence after you have been released, this undertaking may be cancelled and, as a result, you may be detained in custody (subsection 524(4) of the *Criminal Code*).

If you do not comply with this undertaking, the funds or valuable security promised or deposited by you or your surety could be forfeited (subsection 771(2) of the *Criminal Code*).

10 Signatures

ACCUSED:

I understand the contents of this undertaking and agree to comply with the mandatory condition and the conditions that are indicated by a check mark.

I understand that I do not have to accept the conditions and that, if I do not accept the conditions, I will be brought to a justice for a bail hearing.

Signed on (*date*), at (*place*).

.... (*Signature of accused*)

PEACE OFFICER:

Signed on (*date*), at (*place*).

.... (*Signature of peace officer*)

.... (*Name of the peace officer*)

2019, c. 25, s. 337 [To come into force December 18, 2019.]

1997, c. 18, s. 115; 2018, c. 29, s. 70(1)

Form 11 — Recognizance Entered Into Before an Officer in Charge or Other Peace Officer

(Section 493)

Canada,

Province of ....,

(*territorial division*).

I, A.B., of ...., (*occupation*), understand that it is alleged that I have committed (*set out substance of offence*).

In order that I may be released from custody, I hereby acknowledge that I owe $ (*not exceeding $500*) to Her Majesty the Queen to be levied on my real and personal property if I fail to attend court as hereinafter required.

(*or, for a person not ordinarily resident in the province in which the person is in custody or within two hundred kilometers of the place in which the person is in custody*)

In order that I may be released from custody, I hereby acknowledge that I owe $ (*not exceeding $500*) to Her Majesty the Queen and deposit herewith (*money or other valuable security not exceeding in amount or value $500*) to be forfeited if I fail to attend court as hereinafter required.

1. I acknowledge that I am required to attend court on .... day, the.......... day of .... A.D. ...., at .... o'clock in the.......... noon, in courtroom No. ...., at .... court, in the municipality of ...., and to attend thereafter as required by the court, in order to be dealt with according to law.

2. I acknowledge that I am also required to appear on .... day, the.......... day of .... A.D. ...., at .... o'clock in the.......... noon, at (*police station*), (*address*), for the purposes of the *Identification of Criminals Act*. (*Ignore if not filled in*).

I understand that failure without lawful excuse to attend court in accordance with this recognizance to appear is an offence under subsection 145(5) of the *Criminal Code*.

Subsections 145(5) and (6) of the *Criminal Code* state as follows:

"(5) Every person who is named in an appearance notice or promise to appear, or in a recognizance entered into before an officer in charge or another peace officer, that has been confirmed by a justice under section 508 and who fails, without lawful excuse, to appear at the time and place stated in it for the purposes of the *Identification of Criminals Act*, or to attend court in accordance with it, is guilty of

(a) an indictable offence and is liable to imprisonment for a term not exceeding two years; or

(b) an offence punishable on summary conviction.

(6) For the purposes of subsection (5), it is not a lawful excuse that an appearance notice, promise to appear or recognizance states defectively the substance of the alleged offence."

Section 502 of the *Criminal Code* states as follows:

"502. Where an accused who is required by an appearance notice or promise to appear or by a recognizance entered into before an officer in charge or another peace officer to appear at a time and place stated therein for the purposes of the *Identification of Criminals Act* does not appear at that time and place, a justice may, where the appearance notice, promise to appear or recognizance has been confirmed by a justice under section 508, issue a warrant for the arrest of the accused for the offence with which he is charged."

Dated this .... day of .... A.D. ...., at ....

. . . .

(*Signature of accused*)

Proposed Amendment — Form 11 of Part XXVIII

Form 11 — Release Order [Heading amended 2019, c. 25, s. 337. To come into force December 18, 2019.]

(Section 2)

Canada,

Province of ....

(*territorial division*).

1 Identification

Surname: .... Given name(s): ....

Date of Birth: ....

2 Contact Information

....

3 Charge(s)

(*set out briefly the offence in respect of which the accused was charged*)

4 Financial Obligations

❏ You do not have any financial obligations under this release order.

or

In order for you to be released, the obligations that are indicated below by a check mark must be complied with.

> ❏ You promise to pay the amount of .... if you fail to comply with a condition of this release order.
>
> ❏ You must deposit money in the amount of ....or other valuable security whose value does not exceed .... with the clerk of the court.
>
> ❏ The surety (*name*), born on (*date of birth*), (*promises to pay or deposits*) to the court the amount of ....

5 Conditions

You must comply with the conditions that are indicated below by a check mark.

> ❏ You must report to (*name or title*) at (*place*) on (*date or dates*).
>
> ❏ You must remain within the territorial jurisdiction of (*province or territory*).
>
> ❏ You must notify (*name, title and phone number*) of any change of your (*address, employment or occupation*).
>
> ❏ You must not communicate, directly or indirectly, with (*victims, witnesses or other persons*), except in accordance with the following conditions: ....
>
> ❏ You must not go to (*place*) or enter (*geographic area*), except in accordance with the following conditions: ....
>
> ❏ You must deposit all your passports with (*name or title*) at (*place*) before (*date*).

❑ You must not possess a firearm, crossbow, prohibited weapon, restricted weapon, prohibited device, ammunition, prohibited ammunition or explosive substance and you must surrender any of them in your possession and any authorization, licence or registration certificate or other document enabling the acquisition or possession of a firearm to (*name or title*) at (*place*).

❑ You must comply with the following conditions (*conditions for ensuring the safety and security of any victim of or witness to the alleged offence*): ....

❑ You must comply with the following conditions: ....

6 Variation

The conditions of this release order may be varied with the written consent of the prosecutor, yourself and your sureties, if any. In addition, you or the prosecutor may apply to a judge to have any condition in this release order cancelled or changed.

7 Conditions in effect

The conditions indicated by a check mark on this release order (including any obligations imposed on your sureties) remain in effect until they are cancelled or changed or until you have been discharged, sentenced or otherwise detained by the court (sections 763 and 764 of the *Criminal Code*).

8 Consequence for non-compliance

You are warned that, unless you have a lawful excuse, you commit an offence under section 145 of the *Criminal Code* if you fail to follow any of the conditions set out in this release order, including if you fail to attend court as required.

If you commit an offence under section 145 of the *Criminal Code*, a warrant for your arrest may be issued (sections 512 and 512.3 of the *Criminal Code*) and you may be liable to a fine or to imprisonment, or to both.

If you do not comply with this release order or are charged with committing an indictable offence after you have been released, this release order may be cancelled and, as a result, you may be detained in custody (subsection 524(4) of the *Criminal Code*).

If you do not comply with this release order, the money or other valuable security promised or deposited by you or your surety could be forfeited (subsection 771(2) of the *Criminal Code*).

9 Signatures

SURETY: (*if applicable*)

I understand my role and my responsibilities under this release order and I agree to act as a surety.

I agree to (*promise or deposit*) to the court the amount of money described in section 4 of this release order.

❑ Surety Declaration is attached (section 515.1 of the *Criminal Code*).

❑ Surety is excepted from providing Surety Declaration (subsection 515.1(2) of the *Criminal Code*).

Signed on (*date*), at (*place*).

.... (*Signature of the surety*)

ACCUSED:

I understand the contents of this form and agree to comply with the conditions that are indicated by a check mark.

I understand that I do not have to accept the conditions and that, if I do not accept the conditions, I will be detained.

Signed on (*date*), at (*place*).

.... (*Signature of accused*)

JUDGE, JUSTICE OR CLERK OF THE COURT:

Signed on (*date*), at (*place*).

.... (*Signature of judge, justice or clerk of the court*)

.... (*Name of judge or justice who has issued this order*)

2019, c. 25, s. 337 [To come into force December 18, 2019.]

1997, c. 18, s. 115; 2018, c. 29, s. 70(1)

Form 11.1 — Undertaking Given to a Peace Officer or an Officer in Charge [Repealed 2019, c. 25, s. 337. To come into force December 18, 2019.]

(Sections 493, 499 and 503)

Canada,

Province of ....,

(*territorial division*).

I, A.B., of ...., (*occupation*), understand that it is alleged that I have committed (*set out substance of the offence*).

In order that I may be released from custody by way of (a promise to appear *or* a recognizance entered into before an officer in charge), I undertake to (*insert any conditions that are directed*):

(a) remain within (*designated territorial jurisdiction*);

(b) notify (*name of peace officer or other person designated*) of any change in my address, employment or occupation;

(c) abstain from communicating, directly or indirectly, with (*identification of victim, witness or other person*) or from going to (*name or description of place*) except in accordance with the following conditions: (*as the peace officer or other person designated specifies*);

(d) deposit my passport with (*name of peace officer or other person designated*);

(e) to abstain from possession a firearm and to surrender to (*name of peace officer or other person designated*) any firearm in my possession and any authorization, license or registration certificate or other document enabling the acquisition or possession of a firearm;

(f) report at (*state times*) to (*name of peace officer or other person designated*);

(g) to abstain from

(i) the consumption of alcohol or other intoxicating substances, or

(ii) the consumption of drugs except in accordance with a medical prescription; and

(h) comply with any other conditions that the peace officer or officer in charge considers necessary to ensure the safety and security of any victim of or witness to the offence.

I understand that I am not required to give an undertaking to abide by the conditions specified above, but that if I do not, I may be kept in custody and brought before a justice so that the prosecutor may be given a reasonable opportunity to show cause why I should not be released on giving an undertaking without conditions.

I understand that if I give an undertaking to abide by the conditions specified above, then I may apply, at any time before I appear, or when I appear, before a justice pursuant to (a promise to appear *or* a recognizance entered into before an officer in charge or another peace officer), to have this undertaking vacated or varied and that my application will be considered as if I were before a justice pursuant to section 515 of the *Criminal Code*.

I also understand that this undertaking remains in effect until it is vacated or varied.

I also understand that failure without lawful excuse to abide by any of the conditions specified above is an offence under subsection 145(5.1) of the *Criminal Code*.

Subsection 145(5.1) of the *Criminal Code* states as follows:

"(5.1) Every person who, without lawful excuse, fails to comply with any condition of an undertaking entered into under subsection 499(2) or 503(2.1)

(a) is guilty of an indictable offence and is liable to imprisonment for a term not exceeding two years; or

(b) is guilty of an offence punishable on summary conviction."

Dated this .... day of .... A.D. ...., at ....

....

(Signature of accused)

1997, c. 18, s. 115; 1999, c. 25, s. 24; 2018, c. 29, s. 71

Form 12 — Undertaking Given to a Justice or a Judge

(Sections 493 and 679)

Canada,

Province of ....,

(*territorial division*).

I, A.B., of ...., (*occupation*), understand that I have been charged that (*set out briefly the offence in respect of which accused is charged*).

In order that I may be released from custody, I undertake to attend court on .... day, the .... day of .... A.D. ...., and to attend after that as required by the court in order to be dealt with according to law (*or, where date and place of ap-*

pearance before court are not known at the time undertaking is given, to attend at the time and place fixed by the court and after that as required by the court in order to be dealt with according to law).

(*and, where applicable*)

I also undertake to (*insert any conditions that are directed*)

(a) report at (*state times*) to (*name of peace officer or other person designated*);

(b) remain within (*designated territorial jurisdiction*);

(c) notify (*name of peace officer or other person designated*) of any change in my address, employment or occupation;

(d) abstain from communicating, directly or indirectly, with (*identification of victim, witness or other person*) except in accordance with the following conditions: (*as the justice or judge specifies*);

(e) deposit my passport (*as the justice or judge directs*); and

(f) (*any other reasonable conditions*).

I understand that failure without lawful excuse to attend court in accordance with this undertaking is an offence under subsection 145(2) of the *Criminal Code*.

Subsections 145(2) and (3) of the *Criminal Code* state as follows:

"(2) Every person is guilty of an indictable offence and liable to imprisonment for a term of not more than two years or is guilty of an offence punishable on summary conviction who,

(a) being at large on their undertaking or recognizance given to or entered into before a justice or judge, fails, without lawful excuse, to attend court in accordance with the undertaking or recognizance, or

(b) having appeared before a court, justice or judge, fails, without lawful excuse, to attend court as subsequently required by the court, justice or judge or to surrender themselves in accordance with an order of the court, justice or judge, as the case may be.

(3) Every person who is at large on an undertaking or recognizance given to or entered into before a justice or judge and is bound to comply with a condition of that undertaking or recognizance, and every person who is bound to comply with a direction under subsection 515(12) or 522(2.1) or an order under subsection 516(2), and who fails, without lawful excuse, the proof of which lies on them, to comply with the condition, direction or order is guilty of

(a) an indictable offence and is liable to imprisonment for a term not exceeding two years; or

(b) an offence punishable on summary conviction."

Dated this .... day of .... A.D. ...., at ....

....
(*Signature of accused*)

Proposed Amendment — Form 12 of Part XXVIII

Form 12 — Surety Declaration [Heading amended 2019, c. 25, s. 337. To come into force December 18, 2019.]

(Section 515.1)

Canada,

Province of ....,

(*territorial division*).

1 Identification

Surname: .... Given name(s): ....

Date of Birth: ....

Home address: ....

Phone number(s): .... (*primary*) ....(*other*)

Other contact information (*if any*): ....

Employment or occupation (*if any*): ....

Name and contact information for employer (*if any*): ....

2 Information about the Accused

Surname: .... Given name(s): ....

Date of Birth: ....

Court file number: ....

3 Other information required

Relationship to the accused: ....

I am acting as a surety in respect of another accused.

❑ Yes ❑ No

If yes, name and date of birth of any other accused: ....

I have a criminal record or there are outstanding criminal charges against me.

❑ Yes ❑ No

If yes, description of criminal record, if any, and all outstanding criminal charges, specifying offence and year of conviction: ....

4 Charges against the Accused

I understand that the accused has been charged with (*set out briefly the offence in respect of which the accused was charged*).

5 Other Outstanding Charges against the Accused

❑ I understand that the accused does not have any other outstanding criminal charges.

❑ I understand that the accused has also been charged with (*set out briefly the offence in respect of which the accused was charged*), but this declaration does not apply to those charges.

6 Criminal Record of the Accused

❑ I understand that the accused does not have a criminal record.

❑ I understand that the accused has a criminal record, which is described below or a copy of which I have attached and initialled.

....

7 Financial Promise or Deposit

As a surety for the accused, I am willing to (*promise or deposit*) to the court the amount of ....

8 Acknowledgment

I understand that failure on the part of the accused to follow any of the conditions in their release order or recognizance could lead to the forfeiture of the amount of money that has been promised or deposited.

I understand that I may, at any time, ask to no longer be a surety by making an application, by bringing the accused to the court in order to be discharged from my obligation (section 767 of the *Criminal Code*) or by taking and giving the accused into custody (section 768 of the *Criminal Code*).

I voluntarily make this declaration and it is my free choice to take on the responsibilities of a surety.

9 Signature

Signed on (*date*), at (*place*).

.... (*Signature of the surety*)

Sworn before me on (*date*), at (*place*).

.... (*Signature of the person who is authorized to take or receive statements made under oath, solemn declaration or solemn affirmation*)

2019, c. 25, s. 337 [To come into force December 18, 2019.]

1999, c. 25, s. 25; 2008, c. 18, s. 45.1; 2018, c. 29, s. 72

Form 13 — Undertaking by Appellant (Defendant) [Repealed 2019, c. 25, s. 337. To come into force December 18, 2019.]

(Sections 816, 832 and 834)

Canada,

Province of ....,

(*territorial division*).

I, A.B., of ...., (*occupation*), being the appellant against conviction (*or* against sentence *or* against an order *or* by way of stated case) in respect of the following matter (*set out the offence, subject-matter of order or question of law*) undertake to appear personally at the sittings of the appeal court at which the appeal is to be heard.

(*and where applicable*)

I also undertake to (*insert any conditions that are directed*)

(a) report at (*state times*) to (*name of peace officer or other person designated*);

(b) remain within (*designated territorial jurisdiction*);

(c) notify (*name of peace officer or other person designated*) of any change in my address, employment or occupation;

(d) abstain from communicating, directly or indirectly, with (*identification of victim, witness or other person*) except in accordance with the following conditions: (*as the justice or judge specifies*);

(e) deposit my passport (*as the justice or judge directs*); and

(f) (*any other reasonable conditions*).

Dated this .... day of .... A.D ...., at ....

....

(*Signature of appellant*)

1999, c. 25, s. 26

Form 14 — Undertaking by Appellant (Prosecutor) [Repealed 2019, c. 25, s. 337. To come into force December 18, 2019.]

(Section 817)

Canada,

Province of ....

(*territorial division*).

I, A.B., of ...., (*occupation*), being the appellant against an order of dismissal (*or* against sentence) in respect of the following charge (*set out the name of the defendant and the offence, subject-matter of order or question of law*) undertake to appear personally or by counsel at the sittings of the appeal court at which the appeal is to be heard.

Dated this .... day of .... A.D ...., at ....

....

(*Signature of appellant*)

Form 15 — Warrant to Convey Accused Before Justice of Another Territorial Division

(Section 543)

Canada,

Province of ....,

(*territorial division*).

To the peace officers in the said (*territorial division*):

Whereas A.B., of .... hereinafter called the accused, has been charged that (*state place of offence and charge*);

And whereas the deposition of X.Y. in respect of the charge has been taken by me (*or if the signatory is not the justice*, the justice);

And Whereas the charge is for an offence committted in the (*territorial division*);

This is to command you, in Her Majesty's name, to convey the said A.B., before a justice of the (*last mentioned territorial division*).

Dated (*date*).........., at ....(*place*).

(*Signature of justice or clerk of the court*)

....

2019, c. 25, s. 338

Form 16 — Subpoena to a Witness

(Section 699)

Canada,

Province of ....,
(*territorial division*).

To E.F., of ...., (*occupation*);

Whereas A.B. has been charged that (*state offence as in the information*), and it has been made to appear that you are likely to give material evidence for (the prosecution *or* the defence);

This is therefore to command you to attend before (*set out court or justice*), on .... the .... day of .... A.D. ...., at.......... o'clock in the .... noon at .... to give evidence concerning the said charge.[8]

Dated this .... day of .... A.D. ...., at ....

. . . .
A Judge, Justice *or* Clerk of the court

(*Seal if required*) . . . .

1999, c. 5, s. 47

---

8 *Where a witness is required to produce anything, add the following:*

and to bring with you anything in your possession or under your control that relates to the said charge, and more particularly the following: (*specify any documents, objects or other things required*).

Form 16.1 — Subpoena to a witness in the case of proceedings in respect of an offence referred to in s. 278.2(1) of the *Criminal Code*

(Subsections 278.3(5) and 699(7))

Canada,

Province of ....,
(*territorial division*).

To E.F., of ...., (*occupation*);

Whereas A.B. has been charged that (*state offence as in the information*), and it has been made to appear that you are likely to give material evidence for (the prosecution *or* the defence);

This is therefore to command you to attend before (*set out court or justice*), on .... the .... day of .... A.D. ...., at.......... o'clock in the .... noon at .... to give evidence concerning the said charge, and to bring with you anything in your possession or under your control that relates to the said charge, and more particularly the following: (*specify any documents, objects or other things required*).

TAKE NOTE

You are only required to bring the things specified above to the court on the date and at the time indicated, and you are not required to provide the things specified to any person or to discuss their contents with any person unless and until ordered by the court to do so.

If anything specified above is a "record" as defined in section 278.1 of the *Criminal Code*, it may be subject to a determination by the court in accordance with sections 278.1 to 278.91 of the *Criminal Code* as to whether and to what extent it should be produced.

If anything specified above is a "record" as defined in section 278.1 of the *Criminal Code*, the production of which is governed by sections 278.1 to 278.91 of the *Criminal Code*, this subpoena must be accompanied by a copy of an application for the production of the record made pursuant to section 278.3 of the *Criminal Code*, and you will have an opportunity to make submissions to the court concerning the production of the record.

If anything specified above is a "record" as defined in section 278.1 of the *Criminal Code*, the production of which is governed by sections 278.1 to 278.91 of the *Criminal Code*, you are not required to bring it with you until a determination is made in accordance with those sections as to whether and to what extent it should be produced.

As defined in section 278.1 of the *Criminal Code*, "record" means any form of record that contains personal information for which there is a reasonable expectation of privacy and includes, without limiting the generality of the foregoing, medical, psychiatric, therapeutic, counselling, education, employment, child welfare, adoption and social services records, personal journals and diaries, and records containing personal information the production or disclosure of which is protected by any other Act of Parliament or a provincial legislature, but does not include records made by persons responsible for the investigation or prosecution of the offence.

Dated this .... day of .... A.D. ...., at ....

. . . .
Judge, Clerk of the Court
Provincial Court Judge *or* Justice

(Seal if required) . . . .

1997, c. 30, s. 3

Form 17 — Warrant for Witness

(Sections 698 and 705)

Canada,

Province of ....,
(*territorial division*).

To the peace officers in the (*territorial division*):

Whereas A.B. of ...., has been charged that (*state offence as in the information*);

And Whereas it has been made to appear that E.F. of .... hereinafter called the witness, is likely to give material evidence for (the prosecution *or* the defence) and that[9]

This is therefore to command you, in Her Majesty's name, to arrest and bring the witness forthwith before (*set out court or justice*) to be dealt with in accordance with section 706 of the *Criminal Code*.

Dated this .... day of .... A.D. ...., at ....

. . . .
A Justice *or* Clerk of the Court

(Seal, if required)

9 *Insert whichever of the following is appropriate*:

(a) the said E.F. will not attend unless compelled to do so;

(b) the said E.F. is evading service of a subpoena;

(c) the said E.F. was duly served with a subpoena and has neglected (to attend at the time and place appointed therein *or* to remain in attendance);

(d) the said E.F. was bound by a recognizance to attend and give evidence and has neglected (to attend *or* to remain in attendance).

Form 18 — Warrant to Arrest an Absconding Witness

(Section 704)

Canada,

Province of ....,

(*territorial division*).

To the peace officers in the (*territorial division*):

Whereas A.B., of .... has been charged that (*state offence as in the information*);

And whereas I am (*or if the signatory is not the justice*, the justice is) satisfied by information in writing and under oath that C.D., of ...., in this warrant called the witness, is bound by recognizance to give evidence on the trial of the accused on the charge, and that the witness (has absconded or is about to abscond);

This is therefore to command you, in Her Majesty's name, to arrest the witness and bring him forthwith before (*the court, judge, justice or provincial court judge before whom the witness is bound to appear*) to be dealt with in accordance with section 706 of the *Criminal Code*.

Dated (*date*).........., at ....(*place*).

(*Signature of justice or clerk of the court*)

....

R.S.C. 1985, c. 27 (1st Supp.), s. 184(9); 2019, c. 25, s. 339

Form 19 — Warrant Remanding a Prisoner

(Sections 516 and 537)

Canada,

Province of ....,

(*territorial division*).

To the peace officers in the (*territorial division*):

You are hereby commanded forthwith to arrest, if necessary, and convey to the (*prison*) at .... the persons named in the following schedule each of whom has been remanded to the time mentioned in the schedule:

Person charged	Offence	Remanded to

And you, the keeper of the prison, are directed to receive each of the persons into your custody in the prison and keep each person safely until the day when that person's remand expires and then to have that person before me or any other justice (*or if the signatory is not the justice*, before any justice) on ....(*date*),.......... at ....(*hour*), at ....(*place*), there to answer to the charge and to be dealt with according to law, unless you are otherwise directed before that time.

Dated (*date*).........., at ....(*place*).

(*Signature of justice or clerk of the court*)

....

R.S.C. 1985, c. 27 (1st Supp.), s. 184(9); 2019, c. 25, s. 340

Form 20 — Warrant of Committal of Witness for Refusing to Be Sworn or to Give Evidence

(Section 545)

Canada,
Province of ....,
(*territorial division*).

To the peace officers in the (*territorial division*):

Whereas A.B. of ...., in this warrant called the accused, has been charged that (*set out offence as in the information*);

And whereas E.F. of ...., in this warrant called the witness, attending before me (*or if the signatory is not the justice*, before the justice) to give evidence for (the prosecution or the defence) concerning the charge against the accused (refused to be sworn or being duly sworn as a witness refused to answer certain questions concerning the charge that were put to them or refused or failed to produce the following writings, namely .... or refused to sign their deposition) having been ordered to do so, without offering any just excuse for that refusal or failure;

This is therefore to direct you, in Her Majesty's name, to arrest, if necessary, and take the witness and convey them safely to the prison at ...., and there deliver them to the keeper of it, together with the following precept:

You, the keeper, are directed to receive the witness into your custody in the prison and safely keep them there for the term of .... days, unless they sooner consent to do what was required of them, and for so doing this is a sufficient warrant.

Dated (*date*).........., at .... (*place*).

(*Signature of justice or clerk of the court*)

....

R.S.C. 1985, c. 27 (1st Supp.), s. 184(19); 2019, c. 25, s. 341

Form 21 — Warrant of Committal on Conviction

(Sections 570 and 806)

Canada,
Province of ....,
(*territorial division*).

To the peace officers in (*territorial division*) and to the keeper of (*prison*) at ....:

Whereas (*name*), in this Form called the offender, was, on the .... day of .... 20.........., convicted by (*name of judge and court*) of having committed the following offence(s) and it was adjudged that the offender be sentenced as follows:

Offence (*state offence of which offender was convicted*)	Sentence (*state term of imprisonment for the offence and, in case of imprisonment for default of payment of fine, so indicate together with the amount of it and applicable costs and whether payable immediately or within a time fixed*)	Remarks (*state the amount of time spent in custody before sentencing, the term of imprisonment that would have been imposed before any credit was granted under subsection 719(3) or (3.1), the amount of time credited, if any, and whether the sentence is consecutive or concurrent, and specify consecutive to or concurrent with what other sentence*)
1.	....	....
2.	....	....
3.	....	....
4.	....	....

You are hereby commanded, in Her Majesty's name, to arrest the offender if it is necessary to do so in order to take the offender into custody, and to take and convey him or her safely to (*prison*) at .... and deliver him or her to its keeper, who is hereby commanded to receive the accused into custody and to imprison him or her there for the term(s) of his or her imprisonment, unless, if a term of imprisonment was imposed only in default of payment of a fine or costs, those amounts and the costs and charges of the committal and of conveying the offender to that prison are paid sooner, and this is a sufficient warrant for so doing.

Dated this .... day of .... 20.........., at ....

.... Clerk of the Court, Justice, Judge *or* Provincial Court Judge

R.S.C. 1985, c. 27 (1st Supp.), s. 184(10); 1995, c. 22, s. 9; 2009, c. 29, s. 4

Form 22 — Warrant of Committal on an Order for the Payment of Money

(Section 806)

Canada,

Province of ....,
(*territorial division*).

To the peace officers in the (*territorial division*) and to the keeper of the (*prison*) at ....:

Whereas A.B., hereinafter called the defendant, was tried on an information alleging that (*set out matter of complaint*), and it was ordered that (*set out the order made*), and in default that the defendant be imprisoned in the (*prison*) at .... for a term of..........;

You are directed, in Her Majesty's name, to arrest, if necessary, and take the defendant and convey them safely to the (*prison*) at ...., and deliver them to the keeper of the prison, together with the following precept:

You, the keeper of the prison, are directed to receive the defendant into your custody in this prison and keep them safely there for the term of ...., unless the amounts and the costs and charges of the committal and of conveying the defendant to the prison are sooner paid, and for so doing this is a sufficient warrant.

Dated (*date*).........., at ....(*place*).

(*Signature of provincial court judge, justice or clerk of the court*)

....

R.S.C. 1985, c. 27 (1st Supp.), s. 184(19); 2019, c. 25, s. 342

Form 23 — Warrant of Committal for Failure to Furnish Recognizance to Keep the Peace

(Sections 810 and 810.1)

Canada,

Province of ....,

(*territorial division*).

To the peace officers in the (*territorial division*) and to the keeper of the (*prison*) at ....:

Whereas A.B., hereinafter called the accused, has been ordered to enter into a recognizance to keep the peace and be of good behaviour, and has (refused *or* failed) to enter into a recognizance accordingly;

You are hereby commanded, in Her Majesty's name, to arrest, if necessary, and take the accused and convey him safely to the (*prison*) at.......... and deliver him to the keeper thereof, together with the following precept:

You, the said keeper, are hereby commanded to receive the accused into your custody in the said prison and imprison him there until he enters into a recognizance as aforesaid or until he is discharged in due course of law.

Dated this .... day of .... A.D. ...., at ....

. . . .

Clerk of the Court, Justice
or Provincial Court Judge

(*Seal, if required*)

R.S.C. 1985, c. 27 (1st Supp.), ss. 184(19), 206; 1993, c. 45, s. 12

Form 24 — Warrant of Committal of Witness for Failure to Enter into Recognizance

(Section 550)

Canada,
Province of ....,
(*territorial division*).

To the peace officers in the (*territorial division*) and to the keeper of the (prison) at ....:

Whereas A.B., in this warrant called the accused, was committed for trial on a charge that (*state offence as in the information*);

And whereas E.F., in this warrant called the witness, having appeared as a witness on the preliminary inquiry into the charge, and being required to enter into a recognizance to appear as a witness on the trial of the accused on the charge, has (failed or refused) to do so;

This is therefore to direct you, in Her Majesty's name, to arrest, if necessary, and take and safely convey the witness to the (*prison*) at .... and there deliver them to the keeper of it, together with the following precept:

You, the keeper, are directed to receive the witness into your custody in the prison and keep them there safely until the trial of the accused on the charge, unless before that time the witness enters into the recognizance.

Dated (*date*).........., at ....(*place*).

(*Signature of justice or clerk of the court*)

....

R.S.C. 1985, c. 27 (1st Supp.), s. 184(19); 2019, c. 25, s. 343

Form 25 — Warrant of Committal for Contempt

(Section 708)

Canada,

Province of ....,

(*territorial division*).

To the peace officers in the (*territorial division*) and to the keeper of the (*prison*) at (*place*)..........:

Because E.F. of ...., in this warrant called the defaulter, was on (*date*).........., at .... (*place*), convicted before .... for contempt because the defaulter did not attend before .... to give evidence on the trial of a charge that (*state offence as in the information*) against A.B. of ...., although (duly subpoenaed or bound by recognizance to appear and give evidence in that regard, *as the case may be*) and did not show any sufficient excuse for the default;

And because, following the conviction it was ordered that the defaulter (*set out the punishment imposed*);

And because the defaulter has not paid the amounts ordered to be paid; (*delete if not applicable*)

Therefore, you are ordered, in Her Majesty's name, to arrest, if necessary, and take the defaulter and convey them safely to the prison at .... and there deliver them to its keeper, together with the following order:

You, the keeper, are ordered to receive the defaulter into your custody in this prison and keep them safely there[10] and for so doing this is a sufficient warrant.

(a) for the term of ....;

(b) for the term of ...., unless the sums and the costs and charges of the committal and of conveying the defaulter to the prison are sooner paid;

(c) for the term of .... and for the term of (*if consecutive so state*) unless the sums and the costs and charges of the committal and of conveying the defaulter to the prison are sooner paid.

Dated (*date*).........., at ....(*place*).

(*Signature of judge, provincial court judge, justice or clerk of the court*)

(*Seal, if required*)

2019, c. 25, s. 344

Form 26 — Warrant of Committal in Default of Payment of Costs of an Appeal

(Section 827)

Canada,

Province of ....,
(*territorial division*).

To the peace officers of (*territorial division*) and to the keeper of the (*prison*) at ....:

Whereas it appears that on the hearing of an appeal before the (*set out court*), it was adjudged that A.B., of ...., hereinafter called the defaulter, should pay to the Clerk of the Court the sum of .... dollars in respect of costs;

And Whereas the Clerk of the Court has certified that the defaulter has not paid the sum within the time limited therefor;

I do hereby command you, the said peace officers, in Her Majesty's name, to take the defaulter and safely convey him to the (*prison*) at.......... and deliver him to the keeper thereof, together with the following precept:

I do hereby command you, the said keeper, to receive the defaulter into your custody in the said prison and imprison him for the term of ...., unless the said sum and the costs and charges of the committal and of conveying the defaulter to the said prison are sooner paid, and for so doing this is a sufficient warrant.

---

10 *Insert whichever of the following is applicable*:

Dated this .... day of .... A.D. ...., at ....

. . . .

A Justice of the Peace in and for

. . . .

Form 27 — Warrant of Committal on Forfeiture of a Recognizance

(Section 773)

Canada,

Province of ....,

(*territorial division*).

To the sheriff of (*territorial division*) and to the keeper of the (*prison*) at ....:

You are hereby commanded to arrest, if necessary, and take (A.B. and C.D. *as the case may be*) hereinafter called the defaulters, and to convey them safely to the (*prison*) at .... and deliver them to the keeper thereof, together with the following precept:

You, the keeper, are ordered to receive the defaulters into your custody in this prison and keep them safely there for a period of .... or until satisfaction is made of a judgment debt of .... dollars due to Her Majesty the Queen in respect of the forfeiture of a recognizance entered into by .... on (*date*)..........

Dated (*date*).........., at ....(*place*).

(*Signature of judge of the court or clerk of the court*)

(*Seal, if required*)

Proposed Amendment — Form 27 of Part XXVIII

Form 27 — Warrant of Committal on Forfeiture of Amounts [Heading amended 2019, c. 25, s. 345(2). To come into force December 18, 2019.]

(Section 773)

Canada,

Province of ....,

(*territorial division*).

To the sheriff of (*territorial division*) and to the keeper of the (*prison*) at (*place*).

This warrant of committal is issued for the arrest of (*name of person or persons*), referred to in this warrant as the defaulter or defaulters, as the case may be.

You are ordered to arrest the defaulter or defaulters and convey them safely to the (*prison*) at ...., and deliver them to its keeper, with the following order:

You, the keeper, are ordered to receive the defaulter or defaulters into your custody in this prison and keep them safely there for a period of .... or until satisfaction is made of a judgment debt of ...., due to Her Majesty the Queen in respect of the forfeiture of an amount set out in (an undertaking entered into *or* a release order issued *or* a recognizance entered into) on (*date*).

Dated (*date*), at (*place*).

.... (*Signature of judge of the court or clerk of the court*).

.... (*Name of judge who has issued this warrant of committal*)

(*Seal, if required*)

2019, c. 25, s. 345(2) [To come into force December 18, 2019.]

2019, c. 25, s. 345(1)

Form 28 — Endorsement of Warrant

(Section 528)

Canada,

Province of ....,

(*territorial division*).

In accordance with the application this day made to me, I authorize the arrest of the accused (or defendant), within the (*territorial division*).

Dated (*date*).........., at .... (*place*).

.... (*Signature of justice*)

R.S.C. 1985, c. 27 (1st Supp.), s. 184(12); 2019, c. 25, s. 346

Form 28.1 [Repealed 2007, c. 22, s. 26.]

Form 29 — Endorsement of Warrant

(Section 507)

Canada,

Province of ....,

(*territorial division*).

Whereas this warrant is issued under section 507, 508 or 512 of the *Criminal Code* in respect of an offence other than an offence mentioned in section 522 of the *Criminal Code*, I hereby authorize the release of the accused pursuant to section 499 of that Act.

Dated this .... day of .... A.D. ...., at ....

. . . .
A Justice of the Peace in and for
. . . .

Form 30 — Order for Accused to Be Brought Before Justice Prior to Expiration of Period of Remand

(Section 537)

Canada,

Province of ....,

(*territorial division*).

To the keeper of the (*prison*) at ....:

Whereas by warrant dated (*date*), A.B., in this order called the accused, was committed to your custody and you were required to keep them safely until the (*date*).................................., and then to have them before me or any other justice (*or if the signatory is not the justice*, any justice) at (*place*).......... at .... (*hour*) to answer to the charge against the accused and to be dealt with according to law unless you should be ordered otherwise before that time;

Now, therefore, you are directed to have the accused before .... at (*place*).......... at .... (*hour*) to answer to the charge against them and so they may be dealt with according to law.

Dated (*date*).........., at .... (*place*).

(*Signature of justice or clerk of the court*)

....

2019, c. 25, s. 347

Form 31 — Deposition of a Witness

(Section 540)

Canada,

Province of ....,

(*territorial division*).

These are the depositions of X.Y., of ...., and M.N., of ...., taken before me, this .... day of .... A.D., ... at.........., in the presence and hearing of A.B., hereinafter called the accused, who stands charged (*state offence as in the information*).

X.Y., having been duly sworn, deposes as follows: (*insert deposition as nearly as possible in words of witness*).

M.N., having been duly sworn, deposes as follows:

I certify that the depositions of X.Y., and M.N., written on the several sheets of paper hereto annexed to which my signature is affixed, were taken in the presence and hearing of the accused (and signed by them respectively, in is presence, *where they are required to be signed by witness*). In witness whereof I have hereto signed my name.

....

A Justice of the Peace in and for

....

Form 32 — Recognizance

(Sections 493, 550, 679, 706, 707, 810, 810.1 and 817)

Canada,

Province of ....,

(*territorial division*).

Be it remembered that on this day the persons named in the following schedule personally came before me (*or if the signatory is the clerk of the court*, before the judge, provincial court judge or justice, *as the case may be*) and severally acknowledged themselves to owe to Her Majesty the Queen the several amounts set opposite their respective names, namely,

Name	Address	Occupation	Amount
A.B.			
C.D.			
E.F.			

to be made and levied of their several goods and chattels, lands and tenements, respectively, to the use of Her Majesty the Queen, if A.B. fails in any of the conditions set out below.

Taken and acknowledged before me (*or if the signatory is the clerk of the court*, the judge, provincial court judge *or* justice, *as the case may be*) on (*date*).........., at ....(*place*).

Dated (*date*).........., at ....(*place*).

(*Signature of judge, provincial court judge, justice or clerk of the court*)

....

1. Whereas the said ...., hereinafter called the accused, has been charged that (*set out the offence in respect of which the accused has been charged*);

Now, therefore, the condition of this recognizance is that if the accused attends court on .... day, the .... day of .... A.D..........., at .... o'clock in the

.... noon and attends thereafter as required by the court in order to be dealt with according to law (*or, where date and place of appearance before court are not known at the time recognizance is entered into* if the accused attends at the time and place fixed by the court and attends thereafter as required by the court in order to be dealt with according to law) [515, 520, 521, 522, 523, 524, 525, 680];

And further, if the accused (*insert in Schedule of Conditions any additional conditions that are directed*), the said recognizance is void, otherwise it stands in full force and effect.

2. Whereas the said ...., hereinafter called the appellant, is an appellant against his conviction (*or* against his sentence) in respect of the following charge (*set out the offence for which the appellant was convicted*) [679, 680];

Now, therefore, the condition of this recognizance is that if the appellant attends as required by the court in order to be dealt with according to law;

And further, if the appellant (*insert in Schedule of Conditions any additional conditions that are directed*), the said recognizance is void, otherwise it stands in full force and effect.

3. Whereas the said ...., hereinafter called the appellant, is an appellant against his conviction (*or* against his sentence *or* against an order *or* by way of stated case) in respect of the following matter (*set out offence, subject-matter of order or question of law*) [816, 831, 832, 834];

Now, therefore, the condition of this recognizance is that if the appellant appears personally at the sittings of the appeal court at which the appeal is to be heard;

And further, if the appellant (*insert in Schedule of Conditions any additional conditions that are directed*), the said recognizance is void, otherwise it stands in full force and effect.

4. Whereas the said ...., hereinafter called the appellant, is an appellant against an order of dismissal (*or* against sentence) in respect of the following charge (*set out the name of the accused and the offence, subject-matter of order or question of law*) [817, 831, 832, 834];

Now, therefore, the condition of this recognizance is that if the appellant appears personally or by counsel at the sittings of the appeal court at which the appeal is to be heard the said recognizance is void, otherwise it stands in full force and effect.

5. Whereas the said ...., hereinafter called the accused, was ordered to stand trial on a charge that (*set out the offence in respect of which the accused has been charged*);

And whereas A.B. appeared as a witness on the preliminary inquiry into the said charge [550, 706, 707];

Now, therefore, the condition of this recognizance is that if the said A.B. appears at the time and place fixed for the trial of the accused to give evidence on the indictment that is found against the accused, the said recognizance is void, otherwise it stands in full force and effect.

6. The condition of the above written recognizance is that if A.B. keeps the peace and is of good behaviour for the term of .... commencing on.........., the said recognizance is void, otherwise it stands in full force and effect [810 and 810.1].

7. Whereas a warrant was issued under section 462.32 or a restraint order was made under subsection 462.33(3) of the *Criminal Code* in relation to any property (*set out a description of the property and its location*);

Now, therefore, the condition of this recognizance is that A.B. shall not do or cause anything to be done that would result, directly or indirectly, in the disappearance, dissipaton or reduction in value of the property or otherwise affect the property so that all or a part thereof could not be subject to an order of forfeiture under section 462.37 or 462.38 of the *Criminal Code* or any other provision of the *Criminal Code* or any other Act of Parliament [462.34].

Schedule of Conditions

(a) reports at (*state times*) to (*name of peace officer or other person designated*),

(b) remains within (*designated territorial jurisdiction*),

(c) notifies (*name of peace officer or other person designated*) of any change in his address, employment or occupation,

(d) abstains from communicating, directly or indirectly, with (*identification of victim, witness or other person*) except in accordance with the following conditions: (*as the judge, provincial court judge or justice specifies*);

(e) deposits their passport (*as the judge, provincial court judge or justice directs*); and

(f) (*any other reasonable conditions*).

Note: Section 763 and subsections 764(1) to (3) of the Criminal Code state as follows:

"763. Where a person is bound by recognizance to appear before a court, justice or provincial court judge for any purpose and the session or sittings of that court or the proceedings are adjourned or an order is made changing the place of trial, that person and his sureties continue to be bound by the recognizance in like manner as if it had been entered into with relation to the resumed proceedings or the trial at the time and place at which the proceedings are ordered to be resumed or the trial is ordered to be held.

764. (1) Where an accused is bound by recognizance to appear for trial, his arraignment or conviction does not discharge the recognizance, but it continues to bind him and his sureties, if any, for his appearance until he is discharged or sentenced, as the case may be.

(2) Notwithstanding subsection (1), the court, justice or provincial court judge may commit an accused to prison or may require him to furnish new or additional sureties for his appearance until he is discharged or sentenced, as the case may be.

(3) The sureties of an accused who is bound by recognizance to appear for trial are discharged if he is committed to prison pursuant to subsection (2)."

Proposed Amendment — Form 32 of Part XXVIII

Form 32 — Recognizance

(Sections 2, 462.34, 490.9, 550, 683, 706, 707, 779, 810, 810.01, 810.1, 810.2, 817 and 832)

Canada,

Province of ....

(*territorial division*)

1 Identification

Surname: .... Given name(s): ....

Date of birth: ....

Home address: ....

Phone number(s): ....(*primary*).......... (*other*)

Other contact information (*if any*): ....

Employment or Occupation (*if any*): ....

Name and contact information of employer (*if any*): ....

2 Financial Promise or Deposit

Pursuant to .... (*provision*) of the *Criminal Code*, I agree to (*promise or deposit*) the amount of $ ...., or the other valuable security described here:..........

I understand that if I fail to comply with any of the conditions listed below, this amount or security may be forfeited.

3 Conditions

(*List the conditions that have been ordered by the court and indicate the duration for which each condition remains in effect.*)

....

4 Variation

I understand that I may apply to a judge or a justice of the peace to have any condition in this form cancelled or varied.

5 Conditions in effect

I understand that the conditions in this recognizance remain in effect until they are cancelled or changed or until I have been discharged, sentenced or otherwise detained by the court (sections 763 and 764 of the *Criminal Code*).

6 Signatures

PERSON WHO IS GIVING RECOGNIZANCE:

I understand the contents of this form and agree to comply with the conditions that are listed above.

Signed on .... (*date*), at ....(*place*).

.... (*Signature of the person*)

.... (*Print name*)

SURETY (*if applicable*):

I understand my role and my responsibilities under this recognizance and I agree to act as a surety.

I agree to (*promise or deposit*) as security to the court the amount of $..........

I understand that if the person who is giving this recognizance fails to comply with any of the conditions in this recognizance, the money that I have promised or deposited may be forfeited.

Surety Declaration (*if applicable*)

❑ Surety Declaration attached. (Section 515.1 of the *Criminal Code*.)

❑ Surety excepted from providing Surety Declaration. (Subsection 515.1(2) of the *Criminal Code*.)

Signed on .... (*date*), at ....(*place*).

.... (*Signature of the Surety*)

.... (*Print name*)

JUDGE, PROVINCIAL COURT JUDGE, JUSTICE OR CLERK OF THE COURT:

Signed on .... (*date*), at ....(*place*).

.... (*Signature of the judge, provincial court judge, justice or clerk of the court*)

.... (*Print name*)

List of Conditions

(a) has a surety (sections 462.34, 490.9, 550, 779, 810, 817 and 832 of the *Criminal Code*);

(b) agrees to keep the peace and be of good behaviour (sections 83.3, 810, 810.01, 810.1 and 810.2 of the *Criminal Code*);

(c) abstains from possessing a firearm, crossbow, prohibited weapon, restricted weapon, prohibited device, ammunition, prohibited ammunition or explosive substance and surrenders those in their possession and surrenders any authorization, licence or registration certificate or other document enabling the acquisition or possession of a firearm (sections 83.3, 810, 810.01, 810.1 and 810.2 of the *Criminal Code*);

(d) participates in a treatment program (sections 810.01, 810.1 and 810.2 of the *Criminal Code*);

(e) wears an electronic monitoring device (*if the Attorney General makes the request*) (sections 810.01, 810.1 and 810.2 of the *Criminal Code*);

(f) remains within a specified geographic area unless written permission to leave that area is obtained from the judge (sections 810.01 and 810.2 of the *Criminal Code*);

(g) returns to and remains at their place of residence at specified times (sections 810.01, 810.1 and 810.2 of the *Criminal Code*);

(h) abstains from the consumption of drugs, except in accordance with a medical prescription (sections 810.01, 810.1 and 810.2 of the *Criminal Code*);

(i) abstains from the consumption of alcohol or of any other intoxicating substance, except in accordance with a medical prescription (sections 810.01, 810.1 and 810.2 of the *Criminal Code*);

(j) abstains from any contact — including communicating by any means — with a person under the age of 16 years, unless doing so under the supervision of a person whom the judge considers appropriate (section 810.1 of the *Criminal Code*);

(k) abstains from using the Internet or other digital network, unless doing so in accordance with conditions set by the judge (section 810.1 of the *Criminal Code*);

(l) abstains from attending a public park or public swimming area where persons under the age of 16 years are present or can reasonably be expected to be present, or a daycare centre, schoolground or playground (section 810.1 of the *Criminal Code*);

(m) appears personally or by counsel at the sittings of the appeal court at which the appeal is to be heard (sections 817 and 832 of the *Criminal Code*);

(n) appears in court as required (sections 550, 706 and 707 of the *Criminal Code*);

(o) in the case where a warrant was issued under section 462.32 of the *Criminal Code* or a restraint order was made under subsection 462.33(3) of that Act in relation to any property (*set out a description of the property and its location*), refrains from doing or causing anything to be done that would result, directly or indirectly, in the disappearance, dissipation or reduction in value of the property or otherwise affect the property so that all or a part thereof could not be subject to an order of forfeiture under section 462.37 or 462.38 of that Act or any other provision of that Act or any other Act of Parliament (section 462.34 of the *Criminal Code*);

(p) agrees to prosecute the writ of *certiorari* at their own expense, without wilful delay, and, if ordered, to pay to the person in whose favour the conviction, order or other proceeding is affirmed their full costs and charges to be taxed according to the practice of the court where the conviction, order or proceeding is affirmed (section 779 of the *Criminal Code*);

(q) any other reasonable conditions, including:

- reports at specified times to peace officer or other person designated;
- remains within designated territorial jurisdiction;
- notifies peace officer or other person designated of any change in their address, employment or occupation;
- abstains from communicating, directly or indirectly, with victim, witness or other specified person except in accordance with conditions specified by judge, provincial court judge or justice; and
- deposits all their passports as the judge, provincial court judge or justice directs.

2019, c. 25, s. 348(3) [To come into force December 18, 2019.]

R.S.C. 1985, c. 27 (1st Supp.), ss. 101(2), 184(13), 203; R.S.C. 1985, c. 42 (4th Supp.), s. 7; 1993, c. 45, ss. 13, 14; 1999, c. 25, s. 27; 2019, c. 25, s. 348(1), (2)

Form 33 — Certificate of Default to be Endorsed on Recognizance

(Section 770)

It is certified that A.B. (has not appeared as required by this recognizance or has not complied with a condition of this recognizance) and that, as a result, the ends of justice have been (defeated or delayed, *as the case may be*).

The nature of the default is .... and the reason for the default is.......... (*state reason if known*).

The names and addresses of the principal and sureties are as follows:

Dated (*date*).........., at ....(*place*).

(*Signature of judge, provincial court judge, justice, clerk of the court, peace officer or other person*)

(*Seal, if required*)

Proposed Amendment — Form 33 of Part XXVIII

Form 33 — Certificate of Default to Be Endorsed

(Section 770)

It is certified that A.B. (has not appeared as required by this undertaking, release order or recognizance *or* has not complied with a condition of this undertaking, release order or recognizance) and that for this reason the ends of justice have been (defeated *or* delayed, *as the case may be*).

The nature of the default is .... and the reason for the default is .... (*state reason if known*).

The names and addresses of the principal and sureties are as follows:

Dated (*date*).........., at .... (*place*).

....

(*Signature of judge, provincial court judge, justice, clerk of the court, peace officer or other person*)

(*Seal, if required*)

2019, c. 25, s. 349(3) [To come into force December 18, 2019.]

2019, c. 25, s. 349(1), (2)

Form 34 — Writ of Fieri Facias

(Section 771)

Elizabeth II by the Grace of God, etc.

To the sheriff of (*territorial division*), *Greeting*.

You are hereby commanded to levy of the goods and chattels, lands and tenements of each of the following persons the amount set opposite the name of each:

Name	Address	Occupation	Amount

And you are further commanded to make a return of what you have done in execution of this writ.

Dated this .... day of .... A.D. ...., at ....

. . . .
Clerk of the . . . .

(Seal)

Form 34.1 — Statement on Restitution [Heading amended 2015, c. 13, s. 35.]

(Subsection 737.1(4))

Canada,

Province of ....,

(*territorial division*).

To the court that is sentencing (*name the offender*) who was convicted, or was discharged under section 730 of the *Criminal Code*, of an offence under that Act.

I, (*name of declarant*), declare that (*check the appropriate box*):

[ ] (i) I am not seeking restitution for the losses and damages I suffered as the result of the commission of the offence.

[ ] (ii) I am seeking restitution in the amount of $.................................. for the following losses and damages I suffered as the result of the commission of the offence.

I declare that I have suffered the following losses and damages as the result of the commission of the offence:

(*Complete the following table if seeking restitution.*)

Description (*describe each loss and damage*)	Amount of loss and damage (*state the amount of each loss and damage*)
1.	....
2.	....
3.	....
4.	....

I understand that the amount of my losses and damages must be readily ascertainable by the court. For that purpose, I am responsible for providing the court with all necessary documents, including bills, receipts and estimates, in support of my claim for restitution.

Dated this .... day of .... 20................................, at ....

Signature of declarant

2011, c. 6, s. 5; 2015, c. 13, s. 35

Form 34.2 — Victim Impact Statement

(Subsection 722(4))

This form may be used to provide a description of the physical or emotional harm, property damage or economic loss suffered by you as the result of the commission of an offence, as well as a description of the impact of the offence on you. You may attach additional pages if you need more space.

Your statement must not include

- any statement about the offence or the offender that is not relevant to the harm or loss you suffered;
- any unproven allegations;
- any comments about any offence for which the offender was not convicted;
- any complaint about any individual, other than the offender, who was involved in the investigation or prosecution of the offence; or
- except with the court's approval, an opinion or recommendation about the sentence.

You may present a detailed account of the impact the offence has had on your life. The following sections are examples of information you may wish to include in your statement. You are not required to include all of this information.

Emotional impact

Describe how the offence has affected you emotionally. For example, think of

- your lifestyle and activities;
- your relationships with others such as your spouse, family and friends;
- your ability to work, attend school or study; and
- your feelings, emotions and reactions as they relate to the offence.

....

....

....

....

Physical impact

Describe how the offence has affected you physically. For example, think of

- ongoing physical pain, discomfort, illness, scarring, disfigurement or physical limitation;
- hospitalization or surgery you have had because of the offence;

- treatment, physiotherapy or medication you have been prescribed;
- the need for any further treatment or the expectation that you will receive further treatment; and
- any permanent or long-term disability.

....

....

....

....

Economic impact

Describe how the offence has affected you financially. For example, think of

- the value of any property that was lost or damaged and the cost of repairs or replacement;
- any financial loss due to missed time from work;
- the cost of any medical expenses, therapy or counselling;
- any costs or losses that are not covered by insurance.

Please note that this is not an application for compensation or restitution.

....

....

....

....

Fears for security

Describe any fears you have for your security or that of your family and friends. For example, think of

- concerns with respect to contact with the offender; and
- concerns with respect to contact between the offender and members of your family or close friends.

....

....

....

....

Drawing, poem or letter

You may use this space to draw a picture or write a poem or letter if it will help you express the impact that the offence has had on you.

❑ I would like to present my statement in court.

To the best of my knowledge, the information contained in this statement is true.

Dated this .... day of .... 20................................, at ....

Signature of declarant

If you completed this statement on behalf of the victim, please indicate the reasons why you did so and the nature of your relationship with the victim.

....

....

Dated this .... day of .... 20................................, at ....

Signature of declarant

2015, c. 13, s. 35

Form 34.3 — Community Impact Statement

(Subsection 722.2(2))

This form may be used to provide a description of the harm or loss suffered by a community as the result of the commission of an offence, as well as a description of the impact of the offence on the community. You may attach additional pages if you need more space.

Your statement must not include

- any statement about the offence or the offender that is not relevant to the harm or loss suffered by the community;
- any unproven allegations;
- any comments about any offence for which the offender was not convicted;
- any complaint about any individual, other than the offender, who was involved in the investigation or prosecution of the offence; or
- except with the court's approval, an opinion or recommendation about the sentence.

Name of community on whose behalf the statement is made: ....

Explain how the statement reflects this community's views:

....

....

....

....

You may present a detailed account of the impact the offence has had on the community. The following sections are examples of information you may wish to include in your statement. You are not required to include all of this information.

Emotional impact

Describe how the offence has affected community members emotionally. For example, think of

- community members' lifestyles and activities;
- community members' relationships with others in the community and outside it;
- community members' ability to work, attend school or study;
- community members' feelings, emotions and reactions as they relate to the offence; and
- the community's sense of belonging to the region.

....

....

....

....

Physical impact

Describe how the offence has affected community members physically. For example, think of

- the ability of community members to access services; and
- changes in transportation and routes taken to and from school, work, shopping, etc.

....

....

....

....

Economic impact

Describe how the offence has affected the community financially. For example, think of

- any reduction in the number of visitors or tourists to the region;
- the value of any property that was lost or damaged and the cost of repairs or replacement; and
- any costs or losses that are not covered by insurance.

Please note that this is not an application for compensation or restitution.

....

....

....

....

Fears for security

Describe any fears that community members have for their security or that of their family and friends. For example, think of concerns with respect to contact with the offender.

Drawing, poem or letter

You may use this space to draw a picture or write a poem or letter if it will help you express the impact that the offence has had on the community.

❑ I would like to present this statement in court.

To the best of my knowledge, the information contained in this statement is true.

Dated this .... day of .... 20.................................., at ....

Signature of declarant

2015, c. 13, s. 35

Form 35 — Conviction

(Sections 570 and 806)

Canada,

Province of ....,
(*territorial division*).

Be it remembered that on the .... day of .... at ...., A.B., (*date of birth*) hereinafter called the accused, was tried under Part (XIX *or* XXVII) of the *Criminal Code* on the charge that (*state fully the offence of which accused was convicted*), was convicted of the said offence and the following punishment was imposed on him, namely,[11]

Dated this .... day of .... A.D. ...., at ....

. . . .

Clerk of the Court, Justice
or Provincial Court Judge

(Seal, if required)

---

[11] *Use whichever of the following forms of sentence is applicable*:

(a) That the said accused be imprisoned in the (*prison*) at .... for the term of ....;

(b) That the said accused forfeit and pay the sum of .... dollars to be applied according to law and also pay to .... the sum of.......... dollars in respect of costs and in default of payment of the said sums (forthwith *or within a time fixed, if any*) to be imprisoned in the (*prison*) at .... for the term of .... unless the said sums and costs and charges of the committal and of conveying the accused to the said prison are sooner paid;

(c) That the said accused be imprisoned in the (*prison*) at.......... for the term of .... and in addition forfeit and pay the sum of .... dollars to be applied according to law and also pay to .... the sum of .... dollars in respect of costs and in default of payment of the said sums (forthwith *or within a time fixed, if any*), to be imprisoned in the (*prison*) at .... for the term of .... (*if sentence to be consecutive, state accordingly*) unless the said sums and costs and charges of the committal and of conveying the accused to the said prison are sooner paid.

Form 36 — Order Against an Offender

(Sections 570 and 806)

Canada,

Province of ....,
(*territorial division*).

Be it remembered that on the .... day of .... A.D. ...., at ...., A.B., (*date of birth*) of ...., was tried on an information (*indictment*) alleging that (*set out matter of complaint or alleged offence*), and it was ordered and adjudged that (*set out the order made*).

Dated this .... day of .... A.D. ...., at ....

. . . .
Justice *or* Clerk of the Court

R.S.C. 1985, c. 27 (1st Supp.), s. 184(15)

Form 37 — Order Acquitting Accused

(Section 570)

Canada,

Province of ....,
(*territorial division*).

Be it remembered that on the .... day of .... A.D. ...., at ...., A.B., of ...., (*occupation*), (*date of birth*) was tried on the charge that (*state fully the offence of which the accused was acquitted*) and was found not guilty of the said offence.

Dated this .... day of .... A.D. ...., at ....

. . . .
Provincial Court Judge *or* Clerk of the Court

(Seal, if required)

R.S.C. 1985, c. 27 (1st Supp.), ss. 184(16), 203, 206

Form 38 — Conviction for Contempt

(Section 708)

Canada,

Province of ....,

(*territorial division*).

Be it remembered that on (*date*).........., at .... (*place*) in the (*territorial division*), E.F. of ...., in this conviction called the defaulter, is convicted for contempt in that they did not attend before (*set out court or justice*) to give evidence on the trial of a charge that (*state fully offence with which accused was charged*), although (duly subpoenaed or bound by recognizance to attend to give evidence, *as the case may be*) and has not shown any sufficient excuse for their default;

The defaulter is therefore convicted for their default, (*set out punishment as authorized and determined in accordance with section 708 of the* Criminal Code).

Dated (*date*).........., at .... (*place*).

(*Signature of judge, provincial court judge, justice or clerk of the court*)

(*Seal, if required*)

2019, c. 25, s. 350

Form 39 — Order for Discharge of a Person in Custody

(Sections 519 and 550)

Canada,

Province of ....,

(*territorial division*).

To the keeper of the (*prison*) at ....:

You are directed to release E.F., detained by you under a (warrant of committal or order) dated (*date*).........., if E.F. is detained by you for no other cause.

(*Signature of judge, justice or clerk of the court*)

(*Seal, if required*)

2019, c. 25, s. 351

Form 40 — Challenge to Array

(Section 629)

Canada,

Province of . . . .

(territorial division).

The Queen —

v. —

C.D.

The (prosecutor *or* accused) challenges the array of the panel on the ground that X.Y., (sheriff *or* deputy sheriff), who returned the panel, was guilty of (partiality *or* fraud *or* wilful misconduct) on returning it.

Dated this .... day of .... A.D. ...., at ....

. . . .

Counsel for (prosecutor *or* accused)

Form 41 — Challenge for Cause

(Section 639)

Canada,

Province of . . . .
(territorial division).

The Queen —
v. —
C.D.

The (prosecutor *or* accused) challenges G.H. on the ground that (*set out ground of challenge in accordance with s. 638(1) of the Criminal Code*).

. . . .
Counsel for (prosecutor *or* accused)

Form 42 — Certificate of Non-Payment of Costs of Appeal

(Section 827)

In the Court of ....

(*Style of Cause*)

I hereby certify that A.B. (the appellant *or* respondent, *as the case may be*) in this appeal, having been ordered to pay costs in the sum of .... dollars, has failed to pay the said costs within the time limited for the payment thereof.

Dated this .... day of .... A.D. ...., at ....

. . . .
Clerk of the Court of
. . . .

(Seal)

Form 43 — Jailer's Receipt to Peace Officer for Prisoner

(Section 744)

I hereby certify that I have received from X.Y., a peace officer for (*territorial division*), one A.B., together with a (warrant *or* order) issued by (*set out court or justice, as the case may be*).[12]

[12] *Add a statement of the condition of the prisoner*

Dated this .... day of .... A.D. ...., at ....

. . . .

Keeper of *(prison)*

1995, c. 22, s. 18 (Sched. IV, item 22)

Form 44

(Section 667)

I, (*name*), a fingerprint examiner designated as such for the purposes of section 667 of the *Criminal Code* by the Minister of Public Safety and Emergency Preparedness, do hereby certify that (*name*) also known as (*aliases if any*), FPS Number ...., whose fingerprints are shown reproduced below (*reproduction of fingerprints*) or attached hereto, has been convicted, discharged under section 730 of the *Criminal Code* or convicted and sentenced in Canada as follows:

(*record*)

Dated this .... day of .... A.D. ...., at ....

. . . .

Fingerprint Examiner

R.S.C. 1985, c. 27 (1st Supp.), s. 184(17); 1995, c. 22, s. 18 (Sched. IV, item 26); 2005, c. 10, s. 34(1)(f)(xiv)

Form 45

(Section 667)

I, (*name*), a fingerprint examiner designated as such for the purposes of section 667 of the *Criminal Code* by the Minister of Public Safety and Emergency Preparedness, do hereby certify that I have compared the fingerprints reproduced in or attached to exhibit A with the fingerprints reproduced in or attached to the certificate in Form 44 attached marked exhibit B and that they are those of the same person.

Dated this .... day of .... A.D. ...., at ....

. . . .

Fingerprint Examiner

R.S.C. 1985, c. 27 (1st Supp.), s. 184(18); 2005, c. 10, s. 34(1)(f)(xiv)

Form 46 — Probation Order

(Section 732.1)

Canada,

Province of . . . .

(territorial division).

Whereas on the .... day of .... at ...., A.B., hereinafter called the offender, (pleaded guilty to *or* was tried under (*here insert Part XIX, XX or XXVII, as the case may be*) of the *Criminal Code* and was (*here insert convicted or found guilty, as the case may be*) on the charge that (*here state the offence to which the offender pleaded guilty or for which the offender was convicted or found guilty, as the case may be*);

And whereas on the .... day of .... the court adjudged[13]

Now therefore the said offender shall, for the period of .... from the date of this order (*or, where paragraph (d), (e) or (f) is applicable*, the date of expiration of the offender's sentence of imprisonment or conditional sentence order) comply with the following conditions, namely, that the said offender shall keep the peace and be of good behaviour, appear before the court when required to do so by the court and notify the court or probation officer in advance of any change of name or address and promptly notify the court or probation officer of any change of employment or occupation, and, in addition,

(*here state any additional conditions prescribed pursuant to subsection 732.1(3) of the Criminal Code*).

Dated this .... day of .... A.D. ...., at ....

....

Clerk of the Court, Justice
or Provincial Court Judge

R.S.C. 1985, c. 27 (1st Supp.), s. 206; 1995, c. 22, s. 10 (Sched. I, item 35); 2004, c. 12, s. 17

---

[13] *Use whichever of the following forms of disposition is applicable*

(a) that the offender be discharged on the following conditions:

(b) that the passing of sentence on the offender be suspended and that the said offender be released on the following conditions:

(c) that the offender forfeit and pay the sum of .... dollars to be applied according to law and in default of payment of the said sum without delay (*or within a time fixed, if any*), be imprisoned in the (*prison*) at .... for the term of .... unless the said sum and charges of the committal and of conveying the said offender to the said prison are sooner paid, and in addition thereto, that the said offender comply with the following conditions:

(d) that the offender be imprisoned in the (*prison*) at .... for the term of .... and, in addition thereto, that the said offender comply with the following conditions:

(e) that following the expiration of the offender's conditional sentence order related to this or another offence, that the said offender comply with the following conditions:

(f) that following the expiration of the offender's sentence of imprisonment related to another offence, that the said offender comply with the following conditions:

(g) when the offender is ordered to serve the sentence of imprisonment intermittently, that the said offender comply with the following conditions when not in confinement:

Form 47 — Order to Disclose Income Tax Information

(Section 462.48)

Canada,

Province of

. . . . ,

(*territorial division*).

To A.B., of ...., (*office or occupation*):

Whereas, it appears on the oath of C.D., of ...., that there are reasonable grounds for believing that E.F., of ...., has committed or benefited from the commission of the offence of .... and that the information or documents (*describe information or documents*) are likely to be of substantial value to an investigation of that offence or a related matter; and

Whereas there are reasonable grounds for believing that it is in the public interest to allow access to the information or documents, having regard to the benefit likely to accrue to the investigation if the access is obtained;

This is, therefore, to authorize and require you between the hours of (*as the judge may direct*), during the period commencing on .... and ending on ...., to produce all the above-mentioned information and documents to one of the following police officers, namely, (*here name police officers*) and allow the police officer to remove the information or documents, *or* to allow the police officer access to the above-mentioned information and documents and to examine them, *as the judge directs*, subject to the following conditions (*state conditions*): ....

Dated this .... day of .... A.D. ...., at ....

. . . .

Signature of
Judge

R.S.C. 1985, c. 42 (4th Supp.), s. 8

Form 48 — Assessment Order of the Court [Heading amended 2005, c. 22, s. 40.]

(Section 672.13)

Canada,
Province of
(*territorial division*)

Whereas I have (*or if the signatory is the clerk of the court*, the judge or justice has) reasonable grounds to believe that evidence of the mental condition of (*name of accused*), who has been charged with ...., may be necessary to determine[14]

❑ whether the accused is unfit to stand trial

❑ whether the accused suffered from a mental disorder so as to exempt the accused from criminal responsibility by virtue of subsection 16(1) of the *Criminal Code* at the time of the act or omission charged against the accused

❑ whether the balance of the mind of the accused was disturbed at the time of commission of the alleged offence, if the accused is a female person charged with an offence arising out of the death of her newly-born child

❑ if a verdict of unfit to stand trial or a verdict of not criminally responsible on account of mental disorder has been rendered in respect of the accused, the appropriate disposition to be made in respect of the accused under section 672.54, 672.58 or 672.64 of the *Criminal Code* or whether the court should, under subsection 672.84(3) of that Act, revoke a finding that the accused is a high-risk accused

❑ if a verdict of unfit to stand trial has been rendered in respect of the accused, whether the court should order a stay of proceedings under section 672.851 of the *Criminal Code*

An assessment of the mental condition of (*name of accused*) is ordered to be conducted by/at (*name of person or service by which or place where assessment is to be made*) for a period of .... days.

This order is to be in force for a total of .... days, including travelling time, during which time the accused is to remain[15]

❑ in custody at (*place where accused is to be detained*)

❑ out of custody, on the following conditions:

(*set out conditions, if applicable*)

Dated (*date*).........., at .... (*place*).

((*Signature of judge, provincial court judge, justice or clerk of the court*)

1991, c. 43, s. 8; 1995, c. 22, s. 10 (Sched. I, item 36); 2005, c. 22, s. 40; 2014, c. 6, s. 19; 2019, c. 25, s. 352

Form 48.1 — Assessment Order of the Review Board

(Section 672.13)

Canada,
Province of
(*territorial division*)

[14] Check applicable option.

[15] Check applicable option.

Whereas I have reasonable grounds to believe that evidence of the mental condition of (*name of accused*), who has been charged with ...., may be necessary to[16]

- ❑ if a verdict of unfit to stand trial or a verdict of not criminally responsible on account of mental disorder has been rendered in respect of the accused, make a disposition under section 672.54 of the *Criminal Code* or determine whether the Review Board should, under subsection 672.84(1) of that Act, refer to the superior court of criminal jurisdiction for review a finding that the accused is a high-risk accused
- ❑ if a verdict of unfit to stand trial has been rendered in respect of the accused, determine whether the Review Board should make a recommendation to the court that has jurisdiction in respect of the offence charged against the accused to hold an inquiry to determine whether a stay of proceedings should be ordered in accordance with section 672.851 of the *Criminal Code*

I hereby order an assessment of the mental condition of (*name of accused*) to be conducted by/at (*name of person or service by whom or place where assessment is to be made*) for a period of .... days.

This order is to be in force for a total of .... days, including travelling time, during which time the accused is to remain[17]

- ❑ in custody at (*place where accused is to be detained*)
- ❑ out of custody, on the following conditions:

(*set out conditions, if applicable*)

Dated this .... day of .... A.D. ...., at ....

....

(Signature of Chairperson of the Review Board)

2005, c. 22, s. 40; 2014, c. 6, s. 20

Form 48.2 — Victim Impact Statement — Not Criminally Responsible

(Subsection 672.5(14))

This form may be used to provide a description of the physical or emotional harm, property damage or economic loss suffered by you arising from the conduct for which the accused person was found not criminally responsible on account of mental disorder, as well as a description of the impact that the conduct has had on you. You may attach additional pages if you need more space.

Your statement must not include

- any statement about the conduct of the accused that is not relevant to the harm or loss suffered by you;
- any unproven allegations;

---

16 Check applicable option.

17 Check applicable option.

- any comments about any conduct for which the accused was not found not criminally responsible;
- any complaint about any individual, other than the accused, who was involved in the investigation or prosecution of the offence; or
- except with the court's or Review Board's approval, an opinion or recommendation about the disposition.

The following sections are examples of information you may wish to include in your statement. You are not required to include all of this information.

Emotional impact

Describe how the accused's conduct has affected you emotionally. For example, think of

- your lifestyle and activities;
- your relationships with others such as your spouse, family and friends;
- your ability to work, attend school or study; and
- your feelings, emotions and reactions as these relate to the conduct.

....

....

....

....

Physical impact

Describe how the accused's conduct has affected you physically. For example, think of

- ongoing physical pain, discomfort, illness, scarring, disfigurement or physical limitation;
- hospitalization or surgery you have had because of the conduct of the accused;
- treatment, physiotherapy or medication you have been prescribed;
- the need for any further treatment or the expectation that you will receive further treatment; and
- any permanent or long-term disability.

....

....

....

....

Economic impact

Describe how the accused's conduct has affected you financially. For example, think of

- the value of any property that was lost or damaged and the cost of repairs or replacement;
- any financial loss due to missed time from work;
- the cost of any medical expenses, therapy or counselling; and
- any costs or losses that are not covered by insurance.

Please note that this is not an application for compensation or restitution.

....

....

....

....

Fears for security

Describe any fears you have for your security or that of your family and friends. For example, think of

- concerns with respect to contact with the accused; and
- concerns with respect to contact between the accused and members of your family or close friends.

....

....

....

....

Drawing, poem or letter

You may use this space to draw a picture or write a poem or letter if it will help you express the impact that the accused's conduct has had on you.

❑ I would like to read or present my statement (in court *or* before the Review Board).

To the best of my knowledge, the information contained in this statement is true.

Dated this .... day of .... 20...................................., at ....

Signature of declarant

2015, c. 13, s. 36

Form 49 — Warrant of Committal Disposition of Detention

(Section 672.57)

Canada,
Province of

(territorial division)

To the peace officers, in the said (*territorial division*) and to the keeper (*administrator, warden*) of the (*prison, hospital or other appropriate place where the accused is detained*).

This warrant is issued for the committal of A.B., of .... (*occupation*), hereinafter called the accused.

Whereas the accused has been charged that (*set out briefly the offence in respect of which the accused was charged*);

And whereas the accused was found[18]

❑ unfit to stand trial

❑ not criminally responsible on account of mental disorder

This is, therefore, to command you, in Her Majesty's name, to take the accused in custody and convey the accused safely to the (*prison, hospital or other appropriate place*) at .... and there deliver the accused to the keeper (*administrator, warden*) with the following precept:

You, the keeper (*administrator, warden*), are therefore directed to receive the accused in your custody in the (*prison, hospital or other appropriate place*) and to keep the accused safely there until the accused is delivered by due course of law.

The following are the conditions to which the accused shall be subject while in your (*prison, hospital or other appropriate place*):

The following are the powers regarding the restrictions (*and the limits and conditions on these restrictions*) on the liberty of the accused that are hereby delegated to you the said keeper (*administrator, warden*) of the said (*prison, hospital or other appropriate place*):

Dated (*date*).........., at .... (*place*).

(*Signature of judge, provincial court judge, justice, clerk of the court or chairperson of the review board*)

2019, c. 25, s. 353

Form 50 — Warrant of Committal Placement Decision

(Section 672.7(2))

Canada,

Province of

(territorial division)

To the peace officers, in the said (*territorial division*) and to the keeper (*administrator, warden*) of the (*prison, hospital or other appropriate place where the accused is detained*).

---

18 Check applicable option.

This warrant is issues for the committal of A.B., of .... (*occupation*), hereinafter called the accused.

Whereas the accused has been charged that (*set out briefly the offence in respect of which the accused was charged*);

And whereas the accused was found[19]

❑ unfit to stand trial

❑ not criminally responsible on account of mental disorder

And whereas the Review Board has held a hearing and decided that the accused shall be detained in custody;

And whereas the accused is required to be detained in custody pursuant to a warrant of committal issued by (*set out the name of the Judge, Clerk of the Court, Provincial Court Judge or Justice as well as the name of the court and territorial division*), dated the .... day of .... in respect of the offence that (*set out briefly the offence in respect of which the accused was charged or convicted*);

This is, therefore to command you, in Her Majesty's name, to[20]

❑ execute the warrant of committal issued by the court, according to its terms

❑ execute the warrant of committal issued herewith by the Review Board

Dated this .... day of .... A.D. ...., at ....

....

(Signature of chairperson of the Review Board)

Form 51 — Notice of Obligation to Provide Samples of Bodily Substance

(Paragraphs 732.1(3)(c.2), 742.3(2)(a.2), 810(3.02)(c), 810.01(4.1)(g), 810.011(6)(f), 810.1(3.02)(i) and 810.2(4.1)(g))

[Reference amended 2015, c. 20, s. 34(4).]

To A.B., of ...., (*occupation*), (*address in Canada*), (*date of birth*), (*gender*):

Because, on (*date*), you were ordered, under (*applicable provision*) of the *Criminal Code*, to provide samples of a bodily substance prescribed by regulation at regular intervals for the purpose of analysis;

You are provided with this notice to inform you of your obligations with respect to providing samples.

1. On (*specify a day not earlier than 24 hours after the day on which the notice is served*), you must report, at any time from (*time*) to (*time*), at (*address of place at which sample to be taken, as designated by the Attorney General of the province or Minister of Justice of the territory*), to provide a sample of your (*specify type of bodily substance prescribed by regulation*).

---

19 Check applicable option.

20 Check applicable option.

2. Every (*specify a number not less than seven*) days after you first report to provide a sample, you must report, at any time from (*time*) to (*time*), at (*address of place at which sample to be taken, as designated by the Attorney General of the province or Minister of Justice of the territory*), to provide a sample of your (*specify type of bodily substance prescribed by regulation*).

3. You have the right to apply to a court to terminate the obligation to provide samples, and the right to appeal any decision of that court.

4. If you are found to have not complied with your obligation to provide samples as set out in this notice, you may be subject to a fine or imprisonment, or to both (*or, in the case of a conditional sentence*, you may be subject to proceedings under section 742.6 of the *Criminal Code*, the consequences of which may include imprisonment).

5. The results of the analysis of the bodily substances may be used or disclosed in accordance with the *Criminal Code*, including in proceedings against you, the result of which may be that you are subject to a fine or imprisonment, or to both (*or, in the case of a conditional sentence*, including in proceedings under section 742.6 of the *Criminal Code*, the consequences of which may include imprisonment).

Served on (*date*), at (*place the notice is served*).

....

(*Signature of probation officer, supervisor or person designated by the Attorney General or Minister of Justice, as the case may be*)

2005, c. 22, s. 41; 2011, c. 7, s. 13; 2015, c. 20, s. 34(4)

Form 52 — Order to Comply With *Sex Offender Information Registration Act*

(Section 490.012)

Canada,
Province of ....,
(*territorial division*).

To A.B., of ...., (*occupation*), (*address or address of court if no fixed address*), (*date of birth*), (*gender*):

You have been convicted of or found not criminally responsible on account of mental disorder for (*description of offence(s)*) under (*applicable designated offence provision(s) of the Criminal Code*), a designated offence (*or* designated offences) within the meaning of subsection 490.011(1) of the *Criminal Code*.

1. You must report for the first time to the registration centre referred to in section 7.1 of the *Sex Offender Information Registration Act*, whenever required under subsection 4(1) of that Act.

2. You must subsequently report to the registration centre referred to in section 7.1 of the *Sex Offender Information Registration Act*, whenever required under section 4.1 or 4.3 of that Act, for a period of .... years after this order is made (*or if paragraph 490.013(2)(c) or any of subsections 490.013(2.1) to (5) of the Criminal Code* applies, for life).

3. Information relating to you will be collected under sections 5 and 6 of the *Sex Offender Information Registration Act* by a person who collects information at the registration centre.

4. Information relating to you will be registered in a database, and may be consulted, disclosed and used in the circumstances set out in the *Sex Offender Information Registration Act*.

5. If you believe that the information registered in the database contains an error or omission, you may ask a person who collects information at the registration centre referred to in section 7.1 of the *Sex Offender Information Registration Act* or, if applicable, the Canadian Forces Provost Marshal, to correct the information.

6. You have the right to apply to a court to terminate this order, and the right to appeal the decision of that court.

7. If you are found to have contravened this order, you may be subject to a fine or imprisonment, or to both.

8. If you are found to have provided false or misleading information, you may be subject to a fine or imprisonment, or to both.

Dated this .... day of ...., at ....

....

(*Signature of judge or clerk and name of court*)

....

(*Signature of person subject to order*)

2004, c. 10, s. 21; 2007, c. 5, s. 30(2), (3); 2010, c. 17, s. 26

Form 53 — Notice of Obligation to Comply With *Sex Offender Information Registration Act*

(Sections 490.019 and 490.032)

Canada,
Province of ....,
(territorial division).

Because, on .... (*insert date(s)*), you were convicted of, or found not criminally responsible on account of mental disorder for, ... (*insert description of offence(s)*), one or more offences referred to in paragraph (a), (c), (c.1), (d), (d.1) or (e) of the definition “designated offence” in subsection 490.011(1) of the *Criminal Code* or in paragraph (a) or (c) of the definition “designated offence” in section 227 of the *National Defence Act*, under .... (*insert the applicable offence provision(s)*), this is provided to give you notice that you are required to comply with the *Sex Offender Information Registration Act*.

1. You must report for the first time to the registration centre referred to in section 7.1 of the *Sex Offender Information Registration Act*, whenever required under subsection 4(2) of that Act.

2. You must subsequently report to the registration centre referred to in section 7.1 of the *Sex Offender Information Registration Act*, whenever required under section 4.1 or 4.3 of that Act, for a period of .... years after you were sentenced, or

found not criminally responsible on account of mental disorder, for the offence (*or if paragraph 490.022(3)(c) or (d) of the Criminal Code applies*, for life) or for any shorter period set out in subsection 490.022(2) of the *Criminal Code*.

3. Information relating to you will be collected under sections 5 and 6 of the *Sex Offender Information Registration Act* by a person who collects information at the registration centre.

4. Information relating to you will be registered in a database, and may be consulted, disclosed and used in the circumstances set out in the *Sex Offender Information Registration Act.*

5. If you believe that the information registered in the database contains an error or omission, you may ask a person who collects information at the registration centre referred to in section 7.1 of the *Sex Offender Information Registration Act* or, if applicable, the Canadian Forces Provost Marshal, to correct the information.

6. You have the right to apply to a court to exempt you from the obligation to comply with the *Sex Offender Information Registration Act*, and the right to appeal any decision of that court.

7. You have the right to apply to a court to terminate the obligation, and the right to appeal any decision of that court.

8. If you are found to have contravened the obligation, you may be subject to a fine or imprisonment, or to both.

9. If you are found to have provided false or misleading information, you may be subject to a fine or imprisonment, or to both.

Dated this .... day of ...., at ....

2004, c. 10, s. 21; 2007, c. 5, s. 31; 2014, c. 25, s. 33

Form 54 — Obligation to Comply With *Sex Offender Information Registration Act*

(Sections 490.02901 to 490.02903, 490.02905 and 490.032)

To A.B., of ...., (*occupation*), (*address in Canada*), (*date of birth*), (*gender*):

Because, on (*date*), you were convicted of or found not criminally responsible on account of mental disorder for an offence (*or* offences) in (*location of offence(s)*) that the Attorney General of the province, or the minister of justice of the territory, has identified as being equivalent to (*description of offence(s)*) under (*applicable provision(s) of the Criminal Code*), a designated offence (*or* designated offences) as defined in subsection 490.011(1) of the *Criminal Code*;

You are provided with this to inform you that you are required to comply with the *Sex Offender Information Registration Act*.

1. You must report for the first time to the registration centre referred to in section 7.1 of the *Sex Offender Information Registration Act*, whenever required under subsection 4(2) of that Act.

2. You must subsequently report to the registration centre referred to in section 7.1 of the *Sex Offender Information Registration Act*, whenever required under section 4.1 or 4.3 of that Act, for a period of .... years after the day on which you were

sentenced or found not criminally responsible on account of mental disorder for the offence (*or if paragraph 490.02904(3)(c) or (d) of the Criminal Code applies*, for life because you were convicted of or found not criminally responsible on account of mental disorder for (*description of offence(s)*) under (*applicable designated offence provision(s) of the Criminal Code*), a designated offence (*or* designated offences) within the meaning of subsection 490.011(1) of the *Criminal Code*) or for any shorter period determined under subsection 490.02904(2) of the *Criminal Code.*

3. Information relating to you will be collected under sections 5 and 6 of the *Sex Offender Information Registration Act* by a person who collects information at the registration centre.

4. Information relating to you will be registered in a database, and may be consulted, disclosed and used in the circumstances set out in the *Sex Offender Information Registration Act*.

5. If you believe that the information registered in the database contains an error or omission, you may ask a person who collects information at the registration centre referred to in section 7.1 of the *Sex Offender Information Registration Act* to correct the information.

6. You have the right to apply to a court to exempt you from the obligation to comply with the *Sex Offender Information Registration Act*, and the right to appeal the decision of that court.

7. You have the right to apply to a court to terminate the obligation to comply with the *Sex Offender Information Registration Act* and the right to appeal the decision of that court.

8. If you are found to have not complied with the *Sex Offender Information Registration Act*, you may be subject to a fine or imprisonment, or to both.

9. If you are found to have provided false or misleading information, you may be subject to a fine or imprisonment, or to both.

Served on (*date*).

For administrative use only:

Sentence imposed or verdict of not criminally responsible on account of mental disorder rendered on (*date*).

2010, c. 17, s. 27

CAN. REG. SI/85-201 — APPROVED BREATH ANALYSIS INSTRUMENTS ORDER

made under the *Criminal Code*

Order Approving Certain Breath Analysis Instruments as Suitable for the Purposes of Section 258 of the *Criminal Code*

SI/85-201, as am. SI/92-105; SI/92-167; SI/93-61; SI/93-175; SOR/94-422; SOR/94-572; SOR/95-312; SOR/2000-200; SOR/2002-99; SOR/2007-197; SOR/2008-106; SOR/2009-205; SOR/2012-237; SOR/2013-107; SOR/2019-26.

SHORT TITLE

1. This Order may be cited as the *Approved Breath Analysis Instruments Order*.

APPROVED INSTRUMENTS

2. The following instruments, each being an instrument of a kind that is designed to receive and make an analysis of a sample of the breath of a person in order to measure the concentration of alcohol in the blood of that person, are hereby approved as suitable for the purposes of section 258 of the *Criminal Code*:

(a) to (g) [Repealed SOR/2012-237, s. 1(1).]

(h) Intoxilyzer® 5000 C;

(i) [Repealed SOR/2012-237, s. 1(2).]

(j) [Repealed SOR/2013-107, s. 1(2).]

(k) BAC Datamaster C;

(l) Alco-Sensor IV-RBT IV;

(m) [Repealed SOR/2013-107, s. 1(3).]

(n) Alco-Sensor IV/RBT IV-K;

(o) Alcotest 7110 MKIII Dual C;

(p) Intoxilyzer® 8000 C;

(q) DataMaster DMT-C;

(r) Intox EC/IR II; and

(s) Intoxilyzer® 9000.

SI/92-105; SI/92-167; SI/93-61; SI/93-175; SOR/94-422; SOR/94-572; SOR/95-312; SOR/2000-200, s. 1; SOR/2002-99, s. 1; SOR/2007-197, s. 1; SOR/2008-106, s. 1; SOR/2009-205, s. 1; SOR/2012-237, s. 1; SOR/2013-107, s. 1; SOR/2019-26, s. 1

Explanatory Note (This note is not part of the Order.)

This Order approves certain breath analysis instruments as being suitable for the purposes of section 258 of the Criminal Code.

CAN. REG. SI/85-200 — APPROVED SCREENING DEVICES ORDER

made under the *Criminal Code*

Order approving certain screening devices for the purposes of section 238 of the *Criminal Code*

SI/85-200, as am. SI/88-136; SOR/93-263; SOR/94-193; SOR/94-423; SOR/96-81; SOR/97-116; SOR/2009-239; SOR/2011-313; SOR/2012-61; SOR/2019-25.

SHORT TITLE

1. This Order may be cited as the *Approved Screening Devices Order*.

APPROVED SCREENING DEVICES

2. The following devices, each being a device of a kind that is designed to ascertain the presence of alcohol in the blood of a person, are hereby approved for the purposes of section 254 of the *Criminal Code*:

(a) Alcolmeter S-L2;

(b) Alco-Sûr;

(c) Alcotest® 7410 PA3;

(d) Alcotest® 7410 GLC;

(e) Alco-Sensor IV DWF;

(f) Alco-Sensor IV PWF;

(g) Intoxilyzer 400D;

(h) Alco-Sensor FST;

(i) Dräger Alcotest 6810; and

(j) Dräger Alcotest® 6820.

SI/88-136, s. 1; SOR/93-263, s. 2; SOR/94-193, s. 1; SOR/94-423, s. 1; SOR/96-81, s. 1; SOR/97-116, s. 1; SOR/2009-239, s. 1; SOR/2011-313, s. 1; SOR/2012-61, s. 1; SOR/2019-25, s. 1

Explanatory Note (This note is not part of the Order.)

This Order approves certain screening devices for the purposes of section 254 of the Criminal Code.

CAN. REG. 2005-37 — ORDER APPROVING BLOOD SAMPLE CONTAINERS

made under the *Criminal Code*

SOR/2005-37, as am. SOR/2010-64; SOR/2012-60.

APPROVED CONTAINERS

1. The following containers, being containers of a kind that is designed to receive a sample of blood of a person for analysis, are hereby approved as suitable, in respect of blood samples, for the purposes of section 258 of the *Criminal Code*:

(a) Vacutainer® XF947;

(b) BD Vacutainer™ 367001;

(c) Vacutainer® 367001;

(d) Tri-Tech Inc. TUG10;

(e) BD Vacutainer® REF 367001; and

(f) TRITECHFORENSICS TUG10.

SOR/2010-64, s. 1; SOR/2012-60, s. 1

REPEAL

2. The *Approved Blood Sample Container Order*[21] is repealed.

COMING INTO FORCE

3. This Order comes into force on the day on which it is registered.

---

[21] SI/85-199

CAN. REG. 2018-179 — APPROVED DRUG SCREENING EQUIPMENT ORDER

made under the *Criminal Code*

SOR/2018-179, as am. SOR/2019-237.

DRUG SCREENING EQUIPMENT

1. Approved equipment — For the purpose of the definition "approved drug screening equipment" in section 320.11 of the *Criminal Code*, the following equipment that is designed to ascertain the presence of a drug in a person's body is approved:

(a) a Dräger DrugTest® 5000 and a Dräger DrugTest® 5000 STK-CA, when used together; and

(b) a SoToxa™, an Abbot SoToxa™ Test Cartridge and an Abbott SoToxa™ Oral Fluid Collection Device, when used together.

SOR/2019-237, s. 1

COMING INTO FORCE

2. Day made — This Order comes into force on the day on which it is made.

Can. Reg. 2018-148 — Blood Drug Concentration Regulations

made under the *Criminal Code*

SOR/2018-148, as am. SOR/2018-149.

Blood Alcohol Concentration and Blood Drug Concentration

1. Summary offence — For the purpose of subsection 320.14(4) of the *Criminal Code*, the prescribed blood drug concentration for tetrahydrocannabinol (THC) is 2 ng of THC per mL of blood.

SOR/2018-149, s. 1

2. Hybrid offence — drugs — For the purpose of paragraph 320.14(1)(c) of the *Criminal Code*, the prescribed blood drug concentration for each drug set out in column 1 of the table to this section is set out in column 2.

Item	Column 1 Drug	Column 2 Concentration
1	Tetrahydrocannabinol (THC)	5 ng/mL of blood
2	Lysergic acid diethylamide (LSD)	Any detectable level
3	Psilocybin	Any detectable level
4	Psilocin	Any detectable level
5	Phencyclidine (PCP)	Any detectable level
6	6-Monoacetylmorphine	Any detectable level
7	Ketamine	Any detectable level
8	Cocaine	Any detectable level
9	Gamma hydroxybutyrate (GHB)	5 mg/L of blood
10	Methamphetamine	Any detectable level

SOR/2018-149, s. 2

3. Hybrid offence — combination of drugs and alcohol — For the purpose of paragraph 320.14(1)(d) of the *Criminal Code*, the prescribed blood alcohol concentration is 50 mg of alcohol per 100 mL of blood and the prescribed blood drug concentration for tetrahydrocannabinol (THC) is 2.5 ng of THC per mL of blood.

SOR/2018-149, s. 3

Application Before Publication

4. Statutory Instruments Act — For the purpose of paragraph 11(2)(a) of the *Statutory Instruments Act*, these Regulations apply according to their terms before they are published in the *Canada Gazette*.

Coming into Force

5. These Regulations come into force on the day on which they are made.

CAN. REG. 2008-196 — EVALUATION OF IMPAIRED OPERATION (DRUGS AND ALCOHOL) REGULATIONS

made under the *Criminal Code*

SOR/2008-196

QUALIFICATION REQUIRED OF EVALUATING OFFICER

1. An evaluating officer must be a certified drug recognition expert accredited by the International Association of Chiefs of Police.

PHYSICAL COORDINATION TESTS

2. The physical coordination tests to be conducted under paragraph 254(2)(a) of the *Criminal Code* are the following standard field sobriety tests:

(a) the horizontal gaze nystagmus test;

(b) the walk-and-turn test; and

(c) the one-leg stand test.

EVALUATION TESTS AND PROCEDURES

3. The tests to be conducted and the procedures to be followed during an evaluation under subsection 254(3.1) of the *Criminal Code* are

(a) a preliminary examination, which consists of measuring the pulse and determining that the pupils are the same size and that the eyes track an object equally;

(b) eye examinations, which consist of

(i) the horizontal gaze nystagmus test,

(ii) the vertical gaze nystagmus test, and

(iii) the lack-of-convergence test;

(c) divided-attention tests, which consist of

(i) the Romberg balance test,

(ii) the walk-and-turn test referred to in paragraph 2(b),

(iii) the one-leg stand test referred to in paragraph 2(c), and

(iv) the finger-to-nose test, which includes the test subject tilting the head back and touching the tip of their index finger to the tip of their nose in a specified manner while keeping their eyes closed;

(d) an examination, which consists of measuring the blood pressure, temperature and pulse;

(e) an examination of pupil sizes under light levels of ambient light, near total darkness and direct light and an examination of the nasal and oral cavities;

(f) an examination, which consists of checking the muscle tone and pulse; and

(g) a visual examination of the arms, neck and, if exposed, the legs for evidence of injection sites.

COMING INTO FORCE

4. These Regulations come into force on July 2, 2008.

CAN. REG. 98-462 — REGULATIONS PRESCRIBING CERTAIN FIREARMS AND OTHER WEAPONS, COMPONENTS AND PARTS OF WEAPONS, ACCESSORIES, CARTRIDGE MAGAZINES, AMMUNITION AND PROJECTILES AS PROHIBITED, RESTRICTED OR NON-RESTRICTED

made under the *Criminal Code*

SOR/98-462, as am. SOR/98-472, s. 1; SOR/2015-213; SOR/2018-254, s. 1; 2019, c. 9, ss. 19–21 [Not in force at date of publication.].

[Note: The title of this Regulation was changed from "Regulations Prescribing Certain Firearms and Other Weapons, Components and Parts of Weapons, Accessories, CartridgeMagazine, Ammunition and Projectiles as Prohibited or Restricted" to "Regulations Prescribing Certain Firearms and Other Weapons, Components and Parts of Weapons, Accessories, Cartridge Magazines, Ammunition and Projectiles as Prohibited, Restricted or Non-Restricted" by SOR/2015-213, s. 1. The title of this Regulation was changed from "Regulations Prescribing Certain Firearms and Other Weapons, Components and Parts of Weapons, Accessories, Cartridge Magazines, Ammunition and Projectiles as Prohibited, Restricted or Non-Restricted" to "Regulations Prescribing Certain Firearms and Other Weapons, Components and Parts of Weapons, Accessories, Cartridge Magazines, Ammunition and Projectiles as Prohibited or Restricted" by 2019, c. 9, s. 19. Not in force at date of publication.]

His Excellency the Governor General in Council, on therecommendation of the Minister of Justice, pursuant to the definitions "prohibited ammunition"[22], "prohibiteddevice"[23], "prohibitedfirearm"[24], "prohibitedweapon"[25] and "restrictedfirearm"[26] in subsection84(1) and to subsection 117.15(1)[27] of the *Criminal Code*, hereby makesthe annexed *Regulations Prescribing Certain Firearms and other Weapons, Components and Parts of Weapons, Accessories, Cartridge Magazines, Ammunition and Projectiles as Prohibited or Restricted.*

[22] S.C. 1995, c. 39, s. 139

[23] S.C. 1995, c. 39, s. 139

[24] S.C. 1995, c. 39, s. 139

[25] S.C. 1995, c. 39, s. 139

[26] S.C. 1995, c. 39, s. 139

[27] S.C. 1995, c. 39, s. 139

INTERPRETATION

1. In these Regulations, "semi-automatic", in respect of a firearm, means a firearm that is equipped with a mechanism that, following the discharge of a cartridge, automatically operates to complete any part of the reloading cycle necessary to prepare for the discharge of the next cartridge.

PRESCRIPTION

2. The firearms listed in Part 1 of the schedule are prohibited firearms for the purposes of paragraph (d) of the definition "prohibited firearm" in subsection 84(1) of the *Criminal Code*.

3. The firearms listed in Part 2 of the schedule are restricted firearms for the purposes of paragraph (d) of the definition "restricted firearm" in subsection 84(1) of the *Criminal Code*, except for those firearms that are prohibited firearms within the meaning of paragraph (b) or (c) of the definition "prohibited firearm" in that subsection.

SOR/2015-213, s. 2

3.1 The firearms listed in Part 2.1 of the schedule that have a barrel that is less than 470 mm in length, and firearms listed in items 3, 4, 6, 7, 9 and 10 of that Part that do not have a barrel, are restricted firearms for the purposes of paragraph (d) of the definition "restricted firearm" in subsection 84(1) of the *Criminal Code*, except for those firearms that

(a) discharge projectiles in rapid succession during one pressure of the trigger; or

(b) are prohibited firearms within the meaning of paragraph (b) of the definition "prohibited firearm" in subsection 84(1) of the *Criminal Code*.

Proposed Repeal — 3.1

3.1 [Repealed 2019, c. 9, s. 20. Not in force at date of publication.]

SOR/2015-213, s. 2

3.2 The firearms listed in Part 2.1 of the schedule that have a barrel that is at least 470 mm in length, and the firearms listed in items 1, 2, 5, 8 and 11 to 15 of that Part that do not have a barrel, are non-restricted firearms for the purposes of paragraph (b) of the definition "non-restricted firearm" in subsection 84(1) of the *Criminal Code*, except for those firearms that

(a) discharge projectiles in rapid succession during one pressure of the trigger; or

(b) are prohibited firearms within the meaning of paragraph (b) of the definition "prohibited firearm" in subsection 84(1) of the *Criminal Code*.

Proposed Repeal — 3.2

3.2 [Repealed 2019, c. 9, s. 20. Not in force at date of publication.]

SOR/2015-213, s. 2

4. The weapons listed in Part 3 of the schedule are prohibited weapons for the purposes of paragraph (b) of the definition "prohibited weapon" in subsection 84(1) of the *Criminal Code*.

5. The components and parts of weapons, the accessories and the cartridge magazines listed in Part 4 of the schedule are prohibited devices for the purposes of paragraphs (a) and (d) of the definition **"prohibited device"** in subsection 84(1) of the *Criminal Code*.

SOR/2018-254, s. 1

6. The ammunition and projectiles listed in Part 5 of the schedule are prohibited ammunition for the purposes of the definition "prohibited ammunition" in subsection 84(1) of the *Criminal Code*.

Coming Into Force

7. These Regulations come into force on December 1, 1998.

SOR/98-472, s. 1.

Schedule

(Sections 2 to 6)

Part 1 — Prohibited Firearms

Former Prohibited Weapons Order, No. 3

1. Any firearm capable of discharging a dart or other object carrying an electrical current or substance, including the firearm of the design commonly known as the Taser Public Defender and any variant or modified version of it.

Former Prohibited Weapons Order, No. 8

2. The firearm known as the SSS-1 Stinger and any similar firearm designed or of a size to fit in the palm of the hand.

Former Prohibited Weapons Order, No. 11

3. The firearm of the design commonly known as the Franchi SPAS 12 shotgun, and any variant or modified version of it, including the Franchi LAW 12 shotgun.

4. The firearm of the design commonly known as the Striker shotgun, and any variant or modified version of it, including the Striker 12 shotgun and the Sreetsweeper shotgun.

5. The firearm of the design commonly known as the USAS-12 Auto Shotgun, and any variant or modified version of it.

6. The firearm of the design commonly known as the Franchi SPAS-15 shotgun, and any variant or modified version of it.

7. The firearms of the designs commonly known as the Benelli M1 Super 90 shotgun and the Benelli M3 Super 90 shotgun, and any variants or modified versions of them, with the exception of the

(a) M1 Super 90 Field;

(b) M1 Super 90 Sporting Special;

(c) Montefeltro Super 90;

(d) Montefeltro Super 90 Standard Hunter;

(e) Montefeltro Super 90 Left Hand;

(f) Montefeltro Super 90 Turkey;

(g) Montefeltro Super 90 Uplander;

(h) Montefeltro Super 90 Slug;

(i) Montefeltro Super 90 20 Gauge;

(j) Black Eagle;

(k) Black Eagle Limited Edition;

(l) Black Eagle Competition;

(m) Black Eagle Slug Gun;

(n) Super Black Eagle; and

(o) Super Black Eagle Custom Slug.

8. The firearms of the designs commonly known as the Bernardelli B4 shotgun and the Bernardelli B4/B shotgun, and any variants or modified versions of them.

9. The firearm of the design commonly known as the American 180 Auto Carbine, and any variant or modified version of it, including the AM-180 Auto Carbine and the Illinois Arms Company Model 180 Auto Carbine.

10. The firearms of the designs commonly known as the Barrett "Light Fifty" Model 82A1 rifle and the Barrett Model 90 rifle, and any variants or modified versions of them.

11. The firearm of the design commonly known as the Calico M-900 rifle, and any variant or modified version of it, including the M-951 carbine, M-100 carbine and M-105 carbine.

12. The firearm of the design commonly known as the Iver Johnson AMAC long-range rifle, and any variant or modified version of it.

13. The firearm of the design commonly known as the McMillan M87 rifle, and any variant or modified version of it, including the McMillan M87R rifle and the McMillan M88 carbine.

14. The firearms of the designs commonly known as the Pauza Specialties P50 rifle and P50 carbine, and any variants or modified versions of them.

15. The firearm of the design commonly known as the Encom MK-IV carbine, and any variant or modified version of it.

16. The firearms of the designs commonly known as the Encom MP-9 and MP-45 carbines, and any variants or modified versions of them.

17. The firearm of the designs commonly known as the FAMAS rifle, and any variant or modified version of it, including the MAS 223, FAMAS Export, FAMAS Civil and Mitchell MAS/22.

18. The firearm of the design commonly known as the Feather AT-9 Semi-Auto Carbine, and any variant or modified version of it, including the Feather AT-22 Auto Carbine.

19. The firearm of the design commonly known as the Federal XC-450 Auto Rifle, and any variant or modified version of it, including the Federal XC-900 rifle and Federal XC-220 rifle.

20. The firearm of the design commonly known as the Gepard long-range sniper rifle, and any variant or modified version of it.

21. The firearm of the design commonly known as the Heckler and Koch (HK) Model G11 rifle, and any variant or modified version of it.

22. The firearm of the design commonly known as the Research Armament Industries (RAI) Model 500 rifle, and any variant or modified version of it.

23. The firearm of the design commonly known as the Spectre Auto Carbine, and any variant or modified version of it.

24. The firearm of the design commonly known as the US Arms PMAI "Assault" 22 rifle, and any variant or modified version of it.

25. The firearm of the design commonly known as the Weaver Arms Nighthawk Carbine, and any variant or modified version of it.

26. The firearm of the design commonly known as the A.A. Arms AR9 Semi-Automatic Rifle, and any variant or modified version of it.

27. The firearms of the designs commonly known as the Claridge HI-TEC C, LEC-9 and ZLEC-9 carbines, and any variant or modified version of them.

28. The firearm of the design commonly known as the Kimel Industries AR-9 rifle or carbine, and any variant or modified version of it.

29. The firearm of the design commonly known as the Grendel R-31 Auto Carbine, and any variant or modified version of it.

30. The firearms of the designs commonly known as the Maadi Griffin Rifle and the Maadi Griffin Carbine, and any variants or modified versions of them.

31. The firearm of the design commonly known as the AA Arms Model AR-9 carbine, and any variant or modified version of it.

32. The firearm of the design commonly known as the Bushmaster Auto Pistol, and any variant or modified version of it.

33. The firearm of the design commonly known as the Calico M-950 Auto Pistol, and any variant or modified version of it, including the M-110 pistol.

34. The firearm of the design commonly known as the Encom MK-IV assault pistol, and any variant or modified version of it.

35. The firearms of the designs commonly known as the Encom MP-9 and MP-45 assault pistols, and any variant or modified versions of them, including the Encom MP-9 and MP-45 mini pistols.

36. The firearm of the design commonly known as the Federal XP-450 Auto Pistol, and any variant or modified version of it, including the XP-900 Auto Pistol.

37. The firearm of the design commonly known as the Heckler and Koch (HK) SP89 Auto Pistol, and any variant or modified version of it.

38. The firearm of the design commonly known as the Intratec Tec-9 Auto Pistol, and any variant or modified version of it, including the Tec-9S, Tec-9M, Tech-9MS, and any semi-automatic variants of them, including the Tec-DC9, Tec-DC9M, Tech-9A, Tec-Scorpion, Tec-22T and Tec-22TN.

39. The firearms of the designs commonly known as the Iver Johnson Enforcer Model 3000 Auto Pistol and the Iver Johnson Plainfield Super Enforcer Carbine, and any variants or modified versions of them.

40. The firearm of the design commonly known as the Skorpion Auto Pistol, and any variant or modified version of it.

41. The firearm of the design commonly known as the Spectre Auto Pistol, and any variant or modified version of it.

42. The firearm of the design commonly known as the Sterling Mk 7 pistol, and any variant or modified version of it, including the Sterling Mk 7 C4 and Sterling Mk 7 C8.

43. The firearm of the design commonly known as the Universal Enforcer Model 3000 Auto Carbine, and any variant or modified version of it, including the Universal Enforcer Model 3010N, Model 3015G, Model 3020TRB and Model 3025TCO Carbines.

44. The firearm of the design commonly known as the US Arms PMAIP "Assault" 22 pistol, and any variant or modified version of it.

45. The firearm of the design commonly known as the Goncz High-Tech Long Pistol, and any variant or modified version of it, including the Claridge Hi-Tec models S, L, T, ZL-9 and ZT-9 pistols.

46. The firearm of the design commonly known as the Leader Mark 5 Auto Pistol, and any variant or modified version of it.

47. The firearm of the design commonly known as the OA-93 assault pistol, and any variant or modified version of it.

48. The firearm of the design commonly known as the A.A. Arms AP9 Auto Pistol, and any variant or modified version of it.

49. The firearm of the design commonly known as the Patriot pistol, and any variant or modified version of it.

50. The firearm of the design commonly known as the XM 231S pistol, and any variant or modified version of it, including the A1, A2 and A3 Flattop pistols.

51. The firearm of the design commonly known as the AA Arms Model AP-9 pistol, and any variant or modified version of it, including the Target AP-9 and the Mini AP-9 pistols.

52. The firearm of the design commonly known as the Kimel Industries AP-9 pistol, and any variant or modified version of it.

53. The firearms of the designs commonly known as the Grendel P-30, P-30 M, P-30 L and P-31 pistols, and any variant or modified versions of them.

54. The firearms of the designs commonly known as the Claridge HI-TEC ZL-9, HI-TEC S, HI-TEC L, HI-TEC T, HI-TECH ZT-9 and HI-TEC ZL-9 pistols, and any variants of modified versions of them.

55. The firearm of the design commonly known as the Steyr SPP Assault Pistol, and any variant or modified version of it.

56. The firearm of the design commonly known as the Maadi Griffin Pistol, and any variant or modified version of it.

57. The firearm of the design commonly known as the Interdynamics KG-99 Assault Pistol, and any variant or modified version of it.

Former Prohibited Weapons Order, No. 12

58. The firearm of the design commonly known as the Sterling Mk 6 Carbine, and any variant or modified version of it.

59. The firearm of the design commonly known as the Steyr AUG rifle, and any variant or modified version of it.

60. The firearm of the design commonly known as the UZI carbine, and any variant or modified version of it, including the UZI Model A carbine and the Mini-UZI carbine.

61. The firearms of the designs commonly known as the Ingram M10 and M11 pistols, and any variants or modified versions of them, including the Cobray M10 and M11 pistols, the RPB M10, M11, SM10 and SM11 pistols and the SWD M10, M11, SM10 and SM11 pistols.

62. The firearm of the design commonly known as the Partisan Avenger Auto Pistol, and any variant or modified version of it.

63. The firearm of the design commonly known as the UZI pistol, and any variant or modified version of it, including the Micro-UZI pistol.

Former Prohibited Weapons Order, No. 13

64. The firearm of the design commonly known as the AK-47 rifle, and any variant or modified version of it except for the Valmet Hunter, the Valmet Hunter Auto and the Valmet M78 rifles, but including the

(a) AK-74;

(b) AK Hunter;

(c) AKM;

(d) AKM-63;

(e) AKS-56S;

(f) AKS-56S-1;

(g) AKS-56S-2;

(h) AKS-74;

(i) AKS-84S-1;

(j) AMD-65;

(k) AR Model .223;

(l) Dragunov;

(m) Galil;

(n) KKMPi69;

(o) M60;

(p) M62;

(q) M70B1;

(r) M70AB2;

(s) M76;

(t) M77B1;

(u) M78;

(v) M80;

(w) M80A;

(x) MAK90;

(y) MPiK;

(z) MPiKM;

(z.1) MPiKMS-72;

(z.2) MPiKS;

(z.3) PKM;

(z.4) PKM-DGN-60;

(z.5) PMKM;

(z.6) RPK;

(z.7) RPK-74;

(z.8) RPK-87S;

(z.9) Type 56;

(z.10) Type 56-1;

(z.11) Type 56-2;

(z.12) Type 56-3;

(z.13) Type 56-4;

(z.14) Type 68;

(z.15) Type 79;

(z.16) American Arms AKY39;

(z.17) American Arms AKF39;

(z.18) American Arms AKC47;

(z.19) American Arms AKF47;

(z.20) MAM70WS762;

(z.21) MAM70FS762;

(z.22) Mitchell AK-22;

(z.23) Mitchell AK-47;

(z.24) Mitchell Heavy Barrel AK-47;

(z.25) Norinco 84S;

(z.26) Norinco 84S AK;

(z.27) Norinco 56;

(z.28) Norinco 56-1;

(z.29) Norinco 56-2;

(z.30) Norinco 56-3;

(z.31) Norinco 56-4;

(z.32) Poly Technologies Inc. AK-47/S;

(z.33) Poly Technologies Inc. AKS-47/S;

(z.34) Poly Technologies Inc. AKS-762;

(z.35) Valmet M76;

(z.36) Valmet M76 carbine;

(z.37) Valmet M78/A2;

(z.38) Valmet M78 (NATO) LMG;

(z.39) Valmet M82; and

(z.40) Valmet M82 Bullpup.

65. The firearm of the design commonly known as the Armalite AR-180 Sporter carbine, and any variant or modified version of it.

66. The firearm of the design commonly known as the Beretta AR70 assault rifle, and any variant or modified version of it.

67. The firearm of the design commonly known as the BM 59 rifle, and any variant or modified version of it, including

(a) the Beretta

(i) BM 59,

(ii) BM 59R,

(iii) BM 59GL,

(iv) BM 59D,

(v) BM 59 Mk E,

(vi) BM 59 Mk I,

(vii) BM 59 Mk Ital,

(viii) BM 59 Mk II,

(ix) BM 59 Mk III,

(x) BM 59 Mk Ital TA,

(xi) BM 59 Mk Ital Para,

(xii) BM 59 Mk Ital TP, and

(xiii) BM 60CB; and

(b) the Springfield Armory

(i) BM 59 Alpine

(ii) BM 59 Alpine Paratrooper, and

(iii) BM 59 Nigerian Mk IV.

68. The firearm of the design commonly known as the Bushmaster Auto Rifle, and any variant or modified version of it.

69. The firearm of the design commonly known as the Cetme Sport Auto Rifle, and any variant or modified version of it.

70. The firearm of the design commonly known as the Daewoo K1 rife, and any variant or modified version of it, including the Daewoo K1A1, K2, Max 1, Max 2, AR-100, AR 110C, MAXI-II and KC-20.

71. The firearm of the design commonly known as the Demro TAC-1M carbine, and any variant or modified version of it, including the Demro XF-7 Wasp Carbine.

72. The firearm of the design commonly known as the Eagle Apache Carbine, and any variant or modified version of it.

73. The firearm of the design commonly known as the FN-FNC rifle, and any variant or modified version of it, including the FNC Auto Rifle, FNC Auto Paratrooper, FNC-11, FNC-22 and FNC-33.

74. The firearm of the design commonly known as the FN-FAL (FN-LAR) rifle, and any variant or modified version of it, including the FN 308 Model 44, FN-FAL (FN-LAR) Competition Auto, FN-FAL (FN-LAR) Heavy Barrel 308 Match, FN-FAL (FN-LAR) Paratrooper 308 Match 50-64 and FN 308 Model 50-63.

75. The firearm of the design commonly known as the G3 rifle, and any variant or modified version of it, including the Heckler and Koch

(a) HK 91;

(b) HK 91A2;

(c) HK 91A3;
(d) HK G3 A3;
(e) HK G3 A3 ZF;
(f) HK G3 A4;
(g) HK G3 SG/1; and
(h) HK PSG1.

76. The firearm of the design commonly known as the Galil assault rifle, and any variant or modified version of it, including the AP-84, Galil ARM, Galil AR, Galil SAR, Galil 332 and Mitchell Galil/22 Auto Rifle.

77. The firearm of the design commonly known as the Goncz High-Tech Carbine, and any variant or modified version of it,

78. The firearm of the design commonly known as the Heckler and Koch HK 33 rifle, and any variant or modified version of it, including the

(a) HK 33A2;
(b) HK 33A3;
(c) HK 33KA1;
(d) HK 93;
(e) HK 93A2; and
(f) HK 93A3.

79. The firearm of the design commonly known as the J & R Eng M-68 carbine, and any variant or modified version of it, including the PJK M-68 and the Wilkinson Terry carbine.

80. The firearm of the design commonly known as the Leader Mark Series Auto Rifle, and any variant or modified version of it.

81. The firearms of the designs commonly known as the MP5 submachine gun and MP5 carbine, and any variants or modified versions of them, including the Heckler and Koch

(a) HK MP5;
(b) HK MP5A2;
(c) HK MP5A3;
(d) HK MP5K;
(e) HK MP5SD;
(f) HK MP5SD1;
(g) HK MP5SD2;
(h) HK MP5SD3;

(i) HK 94;

(j) HK 94A2; and

(k) HK 94A3.

82. The firearm of the design commonly known as the PE57 rifle, and any variant or modified version of it.

83. The firearm of the design commonly known as the SG-550 rifle and SC-551 carbine, and any variants or modified versions of them.

84. The firearm of the design commonly known as the SIG AMT rifle, and any variant or modified version of it.

85. The firearm of the design commonly known as the Springfield Armory SAR-48 rifle, and any variant or modified version of it, including the SAR-48 Bush, SAR-48 Heavy Barrel, SAR-48 Para and SAR-48 Model 22.

86. The firearm of the design commonly known as the Thompson submachine gun, and any variant or modified version of it, including the

(a) Thompson Model 1921;

(b) Thompson Model 1927;

(c) Thompson Model 1928;

(d) Thompson Model M1;

(e) Auto-Ordnance M27A-1;

(f) Auto-Ordnance M27A-1 Deluxe;

(g) Auto-Ordnance M1927A-3;

(h) Auto-Ordnance M1927A-5;

(i) Auto-Ordnance Thompson M1;

(j) Commando Arms Mk I;

(k) Commando Arms Mk II;

(l) Commando Arms Mk III;

(m) Commando Arms Mk 9; and

(n) Commando Arms Mk 45.

Part 2 — Restricted Firearms

Former Restricted Weapons Order

1. The firearms of the designs commonly known as the High Standard Model 10, Series A shotgun and the High Standard Model 10, Series B shotgun, an any variants or modified versions of them.

2. The firearm of the design commonly known as the M-16 rifle, and any variant or modified version of it, including the

(a) Colt AR-15;

(b) Colt AR-15 SPI;

(c) Colt AR-15 Sporter;

(d) Colt AR-15 Collapsible Stock Model;

(e) Colt AR-15 A2;

(f) Colt AR-15 A2 Carbine;

(g) Colt AR-15 A2 Government Model Rifle;

(h) Colt AR-15 A2 Government Model Target Rifle;

(i) colt AR-15 A2 Government Model Carbine;

(j) Colt AR-15 A2 Sporter II;

(k) Colt AR-15 A2 H-BAR;

(l) Colt AR-15 A2 Delta H-BAR;

(m) Colt AR-15 A2 Delta H-BAR Match;

(n) Colt AR-15 9mm Carbine;

(o) Armalite AR-15;

(p) AAI M15;

(q) AP74;

(r) EAC J-15;

(s) PWA Commando;

(t) SGW XM15A;

(u) SGW CAR-AR;

(v) SWD AR-15; and

(w) any 22-calibre rimfire variant, including the

(i) Mitchell M-16A-1/22,

(ii) Mitchell M-16/22,

(iii) Mitchell CAR-15/22, and

(iv) AP74 Auto Rifle.

Part 2.1 — Firearms for the Purposes of Sections 3.1 and 3.2

[Heading added SOR/2015-213, s. 3. Repealed 2019, c. 9, s. 21. Not in force at date of publication.]

1. Ceská Zbrojovka (CZ) Model CZ858 Tactical-2P rifle

Proposed Repeal — 1

1. [Repealed 2019, c. 9, s. 21. Not in force at date of publication.]

SOR/2015-213, s. 3

2. Ceská Zbrojovka (CZ) Model CZ858 Tactical-2V rifle

Proposed Repeal — 2

2. [Repealed 2019, c. 9, s. 21. Not in force at date of publication.]

SOR/2015-213, s. 3

3. Ceská Zbrojovka (CZ) Model CZ858 Tactical-4P rifle

Proposed Repeal — 3

3. [Repealed 2019, c. 9, s. 21. Not in force at date of publication.]

SOR/2015-213, s. 3

4. Ceská Zbrojovka (CZ) Model CZ858 Tactical-4V rifle

Proposed Repeal — 4

4. [Repealed 2019, c. 9, s. 21. Not in force at date of publication.]

SOR/2015-213, s. 3

5. SAN Swiss Arms Model Classic Green rifle

Proposed Repeal — 5

5. [Repealed 2019, c. 9, s. 21. Not in force at date of publication.]

SOR/2015-213, s. 3

6. SAN Swiss Arms Model Classic Green carbine

Proposed Repeal — 6

6. [Repealed 2019, c. 9, s. 21. Not in force at date of publication.]

SOR/2015-213, s. 3

7. SAN Swiss Arms Model Classic Green CQB rifle

Proposed Repeal — 7

7. [Repealed 2019, c. 9, s. 21. Not in force at date of publication.]

SOR/2015-213, s. 3

8. SAN Swiss Arms Model Black Special rifle

Proposed Repeal — 8

8. [Repealed 2019, c. 9, s. 21. Not in force at date of publication.]

SOR/2015-213, s. 3

9. SAN Swiss Arms Model Black Special carbine

Proposed Repeal — 9

9. [Repealed 2019, c. 9, s. 21. Not in force at date of publication.]

SOR/2015-213, s. 3

10. SAN Swiss Arms Model Black Special CQB rifle

Proposed Repeal — 10

10. [Repealed 2019, c. 9, s. 21. Not in force at date of publication.]

SOR/2015-213, s. 3

11. SAN Swiss Arms Model Black Special Target rifle

Proposed Repeal — 11

11. [Repealed 2019, c. 9, s. 21. Not in force at date of publication.]

SOR/2015-213, s. 3

12. SAN Swiss Arms Model Blue Star rifle

Proposed Repeal — 12

12. [Repealed 2019, c. 9, s. 21. Not in force at date of publication.]

SOR/2015-213, s. 3

13. SAN Swiss Arms Model Heavy Metal rifle

Proposed Repeal — 13

13. [Repealed 2019, c. 9, s. 21. Not in force at date of publication.]

SOR/2015-213, s. 3

14. SAN Swiss Arms Model Red Devil rifle

Proposed Repeal — 14

14. [Repealed 2019, c. 9, s. 21. Not in force at date of publication.]

SOR/2015-213, s. 3

15. SAN Swiss Arms Model Swiss Arms Edition rifle

Proposed Repeal — 15

15. [Repealed 2019, c. 9, s. 21. Not in force at date of publication.]

SOR/2015-213, s. 3

Part 3 — Prohibited Weapons

Former Prohibited Weapons Order, No. 1

1. Any device designed to be used for the purpose of injuring, immobilizing or otherwise incapacitating any person by the discharge therefrom of

(a) tear gas, Mace or other gas, or

(b) any liquid, spray, powder or other substance that is capable of injuring, immobilizing or otherwise incapacitating any person.

Former Prohibited Weapons Order, No. 2

2. Any instrument or device commonly known as "nunchaku", being hard non-flexible sticks, clubs, pipes, or rods linked by a length or lengths of rope, cord, wire or chain, and any similar instrument or device.

3. Any instrument or device commonly known as "shuriken", being a hard non-flexible plate having three or more radiating points with one or more sharp edges in the shape of a polygon, trefoil, cross, star, diamond or other geometrical shape, and any similar instrument or device.

4. Any instrument or device commonly known as "manrikigusari" or "kusari", being hexagonal or other geometrically shaped hard weights or hand grips linked by a length or lengths of rope, cord, wire or chain, and any similar instrument or device.

5. Any finger ring that has one or more blades or sharp objects that are capable of being projected from the surface of the ring.

Former Prohibited Weapons Order, No. 3

6. Any device that is designed to be capable of injuring, immobilizing or incapacitating a person or an animal by discharging an electrical charge produced by means of the amplification or accumulation of the electrical current generated by a battery, where the device is designed or altered so that the electrical charge may be discharged when the device is of a length of less than 480 mm, and any similar device.

7. A crossbow or similar device that

(a) is designed or altered to be aimed and fired by the action of one hand, whether or not it has been redesigned or subsequently altered to be aimed and fired by the action of both hands; or

(b) has a length not exceeding 500 mm.

Former Prohibited Weapons Order, No. 4

8. The device known as the "Constant Companion", being a belt containing a blade capable of being withdrawn from the belt, with the buckle of the belt forming a handle for the blade, and any similar device.

9. Any knife commonly known as a "push-dagger" that is designed in such a fashion that the handle is placed perpendicular to the main cutting edge of the blade and any other similar device other than the aboriginal "ulu" knife.

10. Any device having a length of less than 30 cm and resembling an innocuous object but designed to conceal a knife or blade, including the device commonly known as the "knife-comb", being a comb with the handle of the comb forming a handle for the knife, and any similar device.

Former Prohibited Weapons Order, No. 5

11. The device commonly known as a "Spiked Wristband", being a wristband to which a spike or blade is affixed, and any similar device.

Former Prohibited Weapons Order, No. 6

12. The device commonly known as a "Yaqua Blowgun", being a tube or pipe designed for the purpose of shooting arrows or darts by the breath, and any similar device.

Former Prohibited Weapons Order, No. 7

13. The device commonly known as a "Kiyoga Baton" or "Steel Cobra" and any similar device consisting of a manually triggered telescoping spring-loaded steel whip terminated in a heavy calibre striking tip.

14. The device commonly known as a "Morning Star" and any similar device consisting of a ball of metal or other heavy material, studded with spikes and connected to a handle by a length of chain, rope or other flexible material.

Former Prohibited Weapons Order, No. 8

15. The device commonly known as "Brass Knuckles" and any similar device consisting of a band of metal with one or more finger holes designed to fit over the fingers of the hand.

Part 4 — Prohibited Devices

Former Prohibited Weapons Order, No. 9

1. Any electrical or mechanical device that is designed or adapted to operate the trigger mechanism of a semi-automatic firearm for the purpose of causing the firearm to discharge cartridges in rapid succession.

2. Any rifle, shotgun or carbine stock of the type known as the "bull-pup" design, being a stock that, when combined with a firearm, reduces the overall length of the firearm such that a substantial part f the reloading action or the magazine-well is located behind the trigger of the firearm when it is held in the normal firing position.

Former Cartridge Magazine Control Regulations

3. (1) Any cartridge magazine

(a) that is capable of containing more than five cartridges of the type for which the magazine was originally designed and that is designed or manufactured for use in

(i) a semi-automatic handgun that is not commonly available in Canada,

(ii) a semi-automatic firearm other than a semi-automatic handgun,

(iii) an automatic firearm whether or not it has been altered to discharge only one projectile with one pressure of the trigger,

(iv) the firearms of the designs commonly known as the Ingram M10 and M11 pistols, and any variants or modified versions of them, including the Cobray M10 and M11 pistols, the RPB M10, M11 and SM11 pistols and the SWD M10, M11, SM10 and SM11 pistols,

(v) the firearm of the design commonly known as the Partisan Avenger Auto Pistol, and any variant or modified version of it, or

(vi) the firearm of the design commonly known as the UZI pistol, and any variant or modified version of it, including the Micro-UZI pistol; or

(b) that is capable of containing more than 10 cartridges of the type for which the magazine was originally designed and that is designed or manufactured for use in a semi-automatic handgun that is commonly available in Canada.

(2) Paragraph (1)(a) does not include any cartridge magazine that

(a) was originally designed or manufactured for use in a firearm that

(i) is chambered for, or designed to use, rimfire cartridges,

(ii) is a rifle of the type commonly known as the "Lee Enfield" rifle, where the magazine is capable of containing not more than 10 cartridges of the type for which the magazine was originally designed, or

(iii) is commonly known as the U.S. Rifle M1 (Garand) including the Beretta M1 Garand rifle, the Breda M1 Garand rifle and the Springfield Armoury M1 Garand rifle;

(b) is not a reproduction and was originally designed or manufactured for use in a firearm that

(i) is commonly known as the Charlton Rifle,

(ii) is commonly known as the Farquhar-Hill Rifle, or

(iii) is commonly known as the Huot Automatic Rifle;

(c) is of the "drum" type, is not a reproduction and was originally designed or manufactured for use in a firearm commonly known as

(i) the .303 in. Lewis Mark 1 machine-gun, or any variant or modified version of it, including the Lewis Mark 1*, Mark 2, Mark 2*, Mark 3, Mark 4, Lewis SS and .30 in. Savage-Lewis,

(ii) the .303 in. Vickers Mark 1 machine-gun, or any variant or modified version of it, including the Mark 1*, Mark 2, Mark 2*, Mark 3, Mark 4, Mark 4B, Mark 5, Mark 6, Mark 6* and Mark 7, or

(iii) the Bren Light machine-gun, or any variant or modified version of it, including the Mark 1, Mark 2, Mark 2/1, Mark 3 and Mark 4;

(d) is of the "metallic-strip" type, is not a reproduction and was originally designed or manufactured for use in conjunction with the firearm known as the Hotchkiss machine-gun, Model 1895 or Model 1897, or any variant or modified version of it, including the Hotchkiss machine-gun, Model 1900, Model 1909, Model 1914 and Model 1917, and the Hotchkiss machine-gun (Enfield), Number 2, Mark 1 and Mark 1*;

(e) is of the "saddle-drum" type (*doppeltrommel* or *satteltrommel*), is not a reproduction and was originally designed or manufactured for use in the automatic firearms known as the MG-13, MG-15, MG-17, MG-34, T6-200 or T6-220, or any variant or modified version of it; or

(f) is of the "belt" type consisting of a fabric or metal belt, is not a reproduction and was originally designed or manufactured for the purpose of feeding cartridges into a automatic firearm of a type that was in existence before 1945.

(3) Paragraph (1)(b) does not include any cartridge magazine that

(a) is the "snail-drum" type (*schneckentrommel*) that was originally designed or manufactured for use in a firearm that is a handgun known as the Parabellum-Pistol, System Borchardt-Luger, Model 1900, or "Luger", or any variant or modified version of it, including the Model 1902, Model 1904 (Marine),

Model 1904/06 (Marine), Model 1904/08 (Marine), Model 1906, Model 1908 and Model 1908 (Artillery) pistols;

(b) was originally designed or manufactured for use in a firearm that is a semi-automatic handgun, where the magazine was manufactured before 1910;

(c) was originally designed or manufactured as an integral part of the firearm known as the Mauser Selbstladepistole C/96 ("broomhandle"), or any variant or modified version of it, including the Model 1895, Model 1896, Model 1902, Model 1905, Model 1912, Model 1915, Model 1930, Model 1931, M711 and M712; or

(d) was originally designed or manufactured for use in the semi-automatic firearm that is a handgun known as the Webley and Scott Self-Loading Pistol, Model 1912 or Model 1915.

(4) A cartridge magazine described in subsection (1) that has been altered or re-manufactured so that it is not capable of containing more than five or ten cartridges as the case may be, of the type for which it was originally designed is not a prohibited device as prescribed by that subsection if the modification to the magazine cannot be easily removed and the magazine cannot be easily further altered so that it is so capable of containing more than five or ten cartridges, as the case may be.

(5) For the purposes of subsection (4), altering or re-manufacturing a cartridge magazine includes

(a) the indentation of its casing by forging, casting, swaging or impressing;

(b) in the case of a cartridge magazine with a steel or aluminum casing, the insertion and attachment of a plug, sleeve, rod, pin, flange or similar device, made of steel or aluminum, as the case may be, or of a similar material, to the inner surface of its casing by welding, brazing or any other similar method; or

(c) in the case of a cartridge magazine with a casing made of a material other than steel or aluminum, the attachment of a plug, sleeve, rod, pin, flange or similar device, made of steel or of a material similar to that of the magazine casing, to the inner surface of its casing by welding, brazing or any other similar method or by applying a permanent adhesive substance, such as a cement or an epoxy or other glue.

Part 5 — Prohibited Ammunition

Former Prohibited Weapons Order, No. 10

1. Any cartridge that is capable of being discharged from a commonly available semi-automatic handgun or revolver and that is manufactured or assembled with a projectile that is designed, manufactured or altered so as to be capable of penetrating body armour, including KTW, THV and 5.7 x 28 mm P-90 cartridges.

2. Any projectile that is designed, manufactured or altered to ignite on impact, where the projectile is designed for use in or in conjunction with a cartridge and does not exceed 15 mm in diameter.

3. Any projectile that is designed, manufactured or altered so as to explode on impact, where the projectile is designed for use in or in conjunction with a cartridge and does not exceed 15 mm in diameter.

4. Any cartridge that is capable of being discharged from a shotgun and that contains projectiles known as "fléchettes" or any similar projectiles.

Can. Reg. 98-466 — Regulations Prescribing Public Officers

made under the *Criminal Code*

SOR/98-466, as am. SOR/98-472, s. 5; SOR/2011-68; SOR/2015-166, s. 1.

1. (1) A member of any of the following classes of persons, if employed in the public service of Canada or by the government of a province or municipality, is a public officer for the purposes of paragraph 117.07(2)(g) of the *Criminal Code*:

(a) employees who are responsible for the examination, inventory, storage, maintenance or transportation of court exhibits and evidence;

(b) employees of police force or other public service agencies who are responsible for the acquisition, examination, inventory, storage, maintenance, issuance or transportation of fire fire-arms, prohibited weapons, restricted weapons, prohibited devices, prohibited ammunition or explosive substances;

(c) technicians, laboratory analysts and scientists who work at forensic or research laboratories;

(d) armourers and firearms instructors who work at police academies or similar institutions designated under subparagraph 117.07(2)(e)(ii) of the *Criminal Code*, or are employed by a federal or provincial department of natural resources, fisheries, wildlife, conservation or the environment, or by Revenue Canada;

(e) park wardens and other employees of a federal or provincial department who are responsible for the enforcement of laws and regulations dealing with natural resources, fisheries, wildlife, conservation or the environment;

(f) immigration officers;

(g) security personnel employed by the House of Commons or the Senate or by the Service, as defined in section 79.51 of the *Parliament of Canada Act*; and

(h) aircraft pilots employed by the Department of Transport or other public service agencies.

(2) For the purposes of subsection (1), the expression **"public service agencies"** has the same meaning as in section 1 of the *Public Agents Firearms Regulations*.

SOR/2011-68, s. 1; SOR/2015-166, s. 1

Coming into Force

2. These Regulations come into force on December 1, 1998.

SOR/98-472, s. 5

CAN. REG. 2002-284 — REGULATIONS ESTABLISHING A LIST OF ENTITIES

made under the *Criminal Code*

SOR/2002-284, as am. SOR/2002-434; SOR/2002-454; SOR/2003-53; SOR/2003-127; SOR/2003-235; SOR/2003-365; SOR/2004-135; SOR/2005-159; SOR/2006-62; SOR/2006-257; SOR/2008-214; SOR/2010-51; SOR/2010-312; SOR/2010-313; SOR/2011-144; SOR/2012-162; SOR/2012-299; SOR/2012-300; SOR/2013-93; SOR/2013-194; SOR/2013-195; SOR/2013-257; SOR/2014-97; SOR/2014-147; SOR/2014-211, ss. 1, 2 (Fr.); SOR/2014-246; SOR/2015-87; SOR/2015-175; SOR/2016-320; SOR/2018-103; SOR/2019-45; SOR/2019-231.

LIST

1. The following list is established for the purposes of Part II.1 of the *Criminal Code*.

Al-Gama'a al-Islamiyya (AGAI) (also known as Islamic Group (IG))

Al Qaida (also known among other names as Al Jihad (AJ), Egyptian Islamic Jihad (EIJ), Vanguards of Conquest (VOC), Islamic Army, Islamic Salvation Foundation, The Base, Group for the Preservation of the Holy Sites, Islamic Army for the Liberation of the Holy Places, World Islamic Front for Jihad Against Jews and Crusaders, Usama Bin Ladin Network, Usama Bin Ladin Organization and Qa'idat al-Jihad)

Al Qaeda in the Islamic Maghreb (AQIM) (also known among other names as Tanzim Qaedat bi-Bilad al-Maghrab al-Islami, Tanzim al-Qa'ida fi bilad al-Maghreb al-Islamiya, The Organization of Al-Qaida in the Islamic Maghreb, Al-Qa'ida Organisation in the Lands of the Islamic Maghreb, Al-Qa'ida in the Islamic Maghreb, Al-Qa'ida in the Lands of the Islamic Maghreb, al-Qaïda dans les pays du Maghreb islamique, Salafist Group for Call and Combat (GSPC), Groupe salafiste pour la prédication et le combat, and Salafist Group for Preaching and Combat)

Armed Islamic Group (GIA) (also known as Groupe islamique armé (GIA))

Harakat ul-Mudjahidin (HuM) (also known among other names as Al-Faran, Al-Hadid, Al-Hadith, Harkat-ul-Mujahideen, Harakat ul-Mujahideen, Harakat al-Mujahideen, Harkat-ul-Ansar, Harakat ul-Ansar, Harakat al-Ansar, Harkat-ul-Jehad-e-Islami, Harkat Mujahideen, Harakat-ul-Mujahideen al-Almi, Holy Warriors Movement, Movement of the Mujahideen, Movement of the Helpers, Movement of Islamic Fighters, Al Qanoon and Jamiat ul-Ansar)

Asbat Al-Ansar (AAA) ("The League of Partisans") (also known among other names as God's Partisans, Gathering of Supporters, Partisan's League, Osbat Al Ansar, Usbat Al Ansar, Esbat Al-Ansar, Isbat Al Ansar, Usbat-ul-Ansar, Band of Helpers, Band of Partisans and League of the Followers)

Palestinian Islamic Jihad (PIJ) (also known among other names as Harakat al-Jihad al-Islami fi Filistin, Saraya Al-Quds (The Jerusalem Brigades), Al-Quds Brigades, Islamic Jihad, Palestine Islamic Jihad — Shaqaqi Faction, Palestinian Islamic Jihad — Shaqaqi, PIJ — Shaqaqi Faction, PIJ — Shallah Faction, Islamic Jihad of Palestine, Islamic Jihad in Palestine, Abu Ghunaym Squad of the Hizballah Bayt Al-Maqdis, Al-Quds Squads, Al-Awdah Brigades, Islamic Jihad Palestine (IJP), Islamic Jihad — Palestine Faction and Islamic Holy War)

Jaish-e-Mohammed (JeM) (also known among other names as Jaish-i-Mohammed (Mohammad, Muhammad, Muhammed), Jaish-e-Mohammad (Muhammed), Jaish-e-Mohammad Mujahideen E-Tanzeem, Jeish-e-Mahammed, Army of Mohammed, Mohammed's Army, Tehrik Ul-Furqaan, National Movement for the Restoration of Pakistani Sovereignty and Army of the Prophet)

Hamas (Harakat Al-Muqawama Al-Islamiya) ("Islamic Resistance Movement")

Kurdistan Workers Party (PKK) (also known among other names as Kurdistan Workers Party, Partya Karkeren Kurdistan, Kurdistan Labor Party, Kurdistan Freedom and Democracy Congress, KADEK, Kurdistan People's Congress, Kurdistan Halk Kongresi (KHK), People's Congress of Kurdistan and Kongra-Gel)

Aum Shinrikyo (also known among other names as Aum Shinri Kyo, Aum, Aum Supreme Truth, A. I. C. Comprehensive Research Institute, A. I. C. Sogo Kenkyusho and Aleph)

Hizballah (also known among other names as Hizbullah, Hizbollah, Hezbollah, Hezballah, Hisbu'llah, The Party of God, Islamic Jihad (Islamic Holy War), Islamic Jihad Organization, Islamic Resistance, Islamic Jihad for the Liberation of Palestine, Ansar al-Allah (Followers of God/Partisans of God/God's Helpers), Ansarollah (Followers of God/Partisans of God/God's Helpers), Ansar Allah (Followers of God/Partisans of God/God's Helpers), Al-Muqawamah al-Islamiyyah (Islamic Resistance), Organization of the Oppressed, Organization of the Oppressed on Earth, Revolutionary Justice Organization, Organization of Right Against Wrong and Followers of the Prophet Muhammed)

Abu Nidal Organization (ANO) (also known among other names as Fatah Revolutionary Council, Revolutionary Council, Revolutionary Council of Fatah, Al-Fatah Revolutionary Council, Fatah — the Revolutionary Council, Black June, Arab Revolutionary Brigades, Revolutionary Organization of Socialist Muslims, Black September, Egyptian Revolution, Arab Fedayeen Cells, Palestine Revolutionary Council, Organization of Jund al Haq and Arab Revolutionary Council)

Abu Sayyaf Group (ASG) (also known among other names as Al Harakat Al Islamiyya (AHAI), Al Harakat-ul Al Islamiyya, Al-Harakatul-Islamia, Al Harakat Al Aslamiya, Abou Sayaf Armed Band (ASAB), Abu Sayaff Group, Abu Sayyef Group and Mujahideen Commando Freedom Fighters (MCFF))

Sendero Luminoso (SL) (also known among other names as Shining Path, Partido Comunista del Peru en el Sendero Luminoso de Jose Carlos Mariategui, Communist Party of Peru on the Shining Path of Jose Carlos Mariategui, Partido Comunista del Peru, Communist Party of Peru, The Communist Party of Peru by the Shining Path of Jose Carlos Mariategui and Marxism, Leninism, Maoism and the Thoughts of Chairman Gonzalo, Revolutionary Student Front for the Shining Path of Maritegui, Communist Party of Peru — By Way of the Shining Path of Mariategui, PCP — por el Sendero Luminoso de Mariategui, PCP and PCP-SL)

Jemaah Islamiyyah (JI) (also known among other names as Jemaa Islamiyah, Jema'a Islamiyya, Jema'a Islamiyyah, Jema'ah Islamiyyah, Jema'ah Islamiyyah, Jemaa Islamiya, Jemaa Islamiyya, Jemaah Islamiyya, Jemaa Islamiyyah, Jemaah Islamiah, Jemaah Islamiya, Jemaah Islamiyyah, Jemaah Islamiya, Jamaah Islamiyah, Jamaa Islamiya, Jemaah Islam, Jemahh Islamiyah, Jama'ah Islamiyah, Al-Jama'ah Al Islamiyyah, Islamic Group and Islamic Community)

Islamic Movement of Uzbekistan (IMU) (also known among other names as O'zbekiston Islomiy Harakati, Harakat ul-Islamiyyah, Islamic Movement of Turkestan, Islamic Party of Turkestan (IPT) and IMU-IPT)

Euskadi Ta Askatasuna (ETA) (also known among other names as Basque Homeland and Liberty, Euzkadi Ta Azkatasuna, Euzkadi Ta Askatasuna, Basque Nation and Liberty, Basque Fatherland and Liberty and Basque Homeland and Freedom)

Al-Aqsa Martyrs' Brigade (AAMB) (also known among other names as Al-Asqa Intifada Martyrs' Group, Al-Aqsa Brigades, Martyrs of al-Aqsa group, Al-Aqsa Martyrs Battalion and Armed Militias of the Al-Aqsa Martyr Battalions)

Fuerzas Armadas Revolucionarias de Colombia (FARC) (also known among other names as Revolutionary Armed Forces of Columbia, Revolutionary Armed Forces of Colombia-People's Army (Fuerzas Armadas Revolucionarias de Colombia-Ejército del Pueblo, FARC-EP), National Finance Commission (Comisión Nacional de Finanzas) and Coordinadora Nacional Guerrillera Simon Bolivar (CNGSB))

Ejército de Liberación Nacional (ELN) (also known among other names as National Liberation Army and the Army of National Liberation)

Babbar Khalsa International (BKI) (also known as Babbar Khalsa)

International Sikh Youth Federation (ISYF)

Lashkar-e-Tayyiba (LeT) (also known among other names as Jamaat-ud-Dawa (JuD) (Society for Preaching), al-Anfal Trust, Tehrik-e-Hurmate-e-Rasool, al Mansoorian (The Victorious), Army of the Pure, Paasban-e-Kashmir (Kashmir Brigade), Paasban-i-Ahle-Hadith (Ahle-Hadith Brigade), Falah-i-Insaniat Foundation (FIF), Idara Khidmat-e-Khalq, Lashkar-e-Toiba, Lashkar-i-Toiba (LiT), Lashkar-i-Taiba (Holy Regiment), Lashkar-e-Tayyiba (LT) (Army of the Righteous), Lashkar-e-Taibyya, Lashkar-e-Taiba, Lashkar-e-Tayyiba (Army of the Pure and Righteous), Lashkar-e-Taiba (Righteous Army), Lashkar-Taiba (Army of the Good), Lashkar e Toiba, Lashkar e Taiba, Lashkar-E-Tayyaba, Lashkar e Tayyiba)

Lashkar-e-Jhangvi (LJ) (also known among other names as Lashkar-i-Jhangvi, Lashkar-e-Jhangvie, Laskar-e-Jhangvi, Lashkare Jhangvi, Lashkar-e-Jhangwi, Lashkar-i-Jhangwi, Jhangvi Army, Lashkar-e Jhangvi, Lashkar Jhangvi, Lashkar-e-Jhanvi (LeJ), Lashkar-i-Jangvi, Lashkar e Jhangvi, Lashkar Jangvi, Laskar e Jahangvi)

Palestine Liberation Front (PLF) (also known among other names as PLF — Abu Abbas Faction, Front for the Liberation of Palestine (FLP))

Popular Front for the Liberation of Palestine (PFLP) (Al-Jibha al-Sha'biya lil-Tahrir Filistin) (also known among other names as Halhul Gang, Halhul Squad, Palestinian Popular Resistance Forces, PPRF, Red Eagle Gang, Red Eagle Group, Red Eagles and Abu Ali Mustafa Brigades)

Popular Front for the Liberation of Palestine — General Command (PFLP-GC) (Al-Jibha Sha'biya lil-Tahrir Filistin-al-Qadiya al-Ama)

Ansar al-Islam (AI) (also known among other names as the Partisans of Islam, Helpers of Islam, Supporters of Islam, Soldiers of God, Kurdistan Taliban, Soldiers of Islam, Kurdistan Supporters of Islam, Supporters of Islam in Kurdistan, Followers of Islam in Kurdistan and Ansar al-Sunna)

Gulbuddin Hekmatyar (also known among other names as Gulabudin Hekmatyar, Gulbuddin Khekmatiyar, Gulbuddin Hekmatiar, Gulbuddin Hekmartyar, Gulbudin Hekmetyar, Golboddin Hikmetyar and Gulbuddin Hekmetyar)

Kahane Chai (Kach) (also known among other names as Meir's Youth, No'ar Meir, Repression of Traitors, State of Yehuda, Sword of David, Dikuy Bogdim, DOV, Judea Police, Kahane Lives, Kfar Tapuah Fund, State of Judea, Judean Legion, Judean Voice, Qomemiyut Movement, Way of the Torah and Yeshiva of the Jewish Idea)

The Liberation Tigers of Tamil Eelam (LTTE) (also known among other names as the Tamil Tigers, the Eellalan Force, the Ellalan Force, the Tiger Movement, the Sangilian Force, the Air Tigers, the Black Tigers (Karum Puligal), the Sea Tigers, the Tiger Organization Security Intelligence Service (TOSIS) and the Women's Combat Force of Liberation Tigers (WCFLT))

Gulbuddin Hekmatyar's Faction of the Hezb-e Islami, the Hezb-e Islami Gulbuddin (HIG)

World Tamil Movement (WTM)

Al Shabaab (also known as Harakat Shabaab al-Mujahidin, al-Shabab, Shabaab, the Youth, Mujahidin al Shabaab Movement, Mujahideen Youth Movement, MYM, Mujahidin Youth, Hizbul Shabaab, Hisb'ul Shabaab, al-Shabaab al-Islamiya, Youth Wing, al Shabaab al-Islam, al-Shabaab al-

Jihad, the Unity of Islamic Youth and the Popular Resistance Movement in the Land of the Two Migrations)

Al Qaida in the Arabian Peninsula (AQAP) (also known among other names as Ansar al-Shari'a (AAS), Al-Qaida of Jihad Organization in the Arabian Peninsula, Tanzim Qa'idat al-Jihad fi Jazirat al-Arab, Al-Quaida Organization in the Arabian Peninsula (AQAP), Al-Quaida in the South Arabian Peninsula and Al-Qaida in Yemen (AQY))

Tehrik-e-Taliban Pakistan (TTP) (also known among other names as Tehrik-e-Taliban Pakistan, Tehrik-I-Taliban Pakistan, Tehrik-e-Taliban, Pakistani Taliban, Tehreek-e-Taliban, Tehrik Taliban-I-Pakistan, Tehrik-i-Taliban Pakistan, Tehreek-e-Taliban Pakistan and Mouvement des talibans du Pakistan)

Islamic State (IS) (also known among other names as Daesh, Islamic State in Iraq and the Levant, ISIL, Islamic State of Iraq and Syria, Islamic State of Iraq and al-Sham, ISIS, Al-Dawla Al-Islamiya fi al-Iraq wa al-Sham, Al Qaida in Iraq, al-Qaida in Iraq, Al-Qaeda in Iraq, Al Qaeda in Iraq, AQI, AQI-Zarqawi, al-Tawhid, al-Tawhid and al-Jihad, Kateab al-Tawhid, Brigades of Tawhid, Monotheism and Jihad Group, Al Qaida of the Jihad in the Land of the Two Rivers, Al-Qaida of Jihad in the Land of the Two Rivers, Al-Qaeda in the Land of the Two Rivers, Al-Qaida in the Land of the Two Rivers, Al-Qaida of Jihad Organization in the Land of the Two Rivers, Al-Qaida Group of Jihad in Iraq, Al-Qa'ida of Jihad in Iraq, Al-Qaida Group of Jihad in the Land of the Two Rivers, The Organization of Jihad's Base in the Country of the Two Rivers, The Organization of al-Jihad's Base of Operations in the Land of the Two Rivers, The Organization of al-Jihad's Base of Operations in Iraq, The Organization of al-Jihad's Base in Iraq, The Organization of al-Jihad's Base in the Land of the Two Rivers, The Organization Base of Jihad/Country of the Two Rivers, The Organization Base of Jihad/Mesopotamia, Al-Qaida in Mesopotamia, Tanzim Qa'idat Al-Jihad fi Bilad al-Rafidayn, Tanzim al-Qaeda al-Jihad fi Bilad al-Rafidain, Tanzeem Qa'idat al Jihad/Bilad al Raafidaini, Jama'at Al-Tawhid Wa'al-Jihad, JTJ, Islamic State of Iraq, Islamic State in Iraq, ISI, Mujahidin Shura Council, Unity and Holy Struggle, Unity and Holy War, Unity and Jihad Group and al-Zarqawi Network)

Islamic Revolutionary Guard Corps' Qods Force (also known among other names as Pasdaran-e Enghelab-e Islami (Pasdaran), Sepah-e Qods, Qods/Quds, al Quds, al Quds Force, Qods/Quds Force, Qods Corps, Jerusalem Corps, Jerusalem Force and Qods Force)

Haqqani Network

Taliban (also known among other names as Afghan Taliban, Tahreek-i-Islami-i-Taliban Afghanistan, Movement of Islamic Students, Taleban, Islamic Movement of the Taliban (De Talebano Islami Ghurdzang or Tehrik) and Islamic Emirate of Afghanistan (De Afghanistan Islami Emarat))

Hay'at Tahrir al-Sham (also known among other names as Jabhat al-Nusra (JN), Jabhat Fateh al-Sham, Jabhat Fatah al-Sham, Fath al-Sham Front, al-Jabha, Fath al-Sham, Tanzim al-Qaeda fi Bilad al-Sham, Al-Qaeda in the

Levant, Conquest for al-Sham Front, Conquest of the Levant Front, Fatah al-Sham Front, Fateh al-Sham Front, Front for the Conquest of Syria, Front for the Conquest of Syria/The Levant, Jabhat Fath al-Sham, Jabhat Fath al Sham, Jabhat Fathah al-Sham, Hayat Tahrir al-Sham, Tahrir al-Sham Assembly, Liberation of Syria Assembly, Liberation of the Levant Organisation, Liberation of the Levant Committee, Liberation of al-Sham Commission, Assembly for the Liberation of the Levant, Hay'et Tahrir al-Sham, Tahrir al-Sham, Liwa al-Haqq, the Al-Haqq Brigade, Liwa al-Haq, the Brigade of the Right, the Truth Brigade, the Haqq Brigade of Homs, Lewa' al-Haq, the al-Haq Battalion, Jabhat Ansar al-Din, Ansar al-Din Front, Supporters/Partisans of the Religion Front, Jaish al-Sunnah, Jaysh al-Sunnah, Jaish al-Sunna, Jaysh al-Sunna, Jabhet al-Nusra, The Victory Front, Al-Nusrah Front for the People of the Levant, Jabhat Al-Nusra li-Ahl al-Sham min Mujahedi al-Sham fi Sahat al-Jihad (The Support Front for the People of the Levant by the Levantine Mujahedin on the Battlefields of Jihad), the Front for the Defense of the Syrian People and the Front for the Support of the Syrian People)

al-Muwaqi'un Bil Dima (also known among other names as Al Mouaquioune bi addimaa, Katibat al-Muqaoon bil-Dumaa, al-Muwaqun Bi-Dima, Al-Muawaqqi'un bi 'l-Dima, al-Mouwakoune bi-Dimaa, al-Mua'qi'oon Bid-dam, Those Who Sign With Blood, El Mouwakaoune Bidame, Those Who Have Signed Through Blood, the Signatories for Blood, the Signatories in Blood and Those Who Sign in Blood)

Boko Haram (also known among other names as Jama'atu Ahlis Sunna Lidda'awati Wal-Jihad (People of the Tradition of the Prophet for Preaching and Striving / Group Committed to Propagating the Prophet's Teachings and Jihad))

Caucasus Emirate (also known among other names as Imarat Kavkaz and Islamic Emirate of the Caucasus)

International Relief Fund for the Afflicted and Needy — Canada (also known among other names as International Relief Fund for the Afflicted and Needy, International Relief Fund for the Afflicted and Needy (Canada), IRFAN, IRFAN — Canada and IRFAN Society)

Movement for Oneness and Jihad in West Africa (also known among other names as MOJWA, Mouvement pour l'unicité et le jihad en Afrique de l'Ouest, MUJAO, Jamat Tawhid wal Jihad fi Garbi Afriqqiya and Jamaat Tawhid Wal Jihad Fi Garbi Ifriqiya)

Al-Murabitoun (also known among other names as Mourabitounes, Al-Mourabitoun, Al-Morabitoune, Al-Mourabitoune and Les Almoravides)

Jaysh al-Muhajirin wal-Ansar (JMA) (also known among other names as Jaish al-Muhajireen wal Ansar, Jaysh al-Muhajireen wa'l-Ansar, Army of Migrants and Supporters, Army of Emigrants and Helpers, Muhajireen Brigade and Mujahideen Army)

Islamic State — Sinai Province (ISSP) (also known among other names as Ansar Bayt al-Maqdis, Ansar Jerusalem and Islamic State — Sinai State)

Abdallah Azzam Brigades (AAB) (also known among other names as Abdullah Azzam Brigades, the Brigades of Abdullah Azzam, the Brigades of the

Martyr Abdullah Azzam, the Ziyad al-Jarrah Battalions, the Ziad al-Jarrah Battalion, the Yusuf al-'Uyayri Battalions, the Yusuf al-Ayiri Battalion, the Battalion of Sheikh Yusuf al-'Ayiri and the Marwan Hadid Brigades)

Al Qaida in the Indian Subcontinent (AQIS) (also known among other names as Qaedat al-Jihad in the Indian Subcontinent, and Jamaat Qaidat al Jihad fi Shibh al Qarrah al Hindiyah (Organisation of the Base of Jihad in the Indian Subcontinent))

Indian Mujahideen (IM) (also known among other names as Indian Mujahedeen, Indian Mujahidin, and Islamic Security Force — IM (ISF-IM))

Islamic State — Khorasan Province (ISKP) (also known among other names as Islamic State in the Khorasan Province, Islamic State Khorasan, Islamic State — Khorasan, IS Khorasan, Islamic State of Iraq and the Levant — Khorasan (ISIL-K), Islamic State of Iraq and Syria — Khorasan (ISIS-K), Islamic State of Iraq and al-Sham — Khorasan (ISIS-K), Wilayat Khorasan, Daesh Khorasan, ISIL's South Asia Branch, ISIS Wilayat Khorasan, Islamic State's Khorasan Province, South Asian chapter of ISIL, ISIL Khorasan (ISIL-K), Khorasan Chapter of the Islamic State, Islamic State Wilayat Khorasan (ISWK) and Khorasan branch of ISIS)

HASAM (Harakat Sawa'd Misr) (also known among other names as Hassam, The Hasam Movement, Hasm, Hassm, the Hassm Movement, Harikat Souaid Misr, Harakah Sawa'id Misr, the Movement of Egypt's Arms, the Movement of Egypt's Forearms and the Arms of Egypt Movement)

Al-Ashtar Brigades (AAB) (also known among other names as Saraya al-Ashtar, Al Ashtar Brigades, The Ashtar Brigades, Saraya Waad Allah, Wa'ad Allah Brigades, Islamic Allah Brigades, Imam al-Mahdi Brigades and al-Haydariyah Brigades)

Fatemiyoun Division (FD) (also known among other names as Fatemioun Brigade, Fatemioun Military Division, Fatemiyoun, Fatemiyoun Battalion, Fatemiyoun Force, Fatemiyyun, Liwa Fatemiyoun, Liwa al-Fatemiyon, Fatemiyon Brigade, Fatemiyon Division and Fatemiyoun Brigade)

Harakat al-Sabireen (HaS) (also known among other names as Al-Sabirin Movement for Supporting Palestine, Al-Sabireen Movement for Supporting Palestine, Al-Sabirin, Al-Sabireen, a-Sabrin organization, Al-Sabireen for the Victory of Palestine, HISN, HOSN, The Sabireen Movement, HESN, Movement of Those Who Endure With Patience and Movement of the Patient Ones)

Blood & Honour (B&H)

Combat 18 (C18)

SOR/2002-434, s. 1; SOR/2002-454, s. 1; SOR/2003-53, s. 1; SOR/2003-127, s. 1; SOR/2003-235, s. 1; SOR/2003-365, s. 1; SOR/2004-135, s. 1; SOR/2005-159, s. 1; SOR/2006-62, s. 1; SOR/2006-257, s. 1; SOR/2008-214, s. 1; SOR/2010-51, s. 1; SOR/2010-312, s. 1; SOR/2010-313, s. 1; SOR/2011-144, s. 1; SOR/2012-162, s. 1; SOR/2012-299, s. 1; SOR/2012-300, s. 1; SOR/2013-93, s. 1; SOR/2013-194, s. 1; SOR/2013-195, s. 1; SOR/2013-257, s. 1; SOR/2014-97, s. 1; SOR/2014-147, s. 1; SOR/2014-211, s. 1; SOR/2014-246, s. 1; SOR/2015-87, s. 1; SOR/2015-175, s. 1; SOR/2016-320, s. 1; SOR/2018-103, s. 1; SOR/2019-45, s. 1; SOR/2019-231, s. 1

Coming into Force

2. These Regulations come into force on the day on which they are registered.

Can. Reg. SI/2012-103 — Order Accepting the Recommendation of the Minister of Public Safety and Emergency Preparedness Concerning the Two-year Review of the List of Entities

made under the *Criminal Code*

SI/2012-103

Schedule

Al-Gama'a al-Islamiyya (AGAI) (also known as Islamic Group (IG))

Al-Ittihad Al-Islam (AIAI)

Al Qaida

Al Qaeda in the Islamic Maghreb (AQIM) (also known among other names as Tanzim Qaedat bi-Bilad al-Maghrab al-Islami, Tanzim al-Qa'ida fi bilad al-Maghreb al-Islamiya, The Organization of Al-Qaida in the Islamic Maghreb, Al-Qa'ida Organisation in the Lands of the Islamic Maghreb, Al-Qa'ida in the Islamic Maghreb, Al-Qa'ida in the Lands of the Islamic Maghreb, al-Qaïda dans les pays du Maghreb islamique, Salafist Group for Call and Combat (GSPC), Groupe salafiste pour la prédication et le combat, and Salafist Group for Preaching and Combat)

Al Jihad (AJ) (also known as Egyptian Islamic Jihad (EIJ))

Vanguards of Conquest (VOC)

Armed Islamic Group (GIA) (also known as Groupe islamique armé (GIA))

Islamic Army of Aden (IAA) (also known among other names as the Islamic Army of Aden-Abyan (IAAA), the Aden-Abyan Islamic Army (AAIA), Aden Islamic Army, Islamic Aden Army, Muhammed's Army/Army of Mohammed and the Jaish Adan Al Islami)

Harakat ul-Mudjahidin (HuM) (also known among other names as Al-Faran, Al-Hadid, Al-Hadith, Harkat-ul-Mujahideen, Harakat ul-Mujahideen, Harakat al-Mujahideen, Harkat-ul-Ansar, Harakat ul-Ansar, Harakat al-Ansar, Harkat-ul-Jehad-e-Islami, Harkat Mujahideen, Harakat-ul-Mujahideen al-Almi, Holy Warriors Movement, Movement of the Mujahideen, Movement of the Helpers, Movement of Islamic Fighters and Al Qanoon)

Asbat Al-Ansar ("The League of Partisans") (also known among other names as Osbat Al Ansar, Usbat Al Ansar, Esbat Al-Ansar, Isbat Al Ansar and Usbat-ul-Ansar)

Palestinian Islamic Jihad (PIJ) (also known among other names as Islamic Jihad Palestine (IJP), Islamic Jihad — Palestine Faction and Islamic Holy War)

Jaish-e-Mohammed (JeM) (also known among other names as Jaish-i-Mohammed (Mohammad, Muhammad, Muhammed), Jaish-e-Mohammad (Muhammed), Jaish-e-Mohammad Mujahideen E-Tanzeem, Jeish-e-Mahammed, Army of Mohammed, Mohammed's Army, Tehrik Ul-Furqaan, National Movement for the Restoration of Pakistani Sovereignty and Army of the Prophet)

Hamas (Harakat Al-Muqawama Al-Islamiya) ("Islamic Resistance Movement")

Kurdistan Workers Party (PKK) (also known among other names as Kurdistan Workers Party, Partya Karkeren Kurdistan, Kurdistan Labor Party, Kurdistan Freedom and Democracy Congress, KADEK, Kurdistan People's Congress, Kurdistan Halk Kongresi (KHK), People's Congress of Kurdistan and Kongra-Gel)

Aum Shinrikyo (also known among other names as Aum Shinri Kyo, Aum, Aum Supreme Truth, A. I. C. Comprehensive Research Institute, A. I. C. Sogo Kenkyusho and Aleph)

Hizballah (also known among other names as Hizbullah, Hizbollah, Hezbollah, Hezballah, Hizbu'llah, The Party of God, Islamic Jihad (Islamic Holy War), Islamic Jihad Organization, Islamic Resistance, Islamic Jihad for the Liberation of Palestine, Ansar al-Allah (Followers of God/Partisans of God/God's Helpers), Ansarollah (Followers of God/Partisans of God/God's Helpers), Ansar Allah (Followers of God/Partisans of God/God's Helpers), Al-Muqawamah al-Islamiyyah (Islamic Resistance), Organization of the Oppressed, Organization of the Oppressed on Earth, Revolutionary Justice Organization, Organization of Right Against Wrong and Followers of the Prophet Muhammed)

Abu Nidal Organization (ANO) (also known among other names as Fatah Revolutionary Council, Revolutionary Council, Revolutionary Council of Fatah, Al-Fatah Revolutionary Council, Fatah-the Revolutionary Council, Black June, Arab Revolutionary Brigades, Revolutionary Organization of Socialist Muslims, Black September, Egyptian Revolution, Arab Fedayeen Cells, Palestine Revolutionary Council and Organization of Jund al Haq)

Abu Sayyaf Group (ASG) (also known among other names as Al Harakat Al Islamiyya (AHAI), Al Harakat-ul Al Islamiyya, Al-Harakatul-Islamia, Al Harakat Al Aslamiya, Abou Sayaf Armed Band (ASAB), Abu Sayaff Group, Abu Sayyef Group and Mujahideen Commando Freedom Fighters (MCFF))

Sendero Luminoso (SL) (also known among other names as Shining Path, Partido Comunista del Peru en el Sendero Luminoso de Jose Carlos Mariategui, Communist Party of Peru on the Shining Path of Jose Carlos Mariategui, Partido Comunista del Peru, Communist Party of Peru, The Communist Party of Peru by the Shining Path of Jose Carlos Mariategui and Marxism, Leninism, Maoism and the Thoughts of Chairman Gonzalo, Revolutionary Student Front for the Shining Path of Mariategui, Communist Party of Peru — By Way of the Shining Path of Mariategui, PCP — por el Sendero Luminoso de Mariategui, PCP and PCP-SL)

Jemaah Islamiyyah (JI) (also known among other names as Jemaa Islamiyah, Jema'a Islamiyya, Jema'a Islamiyyah, Jema'ah Islamiyah, Jema'ah Islamiyyah, Jemaa Islamiya, Jemaa Islamiyya, Jemaah Islamiyya, Jemaa Islamiyyah, Jemaah Islamiah, Jemaah Islamiyah, Jemaah Islamiyyah, Jemaah Islamiya, Jamaah Islamiyah, Jamaa Islamiya, Jemaah Islam, Jemahh Islamiyah, Jama'ah Islamiyah, Al-Jama'ah Al Islamiyyah, Islamic Group and Islamic Community)

Islamic Movement of Uzbekistan (IMU)

Euskadi Ta Askatasuna (ETA) (also known among other names as Basque Homeland and Liberty, Euzkadi Ta Azkatasuna, Euzkadi Ta Askatasanu, Basque Nation and Liberty, Basque Fatherland and Liberty and Basque Homeland and Freedom)

Al-Aqsa Martyrs' Brigade (AAMB) (also known among other names as Al-Aqsa Intifada Martyrs' Group, Al-Aqsa Brigades, Martyrs of al-Aqsa group, Al-Aqsa Martyrs Battalion and Armed Militias of the Al-Aqsa Martyr Battalions)

Fuerzas Armadas Revolucionarias de Colombia (FARC) (also known among other names as Revolutionary Armed Forces of Colombia, Revolutionary Armed Forces of Colombia-People's Army (Fuerzas Armadas Revolucionarias de Colombia-Ejército del Pueblo, FARC-EP), National Finance Commission (Comisión Nacional de Finanzas) and Coordinadora Nacional Guerrillera Simon Bolivar (CNGSB))

Autodefensas Unidas de Colombia (AUC) (also known among other names as Autodéfenses unies de Colombie and United Self-Defense Forces of Colombia)

Ejército de Liberación Nacional (ELN) (also known among other names as National Liberation Army and the Army of National Liberation)

Babbar Khalsa (BK)

Babbar Khalsa International (BKI)

International Sikh Youth Federation (ISYF)

Lashkar-e-Tayyiba (LeT) (also known among other names as Lashkar-e-Toiba, Lashkar-i-Toiba (LiT), Lashkar-i-Taiba (Holy Regiment), Lashkar-e-Tayyiba (LT) (Army of the Righteous), Lashkar-e-Taibyya, Lashkar-e-Taiba, Lashkar-e-Tayyiba (Army of the Pure and Righteous), Lashkar-e-Taiba (Righteous Army), Lashkar-Taiba (Army of the Good), Lashkar e Toiba, Lashkar e Taiba, Lashkar-E-Tayyaba, Lashkar e Tayyiba)

Lashkar-e-Jhangvi (LJ) (also known among other names as Lashkar-i-Jhangvi, Lashkar-e-Jhangvie, Laskar-e-Jhangvi, Lashkare Jhangvi, Lashkar-e-Jhangwi, Lashkar-i-Jhangwi, Jhangvi Army, Lashkar-e Jhangvi, Lashkar Jhangvi, Lashkar-e-Jhanvi (LeJ), Lashkar-i-Jangvi, Lashkar e Jhangvi, Lashkar Jangvi, Laskar e Jahangvi)

Palestine Liberation Front (PLF) (also known among other names as PLF — Abu Abbas Faction, Front for the Liberation of Palestine (FLP))

Popular Front for the Liberation of Palestine (PFLP) (Al-Jibha al-Sha'biya lil-Tahrir Filistin)

Popular Front for the Liberation of Palestine — General Command (PFLP-GC) (Al-Jibha Sha'biya lil-Tahrir Filistin-al-Qadiya al-Ama)

Ansar al-Islam (AI) (also known as the Partisans of Islam, Helpers of Islam, Supporters of Islam, Soldiers of God, Kurdistan Taliban, Soldiers of Islam, Kurdistan Supporters of Islam, Supporters of Islam in Kurdistan and Followers of Islam in Kurdistan)

Gulbuddin Hekmatyar (also known among other names as Gulabudin Hekmatyar, Gulbuddin Khekmatiyar, Gulbuddin Hekmatiar, Gulbuddin Hekmartyar, Gulbudin Hekmetyar, Golboddin Hikmetyar and Gulbuddin Hekmetyar)

Kahane Chai (Kach) (also known among other names as Repression of Traitors, State of Yehuda, Sword of David, Dikuy Bogdim, DOV, Judea Police, Kahane Lives, Kfar Tapuah Fund, State of Judea, Judean Legion, Judean Voice, Qomemiyut Movement, Way of the Torah and Yeshiva of the Jewish Idea)

The Liberation Tigers of Tamil Eelam (LTTE) (also known among other names as the Tamil Tigers, the Eellalan Force, the Ellalan Force, the Tiger Movement, the Sangilian Force, the Air Tigers, the Black Tigers (Karum Puligal), the Sea Tigers, the Tiger Organization Security Intelligence Service (TOSIS) and the Women's Combat Force of Liberation Tigers (WCFLT))

Gulbuddin Hekmatyar's Faction of the Hezb-e Islami, the Hezb-e Islami Gulbuddin (HIG)

World Tamil Movement (WTM)

Al Shabaab (also known as Harakat Shabaab al-Mujahidin, al-Shabab, Shabaab, the Youth, Mujahidin al Shabaab Movement, Mujahideen Youth Movement, MYM, Mujahidin Youth, Hizbul Shabaab, Hisb'ul Shabaab, al-Shabaab al-Islamiya, Youth Wing, al Shabaab al-Islam, al-Shabaab al-Jihad, the Unity of Islamic Youth and the Popular Resistance Movement in the Land of the Two Migrations)

Al Qaida in the Arabian Peninsula (AQAP) (also known among other names as Al-Qaida of Jihad Organization in the Arabian Peninsula, Tanzim Qa'idat al-Jihad fi Jazirat al-Arab, Al-Quaida Organization in the Arabian Peninsula (AQAP), Al-Quaida in the South Arabian Peninsula and Al-Qaida in Yemen (AQY))

Tehrik-e-Taliban Pakistan (TTP) (also known among other names as Tehrik-e-Taliban Pakistan, Tehrik-I-Taliban Pakistan, Tehrik-e-Taliban, Pakistani Taliban, Tehreek-e-Taliban, Tehrik Taliban-I-Pakistan, Tehrik-i-Taliban Pakistan, Tehreek-e-Taliban Pakistan and Mouvement des talibans du Pakistan)

Can. Reg. 2015-24 — Order Accepting the Recommendation of the Minister of Public Safety and Emergency Preparedness Concerning the Two-Year Review of the List set out in the Regulations Establishing a List of Entities

made under the *Criminal Code*

SI/2015-24

P.C. 2015-331 March 12, 2015

Whereas, on July 23, 2014, 12 years had elapsed since the establishment of a list by the *Regulations Establishing a List of Entities*[28] pursuant to subsection 83.05(1)[29] of the *Criminal Code*[30];

And whereas, pursuant to subsection 83.05(9)[31] of the Criminal Code[32], the Minister of Public Safety and Emergency Preparedness has reviewed that list, as it existed on July 23, 2014, and has determined that there are still reasonable grounds to believe that each entity listed on that date has knowingly carried out, attempted to carry out, participated in or facilitated a terrorist activity or is knowingly acting on behalf of, at the direction of or in association with such an entity;

Therefore, His Excellency the Governor General in Council, on the recommendation of the Minister of Public Safety and Emergency Preparedness made pursuant to subsection 83.05(9)[33] of the *Criminal Code*[34], accepts that each entity listed as of July 23, 2014 remain a listed entity.

---

28 SOR/2002-284

29 S.C. 2005, c. 10, subpar. 34(1)(f)(iii)

30 R.S., c. C-46

31 S.C. 2005, c. 10, s. 18(3)

32 R.S., c. C-46

33 S.C. 2005, c. 10, s. 18(3)

34 R.S., c. C-46

CAN. REG. 2010-161 — REGULATIONS PRESCRIBING CERTAIN OFFENCES TO BE SERIOUS OFFENCES

made under the *Criminal Code*

SOR/2010-161

1. The following offences under the *Criminal Code* are serious offences that are included in the definition **"serious offence"** in subsection 467.1(1) of that Act:

(a) keeping a common gaming or betting house (subsection 201(1) and paragraph 201(2)(b));

(b) betting, pool-selling and book-making (section 202);

(c) committing offences in relation to lotteries and games of chance (section 206);

(d) cheating while playing a game or in holding the stakes for a game or in betting (section 209); and

(e) keeping a common bawdy-house (subsection 210(1) and paragraph 210(2)(c)).

2. The following offences under the *Controlled Drugs and Substances Act* are serious offences that are included in the definition **"serious offence"** in subsection 467.1(1) of the *Criminal Code*:

(a) trafficking in any substance included in Schedule IV (paragraph 5(3)(c));

(b) trafficking in any substance included in Schedule II in an amount that does not exceed the amount set out for that substance in Schedule VII (subsection 5(4));

(c) importing or exporting any substance included in Schedule IV or V (paragraph 6(3)(c)); and

(d) producing any substance included in Schedule IV (paragraph 7(2)(d)).

COMING INTO FORCE

3. These Regulations come into force on the day on which they are registered.

CAN. REG. 2014-304 — SAMPLES OF BODILY SUBSTANCES REGULATIONS

made under the *Criminal Code*

SOR/2014-304, as am. SOR/2018-254, s. 2 (Fr.).

INTERPRETATION

1. Definitions — The following definitions apply in these Regulations.

"Code" means the *Criminal Code*. *("Code")*

"qualified medical practitioner" means a person duly qualified under provincial law to practise medicine. *("médecin qualifié")*

"qualified technician" means any person or person of a class of persons designated by the Attorney General as being qualified to take samples of blood for the purposes of sections 254, 256 and 258 of the Code. *("technicien qualifié")*

PART 1 — SAMPLES OF BODILY SUBSTANCES PROVIDED IN COMPLIANCE WITH PROBATION ORDER

2. Application — This Part applies in respect of any samples of bodily substances that are provided by offenders in compliance with the conditions of a probation order prescribed by a court under paragraph 732.1(3)(c.1) or (c.2) of the Code.

3. Designations and specifications — If the Attorney General of a province or the minister of justice of a territory proposes to make designations or specifications under subsection 732.1(8) of the Code, they must notify the Attorney General of Canada in writing that the province or territory has the technical and operational capability to take, analyze, store, handle and destroy any samples of bodily substances that are to be provided.

4. Prescribed bodily substances — The following are prescribed bodily substances for the purposes of paragraphs 732.1(3)(c.1) and (c.2) of the Code:

(a) breath;

(b) urine;

(c) blood;

(d) hair; and

(e) saliva.

5. (1) Designation of persons to take blood samples — Only qualified medical practitioners and qualified technicians may be designated for the purposes of taking blood samples.

(2) Medical opinion required — A blood sample may be taken from a person only if a qualified medical practitioner is satisfied that taking the sample would not endanger the person's life or health.

6. Analysis of breath samples — A breath sample must be analyzed either by using an instrument that has been approved under the *Approved Breath Analysis Instruments Order* or by using a screening device that has been approved under the *Approved Screening Devices Order*.

7. Storage of blood samples — A blood sample must be stored in a container that has been approved under the *Order Approving Blood Sample Containers*.

8. Prescribed period for destruction of samples — For the purposes of subsection 732.1(11) of the Code, a sample of a bodily substance must be destroyed within one year after the day on which the sample is provided.

Part 2 — Samples of Bodily Substances Provided in Compliance with Conditional Sentence Order

9. Application — This Part applies in respect of any samples of bodily substances that are provided by offenders in compliance with the conditions of a conditional sentence order prescribed by a court under paragraph 742.3(2)(a.1) or (a.2) of the Code.

10. Designations and specifications — If the Attorney General of a province or the minister of justice of a territory proposes to make designations or specifications under subsection 742.3(6) of the Code, they must notify the Attorney General of Canada in writing that the province or territory has the technical and operational capability to take, analyze, store, handle and destroy any samples of bodily substances that are to be provided.

11. Prescribed bodily substances — The following are prescribed bodily substances for the purposes of paragraphs 742.3(2)(a.1) and (a.2) of the Code:

(a) breath;

(b) urine;

(c) blood;

(d) hair; and

(e) saliva.

12. (1) Designation of persons to take blood samples — Only qualified medical practitioners and qualified technicians may be designated for the purposes of taking blood samples.

(2) Medical opinion required — A blood sample may be taken from a person only if a qualified medical practitioner is satisfied that taking the sample would not endanger the person's life or health.

13. Analysis of breath samples — A breath sample must be analyzed either by using an instrument that has been approved under the *Approved Breath Analysis Instruments Order* or by using a screening device that has been approved under the *Approved Screening Devices Order*.

14. Storage of blood samples — A blood sample must be stored in a container that has been approved under the *Order Approving Blood Sample Containers*.

15. Prescribed period for destruction of samples — For the purposes of subsection 742.3(9) of the Code, a sample of a bodily substance must be destroyed within one year after the day on which the sample is provided.

PART 3 — SAMPLES OF BODILY SUBSTANCES PROVIDED IN COMPLIANCE WITH RECOGNIZANCE TO KEEP THE PEACE

16. Application — This Part applies in respect of any samples of bodily substances that are provided by defendants in compliance with the conditions added to a recognizance to keep the peace under paragraph 810(3.02)(b) or (c), 810.01(4.1)(f) or (g), 810.1(3.02)(h) or (i) or 810.2(4.1)(f) or (g) of the Code.

17. Designations and specifications — If the Attorney General of a province or the minister of justice of a territory proposes to make designations or specifications under subsection 810.3(1) of the Code, they must notify the Attorney General of Canada in writing that the province or territory has the technical and operational capability to take, analyze, store, handle and destroy any samples of bodily substances that are to be provided.

18. Prescribed bodily substances — The following are prescribed bodily substances for the purposes of paragraphs 810(3.02)(b) and (c), 810.01(4.1)(f) and (g), 810.1(3.02)(h) and (i) and 810.2(4.1)(f) and (g) of the Code:

(a) breath;

(b) urine;

(c) blood;

(d) hair; and

(e) saliva.

19. (1) **Designation of persons to take blood samples** — Only qualified medical practitioners and qualified technicians may be designated for the purposes of taking blood samples.

(2) **Medical opinion required** — A blood sample may be taken from a person only if a qualified medical practitioner is satisfied that taking the sample would not endanger the person's life or health.

20. Analysis of breath samples — A breath sample must be analyzed either by using an instrument that has been approved under the *Approved Breath Analysis Instruments Order* or by using a screening device that has been approved under the *Approved Screening Devices Order*.

21. Storage of blood samples — A blood sample must be stored in a container that has been approved under the *Order Approving Blood Sample Containers*.

22. Prescribed period for destruction of samples — For the purposes of subsection 810.3(4) of the Code, a sample of a bodily substance must be destroyed within one year after the day on which the sample is provided.

Coming Into Force

23. S.C. 2011, c. 7 — These Regulations come into force on the day on which the *Response to the Supreme Court of Canada Decision in R. v. Shoker Act* comes into force, but if these Regulations are registered after that day, they come into force on the day on which they are registered.

CANADA EVIDENCE ACT

Editor's note: Current to May 15, 2019.

TABLE OF CONCORDANCE

R.S.C. 1970, c. E-10	R.S.C. 1985, c. C-5	R.S.C. 1970, c. E-10	R.S.C. 1985, c. C-5
1	1	28	28
2	2	29	29
3	3	30	30
4	4	31	31
5	5	32	32
6	6	33	33
7	7	34	34
8	8	35	35
9	79	36	36
10	10	36.1	37
11	11	36.2	38
12	12	36.2	39
13	13	37	40
14	14	38	41
15	15	39	42
16	16	40	43
17	17	41	44
18	18	42	45
19	19	43	46
20	20	44	47
21	21	45	48
22	22	46	49
23	23	47	50
24	24	48	51
25	25	49	52
26	26	50	53
27	27	51	54

CANADA EVIDENCE ACT

An Act respecting Witnesses and Evidence

R.S.C. 1985, c. C-5, as am. R.S.C. 1985, c. 27 (1st Supp.), s. 203; R.S.C. 1985, c. 19 (3rd Supp.), ss. 17, 18; S.C. 1992, c. 1, ss. 142 (Sched. V, item 9), 144 (Sched. VII, item 5) (Fr.); 1992, c. 47, s. 66; 1993, c. 28, s. 78 (Sched. III, item 8); 1993, c. 34, s. 15; 1994, c. 44, ss. 85–93; 1995, c. 28, s. 47; 1997, c. 18, ss. 116–118; 1998, c. 9, s. 1; 1999, c. 18, ss. 89–91; 1999, c. 28, ss. 149, 150; 2000, c. 5, ss. 52–57; 2001, c. 41, ss. 43, 44 (Sched. 2), 124, 140, 141(1), (3)–(7); 2002, c. 1, s. 166; 2002, c. 7, s. 96; 2002, c. 8, ss. 118, 119, 183(1)(b) [s. 119 repealed 2001, c. 41, s. 141(3)(a).]; 2003, c. 22, ss. 104, 105; SOR/2004-19; 2004, c. 12, ss. 18, 19; 2005, c. 32, ss. 26, 27; 2005, c. 46, s. 56 [Amended 2006, c. 9, s. 222.]; SOR/2006-80; SOR/2006-335; 2008, c. 3, s. 11; SOR/2012-220; 2013, c. 9, ss. 17, 18 (Fr.), 19, 20(1), (2), (3) (Fr.), 21–24; 2013, c. 18, ss. 45, 85; 2013, c. 40, s. 448; 2014, c. 2, s. 5; 2014, c. 25, s. 34; 2014, c. 31, s. 27; 2015, c. 3, s. 14 (Fr.); 2015, c. 13, ss. 52, 53; 2015, c. 20, s. 13; 2015, c. 23, s. 20 [Not in force at date of publication. Repealed 2015, c. 13, s. 57(2).]; 2015, c. 36, s. 43; 2017, c. 9, s. 41; 2017, c. 22, s. 2; 2019, c. 13, ss. 20, 61; 2019, c. 15, ss. 48–54 [Not in force at date of publication.]; 2019, c. 18, s. 60.

SHORT TITLE

1. Short title — This Act may be cited as the *Canada Evidence Act*.

PART I — (SS. 2–42)

Application

2. Application — This Part applies to all criminal proceedings and to all civil proceedings and other matters whatever respecting which Parliament has jurisdiction.

Witnesses

3. Interest or crime — A person is not incompetent to give evidence by reason of interest or crime.

4. (1) Accused and spouse — Every person charged with an offence, and, except as otherwise provided in this section, the wife or husband, as the case may be, of the person so charged, is a competent witness for the defence whether the person so charged is charged solely or jointly with any other person.

(2) **Spouse of accused** — No person is incompetent, or uncompellable, to testify for the prosecution by reason only that they are married to the accused.

(3) **Communications during marriage** — No husband is compellable to disclose any communication made to him by his wife during their marriage, and no wife is compellable to disclose any communication made to her by her husband during their marriage.

(4) **and** (5) [Repealed 2015, c. 13, s. 52(2).]

(6) **Failure to testify** — The failure of the person charged, or of the wife or husband of that person, to testify shall not be made the subject of comment by the judge or by counsel for the prosecution.

R.S.C. 1985, c. 19 (3rd Supp.), s. 17; 2002, c. 1, s. 166; 2014, c. 25, s. 34; 2014, c. 31, s. 27; 2015, c. 13, s. 52

5. (1) Incriminating questions — No witness shall be excused from answering any question on the ground that the answer to the question may tend to criminate him, or may tend to establish his liability to a civil proceeding at the instance of the Crown or of any person.

(2) **Answer not admissible against witness** — Where with respect to any question a witness objects to answer on the ground that his answer may tend to criminate him, or may tend to establish his liability to a civil proceeding at the instance of the Crown or of any person, and if but for this Act, or the Act of any provincial legislature, the witness would therefore have been excused from answering the question, then although the witness is by reason of this Act or the provincial Act compelled to answer, the answer so given shall not be used or admissible in evidence against him in any criminal trial or other criminal proceeding against him thereafter taking place, other than a prosecution for perjury in the giving of that evidence or for the giving of contradictory evidence.

1997, c. 18, s. 116

6. (1) Evidence of person with physical disability — If a witness has difficulty communicating by reason of a physical disability, the court may order that the witness be permitted to give evidence by any means that enables the evidence to intelligible.

(2) **Evidence of person with mental disability** — If a witness with a mental disability is determined under section 16 to have the capacity to give evidence and difficulty communicating by reason of disability, the court may order that the witness be permitted to give evidence by any means that enables the evidence to be intelligible.

(3) **Inquiry** — The court may conduct an inquiry to determine if the means by which a witness may be permitted to give evidence under subsection (1) or (2) is necessary and reliable.

1998, c. 9, s. 1

6.1 Identification of accused — For greater certainty, a witness may give evidence as to the identity of an accused whom the witness is able to identify visually or in any other sensory manner.

1998, c. 9, s. 1

7. Expert witnesses — Where, in any trial or other proceeding, criminal or civil, it is intended by the prosecution or the defence, or by any party, to examine as witnesses professional or other experts entitled according to the law or practice to give opinion evidence, not more than five of such witnesses may be called on either side without the leave of the court or judge or person presiding.

8. Handwriting comparison — Comparison of a disputed writing with any writing proved to the satisfaction of the court to be genuine shall be permitted to be made by witnesses, and such writings, and the evidence of witnesses respecting those writings, may be submitted to the court and jury as proof of the genuineness or otherwise of the writing in dispute.

9. (1) Adverse witnesses — A party producing a witness shall not be allowed to impeach his credit by general evidence of bad character, but if the witness, in the opinion of the court, proves adverse, the party may contradict him by other evidence, or, by leave of the court, may prove that the witness made at other times a statement inconsistent with his present testimony, but before the last mentioned proof can be given the circumstances of the supposed statement, sufficient to designate the particular occasion, shall be mentioned to the witness, and he shall be asked whether or not he did make the statement.

(2) Previous statements in writing by witness not proved adverse — Where the party producing a witness alleges that the witness made at other times a statement in writing, reduced to writing, or recorded on audio tape or video tape or otherwise, inconsistent with the witness' present testimony, the court may, without proof that the witness is adverse, grant leave to that party to cross-examine the witness as to the statement and the court may consider the cross-examination in determining whether in the opinion of the court the witness is adverse.

1994, c. 44, s. 85

10. (1) Cross-examination as to previous statements — On any trial a witness may be cross-examined as to previous statements that the witness made in writing, or that have been reduced to writing, or recorded on audio tape or video tape or otherwise, relative to the subject-matter of the case, without the writing being shown to the witness or the witness being given the opportunity to listen to the audio tape or view the video tape or otherwise take cognizance of the statements, but, if it is intended to contradict the witness, the witness' attention must, before the contradictory proof can be given, be called to those parts of the statement that are to be used for the purpose of so contradicting the witness, and the judge, at any time during the trial, may require the production of the writing or tape or other medium for inspection, and thereupon make such use of it for the purposes of the trial as the judge thinks fit.

(2) **Deposition of witness in criminal investigation** — A deposition of a witness, purporting to have been taken before a justice on the investigation of a criminal charge and to be signed by the witness and the justice, returned to and produced from the custody of the proper officer shall be presumed, in the absence of evidence to the contrary, to have been signed by the witness.

1994, c. 44, s. 86

11. **Cross-examination as to previous oral statements** — Where a witness, on cross-examination as to a former statement made by him relative to the subject-matter of the case and inconsistent with his present testimony, does not distinctly admit that he did make the statement, proof may be given that he did in fact make it, but before the proof can be given the circumstances of the supposed statement, sufficient to designate the particular occasion, shall be mentioned to the witness, and he shall be asked whether or not he did make the statement.

12. (1) **Examination as to previous convictions** — A witness may be questioned as to whether the witness has been convicted of any offence, excluding any offence designated as a contravention under the *Contraventions Act*, but including such an offence where the conviction was entered after a trial on an indictment.

(1.1) **Proof of previous convictions** — If the witness either denies the fact or refuses to answer, the opposite party may prove the conviction.

(2) **How conviction proved** — A conviction may be proved by producing

(a) a certificate containing the substance and effect only, omitting the formal part, of the indictment and conviction, if it is for an indictable offence, or a copy of the summary conviction, if it is for an offence punishable on summary conviction, purporting to be signed by the clerk of the court or other officer having the custody of the records of the court in which the conviction, if on indictment, was had, or to which the conviction, if summary, was returned; and

(b) proof of identity.

1992, c. 47, s. 66

Oaths and Solemn Affirmations

13. **Who may administer oaths** — Every court and judge, and every person having, by law or consent of parties, authority to hear and receive evidence, has power to administer an oath to every witness who is legally called to give evidence before that court, judge or person.

14. (1) **Solemn affirmation by witness instead of oath** — A person may, instead of taking an oath, make the following solemn affirmation:

I solemnly affirm that the evidence to be given by me shall be the truth, the whole truth and nothing but the truth.

(2) Effect — Where a person makes a solemn affirmation in accordance with subsection (1), his evidence shall be taken and have the same effect as if taken under oath.

1994, c. 44, s. 87

15. (1) Solemn affirmation by deponent — Where a person who is required or who desires to make an affidavit or deposition in a proceeding or on an occasion on which or concerning a matter respecting which an oath is required or is lawful, whether on the taking of office or otherwise, does not wish to take an oath, the court or judge, or other officer or person qualified to take affidavits or depositions, shall permit the person to make a solemn affirmation in the words following, namely, "I, ..., do solemnly affirm, etc.", and that solemn affirmation has the same force and effect as if that person had taken an oath.

(2) Effect — Any witness whose evidence is admitted or who makes a solemn affirmation under this section or section 14 is liable to indictment and punishment for perjury in all respects as if he had been sworn.

1994, c. 44, s. 88

16. (1) Witness whose capacity is in question — If a proposed witness is a person of fourteen years of age or older whose mental capacity is challenged, the court shall, before permitting the person to give evidence, conduct an inquiry to determine

(a) whether the person understands the nature of an oath or a solemn affirmation; and

(b) whether the person is able to communicate the evidence.

(2) Testimony under oath or solemn affirmation — A person referred to in subsection (1) who understands the nature of an oath or a solemn affirmation and is able to communicate the evidence shall testify under oath or solemn affirmation.

(3) Testimony on promise to tell truth — A person referred to in subsection (1) who does not understand the nature of an oath or a solemn affirmation but is able to communicate the evidence may, notwithstanding any provision of any Act requiring an oath or a solemn affirmation, testify on promising to tell the truth.

(3.1) No questions regarding understanding of promise — A person referred to in subsection (3) shall not be asked any questions regarding their understanding of the nature of the promise to tell the truth for the purpose of determining whether their evidence shall be received by the court.

(4) Inability to testify — A person referred to in subsection (1) who neither understands the nature of an oath or a solemn affirmation nor is able to communicate the evidence shall not testify.

(5) Burden as to capacity of witness — A party who challenges the mental capacity of a proposed witness of fourteen years of age or more has the burden of satisfying the court that there is an issue as to the capacity of the proposed witness to testify under an oath or a solemn affirmation.

R.S.C. 1985, c. 19 (3rd Supp.), s. 18; 1994, c. 44, s. 89; 2005, c. 32, s. 26; 2015, c. 13, s. 53

16.1 (1) Person under fourteen years of age — A person under fourteen years of age is presumed to have the capacity to testify.

(2) No oath or solemn affirmation — A proposed witness under fourteen years of age shall not take an oath or make a solemn affirmation despite a provision of any Act that requires an oath or a solemn affirmation.

(3) Evidence shall be received — The evidence of a proposed witness under fourteen years of age shall be received if they are able to understand and respond to questions.

(4) Burden as to capacity of witness — A party who challenges the capacity of a proposed witness under fourteen years of age has the burden of satisfying the court that there is an issue as to the capacity of the proposed witness to understand and respond to questions.

(5) Court inquiry — If the court is satisfied that there is an issue as to the capacity of a proposed witness under fourteen years of age to understand and respond to questions, it shall, before permitting them to give evidence, conduct an inquiry to determine whether they are able to understand and respond to questions.

(6) Promise to tell truth — The court shall, before permitting a proposed witness under fourteen years of age to give evidence, require them to promise to tell the truth.

(7) Understanding of promise — No proposed witness under fourteen years of age shall be asked any questions regarding their understanding of the nature of the promise to tell the truth for the purpose of determining whether their evidence shall be received by the court.

(8) Effect — For greater certainty, if the evidence of a witness under fourteen years of age is received by the court, it shall have the same effect as if it were taken under oath.

2005, c. 32, s. 27

Judicial Notice

17. Imperial Acts, etc — Judicial notice shall be taken of all Acts of the Imperial Parliament, of all ordinances made by the Governor in Council, or the lieutenant governor in council of any province or colony that, or some portion of which, now forms or hereafter may form part of Canada, and of all the Acts of the legislature of any such province or colony, whether enacted before or after the passing of the *Constitution Act, 1867*.

18. Acts of Canada — Judicial notice shall be taken of all Acts of Parliament, public or private, without being specially pleaded.

Documentary Evidence

19. Copies by Queen's Printer — Every copy of any Act of Parliament, public or private, published by the Queen's Printer, is evidence of that Act and of its contents, and every copy purporting to be published by the Queen's Printer shall be deemed to be so published, unless the contrary is shown.

2000, c. 5, s. 52

20. Imperial proclamations, etc — Imperial proclamations, orders in council, treaties, orders, warrants, licences, certificates, rules, regulations, or other Imperial official records, Acts or documents may be proved

(a) in the same manner as they may from time to time be provable in any court in England;

(b) by the production of a copy of the *Canada Gazette*, or a volume of the Acts of Parliament purporting to contain a copy of the same or a notice thereof; or

(c) by the production of a copy of them purporting to be published by the Queen's Printer.

2000, c. 5, s. 53

21. Proclamations, etc., of Governor General — Evidence of any proclamation, order, regulation or appointment, made or issued by the Governor General or by the Governor in Council, or by or under the authority of any minister or head of any department of the Government of Canada and evidence of a treaty to which Canada is a party, may be given in all or any of the following ways:

(a) by the production of a copy of the *Canada Gazette*, or a volume of the Acts of Parliament purporting to contain a copy of the treaty, proclamation, order, regulation or appointment or a notice thereof;

(b) by the production of a copy of the proclamation, order, regulation or appointment, purporting to be published by the Queen's Printer;

(c) by the production of a copy of the treaty purporting to be published by the Queen's Printer;

(d) by the production, in the case of any proclamation, order, regulation or appointment made or issued by the Governor General or by the Governor in Council, of a copy or extract purporting to be certified to be true by the clerk or assistant or acting clerk of the Queen's Privy Council for Canada; and

(e) by the production, in the case of any order, regulation or appointment made or issued by or under the authority of any minister or head of a department of the Government of Canada, of a copy or extract purporting to be certified to be true by the minister, by his deputy or acting deputy, or by the secretary or acting secretary of the department over which he presides.

2000, c. 5, s. 54

22. (1) Proclamations, etc., of Lieutenant Governor — Evidence of any proclamation, order, regulation or appointment made or issued by a lieutenant governor or lieutenant governor in council of any province, or by or under the authority of any member of the executive council, being the head of any department of the government of the province, may be given in all or any of the following ways:

(a) by the production of a copy of the official gazette for the province, purporting to contain a copy of the proclamation, order, regulation or appointment, or a notice thereof;

(b) by the production of a copy of the proclamation, order, regulation or appointment purporting to be published by the government or Queen's Printer for the province; and

(c) by the production of a copy or extract of the proclamation, order, regulation or appointment purporting to be certified to be true by the clerk or assistant or acting clerk of the executive council, by the head of any department of the government of a province, or by his deputy or acting deputy, as the case may be.

(2) Territories — Evidence of any proclamation, order, regulation or appointment made by the Lieutenant Governor or Lieutenant Governor in Council of the Northwest Territories, as constituted prior to September 1, 1905, or by the Legislature of Yukon, of the Northwest Territories or for Nunavut, may be given by the production of a copy of the *Canada Gazette* purporting to contain a copy of the proclamation, order, regulation or appointment, or a notice of it.

1993, c. 28, s. 78 (Sched. III, item 8); 2000, c. 5, s. 55; 2002, c. 7, s. 96; 2014, c. 2, s. 5

23. (1) Evidence of judicial proceedings, etc. — Evidence of any proceeding or record whatever of, in or before any court in Great Britain, the Supreme Court, the Federal Court of Appeal, the Federal Court or the Tax Court of Canada, any court in any province, any court in any British colony or possession or any court of record of the United States, of a state of the United States or of any other foreign country, or before any justice of the peace or coroner in a province, may be given in any action or proceeding by an exemplification or certified copy of the proceeding or record, purporting to be under the seal of the court or under the hand or seal of the justice, coroner or court stenographer, as the case may be, without any proof of the authenticity of the seal or of the signature of the justice, coroner or court stenographer or other proof whatever.

(2) Certificate where court has no seal — Where any court, justice or coroner or court stenographer referred to in subsection (1) has no seal, or so certifies, the evidence may be given by a copy purporting to be certified under the signature of a judge or presiding provincial court judge or of the justice or coroner or court stenographer, without any proof of the authenticity of the signature or other proof whatever.

R.S.C. 1985, c. 27 (1st Supp.), s. 203; 1993, c. 34, s. 15; 1997, c. 18, s. 117; 2002, c. 8, s. 118

24. Certified copies — In every case in which the original record could be admitted in evidence,

(a) a copy of any official or public document of Canada or of any province, purporting to be certified under the hand of the proper officer or person in whose custody the official or public document is placed, or

(b) a copy of a document, by-law, rule, regulation or proceeding, or a copy of any entry in any register or other book of any municipal or other corporation, created by charter or Act of Parliament or the legislature of any province, purporting to be certified under the seal of the corporation, and the hand of the presiding officer, clerk or secretary thereof,

is admissible in evidence without proof of the seal of the corporation, or of the signature or official character of the person or persons appearing to have signed it, and without further proof thereof.

25. Books and documents — Where a book or other document is of so public a nature as to be admissible in evidence on its mere production from the proper custody, and no other Act exists that renders its contents provable by means of a copy, a copy thereof or extract therefrom is admissible in evidence in any court of justice or before a person having, by law or by consent of parties, authority to hear, receive and examine evidence, if it is proved that it is a copy or extract purporting to be certified to be true by the officer to whose custody the original has been entrusted.

26. (1) Books kept in offices under Government of Canada — A copy of any entry in any book kept in any office or department of the Government of Canada, or in any commission, board or other branch in the federal public administration, shall be admitted as evidence of that entry, and of the matters, transactions and accounts therein recorded, if it is proved by the oath or affidavit of an officer of the office or department, commission, board or other branch in the federal public administration that the book was, at the time of the making of the entry, one of the ordinary books kept in the office, department, commission, board or other branch in the federal public administration, that the entry was made in the usual and ordinary course of business of the office, department, commission, board or other branch in the federal public administration and that the copy is a true copy thereof.

(2) Proof of non-issue of licence or document — Where by any Act of Parliament or regulation made under an Act of Parliament provision is made for the issue by a department, commission, board or other branch in the federal public administration of a licence requisite to the doing or having of any act or thing or for the issue of any other document, an affidavit of an officer of the department, commission, board or other branch in the federal public administration, sworn before any commissioner or other person authorized to take affidavits, setting out that he or she has charge of the appropriate records and that after careful examination and search of those records he or she has been unable to find in any given case that any such licence or other document has been issued, shall be admitted in evidence as proof, in the absence of evidence to the contrary, that in that case no licence or other document has been issued.

(3) Proof of mailing departmental matter — Where by any Act of Parliament or regulation made under an Act of Parliament provision is made for sending by mail any request for information, notice or demand by a department or other branch in the federal public administration, an affidavit of an officer of the department or other branch in the federal public administration, sworn before any commissioner or other person authorized to take affidavits, setting out that he or she has charge of the appropriate records, that he or she has a knowledge of the facts in the particular case, that the request, notice or demand was sent by registered letter on a named date to the person or firm to whom it was addressed (indicating that address) and that he or she identifies as exhibits attached to the affidavit the post office certificate of registration of the letter and a true copy of the request, notice or demand, shall, on production and proof of the post office receipt for the delivery of the registered letter to the addressee, be admitted in evidence as proof, in the absence of evidence to the contrary, of the sending and of the request, notice or demand.

(4) Proof of official character — Where proof is offered by affidavit pursuant to this section it is not necessary to prove the official character of the person making the affidavit if that information is set out in the body of the affidavit.

2003, c. 22, s. 104

27. Notarial acts in Quebec — Any document purporting to be a copy of a notarial act or instrument made, filed or registered in the Province of Quebec, and to be certified by a notary or prothonotary to be a true copy of the original in his possession as such notary or prothonotary, shall be admitted in evidence in the place and stead of the original and has the same force and effect as the original would have if produced and proved, but it may be proved in rebuttal that there is no original, that the copy is not a true copy of the original in some material particular or that the original is not an instrument of such nature as may, by the law of the Province of Quebec, be taken before a notary or be filed, enrolled or registered by a notary in that Province.

28. (1) Notice of production of book or document — No copy of any book or other document shall be admitted in evidence, under the authority of section 23, 24, 25, 26 or 27, on any trial, unless the party intending to produce the copy has before the trial given to the party against whom it is intended to be produced reasonable notice of that intention.

(2) Not less than 7 days — The reasonableness of the notice referred to in subsection (1) shall be determined by the court, judge or other person presiding, but the notice shall not in any case be less than seven days.

29. (1) Copies of entries — Subject to this section, a copy of any entry in any book or record kept in any financial institution shall in all legal proceedings be admitted in evidence as proof, in the absence of evidence to the contrary, of the entry and of the matters, transactions and accounts therein recorded.

(2) Admission in evidence — A copy of an entry in the book or record described in subsection (1) shall not be admitted in evidence under this section unless it is first proved that the book or record was, at the time of the making of the entry, one of the ordinary books or records of the financial institution, that the entry was made in the usual and ordinary course of business, that the book or record is in the custody or control of the financial institution and that the copy is a true copy of it, and such proof may be given by any person employed by the financial institution who has knowledge of the book or record or the manager or accountant of the financial institution, and may be given orally or by affidavit sworn before any commissioner or other person authorized to take affidavits.

(3) Cheques, proof of "no account" — Where a cheque has been drawn on any financial institution or branch thereof by any person, an affidavit of the manager or accountant of the financial institution or branch, sworn before any commissioner or other person authorized to take affidavits, setting out that he is the manager or accountant, that he has made a careful examination and search of the books and records for the purpose of ascertaining whether or not that person has an account with the financial institution or branch and that he has been unable to find such an account, shall be admitted in evidence as proof, in the absence of evidence to the contrary, that that person has no account in the financial institution or branch.

(4) Proof of official character — Where evidence is offered by affidavit pursuant to this section, it is not necessary to prove the signature or official character of the person making the affidavit if the official character of that person is set out in the body of the affidavit.

(5) Compulsion of production or appearance — A financial institution or officer of a financial institution is not in any legal proceedings to which the financial institution is not a party compellable to produce any book or record, the contents of which can be proved under this section, or to appear as a witness to prove the matters, transactions and accounts therein recorded unless by order of the court made for special cause.

(6) Order to inspect and copy — On the application of any party to a legal proceeding, the court may order that that party be at liberty to inspect and take copies of any entries in the books or records of a financial institution for the purposes of the legal proceeding, and the person whose account is to be inspected shall be notified of the application at least two clear days before the hearing thereof, and if it is shown to the satisfaction of the court that he cannot be notified personally, the notice may be given by addressing it to the financial institution.

(7) Warrants to search — Nothing in this section shall be construed as prohibiting any search of the premises of a financial institution under the authority of a warrant to search issued under any other Act of Parliament, but unless the warrant is expressly endorsed by the person under whose hand it is issued as not being limited by this section, the authority conferred by any such warrant to search the premises of a financial institution and to seize and take away anything in it shall, with respect to the books or records of the institution, be construed as limited to the searching of those premises for the purpose of inspecting and taking copies of entries in those books or records, and section 490 of the *Criminal Code* does not apply in respect of the copies of those books or records obtained under a warrant referred to in this section.

(8) Computation of time — Holidays shall be excluded from the computation of time under this section.

(9) Definitions — In this section,

"court" means the court, judge, arbitrator or person before whom a legal proceeding is held or taken;

"financial institution" means the Bank of Canada, the Business Development Bank of Canada and any institution that accepts in Canada deposits of money from its members or the public, and includes a branch, agency or office of any of those Banks or institutions;

"legal proceeding" means any civil or criminal proceeding or inquiry in which evidence is or may be given, and includes an arbitration.

1994, c. 44, s. 90; 1995, c. 28, s. 47(a); 1999, c. 28, s. 149

30. (1) Business records to be admitted in evidence — Where oral evidence in respect of a matter would be admissible in a legal proceeding, a record made in the usual and ordinary course of business that contains information in respect of that matter is admissible in evidence under this section in the legal proceeding on production of the record.

(2) Inference where information not in business record — Where a record made in the usual and ordinary course of business does not contain information in respect of a matter the occurrence or existence of which might reasonably be expected to be recorded in that record, the court may on production of the record admit the record for the purpose of establishing that fact and may draw the inference that the matter did not occur or exist.

(3) Copy of records — Where it is not possible or reasonably practicable to produce any record described in subsection (1) or (2), a copy of the record accompanied by two documents, one that is made by a person who states why it is not possible or reasonably practicable to produce the record and one that sets out the source from which the copy was made, that attests to the copy's authenticity and that is made by the person who made the copy, is admissible in evidence under this section in the same manner as if it were the original of the record if each document is

(a) an affidavit of each of those persons sworn before a commissioner or other person authorized to take affidavits; or

(b) a certificate or other statement pertaining to the record in which the person attests that the certificate or statement is made in conformity with the laws of a foreign state, whether or not the certificate or statement is in the form of an affidavit attested to before an official of the foreign state.

(4) Where record kept in form requiring explanation — Where production of any record or of a copy of any record described in subsection (1) or (2) would not convey to the court the information contained in the record by reason of its having been kept in a form that requires explanation, a transcript of the explanation of the record or copy prepared by a person qualified to make the explanation is admissible in evidence under this section in the same manner as if it were the original of the record if it is accompanied by a document that sets out the person's qualifications to make the explanation, attests to the accuracy of the explanation, and is

(a) an affidavit of that person sworn before a commissioner or other person authorized to take affidavits; or

(b) a certificate or other statement pertaining to the record in which the person attests that the certificate or statement is made in conformity with the laws of a foreign state, whether or not the certificate or statement is in the form of an affidavit attested to before an official of the foreign state.

(5) Court may order other part of record to be produced — Where part only of a record is produced under this section by any party, the court may examine any other part of the record and direct that, together with the part of the record previously so produced, the whole or any part of the other part thereof be produced by that party as the record produced by him.

(6) Court may examine record and hear evidence — For the purpose of determining whether any provision of this section applies, or for the purpose of determining the probative value, if any, to be given to information contained in any record admitted in evidence under this section, the court may, on production of any record, examine the record, admit any evidence in respect thereof given orally or by affidavit including evidence as to the circumstances in which the information contained in the record was written, recorded, stored or reproduced, and draw any reasonable inference from the form or content of the record.

(7) Notice of intention to produce record or affidavit — Unless the court orders otherwise, no record or affidavit shall be admitted in evidence under this section unless the party producing the record or affidavit has, at least seven days before its production, given notice of his intention to produce it to each other party to the legal proceeding and has, within five days after receiving any notice in that behalf given by any such party, produced it for inspection by that party.

(8) Not necessary to prove signature and official character — Where evidence is offered by affidavit under this section, it is not necessary to prove the signature or official character of the person making the affidavit if the official character of that person is set out in the body of the affidavit.

(9) Examination on record with leave of court — Subject to section 4, any person who has or may reasonably be expected to have knowledge of the making or contents of any record produced or received in evidence under this section may, with leave of the court, be examined or cross-examined thereon by any party to the legal proceeding.

(10) Evidence inadmissible under this section — Nothing in this section renders admissible in evidence in any legal proceeding

(a) such part of any record as is proved to be

(i) a record made in the course of an investigation or inquiry,

(ii) a record made in the course of obtaining or giving legal advice or in contemplation of a legal proceeding.

(iii) a record in respect of the production of which any privilege exists and is claimed, or

(iv) a record of or alluding to a statement made by a person who is not, or if he were living and of sound mind would not be, competent and compellable to disclose in the legal proceeding a matter disclosed in the record;

(b) any record the production of which would be contrary to public policy; or

(c) any transcript or recording of evidence taken in the course of another legal proceeding.

(11) Construction of this section — The provisions of this section shall be deemed to be in addition to and not in derogation of

(a) any other provision of this or any other Act of Parliament respecting the admissibility in evidence of any record or the proof of any matter; or

(b) any existing rule of law under which any record is admissible in evidence or any matter may be proved.

(12) Definitions — In this section,

"business" means any business, profession, trade, calling, manufacture or undertaking of any kind carried on in Canada or elsewhere whether for profit or otherwise, including any activity or operation carried on or performed in Canada or elsewhere by any government, by any department, branch, board, commission or agency of any government, by any court or other tribunal or by any other body or authority performing a function of government;

"copy" in relation to any record, includes a print, whether enlarged or not, from a photographic film of the record, and **"photographic film"** includes a photographic plate, microphotographic film or photostatic negative;

"court" means the court, judge, arbitrator or person before whom a legal proceeding is held or taken;

"legal proceeding" means any civil or criminal proceeding or inquiry in which evidence is or may be given, and includes an arbitration;

"record" includes the whole or any part of any book, document, paper, card, tape or other thing on or in which information is written, recorded, stored or reproduced, and, except for the purposes of subsections (3) and (4), any copy or transcript admitted in evidence under this section pursuant to subsection (3) or (4).

1994, c. 44, s. 91

31. (1) Definitions — In this section,

"corporation" means any bank, including the Bank of Canada and the Business Development Bank of Canada, any authorized foreign bank within the meaning of section 2 of the *Bank Act* and each of the following carrying on business in Canada, namely, every railway, express, telegraph and telephone company (except a street railway and tramway company), insurance company or society, trust company and loan company;

"government" means the government of Canada or of any province and includes any department, commission, board or branch of any such government; and

"photographic film" includes any photographic plate, microphotographic film and photostatic negative.

(2) When print admissible in evidence — A print, whether enlarged or not, from any photographic film of

(a) an entry in any book or record kept by any government or corporation and destroyed, lost or delivered to a customer after the film was taken,

(b) any bill of exchange, promissory note, cheque, receipt, instrument or document held by any government or corporation and destroyed, lost or delivered to a customer after the film was taken, or

(c) any record, document, plan, book or paper belonging to or deposited with any government or corporation,

is admissible in evidence in all cases in which and for all purposes for which the object photographed would have been admitted on proof that

(d) while the book, record, bill of exchange, promissory note, cheque, receipt, instrument or document, plan, book or paper was in the custody or control of the government or corporation, the photographic film was taken thereof in order to keep a permanent record thereof, and

(e) the object photographed was subsequently destroyed by or in the presence of one or more of the employees of the government or corporation, or was lost or was delivered to a customer.

(3) Evidence of compliance with conditions — Evidence of compliance with the conditions prescribed by this section may be given by any one or more of the employees of the government or corporation, having knowledge of the taking of the photographic film, of the destruction, loss or delivery to a customer, or of the making of the print, as the case may be, either orally or by affidavit sworn in any part of Canada before any notary public or commissioner for oaths.

(4) Proof by notarial copy — Unless the court otherwise orders, a notarial copy of an affidavit under subsection (3) is admissible in evidence in lieu of the original affidavit.

1992, c. 1, s. 142 (Sched. V, item 9); 1995, c. 28, s. 47(b); 1999, c. 28, s. 150

31.1 Authentication of electronic documents — Any person seeking to admit an electronic document as evidence has the burden of proving its authenticity by evidence capable of supporting a finding that the electronic document is that which it is purported to be.

2000, c. 5, s. 56

31.2 (1) Application of best evidence rule — electronic documents — The best evidence rule in respect of an electronic document is satisfied

(a) on proof of the integrity of the electronic documents system by or in which the electronic document was recorded or stored; or

(b) if an evidentiary presumption established under section 31.4 applies.

(2) Printouts — Despite subsection (1), in the absence of evidence to the contrary, an electronic document in the form of a printout satisfies the best evidence rule if the printout has been manifestly or consistently acted on, relied on or used as a record of the information recorded or stored in the printout.

2000, c. 5, s. 56

31.3 Presumption of integrity — For the purposes of subsection 31.2(1), in the absence of evidence to the contrary, the integrity of an electronic documents system by or in which an electronic document is recorded or stored is proven

(a) by evidence capable of supporting a finding that at all material times the computer system or other similar device used by the electronic documents system was operating properly or, if it was not, the fact of its not operating properly did not affect the integrity of the electronic document and there are no other reasonable grounds to doubt the integrity of the electronic documents system;

(b) if it is established that the electronic document was recorded or stored by a party who is adverse in interest to the party seeking to introduce it; or

(c) if it is established that the electronic document was recorded or stored in the usual and ordinary course of business by a person who is not a party and who did not record or store it under the control of the party seeking to introduce it.

2000, c. 5, s. 56

31.4 Presumptions regarding secure electronic signatures — The Governor in Council may make regulations establishing evidentiary presumptions in relation to electronic documents signed with secure electronic signatures, including regulations respecting

(a) the association of secure electronic signatures with persons; and

(b) the integrity of information contained in electronic documents signed with secure electronic signatures.

2000, c. 5, s. 56

31.5 Standards may be considered — For the purpose of determining under any rule of law whether an electronic document is admissible, evidence may be presented in respect of any standard, procedure, usage or practice concerning the manner in which electronic documents are to be recorded or stored, having regard to the type of business, enterprise or endeavour that used, recorded or stored the electronic document and the nature and purpose of the electronic document.

2000, c. 5, s. 56

31.6 (1) Proof by affidavit — The matters referred to in subsection 31.2(2) and sections 31.3 and 31.5 and in regulations made under section 31.4 may be established by affidavit.

(2) Cross-examination — A party may cross-examine a deponent of an affidavit referred to in subsection (1) that has been introduced in evidence

(a) as of right, if the deponent is an adverse party or is under the control of an adverse party; and

(b) with leave of the court, in the case of any other deponent.

2000, c. 5, s. 56

31.7 Application — Sections 31.1 to 31.4 do not affect any rule of law relating to the admissibility of evidence, except the rules relating to authentication and best evidence.

2000, c. 5, s. 56

31.8 Definitions — The definitions in this section apply in sections 31.1 to 31.6.

"computer system" means a device that, or a group of interconnected or related devices one or more of which,

(a) contains computer programs or other data; and

(b) pursuant to computer programs, performs logic and control, and may perform any other function.

"data" means representations of information or of concepts, in any form.

"electronic document" means data that is recorded or stored on any medium in or by a computer system or other similar device and that can be read or perceived by a person or a computer system or other similar device. It includes a display, printout or other output of that data.

"electronic documents system" includes a computer system or other similar device by or in which data is recorded or stored and any procedures related to the recording or storage of electronic documents.

"secure electronic signature" means a secure electronic signature as defined in subsection 31(1) of the *Personal Information Protection and Electronic Documents Act*.

2000, c. 5, s. 56

32. (1) Order signed by Secretary of State — An order signed by the Secretary of State of Canada and purporting to be written by command of the Governor General shall be admitted in evidence as the order of the Governor General.

(2) Copies published in *Canada Gazette* — All copies of official and other notices, advertisements and documents published in the *Canada Gazette* are admissible in evidence as proof, in the absence of evidence to the contrary, of the originals and of their contents.

2000, c. 5, s. 57

33. (1) Proof of handwriting of person certifying — No proof shall be required of the handwriting or official position of any person certifying, in pursuance of this Act, to the truth of any copy of or extract from any proclamation, order, regulation, appointment, book or other document.

(2) Printed or written — Any copy or extract referred to in subsection (1) may be in print or in writing, or partly in print and partly in writing.

34. (1) Attesting witness — It is not necessary to prove by the attesting witness any instrument to the validity of which attestation is not requisite.

(2) Instrument, how proved — Any instrument referred to in subsection (1) may be proved by admission or otherwise as if there had been no attesting witness thereto.

35. Impounding of forged instrument — Where any instrument that has been forged or fraudulently altered is admitted in evidence, the court or the judge or person who admits the instrument may, at the request of any person against whom it is admitted in evidence, direct that the instrument shall be impounded and be kept in the custody of an officer of the court or other proper person for such period and subject to such conditions as to the court, judge or person admitting the instrument seem meet.

36. Construction — This Part shall be deemed to be in addition to and not in derogation of any powers of proving documents given by any existing Act or existing at law.

Interpretation

[Heading added 2001, c. 41, s. 43.]

36.1 Definition of "official" — In sections 37 to 38.16, **"official"** has the same meaning as in section 118 of the *Criminal Code*.

2001, c. 41, s. 43

Specified Public Interest

[Heading amended 2001, c. 41, s. 43.]

37. (1) Objection to disclosure of information — Subject to sections 38 to 38.16, a Minister of the Crown in right of Canada or other official may object to the disclosure of information before a court, person or body with jurisdiction to compel the production of information by certifying orally or in writing to the court, person or body that the information should not be disclosed on the grounds of a specified public interest.

(1.1) Obligation of court, person or body — If an objection is made under subsection (1), the court, person or body shall ensure that the information is not disclosed other than in accordance with this Act.

(2) Objection made to superior court — If an objection to the disclosure of information is made before a superior court, that court may determine the objection.

(3) Objection not made to superior court — If an objection to the disclosure of information is made before a court, person or body other than a superior court, the objection may be determined, on application, by

(a) the Federal Court, in the case of a person or body vested with power to compel production by or under an Act of Parliament if the person or body is not a court established under a law of a province; or

(b) the trial division or trial court of the superior court of the province within which the court, person or body exercises its jurisdiction, in any other case.

(4) Limitation period — An application under subsection (3) shall be made within 10 days after the objection is made or within any further or lesser time that the court having jurisdiction to hear the application considers appropriate in the circumstances.

(4.1) Disclosure order — Unless the court having jurisdiction to hear the application concludes that the disclosure of the information to which the objection was made under subsection (1) would encroach upon a specified public interest, the court may authorize by order the disclosure of the information.

(5) Disclosure order — If the court having jurisdiction to hear the application concludes that the disclosure of the information to which the objection was made under subsection (1) would encroach upon a specified public interest, but that the public interest in disclosure outweighs in importance the specified public interest, the court may, by order, after considering both the public interest in disclosure and the form of and conditions to disclosure that are most likely to limit any encroachment upon the specified public interest resulting from disclosure, authorize the disclosure, subject to any conditions that the court considers appropriate, of all of the information, a part or summary of the information, or a written admission of facts relating to the information.

(6) Prohibition order — If the court does not authorize disclosure under subsection (4.1) or (5), the court shall, by order, prohibit disclosure of the information.

(6.1) Evidence — The court may receive into evidence anything that, in the opinion of the court, is reliable and appropriate, even if it would not otherwise be admissible under Canadian law, and may base its decision on that evidence.

(7) When determination takes effect — An order of the court that authorizes disclosure does not take effect until the time provided or granted to appeal the order has expired or, if the order is appealed, the time provided or granted to appeal a judgment of an appeal court that confirms the order has expired and no further appeal from a judgment that confirms the order is available.

(8) Introduction into evidence — A person who wishes to introduce into evidence material the disclosure of which is authorized under subsection (5), but who may not be able to do so by reason of the rules of admissibility that apply before the court, person or body with jurisdiction to compel the production of information, may request from the court having jurisdiction under subsection (2) or (3) an order permitting the introduction into evidence of the material in a form or subject to any conditions fixed by that court, as long as that form and those conditions, comply with the order made under subsection (5).

(9) Relevant factors — For the purpose of subsection (8), the court having jurisdiction under subsection (2) or (3) shall consider all the factors that would be relevant for a determination of admissibility before the court, person or body.

2001, c. 41, ss. 43, 140; 2002, c. 8, s. 183(1)(b); 2013, c. 9, s. 17

37.1 (1) Appeal to court of appeal — An appeal lies from a determination under any of subsections 37(4.1) to (6)

(a) to the Federal Court of Appeal from a determination of the Federal Court; or

(b) to the court of appeal of a province from a determination of a trial division or trial court of a superior court of the province.

(2) Limitation period for appeal — An appeal under subsection (1) shall be brought within 10 days after the date of the determination appealed from or within any further time that the court having jurisdiction to hear the appeal considers appropriate in the circumstances.

2001, c. 41, ss. 43, 141(3)(b)

37.2 Limitation periods for appeals to Supreme Court of Canada — Notwithstanding any other Act of Parliament,

(a) an application for leave to appeal to the Supreme Court of Canada from a judgment made under subsection 37.1(1) shall be made within 10 days after the date of the judgment appealed from or within any further time that the court having jurisdiction to grant leave to appeal considers appropriate in the circumstances; and

(b) if leave to appeal is granted, the appeal shall be brought in the manner set out in subsection 60(1) of the *Supreme Court Act* but within the time specified by the court that grants leave.

2001, c. 41, s. 43

37.21 [Repealed 2004, c. 12, s. 18.]

37.3 (1) Protection of right to a fair trial — A judge presiding at a criminal trial or other criminal proceeding may make any order that he or she considers appropriate in the circumstances to protect the right of the accused to a fair trial, as long as that order complies with the terms of any order made under any of subsections 37(4.1) to (6) in relation to that trial or proceeding or any judgment made on appeal of an order made under any of those subsections.

(2) Potential orders — The orders that may be made under subsection (1) include, but are not limited to, the following orders:

(a) an order dismissing specified counts of the indictment or information, or permitting the indictment or information to proceed only in respect of a lesser or included offence;

(b) an order effecting a stay of the proceedings; and

(c) an order finding against any party on any issue relating to information the disclosure of which is prohibited.

2001, c. 41, s. 43

International Relations and National Defence and National Security

[Heading added 2001, c. 41, s. 43.]

38. Definitions — The following definitions apply in this section and in sections 38.01 to 38.15.

"judge" means the Chief Justice of the Federal Court or a judge of that Court designated by the Chief Justice to conduct hearings under section 38.04. *("juge")*

"participant" means a person who, in connection with a proceeding, is required to disclose, or expects to disclose or cause the disclosure of, information. *("participant")*

"potentially injurious information" means information of a type that, if it were disclosed to the public, could injure international relations or national defence or national security. *("renseignements potentiellement préjudiciables")*

"proceeding" means a proceeding before a court, person or body with jurisdiction to compel the production of information. *("instance")*

"prosecutor" means an agent of the Attorney General of Canada or of the Attorney General of a province, the Director of Military Prosecutions under the *National Defence Act* or an individual who acts as a prosecutor in a proceeding. *("poursuivant")*

"sensitive information" means information relating to international relations or national defence or national security that is in the possession of the Government of Canada, whether originating from inside or outside Canada, and is of a type that the Government of Canada is taking measures to safeguard. *("renseignements sensibles")*

2001, c. 41, ss. 43, 141(4)

38.01 (1) Notice to Attorney General of Canada — Every participant who, in connection with a proceeding, is required to disclose, or expects to disclose or cause the disclosure of, information that the participant believes is sensitive information or potentially injurious information shall, as soon as possible, notify, the Attorney General of Canada in writing of the possibility of the disclosure, and of the nature, date and place of the proceeding.

(2) During a proceeding — Every participant who believes that sensitive information or potentially injurious information is about to be disclosed, whether by the participant or another person, in the course of a proceeding shall raise the matter with the person presiding at the proceeding and notify the Attorney General of Canada in writing of the matter as soon as possible, whether or not notice has been given under subsection (1). In such circumstances, the person presiding at the proceeding shall ensure that the information is not disclosed other than in accordance with this Act.

(3) Notice of disclosure from official — An official, other than a participant, who believes that sensitive information or potentially injurious information may be disclosed in connection with a proceeding may notify the Attorney General of Canada in writing of the possibility of the disclosure, and of the nature, date and place of the proceeding.

(4) **During a proceeding** — An official, other than a participant, who believes that sensitive information or potentially injurious information is about to be disclosed in the course of a proceeding may raise the matter with the person presiding at the proceeding. If the official raises the matter, he or she shall notify the Attorney General of Canada in writing of the matter as soon as possible, whether or not notice has been given under subsection (3), and the person presiding at the proceeding shall ensure that the information is not disclosed other than in accordance with this Act.

(5) **Military proceedings** — In the case of a proceeding under Part III of the *National Defence Act*, notice under any of subsections (1) to (4) shall be given to both the Attorney General of Canada and the Minister of National Defence.

Proposed Amendment — 38.01(5)

(5) **Military proceedings** — In the case of a proceeding under Part III of the *National Defence Act*, other than a **"summary hearing"** as defined in subsection 2(1) of that Act, notice under any of subsections (1) to (4) shall be given to both the Attorney General of Canada and the Minister of National Defence.

2019, c. 15, s. 48 [Not in force at date of publication.]

(6) **Exception** — This section does not apply when

(a) the information is disclosed by a person to their solicitor in connection with a proceeding, if the information is relevant to that proceeding;

(b) the information is disclosed to enable the Attorney General of Canada, the Minister of National Defence, a judge or a court hearing an appeal from, or a review of, an order of the judge to discharge their responsibilities under section 38, this section and sections 38.02 to 38.13, 38.15 and 38.16;

(c) disclosure of the information is authorized by the government institution in which or for which the information was produced or, if the information was not produced in or for a government institution, the government institution in which it was first received; or

(d) the information is disclosed to an entity and, where applicable, for a purpose listed in the schedule.

(7) **Exception** — Subsections (1) and (2) do not apply to a participant if a government institution referred to in paragraph (6)(c) advises the participant that it is not necessary, in order to prevent disclosure of the information referred to in that paragraph, to give notice to the Attorney General of Canada under subsection (1) or to raise the matter with the person presiding under subsection (2).

(8) **Schedule** — The Governor in Council may, by order, add to or delete from the schedule a reference to any entity or purpose, or amend such a reference.

2001, c. 41, s. 43

38.02 (1) Disclosure prohibited — Subject to subsection 38.01(6), no person shall disclose in connection with a proceeding

(a) information about which notice is given, under any of subsections 38.01(1) to (4);

(b) the fact that notice is given to the Attorney General of Canada under any of subsections 38.01(1) to (4), or to the Attorney General of Canada and the Minister of National Defence under subsection 38.01(5);

(c) the fact that an application is made to the Federal Court under section 38.04 or that an appeal or review of an order made under any of subsections 38.06(1) to (3) in connection with the application is instituted; or

(d) the fact that an agreement is entered into under section 38.031 or subsection 38.04(6).

(1.1) Entities — When an entity listed in the schedule, for any purpose listed there in relation to that entity, makes a decision or order that would result in the disclosure of sensitive information or potentially injurious information, the entity shall not disclose the information or cause it to be disclosed until notice of intention to disclose the information has been given to the Attorney General of Canada and a period of 10 days has elapsed after notice was given.

(2) Exceptions — Disclosure of the information or the facts referred to in subsection (1) is not prohibited if

(a) the Attorney General of Canada authorizes the disclosure in writing under section 38.03 or by agreement under section 38.031 or subsection 38.04(6); or

(b) a judge authorizes the disclosure under subsection 38.06(1) or (2) or a court hearing an appeal from, or a review of, the order of the judge authorizes the disclosure, and either the time provided to appeal the order or judgment has expired or no further appeal is available.

2001, c. 41, ss. 43, 141(5)

38.03 (1) Authorization by Attorney General of Canada — The Attorney General of Canada may, at any time and subject to any conditions that he or she considers appropriate, authorize the disclosure of all or part of the information and facts the disclosure of which is prohibited under subsection 38.02(1).

(2) Military proceedings — In the case of a proceeding under Part III of the *National Defence Act*, the Attorney General of Canada may authorize disclosure only with the agreement of the Minister of National Defence.

Proposed Amendment — 38.03(2)

(2) Military proceedings — In the case of a proceeding under Part III of the *National Defence Act*, other than a **"summary hearing"** as defined in subsection 2(1) of that Act, the Attorney General of Canada may authorize disclosure only with the agreement of the Minister of National Defence.

2019, c. 15, s. 49 [Not in force at date of publication.]

(3) Notice — The Attorney General of Canada shall, within 10 days after the day on which he or she first receives a notice about information under any of subsections 38.01(1) to (4), notify in writing every person who provided notice under section 38.01 about that information of his or her decision with respect to disclosure of the information.

2001, c. 41, s. 43

38.031 (1) Disclosure agreement — The Attorney General of Canada and a person who has given notice under subsection 38.01(1) or (2) and is not required to disclose information but wishes, in connection with a proceeding, to disclose any facts referred to in paragraphs 38.02(l)(b) to (d) or information about which he or she gave the notice, or to cause that disclosure, may, before the person applies to the Federal Court under paragraph 38.04(2)(c), enter into an agreement that permits the disclosure of part of the facts or information or disclosure of the facts or information subject to conditions.

(2) No application to Federal Court — If an agreement is entered into under subsection (1), the person may not apply to the Federal Court under paragraph 38.04(2)(c) with respect to the information about which he or she gave notice to the Attorney General of Canada under subsection 38.01(1) or (2).

2001, c. 41, ss. 43, 141(6)

38.04 (1) Application to Federal Court — Attorney General of Canada — The Attorney General of Canada may, at any time and in any circumstances, apply to the Federal Court for an order with respect to the disclosure of information about which notice was given under any of subsections 38.01(1) to (4).

(2) Application to Federal Court — general — If, with respect to information about which notice was given under any of subsections 38.01(1) to (4), the Attorney General of Canada does not provide notice of a decision in accordance with subsection 38.03(3) or, other than by an agreement under section 38.031, does not authorize the disclosure of the information or authorizes the disclosure of only part of the information or authorizes the disclosure subject to any conditions,

(a) the Attorney General of Canada shall apply to the Federal Court for an order with respect to disclosure of the information if a person who gave notice under subsection 38.01(1) or (2) is a witness;

(b) a person, other than a witness, who is required to disclose information in connection with a proceeding shall apply to the Federal Court for an order with respect to disclosure of the information; and

(c) a person who is not required to disclose information in connection with a proceeding but who wishes to disclose it or to cause its disclosure may apply to the Federal Court for an order with respect to disclosure of the information.

(3) Notice to Attorney General of Canada — A person who applies to the Federal Court under paragraph (2)(b) or (c) shall provide notice of the application to the Attorney General of Canada.

(4) Court records — Subject to paragraph (5)(a.1), an application under this section is confidential. During the period when an application is confidential, the Chief Administrator of the Courts Administration Service may, subject to section 38.12, take any measure that he or she considers appropriate to protect the confidentiality of the application and the information to which it relates.

(5) Procedure — As soon as the Federal Court is seized of an application under this section, the judge

(a) shall hear the representations of the Attorney General of Canada and, in the case of a proceeding under Part III of the *National Defence Act*, the Minister of National Defence, with respect to making the application public;

Proposed Amendment — 38.04(5)(a)

(a) shall hear the representations of the Attorney General of Canada and, in the case of a proceeding under Part III of the *National Defence Act*, other than a **"summary hearing"** as defined in subsection 2(1) of that Act, the Minister of National Defence, with respect to making the application public;

2019, c. 15, s. 50(1) [Not in force at date of publication.]

(a.1) shall, if he or she decides that the application should be made public, make an order to that effect;

(a.2) shall hear the representations of the Attorney General of Canada and, in the case of a proceeding under Part III of the *National Defence Act*, the Minister of National Defence, concerning the identity of all parties or witnesses whose interests may be affected by either the prohibition of disclosure or the conditions to which disclosure is subject, and concerning the persons who should be given notice of any hearing of the matter;

Proposed Amendment — 38.04(5)(a.2)

(a.2) shall hear the representations of the Attorney General of Canada and, in the case of a proceeding under Part III of the *National Defence Act*, other than a **"summary hearing"** as defined in subsection 2(1) of that Act, the Minister of National Defence, concerning the identity of all parties or witnesses whose interests may be affected by either the prohibition of disclosure or the conditions to which disclosure is subject, and concerning the persons who should be given notice of any hearing of the matter;

2019, c. 15, s. 50(2) [Not in force at date of publication.]

(b) shall decide whether it is necessary to hold any hearing of the matter;

(c) if he or she decides that a hearing should be held, shall

(i) determine who should be given notice of the hearing,

(ii) order the Attorney General of Canada to notify those persons, and

(iii) determine the content and form of the notice; and

(d) if he or she considers it appropriate in the circumstances, may give any person the opportunity to make representations.

(6) Disclosure agreement — After the Federal Court is seized of an application made under paragraph (2)(c) or, in the case of an appeal from, or a review of, an order of the judge made under any of subsections 38.06(1) to (3) in connection with that application, before the appeal or review is disposed of,

(a) the Attorney General of Canada and the person who made the application may enter into an agreement that permits the disclosure of part of the facts referred to in paragraphs 38.02(1)(b) to (d) or part of the information or disclosure of the facts or information subject to conditions; and

(b) if an agreement is entered into, the Court's consideration of the application or any hearing, review or appeal shall be terminated.

(7) Termination of Court consideration, hearing, review or appeal — Subject to subsection (6), after the Federal Court is seized of an application made under this section or, in the case of an appeal from, or a review of, an order of the judge made under any of subsections 38.06(1) to (3), before the appeal or review is disposed of, if the Attorney General of Canada authorizes the disclosure of all or part of the information or withdraws conditions to which the disclosure is subject, the Court's consideration of the application or any hearing, appeal or review shall be terminated in relation to that information, to the extent of the authorization or the withdrawal.

2001, c. 41, ss. 43, 141(7); 2013, c. 9, s. 19

38.05 Report relating to proceedings — If he or she receives notice of a hearing under paragraph 38.04(5)(c), a person presiding or designated to preside at the proceeding to which the information relates or, if no person is designated, the person who has the authority to designate a person to preside may, within 10 days after the day on which he or she receives the notice, provide the judge with a report concerning any matter relating to the proceeding that the person considers may be of assistance to the judge.

2001, c. 41, s. 43

38.06 (1) Disclosure order — Unless the judge concludes that the disclosure of the information or facts referred to in subsection 38.02(1) would be injurious to international relations or national defence or national security, the judge may, by order, authorize the disclosure of the information or facts.

(2) Disclosure — conditions — If the judge concludes that the disclosure of the information or facts would be injurious to international relations or national defence or national security but that the public interest in disclosure outweighs in importance the public interest in non-disclosure, the judge may by order, after considering both the public interest in disclosure and the form of and conditions to disclosure that are most likely to limit any injury to international relations or national defence or national security resulting from disclosure, authorize the disclosure, subject to any conditions that the judge considers appropriate, of all or part of the information or facts, a summary of the information or a written admission of facts relating to the information.

(3) Order confirming prohibition — If the judge does not authorize disclosure under subsection (1) or (2), the judge shall, by order, confirm the prohibition of disclosure.

(3.01) When determination takes effect — An order of the judge that authorizes disclosure does not take effect until the time provided or granted to appeal the order has expired or, if the order is appealed, the time provided or granted to appeal a judgment of an appeal court that confirms the order has expired and no further appeal from a judgment that confirms the order is available.

(3.1) Evidence — The judge may receive into evidence anything that, in the opinion of the judge, is reliable and appropriate, even if it would not otherwise be admissible under Canadian law, and may base his or her decision on that evidence.

(4) Introduction into evidence — A person who wishes to introduce into evidence material the disclosure of which is authorized under subsection (2) but who may not be able to do so in a proceeding by reason of the rules of admissibility that apply in the proceeding may request from a judge an order permitting the introduction into evidence of the material in a form or subject to any conditions fixed by that judge, as long as that form and those conditions comply with the order made under subsection (2).

(5) Relevant factors — For the purpose of subsection (4), the judge shall consider all the factors that would be relevant for a determination of admissibility in the proceeding.

2001, c. 41, s. 43; 2013, c. 9, s. 20(1), (2)

38.07 Notice of order — The judge may order the Attorney General of Canada to give notice of an order made under any of subsections 38.06(1) to (3) to any person who, in the opinion of the judge, should be notified.

2001, c. 41, s. 43

38.08 Automatic review — If the judge determines that a party to the proceeding whose interests are adversely affected by an order made under any of subsections 38.06(1) to (3) was not given the opportunity to make representations under paragraph 38.04(5)(d), the judge shall refer the order to the Federal Court of Appeal for review.

2001, c. 41, s. 43

38.09 (1) Appeal to Federal Court of Appeal — An order made under any of subsections 38.06(1) to (3) may be appealed to the Federal Court of Appeal.

(2) Limitation period for appeal — An appeal shall be brought within 10 days after the day on which the order is made or within any further time that the Court considers appropriate in the circumstances.

2001, c. 41, s. 43

38.1 Limitation periods for appeals to Supreme Court of Canada — Notwithstanding any other Act of Parliament,

(a) an application for leave to appeal to the Supreme Court of Canada from a judgment made on appeal shall be made within 10 days after the day on which the judgment appealed from is made or within any further time that the Supreme Court of Canada considers appropriate in the circumstances; and

(b) if leave to appeal is granted, the appeal shall be brought in the manner set out in subsection 60(1) of the *Supreme Court Act* but within the time specified by the Supreme Court of Canada.

2001, c. 41, s. 43

38.11 (1) Special rules — hearing in private — The judge conducting a hearing under subsection 38.04(5) or the court hearing an appeal or review of an order made under any of subsections 38.06(1) to (3) may make an order that the hearing be held, or the appeal or review be heard, in private.

(1.1) Special rules — hearing in National Capital Region — A hearing under subsection 38.04(5) or an appeal or review of an order made under any of subsections 38.06(1) to (3) shall, at the request of either the Attorney General of Canada or, in the case of a proceeding under Part III of the *National Defence Act*, the Minister of National Defence, be held or heard, as the case may be, in the National Capital Region, as described in the schedule to the *National Capital Act*.

Proposed Amendment — 38.11(1.1)

(1.1) Special rules — hearing in National Capital Region — A hearing under subsection 38.04(5) or an appeal or review of an order made under any of subsections 38.06(1) to (3) shall, at the request of either the Attorney General of Canada or, in the case of a proceeding under Part III of the *National Defence Act*, other than a **"summary hearing"** as defined in subsection 2(1) of that Act, the Minister of National Defence, be held or heard, as the case may be, in the National Capital Region, as described in the schedule to the *National Capital Act*.

2019, c. 15, s. 51 [Not in force at date of publication.]

(2) *Ex parte* representations — The judge conducting a hearing under subsection 38.04(5) or the court hearing an appeal or review of an order made under any of subsections 38.06(1) to (3) may give any person who makes representations under paragraph 38.04(5)(d), and shall give the Attorney General of Canada and, in the case of a proceeding under Part III of the *National Defence Act*, the Minister of National Defence, the opportunity to make representations *ex parte*.

Proposed Amendment — 38.11(2)

(2) *Ex parte* representations — The judge conducting a hearing under subsection 38.04(5) or the court hearing an appeal or review of an order made under any of subsections 38.06(1) to (3) may give any person who makes representations under paragraph 38.04(5)(d), and shall give the Attorney General of Canada and, in the case of a proceeding under Part III of the *National Defence Act*, other than a **"summary hearing"** as defined in subsection 2(1) of that Act, the Minister of National Defence, the opportunity to make representations *ex parte*.

2019, c. 15, s. 51 [Not in force at date of publication.]

(3) *Ex parte* representations — public hearing — If a hearing under subsection 38.04(5) is held, or an appeal or review of an order made under any of subsections 38.06(1) to (3) is heard, in public, any *ex parte* representations made in that hearing, appeal or review shall be made in private.

2001, c. 41, s. 43; 2013, c. 9, s. 21

38.12 (1) Protective order — The judge conducting a hearing under subsection 38.04(5) or the court hearing an appeal or review of an order made under any of subsections 38.06(1) to (3) may make any order that the judge or the court considers appropriate in the circumstances to protect the confidentiality of any information to which the hearing, appeal or review relates.

(2) Court records — The court records relating to a hearing that is held, or an appeal or review that is heard, in private or to any *ex parte* representations are confidential. The judge or the court may order that the court records, or any part of them, relating to a private or public hearing, appeal or review be sealed and kept in a location to which the public has no access.

2001, c. 41, s. 43; 2013, c. 9, s. 22

38.13 (1) Certificate of Attorney General of Canada — The Attorney General of Canada may personally issue a certificate that prohibits the disclosure of information in connection with a proceeding for the purpose of protecting information obtained in confidence from, or in relation to, a foreign entity as defined in subsection 2(1) of the *Security of Information Act* or for the purpose of protecting national defence or national security. The certificate may only be issued after an order or decision that would result in the disclosure of the information to be subject to the certificate has been made under this or any other Act of Parliament.

(2) Military proceedings — In the case of a proceeding under Part III of the *National Defence Act*, the Attorney General of Canada may issue the certificate only with the agreement, given personally, of the Minister of National Defence.

Proposed Amendment — 38.13(2)

(2) Military proceedings — In the case of a proceeding under Part III of the *National Defence Act*, other than a **"summary hearing"** as defined in subsection 2(1) of that Act, the Attorney General of Canada may issue the certificate only with the agreement, given personally, of the Minister of National Defence.

2019, c. 15, s. 52 [Not in force at date of publication.]

(3) Service of certificate — The Attorney General of Canada shall cause a copy of the certificate to be served on

(a) the person presiding or designated to preside at the proceeding to which the information relates or, if no person is designated, the person who has the authority to designate a person to preside;

(b) every party to the proceeding;

(c) every person who gives notice under section 38.01 in connection with the proceeding;

(d) every person who, in connection with the proceeding, may disclose, is required to disclose or may cause the disclosure of the information about which the Attorney General of Canada has received notice under section 38.01;

(e) every party to a hearing under subsection 38.04(5) or to an appeal of an order made under any of subsections 38.06(1) to (3) in relation to the information;

(f) the judge who conducts a hearing under subsection 38.04(5) and any court that hears an appeal from, or review of, an order made under any of subsections 38.06(1) to (3) in relation to the information; and

(g) any other person who, in the opinion of the Attorney General of Canada, should be served.

(4) Filing of certificate — The Attorney General of Canada shall cause a copy of the certificate to be filed

(a) with the person responsible for the records of the proceeding to which the information relates; and

(b) in the Registry of the Federal Court and the registry of any court that hears an appeal from, or review of, an order made under any of subsections 38.06(1) to (3).

(5) Effect of certificate — If the Attorney General of Canada issues a certificate, then, notwithstanding any other provision of this Act, disclosure of the information shall be prohibited in accordance with the terms of the certificate.

(6) *Statutory Instruments Act* does not apply — The *Statutory Instruments Act* does not apply to a certificate issued under subsection (1).

(7) Publication — The Attorney General of Canada shall, without delay after a certificate is issued, cause the certificate to be published in the *Canada Gazette*.

(8) Restriction — The certificate and any matters arising out of it are not subject to review or to be restrained, prohibited, removed, set aside or otherwise dealt with, except in accordance with section 38.131.

(9) Expiry — The certificate expires 10 years after the day on which it is issued and may be reissued.

2001, c. 41, s. 43; 2013, c. 9, s. 23

38.131 (1) Application for review of certificate — A party to the proceeding referred to in section 38.13 may apply to the Federal Court of Appeal for an order varying or cancelling a certificate issued under that section on the grounds referred to in subsection (8) or (9), as the case may be.

(2) Notice to Attorney General of Canada — The applicant shall give notice of the application to the Attorney General of Canada.

(3) Military proceedings — In the case of proceedings under Part III of the *National Defence Act*, notice under subsection (2) shall be given to both the Attorney General of Canada and the Minister of National Defence.

Proposed Amendment — 38.131(3)

(3) Military proceedings — In the case of proceedings under Part III of the *National Defence Act*, other than a **"summary hearing"** as defined in subsection 2(1) of that Act, notice under subsection (2) shall be given to both the Attorney General of Canada and the Minister of National Defence.

2019, c. 15, s. 53 [Not in force at date of publication.]

(4) Single judge — Notwithstanding section 16 of the *Federal Court Act*, for the purposes of the application, the Federal Court of Appeal consists of a single judge of that Court.

(5) **Admissible information** — In considering the application, the judge may receive into evidence anything that, in the opinion of the judge, is reliable and appropriate, even if it would not otherwise be admissible under Canadian law, and may base a determination made under any of subsections (8) to (10) on that evidence.

(6) **Special rules and protective order** — Sections 38.11 and 38.12 apply, with any necessary modifications, to an application made under subsection (1).

(7) **Expedited consideration** — The judge shall consider the application as soon as reasonably possible, but not later than 10 days after the application is made under subsection (1).

(8) **Varying the certificate** — If the judge determines that some of the information subject to the certificate does not relate either to information obtained in confidence from, or in relation to, a foreign entity as defined in subsection 2(1) of the *Security of Information Act*, or to national defence or national security, the judge shall make an order varying the certificate accordingly.

(9) **Cancelling the certificate** — If the judge determines that none of the information subject to the certificate relates to information obtained in confidence from, or in relation to, a foreign entity as defined in subsection 2(1) of the *Security of Information Act*, or to national defence or national security, the judge shall make an order cancelling the certificate.

(10) **Confirming the certificate** — If the judge determines that all of the information subject to the certificate relates to information obtained in confidence from, or in relation to, a foreign entity as defined in subsection 2(1) of the *Security of Information Act*, or to national defence or national security, the judge shall make an order confirming the certificate.

(11) **Determination is final** — Notwithstanding any other Act of Parliament, a determination of a judge under any of subsections (8) to (10) is final and is not subject to review or appeal by any court.

(12) **Publication** — If a certificate is varied or cancelled under this section, the Attorney General of Canada shall, as soon as possible after the decision of the judge and in a manner that mentions the original publication of the certificate, cause to be published in the *Canada Gazette*

(a) the certificate as varied under subsection (8); or

(b) a notice of the cancellation of the certificate under subsection (9).

2001, c. 41, s. 43; 2004, c. 12, s. 19

38.14 (1) **Protection of right to a fair trial** — The person presiding at a criminal proceeding may make any order that he or she considers appropriate in the circumstances to protect the right of the accused to a fair trial, as long as that order complies with the terms of any order made under any of subsections 38.06(1) to (3) in relation to that proceeding, any judgment made on appeal from, or review of, the order, or any certificate issued under section 38.13.

(2) **Potential orders** — The orders that may be made under subsection (1) include, but are not limited to, the following orders:

(a) an order dismissing specified counts of the indictment or information, or permitting the indictment or information to proceed only in respect of a lesser or included offence;

(b) an order effecting a stay of the proceedings; and

(c) an order finding against any party on any issue relating to information the disclosure of which is prohibited.

2001, c. 41, s. 43

38.15 (1) **Fiat** — If sensitive information or potentially injurious information may be disclosed in connection with a prosecution that is not instituted by the Attorney General of Canada or on his or her behalf, the Attorney General of Canada may issue a fiat and serve the fiat on the prosecutor.

(2) **Effect of fiat** — When a fiat is served on a prosecutor, the fiat establishes the exclusive authority of the Attorney General of Canada with respect to the conduct of the prosecution described in the fiat or any related process.

(3) **Fiat filed in court** — If a prosecution described in the fiat or any related process is conducted by or on behalf of the Attorney General of Canada, the fiat or a copy of the fiat shall be filed with the court in which the prosecution or process is conducted.

(4) **Fiat constitutes conclusive proof** — The fiat or a copy of the fiat

(a) is conclusive proof that the prosecution described in the fiat or any related process may be conducted by or on behalf of the Attorney General of Canada; and

(b) is admissible in evidence without proof of the signature or official character of the Attorney General of Canada.

(5) **Military proceedings** — This section does not apply to a proceeding under Part III of the *National Defence Act*.

2001, c. 41, s. 43

38.16 **Regulations** — The Governor in Council may make any regulations that the Governor in Council considers necessary to carry into effect the purposes and provisions of sections 38 to 38.15, including regulations respecting the notices, certificates and the fiat.

2001, c. 41, s. 43

38.17 **Annual report** — Each year the Attorney General of Canada shall prepare and cause to be laid before each House of Parliament a report for the previous year on the operation of sections 38.13 and 38.15 that includes the number of certificates and fiats issued under sections 38.13 and 38.15, respectively.

2013, c. 9, s. 24

Confidences of the Queen's Privy Council for Canada

[Heading added 2001, c. 41, s. 43.]

39. (1) Objection relating to a confidence of the Queen's Privy Council — Where a minister of the Crown or the Clerk of the Privy Council objects to the disclosure of information before a court, person or body with jurisdiction to compel the production of information by certifying in writing that the information constitutes a confidence of the Queen's Privy Council for Canada, disclosure of the information shall be refused without examination or hearing of the information by the court, person or body.

(2) Definition — For the purpose of subsection (1), **"a confidence of the Queen's Privy Council for Canada"** includes, without restricting the generality thereof, information contained in

(a) a memorandum the purpose of which is to present proposals or recommendations to Council;

(b) a discussion paper the purpose of which is to present background explanations, analyses of problems or policy options to Council for consideration by Council in making decisions;

(c) an agendum of Council or a record recording deliberations or decisions of Council;

(d) a record used for or reflecting communications or discussions between ministers of the Crown on matters relating to the making of government decisions or the formulation of government policy;

(e) a record the purpose of which is to brief ministers of the Crown in relation to matters that are brought before, or are proposed to be brought before, Council or that are the subject of communications or discussions referred to in paragraph (d); and

(f) draft legislation.

(3) Definition of "council" — For the purposes of subsection (2), **"Council"** means the Queen's Privy Council for Canada, committees of the Queen's Privy Council for Canada, Cabinet and committees of Cabinet.

(4) Exception — Subsection (1) does not apply in respect of

(a) a confidence of the Queen's Privy Council for Canada that has been in existence for more than twenty years; or

(b) a discussion paper described in paragraph (2)(b)

(i) if the decisions to which the discussion paper relates have been made public, or

(ii) where the decisions have not been made public, if four years have passed since the decisions were made.

Journalistic Sources

[Heading added 2017, c. 22, s. 2.]

39.1 (1) Definitions — The following definitions apply in this section.

"document" has the same meaning as in section 487.011 of the *Criminal Code*. *("document")*

"journalist" means a person whose main occupation is to contribute directly, either regularly or occasionally, for consideration, to the collection, writing or production of information for dissemination by the media, or anyone who assists such a person. *("journaliste")*

"journalistic source" means a source that confidentially transmits information to a journalist on the journalist's undertaking not to divulge the identity of the source, whose anonymity is essential to the relationship between the journalist and the source. *("source journalistique")*

(2) Objection — Subject to subsection (7), a journalist may object to the disclosure of information or a document before a court, person or body with the authority to compel the disclosure of information on the grounds that the information or document identifies or is likely to identify a journalistic source.

(3) Former journalist — For the purposes of subsections (2) and (7), **"journalist"** includes an individual who was a journalist when information that identifies or is likely to identify the journalistic source was transmitted to that individual.

(4) Power of court, person or body — The court, person or body may raise the application of subsection (2) on their own initiative.

(5) Objection of court, person or body — When an objection or the application of subsection (2) is raised, the court, person or body shall ensure that the information or document is not disclosed other than in accordance with this section.

(6) Observations — Before determining the question, the court, person or body must give the parties and interested persons a reasonable opportunity to present observations.

(7) Authorization — The court, person or body may authorize the disclosure of information or a document only if they consider that

(a) the information or document cannot be produced in evidence by any other reasonable means; and

(b) the public interest in the administration of justice outweighs the public interest in preserving the confidentiality of the journalistic source, having regard to, among other things,

(i) the importance of the information or document to a central issue in the proceeding,

(ii) freedom of the press, and

(iii) the impact of disclosure on the journalistic source and the journalist.

(8) Conditions — An authorization under subsection (7) may contain any conditions that the court, person or body considers appropriate to protect the identity of the journalistic source.

(9) Burden of proof — A person who requests the disclosure has the burden of proving that the conditions set out in subsection (7) are fulfilled.

(10) Appeal — An appeal lies from a determination under subsection (7)

(a) to the Federal Court of Appeal from a determination of the Federal Court;

(b) to the court of appeal of a province from a determination of a superior court of the province;

(c) to the Federal Court from a determination of a court, person or body vested with power to compel production by or under an Act of Parliament if the court, person or body is not established under a law of a province; or

(d) to the trial division or trial court of the superior court of the province within which the court, person or body exercises its jurisdiction, in any other case.

(11) Limitation period for appeal — An appeal under subsection (10) shall be brought within 10 days after the date of the determination appealed from or within any further time that the court having jurisdiction to hear the appeal considers appropriate in the circumstances.

(12) Hearing in summary way — An appeal under subsection (10) shall be heard and determined without delay and in a summary way.

2017, c. 22, s. 2

Provincial Laws of Evidence

40. How applicable — In all proceedings over which Parliament has legislative authority, the laws of evidence in force in the province in which those proceedings are taken, including the laws of proof of service of any warrant, summons, subpoena or other document, subject to this Act and other Acts of Parliament, apply to those proceedings.

Statutory Declarations

41. Solemn declaration — Any judge, notary public, justice of the peace, provincial court judge, recorder, mayor or commissioner authorized to take affidavits to be used either in the provincial or federal courts, or any other functionary authorized by law to administer an oath in any matter, may receive the solemn declaration of any person voluntarily making the declaration before him, in the following form, in attestation of the execution of any writing, deed or instrument, or of the truth of any fact, or of any account rendered in writing:

I, ..., solemnly declare that (*state the fact or facts declared to*), and I make this solemn declaration conscientiously believing it to be true, and knowing that it is of the same force and effect as if made under oath.

Declared before me ..... at ..... this ..... day of ..... 19 ...

R.S.C. 1985, c. 27 (1st Supp.), s. 203

Insurance Proofs

42. Affidavits, etc — Any affidavit, solemn affirmation or declaration required by any insurance company authorized by law to do business in Canada, in regard to any loss of or injury to person, property or life insured or assured therein, may be taken before any commissioner or other person authorized to take affidavits, before any justice of the peace or before any notary public for any province, and the commissioner, person, justice of the peace or notary public is required to take the affidavit, solemn affirmation or declaration.

PART II — (SS. 43–51)

Application

43. Foreign courts — This Part applies to the taking of evidence relating to proceedings in courts out of Canada.

Interpretation

44. Definitions — In this Part,

"cause" includes a proceeding against a criminal;

"court" means any superior court in any province;

"judge" means any judge of any superior court in any province;

"oath" includes a solemn affirmation in cases in which, by the law of Canada, or of a province, as the case may be, a solemn affirmation is allowed instead of an oath.

45. Construction — This Part shall not be so construed as to interfere with the right of legislation of the legislature of any province requisite or desirable for the carrying out of the objects hereof.

Procedure

46. (1) Order for examination of witness in Canada — If, on an application for that purpose, it is made to appear to any court or judge that any court or tribunal outside Canada, before which any civil, commercial or criminal matter is pending, is desirous of obtaining the testimony in relation to that matter of a party or witness within the jurisdiction of the first mentioned court, of the court to which the judge belongs or of the judge, the court or judge may, in its or their discretion, order the examination on oath on interrogatories, or otherwise, before any person or persons named in the order, of that party or witness accordingly, and by the same or any subsequent order may command the attendance of that party or witness for the purpose of being examined, and for the production of any writings or other documents mentioned in the order and of any other writings or documents relating to the matter in question that are in the possession or power of that party or witness.

(2) **Video links, etc.** — For greater certainty, testimony for the purposes of subsection (1) may be given by means of technology that permits the virtual presence of the party or witness before the court or tribunal outside Canada or that permits that court or tribunal, and the parties, to hear and examine the party or witness.

1999, c. 18, s. 89

47. Enforcement of the order — On the service on the party or witness of an order referred to in section 46, and of an appointment of a time and place for the examination of the party or witness signed by the person named in the order for taking the examination, or, if more than one person is named, by one of the persons named, and on payment or tender of the like conduct money as is properly payable on attendance at a trial, the order may be enforced in like manner as an order made by the court or judge in a cause pending in that court or before that judge.

48. Expenses and conduct money — Every person whose attendance is required in manner described in section 47 is entitled to the like conduct money and payment for expenses and loss of time as on attendance at a trial.

49. Administering oath — On any examination of parties or witnesses, under the authority of any order made in pursuance of this Part, the oath shall be administered by the person authorized to take the examination, or, if more than one person is authorized, by one of those persons.

50. (1) Right of refusal to answer or produce document — Any person examined under any order made under this Part has the like right to refuse to answer questions tending to criminate himself, or other questions, as a party or witness, as the case may be, would have in any cause pending in the court by which, or by a judge whereof, the order is made.

(1.1) **Laws about witnesses to apply — video links etc.** — Despite subsection (1), when a party or witness gives evidence under subsection 46(2), the evidence shall be given as though they were physically before the court or tribunal outside Canada, for the purposes of the laws relating to evidence and procedure but only to the extent that giving the evidence would not disclose information otherwise protected by the Canadian law of non-disclosure of information or privilege.

(1.2) **Contempt of court in Canada** — When a party or witness gives evidence under subsection 46(2), the Canadian law relating to contempt of court applies with respect to a refusal by the party or witness to answer a question or to produce a writing or document referred to in subsection 46(1), as ordered under that subsection by the court or judge.

(2) Nature of right — No person shall be compelled to produce, under any order referred to in subsection (1), any writing or other document that he could not be compelled to produce at a trial of such a cause.

1999, c. 18, s. 90

51. (1) Rules of court — The court may frame rules and orders in relation to procedure and to the evidence to be produced in support of the application for an order for examination of parties and witnesses under this Part, and generally for carrying this Part into effect.

(2) Letters rogatory — In the absence of any order in relation to the evidence to be produced in support of the application referred to in subsection (1), letters rogatory from a court or tribunal outside Canada in which the civil, commercial or criminal matter is pending, are deemed and taken to be sufficient evidence in support of the application.

1999, c. 18, s. 91

PART III — (SS. 52–54)

Application

52. Application of this Part — This Part extends to the following classes of persons:

(a) officers of any of Her Majesty's diplomatic or consular services while performing their functions in any foreign country, including ambassadors, envoys, ministers, charges d'affaires, counsellors, secretaries, attaches, consuls general, consuls, vice-consuls, pro-consuls, consular agents, acting consuls general, acting consuls, acting vice-consuls and acting consular agents;

(b) officers of the Canadian diplomatic, consular and representative services while performing their functions in any foreign country or in any part of the Commonwealth and Dependent Territories other than Canada, including, in addition to the diplomatic and consular officers mentioned in paragraph (a), high commissioners, permanent delegates, acting high commissioners, acting permanent delegates, counsellors and secretaries;

(c) Canadian Government Trade Commissioners and Assistant Canadian Government Trade Commissioners while performing their functions in any foreign country or in any part of the Commonwealth and Dependent Territories other than Canada;

(d) honorary consular officers of Canada while performing their functions in any foreign country or in any part of the Commonwealth and Dependent Territories other than Canada;

(e) judicial officials in a foreign country in respect of oaths, affidavits, solemn affirmations, declarations or similar documents that the official is authorized to administer, take or receive; and

(f) persons locally engaged and designated by the Deputy Minister of Foreign Affairs or any other persons authorized by that Deputy Minister while performing their functions in any foreign country or in any part of the Commonwealth and Dependent Territories other than Canada.

1994, c. 44, s. 92; 1997, c. 18, s. 118

Oaths and Solemn Affirmations

53. Oaths taken abroad — Oaths, affidavits, solemn affirmations or declarations administered, taken or received outside Canada by any person mentioned in section 52, are as valid and effectual and are of the like force and effect to all intents and purposes as if they had been administered, taken or received in Canada by a person authorized to administer, take or receive oaths, affidavits, solemn affirmations or declarations therein that are valid and effectual under this Act.

Documentary Evidence

54. (1) Documents to be admitted in evidence — Any document that purports to have affixed, impressed or subscribed on it or to it the signature of any person authorized by any of paragraphs 52(a) to (d) to administer, take or receive oaths, affidavits, solemn affirmations or declarations, together with their seal or with the seal or stamp of their office, or the office to which the person is attached, in testimony of any oath, affidavit, solemn affirmation or declaration being administered, taken or received by the person, shall be admitted in evidence, without proof of the seal or stamp or of the person's signature or official character.

(2) Status of statements — An affidavit, solemn affirmation, declaration or other similar statement taken or received in a foreign country by an official referred to in paragraph 52(e) shall be admitted in evidence without proof of the signature or official character of the official appearing to have signed the affidavit, solemn affirmation, declaration or other statement.

1994, c. 44, s. 93

SCHEDULE

(Paragraph 38.01(6)(d) and subsection 38.01(8))

DESIGNATED ENTITIES

1. A judge of the Federal Court, for the purposes of section 21 of the *Canadian Security Intelligence Service Act*

2001, c. 41, s. 44 (Sched. 2)

2. A judge of the Federal Court, for the purposes of sections 6 and 7 of the *Charities Registration (Security Information) Act*, except where the hearing is open to the public

2001, c. 41, ss. 44 (Sched. 2), 124

3. A judge of the Federal Court, the Federal Court of Appeal or the Immigration Division or Immigration Appeal Division of the Immigration and Refugee Board, for the purposes of sections 77 to 87.1 of the *Immigration and Refugee Protection Act*

2001, c. 41, ss. 44 (Sched. 2), 124; 2008, c. 3, s. 11

4. A judge of the Federal Court, for the purposes of section 16 of the *Secure Air Travel Act*.

2001, c. 41, s. 124(3); 2015, c. 20, s. 13

5 to 8. [Repealed 2001, c. 41, s. 124(3).]

9. A board of inquiry convened under section 45 of the *National Defence Act*

2001, c. 41, s. 44 (Sched. 2)

10. A service tribunal or a military judge for the purposes of Part III of the *National Defence Act*

Proposed Amendment — 10

10. A court martial or a military judge for the purposes of Part III of the *National Defence Act*

2019, c. 15, s. 54 [Not in force at date of publication.]

2001, c. 41, s. 44 (Sched. 2)

11. The Federal Public Sector Labour Relations and Employment Board referred to in subsection 4(1) of the *Federal Public Sector Labour Relations and Employment Board Act*, for the purposes of a grievance process under the *Federal Public Sector Labour Relations Act* with respect to an employee of the Canadian Security Intelligence Service, with the exception of any information provided to the Board by the employee

2001, c. 41, s. 44 (Sched. 2); 2003, c. 22, s. 105; 2013, c. 40, s. 448; 2017, c. 9, s. 41

12. The Information Commissioner, for the purposes of the *Access to Information Act*

2001, c. 41, s. 44 (Sched. 2)

13. The Privacy Commissioner, for the purposes of the *Privacy Act*

2001, c. 41, s. 44 (Sched. 2)

14. The Privacy Commissioner, for the purposes of the *Personal Information Protection and Electronic Documents Act*

2001, c. 41, s. 44 (Sched. 2)

15. A judge of the Federal Court, for the purposes of section 41 of the *Access to Information Act*.

2001, c. 41, s. 44 (Sched. 2); 2019, c. 18, s. 60

16. A judge of the Federal Court, for the purposes of sections 41 to 43 of the *Privacy Act*

2001, c. 41, s. 44 (Sched. 2)

17. A judge of the Federal Court, for the purposes of sections 14 to 17 of the *Personal Information Protection and Electronic Documents Act*

2001, c. 41, s. 44 (Sched. 2)

18. The National Security and Intelligence Review Agency, for the purposes of sections 16 to 19 of the *National Security and Intelligence Review Agency Act*, with the exception of any information provided to the Agency by the complainant or an individual who has been denied a security clearance.

2001, c. 41, s. 44 (Sched. 2); 2019, c. 13, s. 20

19. The Public Sector Integrity Commissioner, for the purposes of sections 26 to 35 of the *Public Servants Disclosure Protection Act*

SOR/2004-19, s. 1; SOR/2012-220, s. 1

20. [Repealed 2019, c. 13, s. 61.]

21. A judge of the Federal Court, for the purposes of sections 4 and 6 of the *Prevention of Terrorist Travel Act*.

SOR/2012-220, s. 1; 2015, c. 36, s. 43

22. The Civilian Review and Complaints Commission for the Royal Canadian Mounted Police, for the purposes of the *Royal Canadian Mounted Police Act*, but only in relation to information that is under the control, or in the possession, of the Royal Canadian Mounted Police or the Central Authority, as the case may be.

2013, c. 18, ss. 45, 85

CAN. REG. 2005-30 — SECURE ELECTRONIC SIGNATURE REGULATIONS

made under the *Personal Information Protection and Electronic Documents Act* and the *Canada Evidence Act*

SOR/2005-30, as am. SOR/2011-71.

INTERPRETATION

1. The following definitions apply in these Regulations.

"Act" means the *Personal Information Protection and Electronic Documents Act*. *("Loi")*

"asymmetric cryptography" means a cryptographic system that relies on key pairs. *("système de chiffrement à clé publique")*

"certification authority" means a person or entity that issues digital signature certificates and that is listed as such on the website of the Treasury Board Secretariat. *("autorité de certification")*

"digital signature certificate", in respect of a person, means an electronic document that

(a) identifies the certification authority that issued it and is digitally signed by that certification authority;

(b) identifies, or can be used to identify, the person; and

(c) contains the person's public key.

("certificat de signature numérique")

"entity" includes any federal department, branch, office, board, agency, commission, corporation or body for the administration of the affairs of which a minister of the Crown is accountable to Parliament. *("entité")*

"hash function" means an electronic one-way mathematical process that converts data contained in an electronic document into a message digest that is unique to that data in a way that, were that data changed, it would, on conversion, result in a changed message digest. *("fonction de hachage")*

"key pair" means a pair of keys held by or for a person that includes a private key and a public key that are mathematically related to, but different from, each other. *("biclé")*

"private key" means a string of data that

(a) is used in asymmetric cryptography to encrypt data contained in an electronic document; and

(b) is unique to the person who is identified in, or can be identified through, a digital signature certificate and corresponds only to the public key in that certificate.

("clé privée")

"public key" means a string of data contained in a digital signature certificate that

(a) is used in asymmetric cryptography to decrypt data contained in an electronic document that was encrypted through the application of the private key in the key pair; and

(b) corresponds only to the private key in the key pair.

("clé publique")

SOR/2011-71, s. 1

Technology or Process

2. For the purposes of the definition **"secure electronic signature"** in subsection 31(1) of the Act, a secure electronic signature in respect of data contained in an electronic document is a digital signature that results from completion of the following consecutive operations:

(a) application of the hash function to the data to generate a message digest;

(b) application of a private key to encrypt the message digest;

(c) incorporation in, attachment to, or association with the electronic document of the encrypted message digest;

(d) transmission of the electronic document and encrypted message digest together with either

(i) a digital signature certificate, or

(ii) a means of access to a digital signature certificate; and

(e) after receipt of the electronic document, the encrypted message digest and the digital signature certificate or the means of access to the digital signature certificate,

(i) application of the public key contained in the digital signature certificate to decrypt the encrypted message digest and produce the message digest referred to in paragraph (a),

(ii) application of the hash function to the data contained in the electronic document to generate a new message digest,

(iii) verification that, on comparison, the message digests referred to in paragraph (a) and subparagraph (ii) are identical, and

(iv) verification that the digital signature certificate is valid in accordance with section 3.

3. (1) A digital signature certificate is valid if, at the time when the data contained in an electronic document is digitally signed in accordance with section 2, the certificate

(a) is readable or perceivable by any person or entity who is entitled to have access to the digital signature certificate; and

(b) has not expired or been revoked.

(2) In addition to the requirements for validity set out in subsection (1), when the digital signature certificate is supported by other digital signature certificates, in order for the digital signature certificate to be valid, the supporting certificates must also be valid in accordance with that subsection.

4. (1) Before recognizing a person or entity as a certification authority, the President of the Treasury Board must verify that the person or entity has the capacity to issue digital signature certificates in a secure and reliable manner within the context of these Regulations and paragraphs 48(2)(a) to (d) of the Act.

(2) Every person or entity that is recognized as a certification authority by the President of the Treasury Board shall be listed on the website of the Treasury Board Secretariat.

PRESUMPTION

5. When the technology or process set out in section 2 is used in respect of data contained in an electronic document, that data is presumed, in the absence of evidence to the contrary, to have been signed by the person who is identified in, or can be identified through, the digital signature certificate.

COMING INTO FORCE

6. These Regulations come into force on the day on which they are registered.

CANADIAN BILL OF RIGHTS

R.S.C. 1985, App. III

Preamble

The Parliament of Canada, affirming that the Canadian Nation is founded upon principles that acknowledge the supremacy of God, the dignity and worth of the human person and the position of the family in a society of free men and free institutions;

Affirming also that men and institutions remain free only when freedom is founded upon respect for moral and spiritual values and the rule of law;

And being desirous of enshrining these principles and the human rights and fundamental freedoms derived from them, in a Bill of Rights which shall reflect the respect of Parliament for its constitutional authority and which shall ensure the protection of these rights and freedoms in Canada:

Therefore, Her Majesty, by and with the advice and consent of the Senate and House of Commons of Canada, enacts as follows:

PART I — BILL OF RIGHTS (SS. 1–4)

1. Recognition and declaration of rights and freedoms — It is hereby recognized and declared that in Canada there have existed and shall continue to exist without discrimination by reason of race, national origin, colour, religion or sex, the following human rights and fundamental freedoms, namely,

(a) the right of the individual to life, liberty, security of the person and enjoyment of property, and the right not to be deprived thereof except by due process of law;

(b) the right of the individual to equality before the law and the protection of the law;

(c) freedom of religion;

(d) freedom of speech;

(e) freedom of assembly and association; and

(f) freedom of the press.

2. Construction of law — Every law of Canada shall, unless it is expressly declared by an Act of the Parliament of Canada that it shall operate notwithstanding the *Canadian Bill of Rights*, be so construed and applied as not to abrogate, abridge or infringe or to authorize the abrogation, abridgment or infringement of any of the rights or freedoms herein recognized and declared, and in particular, no law of Canada shall be construed or applied so as to

(a) authorize or effect the arbitrary detention, imprisonment or exile of any person;

(b) impose or authorize the imposition of cruel and unusual treatment or punishment;

(c) deprive a person who has been arrested or detained

(i) of the right to be informed promptly of the reason for his arrest or detention,

(ii) of the right to retain and instruct counsel without delay, or

(iii) of the remedy by way of *habeas corpus* for the determination of the validity of his detention and for his release if the detention is not lawful;

(d) authorize a court, tribunal, commission, board or other authority to compel a person to give evidence if he is denied counsel, protection against self crimination or other constitutional safeguards;

(e) deprive a person of the right to a fair hearing in accordance with the principles of fundamental justice for the determination of his rights and obligations;

(f) deprive a person charged with a criminal offence of the right to be presumed innocent until proved guilty according to law in a fair and public hearing by an independent and impartial tribunal, or of the right to reasonable bail without just cause; or

(g) deprive a person of the right to the assistance of an interpreter in any proceedings in which he is involved or in which he is a party or a witness, before a court, commission, board or other tribunal, if he does not understand or speak the language in which such proceedings are conducted.

3. (1) Duties of Minister of Justice — Subject to subjection (2), the Minister of Justice shall, in accordance with such regulations as may be prescribed by the Governor in Council, examine every regulation transmitted to the Clerk of the Privy Council for registration pursuant to the *Statutory Instruments Act* and every Bill introduced in or presented to the House of Commons by a Minister of the Crown in order to ascertain whether any of the provisions thereof are inconsistent with the purposes and provisions of this Part and he shall report any such inconsistency to the House of Commons at the first convenient opportunity.

(2) Exception — A regulation need not be examined in accordance with subsection (1) if prior to being made it was examined as a proposed regulation in accordance with section 3 of the Statutory Instruments Act to ensure that it was not inconsistent with the purposes and provisions of this Part.

4. Short title — The provisions of this Part shall be known as the *Canadian Bill of Rights*.

PART II — (S. 5)

5. (1) **Savings** — Nothing in Part I shall be construed to abrogate or abridge any human right or fundamental freedom not enumerated therein that may have existed in Canada at the commencement of this Act.

(2) **"Law of Canada" defined** — The expression **"law of Canada"** in Part I means an Act of the Parliament of Canada enacted before or after the coming into force of this Act, any order, rule or regulation thereunder, and any law in force in Canada or in any part of Canada at the commencement of this Act that is subject to be repealed, abolished or altered by the Parliament of Canada.

(3) **Jurisdiction of Parliament** — The provisions of Part I shall be construed as extending only to matters coming within the legislative authority of the Parliament of Canada.

PART II — (s. 5)

5. (1) Savings — Nothing in Part I shall be construed to abrogate or abridge any human right or fundamental freedom not enumerated therein that may have existed in Canada at the commencement of this Act.

(2) "Law of Canada" defined — The expression "law of Canada" in Part I means an Act of the Parliament of Canada enacted before or after the coming into force of this Act, any order, rule or regulation thereunder, and any law in force in Canada or in any part of Canada at the commencement of this Act that is subject to be repealed, abolished or altered by the Parliament of Canada.

(3) Jurisdiction of Parliament — The provisions of Part I shall be construed as extending only to matters coming within the legislative authority of the Parliament of Canada.

Canadian Victims Bill of Rights

An Act for the Recognition of Victims Rights

S.C. 2015, c. 13, s. 2, as am. S.C. 2018, c. 16, s. 187; 2019, c. 15, ss. 61, 62 [Not in force at date of publication.].

Preamble

Whereas crime has a harmful impact on victims and on society;

Whereas victims of crime and their families deserve to be treated with courtesy, compassion and respect, including respect for their dignity;

Whereas it is important that victims' rights be considered throughout the criminal justice system;

Whereas victims of crime have rights that are guaranteed by the *Canadian Charter of Rights and Freedoms*;

Whereas consideration of the rights of victims of crime is in the interest of the proper administration of justice;

Whereas the federal, provincial and territorial governments share responsibility for criminal justice;

Whereas, in 1988, the federal, provincial and territorial governments endorsed the *Canadian Statement of Basic Principles of Justice for Victims of Crime* and, in 2003, the *Canadian Statement of Basic Principles of Justice for Victims of Crime, 2003*;

Now, therefore, Her Majesty, by and with the advice and consent of the Senate and House of Commons of Canada, enacts as follows:

Short Title

1. Short title — This Act may be cited as the *Canadian Victims Bill of Rights*.

Interpretation

2. Definitions — The following definitions apply in this Act.

"offence" means an offence under the *Criminal Code*, the *Youth Criminal Justice Act* or the *Crimes Against Humanity and War Crimes Act*, a **"designated substance offence"** as defined in subsection 2(1) of the *Controlled Drugs and Substances Act*, a **"designated offence"** as defined in subsection 2(1) of the *Cannabis Act* or an offence under section 91 or Part 3 of the *Immigration and Refugee Protection Act*. *("infraction")*

"victim" means an individual who has suffered physical or emotional harm, property damage or economic loss as the result of the commission or alleged commission of an offence. *("victime")*

2018, c. 16, s. 187

3. Acting on victim's behalf — Any of the following individuals may exercise a victim's rights under this Act if the victim is dead or incapable of acting on their own behalf:

(a) the victim's spouse or the individual who was at the time of the victim's death their spouse;

(b) the individual who is or was at the time of the victim's death, cohabiting with them in a conjugal relationship, having so cohabited for a period of at least one year;

(c) a relative or dependant of the victim;

(d) an individual who has in law or fact custody, or is responsible for the care or support, of the victim;

(e) an individual who has in law or fact custody, or is responsible for the care or support, of a dependant of the victim.

4. Exception — An individual is not a victim in relation to an offence, or entitled to exercise a victim's rights under this Act, if the individual is charged with the offence, found guilty of the offence or found not criminally responsible on account of mental disorder or unfit to stand trial in respect of the offence.

5. Criminal justice system — For the purpose of this Act, the criminal justice system consists of

(a) the investigation and prosecution of offences in Canada;

(b) the corrections process and the conditional release process in Canada; and

(c) the proceedings of courts and Review Boards, as those terms are defined in subsection 672.1(1) of the *Criminal Code*, in respect of accused who are found not criminally responsible on account of mental disorder or unfit to stand trial.

RIGHTS

Information

6. General information — Every victim has the right, on request, to information about

(a) the criminal justice system and the role of victims in it;

(b) the services and programs available to them as a victim, including restorative justice programs; and

(c) their right to file a complaint for an infringement or denial of any of their rights under this Act.

7. Investigation and proceedings — Every victim has the right, on request, to information about

(a) the status and outcome of the investigation into the offence; and

(b) the location of proceedings in relation to the offence, when they will take place and their progress and outcome.

8. Information about offender or accused — Every victim has the right, on request, to information about

(a) reviews under the *Corrections and Conditional Release Act* relating to the offender's conditional release and the timing and conditions of that release; and

(b) hearings held for the purpose of making dispositions, as defined in subsection 672.1(1) of the *Criminal Code*, in relation to the accused, if the accused is found not criminally responsible on account of mental disorder or unfit to stand trial, and the dispositions made at those hearings.

Protection

9. Security — Every victim has the right to have their security considered by the appropriate authorities in the criminal justice system.

10. Protection from intimidation and retaliation — Every victim has the right to have reasonable and necessary measures taken by the appropriate authorities in the criminal justice system to protect the victim from intimidation and retaliation.

11. Privacy — Every victim has the right to have their privacy considered by the appropriate authorities in the criminal justice system.

12. Identity protection — Every victim has the right to request that their identity be protected if they are a complainant to the offence or a witness in proceedings relating to the offence.

13. Testimonial aids — Every victim has the right to request testimonial aids when appearing as a witness in proceedings relating to the offence.

Participation

14. Views to be considered — Every victim has the right to convey their views about decisions to be made by appropriate authorities in the criminal justice system that affect the victim's rights under this Act and to have those views considered.

15. Victim impact statement — Every victim has the right to present a victim impact statement to the appropriate authorities in the criminal justice system and to have it considered.

Restitution

16. Restitution order — Every victim has the right to have the court consider making a restitution order against the offender.

17. Enforcement — Every victim in whose favour a restitution order is made has the right, if they are not paid, to have the order entered as a civil court judgment that is enforceable against the offender.

General Provisions

18. (1) Application — This Act applies in respect of a victim of an offence in their interactions with the criminal justice system

(a) while the offence is investigated or prosecuted;

(b) while the offender is subject to the corrections process or the conditional release process in relation to the offence; and

(c) while the accused is, in relation to the offence, under the jurisdiction of a court or a Review Board, as those terms are defined in subsection 672.1(1) of the *Criminal Code*, if they are found not criminally responsible on account of mental disorder or unfit to stand trial.

(2) Reporting of offence — For the purpose of subsection (1), if an offence is reported to the appropriate authorities in the criminal justice system, the investigation of the offence is deemed to begin at the time of the reporting.

(3) National Defence Act — This Act does not apply in respect of offences that are service offences, as defined in subsection 2(1) of the *National Defence Act*, that are investigated or proceeded with under that Act.

Proposed Amendment — 18(3)

(3) National Defence Act — Subject to subsection (4), this Act does not apply in respect of offences that are **"service offences"**, as defined in subsection 2(1) of the *National Defence Act*, that are investigated or proceeded with under that Act.

2019, c. 15, s. 61 [Not in force at date of publication.]

Proposed Addition — 18(4)

(4) Application — This Act applies in respect of an offender who is convicted of a **"service offence"**, as defined in subsection 2(1) of the *National Defence Act* and who is committed to a **"penitentiary"** or a **"civil prison"**, as those terms are defined in that subsection.

2019, c. 15, s. 61 [Not in force at date of publication.]

19. (1) Exercise of rights — The rights of victims under this Act are to be exercised through the mechanisms provided by law.

(2) Connection to Canada — A victim is entitled to exercise their rights under this Act only if they are present in Canada or they are a Canadian citizen or a permanent resident within the meaning of subsection 2(1) of the *Immigration and Refugee Protection Act*.

20. Interpretation of this Act — This Act is to be construed and applied in a manner that is reasonable in the circumstances, and in a manner that is not likely to

(a) interfere with the proper administration of justice, including

(i) by causing interference with police discretion or causing excessive delay in, or compromising or hindering, the investigation of any offence, and

(ii) by causing interference with prosecutorial discretion or causing excessive delay in, or compromising or hindering, the prosecution of any offence;

(b) interfere with ministerial discretion;

(c) interfere with the discretion that may be exercised by any person or body authorized to release an offender into the community;

(d) endanger the life or safety of any individual; or

(e) cause injury to international relations or national defence or national security.

21. Interpretation of other Acts, regulations, etc. — To the extent that it is possible to do so, every Act of Parliament enacted — and every order, rule or regulation made under such an Act — before, on or after the day on which this Act comes into force must be construed and applied in a manner that is compatible with the rights under this Act.

22. (1) Primacy in event of inconsistency — If, after the application of sections 20 and 21, there is any inconsistency between any provision of this Act and any provision of any Act, order, rule or regulation referred to in section 21, the provision of this Act prevails to the extent of the inconsistency.

(2) Exception — Acts and regulations, etc. — Subsection (1) does not apply in respect of the *Canadian Bill of Rights*, the *Canadian Human Rights Act*, the *Official Languages Act*, the *Access to Information Act* and the *Privacy Act* and orders, rules and regulations made under any of those Acts.

Proposed Amendment — 22(2)

(2) Exception — Acts, regulations, etc. — Subsection (1) does not apply in respect of the *Canadian Bill of Rights*, the *Canadian Human Rights Act*, the *Official Languages Act*, the *Access to Information Act* and the *Privacy Act* and in respect of orders, rules and regulations made under any of those Acts. It also does not apply in respect of Division 1.1 of Part III of the *National Defence Act* and in respect of any orders, rules and regulations made under that Act to the extent that they apply in relation to that Division.

2019, c. 15, s. 62 [Not in force at date of publication.]

23. No adverse inference — No adverse inference is to be drawn against a person who is charged with an offence from the fact that an individual has been identified as a victim in relation to the offence.

24. Entering or remaining in Canada — Nothing in this Act is to be construed so as to permit any individual to

(a) enter Canada or to remain in Canada beyond the end of the period for which they are authorized to so remain;

(b) delay any removal proceedings or prevent the enforcement of any removal order; or

(c) delay any extradition proceedings or prevent the extradition of any person to or from Canada.

Remedies

25. (1) Complaint — federal entity — Every victim who is of the opinion that any of their rights under this Act have been infringed or denied by a federal department, agency or body has the right to file a complaint in accordance with its complaints mechanism.

(2) Complaint to authority — Every victim who has exhausted their recourse under the complaints mechanism and who is not satisfied with the response of the federal department, agency or body may file a complaint with any authority that has jurisdiction to review complaints in relation to that department, agency or body.

(3) Complaints mechanism — Every federal department, agency or body that is involved in the criminal justice system must have a complaints mechanism that provides for

(a) a review of complaints involving alleged infringements or denials of rights under this Act;

(b) the power to make recommendations to remedy such infringements and denials; and

(c) the obligation to notify victims of the result of those reviews and of the recommendations, if any were made.

26. Complaint — provincial or territorial entity — Every victim who is of the opinion that their rights under this Act have been infringed or denied by a provincial or territorial department, agency or body may file a complaint in accordance with the laws of the province or territory.

27. Status — Nothing in this Act is to be construed as granting to, or removing from, any victim or any individual acting on behalf of a victim the status of party, intervenor or observer in any proceedings.

28. No cause of action — No cause of action or right to damages arises from an infringement or denial of a right under this Act.

29. No appeal — No appeal lies from any decision or order solely on the grounds that a right under this Act has been infringed or denied.

Related Provision

— 2015, c. 13, s. 2.1:

> 2.1 Review of *Canadian Victims Bill of Rights* — Five years after section 2 comes into force, a committee of Parliament is to be designated or established for the purpose of reviewing the *Canadian Victims Bill of Rights* enacted by that section.

Cannabis Act

An Act respecting cannabis and to amend the Controlled Drugs and Substances Act, the Criminal Code and other Acts

S.C. 2018, c. 16 [s. 193.1 not in force at date of publication.], as am. S.C. 2018, c. 16, ss. 188(2), 189(2), (6), 192, 193.1 [s. 193.1 not in force at date of publication.]; 2019, c. 25, s. 400.1; SOR/2019-207 [Not in force at date of publication.].

Her Majesty, by and with the advice and consent of the Senate and House of Commons of Canada, enacts as follows:

Short Title

1. Short title — This Act may be cited as the *Cannabis Act*.

Interpretation

2. (1) Definitions — The following definitions apply in this Act.

"analyst" means an individual who is designated as an analyst under section 130. *("analyste")*

"Attorney General" means

(a) the Attorney General of Canada, and includes his or her lawful deputy; or

(b) with respect to proceedings commenced at the instance of the government of a province and conducted by or on behalf of that government, the Attorney General of that province, and includes his or her lawful deputy.

("procureur général")

"brand element" includes a brand name, trademark, tradename, distinguishing guise, logo, graphic arrangement, design or slogan that is reasonably associated with, or that evokes,

(a) cannabis, a cannabis accessory or a service related to cannabis; or

(b) a brand of any cannabis, cannabis accessory or service related to cannabis.

("élément de marque")

"brand-preference promotion" means promotion of cannabis by means of its brand characteristics, promotion of a cannabis accessory by means of its brand characteristics or promotion of a service related to cannabis by means of the brand characteristics of the service. *("promotion de marque")*

"cannabis" means a cannabis plant and anything referred to in Schedule 1 but does not include anything referred to in Schedule 2. *("cannabis")*

"cannabis accessory" means

(a) a thing, including rolling papers or wraps, holders, pipes, water pipes, bongs and vaporizers, that is represented to be used in the consumption of cannabis; or

(b) a thing that is deemed under subsection (3) to be represented to be used in the consumption of cannabis.

("accessoire")

"cannabis plant" means a plant that belongs to the genus *Cannabis*. *("plante de cannabis")*

"chemical offence-related property" means offence-related property that is a chemical and includes

(a) anything that contains any offence-related property that is a chemical; or

(b) anything that has any offence-related property on it that is a chemical.

("bien infractionnel chimique")

"chemical property" means

(a) any chemical offence-related property;

(b) a chemical that is not chemical offence-related property; or

(c) anything that contains a chemical referred to in paragraph (b) or anything that has such a chemical on it.

("bien chimique")

"competent authority" means a public authority of a foreign country that is authorized under the laws of that country to approve the importation or exportation of cannabis into or from that country. *("autorité compétente")*

"designated offence" means

(a) an offence under subsection 9(1) or (2), 10(1) or (2), 11(1) or (2), 12(1), (4), (5), (6) or (7), 13(1) or 14(1); or

(b) a conspiracy or an attempt to commit, being an accessory after the fact in relation to, or any counselling in relation to, an offence referred to in paragraph (a).

("infraction désignée")

"distribute" includes administering, giving, transferring, transporting, sending, delivering, providing or otherwise making available in any manner, whether directly or indirectly, and offering to distribute. *("distribuer")*

"dried cannabis" means any part of a cannabis plant that has been subjected to a drying process, other than seeds. *("cannabis séché")*

"dwelling-house" has the same meaning as in section 2 of the *Criminal Code*. *("maison d'habitation")*

"government" means any of the following or their institutions:

(a) the federal government;

(b) a corporation named in Schedule III to the *Financial Administration Act*;

(c) the government of a province or a public body established under an Act of the legislature of a province;

(d) an **"aboriginal government"** as defined in subsection 13(3) of the *Access to Information Act*;

(e) the government of a foreign state or of a subdivision of a foreign state; and

(f) an international organization of states.

("administration")

"illicit cannabis" means cannabis that is or was sold, produced or distributed by a person prohibited from doing so under this Act or any provincial Act or that was imported by a person prohibited from doing so under this Act. *("cannabis illicite")*

"informational promotion" means a promotion by which factual information is provided to the consumer about

(a) cannabis or its characteristics;

(b) a cannabis accessory or its characteristics;

(c) a service related to cannabis; or

(d) the availability or price of cannabis, a cannabis accessory or a service related to cannabis.

("promotion informative")

"inspector" means an individual who is designated as an inspector under section 84. *("inspecteur")*

"judge" means a **"judge"** as defined in section 552 of the *Criminal Code* or a judge of a superior court of criminal jurisdiction. *("juge")*

"justice" has the same meaning as in section 2 of the *Criminal Code*. *("juge de paix")*

"label" includes a legend, word or mark that is, or is to be, applied or attached to or included in, or that accompanies or is to accompany, cannabis or a cannabis accessory or a package. *("étiquette")*

"Minister" means the member of the Queen's Privy Council for Canada who is designated as the Minister under section 4. *("ministre")*

"non-chemical offence-related property" means offence-related property that is not chemical offence-related property. *("bien infractionnel non chimique")*

"offence-related property" means, with the exception of cannabis, any property within or outside Canada

(a) by means of or in respect of which a designated offence is committed;

(b) that is used in any manner in connection with the commission of a designated offence; or

(c) that is intended for use for the purpose of committing a designated offence.

("bien infractionnel")

"organization" has the same meaning as in section 2 of the *Criminal Code*. *("organisation")*

"package" means any inner or outer container or covering. *("emballage")*

"person" means an individual or organization. *("personne")*

"possession" has the same meaning as in subsection 4(3) of the *Criminal Code*. *("possession")*

"prescribed" means prescribed by the regulations. *("Version anglaise seulement")*

"produce", in respect of cannabis, means to obtain it by any method or process, including by

(a) manufacturing;

(b) synthesis;

(c) altering its chemical or physical properties by any means; or

(d) cultivating, propagating or harvesting it or any living thing from which it may be extracted or otherwise obtained.

("production")

"promote", in respect of a thing or service, means to make, for the purpose of selling the thing or service, a representation — other than a representation on a package or label — about the thing or service by any means, whether directly or indirectly, that is likely to influence and shape attitudes, beliefs and behaviours about the thing or service. *("promotion")*

"public place" includes any place to which the public has access as of right or by invitation, express or implied, and any motor vehicle located in a public place or in any place open to public view. *("lieu public")*

"sell" includes offer for sale, expose for sale and have in possession for sale. *("vente")*

"young person" means

(a) for the purposes of sections 8, 9 and 12, an individual who is 12 years of age or older but under 18 years of age; and

(b) for the purposes of any other provision of this Act, an individual who is under 18 years of age.

("jeune")

(2) **Dried cannabis** — For the purposes of this Act, dried cannabis is a class of cannabis.

(3) **Deeming — cannabis accessory** — For the purposes of the definition "cannabis accessory", a thing that is commonly used in the consumption of cannabis is deemed to be represented to be used in the consumption of cannabis if the thing is sold at the same point of sale as cannabis.

(4) **Equivalency** — For the purposes of this Act, a quantity referred to in column 2 of Schedule 3 in respect of any class of cannabis referred to in column 1 of that Schedule is deemed to be equivalent to 1 g of dried cannabis.

3. Interpretation — Every power, duty or function imposed under this Act that may be exercised or performed in respect of an offence under this Act may be exercised or performed in respect of a conspiracy, or an attempt to commit, being an accessory after the fact in relation to, or any counselling in relation to, an offence under this Act.

4. Designation of Minister — The Governor in Council may, by order, designate a member of the Queen's Privy Council for Canada as the Minister for the purposes of this Act.

APPLICATION

5. Youth Criminal Justice Act — The *Youth Criminal Justice Act* applies in respect of contraventions of provisions of this Act or of the regulations.

5.1 For greater certainty — For greater certainty, nothing in this Act is to be construed as limiting the operation of the extrajudicial measures that are provided for under the *Youth Criminal Justice Act*.

HER MAJESTY

6. Act binding on Her Majesty — This Act is binding on Her Majesty in right of Canada or a province.

PURPOSE

7. Purpose — The purpose of this Act is to protect public health and public safety and, in particular, to

(a) protect the health of young persons by restricting their access to cannabis;

(b) protect young persons and others from inducements to use cannabis;

(c) provide for the licit production of cannabis to reduce illicit activities in relation to cannabis;

(d) deter illicit activities in relation to cannabis through appropriate sanctions and enforcement measures;

(e) reduce the burden on the criminal justice system in relation to cannabis;

(f) provide access to a quality-controlled supply of cannabis; and

(g) enhance public awareness of the health risks associated with cannabis use.

PART 1 — PROHIBITIONS, OBLIGATIONS AND OFFENCES (SS. 8–50)

DIVISION 1 — CRIMINAL ACTIVITIES

8. (1) Possession — Unless authorized under this Act, it is prohibited

(a) for an individual who is 18 years of age or older to possess, in a public place, cannabis of one or more classes of cannabis the total amount of which, as determined in accordance with Schedule 3, is equivalent to more than 30 g of dried cannabis;

(b) for an individual who is 18 years of age or older to possess any cannabis that they know is illicit cannabis;

(c) for a young person to possess cannabis of one or more classes of cannabis the total amount of which, as determined in accordance with Schedule 3, is equivalent to more than 5 g of dried cannabis;

(d) for an individual to possess, in a public place, one or more cannabis plants that are budding or flowering;

(e) for an individual to possess more than four cannabis plants that are not budding or flowering; or

(f) for an organization to possess cannabis.

(2) Punishment — Subject to section 51, every person that contravenes subsection (1)

(a) is guilty of an indictable offence and is liable

(i) in the case of an individual who is 18 years of age or older, to imprisonment for a term of not more than five years less a day,

(ii) in the case of a young person, to a youth sentence under the *Youth Criminal Justice Act*, or

(iii) in the case of an organization, to a fine in an amount that is in the discretion of the court; or

(b) is guilty of an offence punishable on summary conviction and is liable

(i) in the case of an individual who is 18 years of age or older, to a fine of not more than $5,000 or imprisonment for a term of not more than six months, or to both,

(ii) in the case of a young person, to a youth sentence under the *Youth Criminal Justice Act*, or

(iii) in the case of an organization, to a fine of not more than $100,000.

8.1 (1) Definition of "medical emergency" — For the purposes of this section, **"medical emergency"** means a physiological event induced by the introduction of a psychoactive substance into the body of a person that results in a life-threatening situation and in respect of which there are reasonable grounds to believe that the person requires emergency medical or law enforcement assistance.

(2) Exemption — medical emergency — No person who seeks emergency medical or law enforcement assistance because that person, or another person, is suffering from a medical emergency is to be charged or convicted of an offence under subsection 8(1) if the evidence in support of that offence was obtained or discovered as a result of that person having sought assistance or having remained at the scene.

(3) Exemption — persons at the scene — The exemption under subsection (2) also applies to any person, including the person suffering from the medical emergency, who is at the scene on the arrival of the emergency medical or law enforcement assistance.

(4) Exemption — evidence — No person who seeks emergency medical or law enforcement assistance because that person, or another person, is suffering from a medical emergency, or who is at the scene on the arrival of the assistance, is to be charged with an offence concerning a violation of any condition of a pre-trial release or probation order relating to an offence under subsection 8(1) if the evidence in support of that offence was obtained or discovered as a result of that person having sought assistance or having remained at the scene.

(5) Deeming — Any condition of a person's pre-trial release, probation order, conditional sentence or parole relating to an offence under subsection 8(1) that may be violated as a result of the person seeking emergency medical or law enforcement assistance for their, or another person's, medical emergency, or as a result of having been at the scene on the arrival of the assistance, is deemed not to be violated.

9. (1) Distribution — Unless authorized under this Act, it is prohibited

(a) for an individual who is 18 years of age or older

(i) to distribute cannabis of one or more classes of cannabis the total amount of which is equivalent, as determined in accordance with Schedule 3, to more than 30 g of dried cannabis,

(ii) to distribute cannabis to an individual who is under 18 years of age,

(iii) to distribute cannabis to an organization, or

(iv) to distribute cannabis that they know is illicit cannabis;

(b) for a young person

(i) to distribute cannabis of one or more classes of cannabis the total amount of which is equivalent, as determined in accordance with Schedule 3, to more than 5 g of dried cannabis,

(ii) to distribute cannabis to an organization;

(c) for an individual

(i) to distribute one or more cannabis plants that are budding or flowering, or

(ii) to distribute more than four cannabis plants that are not budding or flowering; or

(d) for an organization to distribute cannabis.

(2) Possession for purpose of distributing — Unless authorized under this Act, it is prohibited to possess cannabis for the purpose of distributing it contrary to subsection (1).

(3) Defence — subparagraph (1)(a)(ii) — It is not a defence to a charge arising out of the contravention of subparagraph (1)(a)(ii) that the accused believed that the individual referred to in that subparagraph was 18 years of age or older, unless the accused took reasonable steps to ascertain the individual's age.

(4) Defence — subsection (2) — It is not a defence to a charge arising out of the contravention of subsection (2) of possessing cannabis for the purpose of distributing it to an individual referred to in subparagraph (1)(a)(ii) that the accused believed that the individual was 18 years of age or older, unless the accused took reasonable steps to ascertain the individual's age.

(5) Punishment — Subject to section 51, every person that contravenes subsection (1) or (2)

(a) is guilty of an indictable offence and is liable

(i) in the case of an individual who is 18 years of age or older, to imprisonment for a term of not more than 14 years,

(ii) in the case of a young person, to a youth sentence under the *Youth Criminal Justice Act*, or

(iii) in the case of an organization, to a fine in an amount that is in the discretion of the court; or

(b) is guilty of an offence punishable on summary conviction and is liable

(i) in the case of an individual who is 18 years of age or older who contravenes any of subparagraphs (1)(a)(i), (iii) and (iv) and (c)(i) and (ii) — or subsection (2) other than by possessing cannabis for the purpose of distributing it contrary to subparagraph (1)(a)(ii) — to a fine of not more than $5,000 or imprisonment for a term of not more than six months, or to both,

(ii) in the case of an individual who is 18 years of age or older who contravenes subparagraph (1)(a)(ii) — or subsection (2) if the possession was for the purpose of distribution contrary to subparagraph (1)(a)(ii) — to a fine of not more than $15,000 or imprisonment for a term of not more than 18 months, or to both,

(iii) in the case of a young person, to a youth sentence under the *Youth Criminal Justice Act*, or

(iv) in the case of an organization, to a fine of not more than $100,000.

10. (1) Selling — Unless authorized under this Act, it is prohibited to sell cannabis, or any substance represented or held out to be cannabis, to

(a) an individual who is 18 years of age or older;

(b) an individual who is under 18 years of age; or

(c) an organization.

(2) Possession for purpose of selling — Unless authorized under this Act, it is prohibited to possess cannabis for the purpose of selling it contrary to any of paragraphs (1)(a) to (c).

(3) Defence — paragraph (1)(b) — It is not a defence to a charge arising out of the contravention of paragraph (1)(b) that the accused believed that the individual referred to in that paragraph was 18 years of age or older, unless the accused took reasonable steps to ascertain the individual's age.

(4) Defence — subsection (2) — It is not a defence to a charge arising out of the contravention of subsection (2) of possessing cannabis for the purpose of selling it contrary to paragraph (1)(b) that the accused believed that the individual referred to in that paragraph was 18 years of age or older, unless the accused took reasonable steps to ascertain the individual's age.

(5) Punishment — Subject to section 51, every person that contravenes any of paragraphs (1)(a) to (c) or subsection (2)

(a) is guilty of an indictable offence and is liable to imprisonment for a term of not more than 14 years; or

(b) is guilty of an offence punishable on summary conviction and is liable

(i) in the case of an individual who contravenes paragraph (1)(a) or (c) — or subsection (2) other than by possessing cannabis for the purpose of selling it contrary to paragraph (1)(b) — to a fine of not more than $5,000 or imprisonment for a term of not more than six months, or to both,

(ii) in the case of an individual who contravenes paragraph (1)(b) — or subsection (2) if the possession was for the purpose of selling contrary to paragraph (1)(b) — to a fine of not more than $15,000 or imprisonment for a term of not more than 18 months, or to both, or

(iii) in the case of an organization, to a fine of not more than $100,000.

11. (1) Importing and exporting — Unless authorized under this Act, the importation or exportation of cannabis is prohibited.

(2) Possession for purpose of exporting — Unless authorized under this Act, it is prohibited to possess cannabis for the purpose of exporting it.

(3) Punishment — Every person that contravenes subsection (1) or (2)

(a) is guilty of an indictable offence and is liable to imprisonment for a term of not more than 14 years; or

(b) is guilty of an offence punishable on summary conviction and is liable

(i) in the case of an individual, to a fine of not more than $5,000 or imprisonment for a term of not more than six months, or to both, or

(ii) in the case of an organization, to a fine of not more than $300,000.

12. (1) Production — Unless authorized under this Act, it is prohibited

(a) to obtain or offer to obtain cannabis by any method or process, including by manufacturing, by synthesis or by using any means of altering the chemical or physical properties of cannabis; or

(b) to alter or offer to alter the chemical or physical properties of cannabis by the use of an organic solvent.

(2) Authorized alteration — An individual may alter the chemical or physical properties of any cannabis that they are not prohibited by this Act from possessing.

(3) Definition of "organic solvent" — In paragraph (1)(b), **"organic solvent"** means any organic compound that is explosive or highly or extremely flammable, including petroleum naphtha and compressed liquid hydrocarbons such as butane, isobutane, propane and propylene.

(4) Cultivation, propagation and harvesting — 18 years of age or older — Unless authorized under this Act, it is prohibited for an individual who is 18 years of age or older to cultivate, propagate or harvest, or to offer to cultivate, propagate or harvest,

(a) a cannabis plant that is from a seed or plant material that they know is illicit cannabis; or

(b) more than four cannabis plants at any one time in their dwelling-house.

(5) Cultivation, propagation and harvesting — dwelling-house limit — Unless authorized under this Act, if two or more individuals who are 18 years of age or older are ordinarily resident in the same dwelling-house, it is prohibited for any of those individuals to cultivate, propagate or harvest any cannabis plants if doing so results in there being more than four such plants being cultivated, propagated or harvested at any one time in the dwelling-house.

(6) Cultivation, propagation and harvesting — 18 years of age or older — without authorization — Unless authorized under this Act, it is prohibited for an individual who is 18 years of age or older

(a) to cultivate, propagate or harvest any cannabis plant at a place that is not their dwelling-house or to offer to do so; or

(b) to cultivate, propagate or harvest any living thing, other than a cannabis plant, from which cannabis may be extracted or otherwise obtained, or to offer to do so.

(7) Cultivation, propagation and harvesting — young persons and organizations — Unless authorized under this Act, it is prohibited for a young person or an organization to cultivate, propagate or harvest any cannabis plant or any other living thing from which cannabis may be extracted or otherwise obtained, or to offer to do any of those things.

(8) Definition of "dwelling-house" — For the purposes of this section, **"dwelling-house"**, in respect of an individual, means the dwelling-house where the individual is ordinarily resident and includes

(a) any land that is subjacent to it and the immediately contiguous land that is attributable to it, including a yard, garden or any similar land; and

(b) any building or structure on any land referred to in paragraph (a).

(9) Punishment — Subject to section 51, every individual who is 18 years of age or older who contravenes any of subsections (1), (4), (5) and (6) or any organization that contravenes subsection (1) or (7)

(a) is guilty of an indictable offence and is liable to a term of imprisonment of not more than 14 years; or

(b) is guilty of an offence punishable on summary conviction and is liable

(i) in the case of an individual, to a fine of not more than $5,000 or imprisonment for a term of not more than six months, or to both, or

(ii) in the case of an organization, to a fine of not more than $100,000.

(10) Punishment — young person — Every young person who contravenes subsection (1) or (7) is guilty of an indictable offence, or an offence punishable on summary conviction, and is liable to a youth sentence under the *Youth Criminal Justice Act*.

13. (1) Possession, etc., for use in production or distribution of illicit cannabis — It is prohibited to possess, produce, sell, distribute or import anything with the intention that it will be used to produce, sell or distribute illicit cannabis.

(2) Punishment — Every person that contravenes subsection (1)

(a) is guilty of an indictable offence and is liable to imprisonment for a term of not more than seven years; or

(b) is guilty of an offence punishable on summary conviction and is liable

(i) in the case of an individual, to a fine of not more than $5,000 or imprisonment for a term of not more than six months, or to both, or

(ii) in the case of an organization, to a fine of not more than $100,000.

14. (1) Use of young person — It is prohibited to use the services of, or to involve, a young person in the commission of an offence under subsection 9(1) or (2), 10(1) or (2), 11(1) or (2), 12(1), (4), (5), (6) or (7) or 13(1).

(2) Punishment — Every person that contravenes subsection (1)

(a) is guilty of an indictable offence and is liable to imprisonment for a term of not more than 14 years; or

(b) is guilty of an offence punishable on summary conviction and is liable

(i) in the case of an individual, to a fine of not more than $15,000 or imprisonment for a term of not more than 18 months, or to both, or

(ii) in the case of an organization, to a fine of not more than $100,000.

15. (1) Sentencing — Without restricting the generality of the *Criminal Code*, the fundamental purpose of any sentence for an offence under this Division is to contribute to the respect for the law and the maintenance of a just, peaceful and safe society while encouraging rehabilitation, and treatment in appropriate circumstances, of offenders and acknowledging the harm done to victims and to the community.

(2) Factors to take into consideration — If an individual is convicted of a designated offence, the court imposing sentence on the individual must consider any relevant aggravating factors, including that the individual

(a) in relation to the commission of the offence,

(i) carried, used or threatened to use a weapon,

(ii) used or threatened to use violence, or

(iii) sold or distributed cannabis or possessed it for the purpose of sale or distribution, in or near a school, on or near school grounds or in or near any other public place usually frequented by young persons; and

(b) was previously convicted of a **"designated offence"**, as defined in subsection 2(1) of this Act, or a designated substance offence, as defined in subsection 2(1) of the *Controlled Drugs and Substances Act*.

(3) Reasons — If, in the case of an individual who is convicted of a designated offence, the court is satisfied of the existence of one or more of the aggravating factors enumerated in paragraphs (2)(a) and (b), but decides not to sentence the individual to imprisonment, the court must give reasons for that decision.

(4) Drug treatment court program — A court sentencing an individual who is convicted of an offence under this Division may delay sentencing to enable the individual

(a) to participate in a drug treatment court program approved by the Attorney General; or

(b) to attend a treatment program under subsection 720(2) of the *Criminal Code*.

DIVISION 2 — OTHER PROHIBITIONS

Subdivision A — Promotion

16. Non-application — Subject to the regulations, this Subdivision does not apply

(a) to a literary, dramatic, musical, cinematographic, scientific, educational or artistic work, production or performance that uses or depicts cannabis, a cannabis accessory or a service related to cannabis, or a brand element of any of those things, whatever the mode or form of its expression, if no consideration is given, directly or indirectly, for that use or depiction in the work, production or performance;

(b) to a report, commentary or opinion in respect of cannabis, a cannabis accessory or a service related to cannabis or a brand element of any of those things, if no consideration is given, directly or indirectly, for the reference to the cannabis, cannabis accessory, service or brand element in that report, commentary or opinion;

(c) to a promotion, by a person that is authorized to produce, sell or distribute cannabis, that is directed at any person that is authorized to produce, sell or distribute cannabis, but not, either directly or indirectly, at consumers; or

(d) to a promotion, by a person that sells or distributes cannabis accessories or that provides a service related to cannabis, that is directed at any person that sells or distributes cannabis accessories, at any person that is authorized to produce, sell or distribute cannabis, but not, either directly or indirectly, at consumers.

17. (1) Promotion — Unless authorized under this Act, it is prohibited to promote cannabis or a cannabis accessory or any service related to cannabis, including

(a) by communicating information about its price or distribution;

(b) by doing so in a manner that there are reasonable grounds to believe could be appealing to young persons;

(c) by means of a testimonial or endorsement, however displayed or communicated;

(d) by means of the depiction of a person, character or animal, whether real or fictional; or

(e) by presenting it or any of its brand elements in a manner that associates it or the brand element with, or evokes a positive or negative emotion about or image of, a way of life such as one that includes glamour, recreation, excitement, vitality, risk or daring.

(2) Exception — informational promotion — cannabis — Subject to the regulations, a person that is authorized to produce, sell or distribute cannabis may promote cannabis by means of informational promotion or brand-preference promotion if the promotion is

(a) in a communication that is addressed and sent to an individual who is 18 years of age or older and is identified by name;

(b) in a place where young persons are not permitted by law;

(c) communicated by means of a telecommunication, where the person responsible for the content of the promotion has taken reasonable steps to ensure that the promotion cannot be accessed by a young person;

(d) in a prescribed place; or

(e) done in a prescribed manner.

(3) Exception — informational promotion — cannabis accessories and services — Subject to the regulations, a person may promote a cannabis accessory or a service related to cannabis by means of informational promotion or brand-preference promotion if the promotion is

(a) in a communication that is addressed and sent to an individual who is 18 years of age or older and is identified by name;

(b) in a place where young persons are not permitted by law;

(c) communicated by means of a telecommunication, where the person responsible for the content of the promotion has taken reasonable steps to ensure that the promotion cannot be accessed by a young person;

(d) in a prescribed place; or

(e) done in a prescribed manner.

(4) **Exception — point of sale — cannabis** — Subject to the regulations, a person that is authorized to sell cannabis may promote it at the point of sale if the promotion indicates only its availability, its price or its availability and price.

(5) **Exception — point of sale — cannabis accessory and services** — Subject to the regulations, a person that sells a cannabis accessory or provides a service related to cannabis may promote it at the point of sale if the promotion indicates only its availability, its price or its availability and price.

(6) **Exception — brand element on other things** — Subject to the regulations, a person may promote cannabis, a cannabis accessory or a service related to cannabis by displaying a brand element of cannabis, of a cannabis accessory or of a service related to cannabis on a thing that is not cannabis or a cannabis accessory, other than

(a) a thing that is associated with young persons;

(b) a thing that there are reasonable grounds to believe could be appealing to young persons; or

(c) a thing that is associated with a way of life such as one that includes glamour, recreation, excitement, vitality, risk or daring.

18. (1) False promotion — cannabis — It is prohibited to promote cannabis in a manner that is false, misleading or deceptive or that is likely to create an erroneous impression about its characteristics, value, quantity, composition, strength, concentration, potency, purity, quality, merit, safety, health effects or health risks.

(2) **False promotion — cannabis accessory** — It is prohibited to promote a cannabis accessory in a manner that is false, misleading or deceptive or that is likely to create an erroneous impression about its design, construction, performance, intended use, characteristics, value, composition, merit, safety, health effects or health risks.

19. Use of certain terms, etc. — It is prohibited to use any term, expression, logo, symbol or illustration specified in regulations made under paragraph 139(1)(z.1) in the promotion of cannabis, a cannabis accessory or a service related to cannabis.

20. Promotion using foreign media — It is prohibited to promote, in a way that is prohibited by this Part, cannabis, a cannabis accessory, a service related to cannabis or a brand element of any of those things in a publication that is published outside Canada, a broadcast that originates outside Canada or any other communication that originates outside Canada.

21. Sponsorship — It is prohibited to display, refer to or otherwise use any of the following, directly or indirectly in a promotion that is used in the sponsorship of a person, entity, event, activity or facility:

(a) a brand element of cannabis, of a cannabis accessory or of a service related to cannabis; and

(b) the name of a person that

(i) produces, sells or distributes cannabis,

(ii) sells or distributes a cannabis accessory, or

(iii) provides a service related to cannabis.

22. Name of facility — It is prohibited to display on a facility, as part of the name of the facility or otherwise, if the facility is used for a sports or cultural event or activity,

(a) a brand element of cannabis, a cannabis accessory or a service related to cannabis; or

(b) the name of a person that

(i) produces, sells or distributes cannabis,

(ii) sells or distributes a cannabis accessory, or

(iii) provides a service related to cannabis.

23. (1) Publication, etc. of prohibited promotions — It is prohibited to publish, broadcast or otherwise disseminate, on behalf of another person, with or without consideration, any promotion that is prohibited by any of sections 17 to 22.

(2) Exception — Subsection (1) does not apply

(a) in respect of the distribution for sale of an imported publication;

(b) in respect of **"broadcasting"**, as defined in subsection 2(1) of the *Broadcasting Act*, by a **"distribution undertaking"**, as defined in that subsection 2(1), that is lawful under that Act, other than the broadcasting of a promotion that is inserted by the distribution undertaking; and

(c) in respect of a person that disseminates a promotion if they did not know, at the time of the dissemination, that it includes a promotion that is prohibited under any of sections 17 to 22.

24. (1) Inducements — Unless authorized under this Act, it is prohibited for a person that sells cannabis or a cannabis accessory

(a) to provide or offer to provide cannabis or a cannabis accessory if it is provided or offered to be provided without monetary consideration or in consideration of the purchase of any thing or service or the provision of any service;

(b) to provide or offer to provide any thing that is not cannabis or a cannabis accessory, including a right to participate in a game, draw, lottery or contest, if it is provided or offered to be provided as an inducement for the purchase of cannabis or a cannabis accessory; or

(c) to provide or offer to provide any service if it is provided or offered to be provided as an inducement for the purchase of cannabis or a cannabis accessory.

(2) Exception — cannabis — Subject to the regulations, subsection (1) does not apply in respect of a person that is authorized to sell cannabis that provides or offers to provide any thing, including cannabis or a cannabis accessory, or service referred to in any of paragraphs (1)(a) to (c) to a person that is authorized to produce, sell or distribute cannabis.

(3) Exception — cannabis accessory — Subject to the regulations, subsection (1) does not apply in respect of a person that sells a cannabis accessory that provides or offers to provide any thing, including cannabis or a cannabis accessory, or service referred to in any of paragraphs (1)(a) to (c) to a person that is authorized to produce, sell or distribute cannabis.

Subdivision B — Packaging and Labelling

25. Compliance with regulations — It is prohibited for a person that is authorized to sell cannabis to sell cannabis that has not been packaged or labelled in accordance with the regulations.

26. Prohibited packaging and labelling — cannabis — Unless authorized under this Act, it is prohibited for a person that is authorized to sell cannabis to sell it in a package or with a label

(a) if there are reasonable grounds to believe that the package or label could be appealing to young persons;

(b) that sets out a testimonial or endorsement, however displayed or communicated;

(c) that sets out a depiction of a person, character or animal, whether real or fictional;

(d) that associates the cannabis or one of its brand elements with, or evokes a positive or negative emotion about or image of, a way of life such as one that includes glamour, recreation, excitement, vitality, risk or daring; or

(e) that contains any information that is false, misleading or deceptive or that is likely to create an erroneous impression about the characteristics, value, quantity, composition, strength, concentration, potency, purity, quality, merit, safety, health effects or health risks of the cannabis.

27. Prohibited packaging and labelling — cannabis accessory — Unless authorized under this Act, it is prohibited for a person that sells a cannabis accessory to sell it in a package or with a label

(a) if there are reasonable grounds to believe that the package or label could be appealing to young persons;

(b) that sets out a testimonial or an endorsement, however displayed or communicated;

(c) that sets out a depiction of a person, character or animal, whether real or fictional;

(d) that associates the cannabis accessory or one of its brand elements with, or evokes a positive or negative emotion about or image of, a way of life such as one that includes glamour, recreation, excitement, vitality, risk or daring; or

(e) that contains any information that is false, misleading or deceptive or that is likely to create an erroneous impression about the design, construction, performance, intended use, characteristics, value, composition, merit, safety, health effects or health risks of the cannabis accessory.

28. Use of certain terms, etc. — Unless authorized under this Act, it is prohibited to use any term, expression, logo, symbol or illustration specified in regulations made under paragraph 139(1)(z.1) on a package or label of cannabis or a cannabis accessory.

Subdivision C — Display

29. Display of cannabis — Unless authorized under this Act, it is prohibited for a person that is authorized to sell cannabis to display it, or any package or label of cannabis, in a manner that may result in the cannabis, package or label being seen by a young person.

30. Display of cannabis accessory — Unless authorized under this Act, it is prohibited for a person that sells a cannabis accessory to display it, or any package or label of a cannabis accessory, in a manner that may result in the cannabis accessory, package or label being seen by a young person.

Subdivision D — Selling and Distributing

31. Appeal to young persons — Unless authorized under this Act, it is prohibited to sell cannabis or a cannabis accessory that has an appearance, shape or other sensory attribute or a function that there are reasonable grounds to believe could be appealing to young persons.

32. (1) Selling cannabis accessory to young person — Unless authorized under this Act, it is prohibited to sell a cannabis accessory to a young person.

(2) **Defence** — It is not a defence to a charge under subsection (1) that the accused believed that the young person referred to in that subsection was at least 18 years of age, unless the accused took reasonable steps to ascertain the individual's age.

33. **Prohibited sales** — Unless authorized under this Act, it is prohibited for a person that is authorized to sell cannabis to sell cannabis of any class that is not referred to in Schedule 4.

34. (1) **Prohibited substances** — Unless authorized under this Act, it is prohibited to sell any mixture of substances that contains cannabis and any substance that is referred to in column 1 of Schedule 5.

(2) **Non-application of subsection (1)** — Subsection (1) does not apply in respect of a mixture of substances that contains a substance that is referred to in column 1 of Schedule 5 and any cannabis of a class of cannabis that is referred to in column 2 of that Schedule in respect of that substance.

35. **Selling or distributing recalled cannabis** — It is prohibited to sell or distribute cannabis that is the subject of a recall order made under section 76.

36. **Self-service display** — Unless authorized under this Act, it is prohibited to sell or distribute cannabis or a cannabis accessory by means of a display that allows for self-service.

37. **Dispensing device** — Unless authorized under this Act, it is prohibited to sell or distribute cannabis or a cannabis accessory by means of a dispensing device.

Subdivision E — Other Prohibitions

38. (1) **Obstructing inspector** — It is prohibited to obstruct, by act or omission, an inspector who is engaged in the exercise of powers or the performance of duties or functions under this Act.

(2) **False statements** — It is prohibited to knowingly make any false or misleading statement verbally or in writing to an inspector who is engaged in the exercise of powers or the performance of duties or functions under this Act.

(3) **Interference** — It is prohibited, without the authority of an inspector, to move, alter or interfere with, in any way, anything seized, detained or taken under section 86.

39. **False or misleading statement** — It is prohibited to knowingly make, or participate in, assent to or acquiesce in the making of, a false or misleading statement in any record, report, electronic data or document that is required to be prepared, retained or provided by any person under this Act.

Division 3 — Obligations

40. Compliance with conditions — The holder of a licence or permit issued under this Act must comply with its conditions.

41. Suspension — If a licence or permit issued under this Act is suspended in respect of any or all activities, its holder must cease conducting, for the duration of the suspension, the activities to which the suspension relates.

42. Public disclosure — Every person that is authorized under this Act to produce, sell or distribute cannabis must make available to the public, in the prescribed form and manner and within the prescribed time, information about cannabis that is required by the regulations.

43. (1) Promotion-related information — cannabis — Every person that is authorized under this Act to produce, sell or distribute cannabis must provide to the Minister, in the prescribed form and manner and within the prescribed time, information that is required by the regulations about any promotion of cannabis that they conduct, including a promotion referred to in paragraph 16(c).

(2) **Promotion-related information — cannabis accessories and services** — Every person that sells or distributes a cannabis accessory, or that provides a service related to cannabis, must provide to the Minister, in the prescribed form and manner and within the prescribed time, information that is required by the regulations about any promotion of cannabis accessories or their service related to cannabis, as the case may be, that they conduct, including a promotion referred to in paragraph 16(d).

(3) **Inducement information** — Every person that sells cannabis or cannabis accessories must provide to the Minister, in the prescribed form and manner and within the prescribed time, information that is required by the regulations about any thing, including cannabis or a cannabis accessory, or service referred to in any of paragraphs 24(1)(a) to (c) that they provide or offer to provide.

(4) **Additional information** — The Minister may, subject to the regulations, request that a person that has provided information under any of subsections (1) to (3) provide additional information relating to the information they provided under that subsection, and that person must provide the requested information in the form and manner and within the time specified by the Minister.

Division 4 — Miscellaneous

44. Penalty — Subject to section 51, every person that contravenes a provision of this Act for which no punishment is otherwise provided by this Act, or that contravenes a provision of a regulation, an order made under any of sections 73 to 76, an order amended under section 79 or an order made under section 82,

(a) is guilty of an indictable offence and is liable to a fine of not more than $5,000,000 or imprisonment for a term of not more than three years, or to both; or

(b) is guilty of an offence punishable on summary conviction and is liable, for a first offence, to a fine of not more than $250,000 or imprisonment for a term of not more than six months, or to both, and, for any subsequent offence, to a fine of not more than $500,000 or imprisonment for a term of not more than 18 months, or to both.

45. Limitation period — No summary conviction proceedings in respect of an offence under section 44 may be commenced after the expiry of one year after the day on which the subject-matter of the proceedings arose.

46. Offences by corporate officers, etc. — If a person other than an individual commits an offence under section 44, any of the person's directors, officers or agents or mandataries who directed, authorized, assented to, acquiesced in or participated in the commission of the offence is a party to the offence and is liable on conviction to the punishment provided for by this Act, even if the person is not prosecuted for the offence.

47. Continuing offence — If an offence under section 44 is committed or continued on more than one day, it constitutes a separate offence for each day on which it is committed or continued.

48. Employees or agents or mandataries — In a prosecution for an offence under section 44, it is sufficient proof of the offence to establish that it was committed by any employee or agent or mandatary of the accused, even if the employee or agent or mandatary is not identified or is not prosecuted for the offence.

49. Venue — Proceedings in respect of an offence in relation to a contravention of any provision of this Act or of the regulations, or of an order made under any of sections 73 to 76, an order amended under section 79 or an order made under section 82, may be held in the place where the offence was committed or where the subject-matter of the proceedings arose or in any place where the accused is apprehended or happens to be located.

50. (1) Reference to exception, exemption, etc. — No exception, exemption, excuse or qualification prescribed by law is required to be set out or negatived, as the case may be, in an information or indictment for an offence under this Act or under section 463,464 or 465 of the *Criminal Code* in respect of such an offence.

(2) Rebuttal — In any prosecution for an offence under this Act, the prosecutor is not required, except by way of rebuttal, to prove that a certificate, licence, permit, authorization, exemption or qualification does not operate in favour of the accused, whether or not it is referred to in the information or indictment.

PART 2 — TICKETABLE OFFENCES (SS. 51–60)

51. (1) Procedure — In addition to the procedures set out in the *Criminal Code*, proceedings referred to in subsection (2) against an individual who is 18 years of age or older or an organization may be commenced by a peace officer

(a) completing a ticket that consists of a summons portion and an information portion;

(b) in the case of proceedings against an individual, delivering the summons portion of the ticket to the accused;

(c) in the case of proceedings against an organization, sending the summons portion of the ticket, or delivering it, to the organization in accordance with the regulations; and

(d) filing the information portion of the ticket with a court of criminal jurisdiction before or as soon as feasible after the summons portion has been delivered or sent.

(2) Proceedings — The proceedings for the purposes of subsection (1) are the following:

(a) proceedings in respect of an offence arising out of the contravention of paragraph 8(1)(a) or (b) or any of subparagraphs 9(1)(a)(i), (iii) and (iv) in respect of cannabis of one or more classes of cannabis the total amount of which, as determined in accordance with Schedule 3, is equivalent to 50 g or less of dried cannabis;

(b) proceedings against an individual who is 18 years of age or older in respect of an offence arising out of the contravention of paragraph 8(1)(e) or subparagraph 9(1)(c)(ii) in respect of five or six cannabis plants;

(c) proceedings in respect of an offence arising out of the contravention of subsection 9(2) in respect of cannabis of one or more classes of cannabis the total amount of which is, as determined in accordance with Schedule 3, equivalent to 50 g or less of dried cannabis, if its possession was for the purpose of distributing it contrary to any of subparagraphs 9(1)(a)(i), (iii) and (iv);

(d) proceedings against an individual in respect of an offence arising out of the contravention of paragraph 10(1)(a) or (c) in respect of cannabis of one or more classes of cannabis the total amount of which is, as determined in accordance with Schedule 3, equivalent to 50 g or less of dried cannabis;

(e) proceedings against an individual in respect of an offence arising out of the contravention of subsection 10(2) in respect of cannabis of one or more classes of cannabis the total amount of which is, as determined in accordance with Schedule 3, equivalent to 50 g or less of dried cannabis, if its possession was for the purpose of selling it contrary to paragraph 10(1)(a) or (c);

(f) proceedings against an individual in respect of an offence arising out of the contravention of paragraph 12(1)(a) in respect of cannabis of one or more classes of cannabis the total amount of which is, as determined in accordance with Schedule 3, equivalent to 50 g or less of dried cannabis;

(g) proceedings in respect of an offence arising out of the contravention of paragraph 12(4)(b) in respect of five or six cannabis plants;

(h) proceedings in respect of an offence arising out of the contravention of subsection 12(5) in respect of one or two cannabis plants; and

(i) proceedings in respect of an offence arising out of the contravention of section 44 in respect of a contravention of a provision that is specified in regulations made under paragraph 139(1)(z.6).

(3) **Content of ticket** — The summons and information portions of the ticket must set out

(a) a description of the offence and the time and place of its alleged commission;

(b) a statement, signed by the peace officer who completes the ticket, that the peace officer has reasonable grounds to believe that the accused committed the offence;

(c) an amount equal to the amount, determined under subsection (4), to be paid for the offence;

(d) the manner in which and period within which the amount is to be paid;

(d.1) a lesser amount than the amount determined under subsection (4) that may be paid for the offence if it is paid within a specified period that is shorter than the period referred to in paragraph (d);

(e) a statement that if the accused pays the amount within the period referred to in paragraph (d) or (d.1),

(i) a finding of guilt will be entered in the judicial record of the accused and the accused will be deemed to have received an absolute discharge and not to have been convicted of the offence,

(ii) the judicial record of the accused in respect of the offence will not be used for any purpose that would identify the accused as a person dealt with under this Act, and

(iii) if cannabis has been seized in relation to the offence, the cannabis will be forfeited to Her Majesty;

(f) a statement that if the accused wishes to plead not guilty, the accused must appear in the court, at the place, day and time set out in the ticket;

(g) a statement that if the accused pleads not guilty, he or she will be given an opportunity to indicate in which official language he or she wishes to be tried; and

(h) a statement that if the accused does not enter a plea and does not pay the amount within the period referred to in paragraph (d) or (d.1)

(i) a conviction will be entered in the judicial record of the accused, and

(ii) if cannabis has been seized in relation to the offence, the cannabis will be forfeited to Her Majesty.

(4) Amount — For the purpose of paragraph (3)(c), the amount is

(a) for an offence referred to in any of paragraphs (2)(a) to (h), $200 plus a victim surcharge, calculated in accordance with subsection 737(2) of the *Criminal Code*, and any applicable administrative fees; and

(b) for an offence in respect of a contravention of a provision that is specified in regulations made under paragraph 139(1)(z.6), the amount specified in those regulations in respect of that offence plus a victim surcharge, calculated in accordance with subsection 737(2) of the *Criminal Code*, and any applicable administrative fees.

52. Consequences of payment — Payment of the amount set out in the ticket by the accused within the period referred to in paragraph 51(3)(d) or (d.1) constitutes a plea of guilty to the offence described in the ticket and, following the payment,

(a) a finding of guilt is to be entered in the judicial record of the accused and the accused is deemed to have received an absolute discharge and not to have been convicted of the offence;

(b) the judicial record of the accused in relation to the offence must not be used for any purpose that would identify the accused as a person dealt with under this Act; and

(c) if cannabis has been seized in relation to the offence, the cannabis is forfeited to Her Majesty.

53. (1) Consequences of being convicted — If an accused pleads not guilty and the accused is convicted of the offence described in the ticket, the accused is liable to a fine of not more than $200, in the case of an offence referred to in any of paragraphs 51(2)(a) to (h) or, in the case of an offence in respect of a contravention of a provision specified in regulations made under paragraph 139(1)(z.6), to a fine of not more than the amount specified in those regulations in respect of that offence.

(1.1) Non-application of section 731 — If the accused is convicted of the offence, no order is to be made under section 731 of the *Criminal Code* in respect of that conviction.

(2) Effect of payment — If the accused is convicted of the offence and the accused pays the amount owing in respect of the conviction, the judicial record of the accused in relation to the offence must not be used for any purpose that would identify the accused as a person dealt with under this Act.

54. (1) Consequences of failing to pay fine — If an accused fails to pay the amount set out in the ticket within the period referred to in paragraph 51(3)(d) or (d.1), the accused is liable for that amount and

(a) a conviction is to be entered in the judicial record of the accused;

(b) the conviction is deemed to have been pronounced by a court;

(c) if cannabis has been seized in relation to the offence, the cannabis is forfeited to Her Majesty;

(d) the accused has 60 days after the day of the conviction to pay the amount set out in the ticket; and

(e) the amount set out in the ticket, other than the amount in relation to the applicable fees, is deemed to be the fine imposed by the court.

(2) Effect of payment or imprisonment — If, after being convicted, the accused pays the amount set out in the ticket or, if the accused is an individual, the accused has served, in full, any period of imprisonment imposed as a result of a default in payment of the amount of the fine imposed by the court, the judicial record of the accused in relation to the offence must not be used for any purpose that would identify the accused as a person dealt with under this Act.

55. Imprisonment — Only an individual who is unwilling though able to pay a fine or the amount of a victim surcharge imposed in respect of a conviction referred to in subsection 53(1) or a fine imposed in respect of a conviction referred to in section 54 may be imprisoned in default of its payment.

55.1 Licences, permits, etc. — If the amount to be paid under this Part is owed to Her Majesty in right of Canada, the person responsible, by or under an Act or ordinance of the legislature of a territory, for issuing or renewing a licence, permit or other similar instrument in relation to the offender may refuse to issue or renew or may suspend the licence, permit or other instrument until the fine or fee is paid in full, proof of which lies on the offender.

56. Exclusion of laying information — No information under the *Criminal Code* may be laid in respect of an offence for which a summons portion of a ticket is delivered or sent.

57. Application of *Criminal Code* — Except where otherwise provided by this Part, Part XXVII of the *Criminal Code* applies to proceedings commenced under this Part.

58. (1) Election of Attorney General — If a proceeding in respect of an offence referred to in any of paragraphs 51(2)(a) to (j) is commenced by the laying of an information, the Attorney General may elect that the proceeding be dealt with and disposed of as if it had been commenced under section 51.

(2) Notice — If the election is made, the clerk of the court must provide the accused with a notice that sets out

(a) an amount equal to the amount, determined under paragraph 51(4)(a) or (b), as the case may be, to be paid for the offence;

(b) the manner in which and period within which the amount is to be paid;

(b.1) a lesser amount than the amount determined under paragraph 51(4)(a) or (b), as the case may be, that may be paid for the offence if it is paid within a specified period that is shorter than the period referred to in paragraph (b);

(c) a statement that if the accused pays the amount within the period referred to in paragraph (b) or (b.1),

(i) a finding of guilt will be entered in the judicial record of the accused and the accused will be deemed to have received an absolute discharge and not to have been convicted of the offence,

(ii) the judicial record of the accused in respect of the offence will not be used for any purpose that would identify the accused as a person dealt with under this Act, and

(iii) if cannabis has been seized in relation to the offence, the cannabis will be forfeited to Her Majesty;

(d) a statement that if the accused wishes to plead not guilty or fails to pay the amount within the period referred to in paragraph (b) or (b.1), the accused must appear in the court at the place, day and time set out in the notice; and

(e) a statement that if the accused pleads not guilty, an opportunity will be provided for the accused to indicate in which official language the accused wishes to be tried.

(3) **Effect on conditions** — All conditions imposed on the accused in an appearance notice, promise to appear, undertaking or recognizance issued, given or entered into in accordance with Part XVI or XXVII of the *Criminal Code* in relation to the offence cease to have effect when the accused is notified that the Attorney General has made the election.

(4) **Deemed ticket** — The document and the information laid in respect of the offence are deemed to be a ticket delivered or sent under section 51.

59. Agreements — The Attorney General of Canada may enter into an agreement with the government of a province or with any provincial, municipal or local authority or any agent or mandatary of any such authority respecting, in particular, the following matters:

(a) the prosecution of offences commenced under this Part; and

(b) the discharge and enforcement of fines and fees referred to in this Part in respect of offences that are alleged to have been committed in or that are otherwise within the territorial jurisdiction of the courts of the province.

60. (1) Compensation agreements — The Attorney General of Canada may enter into an agreement with the government of a province or with any provincial, municipal or local authority

(a) respecting the sharing with that province or authority of the amounts in respect of fines and fees that are collected in respect of the prosecution of offences commenced under this Part, for the purpose of Canada compensating that province or authority, in whole or in part, for the administration and enforcement of this Part; and

(b) despite subsections 17(1) and (4) of the *Financial Administration Act*, authorizing the government of the province or the authority to withhold amounts, in accordance with the terms and conditions of the agreement, from the fines and fees referred to in paragraph (a) to be remitted to the Receiver General and deposited in the Consolidated Revenue Fund.

(2) Deemed not public money — The fees imposed under the laws of a province in respect of offences under Division 1 of Part 1 are deemed not to be public money for the purposes of the *Financial Administration Act*.

(3) Appropriation by Parliament — All or a portion of the amount of fines and fees referred to in paragraph (1)(a) that are to be shared under an agreement are deemed to be appropriated by Parliament for that purpose.

.....

PART 8 — SEARCH WARRANT (SS. 87, 88)

87. (1) Information for search warrant — A justice who, on *ex parte* application, is satisfied by information on oath that there are reasonable grounds to believe that any of the following is in a place may, at any time, issue a warrant authorizing a peace officer, at any time, to search the place for it and to seize it:

(a) cannabis in respect of which this Act has been contravened;

(b) anything in which cannabis in respect of which this Act has been contravened is contained or concealed;

(c) offence-related property; or

(d) anything that will afford evidence in respect of an offence under this Act or an offence, in whole or in part, in relation to a contravention of this Act, under section 354 or 462.31 of the *Criminal Code*.

(2) Application of section 487.1 of the *Criminal Code* — For the purposes of subsection (1), the information may be submitted by telephone or other means of telecommunication in accordance with section 487.1 of the *Criminal Code*, with any necessary modifications.

(3) Execution of warrant — A warrant issued under subsection (1) may be executed at any place in Canada. Any peace officer who executes the warrant must have authority to act as a peace officer in the place where it is executed.

(4) [Repealed 2019, c. 25, s. 400.1.]

(5) Search of person and seizure — If a peace officer who executes a warrant issued under subsection (1) has reasonable grounds to believe that any individual found in the place referred to in the warrant has on them any cannabis, property or thing referred to in the warrant, the peace officer may search the individual for it and seize it.

(6) Seizure of other things — A peace officer who executes a warrant issued under subsection (1) may seize, in addition to any cannabis, property or thing referred to in the warrant,

(a) any cannabis in respect of which the peace officer believes on reasonable grounds that this Act has been contravened;

(b) anything that the peace officer believes on reasonable grounds contains or conceals cannabis;

(c) anything that the peace officer believes on reasonable grounds is offence-related property; or

(d) anything that the peace officer believes on reasonable grounds will afford evidence in respect of an offence under this Act.

(7) Where warrant not necessary — A peace officer may exercise any of the powers described in subsection (1), (5) or (6) without a warrant if the conditions for obtaining a warrant exist but by reason of exigent circumstances it would be impracticable to obtain one.

(8) Seizure of additional things — A peace officer who executes a warrant issued under subsection (1) or exercises powers under subsection (5) or (7) may seize, in addition to any cannabis, property or thing referred to in the warrant and in subsection (6), anything that the peace officer believes on reasonable grounds has been obtained by or used in the commission of an offence or that will afford evidence in respect of an offence.

2019, c. 25, s. 400.1

88. Assistance and use of force — For the purpose of exercising any of the powers described in section 87, a peace officer may

(a) enlist the assistance that the officer considers necessary; and

(b) use as much force as is necessary in the circumstances.

. . . . .

CAN. REG. 2018-151 — CANNABIS ACT (POLICE ENFORCEMENT) REGULATIONS

made under the *Cannabis Act*

SOR/2018-151

INTERPRETATION

1. Definitions — The definitions in this section apply in these Regulations.

"Act" means the *Cannabis Act. ("Loi")*

"appropriate officer" means

(a) in the case of the RCMP, the Assistant Commissioner of the RCMP in charge of drug enforcement;

(b) in the case of a police force other than the RCMP, the member of the police force who is the most senior officer responsible for operations; and

(c) in the case of the military police, the Canadian Forces Provost Marshal.

("officier compétent")

"chief" means, in respect of a police force other than the RCMP, the senior police officer in charge of the police force. *("chef")*

"military police" means military police that are designated under subsection 2(2). *("policier militaire")*

"particular investigation" means a primary investigation conducted under the Act or any other Act of Parliament and includes any investigation that arises from the primary investigation. *("enquête particulière")*

"police force" means a police force that is designated under subsection 2(1). *("corps policier")*

"provincial minister" means the provincial minister responsible for policing in a province. *("ministre provincial")*

"RCMP" means the Royal Canadian Mounted Police. *("GRC")*

DESIGNATION OF POLICE FORCES AND MILITARY POLICE

2. (1) Authority to designate — police forces — The Minister of Public Safety and Emergency Preparedness and every provincial minister are authorized to designate any police force within the jurisdiction of the Minister or the provincial minister, as the case may be, for the purposes of any or all provisions of these Regulations.

(2) **Authority to designate — military police** — The Minister of National Defence is authorized to designate military police for the purposes of any or all provisions of these Regulations.

General Exemptions

Section 8, 9, 10, 11, 12 or 14 of the Act

3. Offences — general — police — A member of a police force or of the military police is exempt from the application of section 8, 9, 10, 11, 12 or 14 of the Act, as applicable, if the member engages in any activity referred to in those sections involving cannabis — other than cannabis that has been forfeited to Her Majesty, that is imported or exported under the exemption provided for in section 17 of these Regulations or that is produced under the exemption provided for in section 19 of these Regulations — of which the member has come into possession during a particular investigation, if the member

(a) is in active service; and

(b) is acting in the course of the member's responsibilities for the purposes of the particular investigation.

4. Offences — general — direction and control — A person is exempt from the application of section 8, 9, 10, 11, 12 or 14 of the Act, as applicable, if the person engages in any activity referred to in any of those sections involving cannabis — other than cannabis that has been forfeited to Her Majesty, that is imported or exported under the exemption provided for in section 17 of these Regulations or that is produced under the exemption provided for in section 19 of these Regulations — of which the person has come into possession, if the person

(a) acts under the direction and control of a member of a police force or of the military police who meets the conditions set out in paragraphs 3(a) and (b) of these Regulations; and

(b) acts to assist the member in the course of the particular investigation.

5. RCMP notification — importation or exportation — A member of a police force or of the military police who is exempt under section 3 of these Regulations from the application of section 11 of the Act must notify, in written or electronic format, the Assistant Commissioner of the RCMP in charge of drug enforcement of the importation or exportation of cannabis, in respect of which the exemption applies, by the member — or by a person under the member's direction and control who is exempt under section 4 of these Regulations from the application of section 11 of the Act — before the cannabis is imported or exported or, if it is not feasible to do so before the importation or exportation, as soon as feasible after that time.

Section 9 or 10 of the Act — Distribution or Sale

6. Distribution or sale — police — A member of a police force or of the military police who engages in any activity referred to in section 9 or 10 of the Act is exempt from the application of that section if the member

(a) is in active service; and

(b) is acting in the course of the member's responsibilities for the purposes of a particular investigation.

7. Distribution or sale — direction and control — A person who engages in any activity referred to in section 9 or 10 of the Act is exempt from the application of that section if the person

(a) acts under the direction and control of a member of a police force or of the military police who meets the conditions set out in paragraphs 6(a) and (b) of these Regulations; and

(b) acts to assist the member in the course of the particular investigation.

Section 9, 10, 11 or 12 of the Act in Respect of Offering to Engage in Activities

8. Offering to engage in activities — police — A member of a police force or of the military police who engages in any activity referred to in section 9, 10, 11 or 12 of the Act by offering to engage in that activity is exempt, in respect of offering to engage in that activity, from the application of that section, if the member

(a) is in active service; and

(b) is acting in the course of the member's responsibilities for the purposes of a particular investigation.

9. Offering to engage in activities — direction and control — A person who engages in any activity referred to in section 9, 10, 11 or 12 of the Act by offering to engage in that activity is exempt, in respect of offering to engage in that activity, from the application of that section, if the person

(a) acts under the direction and control of a member of a police force or of the military police who meets the conditions set out in paragraphs 8(a) and (b) of these Regulations; and

(b) acts to assist the member in the course of the particular investigation.

Other General Exemptions

10. Conspiracy, etc. — police — A member of a police force or of the military police is exempt from the application of the provisions that create the offence of conspiracy to commit, an attempt to commit, being an accessory after the fact in relation to, or any counselling in relation to, an offence under section 8, 9, 10, 11, 12 or 14 of the Act if the member

(a) is in active service;

(b) is acting in the course of the member's responsibilities for the purposes of a particular investigation; and

(c) engages in any activity that, but for the application of this section, would constitute a conspiracy to commit, an attempt to commit, being an accessory after the fact in relation to, or any counselling in relation to, an offence under section 8, 9, 10, 11, 12 or 14 of the Act.

11. Conspiracy, etc. — direction and control — A person is exempt from the application of the provisions that create the offence of conspiracy to commit, an attempt to commit, being an accessory after the fact in relation to, or any counselling in relation to, an offence under section 8, 9, 10, 11, 12 or 14 of the Act if the person

(a) acts under the direction and control of a member of a police force or of the military police who

(i) is in active service, and

(ii) is acting in the course of the member's responsibilities for the purposes of a particular investigation;

(b) acts to assist the member in the course of the particular investigation; and

(c) engages in any activity that, but for the application of this section, would constitute a conspiracy to commit, an attempt to commit, being an accessory after the fact in relation to, or any counselling in relation to, an offence under section 8, 9, 10, 11, 12 or 14 of the Act.

Other Regulations

12. Other Regulations — police — A member of a police force or of the military police who is exempt under these Regulations from the application of section 8, 9, 10, 11, 12 or 14 of the Act in respect of engaging in any activity referred to in that section is exempt, in respect of engaging in that activity, from the application of the *Cannabis Regulations* and the *Industrial Hemp Regulations*.

13. Other Regulations — direction and control — A person who acts under the direction and control of a member of a police force or of the military police and who is exempt under these Regulations from the application of section 8, 9, 10, 11, 12 or 14 of the Act in respect of engaging in any activity referred to in that section is exempt, in respect of engaging in that activity, from the application of the *Cannabis Regulations* and the *Industrial Hemp Regulations*.

EXEMPTIONS WITH CERTIFICATE

Section 9 or 10 of the Act — Distribution or Sale

14. (1) State cannabis — distribution or sale — Subject to section 8 of these Regulations, a member of a police force or of the military police is exempt from the application of section 9 or 10 of the Act, as applicable, if the member engages in any activity referred to in those sections involving cannabis that has been forfeited to Her Majesty, that is imported under the exemption provided for in section 17 of these Regulations or that is produced under the exemption provided for in section 19 of these Regulations, if the member has been issued a certificate.

(2) Conditions for issuing certificate — The appropriate officer may issue a certificate for a period not exceeding six months for the purposes of subsection (1) to a member of a police force or of the military police, as the case may be, if the member

(a) is in active service; and

(b) is acting in the course of the member's responsibilities for the purposes of a particular investigation.

15. Direction and control — distribution or sale — 15 Subject to section 9 of these Regulations, a person is exempt from the application of section 9 or 10 of the Act, as applicable, if the person engages in any activity referred to in those sections involving cannabis that has been forfeited to Her Majesty, that is imported under the exemption provided for in section 17 of these Regulations or that is produced under the exemption provided for in section 19 of these Regulations, if the person

(a) acts under the direction and control of a member of a police force or of the military police who meets the conditions set out in paragraphs 14(2)(a) and (b) of these Regulations; and

(b) acts to assist the member in the course of the particular investigation.

Section 11 of the Act — Importation or Exportation

16. Interpretation — controlled deliveries — For the purposes of subsection 17(1) and section 18, cannabis requested of and obtained directly from a foreign state does not include cannabis that has, for the purpose of identifying any person involved in the commission of an offence under the Act or any other Act of Parliament or a conspiracy to commit such an offence, been allowed to pass out of or through a foreign state, under the supervision of that state's competent authorities.

17. (1) State cannabis — importation or exportation — A member of a police force or of the military police is exempt from the application of section 11 of the Act if the member engages in any activity referred to in that section involving cannabis that has been forfeited to Her Majesty, that is produced under the exemption provided for in section 19 of these Regulations or that has been requested of and obtained directly from a foreign state, if the member has been issued a certificate.

(2) Conditions for issuing certificate — The Assistant Commissioner of the RCMP in charge of drug enforcement may issue a certificate to a member of a police force or of the military police, as the case may be, for a period not exceeding six months for the purposes of subsection (1) if the member

(a) is in active service;

(b) in the case of a member of a police force, is acting in the course of their responsibilities for the purposes of a particular investigation in which the RCMP participates; and

(c) in the case of a member of the military police, is acting in the course of their responsibilities for the purposes of

(i) a particular investigation in which the RCMP participates, or

(ii) a particular investigation other than one referred to in subparagraph (i).

18. Direction and control — importation or exportation — A person is exempt from the application of section 11 of the Act if the person engages in any activity referred to in that section that involves cannabis that has been forfeited to Her Majesty, that is produced under the exemption provided for in section 19 of these Regulations or that has been requested of and obtained directly from a foreign state, if the person

(a) acts under the direction and control of a member of a police force or of the military police who meets the applicable conditions set out in paragraphs 17(2)(a) to (c) of these Regulations; and

(b) acts to assist the member in the course of the particular investigation.

Section 12 of the Act — Production

19. (1) State cannabis — production — Subject to section 8 of these Regulations, a member of a police force or of the military police is exempt from the application of section 12 of the Act if the member engages in any activity referred to in that section involving cannabis that has been forfeited to Her Majesty or that is imported under the exemption provided for in section 17 of these Regulations, if the member has been issued a certificate.

(2) Conditions for issuing certificate — The appropriate officer may issue a certificate for a period not exceeding one year for the purposes of subsection (1) to a member of a police force or of the military police, as the case may be, if the member

(a) is in active service; and

(b) is acting in the course of the member's responsibilities for the purposes of a particular investigation.

20. Direction and control — production — Subject to section 9 of these Regulations, a person is exempt from the application of section 12 of the Act if the person engages in any activity referred to in that section involving cannabis that has been forfeited to Her Majesty or that is imported under the exemption provided for in section 17 of these Regulations, if the person

(a) acts under the direction and control of a member of a police force or of the military police who meets the conditions set out in paragraphs 19(2)(a) and (b) of these Regulations; and

(b) acts to assist the member in the course of the particular investigation.

Certificate

21. Information in certificate — A certificate issued under section 14, 17 or 19 must identify the member of the police force or of the military police to whom it is issued, the duration of the exemption and the particular investigation to which it relates.

Revocation of Certificate

22. (1) Revocation — A certificate issued under section 14, 17 or 19 to a member of a police force or of the military police is revoked on the earliest of

(a) the date on which the appropriate officer who issued the certificate revokes it,

(b) the date on which the member is no longer in active service,

(c) the date on which the member is no longer acting in the course of their responsibilities for the purposes of the particular investigation to which the certificate relates,

(d) the date on which the particular investigation to which the certificate relates is completed, or

(e) the date on which the certificate expires.

(2) Notice — The appropriate officer must notify the member of the revocation on the day on which the certificate is revoked under paragraph (1)(a), (c) or (d).

DETENTION AND DISPOSAL OF FORFEITED CANNABIS

23. (1) Notice to Minister — cannabis required — The chief or appropriate officer must, as soon as feasible but not later than 60 days after the day on which cannabis that has been forfeited to Her Majesty is no longer required for the preliminary inquiry, trial or other proceeding, under the Act or any other Act of Parliament, in respect of which it was seized, if the cannabis is required for the purposes of conducting investigations under the Act or any other Act of Parliament, inform the Minister in writing that the cannabis is required for those investigations.

(2) **Secure location** — Cannabis referred to in subsection (1) must be kept in a secure location while not being used for the purposes of conducting investigations under the Act or any other Act of Parliament.

(3) **Transfer** — The chief or appropriate officer is exempt from the application of section 9 of the Act if they transfer any cannabis referred to in subsection (1) to another chief or another appropriate officer who requests the transfer for the purposes of a particular investigation.

(4) **Notice to Minister — transfer** — If a transfer is made under subsection (3), the chief or appropriate officer who

(a) makes the transfer of the cannabis must inform the Minister of the transfer, as soon as feasible after receipt of the request for the transfer; and

(b) receives the cannabis must inform the Minister of its receipt, as soon as feasible after the receipt.

(5) **Directions — cannabis not required** — If cannabis referred to in subsection (1) is no longer required for the purposes of conducting investigations under the Act or any other Act of Parliament, the chief or appropriate officer must seek the directions of the Minister and dispose of or otherwise deal with the cannabis in accordance with the Minister's directions.

(6) **Disposal — cannabis not required** — If cannabis that has been forfeited to Her Majesty is not required for the purposes of conducting investigations under the Act or any other Act of Parliament, the chief or appropriate officer must, as soon as feasible,

(a) in writing seek directions from the Minister respecting the disposal of or otherwise dealing with the cannabis, unless the Minister has previously given such directions; and

(b) dispose of or otherwise deal with the cannabis in accordance with the Minister's directions.

24. **Notice to Minister** — The chief or appropriate officer must, within 60 days after the day on which cannabis is disposed of or otherwise dealt with under section 105 of the Act, notify the Minister in writing to that effect.

Reports

25. (1) **Annual report** — The chief or appropriate officer must submit to the Minister of Public Safety and Emergency Preparedness and to the Minister, within three months after the end of every calendar year, a report in written or electronic format containing the information referred to in subsection (4), in respect of cannabis that is imported or exported under the exemption provided for in section 17, cannabis that is produced under the exemption provided for in section 19 and cannabis that is referred to in section 23, that came into the possession of the police force or of the military police in the course of a particular investigation completed during the calendar year.

(2) **Copy of report — police force other than RCMP** — The chief or appropriate officer of a police force other than the RCMP must send a copy of the report to the provincial minister responsible for the police force.

(3) **Copy of report — military police** — The Canadian Forces Provost Marshal must send a copy of the report to the Minister of National Defence.

(4) **Contents of report** — The report must include the following information:

(a) the type of particular investigation in which the cannabis came into the possession of the police force or of the military police;

(b) the dates on which the particular investigation began and ended;

(c) the total quantity of cannabis that was forfeited to Her Majesty, imported, exported, produced or disposed of in the course of the particular investigation, as applicable; and

(d) if applicable, any other detail that is pertinent to describing the law enforcement activities undertaken by the police force or by the military police in the course of the particular investigation.

(5) **Additional report** — The chief or appropriate officer of a police force must submit to the Minister, on the Minister's request, a report in written or electronic format respecting the cannabis as required for the following purposes:

(a) to ensure the protection of the public against potential public health risks caused by the cannabis, including the risk of it being diverted to an illicit market or activity;

(b) to collect data required for studies and research;

(c) to meet international obligations of the Government of Canada; and

(d) to monitor compliance with these Regulations.

26. (1) Report — cannabis no longer in possession — The chief or appropriate officer must submit to the Minister of Public Safety and Emergency Preparedness and to the Minister a report in written or electronic format containing the information referred to in subsection (4), respecting any cannabis referred to in section 23 that is lost, stolen or otherwise no longer in the possession of the police force or of the military police, as soon as feasible after such a situation occurs.

(2) **Copy of report — police force other than RCMP** — The chief or appropriate officer of a police force other than the RCMP must send a copy of the report to the provincial minister responsible for the police force.

(3) **Copy of report — military police** — The Canadian Forces Provost Marshal must send a copy of the report to the Minister of National Defence.

(4) **Contents of report** — The report must include the following information:

(a) the quantity of cannabis;

(b) the date of its forfeiture to Her Majesty or its importation, exportation or production, as applicable; and

(c) the date on which, and an explanation of the circumstances in which, it was lost or stolen or ceased to be in the possession of the police force or of the military police.

Coming into Force

27. Subsection 204(1) of Act or registration — These Regulations come into force on the day on which subsection 204(1) of the *Cannabis Act* comes into force, but if they are registered after that day, they come into force on the day on which they are registered.

Constitution Act, 1982

Canada Act 1982 (U.K.), c. 11 R.S.C. 1985, App. II, No. 44, as am. Constitution Amendment Proclamation, 1983, SI/84-102, Schedule, SI/93-54, Schedule.

. . . . .

Part VII — General

52. (1) **Primacy of Constitution of Canada** — The Constitution of Canada is the supreme law of Canada, and any law that is inconsistent with the provisions of the Constitution is, to the extent of the inconsistency, of no force or effect.

(2) **Constitution of Canada** — The Constitution of Canada includes

(a) the *Canada Act 1982*, including this Act;

(b) the Acts and orders referred to in the schedule; and

(c) any amendment to any Act or order referred to in paragraph (a) or (b).

(3) **Amendments to the Constitution of Canada** — Amendments to the Constitution of Canada shall be made only in accordance with the authority contained in the Constitution of Canada.

Part I — Canadian Charter of Rights and Freedoms

Whereas Canada is founded upon principles that recognize the supremacy of God and the rule of law:

Guarantee of Rights and Freedoms

1. **Rights and freedoms in Canada** — The *Canadian Charter of Rights and Freedoms* guarantees the rights and freedoms set out in it subject only to such reasonable limits prescribed by law as can be demonstrably justified in a free and democratic society.

Fundamental Freedoms

2. **Fundamental freedoms** — Everyone has the following fundamental freedoms:

(a) freedom of conscience and religion;

(b) freedom of thought, belief, opinion and expression, including freedom of the press and other media of communication;

(c) freedom of peaceful assembly; and

(d) freedom of association.

Democratic Rights

3. **Democratic rights of citizens** — Every citizen of Canada has the right to vote in an election of members of the House of Commons or of a legislative assembly and to be qualified for membership therein.

4. (1) **Maximum duration of legislative bodies** — No House of Commons and no legislative assembly shall continue for longer than five years from the date fixed for the return of the writs at a general election of its members.

(2) **Continuation in special circumstances** — In time of real or apprehended war, invasion or insurrection, a House of Commons may be continued by Parliament and a legislative assembly may be continued by the legislature beyond five years if such continuation is not opposed by the votes of more than one-third of the members of the House of Commons or the legislative assembly, as the case may be.

5. **Annual sitting of legislative bodies** — There shall be a sitting of Parliament and of each legislature at least once every twelve months.

Mobility Rights

6. (1) **Mobility of citizens** — Every citizen of Canada has the right to enter, remain in and leave Canada.

(2) **Rights to move and gain livelihood** — Every citizen of Canada and every person who has the status of a permanent resident of Canada has the right

(a) to move to and take up residence in any province; and

(b) to pursue the gaining of a livelihood in any province.

(3) **Limitation** — The rights specified in subsection (2) are subject to

(a) any laws or practices of general application in force in a province other than those that discriminate among persons primarily on the basis of province of present or previous residence; and

(b) any laws providing for reasonable residency requirements as a qualification for the receipt of publicly provided social services.

(4) **Affirmative action programs** — Subsections (2) and (3) do not preclude any law, program or activity that has as its object the amelioration in a province of conditions of individuals in that province who are socially or economically disadvantaged if the rate of employment in that province is below the rate of employment in Canada.

Legal Rights

7. Life, liberty and security of person — Everyone has the right to life, liberty and security of the person and the right not to be deprived thereof except in accordance with the principles of fundamental justice.

8. Search or seizure — Everyone has the right to be secure against unreasonable search or seizure.

9. Detention or imprisonment — Everyone has the right not to be arbitrarily detained or imprisoned.

10. Arrest or detention — Everyone has the right on arrest or detention

(a) to be informed promptly of the reasons therefor;

(b) to retain and instruct counsel without delay and to be informed of that right; and

(c) to have the validity of the detention determined by way of *habeas corpus* and to be released if the detention is not lawful.

11. Proceedings in criminal and penal matters — Any person charged with an offence has the right

(a) to be informed without unreasonable delay of the specific offence;

(b) to be tried within a reasonable time;

(c) not to be compelled to be a witness in proceedings against that person in respect of the offence;

(d) to be presumed innocent until proven guilty according to law in a fair and public hearing by an independent and impartial tribunal;

(e) not to be denied reasonable bail without just cause;

(f) except in the case of an offence under military law tried before a military tribunal, to the benefit of trial by jury where the maximum punishment for the offence is imprisonment for five years or a more severe punishment;

(g) not to be found guilty on account of any act or omission unless, at the time of the act or omission, it constituted an offence under Canadian or international law or was criminal according to the general principles of law recognized by the community of nations;

(h) if finally acquitted of the offence, not to be tried for it again and, if finally found guilty and punished for the offence, not to be tried or punished for it again; and

(i) if found guilty of the offence and if the punishment for the offence has been varied between the time of commission and the time of sentencing, to the benefit of the lesser punishment.

12. Treatment or punishment — Everyone has the right not to be subjected to any cruel and unusual treatment or punishment.

13. Self-crimination — A witness who testifies in any proceedings has the right not to have any incriminating evidence so given used to incriminate that witness in any other proceedings, except in a prosecution for perjury or for the giving of contradictory evidence.

14. Interpreter — A party or witness in any proceedings who does not understand or speak the language in which the proceedings are conducted or who is deaf has the right to the assistance of an interpreter.

Equality Rights

15. (1) Equality before and under law and equal protection and benefit of law — Every individual is equal before and under the law and has the right to the equal protection and equal benefit of the law without discrimination and, in particular, without discrimination based on race, national or ethnic origin, colour, religion, sex, age or mental or physical disability.

(2) Affirmative action programs — Subsection (1) does not preclude any law, program or activity that has as its object the amelioration of conditions of disadvantaged individuals or groups including those that are disadvantaged because of race, national or ethnic origin, colour, religion, sex, age or mental or physical disability.

Official Languages of Canada

16. (1) Official languages of Canada — English and French are the official languages of Canada and have equality of status and equal rights and privileges as to their use in all institutions of the Parliament and government of Canada.

(2) Official languages of New Brunswick — English and French are the official languages of New Brunswick and have equality of status and equal rights and privileges as to their use in all institutions of the legislature and government of New Brunswick.

(3) Advancement of status and use — Nothing in this Charter limits the authority of Parliament or a legislature to advance the equality of status or use of English and French.

16.1 (1) English and French linguistic communities in New Brunswick — The English linguistic community and the French linguistic community in New Brunswick have equality status and equal rights and privileges, including the right to distinct educational institutions and such distinct cultural institutions as are necessary for the preservation and promotion of those communities.

(2) Role of the legislature and government of New Brunswick — The role of the legislature and government of New Brunswick to preserve and promote the status, rights and privileges referred to in subsection (1) is affirmed.

SI/93-54, Sched., s. 1

17. (1) Proceedings of Parliament — Everyone has the right to use English or French in any debates and other proceedings of Parliament.

(2) Proceedings of New Brunswick legislature — Everyone has the right to use English or French in any debates and other proceedings of the legislature of New Brunswick.

18. (1) Parliamentary statutes and records — The statutes, records and journals of Parliament shall be printed and published in English and French and both language versions are equally authoritative.

(2) New Brunswick statutes and records — The statutes, records and journals of the legislature of New Brunswick shall be printed and published in English and French and both language versions are equally authoritative.

19. (1) Proceedings in courts established by Parliament — Either English or French may be used by any person in, or in any pleading in or process issuing from, any court established by Parliament.

(2) Proceedings in New Brunswick courts — Either English or French may be used by any person in, or in any pleading in or process issuing from, any court of New Brunswick.

20. (1) Communications by public with federal institutions — Any member of the public in Canada has the right to communicate with, and to receive available services from, any head or central office of an institution of the Parliament or government of Canada in English or French, and has the same right with respect to any other office of any such institution where

(a) there is a significant demand for communications with and services from that office in such language; or

(b) due to the nature of the office, it is reasonable that communications with and services from that office be available in both English and French.

(2) Communications by public with New Brunswick institutions — Any member of the public in New Brunswick has the right to communicate with, and to receive available services from, any office of an institution of the legislature or government of New Brunswick in English or French.

21. Continuation of existing Constitutional provisions — Nothing in sections 16 to 20 abrogates or derogates from any right, privilege or obligation with respect to the English and French languages, or either of them, that exists or is continued by virtue of any other provision of the Constitution of Canada.

22. Rights and privileges preserved — Nothing in sections 16 to 20 abrogates or derogates from any legal or customary right or privilege acquired or enjoyed either before or after the coming into force of this Charter with respect to any language that is not English or French.

Minority Language Educational Rights

23. (1) Language of instruction — Citizens of Canada

(a) whose first language learned and still understood is that of the English or French linguistic minority population of the province in which they reside, or

(b) who have received their primary school instruction in Canada in English or French and reside in a province where the language in which they received that instruction is the language of the English or French linguistic minority population of the province,

have the right to have their children receive primary and secondary school instruction in that language in that province.

(2) Continuity of language instruction — Citizens of Canada of whom any child has received or is receiving primary or secondary school instruction in English or French in Canada, have the right to have all their children receive primary and secondary school instruction in the same language.

(3) Application where numbers warrant — The right of citizens of Canada under subsections (1) and (2) to have their children receive primary and secondary school instruction in the language of the English or French linguistic minority population of a province

(a) applies wherever in the province the number of children of citizens who have such a right is sufficient to warrant the provision to them out of public funds of minority language instruction; and

(b) includes, where the number of those children so warrants, the right to have them receive that instruction in minority language educational facilities provided out of public funds.

Enforcement

24. (1) Enforcement of guaranteed rights and freedoms — Anyone whose rights or freedoms, as guaranteed by this Charter, have been infringed or denied may apply to a court of competent jurisdiction to obtain such remedy as the court considers appropriate and just in the circumstances.

(2) Exclusion of evidence bringing administration of justice into disrepute — Where, in proceedings under subsection (1), a court concludes that evidence was obtained in a manner that infringed or denied any rights or freedoms guaranteed by this Charter, the evidence shall be excluded if it is established that, having regard to all the circumstances, the admission of it in the proceedings would bring the administration of justice into disrepute.

25. Aboriginal rights and freedoms not affected by Charter — The guarantee in this Charter of certain rights and freedoms shall not be construed so as to abrogate or derogate from any aboriginal treaty or other rights or freedoms that pertain to the aboriginal peoples of Canada including

(a) any rights or freedoms that have been recognized by the Royal Proclamation of October 7, 1763; and

(b) any rights or freedoms that now exist by way of land claims agreements or may be so acquired.

26. Other rights and freedoms not affected by Charter — The guarantee in this Charter of certain rights and freedoms shall not be construed as denying the existence of any other rights or freedoms that exist in Canada.

27. Multicultural heritage — This Charter shall be interpreted in a manner consistent with the preservation and enhancement of the multicultural heritage of Canadians.

28. Rights guaranteed equally to both sexes — Notwithstanding anything in this Charter, the rights and freedoms referred to in it are guaranteed equally to male and female persons.

29. Rights respecting certain schools preserved — Nothing in this Charter abrogates or derogates from any rights or privileges guaranteed by or under the Constitution of Canada in respect of denominational, separate or dissentient schools.

30. Application to Territories and territorial authorities — A reference in this Charter to a province or to the legislative assembly or legislature of a province shall be deemed to include a reference to the Yukon Territory and the Northwest Territories, or to the appropriate legislative authority thereof, as the case may be.

31. Legislative powers not extended — Nothing in this Charter extends the legislative powers of any body or authority.

Application of Charter

32. (1) Application of Charter — This Charter applies

(a) to the Parliament and government of Canada in respect of all matters within the authority of Parliament including all matters relating to the Yukon Territory and Northwest Territories; and

(b) to the legislature and government of each province in respect of all matters within the authority of the legislature of each province.

(2) Exception — Notwithstanding subsection (1), section 15 shall not have effect until three years after this section comes into force.

33. (1) Exception where express declaration — Parliament or the legislature of a province may expressly declare in an Act of Parliament or of the legislature, as the case may be, that the Act or a provision thereof shall operate notwithstanding a provision included in section 2 or sections 7 to 15 of this Charter.

(2) Operation of exception — An Act or a provision of an Act in respect of which a declaration made under this section is in effect shall have such operation as it would have but for the provision of this Charter referred to in the declaration.

(3) Five year limitation — A declaration made under subsection (1) shall cease to have effect five years after it comes into force or on such earlier date as may be specified in the declaration.

(4) Re-enactment — Parliament or a legislature of a province may re-enact a declaration made under subsection (1).

(5) Five year limitation — Subsection (3) applies in respect of a re-enactment made under subsection (4).

Citation

34. Citation — This Part may be cited as the *Canadian Charter of Rights and Freedoms*.

CONTROLLED DRUGS AND SUBSTANCES ACT

TABLE OF CONCORDANCE

[Note: The Controlled Drugs and Substances Act repeals and replaces the Narcotic Control Act and Parts III and IV of the Food and Drugs Act. Note that the Controlled Drugs and Substances Act replaced Parts III and IV of the Food and Drugs Act, however, some of the Controlled Drugs and Substances Act sections pertain to interpretation, administration and enforcement which, while dealt with somewhat in Parts III and IV of the Food and Drugs Act, are also covered in Parts I and II; as such, there are some sections in the Controlled Drugs and Substances Act which equate to section in Parts I and II of the FDA.]

[Editor's Note: Current to May 15, 2019.]

CDA, S.C. 1996, c. 19	NCA, R.S.C. c. N-1	FDA, R.S.C. 1985, c. F-27
1	1	1
2(1)	2	2; 38; 46
2(2)	—	—
2(3)	—	—
3	—	—
4(1)	3(1)	47(1)
4(2)	3.1(1)	38.1(1)
4(3)(a)	3(2)(b)	—
4(3)(b)	3(2)(a)	—
4(4)(a)	3(2)(b)	—
4(4)(b)	3(2)(a)	—
4(5)	—	—
4(6)	—	47(2)
4(7)	3.1(2)	38.1(2)
4(8)	—	—
5(1)	4(1)	39(1); 48(1)
5(2)	4(2)	39(2); 48(2)
5(3)(a)	4(3)	—
5(3)(b)	—	48(3)
5(3)(c)	—	39(3)
5(4)	—	—
5(5)	—	—

CDA, S.C. 1996, c. 19	NCA, R.S.C. c. N-1	FDA, R.S.C. 1985, c. F-27
5(6)	—	—
6(1)	5(1)	39(1); 48(1)
6(2)	—	39(2); 48(2)
6(3)(a)	5(2)	—
6(3)(b)	—	48(3)
6(3)(c)	—	39(3)
7(1)	4(1), (2); 6(1)	39(1); 48(1)
7(2)(a)	4(3); 6(2)	—
7(2)(b)	6(2)	—
7(2)(c)	—	48(3)
7(2)(d)	—	39(3)
8(1)(a), (b)	19.1(1)	44.2(1)(a); 50.1; 50.2(1)
8(1)(c)	—	44.1; 50.1
8(2)	19.1(2)	44.2(2); 50.2(2)
9(1)(a), (b)	—	44.1; 44.3(1); 50.1; 50.3(1)
9(1)(c)	—	44.1
9(2)	19.2(2)	44.3(2); 44.3(1); 50.1; 50.3(1)
10	—	—
11(1)	12	42(3); 51
11(2)-(4)	—	—
11(5), (6)	11	42(2); 51
11(7)	10	42(1); 51
11(8)	11	42(2); 51
12	14	42(5); 51
13	15	43; 51
14-15	—	—
16(1)	16	27; 44; 51
16(2), (3)	—	—
17	—	—
18	—	—
19	—	—
20(1)-(5)	17	—
20(6)	19	—
21	—	—
22	—	—
23	19.3	44.4; 51
24(1)-(4)	15	43; 51
24(5)	—	—

CDA, S.C. 1996, c. 19	NCA, R.S.C. c. N-1	FDA, R.S.C. 1985, c. F-27
25	15(4)	43(4); 51
26	—	—
27	—	—
28	—	27(1)
29	6(3)	—
30	—	22
31(1)	—	23(1)
31(2)	—	23(1.1)
31(3)	—	23(1.2)
31(4)	—	23(1.3)
31(5)	—	23(5)
31(6)	—	25
31(7)	—	—
31(8)	—	26
31(9)	—	—
32	—	24
33-43	—	—
44	21	28
45	—	29
46	—	—
47(1)	3.1(3)	38.1(3)
47(2)	—	33
48	7	41; 50
49, 50	—	—
51	9(1)-(3)	35(1)-(3)
52	9(4), (5)	35(4), (5)
53, 54	—	—
55	20	30; 45(1); 51
56-59	—	—
60	22	45(2); 51

CONTROLLED DRUGS AND SUBSTANCES ACT

An Act respecting the control of certain drugs, their precursors and other substances and to amend certain other Acts and repeal the *Narcotic Control Act* in consequence thereof

S.C. 1996, c. 19, as am. S.C. 1996, c. 8, s. 35(a); 1996, c. 19, s. 93.2; 1997, c. 18, s. 140; SOR/97-230; SOR/98-157; SOR/98-173; 1999, c. 5, ss. 48, 49; SOR/99-371; SOR/99-421; SOR/2000-220; 2001, c. 32, ss. 47–56; SOR/2002-361; SOR/2003-32, ss. 1–3, 4 (Fr.), 5–7; SOR/2003-37; SOR/2003-412; 2005, c. 10, ss. 15, 16, 34(1)(d); SOR/2005-235; SOR/2005-271; 2005, c. 44, s. 13; SOR/2005-337; SOR/2005-364, ss. 1, 2, 3 (Fr.), 4; 2011, c. 14, s. 1; 2012, c. 1, ss. 39–46; SOR/2012-66; SOR/2012-176; 2015, c. 22; SOR/2015-190; SOR/2015-192; SOR/2015-209; SOR/2016-13; SOR/2016-73; SOR/2016-107; SOR/2016-295; SOR/2017-13; SOR/2017-44; 2017, c. 4; 2017, c. 7, ss. 1(1), (2) (Fr.), (3)–(6), 2, 3(1), (2) (Fr.), (3), (4), 4–6, 7(1) (Fr.), (2), (3) (Fr.), (4), (5) (Fr.), 8–25, 26(1), (2) (Fr.), (3)–(8), 27(1), (2), (3) (Fr.), 28–39, 40(1), (2) (Fr.), (3), (4) (Fr.), (5) (Fr.), (6)–(8), (9) (Fr.), (10)–(19), 41–51 [ss. 1(1), 28, 31, 32, 35, 36, 40(12), (13) not in force at date of publication.]; SOR/2017-249; SOR/2017-275; SOR/2017-277; SOR/2018-70, ss. 1, 2, 3 (Fr.), 4; 2018, c. 16, ss. 194–205, 206(6) [s. 199(1) conditions not yet satisified.]; SOR/2019-121; 2019, c. 25, s. 385.

SHORT TITLE

1. Short title — This Act may be cited as the *Controlled Drugs and Substances Act*.

INTERPRETATION

2. (1) Definitions — In this Act,

"adjudicator" means a person appointed or employed under the *Public Service Employment Act* who performs the duties and functions of an adjudicator under this Act and the regulations;

Proposed Repeal — 2(1) "adjudicator"

"adjudicator" [Repealed 2017, c. 7, s. 1(1). Not in force at date of publication.]

"analogue" means a substance that, in relation to a controlled substance, has a substantially similar chemical structure;

"analyst" means a person who is designated as an analyst under section 44;

"Attorney General" means

(a) the Attorney General of Canada, and includes their lawful deputy, or

(b) with respect to proceedings commenced at the instance of the government of a province and conducted by or on behalf of that government, the Attorney General of that province, and includes their lawful deputy;

"chemical offence-related property" means offence-related property that is a chemical or precursor and includes anything that contains such property or has such property on it;

"controlled substance" means a substance included in Schedule I, II, III, IV or V;

"customs office" has the same meaning as in subsection 2(1) of the *Customs Act*;

"designated device" means a device included in Schedule IX;

"designated substance offence" means

(a) an offence under Part I, except subsection 4(1), or

(b) a conspiracy or an attempt to commit, being an accessory after the fact in relation to, or any counselling in relation to, an offence referred to in paragraph (a);

"inspector" means a person who is designated as an inspector under section 30;

"judge" means a judge as defined in section 552 of the *Criminal Code* or a judge of a superior court of criminal jurisdiction;

"justice" has the same meaning as in section 2 of the *Criminal Code*;

"Minister" means the Minister of Health;

"non-chemical offence-related property" means offence-related property that is not chemical offence-related property;

"offence-related property" means, with the exception of a controlled substance, any property, within or outside Canada,

(a) by means of or in respect of which a designated substance offence is committed,

(b) that is used in any manner in connection with the commission of a designated substance offence, or

(c) that is intended for use for the purpose of committing a designated substance offence;

"organization" has the same meaning as in section 2 of the *Criminal Code*.

"person" means an individual or an organization.

"possession" means possession within the meaning of subsection 4(3) of the *Criminal Code*;

"practitioner" means a person who is registered and entitled under the laws of a province to practise in that province the profession of medicine, dentistry or veterinary medicine, and includes any other person or class or persons prescribed as a practitioner;

"precursor" means a substance included in Schedule VI;

"prescribed" means prescribed by the regulations;

"produce" means, in respect of a substance included in any of Schedules I to V, to obtain the substance by any method or process including

(a) manufacturing, synthesizing or using any means of altering the chemical or physical properties of the substance, or

(b) cultivating, propagating or harvesting the substance or any living thing from which the substance may be extracted or otherwise obtained,

and includes offer to produce;

"provide" means to give, transfer or otherwise make available in any manner, whether directly or indirectly and whether or not for consideration;

"sell" includes offer for sale, expose for sale, have in possession for sale and distribute, whether or not the distribution is made for consideration;

"traffic" means, in respect of a substance included in any of Schedules I to V,

(a) to sell, administer, give, transfer, transport, send or deliver the substance,

(b) to sell an authorization to obtain the substance, or

(c) to offer to do anything mentioned in paragraph (a) or (b),

otherwise than under the authority of the regulations.

(2) **Interpretation** — For the purposes of this Act,

(a) a reference to a controlled substance includes a reference to any substance that contains a controlled substance; and

(b) a reference to a controlled substance includes a reference to

(i) all synthetic and natural forms of the substance, and

(ii) any thing that contains or has on it a controlled substance and that is used or intended or designed for use

(A) in producing the substance, or

(B) in introducing the substance into a human body.

(3) **Idem** — For the purposes of this Act, where a substance is expressly named in any of Schedules I to VI, it shall be deemed not to be included in any other of those Schedules.

1996, c. 8, s. 35(a); 2001, c. 32, s. 47; 2017, c. 7, s. 1(3)–(6); 2018, c. 16, s. 194

3. (1) Interpretaton — Every power or duty imposed under this Act that may be exercised or performed in respect of an offence under this Act may be exercised or performed in respect of a conspiracy, or an attempt to commit, being an accessory after the fact in relation to, or any counselling in relation to, an offence under this Act.

(2) [Repealed 2017, c. 7, s. 2.]

1995, c. 22, s. 18 (Sched. IV, item 26); 2017, c. 7, s. 2

Part I — Offences and Punishment (SS. 4–10)

Particular Offences

4. (1) Possession of substance — Except as authorized under the regulations, no person shall possess a substance included in Schedule I, II or III.

(2) Obtaining substance — No person shall seek or obtain

(a) a substance included in Schedule I, II, III or IV, or

(b) an authorization to obtain a substance included in Schedule I, II, III or IV

from a practitioner, unless the person discloses to the practitioner particulars relating to the acquisition by the person of every substance in those Schedules, and of every authorization to obtain such substances, from any other practitioner within the preceding thirty days.

(3) Punishment — Every person who contravenes subsection (1) where the subject-matter of the offence is a substance included in Schedule I

(a) is guilty of an indictable offence and liable to imprisonment for a term not exceeding seven years; or

(b) is guilty of an offence punishable on summary conviction and liable

(i) for a first offence, to a fine not exceeding one thousand dollars or to imprisonment for a term not exceeding six months, or to both, and

(ii) for a subsequent offence, to a fine not exceeding two thousand dollars or to imprisonment for a term not exceeding one year, or to both.

(4) Punishment — Subject to subsection (5), every person who contravenes subsection (1) where the subject-matter of the offence is a substance included in Schedule II

(a) is guilty of an indictable offence and liable to imprisonment for a term not exceeding five years less a day; or

(b) is guilty of an offence punishable on summary conviction and liable

(i) for a first offence, to a fine not exceeding one thousand dollars or to imprisonment for a term not exceeding six months, or to both, and

(ii) for a subsequent offence, to a fine not exceeding two thousand dollars or to imprisonment for a term not exceeding one year, or to both.

(5) [Repealed 2018, c. 16, s. 195(1).]

(6) Punishment — Every person who contravenes subsection (1) where the subject-matter of the offence is a substance included in Schedule III

(a) is guilty of an indictable offence and liable to imprisonment for a term not exceeding three years; or

(b) is guilty of an offence punishable on summary conviction and liable

(i) for a first offence, to a fine not exceeding one thousand dollars or to imprisonment for a term not exceeding six months, or to both, and

(ii) for a subsequent offence, to a fine not exceeding two thousand dollars or to imprisonment for a term not exceeding one year, or to both.

(7) Punishment — Every person who contravenes subsection (2)

(a) is guilty of an indictable offence and liable

(i) to imprisonment for a term not exceeding seven years, where the subject-matter of the offence is a substance included in Schedule I,

(ii) to imprisonment for a term not exceeding five years less a day, where the subject-matter of the offence is a substance included in Schedule II,

(iii) to imprisonment for a term not exceeding three years, where the subject-matter of the offence is a substance included in Schedule III, or

(iv) to imprisonment for a term not exceeding eighteen months, where the subject-matter of the offence is a substance included in Schedule IV; or

(b) is guilty of an offence punishable on summary conviction and liable

(i) for a first offence, to a fine not exceeding one thousand dollars or to imprisonment for a term not exceeding six months, or to both, and

(ii) for a subsequent offence, to a fine not exceeding two thousand dollars or to imprisonment for a term not exceeding one year, or to both.

(8) [Repealed 2018, c. 16, s. 195(2).]

2018, c. 16, s. 195

4.1 (1) Definition of "medical emergency" — For the purposes of this section, **"medical emergency"** means a physiological event induced by the introduction of a psychoactive substance into the body of a person that results in a life-threatening situation and in respect of which there are reasonable grounds to believe that the person requires emergency medical or law enforcement assistance.

(2) Exemption — medical emergency — No person who seeks emergency medical or law enforcement assistance because that person, or another person, is suffering from a medical emergency is to be charged or convicted of an offence under subsection 4(1) if the evidence in support of that offence was obtained or discovered as a result of that person having sought assistance or having remained at the scene.

(3) Exemption — persons at the scene — The exemption under subsection (2) also applies to any person, including the person suffering from the medical emergency, who is at the scene on the arrival of the emergency medical or law enforcement assistance.

(4) **Exemption — evidence** — No person who seeks emergency medical or law enforcement assistance because that person, or another person, is suffering from a medical emergency, or who is at the scene on the arrival of the assistance, is to be charged with an offence concerning a violation of any condition of a pre-trial release or probation order relating to an offence under subsection 4(1) if the evidence in support of that offence was obtained or discovered as a result of that person having sought assistance or having remained at the scene.

(5) **Deeming** — Any condition of a person's pre-trial release, probation order, conditional sentence or parole relating to an offence under subsection 4(1) that may be violated as a result of the person seeking emergency medical or law enforcement assistance for their, or another person's, medical emergency, or as a result of having been at the scene on the arrival of the assistance, is deemed not to be violated.

2017, c. 4, s. 2; 2018, c. 16, s. 195.1

5. (1) **Trafficking in substance** — No person shall traffic in a substance included in Schedule I, II, III, IV or V or in any substance represented or held out by that person to be such a substance.

(2) **Possession for purpose of trafficking** — No person shall, for the purpose of trafficking, possess a substance included in Schedule I, II, III, IV or V.

(3) **Punishment** — Every person who contravenes subsection (1) or (2)

(a) if the subject matter of the offence is a substance included in Schedule I or II, is guilty of an indictable offence and liable to imprisonment for life, and

(i) to a minimum punishment of imprisonment for a term of one year if

(A) the person committed the offence for the benefit of, at the direction of or in association with a criminal organization, as defined in subsection 467.1(1) of the *Criminal Code*,

(B) the person used or threatened to use violence in committing the offence,

(C) the person carried, used or threatened to use a weapon in committing the offence, or

(D) the person was convicted of a designated substance offence, or had served a term of imprisonment for a designated substance offence, within the previous 10 years, or

(ii) to a minimum punishment of imprisonment for a term of two years if

(A) the person committed the offence in or near a school, on or near school grounds or in or near any other public place usually frequented by persons under the age of 18 years,

(B) the person committed the offence in a prison, as defined in section 2 of the *Criminal Code*, or on its grounds, or

(C) the person used the services of a person under the age of 18 years, or involved such a person, in committing the offence;

(a.1) [Repealed 2018, c. 16, s. 196(2).]

(b) if the subject matter of the offence is a substance included in Schedule III or V,

(i) is guilty of an indictable offence and liable to imprisonment for a term not exceeding ten years, or

(ii) is guilty of an offence punishable on summary conviction and liable to imprisonment for a term not exceeding eighteen months; and

(c) where the subject-matter of the offence is a substance included in Schedule IV,

(i) is guilty of an indictable offence and liable to imprisonment for a term not exceeding three years, or

(ii) is guilty of an offence punishable an summary conviction and liable to imprisonment for a term not exceeding one year.

(4) [Repealed 2012, c. 1, s. 39(2).]

(5) Interpretation — For the purposes of applying subsection (3) in respect of an offence under subsection (1), a reference to a substance included in Schedule I, II, III, IV or V includes a reference to any substance represented or held out to be a substance included in that Schedule.

(6) [Repealed 2018, c. 16, s. 196(3).]

2012, c. 1, s. 39; 2017, c. 7, s. 3(1), (3), (4); 2018, c. 16, s. 196

6. (1) Importing and exporting — Except as authorized under the regulations, no person shall import into Canada or export from Canada a substance included in Schedule I, II, III, IV, V or VI.

(2) Possession for the purpose of exporting — Except as authorized under the regulations, no person shall possess a substance included in Schedule I, II, III, IV, V or VI for the purpose of exporting it from Canada.

(3) Punishment — Every person who contravenes subsection (1) or (2)

(a) if the subject matter of the offence is a substance included in Schedule I in an amount that is not more than one kilogram, or in Schedule II, is guilty of an indictable offence and liable to imprisonment for life, and to a minimum punishment of imprisonment for a term of one year if

(i) the offence is committed for the purposes of trafficking,

(ii) the person, while committing the offence, abused a position of trust or authority, or

(iii) the person had access to an area that is restricted to authorized persons and used that access to commit the offence;

(a.1) if the subject matter of the offence is a substance included in Schedule I in an amount that is more than one kilogram, is guilty of an indictable offence and liable to imprisonment for life and to a minimum punishment of imprisonment for a term of two years;

(b) if the subject matter of the offence is a substance included in Schedule III, V or VI,

(i) is guilty of an indictable offence and liable to imprisonment for a term not exceeding ten years, or

(ii) is guilty of an offence punishable on summary conviction and liable to imprisonment for a term not exceeding eighteen months; and

(c) if the subject matter of the offence is a substance included in Schedule IV,

(i) is guilty of an indictable offence and liable to imprisonment for a term not exceeding three years, or

(ii) is guilty of an offence punishable on summary conviction and liable to imprisonment for a term not exceeding one year.

2012, c. 1, s. 40; 2017, c. 7, s. 4

7. (1) Production of substance — Except as authorized under the regulations, no person shall produce a substance included in Schedule I, II, III, IV or V.

(2) Punishment — Every person who contravenes subsection (1)

(a) if the subject matter of the offence is a substance included in Schedule I, is guilty of an indictable offence and liable to imprisonment for life and to a minimum punishment of imprisonment for a term of three years if any of the factors set out in subsection (3) apply and for a term of two years in any other case;

(a.1) if the subject matter of the offence is a substance included in Schedule II, is guilty of an indictable offence and liable to imprisonment for life, and to a minimum punishment of imprisonment

(i) for a term of one year if the production is for the purpose of trafficking, or

(ii) for a term of 18 months if the production is for the purpose of trafficking and any of the factors set out in subsection (3) apply;

(b) [Repealed 2018, c. 16, s. 197(2).]

(c) if the subject matter of the offence is a substance included in Schedule III or V,

(i) is guilty of an indictable offence and liable to imprisonment for a term not exceeding ten years, or

(ii) is guilty of an offence punishable on summary conviction and liable to imprisonment for a term not exceeding eighteen months; and

(d) where the subject-matter of the offence is a substance included in Schedule IV,

(i) is guilty of an indictable offence and liable to imprisonment for a term not exceeding three years, or

(ii) is guilty of an offence punishable on summary conviction and liable to imprisonment for a term not exceeding one year.

(3) Factors — The following factors must be taken into account in applying paragraphs (2)(a) and (a.1):

(a) the person used real property that belongs to a third party in committing the offence;

(b) the production constituted a potential security, health or safety hazard to persons under the age of 18 years who were in the location where the offence was committed or in the immediate area;

(c) the production constituted a potential public safety hazard in a residential area; or

(d) the person set or placed a trap, device or other thing that is likely to cause death or bodily harm to another person in the location where the offence was committed or in the immediate area, or permitted such a trap, device or other thing to remain or be placed in that location or area.

2012, c. 1, s. 41; 2017, c. 7, s. 5; 2018, c. 16, s. 197

7.1 (1) Possession, sale, etc., for use in production of or trafficking in substance — No person shall possess, produce, sell, import or transport anything intending that it will be used

(a) to produce a controlled substance, unless the production of the controlled substance is lawfully authorized; or

(b) to traffic in a controlled substance.

(2) Punishment — Every person who contravenes subsection (1)

(a) if the subject matter of the offence is a substance included in Schedule I, II, III or V,

(i) is guilty of an indictable offence and liable to imprisonment for a term of not more than 10 years, or

(ii) is guilty of an offence punishable on summary conviction and liable to imprisonment for a term of not more than 18 months; and

(b) if the subject matter of the offence is a substance included in Schedule IV,

(i) is guilty of an indictable offence and liable to imprisonment for a term of not more than three years, or

(ii) is guilty of an offence punishable on summary conviction and liable to imprisonment for a term of not more than one year.

2011, c. 14, s. 1; 2017, c. 7, s. 6

Notice

[Heading added 2012, c. 1, s. 42.]

8. Notice — The court is not required to impose a minimum punishment unless it is satisfied that the offender, before entering a plea, was notified of the possible imposition of a minimum punishment for the offence in question and of the Attorney General's intention to prove any factors in relation to the offence that would lead to the imposition of a minimum punishment.

2012, c. 1, s. 42

Report to Parliament

[Heading added 2012, c. 1, s. 42.]

9. (1) Review — Within five years after this section comes into force, a comprehensive review of the provisions and operation of this Act, including a cost-benefit analysis of mandatory minimum sentences, shall be undertaken by any committee of the Senate, of the House of Commons or of both Houses of Parliament that may be designated or established for that purpose.

(2) Report — The committee referred to in subsection (1) shall, within one year after a review is undertaken under that subsection, submit a report to Parliament including a statement of any changes that the committee recommends.

2012, c. 1, s. 42

Sentencing

10. (1) Purpose of sentencing — Without restricting the generality of the *Criminal Code*, the fundamental purpose of any sentence for an offence under this Part is to contribute to the respect for the law and the maintenance of a just, peaceful and safe society while encouraging rehabilitation, and treatment in appropriate circumstances, of offenders and acknowledging the harm done to victims and to the community.

(2) Factors to take into consideration — If a person is convicted of a designated substance offence for which the court is not required to impose a minimum punishment, the court imposing sentence on the person shall consider any relevant aggravating factors including that the person

(a) in relation to the commission of the offence,

(i) carried, used or threatened to use a weapon,

(ii) used or threatened to use violence,

(iii) trafficked in a substance included in Schedule I, II, III, IV or V, or possessed such a substance for the purpose of trafficking, in or near a school, on or near school grounds or in or near any other public place usually frequented by persons under the age of 18 years, or

(iv) trafficked in a substance included in Schedule I, II, III, IV or V, or possessed such a substance for the purpose of trafficking, to a person under the age of 18 years;

(b) was previously convicted of a **"designated substance offence"**, as defined in subsection 2(1) of this Act, or a **"designated offence"**, as defined in subsection 2(1) of the *Cannabis Act*.

(c) used the services of a person under the age of eighteen years to commit, or involved such a person in the commission of, the offence.

(3) Reasons — If, under subsection (1), the court is satisfied of the existence of one or more of the aggravating factors enumerated in paragraphs (2)(a) to (c), but decides not to sentence the person to imprisonment, the court shall give reasons for that decision.

(4) **Drug treatment court program** — A court sentencing a person who is convicted of an offence under this Part may delay sentencing to enable the offender

(a) to participate in a drug treatment court program approved by the Attorney General; or

(b) to attend a treatment program under subsection 720(2) of the *Criminal Code*.

(5) **Minimum punishment** — If the offender successfully completes a program under subsection (4), the court is not required to impose the minimum punishment for the offence for which the person was convicted.

1999, c. 5, s. 49; 2012, c. 1, s. 43; 2017, c. 7, s. 7(2), (4); 2018, c. 16, s. 198

PART II — ENFORCEMENT (SS. 11–12.1)

[Heading repealed 2017, c. 7, s. 8.]

11. (1) **Information for search warrant** — A justice who, on *ex parte* application, is satisfied by information on oath that there are reasonable grounds to believe that

(a) a controlled substance or precursor in respect of which this Act has been contravened,

(b) any thing in which a controlled substance or precursor referred to in paragraph (a) is contained or concealed,

(c) offence-related property, or

(d) any thing that will afford evidence in respect of an offence under this Act or an offence, in whole or in part in relation to a contravention of this Act, under section 354 or 462.31 of the *Criminal Code*

is in a place may, at any time, issue a warrant authorizing a peace officer, at any time, to search the place for any such controlled substance, precursor, property or thing and to seize it.

(2) **Application of s. 487.1 of the *Criminal Code*** — For the purposes of subsection (1), an information may be submitted by telephone or other means of telecommunication in accordance with section 487.1 of the *Criminal Code*, with such modifications as the circumstances require.

(3) **Execution in Canada** — A warrant issued under subsection (1) may be executed at any place in Canada. Any peace officer who executes the warrant must have authority to act as a peace officer in the place where it is executed.

(4) [Repealed 2019, c. 25, s. 385.]

(5) **Search of person and seizure** — Where a peace officer who executes a warrant issued under subsection (1) has reasonable grounds to believe that any person found in the place set out in the warrant has on their person any controlled substance, precursor, property or thing set out in the warrant, the peace officer may search the person for the controlled substance, precursor, property or thing and seize it.

(6) Seizure of things not specified — A peace officer who executes a warrant issued under subsection (1) may seize, in addition to the things mentioned in the warrant,

(a) any controlled substance or precursor in respect of which the peace officer believes on reasonable grounds that this Act has been contravened;

(b) any thing that the peace officer believes on reasonable grounds to contain or conceal a controlled substance or precursor referred to in paragraph (a);

(c) any thing that the peace officer believes on reasonable grounds is offence-related property; or

(d) any thing that the peace officer believes on reasonable grounds will afford evidence in respect of an offence under this Act.

(7) Where warrant not necessary — A peace officer may exercise any of the powers described in subsection (1), (5) or (6) without a warrant if the conditions for obtaining a warrant exist but by reason of exigent circumstances it would be impracticable to obtain one.

(8) Seizure of additional things — A peace officer who executes a warrant issued under subsection (1) or exercises powers under subsection (5) or (7) may seize, in addition to the things mentioned in the warrant and in subsection (6), any thing that the peace officer believes on reasonble grounds has been obtained by or used in the commission of an offence or that will afford evidence in respect of an offence.

2005, c. 44, s. 13; 2017, c. 7, s. 9; 2019, c. 25, s. 385

12. Assistance and use of force — For the purpose of exercising any of the powers described in section 11, a peace officer may

(a) enlist such assistance as the officer deems necessary; and

(b) use as much force as is necessary in the circumstances.

12.1 Report of seizure, finding, etc. — Subject to the regulations, every peace officer, inspector or prescribed person who seizes, finds or otherwise acquires a controlled substance, precursor or chemical offence-related property shall, within 30 days,

(a) prepare a report setting out

(i) the substance, precursor or property,

(ii) the amount of it that was seized, found or acquired,

(iii) the place where it was seized, found or acquired,

(iv) the date on which it was seized, found or acquired,

(v) the name of the police force, agency or entity to which the peace officer, inspector or prescribed person belongs,

(vi) the number of the file or police report related to the seizure, finding or acquisition, and

(vii) any other prescribed information;

(b) cause the report to be sent to the Minister; and

(c) in the case of a seizure made under section 11 of this Act, the *Criminal Code* or a power of seizure at common law, cause a copy of the report to be filed with the justice who issued the warrant or another justice for the same territorial division or, if a warrant was not issued, a justice who would have had jurisdiction to issue a warrant.

2017, c. 7, s. 10

PART III — DISPOSITION (SS. 13–29)

[Heading added 2017, c. 7, s. 10.]

13. (1) Sections 489.1 and 490 of the *Criminal Code* applicable — Subject to subsections (2) and (3), sections 489.1 and 490 of the *Criminal Code* apply to any thing seized under this Act.

(2) Sections 489.1 and 490 of *Criminal Code* applicable — If a thing seized under this Act is non-chemical offence-related property, sections 489.1 and 490 of the *Criminal Code* apply subject to sections 16 to 22 and subsections 31(6) to (9) of this Act.

(3) Provisions of this Act applicable — If a controlled substance, precursor or chemical offence-related property is seized under this Act, any other Act of Parliament or a power of seizure at common law, the provisions of this Act and the regulations apply in respect of that substance, precursor or property.

(4) Recognizance — If, under this section, an order is made in accordance with paragraph 490(9)(c) of the *Criminal Code* for the return of any non-chemical offence-related property seized under this Act, the judge or justice making the order may require the applicant for the order to enter into a recognizance before the judge or justice, with or without sureties, in the amount and with any conditions that the judge or justice directs and, if the judge or justice considers it appropriate, require the applicant to deposit with the judge or justice the sum of money or other valuable security that the judge or justice directs.

(5) and (6) [Repealed 2017, c. 7, s. 11.]

2017, c. 7, s. 11

DIVISION 1 — NON-CHEMICAL OFFENCE-RELATED PROPERTY

[Heading amended 2017, c. 7, s. 12.]

Restraint Orders

[Heading added 2017, c. 7, s. 12.]

14. (1) Application for restraint order — The Attorney General may make an application in accordance with this section for a restraint order in respect of any non-chemical offence-related property.

(2) Procedure — The application for a restraint order may be made *ex parte* and shall be made in writing to a judge and be accompanied by an affidavit of the Attorney General or any other person deposing to the following matters:

(a) the offence to which the property relates;

(b) the person who is believed to be in possession of the property; and

(c) a description of the property.

(3) Restraint order — The judge to whom the application is made may, if satisfied that there are reasonable grounds to believe that the property is non-chemical offence-related property, make a restraint order prohibiting any person from disposing of, or otherwise dealing with any interest in, the property specified in the order other than in the manner that is specified in the order.

(4) Property outside Canada — A restraint order may be issued under this section in respect of property situated outside Canada, with any modifications that the circumstances require.

(5) Conditions — A restraint order made by a judge under this section may be subject to such reasonable conditions as the judge thinks fit.

(6) Order in writing — A restraint order made under this section shall be made in writing.

(7) Service of order — A copy of a restraint order made under this section shall be served on the person to whom the order is addressed in such manner as the judge making the order directs or in accordance with the rules of the court.

(8) Registration of order — A copy of a restraint order made under this section shall be registered against any property in accordance with the laws of the province in which the property is situated.

(9) Order continues in force — A restraint order made under this section remains in effect until

(a) an order is made under subsection 19(3) or 19.1(3) of this Act or subsection 490(9) or (11) of the *Criminal Code* in relation to the property; or

(b) an order of forfeiture of the property is made under subsection 16(1) or 17(2) of this Act or section 490 of the *Criminal Code*.

(10) Offence — Any person on whom a restraint order made under this section is served in accordance with this section and who, while the order is in force, acts in contravention of or fails to comply with the order is guilty of an indictable offence or an offence punishable on summary conviction.

1996, c. 19, s. 93.2; 2001, c. 32, s. 49; 2017, c. 7, s. 13

14.1 [Repealed 2017, c. 7, s. 14.]

15. (1) Sections 489.1 and 490 of *Criminal Code* applicable — Subject to sections 16 to 22, sections 489.1 and 490 of the *Criminal Code* apply, with any modifications that the circumstances require, to any property that is the subject of a restraint order made under section 14.

(2) Recognizance — If, under this section, an order is made in accordance with paragraph 490(9)(c) of the *Criminal Code* for the return of any property that is the subject of a restraint order made under section 14, the judge or justice making the order may require the applicant for the order to enter into a recognizance before the judge or justice, with or without sureties, in the amount and with any conditions that the judge or justice directs and, if the judge or justice considers it appropriate, require the applicant to deposit with the judge or justice the sum of money or other valuable security that the judge or justice directs.

2017, c. 7, s. 14

Management Orders

[Heading added 2017, c. 7, s. 14.]

15.1 (1) Management order — On application of the Attorney General or of any other person with the written consent of the Attorney General, a justice in the case of non-chemical offence-related property seized under section 11 of this Act, the *Criminal Code* or a power of seizure at common law, or a judge in the case of property restrained under section 14, may, if they are of the opinion that the circumstances so require,

(a) appoint a person to take control of and to manage or otherwise deal with all or part of the property in accordance with the directions of the judge or justice; and

(b) require any person having possession of that property to give possession of the property to the person appointed under paragraph (a).

(2) Appointment of Minister of Public Works and Government Services — If the Attorney General of Canada so requests, a judge or justice appointing a person under subsection (1) shall appoint the Minister of Public Works and Government Services.

(3) Power to manage — The power to manage or otherwise deal with property under subsection (1) includes

(a) the power to make an interlocutory sale of perishable or rapidly depreciating property;

(b) the power to destroy, in accordance with subsections (4) to (7), property that has little or no value; and

(c) the power to have property, other than real property or a conveyance, forfeited to Her Majesty in accordance with subsection (8).

(4) Application for destruction order — Before a person who is appointed to manage property destroys property that has little or no value, they shall apply to a court for a destruction order.

(5) Notice required before destruction — Before making a destruction order, a court shall require notice in accordance with subsection (6) to be given to and may hear any person who, in the court's opinion, appears to have a valid interest in the property.

(6) Manner of giving notice — A notice shall

(a) be given in the manner that the court directs or that may be specified in the rules of the court; and

(b) specify the effective period of the notice that the court considers reasonable or that may be set out in the rules of the court.

(7) Destruction order — A court shall order that the property be destroyed if it is satisfied that the property has little or no financial or other value.

(8) Application for forfeiture order — On application by a person who is appointed to manage the property, a court shall order that the property, other than real property or a conveyance, be forfeited to Her Majesty to be disposed of or otherwise dealt with in accordance with the law if

(a) a notice is given or published in the manner that the court directs or that may be specified in the rules of the court;

(b) the notice specifies a period of 60 days during which a person may make an application to the court asserting their interest in the property; and

(c) during that period, no one makes such an application.

(9) When management order ceases to have effect — A management order ceases to have effect when the property that is the subject of the management order is returned in accordance with the law, destroyed or forfeited to Her Majesty.

(10) For greater certainty — For greater certainty, if property that is the subject of a management order is sold, the management order applies to the net proceeds of the sale.

(11) Application to vary conditions — The Attorney General may at any time apply to the judge or justice to cancel or vary any condition to which a management order is subject but may not apply to vary an appointment made under subsection (2).

2017, c. 7, s. 14

Forfeiture

[Heading amended 2017, c. 7, s. 15.]

16. (1) Forfeiture of property — Subject to sections 18 to 19.1, if a person is convicted, or discharged under section 730 of the *Criminal Code*, of a designated substance offence and, on application of the Attorney General, the court is satisfied, on a balance of probabilities, that non-chemical offence-related property is related to the commission of the offence, the court shall

(a) if the prosecution of the offence was commenced at the instance of the government of a province and conducted by or on behalf of that government, order that the property be forfeited to Her Majesty in right of that province to be disposed of or otherwise dealt with in accordance with the law by the Attorney General or Solicitor General of that province; and

(b) in any other case, order that the property be forfeited to Her Majesty in right of Canada to be disposed of or otherwise dealt with in accordance with the law by the member of the Queen's Privy Council for Canada that is designated by the Governor in Council for the purposes of this paragraph.

(2) **Property related to other offences** — Subject to sections 18 to 19.1, if the evidence does not establish to the satisfaction of the court that property in respect of which an order of forfeiture would otherwise be made under subsection (1) is related to the commission of the designated substance offence of which a person is convicted or discharged, but the court is satisfied, beyond a reasonable doubt, that the property is non-chemical offence-related property, the court may make an order of forfeiture under subsection (1) in relation to that property.

(2.1) **Property outside Canada** — An order may be issued under this section in respect of property situated outside Canada, with any modifications that the circumstances require.

(3) **Appeal** — A person who has been convicted or discharged of a designated substance offence or the Attorney General may appeal to the court of appeal from an order or a failure to make an order under subsection (1) as if the appeal were an appeal against the sentence imposed on the person in respect of the offence.

2001, c. 32, s. 51; 2017, c. 7, s. 16

17. (1) **Application for *in rem* forfeiture** — Where an information has been laid in respect of a designated substance offence, the Attorney General may make an application to a judge for an order of forfeiture under subsection (2).

(2) **Order of forfeiture of property** — Subject to sections 18 to 19.1, where an application is made to a judge under subsection (1) and the judge is satisfied

(a) beyond a reasonable doubt that any property is non-chemical offence-related property,

(b) that proceedings were commenced in respect of a designated substance offence to which the property referred to in paragraph (a) is related, and

(c) that the accused charged with the designated substance offence has died or absconded,

the judge shall order that the property be forfeited and disposed of in accordance with subsection (4).

(3) **Accused deemed absconded** — For the purposes of subsection (2), an accused shall be deemed to have absconded in connection with a designated substance offence if

(a) an information has been laid alleging the commission of the offence by the accused,

(b) a warrant for the arrest of the accused has been issued in relation to that information, and

(c) reasonable attempts to arrest the accused pursuant to the warrant have been unsuccessful during a period of six months beginning on the day on which the warrant was issued,

and the accused shall be deemed to have so absconded on the last day of that six month period.

(4) Who may dispose of forfeited property — For the purposes of subsection (2),

(a) if the proceedings referred to in paragraph (2)(b) were commenced at the instance of the government of a province, the judge shall order that the property be forfeited to Her Majesty in right of that province and disposed of or otherwise dealt with in accordance with the law by the Attorney General or Solicitor General of that province; and

(b) in any other case, the judge shall order that the property be forfeited to Her Majesty in right of Canada and disposed of or otherwise dealt with in accordance with the law by the member of the Queen's Privy Council for Canada that is designated by the Governor in Council for the purposes of this paragraph.

(5) Property outside Canada — An order may be issued under this, section in respect of property situated outside Canada, with any modifications that the circumstances require.

2001, c. 32, s. 52; 2017, c. 7, s. 17

18. Voidable transfers — A court may, before ordering that property be forfeited under subsection 16(1) or 17(2), set aside any conveyance or transfer of the property that occurred after the property was seized or restrained, unless the conveyance or transfer was for valuable consideration to a person acting in good faith.

2017, c. 7, s. 18

19. (1) Notice — Before making an order under subsection 16(1) or 17(2) in relation to any property, a court shall require notice in accordance with subsection (2) to be given to, and may hear, any person who, in the opinion of the court, appears to have a valid interest in the property.

(2) Manner of giving notice — A notice shall

(a) be given in the manner that the court directs or that may be specified in the rules of the court;

(b) specify the period that the court considers reasonable or that may be set out in the rules of the court during which a person may make an application to the court asserting their interest in the property; and

(c) set out the designated substance offence charged and a description of the property.

(3) Order of restoration of property — Where a court is satisfied that any person, other than

(a) a person who was charged with a designated substance offence, or

(b) a person who acquired title to or a right of possession of the property from a person referred to in paragraph (a) under circumstances that give rise to a reasonable inference that the title or right was transferred for the purpose of voiding the forfeiture of the property,

is the lawful owner or is lawfully entitled to possession of any property or any part of any property that would otherwise be forfeited pursuant to an order made under subsection 16(1) or 17(2) and that the person appears innocent of any complicity in an offence referred to in paragraph (a) or of any collusion in relation to such an offence, the court may order that the property or part be returned to that person.

2017, c. 7, s. 19

19.1 (1) Notice — If all or part of the property that would otherwise be forfeited under subsection 16(1) or 17(2) is a dwelling-house, before making an order of forfeiture, a court shall require notice in accordance with subsection (2) to be given to and may hear any person who resides in the dwelling-house and is a member of the immediate family of the person charged with or convicted, or discharged under section 730 of the *Criminal Code*, of the indictable offence under this Act in relation to which the property would be forfeited.

(2) Manner of giving notice — A notice shall

(a) be given in the manner that the court directs or that may be specified in the rules of the court;

(b) specify the period that the court considers reasonable or that may be set out in the rules of the court during which a member of the immediate family who resides in the dwelling-house may make themselves known to the court; and

(c) set out the offence charged and a description of the property.

(3) Non-forfeiture of real property — Subject to an order made under subsection 19(3), if a court is satisfied that the impact of an order of forfeiture made under subsection 16(1) or 17(2) in respect of real property would be disproportionate to the nature and gravity of the offence, the circumstances surrounding the commission of the offence and the criminal record, if any, of the person charged with or convicted, or discharged under section 730 of the *Criminal Code*, of the offence, as the case may be, it may decide not to order the forfeiture of the property or part of the property and may revoke any restraint order made in respect of that property or part.

(4) Factors in relation to dwelling-house — Where all or part of the property that would otherwise be forfeited under subsection 16(1) or 17(2) is a dwelling-house, when making a decision under subsection (3), the court shall also consider

(a) the impact of an order of forfeiture on any member of the immediate family of the person charged with or convicted or discharged of the offence, if the dwelling-house was the member's principal residence at the time the charge was laid and continues to be the member's principal residence; and

(b) whether the member referred to in paragraph (a) appears innocent of any complicity in the offence or of any collusion in relation to the offence.

2001, c. 32, s. 53; 2017, c. 7, s. 20

20. (1) Application — If any property is forfeited to Her Majesty under an order made under subsection 16(1) or 17(2), any person who claims an interest in the property, other than

(a) in the case of property forfeited under an order made under subsection 16(1), a person who was convicted, or discharged under section 730 of the

Criminal Code, of the designated substance offence in relation to which the property was forfeited,

(b) in the case of property forfeited pursuant to an order made under subsection 17(2), a person who was charged with the designated substance offence in relation to which the property was forfeited, or

(c) a person who acquired title to or a right of possession of the property from a person referred to in paragraph (a) or (b) under circumstances that give rise to a reasonable inference that the title or right was transferred from that person for the purpose of avoiding the forfeiture of the property,

may, within thirty days after the forfeiture, apply by notice in writing to a judge for an order under subsection (4).

(2) Fixing day for hearing — The judge to whom an application is made under subsection (1) shall fix a day not less than thirty days after the date of the filing of the application for the hearing of the application.

(3) Notice — An applicant shall serve a notice of the application made under subsection (1) and of the hearing of it on the Attorney General at least fifteen days before the day fixed for the hearing.

(4) Order declaring interest not affected by forfeiture — Where, on the hearing of an application made under subsection (1), the judge is satisfied that the applicant

(a) is not a person referred to in paragraph (1)(a), (b) or (c) and appears innocent of any complicity in any designated substance offence that resulted in the forfeiture of the property or of any collusion in relation to such an offence, and

(b) exercised all reasonable care to be satisfied that the property was not likely to have been used in connection with the commission of an unlawful act by the person who was permitted by the applicant to obtain possession of the property or from whom the applicant obtained possession or, where the applicant is a mortgagee or lienholder, by the mortgagor or lien-giver,

the judge may make an order declaring that the interest of the applicant is not affected by the forfeiture and declaring the nature and the extent or value of the interest.

(5) Appeal from order made under subsection (4) — An applicant or the Attorney General may appeal to the court of appeal from an order made under subsection (4), and the provisions of Part XXI of the *Criminal Code* with respect to procedure on appeals apply, with such modifications as the circumstances require, in respect of appeals under this subsection.

(6) Return of property — The Minister shall, on application made to the Minister by any person in respect of whom a judge has made an order under subsection (4), and where the periods with respect to the taking of appeals from that order have expired and any appeal from that order taken under subsection (5) has been determined, direct that

(a) the property, or the part of it to which the interest of the applicant relates, be returned to the applicant; or

(b) an amount equal to the value of the interest of the applicant, as declared in the order, be paid to the applicant.

2017, c. 7, s. 21

21. Appeals from orders under subsection 17(2) — Any person who, in their opinion, is aggrieved by an order made under subsection 17(2) may appeal from the order as if the order were an appeal against conviction or against a judgment or verdict of acquittal, as the case may be, under Part XXI of the *Criminal Code*, and that Part applies, with such modifications as the circumstances require, in respect of such an appeal.

22. Suspension of order pending appeal — Notwithstanding anything in this Act, operation of an order made in respect of property under subsection 16(1), 17(2) or 20(4) is suspended pending

(a) any application made in respect of the property under any of those provisions or any other provision of this or any other Act of Parliament that provides for restoration or forfeiture of the property, or

(b) any appeal taken from an order of forfeiture or restoration in respect of the property,

and the property shall not be disposed of or otherwise dealt with until thirty days have expired after an order is made under any of those provisions.

Division 2 — Controlled Substances, Precursors and Chemical Offence-related Property

[Heading amended 2017, c. 7, s. 22.]

[Heading repealed 2001, c. 32, s. 54.]

23. (1) Return — A peace officer, inspector or prescribed person who seizes, finds or otherwise acquires a controlled substance, precursor or chemical offence-related property may return it to the person who is its lawful owner or who is lawfully entitled to its possession if the peace officer, inspector or prescribed person is satisfied

(a) that there is no dispute as to who is the lawful owner or is lawfully entitled to possession of the substance, precursor or property; and

(b) that the continued detention of the substance, precursor or property is not required for the purposes of a preliminary inquiry, trial or other proceeding under this Act or any other Act of Parliament.

(2) Receipt — When the substance, precursor or property is returned, the peace officer, inspector or prescribed person shall obtain a receipt for it.

(3) Report by peace officer — In the case of a seizure made under section 11 of this Act, the *Criminal Code* or a power of seizure at common law, the peace officer shall make a report about the return to the justice who issued the warrant or another justice for the same territorial division or, if a warrant was not issued, a justice who would have had jurisdiction to issue a warrant.

2017, c. 7, s. 22

24. (1) Application for return — If a controlled substance, precursor or chemical offence-related property has been seized, found or otherwise acquired by a peace officer, inspector or prescribed person, any person may, within 60 days after the date of the seizure, finding or acquisition, on prior notification being given to the Attorney General in the prescribed manner, apply, by notice in writing to a justice in the jurisdiction in which it is being detained, for an order to return it to the person.

(2) Order to return as soon as practicable — If, on the hearing of an application made under subsection (1), a justice is satisfied that an applicant is the lawful owner or is lawfully entitled to possession of the substance, precursor or property and the Attorney General does not indicate that it or a portion of it may be required for the purposes of a preliminary inquiry, trial or other proceeding under this Act or any other Act of Parliament, the justice shall, subject to subsection (5), order that it or the portion be returned as soon as practicable to the applicant.

(3) Order to return at specified time — If, on the hearing of an application made under subsection (1), a justice is satisfied that an applicant is the lawful owner or is lawfully entitled to possession of the substance, precursor or property but the Attorney General indicates that it or a portion of it may be required for the purposes of a preliminary inquiry, trial or other proceeding under this Act or any other Act of Parliament, the justice shall, subject to subsection (5), order that it or the portion be returned to the applicant

(a) on the expiry of 180 days after the day on which the application was made, if no proceeding in relation to it has been commenced before that time; or

(b) on the final conclusion of the proceeding or any other proceeding in relation to it, if the applicant is not found guilty in those proceedings of an offence committed in relation to it.

(4) Forfeiture order — If, on the hearing of an application made under subsection (1), a justice is not satisfied that an applicant is the lawful owner or is lawfully entitled to possession of the substance, precursor or property, and it or a portion of it is not required for the purposes of a preliminary inquiry, trial or other proceeding under this Act or any other Act of Parliament, the justice shall order that it or the portion be forfeited to Her Majesty to be disposed of or otherwise dealt with in accordance with the regulations or, if there are no applicable regulations, in the manner that the Minister directs.

(5) Payment of compensation in lieu — If, on the hearing of an application made under subsection (1), a justice is satisfied that an applicant is the lawful owner or is lawfully entitled to possession of the substance, precursor or property, but it was disposed of or otherwise dealt with under section 26, the justice shall order that an amount equal to its value be paid to the applicant.

2017, c. 7, s. 22

25. Forfeiture if no application — If no application for the return of a controlled substance, precursor or chemical offence-related property has been made under subsection 24(1) within 60 days after the date of the seizure, finding or acquisition by a peace officer, inspector or prescribed person and it or a portion of it is not required for the purposes of a preliminary inquiry, trial or other proceeding under this Act or any other Act of Parliament, it or the portion is forfeited to Her Majesty and may be disposed of or otherwise dealt with in accordance with the regulations or, if there are no applicable regulations, in the manner that the Minister directs.

2017, c. 7, s. 22

26. Expedited disposition — If a precursor or chemical offence-related property — whose storage or handling poses a risk to health or safety — or a controlled substance, or a portion of any of them, is not required for the purposes of a preliminary inquiry, trial or other proceeding under this Act or any other Act of Parliament, it or the portion may be disposed of or otherwise dealt with by the Minister, a peace officer or a prescribed person in accordance with the regulations or, if there are no applicable regulations, in the manner that the Minister directs.

2017, c. 7, s. 22

27. Disposition following proceedings — Subject to section 24, if, in a preliminary inquiry, trial or other proceeding under this Act or any other Act of Parliament, the court before which the proceedings have been brought is satisfied that any controlled substance, precursor or chemical offence-related property that is the subject of proceedings before the court is no longer required by that court or any other court, the court

(a) shall

(i) if it is satisfied that the person from whom the substance, precursor or property was seized came into possession of it lawfully and continued to deal with it lawfully, order that it be returned to the person, or

(ii) if it is satisfied that possession of the substance, precursor or property by the person from whom it was seized is unlawful and the person who is the lawful owner or is lawfully entitled to its possession is known, order that it be returned to the person who is the lawful owner or is lawfully entitled to its possession; and

(b) may, if it is not satisfied that the substance, precursor or property should be returned under subparagraph (a)(i) or (ii) or if possession of it by the person from whom it was seized is unlawful and the person who is the lawful owner or is lawfully entitled to its possession is not known, order that it be forfeited to Her Majesty to be disposed of or otherwise dealt with in accordance with the regulations or, if there are no applicable regulations, in the manner that the Minister directs.

2017, c. 7, s. 23

28. Disposition with consent — If a controlled substance, precursor or chemical offence-related property has been seized, found or otherwise acquired by a peace officer, inspector or prescribed person and it or a portion of it is not required for the purposes of a preliminary inquiry, trial or other proceeding under this Act or any other Act of Parliament, the person who is its lawful owner may consent to its disposition, and when that consent is given, it or the portion is forfeited to Her Majesty and may be disposed of or otherwise dealt with in accordance with the regulations or, if there are no applicable regulations, in the manner that the Minister directs.

2017, c. 7, s. 24

29. (1) Report of disposition — Subject to the regulations, every peace officer, inspector or prescribed person who disposes of or otherwise deals with a controlled substance, precursor or chemical offence-related property under this Division shall, within 30 days, prepare a report setting out the following information and cause the report to be sent to the Minister:

(a) the substance, precursor or property;

(b) the amount of it that was disposed of or otherwise dealt with;

(c) the manner in which it was disposed of or otherwise dealt with;

(d) the date on which it was disposed of or otherwise dealt with;

(e) the name of the police force, agency or entity to which the peace officer, inspector or prescribed person belongs;

(f) the number of the file or police report related to the disposition of it or other dealing with it; and

(g) any other prescribed information.

(2) Interpretation — For the purposes of subsection (1), dealing with a controlled substance, precursor or chemical offence-related property by a peace officer includes using it to conduct an investigation or for training purposes.

2017, c. 7, s. 24

PART IV — ADMINISTRATION AND COMPLIANCE (SS. 30–32)

Inspectors

30. (1) Designation of inspectors — The Minister may designate, in accordance with the regulations made pursuant to paragraph 55(1)(n), any person as an inspector for the purposes of this Act and the regulations.

(2) Certificate — Every inspector shall be provided with a certificate of designation in a form established by the Minister and, on entering any place under subsection 31(1), shall, on request, produce the certificate to the person in charge of the place.

2015, c. 22, s. 2; 2017, c. 7, s. 25

31. (1) Powers of inspector — Subject to subsection (2), an inspector may, for a purpose related to verifying compliance or preventing non-compliance with the provisions of this Act or the regulations, enter any place, including a conveyance, referred to in subsection (1.1) and may for that purpose

(a) open and examine any receptacle or package found in that place in which a controlled substance, precursor or designated device may be found;

(b) examine any thing found in that place that is used or may be capable of being used for the production, preservation, packaging or storage of a controlled substance or a precursor;

(c) examine any labels or advertising material or records, books, electronic data or other documents found in that place with respect to any controlled substance, precursor, or designated device other than the records of the medical condition of persons, and make copies thereof or take extracts therefrom;

(d) use or cause to be used any computer system at that place to examine any electronic data referred to in paragraph (c);

(e) reproduce any document from any electronic data referred to in paragraph (c) or cause it to be reproduced, in the form of a printout or other output;

(f) take the labels or advertising material or records, books or other documents referred to in paragraph (c) or the printout or other output referred to in paragraph (e) for examination or copying;

(g) use or cause to be used any copying equipment at that place to make copies of any document;

(g.1) take photographs and make recordings and sketches;

(h) examine any substance found in that place and take, for the purpose of analysis, such samples thereof as are reasonably required;

(i) seize and detain, in accordance with this Part, any controlled substance, precursor, designated device or conveyance found in that place the seizure and detention of which the inspector believes on reasonable grounds are necessary;

(j) order the owner or person having possession, care or control of any controlled substance, precursor, designated device or other thing to which the provisions of this Act or the regulations apply that is found in that place to move it or, for any time that may be necessary, not to move it or to restrict its movement;

(k) order the owner or person having possession, care or control of any conveyance that is found in that place and that the inspector believes on reasonable grounds contains a controlled substance, precursor or designated device to stop the conveyance, to move it or, for any time that may be necessary, not to move it or to restrict its movement;

(l) order any person in that place to establish their identity to the inspector's satisfaction; and

(m) order a person who, at that place, conducts an activity to which the provisions of this Act or the regulations apply to stop or start the activity.

(1.1) Place — For the purposes of subsection (1), the inspector may only enter a place in which they believe on reasonable grounds

(a) a controlled substance, precursor, designated device or document relating to the administration of this Act or the regulations is located;

(b) an activity could be conducted under a licence, permit, authorization or exemption that is under consideration by the Minister;

(c) an activity to which the provisions of this Act or the regulations apply is being conducted; or

(d) an activity was being conducted under a licence, permit, authorization or exemption before the expiry or revocation of the licence, permit, authorization or exemption, in which case the inspector may enter the place only within 45 days after the day on which it expired or was revoked.

(1.2) Means of telecommunication — For the purposes of subsections (1) and (1.1), an inspector is considered to have entered a place when they access it remotely by a means of telecommunication.

(1.3) Limitation — access by means of telecommunication — An inspector who enters remotely, by a means of telecommunication, a place that is not accessible to the public must do so with the knowledge of the owner or person in charge of the place and only for the period necessary for any purpose referred to in subsection (1).

(1.4) Person accompanying inspector — An inspector may be accompanied by any other person that the inspector believes is necessary to help them exercise their powers or perform their duties or functions under this section.

(1.5) Entering private property — An inspector and any person accompanying them may enter and pass through private property, other than a dwelling-house on that property, in order to gain entry to a place referred to in subsection (1.1).

(2) Warrant to enter dwelling-house — In the case of a dwelling-house, an inspector may enter it only with the consent of an occupant or under the authority of a warrant issued under subsection (3).

(3) Authority to issue warrant — A justice may, on *ex parte* application, issue a warrant authorizing the inspector named in it to enter a place and exercise any of the powers mentioned in paragraphs (1)(a) to (m), subject to any conditions that are specified in the warrant, if the justice is satisfied by information on oath that

(a) the place is a dwelling-house but otherwise meets the conditions for entry described in subsections (1) and (1.1);

(b) entry to the dwelling-house is necessary for the purpose of verifying compliance or preventing non-compliance with the provisions of this Act or the regulations; and

(c) entry to the dwelling-house has been refused or there are reasonable grounds to believe that entry will be refused.

(4) Use of force — In executing a warrant issued under subsection (3), an inspector shall not use force unless the inspector is accompanied by a peace officer and the use of force is specifically authorized in the warrant.

(5) **Assistance to inspector** — The owner or other person in charge of a place entered by an inspector and every person found there shall give the inspector all reasonable assistance in that person's power and provide the inspector with any information that the inspector may reasonably require.

(6) **Storage** — Anything that is seized and detained by an inspector under this section may, at the inspector's discretion, be kept or stored at the place where it was seized or, at the inspector's direction, be removed to any other proper place.

(7) **Notice** — An inspector who seizes anything under this section shall take any measures that are reasonable in the circumstances to give to the owner or other person in charge of the place where the seizure occurred notice of the seizure and of the location where the thing is being kept or stored.

(8) **Return by inspector** — If an inspector determines that to verify compliance or prevent non-compliance with the provisions of this Act or the regulations it is no longer necessary to detain anything seized by the inspector under this section, the inspector shall notify in writing the owner or other person in charge of the place where the seizure occurred of that determination and, on being issued a receipt for it, shall return the thing to that person.

(9) **Return or disposition by Minister** — If a period of 120 days has elapsed after the date of a seizure under this section and the thing has not been returned, disposed of or otherwise dealt with in accordance with subsection (8) or any of sections 24 to 27, it shall be returned, disposed of or otherwise dealt with in accordance with the regulations or, if there are no applicable regulations, in the manner that the Minister directs.

2015, c. 22, s. 3; 2017, c. 7, s. 26(1), (3)–(8)

32. (1) **Obstructing inspector** — No person shall, by act or omission, obstruct an inspector who is engaged in the exercise of their powers or the performance of their duties or functions under this Act or the regulations.

(2) **False statements** — No person shall knowingly make any false or misleading statement verbally or in writing to an inspector who is engaged in the exercise of their powers or the performance of their duties or functions under this Act or the regulations.

(3) **Interference** — No person shall, without the authority of an inspector, remove, alter or interfere in any way with anything seized, detained or taken under section 31.

2017, c. 7, s. 27(1), (2)

PART V — ADMINISTRATIVE ORDERS FOR CONTRAVENTIONS OF DESIGNATED REGULATIONS (SS. 33–43)

[Heading amended to "Administrative Monetary Penalties", 2017, c. 7, s. 28. Not in force at date of publication.]

Violation

[Heading added 2017, c. 7, s. 28. Not in force at date of publication.]

33. Designation of regulations — The Governor in Council may, by regulation, designate any regulation made under this Act (in this Part referred to as a **"designated regulation"**) as a regulation the contravention of which shall be dealt with under this Part.

Proposed Amendment — 33

33. Commission of violation — Every person who contravenes a provision designated by regulations made under paragraph 34(1)(a), or contravenes an order made under section 45.1 or 45.2 or reviewed under section 45.4, commits a violation and is liable to the penalty established in accordance with the provisions of this Act and the regulations.

2017, c. 7, s. 28 [Not in force at date of publication.]

Powers of the Governor in Council and the Minister

[Heading added 2017, c. 7, s. 28. Not in force at date of publication.]

34. Contravention of designated regulation — Where the Minister has reasonable grounds to believe that a person has contravened a designated regulation, the Minister shall

(a) in the prescribed manner, serve a notice to appear on the person; and

(b) send a copy of the notice to appear to an adjudicator and direct the adjudicator to conduct a hearing to determine whether the contravention has occurred and to notify the Minister of the adjudicator's determination.

Proposed Amendment — 34

34. (1) Regulations — The Governor in Council may make regulations

(a) designating as a violation that may be proceeded with in accordance with this Act the contravention of any specified provision of this Act — except a provision of Part I — or the regulations;

(b) fixing a penalty, or a range of penalties, in respect of each violation;

(c) classifying each violation as a minor violation, a serious violation or a very serious violation; and

(d) respecting the circumstances under which, the criteria by which and the manner in which a penalty may be increased or reduced, including a reduction in the amount that is provided for in a compliance agreement.

(2) Maximum penalty — The maximum penalty for a violation is $30,000.

Proposed Amendment — Conditional Amendment — 34(2)

On the coming into force of both S.C. 2017, c. 7, s. 28 [Not in force at date of publication.] and S.C. 2018, c. 16, s. 199(2) [In force June 21, 2018.], subsection 34(2) is replaced by the following:

(2) Maximum penalty — The maximum penalty for a violation is $1,000,000.

2018, c. 16, s. 199(1) [Conditions not yet satisfied.]
2017, c. 7, s. 28 [Not in force at date of publication.]

35. (1) Interim order — Where the Minister has reasonable grounds to believe that a person has contravened a designated regulation and the Minister is of the opinion that, as a result of that contravention, there is a substantial risk of immediate danger to the health or safety of any person, the Minister may, without giving prior notice to the person believed to have contravened the designated regulation, make an interim order in respect of the person

(a) prohibiting the person from doing anything that the person would otherwise be permitted to do under their licence, permit or authorization, or

(b) subjecting the doing of anything under the designated regulation by the person to the terms and conditions specified in the interim order,

and may, for that purpose, suspend, cancel or amend the licence, permit or authorization issued or granted to the person or take any other measures set out in the regulations.

(2) Idem — Where the Minister makes an interim order under subsection (1), the Minister shall forthwith

(a) in the prescribed manner, serve the interim order on the person;

(b) in the prescribed manner, serve a notice to appear on the person; and

(c) send a copy of the interim order and the notice to appear to an adjudicator and direct the adjudicator to conduct a hearing to determine whether the contravention has occurred and to notify the Minister of the adjudicator's determination.

Proposed Amendment — 35

35. Criteria for penalty — Unless a penalty is fixed under paragraph 34(1)(b), the amount of a penalty shall, in each case, be determined taking into account

(a) the history of compliance with the provisions of this Act or the regulations by the person who committed the violation;

(b) the harm to public health or safety that resulted or could have resulted from the violation;

(c) whether the person made reasonable efforts to mitigate or reverse the violation's effects;

(d) whether the person derived any competitive or economic benefit from the violation; and

(e) any other prescribed criteria.

2017, c. 7, s. 28 [Not in force at date of publication.]

36. (1) Hearing by adjudicator — Where an adjudicator receives from the Minister a copy of a notice to appear under paragraph 34(b) or 35(2)(c), the adjudicator shall conduct a hearing on a date to be fixed by the adjudicator at the request of the person on whom the notice was served, on two days notice being given to the adjudicator, which hearing date may not

(a) in the case of a notice served under paragraph 34(a), be less than thirty days, or more than forty-five days, after the day of service of the notice; or

(b) in the case of a notice served under paragraph 35(2)(b), be less than three days, or more than forty-five days, after the day of service of the notice.

(2) Change of hearing date — Where the adjudicator is unable to conduct a hearing on the date referred to in subsection (1), the adjudicator shall forthwith notify the person and fix, for the purpose of holding the hearing, the earliest possible date to which the adjudicator and the person agree.

(3) Proceedings on default — Where an adjudicator has received a copy of a notice to appear referred to in subsection (1) and where the person on whom the notice is served has not requested a date for a hearing within forty-five days after the notice was served on that person, or where the person, having requested a hearing, fails to appear for the hearing, the adjudicator shall proceed to make a determination in the absence of the person.

(4) Time and place — An adjudicator may, subject to the regulations, determine the time and place of any hearing or other proceeding under this Part.

Proposed Amendment — 36

36. Notices of violation — The Minister may

(a) designate individuals, or classes of individuals, who are authorized to issue notices of violation; and

(b) establish, in respect of each violation, a short-form description to be used in notices of violation.

2017, c. 7, s. 28 [Not in force at date of publication.]

Proceedings

[Heading added 2017, c. 7, s. 28. Not in force at date of publication.]

37. Notice to appear — A notice to appear served on a person under paragraph 34(a) or 35(2)(b) shall

(a) specify the designated regulation that the Minister believes the person has contravened;

(b) state the grounds on which the Minister believes the contravention has occurred;

(c) state that the matter has been referred to an adjudicator for a hearing to be conducted on a date within the applicable period described in paragraph 36(1)(a) or (b); and

(d) set out such other information as is prescribed.

Proposed Amendment — 37

37. (1) Issuance of notice of violation — If a person who is designated under paragraph 36(a) believes on reasonable grounds that a person has committed a violation, the designated person may issue, and shall provide the person with, a notice of violation that

(a) sets out the person's name;

(b) identifies the alleged violation;

(c) sets out the penalty for the violation that the person is liable to pay; and

(d) sets out the particulars concerning the time and manner of payment.

(2) Summary of rights — A notice of violation shall clearly summarize, in plain language, the named person's rights and obligations under this section and sections 38 to 43.7, including the right to have the acts or omissions that constitute the alleged violation or the amount of the penalty reviewed and the procedure for requesting that review.

2017, c. 7, s. 28 [Not in force at date of publication.]

Penalties

[Heading added 2017, c. 7, s. 28. Not in force at date of publication.]

38. Proof of service — Proof of service of any notice, order or interim order under this Part shall be given in the prescribed manner.

Proposed Amendment — 38

38. (1) Payment — If the person named in the notice pays, in the prescribed time and manner, the amount of the penalty,

(a) they are deemed to have committed the violation in respect of which the amount is paid;

(b) the Minister shall accept that amount as complete satisfaction of the penalty; and

(c) the proceedings commenced in respect of the violation under section 37 are ended.

(2) Alternatives to payment — Instead of paying the penalty set out in a notice of violation, the person named in the notice may, in the prescribed time and manner,

(a) if the penalty is $5,000 or more, request to enter into a compliance agreement with the Minister that ensures the person's compliance with the order or the provision to which the violation relates; or

(b) request a review by the Minister of the acts or omissions that constitute the alleged violation or the amount of the penalty.

(3) Deeming — If the person named in the notice of violation does not pay the penalty in the prescribed time and manner and does not exercise any right referred to in subsection (2) in the prescribed time and manner, they are deemed to have committed the violation identified in the notice.

2017, c. 7, s. 28 [Not in force at date of publication.]

Compliance Agreements

[Heading added 2017, c. 7, s. 28. Not in force at date of publication.]

39. Powers of adjudicator — For the purposes of this Act, an adjudicator has and may exercise the powers of a person appointed as a commissioner under Part I of the *Inquiries Act*.

Proposed Amendment — 39

39. (1) Compliance agreements — After considering a request under paragraph 38(2)(a), the Minister may enter into a compliance agreement, as described in that paragraph, with the person making the request on any terms and conditions that are satisfactory to the Minister. The terms and conditions may

(a) include a provision for the giving of reasonable security, in a form and in an amount satisfactory to the Minister, as a guarantee that the person will comply with the compliance agreement; and

(b) provide for the reduction, in whole or in part, of the penalty for the violation.

(2) Deeming — A person who enters into a compliance agreement with the Minister is, on doing so, deemed to have committed the violation in respect of which the compliance agreement was entered into.

(3) Notice of compliance — If the Minister is satisfied that a person who has entered into a compliance agreement has complied with it, the Minister shall cause a notice to that effect to be provided to the person, at which time

(a) the proceedings commenced in respect of the violation under section 37 are ended; and

(b) any security given by the person under the compliance agreement shall be returned to the person.

(4) Notice of default — If the Minister is of the opinion that a person who has entered into a compliance agreement has not complied with it, the Minister shall cause a notice of default to be provided to the person to the effect that

(a) instead of the penalty set out in the notice of violation in respect of which the compliance agreement was entered into, the person is liable to pay, in the prescribed time and manner, twice the amount of that penalty, and, for greater certainty, subsection 34(2) does not apply in respect of that amount; or

(b) the security, if any, given by the person under the compliance agreement shall be forfeited to Her Majesty in right of Canada.

(5) Effect of notice of default — Once provided with the notice of default, the person may not deduct from the amount set out in the notice any amount that they spent under the compliance agreement and

(a) the person is liable to pay the amount set out in the notice; or

(b) if the notice provides for the forfeiture of the security given under the compliance agreement, that security is forfeited to Her Majesty in right of Canada and the proceedings commenced in respect of the violation under section 37 are ended.

(6) Effect of payment — If a person pays the amount set out in the notice of default in the prescribed time and manner,

(a) the Minister shall accept the amount as complete satisfaction of the amount owing; and

(b) the proceedings commenced in respect of the violation under section 37 are ended.

2017, c. 7, s. 28 [Not in force at date of publication.]

40. Hearing procedure — An adjudicator shall deal with all matters as informally and expeditiously as the circumstances and considerations of fairness and natural justice permit.

Proposed Amendment — 40

40. (1) Refusal to enter into compliance agreement — If the Minister refuses to enter into a compliance agreement requested under paragraph 38(2)(a), the person who made the request is liable to pay the amount of the penalty in the prescribed time and manner.

(2) Effect of payment — If a person pays the amount referred to in subsection (1),

(a) they are deemed to have committed the violation in respect of which the payment is made;

(b) the Minister shall accept the amount as complete satisfaction of the penalty; and

(c) the proceedings commenced in respect of the violation under section 37 are ended.

(3) Deeming — If a person does not pay the amount referred to in subsection (1) in the prescribed time and manner, they are deemed to have committed the violation identified in the notice of violation.

2017, c. 7, s. 28 [Not in force at date of publication.]

Review by the Minister

[Heading added 2017, c. 7, s. 28. Not in force at date of publication.]

41. (1) Determination by adjudicator — An adjudicator shall, after the conclusion of a hearing referred to in subsection 36(1) or a proceeding referred to in subsection 36(3), within the prescribed time, make a determination that the person who is the subject of the hearing or proceeding contravened or did not contravene the designated regulation.

(2) Notice of determination — Where an adjudicator has made a determination under subsection (1), the adjudicator shall

(a) forthwith notify the person and the Minister of the adjudicator's determination and the reasons; and

(b) where the adjudicator has determined that the person has contravened the designated regulation, notify the person of the opportunity to make representations to the Minister in writing in accordance with the regulations and within the prescribed time.

(3) Ministerial orders — Where an adjudicator has made a determination referred to in paragraph (2)(b) and the Minister has considered the determination and any representations referred to in that paragraph, the Minister shall forthwith make an order

(a) prohibiting the person from doing anything that they would, if they were in compliance with the designated regulation, be permitted to do, or

(b) subjecting the doing of anything under the designated regulation by the person to the terms and conditions specified in the order,

and may, for that purpose, suspend, cancel or amend any licence, permit or authorization issued or granted to the person under the regulations or take any other measures set out in the regulations.

(4) Ministerial orders — An order made under subsection (3) shall be served on the person to whom it is directed in the prescribed manner.

Proposed Amendment — 41

41. (1) Review — facts — On completion of a review requested under paragraph 38(2)(b) with respect to the acts or omissions that constitute the alleged violation, the Minister shall determine whether the person who requested the review committed the violation. If the Minister determines that the person committed the violation but that the amount of the penalty was not established in accordance with the provisions of this Act and the regulations, the Minister shall correct the amount.

(2) **Violation not committed — effect** — If the Minister determines under subsection (1) that the person who requested the review did not commit the violation, the proceedings commenced in respect of it under section 37 are ended.

(3) **Review — penalty** — On completion of a review requested under paragraph 38(2)(b) with respect to the amount of the penalty, the Minister shall determine whether the amount of the penalty was established in accordance with the provisions of this Act and the regulations and, if not, the Minister shall correct the amount.

(4) **Notice of decision** — The Minister shall cause a notice of any decision made under subsection (1) or (3) to be provided to the person who requested the review.

(5) **Payment** — The person is liable to pay, in the prescribed time and manner, the amount of the penalty that is confirmed or corrected in the Minister's decision made under subsection (1) or (3).

(6) **Effect of payment** — If a person pays the amount referred to in subsection (5),

(a) the Minister shall accept the amount as complete satisfaction of the penalty; and

(b) the proceedings commenced in respect of the violation under section 37 are ended.

(7) **Written evidence and submissions** — The Minister shall consider only written evidence and written submissions in determining whether a person committed a violation or whether the amount of a penalty was established in accordance with the provisions of this Act and the regulations.

2017, c. 7, s. 28 [Not in force at date of publication.]

Enforcement

[Heading added 2017, c. 7, s. 28. Not in force at date of publication.]

42. (1) **Effect of order** — An interim order made under subsection 35(1) and an order made under subsection 41(3) have effect from the time that they are served on the person to whom they are directed.

(2) **Cessation of effect** — An interim order that was made in respect of a person believed to have contravened a designated regulation ceases to have effect

(a) where the Minister makes an order under subsection 41(3), at the time the order is served on the person; and

(b) where an adjudicator has determined that the person did not contravene the designated regulation, at the time the adjudicator makes the determination.

(3) **Application to revoke order** — A person in respect of whom an order was made under subsection 41(3) may make an application in writing to the Minister in accordance with the regulations to revoke the order.

(4) **Revocation of order** — The Minister may, in the prescribed circumstances, revoke, in whole or in part, any order made under subsection 41(3).

Proposed Amendment — 42

42. (1) **Debts to Her Majesty** — The following amounts constitute debts due to Her Majesty in right of Canada that may be recovered in the Federal Court:

(a) the amount of a penalty, from the time the notice of violation setting out the penalty is provided;

(b) every amount set out in a compliance agreement entered into with the Minister under subsection 39(1), from the time the compliance agreement is entered into;

(c) the amount set out in a notice of default referred to in subsection 39(4), from the time the notice is provided; and

(d) the amount of a penalty as set out in a decision of the Minister made under subsection 41(1) or (3), from the time the notice of that decision is provided.

(2) **Time limit** — No proceedings to recover a debt referred to in subsection (1) may be commenced later than five years after the debt became payable.

(3) **Debt final** — A debt referred to in subsection (1) is final and not subject to review or to be restrained, prohibited, removed, set aside or otherwise dealt with except to the extent and in the manner provided by sections 38 to 41.

(4) [Repealed 2017, c. 7, s. 28. Not in force at date of publication.]

2017, c. 7, s. 28 [Not in force at date of publication.]

43. **Offence for contravention of order** — Every person commits an offence who contravenes an order or an interim order made under this Part.

Proposed Amendment — 43

43. (1) **Certificate of default** — Any debt referred to in subsection 42(1) in respect of which there is a default of payment, or the part of any such debt that has not been paid, may be certified by the Minister.

(2) **Judgments** — On production to the Federal Court, the certificate shall be registered in that Court and, when registered, has the same force and effect, and all proceedings may be taken on the certificate, as if it were a judgment obtained in that Court for a debt of the amount specified in it and all reasonable costs and charges associated with the registration of the certificate.

2017, c. 7, s. 28 [Not in force at date of publication.]

Proposed Addition — 43.1–43.91

Rules About Violations

[Heading added 2017, c. 7, s. 28. Not in force at date of publication.]

43.1 (1) Certain defences not available — A person named in a notice of violation does not have a defence by reason that the person

(a) exercised due diligence to prevent the violation; or

(b) reasonably and honestly believed in the existence of facts that, if true, would exonerate the person.

(2) Common law principles — Every rule and principle of the common law that renders any circumstance a justification or excuse in relation to a charge for an offence under this Act applies in respect of a violation to the extent that it is not inconsistent with this Act.

2017, c. 7, s. 28 [Not in force at date of publication.]

43.2 Burden of proof — In every case when the facts of a violation are reviewed by the Minister, he or she shall determine, on a balance of probabilities, whether the person named in the notice of violation committed the violation identified in the notice.

2017, c. 7, s. 28 [Not in force at date of publication.]

43.3 Violation by corporate officers, etc. — If a person other than an individual commits a violation under this Act, any of the person's directors, officers, agents or mandataries who directed, authorized, assented to, acquiesced in or participated in the commission of the violation is a party to and liable for the violation whether or not the person who actually committed the violation is proceeded against under this Act.

2017, c. 7, s. 28 [Not in force at date of publication.]

43.4 Vicarious liability — acts of employees and agents — A person is liable for a violation that is committed by any employee, agent or mandatary of the person acting in the course of the employee's employment or the scope of the agent or mandatary's authority, whether or not the employee, agent or mandatary who actually committed the violation is identified or proceeded against under this Act.

2017, c. 7, s. 28 [Not in force at date of publication.]

43.5 Continuing violation — A violation that is continued on more than one day constitutes a separate violation in respect of each day on which it is continued.

2017, c. 7, s. 28 [Not in force at date of publication.]

Other Provisions

[Heading added 2017, c. 7, s. 28. Not in force at date of publication.]

43.6 Evidence — In any proceeding in respect of a violation or a prosecution for an offence, a notice of violation purporting to be issued under this Act is admissible in evidence without proof of the signature or official character of the person appearing to have signed the notice of violation.

2017, c. 7, s. 28 [Not in force at date of publication.]

43.7 Time limit — Proceedings in respect of a violation shall not be commenced later than six months after the Minister becomes aware of the acts or omissions that constitute the alleged violation.

2017, c. 7, s. 28 [Not in force at date of publication.]

43.8 How act or omission may be proceeded with — If an act or omission may be proceeded with either as a violation or as an offence, proceeding in one manner precludes proceeding in the other.

2017, c. 7, s. 28 [Not in force at date of publication.]

43.9 Certification by Minister — A document appearing to have been issued by the Minister, certifying the day on which the acts or omissions that constitute the alleged violation became known to the Minister, is admissible in evidence without proof of the signature or official character of the person appearing to have signed the document and, in the absence of evidence to the contrary, is proof that the Minister became aware of the acts or omissions on that day.

2017, c. 7, s. 28 [Not in force at date of publication.]

43.91 Publication of information — The Minister may, for the purpose of encouraging compliance with the provisions of this Act and the regulations, publish information about any violation after proceedings in respect of it are ended.

2017, c. 7, s. 28 [Not in force at date of publication.]

PART VI — GENERAL (SS. 44–60)

Analysis

44. Designation of Analysts — The Minister may designate, in accordance with the regulations made pursuant to paragraph 55(1)(o), any person as an analyst for the purposes of this Act and the regulations.

45. (1) Analysis — A peace officer, inspector or prescribed person may submit to an analyst for analysis or examination any substance or sample of it taken by the peace officer, inspector or prescribed person.

(2) Report — An analyst who has made an analysis or examination under subsection (1) may prepare a certificate or report stating that the analyst has analysed or examined a substance or a sample thereof and setting out the results of the analysis or examination.

2017, c. 7, s. 29

Ministerial Orders

[Heading added 2017, c. 7, s. 30.]

45.1 Provision of information — The Minister may, by order, require a person who is authorized under this Act to conduct activities in relation to controlled substances or precursors or a person who imports designated devices to provide the Minister, in the time and manner that the Minister specifies, with any information respecting those activities that the Minister considers necessary

Proposed Amendment — 45.1 opening words

45.1 Provision of information — The Minister may, by order, require a person who is authorized under this Act to conduct activities in relation to controlled substances or precursors, who imports designated devices or who conducts other activities referred to in section 46.4 to provide the Minister, in the time and manner that the Minister specifies, with any information respecting those activities that the Minister considers necessary

2017, c. 7, s. 31 [Not in force at date of publication.]

(a) to verify compliance or prevent non-compliance with the provisions of this Act or the regulations; or

(b) to address an issue of public health or safety.

2017, c. 7, s. 30

45.2 Measures — The Minister may, by order, require a person who is authorized under this Act to conduct activities in relation to controlled substances or precursors to take measures, in the time and manner that the Minister specifies, to prevent non-compliance with the provisions of this Act or the regulations or, if the Minister has reasonable grounds to believe that there is such non-compliance, to remedy it.

Proposed Amendment — 45.2

45.2 Measures — The Minister may, by order, require a person who is authorized under this Act to conduct activities in relation to controlled substances or precursors or who conducts activities referred to in section 46.4 in relation to designated devices, to take measures, in the time and manner that the Minister specifies, to prevent non-compliance with the provisions of this Act or the regulations or, if the Minister has reasonable grounds to believe that there is such non-compliance, to remedy it.

2017, c. 7, s. 32 [Not in force at date of publication.]

2017, c. 7, s. 30

45.3 Review officer — The Minister may designate any qualified individual or class of qualified individuals as review officers for the purpose of reviewing orders under section 45.4.

2017, c. 7, s. 30

45.4 (1) Request for review — Subject to any other provision of this section, an order that is made under section 45.1 or 45.2 shall be reviewed on the written request of the person who was ordered to provide information or to take measures — but only on grounds that involve questions of fact alone or questions of mixed law and fact — by a review officer other than the individual who made the order.

(2) Contents of and time for making request — The request shall state the grounds for review and set out the evidence — including evidence that was not considered by the individual who made the order — that supports those grounds and the decision that is sought. It shall be provided to the Minister within seven days after the day on which the order was provided.

(3) No authority to review — The review is not to be done if the request does not comply with subsection (2) or is frivolous, vexatious or not made in good faith.

(4) Reasons for refusal — The person who made the request shall, without delay, be notified in writing of the reasons for not doing the review.

(5) Review initiated by review officer — A review officer — other than the individual who made the order — may review an order, whether or not a request is made under subsection (1).

(6) Order in effect — An order continues to apply during a review unless the review officer decides otherwise.

(7) Completion of review — A review officer shall complete the review no later than 30 days after the day on which the request is provided to the Minister.

(8) Extension of period for review — The review officer may extend the review period by no more than 30 days if they are of the opinion that more time is required to complete the review. They may extend the review period more than once.

(9) Reasons for extension — If the review period is extended, the person who made the request shall, without delay, be notified in writing of the reasons for extending it.

(10) Decision on completion of review — On completion of a review, the review officer shall confirm, amend, terminate or cancel the order.

(11) Written notice — The person who made the request or, if there is no request, the person who was ordered to provide information or to take measures shall, without delay, be notified in writing of the reasons for the review officer's decision under subsection (10).

(12) Effect of amendment — An order that is amended is subject to review under this section.

2017, c. 7, s. 30

45.5 Statutory Instruments Act — The *Statutory Instruments Act* does not apply in respect of an order made under section 45.1 or 45.2.

2017, c. 7, s. 30

Offence and Punishment

46. Penalty — Every person who contravenes a provision of this Act for which punishment is not otherwise provided, a provision of a regulation or an order made under section 45.1 or 45.2

(a) is guilty of an indictable offence and liable to a fine of not more than $5,000,000 or to imprisonment for a term not exceeding three years, or to both; or

(b) is guilty of an offence punishable on summary conviction and liable, for a first offence, to a fine of not more than $250,000 or imprisonment for a term of not more than six months, or to both, and, for any subsequent offence, to a fine of not more than $500,000 or imprisonment for a term of not more than 18 months, or to both.

2017, c. 7, s. 33; 2018, c. 16, s. 200

Prohibitions

[Heading added 2017, c. 7, s. 34.]

46.1 Offence of making false or deceptive statements — No person shall knowingly make, or participate in, assent to or acquiesce in the making of, a false or misleading statement in any book, record, return or other document however recorded, required to be maintained, made or furnished under this Act or the regulations.

2017, c. 7, s. 34

46.2 Compliance with terms and conditions — The holder of a licence, permit, authorization or exemption shall comply with its terms and conditions.

2017, c. 7, s. 34

46.3 (1) Importation of designated device — No person shall import into Canada a designated device unless they register the importation with the Minister.

Proposed Amendment — 46.3(1)

(1) Importation of designated device — No person shall import into Canada a designated device unless they register the importation with the Minister and the person imports it in accordance with the regulations.

2017, c. 7, s. 35(1) [Not in force at date of publication.]

(2) Information for registration — The following information shall be submitted to the Minister for the purpose of registering the importation of a designated device:

(a) the name of the person importing the designated device or, if the person is a corporation, the corporate name and any other name registered with a province, under which the person carries out its activities or identifies itself;

(b) the person's address or, if the person is a corporation, the address of its primary place of business in Canada;

(c) a description of the designated device, including the model number, serial number, and the brand name or trademark associated with it, if any;

(d) the address where the designated device will be delivered as well as the street address of the premises where it will be used by the person importing it;

(e) the name of the customs office where the importation is anticipated; and

Proposed Amendment — 46.3(2)(e)

(e) the name of the customs office where the importation is anticipated;

2017, c. 7, s. 35(2) [Not in force at date of publication.]

(f) the anticipated date of importation.

Proposed Amendment — 46.3(2)(f)

(f) the anticipated date of importation; and

2017, c. 7, s. 35(2) [Not in force at date of publication.]

Proposed Addition — 46.3(2)(g)

(g) any other prescribed information.

2017, c. 7, s. 35(2) [Not in force at date of publication.]

(3) **Registration** — After the Minister receives the information, the Minister shall register the importation and provide proof of the registration to the person importing the designated device.

(4) **Proof of registration** — The person importing the designated device shall provide the proof of the registration of its importation to the customs office at the time specified by the regulations or, if no time is specified by the regulations, at the time of importation.

(5) **Refusal or cancellation** — The Minister may refuse to register or cancel the registration of the importation of a designated device if the Minister believes on reasonable grounds that false or misleading information was provided, or it is necessary to do so to protect public health or safety or for any other prescribed reason.

(6) **Disclosure of information — designated device** — The Minister is authorized to disclose to the Canada Border Services Agency or an **"officer"**, as defined in section 2(1) of the *Customs Act*, any information submitted under subsection (2) for the purpose of verifying compliance with the provisions of this Act or the regulations.

(7) **Disclosure of information to police force** — The Minister is authorized to disclose any information submitted under subsection (2) to a Canadian police force or a member of a Canadian police force who requests the information in the course of an investigation under this Act.

2017, c. 7, s. 34

Evidence and Procedure

Proposed Addition — 46.4

46.4 Designated device — prescribed activity — No person shall conduct a prescribed activity in relation to a designated device except in accordance with the regulations.

2017, c. 7, s. 36 [Not in force at date of publication.]

47. (1) Time limit — No summary conviction proceedings in respect of an offence under subsection 4(2) or 32(2) or the regulations or in respect of a contravention of an order made under section 45.1 or 45.2 shall be commenced after the expiry of one year after the time when the subject matter of the proceedings arose.

(2) Venue — Proceedings in respect of a contravention of any provision of this Act or the regulations or of an order made under section 45.1 or 45.2 may be held in the place where the offence was committed or where the subject matter of the proceedings arose or in any place where the accused is apprehended or happens to be located.

2017, c. 7, s. 37

48. (1) Burden of proving exception, etc. — No exception, exemption, excuse or qualification prescribed by law is required to be set out or negatived, as the case may be, in an information or indictment for an offence under this Act or the regulations or under section 463, 464 or 465 of the *Criminal Code* in respect of such an offence.

(2) Burden of proving exception, etc. — In any prosecution under this Act, the prosecutor is not required, except by way of rebuttal, to prove that a certificate, licence, permit or other qualification does not operate in favour of the accused, whether or not the qualification is set out in the information or indictment.

49. (1) Copies of documents — A copy of any document filed with a department, ministry, agency, municipality or other body established by or pursuant to a law of a province, or of any statement containing information from the records kept by any such department, ministry, agency, municipality or body, purporting to be certified by any official having custody of that document or those records, is admissible in evidence in any prosecution for an offence referred to in subsection 48(1) and, in the absence of evidence to the contrary, is proof of the facts contained in that document or statement, without proof of the signature or official character of the person purporting to have certified it.

(2) Authentication — For the purposes of subsection (1), an engraved, lithographed, photocopied, photographed, printed or otherwise electronically or mechanically reproduced facsimile signature of an official referred to in that subsection is sufficient authentication of any copy referred to in that subsection.

(3) Evidence inadmissible under this section — Nothing in subsection (1) renders admissible in evidence in any legal proceeding such part of any record as is proved to be a record made in the course of an investigation or inquiry.

50. (1) Certificate issued under regulations — Subject to subsection (2), any certificate or other document issued under regulations made under paragraph 55(2)(c) or (2.1)(c) is admissible in evidence in a preliminary inquiry, trial or other proceeding under this or any other Act of Parliament and, in the absence of evidence to the contrary, is proof that the certificate or other document was validly issued and of the facts contained in it, without proof of the signature or official character of the person purporting to have certified it.

(2) Certificate issued pursuant to regulations — The defence may, with leave of the court, require that the person who issued the certificate or other document

(a) produce an affidavit or solemn declaration attesting to any of the matters deemed to be proved under subsection (1); or

(b) appear before the court for examination or cross-examination in respect of the issuance of the certificate or other document.

2018, c. 16, s. 201

51. (1) Certificate or report of analyst — A certificate or report prepared by an analyst under subsection 45(2) is admissible in evidence in any prosecution for an offence under this Act or any other Act of Parliament and, in the absence of evidence to the contrary, is proof of the statements set out in the certificate or report, without proof of the signature or official character of the person appearing to have signed it.

(2) Attendance of analyst — The party against whom a certificate or report of an analyst is produced under subsection (1) may, with leave of the court, require the attendance of the analyst for the purpose of cross-examination.

(3) [Repealed 2017, c. 7, s. 38(2).]

2017, c. 7, s. 38

52. (1) Proof of notice — For the purposes of this Act and the regulations, the giving of any notice, whether orally or in writing, or the service of any document may be proved by the oral evidence of, or by the affidavit or solemn declaration of, the person claiming to have given that notice or served that document.

(2) Proof of notice — Notwithstanding subsection (1), the court may require the affiant or declarant to appear before it for examination or cross-examination in respect of the giving of notice or proof of service.

53. (1) Continuity of possession — In any proceeding under this Act or the regulations, continuity of possession of any exhibit tendered as evidence in that proceeding may be proved by the testimony of, or the affidavit or solemn declaration of, the person claiming to have had it in their possession.

(2) Alternative method of proof — Where an affidavit or solemn declaration is offered in proof of continuity of possession under subsection (1), the court may require the affiant or declarant to appear before it for examination or cross-examination in respect of the issue of continuity of possession.

54. Copies of records, books or documents — Where any record, book, electronic data or other document is examined or seized under this Act or the regulations, the Minister, or the officer by whom the record, book, electronic data or other document is examined or seized, may make or cause to be made one or more copies thereof, and a copy of any such record, book, electronic data or other document purporting to be certified by the Minister or a person authorized by the Minister is admissible in evidence and, in the absence of evidence to the contrary, has the same probative force as the original record, book, electronic data or other document would have had if it had been proved in the ordinary way.

Technical Assistance

[Heading added 2018, c. 16, s. 202.]

54.1 Advice of experts — The Minister may engage the services of persons having technical or specialized knowledge to advise the Minister in respect of his or her powers, duties or functions under this Act and, with the approval of the Treasury Board, fix their remuneration.

2018, c. 16, s. 202

Regulations and Exemptions

[Heading amended 2017, c. 7, s. 39.]

55. (1) Regulations — The Governor in Council may make regulations for carrying out the purposes and provisions of this Act, including the regulation of the medical, scientific and industrial applications and distribution of controlled substances and precursors and the enforcement of this Act, as well as the regulation of designated devices and, without restricting the generality of the foregoing, may make regulations

(a) governing, controlling, limiting, authorizing the importation into Canada, exportation from Canada, production, packaging, sending, transportation, delivery, sale, provision, administration, possession or obtaining of or other dealing in any controlled substances or precursor or any class thereof;

(b) respecting the circumstances in which, the conditions subject to which and the persons or classes of persons by whom any controlled substances or precursor or any class thereof may be imported into Canada, exported from Canada, produced, packaged, sent, transported, delivered, sold, provided, administered, possessed, obtained or otherwise dealt in, as well as the means by which and the persons or classes of persons by whom such activities may be authorized;

(c) respecting the issuance, suspension, cancellation, duration and terms and conditions of any licence or class of licences for the importation into Canada, exportation from Canada, production, packaging, sale, provision or administration of any substance included in Schedule I, II, III, IV, V or VI or any class of those substances;

(d) respecting the issuance, suspension, cancellation, duration and terms and conditions of any permit for the importation into Canada, exportation from

Canada or production of a substance included in Schedule I, II, III, IV, V or VI or any class of those substances as well as the amount of those substances or any class of those substances that may be imported, exported or produced under such a permit;

(d.1) authorizing the Minister to impose terms and conditions on any licence or any permit including existing licences or permits, and to amend those terms and conditions;

(e) prescribing the fees payable on application for any of the licences or permits;

(f) respecting the method of production, preservation, testing, packaging or storage of any controlled substance or precursor or any class thereof;

(g) respecting the premises, processes or conditions for the production or sale of any controlled substance or any class thereof, and deeming such premises, processes or conditions to be or not to be suitable for the purposes of the regulations;

(h) respecting the qualifications of persons who are engaged in the production, preservation, testing, packaging, storage, selling, providing or otherwise dealing in any controlled substance or precursor or any class thereof and who do so under the supervision of a person licensed under the regulations to do any such thing;

(i) prescribing standards of composition, strength, concentration, potency, purity or quality or any other property of any controlled substance or precursor;

(j) respecting the labelling, packaging, size, dimensions, fill and other specifications of packages used for the importation into Canada, exportation from Canada, sending, transportation, delivery, sale or provision of or other dealing in any substance included in Schedule I, II, III, IV, V or VI or any class thereof;

(k) respecting the distribution of samples of any substance included in Schedule I, II, III, IV, V or VI or any class thereof;

(l) controlling and limiting the advertising for sale of any controlled substance or precursor or any class thereof;

(m) respecting records, reports, electronic data or other documents in respect of controlled substances, precursors or designated devices that are required to be kept and provided by any person or class of persons;

(n) respecting the qualifications for inspectors and their powers, duties and functions in relation to verifying compliance or preventing non-compliance with the provisions of this Act or the regulations;

(o) respecting the qualifications for analysts and their powers and duties;

(p) respecting the detention and disposition of or otherwise dealing with any controlled substance, precursor, designated device, offence-related property or conveyance;

(q) [Repealed 2017, c. 7, s. 40(7).]

(r) respecting the taking of samples of substances under paragraph 31(1)(h);

(s) respecting the collection, use, retention, disclosure and disposal of information;

(t) respecting the making, serving, filing and manner of proving service of any notice, order, report or other document required or authorized under this Act or the regulations;

(u) authorizing the Minister to add to or delete from, by order, a schedule to Part J of the *Food and Drug Regulations* any item or portion of an item included in Schedule V;

(v) prescribing forms for the purposes of this Act or the regulations;

(w) establishing classes or groups of controlled substances, precursors or designated devices;

(x) respecting the provision of information under section 45.1;

(y) respecting the measures referred to in section 45.2;

(y.1) respecting the review of orders under section 45.4;

(z) exempting, on any terms and conditions that are specified in the regulations, any person or class of persons or any controlled substance, precursor, designated device or any class of controlled substances, precursors or designated devices from the application of all or any of the provisions of this Act or the regulations;

(z.01) respecting the registration of the importation of any designated device or class of designated devices, including the time that proof of registration must be provided; and

Proposed Amendment — 55(1)(z.01)

(z.01) respecting the registration of the importation of any designated device or class of designated devices, including the time that proof of registration must be provided;

2017, c. 7, s. 40(12) [Not in force at date of publication.]

Proposed Addition — 55(1)(z.02), (z.03)

(z.02) governing, controlling, limiting, authorizing the importation into Canada, exportation from Canada, sale, provision, possession of or other dealing in any designated device or any class of designated devices;

(z.03) respecting the issuance, suspension, cancellation, duration and terms and conditions of any licence or class of licences or of any permit for the importation into Canada, exportation from Canada, sale, provision or possession of any designated device or class of designated devices; and

Proposed Amendment — 55(1)(z.03)

(z.03) respecting the issuance, suspension, cancellation, duration and terms and conditions of any licence or class of licences or of any permit for the importation into Canada, exportation from Canada, sale, provision or possession of any designated device or class of designated devices;

2017, c. 7, s. 40(13) [Not in force at date of publication.]
2017, c. 7, s. 40(12) [Not in force at date of publication.]

Proposed Addition — 55(1)(z.04)–(z.06)

(z.04) prescribing exportation from Canada, sale, provision, or possession of any designated device or any class of designated devices as activities for the purpose of section 46.4;

(z.05) respecting the circumstances in which, the conditions subject to which and the persons or classes of persons by whom any designated device or class of designated devices may be exported from Canada, sold, provided or possessed, as well as the means by which and the persons or classes of persons by whom such activities may be authorized;

(z.06) respecting the registration of activities in relation to any designated device or any class of designated devices for the purpose of section 46.4; and

2017, c. 7, s. 40(13) [Not in force at date of publication.]

(z.1) prescribing anything that, by this Act, is to be or may be prescribed.

(1.1) [Repealed 2017, c. 7, s. 40(14).]

(1.2) Regulations — The Governor in Council may make regulations for carrying out the purposes of section 56.1, including

(a) defining terms for the purposes of that section;

(b) [Repealed 2017, c. 7, s. 40(15).]

(c) respecting any information to be submitted to the Minister and the manner in which it is to be submitted;

(d) respecting the circumstances in which an exemption may be granted;

(e) respecting requirements in relation to an application for an exemption made under subsection 56.1(1); and

(f) respecting terms and conditions in relation to an exemption granted under subsection 56.1(1).

(2) Regulations pertaining to law enforcement — The Governor in Council, on the recommendation of the Minister of Public Safety and Emergency Preparedness, may make regulations that pertain to investigations and other law enforcement activities conducted under this Act by a member of a police force or of the military police and other persons acting under the direction and control of the member and, without restricting the generality of the foregoing, may make regulations

(a) authorizing, for the purposes of this subsection,

(i) the Minister of Public Safety and Emergency Preparedness or the provincial minister responsible for policing in a province, as the case may be, to designate a police force within their jurisdiction, or

(ii) the Minister of National Defence to designate military police;

(b) exempting, on any terms and conditions that are specified in the regulations, a member of a police force or of the military police that has been designated under paragraph (a), and other persons acting under the direction and control of the member, from the application of any provision of Part I or the regulations;

(c) respecting the issuance, suspension, cancellation, duration and terms and conditions of a certificate, other document or, in exigent circumstances, an approval to obtain a certificate or other document, that is issued to a member of a police force or of the military police that has been designated under paragraph (a) for the purpose of exempting the member from the application of any provision of this Act or the regulations;

(d) respecting the detention, storage and disposition of or other dealing with any controlled substance or precursor;

(e) respecting records, reports, electronic data or other documents in respect of a controlled substance or precursor that are required to be kept and provided by any person or class of persons; and

(f) prescribing forms for the purposes of the regulations.

(2.1) Regulations pertaining to law enforcement under other Acts — The Governor in Council, on the recommendation of the Minister of Public Safety and Emergency Preparedness, may, for the purpose of an investigation or other law enforcement activity conducted under another Act of Parliament, make regulations authorizing a member of a police force or of the military police or other person under the direction and control of the member to commit an act or omission — or authorizing a member of a police force or of the military police to direct the commission of an act or omission — that would otherwise constitute an offence under Part I or the regulations and, without restricting the generality of the foregoing, may make regulations

(a) authorizing, for the purposes of this subsection,

(i) the Minister of Public Safety and Emergency Preparedness or the provincial minister responsible for policing in a province, as the case may be, to designate a police force within their jurisdiction, or

(ii) the Minister of National Defence to designate military police;

(b) exempting, on any terms and conditions that are specified in the regulations, a member of a police force or of the military police that has been designated under paragraph (a), and other persons acting under the direction and control of the member, from the application of any provision of Part I or the regulations;

(c) respecting the issuance, suspension, cancellation, duration and terms and conditions of a certificate, other document or, in exigent circumstances, an approval to obtain a certificate or other document, that is issued to a member of a police force or of the military police that has been designated under paragraph (a) for the purpose of exempting the member from the application of any provision of Part I or the regulations;

(d) respecting the detention, storage and disposition of or other dealing with any controlled substance or precursor;

(e) respecting records, reports, electronic data or other documents in respect of a controlled substance or precursor that are required to be kept and provided by any person or class of persons; and

(f) prescribing forms for the purposes of the regulations.

(3) Incorporation by reference — Any regulations made under this Act incorporating by reference a classification, standard, procedure or other specification may incorporate the classification, standard, procedure or specification as amended from time to time, and, in such a case, the reference shall be read accordingly.

2001, c. 32, s. 55; 2005, c. 10, s. 15; 2015, c. 22, s. 4; 2017, c. 7, s. 40(1), (3), (6)–(8), (10), (11), (14)–(19)

56. (1) Exemption by Minister — The Minister may, on any terms and conditions that the Minister considers necessary, exempt from the application of all or any of the provisions of this Act or the regulations any person or class of persons or any controlled substance or precursor or any class of either of them if, in the opinion of the Minister, the exemption is necessary for a medical or scientific purpose or is otherwise in the public interest.

(2) Exception — The Minister is not authorized under subsection (1) to grant an exemption for a medical purpose that would allow activities in relation to a controlled substance or precursor that is obtained in a manner not authorized under this Act to take place at a supervised consumption site.

2015, c. 22, s. 5; 2017, c. 7, s. 41

56.1 (1) Exemption for medical purpose — supervised consumption site — For the purpose of allowing certain activities to take place at a supervised consumption site, the Minister may, on any terms and conditions that the Minister considers necessary, exempt the following from the application of all or any of the provisions of this Act or the regulations if, in the opinion of the Minister, the exemption is necessary for a medical purpose:

(a) any person or class of persons in relation to a controlled substance or precursor that is obtained in a manner not authorized under this Act; or

(b) any controlled substance or precursor or any class of either of them that is obtained in a manner not authorized under this Act.

(2) Application — An application for an exemption under subsection (1) shall include information, submitted in the form and manner determined by the Minister, regarding the intended public health benefits of the site and information, if any, related to

(a) the impact of the site on crime rates;

(b) the local conditions indicating a need for the site;

(c) the administrative structure in place to support the site;

(d) the resources available to support the maintenance of the site; and

(e) expressions of community support or opposition.

(3) Subsequent application — An application for an exemption under subsection (1) that would allow certain activities to continue to take place at a supervised consumption site shall include any update to the information provided to the Minister since the previous exemption was granted, including any information related to the public health impacts of the activities at the site.

(4) Notice — The Minister may give notice, in the form and manner determined by the Minister, of any application for an exemption under subsection (1). The notice shall indicate the period of time — not less than 45 days or more than 90 days — in which members of the public may provide the Minister with comments.

(5) **Public decision** — After making a decision under subsection (1), the Minister shall, in writing, make the decision public and, if the decision is a refusal, include the reasons for it.

(6) [Repealed 2017, c. 7, s. 42.]

2015, c. 22, s. 5; 2017, c. 7, s. 42

56.2 A person who is responsible for the direct supervision, at a supervised consumption site, of the consumption of controlled substances, may offer a person using the site alternative pharmaceutical therapy before that person consumes a controlled substance that is obtained in a manner not authorized under this Act.

2017, c. 7, s. 42

Miscellaneous

[Heading added 2017, c. 7, s. 43.]

57. Powers, duties and functions of Minister or Minister of Public Safety and Emergency Preparedness — The Minister's powers, duties or functions under this Act or the regulations — and those of the Minister of Public Safety and Emergency Preparedness under the regulations — may be exercised or performed by any person designated, or any person occupying a position designated, for that purpose by the relevant Minister.

2005, c. 10, s. 16

58. Paramountcy of this Act and the regulations — In the case of any inconsistency or conflict between this Act or the regulations made under it, and the *Food and Drugs Act* or the regulations made under that Act, this Act and the regulations made under it prevail to the extent of the inconsistency or conflict.

59. [Repealed 2017, c. 7, s. 44.]

Amendments to Schedules

60. Power to amend schedules — The Governor in Council may, by order, amend any of Schedules I to IV, VI and IX by adding to them or deleting from them any item or portion of an item, if the Governor in Council considers the amendment to be necessary in the public interest.

2017, c. 7, s. 45; 2018, c. 16, ss. 203, 206(6)

60.1 (1) Schedule V — The Minister may, by order, add to Schedule V any item or portion of an item for a period of up to one year, or extend that period by up to another year, if the Minister has reasonable grounds to believe that it

(a) poses a significant risk to public health or safety; or

(b) may pose a risk to public health or safety and

(i) is being imported into Canada with no legitimate purpose, or

(ii) is being distributed in Canada with no legitimate purpose.

(2) Deletions — The Minister may, by order, delete any item or portion of an item from Schedule V.

2017, c. 7, s. 45

Part VII — Transitional Provisions, Consequential Amendments, Repeal and Coming into Force (ss. 61–95)

Transitional Provisions

61. References to prior enactments — Any reference in a designation by the Minister of Public Safety and Emergency Preparedness under Part VI of the *Criminal Code* to an offence contrary to the *Narcotic Control Act* or Part III or IV of the *Food and Drugs Act* or any conspiracy or attempt to commit or being an accessory after the fact or any counselling in relation to such an offence shall be deemed to be a reference to an offence contrary to section 5 (trafficking), 6 (importing and exporting) or 7 (production) of this Act, as the case may be, or a conspiracy or attempt to commit or being an accessory after the fact or any counselling in, relation to such an offence.

2001, c. 32, s. 56; 2005, c. 10, s. 34(1)(d)

62. (1) Sentences for prior offences — Subject to subsection (2), where, before the coming into force of this Act, a person has committed an offence under the *Narcotic Control Act* or Part III or IV of the *Food and Drugs Act* but a sentence has not been imposed on the person for that offence, a sentence shall be imposed on the person in accordance with this Act.

(2) Application of increased punishment — Where any penalty, forfeiture or punishment provided by the *Narcotic Control Act* or section 31 or Part III or IV of the *Food and Drugs Act*, as those Acts read immediately before the coming into force of sections 4 to 9 of this Act, is varied by this Act, the lesser penalty, forfeiture or punishment applies in respect of any offence that was committed before the coming into force of those sections.

63. Validation — Every authorization issued by the Minister under subsection G.06.001(1) or J.01.033(1) of the *Food and Drug Regulations* or subsection 68(1) of the *Narcotic Control Regulations* before the coming into force of sections 78 and 90 of this Act is hereby declared to have been validly issued and every such authorization that is in force on the coming into force of sections 78 and 90 of this Act shall continue in force under this Act until it is revoked, as if it were an exemption made under section 56 of this Act.

Consequential Amendments

64. to 93.1 Consequential Amendments — [Note: The Consequential amendments are incorporated into the relevant provisions of the Acts which they affect, including, among others, the *Criminal Code*, the *Food and Drugs Act* and the *Young Offenders Act*.]

Conditional Amendments

93.2 to 93.3 Conditional Amendments — [Note: The Conditional amendments are incorporated into the relevant provisions of this Act and the *Criminal Code*.]

Repeal

Narcotic Control Act

94. Repeal of R.S., c. N-1 — The *Narcotic Control Act* is repealed.

Coming into Force

95. Coming into force — This Act or any of its provisions comes into force on a day or days to be fixed by order of the Governor in Council.

SCHEDULE I

(Sections 2, 4 to 7.1, 10, 29, 55 and 60)

[Reference amended 2017, c. 7, s. 46.]

1. Opium Poppy (*Papaver somniferum*), its preparations, derivatives, alkaloids and salts, including:

(1) Opium

(2) Codeine (methylmorphine)

(3) Morphine (7,8-didehydro-4,5-epoxy-17-methylmorphinan-3,6-diol)

(4) Thebaine (paramorphine),

and the salts, derivatives and salts of derivatives of the substances set out in subitems (1) to (4), including:

(5) Acetorphine (acetyletorphine)

(6) Acetyldihydrocodeine (4,5-epoxy-3-methoxy-17-methylmorphinan-6 -ol acetate)

(7) Benzylmorphine (7,8-didehydro-4,5-epoxy-17-methyl-3 -(phenylmethoxy) morphinan-6-ol)

(8) codoxime (dihydrocodeinone O-(carboxymethyl) oxime)

(9) Desomorphine (dihydrodeoxymorphine)

(10) Diacetylmorphine (heroin)

(11) Dihydrocodeine (4,5-epoxy-3-methoxy-17-methylmorphinan-6-ol)

(12) Dihydromorphine (4,5-epoxy-17-methylmorphinan-3,6-diol)

(13) Ethylmorphine (7,8-didehydro-4,5-epoxy-3-ethoxy-17 -methylmorphinan-6-ol)

(14) Etorphine (tetrahydro-7α-(1-hydroxy-1-methylbutyl) -6,14-endo-ethenooripavine)

(15) Hydrocodone (dihydrocodeinone)

(16) Hydromorphinol (dihydro-14-hydroxymorphine)

(17) Hydromorphone (dihydromorphinone)

(18) Methyldesorphine (δ6-deoxy-6-methylmorphine)

(19) Methyldihydromorphine (dihydro-6-methylmorphine)

(20) Metopon (dihydromethylmorphinone)

(21) Morphine-N-oxide (morphine oxide)

(22) Myrophine (benzylmorphine myristate)

(23) Nalorphine (N-allylnormorphine)

(24) Nicocodine (6-nicotinylcodeine)

(25) Nicomorphine (dinicotinylmorphine)

(26) Norcodeine (N-desmethylcodeine)

(27) Normorphine (N-desmethylmorphine)

(28) Oxycodone (dihydrohydroxycodeinone)

(29) Oxymorphone (dihydrohydroxymorphinone)

(30) Pholcodine (3-[2-(4-morphonlinyl)ethyl]morphine)

(31) Thebacon (acetyldihydrocodeinone)

but not including

(32) Apomorphine (5,6,6a,7-tetrahydro-6-methyl-4H-dibenzo[de,g]quinoline-10,11-diol) and its salts

(33) Cyprenorphine (N-(cyclopropylmethyl)-6,7,8,14-tetrahydro-7α-(1-hydroxy-1-methylethyl)-6,14-endo-ethenonororipavine) and its salts

(34) Nalmefene (17-(cyclopropylmethyl)-4,5α-epoxy-6-methylenemorphinan-3,14-diol) and its salts

(34.1) Naloxone (4,5α-epoxy-3,14-dihydroxy-17-(2-propenyl)morphinan-6-one) and its salts

(34.2) Naltrexone (17-(cyclopropylmethyl)-4,5α-epoxy-3,14-dihydroxymorphinan-6-one) and its salts

(34.3) Methylnaltrexone (17-(cyclopropylmethyl)-4,5α-epoxy-3,14-dihydroxy-17-methyl-6-oxomorphinanium) and its salts

(34.4) Naloxegol (4,5α-epoxy-6α-(3,6,9,12,15,18,21-heptaoxadocos-1-yloxy)-17-(2-propenyl)morphinan-3,14-diol) and its salts

(35) Narcotine (6,7-dimethoxy-3-(5,6,7,8-tetrahydro-4-methoxy-6-methyl-1,3-dioxolo [4,5-g]isoquinolin-5-yl)-1(3H)-isobenzofuranone) and its salts

(36) Papaverine (1-[(3,4-dimethoxyphenyl)methyl]-6,7-dimethoxyisoquinoline) and its salts

(37) Poppy seed

2. Coca (*Erythroxylum*), its preparations, derivatives, alkaloids and salts, including:

(1) Coca leaves

(2) Cocaine (benzoylmethylecgonine)

(3) Ecgonine (3-hydroxy-2-tropane carboxylic acid)

but not including

(4) ^{123}l-ioflupane

3. Phenylpiperidines, their intermediates, salts, derivatives and analogues and salts of intermediates, derivatives and analogues, including:

(1) Allylprodine (3-allyl-1-methyl-4-phenyl-4-piperidinol propionate)

(2) Alphameprodine (α-3-ethyl-1-methyl-4-phenyl-4-piperidinol propionate)

(3) Alphaprodine (α-1,3-dimethyl-4-phenyl-4-piperidi nolpropionate)

(4) Anileridine (ethyl 1-[2-(p-aminophenyl)ethyl]-4-phenylpiperidine-4-carboxylate)

(5) Betameprodine (β-3-ethyl-1-methyl-4-phenyl-4-piperidinol propionate)

(6) Betaprodine (β-1,3-dimethyl-4-phenyl-4-piperidinol propionate)

(7) Benzethidine (ethyl 1-(2-benzyloxyethyl)-4-phenyl-piperidine-4-carboxylate)

(8) Diphenoxylate (ethyl 1-(3-cyano-3,3-diphenyl-propyl)-4-phenylpiperidine-4-carboxylate)

(9) Difenoxin (1-(3-cyno-3,3-diphenylpropyl)-4-phenylpiperidine-4-carboxylate)

(10) Etoxeridine (ethyl 1-[2-(2-hydroxyethoxy) ethyl]-4-phenylpiperidine-4-carboxylate)

(11) Farethidine (ethyl 1-(2-tetrahydrofurfury loxyethyl)-4-phenylpiperidine-4-carboxylate)

(12) Hydroxypethidine (ethyl 4-(m-hydroxyphenyl)-1-methylpiperidine-4-carboxylate)

(13) Ketobemidone (1-[4-(m-hydroxyphenyl)-1-methyl-4- piperidyl]-1-propanone)

(14) Methylphenylisonipecotonitrile (4-cyano-1-methyl-4-phenylpiperidine)

(15) Morpheridine (ethyl 1-(2-morpholinoethyl)-4-phenylpiperidine-4-carboxylate)

(16) Norpethidine (ethyl 4-phenylpiperidine-4-carboxylate)

(17) Pethidine (ethyl 1-methyl-4-phenylpiperidine-4-carboxylate)

(18) Phenoperidine (ethyl 1-(3-hydroxy-3-phenylpropyl)-4-phenylpiperidine-4-carboxylate)

(19) Piminodine (ethyl 1-[3-(phenylamino)propyl]-4-phenylpiperidine-4-carboxylate)

(20) Properidine (isopropyl 1-methyl-4-phenylpiperidine-4-carboxylate)

(21) Trimeperidine (1,2,5-trimethyl-4-phenyl-4-piperidinol propionate)

(22) Pethidine Intermediate C (1-methyl-4-phenylpiperidine-4-4-carboxylate)
but not including

(23) Carperidine (ethyl 1-(2-carbamylethyl)-4-phenylpiperidine-4-carboxylate) and its salts

(24) Oxpheneridine (ethyl 1-(2-hydroxy-2-phenylethyl)-4-phenylpiperidine-4-carboxylate) and its salts

4. Phenazepines, their salts, derivatives and salts of derivatives including:

(1) Proheptazine (hexahydro-1,3-dimethyl-4-phenyl-1H-azepi n-4-ol propionate)
but not including

(2) Ethoheptazine (ethyl hexahydro-1-methyl-4-phenylazepine-4-carboxylate) and its salts

(3) Metethoheptazine (ethyl hexahydro-1,3-dimethyl-4-phenylazepine-4-carboxylate) and its salts

(4) Metheptazine (methylhexahydro-1,2-dimethyl-4-phenylazepine-4-carboxylate) and its salts

5. Amidones, their intermediates, salts, derivatives and salts of intermediates and derivatives including:

(1) Dimethylaminodiphenylbutanonitrile (4-cyano-2-dimethylamino-4,4-diphenylbutane)

(2) Dipipanone (4,4-diphenyl-6-piperidino-3-heptanone)

(3) Isomethadone (6-dimethylamino-5-methyl-4,4-diphenyl-3 -hexanone)

(4) Methadone (6-dimethylamino-4,4-diphenyl-3-heptanone)

(5) Normethadone (6-dimethylamino-4,4-diphenyl-3-hexanone)

(6) Norpipanone (4,4-diphenyl-6-piperidino-3-hexanone)

(7) Phenadoxone (6-morpholino-4,4-diphenyl-3-heptanone)

6. Methadols, their salts, derivatives and salts of derivatives including:

(1) Acetylmethadol (6-dimethylamino-4,4-diphenyl-3-heptanol acetate)

(2) Alphacetylmethadol (α-6-dimethylamino-4,4-diphenyl-3-heptanol acetate)

(3) Alphamethadol (α-6-dimethylamino-4,4-diphenyl-3-heptanol)

(4) Betacetylmethadol (β-6-dimethylamino-4,4-diphenyl-3-heptanol acetate)

(5) Betamethadol (β-6-dimethylamino-4,4-diphenyl-3-heptanol)

(6) Dimepheptanol (6-dimethylamino-4,4-diphenyl-3-heptanol)

(7) Noracymethadol (α-6-methylamino-4,4-diphenyl-3-heptanol acetate)

7. Phenalkoxams, their salts, derivatives and salts of derivatives including:

(1) Dimenoxadol (dimethylaminoethyl 1-ethoxy-1,1-diphenylacetate)

(2) Dioxaphetyl butyrate (ethyl 2,2-diphenyl-4-morpholinobutyrate)

(3) Dextropropoxyphene ([S-(R*,S*)]-α-[2-(di-methylamino)-1-methylethyl]-α-phenylbenzeneethanol, propanoate ester)

8. Thiambutenes, their salts, derivatives and salts of derivatives including:

(1) Diethylthiambutene (N,N-diethyl-1-methyl-3,3-di-2-thienylallylamine)

(2) Dimethylthiambutene (N,N,1-trimethyl-3,3-di-2-thienylallylamine)

(3) Ethylmethylthiambutene (N-ethyl-N,1-dimethyl-3,3-di-2-thie nylallylamine)

9. Moramides, their intermediates, salts, derivatives and salts of intermediates and derivatives including:

(1) Dextromoramide (d-1-(3-methyl-4-morpholino-2,2-diphenylbutyryl)pyrrolidine)

(2) Diphenylmorpholinoisovaleric acid (2-methyl-3-morpholino-1,1-diphenylpropionic acid)

(3) Levomoramide (1-1-(3-methyl-4-morpholino-2,2-diphenylbutyryl)pyrrolidine)

(4) Racemoramide (d,1-1-(3-methyl-4-morpholino-2,2-diphenylbutyryl) pyrrolidine)

10. Morphinans, their salts, derivatives and salts of derivatives including:

(1) Buprenorphine (17-(cyclopropylmethyl)-α-(1,1-dimethylethyl)-4,5-epoxy-18,19-dihydro-3-hydroxy- 6-methoxy-α-methyl-6,14-ethenomorphinan -7-methanol)

(2) Drotebanol (6β,14-dihydroxy-3,4-dimethoxy-17-methylmorphinan)

(3) Levomethorphan (1-3-methoxy-17-methylmorphinan)

(4) Levorphanol (1-3-hydroxy-17-methylmorphinan)

(5) Levophenacylmorphan (1-3-hydroxy-17-phenacyl-morphinan)

(6) Norlevorphanol (1-3-hydroxymorphinan)

(7) Phenomorphan (3-hydroxy-17-(2-phenylethyl) morphinan)

(8) Racemethorphan (d,1-3-methoxy-17-methylmorphinan)

(9) Racemorphan (*d,l*-3-hydroxy-N-methylmorphinan)
but not including

(10) Dextromethorphan (d-1,2,3,9,10, 10a-hexahydro-6-methoxy-11-methyl-4H-10,4a-iminoethanophenanthren) and its salts

(11) Dextrorphan (d-1,2,3,9,10,10a-hexahydro-11-methyl-4H-10,4a-iminoethanophenanthren-6-ol) and its salts

(12) Levallorphan (l-11-allyl-1,2,3,9,10,10a-hexahydro-4H-10,4a-iminoethanophenanthren-6-ol) and its salts

(13) Levargorphan (l-11-propargyl-1,2,3,9,10,10a-hexahydro-4H-10,4a-iminoethanophenanthren-6-ol) and its salts

(14) Butorphanol (l-N-cyclobutylmethyl-3,14-dihydroxymorphinan) and its salts

(15) Nalbuphine (N-cyclobutylmethyl-4,5-epoxy-morphinan-3,6,14-triol) and its salts

11. Benzazocines, their salts, derivatives and salts of derivatives including:

(1) Phenazocine (1,2,3,4,5,6-hexahydro-6,11-dimethyl-3-phenethyl-2,6-methano-3-benzazocin-8-ol)

(2) Metazocine (1,2,3,4,5,6-hexahydro-3,6,11-trimethyl-2,6-methano-3-benzazocin-8-ol)

(3) Pentazocine (1,2,3,4,5,6-hexahydro-6,11-dimethyl-3-(3 -methyl-2-butenyl)-2,6-methano-3-be nzazocin-8-ol)
but not including

(4) Cyclazocine (1,2,3,4,5,6-hexahydro-6,11-dimethyl-3-(cyclopropylmethyl)-2,6-methano-3-benzazocin-8-ol) and its salts

12. Ampromides, their salts, derivatives and salts of derivatives including:

(1) Diampromide (N-[2-(methylphenethylamino) propyl] propionanilide)

(2) Phenampromide (N-(1-methyl-2-piperidino) ethyl) propionanilide)

(3) Propiram (N-(1-methyl-2-piperidinoethyl)-N-2 -pyridylpropionamide)

13. Benzimidazoles, their salts, derivatives and salts of derivatives including:

(1) Clonitazene (2-(p-chlorobenzyl)-1-diethylaminoethyl-5 -nitrobenzimidazole)

(2) Etonitazene (2-(p-ethoxybenzyl)-1-diethylaminoethyl-5 -nitrobenzimidazole)

(3) Bezitramide (1-(3-cyano-3,3-diphenylpropyl)-4-(2 -oxo-3-propionyl-1-benzimidazolinyl)-piperidine)

14. Phencyclidine (1-(1-phenylcyclohexyl)piperidine), its salts, derivatives and analogues and salts of derivatives and analogues, including:

(1) Ketamine (2-(2-chlorophenyl)-2-(methylamino)cyclohexanone)

15. Piritramide (1-(3-cyano-3,3-diphenylpropyl)-4-(1 -piperidino)piperidine-4-carboxylic acid amide), its salts, derivatives and salts of derivatives

16. Fentanyls, their salts, derivatives, and analogues and salts of derivatives and analogues, including:

(1) Acetyl-α-methylfentanyl (N-[1-(α-methylphenethyl)-4-piperidyl] acetanilide)

(2) Alfentanil (N-[1-[2-(4-ethyl-4,5-dihydro-5-oxo-1H-tetrazol-1-yl)ethyl]-4-(methoxymethyl)-4-piperidyl]propionanilide)

(3) Carfentanil (methyl 4-[(1-oxopropyl)phenylamino]-1-(2-phenethyl) -4-piperidinecarboxylate)

(4) p-Fluorofentanyl (4'fluoro-N-(1-phenethyl-4-piperidyl) propionanilide)

(5) Fentanyl (N-(1-phenethyl-4-piperidyl) propionanilide)

(6) β-Hydroxyfentanyl (N-[1-(β-hydroxyphenethyl)-4-piperidyl] propionanilide)

(7) β-Hydroxy-3-methylfentanyl (N-[1-(β-hydroxyphenethyl)-3-methyl- 4-piperidyl] propionanilide)

(8) α-Methylfentanyl (N-[1-(α-methylphenethyl)-4-piperidyl] propionanilide)

(9) α-Methylthiofentanyl (N-[1-[1-methyl-2-(2-thienyl) ethyl]-4-piperidyl] propionanilide)

(10) 3-Methylfentanyl (N-(3-methyl-1-phenethyl-4-piperidyl) propionanilide)

(11) 3-Methylthiofentanyl (N-[3-methyl-1-[2-(2-thienyl) ethyl]-4-piperidyl] propionanilide)

(11.1) Remifentanil (dimethyl 4-carboxy-4-(N-phenylpropionamido)-1-piperidinepropionate)

(12) Sufentanil (N-[4-(methoxymethyl)-1-[2-(2-thienyl)ethyl]-4-piperidyl] propionanilide)

(13) Thiofentanyl (N-[1-[2-(2-thienyl)ethyl]-4-piperidyl]propionilide)

(14) 4-Anilino-N-phenethylpiperidine (ANPP) (N-phenyl-1-(2-phenylethyl)piperidine-4-amine), its derivatives and analogues and salts of derivatives and analogues

17. Tilidine (ethyl2-(dimethylamino)-1-phenyl-3-cyclohexene -1-carboxylate), its salts, derivatives and salts of derivatives

17.1 Methylenedioxypyrovalerone (MDPV), its salts, derivatives, isomers and analogues and salts of derivatives, isomers and analogues

18. Methamphetamine (N, α-dimethylbenzeneethanamine), its salts, derivatives, isomers and analogues and salts of derivatives, isomers and analogues

19. Amphetamines, their salts, derivatives, isomers and analogues and salts of derivatives, isomers and analogues including:

(1) amphetamine (α-methylbenzeneethanamine)

(2) N-ethylamphetamine (N-ethyl-α-methylbenzeneethanamine)

(3) 4-methyl-2,5-dimethoxyamphetamine (STP) (2,5-dimethoxy-4,α-dimethylbenzeneethanamine)

(4) 3,4-methylenedioxyamphetamine (MDA) (α-methyl-1,3-benzodioxole-5-ethanamine)

(5) 2,5-dimethoxyamphetamine (2,5-dimethoxy-α-methylbenzene-ethanamine)

(6) 4-methoxyamphetamine (4-methoxy-α-methylbenzeneethanamine)

(7) 2,4,5-trimethoxyamphetamine (2,4,5-trimethoxy-α-methylbenzeneethanamine)

(8) N-methyl-3,4-methylenedioxyamphetamine (N,α-dimethyl-1,3-benzodioxole-5-ethanamine)

(9) 4-ethoxy-2,5-dimethoxyamphetamine (4-ethoxy-2,5-dimethoxy-α-methylbenzeneethanamine)

(10) 5-methoxy-3,4-methylenedioxyamphetamine (7-methoxy-α-methyl-1,3-benzodioxole-5-ethanamine)

(11) N,N-dimethyl-3,4-methylenedioxyamphetamine (N,N, α-trimethyl-1,3-benzodioxole-5-ethanamine)

(12) N-ethyl-3,4-methylenedioxyamphetamine (N-ethyl-α-methyl-1,3-benzodioxole-5-ethanamine)

(13) 4-ethyl-2,5-dimethoxyamphetamine (DOET) (4-ethyl-2,5-dimethoxy-α-methylbenzeneethanamine)

(14) 4-bromo-2,5-dimethoxyamphetamine (4-bromo-2,5-dimethoxy-α-methylbenzeneethanamine)

(15) 4-chloro-2,5-dimethoxyamphetamine (4-chloro-2,5-dimethoxy-α-methylbenzeneethanamine)

(16) 4-ethoxyamphetamine (4-ethoxy-α-methylbenzeneethanamine)

(17) Benzphetamine (N-benzyl-N,α-dimethylbenzeneethanamine)

(18) N-Propyl-3,4-methylenedioxyamphetamine (α-methyl-N-propyl-1,3-benzodioxole-5-ethanamine)

(19) N-(2-Hydroxyethyl)-α-methylbenzeneethanamine

(20) N-hydroxy-3,4-methylenedioxyamphetamine (N-[α-methyl-3,4-(methylenedioxy)phenethyl] hydroxylamine)

(21) 3,4,5-trimethoxyamphetamine (3,4,5-trimethoxy-α-methylbenzeneethanamine)

20. Flunitrazepam (5-(o-fluorophenyl)-1,3-dihydro-1-methyl-7-nitro-2H-1,4-benzodiazepin-2-one) and any of its salts or derivatives

21. 4-hydroxybutanoic acid (GHB) and any of its salts

22. Tapentadol (3-[(1R,2R)-3-(dimethylamino)-1-ethyl-2-methylpropyl]-phenol), its salts, derivatives and isomers and salts of derivatives and isomers

23. AH-7921 (1-(3,4-dichlorobenzamidomethyl)cyclohexyldimethylamine), its salts, isomers and salts of isomers

24. MT-45 (1-cyclohexyl-4-(1,2-diphenylethyl)piperazine), its salts, derivatives, isomers and analogues and salts of derivatives, isomers and analogues, including

(1) Diphenidine (DEP) (1-(1,2-diphenylethyl)piperidine)

(2) Methoxphenidine (2-MeO-Diphenidine, MXP) (1-[1-(2-methoxyphenyl)-2-phenylethyl]piperidine)

(3) Ephenidine (NEDPA, EPE) (N-ethyl-1,2-diphenylethylamine)

(4) Isophenidine (NPDPA) (N-isopropyl-1,2-diphenylethylamine)

but not including

(5) Lefetamine ((-)-N,N-dimethyl-α-phenylbenzeneethanamine), its salts, derivatives and isomers and salts of derivatives and isomers

25. W-18 (4-chloro-N-[1-[2-(4-nitrophenyl)ethyl]-2-piperidinylidene]benzenesulfonamide), its salts, derivatives, isomers and analogues and salts of derivatives, isomers and analogues

26. U-47700 (3,4-dichloro-N-(2-(dimethylamino)cyclohexyl)-N-methylbenzamide), its salts, derivatives, isomers and analogues, and salts of derivatives, isomers and analogues, including

(1) Bromadoline (4-bromo-N-(2-(dimethylamino)cyclohexyl)benzamide)

(2) U-47109 (3,4-dichloro-N-(2-(dimethylamino)cyclohexyl)benzamide)

(3) U-48520 (4-chloro-N-(2-(dimethylamino)cyclohexyl)-N-methylbenzamide)

(4) U-50211 (N-(2-(dimethylamino)cyclohexyl)-4-hydroxy-N-methylbenzamide)

(5) U-77891 (3,4-dibromo-N-methyl-N-(1-methyl-1-azaspiro[4.5]decan-6-yl)benzamide)

SOR/97-230; SOR/99-371; SOR/99-421; SOR/2005-235, s. 1; SOR/2005-271, s. 1; SOR/2005-337, s. 1; SOR/2012-176, s. 1; 2012, c. 1, s. 44; SOR/2015-190, s. 1; SOR/2016-107, s. 1; SOR/2017-13, ss. 1–5; SOR/2017-275, s. 1; SOR/2017-277, s. 1; SOR/2018-70, ss. 1, 2; SOR/2019-121, s. 1

SCHEDULE II

(Sections 2, 4 to 7.1, 10, 29, 55 and 60)

[Reference amended 2017, c. 7, s. 47.]

1. [Repealed 2018, c. 16, s. 204(1).]

2. Synthetic cannabinoid receptor type 1 agonists, their salts, derivatives, isomers, and salts of derivatives and isomers — with the exception of any substance that is identical to any phytocannabinoid and with the exception of ((3S)-2,3-dihydro-5-methyl-3-(4- morpholinylmethyl)pyrrolo[1,2,3-de]-1,4- benzoxazin-6-yl)-1-naphthalenyl-methanone (WIN 55,212-3) and its salts — including those that fall within the following core chemical structure classes:

(1) Any substance that has a 2-(cyclohexyl)phenol structure with substitution at the 1-position of the benzene ring by a hydroxy, ether or ester group and further substituted at the 5-position of the benzene ring, whether or not further substituted on the benzene ring to any extent, and substituted at the 3'-position of the cyclohexyl ring by an alkyl, carbonyl, hydroxyl, ether or ester, and whether or not further substituted on the cyclohexyl ring to any extent, including

(i) Nabilone ((±)-trans-3-(1,1-dimethylheptyl)-6,6a,7,8,10,10a-hexahydro-1-hydroxy-6,6-dimethyl-9H-dibenzo[b,d]pyran-9-one)

(ii) Parahexyl (3-hexyl-6,6,9-trimethyl-7,8,9,10-tetrahydro-6H-dibenzo[b,d]pyran-1-ol)

(iii) 3-(1,2-dimethylheptyl)-7,8,9,10-tetrahydro-6,6,9-trimethyl-6H-dibenzo[b,d]pyran-1-ol (DMHP)

(iv) 5-(1,1-dimethylheptyl)-2-(5-hydroxy-2-(3-hydroxypropyl)cyclohexyl)phenol (CP 55,940)

(v) 5-(1,1-dimethylheptyl)-2-(3-hydroxycyclohexyl)phenol (CP 47,497)

(2) Any substance that has a 3-(1-naphthoyl)indole structure with substitution at the nitrogen atom of the indole ring, whether or not further substituted on the indole ring to any extent and whether or not substituted on the naphthyl ring to any extent, including

(i) 1-pentyl-3-(1-naphthoyl)indole (JWH-018)

(ii) 1-butyl-3-(1-naphthoyl)indole (JWH-073)

(iii) 1-pentyl-3-(4-methyl-1-naphthoyl)indole (JWH-122)

(iv) 1-hexyl-3-(1-naphthoyl)indole (JWH-019)

(v) 1-(4-pentenyl)-3-(1-naphthoyl)indole (JWH-022)

(vi) 1-butyl-3-(4-methoxy-1-naphthoyl)indole (JWH-080)

(vii) 1-pentyl-3-(4-methoxy-1-naphthoyl)indole (JWH-081)

(viii) 1-(2-morpholin-4-ylethyl)-3-(1-naphthoyl)indole (JWH-200)

(ix) 1-pentyl-3-(4-ethyl-1-naphthoyl)indole (JWH-210)

(x) 1-pentyl-3-(2-methoxy-1-naphthoyl)indole (JWH-267)

(xi) 1-[(N-methylpiperidin-2-yl)methyl]-3-(1-naphthoyl)indole (AM-1220)

(xii) 1-(5-fluoropentyl)-3-(1-naphthoyl)indole (AM-2201)

(xiii) 1-(5-fluoropentyl)-3-(4-methyl-1-naphthoyl)indole (MAM-2201)

(xiv) 1-(5-fluoropentyl)-3-(4-ethyl-1-naphthoyl)indole (EAM-2201)

(xv) ((3R)-2,3-dihydro-5-methyl-3-(4-morpholinylmethyl)pyrrolo[1,2,3-de]-1,4-benzoxazin-6-yl)-1-naphthalenylmethanone (WIN 55,212-2)

(3) Any substance that has a 3-(1-naphthoyl)pyrrole structure with substitution at the nitrogen atom of the pyrrole ring, whether or not further substituted on the pyrrole ring to any extent and whether or not substituted on the naphthyl ring to any extent, including

(i) 1-pentyl-5-(2-fluorophenyl)-3-(1-naphthoyl)pyrrole (JWH-307)

(4) Any substance that has a 3-phenylacetylindole structure with substitution at the nitrogen atom of the indole ring, whether or not further substituted on the indole ring to any extent and whether or not substituted on the phenyl ring to any extent, including

(i) 1-pentyl-3-(2-methoxyphenylacetyl)indole (JWH-250)

(ii) 1-pentyl-3-(2-methylphenylacetyl)indole (JWH-251)

(iii) 1-pentyl-3-(3-methoxyphenylacetyl)indole (JWH-302)

(5) Any substance that has a 3-benzoylindole structure with substitution at the nitrogen atom of the indole ring, whether or not further substituted on the indole ring to any extent and whether or not substituted on the phenyl ring to any extent, including

(i) 1-(1-methylpiperidin-2-ylmethyl)-3-(2-iodobenzoyl)indole (AM-2233)

(6) Any substance that has a 3-methanone(cyclopropyl)indole structure with substitution at the nitrogen atom of the indole ring, whether or not further substituted on the indole ring to any extent and whether or not substituted on the cyclopropyl ring to any extent, including

(i) (1-pentyl-1H-indol-3-yl)(2,2,3,3-tetramethylcyclopropyl)-methanone (UR-144)

(ii) (1-(5-fluoropentyl)-1H-indol-3-yl)(2,2,3,3-tetramethylcyclopropyl)-methanone (5F-UR-144)

(iii) (1-(2-(4-morpholinyl)ethyl)-1H-indol-3-yl)(2,2,3,3-tetramethylcyclopropyl)-methanone (A-796,260)

(7) Any substance that has a quinolin-8-yl 1H-indole-3-carboxylate structure with substitution at the nitrogen atom of the indole ring, whether or not further substituted on the indole ring to any extent and whether or not substituted on the quinolin-8-yl ring to any extent, including

(i) 1-pentyl-8-quinolinyl ester-1H-indole-3-carboxylic acid (PB-22)

(ii) 1-(5-fluoropentyl)-8-quinolinyl ester-1H-indole-3-carboxylic acid (5F-PB-22)

(8) Any substance that has a 3-carboxamideindazole structure with substitution at the nitrogen atom of the indazole ring, whether or not further substituted on the indazole ring to any extent and whether or not substituted at the carboxamide group to any extent, including

(i) N-(adamantan-1-yl)-1-pentyl-1H-indazole-3-carboxamide (AKB48)

(ii) N-(adamantan-1-yl)-1-(5-fluoropentyl)-1H-indazole-3-carboxamide (5F-AKB48)

(iii) N-(1-(aminocarbonyl)-2-methylpropyl)-1-(4-fluorobenzyl)-1H-indazole-3-carboxamide (AB-FUBINACA)

(iv) N-(1-amino-3-methyl-1-oxobutan-2-yl)-1-pentyl-1H-indazole-3-carboxamide (AB-PINACA)

(9) Any substance that has a 3-carboxamideindole structure with substitution at the nitrogen atom of the indole ring, whether or not further substituted on the indole ring to any extent and whether or not substituted at the carboxamide group to any extent, including

(i) N-(adamantan-1-yl)-1-fluoropentylindole-3-carboxamide (STS-135)

(ii) N-(adamantan-1-yl)-1-pentylindole-3-carboxamide (APICA)

SOR/98-157; SOR/2003-32, s. 1; SOR/2015-192, ss. 1, 2; 2018, c. 16, s. 204

SCHEDULE III

(Sections 2, 4 to 7.1, 10, 29, 55 and 60)

[Reference amended 2017, c. 7, s. 48.]

1. [Repealed 2012, c. 1, s. 45.]

2. Methylphenidate (methyl 2-phenyl-2-(piperidin-2-yl)acetate), its salts, derivatives, isomers and analogues and salts of derivatives, isomers and analogues, including

(1) Ethylphenidate (ethyl 2-phenyl-2-(piperidin-2-yl)acetate)

(2) Isopropylphenidate (isopropyl 2-phenyl-2-(piperidin-2-yl)acetate)

(3) Propylphenidate (propyl 2-phenyl-2-(piperidin-2-yl)acetate)

(4) 3,4-Dichloromethylphenidate (methyl 2-(3,4-dichlorophenyl)-2-(piperidin-2-yl)acetate)

(5) 4-Methylmethylphenidate (methyl 2-(4-methylphenyl)-2-(piperidin-2-yl)acetate)

(6) 4-Fluoromethylphenidate (methyl 2-(4-fluorophenyl)-2-(piperidin-2-yl)acetate)

(7) Methylnaphthidate (methyl 2-(naphthalen-2-yl)-2-(piperidin-2-yl)acetate)

(8) Ethylnaphthidate (ethyl 2-(naphthalen-2-yl)-2-(piperidin-2-yl)acetate)

3. Methaqualone (2-methyl-3-(2-methylphenyl)-4(3H)-quinazolinone) and any salt thereof

4. Mecloqualone (2-methyl-3-(2-chlorophenyl)-4(3H)-quinazolinone) and any salt thereof

5. Lysergic acid diethylamide (LSD) (N,N-diethyllysergamide) and any salt thereof

6. N,N-Diethyltryptamine (DET) (3-[(2-diethylamino) ethyl]indole) and any salt thereof

7. N,N-Dimethyltryptamine (DMT) (3-[(2-dimethylamino)ethyl]indole) and any salt thereof

8. N-Methyl-3-piperidyl benzilate (LBJ) (3-[(hydroxydiphenylacetyl)oxy]-1-methylpiperidine) and any salt thereof

9. Harmaline (4,9-dihydro-7-methoxy-1-methyl-3H-pyrido(3,4-b)indole) and any salt thereof

10. Harmalol (4,9-dihydro-1-methyl-3H-pyrido (3,4-b)indol-7-ol) and any salt thereof

11. Psilocin (3-[2-(dimethylamino)ethyl]-4-hydroxyindole) and any salt thereof

12. Psilocybin (3-[2-(dimethylamino)ethyl]-4-phosphoryloxyindole) and any salt thereof

13. N-(1-phenylcyclohexyl)ethylamine (PCE) and any salt thereof

14. 1-[1-(2-Thienyl) cyclohexyl]piperidine (TCP) and any salt thereof

15. 1-Phenyl-N-propylcyclohexanamine and any salt thereof

16. Rolicyclidine (1-(1-phenylcyclohexyl) pyrrolidine) and any salt thereof

17. Mescaline (3,4,5-trimethoxybenzeneethanamine) and any salt thereof, but not peyote (lophophora)

18. [Repealed SOR/2017-249, s. 1.]

19. Cathinone ((-)-α-aminopropiophenone) and its salts

20. Fenetylline (d,1-3,7-dihydro-1,3-dimethyl-7-(2- [(1-methyl-2-phenethyl)amino]ethyl)-1H-purine -2, 6-dione) and any salt thereof

21. 2-Methylamino-1-phenyl-1-propanone and any salt thereof

22. 1-[1-(Phenylmethyl)cyclohexyl]piperidine and any salt thereof

23. 1-[1-(4-Methylphenyl)cyclohexyl]piperidine and any salt thereof

24. [Repealed SOR/2016-73, s. 1.]

25 and 26. [Repealed 2012, c. 1, s. 46.]

27. Aminorex (5-phenyl-4,5-dihydro-1,3-oxazol-2-amine), its salts, derivatives, isomers and analogues and salts of derivatives, isomers and analogues, including

(1) 4-Methylaminorex (4-methyl-5-phenyl-4,5-dihydro-1,3-oxazol-2-amine)

(2) 4,4'-Dimethylaminorex (4-methyl-5-(4-methylphenyl)-4,5-dihydro-1,3-oxazol-2-amine)

SOR/2017-249, s. 2

28. Etryptamine (3-(2-aminobutyl)indole) and any salt thereof

29. Lefetamine ((-)-N,N-dimethyl-α-phenylbenzeneethanamine), its salts, derivatives and isomers and salts of derivatives and isomers

30. Mesocarb (3-(α-methylphenethyl)-N-(phenylcarbamoyl)sydnone imine) and any salt thereof

31. Zipeprol (4-(2-methoxy-2-phenylethyl)-α-(methoxyphenylmethyl)-1-piperazineethanol) and any salt thereof

32. Amineptine (7-[(10,11-dihydro-5H-dibenzo[a,d]cyclohepten-5-yl)amino]heptanoic acid) and any salt thereof

33. Benzylpiperazine [BZP], namely 1-benzylpiperazine and its salts, isomers and salts of isomers

34. Trifluoromethylphenylpiperazine [TFMPP], namely 1-(3-trifluoromethylphenyl)piperazine and its salts, isomers and salts of isomers

35. 2C-phenethylamines and their salts, derivatives, isomers and salts of derivatives and isomers that correspond to the following chemical description:

any substance that has a 1-amino-2-phenylethane structure substituted at the 2' and 5' or 2' and 6' positions of the benzene ring by an alkoxy or haloalkoxy group, or substituted at two adjacent carbon atoms of the benzene ring which results in the formation of a furan, dihydrofuran, pyran, dihydropyran or methylenedioxy group — whether or not further substituted on the benzene ring to any extent, whether or not substituted at the amino group by one or two, or a combination of, methyl, ethyl, propyl, isopropyl, hydroxyl, benzyl (or benzyl substituted to any extent) or benzylene (or benzylene substituted to any extent) groups and whether or not substituted at the 2-ethyl (beta carbon) position by a hydroxyl, oxo or alkoxy group — and its salts and derivatives and salts of derivatives, including

(1) 4-bromo-2,5-dimethoxy-N-(2-methoxybenzyl)phenethylamine (25B-NBOMe)

(2) 4-chloro-2,5-dimethoxy-N-(2-methoxybenzyl)phenethylamine (25C-NBOMe)

(3) 4-iodo-2,5-dimethoxy-N-(2-methoxybenzyl)phenethylamine (25I-NBOMe)

(4) 4-bromo-2,5-dimethoxybenzeneethanamine (2C-B)

SOR/97-230; SOR/98-173; SOR/2000-220, s. 1; SOR/2003-32, ss. 2, 3, 5; SOR/2003-412, s. 1; SOR/2005-235, s. 2; 2012, c. 1, ss. 45, 46; SOR/2012-66, s. 1; SOR/2016-73, s. 2; SOR/2016-107, s. 2; SOR/2017-13, s. 6; SOR/2017-44, s. 1

SCHEDULE IV

(Sections 2, 4 to 7.1, 10, 29, 55 and 60)

[Reference amended 2017, c. 7, s. 49.]

1. Barbiturates, their salts and derivatives including

(1) Allobarbital (5,5-diallylbarbituric acid)

(2) Alphenal (5-allyl-5-phenylbarbituric acid)

(3) Amobarital (5-ethyl-5-(3-methylbutyl) barbituric acid)

(4) Aprobarbital (5-allyl-5-isopropylbarbituric acid)

(5) Barbital (5,5-diethylbarbituric acid)

(6) [Repealed SOR/2017-13, s. 7(1).]

(7) Butabarbital (5-sec-butyl-5-ethylbarbituric acid)

(8) Butalbital (5-allyl-5-isobutylbarbituric acid)

(9) Butallylonal (5-(2-bromoallyl)-5-sec-butylbarbituric acid)

(10) Butethal (5-butyl-5-ethylbarbituric acid)

(11) Cyclobarbital (5-(1-cyclohexen-1-yl)-5-ethylbarbituric acid)

(12) Cyclopal (5-allyl-5-(2-cyclopenten-1-yl)barbituric acid

(13) Heptabarbital (5-(1-cyclohepten-1-yl)-5-ethylbarbituric acid)

(14) Hexethal (5-ethyl-5-hexylbarbituric acid)

(15) Hexobarbital (5-(1-cyclohexen-1-yl)-1,5-dimethylbarbituric acid)

(16) Mephobarbital (5-ethyl-1-methyl-5-phenylbarbituric acid)

(17) Methabarbital (5,5-diethyl-1-methylbarbituric acid)

(18) Methylphenobarbital (5-ethyl-1-methyl-5-phenylbarbituric acid)

(19) Propallylonal(5-(2-bromoally)-5-isopropylbarbituric acid)

(20) Pentobarbital (5-ethyl-5-(1-methylbutyl)barbituric acid)

(21) Phenobarbital (5-ethyl-5-phenylbarbituric acid)

(22) Probarbital (5-ethyl-5-isopropylbarbituric acid)

(23) Phenylmethylbarbituric Acid (5-methyl-5-phenylbarbituric acid)

(24) Secobarbital (5-allyl-5-(1-methylbutyl)barbituric acid)

(25) Sigmodal (5-(2-bromoallyl)-5-(1-methylbutyl)barbituric acid)

(26) Talbutal (5-allyl-5-sec-butylbarbituric acid)

(27) Vinbarbital (5-ethyl-5-(1-methy-1-butenyl)barbituric acid)

(28) Vinylbital (5-(1-methylbutyl)-5-vinylbarbituric acid)
but not including

(29) Barbituric Acid (2,4,6(1H,3H,5H)-pyrimidinetrione) and its salts

(30) 1,3-dimethylbarbituric acid (1,3-dimethyl-2,4,6(1H,3H,5H)-pyrimidinetrione) and its salts

2. Thiobarbiturates, their salts and derivatives including:

(1) Thialbarbital (5-allyl-5-(2-cyclohexen-1-yl)-2-thiobarbituric acid)

(2) Thiamylal (5-allyl-5-(1-methylbutyl)-2-thiobarbituric acid)

(3) Thiobarbituric Acid (2-thiobarbituric acid)

(4) Thiopental (5-ethyl-5-(1-methylbutyl)-2-thiobarbituric acid)

3. Chlorphentermine (1-(p-chlorophenyl)-2-methyl-2-aminopropane) and any salt thereof

4. Diethylpropion (2-(diethylamino)propiophenone) and any salt thereof

5. Phendimetrazine (d-3,4-dimethyl-2-phenylmorpholine) and any salt thereof

6. Phenmetrazine (3-methyl-2-phenylmorpholine) and any salt thereof

7. Pipradol (α,α-diphenyl-2-piperidinemethanol) and its salts

8. Phentermine (α,α-dimethylbenzeneethanamine) and any salt thereof

9. Butorphanol (l-N-cyclobutylmethyl-3,14-dihydroxymorphinan) and its salts

10. Nalbuphine (N-cyclobutylmethyl-4,5-epoxy-morphinan-3,6,14-triol) and its salts

11. Glutethiamide (2-ethyl-2-phenylglutarimide)

12. Clotiazepam (5-(o-chlorophenyl)-7-ethyl-1,3-dihydro-1-methyl-2H-thieno[2,3-e]-1,4-diazepin-2-one) and any salt thereof

13. Ethchlorvynol (ethyl-2-chlorovinyl ethynyl carbinol)

14. Ethinamate (1-ethynylcyclohexanol carbamate)

15. Mazindol (5-(p-chlorophenyl)-2,5-dihydro-3H-imidazo[2,1-a]isoindol-5-ol)

16. Meprobamate (2-methyl-2-propyl-1,3-propanediol dicarbonate)

17. Methyprylon (3,3-diethyl-5-methyl-2,4-piperidinedione)

18. Benzodiazepines, their salts and derivatives, including:

(1) Alprazolam (8-chloro-1-methyl-6-phenyl-4H-s-triazolo[4,3-a][1,4] benzodiazepine)

(2) Bromazepam (7-bromo-1,3-dihydro-5-(2-pyridyl)- 2H-1, 4-benzodiazepin-2-one)

(2.1) Brotizolam (2-bromo-4-(o-chlorophenyl)-9-methyl-6H-thieno[3,2-f]-s-triazolo[4,3-a][1,4]diazepine)

(3) Camazepam (7-chloro-1,3-dihydro-3-(N,N-dimethylcarbamoyl)-1-methyl-5-phenyl-2H-1,4-benzodiazepin-2-one)

(4) Chlodiazepoxide(7-chloro-2-(methylamino)-5-phenyl-3H-1,4-benzodiazepine-4-oxide)

(5) Clobazam(7-chloro-1-methyl-5-phenyl-1H-1,5-benzodiazepine-2,4(3H,5H)-dione)

(6) Clonazepam(5-(o-chlorophenyl)-1,3-dihydro-7-nitro-2H-1,4-benzodiazepin-2-one)

(7) Clorazepate(7-chloro-2,3-dihydro-2,2-dihydroxy-5-phenyl-1H-1,4-benzodiazepine-3-carboxylic acid)

(8) Cloxazolam(10-chloro-11b-(o-chlorophenyl)-2,3,7,11b-tetrahydrooxazolo[3,2-d][1,4]benzodiazepin-6-(5H)-one)

(9) Delorazepam (7-chloro-5-(o-chlorophenyl)-1,3-dihydro-2H-1,4-benzodiazepin-2-one)

(10) Diazepam (7-chloro-1,3-dihydro-1-methyl-5-phenyl-2H-1,4-benzodiazepin-2-one)

(11) Estazolam (8-chloro-6-phenyl-4H-s-triazolo[4,3-a][1,4]benzodiazepine)

(12) Ethyl Loflazepate (ethyl7-chloro-5-(o-flourophenyl)-2,3-dihydro-2-oxo-1H-1,4-benzodiazepine-3-carboxylate)

(13) Fludiazepam(7-chloro-5-(o-flourophenyl)-1,3-dihydro-1-methyl-2H-1,4-benzodiazepin-2-one)

(14) [Repealed SOR/98-173]

(15) Flurazepam(7-chloro-1-[2-(diethylamino)ethyl]-5-(o-flourophenyl)-1,3-dihydro-2H-1,4-benzodiazepin-2-one)

(16) Halazepam(7-chloro-1,3-dihydro-5-phenyl-1-(2,2,2-triflouroethyl)-2H-1,4-benzodiazepin-2-one)

(17) Haloxazolam(10-bromo-11b-(o-flourophenyl)-2,3,7,11b-tetrahydrooxazolo[3,2-d][1,4] benzodiazepin-6(5H)-one)

(18) Ketazolam (11-chloro-8,12b-dihydro-2,8-dimethyl-12b-phenyl-4H-[1,3]-oxazino-[3,2-d][1,4] benzodiazepine-4,7(6H)-dione)

(19) Loprazolam (6-(o-chlorophenyl)-2,4-dihydro-2-[(4-methyl-1-piperazinyl)methylene]-8-nitro-1H-imidazo[1,2-a][1,4]benzodiazepin-1-one)

(20) Lorazepam (7-chloro-5-(o-chlorophenyl)-1,3-dihydro -3-hydroxy-2H-1,4-benzodiazepin-2-one)

(21) Lormetazepam (7-chloro-5(o-chlorophenyl)-1,3-dihydro-3 -hydroxy-1-methyl-2H-1,4-benzodiazepin-2-one)

(22) Medazepam (7-chloro-2,3-dihydro-1-methyl-5-phenyl-1H-1,4-benzodiazepine)

(22.1) Midazolam (8-chloro-6-(o-fluorophenyl)-1-methyl-4H-imidazo[1,5-a][1,4]benzodiazepine)

(23) Nimetazepam (1,3-dihydro-1-methyl-7-nitro-5-phenyl-2H-1,4-benzodiazepin-2-one)

(24) Nitrazepam (1,3-dihydro-7-nitro-5-phenyl-2H-1, 4-benzodiazepin-2-one)

(25) Nordazepam (7-chloro-1,3-dihydro-5-phenyl-2H-1,4-benzodiazepin-2-one)

(26) Oxazepam (7-chloro-1,3-dihydro-3-hydroxy-5-phenyl-2H-1,4-benzodiazepin-2-one)

(27) Oxazolam (10-chloro-2,3,7,11b-tetrahydro-2-methyl-11b-phenyloxazolo[3,2-d] [1,4]benzodiazepin-6(5H)-one)

(28) Pinazepam (7-chloro-1,3-dihydro-5-phenyl-1-(2-propynyl)-2H-1, 4-benzodiazepin-2-one)

(29) Prazepam (7-chloro-1-(cyclopropylmethyl)-1,3-dihydro -5-phenyl-2H-1,4-benzodiazepin-2-one)

(29.1) Quazepam (7-chloro-5-(o-fluorophenyl)-1,3-dihydro-1-(2,2,2-trifluoroethyl)-2H-1,4-benzodiazepine-2-thione)

(30) Temazepam (7-chloro-1,3-dihydro-3-hydroxy-1-methyl-5-phenyl-2H-1,4-benzodiazepin-2-one

(31) Tetrazepam (7-chloro-5-(cyclohexen-1-yl)-1,3-dihydro-1-methyl-2H-1,4-benzodiazepin-2-one)

(32) Triazolam (8-chloro-6-(o-chlorophenyl)-1-methyl -4H-s-triazolo[4,3-a][1,4]benzodiazepine)

but not including

(32.1) Clozapine (8-chloro-11-(4-methyl-1-piperazinyl)-5H-dibenzo[b,e][1,4]diazepine) and any salt thereof

(33) Flunitrazepam (5-(o-fluorophenyl)-1,3-dihydro-1-methyl-7-nitro-2H-1,4-benzodiazepin-2-one) and any salts or derivatives thereof

(34) Olanzapine (2-methyl-4-(4-methyl-1-piperazinyl)-10H-thieno[2,3-b][1,5]benzodiazepine) and its salts

(35) Clozapine N-oxide (8-chloro-11-(4-methyl-4-oxido-1-piperazinyl)-5H-dibenzo[b,e][1,4]diazepine) and its salts

19. *Catha edulis* Forsk, its preparations, derivatives, alkaloids and salts, including:

(1) Cathine (d-threo-2-amino-1-hydroxy-1-phenylpropane)

20. Fencamfamin (d,1-N-ethyl-3-phenylbicyclo[2,2,1] heptan-2-amine) and any salt thereof

21. Fenproporex (d,1-3-[(α-methylphenethyl)amino] propionitrile) and any salt thereof

22. Mefenorex (d,1-N-(3-chloropropyl)-α-methylbenzeneethanamine) and any salt thereof

23. Anabolic steroids and their derivatives including:

(1) Androisoxazole (17β-hydroxy-17α-methylandrostano [3,2-c]isoxazole)

(2) Androstanolone (17β-hydroxy-5α-androstan-3-one)

(3) Androstenediol (androst-5-ene-3β,17β-diol)

(4) Bolandiol (estr-4-ene-3β,17β-diol)

(5) Bolasterone (17β-hydroxy-7α,17-dimethylandrost-4 -en-3-one)

(6) Bolazine (17β-hydroxy-2α-methyl-5α-androstan-3-one azine)

(7) Boldenone (17β-hydroxyandrosta-1,4-dien-3-one)

(8) Bolenol (19-nor-17α-pregn-5-en-17-ol)

(9) Calusterone (17β-hydroxy-7β,17-dimethylandrost-4-en-3-one)

(10) Clostebol (4-chloro-17β-hydroxyandrost-4-en-3-one)

(11) Drostanolone (17β-hydroxy-2α-methyl-5α-androstan-3-one)

(12) Enestebol (4,17β-dihydroxy-17-methylandrosta-1,4-dien-3-one)

(13) Epitiostanol (2α, 3α-epithio-5α-androstan-17β-ol)

(14) Ethylestrenol (19-nor-17α-pregn-4-en-17-ol)

(15) 4-Hydroxy-19-nor testosterone

(16) Fluoxymesterone (9-fluoro-11β,17β-dihydroxy-17-methylandrost-4-en-3-one)

(17) Formebolone (11α,17β-dihydroxy-17-methyl-3-oxoandrosta-1,4 di-en-2-carboxaldehyde)

(18) Furazabol (17-methyl-5α-androstano[2,3-c] furazan-17β-ol)

(19) Mebolazine (17β-hydroxy-2α,17-dimethyl-5α -androstan-3-one azine)

(20) Mesabolone (17β1-[(1-methoxycyclohexyl)oxy]-5α-androst-1-en-3-one)

(21) Mesterolone (17β-hydroxy-1α-methyl-5α-androstan-3-one)

(22) Metandienone (17β-hydroxy-17-methylandrosta-1,4-dien-3-one)

(23) Metenolone (17β-hydroxy-1-methyl-5α-androst-1-en-3-one)

(24) Methandriol (17α-methylandrost-5-ene-3β,17β-diol)

(25) Methyltestosterone (17β-hydroxy-17-methylandrost-4-en-3-one)

(26) Metribolone (17β-hydroxy-17-methylestra-4,9,11-trien-3-one)

(27) Mibolerone (17β-hydroxy-7α,17-dimethylestr-4-en-3-one)

(28) Nandrolone (17β-hydroxyestr-4-en-3-one)

(29) Norboletone (13-ethyl-17β-hydroxy-18,19-dinorpregn-4-en-3-one)

(30) Norclostebol (4-chloro-17β-hydroxyestr-4-en-3-one)

(31) Norethandrolone (17α-ethyl-17β-hydroxyestr-4-en-3-one)

(32) Oxabolone (4,17β-dihydroxyestr-4-en-3-one)

(33) Oxandrolone (17β-hydroxy-17-methyl-2-oxa-5 α-androstan-3-one)

(34) Oxymesterone (4,17β-dihydroxy-17-methylandrost-4-en-3-one)

(35) Oxymetholone (17β-hydroxy-2-(hydroxymethylene)-17-methyl-5α-androstan-3-one)

(36) Prasterone (3β-hydroxyandrost-5-en-17-one)

(37) Quinbolone (17β-(1-cyclopenten-1-yloxy) androsta-1,4-dien-3-one)

(38) Stanozolol (17β-hydroxy-17-methyl-5α-androstano [3,2-c]pyrazole)

(39) Stenbolone (17β-hydroxy-2-methyl-5α-androst-1-en-3-one)

(40) Testosterone (17β-hydroxyandrost-4-en-3-one)

(41) Tibolone ((7α, 17α)-17-hydroxy-7-methyl-19-norpregn-5 (10)en-20-yn-3-one)

(42) Tiomesterone (1α,7α-bis(acetylthio)-17β-hydroxy-17-methylandrost-4-en-3-one)

(43) Trenbolone (17β-hydroxyestra-4,9,11-trien-3-one)

24. Zeranol (3,4,5,6,7,8,9,10,11,12-decahydro-7,14,16- trihydroxy-3-methyl-1H-2-benzoxacyclotetradecin-1-one)

25. Zolpidem (N,N,6-trimethyl-2-(4-methylphenyl)imidazo [1,2-a]pyridine-3-acetamide) and any salt thereof

25.1 Pemoline (2-amino-5-phenyl-oxazolin-4-one) and any salt thereof

26. Pyrovalerone (4'-methyl-2-(1-pyrrolidinyl) valerophenone) and any salt thereof

27. *Salvia divinorum* (*S. divinorum*), its preparations and derivatives, including:

(1) Salvinorin A ((2S,4aR,6aR,7R,9S,10aS,10bR)-9-(acetyloxy)-2-(3-furanyl)dodecahydro-6a,10b-dimethyl-4,10-dioxo-2H-naphtho[2,1-c]pyran-7-carboxylic acid methyl ester)

SOR/97-230; SOR/98-173; SOR/99-371; SOR/99-421; SOR/2000-220, s. 2; SOR/2003-32, s. 6; SOR/2003-37, s. 1; SOR/2015-209, s. 1; SOR/2017-13, ss. 7–12; SOR/2018-70, s. 4

SCHEDULE V

(Sections 2, 5 to 7.1, 10, 55 and 60.1)

[Reference amended 2017, c. 7, s. 50 (Sched. 1).]

1. [Repealed SOR/2002-361, s. 1.]

2. [Repealed 2017, c. 7, s. 50 (Sched. 1).]

3. [Repealed SOR/2003-32, s. 7.]

SOR/2002-361, s. 1; SOR/2003-32, s. 7; 2017, c. 7, s. 50 (Sched. 1)

SCHEDULE VI

(Sections 2, 6, 55 and 60)

Part 1 — Class A Precursors (ss. 1–32)[35]

1. Acetic anhydride

2. N-Acetylanthranilic acid (2-acetamidobenzoic acid) and its salts

3. Anthranilic acid (2-aminobenzoic acid) and its salts

4. Ephedrine (erythro-2-(methylamino)-1-phenylpropan-1-ol), its salts and any plant containing ephedrine or any of its salts

5. Ergometrine (9, 10-didehydro-N-(2-hydroxy-1-methylethyl)-6-methylergoline-8-carboxamide) and its salts

6. Ergotamine (12'-hydroxy-2'-methyl-5'-(phenylmethyl)ergotaman-3',6',18-trione) and its salts

7. Isosafrole (5-(1-propenyl)-1,3-benzodioxole)

8. Lysergic acid (9,10-didehydro-6-methylergoline-8-carboxylic acid) and its salts

9. 3,4-Methylenedioxyphenyl-2-propanone (1-(1,3-benzodioxole)-2-propanone), its derivatives and analogues and salts of derivatives and analogues, including:

(1) methyl 3-(1,3 benzodioxol-5-yl)-2-methyloxirane-2-carboxylate (MMDMG)

10. Norephedrine (Phenylpropanolamine) and its salts

11. 1-Phenyl-2-propanone, its derivatives and analogues and salts of derivatives and analogues, including:

---

35 Each Class A precursor includes synthetic and natural forms.

(1) methyl 2-methyl-3-phenyloxirane-2-carboxylate (BMK methyl glycidate)

(2) 3-oxo-2-phenylbutanamide (α-phenylacetoacetamide-APAA)

12. Phenylacetic acid and its salts

13. Piperidine and its salts

14. Piperonal (1,3-benzodioxole-5-carboxaldehyde)

15. Potassium permanganate

16. Pseudoephedrine (threo-2-(methylamino)-1-phenylpropan-1-ol), its salts and any plant containing pseudoephedrine or any of its salts

17. Safrole (5-(2-propenyl)-1,3-benzodioxole) and any essential oil containing more than 4% safrole

18. Gamma-butyrolactone (dihydro-2(3H)-furanone)

19. 1,4-butanediol

20. Red Phosphorus

21. White Phosphorus

22. Hypophosphorous acid, its salts and derivatives

23. Hydriodic acid

24. Alpha-phenylacetoacetonitrile and its salts, isomers and salts of isomers

25. Propionyl chloride

26. 1-Phenethyl-4-piperidone and its salts

27. 4-Piperidone and its salts

28. Norfentanyl (N-phenyl-N-piperidin-4-ylpropanamide), its salts, derivatives and analogues and salts of derivatives and analogues

29. 1-Phenethylpiperidin-4-ylidenephenylamine and its salts

30. N-Phenyl-4-piperidinamine and its salts

31. N^1,N^1,N^2-trimethylcyclohexane-1,2-diamine and its salts

32. Benzylfentanyl (N-(1-benzylpiperidin-4-yl)-Nphenylpropionamide), its salts, derivatives and analogues and salts of derivatives and analogues

Part 2 — Class B Precursors (ss. 1–6)[36]

1. Acetone

2. Ethyl ether

3. Hydrochloric acid

4. Methyl ethyl ketone

5. Sulphuric acid

6. Toluene

Part 3 — Preparations and Mixtures (s. 1)

1. Any preparation or mixture that contains a precursor set out in Part 1, except items 20 to 23, or in Part 2.

SOR/2002-361, s. 2; SOR/2005-364, ss. 1, 2, 4; SOR/2016-13, s. 1; SOR/2016-295, s. 1; SOR/2017-277, s. 2; SOR/2019-121, ss. 2–5

Schedule VII and VIII [Repealed 2018, c. 16, s. 205.]

Schedule IX

(Sections 2 and 60)

1. Manual, semi-automatic or fully automatic device that may be used to compact or mould powdered, granular or semi-solid material to produce coherent solid tablets

2. Manual, semi-automatic or fully automatic device that may be used to fill capsules with any powdered, granular, semi-solid or liquid material

2017, c. 7, s. 51 (Sched. 2)

[36] Each Class B precursor includes synthetic forms.

CRIMINAL RECORDS ACT

Editor's note: Current to May 15, 2019.

TABLE OF CONCORDANCE

R.S.C. 1970, c. 12 (1st Supp.)	R.S.C. 1985, c. C-47	Remarks
1	1	
2	2, part. 4	
3	3	
4	part. 4	
5	5	
6	6	
7	7	
8	8	
9	9	part. OM
Sch/Ann	Sch/Ann	

CRIMINAL RECORDS ACT

An Act to provide for the suspension of the records of persons who have been convicted of offences and have subsequently rehabilitated themselves

R.S.C. 1985, c. C-47, as am. R.S.C. 1985, c. 1 (4th Supp.), s. 45 (Sched. III, item 7) (Fr.); S.C. 1992, c. 22, ss. 1–10; 1995, c. 22, s. 17 (Sched. III, item 4); 1995, c. 39, ss. 166, 167, 191; 1995, c. 42, ss. 77, 78; 1997, c. 17, s. 38; 1998, c. 37, s. 25; 2000, c. 1, ss. 1 (Fr.), 2–8.1; 2004, c. 10, s. 23; 2004, c. 21, s. 40(1)(b); 2005, c. 10, s. 34(1)(g); 2007, c. 5, s. 50; 2008, c. 6, s. 58; 2010, c. 5, ss. 2–7.2, 7.3–7.5 (Fr.), 8, 9; 2010, c. 17, s. 64; 2012, c. 1, ss. 49, 108–134, 160(d); 2014, c. 25, s. 35; 2018, c. 16, ss. 165, 193; 2018, c. 21, ss. 40–42; 2018, c. 29, ss. 76, 77; 2019, c. 20; 2019, c. 27, s. 37.

[Note: The long title of this Act was changed from "An Act to provide for the relief of persons who have been convicted of offences and have subsequently rehabilitated themselves" to "An Act to provide for the suspension of the records of persons who have been convicted of offences and have subsequently rehabilitated themselves" by 2012, c. 1, s. 108.]

SHORT TITLE

1. Short title — This Act may be cited as the *Criminal Records Act*.

INTERPRETATION

2. (1) Definitions — In this Act,

"Board" means the Parole Board of Canada;

"child" means a person who is less than 18 years of age;

"Commissioner" means the Commissioner of the Royal Canadian Mounted Police;

"Executive Committee" means the Executive Committee of the Board referred to in subsection 151(1) of the *Corrections and Conditional Release Act*;

"Minister" means the Minister of Public Safety and Emergency Preparedness;

"pardon" [Repealed 2012, c. 1, s. 109(1).]

"period of probation" means a period during which a person convicted of an offence was directed by the court that convicted him

(a) to be released on his own recognizance to keep the peace and be of good behaviour, or

(b) to be released on or comply with the conditions prescribed in a probation order;

"possession" means possession within the meaning of subsection 4(3) of the *Criminal Code*.

"record suspension" means a measure ordered by the Board under section 4.1;

"sentence" has the same meaning as in the *Criminal Code*, but does not include an order made under section 109, 110, 161 or 320.24 of that Act or subsection 147.1(1) of the *National Defence Act*.

"service offence" has the same meaning as in subsection 2(1) of the *National Defence Act*.

(2) Termination of period of probation — For the purposes of this Act, the period of probation shall be deemed to have terminated at the time the recognizance or the probation order that relates to the period of probation ceased to be in force.

(3) [Repealed 1992, c. 22, s. 1(3).]

1992, c. 22, s. 1; 1995, c. 39, ss. 166, 191(a); 1995, c. 42, s. 77; 2005, c. 10, s. 34(1)(g); 2010, c. 5, s. 7.1(a); 2012, c. 1, ss. 109, 160(d)(i); 2018, c. 21, s. 40; 2019, c. 20, s. 1

Parole Board of Canada

[Heading amended 2012, c. 1, s. 160(d)(ii).]

2.1 (1) Jurisdiction of the Board — The Board has exclusive jurisdiction and absolute discretion to order, refuse to order or revoke a record suspension.

(2) Employees of Board — The powers, duties and functions of the Board related to an application referred to in subsection 4(3.1) shall be exercised by employees of the Board or any class of its employees.

1992, c. 22, s. 2; 2010, c. 5, s. 7.2; 2012, c. 1, s. 110; 2019, c. 20, s. 2

2.2 (1) Quorum — An application for a record suspension shall be determined, and a decision whether to revoke a record suspension under section 7 shall be made, by a panel that consists of one member of the Board.

(2) Panel of two or more persons — The Chairperson of the Board may direct that the number of members of the Board required to constitute a panel to determine an application for a record suspension, to decide whether to revoke a record suspension under section 7 or to determine any class of those applications or make any class of those decisions shall be greater than one.

1992, c. 22, s. 2; 2012, c. 1, s. 111

Effect of Record Suspension

[Heading added 2012, c. 1, s. 112.]

2.3 Effect of record suspension — A record suspension

(a) is evidence of the fact that

(i) the Board, after making the inquiries referred to in paragraph 4.2(1)(b), was satisfied that the applicant was of good conduct, and

(ii) the conviction in respect of which the record suspension is ordered should no longer reflect adversely on the applicant's character; and

(b) unless the record suspension is subsequently revoked or ceases to have effect, requires that the judicial record of the conviction be kept separate and apart from other criminal records and removes any disqualification or obligation to which the applicant is, by reason of the conviction, subject under any Act of Parliament other than

(i) section 109, 110, 161, 320.24, 490.012, 490.019 or 490.02901 of the *Criminal Code*,

(ii) section 259 of the *Criminal Code*, as it read immediately before the day on which section 14 of *An Act to amend the Criminal Code (offences relating to conveyances) and to make consequential amendments to other Acts* comes into force,

(iii) subsection 147.1(1) or section 227.01 or 227.06 of the *National Defence Act*,

(iv) section 734.5 or 734.6 of the *Criminal Code* or section 145.1 of the *National Defence Act*, in respect of any fine or victim surcharge imposed for any offence referred to in Schedule 3, or

(v) section 36.1 of the *International Transfer of Offenders Act*.

2012, c. 1, s. 112; 2018, c. 21, s. 41; 2019, c. 20, s. 3

Application for Record Suspension

[Heading amended 2012, c. 1, s. 113.]

3. (1) Application for record suspension — Subject to section 4, a person who has been convicted of an offence under an Act of Parliament may apply to the Board for a record suspension in respect of that offence, and a Canadian offender, within the meaning of the *International Transfer of Offenders Act*, who has been transferred to Canada under that Act may apply to the Board for a record suspension in respect of the offence of which he or she has been found guilty.

(2) Transfer of offenders — For the purposes of this Act, the offence of which a Canadian offender within the meaning of the *International Transfer of Offenders Act* who has been transferred to Canada under that Act has been found guilty is deemed to be an offence that was prosecuted by indictment.

1992, c. 22, s. 3; 2004, c. 21, s. 40(1)(b); 2012, c. 1, s. 114

PROCEDURE

4. (1) Restrictions on application for record suspension — Subject to subsections (3.1) and (3.11), a person is ineligible to apply for a record suspension until the following period has elapsed after the expiration according to law of any sentence, including a sentence of imprisonment, a period of probation and the payment of any fine, imposed for an offence:

(a) 10 years, in the case of an offence that is prosecuted by indictment or is a service offence for which the offender was punished by a fine of more than five thousand dollars, detention for more than six months, dismissal from Her Majesty's service, imprisonment for more than six months or a punishment that is greater than imprisonment for less than two years in the scale of punishments set out in subsection 139(1) of the *National Defence Act*; or

(b) five years, in the case of an offence that is punishable on summary conviction or is a service offence other than a service offence referred to in paragraph (a).

(2) Ineligible persons — Subject to subsection (3), a person is ineligible to apply for a record suspension if he or she has been convicted of

(a) an offence referred to in Schedule 1; or

(b) more than three offences each of which either was prosecuted by indictment or is a service offence that is subject to a maximum punishment of imprisonment for life, and for each of which the person was sentenced to imprisonment for two years or more.

(3) Exception — A person who has been convicted of an offence referred to in Schedule 1 may apply for a record suspension if the Board is satisfied that

(a) the person was not in a position of trust or authority towards the victim of the offence and the victim was not in a relationship of dependency with him or her;

(b) the person did not use, threaten to use or attempt to use violence, intimidation or coercion in relation to the victim; and

(c) the person was less than five years older than the victim.

(3.1) Offence referred to in Schedule 3 — A person who has been convicted only of an offence referred to in Schedule 3 may apply for a record suspension in respect of that offence before the expiration of the period referred to in subsection (1).

(3.11) Other offences including at least one offence referred to in Schedule 3 — A person who has been convicted of an offence referred to in Schedule 3 and other offences may only apply for a record suspension after the expiration of the period referred to in subsection (1), without taking into account any offence referred to in Schedule 3.

(3.2) Expiration according to law of sentence — A person is ineligible to make an application for a record suspension referred to in subsection (3.1) or (3.11) until after the expiration according to law of any sentence imposed, other than the payment of any fine or victim surcharge, for any offence referred to in Schedule 3.

(3.21) For greater certainty — For greater certainty, subsection (3.2) does not apply to fines and victim surcharges imposed for both an offence referred to in Schedule 3 and for other offences, in which case a person is ineligible to make an application for a record suspension referred to in subsection (3.11) until after all fines and victim surcharges have been paid.

(3.3) Fee not payable — Despite anything in an order made under the *Financial Administration Act*, a person who makes an application for a record suspension referred to in subsection (3.1) is not required to pay any fee for services provided by the Board in respect of that application if the person has been convicted only of an offence referred to in that subsection.

(4) Onus — exception — The person has the onus of satisfying the Board that the conditions referred to in subsection (3) are met.

(4.1) Onus — person referred to in subsection (3.1) — The person referred to in subsection (3.1) has the onus of satisfying the Board that the person has been convicted only of an offence referred to in that subsection.

(4.11) Information — application referred to in subsection (3.1) — For the purpose of an application referred to in subsection (3.1), the Board may not require a person who makes the application to provide a certified copy of information contained in court records in support of the application unless the certified verification of the applicant's criminal records and information contained in the police records or Canadian Armed Forces records provided in support of the application are not sufficient to demonstrate that the person has been convicted only of an offence referred to in Schedule 3 and that the only sentence imposed for that offence was payment of a fine or victim surcharge or both.

(4.12) Onus — person referred to in subsection (3.11) — For the purpose of subsection (3.11), a person referred to in that subsection has the onus of satisfying the Board that the person has been convicted of an offence referred to in Schedule 3.

(5) Amendment of Schedules 1 and 3 — The Governor in Council may, by order, amend Schedule 1 or 3 by adding or deleting a reference to an offence.

1992, c. 22, s. 4; 2010, c. 5, s. 2; 2012, c. 1, s. 115; 2019, c. 20, s. 4

4.01 Exception — long-term supervision — The period during which a person is supervised under an order for long-term supervision, within the meaning of subsection 2(1) of the *Corrections and Conditional Release Act*, is not included in the calculation of the period referred to in subsection 4(1).

1997, c. 17, s. 38; 2012, c. 1, s. 115

4.1 (1) Record suspension — Subject to subsection (1.1), the Board may order that an applicant's record in respect of an offence be suspended, without taking into account any offence referred to in Schedule 3, if the Board is satisfied that

(a) the applicant, during the applicable period referred to in subsection 4(1), has been of good conduct and has not been convicted of an offence under an Act of Parliament; and

(b) in the case of an offence referred to in paragraph 4(1)(a), ordering the record suspension at that time would provide a measurable benefit to the applicant, would sustain his or her rehabilitation in society as a law-abiding citizen and would not bring the administration of justice into disrepute.

(1.1) Record suspension — person referred to in subsection 4(3.1) — In the case of an application referred to in subsection 4(3.1), the Board shall order that the applicant's record in respect of that offence be suspended if the applicant has been convicted only of an offence referred to in that subsection and has not been convicted of a new offence under an Act of Parliament, other than an offence referred to in that subsection.

(1.2) Exception to revocation — A record suspension ordered under subsection (1.1) may not be revoked by the Board under paragraph 7(b).

(2) Onus on applicant — In the case of an offence referred to in paragraph 4(1)(a), the applicant has the onus of satisfying the Board that the record suspension would provide a measurable benefit to the applicant and would sustain his or her rehabilitation in society as a law-abiding citizen.

(3) Factors — In determining whether ordering the record suspension would bring the administration of justice into disrepute, the Board may consider

(a) the nature, gravity and duration of the offence;

(b) the circumstances surrounding the commission of the offence;

(c) information relating to the applicant's criminal history and, in the case of a service offence, to any service offence history of the applicant that is relevant to the application; and

(d) any factor that is prescribed by regulation.

1992, c. 22, s. 4; 2010, c. 5, s. 3; 2012, c. 1, s. 116; 2019, c. 20, s. 5

4.2 (1) Inquiries — On receipt of an application for a record suspension, the Board

(a) shall cause inquiries to be made to ascertain whether the applicant is eligible to make the application;

(b) if the applicant is eligible, shall cause inquiries to be made to ascertain the applicant's conduct since the date of the conviction; and

(c) may, in the case of an offence referred to in paragraph 4(1)(a), cause inquiries to be made with respect to any factors that it may consider in determining whether ordering the record suspension would bring the administration of justice into disrepute.

(1.1) Restrictions on inquiries — The inquiries referred to in paragraph (1)(a), made with respect to an application referred to in subsection 4(3.1) or (3.11), are not to take into account the non-payment of any fine or victim surcharge imposed for any offence referred to in Schedule 3.

(1.2) Restrictions on inquiries — The inquiries referred to in paragraphs (1)(b) and (c) do not apply to an application referred to in subsection 4(3.1) and, with respect to all other applications for a record suspension, are not to take into account any offence referred to in Schedule 3.

(2) **Entitlement to make representations** — If the Board proposes to refuse to order a record suspension, it shall notify in writing the applicant of its proposal and advise the applicant that he or she is entitled to make, or have made on his or her behalf, any representations to the Board that he or she believes relevant either in writing or, with the Board's authorization, orally at a hearing held for that purpose.

(3) **Board to consider representations** — The Board shall, before making its decision, consider any representations made to it within a reasonable time after the notification is given to the applicant pursuant to subsection (2).

(4) **Waiting period** — An applicant may not re-apply for a record suspension until the expiration of one year after the day on which the Board refuses to order a record suspension.

1992, c. 22, s. 4; 2000, c. 1, s. 2; 2010, c. 5, s. 4; 2012, c. 1, s. 117; 2019, c. 20, s. 6

4.3 Expiration of sentence — For the purposes of section 4, a reference to the expiration according to law of a sentence of imprisonment imposed for an offence shall be read as a reference to the day on which the sentence expires, without taking into account

(a) any period during which the offender could be entitled to statutory release or any period following a statutory release date; or

(b) any remission that stands to the credit of the offender in respect of the offence.

1992, c. 22, s. 4

4.4 Functions of Executive Committee — The Executive Committee shall, after the consultation with Board members that it considers appropriate, adopt policies relating to applications for record suspensions, including related inquiries and proceedings.

2012, c. 1, s. 118

Heading and s. 5. [Repealed 2012, c. 1, s. 119.]

Custody of Records

6. (1) Records to be delivered to Commissioner — The Minister may, by order in writing addressed to a person having the custody or control of a judicial record of a conviction in respect of which a record suspension has been ordered, require that person to deliver that record into the Commissioner's custody.

(2) **Records to be kept separate and not be disclosed** — A record of a conviction in respect of which a record suspension has been ordered that is in the custody of the Commissioner or of any department or agency of the Government of Canada shall be kept separate and apart from other criminal records. Subject to subsection (2.1), no record of a conviction is to be disclosed to any person, nor is the existence of the record or the fact of the conviction to be disclosed to any person, without the prior approval of the Minister.

(2.1) Limited disclosure — The prior approval of the Minister referred to in subsection (2) is not necessary for the purposes of sections 734.5 and 734.6 of the *Criminal Code* or section 145.1 of the *National Defence Act* for non-payment of a fine or victim surcharge that is imposed for an offence referred to in Schedule 3.

(3) Approval for disclosure — The Minister shall, before granting the approval for disclosure referred to in subsection (2), satisfy himself that the disclosure is desirable in the interests of the administration of justice or for any purpose related to the safety or security of Canada or any state allied or associated with Canada.

(4) Information in national DNA data bank — For greater certainty, a judicial record of a conviction includes any information in relation to the conviction that is contained in the convicted offenders index of the national DNA data bank established under the *DNA Identification Act*.

1998, c. 37, s. 25; 2000, c. 1, s. 5; 2010, c. 5, s. 7.1(b); 2012, c. 1, s. 120; 2019, c. 20, s. 6.1

6.1 (1) Discharges — No record of a discharge under section 730 of the *Criminal Code* that is in the custody of the Commissioner or of any department or agency of the Government of Canada shall be disclosed to any person, nor shall the existence of the record or the fact of the discharge be disclosed to any person, without the prior approval of the Minister, if

(a) more than one year has elapsed since the offender was discharged absolutely; or

(b) more than three years have elapsed since the day on which the offender was ordered discharged on the conditions prescribed in a probation order.

(2) Purging C.P.I.C. — The Commissioner shall remove all references to a discharge under section 730 of the *Criminal Code* from the automated criminal conviction records retrieval system maintained by the Royal Canadian Mounted Police on the expiration of the relevant period referred to in subsection (1).

1992, c. 22, s. 6; 1995, c. 22, s. 17 (Sched. III, item 4); 2019, c. 27, s. 37

6.2 Disclosure to police forces — Despite sections 6 and 6.1, the name, date of birth and last known address of a person whose record is suspended under section 4.1 or who has received a discharge referred to in section 6.1 may be disclosed to a police force if a fingerprint, identified as that of the person, is found

(a) at the scene of a crime during an investigation of the crime; or

(b) during an attempt to identify a deceased person or a person suffering from amnesia.

1992, c. 22, s. 6; 2012, c. 1, s. 121

6.3 (1) Definition of "vulnerable person" — In this section, **"vulnerable person"** means a person who, because of his or her age, a disability or other circumstances, whether temporary or permanent,

(a) is in a position of dependency on others; or

(b) is otherwise at a greater risk than the general population of being harmed by a person in a position of trust or authority towards them.

(2) Notation of records — The Commissioner shall make, in the automated criminal conviction records retrieval system maintained by the Royal Canadian Mounted Police, a notation enabling a member of a police force or other authorized body to determine whether there is a record of an individual's conviction for an offence listed in Schedule 2 in respect of which a record suspension has been ordered.

(3) Verification — At the request of any person or organization responsible for the well-being of a child or vulnerable person and to whom or to which an application is made for a paid or volunteer position, a member of a police force or other authorized body shall verify whether the applicant is the subject of a notation made in accordance with subsection (2) if

(a) the position is one of trust or authority towards that child or vulnerable person; and

(b) the applicant has consented in writing to the verification.

(4) Unauthorized use — Except as authorized by subsection (3), no person shall verify whether a person is the subject of a notation made in accordance with subsection (2).

(5) Request to forward record to Minister — A police force or other authorized body that identifies an applicant for a position referred to in paragraph (3)(a) as being a person who is the subject of a notation made in accordance with subsection (2) shall request the Commissioner to provide the Minister with any record of a conviction of that applicant, and the Commissioner shall transmit any such record to the Minister.

(6) Disclosure by Minister — The Minister may disclose to the police force or other authorized body all or part of the information contained in a record transmitted by the Commissioner pursuant to subsection (5).

(7) Disclosure to person or organization — A police force or other authorized body shall disclose the information referred to in subsection (6) to the person or organization that requested a verification if the applicant for a position has consented in writing to the disclosure.

(8) Use of information — A person or organization that acquires information under this section in relation to an application for a position shall not use it or communicate it except in relation to the assessment of the application.

(9) Amendment of Schedule 2 — The Governor in Council may, by order, amend Schedule 2 by adding or deleting a reference to an offence.

2000, c. 1, s. 6; 2010, c. 5, s. 6; 2012, c. 1, s. 122

6.4 Operation of section 6.3 — Section 6.3 applies in respect of a record of a conviction for any offence in respect of which a record suspension has been ordered regardless of the date of the conviction.

2000, c. 1, s. 6; 2010, c. 5, s. 7.1(c); 2012, c. 1, s. 123

Revocation

7. Revocation of record suspension — A record suspension may be revoked by the Board

(a) if the person to whom it relates is subsequently convicted of an offence referred to in paragraph 4(1)(b), other than an offence referred to in subparagraph 7.2(a)(ii);

(b) on evidence establishing to the satisfaction of the Board that the person to whom it relates is no longer of good conduct; or

(c) on evidence establishing to the satisfaction of the Board that the person to whom it relates knowingly made a false or deceptive statement in relation to the application for the record suspension, or knowingly concealed some material particular in relation to that application.

1992, c. 22, s. 7; 2010, c. 5, s. 7.1(d); 2012, c. 1, s. 124

7.1 (1) Entitlement to make representations — If the Board proposes to revoke a record suspension, it shall notify in writing the person to whom it relates of its proposal and advise that person that he or she is entitled to make, or have made on his or her behalf, any representations to the Board that he or she believes relevant either in writing or, with the Board's authorization, orally at a hearing held for that purpose.

(2) Board to consider representations — The Board shall, before making its decision, consider any representations made to it within a reasonable time after the notification is given to a person under subsection (1).

1992, c. 22, s. 7; 2000, c. 1, s. 7; 2010, c. 5, s. 7.1(e); 2012, c. 1, s. 125

7.2 Cessation of effect of record suspension — A record suspension ceases to have effect if

(a) the person to whom it relates is subsequently convicted of

(i) an offence referred to in paragraph 4(1)(a), or

(ii) an offence under the *Criminal Code* other than an offence under subsection 320.14(1) or 320.15(1) of that Act — or under the *Cannabis Act*, the *Controlled Drugs and Substances Act*, the *Firearms Act*, Part III or IV of the *Food and Drugs Act* or the *Narcotic Control Act*, chapter N-1 of the Revised Statutes of Canada, 1985 — that is punishable either on conviction on indictment or on summary conviction; or

(b) the Board is convinced by new information that the person was not eligible for the record suspension when it was ordered.

1992, c. 22, s. 7; 2000, c. 1, s. 7; 2010, c. 5, ss. 6.1, 7.1(f); 2012, c. 1, s. 126; 2018, c. 16, ss. 165, 193; 2018, c. 21, s. 42

General

8. Applications for employment — No person shall use or authorize the use of an application form for or relating to any of the following matters that contains a question that by its terms requires the applicant to disclose a conviction in respect of which a record suspension has been ordered and has not been revoked or ceased to have effect:

(a) employment in any department as defined in section 2 of the *Financial Administration Act*,

(b) employment by any Crown corporation as defined in section 83 of the *Financial Administration Act*,

(c) enrolment in the Canadian Forces, or

(d) employment on or in connection with the operation of any work, undertaking or business that is within the legislative authority of Parliament.

1992, c. 22, s. 8; 2010, c. 5, s. 7.1(g); 2012, c. 1, s. 127

9. Saving of other pardons — Nothing in this Act in any manner limits or affects Her Majesty's royal prerogative of mercy or the provisions of the *Criminal Code* relating to pardons, except that section 6 and 8 apply in respect of any pardon granted pursuant to the royal prerogative of mercy or those provisions.

1992, c. 22, s. 9

9.01 Disclosure of decisions — The Board may disclose decisions that order or refuse to order record suspensions. However, it may not disclose information that could reasonably be expected to identify an individual unless the individual authorizes the disclosure in writing.

2012, c. 1, s. 128

9.1 Regulations — The Governor in Council may make regulations

(a) respecting the making of notations in respect of records of conviction, and the verification of such records, for the purposes of section 6.3;

(b) prescribing the factors that the Minister must have regard to in considering whether to authorize a disclosure under this Act of a record of a conviction;

(c) respecting the consent given by applicants to the verification of records and the disclosure of information contained in them, including the information to be given to applicants before obtaining their consent and the manner in which consent is to be given, for the purposes of subsections 6.3(3) and (7);

(c.1) prescribing factors for the purposes of paragraph 4.1(3)(d);

(c.2) respecting the disclosure of decisions under section 9.01; and

(d) generally for carrying out the purposes and provisions of this Act.

1992, c. 22, s. 9; 2000, c. 1, s. 8; 2010, c. 5, s. 7; 2012, c. 1, s. 129

OFFENCES

10. Offence and punishment — Any person who contravenes any provision of this Act is guilty of an offence punishable on summary conviction.

Report to Parliament

[Heading added 2012, c. 1, s. 130.]

11. (1) Annual report — The Board shall, within three months after the end of each fiscal year, submit to the Minister a report for that year containing the following information:

(a) the number of applications for record suspensions made in respect of the offences referred to in each of paragraphs 4(1)(a) and (b);

(b) the number of record suspensions that the Board ordered or refused to order, in respect of the offences referred to in each of paragraphs 4(1)(a) and (b);

(c) the number of record suspensions ordered, categorized by the offence to which they relate and, if applicable, the province of residence of the applicant; and

(d) any other information required by the Minister.

(2) Tabling of report — The Minister shall cause the report to be laid before each House of Parliament on any of the first 30 days on which that House is sitting after the day on which the Minister receives it.

2012, c. 1, s. 130

Schedule 1

(Subsections 4(2), (3) and (5))

[Reference amended 2012, c. 1, s. 131.]

1. Offences

(a) under the following provisions of the *Criminal Code*:

(i) section 151 (sexual interference with a person under 16),

(ii) section 152 (invitation to a person under 16 to sexual touching),

(iii) section 153 (sexual exploitation of a person 16 or more but under 18),

(iv) subsection 160(3) (bestiality in the presence of a person under 16 or inciting a person under 16 to commit bestiality),

(v) section 163.1 (child pornography),

(vi) section 170 (parent or guardian procuring sexual activity),

(vii) section 171 (householder permitting sexual activity),

(vii.1) paragraph 171.1(1)(a) (making sexually explicit material available to child under 18 for purposes of listed offences),

(vii.2) paragraph 171.1(1)(b) (making sexually explicit material available to child under 16 for purposes of listed offences),

(vii.3) paragraph 171.1(1)(c) (making sexually explicit material available to child under 14 for purposes of listed offences),

(viii) section 172 (corrupting children),

(ix) section 172.1 (luring a child),

(ix.1) paragraph 172.2(1)(a) (agreement or arrangement — listed sexual offence against child under 18),

(ix.2) paragraph 172.2(1)(b) (agreement or arrangement — listed sexual offence against child under 16),

(ix.3) paragraph 172.2(1)(c) (agreement or arrangement — listed sexual offence against child under 14),

(x) subsection 173(2) (exposure),

(xi) to (xiii) [Repealed 2014, c. 25, s. 35(1).]

(xiv) paragraph 273.3(1)(a) (removal of child under 16 from Canada for purposes of listed offences),

(xv) paragraph 273.3(1)(b) (removal of child 16 or more but under 18 from Canada for purpose of listed offence),

(xvi) paragraph 273.3(1)(c) (removal of child under 18 from Canada for purposes of listed offences),

(xvi.1) section 279.011 (trafficking — person under 18 years),

(xvi.2) subsection 279.02(2) (material benefit — trafficking of person under 18 years),

(xvi.3) subsection 279.03(2) (withholding or destroying documents — trafficking of person under 18 years),

(xvi.4) subsection 286.1(2) (obtaining sexual services for consideration from person under 18 years),

(xvi.5) subsection 286.2(2) (material benefit from sexual services provided by person under 18 years),

(xvi.6) subsection 286.3(2) (procuring — person under 18 years),

(xvii) paragraph 348(1)(a) with respect to breaking and entering a place with intent to commit in that place an indictable offence listed in any of subparagraphs (i) to (xvi), and

(xviii) paragraph 348(1)(b) with respect to breaking and entering a place and committing in that place an indictable offence listed in any of subparagraphs (i) to (xvi);

(b) under the following provisions of the *Criminal Code*, R.S.C. 1970, c. C-34, as that Act read before January 1, 1988:

(i) subsection 146(1) (sexual intercourse with a female under 14),

(ii) subsection 146(2) (sexual intercourse with a female 14 or more but under 16),

(iii) section 151 (seduction of a female 16 or more but under 18),

(iv) section 166 (parent or guardian procuring defilement), and

(v) section 167 (householder permitting defilement);

(b.1) under the following provisions of the *Criminal Code*, as they read from time to time before the day on which this paragraph comes into force:

(i) subsection 212(2) (living on the avails of prostitution of person under 18 years),

(ii) subsection 212(2.1) (aggravated offence in relation to living on the avails of prostitution of person under 18 years), and

(iii) subsection 212(4) (prostitution of person under 18 years);

(c) that are referred to in paragraph (a) and that are punishable under section 130 of the *National Defence Act*;

(d) that are referred to in paragraph (b) and that are punishable under section 120 of the *National Defence Act*, R.S.C. 1970, c. N-4; and

(e) of attempt or conspiracy to commit an offence referred to in any of paragraphs (a) to (d).

2010, c. 5, s. 9 (Sched.); 2012, c. 1, ss. 49, 132; 2014, c. 25, s. 35

2. Offences

(a) involving a child under the following provisions of the *Criminal Code*:

(i) section 153.1 (sexual exploitation of a person with a disability),

(ii) section 155 (incest),

(iii) section 162 (voyeurism),

(iv) subsection 163(1) (obscene materials),

(v) paragraph 163(2)(a) (obscene materials),

(vi) section 168 (mailing obscene matter),

(vii) subsection 173(1) (indecent acts),

(viii) section 271 (sexual assault),

(ix) subsection 272(1) and paragraph 272(2)(a) (sexual assault with firearm),

(x) subsection 272(1) and paragraph 272(2)(b) (sexual assault other than with firearm),

(xi) section 273 (aggravated sexual assault),

(xii) paragraph 348(1)(a) with respect to breaking and entering a place with intent to commit in that place an indictable offence listed in any of subparagraphs (i) to (xi), and

(xiii) paragraph 348(1)(b) with respect to breaking and entering a place and committing in that place an indictable offence listed in any of subparagraphs (i) to (xi);

(b) involving a child under the following provisions of the *Criminal Code*, R.S.C. 1970, c. C-34, as that Act read before January 1, 1988:

(i) section 153 (sexual intercourse with stepdaughter, etc., or female employee), and

(ii) section 157 (gross indecency);

(c) involving a child under the following provisions of the *Criminal Code*, R.S.C. 1970, c. C-34, as that Act read before January 4, 1983:

(i) section 144 (rape),

(ii) section 145 (attempt to commit rape),

(iii) section 149 (indecent assault on female),

(iv) section 156 (indecent assault on male),

(v) section 245 (common assault), and

(vi) subsection 246(1) (assault with intent to commit an indictable offence);

(d) that are referred to in paragraph (a) and that are punishable under section 130 of the *National Defence Act*;

(e) that are referred to in paragraph (b) or (c) and that are punishable under section 120 of the *National Defence Act*, R.S.C. 1970, c. N-4; and

(f) of attempt or conspiracy to commit an offence referred to in any of paragraphs (a) to (e).

2010, c. 5, s. 9 (Sched.); 2018, c. 29, s. 76

3. [Repealed 2012, c. 1, s. 133.]

SCHEDULE 2 [Schedule renumbered as Schedule 2: 2010, c. 5, s. 8.]

(Subsections 6.3(2) and (9))

1. Offences

(a) under the following provisions of the *Criminal Code*:

(i) section 153.1 (sexual exploitation of a person with a disability),

(ii) section 155 (incest),

(iii) section 162 (voyeurism),

(iv) subsection 163(1) (obscene materials),

(v) paragraph 163(2)(a) (obscene materials),

(vi) section 168 (mailing obscene matter),

(vii) subsection 173(1) (indecent acts),

(viii) section 271 (sexual assault),

(ix) subsection 272(1) and paragraph 272(2)(a) (sexual assault with firearm),

(x) subsection 272(1) and paragraph 272(2)(b) (sexual assault other than with firearm),

(xi) section 273 (aggravated sexual assault),

(xii) section 280 (abduction of a person under 16),

(xiii) section 281 (abduction of a person under 14),

(xiv) subsection 372(2) (indecent phone calls),

(xv) paragraph 348(1)(a) with respect to breaking and entering a place with intent to commit in that place an indictable offence listed in any of subparagraphs (i) to (xiv), and

(xvi) paragraph 348(1)(b) with respect to breaking and entering a place and committing in that place an indictable offence listed in any of subparagraphs (i) to (xiv); and

(b) of attempt or conspiracy to commit an offence referred to in any of subparagraphs (a)(i) to (xvi).

2000, c. 1, s. 8.1 (Sched.); 2008, c. 6, s. 58; 2012, c. 1, s. 134 (Sched.); 2018, c. 29, s. 77

2. Offences

(a) under the following provisions of the *Criminal Code*, R.S.C. 1970, c. C-34, as that Act read before January 1, 1988:

(i) subsection 146(1) (sexual intercourse with a female under 14),

(ii) subsection 146(2) (sexual intercourse with a female 14 or more but under 16),

(iii) section 151 (seduction of a female 16 or more but under 18),

(iv) section 153 (sexual intercourse with stepdaughter, etc., or female employee), and

(v) section 157 (gross indecency); and

(b) of attempt or conspiracy to commit an offence referred to in any of subparagraphs (a)(i) to (v).

2000, c. 1, s. 8.1 (Sched.); 2012, c. 1, s. 134 (Sched.)

3. Offences

(a) under the following provisions of the *Criminal Code*, R.S.C. 1970, c. C-34, as that Act read before January 4, 1983:

(i) section 144 (rape),

(ii) section 145 (attempt to commit rape),

(iii) section 149 (indecent assault on female),

(iv) section 156 (indecent assault on male),

(v) section 245 (common assault), and

(vi) subsection 246(1) (assault with intent to commit an indictable offence); and

(b) of attempt or conspiracy to commit an offence referred to in any of subparagraphs (a)(i) to (vi).

2000, c. 1, s. 8.1 (Sched.); 2012, c. 1, s. 134 (Sched.)

SCHEDULE 3 — CANNABIS OFFENCES [Heading added 2019, c. 20, s. 7 (Sched.).]

(Subsections 4(3.1) and (5))

1. Offences —

(a) under subsection 4(4) or (5) of the *Controlled Drugs and Substances Act*, as it read from time to time before October 17, 2018, for possession of a substance included in Item 1 of Schedule II to that Act, except for similar synthetic preparations of cannabis, other than any substance that is identical to any phytocannabinoid produced by, or found in, a cannabis (marihuana) plant, regardless of how the substance was obtained;

(b) under subsection 3(2) of the *Narcotic Control Act*, chapter N-1 of the Revised Statutes of Canada, 1985, as it read from time to time before May 14, 1997, for possession of a substance included in Item 3 of the schedule to that Act, except for similar synthetic preparations of cannabis sativa, other than any substance that is identical to any phytocannabinoid produced by, or found in, a cannabis (marihuana) plant, regardless of how the substance was obtained; and

(c) under the *National Defence Act* or any previous version of that Act for an act or omission that constitutes an offence listed in paragraph (a) or (b).

2019, c. 20, s. 7 (Sched.)

Transitional Provisions

— 2010, c. 5, ss. 10–12 [s. 12 added 2012, c. 1, s. 151.]:

10. **New applications for pardons** — Subject to section 11, an application for a pardon under the *Criminal Records Act* in respect of an offence that is referred to in paragraph 4(a) of that Act, as it read immediately before the day on which this Act comes into force, and that is committed before that day shall be dealt with and disposed of in accordance with the *Criminal Records Act*, as amended by this Act.

11. **Pending applications — *Criminal Records Act*** — An application for a pardon under the *Criminal Records Act* that is made before the day on which this Act comes into force shall be dealt with and disposed of in accordance with the *Criminal Records Act*, as it read when the Board received the application, if the application

(a) is made after the period referred to in paragraph 4(a) of that Act, as it read immediately before the day on which this Act comes into force, has elapsed; and

(b) is not finally disposed of on the day on which this Act comes into force.

12. **Pardons in effect — *Criminal Records Act*** — The *Criminal Records Act*, as it read immediately before the day on which this Act comes into force, applies to a pardon that was granted or issued before that day and that has not been revoked or ceased to have effect.

— 2012, c. 1, ss. 161–165:

161. **New applications for pardons** — Subject to section 162, an application for a pardon under the *Criminal Records Act* in respect of an offence that is referred to in paragraph 4(a) or (b) of that Act, as it read immediately before the day on which this section comes into force, and that is committed before that day shall be dealt with and disposed of in accordance with the *Criminal Records Act*, as amended by this Part, as though it were an application for a record suspension.

162. **Pending applications — *Criminal Records Act*** — An application for a pardon under the *Criminal Records Act* that is made on or after the day on which the *Limiting Pardons for Serious Crimes Act*, chapter 5 of the Statutes of Canada, 2010, came into force and before the day on which this section comes into force shall be dealt with and disposed of in accordance with the *Criminal Records Act*, as it read when the Board received the application, if the application is not finally disposed of on the day on which this section comes into force.

163. Pending applications — references in other legislation — A reference to an application for a record suspension in the following provisions, as enacted by this Part, is deemed also to be a reference to an application for a pardon that is not finally disposed of on the day on which this section comes into force:

(a) paragraph 672.35(c) and subsection 750(4) of the *Criminal Code*;

(b) paragraph 202.14(2)(h) of the *National Defence Act*; and

(c) paragraph 82(1)(d) and subparagraphs 119(1)(n)(iii) and 120(4)(c)(iii) of the *Youth Criminal Justice Act*.

164. Pardons in effect — *Criminal Records Act* — The *Criminal Records Act*, as it read immediately before the day on which this section comes into force, applies to a pardon that was granted on or after the day on which the *Limiting Pardons for Serious Crimes Act*, chapter 5 of the Statutes of Canada, 2010, came into force and before the day on which this section comes into force and that has not been revoked or ceased to have effect.

165. Pardons in effect — references in other legislation — A reference to a record suspension in the following provisions, as enacted by this Part, is deemed also to be a reference to a pardon that is granted or issued under the *Criminal Records Act*:

(a) the definition "conviction for an offence for which a pardon has been granted or in respect of which a record suspension has been ordered" in section 25 of the *Canadian Human Rights Act*;

(b) the definition "record suspension" in subsection 490.011(1) of the *Criminal Code*;

(c) subsection 10(8) of the *DNA Identification Act*;

(d) paragraphs 36(3)(b) and 53(f) of the *Immigration and Refugee Protection Act*;

(e) the definition "record suspension" in section 227 of the *National Defence Act*; and

(f) subsection 128(5) of the *Youth Criminal Justice Act*.

— 2019, c. 20, s. 8:

8. (1) Definitions — The following definitions apply in this section.

"Act" means the *Criminal Records Act*. (*"Loi"*)

"application" means an application for a pardon or record suspension. (*"demande"*)

"pardon" has the same meaning as in subsection 2(1) of the Act as it read from time to time before March 13, 2012. (*"réhabilitation"*)

"record suspension" has the same meaning as in subsection 2(1) of the Act. (*"suspension du casier"*)

(2) Pending applications — If an application was made before the day on which this Act comes into force and that application has not been dealt with and disposed of on that day, that application is to be dealt with and disposed of in accordance with the Act, as amended by this Act. However, subsection 4(3.3) of the Act, as enacted by subsection 4(2) of this Act, is not to apply to an application made only with respect to an offence referred to in Schedule 3 of this Act if, on that day, the inquiries referred to in paragraph 4.2(1)(a) of the Act have been completed.

(3) Waiting period — Subsection 4.2(4) of the Act does not apply to an application for a record suspension referred to in subsection 4(3.1) of the Act, as enacted by subsection 4(2) of this Act, if the day on which the Board refuses to grant or issue a pardon or order a record suspension occurs within one year before the day on which this Act comes into force.

(4) Annual report — applications — In its annual report under section 11 of the Act for the year after the year in which this Act comes into force, the Board shall include information on the number of applications dealt with and disposed of in accordance with the Act, as amended by this Act, the associated costs and the number of suspensions that the Board ordered in respect of those applications, as well as the number that it refused to order.

DNA Identification Act

S.C. 1998, c. 37, as am. S.C. 2000, c. 10, ss. 4–12; 2002, c. 1, ss. 187–189; 2005, c. 10, ss. 26, 34(1)(h); 2005, c. 25, ss. 14–22; 2007, c. 22, ss. 27–33; 2012, c. 1, ss. 148, 202, 203; 2014, c. 39, ss. 232, 233, 234(1), (2) (Fr.), 235–238, 239 (Fr.), 240–246.

Short Title

1. Short Title — This Act may be cited as the *DNA Identification Act*.

Interpretation

2. Definitions — The definitions in this section apply in this Act.

"authorization" means an authorization made under section 487.055 or 487.091 of the *Criminal Code* or section 196.24 of the *National Defence Act*. *("autorisation")*

"Commissioner" means the Commissioner of the Royal Canadian Mounted Police.

"designated offence" means a designated offence within the meaning of section 487.04 of the *Criminal Code* or section 196.11 of the *National Defence Act*.

"DNA" means deoxyribonucleic acid.

"DNA profile" means the results of forensic DNA analysis of a bodily substance.

"forensic DNA analysis", in relation to a bodily substance, means forensic DNA analysis of the bodily substance.

"human remains" includes any detached part of the body of a person who may still be alive. *("restes humains")*

"investigating authority" means, as the case may be,

(a) a Canadian law enforcement agency;

(b) a coroner or medical examiner, or a person or organization with similar duties or functions, who is acting in the course of their duties under an Act of Parliament or of a provincial legislature; or

(c) a laboratory.

("autorité chargée de l'enquête")

"order" means an order made under section 487.051 of the *Criminal Code* or section 196.14 of the *National Defence Act*. *("ordonnance")*

"Young Offenders Act" means chapter Y-1 of the Revised Statutes of Canada, 1985. *("Loi sur les jeunes contrevenants")*

"young person" has the meaning assigned by subsection 2(1) of the *Youth Criminal Justice Act* or subsection 2(1) of the *Young Offenders Act*, as the case may be. *("adolescent")*

2000, c. 10, s. 4; 2002, c. 1, s. 187; 2005, c. 25, s. 14; 2007, c. 22, s. 27; 2014, c. 39, s. 232

PURPOSE

3. Purpose — The purpose of this Act is to establish a national DNA data bank to help

(a) law enforcement agencies identify persons alleged to have committed designated offences, including those committed before the coming into force of this Act; and

(b) law enforcement agencies — as well as coroners, medical examiners or persons and organizations with similar duties or functions — find missing persons and identify human remains.

2014, c. 39, s. 233

PRINCIPLES

4. Principles — It is recognized and declared that

(a) the protection of society and the administration of justice are well served by the early detection, arrest and conviction of offenders, which can be facilitated by the use of DNA profiles;

(a.1) society is well served by locating missing persons and identifying human remains, which can be facilitated by the use of DNA profiles;

(b) the DNA profiles, as well as samples of bodily substances from which the profiles are derived, may be used only in accordance with this Act, and not for any unauthorized purpose; and

(c) to protect the privacy of individuals with respect to personal information about themselves, safeguards must be placed on

(i) the use and communication of, and access to, DNA profiles and other information contained in the national DNA data bank, and

(ii) the use of, and access to, bodily substances that are transmitted to the Commissioner for the purposes of this Act.

2000, c. 10, s. 5; 2014, c. 39, s. 234(1)

National DNA Data Bank

Establishment and Contents

[Heading added 2014, c. 39, s. 235.]

5. (1) Establishment — The Minister of Public Safety and Emergency Preparedness shall establish a national DNA data bank, to be maintained by the Commissioner, consisting of

(a) for criminal identification purposes, a crime scene index, a convicted offenders index and a victims index;

(b) for the purposes of finding missing persons and identifying human remains, a missing persons index, a relatives of missing persons index and a human remains index; and

(c) for the purposes set out in paragraphs (a) and (b), a voluntary donors index.

(2) Commissioner's duties — The Commissioner's duties under this Act may be performed on behalf of the Commissioner by any person authorized by the Commissioner to perform those duties.

(3) Crime scene index — The crime scene index shall contain DNA profiles derived from bodily substances that are found

(a) at any place where a designated offence was committed;

(b) on or within the body of the victim of a designated offence;

(c) on anything worn or carried by the victim at the time when a designated offence was committed; or

(d) on or within the body of any person or thing or at any place associated with the commission of a designated offence.

(4) Convicted offenders index — The convicted offenders index shall contain DNA profiles derived from bodily substances that are taken under orders and authorizations.

(4.1) Victims index — The victims index shall contain DNA profiles derived from bodily substances of a victim of a designated offence that

(a) are voluntarily submitted by the victim for the purpose of having their DNA profile added to the index; or

(b) if the victim is unidentified, deceased or unable to consent to submitting their bodily substances or their whereabouts are unknown, are obtained, as the case may be, from

(i) their personal effects,

(ii) any place associated with the commission of the designated offence, and

(iii) if the victim is deceased, their remains.

(4.2) **Missing persons index** — The missing persons index shall contain DNA profiles derived from bodily substances of a missing person, including bodily substances obtained from their personal effects.

(4.3) **Relatives of missing persons index** — The relatives of missing persons index shall contain DNA profiles derived from bodily substances of a person that are voluntarily submitted by them for the purpose of having their DNA profile added to the index, where their profile may assist in confirming the identity of a person whose DNA profile is contained in the missing persons index or human remains index.

(4.4) **Human remains index** — The human remains index shall contain DNA profiles derived from human remains.

(4.5) **Voluntary donors index** — The voluntary donors index shall contain DNA profiles derived from the bodily substances of a person, other than a victim of a designated offence, that are voluntarily submitted by them for the purpose of having their DNA profile added to the index, where their profile may be relevant to an investigation of a designated offence or of a missing person or human remains.

(5) **Other information** — In addition to the DNA profiles referred in subsections (3) to (4.5), the DNA data bank shall contain, in relation to each of the profiles, information from which can be established

(a) in the case of a profile referred to in subsection (3) or any of subsections (4.1) to (4.4), the case number of the investigation associated with the bodily substance from which the profile was derived;

(b) in the case of a profile referred to in any of subsections (4) to (4.5), the identity of the person from whose bodily substance the profile was derived, if that identity is known; and

(c) in the case of a profile referred to in subsection (4.3), the stated biological or other relationship of the person from whose bodily substance the profile was derived with the person whose identity is to be confirmed.

2000, c. 10, s. 6; 2005, c. 10, s. 34(1)(h); 2005, c. 25, s. 15; 2007, c. 22, s. 28; 2014, c. 39, s. 236

5.1 (1) **Review of information transmitted** — The Commissioner shall review the information transmitted under section 487.071 of the *Criminal Code* or section 196.22 of the *National Defence Act* to ensure that the offence referred to in the order or authorization is a designated offence.

(2) **Forensic DNA analysis** — The Commissioner shall conduct a forensic DNA analysis of the bodily substances transmitted if satisfied that the offence referred to in the order or authorization is a designated offence and add the resulting DNA profile in the convicted offenders index.

(3) **Retention of order or authorization** — The Commissioner shall retain the copy of the order or authorization transmitted under subsection 487.071(2) of the *Criminal Code* or subsection 196.22(2) of the *National Defence Act*.

2005, c. 25, s. 16; 2007, c. 22, s. 29; 2014, c. 39, s. 237

5.2 (1) Defect in order or authorization — If the Commissioner is of the opinion that the offence referred to in the order or authorization is not a designated offence, the Commissioner shall retain any bodily substances collected under it and any information transmitted with it, and give notice of the apparent defect to

(a) the Attorney General of the province in which the order or authorization was made, if it was transmitted under section 487.071 of the *Criminal Code*; or

(b) the Director of Military Prosecutions, if the order or authorization was transmitted under section 196.22 of the *National Defence Act*.

(2) Confirmation or correction — If the Attorney General or Director of Military Prosecutions, as the case may be, confirms in writing that the order or authorization is valid or sends a copy of a corrected order or authorization to the Commissioner, the Commissioner shall conduct a forensic DNA analysis of any bodily substances collected under it.

(3) Substantive defect — If the Attorney General or the Director of Military Prosecutions, as the case may be, informs the Commissioner that the offence referred to in the order or authorization is not a designated offence, the Commissioner shall, without delay, destroy the bodily substances collected under the order or authorization and the information transmitted with it.

(4) Destruction of bodily substances — The Commissioner shall destroy any bodily substances and information retained under subsection (1) on the expiry of 180 days after sending a notice under that subsection unless, before the expiry of that period, the Commissioner receives

(a) a confirmation that the order or authorization is valid;

(b) a corrected order or authorization;

(c) a notice that the Attorney General or Director of Military Prosecutions requires an additional period of not greater than 90 days to review the order or authorization; or

(d) a notice that the issue of whether or not the order or authorization is defective is under review by a judge or in proceedings before a court.

2005, c. 25, s. 16; 2007, c. 22, s. 30

5.3 (1) Precondition — victims — A DNA profile and related information shall be added to the victims index only if the Commissioner has reasonable grounds to suspect that the comparison of the profile conducted under subsection 5.5(1) will assist in the investigation of a designated offence with respect to which the profile was obtained.

(2) Preconditions — missing persons and relatives — A DNA profile and related information shall be added to the missing persons index or the relatives of missing persons index only if the Commissioner

(a) has reasonable grounds to suspect that the comparison of the profile conducted under section 5.5 will assist in the investigation of a missing person or human remains; and

(b) is satisfied that other investigative procedures have been tried and have failed or are unlikely to succeed, or that the urgency of the situation requires the comparison of the profile to others.

2014, c. 39, s. 238

5.4 Written consent — A DNA profile and related information shall be added to the relatives of missing persons index or the voluntary donors index, or to the victims index in the circumstances described in paragraph 5(4.1)(a), only if the Commissioner has received the written consent to that addition, provided in accordance with any regulations, of the person who voluntarily provided the bodily substances from which the profile was derived.

2014, c. 39, s. 238

Comparison of Profiles and Communication and Use of Information

[Heading added 2014, c. 39, s. 238.]

5.5 (1) Comparison of DNA profiles — The Commissioner shall compare each DNA profile that is added to the crime scene index, the convicted offenders index, the victims index, the missing person index, the voluntary donors index or the human remains index with the DNA profiles that are already contained in those indices.

(2) Relatives of missing persons index — The Commissioner shall compare each DNA profile that is added to the relatives of missing persons index with the DNA profiles that are already contained in the missing persons index and the human remains index.

2014, c. 39, s. 238

6. (1) Communication — match — If a comparison conducted under subsection 5.5(1) produces a match between DNA profiles, and none of the profiles that match is contained in the missing persons index or the human remains index, the Commissioner may communicate any information in relation to the profiles, to any laboratory or Canadian law enforcement agency that the Commissioner considers appropriate, for the purpose of

(a) if at least one of the profiles is contained in the victims index, the investigation of a designated offence with respect to which that profile was obtained; and

(b) in any other case, the investigation of any designated offence.

(2) Missing persons and human remains indices — If a comparison conducted under subsection 5.5(1) produces a match between DNA profiles, and at least one of the profiles that match is contained in the missing persons index or the human remains index, the Commissioner may communicate any information in relation to the profiles, to any investigating authority that the Commissioner considers appropriate, for the purpose of the investigation of a missing person or human remains.

(3) to (7) [Repealed 2014, c. 39, s. 238.]

2000, c. 10, s. 7; 2005, c. 25, s. 17; 2007, c. 22, s. 31; 2014, c. 39, s. 238

6.1 (1) Communication — similar profile — If a comparison conducted under subsection 5.5(1) indicates that, in the Commissioner's opinion, two or more DNA profiles are similar, the Commissioner may communicate the similar DNA profiles, to any investigating authority that the Commissioner considers appropriate, for the purpose of determining whether the possibility of a match between the profiles can be excluded.

(2) Deemed match — If the investigating authority advises the Commissioner that the profiles are similar and that the possibility of a match between the DNA profiles has not been excluded, the Commissioner may communicate any information in relation to the profiles in accordance with subsection 6(1) or (2), as the case may be, as if there were a match between them.

(3) Relatives of missing persons index — If a comparison conducted under subsection 5.5(2) indicates that a DNA profile that is already contained in the missing persons index or human remains index could be the profile of a biological relative of someone whose DNA profile is added to the relatives of missing persons index, the Commissioner may communicate any information in relation to both DNA profiles, to any investigating authority that the Commissioner considers appropriate, for the purpose of the investigation of a missing person or human remains.

2014, c. 39, s. 238

6.2 Communication — no match — If a comparison conducted under section 5.5 produces neither a match between DNA profiles nor a result referred to in subsection 6.1(1) or (3), the Commissioner may communicate that fact to any investigating authority that the Commissioner considers appropriate.

2014, c. 39, s. 238

6.3 (1) Subsequent communication — paragraph 6(1)(a) — Information that is communicated under paragraph 6(1)(a) may be communicated subsequently to a person to whom it is necessary to communicate the information for the purpose of the investigation or prosecution of a designated offence with respect to which the DNA profile referred to in that paragraph was obtained.

(2) Subsequent communication — different purpose — Information that is communicated under paragraph 6(1)(a) to a law enforcement agency may be communicated subsequently by a member of the agency to a person to whom it is necessary to communicate the information for the purpose of the investigation or prosecution of any designated offence, if the member has reasonable grounds to suspect that the information will assist in the investigation or prosecution.

(3) Further communication — different purpose — Information that is communicated to a person under subsection (2) may be communicated subsequently to another person to whom it is necessary to communicate the information for the purpose of the investigation or prosecution referred to in that subsection.

(4) Subsequent communication — paragraph 6(1)(b) — Information that is communicated under paragraph 6(1)(b) may be communicated subsequently to a person to whom it is necessary to communicate the information for the purpose of the investigation or prosecution of any designated offence.

(5) Subsequent communication — missing person or human remains — Information that is communicated under subsection 6(2) or 6.1(3) may be communicated subsequently to a person to whom it is necessary to communicate the information for the purpose of the investigation of a missing person or human remains.

(6) Subsequent communication — different purpose — Information that is communicated under subsection 6(2) or 6.1(3) to a law enforcement agency may be communicated subsequently by a member of the agency to a person to whom it is necessary to communicate the information for the purpose of the investigation or prosecution of a designated offence, if the member has reasonable grounds to suspect that the information will assist in the investigation or prosecution.

(7) Further communication — different purpose — Information that is communicated to a person under subsection (6) may be communicated subsequently to another person to whom it is necessary to communicate the information for the purpose of the investigation or prosecution referred to in that subsection.

2014, c. 39, s. 238

6.4 (1) Communication — foreign law enforcement agencies — On receipt of a DNA profile from the government of a foreign state, an international organization established by the governments of states or an institution of such a government or international organization, the Commissioner may compare the profile with those already contained in the crime scene index, the convicted offenders index, the missing persons index and the human remains index to determine whether there is a match between profiles and may then communicate any of the following to the government, organization or institution, as the case may be:

(a) if there is no match, that fact;

(b) if there is a match, any information in relation to a matching DNA profile that is already contained in any of those indices;

(c) if there is, in the Commissioner's opinion, a similar DNA profile already contained in an index, the similar DNA profile;

(d) if, after receiving the similar DNA profile referred to in paragraph (c), the government, organization or institution advises the Commissioner that the possibility of a match between the similar profile with the DNA profile it provided has not been excluded, any information in relation to the similar DNA profile.

(2) Crime scene index — The Commissioner may, on the request of a law enforcement agency in the course of the investigation of a designated offence, communicate a DNA profile contained in the crime scene index to the government of a foreign state, an international organization established by the governments of states or an institution of any such government or international organization.

(3) Missing persons or human remains index — The Commissioner may, on the request of an investigating authority in the course of the investigation of a missing person or human remains, communicate a DNA profile contained in the missing persons index or the human remains index to the government of a foreign state, an international organization established by the governments of states or an institution of any such government or international organization.

(4) Agreement or arrangement — Subsections (1) to (3) apply only if the Government of Canada or one of its institutions has entered into an agreement or arrangement, in accordance with any regulations, with that government, international organization or institution, authorizing the communication solely for the purposes of, as the case may be, the investigation or prosecution of a criminal offence or the investigation of a missing person or human remains.

2014, c. 39, s. 238

6.5 Authorized users — Information as to whether a person's DNA profile is contained in the convicted offenders index may be communicated to an authorized user of the automated criminal conviction records retrieval system maintained by the Royal Canadian Mounted Police.

2014, c. 39, s. 238

6.6 Unauthorized communication — Subject to sections 6 to 6.5, no person shall communicate any information that is contained in the DNA data bank or allow the information to be communicated.

2014, c. 39, s. 238

7. Access to information — Access to information contained in the DNA data bank may be granted to

(a) any person or class of persons that the Commissioner considers appropriate for the purposes of the proper operation and maintenance of the DNA data bank; and

(b) the personnel of any laboratories that the Commissioner considers appropriate for training purposes.

8. (1) Unauthorized use of information — Subject to subsection (2), no person to whom information is communicated under any of sections 6, 6.1 and 6.3 or who has access to information under paragraph 7(a) or (b) shall use that information other than for the purposes set out in the applicable provision of those sections.

(2) Use for different purpose — After a law enforcement agency has received information in relation to a DNA profile that was communicated to them under paragraph 6(1)(a) or subsection 6(2) or 6.1(3), a member of the agency may use that information for the purpose of the investigation or prosecution of a designated offence if they have reasonable grounds to suspect that the information will assist in the investigation or prosecution.

(3) Use of results of DNA analysis — order or authorization — No person shall use the results of forensic DNA analysis of bodily substances that are taken in execution of an order or authorization, except in accordance with this Act.

2005, c. 25, s. 17.1; 2014, c. 39, s. 240

Removal of Access to Information

[Heading added 2014, c. 39, s. 240.]

8.1 (1) Removal of access to information — crime scene index — Access to information in the crime scene index shall be removed from that index without delay if the information relates to a DNA profile derived from a bodily substance of

(a) a victim of a designated offence that was the object of the relevant investigation; or

(b) a person who has been eliminated as a suspect in the relevant investigation.

(2) Other indices — Access to information in relation to a DNA profile in the victims index, the missing persons index, the relatives of missing persons index, the human remains index or the voluntary donors index shall be removed from that index without delay if the Commissioner is advised that

(a) the person from whose bodily substances the profile was derived wishes to have access to the information removed; or

(b) the comparison under this Act of the profile with other profiles will not assist in the investigation with respect to which the profile was obtained.

(3) Periodic removal — After each period prescribed by regulation, access to information in relation to a DNA profile in the victims index, the missing persons index, the relatives of missing persons index or the voluntary donors index shall be removed from that index without delay unless the Commissioner is advised before the end of the period, by any investigating authority that the Commissioner considers appropriate, that

(a) the investigating authority has not been advised by the person from whose bodily substances the profile was derived that they wish to have access to the information removed; and

(b) the comparison under this Act of the profile with other profiles may assist in the investigation with respect to which the profile was obtained.

(4) Subsequent DNA profile — Removal of access to information in relation to a DNA profile of a person from an index under this section does not prevent a DNA profile derived from the bodily substances of the same person, and any information in relation to that profile, from subsequently being added to any index in accordance with this Act.

(5) Regulations — requirements — The removal of access to information under any of subsections (1) to (3) shall be done in accordance with the requirements set out in any regulations that apply with respect to that subsection.

2014, c. 39, s. 240

8.2 Transfer to another index — The Commissioner may transfer a DNA profile and information in relation to it from one index — other than the convicted offenders index or the relatives of missing persons index — to another, as long as the addition of the profile to the other index is in accordance with the applicable provisions of this Act.

2014, c. 39, s. 240

9. (1) Information to be kept indefinitely — Subject to subsection (2), section 9.1 and the *Criminal Records Act*, information in the convicted offenders index shall be kept indefinitely.

(2) Information to be permanently removed — Access to information in the convicted offenders index shall be permanently removed

(a) without delay after every order or authorization for the collection of bodily substances from the person to whom the information relates is finally set aside; or

(b) without delay after the person is finally acquitted of every designated offence in connection with which an order was made or an authorization was granted.

(c) [Repealed 2014, c. 39 s. 241.]

(d) and (e) [Repealed 2000, c. 10, s. 8(2).]

[Editor's Note: Section 188 of the Youth Criminal Justice Act, 2002, c. 1, purports to amend ss. 9(2)(c)–(e) of the DNA Identification Act. By the time 2002, c. 1 received Royal Assent, however, ss. 9(2)(c)–(e) had been repealed by 2000, c. 10, s. 8. The proposed amendments would, accordingly, appear to be null.]

2000, c. 10, s. 8; 2005, c. 25, s. 18; 2007, c. 22, s. 32; 2014, c. 39, s. 241

9.1 (1) Young persons — access to information removed — Access to information in the convicted offenders index in relation to a young person who has been found guilty under the *Young Offenders Act* or under the *Youth Criminal Justice Act* of a designated offence shall be permanently removed without delay when the record relating to the same offence is required to be destroyed, sealed or transmitted to the National Archivist of Canada under Part 6 of the *Youth Criminal Justice Act*.

(2) Exception — Section 9 nevertheless applies to information in the convicted offenders index in relation to

(a) a serious violent offence as defined in subsection 2(1) of the *Youth Criminal Justice Act*; or

(b) a record to which subsection 120(6) of that Act applies.

2000, c. 10, s. 9; 2005, c. 25, s. 19; 2012, c. 1, s. 202

Storage and Destruction of Bodily Substances

[Heading added 2014, c. 39, s. 242.]

10. (1) Storage of bodily substances — When bodily substances are transmitted to the Commissioner under section 487.071 of the *Criminal Code* or section

196.22 of the *National Defence Act*, the Commissioner shall, subject to this section and section 10.1, safely and securely store, for the purpose of forensic DNA analysis, the portions of the samples of the bodily substances that the Commissioner considers appropriate and without delay destroy any remaining portions.

(2) **Change in technology** — Forensic DNA analysis of stored bodily substances may be performed if the Commissioner is of the opinion that the analysis is justified because significant technological advances have been made since the time when a DNA profile of the person who provided the bodily substances, or from whom they were taken, was last derived.

(3) [Repealed 2005, c. 25, s. 20(2).]

(4) **Access** — Access to stored bodily substances may be granted to any person or class of persons that the Commissioner considers appropriate for the purpose of preserving the bodily substances.

(5) **Use of bodily substances** — No person shall transmit stored bodily substances to any person or use stored bodily substances except for the purpose of forensic DNA analysis.

(6) **Later destruction** — The Commissioner may at any time destroy any or all of the stored bodily substances if the Commissioner considers that they are no longer required for the purpose of forensic DNA analysis.

(7) **Mandatory destruction in certain cases** — The Commissioner shall destroy the stored bodily substances of a person

(a) without delay after every order or authorization for the collection of bodily substances from the person is finally set aside; or

(b) without delay after the person is finally acquitted of every designated offence in connection with which an order was made or an authorization was granted.

(c) [Repealed 2014, c. 39, s. 243.]

(d) and (e) [Repealed 2000, c. 10, s. 10(2).]

(8) **When record suspension is in effect** — Despite anything in this section, stored bodily substances of a person in respect of whom a record suspension, as defined in subsection 2(1) of the *Criminal Records Act*, is in effect shall be kept separate and apart from other stored bodily substances, and no such bodily substance shall be used for forensic DNA analysis, nor shall the existence of such a bodily substance be communicated to any person.

[Editor's Note: Section 189 of the Youth Criminal Justice Act, 2002, c. 1, purports to amend ss. 10(7)(c)–(e) of the DNA Identification Act. By the time 2002, c. 1 received Royal Assent, however, ss. 10(7)(c)–(e) had been repealed by 2000, c. 10, s. 10. The proposed amendments would, accordingly, appear to be null.]

2000, c. 10, s. 10; 2005, c. 25, s. 20; 2007, c. 22, s. 33; 2012, c. 1, s. 148; 2014, c. 39, s. 243

10.1 (1) **Young persons — destruction of bodily substances** — The Commissioner shall, without delay, destroy stored bodily substances of a young person who has been found guilty of a designated offence under the *Young Offenders Act* or under the *Youth Criminal Justice Act* when the record relating to the same offence is required to be destroyed, sealed or transmitted to the National Archivist of Canada under Part 6 of the *Youth Criminal Justice Act*.

(2) **Exception** — Subsections 10(6) and (7) nevertheless apply to the destruction of stored bodily substances of a young person that relate to

(a) a serious violent offence as defined in subsection 2(1) of the *Youth Criminal Justice Act*; or

(b) a record to which subsection 120(6) of that Act applies.

2000, c. 10, s. 11; 2005, c. 25, s. 21; 2012, c. 1, s. 203

Offence

[Heading added 2014, c. 39, s. 244.]

11. Contravention of sections — Every person who contravenes section 6.6 or 8 or subsection 10(5)

(a) is guilty of an indictable offence and liable to imprisonment for a term not exceeding two years; or

(b) is guilty of an offence punishable on summary conviction and liable to a fine not exceeding $2,000 or to imprisonment for a term not exceeding six months, or to both.

2005, c. 25, s. 22; 2014, c. 39, s. 245

Regulations

12. Regulations — The Governor in Council may make regulations for carrying out the purposes and provisions of this Act, including regulations

(a) respecting the establishment and operation of the national DNA data bank;

(b) respecting the collection and transmission of any information or other thing that is to be received by the Commissioner;

(c) respecting agreements or arrangements referred to in subsection 6.4(4);

(d) respecting access to information that is contained in the national DNA data bank, including removal of access to information and destruction of information;

(e) respecting the establishment of advisory committees to advise on any matter related to the national DNA data bank; and

(f) prescribing anything that by this Act is to be prescribed by regulation.

2014, c. 39, s. 246

Review of Act

13. Review of Act by Parliamentary committee — Within five years after this Act comes into force, a review of the provisions and operation of this Act shall be undertaken by any committee of the Senate, of the House of Commons or of both Houses of Parliament that is designated or established for that purpose.

2000, c. 10, s. 12

REPORT TO PARLIAMENT

13.1 (1) Annual report — The Commissioner shall, within three months after the end of each fiscal year, submit to the Minister of Public Safety and Emergency Preparedness a report on the operations of the national DNA data bank for the year.

(2) Tabling in Parliament — The Minister shall cause the report of the Commissioner to be tabled in each House of Parliament on any of the first 15 days on which that House is sitting after he or she receives it.

2000, c. 10, s. 12; 2005, c. 10, s. 26

EXTRADITION ACT

Editor's note: Current to May 15, 2019.

TABLE OF CONCORDANCE

The *Extradition Act*, R.S.C. 1985, c. E-23, was repealed and replaced by the *Extradition Act*, S.C. 1999, c. 18. The table below traces, to the extent possible, the substantive correspondences between the provisions of both of the former acts, as amended, and those of the new act.

R.S.C. 1970, c. E-21	R.S.C. 1985, c. E-23	Extradition Act, S.C. 1999, c. 18
1	1	1
2	2	2
3	3	10(1), (2)
4	4	—
5	5	—
6	6	—
7	7	8(1), (2)
8	8	8(3)
9(1)	9(1)	2 "court", "judge"; 24
9(2)	9(2)	—
—	9(3)	25
10(1)	10(1)	3
10(2)	—	—
11	11	16(4)
12	12	6
13	13	17; 18(1); 19
14	14	32(1) "evidence otherwise admissible under Canadian law"; 32(2)
15	15	—
16	16	32(1) "evidence otherwise admissible under Canadian law"
17	17	33(4); 35
18(1)	18(1)	29(1)
18(2)	18(2)	29(3)
19	19	38

R.S.C. 1970, c. E-21	R.S.C. 1985, c. E-23	Extradition Act, S.C. 1999, c. 18
—	19.1(1)	43
—	19.1(2)	—
—	19.2	49
—	19.3	50
—	19.4	51
—	19.5	52
—	19.6	53
—	19.7	54
—	19.8	55
—	19.9	56
20	20	2 "extradition partner"
21	21	—
22(1)	22(1)	46; 47
22(2)	22(2)	48(1)
23	23	62(1)
24	24	—
25	25(1)	40(1)
—	25(2)	40(5)
—	25(3)	40(6)
—	25(4)	64(1)
—	25(5)	67
—	25.1	41
—	25.2	57
26	26	60, 61
27	27	39
28	28	69
29	29	—
30	30	78
31	31	79(1)
32	32	81(1)
33	33	80
34–40	34–40	—
Sch. I–III	Sch. I–III	—

EXTRADITION ACT

An Act respecting extradition, to amend the Canada Evidence Act, the Criminal Code, the Immigration Act and the Mutual Legal Assistance in Criminal Matters Act and to amend and repeal other Acts in consequence

S.C. 1999, c. 18, as am. S.C. 2000, c. 24, ss. 47–53; 2001, c. 27, ss. 250–252; 2002, c. 1, ss. 190–194; 2002, c. 7, s. 169; 2002, c. 8, s. 141; 2005, c. 10, s. 34(1)(l); SOR/2005-227.

Her Majesty, by and with the advice and consent of the Senate and House of Commons of Canada, enacts as follows:

SHORT TITLE

1. Short title — This Act may be cited as the *Extradition Act*.

PART 1 — INTERPRETATION (S. 2)

2. Definitions — The definitions in this section apply in this Act.

"Attorney General" means the Attorney General of Canada.

"court" means

(a) in Ontario, the Ontario Court (General Division);

(b) in Quebec, the Superior Court;

(c) in New Brunswick, Manitoba, Alberta and Saskatchewan, the Court of Queen's Bench;

(d) in Nova Scotia, British Columbia, Yukon and the Northwest Territories, the Supreme Court, and in Nunavut, the Nunavut Court of Justice; and

(e) in Prince Edward Island and Newfoundland, the Trial Division of the Supreme Court.

"court of appeal" means

(a) in the Province of Prince Edward Island, the Appeal Division of the Supreme Court; and

(b) in all other provinces, the Court of Appeal.

"extradition agreement" means an agreement that is in force, to which Canada is a party and that contains a provision respecting the extradition of persons, other than a specific agreement.

"extradition partner" means a State or entity with which Canada is party to an extradition agreement, with which Canada has entered into a specific agreement or whose name appears in the schedule.

"International Criminal Court" means the International Criminal Court as defined in subsection 2(1) of the *Crimes Against Humanity and War Crimes Act.*

"judge" means a judge of the court.

"justice" has the same meaning as in section 2 of the *Criminal Code.*

"Minister" means the Minister of Justice.

"specific agreement" means an agreement referred to in section 10 that is in force;

"State or entity" means

(a) a State other than Canada;

(b) a province, state or other political subdivision of a State other than Canada;

(c) a colony, dependency, possession, protectorate, condominium, trust territory or any territory falling under the jurisdiction of a State other than Canada;

(d) an international criminal court or tribunal; or

(e) a territory.

2000, c. 24, s. 47; 2002, c. 7, s. 169

PART 2 — EXTRADITION FROM CANADA (SS. 3–76)

Extraditable Conduct

3. (1) General principle — A person may be extradited from Canada in accordance with this Act and a relevant extradition agreement on the request of an extradition partner for the purpose of prosecuting the person or imposing a sentence on — or enforcing a sentence imposed on — the person if

(a) subject to a relevant extradition agreement, the offence in respect of which the extradition is requested is punishable by the extradition partner, by imprisoning or otherwise depriving the person of their liberty for a maximum term of two years or more, or by a more severe punishment; and

(b) the conduct of the person, had it occurred in Canada, would have constituted an offence that is punishable in Canada,

(i) in the case of a request based on a specific agreement, by imprisonment for a maximum term of five years or more, or by a more severe punishment, and

(ii) in any other case, by imprisonment for a maximum term of two years or more, or by a more severe punishment, subject to a relevant extradition agreement.

(2) Conduct determinative — For greater certainty, it is not relevant whether the conduct referred to in subsection (1) is named, defined or characterized by the extradition partner in the same way as it is in Canada.

(3) Extradition of a person who has been sentenced — Subject to a relevant extradition agreement, the extradition of a person who has been sentenced to imprisonment or another deprivation of liberty may only be granted if the portion of the term remaining is at least six months long or a more severe punishment remains to be carried out.

4. Further proceedings — For greater certainty, the discharge of a person under this Act or an Act repealed by section 129 or 130 does not preclude further proceedings, whether or not they are based on the same conduct, with a view to extraditing the person under this Act unless the judge is of the opinion that those further proceedings would be an abuse of process.

5. Jurisdiction — A person may be extradited

(a) whether or not the conduct on which the extradition partner bases its request occurred in the territory over which it has jurisdiction; and

(b) whether or not Canada could exercise jurisdiction in similar circumstances.

6. Retrospectivity — Subject to a relevant extradition agreement, extradition may be granted under this Act whether the conduct or conviction in respect of which the extradition is requested occurred before or after this Act or the relevant extradition agreement or specific agreement came into force.

6.1 No immunity — Despite any other Act or law, no person who is the subject of a request for surrender by the International Criminal Court or by any international criminal tribunal that is established by resolution of the Security Council of the United Nations and whose name appears in the schedule, may claim immunity under common law or by statute from arrest or extradition under this Act.

2000, c. 24, s. 48

Functions of the Minister

7. Functions of the Minister — The Minister is responsible for the implementation of extradition agreements, the administration of this Act and dealing with requests for extradition made under them.

Publication of Extradition Agreements

8. (1) Publication in Canada Gazette — Unless the extradition agreement has been published under subsection (2), an extradition agreement — or the provisions respecting extradition contained in a multilateral extradition agreement — must be published in the *Canada Gazette* no later than 60 days after it comes into force.

(2) Publication in Canada Treaty Series — An extradition agreement — or the provisions respecting extradition contained in a multilateral extradition agreement — may be published in the *Canada Treaty Series* and, if so published, the publication must be no later than 60 days after it comes into force.

(3) Judicial notice — Agreements and provisions published in the *Canada Gazette* or the *Canada Treaty Series* are to be judicially noticed.

Designated States and Entities

9. (1) Designated extradition partners — The names of members of the Commonwealth or other States or entities that appear in the schedule are designated as extradition partners.

(2) Amendment to the schedule — The Minister of Foreign Affairs, with the agreement of the Minister, may, by order, add to or delete from the schedule the names of members of the Commonwealth or other States or entities.

Specific Agreements

10. (1) Specific agreements — The Minister of Foreign Affairs may, with the agreement of the Minister, enter into a specific agreement with a State or entity for the purpose of giving effect to a request for extradition in a particular case.

(2) Inconsistency — For greater certainty, if there is an inconsistency between this Act and a specific agreement, this Act prevails to the extent of the inconsistency.

(3) Evidence — A certificate issued by or under the authority of the Minister of Foreign Affairs to which is attached a copy of a specific agreement entered into by Canada and a State or entity is conclusive evidence of the agreement and its contents without proof of the signature or official character of the person appearing to have signed the certificate or agreement.

Minister's Power to Receive Requests

11. (1) Request to go to Minister — A request by an extradition partner for the provisional arrest or extradition of a person shall be made to the Minister.

(2) Provisional arrest request to go to Minister — A request by an extradition partner for the provisional arrest of a person may also be made to the Minister through Interpol.

Warrant for Provisional Arrest

12. Minister's approval of request for provisional arrest — The Minister may, after receiving a request by an extradition partner for the provisional arrest of a person, authorize the Attorney General to apply for a provisional arrest warrant, if the Minister is satisfied that

(a) the offence in respect of which the provisional arrest is requested is punishable in accordance with paragraph 3(1)(a); and

(b) the extradition partner will make a request for the extradition of the person.

13. (1) Provisional arrest warrant — A judge may, on *ex parte* application of the Attorney General, issue a warrant for the provisional arrest of a person, if satisfied that there are reasonable grounds to believe that

(a) it is necessary in the public interest to arrest the person, including to prevent the person from escaping or committing an offence;

(b) the person is ordinarily resident in Canada, is in Canada or is on the way to Canada; and

(c) a warrant for the person's arrest or an order of a similar nature has been issued or the person has been convicted.

(2) Contents of the warrant — A provisional arrest warrant must

(a) name or describe the person to be arrested;

(b) set out briefly the offence in respect of which the provisional arrest was requested; and

(c) order that the person be arrested without delay and brought before the judge who issued the warrant or before another judge in Canada.

(3) Execution throughout Canada — A provisional arrest warrant may be executed anywhere in Canada without being endorsed.

14. (1) Discharge if no proceedings — A person who has been provisionally arrested, whether detained or released on judicial interim release, must be discharged

(a) when the Minister notifies the court that an authority to proceed will not be issued under section 15;

(b) if the provisional arrest was made pursuant to a request made under an extradition agreement that contains a period within which a request for extradition must be made and the supporting documents provided,

(i) when the period has expired and the extradition partner has not made the request or provided the documents, or

(ii) when the request for extradition has been made and the documents provided within the period but the Minister has not issued an authority to proceed before the expiry of 30 days after the expiry of that period; or

(c) if the provisional arrest was not made pursuant to a request made under an extradition agreement or was made pursuant to an extradition agreement that does not contain a period within which a request for extradition must be made and the supporting documents provided,

(i) when 60 days have expired after the provisional arrest and the extradition partner has not made the request or provided the documents, or

(ii) when the request for extradition has been made and the documents provided within 60 days but the Minister has not issued an authority to proceed before the expiry of 30 additional days.

(2) **Extension** — On application of the Attorney General, a judge

(a) may extend a period referred to in subsection (1); or

(b) shall, in the case of a person arrested on the request of the International Criminal Court, extend a period referred to in subsection (1) for the period specified by the Attorney General, not to exceed 30 days.

(3) **Release of person** — In extending a period under subsection (2), the judge may also grant the person judicial interim release or vary the conditions of their judicial interim release.

2000, c. 24, s. 49

Authority to Proceed

15. (1) **Minister's power to issue** — The Minister may, after receiving a request for extradition and being satisfied that the conditions set out in paragraph 3(1)(a) and subsection 3(3) are met in respect of one or more offences mentioned in the request, issue an authority to proceed that authorizes the Attorney General to seek, on behalf of the extradition partner, an order of a court for the committal of the person under section 29.

(2) **Competing requests** — If requests from two or more extradition partners are received by the Minister for the extradition of a person, the Minister shall determine the order in which the requests will be authorized to proceed.

(3) **Contents of authority to proceed** — The authority to proceed must contain

(a) the name or description of the person whose extradition is sought;

(b) the name of the extradition partner; and

(c) the name of the offence or offences under Canadian law that correspond to the alleged conduct of the person or the conduct in respect of which the person was convicted, as long as one of the offences would be punishable in accordance with paragraph 3(1)(b).

(4) **Copy of authority to proceed** — A copy of an authority to proceed produced by a means of telecommunication that produces a writing has the same probative force as the original for the purposes of this Part.

Arrest or Summons Following Authority to Proceed

16. (1) Warrant of arrest or summons — The Attorney General may, after the Minister issues an authority to proceed, apply *ex parte* to a judge in the province in which the Attorney General believes the person is or to which the person is on their way, or was last known to be, for the issuance of a summons to the person or a warrant for the arrest of the person.

(2) When provisionally arrested — If the person has been arrested pursuant to a provisional arrest warrant issued under section 13, the Attorney General need not apply for a summons or warrant under subsection (1).

(3) Issuance of summons or warrant of arrest — The judge to whom an application is made shall issue a summons to the person, or a warrant for the arrest of the person, in accordance with subsection 507(4) of the *Criminal Code*, with any modifications that the circumstances require.

(4) Execution throughout Canada — A warrant that is issued under this section may be executed, and a summons issued under this section may be served, anywhere in Canada without being endorsed.

(5) Date of hearing — summons — A summons that is issued under this section must

(a) set a date for the appearance of the person before a judge that is not later than 15 days after its issuance; and

(b) require the person to appear at a time and place stated in it for the purposes of the *Identification of Criminals Act*.

(6) Effect of appearance — A person appearing as required by subsection (5) is considered, for the purposes only of the *Identification of Criminals Act*, to be in lawful custody charged with an indictable offence.

Appearance

17. (1) Appearance — A person who is arrested under section 13 or 16 is to be brought before a judge or a justice within twenty-four hours after the person is arrested, but if no judge or no justice is available during this time, the person shall be brought before a judge or a justice as soon as possible.

(2) Appearance before justice — The justice before whom a person is brought under subsection (1) shall order that the person be detained in custody and brought before a judge.

18. (1) Decision of judge — The judge before whom a person is brought following arrest under section 13 or 16 shall

(a) if the person has been arrested on the request of the International Criminal Court, order the detention in custody of the person unless

(i) the person shows cause, in accordance with subsection 522(2) of the *Criminal Code*, that their detention in custody is not justified, and

(ii) the judge is satisfied that, given the gravity of the alleged offence, there are urgent and exceptional circumstances that justify release — with or without conditions — and that the person will appear as required; or

(b) in any other case, order the release, with or without conditions, or detention in custody of the person.

(1.1) Mandatory adjournment — An application for judicial interim release in respect of a person referred to in paragraph (1)(a) shall, at the request of the Attorney General, be adjourned to await receipt of the recommendations of the Pre-Trial Chamber of the International Criminal Court. If the recommendations are not received within six days, the judge may proceed to hear the application.

(1.2) Recommendations of Pre-Trial Chamber — If the Pre-Trial Chamber of the International Criminal Court submits recommendations, the judge shall consider them before rendering a decision.

(2) Review by court of appeal — A decision respecting judicial interim release may be reviewed by a judge of the court of appeal and that judge may

(a) confirm the decision;

(b) vary the decision; or

(c) substitute any other decision that, in the judge's opinion, should have been made.

2000, c. 24, s. 50

19. Criminal Code — Part XVI of the *Criminal Code* applies, with any modifications that the circumstances require, in respect of a person arrested under section 13 or 16 or to whom a summons has been issued under section 16.

20. Section 679 of the *Criminal Code* — Section 679 of the *Criminal Code* applies, with any modifications that the circumstances require, to the judicial interim release of a person pending

(a) a determination of an appeal from an order of committal made under section 29;

(b) the Minister's decision under section 40 respecting the surrender of the person; or

(c) a determination of a judicial review of the Minister's decision under section 40 to order the surrender of the person.

21. (1) Date of hearing — provisional arrest — If a person has been provisionally arrested, the judge before whom the person is brought shall

(a) order the person to appear before the court from time to time during the period referred to in paragraph 14(1)(b) or (c); and

(b) set a date for the extradition hearing if the Minister has issued an authority to proceed.

(2) **Date of hearing after authority to proceed issued** — If a person has been arrested or is a person to whom a summons has been issued under section 16, the judge before whom the person is brought shall set a date for the extradition hearing.

(3) **Hearing** — The judge shall set an early date for the extradition hearing, whether that date is in or out of the prescribed sessions of the court.

22. (1) **Application for transfer** — On application of the Attorney General or the person arrested or to whom a summons has been issued under section 16, the judge shall, if satisfied that the interests of justice so require, order that the proceedings be transferred to another place in Canada and that the person appear before a judge in that place, and

(a) if the person is detained, that the person be conveyed by a peace officer to the place; and

(b) if the person is not detained or has been released on judicial interim release, that the person be summoned to appear at the place.

(2) **Execution throughout Canada** — A summons issued under paragraph (1)(b) may be served anywhere in Canada without being endorsed.

(3) **Order respecting expenses** — If the order under subsection (1) was made on the application of the Attorney General, the judge may order that the Attorney General pay the person's reasonable travel expenses incurred further to the order.

Substitution and Amendment of Authority to Proceed

23. (1) **Substitution of authority to proceed** — The Minister may substitute another authority to proceed at any time before the extradition hearing begins. All documents issued and orders made by the court apply in respect of the new authority to proceed, unless the court, on application of the person or the Attorney General, orders otherwise.

(1.1) **New date for hearing** — Where the Minister substitutes another authority to proceed under subsection (1) and the person applies for another date to be set for the beginning of the extradition hearing in order to give the person an opportunity to examine the new authority, the judge may set another date for the hearing.

(2) **Amendment of authority to proceed** — The judge may, on application of the Attorney General, amend the authority to proceed after the hearing has begun in accordance with the evidence that is produced during the hearing.

(3) **Withdrawal of the authority to proceed** — The Minister may at any time withdraw the authority to proceed and, if the Minister does so, the court shall discharge the person and set aside any order made respecting their judicial interim release or detention.

Extradition Hearing

24. (1) Extradition hearing — The judge shall, on receipt of an authority to proceed from the Attorney General, hold an extradition hearing.

(2) Application of Part XVIII of the *Criminal Code* — For the purposes of the hearing, the judge has, subject to this Act, the powers of a justice under Part XVIII of the *Criminal Code*, with any modifications that the circumstances require.

25. Competence — For the purposes of the *Constitution Act, 1982*, a judge has, with respect to the functions that the judge is required to perform in applying this Act, the same competence that that judge possesses by virtue of being a superior court judge.

26. Order restricting publication of evidence — Before beginning a hearing in respect of a judicial interim release or an extradition hearing, a judge may, on application by the person or the Attorney General and on being satisfied that the publication or broadcasting of the evidence would constitute a risk to the holding of a fair trial by the extradition partner, make an order directing that the evidence taken not be published or broadcast before the time that the person is discharged or, if surrendered, the trial by the extradition partner has concluded.

27. Exclusion of person from hearing — The presiding judge may make an order excluding any person from the court for all or part of an extradition hearing or hearing in respect of a judicial interim release if the judge is of the opinion that it is in the interest of public morals, the maintenance of order or the proper administration of justice to exclude the person.

28. Power to compel witnesses — A judge who presides over an extradition hearing or a hearing in respect of a judicial interim release may compel a witness to attend the hearing and sections 698 to 708 of the *Criminal Code* apply, with any modifications that the circumstances require.

29. (1) Order of committal — A judge shall order the committal of the person into custody to await surrender if

(a) in the case of a person sought for prosecution, there is evidence admissible under this Act of conduct that, had it occurred in Canada, would justify committal for trial in Canada on the offence set out in the authority to proceed and the judge is satisfied that the person is the person sought by the extradition partner; and

(b) in the case of a person sought for the imposition or enforcement of a sentence, the judge is satisfied that the conviction was in respect of conduct that corresponds to the offence set out in the authority to proceed and that the person is the person who was convicted.

(2) Order of committal — The order of committal must contain

(a) the name of the person;

(b) the offence set out in the authority to proceed for which the committal is ordered;

(c) the place at which the person is to be held in custody; and

(d) the name of the extradition partner.

(3) **Discharge of person** — A judge shall order the person discharged if the judge does not order their committal under subsection (1).

(4) **Relevant date** — The date of the authority to proceed is the relevant date for the purposes of subsection (1).

(5) **Extradition when person not present at conviction** — Subject to a relevant extradition agreement, if a person has been tried and convicted without the person being present, the judge shall apply paragraph (1)(a).

30. (1) **Authority to keep person in custody** — The order of committal constitutes the authority to keep the person in custody, subject to an order of judicial interim release.

(2) **Duration of order** — The order of committal remains in force until the person is surrendered or discharged or until a new hearing is ordered under paragraph 54(a).

Rules of Evidence

31. Definition of "document" — For the purposes of sections 32 to 38, **"document"** means data recorded in any form, and includes photographs and copies of documents.

32. (1) **Evidence** — Subject to subsection (2), evidence that would otherwise be admissible under Canadian law shall be admitted as evidence at an extradition hearing. The following shall also be admitted as evidence, even if it would not otherwise be admissible under Canadian law:

(a) the contents of the documents contained in the record of the case certified under subsection 33(3);

(b) the contents of the documents that are submitted in conformity with the terms of an extradition agreement; and

(c) evidence adduced by the person sought for extradition that is relevant to the tests set out in subsection 29(1) if the judge considers it reliable.

(2) **Exception — Canadian evidence** — Evidence gathered in Canada must satisfy the rules of evidence under Canadian law in order to be admitted.

33. (1) **Record of the case** — The record of the case must include

(a) in the case of a person sought for the purpose of prosecution, a document summarizing the evidence available to the extradition partner for use in the prosecution; and

(b) in the case of a person sought for the imposition or enforcement of a sentence,

(i) a copy of the document that records the conviction of the person, and

(ii) a document describing the conduct for which the person was convicted.

(2) Other documents — record of the case — A record of the case may include other relevant documents, including documents respecting the identification of the person sought for extradition.

(3) Certification of record of the case — A record of the case may not be admitted unless

(a) in the case of a person sought for the purpose of prosecution, a judicial or prosecuting authority of the extradition partner certifies that the evidence summarized or contained in the record of the case is available for trial and

(i) is sufficient under the law of the extradition partner to justify prosecution, or

(ii) was gathered according to the law of the extradition partner; or

(b) in the case of a person sought for the imposition or enforcement of a sentence, a judicial, prosecuting or correctional authority of the extradition partner certifies that the documents in the record of the case are accurate.

(4) Authentication not required — No authentication of documents is required unless a relevant extradition agreement provides otherwise.

(5) Record of the case and supplements — For the purposes of this section, a record of the case includes any supplement added to it.

34. Oath or solemn affirmation — A document is admissible whether or not it is solemnly affirmed or under oath.

35. No proof of signature — A document purporting to have been signed by a judicial, prosecuting or correctional authority, or a public officer, of the extradition partner shall be admitted without proof of the signature or official character of the person appearing to have signed it.

36. Translated documents — A translation of a document into one of Canada's official languages shall be admitted without any further formality.

37. Evidence of identity — The following are evidence that the person before the court is the person referred to in the order of arrest, the document that records the conviction or any other document that is presented to support the request:

(a) the fact that the name of the person before the court is similar to the name that is in the documents submitted by the extradition partner; and

(b) the fact that the physical characteristics of the person before the court are similar to those evidenced in a photograph, finger-print or other description of the person.

Judge's Report

38. (1) Report of the judge — A judge who issues an order of committal of a person to await surrender shall transmit to the Minister the following documents:

(a) a copy of the order;

(b) a copy of the evidence adduced at the hearing that has not already been transmitted to the Minister; and

(c) any report that the judge thinks fit.

(2) Right to appeal — When the judge orders the committal of a person, the judge shall inform the person that they will not be surrendered until after the expiry of 30 days and that the person has a right to appeal the order and to apply for judicial interim release.

Property

39. (1) Property seized — Subject to a relevant extradition agreement, a judge who makes an order of committal may order that any thing that was seized when the person was arrested and that may be used in the prosecution of the person for the offence for which the extradition was requested be transferred to the extradition partner at the time the person is surrendered.

(2) Conditions of order — The judge may include in the order any conditions that the judge considers desirable, including conditions

(a) respecting the preservation and return to Canada of a thing; and

(b) respecting the protection of the interests of third parties.

Powers of Minister

40. (1) Surrender — The Minister may, within a period of 90 days after the date of a person's committal to await surrender, personally order that the person be surrendered to the extradition partner.

(2) When refugee claim — Before making an order under subsection (1) with respect to a person who has made a claim for refugee protection under the *Immigration and Refugee Protection Act*, the Minister shall consult with the minister responsible for that Act.

(3) Powers of the Minister — The Minister may seek any assurances that the Minister considers appropriate from the extradition partner, or may subject the surrender to any conditions that the Minister considers appropriate, including a condition that the person not be prosecuted, nor that a sentence be imposed on or enforced against the person, in respect of any offence or conduct other than that referred to in the order of surrender.

(4) No surrender — If the Minister subjects surrender of a person to assurances or conditions, the order of surrender shall not be executed until the Minister is satisfied that the assurances are given or the conditions agreed to by the extradition partner.

(5) Extension of time — If the person has made submissions to the Minister under section 43 and the Minister is of the opinion that further time is needed to act on those submissions, the Minister may extend the period referred to in subsection (1) as follows:

(a) if the person is the subject of a request for surrender by the International Criminal Court, and an issue has been raised as to the admissibility of the case or the jurisdiction of that Court, for a period ending not more than 45 days after the Court's ruling on the issue; or

(b) in any other case, for one additional period that does not exceed 60 days.

(6) Notice of extension of time — If an appeal has been filed under section 50 and the Minister has extended the period referred to in subsection (1), the Minister shall file with the court of appeal a notice of extension of time before the expiry of that period.

2000, c. 24, s. 51; 2001, c. 27, s. 250

41. (1) When appeal pending — The Minister may postpone the making of the order of surrender if

(a) an appeal has been filed under section 50;

(b) the Minister files a notice of postponement with the court of appeal before the expiry of the period referred to in subsection 40(1); and

(c) the order is made not later than 45 days after the date of the decision of the court of appeal.

(2) No further deferral of appeal — When the Minister has filed a notice of postponement with the court of appeal under paragraph (1)(b), that court may not defer the hearing of the appeal under subsection 51(2).

42. Amendments — The Minister may amend a surrender order at any time before its execution.

Submissions

43. (1) Submissions — The person may, at any time before the expiry of 30 days after the date of the committal, make submissions to the Minister in respect of any ground that would be relevant to the Minister in making a decision in respect of the surrender of the person.

(2) **Late acceptance of submissions** — The Minister may accept submissions even after the expiry of those 30 days in circumstances that the Minister considers appropriate.

Reasons for Refusal

44. (1) **When order not to be made** — The Minister shall refuse to make a surrender order if the Minister is satisfied that

(a) the surrender would be unjust or oppressive having regard to all the relevant circumstances; or

(b) the request for extradition is made for the purpose of prosecuting or punishing the person by reason of their race, religion, nationality, ethnic origin, language, colour, political opinion, sex, sexual orientation, age, mental or physical disability or status or that the person's position may be prejudiced for any of those reasons.

(2) **When Minister may refuse to make order** — The Minister may refuse to make a surrender order if the Minister is satisfied that the conduct in respect of which the request for extradition is made is punishable by death under the laws that apply to the extradition partner.

45. (1) **Refusal in extradition agreement** — The reasons for the refusal of surrender contained in a relevant extradition agreement, other than a multilateral extradition agreement, or the absence of reasons for refusal in such an agreement, prevail over sections 46 and 47.

(2) **Exception — multilateral extradition agreement** — The reasons for the refusal of surrender contained in a relevant multilateral extradition agreement prevail over sections 46 and 47 only to the extent of any inconsistency between either of those sections and those provisions.

46. (1) **When order not to be made** — The Minister shall refuse to make a surrender order if the Minister is satisfied that

(a) the prosecution of a person is barred by prescription or limitation under the law that applies to the extradition partner;

(b) the conduct in respect of which extradition is sought is a military offence that is not also an offence under criminal law; or

(c) the conduct in respect of which extradition is sought is a political offence or an offence of a political character.

(2) **Restriction** — For the purpose of subparagraph (1)(c), conduct that constitutes an offence mentioned in a multilateral extradition agreement for which Canada, as a party, is obliged to extradite the person or submit the matter to its appropriate authority for prosecution does not constitute a political offence or an offence of a political character. The following conduct also does not constitute a political offence or an offence of a political character:

(a) murder or manslaughter;

(b) inflicting serious bodily harm;

(c) sexual assault;

(d) kidnapping, abduction, hostage-taking or extortion;

(e) using explosives, incendiaries, devices or substances in circumstances in which human life is likely to be endangered or serious bodily harm or substantial property damage is likely to be caused; and

(f) an attempt or conspiracy to engage in, counselling, aiding or abetting another person to engage in, or being an accessory after the fact in relation to, the conduct referred to in any of paragraphs (a) to (e).

47. When Minister may refuse to make order — The Minister may refuse to make a surrender order if the Minister is satisfied that

(a) the person would be entitled, if that person were tried in Canada, to be discharged under the laws of Canada because of a previous acquittal or conviction;

(b) the person was convicted in their absence and could not, on surrender, have the case reviewed;

(c) the person was less than eighteen years old at the time of the offence and the law that applies to them in the territory over which the extradition partner has jurisdiction is not consistent with the fundamental principles governing the *Youth Criminal Justice Act*;

(d) the conduct in respect of which the request for extradition is made is the subject of criminal proceedings in Canada against the person; or

(e) none of the conduct on which the extradition partner bases its request occurred in the territory over which the extradition partner has jurisdiction.

2002, c. 1, s. 190

47.1 When grounds for refusal do not apply — The grounds for refusal set out in sections 44, 46 and 47 do not apply in the case of a person who is the subject of a request for surrender by the International Criminal Court.

2000, c. 24, s. 52

48. (1) Discharge — If the Minister decides not to make a surrender order, the Minister shall order the discharge of the person.

(2) When refugee claim — When the Minister orders the discharge of a person and the person has made a claim for refugee protection under the *Immigration and Refugee Protection Act*, the Minister shall send copies of all relevant documents to the minister responsible for that Act.

2001, c. 27, s. 251

Appeal

49. Appeal — A person may appeal against an order of committal — or the Attorney General, on behalf of the extradition partner, may appeal the discharge of the person or a stay of proceedings — to the court of appeal of the province in which the order of committal, the order discharging the person or the order staying the proceedings was made,

(a) on a ground of appeal that involves a question of law alone;

(b) on a ground of appeal that involves a question of fact or a question of mixed law and fact, with leave of the court of appeal or a judge of the court of appeal; or

(c) on a ground of appeal not set out in paragraph (a) or (b) that appears to the court of appeal to be a sufficient ground of appeal, with leave of the court of appeal.

50. (1) Notice of appeal — An appellant who proposes to appeal to a court of appeal or to obtain the leave of that court to appeal must give notice of appeal or notice of the application for leave to appeal not later than 30 days after the decision of the judge with respect to the committal or discharge of the person, or the stay of proceedings, as the case may be, in any manner that may be directed by the rules of court.

(2) Extension of time — The court of appeal or a judge of the court of appeal may, either before or after the expiry of the 30 days referred to in subsection (1), extend the time within which notice of appeal or notice of an application for leave to appeal may be given.

51. (1) Hearing of appeal — An appeal under this Act shall be scheduled for hearing by the court of appeal at an early date whether that date is in or out of the prescribed sessions of that court.

(2) Deferral of appeal — The hearing of an appeal against an order of committal may be deferred by the court of appeal until the Minister makes a decision in respect of the surrender of the person under section 40.

52. (1) Provisions of the *Criminal Code* to apply — Sections 677, 678.1, 682 to 685 and 688 of the *Criminal Code* apply, with any modifications that the circumstances require, to appeals under this Act.

(2) Rules — Unless inconsistent with the provisions of this Act, rules made by the court of appeal under section 482 of the *Criminal Code* in relation to appeals to that court under that Act apply, with any modifications that the circumstances require, to appeals under this Act.

53. Powers of the court of appeal — On the hearing of an appeal against an order of committal of a person, the court of appeal may

(a) allow the appeal, in respect of any offence in respect of which the person has been committed, if it is of the opinion

(i) that the order of committal should be set aside on the ground that it is unreasonable or cannot be supported by the evidence,

(ii) that the order of committal should be set aside on the ground of a wrong decision on a question of law, or

(iii) that, on any ground, there was a miscarriage of justice; or

(b) dismiss the appeal

(i) if it does not allow the appeal on any ground referred to in paragraph (a), or

(ii) even though the court of appeal is of the opinion that on the ground referred to in subparagraph (a)(ii) the appeal may be decided in favour of the appellant, if it is of the opinion that no substantial wrong or miscarriage of justice has occurred and the order of committal should be upheld.

54. Effect of allowing appeal — If the court of appeal allows an appeal under paragraph 53(a), it shall

(a) set aside the order of committal and

(i) discharge the person, or

(ii) order a new extradition hearing; or

(b) amend the order of committal to exclude an offence in respect of which the court is of the opinion that the person has not been properly committed on a ground referred to in subparagraph 53(a)(i), (ii) or (iii).

55. (1) Powers — On the hearing of an appeal against the discharge of a person or against a stay of proceedings, the court of appeal may

(a) allow the appeal and set aside the order of discharge or stay, if it is of the opinion

(i) that the order of discharge should be set aside on the ground that it is unreasonable or cannot be supported by the evidence,

(ii) that the order of discharge or the stay of proceedings should be set aside on the ground of a wrong decision on a question of law, or

(iii) that, on any ground, there was a miscarriage of justice; or

(b) dismiss the appeal.

(2) Order for new extradition hearing or committal — The court of appeal may, if it sets aside a stay of proceedings, order a new extradition hearing. The court of appeal may, if it sets aside an order of discharge, order a new extradition hearing or order the committal of the person.

56. (1) Deferral of Supreme Court appeal — The Supreme Court may defer, until the Minister makes a decision with respect to the surrender of the person under section 40, the hearing of an application for leave to appeal, or the hearing of an appeal, from a decision of the court of appeal on an appeal taken under section 49, or on any other appeal in respect of a matter arising under this Act.

(2) **Deferral of Supreme Court appeal** — The Supreme Court may also, if an application for judicial review is made under section 57 or otherwise, defer the hearing until the court of appeal makes its determination on the application.

Judicial Review of Minister's Order

57. (1) Review of order — Despite the *Federal Courts Act*, the court of appeal of the province in which the committal of the person was ordered has exclusive original jurisdiction to hear and determine applications for judicial review under this Act, made in respect of the decision of the Minister under section 40.

(2) **Application** — An application for judicial review may be made by the person.

(3) **Time limitation** — An application for judicial review shall be made, in accordance with the rules of court of the court of appeal, within 30 days after the time the decision referred to in subsection (1) was first communicated by the Minister to the person, or within any further time that the court of appeal, either before or after the expiry of those 30 days, may fix or allow.

(4) **Section 679 of the *Criminal Code*** — Section 679 of the *Criminal Code* applies, with any modifications that the circumstances require, to an application for judicial review.

(5) **Hearing of application** — An application for judicial review shall be scheduled for hearing by the court of appeal at an early date whether that date is in or out of the prescribed sessions of that court.

(6) **Powers of court of appeal** — On an application for judicial review, the court of appeal may

(a) order the Minister to do any act or thing that the Minister has unlawfully failed or refused to do or has unreasonably delayed in doing; or

(b) declare invalid or unlawful, quash, set aside, set aside and refer back for determination in accordance with any directions that it considers appropriate, prohibit or restrain the decision of the Minister referred to in subsection (1).

(7) **Grounds of review** — The court of appeal may grant relief under this section on any of the grounds on which the Federal Court may grant relief under subsection 18.1(4) of the *Federal Courts Act*.

(8) **Defect in form or technical irregularity** — If the sole ground for relief established in an application for judicial review is a defect in form or a technical irregularity, the court of appeal may

(a) refuse the relief if it finds that no substantial wrong or miscarriage of justice has occurred; or

(b) in the case of a defect in form or a technical irregularity in the decision, make an order validating the order, to have effect from the time and on the terms that it considers appropriate.

(9) **One hearing by court of appeal** — If an appeal under section 49 or any other appeal in respect of a matter arising under this Act is pending, the court of

appeal may join the hearing of that appeal with the hearing of an application for judicial review.

(10) Provincial rules of judicial review apply — Unless inconsistent with the provisions of this Act, all laws, including rules, respecting judicial review in force in the province of the court of appeal apply, with any modifications that the circumstances require, to applications under this section.

2002, c. 8, s. 141

Order of Surrender

58. Contents of the surrender order — An order of surrender must

(a) contain the name of the person who is to be surrendered;

(b) describe the offence in respect of which the extradition is requested, the offence for which the committal was ordered or the conduct for which the person is to be surrendered;

(c) state the extradition partner to which the person is to be conveyed;

(d) direct the person who has custody of the person to be surrendered to deliver them into the custody of the person or a member of the class of persons referred to in paragraph (e);

(e) designate the person or class of persons authorized for the purposes of section 60;

(f) set out any assurances or conditions to which the surrender is subject;

(g) fix, in the case of postponement of surrender under section 64, the period of time at or before the expiry of which the person is to be surrendered; and

(h) fix, in the case of a temporary surrender under section 66,

(i) the period of time at or before the expiry of which the person to be surrendered must be returned to Canada, and

(ii) the period of time at or before the expiry of which final surrender shall take place.

59. Surrender for other offences — Subject to a relevant extradition agreement, the Minister may, if the request for extradition is based on more than one offence, order the surrender of a person for all the offences even if not all of them fulfil the requirements set out in section 3, if

(a) the person is being surrendered for at least one offence that fulfils the requirements set out in section 3; and

(b) all the offences relate to conduct that, had it occurred in Canada, would have constituted offences that are punishable under the laws of Canada.

60. Power to convey — On the execution of a surrender order, the person or persons designated under paragraph 58(e) shall have the authority to receive, hold in custody and convey the person into the territory over which the extradition partner has jurisdiction.

61. (1) Escape — If the person escapes while in custody, the law that applies with respect to a person who is accused or convicted of a crime against the laws of Canada and who escapes applies with respect to the person.

(2) Arrest — If the person escapes while in custody, the person or member of the class of persons having custody of the person has the power to arrest them in fresh pursuit.

62. (1) Delay before surrender — No person may be surrendered

(a) until a period of 30 days has expired after the date of the committal for surrender; or

(b) if an appeal or a judicial review in respect of a matter arising under this Act, or any appeal from an appeal or judicial review, is pending, until after the date of the final decision of the court on the appeal or judicial review.

(2) Waiver of period of time — The person may waive the period referred to in paragraph (1)(a) if they do so in writing.

63. Place of surrender — A surrender may take place at any place within or outside Canada that is agreed to by Canada and the extradition partner.

64. (1) Postponement of surrender — Unless the Minister orders otherwise, a surrender order made in respect of a person accused of an offence within Canadian jurisdiction or who is serving a sentence in Canada after a conviction for an offence, other than an offence with respect to the conduct to which the order relates does not take effect until the person has been discharged, whether by acquittal, by expiry of the sentence or otherwise.

(2) Offence before or after surrender — For greater certainty, the person need not have been accused of the offence within Canadian jurisdiction before the surrender order was made.

65. Return to Canada — If a person returns to Canada after surrender before the expiry of a sentence that they were serving in Canada at the time of surrender, the remaining part of the sentence must be served.

Temporary Surrender

66. (1) Temporary surrender — The Minister may order the temporary surrender to an extradition partner of a person who is ordered committed under section 29 while serving a term of imprisonment in Canada so that the extradition partner may prosecute the person or to ensure the person's presence in respect of appeal proceedings that affect the person, on condition that the extradition partner give the assurances referred to in subsections (3) and (4).

(2) Time limits — An order of temporary surrender is subject to the time limits set out in subsection 40(1) and (5) and paragraph 41(1)(c).

(3) Assurances — The Minister may not order temporary surrender under subsection (1) unless the extradition partner gives an assurance that the person will remain in custody while temporarily surrendered to the extradition partner and

(a) in the case of temporary surrender for a trial, that the person will be returned within 30 days after the completion of the trial, unless a relevant extradition agreement provides for another time limit; and

(b) in the case of temporary surrender for an appeal, that the person will be returned within 30 days after the completion of the proceedings for which the presence of the person was required, unless a relevant extradition agreement provides for another time limit.

(4) Time limit — The Minister may require the extradition partner to give an assurance that the person will be returned no later than a specified date or that the person will be returned on request of the Minister.

(5) Assurances in extradition agreements — Any assurance referred to in subsections (3) and (4) that is included in a relevant extradition agreement need not be repeated as a specific assurance.

(6) Final surrender after temporary surrender — A person shall, subject to subsection (7), be surrendered to the extradition partner without a further request for extradition after the person

(a) has been temporarily surrendered;

(b) has been convicted by the extradition partner and had a term of imprisonment imposed on them;

(c) has been returned to Canada under subsection (4); and

(d) has finished serving the portion of the sentence that they were serving in custody in Canada at the time of the temporary surrender, unless the Minister orders that they be surrendered earlier.

(7) No final surrender if circumstances warrant — The Minister may, in circumstances that the Minister considers appropriate, revoke the surrender order and order the discharge of the person.

(8) Notice — The authority who has custody of the person to be surrendered under subsection (6) shall give the Minister reasonable notice of the time when the portion of the person's sentence to be served in custody is to expire.

(9) Final surrender when Canadian sentence expires — When the sentence that the person is serving in Canada expires during the period during which the person is temporarily surrendered to an extradition partner, the surrender is considered to be a final surrender.

(10) Waiver of return — The Minister may, after consultation with the Minister of Public Safety and Emergency Preparedness or the appropriate provincial minister responsible for corrections, waive the return of the person by the extradition partner.

(11) Final surrender despite subsection 3(3) — A person may be surrendered under subsection (6) even if the term of imprisonment imposed by the extradition partner, or the portion of the term remaining to be served, is less than that required by subsection 3(3).

2005, c. 10, s. 34(1)(l)(i)

67. Order for surrender — An order of surrender prevails over a prior warrant or other order under which the person to whom it applies is otherwise detained in Canada or at liberty under terms and conditions.

68. Calculation of sentence — For the purposes of calculating a sentence that a person to whom an order of temporary surrender applies is serving in Canada at the time of the temporary surrender, the person

(a) is credited with any time that is served in custody outside Canada under a temporary surrender order; and

(b) remains eligible for remission in accordance with the laws of the correctional system under which the person was serving the sentence in Canada.

Remedy

69. Remedy in case of delay — A judge of the superior court of the province in which the person is detained who has the power to grant a writ of *habeas corpus*, may, on application made by or on behalf of the person, and on proof that reasonable notice of the intention to make the application has been given to the Minister, order the person to be discharged out of custody unless sufficient cause is shown against the discharge if

(a) the Minister has not made an order of surrender under section 40

(i) before the expiry of the period referred to in subsection 40(1) and any additional period referred to in subsection 40(5), or

(ii) if a notice of postponement has been filed under paragraph 41(1)(b), before the expiry of 45 days after the date of the decision of the court of appeal referred to in paragraph 41(1)(c); or

(b) the person is not surrendered and conveyed to the extradition partner

(i) within 45 days after the order of surrender is made by the Minister under section 40, or

(ii) if an appeal or judicial review in respect of any matter arising under this Act, or an appeal from such an appeal or judicial review, is pending, within 45 days after the final decision of the court is made,

over and above, in any case referred to in subparagraph (i) or (ii), the time required to convey the person to the extradition partner.

Consent

70. (1) Consent to committal — A person may, at any time after the issuance of an authority to proceed, consent, in writing and before a judge, to committal.

(2) Judge to order committal — A judge before whom a person consents under subsection (1) shall

(a) order the committal of the person into custody to await surrender to the extradition partner; and

(b) transmit a copy of the consent to the Minister.

71. (1) Consent to surrender — A person may, at any time after arrest or appearance, consent, in writing and before a judge, to being surrendered.

(2) Judge to order surrender — A judge before whom a person consents to being surrendered shall

(a) order the committal of the person into custody to await surrender to the extradition partner; and

(b) transmit a copy of the consent to the Minister.

(3) When Minister receives consent — The Minister may, as soon as is feasible after receiving a consent to surrender, personally order that the person be surrendered to the extradition partner.

(4) Sections not applicable — When a person consents to being surrendered to the extradition partner, the following sections do not apply:

(a) section 43 (submissions to the Minister);

(b) section 44 (reasons for refusal);

(c) section 48 (discharge of person);

(d) section 57 (judicial review of Minister's decision); and

(e) paragraph 62(1)(a) (delay before surrender).

Waiver of Extradition

72. (1) Waiving extradition — A person may, at any time after arrest or appearance, waive extradition in writing and before a judge.

(2) Judge to inform person — A judge before whom a person gives a waiver under subsection (1) must inform the person

(a) of the consequences of the waiver including the consequences of waiving the protection of specialty; and

(b) that they will be conveyed without delay to the extradition partner.

(3) Judge to order conveyance — The judge shall

(a) order the conveyance in custody of the person to the extradition partner; and

(b) transmit a copy of the waiver and the order to the Minister.

(4) Conveyance order — The conveyance order must

(a) contain the name of the person who is to be conveyed; and

(b) state the extradition partner to which the person is to be conveyed.

73. (1) Escape — If the person escapes while in custody for conveyance, the law that applies with respect to a person who is accused or convicted of a crime against the laws of Canada and who escapes applies with respect to the person.

(2) Arrest — If the person escapes while in custody for conveyance, the person in whose custody the person is has the power to arrest them in fresh pursuit.

Transit

74. (1) Transit — The Minister may consent to the transit in Canada of a person surrendered by one State or entity to another, subject to any terms and conditions that the Minister considers appropriate.

(2) Consent to transit — A consent to transit constitutes authority to the officer of the surrendering State or entity or the receiving State or entity to keep the person in custody while in Canada.

(3) Sections to apply — Sections 58 (contents of surrender order), 60 (power to convey), 61 (escape) and 69 (remedy in case of delay) apply, with any modifications that the circumstances require, in respect of the consent to transit.

75. (1) Special authorization — The Minister may, in order to give effect to a request for consent to transit, authorize a person in a State or entity who is inadmissible under the *Immigration and Refugee Protection Act* to come into Canada at a place designated by the Minister and to go to and remain in a place in Canada so designated for the period specified by the Minister. The Minister may make the authorization subject to any conditions that the Minister considers desirable.

(2) Variation of authorization — The Minister may vary the terms of an authorization granted under subsection (1) and, in particular, may extend the period of time during which the person is authorized to remain in a place in Canada.

(3) Non-compliance with conditions of authorization — A person in respect of whom an authorization is granted under subsection (1) and who is found in a place in Canada other than the place designated in the authorization or in any place in Canada after the expiry of the period of time specified in the authorization or who fails to comply with some other condition of the authorization is, for the purposes of the *Immigration and Refugee Protection Act*, deemed to be a person who entered Canada as a temporary resident and remains in Canada after the period authorized for their stay.

2001, c. 27, s. 252

76. Unscheduled landing — If a person being extradited or surrendered from one State or entity to another arrives in Canada without prior consent to transit, a peace officer may, at the request of a public officer who has custody of the person while the person is being conveyed,

(a) if the person is being surrendered to the International Criminal Court, hold the person in custody for a maximum period of 96 hours pending receipt by the Minister of a request for a consent to transit from that Court; or

(b) in any other case, hold the person in custody for a maximum period of 24 hours pending receipt by the Minister of a request for a consent to transit from the requesting State or entity.

2000, c. 24, s. 53

PART 3 — EXTRADITION TO CANADA (SS. 77–83)

77. Definition of "competent authority" — In this Part, **"competent authority"** means

(a) in respect of a prosecution or imposition of a sentence — or of a disposition under the *Young Offenders Act*, chapter Y-1 of the Revised Statutes of Canada, 1985 — the Attorney General, or the Attorney General of a province who is responsible for the prosecution of the case; and

(b) in respect of the enforcement of a sentence or a disposition under the *Young Offenders Act*, chapter Y-1 of the Revised Statutes of Canada, 1985,

(i) the Minister of Public Safety and Emergency Preparedness, if the person would serve the sentence in a penitentiary, or

(ii) the appropriate provincial minister responsible for corrections, in any other case.

2002, c. 1, s. 191; 2005, c. 10, s. 34(1)(l)(ii)

78. (1) Request by Canada for extradition — The Minister, at the request of a competent authority, may make a request to a State or entity for the extradition of a person for the purpose of prosecuting the person for — or imposing or enforcing a sentence, or making or enforcing a disposition under the *Young Offenders Act*, chapter Y-1 of the Revised Statutes of Canada, 1985, in respect of — an offence over which Canada has jurisdiction.

(2) Request for provisional arrest — The Minister, at the request of a competent authority, may make a request to a State or entity for the provisional arrest of the person.

2002, c. 1, s. 192

79. (1) Order in respect of evidence — A judge may, for the purposes of acquiring evidence for a request for extradition, on the *ex parte* application of a competent authority, make any order that is necessary to

(a) secure the attendance of a witness at any place designated by the judge;

(b) secure the production as evidence of data that is recorded in any form;

(c) receive and record the evidence; and

(d) certify or authenticate the evidence in a manner and form that is required by the requested State or entity.

(2) Part XXII of the *Criminal Code* to apply — Part XXII of the *Criminal Code* applies, with any modifications that the circumstances require, to orders under subsection (1).

80. Specialty if person is in Canada — Subject to a relevant extradition agreement, a person who has been extradited to Canada by a requested State or entity shall not, unless the person has voluntarily left Canada after surrender or has had a reasonable opportunity of leaving Canada,

(a) be detained or prosecuted, or have a sentence imposed or executed, or a disposition made or executed under the *Young Offenders Act*, chapter Y-1 of the Revised Statutes of Canada, 1985, in Canada in respect of an offence that is alleged to have been committed, or was committed, before surrender other than

(i) the offence in respect of which the person was surrendered or an included offence,

(ii) another offence in respect of which the requested State or entity consents to the person being detained or prosecuted, or

(iii) another offence in respect of which the person consents to being detained or prosecuted; or

(b) be detained in Canada for the purpose of being surrendered to another State or entity for prosecution or for imposition or execution of a sentence in respect of an offence that is alleged to have been committed, or was committed, before surrender to Canada, unless the requested State or entity consents.

2002, c. 1, s. 193

81. (1) Conveyance of surrendered person — A person who is surrendered to Canada by a requested State or entity may be brought into Canada by an agent of the requested State or entity if the Minister so authorizes and be delivered to an appropriate authority to be dealt with according to law.

(2) Power to convey — On the execution of a surrender order, the authorized agent of the requested State or entity shall have the authority to hold the person in custody in Canada until delivery under subsection (1).

(3) Escape — If the person escapes while in custody, the law that applies with respect to a person who is accused or convicted of a crime against the laws of Canada and who escapes applies with respect to the person.

(4) Arrest — If the person escapes, the authorized agent of the requested State or entity has the power to arrest them in fresh pursuit.

82. (1) Order of detention for temporary surrender — Subject to subsection (2), a judge shall, on application of the competent authority made at any time before the temporary surrender, order the detention in custody of a person who is serving a term of imprisonment or has otherwise lawfully been deprived of their liberty in a requested State or entity and whose temporary surrender Canada has requested for the purpose of prosecution or appeal.

(2) Time limit — The order must contain a provision that the person will not be detained in custody after

(a) a date specified in the order;

(b) in the case of surrender for a trial, days after the completion of the trial; or

(c) in the case of surrender for an appeal, 30 days after the completion of the proceedings for which the presence of the person was required.

(3) **Order of detention to prevail** — An order made under subsection (1) prevails over an order made by a Canadian court, a judge of a Canadian court, a Canadian justice of the peace or any other person who has power in Canada to compel the appearance of a person, in respect of anything that occurred before the person is transferred to Canada.

(4) **Variation of detention order** — The judge who made the detention order or another judge may vary its terms and conditions and, in particular, may extend the duration of the detention.

(5) **Return** — Subject to subsection (6), the person shall be returned to the requested State or entity on completion of the proceedings in Canada for which the person was temporarily surrendered or on the expiry of the period set out in the order, whichever is sooner.

(6) **Return if right of appeal** — The person shall not be returned to the requested State or entity

(a) if the person has been convicted in Canada, before 30 days after the conviction, unless the person or the competent authority declares that there will be no appeal; and

(b) if the person has been acquitted, before 30 days after the acquittal, unless the competent authority declares that there will be no appeal.

(7) **Return for appeal** — The court of appeal may, on application, recommend that the Minister request another temporary surrender of a person who has been returned to the requested State or entity after trial, if the court of appeal is satisfied that the interests of justice require their presence for the appeal.

83. (1) Commencement of sentence — Subject to subsection (3), the sentence or disposition of a person who has been temporarily surrendered and who has been convicted and sentenced, or found guilty and sentenced, in Canada, or in respect of whom a disposition has been made under the *Young Offenders Act*, chapter Y-1 of the Revised Statutes of Canada, 1985, does not commence until their final extradition to Canada.

(2) **Warrant of commital** — The warrant of committal issued under the *Criminal Code* in respect of the person must state that the person is to be committed to custody to serve the sentence or disposition immediately on their final extradition to Canada.

(3) **If concurrent sentences ordered** — The sentencing judge may order that the person's sentence, or the disposition under the *Young Offenders Act*, chapter Y-1 of the Revised Statutes of Canada, 1985, be executed concurrently with the sentence they are serving in the requested State or entity, in which case the warrant of committal or order of disposition shall state that the person is to be committed to custody under subsection (2) only for any portion of the sentence or disposition remaining at the time of their final extradition to Canada.

2002, c. 1, s. 194

PART 4 — TRANSITIONAL PROVISIONS, CONSEQUENTIAL AND RELATED AMENDMENTS AND REPEALS (SS. 84–130)

Transitional Provisions

84. Cases pending — former *Extradition Act* — The *Extradition Act* repealed by section 129 of this Act applies to a matter respecting the extradition of a person as though it had not been repealed, if the hearing in respect of the extradition had already begun on the day on which this Act comes into force.

85. Cases pending — *Fugitive Offenders Act* — The *Fugitive Offenders Act* repealed by section 130 of this Act applies to a matter respecting the return under that Act of a person as though it had not been repealed, if the hearing before the provincial court judge in respect of the return had already begun on the day on which this Act comes into force.

Consequential Amendments

86. to 88. Consequential Amendments — [Note: The Consequential amendments are incorporated into the relevant provisions of the Acts which they affect, namely, the *Corrections and Conditional Release Act* and the *Identification of Criminals Act*.]

Related Amendments

89. to 128. Related Amendments — [Note: The Related amendments are incorporated into the relevant provisions of the Acts they affect, namely, the *Canada Evidence Act*, the *Criminal Code*, the *Immigration Act*, R.S.C. 1985, c. I-2, and the *Mutual Legal Assistance in Criminal Matters Act*.]

Repeals

129. Repeal of R.S. c. E-23 — The *Extradition Act* is repealed.

130. Repeal of R.S. c. F-32 — The *Fugitive Offenders Act* is repealed.

SCHEDULE — STATES OR ENTITIES DESIGNATED AS EXTRADITION PARTNERS

(Sections 2 and 9)

Antigua and Barbuda

Australia

The Bahamas

Barbados

Botswana

Costa Rica

Ghana

Grenada

Guyana

International Criminal Court

The International Criminal Tribunal for the Prosecution of Persons Responsible for Genocide and other Serious Violations of International Humanitarian Law Committed in the Territory of Rwanda and Rwandan citizens responsible for genocide and other such violations committed in the territory of neighbouring States, between 1 January 1994 and 31 December 1994, established by Resolution 955 (1994) of the Security Council of the United Nations

The International Tribunal for the Prosecution of Persons Responsible for Serious Violations of International Law Committed in the Territory of the Former Yugoslavia since 1991, established by Resolution 827 (1993) of the Security Council of the United Nations

Jamaica

Japan

Lesotho

Maldives

Malta

Mauritius

Namibia

Nauru

New Zealand

Papua New Guinea

Singapore

Solomon Islands

South Africa

St. Kitts & Nevis

St. Lucia

St. Vincent & The Grenadines

Swaziland

Trinidad and Tobago

Tuvalu

United Kingdom of Great Britain and Northern Ireland

Vanuatu
Zimbabwe

SOR/2005-227, s. 1

FIREARMS ACT–CRIMINAL CODE PART III (PRIOR TO ENACTMENT OF S.C. 1995, C. 39)

Editor's note: Current to May 15, 2019.

TABLE OF CONCORDANCE

The Firearms Act, *S.C. 1995, c. 39 introduced a new legislative regime to govern the licensing, registration, transport, export, import, storage, display, transfer and use of firearms in Canada. In doing so, it repealed and replaced the existing firearms scheme under Part III of the* Criminal Code. *Certain of the matters addressed by the provisions of the former Part III are now addressed under the* Firearms Act *proper. What follows is a table which identifies those provisions of the new* Firearms Act *which correspond, directly or by analogy, to those of the former Part III.*

Firearms Act, S.C. 1995, c. 39	**Criminal Code, R.S.C., c. C-46, Part III (prior to enactment of S.C. 1995, c. 39)**
1	—
2(1) "authorization to carry"	84(1) "permit"
2(2), (3)	—
3	—
4	—
5	106(1), (4)
6	106(2)(b)
7(1)	106(2)(c), (3)
7(2)	—
7(3)	106(2.2)
7(4), (5)	106(2)(c), (2.1)
8	110(6), (7)
9	105(1), (1.2), (4); 107; 109.1
10	—
11	105(1)(b)
12	84(1.2); 109(4), (4.1), (4.3)
13	109(1), (3)(a)
14	106(10); 109(3)(b)
15	92(1)
16	—
17	109(8); 110(3.1), (3.2), (3.3)

Firearms Act, S.C. 1995, c. 39	**Criminal Code, R.S.C., c. C-46, Part III (prior to enactment of S.C. 1995, c. 39)**
18	—
19	109(2); 110(2), (2.1), (3), (3.1), (4)
20	110(2)(a), (2)(b)
21	—
22	94
23	95(1), (4); 97(1); 99; 109(6)
24	95(1), (3)
25-26	—
27	109(6), (7)
28	109(3)(c), (3)(d)
29	109(3)(c); 110(2)(c)
30	84(1) "geniune gun collector"
31	109(7)
32	97(1)
33	93(2); 96(2); 97(2), (4)
34	98(1)
35	96(3); 97(3); 97(4); 110(2.1)
36-39	—
40	95(1); 96(3); 97(3)
41-42	—
43	95(1), (2), (3), (5); 96(3); 97(3), (4); 105
44-53	—
54	106(8), (11); 109(1); 110(1), (2.1), (3), (3.1), (4), (9)
55	106(9), 106(9.1)
56	105(4.1), (5); 106(1); 110(5)
57	110(2.1), (3), (3.1), (4)
58	110(6), (7), (11)
59	110(1)
60	109(7)
61	106(11); 109(7); 110(11)
62	—
63	106(13); 110(10)
64	106(11); 110(5), 110(8)
65	110(1)
66	—
67	106(1.2)

Firearms Act, S.C. 1995, c. 39	Criminal Code, R.S.C., c. C-46, Part III (prior to enactment of S.C. 1995, c. 39)
68	106(5); 112(4)
69	112(3)
70	106(11); 112(2), (2.1)
71	109(4.2); 112(1)
72	106(5); 106(14), 112(5), (6), (7)
73	—
74	90.1; 106(5), (6), (7), (15); 112(8), (9)
75	106(16), (17); 112(12)
76	106(18); 112(11)
76.1	—
77	106(19), (20); 112(13), (14)
78-80	—
81	106(19); 112(13)
82	—
83	114(1)
84-86	—
87	114(1), (3)
88	—
89	114(3)
90	114(3)
91-92	—
93	117
94	114(2)
95	108; 111
96	—
97	90(3.1); 95(4); 105(1.3)
98	84(1) "chief firearms officer"
99	—
100	84(1) "local registrar of firearms"; 84(3)
101	105(1.1)(c)
102	105(1.1)(c)
103	105(1.1)(c)
104-105	—
106	113(1)
107	113(2)
108	—

Firearms Act, S.C. 1995, c. 39	Criminal Code, R.S.C., c. C-46, Part III (prior to enactment of S.C. 1995, c. 39)
109	105(6), (7), (8); 113
110	113(3)
111	113(3)
112-113	—
114	113(4)
115	113(4)
116	—
117	116; 109.1
118	116(2)
119-137	—

FIREARMS ACT

An Act respecting firearms and other weapons

S.C. 1995, c. 39 [ss. 24(2)(d), 37–53 repealed before coming into force 2008, c. 20, s. 3.], as am. S.C. 1995, c. 39, s. 137; 1996, c. 19, s. 76.1; 1999, c. 3, s. 64; 1999, c. 25, s. 31(4)(b); 2000, c. 12, ss. 116–118; 2001, c. 4, s. 85; 2001, c. 41, s. 96; 2003, c. 8, ss. 9–21, 22 (Fr.), 23–52, 53 (Fr.), 54–56 [ss. 26–35, 37, 40(2), 51 repealed before coming into force 2008, c. 20, s. 3.]; 2003, c. 22, s. 224(z.38); 2005, c. 10, s. 29; 2005, c. 38, ss. 139(c), 142(f), 145(2)(j); 2012, c. 6, ss. 9–28, 30 [s. 30(2), (5), (7), (8) conditions not yet satisfied. Repealed 2019, c. 9, s. 24.]; 2015, c. 27, ss. 2(1) (Fr.), (2), 3, 4(1) (Fr.), (2), (3) (Fr.), (4), (5) (Fr.), (6)–(9), 5–11, 12(1), (2) (Fr.), 13–17 [ss. 10, 15 not in force at date of publication.]; 2018, c. 16, s. 182; 2019, c. 9, ss. 1–9, 10(1) (Fr.), (2) (Fr.), (3), (4), 11–15, 23, 24 [ss. 1, 2, 3(2), 4(2), (3), 5–11, 13(1), (3), 14, 15 not in force at date of publication.].

SHORT TITLE

1. Short title — This Act may be cited as the *Firearms Act*.

INTERPRETATION

2. (1) Definitions — In this Act,

"authorization to carry" means an authorization described in section 20;

"authorization to export" means an authorization referred to in section 44 and includes a permit to export goods that is issued under the *Export and Import Permits Act* and that is deemed by regulations made under paragraph 117(a.1) to be an authorization to export;

"authorization to import" means an authorization referred to in section 46;

"authorization to transport" means an authorization described in section 19;

"business" means a person who carries on a business that includes

(a) the manufacture, assembly, possession, purchase, sale, importation, exportation, display, repair, restoration, maintenance, storage, alteration, pawnbroking, transportation, shipping, distribution or delivery of firearms, prohibited weapons, restricted weapons, prohibited devices or prohibited ammunition,

(b) the possession, purchase or sale of ammunition, or

(c) the purchase of cross-bows

and includes a museum;

“carrier” means a person who carries on a transportation business that includes the transportation of firearms, prohibited weapons, restricted weapons, prohibited devices or prohibited ammunition;

“chief firearms officer” means

(a) in respect of a province, the individual who is designated in writing as the chief firearms officer for the province by the provincial minister of that province,

(b) in respect of a territory, the individual who is designated in writing as the chief firearms officer for the territory by the federal Minister, or

(c) in respect of any matter for which there is no chief firearms officer under paragraph (a) or (b), the individual who is designated in writing as the chief firearms officer for the matter by the federal Minister;

“commencement day”, in respect of a provision of this Act or the expression “former Act” in a provision of this Act, means the day on which the provision comes into force;

“Commissioner” means the Commissioner of Firearms appointed under section 81.1;

“common-law partner”, in relation to an individual, means a person who is cohabiting with the individual in a conjugal relationship, having so cohabited for a period of at least one year;

“customs office” has the meaning assigned by subsection 2(1) of the *Customs Act*;

“customs officer” has the meaning assigned to the word “officer” by subsection 2(1) of the *Customs Act*;

“federal Minister” means the Minister of Public Safety and Emergency Preparedness;

“firearms officer” means

(a) in respect of a province, an individual who is designated in writing as a firearms officer for the province by the provincial minister of that province,

(b) in respect of a territory, an individual who is designated in writing as a firearms officer for the territory by the federal Minister, or

(c) in respect of any matter for which there is no firearms officer under paragraph (a) or (b), an individual who is designated in writing as a firearms officer for the matter by the federal Minister;

“former Act” means Part III of the *Criminal Code*, as it read from time to time before the commencement day;

"museum" means a person who operates a museum

(a) in which firearms, prohibited weapons, restricted weapons, prohibited devices or prohibited ammunition are possessed, bought, displayed, repaired, restored, maintained, stored or altered, or

(b) in which ammunition is possessed or bought;

"non-resident" means an individual who ordinarily resides outside Canada;

"prescribed" means

(a) in the case of a form or the information to be included on a form, prescribed by the federal Minister, and

(b) in any other case, prescribed by the regulations;

"provincial minister" means

(a) in respect of a province, the member of the executive council of the province who is designated by the lieutenant governor in council of the province as the provincial minister,

(b) in respect of a territory, the federal Minister, or

(c) in respect of any matter for which there is no provincial minister under paragraph (a) or (b), the federal Minister;

"regulations" means regulations made by the Governor in Council under section 117.

(2) To be interpreted with *Criminal Code* — Unless otherwise provided, words and expressions used in this Act have the meanings assigned to them by section 2 or 84 of the *Criminal Code*. Subsections 117.15(3) and (4) of that Act apply to those words and expressions.

Proposed Amendment — 2(2)

(2) Criminal Code — Unless otherwise provided, words and expressions used in this Act have the meanings assigned to them by section 2 or 84 of the *Criminal Code*.

2019, c. 9, s. 1(1) [Not in force at date of publication.]

(2.1) Deemed references to Registrar — Sections 5, 9, 54 to 58, 67, 68 and 70 to 72 apply in respect of a carrier as if each reference in those sections to a chief firearms officer were a reference to the Registrar and for the purposes of applying section 6 in respect of a carrier, paragraph 113(3)(b) of the *Criminal Code* applies as if the reference in that section to a chief firearms officer were a reference to the Registrar.

(3) Aboriginal and treaty rights — For greater certainty, nothing in this Act shall be construed so as to abrogate or derogate from any existing aboriginal or treaty rights of the aboriginal peoples of Canada under section 35 of the *Constitution Act, 1982*.

Proposed Addition — 2(4)

(4) For greater certainty — For greater certainty, nothing in this Act shall be construed so as to permit or require the registration of nonrestricted firearms.

2019, c. 9, s. 1(2) [Not in force at date of publication.]

2000, c. 12, s. 116; 2001, c. 4, s. 85; 2003, c. 8, s. 9; 2005, c. 10, s. 29; 2015, c. 27, s. 2(2)

Her Majesty

3. (1) Binding on Her Majesty — This Act is binding on Her Majesty in right of Canada or a province.

(2) Canadian Forces — Notwithstanding subsection (1), this Act does not apply in respect of the Canadian Forces.

Purpose

4. Purpose — The purpose of this Act is

(a) to provide, notably by sections 5 to 16 and 54 to 73, for the issuance of

(i) licences for firearms and authorizations and registration certificates for prohibited firearms or restricted firearms, under which persons may possess firearms in circumstances that would otherwise constitute an offence under subsection 91(1), 92(1), 93(1) or 95(1) of the *Criminal Code*,

(ii) licences and authorizations under which persons may possess prohibited weapons, restricted weapons, prohibited devices and prohibited ammunition in circumstances that would otherwise constitute an offence under subsection 91(2), 92(2) or 93(1) of the *Criminal Code*, and

(iii) licences under which persons may sell, barter or give cross-bows in circumstances that would otherwise constitute an offence under subsection 97(1) of the *Criminal Code*;

(b) to authorize,

(i) notably by sections 5 to 12 and 54 to 73, the manufacture of or offer to manufacture, and

(ii) notably by sections 21 to 34 and 54 to 73, the transfer of or offer to transfer,

firearms, prohibited weapons, restricted weapons, prohibited devices, ammunition and prohibited ammunition in circumstances that would otherwise constitute an offence under subsection 99(1), 100(1) or 101(1) of the *Criminal Code*; and

(c) to authorize, notably by sections 35 to 73, the importation or exportation of firearms, prohibited weapons, restricted weapons, prohibited devices, ammunition, prohibited ammunition and components and parts designed exclusively for use in the manufacture of or assembly into automatic firearms in circumstances that would otherwise constitute an offence under subsection 103(1) or 104(1) of the *Criminal Code*.

2012, c. 6, s. 9

Authorized Possession

Eligibility to Hold Licences

General Rules

5. (1) Public safety — A person is not eligible to hold a licence if it is desirable, in the interests of the safety of that or any other person, that the person not possess a firearm, a cross-bow, a prohibited weapon, a restricted weapon, a prohibited device, ammunition or prohibited ammunition.

(2) Criteria — In determining whether a person is eligible to hold a licence under subsection (1), a chief firearms officer or, on a reference under section 74, a provincial court judge shall have regard to whether the person, within the previous five years,

Proposed Amendment — 5(2) opening words

(2) Criteria — In determining whether a person is eligible to hold a licence under subsection (1), a chief firearms officer or, on a reference under section 74, a provincial court judge shall have regard to whether the person

2019, c. 9, s. 2(1) [Not in force at date of publication.]

(a) has been convicted or discharged under section 730 of the *Criminal Code* of

(i) an offence in the commission of which violence against another person was used, threatened or attempted,

(ii) an offence under this Act or Part III of the *Criminal Code*,

(iii) an offence under section 264 of the *Criminal Code* (criminal harassment),

(iv) an offence relating to the contravention of subsection 5(1) or (2), 6(1) or (2) or 7(1) of the *Controlled Drugs and Substances Act*, or

(v) an offence relating to the contravention of subsection 9(1) or (2), 10(1) or (2), 11(1) or (2), 12(1), (4), (5), (6) or (7), 13(1) or 14(1) of the *Cannabis Act*;

(b) has been treated for a mental illness, whether in a hospital, mental institute, psychiatric clinic or otherwise and whether or not the person was confined to such a hospital, institute or clinic, that was associated with violence or threatened or attempted violence on the part of the person against any person; or

Proposed Amendment — 5(2)(b)

(b) has been treated for a mental illness, whether in a hospital, mental institute, psychiatric clinic or otherwise and whether or not the person was confined to such a hospital, institute or clinic, that was associated with violence or threatened or attempted violence on the part of the person against any person;

2019, c. 9, s. 2(2) [Not in force at date of publication.]

(c) has a history of behaviour that includes violence or threatened or attempted violence on the part of the person against any person.

Proposed Amendment — 5(2)(c)

(c) has a history of behaviour that includes violence or threatened or attempted violence or threatening conduct on the part of the person against any person;

2019, c. 9, s. 2(2) [Not in force at date of publication.]

Proposed Addition — 5(2)(d)–(f)

(d) is or was previously prohibited by an order — made in the interests of the safety and security of any person — from communicating with an identified person or from being at a specified place or within a specified distance of that place, and presently poses a threat or risk to the safety and security of any person;

(e) in respect of an offence in the commission of which violence was used, threatened or attempted against the person's intimate partner or former intimate partner, was previously prohibited by a prohibition order from possessing any firearm, cross-bow, prohibited weapon, restricted weapon, prohibited device or prohibited ammunition; or

(f) for any other reason, poses a risk of harm to any person.

2019, c. 9, s. 2(2) [Not in force at date of publication.]

Proposed Addition — 5(2.1)

(2.1) **For greater certainty** — For greater certainty, for the purposes of paragraph (2)(c), threatened violence and threatening conduct include threats or conduct communicated by the person to a person by means of the Internet or other digital network.

2019, c. 9, s. 2(3) [Not in force at date of publication.]

(3) **Exception** — Despite subsection (2), in determining whether a non-resident who is 18 years old or older and by or on behalf of whom an application is made for a 60-day licence authorizing the non-resident to possess non-restricted firearms is eligible to hold a licence under subsection (1), a chief firearms officer or, on a reference under section 74, a provincial court judge may but need not have regard to the criteria described in subsection (2).

1995, c. 39, s. 137; 1996, c. 19, s. 76.1; 2003, c. 8, s. 10; 2015, c. 27, s. 3; 2018, c. 16, s. 182

6. (1) **Court orders** — A person is eligible to hold a licence only if the person is not prohibited by a prohibition order from possessing any firearm, cross-bow, prohibited weapon, restricted weapon, prohibited device or prohibited ammunition.

(2) **Exception** — Subsection (1) is subject to any order made under section 113 of the *Criminal Code* (lifting of prohibition order for sustenance or employment).

7. (1) Successful completion of safety course — An individual is eligible to hold a licence only if the individual

(a) successfully completes the Canadian Firearms Safety Course, as given by an instructor who is designated by a chief firearms officer, and passes the tests, as administered by an instructor who is designated by a chief firearms officer, that form part of that Course;

(b) passed, before the commencement day, the tests, as administered by an instructor who is designated by a chief firearms officer, that form part of that Course;

(c) successfully completed, before January 1, 1995, a course that the attorney general of the province in which the course was given had, during the period beginning on January 1, 1993 and ending on December 31, 1994, approved for the purposes of section 106 of the former Act;

(d) passed, before January 1, 1995, a test that the attorney general of the province in which the test was administered had, during the period beginning on January 1, 1993 and ending on December 31, 1994, approved for the purposes of section 106 of the former Act; or

(e) on the commencement day, was an individual referred to in paragraph 7(4)(c) as it read immediately before that day and held a licence.

(2) Restricted firearms safety course — An individual is eligible to hold a licence authorizing the individual to possess prohibited firearms or restricted firearms only if the individual

(a) successfully completes a restricted firearms safety course that is approved by the federal Minister, as given by an instructor who is designated by a chief firearms officer, and passes any tests, as administered by an instructor who is designated by a chief firearms officer, that form part of that course;

(b) passed, before the commencement day, a restricted firearms safety test, as administered by an instructor who is designated by a chief firearms officer, that is approved by the federal Minister; or

(c) on the commencement day, was an individual referred to in paragraph 7(4)(c) as it read immediately before that day and held a licence authorizing the individual to possess prohibited firearms or restricted firearms.

(3) After expiration of prohibition order — An individual against whom a prohibition order was made

(a) is eligible to hold a licence only if the individual has, after the expiration of the prohibition order,

(i) successfully completed the Canadian Firearms Safety Course, as given by an instructor who is designated by a chief firearms officer, and

(ii) passed the tests, as administered by an instructor who is designated by a chief firearms officer, that form part of that Course; and

(b) is eligible to hold a licence authorizing the individual to possess restricted firearms only if the individual has, after the expiration of the prohibition order,

(i) successfully completed a restricted firearms safety course that is approved by the federal Minister, as given by an instructor who is designated by a chief firearms officer, and

(ii) passed any tests, as administered by an instructor who is designated by a chief firearms officer, that form part of that course.

(4) **Exceptions** — Subsections (1) and (2) do not apply to an individual who

(a) in the prescribed circumstances, has been certified by a chief firearms officer as meeting the prescribed criteria relating to the safe handling and use of firearms and the laws relating to firearms;

(b) is less than eighteen years old and requires a firearm to hunt or trap in order to sustain himself of herself or his or her family;

(c) [Repealed 2015, c. 27, s. 4(8).]

(d) requires a licence merely to acquire cross-bows; or

(e) is a non-resident who is 18 years old or older and by or on behalf of whom an application is made for a 60-day licence authorizing the non-resident to possess non-restricted firearms.

(5) **Further exception** — Subsection (3) does not apply to an individual in respect of whom an order is made under section 113 of the *Criminal Code* (lifting of prohibition order for sustenance or employment) and who is exempted by a chief firearms officer from the application of that subsection.

2003, c. 8, s. 11; 2015, c. 27, s. 4(2), (4), (6)–(9)

Special Cases — Persons

8. (1) **Minors** — An individual who is less than eighteen years old and who is otherwise eligible to hold a licence is not eligible to hold a licence except as provided in this section.

(2) **Minors hunting as a way of life** — An individual who is less than eighteen years old and who hunts or traps as a way of life is eligible to hold a licence if the individual needs to hunt or trap in order to sustain himself or herself or his or her family.

(3) **Hunting, etc.** — An individual who is twelve years old or older but less than eighteen years old is eligible to hold a licence authorizing the individual to possess, in accordance with the conditions attached to the licence, a firearm for the purpose of target practice, hunting or instruction in the use of firearms or for the purpose of taking part in an organized competition.

(4) **No prohibited or restricted firearms** — An individual who is less than eighteen years old is not eligible to hold a licence authorizing the individual to possess prohibited firearms or restricted firearms or to acquire firearms or cross-bows.

(5) **Consent of parent or guardian** — An individual who is less than eighteen years old is eligible to hold a licence only if a parent or person who has custody of the individual has consented, in writing or in any other manner that is satisfactory to the chief firearms officer, to the issuance of the licence.

9. (1) **Businesses** — A business is eligible to hold a licence authorizing a particular activity only if every person who stands in a prescribed relationship to the business is eligible under sections 5 and 6 to hold a licence authorizing that activity or the acquisition of restricted firearms.

(2) **Safety courses** — A business other than a carrier is eligible to hold a licence only if

(a) a chief firearms officer determines that no individual who stands in a prescribed relationship to the business need be eligible to hold a licence under section 7; or

(b) the individuals who stand in a prescribed relationship to the business and who are determined by a chief firearms officer to be the appropriate individuals to satisfy the requirements of section 7 are eligible to hold a licence under that section.

(3) **Employees — firearms** — Subject to subsection (3.1), a business other than a carrier is eligible to hold a licence that authorizes the possession of firearms only if every employee of the business who, in the course of duties of employment, handles or would handle firearms is the holder of a licence authorizing the holder to acquire non-restricted firearms.

(3.1) **Employees — prohibited firearms or restricted firearms** — A business other than a carrier is eligible to hold a licence that authorizes the possession of prohibited firearms or restricted firearms only if every employee of the business who, in the course of duties of employment, handles or would handle firearms is the holder of a licence authorizing the holder to acquire restricted firearms.

(3.2) **Employees — prohibited weapons, restricted weapons, etc.** — A business other than a carrier is eligible to hold a licence that authorizes the possession of prohibited weapons, restricted weapons, prohibited devices or prohibited ammunition only if every employee of the business who, in the course of duties of employment, handles or would handle any of those things is eligible under sections 5 and 6 to hold a licence.

(4) **Exception** — In subsection (3), "firearm" does not include a partially manufactured barrelled weapon that, in its unfinished state, is not a barrelled weapon

(a) from which any shot, bullet or other projectile can be discharged; and

(b) that is capable of causing serious bodily injury or death to a person.

(5) **Exception** — Subsection (1) does not apply in respect of a person who stands in a prescribed relationship to a business where a chief firearms officer determines that, in all the circumstances, the business should not be ineligible to hold a licence merely because of that person's ineligibility.

(6) Exception for museums — Subsection (3) does not apply in respect of an employee of a museum

(a) who, in the course of duties of employment, handles or would handle only firearms that are designed or intended to exactly resemble, or to resemble with near precision, antique firearms, and who has been trained to handle or use such a firearm; or

(b) who is designated, by name, by a provincial minister.

2003, c. 8, s. 12; 2015, c. 27, s. 5

10. [Repealed 2003, c. 8, s. 13.]

Special Cases — Prohibited Firearms, Weapons, Devices and Ammunition

11. (1) Prohibited firearms, weapons, devices and ammunition — businesses — A business that is otherwise eligible to hold a licence is not eligible to hold a licence authorizing the business to possess prohibited firearms, prohibited weapons, prohibited devices or prohibited ammunition except as provided in this section.

(2) Prescribed purposes — A business other than a carrier is eligible to hold a licence authorizing the business to possess prohibited firearms, prohibited weapons, prohibited devices or prohibited ammunition if the business needs to possess them for a prescribed purpose.

(3) Carriers — A carrier is eligible to hold a licence authorizing the carrier to possess prohibited firearms, prohibited weapons, prohibited devices or prohibited ammunition.

12. (1) Prohibited firearms — individuals — An individual who is otherwise eligible to hold a licence is not eligible to hold a licence authorizing the individual to possess prohibited firearms except as provided in this section.

(2) Grandfathered individuals — pre-January 1, 1978 automatic firearms — An individual is eligible to hold a licence authorizing the individual to possess automatic firearms that, on the commencement day, were registered as restricted weapons under the former Act if the individual

(a) on January 1, 1978 possessed one or more automatic firearms;

(b) on the commencement day held a registration certificate under the former Act for one or more automatic firearms; and

(c) beginning on the commencement day was continuously the holder of a registration certificate for one or more automatic firearms.

(3) Grandfathered individuals — pre-August 1, 1992 converted automatic firearms — An individual is eligible to hold a licence authorizing the individual to possess automatic firearms that have been altered to discharge only one projectile during one pressure of the trigger and that, on the commencement day, were registered as restricted weapons under the former Act if the individual

(a) on August 1, 1992 possessed one or more automatic firearms

(i) that had been so altered, and

(ii) for which on October 1, 1992 a registration certificate under the former Act had been issued or applied for;

(b) on the commencement day held a registration certificate under the former Act for one or more automatic firearms that had been so altered; and

(c) beginning on the commencement day was continuously the holder of a registration certificate for one or more automatic firearms that have been so altered.

(4) Grandfathered individuals — Prohibited Weapons Order, No. 12 — An individual is eligible to hold a licence authorizing the individual to possess firearms that were declared to be prohibited weapons under the former Act by the *Prohibited Weapons Order, No. 12*, made by Order in Council P.C. 1992-1690 of July 23, 1992 and registered as SOR/92-471 and that, on October 1, 1992, either were registered as restricted weapons under the former Act or were the subject of an application for a registration certificate under the former Act if the individual

(a) before July 27, 1992 possessed one or more firearms that were so declared;

(b) on the commencement day held a registration certificate under the former Act for one or more firearms that were so declared; and

(c) beginning on the commencement day was continuously the holder of a registration certificate for one or more firearms that were so declared.

(5) Grandfathered individuals — Prohibited Weapons Order, No. 13 — An individual is eligible to hold a licence authorizing the individual to possess firearms that were declared to be prohibited weapons under the former Act by the *Prohibited Weapons Order, No. 13*, made by Order in Council P.C. 1994-1974 of November 29, 1994 and registered as SOR/94-741 and that, on January 1, 1995, either were registered as restricted weapons under the former Act or were the subject of an application for a registration certificate under the former Act if the individual

(a) before January 1, 1995 possessed one or more firearms that were so declared;

(b) on the commencement day held a registration certificate under the former Act for one or more firearms that were so declared; and

(c) beginning on the commencement day was continuously the holder of a registration certificate for one or more firearms that were so declared.

(6) Grandfathered individuals — pre-December 1, 1998 handguns — A particular individual is eligible to hold a licence authorizing that particular individual to possess a handgun referred to in subsection (6.1) if

(a) on December 1, 1998 the particular individual

(i) held a registration certificate under the former Act for that kind of handgun, or

(ii) had applied for a registration certificate that was subsequently issued for that kind of handgun; and

(b) beginning on December 1, 1998 the particular individual was continuously the holder of a registration certificate for that kind of handgun.

(6.1) Grandfathered handguns — pre-December 1, 1998 handguns — Subsection (6) applies in respect of a handgun

(a) that has a barrel equal to or less than 105 mm in length or that is designed or adapted to discharge a 25 or 32 calibre cartridge; and

(b) in respect of which

(i) on December 1, 1998 a registration certificate had been issued to an individual under the former Act,

(ii) on December 1, 1998 a registration certificate had been applied for by an individual under the former Act, if the certificate was subsequently issued to the individual, or

(iii) a record was sent before December 1, 1998 to the Commissioner of the Royal Canadian Mounted Police and received by that officer before, on or after that date.

(7) Next of kin of grandfathered individuals — A particular individual is eligible to hold a licence authorizing the particular individual to possess a particular handgun referred to in subsection (6.1) that was manufactured before 1946 if the particular individual is the spouse or common-law partner or a brother, sister, child or grandchild of an individual who was eligible under this subsection or subsection (6) to hold a licence authorizing the individual to possess the particular handgun.

(8) Grandfathered individuals — regulations re prohibited firearms — An individual is, in the prescribed circumstances, eligible to hold a licence authorizing the individual to possess firearms prescribed by a provision of regulations made by the Governor in Council under section 117.15 of the *Criminal Code* to be prohibited firearms if the individual

(a) on the day on which the provision comes into force possesses one or more of those firearms; and

(b) beginning on

(i) the day on which that provision comes into force, or

(ii) in the case of an individual who on that day did not hold but had applied for a registration certificate for one or more of those firearms, the day on which the registration certificate was issued

was continuously the holder of a registration certificate for one or more of those firearms.

(9) Grandfathered individuals — regulations — An individual is eligible to hold a licence authorizing the individual to possess prohibited firearms of a prescribed class if the individual

(a) possesses one or more firearms of that class on a day that is prescribed with respect to that class;

(b) holds a registration certificate for one or more firearms of that class in the circumstances prescribed with respect to that class; and

(c) was continuously the holder of a registration certificate for one or more firearms of that class beginning on the day that is prescribed — or that is determined under the regulations — with respect to that class.

Proposed Addition — 12(10)–(14)

(10) Grandfathered individuals — CZ rifle — An individual is eligible to hold a licence authorizing the individual to possess one or more firearms referred to in subsection (11) if

(a) the individual possessed one or more such firearms on June 30, 2018;

(b) the individual

(i) held on that day a registration certificate for one or more such firearms, in the case where at least one of those firearms was on that day a restricted firearm, or

(ii) applies, before the first anniversary of the commencement day, for a registration certificate that is subsequently issued for a firearm referred to in subsection (11), in any other case; and

(c) the individual was continuously the holder of a registration certificate for one or more such firearms beginning on

(i) June 30, 2018, in the case where at least one of those firearms was on that day a restricted firearm, or

(ii) the day on which a registration certificate referred to in subparagraph (b)(ii) is issued to the individual, in any other case.

(11) Grandfathered firearms — CZ rifle — Subsection (10) applies in respect of a firearm that

(a) is a

(i) Ceská Zbrojovka (CZ) Model CZ858 Tactical-2P rifle,

(ii) Ceská Zbrojovka (CZ) Model CZ858 Tactical-2V rifle,

(iii) Ceská Zbrojovka (CZ) Model CZ858 Tactical-4P rifle, or

(iv) Ceská Zbrojovka (CZ) Model CZ858 Tactical-4V rifle; and

(b) was registered as a restricted firearm on June 30, 2018 or, in the case of a firearm that was not a restricted firearm on that day, is the subject of an application made before the first anniversary of the commencement day for a registration certificate that is subsequently issued.

(12) For greater certainty — For greater certainty, the firearms referred to in subparagraphs (11)(a)(i) to (iv) include only firearms that are prohibited firearms on the commencement day.

(13) Grandfathered individuals — SAN Swiss Arms — An individual is eligible to hold a licence authorizing the individual to possess one or more firearms referred to in subsection (14) if

(a) the individual possessed one or more such firearms on June 30, 2018;

(b) the individual

(i) held on that day a registration certificate for one or more such firearms, in the case where at least one of those firearms was on that day a restricted firearm, or

(ii) applies, before the first anniversary of the commencement day, for a registration certificate that was subsequently issued for a firearm referred to in subsection (14), in any other case; and

(c) the individual was continuously the holder of a registration certificate for one or more such firearms beginning on

(i) June 30, 2018, in the case where at least one of the firearms was on that day a restricted firearm, or

(ii) the day on which a registration certificate referred to in subparagraph (b)(ii) is issued to the individual, in any other case.

(14) Grandfathered firearms — SAN Swiss Arms — Subsection (13) applies in respect of a firearm that

(a) is a

(i) SAN Swiss Arms Model Classic Green rifle,

(ii) SAN Swiss Arms Model Classic Green carbine,

(iii) SAN Swiss Arms Model Classic Green CQB rifle,

(iv) SAN Swiss Arms Model Black Special rifle,

(v) SAN Swiss Arms Model Black Special carbine,

(vi) SAN Swiss Arms Model Black Special CQB rifle,

(vii) SAN Swiss Arms Model Black Special Target rifle,

(viii) SAN Swiss Arms Model Blue Star rifle,

(ix) SAN Swiss Arms Model Heavy Metal rifle,

(x) SAN Swiss Arms Model Red Devil rifle,

(xi) SAN Swiss Arms Model Swiss Arms Edition rifle,

(xii) SAN Swiss Arms Model Classic Green Sniper rifle,

(xiii) SAN Swiss Arms Model Ver rifle,

(xiv) SAN Swiss Arms Model Aestas rifle,

(xv) SAN Swiss Arms Model Autumnus rifle, or

(xvi) SAN Swiss Arms Model Hiemis rifle; and

(b) was registered as a restricted firearm on June 30, 2018 or, in the case of a firearm that was not a restricted firearm on that day, is the subject of an application made before the first anniversary of the commencement day for a registration certificate that is subsequently issued.

2019, c. 9, s. 3(2) [Not in force at date of publication.]

2000, c. 12, s. 117; 2003, c. 8, s. 14; 2019, c. 9, s. 3(1)

Registration Certificates

12.1 Registration certificate — A registration certificate may only be issued for a prohibited firearm or a restricted firearm.

2012, c. 6, s. 10

13. Registration certificate — A person is not eligible to hold a registration certificate for a firearm unless the person holds a licence authorizing the person to possess that kind of firearm.

14. Serial number — A registration certificate may be issued only for a firearm

(a) that bears a serial number sufficient to distinguish it from other firearms; or

(b) that is described in the prescribed manner.

15. Exempted firearms — A registration certificate may not be issued for a firearm that is owned by Her Majesty in right of Canada or a province or by a police force.

16. (1) Only one person per registration certificate — A registration certificate for a firearm may be issued to only one person.

(2) Exception — Subsection (1) does not apply in the case of a firearm for which a registration certificate referred to in section 127 was issued to more than one person.

AUTHORIZED TRANSPORTATION OF FIREARMS

17. Places where prohibited and restricted firearms may be possessed — Subject to sections 19 and 20, a prohibited firearm or restricted firearm, the holder of the registration certificate for which is an individual, may be possessed only at the dwelling-house of the individual, as recorded in the Canadian Firearms Registry, or at a place authorized by a chief firearms officer.

2003, c. 8, s. 15

18. [Repealed 2003, c. 8, s. 15.]

19. (1) Transporting and using prohibited firearms or restricted firearms — An individual who holds a licence authorizing the individual to possess prohibited firearms or restricted firearms may be authorized to transport a particular prohibited firearm or restricted firearm between two or more specified places for any good and sufficient reason, including, without restricting the generality of the foregoing,

(a) for use in target practice, or a target shooting competition, under specified conditions or under the auspices of a shooting club or shooting range that is approved under section 29; or (a.1) to provide instructions in the use of firearms as part of a restricted firearms safety course that is approved by the federal Minister;

(b) if the individual

(i) changes residence,

(ii) wishes to transport the firearm to a peace officer, firearms officer or chief firearms officer for registration or disposal in accordance with this Act or Part III of the *Criminal Code*,

(iii) wishes to transport the firearm for repair, storage, sale, exportation or appraisal, or

(iv) wishes to transport the firearm to a gun show.

(1.1) **Target practice or competition** — In the case of an authorization to transport issued for a reason referred to in paragraph (1)(a) within the province where the holder of the authorization resides, the specified places must — except in the case of an authorization that is issued for a prohibited firearm referred to in subsection 12(9) — include all shooting clubs and shooting ranges that are approved under section 29 and that are located in that province.

Proposed Amendment — 19(1.1)

(1.1) **Target practice or competition** — In the case of an authorization to transport issued for a reason referred to in paragraph (1)(a) within the province where the holder of the authorization resides, the specified places must — except in the case of an authorization that is issued for a prohibited firearm referred to in subsection 12(9), (11) or (14) — include all shooting clubs and shooting ranges that are approved under section 29 and that are located in that province.

2019, c. 9, s. 4(2) [Not in force at date of publication.]

(2) **Exception for prohibited firearms other than prohibited handguns** — Despite subsection (1), an individual must not be authorized to transport a prohibited firearm — other than a handgun referred to in subsection 12(6.1) or a prohibited firearm referred to in subsection 12(9) — between specified places except for the purposes referred to in paragraph (1)(b).

Proposed Amendment — 19(2)

(2) **Exception for prohibited firearms other than prohibited handguns** — Despite subsection (1), an individual must not be authorized to transport a prohibited firearm — other than a handgun referred to in subsection 12(6.1) or a prohibited firearm referred to in subsection 12(9), (11) or (14) — between specified places except for the purposes referred to in paragraph (1)(b).

2019, c. 9, s. 4(2) [Not in force at date of publication.]

(2.1) **Automatic authorization to transport — licence renewal** — Subject to subsection (2.3), an individual who holds a licence authorizing the individual to possess prohibited firearms or restricted firearms must, if the licence is renewed, be authorized to transport them within the individual's province of residence

(a) to and from all shooting clubs and shooting ranges that are approved under section 29;

(b) to and from any place a peace officer, firearms officer or chief firearms officer is located, for verification, registration or disposal in accordance with this Act or Part III of the *Criminal Code*;

(c) to and from a business that holds a licence authorizing it to repair or appraise prohibited firearms or restricted firearms;

(d) to and from a gun show; and

(e) to a port of exit in order to take them outside Canada, and from a port of entry.

Proposed Amendment — 19(2.1)

(2.1) **Automatic authorization to transport — licence renewal** — An individual who holds a licence authorizing the individual to possess restricted firearms or handguns referred to in subsection 12(6.1) must, if the licence is renewed, be authorized to transport them within the individual's province of residence to and from all shooting clubs and shooting ranges that are approved under section 29. However, the authorization does not apply to a restricted firearm or a handgun referred to in subsection 12(6.1) whose transfer to the individual was approved, in accordance with subparagraph 28(b)(ii), for the purpose of having it form part of a gun collection.

2019, c. 9, s. 4(3) [Not in force at date of publication.]

(2.2) **Automatic authorization to transport — transfer** — Subject to subsection (2.3), if a chief firearms officer has authorized the transfer of a prohibited firearm or a restricted firearm to an individual who holds a licence authorizing the individual to possess prohibited firearms or restricted firearms, the individual must be authorized

(a) to transport the firearm within the individual's province of residence from the place where the individual acquires it to the place where they may possess it under section 17; and

(b) to transport their prohibited firearms and restricted firearms within the individual's province of residence to and from the places referred to in any of paragraphs (2.1)(a) to (e).

Proposed Amendment — 19(2.2)

(2.2) **Automatic authorization to transport — transfer** — If a chief firearms officer has authorized the transfer of a prohibited firearm or a restricted firearm to an individual who holds a licence authorizing the individual to possess prohibited firearms or restricted firearms, the individual must be authorized to transport the firearm within the individual's province of residence from the place where they acquire it to the place where they may possess it under section 17.

2019, c. 9, s. 4(3) [Not in force at date of publication.]

(2.3) **Exceptions** — An individual must not be authorized under subsection (2.1) or (2.2) to transport the following firearms to or from the places referred to in paragraph (2.1)(a):

(a) a prohibited firearm, other than a handgun referred to in subsection 12(6.1); and

(b) a restricted firearm or a handgun referred to in subsection 12(6.1) whose transfer was approved, in accordance with subparagraph 28(b)(ii), for the purpose of forming part of a gun collection.

(3) **Non-residents** — A non-resident may be authorized to transport a particular restricted firearm between specified places in accordance with sections 35 and 35.1.

Proposed Amendment — 19(2.3)

(2.3) **Automatic authorization to transport — transfer** — If a chief firearms officer has authorized the transfer of a restricted firearm or a handgun referred to in subsection 12(6.1) to an individual who holds a licence authorizing the individual to possess a restricted firearm or such a handgun, the individual must be authorized to transport their restricted firearm or handgun within the individual's province of residence to and from all shooting clubs and shooting ranges that are approved under section 29, unless the transfer of the restricted firearm or handgun was approved, in accordance with subparagraph 28(b)(ii), for the purpose of having it form part of a gun collection.

2019, c. 9, s. 4(3) [Not in force at date of publication.]

2003, c. 8, s. 16; 2015, c. 27, s. 6; 2019, c. 9, s. 4(1)

20. Carrying restricted firearms and pre-December 1, 1998 handguns — An individual who holds a licence authorizing the individual to possess restricted firearms or handguns referred to in subsection 12(6.1) (pre-December 1, 1998 handguns) may be authorized to possess a particular restricted firearm or handgun at a place other than the place at which it is authorized to be possessed if the individual needs the particular restricted firearm or handgun

(a) to protect the life of that individual or of other individuals; or

(b) for use in connection with his or her lawful profession or occupation.

2003, c. 8, s. 56(a)

AUTHORIZED TRANSFERS AND LENDING

General Provisions

21. Definition of "transfer" — For the purposes of sections 22 to 32, **"transfer"** means sell, barter or give.

22. Mental disorder, etc. — A person may transfer or lend a firearm to an individual only if the person has no reason to believe that the individual

(a) has a mental illness that makes it desirable, in the interests of the safety of that individual or any other person, that the individual not possess a firearm; or

(b) is impaired by alcohol or a drug.

Authorized Transfers

23. Authorization to transfer non-restricted firearms — A person may transfer a non-restricted firearm if, at the time of the transfer,

(a) the transferee holds a licence authorizing the transferee to acquire and possess that kind of firearm; and

(b) the transferor has no reason to believe that the transferee is not authorized to acquire and possess that kind of firearm.

Proposed Amendment — 23

23. Authorization to transfer non-restricted firearms — **(1)** A person may transfer one or more non-restricted firearms if, at the time of the transfer,

(a) the transferee holds a licence authorizing the transferee to acquire and possess a non-restricted firearm;

(b) the Registrar has, at the transferor's request, issued a reference number for the transfer and provided it to the transferor; and

(c) the reference number is still valid.

(2) Information — transferee's licence — The transferee shall provide to the transferor the prescribed information that relates to the transferee's licence, for the purpose of enabling the transferor to request that the Registrar issue a reference number for the transfer.

(3) Reference number — The Registrar shall issue a reference number if he or she is satisfied that the transferee holds and is still eligible to hold a licence authorizing them to acquire and possess a non-restricted firearm.

(4) Period of validity — A reference number is valid for the prescribed period.

(5) Registrar not satisfied — If the Registrar is not satisfied as set out in subsection (3), he or she may so inform the transferor.

2019, c. 9, s. 5 [Not in force at date of publication.]

2003, c. 8, s. 17; 2012, c. 6, s. 11; 2015, c. 27, s. 7

23.1 (1) Voluntary request to Registrar — A transferor referred to in section 23 may request that the Registrar inform the transferor as to whether the transferee, at the time of the transfer, holds and is still eligible to hold the licence referred to in paragraph 23(a), and if such a request is made, the Registrar or his or her delegate, or any other person that the federal Minister may designate, shall so inform the transferor.

(2) No record of request — Despite sections 12 and 13 of the *Library and Archives of Canada Act* and subsections 6(1) and (3) of the *Privacy Act*, neither the Registrar or his or her delegate nor a designated person shall retain any record of a request made under subsection (1).

Proposed Repeal — 23.1

23.1 [Repealed 2019, c. 9, s. 5. Not in force at date of publication.]

2012, c. 6, s. 11

23.2 (1) Authorization to transfer prohibited or restricted firearms — A person may transfer a prohibited firearm or a restricted firearm if, at the time of the transfer,

(a) the transferee holds a licence authorizing the transferee to acquire and possess that kind of firearm;

(b) the transferor has no reason to believe that the transferee is not authorized to acquire and possess that kind of firearm;

(c) the transferor informs the Registrar of the transfer;

(d) if the transferee is an individual, the transferor informs a chief firearms officer of the transfer and obtains the authorization of the chief firearms officer for the transfer;

(e) a new registration certificate for the firearm is issued in accordance with this Act; and

(f) the prescribed conditions are met.

(2) Notice — If, after being informed of a proposed transfer of a firearm, the Registrar decides to refuse to issue a registration certificate for the firearm, the Registrar shall inform a chief firearms officer of that decision.

2012, c. 6, s. 11

24. (1) Authorization to transfer prohibited weapons, devices and ammunition — Subject to section 26, a person may transfer a prohibited weapon, prohibited device or prohibited ammunition only to a business.

(2) Conditions — A person may transfer a prohibited weapon, prohibited device, ammunition or prohibited ammunition to a business only if

(a) the business holds a licence authorizing the business to acquire and possess prohibited weapons, prohibited devices, ammunition or prohibited ammunition, as the case may be;

(b) [Repealed 2003, c. 8, s. 18.]

(c) the person has no reason to believe that the business is not authorized to acquire and possess prohibited weapons, prohibited devices, ammunition or prohibited ammunition, as the case may be; and

(d) [Repealed before coming into force 2008, c. 20, s. 3.]

2003, c. 8, s. 18

25. Authorization to transfer ammunition to individuals — A person may transfer ammunition that is not prohibited ammunition to an individual only if the individual

(a) until January 1, 2001, holds a licence authorizing him or her to possess firearms or a prescribed document; or

(b) after January 1, 2001, holds a licence authorizing him or her to possess firearms.

26. (1) Authorization to transfer prohibited or restricted firearms to Crown, etc. — A person may transfer a prohibited firearm or a restricted firearm to Her Majesty in right of Canada or a province, to a police force or to a municipality if the person informs the Registrar of the transfer and complies with the prescribed conditions.

(2) Authorization to transfer prohibited weapons, etc., to the Crown, etc. — A person may transfer a prohibited weapon, restricted weapon, prohibited device, ammunition or prohibited ammunition to Her Majesty in right of Canada or a province, to a police force or to a municipality if the person informs a chief firearms officer of the transfer and complies with the prescribed conditions.

2003, c. 8, s. 19; 2012, c. 6, s. 12

27. Chief firearms officer — On being informed of a proposed transfer of a prohibited firearm or restricted firearm under section 23.2, a chief firearms officer shall

(a) verify

(i) whether the transferee or individual holds a licence,

(ii) whether the transferee or individual is still eligible to hold that licence, and

(iii) whether the licence authorizes the transferee or individual to acquire that kind of firearm or to acquire prohibited weapons, prohibited devices, ammunition or prohibited ammunition, as the case may be;

(b) in the case of a proposed transfer of a restricted firearm or a handgun referred to in subsection 12(6.1) (pre-December 1, 1998 handguns), verify the purpose for which the transferee or individual wishes to acquire the restricted firearm or handgun and determine whether the particular restricted firearm or handgun is appropriate for that purpose;

(c) decide whether to approve the transfer and inform the Registrar of that decision; and

(d) take the prescribed measures.

2003, c. 8, s. 20; 2012, c. 6, s. 13

28. Permitted purposes — A chief firearms officer may approve the transfer to an individual of a restricted firearm or a handgun referred to in subsection 12(6.1) (pre-December 1, 1998 handguns) only if the chief firearms officer is satisfied

(a) that the individual needs the restricted firearm or handgun

(i) to protect the life of that individual or of other individuals, or

(ii) for use in connection with his or her lawful profession or occupation; or

(b) that the purpose for which the individual wishes to acquire the restricted firearm or handgun is

(i) for use in target practice, or a target shooting competition, under conditions specified in an authorization to transport or under the auspices of a shooting club or shooting range that is approved under section 29, or

(ii) to form part of a gun collection of the individual, in the case of an individual who satisfies the criteria described in section 30.

2003, c. 8, s. 21

29. (1) Shooting clubs and shooting ranges — No person shall operate a shooting club or shooting range except under an approval of the provincial minister for the province in which the premises of the shooting club or shooting range are located.

(2) Approval — A provincial minister may approve a shooting club or shooting range for the purposes of this Act if

(a) the shooting club or shooting range complies with the regulations made under paragraph 117(e); and

(b) the premises of the shooting club or shooting range are located in that province.

(3) Revocation — A provincial minister who approves a shooting club or shooting range for the purposes of this Act may revoke the approval for any good and sufficient reason including, without limiting the generality of the foregoing, where the shooting club or shooting range contravenes a regulation made under paragraph 117(e).

(4) Delegation — A chief firearms officer who is authorized in writing by a provincial minister may perform such duties and functions of the provincial minister under this section as are specified in the authorization.

(5) Notice of refusal to approve or revocation — Where a provincial minister decides to refuse to approve or to revoke an approval of a shooting club or shooting range for the purposes of this Act, the provincial minister shall give notice of the decision to the shooting club or shooting range.

(6) Material to accompany notice — A notice given under subsection (5) must include reasons for the decision disclosing the nature of the information relied on for the decision and must be accompanied by a copy of sections 74 to 81.

(7) Non-disclosure of information — A provincial minister need not disclose any information the disclosure of which could, in the opinion of the provincial minister, endanger the safety of any person.

30. Gun collectors — The criteria referred to in subparagraph 28(b)(ii) are that the individual

(a) has knowledge of the historical, technological or scientific characteristics that relate or distinguish the restricted firearms or handguns that he or she possesses;

(b) has consented to the periodic inspection, conducted in a reasonable manner, of the premises in which the restricted firearms or handguns are to be kept; and

(c) has complied with such other requirements as are prescribed respecting knowledge, secure storage and the keeping of records in respect of restricted firearms or handguns.

31. (1) Registrar — On being informed of a proposed transfer of a firearm, the Registrar may

(a) issue a new registration certificate for the firearm in accordance with this Act; and

(b) revoke any registration certificate for the firearm held by the transferor.

(2) Transfers of firearms to the Crown, etc. — On being informed of a transfer of a firearm to Her Majesty in right of Canada or a province, to a police force or to a municipality, the Registrar shall revoke any registration certificate for the firearm.

2003, c. 8, s. 23

32. Mail-order transfers of firearms — A person may transfer a firearm by mail only if

(a) the verifications, notifications, issuances and authorizations referred to in sections 21 to 28, 30, 31, 40 to 43 and 46 to 52 take place within a reasonable period before the transfer in the prescribed manner; and

(b) [Repealed 2003, c. 8, s. 24.]

(c) the prescribed conditions are complied with.

2003, c. 8, s. 24

Authorized Lending

33. Authorization to lend — Subject to section 34, a person may lend a firearm only if

(a) the person

(i) has reasonable grounds to believe that the borrower holds a licence authorizing the borrower to possess that kind of firearm, and

(ii) in the case of a prohibited firearm or a restricted firearm, lends the registration certificate for it to the borrower; or

(b) the borrower uses the firearm under the direct and immediate supervision of the person in the same manner in which the person may lawfully use it.

2012, c. 6, s. 14

34. Authorization to lend firearms, etc., to the Crown, etc. — A person may lend a firearm, prohibited weapon, restricted weapon, prohibited device, ammunition or prohibited ammunition to Her Majesty in right of Canada or a province, to a police force or to a municipality if

(a) in the case of a prohibited firearm or a restricted firearm, the transferor lends the registration certificate for it to the borrower; and

(b) the prescribed conditions are complied with.

2003, c. 8, s. 25; 2012, c. 6, s. 15

AUTHORIZED EXPORTATION AND IMPORTATION

Individuals

35. (1) Authorization for non-residents who do not hold a licence to import firearms that are not prohibited firearms — A non-resident who does not hold a licence may import a firearm that is not prohibited firearm if, at the time of the importation,

(a) the non-resident

(i) is eighteen years old or older,

(ii) declares the firearm to a customs officer in the prescribed manner and, in the case of a declaration in writing, completes the prescribed form containing the prescribed information, and

(iii) in the case of a restricted firearm, produces an authorization to transport the restricted firearm; and

(b) a customs officer confirms in the prescribed manner the declaration referred to in subparagraph (a)(ii) and the authorization to transport referred to in subparagraph (a)(iii).

(2) Non-compliances — Where a firearm is declared at a customs office to a customs officer but the requirements of subparagraphs (1)(a)(ii) and (iii) are not complied with, the customs officer may authorize the firearm to be exported from that customs office or may detain the firearm and give the non-resident a reasonable time to comply with those requirements.

(3) Disposal of firearm — Where those requirements are not complied with within a reasonable time and the firearm is not exported, the firearm shall be disposed of in the prescribed manner.

(4) Non-compliance — If a non-restricted firearm is declared at a customs office to a customs officer and

(a) the non-resident has not truthfully completed the prescribed form, or

(b) the customs officer has reasonable grounds to believe that it is desirable, in the interests of the safety of the non-resident or any other person, that the declaration not be confirmed,

the customs officer may refuse to confirm the declaration and may authorize the firearm to be exported from that customs office.

2015, c. 27, s. 8

36. (1) Temporary licence and registration certificate — A declaration that is confirmed under paragraph 35(1)(b) has the same effect after the importation of the firearm as a licence authorizing the non-resident to possess only that firearm and, in the case of a restricted firearm, as a registration certificate for the firearm until

(a) the expiry of 60 days after the importation, in the case of a non-restricted firearm; or

(b) the earlier of the expiry of 60 days after the importation and the expiry of the authorization to transport, in the case of a restricted firearm.

(2) Renewal — A chief firearms officer may renew the confirmation of a declaration for one or more periods of sixty days.

(3) Electronic or other means — For greater certainty, an application for a renewal of the confirmation of a declaration may be made by telephone or other electronic means or by mail and a chief firearms officer may renew that confirmation by electronic means or by mail.

2012, c. 6, s. 16; 2015, c. 27, s. 9

Unproclaimed Text — 37–42.1

37 to 42.1 [Repealed before coming into force 2008, c. 20, s. 3.]

Proposed Addition — 42.2

42.2 (1) Obligation to provide information — A business may import a prohibited firearm or a restricted firearm only if the business completes the prescribed form containing the prescribed information and provides it by electronic or other means to the Registrar before the importation and to a customs officer before or at the time of the importation.

(2) Information sharing — The Registrar and a customs officer may provide each other with any form or information that they receive under subsection (1).

2015, c. 27, s. 10 [Not in force at date of publication.]

Unproclaimed Text — 43–53

Heading and ss. 43 to 53. [Repealed before coming into force 2008, c. 20, s. 3.]

Licences, Registration Certificates and Authorizations

Applications

54. (1) Applications — A licence, registration certificate or authorization, other than an authorization referred to in subsection 19(2.1) or (2.2), may be issued only on application made in the prescribed form — which form may be in writing or electronic — or in the prescribed manner. The application must set out the prescribed information and be accompanied by payment of the prescribed fees.

Proposed Amendment — 54(1)

(1) Applications — A licence, registration certificate or authorization, other than an authorization referred to in subsection 19(2.1), (2.2) or (2.3), may be issued only on application made in the prescribed form — which form may be in writing or electronic — or in the prescribed manner. The application must set out the prescribed information and be accompanied by payment of the prescribed fees.

2019, c. 9, s. 6 [Not in force at date of publication.]

(2) To whom made — An application for a licence, registration certificate or authorization must be made to

(a) a chief firearms officer, in the case of a licence, an authorization to carry or an authorization to transport; or

(b) the Registrar, in the case of a registration certificate, an authorization to export or an authorization to import.

(3) Pre-commencement restricted firearms and handguns — An individual who, on the commencement day, possesses one or more restricted firearms or one or more handguns referred to in subsection 12(6.1) (pre-December 1, 1998 handguns) must specify, in any application for a licence authorizing the individual to possess restricted firearms or handguns that are so referred to,

(a) except in the case of a firearm described in paragraph (b), for which purpose described in section 28 the individual wishes to continue to possess restricted firearms or handguns that are so referred to; and

(b) for which of those firearms was a registration certificate under the former Act issued because they were relics, were of value as a curiosity or rarity or were valued as a memento, remembrance or souvenir.

2003, c. 8, ss. 36, 56(b); 2015, c. 27, s. 11

55. (1) Further information — A chief firearms officer or the Registrar may require an applicant for a licence or authorization to submit such information, in addition to that included in the application, as may reasonably be regarded as relevant for the purpose of determining whether the applicant is eligible to hold the licence or authorization.

(2) Investigation — Without restricting the scope of the inquiries that may be made with respect to an application for a licence, a chief firearms officer may conduct an investigation of the applicant, which may consist of interviews with neighbours, community workers, social workers, individuals who work or live with the applicant, spouse or common-law partner, former spouse or former common-law partner, dependants or whomever in the opinion of the chief firearms officer may provide information pertaining to whether the applicant is eligible under section 5 to hold a licence.

2000, c. 12, s. 118

Issuance

56. (1) Licences — A chief firearms officer is responsible for issuing licences.

(2) Only one licence per individual — Only one licence may be issued to any one individual.

(3) Separate licence for each location — A business other than a carrier requires a separate licence for each place where the business is carried on.

57. Authorizations to carry or transport — A chief firearms officer is responsible for issuing authorizations to carry and authorizations to transport.

58. (1) Conditions — A chief firearms officer who issues a licence, an authorization to carry or an authorization to transport may attach any reasonable condition to it that the chief firearms officer considers desirable in the particular circumstances and in the interests of the safety of the holder or any other person.

(1.1) Exception — licence or authorization — However, a chief firearms officer's power to attach a condition to a licence, an authorization to carry or an authorization to transport is subject to the regulations.

(2) Minors — Before attaching a condition to a licence that is to be issued to an individual who is less than eighteen years old and who is not eligible to hold a licence under subsection 8(2) (minors hunting as a way of life), a chief firearms officer must consult with a parent or person who has custody of the individual.

(3) Minors — Before issuing a licence to an individual who is less than eighteen years old and who is not eligible to hold a licence under subsection 8(2) (minors hunting as a way of life), a chief firearms officer shall have a parent or person who has custody of the individual sign the licence, including any conditions attached to it.

2015, c. 27, s. 12(1)

Proposed Addition — 58.1

58.1 (1) Conditions — licence issued to business — A chief firearms officer who issues a licence to a business must attach the following conditions to the licence:

(a) the business must record and, for the prescribed period, keep the prescribed information that relates to the business' possession and disposal of non-restricted firearms;

(b) the business must record and — for a period of 20 years from the day on which the business transfers a non-restricted firearm, or for a longer period that may be prescribed — keep the following information in respect of the transfer:

(i) the reference number issued by the Registrar,

(ii) the day on which the reference number was issued,

(iii) the transferee's licence number, and

(iv) the firearm's make, model and type and, if any, its serial number; and

(c) the business must, unless otherwise directed by a chief firearms officer, transmit any records containing the information referred to in paragraph (a) or (b) to a prescribed official if it is determined that the business will cease to be a business.

(2) **Destruction of records** — The prescribed official may destroy the records transmitted to them under paragraph (1)(c) at the times and in the circumstances that may be prescribed.

2019, c. 9, s. 7 [Not in force at date of publication.]

59. **Different registered owner** — An individual who holds an authorization to carry or authorization to transport need not be the person to whom the registration certificate for the particular prohibited firearm or restricted firearm was issued.

60. **Registration certificates and authorizations to export or import** — The Registrar is responsible for issuing registration certificates for prohibited firearms and restricted firearms and assigning firearms identification numbers to them and for issuing authorizations to export and authorizations to import.

2012, c. 6, s. 19

61. (1) **Form** — A licence or registration certificate must be issued in the prescribed form — which form may be in writing or electronic — or in the prescribed manner, and include the prescribed information, including any conditions attached to it.

(2) **Form of authorizations** — An authorization to carry, authorization to transport, authorization to export or authorization to import may be issued in the prescribed form — which form may be in writing or electronic — or in the prescribed manner, and include the prescribed information, including any conditions attached to it.

(3) **Condition attached to licence** — An authorization to carry or authorization to transport may take the form of a condition attached to a licence.

(3.1) **Automatic authorization to transport** — An authorization to transport referred to in subsection 19(1.1), (2.1) or (2.2) must take the form of a condition attached to a licence.

Proposed Amendment — 61(3.1)

(3.1) **Automatic authorization to transport** — An authorization to transport referred to in subsection 19(1.1), (2.1), (2.2) or (2.3) must take the form of a condition attached to a licence.

2019, c. 9, s. 8 [Not in force at date of publication.]

(4) **Businesses** — A licence that is issued to a business must specify each particular activity that the licence authorizes in relation to firearms, cross-bows, prohib-

ited weapons, restricted weapons, prohibited devices, ammunition or prohibited ammunition.

2003, c. 8, s. 38; 2015, c. 27, s. 13

62. Not transferable — Licences, registration certificates, authorizations to carry, authorizations to transport, authorizations to export and authorizations to import are not transferable.

63. (1) Geographical extent — Licences, registration certificates, authorizations to transport, authorizations to export and authorizations to import are valid throughout Canada.

(2) [Repealed 2003, c. 8, s. 39.]

(3) Authorizations to carry — Authorizations to carry are not valid outside the province in which they are issued.

2003, c. 8, s. 39

Term

64. (1) Term of licences — A licence that is issued to an individual who is eighteen years old or older expires on the earlier of

(a) five years after the birthday of the holder next following the day on which it is issued, and

(b) the expiration of the period for which it is expressed to be issued.

(1.1) Extension period — Despite subsection (1), if a licence for firearms is not renewed before it expires, the licence is extended for a period of six months beginning on the day on which it would have expired under that subsection.

(1.2) No use or acquisition — The holder of a licence that is extended under subsection (1.1) must not, until the renewal of their licence, use their firearms or acquire any firearms or ammunition.

(1.3) Authorizations — no extension — The extension of a licence under subsection (1.1) does not result in the extension of any authorization to carry or authorization to transport beyond the day on which the licence would have expired under subsection (1).

(1.4) Authorizations — issuance — During the extension period, the following authorizations must not be issued to the holder of the licence:

(a) an authorization to carry; and

(b) an authorization to transport, unless it is issued

(i) for a reason referred to in subparagraph 19(1)(b)(i) or (ii), or

(ii) because the holder wishes to transport a firearm for disposal through sale or exportation.

(2) Minors — A licence that is issued to an individual who is less than eighteen years old expires on the earlier of

(a) the day on which the holder attains the age of eighteen years, and

(b) the expiration of the period for which it is expressed to be issued.

(3) Businesses — A licence that is issued to a business other than a business referred to in subsection (4) expires on the earlier of

(a) three years after the day on which it is issued, and

(b) the expiration of the period for which it is expressed to be issued.

(4) Businesses that sell only ammunition — A licence that is issued to a business that sells ammunition but is not authorized to possess firearms, prohibited weapons, restricted weapons, prohibited devices or prohibited ammunition expires on the earlier of

(a) five years after the day on which it is issued, and

(b) the expiration of the period for which it is expressed to be issued.

(5) and (6) [Repealed before coming into force 2008, c. 20, s. 3.]

(7) Notice to holder — The chief firearms officer shall give notice of every extension under this section to the holder of the licence.

2003, c. 8, s. 40; 2015, c. 27, s. 14

65. (1) Term of authorizations — Subject to subsections (2) to (4), an authorization expires on the expiration of the period for which it is expressed to be issued.

(2) Authorizations to transport — Subject to subsection (3), an authorization to transport that takes the form of a condition attached to a licence expires on the earlier of

(a) the expiration of the period for which the condition is expressed to be attached, and

(b) the expiration of the licence.

(3) Authorizations to transport — An authorization to transport a prohibited firearm, except for an automatic firearm, or a restricted firearm for use in target practice, or a target shooting competition, under specified conditions or under the auspices of a shooting club or shooting range that is approved under section 29, whether or not the authorization takes the form of a condition attached to the licence of the holder of the authorization, expires on the earlier of

(a) the expiration of the period for which the authorization is expressed to be issued, which period may be no more than five years, and

(b) the expiration of the licence.

(4) Authorizations to carry — An authorization to carry expires

(a) in the case of an authorization to carry that takes the form of a condition attached to a licence, on the earlier of

(i) the expiration of the period for which the condition is expressed to be attached, which period may not be more than two years, and

(ii) the expiration of the licence; and

(b) in the case of an authorization to carry that does not take the form of a condition attached to a licence, on the expiration of the period for which the authorization is expressed to be issued, which period may not be more than two years.

2003, c. 8, s. 41

66. Term of registration certificates — A registration certificate for a prohibited firearm or a restricted firearm expires when

(a) the holder of the registration certificate ceases to be the owner of the firearm; or

(b) the firearm ceases to be a firearm.

2012, c. 6, s. 20

67. (1) Renewal — A chief firearms officer may renew a licence, authorization to carry or authorization to transport in the prescribed manner.

(2) Restricted firearms and pre-December 1, 1998 handguns — On renewing a licence authorizing an individual to possess restricted firearms or handguns referred to in subsection 12(6.1) (pre-December 1, 1998 handguns), a chief firearms officer shall decide whether any of those firearms or handguns that the individual possesses are being used for a purpose described in section 28.

(3) Registrar — A chief firearms officer who decides that any restricted firearms or any handguns referred to in subsection 12(6.1) (pre-December 1, 1998 handguns) that are possessed by an individual are not being used for that purpose shall

(a) give notice of that decision in the prescribed form to the individual; and

(b) inform the Registrar of that decision.

(4) Relics — Subsections (2) and (3) do not apply to a firearm

(a) that is a relic, is of value as a curiosity or rarity or is valued as a memento, remembrance or souvenir,

(b) that was specified in the licence application as being a firearm for which a registration certificate under the former Act was issued because the firearm was a relic, was of value as a curiosity or rarity or was valued as a memento, remembrance or souvenir;

(c) for which a registration certificate under the former Act was issued because the firearm was a relic, was of value as a curiosity or rarity or was valued as a memento, remembrance or souvenir; and

(d) in respect of which an individual, on the commencement day, held a registration certificate under the former Act.

(5) Material to accompany notice — A notice given under paragraph (3)(a) must include the reasons for the decision and be accompanied by a copy of sections 74 to 81.

2003, c. 8, ss. 42, 56(c)

Refusal to Issue and Revocation

68. Licences and authorizations — A chief firearms officer shall refuse to issue a licence if the applicant is not eligible to hold one and may refuse to issue an authorization to carry or authorization to transport for any good and sufficient reason.

69. Registration certificates — The Registrar may refuse to issue a registration certificate, authorization to export or authorization to import for any good and sufficient reason including, in the case of an application for a registration certificate, where the applicant is not eligible to hold a registration certificate.

70. (1) Revocation of licence or authorization — A chief firearms officer may revoke a licence, an authorization to carry or an authorization to transport for any good and sufficient reason including, without limiting the generality of the foregoing,

(a) where the holder of the licence or authorization

(i) is no longer or never was eligible to hold the licence or authorization,

Proposed Addition — 70(1)(a)(i.1)

(i.1) transfers, as defined in section 21, a non-restricted firearm other than in accordance with section 23,

2019, c. 9, s. 9 [Not in force at date of publication.]

(ii) contravenes any condition attached to the licence or authorization, or

(iii) has been convicted or discharged under section 730 of the *Criminal Code* of an offence referred to in paragraph 5(2)(a); or

(b) where, in the case of a business, a person who stands in a prescribed relationship to the business has been convicted or discharged under section 730 of the *Criminal Code* of any such offence.

(2) Registrar — The Registrar may revoke an authorization to export or authorization to import for any good and sufficient reason.

1995, c. 39, s. 137; 2003, c. 8, s. 43

71. (1) Revocation of registration certificate — The Registrar

(a) may revoke a registration certificate for a prohibited firearm or a restricted firearm for any good and sufficient reason; and

(b) shall revoke a registration certificate for a firearm held by an individual where the Registrar is informed by a chief firearms officer under section 67 that the firearm is not being used for a purpose described in section 28.

(2) Automatic revocation of registration certificate — A registration certificate for a prohibited firearm referred to in subsection 12(3) (pre-August 1, 1992 converted automatic firearms) is automatically revoked on the change of any alteration in the prohibited firearm that was described in the application for the registration certificate.

2003, c. 8, s. 44; 2012, c. 6, s. 21

72. (1) Notice of refusal to issue or revocation — Subject to subsection (1.1), if a chief firearms officer decides to refuse to issue or to revoke a licence or authorization to transport or the Registrar decides to refuse to issue or to revoke a registration certificate, authorization to export or authorization to import, the chief firearms officer or Registrar shall give notice of the decision in the prescribed form to the applicant for or holder of the licence, registration certificate or authorization.

(1.1) When notice not required — Notice under subsection (1) need not be given in any of the following circumstances:

(a) if the holder has requested that the licence, registration certificate or authorization be revoked; or

(b) if the revocation is incidental to the issuance of a new licence, registration certificate or authorization.

(2) Material to accompany notice — A notice given under subsection (1) must include reasons for the decision disclosing the nature of the information relied on for the decision and must be accompanied by a copy of sections 74 to 81.

(3) Non-disclosure of information — A chief firearms officer or the Registrar need not disclose any information the disclosure of which could, in the opinion of the chief firearms officer or the Registrar, endanger the safety of any person.

(4) Disposal of firearms — A notice given under subsection (1) in respect of a licence must specify a reasonable period during which the applicant for or holder of the licence may deliver to a peace officer or a firearms officer or a chief firearms officer or otherwise lawfully dispose of any firearm, prohibited weapon, restricted weapon, prohibited device or prohibited ammunition that the applicant for or holder of the licence possesses and during which sections 91, 92 and 94 of the *Criminal Code* do not apply to the applicant or holder.

(5) Disposal of firearms — registration certificate — A notice given under subsection (1) in respect of a registration certificate for a prohibited firearm or a restricted firearm must specify a reasonable period during which the applicant for or holder of the registration certificate may deliver to a peace officer or a firearms officer or a chief firearms officer or otherwise lawfully dispose of the firearm to which the registration certificate relates and during which sections 91, 92 and 94 of the *Criminal Code* do not apply to the applicant or holder.

(6) Reference — If the applicant for or holder of the licence or registration certificate refers the refusal to issue it or revocation of it to a provincial court judge under section 74, the reasonable period of time does not begin until after the reference is finally disposed of.

2003, c. 8, s. 45; 2012, c. 6, s. 22

Heading and s. 73. [Repealed 2003, c. 8, s. 46.]

References to Provincial Court Judge

74. (1) Reference to judge of refusal to issue or revocation, etc. — Subject to subsection (2), where

(a) a chief firearms officer or the Registrar refuses to issue or revokes a licence, registration certificate, authorization to transport, authorization to export or authorization to import,

(b) a chief firearms officer decides under section 67 that a firearm possessed by an individual who holds a licence is not being used for a purpose described in section 28, or

(c) a provincial minister refuses to approve or revokes the approval of a shooting club or shooting range for the purposes of this Act,

the applicant for or holder of the licence, registration certificate, authorization or approval may refer the matter to a provincial court judge in the territorial division in which the applicant or holder resides.

(2) Limitation period — An applicant or holder may only refer a matter to a provincial court judge under subsection (1) within thirty days after receiving notice of the decision of the chief firearms officer, Registrar or provincial minister under section 29, 67 or 72 or within such further time as is allowed by a provincial court judge, whether before or after the expiration of those thirty days.

2003, c. 8, s. 47

75. (1) Hearing of reference — On receipt of a reference under section 74, the provincial court judge shall fix a date for the hearing of the reference and direct that notice of the hearing be given to the chief firearms officer, Registrar or provincial minister and to the applicant for or holder of the licence, registration certificate, authorization or approval, in such manner as the provincial court judge may specify.

(2) Evidence — At the hearing of the reference, the provincial court judge shall hear all relevant evidence presented by or on behalf of the chief firearms officer, Registrar or provincial minister and the applicant or holder.

(3) Burden of proof — At the hearing of the reference, the burden of proof is on the applicant or holder to satisfy the provincial court judge that the refusal to issue or revocation of the licence, registration certificate or authorization, the decision or the refusal to approve or revocation of the approval was not justified.

(4) Where hearing may proceed ex parte — A provincial court judge may proceed *ex parte* to hear and determine a reference in the absence of the applicant or holder in the same circumstances as those in which a summary conviction court may, under Part XXVII of the *Criminal Code*, proceed with a trial in the absence of the defendant.

76. Decision by provincial court judge — On the hearing of a reference, the provincial court judge may, by order,

(a) confirm the decision of the chief firearms officer, Registrar or provincial minister,

(b) direct the chief firearms officer or Registrar to issue a licence, registration certificate or authorization or direct the provincial minister to approve a club or shooting range; or

(c) cancel the revocation of the licence, registration certificate, authorization or approval or the decision of the chief firearms officer under section 67.

Appeals to Superior Court and Court of Appeal

76.1 Nunavut — With respect to Nunavut, the following definitions apply for the purposes of sections 77 to 81.

"provincial court judge" means a judge of the Nunavut Court of Justice.

"superior court" means a judge of the Court of Appeal of Nunavut.

1999, c. 3, s. 64

77. (1) Appeal to superior court — Subject to section 78, where a provincial court judge makes an order under paragraph 76(a), the applicant for or holder of the licence, registration certificate, authorization or approval, as the case may be, may appeal to the superior court against the order.

(2) Appeal by Attorney General — Subject to section 78, where a provincial court judge makes an order under paragraph 76(b) or (c),

(a) the Attorney General of Canada may appeal to the superior court against the order, if the order is directed to a chief firearms officer who was designated by the federal Minister, to the Registrar or to the federal Minister; or

(b) the attorney general of the province may appeal to the superior court against the order, in the case of any other order made under paragraph 76(b) or (c).

78. (1) Notice of appeal — An appellant who proposes to appeal an order made under section 76 to the superior court must give notice of appeal not later than thirty days after the order is made.

(2) Extension of time — The superior court may, either before or after the expiration of those thirty days, extend the time within which notice of appeal may be given.

(3) Contents of notice — A notice of appeal must set out the grounds of appeal, together with such further material as the superior court may require.

(4) Service of notice — A copy of any notice of appeal filed with the superior court under subsection (1) and of any further material required to be filed with it shall be served within fourteen days after the filing of the notice, unless before or after the expiration of those fourteen days further time is allowed by the superior court, on

(a) the Attorney General of Canada, in the case of an appeal of an order made under paragraph 76(a) confirming a decision of a chief firearms officer who was designated by the federal Minister, of the Registrar or of the federal Minister;

(b) the attorney general of the province, in the case of an appeal against any other order made under paragraph 76(a);

(c) the applicant for or holder of the licence, registration certificate, authorization or approval, in the case of an appeal against an order made under paragraph 76(b) or (c); and

(d) any other person specified by the superior court.

79. (1) Disposition of appeal — On the hearing of an appeal, the superior court may

(a) dismiss the appeal; or

(b) allow the appeal and, in the case of an appeal against an order made under paragraph 76(a),

(i) direct the chief firearms officer or Registrar to issue a licence, registration certificate or authorization or direct the provincial minister to approve a shooting club or shooting range, or

(ii) cancel the revocation of the licence, registration certificate, authorization or approval or the decision of the chief firearms officer under section 67.

(2) Burden on applicant — A superior court shall dispose of an appeal against an order made under paragraph 76(a) by dismissing it, unless the appellant establishes to the satisfaction of the court that a disposition referred to in paragraph (1)(b) is justified.

80. Appeal to court of appeal — An appeal to the court of appeal may, with leave of that court or of a judge of that court, be taken against a decision of a superior court under section 79 on any ground that involves a question of law alone.

81. Application of Part XXVII of the *Criminal Code* — Part XXVII of the *Criminal Code*, except sections 785 to 812, 816 to 819 and 829 to 838, applies in respect of an appeal under this Act, with such modifications as the circumstances require and as if each reference in that Part to the appeal court were a reference to the superior court.

Commissioner of Firearms

[Heading added 2003, c. 8, s. 48.]

81.1 Appointment — The Governor in Council may appoint a person to be known as the Commissioner of Firearms to hold office during pleasure. The Commissioner shall be paid such remuneration as the Governor in Council may fix.

2003, c. 8, s. 48

81.2 Duties, functions and powers — Subject to any direction that the federal Minister may give, the Commissioner may exercise the powers and shall perform the duties and functions relating to the administration of this Act that are delegated to the Commissioner by the federal Minister.

2003, c. 8, s. 48

81.3 Delegation — federal Minister — The federal Minister may delegate to the Commissioner any duty, function or power conferred on the federal Minister under this Act, except the power to delegate under this section and the power under subsections 97(2) and (3).

2003, c. 8, s. 48

81.4 Incapacity or vacancy — In the event of the absence or incapacity of, or vacancy in the office of, the Commissioner, the federal Minister may appoint a person to perform the duties and functions and exercise the powers of the Commissioner, but no person may be so appointed for a term of more than 60 days without the approval of the Governor in Council.

2003, c. 8, s. 48

81.5 Superannuation and compensation — The Commissioner shall be deemed to be a person employed in the Public Service for the purposes of the *Public Service Superannuation Act* and to be employed in the public service of Canada for the purposes of the *Government Employees Compensation Act* and any regulations made pursuant to section 9 of the *Aeronautics Act*.

2003, c. 8, s. 48

Canadian Firearms Registration System

Registrar of Firearms

82. Registrar of Firearms — An individual to be known as the Registrar of Firearms shall be appointed or deployed in accordance with the *Public Service Employment Act*.

2003, c. 8, s. 49(1)

[Editor's Note: 2003, c. 8, s. 49(1) amended s. 82 to provide for the appointment or deployment of the Registrar of Firearms under the Public Service Employment Act. *2003, c. 8, s. 49(2) provides that the person occupying the position of Registrar of Firearms on the day on which section 82 of the Act, as enacted by 2003, c. 8, s. 49(1) came into force (i.e. on May 30, 2003) is deemed, as of that day, to be appointed as Registrar of Firearms under the* Public Service Employment Act *and continues to occupy that position until another person is appointed or deployed as the Registrar of Firearms under that Act.]*

82.1 Incapacity or vacancy — In the event of the absence or incapacity of, or vacancy in the position of, the Registrar, the Commissioner may perform the duties and functions and exercise the powers of the Registrar.

2003, c. 8, s. 49(1)

Records of the Registrar

83. (1) Canadian Firearms Registry — The Registrar shall establish and maintain a registry, to be known as the Canadian Firearms Registry, in which shall be kept a record of

(a) every licence, every registration certificate for a prohibited firearm or a restricted firearm and every authorization that is issued or revoked by the Registrar;

(b) every application for a licence, a registration certificate for a prohibited firearm or a restricted firearm or an authorization that is refused by the Registrar;

(c) every transfer of a firearm of which the Registrar is informed under section 26 or 27;

(d) every exportation from or importation into Canada of a firearm of which the Registrar is informed under section 42 or 50;

Proposed Addition — 83(1)(d.1)

(d.1) all information provided to the Registrar under section 42.2;

2015, c. 27, s. 15 [Not in force at date of publication.]

(e) every loss, finding, theft or destruction of a firearm of which the Registrar is informed under section 88; and

(f) such other matters as may be prescribed.

(2) Operation — The Registrar is responsible for the day-to-day operation of the Canadian Firearms Registry.

2012, c. 6, s. 23

84. Destruction of records — The Registrar may destroy records kept in the Canadian Firearms Registry at such times and in such circumstances as may be prescribed.

85. (1) Other records of Registrar — The Registrar shall establish and maintain a record of

(a) firearms acquired or possessed by the following persons and used by them in the course of their duties or for the purposes of their employment, namely,

(i) peace officers,

(ii) persons training to become police officers or peace officers under the control and supervision of

(A) a police force, or

(B) a police academy or similar institution designated by the federal Minister or the lieutenant governor in council of a province,

(iii) persons or members of a class of persons employed in the federal public administration or by the government of a province or municipality who are prescribed by the regulations made by the Governor in Council under Part III of the *Criminal Code* to be public officers, and

(iv) chief firearms officers and firearms officers; and

Proposed Amendment — 85(1)(a)(iv)

(iv) chief firearms officers and firearms officers;

2019, c. 9, s. 10(3) [Not in force at date of publication.]

(b) firearms acquired or possessed by individuals on behalf of, and under the authority of, a police force or a department of the Government of Canada or of a province.

Proposed Addition — 85(1)(c), (d)

(c) every request for a reference number made to the Registrar under section 23 and, if the request is refused, the reasons for refusing the request; and

(d) every reference number that is issued by the Registrar under subsection 23(3) and, with respect to each reference number, the day on which it was issued and the licence numbers of the transferor and transferee.

2019, c. 9, s. 10(3) [Not in force at date of publication.]

(2) **Reporting of acquisitions and transfers** — A person referred to in subsection (1) who acquires or transfers a firearm shall have the Registrar informed of the acquisition or transfer.

Proposed Amendment — 85(2)

(2) **Reporting of acquisitions and transfers** — A person referred to in paragraph (1)(a) or (b) who acquires or transfers a firearm shall have the Registrar informed of the acquisition or transfer.

2019, c. 9, s. 10(4) [Not in force at date of publication.]

(3) **Destruction of records** — The Registrar may destroy any record referred to in subsection (1) at such times and in such circumstances as may be prescribed.

2003, c. 22, s. 224(z.38)

86. **Records to be transferred** — The records kept in the registry maintained pursuant to section 114 of the former Act that relate to registration certificates shall be transferred to the Registrar.

Records of Chief Firearms Officers

87. (1) **Records of chief firearms officers** — A chief firearms officer shall keep a record of

(a) every licence and authorization that is issued or revoked by the chief firearms officer;

(b) every application for a licence or authorization that is refused by the chief firearms officer;

(c) every prohibition order of which the chief firearms officer is informed under section 89; and

(d) such other matters as may be prescribed.

(2) Destruction of records — A chief firearms officer may destroy any record referred to in subsection (1) at such times and in such circumstances as may be prescribed.

88. Reporting of loss, finding, theft and destruction — A chief firearms officer to whom the loss, finding, theft or destruction of a prohibited firearm or a restricted firearm is reported shall have the Registrar informed without delay of the loss, finding, theft or destruction.

2012, c. 6, s. 24

Reporting of Prohibition Orders

89. Reporting of prohibition orders — Every court, judge or justice that makes, varies or revokes a prohibition order shall have a chief firearms officer informed without delay of the prohibition order or its variation or revocation.

Access to Records

90. Right of access — The Registrar has a right of access to records kept by a chief firearms officer under section 87 and a chief firearms officer has a right of access to records kept by the Registrar under section 83 or 85 and to records kept by other chief firearms officers under section 87.

90.1 Right of access — subsection 23.1(1) — For the purpose of subsection 23.1(1), the person responding to a request made under that subsection has a right of access to records kept by a chief firearms officer under section 87.

Proposed Repeal — 90.1

90.1 [Repealed 2019, c. 9, s. 11. Not in force at date of publication.]

2012, c. 6, s. 25

Electronic Filing

91. (1) Electronic filing — Subject to the regulations, notices and documents that are sent to or issued by the Registrar pursuant to this or any other Act of Parliament may be sent or issued in electronic or other form in any manner specified by the Registrar.

(2) Time of receipt — For the purposes of this Act and Part III of the *Criminal Code*, a notice or document that is sent or issued in accordance with subsection (1) is deemed to have been received at the time and date provided by the regulations.

92. (1) Records of Registrar — Records required by section 83 or 85 to be kept by the Registrar may

(a) be in bound or loose-leaf form or in photographic film form; or

(b) be entered or recorded by any system of mechanical or electronic data processing or by any other information storage device that is capable of reproducing any required information in intelligible written or printed form within a reasonable time.

(2) **Storage of documents or information in electronic or other form** — Subject to the regulations, a document or information received by the Registrar under this Act in electronic or other form may be entered or recorded by any information storage device, including any system of mechanical or electronic data processing, that is capable of reproducing stored documents or information in intelligible written or printed form within a reasonable time.

(3) **Probative value** — Where the Registrar maintains a record of a document otherwise than in written or printed form, an extract from that record that is certified by the Registrar has the same probative value as the document would have had if it had been proved in the ordinary way.

Reports

93. (1) **Report to federal Minister** — The Commissioner shall, as soon as possible after the end of each calendar year and at any other times that the federal Minister may in writing request, submit to the federal Minister a report, in the form and including the information that the federal Minister may direct, with regard to the administration of this Act.

(2) **Report to be laid before Parliament** — The federal Minister shall have each report laid before each House of Parliament on any of the first 15 days on which that House is sitting after the federal Minister receives it.

2003, c. 8, s. 50

94. **Information to be submitted to Commissioner** — A chief firearms officer shall submit to the Commissioner the prescribed information with regard to the administration of this Act at the prescribed time and in the prescribed form for the purpose of enabling the Commissioner to compile the reports referred to in section 93.

2003, c. 8, s. 50

GENERAL

Agreements with Provinces

95. **Agreements with provinces** — The federal Minister may, with the approval of the Governor in Council, enter into agreements with the governments of the provinces

(a) providing for payment of compensation by Canada to the provinces in respect of administrative costs actually incurred by the provinces in relation to processing licences, registration certificates and authorizations and applications for licences, registration certificates and authorizations and the operation of the Canadian Firearms Registration System; and

(b) notwithstanding subsections 17(1) and (4) of the *Financial Administration Act*, authorizing the governments of the provinces to withhold those costs, in accordance with the terms and conditions of the agreement, from fees under paragraph 117(p) collected or received by the governments of the provinces.

Other Matters

96. Other obligations not affected — The issuance of a licence, registration certificate or authorization under this Act does not affect the obligation of any person to comply with any other Act of Parliament or any regulation made under an Act of Parliament respecting firearms or other weapons.

97. (1) Exemptions — Governor in Council — Subject to subsection (4), the Governor in Council may exempt any class of non-residents from the application of any provision of this Act or the regulations, or from the application of any of sections 91 to 95, 99 to 101, 103 to 107 and 117.03 of the *Criminal Code*, for any period specified by the Governor in Council.

(2) Exemptions — federal Minister — Subject to subsection (4), the federal Minister may exempt any non-resident from the application of any provision of this Act or the regulations, or from the application of any of sections 91 to 95, 99 to 101, 103 to 107 and 117.03 of the *CriminalCode*, for any period not exceeding one year.

(3) Exemptions — provincial minister — Subject to subsection (4), a provincial minister may exempt from the application in that province of any provision of this Act or the regulations or Part III of the *Criminal Code*, for any period not exceeding one year, the employees, in respect of any thing done by them in the course of or for the purpose of their duties or employment, of any business that holds a licence authorizing the business to acquire prohibited firearms, prohibited weapons, prohibited devices or prohibited ammunition.

(4) Public safety — Subsections (1) to (3) do not apply if it is not desirable, in the interests of the safety of any person, that the exemption be granted.

(5) Conditions — The authority granting an exemption may attach to it any reasonable condition that the authority considers desirable in the particular circumstances and in the interests of the safety of any person.

2001, c. 41, s. 96

DELEGATION

98. Authorized chief firearms officer may perform functions of provincial minister — A chief firearms officer of a province who is authorized in writing by a provincial minister may perform the function of the provincial minister of designating firearms officers for the province.

99. Designated officers may perform functions of chief firearms officers — A firearms officer who is designated in writing by a chief firearms officer may perform any of the duties and functions of the chief firearms officer under this Act or Part III of the *Criminal Code* that are specified in the designation.

2003, c. 8, s. 52

100. Designated officers may perform functions of Registrar — A person who is designated in writing by the Registrar for the purpose of this section may perform such duties and functions of the Registrar under this Act or Part III of the *Criminal Code* as are specified in the designation.

INSPECTION

101. Definition of "inspector" — In sections 102 to 105, **"inspector"** means a firearms officer and includes, in respect of a province, a member of a class of individuals designated by the provincial minister.

102. (1) Inspection — Subject to section 104, for the purpose of ensuring compliance with this Act and the regulations, an inspector may at any reasonable time enter and inspect any place where the inspector believes on reasonable grounds a business is being carried on or there is a record of a business, any place in which the inspector believes on reasonable grounds there is a gun collection or a record in relation to a gun collection or any place in which the inspector believes on reasonable grounds there is a prohibited firearm or there are more than 10 firearms and may

(a) open any container that the inspector believes on reasonable grounds contains a firearm or other thing in respect of which this Act or the regulations apply;

(b) examine any firearm and examine any other thing that the inspector finds and take samples of it;

(c) conduct any tests or analyses or take any measurements; and

(d) require any person to produce for examination or copying any records, books of account or other documents that the inspector believes on reasonable grounds contain information that is relevant to the enforcement of this Act or the regulations.

(2) Operation of data processing systems and copying equipment — In carrying out an inspection of a place under subsection (1), an inspector may

(a) use or cause to be used any data processing system at the place to examine any data contained in or available to the system;

(b) reproduce any record or cause it to be reproduced from the data in the form of a print-out or other intelligible output and remove the print-out or other output for examination or copying; and

(c) use or cause to be used any copying equipment at the place to make copies of any record, book of account or other document.

(3) Use of force — In carrying out an inspection of a place under subsection (1), an inspector may not use force.

(4) **Receipt for things taken** — An inspector who takes any thing while carrying out an inspection of a place under subsection (1) must give to the owner or occupant of the place at the time that the thing is taken a receipt for the thing that describes the thing with reasonable precision, including, in the case of a firearm, the serial number if available of the firearm.

(5) **Definition of "business"** — For greater certainty, in this section, "business" has the meaning assigned by subsection 2(1).

103. Duty to assist inspectors — The owner or person in charge of a place that is inspected by an inspector under section 102 and every person found in the place shall

(a) give the inspector all reasonable assistance to enable him or her to carry out the inspection and exercise any power conferred by section 102; and

(b) provide the inspector with any information relevant to the enforcement of this Act or the regulations that he or she may reasonably require.

104. (1) **Inspection of dwelling-house** — An inspector may not enter a dwelling-house under section 102 except

(a) on reasonable notice to the owner or occupant, except where a business is being carried on in the dwelling-house; and

(b) with the consent of the occupant or under a warrant.

(2) **Authority to issue warrant** — A justice who on *ex parte* application is satisfied by information on oath

(a) that the conditions for entry described in section 102 exist in relation to a dwelling-house,

(b) that entry to the dwelling-house is necessary for any purpose relating to the enforcement of this Act or the regulations, and

(c) that entry to the dwelling-house has been refused or that there are reasonable grounds for believing that entry will be refused

may issue a warrant authorizing the inspector named in it to enter that dwelling-house subject to any conditions that may be specified in the warrant.

(3) **Areas that may be inspected** — For greater certainty, an inspector who is carrying out an inspection of a dwelling-house may enter and inspect only

(a) that part of a room of the dwelling-house in which the inspector believes on reasonable grounds there is a firearm, prohibited weapon, restricted weapon, prohibited device, prohibited ammunition, a record in relation to a gun collection or all or part of a device or other thing required by a regulation made under paragraph 117(h) respecting the storage of firearms and restricted weapons; and

(b) in addition, in the case of a dwelling-house where the inspector believes on reasonable grounds a business is being carried on, that part of a room in which the inspector believes on reasonable grounds there is ammunition or a record of the business.

105. Demand to produce firearm — An inspector who believes on reasonable grounds that a person possesses a firearm may, by demand made to that person, require that person, within a reasonable time after the demand is made, to produce the firearm in the manner specified by the inspector for the purpose of verifying the serial number or other identifying features of the firearm and of ensuring that, in the case of a prohibited firearm or a restricted firearm, the person is the holder of the registration certificate for it.

2012, c. 6, s. 26

OFFENCES

106. (1) False statements to procure licences, etc. — Every person commits an offence who, for the purpose of procuring a licence, registration certificate or authorization for that person or any other person, knowingly makes a statement orally or in writing that is false or misleading or knowingly fails to disclose any information that is relevant to the application for the licence, registration certificate or authorization.

(2) False statements to procure customs confirmations — Every person commits an offence who, for the purpose of procuring the confirmation by a customs officer of a document under this Act for that person or any other person, knowingly makes a statement orally or in writing that is false or misleading or knowingly fails to disclose any information that is relevant to the document.

(3) Definition of "statement" — In this section, **"statement"** means an assertion of fact, opinion, belief or knowledge, whether material or not and whether admissible or not.

107. Tampering with licences, etc. — Every person commits an offence who, without lawful excuse the proof of which lies on the person, alters, defaces or falsifies

(a) a licence, registration certificate or authorization; or

(b) a confirmation by a customs officer of a document under this Act.

108. Unauthorized possession of ammunition — Every business commits an offence that possesses ammunition, unless the business holds a licence under which it may possess ammunition.

109. Punishment — Every person who commits an offence under section 106, 107 or 108, who contravenes subsection 29(1) or who contravenes a regulation made under paragraph 117(d), (e), (f), (g), (i), (j), (k.2), (l), (m) or (n) the contravention of which has been made an offence under paragraph 117(o)

(a) is guilty of an indictable offence and liable to imprisonment for a term not exceeding five years; or

(b) is guilty of an offence punishable on summary conviction.

2019, c. 9, s. 12

110. Contravention of conditions of licences, etc. — Every person commits an offence who, without lawful excuse, contravenes a condition of a licence, registration certificate or authorization held by the person.

111. Punishment — Every person who commits an offence under section 110 or who does not comply with section 103

(a) is guilty of an indictable offence and liable to imprisonment for a term not exceeding two years; or

(b) is guilty of an offence punishable on summary conviction.

112. [Repealed 2012, c. 6, s. 27.]

113. Non-compliance with demand to produce firearm — Every person commits an offence who, without reasonable excuse, does not comply with a demand made to the person by an inspector under section 105.

114. Failure to deliver up revoked licence, etc. — Every person commits an offence who, being the holder of a licence, a registration certificate for a prohibited firearm or a restricted firearm or an authorization that is revoked, does not deliver it up to a peace officer or firearms officer without delay after the revocation.

2012, c. 6, s. 28

115. Punishment — Every person who commits an offence under section 113 or 114 is guilty of an offence punishable on summary conviction.

2012, c. 6, s. 28

116. Attorney General of Canada may act — Any proceedings in respect of an offence under this Act may be commenced at the instance of the Government of Canada and conducted by or on behalf of that government.

REGULATIONS

117. Regulations — The Governor in Council may make regulations

(a) regulating the issuance of licences, registration certificates and authorizations, including regulations respecting the purposes for which they may be issued under any provision of this Act and prescribing the circumstances in which persons are or are not eligible to hold licences;

(a.1) deeming permits to export goods, or classes of permits to export goods, that are issued under the *Export and Import Permits Act* to be authorizations to export for the purposes of this Act;

(b) regulating the revocation of licences, registration certificates and authorizations;

(c) prescribing the circumstances in which an individual does or does not need firearms

(i) to protect the life of that individual or of other individuals, or

(ii) for use in connection with his or her lawful profession or occupation;

Proposed Addition — 117(c.1)

(c.1) regulating, for the purpose of issuing a reference number under section 23, the provision of information by a transferor, a transferee and the Registrar;

2019, c. 9, s. 13(1) [Not in force at date of publication.]

(d) regulating the use of firearms in target practice or target shooting competitions;

(e) regulating

(i) the establishment and operation of shooting clubs and shooting ranges,

(ii) the activities that may be carried on at shooting clubs and shooting ranges,

(iii) the possession and use of firearms at shooting clubs and shooting ranges, and

(iv) the keeping and destruction of records in relation to shooting clubs and shooting ranges and members of those clubs and ranges;

(f) regulating the establishment and maintenance of gun collections and the acquisition and disposal or disposition of firearms that form part or are to form part of a gun collection;

(g) regulating the operation of gun shows, the activities that may be carried on at gun shows and the possession and use of firearms at gun shows;

(h) regulating the storage, handling, transportation, shipping, display, advertising and mail-order sale of firearms and restricted weapons and defining the expression "mail-order sale" for the purposes of this Act;

(i) regulating the storage, handling, transportation shipping, possession for a prescribed purpose, transfer, exportation or importation of

(i) prohibited firearms, prohibited weapons, restricted weapons, prohibited devices and prohibited ammunition, or

(ii) components or parts of prohibited firearms, prohibited weapons, restricted weapons, prohibited devices and prohibited ammunition;

(j) regulating the possession and use of restricted weapons;

(j.1) respecting the possession and transportation of firearms during the extension period referred to in subsection 64(1.1);

(k) for authorizing

(i) the possession at any place, or

(ii) the manufacture or transfer, whether or not for consideration, or offer to manufacture or transfer, whether or not for consideration,

of firearms, prohibited weapons, restricted weapons, prohibited devices, ammunition, prohibited ammunition and components and parts designed exclusively for use in the manufacture of or assembly into firearms;

(k.1) respecting the importation or exportation of firearms, prohibited weapons, restricted weapons, prohibited devices, ammunition, prohibited ammunition and components and parts designed exclusively for use in the manufacture of or assembly into firearms;

(k.2) respecting the marking of firearms manufactured in Canada or imported into Canada and the removal, alteration, obliteration and defacing of those markings;

(k.3) respecting the confirmation of declarations and authorizations to transport for the purposes of paragraph 35(1)(d), the confirmation of declarations for the purposes of paragraph 35.1(2)(d) and the confirmation of authorizations to import for the purposes of paragraph 40(2)(e);

(l) regulating the storage, handling, transportation, shipping, acquisition, possession, transfer, exportation, importation, use and disposal or disposition of firearms, prohibited weapons, restricted weapons, prohibited devices, prohibited ammunition and explosive substances

(i) by the following persons in the course of their duties or for the purposes of their employment, namely,

(A) peace officers,

(B) persons training to become police officers or peace officers under the control and supervision of a police force or a police academy or similar institution designated by the federal Minister or the lieutenant governor in council of a province,

(C) persons or members of a class of persons employed in the federal public administration or by the government of a province or municipality who are prescribed by the regulations made by the Governor in Council under Part III of the *Criminal Code* to be public officers, and

(D) chief firearms officers and firearms officers, and

(ii) by individuals on behalf of, and under the authority of, a police force or a department of the Government of Canada or of a province;

(m) regulating the keeping, transmission and destruction of records in relation to firearms, prohibited weapons, restricted weapons, prohibited devices and prohibited ammunition;

(n) regulating the keeping and destruction of records by businesses in relation to ammunition;

Proposed Addition — 117(n.1)

(n.1) regulating the transmission of records under paragraph 58.1(1)(c) by a business to a prescribed official;

2019, c. 9, s. 13(3) [Not in force at date of publication.]

(o) creating offences consisting of contraventions of the regulations made under paragraph (d), (e), (f), (g), (i), (j), (k.1), (k.2), (l), (m) or (n);

(p) prescribing the fees that are to be paid to Her Majesty in right of Canada for licences, registration certificates, authorizations, approvals of transfers and importations of firearms and confirmations by customs officers of documents under this Act;

(q) waiving or reducing the fees payable under paragraph (p) in such circumstances as may be specified in the regulations;

(r) prescribing the charges that are to be paid to Her Majesty in right of Canada in respect of costs incurred by Her Majesty in right of Canada in storing goods that are detained by customs officers or in disposing of goods;

(s) respecting the operation of the Canadian Firearms Registry;

(t) regulating the sending or issuance of notices and documents in electronic or other form, including

(i) the notices and documents that may be sent or issued in electronic or other form,

(ii) the persons or classes of persons by whom they may be sent or issued,

(iii) their signature in electronic or other form or their execution, adoption or authorization in a manner that pursuant to the regulations is to have the same effect for the purposes of this Act as their signature, and

(iv) the time and date when they are deemed to be received;

(u) respecting the manner in which any provision of this Act or the regulations applies to any of the aboriginal peoples of Canada, and adapting any such provision for the purposes of that application;

(v) repealing

(i) section 4 of the *Cartridge Magazine Control Regulations*, made by Order in Council P.C. 1992-1660 of July 16, 1992 and registered as SOR/92-460, and the heading before it,

(ii) the *Designated Areas Firearms Order*, C.R.C., chapter 430,

(iii) section 4 of the *Firearms Acquisition Certificate Regulations*, made by Order in Council P.C. 1992-1663 of July 16, 1992 and registered as SOR/92-461, and the heading before it,

(iv) section 7 of the *Genuine Gun Collector Regulations*, made by Order in Council P.C. 1992-1661 of July 16, 1992 and registered as SOR/92-435, and the heading before it,

(v) sections 8 and 13 of the *Prohibited Weapons Control Regulations*, made by Order in Council P.C. 1991-1925 of October 3, 1991 and registered as SOR/91-572, and the headings before them,

(vi) the *Restricted Weapon Registration Certificate for Classes of Persons other than Individuals Regulations*, made by Order in Council P.C. 1993-766 of April 20, 1993 and registered as SOR/93-200, and

(vii) sections 7, 15 and 17 of the *Restricted Weapons and Firearms Control Regulations*, made by Order in Council P.C. 1978-2572 of August 16, 1978 and registered as SOR/78-670, and the headings before them; and

(w) prescribing anything that by any provision of this Act is to be prescribed by regulation.

2003, c. 8, s. 54; 2003, c. 22, s. 224(z.38); 2015, c. 27, s. 16; 2019, c. 9, s. 13(2)

118. (1) Laying of proposed regulations — Subject to subsection (2), the federal Minister shall have each proposed regulation laid before each House of Parliament.

(2) Idem — Where a proposed regulation is laid pursuant to subsection (1), it shall be laid before each House of Parliament on the same day.

(3) Report by committee — Each proposed regulation that is laid before a House of Parliament shall, on the day it is laid, be referred by that House to an appropriate committee of that House, as determined by the rules of that House, and the committee may conduct inquiries or public hearings with respect to the proposed regulation and report its findings to that House.

(4) Making of regulations — A proposed regulation that has been laid pursuant to subsection (1) may be made

(a) on the expiration of thirty sitting days after it was laid; or

(b) where, with respect to each House of Parliament,

(i) the committee reports to the House, or

(ii) the committee decides not to conduct inquiries or public hearings.

(5) Definition of "sitting day" — For the purpose of this section, **"sitting day"** means a day on which either House of Parliament sits.

119. (1) Exception — No proposed regulation that has been laid pursuant to section 118 need again be laid under that section, whether or not it has been altered.

(2) Exception — minor changes — A regulation made under section 117 may be made without being laid before either House of Parliament if the federal Minister is of the opinion that the changes made by the regulation to an existing regulation are so immaterial or insubstantial that section 118 should not be applicable in the circumstances.

(3) Exception — urgency — A regulation made under paragraph 117(i), (l), (m), (n), (o), (q), (s) or (t) may be made without being laid before either House of Parliament if the federal Minister is of the opinion that the making of the regulation is so urgent that section 118 should not be applicable in the circumstances.

(4) Notice of opinion — Where the federal Minister forms the opinion described in subsection (2) or (3), he or she shall have a statement of the reasons why he or she formed that opinion laid before each House of Parliament.

(5) Exception — prescribed dates — A regulation may be made under paragraph 117(w) prescribing a date for the purposes of the application of any provision of this Act without being laid before either House of Parliament.

(6) **Part III of the *Criminal Code*** — For greater certainty, a regulation may be made under Part III of the *Criminal Code* without being laid before either House of Parliament.

TRANSITIONAL PROVISIONS

Licences

120. (1) **Firearms acquisition certificates** — A firearms acquisition certificate is deemed to be a licence if it

(a) was issued under section 110 or 111 of the former Act;

(b) had not been revoked before the commencement day; and

(c) was valid pursuant to subsection 106(11) of the former Act, or pursuant to that subsection as applied by subsection 107(1) of the former Act, on the commencement day.

(2) **Authorizations** — A firearms acquisition certificate that is deemed to be a licence authorizes the holder

(a) to acquire and possess any firearms other than prohibited firearms that are acquired by the holder on or after the commencement day and before the expiration or revocation of the firearms acquisition certificate;

(b) in the case of an individual referred to in subsection 12(2), (3), (4), (5), (6) or (8), to acquire and possess any prohibited firearms referred to in that subsection that are acquired by the holder on or after the commencement day; and

(c) in the case of a particular individual who is eligible under subsection 12(7) to hold a licence authorizing the particular individual to possess a handgun referred to in subsection 12(6.1) (pre-December 1, 1998 handguns) in the circumstances described in subsection 12(7), to acquire and possess such a handgun in those circumstances, if the particular handgun is acquired by the particular individual on or after the commencement day.

(3) **Expiration** — A firearms acquisition certificate that is deemed to be a licence expires on the earlier of

(a) five years after the day on which it was issued, and

(b) the issuance of a licence to the holder of the firearms acquisition certificate.

(4) **Lost, stolen and destroyed firearms acquisition certificates** — Where a firearms acquisition certificate that is deemed to be a licence is lost, stolen or destroyed before its expiration under subsection (3), a person who has authority under this Act to issue a licence may issue a replacement firearms acquisition certificate that has the same effect as the one that was lost, stolen or destroyed.

2003, c. 8, s. 56(d)

121. (1) Minors' permits — A permit is deemed to be a licence if it

(a) was issued under subsection 110(6) or (7) of the former Act to a person who was under the age of eighteen years;

(b) had not been revoked before the commencement day; and

(c) remained in force pursuant to subsection 110(8) of the former Act on the commencement day.

(2) Authorizations — A permit that is deemed to be a licence authorizes the holder to possess non-restricted firearms.

(3) Geographical extent — A permit that is deemed to be a licence is valid only in the province in which it was issued, unless the permit was endorsed pursuant to subsection 110(10) of the former Act as being valid within the provinces indicated in the permit, in which case it remains valid within those provinces.

(4) Expiration — A permit that is deemed to be a licence expires on the earliest of

(a) the expiration of the period for which it was expressed to be issued,

(b) the day on which the person to whom it was issued attains the age of eighteen years, and

(c) five years after the birthday of the person next following the day on which it was issued, if that fifth anniversary occurs on or after the commencement day.

2015, c. 27, s. 17

122. (1) Museum approvals — An approval of a museum, other than a museum established by the Chief of the Defence Staff, is deemed to be a licence if the approval

(a) was granted under subsection 105(1) of the former Act; and

(b) had not been revoked before the commencement day.

(2) Expiration — An approval of a museum that is deemed to be a licence expires on the earlier of

(a) the expiration of the period for which the approval was expressed to be granted, and

(b) three years after the commencement day.

123. (1) Permits to carry on business — A permit to carry on a business described in paragraph 105(1)(a) or (b) or subparagraph 105(2)(b)(i) of the former Act is deemed to be a licence if it

(a) was

(i) issued under subsection 110(5) of the former Act, or

(ii) continued under subsection 6(2) of the *Criminal Law Amendment Act, 1968-69*, chapter 38 of the Statutes of Canada, 1968-69, or subsection 48(1) of the *Criminal Law Amendment Act, 1977*, chapter 53 of the Statutes of Canada, 1976-77;

(b) had not been revoked before the commencement day;

(c) had not ceased to be in force or have any effect on October 30, 1992 under section 34 of *An Act to amend the Criminal Code and the Customs Tariff in consequence thereof*, chapter 40 of the Statutes of Canada, 1991; and

(d) remained in force pursuant to subsection 110(5) of the former Act on the commencement day.

(2) **Expiration** — A permit that is deemed to be a licence expires on the earlier of

(a) the expiration of the period for which the permit was expressed to be issued, and

(b) one year after the commencement day.

124. **Geographical extent** — A permit or an approval of a museum that is deemed to be a licence under section 122 or 123 is valid only for the location of the business or museum for which it was issued.

125. (1) **Industrial purpose designations** — A designation of a person is deemed to be a licence if it

(a) was made under subsection 90(3.1) or paragraph 95(3)(b) of the former Act; and

(b) had not been revoked before the commencement day.

(2) **Geographical extent** — A designation of a person that is deemed to be a licence is valid only in the province in which it was made.

(3) **Expiration** — A designation of a person that is deemed to be a licence expires on the earliest of

(a) the expiration of the period for which it was expressed to be made,

(b) one year after the commencement day, and

(c) in the case of a designation of a person who holds a permit that is deemed to be a licence under section 123, the expiration of the permit.

126. **Pending applications** — Every application that was pending on the commencement day for a document that would be a document referred to in any of sections 120 to 125 had it been issued before the commencement day shall be dealt with and disposed of under and in accordance with the former Act, except that

(a) a licence shall be issued instead of issuing a firearms acquisition certificate or a permit or making an approval or designation; and

(b) only a person who has authority under this Act to issue a licence may finally dispose of the application.

Proposed Addition — 126.1

126.1 **Licence of business — deemed conditions** — Every licence of a business that is valid on the commencement day is deemed to include the conditions set out in paragraphs 58.1(1)(a) to (c).

2019, c. 9, s. 14 [Not in force at date of publication.]

Registration Certificates

127. (1) Registration certificates — A registration certificate is deemed to be a registration certificate issued under section 60 if it

(a) was

(i) issued under subsection 109(7) of the former Act, or

(ii) continued under subsection 6(2) of the *Criminal Law Amendment Act, 1968-69*, chapter 38 of the Statutes of Canada, 1968-69, or subsection 48(2) of the *Criminal Law Amendment Act, 1977*, chapter 53 of the Statutes of Canada, 1976-77; and

(b) had not been revoked before the commencement day.

(2) Expiration — A registration certificate that is deemed to be a registration certificate issued under section 60 expires on the earlier of

(a) its expiration under section 66, and

(b) December 31, 2002, or such other date as is prescribed.

128. Pending applications — Every application for a registration certificate that was pending on the commencement day shall be dealt with and disposed of under and in accordance with the former Act, except that only a person who has authority under this Act to issue a registration certificate may finally dispose of the application.

Authorized Transportation of Firearms

129. (1) Permit to carry — A permit authorizing a person to possess a particular prohibited firearm or restricted firearm is deemed to be an authorization to carry or authorization to transport if it

(a) was

(i) issued under subsection 110(1) of the former Act, or

(ii) continued under subsection 6(2) of the *Criminal Law Amendment Act, 1968-69*, chapter 38 of the Statutes of Canada, 1968-69, or subsection 48(1) of the *Criminal Law Amendment Act, 1977*, chapter 53 of the Statutes of Canada, 1976-77;

(b) had not been revoked before the commencement day; and

(c) remained in force pursuant to subsection 110(1) of the former Act on the commencement day.

(2) Geographical extent — A permit that is deemed to be an authorization to carry or authorization to transport is valid only in the province in which the permit was issued, unless it was endorsed pursuant to subsection 110(10) of the former Act as being valid within the provinces indicated in the permit, in which case it remains valid within those provinces.

(3) Expiration — A permit that is deemed to be an authorization to carry or authorization to transport expires on the earlier of

(a) the expiration of the period for which it was expressed to be issued, and

(b) two years after the commencement day.

130. Temporary permit to carry — A permit authorizing a person who does not reside in Canada to possess and carry a particular prohibited firearm or restricted firearm is deemed to be an authorization to transport if it

(a) was issued under subsection 110(2.1) of the former Act;

(b) had not been revoked before the commencement day; and

(c) remained in force pursuant to that subsection on the commencement day.

131. Permit to transport or convey — A permit authorizing a person to transport or to convey to a local registrar of firearms a particular prohibited firearm or restricted firearm is deemed to be an authorization to transport if it

(a) was

(i) issued under subsection 110(3) or (4) of the former Act, or

(ii) continued under subsection 6(2) of the *Criminal Law Amendment Act, 1968-69*, chapter 38 of the Statutes of Canada, 1968-69, or subsection 48(1) of the *Criminal Law Amendment Act, 1977*, chapter 53 of the Statutes of Canada, 1976-77;

(b) had not been revoked before the commencement day; and

(c) remained in force pursuant to subsection 110(3) or (4) of the former Act on the commencement day.

132. Expiration — A permit that is deemed to be an authorization to transport under section 130 or 131 expires on the expiration of the period for which the permit was expressed to be issued.

133. Pending applications — Every application that was pending on the commencement day for a document that would be a document referred to in any of sections 129 to 131 had it been issued before the commencement day shall be dealt with and disposed of under and in accordance with the former Act, except that

(a) an authorization to carry or authorization to transport shall be issued or a condition shall be attached to a licence instead of issuing a permit; and

(b) only a person who has authority under this Act to issue an authorization to carry or authorization to transport may finally dispose of the application.

134. (1) Shooting club approvals — An approval of a shooting club is deemed to be an approval granted under this Act if the approval

(a) was granted under subparagraph 109(3)(c)(iii) or paragraph 110(2)(c) of the former Act; and

(b) had not been revoked before the commencement day.

(2) Expiration — An approval of a shooting club that is deemed to be an approval granted under this Act expires on the earlier of

(a) the expiration of the period for which it was expressed to be granted, and

(b) one year after the commencement day.

135. Temporary storage permit — Every permit authorizing a person to temporarily store a particular prohibited firearm or restricted firearm

(a) that was issued under subsection 110(3.1) of the former Act,

(b) that had not been revoked before the commencement day, and

(c) that remained in force pursuant to subsection 110(3.3) of the former Act on the commencement day

continues in force until the expiration of the period for which it was expressd to be issued, unless the permit is revoked by a chief firearms officer for any good and sufficient reason.

Proposed Addition — 135.1

135.1 Revocation of authorization to transport — All of the following authorizations to transport a prohibited firearm or a restricted firearm are revoked:

(a) authorizations issued under any of paragraphs 19(2.1)(b) to (e), as those paragraphs read immediately before the commencement day; and

(b) authorizations issued under paragraph 19(2.2)(b), as that paragraph read immediately before the commencement day, in respect of transportation to and from the places referred to in any of the paragraphs that are set out in paragraph (a).

2019, c. 9, s. 15 [Not in force at date of publication.]

Conditional Amendments to this Act

136. Conditional amendment re Bill C-7 — If Bill C-7, introduced during the first session of the thirty-fifth Parliament and entitled *An Act respecting the control of certain drugs, their precursors and other substances and to amend certain other Acts and repeal the Narcotic Control Act in consequence thereof*, is assented to, then, on the later of the day on which sections 6 and 7 of that Act come into force and the day on which this Act is assented to, subparagraph 5(2)(a)(iv) of this Act is replaced by the following:

(iv) an offence relating to a contravention of subsection 6(1) or (2) or 7(1) or (2) of the *Controlled Drugs and Substances Act*;

137. Conditional amendments re Bill C-41 — If Bill C-41, introduced in the first session of the thirty-fifth Parliament and entitled *An Act to amend the Criminal Code (sentencing) and other Acts is consequence thereof*, is assented to, then, on the later of the day on which section 730 of the *Criminal Code*, as enacted by section 6 of that Act, comes into force and the day on which this Act is assented to, the following provisions of this Act are amended by replacing the expression "section 736 of the *Criminal Code*" with the expression "section 730 of the *Criminal Code*":

(a) paragraph 5(2)(a); and

(b) paragraphs 70(1)(a) and (b).

Editor's Note

[NOTE: ss. 138–192 deal with consequential amendments to other related Acts. Amendments are included in the affected Acts.]

Coming into Force

193. (1) Coming into force — Subject to subsection (2), this Act or any of its provisions or any provision of any other Act enacted or amended by this Act, other than sections 136, 137 and 174, shall come into force on a day or days to be fixed by order of the Governor in Council.

(2) Coming into force if no order made — If no order bringing this Act or any of its provisions or any provision of any other Act enacted or amended by this Act is made before January 1, 2003, this Act, other than sections 136, 137 and 174, comes into force on that date.

Transitional Provisions

— 2012, c. 6, s. 29 [Amended 2019, c. 9, s. 23.]:

29. (1) Destruction of information — Commissioner — The Commissioner of Firearms shall ensure the destruction as soon as feasible of all records in the Canadian Firearms Registry related to the registration of firearms that are neither prohibited firearms nor restricted firearms and all copies of those records under the Commissioner's control.

(2) Destruction of information — chief firearms officers — Each chief firearms officer shall ensure the destruction as soon as feasible of all records under their control related to the registration of firearms that are neither prohibited firearms nor restricted firearms and all copies of those records under their control.

(3) Non-application — Sections 12 and 13 of the *Library and Archives of Canada Act* and subsections 6(1) and (3) of the *Privacy Act* do not apply with respect to the destruction of the records and copies referred to in subsections (1) and (2).

— 2015, c. 27, s. 37:

37. Conversion of possession only licence — A licence that is issued under the *Firearms Act* and that is held by an individual referred to in paragraph 7(4)(c) of that Act, as it read immediately before the day on which this section comes into force, authorizes the holder to acquire any firearms that they are authorized to possess under the licence and that are acquired by the holder on or after that day and before the expiration or revocation of the licence.

— 2019, c. 9, ss. 25–30:

25. Definitions — The following definitions apply in this section and in sections 26 to 28.

"commencement day" means the day on which this Act receives royal assent.

"copy" means a copy referred to in subsection 29(1) or (2) of the *Ending the Long-gun Registry Act*.

"personal information" means any personal information, as defined in section 3 of the *Privacy Act*, that is contained in a record or copy.

"record" means, other than in section 28, a record referred to in subsection 29(1) or (2) of the *Ending the Long-gun Registry Act*.

"specified proceeding" means any request, complaint, investigation, application, judicial review, appeal or other proceeding under the *Access to Information Act* or the *Privacy Act* that is with respect to a record or copy or to personal information and that

(a) was made or initiated on or before June 22, 2015 and was not concluded, or in respect of which no decision was made, on or before that day; or

(b) was made or initiated after June 22, 2015 but before the commencement day.

26. (1) **Non-application — *Access to Information Act*** — Subject to section 27, the Access to *Information Act* does not apply as of the commencement day with respect to records and copies.

(2) **Non-application — *Privacy Act*** — Subject to section 27, the *Privacy Act*, other than its subsections 6(1) and (3), does not apply as of the commencement day with respect to personal information.

(3) **Non-application–subsections 6(1) and (3) of the *Privacy Act*** — For greater certainty, by reason of subsection 29(3) of the *Ending the Long-gun Registry Act*, subsections 6(1) and (3) of the *Privacy Act* do not apply as of April 5, 2012 with respect to personal information.

27. (1) **Continued application** — The *Privacy Act*, other than its subsections 6(1) and (3), and the *Access to Information Act* continue to apply with respect to any specified proceeding and to any complaint, investigation, application, judicial review or appeal that results from a specified proceeding.

(2) **Period running on June 22, 2015 restarts** — A time limit, or other period of time, under the *Access to Information Act* or the *Privacy Act* that was running on June 22, 2015 with respect to a specified proceeding described in paragraph (a) of the definition of that expression in section 25 is deemed to restart, from the beginning, on the commencement day.

(3) **Specified proceeding initiated after June 22, 2015** — A specified proceeding described in paragraph (b) of the definition of that expression in section 25 is deemed to be made or initiated on the commencement day.

(4) **For greater certainty** — For greater certainty, no destruction of records or copies that are the subject of proceedings referred to in subsection (1) is to occur until all proceedings referred to in that subsection are finally disposed of, settled or abandoned.

28. **Permission to view records** — The Commissioner of Firearms shall permit the Information Commissioner to view — for the purpose of settling the Federal Court proceeding *Information Commissioner of Canada v. Minister of Public Safety and Emergency Preparedness*, bearing court file number T-785-15 — any record that was in the Canadian Firearms Registry on April 3, 2015.

29. (1) **Copy to Government of Quebec** — The Commissioner of Firearms shall — for the purpose of the administration and enforcement of the *Firearms Registration Act*, chapter 15 of the Statutes of Quebec, 2016 — provide the Quebec Minister with a copy of all records that were in the Canadian Firearms Registry on April 3, 2015 and that relate to firearms registered, as at that day, as non-restricted firearms, if the Quebec Minister provides the Commissioner with a written request to that effect before the end of the 120th day after the day on which the Commissioner sends written notice under subsection (2).

(2) **Notice** — If no request is provided under subsection (1) before the Commissioner is in a position to proceed with ensuring the destruction of the records referred to in that subsection, the Commissioner shall, as soon as he or she is in that position, send written notice to the Quebec Minister of that fact.

(3) **Destruction of records** — Despite subsection 29(1) of the *Ending the Long-gun Registry Act*, the Commissioner shall proceed with ensuring the destruction of the records referred to in subsection (1) only after

(a) he or she provides the Quebec Minister with a copy of the records, in the case where that Minister provides a written request in accordance with subsection (1); or

(b) the end of the 120th day after the day on which the Commissioner sends written notice under subsection (2), in any other case.

(4) Definition of "Quebec Minister" — In this section, "Quebec Minister" means the minister of the Government of Quebec responsible for public security.

30. Extension — The Minister of Public Safety and Emergency Preparedness may, during the 120-day period referred to in subsection 29(1), make an order extending that period for another 120 days, and in that case the references in subsections 29(1) and (3) to "the 120th day" are to be read as references to "the 240th day".

Can. Reg. 2006-95 — Order Declaring an Amnesty Period (2006)

made under the *Criminal Code*

SOR/2006-95, as am. SOR/2007-101; SOR/2008-147; SOR/2009-139; SOR/2010-104; SOR/2011-102; SOR/2013-96; SOR/2014-123.

Interpretation

1. The following definitions apply in this Order.

"non-restricted firearm" means a firearm other than a prohibited firearm or a restricted firearm. *("arme à feu sans restriction")*

"public service agency" has the same meaning as in section 1 of the *Public Agents Firearms Regulations. ("agence de services publics")*

Non-Restricted Firearms — Individuals

2. (1) The amnesty period set out in subsection (3) is declared under section 117.14 of the *Criminal Code* for an individual who, at any time during the amnesty period,

(a) is in possession of a non-restricted firearm, holds a licence to possess firearms or a licence to possess and acquire firearms but does not hold a registration certificate for the firearm; or

(b) is in possession of a non-restricted firearm, does not hold a registration certificate for the firearm and will have held a licence to possess firearms or a licence to possess and acquire firearms

(i) that expired during the period beginning on January 1, 2004 and ending on May 16, 2006, or

(ii) that will have expired during the period beginning on May 17, 2006 and ending on May 16, 2015.

(2) The purpose of the amnesty period is to permit the individual to

(a) in the case of an individual described in paragraph (1)(a), obtain the registration certificate;

(b) in the case of an individual described in paragraph (1)(b), obtain the licence and registration certificate;

(c) deactivate the firearm so that it is no longer a firearm;

(d) export the firearm in accordance with all applicable legal requirements, including the legal requirements of the country to which the firearm is exported;

(e) turn in the firearm to a police officer or a firearms officer for destruction or other disposal;

(f) sell or give the firearm to a public service agency, to a business, including a museum, that holds a licence authorizing the acquisition of firearms or to an individual who holds a possession and acquisition licence for firearms; or

(g) possess the firearm before doing one of the things described in paragraphs (a) to (f).

(3) The amnesty period begins on May 17, 2006 and ends on May 16, 2015.

SOR/2007-101, s. 1; SOR/2008-147, s. 1; SOR/2009-139, s. 1; SOR/2010-104, s. 1; SOR/2011-102, s. 1; SOR/2013-96, s. 1; SOR/2014-123, s. 1

Coming Into Force

3. This Order comes into force on the day on which it is registered.

Can. Reg. 2014-56 — Order Declaring an Amnesty Period (2014)

made under the *Criminal Code*

SOR/2014-56, as am. SOR/2014-182.

1. Definition of "firearm" — In this Order, **"firearm"** means any of the following prohibited firearms:

(a) a Ceská Zbrojovka (CZ) Model CZ858 Tactical-2P rifle;

(b) a Ceská Zbrojovka (CZ) Model CZ858 Tactical-2V rifle;

(c) a Ceská Zbrojovka (CZ) Model CZ858 Tactical-4P rifle;

(d) a Ceská Zbrojovka (CZ) Model CZ858 Tactical-4V rifle;

(e) a SAN Swiss Arms Model Classic Green rifle;

(f) a SAN Swiss Arms Model Classic Green carbine;

(g) a SAN Swiss Arms Model Classic Green CQB rifle;

(h) a SAN Swiss Arms Model Black Special rifle;

(i) a SAN Swiss Arms Model Black Special carbine;

(j) a SAN Swiss Arms Model Black Special CQB rifle;

(k) a SAN Swiss Arms Model Black Special Target rifle;

(l) a SAN Swiss Arms Model Blue Star rifle;

(m) a SAN Swiss Arms Model Heavy Metal rifle;

(n) a SAN Swiss Arms Model Red Devil rifle; or

(o) a SAN Swiss Arms Model Swiss Arms Edition rifle.

2. (1) Declaration — The amnesty period set out in subsection (3) is declared under section 117.14 of the *Criminal Code* for a person who

(a) on the day before this Order is registered, possessed a firearm and held a licence that was issued under the *Firearms Act*; and

(b) during the amnesty period, continues to hold the licence while in possession of the firearm.

(2) Purpose — The purpose of the amnesty period is to permit the person to do any of the following during that period:

(a) possess the firearm;

(b) deliver the firearm to a peace officer, firearms officer or chief firearms officer;

(c) sell or give the firearm to a business — including a museum — authorized to acquire and possess prohibited firearms;

(d) transport the firearm for the purposes of paragraph (b) or (c);

(e) use the firearm in target practice or at a target shooting competition, under the auspices of a shooting club or shooting range that is approved under section 29 of the *Firearms Act*, and, for that purpose, transport the firearm in accordance with,

(i) in the case of a firearm referred to in any of paragraphs 1(a), (b), (e), (h) and (k) to (o), the requirements set out in section 10 of the *Storage, Display, Transportation and Handling of Firearms by Individuals Regulations* or section 11 of the *Storage, Display and Transportation of Firearms and Other Weapons by Businesses Regulations*, as applicable, or

(ii) in the case of a firearm referred to in any of paragraphs 1(c), (d), (f), (g), (i) and (j), the requirements set out in section 11 of the *Storage, Display, Transportation and Handling of Firearms by Individuals Regulations* or section 12 of the *Storage, Display and Transportation of Firearms and Other Weapons by Businesses Regulations*, as applicable.

(3) Amnesty period — The amnesty period begins on the day on which this Order is registered and ends on March 14, 2016.

SOR/2014-182, s. 1

3. Coming into force — This Order comes into force on the day on which it is registered.

Can. Reg. 2018-46 — Order Declaring an Amnesty Period (2018)

made under the *Criminal Code*

SOR/2018-46

1. Definition of "firearm" — In this Order, **"firearm"** means any of the following prohibited firearms:

(a) a SAN Swiss Arms Model Classic Green Sniper rifle;

(b) a SAN Swiss Arms Model Ver rifle;

(c) a SAN Swiss Arms Model Aestas rifle;

(d) a SAN Swiss Arms Model Autumnus rifle; and

(e) a SAN Swiss Arms Model Hiemis rifle.

2. (1) Amnesty — The amnesty period set out in subsection (3) is declared under section 117.14 of the *Criminal Code* for a person who

(a) on the day before the day on which this Order is registered, possessed a firearm and held a licence that was issued under the *Firearms Act*; and

(b) during the amnesty period, continues to hold a licence while in possession of the firearm.

(2) Purpose — The purpose of the amnesty period is to permit the person to do any of the following during that period:

(a) possess the firearm;

(b) deliver the firearm to a peace officer, firearms officer or chief firearms officer;

(c) sell or give the firearm to a business — including a museum — authorized to acquire and possess prohibited firearms; and

(d) transport the firearm for the purposes of paragraph (b) or (c).

(3) Amnesty period — The amnesty period begins on the day on which this Order is registered and ends on February 28, 2021.

3. Coming into force — This Order comes into force on the day on which it is registered.

IDENTIFICATION OF CRIMINALS ACT

Editor's note: Current to May 15, 2019.

TABLE OF CONCORDANCE

R.S.C. 1970, c. I-1	R.S.C. 1985, c. I-1
1	1
2	2
3	3

IDENTIFICATION OF CRIMINALS ACT

An act respecting the Identification of criminals

R.S.C. 1985, c. I-1, as am. S.C. 1992, c. 47, ss. 73–76 [Amended 1996, c. 7, ss. 39, 40.]; 1999, c. 18, s. 88; 2001, c. 41, ss. 23.1, 35; 2018, c. 16, ss. 166, 167; 2019, c. 25, s. 388 [s. 388(2) to come into force December 18, 2019.].

SHORT TITLE

1. **Short title** — This act may be cited as the *Identification of Criminals Act*.

HER MAJESTY

1.1 **Binding on Her Majesty** — This Act is binding on Her Majesty in right of Canada or a province.

1992, c. 47, s. 73

IDENTIFICATION OF CRIMINALS

2. (1) **Fingerprints and photographs** — The following persons may be fingerprinted or photographed or subjected to such other measurements, processes and operations having the object of identifying persons as are approved by order of the Governor in Council:

(a) any person who is in lawful custody charged with or convicted of

(i) an indictable offence, other than an offence that is designated as a contravention under the *Contraventions Act* in respect of which the Attorney General, within the meaning of that Act, has made an election under section 50 of that Act,

(ii) an offence under the *Security of Information Act*; or

(iii) an offence punishable on summary conviction if that offence may also be prosecuted as an indictable offence described in subparagraph (i);

(b) any person who has been apprehended under the *Extradition Act*;

(c) any person alleged to have committed an indictable offence, other than

(i) an offence that is designated as a contravention under the *Contraventions Act* in respect of which the Attorney General, within the meaning of that Act, has made an election under section 50 of that Act, who is required under subsection 501(3) or 509(5) of the *Criminal*

Code to appear for the purposes of this Act by an appearance notice, promise to appear, recognizance or summons; or

(ii) an offence in respect of which proceedings were commenced by a peace officer under section 51 of the *Cannabis Act*;

Proposed Amendment — 2(1)(c)

(c) any person alleged to have committed an indictable offence, other than an offence that is designated as a contravention under the *Contraventions Act* in respect of which the **"Attorney General"**, within the meaning of that Act, has made an election under section 50 of that Act, who is required under subsection 500(3), 501(4) or 509(5) of the *Criminal Code* to appear for the purposes of this Act by an appearance notice, undertaking or summons; or

2019, c. 25, s. 388(2) [To come into force December 18, 2019.]

(d) any person who is in lawful custody pursuant to section 83.3 of the *Criminal Code*.

(2) Use of force — Such force may be used as is necessary to the effectual carrying out and application of the measurements, processes and operations described under subsection (1).

(3) Publication — The results of the measurements, processes and operations to which a person has been subjected pursuant to subsection (1) may be published for the purpose of affording information to officers and others engaged in the execution or administration of the law.

1992, c. 47, s. 74 [Amended 1996, c. 7, s. 39.]; 1999, c. 18, s. 88; 2001, c. 41, ss. 23.1, 35; 2018, c. 16, s. 166; 2019, c. 25, s. 388(1)

3. No liability for acting under Act — No liability, civil or criminal, for anything lawfully done under this Act shall be incurred by any person

(a) having custody of a person described in subsection 2(1);

(b) acting in the aid or under the direction of a person having such custody; or

(c) concerned in the publication of results under subsection 2(3).

1992, c. 47, s. 75

Destruction of Fingerprints and Photographs

4. Destruction of fingerprints and photographs — Where a person charged with an offence that is designated as a contravention under the *Contraventions Act* is fingerprinted or photographed and the Attorney General, within the meaning of that Act, makes an election under section 50 of that Act, the fingerprints or photographs shall be destroyed.

1992, c. 47, s. 76 [Amended 1996, c. 7, s. 40.]

5. Destruction of fingerprints and photographs — *Cannabis Act* — If a person charged with an offence referred to in any of paragraphs 51(2)(a) to (j) of the *Cannabis Act* is fingerprinted or photographed and the Attorney General, within the meaning of that Act, makes an election under section 58 of that Act, the fingerprints or photographs shall be destroyed.

2018, c. 16, s. 167

meaning of that Act, [illegible] section 9 of that Act, the fingerprints or photographs shall be destroyed.

[illegible]

INTERPRETATION ACT

Editor's note: Current to May 15, 2019.

TABLE OF CONCORDANCE

R.S.C. 1970, c. I-23	R.S.C. 1985, c. I-21	R.S.C. 1970, c. I-23	R.S.C. 1985, c. I-21
1	1	24	25
2	2	25	26
3	3	25	27
4	4	25	28
5	5	25	29
6	6	25	30
7	7	26	31
8	8	26	32
9	9	26	33
10	10	27	34
11	12	28	11, 25, 35, part. 37
12	13	28.1	39
13	14	29	36
14	15	30	38
15	16	31	part. 37
16	17	32	40
17	18	33	41
18	19	34	42
19	20	35	43
20	21	36	44
21	22	37	45
22	23	38	46
23	24	Sch/Ann	Sch/Ann

INTERPRETATION ACT

An Act respecting the interpretation of statutes and regulations

R.S.C. 1985, c. I-21, as am. R.S.C. 1985, c. 11 (1st Supp.), s. 2 (Sched., item 2); R.S.C. 1985, c. 27 (1st Supp.), s. 203; SOR/86-532; R.S.C. 1985, c. 27 (2nd Supp.), s. 10 (Sched., item 14); S.C. 1990, c. 17, s. 26; 1992, c. 1, ss. 87–91; 1992, c. 47, s. 79; 1992, c. 51, s. 56; SOR/93-140; 1993, c. 28, s. 78 (Sched. III, item 82) [Amended 1998, c. 15, s. 28; 1999, c. 3, s. 12 (Sched., item 18).]; 1993, c. 34, s. 88; 1993, c. 38, s. 87; 1995, c. 39, s. 174; SOR/95-366; 1996, c. 31, ss. 86, 87; 1997, c. 39, s. 4; 1998, c. 30, ss. 13(i) (Fr.), 15(i); 1999, c. 3, s. 71; 1999, c. 28, s. 168; 1999, c. 31, ss. 146, 147 (Fr.); 2001, c. 4, s. 8; 2002, c. 7, s. 188; 2002, c. 8, s. 151; 2003, c. 22, s. 224(z.43); 2014, c. 2, s. 14; 2015, c. 3, s. 124.

SHORT TITLE

1. Short title — This Act may be cited as the *Interpretation Act*.

INTERPRETATION

2. (1) Definitions — In this Act,

"Act" means an Act of Parliament;

"enact" includes to issue, make or establish;

"enactment" means an Act or regulation or any portion of an Act or regulation;

"public officer" includes any person in the federal public administration who is authorized by or under an enactment to do or enforce the doing of an act or thing or to exercise a power, or on whom a duty is imposed by or under an enactment;

"regulation" includes an order, regulation, rule, rule of court, form, tariff of costs or fees, letters patent, commission, warrant, proclamation, by-law, resolution or other instrument issued, made or established

(a) in the execution of a power conferred by or under the authority of an Act, or

(b) by or under the authority of the Governor in Council;

"repeal" includes revoke or cancel.

(2) **Expired and replaced enactments** — For the purposes of this Act, an enactment that has been replaced is repealed and an enactment that has expired, lapsed or otherwise ceased to have effect is deemed to have been repealed.

1993, c. 34, s. 88; 1999, c. 31, s. 146; 2003, c. 22, s. 224(z.43)

APPLICATION

3. (1) **Application** — Every provision of this Act applies, unless a contrary intention appears, to every enactment, whether enacted before or after the commencement of this Act.

(2) **Application to this Act** — The provisions of this Act apply to the interpretation of this Act.

(3) **Rules of construction not excluded** — Nothing in this Act excludes the application to an enactment of a rule of construction applicable to that enactment and not inconsistent with this Act.

ENACTING CLAUSE OF ACTS

4. (1) **Enacting clause** — The enacting clause of an Act may be in the following form:

"Her Majesty, by and with the advice and consent of the Senate and House of Commons of Canada, enacts as follows:".

(2) **Order of clauses** — The enacting clause of an Act shall follow the preamble, if any, and the various provisions within the purview or body of the Act shall follow in a concise and enunciative form.

OPERATION

Royal Assent

5. (1) **Royal Assent** — The Clerk of the Parliaments shall endorse on every Act, immediately after its title, the day, month and year when the Act was assented to in Her Majesty's name and the endorsement shall be a part of the Act.

(2) **Date of commencement** — If no date of commencement is provided for in an Act, the date of commencement of that Act is the date of assent to the Act.

(3) **Commencement provision** — Where an Act contains a provision that the Act or any portion thereof is to come into force on a day later than the date of assent to the Act, that provision is deemed to have come into force on the date of assent to the Act.

(4) **Commencement when no date fixed** — Where an Act provides that certain provisions thereof are to come or are deemed to have come into force on a day other than the date of assent to the Act, the remaining provisions of the Act are deemed to have come into force on the date of assent to the Act.

Day Fixed for Commencement or Repeal

6. (1) **Operation when date fixed for commencement or repeal** — Where an enactment is expressed to come into force on a particular day, it shall be construed as coming into force on the expiration of the previous day, and where an enactment is expressed to expire, lapse or otherwise cease to have effect on a particular day, it shall be construed as ceasing to have effect upon the commencement of the following day.

(2) **When no date fixed** — Every enactment that is not expressed to come into force on a particular day shall be construed as coming into force

(a) in the case of an Act, on the expiration of the day immediately before the day the Act was assented to in Her Majesty's name; and

(b) in the case of a regulation, on the expiration of the day immediately before the day the regulation was registered pursuant to section 6 of the *Statutory Instruments Act* or, if the regulation is of a class that is exempted from the application of subsection 5(1) of that Act, on the expiration of the day immediately before the day the regulation was made.

(3) **Judicial notice** — Judicial notice shall be taken of a day for the coming into force of an enactment that is fixed by a regulation that has been published in the *Canada Gazette*.

1992, c. 1, s. 87

Regulation Prior to Commencement

7. **Preliminary proceedings** — Where an enactment is not in force and it contains provisions conferring power to make regulations or do any other thing, that power may, for the purpose of making the enactment effective on its commencement, be exercised at any time before its commencement, but a regulation so made or a thing so done has no effect until the commencement of the enactment except in so far as may be necessary to make the enactment effective on its commencement.

Territorial Operation

8. (1) **Territorial operation** — Every enactment applies to the whole of Canada, unless a contrary intention is expressed in the enactment.

(2) **Amending enactment** — Where an enactment that does not apply to the whole of Canada is amended, no provision in the amending enactment applies to any part of Canada to which the amended enactment does not apply, unless it is provided in the amending enactment that it applies to that part of Canada or to the whole of Canada.

(2.1) **Exclusive economic zone of Canada** — Every enactment that applies in respect of exploring or exploiting, conserving or managing natural resources, whether living or non-living, applies, in addition to its application to Canada, to the exclusive economic zone of Canada, unless a contrary intention is expressed in the enactment.

(2.2) Continental shelf of Canada — Every enactment that applies in respect of exploring or exploiting natural resources that are

(a) mineral or other non-living resources of the seabed or subsoil, or

(b) living organisms belonging to sedentary species, that is to say, organisms that, at the harvestable stage, either are immobile on or under the seabed or are unable to move except in constant physical contact with the seabed or subsoil

applies, in addition to its application to Canada, to the continental shelf of Canada, unless a contrary intention is expressed in the enactment.

(3) Extra-territorial operation — Every Act now in force enacted prior to December 11, 1931 that expressly or by necessary or reasonable implication was intended, as to the whole or any part thereof, to have extra-territorial operation shall be construed as if, at the date of its enactment the Parliament of Canada had full power to make laws having extra-territorial operation as provided by the *Statute of Westminster, 1931*.

1996, c. 31, s. 86

RULES OF CONSTRUCTION

Property and Civil Rights

[Heading added 2001, c. 4, s. 8.]

8.1 Duality of legal traditions and application of provincial law — Both the common law and the civil law are equally authoritative and recognized sources of the law of property and civil rights in Canada and, unless otherwise provided by law, if in interpreting an enactment it is necessary to refer to a province's rules, principles or concepts forming part of the law of property and civil rights, reference must be made to the rules, principles and concepts in force in the province at the time the enactment is being applied.

2001, c. 4, s. 8

8.2 Terminology — Unless otherwise provided by law, when an enactment contains both civil law and common law terminology, or terminology that has a different meaning in the civil law and the common law, the civil law terminology or meaning is to be adopted in the Province of Quebec and the common law terminology or meaning is to be adopted in the other provinces.

2001, c. 4, s. 8

Private Acts

9. Provisions in private Acts — No provision in a private Act affects the rights of any person, except only as therein mentioned or referred to.

Law Always Speaking

10. Law always speaking — The law shall be considered as always speaking, and where a matter or thing is expressed in the present tense, it shall be applied to the circumstances as they arise, so that effect may be given to the enactment according to its true spirit, intent and meaning.

Imperative and Permissive Construction

11. "Shall" and "may" — The expression **"shall"** is to be construed as imperative and the expression **"may"** as permissive.

Enactments Remedial

12. Enactments deemed remedial — Every enactment shall be deemed remedial, and shall be given such fair, large and liberal construction and interpretation as best ensures the attainment of its objects.

Preambles and Marginal Notes

13. Preamble — The preamble of an enactment shall be read as a part of the enactment intended to assist in explaining its purport and object.

14. Marginal notes and historical references — Marginal notes and references to former enactments that appear after the end of a section or other division in an enactment form no part of the enactment, but are inserted for convenience of reference only.

Application of Interpretation Provisions

15. (1) Application of definitions and interpretation rules — Definitions or rules of interpretation in an enactment apply to all of the provisions of the enactment, including the provisions that contain those definitions or rules of interpretation.

(2) Interpretation sections subject to exceptions — Where an enactment contains an interpretation section or provision, it shall be read and construed

(a) as being applicable only if a contrary intention does not appear, and

(b) as being applicable to all other enactments relating to the same subject-matter unless a contrary intention appears.

16. Words in regulations — Where an enactment confers power to make regulations, expressions used in the regulations have the same respective meanings as in the enactment conferring the power.

Her Majesty

17. Her Majesty not bound or affected unless stated — No enactment is binding on Her Majesty or affects Her Majesty or Her Majesty's rights or prerogatives in any manner, except as mentioned or referred to in the enactment.

Proclamations

18. (1) Proclamation — Where an enactment authorizes the issue of a proclamation, the proclamation shall be understood to be a proclamation of the Governor in Council.

(2) Proclamation to be issued on advice — Where the Governor General is authorized to issue a proclamation, the proclamation shall be understood to be a proclamation issued under an order of the Governor in Council, but it is not necessary to mention in the proclamation that it is issued under such an order.

(3) Effective day of proclamations — A proclamation that is issued under an order of the Governor in Council may purport to have been issued on the day of the order or on any subsequent day and, if so, takes effect on that day.

(4) [Repealed 1992, c. 1, s. 88.]

1992, c. 1, s. 88

Oaths

19. (1) Administration of oaths — Where, by an enactment or by a rule of the Senate or House of Commons, evidence under oath is authorized or required to be taken, or an oath is authorized or directed to be made, taken or administered, the oath may be administered, and a certificate of its having been made, taken or administered may be given by

(a) any person authorized by the enactment or rule to take the evidence; or

(b) a judge of any court, a notary public, a justice of the peace or a commissioner for taking affidavits, having authority or jurisdiction within the place where the oath is administered.

(2) Where justice of peace empowered — Where power is conferred on a justice of the peace to administer an oath or solemn affirmation or to take an affidavit or declaration, the power may be exercised by a notary public or a commissioner for taking oaths.

Reports to Parliament

20. Reports to Parliament — Where an Act requires a report or other document to be laid before Parliament and, in compliance with the Act, a particular report or document has been laid before Parliament at a session thereof, nothing in the Act shall be construed as requiring the same report or document to be laid before Parliament at any subsequent session.

CORPORATIONS

21. (1) Powers vested in corporations — Words establishing a corporation shall be construed

(a) as vesting in the corporation power to sue and be sued, to contract and be contracted with by its corporate name, to have a common seal and to alter or change it at pleasure, to have perpetual succession, to acquire and hold personal property for the purposes for which the corporation is established and to alienate that property at pleasure;

(b) in the case of a corporation having a name consisting of an English and a French form or a combined English and French form, as vesting in the corporation power to use either the English or the French form of its name or both forms and to show on its seal both the English and French forms of its name or have two seals, one showing the English and the other showing the French form of its name;

(c) as vesting in a majority of the members of the corporation the power to bind the others by their acts; and

(d) as exempting from personal liability for its debts, obligations or acts such individual members of the corporation who do not contravene the provisions of the enactment establishing the corporation.

(2) Corporate name — Where an enactment establishes a corporation and in each of the English and French versions of the enactment the name of the corporation is in the form only of the language of that version, the name of the corporation shall consist of the form of its name in each of the versions of the enactment.

(3) Banking business — No corporation is deemed to be authorized to carry on the business of banking unless that power is expressly conferred on it by the enactment establishing the corporation.

MAJORITY AND QUORUM

22. (1) Majorities — Where an enactment requires or authorizes more than two persons to do an act or thing, a majority of them may do it.

(2) Quorum of board, court, commission, etc — Where an enactment establishes a board, court, commission or other body consisting of three or more members, in this section called an "association",

(a) at a meeting of the association, a number of members of the association equal to,

(i) if the number of members provided for by the enactment is a fixed number, at least one-half of the number of members, and

(ii) if the number of members provided for by the enactment is not a fixed number but is within a range having a maximum or minimum, at least one-half of the number of members in office if that number is within the range,

constitutes a quorum;

(b) an act or thing done by a majority of the members of the association present at a meeting, if the members present constitute a quorum, is deemed to have been done by the association; and

(c) a vacancy in the membership of the association does not invalidate the constitution of the association or impair the right of the members in office to act, if the number of members in office is not less than a quorum.

Appointment, Retirement and Powers of Officers

23. (1) Public officers hold office during pleasure — Every public officer appointed by or under the authority of an enactment or otherwise is deemed to have been appointed to hold office during pleasure only, unless it is otherwise expressed in the enactment, commission or instrument of appointment.

(2) Effective day of appointments — Where an appointment is made by instrument under the Great Seal, the instrument may purport to have been issued on or after the day its issue was authorized, and the day on which it so purports to have been issued is deemed to be the day on which the appointment takes effect.

(3) Appointment or engagement otherwise than under Great Seal — Where there is authority in an enactment to appoint a person to a position or to engage the services of a person, otherwise than by instrument under the Great Seal, the instrument of appointment or engagement may be expressed to be effective on or after the day on which that person commenced the performance of the duties of the position or commenced the performance of the services, and the day on which it is so expressed to be effective, unless that day is more than sixty days before the day on which the instrument is issued, is deemed to be the day on which the appointment or engagement takes effect.

(4) Remuneration — Where a person is appointed to an office, the appointing authority may fix, vary or terminate that person's remuneration.

(5) Commencement of appointments or retirements — Where a person is appointed to an office effective on a specified day, or where the appointment of a person is terminated effective on a specified day, the appointment or termination is deemed to have been effected immediately on the expiration of the previous day.

24. (1) Implied powers respecting public officers — Words authorizing the appointment of a public officer to hold office during pleasure include, in the discretion of the authority in whom the power of appointment is vested, the power to

(a) terminate the appointment or remove or suspend the public officer;

(b) re-appoint or reinstate the public officer; and

(c) appoint another person in the stead of, or to act in the stead of, the public officer.

(2) Power to act for ministers — Words directing or empowering a minister of the Crown to do an act or thing, regardless of whether the act or thing is administrative, legislative or judicial, or otherwise applying to that minister as the holder of the office, include

(a) a minister acting for that minister or, if the office is vacant, a minister designated to act in the office by or under the authority of an order in council;

(b) the successors of that minister in the office;

(c) his or their deputy; and

(d) notwithstanding paragraph (c), a person appointed to serve, in the department or ministry of state over which the minister presides, in a capacity appropriate to the doing of the act or thing, or to the words so applying.

(3) **Restriction as to public servants** — Nothing in paragraph (2)(c) or (d) shall be construed as authorizing the exercise of any authority conferred on a minister to make a regulation as defined in the *Statutory Instruments Act.*

(4) **Successors to and deputy of public officer** — Words directing or empowering any public officer, other than a minister of the Crown, to do any act or thing, or otherwise applying to the public officer by his name of office, include his successors in the office and his or their deputy.

(5) **Powers of holder of public office** — Where a power is conferred or a duty imposed on the holder of an office, the power may be exercised and the duty shall be performed by the person for the time being charged with the execution of the powers and duties of the office.

1992, c. 1, ss. 89(1), (3), (4)

EVIDENCE

25. (1) **Documentary evidence** — Where an enactment provides that a document is evidence of a fact without anything in the context to indicate that the document is conclusive evidence, then, in any judicial proceedings, the document is admissible in evidence and the fact is deemed to be established in the absence of any evidence to the contrary.

(2) **Queen's Printer** — Every copy of an enactment having printed thereon what purports to be the name or title of the Queen's Printer and Controller of Stationery or the Queen's Printer is deemed to be a copy purporting to be printed by the Queen's Printer for Canada.

COMPUTATION OF TIME

26. **Time limits and holidays** — Where the time limited for the doing of a thing expires or falls on a holiday, the thing may be done on the day next following that is not a holiday.

27. (1) **Clear days** — Where there is a reference to a number of clear days or "at least" a number of days between two events, in calculating that number of days the days on which the events happen are excluded.

(2) **Not clear days** — Where there is a reference to a number of days, not expressed to be clear days, between two events, in calculating that number of days the day on which the first event happens is excluded and the day on which the second event happens is included.

(3) **Beginning and ending of prescribed periods** — Where a time is expressed to begin or end at, on or with a specified day, or to continue to or until a specified day, the time includes that day.

(4) **After specified day** — Where a time is expressed to begin after or to be from a specified day, the time does not include that day.

(5) **Within a time** — Where anything is to be done within a time after, from, of or before a specified day, the time does not include that day.

28. **Calculation of a period of months after or before a specified day** — Where there is a reference to a period of time consisting of a number of months after or before a specified day, the period is calculated by

(a) counting forward or backward from the specified day the number of months, without including the month in which that day falls;

(b) excluding the specified day; and

(c) including in the last month counted under paragraph (a) the day that has the same calendar number as the specified day or, if that month has no day with that number, the last day of that month.

29. **Time of the day** — Where there is a reference to time expressed as a specified time of the day, the time is taken to mean standard time.

30. **Time when specified age attained** — A person is deemed not to have attained a specified number of years of age until the commencement of the anniversary, of the same number, of the day of that person's birth.

MISCELLANEOUS RULES

31. (1) **Reference to provincial court judge, etc** — Where anything is required or authorized to be done by or before a judge, provincial court judge, justice of the peace or any functionary or officer, it shall be done by or before one whose jurisdiction or powers extend to the place where the thing is to be done.

(2) **Ancillary powers** — Where power is given to a person, officer or functionary to do or enforce the doing of any act or thing, all such powers as are necessary to enable the person, officer or functionary to do or enforce the doing of the act or thing are deemed to be also given.

(3) **Powers to be exercised as required** — Where a power is conferred or a duty imposed, the power may be exercised and the duty shall be performed from time to time as occasion requires.

(4) **Power to repeal** — Where a power is conferred to make regulations, the power shall be construed as including a power, exercisable in the same manner, and subject to the same consent and conditions, if any, to repeal, amend or vary the regulations and make others.

R.S.C. 1985, c. 27 (1st Supp.), s. 203

32. **Forms** — Where a form is prescribed, deviations from that form, not affecting the substance or calculated to mislead, do not invalidate the form used.

33. (1) **Gender** — Words importing female persons include male persons and corporations and words importing male persons include female persons and corporations.

(2) **Number** — Words in the singular include the plural, and words in the plural include the singular.

(3) **Parts of speech and grammatical forms** — Where a word is defined, other parts of speech and grammatical forms of the same word have corresponding meanings.

1992, c. 1, s. 90

Offences

34. (1) **Indictable and summary conviction offences** — Where an enactment creates an offence,

(a) the offence is deemed to be an indictable offence if the enactment provides that the offender may be prosecuted for the offence by indictment;

(b) the offence is deemed to be one for which the offender is punishable on summary conviction if there is nothing in the context to indicate that the offence is an indictable offence; and

(c) if the offence is one for which the offender may be prosecuted by indictment or for which he is punishable on summary conviction, no person shall be considered to have been convicted of an indictable offence by reason only of having been convicted of the offence on summary conviction.

(2) ***Criminal Code* to apply** — All the provisions of the *Criminal Code* relating to indictable offences apply to indictable offences created by an enactment, and all the provisions of that Code relating to summary conviction offences apply to all other offences created by an enactment, except to the extent that the enactment otherwise provides.

(3) **Documents similarly construed** — In a commission, proclamation, warrant or other document relating to criminal law or procedure in criminal matters,

(a) a reference to an offence for which the offender may be prosecuted by indictment shall be construed as a reference to an indictable offence; and

(b) a reference to any other offence shall be construed as a reference to an offence for which the offender is punishable on summary conviction.

Powers to Enter Dwelling-houses to Carry out Arrests

34.1 Authorization to enter dwelling-house — Any person who may issue a warrant to arrest or apprehend a person under any Act of Parliament, other than the *Criminal Code*, has the same powers, subject to the same terms and conditions, as a judge or justice has under the *Criminal Code*

(a) to authorize the entry into a dwelling-house described in the warrant for the purpose of arresting or apprehending the person, if the person issuing the warrant is satisfied by information on oath that there are reasonable grounds to believe that the person is or will be present in the dwelling-house; and

(b) to authorize the entry into the dwelling-house without prior announcement if the requirement of subsection 529.4(1) is met.

1997, c. 39, s. 4

Definitions

35. (1) General definitions — In every enactment,

"Act", in respect of an Act of a legislature, includes a law of the Legislature of Yukon, of the Northwest Territories or for Nunavut;

"bank" means a bank listed in Schedule I or II to the *Bank Act*;

"British Commonwealth" or **"British Commonwealth of Nations"** has the same meaning as "Commonwealth";

"broadcasting" means any radiocommunication in which the transmissions are intended for direct reception by the general public;

"Canada", for greater certainty, includes the internal waters of Canada and the territorial sea of Canada;

"Canadian waters" includes the territorial sea of Canada and the internal waters of Canada;

"Clerk of the Privy Council" or **"Clerk of the Queen's Privy Council"** means the Clerk of the Privy Council and Secretary to the Cabinet;

"commencement", when used with reference to an enactment, means the time at which the enactment comes into force;

"Commonwealth" or **"Commonwealth of Nations"** means the association of countries named in the schedule;

"Commonwealth and Dependent Territories" means the several Commonwealth countries and their colonies, possessions, dependencies, protectorates, protected states, condominiums and trust territories;

"contiguous zone",

(a) in relation to Canada, means the contiguous zone of Canada as determined under the *Oceans Act*, and

(b) in relation to any other state, means the contiguous zone of the other state as determined in accordance with international law and the domestic laws of that other state;

"continental shelf",

(a) in relation to Canada, means the continental shelf of Canada as determined under the *Oceans Act*, and

(b) in relation to any other state, means the continental shelf of the other state as determined in accordance with international law and the domestic laws of that other state;

"contravene" includes fail to comply with;

"corporation" does not include a partnership that is considered to be a separate legal entity under provincial law;

"county" includes two or more counties united for purposes to which the enactment relates;

"county court" [Repealed 1990, c. 17, s. 26.]

"diplomatic or consular officer" includes an ambassador, envoy, minister, chargé d'affaires, counsellor, secretary, attaché, consul-general, consul, vice-consul, proconsul, consular agent, acting consul-general, acting consul, acting vice-consul, acting consular agent, high commissioner, permanent delegate, adviser, acting high commissioner, and acting permanent delegate;

"exclusive economic zone",

(a) in relation to Canada, means the exclusive economic zone of Canada as determined under the *Oceans Act* and includes the seabed and subsoil below that zone, and

(b) in relation to any other state, means the exclusive economic zone of the other state as determined in accordance with international law and the domestic laws of that other state;

"Federal Court" [Repealed 2002, c. 8, s. 151(1).]

"Federal Court — Appeal Division" or **"Federal Court of Appeal"** [Repealed 2002, c. 8, s. 151(1).]

"Federal Court — Trial Division" [Repealed 2002, c. 8, s. 151(1).]

"Governor", **"Governor General"**, or **"Governor of Canada"** means the Governor General of Canada, or other chief executive officer or administrator carrying on the Government of Canada on behalf and in the name of the Sovereign, by whatever title that officer is designated;

"Governor General in Council", or **"Governor in Council"** means the Governor General of Canada acting by and with the advice of, or by and with the advice and consent of, or in conjunction with the Queen's Privy Council for Canada;

"Great Seal" means the Great Seal of Canada;

"Her Majesty", **"His Majesty"**, **"the Queen"**, **"the King"** or **"the Crown"** means the Sovereign of the United Kingdom, Canada and Her or His other Realms and Territories, and Head of the Commonwealth;

"Her Majesty's Realms and Territories" or **"His Majesty's Realms and Territories"** means all realms and territories under the sovereignty of Her or His Majesty;

"herein" used in any section shall be understood to relate to the whole enactment, and not to that section only;

"holiday" means any of the following days, namely, Sunday; New Year's Day; Good Friday; Easter Monday; Christmas Day; the birthday or the day fixed by proclamation for the celebration of the birthday of the reigning Sovereign; Victoria Day; Canada Day; the first Monday in September, designated Labour Day; Remembrance Day; any day appointed by proclamation to be observed as a day of general prayer or mourning or day of public rejoicing or thanksgiving; and any of the following additional days, namely:

(a) in any province, any day appointed by proclamation of the lieutenant governor of the province to be observed as a public holiday or as a day of general prayer or mourning or day of public rejoicing or thanksgiving within the province, and any day that is a non-juridical day by virtue of an Act of the legislature of the province, and

(b) in any city, town, municipality or other organized district, any day appointed to be observed as a civic holiday by resolution of the council or other authority charged with the administration of the civic or municipal affairs of the city, town, municipality or district;

"internal waters",

(a) in relation to Canada, means the internal waters of Canada as determined under the *Oceans Act* and includes the airspace above and the bed and subsoil below those waters, and

(b) in relation to any other state, means the waters on the landward side of the baselines of the territorial sea of the other state;

"legislative assembly", **"legislative council"** or **"legislature"** [Repealed 2014, c. 2, s. 14(1).]

"legislative assembly" or **"legislature"** includes the Lieutenant Governor in Council and the Legislative Assembly of the Northwest Territories, as constituted before September 1, 1905, and the Legislature of Yukon, of the Northwest Territories or for Nunavut;

"lieutenant governor" means the lieutenant governor or other chief executive officer or administrator carrying on the government of the province indicated by the enactment, by whatever title that officer is designated, and in Yukon, the Northwest Territories and Nunavut means the Commissioner;

"lieutenant governor in council" means

(a) the lieutenant governor of the province indicated by the enactment acting by and with the advice of, by and with the advice and consent of, or in conjunction with, the executive council,

(b) in Yukon, the Commissioner of Yukon acting with the consent of the Executive Council of Yukon,

(c) in the Northwest Territories, the Commissioner of the Northwest Territories acting with the consent of the Executive Council of the Northwest Territories, and

(d) in Nunavut, the Commissioner;

"local time", in relation to any place, means the time observed in that place for the regulation of business hours;

"military" shall be construed as relating to all or any part of the Canadian Forces;

"month" means a calendar month;

"oath" includes a solemn affirmation or declaration when the context applies to any person by whom and to any case in which a solemn affirmation or declaration may be made instead of an oath, and in the same cases the expression **"sworn"** includes the expression "affirmed" or "declared";

"Parliament" means the Parliament of Canada;

"person" or any word or expression descriptive of a person, includes a corporation;

"proclamation" means a proclamation under the Great Seal;

"province" means a province of Canada, and includes Yukon, the Northwest Territories and Nunavut;

"radio" or **"radiocommunication"** means any transmission, emission or reception of signs, signals, writing, images, sounds or intelligence of any nature by means of electromagnetic waves of frequencies lower than 3,000 GHz propagated in space without artificial guide;

"regular force" means the component of the Canadian Forces that is referred to in the *National Defence Act* as the regular force;

"reserve force" means the component of the Canadian Forces that is referred to in the *National Defence Act* as the reserve force;

"security" means sufficient security, and **"sureties"** means sufficient sureties, and when those words are used one person is sufficient therefor, unless otherwise expressly required;

"standard time", except as otherwise provided by any proclamation of the Governor in Council that may be issued for the purposes of this definition in relation to any province or territory or any part thereof, means

(a) in relation to the Province of Newfoundland and Labrador, Newfoundland standard time, being three hours and thirty minutes behind Greenwich time,

(b) in relation to the Provinces of Nova Scotia, New Brunswick and Prince Edward Island, that part of the Province of Quebec lying east of the sixty-third meridian of west longitude, and that part of Nunavut lying east of the sixty-eighth meridian of west longitude, Atlantic standard time, being four hours behind Greenwich time,

(c) in relation to that part of the Province of Quebec lying west of the sixty-third meridian of west longitude, that part of the Province of Ontario lying between the sixty-eighth and the ninetieth meridians of west longitude, Southampton Island and the islands adjacent to Southampton Island, and that part of Nunavut lying between the sixty-eighth and the eighty-fifth meridians of west longitude, eastern standard time, being five hours behind Greenwich time,

(d) in relation to that part of the Province of Ontario lying west of the ninetieth meridian of west longitude, the Province of Manitoba, and that part of Nunavut, except Southampton Island and the islands adjacent to Southampton Island, lying between the eighty-fifth and the one hundred and second meridians of west longitude, central standard time, being six hours behind Greenwich time,

(e) in relation to the Provinces of Saskatchewan and Alberta, the Northwest Territories and that part of Nunavut lying west of the one hundred and second meridian of west longitude, mountain standard time, being seven hours behind Greenwich time,

[Editor's Note: Pursuant to a proclamation of the Governor in Council issued May 2, 2001, for the purpose of the definition of "standard time" in s. 35(1), "standard time", as applied to Nunavut, means:

> *(a) in relation to that part of Nunavut that is east of the 85th meridian of west longitude, and in Southampton Island and the islands adjacent to Southampton Island, Eastern Standard Time, being five hours behind Greenwich time;*
>
> *(b) in relation to that part of Nunavut that is between the 85th meridian of west longitude and the 102nd meridian of west longitude, except Southampton Island and the islands adjacent to Southampton Island and all areas lying within the Kitikmeot Region, Central Standard Time, being six hours behind Greenwich time;*
>
> *and*
>
> *(c) in relation to that part of Nunavut that is west of the 102nd meridian of west longitude, and all areas lying within the Kitikmeot Region, Mountain Standard Time, being seven hours behind Greenwich time.*

see *SOR/2001-182.]*

(f) in relation to the Province of British Columbia, Pacific standard time, being eight hours behind Greenwich time, and

(g) in relation to Yukon, Yukon standard time, being nine hours behind Greenwich time;

"statutory declaration" means a solemn declaration made pursuant to section 41 of the *Canada Evidence Act*;

"superior court" means

(a) in the Province of Newfoundland and Labrador, the Supreme Court,

(a.1) in the Province of Ontario, the Court of Appeal for Ontario and the Superior Court of Justice

(b) in the Province of Quebec, the Court of Appeal, and the Superior Court in and for the Province,

(c) in the Province of New Brunswick, Manitoba, Saskatchewan or Alberta, the Court of Appeal for the Province and the Court of Queen's Bench for the Province,

(d) in the Provinces of Nova Scotia, British Columbia and Prince Edward Island, the Court of Appeal and the Supreme Court of the Province, and

(e) the Supreme Court of Yukon, the Supreme Court of the Northwest Territories and the Nunavut Court of Justice,

and includes the Supreme Court of Canada, the Federal Court of Appeal, the Federal Court and the Tax Court of Canada;

"telecommunication" means the emission, transmission or reception of signs, signals, writing, images, sounds or intelligence of any nature by any wire, cable, radio, optical or other electromagnetic system, or by any similar technical system;

"territorial sea",

(a) in relation to Canada, means the territorial sea of Canada as determined under the *Oceans Act* and includes the airspace above and the seabed and subsoil below that sea, and

(b) in relation to any other state, means the territorial sea of the other state as determined in accordance with international law and the domestic laws of that other state;

"territory" means Yukon, the Northwest Territories and Nunavut;

"two justices" means two or more justices of the peace, assembled or acting together;

"United Kingdom" means the United Kingdom of Great Britain and Northern Ireland;

"United States" means the United States of America;

"writing", or any term of like import, includes words printed, typewritten, painted, engraved, lithographed, photographed, or represented or reproduced by any mode of representing or reproducing words in visible form.

(2) **Governor in Council may amend schedule** — The Governor in Council may, by order, amend the schedule by adding thereto the name of any country recognized by the order to be a member of the Commonwealth or deleting therefrom

the name of any country recognized by the order to be no longer a member of the Commonwealth.

R.S.C. 1985, c. 11 (1st Supp.), s. 2 (Sched., item 2); R.S.C. 1985, c. 27 (2nd Supp.), s. 10 (Sched., item 14); 1990, c. 17, s. 26; 1992, c. 1, s. 91; 1992, c. 47, s. 79; 1992, c. 51, s. 56; 1993, c. 28, s. 78 (Sched. III, item 82) [Amended 1998, c. 15, s. 28; 1999, c. 3, s. 12 (Sched., item 18).]; 1993, c. 38, s. 87; 1995, c. 39, s. 174; 1996, c. 31, s. 87; 1998, c. 30, s. 15(i); 1999, c. 3, s. 71; 1999, c. 28, s. 168; 2002, c. 7, s. 188; 2002, c. 8, s. 151; 2014, c. 2, s. 14; 2015, c. 3, s. 124

36. Construction of "telegraph" — The expression "telegraph" and its derivatives, in an enactment or in an Act of the legislature of any province enacted before that province became part of Canada on any subject that is within the legislative powers of Parliament, are deemed not to include the word "telephone" or its derivatives.

37. (1) Construction of "year" — The expression **"year"** means any period of twelve consecutive months, except that a reference

(a) to a "calendar year" means a period of twelve consecutive months commencing on January 1;

(b) to a "financial year" or "fiscal year" means, in relation to money provided by Parliament, or the Consolidated Revenue Fund, or the accounts, taxes or finances of Canada, the period beginning on April 1 in one calendar year and ending on March 31 in the next calendar year; and

(c) by number to a Dominical year means the period of twelve consecutive months commencing on January 1 of that Dominical year.

(2) Governor in Council may define year — Where in an enactment relating to the affairs of Parliament or the Government of Canada there is a reference to a period of a year without anything in the context to indicate beyond doubt whether a financial or fiscal year, any period of twelve consecutive months or a period of twelve consecutive months commencing on January 1 is intended, the Governor in Council may prescribe which of those periods of twelve consecutive months shall constitute a year for the purposes of the enactment.

38. Common names — The name commonly applied to any country, place, body, corporation, society, officer, functionary, person, party or thing means the country, place, body, corporation, society, officer, functionary, person, party or thing to which the name is commonly applied, although the name is not the formal or extended designation thereof.

39. (1) Affirmative and negative resolutions — In every Act,

(a) the expression "subject to affirmative resolution of Parliament", when used in relation to any regulation, means that the regulation shall be laid before Parliament within fifteen days after it is made or, if Parliament is not then sitting, on any of the first fifteen days next thereafter that Parliament is sitting and shall not come into force unless and until it is affirmed by a resolution of both Houses of Parliament introduced and passed in accordance with the rules of those Houses;

(b) the expression "subject to affirmative resolution of the House of Commons", when used in relation to any regulation, means that the regulation shall be laid before the House of Commons within fifteen days after it is made or, if the House is not then sitting, on any of the first fifteen days next thereafter that the House is sitting and shall not come into force unless and until it is affirmed by a resolution of the House of Commons introduced and passed in accordance with the rules of that House;

(c) the expression "subject to negative resolution of Parliament", when used in relation to any regulation, means that the regulation shall be laid before Parliament within fifteen days after it is made or, if Parliament is not then sitting, on any of the first fifteen days next thereafter that Parliament is sitting and may be annulled by a resolution of both Houses of Parliament introduced and passed in accordance with the rules of those Houses; and

(d) the expression "subject to negative resolution of the House of Commons", when used in relation to any regulation, means that the regulation shall be laid before the House of Commons within fifteen days after it is made or, if the House is not then sitting, on any of the first fifteen days next thereafter that the House is sitting and may be annulled by a resolution of the House of Commons introduced and passed in accordance with the rules of that House.

(2) **Effect of negative resolution** — Where a regulation is annulled by a resolution of Parliament or of the House of Commons, it is deemed to have been revoked on the day the resolution is passed and any law that was revoked or amended by the making of that regulation is deemed to be revived on the day the resolution is passed but the validity of any action taken or not taken in compliance with a regulation so deemed to have been revoked shall not be affected by the resolution.

References and Citations

40. (1) **Citation of enactment** — In an enactment or document,

(a) an Act may be cited by reference to its chapter number in the Revised Statutes, by reference to its chapter number in the volume of Acts for the year or regnal year in which it was enacted or by reference to its long title or short title, with or without reference to its chapter number; and

(b) a regulation may be cited by reference to its long title or short title, by reference to the Act under which it was made or by reference to the number or designation under which it was registered by the Clerk of the Privy Council.

(2) **Citation includes amendment** — A citation of or reference to an enactment is deemed to be a citation of or reference to the enactment as amended.

41. (1) **Reference to two or more parts, etc** — A reference in an enactment by number or letter to two or more parts, divisions, sections, subsections, paragraphs, subparagraphs, clauses, subclauses, schedules, appendices or forms shall be read as including the number or letter first mentioned and the number or letter last mentioned.

(2) **Reference in enactments to parts, etc** — A reference in an enactment to a part, division, section, schedule, appendix or form shall be read as a reference to a part, division, section, schedule, appendix or form of the enactment in which the reference occurs.

(3) **Reference in enactment to subsections, etc** — A reference in an enactment to a subsection, paragraph, subparagraph, clause or subclause shall be read as a reference to a subsection, paragraph, subparagraph, clause or subclause of the section, subsection, paragraph, subparagraph or clause, as the case may be, in which the reference occurs.

(4) **Reference to regulations** — A reference in an enactment to regulations shall be read as a reference to regulations made under the enactment in which the reference occurs.

(5) **Reference to another enactment** — A reference in an enactment by number or letter to any section, subsection, paragraph, subparagraph, clause, subclause or other division or line of another enactment shall be read as a reference to the section, subsection, paragraph, subparagraph, clause, subclause or other division or line of such other enactment as printed by authority of law.

Repeal and Amendment

42. (1) **Power of repeal or amendment reserved** — Every Act shall be construed as to reserve to Parliament the power of repealing or amending it, and of revoking, restricting or modifying any power, privilege or advantage thereby vested in or granted to any person.

(2) **Amendment or repeal at same session** — An Act may be amended or repealed by an Act passed in the same session of Parliament.

(3) **Amendment part of enactment** — An amending enactment, as far as consistent with the tenor thereof, shall be construed as part of the enactment that it amends.

43. Effect of repeal — Where an enactment is repealed in whole or in part, the repeal does not

(a) revive any enactment or anything not in force or existing at the time when the repeal takes effect,

(b) affect the previous operation of the enactment so repealed or anything duly done or suffered thereunder,

(c) affect any right, privilege, obligation or liability acquired, accrued, accruing or incurred under the enactment so repealed,

(d) affect any offence committed against or contravention of the provisions of the enactment so repealed, or any punishment, penalty or forfeiture incurred under the enactment so repealed, or

(e) affect any investigation, legal proceeding or remedy in respect of any right, privilege, obligation, or liability, referred to in paragraph (*c*) or in respect of any punishment, penalty or forfeiture or referred to in paragraph (*d*), and an investigation, legal proceeding or remedy as described in paragraph (*e*) may be instituted, continued or enforced, and the punishment, penalty or forefeiture may be imposed as if the enactment had not been so repealed.

44. Repeal and substitution — Where an enactment, in this section called the "former enactment", is repealed and another enactment, in this section called the "new enactment", is substituted therefor,

(a) every person acting under the former enactment shall continue to act, as if appointed under the new enactment, until another person is appointed in the stead of that person;

(b) every bond and security given by a person appointed under the former enactment remains in force, and all books, papers, forms and things made or used under the former enactment shall continue to be used as before the repeal in so far as they are consistent with the new enactment;

(c) every proceeding taken under the former enactment shall be taken up and continued under and in conformity with the new enactment in so far as it may be done consistently with the new enactment;

(d) the procedure established by the new enactment shall be followed as far as it can be adapted thereto

(i) in the recovery or enforcement of fines, penalties and forfeitures imposed under the former enactment,

(ii) in the enforcement of rights, existing or accruing under the former enactment, and

(iii) in a proceeding in relation to matters that have happened before the repeal;

(e) when any punishment, penalty or forfeiture is reduced or mitigated by the new enactment, the punishment, penalty or forfeiture if imposed or adjudged after the repeal shall be reduced or mitigated accordingly;

(f) except to the extent that the provisions of the new enactment are not in substance the same as those of the former enactment, the new enactment shall not be held to operate as new law, but shall be construed and have effect as a consolidation and as declaratory of the law as contained in the former enactment;

(g) all regulations made under the repealed enactment remain in force and are deemed to have been made under the new enactment, in so far as they are not inconsistent with the new enactment, until they are repealed or others made in their stead; and

(h) any reference in an unrepealed enactment to the former enactment shall, with respect to a subsequent transaction, matter or thing, be read and construed as a reference to the provisions of the new enactment relating to the same subject-matter as the former enactment, but where there are no provisions in the new enactment relating to the same subject-matter, the former enactment shall be read as unrepealed in so far as is necessary to maintain or give effect to the unrepealed enactment.

45. (1) Repeal does not imply enactment was in force — The repeal of an enactment in whole or in part shall not be deemed to be or to involve a declaration that the enactment was previously in force or was considered by Parliament or other body or person by whom the enactment was enacted to have been previously in force.

(2) Amendment does not imply change in law — The amendment of an enactment shall not be deemed to be or to involve a declaration that the law under that enactment was or was considered by Parliament or other body or person by whom the enactment was enacted to have been different from the law as it is under the enactment as amended.

(3) Repeal does not declare previous law — The repeal or amendment of an enactment in whole or in part shall not be deemed to be or to involve any declaration as to the previous state of the law.

(4) Judicial construction not adopted — A re-enactment, revision, consolidation or amendment of an enactment shall not be deemed to be or to involve an adoption of the construction that has by judicial decision or otherwise been placed on the language used in the enactment or on similar language.

DEMISE OF CROWN

46. (1) Effect of demise — Where there is a demise of the Crown,

(a) the demise does not affect the holding of any office under the Crown in right of Canada; and

(b) it is not necessary by reason of the demise that the holder of any such office again be appointed thereto or, having taken an oath of office or allegiance before the demise, again take that oath.

(2) Continuation of proceedings — No writ, action or other process or proceeding, civil or criminal, in or issuing out of any court established by an Act of the Parliament of Canada is, by reason of a demise of the Crown, determined, abated, discontinued or affected, but every such writ, action, process or proceeding remains in full force and may be enforced, carried on or otherwise proceeded with or completed as though there had been no such demise.

SCHEDULE

(Section 35)

Antigua and Barbuda
Australia
The Bahamas
Bangladesh
Barbados
Belize
Botswana
Brunei Darussalem

Canada
Cyprus
Dominica
Fiji
Gambia
Ghana
Grenada
Guyana
India
Jamaica
Kenya
Kiribati
Lesotho
Malawi
Malaysia
Maldives
Malta
Mauritius
Nauru
New Zealand
Nigeria
Pakistan
Papua New Guinea
St. Christopher and Nevis
St. Lucia
St. Vincent and the Grenadines
Seychelles
Sierra Leone
Singapore
Solomon Islands
South Africa
Sri Lanka
Swaziland
Tanzania
Tonga
Trinidad and Tobago
Tuvalu
Uganda
United Kingdom
Vanuatu
Western Samoa
Zambia
Zimbabwe

SOR/86-532; SOR/93-140; SOR/95-366

An Act Respecting the Mandatory Reporting of Internet Child Pornography by Persons Who Provide an Internet Service

S.C. 2011, c. 4

Her Majesty, by and with the advice and consent of the Senate and House of Commons of Canada, enacts as follows:

Interpretation

1. (1) Definitions — The following definitions apply in this Act.

"child pornography" has the same meaning as in subsection 163.1(1) of the *Criminal Code*. *("pornographie juvénile")*

"child pornography offence" means an offence under any of the following provisions of the *Criminal Code*:

(a) subsection 163.1(2) (making child pornography);

(b) subsection 163.1(3) (distribution, etc., of child pornography);

(c) subsection 163.1(4) (possession of child pornography); or

(d) subsection 163.1(4.1) (accessing child pornography).

("infraction relative à la pornographie juvénile")

"computer data" means representations, including signs, signals or symbols, that are in a form suitable for processing in a computer system. *("données informatiques")*

"Internet Service" means a service providing Internet access, Internet content hosting or electronic mail. *("services Internet")*

"person" means an individual, a corporation, a partnership or an unincorporated association or organization. *("personne")*

(2) Description with cross-reference — The descriptive words in parentheses that follow the reference to a provision of the *Criminal Code* in the definition "child pornography offence" in subsection (1) do not form part of that definition but are inserted for convenience of reference only.

Duties

2. Duty to report Internet address — If a person is advised, in the course of providing an Internet service to the public, of an Internet Protocol address or a Uniform Resource Locator where child pornography may be available to the public, the person must report that address or Uniform Resource Locator to the organization designated by the regulations, as soon as feasible and in accordance with the regulations.

3. Duty to notify police officer — If a person who provides an Internet service to the public has reasonable grounds to believe that their Internet service is being or has been used to commit a child pornography offence, the person must notify an officer, constable or other person employed for the preservation and maintenance of the public peace of that fact, as soon as feasible and in accordance with the regulations.

4. (1) Preservation of computer data — A person who makes a notification under section 3 must preserve all computer data related to the notification that is in their possession or control for 21 days after the day on which the notification is made.

(2) Destruction of preserved computer data — The person must destroy the computer data that would not be retained in the ordinary course of business and any document that is prepared for the purpose of preserving computer data under subsection (1) as soon as feasible after the expiry of the 21-day period, unless the person is required to preserve the computer data by a judicial order made under any other Act of Parliament or the legislature of a province.

5. No disclosure — A person must not disclose that they have made a report under section 2 or a notification under section 3, or disclose the contents of a report or notification, if the disclosure could prejudice a criminal investigation, whether or not a criminal investigation has begun.

6. No seeking out of child pornography — Nothing in this Act requires or authorizes a person to seek out child pornography.

7. Immunity — A civil proceeding cannot be commenced against a person for making a report in good faith under section 2 or for making a notification in good faith under section 3.

8. Self-incrimination — For greater certainty, nothing in this Act affects any right of a person to be protected against self-incrimination.

9. Provincial or foreign jurisdiction — A person who has reported information in compliance with an obligation to report child pornography under the laws of a province or a foreign jurisdiction is deemed to have complied with section 2 of this Act in relation to that information.

OFFENCES AND PUNISHMENT

10. Offence — Every person who knowingly contravenes any of sections 2 to 5 is guilty of an offence and liable on summary conviction,

(a) in the case of an individual,

(i) for a first offence, to a fine of not more than $1,000,

(ii) for a second offence, to a fine of not more than $5,000, and

(iii) for each subsequent offence, to a fine of not more than $10,000 or to imprisonment for a term of not more than six months, or to both; and

(b) in all other cases,

(i) for a first offence, to a fine of not more than $10,000,

(ii) for a second offence, to a fine of not more than $50,000, and

(iii) for each subsequent offence, to a fine of not more than $100,000.

11. Limitation period — A prosecution for an offence under this Act cannot be commenced more than two years after the time when the act or omission giving rise to the prosecution occurred.

REGULATIONS

12. Regulations — The Governor in Council may make regulations

(a) designating an organization for the purpose of section 2;

(b) respecting the role, functions and activities of the designated organization in relation to information received under this Act, including any security measures to be taken;

(c) respecting the making of a report under section 2;

(d) respecting a notification under section 3;

(e) respecting security measures to be taken in relation to computer data preserved under section 4; and

(f) generally, for carrying out the purposes and provisions of this Act.

COMING INTO FORCE

13. Order in council — This Act comes into force on a day to be fixed by order of the Governor in Council.

CAN. REG. 2011-292 — INTERNET CHILD PORNOGRAPHY REPORTING REGULATIONS

made under An Act respecting the mandatory reporting of Internet child pornography by persons who provide an Internet service

SOR/2011-292, as am. SOR/2018-254, ss. 3 (Fr.), 4(1), (2) (Fr.), (3).

INTERPRETATION

1. Definitions — The following definitions apply in these Regulations.

"Act" means *An Act respecting the mandatory reporting of Internet child pornography by persons who provide an Internet service. (""Loi"")*

"designated organization" means the organization named in section 2. *("organisme désigné")*

"Internet address" means an Internet Protocol address or a Uniform Resource Locator. *("adresse Internet")*

"service provider" means a person who provides an Internet service to the public. *("fournisseur de services")*

DESIGNATED ORGANIZATION

2. Designation of organization — For the purpose of section 2 of the Act, the designated organization is the Canadian Centre for Child Protection.

ROLE, FUNCTIONS AND ACTIVITIES OF DESIGNATED ORGANIZATION

3. Online Internet address reporting system — The designated organization must, for the purpose of receiving reports of Internet addresses under section 2 of the Act, maintain a secure online system that

(a) assigns each service provider a unique identifier for the purpose of making reports;

(b) allows a service provider to report only Internet addresses; and

(c) issues to a service provider, for each report they make, a receipt that indicates the incident number assigned to the report, the service provider's name and unique identifier and the date and time of the report.

4. Analysis and communication of findings — As soon as feasible after receiving a report under section 2 of the Act, the designated organization must determine whether any material found at the reported Internet address appears to constitute child pornography and, if so,

(a) determine, if possible, the geographic location of the server that the reported Internet address points to and the geographic location of the server hosting the material that appears to constitute child pornography; and

(b) make available to every appropriate Canadian law enforcement agency by secure means

(i) the reported Internet address,

(ii) a description of any geographic location that the designated organization was able to determine under paragraph (a), and

(iii) any other information in the designated organization's possession that might assist the agency's investigation.

5. Retention of records — For each report received in accordance with section 2 of the Act, the designated organization must retain the reported Internet address and a copy of the receipt issued under paragraph 3(c) for two years after the day on which the report is received.

6. Security measures — The designated organization must take measures to

(a) ensure its continued ability to discharge its role, functions and activities under the Act, including measures relating to the protection of its physical facilities and technical infrastructure, risk prevention and mitigation, emergency management and service resumption;

(b) protect from unauthorized access any information obtained or generated by the designated organization in the course of discharging its role, functions or activities under the Act; and

(c) ensure that its personnel are capable of fulfilling their duties in the discharge of the designated organization's role, functions and activities under the Act, including measures relating to their selection and training.

SOR/2018-254, s. 4(1), (3)

7. Incident: notification of Ministers — The designated organization must notify the Minister of Justice and the Minister of Public Safety and Emergency Preparedness within 24 hours of becoming aware of any incident that jeopardizes the designated organization's ability to discharge its role, functions or activities under the Act.

8. Conflict of interest — The designated organization must take any measures necessary to avoid a conflict of interest in respect of its role, functions and activities under the Act, and must address any such conflict that does arise.

9. Annual report — The designated organization must, not later than June 30 of each year, submit to the Minister of Justice and the Minister of Public Safety and Emergency Preparedness a report on the discharge of its role, functions and activities under the Act for the 12-month period beginning on April 1 of the preceding year. The report must include

(a) the number of reports received under section 2 of the Act and, of those, the number that led the designated organization to make information available to a law enforcement agency under paragraph 4(b);

(b) a description of the measures that the designated organization had in place in accordance with section 6;

(c) a description of any incident referred to in section 7 that occurred and the steps taken in response to the incident;

(d) a description of the measures that the designated organization had in place in accordance with section 8, any conflict of interest that arose and the steps taken to address it; and

(e) any other information that may affect the designated organization's current or future ability to discharge its role, functions or activities under the Act.

Obligations of Service Providers

10. Method of reporting — For the purpose of section 2 of the Act, an Internet address must be reported by a service provider using the online system referred to in section 3.

11. Form and content of notification — For the purpose of section 3 of the Act, a notification from a service provider must be in writing and must include the following information:

(a) the child pornography offence that the service provider has reasonable grounds to believe is being or has been committed using their Internet service;

(b) a description of the material that appears to constitute child pornography, including its format;

(c) the circumstances under which the service provider discovered the alleged offence, including the date and time of discovery;

(d) a description of any other evidence relating to the alleged offence in the possession or control of the service provider; and

(e) contact information of the service provider's representative for the purpose of investigating the matter.

12. Security measures for preserved data — A service provider that is required to preserve computer data under section 4 of the Act must retain a copy of that data in a secure offline location.

Coming Into Force

13. S.C. 2011, c. 4 — These Regulations come into force on the day on which *An Act respecting the mandatory reporting of Internet child pornography by persons who provide an Internet service* comes into force, but if they are registered after that day, they come into force on the day on which they are registered.

MOTOR VEHICLE TRANSPORT ACT

Editor's note: Current to May 15, 2019.

TABLE OF CONCORDANCE

R.S.C. 1970, c. M-14	R.S.C. 1985, c. M-12	R.S.C. 1985, c. 29 (3d Supp.)
1	1	
2	2	
—	—	3
3	3	4
—	—	5
4	4	6
—	—	7
—	—	8
—	—	9
—	—	10
—	—	11
—	—	12
—	—	13
—	—	14
—	—	15
5	6	16
6	5	18
—	—	19
—	—	20
—	—	21
—	—	22
—	—	23
—	—	24
—	—	25
—	—	26
—	—	27
—	—	28
—	—	29
—	—	30
—	—	31

—	—	32
—	—	33
—	—	34
—	—	35

Motor Vehicle Transport Act

An Act respecting motor vehicle transport by extra-provincial undertakings

R.S.C. 1985, c. 29 (3rd Supp.), as am. S.C. 1992, c. 1, s. 143 (Sched. VI, item 18); 1995, c. 5, s. 25(1)(u); 1996, c. 17, s. 19; 2001, c. 4, s. 100; 2001, c. 13, ss. 1–9.

[Note: The title of this Act was changed from "Motor Vehicle Transport Act, 1987" to "Motor Vehicle Transport Act" by 2001, c. 13, s. 1.]

Short Title

1. Short title — This Act may be cited as the *Motor Vehicle Transport Act.*

2001, c. 13, s. 1

Interpretation

2. (1) Definitions — In this Act,

"extra-provincial bus transport" means the transport of passengers or passengers and goods by means of an extra-provincial bus undertaking;

"extra-provincial bus undertaking" means a work or undertaking for the transport of passengers or passengers and goods by a bus, connecting a province with any other or others of the provinces, or extending beyond the limits of a province.

"extra-provincial motor carrier undertaking" means an extra-provincial bus undertaking or an extra-provincial truck undertaking;

"extra-provincial truck transport" [Repealed 2001, c. 13, s. 2(1).]

"extra-provincial truck undertaking" means a work or undertaking for the transport of goods by a motor vehicle other than a bus, connecting a province with any other or others of the province, or extending beyond the limits of a province;

"law of a province" means a law of a province or municipality that provides for the control or regulation of the operation in the province or municipality of local bus undertakings or local truck undertakings;

"local bus transport" means the transport of passengers or passengers and goods by means of a local bus undertaking;

"local bus undertaking" means a work or undertaking for the transport of passengers or passengers and goods by a bus, not being an extra-provincial bus undertaking;

"local truck transport" [Repealed 2001, c. 13, s. 2(1).]

"local truck undertaking" [Repealed 2001, c. 13, s. 2(1).]

"Minister" means the Minister of Transport;

"prescribed" [Repealed 2001, c. 13, s. 2(2).]

"provincial authority" means a person or body that has, under the law of a province, authority to control or regulate motor carrier undertakings that operate exclusively in the province.

"provincial transport board" [Repealed 2001, c. 13, s. 2(1).]

(2) Interpretation — For the purposes of this Act, an extra-provincial bus undertaking or extra-provincial truck undertaking is operated in a province if it is operated into, in, across or out of the province.

2001, c. 13, s. 2

OBJECTIVES

[Heading amended 2001, c. 13, s. 3.]

3. (1) Statement of objectives — The objectives of this Act are to ensure that the National Transportation Policy set out in section 5 of the *Canada Transportation Act* is carried out with respect to extra-provincial motor carrier undertakings, and, more specifically, that

(a) the regulatory regime for those undertakings is focused on safety performance assessments based on the National Safety Code for Motor Carriers; and

(b) the operating standards that apply to those undertakings are applied consistently across Canada.

(2) Statements of policy by Governor in Council — The Governor in Council may, on the recommendation of the Minister, after consultation by the Minister with the provinces, issue transportation policy statements consistent with the objectives set out in subsection (1).

(3) Provincial authority to comply with guidelines — Provincial authorities shall, with respect to extra-provincial motor carrier undertakings, have regard to all transportation policy statements issued under subsection (2).

2001, c. 13, s. 3

3.1 Power to conduct research — The Minister may conduct any research, studies and evaluations that the Minister considers necessary to carry out the objectives of this Act.

2001, c. 13, s. 3

ARRANGEMENTS

[Heading added 2001, c. 13, s. 3.]

3.2 (1) Agreements — The Minister may, after consultation with the provinces and on the terms and conditions that the Minister may specify, enter into agreements in support of the objectives set out in section 3 with provincial governments or with other persons or bodies.

(2) International arrangements — The Minister may, after consultation with the provinces and on the terms and conditions that the Minister may specify, enter into arrangements with foreign states or agencies of those states to promote the objectives of this Act, including the recognition in Canada of documents analogous to safety fitness certificates issued by those states or agencies and the recognition by them of safety fitness certificates.

2001, c. 13, s. 3

BUS TRANSPORT

[Heading amended 2001, c. 13, s. 3.]

Operating Licences

4. Operation without licence prohibited — Where in any province a licence is, by the law of the province, required for the operation of a local bus undertaking, no person shall operate an extra-provincial bus undertaking in that province except under and in accordance with a licence issued under the authority of this Act.

2001, c. 13, s. 4

5. Issue of licence — The provincial authority in each province may, in its discretion, issue a licence to a person to operate an extra-provincial bus undertaking in the province on the like terms and conditions and in the like manner as if the extra-provincial bus undertaking were a local bus undertaking.

2001, c. 13, s. 5

Tariffs and Tolls

6. Tariffs and tolls — Where in any province tariffs and tolls for local bus transport are determined or regulated by the provincial authority, the authority may, in its discretion, determine or regulate the tariffs and tolls for extra-provincial bus transport on the like terms and conditions and in the like manner as if the extra-provincial bus transport were local bus transport.

2001, c. 13, s. 5

EXTRA-PROVINCIAL MOTOR CARRIER SAFETY

[Heading amended 2001, c. 13, s. 5.]

[Heading repealed 2001, c. 13, s. 5.]

7. (1) Operation without safety fitness certificate prohibited — Subject to the regulations, no person or body shall operate an extra-provincial motor carrier undertaking except under a safety fitness certificate issued by a provincial authority under this Act or an analogous document prescribed by the regulations.

(2) Form of certificate — A safety fitness certificate need not be in any particular form.

(3) Applicable safety laws — Laws of a province respecting the safety of motor carrier undertakings apply to an extra-provincial motor carrier undertaking to the extent that those laws are not inconsistent with this Act.

2001, c. 13, s. 5

8. (1) Issuance of safety fitness certificate — The provincial authority in each province may, subject to the regulations, issue a safety fitness certificate to a person or body to operate an extra-provincial motor carrier undertaking, and may revoke any certificate so issued.

(2) Certificate valid throughout Canada — A safety fitness certificate issued under subsection (1) is valid throughout Canada.

(3) Review of decisions with respect to safety fitness certificates — The following rules apply to the review of decisions with respect to the issuance or revocation of safety fitness certificates in a province by a provincial authority:

(a) any rules with respect to the right of review, and any proceedings governing reviews, applicable in that province in respect of such decisions; and

(b) in the absence of rules or procedures established under paragraph (a), the rules with respect to the right of review, and the procedures governing reviews, of decisions with respect to the issuance and revocation of licences of motor carrier undertakings in that province.

(4) to (6) [Repealed 2001, c. 13, s. 5.]

2001, c. 13, s. 5

9. (1) Withdrawal of power to issue safety fitness certificates — If the Minister is satisfied after consultation with the provinces that the provincial authority in a province is not issuing safety fitness certificates in accordance with this Act, the Minister may, by order, withdraw, its power to issue such certificates.

(2) Effective date of withdrawal — An order made under subsection (1) takes effect on the date of its publication in the *Canada Gazette*.

(3) Undertaking that holds a certificate — An extra-provincial motor carrier undertaking that holds a safety fitness certificate issued by a provincial authority whose power to issue certificates under this section has been withdrawn shall, not later than sixty days after publication of an order made under subsection (1), file a declaration with another provincial authority that the undertaking is subject to supervision by it.

2001, c. 4, s. 100; 2001, c. 13, s. 5

10. Reinstatement — If the Minister is satisfied that a provincial authority referred to in subsection 9(3) has remedied its default and established a plan to ensure that the default does not recur, the Minister shall, by order, revoke the order made under subsection 9(1).

2001, c. 13, s. 5

Heading and ss. 11 to 15. [Repealed 1996, c. 17, s. 19.]

EXEMPTIONS, REGULATIONS, FOREIGN CARRIERS AND OFFENCE AND PUNISHMENT

[Heading amended 2001, c. 13, s. 6.]

Exemptions

[Heading amended 2001, c. 13, s. 6.]

16. (1) Exemptions — The Minister may, after consultation with the provinces that would be affected by a proposed exemption, exempt from the application of any provision of this Act or the regulations, either generally or for a limited period or in respect of a limited area, any person, the whole or any part of any extra-provincial motor carrier undertaking or any class of those undertakings, if in the opinion of the Minister the exemption is in the public interest and is not likely to affect motor carrier safety.

(2) Terms and conditions — An exemption under subsection (1) is subject to any terms or conditions that the Minister may specify in it.

2001, c. 13, s. 6

Regulations

[Heading added 2001, c. 13, s. 6.]

16.1 (1) Regulations — The Governor in Council may, on the recommendation of the Minister made after consultation by the Minister with the provinces that would be affected by the proposed regulation, make regulations for the attainment of the objectives of this Act and, in particular, regulations

(a) prescribing classes of extra-provincial motor carrier undertakings for the purposes of this Act, or any or all regulations under this Act;

(b) respecting the criteria according to which provincial authorities may issue safety fitness certificates under section 8;

(c) prescribing analogous documents for the purpose of subsection 7(1);

(d) respecting the safe operation of extra-provincial motor carrier undertakings including regulations respecting audit, inspection, entry on premises and the provision of information;

(e) prescribing the criteria relating to the fitness of an extra-provincial motor carrier undertaking to hold a safety fitness certificate issued under section 8;

(f) prescribing the type, amount and conditions of insurance and bonding coverage required to be held by an extra-provincial motor carrier undertaking;

(g) prescribing the information that applicants, extra-provincial motor carrier undertakings and provincial authorities must provide to the Minister, to other provincial authorities or to foreign states or agencies of those states;

(h) prescribing the conditions of carriage and the limitations of liability that apply with respect to extra-provincial motor carrier undertakings; and

(i) restricting or otherwise governing the release of pollutants into the environment from the operation of vehicles operated by extra-provincial motor carrier undertakings.

(2) Incorporation by reference — A regulation made under subsection (1) may incorporate by reference all or any portion of another document, as amended from time to time, including

(a) a standard relating to the safe operation of a motor carrier undertaking; and

(b) the law of a province relating to motor vehicle undertakings.

2001, c. 13, s. 6

Foreign Carriers

17. (1) Unfair practices — If the Minister is of the opinion that a government in a foreign state has engaged in unfair, discriminatory or restrictive practices with regard to Canadian extra-provincial motor carrier undertakings that operate in that state or between that state and Canada, the Minister shall, with the concurrence of the Minister of Foreign Affairs, seek elimination of those practices through consultations with that state.

(2) Order in Council — If the consultations referred to in subsection (1) fail to result in the elimination of the practices referred to in that subsection, the Governor in Council may, on the recommendation of the Minister and the Minister of Foreign Affairs made after consultation by the Minister with the provinces that would be affected by the proposed order, notwithstanding anything in this Act or any other Act of Parliament, by order, subject to any conditions that may be specified in the order,

(a) prohibit or restrict the issuance of a safety fitness certificate under the authority of this Act to any foreign carrier, all foreign carriers or any class of foreign carrier;

(b) direct any provincial authority to suspend a safety fitness certificate issued under the authority of this Act to any foreign carrier, all foreign carriers or any class of foreign carrier; and

(c) direct any provincial authority to reinstate a safety fitness certificate suspended in accordance with a direction issued under paragraph (b).

(3) **Compliance** — A provincial authority to which an order applies shall comply it.

1995, c. 5, s. 25(1)(u); 2001, c. 13, s. 7

Offence and Punishment

18. (1) Offence — Every person who contravenes or fails to comply with any provision of this Act or any regulation or order made under this Act is guilty of an offence punishable on summary conviction.

(2) **Limitation** — Any proceedings in respect of an offence under this Act may be commenced at any time within, but not later than, twelve months after the time when the subject matter of the proceedings arose.

19. (1) Punishment re individuals — An individual who is convicted of an offence under this Act is liable to a fine not exceeding five thousand dollars.

(2) **Punishment re corporations** — A corporation that is convicted of an offence under this Act is liable to a fine not exceeding twenty-five thousand dollars.

20. Officers, etc., of corporations — Where a corporation commits an offence under this Act, every person who at the time of the commission of the offence was director or officer of the corporation is guilty of the like offence unless the act or omission constituting the offence took place without the person's knowledge or consent or the person exercised all due diligence to prevent the commission of the offence.

20.1 Venue — A prosecution under this Act may be instituted, tried and determined by a court in any territorial jurisdiction in which the accused carries on business, regardless of where the subject-matter of the prosecution arose.

2001, c. 13, s. 8

21. Disposition of fines — A fine imposed under section 19 shall be paid over by the provincial court judge or officer receiving it to the treasurer of the province in which it was imposed.

22. Proof of documents — In any proceedings for an offence under this Act, any document purporting to be certified by a provincial authority to be a true copy of any order or direction made by it is, without proof of the signature or of the official character of the person appearing to have signed the document, evidence of the original document of which it purports to be a copy.

2001, c. 13, s. 9

Transitional Provisions

[Heading amended 2001, c. 13, s. 9.]

[Heading repealed 2001, c. 13, s. 9.]

23. Deeming — If an extra-provincial motor carrier undertaking is, on the day immediately before the coming into force of this section, authorized to operate within a province, the undertaking is deemed to hold a safety fitness certificate issued under section 8.

2001, c. 13, s. 9

[Heading repealed 2001, c. 13, s. 9.]

24. (1) Pending applications — An application for a licence made under section 8, as that section read before the coming into force of this section, and pending on the day immediately before that coming into force, is deemed to have been made under section 8 of this Act.

(2) Pending applications — bus transport — Every application for a licence made under section 5 with respect to bus transport that is pending on the day immediately before the coming into force of this section, is deemed to be an application made under sections 5 and 8.

2001, c. 13, s. 9

Annual Report

[Heading amended 2001, c. 13, s. 9.]

25. (1) Report to Parliament — The Minister shall prepare an annual report and cause a copy of it to be laid before each House of Parliament on any of the first fifteen days on which that House is sitting after the Minister completes it.

(2) Content of annual report — The annual report of the Minister shall contain the following in respect of the year:

(a) the available statistical information respecting trends of highway accidents in Canada involving motor vehicles operated by extra-provincial bus undertakings and extra-provincial truck undertakings reported separately for bus undertakings and truck undertakings; and

(b) a progress report on the implementation of rules and standards respecting the safe operation of extra-provincial bus undertakings and of extra-provincial truck undertakings.

2001, c. 13, s. 9

Review of Provisions

[Heading amended 2001, c. 13, s. 9.]

26. (1) Review — The Minister shall, after the expiry of four years after the coming into force of this section and before the expiry of five years after that coming into force, undertake and complete a comprehensive review of the operation and effect of the amendments to this Act contained in *An Act to amend the Motor Vehicle Transport Act, 1987 and to make consequential amendments to other Acts* and shall, without delay, prepare a report with respect to that review.

(2) Minister to make report available — The Minister shall make the report available to the Council of Ministers Responsible for Transportation and Highway Safety at the next meeting of the council after its completion.

(3) Tabling of report — The Minister shall cause a copy of the report to be laid before each House of Parliament during the first thirty sitting days of that House following its completion.

2001, c. 13, s. 9

Headings and ss. 27 to 35. [Repealed 2001, c. 13, s. 9.]

Review of Provisions

[Heading amended 2001, c. 13, s. 9.]

26. (1) Review — The Minister shall, after the expiry of four years after the coming into force of this section and before the expiry of five years after that coming into force, undertake and complete a comprehensive review of the operation and effect of the amendments to this Act contained in *An Act to amend the Motor Vehicle Transport Act, 1987 and to make consequential amendments to other Acts* and shall, without delay, prepare a report with respect to that review.

(2) Minister to make report available — The Minister shall make the report available to the Council of Ministers Responsible for Transportation and Highway Safety at the next meeting of the council after its completion.

(3) Tabling of report — The Minister shall cause a copy of the report to be laid before each House of Parliament on any of the first thirty sitting days of that House following its completion.

2001, c. 13, s. 9

Heading and ss. 27 to 45 [Repealed 2001, c. 13, s. 9.]

Sex Offender Information Registration Act

An Act respecting the registration of information relating to sex offenders, to amend the *Criminal Code* and to make consequential amendments to other Acts

S.C. 2004, c. 10, as am. S.C. 2007, c. 5, ss. 32, 33(1), (2), (3) (Fr.), (4)–(7), 34, 35, 36(1), (2) (Fr.), (3), 37(1) (Fr.), (2), (3), 38, 39, 40(1), (2) (Fr.), 41, 42, 43(1) (Fr.), (2), 44–46, 47(1)–(4), (5) (Fr.), (6), (7), 48, 49; 2010, c. 17, ss. 28–44; 2013, c. 24, s. 130 (Fr.); 2015, c. 23, ss. 21–28; 2018, c. 11, s. 30; 2019, c. 15, s. 59 [Not in force at date of publication.].

Her Majesty, by and with the advice and consent of the Senate and House of Commons of Canada, enacts as follows:

Short Title

1. Short title — This Act may be cited as the *Sex Offender Information Registration Act.*

Purpose and Principles

2. (1) Purpose — The purpose of this Act is to help police services prevent and investigate crimes of a sexual nature by requiring the registration of certain information relating to sex offenders.

(2) Principles — This Act shall be carried out in recognition of, and in accordance with, the following principles:

(a) in the interest of protecting society through the effective prevention and investigation of crimes of a sexual nature, police services must have rapid access to certain information relating to sex offenders;

(b) the collection and registration of accurate information on an ongoing basis is the most effective way of ensuring that such information is current and reliable; and

(c) the privacy interests of sex offenders and the public interest in their rehabilitation and reintegration into the community as law-abiding citizens require that

(i) the information be collected only to enable police services to prevent or investigate crimes of a sexual nature, and

(ii) access to the information, and use and disclosure of it, be restricted.

2010, c. 17, s. 28

Interpretation

3. (1) Definitions — The following definitions apply in this Act.

"database" means the database that contains the information that is registered under this Act. *("banque de données")*

"finding of not criminally responsible on account of mental disorder" means a verdict of not criminally responsible on account of mental disorder within the meaning of subsection 672.1(1) of the *Criminal Code* or a finding of not responsible on account of mental disorder within the meaning of subsection 2(1) of the *National Defence Act*, as the case may be. *("verdict de non-responsabilité")*

"information" includes characteristics recorded and photographs taken under subsection 5(3) and fingerprints taken under subsection 9(2). *("renseignements")*

"main residence" means the place in Canada where a person lives most often or, if there is no such place, the place in Canada where they may be found most often. *("résidence principale")*

"member of a police service" includes

(a) an officer or non-commissioned member of the Canadian Forces who is appointed for the purposes of section 156 of the *National Defence Act*; and

(b) in an area in which an aboriginal police service is responsible for policing, a member of that police service.

("membre d'un service de police")

"Ontario Act" has the same meaning as in subsection 490.011(1) of the *Criminal Code*. *("loi ontarienne")*

"order" means an order under section 490.012 of the *Criminal Code* or section 227.01 of the *National Defence Act*. *("ordonnance")*

"person who collects information" means a person who is authorized to collect information under paragraph 18(1)(b) or subsection 19(1) of this Act or paragraph 227.2(c) of the *National Defence Act*. *("préposé à la collecte")*

"person who registers information" means a person who is authorized to register information under paragraph 18(1)(c) or subsection 19(1) of this Act or paragraph 227.2(d) of the *National Defence Act*. *("préposé à l'enregistrement")*

"registration centre" means a place that is designated as a registration centre under paragraph 18(1)(d) or subsection 19(1) of this Act or paragraph 227.2(e) of the *National Defence Act*. *("bureau d'inscription")*

"retained" means retained under a contract for services, whether the contract is entered into with an individual, or with their employer or another person to whom the individual provides services. *("agent contractuel")*

"secondary residence" means a place in Canada, other than a main residence, where a person regularly lives. *("résidence secondaire")*

"sex offender" means a person who is subject to an order or to an obligation under section 490.019 or 490.02901 of the *Criminal Code*, section 227.06 of the *National Defence Act* or section 36.1 of the *International Transfer of Offenders Act*. (*"délinquant sexuel"*)

"sexual offence against a child" means

(a) a designated offence as defined in subsection 490.011(1) of the *Criminal Code* that is committed against a person who is under 18 years of age and as a result of which the offender is required to comply with this Act; or

(b) an offence that is committed outside Canada against a person who is under 18 years of age and as a result of which the offender is required to comply with this Act.

(« infraction sexuelle visant un enfant »)

(2) Interpretation — For the purposes of this Act, a crime is of a sexual nature if it consists of one or more acts that

(a) are either sexual in nature or committed with the intent to commit an act or acts that are sexual in nature; and

(b) constitute an offence.

2007, c. 5, s. 32; 2010, c. 17, s. 29; 2015, c. 23, s. 21

OBLIGATIONS OF SEX OFFENDERS

4. (1) First obligation to report — A person who is subject to an order shall report to a registration centre referred to in section 7.1 within seven days — or, if they are required to report to a registration centre designated under the *National Defence Act*, within 15 days — after

(a) the order is made, if they are convicted of the offence in connection with which the order is made and

(i) they are not given a custodial sentence,

(ii) they are ordered to serve a sentence of imprisonment intermittently under subsection 732(1) of the *Criminal Code*, or

(iii) they are the subject of a conditional sentence order made under section 742.1 of the *Criminal Code*;

(b) they receive an absolute or conditional discharge under Part XX.1 of the *Criminal Code*, if they are found not criminally responsible on account of mental disorder for the offence in connection with which the order is made;

(b.1) they receive an absolute or conditional discharge or are released from custody under Division 7 of Part III of the *National Defence Act*, if they are found not criminally responsible on account of mental disorder for the offence in connection with which the order is made;

(b.2) the imprisonment or detention to which they are sentenced for the offence in connection with which the order is made is suspended under section 215 or 216 of the *National Defence Act*;

(c) they are released from custody pending the determination of an appeal relating to the offence in connection with which the order is made; or

(d) they are released from custody after serving the custodial portion of a sentence for the offence in connection with which the order is made.

(2) First obligation to report — A person who is subject to an obligation under section 490.019 or 490.02901 of the *Criminal Code*, section 227.06 of the *National Defence Act* or section 36.1 of the *International Transfer of Offenders Act* shall report to a registration centre referred to in section 7.1

(a) if they are not in custody on the day on which they become subject to the obligation, within seven days — or, if they are required to report to a registration centre designated under the *National Defence Act*, within 15 days — after that day; and

(b) in any other case, within seven days — or, if they are required to report to a registration centre designated under the *National Defence Act*, within 15 days — after

(i) they receive an absolute or conditional discharge under Part XX.1 of the *Criminal Code*,

(i.1) they receive an absolute or conditional discharge or are released from custody under Division 7 of Part III of the *National Defence Act*,

(i.2) an imprisonment or a detention to which they are sentenced is suspended under section 215 or 216 of the *National Defence Act*,

(ii) they are released from custody pending the determination of an appeal, or

(iii) they are released from custody after serving the custodial portion of a sentence.

(3) Means of reporting — If a sex offender is required to report to a registration centre designated under this Act, they shall report in person. If they are required to report to a registration centre designated under the *National Defence Act*, they shall report in person unless regulations are made under paragraph 227.2(a) of that Act, in which case they shall report in accordance with those regulations.

(4) Compliance before leaving Canada — A sex offender shall not leave Canada before they report under this section.

2007, c. 5, s. 33(1), (2), (4)–(7); 2010, c. 17, s. 30

4.1 (1) Subsequent obligation to report — A sex offender shall subsequently report to the registration centre referred to in section 7.1,

(a) within seven days after they change their main residence or any secondary residence or, if they are required to report to a registration centre designated under the *National Defence Act*, within 15 days after the change;

(b) within seven days after they change their given name or surname or, if they are required to report to a registration centre designated under the *National Defence Act*, within 15 days after the change;

(b.1) within seven days after they receive a driver's licence or, if they are required to report to a registration centre designated under the *National Defence Act*, within 15 days after they receive it;

(b.2) within seven days after they receive a passport or, if they are required to report to a registration centre designated under the *National Defence Act*, within 15 days after they receive it; and

(c) at any time between 11 months and one year after they last reported to a registration centre under this Act.

(2) Means of reporting — If a sex offender is required to report to a registration centre designated under this Act, they shall report in person or in accordance with regulations made under paragraph 18(1)(a) or subsection 19(1). If they are required to report to a registration centre designated under the *National Defence Act*, they shall report in person unless regulations are made under paragraph 227.2(a) of that Act, in which case they shall report in accordance with those regulations.

2007, c. 5, s. 34; 2010, c. 17, s. 31; 2015, c. 23, s. 22

4.2 More than one order or obligation — A person shall report on the reporting dates established under only the most recent order or obligation under section 490.019 or 490.02901 of the *Criminal Code*, section 227.06 of the *National Defence Act* or section 36.1 of the *International Transfer of Offenders Act*.

2007, c. 5, s. 35; 2010, c. 17, s. 32

4.3 (1) Temporarily outside Canada — A sex offender who is outside Canada when they are required to report under section 4.1 shall report not later than seven days after they return to Canada.

(2) Canadian Forces — Subsection (1) does not apply to a sex offender who is required to report to a registration centre designated under the *National Defence Act* while they are outside Canada.

2007, c. 5, s. 36(1), (3); 2010, c. 17, s. 33

5. (1) Obligation to provide information — When a sex offender reports to a registration centre, they shall provide the following information to a person who collects information at the registration centre:

(a) their given name and surname, and every alias that they use;

(b) their date of birth and gender;

(c) the address of their main residence and every secondary residence or, if there is no such address, the location of that place;

(d) the address of every place at which they are employed or retained or are engaged on a volunteer basis — or, if there is no address, the location of that place — the name of their employer or the person who engages them on a volunteer basis or retains them and the type of work that they do there;

(d.1) if applicable, their status as an officer or a non-commissioned member of the Canadian Forces within the meaning of subsection 2(1) of the *National Defence Act* and the address and telephone number of their unit within the meaning of that subsection;

(e) the address of every educational institution at which they are enrolled or, if there is no such address, the location of that place;

(f) a telephone number at which they may be reached, if any, for every place referred to in paragraphs (c) and (d), and the number of every mobile telephone or pager in their possession;

(g) their height and weight and a description of every physical distinguishing mark that they have;

(h) the licence plate number, make, model, body type, year of manufacture and colour of the motor vehicles that are registered in their name or that they use regularly;

(i) the licence number and the name of the issuing jurisdiction of every driver's licence that they hold; and

(j) the passport number and the name of the issuing jurisdiction of every passport that they hold.

(2) Additional information — When a sex offender reports to a registration centre, the person who collects the information from them may ask them when and where they were convicted of, or found not criminally responsible on account of mental disorder for, an offence in connection with an order or with an obligation under section 490.019 or 490.02901 of the *Criminal Code*, section 227.06 of the *National Defence Act* or section 36.1 of the *International Transfer of Offenders Act*.

(3) Additional information — When a sex offender reports to a registration centre in person, the person who collects the information referred to in subsection (1) may record any observable characteristic that may assist in identification of the sex offender, including their eye colour and hair colour, and may require that their photograph be taken.

2007, c. 5, s. 37(2), (3); 2010, c. 17, s. 34; 2015, c. 23, s. 23

5.1 Notification of change of information — paragraph 5(1)(d) — A sex offender shall, within seven days after the date of the change, notify a person who collects information at the registration centre referred to in section 7.1 of any change in the information that they have provided under paragraph 5(1)(d).

2010, c. 17, s. 35

6. (1) Notification of absence — Subject to subsection (1.1), a sex offender other than one who is referred to in subsection (1.01) shall notify a person who collects information at the registration centre referred to in section 7.1

(a) before the sex offender's departure — of the dates of their departure and return and of every address or location at which they expect to stay in Canada or outside Canada — if they expect not to be at their main residence or any of their secondary residences for a period of seven or more consecutive days;

(b) within seven days after their departure — of the date of their return and of every address or location at which they are staying in Canada or outside Canada — if they decide, after departure, not to be at their main residence or any of their secondary residences for a period of seven or more consecutive days or if they have not given a notification required under paragraph (a); and

(c) before departure or, if it is later, within seven days after the day on which the change is made — of a change in address, location or date.

(1.01) Sex offender convicted of sex offence against child — Subject to subsection (1.1), a sex offender who is convicted of a sexual offence against a child shall notify a person who collects information at the registration centre referred to in section 7.1

(a) before the sex offender's departure — of the dates of their departure and return and of every address or location at which they expect to stay in Canada — if they expect not to be at their main residence or any of their secondary residences for a period of seven or more consecutive days;

(b) before their departure, of the dates of their departure and return and of every address or location at which they expect to stay outside Canada;

(c) within seven days after their departure — of the date of their return and of every address or location at which they are staying in Canada — if they decide, after departure, not to be at their main residence or any of their secondary residences for a period of seven or more consecutive days or if they have not given a notification required under paragraph (a);

(d) without delay, after their departure — of the date of their return and of every address or location at which they are staying outside Canada — if they decide, after departure, to extend their stay beyond the date of return that they indicated in the notification they gave under paragraph (b) or if they have not given a notification under paragraph (b); and

(e) of a change in address, location or date, before their departure or

(i) if the change is made after their departure and they are staying in Canada, within seven days after the date on which the change is made, or

(ii) if the change is made after their departure and they are staying outside Canada, without delay after the date on which the change is made.

(1.1) Canadian Forces — A sex offender who is required to notify a person who collects information at a registration centre designated under the *National Defence Act* and who requests the Chief of the Defence Staff to make a determination under section 227.16 of that Act shall provide the information relating to the operation within seven days after the date of their departure unless the determination is made during that period.

(2) Means of notification — If a sex offender is required to provide notification to a registration centre designated under this Act, they shall provide the notification by registered mail or in accordance with regulations made under paragraph 18(1)(a) or subsection 19(1). If they are required to provide notification to a registration centre designated under the *National Defence Act*, they shall provide the notification by registered mail unless regulations are made under paragraph 227.2(a) of that Act, in which case they shall provide the notification in accordance with those regulations.

2007, c. 5, s. 38; 2010, c. 17, s. 36; 2015, c. 23, s. 24

7. Young sex offender — A sex offender who is under 18 years of age has the right to have an appropriate adult chosen by them in attendance when they report to a registration centre and when information is collected.

7.1 Registration centre — For the purposes of sections 4, 4.1, 4.3, 5.1 and 6, the registration centre is one that is designated under paragraph 18(1)(d) or subsection 19(1) that serves the area of the province in which the sex offender's main residence is located, unless a registration centre designated under paragraph 227.2(e) of the *National Defence Act* serves a class of persons of which the sex offender is a member or the area in which the unit of the Canadian Forces in which the sex offender is serving is located.

2007, c. 5, s. 39; 2010, c. 17, s. 37

RESPONSIBILITIES OF PERSONS WHO COLLECT AND REGISTER INFORMATION

8. Registration of information — When a police service or the Commissioner of the Royal Canadian Mounted Police receives a copy of an order sent in accordance with paragraph 490.018(1)(d) of the *Criminal Code*, either a person who registers information for the police service or one who registers it for the Commissioner shall

(a) register without delay in the database only the name of the police service and the following information relating to the person who is subject to the order:

(i) their given name and surname,

(ii) the number that identifies a record of fingerprints collected from them under the *Identification of Criminals Act*, if such a record exists,

(iii) every offence to which the order relates,

(iv) when and where the offence or offences were committed,

(v) when and where the person was convicted of, or found not criminally responsible on account of mental disorder for, the offence or offences,

(vi) the age and gender of every victim of the offence or offences, and the victim's relationship to the person,

(vi.1) the person's method of operation in relation to the offence or offences, if that information is available to the person who registers information,

(vii) the date and duration of the order, and

(viii) the court that made the order; and

(b) ensure that the registration of the information is done in a manner and in circumstances that ensure its confidentiality.

2007, c. 5, s. 40(1); 2010, c. 17, s. 38

8.1 (1) Registration of information — obligations — When the Attorney General of a province, or the minister of justice of a territory, receives a copy of an affidavit and a notice sent in accordance with subsection 490.021(6) or 490.02903(3) of the *Criminal Code* — or receives a copy of the Form 1 delivered under subparagraph 8(4)(a)(ii) of the *International Transfer of Offenders Act* — a person who registers information for the Attorney General, or the minister of justice, shall register without delay in the database only the following information, as applicable, relating to the person named in the notice or Form 1, as the case may be:

(a) their given name and surname;

(b) the number that identifies a record of fingerprints collected from them under the *Identification of Criminals Act*, if such a record exists;

(c) the date on which the notice was served;

(d) every offence listed in the notice or form;

(e) when and where the offence or offences were committed;

(f) when and where the person was convicted of, or found not criminally responsible on account of mental disorder for, the offence or offences;

(g) the age and gender of every victim of the offence or offences, and the victim's relationship to the person;

(g.1) the person's method of operation in relation to the offence or offences, if that information is available to the person who registers information;

(h) the expected duration of the obligation; and

(i) in the case of a person referred to in paragraph 490.02(1)(b) of the *Criminal Code*, the date, if any, on which the person last reported under the Ontario Act and the duration of their obligation to comply with section 3 of that Act.

(2) Registration of information — termination orders — When the Attorney General of a province, or the minister of justice of a territory, receives a notice referred to in subsection 490.016(3), 490.017(2), 490.027(3), 490.029(2), 490.02909(3), 490.0291(2), 490.02913(3) or 490.02914(2) of the *Criminal Code*, a person who registers information for the Attorney General, or the minister of justice, shall register without delay in the database the fact that a termination order was made.

(3) Registration of information — exemption orders — A person who registers information for the Attorney General of a province, or the minister of justice of a territory, may register in the database the fact that a person has applied in that jurisdiction for an exemption order under section 490.023 or 490.02905 of the *Criminal Code*.

(4) Registration of information — exemption orders — When the Attorney General of a province, or the minister of justice of a territory, receives a notice referred to in section 490.025 or 490.02907 of the *Criminal Code*, a person who registers information for the Attorney General, or the minister of justice, shall register without delay in the database the fact that the court refused to make an exemption order under subsection 490.023(2) or 490.02905(2) of that Act or that the appeal court dismissed an appeal from such a decision or quashed an exemption order.

(5) Registration of information — A person who registers information for the Attorney General of a province, or the minister of justice of a territory, may register in the database the day on which the custodial portion of a sex offender's sentence or detention in custody begins, the days on which they are or are expected to be outside penitentiary as defined in subsection 2(1) of the *Corrections and Conditional Release Act* or outside the provincial correctional facility, the address or location at which they stay or are expected to stay during that period and the date of their release or discharge if

(a) the sex offender was prosecuted in that jurisdiction for the offence to which the sentence or detention relates; and

(b) the offence was not prosecuted under the *National Defence Act*.

(5.1) **Registration of information — Canada Border Services Agency** — A person who registers information for the Commissioner of the Royal Canadian Mounted Police may register in the database the information disclosed to the Commissioner under subsection 15.2(2).

(6) **Confidentiality and copy of information** — A person who registers information under this section shall

(a) ensure that the registration of the information is done in a manner and in circumstances that ensure its confidentiality; and

(b) once the information is registered, on request, send the sex offender or the person served with a notice under section 490.021 of the *Criminal Code* a copy of all of the information relating to them that is registered in the database, by registered mail, free of charge and without delay.

2007, c. 5, s. 41; 2010, c. 17, s. 39; 2015, c. 23, s. 25

8.2 (1) **Registration of information — Canadian Forces** — When the Canadian Forces Provost Marshal receives a copy of an order sent in accordance with subparagraph 227.05(1)(d)(iii) of the *National Defence Act*, a person who registers information for the Provost Marshal shall register without delay in the database only the following information relating to the person who is subject to the order:

(a) their given name and surname;

(b) the number that identifies a record of fingerprints collected from them under the *Identification of Criminals Act*, if such a record exists;

(c) every offence to which the order relates;

(d) when and where the offence or offences were committed;

(e) when and where the person was convicted of, or found not criminally responsible on account of mental disorder for, the offence or offences;

(f) the age and gender of every victim of the offence or offences, and the victim's relationship to the person;

(f.1) their method of operating in relation to the offence or offences, if that information is available to the person who registers information; and

(g) the date and duration of the order.

(2) **Registration of information — Canadian Forces** — When the Canadian Forces Provost Marshal receives a copy of an affidavit of service and a notice sent in accordance with subsection 227.08(4) of the *National Defence Act*, a person who registers information for the Provost Marshal shall register without delay in the

database only the following information relating to the person who was served with the notice:

(a) their given name and surname;

(b) the number that identifies a record of fingerprints collected from them under the *Identification of Criminals Act*, if such a record exists;

(c) the date on which the notice was served;

(d) every offence listed in the notice;

(e) when and where the offence or offences were committed;

(f) when and where the person was convicted of, or found not criminally responsible on account of mental disorder for, the offence or offences;

(g) the age and gender of every victim of the offence or offences, and the victim's relationship to the person;

(g.1) their method of operating in relation to the offence or offences, if that information is available to the person who registers information; and

(h) the expected duration of the person's obligation under section 227.06 of the *National Defence Act*.

(3) Registration of information — Canadian Forces — When the Canadian Forces Provost Marshal receives a notice referred to in subsection 227.04(3), 227.13(3) or 240.5(3) of the *National Defence Act*, a person who registers information for the Provost Marshal shall register without delay in the database the fact that a termination order was made.

(4) Registration of information — Canadian Forces — A person who registers information for the Canadian Forces Provost Marshal may register in the database the fact that a person has applied for an exemption order under section 227.1 of the *National Defence Act*.

(5) Registration of information — Canadian Forces — When the Canadian Forces Provost Marshal receives a notice referred to in section 227.11 of the *National Defence Act*, a person who registers information for the Provost Marshal shall register without delay in the database the fact that a court martial refused to make an exemption order under subsection 227.1(4) of that Act or that the Court Martial Appeal Court dismissed an appeal from such a decision or quashed an exemption order.

(6) Registration of information — Canadian Forces — If a sex offender was prosecuted under the *National Defence Act* for the offence to which the sentence or detention relates, a person who registers information for the Canadian Forces Provost Marshal may register in the database

(a) the day on which the custodial portion of the sex offender's sentence or detention in custody begins;

(b) the days on which they are or are expected to be outside the service prison or detention barrack as defined in subsection 2(1) of that Act and the address or location at which they stay or are expected to stay during that period; and

(c) the date of their release or discharge.

(7) **Registration of information — Canadian Forces** — A person who registers information for the Canadian Forces Provost Marshal shall register without delay in the database

(a) the fact that a person is the subject of a determination under subsection 227.15(1) of the *National Defence Act*, the effect of the determination on the person, the date on which the suspension of the time limit, proceeding or obligation first applies and the date on which it ceases to apply;

(b) the fact that a person is the subject of a determination under subsection 227.16(1) of the *National Defence Act* and the date on which the determination was made; and

(c) the fact that a person has become, or has ceased to be, subject to a regulation made under paragraph 227.2(a) or (e) of the *National Defence Act*.

(8) **Confidentiality and copy of information** — A person who registers information under this section shall

(a) ensure that the registration of the information is done in a manner and in circumstances that ensure its confidentiality; and

(b) once the information is registered under any of subsections (2) to (7), on request, send the sex offender or the person served with a notice under section 227.08 of the *National Defence Act* a copy of all of the information relating to them that is registered in the database, by registered mail, free of charge and without delay.

2007, c. 5, s. 41; 2010, c. 17, s. 40

9. (1) **Information to be given to sex offender** — When a sex offender reports to a registration centre and provides satisfactory proof of their identity to a person who collects information, that person shall immediately inform them of

(a) the nature of their obligations under sections 4 to 6 and of the information that may be collected under sections 5 and 6; and

(b) the purpose for which the information is being collected.

(2) **Fingerprints** — If a person who collects information has reasonable grounds to suspect that a person who is reporting to the registration centre as a sex offender under this Act is not the sex offender and no other proof of identity is satisfactory in the circumstances, they may take fingerprints from the person in order to confirm their identity.

(3) **Destruction of fingerprints** — Despite any other Act of Parliament, if the fingerprints provided under subsection (2) confirm that the person who is reporting is the sex offender, they shall not be disclosed, or used for any other purpose, and shall be destroyed without delay.

(4) **Privacy and confidentiality** — The person who collects information shall ensure that

(a) the sex offender's privacy is respected in a manner that is reasonable in the circumstances; and

(b) the information is provided and collected in a manner and in circumstances that ensure its confidentiality.

10. Registration of information — A person who registers information collected at a registration centre

(a) shall, subject to paragraph (b) and any regulations made under paragraph 19(3)(c), register without delay in the database only the information collected under sections 5 and 6, the date on which the sex offender reported or provided notification to the registration centre and the province of registration;

(b) may register at any time in the database the number that identifies a record of fingerprints collected from a sex offender under the *Identification of Criminals Act*, if such a record exists; and

(c) shall ensure that the registration of the information is done in a manner and in circumstances that ensure its confidentiality.

2007, c. 5, s. 42

11. Copy of information — A person who collects information at a registration centre shall, free of charge,

(a) either give a copy of the information collected under section 5, dated and signed by the person who collected it, to the sex offender when they report to the registration centre in person and provide information under this Act, or send it to the sex offender by mail or another means agreed to by the sex offender, without delay after it is collected, if they report other than in person;

(b) send the sex offender a copy of the information collected under section 6, dated and signed by the person who collected it, by mail or another means agreed to by the sex offender, without delay after it is collected;

(c) send the sex offender a copy of all of the information relating to them that is registered in the database, by mail or another means agreed to by the sex offender, without delay once the information referred to in paragraph (a) is registered; and

(d) at the request of the sex offender, send them a copy of all of the information relating to them that is registered in the database, by mail or another means agreed to by the sex offender, without delay once the information referred to in paragraph (b) is registered.

2007, c. 5, s. 43(2)

12. (1) Request for correction of information — Subject to subsection (2), a sex offender or a person served with a notice under section 490.021 of the *Criminal Code* or section 227.08 of the *National Defence Act* may, at any time, ask a person who collects information at the registration centre referred to in section 7.1 to correct any information relating to them that is registered in the database and that they believe contains an error or omission.

(2) Request for correction of information — The request shall be made to the Canadian Forces Provost Marshal if the information is registered in the database under section 8.2.

(3) Correction or notation — The person to whom the request is made shall, without delay, ensure that

(a) information in the database is corrected if they are satisfied that the information contains an error or omission; or

(b) a notation is attached to the information in the database that reflects any correction that is requested but not made.

2007, c. 5, s. 44

MANAGEMENT OF INFORMATION

13. (1) Authorization for research — The Commissioner of the Royal Canadian Mounted Police may authorize a person to consult information that is registered in the database, compare the information with other information or, by electronic means, combine the information with, or link it to, any other information contained in a computer system within the meaning of subsection 342.1(2) of the *Criminal Code*, for research or statistical purposes.

(2) Conditions — The Commissioner shall not provide the authorization unless the Commissioner

(a) is satisfied that those purposes cannot reasonably be accomplished without consulting the information or without comparing or combining the information with, or linking it to, the other information, as the case may be; and

(b) obtains from the person a written undertaking that no subsequent disclosure of the information or of any information resulting from the comparison or combination of the information with, or the linking of the information to, other information will be made, or be allowed to be made, in a form that could reasonably be expected to identify any individual to whom it relates.

2007, c. 5, s. 45

14. Administration of database — The database is to be administered by the Royal Canadian Mounted Police.

2010, c. 17, s. 41

15. (1) Retention of information — Subject to subsections (2) and (3) and regulations made under paragraphs 19(3)(b) and (d), information that is registered in the database in accordance with this Act shall be kept in the database indefinitely.

(2) Permanent removal and destruction of information — Despite any other Act of Parliament, all information that is collected under this Act, or registered in the database, in connection with an order shall be destroyed and permanently removed from the database if

(a) the person who is subject to the order is finally acquitted of every offence in connection with which the order was made or receives a free pardon granted under Her Majesty's royal prerogative of mercy or under section 748 of the *Criminal Code* for every such offence or is the subject of an expungement order under the *Expungement of Historically Unjust Convictions Act* for every such offence; or

(b) the sentence for every offence in connection with which the order was made ceases to have force and effect under subsection 249.11(2) of the *National Defence Act*.

(3) Permanent removal and destruction of information — Despite any other Act of Parliament, all information that is collected under this Act, or registered in the database, in connection with an obligation under section 490.019 or 490.02901 of the *Criminal Code* or section 227.06 of the *National Defence Act* shall be destroyed and permanently removed from the database if

(a) the person who is subject to the obligation is finally acquitted of every offence to which it relates or receives a free pardon granted under Her Majesty's royal prerogative of mercy or under section 748 of the *Criminal Code* for every such offence or is the subject of an expungement order under the *Expungement of Historically Unjust Convictions Act* for every such offence;

(b) the sentence for every offence to which the obligation relates ceases to have force and effect under subsection 249.11(2) of the *National Defence Act*; or

(c) the person who is subject to the obligation is granted an exemption order under subsection 490.023(2) or 490.02905(2) of the *Criminal Code* or subsection 227.1(4) of the *National Defence Act* or on an appeal from a decision made under that subsection.

2007, c. 5, s. 46; 2010, c. 17, s. 42; 2018, c. 11, s. 30

AUTHORITY TO COLLECT OR DISCLOSE INFORMATION

[Heading added 2010, c. 17, s. 43. Amended 2015, c. 23, s. 26.]

15.1 (1) Correctional Service of Canada — The Correctional Service of Canada may disclose to a person who registers information

(a) the day on which a sex offender is received into a penitentiary as defined in subsection 2(1) of the *Corrections and Conditional Release Act*;

(b) if a sex offender is expected to be temporarily outside penitentiary for seven or more days, the days on which they are expected to be outside, the days on which they are outside, the address or location at which they are expected to stay and the address or location at which they stay; and

(c) the date of a sex offender's release or discharge.

(2) Provincial correctional authority — The person in charge of a provincial correctional facility may disclose to a person who registers information

(a) the day on which a sex offender is received into the facility;

(b) if a sex offender is expected to be temporarily outside the facility for seven or more days, the days on which they are expected to be outside, the days on which they are outside, the address or location at which they are expected to stay and the address or location at which they stay; and

(c) the date of a sex offender's release or discharge.

(3) Canadian Forces — The person in charge of a service prison or detention barrack as defined in subsection 2(1) of the *National Defence Act* may disclose to a person who registers information

(a) the day on which a sex offender is received into the prison or barrack;

(b) if a sex offender is expected to be temporarily outside the prison or barrack for seven or more days, the days on which they are expected to be outside, the days on which they are outside, the address or location at which they are expected to stay and the address or location at which they stay; and

(c) the date of a sex offender's release or discharge.

2010, c. 17, s. 43

15.2 (1) Canada Border Services Agency — collection of information — The Canada Border Services Agency may assist a member or an employee of, or a person retained by, a police service in the prevention or investigation of a crime of a sexual nature or an offence under section 490.031 or 490.0311 of the *Criminal Code* or in the laying of a charge for such an offence by collecting the information disclosed to it under paragraph 16(4)(j.2) or (j.3) as well as the following information with respect to any sex offender who is the subject of a disclosure made under those paragraphs:

(a) the date of their departure from Canada;

(b) the date of their return to Canada; and

(c) every address or location at which they have stayed outside Canada.

(2) Canada Border Services Agency — disclosure of information — The Canada Border Services Agency may, in assisting the member or employee of, or person retained by, a police service referred to in subsection (1), disclose to the Commissioner of the Royal Canadian Mounted Police any information collected under paragraphs (1)(a) to (c).

2015, c. 23, s. 27

PROHIBITIONS

16. (1) Unauthorized persons — No person shall exercise any function or perform any duty under this Act that they are not authorized under this Act to exercise or perform.

(2) Unauthorized consultation — No person shall consult any information that is collected under this Act or registered in the database, unless they are

(a) a member or employee of, or a person retained by, a police service who consults the information for the purpose of preventing or investigating a crime of a sexual nature or an offence under section 490.031, 490.0311 or 490.0312 of the *Criminal Code*;

(b) a person who collects information at a registration centre designated under this Act in the province in which a sex offender's main residence is located who consults the information to verify compliance by the sex offender with an order or with an obligation under section 490.019 or 490.02901 of the

Criminal Code, section 227.06 of the *National Defence Act* or section 36.1 of the *International Transfer of Offenders Act*;

(b.1) a person who collects information at a registration centre designated under the *National Defence Act* who consults the information to verify compliance by a sex offender who is subject to the Code of Service Discipline — or who is an officer, or non-commissioned member, of the primary reserve as defined in section 227 of the *National Defence Act* — with an order or with an obligation under section 490.019 or 490.02901 of the *Criminal Code*, section 227.06 of the *National Defence Act* or section 36.1 of the *International Transfer of Offenders Act*;

(c) a person who collects or registers information who consults the information in order to exercise the functions or perform the duties assigned to them under an Act of Parliament;

(d) a person who is authorized under section 13 to consult information that is registered in the database for research or statistical purposes and who does so for those purposes;

(e) the Commissioner of the Royal Canadian Mounted Police or a person authorized by the Commissioner who consults information that is collected under this Act or registered in the database in order to perform the duties of the Commissioner under this Act, under subsection 490.03(1) or (2) of the *Criminal Code* or under subsection 227.18(1) or 227.19(1) of the *National Defence Act*; or

(f) a member or employee of, or a person retained by, the Royal Canadian Mounted Police who is authorized to consult the information for the purpose of administering the database and who does so for that purpose.

(3) Unauthorized comparison of information — No person shall compare any information that is collected under this Act or registered in the database with any other information unless

(a) the information was consulted in accordance with paragraph (2)(a) and they compare it with other information for the purpose of preventing or investigating a crime of a sexual nature;

(b) the information was consulted in accordance with paragraph (2)(b) or (b.1) and they compare it with other information for the purpose of verifying compliance by the sex offender with an order or with an obligation under section 490.019 or 490.02901 of the *Criminal Code*, section 227.06 of the *National Defence Act* or section 36.1 of the *International Transfer of Offenders Act* or for the purpose of preventing or investigating an offence under section 490.031, 490.0311 or 490.0312 of the *Criminal Code* — or an offence under any of those provisions that is punishable under section 130 of the *National Defence Act* — or an offence under section 119.1 of that Act;

(b.1) the information was collected under subsection 15.2(1) and they compare it with other information for the purpose of assisting a member or an employee of, or a person retained by, a police service in the prevention or investigation of a crime of a sexual nature or an offence under section 490.031 or 490.0311 of the *Criminal Code* or in the laying of a charge for such an offence; or

(c) they compare the information in accordance with an authorization under section 13.

(3.1) Unauthorized combination or linking of information — No person shall, by electronic means, combine any information that is collected under this Act or registered in the database with, or link it to, any other information contained in a computer system within the meaning of subsection 342.1(2) of the *Criminal Code* unless

(a) they combine the information that is registered in the database with, or link it to, information contained in the sex offender registry established under the Ontario Act, for the purpose of registering information under section 8, 8.1 or 10;

(a.1) the information was consulted in accordance with paragraph (2)(a) and they combine it with, or link it to, law enforcement information for the purpose of preventing or investigating a crime of a sexual nature;

(a.2) the information was consulted in accordance with paragraph (2)(b) or (b.1) and they combine it with, or link it to, law enforcement information for the purpose of verifying the sex offender's compliance with an order or with an obligation under section 490.019 or 490.02901 of the *Criminal Code*, section 227.06 of the *National Defence Act* or section 36.1 of the *International Transfer of Offenders Act* or for the purpose of preventing or investigating an offence under section 490.031 or 490.0311 of the *Criminal Code*, an offence under either of those provisions that is punishable under section 130 of the *National Defence Act* or an offence under section 119.1 of that Act;

(a.3) the information was collected under subsection 15.2(1) and they combine it with information contained in a computer system of the Canada Border Services Agency for the purpose of assisting a member or an employee of, or a person retained by, a police service in the prevention or investigation of a crime of a sexual nature or an offence under section 490.031 or 490.0311 of the *Criminal Code* or in the laying of a charge for such an offence; or

(b) they combine or link information in accordance with an authorization under section 13.

(4) Unauthorized disclosure — No person shall disclose any information that is collected under this Act or registered in the database or the fact that information relating to a person is collected under this Act or registered in the database, or allow it to be disclosed,

(a) unless the disclosure is to the sex offender, or the person served with a notice under section 490.021 of the *Criminal Code* or section 227.08 of the *National Defence Act*, to whom the information relates;

(b) unless the disclosure is expressly authorized under this Act, the *Criminal Code* or the *National Defence Act*;

(c) unless the disclosure is to a member or an employee of, or a person retained by, a police service and is necessary

(i) to enable them to investigate an offence under section 17 or to lay a charge for such an offence,

(ii) to enable them to prevent or investigate a crime of a sexual nature, an offence under section 119.1 of the *National Defence Act*, an offence under section 490.031 or 490.0311 of the *Criminal Code* or an offence under either of those provisions that is punishable under section 130 of the *National Defence Act* or to enable them to lay a charge for such an offence, or

(iii) to enable them to investigate a criminal offence or a service offence within the meaning of subsection 2(1) of the *National Defence Act* or to lay a charge for such an offence, as long as the investigation or charge results from an investigation referred to in subparagraph (ii);

(d) unless the disclosure is to a prosecutor and is necessary to enable the prosecutor to determine whether a charge for an offence resulting from an investigation referred to in paragraph (c) should be laid;

(e) unless the disclosure is to a person who is responsible under the *National Defence Act* for laying, referring or preferring a charge for a service offence and to a person who provides legal advice with respect to the charge, and the disclosure is necessary to enable them to determine whether a charge for a service offence resulting from an investigation referred to in paragraph (c) should be laid, referred or preferred;

(f) unless the disclosure is to a prosecutor, judge or justice in a proceeding relating to an application for a search warrant in connection with an investigation referred to in paragraph (c), and the information is relevant to the application;

(g) unless the disclosure is to a person who is authorized under the *National Defence Act* to issue a search warrant in connection with the investigation of a service offence and to a person who provides legal advice with respect to the issuance of the search warrant, and the information is relevant to an application for a search warrant in connection with an investigation referred to in paragraph (c);

(h) unless the information disclosed is relevant to the proceeding, appeal or review and the disclosure is

(i) to a prosecutor in connection with a proceeding that results from an investigation referred to in paragraph (c) and that is before a court of criminal jurisdiction or superior court of criminal jurisdiction within the meaning of section 2 of the *Criminal Code* or a service tribunal within the meaning of subsection 2(1) of the *National Defence Act*,

Proposed Amendment — 16(4)(h)(i)

(i) to a prosecutor in connection with a proceeding that results from an investigation referred to in paragraph (c) and that is before a **"court of criminal jurisdiction"** or a **"superior court of criminal jurisdiction"**, as defined in section 2 of the *Criminal Code*, or a **"court martial"**, as defined in subsection 2(1) of the *National Defence Act*,

2019, c. 15, s. 59(1) [Not in force at date of publication.]

(ii) to the Attorney General within the meaning of section 2 of the *Criminal Code*, or the Minister of National Defence or counsel instructed by the Minister, in connection with an appeal of a decision made in such a proceeding,

(iii) to the court or service tribunal presiding over the proceeding or appeal and, in the case of a summary trial under the *National Defence Act*, to a person who provides legal advice to the presiding officer, or

Proposed Amendment — 16(4)(h)(iii)

(iii) to the court or military judge presiding over the proceeding or appeal, or

2019, c. 15, s. 59(2) [Not in force at date of publication.]

(iv) to a review authority under section 249 of the *National Defence Act* and to a person who provides legal advice to the review authority in connection with its review of a finding of guilty made or punishment imposed in the proceeding or appeal;

Proposed Amendment — 16(4)(h)(iv)

(iv) to a review authority referred to in section 163.6 of the *National Defence Act* for its review under that section and to a person who provides legal advice to the review authority in connection with that review;

2019, c. 15, s. 59(2) [Not in force at date of publication.]

(i) unless the disclosure to the person is necessary to assist an investigation of any act or omission referred to in subsection 7(4.1) of the *Criminal Code* by a police service in the state where the act or omission was committed;

(j) unless the disclosure is to an employee of, or a person retained by, a person referred to in any of paragraphs (d) to (i) who is authorized by that person to receive information disclosed under that paragraph on their behalf;

(j.1) unless the disclosure is to a member or an employee of, or a person retained by, a police service outside Canada and is necessary to assist them in the prevention or investigation of a crime of a sexual nature;

(j.2) unless the disclosure is to the Canada Border Services Agency, is limited to the information referred to in paragraphs 5(1)(a), (b), (i) and (j) and is necessary to assist a member or an employee of, or a person retained by, a police service in the prevention or investigation of a crime of a sexual nature or an offence under section 490.031 or 490.0311 of the *Criminal Code* or in the laying of a charge for such an offence;

(j.3) unless the disclosure is to the Canada Border Services Agency, relates to a sex offender who is convicted of a sexual offence against a child and who poses a high risk of committing a crime of a sexual nature, is limited to the information referred to in paragraphs 5(1)(a), (b), (i) and (j) and is made for the purpose of assisting a member or an employee of, or a person retained by, a police service in the prevention or investigation of a crime of a sexual nature or an offence under section 490.031 or 490.0311 of the *Criminal Code* or in the laying of a charge for such an offence; or

(k) unless the disclosure is by a person who is authorized under section 13 to consult information that is registered in the database or to compare or combine that information with, or link it to, other information, the disclosure is for research or statistical purposes and it is not made, or allowed to be made, in a form that could reasonably be expected to identify any individual to whom it relates.

(5) Unauthorized use — No person shall use any information that is collected under this Act or registered in the database, or allow it to be used, for a purpose other than that for which it is consulted, compared, combined, linked or disclosed, as the case may be, under this section.

2007, c. 5, s. 47(1)–(4), (6), (7); 2010, c. 17, s. 44; 2015, c. 23, s. 28

OFFENCES

17. Offence — Every person who knowingly contravenes any of subsections 16(1) to (5) is guilty of an offence and liable on summary conviction to a fine of not more than $10,000 or to imprisonment for a term of not more than six months, or to both.

2007, c. 5, s. 48

AUTHORIZATIONS, DESIGNATIONS AND REGULATIONS

18. (1) Regulations — The lieutenant governor in council of a province may, for the purposes of this Act, make regulations

(a) respecting the means by which designated classes of persons may report under section 4.1 or 4.3, or provide notification under section 6, to registration centres designated under paragraph (d);

(b) authorizing persons or classes of persons in the province to collect information;

(c) authorizing persons or classes of persons in the province to register information; and

(d) designating places or classes of places in the province as registration centres, and the area of the province served by each registration centre.

(2) Regulations — Subject to subsection (3), the lieutenant governor in council of a province may, by regulation, exercise the power of the Governor in Council with respect to any matter referred to in paragraph 19(3)(a) if the Governor in Council does not make a regulation with respect to that matter that applies in the province.

(3) Regulations cease to apply — A regulation made with respect to a matter by the lieutenant governor in council of a province under subsection (2) ceases to apply if the Governor in Council makes a regulation with respect to that matter that applies in the province.

2007, c. 5, s. 49

19. (1) Regulations — Subject to subsection (2), the Governor in Council may, by regulation, exercise any power of the lieutenant governor in council of a province under any of paragraphs 18(1)(a) to (d) if the lieutenant governor in council of the province does not make a regulation under that paragraph.

(2) Regulations cease to apply — A regulation made by the Governor in Council under subsection (1) in the exercise of a power under any of paragraphs 18(1)(a) to (d) ceases to apply in a province if the lieutenant governor in council of the province makes a regulation under that paragraph.

(3) Regulations — The Governor in Council may make regulations

(a) respecting the recording, the retention and maintenance, and the protection of information collected under this Act;

(b) respecting the retention and maintenance, and the protection of information that is registered in the database;

(c) respecting the registration of photographs taken under subsection 5(3);

(d) respecting the destruction of information under subsections 9(3) and 15(2) and (3) and the permanent removal of information from the database; and

(e) generally for carrying out the purposes and provisions of this Act.

Related Amendments to the Criminal Code [R.S., c. C-46]

20. and 21. Related Amendments to the *Criminal Code* — [Note: The Related amendments are incorporated into the relevant provisions of the *Criminal Code*.]

Review and Report

21.1 (1) Review by committee — The administration of this Act shall, two years after the coming into force of this Act, be reviewed by the parliamentary committee that may be designated or established by Parliament for that purpose.

(2) Report — The committee designated or established by Parliament for the purpose of subsection (1) shall undertake a review of the provisions and operation of this Act and shall, within six months after the review is undertaken or within any further time that may be authorized, submit a report to Parliament thereon including a statement of any changes to this Act or its administration that the committee would recommend.

Consequential Amendments

22. and 23. Consequential Amendments — [Note: The Consequential amendments are incorporated into the relevant provisions of the Acts which they affect, namely, the *Access to Information Act* and the *Criminal Records Act*.]

Coordinating Provision

24. Bill C-20 — If Bill C-20, introduced in the 2nd Session of the 37th Parliament and entitled *An Act to amend the Criminal Code (protection of children and other* *vulnerable persons) and the Canada Evidence Act* (the “other Act”), receives royal assent, then, on the later of the coming into force of section 6 of the other Act and the coming into force of this Act, subparagraph (b)(i) of the definition “designated offence” in subsection 490.011(1) of the *Criminal Code* is replaced by the following:

(i) section 162 (voyeurism),

(i.1) subsection 173(1) (indecent acts),

Coming Into Force

25. Coming into force — This Act comes into force on a day to be fixed by order of the Governor in Council.

(i) section [illegible]

(ii) subsection [illegible]

Youth Criminal Justice Act

Editor's note: Current to May 15, 2019.

TABLE OF CONCORDANCE

The *Young Offenders Act*, R.S.C. 1985, c. Y-1 was repealed and replaced by the *Youth Criminal Justice Act*, S.C. 2002, c. 1, effective April 1, 2003. What follows is a table of equivalent sections and subsections which identifies, insofar as possible, the substantive correspondence between sections and subsections of the *Young Offenders Act* and the *Youth Criminal Justice Act*. Provisions for which there are significant substantive differences/partial correspondence are denoted by italics and the use of the words "*in part*". Cross-references to more loosely related provisions of the new act are also provided where appropriate, and are denoted by the terms "*see*" and "*see also*".

Young Offenders Act, R.S.C. 1985, c. Y-1	Youth Criminal Justice Act, S.C. 2002, c. 1
1	1
2	2
2.1	22
3	3
4	10
5(1)	14(1)
5(2)	14(3)
5(3)	14(4)
5(4)	14(6)
5(5)	13(4)
6	20(1)
7(1)	30(1)
7(1.1)	30(2)
7(2)	30(3)
7(3)	30(6)
7(4)	30(7)
7(5)	30(8)
7(6)	30(9)
7.1(1)	31(1)
7.1(2)	31(3)
7.1(3)	31(4)
7.1(4)	31(5)

Young Offenders Act, R.S.C. 1985, c. Y-1	Youth Criminal Justice Act, S.C. 2002, c. 1
7.1(5)	31(6)
7.2	139(1)(b), 139(2)
8(1)	—
8(2)	33(1)
8(3)	33(2)
8(4)	33(3)
8(5)	33(4)
8(6)	33(5)
8(6.1)	33(6)
8(7)	33(7)
8(8)	33(8)
8(9)	33(9)
9(1)	26(1)
9(2)	26(2)
9(2.1)	26(3)
9(3)	26(4)
9(4)	—
9(5)	26(5)
9(6)	26(6)
9(6.1)	26(7)
9(7)	26(8)
9(8)	26(9)
9(9)	26(10)
9(10)	26(11)
—	26(12)
10(1)	27(1)
10(1.1)	27(2)
10(2)	27(3)
10(3)	27(4)
10(4)	37(3)
10(5)	27(5)
11(1)	25(1), 88
11(2)	25(2), 88
11(3)	25(3), 88
11(4)	25(4), 88
11(5)	25(5), 88
11(6)	25(6), 88
11(7)	25(7), 88
11(8)	25(8), 88
11(9)	25(9), 88

Young Offenders Act, R.S.C. 1985, c. Y-1	**Youth Criminal Justice Act, S.C. 2002, c. 1**
—	25(10), 88
—	25(11), 88
12(1)(a)–(c)	32(1)(a)–(c)
—	32(1)(d)
12(2)	32(2)
12(3)(a)	32(3)(a)
—	32(3)(b)
12(3)(b)	32(3)(c)
12(3.1)	—
12(4)	32(4)
12(5)	32(5)
13(1)	34(1)
—	34(2)(a)
13(2)(a)	34(2)(b)
13(2)(b)	34(2)(c)
13(2)(c)	34(2)(d)
13(2)(d)	34(2)(e)
13(2)(e)	34(2)(f)
13(2)(f)	34(2)(g)
13(3)	34(3)
13(3.1)	34(4)
13(3.2)	34(5)
13(3.3)	34(6)
13(4)	34(7)
13(5)	34(8)
13(6)	34(9)
13(7)	34(10)
13(8)	34(11)
13(9)	34(12)
13(10)	34(13)
13(11)	34(14)
13.1	147
13.2(1)–(11)	141(1)–(11)
—	141(12)
14(1)	40(1)(a)–(b)
14(2)(a)(i)–(iii)	40(2)(a)
14(2)(b)	40(2)(b)
—	40(2)(c)
14(2)(c)	40(2)(d)
—	40(2)(e)

Young Offenders Act, R.S.C. 1985, c. Y-1	**Youth Criminal Justice Act, S.C. 2002, c. 1**
14(2)(d)	40(2)(f)
14(3)–(10)	40(3)–(10)
15	130
16(1)	*61, 62(b)*
16(1.01)	*61, 62(a)*
16(1.02)	*63(1), 64(2)–(4), 81*
16(1.03)	*64(2)–(4)*
16(1.04)	*63(2)*
16(1.05)	—
16(1.06)	—
16(1.1)	*71, 72(1), 73*
16(1.11)	*72(2)*
16(2)	*72(1)*
16(3)	*72(3)*
16(4)	—
16(5)	*72(4)*
16(6)	—
16(7)	—
16(7.1)	—
16(8)	—
16(9)	*37(1), (4), 72(5); CC 675(1)(b), 675(2)–(4), 676(1)(d), 676(4)–(5)*
16(10)	*37(1), (4); CC 678(2)*
16(11)	*37(1), (4); CC 678(1)*
16(12)	—
16.1	*see 28, 29, 30*
16.2(1)	*76(1)*
16.2(2)	*76(2) in part*
—	*76(3)*
16.2(3)	*76(4)*
—	*76(5)*
16.2(4)–(6)	*76(6)–(8)*
—	*76(9)*
17	*see 65, 75, 110*
18	133
19(1)	36(1)
19(2)	36(2)
19(3)	19(3)
19(4)	67(1)(c)
19(5)	67(8), (9); CC 536(4), 565(1)

Young Offenders Act, R.S.C. 1985, c. Y-1	**Youth Criminal Justice Act, S.C. 2002, c. 1**
19(5.1)	67(7)(a)
19(5.2)	67(8)
19(6)	67(9)
19.1(1)	36(1)
19.1(2)	36(2)
19.1(3)	—
19.1(4)	67(3)(c), 67(4)
19.1(5)	67(8), (9); CC 536.1(4), 565(1.1)
19.1(6)	67(7)(b)
19.1(7)	67(8)
19.1(8)	67(9)
19.1(9)	—
20(1)(a)	42(2)(b)
—	42(2)(a)
20(1)(a.1)	42(2)(c)
20(1)(b)	42(2)(d)
20(1)(c)	42(2)(e)
20(1)(d)	42(2)(f)
20(1)(e)	42(2)(g)
20(1)(f)	42(2)(h)
20(1)(g)	42(2)(i)
20(1)(h)	42(2)(j)
20(1)(i)	—
20(1)(j)	42(2)(k)
—	42(2)(l)
—	42(2)(m)
20(1)(k)	42(2)*(n), see also 47*
—	42(2)(o)
—	42(2)(p)
20(1)(k.1)	42(2)(q)
—	42(2)(r)
20(1)(l)	42(2)(s)
20(2)	42(12)
20(3)	42(14)
20(4)	42(15)
20(4.1)	42(16)
20(4.2)	45
20(4.3)	45
20(5)	42(17)
20(6)	48

Young Offenders Act, R.S.C. 1985, c. Y-1	Youth Criminal Justice Act, S.C. 2002, c. 1
20(7)	38(2)(a)
20(8)	50(1)
20(9)	50(2)
20(10)	—
20(11)	42(2)(i)
20.1(1)–(4)	51(1)–(4)
20.1(5)	—
20.1(6)–(9)	51(5)–(8)
21	54
23(1)	55(1)
23(2)(a)–(g)	55(2)(a)–(h)
—	55(2)(i)
23(3)	56(1)
23(4)	56(2)
23(5)	56(3)
23(6)	56(4)
23(7)	56(5)
23(8)	56(7)
23(9)	56(8)
24(1)	39(1)
24(1.1)(a)	39(5)
24(1.1)(b)	—
24(1.1)(c)	39(2)
—	39(3)–(4)
24(2)	39(6)
24(3)	39(7)
—	39(8)
24(4)	39(9)
24.1(1)	85(1), 88
24.1(2)	88
24.1(3)	85(3), 88
24.1(4)	85(5), 88
24.2(1)	85(6), 88
24.2(2)	49(1), 88
24.2(3)	49(2), 88
24.2(4)	84, 88
24.2(5)	49(3), 88
24.2(6)	85(4), 85(6), 88
24.2(7)	88
24.2(8)	88

Young Offenders Act, R.S.C. 1985, c. Y-1	**Youth Criminal Justice Act, S.C. 2002, c. 1**
24.2(9)	88
24.2(10)	85(4), 88
24.2(11)	85(4), 88
24.2(12)	85(7), 88
24.2(13)	88
24.2(14)	88
24.3	88
24.4(1)	47(1)
—	47(2)
24.4(2)	47(3)
24.5(1)	92(1)
—	92(2)–(4)
24.5(2)	92(5)
25	57
25.1	58
26	137
26.1(1)	*104(1) in part; see also 98(1), 98(3)*
26.1(1.1)	104(2) *see also 98(2)*
26.1(2)	104(3) *see also 98(4)*
26.1(3)	104(4)
26.1(4)	99(1), 104(5)
26.1(5)	99(2), 104(5)
26.1(6)	99(3), 104(5)
26.1(7)	99(4), 104(5)
26.1(8)	99(5), 104(5)
26.1(9)	99(6), 104(5)
26.1(10)	99(7), 104(5)
26.1(11)	100, 104(5)
26.1(12)	101, 104(5)
26.1(13)	104(6)
26.2(1)–(2)	105(1)–(2)
26.2(3)(a)–(f)	105(3)(a)–(f)
—	105(3)(g)
26.2(3)(g)	105(3)(h)
26.2(4)–(8)	105(4)–(8)
26.3	106
26.4	107
26.5	108
26.6(1)	109(1)
26.6(2)(a)–(b)	109(2)(a)–(b)

Young Offenders Act, R.S.C. 1985, c. Y-1	Youth Criminal Justice Act, S.C. 2002, c. 1
—	109(2)(c)
—	109(3)–(4)
26.6(3)	109(5)
—	109(6)
26.6(4)	109(7) *in part*
26.6(5)	109(8) *in part*
27(1)	37(1)
—	37(4)
27(1.1)	37(5)
27(1.2)	37(6)
27(2)	37(7)
27(3)	37(8)
27(3.1)	37(9)
27(4)	—
27(5)	37(10)
27(6)	37(11)
28(1)–(2)	94(1)–(2), 88
28(3)	94(3)–(5), 88
28(4)(a)–(c)	94(6)(a)–(c), 88
28(4)(c.1)	94(6)(d), 88
28(4)(d)	94(6)(e), 88
28(5)–(16)	94(7)–(18), 88
28(17)(a)	94(19)(a)
28(17)(b)	—
28(17)(c)(i)	—
28(17)(c)(ii)	94(19)(b)
—	94(19(c)
28.1	87, 88
29(1)	96(1) *in part, 96(2) in part*, 88
29(1.1)	96(2) *in part*, 88
29(2)–(3)	96(3)–(4), 88
29(4)	96(5) *in part*, 88
29(4.1)	88
29(4.2)	96(6)
29(4.3)	96(7)
29(5)	96(8)
29(6)	—
30	88
31	88
32(1)	59(1)

Young Offenders Act, R.S.C. 1985, c. Y-1	**Youth Criminal Justice Act, S.C. 2002, c. 1**
32(2)(a)–(b)	59(2)(a)–(b)
—	59(2)(c)
32(2)(c)–(d)	59(2)(d)–(e)
32(3)–(9)	59(3)–(9)
33	52
34(1)	60 *in part*
34(2)	95 *in part*
35(1)–(4)	91(1)–(4)
35(5)	—
36(1)–(3)	82(1)–(3)
36(4)	139(3)
36(5)	82(4) *in part*
37	90
38(1)	65, 110(1), 110(2)(a), 111(1)
38(1.1)	110(2)(c)
38(1.11)	125(5)
38(1.12)	129
38(1.13)	125(6)(a)–(b)
—	125(6)(c)
38(1.14)	129
38(1.15)	125(7)
38(1.2)–(1.3)	110(4)–(5)
38(1.4)	110(6), 111(3)
38(1.5)–(1.8)	127(1)–(4)
38(2)	138(1) *in part*
38(3)	138(2)
39	132
40(1)	114
40(2)	117
40(3)	119(10)
41(1)	115(3)
41(2)	115(2) *in part*
41(3)	115(2) *in part*
42	115(1)
43	116
44	113
44.1(1)(a)	119(1)(a), 120(1)(a)
44.1(1)(b)	119(1)(b), 120(1)(b)
44.1(1)(c)	119(1)(c), *120(1)(e)–(f) in part*
44.1(1)(d)	119(1)(e),(f)

Young Offenders Act, R.S.C. 1985, c. Y-1	**Youth Criminal Justice Act, S.C. 2002, c. 1**
44.1(1)(e)	119(1)(h)
—	119(1)(i)
44.1(1)(f)(i)	*119(1)(g)(i), 120(1)(e) in part*
44.1(1)(f)(ii)	119(1)(g)(ii)
44.1(1)(f)(iii)–(iv)	*119(1)(g)(i), 120(1)(f)*
44.1(1)(g)(i)	*119(1)(j) in part*
—	119(1)(k)–(l)
44.1(1)(g)(ii)	*119(1)(n)(i)*
44.1(1)(g)(iii)	119(1)(n)(ii)
44.1(1)(g)(iv)	119(1)(n)(iii)
44.1(1)(h)	119(1)(r)
44.1(1)(i)	*119(1)(o) in part*
44.1(1)(i.1)	119(1)(m), 120(1)(g)
44.1(1)(j)	119(1)(p), 120(1)(c)
—	119(1)(q)
44.1(1)(k)	119(1)(s), 120(1)(d)
44.1(2)	119(5)
44.1(2.1)	119(6)
44.1(3)	119(7)
44.1(4)	119(8), 120(5)
44.1(5)	119(1)(d)
44.1(6)	*122 in part*
44.2(1)	*125(1) in part*
44.2(2)	*125(4) in part*
45(1) before (a)	*118(1)*
45(1)(a)–(c)	*119(2)(b)–(d)*
45(1)(d)	*119(2)(a)*
45(1)(d.1)–(f)	*119(2)(e)–(h)*
45(1)(g)(i)	*119(2)(i) in part*
45(1)(g)(ii)	*119(2)(j)*
45(2)	*128(2)–(4)*
45(2.1)	*115(2),(3)*
45(2.2)	*115(2),(3)*
45(2.3)	128(7)
45(3)	*128(2) in part*
45(4)	*82(1) but see 119(9)*
45(5)	121
45(5.1)	119(3)
45(6)	163
45.01	120(5)

Young Offenders Act, R.S.C. 1985, c. Y-1	**Youth Criminal Justice Act, S.C. 2002, c. 1**
45.02	*115(3), 120 (1), (3), (4)*
45.03	*115(3), 119(3), (10), 120(2), 128(3), (5)*
45.1(1)	123(1)(a)
—	123(1)(b)
45.1(1.1)	123(2)
45.1(2)	123(3)
45.1(2.1)	123(4)
45.1(3)	123(5)
45.2	126
46	118, 128(1), *138 in part*
47(1)–(5)	15(1)–(5)
47(6)	37(2)
48	134
49	135
50	136
51	140
52(1)	*142(1) in part*
—	142(1)(a)
52(2)–(5)	142(2)–(5)
53	143
54	144
55	145
56(1)–(3)	146(1)–(3)
56(4)	*146(4) in part*
—	146(5)–(6)
56(5)	146(7)
56(5.1)	146(8)
56(6)	146(9)
57	148
58	149
59	150
60	151
62	152
63	153
64	131
65	21
66	154
67	155
68	17

Young Offenders Act, R.S.C. 1985, c. Y-1	**Youth Criminal Justice Act, S.C. 2002, c. 1**
69	18(1)
70	156
Schedule	*Schedule in part*

YOUTH CRIMINAL JUSTICE ACT

An Act in respect of criminal justice for young persons and to amend and repeal other Acts

S.C. 2002, c. 1, as am. S.C. 2002, c. 7, s. 274; 2002, c. 13, s. 91; 2004, c. 11, ss. 48, 49; 2005, c. 22, s. 63; 2012, c. 1, ss. 156–159, 160(l), 167–187, 188(1), (2), (3) (Fr.), 189, 190, 191 (Fr.), 192–194; 2014, c. 2, s. 52; 2014, c. 25, s. 43; 2015, c. 20, ss. 32, 33, 36(8), (9); 2015, c. 29, ss. 14, 15; 2018, c. 16, s. 184; 2019, c. 13, ss. 159–167; 2019, c. 25, ss. 361–383 [ss. 361–365, 367–369, 370(2), 371–375, 380, 381 to come into force December 18, 2019.] [s. 366 repealed before coming into force 2019, c. 25, s. 404(5).].

Preamble

WHEREAS members of society share a responsibility to address the developmental challenges and the needs of young persons and to guide them into adulthood;

WHEREAS communities, families, parents and others concerned with the development of young persons should, through multi-disciplinary approaches, take reasonable steps to prevent youth crime by addressing its underlying causes, to respond to the needs of young persons, and to provide guidance and support to those at risk of committing crimes;

WHEREAS information about youth justice, youth crime and the effectiveness of measures taken to address youth crime should be publicly available;

WHEREAS Canada is a party to the United Nations Convention on the Rights of the Child and recognizes that young persons have rights and freedoms, including those stated in the *Canadian Charter of Rights and Freedoms* and the *Canadian Bill of Rights*, and have special guarantees of their rights and freedoms;

AND WHEREAS Canadian society should have a youth criminal justice system that commands respect, takes into account the interests of victims, fosters responsibility and ensures accountability through meaningful consequences and effective rehabilitation and reintegration, and that reserves its most serious intervention for the most serious crimes and reduces the over-reliance on incarceration for non-violent young persons;

NOW, THEREFORE, Her Majesty, by and with the advice and consent of the Senate and House of Commons of Canada, enacts as follows:

SHORT TITLE

1. Short title — This Act may be cited as the *Youth Criminal Justice Act*.

INTERPRETATION

2. (1) Definitions — The definitions in this subsection apply in this Act.

"adult" means a person who is neither a young person nor a child. *("adulte")*

"adult sentence", in the case of a young person who is found guilty of an offence, means any sentence that could be imposed on an adult who has been convicted of the same offence. *("peine applicable aux adultes")*

"Attorney General" means the Attorney General as defined in section 2 of the *Criminal Code*, read as if the reference in that definition to "proceedings" were a reference to "proceedings or extrajudicial measures", and includes an agent or delegate of the Attorney General. *("procureur général")*

"child" means a person who is or, in the absence of evidence to the contrary, appears to be less than twelve years old. *("enfant")*

"conference" means a group of persons who are convened to give advice in accordance with section 19. *("groupe consultatif")*

"confirmed delivery service" means certified or registered mail or any other method of service that provides proof of delivery. *("service de messagerie")*

"custodial portion", with respect to a youth sentence imposed on a young person under paragraph 42(2)(n), (o), (q) or (r), means the period of time, or the portion of the young person's youth sentence, that must be served in custody before he or she begins to serve the remainder under supervision in the community subject to conditions under paragraph 42(2)(n) or under conditional supervision under paragraph 42(2)(o), (q) or (r). *("période de garde")*

"disclosure" means the communication of information other than by way of publication. *("communication")*

"extrajudicial measures" means measures other than judicial proceedings under this Act used to deal with a young person alleged to have committed an offence and includes extrajudicial sanctions. *("mesures extrajudiciaires")*

"extrajudicial sanction" means a sanction that is part of a program referred to in section 10. *("sanction extrajudiciaire")*

"offence" means an offence created by an Act of Parliament or by any regulation, rule, order, by-law or ordinance made under an Act of Parliament other than a law of the Legislature of Yukon, of the Northwest Territories or for Nunavut. *("infraction")*

"parent" includes, in respect of a young person, any person who is under a legal duty to provide for the young person or any person who has, in law or in fact, the custody or control of the young person, but does not include a person who has the custody or control of the young person by reason only of proceedings under this Act. *("père ou mère")* ou *("père et mère")*

"pre-sentence report" means a report on the personal and family history and present environment of a young person made in accordance with section 40. *("rapport prédécisionnel")*

"presumptive offence" [Repealed 2012, c. 1, s. 167(1).]

"provincial director" means a person, a group or class of persons or a body appointed or designated by or under an Act of the legislature of a province or by the lieutenant governor in council of a province or his or her delegate to perform in that province, either generally or in a specific case, any of the duties or functions of a provincial director under this Act. *("directeur provincial")* ou *("directeur")*

"publication" means the communication of information by making it known or accessible to the general public through any means, including print, radio or television broadcast, telecommunication or electronic means. *("publication")*

"record" includes any thing containing information, regardless of its physical form or characteristics, including microform, sound recording, videotape, machine-readable record, and any copy of any of those things, that is created or kept for the purposes of this Act or for the investigation of an offence that is or could be prosecuted under this Act. *("dossier")*

"review board" means a review board referred to in subsection 87(2). *("commission d'examen")*

"serious offence" means an indictable offence under an Act of Parliament for which the maximum punishment is imprisonment for five years or more. *(« infraction grave »)*

"serious violent offence" means an offence under one of the following provisions of the *Criminal Code*:

(a) section 231 or 235 (first degree murder or second degree murder);

(b) section 239 (attempt to commit murder);

(c) section 232, 234 or 236 (manslaughter); or

(d) section 273 (aggravated sexual assault).

(« infraction grave avec violence »)

"violent offence" means

(a) an offence committed by a young person that includes as an element the causing of bodily harm;

(b) an attempt or a threat to commit an offence referred to in paragraph (a); or

(c) an offence in the commission of which a young person endangers the life or safety of another person by creating a substantial likelihood of causing bodily harm.

(« infraction avec violence »)

"young person" means a person who is or, in the absence of evidence to the contrary, appears to be twelve years old or older, but less than eighteen years old and, if the context requires, includes any person who is charged under this Act with having committed an offence while he or she was a young person or who is found guilty of an offence under this Act. *("adolescent")*

"youth custody facility" means a facility designated under subsection 85(2) for the placement of young persons and, if so designated, includes a facility for the secure restraint of young persons, a community residential centre, a group home, a child care institution and a forest or wilderness camp. *("lieu de garde")*

"youth justice court" means a youth justice court referred to in section 13. *("tribunal pour adolescents")*

"youth justice court judge" means a youth justice court judge referred to in section 13. *("juge du tribunal pour adolescents")*

"youth sentence" means a sentence imposed under section 42, 51 or 59 or any of sections 94 to 96 and includes a confirmation or a variation of that sentence. *("peine spécifique")*

"youth worker" means any person appointed or designated, whether by title of youth worker or probation officer or by any other title, by or under an Act of the legislature of a province or by the lieutenant governor in council of a province or his or her delegate to perform in that province, either generally or in a specific case, any of the duties or functions of a youth worker under this Act. *("délégué à la jeunesse")*

(2) **Words and expressions** — Unless otherwise provided, words and expressions used in this Act have the same meaning as in the *Criminal Code*.

(3) **Descriptive cross-references** — If, in any provision of this Act, a reference to another provision of this Act or a provision of any other Act is followed by words in parentheses that are or purport to be descriptive of the subject-matter of the provision referred to, those words form no part of the provision in which they occur but are inserted for convenience of reference only.

2002, c. 7, s. 274; 2012, c. 1, s. 167; 2014, c. 2, s. 52

DECLARATION OF PRINCIPLE

3. (1) **Policy for Canada with respect to young persons** — The following principles apply in this Act:

(a) the youth criminal justice system is intended to protect the public by

(i) holding young persons accountable through measures that are proportionate to the seriousness of the offence and the degree of responsibility of the young person,

(ii) promoting the rehabilitation and reintegration of young persons who have committed offences, and

(iii) supporting the prevention of crime by referring young persons to programs or agencies in the community to address the circumstances underlying their offending behaviour;

(b) the criminal justice system for young persons must be separate from that of adults, must be based on the principle of diminished moral blameworthiness or culpability and must emphasize the following:

(i) rehabilitation and reintegration,

(ii) fair and proportionate accountability that is consistent with the greater dependency of young persons and their reduced level of maturity,

(iii) enhanced procedural protection to ensure that young persons are treated fairly and that their rights, including their right to privacy, are protected,

(iv) timely intervention that reinforces the link between the offending behaviour and its consequences, and

(v) the promptness and speed with which persons responsible for enforcing this Act must act, given young persons' perception of time;

(c) within the limits of fair and proportionate accountability, the measures taken against young persons who commit offences should

(i) reinforce respect for societal values,

(ii) encourage the repair of harm done to victims and the community,

(iii) be meaningful for the individual young person given his or her needs and level of development and, where appropriate, involve the parents, the extended family, the community and social or other agencies in the young person's rehabilitation and reintegration, and

(iv) respect gender, ethnic, cultural and linguistic differences and respond to the needs of aboriginal young persons and of young persons with special requirements; and

(d) special considerations apply in respect of proceedings against young persons and, in particular,

(i) young persons have rights and freedoms in their own right, such as a right to be heard in the course of and to participate in the processes, other than the decision to prosecute, that lead to decisions that affect them, and young persons have special guarantees of their rights and freedoms,

(ii) victims should be treated with courtesy, compassion and respect for their dignity and privacy and should suffer the minimum degree of inconvenience as a result of their involvement with the youth criminal justice system,

(iii) victims should be provided with information about the proceedings and given an opportunity to participate and be heard, and

(iv) parents should be informed of measures or proceedings involving their children and encouraged to support them in addressing their offending behaviour.

(2) **Act to be liberally construed** — This Act shall be liberally construed so as to ensure that young persons are dealt with in accordance with the principles set out in subsection (1).

2012, c. 1, s. 168

PART 1 — EXTRAJUDICIAL MEASURES (SS. 4–12)

Principles and Objectives

4. Declaration of principles — The following principles apply in this Part in addition to the principles set out in section 3:

(a) extrajudicial measures are often the most appropriate and effective way to address youth crime;

(b) extrajudicial measures allow for effective and timely interventions focused on correcting offending behaviour;

(c) extrajudicial measures are presumed to be adequate to hold a young person accountable for his or her offending behaviour if the young person has committed a non-violent offence and has not previously been found guilty of an offence; and

(d) extrajudicial measures should be used if they are adequate to hold a young person accountable for his or her offending behaviour and, if the use of extrajudicial measures is consistent with the principles set out in this section, nothing in this Act precludes their use in respect of a young person who

(i) has previously been dealt with by the use of extrajudicial measures, or

(ii) has previously been found guilty of an offence.

Proposed Addition — 4.1

4.1 (1) **Certain offences — extrajudicial measures deemed adequate** — Extrajudicial measures are presumed to be adequate to hold a young person accountable for a failure or refusal referred to in section 137 and for a failure referred to in section 496 of the *Criminal Code* unless

(a) the young person has a history of repetitive failures or refusals; or

(b) the young person's failure or refusal caused harm, or a risk of harm, to the safety of the public.

(2) **Certain offences — various measures** — In the cases referred to in paragraphs (1)(a) and (b),

(a) extrajudicial measures should be used if they are adequate to hold the young person accountable for the failure or refusal; and

(b) if the use of extrajudicial measures would not be adequate under paragraph (a), but issuing an appearance notice under section 496 (judicial referral hearing) of the *Criminal Code* or making an application for review of the youth sentence referred to in section 59(1) as an alternative to proceeding by charge would be adequate, then the applicable alternative should be used.

2019, c. 25, s. 361 [To come into force December 18, 2019.]

5. Objectives — Extrajudicial measures should be designed to

(a) provide an effective and timely response to offending behaviour outside the bounds of judicial measures;

(b) encourage young persons to acknowledge and repair the harm caused to the victim and the community;

(c) encourage families of young persons — including extended families where appropriate — and the community to become involved in the design and implementation of those measures;

(d) provide an opportunity for victims to participate in decisions related to the measures selected and to receive reparation; and

(e) respect the rights and freedoms of young persons and be proportionate to the seriousness of the offence.

Warnings, Cautions and Referrals

6. (1) Warnings, cautions and referrals — A police officer shall, before starting judicial proceedings or taking any other measures under this Act against a young person alleged to have committed an offence, consider whether it would be sufficient, having regard to the principles set out in section 4, to take no further action, warn the young person, administer a caution, if a program has been established under section 7, or, with the consent of the young person, refer the young person to a program or agency in the community that may assist the young person not to commit offences.

Proposed Amendment — 6(1)

(1) Warnings, cautions and referrals — A police officer shall, before starting judicial proceedings or taking any other measures under this Act against a young person alleged to have committed an offence, consider whether it would be sufficient, having regard to the principles set out in sections 4 and 4.1, to take no further action, warn the young person, administer a caution, if a program has been established under section 7, or, with the consent of the young person, refer the young person to a program or agency in the community that may assist the young person not to commit offences.

2019, c. 25, s. 362 [To come into force December 18, 2019.]

(2) Saving — The failure of a police officer to consider the options set out in subsection (1) does not invalidate any subsequent charges against the young person for the offence.

7. Police cautions — The Attorney General, or any other minister designated by the lieutenant governor of a province, may establish a program authorizing the police to administer cautions to young persons instead of starting judicial proceedings under this Act.

8. Crown cautions — The Attorney General may establish a program authorizing prosecutors to administer cautions to young persons instead of starting or continuing judicial proceedings under this Act.

9. Evidence of measures is inadmissible — Evidence that a young person has received a warning, caution or referral mentioned in section 6, 7 or 8 or that a police officer has taken no further action in respect of an offence, and evidence of the offence, is inadmissible for the purpose of proving prior offending behaviour in any proceedings before a youth justice court in respect of the young person.

Extrajudicial Sanctions

10. (1) Extrajudicial sanctions — An extrajudicial sanction may be used to deal with a young person alleged to have committed an offence only if the young person cannot be adequately dealt with by a warning, caution or referral mentioned in section 6, 7 or 8 because of the seriousness of the offence, the nature and number of previous offences committed by the young person or any other aggravating circumstances.

(2) Conditions — An extrajudicial sanction may be used only if

(a) it is part of a program of sanctions that may be authorized by the Attorney General or authorized by a person, or a member of a class of persons, designated by the lieutenant governor in council of the province;

(b) the person who is considering whether to use the extrajudicial sanction is satisfied that it would be appropriate, having regard to the needs of the young person and the interests of society;

(c) the young person, having been informed of the extrajudicial sanction, fully and freely consents to be subject to it;

(d) the young person has, before consenting to be subject to the extrajudicial sanction, been advised of his or her right to be represented by counsel and been given a reasonable opportunity to consult with counsel;

(e) the young person accepts responsibility for the act or omission that forms the basis of the offence that he or she is alleged to have committed;

(f) there is, in the opinion of the Attorney General, sufficient evidence to proceed with the prosecution of the offence; and

(g) the prosecution of the offence is not in any way barred at law.

(3) Restriction on use — An extrajudicial sanction may not be used in respect of a young person who

(a) denies participation or involvement in the commission of the offence; or

(b) expresses the wish to have the charge dealt with by a youth justice court.

(4) **Admissions not admissible in evidence** — Any admission, confession or statement accepting responsibility for a given act or omission that is made by a young person as a condition of being dealt with by extrajudicial measures is inadmissible in evidence against any young person in civil or criminal proceedings.

(5) **No bar to judicial proceedings** — The use of an extrajudicial sanction in respect of a young person alleged to have committed an offence is not a bar to judicial proceedings under this Act, but if a charge is laid against the young person in respect of the offence,

(a) the youth justice court shall dismiss the charge if it is satisfied on a balance of probabilities that the young person has totally complied with the terms and conditions of the extrajudicial sanction; and

(b) the youth justice court may dismiss the charge if it is satisfied on a balance of probabilities that the young person has partially complied with the terms and conditions of the extrajudicial sanction and if, in the opinion of the court, prosecution of the charge would be unfair having regard to the circumstances and the young person's performance with respect to the extrajudicial sanction.

(6) **Laying of information, etc.** — Subject to subsection (5) and section 24 (private prosecutions only with consent of Attorney General), nothing in this section shall be construed as preventing any person from laying an information or indictment, obtaining the issue or confirmation of any process or proceeding with the prosecution of any offence in accordance with law.

11. **Notice to parent** — If a young person is dealt with by an extrajudicial sanction, the person who administers the program under which the sanction is used shall inform a parent of the young person of the sanction.

12. **Victim's right to information** — If a young person is dealt with by an extrajudicial sanction, a police officer, the Attorney General, the provincial director or any organization established by a province to provide assistance to victims shall, on request, inform the victim of the identity of the young person and how the offence has been dealt with.

PART 2 — ORGANIZATION OF YOUTH CRIMINAL JUSTICE SYSTEM (SS. 13–22)

Youth Justice Court

13. (1) **Designation of youth justice court** — A youth justice court is any court that may be established or designated by or under an Act of the legislature of a province, or designated by the Governor in Council or the lieutenant governor in council of a province, as a youth justice court for the purposes of this Act, and a youth justice court judge is a person who may be appointed or designated as a judge of the youth justice court or a judge sitting in a court established or designated as a youth justice court.

(2) **Deemed youth justice court** — When a young person elects to be tried by a judge without a jury, the judge shall be a judge as defined in section 552 of the *Criminal Code*, or if it is an offence set out in section 469 of that Act, the judge shall be a judge of the superior court of criminal jurisdiction in the province in which the election is made. In either case, the judge is deemed to be a youth justice court judge and the court is deemed to be a youth justice court for the purpose of the proceeding.

(3) **Deemed youth justice court** — When a young person elects or is deemed to have elected to be tried by a court composed of a judge and jury, the superior court of criminal jurisdiction in the province in which the election is made or deemed to have been made is deemed to be a youth justice court for the purpose of the proceeding, and the superior court judge is deemed to be a youth justice court judge.

(4) **Court of record** — A youth justice court is a court of record.

14. (1) Exclusive jurisdiction of youth justice court — Despite any other Act of Parliament but subject to the *Contraventions Act* and the *National Defence Act*, a youth justice court has exclusive jurisdiction in respect of any offence alleged to have been committed by a person while he or she was a young person, and that person shall be dealt with as provided in this Act.

(2) **Orders** — A youth justice court has exclusive jurisdiction to make orders against a young person under sections 83.3 (recognizance — terrorist activity), 810 (recognizance — fear of injury or damage), 810.01 (recognizance — fear of certain offences), 810.011 (recognizance — fear of terrorism offence), 810.02 (recognizance — fear of forced marriage or marriage under age of 16 years) and 810.2 (recognizance — fear of serious personal injury offence) of the *Criminal Code* and the provisions of this Act apply, with any modifications that the circumstances require. If the young person fails or refuses to enter into a recognizance referred to in any of those sections, the court may impose any one of the sanctions set out in subsection 42(2) (youth sentences) except that, in the case of an order under paragraph 42(2)(n) (custody and supervision order), it shall not exceed 30 days.

(3) **Prosecution prohibited** — Unless the Attorney General and the young person agree, no extrajudicial measures shall be taken or judicial proceedings commenced under this Act in respect of an offence after the end of the time limit set out in any other Act of Parliament or any regulation made under it for the institution of proceedings in respect of that offence.

(4) **Continuation of proceedings** — Extrajudicial measures taken or judicial proceedings commenced under this Act against a young person may be continued under this Act after the person attains the age of eighteen years.

(5) **Young persons over the age of eighteen years** — This Act applies to persons eighteen years old or older who are alleged to have committed an offence while a young person.

(6) **Powers of youth justice court judge** — For the purpose of carrying out the provisions of this Act, a youth justice court judge is a justice and a provincial court judge and has the jurisdiction and powers of a summary conviction court under the *Criminal Code*.

(7) **Powers of a judge of a superior court** — A judge of a superior court of criminal jurisdiction, when deemed to be a youth justice court judge for the purpose of a proceeding, retains the jurisdiction and powers of a superior court of criminal jurisdiction.

2015, c. 20, ss. 32, 36(8); 2015, c. 29, s. 14; 2019, c. 13, s. 159

15. (1) **Contempt against youth justice court** — Every youth justice court has the same power, jurisdiction and authority to deal with and impose punishment for contempt against the court as may be exercised by the superior court of criminal jurisdiction of the province in which the court is situated.

(2) **Jurisdiction of youth justice court** — A youth justice court has jurisdiction in respect of every contempt of court committed by a young person against the youth justice court whether or not committed in the face of the court, and every contempt of court committed by a young person against any other court otherwise than in the face of that court.

(3) **Concurrent jurisdiction of youth justice court** — A youth justice court has jurisdiction in respect of every contempt of court committed by a young person against any other court in the face of that court and every contempt of court committed by an adult against the youth justice court in the face of the youth justice court, but nothing in this subsection affects the power, jurisdiction or authority of any other court to deal with or impose punishment for contempt of court.

(4) **Youth sentence — contempt** — When a youth justice court or any other court finds a young person guilty of contempt of court, it may impose as a youth sentence any one of the sanctions set out in subsection 42(2) (youth sentences), or any number of them that are not inconsistent with each other, but no other sentence.

(5) **Section 708 of *Criminal Code* applies in respect of adults** — Section 708 (contempt) of the *Criminal Code* applies in respect of proceedings under this section in youth justice court against adults, with any modifications that the circumstances require.

16. **Status of offender uncertain** — When a person is alleged to have committed an offence during a period that includes the date on which the person attains the age of eighteen years, the youth justice court has jurisdiction in respect of the offence and shall, after putting the person to their election under section 67 (adult sentence) if applicable, and on finding the person guilty of the offence,

(a) if it has been proven that the offence was committed before the person attained the age of eighteen years, impose a sentence under this Act;

(b) if it has been proven that the offence was committed after the person attained the age of eighteen years, impose any sentence that could be imposed under the *Criminal Code* or any other Act of Parliament on an adult who has been convicted of the same offence; and

(c) if it has not been proven that the offence was committed after the person attained the age of eighteen years, impose a sentence under this Act.

17. (1) Youth justice court may make rules — The youth justice court for a province may, subject to the approval of the lieutenant governor in council of the province, establish rules of court not inconsistent with this Act or any other Act of Parliament or with any regulations made under section 155 regulating proceedings within the jurisdiction of the youth justice court.

(2) Rules of court — Rules under subsection (1) may be made

(a) generally to regulate the duties of the officers of the youth justice court and any other matter considered expedient to attain the ends of justice and carry into effect the provisions of this Act;

(b) subject to any regulations made under paragraph 155(b), to regulate the practice and procedure in the youth justice court; and

(c) to prescribe forms to be used in the youth justice court if they are not otherwise provided for by or under this Act.

(3) Publication of rules — Rules of court that are made under the authority of this section shall be published in the appropriate provincial gazette.

Youth Justice Committees

18. (1) Youth justice committees — The Attorney General of Canada or a province or any other minister that the lieutenant governor in council of the province may designate may establish one or more committees of citizens, to be known as youth justice committees, to assist in any aspect of the administration of this Act or in any programs or services for young persons.

(2) Role of committee — The functions of a youth justice committee may include the following:

(a) in the case of a young person alleged to have committed an offence,

(i) giving advice on the appropriate extrajudicial measure to be used in respect of the young person,

(ii) supporting any victim of the alleged offence by soliciting his or her concerns and facilitating the reconciliation of the victim and the young person,

(iii) ensuring that community support is available to the young person by arranging for the use of services from within the community, and enlisting members of the community to provide short-term mentoring and supervision, and

(iv) when the young person is also being dealt with by a child protection agency or a community group, helping to coordinate the interaction of the agency or group with the youth criminal justice system;

(b) advising the federal and provincial governments on whether the provisions of this Act that grant rights to young persons, or provide for the protection of young persons, are being complied with;

(c) advising the federal and provincial governments on policies and procedures related to the youth criminal justice system;

(d) providing information to the public in respect of this Act and the youth criminal justice system;

(e) acting as a conference; and

(f) any other functions assigned by the person who establishes the committee.

Conferences

19. (1) Conferences may be convened — A youth justice court judge, the provincial director, a police officer, a justice of the peace, a prosecutor or a youth worker may convene or cause to be convened a conference for the purpose of making a decision required to be made under this Act.

(2) Mandate of a conference — The mandate of a conference may be, among other things, to give advice on appropriate extrajudicial measures, conditions for judicial interim release, sentences, including the review of sentences, and reintegration plans.

(3) Rules for conferences — The Attorney General or any other minister designated by the lieutenant governor in council of a province may establish rules for the convening and conducting of conferences other than conferences convened or caused to be convened by a youth justice court judge or a justice of the peace.

(4) Rules to apply — In provinces where rules are established under subsection (3), the conferences to which those rules apply must be convened and conducted in accordance with those rules.

Justices of the Peace

20. (1) Certain proceedings may be taken before justices — Any proceeding that may be carried out before a justice under the *Criminal Code*, other than a plea, a trial or an adjudication, may be carried out before a justice in respect of an offence alleged to have been committed by a young person, and any process that may be issued by a justice under the *Criminal Code* may be issued by a justice in respect of an offence alleged to have been committed by a young person.

(2) Orders under section 810 of *Criminal Code* — Despite subsection 14(2), a justice has jurisdiction to make an order under section 810 (recognizance — fear of injury or damage) of the *Criminal Code* in respect of a young person. If the young person fails or refuses to enter into a recognizance referred to in that section, the justice shall refer the matter to a youth justice court.

2019, c. 13, s. 160

Clerks of the Court

21. Powers of clerks — In addition to any powers conferred on a clerk of a court by the *Criminal Code*, a clerk of the youth justice court may exercise the powers ordinarily exercised by a clerk of a court, and, in particular, may

(a) administer oaths or solemn affirmations in all matters relating to the business of the youth justice court; and

(b) in the absence of a youth justice court judge, exercise all the powers of a youth justice court judge relating to adjournment.

Provincial Directors

22. Powers, duties and functions of provincial directors — The provincial director may authorize any person to exercise the powers or perform the duties or functions of the provincial director under this Act, in which case the powers, duties or functions are deemed to have been exercised or performed by the provincial director.

PART 3 — JUDICIAL MEASURES (SS. 23–37)

Consent to Prosecute

23. (1) Pre-charge screening — The Attorney General may establish a program of pre-charge screening that sets out the circumstances in which the consent of the Attorney General must be obtained before a young person is charged with an offence.

(2) Pre-charge screening program — Any program of pre-charge screening of young persons that is established under an Act of the legislature of a province or by a directive of a provincial government, and that is in place before the coming into force of this section, is deemed to be a program of pre-charge screening for the purposes of subsection (1).

24. Private prosecutions — No prosecutions may be conducted by a prosecutor other than the Attorney General without the consent of the Attorney General.

Proposed Addition — 24.1

Certain Offences — Review of Charges by Attorney General

[Heading added 2019, c. 25, s. 363. To come into force December 18, 2019.]

24.1 Review required — If a charge for which an appearance notice, summons or release order was issued, or an undertaking was given, is dismissed, withdrawn or stayed, or the young person is acquitted of that charge, the Attorney General must review any charge pending against the young person under any of subsections 145(2) to (5) of the *Criminal Code* for failure to comply with the appearance notice, summons, release order or undertaking in order to determine whether the prosecution of the charge should proceed.

2019, c. 25, s. 363 [To come into force December 18, 2019.]

Right to Counsel

25. (1) Right to counsel — A young person has the right to retain and instruct counsel without delay, and to exercise that right personally, at any stage of proceedings against the young person and before and during any consideration of whether, instead of starting or continuing judicial proceedings against the young person under this Act, to use an extrajudicial sanction to deal with the young person.

(2) Arresting officer to advise young person of right to counsel — Every young person who is arrested or detained shall, on being arrested or detained, be advised without delay by the arresting officer or the officer in charge, as the case may be, of the right to retain and instruct counsel, and be given an opportunity to obtain counsel.

Proposed Amendment — 25(2)

(2) Arresting officer to advise young person of right to counsel — Every young person who is arrested or detained shall, on being arrested or detained, be advised without delay by the arresting officer of the right to retain and instruct counsel, and be given an opportunity to obtain counsel.

2019, c. 25, s. 364(1) [To come into force December 18, 2019.]

(3) Justice, youth justice court or review board to advise young person of right to counsel — When a young person is not represented by counsel

(a) at a hearing at which it will be determined whether to release the young person or detain the young person in custody,

(a.1) at a hearing held in relation to an order referred to in subsection 14(2) or 20(2),

(b) at a hearing held under section 71 (hearing — adult sentences),

(c) at trial,

(d) at any proceedings held under subsection 98(3) (continuation of custody), 103(1) (review by youth justice court), 104(1) (continuation of custody), 105(1) (conditional supervision) or 109(1) (review of decision),

(e) at a review of a youth sentence held before a youth justice court under this Act, or

(f) at a review of the level of custody under section 87,

the justice or youth justice court before which the hearing, trial or review is held, or the review board before which the review is held, shall advise the young person of the right to retain and instruct counsel and shall give the young person a reasonable opportunity to obtain counsel.

(4) Trial, hearing or review before youth justice court or review board — When a young person at trial or at a hearing or review referred to in subsection (3) wishes to obtain counsel but is unable to do so, the youth justice court before which the hearing, trial or review is held or the review board before which the review is held

(a) shall, if there is a legal aid program or an assistance program available in the province where the hearing, trial or review is held, refer the young person to that program for the appointment of counsel; or

(b) if no legal aid program or assistance program is available or the young person is unable to obtain counsel through the program, may, and on the request of the young person shall, direct that the young person be represented by counsel.

(5) Appointment of counsel — When a direction is made under paragraph (4)(b) in respect of a young person, the Attorney General shall appoint counsel, or cause counsel to be appointed, to represent the young person.

(6) Release hearing before justice — When a young person, at a hearing referred to in paragraph (3)(a) or (a.1) that is held before a justice who is not a youth justice court judge, wishes to obtain counsel but is unable to do so, the justice shall

(a) if there is a legal aid program or an assistance program available in the province where the hearing is held,

(i) refer the young person to that program for the appointment of counsel, or

(ii) refer the matter to a youth justice court to be dealt with in accordance with paragraph (4)(a) or (b); or

(b) if no legal aid program or assistance program is available or the young person is unable to obtain counsel through the program, refer the matter without delay to a youth justice court to be dealt with in accordance with paragraph (4)(b).

(7) Young person may be assisted by adult — When a young person is not represented by counsel at trial or at a hearing or review referred to in subsection (3), the justice before whom or the youth justice court or review board before which the proceedings are held may, on the request of the young person, allow the young person to be assisted by an adult whom the justice, court or review board considers to be suitable.

(8) Counsel independent of parents — If it appears to a youth justice court judge or a justice that the interests of a young person and the interests of a parent are in conflict or that it would be in the best interests of the young person to be represented by his or her own counsel, the judge or justice shall ensure that the young person is represented by counsel independent of the parent.

(9) Statement of right to counsel — A statement that a young person has the right to be represented by counsel shall be included in

(a) any appearance notice or summons issued to the young person;

(b) any warrant to arrest the young person;

(c) any promise to appear given by the young person;

Proposed Amendment — 25(9)(c)

(c) any undertaking entered into before a peace officer by the young person;
2019, c. 25, s. 364(2) [To come into force December 18, 2019.]

(d) any undertaking or recognizance entered into before an officer in charge by the young person;

Proposed Repeal — 25(9)(d)

(d) [Repealed 2019, c. 25, s. 364(2). To come into force December 18, 2019.]

(e) any notice given to the young person in relation to any proceedings held under subsection 98(3) (continuation of custody), 103(1) (review by youth justice court), 104(1) (continuation of custody), 105(1) (conditional supervision) or 109(1) (review of decision); or

(f) any notice of a review of a youth sentence given to the young person.

(10) **Recovery of costs of counsel** — Nothing in this Act prevents the lieutenant governor in council of a province or his or her delegate from establishing a program to authorize the recovery of the costs of a young person's counsel from the young person or the parents of the young person. The costs may be recovered only after the proceedings are completed and the time allowed for the taking of an appeal has expired or, if an appeal is taken, all proceedings in respect of the appeal have been completed.

(11) **Exception for persons over the age of twenty** — Subsections (4) to (9) do not apply to a person who is alleged to have committed an offence while a young person, if the person has attained the age of twenty years at the time of his or her first appearance before a youth justice court in respect of the offence; however, this does not restrict any rights that a person has under the law applicable to adults.
2019, c. 13, s. 161

Notices to Parents

26. (1) **Notice in case of arrest or detention** — Subject to subsection (4), if a young person is arrested and detained in custody pending his or her appearance in court, the officer in charge at the time the young person is detained shall, as soon as possible, give or cause to be given to a parent of the young person, orally or in writing, notice of the arrest stating the place of detention and the reason for the arrest.

Proposed Amendment — 26(1)

(1) **Notice in case of arrest and detained** — Subject to subsection (4), if a young person is arrested and detained in custody pending their appearance in court, a peace officer shall, as soon as possible after the young person is detained, give or cause to be given to a parent of the young person, orally or in writing, notice of the arrest stating the place of detention and the reason for the arrest.
2019, c. 25, s. 365 [To come into force December 18, 2019.]

(2) Notice in other cases — Subject to subsection (4), if a summons or an appearance notice is issued in respect of a young person, the person who issued the summons or appearance notice, or, if a young person is released on giving a promise to appear or entering into an undertaking or recognizance, the officer in charge, shall, as soon as possible, give or cause to be given to a parent of the young person notice in writing of the summons, appearance notice, promise to appear, undertaking or recognizance.

Proposed Amendment — 26(2)

(2) Notice in other cases — Subject to subsection (4), if a summons or an appearance notice is issued in respect of a young person, the person who issued the summons or appearance notice, or, if a young person is released on an undertaking, a peace officer, shall, as soon as possible, give or cause to be given to a parent of the young person notice in writing of the summons, appearance notice or undertaking.

2019, c. 25, s. 365 [To come into force December 18, 2019.]

(3) Notice to parent in case of ticket — Subject to subsection (4), a person who serves a ticket under the *Contraventions Act* on a young person, other than a ticket served for a contravention relating to parking a vehicle, shall, as soon as possible, give or cause to be given notice in writing of the ticket to a parent of the young person.

(4) Notice to relative or other adult — If the whereabouts of the parents of a young person are not known or it appears that no parent is available, a notice under this section may be given to an adult relative of the young person who is known to the young person and is likely to assist the young person or, if no such adult relative is available, to any other adult who is known to the young person and is likely to assist the young person and who the person giving the notice considers appropriate.

(5) Notice on direction of youth justice court judge or justice — If doubt exists as to the person to whom a notice under this section should be given, a youth justice court judge or, if a youth justice court judge is, having regard to the circumstances, not reasonably available, a justice may give directions as to the person to whom the notice should be given, and a notice given in accordance with those directions is sufficient notice for the purposes of this section.

(6) Contents of notice — Any notice under this section shall, in addition to any other requirements under this section, include

(a) the name of the young person in respect of whom it is given;

(b) the charge against the young person and, except in the case of a notice of a ticket served under the *Contraventions Act*, the time and place of appearance; and

(c) a statement that the young person has the right to be represented by counsel.

(7) Notice of ticket under *Contraventions Act* — A notice under subsection (3) shall include a copy of the ticket.

(8) **Service of notice** — Subject to subsections (10) and (11), a notice under this section that is given in writing may be served personally or be sent by confirmed delivery service.

(9) **Proceedings not invalid** — Subject to subsections (10) and (11), failure to give a notice in accordance with this section does not affect the validity of proceedings under this Act.

(10) **Exception** — Failure to give a notice under subsection (2) in accordance with this section in any case renders invalid any subsequent proceedings under this Act relating to the case unless

(a) a parent of the young person attends court with the young person; or

(b) a youth justice court judge or a justice before whom proceedings are held against the young person

(i) adjourns the proceedings and orders that the notice be given in the manner and to the persons that the judge or justice directs, or

(ii) dispenses with the notice if the judge or justice is of the opinion that, having regard to the circumstances, the notice may be dispensed with.

(11) **Where notice is not served** — Where there has been a failure to give a notice under subsection (1) or (3) in accordance with this section and none of the persons to whom the notice may be given attends court with the young person, a youth justice court judge or a justice before whom proceedings are held against the young person may

(a) adjourn the proceedings and order that the notice be given in the manner and to the persons that the judge or justice directs; or

(b) dispense with the notice if the judge or justice is of the opinion that, having regard to the circumstances, the notice may be dispensed with.

(12) **Exception for persons over the age of twenty** — This section does not apply to a person who is alleged to have committed an offence while a young person, if the person has attained the age of twenty years at the time of his or her first appearance before a youth justice court in respect of the offence.

27. (1) **Order requiring attendance of parent** — If a parent does not attend proceedings held before a youth justice court in respect of a young person, the court may, if in its opinion the presence of the parent is necessary or in the best interests of the young person, by order in writing require the parent to attend at any stage of the proceedings.

(2) **No order in ticket proceedings** — Subsection (1) does not apply in proceedings commenced by filing a ticket under the *Contraventions Act*.

(3) **Service of order** — A copy of the order shall be served by a peace officer or by a person designated by a youth justice court by delivering it personally to the parent to whom it is directed, unless the youth justice court authorizes service by confirmed delivery service.

(4) Failure to attend — A parent who is ordered to attend a youth justice court under subsection (1) and who fails without reasonable excuse, the proof of which lies on the parent, to comply with the order

(a) is guilty of contempt of court;

(b) may be dealt with summarily by the court; and

(c) is liable to the punishment provided for in the *Criminal Code* for a summary conviction offence.

(5) Warrant to arrest parent — If a parent who is ordered to attend a youth justice court under subsection (1) does not attend when required by the order or fails to remain in attendance as required and it is proved that a copy of the order was served on the parent, a youth justice court may issue a warrant to compel the attendance of the parent.

Detention and Release

[Heading amended 2019, c. 13, s. 162.]

28. Application of Part XVI of *Criminal Code* — Except to the extent that they are inconsistent with or excluded by this Act, the provisions of Part XVI (compelling appearance of an accused and interim release) of the *Criminal Code* apply to the detention and release of young persons under this Act.

Proposed Addition — 28.1

28.1 Substitute for social measures prohibited — A peace officer, youth justice court judge or justice shall not detain a young person in custody, or impose a condition in respect of a young person's release by including it in an undertaking or release order, as a substitute for appropriate child protection, mental health or other social measures.

2019, c. 25, s. 367 [To come into force December 18, 2019.]

29. (1) Detention as social measure prohibited — A youth justice court judge or a justice shall not detain a young person in custody as a substitute for appropriate child protection, mental health or other social measures.

Proposed Amendment — 29(1)

(1) Release order with conditions — A youth justice court judge or a justice may impose a condition set out in subsections 515(4) to (4.2) of the *Criminal Code* in respect of a release order only if they are satisfied that

(a) the condition is necessary to ensure the young person's attendance in court or for the protection or safety of the public, including any victim of or witness to the offence;

(b) the condition is reasonable having regard to the circumstances of the offending behaviour; and

(c) the young person will reasonably be able to comply with the condition.

2019, c. 25, s. 368 [To come into force December 18, 2019.]

(2) Justification for detention in custody — A youth justice court judge or a justice may order that a young person be detained in custody only if

(a) the young person has been charged with

(i) a serious offence, or

(ii) an offence other than a serious offence, if they have a history that indicates a pattern of either outstanding charges or findings of guilt;

(b) the judge or justice is satisfied, on a balance of probabilities,

(i) that there is a substantial likelihood that, before being dealt with according to law, the young person will not appear in court when required by law to do so,

(ii) that detention is necessary for the protection or safety of the public, including any victim of or witness to the offence, having regard to all the circumstances, including a substantial likelihood that the young person will, if released from custody, commit a serious offence, or

(iii) in the case where the young person has been charged with a serious offence and detention is not justified under subparagraph (i) or (ii), that there are exceptional circumstances that warrant detention and that detention is necessary to maintain confidence in the administration of justice, having regard to the principles set out in section 3 and to all the circumstances, including

(A) the apparent strength of the prosecution's case,

(B) the gravity of the offence,

(C) the circumstances surrounding the commission of the offence, including whether a firearm was used, and

(D) the fact that the young person is liable, on being found guilty, for a potentially lengthy custodial sentence; and

(c) the judge or justice is satisfied, on a balance of probabilities, that no condition or combination of conditions of release would, depending on the justification on which the judge or justice relies under paragraph (b),

(i) reduce, to a level below substantial, the likelihood that the young person would not appear in court when required by law to do so,

(ii) offer adequate protection to the public from the risk that the young person might otherwise present, or

(iii) maintain confidence in the administration of justice.

(3) Onus — The onus of satisfying the youth justice court judge or the justice as to the matters referred to in subsection (2) is on the Attorney General.

2012, c. 1, s. 169; 2019, c. 13, s. 163

30. (1) Designated place of temporary detention — Subject to subsection (7), a young person who is detained in custody in relation to any proceedings against the young person shall be detained in a safe, fair and humane manner in any place of temporary detention that may be designated by the lieutenant governor in council of the province or his or her delegate or in a place within a class of places so designated.

(2) Exception — A young person who is detained in a place of temporary detention under subsection (1) may, in the course of being transferred from that place to the court or from the court to that place, be held under the supervision and control of a peace officer.

(3) Detention separate from adults — A young person referred to in subsection (1) shall be held separate and apart from any adult who is detained or held in custody unless a youth justice court judge or a justice is satisfied that, having regard to the best interests of the young person,

(a) the young person cannot, having regard to his or her own safety or the safety of others, be detained in a place of detention for young persons; or

(b) no place of detention for young persons is available within a reasonable distance.

(4) Transfer to adult facility — When a young person is detained under subsection (1), the youth justice court may, on application of the provincial director made at any time after the young person attains the age of eighteen years, after giving the young person an opportunity to be heard, authorize the provincial director to direct, despite subsection (3), that the young person be temporarily detained in a provincial correctional facility for adults, if the court considers it to be in the best interests of the young person or in the public interest.

(5) When young person is twenty years old or older — When a young person is twenty years old or older at the time his or her temporary detention under subsection (1) begins, the young person shall, despite subsection (3), be temporarily detained in a provincial correctional facility for adults.

(6) Transfer by provincial director — A young person who is detained in custody under subsection (1) may, during the period of detention, be transferred by the provincial director from one place of temporary detention to another.

(7) Exception relating to temporary detention — Subsections (1) and (3) do not apply in respect of any temporary restraint of a young person under the supervision and control of a peace officer after arrest, but a young person who is so restrained shall be transferred to a place of temporary detention referred to in subsection (1) as soon as is practicable, and in no case later than the first reasonable opportunity after the appearance of the young person before a youth justice court judge or a justice under section 503 of the *Criminal Code*.

(8) Authorization of provincial authority for detention — In any province for which the lieutenant governor in council has designated a person or a group of persons whose authorization is required, either in all circumstances or in circumstances specified by the lieutenant governor in council, before a young person who has been arrested may be detained in accordance with this section, no young person shall be so detained unless the authorization is obtained.

(9) Determination by provincial authority of place of detention — In any province for which the lieutenant governor in council has designated a person or a group of persons who may determine the place where a young person who has been arrested may be detained in accordance with this section, no young person may be so detained in a place other than the one so determined.

2019, c. 13, s. 164

Proposed Addition — 30.1

30.1 Review of detention — 30-day period — For the purposes of section 525 of the *Criminal Code* with respect to a young person who has been charged with an offence for which they are being prosecuted in proceedings by way of summary conviction, every reference in that provision to "90 days" or "90-day" is to be read and construed as a reference to "30 days" or "30-day" respectively.

2019, c. 25, s. 369 [To come into force December 18, 2019.]

31. (1) Placement of young person in care of responsible person — A young person who has been arrested may be placed in the care of a responsible person instead of being detained in custody if a youth justice court or a justice is satisfied that

(a) the young person would, but for this subsection, be detained in custody under section 515 (judicial interim release) of the *Criminal Code*;

(b) the person is willing and able to take care of and exercise control over the young person; and

(c) the young person is willing to be placed in the care of that person.

(2) Inquiry as to availability of a responsible person — If a young person would, in the absence of a responsible person, be detained in custody, the youth justice court or the justice shall inquire as to the availability of a responsible person and whether the young person is willing to be placed in that person's care.

(3) Condition of placement — A young person shall not be placed in the care of a person under subsection (1) unless

(a) that person undertakes in writing to take care of and to be responsible for the attendance of the young person in court when required and to comply with any other conditions that the youth justice court judge or the justice may specify; and

(b) the young person undertakes in writing to comply with the arrangement and to comply with any other conditions that the youth justice court judge or the justice may specify.

(4) Removing young person from care — A young person, a person in whose care a young person has been placed or any other person may, by application in writing to a youth justice court judge or a justice, apply for an order under subsection (5) if

(a) the person in whose care the young person has been placed is no longer willing or able to take care of or exercise control over the young person; or

(b) it is, for any other reason, no longer appropriate that the young person remain in the care of the person with whom he or she has been placed.

(5) Order — When a youth justice court judge or a justice is satisfied that a young person should not remain in the custody of the person in whose care he or she was placed under subsection (1), the judge or justice shall

(a) make an order relieving the person and the young person of the obligations undertaken under subsection (3); and

(b) issue a warrant for the arrest of the young person.

(6) Effect of arrest — If a young person is arrested in accordance with a warrant issued under paragraph (5)(b), the young person shall be taken before a youth justice court judge or a justice without delay and dealt with under this section and sections 28 to 30.

Appearance

32. (1) Appearance before judge or justice — A young person against whom an information or indictment is laid must first appear before a youth justice court judge or a justice, and the judge or justice shall

(a) cause the information or indictment to be read to the young person;

(b) if the young person is not represented by counsel, inform the young person of the right to retain and instruct counsel; and

(c) if notified under subsection 64(2) (intention to seek adult sentence) or if section 16 (status of accused uncertain) applies, inform the young person that the youth justice court might, if the young person is found guilty, order that an adult sentence be imposed.

(d) [Repealed 2012, c. 1, s. 170.]

(2) Waiver — A young person may waive the requirements of subsection (1) if the young person is represented by counsel and counsel advises the court that the young person has been informed of that provision.

(3) Young person not represented by counsel — When a young person is not represented by counsel, the youth justice court, before accepting a plea, shall

(a) satisfy itself that the young person understands the charge;

(b) if the young person is liable to an adult sentence, explain to the young person the consequences of being liable to an adult sentence and the procedure by which the young person may apply for an order that a youth sentence be imposed; and

(c) explain that the young person may plead guilty or not guilty to the charge or, if subsection 67(1) (election of court for trial — adult sentence) or (3) (election of court for trial in Nunavut — adult sentence) applies, explain that the young person may elect to be tried by a youth justice court judge without a jury and without having a preliminary inquiry, or to have a preliminary inquiry and be tried by a judge without a jury, or to have a preliminary inquiry and be tried by a court composed of a judge and jury and, in either of the latter two cases, a preliminary inquiry will only be conducted if requested by the young person or the prosecutor.

(4) **If youth justice court not satisfied** — If the youth justice court is not satisfied that a young person understands the charge, the court shall, unless the young person must be put to his or her election under subsection 67(1) (election of court for trial — adult sentence) or, with respect to Nunavut, subsection 67(3) (election of court for trial in Nunavut — adult sentence), enter a plea of not guilty on behalf of the young person and proceed with the trial in accordance with subsection 36(2) (young person pleads not guilty).

(5) **If youth justice court not satisfied** — If the youth justice court is not satisfied that a young person understands the matters set out in subsection (3), the court shall direct that the young person be represented by counsel.

2002, c. 13, s. 91(1)(a); 2012, c. 1, s. 170

Application for Release from or Detention in Custody

[Heading amended 2019, c. 13, s. 165.]

33. (1) **Application for release from or detention in custody** — If an order is made under section 515 (judicial interim release) of the *Criminal Code* in respect of a young person by a justice who is not a youth justice court judge, an application may, at any time after the order is made, be made to a youth justice court for the release from or detention in custody of the young person, as the case may be, and the youth justice court shall hear the matter as an original application.

(2) **Notice to prosecutor** — An application under subsection (1) for release from custody shall not be heard unless the young person has given the prosecutor at least two clear days notice in writing of the application.

(3) **Notice to young person** — An application under subsection (1) for detention in custody shall not be heard unless the prosecutor has given the young person at least two clear days notice in writing of the application.

(4) **Waiver of notice** — The requirement for notice under subsection (2) or (3) may be waived by the prosecutor or by the young person or his or her counsel, as the case may be.

(5) **Application for review under section 520 or 521 of *Criminal Code*** — An application under section 520 or 521 of the *Criminal Code* for a review of an order made in respect of a young person by a youth justice court judge who is a judge of a superior court shall be made to a judge of the court of appeal.

(6) **Nunavut** — Despite subsection (5), an application under section 520 or 521 of the *Criminal Code* for a review of an order made in respect of a young person by a youth justice court judge who is a judge of the Nunavut Court of Justice shall be made to a judge of that court.

(7) **No review** — No application may be made under section 520 or 521 of the *Criminal Code* for a review of an order made in respect of a young person by a justice who is not a youth justice court judge.

(8) Interim release by youth justice court judge only — If a young person against whom proceedings have been taken under this Act is charged with an offence referred to in section 522 of the *Criminal Code*, a youth justice court judge, but no other court, judge or justice, may release the young person from custody under that section.

(9) Review by court of appeal — A decision made by a youth justice court judge under subsection (8) may be reviewed in accordance with section 680 of the *Criminal Code* and that section applies, with any modifications that the circumstances require, to any decision so made.

Medical and Psychological Reports

34. (1) Medical or psychological assessment — A youth justice court may, at any stage of proceedings against a young person, by order require that the young person be assessed by a qualified person who is required to report the results in writing to the court,

(a) with the consent of the young person and the prosecutor; or

(b) on its own motion or on application of the young person or the prosecutor, if the court believes a medical, psychological or psychiatric report in respect of the young person is necessary for a purpose mentioned in paragraphs (2)(a) to (g) and

(i) the court has reasonable grounds to believe that the young person may be suffering from a physical or mental illness or disorder, a psychological disorder, an emotional disturbance, a learning disability or a mental disability,

(ii) the young person's history indicates a pattern of repeated findings of guilt under this Act or the *Young Offenders Act*, chapter Y-1 of the Revised Statutes of Canada, 1985, or

(iii) the young person is alleged to have committed a serious violent offence.

(2) Purpose of assessment — A youth justice court may make an order under subsection (1) in respect of a young person for the purpose of

(a) considering an application under section 33 (release from or detention in custody);

(b) making its decision on an application heard under section 71 (hearing — adult sentences);

(c) making or reviewing a youth sentence;

(d) considering an application under subsection 104(1) (continuation of custody);

(e) setting conditions under subsection 105(1) (conditional supervision);

(f) making an order under subsection 109(2) (conditional supervision); or

(g) authorizing disclosure under subsection 127(1) (information about a young person).

(3) Custody for assessment — Subject to subsections (4) and (6), for the purpose of an assessment under this section, a youth justice court may remand a young person to any custody that it directs for a period not exceeding thirty days.

(4) Presumption against custodial remand — A young person shall not be remanded in custody in accordance with an order made under subsection (1) unless

(a) the youth justice court is satisfied that

(i) on the evidence custody is necessary to conduct an assessment of the young person, or

(ii) on the evidence of a qualified person detention of the young person in custody is desirable to conduct the assessment of the young person, and the young person consents to custody; or

(b) the young person is required to be detained in custody in respect of any other matter or by virtue of any provision of the *Criminal Code*.

(5) Report of qualified person in writing — For the purposes of paragraph (4)(a), if the prosecutor and the young person agree, evidence of a qualified person may be received in the form of a report in writing.

(6) Application to vary assessment order if circumstances change — A youth justice court may, at any time while an order made under subsection (1) is in force, on cause being shown, vary the terms and conditions specified in the order in any manner that the court considers appropriate in the circumstances.

(7) Disclosure of report — When a youth justice court receives a report made in respect of a young person under subsection (1),

(a) the court shall, subject to subsection (9), cause a copy of the report to be given to

(i) the young person,

(ii) any parent of the young person who is in attendance at the proceedings against the young person,

(iii) any counsel representing the young person, and

(iv) the prosecutor; and

(b) the court may cause a copy of the report to be given to

(i) a parent of the young person who is not in attendance at the proceedings if the parent is, in the opinion of the court, taking an active interest in the proceedings, or

(ii) despite subsection 119(6) (restrictions respecting access to certain records), the provincial director, or the director of the provincial correctional facility for adults or the penitentiary at which the young person is serving a youth sentence, if, in the opinion of the court, withholding the report would jeopardize the safety of any person.

(8) Cross-examination — When a report is made in respect of a young person under subsection (1), the young person, his or her counsel or the adult assisting the young person under subsection 25(7) and the prosecutor shall, subject to subsection

(9), on application to the youth justice court, be given an opportunity to cross-examine the person who made the report.

(9) Non-disclosure in certain cases — A youth justice court shall withhold all or part of a report made in respect of a young person under subsection (1) from a private prosecutor, if disclosure of the report or part, in the opinion of the court, is not necessary for the prosecution of the case and might be prejudicial to the young person.

(10) Non-disclosure in certain cases — A youth justice court shall withhold all or part of a report made in respect of a young person under subsection (1) from the young person, the young person's parents or a private prosecutor if the court is satisfied, on the basis of the report or evidence given in the absence of the young person, parents or private prosecutor by the person who made the report, that disclosure of the report or part would seriously impair the treatment or recovery of the young person, or would be likely to endanger the life or safety of, or result in serious psychological harm to, another person.

(11) Exception — interests of justice — Despite subsection (10), the youth justice court may release all or part of the report to the young person, the young person's parents or the private prosecutor if the court is of the opinion that the interests of justice make disclosure essential.

(12) Report to be part of record — A report made under subsection (1) forms part of the record of the case in respect of which it was requested.

(13) Disclosure by qualified person — Despite any other provision of this Act, a qualified person who is of the opinion that a young person held in detention or committed to custody is likely to endanger his or her own life or safety or to endanger the life of, or cause bodily harm to, another person may immediately so advise any person who has the care and custody of the young person whether or not the same information is contained in a report made under subsection (1).

(14) Definition of "qualified person" — In this section, **"qualified person"** means a person duly qualified by provincial law to practice medicine or psychiatry or to carry out psychological examinations or assessments, as the circumstances require, or, if no such law exists, a person who is, in the opinion of the youth justice court, so qualified, and includes a person or a member of a class of persons designated by the lieutenant governor in council of a province or his or her delegate.

Referral to Child Welfare Agency

35. Referral to child welfare agency — In addition to any order that it is authorized to make, a youth justice court may, at any stage of proceedings against a young person, refer the young person to a child welfare agency for assessment to determine whether the young person is in need of child welfare services.

Adjudication

36. (1) When young person pleads guilty — If a young person pleads guilty to an offence charged against the young person and the youth justice court is satisfied that the facts support the charge, the court shall find the young person guilty of the offence.

(2) When young person pleads not guilty — If a young person charged with an offence pleads not guilty to the offence or pleads guilty but the youth justice court is not satisfied that the facts support the charge, the court shall proceed with the trial and shall, after considering the matter, find the young person guilty or not guilty or make an order dismissing the charge, as the case may be.

Appeals

37. (1) Appeals — An appeal in respect of an indictable offence or an offence that the Attorney General elects to proceed with as an indictable offence lies under this Act in accordance with Part XXI (appeals — indictable offences) of the *Criminal Code*, which Part applies with any modifications that the circumstances require.

(2) Appeals for contempt of court — A finding of guilt under section 15 for contempt of court or a sentence imposed in respect of the finding may be appealed as if the finding were a conviction or the sentence were a sentence in a prosecution by indictment.

(3) Appeal — Section 10 of the *Criminal Code* applies if a person is convicted of contempt of court under subsection 27(4) (failure of parent to attend court).

(4) Appeals heard together — An order under subsection 72(1) or (1.1) (adult or youth sentence) or 76(1) (placement when subject to adult sentence) may be appealed as part of the sentence and, unless the court to which the appeal is taken otherwise orders, if more than one of these is appealed they must be part of the same appeal proceeding.

(5) Appeals for summary conviction offences — An appeal in respect of an offence punishable on summary conviction or an offence that the Attorney General elects to proceed with as an offence punishable on summary conviction lies under this Act in accordance with Part XXVII (summary conviction offences) of the *Criminal Code*, which Part applies with any modifications that the circumstances require.

(6) Appeals where offences are tried jointly — An appeal in respect of one or more indictable offences and one or more summary conviction offences that are tried jointly or in respect of which youth sentences are jointly imposed lies under this Act in accordance with Part XXI (appeals — indictable offences) of the *Criminal Code*, which Part applies with any modifications that the circumstances require.

(7) Deemed election — For the purpose of appeals under this Act, if no election is made in respect of an offence that may be prosecuted by indictment or proceeded with by way of summary conviction, the Attorney General is deemed to have elected to proceed with the offence as an offence punishable on summary conviction.

(8) **If the youth justice court is a superior court** — In any province where the youth justice court is a superior court, an appeal under subsection (5) shall be made to the court of appeal of the province.

(9) **Nunavut** — Despite subsection (8), if the Nunavut Court of Justice is acting as a youth justice court, an appeal under subsection (5) shall be made to a judge of the Nunavut Court of Appeal, and an appeal of that judge's decision shall be made to the Nunavut Court of Appeal in accordance with section 839 of the *Criminal Code*.

(10) **Appeal to the Supreme Court of Canada** — No appeal lies under subsection (1) from a judgment of the court of appeal in respect of a finding of guilt or an order dismissing an information or indictment to the Supreme Court of Canada unless leave to appeal is granted by the Supreme Court of Canada.

(11) **No appeal from youth sentence on review** — No appeal lies from a youth sentence under section 59 or any of sections 94 to 96.

Proposed Amendment — 37(11)

(11) **No appeal from youth sentence on review** — No appeal lies from a youth sentence under section 59 — other than subsection 59(10) — or under any of sections 94 to 96.

2019, c. 25, s. 370(2) [To come into force December 18, 2019.]

2012, c. 1, s. 171; 2019, c. 25, s. 370(1)

PART 4 — SENTENCING (SS. 38–82)

Purpose and Principles

38. (1) **Purpose** — The purpose of sentencing under section 42 (youth sentences) is to hold a young person accountable for an offence through the imposition of just sanctions that have meaningful consequences for the young person and that promote his or her rehabilitation and reintegration into society, thereby contributing to the long-term protection of the public.

(2) **Sentencing principles** — A youth justice court that imposes a youth sentence on a young person shall determine the sentence in accordance with the principles set out in section 3 and the following principles:

(a) the sentence must not result in a punishment that is greater than the punishment that would be appropriate for an adult who has been convicted of the same offence committed in similar circumstances;

(b) the sentence must be similar to the sentences imposed in the region on similar young persons found guilty of the same offence committed in similar circumstances;

(c) the sentence must be proportionate to the seriousness of the offence and the degree of responsibility of the young person for that offence;

(d) all available sanctions other than custody that are reasonable in the circumstances should be considered for all young persons with particular attention to the circumstances of aboriginal young persons;

(e) subject to paragraph (c), the sentence must

(i) be the least restrictive sentence that is capable of achieving the purpose set out in subsection (1),

(ii) be the one that is most likely to rehabilitate the young person and reintegrate him or her into society, and

(iii) promote a sense of responsibility in the young person, and an acknowledgement of the harm done to victims and the community; and

Proposed Amendment — 38(2)(e)

(e) subject to paragraph (c), the sentence must

(i) be the least restrictive sentence that is capable of achieving the purpose set out in subsection (1),

(ii) be the one that is most likely to rehabilitate the young person and reintegrate him or her into society, and

(iii) promote a sense of responsibility in the young person, and an acknowledgement of the harm done to victims and the community;

2019, c. 25, s. 371 [To come into force December 18, 2019.]

Proposed Addition — 38(2)(e.1)

(e.1) if this Act provides that a youth justice court may impose conditions as part of the sentence, a condition may be imposed only if

(i) the imposition of the condition is necessary to achieve the purpose set out in subsection 38(1),

(ii) the young person will reasonably be able to comply with the condition, and

(iii) the condition is not used as a substitute for appropriate child protection, mental health or other social measures; and

2019, c. 25, s. 371 [To come into force December 18, 2019.]

(f) subject to paragraph (c), the sentence may have the following objectives:

(i) to denounce unlawful conduct, and

(ii) to deter the young person from committing offences.

(3) Factors to be considered — In determining a youth sentence, the youth justice court shall take into account

(a) the degree of participation by the young person in the commission of the offence;

(b) the harm done to victims and whether it was intentional or reasonably foreseeable;

(c) any reparation made by the young person to the victim or the community;

(d) the time spent in detention by the young person as a result of the offence;

(e) the previous findings of guilt of the young person; and

(f) any other aggravating and mitigating circumstances related to the young person or the offence that are relevant to the purpose and principles set out in this section.

2012, c. 1, s. 172

39. (1) Committal to custody — A youth justice court shall not commit a young person to custody under section 42 (youth sentences) unless

(a) the young person has committed a violent offence;

(b) the young person has failed to comply with non-custodial sentences;

Proposed Amendment — 39(1)(b)

(b) the young person has previously been found guilty of an offence under section 137 in relation to more than one sentence and, if the court is imposing a sentence for an offence under subsections 145(2) to (5) of the *Criminal Code* or section 137, the young person caused harm, or a risk of harm, to the safety of the public in committing that offence;

2019, c. 25, s. 372 [To come into force December 18, 2019.]

(c) the young person has committed an indictable offence for which an adult would be liable to imprisonment for a term of more than two years and has a history that indicates a pattern of either extrajudicial sanctions or of findings of guilt or of both under this Act or the *Young Offenders Act*, chapter Y-1 of the Revised Statutes of Canada, 1985; or

(d) in exceptional cases where the young person has committed an indictable offence, the aggravating circumstances of the offence are such that the imposition of a non-custodial sentence would be inconsistent with the purpose and principles set out in section 38.

(2) Alternatives to custody — If any of paragraphs (1)(a) to (c) apply, a youth justice court shall not impose a custodial sentence under section 42 (youth sentences) unless the court has considered all alternatives to custody raised at the sentencing hearing that are reasonable in the circumstances, and determined that there is not a reasonable alternative, or combination of alternatives, that is in accordance with the purpose and principles set out in section 38.

(3) Factors to be considered — In determining whether there is a reasonable alternative to custody, a youth justice court shall consider submissions relating to

(a) the alternatives to custody that are available;

(b) the likelihood that the young person will comply with a non-custodial sentence, taking into account his or her compliance with previous non-custodial sentences; and

(c) the alternatives to custody that have been used in respect of young persons for similar offences committed in similar circumstances.

(4) Imposition of same sentence — The previous imposition of a particular non-custodial sentence on a young person does not preclude a youth justice court from imposing the same or any other non-custodial sentence for another offence.

(5) **Custody as social measure prohibited** — A youth justice court shall not use custody as a substitute for appropriate child protection, mental health or other social measures.

(6) **Pre-sentence report** — Before imposing a custodial sentence under section 42 (youth sentences), a youth justice court shall consider a pre-sentence report and any sentencing proposal made by the young person or his or her counsel.

(7) **Report dispensed with** — A youth justice court may, with the consent of the prosecutor and the young person or his or her counsel, dispense with a pre-sentence report if the court is satisfied that the report is not necessary.

(8) **Length of custody** — In determining the length of a youth sentence that includes a custodial portion, a youth justice court shall be guided by the purpose and principles set out in section 38, and shall not take into consideration the fact that the supervision portion of the sentence may not be served in custody and that the sentence may be reviewed by the court under section 94.

(9) **Reasons** — If a youth justice court imposes a youth sentence that includes a custodial portion, the court shall state the reasons why it has determined that a non-custodial sentence is not adequate to achieve the purpose set out in subsection 38(1), including, if applicable, the reasons why the case is an exceptional case under paragraph (1)(d).

2012, c. 1, s. 173

Pre-sentence Report

40. (1) **Pre-sentence report** — Before imposing sentence on a young person found guilty of an offence, a youth justice court

(a) shall, if it is required under this Act to consider a pre-sentence report before making an order or a sentence in respect of a young person, and

(b) may, if it considers it advisable,

require the provincial director to cause to be prepared a pre-sentence report in respect of the young person and to submit the report to the court.

(2) **Contents of report** — A pre-sentence report made in respect of a young person shall, subject to subsection (3), be in writing and shall include the following, to the extent that it is relevant to the purpose and principles of sentencing set out in section 38 and to the restrictions on custody set out in section 39:

(a) the results of an interview with the young person and, if reasonably possible, the parents of the young person and, if appropriate and reasonably possible, members of the young person's extended family;

(b) the results of an interview with the victim in the case, if applicable and reasonably possible;

(c) the recommendations resulting from any conference referred to in section 41;

(d) any information that is applicable to the case, including

(i) the age, maturity, character, behaviour and attitude of the young person and his or her willingness to make amends,

(ii) any plans put forward by the young person to change his or her conduct or to participate in activities or undertake measures to improve himself or herself,

(iii) subject to subsection 119(2) (period of access to records), the history of previous findings of delinquency under the *Juvenile Delinquents Act*, chapter J-3 of the Revised Statutes of Canada, 1970, or previous findings of guilt for offences under the *Young Offenders Act*, chapter Y-1 of the Revised Statutes of Canada, 1985, or under this or any other Act of Parliament or any regulation made under it, the history of community or other services rendered to the young person with respect to those findings and the response of the young person to previous sentences or dispositions and to services rendered to him or her,

(iv) subject to subsection 119(2) (period of access to records), the history of alternative measures under the *Young Offenders Act*, chapter Y-1 of the Revised Statutes of Canada, 1985, or extrajudicial sanctions used to deal with the young person and the response of the young person to those measures or sanctions,

(v) the availability and appropriateness of community services and facilities for young persons and the willingness of the young person to avail himself or herself of those services or facilities,

(vi) the relationship between the young person and the young person's parents and the degree of control and influence of the parents over the young person and, if appropriate and reasonably possible, the relationship between the young person and the young person's extended family and the degree of control and influence of the young person's extended family over the young person, and

(vii) the school attendance and performance record and the employment record of the young person;

(e) any information that may assist the court in determining under subsection 39(2) whether there is an alternative to custody; and

(f) any information that the provincial director considers relevant, including any recommendation that the provincial director considers appropriate.

(3) Oral report with leave — If a pre-sentence report cannot reasonably be committed to writing, it may, with leave of the youth justice court, be submitted orally in court.

(4) Report forms part of record — A pre-sentence report shall form part of the record of the case in respect of which it was requested.

(5) Copies of pre-sentence report — If a pre-sentence report made in respect of a young person is submitted to a youth justice court in writing, the court

(a) shall, subject to subsection (7), cause a copy of the report to be given to

(i) the young person,

(ii) any parent of the young person who is in attendance at the proceedings against the young person,

(iii) any counsel representing the young person, and

(iv) the prosecutor; and

(b) may cause a copy of the report to be given to a parent of the young person who is not in attendance at the proceedings if the parent is, in the opinion of the court, taking an active interest in the proceedings.

(6) **Cross-examination** — If a pre-sentence report made in respect of a young person is submitted to a youth justice court, the young person, his or her counsel or the adult assisting the young person under subsection 25(7) and the prosecutor shall, subject to subsection (7), on application to the court, be given the opportunity to cross-examine the person who made the report.

(7) **Report may be withheld from private prosecutor** — If a pre-sentence report made in respect of a young person is submitted to a youth justice court, the court may, when the prosecutor is a private prosecutor and disclosure of all or part of the report to the prosecutor might, in the opinion of the court, be prejudicial to the young person and is not, in the opinion of the court, necessary for the prosecution of the case against the young person,

(a) withhold the report or part from the prosecutor, if the report is submitted in writing; or

(b) exclude the prosecutor from the court during the submission of the report or part, if the report is submitted orally in court.

(8) **Report disclosed to other persons** — If a pre-sentence report made in respect of a young person is submitted to a youth justice court, the court

(a) shall, on request, cause a copy or a transcript of the report to be supplied to

(i) any court that is dealing with matters relating to the young person, and

(ii) any youth worker to whom the young person's case has been assigned; and

(b) may, on request, cause a copy or a transcript of all or part of the report to be supplied to any person not otherwise authorized under this section to receive a copy or a transcript of the report if, in the opinion of the court, the person has a valid interest in the proceedings.

(9) **Disclosure by the provincial director** — A provincial director who submits a pre-sentence report made in respect of a young person to a youth justice court may make all or part of the report available to any person in whose custody or under whose supervision the young person is placed or to any other person who is directly assisting in the care or treatment of the young person.

(10) **Inadmissibility of statements** — No statement made by a young person in the course of the preparation of a pre-sentence report in respect of the young person is admissible in evidence against any young person in civil or criminal proceedings except those under section 42 (youth sentences), 59 (review of non-custodial sen-

tence) or 71 (hearing — adult sentences) or any of sections 94 to 96 (reviews and other proceedings related to custodial sentences).

Youth Sentences

41. Recommendation of conference — When a youth justice court finds a young person guilty of an offence, the court may convene or cause to be convened a conference under section 19 for recommendations to the court on an appropriate youth sentence.

42. (1) Considerations as to youth sentence — A youth justice court shall, before imposing a youth sentence, consider any recommendations submitted under section 41, any pre-sentence report, any representations made by the parties to the proceedings or their counsel or agents and by the parents of the young person, and any other relevant information before the court.

(2) Youth sentence — When a youth justice court finds a young person guilty of an offence and is imposing a youth sentence, the court shall, subject to this section, impose any one of the following sanctions or any number of them that are not inconsistent with each other and, if the offence is first degree murder or second degree murder within the meaning of section 231 of the *Criminal Code*, the court shall impose a sanction set out in paragraph (q) or subparagraph (r)(ii) or (iii) and may impose any other of the sanctions set out in this subsection that the court considers appropriate:

(a) reprimand the young person;

(b) by order direct that the young person be discharged absolutely, if the court considers it to be in the best interests of the young person and not contrary to the public interest;

(c) by order direct that the young person be discharged on any conditions that the court considers appropriate and may require the young person to report to and be supervised by the provincial director;

Proposed Amendment — 42(2)(c)

(c) by order direct that the young person be discharged on any conditions imposed by the court in accordance with paragraph 38(2)(e.1) and may require the young person to report to and be supervised by the provincial director;

2019, c. 25, s. 373(1) [To come into force December 18, 2019.]

(d) impose on the young person a fine not exceeding $1,000 to be paid at the time and on the terms that the court may fix;

(e) order the young person to pay to any other person at the times and on the terms that the court may fix an amount by way of compensation for loss of or damage to property or for loss of income or support, or an amount for, in the Province of Quebec, pre-trial pecuniary loss or, in any other province, special damages, for personal injury arising from the commission of the offence if the value is readily ascertainable, but no order shall be made for other damages in the Province of Quebec or for general damages in any other province;

(f) order the young person to make restitution to any other person of any property obtained by the young person as a result of the commission of the offence within the time that the court may fix, if the property is owned by the other person or was, at the time of the offence, in his or her lawful possession;

(g) if property obtained as a result of the commission of the offence has been sold to an innocent purchaser, where restitution of the property to its owner or any other person has been made or ordered, order the young person to pay the purchaser, at the time and on the terms that the court may fix, an amount not exceeding the amount paid by the purchaser for the property;

(h) subject to section 54, order the young person to compensate any person in kind or by way of personal services at the time and on the terms that the court may fix for any loss, damage or injury suffered by that person in respect of which an order may be made under paragraph (e) or (g);

(i) subject to section 54, order the young person to perform a community service at the time and on the terms that the court may fix, and to report to and be supervised by the provincial director or a person designated by the youth justice court;

(j) subject to section 51 (mandatory prohibition order), make any order of prohibition, seizure or forfeiture that may be imposed under any Act of Parliament or any regulation made under it if an accused is found guilty or convicted of that offence, other than an order under section 161 of the *Criminal Code*;

(k) place the young person on probation in accordance with sections 55 and 56 (conditions and other matters related to probation orders) for a specified period not exceeding two years;

(l) subject to subsection (3) (agreement of provincial director), order the young person into an intensive support and supervision program approved by the provincial director;

(m) subject to subsection (3) (agreement of provincial director) and section 54, order the young person to attend a non-residential program approved by the provincial director, at the times and on the terms that the court may fix, for a maximum of two hundred and forty hours, over a period not exceeding six months;

(n) make a custody and supervision order with respect to the young person, ordering that a period be served in custody and that a second period — which is one half as long as the first — be served, subject to sections 97 (conditions to be included) and 98 (continuation of custody), under supervision in the community subject to conditions, the total of the periods not to exceed two years from the date of the coming into force of the order or, if the young person is found guilty of an offence for which the punishment provided by the *Criminal Code* or any other Act of Parliament is imprisonment for life, three years from the date of coming into force of the order;

(o) in the case of an offence set out in section 239 (attempt to commit murder), 232, 234 or 236 (manslaughter) or 273 (aggravated sexual assault) of the *Criminal Code*, make a custody and supervision order in respect of the young person for a specified period not exceeding three years from the date of committal that orders the young person to be committed into a continuous period of custody for the first portion of the sentence and, subject to subsection 104(1) (continuation of custody), to serve the remainder of the sentence under conditional supervision in the community in accordance with section 105;

(p) subject to subsection (5), make a deferred custody and supervision order that is for a specified period not exceeding six months, subject to the conditions set out in subsection 105(2), and to any conditions set out in subsection 105(3) that the court considers appropriate;

(q) order the young person to serve a sentence not to exceed

(i) in the case of first degree murder, ten years comprised of

(A) a committal to custody, to be served continuously, for a period that must not, subject to subsection 104(1) (continuation of custody), exceed six years from the date of committal, and

(B) a placement under conditional supervision to be served in the community in accordance with section 105, and

(ii) in the case of second degree murder, seven years comprised of

(A) a committal to custody, to be served continuously, for a period that must not, subject to subsection 104(1) (continuation of custody), exceed four years from the date of committal, and

(B) a placement under conditional supervision to be served in the community in accordance with section 105;

(r) subject to subsection (7), make an intensive rehabilitative custody and supervision order in respect of the young person

(i) that is for a specified period that must not exceed

(A) two years from the date of committal, or

(B) if the young person is found guilty of an offence for which the punishment provided by the *Criminal Code* or any other Act of Parliament is imprisonment for life, three years from the date of committal,

and that orders the young person to be committed into a continuous period of intensive rehabilitative custody for the first portion of the sentence and, subject to subsection 104(1) (continuation of custody), to serve the remainder under conditional supervision in the community in accordance with section 105,

(ii) that is for a specified period that must not exceed, in the case of first degree murder, ten years from the date of committal, comprising

(A) a committal to intensive rehabilitative custody, to be served continuously, for a period that must not exceed six years from the date of committal, and

(B) subject to subsection 104(1) (continuation of custody), a placement under conditional supervision to be served in the community in accordance with section 105, and

(iii) that is for a specified period that must not exceed, in the case of second degree murder, seven years from the date of committal, comprising

(A) a committal to intensive rehabilitative custody, to be served continuously, for a period that must not exceed four years from the date of committal, and

(B) subject to subsection 104(1) (continuation of custody), a placement under conditional supervision to be served in the community in accordance with section 105; and

(s) impose on the young person any other reasonable and ancillary conditions that the court considers advisable and in the best interests of the young person and the public.

Proposed Amendment — 42(2)(s)

(s) impose on the young person, in accordance with paragraph 38(2)(e.1), any other conditions that the court considers appropriate.

2019, c. 25, s. 373(2) [To come into force December 18, 2019.]

(3) Agreement of provincial director — A youth justice court may make an order under paragraph (2)(l) or (m) only if the provincial director has determined that a program to enforce the order is available.

(4) Youth justice court statement — When the youth justice court makes a custody and supervision order with respect to a young person under paragraph (2)(n), the court shall state the following with respect to that order:

You are ordered to serve (*state the number of days or months to be served*) in custody, to be followed by (*state one-half of the number of days or months stated above*) to be served under supervision in the community subject to conditions.

If you breach any of the conditions while you are under supervision in the community, you may be brought back into custody and required to serve the rest of the second period in custody as well.

You should also be aware that, under other provisions of the *Youth Criminal Justice Act*, a court could require you to serve the second period in custody as well.

The periods in custody and under supervision in the community may be changed if you are or become subject to another sentence.

(5) Deferred custody and supervision order — The court may make a deferred custody and supervision order under paragraph (2)(p) if

(a) the young person is found guilty of an offence other than one in the commission of which a young person causes or attempts to cause serious bodily harm; and

(b) it is consistent with the purpose and principles set out in section 38 and the restrictions on custody set out in section 39.

(6) Application of sections 106 to 109 — Sections 106 to 109 (suspension of conditional supervision) apply to a breach of a deferred custody and supervision order made under paragraph (2)(p) as if the breach were a breach of an order for conditional supervision made under subsection 105(1) and, for the purposes of sections 106 to 109, supervision under a deferred custody and supervision order is deemed to be conditional supervision.

(7) Intensive rehabilitative custody and supervision order — A youth justice court may make an intensive rehabilitative custody and supervision order under paragraph (2)(r) in respect of a young person only if

(a) either

(i) the young person has been found guilty of a serious violent offence, or

(ii) the young person has been found guilty of an offence, in the commission of which the young person caused or attempted to cause serious bodily harm and for which an adult is liable to imprisonment for a term of more than two years, and the young person had previously been found guilty at least twice of such an offence;

(b) the young person is suffering from a mental illness or disorder, a psychological disorder or an emotional disturbance;

(c) a plan of treatment and intensive supervision has been developed for the young person, and there are reasonable grounds to believe that the plan might reduce the risk of the young person repeating the offence or committing a serious violent offence; and

(d) the provincial director has determined that an intensive rehabilitative custody and supervision program is available and that the young person's participation in the program is appropriate.

(8) Safeguard of rights — Nothing in this section abrogates or derogates from the rights of a young person regarding consent to physical or mental health treatment or care.

(9) and (10) [Repealed 2012, c. 1, s. 174(4).]

(11) Inconsistency — An order may not be made under paragraphs (2)(k) to (m) in respect of an offence for which a conditional discharge has been granted under paragraph (2)(c).

(12) Coming into force of youth sentence — A youth sentence or any part of it comes into force on the date on which it is imposed or on any later date that the youth justice court specifies.

(13) Consecutive youth sentences — Subject to subsections (15) and (16), a youth justice court that sentences a young person may direct that a sentence imposed on the young person under paragraph (2)(n), (o), (q) or (r) be served consecutively if the young person

(a) is sentenced while under sentence for an offence under any of those paragraphs; or

(b) is found guilty of more than one offence under any of those paragraphs.

(14) Duration of youth sentence for a single offence — No youth sentence, other than an order made under paragraph (2)(j), (n), (o), (q) or (r), shall continue in force for more than two years. If the youth sentence comprises more than one sanction imposed at the same time in respect of the same offence, the combined duration of the sanctions shall not exceed two years, unless the sentence includes a sanction under paragraph (2)(j), (n), (o), (q) or (r) that exceeds two years.

(15) Duration of youth sentence for different offences — Subject to subsection (16), if more than one youth sentence is imposed under this section in respect of a young person with respect to different offences, the continuous combined duration of those youth sentences shall not exceed three years, except if one of the offences is first degree murder or second degree murder within the meaning of section 231 of the *Criminal Code*, in which case the continuous combined duration of those youth sentences shall not exceed ten years in the case of first degree murder, or seven years in the case of second degree murder.

(16) Duration of youth sentences made at different times — If a youth sentence is imposed in respect of an offence committed by a young person after the commencement of, but before the completion of, any youth sentences imposed on the young person,

(a) the duration of the sentence imposed in respect of the subsequent offence shall be determined in accordance with subsections (14) and (15);

(b) the sentence may be served consecutively to the sentences imposed in respect of the previous offences; and

(c) the combined duration of all the sentences may exceed three years and, if the offence is, or one of the previous offences was,

(i) first degree murder within the meaning of section 231 of the *Criminal Code*, the continuous combined duration of the youth sentences may exceed ten years, or

(ii) second degree murder within the meaning of section 231 of the *Criminal Code*, the continuous combined duration of the youth sentences may exceed seven years.

(17) Sentence continues when adult — Subject to sections 89, 92 and 93 (provisions related to placement in adult facilities) of this Act and section 743.5 (transfer of jurisdiction) of the *Criminal Code*, a youth sentence imposed on a young person continues in effect in accordance with its terms after the young person becomes an adult.

2012, c. 1, s. 174

43. Additional youth sentences — Subject to subsection 42(15) (duration of youth sentences), if a young person who is subject to a custodial sentence imposed under paragraph 42(2)(n), (o), (q) or (r) that has not expired receives an additional youth sentence under one of those paragraphs, the young person is, for the purposes of the *Corrections and Conditional Release Act*, the *Criminal Code*, the *Prisons and Reformatories Act* and this Act, deemed to have been sentenced to one youth sentence commencing at the beginning of the first of those youth sentences to be served and ending on the expiry of the last of them to be served.

44. Custodial portion if additional youth sentence — Subject to subsection 42(15) (duration of youth sentences) and section 46 (exception when youth sentence in respect of earlier offence), if an additional youth sentence under paragraph 42(2)(n), (o), (q) or (r) is imposed on a young person on whom a youth sentence had already been imposed under one of those paragraphs that has not expired and the expiry date of the youth sentence that includes the additional youth sentence, as determined in accordance with section 43, is later than the expiry date of the youth sentence that the young person was serving before the additional youth sentence was imposed, the custodial portion of the young person's youth sentence is, from the date the additional sentence is imposed, the total of

(a) the unexpired portion of the custodial portion of the youth sentence before the additional youth sentence was imposed, and

(b) the relevant period set out in subparagraph (i), (ii) or (iii):

(i) if the additional youth sentence is imposed under paragraph 42(2)(n), the period that is two thirds of the period that constitutes the difference between the expiry of the youth sentence as determined in accordance with section 43 and the expiry of the youth sentence that the young person was serving before the additional youth sentence was imposed,

(ii) if the additional youth sentence is a concurrent youth sentence imposed under paragraph 42(2)(o), (q) or (r), the custodial portion of the youth sentence imposed under that paragraph that extends beyond the expiry date of the custodial portion of the sentence being served before the imposition of the additional sentence, or

(iii) if the additional youth sentence is a consecutive youth sentence imposed under paragraph 42(2)(o), (q) or (r), the custodial portion of the additional youth sentence imposed under that paragraph.

45. (1) Supervision when additional youth sentence extends the period in custody — If a young person has begun to serve a portion of a youth sentence in the community subject to conditions under paragraph 42(2)(n) or under conditional supervision under paragraph 42(2)(o), (q) or (r) at the time an additional youth sentence is imposed under one of those paragraphs, and, as a result of the application of section 44, the custodial portion of the young person's youth sentence ends on a day that is later than the day on which the young person received the additional youth sentence, the serving of a portion of the youth sentence under supervision in the community subject to conditions or under conditional supervision shall become inoperative and the young person shall be committed to custody under paragraph 102(1)(b) or 106(b) until the end of the extended portion of the youth sentence to be served in custody.

(2) Supervision when additional youth sentence does not extend the period in custody — If a youth sentence has been imposed under paragraph 42(2)(n), (o), (q) or (r) on a young person who is under supervision in the community subject to conditions under paragraph 42(2)(n) or under conditional supervision under paragraph 42(2)(o), (q) or (r), and the additional youth sentence would not modify the expiry date of the youth sentence that the young person was serving at the time the additional youth sentence was imposed, the young person may be remanded to the youth custody facility that the provincial director considers appropriate. The provincial director shall review the case and, no later than forty-eight hours after the remand of the young person, shall either refer the case to the youth justice court for a review under section 103 or 109 or release the young person to continue the supervision in the community or the conditional supervision.

(3) **Supervision when youth sentence additional to supervision** — If a youth sentence has been imposed under paragraph 42(2)(n), (o), (q) or (r) on a young person who is under conditional supervision under paragraph 94(19)(b) or subsection 96(5), the young person shall be remanded to the youth custody facility that the provincial director considers appropriate. The provincial director shall review the case and, no later than forty-eight hours after the remand of the young person, shall either refer the case to the youth justice court for a review under section 103 or 109 or release the young person to continue the conditional supervision.

46. Exception when youth sentence in respect of earlier offence — The total of the custodial portions of a young person's youth sentences shall not exceed six years calculated from the beginning of the youth sentence that is determined in accordance with section 43 if

(a) a youth sentence is imposed under paragraph 42(2)(n), (o), (q) or (r) on the young person already serving a youth sentence under one of those paragraphs; and

(b) the later youth sentence imposed is in respect of an offence committed before the commencement of the earlier youth sentence.

47. (1) Committal to custody deemed continuous — Subject to subsections (2) and (3), a young person who is sentenced under paragraph 42(2)(n) is deemed to be committed to continuous custody for the custodial portion of the sentence.

(2) **Intermittent custody** — If the sentence does not exceed ninety days, the youth justice court may order that the custodial portion of the sentence be served intermittently if it is consistent with the purpose and principles set out in section 38.

(3) **Availability of place of intermittent custody** — Before making an order of committal to intermittent custody, the youth justice court shall require the prosecutor to make available to the court for its consideration a report of the provincial director as to the availability of a youth custody facility in which an order of intermittent custody can be enforced and, if the report discloses that no such youth custody facility is available, the court shall not make the order.

48. Reasons for the sentence — When a youth justice court imposes a youth sentence, it shall state its reasons for the sentence in the record of the case and shall, on request, give or cause to be given a copy of the sentence and the reasons for the sentence to

(a) the young person, the young person's counsel, a parent of the young person, the provincial director and the prosecutor; and

(b) in the case of a committal to custody under paragraph 42(2)(n), (o), (q) or (r), the review board.

49. (1) Warrant of committal — When a young person is committed to custody, the youth justice court shall issue or cause to be issued a warrant of committal.

(2) Custody during transfer — A young person who is committed to custody may, in the course of being transferred from custody to the court or from the court to custody, be held under the supervision and control of a peace officer or in any place of temporary detention referred to in subsection 30(1) that the provincial director may specify.

(3) Subsection 30(3) applies — Subsection 30(3) (detention separate from adults) applies, with any modifications that the circumstances require, in respect of a person held in a place of temporary detention under subsection (2).

50. (1) Application of Part XXIII of *Criminal Code* — Subject to section 74 (application of *Criminal Code* to adult sentences), Part XXIII (sentencing) of the *Criminal Code* does not apply in respect of proceedings under this Act except for paragraph 718.2(e) (sentencing principle for aboriginal offenders), sections 722 (victim impact statements), 722.1 (copy of statement) and 722.2 (inquiry by court), subsection 730(2) (court process continues in force) and sections 748 (pardons and remissions), 748.1 (remission by the Governor in Council) and 749 (royal prerogative) of that Act, which provisions apply with any modifications that the circumstances require.

(2) Section 787 of *Criminal Code* does not apply — Section 787 (general penalty) of the *Criminal Code* does not apply in respect of proceedings under this Act.

51. (1) Mandatory prohibition order — Despite section 42 (youth sentences), when a young person is found guilty of an offence referred to in any of paragraphs 109(1)(a) to (d) of the *Criminal Code*, the youth justice court shall, in addition to imposing a sentence under section 42 (youth sentences), make an order prohibiting the young person from possessing any firearm, cross-bow, prohibited weapon, restricted weapon, prohibited device, ammunition, prohibited ammunition or explosive substance during the period specified in the order as determined in accordance with subsection (2).

(2) Duration of prohibition order — An order made under subsection (1) begins on the day on which the order is made and ends not earlier than two years after the young person has completed the custodial portion of the sentence or, if the young person is not subject to custody, after the time the young person is found guilty of the offence.

(3) Discretionary prohibition order — Despite section 42 (youth sentences), where a young person is found guilty of an offence referred to in paragraph 110(1)(a) or (b) of the *Criminal Code*, the youth justice court shall, in addition to imposing a sentence under section 42 (youth sentences), consider whether it is desirable, in the interests of the safety of the young person or of any other person, to make an order prohibiting the young person from possessing any firearm, cross-bow, prohibited weapon, restricted weapon, prohibited device, ammunition, prohibited ammunition or explosive substance, or all such things, and where the court decides that it is so desirable, the court shall so order.

(4) Duration of prohibition order — An order made under subsection (3) against a young person begins on the day on which the order is made and ends not later than two years after the young person has completed the custodial portion of the sentence or, if the young person is not subject to custody, after the time the young person is found guilty of the offence.

(5) Reasons for the prohibition order — When a youth justice court makes an order under this section, it shall state its reasons for making the order in the record of the case and shall give or cause to be given a copy of the order and, on request, a transcript or copy of the reasons to the young person against whom the order was made, the counsel and a parent of the young person and the provincial director.

(6) Reasons — When the youth justice court does not make an order under subsection (3), or when the youth justice court does make such an order but does not prohibit the possession of everything referred to in that subsection, the youth justice court shall include in the record a statement of the youth justice court's reasons.

(7) Application of *Criminal Code* — Sections 113 to 117 (firearm prohibition orders) of the *Criminal Code* apply in respect of any order made under this section.

(8) Report — Before making an order referred to in section 113 (lifting firearms order) of the *Criminal Code* in respect of a young person, the youth justice court may require the provincial director to cause to be prepared, and to submit to the youth justice court, a report on the young person.

52. (1) Review of order made under section 51 — A youth justice court may, on application, review an order made under section 51 at any time after the end of the period set out in subsection 119(2) (period of access to records) that applies to the record of the offence that resulted in the order being made.

(2) Grounds — In conducting a review under this section, the youth justice court shall take into account

(a) the nature and circumstances of the offence in respect of which the order was made; and

(b) the safety of the young person and of other persons.

(3) Decision of review — When a youth justice court conducts a review under this section, it may, after giving the young person, a parent of the young person, the Attorney General and the provincial director an opportunity to be heard,

(a) confirm the order;

(b) revoke the order; or

(c) vary the order as it considers appropriate in the circumstances of the case.

(4) New order not to be more onerous — No variation of an order made under paragraph (3)(c) may be more onerous than the order being reviewed.

(5) Application of provisions — Subsections 59(3) to (5) apply, with any modifications that the circumstances require, in respect of a review under this section.

53. (1) Funding for victims — The lieutenant governor in council of a province may order that, in respect of any fine imposed in the province under paragraph 42(2)(d), a percentage of the fine as fixed by the lieutenant governor in council be used to provide such assistance to victims of offences as the lieutenant governor in council may direct from time to time.

(2) Victim fine surcharge — If the lieutenant governor in council of a province has not made an order under subsection (1), a youth justice court that imposes a fine on a young person under paragraph 42(2)(d) may, in addition to any other punishment imposed on the young person, order the young person to pay a victim fine surcharge in an amount not exceeding fifteen per cent of the fine. The surcharge shall be used to provide such assistance to victims of offences as the lieutenant governor in council of the province in which the surcharge is imposed may direct from time to time.

54. (1) Where a fine or other payment is ordered — The youth justice court shall, in imposing a fine under paragraph 42(2)(d) or in making an order under paragraph 42(2)(e) or (g), have regard to the present and future means of the young person to pay.

(2) Discharge of fine or surcharge — A young person on whom a fine is imposed under paragraph 42(2)(d), including any percentage of a fine imposed under subsection 53(1), or on whom a victim fine surcharge is imposed under subsection 53(2), may discharge the fine or surcharge in whole or in part by earning credits for work performed in a program established for that purpose

(a) by the lieutenant governor in council of the province in which the fine or surcharge was imposed; or

(b) by the lieutenant governor in council of the province in which the young person resides, if an appropriate agreement is in effect between the government of that province and the government of the province in which the fine or surcharge was imposed.

(3) Rates, crediting and other matters — A program referred to in subsection (2) shall determine the rate at which credits are earned and may provide for the manner of crediting any amounts earned against the fine or surcharge and any other matters necessary for or incidental to carrying out the program.

(4) Representations respecting orders under paragraphs 42(2)(e) to (h) — In considering whether to make an order under any of paragraphs 42(2)(e) to (h), the youth justice court may consider any representations made by the person who would be compensated or to whom restitution or payment would be made.

(5) Notice of orders under paragraphs 42(2)(e) to (h) — If the youth justice court makes an order under any of paragraphs 42(2)(e) to (h), it shall cause notice of the terms of the order to be given to the person who is to be compensated or to whom restitution or payment is to be made.

(6) Consent of person to be compensated — No order may be made under paragraph 42(2)(h) unless the youth justice court has secured the consent of the person to be compensated.

(7) Orders under paragraph 42(2)(h), (i) or (m) — No order may be made under paragraph 42(2)(h), (i) or (m) unless the youth justice court is satisfied that

(a) the young person against whom the order is made is a suitable candidate for such an order; and

(b) the order does not interfere with the normal hours of work or education of the young person.

(8) Duration of order for service — No order may be made under paragraph 42(2)(h) or (i) to perform personal or community services unless those services can be completed in two hundred and forty hours or less and within twelve months after the date of the order.

(9) Community service order — No order may be made under paragraph 42(2)(i) unless

(a) the community service to be performed is part of a program that is approved by the provincial director; or

(b) the youth justice court is satisfied that the person or organization for whom the community service is to be performed has agreed to its performance.

(10) Application for further time to complete youth sentence — A youth justice court may, on application by or on behalf of the young person in respect of whom a youth sentence has been imposed under any of paragraphs 42(2)(d) to (i), allow further time for the completion of the sentence subject to any regulations made under paragraph 155(b) and to any rules made by the youth justice court under subsection 17(1).

55. (1) Conditions that must appear in orders — The youth justice court shall prescribe, as conditions of an order made under paragraph 42(2)(k) or (l), that the young person

(a) keep the peace and be of good behaviour; and

(b) appear before the youth justice court when required by the court to do so.

Proposed Amendment — 55(1)

(1) Condition that must appear in orders — The youth justice court shall prescribe, as a condition of an order made under paragraph 42(2)(k) or (l), that the young person appear before the youth justice court when required by the court to do so.

2019, c. 25, s. 374(1) [To come into force December 18, 2019.]

(2) Conditions that may appear in orders — A youth justice court may prescribe, as conditions of an order made under paragraph 42(2)(k) or (l), that a young person do one or more of the following that the youth justice court considers appropriate in the circumstances:

Proposed Amendment — 55(2) opening words

(2) Conditions that may appear in orders — A youth justice court may, in accordance with paragraph 38(2)(e.1), prescribe as conditions of an order made under paragraph 42(2)(k) or (l) that a young person do one or more of the following:

2019, c. 25, s. 374(2) [To come into force December 18, 2019.]

(a) report to and be supervised by the provincial director or a person designated by the youth justice court;

(b) notify the clerk of the youth justice court, the provincial director or the youth worker assigned to the case of any change of address or any change in the young person's place of employment, education or training;

(c) remain within the territorial jurisdiction of one or more courts named in the order;

(d) make reasonable efforts to obtain and maintain suitable employment;

(e) attend school or any other place of learning, training or recreation that is appropriate, if the youth justice court is satisfied that a suitable program for the young person is available there;

(f) reside with a parent, or any other adult that the youth justice court considers appropriate, who is willing to provide for the care and maintenance of the young person;

(g) reside at a place that the provincial director may specify;

(h) comply with any other conditions set out in the order that the youth justice court considers appropriate, including conditions for securing the young person's good conduct and for preventing the young person from repeating the offence or committing other offences; and

Proposed Amendment — 55(2)(h)

(h) comply with any other conditions set out in the order that the youth justice court considers appropriate; and

2019, c. 25, s. 374(3) [To come into force December 18, 2019.]

(i) not own, possess or have the control of any weapon, ammunition, prohibited ammunition, prohibited device or explosive substance, except as authorized by the order.

56. (1) Communication of order — A youth justice court that makes an order under paragraph 42(2)(k) or (l) shall

(a) cause the order to be read by or to the young person bound by it;

(b) explain or cause to be explained to the young person the purpose and effect of the order, and confirm that the young person understands it; and

(c) cause a copy of the order to be given to the young person, and to any parent of the young person who is in attendance at the sentencing hearing.

(2) Copy of order to parent — A youth justice court that makes an order under paragraph 42(2)(k) or (l) may cause a copy to be given to a parent of the young person who is not in attendance at the proceedings if the parent is, in the opinion of the court, taking an active interest in the proceedings.

(3) Endorsement of order by young person — After the order has been read and explained under subsection (1), the young person shall endorse on the order an acknowledgement that the young person has received a copy of the order and had its purpose and effect explained.

(4) Validity of order — The failure of a young person to endorse the order or of a parent to receive a copy of the order does not affect the validity of the order.

(5) Commencement of order — An order made under paragraph 42(2)(k) or (l) comes into force

(a) on the date on which it is made; or

(b) if a young person receives a sentence that includes a period of continuous custody and supervision, at the end of the period of supervision.

(6) Effect of order in case of custody — If a young person is subject to a sentence that includes both a period of continuous custody and supervision and an order made under paragraph 42(2)(k) or (l), and the court orders under subsection 42(12) a delay in the start of the period of custody, the court may divide the period that the order made under paragraph 42(2)(k) or (l) is in effect, with the first portion to have effect from the date on which it is made until the start of the period of custody, and the remainder to take effect at the end of the period of supervision.

(7) Notice to appear — A young person may be given notice either orally or in writing to appear before the youth justice court under paragraph 55(1)(b).

(8) Warrant in default of appearance — If service of a notice in writing is proved and the young person fails to attend court in accordance with the notice, a youth justice court may issue a warrant to compel the appearance of the young person.

57. (1) Transfer of youth sentence — When a youth sentence has been imposed under any of paragraphs 42(2)(d) to (i), (k), (l) or (s) in respect of a young person and the young person or a parent with whom the young person resides is or becomes a resident of a territorial division outside the jurisdiction of the youth justice court that imposed the youth sentence, whether in the same or in another province, a youth justice court judge in the territorial division in which the youth sentence was imposed may, on the application of the Attorney General or on the application of the young person or the young person's parent, with the consent of the Attorney General, transfer to a youth justice court in another territorial division the youth sentence and any portion of the record of the case that is appropriate. All subsequent proceedings relating to the case shall then be carried out and enforced by that court.

(2) No transfer outside province before appeal completed — No youth sentence may be transferred from one province to another under this section until the time for an appeal against the youth sentence or the finding on which the youth sentence was based has expired or until all proceedings in respect of any such appeal have been completed.

(3) Transfer to a province when person is adult — When an application is made under subsection (1) to transfer the youth sentence of a young person to a province in which the young person is an adult, a youth justice court judge may, with the consent of the Attorney General, transfer the youth sentence and the record of the case to the youth justice court in the province to which the transfer is sought, and the youth justice court to which the case is transferred shall have full jurisdiction in respect of the youth sentence as if that court had imposed the youth sentence. The person shall be further dealt with in accordance with this Act.

58. (1) Interprovincial arrangements — When a youth sentence has been imposed under any of paragraphs 42(2)(k) to (r) in respect of a young person, the youth sentence in one province may be dealt with in any other province in accordance with any agreement that may have been made between those provinces.

(2) Youth justice court retains jurisdiction — Subject to subsection (3), when a youth sentence imposed in respect of a young person is dealt with under this section in a province other than that in which the youth sentence was imposed, the youth justice court of the province in which the youth sentence was imposed retains, for all purposes of this Act, exclusive jurisdiction over the young person as if the youth sentence were dealt with within that province, and any warrant or process issued in respect of the young person may be executed or served in any place in Canada outside the province where the youth sentence was imposed as if it were executed or served in that province.

(3) Waiver of jurisdiction — When a youth sentence imposed in respect of a young person is dealt with under this section in a province other than the one in which the youth sentence was imposed, the youth justice court of the province in which the youth sentence was imposed may, with the consent in writing of the Attorney General of that province and the young person, waive its jurisdiction, for the purpose of any proceeding under this Act, to the youth justice court of the province in which the youth sentence is dealt with, in which case the youth justice court in the province in which the youth sentence is dealt with shall have full jurisdiction in respect of the youth sentence as if that court had imposed the youth sentence.

59. (1) Review of youth sentences not involving custody — When a youth justice court has imposed a youth sentence in respect of a young person, other than a youth sentence under paragraph 42(2)(n), (o), (q) or (r), the youth justice court shall, on the application of the young person, the young person's parent, the Attorney General or the provincial director, made at any time after six months after the date of the youth sentence or, with leave of a youth justice court judge, at any earlier time, review the youth sentence if the court is satisfied that there are grounds for a review under subsection (2).

Proposed Amendment — 59(1)

(1) Review of youth sentences not involving custody — When a youth justice court has imposed a youth sentence in respect of a young person, other than a youth sentence under paragraph 42(2)(n), (o), (q) or (r), the youth justice court shall, on the application of the young person, the young person's parent, the Attorney General or the provincial director, review the youth sentence if the court is satisfied that there are grounds for a review under subsection (2).

2019, c. 25, s. 375(1) [To come into force December 18, 2019.]

(2) **Grounds for review** — A review of a youth sentence may be made under this section

(a) on the ground that the circumstances that led to the youth sentence have changed materially;

(b) on the ground that the young person in respect of whom the review is to be made is unable to comply with or is experiencing serious difficulty in complying with the terms of the youth sentence;

(c) on the ground that the young person in respect of whom the review is to be made has contravened a condition of an order made under paragraph 42(2)(k) or (l) without reasonable excuse;

(d) on the ground that the terms of the youth sentence are adversely affecting the opportunities available to the young person to obtain services, education or employment; or

(e) on any other ground that the youth justice court considers appropriate.

(3) **Progress report** — The youth justice court may, before reviewing under this section a youth sentence imposed in respect of a young person, require the provincial director to cause to be prepared, and to submit to the youth justice court, a progress report on the performance of the young person since the youth sentence took effect.

(4) **Subsections 94(10) to (12) apply** — Subsections 94(10) to (12) apply, with any modifications that the circumstances require, in respect of any progress report required under subsection (3).

(5) **Subsections 94(7) and (14) to (18) apply** — Subsections 94(7) and (14) to (18) apply, with any modifications that the circumstances require, in respect of reviews made under this section and any notice required under subsection 94(14) shall also be given to the provincial director.

(6) **Compelling appearance of young person** — The youth justice court may, by summons or warrant, compel a young person in respect of whom a review is to be made under this section to appear before the youth justice court for the purposes of the review.

(7) **Decision of the youth justice court after review** — When a youth justice court reviews under this section a youth sentence imposed in respect of a young person, it may, after giving the young person, a parent of the young person, the Attorney General and the provincial director an opportunity to be heard,

(a) confirm the youth sentence;

(b) terminate the youth sentence and discharge the young person from any further obligation of the youth sentence; or

(c) vary the youth sentence or impose any new youth sentence under section 42, other than a committal to custody, for any period of time, not exceeding the remainder of the period of the earlier youth sentence, that the court considers appropriate in the circumstances of the case.

(8) **New youth sentence not to be more onerous** — Subject to subsection (9), when a youth sentence imposed in respect of a young person is reviewed under

this section, no youth sentence imposed under subsection (7) shall, without the consent of the young person, be more onerous than the remainder of the youth sentence reviewed.

Proposed Amendment — 59(8)

(8) New youth sentence not to be more onerous — Subject to subsections (9) and (10), when a youth sentence imposed in respect of a young person is reviewed under this section, no youth sentence imposed under subsection (7) shall, without the consent of the young person, be more onerous than the remainder of the youth sentence reviewed.

2019, c. 25, s. 375(2) [To come into force December 18, 2019.]

(9) Exception — A youth justice court may under this section extend the time within which a youth sentence imposed under paragraphs 42(2)(d) to (i) is to be complied with by a young person if the court is satisfied that the young person requires more time to comply with the youth sentence, but in no case shall the extension be for a period of time that expires more than twelve months after the date the youth sentence would otherwise have expired.

Proposed Addition — 59(10)

(10) Exception — paragraph (2)(c) — In the case of a review of a youth sentence made on the ground set out in paragraph (2)(c), the youth justice court may, in accordance with paragraph 38(2)(e.1), impose on the young person additional or more onerous conditions if it is of the opinion that the conditions

(a) would better protect against the risk of harm to the safety of the public that the young person might otherwise present; or

(b) would assist the young person to comply with any conditions previously imposed as part of that sentence.

2019, c. 25, s. 375(3) [To come into force December 18, 2019.]

60. Provisions applicable to youth sentences on review — This Part and Part 5 (custody and supervision) apply with any modifications that the circumstances require to orders made in respect of reviews of youth sentences under sections 59 and 94 to 96.

Adult Sentence and Election

61 to 63. [Repealed 2012, c. 1, s. 175.]

64. (1) Application by Attorney General — The Attorney General may, before evidence is called as to sentence or, if no evidence is called, before submissions are made as to sentence, make an application to the youth justice court for an order that a young person is liable to an adult sentence if the young person is or has been found guilty of an offence for which an adult is liable to imprisonment for a term of more than two years and that was committed after the young person attained the age of 14 years.

(1.1) and (1.2) [Repealed 2019, c. 25, s. 376.]

(2) Notice of intention to seek adult sentence — If the Attorney General intends to seek an adult sentence for an offence by making an application under subsection (1), the Attorney General shall, before the young person enters a plea or with leave of the youth justice court before the commencement of the trial, give notice to the young person and the youth justice court of the intention to seek an adult sentence.

(3) Included offences — A notice of intention to seek an adult sentence given in respect of an offence is notice in respect of any included offence of which the young person is found guilty for which an adult is liable to imprisonment for a term of more than two years.

(4) and (5) [Repealed 2012, c. 1, s. 176(2).]

2012, c. 1, s. 176; 2019, c. 25, s. 376

65 and 66. [Repealed 2012, c. 1, s. 177.]

67. (1) Election — adult sentence — The youth justice court shall, before a young person enters a plea, put the young person to his or her election in the words set out in subsection (2) if

(a) [Repealed 2012, c. 1, s. 178(1).]

(b) the Attorney General has given notice under subsection 64(2) of the intention to seek an adult sentence for an offence committed after the young person has attained the age of fourteen years;

(c) the young person is charged with first or second degree murder within the meaning of section 231 of the *Criminal Code*; or

(d) the person to whom section 16 (status of accused uncertain) applies is charged with having, after attaining the age of fourteen years, committed an offence for which an adult would be entitled to an election under section 536 of the *Criminal Code*, or over which a superior court of criminal jurisdiction would have exclusive jurisdiction under section 469 of that Act.

(2) Wording of election — The youth justice court shall put the young person to his or her election in the following words:

> You have the option to elect to be tried by a youth justice court judge without a jury and without having had a preliminary inquiry; or you may elect to be tried by a judge without a jury; or you may elect to be tried by a court composed of a judge and jury. If you do not elect now, you are deemed to have elected to be tried by a court composed of a judge and jury. If you elect to be tried by a judge without a jury or by a court composed of a judge and jury or if you are deemed to have elected to be tried by a court composed of a judge and jury, you will have a preliminary inquiry only if you or the prosecutor requests one. How do you elect to be tried?

(3) Election — Nunavut — In respect of proceedings in Nunavut, the youth justice court shall, before a young person enters a plea, put the young person to his or her election in the words set out in subsection (4) if

(a) [Repealed 2012, c. 1, s. 178(2).]

(b) the Attorney General has given notice under subsection 64(2) of the intention to seek an adult sentence for an offence committed after the young person has attained the age of fourteen years;

(c) the young person is charged with first or second degree murder within the meaning of section 231 of the *Criminal Code*; or

(d) the person to whom section 16 (status of accused uncertain) applies is charged with having, after attaining the age of fourteen years, committed an offence for which an adult would be entitled to an election under section 536.1 of the *Criminal Code*.

(4) Wording of election — The youth justice court shall put the young person to his or her election in the following words:

> You have the option to elect to be tried by a judge of the Nunavut Court of Justice alone, acting as a youth justice court without a jury and without a preliminary inquiry; or you may elect to be tried by a judge of the Nunavut Court of Justice, acting as a youth justice court without a jury; or you may elect to be tried by a judge of the Nunavut Court of Justice, acting as a youth justice court with a jury. If you elect to be tried by a judge without a jury or by a judge, acting as a youth justice court, with a jury or if you are deemed to have elected to be tried by a judge, acting as a youth justice court, with a jury, you will have a preliminary inquiry only if you or the prosecutor requests one.How do you elect to be tried?

(5) Mode of trial where co-accused are young persons — When two or more young persons who are charged with the same offence, who are jointly charged in the same information or indictment or in respect of whom the Attorney General seeks joinder of counts that are set out in separate informations or indictments are put to their election, then, unless all of them elect or re-elect or are deemed to have elected, as the case may be, the same mode of trial, the youth justice court judge

(a) may decline to record any election, re-election or deemed election for trial by a youth justice court judge without a jury, a judge without a jury or, in Nunavut, a judge of the Nunavut Court Justice without a jury; and

(b) if the judge declines to do so, shall hold a preliminary inquiry, if requested to do so by one of the parties, unless a preliminary inquiry has been held prior to the election, re-election or deemed election.

(6) Attorney General may require trial by jury — The Attorney General may, even if a young person elects under subsection (1) or (3) to be tried by a youth justice court judge without a jury or a judge without a jury, require the young person to be tried by a court composed of a judge and jury.

(7) Preliminary inquiry — When a young person elects to be tried by a judge without a jury, or elects or is deemed to have elected to be tried by a court composed of a judge and jury, the youth justice court referred to in subsection 13(1) shall, on the request of the young person or the prosecutor made at the time or within the period fixed by rules of court made under section 17 or 155 or, if there are no such rules, by the youth justice court judge, conduct a preliminary inquiry and if, on its conclusion, the young person is ordered to stand trial, the proceedings shall be conducted

(a) before a judge without a jury or a court composed of a judge and jury, as the case may be; or

(b) in Nunavut, before a judge of the Nunavut Court of Justice acting as a youth justice court, with or without a jury, as the case may be.

(7.1) Preliminary inquiry if two or more accused — If two or more young persons are jointly charged in an information and one or more of them make a request for a preliminary inquiry under subsection (7), a preliminary inquiry must be held with respect to all of them.

(7.2) When no request for preliminary inquiry — If no request for a preliminary inquiry is made under subsection (7), the youth justice court shall fix the date for the trial or the date on which the young person must appear in the trial court to have the date fixed.

(8) Preliminary inquiry provisions of *Criminal Code* — The preliminary inquiry shall be conducted in accordance with the provisions of Part XVIII (procedure on preliminary inquiry) of the *Criminal Code*, except to the extent that they are inconsistent with this Act.

(9) Parts XIX and XX of *Criminal Code* — Proceedings under this Act before a judge without a jury or a court composed of a judge and jury or, in Nunavut, a judge of the Nunavut Court of Justice acting as a youth justice court, with or without a jury, as the case may be, shall be conducted in accordance with the provisions of Parts XIX (indictable offences — trial without jury) and XX (procedure in jury trials and general provisions) of the *Criminal Code*, with any modifications that the circumstances require, except that

(a) the provisions of this Act respecting the protection of privacy of young persons prevail over the provisions of the *Criminal Code*; and

(b) the young person is entitled to be represented in court by counsel if the young person is removed from court in accordance with subsection 650(2) of the *Criminal Code*.

2002, c. 13, s. 91(1)(b)–(e); 2012, c. 1, s. 178; 2019, c. 13, s. 166

68. [Repealed 2012, c. 1, s. 179.]

69. (1) [Repealed 2012, c. 1, s. 180(1).]

(2) Included offences — If the Attorney General has given notice under subsection 64(2) of the intention to seek an adult sentence and the young person is found guilty of an included offence for which an adult is liable to imprisonment for a term of more than two years, committed after he or she has attained the age of 14 years, the Attorney General may make an application under subsection 64(1) (application for adult sentence).

2012, c. 1, s. 180

70. [Repealed 2012, c. 1, s. 181.]

71. Hearing — adult sentences — The youth justice court shall, at the commencement of the sentencing hearing, hold a hearing in respect of an application under subsection 64(1) (application for adult sentence), unless the court has received notice that the application is not opposed. Both parties and the parents of the young person shall be given an opportunity to be heard at the hearing.

2012, c. 1, s. 182

72. (1) Order of adult sentence — The youth justice court shall order that an adult sentence be imposed if it is satisfied that

(a) the presumption of diminished moral blameworthiness or culpability of the young person is rebutted; and

(b) a youth sentence imposed in accordance with the purpose and principles set out in subparagraph 3(1)(b)(ii) and section 38 would not be of sufficient length to hold the young person accountable for his or her offending behaviour.

(1.1) Order of youth sentence — If the youth justice court is not satisfied that an order should be made under subsection (1), it shall order that the young person is not liable to an adult sentence and that a youth sentence must be imposed.

(2) Onus — The onus of satisfying the youth justice court as to the matters referred to in subsection (1) is on the Attorney General.

(3) Pre-sentence report — In making an order under subsection (1) or (1.1), the youth justice court shall consider the pre-sentence report.

(4) Court to state reasons — When the youth justice court makes an order under this section, it shall state the reasons for its decision.

(5) Appeal — For the purposes of an appeal in accordance with section 37, an order under subsection (1) or (1.1) is part of the sentence.

2012, c. 1, s. 183

73. (1) Court must impose adult sentence — When the youth justice court makes an order under subsection 72(1) in respect of a young person, the court shall, on a finding of guilt, impose an adult sentence on the young person.

(2) Court must impose youth sentence — When the youth justice court makes an order under subsection 72(1.1) in respect of a young person, the court shall, on a finding of guilt, impose a youth sentence on the young person.

2012, c. 1, s. 184

74. (1) Application of Parts XXIII and XXIV of *Criminal Code* — Parts XXIII (sentencing) and XXIV (dangerous and long-term offenders) of the *Criminal Code* apply to a young person in respect of whom the youth justice court has ordered that an adult sentence be imposed.

(2) Finding of guilt becomes a conviction — A finding of guilt for an offence in respect of which an adult sentence is imposed becomes a conviction once the time allowed for the taking of an appeal has expired or, if an appeal is taken, all proceedings in respect of the appeal have been completed and the appeal court has upheld an adult sentence.

(3) Interpretation — This section does not affect the time of commencement of an adult sentence under subsection 719(1) of the *Criminal Code*.

75. [Repealed 2019, c. 25, s. 377.]

76. (1) Placement when subject to adult sentence — Subject to subsections (2) and (9) and sections 79 and 80 and despite anything else in this Act or any other Act of Parliament, when a young person who is subject to an adult sentence in respect of an offence is sentenced to a term of imprisonment for the offence, the youth justice court shall order that the young person serve any portion of the imprisonment in

(a) a youth custody facility separate and apart from any adult who is detained or held in custody;

(b) a provincial correctional facility for adults; or

(c) if the sentence is for two years or more, a penitentiary.

(2) Young person under age of 18 — No young person who is under the age of 18 years is to serve any portion of the imprisonment in a provincial correctional facility for adults or a penitentiary.

(3) Opportunity to be heard — Before making an order under subsection (1), the youth justice court shall give the young person, a parent of the young person, the Attorney General, the provincial director and representatives of the provincial and federal correctional systems an opportunity to be heard.

(4) Report — Before making an order under subsection (1), the youth justice court may require that a report be prepared for the purpose of assisting the court.

(5) Appeals — For the purposes of an appeal in accordance with section 37, an order under subsection (1) is part of the sentence.

(6) Review — On application, the youth justice court shall review the placement of a young person under this section and, if satisfied that the circumstances that resulted in the initial order have changed materially, and after having given the young person, a parent of the young person, the Attorney General, the provincial director and the representatives of the provincial and federal correctional systems an opportunity to be heard, the court may order that the young person be placed in

(a) a youth custody facility separate and apart from any adult who is detained or held in custody;

(b) a provincial correctional facility for adults; or

(c) if the sentence is for two years or more, a penitentiary.

(7) Who may make application — An application referred to in this section may be made by the young person, one of the young person's parents, the provincial director, representatives of the provincial and federal correctional systems and the Attorney General, after the time for all appeals has expired.

(8) Notice — When an application referred to in this section is made, the applicant shall cause a notice of the application to be given to the other persons referred to in subsection (7).

(9) Limit — age twenty — No young person shall remain in a youth custody facility under this section after the young person attains the age of twenty years, unless the youth justice court that makes the order under subsection (1) or reviews the placement under subsection (6) is satisfied that remaining in the youth custody facility would be in the best interests of the young person and would not jeopardize the safety of others.

2012, c. 1, s. 186; 2019, c. 25, s. 378

77. (1) Obligation to inform — parole — When a young person is ordered to serve a portion of a sentence in a youth custody facility under paragraph 76(1)(a) (placement when subject to adult sentence), the provincial director shall inform the appropriate parole board.

(2) Applicability of *Corrections and Conditional Release Act* — For greater certainty, Part II of the *Corrections and Conditional Release Act* applies, subject to section 78, with respect to a young person who is the subject of an order under subsection 76(1) (placement when subject to adult sentence).

(3) Appropriate parole board — The appropriate parole board for the purposes of this section is

(a) if subsection 112(1) of the *Corrections and Conditional Release Act* would apply with respect to the young person but for the fact that the young person was ordered into a youth custody facility, the parole board mentioned in that subsection; and

(b) in any other case, the Parole Board of Canada.

2012, c. 1, s. 160(l)(i)

78. (1) Release entitlement — For greater certainty, section 6 of the *Prisons and Reformatories Act* applies to a young person who is ordered to serve a portion of a sentence in a youth custody facility under paragraph 76(1)(a) (placement when subject to adult sentence) only if section 743.1 (rules respecting sentences of two or more years) of the *Criminal Code* would direct that the young person serve the sentence in a prison.

(2) Release entitlement — For greater certainty, section 127 of the *Corrections and Conditional Release Act* applies to a young person who is ordered to serve a portion of a sentence in a youth custody facility under paragraph 76(1)(a) (placement when subject to adult sentence) only if section 743.1 (rules respecting sentences of two or more years) of the *Criminal Code* would direct that the young person serve the sentence in a penitentiary.

79. If person convicted under another Act — If a person who is serving all or a portion of a sentence in a youth custody facility under paragraph 76(1)(a) (placement when subject to adult sentence) is sentenced to a term of imprisonment under an Act of Parliament other than this Act, the remainder of the portion of the sentence being served in the youth custody facility shall be served in a provincial correctional facility for adults or a penitentiary, in accordance with section 743.1 (rules respecting sentences of two or more years) of the *Criminal Code*.

80. If person who is serving a sentence under another Act is sentenced to an adult sentence — If a person who has been serving a sentence of imprisonment under an Act of Parliament other than this Act is sentenced to an adult sentence of imprisonment under this Act, the sentences shall be served in a provincial correctional facility for adults or a penitentiary, in accordance with section 743.1 (rules respecting sentences of two or more years) of the *Criminal Code*.

81. Procedure for application or notice — An application or a notice to the court under section 64 or 76 must be made or given orally, in the presence of the other party, or in writing with a copy served personally on the other party.

2012, c. 1, s. 187

Effect of Termination of Youth Sentence

82. (1) Effect of absolute discharge or termination of youth sentence — Subject to section 12 (examination as to previous convictions) of the *Canada Evidence Act*, if a young person is found guilty of an offence, and a youth justice court directs under paragraph 42(2)(b) that the young person be discharged absolutely, or the youth sentence, or any disposition made under the *Young Offenders Act*, chapter Y-1 of the Revised Statutes of Canada, 1985, has ceased to have effect, other than an order under section 51 (mandatory prohibition order) of this Act or section 20.1 (mandatory prohibition order) of the *Young Offenders Act*, the young person is deemed not to have been found guilty or convicted of the offence except that

(a) the young person may plead *autrefois convict* in respect of any subsequent charge relating to the offence;

(b) a youth justice court may consider the finding of guilt in considering an application under subsection 64(1) (application for adult sentence);

(c) any court or justice may consider the finding of guilt in considering an application for judicial interim release or in considering what sentence to impose for any offence; and

(d) the Parole Board of Canada or any provincial parole board may consider the finding of guilt in considering an application for conditional release or for a record suspension under the *Criminal Records Act*.

(2) Disqualifications removed — For greater certainty and without restricting the generality of subsection (1), an absolute discharge under paragraph 42(2)(b) or the termination of the youth sentence or disposition in respect of an offence for which a young person is found guilty removes any disqualification in respect of the offence to which the young person is subject under any Act of Parliament by reason of a finding of guilt.

(3) Applications for employment — No application form for or relating to the following shall contain any question that by its terms requires the applicant to disclose that he or she has been charged with or found guilty of an offence in respect of which he or she has, under this Act or the *Young Offenders Act*, chapter Y-1 of the Revised Statutes of Canada, 1985, been discharged absolutely, or has completed the youth sentence under this Act or the disposition under the *Young Offenders Act*:

(a) employment in any department, as defined in section 2 of the *Financial Administration Act*;

(b) employment by any Crown corporation, as defined in section 83 of the *Financial Administration Act*;

(c) enrolment in the Canadian Forces; or

(d) employment on or in connection with the operation of any work, undertaking or business that is within the legislative authority of Parliament.

(4) Finding of guilt not a previous conviction — A finding of guilt under this Act is not a previous conviction for the purposes of any offence under any Act of Parliament for which a greater punishment is prescribed by reason of previous convictions, except for

(a) [Repealed 2012, c. 1, s. 188(2).]

(b) the purpose of determining the adult sentence to be imposed.

2012, c. 1, ss. 156, 160(l)(ii), 188(1), (2)

PART 5 — CUSTODY AND SUPERVISION (SS. 83–109)

83. (1) Purpose — The purpose of the youth custody and supervision system is to contribute to the protection of society by

(a) carrying out sentences imposed by courts through the safe, fair and humane custody and supervision of young persons; and

(b) assisting young persons to be rehabilitated and reintegrated into the community as law-abiding citizens, by providing effective programs to young persons in custody and while under supervision in the community.

(2) Principles to be used — In addition to the principles set out in section 3, the following principles are to be used in achieving that purpose:

(a) that the least restrictive measures consistent with the protection of the public, of personnel working with young persons and of young persons be used;

(b) that young persons sentenced to custody retain the rights of other young persons, except the rights that are necessarily removed or restricted as a consequence of a sentence under this Act or another Act of Parliament;

(c) that the youth custody and supervision system facilitate the involvement of the families of young persons and members of the public;

(d) that custody and supervision decisions be made in a forthright, fair and timely manner, and that young persons have access to an effective review procedure; and

(e) that placements of young persons where they are treated as adults not disadvantage them with respect to their eligibility for and conditions of release.

84. Young person to be held apart from adults — Subject to subsection 30(3) (pre-trial detention), paragraphs 76(1)(b) and (c) (placement in adult facilities with adult sentence) and sections 89 to 93 (placement in adult facilities with youth sentence), a young person who is committed to custody shall be held separate and apart from any adult who is detained or held in custody.

85. (1) Levels of custody — In the youth custody and supervision system in each province there must be at least two levels of custody for young persons distinguished by the degree of restraint of the young persons in them.

(2) Designation of youth custody facilities — Every youth custody facility in a province that contains one or more levels of custody shall be designated by

(a) in the case of a youth custody facility with only one level of custody, being the level of custody with the least degree of restraint of the young persons in it, the lieutenant governor in council or his or her delegate; and

(b) in any other case, the lieutenant governor in council.

(3) Provincial director to specify custody level — committal to custody — The provincial director shall, when a young person is committed to custody under paragraph 42(2)(n), (o), (q) or (r) or an order is made under subsection 98(3), paragraph 103(2)(b), subsection 104(1) or paragraph 109(2)(b), determine the level of custody appropriate for the young person, after having taken into account the factors set out in subsection (5).

(4) Provincial director to specify custody level — transfer — The provincial director may determine a different level of custody for the young person when the provincial director is satisfied that the needs of the young person and the interests of society would be better served by doing so, after having taken into account the factors set out in subsection (5).

(5) Factors — The factors referred to in subsections (3) and (4) are

(a) that the appropriate level of custody for the young person is the one that is the least restrictive to the young person, having regard to

(i) the seriousness of the offence in respect of which the young person was committed to custody and the circumstances in which that offence was committed,

(ii) the needs and circumstances of the young person, including proximity to family, school, employment and support services,

(iii) the safety of other young persons in custody, and

(iv) the interests of society;

(b) that the level of custody should allow for the best possible match of programs to the young person's needs and behaviour, having regard to the findings of any assessment in respect of the young person; and

(c) the likelihood of escape.

(6) Placement and transfer at appropriate level — After the provincial director has determined the appropriate level of custody for the young person under subsection (3) or (4), the young person shall be placed in the youth custody facility that contains that level of custody specified by the provincial director.

(7) Notice — The provincial director shall cause a notice in writing of a determination under subsection (3) or (4) to be given to the young person and a parent of the young person and set out in that notice the reasons for it.

86. (1) Procedural safeguards — The lieutenant governor in council of a province shall ensure that procedures are in place to ensure that the due process rights of the young person are protected with respect to a determination made under subsection 85(3) or (4), including that the young person be

(a) provided with any relevant information to which the provincial director has access in making the determination, subject to subsection (2);

(b) given the opportunity to be heard; and

(c) informed of any right to a review under section 87.

(2) Withholding of information — Where the provincial director has reasonable grounds to believe that providing the information referred to in paragraph (1)(a) would jeopardize the safety of any person or the security of a facility, he or she may authorize the withholding from the young person of as much information as is strictly necessary in order to protect such safety or security.

87. (1) Review — A young person may apply for a review under this section of a determination

(a) under subsection 85(3) that would place the young person in a facility at a level of custody that has more than a minimal degree of restraint; or

(b) under subsection 85(4) that would transfer a young person to a facility at a level of custody with a higher degree of restraint or increase the degree of restraint of the young person in the facility.

(2) Procedural safeguards — The lieutenant governor in council of a province shall ensure that procedures are in place for the review under subsection (1), including that

(a) the review board that conducts the review be independent;

(b) the young person be provided with any relevant information to which the review board has access, subject to subsection (3); and

(c) the young person be given the opportunity to be heard.

(3) Withholding of information — Where the review board has reasonable grounds to believe that providing the information referred to in paragraph (2)(b) would jeopardize the safety of any person or the security of a facility, it may authorize the withholding from the young person of as much information as is strictly necessary in order to protect such safety or security.

(4) Factors — The review board shall take into account the factors referred to in subsection 85(5) in reviewing a determination.

(5) Decision is final — A decision of the review board under this section in respect of a particular determination is final.

88. Functions to be exercised by youth justice court — The lieutenant governor in council of a province may order that the power to make determinations of the level of custody for young persons and to review those determinations be exercised in accordance with the *Young Offenders Act*, chapter Y-1 of the Revised Statutes of Canada, 1985. The following provisions of that Act apply, with any modifications that the circumstances require, to the exercise of those powers:

(a) the definitions "review board" and "progress report" in subsection 2(1);

(b) section 11;

(c) sections 24.1 to 24.3; and

(d) sections 28 to 31.

89. (1) Exception if young person is twenty years old or older — When a young person is twenty years old or older at the time the youth sentence is imposed on him or her under paragraph 42(2)(n), (o), (q) or (r), the young person shall, despite section 85, be committed to a provincial correctional facility for adults to serve the youth sentence.

(2) If serving youth sentence in a provincial correctional facility — If a young person is serving a youth sentence in a provincial correctional facility for adults pursuant to subsection (1), the youth justice court may, on application of the provincial director at any time after the young person begins to serve a portion of the youth sentence in a provincial correctional facility for adults, after giving the young person, the provincial director and representatives of the provincial and federal correctional systems an opportunity to be heard, authorize the provincial director to direct that the young person serve the remainder of the youth sentence in a penitentiary if the court considers it to be in the best interests of the young person or in the public interest and if, at the time of the application, that remainder is two years or more.

(3) Provisions to apply — If a young person is serving a youth sentence in a provincial correctional facility for adults or a penitentiary under subsection (1) or (2), the *Prisons and Reformatories Act* and the *Corrections and Conditional Release Act*, and any other statute, regulation or rule applicable in respect of prisoners or offenders within the meaning of those Acts, statutes, regulations and rules, apply in respect of the young person except to the extent that they conflict with Part 6 (publication, records and information) of this Act, which Part continues to apply to the young person.

90. (1) Youth worker — When a youth sentence is imposed committing a young person to custody, the provincial director of the province in which the young person received the youth sentence and was placed in custody shall, without delay, designate a youth worker to work with the young person to plan for his or her reintegration into the community, including the preparation and implementation of a reintegration plan that sets out the most effective programs for the young person in order to maximize his or her chances for reintegration into the community.

(2) **Role of youth worker when young person in the community** — When a portion of a young person's youth sentence is served in the community in accordance with section 97 or 105, the youth worker shall supervise the young person, continue to provide support to the young person and assist the young person to respect the conditions to which he or she is subject, and help the young person in the implementation of the reintegration plan.

91. (1) Reintegration leave — The provincial director of a province may, subject to any terms or conditions that he or she considers desirable, authorize, for a young person committed to a youth custody facility in the province further to an order under paragraph 76(1)(a) (placement when subject to adult sentence) or a youth sentence imposed under paragraph 42(2)(n), (o), (q) or (r),

(a) a reintegration leave from the youth custody facility for a period not exceeding thirty days if, in the opinion of the provincial director, it is necessary or desirable that the young person be absent, with or without escort, for medical, compassionate or humanitarian reasons or for the purpose of rehabilitating the young person or reintegrating the young person into the community; or

(b) that the young person be released from the youth custody facility on the days and during the hours that the provincial director specifies in order that the young person may

(i) attend school or any other educational or training institution,

(ii) obtain or continue employment or perform domestic or other duties required by the young person's family,

(iii) participate in a program specified by the provincial director that, in the provincial director's opinion, will enable the young person to better carry out employment or improve his or her education or training, or

(iv) attend an out-patient treatment program or other program that provides services that are suitable to addressing the young person's needs.

(2) **Renewal of reintegration leave** — A reintegration leave authorized under paragraph (1)(a) may be renewed by the provincial director for one or more thirty-day periods on reassessment of the case.

(3) **Revocation of authorization** — The provincial director of a province may, at any time, revoke an authorization made under subsection (1).

(4) **Arrest and return to custody** — If the provincial director revokes an authorization under subsection (3) or if a young person fails to comply with any term or condition of a reintegration leave or a release from custody under this section, the young person may be arrested without warrant and returned to custody.

92. (1) Transfer to adult facility — When a young person is committed to custody under paragraph 42(2)(n), (o), (q) or (r), the youth justice court may, on application of the provincial director made at any time after the young person attains the age of eighteen years, after giving the young person, the provincial director and representatives of the provincial correctional system an opportunity to be heard, authorize the provincial director to direct that the young person, subject to subsection (3), serve the remainder of the youth sentence in a provincial correctional facility for adults, if the court considers it to be in the best interests of the young person or in the public interest.

(2) If serving youth sentence in a provincial correctional facility — The youth justice court may authorize the provincial director to direct that a young person, subject to subsection (3), serve the remainder of a youth sentence in a penitentiary

(a) if the youth justice court considers it to be in the best interests of the young person or in the public interest;

(b) if the provincial director applies for the authorization at any time after the young person begins to serve a portion of a youth sentence in a provincial correctional facility for adults further to a direction made under subsection (1);

(c) if, at the time of the application, that remainder is two years or more; and

(d) so long as the youth justice court gives the young person, the provincial director and representatives of the provincial and federal correctional systems an opportunity to be heard.

(3) Provisions to apply — If the provincial director makes a direction under subsection (1) or (2), the *Prisons and Reformatories Act* and the *Corrections and Conditional Release Act*, and any other statute, regulation or rule applicable in respect of prisoners and offenders within the meaning of those Acts, statutes, regulations and rules, apply in respect of the young person except to the extent that they conflict with Part 6 (publication, records and information) of this Act, which Part continues to apply to the young person.

(4) Placement when adult and youth sentences — If a person is subject to more than one sentence, at least one of which is a youth sentence imposed under paragraph 42(2)(n), (o), (q) or (r) and at least one of which is a sentence referred to in either paragraph (b) or (c), he or she shall serve, in a provincial correctional facility for adults or a penitentiary in accordance with section 743.1 (rules respecting sentences of two or more years) of the *Criminal Code*, the following:

(a) the remainder of any youth sentence imposed under paragraph 42(2)(n), (o), (q) or (r);

(b) an adult sentence to which an order under paragraph 76(1)(b) or (c) (placement in adult facility) applies; and

(c) any sentence of imprisonment imposed otherwise than under this Act.

(5) Youth sentence and adult sentence — If a young person is committed to custody under a youth sentence under paragraph 42(2)(n), (o), (q) or (r) and is also already subject to an adult sentence to which an order under paragraph 76(1)(a) (placement when subject to adult sentence) applies, the young person may, in the discretion of the provincial director, serve the sentences, or any portion of the sentences, in a youth custody facility, in a provincial correctional facility for adults or, if the unexpired portion of the sentence is two years or more, in a penitentiary.

93. (1) When young person reaches twenty years of age — When a young person who is committed to custody under paragraph 42(2)(n), (o), (q) or (r) is in a youth custody facility when the young person attains the age of twenty years, the young person shall be transferred to a provincial correctional facility for adults to serve the remainder of the youth sentence, unless the provincial director orders that the young person continue to serve the youth sentence in a youth custody facility.

(2) If serving youth sentence in a provincial correctional facility — If a young person is serving a portion of a youth sentence in a provincial correctional facility for adults pursuant to a transfer under subsection (1), the youth justice court may, on application of the provincial director after the transfer, after giving the young person, the provincial director and representatives of the provincial and federal correctional systems an opportunity to be heard, authorize the provincial director to direct that the young person serve the remainder of the youth sentence in a penitentiary if the court considers it to be in the best interests of the young person or in the public interest and if, at the time of the application, that remainder is two years or more.

(3) Provisions to apply — If the provincial director makes the direction, the *Prisons and Reformatories Act* and the *Corrections and Conditional Release Act*, and any other statute, regulation or rule applicable in respect of prisoners and offenders within the meaning of those Acts, statutes, regulations and rules, apply in respect of the young person except to the extent that they conflict with Part 6 (publication, records and information) of this Act, which Part continues to apply to the young person.

94. (1) Annual review — When a young person is committed to custody pursuant to a youth sentence under paragraph 42(2)(n), (o), (q) or (r) for a period exceeding one year, the provincial director of the province in which the young person is held in custody shall cause the young person to be brought before the youth justice court without delay at the end of one year from the date of the most recent youth sentence imposed in respect of the offence — and at the end of every subsequent year from that date — and the youth justice court shall review the youth sentence.

(2) Annual review — When a young person is committed to custody pursuant to youth sentences imposed under paragraph 42(2)(n), (o), (q) or (r) in respect of more than one offence for a total period exceeding one year, the provincial director of the province in which the young person is held in custody shall cause the young person to be brought before the youth justice court without delay at the end of one year from the date of the earliest youth sentence imposed — and at the end of every subsequent year from that date — and the youth justice court shall review the youth sentences.

(3) Optional review — When a young person is committed to custody pursuant to a youth sentence imposed under paragraph 42(2)(n), (o), (q) or (r) in respect of an offence, the provincial director may, on the provincial director's own initiative, and shall, on the request of the young person, the young person's parent or the Attorney General, on any of the grounds set out in subsection (6), cause the young person to be brought before a youth justice court to review the youth sentence,

(a) when the youth sentence is for a period not exceeding one year, once at any time after the expiry of the greater of

(i) thirty days after the date of the youth sentence imposed under subsection 42(2) in respect of the offence, and

(ii) one third of the period of the youth sentence imposed under subsection 42(2) in respect of the offence; and

(b) when the youth sentence is for a period exceeding one year, at any time after six months after the date of the most recent youth sentence imposed in respect of the offence.

(4) **Time for optional review** — The young person may be brought before the youth justice court at any other time, with leave of the youth justice court judge.

(5) **Review** — If a youth justice court is satisfied that there are grounds for review under subsection (6), the court shall review the youth sentence.

(6) **Grounds for review** — A youth sentence imposed in respect of a young person may be reviewed under subsection (5)

(a) on the ground that the young person has made sufficient progress to justify a change in the youth sentence;

(b) on the ground that the circumstances that led to the youth sentence have changed materially;

(c) on the ground that new services or programs are available that were not available at the time of the youth sentence;

(d) on the ground that the opportunities for rehabilitation are now greater in the community; or

(e) on any other ground that the youth justice court considers appropriate.

(7) **No review if appeal pending** — Despite any other provision of this section, no review of a youth sentence in respect of which an appeal has been taken shall be made under this section until all proceedings in respect of any such appeal have been completed.

(8) **Youth justice court may order appearance of young person for review** — When a provincial director is required under subsections (1) to (3) to cause a young person to be brought before the youth justice court and fails to do so, the youth justice court may, on application made by the young person, his or her parent or the Attorney General, or on its own motion, order the provincial director to cause the young person to be brought before the youth justice court.

(9) **Progress report** — The youth justice court shall, before reviewing under this section a youth sentence imposed in respect of a young person, require the provincial director to cause to be prepared, and to submit to the youth justice court, a progress report on the performance of the young person since the youth sentence took effect.

(10) Additional information in progress report — A person preparing a progress report in respect of a young person may include in the report any information relating to the personal and family history and present environment of the young person that he or she considers advisable.

(11) Written or oral report — A progress report shall be in writing unless it cannot reasonably be committed to writing, in which case it may, with leave of the youth justice court, be submitted orally in court.

(12) Subsections 40(4) to (10) to apply — Subsections 40(4) to (10) (procedures respecting pre-sentence reports) apply, with any modifications that the circumstances require, in respect of progress reports.

(13) Notice of review from provincial director — When a youth sentence imposed in respect of a young person is to be reviewed under subsection (1) or (2), the provincial director shall cause any notice that may be directed by rules of court applicable to the youth justice court or, in the absence of such a direction, at least five clear days notice of the review to be given in writing to the young person, a parent of the young person and the Attorney General.

(14) Notice of review from person requesting it — When a review of a youth sentence imposed in respect of a young person is requested under subsection (3), the person requesting the review shall cause any notice that may be directed by rules of court applicable to the youth justice court or, in the absence of such a direction, at least five clear days notice of the review to be given in writing to the young person, a parent of the young person and the Attorney General.

(15) Statement of right to counsel — A notice given to a parent under subsection (13) or (14) shall include a statement that the young person whose youth sentence is to be reviewed has the right to be represented by counsel.

(16) Service of notice — A notice under subsection (13) or (14) may be served personally or may be sent by confirmed delivery service.

(17) Notice may be waived — Any of the persons entitled to notice under subsection (13) or (14) may waive the right to that notice.

(18) If notice not given — If notice under subsection (13) or (14) is not given in accordance with this section, the youth justice court may

(a) adjourn the proceedings and order that the notice be given in the manner and to the persons that it directs; or

(b) dispense with the notice if, in the opinion of the court, having regard to the circumstances, notice may be dispensed with.

(19) Decision of the youth justice court after review — When a youth justice court reviews under this section a youth sentence imposed in respect of a young person, it may, after giving the young person, a parent of the young person, the Attorney General and the provincial director an opportunity to be heard, having regard to the needs of the young person and the interests of society,

(a) confirm the youth sentence;

(b) release the young person from custody and place the young person under conditional supervision in accordance with the procedure set out in section 105, with any modifications that the circumstances require, for a period not exceeding the remainder of the youth sentence that the young person is then serving; or

(c) if the provincial director so recommends, convert a youth sentence under paragraph 42(2)(r) to a youth sentence under paragraph 42(2)(q) if the offence was murder or to a youth sentence under paragraph 42(2)(n) or (o), as the case may be, if the offence was an offence other than murder.

95. Orders are youth sentences — Orders under subsections 97(2) (conditions) and 98(3) (continuation of custody), paragraph 103(2)(b) (continuation of custody), subsections 104(1) (continuation of custody) and 105(1) (conditional supervision) and paragraph 109(2)(b) (continuation of suspension of conditional supervision) are deemed to be youth sentences for the purposes of section 94 (reviews).

96. (1) Recommendation of provincial director for conditional supervision of young person — When a young person is held in custody pursuant to a youth sentence under paragraph 42(2)(n), (o), (q) or (r), the provincial director may, if satisfied that the needs of the young person and the interests of society would be better served by doing so, make a recommendation to the youth justice court that the young person be released from custody and placed under conditional supervision.

(2) Notice — If the provincial director makes a recommendation, the provincial director shall cause a notice to be given in writing that includes the reasons for the recommendation and the conditions that the provincial director would recommend be set under section 105 to the young person, a parent of the young person and the Attorney General and give a copy of the notice to the youth justice court.

(3) Application to court for review of recommendation — If notice of a recommendation is made under subsection (2) with respect to a youth sentence imposed on a young person, the youth justice court shall, if an application for review is made by the young person, the young person's parent or the Attorney General within ten days after service of the notice, review the youth sentence without delay.

(4) Subsections 94(7), (9) to (12) and (14) to (19) apply — Subject to subsection (5), subsections 94(7) (no review of appeal pending), (9) to (12) (progress reports) and (14) to (19) (provisions respecting notice and decision of the youth justice court) apply, with any modifications that the circumstances require, in respect of reviews made under this section and any notice required under subsection 94(14) shall also be given to the provincial director.

(5) If no application for review made under subsection (3) — A youth justice court that receives a notice under subsection (2) shall, if no application for a review is made under subsection (3),

(a) order the release of the young person and place the young person under conditional supervision in accordance with section 105, having regard to the recommendations of the provincial director; or

(b) if the court considers it advisable, order that the young person not be released.

For greater certainty, an order under this subsection may be made without a hearing.

(6) Notice when no release ordered — When a youth justice court orders that the young person not be released under paragraph (5)(b), it shall cause a notice of its order to be given to the provincial director without delay.

(7) Provincial director may request review — When the provincial director is given a notice under subsection (6), he or she may request a review under this section.

(8) When provincial director requests a review — When the provincial director requests a review under subsection (7),

(a) the provincial director shall cause any notice that may be directed by rules of court applicable to the youth justice court or, in the absence of such a direction, at least five clear days notice of the review to be given in writing to the young person, a parent of the young person and the Attorney General; and

(b) the youth justice court shall review the youth sentence without delay after the notice required under paragraph (a) is given.

97. (1) Conditions to be included in custody and supervision order — Every youth sentence imposed under paragraph 42(2)(n) shall contain the following conditions, namely, that the young person, while serving the portion of the youth sentence under supervision in the community,

(a) keep the peace and be of good behaviour;

(b) report to the provincial director and then be under the supervision of the provincial director;

(c) inform the provincial director immediately on being arrested or questioned by the police;

(d) report to the police, or any named individual, as instructed by the provincial director;

(e) advise the provincial director of the young person's address of residence and report immediately to the provincial director any change

(i) in that address,

(ii) in the young person's normal occupation, including employment, vocational or educational training and volunteer work,

(iii) in the young person's family or financial situation, and

(iv) that may reasonably be expected to affect the young person's ability to comply with the conditions of the sentence; and

(f) not own, possess or have the control of any weapon, ammunition, prohibited ammunition, prohibited device or explosive substance, except as authorized in writing by the provincial director for the purposes of the young person participating in a program specified in the authorization.

(2) Other conditions — The provincial director may set additional conditions that support and address the needs of the young person, promote the reintegration of the young person into the community and offer adequate protection to the public from the risk that the young person might otherwise present. The provincial director shall, in setting the conditions, take into account the needs of the young person, the most effective programs for the young person in order to maximize his or her chances for reintegration into the community, the nature of the offence and the ability of the young person to comply with the conditions.

(3) Communication of conditions — The provincial director shall

(a) cause the conditions to be read by or to the young person bound by them;

(b) explain or cause to be explained to the young person the purpose and effect of the conditions, and confirm that the young person understands them; and

(c) cause a copy of the conditions to be given to the young person, and to a parent of the young person.

(4) Provisions to apply — Subsections 56(3) (endorsement of order by young person) and (4) (validity of order) apply, with any modifications that the circumstances require, in respect of conditions under this section.

98. (1) Application for continuation of custody — Within a reasonable time before the expiry of the custodial portion of a young person's youth sentence, the Attorney General or the provincial director may apply to the youth justice court for an order that the young person remain in custody for a period not exceeding the remainder of the youth sentence.

(2) Continuation of custody — If the hearing for an application under subsection (1) cannot be completed before the expiry of the custodial portion of the youth sentence, the court may order that the young person remain in custody pending the determination of the application if the court is satisfied that the application was made in a reasonable time, having regard to all the circumstances, and that there are compelling reasons for keeping the young person in custody.

(3) Decision — The youth justice court may, after giving both parties and a parent of the young person an opportunity to be heard, order that a young person remain in custody for a period not exceeding the remainder of the youth sentence, if it is satisfied that there are reasonable grounds to believe that

(a) the young person is likely to commit a serious violent offence before the expiry of the youth sentence he or she is then serving; and

(b) the conditions that would be imposed on the young person if he or she were to serve a portion of the youth sentence in the community would not be adequate to prevent the commission of the offence.

(4) Factors — For the purpose of determining an application under subsection (1), the youth justice court shall take into consideration any factor that is relevant to the case of the young person, including

(a) evidence of a pattern of persistent violent behaviour and, in particular,

(i) the number of offences committed by the young person that caused physical or psychological harm to any other person,

(ii) the young person's difficulties in controlling violent impulses to the point of endangering the safety of any other person,

(iii) the use of weapons in the commission of any offence,

(iv) explicit threats of violence,

(v) behaviour of a brutal nature associated with the commission of any offence, and

(vi) a substantial degree of indifference on the part of the young person as to the reasonably foreseeable consequences, to other persons, of the young person's behaviour;

(b) psychiatric or psychological evidence that a physical or mental illness or disorder of the young person is of such a nature that the young person is likely to commit, before the expiry of the youth sentence the young person is then serving, a serious violent offence;

(c) reliable information that satisfies the youth justice court that the young person is planning to commit, before the expiry of the youth sentence the young person is then serving, a serious violent offence;

(d) the availability of supervision programs in the community that would offer adequate protection to the public from the risk that the young person might otherwise present until the expiry of the youth sentence the young person is then serving;

(e) whether the young person is more likely to reoffend if he or she serves his or her youth sentence entirely in custody without the benefits of serving a portion of the youth sentence in the community under supervision; and

(f) evidence of a pattern of committing violent offences while he or she was serving a portion of a youth sentence in the community under supervision.

99. (1) Report — For the purpose of determining an application under section 98 (application for continuation of custody), the youth justice court shall require the provincial director to cause to be prepared, and to submit to the youth justice court, a report setting out any information of which the provincial director is aware with respect to the factors set out in subsection 98(4) that may be of assistance to the court.

(2) Written or oral report — A report referred to in subsection (1) shall be in writing unless it cannot reasonably be committed to writing, in which case it may, with leave of the youth justice court, be submitted orally in court.

(3) Provisions apply — Subsections 40(4) to (10) (procedures respecting pre-sentence reports) apply, with any modifications that the circumstances require, in respect of a report referred to in subsection (1).

(4) **Notice of hearing** — When an application is made under section 98 (application for continuation of custody) in respect of a young person, the provincial director shall cause to be given, to the young person and to a parent of the young person, at least five clear days notice of the hearing in writing.

(5) **Statement of right to counsel** — Any notice given to a parent under subsection (4) shall include a statement that the young person has the right to be represented by counsel.

(6) **Service of notice** — A notice under subsection (4) may be served personally or may be sent by confirmed delivery service.

(7) **When notice not given** — When notice under subsection (4) is not given in accordance with this section, the youth justice court may

(a) adjourn the hearing and order that the notice be given in any manner and to any person that it directs; or

(b) dispense with the giving of the notice if, in the opinion of the youth justice court, having regard to the circumstances, the giving of the notice may be dispensed with.

100. Reasons — When a youth justice court makes an order under subsection 98(3) (decision for continued custody), it shall state its reasons for the order in the record of the case and shall provide, or cause to be provided, to the young person in respect of whom the order was made, the counsel and a parent of the young person, the Attorney General and the provincial director

(a) a copy of the order; and

(b) on request, a transcript or copy of the reasons for the order.

101. (1) Review of youth justice court decision — An order made under subsection 98(3) (decision for continued custody) in respect of a young person, or the refusal to make such an order, shall, on application of the young person, the young person's counsel, the Attorney General or the provincial director made within thirty days after the decision of the youth justice court, be reviewed by the court of appeal, and that court may, in its discretion, confirm or reverse the decision of the youth justice court.

(2) **Extension of time to make application** — The court of appeal may, at any time, extend the time within which an application under subsection (1) may be made.

(3) **Notice of application** — A person who proposes to apply for a review under subsection (1) shall give notice of the application in the manner and within the period of time that may be directed by rules of court.

102. (1) Breach of conditions — If the provincial director has reasonable grounds to believe that a young person has breached or is about to breach a condition to which he or she is subject under section 97 (conditions to be included in custody and supervision orders), the provincial director may, in writing,

(a) permit the young person to continue to serve a portion of his or her youth sentence in the community, on the same or different conditions; or

(b) if satisfied that the breach is a serious one that increases the risk to public safety, order that the young person be remanded to any youth custody facility that the provincial director considers appropriate until a review is conducted.

(2) **Provisions apply** — Sections 107 (apprehension) and 108 (review by provincial director) apply, with any modifications that the circumstances require, to an order under paragraph (1)(b).

103. (1) Review by youth justice court — When the case of a young person is referred to the youth justice court under section 108 (review by provincial director), the provincial director shall, without delay, cause the young person to be brought before the youth justice court, and the youth justice court shall, after giving the young person an opportunity to be heard,

(a) if the court is not satisfied on reasonable grounds that the young person has breached or was about to breach one of the conditions under which he or she was being supervised in the community, order that the young person continue to serve a portion of his or her youth sentence in the community, on the same or different conditions; or

(b) if the court is satisfied on reasonable grounds that the young person has breached or was about to breach one of the conditions under which he or she was being supervised in the community, make an order under subsection (2).

(2) **Order** — On completion of a review under subsection (1), the youth justice court

(a) shall order that the young person continue to serve the remainder of the youth sentence the young person is then serving in the community, and when the court does so, the court may vary the existing conditions or impose new conditions; or

(b) shall, despite paragraph 42(2)(n) (custody and supervision order), order that the young person remain in custody for a period that does not exceed the remainder of the youth sentence the young person is then serving, if the youth justice court is satisfied that the breach of the conditions was serious.

(3) **Provisions apply** — Subsections 109(4) to (8) apply, with any modifications that the circumstances require, in respect of a review under this section.

104. (1) Continuation of custody — When a young person on whom a youth sentence under paragraph 42(2)(o), (q) or (r) has been imposed is held in custody and an application is made to the youth justice court by the Attorney General, within a reasonable time before the expiry of the custodial portion of the youth sentence, the provincial director of the province in which the young person is held in custody shall cause the young person to be brought before the youth justice court and the youth justice court may, after giving both parties and a parent of the young person an opportunity to be heard and if it is satisfied that there are reasonable grounds to believe that the young person is likely to commit an offence causing the death of or serious harm to another person before the expiry of the youth sentence the young person is then serving, order that the young person remain in custody for a period not exceeding the remainder of the youth sentence.

(2) **Continuation of custody** — If the hearing of an application under subsection (1) cannot be completed before the expiry of the custodial portion of the youth sentence, the court may order that the young person remain in custody until the determination of the application if the court is satisfied that the application was made in a reasonable time, having regard to all the circumstances, and that there are compelling reasons for keeping the young person in custody.

(3) **Factors** — For the purpose of determining an application under subsection (1), the youth justice court shall take into consideration any factor that is relevant to the case of the young person, including

(a) evidence of a pattern of persistent violent behaviour and, in particular,

(i) the number of offences committed by the young person that caused physical or psychological harm to any other person,

(ii) the young person's difficulties in controlling violent impulses to the point of endangering the safety of any other person,

(iii) the use of weapons in the commission of any offence,

(iv) explicit threats of violence,

(v) behaviour of a brutal nature associated with the commission of any offence, and

(vi) a substantial degree of indifference on the part of the young person as to the reasonably foreseeable consequences, to other persons, of the young person's behaviour;

(b) psychiatric or psychological evidence that a physical or mental illness or disorder of the young person is of such a nature that the young person is likely to commit, before the expiry of the youth sentence the young person is then serving, an offence causing the death of or serious harm to another person;

(c) reliable information that satisfies the youth justice court that the young person is planning to commit, before the expiry of the youth sentence the young person is then serving, an offence causing the death of or serious harm to another person; and

(d) the availability of supervision programs in the community that would offer adequate protection to the public from the risk that the young person might otherwise present until the expiry of the youth sentence the young person is then serving.

(4) **Youth justice court to order appearance of young person** — If a provincial director fails to cause a young person to be brought before the youth justice court under subsection (1), the youth justice court shall order the provincial director to cause the young person to be brought before the youth justice court without delay.

(5) Provisions to apply — Sections 99 to 101 apply, with any modifications that the circumstances require, in respect of an order made, or the refusal to make an order, under this section.

(6) If application denied — If an application under this section is denied, the court may, with the consent of the young person, the Attorney General and the provincial director, proceed as though the young person had been brought before the court as required under subsection 105(1).

105. (1) Conditional supervision — The provincial director of the province in which a young person on whom a youth sentence under paragraph 42(2)(o), (q) or (r) has been imposed is held in custody or, if applicable, with respect to whom an order has been made under subsection 104(1) (continuation of custody), shall cause the young person to be brought before the youth justice court at least one month before the expiry of the custodial portion of the youth sentence. The court shall, after giving the young person an opportunity to be heard, by order, set the conditions of the young person's conditional supervision.

(2) Conditions to be included in order — The youth justice court shall include in the order under subsection (1) the following conditions, namely, that the young person

(a) keep the peace and be of good behaviour;

(b) appear before the youth justice court when required by the court to do so;

(c) report to the provincial director immediately on release, and then be under the supervision of the provincial director or a person designated by the youth justice court;

(d) inform the provincial director immediately on being arrested or questioned by the police;

(e) report to the police, or any named individual, as instructed by the provincial director;

(f) advise the provincial director of the young person's address of residence on release and after release report immediately to the clerk of the youth justice court or the provincial director any change

(i) in that address,

(ii) in the young person's normal occupation, including employment, vocational or educational training and volunteer work,

(iii) in the young person's family or financial situation, and

(iv) that may reasonably be expected to affect the young person's ability to comply with the conditions of the order;

(g) not own, possess or have the control of any weapon, ammunition, prohibited ammunition, prohibited device or explosive substance, except as authorized by the order; and

(h) comply with any reasonable instructions that the provincial director considers necessary in respect of any condition of the conditional supervision in order to prevent a breach of that condition or to protect society.

(3) Other conditions — In setting conditions for the purposes of subsection (1), the youth justice court may include in the order the following conditions, namely, that the young person

(a) on release, travel directly to the young person's place of residence, or to any other place that is noted in the order;

(b) make reasonable efforts to obtain and maintain suitable employment;

(c) attend school or any other place of learning, training or recreation that is appropriate, if the court is satisfied that a suitable program is available for the young person at such a place;

(d) reside with a parent, or any other adult that the court considers appropriate, who is willing to provide for the care and maintenance of the young person;

(e) reside in any place that the provincial director may specify;

(f) remain within the territorial jurisdiction of one or more courts named in the order;

(g) comply with conditions set out in the order that support and address the needs of the young person and promote the reintegration of the young person into the community; and

(h) comply with any other conditions set out in the order that the court considers appropriate, including conditions for securing the young person's good conduct and for preventing the young person from repeating the offence or committing other offences.

(4) Temporary conditions — When a provincial director is required under subsection (1) to cause a young person to be brought before the youth justice court but cannot do so for reasons beyond the young person's control, the provincial director shall so advise the youth justice court and the court shall, by order, set any temporary conditions for the young person's conditional supervision that are appropriate in the circumstances.

(5) Conditions to be set at first opportunity — When an order is made under subsection (4), the provincial director shall bring the young person before the youth justice court as soon after the order is made as the circumstances permit and the court shall then set the conditions of the young person's conditional supervision.

(6) Report — For the purpose of setting conditions under this section, the youth justice court shall require the provincial director to cause to be prepared, and to submit to the youth justice court, a report setting out any information that may be of assistance to the court.

(7) Provisions apply — Subsections 99(2) to (7) (provisions respecting reports and notice) and 104(4) (ordering appearance of young person) apply, with any modifications that the circumstances require, in respect of any proceedings held under subsection (1).

(8) Provisions apply — Subsections 56(1) to (4) (provisions respecting probation orders), (7) (notice to appear) and (8) (warrant in default) and section 101 (review of youth justice court decision) apply, with any modifications that the circumstances require, in respect of an order made under subsection (1).

106. Suspension of conditional supervision — If the provincial director has reasonable grounds to believe that a young person has breached or is about to breach a condition of an order made under subsection 105(1), the provincial director may, in writing,

(a) suspend the conditional supervision; and

(b) order that the young person be remanded to any youth custody facility that the provincial director considers appropriate until a review is conducted under section 108 and, if applicable, section 109.

107. (1) Apprehension — If the conditional supervision of a young person is suspended under section 106, the provincial director may issue a warrant in writing, authorizing the apprehension of the young person and, until the young person is apprehended, the young person is deemed not to be continuing to serve the youth sentence the young person is then serving.

(2) Warrants — A warrant issued under subsection (1) shall be executed by any peace officer to whom it is given at any place in Canada and has the same force and effect in all parts of Canada as if it had been originally issued or subsequently endorsed by a provincial court judge or other lawful authority having jurisdiction in the place where it is executed.

(3) Peace officer may arrest — If a peace officer believes on reasonable grounds that a warrant issued under subsection (1) is in force in respect of a young person, the peace officer may arrest the young person without the warrant at any place in Canada.

(4) Requirement to bring before provincial director — If a young person is arrested under subsection (3) and detained, the peace officer making the arrest shall cause the young person to be brought before the provincial director or a person designated by the provincial director

(a) if the provincial director or the designated person is available within a period of twenty-four hours after the young person is arrested, without unreasonable delay and in any event within that period; and

(b) if the provincial director or the designated person is not available within that period, as soon as possible.

(5) Release or remand in custody — If a young person is brought before the provincial director or a person designated by the provincial director under subsection (4), the provincial director or the designated person

(a) if not satisfied that there are reasonable grounds to believe that the young person is the young person in respect of whom the warrant referred to in subsection (1) was issued, shall release the young person; or

(b) if satisfied that there are reasonable grounds to believe that the young person is the young person in respect of whom the warrant referred to in subsection (1) was issued, may remand the young person in custody to await execution of the warrant, but if no warrant for the young person's arrest is executed within a period of forty-eight hours after the time the young person is remanded in custody, the person in whose custody the young person then is shall release the young person.

108. Review by provincial director — Without delay after the remand to custody of a young person whose conditional supervision has been suspended under section 106, or without delay after being informed of the arrest of such a young person, the provincial director shall review the case and, within forty-eight hours, cancel the suspension of the conditional supervision or refer the case to the youth justice court for a review under section 109.

109. (1) Review by youth justice court — If the case of a young person is referred to the youth justice court under section 108, the provincial director shall, without delay, cause the young person to be brought before the youth justice court, and the youth justice court shall, after giving the young person an opportunity to be heard,

(a) if the court is not satisfied on reasonable grounds that the young person has breached or was about to breach a condition of the conditional supervision, cancel the suspension of the conditional supervision; or

(b) if the court is satisfied on reasonable grounds that the young person has breached or was about to breach a condition of the conditional supervision, review the decision of the provincial director to suspend the conditional supervision and make an order under subsection (2).

(2) Order — On completion of a review under subsection (1), the youth justice court shall order

(a) the cancellation of the suspension of the conditional supervision, and when the court does so, the court may vary the conditions of the conditional supervision or impose new conditions;

(b) in a case other than a deferred custody and supervision order made under paragraph 42(2)(p), the continuation of the suspension of the conditional supervision for any period of time, not to exceed the remainder of the youth sentence the young person is then serving, that the court considers appropriate, and when the court does so, the court shall order that the young person remain in custody; or

(c) in the case of a deferred custody and supervision order made under paragraph 42(2)(p), that the young person serve the remainder of the order as if it were a custody and supervision order under paragraph 42(2)(n).

(3) Custody and supervision order — After a court has made a direction under paragraph (2)(c), the provisions of this Act applicable to orders under paragraph 42(2)(n) apply in respect of the deferred custody and supervision order.

(4) Factors to be considered — In making its decision under subsection (2), the court shall consider the length of time the young person has been subject to the order, whether the young person has previously contravened it, and the nature of the contravention, if any.

(5) Reasons — When a youth justice court makes an order under subsection (2), it shall state its reasons for the order in the record of the case and shall give, or cause to be given, to the young person in respect of whom the order was made, the counsel and a parent of the young person, the Attorney General and the provincial director,

(a) a copy of the order; and

(b) on request, a transcript or copy of the reasons for the order.

(6) Report — For the purposes of a review under subsection (1), the youth justice court shall require the provincial director to cause to be prepared, and to submit to the youth justice court, a report setting out any information of which the provincial director is aware that may be of assistance to the court.

(7) Provisions apply — Subsections 99(2) to (7) (provisions respecting reports and notice) and 105(6) (report for the purpose of setting conditions) apply, with any modifications that the circumstances require, in respect of a review under this section.

(8) Provisions apply — Section 101 (review of youth justice court decision) applies, with any modifications that the circumstances require, in respect of an order made under subsection (2).

PART 6 — PUBLICATION, RECORDS AND INFORMATION (SS. 110–129)

Protection of Privacy of Young Persons

110. (1) Identity of offender not to be published — Subject to this section, no person shall publish the name of a young person, or any other information related to a young person, if it would identify the young person as a young person dealt with under this Act.

(2) Limitation — Subsection (1) does not apply

(a) in a case where the information relates to a young person who has received an adult sentence; or

(b) [Repealed 2019, c. 25, s. 379.]

(c) in a case where the publication of information is made in the course of the administration of justice, if it is not the purpose of the publication to make the information known in the community.

(3) Exception — A young person referred to in subsection (1) may, after he or she attains the age of eighteen years, publish or cause to be published information that would identify him or her as having been dealt with under this Act or the *Young Offenders Act*, chapter Y-1 of the Revised Statutes of Canada, 1985, provided that he or she is not in custody pursuant to either Act at the time of the publication.

(4) *Ex parte* application for leave to publish — A youth justice court judge shall, on the *ex parte* application of a peace officer, make an order permitting any person to publish information that identifies a young person as having committed or allegedly committed an indictable offence, if the judge is satisfied that

(a) there is reason to believe that the young person is a danger to others; and

(b) publication of the information is necessary to assist in apprehending the young person.

(5) Order ceases to have effect — An order made under subsection (4) ceases to have effect five days after it is made.

(6) Application for leave to publish — The youth justice court may, on the application of a young person referred to in subsection (1), make an order permitting the young person to publish information that would identify him or her as having been dealt with under this Act or the *Young Offenders Act*, chapter Y-1 of the Revised Statutes of Canada, 1985, if the court is satisfied that the publication would not be contrary to the young person's best interests or the public interest.

2012, c. 1, s. 189; 2019, c. 25, s. 379

111. (1) Identity of victim or witness not to be published — Subject to this section, no person shall publish the name of a child or young person, or any other information related to a child or a young person, if it would identify the child or young person as having been a victim of, or as having appeared as a witness in connection with, an offence committed or alleged to have been committed by a young person.

(2) Exception — Information that would serve to identify a child or young person referred to in subsection (1) as having been a victim or a witness may be published, or caused to be published, by

(a) that child or young person after he or she attains the age of eighteen years or before that age with the consent of his or her parents; or

(b) the parents of that child or young person if he or she is deceased.

(3) Application for leave to publish — The youth justice court may, on the application of a child or a young person referred to in subsection (1), make an order permitting the child or young person to publish information that would identify him or her as having been a victim or a witness if the court is satisfied that the publication would not be contrary to his or her best interests or the public interest.

112. Non-application — Once information is published under subsection 110(3) or (6) or 111(2) or (3), subsection 110(1) (identity of offender not to be published) or 111(1) (identity of victim or witness not to be published), as the case may be, no longer applies in respect of the information.

Fingerprints and Photographs

113. (1) *Identification of Criminals Act* applies — The *Identification of Criminals Act* applies in respect of young persons.

(2) Limitation — No fingerprint, palmprint or photograph or other measurement, process or operation referred to in the *Identification of Criminals Act* shall be taken of, or applied in respect of, a young person who is charged with having committed an offence except in the circumstances in which an adult may, under that Act, be subjected to the measurements, processes and operations.

Records That May Be Kept

114. Youth justice court, review board and other courts — A youth justice court, review board or any court dealing with matters arising out of proceedings under this Act may keep a record of any case that comes before it arising under this Act.

115. (1) Police records — A record relating to any offence alleged to have been committed by a young person, including the original or a copy of any fingerprints or photographs of the young person, may be kept by any police force responsible for or participating in the investigation of the offence.

(1.1) Extrajudicial measures — The police force shall keep a record of any extrajudicial measures that they use to deal with young persons.

(2) Police records — When a young person is charged with having committed an offence in respect of which an adult may be subjected to any measurement, process or operation referred to in the *Identification of Criminals Act*, the police force responsible for the investigation of the offence may provide a record relating to the offence to the Royal Canadian Mounted Police. If the young person is found guilty of the offence, the police force shall provide the record.

(3) Records held by R.C.M.P. — The Royal Canadian Mounted Police shall keep the records provided under subsection (2) in the central repository that the Commissioner of the Royal Canadian Mounted Police may, from time to time, designate for the purpose of keeping criminal history files or records of offenders or keeping records for the identification of offenders.

2012, c. 1, s. 190

116. (1) Government records — A department or an agency of any government in Canada may keep records containing information obtained by the department or agency

(a) for the purposes of an investigation of an offence alleged to have been committed by a young person;

(b) for use in proceedings against a young person under this Act;

(c) for the purpose of administering a youth sentence or an order of the youth justice court;

(d) for the purpose of considering whether to use extrajudicial measures to deal with a young person; or

(e) as a result of the use of extrajudicial measures to deal with a young person.

(2) Other records — A person or organization may keep records containing information obtained by the person or organization

(a) as a result of the use of extrajudicial measures to deal with a young person; or

(b) for the purpose of administering or participating in the administration of a youth sentence.

Access to Records

117. Exception — adult sentence — Sections 118 to 129 do not apply to records kept in respect of an offence for which an adult sentence has been imposed once the time allowed for the taking of an appeal has expired or, if an appeal is taken, all proceedings in respect of the appeal have been completed and the appeal court has upheld an adult sentence. The record shall be dealt with as a record of an adult and, for the purposes of the *Criminal Records Act*, the finding of guilt in respect of the offence for which the record is kept is deemed to be a conviction.

118. (1) No access unless authorized — Except as authorized or required by this Act, no person shall be given access to a record kept under sections 114 to 116, and no information contained in it may be given to any person, where to do so would identify the young person to whom it relates as a young person dealt with under this Act.

(2) Exception for employees — No person who is employed in keeping or maintaining records referred to in subsection (1) is restricted from doing anything prohibited under subsection (1) with respect to any other person so employed.

119. (1) Persons having access to records — Subject to subsections (4) to (6), from the date that a record is created until the end of the applicable period set out in subsection (2), the following persons, on request, shall be given access to a record kept under section 114, and may be given access to a record kept under sections 115 and 116:

(a) the young person to whom the record relates;

(b) the young person's counsel, or any representative of that counsel;

(c) the Attorney General;

(d) the victim of the offence or alleged offence to which the record relates;

(e) the parents of the young person, during the course of any proceedings relating to the offence or alleged offence to which the record relates or during the term of any youth sentence made in respect of the offence;

(f) any adult assisting the young person under subsection 25(7), during the course of any proceedings relating to the offence or alleged offence to which the record relates or during the term of any youth sentence made in respect of the offence;

(g) any peace officer for

(i) law enforcement purposes, or

(ii) any purpose related to the administration of the case to which the record relates, during the course of proceedings against the young person or the term of the youth sentence;

(h) a judge, court or review board, for any purpose relating to proceedings against the young person, or proceedings against the person after he or she becomes an adult, in respect of offences committed or alleged to have been committed by that person;

(i) the provincial director, or the director of the provincial correctional facility for adults or the penitentiary at which the young person is serving a sentence;

(j) a person participating in a conference or in the administration of extrajudicial measures, if required for the administration of the case to which the record relates;

(k) a person acting as ombudsman, privacy commissioner or information commissioner, whatever his or her official designation might be, who in the course of his or herduties under an Act of Parliament or the legislature of a province is investigating a complaint to which the record relates;

(l) a coroner or a person acting as a child advocate, whatever his or her official designation might be, who is acting in the course of his or her duties under an Act of Parliament or the legislature of a province;

(m) a person acting under the *Firearms Act*;

(n) a member of a department or agency of a government in Canada, or of an organization that is an agent of, or under contract with, the department or agency, who is

(i) acting in the exercise of his or her duties under this Act,

(ii) engaged in the supervision or care of the young person, whether as a young person or an adult, or in an investigation related to the young person under an Act of the legislature of a province respecting child welfare,

(iii) considering an application for conditional release, or for a record suspension under the *Criminal Records Act*, made by the young person, whether as a young person or an adult,

(iv) administering a prohibition order made under an Act of Parliament or the legislature of a province, or

(v) administering a youth sentence, if the young person has been committed to custody and is serving the custody in a provincial correctional facility for adults or a penitentiary;

(o) a person, for the purpose of carrying out a criminal record check required by the Government of Canada or the government of a province or a municipality for purposes of employment or the performance of services, with or without remuneration;

(p) an employee or agent of the Government of Canada, for statistical purposes under the *Statistics Act*;

(p.1) an employee of a department or agency of the Government of Canada, for the purpose of administering the *Canadian Passport Order*;

(q) an accused or his or her counsel who swears an affidavit to the effect that access to the record is necessary to make a full answer and defence;

(r) a person or a member of a class of persons designated by order of the Governor in Council, or the lieutenant governor in council of the appropriate province, for a purpose and to the extent specified in the order; and

(s) any person or member of a class of persons that a youth justice court judge considers has a valid interest in the record, to the extent directed by the judge, if the judge is satisfied that access to the record is

(i) desirable in the public interest for research or statistical purposes, or

(ii) desirable in the interest of the proper administration of justice.

(2) **Period of access** — The period of access referred to in subsection (1) is

(a) if an extrajudicial sanction is used to deal with the young person, the period ending two years after the young person consents to be subject to the sanction in accordance with paragraph 10(2)(c);

(b) if the young person is acquitted of the offence otherwise than by reason of a verdict of not criminally responsible on account of mental disorder, the period ending two months after the expiry of the time allowed for the taking of an appeal or, if an appeal is taken, the period ending three months after all proceedings in respect of the appeal have been completed;

(c) if the charge against the young person is dismissed for any reason other than acquittal, the charge is withdrawn, or the young person is found guilty of the offence and a reprimand is given, the period ending two months after the dismissal, withdrawal, or finding of guilt;

(d) if the charge against the young person is stayed, with no proceedings being taken against the young person for a period of one year, at the end of that period;

(d.1) if an order referred to in subsection 14(2) or 20(2) is made against a young person, the period ending six months after the expiry of the order;

(e) if the young person is found guilty of the offence and the youth sentence is an absolute discharge, the period ending one year after the young person is found guilty;

(f) if the young person is found guilty of the offence and the youth sentence is a conditional discharge, the period ending three years after the young person is found guilty;

(g) subject to paragraphs (i) and (j) and subsection (9), if the young person is found guilty of the offence and it is a summary conviction offence, the period ending three years after the youth sentence imposed in respect of the offence has been completed;

(h) subject to paragraphs (i) and (j) and subsection (9), if the young person is found guilty of the offence and it is an indictable offence, the period ending five years after the youth sentence imposed in respect of the offence has been completed;

(i) subject to subsection (9), if, during the period calculated in accordance with paragraph (g) or (h), the young person is found guilty of an offence punishable on summary conviction committed when he or she was a young person, the latest of

(i) the period calculated in accordance with paragraph (g) or (h), as the case may be, and

(ii) the period ending three years after the youth sentence imposed for that offence has been completed; and

(j) subject to subsection (9), if, during the period calculated in accordance with paragraph (g) or (h), the young person is found guilty of an indictable offence committed when he or she was a young person, the period ending five years after the sentence imposed for that indictable offence has been completed.

(3) **Prohibition orders not included** — Prohibition orders made under an Act of Parliament or the legislature of a province, including any order made under section 51, shall not be taken into account in determining any period referred to in subsection (2).

(4) **Extrajudicial measures** — Access to a record kept under section 115 or 116 in respect of extrajudicial measures, other than extrajudicial sanctions, used in respect of a young person shall be given only to the following persons for the following purposes:

(a) a peace officer or the Attorney General, in order to make a decision whether to again use extrajudicial measures in respect of the young person;

(b) a person participating in a conference, in order to decide on the appropriate extrajudicial measure;

(c) a peace officer, the Attorney General or a person participating in a conference, if access is required for the administration of the case to which the record relates; and

(d) a peace officer for the purpose of investigating an offence.

(5) **Exception** — When a youth justice court has withheld all or part of a report from any person under subsection 34(9) or (10) (nondisclosure of medical or psychological report) or 40(7) (nondisclosure of pre-sentence report), that person shall not be given access under subsection (1) to that report or part.

(6) **Records of assessments or forensic DNA analysis** — Access to a report made under section 34 (medical and psychological reports) or a record of the results of forensic DNA analysis of a bodily substance taken from a young person in execution of a warrant issued under section 487.05 of the *Criminal Code* may be given only under paragraphs (1)(a) to (c), (e) to (h) and (q) and subparagraph (1)(s)(ii).

(7) **Introduction into evidence** — Nothing in paragraph (1)(h) or (q) authorizes the introduction into evidence of any part of a record that would not otherwise be admissible in evidence.

(8) **Disclosures for research or statistical purposes** — When access to a record is given to a person under paragraph (1)(p) or subparagraph (1)(s)(i), the person may subsequently disclose information contained in the record, but shall not disclose the information in any form that would reasonably be expected to identify the young person to whom it relates.

(9) Application of usual rules — If, during the period of access to a record under any of paragraphs (2)(g) to (j), the young person is convicted of an offence committed when he or she is an adult,

(a) section 82 (effect of absolute discharge or termination of youth sentence) does not apply to the young person in respect of the offence for which the record is kept under sections 114 to 116;

(b) this Part no longer applies to the record and the record shall be dealt with as a record of an adult; and

(c) for the purposes of the *Criminal Records Act*, the finding of guilt in respect of the offence for which the record is kept is deemed to be a conviction.

(10) Records of offences that result in a prohibition order — Despite anything in this Act, when a young person is found guilty of an offence that results in a prohibition order being made, and the order is still in force at the end of the applicable period for which access to a record kept in respect of the order may be given under subsection (2),

(a) the record kept by the Royal Canadian Mounted Police pursuant to subsection 115(3) may be disclosed only to establish the existence of the order for purposes of law enforcement; and

(b) the record referred to in section 114 that is kept by the youth justice court may be disclosed only to establish the existence of the order in any offence involving a breach of the order.

2012, c. 1, s. 157; 2019, c. 13, s. 167

120. (1) Access to R.C.M.P. records — The following persons may, during the period set out in subsection (3), be given access to a record kept under subsection 115(3) in respect of an offence set out in the schedule:

(a) the young person to whom the record relates;

(b) the young person's counsel, or any representative of that counsel;

(c) an employee or agent of the Government of Canada, for statistical purposes under the *Statistics Act*;

(d) any person or member of a class of persons that a youth justice court judge considers has a valid interest in the record, to the extent directed by the judge, if the judge is satisfied that access is desirable in the public interest for research or statistical purposes;

(e) the Attorney General or a peace officer, when the young person is or has been charged with another offence set out in the schedule or the same offence more than once, for the purpose of investigating any offence that the young person is suspected of having committed, or in respect of which the young person has been arrested or charged, whether as a young person or as an adult;

(f) the Attorney General or a peace officer to establish the existence of an order in any offence involving a breach of the order; and

(g) any person for the purposes of the *Firearms Act*.

(2) Access for identification purposes — During the period set out in subsection (3), access to the portion of a record kept under subsection 115(3) that contains the name, date of birth and last known address of the young person to whom the fingerprints belong, may be given to a person for identification purposes if a fingerprint identified as that of the young person is found during the investigation of an offence or during an attempt to identify a deceased person or a person suffering from amnesia.

(3) Period of access — For the purposes of subsections (1) and (2), the period of access to a record kept under subsection 115(3) in respect of an offence is the following:

(a) if the offence is an indictable offence, other than an offence referred to in paragraph (b), the period starting at the end of the applicable period set out in paragraphs 119(2)(h) to (j) and ending five years later; and

(b) if the offence is a serious violent offence for which the Attorney General has given notice under subsection 64(2) (intention to seek adult sentence), the period starting at the end of the applicable period set out in paragraphs 119(2)(h) to (j) and continuing indefinitely.

(4) Subsequent offences as young person — If a young person was found guilty of an offence set out in the schedule is, during the period of access to a record under subsection (3), found guilty of an additional offence set out in the schedule, committed when he or she was a young person, access to the record may be given to the following additional persons:

(a) a parent of the young person or any adult assisting the young person under subsection 25(7);

(b) a judge, court or review board, for a purpose relating to proceedings against the young person under this Act or any other Act of Parliament in respect of offences committed or alleged to have been committed by the young person, whether as a young person or as an adult; or

(c) a member of a department or agency of a government in Canada, or of an organization that is an agent of, or is under contract with, the department or agency, who is

(i) preparing a report in respect of the young person under this Act or for the purpose of assisting a court in sentencing the young person after the young person becomes an adult,

(ii) engaged in the supervision or care of the young person, whether as a young person or as an adult, or in the administration of a sentence in respect of the young person, whether as a young person or as an adult, or

(iii) considering an application for conditional release, or for a record suspension under the *Criminal Records Act*, made by the young person after the young person becomes an adult.

(5) Disclosure for research or statistical purposes — A person who is given access to a record under paragraph (1)(c) or (d) may subsequently disclose information contained in the record, but shall not disclose the informationin any form that would reasonably be expected to identify the young person to whom it relates.

(6) Subsequent offences as adult — If, during the period of access to a record under subsection (3), the young person is convicted of an additional offence set out in the schedule, committed when he or she was an adult,

(a) this Part no longer applies to the record and the record shall be dealt with as a record of an adult and may be included on the automated criminal conviction records retrieval system maintained by the Royal Canadian Mounted Police; and

(b) for the purposes of the *Criminal Records Act*, the finding of guilt in respect of the offence for which the record is kept is deemed to be a conviction.

2012, c. 1, ss. 158, 192

121. Deemed election — For the purposes of sections 119 and 120, if no election is made in respect of an offence that may be prosecuted by indictment or proceeded with by way of summary conviction, the Attorney General is deemed to have elected to proceed with the offence as an offence punishable on summary conviction.

122. Disclosure of information and copies of record — A person who is required or authorized to be given access to a record under section 119, 120, 123 or 124 may be given any information contained in the record and may be given a copy of any part of the record.

123. (1) Where records may be made available — A youth justice court judge may, on application by a person after the end of the applicable period set out in subsection 119(2), order that the person be given access to all or part of a record kept under sections 114 to 116 or that a copy of the record or part be given to that person,

(a) if the youth justice court judge is satisfied that

(i) the person has a valid and substantial interest in the record or part,

(ii) it is necessary for access to be given to the record or part in the interest of the proper administration of justice, and

(iii) disclosure of the record or part or the information in it is not prohibited under any other Act of Parliament or the legislature of a province; or

(b) if the youth court judge is satisfied that access to the record or part is desirable in the public interest for research or statistical purposes.

(2) Restriction for paragraph (1)(a) — Paragraph (1)(a) applies in respect of a record relating to a particular young person or to a record relating to a class of young persons only if the identity of young persons in the class at the time of the making of the application referred to in that paragraph cannot reasonably be ascertained and the disclosure of the record is necessary for the purpose of investigating any offence that a person is suspected on reasonable grounds of having committed against a young person while the young person is, or was, serving a sentence.

(3) **Notice** — Subject to subsection (4), an application for an order under paragraph (1)(a) in respect of a record shall not be heard unless the person who makes the application has given the young person to whom the record relates and the person or body that has possession of the record at least five days notice in writing of the application, and the young person and the person or body that has possession have had a reasonable opportunity to be heard.

(4) **Where notice not required** — A youth justice court judge may waive the requirement in subsection (3) to give notice to a young person when the judge is of the opinion that

(a) to insist on the giving of the notice would frustrate the application; or

(b) reasonable efforts have not been successful in finding the young person.

(5) **Use of record** — In any order under subsection (1), the youth justice court judge shall set out the purposes for which the record may be used.

(6) **Disclosure for research or statistical purposes** — When access to a record is given to any person under paragraph (1)(b), that person may subsequently disclose information contained in the record, but shall not disclose the information in any form that would reasonably be expected to identify the young person to whom it relates.

124. Access to record by young person — A young person to whom a record relates and his or her counsel may have access to the record at any time.

Disclosure of Information in a Record

125. (1) **Disclosure by peace officer during investigation** — A peace officer may disclose to any person any information in a record kept under section 114 (court records) or 115 (police records) that it is necessary to disclose in the conduct of the investigation of an offence.

(2) **Disclosure by Attorney General** — The Attorney General may, in the course of a proceeding under this Act or any other Act of Parliament, disclose the following information in a record kept under section 114 (court reports) or 115 (police records):

(a) to a person who is a co-accused with the young person in respect of the offence for which the record is kept, any information contained in the record; and

(b) to an accused in a proceeding, if the record is in respect of a witness in the proceeding, information that identifies the witness as a young person who has been dealt with under this Act.

(3) **Information that may be disclosed to a foreign state** — The Attorney General or a peace officer may disclose to the Minister of Justice of Canada information in a record that is kept under section 114 (court records) or 115 (police records) to the extent that it is necessary to deal with a request to or by a foreign state under the *Mutual Legal Assistance in Criminal Matters Act*, or for the purposes of any extradition matter under the *Extradition Act*. The Minister of Justice of

Canada may disclose the information to the foreign state in respect of which the request was made, or to which the extradition matter relates, as the case may be.

(4) **Disclosure to insurance company** — A peace officer may disclose to an insurance company information in a record that is kept under section 114 (court records) or 115 (police records) for the purpose of investigating a claim arising out of an offence committed or alleged to have been committed by the young person to whom the record relates.

(5) **Preparation of reports** — The provincial director or a youth worker may disclose information contained in a record if the disclosure is necessary for procuring information that relates to the preparation of a report required by this Act.

(6) **Schools and others** — The provincial director, a youth worker, the Attorney General, a peace officer or any other person engaged in the provision of services to young persons may disclose to any professional or other person engaged in the supervision or care of a young person — including a representative of any school board or school or any other educational or training institution — any information contained in a record kept under sections 114 to 116 if the disclosure is necessary

(a) to ensure compliance by the young person with an authorization under section 91 or an order of the youth justice court;

(b) to ensure the safety of staff, students or other persons; or

(c) to facilitate the rehabilitation of the young person.

(7) **Information to be kept separate** — A person to whom information is disclosed under subsection (6) shall

(a) keep the information separate from any other record of the young person to whom the information relates;

(b) ensure that no other person has access to the information except if authorized under this Act, or if necessary for the purposes of subsection (6); and

(c) destroy their copy of the record when the information is no longer required for the purpose for which it was disclosed.

(8) **Time limit** — No information may be disclosed under this section after the end of the applicable period set out in subsection 119(2) (period of access to records).

126. **Records in the custody, etc., of archivists** — When records originally kept under sections 114 to 116 are under the custody or control of the Librarian and Archivist of Canada or the archivist for any province, that person may disclose any information contained in the records to any other person if

(a) a youth justice court judge is satisfied that the disclosure is desirable in the public interest for research or statistical purposes; and

(b) the person to whom the information is disclosed undertakes not to disclose the information in any form that could reasonably be expected to identify the young person to whom it relates.

2004, c. 11, s. 48

127. (1) Disclosure with court order — The youth justice court may, on the application of the provincial director, the Attorney General or a peace officer, make an order permitting the applicant to disclose to the person or persons specified by the court any information about a young person that is specified, if the court is satisfied that the disclosure is necessary, having regard to the following circumstances:

(a) the young person has been found guilty of an offence involving serious personal injury;

(b) the young person poses a risk of serious harm to persons; and

(c) the disclosure of the information is relevant to the avoidance of that risk.

(2) Opportunity to be heard — Subject to subsection (3), before making an order under subsection (1), the youth justice court shall give the young person, a parent of the young person and the Attorney General an opportunity to be heard.

(3) *Ex parte* application — An application under subsection (1) may be made *ex parte* by the Attorney General where the youth justice court is satisfied that reasonable efforts have been made to locate the young person and that those efforts have not been successful.

(4) Time limit — No information may be disclosed under subsection (1) after the end of the applicable period set out in subsection 119(2) (period of access to records).

Disposition or Destruction of Records and Prohibition on Use and Disclosure

128. (1) Effect of end of access periods — Subject to sections 123, 124 and 126, after the end of the applicable period set out in section 119 or 120 no record kept under sections 114 to 116 may be used for any purpose that would identify the young person to whom the record relates as a young person dealt with under this Act or the *Young Offenders Act*, chapter Y-1 of the Revised Statutes of Canada, 1985.

(2) Disposal of records — Subject to paragraph 125(7)(c), any record kept under sections 114 to 116, other than a record kept under subsection 115(3), may, in the discretion of the person or body keeping the record, be destroyed or transmitted to the Librarian and Archivist of Canada or the archivist for any province, at any time before or after the end of the applicable period set out in section 119.

(3) Disposal of R.C.M.P. records — All records kept under subsection 115(3) shall be destroyed or, if the Librarian and Archivist of Canada requires it, transmitted to the Librarian and Archivist, at the end of the applicable period set out in section 119 or 120.

(4) Purging CPIC — The Commissioner of the Royal Canadian Mounted Police shall remove a record from the automated criminal conviction records retrieval system maintained by the Royal Canadian Mounted Police at the end of the applicable period referred to in section 119; however, information relating to a prohibition order made under an Act of Parliament or the legislature of a province shall be removed only at the end of the period for which the order is in force.

(5) Exception — Despite subsections (1), (2) and (4), an entry that is contained in a system maintained by the Royal Canadian Mounted Police to match crime scene information and that relates to an offence committed or alleged to have been committed by a young person shall be dealt with in the same manner as information that relates to an offence committed by an adult for which a record suspension ordered under the *Criminal Records Act* is in effect.

(6) Authority to inspect — The Librarian and Archivist of Canada may, at any time, inspect records kept under sections 114 to 116 that are under the control of a government institution as defined in section 2 of the *Library and Archives of Canada Act*, and the archivist for a province may at any time inspect any records kept under those sections that the archivist is authorized to inspect under any Act of the legislature of the province.

(7) Definition of "destroy" — For the purposes of subsections (2) and (3), **"destroy"**, in respect of a record, means

(a) to shred, burn or otherwise physically destroy the record, in the case of a record other than a record in electronic form; and

(b) to delete, write over or otherwise render the record inaccessible, in the case of a record in electronic form.

2004, c. 11, s. 49; 2012, c. 1, s. 159

129. No subsequent disclosure — No person who is given access to a record or to whom information is disclosed under this Act shall disclose that information to any other person unless the disclosure is authorized under this Act.

PART 7 — GENERAL PROVISIONS (SS. 130–157)

Disqualification of Judge

130. (1) Disqualification of judge — Subject to subsection (2), a youth justice court judge who, prior to an adjudication in respect of a young person charged with an offence, examines a pre-sentence report made in respect of the young person in connection with that offence or has, after a guilty plea or a finding of guilt, heard submissions as to sentence and then there has been a change of plea, shall not in any capacity conduct or continue the trial of the young person for the offence and shall transfer the case to another judge to be dealt with according to law.

(2) Exception — A youth justice court judge may, in the circumstances referred to in subsection (1), with the consent of the young person and the prosecutor, conduct or continue the trial of the young person if the judge is satisfied that he or she has not been predisposed by a guilty plea or finding of guilt, or by information contained in the pre-sentence report or submissions as to sentence.

Substitution of Judge

131. (1) Powers of substitute youth justice court judge — A youth justice court judge who acts in the place of another youth justice court judge under subsection 669.2(1) (continuation of proceedings) of the *Criminal Code* shall

(a) if an adjudication has been made, proceed to sentence the young person or make the order that, in the circumstances, is authorized by law; or

(b) if no adjudication has been made, recommence the trial as if no evidence had been taken.

(2) Transcript of evidence already given — A youth justice court judge who recommences a trial under paragraph (1)(b) may, if the parties consent, admit into evidence a transcript of any evidence already given in the case.

Exclusion from Hearing

132. (1) Exclusion from hearing — Subject to subsection (2), a court or justice before whom proceedings are carried out under this Act may exclude any person from all or part of the proceedings if the court or justice considers that the person's presence is unnecessary to the conduct of the proceedings and the court or justice is of the opinion that

(a) any evidence or information presented to the court or justice would be seriously injurious or seriously prejudicial to

(i) the young person who is being dealt with in the proceedings,

(ii) a child or young person who is a witness in the proceedings, or

(iii) a child or young person who is aggrieved by or the victim of the offence charged in the proceedings; or

(b) it would be in the interest of public morals, the maintenance of order or the proper administration of justice to exclude any or all members of the public from the court room.

(2) Exception — Subject to section 650 (accused to be present) of the *Criminal Code* and except if it is necessary for the purposes of subsection 34(9) (nondisclosure of medical or psychological report) of this Act, a court or justice may not, under subsection (1), exclude from proceedings under this Act

(a) the prosecutor;

(b) the young person who is being dealt with in the proceedings, the counsel or a parent of the young person or any adult assisting the young person under subsection 25(7);

(c) the provincial director or his or her agent; or

(d) the youth worker to whom the young person's case has been assigned.

(3) Exclusion after adjudication or during review — A youth justice court, after it has found a young person guilty of an offence, or a youth justice court or a review board, during a review, may, in its discretion, exclude from the court or from a hearing of the review board any person other than the following, when it is being presented with information the knowledge of which might, in its opinion, be seriously injurious or seriously prejudicial to the young person:

(a) the young person or his or her counsel;

(b) the provincial director or his or her agent;

(c) the youth worker to whom the young person's case has been assigned; and

(d) the Attorney General.

(4) Exception — The exception set out in paragraph (3)(a) is subject to subsection 34(9) (nondisclosure of medical or psychological report) of this Act and section 650 (accused to be present) of the *Criminal Code*.

Transfer of Charges

133. Transfer of charges — Despite subsections 478(1) and (3) of the *Criminal Code*, a young person charged with an offence that is alleged to have been committed in one province may, if the Attorney General of the province consents, appear before a youth justice court of any other province and

(a) if the young person pleads guilty to that offence and the youth justice court is satisfied that the facts support the charge, the court shall find the young person guilty of the offence alleged in the information or indictment; and

(b) if the young person pleads not guilty to that offence, or pleads guilty but the court is not satisfied that the facts support the charge, the young person shall, if he or she was detained in custody prior to the appearance, be returned to custody and dealt with according to law.

Forfeiture of Recognizances

134. Applications for forfeiture of recognizances — Applications for the forfeiture of recognizances of young persons shall be made to the youth justice court.

Proposed Amendment — 134

134. Applications for forfeiture — Applications for the forfeiture of amounts set out in undertakings, release orders or recognizances binding young persons shall be made to the youth justice court.

2019, c. 25, s. 380 [To come into force December 18, 2019.]

135. (1) Proceedings in case of default — When a recognizance binding a young person has been endorsed with a certificate under subsection 770(1) of the *Criminal Code*, a youth justice court judge shall

(a) on the request of the Attorney General, fix a time and place for the hearing of an application for the forfeiture of the recognizance; and

(b) after fixing a time and place for the hearing, cause to be sent by confirmed delivery service, not less than ten days before the time so fixed, to each principal and surety named in the recognizance, directed to his or her latest known address, a notice requiring him or her to appear at the time and place fixed by the judge to show cause why the recognizance should not be forfeited.

Proposed Amendment — 135(1)

(1) Proceedings in case of default — If an undertaking, release order or recognizance binding a young person has been endorsed with a certificate under subsection 770(1) of the *Criminal Code*, a youth justice court judge shall

(a) on the request of the Attorney General, fix a time and place for the hearing of an application for the forfeiture of the amount set out in the undertaking, release order or recognizance; and

(b) after fixing a time and place for the hearing, cause to be sent by confirmed delivery service, not less than 10 days before the time so fixed, to each principal and surety named in the undertaking, release order or recognizance, directed to their latest known address, a notice requiring them to appear at the time and place fixed by the judge to show cause why the amount set out in the undertaking, release order or recognizance should not be forfeited.

2019, c. 25, s. 381(1) [To come into force December 18, 2019.]

(2) Order for forfeiture of recognizance — When subsection (1) is complied with, the youth justice court judge may, after giving the parties an opportunity to be heard, in his or her discretion grant or refuse the application and make any order with respect to the forfeiture of the recognizance that he or she considers proper.

Proposed Amendment — 135(2)

(2) Order for forfeiture — When subsection (1) is complied with, the youth justice court judge may, after giving the parties an opportunity to be heard, in the judge's discretion grant or refuse the application and make any order with respect to the forfeiture of the amount that the judge considers proper.

2019, c. 25, s. 381(1) [To come into force December 18, 2019.]

(3) Judgment debtors of the Crown — If, under subsection (2), a youth justice court judge orders forfeiture of a recognizance, the principal and his or her sureties become judgment debtors of the Crown, each in the amount that the judge orders him or her to pay.

Proposed Amendment — 135(3)

(3) Judgment debtors of the Crown — If, under subsection (2), a youth justice court judge orders the forfeiture of the amount, the principal and their sureties become judgment debtors of the Crown, each in the amount that the judge orders them to pay.

2019, c. 25, s. 381(1) [To come into force December 18, 2019.]

(4) Order may be filed — An order made under subsection (2) may be filed with the clerk of the superior court or, in the province of Quebec, the prothonotary and, if an order is filed, the clerk or the prothonotary shall issue a writ of *fieri facias* in Form 34 set out in the *Criminal Code* and deliver it to the sheriff of each of the territorial divisions in which any of the principal and his or her sureties resides, carries on business or has property.

(5) **If a deposit has been made** — If a deposit has been made by a person against whom an order for forfeiture of a recognizance has been made, no writ of *fieri facias* shall issue, but the amount of the deposit shall be transferred by the person who has custody of it to the person who is entitled by law to receive it.

Proposed Amendment — 135(5)

(5) **If a deposit has been made** — If a deposit has been made by a person against whom an order for forfeiture has been made, no writ of *fieri facias* shall issue, but the amount of the deposit shall be transferred by the person who has custody of it to the person who is entitled by law to receive it.

2019, c. 25, s. 381(2) [To come into force December 18, 2019.]

(6) **Subsections 770(2) and (4) of *Criminal Code* do not apply** — Subsections 770(2) (transmission of recognizance) and (4) (transmission of deposit) of the *Criminal Code* do not apply in respect of proceedings under this Act.

Proposed Amendment — 135(6)

(6) **Subsections 770(2) and (4) of *Criminal Code* do not apply** — Subsections 770(2) (transmission to clerk of the court) and (4) (transmission of deposit) of the *Criminal Code* do not apply in respect of proceedings under this Act.

2019, c. 25, s. 381(2) [To come into force December 18, 2019.]

(7) **Sections 772 and 773 of *Criminal Code* apply** — Sections 772 (levy under writ) and 773 (committal when writ not satisfied) of the *Criminal Code* apply in respect of writs of *fieri facias* issued under this section as if they were issued under section 771 (proceedings in case of default) of that Act.

Offences and Punishment

136. (1) **Inducing a young person, etc.** — Every person who

(a) induces or assists a young person to leave unlawfully a place of custody or other place in which the young person has been placed in accordance with a youth sentence or a disposition imposed under the *Young Offenders Act*, chapter Y-1 of the Revised Statutes of Canada, 1985,

(b) unlawfully removes a young person from a place referred to in paragraph (a),

(c) knowingly harbours or conceals a young person who has unlawfully left a place referred to in paragraph (a),

(d) wilfully induces or assists a young person to breach or disobey a term or condition of a youth sentence or other order of the youth justice court, or a term or condition of a disposition or other order under the *Young Offenders Act*, chapter Y-1 of the Revised Statutes of Canada, 1985, or

(e) wilfully prevents or interferes with the performance by a young person of a term or condition of a youth sentence or other order of the youth justice court, or a term or condition of a disposition or other order under the *Young Offenders Act*, chapter Y-1 of the Revised Statutes of Canada, 1985,

is guilty of an indictable offence and liable to imprisonment for a term not exceeding two years or is guilty of an offence punishable on summary conviction.

(2) **Absolute jurisdiction of provincial court judge** — The jurisdiction of a provincial court judge to try an adult charged with an indictable offence under this section is absolute and does not depend on the consent of the accused.

137. **Failure to comply with sentence or disposition** — Every person who is subject to a youth sentence imposed under any of paragraphs 42(2)(c) to (m) or (s) of this Act, to a victim fine surcharge ordered under subsection 53(2) of this Act or to a disposition made under any of paragraphs 20(1)(a.1) to (g), (j) or (l) of the *Young Offenders Act*, chapter Y-1 of the Revised Statutes of Canada, 1985, and who wilfully fails or refuses to comply with that sentence, surcharge or disposition is guilty of an offence punishable on summary conviction.

138. (1) **Offences** — Every person who contravenes subsection 110(1) (identity of offender not to be published), 111(1) (identity of victim or witness not to be published), 118(1) (no access to records unless authorized) or 128(3) (disposal of R.C.M.P. records) or section 129 (no subsequent disclosure) of this Act, or subsection 38(1) (identity not to be published), (1.12) (no subsequent disclosure), (1.14) (no subsequent disclosure by school) or (1.15) (information to be kept separate), 45(2) (destruction of records) or 46(1) (prohibition against disclosure) of the *Young Offenders Act*, chapter Y-1 of the Revised Statutes of Canada, 1985,

(a) is guilty of an indictable offence and liable to imprisonment for a term not exceeding two years; or

(b) is guilty of an offence punishable on summary conviction.

(2) **Provincial court judge has absolute jurisdiction on indictment** — The jurisdiction of a provincial court judge to try an adult charged with an offence under paragraph (1)(a) is absolute and does not depend on the consent of the accused.

139. (1) **Offence and punishment** — Every person who wilfully fails to comply with section 30 (designated place of temporary detention), or with an undertaking entered into under subsection 31(3) (condition of placement),

(a) is guilty of an indictable offence and liable to imprisonment for a term not exceeding two years; or

(b) is guilty of an offence punishable on summary conviction.

(2) **Offence and punishment** — Every person who wilfully fails to comply with section 7 (designated place of temporary detention) of the *Young Offenders Act*, chapter Y-1 of the Revised Statutes of Canada, 1985, or with an undertaking entered into under subsection 7.1(2) (condition of placement) of that Act is guilty of an offence punishable on summary conviction.

(3) Punishment — Any person who uses or authorizes the use of an application form in contravention of subsection 82(3) (application for employment) is guilty of an offence punishable on summary conviction.

Application of Criminal Code

140. Application of *Criminal Code* — Except to the extent that it is inconsistent with or excluded by this Act, the provisions of the *Criminal Code* apply, with any modifications that the circumstances require, in respect of offences alleged to have been committed by young persons.

141. (1) Sections of *Criminal Code* applicable — Except to the extent that they are inconsistent with or excluded by this Act, section 16 (defence of mental disorder) and Part XX.1 (mental disorder) of the *Criminal Code* apply, with any modifications that the circumstances require, in respect of proceedings under this Act in relation to offences alleged to have been committed by young persons.

(2) Notice and copies to counsel and parents — For the purposes of subsection (1),

(a) wherever in Part XX.1 (mental disorder) of the *Criminal Code* a reference is made to a copy to be sent or otherwise given to an accused or a party to the proceedings, the reference shall be read as including a reference to a copy to be sent or otherwise given to

(i) any counsel representing the young person,

(ii) a parent of the young person who is in attendance at the proceedings against the young person, and

(iii) a parent of the young person not in attendance at the proceedings who is, in the opinion of the youth justice court or Review Board, taking an active interest in the proceedings; and

(b) wherever in Part XX.1 (mental disorder) of the *Criminal Code* a reference is made to notice to be given to an accused or a party to proceedings, the reference shall be read as including a reference to notice to be given to a parent of the young person and any counsel representing the young person.

(3) Proceedings not invalid — Subject to subsection (4), failure to give a notice referred to in paragraph (2)(b) to a parent of a young person does not affect the validity of proceedings under this Act.

(4) Exception — Failure to give a notice referred to in paragraph (2)(b) to a parent of a young person in any case renders invalid any subsequent proceedings under this Act relating to the case unless

(a) a parent of the young person attends at the court or Review Board with the young person; or

(b) a youth justice court judge or Review Board before whom proceedings are held against the young person

(i) adjourns the proceedings and orders that the notice be given in the manner and to the persons that the judge or Review Board directs, or

(ii) dispenses with the notice if the youth justice court or Review Board is of the opinion that, having regard to the circumstances, the notice may be dispensed with.

(5) [Repealed 2005, c. 22, s. 63(2).]

(6) Considerations of court or Review Board making a disposition — Before making or reviewing a disposition in respect of a young person under Part XX.1 (mental disorder) of the *Criminal Code*, a youth justice court or Review Board shall consider the age and special needs of the young person and any representations or submissions made by a parent of the young person.

(7) to (9) [Repealed 2005, c. 22, s. 63(3).]

(10) Prima facie case to be made every year — For the purpose of applying subsection 672.33(1) (fitness to stand trial) of the *Criminal Code* to proceedings under this Act in relation to an offence alleged to have been committed by a young person, wherever in that subsection a reference is made to two years, there shall be substituted a reference to one year.

(11) Designation of hospitals for young persons — A reference in Part XX.1 (mental disorder) of the *Criminal Code* to a hospital in a province shall be construed as a reference to a hospital designated by the Minister of Health for the province for the custody, treatment or assessment of young persons.

(12) Definition of "Review Board" — In this section, **"Review Board"** has the meaning assigned by section 672.1 of the *Criminal Code*.

2005, c. 22, s. 63

142. (1) Part XXVII and summary conviction trial provisions of *Criminal Code* to apply — Subject to this section and except to the extent that they are inconsistent with this Act, the provisions of Part XXVII (summary conviction offences) of the *Criminal Code*, and any other provisions of that Act that apply in respect of summary conviction offences and relate to trial proceedings, apply to proceedings under this Act

(a) in respect of an order under section 83.3 (recognizance — terrorist activity), 810 (recognizance — fear of injury or damage), 810.01 (recognizance — fear of certain offences), 810.011 (recognizance — fear of terrorism offence), 810.02 (recognizance — fear of forced marriage or marriage under age of 16 years) or 810.2 (recognizance — fear of serious personal injury offence) of that Act or an offence under section 811 (breach of recognizance) of that Act;

(b) in respect of a summary conviction offence; and

(c) in respect of an indictable offence as if it were defined in the enactment creating it as a summary conviction offence.

(2) **Indictable offences** — For greater certainty and despite subsection (1) or any other provision of this Act, an indictable offence committed by a young person is, for the purposes of this Act or any other Act of Parliament, an indictable offence.

(3) **Attendance of young person** — Section 650 of the *Criminal Code* applies in respect of proceedings under this Act, whether the proceedings relate to an indictable offence or an offence punishable on summary conviction.

(4) **Limitation period** — In proceedings under this Act, subsection 786(2) of the *Criminal Code* does not apply in respect of an indictable offence.

(5) **Costs** — Section 809 of the *Criminal Code* does not apply in respect of proceedings under this Act.

2015, c. 20, ss. 33, 36(9); 2015, c. 29, s. 15

Procedure

143. Counts charged in information — Indictable offences and offences punishable on summary conviction may under this Act be charged in the same information or indictment and tried jointly.

144. (1) Issue of subpoena — If a person is required to attend to give evidence before a youth justice court, the subpoena directed to that person may be issued by a youth justice court judge, whether or not the person whose attendance is required is within the same province as the youth justice court.

(2) **Service of subpoena** — A subpoena issued by a youth justice court and directed to a person who is not within the same province as the youth justice court shall be served personally on the person to whom it is directed.

145. Warrant — A warrant issued by a youth justice court may be executed anywhere in Canada.

Evidence

146. (1) General law on admissibility of statements to apply — Subject to this section, the law relating to the admissibility of statements made by persons accused of committing offences applies in respect of young persons.

(2) **When statements are admissible** — No oral or written statement made by a young person who is less than eighteen years old, to a peace officer or to any other person who is, in law, a person in authority, on the arrest or detention of the young person or in circumstances where the peace officer or other person has reasonable grounds for believing that the young person has committed an offence is admissible against the young person unless

(a) the statement was voluntary;

(b) the person to whom the statement was made has, before the statement was made, clearly explained to the young person, in language appropriate to his or her age and understanding, that

(i) the young person is under no obligation to make a statement,

(ii) any statement made by the young person may be used as evidence in proceedings against him or her,

(iii) the young person has the right to consult counsel and a parent or other person in accordance with paragraph (c), and

(iv) any statement made by the young person is required to be made in the presence of counsel and any other person consulted in accordance with paragraph (c), if any, unless the young person desires otherwise;

(c) the young person has, before the statement was made, been given a reasonable opportunity to consult

(i) with counsel, and

(ii) with a parent or, in the absence of a parent, an adult relative or, in the absence of a parent and an adult relative, any other appropriate adult chosen by the young person, as long as that person is not a co-accused, or under investigation, in respect of the same offence; and

(d) if the young person consults a person in accordance with paragraph (c), the young person has been given a reasonable opportunity to make the statement in the presence of that person.

(3) **Exception in certain cases for oral statements** — The requirements set out in paragraphs (2)(b) to (d) do not apply in respect of oral statements if they are made spontaneously by the young person to a peace officer or other person in authority before that person has had a reasonable opportunity to comply with those requirements.

(4) **Waiver of right to consult** — A young person may waive the rights under paragraph (2)(c) or (d) but any such waiver

(a) must be recorded on video tape or audio tape; or

(b) must be in writing and contain a statement signed by the young person that he or she has been informed of the right being waived.

(5) **Waiver of right to consult** — When a waiver of rights under paragraph (2)(c) or (d) is not made in accordance with subsection (4) owing to a technical irregularity, the youth justice court may determine that the waiver is valid if it is satisfied that the young person was informed of his or her rights, and voluntarily waived them.

(6) **Admissibility of statements** — When there has been a technical irregularity in complying with paragraphs (2)(b) to (d), the youth justice court may admit into evidence a statement referred to in subsection (2), if satisfied that the admission of the statement would not bring into disrepute the principle that young persons are entitled to enhanced procedural protection to ensure that they are treated fairly and their rights are protected.

(7) Statements made under duress are inadmissible — A youth justice court judge may rule inadmissible in any proceedings under this Act a statement made by the young person in respect of whom the proceedings are taken if the young person satisfies the judge that the statement was made under duress imposed by any person who is not, in law, a person in authority.

(8) Misrepresentation of age — A youth justice court judge may in any proceedings under this Act rule admissible any statement or waiver by a young person if, at the time of the making of the statement or waiver,

(a) the young person held himself or herself to be eighteen years old or older;

(b) the person to whom the statement or waiver was made conducted reasonable inquiries as to the age of the young person and had reasonable grounds for believing that the young person was eighteen years old or older; and

(c) in all other circumstances the statement or waiver would otherwise be admissible.

(9) Parent, etc., not a person in authority — For the purpose of this section, a person consulted under paragraph (2)(c) is, in the absence of evidence to the contrary, deemed not to be a person in authority.

147. (1) Statements not admissible against young person — Subject to subsection (2), if a young person is assessed in accordance with an order made under subsection 34(1) (medical or psychological assessment), no statement or reference to a statement made by the young person during the course and for the purposes of the assessment to the person who conducts the assessment or to anyone acting under that person's direction is admissible in evidence, without the consent of the young person, in any proceeding before a court, tribunal, body or person with jurisdiction to compel the production of evidence.

(2) Exceptions — A statement referred to in subsection (1) is admissible in evidence for the purposes of

(a) making a decision on an application heard under section 71 (hearing — adult sentences);

(b) determining whether the young person is unfit to stand trial;

(c) determining whether the balance of the mind of the young person was disturbed at the time of commission of the alleged offence, if the young person is a female person charged with an offence arising out of the death of her newly-born child;

(d) making or reviewing a sentence in respect of the young person;

(e) determining whether the young person was, at the time of the commission of an alleged offence, suffering from automatism or a mental disorder so as to be exempt from criminal responsibility by virtue of subsection 16(1) of the *Criminal Code*, if the accused puts his or her mental capacity for criminal intent into issue, or if the prosecutor raises the issue after verdict;

(f) challenging the credibility of a young person in any proceeding if the testimony of the young person is inconsistent in a material particular with a statement referred to in subsection (1) that the young person made previously;

(g) establishing the perjury of a young person who is charged with perjury in respect of a statement made in any proceeding;

(h) deciding an application for an order under subsection 104(1) (continuation of custody);

(i) setting the conditions under subsection 105(1) (conditional supervision);

(j) conducting a review under subsection 109(1) (review of decision); or

(k) deciding an application for a disclosure order under subsection 127(1) (information about a young person).

148. (1) Testimony of a parent — In any proceedings under this Act, the testimony of a parent as to the age of a person of whom he or she is a parent is admissible as evidence of the age of that person.

(2) Evidence of age by certificate or record — In any proceedings under this Act,

(a) a birth or baptismal certificate or a copy of it purporting to be certified under the hand of the person in whose custody those records are held is evidence of the age of the person named in the certificate or copy; and

(b) an entry or record of an incorporated society that has had the control or care of the person alleged to have committed the offence in respect of which the proceedings are taken at or about the time the person came to Canada is evidence of the age of that person, if the entry or record was made before the time when the offence is alleged to have been committed.

(3) Other evidence — In the absence of any certificate, copy, entry or record mentioned in subsection (2), or in corroboration of that certificate, copy, entry or record, the youth justice court may receive and act on any other information relating to age that it considers reliable.

(4) When age may be inferred — In any proceedings under this Act, the youth justice court may draw inferences as to the age of a person from the person's appearance or from statements made by the person in direct examination or cross-examination.

149. (1) Admissions — A party to any proceedings under this Act may admit any relevant fact or matter for the purpose of dispensing with proof of it, including any fact or matter the admissibility of which depends on a ruling of law or of mixed law and fact.

(2) Other party may adduce evidence — Nothing in this section precludes a party to a proceeding from adducing evidence to prove a fact or matter admitted by another party.

150. Material evidence — Any evidence material to proceedings under this Act that would not but for this section be admissible in evidence may, with the consent of the parties to the proceedings and if the young person is represented by counsel, be given in such proceedings.

151. Evidence of a child or young person — The evidence of a child or a young person may be taken in proceedings under this Act only after the youth justice court judge or the justice in the proceedings has

(a) if the witness is a child, instructed the child as to the duty to speak the truth and the consequences of failing to do so; and

(b) if the witness is a young person and the judge or justice considers it necessary, instructed the young person as to the duty to speak the truth and the consequences of failing to do so.

152. (1) Proof of service — For the purposes of this Act, service of any document may be proved by oral evidence given under oath by, or by the affidavit or statutory declaration of, the person claiming to have personally served it or sent it by confirmed delivery service.

(2) Proof of signature and official character unnecessary — If proof of service of any document is offered by affidavit or statutory declaration, it is not necessary to prove the signature or official character of the person making or taking the affidavit or declaration, if the official character of that person appears on the face of the affidavit or declaration.

153. Seal not required — It is not necessary to the validity of any information, indictment, summons, warrant, minute, sentence, conviction, order or other process or document laid, issued, filed or entered in any proceedings under this Act that any seal be attached or affixed to it.

Forms, Regulations and Rules of Court

154. (1) Forms — The forms prescribed under section 155, varied to suit the case, or forms to the like effect, are valid and sufficient in the circumstances for which they are provided.

(2) If forms not prescribed — In any case for which forms are not prescribed under section 155, the forms set out in Part XXVIII of the *Criminal Code*, with any modifications that the circumstances require, or other appropriate forms, may be used.

155. Regulations — The Governor in Council may make regulations

(a) prescribing forms that may be used for the purposes of this Act;

(b) establishing uniform rules of court for youth justice courts across Canada, including rules regulating the practice and procedure to be followed by youth justice courts; and

(c) generally for carrying out the purposes and provisions of this Act.

Agreements with Provinces

156. Agreements with provinces — Any minister of the Crown may, with the approval of the Governor in Council, enter into an agreement with the government of any province providing for payments by Canada to the province in respect of costs incurred by the province or a municipality in the province for care of and services provided to young persons dealt with under this Act.

Programs

157. Community-based programs — The Attorney General of Canada or a minister designated by the lieutenant governor in council of a province may establish the following types of community-based programs:

(a) programs that are an alternative to judicial proceedings, such as victim-offender reconciliation programs, mediation programs and restitution programs;

(b) programs that are an alternative to detention before sentencing, such as bail supervision programs; and

(c) programs that are an alternative to custody, such as intensive support and supervision programs, and programs to carry out attendance orders.

PART 8 — TRANSITIONAL PROVISIONS (SS. 158–165)

158. Prohibition on proceedings — On and after the coming into force of this section, no proceedings may be commenced under the *Young Offenders Act*, chapter Y-1 of the Revised Statutes of Canada, 1985, in respect of an offence within the meaning of that Act, or under the *Juvenile Delinquents Act*, chapter J-3 of the Revised Statutes of Canada, 1970, in respect of a delinquency within the meaning of that Act.

159. (1) Proceedings commenced under *Young Offenders Act* — Subject to section 161, where, before the coming into force of this section, proceedings are commenced under the *Young Offenders Act*, chapter Y-1 of the Revised Statutes of Canada, 1985, in respect of an offence within the meaning of that Act alleged to have been committed by a person who was at the time of the offence a young person within the meaning of that Act, the proceedings and all related matters shall be dealt with in all respects as if this Act had not come into force.

(2) Proceedings commenced under *Juvenile Delinquents Act* — Subject to section 161, where, before the coming into force of this section, proceedings are commenced under the *Juvenile Delinquents Act*, chapter J-3 of the Revised Statutes of Canada, 1970, in respect of a delinquency within the meaning of that Act alleged to have been committed by a person who was at the time of the delinquency a child as defined in that Act, the proceedings and all related matters shall be dealt with under this Act as if the delinquency were an offence that occurred after the coming into force of this section.

160. [Repealed 2012, c. 1, s. 193.]

161. (1) Applicable sentence — A person referred to in section 159 who is found guilty of an offence or delinquency, other than a person convicted of an offence in ordinary court, as defined in subsection 2(1) of the *Young Offenders Act*, chapter Y-1 of the Revised Statutes of Canada, 1985, shall be sentenced under this Act, except that

(a) [Repealed 2019, c. 25, s. 382.]

(b) paragraph 42(2)(r) applies in respect of the offence or delinquency only if the young person consents to its application.

The provisions of this Act applicable to sentences imposed under section 42 apply in respect of the sentence.

(2) Dispositions under paragraph 20(1)(k) or (k.1) of *Young Offenders Act* — Where a young person is to be sentenced under this Act while subject to a disposition under paragraph 20(1)(k) or (k.1) of the *Young Offenders Act*, chapter Y-1 of the Revised Statutes of Canada, 1985, on the application of the Attorney General or the young person, a youth justice court shall, unless to do so would bring the administration of justice into disrepute, order that the remaining portion of the disposition made under that Act be dealt with, for all purposes under this Act or any other Act of Parliament, as if it had been a sentence imposed under paragraph 42(2)(n) or (q) of this Act, as the case may be.

(3) Review of sentence — For greater certainty, for the purpose of determining when the sentence is reviewed under section 94, the relevant date is the one on which the disposition came into force under the *Young Offenders Act*, chapter Y-1 of the Revised Statutes of Canada, 1985.

2019, c. 25, s. 382

162. Commencement of proceedings — For the purposes of sections 158 and 159, proceedings are commenced by the laying of an information or indictment.

2012, c. 1, s. 194

163. Application to delinquency and other offending behaviour — Sections 114 to 129 apply, with any modifications that the circumstances require, in respect of records relating to the offence of delinquency under the *Juvenile Delinquents Act*, chapter J-3 of the Revised Statutes of Canada, 1970, and in respect of records kept under sections 40 to 43 of the *Young Offenders Act*, chapter Y-1 of the Revised Statutes of Canada, 1985.

164. Agreements continue in force — Any agreement made under the *Young Offenders Act*, chapter Y-1 of the Revised Statutes of Canada, 1985, remains in force until it expires, unless it is amended or a new agreement is made under this Act.

165. (1) Designation of youth justice court — Any court established or designated as a youth court for the purposes of the *Young Offenders Act*, chapter Y-1 of the Revised Statutes of Canada, 1985, is deemed, as of the coming into force of this section, to have been established or designated as a youth justice court for the purposes of this Act.

(2) Designation of youth justice court judges — Any person appointed to be a judge of the youth court for the purposes of the *Young Offenders Act*, chapter Y-1 of the Revised Statutes of Canada, 1985, is deemed, as of the coming into force of this section, to have been appointed as a judge of the youth justice court for the purposes of this Act.

(3) Designation of provincial directors and youth workers — Any person, group or class of persons or body appointed or designated as a provincial director for the purposes of the *Young Offenders Act*, chapter Y-1 of the Revised Statutes of Canada, 1985, and any person appointed or designated as a youth worker for the purposes of that Act is deemed, as of the coming into force of this section, to have been appointed or designated as a provincial director or youth worker, as the case may be, for the purposes of this Act.

(4) Designation of review boards and youth justice committees — Any review board established or designated for the purposes of the *Young Offenders Act*, chapter Y-1 of the Revised Statutes of Canada, 1985, and any youth justice committee established for the purposes of that Act is deemed, as of the coming into force of this section, to have been established or designated as a review board or a youth justice committee, as the case may be, for the purposes of this Act.

(5) Alternative measures continued as extrajudicial sanctions — Any program of alternative measures authorized for the purposes of the *Young Offenders Act*, chapter Y-1 of the Revised Statutes of Canada, 1985, is deemed, as of the coming into force of this section, to be a program of extrajudicial sanctions authorized for the purposes of this Act.

(6) Designation of places of temporary detention and youth custody — Subject to subsection (7), any place that was designated as a place of temporary detention or open custody for the purposes of the *Young Offenders Act*, chapter Y-1 of the Revised Statutes of Canada, 1985, and any place or facility designated as a place of secure custody for the purposes of that Act is deemed, as of the coming into force of this section, to have been designated for the purposes of this Act as

(a) in the case of a place of temporary detention, a place of temporary detention; and

(b) in the case of a place of open custody or secure custody, a youth custody facility.

(7) Exception — If the lieutenant governor in council of a province makes an order under section 88 that the power to make determinations of the level of custody for young persons and to review those determinations be exercised in accordance with the *Young Offenders Act*, chapter Y-1 of the Revised Statutes of Canada, 1985, the designation of any place as a place of open custody or secure custody for the purposes of that Act remains in force for the purposes of section 88, subject to revocation or amendment of the designation.

(8) **Designation of other persons** — Any person designated as a clerk of the youth court for the purposes of the *Young Offenders Act*, chapter Y-1 of the Revised Statutes of Canada, 1985, or any person or group of persons who were designated under that Act to carry out specified functions and duties are deemed, as of the coming into force of this section, to have been designated as a clerk of the youth justice court, or to carry out the same functions and duties, as the case may be, under this Act.

PART 9 — CONSEQUENTIAL AMENDMENTS, REPEAL AND COMING INTO FORCE (SS. 166–200)

Consequential Amendments

166. to 198. Consequential Amendments — [Note: The Consequential amendments are incorporated into the relevant provisions of the Acts which they affect, namely, the *Canada Evidence Act*, the *Contraventions Act*, the *Corrections and Conditional Release Act*, the *Criminal Code*, the *DNA Identification Act*, the *Extradition Act*, the *Mutual Assistance in Criminal Matters Act*, the *Prisons and Reformatories Act*, and the *Transfer of Offenders Act*.]

Repeal

199. Repeal of R.S., c. Y-1 — The *Young Offenders Act* is repealed.

Coming into Force

200. Coming into force — The provisions of this Act come into force on a day or days to be fixed by order of the Governor in Council.

SCHEDULE

(Subsections 120(1), (4) and (6))

1. An offence under any of the following provisions of the *Criminal Code*:

(a) paragraph 81(2)(a) (using explosives);

(b) subsection 85(1) (using firearm in commission of offence);

(c) section 151 (sexual interference);

(d) section 152 (invitation to sexual touching);

(e) section 153 (sexual exploitation);

(f) section 155 (incest);

(g) [Repealed 2019, c. 25, s. 383.]

(h) section 170 (parent or guardian procuring sexual activity by child);

(i) and (j) [Repealed 2014, c. 25, s. 43(1).]

(k) section 231 or 235 (first degree murder or second degree murder within the meaning of section 231);

(l) section 232, 234 or 236 (manslaughter);

(m) section 239 (attempt to commit murder);

(n) section 267 (assault with a weapon or causing bodily harm);

(o) section 268 (aggravated assault);

(p) section 269 (unlawfully causing bodily harm);

(q) section 271 (sexual assault);

(r) section 272 (sexual assault with a weapon, threats to a third party or causing bodily harm);

(s) section 273 (aggravated sexual assault);

(t) section 279 (kidnapping);

(t.1) section 279.011 (trafficking — person under 18 years);

(t.2) subsection 279.02(2) (material benefit — trafficking of person under 18 years);

(t.3) subsection 279.03(2) (withholding or destroying documents — trafficking of person under 18 years);

(t.4) subsection 286.1(2) (obtaining sexual services for consideration from person under 18 years);

(t.5) subsection 286.2(2) (material benefit from sexual services provided by person under 18 years);

(t.6) subsection 286.3(2) (procuring — person under 18 years);

(u) section 344 (robbery);

(v) section 433 (arson — disregard for human life);

(w) section 434.1 (arson — own property);

(x) section 436 (arson by negligence); and

(y) paragraph 465(1)(a) (conspiracy to commit murder).

1.1 An offence under one of the following provisions of the *Criminal Code*, as they read from time to time before the day on which this section comes into force:

(a) subsection 212(2) (living on the avails of prostitution of person under 18 years); and

(b) subsection 212(4) (prostitution of person under 18 years).

2. An offence under any of the following provisions of the *Criminal Code*, as they read immediately before July 1, 1990:

(a) section 433 (arson);

(b) section 434 (setting fire to other substance); and

(c) section 436 (setting fire by negligence).

3. An offence under any of the following provisions of the *Criminal Code*, chapter C-34 of the Revised Statutes of Canada, 1970, as they read immediately before January 4, 1983:

(a) section 144 (rape);

(b) section 145 (attempt to commit rape);

(c) section 149 (indecent assault on female);

(d) section 156 (indecent assault on male); and

(e) section 246 (assault with intent).

4. An offence under any of the following provisions of the *Controlled Drugs and Substances Act*:

(a) section 5 (trafficking);

(b) section 6 (importing and exporting); and

(c) section 7 (production of substance).

5. An offence under any of the following provisions of the *Cannabis Act*:

(a) section 9 (distribution and possession for purpose of distributing);

(b) section 10 (selling and possession for purpose of selling);

(c) section 11 (importing and exporting and possession for purpose of exporting);

(d) section 12 (production); and

(e) section 14 (use of young person).

2014, c. 25, s. 43; 2018, c. 16, s. 184; 2019, c. 25, s. 383

Transitional Provisions

— 2012, c. 1, ss. 163, 195:

163. Pending applications — references in other legislation — A reference to an application for a record suspension in the following provisions, as enacted by this Part, is deemed also to be a reference to an application for a pardon that is not finally disposed of on the day on which this section comes into force:

(a) paragraph 672.35(c) and subsection 750(4) of the *Criminal Code*;

(b) paragraph 202.14(2)(h) of the *National Defence Act*; and

(c) paragraph 82(1)(d) and subparagraphs 119(1)(n)(iii) and 120(4)(c)(iii) of the *Youth Criminal Justice Act*.

195. Offences committed before this section in force — Any person who, before the coming into force of this section, while he or she was a young person, committed an offence in respect of which no proceedings were commenced before that coming into force shall be dealt with under the *Youth Criminal Justice Act* as amended by this Part as if the offence occurred after that coming into force, except that

(a) the definition "violent offence" in subsection 2(1) of the *Youth Criminal Justice Act*, as enacted by subsection 167(3), does not apply in respect of the offence;

(b) paragraph 3(1)(a) of that Act, as enacted by subsection 168(1), does not apply in respect of the offence;

(c) paragraph 38(2)(f) of that Act, as enacted by section 172, does not apply in respect of the offence;

(d) paragraph 39(1)(c) of that Act, as enacted by section 173, does not apply in respect of the offence; and

(e) section 75 of that Act, as enacted by section 185, does not apply in respect of the offence.

— 2019, c. 25, s. 384:

384. Subsection 59(10) — Subsection 59(10) of the *Youth Criminal Justice Act* does not apply to the sentence for an offence committed before the coming into force of that subsection.

FORMS OF CHARGES

From *The Police Officers Manual* by Gary P. Rodrigues, B.A., LL.B., of the Ontario Bar

Criminal Code

[Editor's Note: These Forms of Charges reflect the state of the law prior to the legislative amendments introduced on June 21, 2019. When consulting these precedents, please keep in mind the changes made on that date, as well as subsequent to then, to the applicable offence provisions.]

Part II — Offences Against Public Order

Section 47(1) High treason

A.B., on the (day) of (month), (year) at (specify time) in (specify place), in Canada, did kill [or did maim or did wound or did imprison or did restrain] Her Majesty the Queen and did thereby commit high treason, contrary to s. 47(1) of the *Criminal Code*.

Section 47(2) Treason

A.B., on the (day) of (month), (year) at (specify time) in (specify place), in Canada, used force or violence for the purpose of overthrowing the government of Canada [or (specify the government of the province of Canada)], to wit: (specify the particulars of the offence), contrary to s. 47(2) of the *Criminal Code*.

Section 49(a) Alarming the Queen

A.B., on the (day) of (month), (year), at (specify time) in (specify place), wilfully, in the presence of Her Majesty the Queen, did an act with intent to alarm Her Majesty [or did an act with intent to break the public peace], to wit: (specify the particulars of the offence), contrary to s. 49(a) of the *Criminal Code*.

Section 49(b) Causing bodily harm to the Queen

A.B., on the (day) of (month), (year) at (specify time) in (specify place), in Canada, wilfully, in the presence of Her Majesty the Queen, did an act with intent to cause bodily harm to [or did an act likely to cause bodily harm to] Her Majesty the Queen, to wit: (specify the particulars of the offence), contrary to s. 49(b) of the *Criminal Code*.

Section 50(1)(a) Assisting alien enemy to leave Canada

A.B., on the (day) of (month), (year) at (specify time) in (specify place)

..........incited [or wilfully assisted] C.D., a subject of (specify the country), a state at war with Canada, to leave Canada without the consent of the Crown and without establishing that assistance to (specify the country) was not intended thereby, to wit: (specify the particulars of the offence), contrary to s. 50(1)(a)(i) of the *Criminal Code*.

..........incited [or wilfully assisted] C.D., a subject of (specify the country), a state against whose forces Canadian Forces were engaged in hostilities, to leave Canada with out the consent of the Crown and without establishing that assistance to the forces of (specify the country) was not intended thereby, to wit: (specify the particulars of the offence), contrary to s. 50(1)(a)(ii) of the *Criminal Code*.

Section 50(1)(b) Omitting to prevent treason

A.B., on the (day) of (month), (year) at (specify time) in (specify place), knowing that C.D. was about to commit high treason [or treason], did not, with all reasonable dispatch, inform a justice of the peace [or peace officer] [or did not make reasonable efforts to prevent C.D. from committing high treason (or treason)], to wit: (specify the particulars of the offence), contrary to s. 50(1)(b) of the *Criminal Code*.

Section 51 Intimidation of Parliament or legislature

A.B., on the (day) of (month), (year) at (specify time) in (specify place), did an act of violence in order to intimidate the Parliament of Canada [or (specify the legislative of a Province)], to wit: (specify the particulars of the offence), contrary to s. 51 of the *Criminal Code*.

Section 52 Sabotage

A.B., on the (day) of (month), (year), at (specify time) in (specify place), did a prohibited act for a purpose prejudicial to the safety [or security or defence] of Canada [or the safety (or security) of the naval or army or air)] forces of (specify the country other than Canada), that were lawfully present in Canada], to wit: (specify the particulars of the offence), contrary to s. 52 of the *Criminal Code*.

Section 53 Inciting to mutiny

A.B., on the (day) of (month), (year), at (specify time) in (specify place),

..........did attempt to seduce for a traitorous [or mutinous] purpose C.D., a member of the Canadian Forces, from his [or her] duty and allegiance to Her Majesty, to wit: (specify the particulars of the offence), contrary to s. 53(a) of the *Criminal Code*.

..........did attempt to incite [or to induce] C.D., a member of the Canadian Forces, to commit a traitorous [or mutinous] act, to wit: (specify the particulars of the offence), contrary to s. 53(b) of the *Criminal Code*.

Section 54 Aiding Canadian Forces deserter

A.B., on the (day) of (month), (year), at (specify time) in (specify place), did aid [or assist or harbour or conceal] C.D., knowing the said C.D. to be a deserter [or absent without leave] from the Canadian Forces, to wit: (specify the particulars of the offence), contrary to s. 54 of the *Criminal Code*.

Section 56 Assisting R.C.M.P. deserter

A.B., on the (day) of (month), (year), at (specify time) in (specify place), wilfully

..........did persuade [or counsel] C.D., a member of the Royal Canadian Mounted Police, to desert [or absent himself (or herself) without leave] to wit: (specify the particulars of the offence), contrary to s. 56(a) of the *Criminal Code*.

..........did aid [or assist or harbour or conceal] C.D., a member of the Royal Canadian Mounted Police, who A.B. knew was a deserter [or absent without leave], to wit: (specify the particulars of the offence), contrary to s. 56(b) of the *Criminal Code*.

..........did aid [or assist] C.D., a member of the Royal Canadian Mounted Police, to desert [or absent himself (or herself) without leave], knowing that C.D. was about to desert [or absent himself (or herself) without leave], to wit: (specify the particulars of the offence), contrary to s. 56(c) of the *Criminal Code*.

Section 56.1 Identity document

A.B., on the (day) of (month), (year) at (specify time) in (specify place), without lawful excuse,

..........did procure to be made [or transfer or sell or offer for sale] (specify identity document), an identity document that relates to [or purports to relate to] C.D., to wit: (specify the particulars of the offence), contrary to s. 56.1(1) of the *Criminal Code*.

..........did possess (specify identity document), an identity document that relates to [or purports to relate to] C.D., to wit: (specify the particulars of the offence), contrary to s. 56.1(1) of the *Criminal Code*.

Section 57(1)(a) Forgery of passport

A.B., on the (day) of (month), (year), at (specify time) in (specify place), did forge a passport, to wit: (specify the particulars of the offence), contrary to s. 57(1)(a) of the *Criminal Code*.

..........did cause [or attempt to cause] C.D. to use [or deal with or act on] a forged passport as if the passport were genuine, to wit: (specify the particulars of the offence), contrary to s. 57(1)(b)(ii) of the *Criminal Code*.

Section 57(1)(b) Uttering or using forged passport

A.B., on the (day) of (month), (year), at (specify time) in (specify place), knowing that a passport was forged,

..........did use [or deal with or act on] it as if the passport were genuine, to wit: (specify the particulars of the offence), contrary to s. 57(1)(b)(i) of the *Criminal Code*.

Section 57(2) False statement to procure passport

A.B., on the (day) of (month), (year), at (specify time) in (specify place),

..........did make a written [or oral] statement that A.B. knew was false [or misleading], for the purpose of procuring a passport for A.B. [or C.D.], to wit: (specify the particulars of the offence), contrary to s. 57(2) of the *Criminal Code*.

..........did make a written [or oral] statement that A.B. knew was false [or misleading] for the purpose of procuring a material alteration [or addition] to a passport for A.B. [or C.D.], to wit: (specify the particulars of the offence), contrary to s. 57(2) of the *Criminal Code*.

Section 57(3) Possession of forged passport or passport obtained by false statement

A.B., on the (day) of (month), (year), at (specify time) in (specify place), without lawful excuse,

..........did have in his [or her] possession a forged passport, to wit: (specify the particulars of the offence) contrary to 57(3) of the *Criminal Code*.

..........did have in his [or her] possession a passport procured by making a false or misleading statement [or containing a material alteration or addition obtained by making a false or misleading statement], to wit: (specify the particulars of the offence), contrary to s. 57(3) of the *Criminal Code*.

Section 58(1) Fraudulent use of certificate of citizenship or certificate of naturalization

A.B., on the (day) of (month), (year), at (specify time) in (specify place),

..........did use a certificate of citizenship [or a certificate of naturalization] for a fraudulent purpose, to wit: (specify the particulars of the offence), contrary to s. 58(1)(a) of the *Criminal Code*.

..........being a person to whom a certificate of a citizenship [or a certificate of naturalization] had been granted under the provisions of the *Canadian Citizenship Act*, did knowingly part with possession of that certificate with intent that it be used for a fraudulent purpose, to wit: (specify the particulars of the offence), contrary to s. 58(1)(b) of the *Criminal Code*.

Section 61 Seditious offences

A.B., on the (day) of (month), (year), at (specify time) in (specify place), did speak seditious words [or did publish a seditious libel or was a party to a seditious conspiracy], to wit: [specify the particulars of the offence], contrary to s. 61(a) [or (b) or (c)] of the *Criminal Code*.

Section 62(1) Offences in relation to members of military forces

A.B., on the (day) of (month), (year), at (specify time) in (specify place), wilfully

..........did interfere with [or impair or influence] the loyalty [or discipline] of C.D., a member of the Canadian forces [or a member of the naval (or army or air) forces of (specify a state other than Canada) lawfully present in Canada], to wit: specify the particulars of the offence), contrary to s. 62(1)(a) of the *Criminal Code*.

..........did publish [or edit or issue or circulate or distribute] a writing that advises [or counsels or urges] insubordination [or disloyalty or mutiny or refusal of duty] by

C.D., a member of the Canadian forces [or a member of the naval (or army or air) forces of (specify a state other than Canada) lawfully present in Canada] to wit: (specify the particulars of the offence), contrary to s. 62(1)(b) of the *Criminal Code*.

..........did advise [or counsel or urge or cause] insubordination [or disloyalty or mutiny or refusal of duty] by C.D., a member of the Canadian forces [or a member of the naval (or army or air) forces of (specify a state other than Canada) lawfully present in Canada], to wit: (specify the particulars of the offence), contrary to s. 62(1)(c) of the *Criminal Code*.

Section 65(1) Rioting

A.B., on the (day) of (month), (year), at (specify time) in (specify place),

..........was a member of a lawful assembly that had begun to disturb the peace tumultuously, and did thereby take part in a riot, to wit: (specify the particulars of the offence), contrary to s. 65(1) of the *Criminal Code*.

..........did take part in a riot, to wit: (specify the particulars of the offence), contrary to s. 65(1) of the *Criminal Code*.

Section 65(2) Concealment of identity while rioting

A.B., on the (day) of (month), (year), at (specify time) in (specify place),

..........while wearing a mask [or other disguise] to conceal A.B.'s identity, without lawful excuse, was a member of a lawful assembly that had begun to disturb the peace tumultuously, and did thereby take part in a riot, to wit: (specify the particulars of the offence), contrary to s. 65(1) of the *Criminal Code*.

..........while wearing a mask [or other disguise] to conceal A.B.'s identity, without lawful cause, did take part in a riot, to wit: (specify the particulars of the offence), contrary to s. 65(1) of the *Criminal Code*.

Section 66(1) Unlawful assembly

A.B., on the (day) of (month), (year), at (specify time) in (specify place),

..........was a member of an unlawful assembly, to wit: (specify the particulars of the offence), contrary to s. 66(1) of the *Criminal Code*.

..........with C.D. and E.F., with intent to carry out (specify a common purpose), did assemble themselves in such a manner [or conduct themselves in such a manner], as to cause persons in the neighbourhood to fear on reasonable grounds that A.B. would disturb the peace tumultuously, to wit: (specify the particulars of the offence), contrary to s. 66(1) of the *Criminal Code*.

..........with C.D. and E.F., with intent to carry out (specify a common purpose), did assemble themselves in such a manner [or conduct themselves in such a manner], as to cause persons in the neighbourhood to fear on reasonable grounds that A.B. would needlessly and without reasonable cause provoke other persons to disturb the peace tumultuously, to wit: (specify the particulars of the offence), contrary to s. 66(1) of the *Criminal Code*.

Section 66(2) Concealment of identity at unlawful assembly

A.B., on the (day) of (month), (year), at (specify time) in (specify place),

..........while wearing a mask [or other disguise] to conceal A.B.'s identity, without lawful cause, was a member of an unlawful assembly, to wit: (specify the particulars of the offence), contrary to s. 66(2) of the *Criminal Code*.

..........while wearing a mask [or other disguise] to conceal A.B.'s identity, without lawful cause, with C.D. and E.F., and with intent to carry out (specify a common purpose), did assemble themselves in such a manner [or conduct themselves in such a manner], as to cause persons in the neighbourhood to fear on reasonable grounds that A.B. would disturb the peace tumultuously, to wit: (specify the particulars of the offence), contrary to s. 66(2) of the *Criminal Code*.

..........while wearing a mask [or other disguise] to conceal A.B.'s identity, without lawful cause, with C.D. and E.F., and with intent to carry out (specify a common purpose), did assemble themselves in such a manner [or conduct themselves in such a manner], as to cause persons in the neighbourhood to fear on reasonable grounds that A.B. would needlessly and without reasonable cause provoke other persons to disturb the peace tumultuously, to wit: (specify the particulars of the offence), contrary to s. 66(2) of the *Criminal Code*.

Section 68 Offences relating to proclamation to disperse

A.B., on the (day) of (month), (year), at (specify time) in (specify place),

..........did oppose [or hinder or assault] wilfully and with force C.D., a person who began to make [or was about to begin to make or was making] a proclamation to disperse pursuant to s. 67, so that it was not made, to wit: (specify the particulars of the offence), contrary to s. 68(a) of the *Criminal Code*.

..........did not peaceably disperse and depart from a place where a proclamation to disperse pursuant to s. 67 was made within 30 minutes after it was made, to wit: (specify the particulars of the offence), contrary to s. 68(b) of the *Criminal Code*.

..........did not depart from a place within 30 minutes when A.B. had reasonable grounds to believe that the proclamation to disperse pursuant to s. 67 would have been made in that place if A.B. [or C.D.] had not opposed [or hindered or assaulted], wilfully and with force, E.F., the person who would have made it, to wit: (specify the particulars of the offence), contrary to s. 68(c) of the *Criminal Code*.

Section 69 Peace officer failing to suppress riot

A.B., on the (day) of (month), (year), at (specify time) in (specify place), being a peace officer who had received notice that there was a riot within his [or her] jurisdiction, without reasonable excuse, did fail to take all reasonable steps to suppress the riot, to wit: (specify the particulars of the offence), contrary to s. 69 of the *Criminal Code*.

Section 70(3) Contravention of orders prohibiting unlawful drilling

A.B., on the (day) of (month), (year), at (specify time) in (specify place), without lawful authority, did contravene an order made under s. 70(1) prohibiting assemblies, for the purpose of training or drilling [or of being trained or drilled to the use of arms or of practising military exercises], to wit: (specify the particulars of the offence), contrary to s. 70(3) of the *Criminal Code*.

Section 73 Forcible entry and detainer

A.B., on the (day) of (month), (year), at (specify time) in (specify place),

..........did commit forcible entry, to wit: (specify the particulars of the offence), contrary to s. 73 of the *Criminal Code*.

..........did enter (specify address), real property in the actual and peaceable possession of C.D., in a manner that was likely to cause a breach of the peace [or reasonable apprehension of a breach of the peace], to wit: (specify the particulars of the offence), contrary to s. 73 of the *Criminal Code*.

..........did commit forcible detainer, to wit: (specify the particulars of the offence), contrary to s. 73 of the *Criminal Code*.

..........being in actual possession of (specify real property), without colour of right, did detain it in a manner that was likely to cause a breach of the peace [or reasonable apprehension of a breach of the peace], against C.D., a person who was entitled by law to possess it, to wit: (specify the particulars of the offence), contrary to s. 73 of the *Criminal Code*.

Section 74 Piracy

A.B., on the (day) of (month), (year), at (specify time) in (specify place), did commit piracy, to wit: (specify the particulars of the offence), contrary to s. 74 of the *Criminal Code*.

Section 75 Offences in connection with Canadian ships

A.B., on the (day) of (month), (year), at (specify time) in (specify place),

..........did steal [or counsel C.D. to steal] a Canadian ship [or part of the cargo (or part of the supplies or part of the fittings) in a Canadian ship], to wit: (specify the particulars of the offence), contrary to s. 75 of the *Criminal Code*.

..........without lawful authority, did throw overboard [or damage or destroy] part of the cargo [or part of the supplies or part of the fittings] in a Canadian ship, to wit: (specify the particulars of the offence), contrary to s. 75 of the *Criminal Code*.

..........without lawful authority, did counsel C.D. to throw overboard [or damage or destroy] part of the cargo [or part of the supplies or part of the fittings] in a Canadian ship, to wit: (specify the particulars of the offence), contrary to s. 75 of the *Criminal Code*.

..........did [or did attempt or did counsel C.D. to do] a mutinous act on a Canadian ship, to wit: (specify the particulars of the offence), contrary to s. 75 of the *Criminal Code*.

Section 76 Aircraft hijacking

A.B., on the (day) of (month), (year), at (specify time) in (specify place), unlawfully, by force [or threat of force or (specify other form of intimidation)]

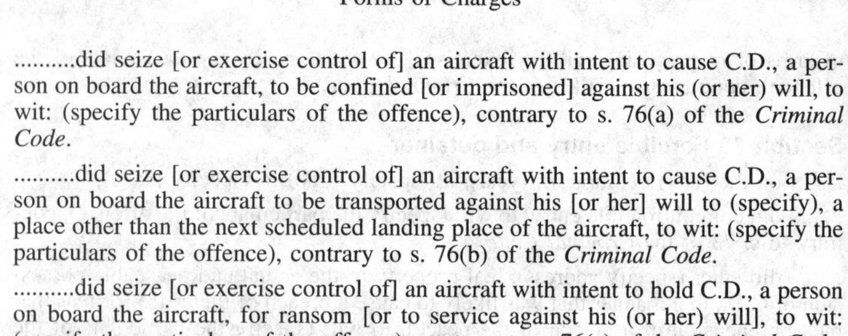

..........did seize [or exercise control of] an aircraft with intent to cause C.D., a person on board the aircraft, to be confined [or imprisoned] against his (or her) will, to wit: (specify the particulars of the offence), contrary to s. 76(a) of the *Criminal Code*.

..........did seize [or exercise control of] an aircraft with intent to cause C.D., a person on board the aircraft to be transported against his [or her] will to (specify), a place other than the next scheduled landing place of the aircraft, to wit: (specify the particulars of the offence), contrary to s. 76(b) of the *Criminal Code*.

..........did seize [or exercise control of] an aircraft with intent to hold C.D., a person on board the aircraft, for ransom [or to service against his (or her) will], to wit: (specify the particulars of the offence), contrary to s. 76(c) of the *Criminal Code*.

..........did seize [or exercise control of] an aircraft with intent to cause the aircraft to deviate in a material respect from its flight plan, to wit: (specify the particulars of the offence), contrary to s. 76(d) of the *Criminal Code*.

Section 77 Endangering safety of airport or aircraft

A.B., on the (day) of (month), (year), at (specify time) in (specify place),

..........did commit an act of violence against C.D., a person on board an aircraft in flight, that was likely to endanger the safety of the aircraft, to wit: (specify the particulars of the offence), contrary to s. 77(a) of the *Criminal Code*.

..........using a weapon, did commit an act of violence against C.D., a person at an airport serving international civil aviation, that caused [or was likely to cause] serious injury [or death] that endangered [or was likely to endanger] safety at the airport, to wit: (specify the particulars of the offence), contrary to s. 77(b) of the *Criminal Code*.

..........did cause damage to an aircraft in service that rendered the aircraft incapable of flight [or was likely to endanger the safety of the aircraft in flight], to wit: (specify the particulars of the offence), contrary to s. 77(c) of the *Criminal Code*.

..........did place [or cause to be placed] on board an aircraft in service a (specify the thing placed on board) which was likely to cause damage to an aircraft that would render it incapable of flight [or was likely to endanger the safety of an aircraft in flight], to wit: (specify the particulars of the offence), contrary to s. 77(d) of the *Criminal Code*.

..........did damage to [or interfere with the operation of] an air navigation facility, which damage [or interference] was likely to endanger the safety of an aircraft in flight, to wit: (specify the particulars of the offence), contrary to s. 77(e) of the *Criminal Code*.

..........using a weapon [or substance or device] did destroy [or cause serious damage to] the facilities of an airport serving international civil aviation [or to an aircraft not in service located there or did cause disruption of services of the airport] that endangered [or was likely to endanger] safety at the airport, to wit: (specify the particulars of the offence), contrary to s. 77(f) of the *Criminal Code*.

..........did endanger the safety of an aircraft in flight by communicating information to C.D. that A.B. knew to be false, to wit: (specify the particulars of the offence), contrary to s. 77(g) of the *Criminal Code*.

Section 78 Offensive weapons and explosive substances on board an aircraft

A.B., on the (day) of (month), (year), at (specify time) in (specify place),

..........did take on board a civil aircraft an offensive weapon [or an explosive substance] without the consent of C.D., the owner [or the operator or a person duly authorized by E.F., the owner (or the operator) to consent thereto] to wit: (specify the particulars of the offence), contrary to s. 78(1)(a) of the *Criminal Code*.

..........did take on board a civil aircraft an offensive weapon [or an explosive substance] with the consent of C.D., the owner [or the operator or a person duly authorized by E.F., the owner (or the operator) to consent thereto] but without complying with the terms and conditions on which consent was given, to wit: (specify the particulars of the offence), contrary to s. 78(1)(b) of the *Criminal Code*.

Section 78.1(1) Seizing control of ship or fixed platform

A.B., on the (day) of (month), (year), at (specify time) in (specify place), did seize [or exercise control over] a ship [or fixed platform] by force [or by threat of force or by intimidation], to wit: (specify the particulars of the offence), contrary to s. 78.1(1) of the *Criminal Code*.

Section 78.1(2) Endangering safety of ship or fixed platform by committing an act of violence on board

A.B., on the (day) of (month), (year), at (specify time) in (specify place), did commit an act of violence against C.D., a person on board a ship [or fixed platform], where that act was likely to endanger the safe navigation of the ship [or the safety of the fixed platform], to wit: (specify the particulars of the offence), contrary to s. 78.1(2)(a) of the *Criminal Code*.

Section 78.1(2)(b) Destroying or causing damage to ship or platform

A.B., on the (day) of (month), (year), at (specify time) in (specify place), did destroy [or cause damage] to a ship [or the cargo of a ship or to a fixed platform], where that act was likely to endanger the safe navigation of the ship [or the safety of the fixed platform], to wit: (specify the particulars of the offence), contrary to s. 78.1(2)(b) of the *Criminal Code*.

Section 78.1(2)(c) Destroying or causing damage to maritime navigational facility

A.B., on the (day) of (month), (year), at (specify time) in (specify place), did destroy [or cause damage to or interfere with the operation of] (specify), a maritime navigational facility, where that act was likely to endanger the safe navigation of the ship [or the safety of the fixed platform], to wit: (specify the particulars of the offence), contrary to s. 78.1(2)(c) of the *Criminal Code*.

Section 78.1(2)(d) Placing on board a ship or fixed platform anything likely to cause damage

A.B., on the (day) of (month), (year), at (specify time) in (specify place), did place [or cause to be placed] on board a ship [or fixed platform] a thing that was likely to cause damage to the ship [or to the cargo of a ship or to the fixed platform], where that act was likely to endanger the safe navigation of the ship [or the safety of the fixed platform], to wit: (specify the particulars of the offence), contrary to s. 78.1(2)(d) of the *Criminal Code*.

Section 78.1(3) False communication endangering safe navigation

A.B., on the (day) of (month), (year), at (specify time) in (specify place), did communicate information that endangered the safe navigation of a ship, knowing the information to be false, to wit: (specify the particulars of the offence), contrary to s. 78.1(3) of the *Criminal Code*.

Section 78.1(4) Threats causing damage or injury on ship or fixed platform

A.B., on the (day) of (month), (year), at (specify time) in (specify place), did threaten to commit an offence under s. 78.1(2)(a) [or (b) or (c)] of the *Criminal Code* in order to compel a person to do [or refrain from doing] any act, where the threat is likely to endanger the safe navigation of a ship [or the safety of a fixed platform], to wit: (specify the particulars of the offence), contrary to s. 78.1(4) of the *Criminal Code*.

Section 80 Breach of duty of care with explosive substances

A.B., on the (day) of (month), (year), at (specify time) in (specify place), being a person who had an explosive substance in his [or her] possession [or under his (or her) care and control], did fail without lawful excuse to perform his [or her] legal duty to use reasonable care to prevent bodily harm to C.D. [or death to C.D. or damage to property] by that explosive substance, to wit: (specify the particulars of the offence), contrary to s. 80 of the *Criminal Code*.

Section 81(1) Explosive substances offences

A.B., on the (day) of (month), (year), at (specify time) in (specify place),

..........with intent to cause an explosion of (specify the type of explosive substance), an explosive substance that was likely to cause serious bodily harm to C.D. [or death to C.D. or damage to (specify the property)] did (specify the act), to wit: (specify the particulars of the offence), contrary to s. 81(1)(a) of the *Criminal Code*.

..........with intent to do bodily harm to C.D., did cause (specify the type of explosive substance). an explosive substance, to explode, to wit: (specify the particulars of the offence), contrary to s. 81(1)(b)(i) of the *Criminal Code*.

..........with intent to do bodily harm to C.D., did send [or deliver] to C.D. [or cause C.D. to take (or receive)](specify the type of explosive substance or other dangerous substance or thing), an explosive substance [or a dangerous substance (or thing)], to wit: (specify the particulars of the offence), contrary to s. 81(1)(b)(ii) of the *Criminal Code*.

..........with intent to do bodily harm to C.D., did place on C.D. [or throw at C.D. or throw on C.D. or throw (specify where thrown)](specify the type of substance or thing thrown), a corrosive fluid [or an explosive substance or a dangerous substance or a dangerous thing], to wit: (specify the particulars of the offence), contrary to s. 81(1)(b)(iii) of the *Criminal Code*.

..........with intent to destroy [or damage] property without lawful excuse, did place [or throw] (specify the type of explosive substance), an explosive substance (specify where), to wit: (specify the particulars of the offence), contrary to s. 81(1)(c) of the *Criminal Code*.

..........did make [or have in his [or her] possession or have under his [or her] care or have under his [or her] control] (specify the type of explosive substance), an explosive substance, with intent thereby to endanger the life of C.D. [or to cause serious damage to property or to enable E.F. to endanger the life of C.D. or to enable E.F. to cause serious damage to property], to wit: (specify the particulars of the offence), contrary to s. 81(1)(d) of the *Criminal Code*.

Section 82(1) Possession of explosive substance without lawful excuse

A.B., on the (day) of (month), (year), at (specify time) in (specify place), without lawful excuse, did make [or have in his (or her) possession or have under his (or her) care or control] an explosive substance, to wit: (specify the particulars of the offence), contrary to s. 82(1) of the *Criminal Code*.

Section 82(2) Criminal organizations and explosive substances

A.B., on the (day) of (month), (year), at (specify time) in (specify place), without lawful excuse, did make [or have in his (or her) possession or have under his (or her) care or control] an explosive substance for the benefit of [or at the direction of or in association with] a criminal organization, to wit: (specify the particulars of the offence), contrary to s. 82(2) of the *Criminal Code*.

Section 82.3 Possession of nuclear material, radioactive material or device

A.B., on the (day) of (month), (year), at (specify time) in (specify place), with intent to cause death [or serious bodily harm or damage to property or damage to the environment], did make [or possess or use or transfer or export or import or alter or dispose of] nuclear material [or radioactive material or a device], to wit: (specify the particulars of the offence), contrary to s. 82.3 of the *Criminal Code*.

Section 82.3 Interference with or disruption of the operations of a nuclear facility

A.B., on the (day) of (month), (year), at (specify time) in (specify place), with intent to cause death [or serious bodily harm or damage to property or damage to the environment], did commit an act against a nuclear facility [or an act that causes serious interference with or disruption of the operations of a nuclear facility], to wit: (specify the particulars of the offence), contrary to s. 82.3 of the *Criminal Code*.

Section 82.4 Use or alteration of nuclear material, radioactive material or device to compel a government or agency

A.B., on the (day) of (month), (year), at (specify time) in (specify place), with intent to compel C.D. (or specify a government or an international organization) to do [or refrain from doing] (specify any act), did use [or alter nuclear material or radioactive material or a device], to wit: (specify the particulars of the offence), contrary to s. 82.4 of the *Criminal Code*.

Section 82.4 Interference with or disruption of a nuclear facility to compel a government or agency

A.B., on the (day) of (month), (year), at (specify time) in (specify place), with intent to compel C.D. (or specify a government or an international organization) to do [or refrain from doing] (specify any act), did commit an act against a nuclear facility [or an act that causes serious interference with or disruption of the operations of a nuclear facility], to wit: (specify the particulars of the offence), contrary to s. 82.4 of the *Criminal Code*.

Section 82.5 Commission of indictable offence to obtain nuclear material

A.B., on the (day) of (month), (year), at (specify time) in (specify place), did commit an indictable offence under the *Criminal Code* [or an Act of Parliament], with intent to obtain nuclear material [or radioactive material or a device], to wit: (specify the particulars of the offence), contrary to s. 82.5 of the *Criminal Code*.

Section 82.5 Commission of an indictable offence to obtain access to a nuclear facility

A.B., on the (day) of (month), (year), at (specify time) in (specify place), did commit an indictable offence under the *Criminal Code* [or an Act of Parliament], with intent to obtain access to a nuclear facility, to wit: (specify the particulars of the offence), contrary to s. 82.5 of the *Criminal Code*.

Section 82.6 Threats to commit an act of nuclear terrorism

A.B., on the (day) of (month), (year) at (specify time) in (specify place), did commit (specify an offence under s. 82.3, s. 82.4 or s. 82.5), to wit: (specify the particulars of the offence), contrary to s. 82.6 of the *Criminal Code*.

Section 83(1) Prize fights

A.B., on the (day) of (month), (year), at (specify time) in (specify place),

..........did engage as a principal in a prize fight, to wit: (specify the particulars of the offence), contrary to s. 83(1)(a) of the *Criminal Code*.

..........did advise [or encourage or promote] a prize fight, to wit: (specify the particulars of the offence), contrary to s. 83(1)(b) of the *Criminal Code*.

..........was present at a prize fight as an aid [or as a second or as a surgeon or as an umpire or as a backer or as a reporter] to wit: (specify the particulars of the offence), contrary to s. 83(1)(c) of the *Criminal Code*.

Part II.1 — Terrorism

Section 83.02 Financing of terrorism

A.B., on the (day) of (month), (year), at (specify time) in (specify place),

..........wilfully and without lawful justification or excuse, provided [or did collect] property intending that it be used [or knowing that it will be used] in order to carry out a terrorist activity, to wit: [specify the particulars of the offence], contrary to s. 83.02 of the *Criminal Code*.

..........wilfully and without lawful justification or excuse, did provide [or did collect] property intending that it be used [or knowing that it will be used] in order to carry out an act [or omission] intended to cause death or serious bodily harm to C.D., a civilian [or to a person not taking an active part in the hostilities in a situation of armed conflict] for the purpose of intimidating the public [or compelling a government (or an international organization)] to do [or refrain from doing] (specify an act), to wit: [specify the particulars of the offence], contrary to s. 83.02 of the *Criminal Code*.

Section 83.03 Providing property or services for terrorist purposes

A.B., on the (day) of (month), (year), at (specify time) in (specify place),

..........did collect [or did provide or did invite C.D. to provide or make available] property [or financial services or services] intending that they be used [or knowing that they will be used] for the purpose of facilitating [or carrying out] a terrorist activity [or for the purpose of benefiting C.D., a person who is facilitating (or carrying out) a terrorist activity], to wit: [specify the particulars of the offence], contrary to s. 83.03 of the *Criminal Code*.

..........did collect [or did provide or did invite C.D. to provide or make available] property [or financial services or services] knowing that they will be used by [or will benefit] a terrorist group, to wit: [specify the particulars of the offence], contrary to s. 83.03 of the *Criminal Code*.

Section 83.04 Using or possessing property for terrorist purposes

A.B., on the (day) of (month), (year), at (specify time) in (specify place),

..........did use property for the purpose of facilitating or carrying out a terrorist activity, to wit [specify the particulars of the offence], contrary to s. 83.04 of the *Criminal Code*.

..........did possess property intending that it be used [or knowing that it will be used] for the purpose of facilitating or carrying out a terrorist activity, to wit: [specify the particulars of the offence], contrary to s. 83.04 of the *Criminal Code*.

Section 83.08 Freezing of property

A.B., on the (day) of (month), (year), at (specify time) in (specify place),

..........knowingly dealt in property that was owned [or controlled] by [or on behalf of] a terrorist group, to wit [specify the particulars of the offence], contrary to s. 83.08 of the *Criminal Code*.

..........knowingly entered into [or facilitated] a transaction in respect of property that was owned [or controlled] by [or on behalf of] a terrorist group, to wit [specify the particulars of the offence], contrary to s. 83.08 of the *Criminal Code.*

..........knowingly provided a financial service [or specify other service] in respect of property that was owned [or controlled] by [or on behalf of] a terrorist group, to wit [specify the particulars of the offence], contrary to s. 83.08 of the *Criminal Code.*

Section 83.1 Disclosure

A.B., on the (day) of (month), (year), at (specify time) in (specify place), being resident in Canada [or being a Canadian citizen] failed to disclose forthwith to the R.C.M.P. Commissioner or to the C.S.I.S. Director, the existence of property and information about a transaction in respect of such property in A.B.'s possession or control that A.B. knew was owned or controlled on behalf of a terrorist group, to wit: (specify the particulars of the offence), contrary to s. 83.1 of the *Criminal Code.*

Section 83.18(1) Participating in activity of terrorist group

A.B., on the (day) of (month), (year), at (specify time) in (specify place), knowingly participated in [or contributed to] an activity of a terrorist group for the purpose of enhancing the ability of the terrorist group to facilitate or carry out a terrorist activity, to wit: (specify the particulars of the offence), contrary to s. 83.18(1) of the *Criminal Code.*

Section 83.181 Leaving Canada to participate in activity of terrorist group

A.B., on the (day) of (month), (year), at (specify time) in (specify place),

..........did leave [or attempt to leave] Canada for the purpose of committing outside Canada (specify an act or omission that would be an offence under s. 83.18(1)), to wit: (specify the particulars of the offence), contrary to s. 83.181 of the *Criminal Code.*

..........did go [or attempt to go] on board a conveyance with intent to leave Canada for the purpose of committing outside Canada (specify an act or omission that would be an offence under s. 83.18(1)), to wit: (specify the particulars of the offence), contrary to s. 83.181 of the *Criminal Code.*

Section 83.19(1) Facilitating terrorist activity

A.B., on the (day) of (month), (year), at (specify time) in (specify place), knowingly facilitated a terrorist activity, to wit: (specify the particulars of the offence), contrary to s. 83.19(1) of the *Criminal Code.*

Section 83.191 Leaving Canada to facilitate terrorist activity

A.B., on the (day) of (month), (year), at (specify time) in (specify place),

..........did leave [or attempt to leave] Canada for the purpose of committing outside Canada (specify an act or omission that would be an offence under s. 83.19(1)), to wit: (specify the particulars of the offence), contrary to s. 83.191 of the *Criminal Code*.

..........did go [or attempt to go] on board a conveyance with intent to leave Canada for the purpose of committing outside Canada (specify an act or omission that would be an offence under s. 83.19(1)), to wit: (specify the particulars of the offence), contrary to s. 83.191 of the *Criminal Code*.

Section 83.2 Commission of offence for terrorist group

A.B., on the (day) of (month), (year), at (specify time) in (specify place), committed (specify an indictable offence under the *Criminal Code* or specify another Act of Parliament) for the benefit of [or at the direction of or in association with] a terrorist group, to wit: (specify the particulars of the offence), contrary to s. 83.2 of the *Criminal Code*.

Section 83.201 Leaving Canada to commit offence for terrorist group

A.B., on the (day) of (month), (year), at (specify time) in (specify place),

..........did leave [or attempt to leave] Canada for the purpose of committing outside Canada (specify an indictable offence under the *Criminal Code* or an Act of Parliament), for the benefit of [or at the direction of or in association with] a terrorist group, to wit: (specify the particulars of the offence), contrary to s. 83.201 of the *Criminal Code*.

..........did go [or attempt to go] on board a conveyance with intent to leave Canada for the purpose of committing outside Canada (specify an indictable offence under the *Criminal Code* or an Act of Parliament), for the benefit of [or at the direction of or in association with] a terrorist group, to wit: (specify the particulars of the offence), contrary to s. 83.201 of the *Criminal Code*.

Section 83.202 Leaving Canada to commit offence that is a terrorist activity

A.B., on the (day) of (month), (year), at (specify time) in (specify place),

..........did leave [or attempt to leave] Canada for the purpose of committing outside Canada (specify an indictable offence under the *Criminal Code* or an Act of Parliament), an act or omission that constitutes a terrorist activity, to wit: (specify the particulars of the offence), contrary to s. 83.202 of the *Criminal Code*.

..........did go [or attempt to go] on board a conveyance with intent to leave Canada for the purpose of committing outside Canada (specify an indictable offence under the *Criminal Code* or an Act of Parliament), an act or omission that constitutes a terrorist activity, to wit: (specify the particulars of the offence), contrary to s. 83.202 of the *Criminal Code*.

Section 83.21(1) Instruction to carry out activity for terrorist group

A.B., on the (day) of (month), (year), at (specify time) in (specify place), knowingly instructed C.D. to carry out an activity for the benefit of [or at the direction of or in association with] a terrorist group for the purpose of enhancing the ability of a terrorist group to facilitate or carry out a terrorist activity, to wit: (specify the particulars of the offence), contrary to s. 83.21(1) of the *Criminal Code*.

Section 83.22(1) Instruction to carry out terrorist activity

A.B., on the (day) of (month), (year), at (specify time) in (specify place), knowingly instructed C.D. to carry out a terrorist activity, to wit: (specify the particulars of the offence), contrary to s. 83.22(1) of the *Criminal Code*.

Section 83.23(1) Concealing person who carried out terrorist activity

A.B., on the (day) of (month), (year), at (specify time) in (specify place), did knowingly harbour [or conceal] C.D., a person A.B. knew had carried out a terrorist activity, for the purpose of enabling C.D. to facilitate [or carry out a terrorist activity], to wit: (specify the particulars of the offence), contrary to s. 83.23(1) of the *Criminal Code*.

Section 83.23(2) Concealing person who is likely to carry out terrorist activity

A.B., on the (day) of (month), (year), at (specify time) in (specify place), did knowingly harbour [or conceal] C.D., a person A.B. knew was likely to carry out a terrorist activity, for the purpose of enabling C.D. to facilitate [or carry out a terrorist activity], to wit: (specify the particulars of the offence), contrary to s. 83.23(2) of the *Criminal Code*.

Section 83.231 Hoax regarding terrorist activity

A.B., on the (day) of (month), (year), at (specify time) in (specify place), without lawful excuse and with intent to cause C.D. to fear death [or bodily harm or substantial damage to property or serious interference with the lawful use or operation of property],

..........did convey [or cause or procure to be conveyed] information that is likely to cause a reasonable apprehension that terrorist activity is occurring [or will occur] without believing that the information is true, to wit: (specify the particulars of the offence), contrary to s. 83.231(a) of the *Criminal Code*.

..........did commit the act of (specify the act) that is likely to cause a reasonable apprehension that terrorist activity is occurring [or will occur] without believing that such activity is occurring [or will occur], to wit: (specify the particulars of the offence), contrary to s. 83.231(b) of the *Criminal Code*.

Section 83.231 Hoax regarding terrorist activity causing bodily harm

A.B., on the (day) of (month), (year), at (specify time) in (specify place), without lawful excuse and with intent to cause C.D. to fear death [or bodily harm or substantial damage to property or serious interference with the lawful use or operation of property],

..........did convey [or cause or procure to be conveyed] information that is likely to cause a reasonable apprehension that terrorist activity is occurring [or will occur] without believing that the information is true, and thereby caused bodily harm to

C.D., to wit: (specify the particulars of the offence), contrary to s. 83.231(a) of the *Criminal Code*.

..........did commit the act of (specify the act) that is likely to cause a reasonable apprehension that terrorist activity is occurring [or will occur] without believing that the information is true, and thereby caused bodily harm to C.D., to wit: (specify the particulars of the offence), contrary to s. 83.231(a) of the *Criminal Code*.

Part III — Firearms and Other Offensive Weapons

Section 85(1) Using a firearm committing or attempting to commit an offence, or during flight

A.B., on the (day) of (month), (year), at (specify time) in (specify place),

.... did use a firearm while committing [or attempting to commit] the indictable offence of (specify), to wit: (specify the particulars of the offence), contrary to s. 85(1)(a)[or (b)] of the *Criminal Code*.

.... did use a firearm during his [or her] flight after committing [or attempting to commit] the indictable offence of (specify), to wit: (specify the particulars of the offence), contrary to s. 85(1)(c) of the *Criminal Code*.

Section 85(2) Using an imitation firearm while committing or attempting to commit an offence, or during flight

A.B., on the (day) of (month), (year), at (specify time) in (specify place),

.... did use an imitation firearm while committing [or attempting to commit] the indictable offence of (specify), to wit: (specify the particulars of the offence), contrary to s. 85(2)(a)[or (b)] of the *Criminal Code*.

.... did use an imitation firearm during his [or her] flight after committing [or attempting to commit] the indictable offence of (specify), to wit: (specify the particulars of the offence), contrary to s. 85(2)(c) of the *Criminal Code*.

Section 86(1) Careless use of firearm, prohibited weapon, restricted weapon, prohibited device, ammunition or prohibited ammunition

A.B., on the (day) of (month), (year), at (specify time) in (specify place), without lawful excuse, did use [or carry or handle or ship or transport or store] a firearm [or a prohibited weapon or a restricted weapon or a prohibited device or ammunition or prohibited ammunition] in a careless manner [or without reasonable precautions for the safety of C.D.], to wit: (specify the particulars of the offence), contrary to s. 86(1) of the *Criminal Code*.

Section 86(2) Contravention of storage regulations made under the *Firearms Act* respecting firearms and restricted weapons

A.B., on the (day) of (month), (year), at (specify time) in (specify place), did contravene (specify the regulation made under s. 117(h) of the *Firearms Act*) respecting the storage [or handling or transportation or shipping or display or advertising or mail order sale] of firearms [or restricted weapons], to wit: (specify the particulars of the offence), contrary to s. 86(2) of the *Criminal Code*.

Section 87(1) Pointing a firearm

A.B., on the (day) of (month), (year), at (specify time) in (specify place), without lawful excuse, did point a firearm at C.D., to wit: (specify the particulars of the offence), contrary to s. 87(1) of the *Criminal Code*.

Section 88(1) Possession of weapon, imitation of weapon, prohibited device, ammunition or prohibited ammunition for a dangerous purpose

A.B., on the (day) of (month), (year), at (specify time) in (specify place), did carry [or possess] a weapon [or an imitation of a weapon or a prohibited device or ammunition or prohibited ammunition] for a purpose dangerous to the public peace [or for the purpose of committing an offence], to wit: (specify the particulars of the offence), contrary to s. 88(1) of the *Criminal Code*.

Section 89(1) Carrying a weapon, prohibited device, ammunition or prohibited ammunition while attending public meeting

A.B., on the (day) of (month), (year), at (specify time) in (specify place), without lawful excuse, did carry a weapon [or a prohibited device or ammunition or prohibited ammunition] while attending [or while on the way to attend] a public meeting, to wit: (specify the particulars of the offence), contrary to s. 89(1) of the *Criminal Code*.

Section 90(1) Carrying a concealed weapon, prohibited device or prohibited ammunition without authorization

A.B., on the (day) of (month), (year), at (specify time) in (specify place), did carry a concealed weapon [or a prohibited device or prohibited ammunition] without being authorized under the *Firearms Act*, to wit: (specify the particulars of the offence), contrary to s. 90(1) of the *Criminal Code*.

Section 91(1) Unauthorized possession of a firearm or a prohibited or restricted firearm

A.B., on the (day) of (month), (year), at (specify time) in (specify place),

..........not being the holder of a licence and a registration certificate for a prohibited (or restricted) firearm, did possess a prohibited [or restricted] firearm, to wit: (specify the particulars of the offence), contrary to s. 91(1) of the *Criminal Code*.

..........not being the holder of a licence for a firearm other than a prohibited or restricted weapon, did possess a firearm, to wit: (specify the particulars of the offence), contrary to s. 91(1) of the *Criminal Code*.

Section 91(2) Unauthorized possession of a prohibited weapon, restricted weapon, prohibited device or prohibited ammunition

A.B., on the (day) of (month), (year), at (specify time) in (specify place), not being the holder of a licence, did possess a prohibited weapon [or a restricted weapon or a prohibited device or prohibited ammunition], to wit: (specify the particulars of the offence), contrary to s. 91(2) of the *Criminal Code*.

Section 92(1) Possession of a firearm or a prohibited or restricted firearm knowing its possession is unauthorized

A.B., on the (day) of (month), (year), at (specify time) in (specify place),

..........did possess a restricted [or prohibited] firearm, knowing that he [or she] was not the holder of a licence to possess it or a registration certificate for it, to wit: (specify the particulars of the offence), contrary to s. 92(1) of the *Criminal Code.*

..........did possess a firearm other than a prohibited or restricted weapon, knowing that he (or she) was not the holder of a licence to possess it, to wit: (specify the particulars of the offence), contrary to s. 92(1) of the *Criminal Code*.

Section 92(2) Unauthorized possession of prohibited weapon, restricted weapon, prohibited device or prohibited ammunition

A.B., on the (day) of (month), (year), at (specify time) in (specify place), did possess a prohibited weapon [or a restricted weapon or a prohibited device or prohibited ammunition] knowing that A.B. was not the holder of a licence to possess it, to wit: (specify the particulars of the offence), contrary to s. 92(2) of the *Criminal Code*.

Section 93(1) Possession of firearm, prohibited weapon, restricted weapon, prohibited device or prohibited ammunition at unauthorized place

A.B., on the (day) of (month), (year), at (specify time) in (specify place), being the holder of an authorization [or a licence] under which A.B. may possess a firearm [or a prohibited weapon or a restricted weapon or a prohibited device or prohibited ammunition], did possess the firearm [or prohibited weapon or restricted weapon or prohibited device or prohibited ammunition] at an unauthorized place, to wit: (specify the particulars of the offence), contrary to s. 93(1) of the *Criminal Code*.

Section 94(1) Unauthorized possession in a motor vehicle

A.B., on the (day) of (month), (year), at (specify time) in (specify place),

..........was an occupant of a motor vehicle in which A.B. [or C.D., another occupant] did possess a restricted [or prohibited] firearm, knowing that A.B. (or C.D.) was not the holder of a licence to possess it and an authorization or registration certificate for it, to wit: (specify the particulars of the offence), contrary to s. 94(1) of the *Criminal Code*.

..........was an occupant of a motor vehicle in which A.B. [or C.D., another occupant] did possess a firearm other than restricted [or prohibited] firearm, knowing that A.B. (or C.D.) was not the holder of a licence to possess it, to wit: (specify the particulars of the offence), contrary to s. 94(1) of the *Criminal Code*.

..........was an occupant of a motor vehicle in which A.B. [or C.D., another occupant] did possess a restricted [or prohibited] firearm, without having reasonable grounds to believe that A.B. (or C.D.) was the holder of a licence to possess it and an authorization or registration certificate for it, to wit: (specify the particulars of the offence), contrary to s. 94(1) of the *Criminal Code*.

..........was an occupant of a motor vehicle in which A.B. [or C.D., another occupant] did possess a firearm other than restricted [or prohibited] firearm, without having reasonable grounds to believe that A.B. (or C.D.) was the holder of a licence to possess it, to wit: (specify the particulars of the offence), contrary to s. 94(1) of the *Criminal Code*.

Section 95(1) Possession of prohibited or restricted firearm with ammunition

A.B., on the (day) of (month), (year), at (specify time) in (specify place),

..........did possess a loaded prohibited firearm [or restricted firearm] without an authorization or a licence and a registration certificate to possess the firearm, to wit: (specify the particulars of the offence), contrary to s. 95(1) of the *Criminal Code*.

..........did possess an unloaded prohibited firearm [or restricted firearm] together with readily accessible ammunition that is capable of being discharged in the firearm, without an authorization or a licence and a registration certificate to possess the firearm, to wit: (specify the particulars of the offence), contrary to s. 95(1) of the *Criminal Code*.

Section 96(1) Possession of firearm, prohibited weapon, restricted weapon, prohibited device or prohibited ammunition obtained by commission of offence

A.B., on the (day) of (month), (year), at (specify time) in (specify place), did possess a firearm [or a prohibited weapon or a restricted weapon or a prohibited device or prohibited ammunition] that A.B. knew was obtained by the commission of an offence [or was obtained by an act or omission that would have been an offence if it had occurred in Canada], to wit: (specify the particulars of the offence), contrary to s. 96(1) of the *Criminal Code*.

Section 98(1) Breaking and entering to steal firearm

A.B., on the (day) of (month), (year), at (specify time) in (specify place),

..........did break and enter a building [or structure or motor vehicle or vessel or aircraft or railway vehicle or container or trailer] with intent to steal a firearm located in it, to wit: (specify the particulars of the offence), contrary to s. 98(1)(a) of the *Criminal Code*.

..........did break and enter a building [or structure or motor vehicle or vessel or aircraft or railway vehicle or container or trailer] and did steal a firearm located in it, to wit: (specify the particulars of the offence), contrary to s. 98(1)(b) of the *Criminal Code*.

..........did break out of a building [or structure or motor vehicle or vessel or aircraft or railway vehicle or container or trailer] after stealing a firearm located in it, to wit: (specify the particulars of the offence), contrary to s. 98(1)(c) of the *Criminal Code*.

..........did break out of a building [or structure or motor vehicle or vessel or aircraft or railway vehicle or container or trailer] after entering the place with intent to steal a firearm located in it, to wit: (specify the particulars of the offence), contrary to s. 98(1)(c) of the *Criminal Code*.

Section 98.1 Robbery to steal firearm

A.B., on the (day) of (month), (year), at (specify time) in (specify place),

..........did steal a firearm from C.D., and for the purpose of extorting [or to prevent resistance to the stealing of or to overcome resistance to the stealing of] the firearm did use violence [or the threat of violence] to C.D. [or to the property of C.D.] and did thereby commit robbery, to wit: (specify the particulars of the offence), contrary to s. 98.1 of the *Criminal Code*.

..........did steal a firearm from C.D., and at the same time [or immediately before or immediately thereafter] did wound [or beat or strike or use personal violence to] C.D. and did thereby commit robbery, to wit: (specify the particulars of the offence), contrary to s. 98.1 of the *Criminal Code*.

..........did assault C.D. with intent to steal a firearm from C.D. and did thereby commit robbery, to wit: (specify the particulars of the offence), contrary to s. 98.1 of the *Criminal Code*.

..........did steal a firearm from C.D. while armed with an offensive weapon [or an imitation of an offensive weapon], to wit: (specify the particulars of the offence), contrary to s. 98.1 of the *Criminal Code*.

Section 99(1) Trafficking in firearms, prohibited weapons, restricted weapons, prohibited device, ammunition or prohibited ammunition

A.B., on the (day) of (month), (year), at (specify time) in (specify place), did manufacture [or transfer or offer to manufacture or offer to transfer] a firearm [or a prohibited weapon or a restricted weapon or a prohibited device or ammunition or prohibited ammunition] for [or to] C.D., without authorization, to wit: (specify the particulars of the offence), contrary to s. 99(1) of the *Criminal Code*.

Section 100 Possession of firearm, prohibited weapon, restricted weapon, prohibited device, ammunition or prohibited ammunition for purpose of trafficking

A.B., on the (day) of (month), (year), at (specify time) in (specify place), did possess a firearm [or a prohibited weapon or a restricted weapon or a prohibited device or ammunition or prohibited ammunition] for the purpose of transferring it [or offering to transfer it] to C.D., without authorization, to wit: (specify the particulars of the offence), contrary to s. 100 of the *Criminal Code*.

Section 101 Transfer of firearm, prohibited weapon, ammunition or prohibited ammunition without authority

A.B., on the (day) of (month), (year), at (specify time) in (specify place), did transfer a firearm [or a prohibited weapon or a restricted weapon or a prohibited device or ammunition or prohibited ammunition] to C.D. without being authorized by law to do so, to wit: (specify the particulars of the offence), contrary to s. 101 of the *Criminal Code*.

Section 102(1) Making automatic firearm

A.B., on the (day) of (month), (year), at (specify time) in (specify place), without lawful excuse,

..........did alter a firearm so that it is capable of discharging projectiles in rapid succession during one pressure of the trigger, to wit: (specify the particulars of the offence), contrary to s. 102(1) of the *Criminal Code*.

..........did manufacture [or assemble] a firearm that is capable of discharging projectiles in rapid succession during one pressure of the trigger, to wit: (specify the particulars of the offence), contrary to s. 102(1) of the *Criminal Code*.

Section 103(1) Importing or exporting of firearm, prohibited weapon, restricted weapon, prohibited device or prohibited ammunition knowing that it is not authorized

A.B., on the (day) of (month), (year), at (specify time) in (specify place), did import [or export] a firearm [or a prohibited weapon or a restricted weapon or a prohibited device or prohibited ammunition], knowing that A.B. is not authorized by law, to wit: (specify the particulars of the offence), contrary to s. 103(1) of the *Criminal Code*.

Section 103(1) Unauthorized importing or exporting component or part for automatic firearm knowing it is not authorized

A.B., on the (day) of (month), (year), at (specify time) in (specify place), did import [or export], a component [or part] designed exclusively for use in the manufacture of [or the assembly into] an automatic firearm, knowing that A.B. is not authorized by law, to wit: (specify the particulars of the offence), contrary to s. 103(1) of the *Criminal Code*.

Section 104(1)(a) Unauthorized importing or exporting of firearm, prohibited weapon, restricted weapon, prohibited device or prohibited ammunition

A.B., on the (day) of (month), (year), at (specify time) in (specify place), did import [or export], a firearm [or a prohibited weapon or a restricted weapon or a prohibited device or prohibited ammunition], without authorization by law, to wit: (specify the particulars of the offence), contrary to s. 104(1) of the *Criminal Code*.

Section 104(1)(b) Unauthorized importing or exporting component or part for automatic firearm

A.B., on the (day) of (month), (year), at (specify time) in (specify place), did import [or export], a component [or a part] designed exclusively for use in the manufacture of [or the assembly into] an automatic firearm, to wit: (specify the particulars of the offence), contrary to s. 104(1) of the *Criminal Code*.

Section 105(1)(a) Failure to report the loss of a firearm, prohibited weapon, restricted weapon, prohibited device, prohibited ammunition, authorization, licence, or registration certificate

A.B., on the (day) of (month), (year), at (specify time) in (specify place), did not with reasonable dispatch, report the loss of a firearm [or a prohibited weapon or a restricted weapon or a prohibited device or prohibited ammunition or an authorization or a licence or a registration certificate] to a peace officer or firearms officer or chief firearms officer, to wit: (specify the particulars of the offence), contrary to s. 105(1) of the *Criminal Code*.

Section 105(1)(a) Reporting that firearm, prohibited weapon, restricted weapon, prohibited device, prohibited ammunition, authorization, licence, or registration certificate had been stolen

A.B., on the (day) of (month), (year), at (specify time) in (specify place), did not with reasonable dispatch report that a firearm [or a prohibited weapon or a restricted weapon or a prohibited device or prohibited ammunition or an authorization or a licence or a registration certificate] had been stolen to a peace officer or firearms officer or chief firearms officer, to wit: (specify the particulars of the offence), contrary to s. 105(1) of the *Criminal Code*.

Section 105(1)(b) Failure to deliver or report the finding of a firearm, prohibited weapon, restricted weapon, prohibited device or prohibited ammunition

A.B., on the (day) of (month), (year), at (specify time) in (specify place), did not with reasonable dispatch deliver [or report finding] a firearm [or prohibited weapon or restricted weapon or prohibited device or prohibited ammunition] that A.B. has reasonable grounds to believe has been lost or abandoned, to wit: (specify the particulars of the offence), contrary to s. 105(1) of the *Criminal Code*.

Section 106(1) Failure to report on destruction of prohibited or restricted weapons

A.B., on the (day) of (month), (year), at (specify time) in (specify place),

..........after destroying a prohibited firearm [or restricted firearm or prohibited weapon or restricted weapon or prohibited device or prohibited ammunition] did possess a restricted [or prohibited] firearm, did not with reasonable dispatch report its destruction to a peace officer, firearms officer or chief firearms officer, to wit: (specify the particulars of the offence), contrary to s. 106(1) of the *Criminal Code*.

..........on becoming aware of the destruction of a prohibited firearm [or restricted firearm or prohibited weapon or restricted weapon or prohibited device or prohibited ammunition] that was in the possession of A.B. before its destruction, did not with reasonable dispatch report its destruction to a peace officer, firearms officer or chief firearms officer, to wit: (specify the particulars of the offence), contrary to s. 106(1) of the *Criminal Code*.

Section 107(1) False statements regarding loss, theft or destruction of firearm, prohibited weapon, restricted weapon, prohibited device, prohibited ammunition, authorization, licence or registration certificate

A.B., on the (day) of (month), (year), at (specify time) in (specify place), knowingly, did make a false report [or statement] concerning the loss [or theft or destruction] of a firearm [or a prohibited weapon or a restricted weapon or a prohibited device or prohibited ammunition or authorization or a licence or a registration certificate] before C.D. [a peace officer or firearms officer or chief firearms officer], to wit: (specify the particulars of the offence), contrary to s. 107(1) of the *Criminal Code*.

Section 108(1) Altering, defacing or removing a serial number

A.B., on the (day) of (month), (year), at (specify time) in (specify place), without lawful excuse,

..........did alter [or deface or remove] a serial number on a firearm, to wit: (specify the particulars of the offence), contrary to s. 108(1)(a) of the *Criminal Code*.

..........did possess a firearm knowing that the serial number on it had been altered [or defaced or removed], to wit: (specify the particulars of the offence), contrary to s. 108(1)(b) of the *Criminal Code*.

Section 117.01(1) Possession of firearm, cross-bow, prohibited weapon, restricted weapon, prohibited device, ammunition, prohibited ammunition or explosive substance while prohibited

A.B., on the (day) of (month), (year), at (specify time) in (specify place), did possess a firearm [or a cross-bow or a prohibited weapon or a restricted weapon or a prohibited device or ammunition or prohibited ammunition or an explosive substance] while prohibited from doing so by (specify an order made under an Act of Parliament), to wit: (specify the particulars of the offence), contrary to s. 117.01(1) of the *Criminal Code*.

Section 117.01(2) Failure to surrender authorization of licence or registration certificate

A.B., on the (day) of (month), (year), at (specify time) in (specify place), wilfully failed to surrender an authorization [or a licence or a registration certificate] to C.D., a peace officer [or firearms officer or chief firearms officer] when required to do so by (specify an order made pursuant to an Act of Parliament), to wit: (specify the particulars of the offence), contrary to s. 117.01(2) of the *Criminal Code*.

Part IV — Offences Against the Administration of Law and Justice

Section 119(1)(a) Corruption of judges, members of Parliament and members of provincial legislatures — accepting bribes

A.B., on the (day) of (month), (year), at (specify time) in (specify place), being the holder of a judicial office [or being a member of Parliament (or of the legislature of a province)] corruptly did accept [or obtain or agree to accept or attempt to obtain] money [or valuable consideration or office or place or employment] for himself [or herself or C.D.] in respect of (specify anything done or omitted or to be done or to be omitted) by C.D. in his [or her] official capacity, to wit: (specify the particulars of the offence), contrary to s. 119(1)(a) of the *Criminal Code*.

Section 119(1)(b) Corruption of judges, members of Parliament and members of provincial legislature — offering bribes

A.B., on the (day) of (month), (year), at (specify time) in (specify place), corruptly did give [or offer] to C.D., a person who holds a judicial office [or is a member of Parliament (or of the legislature of a province)] money [or valuable consideration or office or place or employment] in respect of (specify anything done or omitted or to be done or to be omitted) by C.D. in his [or her] official capacity for A.B. [or C.D.], to wit: (specify the particulars of the offence), contrary to s. 119(1)(b) of the *Criminal Code*.

Section 120(a) Corruption of person employed in the administration of criminal law — accepting bribes

A.B., on the (day) of (month), (year), at (specify time) in (specify place), being a justice [or a police commissioner or a peace officer or a public officer or an officer of a juvenile court or a person who employed in the administration of criminal law] corruptly did accept [or did obtain or did agree to accept or did attempt to obtain] for A.B. [or C.D.] money [or valuable consideration or an office or a place or employment] with intent to interfere with the administration of justice [or with intent to procure or facilitate the commission of an offence or with intent to protect from detection (or punishment) E.F., a person who has committed (or who intends to commit) an indictable offence], to wit: (specify the particulars of the offence), contrary to s. 120(a) of the *Criminal Code*.

Section 120(b) Corruption of persons employed in the administration of criminal law — offering bribes

A.B., on the (day) of (month), (year), at (specify time) in (specify place), corruptly did give [or offer] to C.D., a justice [or police commissioner or peace officer or public officer or officer of a juvenile court or a person who was employed in the administration of criminal law] money [or valuable consideration or office or place or employment] with intent that C.D. should interfere with the administration of justice [or procure (or facilitate) the commission of an offence or protect from detection (or punishment) E.F., a person who has committed (or who intends to commit) an offence], to wit: (specify the particulars of the offence), contrary to s. 120(b) of the *Criminal Code*.

Section 121(1)(a)–(e) Frauds on the government and influence peddling

A.B., on the (day) of (month), (year), at (specify time) in (specify place),

.... directly [or indirectly] did give [or offer or agree to give (or offer)] to C.D., an official [or a member of the family of E.F., an official, or for the benefit of E.F., an official], a loan [or a reward or an advantage or a benefit] as consideration for cooperation [or assistance or the exercise of influence or an act or an omission] in connection with the transaction of business with the government [or matter of business relating to the government or a claim against Her Majesty or any benefit that Her Majesty is entitled to bestow], to wit: (specify the particulars of the offence), contrary to s. 121(1)(a) of the *Criminal Code*.

..........having dealings of any kind with the government, did pay a commission [or reward] to [or confer an advantage (or benefit) on] C.D., an employee [or official] of the government with which A.B. dealt [or to any member of the family of C.D. or to E.F. for the benefit of the employee (or official)] with respect to those dealings without the consent in writing of the head of the branch of government with which A.B. dealt, to wit: (specify the particulars of the offence), contrary to s. 121(1)(b) of the *Criminal Code*.

..........being an official [or employee] of the government, did demand [or accept or offer (or agree) to accept] from C.D., a person who had dealings with the government, a commission [or reward or advantage or benefit] directly [or indirectly] by himself [or by herself or through any one for his (or her) benefit] without the consent in writing of the head of the branch of government that employed A.B. [or of which A.B. was an official], to wit: (specify the particulars of the offence), contrary to s. 121(1)(c) of the *Criminal Code*.

..........having [or pretending to have] influence with the government [or with a minister of the government or an official] did demand [or accept or offer or agree to accept] for A.B. [or for C.D.] a reward [or advantage or benefit] as consideration for cooperation [or assistance or exercise of influence or an act (or omission)] in connection with the transaction of business with [or a matter of business relating to] the government [or a claim against Her Majesty or a benefit that Her Majesty is authorized (or is entitled) to bestow or the appointment of A.B. (or E.F.) to an office], to wit: (specify the particulars of the offence), contrary to s. 121(1)(d) of the *Criminal Code*.

..........did give [or offer or agree to give (or offer)] to C.D., a minister of the government [or an official] a reward [or advantage or benefit] as consideration for cooperation [or assistance or exercise of influence or an act (or omission)] in connection with the transaction of business with [or a matter of business relating to] the government [or a claim against Her Majesty or a benefit that Her Majesty is authorized (or is entitled) to bestow or the appointment of A.B. (or E.F.) to an office], to wit: (specify the particulars of the offence), contrary to s. 121(1)(e) of the *Criminal Code*.

Section 121(1)(f) Frauds on the government — In connection with tenders

A.B., on the (day) of (month), (year), at (specify time) in (specify place),

..........having made a tender to obtain a contract with the government, did give [or offer or agree to give (or offer)] to C.D., a person who had made a tender [or to a member of his (or her) family or to E.F. for the benefit of C.D.] a reward [or advantage or benefit] as consideration for the withdrawal of the tender of that person, to wit: (specify the particulars of the offence), contrary to s. 121(1)(f) of the *Criminal Code*.

..........having made a tender to obtain a contract with the government, did demand [or accept or offer (or agree) to accept] from C.D., a person who had made a tender, a reward [or advantage or benefit] as consideration for the withdrawal of his (or her) tender, to wit: (specify the particulars of the offence), contrary to s. 121(1)(f) of the *Criminal Code*.

Section 121(2) Frauds on the government — In connection with elections

A.B., on the (day) of (month), (year), at (specify time) in (specify place), in order to obtain [or retain] a contract with the government [or as a term of a contract with the government, whether express or implied] directly [or indirectly] did subscribe [or give or agree to subscribe (or give)] to C.D., valuable consideration for the purpose of promoting the election of a candidate [or class (or party) of candidates] to Parliament [or the legislature of a province] [or with intent to influence (or affect) in any way the result of an election conducted for the purpose of electing persons to serve in Parliament (or the legislature of a province)], to wit: (specify the particulars of the offence), contrary to s. 121(2) of the *Criminal Code*.

Section 121.1(1) Selling tobacco products and raw leaf tobacco products

A.B., on the (day) of (month), (year), at (specify time) in (specify place), did sell [or did offer for sale or did transport or did deliver or did have in possession for the purpose of sale] a tobacco product [or unpackaged raw leaf tobacco] that is not stamped, to wit: (specify the particulars of the offence), contrary to s. 121.1 of the *Criminal Code*.

Section 122 Fraud or breach of trust by public officer

A.B., on the (day) of (month), (year), at (specify time) in (specify place), did commit fraud [or a breach of trust] in connection with the duties of his [or her] office, to wit: (specify the particulars of the offence), contrary to s. 122 of the *Criminal Code*.

Section 123(1)(a) Corrupting a municipal official

A.B., on the (day) of (month), (year), at (specify time) in (specify place), did give [or offer or agree to give (or offer)] to C.D., a municipal official, a loan [or reward or advantage or benefit] as consideration for C.D. to abstain from voting at a meeting [or a committee] of the municipal council [or to vote in favour of (or against) a measure (or motion or resolution) or to aid in procuring (or preventing) the adoption of a measure (or motion or resolution) or to perform (or fail to perform) an official act], to wit: (specify the particulars of the offence), contrary to s. 123(1)(a) of the *Criminal Code*.

Section 123(1)(b) Being a corrupt municipal official

A.B., on the (day) of (month), (year), at (specify time) in (specify place), being a municipal official, did demand [or accept or offer (or agree) to accept] from C.D. a loan [or reward or advantage or benefit] as consideration for A.B. to abstain from voting at a meeting [or a committee] of the municipal council [or to vote in favour of (or against) a measure (or motion or resolution) or to perform (or fail to perform) an official act], to wit: (specify the particulars of the offence), contrary to s. 123(1)(b) of the *Criminal Code*.

Section 123(2) Influencing municipal official

A.B., on the (day) of (month), (year), at (specify time) in (specify place),

..........being a person who was under a duty to disclose the truth, did influence [or attempt to influence] C.D., a municipal official, by suppression of the truth, to abstain from voting at a meeting [or at a committee] of the municipal council [or to vote in favour of (or against) a measure (or motion or resolution)] [or to aid in procuring (or preventing) the adoption of a measure (or motion or resolution)] [or to perform (or fail to perform) an official act], to wit: (specify the particulars of the offence), contrary to s. 123(2) of the *Criminal Code*.

..........did influence [or attempt to influence] C.D., a municipal official, by threats [or by deceit or by (specify other unlawful means)], to abstain from voting at a meeting [or at a committee] of the municipal council [or to vote in favour of (or against) a measure (or motion or resolution)] [or to aid in procuring (or preventing) the adoption of a measure (or motion or resolution)] [or to perform (or fail to perform) an official act], to wit: (specify the particulars of the offence), contrary to s. 123(2) of the *Criminal Code*.

Section 124(a) Selling office

A.B., on the (day) of (month), (year), at (specify time) in (specify place),

..........did purport to sell [or agree to sell] the appointment of C.D. to [or the resignation of C.D. from or the consent to the appointment of C.D. to or the consent to the resignation of C.D. from] (specify the office), to wit: (specify the particulars of the offence), contrary to s. 124(a) of the *Criminal Code*.

..........did receive [or agree to receive] a reward [or profit] from the purported sale of the appointment of C.D. to [or the resignation of C.D. from or the consent to the appointment of C.D. to [or the consent to the resignation of C.D. from] (specify the office), to wit: (specify the particulars of the offence), contrary to s. 124(a) of the *Criminal Code*.

Section 124(b) Purchasing office

A.B., on the (day) of (month), (year), at (specify time) in (specify place), did purport to [or agree to or promise to] purchase [or give a reward (or profit) for] the appointment of C.D. to [or the resignation of C.D. from or the consent to the appointment of C.D. to or the consent to the resignation of C.D. from] (specify the office), to wit: (specify the particulars of the offence), contrary to s. 124(b) of the *Criminal Code*.

Section 125(a) Influencing appointments

A.B., on the (day) of (month), (year), at (specify time) in (specify place), did receive [or agree to receive] [or give or procure to be given] directly [or indirectly] a reward [or advantage or benefit of any kind] as consideration for cooperation [or assistance or exercise of influence] to secure the appointment of C.D. to (specify the office), to wit: (specify the particulars of the offence), contrary to s. 125(a) of the *Criminal Code*.

Section 125(b) Negotiating appointments

A.B., on the (day) of (month), (year), at (specify time) in (specify place), did solicit [or recommend or negotiate] with respect to the appointment of C.D. to [or resignation of C.D. from] (specify the office) in expectation of a direct [or indirect] reward [or advantage or benefit], to wit: (specify the particulars of the offence), contrary to s. 125(b) of the *Criminal Code*.

Section 125(c) Keeping a place for dealing in offices

A.B., on the (day) of (month), (year), at (specify time) in (specify place), without lawful authority did keep a place for transacting [or negotiating] business relating to the filling of vacancies in offices [or the sale (or purchase) of offices or appointments to (or resignations from) offices], to wit: (specify the particulars of the offence), contrary to s. 125(c) of the *Criminal Code*.

Section 126 Disobeying a statute

A.B., on the (day) of (month), (year), at (specify time) in (specify place), without a lawful excuse, did contravene (specify an Act of Parliament) by wilfully doing (specify a thing it forbids) [or by wilfully omitting to do (specify a thing it requires to be done)], to wit: (specify the particulars of the offence), contrary to s. 126 of the *Criminal Code*.

Section 127 Disobeying an order of court

A.B., on the (day) of (month), (year), at (specify time) in (specify place), without lawful excuse, did disobey a lawful order made by (specify a court of justice) [or by C.D., a person (or body of persons) authorized by (specify an Act of Parliament) to make (or give) the order], to wit: (specify the particulars of the offence), contrary to s. 127 of the *Criminal Code*.

Section 128 Misconduct in the execution of process

A.B., on the (day) of (month), (year), at (specify time) in (specify place), being a peace officer [or coroner], being entrusted with the execution of a process, wilfully, did misconduct himself [or herself] in the execution of the process [or did make a false return to the process], to wit: (specify the particulars of the offence), contrary to s. 128 of the *Criminal Code*.

Section 129(a) Resisting or obstructing peace officer

A.B., on the (day) of (month), (year), at (specify time) in (specify place), did resist [or wilfully obstruct] C.D., a peace officer [or a public officer] in the execution of his [or her] duty, to wit: (specify the particulars of the offence), contrary to s. 129(a) of the *Criminal Code*.

Section 129(b) Omitting to assist public officer or peace officer

A.B., on the (day) of (month), (year), at (specify time) in (specify place), without reasonable excuse, did omit to assist C.D., a public [or peace] officer, in the execution of his [or her] duty in arresting E.F. [or in preserving the peace] after having reasonable notice that A.B. was required to do so, to wit: (specify the particulars of the offence), contrary to s. 129(b) of the *Criminal Code*.

Section 129(c) Execution of process

A.B., on the (day) of (month), (year), at (specify time) in (specify place),

..........did resist [or wilfully obstruct] C.D. in the lawful execution of a process against land [or goods], to wit: (specify the particulars of the offence), contrary to s. 129(c) of the *Criminal Code*.

..........did resist [or wilfully obstruct] C.D. in making a lawful distress [or seizure], to wit: (specify the particulars of the offence), contrary to s. 129(c) of the *Criminal Code*.

Section 130 Personating a peace officer or a public officer

A.B., on the (day) of (month), (year), at (specify time) in (specify place),

..........did falsely represent himself [or herself] to be a peace officer [or public officer], to wit: (specify the particulars of the offence), contrary to s. 130(a) of the *Criminal Code*.

..........not being a peace officer [or public officer], did use a badge [or article of uniform or equipment] in a manner that was likely to cause C.D. to believe that A.B. was a peace officer [or public officer], to wit: (specify the particulars of the offence), contrary to s. 130(b) of the *Criminal Code*.

Section 132 Perjury

A.B., on the (day) of (month), (year), at (specify time) in (specify place),

..........did commit perjury, to wit: (specify the particulars of the offence), contrary to s. 132 of the *Criminal Code*.

..........being specially permitted [or authorized or required] by law to make a statement under oath or solemn affirmation, did make a false statement by affidavit [or solemn declaration or deposition or orally] before C.D., a person authorized by law to permit it to be made before him [or her], knowing that the statement was false, to wit: (specify the particulars of the offence), contrary to s. 132 of the *Criminal Code*.

Section 134(1) False statements

A.B., on the (day) of (month), (year), at (specify time) in (specify place), not being specially permitted, authorized or required by law to make a statement under oath or solemn affirmation, did make a statement by affidavit [or solemn declaration or deposition or orally] before C.D., a person authorized by law to permit it to be made before him, knowing that the statement was false, to wit: (specify the particulars of the offence), contrary to s. 134(1) of the *Criminal Code*.

Section 136(1) Witness giving contradictory evidence with intent to mislead

A.B., on the (day) of (month), (year), at (specify time) in (specify place), being a witness in a judicial proceeding, with intent to mislead gave evidence with respect to a matter of fact [or knowledge] and subsequently, in a judicial proceeding, gave evidence that was contrary to his [or her] previous evidence, to wit: (specify the particulars of the offence), contrary to s. 136(1) of the *Criminal Code*.

Section 137 Fabricating evidence

A.B., on the (day) of (month), (year), at (specify time) in (specify place), with intent to mislead, did fabricate (specify the thing fabricated) with intent that it should be used as evidence in a judicial proceeding, by a means other than perjury or incitement to perjury, to wit: (specify the particulars of the offence), contrary to s. 137 of the *Criminal Code*.

Section 138(a) Offences relating to affidavits

A.B., on the (day) of (month), (year), at (specify time) in (specify place), did sign a writing that purported to be an affidavit [or statutory declaration] and to have been sworn [or declared] before him [or her] when the writing was not so sworn [or when the writing was not so declared or when he (or she) knew that he (or she) had no authority to administer the oath (or declaration)], to wit: (specify the particulars of the offence), contrary to s. 138(a) of the *Criminal Code*.

..........did use [or offered for use] writing purporting to be an affidavit [or statutory declaration] that he (or she) knew was not sworn [or declared] by the affiant [or declarant or before a person authorized], to wit: (specify the particulars of the offence), contrary to s. 138(b) of the *Criminal Code*.

..........did sign as affiant [or declarant] a writing that purported to be an affidavit [or statutory declaration] and to have been sworn [or declared] by A.B. when the writing was not so sworn [or declared], to wit: (specify the particulars of the offence), contrary to s. 138(c) of the *Criminal Code*.

Section 139(1) Obstructing justice

A.B., on the (day) of (month), (year), at (specify time) in (specify place),

..........did wilfully attempt to obstruct [or pervert or defeat] the course of justice in a judicial proceeding, by indemnifying [or by agreeing to indemnify] C.D., a surety, to wit: (specify the particulars of the offence), contrary to s. 139(1)(a) of the *Criminal Code*.

..........being a surety, did wilfully attempt to obstruct [or pervert or defeat] the course of justice in a judicial proceeding, by accepting [or by agreeing to accept] a fee [or an indemnity] from [or in respect of] C.D., a person who was released [or who was to be released] from custody, to wit: (specify the particulars of the offence), contrary to s. 139(1)(b) of the *Criminal Code*.

Section 140(1)(a) Public mischief

A.B., on the (day) of (month), (year), at (specify time) in (specify place),

..........with intent to mislead, did cause C.D., a peace officer, to enter on [or continue] an investigation by making a false statement that accused E.F. of having committed an offence, to wit: (specify the particulars of the offence), contrary to s. 140(1)(a) of the *Criminal Code*.

..........with intent to mislead, did cause C.D., a peace officer, to enter on [or continue] an investigation by (specify anything), with the intention of causing E.F. to be suspected of having committed an offence which E.F. had not committed [or with the intention of diverting suspicion from himself (or herself)], to wit: (specify the particulars of the offence), contrary to s. 140(1)(b) of the *Criminal Code*.

..........with intent to mislead, did cause C.D., a peace officer, to enter on [or continue] an investigation by reporting that the offence of (specify an offence) had been committed when it had not been committed, to wit: (specify the particulars of the offence), contrary to s. 140(1)(c) of the *Criminal Code*.

..........with intent to mislead, did cause C.D., a peace officer, to enter on [or continue] an investigation by reporting [or by making it known or by causing it to be made known] that A.B. [or E.F.] had died, when A.B. [or E.F.] had not died, to wit: (specify the particulars of the offence), contrary to s. 140(1)(d) of the *Criminal Code*.

Section 141(1) Compounding indictable offence

A.B., on the (day) of (month), (year), at (specify time) in (specify place), did ask for [or obtain or agree to receive or agree to obtain] valuable consideration for himself [or for herself or for C.D.] by agreeing to compound [or conceal] an indictable offence of (specify the indictable offence), to wit: (specify the particulars of the offence), contrary to s. 141(1) of the *Criminal Code*.

Section 142 Corruptly taking reward for recovery of goods

A.B., on the (day) of (month), (year), at (specify time) in (specify place), corruptly did accept valuable consideration under pretence [or upon account] of helping C.D. to recover (specify the thing recovered) obtained by the commission of an indictable offence of (specify the indictable offence), to wit: (specify the particulars of the offence), contrary to s. 142 of the *Criminal Code*.

Section 143 Advertising reward and immunity

A.B., on the (day) of (month), (year), at (specify time) in (specify place),

..........publicly did advertise a reward for the return of (specify thing) that had been stolen [or lost] and in the advertisement did use words to indicate that no questions would be asked if it was returned, to wit: (specify the particulars of the offence), contrary to s. 143(a) of the *Criminal Code*.

..........in a public advertisement did use words to indicate that a reward would be given [or paid] for (specify thing) that had been stolen [or lost] without interference with [or inquiry about] the person who produced it, to wit: (specify the particulars of the offence), contrary to s. 143(b) of the *Criminal Code*.

..........in a public advertisement did promise [or offer] to return to a person who had advanced money by way of loan on [or had bought] (specify thing) that had been stolen [or lost] the money so advanced [or paid or any other sum of money] for the return of that thing, to wit: (specify the particulars of the offence), contrary to s. 143(c) of the *Criminal Code*.

..........did print [or publish] an advertisement (specify as provided in s. 143(a) [or s. 143(b) or s. 143(c)), to wit: (specify the particulars of the offence), contrary to s. 143(d) of the *Criminal Code*.

Section 144 Prison breach

A.B., on the (day) of (month), (year), at (specify time) in (specify place),

..........by force [or violence] did break a prison, with intent to set at liberty himself [or herself or C.D., a person confined therein], to wit: (specify the particulars of the offence), contrary to s. 144(a) of the *Criminal Code*.

..........with intent to escape did forcibly break out of [or make a breach in] the cell [or (specify what other place) within the prison in which A.B. was confined], to wit: (specify the particulars of the offence), contrary to s. 144(b) of the *Criminal Code*.

Section 145(1)(a) Escaping lawful custody

A.B., on the (day) of (month), (year), at (specify time) in (specify place), did escape from lawful custody, to wit: (specify the particulars of the offence), contrary to s. 145(1)(a) of the *Criminal Code*.

Section 145(1)(b) Being at large without lawful excuse

A.B., on the (day) of (month), (year), at (specify time) in (specify place), was at large within [or outside] Canada without lawful excuse before the expiration of a term of imprisonment to which A.B. was sentenced, to wit: (specify the particulars of the offence), contrary to s. 145(1)(b) of the *Criminal Code*.

Section 145(2)(a) Failure to attend at court when at large on undertaking or recognizance

A.B., on the (day) of (month), (year), at (specify time) in (specify place), being at large on an undertaking [or recognizance] given to [or entered into before] C.D., a justice [or judge], did fail without lawful excuse to attend at court in accordance therewith [or to surrender himself (or herself) in accordance with the order of C.D.], to wit: (specify the particulars of the offence), contrary to s. 145(2)(a) of the *Criminal Code*.

Section 145(2)(b) Failure to attend at court after appearing before court, justice or judge

A.B., on the (day) of (month), (year), at (specify time) in (specify place), having appeared before a court [or C.D., a justice or C.D., a judge], did fail without lawful excuse to attend court as thereafter required by the court [or C.D.] [or to surrender himself in accordance with the order of the court (or C.D.)], to wit: (specify the particulars of the offence), contrary to s. 145(2)(b) of the *Criminal Code*.

Section 145(3) Failure to comply with condition of undertaking or recognizance

A.B., on the (day) of (month), (year), at (specify time) in (specify place), being at large on an undertaking [or recognizance] given to [or entered into before] C.D., a justice [or judge], did fail without lawful excuse to comply with a condition of that undertaking [or recognizance (or a direction ordered under s. 515(12) or s. 522(2.1) prohibiting communication with a witness or other person)] directed by C.D., to wit: (specify the particulars of the offence), contrary to s. 145(3) of the *Criminal Code*.

Section 145(4) Failure to appear or to comply with summons

A.B., on the (day) of (month), (year), at (specify time) in (specify place), having being served with a summons,

..........did fail without lawful excuse to appear at the time and place stated therein for the purposes of the *Identification of Criminals Act*, to wit: (specify the particulars of the of fence), contrary to s. 145(4) of the *Criminal Code*.

..........did fail without lawful excuse to attend at court in accordance therewith, to wit: (specify the particulars of the offence), contrary to s. 145(4) of the *Criminal Code*.

Section 145(5) Failure to appear or to comply with appearance notice or promise to appear

A.B., on the (day) of (month), (year), at (specify time) in (specify place), having been named in an appearance notice [or a promise to appear or a recognizance entered into before C.D., an officer in charge], that was confirmed by E.F., a justice, under s. 508,

..........did fail without lawful excuse to appear at the time and place stated therein for the purposes of the *Identification of Criminals Act*, to wit: (specify the particulars of the offence), contrary to s. 145(5) of the *Criminal Code*.

..........did fail without lawful excuse to attend court in accordance therewith, to wit: (specify the particulars of the offence), contrary to s. 145(5) of the *Criminal Code*.

Section 145(5.1) Failure to comply with conditions of an undertaking

A.B., on the (day) of (month), (year), at (specify time) in (specify place),

..........did fail without lawful excuse to comply with a condition of an undertaking entered into pursuant to s. 499(2) [or s. 503(2.1)], to wit: (specify the particulars of the offence), contrary to s. 145(5.1) of the *Criminal Code*.

Section 146 Permitting or assisting escape

A.B., on the (day) of (month), (year), at (specify time) in (specify place),

..........did permit C.D., a person who A.B. had in lawful custody, to escape such custody by failing to perform a legal duty, to wit: (specify the particulars of the offence), contrary to s. 146(a) of the *Criminal Code*.

..........did convey [or cause to be conveyed] into a prison a (specify the thing conveyed), with intent to facilitate the escape of C.D., a person imprisoned therein, to wit: (specify the particulars of the offence), contrary to s. 146(b) of the *Criminal Code*.

..........did direct [or procure], under colour of pretended authority, the discharge of C.D., a prisoner who was not entitled to be discharged, to wit: (specify the particulars of the offence), contrary to s. 146(c) of the *Criminal Code*.

Section 147 Rescue or permitting escape

A.B., on the (day) of (month), (year), at (specify time) in (specify place),

..........did rescue C.D. in escaping [or in attempting to escape] from lawful custody, to wit: (specify the particulars of the offence), contrary to s. 147(a) of the *Criminal Code*.

..........did assist C.D. in escaping [or in attempting to escape] from lawful custody, to wit: (specify the particulars of the offence), contrary to s. 147(a) of the *Criminal Code*.

..........did wilfully permit C.D., a person his [or her] in lawful custody to escape, to wit: (specify the particulars of the offence), contrary to s. 147(b) of the *Criminal Code*.

..........being an officer of [or an employee in] a prison, did lawfully permit C.D. to escape from lawful custody therein, to wit: (specify the particulars of the offence), contrary to s. 147(c) of the *Criminal Code*.

Part V — Sexual Offences, Public Morals and Disorderly Conduct

Section 151 Sexual interference — Person under 16 years

A.B., on the (day) of (month), (year), at (specify time) in (specify place), for a sexual purpose, did touch, directly or indirectly, with a part of the body of A.B. [or with an object], a part of the body of C.D., a person under the age of 16 years, to wit: (specify the particulars of the offence), contrary to s. 151 of the *Criminal Code*.

Section 152 Invitation to sexual touching — Person under 16 years

A.B., on the (day) of (month), (year), at (specify time) in (specify place), for a sexual purpose, did invite [or counsel or incite] C.D., a person under the age of 16 years, to touch, directly or indirectly, with a part of the body [or with an object] the body of A.B. (or C.D. or E.F.), to wit: (specify the particulars of the offence), contrary to s. 152 of the *Criminal Code*.

Section 153 Sexual exploitation of a young person by a person in a position of trust or authority

A.B., on the (day) of (month), (year), at (specify time) in (specify place), being in a position of trust or authority towards C.D., a young person, and who

..........for a sexual purpose, did touch, directly or indirectly, with a part of the body of A.B., [or with a part of the body of E.F. or with an object] a part of the body of

C.D., to wit: (specify the particulars of the offence), contrary to s. 153(1)(a) of the *Criminal Code*.

..........for a sexual purpose, did invite [or counsel or incite] C.D. to touch, directly or indirectly, with a part of the body of A.B. [or with a part of the body of E.F. or with an object] the body of A.B. or C.D. or E.F., to wit: (specify the particulars of the offence), contrary to s. 153(1)(b) of the *Criminal Code*.

Section 153 Sexual exploitation of a young person by a person with whom the young person is in a relationship of dependency

A.B., on the (day) of (month), (year), at (specify time) in (specify place), being a person with whom C.D., a young person, was in a relationship of dependency and who

..........for a sexual purpose, did touch, directly or indirectly, with a part of the body of A.B., [or with a part of the body of E.F. or with an object] a part of the body of C.D., to wit: (specify the particulars of the offence), contrary to s. 153(1)(a) of the *Criminal Code*.

..........for a sexual purpose, did invite [or counsel or incite] C.D. to touch, directly or indirectly, with a part of the body of A.B. [or with a part of the body of E.F. or with an object] the body of A.B. or C.D. or E.F., to wit: (specify the particulars of the offence), contrary to s. 153(1)(b) of the *Criminal Code*.

Section 153 Sexual exploitation of a young person by a person who is in an exploitative relationship with the young person

A.B., on the (day) of (month), (year), at (specify time) in (specify place), being a person who is in a relationship that is exploitative of C.D., a young person and who

..........for a sexual purpose, did touch, directly [or indirectly], with a part of the body of A.B, [or with a part of the body of E.F. or with an object] a part of the body of C.D., to wit: (specify the particulars of the offence), contrary to s. 153(1)(a) of the *Criminal Code*.

..........for a sexual purpose, did invite [or counsel or incite] C.D. to touch, directly [or indirectly], with a part of the body of A.B. [or with a part of the body of E.F. or with an object] the body of A.B. or C.D. or E.F., to wit: (specify the particulars of the offence), contrary to s. 153(1)(b) of the *Criminal Code*.

Section 153.1 Sexual exploitation of person with a disability

A.B., on the (day) of (month), (year), at (specify time) in (specify place),

..........being in a position of trust [or authority] towards C.D., a person with a mental [or physical] disability without the consent of C.D. and for a sexual purpose, did counsel [or incite] C.D. to touch directly [or indirectly] with (specify a part of C.D.'s body or an object) the body of A.B. [or C.D. or E.F.], to wit: (specify the particulars of the offence), contrary to s. 153.1 of the *Criminal Code*.

..........being a person with whom C.D., a person with a mental [or physical] disability was in a relationship of dependency, without the consent of C.D. and for a sexual purpose, did counsel [or incite] C.D. to touch directly [or indirectly] with (specify a part of C.D.'s body or an object) the body of A.B. [or C.D. or E.F.], to wit: (specify the particulars of the offence), contrary to s. 153.1 of the *Criminal Code.*

Section 155(1) Incest

A.B., on the (day) of (month), (year), at (specify time) in (specify place), knowing that C.D. was by blood relationship A.B.'s parent [or child or brother or sister or grandparent or grandchild] had sexual intercourse with C.D. and did thereby commit incest, to wit: (specify the particulars of the offence), contrary to s. 155(1) of the *Criminal Code.*

Section 159(1) Anal intercourse in public

A.B., on the (day) of (month), (year), at (specify time) in (specify place), did engage in an act of anal intercourse in public [or in the presence of more than two persons] with C.D., to wit: (specify the particulars of the offence), contrary to s. 159(1) of the *Criminal Code.*

Section 159(1) Anal intercourse by persons under 18 years of age

A.B., on the (day) of (month), (year) at (specify time) in (specify place), not being 18 years of age, did engage in an act of anal intercourse with C.D., to wit: (specify the particulars of the offence), contrary to s. 159(1) of the *Criminal Code.*

Section 160(1) Bestiality

A.B., on the (day) of (month), (year) at (specify time) in (specify place), did carry out intercourse with a beast [or bird] and thereby commit bestiality, to wit: (specify the particulars of the offence), contrary to s. 160(1) of the *Criminal Code.*

Section 160(2) Compulsion to commit bestiality

A.B., on the (day) of (month), (year), at (specify time) in (specify place), did compel C.D. to commit bestiality with (specify the animal or bird), to wit: (specify the particulars of the offence), contrary to s. 160(2) of the *Criminal Code.*

Section 160(3) Bestiality in the presence of person under 16 years or by person under 16 years

A.B., on the (day) of (month), (year), at (specify time) in (specify place),

..........did commit bestiality in the presence of C.D., a person who was under the age of 16 years, to wit: (specify the particulars of the offence), contrary to s. 160(3) of the *Criminal Code.*

..........did incite CD., a person under the age of 16 years, to commit bestiality, to wit: (specify the particulars of the offence), contrary to s. 160(3) of the *Criminal Code.*

Section 161 Order of prohibition

A.B., on the (day) of (month), (year), at (specify time) in (specify place),

..........being bound by an order prohibiting A.B. from attending a public park or swimming area where persons under the age of 16 are present or can be reasonably be expected to be present [or a daycare center or a schoolground or a playground or a community center] did not comply with the order, to wit: (specify the particulars of the offence), contrary to s. 161(4) of the *Criminal Code*.

..........being bound by an order prohibiting A.B. from seeking or obtaining or continuing any employment whether or not the employment is remunerated [or becoming a volunteer in a capacity] that involves a position of trust towards persons under the age of 16 years, to wit: (specify the particulars of the offence), contrary to s. 161(4) of the *Criminal Code*.

..........being bound by an order prohibiting A.B. from using a computer system for the purpose of communicating with a person under the age of 16 years, to wit: (specify the particulars of the offence), contrary to s. 161(4) of the *Criminal Code*.

Section 162(1) Voyeurism

A.B., on the (day) of (month), (year), at (specify time) in (specify place), did surreptitiously observe [or make a visual recording of] C.D., in circumstances that give rise to a reasonable expectation of privacy, when C.D. was in a place in which C.D. could reasonably be expected to be nude [or to expose his or her genital organs or anal region or her breasts or to engage in explicit sexual activity], to wit: (specify the particulars of the offence), contrary to s. 162(1)(a) of the *Criminal Code*.

A.B., on the (day) of (month), (year), at (specify time) in (specify place), did surreptitiously observe [or make a visual recording of] C.D., in circumstances that give rise to a reasonable expectation of privacy, when C.D. was nude [or was exposing his or her genital organs or anal region or her breasts] and the observation [or recording] was done for the purpose of observing [or recording] C.D. in such a state [or engaged in such an activity], to wit: (specify the particulars of the offence), contrary to s. 162(1)(b) of the *Criminal Code*.

A.B., on the (day) of (month), (year), at (specify time) in (specify place), did surreptitiously observe [or make a visual recording of] C.D., in circumstances that give rise to a reasonable expectation of privacy and the observation [or recording] was done for a sexual purpose, to wit: (specify the particulars of the offence), contrary to s. 162(1)(c) of the *Criminal Code*.

Section 162(4) Voyeuristic Materials

A.B., on the (day) of (month), (year), at (specify time) in (specify place), knowing that a recording was obtained by the commission of an offence under s. 162(1), did print [or copy or publish or distribute or circulate or sell or advertise or make available] the recording, to wit: (specify the particulars of the offence), contrary to s. 162(4) of the *Criminal Code*.

A.B., on the (day) of (month), (year), at (specify time) in (specify place), knowing that a recording was obtained by the commission of an offence under s. 162(1), had the recording in his [or her] possession for the purpose of printing [or copying or publishing or distributing or circulating or selling or advertising or making it available], to wit: (specify the particulars of the offence), contrary to s. 162(4) of the *Criminal Code*.

Section 162.1(1) Publication of an intimate image without consent

A.B., on the (day) of (month), (year), at (specify time) in (specify place),

..........knowing that C.D.did not give consent, did publish [or distribute or transmit or sell or make available or advertise] an intimate image [or a visual image or photograph or film or video recording] of C.D., to wit: (specify the particulars of the offence), contrary to s. 162.1(1) of the *Criminal Code*.

..........being reckless as to whether or not C.D. gave his [or her] consent, did publish [or distribute or transmit or sell or make or advertise] an intimate image of C.D., to wit: (specify the particulars of the offence), contrary to s. 162.1(1) of the *Criminal Code*.

Section 162.2(1) Order of prohibition from using the internet or other digital network

A.B., on the (day) of (month), (year), at (specify time) in (specify place), being bound by an order prohibiting A.B. from using the internet [or specify other digital network], did not comply with the order [or with the terms and conditions of the order], to wit: (specify the particulars of the offence), contrary to s. 162.2(1) of the *Criminal Code*.

Section 163(1)(a) Making, printing, publishing, distributing, circulating or having in possession obscene matter

A.B., on the (day) of (month), (year), at (specify time) in (specify place), did make [or print or publish or distribute or circulate or have in his (or her) possession for the purpose of publication (or distribution or circulation)] obscene written matter [or an obscene picture or an obscene model or an obscene phonograph record or (specify any other obscene thing)], to wit: (specify the particulars of the offence), contrary to s. 163(1)(a) of the *Criminal Code*.

Section 163(1)(b) Offences in connection with crime comics

A.B., on the (day) of (month), (year), at (specify time) in (specify place),

..........did make [or print or publish or distribute or sell] a crime comic, to wit: (specify the particulars of the offence), contrary to s. 163(1)(b) of the *Criminal Code*.

..........did have in his [or her] possession for the purpose of publication [or distribution or circulation] a crime comic, to wit: (specify the particulars of the offence), contrary to s. 163(1)(b) of the *Criminal Code*.

Section 163(2)(a) Selling, exposing to public view or having in possession obscene matter

A.B., on the (day) of (month), (year), at (specify time) in (specify place), knowingly and without lawful justification or excuse, did sell [or expose to public view or have in his [or her] possession for the purpose of sale], obscene written matter [or an obscene picture or an obscene model or an obscene phonograph record or (specify any other obscene thing)], to wit: (specify the particulars of the offence), contrary to s. 163(2)(a) of the *Criminal Code*.

Section 163(2)(b) Exhibiting disgusting objects or indecent show

A.B., on the (day) of (month), (year), at (specify time) in (specify place), knowingly and without lawful justification or excuse, did publicly exhibit a disgusting object [or an indecent show], to wit: (specify the particulars of the offence), contrary to s. 163(2)(b) of the *Criminal Code*.

Section 163(2)(c) Advertising means of causing abortion or miscarriage

A.B., on the (day) of (month), (year), at (specify time) in (specify place), did knowingly and without lawful justification or excuse, offer to sell [or advertise or publish an advertisement of or have for sale or have for disposal] means [or instructions or medicine or a drug or an article] intended [or represented] as a method of causing an abortion [or miscarriage], to wit: (specify the particulars of the offence), contrary to s. 163(2)(c) of the *Criminal Code*.

Section 163(2)(d) Advertising means of restoring sexual virility or curing venereal disease

A.B., on the (day) of (month), (year), at (specify time) in (specify place), knowingly and without lawful excuse, did advertise [or publish an advertisement] of means [or instructions or medicine or a drug or an article] intended [or represented] as a method for restoring sexual virility [or curing venereal diseases or curing diseases of the generative organs], to wit: (specify the particulars of the offence), contrary to s. 163(2)(d) of the *Criminal Code*.

Section 163.1(2) Making, printing, publishing or possessing child pornography for purposes of publication

A.B., on the (day) of (month), (year), at (specify time) in (specify place), knowingly, did make [or print or publish or possess for the purpose of publication] child pornography, to wit: (specify the particulars of the offence), contrary to s. 163.1(2) of the *Criminal Code*.

Section 163.1(3) Importing, distributing, selling or possessing for purpose of distribution or sale

A.B., on the (day) of (month), (year), at (specify time) in (specify place), did transmit [or make available or distribute or sell or import or export or possess for the purpose of transmission (or making available or distribution or sale or exportation)] child pornography, to wit: (specify the particulars of the offence), contrary to s. 163.1(3) of the *Criminal Code*.

Section 163.1(4) Possession of child pornography

A.B., on the (day) of (month), (year), at (specify time) in (specify place), did possess child pornography, to wit: (specify the particulars of the offence), contrary to s. 163.1(4) of the *Criminal Code*.

Section 163.1(4.1) Accessing child pornography

A.B., on the (day) of (month), (year), at (specify time) in (specify place), accessed child pornography [or knowingly caused child pornography to be viewed by A.B. or knowingly caused child pornography to be transmitted to A.B.], to wit: (specify the particulars of the offence), contrary to s. 163.1(4.1) of the *Criminal Code*.

Section 165 Tied sales

A.B., on the (day) of (month), (year), at (specify time) in (specify place), did refuse to sell [or supply] to C.D., copies of a publication for the reason only that C.D. refused to purchase [or acquire] from A.B. copies of any other publication that C.D. was apprehensive might be obscene [or a crime comic], to wit: (specify the particulars of the offence), contrary to s. 165 of the *Criminal Code*.

Section 167(1) Presenting or giving immoral theatrical performance

A.B., on the (day) of (month), (year), at (specify time) in (specify place), being the lessee [or manager or agent or person in charge] of a theatre, did present [or give or allow to be presented or allow to be given] therein an immoral [or indecent or obscene] performance [or entertainment or representation] to wit: (specify the particulars of the offence), contrary to s. 167(1) of the *Criminal Code*.

Section 167(2) Taking part or appearing in immoral theatrical performance

A.B., on the (day) of (month), (year), at (specify time) in (specify place), did take part [or appear] as an actor [or a performer or an assistant], in an immoral [or indecent or obscene] performance [or entertainment or representation] in a theatre, to wit: (specify the particulars of the offence), contrary to s. 167(2) of the *Criminal Code*.

Section 168 Mailing obscene matter

A.B., on the (day) of (month), (year), at (specify time) in (specify place), did make use of the mails for the purpose of transmitting [or delivering] (specify the thing transmitted or delivered), that was obscene [or indecent or immoral or scurrilous], to wit: (specify the particulars of the offence), contrary to s. 168 of the *Criminal Code*.

Section 170 Parent or guardian procuring sexual activity

A.B., on the (day) of (month), (year), at (specify time) in (specify place), being the parent [or guardian] of C.D., a person under the age of 18 years, did procure C.D. to engage in prohibited sexual activity with E.F., to wit: (specify the particulars of the offence), contrary to s. 170 of the *Criminal Code*.

Section 171 Householder permitting sexual activity

A.B., on the (day) of (month), (year), at (specify time) in (specify place), being the owner [or the occupier or the manager or a person having control of premises or a person assisting in the management (or control)], of premises knowingly did permit C.D., a person under the age of 18 years to resort to [or to be in or to be upon] the premises for the purpose of engaging in prohibited sexual activity with E.F., to wit: (specify the particulars of the offence), contrary to s. 171 of the *Criminal Code*.

Section 171.1 Making sexually explicit material available to a child

A.B., on the (day) of (month), (year), at (specify time) in (specify place), did

..........transmit [or make available or distribute or sell] sexually explicit material to C.D., a person under the age of 18 years of age [or a person A.B. believed to be under 18 years of age], for the purpose of facilitating an offence with respect to C.D. under s. 153(1) [or s. 155 or s. 163.1 or s. 170 or s. 171 or s. 279.011 or s. 279.02(2) or s. 279.03(2) or s. 286.1(2) or s. 286.2(2) or s. 286.3(2)], to wit: (specify the particulars of the offence), contrary to s. 171.1(a) of the *Criminal Code*.

..........transmit [or make available or distribute or sell] sexually explicit material to C.D., a person under the age of 16 years of age [or a person A.B. believed to be under 16 years of age], for the purpose of facilitating an offence with respect to C.D. under s. 151 [or s. 152 or s. 160.3 or s. 173(2) or s. 271 or s. 272 or s. 273 or s. 280], to wit: (specify the particulars of the offence), contrary to s. 171.1(b) of the *Criminal Code*.

..........transmit [or make available or distribute or sell] sexually explicit material to C.D., a person under the age of 14 years of age [or a person A.B. believed to be under 14 years of age], for the purpose of facilitating a offence under s. 281 with respect to C.D., to wit: (specify the particulars of the offence), contrary to s. 171.1(c) of the *Criminal Code*.

Section 172(1) Corrupting children

A.B., on the (day) of (month), (year), at (specify time) in (specify place), while in the home of C.D., a child, did participate in adultery [or sexual immorality or did indulge in habitual drunkenness (or specify any other form of vice)] and thereby endangered the morals of C.D. [or rendered the home an unfit place for C.D. to be in], to wit: (specify the particulars of the offence), contrary to s. 172(1) of the *Criminal Code*.

Section 172.1 Luring a child

A.B., on the (day) of (month), (year), at (specify time) in (specify place), by means of a telecommunication did

..........communicate with C.D., a person under the age of 18 years of age [or a person A.B. believed to be under 18 years of age], for the purpose of facilitating the commission of an offence with respect to C.D. under s. 153(1) [or s. 155 or s. 163.1 or s. 170 or s. 171 or s. 279.011 or s. 279.02(2) or s. 279.03(2) or s. 286.1(2) or s. 286.2(2) or s. 286.3(2)], to wit: (specify the particulars of the offence), contrary to s. 172.2(a) of the *Criminal Code*.

..........communicate with C.D., a person under the age of 16 years of age [or a person A.B. believed to be under 16 years of age], for the purpose of facilitating the commission of an offence with respect to C.D. under s. 151 [or s. 152 or s. 160(3) or 173(2) or s. 271 or s. 272 or s. 273 or s. 280], to wit: (specify the particulars of the offence), contrary to s. 172.1(b) of the *Criminal Code*.

..........transmit [or make available or distribute or sell] sexually explicit material to C.D., a person under the age of 14 years of age [or a person A.B. believed to be under 14 years of age], for the purpose of facilitating the commission of an offence under s. 281 with respect to C.D., to wit: (specify the particulars of the offence), contrary to s. 172.1(c) of the *Criminal Code*.

Section 172.2 Agreements and arrangements regarding sexual offences against a child

A.B., on the (day) of (month), (year), at (specify time) in (specify place), by means of a telecommunication did

..........agree [or make an arrangement] with C.D., a person under the age of 18 years of age [or a person A.B. believed to be under 18 years of age], to commit an offence with respect to C.D. under s. 153(1) [or s. 155 or s. 163.1 or s. 170 or s. 171 or s. 279.011 or s. 279.02(2) or s. 279.03(2) or s. 286.1(2) or s. 286.2(2) or s. 286.3(2)], to wit: (specify the particulars of the offence), contrary to s. 172.2(a) of the *Criminal Code*.

..........agree [or make an arrangement] with C.D., a person under the age of 16 years of age [or a person A.B. believed to be under 16 years of age], to commit an offence with respect to C.D. under s. 151 [or s. 152 or s. 160(3) or s. 173(2) or s. 271 or s. 272 or s. 273 or s. 280], to wit: (specify the particulars of the offence), contrary to s. 172.2(b) of the *Criminal Code*.

..........agree [or make an arrangement] with C.D., a person under the age of 14 years of age [or a person A.B. believed to be under 14 years of age], to commit an offence under s. 281 with respect to C.D., to wit: (specify the particulars of the offence), contrary to s. 172.2(c) of the *Criminal Code*.

Section 173(1) Indecent acts

A.B., on the (day) of (month), (year), at (specify time) in (specify place), wilfully

..........did an indecent act in a public place in the presence of C.D., to wit: (specify the particulars of the offence), contrary to s. 173(1)(a) of the *Criminal Code*.

..........did an indecent act with intent thereby to insult or offend C.D., to wit: (specify the particulars of the offence), contrary to s. 173(1)(b) of the *Criminal Code*.

Section 173(2) Exposure of genital organs to person under 16 years

A.B., on the (day) of (month), (year), at (specify time) in (specify place), for a sexual purpose, did expose his (or her) genital organs to C.D., a person under the age of 16 years, to wit: (specify the particulars of the offence), contrary to s. 173(2) of the *Criminal Code*.

Section 174(1) Nudity

A.B., on the (day) of (month), (year), at (specify time) in (specify place), without lawful excuse,

..........was nude in a public place, to wit: (specify the particulars of the offence), contrary to s. 174(1)(a) of the *Criminal Code*.

..........was nude and exposed to public view while on private property, to wit: (specify the particulars of the offence), contrary to s. 174(1)(b) of the *Criminal Code*.

Section 175(1)(a) Causing a disturbance

A.B., on the (day) of (month), (year), at (specify time) in (specify place), not being in a dwelling-house, did cause a disturbance in [or near] a public place by fighting [or screaming or shouting or swearing or singing or using insulting language or using obscene language or impeding C.D. or molesting C.D. or being drunk], to wit: (specify the particulars of the offence), contrary to s. 175(1)(a) of the *Criminal Code*.

Section 175(1)(b) Indecent exhibition

A.B., on the (day) of (month), (year), at (specify time) in (specify place), did openly expose [or exhibit] an indecent exhibition in a public place, to wit: (specify the particulars of the offence), contrary to s. 175(1)(b) of the *Criminal Code*.

Section 175(1)(c) Loitering and obstructing

A.B., on the (day) of (month), (year), at (specify time) in (specify place), did loiter in a public place and did obstruct C.D., a person who was there, to wit: (specify the particulars of the offence), contrary to s. 175(1)(c) of the *Criminal Code*.

Section 175(1)(d) Disturbing the occupants of a dwelling-house

A.B., on the (day) of (month), (year), at (specify time) in (specify place), did disturb the peace and quiet of C.D., the occupant of a dwelling-house,

..........by discharging firearms [or by disorderly conduct] in a public place, to wit: (specify the particulars of the offence), contrary to s. 175(1)(d) of the *Criminal Code*.

..........in a particular building [or structure] in which A.B. was not himself [or herself] an occupant, by discharging a firearm [or by disorderly conduct] in a part of the building [or structure] to which other occupants of dwelling-houses in the building [or structure] have access, to wit: (specify the particulars of the offence), contrary to s. 175(1)(d) of the *Criminal Code*.

Section 176(1) Obstructing officiating clergyman

A.B., on the (day) of (month), (year), at (specify time) in (specify place),

..........by threats [or force] unlawfully did obstruct [or prevent or endeavour to obstruct or endeavour to prevent] C.D., a clergyman [or minister] from celebrating divine service [or from performing a function in connection with his (or her) calling], to wit: (specify the particulars of the offence), contrary to s. 176(1)(a) of the *Criminal Code*.

..........knowing that C.D., a clergyman [or minister] was about to perform [or was on his (or her) way to perform or was returning from the performance of] divine service [or from a function in connection with his (or her) calling], did assault [or offer violence to or arrest upon a civil process or arrest under the pretence of executing a civil process] C.D., to wit: (specify the particulars of the offence), contrary to s. 176(1)(b) of the *Criminal Code*.

Section 176(2), (3) Disturbing religious worship

A.B., on the (day) of (month), (year), at (specify time) in (specify place),

..........did wilfully disturb [or interrupt] an assemblage of persons meeting for religious worship [or for a moral purpose or for a social purpose or for a benevolent purpose], to wit: (specify the particulars of the offence), contrary to s. 176(2) of the *Criminal Code*.

..........being at [or near] a meeting for religious worship [or for a moral purpose or for a social purpose or for a benevolent purpose], by (specify action), disturbed the order [or solemnity] of the meeting, to wit: (specify the particulars of the offence), contrary to s. 176(3) of the *Criminal Code*.

Section 177 Trespassing at night

A.B., on the (day) of (month), (year), at (specify time) in (specify place), without lawful excuse, did loiter [or prowl] at night upon the property of C.D. near the dwelling-house situated on that property, to wit: (specify the particulars of the offence), contrary to s. 177 of the *Criminal Code*.

Section 178 Stink or stench bombs

A.B., on the (day) of (month), (year), at (specify time) in (specify place), not being a peace officer engaged in the discharge of his [or her] duty, did have in his [or her] possession in a public place [or did deposit or throw or inject or cause to be deposited (or thrown or injected) in (or into or near) (specify any place)]

..........an offensive volatile substance that was likely to harm [or inconvenience or discommode or cause discomfort to] C.D. [or to cause damage to property], to wit: (specify the particulars of the offence), contrary to s. 178 of the *Criminal Code*.

..........a stink bomb [or stench bomb or a device from which such substance is capable of being liberated], to wit: (specify the particulars of the offence), contrary to s. 178 of the *Criminal Code*.

Section 179(1)(a) Supporting oneself by gaming or crime and committing vagrancy

A.B., on the (day) of (month), (year), at (specify time) in (specify place), having no lawful profession or calling by which to maintain himself [or herself], did support himself [or herself] in whole [or in part] by gaming [or crime], and did thereby commit vagrancy, to wit: (specify the particulars of the offence), contrary to s. 179(1)(a) of the *Criminal Code*.

Section 179(1)(b) Person convicted of sexual offence and committing vagrancy

A.B., on the (day) of (month), (year), at (specify time) in (specify place), having been convicted of the offence of (specify an offence mentioned in s. 179(1)(b)), was found loitering in [or near] a school ground [or playground or public park or bathing area], and did thereby commit vagrancy, to wit: (specify the particulars of the offence), contrary to s. 179(1)(b) of the *Criminal Code*.

Section 180 Common nuisance

A.B., on the (day) of (month), (year), at (specify time) in (specify place),

..........did commit a common nuisance by (specify how the common nuisance was committed) and did thereby endanger the lives [or safety or health] of the public, to wit: (specify the particulars of the offence), contrary to s. 180 of the *Criminal Code.*

..........did commit a common nuisance by (specify how the common nuisance was committed) and did thereby cause physical injury to C.D., to wit: (specify the particulars of the offence), contrary to s. 180 of the *Criminal Code.*

Section 181 Spreading false news

A.B., on the (day) of (month), (year), at (specify time) in (specify place), wilfully did publish a statement [or tale or news] that A.B. knew was false and that did cause [or was likely to cause] injury [or mischief] to a public interest, to wit: (specify the particulars of the offence), contrary to s. 181 of the *Criminal Code.*

Section 182 Neglect of or indignity to dead human body

A.B., on the (day) of (month), (year), at (specify time) in (specify place),

..........did without lawful excuse, neglect to perform a duty imposed upon A.B. by law [or undertaken by A.B.] with reference to a dead human body [or human remains], to wit: (specify the particulars of the offence), contrary to s. 182(a) of the *Criminal Code.*

..........did improperly [or indecently] interfere with [or offer an indignity to] a dead human body [or human remains], to wit: (specify the particulars of the offence), contrary to s. 182(b) of the *Criminal Code.*

Part VI — Invasion of Privacy

Section 184(1) Interception of private communication

A.B., on the (day) of (month), (year), at (specify time) in (specify place), by means of an electro-magnetic [or an acoustic or a mechanical or (specify other device)] device, did wilfully intercept a private communication, to wit: (specify the particulars of the offence), contrary to s. 184(1) of the *Criminal Code.*

Section 184.5(1) Interception of radio-based telephone communication

A.B., on the (day) of (month), (year), at (specify time) in (specify place), maliciously [or for gain], did intercept by means of a electro-magnetic [or acoustic or mechanical or specify other type of device] device, a radio-based telephone communication, while C.D., the originator of the communication [or the person intended by E.F., the originator of the communication to receive it] was in Canada, to wit: (specify the particulars of the offence), contrary to s. 184.5(1) of the *Criminal Code.*

Section 191(1) Possession of devices for interception of private communications

A.B., on the (day) of (month), (year), at (specify time) in (specify place), did possess [or sell or purchase] an electro-magnetic [or an acoustic or a mechanical or (specify other type of device)] device, knowing that the design thereof did render it primarily useful for surreptitious interception of private communications, to wit: (specify the particulars of the offence), contrary to s. 191(1) of the *Criminal Code.*

Section 193(1) Disclosure of information from private communication

A.B., on the (day) of (month), (year), at (specify time) in (specify place), wilfully did use [or disclose or disclose the existence of] a private communication [or a part of a private communication or the substance (or meaning or purport) of a private communication] that had been intercepted by means of an electro-magnetic [or an acoustic or a mechanical or (specify other type of device) device], without the consent, express or implied, of C.D., the originator of the private communication [or E.F., the person intended by C.D. to receive it], to wit: (specify the particulars of the offence), contrary to s. 193(1) of the *Criminal Code.*

Section 193.1(1) Disclosure of information received from interception of radio-based telephone communication

A.B., on the (day) of (month), (year), at (specify time) in (specify place), without the express [or implied] consent of A.B., the originator of the communication [or E.F., the person intended by the originator of the communication] wilfully did use [or disclose or disclose the existence] of a radio-based telephone communication that was intercepted by means of an electromagnetic [or acoustic or mechanical or (specify other type of device)], to wit: (specify the particulars of the offence), contrary to s. 193.1(1) of the *Criminal Code.*

Part VII — Disorderly Houses, Gaming and Betting

Section 201(1) Keeping a gaming house or betting house

A.B., on the (day) of (month), (year), at (specify time) in (specify place), did keep a common gaming house [or common betting house], to wit: (specify the particulars of the offence), contrary to s. 201(1) of the *Criminal Code.*

Section 201(2)(a) Found in gaming house or betting house

A.B., on the (day) of (month), (year), at (specify time) in (specify place), was found, without lawful excuse, in a common gaming [or betting] house, to wit: (specify the particulars of the offence), contrary to s. 201(2) of the *Criminal Code.*

Section 201(2)(b) Allowing premises to be used as gaming house or betting house

A.B., on the (day) of (month), (year), at (specify time) in (specify place), being the owner [or landlord or lessor or tenant or occupier or agent] of (specify the place), did knowingly permit such place to be let [or used] for the purposes of a common gaming [or betting] house, to wit: (specify the particulars of the offence), contrary to s. 201(2)(b) of the *Criminal Code*.

Section 202(1) Betting, pool-making and book-making

A.B., on the (day) of (month), (year), at (specify time) in (specify place),

..........did use [or knowingly allow to be used], a place under his [or her] control, for the purpose of recording bets [or registering bets or selling a pool], to wit: (specify the particulars of the offence), contrary to s. 202(1)(a) of the *Criminal Code*.

..........did import [or make or buy or sell or rent or lease or hire or keep or exhibit or employ or knowingly allow to be kept (or exhibited or employed)] a device [or apparatus] for the purpose of recording bets [or registering bets or selling a pool], to wit: (specify the particulars of the offence), contrary to s. 202(1)(b) of the *Criminal Code*.

..........did import [or make or buy or sell or rent or lease or hire or keep or exhibit or employ or knowingly allow to be kept (or exhibited or employed)] a machine [or device] for gambling [or betting] to wit: (specify the particulars of the offence), contrary to s. 202(1)(b) of the *Criminal Code*.

..........did record bets [or register bets or sell a pool], to wit: (specify the particulars of the offence), contrary to s. 202(1)(d) of the *Criminal Code*.

..........did engage in pool-selling [or book-making or in the business (or occupation) of betting], to wit: (specify the particulars of the offence), contrary to s. 202(1)(e) of the *Criminal Code*.

..........did make an agreement for the purchase [or sale] of betting [or gaming] privileges, to wit: (specify the particulars of the offence), contrary to s. 202(1)(e) of the *Criminal Code*.

..........did make an agreement for the purchase [or sale] of information that is intended to assist in book-making [or pool-selling or betting], to wit: (specify the particulars of the offence), contrary to s. 202(1)(e) of the *Criminal Code*.

..........did print [or provide or offer to print (or provide)] information intended for use in connection with book-making [or pool-selling or betting] on a horse-race [or fight or game or (specify a sport)] that has [or has not yet] taken place in [or outside] Canada, to wit: (specify the particulars of the offence), contrary to s. 202(1)(f) of the *Criminal Code*.

..........did import [or bring] into Canada information [or writing] that was intended [or was likely] to promote [or to be of use in] gambling [or book-making or pool-selling or betting] upon a horse-race [or fight or game or (specify a sport)], to wit: (specify the particulars of the offence), contrary to s. 202(1)(g) of the *Criminal Code*.

..........did advertise [or print or publish or exhibit or post up or give notice of] an offer [or invitation or inducement] to be on [or guess or foretell] the results of a contest [or a result of (or contingency relating to) a contest], to wit: (specify the particulars of the offence), contrary to s. 202(1)(h) of the *Criminal Code*.

..........did wilfully and knowingly send [or transmit or deliver or receive] a message by radio [or telegraph or telephone or mail or express] that conveyed information relating to book-making [or pool-selling or betting or wagering], to wit: (specify the particulars of the offence), contrary to s. 202(1)(i) of the *Criminal Code*.

..........did wilfully and knowingly send [or transmit or deliver or receive] a message by radio [or telegraph or telephone or mail or express] that conveyed information that was intended to assist in book-making [or pool-selling or betting or wagering], to wit: (specify the particulars of the offence), contrary to s. 202(1)(i) of the *Criminal Code*.

..........did aid [or assist] in the committing of an offence under s. 202 of the *Criminal Code* of Canada, to wit: (specify the particulars of the offence), contrary to s. 202(1)(j) of the *Criminal Code*.

Section 203 Placing bets on behalf of others

A.B., on the (day) of (month), (year), at (specify time) in (specify place),

..........did place [or offer to place or agree to place] a bet on behalf of C.D. for a consideration paid [or to be paid] by [or on behalf of] C.D., to wit: (specify the particulars of the offence), contrary to s. 203(a) of the *Criminal Code*.

..........did engage in the business [or practice] of placing [or of agreeing to place] bets on behalf of C.D., to wit: (specify the particulars of the offence) contrary to s. 203(b) of the *Criminal Code*.

..........did hold himself [or herself] out [or allow himself (or herself) to be held out] as engaging in the business [or practice] of placing [or of agreeing to place] bets on behalf of C.D., to wit: (specify the particulars of the offence), contrary to s. 203(c) of the *Criminal Code*.

Section 204(10) Pari-mutuel betting

A.B., on the (day) of (month), (year), at (specify time) in (specify place), did contravene [or fail to comply with] (specify provisions of s. 204 (pari-mutuel betting)), to wit: (specify the particulars of the offence), contrary to s. 204(10) of the *Criminal Code*.

Section 204(10) Violation or non-compliance with race-track regulations

A.B., on the (day) of (month), (year), at (specify time) in (specify place), did contravene [or fail to comply with] (specify a regulation made under s. 204 (race-track regulations)), to wit: (specify the particulars of the offence), contrary to s. 204(10) of the *Criminal Code*.

Section 206, 207 Lotteries and games of chance prohibited by law

A.B., on the (day) of (month), (year), at (specify time) in (specify place),

..........did make [or print or advertise or publish or cause (or procure) to be made (or printed or advertised or published)] a proposal [or scheme or plan] for advancing [or lending or giving or selling or disposing of] property by lots [or cards or tickets or a mode of chance)], to wit: (specify the particulars of the offence), contrary to s. 206(1)(a) of the *Criminal Code*.

..........did sell [or barter or exchange or dispose of or cause (or procure or aid or assist in), the sale (or barter or exchange or disposal of or offer for sale or offer for barter or offer for exchange)] a lot [or card or ticket or (specify other means or device)] for advancing [or lending or giving or selling or otherwise disposing of] property by lots [or tickets or (specify a mode of chance)] to wit: (specify the particulars of the offence), contrary to s. 206(1)(b) of the *Criminal Code.*

..........knowingly, did send [or transmit or mail or ship or deliver or allow to be sent (or transmitted or mailed or shipped or delivered) or accept for carriage or transport or convey] (specify an article) that was used [or intended for use] in carrying out a device [or proposal or scheme or plan] for advancing [or lending or giving or selling or disposing of] (specify property) by (specify a mode of chance), to wit: (specify the particulars of the offence), contrary to s. 206(1)(c) of the *Criminal Code.*

..........did conduct [or manage] a scheme [or contrivance or operation] for the purpose of determining who [or the holders of what lots (or tickets or numbers or chances)] were the winners of (specify property) so proposed to be advanced [or lent or given or sold or disposed of], to wit: (specify the particulars of the offence), contrary to s. 206(1)(d) of the *Criminal Code.*

..........did conduct [or manage or was a party to] a scheme [or contrivance or operation] by which a C.D. became entitled under the scheme [or contrivance or operation] on payment of any sum of money [or the giving of any valuable security or by obligating himself (or herself) to pay any sum of money (or give any valuable security)] to receive from A.B., the person conducting the scheme [or contrivance or operation] [or from E.F.] a larger sum of money [or amount of valuable security] than the sum [or amount] paid [or given or to be paid (or given)] by reason of the fact that E.F. and G.H. have paid [or given or obligated themselves to pay (or give)] a sum of money [or valuable security] under the scheme [or contrivance or operation], to wit: (specify the particulars of the of-fence), contrary to s. 206(1)(e) of the *Criminal Code.*

..........did dispose of goods [or wares or merchandise] by a game of chance [or a game of mixed chance and skill] in which C.D., the contestant [or competitor] paid money [or (specify other valuable consideration)], to wit: (specify the particulars of the offence), contrary to s. 206(1)(f) of the *Criminal Code.*

..........did induce C.D. to stake [or hazard] money [or other valuable property (or specify other thing)] on the result of a dice game [or three-card monte or punch board or coin table or on the operation of a wheel of fortune], to wit: (specify the particulars of the offence), contrary to s. 206(1)(g) of the *Criminal Code.*

..........for valuable consideration, did carry on [or play or offer to carry on (or play) or employ C.D. to carry on (or play)], in a public place [or a place to which the public had access], the game of three-card monte, to wit: (specify the particulars of the offence), contrary to s. 206(1)(h) of the *Criminal Code.*

..........did receive bets on the outcome of a game of three-card monte, to wit: (specify the particulars of the offence), contrary to s. 206(1)(i) of the *Criminal Code.*

..........being the owner of a place, did permit C.D. to play the game of three-card monte therein, to wit: (specify the particulars of the offence), contrary to s. 206(1)(j) of the *Criminal Code.*

..........did buy [or take or receive] (specify a lot or ticket or other device mentioned in s. 206(1) of the *Criminal Code*), to wit: (specify the particulars of the offence), contrary to s. 206(4) of the *Criminal Code*.

Section 207 Lottery schemes

A.B., on the (day) of (month), (year), at (specify time) in (specify place),

..........for the purposes of a lottery scheme, did (specify a thing that was not authorized pursuant to a provision of s. 207 of the *Criminal Code*) in the case of the conduct [or management or operation] of that lottery scheme, to wit: (specify the particulars of the offence), contrary to s. 207(3) of the *Criminal Code*.

..........for the purposes of a lottery scheme, did (specify anything that was not authorized pursuant to a provision of s. 207 of the *Criminal Code*), in the course of participating in that lottery scheme, to wit: (specify the particulars of the offence), contrary to s. 207(3) of the *Criminal Code*.

Section 209 Cheating at play

A.B., on the (day) of (month), (year), at (specify time) in (specify place), with intent to defraud C.D., did cheat while playing a game [or in holding the stakes for a game or in betting], to wit: (specify the particulars of the offence), contrary to s. 209 of the *Criminal Code*.

Section 210(1) Keeping common bawdy-house

A.B., on the (day) of (month), (year), at (specify time) in (specify place), did keep a common bawdy-house, to wit: (specify the particulars of the offence), contrary to s. 210(1) of the *Criminal Code*.

Section 210(2)(a), (b) Being an inmate or being found in a common bawdy-house

A.B., on the (day) of (month), (year), at (specify time) in (specify place),

..........was an inmate of a common bawdy-house, to wit: (specify the particulars of the offence), contrary to s. 210(2)(a) of the *Criminal Code*.

..........was found, without lawful excuse, in a common bawdy-house, to wit: (specify the particulars of the offence), contrary to s. 210(2)(b) of the *Criminal Code*.

Section 210(2)(c) Having charge or control of place used for common bawdy-house

A.B., on the (day) of (month), (year), at (specify time) in (specify place), being the owner [or landlord or lessor or tenant or occupier or agent or having charge or control] of (specify the place) did knowingly permit the place [or part of the place], to be let [or used] for the purposes of a common bawdy-house, to wit: (specify the particulars of the offence), contrary to s. 210(2)(c) of the *Criminal Code*.

Section 211 Transporting person to bawdy-house

A.B., on the (day) of (month), (year), at (specify time) in (specify place), did knowingly take [or transport or direct or offer to take or offer to transport or offer to direct] C.D. to a common bawdy-house, to wit: (specify the particulars of the offence), contrary to s. 211 of the *Criminal Code*.

Section 212(1) Procuring offences

A.B., on the (day) of (month), (year), at (specify time) in (specify place),

..........did procure [or attempt to procure or solicit] C.D., to have illicit sexual intercourse with E.F., to wit: (specify the particulars of the offence), contrary to s. 212(1)(a) of the *Criminal Code*.

..........did inveigle [or entice] C.D., a person who is not a prostitute, to a common bawdy-house for the purpose of illicit sexual intercourse [or prostitution], to wit: (specify the particulars of the offence), contrary to s. 212(1)(b) of the *Criminal Code*.

..........did knowingly conceal C.D. in a common bawdy-house, to wit: (specify the particulars of the offence), contrary to s. 212(1)(c) of the *Criminal Code*.

..........did procure [or attempt to procure] C.D. to become a prostitute, to wit: (specify the particulars of the offence), contrary to s. 212(1)(d) of the *Criminal Code*.

..........did procure [or attempt to procure] C.D. to leave the usual place of abode of that person with intent that C.D. become an inmate [or frequenter] of a common bawdy-house, to wit: (specify the particulars of the offence), contrary to s. 212(1)(e) of the *Criminal Code*.

..........did direct C.D. [or cause C.D. to be directed or take C.D. or cause C.D. to be taken] to a common bawdy-house on his [or her] arrival in Canada, to wit: (specify the particulars of the offence), contrary to s. 212(1)(f) of the *Criminal Code*.

..........did procure C.D. to enter [or leave] Canada, for the purpose of prostitution, to wit: (specify the particulars of the offence), contrary to s. 212(1)(g) of the *Criminal Code*.

..........for the purpose of gain, did exercise control [or direction or influence] over the movements of C.D. in such a manner as to show that A.B. was aiding [or abetting or compelling] C.D. to engage in [or carry on] prostitution with E.F. [or generally], to wit: (specify the particulars of the offence), contrary to s. 212(1)(h) of the *Criminal Code*.

..........did apply to C.D. [or administer to C.D. or cause C.D. to take] a drug [or intoxicating liquor or (specify a matter or thing)] with intent to stupefy [or overpower] C.D. in order thereby to enable E.F. to have illicit sexual intercourse with C.D., to wit: (specify the particulars of the offence), contrary to s. 212(1)(i) of the *Criminal Code*.

Section 212(1)(j) Living on avails of prostitution

A.B., on the (day) of (month), (year), at (specify time) in (specify place), did live wholly [or in part] on the avails of prostitution of C.D., to wit: (specify the particulars of the offence), contrary to s. 212(1)(j) of the *Criminal Code*.

Section 212(2) Living on the avails of prostitution of a person under the age of eighteen years

A.B., on the (day) of (month), (year), at (specify time) in (specify place), did live wholly [or in part] on the avails of prostitution of C.D., a person under the age of 18 years, to wit: (specify the particulars of the offence), contrary to s. 212(2) of the *Criminal Code.*

Section 212(2.1) Aggravated offence in relation to living on the avails of a person under the age of eighteen years

A.B., on the (day) of (month), (year), at (specify time) in (specify place), did live wholly [or in part] on the avails of prostitution by C.D., a person under the age of 18 years and, for the purpose of profit, did aid [or abet or counsel or compel] C.D. to engage in [or carry on] prostitution with E.F. and did use [or threaten to use or attempt to use] violence [or intimidation or coercion] with C.D., to wit: (specify the particulars to the offence), contrary to s. 212(2.1) of the *Criminal Code.*

Section 212(4) Offence in relation to juvenile prostitution

A.B., on the (day) of (month), (year), at (specify time) in (specify place), did obtain [or attempt to obtain] for consideration the sexual services of C.D., a person who was under the age of 18 years [or a person that A.B. believed was under the age of 18 years], to wit: (specify the particulars of the offence), contrary to s. 212(4) of the *Criminal Code.*

Section 213(1) Offence in relation to prostitution

A.B., on the (day) of (month), (year), at (specify time) in (specify place),

..........did stop a motor vehicle [or attempt to stop a motor vehicle] in a public place [or in a place open to public view] for the purpose of engaging in prostitution [or of obtaining the sexual services of a prostitute], to wit: (specify the particulars of the offence), contrary to s. 213(1) of the *Criminal Code.*

..........did impede the free flow of pedestrian [or vehicular] traffic in a public place [or a place open to public view] from premises adjacent to that place, for the purpose of engaging in prostitution [or of obtaining the sexual services of a prostitute], to wit: (specify the particulars of the offence), contrary to s. 213(1)(b) of the *Criminal Code.*

..........did impede the ingress to [or egress from] a public place [or a place open to public view] from premises adjacent to that place, for the purpose of engaging in prostitution [or of obtaining the sexual services of a prostitute], to wit: (specify the particulars of the offence), contrary to s. 213(1)(b) of the *Criminal Code.*

..........stopped [or attempted to stop or communicated with or attempted to communicate with] C.D. in a public place [or a place open to public view] for the purpose of engaging in prostitution [or of obtaining the sexual services of a prostitute], to wit: (specify the particulars of the offence), contrary to s. 213(1)(c) of the *Criminal Code.*

Part VIII — Offences Against the Person and Reputation

Section 215 Parent, foster parent, guardian or head of family failing in duties

A.B., on the (day) of (month), (year), at (specify time) in (specify place), being the parent of C.D. [or the foster parent of C.D., or the guardian of C.D., or the head of a family of which C.D. was a member], without lawful excuse

..........did fail to provide the necessaries of life to C.D., a child under the age of 16 years, who was in destitute or necessitous circumstances, to wit: (specify the particulars of the offence), contrary to s. 215 of the *Criminal Code*.

..........did fail to provide the necessaries of life to C.D., a child under the age of 16 years, thereby endangering the life of C.D. [or causing the health of C.D. to be endangered permanently], to wit: (specify the particulars of the offence contrary to s. 215 of the *Criminal Code*.

Section 215(2)(a) Married person failing in duties

A.B., on the (day) of (month), (year), at (specify time) in (specify place), being married to C.D., without lawful excuse

..........did fail to provide the necessaries of life to C.D., who was in destitute or necessitous circumstances, to wit: (specify the particulars of the offence), contrary to s. 215(2)(a) of the *Criminal Code*.

..........did fail to provide the necessaries of life to C.D., thereby endangering the life of C.D. [or causing the health of C.D. to be endangered permanently], to wit: (specify the particulars of the offence) contrary to s. 215(2)(a) of the *Criminal Code*.

Section 215(2)(b) Person under the charge of another person failing in duties

A.B., on the (day) of (month), (year), at (specify time) in (specify place), being under a legal duty to provide the necessaries of life to C.D., a person in his [or her] charge unable to withdraw from that charge and unable to provide himself [or herself] with the necessaries of life, did fail to perform that duty thereby endangering the life of C.D. [or causing or being likely to cause permanent injury to the health of C.D.], to wit: (specify the particulars of the offence, contrary to s. 215(2)(b) of the *Criminal Code*.

Section 218 Abandoning child

A.B., on the (day) of (month), (year), at (specify time) in (specify place), unlawfully

..........did abandon [or expose] C.D., a child under the age of 10 years, so that the life of C.D. was endangered [or was likely to be endangered], to wit: (specify the particulars of the offence), contrary to s. 218 of the *Criminal Code*.

..........did abandon [or expose] C.D., a child under the age of 10 years, so that the health of C.D. was permanently injured [or was likely to be permanently injured], to wit: (specify the particulars of the offence), contrary to s. 218 of the *Criminal Code*.

Section 220 Causing death by criminal negligence

A.B., on the (day) of (month), (year), at (specify time) in (specify place), by criminal negligence, did cause death to C.D., to wit: (specify the particulars of the offence), contrary to s. 220 of the *Criminal Code*.

Section 221 Causing bodily harm by criminal negligence

A.B., on the (day) of (month), (year), at (specify time) in (specify place), by criminal negligence, did cause bodily harm to C.D., to wit: (specify the particulars of the offence), contrary to s. 221 of the *Criminal Code*.

Section 235(1) Murder

A.B., on the (day) of (month), (year), at (specify time) in (specify place), did cause the death of C.D. and thereby commit murder in the first degree [or murder in the second degree], to wit: (specify the particulars of the offence), contrary to s. 235(1) of the *Criminal Code*.

Section 236 Manslaughter

A.B., on the (day) of (month), (year), at (specify time) in (specify place), did cause the death of C.D. and thereby commit manslaughter, to wit: (specify the particulars of the offence), contrary to s. 236 of the *Criminal Code*.

Section 237 Infanticide

A.B., on the (day) of (month), (year), at (specify time) in (specify place), being a female person, did commit infanticide, to wit: (specify the particulars of the offence), contrary to s. 237 of the *Criminal Code*.

Section 238(1) Killing unborn child in act of birth

A.B., on the (day) of (month), (year), at (specify time) in (specify place), did cause the death, in the act of birth, of a child that had not become a human being in such a manner that if the child were a human being, A.B. would be guilty of murder, to wit: (specify the particulars of the offence), contrary to s. 238(1) of the *Criminal Code*.

Section 239 Attempt to commit murder by any means

A.B., on the (day) of (month), (year), at (specify time) in (specify place), did attempt to cause the death of C.D. and thereby commit murder, to wit: (specify the particulars of the offence), contrary to s. 239 of the *Criminal Code*.

Section 240 Accessory after the fact to murder

A.B., on the (day) of (month), (year), at (specify time) in (specify place), was an accessory after the fact to murder, to wit: (specify the particulars of the offence), contrary to s. 240 of the *Criminal Code*.

Section 241 Counselling or aiding suicide

A.B., on the (day) of (month), (year), at (specify time) in (specify place),

..........without an exemption for medical assistance in dying, did counsel C.D. to die by suicide, to wit: (specify the particulars of the offence), contrary to s. 241(a) of the *Criminal Code.*

..........without an exemption for medical assistance in dying, did abet C.D. in dying by suicide, to wit: (specify the particulars of the offence), contrary to s. 241(a) of the *Criminal Code.*

..........without an exemption for medical assistance in dying, did aid C.D. to die by suicide, to wit: (specify the particulars of the offence), contrary to s. 241(a) of the *Criminal Code.*

Section 241.2(3) Failure to comply with safeguards in providing medical assistance in dying

A.B., on the (day) of (month), (year), at (specify time) in (specify place), being a medical practitioner (or a nurse practitioner) who, in providing medical assistance in dying,

..........did fail to ensure that C.D.'s request for medical assistance in dying was made in writing and signed and dated by C.D. (or by E.F., a person authorized under s. 241(4)), and signed and dated after C.D. (or E.F.) was informed by A.B. that C.D. has a grievous and irremediable medical condition, to wit: (specify the particulars of the offence), contrary to s. 241.2(3)(b) of the *Criminal Code.*

..........did fail to be satisfied that the request for medical assistance in dying was signed and dated by C.D. (or by E.F., a person authorized under s. 241(4)) before two independent witnesses who also signed and dated the request, to wit: (specify the particulars of the offence), contrary to s. 241.2(3)(c) of the *Criminal Code.*

..........did fail to ensure that C.D., a person who has made a request for medical assistance in dying has been informed that C.D. may at any time and in any manner withdraw the request, to wit: (specify the particulars of the offence), contrary to s. 241.2(3)(d) of the *Criminal Code.*

..........did fail to ensure that another medical practitioner or nurse practitioner has provided a written opinion that C.D. meets all of the criteria for eligibility for medical assistance in dying set out in s. 241.2(1), to wit: (specify the particulars of the offence), contrary to s. 241.2(3)(e) of the *Criminal Code.*

..........did fail to be satisfied that A.B. and C.D., a medical practitioner (or a nurse practitioner) provided a written opinion that E.F. meets all of the criteria for medical assistance in dying set out in s. 241.2(1), to wit: (specify the particulars of the offence), contrary to s. 241.2(3)(f) of the *Criminal Code.*

..........did fail to ensure that there were at least 10 clear days between the day on which the request for medical assistance in dying was signed by (or on behalf of) C.D. and the day on which the medical assistance is provided, to wit: (specify the particulars of the offence), contrary to s. 241.2(3)(g) of the *Criminal Code.*

..........did fail to ensure that there were an appropriate number of clear days between the day on which the request for medical assistance in dying was signed by (or on behalf of) C.D. and the day on which the medical assistance is provided when

C.D.'s death (or the loss of C.D.'s capacity to provide informed consent) is imminent, to wit: (specify the particulars of the offence), contrary to s. 241.2(3)(g) of the *Criminal Code*.

..........did fail to give C.D an opportunity to withdraw their request and ensure that C.D. has given express consent to receive medical assistance in dying, to wit: (specify the particulars of the offence), contrary to s. 241.2(3)(h) of the *Criminal Code*.

..........did fail to take all necessary measures to provide a reliable means by which C.D., a person who has difficulty communicating, may understand that the information provided to C.D. and communicate C.D.'s decision, to wit: (specify the particulars of the offence), contrary to s. 241.2(3)(i) of the *Criminal Code*.

Section 241.2(8) Failure to provide safeguards in prescribing substance for use in providing medical assistance in dying

A.B., on the (day) of (month), (year) at (specify time) in (specify place), being a medical practitioner (or nurse practitioner) who, in providing medical assistance to the dying, did prescribe (or obtain) a substance for that purpose and failed to inform C.D., a pharmacist, that the substance was intended for that purpose before C.D. dispenses the substance, to wit: (specify the particulars of the offence), contrary to s. 241.2(8) of the *Criminal Code*.

Section 241.4(1) Forgery in relation to a request for medical assistance in dying

A.B., on the (day) of (month), (year) at (specify time) in (specify place), did commit forgery in relation to a request for medical assistance in dying, to wit: (specify the particulars of the offence), contrary to s. 241.4(1) of the *Criminal Code*.

Section 241.4(2) Destruction of documents relating to a request for medical assistance in dying

A.B., on the (day) of (month), (year) at (specify time) in (specify place), did destroy a document that relates to a request for medical assistance in dying with intent to interfere with C.D.'s request for medical assistance in dying (or the lawful assessment of C.D.'s request for medical assistance in dying or E.F.'s invoking of an authorized exemption), to wit: (specify the particulars), contrary to s. 241.4(2) of the *Criminal Code*.

Section 242 Neglect in childbirth

A.B., on the (day) of (month), (year), at (specify time) in (specify place), being a pregnant female person about to be delivered, did fail to make provision for reasonable assistance in respect of her delivery, with intent that her child should not live [or with intent to conceal the birth of the child], resulting in permanent injury to her child [or resulting in the death of her child] before [or during or a short time after] birth, to wit: (specify the particulars of the offence), contrary to s. 242 of the *Criminal Code*.

Section 243 Concealing dead body of child

A.B., on the (day) of (month), (year), at (specify time) in (specify place), did dispose of the dead body of the child of A.B. [or C.D.] with intent to conceal the fact that A.B. [or C.D.] had been delivered of it, to wit: (specify the particulars of the offence), contrary to s. 243 of the *Criminal Code*.

Section 244 Discharging a firearm

A.B., on the (day) of (month), (year), at (specify time) in (specify place), with intent to wound [or maim or disfigure or endanger the life of or prevent the arrest (or detention) of] C.D., did discharge a firearm at C.D. [or E.F.], to wit: (specify the particulars of the offence), contrary to s. 244 of the *Criminal Code*.

Section 244.1 Discharging an air gun with intent

A.B., on the (day) of (month), (year), at (specify time) in (specify place), with intent to wound [or maim or disfigure or endanger the life of or prevent the arrest (or detention) of] C.D., did discharge an air gun [or air pistol or compressed gas gun or compressed gas pistol] at C.D. [or E.F.], to wit: specify the particulars of the offence), contrary to s. 244.1 of the *Criminal Code*.

Section 244.2 Reckless discharge of firearm

A.B., on the (day) of (month), (year), at (specify time) in (specify place),

..........intentionally did discharge a firearm into [or at] the place knowing that C.D. was present [or being reckless as to whether C.D. was present], to wit: (specify the particulars of the offence), contrary to s. 244.2 of the *Criminal Code*.

..........intentionally did discharge a firearm while being reckless as to the life or safety of C.D., to wit: (specify the particulars of the offence), contrary to s. 244.2 of the *Criminal Code*.

Section 245 Administering poison or other destructive or noxious thing

A.B., on the (day) of (month), (year), at (specify time) in (specify place), did administer to C.D. [or cause to be administered to C.D. or cause C.D. to take] poison [or specify a destructive or noxious thing] with intent thereby to endanger the life of [or cause bodily harm to or grieve or annoy] C.D., to wit: (specify the particulars of the offence), contrary to s. 245 of the *Criminal Code*.

Section 246 Overcoming resistance to commission of offence

A.B., on the (day) of (month), (year), at (specify time) in (specify place), with intent to enable [or assist] himself [or herself or E.F.] to commit the indictable offence of (specify),

..........did attempt to choke [or suffocate or strangle] C.D., to wit: (specify the particulars of the offence), contrary to s. 246(a) of the *Criminal Code*.

..........did attempt to render C.D. insensible [or unconscious or incapable of resistance] by a means calculated to choke [or suffocate or strangle] C.D., to wit: (specify the particulars of the offence), contrary to s. 246(a) of the *Criminal Code*.

..........did administer [or cause to be administered or attempt to administer] to C.D., (specify a stupefying or overpowering drug or matter or thing), to wit: (specify the particulars of the offence), contrary to s. 246(b) of the *Criminal Code*.

..........did cause [or attempt to cause] C.D. to take (specify a stupefying or overpowering drug or matter or thing) to wit: (specify the particulars of the offence), contrary to s. 246(b) of the *Criminal Code*.

Section 247(1)(a) Traps likely to cause bodily harm

A.B., on the (day) of (month), (year), at (specify time) in (specify place), with intent to cause the death of [or bodily harm to] C.D., did set [or place] a trap [or device] that was likely to cause death or bodily harm to C.D. [or C.D. and E.F.], to wit: (specify the particulars of the offence), contrary to s. 247(1) of the *Criminal Code*.

Section 248 Interfering with transportation facilities

A.B., on the (day) of (month), (year), at (specify time) in (specify place), with intent to endanger the safety of C.D.,

..........did place a (specify the thing placed) upon property that was used for [or in connection with] the transportation of persons [or goods] by land [or water or air], that was likely to cause the death of [or bodily harm to] C.D. [or E.F.], to wit: (specify the particulars of the offence), contrary to s. 248 of the *Criminal Code*.

..........did (specify the thing done) to property that was used for [or in connection with] the transportation of persons [or goods] by land [or water or air], that was likely to cause the death of [or bodily harm to] C.D. [or E.F.], to wit: (specify the particulars of the offence), contrary to s. 248 of the *Criminal Code*.

Section 262 Impeding attempt to save life

A.B., on the (day) of (month), (year), at (specify time) in (specify place),

..........did prevent [or impede or attempt to prevent or attempt to impede] C.D., who was attempting to save his C.D.'s own life, to wit: (specify the particulars of the offence), contrary to s. 262(a) of the *Criminal Code*.

..........without reasonable cause, did prevent [or impede or attempt to prevent or attempt to impede] C.D., who was attempting to save the life of E.F., to wit: (specify the particulars of the offence), contrary to s. 262(b) of the *Criminal Code*.

Section 263(1) Opening in ice

A.B., on the (day) of (month), (year), at (specify time) in (specify place), having made an opening in ice that is open to [or frequented by] the public, did fail to perform his [or her] legal duty to guard it in a manner adequate to prevent persons from falling in by accident and adequate to warn persons that the opening existed, to wit: (specify the particulars of the offence), contrary to s. 263(1) of the *Criminal Code*.

Section 263(3) Excavation

A.B., on the (day) of (month), (year), at (specify time) in (specify place), having left an excavation on land that A.B. owned [or on land of which A.B. had charge (or supervision)], did fail to perform his [or her] legal duty to guard it in a manner that was adequate to prevent persons from falling in by accident and adequate to warn persons that the excavation existed, to wit: (specify the particulars of the offence), contrary to s. 263(3) of the *Criminal Code.*

Section 264(3) Criminal harassment

A.B., on the (day) of (month), (year), at (specify time) in (specify place), without lawful authority and knowing that C.D. was harassed [or reckless as to whether C.D. was harassed]

..........did engage in conduct consisting of repeatedly following C.D. from place to place [or E.F. a person known to C.D.], to wit: (specify the particulars of the offence), contrary to s. 264(3) of the *Criminal Code.*

..........did engage in contact consisting of repeatedly communicating with C.D., [or E.F., a person known to them], to wit: (specify the particulars of the offence), contrary to s. 264(3) of the *Criminal Code.*

..........did encourage conduct consisting of besetting [or watching] the dwelling-house [or place] where C.D. [or E.F. a person known to C.D.] resided [or worked or carried on business or happened to be], to wit: (specify the particulars of the offence, contrary to s. 264(3) of the *Criminal Code.*

..........did engage in threatening conduct directed at C.D. [or E.F., a member of the family of C.D.], that causes C.D. reasonably in all the circumstances, to fear for his [or her] safety [or E.F., a person known to C.D.], to wit: (specify the particulars of the offence, contrary to 264(3) of the *Criminal Code.*

Section 264.1(1)(a) Uttering threats relating to persons

A.B., on the (day) of (month), (year), at (specify time) in (specify place), knowingly did utter [or convey or cause C.D. to receive] a threat to cause death [or bodily harm] to C.D. [or E.F.], to wit: (specify the particulars of the offence), contrary to s. 264.1(1)(a) of the *Criminal Code.*

Section 264.1(1)(b) Uttering threats relating to property

A.B., on the (day) of (month), (year), at (specify time) in (specify place), knowingly did utter [or convey or cause C.D. to receive] a threat to burn [or destroy or damage] real [or personal] property, to wit: (specify the particulars of the offence), contrary to s. 264.1(1)(b) of the *Criminal Code.*

Section 264.1(1)(c) Uttering threats relating to animals

A.B., on the (day) of (month), (year), at (specify time) in (specify place), knowingly did utter [or convey or cause C.D. to receive] a threat to kill [or poison or injure] an animal belonging to C.D. [or E.F.], to wit: (specify the particulars of the offence), contrary to s. 264.1(1)(c) of the *Criminal Code.*

Section 266 Assault

A.B., on the (day) of (month), (year), at (specify time) in (specify place), did commit an assault on C.D., to wit: (specify the particulars of the offence), contrary to s. 266 of the *Criminal Code.*

Section 267(a) Assault with a weapon

A.B., on the (day) of (month), (year), at (specify time) in (specify place), while committing an assault on C.D., did carry [or use or threaten to use] a weapon [or an imitation of a weapon], to wit: (specify the particulars of the offence), contrary to s. 267(a) of the *Criminal Code.*

Section 267(b) Assault causing bodily harm

A.B., on the (day) of (month), (year), at (specify time) in (specify place), while committing an assault against C.D., did cause bodily harm to C.D., to wit: (specify the particulars of the offence), contrary to s. 267(b) of the *Criminal Code.*

Section 268(2) Aggravated assault

A.B., on the (day) of (month), (year), at (specify time) in (specify place), did wound [or maim or disfigure or endanger the life of] C.D. and thereby commit an aggravated assault to wit: (specify the particulars of the offence), contrary to s. 268(2) of the *Criminal Code.*

Section 269 Unlawfully causing bodily harm

A.B., on the (day) of (month), (year), at (specify time) in (specify place), did unlawfully cause bodily harm to C.D., to wit: (specify the particulars of the offence), contrary to s. 269 of the *Criminal Code.*

Section 269.1(1) Torture

A.B., on the (day) of (month), (year), at (specify time) in (specify place), being an official [or being a person acting at the instigation of or with the consent or acquiescence of C.D., an official], did inflict torture on E.F., to wit: (specify the particulars of the offence), contrary to s. 269.1(1) of the *Criminal Code.*

Section 270(1)(a) Assaulting a public officer or a peace officer

A.B., on the (day) of (month), (year), at (specify time) in (specify place), did assault C.D., a public officer [or peace officer or person acting in aid of E.F., a public (or peace) officer], engaged in the execution of his [or her] duty, to wit: (specify the particulars of the offence), contrary to s. 270(1)(a) of the *Criminal Code.*

Section 270(1)(b) Assault with intent to resist arrest

A.B., on the (day) of (month), (year), at (specify time) in (specify place), did assault C.D., with intent to resist [or prevent] the lawful arrest [or detention] of A.B. [or E.F.], to wit: (specify the particulars of the offence), contrary to s. 270(1)(b) of the *Criminal Code.*

Section 270(1)(c)(i) Assault during execution of process or making a distress or seizure

A.B., on the (day) of (month), (year), at (specify time) in (specify place),

..........did assault C.D., a person engaged in the lawful execution of a process against the lands [or goods] of A.B. [or E.F.], to wit: (specify the particulars of the assault as well as the particulars of the process being lawfully executed), contrary to s. 270(1)(c)(i) of the *Criminal Code.*

..........did assault C.D., a person engaged in making a lawful distress [or seizure], to wit: (specify the particulars of the assault as well as the particulars of the lawful distress or seizure), contrary to s. 270(1)(c)(i) of the *Criminal Code.*

Section 270(1)(c)(ii) Assault with intent to rescue thing taken under lawful process

A.B., on the (day) of (month), (year), at (specify time) in (specify place), did assault C.D., with intent to rescue property that had been taken under a lawful process [or distress or seizure], to wit: (specify the particulars of the offence), contrary to s. 270(1)(c)(ii) of the *Criminal Code.*

Section 270.01 Assaulting peace office with a weapon or causing bodily harm

A.B., on the (day) of (month), (year), at (specify time) in (specify place),

..........did carry [or use or threaten to use] a weapon [or an imitation of a weapon] in committing an assault on a peace [or public] officer, to wit: (specify the particulars of an offence contrary to s. 270), contrary to s. 270.01 of the *Criminal Code.*

...........did cause bodily harm to C.D. in committing an assault on a peace [or public] officer, to wit: (specify the particulars of an offence contrary to s. 270), contrary to s. 270.01 of the *Criminal Code.*

Section 270.02 Aggravated assault of peace officer

A.B., on the (day) of (month), (year), at (specify time) in (specify place), did wound [or maim or disfigure or endanger the life of] C.D. in committing an assault on a peace [or public] officer, to wit: (specify the particulars of an offence contrary to s. 270), contrary to s. 270.02 of the *Criminal Code.*

Section 270.1 Disarming a peace officer

A.B., on the (day) of (month) (year), at (specify time) in (specify place), without the consent of C.D., a peace officer, did take [or did attempt to take] a weapon that was in the possession of C.D., when C.D. was engaged in the execution of his [or her] duty, to wit: (specify the particulars of the offence), contrary to s. 270.1 of the *Criminal Code.*

Section 271(1) Sexual assault

A.B., on the (day) of (month), (year), at (specify time) in (specify place), did commit a sexual assault on C.D., to wit: (specify the particulars of the offence), contrary to s. 271(1) of the *Criminal Code.*

Section 272(1)(a) Sexual assault with a weapon

A.B., on the (day) of (month), (year), at (specify time) in (specify place), while committing a sexual assault on C.D., did carry [or use or threaten to use] a weapon [or an imitation of a weapon], to wit: (specify the particulars of the offence), contrary to s. 272(1)(a) of the *Criminal Code*.

Section 272(1)(b) Sexual assault with threats to a third party

A.B., on the (day) of (month), (year), at (specify time) in (specify place), while committing a sexual assault on C.D., did threaten to cause bodily harm to E.F., to wit: (specify the particulars of the offence), contrary to s. 272(1)(b) of the *Criminal Code*.

Section 272(1)(c) Sexual assault causing bodily harm

A.B., on the (day) of (month), (year), at (specify time) in (specify place), while committing a sexual assault on C.D., did cause bodily harm to C.D., to wit: (specify the particulars of the offence), contrary to s. 272(1)(c) of the *Criminal Code*.

Section 272(1)(d) Sexual assault — Party to the offence

A.B., on the (day) of (month), (year), at (specify time) in (specify place), was a party to the commission of a sexual assault on C.D. by E.F., to wit: (specify the particulars of the offence), contrary to s. 272(1)(d) of the *Criminal Code*.

Section 273(2) Aggravated sexual assault

A.B., on the (day) of (month), (year), at (specify time) in (specify place), did wound [or maim or disfigure or endanger the life of] C.D., while committing an aggravated sexual assault on C.D., to wit: (specify the particulars of the offence), contrary to s. 273(2) of the *Criminal Code*.

Section 273.3(1) Removal of child from Canada

A.B., on the (day) of (month), (year), at (specify time) in (specify place),

..........did (specify thing done) for the purpose of removing from Canada C.D., a person under 16 years of age who was ordinarily resident in Canada, with the intention of committing an act outside Canada that would be an offence under s. 151 [or s. 152 or s. 160(3) or s. 173(2)] if it were committed inside Canada, to wit: (specify the particulars of the offence), contrary to s. 273.3(1)(a) of the *Criminal Code*.

..........did (specify thing done) for the purpose of removing from Canada C.D., a person over 16 years of age but under 18 years of age, who was ordinarily resident in Canada, with the intention of committing an act outside Canada that would be an offence under s. 153 if it were committed inside Canada, to wit: (specify the particulars of the offence), contrary to s. 273.3(1)(b) of the *Criminal Code*.

..........did (specify thing done) for the purpose of removing from Canada C.D., a person under 18 years of age who was ordinarily resident in Canada, with the intention of committing an act outside Canada that would be an offence under s. 155 [or s. 159 or s. 160(2) or s. 170 or s. 171 or s. 267 or s. 268 or s. 269 or s. 271 or s. 272

or s. 273], to wit: (specify the particulars of the offence), contrary to s. 273.3(1)(c) of the *Criminal Code*.

Section 276.3(2) Publishing evidence of sexual activity

A.B., on the (day) of (month), (year), at (specify time) in (specify place),

..........did publish in a newspaper [or in a broadcast] the contents of an application made under s. 276.1, to wit: (specify the particulars of the offence), contrary to s. 276.3(2)(a) of the *Criminal Code*.

..........did publish in a newspaper [or in a broadcast] evidence taken [or the information given or the representations made] at an application under s. 276.1 [or at a hearing under s. 276.2], to wit: (specify the particulars of the offence), contrary to s. 276.3(2)(b) of the *Criminal Code*.

..........did publish in a newspaper [or in a broadcast] the decision of the judge [or justice] under s. 276.1(4), without an order permitting publication, to wit: (specify the particulars of the offence), contrary to s. 276.3(2)(c) of the *Criminal Code*.

..........did publish in a newspaper [or in a broadcast] the determination made and the reasons provided under s. 276.2, without a determination that evidence is admissible [or without an order] permitting publication, to wit: (specify the particulars of the offence), contrary to s. 276.3(2)(d) of the *Criminal Code*.

Section 278.9(2) Publishing records in sexual offence proceedings

A.B., on the (day) of (month), (year), at (specify time) in (specify place),

..........did publish in a document [or broadcast or transmit] the contents of an application made under s. 278.3, to wit: (specify the particulars of the offence), contrary to s. 278.9(a) of the *Criminal Code*.

..........did publish in a document [or broadcast or transmit] evidence taken [or information given or submissions made] at a hearing under s. 278.4(1) [or s. 278.6(2)], to wit: (specify the particulars of the offence), contrary to s. 278.9(b) of the *Criminal Code*.

..........did publish in a document [or broadcast or transmit] the determination of a judge pursuant to s. 278.5(1) [or s. 278.7(1)] and the reasons provided pursuant to s. 278.8, without an order of the judge permitting publication, to wit: (specify the particulars of the of fence), contrary to s. 278.9(2)(c) of the *Criminal Code*.

Section 279(1) Kidnapping

A.B., on the (day) of (month), (year), at (specify time) in (specify place),

..........did kidnap C.D. with intent to cause C.D. to be confined [or imprisoned] against his [or her] will, to wit: (specify the particulars of the offence), contrary to s. 279(1)(a) of the *Criminal Code*.

..........did kidnap C.D. with intent to cause C.D. to be unlawfully sent or transported out of Canada against his [or her] will, to wit: (specify the particulars of the offence), contrary to s. 279(1)(b) of the *Criminal Code*.

..........did kidnap C.D. with intent to hold C.D. to ransom [or to service] against his [or her] will, to wit: (specify the particulars of the offence), contrary to s. 279(1)(c) of the *Criminal Code*.

Section 279(2) Forcible confinement

A.B., on the (day) of (month), (year), at (specify time) in (specify place), did without lawful authority confine [or imprison or forcibly seize] C.D., to wit: (specify the particulars of the offence), contrary to s. 279(2) of the *Criminal Code*.

Section 279.01(1) Trafficking in persons

A.B., on the (day) of (month), (year), at (specify time) in (specify place),

..........did recruit [or transport or transfer or receive or hold or conceal or harbour] C.D. for the purpose of exploiting [or facilitating the exploitation of] C.D., to wit: (specify the particulars of the offence), contrary to s. 279.01(1) of the *Criminal Code*.

..........did exercise control [or exercise direction or exercise influence] over C.D. for the purpose of exploiting [or facilitating the exploitation of] C.D. to wit: (specify the particulars of the offence), contrary to s. 279.01(1) of the *Criminal Code*.

Section 279.011 Trafficking in persons under the age of eighteen years

A.B., on the (day) of (month), (year), at (specify time) in (specify place),

..........did recruit [or transport or transfer or receive or hold or conceal or harbour] C.D., a person under 18 years of age, for the purpose of exploiting [or facilitating the exploitation of] C.D., to wit: (specify the particulars of the offence), contrary to s. 279.011 of the *Criminal Code*.

..........did exercise control [or exercise direction or influence] over the movements of C.D., a person under 18 years of age for the purpose of exploiting [or facilitating the exploitation of] C.D. to wit: (specify the particulars of the offence), contrary to s. 279.011 of the *Criminal Code*.

Section 279.02 Receiving a material benefit from trafficking in persons

A.B., on the (day) of (month), (year), at (specify time) in (specify place), did receive a financial benefit [or a material benefit] knowing that it resulted from the commission of an offence under s. 279.01(1) [or s. 279.011(1)] of the *Criminal Code*, to wit: (specify the particulars of the offence), contrary to s. 279.02 of the *Criminal Code*.

Section 279.03 Withholding or destroying documents related to trafficking in persons

A.B., on the (day) of (month), (year), at (specify time) in (specify place),

..........for the purpose of committing [or facilitating] an offence under s. 279.01(1) [or s. 279.011(1)], did conceal [or remove or withhold or destroy] a travel document that belongs to C.D., to wit: (specify the particulars of the offence), contrary to s. 279.03 of the *Criminal Code*.

..........for the purpose of committing [or facilitating] an offence under s. 279.01(1) [or s. 279.011(1)], did conceal [or remove or withhold or destroy] a travel document that establishes [or purports to establish] the identity of [or the immigration status of] C.D., to wit: (specify the particulars of the offence), contrary to s. 279.03 of the *Criminal Code.*

Section 279.1(2) Hostage taking

A.B., on the (day) of (month), (year), at (specify time) in (specify place),

..........did confine [or imprison or forcibly seize or detain] C.D. and did utter [or convey or cause a person to receive] a threat that the death of [or bodily harm to] C.D. would be caused, with intent to induce (specify an act or omission) as a condition of the release of C.D., to wit: (specify the particulars of the offence), contrary to s. 279.1(2) of the *Criminal Code.*

..........did confine [or imprison or forcibly seize or detain] C.D. and did utter [or convey or cause a person to receive] a threat that the confinement [or imprisonment or detention] of C.D. would be continued, with intent to induce (specify an act or omission) as a condition of the release of C.D., to wit: (specify the particulars of the offence), contrary to s. 279.1(2) of the *Criminal Code.*

Section 280(1) Abduction of person under sixteen

A.B., on the (day) of (month), (year), at (specify time) in (specify place), did without lawful authority take [or cause to be taken] C.D., an unmarried person under the age of 16 years, out of the possession of and against the will of E.F., her [or his] parent [or guardian or person] then having the lawful care or charge of C.D., to wit: (specify the particulars of the offence), contrary to s. 280(1) of the *Criminal Code.*

Section 281 Abduction of person under fourteen

A.B., on the (day) of (month), (year), at (specify time) in (specify place), not being a parent or guardian or person having the lawful care or charge of C.D., a person under the age of 14 years, did unlawfully take [or entice away or conceal or detain or receive or harbour] C.D. with intent to deprive E.F., the parent [or guardian or person having the lawful care or charge] of C.D., of the possession of C.D., to wit: (specify the particulars of the offence), contrary to s. 281 of the *Criminal Code.*

Section 282(1) Abduction in contravention of custody order

A.B., on the (day) of (month), (year), at (specify time) in (specify place), being the parent, guardian or person having the lawful care or charge of C.D., a person under the age of 14 years, did take [or entice away or conceal or detain or receive or harbour] C.D. in contravention of the custody provisions of a custody order in relation to C.D. made by (specify the name of the court) at (specify the location of the court) on (specify the date that the order was made), with intent to deprive E.F., the parent [or guardian or person having the lawful care or charge] of C.D., of the possession of C.D., to wit: (specify the particulars of the offence), contrary to s. 282(1) of the *Criminal Code.*

Section 283(1) Abduction where no custody order

A.B., on the (day) of (month), (year), at (specify time) in (specify place), being the parent, guardian or person having the lawful care or charge of C.D., a person under the age of 14 years, did unlawfully take [or entice away or conceal or detain or receive or harbour] C.D., with intent to deprive E.F., the parent [or guardian or person who has the lawful care or charge of] C.D., of the possession of C.D., to wit: (specify the particulars of the offence), contrary to s. 283(1) of the *Criminal Code.*

Section 286.1(1) Obtaining sexual services for consideration

A.B., on the (day) of (month), (year), at (specify time) in (specify place),

..........did obtain for consideration [or did communicate with C.D. for the purpose of obtaining] the sexual services of C.D., to wit: (specify the particulars of the offence), contrary to s. 286.1(1) of the *Criminal Code.*

..........in a public place [or a place open to public view or a place that is next to a park or a place that is next to the grounds of a school or religious institution or a place where persons under the age of 18 can reasonably be expected to be present], did obtain for consideration [or did communicate with C.D. for the purpose of obtaining] the sexual services of C.D., to wit: (specify the particulars of the offence), contrary to s. 286.1(1) of the *Criminal Code.*

Section 286.1(2) Obtaining sexual services for consideration from person under 18 years

A.B., on the (day) of (month), (year), at (specify time) in (specify place),

..........did obtain for consideration [or did communicate with C.D., a person under the age of 18 years, for the purpose of obtaining] the sexual services of C.D., a person under the age of 18 years, to wit: (specify the particulars of the offence), contrary to s. 286.1(2) of the *Criminal Code.*

..........in a public place [or a place open to public view or a place that is next to a park or a place that is next to the grounds of a school or religious institution or a place where persons under the age of 18 can reasonably be expected to be present], did obtain for consideration [or did communicate with C.D. for the purpose of obtaining] the sexual services of C.D., a person under the age of 18 years, to wit: (specify the particulars of the offence), contrary to s. 286.1(2) of the *Criminal Code.*

Section 286.2(1) Financial or material benefit from sexual services

A.B., on the (day) of (year), at (specify time) in (specify place), did receive a financial benefit [or other material benefit] from C.D., knowing that it was obtained by or derived from the commission of an offence under s. 286.1(1), to wit: (specify the particulars of the offence), contrary to s. 286.2(1) of the *Criminal Code.*

Section 286.2(2) Financial or material benefit from sexual services provided by persons under 18 years

A.B., on the (day) of (year), at (specify time) in (specify place), did receive a financial benefit [or other material benefit] from C.D., a person under the age of 18 years, knowing that it was obtained by or derived from the commission of an offence under s. 286.1(2), to wit: (specify the particulars of the offence), contrary to s. 286.2(1) of the *Criminal Code*.

Section 286.3(1) Procuring

A.B., on the (day) of (month), (year), at (specify time) in (specify place), did

..........procure C.D. to offer [or provide] sexual services for consideration, to wit: (specify the particulars of the offence), contrary to s. 286.3(1) of the *Criminal Code*.

..........for the purpose of facilitating an offence under s. 286.1(1), did recruit [or hold or conceal or harbour] C.D., a person who offers [or provides] sexual services for consideration, to wit: (specify the particulars of the offence), contrary to s. 286.3(1) of the *Criminal Code*.

..........for the purpose of facilitating an offence under s. 286.1(1), did exercise control [or direction or influence] over the movements of C.D., a person who offers [or provides] sexual services for consideration, to wit: (specify the particulars of the offence), contrary to s. 286.3(1) of the *Criminal Code*.

Section 286.3(2) Procuring a person under the age of 18 years

A.B., on the (day) of (month), (year), at (specify time) in (specify place), did

..........procure C.D., a person under the age of 18 years, to offer [or provide] sexual services for consideration, to wit: (specify the particulars of the offence), contrary to s. 286.3(2) of the *Criminal Code*.

..........for the purpose of facilitating an offence under s. 286.1(2), did recruit [or hold or conceal or harbour] C.D., a person under the age of 18 years who offers [or provides] sexual services for consideration, to wit: (specify the particulars of the offence), contrary to s. 286.3(2) of the *Criminal Code*.

..........for the purpose of facilitating an offence under s. 286.1(2), did exercise control [or direction or influence] over the movements of C.D., a person under the age of 18 years who offers [or provides] sexual services for consideration, to wit: (specify the particulars of the offence), contrary to s. 286.3(2) of the *Criminal Code*.

Section 286.4 Advertising sexual services

A.B., on the (day) of (month), (year), at (specify time) in (specify place), knowingly did advertise an offer to provide sexual services for consideration, to wit: (specify the particulars of the offence), contrary to s. 286.4 of the *Criminal Code*.

Section 288 Supplying noxious things for purposes of miscarriage

A.B., on the (day) of (month), (year), at (specify time) in (specify place), did unlawfully supply [or procure] a drug [or noxious thing or instrument), knowing it was intended to be used [or employed] to procure the miscarriage of C.D. [or E.F.], a female person, to wit: (specify the particulars of the offence), contrary to s. 288 of the *Criminal Code*.

Section 291(1) Bigamy

A.B., on the (day) of (month), (year), at (specify time) in (specify place),

..........being married [or knowing C.D. to be then married] did go through a form of marriage with C.D., and did thereby commit bigamy, to wit: (specify the particulars of the offence), contrary to s. 291(1) of the *Criminal Code*.

..........did go through a form of marriage with C.D. and E.F. on the same day [or simultaneously] and did thereby commit bigamy, to wit: (specify the particulars of the offence), contrary to s. 291(1) of the *Criminal Code*.

Section 291(1) Leaving Canada to commit bigamy

A.B., on the (day) of (month), (year), at (specify time) in (specify place), being a Canadian citizen resident in Canada,

..........being married [or knowing that C.D. was married], did leave Canada with intent to go through a form of marriage with C.D., and thereby commit bigamy, to wit: (specify the particulars of the offence), contrary to s. 291(1) of the *Criminal Code*.

..........did leave Canada with intent to go through a form of marriage with C.D. and E.F. on the same day [or simultaneously and thereby commit bigamy to wit: (specify the particulars of the offence), contrary to s. 291(1) of the *Criminal Code*.

Section 292(1) Procuring a feigned marriage

A.B., on the (day) of (month), (year), at (specify time) in (specify place), did procure a feigned marriage to be performed between himself [or herself] and C.D., [or did assist E.F. in procuring a feigned marriage between E.F. and C.D.], to wit: (specify the particulars of the offence), contrary to s. 292(1) of the *Criminal Code*.

Section 293(1)(a) Practising or agreeing to practise polygamy

A.B., on the (day) of (month), (year), at (specify time) in (specify place), did practise [or enter into or agrees to practise or agrees to enter into] a form of polygamy [or a conjugal union with more than one person at the same time], to wit: (specify the particulars of the offence), contrary to s. 293 of the *Criminal Code*.

Section 293(1)(b) Being a party to the offence of polygamy

A.B., on the (day) of (month), (year), at (specify time) in (specify place), celebrated [or did assist or was a party to] a rite [or ceremony or contract or consent] that purported to sanction a form of polygamy [or a conjugal union with more than one person at the same time], to wit: (specify the particulars of the offence), contrary to s. 293 of the *Criminal Code*.

Section 294 Pretending to solemnize marriage

A.B., on the (day) of (month), (year), at (specify time) in (specify place),

..........without lawful authority did solemnize [or pretend to solemnize] a marriage between C.D. and E.F., to wit: (specify the particulars of the offence), contrary to s. 294(a) of the *Criminal Code*.

.... did procure C.D. to solemnize a marriage between E.F. and G.H., knowing that C.D. was not lawfully authorized to solemnize a marriage, to wit: (specify the particulars of the offence), contrary to s. 294(b) of the *Criminal Code*.

Section 295 Solemnizing a marriage contrary to law

A.B., on the (day) of (month), (year), at (specify time) in (specify place), being lawfully authorized to solemnize marriage, knowingly and wilfully, did solemnize a marriage in contravention of the laws of the province of (specify the province) in which the marriage was solemnized), to wit: (specify the particulars of the offence), contrary to s. 295 of the *Criminal Code*.

Section 296(1) Publishing a blasphemous libel

A.B., on the (day) of (month), (year), at (specify time) in (specify place), did publish a blasphemous libel, to wit: (specify the particulars of the offence), contrary to s. 296(1) of the *Criminal Code*.

Section 300 Publishing a defamatory libel known to be false

A.B., on the (day) of (month), (year), at (specify time) in (specify place), did publish a defamatory libel that A.B. knew was false, to wit: (specify the particulars of the offence), contrary to s. 300 of the *Criminal Code*.

Section 301 Publishing a defamatory libel

A.B., on the (day) of (month), (year), at (specify time) in (specify place), did publish a defamatory libel, to wit: (specify the particulars of the offence), contrary to s. 301 of the *Criminal Code*.

Section 302(1) and (2) Extortion by libel

A.B., on the (day) of (month), (year), at (specify time) in (specify place),

..........with intent to extort money from C.D. [or to induce C.D. to confer on (or procure for) E.F. an appointment (or office or profit or trust)] did publish [or threaten to publish or offer to abstain from publishing (or prevent the publication of)] a defamatory libel, to wit: (specify the particulars of the offence), contrary to s. 302(2) of the *Criminal Code*.

..........as the result of the refusal of C.D. to permit money to be extorted [or to confer (or procure) an appointment (or office or profit or trust)] did publish [or threaten to publish] a defamatory libel, to wit: (specify the particulars of the offence), contrary to s. 302(2) of the *Criminal Code*.

Section 318(1) Advocating genocide

A.B., on the (day) of (month), (year), at (specify time) in (specify place), did advocate [or promote] genocide, to wit: (specify the particulars of the offence), contrary to s. 318(1) of the *Criminal Code*.

Section 319(1) Public incitement of hatred

A.B., on the (day) of (month), (year), at (specify time) in (specify place), by communicating statements in a public place did incite hatred against (specify an identifiable group) where such incitement was likely to lead to a breach of the peace, to wit: (specify the particulars of the offence), contrary to s. 319(1) of the *Criminal Code*.

Section 319(2) Wilful promotion of hatred

A.B., on the (day) of (month), (year), at (specify time) in (specify place), by communicating statements wilfully did promote hatred against (specify an identifiable group), to wit: (specify the particulars of the offence), contrary to s. 319(2) of the *Criminal Code*.

Part VIII.1 — Offences Relating to Conveyances

Section 320.13(1) Dangerous operation of conveyance

A.B., on the (day) of (month), (year) at (specify time) in (specify place), did operate a conveyance in a manner dangerous to the public, to wit: (specify the particulars of the offence), contrary to s. 320.13(1) of the *Criminal Code*.

Section 320.13(2) Dangerous operation of conveyance causing bodily harm

A.B., on the (day) of (month), (year) at (specify time) in (specify place), did operate a conveyance in a manner dangerous to the public, thereby causing bodily harm to C.D., to wit: (specify the particulars of the offence), contrary to s. 320.13(2) of the *Criminal Code*.

Section 320.13(3) Dangerous operation of conveyance causing death

A.B., on the (day) of (month), (year) at (specify time) in (specify place), did operate a conveyance in a manner dangerous to the public, thereby causing the death of C.D., to wit: (specify the particulars of the offence), contrary to s. 320.13(3) of the *Criminal Code*.

Section 320.14(1)(a) Operation of conveyance while impaired

A.B., on the (day) of (month), (year) at (specify time) in (specify place), did operate a conveyance while the person's ability to operate the conveyance was impaired by alcohol [or by a drug or by a combination of alcohol and a drug], to wit: (specify the particulars of the offence), contrary to s. 320.14(1)(a) of the *Criminal Code*.

Section 320.14(1)(b) Blood alcohol concentration after ceasing to operate a conveyance

A.B., on the (day) of (month), (year) at (specify time) in (specify place), had, within two hours after ceasing to operate a conveyance, a blood alcohol concentration that is equal to or exceeds 80 mg of alcohol in 100 ml of blood, to wit: (specify the particulars of the offence), contrary to s. 320.14(1)(b) of the *Criminal Code*.

Section 320.14(1)(c) Blood drug concentration after ceasing to operate a conveyance

A.B., on the (day) of (month), (year) at (specify time) in (specify place), within two hours after ceasing to operate a conveyance had a blood drug concentration that was equal to or exceeded the prescribed blood drug concentration, to wit: (specify the particulars of the offence), contrary to s. 320.14 (1)(c) of the *Criminal Code*.

Sections 320.14(1)(d), (2) and (3) Blood alcohol and blood drug concentration after ceasing to operate a conveyance

A.B., on the (day) of (month), (year) at (specify time) in (specify place), within two hours after ceasing to operate a conveyance, had a blood alcohol concentration and a blood drug concentration that was equal to or exceeded the prescribed blood alcohol concentration and blood drug concentration where alcohol and the drug are combined, to wit: (specify the particulars of the offence), contrary to s. 320.14(1)(d) of the *Criminal Code.*

A.B., on the (day) of (month), (year) at (specify time) in (specify place), within two hours after ceasing to operate a conveyance, had a blood alcohol concentration and a blood drug concentration that was equal to or exceeded the prescribed blood alcohol concentration and blood drug concentration where alcohol and the drug were combined and who while operating the conveyance caused bodily harm to C.D., to wit: (specify the particulars of the offence), contrary to s. 320.14(2) of the *Criminal Code.*

A.B., on the (day) of (month), (year) at (specify time) in (specify place), within two hours after ceasing to operate a conveyance, a blood alcohol concentration and a blood drug concentration that was equal to or exceeded the prescribed blood alcohol concentration and blood drug concentration where alcohol and the drug are combined and who while operating the conveyance, caused the death of C.D., to wit: (specify the particulars of the offence), contrary to s. 320.14(3) of the *Criminal Code.*

Section 320.14(4) Operation — low blood drug concentration

A.B., on the (day) of (month), (year) at (specify time) in (specify place), within two hours after ceasing to operate a conveyance, had a blood drug concentration that was equal to or exceeded the prescribed blood drug concentration for the drug and that is less than the concentration prescribed for the purpose of s. 320(1)(c), to wit: (specify the particulars of the office), contrary to s. 320.14(4) of the *Criminal Code.*

Section 320.15(1) Failure or refusal to comply with demand

A.B., on the (day) of (month), (year) at (specify time) in (specify place),

..........knowing that a demand made to A.B. by C.D., pursuant to s. 320.27 for a physical coordination test [or a breath test or a sample of a bodily substance] has been made, did fail or refuse to comply, without reasonable excuse, to wit: (specify the particulars of the offence), contrary to s. 320.15(1) of the *Criminal Code.*

..........knowing that a demand pursuant to s. 320.28 has been made to A.B. by C.D., did fail or refuse to comply, without reasonable excuse, to wit: (specify the particulars of the offence), contrary to s. 320.15(1) of the *Criminal Code.*

Section 320.15(2) Accident resulting in bodily harm

A.B., on the (day) of (month), (year) at (specify time) in (specify place), having failed or refused to provide a lawful demand pursuant to s. 320.15(1), knew that [or was reckless as to whether] the accident resulted in the bodily harm to C.D., to wit: (specify the particulars of the offence), contrary to s. 320.15(2) of the *Criminal Code.*

Section 320.15(3) Accident resulting in death

A.B., on the (day) of (month), (year) at (specify time) in (specify place), having failed or refused to provide a lawful demand pursuant to s. 320.15(1), knew that [or was reckless as to whether] the accident resulted in the death of C.D., to wit: (specify the particulars of the offence), contrary to s. 320.15(3) of the *Criminal Code*.

Section 320.17 Flight from peace officer

A.B., on the (day) of (month), (year) at (specify time) in (specify place), while being pursued by C.D., a peace officer, did operate a motor vehicle or vessel in order to evade C.D., and without reasonable excuse did fail to stop his vehicle as soon as was reasonable in the circumstances, to wit: (specify the particulars of the offence), contrary to s. 320.17 of the *Criminal Code*.

Section 320.18 Operation of a conveyance while prohibited

A.B., on the (day) of (month), (year) at (specify time) in (specify place), did operate a conveyance while prohibited from doing so by an order made under the *Criminal Code* [or a legal restriction imposed by an Act of Parliament or a provincial law in respect of a conviction under the *Criminal Code* or a discharge under s. 730], to wit: (specify the particulars of the offence), contrary to s. 320.18 of the *Criminal Code*.

Part IX — Offence Against Rights of Property

Section 327 Instrument or device to obtain telecommunication service without payment

A.B., on the (day) of (month), (year), at (specify time) in (specify place), did manufacture [or possess or sell or offer for sale or distribute] an instrument [or device or component of an instrument or component of a device] the design of which renders it primarily useful for obtaining the use of a telecommunication service [or facility], under circumstances that gave rise to a reasonable inference that the device had been used [or was intended to be used or had been intended to be used] to obtain the use of any telecommunication service [or facility] without payment of a lawful charge therefor, to wit: (specify the particulars of the offence), contrary to s. 327 of the *Criminal Code*.

Section 333.1 Motor vehicle theft

A.B., on the (day) of (month), (year), at (specify time) in (specify place), did commit theft of a motor vehicle, to wit: (specify the particulars of the offence), contrary to s. 333.1 of the *Criminal Code*.

Section 334 Theft

A.B., on the (day) of (month), (year), at (specify time) in (specify place), did commit theft, to wit: (specify the particulars of the offence), contrary to s. 334 of the *Criminal Code*.

Section 335 Taking motor vehicle or vessel without consent

A.B., on the (day) of (month), (year), at (specify time) in (specify place),

..........did take a motor vehicle [or vessel] without the consent of C.D., the owner of a motor vehicle [or vessel], with intent to drive [or use or navigate or operate] to wit: (specify the particulars of the offence), contrary to s. 335 of the *Criminal Code*.

..........did take a motor vehicle [or vessel] without the consent of C.D., the owner of the motor vehicle [or vessel], with intent to cause it to be driven [or used or navigated or operated], to wit: (specify the particulars of the offence), contrary to s. 335 of the *Criminal Code*.

..........was the occupant of a motor vehicle [or vessel] knowing that it was taken without the consent of the owner, to wit: (specify the particulars of the offence), contrary to s. 335 of the *Criminal Code*.

Section 336 Criminal breach of trust

A.B., on the (day) of (month), (year), at (specify time) in (specify place), being a trustee of (specify) for the use [or benefit], of C.D. [or specify a public (or charitable purpose)], with intent to defraud and in contravention of his [or her] trust, did convert (specify) to a use that was not authorized by the trust, to wit: (specify the particulars of the offence), contrary to s. 336 of the *Criminal Code*.

Section 337 Public servant refusing to deliver property

A.B., on the (day) of (month), (year), at (specify time) in (specify place), being [or having been] employed in the service of Her Majesty in right of Canada [or in right of a province or in the service of a municipality] and entrusted by virtue of that employment with the receipt [or custody or management or control] of (specify) did refuse [or fail] to deliver it to C.D., a person who was authorized to demand it and did demand it, to wit: (specify the particulars of the offence), contrary to s. 337 of the *Criminal Code*.

Section 338(1) Fraudulently taking cattle or defacing brand

A.B., on the (day) of (month), (year), at (specify time) in (specify place),

..........without the consent of C.D., fraudulently, did take [or hold or keep in his (or her) possession or conceal or receive or appropriate or purchase or sell] cattle owned by C.D. that were found astray, to wit: (specify the particulars of the offence), contrary to s. 338(1)(a) of the *Criminal Code*.

..........without the consent of C.D., fraudulently, did obliterate [or alter or deface] a brand [or mark] on cattle owned by C.D., to wit: (specify the particulars of the offence), contrary to s. 338(1)(b) of the *Criminal Code*.

..........without the consent of C.D., fraudulently, did make a false [or counterfeit] brand [or mark] on cattle owned by C.D., to wit: (specify the particulars of the offence), contrary to s. 338(1)(b) of the *Criminal Code*.

Section 338(2) Theft of cattle

A.B., on the (day) of (month), (year), at (specify time) in (specify place), did commit theft of cattle, to wit: (specify the particulars of the offence), contrary to s. 338(2) of the *Criminal Code*.

Section 339(1) Lumber and lumbering equipment

A.B., on the (day) of (month), (year), at (specify time) in (specify place), without the consent of the owner.

..........fraudulently did take [or hold or keep in his (or her) possession or conceal or receive or appropriate or purchase or sell] lumber [or lumbering equipment] that was found adrift [or cast ashore or lying] on or embedded in the bed [or bottom or bank or beach] of a river [or stream or lake] in Canada [or in a harbour (or the coastal waters) of Canada], to wit: (specify the particulars of the offence), contrary to s. 339(1)(a) of the *Criminal Code*.

..........did remove [or alter or obliterate or deface] a mark [or number] on lumber [or lumbering equipment] that was found adrift [or cast ashore or lying] on or embedded in the bed [or bottom or bank or beach] of a river [or stream or lake] in Canada [or in the harbour or the coastal waters of Canada], to wit: (specify the particulars of the offence), contrary to s. 339(1)(b) of the *Criminal Code*.

..........did refuse to deliver up to C.D. the owner [or to E.F., the person in charge thereof on behalf of the owner or to a person authorized by the owner to receive it] lumber [or lumbering equipment] that was found adrift [or cast ashore or lying] on or embedded in the bed [or bottom or bank or beach] of a river [or stream or lake] in Canada [or in the harbour (or the coastal waters) of Canada], to wit: (specify the particulars of the offence), contrary to s. 339(1)(c) of the *Criminal Code*.

Section 339(2) Dealing in marked lumbering equipment

A.B., on the (day) of (month), (year), at (specify time) in (specify place), being a dealer in second-hand goods, did trade in [or traffic in or have in his (or her) possession for sale (or traffic)] lumbering equipment that was marked with a mark [or brand or registered timber mark or name or initials] of C.D., without the written consent of C.D., to wit: (specify the particulars of the offence), contrary to s. 339(2) of the *Criminal Code*.

Section 340 Destroying documents of title

A.B., on the (day) of (month), (year), at (specify time) in (specify place), for a fraudulent purpose, did destroy [or cancel or conceal or obliterate] a document of title to goods [or a document of title to lands or a valuable security or a testamentary instrument or a judicial (or official) document], to wit: (specify the particulars of the offence), contrary to s. 340 of the *Criminal Code*.

Section 341 Fraudulent concealment

A.B., on the (day) of (month), (year), at (specify time) in (specify place), for a fraudulent purpose, did take [or obtain or remove or conceal] (specify the thing), to wit: (specify the particulars of the offence), contrary to s. 341 of the *Criminal Code*.

Section 342(1) Credit card offences

A.B., on the (day) of (month), (year) at (specify time) in (specify place),

..........did steal a credit card, to wit: (specify the particulars of the offence), contrary to s. 342(1)(a) of the *Criminal Code*.

..........did forge [or falsify] a credit card, to wit: (specify the particulars of the offence), contrary to s. 342(1)(b) of the *Criminal Code*.

..........did possess [or use or traffic in] a credit card [or a forged credit card or a falsified credit card] knowing that it was obtained [or made or altered] by the commission of (specify an offence committed in Canada), to wit: (specify the particulars of the offence), contrary to s. 342(1)(c) of the *Criminal Code*.

..........did possess [or use or traffic in] a credit card [or a forged credit card or a falsified credit card] knowing that it was obtained [or made or altered] by the commission of (specify an act or omission committed anywhere that would have been an offence if committed in Canada), to wit: (specify the particulars of the offence), contrary to s. 342(1)(c) of the *Criminal Code*.

..........did use a credit card knowing that it has been revoked [or cancelled], to wit: (specify the particulars of the offence), contrary to s. 342(1)(d) of the *Criminal Code*.

Section 342(3) Unauthorized use of credit card data

A.B., on the (day) of (month), (year) at (specify time) in (specify place), fraudulently and without colour of right, did possess [or use or traffic in or permit C.D. to use] credit card data [or personal authentication information] that would enable E.F. to use a credit card [or to obtain the services that are provided by the issuer of a credit card to credit card holders], to wit: (specify the particulars of the offence), contrary to s. 342(3) of the *Criminal Code*.

Section 342.01 Instruments for copying credit card data or forging or falsifying credit cards

A.B., on the (day) of (month), (year) at (specify time) in (specify place), without lawful justification or excuse,

..........did make [or repair or buy or sell or export from Canada or import into Canada or possess] an instrument [or device or apparatus or material or thing] that they know has been used [or know is adapted or know is intended for use] in the copying of credit card data for use in the commission of the offence of (specify an offence under s. 342(3)), to wit: (specify the particulars of the offence), contrary to s. 342.01 of the *Criminal Code*.

..........did make [or repair or buy or sell or export from Canada or import into Canada or possess] an instrument [or device or apparatus or material or thing] that they know has been used [or know is adapted or know is intended for use] in the copying of credit card data for use in the forging [or falsifying] of credit cards, to wit: (specify the particulars of the offence), contrary to s. 342.01 of the *Criminal Code*.

Section 342.1 Unauthorized use of computer

A.B., on the (day) of (month), (year), at (specify time) in (specify place), fraudulently and without colour of right, did

.... obtain a computer service, to wit: (specify the particulars of the offence), contrary to s. 342.1(a) of the *Criminal Code*.

..........intercept [or cause to be intercepted] a function of a computer system by means of an electromagnetic [or acoustic or mechanical] device, to wit: (specify the particulars of the offence), contrary to s. 342.1(b) of the *Criminal Code*.

..........use [or cause to be used] a computer system with intent to commit an offence under s. 430(a) [or s. 430(b)] in relation to computer data [or a computer system] of the *Criminal Code*, to wit: (specify the particulars of the offence), contrary to s. 342.1(c) of the *Criminal Code*.

..........use [or possess or traffic in or permit C.D. to have access to] a computer password that would enable C.D. to have access to a computer password, that would enable C.D. to commit an offence under s. 342.1(a) [or s. 342.1(b) or s. 342.1(c)] of the *Criminal Code*, to wit: (specify the particulars of the offence), contrary to s. 342.1(d) of the *Criminal Code*.

Section 342.2 Possession of device to obtain unauthorized use of a computer system or to commit mischief

A.B., on the (day) of (month), (year), at (specify time) in (specify place), without lawful excuse, did make [or possess or sell or offer for sale or import or obtain for use or distribute or make available] a device that is designed for [or adapted primarily] to commit an offence under s. 342.1 [or s. 430] of the *Criminal Code*, under circumstances that give rise to an inference that the device has been used [or was intended to be used] to commit such an offence, to wit: (specify the particulars of the offence), contrary to s. 342.2 of the *Criminal Code*.

Section 343 Robbery

A.B., on the (day) of (month), (year), at (specify time) in (specify place),

..........did steal (specify) from C.D., and for the purpose of extorting what was stolen [or to prevent resistance to the stealing or to overcome resistance to the stealing] used violence [or threats of violence] to C.D. [or to the property of C.D.], and did thereby commit robbery, to wit: (specify the particulars of the offence), contrary to s. 343(a) of the *Criminal Code*.

..........did steal (specify) from C.D., and at the same time [or immediately before or immediately thereafter] did wound [or beat or strike or use personal violence to] C.D., and did thereby commit robbery, to wit: (specify the particulars of the offence), contrary to s. 343(b) of the *Criminal Code*.

..........did assault C.D. with intent to steal from C.D., and did thereby commit robbery, to wit: (specify the particulars of the offence), contrary to s. 343(d) of the *Criminal Code*.

..........did rob C.D. of (specify), to wit: (specify the particulars of the offence), contrary to s. 344 of the *Criminal Code*.

Section 345 Stopping mail with intent to rob or search

A.B., on the (day) of (month), (year), at (specify time) in (specify place), did stop a mail conveyance with the intent to rob [or search] it, to wit: (specify the particulars of the offence), contrary to s. 345 of the *Criminal Code*.

Section 346(1.1) Extortion

A.B., on the (day) of (month), (year), at (specify time) in (specify place), without reasonable justification or excuse and with intent to obtain (specify), by threats [or accusations or menaces or violence] did induce [or attempt to induce] C.D., the person threatened [or the person accused or the person menaced or the person to whom violence was shown], to do [or cause to be done] (specify the thing done (specify), to wit: (specify the particulars of the offence), contrary to s. 346(1.1) of the *Criminal Code*.

Section 347(1) Criminal interest rates

A.B., on the (day) of (month), (year), at (specify time) in (specify place),

..........did enter into an agreement [or arrangement] to receive interest at a criminal rate, to wit: (specify the particulars of the offence), contrary to s. 347(1)(a) of the *Criminal Code*.

..........did receive a payment [or partial payment] of interest at a criminal rate, to wit: (specify the particulars of the offence), contrary to s. 347(1)(b) of the *Criminal Code*.

Section 348(1)(a) Breaking and entering with intent

A.B., on the (day) of (month), (year), at (specify time) in (specify place), did break and enter (specify a place) with intent to commit therein the indictable offence of (specify the indictable offence), to wit: (specify the particulars of the break-in and entry), contrary to s. 348(1)(a) of the *Criminal Code*.

Section 348(1)(b) Breaking and entering and committing offence

A.B., on the (day) of (month), (year), at (specify time) in (specify place), did break and enter (specify a place) and did commit therein the indictable offence of (specify the indictable offence committed), to wit: (specify the particulars of the break-in and entry), contrary to s. 348(1)(b) of the *Criminal Code*.

Section 348(1)(c) Breaking out

A.B., on the (day) of (month), (year), at (specify time) in (specify place),

..........did break out of (specify a place) after having committed therein the indictable offence of (specify the indictable offence committed), to wit: (specify the particulars of the breaking-out), contrary to s. 348(1)(c) of the *Criminal Code*.

..........did break out of (specify a place) after having entered the place with the intention to commit therein the indictable offence of (specify the indictable offence), to wit: (specify the particulars of the breaking-out), contrary to s. 348(1)(c) of the *Criminal Code*.

Section 349(1) Being unlawfully in dwelling-house

A.B., on the (day) of (month), (year), at (specify time) in (specify place), without lawful excuse, did enter [or was in] the dwelling-house of C.D. with intent to commit therein the indictable offence of (specify the indictable offence), to wit: (specify the particulars of the offence), contrary to s. 349(1) of the *Criminal Code*.

Section 351(1) Possession of break-in instrument

A.B., on the (day) of (month), (year), at (specify time) in (specify place), without lawful excuse, did have in his [or her] possession an instrument suitable for breaking into a place [or motor vehicle or vault or safe] under circumstances that gave rise to a reasonable inference that the instrument had been used [or was intended to be used or had been intended to be used] for breaking into (specify a place) [or a motor vehicle or a vault or a safe], to wit: (specify the particulars of the offence), contrary to s. 351(1) of the *Criminal Code*.

Section 351(2) Being in disguise

A.B., on the (day) of (month), (year), at (specify time) in (specify place), with intent to commit the indictable offence of (specify the indictable offence),

..........did have his [or her] face masked [or coloured], to wit: (specify the particulars of the offence), contrary to s. 351(2) of the *Criminal Code*.

..........was disguised, to wit: (specify the particulars of the offence), contrary to s. 351(2) of the *Criminal Code*.

Section 352 Possession of instruments for breaking into coin-operated device or currency exchange device

A.B., on the (day) of (month), (year), at (specify time) in (specify place),

..........did have in his [or her] possession an instrument suitable for breaking into a currency exchange device under circumstances that gave rise to a reasonable inference that the instrument had been used [or was (or had been) intended to be used] for breaking into a currency exchange device, to wit: (specify the particulars of the offence), contrary to s. 352 of the *Criminal Code*.

..........did have in his [or her] possession an instrument suitable for breaking into a coin-operated device under circumstances that gave rise to a reasonable inference that the instrument had been used [or was (or had been) intended to be used] for breaking into a coin-operated device, to wit: (specify the particulars of the offence), contrary to s. 352 of the *Criminal Code*.

Section 353(1) Automobile master keys

A.B., on the (day) of (month), (year), at (specify time) in (specify place),

..........did sell [or offer for sale or advertise] in the province of (specify), an automobile master key without the authority of a licence issued by the Attorney General of (specify), to wit: (specify the particulars of the offence), contrary to s. 353(1) of the *Criminal Code*.

..........did purchase [or have in his [or her] possession] in the province of (specify), an automobile master key without the authority of a licence issued by the Attorney General of (specify), to wit: (specify the particulars of the offence), contrary to s. 353(1) of the *Criminal Code*.

Section 353(4) Records of sales of automobile master keys

A.B., on the (day) of (month), (year), at (specify time) in (specify place),

..........did fail to keep a record of the sale of the automobile master key showing the name and address of the purchaser and the particulars of the licence issued to the purchaser as described in s. 353(1)(b) of the *Criminal Code* of Canada, contrary to s. 353(3) of the *Criminal Code*.

..........did fail to produce for inspection at the request of C.D., a peace officer, the record of the sale of an automobile master key required by law to be kept by anyone who sells an automobile master key, to wit: (specify the particulars of the offence), contrary to s. 353(4) of the *Criminal Code*.

Section 353.1 Tampering with motor vehicle identification number

A.B., on the (day) of (month), (year), at (specify time) in (specify place), without lawful excuse, did wholly or partially, alter [or remove or obliterate] a motor vehicle identification number on a motor vehicle, to wit: (specify the particulars of the offence), contrary to s. 353.1 of the *Criminal Code*.

Section 354(1) Possession of property obtained by crime

A.B., on the (day) of (month), (year), at (specify time) in (specify place),

..........did have in his [or her] possession (specify the property or thing or the proceeds of any property or thing) of a value of more than [or less than] $5,000, knowing that the property [or thing or proceeds] was [or were] obtained by [or derived from] the commission in Canada of an offence punishable by indictment, to wit: (specify the particulars of the offence), contrary to s. 354(1) of the *Criminal Code*.

..........did have in his [or her] possession (specify the property or thing or the proceeds of any property or thing) of a value of more than [or less than] $5,000, knowing that the property [or thing or proceeds] was [or were] obtained by [or derived from] an act [or omission] that would have constituted an offence punishable by indictment if it had occurred in Canada, to wit: (specify the particulars of the offence), contrary to s. 354(1) of the *Criminal Code*.

Section 355.2 Trafficking in property obtained by crime

A.B., on the (day) of (month), (year), at (specify time) in (specify place),

..........did traffic in property [or proceeds of property] knowing that all or part of the property [or proceeds] was obtained by or derived from directly or indirectly the commission of an offence punishable by indictment [or by an act or omission that would have consituted an offence punishable by indictment if it had occurred in Canada], to wit: (specify the particulars of the offence), contrary to s. 355.2 of the *Criminal Code*.

..........did traffic in (specify a thing) (or specify proceeds of a thing) knowing that all or part (specify the thing or the proceeds of the thing) was obtained by or derived from directly or indirectly the commission of an offence punishable by indictment [or by an act or omission that would have constituted an offence punishable by indictment if it had occurred in Canada], to wit: (specify the particulars of the offence), contrary to s. 355.2 of the *Criminal Code*.

Section 355.4 Possession of property obtained by crime for the purpose of trafficking

A.B., on the (day) of (month), (year), at (specify time) in (specify place),

..........did have in his [or her] possession property [or proceeds of property] for the purpose of trafficking knowing that all or part of the property [or proceeds of property] was obtained by or derived from directly or indirectly the commission of an offence punishable by indictment [or by an act or omission that would have constituted an offence punishable by indictment if it had occurred in Canada], to wit: (specify the particulars of the offence), contrary to s. 355.4 of the *Criminal Code*.

..........did have in his [or her] possession (specify a thing) (or specify proceeds of a thing) for the purpose of trafficking knowing that all or part of the (specify the thing or the proceeds of the thing) was obtained by or derived from directly or indirectly the commission of an offence punishable by indictment [or by an act or omission that would have constituted an offence punishable by indictment if it had occurred in Canada], to wit: (specify the particulars of the offence), contrary to s. 355.4 of the *Criminal Code*.

Section 356 Theft from mail

A.B., on the (day) of (month), (year) at (specify time) in (specify place),

..........did steal (specify anything) sent by post after it had been deposited at a post office and before it was delivered, to wit: (specify the particulars of the offence), contrary to s. 356(1)(a) of the *Criminal Code*.

..........did steal (specify anything) sent by post after it was delivered but before it was in the possession of C.D., the addressee [or a person who may reasonably be considered by the addressee to receive mail], to wit: (specify the particulars of the offence), contrary to s. 356(1)(a) of the *Criminal Code*.

..........did steal a bag [or sack or container or covering] in which mail is conveyed, to wit: (specify the particulars of the offence), contrary to s. 356(1)(a) of the *Criminal Code*.

..........did steal a key suited to a lock adopted for use by the Canada Post Corporation, to wit: (specify the particulars of the offence), contrary to s. 356(1)(a) of the *Criminal Code*.

..........with an intent to commit an offence under s. 356(1)(a) of the *Criminal Code*, did make [or possess or use] a copy of a key suited for use by the Canada Post Corporation [or a key suited to obtaining access to a receptacle or device provided for the receipt of mail], to wit: (specify the particulars of the offence), contrary to s. 356(1)(a.1) of the *Criminal Code*.

..........did have in their possession (specify anything) that A.B. knew had been used to commit an offence under s. 356(1)(a) or s. 356(1)(a.1) of the *Criminal Code* [or (specify anything) in respect of which they know an offence has been committed], to wit: (specify the particulars of the offence), contrary to s. 356(1)(a) of the *Criminal Code*.

..........did fraudulently redirect [or cause to be redirected] (specify anything) sent by post, to wit: (specify the particulars of the offence), contrary to s. 356(1)(a) of the *Criminal Code*.

Section 356(1)(b) Possession of stolen mail

A.B., on the (day) of (month), (year), at (specify time) in (specify place), did have in his possession (specify), in respect of which A.B. knew that an offence had been committed under s. 356(1)(a) of the *Criminal Code*, to wit: (specify the particulars of the offence), contrary to s. 356(1)(b) of the *Criminal Code*.

Section 357 Bringing into Canada property obtained by crime

A.B., on the (day) of (month), (year), at (specify time) in (specify place), did bring into [or have in] Canada (specify) that A.B. had obtained outside Canada by an act that would have been the offence of theft [or an offence under s. 342 of the *Criminal Code* or an offence under s. 354 of the *Criminal Code*] if it had been committed in Canada, to wit: (specify the particulars of the offence), contrary to s. 357 of the *Criminal Code*.

Section 362(1)(a) Obtaining anything by false pretences that may be the object of theft

A.B., on the (day) of (month), (year), at (specify time) in (specify place), by a false pretence did obtain [or cause to be delivered to C.D.] (specify) in respect of which the offence of theft may be committed, to wit: (specify the particulars of the offence), contrary to s. 362(1)(a) of the *Criminal Code*.

Section 362(1)(b) Obtaining credit by false pretences or fraud

A.B., on the (day) of (month), (year), at (specify time) in (specify place), did obtain credit by false pretence [or fraud] to wit: (specify the particulars of the offence), contrary to s. 362(1)(b) of the *Criminal Code*.

Section 362(1)(c), (d) False statement in writing

A.B., on the (day) of (month), (year), at (specify time) in (specify place),

..........knowingly, did make [or cause to be made], a false statement in writing with intent that it should be relied on with respect to the financial condition [or means or ability to pay] of A.B. [a person or organization] that A.B. was interested in [or that A.B. acts for] for the purpose of procuring the delivery of personal property, to wit: (specify the particulars of the offence), contrary to s. 362(1)(c) of the *Criminal Code*.

..........knowingly, did make [or cause to be made], a false statement in writing with intent that it should be relied on with respect to the financial condition [or means or ability to pay] of A.B. [a person or organization] that A.B. was interested in [or that A.B. acts for] for the purpose of procuring the payment of money, to wit: (specify the particulars of the offence), contrary to s. 362(1)(c) of the *Criminal Code*.

..........knowingly, did make [or cause to be made], a false statement in writing with intent that it should be relied on with respect to the financial condition [or means or ability to pay] of A.B. [a person or organization] that A.B. was interested in [or that A.B. acts for] for the purpose of procuring the making of a loan, to wit: (specify the particulars of the offence), contrary to s. 362(1)(c) of the *Criminal Code*.

..........knowingly, did make [or cause to be made], a false statement in writing with intent that it should be relied on with respect to the financial condition [or means or ability to pay] of A.B. [a person or organization] that A.B. was interested in [or that A.B. acts for] for the purpose of procuring the grant [or extension] of credit, to wit: (specify the particulars of the offence), contrary to s. 362(1)(c) of the *Criminal Code*.

..........knowingly, did make [or cause to be made], a false statement in writing with intent that it should be relied on with respect to the financial condition [or means or ability to pay] of A.B. [a person or organization] that A.B. was interested in [or that A.B. acts for] for the purpose of procuring the discount of an account receivable, to wit: (specify the particulars of the offence), contrary to s. 362(1)(c) of the *Criminal Code*.

..........knowingly, did make [or cause to be made], a false statement in writing with intent that it should be relied on with respect to the financial condition [or means or ability to pay] of A.B. [a person or organization] that A.B. was interested in [or that A.B. acts for] for the purpose of procuring the making (or accepting or discounting or endorsing) of a bill of exchange [or cheque or draft or promissory note], to wit: (specify the particulars of the offence), contrary to s. 362(1)(c) of the *Criminal Code*.

..........knowing that a false statement in writing had been made with respect to the financial condition [or means or ability to pay] of A.B. [a person or organization] that A.B. was interested in [or that A.B. acts for] did procure on the faith of that statement the delivery of personal property [or the payment of money or the making of a loan or the grant (or extension) of credit or the discount of an account receivable or the making (or accepting or discounting or endorsing) of a bill of exchange (or cheque or draft or promissory note)] for the benefit of A.B., to wit: (specify the particulars of the offence), contrary to s. 362(1)(d) of the *Criminal Code*.

Section 363 Obtaining execution of valuable security by fraud

A.B., on the (day) of (month), (year), at (specify time) in (specify place),

..........with intent to defraud [or injure] C.D., by a false pretence did cause [or induce] C.D. to execute [or make or accept or endorse or destroy] the whole of [or a part of] a valuable security, to wit: (specify the particulars of the offence), contrary to s. 363(a) of the *Criminal Code*.

..........with intent to defraud [or injure] C.D., by a false pretence did cause [or induce] C.D. to write [or impress or affix] a name [or seal] on paper [or parchment] in order that it may be made [or converted into or used or dealt with] as a valuable security, to wit: (specify the particulars of the offence), contrary to s. 363(b) of the *Criminal Code*.

Section 364(1) Fraudulently obtaining food and lodging

A.B., on the (day) of (month), (year), at (specify time) in (specify place), did fraudulently obtain food [or a beverage or accommodation] at a place that is in the business of providing it, to wit: (specify the particulars of the offence), contrary to s. 364(1) of the *Criminal Code*.

Section 365 Witchcraft and fortune-telling

A.B., on the (day) of (month), (year), at (specify time) in (specify place),

..........fraudulently did pretend to use [or to exercise] witchcraft [or sorcery or an enchantment or a conjuration], to wit: (specify the particulars of the offence), contrary to s. 365(a) of the *Criminal Code*.

..........fraudulently did undertake, for a consideration, to tell fortunes, to wit: (specify the particulars of the offence), contrary to s. 365(b) of the *Criminal Code*.

..........did pretend from his [or her] skill in [or knowledge of] an occult [or crafty] science to discover where [or in what manner] (specify a thing), that was supposed to have been stolen [or lost], may be found, to wit: (specify the particulars of the offence), contrary to s. 365(c) of the *Criminal Code*.

Section 366(1)(a) Forgery

A.B., on the (day) of (month), (year), at (specify time) in (specify place),

..........did make a false document, knowing it to be false, with intent that it should be acted on [or used] as genuine, to the prejudice of C.D., and did thereby commit forgery, to wit: (specify the particulars of the offence), contrary to s. 366(1)(a) of the *Criminal Code*.

..........did make a false document, knowing it to be false, with intent that C.D. should be induced by the belief that it was genuine, to do [or refrain from doing (specify), to wit: (specify the particulars of the offence), contrary to s. 366(1(b) of the *Criminal Code*.

Section 368(1) Use, trafficking or possession of forged document

A.B., on the (day) of (month), (year) at (specify time) in (specify place), knowing or believing a document was forged,

..........did use it [or deal with it or act upon it] as if the document were genuine, to wit: (specify the particulars of the offence), contrary to s. 368(1) of the *Criminal Code*.

..........did cause C.D. [or attempt to cause C.D.] to use it [or deal with it or act upon it] as if the document were genuine, to wit: (specify the particulars of the offence), contrary to s. 368(1) of the *Criminal Code*.

..........did transfer [or sell or offer to sell] the document [or make the document available] to C.C., knowing that [or being reckless as to whether] an offence will be committed under s. 368(1)(a) [or s. 368(1)(b)], to wit: (specify the particulars of the offence), contrary to s. 368(1) of the *Criminal Code*.

..........did possess the document with an intent to commit an offence under s. 368(1)(a) [or s. 368(1)(b) or s. 368(1)(c)], to wit: (specify the particulars of the offence), contrary to s. 368(1) of the *Criminal Code*.

Section 368.1 Forgery instruments

A.B., on the (day) of (month), (year) at (specify time) in (specify place), without lawful authority or excuse,

..........did make [or repair or buy or sell or export from Canada or import into Canada] an instrument [or an apparatus or a material or a thing] that A.B. knew has been used [or knows is adapted for use or is intended for use] by C.D. to commit forgery, to wit: (specify the particulars of the offence), contrary to s. 368.1 of the *Criminal Code*.

..........did possess an instrument [or an apparatus or a material or a thing] that A.B. knew has been used [or knows is adapted for use or is intended for use] by C.D. to commit forgery, to wit: (specify the particulars of the offence), contrary to s. 368.1 of the *Criminal Code*.

Section 369 Exchequer bill paper, revenue paper and public seals

A.B., on the (day) of (month), (year) at (specify time) in (specify place), without lawful authority or excuse,

..........did make or use exchequer bill paper [or revenue paper or paper that is used to make bank notes], to wit: (specify the particulars of the offence), contrary to s. 369 of the *Criminal Code*.

..........did make or use paper that is intended to resemble exchequer bill paper [or revenue paper or paper that is used to make bank notes], to wit: (specify the particulars of the offence), contrary to s. 369 of the *Criminal Code*.

..........did possess exchequer bill paper [or revenue paper or paper that is used to make bank notes], to wit: (specify the particulars of the offence), contrary to s. 369 of the *Criminal Code*.

...........did possess paper that is intended to resemble exchequer bill paper [or revenue paper or paper that is used to make bank notes], to wit: (specify the particulars of the offence), contrary to s. 369 of the *Criminal Code*.

..........did make [or reproduce or use] the public seal of Canada [or of the province of (specify) or of (specify a public body or authority) or of (specify a court of law)], to wit: (specify the particulars of the offence), contrary to s. 369 of the *Criminal Code*.

Section 370 Counterfeit proclamation, order, regulation or appointment

A.B., on the (day) of (month), (year), at (specify time) in (specify place), knowingly,

..........did print a proclamation [or notice] and did cause it falsely to purport to have been printed by the Queen's Printer for Canada [or the Queen's Printer of the province of (specify)], to wit: (specify the particulars of the offence), contrary to s. 370 of the *Criminal Code*.

..........did tender in evidence a copy of a proclamation [or an order or a regulation or an appointment] that did falsely purport to have been printed by the Queen's Printer for Canada [or the Queen's Printer for the province of (specify)], to wit: (specify the particulars of the offence), contrary to s. 370 of the *Criminal Code*.

Section 371 Message in false name

A.B., on the (day) of (month), (year), at (specify time) in (specify place), with intent to defraud, did cause a message to be sent as if it were sent under the authority of

C.D., knowing that it was not sent under that authority and with intent that it should be acted on as if it were, to wit: (specify the particulars of the offence), contrary to s. 371 of the *Criminal Code.*

Section 372(1) False information

A.B., on the (day) of (month), (year), at (specify time) in (specify place), with intent to injure [or alarm] C.D., did convey information that A.B. knew was false [or cause false information to be conveyed by letter or cause false information to be conveyed by a means of telecommunication], to wit: (specify the particulars of the offence), contrary to s. 372(1) of the *Criminal Code.*

Section 372(2) Indecent communications

A.B., on the (day) of (month), (year), at (specify time) in (specify place), with intent to alarm [or annoy] C.D., did make an indecent communication to C.D. [or E.F.] by a means of telecommunication, to wit: (specify the particulars of the offence), contrary to s. 372(2) of the *Criminal Code.*

Section 372(3) Harassing communications

A.B., on the (day) of (month), (year), at (specify time) in (specify place), without lawful excuse and with intent to harass C.D., did repeatedly communicate [or cause repeated communications to be made] with C.D. by a means of telecommunication, to wit: (specify the particulars of the offence), contrary to s. 372(3) of the *Criminal Code.*

Section 374 Drawing or using documents without authority

A.B., on the (day) of (month), (year), at (specify time) in (specify place),

..........with intent to defraud and without lawful authority, did make [or execute or draw or sign or accept or endorse] a document in the name [or on the account] of C.D. by procuration, to wit: (specify the particulars of the offence), contrary to s. 374(a) of the *Criminal Code.*

..........with intent to defraud and without lawful authority, did make use of [or utter] a document, knowing that it had been made [or executed or signed or accepted or endorsed] in the name [or on the account] of C.D. by procuration, to wit: (specify the particulars of the offence), contrary to s. 374(b) of the *Criminal Code.*

Section 375 Obtaining anything by instrument based on forged document

A.B., on the (day) of (month), (year), at (specify time) in (specify place), did demand [or receive or obtain] (specify) [or did cause or procure (specify) to be delivered (or paid) to C.D.] under [or on or by] virtue of an instrument issued under the authority of law knowing that it was based on a forged document, to wit: (specify the particulars of the offence), contrary to s. 375 of the *Criminal Code.*

Section 376(1) Counterfeiting stamp

A.B., on the (day) of (month), (year), at (specify time) in (specify place),

..........fraudulently, did use [or mutilate or affix or remove or counterfeit] a stamp [or a part of a stamp], to wit: (specify the particulars of the offence), contrary to s. 376(1)(a) of the *Criminal Code*.

..........knowingly and without lawful excuse, had in his [or her] possession a counterfeit stamp [or a stamp that had been fraudulently mutilated or (specify), a thing bearing a stamp of which a part had been fraudulently erased (or removed or concealed)], to wit: (specify the particulars of the offence), contrary to s. 376(1)(b) of the *Criminal Code*.

..........without lawful excuse, did make [or knowingly have in his (or her) possession] a die [or an instrument] that was capable of making the impression of a stamp [or part of a stamp], to wit: (specify the particulars of the offence), contrary to s. 376(1)(c) of the *Criminal Code*.

Section 376(2) Counterfeiting mark

A.B., on the (day) of (month), (year), at (specify time) in (specify place),

..........without lawful authority, did make a mark, to wit: (specify the particulars of the offence), contrary to s. 376(2) of the *Criminal Code*.

..........without lawful authority, did sell or expose for sale or have in his [or her] possession, a counterfeit mark, to wit: (specify the particulars of the offence), contrary to s. 376(2) of the *Criminal Code*.

..........did affix a mark to (specify), a thing that was required by law to be marked [or branded or sealed or wrapped] other than the thing to which the mark was originally affixed [or was intended to be affixed], to wit: (specify the particulars of the offence), contrary to s. 376(2) of the *Criminal Code*.

..........did affix a counterfeit mark to (specify) a thing that was required by law to be marked (or branded or sealed or wrapped), to wit: (specify the particulars of the offence, contrary to s. 376(2) of the *Criminal Code*.

Section 377 Damaging registers

A.B., on the (day) of (month), (year), at (specify time) in (specify place),

..........unlawfully did destroy [or deface or injure] a register [or part of a register] of birth [or baptism or marriages or deaths or burials] that was required [or authorized] by law to be kept in Canada [or a copy (or any part of a copy) of a register that was required by law to be transmitted to a registrar (or other officer)], to wit: (specify the particulars of the offence), contrary to s. 377(1)(a) of the *Criminal Code*.

..........unlawfully did insert [or cause to be inserted] in a register [or part of a register] of birth [or baptism or marriages or deaths or burials] that was required [or authorized] by law to be kept in Canada [or a copy (or any part of a copy) of such a register that was required by law to be transmitted to a registrar (or other officer)], an entry that A.B. knew was false of a matter relating to a birth [or baptism or marriage or death or burial] [or did erase a material part from that register (or copy)], to wit: (specify the particulars of the offence), contrary to s. 377(1)(b) of the *Criminal Code*.

..........unlawfully did destroy [or damage or obliterate or cause to be destroyed (or damaged or obliterated)] an election document, to wit: (specify the particulars of the offence), contrary to s. 377(1)(c) of the *Criminal Code*.

..........unlawfully did make [or cause to be made] an erasure [or alteration or interlineation] in [or on] an election document, to wit: (specify the particulars of the offence), contrary to s. 377(1)(d) of the *Criminal Code*.

Section 378(a) False certified copies of registers by authorized persons

A.B., on the (day) of (month), (year), at (specify time) in (specify place), being authorized [or required] by law to make [or issue] a certified copy of [or an extract from or a certificate in respect of] a register [or record or document], knowingly, did make [or issue] a false certified copy [or extract or certificate], to wit: (specify the particulars of the offence), contrary to s. 378(a) of the *Criminal Code*.

Section 378(b) False certified copies of registers by unauthorized persons

A.B., on the (day) of (month), (year), at (specify time) in (specify place), not being authorized or required by law to make [or issue] a certified copy of [or extract from or certificate in respect of] a register] [or record or document], fraudulently did make [or issue] a copy [or an extract or a certificate] that purported to be certified as authorized [or required] by law, to wit: (specify the particulars of the offence), contrary to s. 378(b) of the *Criminal Code*.

Section 378(c) False certificate or declaration regarding entries in registers

A.B., on the (day) of (month), (year), at (specify time) in (specify place), being authorized or required by law to make a certificate [or declaration] concerning a particular required for the purpose of making entries in a register [or record or document], knowingly and falsely, did make the certificate [or declaration], to wit: (specify the particulars of the offence), contrary to s. 378(c) of the *Criminal Code*.

Part X — Fraudulent Transactions Relating to Contracts and Trade

Section 380(1) Fraud

A.B., on the (day) of (month), (year), at (specify time) in (specify place), by deceit [or by falsehood or by fraudulent means], did defraud the public [or C.D.] of property [or of money or of a valuable security], to wit: (specify the particulars of the offence), contrary to s. 380(1) of the *Criminal Code*.

Section 380(2) Frauds affecting public market price

A.B., on the (day) of (month), (year), at (specify time) in (specify place), by deceit [or by falsehood or by fraudulent means], with intent to defraud, did affect the public market price of stocks [or shares or merchandise or (specify a thing that was offered for sale to the public)], to wit: (specify the particulars of the offence), contrary to s. 380(2) of the *Criminal Code*.

Section 380.2 Failure to comply with an order of prohibition

A.B., on the (day) of (month), (year), at (specify time) in (specify place), being bound by an order of prohibition prohibiting an offender from seeking [or obtaining or continuing] any employment [or being or becoming a volunteer] that involves having authority over the real property [or money or valuable security] of another person pursuant to s. 380.2 of the *Criminal Code*, did fail to comply with the order, to wit: (specify the particulars of the offence), contrary to s. 380.2 of the *Criminal Code*.

Section 381 Using mails to defraud

A.B., on the (day) of (month), (year), at (specify time) in (specify place), did make use of the mails for the purpose of transmitting [or delivering] letters [or circulars] concerning schemes devised [or intended] to deceive the public [or to defraud the public or for the purpose of obtaining money under false pretences], to wit: (specify the particulars of the offence), contrary to s. 381 of the *Criminal Code*.

Section 382 Fraudulent manipulation of stock exchange transactions

A.B., on the (day) of (month), (year), at (specify time) in (specify place), through the facility of a stock exchange [or curb market or market], with intent to create a false [or misleading] appearance of active public trading in a security [or with intent to create a false or misleading appearance with respect to the market price of a security], did effect a transaction in the security that involved no change in the beneficial ownership, to wit: (specify the particulars of the offence), contrary to s. 382 of the *Criminal Code*.

A.B. on the (day) of (month), (year), in (specify place), through the facility of a stock exchange [or curb market or market] with intent to create a false [or misleading] appearance of active public trading in a security [or with intent to create a false or misleading appearance with respect to the market price of a security] did enter an order for the purchase of the security knowing that an order of substantially the same size at substantially the same time and at substantially the same price for the sale of the security had been [or would be] entered by [or for] the same [or different] persons, to wit: (specify the particulars of the offence), contrary to s. 382 of the *Criminal Code*.

A.B., on the (day) of (month), (year) at (specify time) in (specify place), through the facility of a stock exchange [or curb market or market], with intent to create a false [or misleading] appearance of active public trading in a security [or with intent to create a false or misleading appearance with respect to the market price of a security] did enter an order for the sale of a security knowing that an order of substantially the same size at substantially the same time and at substantially the same price for the purchase of the security had been [or would be] entered by [or for] the same [or different] persons, to wit: (specify the particulars of the offence), contrary to s. 382 of the *Criminal Code*.

Section 382.1(1) Prohibited insider trading

A.B., on the (day) of (month), (year), at (specify time) in (specify place),

..........did buy [or sell] a security knowingly using insider information that they possessed by virtue of being a shareholder of the issuer of that security, to wit: (specify the particulars of the offence), contrary to s. 382.1(1) of the *Criminal Code*.

..........did buy [or sell] a security knowingly using insider information that they possessed by virtue of [or obtained in the course of] their business [or professional] relationship with that issuer, to wit: (specify the particulars of the offence), contrary to s. 382.1(1) of the *Criminal Code*.

..........did buy [or sell] a security knowingly using insider information that they possessed by virtue of {or obtained in the course of] a proposed takeover [or reorganization of or amalgamation with or merger with or business combination with] the issuer of the security, to wit: (specify the particulars of the offence), contrary to s. 382.1(1) of the *Criminal Code*.

..........did buy [or sell] a security knowingly using insider information that they possessed by virtue of [or obtained in the course of their employment [or office or duties or occupation] with that issuer [or with a person referred to in s. 382.1(1)(a), (b) or (c)], to wit: (specify the particulars of the offence), contrary to s. 382.1(1) of the *Criminal Code*.

..........did buy [or sell] a security knowingly using insider information that they obtained from a person who possess [or obtained] the information [specify a manner referred to in s. 382.1(1)(a), (b), (c) or (d)], to wit: (specify the particulars of the offence), contrary to s. 382.1(1) of the *Criminal Code*.

Section 382.1(2) Tipping — conveying inside information

A.B., on the (day) of (month), (year), at (specify time) in (specify place), knowingly did convey inside information that A.B. possessed [or obtained in a manner referred to in s. 382.1(1) to C.D., knowing that there was a risk that C.D. would use the information to buy [or sell] a security to which the information relates [or that C.D. would convey the information to E.F. who may buy or sell such a security], to wit: (specify the particulars of the offence), contrary to s. 382.1(2) of the *Criminal Code*.

Section 383(1) Gaming in stocks or merchandise

A.B., on the (day) of (month), (year), at (specify time) in (specify place), with intent to make gain [or profit] by the rise [or fall] in price of the stock of an incorporated [or unincorporated] company [or undertaking], [or of any goods or wares or merchandise], did make [or sign or authorize to be made or signed] a contract [or an agreement], purporting to be for the purchase [or sale] of shares of stock [or goods or wares or merchandise] without the bona fide intention of acquiring [or selling] the shares [goods or wares or merchandise], to wit: (specify the particulars of the offence), contrary to s. 383(1) of the *Criminal Code*.

A.B., on the (day) of (month), (year), at (specify time) in (specify place), with intent to make gain [or profit] by the rise [or fall] in price of the stock of an incorporated [or unincorporated] company [or undertaking], [or of any goods or wares or merchandise], did make [or sign or authorize to be made or signed] a contract [or an agreement] purporting to be for the purchase [or sale] of shares of stock [or goods or wares or merchandise] in respect of which no delivery of the thing sold [or purchased] was made [or received] and without the bona fide intention of making or receiving delivery thereof], to wit: (specify the particulars of the offence), contrary to s. 383(1) of the *Criminal Code*.

Section 384 Broker reducing stock by selling for his own account

A.B., on the (day) of (month), (year), at (specify time) in (specify place), being an individual [or a member or an employee of a partnership or a director or officer or an employee of a corporation] where A.B. [or the partnership or corporation] is employed as a broker by a customer to buy and carry on margin any shares of an incorporated [or unincorporated] company [or undertaking], thereafter did sell [or cause to be sold] shares of the company [or undertaking] for any account in which A.B. [or his or her firm or a partner or the corporation or a director thereof] had a direct [or an indirect] interest, if the intentional effect of the sale was to reduce the amount of those shares in the hands of the broker [or under his (or her) control in the ordinary course of business] below the amount of those shares that the broker should be carrying for all customers, to wit: (specify the particulars of the offence), contrary to s. 384 of the *Criminal Code*.

Section 385(1) Fraudulent concealment of title documents

A.B., on the (day) of (month), (year), at (specify time) in (specify place), being a vendor [or mortgagor] of property [or of a chose in action] [or being a solicitor for or agent of a vendor or mortgagor of property or a chose in action] was served with a written demand for an abstract of title by [or on behalf of] the purchaser [or mortgagee] before the completion of the purchase [or mortgage], and with intent to defraud and for the purpose of inducing the purchaser [or mortgagee] to accept the title offered [or produced] to him [or her], did conceal from him [or her] a settlement [or deed or will or other instrument] material to the title [or any encumbrance on the title] [or did falsify any pedigree on which the title depended], to wit: (specify the particulars of the offence), contrary to s. 385(1) of the *Criminal Code*.

Section 386 Fraudulent registration of title

A.B., on the (day) of (month), (year), at (specify time) in (specify place),

..........as principal [or agent] in a proceeding to register title to real property [or in a transaction relating to real property that was (or was proposed) to be registered], knowingly and with intent to deceive, did make a material false statement [or representation], to wit: (specify the particulars of the offence), contrary to s. 386 of the *Criminal Code*.

..........as principal [or agent] in a proceeding to register title to real property [or in a transaction relating to real property that was (or was proposed) to be registered], knowingly and with intent to deceive, did suppress [or conceal] from a judge [or registrar or any person employed by or assisting the registrar] a material document [or fact or matter or information or was privy to anything just mentioned], to wit: (specify the particulars of the offence), contrary to s. 386 of the *Criminal Code*.

Section 387 Fraudulent sale of real property

A.B., on the (day) of (month), (year), at (specify time) in (specify place), knowing of an unregistered prior sale [or of an existing unregistered grant or mortgage or hypothec or privilege or encumbrance] of [or on] real property, fraudulently did sell the property [or part of the property], to wit: (specify the particulars of the offence), contrary to s. 387 of the *Criminal Code*.

Section 388 Misleading receipt

A.B., on the (day) of (month), (year), at (specify time) in (specify place), wilfully

..........with intent to mislead [or injure or defraud] C.D., whether or not C.D. was known to A.B., did give C.D. (specify) that purported to be a receipt for [or an acknowledgment of] property that had been delivered to [or received by] A.B. before the property referred to in the purported receipt [or acknowledgment] had been delivered to [or received by] A.B., to wit: (specify the particulars of the offence), contrary to s. 388(a) of the *Criminal Code*.

..........did accept [or transmit or use] a purported receipt [or acknowledgment] referred to in s. 388(a), to wit: (specify the particulars of the offence), contrary to s. 388(b) of the *Criminal Code*.

Section 389(1) Fraudulent disposal of goods on which money advanced

A.B., on the (day) of (month), (year), at (specify time) in (specify place),

..........having shipped [or delivered] to C.D., the keeper of a warehouse [or to a factor or agent or carrier] (specify) thereafter on which E.F., the consignee thereof had advanced money [or had given valuable security], thereafter, with intent to deceive [or defraud or injure] the consignee, did dispose of it in a manner that was different from and inconsistent with the agreement that had been made in that behalf between A.B. and the consignee, to wit: (specify the particulars of the offence), contrary to s. 389(1)(a) of the *Criminal Code*.

..........knowingly and wilfully, did aid [or assist] C.D. to make a disposition of (specify anything mentioned in s. 389(1)(a) of the *Criminal Code*) for the purpose of deceiving [or defrauding or injuring] the consignee, to wit: (specify the particulars of the offence), contrary to s. 389(1)(b) of the *Criminal Code*.

Section 390 Fraudulent receipts under *Bank Act*

A.B., on the (day) of (month), (year), at (specify time) in (specify place), wilfully,

..........did make a false statement in a receipt [or certificate or acknowledgment] for (specify) that might be used for a purpose mentioned in the *Bank Act*, to wit: (specify the particulars of the offence), contrary to s. 390(a) of the *Criminal Code*.

..........after giving to C.D. [or after C.D. employed by A.B. to his (or her) knowledge has given to E.F. or after obtaining and endorsing or assigning to E.F.] a receipt [or certificate or acknowledgment] for (specify) that might be used for a purpose mentioned in the *Bank Act*, without the consent in writing of the holder [or endorsee] [or without the production and delivery of the receipt or certificate or acknowledgment] did alienate [or part with or did not deliver to the holder or owner] the property mentioned in the receipt [or certificate or acknowledgment], to wit: (specify the particulars of the offence), contrary to s. 390(b) of the *Criminal Code*.

Section 392 Disposal of property to defraud creditors

A.B., on the (day) of (month), (year), at (specify time) in (specify place),

..........with intent to defraud his [or her] creditors did make [or cause to be made] a gift [or conveyance or assignment or sale or transfer or delivery] of his [or her] property [or did remove (or conceal or dispose of) any of his (or her) property], to wit: (specify the particulars of the offence), contrary to s. 392(a) of the *Criminal Code*.

..........with intent that C.D. should defraud his [or her] creditors, did receive property by means of [or in relation to] which such an offence had been committed, to wit: (specify the particulars of the offence), contrary to s. 392(b) of the *Criminal Code*.

Section 393 Fraud in relation to fares

A.B., on the (day) of (month), (year), at (specify time) in (specify place),

..........whose duty it was to collect a fare [or toll or ticket or admission] wilfully did fail to collect it [or did collect less than the proper amount payable in respect thereof or did accept to collect it (or for collecting less than the proper amount payable in respect thereof)], to wit: (specify the particulars of the offence), contrary to s. 393(1) of the *Criminal Code*.

..........did give [or offer] valuable consideration to C.D., a person whose duty it was to collect a fare [or toll or ticket or admission fee], for failing to collect it [or for collecting an amount less than the amount payable in respect thereof], to wit: (specify the particulars of the offence), contrary to s. 393(2) of the *Criminal Code*.

Section 393(3) Fraudulently obtaining transportation

A.B., on the (day) of (month), (year), at (specify time) in (specify place), by any false pretence [or fraud] unlawfully did obtain transportation by land [or water or air], to wit: (specify the particulars of the offence), contrary to s. 393(3) of the *Criminal Code*.

Section 394 Fraud in relation to minerals

A.B., on the (day) of (month), (year), at (specify time) in (specify place),

..........being the holder of a lease [or licence] issued under (specify an Act relating to the mining of precious metals) [or by the owner of land] that was supposed to contain valuable minerals, by a fraudulent device [or contrivance], did defraud [or attempt to defraud] C.D. of valuable minerals obtained under [or reserved by] the lease [or licence], to wit: (specify the particulars of the offence), contrary to s. 394(1)(a) of the *Criminal Code*.

..........being the holder of a lease [or licence] issued under (specify an Act relating to the mining of precious metals) [or by the owner of land] that was supposed to contain valuable minerals, by a fraudulent device [or contrivance], did defraud [or attempt to defraud] C.D. of money [or a valuable interest or thing] payable in respect of the lease [or licence], to wit: (specify the particulars of the offence), contrary to s. 394(1)(a) of the *Criminal Code*.

..........not being the owner [or the owner's agent or a person acting under lawful authority], did sell a valuable mineral that was unrefined [or partly refined or uncut or unprocessed], to wit: (specify the particulars of the offence), contrary to s. 394(2) of the *Criminal Code*.

..........did buy a valuable mineral that was unrefined [or partly refined or uncut or unprocessed] from C.D., a person A.B. had reason to believe was not the owner [or the owner's agent or a person acting under lawful authority], to wit: (specify the particulars of the offence), contrary to s. 394(3) of the *Criminal Code*.

Section 394.1 Possession of stolen or fraudulently obtained valuable minerals

A.B., on the (day) of (month), (year), at (specify time) in (specify place), did possess a valuable mineral that was unrefined [or partly refined or uncut or unprocessed] that had been stolen [or dealt with contrary to s. 394], to wit: (specify the particulars of the offence), contrary to s. 394.1(1) of the *Criminal Code*.

Section 396(1) Fraud in relation to mines

A.B., on the (day) of (month), (year), at (specify time) in (specify place),

..........did add (specify) to [or remove (specify) from] an existing [or a prospective] mine [or mining claim or oil well] with a fraudulent intent to affect the result of an assay [or a test or a valuation] that had been made [or was to be made] with respect to the mine [or mining claim or oil well], to wit: (specify the particulars of the offence), contrary to s. 396(1)(a) of the *Criminal Code*.

..........did add (specify) to [or remove (specify) from or tamper with] a sample [or material] that had been taken [or was being or was about to be taken] from a existing [or prospective] mine [or mining claim or oil well] for the purpose of being assayed [or tested or otherwise valued] with a fraudulent intent to affect the result of the assay [or test or valuation], to wit: (specify the particulars of the offence), contrary to s. 396(1)(b) of the *Criminal Code*.

Section 397(1) Falsification of book, paper, writing, valuable security or document

A.B., on the (day) of (month), (year), at (specify time) in (specify place),

..........with intent to defraud, did destroy [or mutilate or alter or falsify or made a false entry in] a book [or a paper or a writing or a valuable security or a document], to wit: (specify the particulars of the offence), contrary to s. 397(1)(a) of the *Criminal Code*.

..........with intent to defraud, did omit a material particular from [or alter a material particular in] a book [or a paper or a writing or a valuable security or a document], to wit: (specify the particulars of the offence), contrary to s. 397(1)(b) of the *Criminal Code*.

Section 397(2) Being privy to the falsification of a book, paper, writing, valuable security or document

A.B., on the (day) of (month), (year), at (specify time) in (specify place), with intent to defraud A.B.'s creditors.

..........was privy to the destruction of [or mutilation of or alteration of or falsification of or making of a false entry in] (specify a book or a paper or a writing or a valuable security or a document), to wit: (specify the particulars of the offence), contrary to s. 397(2) of the *Criminal Code*.

..........was privy to the omission of a material particular from [or alteration of a material particular in] (specify a book or a paper or a writing or a valuable security or a document), to wit: (specify the particulars of the offence), contrary to s. 397(2) of the *Criminal Code*.

Section 398 Falsification of employment record

A.B., on the (day) of (month), (year), at (specify time) in (specify place), with intent to deceive, did falsify an employment record by (specify the means), to wit: (specify the particulars of the offence), contrary to s. 398 of the *Criminal Code*.

Section 399 Falsification of statement or return of public officer

A.B., on the (day) of (month), (year), at (specify time) in (specify place), being entrusted with the receipt [or custody or management] of any part of the public statement [or return] of any sum of money collected by A.B. [or entrusted to his (or her) care] [or any balance of money in his hands (or under his (or her) control)], to wit: (specify the particulars of the offence), contrary to s. 399 of the *Criminal Code*.

Section 400(1) Falsification of prospectus

A.B., on the (day) of (month), (year), at (specify time) in (specify place), did make [or circulate or publish] a written [or oral] prospectus [or statement or an account], that A.B. knew was false in a material particular with intent to induce C.D. and E.F., to become shareholders [or partners] in a company [or to deceive (or defraud) the members (or shareholder or creditors), of a company or to induce C.D. to entrust (or advance) a thing to a company or to induce C.D. to enter into a security for the benefit of a company], to wit: (specify the particulars of the offence), contrary to s. 400(1) of the *Criminal Code*.

Section 401(1) Obtaining carriage by false billing

A.B., on the (day) of (month), (year), at (specify time) in (specify place), by means of a false [or misleading] representation, knowingly did obtain [or attempt to obtain] the carriage of (specify a thing) by C.D. into a country [or province or district or other place], where the importation [or transportation] of it was, in the circumstances of the case, unlawful, to wit: (specify the particulars of the offence), contrary to s. 401(1) of the *Criminal Code*.

Section 402(1) Trader or businessman failing to keep accounts

A.B., on the (day) of (month), (year), at (specify time) in (specify place), being a trader [or in business], was indebted in an amount exceeding $1,000 and was unable to pay his [or her] creditors in full and had not kept books of account that, in the ordinary course of the trade [or business] in which A.B. was engaged, were necessary to exhibit [or explain] his [or her] transactions, to wit: (specify the particulars of the offence), contrary to s. 402(1) of the *Criminal Code*.

Section 402.2(1) Identity theft

A.B., on the (day) of (month), (year) at (specify time) in (specify place), knowingly

...........did obtain the identity information of C.D. in circumstances that gave rise to a reasonable inference that the identity information was intended to be used to commit the offence of (specify an offence that includes fraud or deceit or falsehood as an element of the offence), to wit: (specify the particulars of the offence), contrary to s. 402.2(1) of the *Criminal Code*.

...........did possess the identity information of C.D. in circumstances that gave rise to a reasonable inference that the identity information was intended to be used to commit the offence of (specify an offence that includes fraud or deceit or falsehood as an element of the offence), to wit: (specify the particulars of the offence), contrary to s. 402.2(1) of the *Criminal Code*.

Section 402.2(2) Trafficking in identity information

A.B., on the (day) of (month), (year) at (specify time) in (specify place),

..........did transmit [or make available or distribute or sell or offer for sale] the identity information of C.D. knowing that [or being reckless whether] the information was intended to be used to commit the offence of (specify an offence that includes fraud or deceit or falsehood as an element of the offence), to wit: (specify the particulars of the offence), contrary to s. 402.2(1) of the *Criminal Code*.

..........did possess the identity information of C.D. knowing that [or being reckless whether] the information was intended to be used to commit the offence of (specify an offence that includes fraud or deceit or falsehood as an element of the offence), to wit: (specify the particulars of the offence), contrary to s. 402.2(1) of the *Criminal Code*.

Section 403(1) Identity fraud

A.B., on the (day) of (month), (year) at (specify time) in (specify place), fraudulently

..........did personate C.D. with intent to gain advantage for C.D. [or E.F.], to wit: (specify the particulars of the offence), contrary to s. 403 of the *Criminal Code*.

..........did personate C.D. with intent to obtain property [or an interest in property], to wit: (specify the particulars of the offence), contrary to s. 403 of the *Criminal Code*.

..........did personate C.D. with intent to cause disadvantage to C.D. [or E.F.], to wit: (specify the particulars of the offence), contrary to s. 403 of the *Criminal Code*.

..........did personate C.D. with intent to avoid arrest [or prosecution], to wit: (specify the particulars of the offence), contrary to s. 403 of the *Criminal Code*.

..........did personate C.D. with intent to obstruct [or defeat or pervert] the course of justice, to wit: (specify the particulars of the offence), contrary to s. 403 of the *Criminal Code*.

Section 404 Personation at an examination

A.B., on the (day) of (month), (year), at (specify time) in (specify place),

..........falsely, with intent to gain advantage for himself [or herself or C.D.], did personate C.D., a candidate at a competitive [or a qualifying] examination held under the authority of law [or in connection with a university (or a college or a school)], to wit: (specify the particulars of the offence), contrary to s. 404 of the *Criminal Code*.

..........did knowingly avail himself of the results of the personation of himself [or herself or C.D.], a candidate at a competitive [or a qualifying] examination held under the authority of law [or in connection with a university (or a college or a school)], to wit: (specify the particulars of the offence), contrary to s. 404 of the *Criminal Code*.

Section 405 Acknowledging instrument in false name

A.B., on the (day) of (month), (year), at (specify time) in (specify place), without lawful authority or excuse, did acknowledge, in the name of C.D., before a court [or a judge or (specify another person authorized to receive the acknowledgment)] a recognizance of bail [or a confession of judgment or a consent to judgment or a judgment or a deed or (specify other instrument)], to wit: (specify the particulars of the offence), contrary to s. 405 of the *Criminal Code*.

Section 407 Forging a trademark

A.B., on the (day) of (month), (year), at (specify time) in (specify place), with intent to deceive [or defraud] the public [or a person (whether ascertained or not)], did forge a trademark, to wit: (specify the particulars of the offence), contrary to s. 407 of the *Criminal Code*.

Section 408 Passing off

A.B., on the (day) of (month), (year), at (specify time) in (specify place),

..........with intent to deceive [or defraud] the public [or C.D.], did pass off other wares [or services] as and for those ordered [or required], to wit: (specify the particulars of the offence), contrary to s. 408(a) of the *Criminal Code*.

..........with intent to deceive or defraud the public [or C.D.], did make use, in association with wares [or with services] of a description that was false in a material aspect as to the kind [or the quality or the quantity or the composition or the geographical origin or the mode of manufacture or the mode of production or the mode of performance] of such wares [or services], to wit: (specify the particulars of the offence), contrary to s. 408(b) of the *Criminal Code*.

Section 409(1) Possession of instruments for forging trademark

A.B., on the (day) of (month), (year), at (specify time) in (specify place), did make [or have in his [or her] possession or dispose of] a die [or a block or a machine or (specify some other instrument)], designed [or intended] to be used in forging a trademark, to wit: (specify the particulars of the offence), contrary to s. 409(1) of the *Criminal Code*.

Section 410(a) Defacing, concealing or removing trademark

A.B., on the (day) of (month), (year), at (specify time) in (specify place), with intent to deceive [or to defraud], did deface [or conceal or remove] a trademark [or the name of C.D. from (specify the thing) without the consent of C.D.], to wit: (specify the particulars of the offence), contrary to s. 410(a) of the *Criminal Code*.

Section 410(b) Using bottle or siphon bearing trademark

A.B., on the (day) of (month), (year), at (specify time) in (specify place), being a manufacturer [or dealer or trader or bottler] with intent to deceive [or defraud], did fill any bottle [or siphon] that bore the trademark [or name] of C.D. without the consent of that C.D. with a beverage [or milk or by-product of milk or specify other liquid commodity] for the purpose of sale [or traffic], to wit: (specify the particulars of the offence), contrary to s. 410(b) of the *Criminal Code*.

Section 411 Reconditioned goods

A.B., on the (day) of (month), (year), at (specify time) in (specify place), did sell [or expose (or have in his [or her] possession) for sale or advertise for sale] goods that had been used [or reconditioned or remade] and that bore the trademark [or the trade-name] of A.B. without making full disclosure that the goods had been reconditioned [or rebuilt or remade] for sale and that they were not in the condition in which they were originally made [or produced], to wit: (specify the particulars of the offence), contrary to s. 411 of the *Criminal Code*.

Section 413 Falsely claiming royal warrant

A.B., on the (day) of (month), (year), at (specify time) in (specify place), did falsely represent that goods were made by A.B., a person holding a royal warrant [or for the service of Her Majesty (or a member of the Royal Family or a public department)], to wit: (specify the particulars of the offence), contrary to s. 413 of the *Criminal Code*.

Section 415 Offences in relation to wreck

A.B., on the (day) of (month), (year), at (specify time) in (specify place),

..........did secrete a wreck [or deface (or obliterate) the marks on a wreck or use any means to disguise (or conceal) the fact that anything is a wreck or in any manner conceal the character of a wreck] from C.D., a person entitled to inquire into the wreck, to wit: (specify the particulars of the offence), contrary to s. 415(a) of the *Criminal Code*.

..........did receive a wreck, knowing that it was a wreck, from C.D., a person other than the owner thereof [or a receiver of the wreck] and did not within 48 hours thereafter inform the receiver of the wreck, to wit: (specify the particulars of the offence), contrary to s. 415(b) of the *Criminal Code*.

..........did offer a wreck for sale [or otherwise deal with it] knowing that it was a wreck and not having a lawful authority to sell [or deal with] it, to wit: (specify the particulars of the offence), contrary to s. 415(c) of the *Criminal Code*.

..........did keep a wreck in his [or her] possession knowing that it was a wreck without lawful authority, to keep it for any time longer than the time reasonably necessary to deliver it to the receiver of the wreck, to wit: (specify the particulars of the offence), contrary to s. 415(d) of the *Criminal Code*.

..........did board a vessel that was wrecked [or stranded or in distress] against the will of C.D., the master, unless A.B. was a receiver of the wreck [or a person acting under orders of a receiver of the wreck], to wit: (specify the particulars of the offence), contrary to s. 415(e) of the *Criminal Code*.

Section 417(1) Applying or removing marks without authority

A.B., on the (day) of (month), (year), at (specify time) in (specify place),

..........without lawful authority, did apply a distinguishing mark to (specify the thing), to wit: (specify the particulars of the offence), contrary to s. 417(1)(a) of the *Criminal Code*.

..........with intent to conceal the property of Her Majesty in public stores, did remove [or destroy or obliterate] a distinguishing mark in whole [or in part], to wit: (specify the particulars of the offence), contrary to s. 417(1)(b) of the *Criminal Code*.

Section 417(2) Unlawful transactions in public stores

A.B., on the (day) of (month), (year), at (specify time) in (specify place), without lawful authority, did receive [or possess or keep or sell or deliver public stores that A.B. knew bore a distinguishing mark, to wit: (specify the particulars of the offence), contrary to s. 417(2) of the *Criminal Code*.

Section 418(1) Selling defective stores to the government

A.B., on the (day) of (month), (year), at (specify time) in (specify place),

..........did knowingly sell [or deliver] to Her Majesty defective stores, to wit: (specify the particulars of the offence), contrary to s. 418(1) of the *Criminal Code*.

..........did commit an act of fraud upon Her Majesty [or an officer in Her Majesty's service] in connection with the sale [or lease or delivery or manufacture] of certain stores, to wit: (specify the particulars of the offence), contrary to s. 418(1) of the *Criminal Code*.

Section 418(2) Being a party to the selling of defective stores to the government

A.B., on the (day) of (month), (year), at (specify time) in (specify place),

..........being a director [or an officer or an agent or an employee] of (specify the corporation) that did commit, by fraud, the offence of selling defective stores to the government, knowingly did take part in the fraud, to wit: (specify the particulars of the offence), contrary to s. 418(2)(a) of the *Criminal Code.*

..........being a director [or an officer or an agent or an employee] of (specify the corporation) that did commit, by fraud, the offence of selling defective stores to the government, did know [or had reason to suspect] that the fraud was being committed [or had been (or was about to be) committed] and did not inform the responsible government [or a department thereof] of Her Majesty, to wit: (specify the particulars of the offence), contrary to s. 418(2)(b) of the *Criminal Code.*

Section 419 Unlawful use of military uniforms or certificates

A.B., on the (day) of (month), (year), at (specify time) in (specify place), without lawful authority,

..........did wear a uniform of the Canadian Forces [or specify other naval or army or air force or a uniform that was so similar to the uniform of any of those forces that it was likely to be mistaken therefor], to wit: (specify the particulars of the offence), contrary to s. 419(a) of the *Criminal Code.*

..........did wear a distinctive mark relating to wound received [or service performed] in war [or a military medal (or ribbon or badge or chevron or any decoration or order) that was awarded for war services or any imitation thereof or any mark (or device or thing) that was likely to be mistaken for any such mark (or medal or ribbon or badge or chevron or decoration or order)], to wit: (specify the particulars of the offence), contrary to s. 419(b) of the *Criminal Code.*

..........did have in his [or her] possession a certificate of discharge [or certificate of release or statement of service or identity card] from the Canadian Forces [or specify other naval (or army or air) force] that had not been issued to and does not belong to him, to wit: (specify the particulars of the offence), contrary to s. 419(c) of the *Criminal Code.*

..........did have in his [or her] possession a commission [or warrant or a certificate of discharge or certificate of release or statement of service or identity card] issued to A.B., an officer [or a person] in [or who has been in] the Canadian Forces [or specify other naval (or army or air) force] that contained any alteration that was not verified by the initials of the officer who issued it [or by the initials of an officer thereto lawfully authorized], to wit: (specify the particulars of the offence), contrary to s. 419(d) of the *Criminal Code.*

Section 420(1) Buying military stores from members of Canadian Forces or from deserter

A.B., on the (day) of (month), (year), at (specify time) in (specify place), did buy [or receive or detain] from C.D., a member of the Canadian Forces [or a deserter or an absentee without leave therefrom] military stores that were owned by Her Majesty [or for which the member (or deserter or absentee without leave) was accountable to Her Majesty] to wit: (specify the particulars of the offence), contrary to s. 420(1) of the *Criminal Code.*

Section 422(1) Breach of contract endangering human life

A.B., on the (day) of (month), (year), at (specify time) in (specify place), wilfully did break a contract knowing [or having reasonable cause to believe] that the probable consequences of doing so would be to endanger human life [or to cause bodily injury or to expose valuable property to destruction (or to serious injury) or to deprive the inhabitants of a city (or a place or part of a city or part of a place) wholly (or to a great extent) of their supply of light (or power or gas or water) or to delay (or prevent) the running of a locomotive engine (or tender or freight train or passenger train or car) on a railway that was a common carrier], to wit: (specify the particulars of the offence), contrary to s. 422(1) of the *Criminal Code*.

Section 423(1) Intimidation

A.B., on the (day) of (month), (year) at (specify time) in (specify place), wrongfully and without lawful authority, for the purpose of compelling C.D. to (specify anything done or not done),

..........used violence to [or used threats of violence to or injured] C.D. [or E.F., the spouse (or common law partner or child) of C.D. or the property of C.D.], to wit: (specify the particulars of the offence), contrary to s. 423(1) of the *Criminal Code*.

..........intimidated [or attempted to intimidate] C.D. [or E.F., a relative of C.D.] by threats that violence [or injury or damage or punishment] would be done to [or inflicted upon] C.D. [or E.F., a relative of C.D. or the property of C.D. (or E.F.)], to wit: (specify the particulars of the offence), contrary to s. 423(1) of the *Criminal Code*.

..........persistently followed C.D., to wit: (specify the particulars of the offence), contrary to s. 423(1) of the *Criminal Code*.

..........hid [or deprived C.D. of the use of or hindered C.D. in the use of] tools [or clothes or property] owned [or used] by C.D., to wit: (specify the particulars of the offence), contrary to s. 423(1) of the *Criminal Code*.

..........with E.F, followed C.D., in a disorderly manner on a highway, to wit: (specify the particulars of the offence), contrary to s. 423(1) of the *Criminal Code*.

..........did beset [or watched] the place where C.D. resided [or worked or carried on business or happened to be], to wit: (specify the particulars of the offence), contrary to s. 423(1) of the *Criminal Code*.

..........blocked [or obstructed] a highway, to wit: (specify the particulars of the offence), contrary to s. 423(1) of the *Criminal Code*.

Section 423.1 Intimidation of a justice system participant

A.B., on the (day) of (month), (year), at (specify time) in (specify place), without lawful authority and with intent to provoke a state of fear in C.D. and E.F. [or the general pubic in order to impede the administration of justice or C.D. a justice system participant in order to impede C.D. in the performance of his (or her) duties) or C.D., a journalist in order to impede C.D. in the transmission of information in relation to a criminal organization]

..........used violence against [or destroyed or caused damage to the property of] C.D., a justice system participant [or a journalist or E.F., a person known to C.D., a justice system participant (or a journalist)], to wit: (specify the particulars of the offence), contrary to s. 423.1(1) of the *Criminal Code.*

..........threatened to use violence against [or destroyed or caused damage to the property of] C.D., a justice system participant [or a journalist or E.F., a person known to C.D., a justice system participant (or a journalist)], to wit: (specify the particulars of the offence), contrary to s. 423.1(1) of the *Criminal Code.*

..........persistently or repeatedly followed C.D., a justice system participant [or a journalist or E.F., a person known to C.D., a justice system participant (or a journalist)][in a disorderly manner on a highway], to wit: (specify the particulars of the offence), contrary to s. 423.1(1) of the *Criminal Code.*

..........repeatedly communicated with C.D., a justice system participant [or a journalist or E.F., a person known to C.D., a justice system participant (or a journalist)], to wit: (specify the particulars of the offence), contrary to s. 423.1(1) of the *Criminal Code.*

..........beset [or watched] the place where C.D., a justice system participant [or a journalist or E.F., a person known to C.D., a justice system participant (or a journalist)] resided [or worked or attended school or carried on business or happened to be], to wit: (specify the particulars of the offence), contrary to s. 423.1(1) of the *Criminal Code.*

Section 424 Threat against internationally protected person

A.B., on the (day) of (month), (year), at (specify time) in (specify place), threatened to commit (specify an offence under s. 235, 236, 266, 267, 268, 269, 269.1, 271, 272, 273, 279 or 279.1), against C.D., an internationally protected person], to wit: (specify the particulars of the offence), contrary to s. 424 of the *Criminal Code.*

A.B., on the (day) of (month), (year), at (specify time) in (specify place), threatened to commit (specify an offence under s. 431) against the premises [or the residence or transport] of C.D., an internationally protected person, to wit: (specify the particulars of the offence), contrary to s. 424 of the *Criminal Code.*

Section 424.1 Threat against United Nations or associated personnel

A.B., on the (day) of (month), (year), at (specify time) in (specify place), with intent to compel C.D. [or C.D. and E.F. or (specify a state or international or intergovernmental organization)] to (specify an act done or refrained from being done), threatened to commit (specify an offence under s. 235, 236, 266, 267, 268, 269, 269.1, 271, 272, 273, 279 or 279.1), against C.D., United Nations personnel, to wit: (specify the particulars of the offence), contrary to s. 424.1 of the *Criminal Code.*

A.B., on the (day) of (month), (year), at (specify time) in (specify place), with intent to compel C.D. [or C.D. and E.F. or (specify a state or international organization or inter-governmental organization)] to (specify an act done or refrained from being done), threatened to commit (specify an offence under s. 431) against the premises [or the residence or transport] of C.D., United Nations personnel, to wit: (specify the particulars of the offence), contrary to s. 424.1 of the *Criminal Code.*

Section 425(a) Refusing to employ trade union members

A.B., on the (day) of (month), (year), at (specify time) in (specify place), being an employer [or the agent of C.D., an employer] wrongfully and without lawful authority refused to employ E.F. [or dismissed E.F. from his employment] for the reason only that the said E.F. was a member of a lawful trade union [or a lawful association (or combination) of workmen (or employees)] formed for the purpose of advancing, in a lawful manner, their interests and organized for their protection in the regulation of wages and conditions of work, to wit: (specify the particulars of the offence), contrary to s. 425(a) of the *Criminal Code*.

Section 425(b) Intimidation of employees

A.B., on the (day) of (month), (year), at (specify time) in (specify place), being an employer [or the agent of C.D. an employer] wrongfully and without lawful authority did seek by intimidation [or by threat of loss of position (or employment) or by causing actual loss of position (or employment) or by threatening (or imposing) a pecuniary penalty] to compel E.F. and F.G., workmen [or employees], in the employ of C.D., to abstain from belonging to a trade union [or an association (or combination) of workmen (or employees)] to which they had a lawful right to belong, to wit: (specify the particulars of the offence), contrary to s. 425(b) of the *Criminal Code*.

Section 425(c) Employer conspiring to refuse to employ or intimidate

A.B., on the (day) of (month), (year), at (specify time) in (specify place),

..........being an employer [or the agent of an employer], wrongfully and without lawful authority, did conspire [or combine or agree or arrange] with C.D., another employer [or his agent], to refuse to employ [or to dismiss from his employment] E.F., for the reason only that E.F. was a member of a lawful trade union [or of a lawful association (or combination) of workmen] formed for the purpose of advancing, in a lawful manner, their interests and organized for their protection in the regulation of wages and conditions of work, to wit: (specify the particulars of the offence), contrary to s. 425(c) of the *Criminal Code*.

..........being an employer [or the agent of an employer], wrongfully and without lawful authority, did conspire [or combine or agree or arrange] with C.D., another employer [or his agent], by intimidation [or threat of loss of position (or employment) or by causing actual loss of position (or employment) or by threatening (or imposing) any pecuniary penalty] did seek to compel workmen [or employees] to abstain from belonging to a trade union [or association or combination] to which they had a lawful right to belong, to wit: (specify the particulars of the offence), contrary to s. 425(c) of the *Criminal Code*.

Section 425.1(1) Threats and retaliation against employees

A.B., on the (day) of (month), (year), at (specify time) in (specify place),

..........being an employer [or person acting on behalf of an employer or in a position of authority in respect of an employee] did take a disciplinary measure against [or terminate or adversely affect or threaten to terminate] the employment of C.D. with intent to compel C.D. from providing information to E.F., a person whose duties include enforcing federal and provincial law, respecting an offence C.D. believes has been committed by his employer, to wit: (specify the particulars of the offence), contrary to s. 425.1(1) of the *Criminal Code*.

..........being an employer [or person acting on behalf of an employer or in a position of authority in respect of an employee] did take a disciplinary measure against [or terminate or adversely affect or threaten to terminate] the employment of C.D. with intent to retaliate against C.D. because C.D. has provided information to E.F., a person whose duties include the enforcement of federal and provincial law, to wit: (specify the particulars of the offence), contrary to s. 425.1(1) of the *Criminal Code*.

Section 426(1)(a) Giving or offering secret commissions

A.B., on the (day) of (month), (year), at (specify time) in (specify place), directly or indirectly and corruptly, did give [or offer or agree to give or agree to offer] to C.D., an agent, a reward [or an advantage or a benefit] as consideration for doing [or for forbearing to do or for having done or for having forborne to do] an act relating to the affairs [or business] of E.F., his (or her) principal [or as consideration for showing (or forbearing to show) favour or disfavour) to G.H with relation to the affairs (or business) of E.F.], to wit: (specify the particulars of the offence), contrary to s. 426(1)(a) of the *Criminal Code*.

Section 426(1)(a) Demanding or accepting secret commissions

A.B., on the (day) of (month), (year), at (specify time) in (specify place), being an agent, directly (or indirectly) corruptly did demand (or accept or offer to accept or agree to accept) from C.D. a reward [or an advantage or a benefit] as consideration for doing [or forbearing to do or for having done (or forborne to do)] an act relating to the affairs [or business] of E.F., his (or her) principal [or as consideration for showing (or forbearing to show) favour or disfavour) to G.H. with relation to the affairs (or business) of E.F.], to wit: (specify the particulars of the offence), contrary to s. 426(1)(a) of the *Criminal Code*.

Section 426(1)(b) Deceiving a principal

A.B., on the (day) of (month), (year), at (specify time) in (specify (place),

..........with intent to deceive C.D., a principal, did give to E.F., an agent of that principal, a receipt [or an account or other writing] in which the principal had an interest and that contained a statement that was false [or erroneous or defective] in a material particular and that was intended to mislead C.D., to wit: (specify the particulars of the offence), contrary to s. 426(1)(b) of the *Criminal Code*.

..........being the agent of C.D., with intent to deceive C.D. did use a receipt [or an account or writing] in which C.D. had an interest and that contained a statement that was false [or erroneous or defective] in a material particular and that was intended to mislead C.D., to wit: (specify the particulars of the offence), contrary to s. 426(1)(b) of the *Criminal Code*.

Section 426(2) Privy to the commission of a secret commission offence

A.B., on the (day) of (month), (year), at (specify time) in (specify place), knowingly, was privy to the commission of an offence under s. 426(1) of the *Criminal*

Code, to wit: (specify the particulars of the offence), contrary to s. 426(2) of the *Criminal Code*.

Section 427(1) Issuing trading stamps

A.B., on the (day) of (month), (year), at (specify time) in (specify place), by himself [or by herself or by C.D., his (or her) employee, or by C.D., his (or her) agent] directly [or indirectly] did issue [or give or sell or dispose of or offer to issue or offer to sell or offer to dispose of] trading stamps to E.F., a merchant [or dealer in goods] for use in his [or her] business, to wit: (specify the particulars of the offence), contrary to s. 427(1) of the *Criminal Code*.

Section 427(2) Giving trading stamps to purchaser of goods

A.B., on the (day) of (month), (year), at (specify time) in (specify place), being a merchant [or a dealer in goods] by himself [or by herself or by C.D., his (or her) employee, or by C.D., his (or her) agent] directly [or indirectly] did give [or dispose of or offer to dispose of] trading stamps to E.F., a person who purchased goods from him, to wit: (specify the particulars of the offence), contrary to s. 427(2) of the *Criminal Code*.

Part XI — Wilful and Forbidden Acts in Respect of Certain Property

Section 430(1.1) Mischief in relation to computer data

A.B., on the (day) of (month), (year), at (specify time) in (specify place), wilfully did

..........destroy [or alter] computer data, to wit: (specify the particulars of the offence), contrary to s. 430(1.1)(a) of the *Criminal Code*.

..........render computer data meaningless [or useless or ineffective], to wit: (specify the particulars of the offence), contrary to s. 430(1.1)(b) of the *Criminal Code*.

..........obstruct [or interrupt or interfere] with the lawful use of computer data, to wit: (specify the particulars of the offence), contrary to s. 430(1.1)(c) of the *Criminal Code*.

..........obstruct [or interrupt or interfere] with C.D. in the lawful use of computer data, to wit: (specify the particulars of the offence), contrary to s. 430(1.1)(d) of the *Criminal Code*.

..........deny access to computer data to C.D., a person who was entitled to have access to it, to wit: (specify the particulars of the offence), contrary to s. 430(1.1)(d) of the *Criminal Code*.

Section 430(2) Mischief causing danger to life

A.B., on the (day) of (month), (year), at (specify time) in (specify place), wilfully did destroy [or damage] property [or render property dangerous (or useless or inoperative or ineffective) or obstruct (or interrupt or interfere with) the lawful use (or enjoyment or operation) of property or obstruct (or interfere with or interrupt) C.D. in the lawful use (or enjoyment or operation) of property], and thereby commit mischief that caused actual danger to life, to wit: (specify the particulars of the offence), contrary to s. 430(2) of the *Criminal Code*.

Section 430(3) Mischief in relation to testamentary instrument

A.B., on the (day) of (month), (year), at (specify time) in (specify place), did commit mischief in relation to a testamentary instrument, to wit: (specify the particulars of the offence), contrary to s. 430(3) of the *Criminal Code*.

Section 430(3) Mischief in relation to property worth more than $5,000

A.B., on the (day) of (month), (year), at (specify time) in (specify place), did commit mischief in relation to property the value of which exceeded $5,000, to wit: (specify the particulars of the offence), contrary to s. 430(3) of the *Criminal Code*.

Section 430(4) Mischief in relation to other property

A.B., on the (day) of (month), (year), at (specify time) in (specify place), did commit mischief in relation to (specify property other than property that was a testamentary instrument or the value of which exceeds $5,000), to wit: (specify the particulars of the offence), contrary to s. 430(4) of the *Criminal Code*.

Section 430(4.1) Mischief in relation to religious property

A.B., on the (day) of (month), (year), at (specify time) in (specify place), committed mischief in relation to (specify property that is a building structure or part thereof) that is primarily used for religious worship, that was motivated by bias [or prejudice or hate] based on religion [or race or colour or national origin or ethnic origin], to wit: (specify the particulars of the offence), contrary to s. 430(4.1) of the *Criminal Code*.

A.B., on the (day) of (month), (year), at (specify time) in (specify place), committed mischief in relation to (specify an object associated with religious worship located in or on the grounds of property that is a building structure or part thereof) that is primarily used for religious worship, that was motivated by bias [or prejudice or hate] based on religion [or race or colour or national origin or ethnic origin], to wit: (specify the particulars of the offence), contrary to s. 430(4.1) of the *Criminal Code*.

Section 430(4.1)(a) Mischief relating to religious property including a church, mosque, synagogue or temple

A.B., on the (day) of (month), (year), at (specify time) in (specify place),

..........did commit mischief in relation to a building [or structure or part of a building or part of a structure] that is primarily used for religious worship, where the commission of the mischief was motivated by bias [or prejudice or hate] based on colour [or race or religion or national origin or ethnic origin], to wit: (specify the particulars of the offence), contrary to s. 430(4.1)(a) of the *Criminal Code*.

..........did commit mischief in relation to an object associated with religious worship located in [or on the grounds of] a building [or structure or part of a building or part of a structure] that is primarily used for religious worship, where the commission of the mischief was motivated by bias [or prejudice or hate] based on colour [or race or religion or national origin or ethnic origin], to wit: (specify the particulars of the offence), contrary to s. 430(4.1)(a) of the *Criminal Code*.

..........did commit mischief in relation to an object associated with religious worship located in a cemetery, where the commission of the mischief was motivated by bias [or prejudice or hate] based on colour [or race or religion or national origin or ethnic origin], to wit: (specify the particulars of the offence), contrary to s. 430(4.1)(a) of the *Criminal Code*.

Section 430(4.1)(b) Mischief relating to building or structure used by an identifiable group as an educational institution, including a school, daycare centre, college or university

A.B., on the (day) of (month), (year), at (specify time) in (specify place),

..........did commit mischief in relation to a building [or structure or part of a building or part of a structure] that is primarily used by an identifiable group as an education institution, where the commission of the mischief was motivated by bias [or prejudice or hate] based on colour [or race or or religion or national origin or ethnic origin], to wit: (specify the particulars of the offence], contrary to s. 430(4.1)(b) of the *Criminal Code*.

..........did commit mischief in relation to an object associated with an educational institution located in [or on the grounds of] a building [or structure or part of a building or part of a structure] that is primarily used as an educational institution, where the commission of the mischief was motivated by bias [or prejudice or hate] based on colour [or race or or religion or national origin or ethnic origin], to wit: (specify the particulars of the offence], contrary to s. 430(4.1)(b) of the *Criminal Code*.

Section 430(4.1)(c) Mischief relating to building or structure used by an identifiable group for administrative, social, cultural or sports events

A.B., on the (day) of (month), (year), at (specify time) in (specify place),

..........did commit mischief in relation to a building [or structure or part of a building or part of a structure] that is primarily used by an identifiable group for administrative [or social or cultural or sports] activities or events, where the commission of the mischief was motivated by bias [or prejudice or hate] based on colour [or race or religion or national origin or ethnic origin], to wit: (specify the particulars of the offence), contrary to s. 430(4.1)(c) of the *Criminal Code*.

..........did commit mischief in relation to an object associated with an activity or event located in or on the grounds of a building [or structure or part of a building or part of a structure] that is primarily used by an identifiable group for administrative [or social or cultural or sports] activities or events, where the commission of the mischief was motivated by bias [or prejudice or hate] based on colour [or race or religion or national origin or ethnic origin], to wit: (specify the particulars of the offence), contrary to s. 430(4.1)(c) of the *Criminal Code*.

Section 430(4.1)(d) Mischief relating to building or structure used by an identifiable group as a residence for seniors

A.B., on the (day) of (month), (year), at (specify time) in (specify place),

..........did commit mischief in relation to a building [or structure or part of a building or part of a structure] that is primarily used by an identifiable group as a residence for seniors, where the commission of the mischief was motivated by bias [or prejudice or hate] based on colour [or race or religion or national origin or ethnic origin], to wit: (specify the particulars of the offence), contrary to s. 430(4.1)(d) of the *Criminal Code*.

..........did commit mischief in relation to an object located in or on the grounds of a building [or structure or part of a building or part of a structure] that is primarily used by an identifiable group as a residence for seniors, where the commission of the mischief was motivated by bias [or prejudice or hate] based on colour [or race or religion or national origin or ethnic origin], to wit: (specify the particulars of the offence), contrary to s. 430(4.1)(d) of the *Criminal Code*.

Section 430(4.11) Mischief relating to war memorials

A.B., on the (day) of (month), (year), at (specify time) in (specify (place), did commit mischief in relation to

..........a building [or structure or part thereof] that primarily serves as a monument to honour persons who were killed or died in consequence of a war, to wit: (specify the particulars of the offence), contrary to s. 430(4.11) of the *Criminal Code*.

..........an object [or war memorial or cenotaph] associated with honouring persons who were killed or died as a consequence of a war that is located on the grounds of a building (or structure or part thereof or a cemetery), to wit: (specify the particulars of the offence), contrary to s. 430(4.11) of the *Criminal Code*.

Section 430(4.2) Mischief in relation to cultural property

A.B., on the (day) of (month), (year), at (specify time) in (specify place), committed mischief in relation to cultural property, to wit: (specify the particulars of the offence), contrary to s. 430(4.2) of the *Criminal Code*.

Section 430(5.1) Acts or omissions likely to cause mischief

A.B., on the (day) of (month), (year), at (specify time) in (specify place), wilfully

..........did an act likely to constitute mischief causing actual danger to life [or mischief in relation to property or mischief in relation to computer data], to wit: (specify the particulars of the offence), contrary to s. 430(5.1) of the *Criminal Code*.

..........did omit to do an act that is his [or her] duty to do, that was likely to constitute mischief causing actual danger to life [or mischief in relation to property or mischief in relation to computer data], to wit: (specify the particulars of the offence), contrary to s. 430(5.1) of the *Criminal Code*.

Section 431 Violent attack on premises, residence or transport of internationally protected person

A.B., on the (day) of (month), (year), at (specify time) in (specify place), committed an attack on the official premises [or private accommodation or means of transport] of C.D., an internationally protected person, that was likely to endanger the life [or liberty] of C.D., to wit: (specify the particulars of the offence), contrary to s. 431 of the *Criminal Code*.

Section 431.1 Violent attack on premises, accommodation or transport of United Nations or associated personnel

A.B., on the (day) of (month), (year), at (specify time) in (specify place), committed a violent attack on the official premises [or private accommodation or means of transport] of C.D., (specify relationship with the United Nations), to wit: (specify the particulars of the offence), contrary to s. 431.1 of the *Criminal Code*.

Section 431.2(2) Explosive or other lethal device

A.B., on the (day) of (month), (year), at (specify time) in (specify place), delivered [or placed or discharged or detonated] an explosive [or specify other lethal device] to [or into or in or against] (specify a place of public use or a government facility or a public facility or a public transportation system or an infrastructure facility) with intent to cause death [or serious bodily injury or extensive destruction] that resulted in [or was likely to result in] major economic loss, to wit: (specify the particulars of the offence), contrary to s. 431.2(2) of the *Criminal Code*.

Section 432(1) Unauthorized recording of a movie

A.B., on the (day) of (month), (year), at (specify time) in (specify place), without the consent of the theatre manager, did record a performance of a cinematographic work [or the sound-track of a cinematographic work] in a movie theatre, to wit: (specify the particular of the offence), contrary to s. 432(1) of the *Criminal Code*.

Section 432(2) Unauthorized recording for the purpose of sale

A.B., on the (day) of (month), (year), at (specify time) in (specify place), without the consent of the theatre manager, did record a performance of a cinematographic work [or the sound-track of a cinematographic work] for the purpose of the sale [or rental or commercial distribution] of a copy of the cinematographic work to wit: (specify the particulars of the offence), contrary to s. 432(2) of the *Criminal Code*.

Section 433(a) Arson with disregard for human life

A.B., on the (day) of (month), (year), at (specify time) in (specify place), intentionally [or recklessly] did cause damage by fire [or explosion] to property, where A.B. knew that [or was reckless with respect to whether] the property was inhabited [or occupied], to wit: (specify the particulars of the offence), contrary to s. 433(a) of the *Criminal Code*.

Section 433(b) Arson causing bodily harm

A.B., on the (day) of (month), (year), at (specify time) in (specify place), intentionally [or recklessly] did cause damage by fire [or explosion] to property where the fire [or explosion] causes bodily harm to C.D., to wit: (specify the particulars of the offence), contrary to s. 433(b) of the *Criminal Code*.

Section 434 Arson with damage to property

A.B., on the (day) of (month), (year), at (specify time) in (specify place), did intentionally [or recklessly] cause damage by fire [or explosion] to property not wholly owned by A.B., to wit: (specify the particulars of the offence), contrary to s. 434 of the *Criminal Code*.

Section 434.1 Arson of own property

A.B., on the (day) of (month), (year), at (specify time) in (specify place), did intentionally [or recklessly] cause damage by fire [or explosion] to property owned in whole [or in part] by A.B. thereby threatening the health [or safety or property] of C.D., to wit: (specify the particulars of the offence), contrary to s. 434.1 of the *Criminal Code*.

Section 435(1) Arson for fraudulent purpose

A.B., on the (day) of (month), (year), at (specify time) in (specify place), did with intent to defraud C.D. cause damage by fire [or explosion] to property, to wit: (specify the particulars of the offence), contrary to s. 435(1) of the *Criminal Code*.

Section 436(1) Arson due to negligence

A.B., on the (day) of (month), (year), at (specify time) in (specify place), being the owner [or part owner or person in control] of (specify property owned or controlled), did cause a fire [or explosion] in the said property, as a result of a marked departure from the standard of care that a reasonably prudent person would use to prevent or control the spread of fires [or explosions], that caused bodily harm to C.D. [or damage to property], to wit: (specify the particulars of the offence), contrary to s. 436(1) of the *Criminal Code*.

Section 436.1 Possession of incendiary material

A.B., on the (day) of (month), (year), at (specify time) in (specify place), did have in his possession incendiary material [or an incendiary device or an explosive substance] for the purpose of committing an offence under s. 433 [or s. 434 or s. 435 or s. 436] of the *Criminal Code*, to wit: (specify the particulars of the offence), contrary to s. 436.1 of the *Criminal Code*.

Section 437 False alarm of fire

A.B., on the (day) of (month), (year), at (specify time) in (specify place), wilfully and without reasonable cause, did not make [or circulate or cause to be made or cause to be circulated] an alarm of fire by outcry [or ringing bells or using a fire alarm (or telephone or telegraph) or (specify other manner in which the alarm was made)], to wit: (specify the particulars of the offence), contrary to s. 437 of the *Criminal Code*.

Section 438(1) Preventing or impeding the saving of a vessel

A.B., on the (day) of (month), (year), at (specify time) in (specify place), willfully

..........did prevent or impede [or wilfully did endeavour to prevent or impede] the saving of a vessel that was wrecked [or stranded or abandoned or in distress], to wit: (specify the particulars of the offence), contrary to s. 438(1)(a) of the *Criminal Code*.

..........did prevent or impede [or wilfully did endeavour to prevent or impede] C.D., a person who attempted to save a vessel that was wrecked [or stranded or abandoned or in distress], to wit: (specify the particulars of the offence), contrary to s. 438(1)(b) of the *Criminal Code*.

Section 438(2) Preventing or impeding the saving of wreck

A.B., on the (day) of (month), (year), at (specify time) in (specify place), wilfully did prevent or impede [or wilfully did endeavour to prevent or impede] the saving of a wreck, to wit: (specify the particulars of the offence), contrary to s. 438(2) of the *Criminal Code*.

Section 439(1) Making fast a vessel or boat to a marine signal

A.B., on the (day) of (month), (year), at (specify time) in (specify place), did make fast a vessel [or boat] to a signal [or buoy or (specify other seamark)] that was used for purposes of navigation, to wit: (specify the particulars of the offence), contrary to s. 439(1) of the *Criminal Code*.

Section 439(2) Altering, removing or concealing marine signal

A.B., on the (day) of (month), (year), at (specify time) in (specify place), wilfully did alter [or remove or conceal] a signal [or buoy or specify other seamark] that was used for the purposes of navigation, to wit: (specify the particulars of the offence), contrary to s. 439(2) of the *Criminal Code*.

Section 440 Public harbours

A.B., on the (day) of (month), (year), at (specify time) in (specify place), wilfully and without the written permission of the Minister of Transport did remove a stone [or wood or earth or other material] that formed a natural bar necessary to the existence of a public harbour [or that forms a natural protection to such a bar], to wit: (specify the particulars of the offence), contrary to s. 440 of the *Criminal Code*.

Section 441 Demolishing or damaging building

A.B., on the (day) of (month), (year), at (specify time) in (specify place), wilfully and to the prejudice of a mortgagee [or an owner]

..........did pull down [or demolish or remove all (or any part) of a dwelling-house (or other building)] of which he was in possession [or occupation], to wit: (specify the particulars of the offence), contrary to s. 441 of the *Criminal Code*.

..........did sever from the freehold any fixture fixed therein [or thereto], to wit: (specify the particulars of the offence), contrary to s. 441 of the *Criminal Code*.

Section 442 Interfering with boundary lines of land

A.B., on the (day) of (month), (year), at (specify time) in (specify place), wilfully did pull down [or deface or alter or remove] anything planted [or set up] as the boundary line [or part of the boundary line] of land, to wit: (specify the particulars of the offence), contrary to s. 442 of the *Criminal Code*.

Section 443(1)(a) Interfering with international, provincial, county or municipal boundary line

A.B., on the (day) of (month), (year), at (specify time) in (specify place), wilfully did pull down [or deface or alter or remove] a boundary mark lawfully placed to mark an international [or provincial or county or municipal] boundary, to wit: (specify the particulars of the offence), contrary to s. 443(1)(a) of the *Criminal Code*.

Section 443(1)(b) Interfering with boundary marks placed by land surveyors

A.B., on the (day) of (month), (year), at (specify time) in (specify place), wilfully did pull down [or deface or alter or remove] a boundary mark lawfully placed by a land surveyor to mark any limit [or boundary or angle of a concession or range or lot or parcel of land], to wit: (specify the particulars of the offence), contrary to s. 443(1)(b) of the *Criminal Code*.

Section 444 Injuring or endangering cattle

A.B., on the (day) of (month), (year), at (specify time) in (specify place), wilfully

..........did kill [or maim or wound or poison or injure] certain cattle, to wit: (specify the particulars of the offence), contrary to s. 444(a) of the *Criminal Code*.

..........did place poison in such a position as to be easily consumed by certain cattle, to wit: (specify the particulars of the offence), contrary to s. 444(b) of the *Criminal Code*.

Section 445 Injuring or endangering animals other than cattle

A.B., on the (day) of (month), (year), at (specify time) in (specify place), wilfully and without lawful excuse

..........did kill [or maim or wound or poison or injure] a dog [or a bird or (specify animal other than cattle)], that was kept for a lawful purpose to wit: (specify the particulars of the offence), contrary to s. 445(a) of the *Criminal Code*.

..........did place poison in such a position as to be easily consumed by dogs [or birds or (specify animals other than cattle)] that were kept for a lawful purpose, to wit: (specify the particulars of the offence), contrary to s. 445(b) of the *Criminal Code*.

Section 446(1) Cruelty to animals

A.B., on the (day) of (month), (year), at (specify time) in (specify place),

..........did wilfully cause [or being the owner, did wilfully permit to be caused] unneccessary pain [or suffering or injury] to a bird [or an animal], to wit: (specify the particulars of the offence), contrary to s. 446(1)(a) of the *Criminal Code*.

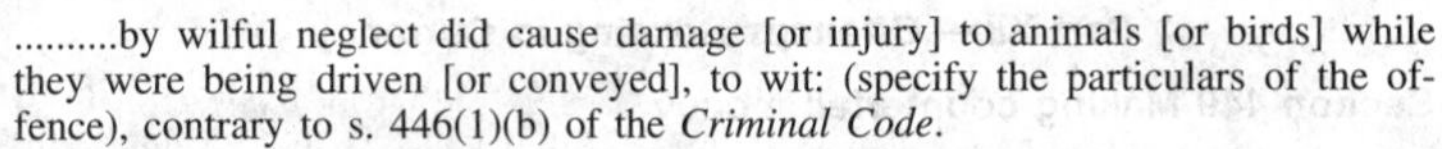

..........by wilful neglect did cause damage [or injury] to animals [or birds] while they were being driven [or conveyed], to wit: (specify the particulars of the offence), contrary to s. 446(1)(b) of the *Criminal Code*.

..........being the owner [or the person having the custody or control] of a domestic animal [or bird or an animal or a bird wild by nature that was in captivity] did abandon it in distress [or wilfully neglect (or fail) to provide suitable and adequate food and water and shelter and care for such animal (or bird)], to wit: (specify the particulars of the offence), contrary to s. 446(1)(c) of the *Criminal Code*.

..........did encourage [or aid or assist] at the fighting [or baiting] of an animal [or bird], to wit: (specify the particulars of the offence), contrary to s. 446(1)(d) of the *Criminal Code*.

..........did wilfully and without reasonable excuse, administer [or being the owner thereof did permit to be administered] a poisonous [or an injurious] drug [or substance] to a domestic animal [or bird or an animal or a bird wild by nature that was kept in captivity], to wit: (specify the particulars of the offence), contrary to s. 446(1)(e) of the *Criminal Code*.

..........did promote [or arrange or conduct or assist in or receive money for or take part in] any meeting [or competition or exhibition or pastime or practice or display or event] at [or in the course of] which captive birds were liberated by hand [or trap or contrivance or (specify other means)] for the purpose of being shot while they were liberated, to wit: (specify the particulars of the offence), contrary to s. 446(1)(f) of the *Criminal Code*.

..........being the owner [or occupier or person in charge] of (specify the premises) did permit the said [or part of the said] premises to be used for any meeting [or competition or exhibition or pastime or practice or display or event] at [or in the course of] which captive birds were liberated for the purpose of being shot while they were liberated, to wit: (specify the particulars of the offence), contrary to s. 446(1)(g) of the *Criminal Code*.

Section 446(6) Owning or having custody of animal or bird while prohibited

A.B., on the (day) of (month), (year), at (specify time) in (specify place), did own [or have the custody (or control) of an animal [or bird] while prohibited from doing so by an order of the court made under s. 446(5) of the *Criminal Code*, to wit: (specify the particulars of the offence), contrary to s. 446(6) of the *Criminal Code*.

Section 447(1) Keeping cockpit

A.B., on the (day) of (month), (year), at (specify time) in (specify place),

..........did build [or make or maintain or keep] a cockpit on premises that A.B. owned [or occupied], to wit: (specify the particulars of the offence), contrary to s. 447(1) of the *Criminal Code*.

..........did allow a cockpit to be built [or made or maintained or kept] on premises that A.B. owned [or occupied] to wit: (specify the particulars of the offence), contrary to s. 447(1) of the *Criminal Code*.

Part XII — Offences Relating to Currency

Section 449 Making counterfeit money

A.B., on the (day) of (month), (year), at (specify time) in (specify place), did make [or begin to make] counterfeit money, to wit: (specify the particulars of the offence), contrary to s. 449 of the *Criminal Code*.

Section 450 Possession of counterfeit money

A.B., on the (day) of (month), (year), at (specify time) in (specify place), without lawful justification or excuse,

..........did buy [or receive or offer to buy or offer to receive] counterfeit money, to wit: (specify the particulars of the offence), contrary to s. 450(a) of the *Criminal Code*.

..........did have in his [or her] custody [or did have in his [or her] possession] counterfeit money, to wit: (specify the particulars of the offence), contrary to s. 450(b) of the *Criminal Code*.

..........did introduce into Canada counterfeit money, to wit: (specify the particulars of the offence), contrary to s. 450(c) of the *Criminal Code*.

Section 451 Possession of filings or clippings

A.B., on the (day) of (month), (year), at (specify time) in (specify place), without lawful justification or excuse, did have in his [or her] custody or possession gold [or silver] filings [or clippings or bullion or in dust or in solution or (specify)], produced or obtained by impairing [or diminishing or lightening] a current gold [or silver] coin, knowing that it has been so produced [or obtained], to wit: (specify the particulars of the offence), contrary to s. 451 of the *Criminal Code*.

Section 452 Uttering or exporting counterfeit money

A.B., on the (day) of (month), (year), at (specify time) in (specify place), without lawful justification or excuse,

..........did utter [or offer to utter or use as if it were genuine] counterfeit money, to wit: (specify the particulars of the offence), contrary to s. 452(a) of the *Criminal Code*.

..........did export [or send or take] counterfeit money out of Canada, to wit: (specify the particulars of the offence), contrary to s. 452(b) of the *Criminal Code*.

Section 453 Fraudulently uttering coins

A.B., on the (day) of (month), (year), at (specify time) in (specify place), with intent to defraud, knowingly

..........did utter a coin that was not current, to wit: (specify the particulars of the offence), contrary to s. 453(a) of the *Criminal Code*.

..........did utter a piece of metal [or mixed metals] that resembles in size [or figure or colour] a current coin for which it was uttered, to wit: (specify the particulars of the offence), contrary to s. 453(b) of the *Criminal Code*.

Section 454 Slugs and tokens

A.B., on the (day) of (month), (year), at (specify time) in (specify place), without lawful justification or excuse, did manufacture [or produce or sell or have in his (or her) possession] (specify the thing), that was intended to be fraudulently used in substitution for a coin [or token of value] that a coin [or token-operated] device was designed to receive, to wit: (specify the particulars of the offence), contrary to s. 454 of the *Criminal Code*.

Section 455 Clipping or uttering clipped coins

A.B., on the (day) of (month), (year), at (specify time) in (specify place),

..........did impair [or diminish or lighten] a current gold [or silver] coin with intent that it should pass for a current gold [or silver] coin, to wit: (specify the particulars of the offence), contrary to s. 455(a) of the *Criminal Code*.

..........did utter a current gold [or silver] coin, knowing that it had been impaired [or diminished or lightened] with intent to pass for a current gold [or silver] coin, to wit: (specify the particulars of the offence), contrary to s. 455(b) of the *Criminal Code*.

Section 456 Defacing current coin or uttering defaced coin

A.B., on the (day) of (month), (year), at (specify time) in (specify place), did deface a current coin [or utter a current coin that had been defaced], to wit: (specify the particulars of the offence), contrary to s. 456 of the *Criminal Code*.

Section 457(1) Making or distributing likeness of bank note or security, including by electronic or computer-assisted means

A.B., on the (day) of (month), (year), at (specify time) in (specify place), did make [or publish or print or execute or issue or distribute or circulate] (specify anything) in the likeness of a current bank-note [or an obligation or a security] of (specify a government or bank), to wit: (specify the particulars of the offence), contrary to s. 457(1) of the *Criminal Code*.

Section 458 Making, having or dealing in instruments for counterfeiting

A.B., on the (day) of (month), (year), at (specify time) in (specify place), without lawful justification or excuse, did make [or repair or begin to make or begin to repair or proceed to make or proceed to repair or buy or sell or have in his (or her) custody or have in his (or her) possession] a machine [or an engine or a tool or an instrument or material or a thing] that A.B. knew had been used [or that A.B. knew was adapted and intended for use] in making counterfeit money [or counterfeit tokens of value], to wit: (specify the particulars of the offence), contrary to s. 458 of the *Criminal Code*.

Section 459 Conveying instruments for coining or metals out of mint

A.B., on the (day) of (month), (year), at (specify time) in (specify place), without lawful justification or excuse, knowingly

..........did convey out of Her Majesty's mints in Canada, a machine [or part of a machine or an engine or part of an engine or a tool or a part of a tool or an instrument or part of an instrument or material or thing] used or employed in connection with the manufacture of coins, to wit: (specify the particulars of the offence), contrary to s. 459(a) [or (b)] of the *Criminal Code*.

..........did convey out of Her Majesty's mints in Canada, coin [or bullion or metal or a mixture of metals], to wit: specify the particulars of the offence), contrary to s. 459(c) of the *Criminal Code*.

Section 460(1)(a) Advertising counterfeit money or tokens of value

A.B., on the (day) of (month), (year), at (specify time) in (specify place),

..........did by an advertisement [or a writing] offer to sell [or procure or dispose of] counterfeit money [or counterfeit tokens of value], to wit: (specify the particulars of the offence), contrary to s. 460(1)(a) of the *Criminal Code*.

..........did by an advertisement [or a writing] offer to give information with respect to the manner in which [or the means by which] counterfeit money [or counterfeit tokens of value] may be sold [or procured or disposed of], to wit: (specify the particulars of the offence), contrary to s. 460(1)(a) of the *Criminal Code*.

Section 460(1)(b) Trafficking or dealing in counterfeit money or tokens of value

A.B., on the (day) of (month), (year), at (specify time) in (specify place),

..........did purchase [or obtain or negotiate or deal with] counterfeit tokens of value, to wit: (specify the particulars of the offence), contrary to s. 460(1)(b) of the *Criminal Code*.

..........did offer to negotiate with a view to purchasing [or obtaining] counterfeit tokens of value, to wit: (specify the particulars of the offence), contrary to s. 460(1)(b) of the *Criminal Code*.

Part XII.1 — Instruments and Literature for Illicit Drug Use

Section 462.2 Instruments or literature for illicit drug use

A.B., on the (day) of (month), (year), at (specify time) in (specify place), did import into Canada [or export from Canada or manufacture or promote or sell] (specify), an instrument [or literature], for illicit drug use, to wit: (specify the particulars of the offence), contrary to s. 462.2 of the *Criminal Code*.

Part XII.2 — Proceeds of Crime

Section 462.31 Laundering proceeds of crime

A.B., on the (day) of (month), (year), at (specify time) in (specify place), did use [or transfer the possession of or send (or deliver) to C.D. (or specify a place) or transport or alter or dispose of or otherwise deal with], property [or proceeds of property] with intent to conceal [or convert] that property [or those proceeds] and knowing that all [or a part] of that property [or of those proceeds] was obtained [or derived] directly [or indirectly] as a result of the commission in Canada of an enterprise crime offence [or a designated drug offence or an act (or omission) that, if it had occurred in Canada, would have constituted an enterprise crime offence (or a designated drug offence)], to wit: (specify the particulars of the offence), contrary to s. 462.31 of the *Criminal Code.*

Part XIII — Attempts, Conspiracies, Accessories

Section 463 Attempts

A.B., on the (day) of (month), (year), at (specify time) in (specify place), did attempt to (specify the particulars using form of charge for the offence attempted).

Section 463 Accessory after the fact

A.B., on the (day) of (month), (year), at (specify time) in (specify place), knowing that C.D. had been a party to the offence of (specify the offence to which C.D. had been a party), did receive [or comfort or assist] C.D. for the purpose of enabling C.D. to escape, to wit: (specify the particulars of the offence), contrary to s. 463 of the *Criminal Code.*

Section 464 Counselling commission of offence which is not committed

A.B., on the (day) of (month), (year), at (specify time) in (specify place), did counsel C.D. to commit the offence of (specify an indictable or summary conviction offence), to wit: (specify the particulars of the offence), contrary to s. 464 of the *Criminal Code.*

Section 465(1)(a) Conspiracy to commit murder

A.B., on the (day) of (month), (year), at (specify time) in (specify place), did conspire with C.D. to commit murder [or to cause E.F. to be murdered], to wit: (specify the particulars of the offence), contrary to s. 465(1)(a) of the *Criminal Code.*

Section 465(1)(b) Conspiracy to prosecute innocent person

A.B., on the (day) of (month), (year), at (specify time) in (specify place), did conspire with C.D. to prosecute E.F. for an alleged offence, knowing that E.F. did not commit that offence, to wit: (specify the particulars of the offence), contrary to s. 465(1)(b) of the *Criminal Code.*

Section 465(1)(c) Conspiracy to commit an indictable offence

A.B., on the (day) of (month), (year), at (specify time) in (specify place), did conspire with C.D. to commit the indictable offence of (specify the indictable offence), to wit: (specify the particulars of the offence), contrary to s. 465(1)(c) of the *Criminal Code.*

Section 465(1)(d) Conspiracy to commit an offence punishable on summary conviction

A.B., on the (day) of (month), (year), at (specify time) in (specify place), did conspire with C.D. to commit the offence of (specify the offence punishable on summary conviction), such offence being punishable on summary conviction, to wit: (specify the particulars of the offence), contrary to s. 465(1)(d) of the *Criminal Code*.

Section 467.1 Participation in criminal organization

A.B., on the (day) of (month), (year), at (specify time) in (specify place),

..........did participate in [or substantially contribute to] the activities of a criminal organization knowing that C.D. [or C.D. and E.F.], who were members of the organization, engaged in the commission of a series of indictable offences within the preceding five years, to wit: (specify the particulars of the offence), contrary to s. 467.1(a) of the *Criminal Code*.

..........was a party to the commission of an indictable offence for the benefit of [or at the direction of or in association with] a criminal organization, to wit: (specify the particulars of the offence including a reference to the indictable offence to which A.B. was a party), contrary to s. 467.1(b) of the *Criminal Code*.

Section 467.11 Participation in activities of criminal organization

A.B., on the (day) of (month), (year), at (specify time) in (specify place), for the purpose of enhancing the ability of a criminal organization to facilitate [or commit] (specify an indict-able offence) knowingly participated in [or contributed to] an activity of a criminal organization, to wit: (specify the particulars of the offence), contrary to s. 467.11 of the *Criminal Code*.

Section 467.111 Recruitment of members by a criminal organization

A.B., on the (day) of (month), (year), at (specify time) in (specify place), for the purpose of enhancing the ability of a criminal organization, did recruit [or solicit or encourage or invite] C.D., a person under [or over] the age of 18 years, for the purpose of enhancing the ability of a criminal organization to commit an indictable offence, to wit: (specify the particulars of the offence), contrary to s. 467.111 of the *Criminal Code*.

Section 467.13 Instructing commission of offence for criminal organization

A.B., on the (day) of (month), (year), at (specify time) in (specify place), being one of the persons constituting a criminal organization, knowingly instructed C.D. to commit (specify an offence) for the benefit of [or at the direction of or in association with] the criminal organization, to wit: (specify the particulars of the offence), contrary to s. 467.13(1) of the *Criminal Code*.

Part XV — Special Procedure and Powers

Section 487.017 Failure to comply with production order

A.B., on the (day) of (month), (year), at (specify time), in (specify place), did fail to comply with a production order made under s. 487.012 [or s. 487.013], to wit: (specify the particulars of the offence), contrary to s. 487.017 of the *Criminal Code*.

Section 487.0197 Contravention of a preservation demand

A.B., on the (day) of (month), (year), at (specify time) in (specify place), did contravene a preservation demand made under s. 487.012 without lawful excuse, to wit: (specify the particulars of the offence), contrary to s. 487.0197 of the *Criminal Code*.

Section 487.0198 Contravention of preservation or production order

A.B., on the (day) of (month), (year), at (specify time) in (specify place), a person [or financial institution or entity] did contravene a preservation [or production] order made pursuant to s. 487.013 [or any of sections 487.013 to 487.018] without lawful excuse, to wit: (specify the particulars of the offence), contrary to s. 487.0198 of the *Criminal Code*.

Section 487.0198 Destruction of preserved data

A.B., on the (day) of (month), (year), at (specify time) in (specify place), did contravene s. 487.0194 without lawful excuse, to wit: (specify the particulars of the offence), contrary to s. 487.0194 of the *Criminal Code*.

Section 487.08(3) Failure to observe limitations on the use of results of forensic DNA analysis

A.B., on the (day) of (month), (year), at (specify time) in (specify place), did use bodily substances [or the results of forensic DNA analysis of a bodily substance], for a purpose not authorized by the warrant by which it was obtained, to wit: (specify the particulars of the offence), contrary to s. 487.08(3) of the *Criminal Code*.

Section 487.08(4) Failure to observe limitations on use of bodily substances obtained for forensic DNA analysis

A.B., on the (day) of (month), (year), at (specify time) in (specify place), did use bodily substances [or the results of forensic DNA analysis of a bodily substance] for a purpose not authorized by the order by which it was obtained, to wit: (specify the particulars of the offence), contrary to s. 487.08(4) of the *Criminal Code*.

Section 490.031 Failure to comply with an order made under s. 490.012 requiring compliance with the *Sex Offender Information Registration Act*

A.B., on the (day) of (month), (year) in (specify place), without reasonable excuse, failed to comply with an order made under s. 490.012 of the *Criminal Code* (or under s. 227.01 of the *National Defence Act*), to comply with the *Sex Offender Information Registration Act*, to wit: (specify the particulars of the offence), contrary to s. 490.031 of the *Criminal Code*.

Section 490.031 Failure to comply with an obligation under s. 490.019 requiring compliance with the *Sex Offender Information Registration Act*

A.B., on the (day) of (month), (year), at (specify time) in (specify place), without reasonable excuse, failed to comply with (specify an obligation under s. 490.019 of the *Criminal Code*), to comply with the *Sex Offender Information Registration Act*, to wit: (specify the particulars of the offence), contrary to s. 490.031 of the *Criminal Code*.

Section 490.0311 Providing false or misleading information under the *Sex Offender Information Registration Act*

A.B., on the (day) of (month), (year), at (specify time) in (specify place), knowingly did provide false or misleading information under s. 5.1 (or s. 6.1) of the *Sex Offender Information Act*, to wit: (specify the particulars of the offence), contrary to s. 490.0311 of the *Criminal Code*.

Section 490.8(9) Failure to comply with restraint order

A.B., on the (day) of (month), (year), at (specify time) in (specify place), acted in contravention of [or failed to comply with] a restraint order in respect of offence-related property that had been served on A.B., to wit: (specify the particulars of the offence), contrary to s. 490.8(9) of the *Criminal Code*.

Part XVI — Compelling Appearance of Accused Before a Justice and Interim Release

Section 517(2) Failure to comply with publication ban at judicial interim release proceeding

A.B., on the (day) of (month), (year), at (specify time) in (specify place), without lawful excuse did fail to comply with an order directing that evidence taken [or information given or representations made or the reasons given] in proceedings under s. 515 regarding judicial interim release, not be published [or broadcast or transmitted] without the accused having been discharged [or the accused having been committed for trial, the trial having ended], to wit: (specify the particulars of the offence), contrary to s. 517(2) of the *Criminal Code*.

Part XVIII — Procedure on Preliminary Inquiry

Section 539(3) Failure to comply with publication ban regarding evidence at preliminary inquiry

A.B., on the (day) of (month), (year), at (specify time) in (specify place), did fail to comply with an order of a justice at a preliminary inquiry directing that the evidence not be published [or broadcast or transmitted] without the accused having been discharged [or the accused having been ordered to stand trial, the trial having ended], to wit: (specify the particulars of the offence), contrary to s. 539(3) of the *Criminal Code*.

Section 542(2) Failure to comply with publication ban regarding an admission or a confession at preliminary inquiry

A.B., on the (day) of (month), (year), at (specify time) in (specify place), did publish [or broadcast or transmit] a report that an admission [or confession] was tendered in evidence at a preliminary inquiry [or a report of the nature of an admission (or a confession) tendered in evidence] without the accused having been discharged [or the accused having been committed for trial, the trial having ended], to wit: (specify the particulars of the offence), contrary to s. 542(2) of the *Criminal Code.*

Part XX — Procedure in Jury Trials and General Provisions

Section 648(2) Failure to comply with publication ban regarding portion of trial when jury not present

A.B., on the (day) of (month), (year), at (specify time) in (specify place), did publish [or broadcast or transmit] information regarding a portion of a trial at which a jury is not present before the jury has retired to consider its verdict, to wit: (specify the particulars of the offence), contrary to s. 648(2) of the *Criminal Code.*

Part XXII — Procuring Attendance

Section 708 Contempt of court where witness fails to attend or remain in attendance

A.B., on the (day) of (month), (year), at (specify time) in (specify place), being a person required by law to attend [or remain in attendance] for the purpose of giving evidence did fail without lawful excuse to attend [or remain in attendance] to wit: (specify the particulars of the offence), contrary to s. 708 of the *Criminal Code.*

Part XXIII — Sentencing

Section 733.1(1) Breach of probation order

A.B., on the (day) of (month), (year), at (specify time) in (specify place), being a person bound by a probation order made (specify where and when the order was made), without reasonable excuse failed [or refused] to comply with that order, to wit: (specify the particulars of the offence), contrary to s. 733.1(1) of the *Criminal Code.*

Part XXVII — Summary Convictions

Section 811 Breach of recognizance where injury or damage feared

A.B., on the (day) of (month), (year), at (specify time) in (specify place),

..........being bound by a recognizance that was entered into because A.B in order to prevent the carrying out of a terrorist activity, did commit a breach of the recognizance, to wit: (specify the particulars of the offence), contrary to s. 811 of the *Criminal Code.*

..........being bound by a recognizance that was entered into by A.B. because A.B. uttered certain words [or did things] so as to cause fear on the part of C.D. that A.B. would cause personal injury to C.D. [or the spouse of C.D. or the children of C.D.], did commit a breach of the recognizance, to wit: (specify the particulars of the offence), contrary to s. 811 of the *Criminal Code.*

..........being bound by a recognizance that was entered into by A.B. because A.B. uttered certain words [or did things] so as to cause fear on the part of C.D. that A.B. would damage the property of C.D., did commit a breach of the recognizance, to wit: (specify the particulars of the offence), contrary to s. 811 of the *Criminal Code.*

..........being bound by a recognizance that was entered into by A.B. because A.B. uttered certain words [or did things] so as to cause fear on the part of C.D. that A.B. would commit an offence under s. 151 [or s. 152, s. 155, s. 159, s. 160(2), s. 160(3), s. 170, s. 171, s. 173(2), s. 271, s. 272, or s. 273], in respect of one or more persons who were under the age of 14 years, did commit a breach of the recognizance, to wit: (specify the particulars of the offence), contrary to s. 811 of the *Criminal Code*.

..........being bound by a recognizance that was entered into by A.B. because there were reasonable grounds to believe that A.B. would commit a criminal organization offence, did commit a breach of the recognizance, to wit: (specify the particulars of the offence), contrary to s. 811 of the *Criminal Code*.

..........being bound by a recognizance that was entered into by A.B. because there were reasonable grounds to believe that A.B. would commit a serious personal injury offence, did commit a breach of the recognizance, to wit: (specify the particulars of the offence), contrary to s. 811 of the *Criminal Code*.

Cannabis Act

Section 8(1)(a) Possession of cannabis when prohibited in a public place

A.B., on the (day) of (month), (year) at (specify time) in (specify public place), being 18 years of age [or older than 18 years of age] did possess cannabis the total amount of which is equivalent to more than 30 g of dried cannabis, to wit: (specify the particulars of the offence), contrary to s. 8(1)(a) of the *Cannabis Act*.

Section 8(1)(b) Possession of illicit cannabis

A.B., on the (day) of (month), (year) at (specify time) in (specify place), being 18 years of age [or older than 18 years of age] did possess cannabis that A.B. knew was illicit cannabis, to wit: (specify the particulars of the offence), contrary to s. 8(1)(b) of the *Cannabis Act*.

Section 8(1)(c) Possession of cannabis by a young person

A.B., on the (day) of (month), (year) at (specify time) in (specify place), being a young person (specify years more than 12 years but less than 18 years) years of age, did possess cannabis equivalent to more than 5 g of dried cannabis, to wit: (specify the particulars of the offence), contrary to s. 8(1)(c) of the *Cannabis Act*.

Section 8(1)(d) Possession of budding or flowering cannabis plants in a public place

A.B., on the (day) of (month), (year) at (specify time) in (specify public place), did possess one or more cannabis plants that were budding or flowering, to wit: (specify the particulars of the offence), contrary to s. 8(1)(d) of the *Cannabis Act*.

Section 8(1)(e) Possession of cannabis plants not budding or flowering

A.B., on the (day) of (month), (year) at (specify time) in (specify place), did possess more than four cannabis plants that were not flowering or budding, to wit: (specify the particulars of the offence), contrary to s. 8(1)(e) of the *Cannabis Act*.

Section 8(1)(f) Possession by an organization

A.B., on the (day) of (month), (year) at (specify time) in (specify place), being an organization, did possess cannabis, to wit: (specify the particulars of the offence), contrary to s. 8(1)(f) of the *Cannabis Act*.

Section 9(1)(a) Unauthorized distribution of cannabis

A.B., on the (day) of (month), (year) at (specify time) in (specify place), being 18 years of age (or older than 18 years of age)

..........did distribute cannabis the total amount of which is equivalent to more than 30 g of dried cannabis, to wit: (specify the particulars of the offence), contrary to s. 9(1)(a)(i) of the *Cannabis Act*.

..........did distribute cannabis to C.D., an individual under 18 years of age, to wit: (specify the particulars of the offence), contrary to s. 9(1)(ii) of the *Cannabis Act*.

..........did distribute cannabis to C.D., an organization, to wit: (specify the particulars of the offence), contrary to s. 9(1)(iii) of the *Cannabis Act*.

..........did distribute cannabis that A.B. knew was illicit cannabis, to wit: (specify the particulars of the offence), contrary to s. 9(1)(iv) of the *Cannabis Act*.

Section 9(1)(b) Unauthorized distribution by a young person

A.B., on the (day) of (month), (year) at (specify time) in (specify place), being a young person (specify years more than 12 but less than 18) years of age

..........did distribute cannabis the amount of which was equivalent to more than 5 g of dried cannabis, to wit: (specify the particulars of the offence), contrary to s. 9(1)(b)(i) of the *Cannabis Act*.

..........did distribute cannabis to C.D., an organization, to wit: (specify the particulars of the offence), contrary to s. 9(1)(b)(ii) of the *Cannabis Act*.

Section 9(1)(c) Unauthorized distribution of cannabis plants by individual

A.B., on the (day) of (month), (year) at (specify time) in (specify place), an individual

..........did distribute one or more cannabis plants that were budding or flowering, to wit: (specify the particulars of the offence), contrary to s. 9(1)(c)(i) of the *Cannabis Act*.

..........did distribute more than four cannabis plants that were not budding or flowering, to wit: (specify the particulars of the offence), contrary to s. 9(1)(c)(ii) of the *Cannabis Act*.

Section 9(1)(d) Unauthorized distribution of cannabis by an organization

A.B., on the (day) of (month), (year) at (specify time) in (specify place), being an organization, did distribute cannabis, to wit: (specify the particulars of the offence), contrary to s. 9(1)(d) of the *Cannabis Act*.

Section 9(2) Possession of cannabis for the purpose of unauthorized distribution

A.B., on the (day) of (month), (year) at (specify time) in (specify place), did possess cannabis for the purpose of unauthorized distribution, to wit: (specify the particulars of the offence), contrary to s. 9(2) of the *Cannabis Act*.

Section 10(1) Unauthorized selling of cannabis

A.B., on the (day) of (month), (year) at (specify time) in (specify place), without authorization did sell cannabis [or a substance represented or held out to be cannabis] to C.D., an individual who was 18 years of age or older [or an individual who was under 18 years of age or an organization], to wit: (specify the particulars of the offence), contrary to s. 10(1) of the *Cannabis Act*.

Section 10(2) Possession for unauthorized selling of cannabis

A.B., on the (day) of (month), (year) at (specify time) in (specify place), without authorization did possess cannabis [or a substance represented or held out to be cannabis] for the purpose of selling it to C.D., an individual who was 18 years of age or older [or an individual who was under 18 years of age or an organization], to wit: (specify the particulars of the offence), contrary to s. 10(2) of the *Cannabis Act*.

Section 11(1) Unauthorized importing or exporting of cannabis

A.B., on the (day) of (month), (year) at (specify time) in (specify place), did import [or export] cannabis, to wit: (specify the particulars of the offence), contrary to s. 11(1) of the *Cannabis Act*.

Section 11(2) Unauthorized possession of cannabis for the purpose of exporting

A.B., on the (day) of (month), (year) at (specify time) in (specify place), did possess cannabis for the purpose of exporting it, to wit: (specify the particulars of the offence), contrary to s. 11(2) of the *Cannabis Act*.

Section 12(1) Unauthorized production of cannabis

A.B., on the (day) of (month), (year) at (specify time) in (specify place), without authorization did

..........obtain [or offer to obtain] cannabis by manufacturing [or by synthesis or by using a means of altering the chemical or altering the physical properties of cannabis, to wit: (specify the particulars of the offence), contrary to s. 12(1)(a) of the *Cannabis Act*.

..........did alter [or offer to alter] the chemical [or physical] properties of cannabis by use of an organic solvent, to wit: (specify the particulars of the offence), contrary to s. 12(1)(b) of the *Cannabis Act*.

Section 12(4) Unauthorized cultivation, propagation and harvesting cannabis by person 18 year or older

A.B., on the (day) of (month), (year) at (specify time) in (specify place), being 18 years of age (or specify other age over 18), without authorization did cultivate (or propagate or harvest or offer to cultivate or offer to propagate or offer to harvest)

..........a cannabis plant from seed [or plant material] that A.B. knows is illicit cannabis, to wit: (specify the particulars of the offence), contrary to s. 12(4)(a) of the *Cannabis Act*.

..........more than four cannabis plants in the dwelling house of A.B, to wit: (specify the particulars of the offence), contrary to s. 12(4)(b) of the *Cannabis Act*.

Section 12(5) Exceeding dwelling house limit for cultivation, propagation and harvesting cannabis plants without authorization.

A.B. and C.D. on the (day) of (month), (year) at (specify time) in (specify place), being 18 years of age or older, and who were ordinarily resident in the same dwelling house, without authorization, did cultivate [or propagate or harvest] more than four cannabis plants at one time in the dwelling house, to wit: (specify the particulars of the offence), contrary to s. 12(5) of the *Cannabis Act*.

Section 12(6) Unauthorized cultivation, propagation and harvesting of cannabis plant by individual 18 years of age or older

A.B., on the (day) of (month), (year) at (specify time) in (specify place), being 18 years of age or older, without authorization did

..........cultivate [or propagate or harvest or offer to cultivate or offer to propagate or offer to harvest] a cannabis plant at a place that was not their dwelling house, to wit: (specify the particulars of the offence), contrary to s. 12(6)(a) of the *Cannabis Act*.

..........cultivate [or propagate or harvest or offer to cultivate or offer to propagate or offer to harvest] a living thing from which cannabis can be extracted [or obtained], to wit: (specify the particulars of the offence), contrary to s. 12(6)(b) of the *Cannabis Act*.

Section 12(7) Unauthorized cultivation, propagation and harvesting of cannabis plant by a young person or organization

A.B. and C.D. on the (day) of (month), (year) at (specify time) in (specify place), being a young person [or an organization] did cultivate [or propagate or harvest or offer to cultivate or offer to propagate or offer to harvest] a cannabis plant [or specify a living thing from which cannabis can be extracted or obtained], to wit: (specify the particulars of the offence), contrary to s. 12(7) of the *Cannabis Act*.

Section 13(1) Possession for use in production or distribution of illicit cannabis

A.B., on the (day) of (month), (year) at (specify time) in (specify place), did possess [or produce or sell or distribute or import] (specify a thing) with the intention that it be used to produce [or sell or distribute] illicit cannabis, to wit: (specify the particulars of the offence), contrary to s. 13(1) of the *Cannabis Act*.

Section 14(1) Using the services of a young person

A.B., on the (day) of (month), (year) at (specify time) in (specify place), did use the services of C.D., a young person (specify an age between 12 years and 18 years) of age, in the commission of an offence under (specify subsection 9(1) or (2), 10(1) or (2), 11(1) or (2), 12(1), (4), (5), (6), or (7) or 13(1), to wit: (specify the particulars of the offence), contrary to s. 14(1) of the *Cannabis Act*.

Section 17(1) Unauthorized promotion of cannabis, accessory or service related to cannabis

A.B., on the (day) of (month), (year) at (specify time) in (specify place), without authorization did promote cannabis [or a cannabis accessory or a service related to cannabis]

..........by communicating information about its price [or distribution], to wit: (specify the particulars of the offence), contrary to s. 17(1)(a) of the *Cannabis Act*.

..........by doing so in a manner that there were reasonable grounds to believe were appealing to young people, to wit: (specify the particulars of the offence), contrary to s. 17(1)(b) of the *Cannabis Act*.

..........by means of a testimonial [or endorsement], to wit: (specify the particulars of the offence), contrary to s. 17(1)(c) of the *Cannabis Act*.

..........by means of the depiction of C.D., a real [or fictional] person [or character or animal], to wit: (specify the particulars of the offence), contrary to s. 17(1)(d) of the *Cannabis Act*.

..........by presenting it [or a brand element] in a manner that associates it with [or evokes a positive or negative emotion about or image of] a way of life that includes glamour [or recreation or excitement or vitality or risk or daring], to wit: (specify the particulars of the offence), contrary to s. 17(1)(e) of the *Cannabis Act*.

Section 18(1) False promotion of cannabis

A.B., on the (day) of (month), (year) at (specify time) in (specify place), did promote cannabis in a manner

..........that was false [or misleading or deceptive], to wit: (specify the particulars of the offence), contrary to s. 18(1) of the *Cannabis Act*.

..........that was likely to create an erroneous impression about its characteristics [or value or quantity or composition or strength or concentration or potency or purity or quality or merit or safety or health effects or health risks], to wit: (specify the particulars of the offence), contrary to s. 18(1) of the *Cannabis Act*.

Section 18(2) False promotion of cannabis accessory

A.B., on the (day) of (month), (year) at (specify time) in (specify place), did promote a cannabis accessory in a manner

..........that was false [or misleading or deceptive], to wit: (specify the particulars of the offence), contrary to s. 18(2) of the *Cannabis Act*.

..........that was likely to create an erroneous impression about its characteristics [or value or quantity or composition or strength or concentration or potency or purity or quality or merit or safety or health effects or health risks], to wit: (specify the particulars of the offence), contrary to s. 18(2) of the *Cannabis Act*.

Section 19 Use of prohibited terms in promotion of cannabis

A.B., on the (day) of (month), (year) at (specify time) in (specify place), used a prohibited term [or expression or logo or symbol or illustration], in the promotion of cannabis [or a cannabis accessory or a service related to cannabis] that was prohibited by a regulation made under s. 139(1)(z.1) of the *Cannabis Act*, to wit: (specify the particulars of the offence), contrary to s. 19 of the *Cannabis Act*.

Section 20 Promotion using foreign media

A.B., on the (day) of (month), (year) at (specify time) in (specify place), did promote cannabis (or a cannabis accessory or a service related to cannabis or a brand element) in a publication that was published outside Canada [or a broadcast that originates outside Canada or a communication that originated outside Canada] in a way prohibited by the *Cannabis Act*, to wit: (specify the particulars of the offence), contrary to s. 20 of the *Cannabis Act*.

Section 21 Prohibited sponsorship of cannabis, cannabis accessory or cannabis service

A.B., on the (day) of (month), (year) at (specify time) in (specify place), did display [or refer to or use] in a promotion that is used in the sponsorship of a person [or entity or event or activity or facility] a brand element of cannabis [or of a cannabis accessory or a service related to cannabis] and the name of a person that produced, sold or distributed cannabis [or sold or distributed a cannabis accessory or provided a service related to cannabis], to wit: (specify the particulars of the offence), contrary to s. 21 of the *Cannabis Act*.

Section 22 Name of facility

A.B., on the (day) of (month), (year) at (specify time) in (specify place), did display on a facility used for sports [or cultural event activity]

..........a brand element of cannabis [or a cannabis accessory or a service related to cannabis], to wit: (specify the particulars of the offence), contrary to s. 22(a) of the *Cannabis Act*.

..........the name of a person that produced, sold or distributed cannabis [or sold or distributed a cannabis accessory or provided a service related to cannabis], contrary to s. 22(b) of the *Cannabis Act*.

Section 23(1) Publication of prohibited promotions

A.B., on the (day) of (month), (year) at (specify time) in (specify place), did publish [or broadcast or disseminate] a promotion prohibited by the *Cannabis Act*, on behalf of C.D., to wit: (specify the particulars of the offence), contrary to s. 23(1) of the *Cannabis Act*.

Section 24(1) Inducement

A.B., on the (day) of (month), (year) at (specify time) in (specify place), being a person who did sells cannabis [or a cannabis accessory] without authorization, did

..........provide [or offer to provide] cannabis [or a cannabis accessory] without monetary consideration [or in consideration of the purchase of a thing or service or the provision of a service], to wit: (specify the particulars of the offence), contrary to s. 24(1)(a) of the *Cannabis Act*.

..........provide [or offer to provide] (specify a thing) [or a right to participate in a game or draw or lottery or contest] that was provided as an inducement for the purchase of cannabis [or a cannabis accessory], to wit: (specify the particulars of the offence), contrary to s. 24(1)(b) of the *Cannabis Act*.

..........provide [or offer to provide] a service provided [or offered to be provided] as an inducement for the purchase of cannabis [or a cannabis accessory], to wit: (specify the particulars of the offence), contrary to s. 24(1)(c) of the *Cannabis Act*.

Section 25 Unauthorized packaging or labelling

A.B., on the (day) of (month), (year) at (specify time) in (specify place), being a person authorized to sell cannabis, did sell cannabis that had not been packaged or labelled in the required manner, to wit: (specify the particulars of the offence), contrary to s. 25 of the *Cannabis Act*.

Section 26 Prohibited packaging and labelling of cannabis

A.B., on the (day) of (month), (year) at (specify time) in (specify place), being a person authorized to sell cannabis, did sell it in a package [or with a label] without authorization

..........when there were reasonable grounds to believe that the package [or label] could be appealing to young people, to wit: (specify the particulars of the offence), contrary to s. 26(a) of the *Cannabis Act*.

..........that set out a testimonial or endorsement, to wit: (specify the particulars of the offence), contrary to s. 26(b) of the *Cannabis Act*.

..........that set out a depiction of C.D., a person [or a character or an animal] to wit: (specify the particulars of the offence), contrary to s. 26(c) of the *Cannabis Act*.

..........that associated the cannabis or one of its brand elements with a way of life that included glamour [or recreation or excitement or vitality or risk or daring], to wit: (specify the particulars of the offence), contrary to s. 26(d) of the *Cannabis Act*.

..........that evoked a positive [or negative emotion] about [or image of] a way of life that included glamour [or recreation or excitement or vitality or risk or daring], to wit: (specify the particulars of the offence), contrary to s. 26(d) of the *Cannabis Act*.

..........that contained information that was false [or misleading or deceptive], to wit: (specify the particulars of the offence), contrary to s. 26(e) of the *Cannabis Act*.

..........that was likely to create an erroneous impression about the characteristics [or value or quantity or composition or strength or concentration or potency or purity of quality or merit or safety or health effect or health risks] of the cannabis, to wit: (specify the particulars of the offence), contrary to s. 26(e) of the *Cannabis Act*.

Section 27 Prohibited packaging and labelling of cannabis accessory

A.B., on the (day) of (month), (year) at (specify time) in (specify place), without authorization did sell a cannabis accessory in a package [or with a label]

..........when there were reasonable grounds to believe that the package [or label] could be appealing to young people, to wit: (specify the particulars of the offence), contrary to s. 27(a) of the *Cannabis Act*.

..........that set out a testimonial or endorsement, to wit: (specify the particulars of the offence), contrary to s. 27(b) of the *Cannabis Act*.

..........that set out a depiction of C.D., a person [or a character or an animal] to wit: (specify the particulars of the offence), contrary to s. 27(c) of the *Cannabis Act*.

..........[or one of its brand elements] a way of life that included glamour [or recreation or excitement or vitality or risk or daring], to wit: (specify the particulars of the offence), contrary to s. 27(d) of the *Cannabis Act*.

..........that evoked a positive [or negative emotion] about [or image of] a way of life that included glamour [or recreation or excitement or vitality or risk or daring], to wit: (specify the particulars of the offence), contrary to s. 27(d) of the *Cannabis Act*.

..........that contained information that was false [or misleading or deceptive], to wit: (specify the particulars of the offence), contrary to s. 27(e) of the *Cannabis Act*.

..........that was likely to create an erroneous impression about the characteristics [or value or quantity or composition or strength or concentration or potency or purity of quality or merit or safety or health effect or health risks] of the cannabis, to wit: (specify the particulars of the offence), contrary to s. 27(e) of the *Cannabis Act*.

Section 28 Use of prohibited terms

A.B., on the (day) of (month), (year) without authorization did use a prohibited term [or expression or logo or symbol of illustration] on a package [or label] of cannabis [or a cannabis accessory], to wit: (specify the particulars of the offence), contrary to s. 28 of the *Cannabis Act*.

Section 29 Unauthorized display of cannabis

A.B., on the (day) of (month), (year) being a person authorized to sell cannabis, without authorization, did display it [or a package or label of cannabis] in a manner that resulted in the cannabis [or package or label of cannabis] being seen by C.D., a young person, to wit: (specify the particulars of the offence), contrary to s. 29 of the *Cannabis Act*.

Section 30 Unauthorized display of cannabis accessory

A.B., on the (day) of (month), (year) without authorization, being a seller of a cannabis accessory, did display it [or a package or label of a cannabis accessory] in a manner that may result in the cannabis accessory [or package or label] being seen by C.D., a young person, to wit: (specify the particulars of the offence), contrary to s. 30 of the *Cannabis Act*.

Section 31 Appeal to young persons

A.B., on the (day) of (month), (year) without authorization, did sell cannabis [or a cannabis accessory] that had an appearance [or shape or sensory attribute or a function] that there were reasonable grounds to believe could be appealing to young persons, to wit: (specify the particulars of the offence), contrary to s. 31 of the *Cannabis Act*.

Section 32(1) Selling cannabis to a young person

A.B., on the (day) of (month), (year), without authorization, did sell a cannabis accessory to C.D., a young person under 18 years of age, to wit: (specify the particulars of the offence), contrary to s. 32(1) of the *Cannabis Act*.

Section 33 Prohibited Sales

A.B., on the (day) of (month), (year) being a person authorized to sell cannabis, did sell cannabis of a class not referred to in s. 4 of the *Cannabis Act* without authorization, to wit: (specify the particulars of the offence), contrary to s. 33 of the *Cannabis Act*.

Section 34(1) Prohibited Substances

A.B., on the (day) of (month), (year), without authorization did sell a mixture of substances that contained cannabis and (specify a substance referred to in column 1 of Schedule 5 of the *Cannabis Act*), to wit: (specify the particulars of the offence), contrary to s. 34(1) of the *Cannabis Act*.

Section 35 Selling or distributing recalled cannabis

A.B., on the (day) of (month), (year) did sell [or distribute] cannabis that was the subject of a recall order made under s. 76 of the *Cannabis Act*, to wit: (specify the particulars of the offence), contrary to s. 35 of the *Cannabis Act*.

Section 36 Self service display

A.B., on the (day) of (month), (year) did sell [or distribute] cannabis [or a cannabis accessory] that allowed for self service, to wit: (specify the particulars of the offence), contrary to s. 36 of the *Cannabis Act*.

Section 37 Dispensing service

A.B., on the (day) of (month), (year) did sell [or distribute] cannabis [or a cannabis accessory] by means of a dispensing service, to wit: (specify the particulars of the offence), contrary to s. 37 of the *Cannabis Act*.

Section 38(1) Obstructing inspector by act or omission

A.B., on the (day) of (month), (year) at (specify time) in (specify place), did obstruct C.D., an inspector who was engaged in the exercise of powers [or in the performance or duties or functions] under that *Cannabis Act*, to wit: (specify the particulars of the offence), contrary to s. 38(1) of the *Cannabis Act*.

Section 38(2) False statements to inspector

A.B., on the (day) of (month), (year) at (specify time) in (specify place), did knowingly make a false or misleading statement verbally [or in writing] to C.D., an inspector, who was engaged in the exercise of power [or the performance of duties or functions] under the *Cannabis Act*.

Section 38(3) Interference

A.B., on the (day) of (month), (year) at (specify time) in (specify place), without the authority of an inspector, did move [or alter or interfere with] (specify a thing) that had been seized [or detained or taken] under s. 86 of the *Cannabis Act*, to wit: (specify the particulars of the offence), contrary to s. 38(3) of the *Cannabis Act*.

Section 39 False or misleading statement

A.B., on the (day) of (month), (year) at (specify time) in (specify place), did knowingly make [or participate in or assent to or acquiesce in] the making of a false [or misleading statement] in a record [or report or electronic data or document] that was required to be prepared [or retained or provided by A.B [or C.D] under the *Cannabis Act*, to wit: (specify the particulars of the offence), contrary to s. 39 of the *Cannabis Act*.

Controlled Drugs and Substances Act

Section 4(1) Possession of controlled substance

A.B., on the (day) of (month), (year), at (specify time) in (specify place), had in his [or her] possession (specify a substance included in Schedule I, II, III, IV or V), a controlled substance, without being authorized by the *Controlled Drugs and Substances Act Regulations*, to wit: (specify the particulars of the offence), contrary to s. 4(l) of the *Controlled Drugs and Substances Act*.

Section 4(2)(a) Obtaining controlled substance

A.B., on the (day) of (month), (year), at (specify time) in (specify place), had in his [or her] possession (specify a substance included in Schedule I, II, III, IV or V), a controlled substance, without being authorized by the *Controlled Drugs and Substances Act Regulations*, to wit: (specify the particulars of the offence), contrary to s. 4(2)(a) of the *Controlled Drugs and Substances Act*.

Section 4(2)(b) Obtaining authorization to obtain a controlled substance

A.B., on the (day) of (month), (year), at (specify time) in (specify place), sought [or obtained] an authorization to obtain (specify a substance included in Schedules I, II, III, IV or V), a controlled substance, from C.D., a medical [or dental or veterinary] professional, without disclosing to C.D. the particulars relating to the acquisition by A.B. of every controlled substance, or of every authorization to obtain a controlled substance, from any other practitioner in the preceding 30 days, to wit: (specify the particulars of the offence), contrary to s. 4(2)(b) of the *Controlled Drugs and Substances Act*.

Section 5(1) Trafficking in controlled substance

A.B., on the (day) of (month), (year), at (specify time) in (specify place),

..........trafficked in (specify a controlled substance included in Schedule I, II, III, IV or V), a controlled substance, to wit: (specify the particulars of the offence), contrary to s. 5(1) of the *Controlled Drugs and Substances Act.*

A.B., on the (day) of (month), (year) at (time) in (place),

..........trafficked in a substance represented [or held out] to be a controlled substance, to wit: (specify the particulars of the offence), contrary to s. 5(l) of the *Controlled Drugs and Substances Act.*

Section 5(2) Possession for the purpose of trafficking

A.B., on the (day) of (month), (year), at (specify time) in (specify place), possessed (specify a substance included in Schedule I, II, III, IV or V), a controlled substance, for the purpose of trafficking, to wit: (specify the particulars of the offence), contrary to s. 5(2) of the *Controlled Drugs and Substances Act.*

Section 6(1) Importing and exporting

A.B., on the (day) of (month), (year), at (specify time) in (specify place), imported into Canada [or exported from Canada] (specify a substance included in Schedule I, II, III, IV, V or VI), a controlled substance without authorization, to wit: (specify the particulars of the offence), contrary to s. 6(l) of the *Controlled Drugs and Substances Act.*

Section 6(2) Possession for the purpose of exporting

A.B., on the (day) of (month), (year), at (specify time) in (specify place), possessed (specify a substance included in Schedule I, II, III, IV, V or VI), a controlled substance, for the purpose of exporting it from Canada, without authorization, to wit: (specify the particulars of the offence), contrary to s. 6(2) of the *Controlled Drugs and Substances Act.*

Section 7(1) Production of substance

A.B., on the (day) of (month), (year), at (specify time) in (specify place), produced [or offered to produce] (specify a substance included in Schedule I, II, III, IV, V or VI), a controlled substance, without authorization, to wit: (specify the particulars of the offence), contrary to s. 7(1) of the *Controlled Drugs and Substances Act.*

Section 7.1 Possession for use in production of or trafficking in substances

A.B., on the (day) of (month), (year), at (specify time) in (specify place), did possess [or produce or sell or import or transport] (specify anything) intending that it will be used to produce a controlled substance without authorization, to wit: (specify the particulars of the offence), contrary to s. 7.1 of the *Controlled Drugs and Substances Act.*

A.B., on the (day) of (month), (year), at (specify time) in (specify place), did possess [or produce or sell or import or transport] (specify anything) to traffic in a controlled substance, to wit: (specify the particulars of the offence), contrary to s. 7.1 of the *Controlled Drugs and Substances Act*.

Section 14(10) Failure to comply with restraint order

A.B., on the (day) of (month), (year), at (specify time) in (specify place), acted in contravention of [or did fail to comply with] a duly served valid restraint order made pursuant to s. 14 of the *Controlled Drugs and Substances Act*, to wit: (specify the particulars of the offence including particulars of the restraint order), contrary to s. 14(10) of the *Controlled Drugs and Substances Act*.

Section 32(1) Obstructing inspector

A.B., on the (day) of (month), (year), at (specify time) in (specify place), obstructed C.D., an inspector, in in the exercise of C.D.'s powers or the performance of his [or her] duties under the *Controlled Drugs and Substances Act* [or specify a particular regulation], contrary to s. 32(1) of the *Controlled Drugs and Substances Act*.

Section 32(2) Making false statements to inspector

A.B., on the (day) of (month), (year), at (specify time) in (specify place), knowingly made a false [or misleading] statement verbally [or in writing] to C.D., an inspector engaged in the exercise of C.D.'s powers or the performance of his [or her] duties under the *Controlled Drugs and Substances Act* [or specify the regulation], to wit: (specify the particulars of the offence), contrary to s. 32(2) of the *Controlled Drugs and Substances Act*.

Section 32(3) Interference

A.B., on the (day) of (month), (year), at (specify time) in (specify place), without authorization, removed [or altered or interfered with] (specify the thing), which had been duly seized [or detained or taken] by C.D., an inspector pursuant to the *Controlled Drugs and Substances Act*, to wit: (specify the particulars of the offence), contrary to s. 32(3) of the *Controlled Drugs and Substances Act*.

Section 43 Contravention of administrative order

A.B., on the (day) of (month), (year), at (specify time) in (specify place), contravened (specify the order or interim order made under Part V), to wit: (specify the particulars of the offence), contrary to s. 43 of the *Controlled Drugs and Substances Act*.

Firearms Act

Section 29(1) Operating a shooting club or shooting range without approval

A.B., on the (day) of (month), (year), at (specify time) in (specify place), operated a shooting club [or a shooting range] without the approval of the Minister of (specify designated provincial Ministry), to wit: (specify the particulars of the offence), contrary to s. 29(1) of the *Firearms Act*.

Section 103 Failure to assist inspectors

A.B., on the (day) of (month), (year), at (specify time) in (specify place), being the owner of [or person in charge of or person found in] (specify place), failed to give to C.D., an inspector, all reasonable assistance to enable C.D. to carry out an inspection and exercise a lawful power [or failed to give C.D., an inspector, required information], to wit: (specify the particulars of the offence), contrary to s. 103 of the *Firearms Act*.

Section 106(1) False statements to procure a licence, registration certificate or authorization

A.B., on the (day) of (month), (year), at (specify time) in (specify place), for the purpose of procuring a licence [or a registration certificate or an authorization] for A.B., knowingly made a false misleading statement [or failed to disclose relevant information], to wit: (specify the particulars of the offence), contrary to s. 106(1) of the *Firearms Act*.

Section 106(2) False statements to procure a customs confirmation

A.B., on the (day) of (month), (year), at (specify time) in (specify place), for the purpose of procuring the confirmation of (specify document), by C.D., a customs officer, for A.B. [or E.F.], knowingly made a false or misleading statement [or failed to disclose relevant information], to wit: (specify the particulars of the offence), contrary to s. 106(2) of the *Firearms Act*.

Section 107 Tampering with a licence, registration certificate, authorization or confirmation

A.B., on the (day) of (month), (year), at (specify time) in (specify place), without lawful excuse, altered [or defaced or falsified] a licence [or registration certificate or authorization or confirmation], to wit: (specify the particulars of the offence), contrary to s. 107 of the *Firearms Act*.

Section 108 Unauthorized use of ammunition

A.B., on the (day) of (month), (year), at (specify time) in (specify place), did possess ammunition without holding a licence under which the business is permitted to possess ammunition, to wit: (specify the particulars of the offence), contrary to s. 108 of the *Firearms Act*.

Section 110 Contravention of conditions of a licence, registration certificate or authorization

A.B., on the (day) of (month), (year), at (specify time) in (specify place), without lawful excuse, contravened a condition of a licence [or registration certificate or authorization] held by A.B., that required A.B. to (specify condition), to wit: (specify the particulars of the offence), contrary to s. 110 of the *Firearms Act*.

Section 112(1) Possession of unregistered firearm

A.B., on the (day) of (month), (year), at (specify time) in (specify place), possessed a firearm without holding a registration certificate, to wit: (specify the particulars of the offence), contrary to s. 112(1) of the *Firearms Act*.

Section 113 Non-compliance with demand to produce a firearm

A.B., on the (day) of (month), (year), at (specify time) in (specify place), without reasonable excuse, failed to comply with a lawful demand made by C.D., an inspector, pursuant to s. 105 of the *Firearms Act*, to wit: (specify the particulars of the offence), contrary to s. 113 of the *Firearms Act*.

Section 114 Failure to deliver up a licence, certificate or authorization that is revoked

A.B., on the (day) of (month), (year), at (specify time) in (specify place), being the holder of a licence or a registered certificate for a prohibited firearm (or a restricted firearm or an authorization) that is revoked, did not deliver it up to a peace office or firearms officer without delay following its revocation, to wit (specify the particulars of the office), contrary to s. 114 of the *Firearms Act*.

An Act Respecting the Mandatory Reporting of Internet Child Pornography by Persons Who Provide an Internet Service

Section 2 Duty to report Internet address

A.B., on the (day) of (month), (year), at (specify time), in (specify place), in the course of providing an Internet service to the public, being advised of an Internet protocol or address (or a Uniform Resource Locator), where child pornography may be available to the public, did not report that address (or Uniform Resource Locator) to the authorized organization as soon as feasible, to wit: (specify the particulars of the offence), contrary to s. 10 of the *Act respecting the Mandatory Reporting of Internet Child Pornography by Persons who provide an Internet Service.*

Section 3 Duty to report to police officer

A.B., on the (day) of (month), (year), at (specify time), in (specify place), being a person who provides an Internet service to the public, having reasonable grounds to believe that the Internet service is being (or has been) used to commit a child pornography offence, did fail to notify an officer or constable or person employed for the preservation of the public peace, to wit: (specify the particulars of the offence), contrary to s. 10 of the *Act respecting the Mandatory Reporting of Internet Child Pornography by Persons who provide an Internet Service.*

Section 4(1) Preservation of computer data

A.B., on the (day) of (month), (year), at (specify time), in (specify place), being a person who provides an Internet service to the public, having reasonable grounds to believe that the Internet service is being (or has been) used to commit a child pornography offence, did notify an officer (or constable or person employed for the preservation of the public peace), and did fail to preserve all computer data relating to that notification in their possession or control, for 21 days after the notification, to wit: (specify the particulars of the offence), contrary to s. 10 of the *Act respecting the Mandatory Reporting of Internet Child Pornography by Persons who provide an Internet Service.*

Section 4(2) Destruction of preserved computer data

A.B., on the (day) of (month), (year), at (specify time), in (specify place), being a person who provides an Internet service to the public, having reasonable grounds to believe that the Internet service is being (or has been) used to commit a child pornography offence, did notify an officer (or constable or person employed for the preservation of the public peace), and did fail to destroy all computer data relating to that notification in their possession or control, on the expiry of 21 days after the notification, to wit: (specify the particulars of the offence), contrary to s. 10 of the *Act respecting the Mandatory Reporting of Internet Child Pornography by Persons who provide an Internet Service.*

Section 5 Disclosure of preserved computer data

A.B., on the (day) of (month), (year), at (specify time), in (specify place), being a person who provides an Internet service to the public, having reasonable grounds to believe that the Internet service is being (or has been) used to commit a child pornography offence, did disclose that they made a report under s. 2 or a notification under s. 3, contrary to s. 10 of the *Act respecting the Mandatory Reporting of Internet Child Pornography by Persons who provide an Internet Service.*

Youth Criminal Justice Act

Section 136(1)(a) Inducing or assisting young person to leave place of custody

A.B., on the (day) of (month), (year), at (specify time) in (specify place), induced [or assisted] C.D., a young person, to leave lawfully a place of custody [or (specify other place)], in which C.D. had been placed in accordance with a youth sentence [or a disposition imposed under the *Young Offenders Act*], to wit: (specify the particulars of the offence), contrary to s. 136(1)(a) of the *Youth Criminal Justice Act.*

Section 136(1)(b) Unlawfully removing person from place of custody

A.B., on the (day) of (month), (year), at (specify time) in (specify place), unlawfully removed C.D., a young person, from a place of custody [or specify other place] in which a young person had been placed in accordance with a youth sentence [or a disposition imposed under the *Young Offenders Act*], to wit: (specify the particulars of the offence), contrary to s. 136(1)(b) of the *Youth Criminal Justice Act.*

Section 136(1)(c) Harbouring or concealing young person who has left place of custody

A.B., on the (day) of (month), (year), at (specify time) in (specify place), knowingly harboured [or concealed] C.D., a young person, who unlawfully left a place of custody [or specify other place] in which C.D. had been placed in accordance with a youth sentence [or a disposition imposed under the *Young Offenders Act*], to wit: (specify the particulars of the offence), contrary to s. 136(1)(c) of the *Youth Criminal Justice Act*.

Section 136(1)(d) Assisting young person to disobey condition of youth sentence or disposition

A.B., on the (day) of (month), (year), at (specify time) in (specify place), wilfully induced [or assisted] C.D., a young person, to breach [or disobey] a term [or condition] of a youth sentence [or order of the youth justice court or of a disposition (or order) under the *Young Offenders Act*], to wit: (specify the particulars of the offence), contrary to s. 136(1)(d) of the *Youth Criminal Justice Act*.

Section 136(1)(e) Preventing young person from performing condition of youth sentence or disposition

A.B., on the (day) of (month), (year), at (specify time) in (specify place), wilfully prevented [or interfered with] the performance by C.D., a young person, of a term [or condition of a youth sentence (or order of the youth justice court or of a disposition (or order) under the *Young Offenders Act*], to wit: (specify the particulars of the offence), contrary to s. 136(1)(e) of the *Youth Criminal Justice Act*.

Section 137 Failure to comply with youth sentence, victim fine surcharge or disposition

A.B., on the (day) of (month), (year), at (specify time) in (specify place),

..........being a person subject to a youth sentence imposed under s. 42(2)(c) [or (d), or (e), or (f), or (g), or (h), or (I), or (j), or (k), or (l), or (m), or (s)] of the *Youth Criminal Justice Act*, wilfully failed [or refused] to comply with that sentence, to wit: (specify the particulars of the offence), contrary to s. 137 of the *Youth Criminal Justice Act*.

..........being a person subject to a victim fine charge ordered under s. 53(2) of the *Youth Criminal Justice Act*, wilfully failed [or refused] to comply with that surcharge, to wit: (specify the particulars of the offence), contrary to s. 137 of the *Youth Criminal Justice Act*.

..........being a person subject to a disposition made under s. 20(1)(a.1) [or (b), or (c), or (d), or (e), or (f), or (g), or (j) or (l)] of the *Young Offenders Act*, wilfully failed [or refused] to comply with that disposition, to wit: (specify the particulars of the offence), contrary to s. 137 of the *Youth Criminal Justice Act*.

Section 138(1) Information and records relating to a young person

A.B., on the (day) of (month), (year), at (specify time) in (specify place),

..........published the name of [or information related to] C.D. a young person, that would identify the young person as a young person dealt with under the *Youth Criminal Justice Act* in contravention of s. 110(1) of the Act, to wit: (specify the particulars of the offence), contrary to s. 138(1) of the *Youth Criminal Justice Act*.

..........did publish the name of [or information related to] C.D., a child, [or young person] that would identify the child [or young person] as having been a victim of [or as having appeared as a witness in connection with] an office committed [or alleged to have been committed] by a young person in contravention of s. 111(1) of the *Youth Criminal Justice Act*, to wit: (specify the particulars of the offence), contrary to s. 138(1) of the *Youth Criminal Justice Act*.

..........without authorization, gave information contained in a record kept by a youth justice court [or review board or court or police force or the R.C.M.P., or (specify a government department or agency)] so as to identify the young person to whom it relates as a young person dealt with under the *Youth Criminal Justice Act* in contravention of s. 118(1) of the Act, to wit: (specify the particulars of the offence), contrary to s. 138(1) of the *Youth Criminal Justice Act*.

..........as required by the *Youth Criminal Justice Act*, did fail to destroy [or fail to transmit to the National Archivist of Canada] records kept by the R.C.M.P. of a young person charged with an offence, to wit: (specify the particulars of the offence), contrary to s. 138(1) of the *Youth Criminal Justice Act*.

..........being a person given access to the record [or to information contained in a record] of a young person dealt with under the *Youth Criminal Justice Act*, disclosed information contained in the record without authorization to C.D. in contravention of s. 129 of the Act, to wit: (specify the particulars of the offence), contrary to s. 138(1) of the *Youth Criminal Justice Act*.

..........published a report of a hearing [or an adjudication or a disposition or an appeal] concerning C.D., a young person, who committed [or who is alleged to have committed] an offence in which the name of the young person [or a child (or a young person) either who was the victim of an offence, or who appeared as a witness in connection with the offence] was disclosed in contravention of s. 38(1) of the *Young Offenders Act*, to wit: (specify the particulars of the offence), contrary to s. 138(1) of the *Youth Criminal Justice Act*.

..........published a report of a hearing [or an adjudication or a disposition or an appeal] concerning C.D., a young person who committed [or who is alleged to have committed] an offence in which information serving to identify the name of the young person [or a child (or a young person) either who was the victim of an offence, or who appeared as a witness in connection with the offence] was disclosed in contravention of s. 38(1) of the *Youth Criminal Justice Act*, to wit: (specify the particulars of the offence), contrary to s. 138(1) of the *Youth Criminal Justice Act*.

..........published without authorization a report of an offence committed [or alleged to have been committed] in which the name of C.D., a young person [or a child (or a young person) either who was the victim of an offence, or who appeared as a witness in connection with the offence] was disclosed in contravention of s. 38(1) of the *Young Offenders Act*, to wit: (specify the particulars of the offence), contrary to s. 138(1) of the *Youth Criminal Justice Act*.

..........published without authorization a report of an offence committed [or alleged to have been committed] in which information serving to identify the name of C.D., a young person [or a child (or a young person) either who was the victim of an offence, or who appeared as a witness in connection with the offence] was disclosed in contravention of s. 38(1) of the *Young Offenders Act*, to wit: (specify the particulars of the offence), contrary to s. 138(1) of the *Youth Criminal Justice Act*.

..........being a provincial director [or youth worker], to whom information has been disclosed for the preparation of a report required by the *Young Offenders Act*, did disclose that information to C.D. when it was not necessary for the purpose of preparing the report in contravention of s. 38(1.12) of the *Young Offenders Act*, to wit: (specify the particulars of the offence), contrary to s. 138(1) of the *Youth Criminal Justice Act*.

..........being a representative of (specify a school board or school or educational institution or training institution), to whom information was disclosed to ensure compliance by C.D., a young person, with an authorization pursuant to s. 35 of the *Young Offenders Act* [or to court order concerning bail (or probation or conditional supervision) or to ensure the safety of staff (or students, or C.D.)] disclosed that information to E.F. when it was not necessary to do in contravention of s. 38(1.14) of the *Young Offenders Act*, to wit: (specify the particulars of the offence), contrary to s. 138(1) of the *Youth Criminal Justice Act*.

..........being a provincial director [or youth worker], to whom information has been disclosed for the purpose of the preparation of a report required by the *Young Offenders Act*, failed to keep the information separate from any other record of C.D., the young person to whom the information relates [or to ensure that no other person had access to the information or to destroy the information when the information was no longer required for the purpose for which it was disclosed] in contravention of s. 38(1.15) of the *Young Offenders Act*, to wit: (specify the particulars of the offence), contrary to s. 138(1) of the *Youth Criminal Justice Act*.

..........failed to destroy a record kept pursuant to s. 41 of an offence that C.D., a young person, is charged with having committed when required by s. 45(1) of the *Young Offenders Act*, to wit: (specify the particulars of the offence), contrary to s. 138(1) of the *Youth Criminal Justice Act*.

..........without authorization or direction gave a record kept for inspection pursuant to s. 40, [or s. 41, or s. 42, or s. 43] of the *Young Offenders Act* [or copy or print or a negative or information contained therein] to C.D., thereby serving to identify C.D., the young person to whom it relates as a young person dealt with under the *Young Offenders Act* in contravention of s. 46(1) of the *Young Offenders Act*, to wit: (specify the particulars of the offence), contrary to s. 138(1) of the *Youth Criminal Justice Act*.

Section 139(1) Failure of young person to remain in designated place of temporary detention

A.B., on the (day) of (month), (year), at (specify time) in (specify place), a young person, who was arrested and detained prior to being sentenced [or who was detained in accordance for review of sentence], wilfully failed remain in the designated place of temporary detention, to wit: (specify the particulars of the offence), contrary to s. 139(1) of the *Youth Criminal Justice Act*.

Section 139(1) Failure of person responsible for young person

A.B., on the (day) of (month), (year), at (specify time) in (specify place), a person who has undertaken in writing to take care of and be responsible for the attendance in court when required of C.D., a young person, failed to comply with that undertaking, to wit: (specify the particulars of the offence), contrary to s. 139(1) of the *Youth Criminal Justice Act*.

Section 139(1) Failure of person responsible for young person

A.B., on the (day) of (month), (year), at (specify time) in (specify place), a person who has undertaken in writing to take care of and be responsible for the compliance by C.D. of conditions placed on C.D., a young person, by a youth court justice [or justice], failed to ensure compliance with those conditions, to wit: (specify the particulars of the offence), contrary to s. 139(1) of the *Youth Criminal Justice Act.*

Section 139(2) Failure of young person to remain in designated place of temporary detention

A.B., on the (day) of (month), (year), at (specify time) in (specify place), a young person, who was arrested and detained prior to the making of a disposition respecting the young person [or who was detained in accordance with a review of the disposition respecting the young person], under s. 7 of the *Young Offenders Act* wilfully failed to remain in the designated place of temporary detention to wit: (specify the particulars of the offence), contrary to s. 139(2) of the *Youth Criminal Justice Act.*

Section 139(2) Failure of young person to comply with undertaking

A.B., on the (day) of (month), (year), at (specify time) in (specify place), a young person who was arrested and placed in the care of C.D., under the *Young Offenders Act*, instead of being detained in custody, failed to comply with an undertaking in writing to comply with the arrangement [or with conditions specified by the youth court judge (or justice)], to wit: (specify the particulars of the offence), contrary to s. 139(2) of the *Youth Criminal Justice Act.*

Section 139(2) Failure of person responsible for young person

A.B., on the (day) of (month), (year), at (specify time) in (specify place), a young person who has undertaken in writing under the *Young Offenders Act*, to take care of and be responsible for the attendance in court when required of C.D., a young person, failed to comply with that undertaking, to wit: (specify the particulars of the offence), contrary to s. 139(2) of the *Youth Criminal Justice Act.*

Section 139(2) Failure of person responsible for young person

A.B., on the (day) of (month), (year), at (specify time) in (specify place), a person who has undertaken in writing under the *Young Offenders Act*, to take care of and be responsible for the compliance by C.D., a young person, with conditions placed on C.D., failed to ensure compliance with those conditions, to wit: (specify the particulars of the offence), contrary to s. 139(2) of the *Youth Criminal Justice Act.*

INDEX

Canadian Bill of Rights, CBR*; Canadian Victims Bill of Rights,* CVBR*; Criminal Code,* CC*; Constitution Act,* CA*; Controlled Drugs and Substances Act,* CDA*; Criminal Records Act,* CRA*; Canada Evidence Act,* CEA*;* CannA, *Cannabis Act; DNA Identification Act,* DNA*; Extradition Act,* EXA*; Firearms Act,* FA*; Identification of Criminals Act,* ICA*; Interpretation Act,* IA*; An Act respecting the mandatory reporting of Internet child pornography by persons who provide an Internet service,* MRICP*; Motor Vehicle Transport Act,* MVTA*; Sex Offender Information Registration Act,* SOIRA*; Youth Criminal Justice Act,* YCJA